EDWIN A. FLEISHER

The Edwin A. Fleisher Collection
of Orchestral Music
in the Free Library of Philadelphia

a cumulative catalog, 1929-1977

With highest regards and best wishes — Sam Dennison

The Edwin A. Fleisher Collection
of Orchestral Music
in the Free Library of Philadelphia

a cumulative catalog, 1929-1977

THE FLEISHER COLLECTION IN THE FREE LIBRARY
OF PHILADELPHIA

G.K.HALL&CO.
70 LINCOLN STREET, BOSTON, MASS.

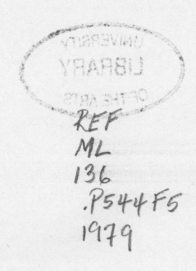

Library of Congress Cataloging in Publication Data

Philadelphia.   Free Library.   Edwin A. Fleisher Music Collection.
   The Edwin A. Fleisher Collection of Orchestral Music in the Free
Library of Philadelphia.

   Includes index.
   1.   Orchestral music--Bibliography--Catalogs.
I.   Title.
ML136.P4F68   016.785   78-24557
IBSN 0-8161-7942-5

This publication is printed on permanent/durable acid-free paper
MANUFACTURED IN THE UNITED STATES OF AMERICA

Catalog Project Staff

SAM DENNISON, CURATOR

HARRY L. KOWNATSKY, CATALOG PROJECT DIRECTOR   (1975–1976)

STANLEY GLOWACKI, MUSIC COLLECTION ASSISTANT   (1975–1977)

MARY L. FRORER, CATALOGER–EDITOR   (1977–1978)

STEPHEN F. HENNER, CATALOGER–BIBLIOGRAPHER   (1975–1977)

SUSAN R. MORRIS, CATALOGER–BIBLIOGRAPHER   (1975–1978)

SADIE J. MORGAN, INCIPITS COPYIST   (1975–1978)

BARBARA L. DACHOWSKI, TYPIST   (1975–1977)

MARSHA H. RICHARDSON, TYPIST   (1977–1978)

Fleisher Collection Staff

SAM DENNISON, CURATOR

ROMULUS FRANCESCHINI, MUSIC COLLECTION ASSISTANT

SUSAN R. MORRIS, MUSIC COLLECTION ASSISTANT

SADIE J. MORGAN, STAFF COPYIST

WILLIAM A. DANIELS, STAFF COPYIST

FRANK DEODATO, PHOTOGRAPHIC MACHINE OPERATOR

Contents

Introduction

Edwin A. Fleisher, aptly characterized as "a musical philanthropist of the first order," began his collection of orchestral music in 1909 in order to provide performance materials for the Symphony Club, an amateur orchestra in Philadelphia of which he was both founder and patron. In time his collection grew to more than 4,000 works, each with score, and complete set of parts. In 1929, he presented his magnificent collection to The Free Library of Philadelphia because, as legend has it, the Fire Marshall had informed Mr. Fleisher that the collection had grown too large to be stored safely in the house he had purchased for the use of the Symphony Club.

From the outset, Mr. Fleisher took a personal interest in the growth, development and care of the collection now housed in The Free Library. He made provisions for the acquisition of new works and oversaw the preservation of material already in the collection, even to the extent of designing a special box for separate storage of each work. It is to his eternal credit that he envisioned the collection as a living, continually growing entity, intended for use as an active performance resource while still functioning as an archive of our musical heritage.

Beginning in 1937 music in the Fleisher Collection was made available on loan to orchestras throughout the world, because of a great number of requests for works unobtainable elsewhere. Since that time, music has been loaned to orchestras in virtually every country in which symphony orchestras exist. Major symphony orchestras, conservatories, music schools, and universities have come to view the Fleisher Collection as a prime source of music. Many smaller orchestras, community orchestras and the like, depend upon the collection for all their music needs, because maintenance of their own libraries would be prohibitively expensive. Many summer music festivals obtain music for their entire season from the Fleisher Collection.

It has been said that Edwin A. Fleisher was interested in the acquisition of every available orchestral work. He was certainly universal in his musical tastes, not only acquiring works of the past but actively searching for excellent contemporary works as well. He personally commissioned Nicolas Slonimsky in 1941 to undertake the acquisition of contemporary music of Latin American composers, with the happy result that his collection became among the richest in holdings in the United States of Latin American composers. The same effort was made with respect to composers of other countries as well: Sweden, Great Britain, and Canada are only a few of the countries represented by large holdings in the collection. Recent efforts to acquire contemporary works have involved such countries as Israel and Poland, while acquisition of new works by composers in the United States goes on continually.

New editions of older works are produced by the Fleisher Collection staff in order to provide performing versions of works which otherwise might remain unknown to today's audiences. A number of rare and early works have thus been reconstructed in modern performing editions, including those of Paer, Gehra, Gossec, and Gyrowetz.

In order to make the collection accessible to potential borrowers, Edwin A. Fleisher published a descriptive catalog in 1933, with a second volume appearing in 1945. A supplementary list was issued in 1966, but lacking the descriptive cataloging of the first two volumes its use was limited. The present catalog is the result of a project begun in 1975 to recatalog the entire collection, now grown to almost 13,000 works, each complete with score and full performance materials. It corrects many errors in the previous volumes, fully catalogs the works entered in the supplementary list, and provides entries for those works added to the collection since 1966. The classified format of the older volumes has been abandoned in favor of dictionary entry under the composer's name, with an index provided to define even more precisely than before various types of works in the collection. Thus it will be possible for the user of the present volume to locate works, for example, specifically for piano solo with string orchestra accompaniment, or for viola solo with percussion ensemble accompaniment.

In cataloging a collection of the size and scope of the Edwin A. Fleisher Collection, one frequently has to confront questions of judgment with regard to classification, format, translation of titles, or transliteration from other alphabets. Bearing in mind the fact that the collection consists mainly of orchestral music for performance as well as research purposes, the catalogers had to strike a balance between strict adherence to standard cataloging rules and common usage among performing musicians. The English language was preferred from the beginning, although many titles such as "Aubade," or "Berceuse," and many titles of indigenous dances were left untranslated. The use of diacritical marks in transliterations was avoided wherever possible since they do not appear in the English language and offer little help in pronunciation. Ch has replaced Tch or Tsch for Chaikovsky; but Tch has been retained for Tcherepnin since the composer himself expressed a preference for this spelling. Ks was discarded in favor of X in transliteration of "Alexander," the former giving the appearance of intellectual posturing, as did the double I for Y. In judging the wisdom of such editorial decisions, one should bear in mind that this catalog is designed primarily for those who use the Collection as a resource: conductors, programmers, orchestra librarians, and researchers. All modifications to cataloging rules were made with a view to making the catalog easier for such persons to use, and a mechanical following of the latest rules of music cataloging was avoided.

In line with this principle, some changes will require explanation. Opera overtures, for example, appear before other excerpts from the same opera, regardless of whether or not this violates alphabetical order. This change was deemed necessary on musical grounds, since the overture is often the only part of an opera in the Collection and is usually the only part requested from the Collection. Similarly, Haydn symphonies with almost identical bibliographical details, as well as other examples that fall in the same category, have been given abbreviated entries not only to save space but to spare the reader endless repetition of the same information. For many composers, thematic catalog numbers, or catalogue raisonné numbering systems have been utilized as an aid to identification. For most compositions before 1800, incipits have been provided if no thematic catalog exists.

Even the most careful editing and proofreading cannot guarantee the elimination of all errors in a catalog such as this. We would appreciate and welcome suggestions and corrections. These may be sent directly to: The Free Library of Philadelphia, Logan Square, Philadelphia, Pennsylvania, 19103.

Acknowledgments

The Fleisher Collection owes an enormous debt of gratitude to the many persons whose efforts, interest and cooperation were essential to successful completion of this catalog. While everyone cannot be named, there are those who contributed so much in terms of time and devotion that they must be recognized.

Harry L. Kownatsky, retired Curator of the Fleisher Collection, initiated the catalog project, saw to its funding and laid the groundwork for actual cataloging to begin.

Dr. Sol Schoenbach, Executive Director of Settlement Music School, and Richard Kapp, Program Officer in the Division of Humanities and the Arts of the Ford Foundation, deserve special thanks for their efforts in obtaining initial funding for the project. The grant from the Ford Foundation, covering the first two years of the catalog project, contributed materially by providing for the special staff necessary to catalog works acquired since 1945.

The unhesitating cooperation and support of The Free Library of Philadelphia administration were essential ingredients in the success of the project. In particular, Keith Doms, Director; Marie Davis, Associate Director; and Henry Kapenstein, Chief, Central Public Services Division, gave endlessly of their time and support.

Throughout the project, Frederick James Kent, Head of the Music Department of The Free Library of Philadelphia and his staff provided essential research resources and assistance while demonstrating remarkable patience as the project staff rummaged for information in the music reference section.

The staff of the Fleisher Collection deserves a great deal of credit for keeping the Collection functioning despite the turbulence of a major cataloging project being conducted in the same room.

Technical assistance and support from the staff of the publisher, G. K. Hall, have proved invaluable to the project and have been much appreciated by a staff more accustomed to cataloging music than to having the resulting catalog published.

Specific words of praise and appreciation must be added to highlight the dedication, skill, and teamwork of the members of the Catalog Project Staff. Their exemplary work produced this long-awaited reference catalog. Their contributions are here presented as a group effort, but their individual contributions are bright examples of scholars at productive and creative work.

Finally, a vote of thanks is due to all those composers whose many works make the Edwin A. Fleisher Collection of Orchestral Music what it is: one of the most important repositories of orchestral music in the world.

September 12, 1978

How to Use the Catalog

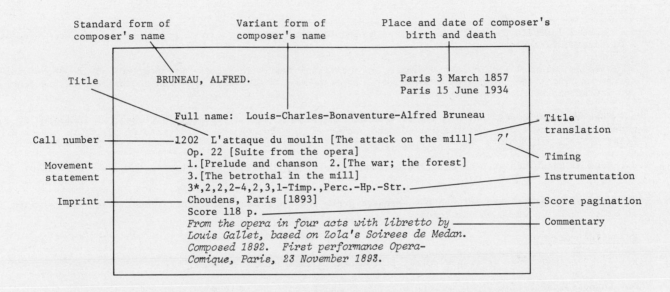

Standard form of composer's name   Variant form of composer's name   Place and date of composer's birth and death

Title

BRUNEAU, ALFRED.

Paris 3 March 1857
Paris 15 June 1934

Full name: Louis-Charles-Bonaventure-Alfred Bruneau — Title

Call number —— 1202 L'attaque du moulin [The attack on the mill] 7' translation
Op. 22 [Suite from the opera]
Movement statement —— 1.[Prelude and chanson 2.[The war; the forest] Timing
3.[The betrothal in the mill]
3*,2,2,2-4,2,3,1-Timp.,Perc.-Hp.-Str. —— Instrumentation
Imprint —— Choudens, Paris [1893] Score pagination
Score 118 p. ——
From the opera in four acts with libretto by —— Commentary
Louis Gallet, based on Zola's Soirees de Medan.
Composed 1892. First performance Opera-
Comique, Paris, 23 November 1893.

Compositions and arrangements are entered under the name of the composer or, in the case of medleys or arrangements of anonymous works only, the editor or transcriber. Works which were composed as a joint effort are entered under title unless a principal contributor to the work can be identified, in which case the work is entered under that composer's name.

Variant forms of the composer's name are given as well as the place and date of birth and death when these can be determined. Russian dates have been given in New Style (Gregorian calendar) wherever possible.

Titles appear in the original language with translation into English or, as in the case of indigenous dances or well-known foreign titles, without translation. This practice follows the reasoning of Ernst Roth who says in his The Business of Music; Reflections of a Music Publisher:

> The titles of musical works always raise certain problems in translation and the reader may forgive apparent inconsistencies. No one would think of translating Rosenkavalier or Così fan tutte.... And to refer to The Bartered Bride by its original Czech title would be pure musical snobbery....

He rightly concludes that in the final analysis it is a matter of musical taste.

The use of the editorial sic has been avoided. Misspelled words in titles have been left unchanged in most instances in which the meanings are clear. Also included where applicable in the title statement are: form, medium, opus number, key signature, and transcriber. Brackets [ ] are used (1) to indicate translations, (2) to indicate information not on the title page, and (3) to indicate the use of a conventional title.

Conventional titles are constructed in order to bring together works belonging to the same class. In addition to the elements listed above, conventional titles may include: popular name, thematic catalog number, specific excerpt, transcriber, or arranger.

Durations appear in italics at the far right of the first line of the title statement. They are determined by consulting composers, examining scores, timing actual performances, or consulting the numerous catalogs which contain timings.

The movement statement identifies individual movements by title, if any, or by tempo indication. Where a movement lacks a title or tempo marking, the statement reads "no tempo indicated" or [-----]. As in the case of titles, translations of movement titles appear within brackets.

Instrumentation is indicated by dividing the orchestra into groups in scoring order:

1st group	=	Woodwinds
2nd group	=	Brass instruments
3rd group	=	Timpani and Percussion
4th group	=	Keyboard and Plucked instruments
5th group	=	Voices
6th group	=	Strings

The groups are separated by hyphens. Numbers indicate the number of players needed for performance.

1. Woodwinds

   a. Numbers indicate the number of players needed for performance: 2,2,2,2 indicates: 2 Flutes; 2 Oboes; 2 Clarinets; 2 Bassoons.

   b. When an asterisk (*) follows a number, an additional family instrument is required: 3*,3*,3*,3* indicates: 2 Flutes and 1 Piccolo; 2 Oboes and 1 English Horn; 2 Clarinets and 1 Bass Clarinett; 2 Bassoons and 1 Contrabassoon.

   c. When one instrumentalist plays more than one instrument, the alternating instrument is indicated in parentheses. The first number specifies the number of players needed: 2(2nd alt. Picc.),2(2nd alt. E.H.), 2(1st alt. Cl. in E-flat; 2nd alt. B.Cl.),2(2nd alt. C.Bn.).

   d. Unusual woodwinds such as Alto Flute, Oboe d'Amore, and Clarinet in E-flat are always specified by name.

   e. Saxophones are listed between the Woodwind group and the Brass Instruments group. They are itemized if other than the usual AATBar. choir.

2. Brass Instruments

   a. 4,2,3,1 indicates: 4 French Horns; 2 Trumpets; 3 Trombones; 1 Tuba.

   b. Cornet, Ophicleide, Euphonium and other such instruments are entered within the brasses, in abbreviated form: 4,2,Cnt.,3,Euph.,Ophicl.

3. Percussion

   Timpani are always entered first as Timp., followed either by Perc. or by listing of percussion instruments required.

4. Keyboard and Plucked Instruments

   a. Specified by abbreviations in the following order:
   Piano--Pno.
   Cembalo--Cemb.
   Harpsichord--Hpscd.
   Organ--Org.
   Celesta--Cel.
   Harp--Hp.
   Harmonium--Harm.
   Mandolin--Mand.
   Guitar--Guit.

   b. All others are spelled out in full.

5. Voices

   a. Listed in order by range, beginning with the highest:
   Soprano--Sop.
   Mezzo-soprano--Mezzo-sop.
   Tenor--Ten.

Baritone--Bar.
Bass--Bass

    b. Chorus is indicated by voices: Chorus(SATB).

6. <u>Strings</u>

    a. The abbreviation Str. indicates a full complement of strings: Violin I; Violin II; Viola; Violon-cello; Contrabass.

    b. Variations from normal string instrumentation are indicated: Str.(without Cb.); or Str.(without Va.); or spelled out; Vn.I,Vn.II,Vn.III,Vc.,Cb.

Solo instruments are specified at the beginning of the instrumentation statement. Example of a complete instrumentation statement:

        Solo Vn.-2(2nd alt. Picc.),3*,2,2-2Alto Sax.-5,2,3,1-Timp.,Perc.-Pno.,Hp.-Chorus(SATB)-Str.

Unconventional instrumentation, including percussion ensemble, is spelled out:

        6Hn.,4Tpt.,3Tbn.,Tuba-Timp.

or:

    HARRISON, LOU.

        991m Bomba, for twenty instruments, five players
            1st--2 Maracas, 3 Flower Pots;
            2nd--2 Metal Rattles, 3 Large Bells;
            3rd--3 Dragon's Mouths, Thundersheet;
            4th--Rasp, 3 Chinese Woodblocks;
            5th--Low Tam-tam, Bass Drum

The imprint (publisher, place and date of edition) is taken from the score. Agents are not listed, owing to the rapid changes in this field; the Fleisher Collection can supply this information upon request. Dates of publication are determined from plate numbers or bibliographic research when not on the scores.

Pagination is given to provide the conductor with an idea of what length score is involved in performance. If the score is a large folio or miniature score, this size information is also recorded.

The commentary includes any or all of the following information:

    Literary or other inspiration

    Commissioning person or institution

    Date of composition

    First performance information: place, date, festival or symposium, performing group or orchestra, conductor, and soloist, if any

    Information concerning transcriptions of the work

    Prizes or awards given for the work

    Relevant quotations

<u>Incipits</u> are provided for most eighteenth-century works not identified by thematic catalog number. The following thematic catalogs were used:

ABEL, KARL FRIEDRICH.
Knape, Walter. <u>Bibliographisch-thematisches Verzeichnis der Kompositionen von Karl Friedrich Abel (1723-1787)</u>.
   Cuxhaven: W. Knape, 1971.

BACH, CARL PHILIPP EMANUEL.
Wotquenne, Alfred. <u>Thematisches Verzeichnis der Werke von C.P.E. Bach</u>. Leipzig: Breitkopf and Härtel, 1905.

BACH, JOHANN CHRISTIAN.
Terry, Charles Sanford. <u>John Christian Bach</u>. 2nd ed., with a foreword by H.C. Robbins Landon. London,
   New York: Oxford, 1967. Thematic Catalogue, pp. 193-361.

BACH, JOHANN SEBASTIAN.
Schmieder, Wolfgang. Thematisch-systematisches Verzeichnis der musikalischen Werke von Johann Sebastian Bach.
    Bach-Werke-Verzeichnis. Leipzig: Breitkopf and Härtel, 1950. Unchanged re-edition, 1958. Abbreviated
    BWV.

BEETHOVEN, LUDWIG VAN.
Kinsky, Georg. Das Werk Beethovens: Thematische-bibliographisches Verzeichnis seiner sämtlichen vollendeten
    Kompositionen. Completed and edited by Hans Halm.
        Used to identify those of Beethoven's works for which opus numbers do not exist.

BOCCHERINI, LUIGI.
Gérard, Yves. Catalogue of the Works of Luigi Boccherini. London: Oxford, 1969.

CLEMENTI, MUZIO.
Tyson, Alan. Thematic Catalogue of the Works of Muzio Clementi. Tutzing: Hans Schneider, 1967.

COUPERIN, FRANÇOIS (LE GRAND).
Cauchie, Maurice. Thematic Index of the Works of François Couperin. Monaco: Lyrebird Press, Louise B. M.
    Dyer, 1949.

DITTERSDORF, KARL DITTERS VON.
Krebs, Carl. Dittersdorfiana. Berlin: Paetel, 1900. Verzeichniss der Werke Ditters v. Dittersdorfs,
    pp. 55-144.

GLUCK, CHRISTOPH WILLIBALD.
Wotquenne, Alfred. Catalogue thématique des oeuvres de Chr. W. v. Gluck. Leipzig: Breitkopf and Härtel,
    1904.

GOTTSCHALK, LOUIS MOREAU.
Offergeld, Robert. The Centennial Catalogue of the Published and Unpublished Compositions of Louis Moreau
    Gottschalk. New York: Stereo Review, 1970.

HANDEL, GEORGE FRIDERIC.
Bell, A. Craig. Handel: Chronological thematic catalogue. Darley: The Grian-Aig Press, 1972.

HAYDN, JOSEPH.
Hoboken, Anthony van. Joseph Haydn: Thematisch-bibliographisches Werkeverzeichnis. I. Instrumentalwerke.
    Mainz: B. Schott's Söhne, 1957.

LOCKE, MATTHEW.
Harding, Rosamond E.M. A Thematic Catalogue of the Works of Matthew Locke. Oxford: Blackwell, 1972.

MOZART, WOLFGANG AMADEUS.
Köchel, Ludwig Ritter von. Chronologisch-thematisches Verzeichnis sämmtlicher Tonwerke W.A. Mozart's. 6th ed.
    Edited by Franz Giegling, Alexander Weinmann, and Gerd Sievers. Wiesbaden: Breitkopf and Härtel, 1964.

PURCELL, HENRY.
Zimmerman, Franklin B. Henry Purcell, 1659-1695, an Analytical Catalogue of his Music. New York: St. Mar-
    tin's Press, 1963.

SCARLATTI, DOMENICO.
Kirkpatrick, Ralph. Domenico Scarlatti. 6th corrected printing. Princeton: Princeton U. Press, 1970.
    Catalogue of Scarlatti Sonatas, pp. 442-59.
        The numbers assigned by Alessandro Longo in his Indice Tematico are also given in Kirkpatrick and
    cited in Fleisher catalog entries.

SCHUBERT, FRANZ.
Deutsch, Otto Erich, and Donald R. Wakeling. Schubert: Thematic Catalogue of all his Works in Chronological
    Order. New York: Kalmus, n.d.

VIOTTI, GIOVANNI BATTISTA.
Giazotto, Remo. Giovanni Battista Viotti. Milan: Curci, 1956.

VIVALDI, ANTONIO LUCIO.
Fanna, Antonio. Antonio Vivaldi: Catalogo numerico-tematico delle opere strumentali. Milan: Ricordi, 1968.

    The index is designed to aid the reader in finding specific types of works. It is divided into two sec-
tions: (1) ensembles without solo instrument (BAND, BRASS ENSEMBLE, STRING ORCHESTRA, etc.) and (2) works
with solo instrument or instruments. Categories for large and small orchestra are not included since the
designation is too broad to be useful.

Works without solo instruments appear under headings arranged alphabetically. Fanfares, for example, may be found by looking under the letter F.

Works with one solo instrument appear first in the second section arranged alphabetically under the solo instrument which is the first word of the heading. Accompaniments are specified (VIOLA-ORCHESTRA, VIOLA-PERCUSSION or VIOLA-STRING ORCHESTRA).

Works for more than one solo instrument follow in numerical sequence. Multiple entries are made for works with different solo entries, thus a work for solo clarinet and bassoon will be found under two headings: (1) CLARINET, BASSOON-ORCHESTRA, or (2) BASSOON, CLARINET-ORCHESTRA.

The heading CONCERTI GROSSI does not specify the makeup of the concertino group but this may be found by consulting the various combinations of solo groups, such as: VIOLIN, VIOLA, VIOLONCELLO--ORCHESTRA.

Under each heading appears the composer's name, page number in brackets, and the call number for the appropriate work. Thus, #473p, J.S. Bach's CONCERTO, Three Cembali, no. 1, D minor, BWV 1063, entered on page 41 in the Catalog, will appear in the index under:

> THREE CEMBALI-STRINGS
> Bach, J.S. [41]473p.

In order to locate the full entry for the work, turn to page 41 (the number in brackets); scan down the left hand side of each column until the call number 473p is found.

How to Borrow Music

The Fleisher Collection is not intended to supplant commercial sources from which orchestras may buy or rent orchestrations, but it can lend those in the public domain. Music protected by copyright or under contract to a publisher can be lent only upon clearance from the publisher or, in the case of unpublished music, the composer or his accredited representative. It is the responsibility of the borrowing organization to obtain clearances and to forward them to the Collection. The Fleisher Collection, while performing the service of lending music, does not grant or imply the right of performance in the case of music protected by law.

Music may be lent to recognized orchestras, universities, colleges, conservatories, and other organizations interested in the furtherance of music. In no case is music lent to individuals.

An organization wishing to borrow music must submit a written request on its official stationery over the signature of the music director, business manager, or president who assumes responsibility for its care and prompt return. A nominal fee to cover shipping and handling is levied for each work to be borrowed.

As a preliminary to possible performance, scores otherwise unavailable may be lent to conductors for perusal upon receipt of a written request as above.

Information in the written request should include: Composer and title of the work requested; date of first rehearsal and performance date; and the number of string parts required. The request should be sent directly to:

> The Edwin A. Fleisher Music Collection
> The Free Library of Philadelphia
> Logan Square
> Philadelphia, Pennsylvania 19103

The complete conditions of loan and a brochure describing the Collection are available upon request.

Abbreviations

Instruments

Piccolo	Picc.
Flute	Fl.
Oboe	Ob.
English horn	E.H.
Bass clarinet	B.Cl.
Contrabass Clarinet	Cb.Cl.
Bassoon	Bn.
Contrabassoon	C.Bn.
Sarrusophone	Sarrus.
Saxophone	Sax.
Horn	Hn.
Trumpet	Tpt.
Cornet	Cnt.
Trombone	Tbn.
Baritone	Bar.
Tuba	Tuba
Euphonium	Euph.
Ophicleide	Ophicl.
Bass drum	B.Dr.
Snare drum	S.Dr.
Tenor drum	T.Dr.
Timpani	Timp.
Castanets	Cast.
Cymbals	Cym.
Tambourine	Tamb.
Xylophone	Xyl.
Gong	Gong
Triangle	Trgl.
Glockenspiel (Chime bells)	Glock.

Piano	Pno.
Cembalo	Cemb.
Harpischord	Hpscd.
Organ	Org.
Celesta	Cel.
Harp	Hp.
Harmonium	Harm.
Mandolin	Mand.
Guitar	Guit.
Soprano	Sop.
Tenor	Ten.
Baritone	Bar.
Strings	Str.
Violin	Vn.
Viola	Va.
Violoncello	Vc.
Contrabass	Cb.

General

Ad lib.	ad libitum
alt.	alternating; alternate
b.	born
c	copyright
ca.	circa; about
d.	died
DTÖ	Denkmäler der Tonkunst in Oesterreich
fl.	flourished
Ms.	manuscript
no.	number
op.	opus
p.	page
Tr.	translation; translated

The Edwin A. Fleisher Collection of Orchestral Music

A

ABACO, EVARISTO FELICE DALL'.
See: DALL'ABACO, EVARISTO FELICE.

ABBIATE, LOUIS.   Monaco 1866
                                        Monaco 1933

    640c Lamento, Op. 109
    Solo Vc.-2,2,2,2-4Hn.-Timp.-Hp.-Str.
    Score: Ms. 18 p.
    Parts: Durdilly, Paris, ᶜ1929

    688m Villanelle, Op. 2
    Solo Ob.-1,1,1,2-2Hn.-Trgl.-Str.
    Score: Ms. 23 p.
    Parts: Durdilly, Paris, ᶜ1929

ABEL, KARL FRIEDRICH.
        Köthen, Germany 22 December 1723
              London 20 June 1787

    1986s [Quartet, strings, no. 17, Op. 15   *7'30"*
    no. 5, F major. Knape no. 77] Arranged for
    string orchestra by Karl Geiringer
    1.Moderato 2.Andante ma non troppo adagio
    3.Un poco vivace
    Str.
    Ms.
    Score 15 p.
    Composed 1770-71. First published 1781.

    2267 [Symphony no. 18, Op. 7 no. 6,   *13'*
    E-flat major. Knape no. 18] Orchestrated by
    W.A. Mozart
    0,0,2,1-2Hn.-Str.
    Breitkopf & Härtel, Leipzig [n.d.]
    Score 14 p.
    At head of published title: "W. A. Mozart."
    Actually composed by K. F. Abel. Copied and

orchestrated by Mozart in 1764. Cf. Köchel
6 Aufl., Anh. A51, p. 762.

    6129 [Symphony no. 19, Op. 10 no. 1,   *11'50"*
    E major. Knape no. 19]
    1.Allegro 2.Andante 3.Allegro (Rondo)
    2Ob.-2Hn.-Cemb.-Str.
    Ms. ᶜ1976 by The Fleisher Collection of Orches-
    tral Music, Free Library of Philadelphia
    Score 25 p. Large folio
    Composed 1771. This and the following Fleisher
    Collection editions were edited from parts
    first published by R. Bremner, London [1771-
    1785].

    6197 [Symphony no. 20, Op. 10 no. 2,   *12'*
    B-flat major. Knape no. 20]
    1.Allegro assai 2.Andantino 3.Minuetto
    2Ob.-2Hn.-Cemb.-Str.
    Ms. ᶜ1976 by The Fleisher Collection of Orches-
    tral Music, Free Library of Philadelphia
    Score 19 p. Large folio
    Composed 1771.

    4626 [Symphony no. 21, Op. 10 no. 3,   *14'*
    E-flat major. Knape no. 21] Edited by Adam
    Carse
    1.Allegro 2.Andante 3.Presto
    2Ob.(or 2Fl.)-2Hn.-Str.
    Augener, London, ᶜ1935
    Score 12 p.
    Composed 1771. First published 1771 or 1772.

Abel, Karl Friedrich

6312 [Symphony no. 22, Op. 10 no. 4,   *12'*
C major. Knape no. 22]
1.Presto 2.Andante 3.Allegro
2Ob.-2Hn.-Cemb.-Str.
Ms. c1976 by The Fleisher Collection of
Orchestral Music, Free Library of Philadelphia
Score 27 p. Large folio
Composed 1771.

2451 [Symphony no. 23, Op. 10 no. 5, D major.
Knape no. 23]
1.Overture 2.Andantino 3.Tempo di minuetto
2Ob.-2Hn.-Str.
Ms.
Score 26 p.
Original edition published by Bremner in London as Six Symphonies, Op. 10.

6313 [Symphony no. 24, Op. 10 no. 6,   *12'*
A major. Knape no. 24]
1.Allegro 2.Andante un poco adagio 3.Allegro
assai (Presto)
2Ob.-2Hn.-Cemb.-Str.
Ms. c1976 by The Fleisher Collection of
Orchestral Music, Free Library of Philadelphia
Score 26 p. Large folio
Composed 1771.

6248 [Symphony no. 31, Op. 17 no. 1,   *7'*
E-flat major. Knape no. 31]
1.Allegro maestoso 2.Andante 3.Allegro assai
2Ob.-2Hn.-Cemb.-Str.
Ms. c1976 by The Fleisher Collection of
Orchestral Music, Free Library of Philadelphia
Score 26 p. Large folio
Composed 1780 or later.

6459 [Symphony no. 32, Op. 17 no.2,   *8'40"*
B-flat major. Knape no. 32]
1.Allegro 2.Andante 3.Allegro assai (quasi
presto)
2Ob.-2Hn.-Cemb.-Str.
Ms. c1976 by The Fleisher Collection of Orchestral Music, Free Library of Philadelphia
Score 39 p. Large folio
Composed ca.1780.

6792 [Symphony no. 33, Op. 17 no. 3,   *9'30"*
D major. Knape no. 33]
1.Allegro maestoso 2.Andante 3.Allegro vivace
2Ob.-2Hn.-Cemb.-Str.
Ms. c1976 by The Fleisher Collection of Orchestral Music, Free Library of Philadelphia
Score 39 p. Large folio
Composed 1780.

6811 [Symphony no. 34, Op. 17 no. 4,   *9'*
C major. Knape no. 34]
1.Allegro maestoso 2.Andante 3.Allegro ma
non troppo presto
2Ob.-2Hn.-Cemb.-Str.
Ms. c1976 by The Fleisher Collection of Orchestral Music, Free Library of Philadelphia
Score 32 p. Large folio
Composed 1780 or later.

6802 [Symphony no. 35, Op. 17 no. 5,   *10'*
B-flat major. Knape no. 35]
1.Allegro 2.Andante 3.Tempo di minuetto
2Ob.-2Hn.-Cemb.-Str.
Ms. c1976 by The Fleisher Collection of Orchestral Music, Free Library of Philadelphia
Score 28 p. Large folio
Composed 1780.

6837 [Symphony no. 36, Op. 17 no. 6,   9'
G major. Knape no. 36]
1.Allegro molto 2.Andante 3.Allegro non
troppo presto
2Ob.-2Hn.-Cemb.-Str.
Ms. ᶜ1976 by The Fleisher Collection of
Orchestral Music, Free Library of Philadelphia
Score 37 p.
Composed ca.1780.

ABEL, PAUL LOUIS.
b. Clarksdale, Mississippi 23 November 1926

6237 Vignette for orchestra   5'15"
2,2(2nd alt. E.H.),2,2-4,2,3,1-Hp.-Str.
Ms.
Score 14 p. Large folio
*Composed 1962. First performance Rochester,
13 April 1962, Eastman-Rochester Orchestra,
Howard Hanson conductor. Received the Edward
Benjamin award, 13 April 1962.*

ĀBELE, ĀDOLFS.   Blome, Latvia 1889

5119 [Meditation]   8'
2,3*,2(2nd alt. B.Cl.),2-4,2,3,1-Timp.,Cym.-
Cel.,Hp.-Str.
Universal Edition, Vienna, ᶜ1937
Score 33 p.

4873 [The tomb of the hero Lahtschplehsis]   4'
2,2,2,2-4,2,3,1-Timp.,Perc.-Str.
Universal Edition, Vienna, ᶜ1936
Score 17 p.
Lahtschplehsis is a hero in Latvian folklore.

ABERT, JOHANN JOSEPH.
Kochovice, Bohemia 20 September 1832
Stuttgart, Germany 1 April 1915

2160 [Columbus, a musical sea-piece in the   40'
form of a symphony, Op. 31, D major]
1.Empfindungen bei der Abfahrt 2.Seemann-
streiben 3.Abends auf dem Meere 4.Finale:
Gute Zeichen, Empörung, Sturm, Land!
2,2,2,2-4,2,3,Ophicl.-Timp.,B.Dr.-Str.
Schott, Mainz [1865]
Score 197 p.
*Composed 1864. First performance Stuttgart,
26 January 1864, Karl A. Eckert conductor.*

913 [Symphony, Spring, C major]   45'
1.[Spring awakening] 2.[Young spring]
3.[Spring and love] 4.[Spring's victory]

2,2,2,2-4,2,3-Timp.-Str.
Breitkopf & Härtel, Leipzig [1894]
Score 148 p.
*Composed 1893. First performance Stuttgart,
31 January 1894, Hermann Zumpe conductor.*

ABSIL, JEAN.   Péruwelz, Belgium 23 October 1893
Brussels 2 February 1974

6558 [Bulgarian rhapsody for orchestra,
Op. 104]
2(2nd alt. Picc.),2,2,2-4,2,2,1-Timp.,Perc.-
Hp.-Str.
CeBeDem, Brussels, ᶜ1960
Score 32 p.
Based on Bulgarian themes. Composed 1960.

814p [Concerto, piano, Op. 30]   13'
1.Allegro moderato ma energico 2.Andante
3.Final: Molto vivo
Solo Pno.-2,2,2,2-4,2,2,1-Timp.,Perc.-Str.
Ms. ᶜby Jean Absil
Score 72 p. Large folio
*Composed 1937. Entered in competition for Le
Prix Ysaÿe (later called the Concours-Reine
Elisabeth). First performance Brussels, May
1938, L'Orchestre National de Belgique, Franz
André conductor, the composer as soloist.*

1195v [Concerto, violin, Op. 11]   15'
1.Andante moderato 2.Chant funèbre 3.Final
Solo Vn.-2,2,4,3-3,1,1,1-Timp.,Perc.-Cel.,Hp.-
Va.,Vc.,Cb.
Ms. ᶜby Jean Absil
Score 71 p. Large folio
*Composed 1933. First performance Brussels,
1939(?), Orchestre de l'Institut National
Belge de Radiodiffusion (INR), Franz André
conductor, Henri Desclin soloist.*

4899 [Flemish rhapsody, Op. 4]   14'
3*,3*,2,3*-4,2,2,1-Timp.,Perc.-Pno.,Hp.-Str.
Ms. ᶜby Jean Absil
Score 56 p. Large folio
*Based on popular Flemish themes. Composed
1928.*

4678 [Little suite, Op. 20]   9'
1.March 2.Story 3.Carrousel
1,1,1,1-2Hn.-Timp.,Perc.-Str.
Ms. ᶜ1953 by Jean Absil
Score 20 p.
Composed 1935.

4900 [Rhapsody no. 2, Op. 34]   15'
2*,2(2nd alt. E.H.),3,2-4,2,2,1-Timp.,Perc.-
Cel.,Hp.-Str.
Ms.,ᶜ1958 by Jean Absil
Score 44 p. Large folio
Composed 1938.

4905 [Symphonic variations, Op. 50]   18'
3*,3*,4*(1Cl. in E-flat),3*-4,2,2,1-Timp.,
Perc.-Cel.,Hp.-Str.
Ms. ᶜby Jean Absil
Score 96 p. Large folio
*Composed 1942. First performance Brussels,
Orchestre National de Belgique, Charles Münch
conductor.*

Absil, Jean

4901 [Symphony no. 2, Op. 25]   18'
1.Allegro giocoso 2.Andante moderato
3.Molto vivo
3*,3*,4*,3*-4,2,2,1-Timp.,Perc.-Cel.,Hp.-Str.
Ms. ᶜby Jean Absil
Score 134 p.
*Composed 1936. First performance Brussels,
April 1939, Société Philharmonique de Bruxelles, Franz André conductor.*

ACHRON, JOSEPH.   Losdzeye, Lithuania 13 May 1886
                     Hollywood, California 29 April 1943

3463 [Belshazzar. Two excerpts from the   16'
music to Roche's play, Op. 58]
1.Introduction and dance of the priestesses
2.Belshazzar's feast
3*,3*,4*(1Cl. in D),3*-4Sax.(ATBar.B)-4,3,3,1-
Timp.,Perc.-Pno.,Cel.-Str.
Ms.
Score 96 p.
*Commissioned by the Palestine Theatre, 1923.
Originally composed for small orchestra, 1924;
these excerpts reorchestrated, 1931. First
performance Los Angeles, 16 May 1939, Los
Angeles Federal Symphony Orchestra of the WPA,
Gastone Usigli conductor.*

4553 Children's suite, Op. 57. Transcribed   23'
for large orchestra by David Tamkin
In 20 movements
3(2nd&3rd alt. Picc.),3*,3*,3*-4,3,3,1-Timp.,
Perc.-Pno.,Cel.,Hp.-Str.
Ms. ᶜby David Tamkin
Score 94 p. Large folio
Composed 1923. Transcribed 1942.

1071v [Concerto, violin, no. 2, Op. 68]   26'
1.Moderato - Allegro moderato 2.Lento
3.Burla (Allegro molto)
Solo Vn.-3*,2,2,2-Alto Sax.-4Hn.,2Tpt.-Perc.-
Pno.,Cel.-Str.
Ms.
Score 161 p.
*Composed 1932-33; orchestrated 1934. First
performance Los Angeles, 19 December 1936, Los
Angeles Philharmonic Orchestra, Otto Klemperer
conductor, the composer as soloist.*

1129v [Concerto, violin, no. 3, Op. 72]   22'
1.Allegro non troppo 2.Cantabile 3.Dance
(giocoso)
Solo Vn.-3*,2,2,2-4,2,3,1-Timp.,Perc.-Pno.,Hp.
-Str.
Ms.
Score 150 p.
*Commissioned by Jascha Heifetz, 1931 or 1932.
Composed 1936-37. First performance Los
Angeles, 31 March 1939, Los Angeles Philhar-
monic Orchestra, Otto Klemperer conductor, the
composer as soloist.*

2582 Dance improvisation, Op. 37   3'
3*,3*,3*,2-4,2,3,1-Timp.,Perc.-Hp.-Str.
Ms.
Score 25 p.
*Written for the Society for Hebrew Music of
St. Petersburg. Originally composed for*

violin and piano, 1913; orchestrated 1916.
*First performance Petrograd, ca.1916, Pav-
lovsk Summer Symphony Orchestra, the composer
conducting.*

2583 [Golem. Suite from the music to   11'
the play]
1.Creation of the Golem 2.The Golem's rampage
3.The fatigued wanderer (Lullaby) 4.Dance of
the phantom spirits 5.Petrifying of the Golem
2*,2*,2*,2*-2,3,1,1-Perc.-Pno.,Hp.-Vc.,Cb.
Ms.
Score 57 p.
*From the incidental music to Leivick's play.
Originally composed for trumpet, French horn,
violoncello and piano, 1931, on commission
from a private group of actors. Reorchestrated
for the play, 1932. First performance, Second
International Music Festival, Venice, 8 September 1932, Fritz Reiner conductor.*

2584 Hebrew dance, Op. 35 no. 1   5'30"
3*,2,3(1Cl. in E-flat),2-4,2,3,1-Timp.,Perc.-
Pno.,Hp.-Str.
Ms.
Score 47 p.
*Written for the Society for Hebrew Music of St.
Petersburg. Originally composed for violin and
piano, 1912; orchestrated, 1913. First per-
formance Kharkov, Russia, 1913, Kharkov Sym-
phony Orchestra, L. Zeitlin conductor.*

2585 Hebrew lullaby, for small orchestra,   3'
Op. 35 no. 2
1,1*,1,1-Hn.-Hp.-Str.
Ms.
Score 8 p.
*Written for the Society for Hebrew Music of St.
Petersburg. Originally composed for violin and
piano, 1912; orchestrated, 1913. First per-
formance Kharkov, Russia, 1913, Kharkov Sym-
phony Orchestra, L. Zeitlin conductor.*

1856s Improvisation on Jeanie with the   7'
Light Brown Hair, by Stephen C. Foster
Str.
Ms.
Score 13 p.
*Written at the request of Alfred Newman. Com-
posed and orchestrated, 1939. First perform-
ance broadcast over CBS, Los Angeles, 28 May
1939, Los Angeles Philharmonic Orchestra,
Alfred Newman conductor.*

1852s Improvisation on Tambourin, by   3'
Jean-Philippe Rameau
Str.
Ms. ᶜ1940 by Joseph Achron
Score 13 p.
*Originally composed for violin and piano, 1910;
arranged 1938. First performance at a private
concert, 1938 or 1939, Alfred Newman conductor.*

ACKERMANS, H.

1391s Sous ta fenêtre pour orchestre à cordes
Str.
Score: Ms. [6] p.
Parts: Grus, Paris [n.d.]

4

ADALID Y GAMERO, M. DE.   Danlí, Honduras 1872

    3664 Funeral of a rabbit, symphonic poem   7'
    3*,3*,3*,2-4,2,3,1-Timp.,Perc.-Hp.-Str.
    Ms.
    Score 21 p.
    *Composed 1936. First performance Washington,
    D.C., 14 April 1936, United Service Orchestra,
    Lt. Charles Benter conductor.*

ADAM, ADOLPHE CHARLES.   Paris 24 July 1803
                                 Paris 3 May 1856

    4320 [If I were king. Overture]   8'
    2*,2,2,2-4,2Cnt.,3-Timp.,Perc.-Hp.-Str.
    Leduc, Paris [19-?]
    Score 31 p.
    *From the opera in three acts with libretto by
    A. P. d'Ennery and Jules Brésil. First per-
    formance Paris, 4 September 1852.*

    4531 Le toréador, ou L'accord parfait. Overture
    2*,2,2,2-4,2,3-Trgl.-Str.
    Bernard Latte, Paris [1849]
    Score 28 p.
    *From the opera in two acts with libretto by
    Thomas Marie François Sauvage. First perform-
    ance Paris, 18 May 1849.*

ADAME, RAFAEL G. Jalisco, Mexico 11 September 1906

    988m [Concertino no. 1, guitar and orchestra,
    Estilo mariache]
    1.Estilo mariache 2.Estilo, canción mescicana
    3.Estilo mariachi
    Solo Guit.-1,1,1,1-Perc.-Str.
    Ms.
    Score 48 p.

    985m [Concertino no. 3, guitar and orchestra,
    Estilo mariache]
    1.Preludio 2.Andantino - Fuga
    Solo Guit.-1,1,1,1-Str.
    Ms.
    Score 29 p.

ADAMS, GEORGE.   Los Angeles 1917

    3397 Suite for orchestra   11'
    1.Prelude 2.Andante 3.Scherzo
    2(2nd alt. Picc.),2,2,2-4,2,2,1-Timp.,S.Dr.,
    Cym.-Hp.-Str.
    Ms.
    Score 58 p. Large folio
    *Composed 1939-40. First performance Rochester,
    April 1940, Rochester Civic Orchestra, Howard
    Hanson conductor.*

ADJIP, HARRY.   Honolulu 15 January 1888

    3031 Evening (Meditation)   6'
    1,1,2,1-2,2,1-Timp.,Bells-Hp.-Str.
    Ms.
    Score 16 p.
    *Composed 1937. First performance Philadelphia,
    1937, Rittenhouse Concert Orchestra of the WPA,
    Guglielmo Sabatini conductor.*

    2796 A night in Arphah   8'
    2,2,3*,2-4,3,2,1-Timp.,Perc.-Str.
    Ms.
    Score 31 p.
    *Composed 1915-36. First performance Philadel-
    phia, 11 May 1937, Rittenhouse Concert Orches-
    tra of the WPA, Guglielmo Sabatini conductor.*

    2992 To Maalah, suite, Op. 2   35'
    1.Approach of the shepherds 2.Horma, the
    Arabian girl 3.Jedah
    3*,3*,3*,2-4,2,3,1-Timp.,Perc.-Hp.-Str.
    Ms.
    Score 124 p.
    *Composed 1917-38. First performance broadcast
    over Station KYW, Philadelphia, 5 March 1939,
    Senior Orchestra of the Symphony Club of Phila-
    delphia, William F. Happich conductor.*

ADLER, JAMES.   Chicago 19 November 1950

    7212 The classic rag-time suite. A tribute   10'
    to Scott Joplin
    1.Maple-leaf rag 2.The entertainer *and* Cas-
    cade 3.Pleasant moments - Rag-time waltz
    4.The chrysanthemum 5.Rag-time dance (with
    stop-time scherzo) 6.Finale: Maple-leaf rag
    2(2nd alt. Picc.),2,3*,2-4,2,2,1-Perc.-Banjo-
    Str.
    Chappell Music, New York, c1974 by James Adler
    Score 37 p.
    *Based on Scott Joplin's rags for piano. This
    work composed 1973. First performance Chau-
    tauqua, New York, 14 August 1974, Chautauqua
    Festival Orchestra, Everett Lee conductor.*

    2394s A suite for strings   15'
    1.Overture and fugue: Boldly 2.Intermezzo:
    Flowing and songful 3.Scherzo: Very fast and
    agitated 4.Epilogue: Introspective
    Str.
    Ms. c1975 by James Adler
    Score 38 p.
    *Composed 1975. First performance Curtis Insti-
    tute of Music, Philadelphia, 18 February 1976,
    the composer conducting.*

ADLER, SAMUEL H.   Mannheim, Germany 4 March 1928

    6630 [Symphony no. 1]   27'
    1.Gently moving 2.Very slowly 3.Vigorous and
    very rhythmic
    3*,3*,3*,3-4,3,3,1-Timp.,Perc.-Hp.-Str.
    Ms. cby Mercury Music
    Score 187 p. Large folio
    *Commissioned by the University of Texas for
    the Dallas Symphony Orchestra. Composed 1953.
    First performance Dallas, 7 December 1953,
    Dallas Symphony Orchestra, Walter Hendl con-
    ductor.*

    6631 [Symphony no. 2]   25'
    1.Quite slowly 2.Slowly 3.Quite fast and
    triumphant
    3*,3*,3*,3-4,3,3,1-Timp.,Perc.-Pno.-Str.
    Ms. cby Mercury Music
    Score 134 p. Large folio
    Composed 1957. First performance Dallas,

Adlington, Fred

12 February 1958, Dallas Symphony Orchestra, Walter Hendl conductor.

ADLINGTON, FRED.

1331s Three English folk tunes, suite for
string orchestra
1.Three merry men of Kent 2.The keys of Canterbury 3.A clown's dance
Pno.(optional)-Str.
Goodwin & Tabb, London, ᶜ1930
Score 14 p.

ADOLPHUS, MILTON.   New York 27 January 1913

916m Adagio, for solo violin, solo   *10'*
violoncello and sinfonietta, Op. 42
Solo Vn., Solo Vc.-1,1,2,1-Str.
Ms.
Score 14 p.
*Originally composed for violin solo with
string orchestra, 1935. This version commis-
sioned by the Philadelphia Music Center, 1938.
First performance Philadelphia, 8 May 1938,
Philadelphia Music Center Orchestra, Sidney
Fox conductor, Oscar Langman violinist,
Bernard Drossin cellist.*

2758 Four poems, Op. 38   *30'*
1.Allegro 2.Allegretto grazioso 3.Presto
4.Andante affannato
3*,3*,3*,3*-6,4,4,1-Timp.(2 players)-Str.
Ms.
Score 86 p.
Composed 1935.

1761s Prelude and allegro, for string   *6'*
orchestra, Op. 51
Str.
Ms.
Score 12 p.
*Originally composed for two pianos, 1936;
arranged for string orchestra, 1936. First
performance Philadelphia, 8 August 1937, Philadelphia Music Center Orchestra, the composer
conducting.*

1719s Suite, for string orchestra, Op. 47   *25'*
1.Allegro assai 2.Andante molto 3.Valse
burlando 4.Finale: Molto moderato e rigoroso
Str.
Ms.
Score 32 p.
*Originally composed for piano 4-hands, 1935;
arranged for string orchestra, 1936. First
performance Philadelphia, 12 February 1937,
Philadelphia Music Center Orchestra, Arthur
Cohn conductor.*

3058 [Suite no. 2, for orchestra, Op. 62]   *20'*
1.Prelude 2.Gavotte 3.Nocturne 4.Fantasia
2,2,3,2-4,4,4-Timp.-Str.
Ms.
Score 63 p.
Composed 1937.

2764 [Symphony no. 8, Op. 50, B minor]   *30'*
1.Allegro moderato 2.Andante mistico

3.Allegro assai 4.Largo
3*,3*,4*,3*-4,4,4,1-Timp.-Str.
Ms.
Score 130 p.
Composed 1936.

3068 Ulalume, Op. 39b   *10'*
1,2(1st alt. E.H.),3*,3*-4Hn.-Timp.-Str.
Ms.
Score 28 p.
Composed 1935.

2754 War sketches, Op. 35   *25'*
1.Prelude 2.General Pomposen 3.The sentinel
4.Allegro bellicoso 5.Aftermath
3*,2,2,2-4,4,3,1-Timp.(2 players),Perc.-Str.
Ms.
Score 90 p.
*Composed 1935. First performance Philadelphia,
18 May 1938, Philadelphia Music Center Orchestra, Sylvan Levin conductor.*

ADOMIAN, LAN.   Moghilev-Podolsk, Russia 1905

3518 Prelude, Op. 2 [Stage music no. 1]   *7'*
3(3rd alt. Picc.),3*,3*,3*-4,4,3,1-Timp.,Perc.
-2Pno.,Cel.,2Hp.-Str.
Ms.
Score 35 p. Large folio
Composed 1929.

AFFERNI, UGO.   Florence 1 January 1871
                       Leghorn 9 October 1931

1506s [Mandolinata, Italian serenade]
Hp.(ad lib.)-Str.
Score: Ms. 5 p.
Parts: Reinecke, Leipzig, ᶜ1903

1115 [Prince Potemkin. Overture]   *8'*
3*,3*,3*,2-4,3(3rd ad lib.),3,1-Timp.,Perc.-
Hp.-Str.
Oertel, Hannover, ᶜ1911
Score 43 p.
*Opera composed 1897. First performance of
opera Annaberg, Saxony, 1897, the composer
conducting.*

627s [Sweet happiness, Op. 30 *and* The siren,
Op. 20]
Str.(Cb. in no. 2 only)
Bosworth, Leipzig, ᶜ1899
Score 7 p.

AFFROSSIMOV, JOAS VON SELDENECK.

298s Serenade for string orchestra, Op. 4,
D major
1.Marcia 2.Andante (Romanza) 3.Scherzo
4.Finale
Str.
Challier, Berlin [n.d.]
Score 39 p.

AGRÈVES, ERNEST D'.   Belgium 31 March 1880

Also known as: E. van Nieuwenhove

5550 [Nocturne for orchestra, no. 2]
2,2,2,2-3,2,3,1-Hp.-Str.
Édition Buyst, Brussels [n.d.]
Score 13 p.

AGUIRRE, JULIÁN.   Buenos Aires 28 January 1868
                       Buenos Aires 13 August 1924

Suite, De mi país [Of my country]
3798 I.   Preámbulo [Prelude]
3799 II. De mi país [Of my country]
3800 III. Gato [The cat]
2,3*,2,2-2Hn.-Hp.-Str.
Ms.
Scores: 50 p., 53 p., 38 p.
*First performance Conciertos Sinfónicos,
Buenos Aires, 9 September 1910, Alberto Williams conductor.*

3721 [Two Argentine dances. Orchestrated   6'
by Ernest Ansermet]
1.La huella 2.El gato
3*,3*,2,2-4,2,3,1-Timp.,Perc.-Cel.,Hp.-Str.
Ricordi, Milan, ᶜ1938
Miniature score 43 p.

[Two Argentine dances] Transcribed for band
by Mark H. Hindsley
5933 No. 1. La huella [The dance step]
5934 No. 2. El gato [The cat]
3*,2*,5*(1 Alto Cl.),1-4Sax.-4,2,3Cnt.,3,Bar.,
Euph.,2-Timp.,Perc.-Cel.(or Bells or Pno.),
Hp.(or Marimba or Pno.)-Cb.
Ricordi, New York, ᶜ1952
Scores: 12 p., 19 p.
*First performance of transcription, University
of Illinois Concert Band, Mark H. Hindsley
conductor.*

AHN, EAK TAI.   Pyengyang, Korea 1911
                     Barcelona 1965

2812 Pastorale for orchestra, from Korean   10'
life, no. 3
3*,2,2,2-2,2,2-Timp.,Perc.-2Hp.-Str.
Ms.
Score 18 p.
*First performance Budapest, 14 September 1936,
Budapest Radio Symphony Orchestra, the com-
poser conducting.*

AHRENDT, KARL.   Toledo, Ohio 1904

4888 Dance overture   8'
2(2nd alt. Picc.),2,2,2-4,3,3,1-Timp.,Perc.-
Str.
Ms.
Score 54 p. Large folio
*Composed 1946. First performance Urbana,
Illinois, 21 March 1950, University of Illi-
nois Symphony Orchestra, George Kuyper con-
ductor.*

2241s Pastoral for strings   6'
Str.
Ms.
Score 7 p.
Composed 1956. First performance Hamilton,

*Ohio, 1 December 1957, Hamilton Symphony
Orchestra, Joseph Bein conductor.*

6393 Prelude for orchestra   7'
1,1,2,1-2,3,3-Timp.,Perc.-Str.
Ms.
Score 17 p.
*Commissioned by the Ohio University Summer
Music Clinic Orchestra. Composed 1956. First
performance Athens, Ohio, 29 June 1957, Ohio
University Summer Orchestra, the composer con-
ducting.*

AISBERG, ILYA SIMEON.   Odessa 1872

721p [Hebrew caprice, piano and orchestra,   9'
Op. 20]
Solo Pno.-3*,3*,2,2-4,2,3,1-Timp.,Perc.-Str.
Mussektor, Moscow, ᶜ1930
Score 63 p.
*First performance Leningrad, December 1931,
Leningrad Philharmonic Orchestra, A. V. Hauk
conductor, Schmidt soloist.*

AKIMENKO, FEODOR STEPANOVICH.
                    Kharkov 20 February 1876
                    Paris 8 January 1945

808 [Angel, nocturnal poem after Lermontov] 11'
3*,3*,2,2-4,2,3,1-Timp.-Pno.,Hp.-Str.
Leduc, Paris, ᶜ1924
Score 35 p.
*Composed 1912-17. First performance Leningrad,
1922, the composer conducting.*

1346s [Nocturne, for string orchestra]
Str.
Score: Ms. 6 p.
Parts: Bessel, St. Petersburg [n.d.]

1862 [Nocturne no. 2, for orchestra]   8'
3(1st alt. Picc.),2,2,2-4,2,1,1-Hp.-Str.
Ms.
Score 30 p.
Composed 1920.

555 Poème lyrique [Lyric poem] Op. 20   12'
2,2,2,2-4,2,3,1-Timp.-Str.
Belaieff, Leipzig, 1903
Score 73 p.
*Composed 1899. First performance St. Peters-
burg, 1901, N. Rimsky-Korsakov conductor.*

955 [Suite, Op. 28, G minor]   10'
1.Elégie 2.Rêverie 3.Berceuse 4.Petite
valse
1,1,2,1-2Hn.-Str.
Jurgenson, Moscow [n.d.]
Score 28 p.
*Originally composed for piano 1903; arranged
by the composer's brother. First performance
Paris, 1905, the composer conducting.*

1861 Suite de ballet   12'
1.Andantino 2.Carillon céleste 3.Danse
génerale
3*,3*,2,2-4,2,3,1-Glock.-Cel.,2Hp.(2nd ad lib.)
-Str.

Akimenko, Feodor Stepanovich

Ms.
Score 56 p.
*Composed 1916. First performance at a Siloti
concert, Leningrad, 1917, the composer conducting.*

ALALEONA, DOMENICO.
Montegiorgio, Italy 16 November 1881
Montegiorgio 28 December 1928

[Two Italian songs for string orchestra] *10'*
1169s   I. La mamma lontana [The absent mother]
1119s   II. Canzone a ballo [Dance song]
Timp.-Cel.,Hp.-Str.
Ricordi, Milan, ^c1920
Scores: 14 p. Large folio; 22 p.   Miniature
score
*Composed 1917. First performance Rome, 15
June 1917, the composer conducting.*

ALARD, DELPHIN JEAN.   Bayonne 8 March 1815
Paris 22 February 1888

1574s   [Berceuse, for violin with string
orchestra, Op. 49 no. 8]
Solo Vn.-Str.
Score: Ms. [6] p.
Parts: André, Offenbach a.M. [1902?]

999v   [Concerto, violin, no. 2, Op. 34,   *8'*
A major]
1.Allegro maestoso 2.Larghetto 3.Final
Solo Vn.-2,2,2,2-2,2,3-Str.
Score: Ms. 75 p.
Parts: Schott, London [1859]

ALAYRAC, NICOLAS-MARIE D'.
See: DALAYRAC, NICOLAS-MARIE.

ALBÉNIZ, ISAAC MANUEL FRANCISCO.
Camprodón, Catalonia 29 May 1860
Cambo-les-Bains, Pyrenees 18 May 1909

562   [Catalonia, suite for orchestra in   *7'*
three parts. No. 1]
3*,3*,3*,3-4,4,3,1-Timp.,Perc.-2Hp.-Str.
Durand, Paris, ^c1908
Score 58 p.
*Originally composed for piano; orchestrated by
the composer, 1899. First performance Société
Nationale, Paris, 1899.*

1428   Iberia [Book I, no. 1]. Evocation.   *5'*
Transcribed by E. Fernandez Arbós
3*,3*,3*,2-4,2,3-Timp.,Perc.-Hp.-Str.
Eschig, Paris, ^c1927
Score 23 p.
*Iberia in four books originally composed for
piano, 1906-09. Orchestrated 1909. First
performance Madrid, 1909, Orquesta Sinfónica,
E. Fernandez Arbós conductor.*

1477   Iberia [Book I, no. 2]. El puerto.   *5'*
Orchestrated by E. Fernandez Arbós
3*,3*,2,2-4,3,3,1-Timp.,Perc.-Hp.-Str.
Eschig, Paris, ^c1927
Score 35 p.
Orchestrated 1908. First performance Madrid,

*1908, Orquesta Sinfónica, E. Fernandez Arbós
conductor.*

1289   Iberia [Book I, no. 3]. Fête Dieu à   *6'*
Séville. Transcribed by E. Fernandez Arbós
3*,3*,4*(1Cl. in D),3*-4,4,3,1-Timp.,Perc.-Cel.,
2Hp.-Str.
Eschig, Paris, ^c1927
Score 43 p.
*Orchestrated 1909 at the composer's request.
First performance Madrid, 1909, Orquesta Sin-
fónica, E. Fernandez Arbós conductor.*

6227   Iberia [Book II, no. 4]. Rondeña.   *7'*
Transcribed by Carlos Surinach
2(both alt. Picc.),2(2nd alt. E.H.),2,2-4,2,3,
1-Timp.,Perc.-Cel.,Hp.-Str.
Associated Music Publishers, New York, ^c1956
Score 45 p. Large folio
*Transcribed 1954. First performance Philadel-
phia, 5 January 1956, Philadelphia Orchestra,
Eugene Ormandy conductor.*

6228   Iberia [Book II, no. 5]. Almería.   *7'*
Transcribed by Carlos Surinach
2(both alt. Picc.),2(2nd alt. E.H.),2,2-4,2,3,
1-Timp.,Perc.-Hp.-Str.
Associated Music Publishers, New York, ^c1956
Score 41 p. Large folio
*Transcribed 1955. First performance Philadel-
phia, 5 January 1956, Philadelphia Orchestra,
Eugene Ormandy conductor.*

1516   Iberia [Book II, no. 6]. Triana.   *5'*
Orchestrated by E. Fernandez Arbós
3*,3*,3*,3-4,3,3,1-Timp.,Perc.-Cel.,2Hp.-Str.
Eschig, Paris, ^c1927
Score 37 p.
*Orchestrated 1916. First performance Madrid,
1919, Orquesta Sinfónica, E. Fernandez Arbós
conductor.*

1929   Iberia [Book III, no. 7]. El   *5'*
Albaicin. Orchestrated by E. Fernandez Arbós
3*,3*,3*,3-Ten.Sax.(or B.Cl.)-4,3,3,1-Timp.,
Perc.-Cel.,2Hp.-Str.
Eschig, Paris, ^c1927
Score 42 p.
*Orchestrated 1919. First performance Madrid,
1919, Orquesta Sinfónica, E. Fernandez Arbós
conductor.*

6236   Iberia [Book III, no. 8]. El polo.   *9'*
Transcribed by Carlos Surinach
2(both alt. Picc.),2(2nd alt. E.H.),2,2-4,2,3,
1-Timp.,Perc.-Hp.-Str.
Associated Music Publishers, New York, ^c1956
Score 53 p. Large folio
*Transcribed 1955. First performance Philadel-
phia, 26 March 1956, Philadelphia Orchestra,
Eugene Ormandy conductor.*

6229   Iberia [Book III, no. 9]. Lavapies.   *7'*
Transcribed by Carlos Surinach
2(both alt. Picc.),2(2nd alt. E.H.),2,2-4,2,3,
1-Timp.,Perc.-Hp.-Str.
Associated Music Publishers, New York, ^c1956
Score 46 p. Large folio

Transcribed 1955. First performance Philadelphia, 16 February 1956, Philadelphia Orchestra, Eugene Ormandy conductor.

6230 Iberia [Book IV, no. 10]. Málaga.   5'
Transcribed by Carlos Surinach
2(both alt. Picc.),2(2nd alt. E.H.),2,2-4,2,3,
1-Timp.,Perc.-Hp.-Str.
Associated Music Publishers, New York, ᶜ1956
Score 51 p. Large folio
Transcribed 1955. First performance Philadelphia, 16 February 1956, Philadelphia Orchestra, Eugene Ormandy conductor.

6226 Iberia [Book IV, no. 11]. Jérez.   8'
Transcribed by Carlos Surinach
2(both alt. Picc.),2(2nd alt. E.H.),2,2-4,2,3,
1-Timp.,Perc.-Hp.-Str.
Associated Music Publishers, New York, ᶜ1956
Score 45 p. Large folio
Transcribed 1955. First performance Philadelphia, 16 February 1956, Philadelphia Orchestra, Eugene Ormandy conductor.

6235 Iberia [Book IV, no. 12]. Eritaña.   7'
Transcribed by Carlos Surinach
2(both alt. Picc.),2(2nd alt. E.H.),2,2-4,2,3,
1-Timp.,Perc.-Hp.-Str.
Associated Music Publishers, New York, ᶜ1956
Score 42 p. Large folio
Transcribed 1955. First performance Philadelphia, 16 February 1956, Philadelphia Orchestra, Eugene Ormandy conductor.

6066 [Merlin. Symphonic suite. Arranged for
orchestra by Manuel M. Ponce]
1.Preludio 2.Andante 3.Danza 4.Final
3*,3*,3*,3-4,4,3,1-Timp.,Cym.-2Hp.-Str.
Ms.
Score 59 p. Large folio
Originally composed 1897-1906 as the first part of a dramatic trilogy (never completed), with a libretto by Francis Coutts, based on the Arthurian legends of Thomas Malory.

1389 [Pepita Jiménez. Interlude]
3*,3*,3*,2-4,2,4-Timp.-2Hp.-Str.
Breitkopf & Härtel, Leipzig, ᶜ1896, 1904
Score 18 p.
First performance Barcelona, 1896.

255p [Spanish rhapsody for two pianos,   12'
Op. 70. Transcribed for piano and orchestra
by Cristóbal Halffter]
Solo Pno.-3*,3*,2-4,2,3,1-Timp.,Perc.-Cel.,
Hp.-Str.
Unión Musical Española, Madrid, ᶜ1962
Score 105 p.
Originally composed for two pianos ca.1886.

6721 [Suite española, suite no. 1. No. 5.
Asturias (Leyenda). Transcribed for orchestra]
3*,3*,2,2-4,2-Timp.,S.Dr.-Str.
Ms.
Score 29 p. Large folio
Originally composed for piano. Transcriber not known.

ALBERSTOETTER, CARL.

555m Ballade (Koncertstück) [for solo   12'
harp and orchestra] Op. 3
Solo Hp.-2,2,2,2-4,2,3-Str.
Zimmermann, Leipzig, ᶜ1900
Score 26 p.

ALBERT, EUGEN D'.   Glasgow 10 April 1864
                             Riga, Latvia 3 March 1932

Full name: Eugene Francis Charles d'Albert.

6306 [Cain. Prelude]   9'
3(3rd alt. Picc.),3*,3,3*-4,3,3,1-Timp.,B.Dr.-
Str.
Bote & Bock, Berlin, ᶜ1901
Score 47 p.
From the opera in one act with libretto by Heinrich Bulthaupt. First performance Berlin, 17 February 1900.

1799 [Cinderella, a little suite for   25'
orchestra in five movements, Op. 33]
1.[Cinderella on the hearth] 2.[Pigeon in the
ashes] 3.[Ball in the king's castle] 4.[The
prince and the ride with the wicked sisters]
5.[Cinderella's wedding]
3(3rd alt. Picc.),2(2nd alt. E.H.),2(2nd alt.
B.Cl.),2(2nd alt. C.Bn.)-2,3-Timp.,Perc.-Cel.,
Hp.-Str.
Forberg, Leipzig, ᶜ1924
Score 48 p.
Composed 1924. First performance Essen, 15 December 1924, Max Fiedler conductor.

600p [Concerto, piano, no. 1, Op. 2,   46'
B minor]
In one movement
Solo Pno.-2(2nd alt. Picc.),2,2,2-4,2,3,1-
Timp.-Str.
Bote & Bock, Berlin [1884]
Score 141 p.
Composed 1883-84. First performance Berlin, 1884, Karl Klindworth conductor, the composer as soloist.

498p [Concerto, piano, no. 2, Op. 12,   20'
E major]
In one movement
Solo Pno.-2,2,2,2-4,2-Timp.-Str.
Bote & Bock, Berlin, ᶜ1893
Score 58 p.
Composed 1892. First performance Bremen, 29 November 1892, the composer as soloist.

571c [Concerto, violoncello, Op. 20,   24'
C major]
In one movement
Solo Vc.-2,2,2,2-4,2-Timp.-Str.
Forberg, Leipzig, ᶜ1900
Score 55 p.
Composed 1879. First performance Frankfurt, 1880, Hugo Becker soloist.

1155s [Evening's serenade]
Arranged by Arnaud
Str.

Albert, Eugen d'

Score: Ms. 7 p.
Parts: Decourcelle, Nice, c1913, 1922

1004 [Ghismonda. Introduction to Act III]   4'
3,3*,3*,3-4,3,3,1-Timp.-Hp.-Str.
Breitkopf & Härtel, Leipzig, c1897
Score 11 p.
*From the opera first performed Dresden, 28
November 1895, Ernst von Schuch conductor.*

1810 Der Improvisator. [Overture]   3'
3*,2,2,2-4,3,3,1-Timp.,Perc.-Hp.-Str.
Bote & Bock, Berlin, c1901
Score 44 p.
*From the opera composed 1900. First perform-
ance Berlin, 2 February 1902, Karl Muck conductor.*

1055 Ouvertüre für grosses Orchester zu   14'
Grillparzer's Esther, Op. 8
3*,2,2,2-4,2,3,1-Timp.,Perc.-Str.
Bote & Bock, Berlin [1888]
Score 72 p.
*From the opera composed 1887. First perform-
ance at a Philharmonic Concert, Vienna, 1887.*

ALBINONI, TOMASO.   Venice 8 June 1671
    Venice 17 January 1750

241m [Concerto, oboe and string orchestra,   8'
Concerto a cinque, Op. 7 no. 3, B-flat major]
Edited by Bernhard Paumgartner
1.Allegro 2.Adagio 3.Allegro
Solo Ob.-Cemb.-Str.
Boosey & Hawkes, London, c1948
Score 25 p.
Composed ca.1710.

240m [Concerto, oboe and string orchestra,   7'
Concerto a cinque, Op. 7 no. 6, D major]
Edited by Bernhard Paumgartner
1.Allegro 2.Adagio 3.Allegro
Solo Ob.-Cemb.-Str.
Boosey & Hawkes, London, c1948
Score 25 p.
Composed ca.1710.

228m [Concerto, oboe and string orchestra,
Concerto a cinque, Op. 9 no. 2, D minor]
Edited by Fritz Kneusslin
1.Allegro e non presto 2.Adagio 3.Allegro
Solo Ob.-Cemb.-Str.
Kneusslin, Basel, 1955

Score 19 p.
Composed ca.1720.

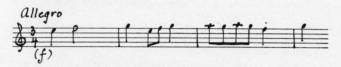

255m [Concerto, 2 oboes and string orchestra,
Concerto a cinque, Op. 7 no. 5, C major]
Edited by Fritz Kneusslin
1.Allegro 2.Adagio 3.Allegro
2 Solo Ob.-Cemb.-Str.
Kneusslin, Basel, c1954
Score 8 p.
Composed ca.1710.

282m [Concerto, 2 oboes and string   11'
orchestra, Concerto a cinque, Op. 9 no. 9,
C major] Edited by Remo Giazotto
1.Allegro 2.Adagio 3.Allegro
2 Solo Ob.-Hpscd.-Str.
Ricordi, Milan, c1959
Score 40 p.
Composed ca.1720.

2101s [Concerto, string orchestra,   10'
Concerto a cinque, Op. 5 no. 7, D minor]
Edited by Ettore Bonelli
1.Allegro 2.Adagio 2a.Adagio (ossia)
3.Allegro
Solo Vn.-Str.
Zanibon, Padua, c1948
Score 12 p.
*Composed 1710. The second Adagio is from the
eighth concerto by Albinoni.*

732v [Concerto, violin, A major] Edited   8'
by Emilio Pente
1.Allegro 2.Adagio 3.Allegro moderato
Solo Vn.-1,1,1,1-2Hn.-Str.
Schott, Mainz, c1926
Score 24 p.

Albrechtsberger, Johann Georg

940v [Concerto, violin and string orchestra,
C major] Edited by Walter Upmeyer
1.Allegro 2.Adagio 3.Allegro
Solo Vn.-Cemb.(or Org.)-Str.
Vieweg, Berlin, 1930
Score 11 p.
*First published ca.1718 in a collection of
Concerti a Cinque.*

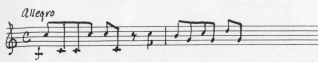

283v [Concerto, violin and string orchestra,
Concerto a cinque, Op. 9 no. 7, D major]
Edited by Fritz Kneusslin
1.Allegro 2.Andante e sempre piano 3.Allegro
Solo Vn.-Str.
Kneusslin, Basel, c1973
Score 22 p.
Composed ca.1720.

331v [Concerto, violin and string   11'
orchestra, Concerto a cinque, Op. 9 no. 10,
F major] Edited by Remo Giazotto
1.Allegro 2.Adagio 3.Allegro
Solo Vn.-Hpscd.-Str.
Ricordi, Milan, c1961
Score 39 p.
Composed ca.1720.

2293s [Concerto, 2 violins and string
orchestra, Concerto a cinque, Op. 5 no. 5,
A minor] Edited by Fritz Kneusslin
1.Allegro 2.Adagio 3.Allegro
2 Solo Vn.-Cemb.-Str.
Kneusslin, Basel, c1954
Score 10 p.
Composed 1710.

2259s [Sinfonia a quattro, no. 3, string   11'
orchestra, G major] Edited by Remo Giazotto
1.Allegro 2.Minuetto 3.Allegro
Str.
Ricordi, Milan, c1961
Score 12 p.

2258s [Sinfonia a quattro, no. 5, string   9'
orchestra, D major] Edited by Remo Giazotto
1.Allegro 2.Minuetto 3.Allegro
Str.
Ricordi, Milan, c1961
Score 10 p.
Composed ca.1735.

2257s [Sonata (Sinfonia) a cinque, Op. 2   9'
no. 3, A major] Edited by Remo Giazotto
1.Grave - Allegro 2.Adagio 3.Allegro
Cemb.-Str.(without Cb.)
Ricordi, Milan, c1959
Score 23 p.
Composed 1707.

ALBRECHTSBERGER, JOHANN GEORG.
            Klosterneuberg, near Vienna 3 February 1736
                    Vienna 7 March 1809

4403 Sinfonia concertino in D major
      1.Allegro 2.Andante 3.Menuetto 4.Presto
      2,2,0,2-2,2-Timp.-Str.
      Score: Denkmäler der Tonkunst in Österreich,
      XVI/2. Breitkopf & Härtel, Leipzig, 1909.
      Edited by Oskar Kapp. 45 p.
      Parts: Ms. c1976 by The Fleisher Collection of
      Orchestral Music, Free Library of Philadelphia

Alfvén, Hugo

6183 [Gustav II Adolf suite, Op. 49.   4'
I: Vision]
3,3*,3*,3*-4,3,3,1-Timp.,Perc.-Str.
Carl Gehrmans, Stockholm, C1943
Score 8 p.
*Suite commissioned by the Royal Opera, Stock-
holm. Composed 1932. First complete performance Stockholm, 1932, Royal Opera Orchestra.*

6184 [Gustav II Adolf suite, Op. 49.   3'
II: Intermezzo]
3*,3*,3*,3*-4,3,3,1-Timp.,Cym.,B.Dr.-Str.
Carl Gehrmans, Stockholm, C1943
Score 12 p.

6186 [Gustav II Adolf suite, Op. 49.   6'
III: Chapel Imperial]
3,1,3*,3*(or 2,2,2,3*)-4,3,3,1-Timp.,Gong,
B.Dr.-Cel.-Str.
Carl Gehrmans, Stockholm, C1943
Score 12 p.

2201s [Gustav II Adolf suite, Op. 49.   3'
IVa: Saraband]
Str.
Carl Gehrmans, Stockholm, C1938
Score 3 p.

226m [Gustav II Adolf suite, Op. 49.   1'30"
IVb: Bourrée]
3Bn.(or 2Bn. and Vc.)
Carl Gehrmans, Stockholm, C1938
Score 3 p.

4992 [Gustav II Adolf suite, Op. 49.   3'
IVc: Minuet]
2,2,2,2-2,2-Timp.-Str.
Carl Gehrmans, Stockholm, C1938
Score 7 p.

6188 [Gustav II Adolf suite, Op. 49.   4'
V: Elegy]
0,1,2,1-Str.
Carl Gehrmans, Stockholm, C1938
Score 4 p.

6189 [Gustav II Adolf suite, Op. 49.   10'
VI: Breitenfeld, a battle painting]
3(3rd alt. Picc. ad lib.),3*(E.H. ad lib.),3*
(B.Cl. ad lib.),3*(C.Bn. ad lib.)-4,3(3rd ad
lib.),3,1-Timp.,Perc.-Str.
Carl Gehrmans, Stockholm, C1942
Score 49 p.

762 [Swedish rhapsody no. 1, Midsummer   13'
vigil, Op. 19]
3(3rd alt. Picc.),3(3rd alt. E.H.),3*(2nd alt.
Cl. in E-flat),3-4,2,3,1-Timp.,Perc.-2Hp.-Str.
Hansen, Copenhagen [n.d.]
Score 66 p.
*Composed 1903. First performance Stockholm,
1904, the composer conducting.*

6182 [Swedish rhapsody no. 3, Dalecarlian   18'
rhapsody, Op. 48]
3(2nd&3rd alt. Picc.),3*,3*(1st alt. Sop.Sax.),
3*-4,2,3,1-Timp.,Cym.,B.Dr.-Hp.-Str.

Wilhelm Hansen, Copenhagen, C1941
Score 63 p.
Composed 1932.

1129 [Symphony no. 2, Op. 11, D major]   40'
1.Moderato 2.Allegro 3.Fuga: Allegro
energico
3(3rd alt. Picc.),2(2nd alt. E.H.),3*,3*-4,2,
3,1-Timp.,Perc.-Str.
Schott, London [1900]
Score 213 p.
Composed 1900. First performance Mainz, 1900.

4866 [Symphony no. 3, Op. 23, E major]   35'
1.Allegro con brio 2.Andante 3.Presto
4.Allegro con brio
3(3rd alt. Picc.),3(3rd alt. E.H.),4*,3-6,3,3,
1-Timp.-Str.
Abr. Hirsch, Stockholm [n.d.]
Score 165 p.
Composed 1905.

1564 [Symphony no. 4, Op. 39, C minor]   45'
In one movement
4*,4*,4*(1Cl. in E-flat),4*-8,4,3,1-Timp.,
Perc.-Pno.,Cel.,2Hp.-Sop.&Ten. Solos without
words-Str.
Universal Edition, Vienna, C1922
Score 192 p.
*Composed 1918. First performance Stockholm,
4 October 1919, the composer conducting.*

6086 [Synnöve Solbakken, suite from the   22'
film music, Op. 50]
1.Sunday morning in the wood 2.Young love
3.Heartache 4.Torbjörn and Synnöve 5.Longing
6.At Solbakken
2,2,2,2-2Hn.-Pno.,Hp.-Str.
Nordiska Musikförlaget, Stockholm, C1935
Score 87 p.
*Based on Norwegian folk melodies and themes
by Ole Bull and Halfdan Kjerulf. Composed
1934 for the Björnson film.*

ALLAGA, GÉZA.

1612s [Rákóczi march. Transcribed by Géza
Allaga]
Str.(Cb. ad lib.)
Rozsnyai, Budapest [n.d.]
Score 5 p.

ALLEN, FRANCIS BERTRAND.
                    b. Philadelphia 17 December 1906

1073v Suite marihuana, for solo violin   14'
and orchestra, Op. 1
1.Muggle I 2.Muggle II 3.Muggle III
Solo Vn.-2,2,2,2-4,2-Hp.-Str.
Ms.
Score 65 p.
*Composed 1935. First performance of Muggle II
only broadcast over Station KYW, Philadelphia,
1936, Senior Orchestra of the Symphony Club
of Philadelphia, William F. Happich conductor, Frank Costanzo soloist.*

ALLENDE SARÓN, PEDRO HUMBERTO.
Santiago, Chile 29 June 1885
Santiago 16 August 1959

1149v [Concerto, violin, Sinfónico, D major]
1.Allegro moderato 2.Andantino con moto, ada-
gio 3.Allegro mosso
Solo Vn.-2,2(2nd alt. E.H.),2,2-4,2-Timp.-Hp.-
Str.
Ms.
Score 64 p. Large folio
*First performance Santiago, 27 November 1942,
Orquesta Sinfónica de Chile, Armando Carvajal
conductor, Fredy Wang soloist. Awarded Second
Prize at the Music Festival, Santiago, 1941.*

261 [Three melodies of national Chilean   12'
character]
1.X Tonada 2.XI Tonada 3.XII Tonada
3*(3rd alt. Picc.),3*,3*,3*-4,3,3,1-Timp.-Cel.,
2Hp.-Vocal chorus in no. 1(Sop.& Contralto
ad lib.)-Str.
Senart, Paris, c1930
Score 34 p.
*Composed 1929. First performance Paris, 30
January 1930, Walther Straram conductor.*

3514 [The voice of the streets, symphonic poem]
3*(3rd alt. Picc.),3*,3*,3*-4,3,3,1-Timp.-Cel.,
Hp.-Str.
Ms.
Score 55 p.
*Composed 1920. First performance Santiago,
20 May 1921, Juan Casanova conductor.*

ALMAND, CLAUDE.   Winnsboro, Louisiana 31 May 1915
Jacksonville, Florida 12 September 1957

4326 Chorale for chamber orchestra   5'
1,1,2-2Hn.-Str.
Ms.
Score 15 p.
*Originally composed for string quartet 1942.
Transcribed 1943. First performance Nashville,
May 1943, Peabody College Orchestra, C. B.
Hunt conductor.*

3395 Symphony, The waste land   29'
1.Andante moderato 2.Largo 3.Presto
4.Allegro moderato con energia
3*,3*,2,2-4,3,3,1-Timp.,Perc.-Str.
Ms.
Score 135 p. Large folio
*Composed 1940. First performance Rochester,
19 April 1940, Rochester Civic Orchestra,
Howard Hanson conductor.*

4327 Toccata   5'
1,1,2,1-2,1-Timp.-Pno.-Str.
Ms.
Score 36 p.
*Originally composed for piano, 1941. Tran-
scribed 1943. First performance Louisville,
March 1945, Louisville Orchestra, Robert
Whitney conductor.*

ALNAR, HASSAN FERID.
b. Constantinople 11 March 1906

4994 [Prelude and two dances]   12'
2,2,2,2-2,2-Timp.,Perc.-Str.
Universal-Edition, Vienna, c1935
Score 70 p.
Composed 1935.

ALPAERTS, FLOR. Antwerp, Belgium 12 September 1876
Antwerp 5 October 1954

758m [Concert piece for trumpet and string
orchestra, B minor]
Solo Tpt.-Str.
Ms.
Score 11 p.

ALTEMARK, JOACHIM.

4357 [Old military music, suite transcribed
for wind orchestra by Joachim Altemark]
In 9 movements
2*,2,3(1Cl. in E-flat),1-2Cornettino,2Alto Hn.
2Flügelhn.,2Ten. Hn.,2Waldhn.,2Tpt.,2Tbn.,Bar.,
2Tuba-Perc.
Chr. Friedrich Vieweg, Berlin, c1941
Score 19 p.
*Based on seven manuscript instrumental parts
in the Bavarian State Library*

4363 [Two old Saxon fanfare marches. Transcribed for 3 trumpets, timpani, and wind
orchestra by Joachim Altemark]
2*,2,4(1Cl. in E-flat),1-2Flügelhn.,2Cnt.,
2Alto Hn.,2Ten. Hn.,2Waldhn.4Tpt.)1Tpt. in
E-flat),2Tbn.,Bar.,2Tuba-Timp.
Chr. Friedrich Vieweg, Berlin [1940/41]
Score in reduction 11 p.
Based on old manuscripts.

ALTENBURG, JOHANN ERNST.
Weissenfels, Germany 15 June 1734
Bitterfeld, Germany 14 May 1801

4338 Concerto for clarini and timpani.   4'30"
Edited by Robert D. King
1.Allegro 2.Andante 3.Vivace
7Cnt.(2Hn. may substitute for Cnt.VI/VII)-Timp.
Music for Brass, North Easton, Mass., 1947
Score 11 p.
*This work appears among the examples given in
the back of Altenburg's Versuch einer Anlei-
tung zur Heroisch-Musikalischen Trompeter -
und Pauker-Kunst (Halle, 1795). This edition
lowers the music a major third and adds tempo,
dynamic and phrase markings.*

Alter, Martha

ALTER, MARTHA.　　New Bloomfield, Pennsylvania 1904

　3008　[Anthony Comstock, or a puritan's　　24'
　　progress. Suite from the ballet]
　　1.Prelude: Comstock's prayer　2.Dances from
　　Scene of the Seventies　3.Dance of the satyr
　　4.Comstock's vision　5.Dance of conflict
　　3*,3*,3*(2nd alt. Cl. in E-flat),3*-4,3,3,1-
　　Timp.,Perc.-Pno.,Cel.,Hp.-Str.
　　Ms.
　　Score 148 p.
　　*Composed 1934.　First performance of complete
　　ballet Festival of American Music, Rochester,
　　4 May 1934, Rochester Civic Orchestra, Howard
　　Hanson conductor.*

ALWYN, WILLIAM.
　　　　　　　b. Northampton, England 7 November 1905

　7094　Fanfare for a joyful occasion　　　5'
　　4Hn.,3Tpt.,3Tbn.,Tuba-Timp.,Perc.
　　Oxford University Press, London, ᶜ1964
　　Score 13 p.

AMANI, NIKOLAI NIKOLAYEVICH.
　　　　　　　　　St. Petersburg 4 April 1872
　　　　　　　　　Yalta, Crimea 4 October 1904

　1067v　Orientale. Arranged for violin and　　4'
　　orchestra by Mischa Elman
　　Solo Vn.-3*,3*,3*,2-4Hn.-Timp.,Perc.-Cimbalon,
　　Cel.,Hp.-Str.
　　Ms.
　　Score 16 p.
　　*Originally composed for piano; arranged 1917.
　　First performance Philadelphia, 16 November
　　1917, Philadelphia Orchestra, Leopold Stokow-
　　ski conductor, Mischa Elman soloist.*

AMBERG, JOHAN.　　　　Copenhagen 20 October 1846
　　　　　　　　　　　　　Copenhagen 1914

　549p　[Mazurka, piano and string orchestra,
　　C minor]
　　Solo Pno.-Str.
　　Hansen, Copenhagen [n.d.]
　　Score 25 p.

　398s　[A midnight chat, humorous sketch]
　　Str.
　　Hansen, Copenhagen [n.d.]
　　Score 13 p.

　1341s　Three sketches, for flute and string
　　orchestra, Op. 13
　　1.Pastorale　2.Remembrance　3.Tarantelle
　　Solo Fl.-Str.
　　Score: Ms. 20 p.
　　Parts: Hansen, Copenhagen [n.d.]

AMBROSIO, ALFREDO D'.　　　Naples 13 June 1871
　　　　　　　　　　　　　　　Nice 29 December 1914

　639v　[Aria, violin and orchestra, Op. 22]
　　Solo Vn.-1,1*,2,2-2Hn.-Hp.-Str.
　　Decourcelle, Nice, ᶜ1904
　　Score 13 p.

　1066s　[Berceuse, Op. 30, F major]
　　Solo Vn.-Str.
　　Score: Ms. 6 p.
　　Parts: Decourcelle, Nice, ᶜ1920

　511v　[Canzonetta, violin and string　　　2'
　　orchestra, no. 1, Op. 6]
　　Solo Vn.-Str.
　　Decourcelle, Nice, ᶜ1898, 1907
　　Score 3 p.
　　*Composed 1898.　First performance Nice, 1898,
　　N. Gervasio conductor.*

　895v　[Canzonetta, violin and string　　　3'
　　orchestra, no. 2, Op. 28]
　　Solo Vn.-Str.
　　Score: Ms. 5 p.
　　Parts: Decourcelle, Nice, ᶜ1911
　　*Composed 1911.　First performance Nice, October
　　1911, N. Gervasio conductor.*

　961v　[Canzonetta, violin and orchestra,　　4'
　　no. 3, Op. 47]
　　Solo Vn.-2,1,2,1-Hn.-Str.
　　Score: Ms. 18 p.
　　Parts: Decourcelle, Nice, ᶜ1911
　　*Composed 1911.　First performance Nice, Janu-
　　ary 1912, N. Gervasio conductor.*

　437v　[Concerto, violin, no. 1, Op. 29,　　25'
　　B minor]
　　1.Grandioso, moderato e sostenuto　2.Andante
　　3.Final: Allegro
　　Solo Vn.-3*,2,2,2-4,2,3-Timp.-Hp.-Str.
　　Decourcelle, Nice, ᶜ1904
　　Score 111 p.
　　*Composed 1903.　First performance Berlin, 29
　　October 1904, Arrigo Serato soloist.*

　493v　[Concerto, violin, no. 2, Op. 51,　　29'
　　G minor]
　　1.Allegro moderato　2.Andante moderato
　　3.Allegro energico
　　Solo Vn.-2,2,2,2-4,2,3-Timp.,Trgl.-Hp.-Str.
　　Decourcelle, Nice, ᶜ1913
　　Score 151 p.
　　*Composed 1912.　First performance Paris, 6
　　April 1913, the composer conducting, Georges
　　Enesco soloist.*

　960v　[Confession, violin and orchestra,　　4'
　　Op. 38 no. 1]
　　Solo Vn.-1,1,2,1-2Hn.-Str.
　　Score: Ms. 22 p.
　　Parts: Decourcelle, Nice, ᶜ1930
　　*Composed 1908.　First performance Nice, Decem-
　　ber 1909.*

　68s　[Dream, string orchestra, E-flat major]
　　Str.
　　Decourcelle, Nice, ᶜ1898
　　Score 6 p.

　674　[Four orchestral pieces, Op. 3]　　　14'
　　1.Andantino　2.Peasant's wife　3.Round dance
　　of the elves　4.Tarantella
　　3*,2,2,2-2,2,3-Timp.,Perc.-Hp.(ad lib.)-Str.
　　Decourcelle, Nice, ᶜ1897

Ambrosius, Hermann

Score 48 p.
Composed 1896. First performance Nice, 1896,
N. Gervasio conductor.

520s [Frolicking, scherzino for string
orchestra]
Str.
Decourcelle, Nice, ^c1896
Score 3 p.

735 [Hersilia, suite from the ballet on   20'
M. Alfred Mortier's libretto]
1.Introduction, apparition and dance of the
Ondines 2.Larghetto 3.Scherzino 4.Dance of
the Naiades 5.Waltz of the sirens 6.Fantas-
tic round
2(2nd alt. Picc.),2,2,2-4,2,3,1-Timp.,Perc.-
Hp.-Str.
Decourcelle, Nice, ^c1905
Score 124 p.
Composed 1904. First performance Nice, 1905.

495v Introduction et humoresque [violin   5'
and orchestra] Op. 25
Solo Vn.-2,2,2,2-2Hn.-Str.
Decourcelle, Nice, ^c1905
Score 15 p.
Composed 1904. First performance Nice, March
1905, N. Gervasio conductor.

666c Légende, pour violoncelle avec   4'
accompagnement d'orchestre, Op. 32
Solo Vc.-2,2,2,2-2Hn.-Str.
Score: Ms. 16 p.
Parts: Decourcelle, Nice, ^c1905, 1911
First performance Nice, February 1911, N.
Gervasio conductor.

1131s Madrigal [for string orchestra] Op. 26
Solo Vn.-Str.
Score: Ms. 6 p.
Parts: Decourcelle, Nice, ^c1920

612v Mazurka [for violin and orchestra]   8'
Op. 11
Solo Vn.-2,1,2,1-2,2,3-Timp.-Str.
Decourcelle, Nice, ^c1899
Score 19 p.
Composed 1899. First performance Nice, Octo-
ber 1899, N. Gervasio conductor.

1077s [Novelletta, string orchestra, no. 1,
Op. 16, G major]
Solo Vn.-Str.
Score: Ms. 5 p.
Parts: Decourcelle, Nice, ^c1920

1154s [Novelletta, string orchestra, no. 2,
Op. 20, E-flat major]
Solo Vn.-Str.
Score: Ms. 9 p.
Parts: Decourcelle, Nice, ^c1920

1070s Pavane [for string orchestra] G major
Str.
Score: Ms. 8 p.
Parts: Decourcelle, Nice, ^c1911

494v Romance [for violin and orchestra]   5'
Op. 9
Solo Vn.-2,1,2,1-2Hn.-Timp.-Hp.(or Pno.)-Str.
Decourcelle, Nice, ^c1899
Score 11 p.
Composed 1899. First performance Nice, March
1899, N. Gervasio conductor.

736 [Scattered leaves, suite, Op. 33]   14'
1.Nocturne 2.Gavotte et musette 3.Intermezzo
4.Waltz
2,2,2,2-2Hn.-Str.
Decourcelle, Nice, ^c1906
Score 32 p.
Originally composed for piano; orchestrated by
the composer in 1906. First performance Nice,
1906, N. Gervasio conductor.

971v [Serenade, violin and orchestra,   4'
Op. 4, D major]
Solo Vn.-2,1,2,1-2Hn.-Timp.-Str.
Score: Ms. 21 p.
Parts: Decourcelle, Nice [n.d.]
Composed 1898. First performance Nice, Febru-
ary 1899, N. Gervasio conductor.

444c Spleen, pour violoncelle solo et orchestre
à cordes
Solo Vc.-Str.
Decourcelle, Nice, ^c1926
Score 6 p.

AMBROSIUS, HERMANN.   Hamburg 25 July 1897

344p [Concerto, piano and string   20'
orchestra, G minor]
1.Allegro 2.Largo e con espressivo 3.Allegro
giocoso
Solo Pno.-Str.
Ms.
Score 23 p.
Composed 1946. First performance Leipzig,
1949, Laien-Orchester, Kurt Beilschmidt con-
ductor, Kurt Prinz soloist.

676c [Concerto, violoncello, D minor]   25'
1.Allegro moderato 2.Andante moderato
3.Allegro vivace
Solo Vc.-2(2nd alt. Picc.),2,2,2-2,2,3-Timp.,
Perc.-Str.
Filser, Augsburg [n.d.]
Score 48 p.
Composed ca.1927. First performance ca.1928,
Berliner Sinfonieorchester, Alfred Szendrei
conductor, Afrem Kinkulkin soloist.

2127s Divertimento für Streichorchester   20'
1.Andante con moto 2.Molto vivace 3.Andante
con espressione 4.Vivace
Str.
Ms.
Score 24 p.
Composed 1953. First performance Tübinger
Musiktage, Tübingen, Germany, 1954, Johann
Nepomuk David conductor.

Ambrosius, Hermann

5703 [The star of promise, musical   *15'*
legend for small orchestra]
1.Die Heimatlosen [The homeless ones] 2.In
der Herberge [At the inn] 3.Sternenbotschaft
[Message of the star]
2,2,2,2-2Hn.-Str.(without Cb.)
Ms.
Score 19 p.
Composed 1947. First performance Freiburg,
1950, Rundfunk Freiburg im Breisgau Städt
Orchester, Krämer conductor.

2180 [Suite no. 2, Op. 64a, G minor]   *30'*
1.Overture 2.Courante 3.Musette 4.Bourrée
5.Sarabande 6.Gigue
2,2,0,2-2Hn.-Timp.-Str.
Filser, Augsburg [n.d.]
Score 37 p.
Composed ca.1926. First performance ca.1926,
Leipzig Rundfunkorchester, Theodor Blumer
conductor.

AMES, JOHN CARLOWITZ.
    Westbury-on-Trym, near Bristol, England 1860
    Torquay, England 21 July 1924

1314s The seasons, suite for strings
1.Dawn of spring 2.On summer seas, barcarole
3.Harvest festival
Str.
Score: Ms. 20 p.
Parts: Hawkes, London, ᶜ1915

AMES, WILLIAM T.
    b. Cambridge, Massachusetts 20 March 1901

317m Concertino for clarinet and small   *18'30"*
orchestra
1.Fairly fast 2.Slow 3.Moderately fast
Solo Cl.-1(alt. Picc.),1,1,1-1,1,1-Timp.-Str.
Ms.
Score 77 p.
Composed 1958-59.

AMON, JOHANN ANDREAS.   Bamberg 1763
    Wallerstein, Bavaria 29 March 1825

2214 [Symphony, Op. 10 no. 1, F major]
1.Adagio - Allegro vivace 2.Adagio 3.Menuetto
4.Rondo
1,2(or 2Cl.),0,1-2Hn.-Str.
Ms.
Score 136 p.
Copied from an edition published by J. Amon
& Cie, Heilbronn as no. 1 of Trois Sinfonies
à grand Orchestre. According to Fétis, Op.
10 is Premier Concerto pour l'Alto published
by Pleyel, Paris; the above symphony is not
mentioned in his article.

4093 [Symphony, Op. 25, C major]
1.Allegro assai 2.Adagio 3.Menuetto alle-
gretto 4.Rondo allegro
1,2,0,1-Hn.-Str.
Ms.
Score 55 p.
Composed for the celebration of the Fête
Heilbronn, 29 July 1805.

ANDERS, ERICH FREIHERR WOLFF VON GUDENBERG.
    Teutschenthal, Germany 29 August 1883
    Hamburg 8 January 1955

4329 [A little courting music, Op. 83]   *14'*
1.Sehr lebhaft 2.Cantabile 3.Lento assai,
espressivo
1,1,2,1-2,1,1-Timp.,Perc.-Str.
Wilhelm Zimmermann, Leipzig, ᶜ1939
Score 48 p.

4650 [Rococo miniatures, Op. 82]   *14'*
2,2,2,2-4,2-Timp.,Perc.-Hp.-Str.
Wilhelm Zimmermann, Leipzig, ᶜ1939
Score 38 p.

ANDERSEN, KARL JOACHIM.   Copenhagen 29 April 1847
    Copenhagen 7 May 1909

903m Allegro militaire, Op. 48
2 Solo Fl.-2*,2,2,2-2,2,3-Timp.,Perc.-Str.
Score: Ms. 76 p.
Parts: J.H. Zimmermann, Leipzig, ᶜ1894

680m [Concert piece no. 2, for flute and
orchestra, Op. 61]
Solo Fl.-1,2,2,2-2,2-Timp.-Str.
Ms.
Score 33 p.

583m Fantaisie caractéristique, Op. 16
Solo Fl.-Str.
Ms.
Score 35 p.

883m [Hungarian fantasy, flute and orchestra,
Op. 2]
Solo Fl.-2(2nd alt. Picc.),2,2,2-2,2,1-Timp.,
Trgl.,Tamb.-Str.
Score: Ms. 64 p.
Parts: Rühle & Wendling, Leipzig [n.d.]

ANDERSEN-WINGAR, ALFRED.   Oslo October 1869
    Oslo 21 April 1952

694m [Concert piece, clarinet and orchestra,
Op. 23]
Solo Cl.-2(2nd alt. Picc.),2,0,2-2,2,1-Timp.-
Str.
Ms.
Score 62 p.

ANDERSON, FLORENCE.
See: DU PAGE, FLORENCE.

ANDERSON, LEROY.
    Cambridge, Massachusetts 29 June 1908
    Woodbury, Connecticut 18 May 1975

2023s Fiddle-faddle   *3'*
Pno.(optional)-Str.
Mills Music, New York, ᶜ1947
Score 18 p.
Composed 1947. First performance Boston,
March 1947, Boston Pops Orchestra, Arthur
Fiedler conductor.

2017s Jazz legato   *1'30"*
Pno.(optional)-Str.
Mills Music, New York, ᶜ1944
Score 7 p.
*Composed at the suggestion of Arthur Fiedler.
First performance Boston, 16 June 1939, Boston
Pops Orchestra, Arthur Fiedler conductor.*

2001s Jazz pizzicato   *1'30"*
Str.
Mills Music, New York, ᶜ1939
Score 5 p.
*Composed 1937. First performance Boston, 15
May 1939, Boston Pops Orchestra, the composer
conducting.*

ANDRÉ, CARL.   Coblenz 24 August 1853
                               Coblenz 29 June 1914

469s [Dance of the elves, pizzicato-capriccio,
Op. 10]
2Fl.(ad lib.)-Hp.(ad lib.)-Str.
Joh. André, Offenbach a.M., ᶜ1897
Score 7 p.

ANDRÉ, JOHANN ANTON.
        Offenbach am Main, Germany 6 October 1775
                          Offenbach 6 April 1842

4097 Ouverture militaire à grande orchestre,
Op. 24
3*,2,2,1-2Hn.-Str.
Ms.
Score 80 p.
Composed ca.1801.

4098 [Rinaldo and Alcina, or The island of
seduction, Op. 16. Overture]
2,2,2,2-2Hn.-Timp.-Str.
Ms.
Score 34 p.
First performance of opera Dresden, 1799.

4094 [Symphony, Op. 5, F major]
1.Adagio 2.Andantino 3.Menuetto 4.Allegro
vivace
2,2,0,2-2Hn.-Str.
Ms.
Score 134 p.
Composed 1795.

4095 [Symphony, Op. 6, C major]
1.Adagio 2.Adagio con moto 3.Menuetto
4.Rondo
1,2,2,2-2Hn.-Str.
Ms.
Score 149 p.
Composed 1795.

4096 [Symphony, Op. 13, G major]
1.Grave 2.Andante 3.Allegretto vivace ma non
troppo 4.Menuetto secondo
1,2,0,1-2Hn.-Str.
Ms.
Score 178 p.
Composed ca.1801.

4282 [Symphony, Op. 25, E-flat]
1.Adagio - Allegro con fuoco 2.Adagio -
Andantino moderato quasi larghetto con moto
3.Menuetto: Allegro non molto 4.Finale: Presto
1,2,2-4,2,1-Timp.-Str.
Joh. André, Offenbach a.M. [n.d.]
Score 60 p.

ANDRÉ, LUDWIG.   Minden, Westphalia 1 February 1858
                          Offenbach 8 June 1924

6873 [Amorous whisper, waltz poem, Op. 146]
2Fl.-Timp.,Bells-Hp.(ad lib.)-Str.
Hansen, Copenhagen, ᶜ1895
Score 15 p.

1272s [Mountain violet, two solo violins and
string orchestra, Op. 100]
2 Solo Vn.-Str.
Score: Ms. 11 p.
Parts: Joh. André, Offenbach a.M. [1889]

ANDREAE, VOLKMAR.   Berne 5 July 1879
                               Zurich 18 June 1962

1249 [Little suite, for orchestra, Op. 27] *20'*
3(3rd alt. Picc.),3*,3*,3*-4,2,3,1-Timp.,Perc.
-Cel.,Hp.-Str.
Leuckart, Leipzig [n.d.]
Score 46 p.
*Composed 1916-17. First performance Basel, 20
October 1917, the composer conducting.*

1345 Notturno und Scherzo für Orchester,   *12'*
Op. 30
3(3rd alt. Picc.),3*,3*,3*-4,2,3,1-Timp.,Perc.-
Cel.,Hp.-Str.
Leuckart, Leipzig [n.d.]
Score 37 p.

Andreae, Volkmar

> Composed 1918. First performance Zurich, 16
> December 1918, the composer conducting.

748v Rhapsodie für Violine und Orchester,   10'
Op. 32
Solo Vn.-2,2,2,2-3,2,3-Timp.,Perc.-Str.
Hug, Leipzig, ᶜ1920
Score 34 p.

1165 [Symphony, Op. 31, C major]   30'
4*,3*,4*(1Cl. in E-flat),3*-4,4,3,1-Timp.,
Perc.-Cel.,Hp.-Str.
Hug, Leipzig, ᶜ1920
Score 95 p.
*Composed 1919. First performance Zurich, 3
November 1919, the composer conducting.*

ANDREOLI, GUGLIELMO.   Modena, Italy 22 April 1835
                        Nice 13 March 1860

673s [Prelude and minuet, Op. 12]   8'
Pno.&Cb.(ad lib.)-Str.
Ricordi, Milan [n.d.]
Score 11 p.

ANDRESS, WALTER.   Vienna 2 February 1904

5981 [Symphony no. 1, Op. 68, F major]   35'
1.Lebhaft, doch nicht zu schnell 2.Sehr
langsam 3.Scherzo: Lebhaft 4.Langsam –
Ruhig – Fliessend
2(2nd alt. Picc.),3*,2,2-4,3,3,1-Timp.,Perc.-
Hp.-Str.
Ms. ᶜ1950
Score 147 p. Large folio
*Composed 1949. First performance Vienna, 14
May 1950, Vienna Symphony Orchestra, Karl Etti
conductor.*

5992 [Symphony no. 2, Op. 71, A minor]   39'
1.Langsam – Mässige 2 Schläge 2.Langsam
3.Sehr lebhaft 4.Bewegt
2(2nd alt. Picc.),2*,2(2nd alt. B.Cl.),2-4,3,3,
1-Timp.,Perc.-Hp.-Str.
Ms.
Score 177 p.
*Commissioned by the AKM [Staatlich Genehmigte
Gesellschaft der Autoren, Komponisten, und
Musik-Verlage], Vienna. Composed 1952. First
performance Vienna Radio, 15 December 1952,
Full Symphony Orchestra of the Vienna Radio,
Max Schönherr conductor.*

5993 [Symphony no. 3, Op. 77, E-flat major] 34'
1.Mässig bewegt 2.Sehr langsam 3.Allegro
moderato 4.Lebhaft
2(2nd alt. Picc.),2*,2,2-4,3,3,1-Timp.,Perc.-
Hp.-Str.
Ms., ᶜ[n.d.]
Score 135 p.
*Commissioned by the AKM, Vienna. First per-
formance Vienna Radio, 4 January 1956, Full
Symphony Orchestra of the Vienna Radio, Max
Schönherr conductor.*

3464 [Viennese rhapsody, Op. 39]   13'30"
2(2nd alt. Picc.),2*,2,2-3,2,3-Timp.,Perc.-Str.
Universal Edition, Vienna, ᶜ1939

Score 86 p.
*Commissioned by the AKM, Vienna. Composed
1937. First performance Vienna Radio, 25
January 1938, Full Symphony Orchestra of the
Vienna Radio, Max Schönherr conductor.*

ANDREWS, R.

3862 Fanfare to confound a Philistine   15"
3Tpt.,Ten.Tbn.,B.Tbn.,Tuba
Ms.
Score 4 p.

ANGELOFF, BORIS. pseudonym.
See: KREMENLIEV, BORIS ANGELOFF.

ANGLÈS, RAFAEL.   Rafales, Teruel, Spain 1731
                   Valencia 19 February 1816

7301 Aria in D minor. Free transcription ca.3'
[for orchestra] by Arthur Bosmans
2,1,2,1-Hn.-Pno.(ad lib.)-Str.
Ms. ᶜ1976 by Arthur Bosmans
Score 10 p.
Originally composed for organ or spinet.

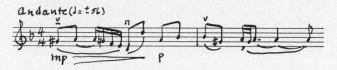

ANROOIJ, PETER G. VAN.
            Zalt-Bommel, Holland 13 October 1879
            The Hague 13 October 1954

2096 [Piet Hein, Dutch rhapsody for   9'
orchestra]
3*,2,2,2-4,2,3,1-Timp.,Perc.-Str.
Alsbach, Amsterdam [n.d.]
Score 63 p.
*Piet Hein (1577-1629) was a Dutch admiral in
the wars between Spain and the Netherlands.
Composed 1901, using J. J. Viotta's song The
Silver Flute. First performance Utrecht,
March 1901, the composer conducting.*

ANTHIOME, EUGÈNE.   Lorient 19 August 1836

17s Souvenir d'antan [Souvenir of yesteryear]
Str.(without Cb.)
Score: Ms. 4 p.
Parts: DuPont, Paris [n.d.]

ANTIPOV, KONSTANTIN ATHANASIEVICH.
            b. St. Petersburg 18 January 1859

554 Allegro symphonique, pour orchestre,   10'
Op. 7
2,2,2,2-4,2,3-Timp.-Str.
Belaieff, Leipzig, ᶜ1890
Score 68 p.
*Composed 1889. First performance St. Peters-
burg, 1890.*

ANTRÉAS, EDMOND.

513s Est-ce bien vrai? [Can it be true?,
intermezzo for string orchestra]
Str.
Score: Ms. 7 p.
Parts: Leduc, Paris, ᶜ1902

747s Galanterie [intermezzo for string
orchestra, Op. 36]
Str.
Score: Ms. 11 p.
Parts: Leduc, Paris, ᶜ1904

365s Rêve d'enfant [Child's dream, for string
orchestra]
Str.
Leduc, Paris [1902?]
Score 4 p.

APITIUS, C. the younger.

804m [Concertino with variations, for trumpet
and orchestra, E-flat major]
Solo Tpt.-1,1,2,1-2,2,1-B.Dr.,S.Dr.-Str.
Score: Ms. 40 p.
Parts: Linsdorf, Dessau [n.d.]/Lehne,
Hannover [n.d.]

APPELMEYER, FRANZ.
See: ASPELMAYR, FRANZ.

ARAGUARI, ERICH KROPSCH.   near Trieste 1903

5342 Pequeña sinfonia, Op. 80   35'
1.Moderato, e accelerando molto gradualmente
2.Adagio 3.Andantino 4.Allegro ma non troppo
2*,3*,4*,3*-1,2,3,1-Timp.,Perc.-Cel.,2Hp.-Str.
Ms.
Score 145 p.
Composed 1954.

ARAKISHVILI, DMITRI.
Vladikavkaz, Georgia 23 February 1873
Tiflis 13 August 1953

3993 [The legend of Shola Rustavelli.   10'
Suite from the opera]
1.Introduction. Georgian dances 2.Aavouri
[dance] 3.Satamasho
3*,3*,2,2-4,2,3,1-Timp.,Perc.-Hp.-Str.
Mussektor, Moscow, ᶜ1937
Score 71 p.
First performance of the opera, Tiflis, 1919.

ARAÚJO, JOÃO GOMES DE.
See: GOMES DE ARAÚGO, JOÃO.

ARBEAU, PIERRE.

297v Berceuse
Solo Vn.-Str.
Score: Ms. 3 p.
Parts: Durand, Paris, ᶜ1924

ARCADELT, JACOB.   Liège ca.1505
Paris 14 October 1568

3009 Ave Maria. Freely transcribed for   4'30"
orchestra by Harl McDonald
2,3*,3,3*-3,3,3-Timp.,Perc.-Str.
Elkan-Vogel, Philadelphia, ᶜ1938
Score 6 p. Large folio
*Originally composed for three women's voices
or three part women's chorus. Transcribed
1938. First performance Boston, 28 June 1938,
Boston Pops Orchestra, Charles O'Connell
conductor.*

ARCHER, VIOLET.   Montreal, Quebec 24 April 1913

5840 Britannia, a joyful overture   6'45"
3*,2,2,2-4,3,3,1-Timp.,Perc.-Str.
Ms.
Score 47 p.
*Includes allusions to the melody Rule Britan-
nia and two Canadian folk songs: V'la l'Bon
Vent and Vive la Canadienne. Composed 1941.
First performance London, 10 March 1942, BBC
Orchestra, Adrian Boult conductor.*

339p [Concerto, piano, no. 1]   17'
1.Allegro energico 2.Adagio molto, espressivo
e cantabile 3.Allegro ma non troppo,
scherzoso
Solo Pno.-2,2,2,2-2Hn.,2Tpt.-Timp.,Cym.-Str.
Ms.
Score 130 p. Large folio
*Composed 1956. First performance Toronto, 28
December 1958, CBC Orchestra, Victor Feldbrill
conductor, William Stevens soloist.*

5912 Fanfare and passacaglia for orchestra   8'
2,2,2,2-4,3,3,1-Timp.-Str.
Ms.
Score 29 p.
*Composed 1949. First performance Symposium
for the International Federation of Music
Students, Boston, 18 March 1949, Malcolm. H.
Holmes conductor.*

5839 Fantasy on a ground, a piece for   8'
orchestra
3*,2,2,2-4,2,3,1-Timp.-Str.
Ms.
Score 34 p.
*Composed 1946. Revised 1956. First perform-
ance Austin, Texas, 14 April 1956, University
of Texas Symposium Orchestra, Guy Fraser Harrison conductor.*

5850 Poem for orchestra   7'
2,2,2,2-4,2,3-Timp.-Hp.-Str.
Ms.
Score 42 p.
*Composed 1944. First performance Oklahoma
City University, 9 December 1956, Oklahoma
City Symphony, Guy Fraser Harrison conductor.
A recording of this performance was later
broadcast over Voice of America.*

5838 Scherzo sinfonico, a symphonic jest   4'
3*,2,3*(2nd alt. B.Cl.,1Cb.Cl.),2-4,2,3,1-
Timp.,Perc.-Hp.-Str.
Ms.
Score 31 p.

Ardévol, José

Composed 1940. First performance Montreal, 24 February 1940, Montreal Symphony Orchestra, Douglas Clarke conductor.

ARDÉVOL, JOSÉ.   Barcelona 13 March 1911

5975 Música para pequeña orquesta   *24'30"*
1.Himno 2.Rondo 3.Variaciones
2Hn.-Timp.,Perc.-Pno.,Hpscd.,Cel.,Hp.-Str.
Ms.
Score 56 p. Large folio
Commissioned by International House of New Orleans. Composed 1957. First performance Washington, D.C., 19 April 1958, Orquesta Sinfónica Nacional de México, Luis Herrera de la Fuente conductor.

5674 Tríptico de Santiago, para orquesta   *29'*
1.El Morro 2.El Caney 3.Puerto Boniato
3(3rd alt. Picc.),3(3rd alt. E.H.),4(1Cl. in E-flat),3*-4,4,4,1-Timp.,Perc.-Pno.,Cel.,2Hp.-Str.
Ms.
Score 82 p. Large folio
Composed 1949. First performance Cologne, 25 May 1953, Symphony Orchestra of Hamburg Radio, Hans Schmidt-Isserstedt conductor.

AREL, BÜLENT.   Constantinople 23 April 1919

2215s [Six bagatelles for string   *8'30"*
orchestra]
Str.
Impero-Verlag, Wiesbaden, c1958
Score 28 p.
Composed 1954.

ARENDS, H.   Moscow 1855
                                        Moscow 1924

492v [Concertino, viola and orchestra,   *13'*
Op. 7, C major]
Solo Va.-2,2,2,2-2,2-Timp.-Str.
Jurgenson, Moscow [n.d.]
Score 43 p.

1367 Salammbô, suite de ballet   *30'*
In 12 movements
3(3rd alt. Picc.),3*,2,3*(C.Bn. ad lib.)-4,2,2Cnt.,3,1-Timp.,Perc.-Hp.-Str.
Jurgenson, Moscow [n.d.]
Score 162 p.

ARENSON, ADOLF.   Altona, Germany 1855

11s Menuett und Habanera für Streichorchester
Str.
Fritz Schuberth, Leipzig, c1893
Score 6 p.

ARENSKY, ANTON STEPANOVICH.
                Novgorod, Russia 12 July 1861
                Terijoki, Finland 25 February 1906

404p [Concerto, piano, Op. 2, F major]   *25'*
Edited by Paul Pabst
1.Allegro maestoso 2.Andante con moto
3.Allegro molto
Solo Pno.-2,2,2,2-4,2,3-Timp.,Perc.-Str.

Rahter, Leipzig [n.d.]
Score 127 p.

768v [Concerto, violin, Op. 54, A minor]   *25'*
In one movement
Solo Vn.-2,2,2,2-4,2-Timp.-Str.
Jurgenson, Moscow, c1902
Score 71 p.

1206 [A dream on the Volga, Op. 16.   *7'30"*
Overture]
3*,2,2,2-4,2,3,1-Timp.,Perc.-2Hp.(2nd ad lib.),Pno.-Str.
Jurgenson, Moscow [1892?]
Score 33 p.
From the opera in four acts with libretto from the drama by Alexander Nikolayevich Ostrovsky (same as for Chaikovsky's opera Voyevoda). First performance Moscow, 2 January 1891.

425p [Fantasy on Russian epic themes, piano   *9'*
and orchestra, Op. 48]
Solo Pno.-2,2,2,2-4,2,3,1-Timp.,Perc.-Str.
Jurgenson, Moscow [n.d.]
Score 50 p.

665 [Intermezzo for orchestra, Op. 13]   *3'*
2,2,2,2-2Hn.-Str.
Jurgenson, Moscow [1898]
Score 15 p.

1472 [March for orchestra, in memory of   *4'*
Suvorov]
3*,2,2,2-4,2,3,1-Timp.,Perc.-Str.
Jurgenson, Moscow, c1900
Score 19 p.
First performance St. Petersburg, 1899.

732 [Nal and Damajanti. Overture]   *4'30"*
3*,2,3*,2-4,2,3,1-Timp.,Perc.-Pno.,Hp.-Str.
Jurgenson, Moscow [n.d.]
Score 37 p.
Opera completed 1899. First performance Moscow, 22 January 1904.

964 [Night in Egypt. Suite from the   *20'*
ballet, Op. 50a]
1.[Overture] 2.[Dance of Arsinoe and the slaves] 3.[Dance of the Jews] 4.[Dance of the Ghazies] 5.[The snake charmer] 6.[Pas de deux. Waltz] 7.[Solemn entrance of Anthony]
3*,3*,2,2-4,2,3,1-Timp.,Perc.-Hp.-Str.
Jurgenson, Moscow [n.d.]
Score 117 p.
First performance of ballet, St. Petersburg, 1900.

776v Sérénade pour violon avec accompagne-   *2'*
ment d'orchestre à cordes, Op. 30 no. 2
Solo Vn.-2,0,2,0-Trgl.-Str.
Score: Mussektor, Moscow, 1926. 9 p.
Parts: Jurgenson, Moscow [n.d.]

4391 Suite, Op. 15. Transcribed for orchestra
by Modest Altschuler
1.Romance 2.Valse 3.Polonaise

3,2,2,2-4,3,3,1-Timp.,Perc.-Str.
Ms.
Score 74 p.
*Originally composed for two pianos and
published 1908.*

318 [Suite no. 1, Op. 7, G minor] Arranged by
the composer
1.[Variations on a Russian theme] 2.Air de
danse 3.Scherzo 4.Basso ostinato 5.Marche
3*,2,2,2-4,2,3,1-Timp.,Perc.-Hp.-Str.
Jurgenson, Moscow, 1896
Score 127 p.
Originally composed for two pianos.

658 [Suite no. 2, Silhouettes, Op. 23,   *14'*
C minor] Arranged by the composer
1.Le savant 2.La coquette 3.Polichinelle
4.Le rêveur 5.La danseuse
3*,2*,2,2-4,2,3,1-Timp.,Perc.-Hp.-Str.
Jurgenson, Moscow [n.d.]
Score 77 p.
*Originally composed for two pianos and
published 1901.*

1001 [Suite no. 3, Variations, Op. 33,   *21'*
C major] Arranged by the composer
Theme 1.Dialogue 2.[Waltz] 3.[Triumphal
march] 4.Menuet 5.Gavotte 6.Scherzo
7.[Funeral march] 8.Nocturne 9.Polonaise
3*,3(3rd alt. E.H.),2,2-4,2,3,1-Timp.,Perc.-
Pno.(or Cel.)-Str.
Jurgenson, Moscow [n.d.]
Score 73 p.
Originally composed for two pianos.

74 [Symphony no. 1, Op. 4, B minor]   *33'*
1.Adagio - Allegro patetico 2.Andante pastorale con moto 3.Scherzo 4.Finale: Allegro
giocoso
3*,2,2,2-4,2,3,1-Timp.,Perc.-Str.
Jurgenson, Moscow [n.d.]
Score 145 p.
*First performance Moscow, 21 December 1889,
the composer conducting.*

407s [Variations on a theme by Chaikovsky, *15'*
for string orchestra, Op. 35a]
Str.
Forberg, Leipzig, [n.d.]
Score 14 p.
*Originally the slow movement of Arensky's
Quartet, Op. 35, and subsequently orches-
trated by the composer.*

ARGENTO, DOMINICK.
        b. York, Pennsylvania 27 October 1927

6744 [The boor. Overture]   *6'*
1,1,2(2nd alt. B.Cl.),1-2,1-Timp.,Perc.-Pno.-
Str.
Boosey & Hawkes, New York, c1965
Score 31 p.
*From the opera buffa in one act with libretto
by John Olon, adapted from the play of Anton
Chekhov. Composed 1957. First performance
Eastman School of Music, Rochester, 6 May
1957, Frederick Fennell conductor.*

265p Divertimento for piano and string   *15'*
orchestra
1.Veloce e giocoso 2.Moderato cantabile
3.Allegro energico
Solo Pno.-Str.
Score: Ms. 30 p. Large folio
Parts: Boosey & Hawkes, New York, c1967
*Composed 1954-55. First performance Rochester,
2 July 1958, Kilbourn Hall Chamber Orchestra,
Eastman School of Music, Frederick Fennell
conductor, Richard Woitach soloist.*

6759 Ode to the west wind, concerto for   *28'*
soprano and orchestra
In one movement
Sop. Voice Solo-3(3rd alt. Picc.),3(3rd alt.
E.H.),3*,3(3rd alt. C.Bn.)-4,3,3,1-Timp.,Perc.-
Hp.-Str.
Score: Ms. 94 p. Large folio
Parts: Boosey & Hawkes, New York, c1957
*Text is the poem by Percy Bysshe Shelley.
Composed 1956. First performance Eastman
School of Music, Rochester, 29 April 1957,
Howard Hanson conductor, Carolyn Bailey soloist.*

5410 The resurrection of Don Juan.   *18-20'*
Concert suite from the ballet
1.Paseo 2.Serenade and pas de deux 3.The
combat 4.Tributes to the dead Don Juan
5.Pas d'action
2(2nd alt. Picc.),2,2,2-4,2,2,1-Timp.,Perc.-
Hp.-Str.
Score: Ms. 57 p. Large folio
Parts: Boosey & Hawkes, New York, c1967
*Originally composed as a ballet in one act
with scenario by Richard Hart. Composed 1955.
First performance Rochester, 2 May 1956,
Eastman-Rochester Orchestra, Howard Hanson
conductor.*

6739 Royal invitation, or Homage to the   *23'*
queen of Tonga
1.Proclamation and minuet 2.Theme and variations 3.Fanfare and fox-trot 4.March and
interruption 5.Oh, to be in England
1,2,0,2-2Hn.-Str.
Score: Ms. 53 p. Large folio
Parts: Boosey & Hawkes, New York, c1966
*Suggested by a newspaper account of the spec-
tacular appearance of Her Majesty Salota,
Queen of Tonga, during the Coronation Ceremonies of Elizabeth II of England. Commissioned by the St. Paul Chamber Orchestra.
Composed 1964. First performance St. Paul,
Minnesota, 22 March 1964, St. Paul Chamber
Orchestra, Leopold Sipe conductor.*

6738 Variations for orchestra (The mask   *28'*
of night)
1.Nocturne 2.Barcarolle 3.Burlesca
4.Serenade 5.Toccata 6.Recitative and aria
2(2nd alt. Picc.),2,2(2nd alt. B.Cl.),2-4,3,
3,1-Timp.,Perc.-Hp.-Sop. Voice(in Var. 6)-Str.
Score: Ms. 86 p. Large folio
Parts: Boosey & Hawkes, New York, c1967
*Text (in Variation 6) from Romeo and Juliet
by Shakespeare. Commissioned by the Civic
Orchestra of Minneapolis. Composed 1965.*

Ariosti, Attilio

First performance Minneapolis, 26 January 1966, Civic Orchestra of Minneapolis, Thomas Nee conductor, Carolyn Bailey soprano.

ARIOSTI, ATTILIO.　　　　Bologna 5 November 1666
　　　　　　　　　　　　　(?)Spain ca.1740

538c [Concertino, violoncello and string　　*10'*
orchestra, no. 3, E minor] Transcribed by
Albert Elkus
Andantino espressivo - Allemanda - Andantino -
Giga
Solo Vc.-Timp.(ad lib.)-Str.
Universal-Edition, ᶜ1921
Score 24 p.
*First published as Cantatas and a Collection
of Lessons for the Viol d'Amore in London,
ca.1724. Transcribed 1916. First performance
of transcription probably in a broadcast,
Stockholm.*

749c [Same as above. Revised edition]　　*14'*
Revised ca.1942.

375v [Sonata, viola, no. 2, A major]　　*10'30"*
Transcribed for viola and chamber orchestra by
Guido Santórsola
1.Cantabile 2.Vivace 3.Adagio 4.Minuetto
Solo Va.-1,1,1,1-Hp.-Va.,Vc.
Score: Ms. 23 p.
Parts: Asociación General de Autores del
Uruguay, ᶜ1942
*First published as Cantatas and a Collection
of Lessons for the Viol d'Amore in London,
ca.1724. This transcription 1934. First per-
formance Belo Horizonte, Brazil, 17 January
1945, Sinfônica de Belo Horizonte, Arthur Bos-
mans conductor, Guido Santórsola soloist.*

ARMÁNDOLA, JOSÉ. pseudonym.
　See: LAUTENSCHLÄGER, WILLI.

ARNE, THOMAS AUGUSTINE.　　London 12 March 1710
　　　　　　　　　　　　　　London 5 March 1778

2509 [Comus. Overture] Edited by Bernard　　*7'*
Herrmann
1,2,0,1-2Tpt.-Str.
Kalmus, New York, ᶜ1933
Score 11 p.
*From the masque based on Milton's Comus,
adapted by John Dalton. Originally composed
1738. First performance of masque Drury Lane
Theatre, London, 4 March 1738. First*

*performance of this arrangement, New York, 3
December 1933, New Chamber Orchestra, Bernard
Herrmann conductor.*

1907s [Comus. Dance, F major] Arranged by　　*2'*
Adam Carse
1,1,1,1(all optional)-Str.
Ms.
Score 7 p.
This arrangement 1923.

2322s [Comus. Three dances] Transcribed by
W. Gillies Whittaker
1.Moderate gigue tempo 2.[Largo] 3.[Presto]
Fl.,2Ob.(optional)-Pno.or Hpscd.(optional)-
Str.
Oxford University Press, London, ᶜ1938
Score 8 p.

1906s [Comus. Two dances, A major]　　*3'*
Arranged by Adam Carse
1,1,1,1(all optional)-Str.
Ms.
Score 10 p.
This arrangement 1923.

7228 [The guardian outwitted. Overture]　　*10'*
Edited by Gwilym Beechey
1.Con spirito 2.Andante larghetto 3.Andante
amoroso
2,2,0,2-2Hn.-Cemb.-Str.
Oxford University Press, London, ᶜ1973
Score 16 p.
*From the opera with libretto by the composer.
First performance London, 12 December 1764.
This edition based on parts first published by
R. Bremner, London, probably 1765.*

4639 [The judgement of Paris. Overture]
Transcribed by Adam Carse
1.Largo 2.Allegro moderato 3.Minuet 4.Giga
2,2,2,2(all optional)-Str.
Augener, London, ᶜ1939
Score 10 p.
*From the masque with libretto altered from
William Congreve. Composed 1740. First per-
formance London, 1740.*

4627 [Symphony no. 4, F major] Transcribed by
Adam Carse
1.Con spirito (Moderato) 2.Con spirito
(Allegro moderato) 3.Andantino
2Ob.(or 2Fl.)-2Hn.-Hpscd.or Pno.-Str.
Augener, London, ᶜ1935
Score 8 p.
Composed 1740, as Overture in eight parts.

ARNELL, RICHARD.　　　　London 15 September 1917

2073s Abstract forms, suite for string　　*13-15'*
orchestra, Op. 50

1.Andante con moto 2.Andante sostenuto
3.Adagio 4.Allegro vivace
Str.
Ms.
Score 24 p.
*Composed 1946-47. First performance Bath
Assembly, England, 2 June 1951, Boyd Neel
Orchestra, Boyd Neel conductor.*

1132v [Concerto, violin, in one   *20'*
movement, Op. 9]
Solo Vn.-3*,2,2,2-4,3,3,1-Timp.-Str.
Ms. [Schott, London, ᶜ1950]
Score 151 p.
*Composed 1940. First performance New York,
22 April 1946, National Orchestral Association,
Leon Barzin conductor, Harold Kohon soloist.
Revised 1947 and 1950.*

391v [Concerto capriccioso, violin,   *20'*
Op. 70]
1.Allegro maestoso 2.Andante, non troppo
3.Poco vivace
Solo Vn.-2(2nd alt. Picc.),1,2,1-2,2,2-Perc.
Str.
Ms. [ᶜ1954 by C.F. Peters, New York]
Score 88 p. Large folio
Composed 1950. Revised 1954.

829p [Divertimento, piano and chamber   *16-18'*
orchestra, no. 1, Op. 5]
1.Moderato 2.Andante con moto 3.Allegro
Solo Pno.-1,1,2,1-2,2-Str.
Ms.
Score 56 p.
Composed 1939.

3949 Fantasia for orchestra [Op. 17]   *14'*
3*,2,2,3*-4,3,3,1-Timp.-Str.
Ms.
Score 76 p. Large folio
Composed 1941.

5190 Harlequin in April, ballet [complete] *31'*
Op. 63
2,2,2,2-4,2,2-Timp.,Perc.-Str.
Ms.
Score 146 p. Large folio
*Ballet suggested by T. S. Eliot's The Waste
Land, 'April is the cruellest month...'. Com-
missioned by The Arts Council of Great Britain
for the Festival of Britain, 1951. Composed
1951. First performance London, 8 May 1951,
John Larchberg conductor, choreography by
John Cranko.*

4208 The land, complete film music, Op. 12 *37'*
Prelude - Reminiscence - Machines - Interlude
- Finale
3*,2,2,2-4,3,3,1-Timp.,B.Dr.-Str.
Ms.
Score 116 p.
*Commissioned by the United States Department
of Agriculture for the film by Robert Flaherty.
Composed 1941. First performance of Suite,
Station WNYC, New York, 30 July 1941, National
Youth Administration Orchestra, Robert Huf-
stader conductor.*

5193 Lord Byron, a symphonic portrait,   *20'*
Op. 67
1.Prelude 2.Newstead 3.Augusta 4.Success and
disgrace 5.Voyage 6.Serenade 7.Battles
8.Epilogue
3*,3*,3*,3*-4,3,3,1-Timp.,Perc.-Cel.-Str.
Ms.
Score 114 p. Large folio
*Commissioned by Thomas Beecham. Composed 1952.
First performance London, 19 November 1952,
Royal Philharmonic Society, Thomas Beecham
conductor.*

3349 Overture, the new age [Op. 2]   *10'*
3*,2,2,2-4,3,3,1-Timp.,B.Dr.-Str.
Ms.
Score 95 p.
*Composed 1939. First performance New York,
13 January 1941, National Orchestral Association, Leon Barzin conductor.*

3378 Overture 1940 [Op. 6]   *13'*
3*,2,2,2-4,3,3,1-Timp.,B.Dr.-Str.
Ms.
Score 112 p.
Composed 1940.

3517 Sinfonia (1941), Quasi variazioni   *17'*
[Op. 13]
3*,2,2,2-4,3,3,1-Timp.,B.Dr.-Str.
Ms.
Score 60 p. Large folio
*Composed 1941. First performance New York, 15
March 1942, New York Civic Orchestra of the
WPA, Thomas Beecham conductor.*

5392 [Symphony no. 4, Op. 52]   *27'*
1.Andante - Allegro 2.Andante 3.Allegro
vivace
3*,2,2,2-4,3,3,1-Timp.-Str.
Ms.
Score 137 p. Large folio
*Composed 1947-48. First concert performance
Cheltenham Festival, England, 29 June 1949,
Halle Orchestra, John Barbirolli conductor.*

ARNOLD, GEORGE.

1015v Romance, pour violon ou violoncelle avec
accompagnement d'orchestre, Op. 13 no. 4
Solo Vn.-2,2,2,2-2Hn.-Hp.(or Pno.)-Str.
Breitkopf & Härtel, Brussels, ᶜ1910
Score 19 p.

1008v Rêve de sorcière [Witch's dream, Op. 13
no. 1]
Solo Vn.-2,2,2,2-2,2,3-Timp.,Cym.-Hp.(ad lib.)
-Str.
Score: Ms. 29 p.
Parts: Breitkopf & Härtel, Brussels, ᶜ1910

ARNOLD, MALCOLM HENRY.
                    Northampton, England 21 October 1921

357m Concerto for oboe and strings, Op. 39 *11'*
1.Cantabile 2.Vivace 3.Quasi allegretto
Solo Ob.-Str.
Paterson's Publications, London, ᶜ1952, 1957

Arnold, Malcolm

Score 28 p. Large folio
Composed 1952. First performance London, 26 June 1953, Boyd Neel Orchestra, Boyd Neel conductor, Leon Goossens soloist.

6210 A grand grand festival overture, *8'*
Op. 57
3*,2,2,2-4,3,3,1-Timp.,Perc.-Chimes-3Vacuum Cleaners, 1Electric Polisher,4Rifles-Org.-Str.
Paterson's Publications, London, c1956
Score 63 p. Large folio
Commissioned by the Hoffnung Music Festival. Composed 1956. First performance London, 13 November 1956, Hoffnung Festival Orchestra, the composer conducting.

ARNOLD, YURI KARLOVICH VON.
St. Petersburg 13 November 1811
Karakash, Crimea 20 July 1898

4274 [Overture to Boris Godunov]
2*,2,2,2-4,2,3,Ophicl.-Timp.,Perc.-Str.
Gustav Heinze, Leipzig [1869?]
Score 33 p.
From the incidental music to Pushkin's poem.

ARRIAGA, JUAN CRISÓSTOMO JACOBO ANTONIO DE.
Rigoitia near Bilbao, Spain 27 January 1806
Paris 17 January 1826

5659 [The happy slaves. Overture] *8'*
2,2,2,2-2Hn.-Timp.-Str.
Junta de Cultura de Vizcaya [n.d.]
Score 30 p.
From the opera composed at age thirteen (1819).

5515 [Nothing and yet much, essay for octet]
Hn.-Pno.,Guit.-Str.
Comisión Permanente Arriaga, Bilbao, Spain, 1929
Score 22 p.
Composed at age eleven (1817).

5519 Pastoral
3*,2,2,2-4,2Cnt.,3,1-Timp.,Perc.-Str.
[n.p., n.d.]
Score 15 p.

5654 [Symphony for large orchestra] *25'*
1.Adagio - Allegro vivace 2.Andante
3.Minuetto; Allegro 4.Allegro con moto
2,2,2,2-2,2-Timp.-Str.
Junta de Cultura de Vizcaya [Bilbao, Spain, 1953?]
Score 90 p.
Composed in Paris ca.1821-26.

ARROYO, JOÃO MARCELLINO.
Oporto, Portugal 4 October 1861
Oporto, Portugal 18 May 1930

1350 [Symphonic poem no. 2, Op. 26]
1.Récit dramatique 2.La grâce consolatrice
3.Révolte et apaisement
4*,3*,4*(1Cl. in F),4*-4,3,3,1-Timp.,Perc.-2Hp.-Str.
Schott, Mainz, c1914 by João Marcellino Arroyo
Score 152 p.

ARTSYBUSHEV, NIKOLAI VASSILIEVICH.
Tsarskoe Selo 7 March 1858
Paris 15 April 1937

1414 Polka caractéristique pour orchestre, *5'*
Op. 4
2,2,2,2-4,2-Timp.,Perc.-Str.
Belaieff, Leipzig, 1890
Score 21 p.
First performance Moscow, 1890.

1398 Valse-fantasia pour orchestre, Op. 9 *7'*
3*,2,2,2-4,2,3-Timp.-Hp.-Str.
Belaieff, Leipzig, 1897
Score 23 p.
First performance Moscow, 1897.

ASAFIEV, BORIS VLADIMIROVICH.
St. Petersburg 29 June 1884
Moscow 27 January 1949

Also known by the pseudonym Igor Glebov.

1563 [The hunchback pony. Adagio and six variations from the ballet]
2,2(2nd alt. E.H.),2,2-4,2,3,1-Timp.,Perc.-2Hp.-Str.
Bessel, St. Petersburg [n.d.]
Score 69 p.

ASCONE, VICENTE. Montevideo, Uruguay 1897

3281 [Songs of eventide, symphonic *14'*
impressions]
3(3rd alt. Picc.),3*,3*,4*-2Sax.(SA)-4,3,3,1-Timp.,Perc.-Pno.,Cel.,Hp.-Str.
Ms.
Score 67 p.
Composed 1932. First performance Montevideo, Uruguay, 14 October 1933, Orchestra of the Servicio Oficial de Difusion Radio Electrica (SODRE), Lamberto Baldi conductor.

ASPELMAYR, FRANZ. (?)Vienna 1728
Vienna 29 July 1786

1980s [Divertimento, E major] Edited by Karl Geiringer
1.Molto allegro 2.Minuetto 3.Andante poco adagio 4.Allegro assai
Str.
Ms.
Score 11 p.

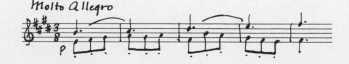

ASSIS REPUBLICANO, ANTONIO DE.
Pôrto Alegre, Brazil 1897

754c [Improvisation on a Brazilian theme, for violoncello and orchestra]
Solo Vc.-2(2nd alt. Picc.),2,2,2-2,2,2,1-Timp.,Trgl.-Hp.-Str.

Ms. ᶜ1925
Score 23 p. Large folio
*Composed 1925. First performance Rio de
Janeiro, 21 June 1925, Symphony Society of Rio
de Janeiro, Francisco Braga conductor.*

ATTERBERG, KURT. Göteborg, Sweden 12 December 1887
Stockholm 15 February 1974

3912 [Ballade and passacaglia on a theme   9'
in Swedish folk style]
2(2nd alt. Picc.),2,2,2(2nd alt. C.Bn.)-4,2,3
1-Timp.,Perc.-Hp.-Str.
Eulenburg, Leipzig, ᶜ1937
Score 56 p.
*Composed 1925-37. First performance 17 Sep-
tember 1937, Concert Society of Stockholm,
Eugene Ormandy conductor.*

626m [Concerto, horn, Op. 28, A minor]   23'
1.Allegro pathetico 2.Adagio 3.Allegro molto
Solo Hn.-Perc.-Pno.-Str.
Breitkopf & Härtel, Leipzig, ᶜ1928
Score 47 p.
*Composed 1926. First performance Stockholm,
20 March 1927, Adolf Wiklund conductor, Axel
Malm soloist.*

285p [Concerto, piano, Op. 37]   36'
1.Pesante allegro 2.Andante 3.Furioso
Solo Pno.-2(2nd alt. Picc.),2,2,2-4(3rd&4th
ad lib.),2,3(3rd ad lib.),1(ad lib.)-Timp.,
Perc.-Str.
Breitkopf & Härtel, Leipzig, ᶜ1938
Score 132 p.
*Composed 1935-36. First performance Stockholm,
12 January 1936, Stockholm Philharmonic
Orchestra, the composer conducting, Olaf
Wibergh soloist.*

601v [Concerto, violin, Op. 7, E minor]   32'
1.Moderato 2.Adagio cantabile 3.Allegro
molto
Solo Vn.-2,2,2,2-2,2,1-Timp.-Str.
Nordiska, Stockholm, ᶜ1924
Score 70 p.
*Composed 1913. First performance Göteborg, 11
February 1914, the composer conducting, Sven
Kjellström soloist.*

576c [Concerto, violoncello, Op. 21, C   30'
minor]
1.Andante cantabile 2.Allegro molto 3.Adagio
4.Allegro
Solo Vc.-2(2nd alt. Picc.),2(2nd ad lib.),2,
2(2nd ad lib.)-2,2,2(2nd ad lib.)-Timp.-Str.
Breitkopf & Härtel, Leipzig, ᶜ1923
Score 58 p.
*Composed 1917-22. First performance Berlin, 6
January 1923, Berlin Philharmonic Orchestra,
the composer conducting, Hans Bottermund
soloist.*

605m [Suite no. 3, violin, viola and   12'
string orchestra, Op. 19 no. 1]
1.Prelude 2.Pantomim 3.Vision
Solo Vn., Solo Va.-Str.
Leuckart, Leipzig [n.d.]
Score 15 p.

*Composed 1918. First performance Göteborg,
28 August 1923, Göteborg Symphony Orchestra,
Tor Mann conductor.*

1528 [Suite no. 4, Turandot-suite on old   16'
Chinese melodies, Op. 19 no. 2]
1.[Kalaf sees Turandot's portrait] 2.Altoum -
Truffaldino - Marsch 3.[Room in the serail]
4.[Kalaf's night in the serail] 5.Turandot -
Marsch
2(2nd ad lib.,both alt. Picc.),0,1(alt. B.Cl.)
-1(ad lib.),2(ad lib.)-Perc.-Cel.,Glock.(or
Pno.)-Str.
Leuckart, Leipzig [n.d.]
Score 17 p.
*Composed 1920-21. First performance Stockholm,
4 January 1921, the composer conducting.*

1116 [Suite no. 5, Barocco, Op. 23]   18'
1.Entrata 2.Sarabanda 3.Gavotta 4.Pastorale
e gagliarda 5.Siciliana 6.Giga
1,1(alt. E.H.),1-Str.
Breitkopf & Härtel, Leipzig, ᶜ1925
Score 15 p.
*Composed 1922-23 as incidental music to Shake-
speare's A Winter's Tale. First performance
Norrköping, Sweden, 2 April 1924, Ivar Hellman
conductor.*

1941 [Symphony no. 2, Op. 6, F major]   40'
1.Allegro con moto 2.Adagio 3.Allegro con
fuoco
3(3rd alt. Picc.),2(2nd alt. E.H.),3*,2-4,2,3,
1-Timp.,Cym.-Pno.-Str.
Nordiska, Stockholm, ᶜ1916
Score 195 p.
*Composed 1911-13. First complete performance
Sondershausen, Germany, 26 July 1913, Carl
Corbach conductor.*

1815 [Symphony no. 3, Sea, Op. 10,   38'
D major]
1.Sun-smoke 2.Storm 3.Summer night
4(3rd alt. Picc.,1Alto Fl. ad lib.),3(3rd alt.
E.H.),3*,3*-4,3,3,1-Timp.,Perc.-Cel.(ad lib.),
Hp.-Str.
Leuckart, Leipzig [n.d.]
Score 157 p.
*Composed 1914-46. First complete performance
Stockholm, 28 November 1916, Court Orchestra,
Armas Järnefelt conductor.*

1403 [Symphony no. 4, Little, Op. 14,   22'
G minor]
1.Con forza 2.Andante 3.Scherzo
2(2nd alt. Picc.),2,2,2-4,2,2,1-Timp.-Str.
Leuckart, Leipzig [n.d.]
Score 82 p.
*Composed 1918. First performance Konsert
Foreningen, Stockholm, 27 March 1919, Georg
Schnéevoigt conductor.*

1831 [Symphony no. 5, Funeral, Op. 20,   30'
D minor]
1.Pesante allegro 2.Lento
3(3rd alt. Picc.),3(3rd alt. E.H.),3,2-4,3,3,
1-Timp.,Perc.-Pno.-Str.
Leuckart, Leipzig [n.d.]

Atterberg, Kurt

Score 106 p.
*Composed 1917-22. First performance Berlin,
6 January 1923, Berlin Philharmonic Orchestra,
the composer conducting.*

1566 [Symphony no. 6, Op. 31, C major]   25'
1.Moderato 2.Adagio 3.Vivace
3(3rd alt. Picc.),2,2,2-4,3,3,1-Timp.,Perc.-
Hp.-Str.
Universal Edition, Vienna, c1928
Score 140 p.
*Composed 1927-28. First performance Cologne,
15 October 1928, Cologne Symphony Orchestra,
Hermann Abendroth conductor. Awarded first
prize at the International Schubert Centenary
Contest arranged by the Columbia Gramophone
Co. of New York, 1928.*

6149 [Symphony no. 7, Romantic, Op. 45]   32'
1.Drammatico 2.Semplice 3.Feroce
2(2nd alt. Picc.),2(2nd alt. E.H.),2,2-4,3,3,1
-Timp.,Perc.-Cel.(ad lib.),Hp.-Str.
Ms.
Score 131 p.
*Composed 1942, originally in four movements.
Fourth movement withdrawn by composer. First
performance Frankfurt a.M., 14 February 1943,
Hermann Abendroth conductor.*

5965 [Symphony no. 8, on Swedish national   33'
melodies, Op. 48]
1.Largo 2.Adagio 3.Molto vivace 4.Con moto
2(1st alt. Picc.),2(1st alt. E.H.,2nd ad lib.),
2,2(2nd ad lib.)-2,2,3(1st&2nd ad lib.)-
Timp.-Str.
Ms. c1945 by Kurt Atterberg
Score 156 p.
*Composed 1944. First performance Helsinki,
9 February 1945, State Orchestra, the composer conducting.*

ATTRUP, CARL.   Copenhagen 1848
                                       Copenhagen 1892

781v [Romance, violin and orchestra, Op. 18]
Solo Vn.-1,1,2,1-2Hn.-Str.
Simrock, Berlin, 1888
Score 30 p.

AUBEL, HENRI D'.

370s Menuet nuptial, XVIIIe siècle, Op. 24
Str.(Cb. ad lib.)
Leduc, Paris [n.d.]
Score 7 p.

AUBER, DANIEL FRANÇOIS ESPRIT.
                     Caen, France 29 January 1782
                     Paris 12 May 1871

6832 Le cheval de bronze. Ouverture   7'
2*,2,2,2-4,2,3-Timp.,Perc.-Str.
[n.p., n.d.]
Score 56 p.
*From the opera in three acts with libretto by
Augustin Eugène Scribe. First performance of
original version Paris, 23 March 1835.*

4389 La circassienne. [Overture]
2*,2,2,2-4,2Cnt.,3-Timp.,Perc.-Hp.-Str.
Colombier, Paris [n.d.]
Score 48 p.
*From the opera in three acts with libretto by
Augustin Eugène Scribe. First performance
Paris, 2 February 1861.*

289v [Concerto, violin, D major]
1.Allegro ma non troppo 2.Andante 3.Presto
Solo Vn.-1,2,0,2-2Hn.-Str.
New York Public Library, New York, 1938
Score 37 p.
*Composed 1806. First performance Élèves du
Conservatoire, Jacques-Féréol Mazas soloist.*

5291 Les diamants de la couronne.   7'
Ouverture
2*,2,2,2-4,2Cnt.,3-Timp.,Perc.-Str.
(?)Troupenas, Paris [n.d.]
Score 40 p.
*From the opera in three acts with libretto by
Augustin Eugène Scribe and Vernoy de Saint-
Georges. First performance Paris, 6 March
1841.*

4257 Le duc d'Olonne. Ouverture   8'
2(2nd alt. Picc.),2,2,2-4,2,3-Timp.,Perc.-Str.
Troupenas, Paris [n.d.]
Score 31 p.
*From the opera in three acts with libretto by
Augustin Eugène Scribe and Xavier Boniface
Saintine. First performance Paris, 4 February
1842.*

6578 [Fiorella. Overture]
2*,2,2,2-2,2,1-Timp.,Perc.-Hp.-Str.
Pleyel et Fils, Paris [n.d.]
Score 48 p.
*From the opera in three acts with libretto by
Augustin Eugène Scribe. First performance
Paris, 28 November 1826.*

6840 [Fra Diavolo, or The inn of Terra-   7'30"
cina. Overture]
2*,2,2,2-4,2,3-Timp.,Perc.-Str.
Luck's Music Library, Detroit [n.d.]
Score 47 p.
*From the opera in three acts with libretto by
Augustin Eugène Scribe. First performance
Paris, 28 January 1830.*

5319 [Grand overture for the inauguration   11'
of the London Exposition (i.e., International
Exposition at the Crystal Palace-1862)]
2*,2,2,2-4,2,2Cnt.,4,Ophicl.-Timp.,Perc.-Str.
Brandus & Dufour [n.d.]
Score 39 p.
First performance 1862.

4092 Gustave, ou Le bal masqué. Ouverture   9'
2*,2,2,2-4,2,3,Ophicl.-Timp.,Perc.-Str.
B. Schott, Mayence [n.d.]
Score 94 p.
*First performance of opera, Paris, 27 February
1833.*

5196 [Manon Lescaut. Overture]
2*,2,2,2-4,2Cnt.,3-Timp.,Perc.-Str.
Boieldieu, Paris [n.d.]
Score 34 p.
*From the opera in three acts with libretto by
Augustin Eugène Scribe based on the novel by
Antoine François Prévost. First performance
Paris, 23 February 1856.*

5209 [The mute girl of Portici   7'30"
(Masaniello). Overture]
3*,2,2,4-4,2,3,Ophicl.-Timp.,Perc.-Str.
Joh. André, Offenbach a.M. [1875]
Score 60 p.
*From the opera in five acts with libretto by
Augustin Eugène Scribe and Casimir Delavigne.
First performance Paris, 29 February 1828.*

5644 Le serment, ou Les faux-monnayeurs   7'
[Overture]
2*,2,2,2-4,2,3,Ophicl.-Timp.,Perc.-Str.
[n.p.,n.d.]
Score 43 p.
*From the opera in three acts with libretto by
Augustin Eugène Scribe and Edouard Joseph
Ennemond Mazères. First performance Paris, 1
October 1832.*

5246 La sirène [Overture]   8'
2*,2,2,2-4,2Cnt.,3-Timp.,Perc.-Str.
Maison Troupenas, Paris [n.d.]
Score 36 p.
*From the opera in three acts with libretto by
Augustin Eugène Scribe. First performance
Paris, 26 March 1844.*

4353 [Zanetta, or Playing with fire.   9'
Overture] Arranged by Aubrey Winter
2*,2,2,2-4,2,3-Timp.,Perc.-Str.
Boosey & Hawkes, London, C1933
Score 45 p.
*From the opera in three acts with libretto by
Augustin Eugène Scribe and Jules Henri Vernoy
de Saint-Georges. First performance Paris 18
May 1840.*

AUBERT, LOUIS FRANÇOIS MARIE.
                Paramé, France 19 February 1877
                Paris 9 January 1968

621v Caprice, pour violon et orchestre
Solo Vn.-2,2*,2,2-2,2-Timp.,Trgl.-Hp.-Str.
Durand, Paris, C1925
Score 59 p.
Composed 1925.

811 Dryade, tableau musical   9'
2,2*,2,2-4,2,3-Timp.,Perc.-Hp.-Str.
Durand, Paris, C1924
Score 53 p.
*Composed 1921. First performance Paris,
November 1923, Concerts Colonne, Gabriel
Pierné conductor.*

513p [Fantasy, piano and orchestra, Op. 8,
B minor]
Solo Pno.-2,2,2,2-4,2,3,1-Timp.-Str.
Durand, Paris, C1908

Score 64 p.
*Composed 1899. First performance Paris, 17
November 1901, Concerts Colonne, Louis Diémer
soloist.*

506 Habanera   12'
3*,3*,3*,2,Sarrus.(or C.Bn.)-4,3,3,1-Timp.,
Perc.-2Hp.-Str.
Durand, Paris, C1919
Score 39 p.
*Composed 1918. First performance Paris, 22
March 1919, Concerts Pasdeloup, Rhené-Baton
conductor.*

2911 [Picture album, five children's   12'
pieces for orchestra]
1.Confidence 2.Chanson de route 3.Sérénade
4.Des pays lointains [From distant lands]
5.Danse de l'ours en peluche [Dance of the
teddy bear]
2(2nd alt. Picc.),2(2nd alt. E.H.),2,2(2nd alt.
C.Bn.)-2,2,1-Timp.,Perc.-Cel.,Hp.-Str.
Durand, Paris, C1932
Score 50 p.
First performance Paris, 7 March 1931.

505 Suite brève, Op. 6, B minor   10'
1.Minuet 2.Berceuse 3.Air de ballet
2,2(2nd alt. E.H.),2,2-4,2,3,1-Timp.,Perc.-
Hp.-Str.
Durand, Paris, C1913
Score 58 p.
*Originally composed for two pianos, 1900.
First performance Paris Exposition, 1900.
Orchestral version by composer, 1913. First
performance Paris, 27 April 1916, Concerts
Lamoureux, Camille Chevillard conductor.*

AUER, LEOPOLD.   Veszprém, Hungary 7 June 1845
                Loschwitz, near Dresden 15 July 1930

714v [Hungarian rhapsody, violin and orchestra,
Op. 5]
Solo Vn.-3*,2,2,2-2,2,3-Timp.,Perc.-Str.
Kistner, Leipzig [1881]
Score 34 p.

AULIN, TOR.   Stockholm 10 September 1866
                Stockholm 1 March 1914

604v [Concerto, violin, no. 3, Op. 14,   30'
C minor]
1.Molto moderato 2.Andante con moto 3.Finale
Solo Vn.-2,2,2,2-2,2-Timp.-Str.
Zimmermann, Leipzig, C1905
Score 99 p.

      [Four Swedish dances, Op. 32 nos. 1-4]   22'
1068 No. 1.   5'
2(2nd alt. Picc.),2,2,2-4,2-Timp.,Perc.-Str.
1117 No. 2.   6'
2(2nd alt. Picc.),2,2,2-4,2-Timp.-Str.
1128 No. 3.   5'
2,2(2nd alt. E.H.),2,2-4Hn.-Hp.-Str.
1096 No. 4.   6'
2*,2,2,2-4,2-Timp.,Glock.-Str.
Zimmermann, Leipzig, C1913
Scores: 13 p., 23 p., 13 p., 27 p.

Aulin, Tor

First performance of nos. 1, 2, and 3 Dort-mund, 1913, Georg Hüttner conductor. First performance of no. 4, Göteborg, 1912.

29s Idyll. Arranged for string orchestra by William F. Happich
Str.
Ms.
Score 7 p.
Originally composed for violin and piano as no. 1 of Four Aquarelles [published by C. Fischer, ᶜ1912]. Arranged 1920.

391 [Mäster Olof. Suite from Strindberg's   26'
drama, Op. 22]
1.[The reformer (in Stregnäs' convent)]
2.[His wife and child] 3.[In the town church]
4.[At mother's death bed] 5.[The feast at Norreport]
2(2nd alt. Picc.),2,2,2-4,2,3-Timp.,Perc.-Str.
Zimmermann, Leipzig, ᶜ1909
Score 111 p.
First performance Göteborg, 1909.

[Three Gottland dances, Op. 28 nos. 1-3]   14'
1162 No. 1.   4'
2,2,2,2-4Hn.-Timp.,Bells-Str.
1183 No. 2.   6'
2(2nd alt. Picc.),2,2,2-4Hn.-Trgl.-Str.
1218 No. 3.   4'
2*,2,2,2-4,2-Timp.,B.Dr.,Trgl.-Str.
Zimmermann, Leipzig, ᶜ1912
Scores: 15 p., 12 p., 16 p.
First performance Göteborg, 1912.

AURIC, GEORGES.
                    Lodève, Hérault, France 15 February 1899

5756 [Malborough [sic] s'en va-t'en guerre! 17'
Suite for six instruments]
1.Ouverture 2.La chemin de tous 3.La tente de Malborough 4.Le haut de la tour 5.La bataille
Cl.,Bn.-Tpt.-Pno.-Vn.,Vc.
Heugel, Paris, ᶜ1925
Score 35 p.
The title is the name of a popular French bal-lad from the 18th century. Composed 1924 as incidental music for the play by Marcel Achard.

AUSTIN, ERNEST.   London 31 December 1874

531s The vicar of Bray, variations for   18'
string orchestra, Op. 35
Str.
Novello, London, ᶜ1911
Score 26 p.
First performance at a Queen's Hall Promenade Concert, London, 1910.

AUZENDE, A. M.

1533s [Cantabile, string orchestra, G minor]
Str.
Score: Ms. 11 p.
Parts: Richault, Paris [n.d.]

AVALLE, LOUIS.

1206s Menuet des Muscadens [Minuet of the dandies]
Str.
Score: Ms. 8 p.
Parts: Decourcelle, Nice, ᶜ1911

AVENA, RENATO.   Ancona 19 October 1870
                              Milan 6 March 1927

1068s Danza, nonnina! [Dance, grandmother dear! Minuet for string orchestra]
Str.
Score: Ms. 8 p.
Parts: Ricordi, Milano, ᶜ1921

AVIDOM, MENAHEM. Stanislawow, Poland 6 January 1908

Born: Mahler-Kalkstein

6295 Symphony no. 2, David   28'
1.Childhood 2.Adolescence 3.Exile 4.Finale
3*,3*,3*,3*-4,2,3,1-Timp.,Perc.-Pno.,Cel.,Hp.-Str.
Ms. [ᶜby Israeli Music Publications, Tel Aviv, n.d.]
Score 85 p. Large folio
Composed 1948. First performance on the occa-sion of the transfer to Israel of Theodor Herzl's remains, Vienna, 20 August 1949, Wie-ner Tonkünstlerverein Orchester, Georg Singer conductor.

6563 [Symphony no. 5, The song of Eilat]   28'
1.The first who dared 2.Eilat 3.With Petra lying yonder 4.A prayer and hymn for Eilat
Medium Voice Solo-2(2nd alt. Picc.),2,2,2-4,2,3,1-Timp.,Perc.-Str.
Ms. ᶜ1956, 1957 by Israeli Music Publications, Tel Aviv
Score 94 p.
Text consists of four Hebrew poems (with English and German translations) by Ora Attaria. Composed 1956. An alternate English title for this work is Four Songs of Eilat.

6574 Symphony no. 6   24'
1.Andante 2.Scherzo 3.Lied 4.Finale
2(2nd alt. Picc.),3*,2,2-4,2,3,1-Timp.,Perc.-Pno.,Cel.-Str.
Ms. [ᶜ1958 by Israeli Music Publications, Tel Aviv]
Score 69 p.
Composed 1958. First performance Tel Aviv, autumn 1959, Israel Philharmonic Orchestra, Jean Martinon conductor.

AVISON, CHARLES.
        Newcastle-on-Tyne baptized 16 February 1709
                Newcastle-on-Tyne 9 May 1770

1329s [Concerto, string orchestra,   8'
E minor] Edited by Peter Warlock
1.Adagio - Allegro 2.Amoroso 3.Allegro
Str.
Augener, London, ᶜ1930
Score 9 p.
Originally published 1755.

Avshalomov, Jacob

2338s [Concerto, string orchestra, G minor]
Edited by Arthur Milner
1.Adagio 2.Allegro 3.Adagio 4.Allegro
Str.
Oxford University Press, London, ᶜ1953
Score 8 p.
Original version first published in 1758.
Published as no. 1.

AVSHALOMOV, AARON.
        Nikolayevsk, Siberia 12 November 1894
        New York City 26 April 1965

352m Concerto, flute and orchestra   *15'*
1.Andante - Allegro 2.Andante 3.Allegretto
Solo Fl.-0,2,2,2-2,2,3,1-Timp.,Perc.-Hp.-Str.
Ms. [ᶜ1960]
Score 139 p. Large folio
Composed 1948.

722p [Concerto, piano, Upon Chinese   *35'*
themes and rhythms, in G]
1.Allegro moderato 2.Adagio 3.Allegro non
troppo (Finale)
Solo Pno.-3(3rd alt. Picc.),2(2nd alt. E.H.),
2,2-4,2,3,1-Timp.,Perc.-Cel.,Hp.-Str.
Ms.
Score 156 p.
Composed 1935. First performance Shanghai,
19 January 1936, Shanghai Municipal Orchestra,
the composer conducting, Gregory Singer
soloist.

353v [Concerto, violin, Upon Chinese   *30'*
themes and rhythms, in D]
1.Allegro moderato 2.Adagio, con dolore
3.Finale
Solo Vn.-2(2nd alt. Picc.),2(2nd alt. E.H.),
2,1-2,2-Timp.,Perc.-Cel.,Hp.-Str.
Ms.
Score 181 p.
Composed 1937. First performance Shanghai,
16 January 1938, Shanghai Municipal Symphony
Orchestra, Mario Paci conductor, Gregory
Fidlon soloist.

2994 Peiping hutungs, a sketch in sounds   *12'*
upon Chinese themes and rhythms for symphonic
orchestra
3(3rd alt. Picc.),3*,3(E-flat Cl. alt. B.Cl.),
3*-4,3,3,1-Perc.-Pno.,Cel.,Hp.-Banjo(ad lib.)-
Str.
Ms.
Score 80 p.

The term hutung is confined to North China,
and is used largely in Peking, referring to
certain streets outside the Forbidden City.
Composed 1931-32. First performance under
original title In Hutungs of Peking, *Shanghai,*
24 April 1932, Shanghai Municipal Symphony
Orchestra, Mario Paci conductor. First per-
formance (under revised title) Philadelphia, 8
November 1935, Philadelphia Orchestra, Leopold
Stokowski conductor.

6272 The soul of the ch'in, symphonic   *20'*
suite for orchestra, [or] Four episodes for
grand orchestra from [a] Chinese pantomime
ballet
1.Go Chai's war cry 2.Ming's despair 3.Sai
Hu's dance 4.Kinsei's death
3(3rd alt. Picc.),2,2,2-4,3,3,1-Timp.,Perc.-
Hp.-Str.
Ms.
Score 104 p. Large folio
The ch'in or chyn or guuchyn is an ancient
Chinese seven-stringed zither made of hollowed
wood. The ballet pantomime is an adaptation
of a Chinese story by S. M. Sung. Composed
1926. First performance of no. 4 only New York,
1928, Jacob Gershkovich conductor. First
performance of suite Portland, Oregon, 21 Jan-
uary 1929, Portland Symphony Orchestra, Willem
van Hoogstraten conductor.

6257 [Symphony no. 1, C minor]   *40'*
1.Lento - Allegro non troppo 2.Adagio
3.Scherzo 4.Finale
3(3rd alt. Picc.),3*,2,2-4,3,3,1-Timp.,Perc.-
Pno.,Cel.,Hp.-Str.
Ms. ᶜ1960 by Aaron Avshalomov
Score 237 p. Large folio
Composed 1938-39. First performance Shanghai,
17 March 1940, Shanghai Municipal Orchestra,
Mario Paci conductor.

6232 [Symphony no. 2, Chinese, E minor]   *35'*
1.Largo - Allegro moderato 2.Andante
3.Scherzo 4.Finale
3(3rd alt. Picc.),3*,3*,3*-4,3,3,1-Timp.,Perc.-
Pno.,Cel.,Hp.-Str.
Ms. ᶜ1960 by Aaron Avshalomov
Score 218 p. Large folio
Commissioned by Thor Johnson for the Cincinnati
Symphony Orchestra, 1949. First performance
Cincinnati, 30 December 1949, Cincinnati Sym-
phony Orchestra, Thor Johnson conductor.

6300 Symphony no. 3, B minor   *26'*
1.Andante sostenuto - Allegro moderato
2.Adagio 3.Allegro vivace 4.Finale
3(2nd&3rd alt. Picc.),3*,4(1Cl. in E-flat),3*-
4,3,3,1-Timp.,Perc.-Pno.,Cel.,Hp.-Str.
Ms.
Score 169 p. Large folio
Commissioned by the Serge Koussevitzky Founda-
tion. Composed 1953.

AVSHALOMOV, JACOB.   Tsingtao, China 28 March 1919

5892 Cues from The little clay cart, an   *12'*
ancient Hindu farce

Avshalomov, Jacob

1.Pro & epilogue 2.Maitreya: Be not thus cast
down 3.Shampooer: Ah, the rattle of dice is a
charming thing 4.Illusion of a storm
5.Sharvilaka: May all six seasons bring you
joy
2(2nd alt. Picc.),1,2-Perc.-Hp.,Banjo-Str.
Composers Facsimile Edition, c1954 by Jacob
Avshalomov
Score 44 p.
*Originally composed 1942 as incidental music
to a Hindu farce. First stage performance
Reed College, Portland, Oregon. First performance as a suite, Columbia University, New
York, February 1949. This version revised
1953.*

419m Evocations, concerto for clarinet   *17'*
(or viola) and chamber orchestra
1.Allegro giocoso - Andantino - Allegro gio-
coso 2.Lento 3.Allegro con grazia - Andante
liberamente
Solo Cl.(or Solo Va.)-Picc.(alt. Fl.)-Timp.,
Perc.-Pno.-Str.
Composers Facsimile Edition, c1956 by Jacob
Avshalomov
Score 42 p. Large folio
*Composed 1947. First performance Saratoga
Springs, New York, 17 August 1950, Yaddo Fes-
tival Orchestra, Dean Dixon conductor.
Revised 1952.*

5894 Sinfonietta   *18'*
1.Movendo 2.Andantino 3.Vivo
2(1st alt. Picc.,2nd ad lib.),2(2nd ad lib.),
2(2nd alt. B.Cl.),1-2,2,1-Timp.,Perc.-Pno.-Str.
Composers Facsimile Edition, c1955 by Jacob
Avshalomov
Score 86 p.
*Composed 1946. First performance New York, 29
November 1949, Little Orchestra Society of New
York, Thomas Sherman conductor. Revised 1953.
Winner of Naumburg Recording Award for 1956.*

5893 The taking of T'ung Kuan   *7'*
Allegro furioso - A tempo marziale
3*,2,3(2nd alt. B.Cl.,1Cl. in E-flat),2-4,3,3,
1-Timp.,Perc.-Str.
Composers Facsimile Edition, c1954 by Jacob
Avshalomov
Score 47 p.
*Composed 1943. Revised 1953. First perform-
ance 20 November 1953, Detroit Symphony, Leo-
pold Stokowski conductor.*

AYALA PEREZ, DANIEL.
b. Pueblo de Abalá, Yucatán 21 July 1908

Also known as Daniel Ayala

4024 Tribu [The tribe, suite for symphony
orchestra]
1.En la llanura [On the plain] 2.La serpienta
negra [The black serpent] 3.Danza de fuego
[Fire dance]
4(2Picc.),3*,2,2-4,2,2,1-Timp.,Perc.-Str.
Ms.
Score 39 p.
Composed 1934. First performance Mexico, 18

*October 1935, Orquesta Sinfónica de México,
Carlos Chavez conductor.*

6782 [Uchben X'Coholté (an ancient cemetery),
a Mayan legend, music for ballet in 2 acts,
for orchestra and soprano]
1.Época precortesiana [The pre-Cortez era]
2.Época actual [The present day]
Sop. Voice Solo-2*,1,1-2,1,1,1(or Bn.)-Timp.,
Perc.-Str.
Ms. c1937 by Daniel Ayala Perez
Score 52 p.
*Composed 1936. First performance Mexico City,
March 1936, pupils of the Escuela de Danza.*

AZÉMARD, ALFRED.

1186s Gavotte Louis XIII, pour orchestre à
cordes
Str.
Score: Ms. 7 p.
Parts: Decourcelle, Nice [n.d.]

B

BABER, JOSEPH.
b. Richmond, Virginia 11 September 1937

329v Rhapsody for viola and orchestra   *12'*
Solo Va.-2,2,2,2-4,2,3,1-Timp.-Str.
Ms.
Score 44 p. Large folio
*Composed 1964. First performance Rochester,
15 April 1964, Eastman-Rochester Symphony
Orchestra, Howard Hanson conductor, the com-
poser as soloist. Awarded the Louis Lane
Prize, April 1964.*

BACARISSE, SALVADORE.   Madrid 12 September 1898

962m Tres movimientos concertantes, para
violin, viola, violoncello y orquesta
1.Grave - Allegro 2.Andante quasi adagio
3.Allegro molto vivace
Solo Vn., Solo Va., Solo Vc.-3(3rd alt. Picc.),
3*,3*,3(3rd alt. C.Bn.)-4,3,3,1-Timp.-Hp.-Str.
Ediciones del Consejo Central de la Música,
Barcelona, c1938
Score 139 p. Large folio
Composed 1934.

BACEWICZ, GRAŻYNA.   Łódź, Poland 5 February 1913
Warsaw 17 January 1969

2218s [Concerto, string orchestra]   *15'*
1.Allegro 2.Andante 3.Vivo
Str.
Polskie Wydawnictwo Muzyczne, Cracow, c1951
Score 62 p.
*Composed 1948. First performance Warsaw,
1950, Great Symphony Orchestra of Polish Radio,
Gregor Fitelberg conductor. Awarded the
Polish State Prize in 1950.*

BACH, CARL PHILIPP EMANUEL.   Weimar 8 March 1714
                               Hamburg 14 December 1788

Also known as the "Berlin" or "Hamburg" Bach.

499p [Concerto, cembalo and string orchestra,
      D minor. Wotquenne no. 23]
      1.Allegro 2.Poco andante 3.Allegro assai
      Solo: Cemb.
      Ripieno: Cemb.-Str.
      Score: Denkmäler deutscher Tonkunst, XXIX/XXX.
      Breitkopf & Härtel, Leipzig, 1905. Edited by
      A. Schering. 42 p.
      Parts: Ms.
      Composed 1748.

442p [Concerto, cembalo and string   *23'*
      orchestra, A minor. Wotquenne no. 26] Edited
      by Georg Amft
      1.[Allegro assai] 2.Andante 3.Allegro assai
      Solo: Cemb.
      Ripieno: Cemb.-Str.
      C.F. Kahnt, Leipzig, ᶜ1905
      Score 61 p.
      Composed 1750.

433p [Concerto, 2 pianos and orchestra,   *20'*
      F major. Wotquenne no. 46] Edited by Heinrich
      Schwartz
      1.Allegro 2.Largo 3.Allegro assai
      2 Solo Pno.(or Cemb.&Pno.)-0,2,0,2-2Hn.-Str.
      No score
      Parts: Steingräber, Leipzig, ᶜ1914
      Composed 1740.

432p [Concerto, 2 pianos and orchestra, E-flat
      major. Wotquenne no. 47]
      1.Allegro di molto 2.Larghetto 3.Presto
      2 Solo Pno.-2,0,0,2-2Hn.-Str.
      Score: Ms. ᶜ1976 by The Fleisher Collection of
      Orchestral Music, Free Library of Philadelphia
      145 p.
      Parts: Steingräber, Leipzig, ᶜ1914. Edited by
      Heinrich Schwartz
      Composed 1788.

813   [Concerto, 4 stringed instruments,   *15'*
      D major. (Not in Wotquenne catalog). Tran-
      scribed for small orchestra by Maximilian
      Steinberg]
      1.Allegro moderato 2.Andante lento molto
      3.Allegro
      1,2(2nd alt. E.H.),0,1-Hn.-Str.
      Russischer Musikverlag, Berlin [n.d.]
      Score 26 p.
      *This transcription 1909. First performance St.
      Petersburg, 23 October 1909, Alexander Siloti
      conductor.*

388c [Concerto, violoncello (or viola da gamba,
      or viola) and string orchestra, B-flat major.
      Wotquenne no. 171] Edited by Walter Schulz
      Solo Vc.-Cemb.-Str.
      Breitkopf & Härtel, Leipzig, ᶜ1938
      Score 44 p.
      *Composed 1751. Original title: Concerto a
      Violoncello Concertato, Accompagnato de Due
      Violini, Violetta e Basso.*

3321 [Six little pieces or marches for 2 horns,
      2 oboes, 2 clarinets and bassoon. Wotquenne
      no. 185]
      0,2,2,1-2Hn.
      Ms.
      Score 13 p.
      *Copied from the autograph in the Library of the
      National Conservatory in Brussels.*

1627s [Symphony, C major. Wotquenne no. 182/3]
      Edited by Ernst Fritz Schmid
      Allegro assai - Adagio - Allegretto
      Cemb.-Str.
      Adolph Nagel, Hannover, ᶜ1931
      Score 17 p.
      *No. 3 of six symphonies composed 1773 for
      Baron van Swieten.*

3244 [Symphony, D major. Wotquenne   *12'*
      no. 183/1]
      Allegro di molto - Largo - Presto
      2,2,0,2-2,2(ad lib.)-Timp.(ad lib.)-Str.
      Breitkopf & Härtel, Leipzig [1893]
      Score 28 p.
      Composed ca.1776.

339   [Symphony, E-flat major. Wotquenne   *10'*
      no. 183/2]
      Allegro di molto - Larghetto - Allegretto
      2,2,0,1-2Hn.-Cemb.-Str.
      C.F. Peters, Leipzig [n.d.]
      Score 28 p.
      *Composed ca.1776. This edition from the auto-
      graph in the Royal Library of Berlin.*

340   [Symphony, F major. Wotquenne   *11'*
      no. 183/3]
      Allegro di molto - Larghetto - Presto
      2,2,0,1-2Hn.-Cemb.-Str.
      C.F. Peters, Leipzig [n.d.]
      Score 33 p.
      *Composed ca.1776. This edition from the auto-
      graph in the Royal Library of Berlin.*

BACH. E.

754m Das Abendglöcklein [The evening bell,
      idyll for oboe and orchestra]
      Solo Ob.-0,0,2,1-2,2,1-Bells-Str.
      Score: Ms. 12 p.
      Parts: C.F. Schmidt, Heilbronn [n.d.]

83s   Frühlings Erwachen [Awakening of spring,
      romance for string orchestra]
      Str.
      Score: Ms. 8 p.
      Parts: C.F. Schmidt, Heilbronn [n.d.]

Bach, Johann Bernhard

BACH, JOHANN BERNHARD.
        Erfurt, Germany 23 November 1676
        Eisenach, Germany 11 June 1749

942s [Overture (Suite), string orchestra,   *19'*
no. 1, G minor] Edited by Alexander Fareanu
1.Maestoso - Allegro - Maestoso 2.Air
(Andante) 3.Rondeau (Allegro moderato)
4.Loure (Andante) 5.Fantaisie (Largo)
6.Passepied (Allegro giocoso)
Vn. Concertato-Cemb.-Str.
Breitkopf & Härtel, Leipzig [n.d.]
Score 21 p.
This edition 1920.

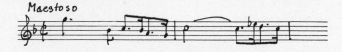

BACH, JOHANN CHRISTIAN.   Leipzig 5 September 1735
        London 1 January 1782

Also known as: John Christian Bach, Jean Bach,
Giovanni Bach, the "London" or "English" Bach,
the "Milan" Bach.

332m [Concerto, bassoon and orchestra,   *21'*
B-flat major] Edited by Johannes Wojciech-
owski
1.Allegro 2.Adagio 3.Presto
Solo Bn.-2Ob.-Cemb.(ad lib.,part not provided)
-Str.
Hans Sikorski, Hamburg, c1953
Score 40 p.
*This edition 1952. The inclusion of a cem-
balo ad lib. is the editor's suggestion. This
work not in the Terry thematic catalog.*

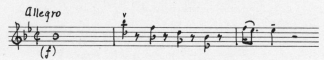

322m [Concerto, bassoon and orchestra,   *16'*
E-flat major. Terry, p.288, no.10] Edited by
Johannes Wojciechowski
1.Allegro spirituoso 2.Largo ma non tanto
3.Tempo di menuetto, più tosto allegro
Solo Bn.-2Ob.-2Hn.-Str.
Hans Sikorski, Hamburg, c1953
Score 41 p.

347p [Concerto, cembalo or piano, 2 violins and
violoncello, Op. 7 no. 2, F major. Terry,
p.293, no.2] Edited by Thor Johnson and Donald
M. McCorkle
1.Allegro con spirito 2.Tempo di minuetto
Solo Hpscd.(or Solo Pno.)-Str.(without Va. or
Cb.)
Ms.
Score 26 p. Large folio
*First published ca.1775. This edition after a
manuscript copied by the Moravian J. F. Peter*

*and now in the Moravian Music Foundation
Archives. First modern performance at the
Fourth Early American Moravian Music Festival
and Seminar, Moravian College, Bethlehem,
Pennsylvania, 25 June 1957, The Festival
Orchestra, Thor Johnson conductor, Mayne Miller
soloist.*

646p [Concerto, cembalo or piano, 2 violins and
violoncello, Op. 7 no. 5, E-flat major. Terry,
p.294, no.5] Edited by Christian Döbereiner
1.Allegro di molto 2.Andante 3.Allegro
Solo Hpscd. (or Solo Pno.)-Str.(without Va. or
Cb.)
C.F. Peters, Leipzig, c1927
Score 38 p.
First published ca.1775.

566p [Concerto, harpsichord or piano and
orchestra, Op. 13 no. 4, B-flat major. Terry,
p.296, no.4] Edited by Ludwig Landshoff
1.Allegro 2.Andante 3.Andante con moto
Solo Hpscd. (or Solo Pno.)-2Ob.-2Hn.-Str.(without Va.)
C.F. Peters, Leipzig, c1931
Score 32 p.
*First published London, 1777, in A Third Set
of Six Concertos for the Harpsichord or Piano
Forte.*

Endimione. Overture to the opera
  See: [Symphony, Op. 18 no. 3, D major]

Lucio Silla. Overture to the opera
  See: [Symphony, Op. 18 no. 2, B-flat major]

3507 [Quintet, flute, oboe, violin,   *12'30"*
tenor instrument and bass, Op. 11 no. 2,
G major. Terry, p.303, no.2. Transcribed for
flute, oboe and string orchestra by Karl
Geiringer]
1.Allegro 2.Allegro assai [3rd movement
lacking]
1,1-Str.
Ms.
Score 24 p.
*First published in London between 1772 and
1777 by Peter Welcker.*

358m [Sinfonia concertante, violin,   *21'*
violoncello and orchestra, A major. Terry,
p.284, no.2] Edited by Alfred Einstein
1.Andante di molto 2.Rondeau: Allegro assai
Solo Vn., Solo Vc.-2Ob.-2Hn.-Cemb.-Str.
Horst Sander, Leipzig [c1949 by Ernst Eulen-
burg]
Score 38 p.
*First published in Paris by J. G. Sieber
ca.1771.*

3245 [Symphony, Op. 3 no. 4, B-flat   *9'*
major. Terry, p.263, no.4] Edited by Fritz
Kneusslin
1.Allegro con spirito 2.Andantino 3.Tempo di
menuetto più tosto allegro
2Ob.(or 2Fl.,or 2Cl.)-2Hn.-Str.
Kneusslin, Basel, c1953
Score 16 p.
First published in London, 1765.

6887 [Symphony, Op. 8 no. 1, E-flat major.
Terry, p.266, no.1]
1.Allegro 2.Andante 3.Allegro assai
2Ob.-2Hn.-Str.
Ms. C1976 by The Fleisher Collection of Orches-
tral Music, Free Library of Philadelphia
Score 26 p.
This symphony is the same as Op. 6 no. 3.
Edited from parts of the original edition
published by S. Markordt, Amsterdam [ca.1775].

6888 [Symphony, Op. 8 no. 2, G major. Terry,
p.267, no.2]
1.Allegro 2.Andante 3.Presto assai
2Ob.-2Hn.-Str.
Ms. C1976 by The Fleisher Collection of Orchestral Music, Free Library of Philadelphia
Score 23 p.
Edited from parts of the original edition
published by S. Markordt, Amsterdam [ca.1775].

6889 [Symphony, Op. 8 no. 3, D major. Terry,
p.267, no.3]
1.Allegro assai 2.Andante 3.Presto
2Ob.-2Hn.-Str.
Ms. C1976 by The Fleisher Collection of Orchestral Music, Free Library of Philadelphia
Score 19 p.
See commentary above.

6190 [Symphony, Op. 9 no. 1, B-flat major. 15'
Terry, p.268, no.1] Edited by Fritz Stein
1.Allegro con spirito 2.Andante 3.[No tempo
indicated]
2Ob.-2Hn.-Cemb.-Str.
Breitkopf & Härtel, Wiesbaden, C1959
Score 27 p.
Also published as Op. 21 no. 1. Used as the
overture to the composer's opera Temistocle.
Composed ca.1767.

4674 [Same as above. Movement I] Edited by Adam
Carse
2,2,0,2-2,2-Timp.-Str.
Augener, London, C1940
Score 15 p.

4636 [Symphony, Op. 9 no. 3, B-flat 10'30"
major. Terry, p.269, no.3] Edited by Adam
Carse
1.Allegro 2.Andante 3.Allegro
2Ob.(or 2Fl.)-2Hn.-Str.
Augener, London, C1935
Score 11 p.
Also published as Op. 21 no. 3. Used as the
overture to the composer's opera Zanaida.

6009 [Symphony, Op. 18 no. 1, E-flat 15'
major. Terry, p.269, no.1] Edited by Fritz
Stein
1.[Allegro spiritoso] 2.Andante 3.Allegro
Orchestra I: 2Ob.,2Bn.-2Hn.-Str.
Orchestra II: 2Fl.-Cemb.(ad lib.)-Str.
Edition Peters, Leipzig, C1932
Score 35 p.
Composed between 1774 and 1777. Op. 18, a set
of six Grand Overtures, first published in Lon-
don by William Forster ca.1781. First

performance of this edition Berlin, 1932, Kam-
merorchester der Hochschule für Musik, Fritz
Stein conductor.

588 [Symphony, Op. 18 no. 2, B-flat 20'
major. Terry, p.270, no.2] Edited by Fritz
Stein
1.Allegro assai 2.Andante 3.Presto
2,2,2,2-2Hn.-Str.
C.F. Peters, New York, C1925
Score 29 p.
Originally composed as the overture to the
composer's opera Lucio Silla, with libretto by
Mattia Verazi after Giovanni da Camera. First
performance Mannheim, 20 November 1776. First
modern performance of the symphony alone, Kiel,
Germany, 1925, Fritz Stein conductor.

2446 [Symphony, Op. 18 no. 3, D major. Terry,
p.270, no.3] Edited by Fritz Stein
1.Allegro 2.Andante 3.Allegro assai
Orchestra I: 0,2,0,1-2Hn.-Str.
Orchestra II: 2Fl.-Str.
C.F. Peters, Leipzig, C1930
Score 28 p.
Originally composed as the overture to the com-
poser's opera Endimione of 1772, now lost.

3401 [Symphony, Op. 18 no. 4, D major. Terry,
p.270, no.4] Edited by Alfred Einstein
1.Allegro con spirito 2.Andante 3.Rondo:
Presto
2(optional),2,0,1-2,2-Timp.-Cemb.(ad lib.)-Str.
Ernst Eulenburg, Leipzig [1934?]
Miniature score 34 p.

3402 [Symphony, 2 clarinets, 2 horns and
bassoon, E-flat major. Terry, p.285, no.1]
1.Allegro 2.Andante 3.March 4.Allegro assai
2Cl.(Ob. may substitute for Cl.I),Bn.-2Hn.
Ms.
Score 33 p.

3403 [Symphony, 2 clarinets, 2 horns and
bassoon, E-flat major. Terry, p.285, no.5]
1.Allegro 2.Andantino 3.Menuetto 4.Allegro
assai
2Cl.(Ob. may substitute for Cl.I),Bn.-2Hn.
Ms.
Score 6 p.

3404 [Symphony, 2 clarinets, 2 horns and 2
bassoons, B-flat major. Terry, p.285, no.6]
1.Allegro 2.Andante 3.Grazioso 4.Allegretto
2Cl.(Ob. may substitute for Cl.I),2Bn.-2Hn.
Ms.
Score 12 p.
First modern performance Sheffield, England, 6
January 1940, John Parr Chamber Concerts, O. C.
Owrid conductor.

Temistocle. Overture
See: [Symphony, Op. 9 no. 1, B-flat major.
Movement 1]

Zanaida. Overture
See: [Symphony, Op. 9 no. 3, B-flat major]

Bach, Johann Christoph.

BACH, JOHANN CHRISTOPH.
     Arnstadt, Germany 8 December 1642
     Eisenach, Germany 31 March 1703

1721s [Lament, Ach, dass ich Wassers g'nug *9'*
hätte, contralto voice, organ and strings.
Transcribed for solo violin and string
orchestra by Quinto Maganini]
Solo Vn.-Str.
Affiliated Music Corp., New York, ^c1936
Score 8 p.
Formerly attributed to Johann Christoph Bach's
father, Heinrich. This transcription, 1931.
First performance New York, 22 December 1931,
New York Sinfonietta, Quinto Maganini con-
ductor.

BACH, JOHANN ERNST. Eisenach 28 January 1722
        Eisenach 1 September 1777

5575 [Symphony, B-flat major] Edited by *7'*
Donald M. McCorkle
1.Allegro 2.Andante 3.Allegro
2Bn.-Str.
Ms. ^c[n.d.] by The Moravian Music Foundation,
Inc., Winston-Salem, North Carolina
Score 16 p. Large folio
This edition based on a manuscript copied by
the Moravian Johann Friedrich Peter and now in
the Moravian Music Foundation Archives. First
modern performance at the Fourth Early Ameri-
can Moravian Music Festival and Seminar, Mora-
vian College, Bethlehem, Pennsylvania, 25 June
1957, The Festival Orchestra, Thor Johnson
conductor.

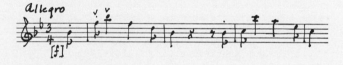

BACH, JOHANN LUDWIG.
   (?)Thal, Thuringia, Germany 4 February 1677
   Meiningen, Germany buried 1 May 1731

Also known as the "Meiningen" Bach

1862s [Overture, cembalo and string *8'*
orchestra, G major] Adapted by Karl Geiringer
In one movement: Lentement - Allegro
Cemb.-Str.
Ms.
Score 12 p.
Composed 1715. This and an accompanying suite
of dances are Johann Ludwig Bach's only extant
instrumental works.

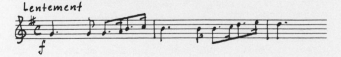

BACH, JOHANN SEBASTIAN.
     Eisenach, Germany 21 March 1685
     Leipzig 28 July 1750

Adagio for chamber orchestra
 See: [Sonata, violin and clavier (or
    cembalo), no. 4, C minor. BWV 1017.
    Adagio]

Adagio for orchestra
 See: [Toccata and fugue for organ, C major.
    BWV 564. Adagio]

Adagio from the Easter oratorio
 See: [Easter oratorio. BWV 249. No. 2,
    Adagio]

Air on the G string
 See: [Overture (Suite), orchestra, no. 3,
    D major. BWV 1068. Air]

Anna Magdalena Bach notebook
 See: [Notebook for Anna Magdalena Bach]

963s A Bach suite. Movements from the English
and French suites. Selected and arranged by
Gerrard Williams
1.Prelude (3rd English suite) 2.Allemande
(2nd French suite) 3.Sarabande (4th English
suite) 4.Gavotte (5th French suite) 5.Minuet
(no. 2, 1st French suite) 6.Bourrée I (2nd
English suite) 7.Bourrée II (2nd English
suite) 8.Gigue (5th French suite)
1,1,1,1(all ad lib.)-Tpt.(ad lib.)-Timp.(ad
lib.)-Str.
Oxford University Press, London, ^c1926
Score 36 p.

Bist du bei mir (BWV 508)
 See: [Notebook for Anna Magdalena Bach,
    vol. 2. Selections] Transcribed by
    Thomas T. Frost

Brandenburg concerti
 See: [Concerto grosso, Brandenburg...]

1949s [Cantata no. 2, Ach Gott vom Himmel *4'*
sieh' darein. BWV 2. Chorale, O God from
heaven look below] Transcribed by Harl
McDonald
Str.
Ms.
Score 4 p.
The melody is an old German hymn tune, to
which Martin Luther added his paraphrase of
Psalm 12 in 1524.

5000 [Cantata no. 4, Easter cantata. *3'45"*
BWV 4. Movement 4, Christ lag in Todesbanden]
Transcribed by Leopold Stokowski
4,4*,3*,3*-6,4,4,1-Timp.-Str.
Broude Brothers, New York, ^c1950
Score 17 p.
Melody and text of the chorale are Martin
Luther's correction and arrangement in 1524 of
a 12th century German hymn, Christ ist ufer-
standen. Cantata composed 1724.

Bach, Johann Sebastian

1149s [Cantata no. 12, Weinen, Klagen, Sorgen, Zagen. BWV 12. Sinfonia] Edited by W.G. Whittaker
Ob.(or Solo Vn.),Bn.(ad lib.)-Str.
Oxford University Press, London, c1925
Score 3 p.
Bound with Cantatas nos. 21, 156.

1149s [Cantata no. 21, Ich hatte viel Bekümmernis. BWV 21. Sinfonia] Edited by W.G. Whittaker
Ob.(or Solo Vn.),Bn.(ad lib.)-Str.
Oxford University Press, London, c1925
Score 3 p.
Bound with Cantatas nos. 12, 156.

2726 [Cantata no. 26, Ach wie flüchtig,   *4'*
ach wie nichtig. BWV 26. No. 1, Overture]
Transcribed by Leonid Leonardi
2,2,3*,2-4,3,3,1-Timp.-Str.
Ms.
Score 24 p.
Transcribed 1935. First performance St. Louis, 25 November 1938, St. Louis Symphony Orchestra, Vladimir Golschmann conductor.

1488 [Cantata no. 29, Wir danken dir Gott, wir danken dir (Ratswahl cantata). BWV 29. Sinfonia] Edited by A. Siloti
0,3*,0,3*-3Tpt.-Timp.-Str.
Jurgenson, Moscow [n.d.]
Score 31 p.

1496 [Cantata no. 31, Der Himmel lacht,   *3'*
die Erde jubilieret. BWV 31. Sonata] Arranged by W.G. Whittaker
0,4*,0,1(ad lib.)-3Tpt.-Timp.-Str.
Oxford University Press, London, c1928
Score 14 p.

1107s [Cantata no. 35, Geist und Seele   *3'*
wird verwirret. BWV 35. Sinfonia no. 1] Edited by W.G. Whittaker
2Ob.,E.H.(or Vn.III)-Org.(or Pno.,obbligato)-Str.
Oxford University Press, London, c1929
Score 18 p.

1109s [Cantata no. 35, Geist und Seele   *3'*
wird verwirret. BWV 35. Sinfonia no. 2] Edited by W.G. Whittaker
2Ob.(optional),E.H.(optional)-Org.(or Pno., obbligato)-Str.
Oxford University Press, London, c1928
Score 6 p.

1147s [Cantata no. 42, Am Abend aber desselbigen Sabbats. BWV 42. Sinfonia] Edited by W.G. Whittaker
2Ob.(or 2Solo Vn.),Bn.(or Solo Vc.)-Str.
Oxford University Press, London, c1925
Score 10 p.

571s [Cantata no. 75, Die Elenden sollen essen. BWV 75. Sinfonia] Edited by W.G. Whittaker
Tpt.(extra Vn.,Fl.,Ob.,Cl.,Voices, all ad lib.)-Str.
Oxford University Press, London, c1925
Score 4 p.

663s [Cantata no. 76, Die Himmel erzählen die Ehre Gottes. BWV 76. Sinfonia] Edited by W.G. Whittaker
Ob.d'Amore(or Ob. or Vn.I),Va.da Gamba(or Vn.II or Va.or Vc.),Vc.,Cb.(optional)-Pno.(or Org.) (ad lib.)
Oxford University Press, London, c1925
Score 5 p.

1374s [Cantata no. 140, Wachet auf, ruft uns die Stimme. BWV 140. No. 4, Chorale] Arranged by Michele Esposito
1,1,1,1-1,1-Str.
Oxford University Press, London, c1925
Score 9 p.
Woodwinds may be doubled; horn is optional if there is a trumpet playing the part.

1232s [Cantata no. 142, Uns ist ein Kind geboren. BWV 142. Concerto] Edited by W.G. Whittaker
2Fl.(or Solo Vn.I&II),2Ob.(or Solo Vn.III&IV)-Str.
Oxford University Press, London, c1925
Score 6 p.

5882 [Cantata no. 147, Herz und Mund und   *3'*
Tat und Leben. BWV 147. Chorale, Jesu, joy of man's desiring] Transcribed by Richard G. Appel
2,2,2,2-4,2,3,1-Hpscd.(or Hp.),Org.-Str.
Ms. c1941 by Richard G. Appel
Score 15 p. Large folio
Basic melody of the Chorale is by Johann Schop, first published to the text of Werde Munter, Mein Gemüthe in Johann Rist's Himmlische Lieder, 1642. Text of Bach's Chorale is from Martin Jahn's hymn, Jesu, Meiner Seelen Wonne. Cantata composed 1716 and revised by Bach, possibly 1727. First performance of this transcription Boston, 20 June 1941, Boston Pops Orchestra, Arthur Fiedler conductor.

5990 [Same as above] Transcribed by   *3'*
Lucien Cailliet
3(3rd alt. Picc.),3*,4*(1Cb.Cl.),4*-4,3,3,1-Timp.-Hp.-Str.
Ms.
Score 13 p.
This transcription commissioned by Eugene Ormandy for the Philadelphia Orchestra. Transcribed 1934-36. First performance Philadelphia, 9 October 1936, Philadelphia Orchestra, Eugene Ormandy conductor.

862s [Same as above] Transcribed by W.G. Whittaker
Str.(with Ob.I,II-Tpt.-Vocal Chorus, all ad lib.)
Oxford University Press, London, c1928
Score 4 p.

851s [Cantata no. 152, Tritt auf die Glaubensbahn. BWV 152. Concerto] Edited by W.G. Whittaker
Fl.(or Vn.),Ob.(or Vn.)-Va.d'Amore(or Va.),Va. da Gamba(or Vc.I),Vc.II,Cb.(ad lib.)
Oxford University Press, London, c1925
Score 8 p.

Bach, Johann Sebastian

1303s [Cantata no. 156, Ich steh' mit einem
Fuss im Grabe. BWV 156. Sinfonia] Transcribed
by Sam Franko
Str.
G. Schirmer, New York, c1915
Score 5 p.
Also known popularly as Arioso.

1149s [Same as above] Edited by W.G. Whittaker
Ob.(or Solo Vn.),Bn.(ad lib.)-Str.
Oxford University Press, London, c1925
Score 2 p.
Bound with Cantatas nos. 12, 21.

6896 [Cantata no. 175, Er rufet seinen Schafen
mit Namen. BWV 175. No. 2, Aria, Komm, leite
mich] Edited by Hans Fischer
Solo Vn.(or Solo Va. or Voice Solo)-3Alto
Recorders(or 3 Vn.)-Cemb.(or Org.)
Vieweg, Berlin-Lichterfelde, c1962
Score 11 p.

1025s [Cantata no. 207 (Dramma per musica)
Vereinigte Zwietracht der wechselnden Saiten.
BWV 207. Marcia] Edited by W.G. Whittaker
3Tpt.(or Fl.,Ob.,Cl.)-Timp.-Str.
Oxford University Press, London, c1925
Score 3 p.
*Bound with Cantatas nos. 208, 212. Based on
the opening number of a cantata composed 1726
in honor of Gottlieb Korte, University of
Leipzig, upon his promotion to professor.*

2323s [Cantata no. 208, Was mir behagt,   4'
ist nur die muntre Jagd (Hunt cantata). BWV
208. No. 9, Aria, Sheep may safely graze]
Transcribed by Reginald Jacques
2Solo Vn.(or 2Solo Fl.)-Str.
Oxford University Press, London, c1947
Score 4 p.

1025s [Same as above. Number 13, Aria] Edited
by W.G. Whittaker
Ob.(or Vn.II)-Pno.-Vn.,Vc.
Oxford University Press, London, c1925
Score 3 p.
*Bound with Cantatas nos. 207, 212. Last num-
ber of the secular Cantata, Was mir behagt,
ist nur die muntre Jagd, first performed at
the birthday hunting party of Duke Christian
of Saxe-Weissenfels, 23 February 1716.*

558s [Cantata no. 209, Non sa che sia dolore.
BWV 209. Sinfonia] Edited by W.G. Whittaker
Fl.(or Solo Vn.)-Str.
Oxford University Press, London, c1925
Score 8 p.

1025s [Cantata no. 212, Mer hahn en neue
Oberkeet (Peasant cantata). BWV 212. Prelude]
Edited by W.G. Whittaker
Cemb.or Pno.(optional)-Str.
Oxford University Press, London, c1925
Score 4 p.
*Bound with Cantatas nos. 207, 208. Commis-
sioned by Carl Heinrich von Dieskau in honor
of his ennoblement. First performance Dresden,
30 August 1742.*

4938 [Capriccio for clavier, 'Sopra la   12'
lontananza del suo fratello dilettissimo',
B major. BWV 992] Transcribed by Ralph
Berkowitz
In 6 movements
2,2,2,2-2,2-Timp.-Str.
Ms.
Score 32 p. Large folio
*Composed 1704 when the composer's brother
Johann Jakob Bach entered Swedish military
service as an oboist under Charles XII of
Sweden.*

Chaconne (no. 2) in D minor for unaccompanied
violin. Transcribed for orchestra
See: [Partita for unaccompanied violin, no. 2,
D minor. BWV 1004. Chaconne]

4742 [Chorale, Gott, der du selber bist das
Licht. BWV 316] Transcribed for winds and
timpani by Harl McDonald
2,3*,4*,3*-0,3,3,1-Timp.
Ms.
Score 4 p.
*Text of the chorale by Johann Rist (1641).
Melody by Johann Crüger (1648). Bach's setting was for four mixed voices. First published posthumously by Fr. W. Birnstiel, Berlin, 1765, in the first volume of a collection
of the four-part chorales made by the composer's son, Carl Philipp Emanuel Bach.*

2030 [Chorale-prelude, organ, An Wasserflüssen
Babylon. BWV 653] Transcribed by M. Wood-Hill
1,1,1,2-Hn.-Hp.-Str.
Goodwin & Tabb, London, c1926
Score 16 p.

507s [Chorale-prelude, organ, Aus tiefer Not
schrei' ich zu dir. BWV 687] Transcribed by
Hugo Kaun
Str.
Vieweg, Berlin [n.d.]
Score 5 p.

505s [Chorale-prelude, organ, Erbarm' dich
mein, o Herre Gott. BWV 721] Transcribed by
Hugo Kaun
Str.
Vieweg, Berlin [n.d.]
Score 5 p.

2514 [Chorale-prelude, organ, Herzlich   4'
tut mich verlangen. BWV 727] Transcribed by
Lucien Cailliet
2,3*,3*,3*-3Sax.(AAT, ad lib.)-4,3,3,1-Timp.-
Pno.(ad lib.)-Str.
Elkan-Vogel, Philadelphia, c1934
Score 4 p.
*First performance Minneapolis, 18 January
1935, Minneapolis Symphony Orchestra, Eugene
Ormandy conductor.*

1172s [Same as above] Transcribed by Fabien
Sevitzky
Str.
Ms.
Score 3 p.

6467 [Chorale-prelude, organ, In dir ist   *5'*
Freude. BWV 615] Transcribed by Frederic
Balazs
3*,2,2,2-4,2,3,1-Timp.-Str.
Ms.
Score 15 p.
*Theme by Giovanni Gastoldi, first published as
A Lieta Vita in his Canzonette a 3 Voci (1592-
96). This theme was adapted as a hymn tune by
Johannes Lindemann in 1597 to the words In Dir
Ist Freude. This transcription, 1954. First
performance El Paso, 1959-60 season, El Paso
Symphony, Orlando Barera conductor.*

1570 [Chorale-prelude, organ, Komm, Gott
Schöpfer, heiliger Geist. BWV 667] Transcribed
by Arnold Schoenberg
4*,4*,6*,4*-4,4,4,1-Timp.,Perc.-2Hp.-Str.
Universal Edition, Vienna, ᶜ1925
Score 11 p.
*Transcribed Vienna, summer 1922. First per-
formance New York, 7 December 1922, Philhar-
monic Orchestra, Josef Stransky conductor.
Bound with BWV 654.*

4660 [Chorale-prelude, organ, Kyrie,   *4'30"*
Gott heiliger Geist. BWV 671] Transcribed for
wind orchestra by Hershey Kay
4(4th alt. Picc.),4*,4*,4-4,0,0,1
Ms.
Score 15 p. Large folio
*This transcription 1941. First performance
Philadelphia, 28 April 1942, Curtis Institute
Woodwind Ensemble, Marcel Tabuteau conductor.
First public performance New York, 17 January
1948, New York Philharmonic, Walter Hendl
conductor.*

510s [Chorale-prelude, organ, Liebster Jesu,
wir sind hier. BWV 706] Transcribed by
Maurice Besly
Solo Vn.-Fl.,Ob.-Str.
Boosey, London, ᶜ1924
Score 8 p.

389s [Chorale-prelude, organ, O Mensch, bewein'
dein' Sünde gross. BWV 622] Transcribed by
Max Reger
Str.
Breitkopf & Härtel, Leipzig, ᶜ1915
Score 5 p.
*This transcription transposed from the original
key of E-flat major to D major.*

1567 [Chorale-prelude, organ, O Mensch,
bewein' dein' Sünde gross. BWV 622 *and* In dir
ist Freude. BWV 615] Transcribed by Vittorio
Gui
4,2*,0,2-4,3-Timp.,Bells-Str.
Universal Edition, Vienna, ᶜ1925
Score 12 p.
*Transcribed 1923. First performance Politeana
Fiorentino, Florence, May 1923, Vittorio Gui
conductor.*

1570 [Chorale-prelude, organ, Schmücke dich, o
liebe Seele. BWV 654] Transcribed by Arnold
Schoenberg

4*,4*,6*,4*-4,4,4,1-Timp.,Perc.-Cel.,Hp.-Str.
Universal Edition, Vienna, ᶜ1925
Score 16 p.
*Transcribed Vienna, summer 1922. First per-
formance New York, 7 December 1922, New York
Philharmonic, Josef Stransky conductor. Bound
with BWV 667.*

6831 [Chorale-prelude, organ, Vor deinen   *3'*
Thron tret' ich (Wenn wir in höchsten Nöten
sein). BWV 668] Transcribed by John Barbirolli
4Hn.(or 2Hn.),Tpt.-Str.(without Vn.)
Oxford University Press, London, ᶜ1950
Score 4 p.
*Bach wrote several chorales and chorale pre-
ludes on the melody Wenn Wir in Höchsten Nöten
Sein, but this version is apparently his last
piece of music. Composed 1750.*

3429 [Chorale-prelude, organ, Wir glauben   *3'*
all' an einen Gott (Giant fugue). BWV 680]
Transcribed by Herman Boessenroth
3*,3*,3*,4*-4,4,3,1-Timp.-Org.(ad lib.)-Str.
Ms.
Score 19 p.
*First performance Minneapolis, 20 December
1935, Minneapolis Symphony Orchestra, Eugene
Ormandy conductor. The text of the hymn is a
free version by Martin Luther of the Nicene
Creed. Origin of the basic musical theme
uncertain. Possibly derived from the traditional plain chant melody with German words
used by Luther ca.1524 to replace the Latin
Credo in Unum Deum of the Mass. Bach composed
several versions of Wir Glauben All' an Einen
Gott. This version is taken from Part III of
the Clavierübung, or Exercises for the Clavier.*

4926 [Same as above] Transcribed by   *6'*
Leopold Stokowski
3(3rd alt. Picc.),3*,5*(1Cl. in E-flat,1Cb.Cl.),
3*-4,3,3,2-Timp.-Str.
Broude Brothers, New York, ᶜ1948
Score 18 p.

559s [Same as above] Transcribed by Ralph
Vaughan Williams and Arnold Foster
Str.
Oxford University Press, London, ᶜ1925
Score 4 p.

1446 Chorale-variation, organ, Wachet auf, ruft
uns die Stimme (after Cantata no. 140).
BWV 645] Transcribed by Granville Bantock
0,0,2,2-2Hn.-Str.
Breitkopf & Härtel, Leipzig [n.d.]
Score 8 p.

Christ lag in Todesbanden
   See: [Cantata no. 4, Easter cantata. BWV 4.
      Movement 4, Christ lag in Todesbanden]

1342 [Christmas oratorio. BWV 248.   *5'*
Sinfonia] Transcribed by Robert Franz
2,4(2 are E.H.),2,2-2Hn.-Pno.-Str.
Leuckart, Leipzig [n.d.]
Score 18 p.
Originally composed 1733-34. First performance

Bach, Johann Sebastian

of oratorio by the choir of St. Thomas' Church, Leipzig, 1734.

1364s [Same as above] Transcribed by Hermann Schröder
Org.-Str.
Vieweg, Berlin [n.d.]
Score 7 p.

5653 [Chromatic fantasy and fugue for   10-14'
clavier, D minor. BWV 903] Transcribed by
George F. Bristow as his Op. 53.
2,2,3*,2-4,2,3-Timp.-Str.
Ms.
Score 48 p.
*Composed probably 1720. This transcription
ca.1879.*

Come sweet death
See: [Komm, süsser Tod. BWV 478]

464p [Concerto, cembalo, no. 1, D minor.   23'
BWV 1052]
1.Allegro 2.Adagio 3.Allegro
Solo Cemb.-Str.
Breitkopf & Härtel, Leipzig [n.d.]
Score 42 p.
*Composed between 1730 and 1731. First perform-
ance Leipzig, at the Telemann Collegium
Musicum.*

465p [Concerto, cembalo, no. 2, E major.   18'
BWV 1053]
1.[No tempo indicated] 2.Siciliano 3.Allegro
Solo Cemb.-Str.
Breitkopf & Härtel, Leipzig [n.d.]
Score 34 p.
*Composed before 1731. First performance Leip-
zig, at the Telemann Collegium Musicum.*

466p [Concerto, cembalo, no. 3, D major.   27'
BWV 1054]
1.[No tempo indicated] 2.Adagio e sempre
piano 3.Allegro
Solo Cemb.-Str.
Peters, Leipzig [n.d.]
Score 28 p.
*Composed between 1729 and 1736. First per-
formance Leipzig, at the Telemann Collegium
Musicum.*

467p [Concerto, cembalo, no. 4, A major.   16'
BWV 1055]
1.Allegro 2.Larghetto 3.Allegro ma non tanto
Solo Cemb.-Str.
Breitkopf & Härtel, Wiesbaden [n.d.]
Score 24 p.
*Composed between 1729 and 1736. First per-
formance Leipzig, at the Telemann Collegium
Musicum.*

468p [Concerto, cembalo, no. 5, F minor.   12'
BWV 1056]
1.[No tempo indicated] 2.Largo 3.Presto
Solo Cemb.-Str.
Breitkopf & Härtel, Leipzig [n.d.]
Score 16 p.

*Composed ca.1730. First performance Leipzig,
at the Telemann Collegium Musicum.*

787v [Same as above] Reconstructed as   12'
a concerto for violin in G minor by J.
Bernard Jackson
1.Moderato con moto 2.Largo, ma non troppo
3.Allegro vivace
Solo Vn.-Pno.(ad lib.)-Str.
Oxford University Press, London, ᶜ1925
Score 28 p.
Reconstructed in 1924.

574v [Same as above] Reconstructed as   12'
a concerto for violin in G minor by Gustav
Schreck
1.Moderato 2.Largo 3.Presto
Solo Vn.-Pno.(or Cemb.)-Str.
Peters, Leipzig [n.d.]
Score 23 p.
*Reconstructed in 1903. First performance
Leipzig, 1904.*

490p [Concerto, cembalo, no. 6, F major.   15'
BWV 1057]
1.[No tempo indicated] 2.Andante 3.Allegro
assai
Solo Cemb.-2Fl.-Str.
Breitkopf & Härtel, Leipzig [n.d.]
Score 44 p.
*A transcription of the Brandenburg Concerto
IV, composed between 1717 and 1721. Tran-
scribed after 1729. First performance Leipzig,
at the Telemann Collegium Musicum.*

469p [Concerto, cembalo, no. 7, G minor.   12'
BWV 1058]
1.[No tempo indicated] 2.Andante 3.Allegro
assai
Solo Cemb.-Str.
Breitkopf & Härtel, [n.p., n.d.]
Score 24 p.
*A transcription of the Violin Concerto in A
Minor, BWV 1041, composed between 1717 and
1723. Transcribed between 1729 and 1736.
First performance Leipzig, at the Telemann
Collegium Musicum.*

470p [Concerto, 2 cembali, no. 1,   15'
C minor. BWV 1060]
1.Allegro 2.Adagio 3.Allegro
2 Solo Cemb.-Str.
Breitkopf & Härtel, Leipzig [n.d.]
Score 34 p.
*Composed between 1729 and 1736. First per-
formance Leipzig, at the Telemann Collegium
Musicum.*

575v [Same as above] Transcribed for   17'
2 violins and string orchestra by Ossip
Schnirlin
1.Allegro 2.Largo [Bach: Adagio] 3.Allegro
2 Solo Vn.-Str.
Simrock, Berlin, ᶜ1923
Score 27 p.
*Transcribed by J. S. Bach for two cembali
ca.1730, from the composer's concerto for two
violins or oboe and violin, now lost.*

Bach, Johann Sebastian

471p [Concerto, 2 cembali, no. 2,   20'
C major. BWV 1061]
1.[No tempo indicated] 2.Adagio ovvero largo
3.Fuga
2 Solo Cemb.-Str.
Breitkopf & Härtel, Leipzig [n.d.]
Score 42 p.
Composed between 1727 and 1730. First per-
formance Leipzig, at the Telemann Collegium
Musicum.

472p [Concerto, 2 cembali, no. 3,   14'
C minor. BWV 1062]
1.[No tempo indicated] 2.Andante 3.Allegro
assai
2 Solo Cemb.-Str.
Breitkopf & Härtel, Leipzig [n.d.]
Score 35 p.
Composed between 1729 and 1736. First per-
formance Leipzig, at the Telemann Collegium
Musicum.

473p [Concerto, 3 cembali, no. 1,   15'
D minor. BWV 1063]
1.[No tempo indicated] 2.Alla siciliana
3.Allegro
3 Solo Cemb.-Str.
Peters, Leipzig [1845]
Score 43 p.
Composed between 1730 and 1733. First per-
formance Leipzig, at the Telemann Collegium
Musicum.

474p [Concerto, 3 cembali, no. 2,   14'
C major. BWV 1064]
1.[Allegro] 2.Adagio 3.Allegro
3 Solo Cemb.-Str.
Peters, Leipzig [1850]
Score 47 p.
Bach apparently adapted this from a concerto
for three violins, now lost, which may not
have been his own. Composed between 1730 and
1733 for performance by J.S., W.F. and C.P.E.
Bach.

1339s [Same as above. Movement I] Transcribed
for string orchestra by Adolf Lotter
1.Allegro moderato [Bach: Allegro]
Str.
Hawkes & Son, London, ᶜ1929
Score 27 p.

475p [Concerto, 4 cembali, A minor.   11'
BWV 1065]
1.[No tempo indicated] 2.Largo 3.Allegro
4 Solo Cemb.-Str.
Breitkopf & Härtel, Leipzig [n.d.]
Score 28 p.
After a B minor concerto for four violins by
A. Vivaldi

588m [Concerto, flute, violin, cembalo,   23'
A minor. BWV 1044]
1.Allegro 2.Adagio ma non tanto e dolce
3.Alla breve
Solo Fl., Solo Vn., Solo Cemb.-Str.
Breitkopf & Härtel, Wiesbaden [n.d.]
Score 50 p.

From a Prelude and Fugue composed before 1725;
arranged as a Concerto between 1730 and 1736.

572v [Concerto, violin, no. 1, A minor.   15'
BWV 1041]
1.[No tempo indicated] 2.Andante 3.Allegro
assai
Solo Vn.-Str.
Breitkopf & Härtel, Leipzig [n.d.]
Score 18 p.

573v [Concerto, violin, no. 2, E major.   24'
BWV 1042]
1.Allegro 2.Adagio 3.Allegro assai
Solo Vn.-Str.
Breitkopf & Härtel [n.p., n.d.]
Score 18 p.

576v [Concerto, 2 violins, D minor. BWV 1043]
1.Vivace 2.Largo, ma non tanto 3.Allegro
2 Solo Vn.-Str.
Breitkopf & Härtel, Wiesbaden [n.d.]
Score 22 p.

965v [Concerto grosso, Brandenburg no. 1,   16'
F major. BWV 1046]
1.[No tempo indicated] 2.Adagio 3.Allegro
4.Menuetto - Trio 5.Polacca 6.Trio
Soli: Vn.,3Ob.,1Bn.-2Hn.-Cemb.-Str.
Breitkopf & Härtel, Wiesbaden [n.d.]
Score 30 p.

1356s [Same as above. Menuet, Polacca, Trio]
Transcribed for string orchestra by W.G.
Whittaker
1.Menuetto 2.Trio I 3.Polacca - Menuetto da
capo 4.Trio II - Menuetto da capo
Str.
Oxford University Press, London, ᶜ1927
Score 4 p.

712m [Concerto grosso, Brandenburg no. 2,   15'
F major. BWV 1047]
1.[No tempo indicated] 2.Andante 3.Allegro
assai
Soli: Vn.,Fl.,Ob.,Tpt.-Cemb.-Str.
Breitkopf & Härtel, Leipzig [n.d.]
Score 26 p.

1445 [Same as above] Arranged by F. Mottl   15'
1.Allegro moderato 2.Andante 3.Allegro
Solo Vn.-3,3,2,2-2,2-Str.
Breitkopf & Härtel, Leipzig ᶜ1901
Score 53 p.

78s [Concerto grosso, Brandenburg no. 3,   9'
G major. BWV 1048]
1.[No tempo indicated] 2.Allegro
Cemb.-Str.
Kalmus, New York [n.d.]
Score 23 p.

991v [Concerto grosso, Brandenburg no. 4,   19'
G major. BWV 1049]
1.Allegro 2.Andante 3.Presto
Soli: 2Fl.,Vn.-Str.
Breitkopf & Härtel, Wiesbaden [n.d.]
Score 40 p.

Bach, Johann Sebastian

743m [Concerto grosso, Brandenburg no. 5,   24'
D major. BWV 1050]
1.Allegro 2.Affettuoso 3.Allegro
Soli: Fl.,Cemb.,Vn.-Str.
Breitkopf & Härtel, Wiesbaden [n.d.]
Score 38 p.

825m [Same as above] Transcribed by   24'
A. Siloti
1.Moderato 2.Affettuoso 3.Allegro
Soli: 2Fl.,Vn.-Pno.-Str.
Breitkopf & Härtel, Leipzig [n.d.]
Score 35 p.

535s [Concerto grosso, Brandenburg no. 6,   16'
B-flat major. BWV 1051]
1.[No tempo indicated] 2.Adagio ma non tanto
3.Allegro
Cemb.-2Va.da Braccio,2Va.da Gamba,Vc.,Violone
Breitkopf & Härtel, Leipzig [n.d.]
Score [25] p.

2363s [Same as above] Transcribed for   18'
string orchestra by Michele Esposito
1.Allegro 2.Adagio, ma non troppo 3.Allegro
Str.
Oxford University Press, London, c1929
Score 24 p.

Dorian prelude (Toccata) and fugue, organ,
D minor
See: [Prelude (Toccata) and fugue, organ,
        Dorian, D minor. BWV 538]

7085 [Easter oratorio. BWV 249. No. 1,   4'
Sinfonia] Edited by W. Gillies Whittaker
2Ob.,Bn.(optional)-3Tpt.-Timp.-Str.
Oxford University Press, London, c1928
Score 14 p.

209m [Easter oratorio. BWV 249. No. 2,
Adagio] Edited by W. Gillies Whittaker
Solo Ob.(or Solo Vn.)-Bn.(optional)-Str.
Oxford University Press, London, c1928
Score 3 p.

1891 [English suite no. 2. BWV 807.   5'
Bourrée I] Transcribed by François Auguste
Gevaert
2,2,0,2-2Hn.-Str.
Durand, Paris [n.d.]
Score 7 p.
Orchestrated and first performed Paris, 1875.

508s [Same as above] Transcribed by Hugo Kaun
Solo Vn.-Str.
Vieweg, Berlin [n.d.]
Score 7 p.

504s [English suite no. 2. BWV 807. Sarabande]
Transcribed by Hugo Kaun
Solo Vn.-Str.
Vieweg, Berlin [n.d.]
Score 5 p.

702s [English suite no. 2. BWV 807. Sarabande
and English suite no. 3. BWV 808. Gavotte I]
Arranged by Georg Kramm

Solo Ob.-Str.
Heinrichshofen, Magdeburg [n.d.]
Score 3 p.

1318 [English suite no. 3. BWV 808]   25'
Orchestrated by Joachim Raff; revised by Max
Erdmannsdörfer
1.Prelude 2.Allemande 3.Courante 4.Sara-
bande 5.Gavotte
2,2,2,2-2,2-Timp.-Str.
Ries & Erler, Berlin [n.d.]
Score 40 p.
*The final movement of Bach's suite, a Gigue,
is lacking from this arrangement. Revised
1890. First performance Bremen, 1891, Max
Erdmannsdörfer conductor.*

754v [Same as above. Sarabande] Transcribed
for violin and orchestra by C. Saint-Saëns
Solo Vn.-0,2,2,2-Timp.-Str.
Durand, Paris [n.d.]
Score 12 p.

683s [English suite no. 5. BWV 810. Prelude]
Transcribed by Gerrard Williams
1,1,1,1(ad lib.)-Tpt.(or Cnt.,ad lib.)-Str.
Oxford University Press, London, c1925
Score 19 p.

1008s [English suite no. 6. BWV 811.
Gavotte I] Transcribed by Fernand Pollain
Str.
Score: Ms. 6 p.
Parts: Senart, Paris [n.d.]

1401 [English suite no. 6. BWV 811.   5'
Gavotte I and II] Transcribed by A. Gevaert
1,2,0,2-2Hn.-Str.
Durand, Paris [n.d.]
Score 6 p.
*Orchestrated 1874. First performance Paris,
1875.*

Fantasia and fugue
See: [Prelude (Fantasy) and fugue, organ]

2438 [French suite no. 5. BWV 816]   20'
Transcribed by Eugene Goossens
1.Courante 2.Allemande 3.Bourrée 4.Menuet
5.Gavotte 6.Sarabande 7.Gigue
3,2,2,2-2,3-Timp.-Str.
J.& W. Chester [London, n.d.]
Score 34 p.
*In place of the Loure of French suite no. 5
this transcription has the Menuet from Suite
no. 3, BWV 814. This suite specially arranged
and scored for a 'Ballet divertissement' in
Thomas Beecham's production of Bach's cantata
Phoebus and Pan, London, 1917.*

936s [Fugue, clavier, A minor. BWV 944]
Freely arranged by Joseph Hellmesberger
Str.
Universal Edition [n.p., n.d.]
Score 18 p.

2367s [Fugue, clavier, A minor.   3'30"
BWV 947] Transcribed by Ralph Nicholson

Str.
Oxford University Press, London, c1952
Score 8 p.

2247 [Fugue, organ, G major. BWV 577]
Transcribed by Gustav Holst
2,2,2,2-2,2,2,1-Str.
Hawkes & Son, London, c1929
Score 11 p.

5001 [Fugue, organ, G minor (The   3'45"
shorter). BWV 578] Transcribed by Leopold
Stokowski
4*(1Alto Fl.),3*,4*(1Cl. in E-flat),3*-5,4,4,
2-Timp.,B.Dr.-Hp.-Str.
Broude Brothers, New York, c1950
Score 21 p.

Giant fugue
    See: [Chorale-prelude, organ, Wir glauben
        all' an einen Gott (Giant fugue).
        BWV 680]

3565 [Goldberg variations. BWV 988. Aria and
17 variations] Transcribed by Nicolas Nabokov
2,2,0,2-2Tpt.,2Tbn.-Cemb.(or Pno.,ad lib.)-
Str.
Ms.
Score 110 p.
*This arrangement completed 1938. Bach's
original includes thirty variations.*

466v [Italian concerto, clavier, F major.
BWV 971. Andante] Arranged by Louis Maas
Solo Vn.(or Vc.)-Str.
Schirmer, New York, c1882
Score 7 p.

Jesu, joy of man's desiring
    See: [Cantata no. 147, Herz und Mund und Tat
        und Leben. BWV 147. Chorale, Jesu, joy
        of man's desiring]

1720s [Komm, süsser Tod. BWV 478] Arranged   4'
by Henri Elkan
Pno.(ad lib.)-Str.
Elkan-Vogel, Philadelphia, c1936
Score 4 p.
*The source of the text is unknown. Composed
ca.1736. First published in Georg Christian
Schemelli's Musicalisches Gesangbuch, 1736,
for which Bach was musical editor and contri-
butor. First performance of this arrangement
Philadelphia, 3 August 1936, Civic Symphony
Orchestra of the WPA, Emil Folgmann conductor.*

1770s [Komm, süsser Tod. BWV 478] Chorale   8'
and variation for string orchestra transcribed
by Clair Leonard
Vn.I(or Solo Fl.),Vn.II,Va.,Vc.
Ms.
Score 5 p.
*First performance Poughkeepsie, New York, 18
May 1939, Vassar College Orchestra, Homer
Pearson conductor, Hilda Sizer flautist.*

4927 [Komm, süsser Tod. BWV 478]   4'
Transcribed by Leopold Stokowski

3*,3*,1*,2*-4,3,4,1-Timp.-Hp.-Str.
Broude Brothers, New York, c1946
Score 6 p.

2038s [Mein Jesu, was für Seelenweh.   5'30"
BWV 487] Transcribed by Leopold Stokowski
Str.
Broude Brothers, New York, c1949
Score 4 p.
*Text probably by Georg Christian Schemelli
(b.1676). Melody composed ca.1725, and first
published in Schemelli's Musicalisches Gesang-
buch, 1736.*

948s [Musical offering. BWV 1079. No. 5,
Ricercare] Arranged by G. Lenzewski, Sr.
Str.
Vieweg, Berlin [1926?]
Score 11 p.

2399 [Same as above] Transcribed by Eliot B.
Wheaton
4*,4*,4*,4*-8,4,3,1-Timp.-Str.
Kalmus, New York, c1931
Score 48 p.

898s [Notebook for Anna Magdalena Bach,
vol. 2. Selections] Transcribed by Thomas F.
Dunhill
1.March (BWV Anh.122) 2.First polonaise (BWV
Anh.125) 3.Two minuets (BWV Anh.114,115)
4.Second polonaise (BWV Anh.119) 5.Musette
(BWV Anh.126)
Str.
Oxford University Press, London, c1929
Score 6 p.
*Nos. 16, 19, 4&5, 10, 22 of the Notebook. None
actually composed by Bach; all originally for
keyboard.*

6898 [Notebook for Anna Magdalena Bach,   8'
vol. 2. Selections] Transcribed by Thomas T.
Frost
1.Minuet (BWV Anh.114) 2.Musette (BWV Anh.126)
3.Aria, Bist du bei mir (BWV 508) 4.March
(BWV Anh.122)
2,2,2(optional),2-2,1-Timp.,Trgl.-Str.
A. Broude, New York, c1970 by Tetra Music Co.
Score 16 p.
*All originally for keyboard. According to the
J.S. Bach Neue Ausgabe Sämtlicher Werke, V/4,
1957 (Georg von Dadelsen, editor) none of the
pieces in this suite were composed by J.S.
Bach. Nos. 1 and 2 are by unknown composers.
No. 3 is most probably by Gottfried Heinrich
Stölzel (1690-1749). No. 4 is by Carl Philipp
Emanuel Bach (1714-1788).*

91s [Notebook for Anna Magdalena Bach, vol. 2.
Aria. BWV 509] Arranged by Hugo Wehrle
Str.
Breitkopf & Härtel, Leipzig [n.d.]
Score 3 p.
*This arrangement transposed from the original
key of E-flat major to E major.*

1246 [Overture (Suite), orchestra, no. 1,   34'
C major. BWV 1066] Edited by Felix Weingartner
1.Grave - Vivace 2.Courante 3.Gavotte

Bach, Johann Sebastian

4.Forlane (Danza veneziana) 5.Menuetto
(Alternativo) 6.Bourrée 7.Passepied
2Ob.,Bn.-Str.
Breitkopf & Härtel, Leipzig, C1905
Score 22 p.

1352s [Same as above] Transcribed for   23'
string orchestra by W.G. Whittaker
1.Courante 2.Gavotte I and II 3.Forlane
4.Menuet I and II 5.Bourrée I and II
6.Passepied I and II
Str.
Oxford University Press, London, C1927
Score 12 p.
*First movement of Overture not included in
this transcription.*

1449s [Overture (Suite), orchestra, no. 2,
B minor. BWV 1067]
1.Ouverture 2.Rondeau 3.Sarabande 4.Bourrée
I 5.Bourrée II 6.Polonaise 7.Double
8.Menuet 9.Badinerie
Fl.-Str.
Breitkopf & Härtel, Wiesbaden, C1962
Score 16 p.

565m [Same as above] Transcribed by Hans   17'
von Bülow
1.Ouverture 2.Rondo 3.Sarabande 4.Bourrée
5.Polonaise 6.Menuet 7.Badinerie
Fl.-Str.
Universal Edition, Vienna [n.d.]
Score 16 p.

1353s [Same as above] Transcribed by W.G.   17'
Whittaker
1.Rondeau 2.Sarabande 3.Bourrée 4.Polonaise
5.Menuet 6.Badinerie
Solo Vn.(Fl. optional)-Str.
Oxford University Press, London, C1927
Score 11 p.
*First movement of Overture not included in
this transcription.*

531 [Overture (Suite), orchestra, no. 3,   16'
D major. BWV 1068] Transcribed by Ferdinand
David and Felix Mendelssohn-Bartholdy
1.Overture 2.Air 3.Gavotte 4.Bourrée
5.Gigue
2Ob.-3Tpt.-Timp.-Str.
Breitkopf & Härtel, Leipzig, C1942
Score 26 p.
*This transcription first performed 15 February
1838, Felix Mendelssohn conductor.*

6067 [Same as above] Edited by Kurt   24'
Soldan
1.Ouverture: [Grave - Vivace] 2.Air
3.Gavotte I 4.Gavotte II 5.Bourrée 6.Gigue
2Ob.-3Tpt.-Timp.-Cemb.-Str.
C.F. Peters, Frankfurt, C1934
Score 27 p.
*This edition based on manuscript copies in the
Preussische Staatsbibliothek.*

1354s [Same as above] Transcribed by   19'
W.G. Whittaker
1.Gavotte I and II 2.Bourrée 3.Air 4.Gigue
Timp.(optional)-Str.

Oxford University Press, London, C1927
Score 9 p.
*The first movement of the Overture is not
included in this transcription, and the order
of the other movements has been changed.*

920s [Same as above] Transcribed for string
orchestra by Charles Woodhouse
1.Gavotte 2.Bourrée 3.Air 4.Gigue
Str.
Hawkes & Son, London, C1924
Score 12 p.

824v [Same as above. Air] Transcribed for vio-
lin and string orchestra by Josef Bloch
Solo Vn.-Str.
Rozsnyai, Budapest [n.d.]
Score 5 p.

2036s [Same as above. Air] Transcribed   5'45"
by Leopold Stokowski
Str.
Broude Brothers, New York, C1949
Score 8 p.

138s [Same as above. Gavotte I and II]
Transcribed anonymously
Str.
Ms.
Score 39 p.
*Bound with Gluck's Iphigenia overture, Mozart's
Canzonetta from Don Giovanni and Schubert's
March, Op. 51 no. 1.*

1052 [Overture (Suite), orchestra, no. 4,   16'
D major. BWV 1069]
0,3,0,1-3Tpt.-Timp.-Pno.-Str.
Breitkopf & Härtel, Leipzig [n.d.]
Score 31 p.

1355s [Same as above] Transcribed for   19'
string orchestra with optional timpani by
W.G. Whittaker
1.Bourrée I and II 2.Gavotte 3.Menuet
4.Réjouissance
Timp.(optional)-Str.
Oxford University Press, London, C1927
Score 11 p.
*First movement of the Overture not included in
this transcription.*

1981 [Overtures (Suites), orchestra,   8'
nos. 2 and 3. BWV 1067 and 1068. Excerpts]
Selected and edited by Gustav Mahler
1.Ouverture 2.Rondeau - Badinerie 3.Air
4.Gavotte I and II
1,2,1(ad lib.)-3Tpt.-Timp.-Pno.,Org.-Str.
G. Schirmer, New York, C1910
Score 37 p.
*Movements 1 and 2 from BWV 1067. Movements 3
and 4 from BWV 1068.*

2070s [Partita for unaccompanied violin,   9'
no. 1, B minor. BWV 1002. Sarabande *and*
Tempo di Bourrée] Transcribed by Norman Black
Str.
Ms.
Score 4 p.
This transcription 1939.

Bach, Johann Sebastian

537s [Partita for unaccompanied violin, no. 1,
B minor. BWV 1002. Sarabande *and* Tempo di
Bourrée *with* Sonata, flute and figured bass,
no. 2, E minor. BWV 1034. Andante] Transcribed
by S. Bachrich
Str.
Doblinger, Vienna [n.d.]
Score 7 p.

2914 [Partita for unaccompanied violin,   *12'*
no. 2, D minor. BWV 1004. Chaconne] Transcribed by Jenö Hubay
3*,3*,3*,3*-4,3,3,1-Timp.,Bells-Str.
Universal Edition [n.p.] ᶜ1931
Score 60 p.
*First performance of this transcription Buda-
pest, 8 January 1932, Budapest Philharmonic
Orchestra, Joseph Krips conductor.*

3178 [Same as above] Transcribed by Burle   *16'*
Marx
3*,2,2,2-4,2,3-Timp.-Str.
Ms.
Score 48 p.
*First performance Rio de Janeiro, 4 August
1932, Philharmonic Orchestra of Rio de Janeiro,
Burle Marx conductor.*

4388 [Same as above] Transcribed by   *13-15'*
Joachim Raff
2,2,2,2-4,2,3-Timp.-Str.
Robert Seitz, Leipzig [187-?]
Score 47 p.

2145 [Same as above] Arranged from   *13'*
F. Busoni's piano transcription by Maximilian
Steinberg
2,2*,2,2-4,2,3,1-Timp.-Str.
Russischer Musikverlag, Berlin [n.d.]
Score 41 p.
*Orchestrated 1911. First performance St.
Petersburg, 5 November 1911, Alexander Siloti
conductor.*

803v [Same as above] Transcribed by   *12'*
August Wilhelmj
Solo Vn.-2,2,2,2-Timp.-Str.
Schlesinger, Berlin [n.d.]
Score 37 p.

56s [Partita for unaccompanied violin, no. 3,
E major. BWV 1006. Gavotte en rondeau]
Transcribed by Cecil Forsyth
Str.
Goodwin & Tabb, London, ᶜ1907
Score 7 p.

3341 [Same as above. Preludio] Transcribed   *4'*
by Herman Boessenroth
3*,3*,3*,3*-4,3,3,1-Timp.-Hp.-Str.
Ms.
Score 30 p.
*First performance Minneapolis, 12 March 1936,
Minneapolis Symphony Orchestra, Paul Lemay
conductor.*

2916 [Same as above. Preludio] Transcribed   *4'*
by Leo Weiner

2,2,2,2-2,2-Timp.-Str.
Rózsavölgyi, Budapest, ᶜ1937
Score 16 p.

1116s [Partita for unaccompanied violin, no. 3,
E major. BWV 1006. Preludio *and* Gavotte en
rondeau *with* Sonata for unaccompanied violin,
no. 2, A minor. BWV 1003. Andante] Transcribed
by S. Bachrich
Str.
Universal Edition, Vienna, ᶜ1895
Score 26 p.

2261s [Partitas on 'Christ, der du bist der
helle Tag', for organ, F minor. BWV 766]
Transcribed for string orchestra by Fabien
Sevitzky
1.Grave 2.Andante 3.Andante 4.Allegro
5.Pastorale 6.Molto pesante
Str.
Ms.
Score 12 p.
*Text of the original hymn by Erasmus Alber
ca.1556. Composer of the original melody
(1568) unknown. This transcription, 1930, does
not include no. 5 of the original seven partitas.*

4822 [Passacaglia, organ, C minor.   *13'*
BWV 582] Transcribed by Herman
Boessenroth
3(3rd alt. Picc.),3*,3*,3-4,4,4,1-Timp.,Perc.-
Org.(ad lib.),Hp.-Str.
Ms.
Score 34 p. Large folio
*The first four measures of the Passacaglia are
a quotation from a Short Passacaglia composed
by André Raison ca.1700. Composed 1716-17.
This transcription commissioned by Eugene
Ormandy for the Minneapolis Symphony Orchestra.
First performance Minneapolis, 12 April 1935,
Minneapolis Symphony Orchestra, Eugene
Ormandy conductor.*

1569 [Same as above] Transcribed by   *20'*
A. Goedicke
3*,2*,3*,3*-4,3,3,1-Timp.,Perc.-Str.
Universal Edition & Mussektor, Moscow, ᶜ1929
Score 49 p.

2201 [Same as above] Transcribed by   *15'*
Ottorino Respighi
4*,4*,4*,4*-6,4,3,1-Timp.-Org.-Str.
Ricordi, Milan, ᶜ1930
Score 56 p.
*Orchestrated 1930. First performance New York,
16 April 1930, Arturo Toscanini conductor.*

4989 [Same as above] Transcribed by   *13'*
Leopold Stokowski
5(1Alto Fl.),4*,4*,4*-8,4,4,2-Timp.-Str.
Broude Brothers, New York, ᶜ1951
Score 69 p.

2912 [Pastorale, organ, F major. BWV 590]   *14'*
Transcribed by Vittorio Gui
2,3*,0,2-2Hn.,2Tpt.-Str.
Universal Edition, Vienna, ᶜ1931

Bach, Johann Sebastian

Score 40 p.
First performance of this transcription Rome,
January 1928.

5853 [Pastorale, organ, F major. BWV 590 *with*
Prelude and fugue for organ, F major. BWV 556]
Transcribed for wind orchestra by Archer
Gibson
1.Pastorale 2.Musette [Bach: untitled] 3.
Aria [Bach: untitled] 4.Prelude and fugue
2,2*,3*,2-2Hn.
Ms.
Score 27 p.
The Pastorale composed between 1703 and 1707;
authenticity not certain. The Prelude and
Fugue is no. 4 of Eight Little Preludes and
Fugues for organ composed before 1710. All
eight may possibly be by Johann Ludwig Krebs
or by his father Johann Tobias Krebs. This
transcription 1911. First performance Boston,
25 November 1914, Longy Club, Georges Longy
conductor.

7192 [Prelude and fugue, organ, C major.
BWV 545] Transcribed for brass choir by
Irving Rosenthal
4Hn.,3Tpt.,3Tbn.,Bar.,Tuba
Western International Music, Los Angeles,
^c1970
Score 44 p.

2221 [Prelude and fugue, organ, C major.   6'
BWV 547. Prelude only] Transcribed by Bernard
Jackson
2Fl.,2Ob.-Str.
Oxford University Press, London, ^c1925
Score 8 p.
First performance Birmingham, 1925, City
Orchestra, Adrian C. Boult conductor.

966s [Prelude and fugue, organ, D minor.   9'
BWV 539 *with* Partita for unaccompanied violin,
no. 3, E major. BWV 1006] Transcribed by
Riccardo Pick-Mangiagalli
Str.
Ricordi, Milan, ^c1930
Score 14 p.
Transcribed 1930. First performance Boston,
17 October 1930, Serge Koussevitsky conductor.

1949 [Prelude and fugue, organ, E-flat   12'
major. BWV 552] Transcribed by Arnold Schoenberg
4(3rd&4th alt. Picc.),4(3rd&4th alt. E.H.),6*,
4*-4,4,4,1-Timp.,Perc.-Cel.,Hp.-Str.
Universal Edition, Vienna, ^c1929
Score 61 p.
Orchestrated 1928. First performance Vienna,
10 November 1929, Anton von Webern conductor.

2475 [Prelude and fugue, organ, E-flat major.
BWV 552. Prelude only] Transcribed by Bernhard
Scholz
2,2,2,3(C.Bn. ad lib.)-2,2,3-Timp.-Str.
Rieter-Biedermann, Leipzig, 1874
Score 43 p.

2725 [Prelude and fugue, organ (Cathedral),   5'
E minor. BWV 536] Transcribed by Leonid
Leonardi
2,3,3,3-4,3,3,1-Timp.-Hp.-Str.
Ms.
Score 30 p.
Transcribed 1935. First performance Pasadena,
22 January 1938, Pasadena Civic Orchestra,
Richard Lert conductor.

1754s [Prelude and fugue, organ, E minor.   4'
BWV 555. Prelude only] Transcribed by
Christian L. Thaulow
Str.
Sprague-Coleman [n.p.] ^c1938
Score 4 p.
From no. 3 of the Eight Preludes and Fugues
for organ. Transcribed 1938. First perform-
ance New York, 10 July 1938, New York Philhar-
monic, Macklin Marrow conductor.

2884 [Prelude and fugue, organ, B minor.   12'
BWV 544] Transcribed by Gardner Read
4*(1Alto Fl. in G),3*,3*,3*-4,4(4th optional),
4(4th optional),1-Timp.-Str.
Ms.
Score 62 p.
Transcribed 1937. First performance Chicago,
2 November 1939, Chicago Symphony Orchestra,
Frederick Stock conductor.

1568 [Prelude (Fantasy) and fugue,   10'
organ, C minor. BWV 537] Transcribed by
Edward Elgar
3*,3*,3*,3*-4,3,3,1-Timp.,Perc.-Glock.,2Hp.-
Str.
Novello, London, ^c1922
Scores: 15 p., 22 p.
Fantasia orchestrated 1922. First performance
Gloucester Festival, September 1922, Edward
Elgar conductor. Fugue orchestrated 1921.
First performance London, 27 October 1921,
Eugene Goossens conductor.

3428 [Prelude (Fantasy) and fugue, organ, G
minor. BWV 542] Transcribed by A. Goedicke
3,3,3,3-4,3,3,1-Timp.,Perc.-Str.
Mussektor, Moscow, 1937
Score 47 p.

6502 [Same as above] Transcribed by Fabien
Sevitzky
3(3rd alt. Picc.&Alto Fl.),3*,3*,3*-4,3,3,1-
Timp.,Perc.-Hp.-Str.
Ms.
Score 48 p.
Composed ca.1720. This transcription, 1952.
First performance Indianapolis, 25 October
1952, Indianapolis Symphony Orchestra, Fabien
Sevitzky conductor.

5070 [Prelude (Toccata) and fugue, organ,   13'
Dorian, D minor. BWV 538] Transcribed by
Alexandre Tansman
2,2,2,2-4,3,3,1-Timp.,B.Dr.,Cym.-Str.
Max Eschig, Paris, c1937
Score 40 p.

COLLECTION OF ORCHESTRAL MUSIC

Bach, Johann Sebastian

1769 [Prelude (Toccata) and fugue, organ, 11'
F major. BWV 540. Prelude only] Transcribed by
H. Esser. Coda by Edward Elgar
3,2,2,3*-4,3,3,1-Timp.,B.Dr.-Str.
Score: Ms. 50 p.
Parts: Schott, Mainz [n.d.]
Transcribed 1856. First performance Vienna,
1856, at the Philharmonic concerts, H. Esser
conductor. Elgar's coda added later.

Ratswahl cantata, no. 29. Sinfonia
See: [Cantata no. 29, Wir danken dir Gott,
wir danken dir...BWV 29. Sinfonia]

Sheep may safely graze (Was mir behagt ist nur
die muntre Jagd)
See: [Cantata no. 208...BWV 208]

2440 [Sinfonia, F major. BWV 1071] 10'
3Ob.,1Bn.-2Hn.-Str.
Breitkopf & Härtel, Leipzig, [n.d.]
Score 17 p.
The Sinfonia is an arrangement of the First
Brandenburg Concerto (BWV 1046), without the
Allegro and Polacca movements; probably
arranged between 1729 and 1736 for performance
in the Telemann Collegium Musicum.

7105 [Sinfonia no. 9, from 3-part 4'
sinfonias. BWV 795] Transcribed by Burle Marx
2Recorders-1,1,1,1-Str.
Ms. c1975 by Burle Marx
Score 5 p. Large folio
Transcribed 1975. First performance Philadel-
phia, 9 March 1975, Orchestra Society of Phil-
adelphia, Sidney Rothstein conductor.

522v Sinfonie-Satz für concertante Violine, 5'
Nr. 4 in D dur [BWV 1045]
Solo Vn.-2Ob.-3Tpt.-Timp.-Str.
Breitkopf & Härtel, Leipzig [n.d.]
Score 17 p.
From a church cantata now lost.

4404 [Sonata, flute and clavier, no. 2, E-flat
major. BWV 1031. Siciliano] Transcribed by
François Auguste Gevaert
1,1,1,1-Hn.-Str.
[Durand, Schoenewerk & Cie., Paris, 1875?]
Score 4 p.
Composed possibly 1720.

1372 [Sonata, organ, no. 1, E-flat major. 12'
BWV 525] Transcribed by H.H. Wetzler
2,2,2,2-2,3,3-Timp.-Str.
Novello, London [1903?]
Score 43 p.

5451 [Sonata, violin and clavier (or 4'
cembalo), no. 4, C minor. BWV 1017. Adagio]
Transcribed by Heinrich Urban
0,0,2,2-3Tbn.-Str.
Adolph Fürstner, Berlin [n.d.]
Score 7 p.

2044s [Sonata, violin and clavier (or 3'
cembalo), no. 4, C minor. BWV 1017. Siciliano]
Transcribed by Leopold Stokowski
Str.
Broude Brothers, New York, c1949
Score 6 p.

1115s [Sonata, violin and figured bass, E minor.
BWV 1023] Transcribed by Josef Hellmesberger
Str.
Universal Edition, Vienna, c1890
Score 21 p.
Allemande omitted in this arrangement.

967v [Same as above] Transcribed by Ottorino
Respighi
Solo Vn.-Org.-Str.
Schmidl, Leipzig, c1911
Score 15 p.

1746s [Sonata, unaccompanied violin, no. 2, A
minor. BWV 1003. Andante only] Transcribed by
Leo Weiner
Str.
Rózsavölgyi, Budapest, c1937
Score 3 p.

1684s [Same as above] Transcribed by Frederick
Stock
Str.
G. Schirmer, New York, c1931
Score 7 p.

2504 [Sonata, unaccompanied violin, no. 3, 10'
C major. BWV 1005. Fuga] Transcribed by Otto
Mueller
2*,2,2,2-4,2,3,1-Timp.-Str.
Ms.
Score 59 p.
First performance Philadelphia, 6 May 1934,
Philadelphia City Symphony Orchestra of the
Local Works Division, State Emergency Relief
Administration, Thaddeus Rich conductor.

1473s [Stücke (Pieces) arranged in form of a
suite for string orchestra by Ludwig Schmutzler]
1.Allemande 2.Sarabande 3a.Menuett 3b.
Menuett 4.Allegretto 5.Larghetto 6.Gavotte
7.Gigue
Str.
C.F. Schmidt, Heilbron a.N. [n.d.]
Score 15 p.
Nos. 1, 2, 3b, 7 from French suite no. 1, BWV
1812; 3a from French suite no. 6, BWV 817; no.
4 is Sinfonia 3, BWV 789; no. 5 is Sinfonia
9, BWV 795; no. 6 from French suite no. 5,
BWV 816.

919s [Suite, unaccompanied violoncello, no. 3,
C major. BWV 1009. Bourrée I and II] Tran-
scribed by Charles Woodhouse
Str.
Hawkes & Son, London, c1929
Score 5 p.

904s Suite of six pieces from the lesser known
piano works. Transcribed for string quartet or
string orchestra by Charles Woodhouse
1.March 2.Menuet and trio 3.Aria 4.Musette
5.Adagio 6.Gigue

Bach, Johann Sebastian

Str.
Hawkes & Son, London, c1929
Score 15 p.
Nos. 1 and 4 from the second Notebook for Anna Magdalena Bach of 1725; neither is by J. S. Bach. No. 2 from Overture (Suite) for clavier, F major (BWV 820). No. 3 is the Aria Variata Alla Maniera Italiana, A minor (BWV 989). No. 5 from Toccata, G major (BWV 916). Nos. 2, 3, and 5 all composed ca.1709. No. 6 from the fragmentary Suite, A major (BWV 824), in the Notebook for Wilhelm Friedemann Bach of 1720-21; possibly by Georg Philipp Telemann.

2243 [Toccata and fugue, organ, C major.   16'
BWV 564] Orchestrated by Leo Weiner
1.Allegro non troppo 2.Adagio 3.Fuga. Allegretto ma poco moderato, molto deciso
3*,3,3*,3*-6,4,3,1-Timp.-Hp.-Str.
Universal Edition, Vienna, c1930
Score 64 p.
Orchestrated 1929. First performance Trieste, April 1930, George Sebastian conductor.

1211s [Same as above. Adagio] Transcribed by Alexander Siloti
Str.
C. Fischer, New York, c1925
Score 3 p.

4986 [Same as above. Adagio] Transcribed   4'
by Leopold Stokowski
3,3*,2*,3*-4,4,4,1-Timp.,B.Dr.,Glock.-Hp.-Str.
Broude Brothers, New York, c1946
Score 9 p.

4699 [Toccata and fugue, organ, D minor.   8'30"
BWV 565] Transcribed for band by Hans Felix Husadel
3*,3*,8*(1Cl. in A-flat,1Cl. in E-flat,1Alto Cl.,1Cb.Cl.),2-5Sax.(SAAT,Bar.)-4,Sopranino,3Tpt.,2Cnt.,3Tbn.,6Tuba(TTT,Bar.,BB)-Timp.
Friederich Friede, Berlin, c1943
Score 32 p.

2724 [Same as above] Transcribed by   9'
Leonid Leonardi
3*,3*,4*,3*-4,3,3,1-Timp.-Cel.,Hp.-Str.
Ms.
Score 56 p.
First performance Philadelphia, 2 December 1936, broadcast from the Curtis Institute of Music over CBS, Curtis Orchestra, Fritz Reiner conductor.

5011 [Same as above] Transcribed by   9'
Leopold Stokowski
4(3rd&4th alt. Picc.I&II),4*,4*,4*-6,4,4,1-Timp.-Cel.,2Hp.-Str.
Broude Brothers, New York, c1952
Score 63 p.

2915 [Same as above] Transcribed by
Henry J. Wood
4*,4*,4*,4*-6,4,4,1-Timp.,Perc.-Cel.,Org.,2Hp.-Str.
Oxford University Press, London, c1934
Score 44 p.
First performance at a Promenade Concert,

London, 5 October 1929, BBC Symphony Orchestra, Henry Wood conductor.

Toccata and fugue for organ
See also: [Prelude (Toccata) and fugue...]

1543 [Trio, organ, C minor. BWV 585]   5'
Transcribed by Maurice Besly
1.Adagio 2.Allegro
Solo Ob., Solo Vn.-1,1,2,2-2,1-Timp.-Str.
Boosey, London, c1924
Score 25 p.
Composition also ascribed to Johann Ludwig Krebs. Arranged 1924. First performance London, 1924, Maurice Besly conductor.

676s Two pieces for string orchestra
1.Air on the G string from [Overture (Suite), orchestra, no. 3, D major. BWV 1068] Transcribed by A. Wilhelmj 2.Gavotte from [Partita, unaccompanied violin, no. 3, E major. BWV 1006] Transcribed by Karl Rissland
Pno.(ad lib.)-Str.
Ditson, Boston, c1928
Score 9 p.

5473 [Well-tempered clavier. Part I. Prelude no. 4. (BWV 849) *with* Fugue for organ, G minor, from the Prelude (Fantasy) and fugue (BWV 542)] Transcribed with the addition of a Chorale by Johann Joseph Abert
1.Präludium 2.Chorale 3.Fuga
2,2,2,2-4,2,3-Timp.-Str.
Robert Seitz, Leipzig [n.d.]
Score 55 p.
The Prelude is transposed from C-sharp minor to D minor. The Chorale is an original composition by J. J. Abert.

1328s [Well-tempered clavier. Part I. Prelude and fugue no. 4. BWV 849 *with* Prelude and fugue no. 22. BWV 867] Arranged by Mabel Wood-Hill
Str.
Gray, New York, c1923
Score 17 p.

2713 [Well-tempered clavier. Part I.   7'
Prelude no. 8. BWV 853] Arranged by Louis Vyner
1Cl.,2Bn.-3Tbn.-Timp.-Hp.-Str.
Ms.
Score 9 p.
May be performed without woodwinds or brass. First performance Wilmington, Delaware, 27 January 1936, Wilmington Music School, Louis Vyner conductor.

1830 [Well-tempered clavier, Part I.   10'
Prelude no. 8. BWV 853; Prelude no. 22. BWV 867; Prelude no. 3. BWV 848] Transcribed by W. Kes
2,2,2,2-2Hn.-Bells,Trgl.-Hp.-Str.
Leuckart, Leipzig, c1916
Score 14 p.
Transcribed 1912. First performance Coblenz, 1912, Willem Kes conductor.

Bach, Wilhelm Friedemann

2437 [Well-tempered clavier. Part I.   8'
Prelude no 22. BWV 867 *and* Part II. Fugue no.
22. BWV 891] Transcribed by Edvin Kallstenius
2,2(2nd alt. E.H.),0,2-2,2,1-Str.
Ries & Erler, Berlin, ^c1931
Score 27 p.

2037s [Well-tempered clavier. Part I.   4-5'
Prelude no. 24. BWV 869] Transcribed by
Leopold Stokowski
Str.
Broude Brothers, New York, ^c1949
Score 6 p.

1297 [Well-tempered clavier. Part I.   9'
Prelude no. 24. BWV 869 *and* Fugue no. 15.
BWV 860] Transcribed by J.J. Abert
2,2,2,2-4,2,1-Timp.-Str.
Ries & Erler, Berlin [n.d.]
Score 18 p.
First performance of this transcription at a
Philharmonic concert, Vienna, January 1875,
Otto Dessoff conductor.

804s [Well-tempered clavier. Part II. Prelude
and fugue no. 16. BWV 885] Arranged by Julius
Harrison
Str.
Novello, London, ^c1924
Score 13 p.

BACH, OTTO.   Vienna 9 February 1833
Unterwaltersdorf, near Vienna 3 July 1893

260 Frühlings-Nahen [Approach of spring,   10'
tone picture for orchestra]
2,2,2,2-2,2,3-Timp.-Str.
J. André, Offenbach a.M. [1879?]
Score 56 p.
Composed 1877. First performance Vienna, 1878.

BACH, WILHELM FRIEDEMANN.   Weimar 22 November 1710
Berlin 1 July 1784

Also known as: the "Halle" Bach

462p [Concerto, cembalo and string orchestra,
E minor] Edited by Walter Upmeyer
1.Allegretto 2.Adagio 3.Allegro assai
Solo Cemb.-Str.
Vieweg, Berlin [1931]
Score 39 p.
Composed between 1733 and 1747. Published for
the first time 1931.

330p [Concerto, cembalo (or piano) and   17'
string orchestra, F minor] Edited by Werner
Smigelski
1.Allegro di molto 2.Andante 3.Prestissimo
Solo Hpscd.(or Solo Pno.)-Str.
Hans Sikorski, Hamburg, ^c1959

Score 35 p.
Often erroneously attributed to the composer's
brother Carl Philipp Emanuel Bach, since there
exists one manuscript copy bearing his name.
Composed ca.1769. This first published edition
1958, based on a manuscript in the Berlin State
Library. First performance of this edition
Hanover, 9 November 1958, Norddeutscher Rund-
funkorchester, Mathieu Lange conductor, Werner
Smigelski soloist.

489p [Concerto, 2 pianos, E-flat major] Arranged
by Heinrich Schwartz
1.Un poco allegro 2.Andante cantabile
3.Vivace
2 Solo Pno.-2Hn.,2Tpt.-Timp.-Str.
Ms.
Score 40 p.
Composed ca.1761.

976m [Prelude and fugue, 2 flutes and string
quartet]
1.Adagio 2.Allegro e forte
2Fl.-Str.
Ms.
Score 23 p.
Also published as Sinfonia, D minor below.

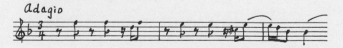

1419s [Sinfonia, D minor] Edited by Ludwig
Schittler
1.Adagio 2.Allegro e forte
2Fl.-Str.
Wunderhorn, Munich, 1910
Score 11 p.

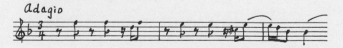

2264s [Symphony, cembalo and string   15'
orchestra, F major] Edited by Max Schneider
1.Vivace - Allegro 2.Andante 3.Allegro
4.Menuetto I - Menuetto II
Cemb.-Str.

Bachelet, Alfred Georges

Breitkopf & Härtel, Leipzig [n.d.]
Score 11 p.
Composed before 1745. This is the first pub-
lished edition of the work, also known as a
Quartet.

BACHELET, ALFRED GEORGES.   Paris 26 February 1864
                                Nancy 10 February 1944

622v Ballade, pour violon et orchestre
      Solo Vn.-3*,3*,2,2-4,2,3,1-Timp.,Cym.,Trgl.-
      Cel.,Hp.-Str.
      Durand, Paris, ᶜ1920
      Score 75 p.
      First performance Paris, 14 May 1919, Société
      Nationale de Musique.

541c Barcarolle nocturne, et petite histoire,
      [deux] pieces inséparables pour violon, ou
      violoncelle, ou alto, et orchestre
      Solo Vc.-2(2nd alt. Picc.),2*,2,2-2,2-Timp.,
      Perc.-Cel.,Hp.-Str.
      Durand, Paris, ᶜ1927
      Score 27 p.

BÄCK, SVEN-ERIK.   Stockholm 16 September 1919

5885 [Chamber symphony]   12'
      1.Adagio - Allegro 2.Largo sostenuto
      3.Allegro molto
      1(alt. Picc.),0,1,1-1,1,1-Timp.,Perc.-Str.
      (without Vn.)
      [Wilhelm Hansen, Copenhagen, ᶜ1959]
      Score 52 p.
      Composed 1955. First performance Stockholm,
      May 1955, Fylkingen Chamber Music Society,
      Herbert Blomstedt conductor. Awarded the
      International Society for Contemporary Music
      Prize in June 1956 at Stockholm. Awarded
      South African prize for the best "avant'
      gardism composition."

BACON, ERNST.   Chicago 26 May 1898

5385 The enchanted isle   24'
      1.Shipwreck 2.Ariel 3.Miranda 4.Caliban
      5.Ariel and the conspirators 6.The shapes
      7.Ariel 8.Danse of certain reapers and
      nymphs 9.Prospero's farewell 10.Marriage
      blessing
      2,2,2,2-4,3,3,1-Timp.(2 players),Perc.-Pno.,
      Cel.,Hp.,Accordion-Str.
      Ms.
      Score 77 p.
      Commissioned by the Louisville Symphony. Ori-
      ginally composed as incidental music for pro-
      ductions of Shakespeare's The Tempest at
      Converse College, Spartanburg, South Carolina,
      and at Syracuse University. This suite, 1954.
      First concert performance Louisville, 26 June
      1954, Louisville Symphony Orchestra, Robert
      Whitney conductor.

3188 Ford's theatre, a few glimpses of   34'
      Easter week, 1865
      1.Preamble 2.Walt Whitman and the dying sol-
      dier 3.Passing troops 4.The telegraph fugue
      (an etude for strings with timpani) 5.Moon-
      light on the Savannah 6.The theatre 7.The
      River Queen 8.Premonitions (a duet with a
      hall-clock) 9.Pennsylvania Avenue, April 9,
      1865 10.Good Friday, 1865 11.The long rain
      12.Conclusion
      3*(2nd alt. 2nd Picc.),3*,3*,3*-4,3,3,1-Timp.,
      Perc.-Cel.,Hp.-Str.
      Ms.
      Score 113 p.
      Composed 1939-43. Some portions originally
      composed for two pianos as incidental music to
      Paul Horgan's play, Yours, A. Lincoln. First
      performance Detroit, ca.1948, Detroit Sym-
      phony, the composer conducting.

4570 From these States, a geographical   20'
      excursion
      1.Laying the rails (A sledge-hammer song)
      2.Source of the Tennessee 3.The sunless
      pines 4.The Saluda barn dance 5.The cliff
      dwellers (No ancient cliffs, these) 6.Wizard
      oil 7.Storm over Huron 8.Lullaby to a sick
      child 9.Polly's murder 10.Hickory Gap
      11.The Timberline Express (A.D. & R.G. fantasy)
      3*(all alt. Picc.),3*,3*,3*-4,3,3,1-Timp.,
      Perc.-Cel.-Str.
      Ms. [ᶜ1951]
      Score 87 p.
      Composed ca.1943.

5481 Great River: The Rio Grande, for   40'
      symphony orchestra with narrator
      Preface 1.A river created 2.The peaks-Colo-
      rado 3.Pastoral valleys, New Mexico 4.Desert
      and canyon (Texas-Mexico) 5.Mexico Bay (The
      Gulf) 6.A pueblo dance prayer 7.An Indian
      death 8.Spanish soldiers before battle (New
      Mexico, 1599) 9.Mountain man (Taos, 1820-
      1830) 10.Soldiers by firelight (Texas, 1846)
      11.The honey-eaters 12.American visions
      2(both alt. Picc.),2(2nd alt. E.H.),2(2nd
      alt. B.Cl.),2-4,2,3,1-Timp.,Perc.-Pno.,Hp.-
      Narrator-Str.
      Ms.
      Score 104 p.
      Text by Paul Horgan, from Great River: The
      Rio Grande in North American History, 1954.
      Composed 1955-56. First performance Dallas,
      11 February 1957, Dallas Symphony Orchestra,
      Walter Hendl conductor.

2829 Prelude and fugue [first version]   8'
      3*,2,2,3*-4,2,3,1-Timp.,Perc.-Cel.-Str.
      Ms.
      Score 35 p. Large folio
      Composed 1926. The Fugue was originally com-
      posed for piano, the Prelude was added at time
      of scoring. First performance Rochester, 23
      April 1926, Rochester Philharmonic Orchestra,
      Howard Hanson conductor.

2896 Prelude and fugue [second version]   8'
      3*,2,2,3*-4,3,3,1-Timp.-Cel.-Str.

Ms.
Score 28 p.
Composed 1926; revised 1927.

303p Riolama, ten places for piano and   *25'*
orchestra
1.Salem, Mass[achussetts] 2.The Chama River,
N[ew] M[exico] 3.Creede, Colo[rado] 4.Nan-
tahala, N[orth] C[arolina] 5.Ruwenzori,
Africa 6.Gnaw Bone,Ind[iana] 7.Gaspé,
Ontario 8.Nicasio Valley, Calif[ornia] 9.Rio-
lama, Venezuela 10.Pico Perdida, Spain [11.]
Supplement. 156 W. 55th Street, N[ew] Y[ork]
Solo Pno.-2(both alt. Picc.),2(2nd alt. E.H.),
2(2nd alt. B.Cl.),2(2nd alt. C.Bn.)-4,3,3,1-
Timp.,Perc.-Str.
Ms.
Score 152 p. Large folio
*Commissioned by the Syracuse Symphony Orches-
tra. Composed 1962. First performance Syra-
cuse, New York, 18 January 1963, Syracuse Sym-
phony Orchestra, Karl Kritz conductor, the
composer as soloist.*

2786 [Symphony no. 1, in four movements] *36'*
1.Allegro 2.Andante sostenuto 3.Allegretto
moderato 4.Finale: Maestoso
3*,3*,3*,3*-2Sax.-4,4,3,1-Timp.,Perc.-Pno.,
Cel.,Hp.-Str.
Ms.
Score 236 p.
*Composed 1931. First performance (of last
three movements only) San Francisco, 5 Jan-
uary 1934, San Francisco Symphony Orchestra,
Issay Dobrowen conductor. Awarded the Pulitzer
Prize in 1932.*

3091 Symphony no. 2   *26'*
1.Grave and agitato 2.Interlude and diversion
3.Air 4.Fugue
2(both alt. Picc.),2(2nd alt. E.H.),2,2(2nd
alt. C.Bn.)-4,3,3,1-Timp.,Perc.-Cel.,Hp.-Str.
Ms.
Score 185 p.
*Composed 1937. First performance Chicago, 5
February 1940, Illinois Symphony Orchestra of
the WPA, the composer conducting.*

BADINGS, HENK.   Bandung, Java 17 January 1907

2057s [Largo and allegro for string   *11'*
orchestra]
Str.
Universal Edition, Vienna, ᶜ1938
Score 21 p.
Composed 1935.

3996 [Remembered melodies, suite for   *28'*
orchestra on Dutch melodies]
1.Intrada - Marcia - Siciliano - Marcia 2.
Pavane 3.Gagliarda 4.Saltarello 5.Sara-
bande 6.Rondeau 7. Finale: Tema con variazioni
3*,3*,3*,2-4,3,2-Timp.,Perc.-Pno.,Cel.,Hp.(ad
lib.)-Str.
Universal Edition, Vienna, ᶜ1939
Score 123 p.
Composed 1938. Based on an edition of Dutch

*folksongs, collected and published in the early
17th century by Adrianus Valerius.*

3932 [Symphonic variations]   *16'*
3*,3*,3*,3*-4,3,3,1-Timp.,Perc.-Cel.-Str.
Universal Edition, Vienna, ᶜ1938
Score 45 p.
Composed 1936.

5184 [Symphony no. 3]   *30'*
1.Allegro 2.Scherzo 3.Adagio 4.Allegro assai
3*,3*,3*,3*-4,5(1small Tpt. in D),3,1-Timp.,
Perc.-Cel.-Str.
Universal Edition, Vienna, ᶜ1935
Score 80 p.
Composed 1934.

6023 [Symphony no. 4]   *32'*
1.Lento - Allegro 2.Scherzo presto 3.Largo e
mesto 4.Allegro
3(3rd alt. Picc.),3*,3*,3*-4,3,3,1-Timp.,Perc.
-Cel.-Str.
Donemus, Amsterdam [ᶜ1943]
Score 114 p.
*Composed 1943. First performance Rotterdam,
13 October 1947, Rotterdam Philharmonisch
Orkest, Eduard Flipse conductor.*

BAER, FREDERIC.
See: PAER, FERDINANDO.

BAERMANN, CARL, SR.   Munich 24 October 1811
                           Munich 24 May 1885

389m [Concert piece, clarinet, Op. 44, D minor]
Solo Cl.-2,2,2,2-4,2,3-Timp.,B.Dr.-Str.
Score: Ms. 125 p. Large folio
Parts: Joh. André, Offenbach a.M. [n.d.]

874m [Concert piece, clarinet, Op. 49, E-flat
major]
Solo Cl.-2,2,2,2-4,2,2-Timp.-Str.
Score: Ms. 108 p.
Parts Joh. André, Offenbach a.M. [1878]
Published as no. 1.

BAGGE, GUSTAVE.

1157s Svea (Sweden). Suite pour orchestre à
cordes sur des danses et chants populaires
suèdois
Str.
Score: Ms. 7 p.
Parts: Decourcelle, Nice, ᶜ1926

BAGRINOVSKY, M.

2186 [From Russian fairy tales, suite,   *15'*
Op. 1. Movements 1-4]
1.Domovoi [Hobgoblin] 2.Baba-yaga [Old hag]
3.Russalka [Water-nymph] 4.Lieshii [Spirit of
the forest]
3(3rd alt. Picc.),3*,2,2-4,2,2Cnt.,3,1-Timp.,
Perc.-Hp.-Str.
Gutheil, Moscow, ᶜ1910
Score 43 p.

Bagrinovsky, M.

41 [From Russian fairy tales, Suite,   5'
Op. 1. Finale: Morning]
3*,3*,2,2-4,3,3,1-Timp.,Perc.-Str.
Gutheil, Moscow, c1911
Score 29 p.

BAILLE, GABRIEL.

933v [Concerto, violin, no. 1, Op. 120.
Romance]
Solo Vn.-Fl.,2Cl.-Str.
Score: Ms. 6 p.
Parts: Enoch, Paris [n.d.]

BAILLOT, PIERRE MARIE FRANÇOIS DE SALES.
Passy, near Paris 1 October 1771
Paris 15 September 1842

1103v [Andante, violin and orchestra, Op. 29]
Solo Vn.-2Ob.,Bn.(ad lib.)-Str.
Score: Ms. 27 p.
Parts: Breitkopf & Härtel, Leipzig [n.d.]
Composed 1817.

1101v [Concerto, violin, no. 1, Op. 3, A minor]
1.Allegro non troppo 2.Adagio 3.Rondo:
Presto ma non troppo
Solo Vn.-1,2,0,2-2Hn.-Str.
Score: Ms. 64 p.
Parts: Conservatoire Faubourg Poissoniere,
Paris [n.d.]
Composed 1802.

1105v [Concerto, violin, no. 3, Op. 7, F major]
1.Maestoso 2.Andante 3.Rondo. Animé
Solo Vn.-1,0,2,2-2Hn.-Str.
Score: Ms. 65 p.
Parts: Breitkopf & Härtel, Leipzig [n.d.]

1083v [Concerto, violin, no. 5, Op. 13, G minor]
1.Allegro risoluto 2.Un poco adagio 3.Rondo
russe
Solo Vn.-1,2,0,2-2Hn.-Str.
Score: Ms. 57 p.
Parts: Bureau des Arts et d'Industrie, Leipzig
[n.d.]
Composed 1807.

1104v [Concerto, violin, no. 6, Op. 18, A major]
1.Moderato 2.Romance: Andante 3.Rondeau
Solo Vn.-1,2,0,2-2Hn.-Timp.-Str.
Score: Ms. 84 p.
Parts: Pleyel, Paris [n.d.]
Composed 1811.

1084v [Concerto, violin, no. 7, Op. 21, D major]
1.Allegro risoluto 2.Andantino con moto
3.Rondo polonais
Solo Vn.-1,2,0,2-2Hn.-Timp.-Str.
Score: Ms. 61 p.
Parts: Pleyel, Paris [n.d.]
Composed 1809.

1085v [Concerto, violin, no. 8, Op. 22, C major]
1.Maestoso 2.Adagio non troppo 3.Rondo:
Tempo di polacca
Solo Vn.-1,2,0,2-2Hn.-Timp.-Str.
Score: Ms. 61 p.

Parts: Pleyel, Paris [n.d.]
Composed 1809.

1090v Menuet favori de Pugnani, variations
Solo Vn.-1,2,0,1-2,1-Timp.-Str.
Ms.
Score 24 p.

984v [Russian air with variations, violin and
string orchestra, Op. 24]
Solo Vn.-Str.
Score: Ms. 32 p.
Parts: Besozzi, Paris [n.d.]
Composed 1807. First performance Paris, the
composer as soloist. The air for these variations is the same as that in no. 1099v, Variations Pour le Violon. The variations for solo
violin are the same in both; the orchestration
differs throughout.

1109v [Theme and variations, violin and
orchestra, Op. 17]
Solo Vn.-1,0,2,2-2Hn.-Timp.-Str.
Score: Ms. 28 p.
Parts: Pleyel, Paris [n.d.]
Composed 1807.

1099v [Variations, violin and orchestra]
Solo Vn.-1,2,0,2-2Hn.-Timp.-Str.
Score: Ms. 41 p.
Parts: Breitkopf & Härtel, Leipzig [ca.1815]

1164v Vive Henri 4! Air varié [after Handel]
pour le violon, Op. 27
Solo Vn.-1,2,2,2-2,0,1-Timp.-Str.
Score: Ms. 22 p.
Parts: Breitkopf & Härtel, Leipzig [n.d.]

BAINTON, EDGAR LESLIE.   London 14 February 1880
Sydney, Australia 8 December 1956

648p Concerto-fantasia, pianoforte and   26'
orchestra, D major
1.Quasi cadenza 2.Scherzo 3.Improvisation
4.Finale 5.Epilogue
Solo Pno.-3*,2*,2,2-4,2,3,1-Timp.-Str.
Stainer & Bell, London, c1922
Score 123 p.
Received the Carnegie Trust Award, 1920.
First performance London, 26 January 1922,
Royal Philharmonic Society, Winifred Christie
soloist.

561s Pavane, idyll and bacchanal   11'
Solo Vn., Solo Fl.-Tamb.(ad lib.)-Str.
Oxford University Press, London, c1925
Score 16 p.

BAIRD, TADEUSZ.   Grodzisk Mazowiecki,
near Warsaw 26 July 1928

184m [Colas Breugnon, suite in ancient   15'
style for string orchestra with flute]
1.Preludium 2.[A pleasant cantilena] 3.Tan-
iec I (Basse-danse) 4.[A sad song]
Solo Fl.-Str.
Polskie Wydawnictwo Muzycne, Cracow, c1953
Score 21 p.

Suggested by Colas Breugnon, a character in Romain Rolland's novel Le Maître de Clamecy. Composed 1951.

6287 [Four essays for orchestra]   19'
1.Molto adagio 2.Allegretto grazioso 3.Allegro 4.Molto adagio
1,2*,2*,1-2,2,2-Timp.,Perc.-2Pno.,Cel.,2Hp.-Str.
Polskie Wydawnictwo Muzyczne, Crakow, ᶜ1959
Score 31 p.
Composed 1958. First performance Warsaw Autumn Festival, Warsaw, 27 September 1958, National Philharmonic, Witold Rowicki conductor. Awarded first prize in the Grzegorz Fitelberg Competition, 1958, by the International Tribune of Composers, UNESCO, Paris, 1959. This work was also produced as a ballet and played in the film Essays.

BAKER, LANCE.   Birmingham, England 24 May 1947

5817 Symphonic overture "ABFE"   15'
4*(2nd alt. Picc.II),4*(1Ob. d'Amore),4(3rd alt. Cl. in E-flat,4th alt. B.Cl.),4*-6,4,4,2-Timp.,Perc.-Org.,Hp.-Str.
Ms.
Score 48 p.
Composed 1972. First performance Croydon, England, 22 April 1974, London Repertoire Orchestra, Ruth Gipps conductor. Awarded the Royal Philharmonic Society Composition Prize, 1973.

BASKA, ROBERT FRANK. New York City 7 February 1938

7152 Meditation for orchestra   6'30"
3,1,2,2-4,0,3-Str.
Shawnee Press, Delaware Water Gap, Pa., ᶜ1958
Score 12 p.

BALAKIREV, MILI ALEXEYEVICH.
                  Nizhny-Novgorod 2 January 1837
                  St. Petersburg 29 May 1910

583p [Concerto, piano, no. 2, E-flat   35'
major]
1.Allegro non troppo 2.Adagio 3.Allegro risoluto
Solo Pno.-3(3rd alt. Picc.),2*,2,2-4,2,3,1-Timp.,Perc.-Str.
Zimmermann, Leipzig, ᶜ1911
Score 164 p.
Composed 1861-1909. Third movement completed by Sergei Liapunov.

1476 [In Bohemia, symphonic poem on three   12'
Czech folksongs]
3(3rd alt. Picc.),2*,3,2-4,2,3,1-Timp.,Perc.-Hp.-Str.
Zimmermann, Leipzig, ᶜ1906
Score 74 p.
Composed 1867. Original title Overture on Czech Themes. Revised and rescored in 1906. First performance St. Petersburg, 24 May 1867, the composer conducting.

523 [Islamey, Oriental fantasy for piano]   12'
Transcribed by Alfredo Casella

4(4th alt. Picc.),3*,3(1Cl. in E-flat),4*-4,4,3,1-Timp.,Perc.-2Hp.-Str.
Rahter, Leipzig [n.d.]
Score 67 p.
Originally composed for piano in 1869. Transcribed 1907. First performance Paris, April 1908, Alfredo Casella conductor.

1529 [Same as above] Transcribed by   12'
S. Liapunov
4*,2*,3(1Cl. in E-flat),2-4,4,3,1-Timp.,Perc.-2Hp.-Str.
Jurgenson, Moscow [n.d.]
Score 60 p.

1572 [King Lear, music to Shakespeare's   35'
tragedy]
1.[Overture] 2.[Act I. Lear's train] 3.[Music for a festive procession] 4.[Prelude to Act II] 5.[Act II, Scene 1, Gloucester. Scene 2, Kent] 6.[Prelude to Act III] 7.[Prelude to Act IV] 8.[Act IV, Scenes 6 and 7] 9.[Prelude to Act V] 10.[Act V, Scenes 1, 2, and 3]
3(3rd alt. Picc.),2*,3,2-4,4,3,1-Timp.,Perc.-Hp.-Str.
Zimmermann, Leipzig [n.d.]
Score 163 p.
Composed 1858-61. First performance St. Petersburg, 1861.

317 [Overture on a Spanish march theme]   12'
3*,2*,2,2-4,2,3,1-Timp.,Perc.-Str.
Zimmermann, Leipzig, ᶜ1907
Score 85 p.
Composed 1857 on a theme given to the composer by M. I. Glinka. Orchestration revised in 1886.

1416 [Overture on three Russian themes]   8'
2,2,2,2-2,2,3-Timp.-Str.
Jurgenson, Moscow [n.d.]
Score 36 p.
Composed 1858. First performance St. Petersburg, 1858.

72 [Russia, symphonic poem, Op. 10]   13'
3(3rd alt. Picc.),2,2,2-4,2,3,1-Timp.,Perc.,-2Hp.-Str.
Bessel, St. Petersburg [ca.1887]
Score 69 p.
Composed 1864 for the inauguration of the Russian millenium monument in Novgorod under the title Musical Picture, 1000 Years. Revised and retitled in 1884. Also known as Second Overture on Russian Themes.

1064 [Symphony no. 1, C major]   37'
1.Largo - Allegro vivo 2.Scherzo 3.Andante 4.Finale: Allegro moderato
3(3rd alt. Picc.),2*,3,2-4,2,3,1-Timp.,Perc.-Hp.-Str.
Zimmermann, Leipzig [n.d.]
Score 222 p.
Composed 1866-97. First performance St. Petersburg, 23 April 1898, the composer conducting.

390 [Symphony no. 2, D minor]   33'
1.Allegro ma non troppo 2.Scherzo alla cosacca 3.Romanza 4.Finale: Tempo di polacca

Balakirev, Mili Alexeyevich

3(3rd alt. Picc.),2*,3,2-4,2,3,1-Timp.,Perc.-Hp.-Str.
Zimmermann, Leipzig, ᶜ1909
Score 171 p.
Composed 1908. First performance St. Petersburg, 1909, the composer conducting.

659 [Tamara, symphonic poem after Mikhail   *18'*
Lermontov]
3(3rd alt. Picc.),2*,3,2-4,2,3,1-Timp.,Perc.-2Hp.-Str.
Jurgenson, Moscow [ca.1884]
Score 177 p.
Composed 1867-82. First performance St. Petersburg, 1882, the composer conducting.

BÀLAN, JOAN.   Bratovocoti, Romania 14 November 1892

729c [Capriccio, violoncello, with chamber orchestra]
Solo Vc.-0,1,2,1-2Hn.-Str.
Benno Balan, Berlin, ᶜ1931
Score 12 p.

892s [Lyric suite for string orchestra, no. 1]
1.[Melancholy] 2.[Solitude] 3.[The dancer]
4.[Joy]
Str.
Benno Balan, Berlin, ᶜ1931
Score 16 p.
Composed 1930.

BALANCHIVADZE, ANDREI.   St. Petersburg 1 June 1906

5866 [Symphony no. 1, Op. 51, B major]   *45'*
1.Allegro vivo 2.Andantino 3.Allegro
4.Adagio - Allegro
4*(3rd alt. Picc.II),3(3rd alt. E.H.),4(3rd alt. B.Cl.,1Cl. in E-flat,4th alt. Cl. in E-flat II),2-4,4,3,1-Timp.,Perc.-Org.,Cel.,2Hp.-Str.
State Music Publishers, Moscow, 1946 [ᶜ1945]
Score 134 p.
Composed 1944. First performance Tbilisi (Tiflis), Georgian Republic, USSR, November 1944, Orchestra of the State Philharmonic Society, Odissey Dymitriadi conductor. Awarded the Stalin Prize.

BALAZS, FREDERIC.   Budapest 12 December 1919

415c [Concerto, violoncello, In memoriam] *25'*
In one movement
Solo Vc.-2(2nd alt. Picc.),2,2,2-4,2,3,1-Timp.,Perc.-Hp.-Str.
Composers Facsimile Edition, New York, ᶜ1963
by Frederic Balazs
Score 45 p. Large folio
Composed 1962. First performance, in memory of President John F. Kennedy, Tucson, 10 December 1963, Tucson Symphony Orchestra, the composer conducting, Gabor Rejto soloist.

2265s Kentuckia, for string orchestra   *12'*
Str.
Composers Facsimile Edition, New York, ᶜ1957
by Frederic Balazs
Score 28 p. Large folio

Originally composed for violin and piano. Transcribed 1956.

6521 Song for Pablito   *7'*
2,2,2,2-4,2,3,1-Perc.-Hp.-Str.
Composers Facsimile Edition, New York, ᶜ1960
by Frederic Balazs
Score 12 p. Large folio
Composed 1960 in memory of the composer's young friend Pablito, age three. First performance Mexico City, May 1961, National Symphony Orchestra, the composer conducting.

6506 A statement of faith, music for   *10'*
orchestra
3*,2,2,2-4,2,3,1-Timp.,Perc.-Hp.-Str.
Composers Facsimile Edition, New York, ᶜ1961
by Frederic Balazs
Score 42 p. Large folio
Inspired by the Gregorian chant, Adoro Te Devote, Latens Deitas, the words attributed to St. Thomas Aquinas. Composed 1961. First performance Tucson, Arizona, April 1962, Tucson Symphony Orchestra, the composer conducting.

6450 [Symphony, American, after Walt   *25'*
Whitman]
1.Allegro moderato, con brio 2.Andantino, dolce e cantabile 3.Vivace 4.Triumphal music: Fanfares - Allegro moderato - Tempo di marciale, con maestoso
3*(2nd alt. Picc.II),3*,3*,3*-4,3,3,1-Timp.,Perc.-Hp.-Str.
Ms.
Score 102 p. Large folio
Composed 1945. First three movements originally a string quartet. First performance of the symphony New York, summer 1950, New York Philharmonic, the composer conducting.

6520 The trail, a ballad for orchestra   *6'*
2,3*(2nd Ob. optional),2(2nd optional),2-Ten. Sax.-4(2nd&3rd optional),2,3(1st optional),1-Hp.(1 or more, or Pno.)-Str.
Composers Facsimile Edition, New York, ᶜ1957
by Frederic Balazs
Score 10 p. Large folio
Composed 1956.

279m Two dances after David, for flute   *18'*
and orchestra
1.Lontano 2.Prestissimo - Molto ritmico
Solo Fl.-2(2nd alt. Picc.),2,2,2-4,2,3,1-Timp.,Perc.-Cel.,Hp.-Str.
Composers Facsimile Edition, New York, ᶜ1958
Score 42 p. Large folio
The trio theme of the second movement is based on the plainchants Per Omnia Saecula Saeculorum, Dominus Vobiscum, Et Cum Spiritu Tuo, etc., of the High Mass. Composed 1957. First performance Hamburg, Germany, May 1963, Philharmonic Hungarica, the composer conducting, Peter Pazmandy soloist.

BALENDONCK, ARMAND.   Liège, Belgium 9 August 1893

3004 The donkey   *5'*
2,2,2,2-2-2,2-Timp.,Perc.-Hp.-Str.

Ms.
Score 26 p.
Composed 1935. First performance New York, 18 August 1935, Greenwich Sinfonietta, Gerald McGarrahan conductor.

3483 Overture, In the autumn   14'
2,2,2,2-4,2,3,1-Timp.,Perc.-Hp.-Str.
Ms.
Score 90 p.
Composed 1940.

747c Poem, for violoncello and orchestra   10'
Solo Vc.-3,3*,3*,3*-4,3,3,1-Timp.-Hp.-Str.
Ms.
Score 47 p.
Composed 1938-39. First performance Schenectady, New York, 25 November 1941, Schenectady Philharmonic Orchestra, the composer conducting, A. Catricala soloist.

3782 Procession of the Scots Guards, for   6'
symphonic band
3*,2,7*(2Cl. in E-flat,Alto Cl.),2-4Sax.(AAT Bar)-4,2,3Cnt.,3,2Bar.,2Euph.,2-Timp.,Perc.
Pro-Art Publications, New York, ᶜ1938
Score 16 p.
Originally composed for symphony orchestra, 1937. Arranged for band 1937. First performance Brooklyn, 19 November 1938, New York State Symphonic Band, George Allen Foster conductor.

3048 Procession of the Scots Guards,   6'
for symphony orchestra
3*,2,2,2-4,3,3,1-Timp.,Perc.-Str.
Ms.
Score 24 p.
Composed 1937; revised 1938. First performance Philadelphia, 8 July 1937, Philadelphia Civic Orchestra of the WPA, the composer conducting.

1757s Suite for string orchestra (1937)   14'
1.Minuetto 2.Gavotte 3.Sarabande 4.Gigue
Str.
Ms.
Score 25 p.
Composed 1937. First performance of first three movements only, New York, 23 May 1938, WOR Symphonic Strings, Alfred Wallenstein conductor.

3825 To a departed friend, symphonic poem   10'
2,2,2,2-4,2,3,1-Timp.,Tam-tam,B.Dr.-Str.
Ms.
Score 39 p.
Composed 1936. First performance Philadelphia, 25 April 1937, Philadelphia Civic Orchestra of the WPA, the composer conducting.

BALES, RICHARD.
        b. Alexandria, Virginia 3 February 1915

4945 Episodes from A Lincoln ballet   14'
1.Youth and dreams 2.Country dances 3.The presidency 4.Fame everlasting
1,1,2,1-2,2,1-Timp.,Perc.-Pno.-Speaking Voice -Str.
Ms.

Score 57 p. Large folio
Text is from Lincoln's Second Inaugural Address, 4 March 1865. Originally composed for piano 1946. This orchestral version (four extracts), 1947. First performance Washington, D.C., 29 May 1949, National Gallery Orchestra, the composer conducting, Noel Smith speaker.

1960s Music for strings [revised version]   6'
Str.
Ms. ᶜ1942 by Richard Bales
Score 11 p.
Originally composed for string quartet, 1936 (now withdrawn). Transcribed for string orchestra 1939. Revised 1942. First performance of revised version, Washington, D.C., 25 February 1942, National Symphony Orchestra, the composer conducting. Received First Prize, the Arts Club of Washington Contest for a String Work, 1941.

1969s [Music of the American Revolution.   10'
Suite no. 1, for string orchestra]
1.Washington's march (Philip Phile) 2.Minuet danced before George Washington (Pierre Duport) 3.Brandywine quickstep (Anonymous) 4.Beneath a weeping willow's shade (Francis Hopkinson) 5.The wayworn traveller (Samuel Arnold) 6.The toast to George Washington (Francis Hopkinson)
Str.
Ms. [ᶜ1953. Now published by Peer International, New York]
Score 10 p.
Original title of this suite: From Washington's Time.

1044s [Music of the American Revolution.   10'
Suite no. 2, for string orchestra]
1.General Burgoyne's march (Anonymous) 2.Minuet (Alexander Reinagle) 3.Gavotte (Alexander Reinagle) 4.Roslin Castle (Harmonized by James Hewitt) 5.Delia (Henri Capron) 6.Yankee Doodle with quicksteps
Str.
Peer International, New York, ᶜ1956
Score 16 p.
All of the movements originally composed in the 18th century, for harpsichord and voice. This transcription 1952. First performance Washington, D.C., 27 April 1952, National Gallery Orchestra, Richard Bales conductor.

4670 The National Gallery of Art. Suite   14'
[no. 1] from the film score
1.Prelude 2.The rotunda 3.Gallery views 4.The courts 5.Mechanics 6.Life of Christ 7.Transition 8.Two women 9.Finale
1,1,1,1-2,2-Timp.,Perc.-Str.
Ms.
Score 74 p. Large folio
Commissioned by the National Gallery of Art for the film Your National Gallery. Composed 1943. First performance Washington, D.C., 26 September 1943, United States Navy Band Symphony Orchestra, Charles Brendler conductor.

Bales, Richard

4671 National Gallery [of Art] suite no. 2, *11'*
after 3 paintings in the Kress Collection
1.Passacaglia: Giorgione, 'Adoration of the
shepherds' 2.Interlude: Veneziano, 'Saint
John in the desert' 3.Scherzo: Watteau,
'Italian comedians'
1,1,3*,1-2,2,1-Timp.,Perc.-Pno.-Str.
Ms.
Score 57 p. Large folio
*Composed 1944. First performance Washington,
D.C., 25 March 1945, National Gallery Orches-
tra, the composer conducting.*

5628 National Gallery [of Art] suite no. 3, *18'*
after watercolor renderings from The Index
of American Design
1.Sign from Black Horse Inn, Saybrook, Connecticut 2.Ship's figurehead, 'Jenny Lind,'
from the ship Nightingale 3.Black mammy doll
4.Weather vane, 'The angel Gabriel' 5.Cigar
store Indian 6.Whiskey flask 7.Dowry chest
8.Baseball player
1,1(alt. E.H.),2,1-2,2,1-Timp.,Perc.-Str.
Ms. C1957 by Richard Bales
Score 134 p. Large folio
*Commissioned by the American Institute of
Architects. Composed 1957. First performance Washington, D.C., 26 May 1957, National
Gallery Orchestra, the composer conducting.
Later published [n.d.] by Alexander Broude
under the title American Design.*

4687 Primavera, for chamber orchestra   *5'*
1,1,2,1-2,2,1-Timp.,Perc.-Str.
Ms.
Score 17 p.
*Originally composed as Poem for Violin and
Piano, 1937. Transcribed for chamber orches-
tra by the composer, 1946. First performance
Washington, D.C., 30 March 1947, National
Gallery Orchestra, the composer conducting.*

1961s Theme and variations for string   *10'*
orchestra
Str.
Ms.
Score 9 p.
*Originally composed for string quartet, 1935
(withdrawn). Transcribed 1944. First per-
formance Washington, D.C., 26 August 1944,
National Gallery Orchestra.*

4911 Three songs of early America.   *7'*
[Transcribed] for small orchestra
1.David's lament[ation] (William Billings)
2.Poor wayfaring stranger (Folk) 3.Bunker
Hill (Andrew Law)
1,1,2,1-2,2,1-Timp.,Perc.-Str.
Ms.
Score 24 p. Large folio
*David's Lamentation was originally published
in the first edition of Billings' The Singing
Master's Assistant, Boston, 1778. Bunker Hill
was originally published in Law's A Select
Number of Plain Tunes Adapted to Congregational Worship, ca.1775. This transcription
1946. First performance Washington, D.C.,
6 October 1946, National Gallery Orchestra,
Richard Bales conductor.*

BALLOU, ESTHER WILLIAMSON.
Elmira, New York 17 July 1915
London 12 March 1973

294m Concertino for oboe and strings,   *12'*
Op. 1
1.Allegro non troppo 2.Adagio espressivo
3.Vivace
Solo Ob.-Str.
Composers Facsimile Edition, New York, C1953
by Esther Williamson Ballou
Score 35 p.
*Composed 1953. First performance Composers'
Conference at Bennington College, Bennington,
Vermont, August 1953, Composers' Conference
Orchestra, Roger Goeb conductor, Robert Bloom
soloist. Second movement, Adagio, rewritten,
1960, as In Memoriam.*

268p Concerto for piano and orchestra   *32'*
1.Maestoso - Allegro moderato 2.Scherzo
3.Molto lento 4.Allegro ritmico
Solo Pno.-2(1st alt. Picc.),2,2,2-4,2,2,1-
Timp.,Perc.-Cel.-Str.
Composers Facsimile Edition, New York, C1965
by Esther Williamson Ballou
Score 92 p. Large folio
*Commissioned for the 1,000th concert of the
National Gallery of Art Orchestra, Washington,
D.C. Composed 1964. First performance Wash-
inton, D.C., 12 June 1964, National Gallery
Orchestra, Richard Bales conductor, Charles
Crowder soloist.*

242p Prelude and allegro for string   *7'*
orchestra and piano
Solo Pno.-Str.
Composers Facsimile Edition, New York, C1952
by Esther Williamson Ballou
Score 18 p.
*Composed 1951. First performance Composers'
Conference, Middlebury, Vermont, August 1951,
Alan Carter conductor, the composer as soloist.*

BALOUGH, ERNO.   Budapest 4 April 1897

4019 Pastorale and capriccio, Op. 21   *5'*
Fl.,Cl.-Pno.-Str.
Ms.
Score 29 p.
*Commissioned by Radio Station WQXR, New York.
Composed 1943. First performance in a broad-
cast, New York, 11 June 1943, WQXR Orchestra,
the composer as pianist, Milton Wittgenstein
flautist, D. Webber clarinetist.*

1884s Portrait of a city from morning to   *24'*
midnight, suite for strings and piano, Op. 19
1.Morning call 2.Awakening 3.Prayer 4.
Factory: At the assembly lines 5.Resting 6.
Chatting 7.Children's bedtime 8.Merrymaking
Pno.-Str.
Ms.
Score 25 p. Large folio
*Composed 1939. First performance of 4th, 5th
and 8th movements broadcast over Station WNYC,
New York, 14 December 1940, Washington Square
College String Orchestra, Martin Bernstein*

COLLECTION OF ORCHESTRAL MUSIC

conductor. *First performance of 1st, 2nd, and 3rd movements broadcast over Station WQXR, New York, 22 April 1941, Eddy Brown conductor.*

BALTHASAR-FLORENCE, HENRI MATHIAS.
Arlon, Belgium 1844
Paris 1915

937v [Concerto, violin, A minor]
1.Moderato 2.Scherzino 3.Contemplation
4.Finale
Solo Vn.-2(1st alt. Picc.),2,2,2-4,2,3-Timp.,
Perc.-Str.
Score: Ms. 132 p.
Parts: Schott Frères, Brussels, 1885

BANÈS, ANTOINE.
Paris 1856
Paris 1924

1518s Les bons vieux [The good old folks, duet for violin and violoncello with accompaniment of string orchestra]
Solo Vn., Solo Vc.-Str.
Score: Ms. 15 p.
Parts: Costallat, Paris [n.d.]

BANGERT, EMILIUS.
Copenhagen 19 August 1883
Roskilde, near Copenhagen 19 August 1962

5937 [I, myself, choose April, concert overture, Op. 7]
2(2nd alt. Picc.),2,2,2-4,2,3,1-Timp.,Perc.-Str.
Edition Dania, Copenhagen, c1936
Score 24 p.
The motif of this overture was suggested by a poem of Bjørnstjerne Bjørnson, 1870. Composed 1913.

BANISTER, JOHN. the younger.
London ca.1663
London 1735

2181s Two suites for strings and   3'
continuo. Edited by Michael Tilmouth   4'
Suite I: 1.Allemanda 2.Boree 3.Roundo
Suite II: 1.Simphony 2.Gavot 3.Minuet
4.Hornpipe
Cemb.-Str.
Oxford University Press, London, c1960
Score 10 p.
Original version first published in A Sett of Ayres in Four Parts, by J. Banister, J. Carr, and H. Playford, London, 1691. This edition prepared from the unique surviving copy of the above in Durham Cathedral.

BANTOCK, GRANVILLE.
London 7 August 1868
London 16 October 1946

[The curse of Kehama. Two orchestral   20'
scenes, after Southey]

1146 No. 1. Processional, Canto I   10'
3*,2*,3*,3*-4,2,2Cnt.,3,1-Timp.,Perc.-2Hp.-
(2nd ad lib.)-Str.
Breitkopf & Härtel, Leipzig, c1911
Score 52 p.

1130 No. 2. Jaga-Naut, Canto XIV   10'
3*,2*,3*,3*-4,2,2Cnt.,3,1-Timp.,Perc.-2Hp.
(2nd ad lib.)-Str.
Breitkopf & Härtel, Leipzig, c1912
Score 59 p.
Both composed 1896. First performance London, 1896, the composer conducting.

1200 Dante and Beatrice, poem for orchestra 20'
3*,3*,3*,3*-4,2,2Cnt.,3,1-Timp.,Perc.-Hp.-Str.
Breitkopf & Härtel, Leipzig, c1911
Score 91 p.
Originally composed as Tone Poem no. 2, Dante, ca.1901. Revised and retitled, 1910. First performance at the London Musical Festival, 1911, the composer conducting.

584c Elegiac poem, for violoncello and   7'
orchestra
Solo Vc.-2,2,2,2-2Hn.-Str.
Joseph Williams, London, c1908
Score 11 p.
Composed 1898.

1097 [English scenes, suite for   27'
orchestra]
1.Pastorale: In the country 2.Romance: The trysting place 3.Intermezzo: Fairyland 4. Benedictus: In church 5.Hornpipe: Sailors dance
3*,2,2,2-4,0,2Cnt.,3,1-Timp.,Perc.-Hp.-Str.
Bosworth, Leipzig, c1904
Score 100 p.

3975 Fanfare, for 4 trumpets
4Tpt.
Ms.
Score 1 p.
Composed ca.1921.

1805 Fifine at the fair (A defence of   30'
inconstancy), an orchestral drama with a prologue [After Browning]
4*,2*,4*,4*-6,3(or 3Cnt.),3,1-Timp.,Perc.-2Hp.-Str.
Novello, London, c1912
Score 124 p. Large folio
Composed 1911. First performance Birmingham Music Festival, 1912, the composer conducting.

667c Hamabdil, Hebrew melody for violoncello 5'
Solo Vc.-Timp.-Hp.(or Pno.)-Str.
J.&W. Chester, London, c1919
Score 5 p.
Composed 1918. First performance Birmingham, 5 November 1919, the composer conducting.

1250 [Old English suite. Arranged for   15'
small orchestra]
1.Fantasia (Orlando Gibbons) 2.Lachrymae pavan (John Dowland) 3.The king's hunt (John Bull) 4.Quodling's delight (Giles Farnaby) 5.Sellenger's round (William Byrd)

THE EDWIN A. FLEISHER

Bantock, Granville

2,2,2,2-4(3rd&4th ad lib.),2-Timp.-Str.
Novello, London, ^c1909
Score 55 p.
*Arranged 1908 from music in the Parthenia and
the Fitzwilliam Virginal Book. First performance Hereford Festival, 1909, the composer
conducting.*

1440 [Overture to a Greek tragedy,   15'
Oedipus at Colones]
3*,3*,3*,3*-4,2,2Cnt.,3,1-Timp.,Perc.-2Hp.-
Str.
Leuckart, Leipzig, ^c1912
Score 58 p.
*Composed 1911. First performance Worcester
Festival, 1911, the composer conducting.*

683 The pierrot of the minute, a comedy   11'
overture
3*,1,2,1-3,2,1-Timp.,Perc.-Hp.-Str.
Breitkopf & Härtel, Leipzig, ^c1909
Score 54 p.
*Composed 1908 for the dramatic fantasy by
Ernest Dowson.*

5789 [Russian scenes, a suite]   21'
1.At the fair (Nijni Novgorod) 2.Mazurka
3.Polka 4.Valse 5.Cossack dance
2(2nd alt. Picc.),2,2,2-2,2Cnt.,3-Timp.,Perc.-
Str.
Bosworth, London, ^c1902
Score 100 p.

597c Sapphic poem, for violoncello and orchestra
Solo Vc.-2,1,2,2-2,1-Timp.,Trgl.-Str.
Novello, London, ^c1909
Score 48 p.
Composed 1906.

5167 Sappho. Prelude   9'
2,2*,2,2-3,1,3,1-Timp.,Perc.-Hp.-Str.
Breitkopf & Härtel, Leipzig, ^c1906
Score 43 p.
*Prelude to Sappho, Nine Fragments for Con-
tralto, a vocal work consisting of translations by Helen F. Bantock of poems by Sappho.*

246s Scenes from the Scottish Highlands,   18'
suite for string orchestra
1.Strathspey, The braes o' Tullymet 2.Dirge,
The Isle of Mull 3.Quickstep, Inverness
gathering 4.Gaelic melody, Baloo, baloo
5.Reel, The de'il among the tailors
Str.
Breitkopf & Härtel, Leipzig, ^c1914
Score 28 p.

245s Serenade, In the far west   7'
Str.
Breitkopf & Härtel, Leipzig, ^c1912
Score 37 p.
*Originally composed for string quartet in
1900; for string orchestra in 1912.*

1571 The witch of Atlas, tone poem no. 5   15'
(after Shelley)
3*,2*,3*,2-4,3,3,1-Timp.,Perc.-Hp.-Str.
Novello, London, ^c1903

Score 48 p.
*Composed 1902. First performance Worcester
Festival, 1902, the composer conducting.*

BAQUEIRO FOSTER, GERÓNIMO.   Mexico 1898

4049 Huapangos, no. 3, Balajú
2(2nd alt. Picc.),1,2(1Cl. in E-flat),1-Tpt.,
Tbn.-Timp.,Perc.-Hp.,Guit.,B.Guit.-Str.
Ms.
Score 72 p.
Composed 1940.

BARATI, GEORGE.   Györ, Hungary 3 April 1913

429m Chamber concerto, for flute, oboe,   23'
clarinet, bassoon and strings
1.Energico non troppo allegro 2.Andante
tranquillo 3.Allegretto e grottesco 4.Allegro
pressando
1,1,1,1-Str.(or Str. only)
Composers Facsimile Edition, New York, ^c1952
Score 36 p. Large folio
*First two movements composed 1950. Work com-
pleted 1952. First performance of completed
version Heidelberg, 18 August 1955, Pfalz
Orchestra of Ludwigshafen, the composer conducting. Winner of the Naumberg Award for
1959.*

5478 Scherzo from the Suite (1946) for   6'
orchestra
2(2nd alt. Picc.),2,2,2-4,2,3,1-Perc.-Hp.-Str.
Ms.
Score 28 p. Large folio
*Composed 1946. First performance Honolulu, 19
March 1950, Honolulu Symphony, the composer
conducting.*

BARATTA, MARÍA M. DE.
b. Barrio del Calvario, San Salvador,
El Salvador 27 February 1894

3749 Danza del incienso [Native ballet,   12'
in the Teocalli] Orchestrated by Alejandro
Muñoz
2(2nd alt. Picc.),1,2,2-2,2,1-Timp.,Perc.-Str.
Ms.
Score 33 p.
*Commissioned by the Municipality of San Salva-
dor. Originally composed for piano, 1937.
Orchestrated 1937. First performance San Salvador, 3 August 1937, Orquesta de los Supremos Poderes, Alejandro Muñoz conductor.*

3282 Nahualismo, Diábolus in musica.   12'
Orchestrated by Ricardo Hüttenrauch
[Prophecy] - [Incantation] - [Sorcery] -
[Prophecy] - [Dance of the Cabal] - [Bewitch-
ment] - [The onslaught of Nahual] - [Loud
laughter]
2(2nd alt. Picc.),2,2,2-4,2,3,1-Timp.,Perc.-
Str.
Ms.
Score 52 p.
*Originally composed for piano, 1934. Orches-
trated ca.1935. First performance Radio
Difusora Nacional, San Salvador, 19 April 1936,*

Banda de los Supremos Poderes de El Salvador, Ricardo Hüttenrauch conductor.

BARBER, SAMUEL.
            b. West Chester, Pennsylvania 9 March 1910

2000s Adagio for string orchestra, Op. 11 *7'30"*
Str.
G. Schirmer, New York, c1939
Score 7 p.
Originally composed as the Molto Adagio movement from String Quartet, Op. 11, 1936. Transcribed 1936. First performance New York, 5 November 1938, NBC Symphony, Arturo Toscanini conductor.

1072m Capricorn concerto, for flute,   *14'*
oboe, trumpet and strings, Op. 21
1.Allegro ma non troppo 2.Allegretto
3.Allegro con brio
1,1-Tpt.-Str.
G. Schirmer, New York, c1945
Score 35 p.
Capricorn is the name of the composer's home near Mt. Kisco, New York. Composed 1944. First performance New York, 8 October 1944, Saidenberg Little Symphony, Daniel Saidenberg conductor.

7167 Chorale prelude on Silent Night,   *3'*
from Die Natali, Op. 37
1,2*(E.H. optional),3*(B.Cl. optional),1-4(3rd &4th optional),0,3(2nd&3rd optional),1(optional)-Cel.,Hp.-Str.
G. Schirmer, New York, c1961
Score 8 p.
First performance Boston, 22 December 1960, Boston Symphony, Charles Munch conductor.

7060 Fadograph of a yestern scene, Op. 44 *7'*
3*,3*,3*,2-4,3,3,1-Timp.,Perc.-Pno.,Cel.,2Hp.
(2nd ad lib.)-Str.
G. Schirmer, New York, c1972
Score 26 p.
The title is from James Joyce's Finnegans Wake.

7168 First essay for orchestra, Op. 12   *8'*
2,2,2,2-4,3,3,1-Timp.-Pno.-Str.
G. Schirmer, New York, c1941
Score 23 p.
Composed 1937. Originally published as Essay for Orchestra. First performance New York, 5 November 1938, NBC Symphony, Arturo Toscanini conductor.

6893 Mutations from Bach, for brass choir and
timpani
4Hn.,3Tpt.,3Tbn.,Tuba-Timp.
G. Schirmer, Inc., New York, c1968
Score 11 p.
Based on the plainsong, Christe, Du Lamm Gottes, first as harmonized by Joachim Decker (1604), then in various versions by J.S. Bach (BWV 23, BWV 619).

7161 Night flight, Op. 19a   *7'30"*
3(3rd alt. Picc.),3*,4*(1Cl. in E-flat),2-4,3,
3,1-Perc.-Pno.-Str.

G. Schirmer, New York, c1950, c1964
Score 21 p.
Originally the second movement of the composer's Symphony no. 2, Op. 19, commissioned by the USA Army Air Forces and composed in 1944. The symphony now withdrawn. This movement revised as a separate work ca.1967 and retitled after Antoine de Saint Exupéry's novel.

7170 Overture to The school for   *7'30"*
scandal [Op. 5]
3*,3*,3*,2-4,3,3,1-Timp.,Perc.-Cel.,Hp.-Str.
G. Schirmer, New York, c1941
Score 36 p.
Suggested by Richard Sheridan's play. Composed 1931-33. First performance Philadelphia, 30 August 1933, Philadelphia Orchestra, Alexander Smallens conductor. Awarded the Bearns Prize by Columbia University.

7169 Second essay for orchestra, Op. 17 *9'30"*
3*,3*,2(2nd alt. B.Cl.),2-4,3,3,1-Timp.,Perc.-
Str.
G. Schirmer, New York, c1942
Score 45 p.
Composed 1942. First performance New York, 16 April 1942, New York Philharmonic, Bruno Walter conductor.

189m Toccata festiva, Op. 36a [reduced   *14'*
orchestration]
Solo Org.-Tpt.-Timp.-Str.
G. Schirmer, New York, c1961
Score 46 p.
Commissioned by Mary Curtis Zimbalist for the dedication of the new organ at the Academy of Music in Philadelphia. Originally composed for organ and full orchestra, 1960. First performance of this version Church of the Incarnation, New York, 10 December 1961, Thomas Dunn conductor.

7171 [Vanessa. Intermezzo]   *4'*
3(3rd alt. Picc.),3*,3*,2-4,2,3,1-Timp.,Perc.-
Hp.(or Pno.)-Str.
G. Schirmer, New York, c1958
Score 13 p.
From the opera in four acts with libretto by Gian Carlo Menotti. The intermezzo is played between the scenes of the last act. Composed 1957-58. First performance of opera New York, 15 January 1958, Metropolitan Opera Company, Dimitri Mitropoulos conductor.

BARBERÁ, JOSÉ.   Barcelona 27 January 1874
            Barcelona 19 February 1947

3772 Soldatini in marcia [Toy soldiers   *4'*
on parade, for small orchestra]
3*,2,2,2-2,1-Perc.-Hp.-Str.
Ricordi, Milan, c1940
Score 26 p.
Composed 1939.

BARBIER, RENÉ AUGUST-ERNEST.
            b. Namur, Belgium 12 July 1890

2290s [Three symphonic movements, for   *18'*
string orchestra, Op. 104]

Barbirolli, A.

Str.
CeBeDem, Brussels, ^c1963
Score 34 p.
Composed 1962. First performance Namur, Belgium, 14 March 1963, Orchestre du Conservatoire de Namur, the composer conducting.

BARBIROLLI, A.

1065s Fremito d'amore [Trembling with love]
valse lente. Arranged for strings
Str.
Score: Ms. 11 p.
Parts: Emile Gallet, Paris [n.d.]

BARCLAY, ROBERT LENARD.
        b. Penticton, British Columbia, Canada 1918

Born: Leonard Edwin Basham

4909 Ballade for orchestra   9'
4*,3*,3*,3*-4,3,3,1-Timp.,Perc.-Hp.-Str.
Ms. ^c1947 by Robert Barclay
Score 45 p. Large folio
Composed 1946.

2029s Caprice for strings   5'
Str.
Ms. ^c1952 by Robert Barclay
Score 15 p.
Composed 1950.

1948s Elegy for strings, Op. 10   3'30"
Str.
Ms. ^c1948 by Leonard Basham
Score 7 p.
Composed 1941. First performance Toronto, 2 April 1942, CBC String Orchestra, Alexander Chuhaldin conductor.

4562 Legend for orchestra   5'
2,2,2,2-2,2,3-Timp.,Perc.-Str.
Ms. ^c1948 by Leonard Basham
Score 21 p.
Composed 1940. First performance a CBC Broadcast, 7 February 1941, Vancouver Promenade Symphony Orchestra, Arthur Benjamin conductor.

1946s Night scene, for strings [1950   5'
version]
Str.
Ms. ^c1950 by Leonard Basham
Score 12 p.
Originally composed 1940. First performance Rochester, 28 October 1942, Eastman-Rochester Symphony Orchestra, Howard Hanson conductor. Revised 1950. The 1950 version is for reference only. The composer now wishes only the original 1940 version to be performed.

Nocturne and scherzo [1947 version]
5077 Nocturne   5'30"
2,2,2,2-Timp.-Hp.-Str.
4913 Scherzo   5'
1,1,1,1-Timp.-Str.
Ms. ^c1947, 1956 by Robert Barclay
Scores: 28 p., 46 p.
Originally composed 1942. Revised 1947. First

performance of revised version at a meeting of the National Association for American Composers and Conductors, Columbia University, New York, 21 January 1951, Teachers College Little Symphony, Ernest E. Harris conductor.

5328 Prelude for orchestra   3'
2,2,2,2-3,3,3-Timp.,Perc.-Hp.-Str.
Ms. ^c1955 by Robert Barclay
Score 18 p.
Composed 1955.

4902 Rhapsody for orchestra [1947 version] 8'
2(2nd alt. Picc.),2(2nd alt. E.H.),2,2-4,2,3,1-
Timp.,Perc.-Pno.,Hp.-Str.
Ms. ^c1947 by Leonard Basham
Score 53 p.
Originally composed 1942, and titled Pastoral Overture. First performance Vancouver, British Columbia, 26 July 1942, Vancouver Symphony Orchestra, Ernest MacMillan conductor. Revised 1947.

4569 Seaport town overture   6'
4*,3*,3*,3*-4,3,3,1-Timp.,Perc.-Pno.,Hp.-Str.
Ms. ^c1950 by Leonard Basham
Score in reduction 18 p.
Composed 1950. First performance Vancouver, British Columbia, 14 March 1950, Vancouver Symphony Orchestra, the composer conducting.

4567 Symphony in one movement, Op. 9   15'
[1950 version]
2,2,2,2-4,2-Timp.-Str.
Ms. ^c1950 by Leonard Basham
Score 72 p.
Originally composed 1942 under the title Symphony for Radio Orchestra. Revised 1949, 1950. First performance of revised version Contemporary Arts Festival, Urbana, Illinois, 3 March 1950, University of Illinois Symphony Orchestra, John M. Kuypers conductor.

4910 Two pieces for small orchestra,   7'30"
music for a film [revised version]
1.Outdoor scene 2.Dance
1(alt. Picc.),1,2,1-2,2,1-Timp.,Perc.-Pno.,Hp.
-Str.
Ms. ^c1952 by Robert Barclay
Score 51 p.
Composed 1939. Revised 1950.

BARGIEL, WOLDEMAR.   Berlin 3 October 1828
                          Berlin 23 February 1897

759c [Adagio for violoncello and orchestra,
Op. 38]
Solo Vc.-2,2,2,2-2Hn.-Str.
Breitkopf & Härtel, Leipzig [1871]
Score 11 p.

591 Intermezzo für Orchester, Op. 46   9'
2,2,2,2-2,2-Timp.-Str.
Breitkopf & Härtel, Leipzig [ca.1880-81]
Score 34 p.
Composed 1879. First performance Berlin, 1880.

5721 [Medea, Op. 22. Overture]   *9'*
2,2,2,2-4,2,3-Timp.-Str.
Leuckart, Leipzig [ca.1861]
Score 73 p.
For the tragedy by Euripides.

2150 [Overture to a tragedy, Op. 18]   *10'*
2,2,2,2-4,2,3-Timp.-Str.
Senff, Leipzig [1859]
Score 65 p.

5425 [Prometheus, Op. 16. Overture]   *16'*
3*,2,2,2-4,2,3-Timp.-Str.
Breitkopf & Härtel, Leipzig [1865]
Score 84 p.
For Aeschylus' tragedy Prometheus Bound.

5004 [Symphony, Op. 30, C major]
1.Allegro energico 2.Andante con moto
3.Menuetto 4.Allegro molto
2,2,2,2-4,2,3-Timp.-Str.
Breitkopf & Härtel, Leipzig [ca.1880-81]
Score 200 p.

BARLOW, WAYNE.   Elyria, Ohio 6 September 1912

2905 De profundis, poem for orchestra,   *8'*
Op. 6
2,2(2nd alt. E.H.),2,2-4,2,3,1-Timp.,Perc.-
Sop. Voice(cued for Fl.I)-Str.
Ms.
Score 34 p.
*Based on a poem by Amy Lowell. Composed 1934.
First performance Rochester, 8 April 1934,
Rochester Civic Orchestra, Howard Hanson con-
ductor.*

3513 Three moods for dancing, Op. 12   *12'*
1.Neo-classic 2.Impressionist 3.Cubist
3(3rd alt. Picc.),3*,3*,3*-4,3,3,1-Timp.,Perc.
-Cel.,Hp.-Str.
Ms.
Score 62 p.
*Written for Thelma Biracree, choreographer for
the first ballet performance. Composed 1940.
First ballet performance Rochester, 26 April
1940, Rochester Civic Orchestra, Howard Hanson
conductor. First concert performance Rochester, 28 April 1942, Eastman School Senior Symphony, Howard Hanson conductor.*

933m The winter's passed, rhapsody for   *5'*
oboe and strings, Op. 11
Solo Ob., Solo Vn.-Str.
Ms.
Score 11 p.
*Based on two Carolina mountain songs. Com-
posed 1938. First performance Rochester, 28
October 1938, Rochester Civic Orchestra,
Howard Hanson conductor, Robert Sprenkle
soloist.*

BARNEKOW, CHRISTIAN.
        St. Sauveur, Pyrenees, France 28 July 1837
                        Copenhagen 20 March 1913

356s [Idylls for string orchestra, Op. 29]
1.Allegro non troppo 2.Andantino

3.Allegretto 4.Allegro moderato
Str.
W. Hansen, Copenhagen [1911]
Score 43 p.
Composed 1910.

BARNETT, JOHN FRANCIS.   London 16 October 1837
                        London 24 November 1916

855s Fairyland, pizzicato
Str.
Score: Ms. 9 p.
Parts: Joseph Williams, London [n.d.]
*From Two Sketches. First performance London,
1891.*

271s [Two pieces for string orchestra]
1.Pensée mélodique 2.Gavotte
Str.
Breitkopf & Härtel, Leipzig, c1899
Score 9 p.
First performance London, 1899.

BARNS, ETHEL.   London 1880
                        Maidenhead 31 December 1948

934s L'escarpolette [Seesaw] Transcribed for
string orchestra by F. Louis Schneider
Str.
Score: Ms. 6 p.
Parts: Schott, Mainz, c1908

BARRAUD, HENRI.   Bordeaux 23 April 1900

6140 [Poem for orchestra]   *9'*
3*,3*,3*,3*-4,3,3,1-Timp.,Perc.-Hp.-Str.
Eulenburg, Leipzig, c1938
Score 59 p.
*Composed 1933. First performance Paris, Feb-
ruary 1934, Orchestre Symphonique de Paris,
Pierre Monteux conductor.*

6277 Symphony no. 3   *25'*
1.Pesante e marcato 2.Presto 3.Adagio
4.Energico
3*(2nd alt. Picc.II),3*,3*,3*-4,3,3,1-Timp.,
Perc.-Pno.,Cel.,Hp.-Str.
Hawkes & Son, London, c1958
Score 143 p.
*Composed 1956. First performance Boston, 7
March 1958, Boston Symphony Orchestra, Charles
Munch conductor.*

BARROZO NETTO, JOAQUIM ANTONIO.
                Rio de Janeiro 30 January 1881
                Rio de Janeiro 1 September 1941

1849s Berceuse
Str.
Ms.
Score 5 p.

1850s Dansa caracteristica
Str.
Ms.
Score 8 p.

Barrozo Netto, Joachim Antonio

1846s Ideal
Str.
Ms.
Score 5 p.

793p Minha terra [My country, for piano and
string orchestra]
Solo Pno.-Str.
Ms.
Score 20 p.
Originally composed for solo piano.

BARRYMORE, LIONEL.   Philadelphia 28 April 1878
              Chatsworth, California 15 November 1954

4352 Piranesi suite   20'
1.Pantheon 2.Carceri imagineri [Imaginary
prisons] 3.The falls of Tivoli 4.Colloseum
3(3rd alt. Picc.),2(2nd alt. E.H.),3*,3*-4,3,
3,1-Timp.,Perc.-Pno.(alt. Cel.),Hp.-Str.
Ms. c1946
Score 154 p.
*After the engravings of Giovanni Battista
Piranesi. First performance Indianapolis,
23 November 1946, Indianapolis Symphony Orchestra, Fabien Sevitzky conductor.*

5079 Preludium and fugue   13'
3(3rd alt. Picc.),2(2nd alt. E.H.),2,3*-4,3,
3,1-Timp.,Perc.-Pno.(alt. Cel. or Hpscd.),
Org.,Hp.-Str.
Ms.
Score 50 p.
*First performance Indianapolis, 28 October
1944, Indianapolis Symphony Orchestra, Fabien
Sevitzky conductor.*

BARSAM, YIZHAK.   Vienna 7 March 1922

6458 Toccata and capriccio for strings   12'
and brass, Op. 20
4Hn.,2Tpt.-Str.
Israeli Music Publications, Tel Aviv, c1964
Score 31 p. Large folio
*Composed 1959. First performance Jerusalem,
12 June 1962, Kol Yisrael Symphony Orchestra,
Mendi Rodan conductor.*

BARTELS, WOLFGANG VON.   Hamburg 21 July 1883
                            Munich 19 April 1938

681m [Suite for flute and string orchestra,
Op. 14]
Solo Fl.-Str.
Tischer & Jagenberg, Cologne, c1926
Score 40 p.

BARTH, HANS.   Leipzig 25 June 1897
              Jacksonville, Florida 9 December 1956

706p [Concerto, piano, Op. 11 no. 1]   10'
Allegro con moto - Andante - Allegro
Solo Pno.-2(2nd alt. Picc.),2,2,2-4,2,3-Timp.,
Glock.-Str.
Ms.
Score 59 p.
*This and Op. 11 no. 2 were originally a single
concerto, composed 1925. This version, 1928.*

707p [Concerto, piano, Op. 11 no. 2]   9'
In one movement
Solo Pno.-2(2nd alt. Picc.),2,2,2-4,2,3-Timp.,
Perc.-Str.
Ms.
Score 60 p.

BARTHELSON, JOYCE.   Yakima, Washington 1905

4784 Ode to Franklin Delano Roosevelt
1.Moderato - Very slow - Moderato 2.Adagio
3.Allegro - Slower - Very slow
3,3*,3*,3*-4,3,3,1-Timp.,Perc.-Hp.-Str.
Ms.
Score 64 p. Large folio
*Withdrawn from circulation at composer's
request.*

3319 Overture in A minor   6'30"
2(2nd alt. Picc.),2(2nd alt. E.H.),2,2-4,3,2-
Timp.,Cym.-Pno.(optional)-Str.
Ms.
Score 19 p.
*Composed 1940. First performance Oakland,
California, 19 November 1940, Oakland Symphony
Orchestra, Orley See conductor.*

BARTHOLDY, CONRAD JOHAN.
              Frijsenborg, Denmark 12 March 1853
                    Copenhagen 6 December 1904

970s [Strophe, for string orchestra and piano,
Op. 30]
Pno.,Harm.(ad lib.),Hp.(ad lib.)-Str.
W. Hansen, Copenhagen [n.d.]
Score 17 p.

BARTÓK, BÉLA.
              Nagyszentmiklós, Hungary 25 March 1881
                    New York 26 September 1945

Full name: Béla Viktor János Bartók

4885 Concerto for orchestra   37'
1.Introduzione 2.Giuocco delle coppie
3.Elegia 4.Intermezzo interrotto 5.Finale:
Pesante - Presto
3(3rd alt. Picc.),3(3rd alt. E.H.),3(3rd alt.
B.Cl.),3(3rd alt. C.Bn.)-4,3,3,1-Timp.,Perc.-
2Hp.-Str.
Boosey & Hawkes, London, c1946
Score 147 p.
*Commissioned by the Koussevitzky Foundation in
memory of Natalie Koussevitzky. Composed 1943.
First performance New York, 1 December 1944,
Boston Symphony Orchestra, Serge Koussevitzky
conductor.*

620p [Concerto, piano, no. 1]   23'
1.Allegro moderato 2.Andante 3.Allegro molto
Solo Pno.-2(2nd alt. Picc.),2(2nd alt. E.H.),
2(2nd alt. B.Cl.),2-4,2,3-Timp.,Perc.-Str.
Universal Edition, Vienna, c1927
Score 112 p.
*Composed 1926. First performance Frankfurt,
1 July 1927, Wilhelm Furtwängler conductor,
the composer as soloist.*

Bartók, Béla

359p [Concerto, piano, no. 2]   25'
1.Allegro 2.Adagio - Presto - Adagio
3.Allegro molto
Solo Pno.-3(3rd alt. Picc.),2(2nd alt. E.H.),2
(2nd alt. B.Cl.),3(3rd alt. C.Bn.)-4,3,3,1-
Timp.,Perc.-Str.
Universal Edition, Vienna, ᶜ1932
Score 98 p.
Composed 1930-31. First performance Frankfurt,
23 January 1933, Frankfurt Radio Symphony, Hans
Rosbaud conductor, the composer as soloist.

830p [Concerto, piano, no. 3]   23'
1.Allegretto 2.Adagio religioso - Poco più
mosso - Tempo I 3.Allegro vivace
Solo Pno.-2(2nd alt. Picc.),2(2nd alt. E.H.),
2(2nd alt. B.Cl.),2-4,2,3,1-Timp.,Perc.-Str.
Boosey & Hawkes, London, ᶜ1947
Score 91 p.
Composed 1945; last 17 bars orchestrated by
Tibor Serly. First performance Philadelphia,
8 February 1946, Philadelphia Orchestra,
Eugene Ormandy conductor, György Sándor
soloist.

784p [Concerto, 2 pianos, percussion   24'30"
and orchestra]
1.Assai lento - Allegro molto - Vivo - Meno
mosso tranquillo - Vivo 2.Lento, ma non
troppo - Allegro non troppo
2 Solo Pno.-2(2nd alt. Picc.),2(2nd alt. E.H.),
2,2(2nd alt. C.Bn.)-4,2,3-Perc.-Cel.-Str.
Ms.
Score 171 p.
Originally composed 1937 as Sonata for Two
Pianos and Percussion. Transcribed 1940.
First performance London, 14 October 1942,
Royal Philharmonic Orchestra, Adrian Boult
conductor, Louis Kentner and Ilona Kabos
soloists.

1159v [Concerto, violin, no. 2]   32'
1.Allegro non troppo 2.Andante tranquillo
(Theme and variations) 3.Allegro molto (Rondo)
Solo Vn.-2(2nd alt. Picc.),2(2nd alt. E.H.),2
(2nd alt. B.Cl.),2(2nd alt. C.Bn.)-4,2,3-Timp.,
Perc.-Cel.,Hp.-Str.
Ms.
Score 98 p.
Composed 1937-38. First performance Amsterdam,
23 April 1939, Concertgebouw Orchestra, Willem
Mengelberg conductor, Zoltán Székely soloist.

1574 [Dance suite]   16'
1.Moderato 2.Allegro molto 3.Allegro vivace
4.Molto tranquillo 5.Comodo 6.Finale
2(1st alt. Picc.II,2nd alt. Picc.I),2(2nd alt.
E.H.),2(2nd alt. B.Cl.),2(2nd alt. C.Bn.)-4,2,
2,1-Timp.,Perc.-Pno.,Cel.,Hp.-Str.
Universal Edition, Vienna, ᶜ1924
Score 80 p.
Composed 1923 for the fiftieth anniversary of
the union of Buda and Pest. First performance
Budapest, 19 November 1923, Budapest Philhar-
monic Society, Ernö Dohnányi conductor.

1800s Divertimento, for string orchestra   22'
1.Allegro non troppo 2.Molto adagio

3.Allegro assai
Str.
Boosey & Hawkes, London, ᶜ1940
Score 42 p.
Commissioned by the Chamber Orchestra of Basel,
Switzerland, and its conductor, Paul Sacher,
1939. First performance 10 June 1940, Chamber
Orchestra of Basel, Paul Sacher conductor.

5307 [Four orchestral pieces, Op. 12]   25'
1.Preludio 2.Scherzo 3.Intermezzo 4.Marcia
funebre
4(3rd alt. Picc.II,4th alt. Picc.I),3(3rd alt.
E.H.),4*(B.Cl. alt. Cl. in E-flat),4(4th alt.
C.Bn.)-4,4,4,1-Timp.,Perc.-Pno.,Cel.,2Hp.-Str.
Universal Edition, Vienna, ᶜ1923
Score 111 p.
Composed ca.1912. Orchestrated 1921. First
performance Budapest, 9 January 1922, Budapest
Philharmonic Society, Ernö Dohnányi conductor.

5165 Hungarian peasant songs   9'
1.Ballad (Theme with variations) 2.Hungarian
peasant dances
2(2nd alt. Picc.),2(2nd alt. E.H.),2(2nd alt.
B.Cl.),2-2,2,2,1-Timp.,B.Dr.-Hp.-Str.
Score: Boosey & Hawkes, London, ᶜ1939. 36 p.
Parts: Universal Edition, Vienna, ᶜ1933
Originally composed for piano from fifteen Hun-
garian Peasant Songs, 1914-17. Nos. 6-12, 14
and 15 transcribed for orchestra in 1933.
First performance Szombathely, Hungary, 18
March 1934, Gyula Baranyai conductor.

4061 Mikrokosmos. Suite arranged for   16'30"
orchestra by Tibor Serly
1.Prelude 2.Scherzando (Jack in the box)
3.Unisono 4.Bourrée 5.Moto perpetuo (From the
diary of a fly) 6.Contrasts over pedal (Study
in overtones) 7.Bulgarian rhythm no. 4
8.Bulgarian rhythm no. 6
3(3rd alt. Picc.),2(2nd alt. E.H.),2(2nd alt.
B.Cl.),2(2nd alt. C.Bn.)-4,3,3,1-Timp.,Perc.-
Cel.,Hp.-Str.
Boosey & Hawkes, New York, ᶜ1943
Score 92 p.
Tibor Serly arranged this suite ca.1943. No. 1
is an orchestration of a piano composition
included in the album Homage to Paderewski.
Nos. 2-8 are arrangements based on pieces from
Mikrokosmos, 153 Progressive Piano Pieces. The
movements may be performed separately. First
performance of six movements only St. Louis, 20
November 1943, St. Louis Symphony Orchestra,
Vladimir Golschmann conductor.

2084s [Music for strings, percussion   26'
and celesta]
1.Andante tranquillo 2.Allegro 3.Adagio
4.Allegro molto
Timp.,Perc.-Pno.,Cel.,Hp.-Str.(in 2 groups)
Universal Edition, Vienna, ᶜ1937
Score 144 p.
Commissioned by the Basel Chamber Orchestra and
Paul Sacher. Composed 1936. First performance
Basel, 21 January 1937, Basel Chamber Orchestra,
Paul Sacher conductor.

Bartók, Béla

441p Rhapsodie, pour le piano et   17'
1'orchestre, Op. 1
Solo Pno.-3*,2,2,2-4,2,3-Timp.,Perc.-Str.
Rózsavölgyi, Budapest, c1910
Score 60 p.
Composed 1904.

935v [Rhapsody, violin and orchestra,   11'
Folk dances, no. 1]
Part I.Lassú Part II.Friss
Solo Vn.-2(2nd alt. Picc.),2,2(2nd alt. B.Cl.),
2(2nd alt. C.Bn.)-2,2,1,1-Trgl.-Cimbalon(or Hp.
&Pno.)-Str.
Universal Edition, Vienna, c1931
Score 52 p.
*Originally composed for violin and piano, 1928.
First performance of this version Zurich, 19
November 1929, Volkmar Andreae conductor,
Joseph Szigeti soloist. Each part may be per-
formed separately.*

624v [Rhapsody, violin and orchestra,   12'
Folk dances, no. 2]
Part I.Lassú Part II.Friss
Solo Vn.-2(2nd alt. Picc.),2,2(2nd alt. E.H.),2
(2nd alt. B.Cl.),2(2nd alt. C.Bn.)-2,2,1,1-
Timp.,Perc.-Pno.,Cel.,Hp.-Str.
Universal Edition, Vienna, c1931
Score 65 p.
*Originally composed for violin and piano, 1928.
Transcribed for violin and orchestra by the
composer, 1928. First performance of this ver-
sion, Budapest, 23 November 1929, Ernö Dohnányi
conductor, Zoltán Székely soloist.*

4806 [Romanian folk dances. Transcribed for
orchestra by Arnold Wilke]
1.[Jocul cu bâtă, from Mezöszabad] 2.[Buciu-
meana, from Bisztra] 3.[Mărunţel, from Belén-
yes]
1(alt. Picc.),1,2,1-2,2,1-Timp.,Perc.-Harm.-
Str.
Score: Ms. 33 p.
Parts: Universal Edition, Vienna, c1928
*Originally composed for piano, 1915, as Roma-
nian Folk Dances from Hungary. This transcription contains only three of the original
seven dances.*

1114s [Romanian folk dances. Transcribed   6'
for string orchestra by Arthur Willner]
1.Jocul cu bâtă [from Mezöszabad] 2.Brâul
[from Egres] 3.Pe loc [from Egres] 4.Buciu-
meana [from Bisztra] 5.Poarga românească
[from Belényes] 6.Mărunţel [from Belényes]
7.Mărunţel [from Nyágra]
Str.
Universal Edition, Vienna, c1929
Score 15 p.
*Originally composed for piano, 1915, as Roma-
nian Folk Dances from Hungary. This transcription includes all seven dances.*

783p Sonata for two pianos and   24'30"
percussion
1.Assai lento - Allegro molto 2.Lento, ma non
troppo 3.Allegro non troppo
2Pno.-Perc.(2 players):3Timp.,Xyl.,2S.Dr.,

Susp.Cym.,2Cym.,B.Dr.,Trgl.,Tam-tam
Boosey & Hawkes, London, c1942
Miniature score 96 p.
*Composed 1937. First performance Basel, 16
January 1938, Ditta and Béla Bartók pianists.
Later transcribed as Concerto for Two Pianos,
Percussion and Orchestra, Catalog no. 784p.*

857 [Suite for orchestra, no. 1, Op. 3]   45'
1.Allegro vivace 2.Poco adagio 3.Presto
4.Moderato 5.Molto vivace
4*,3*,4*,4*-4,3,3,1-Timp.,Perc.-2Hp.-Str.
Rózsavölgyi, Budapest [1905]
Score 188 p.
*Composed 1905. First complete performance
Budapest, 1 March 1909, Conservatory Orchestra,
Jenö Hubay conductor.*

1575 [Suite for orchestra, no. 2, Op. 4]   30'
1.Comodo 2.Allegro scherzando 3.Andante
4.Comodo
2(1st alt. Picc.),2(2nd alt. E.H.),2(2nd alt.
B.Cl.),2(2nd alt. C.Bn.)-3,2-Timp.,Perc.-2Hp.-
Str.
Universal Edition, Vienna, c1921
Score 110 p.
*Composed 1905-07. First performance Budapest,
22 November 1909, Philharmonic Society, István
Kerner conductor.*

2494 [Two pictures for orchestra, Op. 10]   20'
1.En pleine fleur [In full bloom] 2.Danse
villageoise
3(3rd alt. Picc.),3*,3(3rd alt. B.Cl.),3(3rd
alt. C.Bn.)-4,4,3,1-Timp.,Perc.-Cel.,2Hp.-
Str.
Rózsavölgyi, Budapest, c1912
Score 61 p.
*Composed 1910. First performance Budapest, 5
October 1912, Philharmonic Orchestra, Stephan
Kerner conductor.*

1573 [Two portraits for orchestra, Op. 5]   12'
1.Egy ideális [Ideal] 2.Egy torz [Distortion]
Solo Vn.-2,2(2nd alt. E.H.),2(2nd alt. B.Cl.),
2-4,2,2,1-Timp.,Perc.-2Hp.-Str.
Rozsnyai, Budapest [1912]
Score 39 p.
*The first portrait is identical with the first
movement of the Concerto for Violin, no. 1,
Op. posth., composed 1907-08. The second por-
trait is a transcription of Bagatelle Op. 6
no. 14, Ma Mie qui Danse..., composed 1908.
First performance in this form, Budapest, 1909,
Budapest Symphony, László Kún conductor, Imre
Waldbauer soloist.*

BÄRWOLF, LOUIS.   d. (?)1899

725m Cavatine [for flute and orchestra]
Solo Fl.-0,1,2,2-Hn.-Str.
Ms.
Score 14 p.

BASHAM, LEONARD EDWIN.
See: BARCLAY, ROBERT LENARD.

BASSERMANN, ERNST.

5128 [Overture, F major]
3*,2,2,2-4,2,3,1-Timp.-Str.
Breitkopf & Härtel, Leipzig [ca.1884]
Score 51 p.

BASSETT, LESLIE.
        b. Hanford, California 22 January 1923

6158 [Symphony no. 2]   25'
1.Moderato 2.Allegro brillante 3.Adagio
espressivo 4.Allegro energico
3*,3*,3*,3*-4,3,3,1-Timp.,Perc.-Str.
Composer's Facsimile Edition, New York, c1957
by Leslie Bassett
Score 148 p. Large folio
Composed 1955-56. First performance Asilomar,
California, July 1959, American Symphony
Orchestra League, Erno Daniel conductor.

BATE, STANLEY.
        Plymouth, Devonshire 12 December 1912
        London 19 October 1959

786p Concertante, for piano and string
orchestra, Op. 24
1.Allegro risoluto 2.Andante sostenuto 3.
Finale: Andante maestoso - Allegro vivace
Solo Pno.-Str.
Ms. [Schott & Co., London, c1941]
Score 54 p. Large folio
Composed 1938. First performance London, 5
June 1939, London Women's String Orchestra,
Kathleen Riddick conductor, Lloyd Powell
soloist.

785p Concertino, for piano and chamber   11'
orchestra, Op. 21
1.Toccata 2.Romanza 3.Rondo
Solo Pno.-1,1,1,1-2,1-Timp.,Perc.-Str.
Ms.
Score 84 p.
Commissioned by the Eastbourne Music Festival
Committee, Eastbourne, Sussex, 1937. Com-
posed 1937. First performance Eastbourne
Music Festival, 8 February 1938, Eastbourne
Municipal Orchestra, Kneale Kelly conductor,
the composer as soloist.

4066 Sinfonietta no. 1, Op. 22   15'
1.Allegro molto 2.Andante 3.Alla marcia
4.Finale
2,2,2,2-4,2,2-Timp.,S.Dr.-Str.
Ms. [Schott & Co., London, c1941]
Score 100 p. Large folio
Composed for Universal Editions, London Ltd.,
1938. First performance Sydney, Australia,
8 December 1940, Sydney Symphony Orchestra of
the Australian Broadcasting Commission, Percy
Code conductor.

4559 Sinfonietta no. 2, Op. 39   15'
1. ♩=100 2.Adagio 3.Finale: Allegro
2(2nd alt. Picc.),2,2,2-4,3,3,1-Timp.-Pno.-Str.
Ms.
Score 125 p. Large folio

4551 Symphony no. 3, Op. 29   28'
1.Moderato 2.Lento 3.Finale: Presto
3(2nd alt. Picc.),3*,3*,3*-4,3,3,1-Timp.,Perc.
-Pno.-Str.
Ms. [c1942 by Schott & Co., London]
Score 180 p. Large folio
Composed 1941-42. First performance Chelten-
ham Festival, 14 July 1954.

BATON, RENÉ.
    See: RHENÉ-BATON.

BATTANCHON, FELIX.   Paris 9 April 1814
                          Paris July 1893

703c [Concerto, violoncello, no. 1, Op. 20,
E minor]
1.Allegro 2.Andante cantabile 3.Allegro non
troppo
Solo Vc.-2,0,2-2Hn.-Timp.-Str.
Score: Ms. 91 p.
Parts: Fréderic Hofmeister, Leipzig [ca.1860-
66]

BAUER, MARION.
        Walla Walla, Washington 15 August 1887
        South Hadley, Massachusetts 9 August 1955

6553 Aquarelle, Op. 39 no. 2   4'
2(2nd alt. Picc.),2,2,2-2Hn.-2Cb.
Ms.
Score 7 p.
Originally composed for piano, ca.1950.

3511 Indian pipes, Op. 12 no. 2.   2'30"
Orchestrated by Martin Bernstein
2,2*,2,2-4,2,3-Hp.-Str.
Ms.
Score 15 p.
Originally part of a group of three pieces for
piano, From New Hampshire Woods, composed
1921. Orchestrated 1927-28. First performance Chautauqua, summer 1928, Chautauqua Symphony Orchestra, Albert Stoessel conductor.

1825s A lament on an African theme, Op. 20. 6'
Arranged by Martin Bernstein
Str.
Ms.
Score 10 p.
The theme is an African lament from the col-
lection of Natalie Curtis, Songs and Tales
from the Dark Continent. Originally the slow
movement of String Quartet, Op. 20, composed
1925-57. This arrangement, 1926-27. First
performance New York University, April 1935,
Washington Square String Orchestra, Martin
Bernstein conductor.

6554 Patterns [for chamber orchestra]   2'
Op. 41 no. 2
2(2nd alt. Picc.),2,2,2-2Hn.-Cb.
Ms.
Score 7 p.
Originally composed for piano ca.1951.

1920s Symphonic suite for string   15'
orchestra, Op. 33

Baussart, A.

1.Prelude   2.Interlude   3.Finale: Fugue
Str.
Ms.
Score 14 p.
Composed 1940.

BAUSSART, A.

1642s Les yeux, romance pour violon solo et
orchestre à cordes
Solo Vn.-Str.
Score: Ms. 4 p.
Parts: Gaudet, Paris [n.d.]

BAUSSNERN, WALDEMAR VON.   Berlin 29 November 1866
                             Potsdam 20 August 1931

[Hymnic hours, three pieces for string
orchestra]
553s No. 1. Prolog
554s No. 2. Evangelium [Gospel]
518s No. 3. Dithyrambus
Str.
Vieweg, Berlin, ᶜ1925
Scores: 11 p., 9 p., 13 p.

BAUTISTA, JULIÁN.   Madrid 21 April 1901
                             Buenos Aires 8 July 1961

1021m Suite all'antica, para orquesta,   *20'*
Op. 11
1.Overtura 2.Adagietto 3.Rigodón 4.Finale
Soli: Vn.I,Vn.II,Va.,Vc.-1,1,1,1-1,1,1-Timp.,
S.Dr.-Str.
Ministerio de Instruction Pública, Barcelona,
1938
Score 99 p.
*Originally composed 1932 for medium-sized
orchestra without soloists. Arranged in pre-
sent form 1933. First performance Barcelona,
30 December 1938, Orquesta Nacional de Con-
ciertos, the composer conducting, Cuarteto
A.M.I.S. soloists.*

BAVICCHI, JOHN.   Boston 25 April 1922

355m Fantasy for harp and chamber   *10'*
orchestra, Op. 36
In two movements
Solo Hp.-1,1,1,1-Hn.-Str.
Ms.
Score 34 p.
*Composed 1959. First performance New York, 18
March 1960, Music In Our Time orchestra,
Howard Shanet conductor, Assunta dell'Aguila
soloist.*

6168 Farewell and hail, Op. 28   *20'*
Sop. Voice Solo-Tpt.-Str.
Ms.
Score 31 p.
Words by Norma Farber. Composed 1957.

6196 Four songs for contralto and   *14'*
chamber orchestra, Op. 6
1.To Lorna (poem by Eric Wilson Barker) 2.
In memoriam (poem by Rose Nolfi) 3.Lament
(poem by Dorothy Berg Bavicchi)

4.The search (poem by Marybelle Tyree Schwert-
man)
Contralto Voice Solo-2,1,2*-2Hn.-Str.
Ms.
Score 55 p.
*Composed 1952. First performance Cambridge,
Massachusetts, 17 December 1952, Harvard
Music Club, Herbert Blomstedt conductor,
Valentina Sobalvarro soloist.*

6065 Suite for orchestra, Op. 19   *24'*
1.Spiritoso 2.Scherzoso 3.Allegro molto
4.Serioso 5.Molto allegro
3*,3*,3*,3*-4,3,3,1-Timp.,Perc.-Str.
Ms.
Score 94 p. Large folio
*Movements 1, 4 and 5 originally composed as
Sonata for Two Pianos, 1953. This work com-
posed 1955-59. First performance Cambridge,
Massachusetts, 16 April 1961, Cambridge Civic
Symphony Orchestra, the composer conducting.*

6240 Tobal, a fantasy concert-piece for
orchestra, Op. 5
2,2,3*,2-4,3,3-Timp.,Perc.-Str.
Ms.
Score 55 p. Large folio
Composed 1952.

BAX, ARNOLD EDWARD TREVOR.   London 8 November 1883
                             Cork, Ireland 3 October 1953

4029 Fanfare (Hasting at dawn). Edited and
arranged by Arthur Cohn
1,0,2-2,3,2(2nd ad lib.),1-Cym.,B.Dr.
Ms.
Score 5 p.
Composed ca.1921.

974 Mediterranean   *4'*
2,3*,2,2-4Hn.-Timp.,Perc.-Hp.-Str.
Murdoch, London, ᶜ1923
Score 19 p.
Composed 1921. First performance London, 1922.

BAXTER, LINCOLN ARTHUR.
        b. Winchester, Massachusetts 6 July 1951

7321 Land blowing out to sea   *12'*
Solo Bar. Voice-Ob.,Bn.-Perc.-Hpscd.-Vn.,Vc.
Ms. ᶜ1977 by Lincoln A. Baxter
Score 42 p.
*Text is the poem by Eric Edwards, from his
collection Ancestors to Come. Composed 1977.
First performance Temple University, Phila-
delphia, 4 April 1978, Contemporary Players
and Singers, the composer conducting, Scott
Conlan soloist.*

2409s Movement for string orchestra   *3'30"*
Str.
Ms. ᶜ1977 by Lincoln A. Baxter
Score 24 p.
*Originally composed for string quartet, 1973.
This transcription 1976. Selected for per-
formance by the Orchestra Society of Phila-
delphia as part of its Pennsylvania Composers
Project 1977, made possible by grants from*

*the National Endowment for the Arts and the
Pennsylvania Council on the Arts with perform-
ance materials prepared by the Fleisher Col-
lection of Orchestral Music. First performance
Drexel University, Philadelphia, 24 April 1977,
Orchestra Society of Philadelphia, William
Smith conductor.*

BAZELAIRE, PAUL.   Sedan, France 4 March 1886
                             Paris 11 December 1958

459c [Rhapsody in the Russian style for
   violoncello and orchestra, Op. 117]
   Solo Vc.-3*,2,2,2-4,2-Timp.,Perc.-Hp.-Str.
   Durand, Paris, C1939
   Score 64 p.
   *Composed 1938. First performance Paris, 2
   February 1941.*

BAZZINI, ANTONIO.   Brescia, Italy 11 March 1818
                           Milan 10 February 1897

863v [Concertino, violin and orchestra, Op. 14,
   E major]
   Solo Vn.-2(2nd alt. Picc.),2,2,2-4,2,3,Ophicl.
   -Timp.,Perc.-Str.
   Score: Ms. 111 p.
   Parts: Breitkopf & Härtel, Leipzig [n.d.]

5760 Francesca da Rimini, poème symphonique,
   Op. 77
   3(3rd alt. Picc.),3,3,2-4,2,3,1-Timp.,Perc.-
   Hp.-Str.
   Adolph Fürstner, Berlin [n.d.]
   Score 69 p.
   After the poem by Dante.

996v Grand allegro de concert [violin and
   orchestra] Op. 15, D major
   Solo Vn.-2,2,2,2-4,2,3,Ophicl.-Timp.-Str.
   Score: Ms. 75 p.
   Parts: Litolff, Braunschweig [n.d.]

949v Rêverie [for violin and orchestra.
   Arranged by V. Ranzato]
   Solo Vn.-2,2,2-4Hn.-Str.
   Score: Ms. 11 p.
   Parts: Carisch, Milan, C1906

BEACH, ALDEN.   Rome, New York (?)19--

Real name: Priscilla A. Beach

3007 City trees, Op. 5   6'
   2(2nd alt. Picc.),2,2,2-4,3,3,1-Timp.,Cym.-Str.
   Ms.
   Score 18 p.
   *Originally composed for piano 1928. Orches-
   trated 1928. First performance Rochester, 8
   June 1928, Rochester Philharmonic Orchestra,
   Howard Hanson conductor.*

BEACH, BRUCE CRESSWELL.   Philadelphia 1903

3640 Plaza, a ballet in the form of a   26'
   symphony
   1.Urchins 2.Nuances 3.Escapade 4.Grotesque
   3*,2,2,2-4,2,3,1-Timp.,Perc.-Hp.-Str.

Ms.
Score 169 p.
Composed 1937-38.

BEACH, MRS. H. H. A.
      Henniker, New Hampshire 5 September 1867
               New York City 27 December 1944

Born: Amy Marcy Cheney

6181 Bal masqué for orchestra   4'
   2,2,2,2-4,2-Timp.,Perc.-Hp.-Str.
   Ms.
   Score 28 p.

320p [Concerto, piano, Op. 45, C-sharp minor]
   1.Allegro moderato 2.Scherzo (Perpetuum
   mobile) 3.Largo 4.Allegro con scioltezza
   Solo Pno.-3*,2,3*,2-4,2,3,1-Timp.,Perc.-Str.
   Ms.
   Score 141 p.

5439 [Symphony, Gaelic, Op. 32, E minor]
   1.Allegro con fuoco 2.Alla siciliana - Allegro
   vivace 3.Lento con molto espressione
   4.Allegro di molto
   3*,3*,3*,2-4,2,3,1-Timp.,Trgl.-Str.
   Arthur P. Schmidt, Leipzig, C1897
   Score 220 p.

BEACH, JOHN PARSONS.
      Gloversville, New York 11 October 1877
          Pasadena, California 6 November 1953

3267 The Asolani (after Bembo)   20'
   1.Sentimental conversation 2.Enter buffoon
   3.Distant revelry (nocturne)
   3(3rd alt. Picc.),3*,2,2-4,3,3-Timp.,Perc.-
   Cel.,Hp.-Str.
   Ms.
   Score 94 p.
   *Composed 1922. First performance Minneapolis,
   12 November 1926, Minneapolis Symphony
   Orchestra, Henri Verbrugghen conductor.*

3189 Mardi Gras, ballet pantomime   30'
   (dramatic episode of a carnival in New Orleans)
   1(alt. Picc.),1(alt. E.H.),1,1-Sax. in E-flat
   -1,1-Timp.,Perc.-Pno.-Bar. Voice - Str.
   Ms.
   Score 136 p.
   *Composed 1925. First performance New Orleans,
   15 February 1926, Henri Wehrman conductor,
   William Broussard baritone.*

3110 Orleans alley, New Orleans street   12'
   cries at dawn
   3,2*,2,2-4,2,3-Timp.,Perc.-Pno.,Hp.-Str.
   Ms.
   Score 45 p.
   *Composed 1926. Original title: New Orleans
   Street Cries at Dawn. First performance under
   original title Philadelphia, 22 April 1927,
   Philadelphia Orchestra, Leopold Stokowski con-
   ductor.*

3128 The phantom satyr, ballet pantomime   12'
   3(3rd alt. Picc.),3*,2,2-4,3,3-Timp.,Perc.,

BEACH, PRISCILLA A.

    Eoliphone(ad lib.)-Cel.,Hp.-Str.
    Ms.
    Score 55 p.
    Composed 1923. First concert performance
    Rochester, 28 December 1926, Rochester Little
    Symphony Orchestra, Howard Hanson conductor.

BEACH, PRISCILLA A.
    See: BEACH, ALDEN.

BEAUME, P.

    1072s Au fil de l'eau, bluette
    Str.
    Score: Ms. 4 p.
    Parts: Choudens, Paris, c1923

    1122s Bonheur, meditation
    Timp.-Str.
    Score: Ms. 2 p.
    Parts: Choudens, Paris, c1923

    1080s Romance sans paroles
    Solo Vn.-Str.
    Score: Ms. 4 p.
    Parts: Choudens, Paris, c1923

BEAUMONT, L.

    5226 [General Hoche, quickstep for trumpet
    fanfare (percussion ad lib.)]
    4Tpt.(1B.Tpt.)-Perc.(ad lib.)
    Editions Musicales Andrieu Frères, Paris [n.d.]
    Score 2 p.

BECK, CONRAD.   Lohn, Switzerland 16 June 1901

    1096m [Concert music for oboe and string   *20'*
    orchestra]
    Largo - Andante con moto - Lento - Allegro
    Solo Ob.-Str.
    Schott's Söhne, Mainz, c1932
    Score 26 p.
    Composed 1932. First performance Basel, 30
    April 1933.

    1031m [Concerto for string quartet and   *18'*
    orchestra]
    1.Allegro energico 2.Lento - Allegretto
    3.Allegro moderato 4.Largo - Presto
    Solo Str. Quartet-2,3*,3*,2-4,2-Timp.,Perc.-
    Str.
    Schott's Söhne, Mainz, c1930
    Score 63 p.
    Commissioned by Elizabeth Sprague Coolidge.
    Composed 1929. First performance Chicago,
    Leopold Stokowski conductor. Awarded the
    Elizabeth Sprague Coolidge Prize.

    4307 Innominata für Orchester   *10'*
    2,3*,3*,3*-4,3,3,1-Timp.,Perc.-Str.
    Schott's Söhne, Mainz, c1932
    Score 29 p.
    Composed 1931. First performance Tenth Fes-
    tival of the International Society for Con-
    temporary Music, Vienna, 16 June 1932.

    1928s [Little suite for string orchestra]   *13'*
    1.Tempo di marcia 2.Andante 3.Allegro ma non

troppo 4.Andante sostenuto 5.Allegro
6.Presto
Str.
Schott's Söhne, Mainz, c1931
Score 14 p.
Composed 1930.

    568s [Symphony no. 3, for string   *25'*
    orchestra]
    Str.
    Schott, Mainz, c1928
    Score 30 p.
    First performance at the Schweizer Tonkünstler-
    fest, 1928.

BECK, FRANZ.   Mannheim 15 February 1723
                          Bordeaux 31 December 1809

    6877 [Symphony, Op. 4 no. 1, D major] Edited by
    Hugo Riemann
    1.Allegro maestoso 2.Andante, sempre piano
    3.Menuetto 4.Presto assai
    2Ob.-2Hn.-Str.
    Score: Denkmäler der Tonkunst in Bayern VIII/2.
    Breitkopf & Härtel, Leipzig [1908] 37 p.
    Parts: Ms. c1976 by The Fleisher Collection of
    Orchestral Music, Free Library of Philadelphia
    Composed 1773.

BECK, PAUL B.   d. Hanover 1893

    1282s Plauderei [Chattering] pour orchestre à
    cordes, Op. 40. Edited by Reinhold I. Beck
    Str.
    Score: Ms. 5 p.
    Parts: Gries & Schornagel, Hannover [n.d.]

BECKER, ALBERT ERNST ANTON.
                      Quedlinburg 13 June 1834
                      Berlin 10 January 1899

    414v [Adagio no. 3, for solo violin and
    orchestra, Op. 70, E major]
    Solo Vn.-0,1,2,2-2Hn.-Str.
    Breitkopf & Härtel, Leipzig, c1893
    Score 11 p.

    415v Concertstück für Violine und Orchester,
    Op. 66 [G major]
    Solo Vn.-2,2,2,2-2,2-Timp.-Str.
    Breitkopf & Härtel, Leipzig, c1893
    Score 31 p.

BECKER, HUGO.   Strasbourg 13 February 1863
           Geiselgastag, near Munich 30 July 1941

    614c [Concerto, violoncello, Op. 10,   *12'*
    A major]
    In one movement
    Solo Vc.-2,2,2,2-3,2-Timp.-Str.
    Schott, Mainz, c1896
    Score 106 p.

Composed 1896. First performance Frankfurt 1896, the composer as soloist.

1549s Minuetto, Op. 3 no. 3
Solo Vc.-Str.
Score: Ms. 6 p.
Parts: Schott, Mainz [ca.1889]

BECKER, JEAN.   Mannheim 11 May 1833
                                 Mannheim 10 October 1884

1009v Concertstück [violin and orchestra,
Op. 10, D major]
1.[Prelude] 2.[Rhapsody] 3.[Rondo]
Solo Vn.-2,2,2,2-2,2-Timp.-Str.
Score: Ms. 120 p.
Parts: Leuckart, Leipzig [ca.1872]

BECKER, JOHN J. Henderson, Kentucky 22 January 1886
                 Wilmette, Illinois 21 January 1961

1061m Abongo, stage work no. 2, a primitive 10'
dance for percussion instruments, two solo
dancers and dance-group
3Timp.,4Dr.(2 small, 1 med., 1 large) Water Dr.,
2Tin pans, 2Barrels,2Tam-tams(small&large),
S.Dr.,B.Dr.,Small Cym.,Large Cym.,Large Gong,
Hand-claps,Voice
Ms. [now published by Autograph Editions,
Hackensack, New Jersey]
Score 20 p.
Composed 1933.

923m Concertino pastorale, a forest   8'
rhapsody, for two flutes and orchestra
Noises of the night - Noises of the day -
Noises of space
2 Solo Fl.-0,2,2,2-2,2-Timp.-Str.
Ms.
Score 38 p.
Composed 1933.

930m [Concerto, horn and orchestra]   15'
Slowly and dramatically - A poem - A satire -
A song - A choral - A choral fugue
Solo Hn.-2,2,2,2-2Tpt.-Timp.-Str.
New Music Orchestra Series, San Francisco,
c1936 by John J. Becker
Score 19 p.
Composed 1935.

700p [Concerto, piano, no. 1, Arabesque]   10'
In one movement
Solo Pno.-1,1,1,2*-1,1-Str.
New Music Orchestra Series [San Francisco,
n.d.]
Score 41 p.
*Composed 1930. First performance New York, 16
February 1932, Pan American Chamber Orchestra,
the composer conducting, Georgia Kober
soloist.*

771p [Concerto, piano, no. 2, Satirico]   20'
In one movement
Solo Pno.-2,2,2,2-4,2,2-Timp.,Perc.-Str.
Ms.
Score 66 p.
*Completed 1938. First performance St. Paul,
Minnesota, 28 March 1939, Minnesota Symphony*

*Orchestra of the WPA, John M. Kuypers con-
ductor, John Verrall soloist.*

1135v [Concerto, viola]   18'
In one movement
Solo Va.-2,2,2,2-2,2-Timp.-Str.(without Va.)
Ms.
Score 68 p.
Composed 1937.

361v [Concerto, violin]   15'
In one movement
Solo Vn.-2,2,2,3-4,2,3,1-Timp.-Str.
Composers Facsimile Edition, New York, c1953
by John Becker
Score 48 p.
Composed 1948.

997m A dance, for percussion orchestra   12'
S.Dr.,Small Tam-tam,Large Tam-tam,B.Dr.,Cym.,
Gong-Pno.
Ms.
Score 14 p.
*Commissioned by Diana Huebert and Carleton Col-
lege, 1938. Composed 1938. First performance
Northfield, Minnesota, 12 December 1938, by a
Carleton College group, the composer con-
ducting, Diana Huebert dancer.*

6823 Dance figure
Solo Voice-4*(2nd Picc. ad lib.),2,2,2-2,2-
Timp.,Perc.-Pno.-Str.
Ms.
Score 55 p.
*Text by Ezra Pound. Composed 1932 as a ballet
with poem.*

A marriage with space
See: Stage work no. 3...

Out of bondage, a symphony of democracy...
See: Symphony no. 6, Out of bondage...

1877s Soundpiece no. 1, for piano and   12'
string orchestra
Pno.-Str.
Ms.
Score 20 p.
*Composed 1933. Original number designated as
I-B. First performance in this form, St. Paul,
Minnesota, 14 May 1936, Twin Cities Civic
Orchestra of the WPA, Paul Lemay conductor,
Winifred Reichmuth-Bolle pianist.*

1735s Soundpiece no. 2, Homage to Haydn,   12'
for string orchestra
Str.
Ms.
Score 23 p.
*Composed 1938. Original number designated as
2-B.*

Stage work no. 2
See: Abongo, stage work no. 2...

6043 Stage work no. 3, A marriage with space, a
drama in color, light and sound for solo and
mass dramatization, solo and dance group and
large orchestra

Becker, John J.

1.The builder 2.The bridge of days
Speakers-3*,3*,2,4*-4,4,3,1-Timp.,Perc.-2Pno.,
2Hp.-Str.
Ms.
Score 106 p.
Poem by Mark Turbyfill. Composed 1935.

3907 [Stage work no. 5-b, When the willow   *15'*
nods, second orchestral suite in one movement]
1,1,1,1-1,1-Timp.,Gong-Pno.-Str.
Ms.
Score 107 p.
*Stage work no. 5-B is the second of three plays
with music written in collaboration with Alfred
Kreymborg. First performance Albert Lea,
Minnesota, 7 January 1940, Minnesota Sym-
phony Orchestra, the composer conducting.*

3573 Symphony no. 1, Etude primitive   *20'*
1.An Indian hymn 2.A circus clown 3.Deep
forests 4.Symphonic movement (Americana)
3*,3*,3*,4*-4,2,3,1-Timp.,Perc.-Pno.,Hp.-Str.
Ms.
Score 84 p.
*Completed 1912. First performance University
of Minnesota, 17 June 1936, Twin Cities Civic
Orchestra of the WPA, Gabriel Fenyves conductor.*

3856 Symphony no. 2, Fantasia tragica, a   *25'*
short symphony in one movement
3*,2,2,4*,Sarrus.-4,4,3,1-Timp.,Perc.-Pno.-
Male Choir (ad lib.)-Str.
Ms.
Score 50 p.
This version completed 1920.

2848 [Symphony no. 3, Symphonia brevis]   *20'*
1.A scherzo in the spirit of mockery 2.Must
life forever be a struggle?
3*,3*,2,4*-4,4,3,1-Timp.,Perc.-Pno.-Str.
Ms.
Score 75 p.
*Completed 1931. First performance St. Paul,
Minnesota, 14 May 1936, Minnesota Symphony
Orchestra of the WPA, Paul Lemay conductor.*

4652 Symphony no. 5 (Homage to Mozart)   *15'*
in two movements
1.Slowly and expressively 2.Moderately fast
Fl.,Ob.-2Hn.-2Tpt.-Str.
Ms.
Score 15 p. Large folio
Composed 1942.

4760 Symphony no. 6, Out of bondage, a   *30'*
symphony of democracy suggested by Lincoln's
Gettysburg address
1.With brooding uncertainty 2.Kreymborg's
ballad of fallen France 3.Lincoln's Gettys-
burg address - Victory march
3*,2,2,4*-4,2,3,1-Timp.,Perc.-Speaker,
Chorus(SATB)-Str.
Ms.
Score 82 p.
*Victory march in third movement written for
Efrem Kurtz at his request. Composed 1941-42.*

Two pieces for orchestra
3609 1.Among the reeds and rushes   *3'*
1,1,2,1-Hn.,Tpt.-Timp.-Hp.-Str.
Ms.
Score 12 p.
3610 2.The mountains   *3'*
3*,2,2,1-2,2,2,1-Timp.,Perc.-Str.
Ms.
Score 17 p.
*Composed 1912. First performance Minneapolis,
8 August 1940, Minnesota Symphony Orchestra of
the WPA, Bernhard Andersen conductor.*

4744 Victory march for large orchestra   *6'*
3*,2,2,4*-4,2,3,1-Timp.,Perc.-Pno.-Str.
Ms.
Score 12 p.
*From the third movement of Symphony no. 6.
Composed for Efrem Kurtz, 1942.*

When the willow nods
See: [Stage work no. 5-b, When the willow
      nods, second orchestral suite in one
      movement]

BECKER, REINHOLD.   Adorf, Saxony 11 August 1842
                         Dresden 7 December 1924

1058v [Concerto, violin, Op. 4, A minor]
Solo Vn.-2,2,2,2-2,2,1-Timp.-Str.
Score: Ms. 181 p.
Parts: [n.p., n.d.]

BECKERATH, ALFRED VON.
              b. Hagenau, Germany 4 October 1901

4354 [Happy suite for wind orchestra]
1.[Joyous entrance music] 2.[Evening music]
3.[Festive dance]
1,1,3(1Cl. in E-flat),2-0,2,2Ten.Hn.,2Flugel-
hn.,2Waldhn.,2,Bar.,2-Timp.,Perc.
C.F. Vieweg, Berlin, ᶜ1940
Score 16 p.

BECKWITH, JOHN.
              b. Victoria, British Columbia 9 March 1927

5834 Montage [revised version]   *4'30"*
2,2,2,2-2,2,2-Timp.,Perc.-Pno.-Str.
Ms.
Score 12 p.
*Commissioned by the Canadian Broadcasting Cor-
poration. Composed 1953. First performance
Toronto, October 1953, CBC Studio Orchestra,
John Adaskin conductor. Revised 1955. First
performance of revised version Montreal, 1956,
Canadian League of Composers, Jean-Marie Beau-
det conductor.*

BEDFORD, HERBERT.   London 23 January 1867
                            London 13 March 1945

701p Divertimento for piano and string   *11'*
orchestra, Op. 44
Solo Pno.-Str.
J.&W. Chester, London, ᶜ1926
Score 31 p.
First performance probably at the Festival of

Beethoven, Ludwig van

Contemporary Music, Bath, England, 1930,
Edward Dunn conductor.

453 The lonely dancer of Gedār, oriental   4'
dance for small orchestra, Op. 36
1,1,0,1-Hn.-Timp.,Perc.-Str.
J.&W. Chester, London, c1926
Score 23 p.
Composed 1926.

BEEMT, HEDDA VAN DEN.
  See: VAN DEN BEEMT, HEDDA.

BEER, MAX JOSEF.   Vienna 25 August 1851
                             Vienna 25 November 1908

1464s [Serenade, string orchestra, Op. 54]
  1.Alla marcia 2.Largo 3.Intermezzo
  4.Andante e interludium 5.Finale (Alla marcia)
2Hn.-Timp.-Str.
Schott, Mainz [1898]
Score 29 p.

BEETHOVEN, LUDWIG VAN.
              Bonn, probably 16 December
              (baptized 17 December) 1770
                   Vienna 26 March 1827

366p [Concerto, piano, no. 1, Op. 15,   37'
  C major]
  1.Allegro con brio 2.Largo 3.Rondo: Allegro
Solo Pno.-1,2,2,2-2,2-Timp.-Str.
Score: Kalmus, New York [n.d.] 75 p.
Parts: Breitkopf & Härtel, Leipzig [195-?]
Composed ca.1798. First performance Prague,
1798, the composer as soloist. Julius Rönt-
gen's cadenza to the first movement is also
available.

377p [Concerto, piano, no. 2, Op. 19,   28'
  B-flat major]
  1.Allegro con brio 2.Adagio 3.Rondo: Molto
  allegro
Solo Pno.-1,2,0,2-2Hn.-Str.
Breitkopf & Härtel, Wiesbaden [195-?]
Score 50 p.
Composed 1794-95. First performance Vienna,
29 March 1795, Antonio Salieri conductor,
the composer as soloist. Revised 1798. First
performance Prague, 1798, the composer as
soloist. Julius Röntgen's cadenza to the
first movement is also available.

368p [Concerto, piano, no. 3, Op. 37,   39'
  C minor]
  1.Allegro con brio 2.Largo 3.Rondo: Allegro
Solo Pno.-2,2,2,2-2,2-Timp.-Str.
Luck's Music Library, Detroit [n.d.]
Score 68 p.
Composed 1800. First performance Vienna, 5
April 1803, Ignaz von Seyfried conductor, the
composer as soloist. Cadenzas by Julius Rönt-
gen and Gabriel Fauré are available.

369p [Concerto, piano, no. 4, Op. 58,   30'
  G major]
  1.Allegro moderato 2.Andante con moto, segue
  3.Rondo: Vivace

Solo Pno.-1,2,2,2-2,2-Timp.-Str.
Breitkopf & Härtel, Leipzig, c1962
Score 68 p.
Composed 1805-06. First performance privately
March 1807; in public, Vienna, 22 December
1808, Ignaz von Seyfried conductor, the com-
poser as soloist. Cadenzas by Julius Röntgen
and Wilhelm Backhaus are also available.

363p [Concerto, piano, no. 5, Emperor,   36'
  Op. 73, E-flat major]
  1.Allegro 2.Adagio un poco mosso, attacca
  3.Rondo: Allegro
Solo Pno.-2,2,2,2-2,2-Timp.-Str.
Breitkopf & Härtel, Leipzig [1893]
Score 88 p.
Composed 1809. First performance Leipzig, 28
November 1811, Gewandhaus Orchestra, Johann
Philipp Christian Schulz conductor, Friedrich
Schneider soloist.

795p [Concerto, piano, D major,   41'
  transcribed from the violin concerto, Op. 61]
  1.Allegro, ma non troppo 2.Larghetto 3.Rondo
Solo Pno.-1,2,2,2-2,2-Timp.-Str.
Breitkopf & Härtel, Leipzig [n.d.]
Score 116 p.
(Score and solo part only) For parts see
[Concerto, violin, Op. 61, D major]

452p [Concerto, piano, D major. Kinsky   12'
  Anh. 7. First movement]
Solo Pno.-1,2,0,2-2,2-Timp.-Str.
Breitkopf & Härtel, Leipzig [n.d.]
Score 28 p.
Posthumous work.

419v [Concerto, violin, Op. 61, D major]   41'
  1.Allegro ma non troppo 2.Larghetto 3.Rondo
  (Allegro)
Solo Vn.-1,2,2,2-2,2-Timp.-Str.
Breitkopf & Härtel, Wiesbaden [n.d.]
Score 64 p.
Cadenzas by Auer, Besekirsky, Busoni, Joachim,
Kreisler, Edmund Singer, Vieuxtemps, Wilhelmj
are available. Composed 1806. First perform-
ance Vienna, 23 December 1806, Franz Clement
soloist.

938v [Concerto, violin, C major. WoO 5]   10'
  Edited by Josef Hellmesberger
Solo Vn.-1,2,0,2-2,2-Timp.-Str.
Friedrich Schreiber, Vienna [1879?]
Score 98 p.
Composed ca.1790-92.

603m [Concerto, violin, violoncello,   35'
  piano and orchestra, Op. 56, C major]
  1.Allegro 2.Largo, attacca 3.Rondo alla
  polacca
Solo Pno., Solo Vn., Solo Vc.-1,2,2,2-2,2-Timp.
  -Str.
Score: Kalmus, New York [n.d.] 100 p.
Parts: Breitkopf & Härtel, Leipzig [189-?]
Composed ca.1804. First performance in
public at a summer concert in the Augarten,
Vienna, May 1808.

Beethoven, Ludwig van

78 [Consecration of the house, overture,   *12'*
Op. 124, C major]
2,2,2,2-4,2,3-Timp.-Str.
Breitkopf & Härtel, Wiesbaden [n.d.]
Score 52 p.
Composed 1822 for the opening of the Vienna
Josephstädter Theater, and first performed
there, 3 October 1822, the composer conducting.

16 [Coriolan overture, Op. 62, C minor]   *7'*
2,2,2,2-2,2-Timp.-Str.
Breitkopf & Härtel, Leipzig [1894]
Score 38 p.
Composed 1807. First performance at Prince
Lobkowitz' palace, Vienna, March 1807, the
composer conducting.

6475 [The creatures of Prometheus,   *53'*
Op. 43. Complete ballet]
2,2,2,Corno di Bassetto,2-2,2-Timp.-Hp.-Str.
Kalmus, New York [n.d.]
Score 162 p.
Ballet designed by Salvatore Viganò. Com-
posed 1800-01. First performance Vienna, 28
March 1801.

9 [The creatures of Prometheus, Op. 43.   *5'*
Overture]
2,2,2,2-2,2-Timp.-Str.
Breitkopf & Härtel [Leipzig, n.d.]
Score 30 p.

6918 [Ecossaise, military band, D major.   *1'30"*
WoO 22]
1,2,2,3*-2,1-Perc.
Score: Collected Works, Series 25, no. 27.
Breitkopf & Härtel, Leipzig [1888] 2 p.
Parts: Ms.
Composed 1810.

149 [Egmont, Op. 84. Overture]   *8'*
2(2nd alt. Picc.),2,2,2-4,2-Timp.-Str.
Breitkopf & Härtel [Leipzig, n.d.]
Score 32 p.
From the incidental music to Goethe's play.
Composed 1810. First performance Vienna, 24
May 1810.

4399 [Eleven dance (Mödling dances) for seven
wind instruments and strings. WoO 17] Edited
by Hugo Riemann
2,0,2,1-2Hn.-Str.(Vn.I,Vn.II,Cb.)
Breitkopf & Härtel, Leipzig [1907]
Score 12 p.
Composed 1819. This first edition from Ms.
parts in Archiv der Thomasschule, Leipzig.

590p [Fantasy, piano, chorus, and   *19'*
orchestra, Op. 80, C minor]
1.Adagio 2.Finale: Allegro - Allegretto ma
non troppo, quasi andante con moto
Solo Pno.-2,2,2,2-2,2-Timp.-SATB Chorus-Str.
Kalmus, New York [n.d.]
Score 56 p.
Composed 1808. First performance Vienna, 22
December 1808, Ignaz von Seyfried conductor,
the composer as soloist.

189 [Fidelio, Op. 72. Overture, E major]   *7'*
2,2,2,2-4,2,2-Timp.-Str.
Luck's Music Library, Detroit [n.d.]
Score 20 p.
Composed 1814 for the third and final version
of the opera. First performance Kärnthnerthor
Theater, Vienna, 26 May 1814.

Die Geschöpfe des Prometheus, Op. 43
  See: [The creatures of Prometheus...]

86s [Grosse Fuge, string quartet, Op. 133,
B-flat major. Edited for string quartet or
string orchestra by Felix Weingartner]
Str.
Breitkopf & Härtel, Leipzig [190-?]
Score 22 p.
Originally the final movement of String Quartet
Op. 130, B-flat major, which was composed in
1825 and first performed Vienna, 21 March 1826.
Beethoven replaced the fugue with a new finale
in 1826. Fugue first published as a separate
work by Artaria, Vienna, 1827.

29 [King Stephen, Op. 117, E-flat major.   *8'*
Overture]
2,2,2,3*-4,2-Timp.-Str.
Kalmus, New York [n.d.]
Score 40 p.
Composed 1811 for the opening of the new the-
ater at Pest on February 1812.

Là ci darem la mano, variations
  See: [Variations on Mozart's Là ci darem la
  mano...]

23 [Leonore overture no. 1, Op. 138,   *10'*
C major]
2,2,2,2-4,2-Timp.-Str.
Breitkopf & Härtel, Leipzig [n.d.]
Score 44 p.
Composed ca.1807 for an unrealized production
of the opera Fidelio. First performance of
this overture Vienna, 7 February 1828.

79 [Leonore overture no. 2, Op. 72a,   *13'*
C major]
2,2,2,2-4,2,3-Timp.-Str.
Kalmus, New York [n.d.]
Score 58 p.
Composed 1805 for the first version of the
opera Fidelio. First performance Theater an
der Wien, Vienna, 20 November 1805, the com-
poser conducting.

112 [Leonore overture no. 3, Op. 72b,   *14'*
C major]
2,2,2,2-4,2,3-Timp.-Str.
Breitkopf & Härtel [Leipzig,n.d.]
Score 64 p.
Composed 1806 for the second version of the
opera Fidelio. First performance Theater an
der Wien, Vienna, 29 March 1806, Ignaz von
Seyfried conductor.

1642 [Leonore Prohaska. WoO 96. No. 4,   *5'*
Funeral march]
2,0,2,2-4Hn.-Timp.-Str.

Beethoven, Ludwig van

Breitkopf & Härtel, Leipzig [n.d.]
Score 7 p.
From the incidental music to Friedrich Duncker's play. Composed 1814. March transcribed from the Marcia Funebre in the Piano Sonata, Op. 26.

2522 [Military march, band, D major. WoO 24]
2Picc.,2,5(1Cl. in F),3*-6,8,2,Serp.-Perc.
Breitkopf & Härtel, Leipzig [1864?]
Score 24 p.
Composed as Marsch zur Grossen Wachtparade [March for the Grand Guard Parade], 3 June 1816.

6845 [Military march, band, Taps no. 2,   *3'40"*
C major. WoO 20]
1,2,2,3*-2,2-Perc.
Score: Collected Works. Series 25, no. 25.
Breitkopf & Härtel, Leipzig [1888] 7 p.
Parts: Ms.
Composed 1809-10.

6817 [Military marches, band, F major.   *6'25"*
WoO 18 *and* WoO 19]
3*(in F),0,3(1Cl. in F,2Cl. in C),3*-2,2-S.Dr.,
B.Dr.
Score: Collected Works. Series 25, no. 24, I
and II. Breitkopf & Härtel, Leipzig [1888] 7 p.
Parts: Ms.
Composed 1810 for the tournament at Laxenburg held in honor of the birthday of Empress Maria Ludovica, 25 August 1810. No. 1 is known as York'scher Marsch, No. 2 is Taps no. 3.

1641 [Minuet of congratulation, E-flat   *3'*
major. WoO 3]
2,0,2,2-2,2-Timp.-Str.
Breitkopf & Härtel, Leipzig [n.d.]
Score 8 p.
First performance 3 November 1822.

1338s [Minuets. WoO 82 *and* WoO 10/2. Transcribed for string orchestra by Charles Woodhouse]
1.Allegretto 2.Quasi andantino
Str.
Hawkes, London, ᶜ1930
Score 7 p.
No. 1 originally composed for piano, probably ca.1803 rather than ca.1785 as has been supposed; first published 1805. No. 2, the Minuet in G, composed for orchestra, 1795.

844 [Missa solemnis, Op. 123. Benedictus.   *12'*
Arranged for orchestra by Ferruccio Busoni]
Soli: Ob.,Vn.,Va.,Vc.-2,0,2,2-2,2,3-Timp.-Str.
Breitkopf & Härtel, Leipzig, 1916
Score 18 p.
Originally composed 1818-23 for voices and orchestra. First performance of Benedictus Frankfurt-am-Main, 14 May 1827, J. N. Schelble conductor.

Mödling dances
See: [Eleven dances (Mödling dances) for
seven wind instruments and strings.
WoO 17]

1106 [Music to a ballet of knighthood.   *15'*
WoO 1]
1.[March] 2.[German song] 3.[Hunting song]
4.[Romance] 5.[War song] 6.[Drinking song]
7.[German dance] 8.[Coda]
Picc.,2Cl.-2Hn.,2Tpt.-Timp.-Str.
Breitkopf & Härtel, Leipzig [n.d.]
Score 19 p.
Composed ca.1790. First performance Bonn, 6 March 1791.

764 Namensfeier-Ouverture, Op. 115   *6'*
[C major]
2,2,2,2-4,2-Timp.-Str.
Breitkopf & Härtel, Leipzig [n.d.]
Score 40 p.
Begun 1809; completed October 1814. First performance Vienna, 25 December 1815, the composer conducting.

6919 [Polonaise, military band, D major.   *2'20"*
WoO 21]
1,2,2,3*-2,1-Perc.
Score: Collected Works. Series 25, no. 26.
Breitkopf & Härtel, Leipzig [1888] 3 p.
Parts: Ms.
Composed 1810.

5648 [Quartet, strings, Op. 95, F   *21'30"*
minor. Transcribed for orchestra by Alexander Friedrich, Landgrave of Hesse]
1.Allegro con brio 2.Allegretto ma non troppo
3.Allegro assai vivace, ma serioso 4.Larghetto
espressivo - Allegretto agitato - Allegro
2,2,2,2-2,2-Timp.-Str.
Ries & Erler, Berlin [188-?]
Score 54 p.
Composed 1810.

5804 [Quartet, strings, Op. 131, C-sharp   *38'*
minor. Transcribed as a symphony by Karl Müller-Berghaus]
1.Adagio ma non troppo e molto espressivo
2.Allegro molto vivace 3.Allegro moderato -
Adagio 4.Andante ma non troppo, molto cantabile - [Six variations] 5.Presto 6.Adagio,
quasi un poco andante 7.Allegro
2,3*,2,2-4,2,3-Timp.-Str.
Hugo Pohle, Hamburg [1884?]
Score 101 p. Large folio
Originally composed 1826.

417v [Romance, violin and orchestra,   *8'*
Op. 40, G major]
Solo Vn.-1,2,0,2-2Hn.-Str.
Breitkopf & Härtel, Leipzig [1893]
Score 8 p.
Composed 1802 at the latest. Parts bound with Op. 50 below.

279v [Same as above]   *8'*
Solo Vn.-1,2,0,2-2Hn.-Str.
Kalmus, New York [n.d.]
Score 8 p.

417v [Romance, violin and orchestra,   *6'*
Op. 50, F major]
Solo Vn.-1,2,0,2-2Hn.-Str.

Beethoven, Ludwig van

Breitkopf & Härtel, Leipzig [1893]
Score 12 p.
Composed 1803. Parts bound with Op. 40 above.

278v [Same as above]   8'30"
Solo Vn.-1,2,0,2-2Hn.-Str.
Kalmus, New York [n.d.]
Score 12 p.

2460 [Rondino, E-flat major. WoO 25]
0,2,2,2-2
Score: Ms. 16 p.
Parts: Breitkopf & Härtel, Leipzig [n.d.]

591p [Rondo, piano and orchestra,   10'
B-flat major. WoO 6]
Solo Pno.-1,2,0,2-2Hn.-Str.
Breitkopf & Härtel, Leipzig [1893]
Score 26 p.
Composed 1795. First published 1829.

347 [The ruins of Athens, Op. 113.   6'
Overture]
2,2,2,2-4,2-Timp.-Str.
Breitkopf & Härtel, Leipzig [n.d.]
Score 26 p.
*From the incidental music to Kotzebue's play.
Composed 1811 for the opening of the new the-
ater at Pest on 9 February 1812.*

867 [The ruins of Athens, Op. 113.   4'
No. 4, Turkish march]
1(Picc.),2,2,3*-2,2-Perc.-Str.
Breitkopf & Härtel, Leipzig [n.d.]
Score 11 p.

1260s [Serenade, violin, viola and violoncello,
Op. 8, D major. Arranged for string orchestra
by J. Cleuver]
1.Marcia 2.Menuet 3.Allegretto alla polacca
4.Andante quasi allegretto (Theme with varia-
tions)
Str.
Oppenheimer, Hameln [n.d.]
Score 20 p.
*Publication announced in the newspaper Wiener
Zeitung of 7 October 1797; probably composed
same year.*

1548 [Sonata, piano, Hammerklavier,   26'
Op. 106, B major. Transcribed for orchestra by
Felix Weingartner]
1.Allegro 2.Scherzo 3.Adagio sostenuto
4.Largo - Allegro risoluto
3*,2,2,3*-4,2,3-Timp.-Str.
Breitkopf & Härtel, Leipzig, c1926
Score 125 p.
*Composed 1818-19. Transcribed 1926. First
performance Essen, 14 November 1926, Max
Fiedler conductor.*

138 [Symphony no. 1, Op. 21, C major]   28'
1.Adagio molto - Allegro con brio 2.Andante
cantabile con moto 3.Menuetto 4.Finale:
Adagio - Allegro molto e vivace
2,2,2,2-2,2-Timp.-Str.
Breitkopf & Härtel, Wiesbaden [n.d.]
Score 44 p.

*First performance Burgtheater, Vienna, 2 April
1800, the composer conducting.*

139 [Symphony no. 2, Op. 36, D major]   36'
1.Adagio molto - Allegro con brio 2.Larghetto
3.Scherzo: Allegro 4.Allegro molto
2,2,2,2-2,2-Timp.-Str.
Breitkopf & Härtel, Wiesbaden [n.d.]
Score 64 p.
*Composed 1802. First performance Theater an
der Wien, Vienna, 5 April 1803, the composer
conducting.*

140 [Symphony no. 3, Eroica, Op. 55,   50'
E-flat major]
1.Allegro con brio 2.Marcia funebre: Adagio
assai 3.Scherzo: Allegro vivace 4.Finale:
Allegro molto
2,2,2,2-3,2-Timp.-Str.
Breitkopf & Härtel, Wiesbaden [n.d.]
Score 96 p.
*Composed 1803-04. First performance Vienna,
summer 1804, Prince Lobkowitz' orchestra.*

141 [Symphony no. 4, Op. 60, B-flat   34'
major]
1.Adagio - Allegro vivace 2.Adagio 3.Allegro
vivace 4.Allegro ma non troppo
1,2,2,2-2,2-Timp.-Str.
Breitkopf & Härtel, Wiesbaden, c1965
Score 80 p.
*Composed 1806. First performance Prince Lob-
kowitz' palace, Vienna, March 1807, the composer conducting.*

142 [Symphony no. 5, Op. 67, C minor]   29'
1.Allegro con brio 2.Andante con moto
3.Allegro 4.Allegro
3*,2,2,3*-2,2,3-Timp.-Str.
Breitkopf & Härtel, Wiesbaden [n.d.]
Score 100 p.
*Begun ca.1805. First performance Theater an
der Wien, Vienna, 22 December 1808, the composer conducting.*

143 [Symphony no. 6, Pastorale, Op. 68, 36'
F major]
1.Allegro ma non troppo [Awakening of happy
feelings on getting out into the country]
2.Andante molto moto [By the brookside] 3.
Allegro [Merry gathering of the country folk]
4.Allegro [Thunderstorm] 5.Allegretto [Happy
and thankful feelings after the storm]
3*,2,2,2-2,2-Timp.-Str.
Breitkopf & Härtel, Leipzig [n.d.]
Score 86 p.
*Composed 1808. First performance Theater an
der Wien, Vienna, 22 December 1808, the composer conducting.*

144 [Symphony no. 7, Op. 92, A major]   40'
1.Poco sostenuto - Vivace 2.Allegretto
3.Presto 4.Allegro con brio
2,2,2,2-2,2-Timp.-Str.
Breitkopf & Härtel, Wiesbaden [n.d.]
Score 90 p.
*Composed 1812. First performance University
Hall, Vienna, 8 December 1813, the composer
conducting.*

145 [Symphony no. 8, Op. 93, F major]   25'
1.Allegro vivace con brio 2.Allegretto scherzando 3.Tempo di menuetto 4.Allegro vivace
2,2,2,2-2,2-Timp.-Str.
Breitkopf & Härtel, Wiesbaden [n.d.]
Score 66 p.
*Composed 1812. First performance Redoutensaal,
Vienna, 27 February 1814, the composer conducting.*

164 [Symphony no. 9, Choral, Op. 125,   70'
D minor]
1.Allegro ma non troppo, un poco maestoso 2.
Molto vivace 3.Adagio molto e cantabile 4.
Presto - Allegro assai 5.Allegro assai vivace
3*,2,3*-4,2,3-Timp.,Perc.-Solo Voices(SATB),
SATB Chorus-Str.
Breitkopf & Härtel, Wiesbaden [n.d.]
Score 276 p.
*Composed 1817-23. First performance Kärnth-
nerthor Theater, Vienna, 7 May 1824, conducted
principally by Beethoven, assisted by Umlauf
and Schuppanzigh.*

146 [Symphony, Jena, C major. Kinsky Anh. 1]
See: WITT, FRIEDRICH.
    [Symphony, Jena, C major]

4334 [Tarpeja. Introduction to Act 2.   4'
WoO 2b *and* Triumphal march. WoO 2a]
2,2,2,2-4,2-Timp.-Str.
Schott's Söhne, Mainz, c1939
Score 24 p.
*Incidental music for Christoph Kuffner's
tragedy, Tarpeja. Composed 1813.*

1049 [Tarpeja. Triumphal march. WoO 2a]   2'
2,2,2,2-2,2-Timp.-Str.
Breitkopf & Härtel, Leipzig [n.d.]
Score 6 p.
*Composed 1813. First performance Vienna, 26
March 1813.*

2972 [Three equales for four trombones.
WoO 30]
1.Andante [D minor] 2.Poco adagio [D major]
3.Poco sostenuto [B-flat major]
4Tbn.
Score: Ms. 9 p.
Parts: Breitkopf & Härtel, Leipzig [1888]
*Equales are short, solemn compositions for
equal voices or instruments. Composed 1812,
at the suggestion of the chapelmaster of the
cathedral in Linz, F. X. Glöggl. First performance Linz, Austria, on All Soul's Day, 2
November 1812. An arrangement by Ignaz Seyfried, for trombones and male chorus, was performed at Beethoven's funeral, 29 March 1827.*

3 [Twelve country dances for orchestra.   15'
WoO 14]
1,2,2,2-2Hn.-Side Dr.-Str.
Breitkopf & Härtel, Leipzig [1893]
Score 10 p.
*Composed 1802 (nos. 7 and 11 from Finale of
The Creatures of Prometheus).*

4 [Twelve German dances for orchestra.   20'
WoO 8]
3*,2,2,2-2(1Hn. is a Cornetto in C, i.e., Post-
hn.),2-Timp.-Str.
Breitkopf & Härtel, Leipzig [1893]
Score 26 p.
*Composed for the masked ball given by the
Pension-Fund Society of the Fine Artists of
Vienna, 22 November 1795.*

1443 [Twelve minuets for orchestra.   20'
WoO 7]
3*,2,2,2-2,2-Timp.-Str.
Breitkopf & Härtel, Leipzig [1893]
Score 22 p.
*Composed for the masked ball given by the
Pension-Fund Society of the Fine Artists of
Vienna, 22 November 1795.*

1210s [Variations on Mozart's Là ci   11'
darem la mano, 2 oboes and English horn,
C major. WoO 28. Transcribed for string
orchestra by Michael Press]
Str.
C. Fischer, New York, c1925
Score 23 p.
*Composed 1796-97. First performance Vienna,
23 December 1797, Wiener Tonkünstlergesell-
schaft benefit concert, Joseph Czerwenka,
Reuter (first name unknown), and Philipp
Mathias Teimer performers.*

705 [Wellington's victory, or The battle   14'
of Vittoria, Op. 91]
1.[Battle] 2.[Symphony of victory]
3*,2,2,2-4,6,3-Timp.,Perc.-Str.(In Part I,2Tpt.
(E-flat&C),B.Dr.,Side Dr.,Rattles are divided
to left and right behind the scene)
Breitkopf & Härtel, Leipzig [n.d.]
Score 82 p.
*Composed 1813. First performance Vienna, 8
December 1813.*

BÉHAULT, E. R. DE.

1216s Les mois et les saisons [The months and
the seasons] Berceuse pour violon solo,
violoncelle solo et quintette
Solo Vn., Solo Vc.-Str.
Score: Ms. 7 p.
Parts: Decourcelle, Nice, c1920

BEHR, C. VON.

490s Sechs Kinderlieder, Op. 9
1.[Blissful childhood] 2.[Forget-me-not]
3.[Little bee] 4.[Cradle song] 5.[At
harvest-time] 6.[Dream]
Str.
Raabe & Plothow, Berlin [n.d.]
Score 5 p.

BEHR, FRANZ FRANÇOIS.
                Lübtheen, Mecklenburg 22 July 1837
                Dresden 15 February 1898

Also known by pseudonyms: Charles Morley,
Francesco d'Orso, William Cooper, and Georges
Bachmann

Behr, Franz

200s Meditation, Op. 378
Str.
Kistner, Leipzig [n.d.]
Score 5 p.

668s Mon petit coeur [My darling, pizzicato
waltz for string orchestra by Charles Morley]
Str.
Score: Ms. 9 p.
Parts: Durand, Paris [n.d.]

1142s Rosenlied [The flower song, melodic tone
piece for string orchestra, Op. 60, by Charles
Morley]
Str.
Score: Ms. 4 p.
Parts:Forberg, Leipzig [n.d.]

1481s Schlummerlied [Slumber song, solo violin
and string orchestra, Op. 295 no. 1] Arranged
by Bernhard Triebel
Solo Vn.-Str.
André, Offenbach a.M. [ca.1893]
Score 6 p.

1410s Silence! pour orchestre à cordes
Str.
Score: Ms. 5 p.
Parts: Ende, Cologne [n.d.]

BEHREND, JEANNE.   Philadelphia 11 May 1911

7136 Festival fanfare prelude to The   *1'30"*
Star-Spangled Banner [in B-flat]
2,2,2,2-4,3,3,1-Timp.,Perc.-Str.
Ms.
Score 7 p. Large folio
*Composed 1959. First performance Philadelphia,
27 September 1959, members of the Philadelphia
Orchestra, William R. Smith conductor.*

3515 From dawn until dusk, suite, seven   *15'*
scenes depicting a child's day from dawn until
dusk, Op. 6
1.A birdie with a yellow bill...2.Mother is
sad 3....because I'm bad! 4.Let's go out and
play 5.Please tell us a story...6.Father
comes home 7.Bird at evening
3*,3*,4*(1Cl. in E-flat),3*-2,2,2,1-Timp.,
Perc.-Cel.,2Hp.,2Harmonica-Str.
Ms.
Score 72 p.
*Originally composed for piano, 1934; orches-
trated 1939. The piano suite was awarded the
Bearns Prize by Columbia University, 1936.
First performance Oakland, California, 25
October 1940, Northern California Symphony
Orchestra of the WPA, Nathan Abas conductor.*

BELICZAY, JULIUS VON *or* JULES DE.
Komorn, Hungary 10 August 1835
Budapest 30 April 1893

96s Andante, Op. 25 [E-flat major]
Str.
Breitkopf & Härtel, Leipzig [ca.1883]
Score 9 p.

612s [Serenade, string orchestra, Op. 36,
D minor]
1.Moderato ma non troppo 2.Allegretto vivace
3.Adagio cantabile 4.Allegro con fuoco
Str.
Durdilly, Paris [n.d.]
Score 40 p.

BELLINI, FRANÇOIS.   Cassano near Bari, Italy 1836
Monaco ca.1910

673c Sous les palmiers [Under the palm trees]
Solo Vc.-Fl.,2Cl.-Str.
Score: Ms. 6 p.
Parts: Decourcelle [Nice, n.d.]

BELLINI, VINCENZO. Catania, Sicily 3 November 1801
Puteaux near Paris 23 September 1835

287m [Concerto, oboe and strings, E-flat   *9'30"*
major] Edited by Terenzio Gargiulo
Maestoso e deciso - Larghetto cantabile -
Allegro [alla polonese)
Solo Ob.-Str.
Ricordi, Milan, ᶜ1961
Score 25 p.

BENDA, JAN JIŘÍ.   Stáre Benátky, Bohemia
baptized 30 August 1713
Berlin 1752

Also known as: Johann Benda, Giovanni Benda

392v [Concerto, violin and strings,   *10'*
G major] Edited by Samuel Dushkin
1.Allegro 2.Grave 3.Allegro
Solo Vn.-Str.
Schott's Söhne, Mainz, ᶜ1932
Score 15 p.

BENDA, JIŘÍ ANTONÍN.
Stáre Benátky, Bohemia, baptized 30 June 1722
Köstritz, Thuringia 6 November 1795

Also known as: Georg Benda, Georges Benda

348p [Concerto, piano and strings,   *18'*
G minor] String parts edited by Viktor Nopp
1.Allegro non troppo 2.Andante 3.Presto
Solo Pno.-Str.
Národní Hudební Vydavatelství, Orbis, Prague,
ᶜ1950
Score 48 p.
*Listed in The Breitkopf Thematic Catalog, Sup-
plement V, Leipzig, 1770.*

Ben-Haim, Paul

6517 [Symphony, F major] Edited by   *9-11'*
Max Schneider
1.Allegro 2.Larghetto 3.Allegro
2Hn.-Cemb.-Str.
Breitkopf & Härtel, Leipzig [1957]
Score 12 p.
*Listed in The Breitkopf Thematic Catalog,
Part I, Leipzig, 1762.*

BENDEL, FRANZ.
                Schönlinde, North Bohemia 23 March 1833
                            Berlin 3 July 1874

5271 [Cinderella, from Six German fairy tale
pictures, Op. 135 no. 3. Transcribed by Karl
Müller-Berghaus]
3*,3*(E.H. alt. 3rd Ob.),2,2-4,3(3rd ad lib.),
3,1-Timp.,Perc.-Hp.(ad lib.)-Str.
Hugo Pohle, Hamburg [188-?]
Score 49 p.
*After Charles Perrault's fairy tale, Cinder-
ella. Op. 135 originally composed for piano
solo.*

5273 [Hans in luck, from Six German fairy tale
pictures, Op. 135 no. 6. Transcribed by Karl
Müller-Berghaus]
3*,2,2,2-4,2,3,1-Timp.,Perc.-Str.
Hugo Pohle, Hamburg [188-?]
Score 21 p.
*After the Brothers Grimm fairy tale, Hans in
Luck.*

5272 [Little Red Riding Hood, from Six German
fairy tale pictures, Op. 135 no. 5. Tran-
scribed by Karl Müller-Berghaus]
3*,2,3*(B.Cl.ad lib.),2-4,2,3,1-Timp.,Perc.-
Hp.-Str.
Hugo Pohle, Hamburg [188-?]
Score 35 p.
After the Brothers Grimm fairy tale.

5270 [Snow White, from Six German fairy tale
pictures, Op. 135 no. 2. Transcribed by
Karl Müller-Berghaus]
3*,2,2,2-4,3,3,1-Timp.,Trgl.-Hp.-Str.
Hugo Pohle, Hamburg [188-?]
Score 53 p.
After the Brothers Grimm fairy tale.

BENDL, KAREL.   Prague 16 April 1838
                        Prague 20 September 1897

2053 Südslavische Rhapsodie [Southern Slavic
rhapsody] Op. 60
4*,2,2,2-4,2,3,1-Timp.,Perc.-Hp.-Str.
Simrock, Berlin, c1896
Score 142 p.

BENEDICT, JULIUS *or* JULES.
                    Stuttgart 27 November 1804
                            London 5 June 1885

689p [Concertino, piano and orchestra, Op. 18,
A-flat major]
Solo Pno.-2,2,2,2-2,2-Timp.-Str.
Score: Ms. 111 p.
Parts: Hofmeister, Leipzig [ca.1831]

BEN-HAIM, PAUL.   Munich 5 July 1897

Born: Paul Frankenburger

281p Capriccio for piano and orchestra   *12'*
Solo Pno.-2(both alt. Picc.),2,2,2-4,2-Timp.,
Perc.-Hp.-Str.
Israeli Music Publications, Tel Aviv, c1961
Score 62 p.
*Commissioned by the Israeli Composers' Fund,
Jerusalem, and the Israel Philharmonic
Orchestra. Composed 1960. First performance
Tel Aviv, 25 September 1960, Israel Philhar-
monic Orchestra, Carlo Maria Giulini conductor,
Pnina Saltzman soloist.*

2211s Concerto for string orchestra,   *18'*
Op. 40
1.Preambolo 2.Capriccio 3.Intermezzo lirico
4.Finale
Str.
Israeli Music Publications, Tel Aviv, c1949
Score 46 p.
*Composed 1947. First performance Jerusalem,
5 July 1947, Orchestra of the Israel Broad-
casting Service, the composer conducting.*

333v Concerto for violin and orchestra   *21'*
(1960)
1.Allegro 2.Andante affettuoso 3.Vivo
Solo Vn.-2(2nd alt. Picc.),2(2nd alt. E.H.),2,
2-2,2-Timp.,Perc.-Cel.,Hp.-Str.
Israeli Music Publications, Tel Aviv, c1960
Score 93 p.
*Commissioned by Mrs. Lionello Perera for Zvi
Zeitlin. Composed 1960. First performance
Tel Aviv, 20 March 1962, Israel Philharmonic
Orchestra, Istvan Kertesz conductor, Zvi Zeit-
lin soloist.*

422c Concerto for violoncello and   *22'*
orchestra (1962)
1.Allegro giusto 2.Sostenuto e languido
3.Allegro gioioso
Solo Vc.-2(2nd alt. Picc.),2,2,2-Alto Sax.-2,2
-Timp.,Perc.-Cel.,Hp.-Str.
Israeli Music Publications, Tel Aviv, c1962
Score 101 p.
Composed 1962.

6661 The eternal theme, concert music for   *20'*
orchestra
Intrada (Sostenuto e solemne - Allegro) -
Fanfare (Allegro) - Prayer for the innocent
(Adagio) - Meditation (Grave e serio) - Rondo,
conclusion (Allegro moderato)
3(all alt. Picc.,3rd also alt. Alto Fl.),3*,3*
(2nd alt. Cl. in E-flat),3*-4,6-Perc.Cel.,2Hp.,

Ben-Haim, Paul

Hpscd.-Str.
Israeli Music Publications, Tel Aviv, c1965
Score 81 p. Large folio
*Composed 1963-65. First performance Tel Aviv,
11 February 1966, Israel Philharmonic Orchestra, Paul Kletski conductor.*

6285 From Israel [suite]   16'
1.Prologue 2.Song of songs 3.Yemenite
melody 4.Siesta 5.Celebration
2(2nd alt. Picc.),1,2,2-2,2-Timp.,Perc.-Cemb.,
Hp.-Str.
Israeli Music Publications, Tel Aviv, c1951
Score 69 p.
*Commissioned by Kol Zion Lagola (The Voice
of Zion to the Dispersed), a branch of Israel
Broadcasting Service. Composed 1951. First
performance Zurich, spring 1952, The Orchestra
of Radio Beromuenster, George Singer conductor.*

249p Rhapsody for piano and strings (1971)
Solo Pno.-Str.
Ms. c1972 by Israeli Music Publications
Score 17 p.
*Commissioned by Vishay Intertechnology, Inc.,
for Ruth Apfel Zandman, pianist, and the Concerto Soloists of Philadelphia. First performance Philadelphia, 6 December 1971, Concerto Soloists of Philadelphia, Marc Mostovoy
conductor, Monroe Levin soloist.*

6262 Symphony no. 1 (1940), Op. 25   30'
1.Allegro energico 2.Molto calmo e cantabile
(may be performed separately under the title
Psalm for Orchestra) 3.Finale: Presto con
fuoco
3*(Picc. alt. 3rd Fl.),3*,3*,3*-4,3,3,1-Timp.,
Perc.-Hp.-Str.
Israeli Music Publications, Tel Aviv, c1950
Score 121 p. Large folio
*Composed 1939-40. First performance Tel Aviv,
January 1941, Israeli Philharmonic Orchestra,
the composer conducting. Awarded the Engel
Prize of the Tel Aviv Municipality, 1945.*

6263 [Symphony no. 2, Op. 36]   36'
1.Molto moderato 2.Allegretto vivace 3.
Andante affettuoso e languendo 4.Finale:
Allegro deciso
3*(Picc. alt. 3rd Fl.),3*(E.H. alt. 3rd Ob.),
3*,2-4,3,3,1-Timp.,Perc.-Hp.-Str.
Israeli Music Publications, Tel Aviv, c1949
Score 207 p. Large folio
*Composed 1943-45. First performance Tel Aviv,
4 February 1948, Israel Philharmonic Orchestra, George Singer conductor. Awarded the
Engel Prize of the Tel Aviv Municipality, 1953.*

6251 To the chief musician, metamorphoses 15'
for orchestra
Broad and solemn - March - Toccata - Very fast
- Epilogue
2(both alt. Picc.),2*,2(2nd alt. Cl. in
E-flat),2-3,2,2,1-Timp.,Perc.-Cemb.,Hp.-Str.
Israeli Music Publications, Tel Aviv, c1958
Score 93 p. Large folio
*Commissioned by the Louisville Orchestra,
1957. Composed 1958. First performance*

*Louisville, 28 October 1958, Louisville
Orchestra, Robert Whitney conductor.*

BENJAMIN, ARTHUR.
              Sydney, Australia 18 September 1893
                           London 10 April 1960

960m Concerto for oboe, accompanied by string
orchestra, on themes by Cimarosa. Freely
adapted by Arthur Benjamin
1.Introduzione 2.Allegro 3.Siciliana
4.Allegro giusto
Solo Ob.-Str.
Ms.
Score 15 p. Large folio
Composed 1940.

3287 Cotillon, a suite of dance tunes for   11'
full orchestra
1.Lord Hereford's delight 2.Daphne's delight
3.Marlborough's victory 4.Love's triumph
5.Jigg it e foot 6.The charmer 7.Nymph
divine 8.The tattler 9.Argyle
3(3rd alt. Picc.),2,2,2-4,2,3,1-Timp.,Perc.-
Hp.-Str.
Boosey & Hawkes, London, c1939
Score 30 p.
*Composed 1938. This orchestral suite is based
upon original melodies found in The Dancing
Master, published by W. Pearson and John
Young, London, 1719. First performance in a
broadcast, London, 3 February 1939, BBC
Orchestra, Clarence Raybould conductor. First
public performance England, 5 February 1939,
New Metropolitan Symphony Orchestra, the composer conducting.*

3512 Jamaican rumba   2'
1,1,2(2nd ad lib.),1-Alto Sax.(ad lib.)-2,1-
Timp.(ad lib.),Perc.-Pno.-Str.
Ms.
Score 22 p.
*Originally written for two pianos as the
second piece of the composer's Two Jamaican
Pieces.*

3336 Light music, suite for orchestra   13'30"
1.March 2.Pastorale 3.Viennese waltz
4.Introduction and final dance
2(2nd alt. Picc.),1,1,1-2,2,1-Timp.,Perc.-Pno.,
Cel.-Str.
Boosey & Hawkes, London, c1934
Score 71 p.
*Movements 1 and 2 originally composed for two
pianos, 1928. Movements 3 and 4 composed
1932. First performance Hastings, England,
28 October 1933, Hastings Municipal Orchestra,
Julius Harrison conductor.*

3288 Overture to an Italian comedy, Ah,   6'
perdona se ti inganno [Sorry you've been
deceived]
2(2nd alt. Picc.),2,2,2-4,2,3-Timp.,Perc.-Pno.,
Hp.-Str.
Boosey & Hawkes, London, c1938
Score 43 p.
*Composed 1936 as an addition to the composer's
second opera, Prima Donna. First performance*

at a Patron's Fund concert, London, 2 March 1937, Royal College of Music, Gordon Jacob conductor.

3629 Prelude to holiday, a rondo for   *11'*
orchestra
3*,2,2,2-4,2,3,1-Timp.,Perc.-Cel.,Hp.-Str.
Boosey & Hawkes, London, ᶜ1941
Score 52 p.
Composed 1940. First performance Indianapolis, 17 January 1941, Indianapolis Symphony Orchestra, Fabien Sevitzky conductor.

1018m Romantic fantasy, for solo violin,   *20'*
solo viola and orchestra
1.Nocturne 2.Scherzino 3.Finale: Sonata
Solo Vn., Solo Va.-2(2nd alt. Picc.),2,2,2-4,
2-Timp.,Perc.-Pno.-Str.
Ms.
Score 114 p.
Composed 1936-37. First performance London, 24 March 1938, Royal Philharmonic Society, the composer conducting, Eda Kersey violinist, Bernard Shore violist.

BENNETT, GEORGE JOHN.   Andover, England 5 May 1863
Lincoln, England 20 August 1930

1052s Eventide, melody for harp and string
orchestra
Hp.(Org. or Harm. ad lib.)-Str.
Novello, London [n.d.]
Score 8 p.
From his suite in D minor for orchestra.

BENNETT, ROBERT RUSSELL.
b. Kansas City, Missouri 15 June 1894

2761 Abraham Lincoln, a likeness in   *30'*
symphony form
1.His simplicity and his sadness 2.His affection and his faith 3.His humor and his weakness 4.His greatness and his sacrifice
4(3rd alt. Picc.),3(3rd alt. E.H.),4(4th alt. B.Cl.),4*-6,4,3,1-Timp.,Perc.-Cel.,2Hp.-Str.
Harms, New York, ᶜ1931
Score 135 p.
Composed 1927. Awarded a prize in the Victor Talking Machine Co. Competition, 1929-30, as one of five outstanding works. First performance Philadelphia, 24 October 1931, Philadelphia Orchestra, Leopold Stokowski conductor.

3239 Concerto grosso, for small dance band *12'*
and symphony orchestra in the form of sketches
from an American theatre
1.Praeludium (Opening chorus, vigoroso e con brio) 2.Moderato con anima (Dialog, ingenue and juvenile) 3.Andante con moto (Theme song) 4.Allegro scherzando (Comedy scene and blackout) 5.Marcia (Finale with flags)
Soli(Small Dance Band): 2Alto Sax.(alt. 1st& 2nd Cl.),Ten.Sax.(alt. 3rd Cl.)-2Tpt.,Tbn.-Pno.,Guit.
Orchestra: 2(2nd alt. Picc.),2,3,1-3,2,2-Timp.,Perc.-Str.
Ms.
Score 114 p.

Composed 1931. *First performance Rochester, New York, 9 December 1932, Rochester Philharmonic Orchestra, Howard Hanson conductor.*

3166 Hollywood   *15'*
3*,3*,3*,2-4,3,3,1-Timp.,Perc.-2Pno.(2nd alt. Cel.),Hp.-Str.
Ms.
Score 127 p.
Commissioned by the League of Composers, 1936. Composed 1936. First performance New York, 15 November 1936, in a nation-wide broadcast, NBC Symphony Orchestra, Frank Black conductor.

2762 Sights and sounds, an orchestral   *28'*
entertainment
1.Union Station 2.Highbrows 3.Lowbrows 4.Electric signs 5.Night club 6.Skyscraper 7.Speed
4(2Picc.),4*,4*,4*-4Sax.-6,4,3,2-Timp.,Perc.-Pno.,Cel.,Hp.-Str.
Harms, New York, ᶜ1931
Score 121 p.
Composed in Berlin and Paris on a Guggenheim Fellowship, 1928. Awarded a prize in the Victor Talking Machine Co. Competition, 1929-30, as one of five outstanding works. First performance Chicago, 13 December 1938, Illinois Symphony Orchestra of the WPA, Izler Solomon conductor.

BENNETT, WILLIAM STERNDALE.
Sheffield, England 13 April 1816
London 1 February 1875

668p [Capriccio, piano and orchestra,   *8'*
Op. 22, E major]
Solo Pno.-2,2,2,2-2,2-Timp.-Str.
Score: Ms. 103 p.
Parts: Kistner, Leipzig [n.d.]
Composed at Leipzig 1840-41.

669p [Concerto, piano, no. 4, Op. 19,   *22'*
F minor]
1.Allegro con maesta 2.Barcarole 3.Presto
Solo Pno.-2,2,2,2-2,2-Timp.-Str.
Score: Ms. 207 p.
Parts: Kistner, Leipzig [n.d.]
First performance Gewandhaus, Leipzig, 17 January 1838, the composer as soloist.

5390 [The naiads overture, Op. 15]   *13'*
2,2,2,2-2-2,1-Timp.-Str.
Kistner, Leipzig [1842?]
Score 83 p.
Composed 1836. First performance Gewandhaus, Leipzig, 13 February 1837, the composer conducting.

BENOIT, GERD.

4375 [German dances from Poland, Banat and North Germany. Transcribed for small wind ensemble by Gerd Benoit and Georg Blumensaat]
3Cl.-Ten.Hn.,Hn.(or Alto Hn.),Bar.Hn.(or Tbn.),2Tpt.,Tuba-Vn.I(or Fl. or Cl. in C),Vn.II(or Cl. in C)
Ludwig Voggenreiter, Potsdam [ca.1940]
Score 13 p.

Benoît, Peter

The Banat was an Austro-Hungarian possession settled by Serbs and Germans and now divided among Hungary, Romania and Yugoslavia. Movements 1 and 2 transcribed by Gerd Benoit; Movements 3 and 4 by Georg Blumensaat.

BENOÎT, PETER.
　　　　　　Harlebeke, Belgium 17 August 1834
　　　　　　Antwerp 8 March 1901

864m Andante, for trombone and string
orchestra, C minor
Solo Tbn.-Str.
Ms.
Score 5 p.

756m Humoresque, for 2 clarinets and string
orchestra, B-flat major
2Cl.-Str.
Ms.
Score 7 p.

1057m [In the fields, song for oboe and strings]
Solo Ob.-Str.
A. Mertens, Antwerp [n.d.]
Score 8 p.
Composed 1869.

727m [Symphonic poem, for flute and orchestra
in three parts]
1.[Will o' the wisps] 2.[Melancholy] (Andante)
3.[Will o' the wisps' dance] (Finale)
Solo Fl.-2,2,2,2-4,2-Timp.-Str.
Score: Ms. 123 p.
Parts: Schott Frères, Brussels [n.d.]

BENOÎT-BERBIGUIER, TRANQUILLE.
See: BERBIGUIER, BENOÎT-TRANQUILLE.

BÉON, ALEXANDRE.

440s Suite Louis XV [for string orchestra]
1.Pavane 2.Rigodon 3.Passe-pied 4.Sarabande
5.Gavotte
Str.
Costallat, Paris, ᶜ1907
Score 25 p.

BERBIGUIER, BENOÎT-TRANQUILLE.
　　　　Caderousse, Vaucluse 21 December 1782
　　　　Pont-Levoy near Blois, France 20 January 1838

891m [Concerto, flute, no. 1, D major]
1.Maestoso 2.Adagio 3.Polacca
Solo Fl.-2Ob.,2Bn.-2Hn.-Str.
Score: Ms. 69 p.
Parts: Decombe, Paris [n.d.]
Composed and published before 1813.

371m [Concerto, flute, no. 7, E-flat major]
1.Introduction: Maestoso - Allegro non troppo
2.Romanza: Lento 3.Rondo montagnard: Allegro
poco spiritoso
Solo Fl.-0,2,1,1-2Hn.-Str.
Score: Ms. 104 p. Large folio
Parts: Breitkopf & Härtel, Leipzig [1819]

817m [Concerto, flute, no. 8, Op. 44]　　　*15'*
Spiritoso - Adagio mosso - Polonaise
Solo Fl.-0,2,0,2-2Hn.-Str.
Score: Ms. 73 p.
Parts: Breitkopf & Härtel, Leipzig [ca.1820]

892m [Fantasy, flute and orchestra, Op. 78]
1.Intrada 2.Thêma 3.[Five variations]
Solo Fl.-2Ob.,2Bn.-2Hn.-Str.
Score: Ms. 47 p.
Parts: Janet et Cotelle, Paris [n.d.]
*Based on the romance of Charlemagne called Les
Chevaliers de la Fidêlitê.*

893m [Theme with variations, for solo flute and
orchestra]
Solo Fl.-2Ob.(ad lib.)-2Hn.(ad lib.)-Str.
Score: Ms. 25 p.
Parts: Janet et Cotelle, Paris [n.d.]

BERCKMAN, EVELYN.　　　　　　Philadelphia 1900

3274 [Dances from county fair, ballet]　　　*7'*
1.Curtain music, Crowd music 2.Dance of
balloon man and children 3.Country dances
3(3rd alt. Picc.),3,3,2-2Hn.,2Cnt.,Tbn.-Timp.,
Perc.-Hp.-Str.
Ms.
Score 146 p. Large folio
*Composed 1936. First performance Philadelphia,
9 February 1937, Civic Symphony Orchestra of
the WPA, Guglielmo Sabatini conductor, with
the Mary Binney Montgomery Dancers.*

3054 The return of song (after a fable of　　*6'*
Lord Dunsany)
3,3*,3*,2-4,3-Timp.-Pno.,2Hp.-Str.
Ms.
Score 42 p.
*Composed ca.1927. First performance Rochester,
New York, 29 April 1927, Rochester Philhar-
monic Orchestra, Howard Hanson conductor.*

3279 Tours (XVth century)　　　　　　*5'30"*
2,2,2,2-4,4,3-Timp.,Perc.-Cel.,2Hp.-Str.
Ms.
Score 25 p. Large folio
Composed 1935.

BEREZOWSKY, NICOLAI T.
　　　　St. Petersburg, Russia 17 May 1900
　　　　New York City 27 August 1953

4072 [Christmas festival overture,　　　　*7'30"*
Op. 30 no. 2]
3*,3,3(1Cl. in E-flat),2-4,4,3,1-Timp.,Perc.-
Pno.-Str.
Ms.
Score 33 p. Large folio
*Commissioned by Howard Barlow. Composed 1943.
First performance New York, 23 December 1943,
New York Philharmonic, Howard Barlow con-
ductor.*

Berezowsky, Nicolai T.

1073m [Concerto, harp, Op. 31]
1.Moderato 2.Adagio 3.Allegro non tanto
Solo Hp.-3*,2,3*,2-4,2,3,1-Timp.,Perc.-Str.
Ms. c1944 by Elkan-Vogel, Philadelphia
Score 59 p. Large folio
*Composed 1944. Written for and dedicated to
Edna Philipps.*

1133v [Concerto, viola or clarinet,   24'
Op. 28]
1.Introduction - Recitativo - Variations
2.Allegretto, rubato 3.Andante sostenuto
4.Allegro commodo, con brio
Solo Va.(or Cl.)-3*,2,0,2-2,2,1,1-Timp.,Perc.-
Str.
Ms.
Score 93 p. Large folio
*Composed 1941. First performance New York,
11 October 1941, broadcast over WABC, CBS
Orchestra, Howard Barlow conductor, the com-
poser as soloist. First concert performance
Chicago, 29 January 1942, Chicago Symphony
Orchestra, Frederick Stock conductor, William
Primrose soloist.*

1081v [Concerto, violin, Op. 14]   16'
1.Allegro di bravuro, ma non troppo 2.Adagio
sostenuto 3.Allegro giusto
Solo Vn.-2,2,2,2-2,2-Timp.,Perc.-Str.
Ms.
Score 94 p.
*Composed 1929-30. First performance Dresden,
Germany, 29 April 1930, Dresden Philharmonic
Orchestra, the composer conducting, Carl
Flesch soloist.*

737c [Concerto, violoncello, Lyric,Op. 19] 22'
In one movement
Solo Vc.-1,1,2*,1-2,2,1,1-Timp.,Perc.-Pno.,
Hp.-Str.(without Vc.)
Ms.
Score 83 p.
*Composed 1935. First performance Boston, 22
February 1935, Boston Symphony Orchestra,
Serge Koussevitzky conductor, Gregor
Piatigorsky soloist.*

718p Fantasie, for 2 pianos and   11'
orchestra, Op. 9
2 Solo Pno.-3*,2,2,2-4,2,3,1-Timp.,Perc.-Str.
Ms.
Score 93 p.
*Originally composed for two pianos, 1929;
orchestrated 1932. First performance New York,
14 February 1933, National Orchestral Association, Leon Barzin conductor, Vera Brodsky
and Harold Triggs soloists.*

1780s Introduction and waltz, Op. 25   10'
Str.
Ms.
Score 28 p.
*Composed 1939. First broadcast performance,
New York, 15 October 1939, NBC Symphony
Orchestra, Frank Black conductor. First*

*concert performance New York, 27 March 1941,
New York Philharmonic, John Barbirolli conductor.*

3837 Sinfonietta, for orchestra, Op. 17   13'
3*,2,2,2-4,2,3,1-Timp.,Perc.-Str.
Birchard [n.p.] c1934 by Juilliard Musical
Foundation
Score 72 p.
*Composed 1931. Awarded fifth prize in the
NBC Competition, 1932. First performance New
York, 1 May 1932, in a broadcast by the NBC
Symphony Orchestra, Eugene Goossens conductor.*

4073 Soldiers on the town, Op. 30   3'30"
no. 1
3*,2,3*,2-4,3,3,1-Timp.,Perc.-Str.
Ms. c1943 by Nicolai Berezowsky
Score 12 p.
*Commissioned by the League of Composers, 1943.
Composed 1943. First performance New York,
25 November 1943, New York Philharmonic, Artur
Rodzinski conductor.*

3029 Symphony no. 2, Op. 18   30'
1.Allegro ma non tanto 2.Allegro giocoso 3.
Largo assai 4.Allegro con brio
3*,3*,4*,3*-6,4,3,1-Timp.,Perc.-Cel.-Str.
Ms.
Score 180 p.
*Composed 1933. First performance Boston,
16 February 1934, Boston Symphony Orchestra,
Serge Koussevitzky conductor.*

3049 Symphony no. 3, Op. 21   28'
1.Adagio 2.Allegro 3.Lento
3*,2,3*,3*-4,3,3,1-Timp.,Perc.-Str.
Ms.
Score 155 p.
*Composed 1936. First performance Rochester,
New York, 21 January 1937, Rochester Philhar-
monic Orchestra, José Iturbi conductor.*

4057 Symphony no. 4, Op. 29   35'
1.Allegro non troppo, cantabile 2.Vivace
3.Adagio 4.Allegro commodo, ma bravura
3*,3*,4*(1Cl. in E-flat),3*-4,4,3,1-Timp.,
Perc.-Cel.-Str.
Ms.
Score 150 p. Large folio
*Commissioned by the Koussevitzky Music Founda-
tion, 1942. Composed 1942. First performance
Boston, 22 October 1943, Boston Symphony
Orchestra, the composer conducting.*

928m Toccata, variations and finale,   23'
for string quartet and orchestra, Op. 23
1.Allegro moderato e risoluto 2.Andante
sostenuto 3.Allegro con fuoco
Solo Vn.I/II, Solo Va., Solo Vc.-3*,2,3*,2-
4,2,3,1-Timp.,Perc.-Str.
Ms.
Score 124 p. Large folio

Berg, Alban

Composed 1938. First performance Boston, 21 October 1938, Boston Symphony Orchestra, Serge Koussevitzky conductor, the Coolidge String Quartet: William Kroll (1st violin), the composer (2nd violin), Nicolas Moldavan (viola), Victor Gottlieb (cello), soloists.

BERG, ALBAN.   Vienna 9 February 1885
                  Vienna 24 December 1935

397v [Concerto, violin]   *24'*
1.Andante - Allegretto 2.Allegro - Adagio
Solo Vn.-2(both alt. Picc.),2(2nd alt. E.H.),
4*(3rd alt. Alto Sax.),3*-4,2,2,1-Timp.,Perc.-
Hp.-Str.
Universal Edition, Vienna, ᶜ1936
Score 99 p.
Composed 1935. First performance Fourteenth Festival of the International Society for Contemporary Music, Barcelona, 19 April 1936, Hermann Scherchen conductor, Louis Krassner soloist. Written for Louis Krassner.

6894 [Five orchestral songs on picture *15'30"*
postcard texts by Peter Altenberg, Op. 4]
1.Seele, wie bist du schöner 2.Sahst du nach dem Gewitterregen dem Wald?!?! 3.Über die Grenzen des All 4.Nichts ist Friede 5.Hier ist Friede
High Voice Solo-3*,3(3rd alt. E.H.),4*(3rd alt. Cl. in E-flat),3(3rd alt. C.Bn.)-4,3,4,
1-Timp.,Perc.-Pno.,Cel.,Hp.,Harm.-Str.
Universal Edition, Vienna, ᶜ1953
Score 28 p. Large folio
Text by Peter Altenberg (1859-1919). Composed 1912. First complete performance Rome, 1952, Jascha Horenstein conductor.

901s [Lyric suite. Three pieces for   *15'*
string orchestra]
1.Andante amoroso 2.Allegro misterioso
3.Adagio appassionato
Str.
Universal Edition, Vienna, ᶜ1928
Score 39 p.
Originally composed for string quartet, 1926. Transcribed 1928.

BERG, NATANAEL.   Stockholm 9 February 1879
                Stockholm 14 October 1957

Baptized: Carl Natanael Berg
Also known as: Carl Natanael Rexroth-Berg

4981 [Powers, a symphonic poem]   *25'*
1.Mannen. Selbst ist der Mann: Prestissimo -
Andante - Grave - Allegro moderato - Adagio -
Allegro energico - Lento 2.Kvinnan [Women]
Andante - Moderato - Allegro moderato -
Andante
3*,3*,3*,3*-4,3,3,1-Timp.,Perc.Hp.-Str.
Ms.
Score 95 p.
Composed 1917. First performance 1917, Concert Society of Stockholm, Georg Schnéevoigt conductor.

5030 [Suite for orchestra]   *15'*
1.Introduction: Adagio 2.Rondo: Allegro 3.
Serenade: Allegretto 4.Menuett 5.Final: Allegro molto e con brio
2,2,2(2nd alt. B.Cl.),2-4,0,1(ad lib.)-Timp.-
Hp.(ad lib.)-Str.
Ms.
Score 46 p.
Composed 1930.

6077 [Symphonic piece for large orchestra] *22'*
1.Andantino 2.Quasi presto grazioso 3.Andante non troppo 4.Presto
2(2nd alt. Picc.),3,2,2-4,2,3,1-Timp.,Perc.-Hp.
Str.
A.B. Nordiska Musikförlaget, Stockholm [n.d.]
Score 100 p.
Composed 1918.

BERGÉ, IRÉNÉE.   Toulouse 1 February 1867
              Jersey City 30 July 1936

773s Nocturne [for solo flute, solo harp, and
string quartet, D major]
Solo Fl., Solo Hp.-Str.(without Cb.)
Leduc, Paris, ᶜ1902
Score 7 p.
The flute solo may be replaced by a violin solo, and the harp by a piano.

BERGEL, BERND.
  b. Hohensalza, Posen, Germany 24 November 1909

2251s Two movements for strings   *15'*
1.Andantino - Allegro 2.Andantino - Allegro poco maestoso
Str.
Israeli Music Publications, Tel Aviv, ᶜ1963
Score 59 p.
Commissioned by Omanut, Zurich and Israeli Music Publications, Ltd. Composed 1963.

BERGER, PETER.

7179 Manifest destiny, march for symphonic band
3*,2,7*(1 in E-flat,Alto Cl.,B.Cl.,Cb.Cl.),2-
5Sax.(2Alto,2Ten.,Bar.)-4,3,3,2Bar.,Tuba-Timp.,
Perc.-Cb.
Avant Music, Los Angeles, ᶜ1962
Score in reduction 13 p.

7180 Plaintive song for orchestra
1,1,2,1-Alto Sax.,Ten.Sax.-2,2,2,1-Timp.,Perc.-
Hp.-Str.
Avant Music, Los Angeles, ᶜ1960
Score 14 p.

BERGER, THEODOR.
   b. Traismauer, Lower Austria 18 May 1905

2058s [Two pieces for string orchestra. *1.16'*
1.Malinconia, Op. 5 2.Rondino giocoso, *2. 5'*
Op. 4]
Str.
Ries & Erler, Berlin, ᶜ1939
Score 140 p.
Composed 1933.

Bériot, Charles Auguste de

BERGHESE, HANS.   Freiburg 24 May 1910

1005m [Pieces for small percussion instruments.
Spielstück: As quickly as possible (from
Orff's Schulwerk)]
3Small Timp.,Glock.,Small Gong,Cym.,Small Hand
Dr.,Small Xyl.
Ms. [Hansen,, n.p., ᶜ1932]
Score 7 p.

BERGHOUT, JOHAN CORNELIS.
                    Rotterdam 2 September 1869
                    Amsterdam 20 May 1963

300s [Suite for string orchestra, Op. 52]
1.[Prelude] 2.[Impromptu] 3.[Intermezzo]
4.[Evensong] 5.[Moment musical]
Str.
Steingräber, Leipzig, c1913
Score 22 p.

BERGSMA, WILLIAM. Oakland, California 1 April 1921

1997s The fortunate islands, for string   19'
orchestra [original version]
Str.
Ms. [This version withdrawn from circulation
at composer's request]
Score 40 p. Large folio
*Composed in reaction against Walter Raleigh's
statement that the artist "does not guide the
ship... nor discover the Fortunate Islands."
Commissioned by Carl Fischer, Inc. in honor of
the 25th anniversary of the League of Composers.
Composed 1947. First performance 1948, CBS
Symphony Orchestra, Sylvan Levin conductor.
This version withdrawn; revised version, 1956.*

3669 [Gold and the Señor Commandante.   20'
Complete music to the ballet]
1.Siesta and parade - Interlude I: Entrance of
the travellers 2.Greetings and local dances:
(a)Elegant dance of the señors and señoritas
(b)Furious dance of the bearded Russians (c)
Sinister dance of the Digger Indians 3.Dis-
putations and theology: Interlude II - Chinese
dance - Tender dance of the Commandante's
daughter - Interlude III: Discovery 4.Chase
music 5.Happy dance, in which the characters
fall asleep
2(2nd alt. Picc.),1,2,2-2,2,2-Timp.,Perc.-Pno.
-Str.
Ms.
Score 96 p. Large folio
*The story of the ballet is freely expanded
from three characters and the locale of Bret
Harte's The Right Eye of the Commander. Composed 1941. First performance Rochester, 1
May 1942, Rochester Civic Orchestra, Howard
Hanson conductor.*

3954 Music on a quiet theme   7'30"
2*,2*,2,2-4,2,3,1-Timp.,Cym.-Str.
Ms.
Score 20 p. Large folio
*Composed 1942-43. First performance in a CBS
broadcast, Rochester, April 1943, Eastman-
Rochester Symphony Orchestra, Howard Hanson*

conductor.

4048 Paul Bunyan. Suite from the ballet   12'
for puppets and solo dancers
1.The dance of the Blue Ox 2.Night 3.Country
dance 4.Finale
3(3rd alt. Picc.),3*,3(3rd alt. B.Cl.),2-4,3,3,
1-Timp.-Pno.-Str.
Ms.
Score 41 p.
*Composed 1937. First performance of ballet
under the title Pioneer Saga, Rochester, New
York, 28 April 1939, Rochester Civic Orchestra,
Howard Hanson conductor. First performance of
suite San Francisco, 22 June 1939, San Francisco Symphony Orchestra, Pierre Monteux conductor.*

4783 [Symphony no. 1]   25'
1.Prologue 2.March 3.Interlude 4.Aria 5.
Epilogue
3*(Picc. alt. 3rd Fl.),3*(E.H. alt. 3rd Ob.),3*
(B.Cl. alt. 3rd Cl.),2-4,3,3,1-Timp.,Perc.-Str.
Ms.
Score 129 p. Large folio
Composed 1949.

3758 Symphony, for chamber orchestra   14'
1.Free, moving 2.Pastorale 3.Quick, driving
1(alt. Picc.),0,1-2,1-Timp.(alt. B.Dr.)-Pno.-
Str.
Ms.
Score 67 p. Large folio
*Composed 1942 for the Saidenberg Little Sym-
phony, on commission from Town Hall, New York.
First performance Rochester, 14 April 1943,
Eastman School Little Symphony Orchestra, the
composer conducting.*

3521 Trumpet sing jubilee   8'30"
2(2nd alt. Picc.),2,2,2-4,2,3,1-Timp.,Susp.
Cym.-Str.
Ms.
Score 40 p. Large folio
*Expresses the delight of a revival meeting at
the prospect of Paradise. Composed 1940.
First performance Rochester, 23 April 1941,
Eastman-Rochester Symphony Orchestra, Howard
Hanson conductor.*

3585 Variations on a sea chantey: High   8'30"
Barbaree
3(3rd alt. Picc.),2,3*,2-4,3(3rd ad lib.),3,1-
Timp.-Str.
Ms.
Score 16 p. Large folio
*Composed 1939. This work is the slow movement
of Symphony, (1940). First performance at a
symposium, Rochester, New York, 22 April 1942,
Rochester Civic Orchestra, Howard Hanson con-
ductor.*

BÉRIOT, CHARLES AUGUSTE DE.
                    Louvain, Belgium 20 February 1802
                    Brussels 8 April 1870

354v [Air with variations, violin and orchestra,
no. 10, Op. 67]

Bériot, Charles

Solo Vn.-1,2,2,2-2,2,3-Timp.-Str.
Score: Ms. 75 p. Large folio
Parts: Schott's Söhne, Mainz [ca.1849]

504v [Concerto, violin, no. 1, Op. 16, D major]
In one movement
Solo Vn.-2,2,2,2-4,2,3-Timp.,Perc.-Str.
Schott's Söhne, Mainz [ca.1836]
Score in reduction 15 p.
This concerto also known as the Military Concerto.

1169v [Concerto, violin, no. 5, Op. 55, D major]
1.Allegro moderato 2.Adagio 3.Allegro
Solo Vn.-1,2,2,2-2,2,2-Timp.-Str.
Schott's Söhne, Mainz [ca.1846]
Score in reduction 17 p.

505v [Concerto, violin, no. 7, Op. 76,   *8'*
G major]
Allegro maestoso - Allegro moderato - Allegro assai
Solo Vn.-1,2,2,2-2,2,3-Timp.-Str.
Schott's Söhne, Mainz [ca.1852]
Score in reduction 19 p.

506v [Concerto, violin, no. 9, Op. 104,   *7'*
A minor]
Allegro maestoso - Allegro grazioso - Rondo: Allegretto moderato
Solo Vn.-1,0,2,2-2Hn.-Timp.-Str.
Schott's Söhne, Mainz [ca.1860]
Score in reduction 16 p.

1173v [Fantasy, or Scène de ballet, violin and orchestra, Op. 100]
Solo Vn.-2,2,2,2-4,2,3-Timp.-Str.
Score in reduction: Carl Fischer, New York, c1912. 19 p.
Parts: Schott's Söhne, Mainz [ca.1858]

BERKELEY, LENNOX.   Boar's Hill near Oxford England 12 May 1903

3295 Mont Juic, suite of Catalan dances   *12'*
for orchestra
2(2nd alt. Picc.),2,2,2(2nd alt. C.Bn.)-2Sax.
(AT; ad lib.)-4,2,3,1-Timp.,Perc.-Hp.-Str.
Hawkes & Son, London, c1938
Score 64 p.
Composed 1937. First performance London, 8 January 1938, BBC Orchestra, Joseph Lewis conductor.

1821s Serenade, for string orchestra   *14'*
1.Vivace 2.Andantino 3.Allegro moderato 4. Lento
Str.
J.&W. Chester, London, c1940
Score 22 p.
Composed 1939. First performance at a Concert of the Contemporary Music Society, London, 30 January 1940, Boyd Neel String Orchestra, Boyd Neel conductor.

BERLIN, DAVID N.   b. Pittsburgh, Pennsylvania 23 January 1943

7156 Structures for chamber orchestra   *8'*
1.Allegro marcato 2.Moderato 3.Alla marcia
1(alt. Picc.),1,1,1-1,1,2-Perc.-Str.
Ms. c1976 by David Berlin
Score 45 p. Large folio
Composed 1975.

7111 Variants for orchestra   *15'*
2(2nd alt. Picc.),2,2,2-3,3,3-Perc.-Str.
Ms. c1974 by David N. Berlin
Score 58 p. Large folio
Composed 1973. First performance Carnegie-Mellon University, Pittsburgh, Pennsylvania, April 1974, University Symphony Orchestra, the composer conducting. Selected for performance by the Orchestra Society of Philadelphia as part of its Pennsylvania Composers Project 1975, made possible by a grant from the Pennsylvania Council on the Arts with performance materials prepared by the Fleisher Collection of Orchestral Music. The award performance at Mandell Theater, Drexel University, Philadelphia, 1 June 1975, Orchestra Society of Philadelphia, Sidney Rothstein conductor.

BERLIOZ, HECTOR.   La Côte-Saint-André, Isère 11 December 1803 Paris 8 March 1869

Born: Louis-Hector Berlioz

6595 [Beatrice and Benedict. Overture]   *7'*
2*,2,2,2-4,2,Cnt.,3-Timp.-Str.
Luck's, Detroit [n.d.]
Score 38 p.
From the opera in 2 acts with libretto by Berlioz based on Shakespeare's Much Ado About Nothing. Composed 1860-62. First performance of opera (in German) Baden-Baden, 9 August 1862, the composer conducting.

733 [Benvenuto Cellini, Op. 23. Overture]   *11'*
2(2nd alt. Picc.),2,2(2nd alt. B.Cl.),4(3rd& 4th ad lib.)-4,4,2Cnt.,3,1-Timp.,Perc.-Str.
Breitkopf & Härtel, Leipzig [n.d.]
Score 44 p.
From the opera composed 1834-38. First performance Paris, 10 September 1838, Antoine Habeneck conductor.

1843 [The childhood of Christ, Op. 25.   *3'*
Part 2, The flight into Egypt. Overture]
2Fl.,Ob.,E.H.-Str.
Breitkopf & Härtel, Leipzig [n.d.]
Score 8 p.
Flight into Egypt composed 1850. First performance Leipzig, 1853, the composer conducting. Later included as Part 2 of the oratorio The Childhood of Christ.

765 [Le corsaire overture, Op. 21]   *8'*
2,2,2,2-4-4,2,2Cnt.,3,1(Ophicl.)-Timp.-Str.
Costallat, Paris [n.d.]
Score 63 p.
Composed 1855. From overture La Tour de Nice,

sketched ca.1831 and composed 1844. First performance as La Tour de Nice, Paris, 19 January 1845. First performance of this revised version Paris, 1 April 1855, the composer conducting.

767 [The damnation of Faust, Op. 24.   3'
   Scene VII. Dance of the sylphs]
   3Fl.,2Cl.-Timp.-2Hp.-Str.
   Kalmus, New York [n.d.]
   Score 6 p.
   From the secular cantata after Goethe. Dance of the Sylphs composed 1845; cantata completed 1846. First performance Paris, 6 December 1846, Opéra-Comique, the composer conducting.

130 [The damnation of Faust, Op. 24.   4'
   Scene III. Hungarian march]
   3*,2,2,4-4,2,2Cnt.,3,1-Timp.,Perc.-Str.
   Breitkopf & Härtel, Leipzig [1900]
   Score 19 p.
   Based on the traditional Rákóczi March. Composed 1845. First performance Pest, 20 February 1846, the composer conducting. Later included in The Damnation of Faust.

686 [The damnation of Faust, Op. 24.   6'
   Scene XII. Minuet of the will o' the wisps]
   3(2Picc.),2,3*,4-4,2,2Cnt.,3-Timp.,Perc.-Str.
   Score: Breitkopf & Härtel, Leipzig, c1900.
   25 p.
   Parts: Costallat, Paris [n.d.]

Dance of the sylphs
   See: [The damnation of Faust, Op. 24. Scene
      VII. Dance of the sylphs]

Festival at the Capulets, from Romeo and Juliet
   See: [Romeo and Juliet, dramatic symphony,
      Op. 17. Part II, no. 1. Romeo alone...]

The flight into Egypt, Op. 25. Overture
   See: [The childhood of Christ, Op. 25. Part 2,
      The flight into Egypt. Overture]

5651 [Funeral and triumphal symphony,   18'
   Op. 15]
   1.Funeral march 2.Funeral sermon 3.Apotheosis
   3*,2,4*(1Cl. in E-flat),3*(C.Bn. ad lib.)-6,4,
   2Cnt.,4(B.Tbn. ad lib.),2-Timp.,Perc.-Chorus
   (SATB ad lib.)-Str.(ad lib.) (Winds are
   expanded in number as noted in the score)
   Score: Kalmus, New York [n.d.] 76 p.
   Parts: Ms. Copied from Breitkopf & Härtel
   edition of Berlioz' Complete Works [n.d.]
   Commissioned by the French Government. Text by Antony Deschamps. Composed 1840, for the transferral of the remains of those who fell in the July revolution of 1830 and for the dedication of the Bastille column. First performances Paris, 28 July 1840 (without strings) and 6 August 1840 (with strings), the composer conducting.

707 [Harold in Italy, symphony in 4   47'
   parts with a viola solo, Op. 16]
   1.Harold in the mountains (Scenes of

melancholy, happiness and joy) 2.Procession of
pilgrims singing the evening hymn 3.Serenade
of an Abruzzi mountaineer to his sweetheart
4.The brigand's orgies (Reminiscences of the
preceding scenes)
Solo Va.-2(2nd alt. Picc.),2(1st alt. E.H.),2,
4-4,2,2Cnt.,3,1-Timp.,Perc.-Hp.-Str.
Kalmus, New York [n.d.]
Score 170 p.
Based on Byron's Childe Harold. Composed 1834. First performance Paris, 23 November 1834, Narcisse Girard conductor.

Hungarian march
   See: [The damnation of Faust, Op. 24. Scene
      III. Hungarian march]

1047 [Judges of the secret court.   12'
   Overture, Op. 3]
   2(alt. Picc.),2,2,3*-4,3,3,2-Timp.,Perc.-Str.
   Breitkopf & Härtel, Leipzig [n.d.]
   Score 48 p.
   From an early unfinished opera. Composed ca. 1827. First performance Paris, 26 May 1828, Conservatoire, Bloc conductor.

173 [King Lear overture, Op. 4]   12'
   2(2nd alt. Picc.),2,2,2-4,2,3,1(Ophicl.)-Timp.
   -Str.
   Score: Luck's, Detroit [n.d.] 56 p.
   Parts: Breitkopf & Härtel, Leipzig [n.d.]
   Composed 1831. First performance Paris, 9 November 1834, Narcisse Girard conductor.

March for the presentation of the colors
   See: [Te Deum, Op. 22. March for the
      presentation of the colors]

Minuet of the will o' the wisps
   See: [The damnation of Faust, Op. 24. Scene
      XII. Minuet of the will o' the wisps]

6596 Les nuits d'été [Summer nights]   32'
   Op. 7
   1.Villanelle, for Mezzo-Soprano or Tenor Voice
   2.[The spectre of the rose, for Contralto
   Voice] 3.[On the lagoons, lament for Baritone
   or Contralto or Mezzo-Soprano Voice] 4.Absence
   [for Mezzo-Soprano or Tenor Voice] 5.[At the
   cemetery, moonlight, for Tenor Voice] 6.[Unknown island, for Mezzo-Soprano or Tenor
   Voice]
   Various Solo Voices(as indicated)-2,1,2,2-3Hn.-
   Hp.-Str.
   Kalmus, New York [n.d.]
   Score 71 p.
   Poems by Théophile Gautier. Originally composed for voice and piano 1834-41. Transcribed for orchestra 1843-56.

Queen Mab scherzo
   See: [Romeo and Juliet, dramatic symphony,
   Op. 17. Part II, no. 3. Queen Mab...]

Rákóczi march from La damnation de Faust
   See: [The damnation of Faust, Op. 24. Scene
   III. Hungarian march]

Berlioz, Hector

462v [Reverie and caprice, Op. 8]   9'
Solo Vn.-2*,2,2,2-2Hn.-Str.
Breitkopf & Härtel, Leipzig [n.d.]
Score 14 p.
*Composed 1839. First performance Paris, 1
February 1839, the composer conducting, Del-
phin Alard soloist.*

1100 [Rob Roy overture]   12'
2(2nd alt. Picc.),2,2,2-4,2,Cnt.,3-Timp.-Hp.-
Str.
Breitkopf & Härtel, Leipzig [n.d.]
Score 68 p.
*Composed 1831. First performance Paris, 14
April 1838, François Antoine Habeneck con-
ductor.*

171 Roman carnival overture, Op. 9   6'
2(2nd alt. Picc.),2(2nd alt. E.H.),2,2-4,2,
2Cnt.,3-Timp.,Perc.-Str.
Breitkopf & Härtel, Leipzig [n.d.]
Score 44 p.
*Composed 1843. First performance Paris, 3
February 1844, the composer conducting.*

768 [Romeo and Juliet, dramatic symphony,   100'
Op. 17. Complete]
1.First act: Introduction, Prologue 2.Second
act: Romeo alone, Night scene, Queen Mab 3.
Third act: Juliet's funeral march, Romeo at the
tomb of the Capulets, Finale
3*,2(2nd alt. E.H.),2,4-4,2,2Cnt.,3,1-Timp.,
Perc.-2Hp.-Solo Voices(ATB),Small Chorus(ATB),
Men's Choruses I and II-Str.
Score: Broude Bros., New York [n.d.]. 241 p.
Parts: Kalmus, New York [n.d.]
*Text by d'Emile Deschamps, based on Shakespeare.
Composed 1839. First performance Paris, 24 No-
vember 1839, Conservatoire, the composer con-
ducting.*

7147 [Romeo and Juliet, dramatic symphony,   12'
Op. 17. Part II, no. 1. Romeo alone - Sadness -
Distant sounds of music and dancing - Great
festivities in Capulet's palace]
3*,2(2nd alt. E.H.),2,4-4,2,2Cnt.,3-Timp.,Perc.
-2Hp.-Str.
Edwin F. Kalmus, New York [n.d.]
Score 50 p.

7146 [Romeo and Juliet, dramatic symphony,   16'
Op. 17. Part II, no. 2. Star-lit night - Capu-
let's garden, silent and deserted - The young
Capulets, leaving the hall, pass by singing
fragments of the dance-music - Love scene]
2,2*,2,4-4Hn.-Double Men's Chorus-Str.
Edwin F. Kalmus, New York [n.d.]
Score 29 p.

7145 [Romeo and Juliet, dramatic symphony,   8'
Op. 17. Part II, no. 3. Queen Mab or the fairy
of dreams: Scherzo]
3*,2*,2,4-4Hn.-Timp.,Perc.-2Hp.-Str.
Edwin F. Kalmus, New York [n.d.]
Score 32 p.

586 [Symphonie fantastique, an episode in   52'
the life of an artist, Op. 14]

1.Visions and passions 2.A ball 3.In the
country 4.The procession to the stake 5.The
witches' sabbath
2(2nd alt. Picc.),2(2nd alt. E.H.),2,4-4,2,
2Cnt.,3,2-Timp.,Perc.-2Hp.-Str.
Breitkopf & Härtel, Leipzig [n.d.]
Score 150 p.
*Program by the composer. Composed 1830.
Revised 1831 and performed Paris Conservatoire,
9 December 1832, François Antoine Habeneck
conductor.*

965 [Te Deum, Op. 22. March for the   8'
presentation of the colors]
4,4,4,4-Picc.Saxhn. in B-flat(may be replaced
by an E-flat Cl.&Ob. in unison)-4,2,2Cnt.,6,
2-Timp.,4Dr.-Org.,12Hp.-Str.
Breitkopf & Härtel, Leipzig [n.d.]
Score 21 p.
*Te Deum composed 1849-55. First performance
Paris, 30 April 1855, upon the opening of the
Paris Exhibition, the composer conducting.
This is part 8 of Op. 22.*

4254 [Tristia, Op. 18. No. 3, Funeral march for
the last scene of Hamlet]
2,2,2,4(2 ad lib.)-4,2,2Cnt.,3,1-Timp.,Perc.
(including Volley firing)-Chorus(SATB)-Str.
Breitkopf & Härtel, Leipzig [n.d.]
Score 16 p.
*Suggested by Shakespeare's Hamlet. Composed
1848.*

823 [The Trojans in Carthage. Ballets]   12'
[a)Dance of the Egyptian dancing girls
b)Dance of the slaves c)Dance of the Nubian
slaves]
3*,2,2,2-4,2,2Cnt.,3,1(Ophicl.)-Timp.,Perc.-
Str.
Choudens, Paris [n.d.]
Score 42 p.
*From Part II of the opera in five acts, The
Trojans, with libretto by the composer, based
on Virgil. Composed 1856-59. First performance of Part II, Paris, 4 November 1863, the
composer conducting. First performance of the
complete opera, in German, Karlsruhe, 6 December 1890.*

5158 [The Trojans in Carthage. Prelude]
2,2,2*,2-4,2,2Cnt.,3-Timp.-Str.
Breitkopf & Härtel, Leipzig [n.d.]
Score 12 p.
*This prelude, not in the original version, was
composed for the first performance of Part II.*

734 [The Trojans in Carthage. Royal   7'
hunt and tempest]
3*,2,2,2-4,2,2Cnt.,3,1(Ophicl.)-Timp.,B.Dr.-
Small Chorus(STB)-Str. Backstage: Timp.(2
players)
Score: Kalmus, New York [n.d.] 33 p.
Parts: Choudens, Paris [n.d.]

822 [The Trojans in Carthage. Act IV.   6'
Intermezzo, Trojan march]
2,2,2,2-4,2,2Cnt.,3,1(Ophicl. or Tuba)-Timp.,
Perc.-2Hp.-Str.

Score: Kalmus, New York [n.d.] 32 p.
Parts: Choudens, Paris, 1865
This intermezzo, not in the original version, was composed for the first performance of Part II.

766 [Waverly overture, Op. 1b]   *9'*
2,2,2,4-4,2,Cnt.,3,1(Ophicl.)-Timp.-Str.
Costallat, Paris [n.d.]
Score 50 p.
Composed ca.1827. First performance Paris, 26 May 1828, Conservatoire, Bloc conductor.

BERLYN, ANTON.   Amsterdam 2 May 1817
                        Amsterdam 6 January 1870

Also known as: Berlŷn

990v Nocturne for viola, or violin, or violon-
cello and orchestra, Op. 161
Solo Va.(or Vn.,or Vc.)-1,2,2,2-2,2,3-Timp.-
Str.
Score: Ms. 12 p.
Parts: Joh. André, Offenbach a.M. [n.d.]

BERMÚDEZ-SILVA, JESÚS.
          b. Bogotá, Colombia 24 December 1884

3991 Torbellino, poema sinfónico
3(3rd alt. Picc.),3*,3*,2-4,3,3,1-Timp.,Perc.-
Str.
Ms.
Score 70 p.
Based on the poem, La Voragine [The Abyss] by José Eustacio Rivera. Composed 1932. First performance Madrid, 24 March 1933, the Orquesta Filarmónica, the composer conducting.

BERN, BEN. pseudonym.
See: WINKLER, GERHARD.

BERNAL JIMÉNEZ, MIGUEL.
     Morelia, Michoacán, Mexico 16 February 1910
          León, Mexico 26 July 1956

6153 [Michoacán, symphonic suite]
1.Alborada [Morning music] 2.Canción
3.Corrido
3*,3*,3*,3*-4,4,3,1-Timp.,Perc.-Pno.,2Hp.-Str.
Ms.
Score 96 p.
Composed 1940.

6044 [Night in Morelia]
3*,3*,3*,3*-4,4,3,1-Timp.,Perc.-Pno.,Hp.-Str.
Ms.
Score 47 p. Large folio
Composed 1941. First performance Mexico City, 1 August 1941, Orquesta Sinfónica de Mexico, Carlos Chávez conductor.

BERNARD, JEAN EMILE AUGUSTE.
          Marseilles 28 November 1843
          Paris 11 September 1902

1033v [Concerto, violin, Op. 29, G minor]
1.Molto moderato 2.Allegro 3.Moderato -
Scherzando e con spirito

Solo Vn.-2,2,2,2-2,2,3-Timp.-Str.
Score: Ms. 86 p.
Parts: Ries & Erler, Berlin [n.d.]

2338 [Divertissement for wind instruments, *21'*
Op. 36, F major]
1.Andante sostenuto 2.Allegro vivace
3.Andante - Allegro non troppo
2,2,2-2Hn.
Durand, Paris [n.d.]
Score 76 p.
Composed 1893. First performance Paris, 1894.

538p Fantaisie, Op. 31 [E major]   *30'*
1.Maestoso 2.Allegro
Solo Pno.-2,2,2,2-4,2,3-Timp.-Str.
Ries & Erler, Berlin [n.d.]
Score 150 p.
First performance Paris, 23 December 1888, Concerts Lamoureux, Berthe Max soloist.

BERNERS, LORD.   Arley Park, Bridgnorth,
                 England 18 September 1883
                        London 19 April 1950

Born: Gerald Hugh Tyrwhitt

4010 Fugue for orchestra
3(3rd alt. Picc.),2,2,3*-4,2,2-Perc.-Org.(ad
lib.),Hp.-Str.
J. & W. Chester, London, 1928
Score 63 p.
Composed 1924.

887 [Spanish fantasy] Fantaisie espagnole   *7'*
1.Prélude 2.Fandango 3.Paso doble
4*(3rd alt. 2nd Picc.),3*,4*,4*-4,3,3,1-Timp.,
Perc.-Cel.,2Hp.-Str.
J.&W. Chester, London, c1920
Score 47 p.
Composed 1919. First performance London, 13 September 1919, the composer conducting.

2197 [Three pieces for orchestra]   *8'*
1.Chinoiserie [Knick-knacks] 2.Valse senti-
mentale 3.Kasatchok [Cossack-dance]
3(3rd alt. Picc.),3*,3,3*-4,3,2,1-Timp.,Perc.-
Cel.,Hp.-Str.
J. & W. Chester, London, c1921
Score 45 p.
Composed 1919. First performance Manchester, 8 March 1919, Hallé Concerts, Eugene Goossens conductor.

BERNIER, RENÉ. Saint-Gilles, Belgium 10 March 1905

2246s [Sinfonietta for string orchestra]   *12'*
1.Divertimento 2.Arioso 3.Rondino
Str.
A. Cranz, Brussels, c1960
Score 25 p.
Composed 1954. First performance Brussels, 15 April 1958, Grand Orchestra of the Belgian Radio-Television, Daniël Sternfeld conductor. Awarded the Koopal Prize by the Department of Fine Arts and Literature, the Belgian Ministry for National Education and Culture, 1958.

Bernstein, Arthur

BERNSTEIN, ARTHUR.

1269s Ball-Episode, Waltz-Intermezzo, Op. 41.
Arranged by August Oertel
Str.
Lehne, Hannover [n.d.]
Score 4 p.

BERRY, WALLACE.   b. La Crosse, Wisconsin 10 January 1928

6719 Five pieces for small orchestra   18'
1.Evocation: Very slow 2.Variation: Fast
3.Fantasy: Slow and Fast 4.Chorale: Slow
5.Fugue: Fast
1,1,1,1-1,1,1-Timp.,Cym.-Hp.-Str.
Carl Fischer, New York, c1965
Score 70 p.
*Commissioned by the Chicago Little Symphony.
Composed 1961. First performance Peninsula
Music Festival, Fish Creek, Wisconsin, August
1962, Peninsula Festival Orchestra, Thor
Johnson conductor.*

BERTOLYS.

1158s [Phryne's dream, elegiac serenade]
Str.
Score: Ms. 7 p.
Parts: Decourcelle, Nice, c1921

1606s Zaragoza, habanera
Fl.,Cl.-Str.
Score: Ms. 6 p.
Parts: Decourcelle, Nice, c1921

BERWALD, FRANZ.   Stockholm 23 July 1796
                          Stockholm 3 April 1868

842v [Concerto, violin, Op. 2, C-sharp minor.
Revised by Henri Marteau]
1.Allegro moderato 2.Adagio 3.Allegretto:
Rondo
Solo Vn.-1,0,2,2-2,2-Timp.-Str.
Zimmermann, Leipzig, c1911
Score 73 p.
Composed 1820.

6020 [Estrella de Soria. Overture]   8'
2,2,2,2-4,2,3-Timp.-Str.
Abr. Hirschs Förlag, Stockholm [n.d.]
Score 41 p.
*From the opera in four acts. Composed 1841-
42. First public performance Royal Theatre,
Stockholm, 9 April 1862.*

2171 [Symphony, Singulière, C major]   30'
1.Allegro fuocoso 2.Adagio 3.Finale: Presto
2,2,2,2-4,2,3-Timp.-Str.
Hansen, Copenhagen [n.d.]
Score 71 p.
Composed Stockholm, 1845.

BETTINELLI, BRUNO.   Milan 4 June 1913

4809 [Chamber symphony]   17'
1.Allegro vigoroso ed irrequieto 2.Tranquillo
3.Allegro bizzarro 4.Corale ostinato

2,2,2,2-2,1-Timp.-Str.
Ricordi, Milan, c1940
Score 53 p.
Composed 1939. Now known as Symphony no. 1.

4827 [Concerto for orchestra]   20'
1.Allegro moderato, ma vigoroso 2.Largo (non
troppo) 3.Scherzo fuga
3*,2,3*,2-4,3,3-Timp.,Perc.-Pno.-Str.
Ricordi, Milan, c1941
Score 140 p.
Composed 1940. Won the Saint Cecilia prize.

BEUGER, OTTO.

1004s [Gnomish pranks, character piece, Op. 17]
1.[Dance of the goblins] 2.[The sovereign is
approaching] 3.[General dance]
Str.
Score: Ms. 13 p.
Parts: C.F. Schmidt, Heilbronn [n.d.]

299s Souvenir du bal, intermezzo, Op. 27
Str.
Wernthal, Magdeburg, c1896
Score 3 p.

BEVERSDORF, THOMAS.   Yoakum, Texas 8 August 1924

1105m Concerto grosso for chamber orchestra
with solo oboe
1.Adagio 2.Allegro 3.Largo 4.Allegro
Solo Ob.-1,1,1,1-1,1,1-Timp.-Hp.-Str.
Ms.
Score 40 p.
*Composed 1950. First performance Pittsburgh,
28 April 1950, Pittsburgh Symphony Orchestra,
Vladimir Bakaleinikoff conductor, Arno Mari-
otti soloist.*

5147 New frontiers
3*(2nd alt. 2nd Picc.),3*,3*(2nd alt. Cl. in
E-flat),3*-4,3,3,1-Timp.,Perc.-Cel.,Hp.-Str.
Ms.
Score 78 p. Large folio
*Commissioned by the Houston Symphony Orches-
tra. Composed 1952. First performance Houston, 31 March 1953, Houston Symphony Orchestra,
the composer conducting.*

5142 Ode for orchestra
3*,3*,3*,3*-4,3,3,1-Timp.,Perc.-Hp.-Str.
Ms.
Score 43 p. Large folio
*Suggested by an ode from the Bacchae of
Euripides. Commissioned by the Cincinnati
Symphony Orchestra. Composed 1952.*

5145 Reflections
2(2nd alt. Picc.),2,2,2-2,2,2-Timp.,Perc.-Hp.-
Str.
Ms.
Score 27 p.
Composed 1947.

1102m Suite for clarinet, violoncello and
strings
1.Andante con moto 2.Allemande 3.Sarabande

4.Minuet 5.Gigue
Solo Cl., Solo Vc.-Str.
Ms.
Score 31 p.
Originally composed 1947 as Suite on Baroque Themes for clarinet (or violin), violoncello (or bassoon) and piano. Transcribed for clarinet, violoncello and strings, 1949.

5186 Symphony no. 2
1.Grave maestoso - Un poco allegretto e grazioso 2.Andante cantabile 3.Vivace - Andantino - Vivace 4.Adagio - Andante con moto - Adagio
3*,3*,3*,3*-4,3,3,1-Timp.,Perc.-Pno.,Hp.-Str.
Ms.
Score 193 p. Large folio
Composed 1950.

BEYER, JOHANNA M.   Leipzig 1888
                                New York 1944

982m IV, for percussion
For nine percussion players; percussion instruments not specified.
New Music Orchestra Series, San Francisco, c1936
Score 4 p.
Composed 1935.

2875 Fragment, for chamber orchestra   7'
1,1,1,1-Hn.-Perc.-Pno.-Str.
Ms.
Score 14 p.
Composed 1937.

1034m March for 30 percussion   4'30"
instruments
3Trgl.,2High-pitched Metal Bowls,2Wood Blocks,
4Rice Bowls,1Dragon's Mouth,Tamb.,4Tom-toms,
2Cym.,Anvil,4Temple Gongs,Gong,S.Dr.,B.Dr.,
Thunder Sheet,Lion's Roar
Ms.
Score 4 p.
Composed 1939.

1014m Percussion, Op. 14   4'
1st-Timp.
2nd-2Metal Bowls (High,Low)
3rd-4Dragon's Mouths,Tom-tom
4th-Cym.,Anvil,Gong
5th-Trgl.,Lion's Roar
6th-S.Dr.,B.Dr.
Ms.
Score 3 p.
Composed 1939.

996m Percussion suite in 3 movements
1st-Chinese Blocks,Large Xyl.
2nd-Trgl.
3rd-Tamb.,Rattle
4th-Cym.,Cast.
5th-B.Dr.,Tam-tam
Ms.
Score 17 p.
Composed 1933.

3170 Symphonic movement [no. 1]   5'
3*,2*,2*,2*-2,2,1,1-Timp.,Perc.-Str.
Ms.
Score 12 p. Large folio
Composed 1939.

3646 Symphonic movement no. 2   6'
3*,3*,3*,1-2,2,2,1-Timp.,Perc.-Str.
Ms.
Score 11 p. Large folio
Composed 1941.

3147 Symphonic opus 3   16'
1.Andante 2.Moderato-ritmico 3.Largo 4.Presto
4*,3*,3*,1-2,2,1-Timp.,Perc.-Str.
Ms.
Score 52 p. Large folio
Composed 1939.

3666 Symphonic opus 5   10'
1.Moderato 2.Andante 3.Allegro
2(2nd alt. Picc.),3*,3*,1-3,4,3,1-Timp.,Perc.-Hp.-Str.
Ms.
Score 21 p. Large folio
Composed 1940.

3770 Symphonic suite   24'
1.Grave 2.Allegretto scherzando 3.Lentamente 4.Presto
2*,2*,1,2*-1,1,2,1-Timp.,Perc.-Pno.-Str.
Ms.
Score 81 p.
Composed 1937.

1036m Three movements for percussion
1.Restless 2.Endless 3.Tactless
2Timp.,2Trgl.(High, Low),Bells,2Wood Blocks,
Tamb.,2Cym.,Tom-tom,S.Dr.,Gong,Lion's Roar,
B.Dr.
Ms.
Score 4 p.
Composed 1939.

1058m Waltz for percussion   4'
Timp.,2Trgl.(High, Low),Bell, Dragon's Mouth,
Tom-tom,Cym.,Gong,B.Dr.
Ms.
Score 4 p.
Composed 1939.

BEYNON, JARED.
        b. Pittsburgh, Pennsylvania 25 April 1949

7205 Windfall   6'
3(all alt. Picc.),3*,4*(1Cl. in E-flat),3-4,4,
3,1-Timp.,Perc.-Cel.,2Hp.-Str.
Ms. c1975 by Jared Beynon
Score 32 p. Large folio
Composed 1974-75. First performance Ann Arbor, 15 April 1975, University of Michigan Philharmonia, Uri Mayer conductor. Selected for performance by the Orchestra Society of Philadelphia as part of its Pennsylvania Composers Project 1976, made possible by a grant from the Pennsylvania Council on the Arts with performance materials prepared by the Fleisher

Bezekirsky, Vassili

Collection of Orchestral Music. The award performance Drexel University, Philadelphia, 16 May 1976, Orchestra Society of Philadelphia, Sidney Rothstein conductor.

BEZEKIRSKY, VASSILI.   Moscow 26 January 1835
                              Moscow 8 November 1919

   1029v [Concerto, violin, Op. 3, A minor]
   1.Allegro 2.Andante 3.Finale: Allegro
   Solo Vn.-2,2,2,2-2,2,3-Timp.-Str.
   Score: Ms. 109 p.
   Parts: Kistner, Leipzig [n.d.]

BIANCHINI, GUIDO.   Venice 27 April 1888

   3926 [Chimeras, symphonic poem]   *23'*
   3(3rd alt. Picc.),3*,3*,3*-4,3,3,1-Timp.,Perc.-
   Hp.-Str.
   Ricordi, Milan, ᶜ1935
   Miniature score 141 p.
   First performance Monte Carlo, April 1925,
   G. Lauwergne conductor.

BICHELS, H.

   713c Concertino (Variations brillantes) [for
   contrabass and orchestra, Op. 4]
   Solo Cb.-1,2,2,2-2,2,1-Timp.-Str.
   Score: Ms. 47 p.
   Parts: Oertel, Hannover [n.d.]

BIEBL, FRANZ.   Pursruck, Bavaria 1 September 1906

   4648 Wem Gott will rechte Gunst erweisen
   [To whomever God shows true grace (Songs of
   the year). Ten folksongs for strings, flute,
   oboe or clarinet and trumpet (ad lib.)]
   1.[Ah, bitter winter] 2.[Toward spring]
   3.[Winter is gone] 4.[Greetings, fair May]
   5.[May, May, lusty May] 6.Wem Gott will
   rechte Gunst erweisen 7.[You little birds]
   8.[The woods are already gay] 9.[Still]
   10.[My children]
   Fl.,Ob.(or Cl.)-Tpt.(or Cl.)-Voice-Str.
   Ludwig Voggenreiter Verlag, Potsdam, ᶜ1943
   Score 17 p.

BIELFELD, AUGUST.   Hamburg 20 May 1847
                           Hamburg 14 February 1924

   875m [Divertimento, bassoon and orchestra,
   D minor]
   Solo Bn.-1,0,2,1-2Hn.-Str.
   Score: Ms. 17 p.
   Parts: A.E. Fischer, Bremen [n.d.]

BIGGS, JOHN.   Los Angeles 18 October 1932

   6941 Symphonic ode   *5'*
   2*,2*,2,2-4,3,3,1-Timp.,Perc.-Hp.-Str.
   Ms.
   Score 32 p. Large folio
   Commissioned by the Peter Britt Festival
   Orchestra. Composed 1971. First performance
   Jacksonville, Oregon, August 1971, Britt Fes-
   tival Orchestra, John Trudeau conductor.

   6926 Symphony no. 1   *27'*
   1.Andante sostenuto – Allegro moderato 2.Ada-
   gio mesto (Passacaglia) 3.Allegro energico
   2,2,2,2-4,2,2,1-Timp.,Perc.-Str.
   Ms.
   Score 140 p.
   Composed 1964. First performance Antwerp, 15
   May 1965, Antwerp Philharmonic, the composer
   conducting. Second movement in memoriam
   John Fitzgerald Kennedy.

BILANTER, M.
   See: BLANTER, MATVEI ISAACOVICH.

BILLI, VINCENZO.
                 b. Brisighella (Romagna) 4 April 1869

   1563s Chant du ruisseau [The brook song,
   character piece, Op. 191]
   Str.
   Score: Ms. 8 p.
   Parts: Carisch & Jänichen, Milan, ᶜ1909

   813s Mon dernier rêve [My last dream, slow
   waltz, Op. 100]
   Str.
   Ricordi, Milan [n.d.]
   Score 8 p.

BILOTTI, ANTON.   New York 17 January 1906
                         New York 10 November 1963

   724p [Concerto, piano]   *28'*
   1.Maestoso 2.Allegro 3.Andante 4.Rondo –
   Allegro
   Solo Pno.-3*,2,3*,3*-4,3,3,1-Timp.,Perc.-Cel.,
   Hp.-Str.
   Ms.
   Score 218 p. Large folio
   Composed 1936. First performance New York, 21
   March 1938, National Orchestral Association,
   Leon Barzin conductor, the composer as soloist.

BIMBONI, ORESTE.   Florence 1846
                          Florence August 1905

   1505s [Pizzicato, figure polka from the opera
   La Modella]
   Str.
   Score: Ms. 5 p.
   Parts: Hansen, Copenhagen [n.d.]

BINDER, ABRAHAM WOLFE.
                    New York City 13 January 1895
                    New York City 10 October 1966

   1820s Concertante, for string orchestra   *12'*
   1.Largo 2.Menuetto 3.Hora
   Str.
   Ms.
   Score 28 p. Large folio
   Composed 1938. First performance Town Hall,
   New York, 22 November 1938, Moritz chamber
   Orchestra, Edvard Moritz conductor.

   826p King David, rhapsody for piano and   *15'*
   orchestra
   Solo Pno.-3*,2,2,2-4,2,3,1-Timp.,Perc.-Str.
   Ms.

Score 55 p. Large folio
Composed 1941-42.

3113 Symphonic suite no. 2   *12'*
1.Work (Road workers) 2.Prayer 3.Dance (hora)
4*,3*,3*,2-4,2,3,1-Timp.,Perc.-Pno.-Str.
Ms.
Score 55 p.
*First movement originally composed for piano,
1934. Entire suite composed 1935.*

3379 Theodore Herzl, overture-fantasy   *17'*
for symphony orchestra
3*,2,2,2-4,2,3,1-Timp.,Perc.-Str.
Ms.
Score 46 p. Large folio
*Theodore Herzl was the founder and first
leader of the modern Zionist movement, born
Budapest, 1860, died Vienna, 1904. Composed
1938-39. First performance New York, March
1942, Y.M.H.A. Symphony Orchestra, Boris
Schwarz conductor.*

3612 Three Palestinian pioneer pictures,   *15'*
symphonic suite no. 3
1.Watchman's song 2.Aspiration 3.To the land!
3*,2(2nd alt. E.H.),2,2-4,2,4,1-Timp.,Perc.-
Cel.,Hp.-Str.
Ms.
Score 60 p. Large folio
*Second movement originally composed for piano,
1932. Entire suite composed 1936-38.*

BINGE, RONALD.   Derby, England 15 July 1910

7234 Simple serenade, for string   *4'*
orchestra, guitar and piano
Pno.,Guit.-Str.
Edward B. Marks Music Corporation, New York,
c1974
Score 12 p.
Composed 1973.

BINGHAM, SETH. Bloomfield, New Jersey 16 April 1882
                    New York City 21 June 1972

3114 Memories of France   *13'*
1.Carillon de Chateau Thierry 2.Love in the
fields 3.Mid-Lent in Paris
3(3rd alt. Picc.),3*,3*,2-4,4,3,1-Timp.,Perc.
Org.(or Harm.),Cel.,Hp.-Str.
Ms.
Score 82 p.
Composed 1921.

3186 Pioneer America   *17'*
1.Redskin rhapsody 2.Sailing over Jordan
3.Along the frontier 4.Puritan procession
2(2nd alt. Picc.),2(2nd alt. E.H.),3*,2-4,4,3,
1-Timp.,Perc.-Cel.,Hp.-Str.
Ms.
Score 76 p.
*Composed 1919. First performance New York,
1924, Columbia University Orchestra, Douglas
Moore conductor.*

6973 Tame animal tunes, Op. 20   *19'*
1.Duck a la barcarolle: Andantino 2.Rabbit-
occatina: Vivace e leggiero (quick and slick)

3.New kittens: Smooth and velvety 4.Caper the
billy-goat: Allegro vigoroso 5.Pig in slumber:
Andante, with well-fed, dreamy movement 6.
Love-sick rooster: Moderato e tranquillo 7.
Puppy song: Allegretto, very friendly 8.
Dignified ruminations of a cow: Lento, con
moto tranquillo - Without climax 9.Variations
on a turkey (interlarded with goose-step)
Rather fast, poco pomposo
1(alt. Picc.),1(alt. E.H.),1,1-1,1-Timp.,Perc.-
Str.
Ms.
Score 84 p.

BINKERD, GORDON.   Lynch, Nebraska 22 May 1916

263m Studenten-Schmauss [Student's ban-   *11'*
quet] for organ solo and double brass choir
1.Intrada 2.Passamezzo antico 3.Canzona
Solo Org.-Choir I: 2Sax.(AT)-2Hn.,Tuba; Choir
II: 2Tpt.,3Tbn.,Tuba
Ms. Composers Facsimile Edition, New York,
c1962 by Gordon Binkerd
Score 68 p.
*Based on the following: 1.Intrada from Ban-
chetto Musicale by Johann Hermann Schein, 1617;
2.Passamezzo Antico from Orgel oder Instrument
Tabulatur by Elias Nikolaus Ammerbach, 1571;
3.Canzona XIII from Sacrae Symphoniae by Giovanni Gabrieli, 1597. Composed 1962. First
performance Urbana, Illinois, 11 November 1962,
University of Illinois Wind Ensemble, Robert
Gray conductor, Paul Pettinga soloist.*

6126 Sun singer for large orchestra   *13'*
3(3rd alt. Picc.),3*,3(3rd alt. B.Cl.),3*-4,3,
3,1-Timp.,Perc.-Hp.-Str.
Ms. Composers Facsimile Edition, New York,
c1956 by Gordon Binkerd
Score 79 p. Large folio
*Commissioned by the University of Illinois.
Composed 1952 for the Festival of Contemporary
Arts, University of Illinois. First perform-
ance Urbana, Illinois, University of Illinois
Symphony Orchestra, Rafael Kubelik conductor.*

6127 Symphony no. 1   *23'*
1.Allegretto 2.Adagio 3.Allegro
3*,3*,3*,3*-4,3,3,1-Timp.,Perc.-Hp.-Str.
Ms.
Score 167 p. Large folio
*Commissioned by the University of Illinois for
the 1955 Festival of Contemporary Arts. Composed 1955. First performance Urbana, Illinois,
20 March 1955, University of Illinois Symphony
Orchestra, Bernard Goodman conductor.*

6135 Symphony no. 2   *30'*
1.Allegro moderato e risoluto 2. ♪ =69
3*(2nd alt. Alto Fl.),3*,3*,3*-3,3,3,1-Str.
Ms. Composers Facsimile Edition, New York,
c1957 by Gordon Binkerd
Score 95 p. Large folio
*Commissioned by the Fromm Musical Foundation
and the University of Illinois for the 1957
Festival of Contemporary Arts. Composed 1956-
57. First performance Urbana, Illinois, 13
April 1957, University of Illinois Symphony
Orchestra, Bernard Goodman conductor.*

Binkerd, Gordon

6136 Symphony no. 3   *13'*
Maestoso - Allegro moderato - Andante - Allegro
moderato - Andante - Allegro moderato -
Maestoso - Allegro
3*,2,2,2-3,3,3,1-Timp.-Str.
Ms. Composers Facsimile Edition, New York,
c1968 by Gordon Binkerd
Score 90 p. Large folio
Composed 1959. First performance New York, 6
January 1961, Music in the Making Concert,
Howard Shanet conductor.

6436 Symphony no. 4   *23'*
1.Adagio 2. ♩.♩. =76
2(2nd alt. Picc.),2,2,2-3,2,2-Timp.-Str.
Ms. Composers Facsimile Edition, New York,
c1963 by Gordon Binkerd
Score 190 p. Large folio
Commissioned by the Women's Association of the
St. Louis Symphony Orchestra. Composed 1963.
First performance St. Louis, 12 October 1963,
St. Louis Symphony Orchestra, Eleazar de
Carvalho conductor.

6566 Three canzonas for brass choir   *9'*
3Hn.,3Tpt.,3Tbn.,Tuba
Ms. Composers Facsimile Edition, New York,
c1960 by Gordon Binkerd
Score 18 p.
Original title: Canzone 1, 2, 3. Composed
1960. First performance University of Illi-
nois, Urbana, 3 May 1960, University of Illi-
nois Wind Ensemble, Robert Gray conductor.

BIRD, ARTHUR.   Belmont, Massachusetts 23 July 1856
                Berlin 22 December 1923

300 [A carnival scene, Op. 5]   *10'*
3*,3*,2,2-4,3,3,1-Timp.,Perc.-Hp.-Str.
Hainauer, Breslau, 1887
Score 46 p.
Composed 1886. First American performance
26 July 1886, Theodore Thomas conductor.

7207 Galop for military band
3*,2,4(1 Cl. in E-flat),3*-4,4,4,Alto Hn.,2Ten.
Hn.,Bar.,2Tuba-S.Dr.,B.Dr.
Ms.
Score 27 p.

610s [Gavotte, for string orchestra,   *4'*
from Op. 7, C major]
Str.
Dörffel, Leipzig [n.d.]
Score 11 p.

7101 [Introduction and fugue for orchestra and
organ, Op. 16, D minor]
3*,2,2,3*-4,2,3,1-Timp.-Org.-Str.
Ms.
Score 52 p.
Composed 1886, originally for orchestra. Bird
added the organ part to the score after tran-
scribing this for piano 4-hands. Dedicated to
Georg Vierling.

201m [Meditation, for harmonium and strings,
Op. 43. Arranged by Richard Francke]

Solo Harm.-Str.
Paul Koeppen, Berlin. c1898 by Breitkopf &
Härtel, Leipzig
Score 7 p.
Composed 1898 for string orchestra. First
performance Berlin, 1898, C. Zimmer conductor.

5762 [Symphony no. 1, Op. 8, A major]   *33'*
1.Allegro moderato 2.Andante ma non troppo
3.Vivo 4.Andante sostenuto
2,2,2,2-4,2,3-Timp.,Trgl.,Cym.-Str.
G. Schirmer, New York, c1886
Score 67 p.
Composed 1885. First performance Singakademie
Concert, Berlin, 4 February 1886, the composer
conducting. Dedicated to Count Curt von
Seckendorff.

5261 [Third little suite for large   *22'*
orchestra, Op. 32, C major]
1.Allegretto 2.Andante 3.Allegro con brio
4.Allegretto
3*,2,2,2-4,2,3,1-Timp.,B.Dr.,Trgl.-Hp.-Str.
Arthur P. Schmidt, Boston, c1892
Score 86 p.
This work is also known as Souvenirs of Sum-
mer Saturdays. Composed 1890. First per-
formance Chicago, 12 June 1893, Columbia
Exposition Orchestra, Theodore Thomas con-
ductor.

204m Two pieces for solo flute and small
orchestra, Op. 17
1.Oriental scene 2.Oriental caprice
No. 1: Solo Fl.-E.H.-Hp.-Str.
No. 2: Solo Fl.-0,2,2,2-2Hn.-Perc.-Str.
Ms.
Score 54 p.
Composed 1887 for Joachim Andersen.

373m [Variations on an American folksong, for
flute and orchestra, Op. 34]
Solo Fl.-1,2,2,2-2-Timp.,Perc.-Str.
Score: Ms. 44 p. Large folio
Parts: Max Leichssenring, Hamburg [n.d.]
The theme is Stephen Foster's Old Folks at
Home. Composed 1891.

301s [Waltz minuet, string orchestra, Op. 39
no. 2, A major]
Str.
Breitkopf & Härtel, Leipzig, c1903
Score 5 p.

BISCHOFF, HERMANN.
                Duisburg, Germany 7 January 1868
                Berlin 25 January 1936

6997 [Symphony no. 1, Op. 16, E major]   *45'*
1.Sehr schnell und feurig 2.Sehr ruhig und
getragen 3.Presto 4.Allegro moderato
3(3rd alt. Picc.),3*,3(1Cl. in D),3*-6,3,3,1-
Timp.,Perc.-Hp.-Str.
Leuckart, Leipzig, c1906
Score 235 p.
First performance Essen, Germany, 24 May 1906,
Boston Symphony Orchestra, Karl Muck conductor.

6972 [Symphony no. 2, D minor]   40'
1.Allegro non troppo 2.Intermezzo 3.Adagio
4.Allegro molto vivace e con brio
3(2nd&3rd alt. Picc.),3*,3*,3*-4,3,3,1-Timp.,
Perc.-Hp.-Str.
Leuckart, Leipzig [c1901]
Score 150 p.

BISCHOFF, KASPAR JAKOB.   Ansbach 7 April 1823
                              Munich 26 October 1893

671c [Concert piece in the form of a vocal
  scene, Op. 40, F major]
Solo Vc.-2,2,2,2-2,2,1(ad lib.)-Timp.-Str.
Score: Ms. 89 p.
Parts: Breitkopf & Härtel, Leipzig [1873]

698c [Concerto, violoncello, no. 2, Op. 43,
  A minor]
1.Allegro appassionato 2.Andante sostenuto
3.Rondo: Allegro capriccio molto vivace
Solo Vc.-2,2,2,2-4,2,1-Timp.-Hp.-Str.
Score: Ms. 199 p.
Parts: Joh. André, Offenbach am Main [1875]

BISQUERTT PRADO, PROSPERO.
            Santiago de Chile 8 June 1881
            Santiago de Chile 2 August 1959

4149 Noche buena [Christmas Eve, symphonic
  triptych]
1.[About the poor child] 2.[About the rich
child] 3.[On the mall]
3*,3*,3*,2-4,3,3,1-Timp.,Perc.-Pno.,Cel.,Hp.-
Str.
Ms.
Score 56 p.
Composed 1936. First performance 10 May 1937,
Orquesta Sinfónico de Santiago, Armando Carvajal conductor.

BITTNER, JULIUS.   Vienna 9 April 1874
                        Vienna 10 January 1939

2389 [Dances from Austria]   26'
1.Andantino 2.Polka rhythmus 3.Rühiges Länd-
lerzeitmass 4.Flott und feurig 5.Geschwind
6.Ziemlich langsam
3(all alt. Picc.),2,2,2-4,3,3,1-Timp.,Perc.-
Hp.-Str.
Ms.
Score 91 p.
Composed 1919. First performance Vienna, 1919,
Rudolf Nilius conductor.

2345 [Fatherland, symphonic poem]   16'
3(3rd alt. Picc.),3(3rd alt. Alto Ob.),4*,4*-
6,4,B.Tpt.,3,1-Timp.,Perc.-Org.,2Hp.-Str.
Universal Edition, Vienna, c1916
Score 74 p.
Composed 1912. First performance Vienna, 19
December 1915.

912 Der Musikant. Vorspiel   6'
Soli: 3Vn.,Va.,Vc.-3,3,3,3-4,3,3,1-Timp.-2Hp.-
Str.
Schott's Söhne, Mainz, c1911
Score 8 p.

From the opera composed 1907-08. First performance Vienna, 12 April 1910, Bruno Walter
conductor.

1131 Der Musikant. Serenade   4'
1,1,2,1-2Hn.-Str.
Schott's Söhne, Mainz, c1911
Score 6 p.

2119 [Symphony, F minor]   45'
1.Allegro 2.Sehr langsam 3.Sehr rasch (ganze
Takte schlagen) 4.Scherzo
3(3rd alt. Picc.),2(2nd alt. E.H.),3,3(3rd alt.
C.Bn.)-4,3,3,1-Timp.,Perc.-Str.
Universal Edition, Vienna, c1923
Score 110 p.
Composed 1922. First performance Vienna, De-
cember 1923, at a Philharmonic concert, Felix
Weingartner conductor.

BIZET, GEORGES.   Paris 25 October 1838
                Bougival, near Paris 3 June 1875

Born: Alexandre César Léopold Bizet

56 [L'Arlésienne, incidental music to   20'
Alphonse Daudet's play. Orchestra suite no. 1]
Revised by Fritz Hoffmann
1.Ouverture 2.Minuetto 3.Adagietto 4.Carillon
2,2(1st alt. E.H.),2,2-Alto Sax. in E-flat-4,4,
3-Timp.,S.Dr.-Hp.(or Pno.)-Str.
Breitkopf & Härtel, Leipzig [n.d.]
Score 55 p.

57 [L'Arlésienne, incidental music to   25'
Alphonse Daudet's play. Orchestra suite no. 2]
Revised by Fritz Hoffmann
1.Pastorale 2.Intermezzo 3.Menuetto 4.Faran-
dole
2(2nd alt. Picc.),2(1st alt. E.H.),2,2-Sax.-4,
4,3-Timp.,S.Dr.-Hp.(or Pno.)-Str.
Breitkopf & Härtel, Leipzig [n.d.]
Score 60 p.
Both suites composed 1872. First performance
Paris, 1 October 1872.

471 [Carmen. Orchestral suite no. 1]   11'
1.Prelude 1a.Aragonaise 2.Intermezzo 3.Seque-
dille 4.Les dragons d'Alcala 5.Les toréadors
2*,2*,2,2-4Hn.,2Cnt.,3Tbn.-Timp.,Perc.-2Hp.-Str.
Score: Kalmus, New York [n.d.]. 47 p.
Parts: Luck's Music Library, Detroit [n.d.]

472 [Carmen. Orchestral suite no. 2]   19'
6.Marche des contrebandiers 7.Habañera 8.Noc-
turne 9.Chanson de toréador 10.La garde mon-
tante 11.Danse bohême
2*,2*,2,2-4,0,2Cnt.,3,1-Timp.,Perc.-2Hp.-Str.
Broude Bros., New York, c1952
Score 87 p.
Both suites from the opera based on Prosper
Mérimée's story, composed 1873. First performance Opéra-Comique, Paris, 3 March 1875.

5236 [Chromatic variations. Transcribed for
  orchestra by Felix Weingartner]
2(2nd alt. Picc.),2*(E.H. alt. 2nd Ob.),2,2-4,
2,3-Timp.,Perc.-Hp.-Str.

Bizet, Georges

Choudens, Paris, ^c1933
Score 54 p.
*Original title: Variations Chromatiques de
Concert. Composed for piano solo, 1868.*

4264 [Djamileh. Overture]   5'
2(2nd alt. Picc.),2,2,2-4,2,3-Timp.,Perc.-Hp.-
Str.
Simrock, Berlin [1892]
Score 39 p.
*From the opera in one act with libretto by
Louis Gallet based on Alfred de Musset's
Namouna. Composed 1871. First performance
Opéra Comique, Paris, 22 May 1872.*

489 [Jeux d'enfants, Op. 22. Petite   10'
suite d'orchestre]
1.March 2.Berceuse 3.Impromptu 4.Duo
5.Gallop
2(2nd alt. Picc.),2,2,2-4,2-Timp.,Perc.-Str.
Kalmus, New York [n.d.]
Score 55 p.
*Jeux d'enfants originally composed for piano
duet; five pieces from it arranged for orchestra by the composer, 1872. First performance
Paris, 2 March 1873, Edouard Colonne conductor.*

825 [La jolie fille de Perth. Scènes   12'
bohémiennes, ballet et fragments symphoniques]
1.Prélude 2.Sérénade 3.Marche 4.[Bohemian
dance]
2(2nd alt. Picc.),2,2,2-4,2,3-Timp.,Perc.-Hp.-
Str.
Choudens, Paris [n.d.]
Score 56 p.

895 Patrie [Fatherland, dramatic overture,   12'
Op. 19]
2(alt. Picc.),2,2,2-4,2,2Cnt.,3,1(Ophicl.)-
Timp.,Perc.-2Hp.-Str.
Choudens, Paris [n.d.]
Score 59 p.
Composed 1873. First performance Paris, 1874.

4310 [The pearl fishers. Prelude]
2,2,2,2-4Hn.-Timp.-Str.
Simrock, Berlin [1892]
Score 10 p.
*From the opera in three acts with libretto by
Eugène Cormon and Michel Carré. Composed
1862-63. First performance Paris, 30 Septem-
ber 1863.*

4344 [The pearl fishers. Hindu dance]
2(2nd alt. Picc.),2,2,2-4,2,3-Timp.,Perc.-Str.
Simrock, Berlin [1892]
Score 30 p.

685 [Roma, third orchestral suite]   25'
1.Andante tranquillo 2.Allegretto vivace
3.Andante molto 4.Allegro vivacissimo
2(2nd alt. Picc.),3*,2,2-4,2,3-Timp.-2Hp.-Str.
Choudens, Paris [n.d.]
Score 147 p.
*Composed 1866-68. First performance Paris,
1869.*

2917 [Symphony no. 1, C major]   40'
1.Allegro vivo 2.Adagio 3.Allegro vivace
4.Allegro vivace
2,2,2,2-4,2-Timp.-Str.
Universal Edition, Vienna, ^c1935
Score 91 p.
*Composed 1855. First performance Basel, 26
February 1935, Felix Weingartner conductor.*

BJÖRKANDER, NILS.   Stockholm 28 June 1893
                    Södertälje, Sweden 5 March 1972

5113 [Sketches from the Swedish archi-   11'
pelago. Transcribed for orchestra by Tor Mann]
1.Allegro giocoso 2.Vivace ma non troppo
3.Lento sostenuto 4.Poco lento
2(both alt. Picc.),2,2,2-2Hn.-Timp.,Perc.-Hp.-
Str.
Nordiska Musikförlaget, Stockholm, ^c1943
Score 23 p.
*Originally composed for piano as Fyra Skärgårds-
skisser [Four Sketches from the Swedish Archi-
pelago]. This orchestration 1923.*

BLACHER, BORIS.   Newchwang (Niu-chuang),
                    Manchuria 6 January 1903
                         Berlin 30 January 1975

4335 [Concertante music for orchestra,   15'
Op. 10]
2(2nd alt. Picc.),2,2,2-4,2,3,1-Timp.-Str.
Bote & Bock, Berlin, ^c1938
Score 33 p.
*Composed 1937. First performance Berlin, 12
June 1937, Berlin Philharmonic Orchestra, Carl
Schuricht conductor. Dedicated to Carl
Schuricht.*

326p [Concerto, piano, no. 1, Op. 28]   22'
1.Adagio - Presto 2.Andante 3.Allegro
Solo Pno.-1,1,1,1-2,1,1-Str.
Bote & Bock, Berlin, ^c1948
Score 95 p.
*Composed 1947. First performance Göttingen,
Germany, 20 March 1948, Municipal Orchestra of
Göttingen, Fritz Lehmann conductor, Gerty Her-
zog soloist.*

2169s [Concerto for strings, Op. 20]   20'
1.Sonate 2.Scherzo 3.Thema con variazioni
Str.
Ms.
Score 38 p.
*Composed 1940. First performance Hamburg, 18
October 1942, Hamburg Philharmonic Orchestra,
Eugen Jochum conductor.*

6027 [Festival in the South. Suite from   24'
the ballet, Op. 6a]
1.Ouvertüre 2.Tango 3.Dorfwalzer [Village
waltz] 4.Nachtstück 5.Eifersuchtstanz
[Jealous dance] 6.Liebesduett 7.Finale
2(2nd alt. Picc.),2,2,2-2,2,2-Timp.,Perc.-
Accordion(ad lib.)-Str.
Bote & Bock, Berlin, ^c1938
Score 65 p.
From the dance drama in one act, with scenario

by Ellen Petz. Composed 1935. First performance Berlin, Deutscher Kurzwellensender Broadcast, December 1935, Erich Hannemann conductor.

6118 Music for Cleveland, Op. 53   10'
3*(Picc. alt. 3rd Fl.),3*,3*(B.Cl. alt. 3rd
Cl.),3*(C.Bn. alt. 3rd Bn.)-4,4,3,1-Timp.,
Perc.-Hp.-Str.
Bote & Bock, Berlin, c1957
Score 75 p.
Commissioned by the Cleveland Orchestra. Composed 1957. First performance Cleveland, 21 November 1957, Cleveland Orchestra, George Szell conductor.

6025 [Orchestra variations on a theme of   17'
Paganini, Op. 26]
3(3rd alt. Picc.),3*,3(3rd alt. B.Cl.),3(3rd
alt. C.Bn.)-4,3,3,1-Timp.-Str.
Bote & Bock, Berlin, c1947
Score 81 p.
Based on Paganini's Caprice, Op. 1 no. 24. Composed 1946. First performance Leipzig, 27 November 1947, Gewandhaus-Orchester, Herbert Albert conductor.

BLACKWOOD, EASLEY.   Indianapolis 21 April 1933

6331 Chamber symphony for fourteen wind   17'
instruments, Op. 2
1.Sonata 2.Romanza 3.Toccata
2(2nd alt. Picc.),2,3*,3*-4Hn.
Elkan-Vogel, Philadelphia, c1958
Score 116 p.
Composed 1954.

5927 Symphony no. 1, Op. 3   30'
1.Andante maestoso 2.Andante comodo 3.Scherzo:
Allegretto grotesco, molto rigoroso il tempo
4.Andante sostenuto
4(3rd & 4th alt. Picc.),3(3rd alt. E.H.),4*(3rd
alt. Cl. in E-flat),4*-6,4(1Tpt. in D),3,1-
Timp.,Perc.-Cel.-Str.
Elkan-Vogel, Philadelphia, c1958
Score 121 p. Large folio
Composed 1955.

BLAIR-OLIPHANT, LILIAN.

766s Suite in G minor, for string orchestra
1.Prelude 2.Allemande 3.Sarabande
4.Bourrée I 5.Bourrée II 6.Courant 7.Gigue
Str.
Ms.
Score 18 p.

BLANC, ADOLPHE.
                Manosque, Basses-Alpes 24 June 1828
                            Paris May 1885

951m [Romance for oboe and horn, with string
orchestra accompaniment, Op. 43 no. 2]
Solo Ob., Solo Hn.-Str.
Score: Ms. 7 p.
Parts: Costallat, Paris [n.d.]
Originally composed for horn (or violoncello) and piano.

BLANCAFORT DE ROSELLÓ, MANUEL.
                            b. Barcelona 12 August 1897

4421 [Morning of the festival at Puig-   14'
Graciós, symphonic tableau]
3*,3*,2,2-4,2,2-Timp.,Cym.,Trgl.-Cel.-Hp.-Str.
Senart, Paris, c1930
Score 62 p.
Composed 1927. First performance Barcelona, 1929.

BLANCHET, EMILE R.   Lausanne 17 July 1877
                          Pully 27 March 1943

491p [Concert piece, piano and orchestra,
Op. 14, A-flat major]
Solo Pno.-2(2nd alt. Picc.),2(2nd alt. E.H.),2,
2-4,2,3-Timp.,Perc.-Str.
Rózsavölgyi, Budapest, c1912
Score 63 p.

BLANTER, MATVEI ISAACOVICH.
                b. Pochep, district of Chernigov,
                        Russia 10 February 1903

Also transliterated as Bilanter

5139 [Song of Shchors. Transcribed for orchestra
by V. Knushevich]
Voice Solo-1,0,1-Sax.(AAT)-0,2,1,1-S.Dr.,
B.Dr.-Banjo-Str.
[Moscow State Publishers, Moscow, n.d.]
Score in reduction 9 p.
Text by M. Golodny.

BLARAMBERG, PAVEL IVANOVICH.
                Orenburg, Russia 26 September 1841
                            Nice 28 March 1907

5292 [Phantasmagoria, sinfonietta]
1.Moderato - Allegro 2.Andante 3.Quasi
andante - Allegro molto
2(2nd alt. Picc.),2,2,2-4,2,3,1-Timp.,Cym.-
Str.
W. Bessel, St. Petersburg [n.d.]
Score 103 p.

BLASIUS, MATHIEU-FRÉDÉRIC.
                Lauterburg, Alsace 27 April 1758
                            Versailles 1829

887m [Concerto, clarinet, no. 2, F major]
1.[No tempo indicated] 2.Romanza 3.[No tempo
indicated]
Solo Cl.-2Ob.-2Hn.-Str.
Score: Ms. 83 p.
Parts: Magasin de Musique, Paris [n.d.]

BLASSER, GUSTAV.   Vienna 12 April 1857

400s Aufblick zu den Sternen, Op. 84 [Nocturne
for string orchestra and harp. Arranged by
William Happich]
Hp.-Str.
Ms.
Score 13 p.

Blasser, Gustav

585s [Bagatelles, string quartet or string
orchestra, Op. 68]
1.Traumverloren 2.Frühling ist da 3.Unter
den Linden 4.Heitere Kahnfahrt 5.Im grünen
Kranze 6.Bauerntanz
Str.
André, Offenbach a.M. [n.d.]
Score 31 p.

2048 Ballade, Op. 82   4'
3*,2,2,2-4,2,3-Timp.,Perc.-Hp.-Str.
Doblinger, Vienna [n.d.]
Score 7 p.
*Composed 1889. First performance Vienna,
November 1889, Eduard Strauss conductor.*

800s Idyllen, Op. 105
1.Müllerin träumt [The miller's wife is dream-
ing] 2.Morgenständchen [Morning serenade] 3.
Neckerei [Bantering]
Hp.(ad lib.)-Str.
André, Offenbach a.M. [n.d.]
Score 11 p.

609s [Little serenade, string orchestra, Op.
88, D major]
1.Prelude 2.Adagio 3.Tempo di valse
Str.
André, Offenbach a.M. [n.d.]
Score 23 p.

681 [Suite, Op. 76, D major]   25'
1.Prelude 2.Ballade 3.Tambourin 4.Inter-
mezzo 5.Gavotte 6.Finale
1,1,2,1-2,2,1-Timp.,Perc.-Str.
André, Offenbach a.M. [n.d.]
Score 71 p.
*Composed 1888. First performance Dresden,
December 1893, August Trenkler conductor.*

BLÄTTERMAN, H.

1426s Am Springquell [At the spring] Inter-
mezzo
Solo String Sextet-Hp.-Vn.I,II,III(ad lib.),
Va.,Vc.
Louis Oertel, London [n.d.]
Score 19 p.

803m [Concertino, trumpet (cornet à pistons)
E-flat major]
Solo Tpt.(Cnt.)-2,2,2,2-2,2,3-Timp.-Str.
Score: Ms. 99 p.
Parts: Louis Oertel, London [n.d.]

BLECH, LEO.   Aachen 21 April 1871
                                     Berlin 24 August 1958

44s [Gondellied (Barcarole) from Op. 11.
Arranged by Leo Blech]
Str.
Süddeutscher Musikverlag, Strassburg, c1902
Score 5 p.

1379 Waldwanderung, tone poem, Op. 8   24'
3*,3*,3*,3*-4,3,3,1-Timp.-Hp.-Str.
Schott, London [n.d.]
Score 33 p.

*Composed 1904. First performance at a Philhar-
monic Concert, Prague, the composer conducting.*

BLEICHMANN, YULY IVANOVICH.
                          St. Petersburg 6 December 1868
                          St. Petersburg 8 January 1910

2429 Baletnaia suita, Op. 22
1.[Overture] 2.[Dance of the buffoons]
3.[Oriental dance] 4.[Dance of the will-o'-
the-wisps] 5.[Vision] 6.[Waltz]
3*,3*,2,2-4,2,3,1-Timp.,Perc.-Hp.-Str.
Jurgenson, Moscow [n.d.]
Score 36 p.

2248 [Suite no. 2, Op. 38]
1.Intermezzo (Panorama) 2.Valse des dryades
3.Dans les champs 4.Danse russe 5.Cortège
héroïque
3*,3*,3*,2-4,2,3,1-Timp.,Perc.-Hp.-Str.
Jurgenson, Moscow [n.d.]
Score 119 p.

3829 [Symphony, Op. 18, A major]
1.Grave maestoso – Allegro non troppo 2.Andan-
te elegiaco 3.Allegro non troppo 4.Allegro
giusto
3*,3*,2,2-4,2,3,1-Timp.-Str.
Wispolsky, St. Petersburg [n.d.]
Score 206 p.
Composed ca.1892.

BLEYLE, KARL.
            Feldkirch, Vorarlberg, Austria 7 May 1880
                   Stuttgart, Germany 5 June 1969

795v [Concerto, violin, Op. 10, C major]
1.Allegro moderato 2.Larghetto 3.Allegro
giojoso
Solo Vn.-3*,2,2,2-4,3,3,1-Timp.,Trgl.-Hp.-Str.
Breitkopf & Härtel, Leipzig [n.d.]
Score 72 p.

2230 Gnomentanz [Gnome's dance], Op. 16   13'
3*,2,2,2-4,3,3-Timp.,Trgl.-Hp.-Str.
Kistner, Leipzig, c1910
Score 43 p.
Composed 1908. First performance Munich, 1910.

5086 [Overture to Goethe's Reynard the Fox,   7'
Op. 23]
3(all alt. Picc.),2,2,2-3,3,1-Timp.,Cym.,Trgl.
-Hp.(ad lib.)-Str.
Breitkopf & Härtel, Leipzig, c1914
Score 51 p.

BLISS, ARTHUR EDWARD DRUMMOND. London 2 August 1891
                               London 27 March 1975

5169 A colour symphony [original version]   35'
1.Purple 2.Red 3.Blue 4.Green
3(all alt. Picc.),3*,3*,3*-4,3,3,1-Timp.(2
players),Perc.-Hp.-Str.
J. Curwen, London, c1924
Score 133 p.
*Composed 1921-22 for the Gloucester Festival.
First performance Gloucester, 7 September 1922,
the composer conducting. Later revised, 1932,
and published by Boosey, London.*

Bloch, Ernest

3865 Fanfare for a political address
2Cl.-Tpt.-Speaker
Ms.
Score 1 p.
Composed ca.1921.

3816 Introduction and allegro   12'
3*,3*,3*,3*-4,3,3,1-Timp.,Perc.-Hp.-Str.
Universal Edition, London, c1937
Score 78 p.
First performance London, 8 September 1926,
the composer conducting.

4961 Mêlée fantasque   14'
3*,3*,3*,3*-4,3,3,1-Timp.,Perc.-Str.
J. Curwen, London, c1924
Score 51 p.
Composed 1921.

4238 Rout   6'
Sop. Voice Solo-Fl.,Cl.-S.Dr.,Glock.-Hp.-Str.
Goodwin & Tabb, London, c1921
Score 23 p.
Composed 1920. First performance First Inter-
national Festival of Modern Music, Salzburg,
7 August 1922.

6022 Two royal fanfares   4'
3Tpt.,3Tbn.,Tuba
Novello, London, c1960
Score in reduction 4 p.
Composed for the wedding of Her Royal Highness
Princess Margaret. First performance West-
minster Abbey, 6 May 1960, trumpeters of the
Royal Military School of Music.

BLITZSTEIN, MARC.   Philadelphia 2 March 1905
                             Martinique 22 January 1964

769p [Concerto, piano]   24'
1.Moderato molto - Allegro 2.Largo assai 3.
Allegro non troppo
Solo Pno.-3*,2,2,3*-4,2,3,1-Str.
Ms.
Score 127 p.
First performance New York, 1935 or 1936, at
a Composer's Forum Laboratory Concert.

3623 Orchestra variations   15'
3*,3*,4*(1Cl. in E-flat),3*-4,2,2Cnt.,3,1-
Timp.,Perc.-Pno.-Str.
Ms.
Score 60 p.
Composed 1934. This work, among others, was
the basis for the award of Guggenheim Fellow-
ships, 1940-41, 1941-42.

3689 [Surf and seaweed. Suite for the   16'
film]
1.Giocoso 2.Moderato 3.Allegro vivace
4.Andante 5. ♩=69
1,1,1,1(alt. C.Bn.)-Tpt.-Pno.-Str.(without
Cb.)
Ms.
Score 94 p.
Film by Ralph Steiner. Suite first performed
New York, 15 March 1931, at a Copland-Sessions
concert, An Evening of Music and Films,

members of the New York Philharmonic, Hugh
Ross conductor.

BLOCH, ERNEST.   Geneva 24 July 1880
                        Portland, Oregon 15 July 1959

1956 America, an epic rhapsody   45'
1. ...1620 (The soil - the Indians - England
- the Mayflower - the landing of the pilgrims)
2. ...1861-1865 (Hours of joy - hours of sorrow) 3.1926...(The present - the future)
3*,3*,3*,3*-4,3,3,1-Timp.,Perc.-Org.(ad lib.),
Cel.,2Hp.-Chorus-Str.
Birchard, Boston, c1928
Score 181 p.
Composed 1926-27. First performance simultan-
eously in Boston, Chicago, Cincinnati, Los
Angeles, New York, Philadelphia, San Francisco,
21 December 1928, after winning the prize
offered by the magazine Musical America for
the best American symphonic work.

1120v Baal Shem, three pictures of   12'
Chassidic life, for violin solo and orchestra
1.Vidui (Contrition) 2.Nigun (Improvisation)
3.Simchas Torah (Rejoicing)
Solo Vn.-2(2nd alt. Picc.),2,2,2-4,3-Timp.,
Perc.-Cel.,Hp.-Str.
Ms.
Score 52 p.
Originally composed for violin and piano, 1923;
orchestrated 1939. First performance New
York, 19 October 1941, New York City Symphony
of the WPA, Reginald Stewart conductor,
Joseph Szigeti soloist.

1113v [Concerto, violin and orchestra]   35'
1.Allegro deciso 2.Andante 3.Deciso
Solo Vn.-3*,3*,3*,3*-4,3,3,1-Timp.,Perc.-Cel.,
Hp.-Str.
Boosey & Hawkes, London, c1938
Score 154 p. Large folio
Composed 1937-38. First performance Cleveland,
15 December 1938, Cleveland Symphony Orchestra,
Dimitri Mitropoulos conductor, Joseph Szigeti
soloist.

1117s Concerto grosso, for string orchestra
with piano obbligato
1.Prelude 2.Dirge 3.Pastorale and rustic
dances 4.Fugue
Pno.(obbligato)-Str.
Summy-Birchard, Evanston, c1925
Score 48 p.
Composed 1924-25. First performance Los Angeles,
15 August 1925, the composer conducting.

2311s Concerto grosso II   18'
1.Maestoso - Allegro 2.Andante 3.Allegro 4.
Variations
4Soli(2Vn.,Va.,Vc.)-Str.
G. Schirmer, New York, c1952, 1953
Score 42 p.
Composed 1952. First performance BBC broad-
cast, 11 April 1953, BBC Symphony Orchestra,
Malcolm Sargent conductor. Won the New York
Music Critics Circle Award for symphonic music,
1953.

Bloch, Ernest

6756 Evocations, symphonic suite for   *16-17'*
orchestra
1.Contemplation 2.Houang Ti (God of War)
3.Renouveau [Springtime]
3(3rd alt. Picc.),2(2nd alt. E.H.),2,2-4,2,3,1-
Timp.,Perc.-Pno.,Cel.,Hp.-Str.
G. Schirmer, New York, c1937
Score 79 p.
Composed 1937. First performance 11 February
1938.

1993 Four episodes for chamber orchestra   *14'*
1.Humoresque macabre 2.Obsession 3.Calm 4.
Chinese
1,1,1,1-Hn.-Pno.-Str.
Birchard, Boston, c1929
Score 87 p.
Completed May, 1926. First performance New
York, 20 March 1927, New York Chamber Music
Society, Carolyn Beebe conductor.

2586 Helvetia, the land of mountains   *25'*
and its people; a symphonic fresco for
orchestra
4(3rd and 4th alt. Picc.),4*,4*,4*-6,4,3,1-
Timp.(2 players),Perc.-Cel.,2Hp.-Str.
Birchard, Boston, c1931
Score 88 p.
Composed 1900-29. Awarded a prize in the Vic-
tor Talking Machine Company competition, 1929-
30, as one of five outstanding works. First
performance Chicago, 18 February 1932, Chicago
Symphony Orchestra, Frederick Stock conductor.

1982 Hiver-printemps [Winter-spring] deux
poèmes
2(2nd alt. Picc.),2(2nd alt. E.H.),2,2-4,2,3,
1-Timp.,Trgl.-Hp.-Str.
G. Schirmer, New York, c1918
Score 41 p.
Composed 1905.

6771 Israel, symphony for orchestra   *30'*
4(3rd and 4th alt. Picc.),4*,4*,4*-6,4,3,1-
Timp.,Perc.-Cel.,2Hp.-Bass Voice Solo,4 Female
Voices(2Sop.,2Alto)-Str.
G. Schirmer, New York, c1924, 1925
Score 96 p.
Composed 1912-16. First performance New York,
3 May 1917, Society of the Friends of Music,
the composer conducting.

504c [Schelomo (Solomon), Hebrew rhapsody, *20'*
violoncello solo and orchestra]
Solo Vc.-3*,3*,3*,3*-4,3,3,1-Timp.,Perc.-Cel.,
2Hp.-Str.
G. Schirmer, New York, c1918
Score 77 p.
Composed 1916.

264p Scherzo fantasque for piano and   *9'*
orchestra
Solo Pno.-3*,3*,3*,3*-4,3,3,1-Timp.,Perc.-Hp.-
Str.
G. Schirmer, New York, c1950
Score 74 p.
Composed 1948. First performance, 2 December
1950.

6772 Sinfonia breve   *18'*
1.Moderato - Allegro 2.Andante 3.Allegro molto
4.Allegro deciso
3*,3*,3*,3*-4,3,3,1-Timp.,Perc.-Cel.,Hp.-Str.
G. Schirmer, New York, c1955
Score 82 p.
Composed 1952. First performance London, 11
April 1953, BBC Symphony Orchestra, Malcolm
Sargent conductor.

304v Suite hébraïque, for viola (or violin) and
orchestra
1.Rhapsodie 2.Processional 3.Affirmation
Solo Va.-2,2,2,2-4,3-Timp.,Perc.-Hp.-Str.
Ms.
Score 43 p.
Composed 1951.

4891 Suite symphonique   *20'*
1.Overture 2.Passacaglia 3.Finale
3(3rd alt. Picc.),3*,3*,3*-4,3,3,1-Timp.,Perc.-
Str.
Boosey & Hawkes, London, c1947
Score 120 p.
Composed 1944. First performance Philadelphia,
26 October 1945, Philadelphia Orchestra, Pierre
Monteux conductor.

1219 [Symphony, C-sharp minor]   *56'*
1.Lento - Allegro agitato ma molto energico 2.
Andante molto moderato 3.Vivace 4.Allegro en-
ergico e molto marcato
4(3rd and 4th alt. Picc.),3*,4,3*-4,4,3,2-
Timp.,Perc.-Pno.,2Hp.-Str.
Leuckart, Leipzig [n.d.]
Score 231 p.
Composed 1901-02. First performance Lausanne,
1910.

963 Trois poèmes juifs (Three Jewish   *23'*
poems)
1.Dance 2.Rite 3.Funeral procession
3*,3*,2,3*-4,3,3,1-Timp.,Perc.-Cel.,Hp.-Str.
G. Schirmer, New York, c1918
Score 87 p.
Composed 1913. First performance Boston, 1917.

420c Voice in the wilderness (Voix dans   *25'*
le désert), symphonic poem with violoncello
obbligato
1.Moderato (poco lento) 2.Poco lento 3.Mod-
erato 4.Adagio piacevole 5.Poco agitato 6.
Allegro
3(3rd alt. Picc.),3*,3*,3*-4,3,3,1-Timp.,Perc.
-Cel.,2Hp.-Str.
G. Schirmer, New York, c1936
Score 87 p. Large folio
Composed 1934-36.

BLOCH, JOSEF.   Budapest 5 January 1862
                               Budapest 6 May 1922

816v [Concerto, violin, Op. 64, A minor]
1.Allegro maestoso 2.Adagio cantabile 3.Moto
perpetuo: Allegro vivace ma non troppo
Solo Vn.-2(2nd alt. Picc.),2,2,2-4,2-Timp.-
Str.
Rozsnyai, Budapest [n.d.]
Score 61 p.

822v [Hungarian airs, one or two solo violins
and orchestra, Op. 49]
Solo Vn.-2(2nd alt. Picc.),2,2,2-2,2-Timp.-Str.
Rozsnyai, Budapest [n.d.]
Score 28 p.

2454 [Hungarian overture, Op. 20]
3*,3*,3*,3*-4,3,3,1-Timp.,Perc.-Hp.-Str.
Seemann, Leipzig [n.d.]
Score 65 p.

2455 [Hungarian rhapsody, Op. 31]
3*,2,2,3-4,3,3,1-Timp.,Perc.-Hp.-Str.
Seemann, Leipzig [n.d.]
Score 43 p.

1577 Ouverture solennelle, Op. 57, F major
3*,3*(E.H. or Tárogató),2,3*-4,4,3,1-Timp.,
Perc.-Hp.-Str.
Rozsnyai, Budapest [n.d.]
Score 51 p.
*Composed for inauguration of the new building
of the Royal Academy of Music, Budapest, 1907.*

1576 Suite idyllique, Op. 35
1.[In the open air] 2.[In the forest] 3.[In
the mountains] 4.[Homeward] 5.[The cabaret]
2(2nd alt. Picc.),2,2,2-2,2-Timp.,Trgl.-Str.
Rozsnyai, Budapest [n.d.]
Score 61 p.

631 Suite poétique, Op. 26   15'
1.Souvenir 2.Gavotte 3.Berceuse 4.March
2,1,2,2-2,1,Cnt.(ad lib.)-Timp.-Str.
Hawkes, London, c1901
Score 57 p.
Composed 1905. First performance Budapest, 1906.

164s [Suite for string orchestra, no. 1, Op. 6
D major]
1.Allegro con brio 2.Andante 3.Scherzo: Viva-
ce 4.Adagio - Allegro vivace
Str.
Ries & Erler, Berlin [n.d.]
Score 28 p.

173s [Suite for string orchestra, no. 2,
Op. 10, A major]
1.Allegro ma non troppo 2.Scherzo: Presto 3.
Adagio molto 4.Allegro vivace
Str.
Ries & Erler, Berlin [n.d.]
Score 39 p.

BLOCKX, JAN.   Antwerp 25 January 1851
                      Antwerp 26 May 1912

1682s Albumleaf
Str.
Ms.
Score 7 p.

5463 [Flemish dances, Op. 26]   22'
1.Allegretto 2.Scherzo 3.Un poco maestoso
4.Scherzo 5.Tempo risoluto
3*,2,2,2-4,3,3,1-Timp.,Perc.-Str.
Ménestrel-Heugel, Paris, c1898
Score 102 p.

BLOHM, SVEN.   Sweden 1907
                      Sweden 1956

1930s [Little partita for string orchestra]
1.Moderato un poco maestoso 2.Tempo alla sara-
banda 3.Molto vivace
Str.
Carl Gehrmans, Stockholm, c1942
Score 12 p.
Composed 1937.

BLOMDAHL, KARL-BIRGER.
          Växjö, Sweden 19 October 1916
          Kungsängen, near Stockholm 14 June 1968

1200v [Concerto, violin and string   16'
orchestra]
1.Allegro energico 2.Andante, molto tranquillo
3.Allegro giocoso
Solo Vn.-Str.
Ms.
Score 45 p.
*Composed 1946. First performance Stockholm,
1 October 1947, Concert Society of Stockholm,
Carl Garaguly conductor, Joseph Grünfarb soloist.*

5051 [Symphony no. 2]   21'
1.Maestoso - Allegro giusto 2.Molto tranquillo
3.Allegro assai
3*,2,3(2nd alt. B.Cl.;3rd alt. Cl. in E-flat),
2-4,3,3,1-Str.
Ms.
Score 98 p.
Composed 1947.

BLON, FRANZ VON.   Berlin 16 July 1861

1322s Auf Capri [barcarole for string orchestra]
Op. 55
Str.
Score: Ms. 5 p.
Parts: Oertel, Hannover [n.d.]

354s La danseuse [intermezzo]
Str.
Rühle & Wendling, Leipzig [n.d.]
Score 4 p.

352s Darf ich bitten [May I have the pleasure]
Op. 105
Str.
Zimmermann, Leipzig, c1910
Score 7 p.

353s Liebeständelei [Flirtation]
Str.
Rühle & Wendling [n.d.]
Score 4 p.

552s Puppen-Menuett [Doll-minuet]
Str.
Wernthal, Berlin, c1906
Score 4 p.

1228s Schlummerliedchen [Lullaby], Op. 106
Str.
Zimmermann, Leipzig, c1912
Score 3 p.

Blon, Franz von

613s Traumbild, Charakterstück, Op. 63
Str.(Final Chord: 2,2,2,2-4,2,3-Timp.,Perc.-
Str.)
Heinrichshofen's Verlag, Magdeburg, c1899
Score 7 p.

355s Traumverloren [Lost in dreams, study to
the painting by H. v. Bodenhausen]
Str.
Rühle & Wendling, Leipzig [n.d.]
Score 3 p.

BLOW, JOHN. Newark-on-Trent, Nottinghamshire
baptized 23 February 1648 or 1649
London 1 October 1708

1951s Venus and Adonis; a short suite   10'
transcribed for string orchestra with optional
woodwinds by Julius Harrison
1.Overture 2.Sarabande of the graces
3.Gavatt 4.Entr'acte 5.Dance of cupids and
music of the hunt
1,1,1,1(all optional)-Str.
Joseph Williams, London, c1931
Score 15 p.
*From the Masque for the Entertainment of the
King, Charles II. Composed ca.1682.*

2362s The Whitehall suite. Transcribed for
strings by Harold Watkins Shaw
1.Overture 2.Allegro vivace 3.Ground
Str.
Oxford University Press, London, c1947
Score 13 p.
*From the Odes and Welcome Songs composed be-
tween 1685 and 1687 for either Charles II or
James II. They were performed in the Palace
of Whitehall. The Overture and Ground are
from the ode, Hail, Monarch, Sprung of Race
Divine. The Allegro Vivace is from the ode
How Does the New-born Infant Year?*

BLUMENFELD, FELIX MICHAILOVICH.
Kovalevka, Govt. of Kherson 19 April 1863
Moscow 21 January 1931

517p [Allegro de concert, piano and orchestra,
Op. 7, A major]
Solo Pno.-2,2,2,2-2,2,3-Timp.-Str.
Belaieff, Leipzig [1887?]
Score 88 p.

BLUMENTHAL, SANDRO.   Venice 30 June 1874
Berlin 1 August 1919

881s Gavotte [G major]
Str.
Decourcelle, Nice [n.d.]
Score 5 p.

BLUMER, THEODOR. Dresden, Germany 24 March 1881
Berlin 21 September 1964

700v [Capriccio, violin and small orchestra,
Op. 42]
Solo Vn.-2(2nd alt. Picc.),2,2,2-2Hn.-Hp.(ad
lib.)-Str.
Simrock, Berlin, c1921
Score 31 p.

2432 Heiteres Spiel für Orchester [Happy   8'
music for orchestra, Op. 68, F major]
2(2nd alt. Picc.),2,2,2-2,2,1-Timp.,Perc.-Str.
Zimmermann, Leipzig, c1931
Score 20 p.
*Completed in Leipzig, 1931. First performance
Cologne, 18 December 1931, Wilhelm Buschkötter
conductor.*

4372 [Lyric intermezzo for small   6'
orchestra, Op. 82]
1,1,2,1-2,2,1-Timp.,Perc.-Cel.(ad lib.),Hp.(ad
lib.)-Str.
Wilhelm Zimmermann, Leipzig, c1939
Score 27 p.

1286s Ein seliger Augenblick [Blissful moment,
intermezzo from Der Fünfuhrtee (Five-o'clock-
tea). Arranged by C. Morena]
Bells(ad lib.)-Hp.(ad lib.)-Str.
Ahn & Simrock, Berlin, c1912
Score 16 p.

BLYTON, CAREY.
b. Beckenham, Kent, England 14 March 1932

7121 [Cinque ports. Suite from the music   15'
for an opera, Op. 28]
1.Prelude (Daybreak over the harbour) 2.Song
I (Captain Bowsprit's blues) 3.Interlude (The
beach - Midwinter) 4.Song II (The sea-dog's
song) 5.Postlude (Dusk over the harbour)
2(2nd alt. Picc.),2(2nd alt. E.H.),2,2-4,2,3,1
-Timp.,Perc.-Pno.-Str.
Ms. c1957 by Carey Blyton
Score 90 p. Large folio
*Music from an unfinished one-act opera, com-
posed 1957-58. First performance Manchester,
England, 24 January 1962, The Hallé Orchestra,
Maurice Handford conductor.*

7122 Overture: The Hobbit, or There and   5'
back again, Op. 52
2(2nd alt. Picc.),1,2,1-2,2,1-Perc.-Hp.
(optional)-Str.
Ms. c1967 by Carey Blyton
Score 34 p. Large folio
*Based on J.R.R. Tolkien's The Hobbit. Com-
posed 1967. First performance Bristol, England, 18 December 1968, Bristol Sinfonia,
Sidney Sager conductor.*

BOBINSKY, HENRYK ANFONOVICH. Warsaw 19 January 1861
Warsaw 24 April 1914

606p [Concerto, piano, Op. 8, E minor]
1.Andantino - Molto animato 2.Andante cantabile
3.Allegro vivace
Solo Pno.-2,2,2,2-4,2,3-Timp.-Str.
Jurgenson, Moscow, 1896
Score 143 p.

BOCCHERINI, LUIGI. Lucca, Italy 19 February 1743
Madrid 28 May 1805

743v [Concerto, violin, D major. Gérard   10'
no. 486. Revised and edited by Samuel Dushkin]

1.Allegro giusto 2.Andante tranquillo
3.Allegretto gentile
Solo Vn.-2,2-2Hn.-Str.
Schott, Mainz, c1927
Score 27 p.
*Cadenza added by Samuel Dushkin. Attribution
to Boccherini is probably incorrect.*

455c [Concerto, violoncello, A major. Gérard
no. 475. Transcribed by Roberto Lupi]
1.Allegro 2.Adagio 3.Rondo
Solo Vc.-2Ob.-2Hn.-Str.
Edizioni Piccinelli, Rome, c1946
Score 27 p.
*Composed ca.1763(?). Attribution of this
work is not certain. The first theme of the
first movement was used by Boccherini in his
Sonata No. 13 for solo violoncello and bass,
A major.*

494c [Concerto, violoncello, no. 9, B-flat
major. Gérard no. 482. Edited by Friedrich
Grützmacher]
1.Allegro moderato 2.Adagio non troppo
3.Rondo: Allegro
Solo Vc.-2Ob.-2Hn.-Str.
Breitkopf & Härtel, Wiesbaden [n.d.]
Score 33 p.

2107s [Quartet, strings, Op. 2 no. 2, B-flat
major. Gérard no. 160. Arranged for string
orchestra] Edited by Thor Johnson and Donald
M. McCorkle
1.Andante [Allegro non tanto] 2.Largo assai
[Largo] 3.Fuga: Allegro [Fuga con spirito]
Str.
Ms.
Score 20 p.
*Composed 1761. This edition after a J.F. Peter
autograph copied in 1771, now in the Moravian
Music Foundation Archives. First modern per-
formance at the Fourth Early American Moravian
Music Festival and Seminar, Moravian College,
Bethlehem, Pennsylvania, 29 June 1957, The
Festival Orchestra, Thor Johnson conductor.*

6209 [Quartet, strings, Op. 15 no. 6, C minor.
Gérard no. 182] Transcribed for small
orchestra
1.Larghetto 2.Menuett
Ob.(or Fl.)-2Hn.-Pno.(ad lib.)-Str.
Robert Lienau, Berlin-Lichterfelde, c1941
Score 10 p.
*Composed 1772. Bound with Symphony in G
major by Johann Georg Lang.*

495c [Quintet, strings, no. 46, Op. 28 no. 4,
C major. Gérard no. 310. Rondo] Transcribed
for violoncello and string orchestra by Paul
Bazelaire
Solo Vc.-Str.
Leduc, Paris, c1924
Score 8 p.
Composed 1779.

883s [Quintet, strings, no. 54, Op. 29 no. 6,
G minor. Gérard no. 318. Minuetto, G major]
Str.

Decourcelle, Nice [n.d.]
Score 5 p.
Composed 1779. First edition published 1813.

615s [Quintet, strings, no. 105, Op. 49 no. 5,
E-flat major. Gérard no. 369. Number 3,
Larghetto]
Str.
Ricordi, Milan [n.d.]
Score 3 p.
Composed 1794.

529c [Sonata, violoncello, no. 4, A major.
Gérard no. 4. Adagio and Allegro. Arranged for
violoncello and string orchestra by Franz
Köhler]
Solo Vc.-Str.
Joh. André, Offenbach a.M. [n.d.]
Score 13 p.
*Movements 1 and 2 of the original composition
are reversed in this arrangement, and move-
ment 3 is omitted.*

1247 [Symphony no. 3, Op. 12 no. 3, C major.
Gérard no. 505] Edited by Robert Sondheimer
1.Allegro, ma non molto 2.Andante amoroso
3.Tempo di menuetto 4.Presto, ma non tanto
4Fl.-4Hn.-Str.
Bernoulli, Basel, c1922
Score 24 p.
*Composed 1771. First performance of this
edition Berlin, 11 November 1920, Robert Sondheimer conductor.*

6689 [Symphony no. 10, Op. 35, no. 4, 15'
F major. Gérard no. 512] Edited by Newell
Jenkins
1.Allegro assai 2.Andantino 3.Allegro viva-
ce - Tempo di minuetto - Allegro vivace
0,2,0,1-2Hn.-Str.
G. Schirmer, New York, c1965
Score 28 p.
Composed 1782.

4552 [Symphony no. 16, Op. 37, no. 4, 22'
A major. Gérard no. 518] Revised by Karl
Geiringer
1.Allegro assai [Allegro spiritoso] 2.Minu-
etto 3.Andante 4.Finale
1,2,0,2-2Hn.-Str.
Universal Edition, Vienna, c1937
Score 75 p.
Composed 1787.

769 [Symphony no. 19, Op. 43, D major. 4'
Gérard no. 521]
1.Allegro con molto spirito 2.Andantino
3.Allegro come prima
2Fl.,Bn.-2Hn.-Str.
Breitkopf & Härtel, Leipzig [n.d.]
Score 32 p.
Composed 1790.

1366s [Two minuets. Arranged by Joseph
Hellmesberger]
1.[From Quintet no. 2, Op. 10 no. 2, E-flat
major. Gérard no. 266] 2.[From Quintet no.
101, Op. 49 no. 1, D major. Gérard no. 365]

Boccherini, Luigi

Str.
Universal Edition, Vienna [n.d.]
Score 15 p.
Minuet in E-flat major composed 1771; D major, 1794.

BOCHAU, CHARLES H.　　　Grafschaft Rantzau,
　　　　　　　Holstein, Germany 7 July 1870
　　　　　　　Baltimore, Maryland 8 June 1932

5842　Symphonic fantasy
1.Lento assai - Allegro energico - Presto
2.Adagio - Allegro scherzando
3(3rd alt. Picc.),2(1st alt. E.H.),2,2-4,3,3,1
-Timp.,Cym.,Trgl.-Hp.-Str.
Ms.
Score 71 p.
Composed 1923. First performance Baltimore, 17 March 1924, Baltimore Symphony, the composer conducting.

BOECKX, P. L.

580m　Une pensée de nuit [A nocturnal thought, melody for flute]
Solo Fl.-1,2,2,2-2,2,3-Str.
Ms.
Score 13 p.

BOEHE, ERNST.　　　　Munich 27 December 1880
　　　　　　　Ludwigshafen, Germany 16 November 1938

5910　[Odysseus' voyages, Op. 6.　　　25'
No. 4, Odysseus' homecoming]
4(4th alt. Picc.I; 3rd alt. Picc.II),4*,4(3rd
alt. Cl. in E-flat),4*-6,5(1 is a B.Tpt. which
can alt. with 4th),4-Timp.,Perc.-2Hp.-Str.
L. Staackmann, Leipzig, ᶜ1905
Score 114 p. Large folio
This is no. 4 of an orchestral tetralogy suggested by Homer's Odyssey.

5782　[Taormina, tone poem for large　　28'
orchestra, Op. 9]
4,4*,4*,4*-4,4(1B.Tpt.),3,1-Timp.,Perc.-2Hp.-Str.
Rob. Forberg, Leipzig, ᶜ1906
Score 79 p.
Composed 1905-06. First performance Essen, 1906.

BOEHM, THEOBALD.　　　Munich 9 April 1794
　　　　　　　Munich 25 November 1881

363m　[Fantasy on Swiss themes, for flute and orchestra, Op. 23]
1.Allegro - Recitativo adagio - Allegretto
2.Larghetto con espressivo - Allegro
3.Allegretto　4.Più presto
Solo Fl.-1,2,2,2-2Hn.-Str.
Score: Ms. ᶜ1976 by The Fleisher Collection of Orchestral Music, Free Library of Philadelphia
49 p. Large folio
Parts: B. Schott, Mainz [1845]
Composed 1845.

BOEHM, YOHANAN.　　　　Breslau 21 July 1914

6484　Divertimento for 10 wind instruments,　21'
Op. 20
1.Moderato　2.Allegro　3.Tranquillo　4.Allegro
molto　5.Intermezzo　6.A modo di parodia
2,2(2nd alt. E.H.),2,2-2Hn.
Israeli Music Publication, Tel-Aviv, ᶜ1958
Score 24 p.
Composed 1957. First performance Jerusalem, Kol Israel Broadcasting Station, 1957, Kol Israel Symphony Orchestra, Heinz Freudenthal conductor.

BOEKELMAN, BERNARDUS.　　Utrecht, Holland 9 June 1838
　　　　　　　New York City 2 August 1930

7009　Ballabile, Op. 3. Orchestrated by Valentin Frank
1,0,2,1-2,2,1-Timp.,Trgl.,Glock.-Str.
Schuberth, New York, ᶜ1894 by Bernardus Boekelman
Score in reduction 4 p.

302s　In der Einsamkeit [Solitude] Op. 7
Str.
Schuberth, Leipzig, ᶜ1888
Score 6 p.

BOËLLMANN, LÉON.
　　　　　　Ensisheim, Alsace 25 September 1862
　　　　　　Paris 11 October 1897

954v　Fantaisie sur des airs hongrois [Fantasy on Hungarian airs, for violin solo and orchestra, Op. 7, B-flat major]
Solo Vn.-2,2,2,2-4,2-Timp.-Str.
Score: Ms. 57 p.
Parts: Hamelle, Paris [n.d.]

5164　[Gavotte, for piano. Transcribed for small orchestra]
2,2,2,2-4Hn.-Timp.-Str.
J. Hamelle, Paris [n.d.]
Score 23 p.

303s　Quatre pièces brèves [from] Heures mystiques
1.Allegro　2.Moderato　3.Andantino　4.Allegro
Str.
Enoch, Paris, ᶜ1896
Score 26 p.
Originally composed for organ.

464c　Variations symphoniques pour　　13'
violoncelle solo et orchestre, Op. 23
Solo Vc.-2,2,2,2-4,2,3,1-Timp.-Hp.-Str.
Durand, Paris [n.d.]
Score 75 p.

BOHM, KARL.　　　Berlin 11 September 1844
　　　　　　　Berlin 4 April 1920

542m　An die Nacht [for trumpet or trombone solo and orchestra. Arranged by Aug. Fürstenberg]
Solo Tpt.(or Tbn.)-2,2,2,2(or 1,1,2,1)-2,1,1-Timp.-Str.

Simrock, Berlin, 1899
Score 7 p.

518v [Cavatina, violin and orchestra, Op. 314
no. 2]
Solo Vn.-0,0,2,2-2Hn.-Timp.-Str.
Simrock, Berlin, 1887
Score 18 p.

546v [Legend, violin and orchestra, Op. 314
no. 7]
Solo Vn.-0,2,2,2-2,0,3-Timp.-Str.
Simrock, Berlin, 1887
Score 22 p.

429v [Papillon, capriccio for violin and
orchestra, Op. 314 no. 4]
Solo Vn.-2,2,2,2-4Hn.-Str.
Simrock, Berlin, 1887
Score 34 p.

828s Un petit rien [A small trifle] petit
valse
Str.
Score: Ms. 13 p.
Parts: Simrock, Berlin, C1896

304s Petite bijouterie [Small gems, waltz]
Op. 337. Edited by O.B. Boise
Str.
Bote & Bock, Berlin, C1890
Score 4 p.

543m Still wie die Nacht [for trumpet or
trombone solo and orchestra] Arranged by Aug.
Fürstenberg
Solo Tpt.(or Tbn.)-2(2nd ad lib.),2,2,2-2,1,1-
Timp.-Str.
Simrock, Berlin [1899?]
Score 7 p.

BÖHME, OSKAR.
              b. Potschappel, Dresden 24 February 1870

666m Ballet-scene for cornet à pistons,   6'
Op. 31
Solo Tpt.-2(2nd alt. Picc.),2,2,2-2,0,3-Timp.,
Perc.-Str.
Score in reduction: Ms. 15 p.
Parts: Zimmermann, Leipzig, C1907
First performance St. Petersburg, 1905.

895m [Concerto, trumpet in A, Op. 18, E minor]
1.Allegro moderato 2.Adagio religioso
3.Rondo: Allegro scherzando
Solo Tpt.-2,2,2,2-4,2,3-Timp.-Str.
Jurgenson, Moscow, 1896
Score 73 p.

649m La Napolitaine [tarantella for   4'
trumpet in B-flat, Op. 25]
Solo Tpt.-2(2nd alt. Picc.),2,2,2-4,2,3-Timp.,
Perc.-Str.
Zimmermann, Leipzig, 1903
Score in reduction 11 p.

BÖHME, WALTHER.   Leipzig 6 September 1884

1257s [Sostenuto, for string orchestra and
organ (harmonium), Op. 8]
Org.-Str.
Oppenheimer, Hameln [n.d.]
Score 11 p.

BOHNE, R.

814m [Serenade for horn and clarinet soli with
orchestra, Op. 35]
Solo Cl., Solo Hn.-1,1,1,1-1,2,1-Str.
Score: Ms. 19 p.
Parts: Engelmann & Mühlberg, Leipzig [n.d.]
Bound with M. Carl, In Einsamen Stunden, for
trombone.

BOHNKE, EMIL. Zduńska Wola, Poland 11 October 1888
                Pasewalk, Pomerania 11 May 1928

4597 [Theme with variations, Op. 9]   18'
2(2nd alt. Picc.),3*,3*,3*-4,3,3,1-Timp.,Perc.
-Hp.-Str.
Simrock, Berlin, C1921
Score 44 p.
First performance Gotha, 24 November 1920.

BOIELDIEU, FRANÇOIS-ADRIEN.
                Rouen, France 16 December 1775
                Jarcy, near Grosbois 8 October 1834

6866 [The caliph of Bagdad. Overture]   8'
Edited by Antonio de Almeida
2(alt. Picc.),2,2,2-2Hn.-Timp.,Perc.-Str.
Heugel, Paris, C1962
Score 44 p.
From the opera in one act. First performance
of the opera, Paris, 16 September 1800.

970m [Concerto in tre tempi, harp and   22'
orchestra, C major. Elaborated by Carlo
Steuber]
1.Allegro brillante 2.Andante lento 3.Ron-
deau: Allegro agitato
Solo Hp.-2,2,0,2-2Hn.-Str.
Ricordi, Milan, C1939
Score 66 p.

5163 La dame blanche [The white lady]   9'
Overture
2,2,2,2-2,2,1-Timp.-Str.
Score: Cranz, Leipzig [n.d.] 51 p.
Parts: Breitkopf & Hartel, Leipzig [n.d.]
From the opera in three acts after Walter
Scott's two novels, The Monastery and Guy
Mannering. First performance Opéra-Comique,
Paris, 10 December 1825.

3024 [Ma tante Aurore. Overture]
2,2,2,2-Hn.-Timp.-Str.
Ms.
Score 36 p.
From the opera composed 1802. First complete
performance, Opéra Comique, Paris, 13 January
1803.

Boisdeffre, Charles

BOISDEFFRE, CHARLES HENRI RENÉ DE.
                    Vesoul, Haute-Savoie 3 April 1838
          Vézelise, Meurthe-et-Moselle 25 November 1906

241s [Adagietto for stringed orchestra,
Op. 15 no. 4, C major]
Str.
Score: Ms. 7 p.
Parts: Hamelle, Paris, c1905

1328 Au bord d'un ruisseau [At the edge   4'
of a brook, rural serenade] Op. 52
2,2,2,2-Hn.-Hp.(or Pno.)-Str.
Hamelle, Paris [n.d.]
Score 21 p.
Composed 1898. First performance Paris, 1899.

1179v [Reverie, for viola d'amore, or violin,
or viola, or violoncello, Op. 55]
Solo Viola d'Amore(or Vn.,Va. or Vc.)-Hp.-Str.
J. Hamelle, Paris [n.d.]
Score 7 p.

649v Romance et canzonetta, Op. 21
Solo Vn.-2,2,2,2-2Hn.-Timp.,Trgl.-Hp.-Str.
Enoch Frères & Costallat, Paris [n.d.]
Score 52 p.

1293 Suite lorraine, Op. 92   19'
1.[The banks of the Moselle] 2.[Shepherd's
song] 3.Idylle 4.[Festival in the village
Lorrain]
3*,2,2,2-4,2,3-Timp.,Trgl.-Hp.-Str.
Hamelle, Paris [n.d.]
Score 110 p.
Composed 1909. First performance Paris, 1909.

BOLCK, OSKAR.   Hohenstein 4 March 1837
                       Bremen, Germany 2 May 1888

5204 [Gudrun, Op. 50. Overture]
2,2,2,2-4,4,3-Timp.-Str.
E.W. Fritzsch, Leipzig, 1876
Score 27 p.

BOLLMACHER, PAUL.

4484 [Cheerful waltzes, Op. 33. Transcribed
for band by Carl Herbst]
2,2,4(1Cl. in E-flat),2-4Sax(AATBar.)-4,4Tpt.
in B-flat,2Tpt. in E-flat,2Flugelhn.,3Tbn.,
3Ten.Hn.,Bar.Hn.,2Tuba-Perc.
Fr. Portius, Leipzig [n.d.]
Score in reduction 4 p.

BOLZONI, GIOVANNI.   Parma 14 May 1841
                            Turin 21 February 1919

640s Aggirandomi fra i meandri dell'armonia
[Wandering through the meanders of harmony,
a romance without words, D major]
Str.(without Cb.)
Ricordi, Milan, c1917
Score 4 p.

852s Al castello medioevale [At the medieval
castle, romantic serenade no. 2]
Str.
Ricordi, Milan [n.d.]
Score 11 p.

1465s Un corno inopportuno, Op. 120
Hn.-Str.
Ricordi, Milan, c1907
Score 17 p.

999s D'inverno in soffitta [Winter in the attic,
character sketch]
Str.
Ricordi, Milan, c1917
Score 14 p.

693s Dolce sogno [Sweet dream, romance without
words]
Str.(without Cb.)
Ricordi, Milan [n.d.]
Score 8 p.

703s E canto quello che mi detta l'estro
[It's the song that gave me the inspiration,
romance without words]
Str.(without Cb.)
Ricordi, Milan, c1917
Score 6 p.

762s Gavotta, Op. 158 [D major]
Str.
Ricordi, Milan, c1913
Score 6 p.

1041s Gavotta [F major]
Str.
Ricordi, Milan [n.d.]
Score 8 p.

742s J'ai tant souffert [I have suffered so
much, romance without words]
Str.(without Cb.)
Ricordi, Milan, c1917
Score 8 p.

772s Maggiolata [Maysong] Op. 130
Fl.,Cl.-Str.
Ricordi, Milan, c1907
Score 10 p.

667s Mamma brontola perchè amo Beppe [Mother
scolds me for loving Beppe, romance without
words]
Str.(without Cb.)
Ricordi, Milan, c1917
Score 6 p.

177s Menuet lent [Slow minuet] Op. 157
Str.
Ricordi, Milan, c1913
Score 9 p.

656s Minuetto [B-flat major. Arranged by Karl
Rissland]
Pno.(ad lib.)-Str.
Ditson, Boston [n.d.]
Score 7 p.
Bound with Georges Valensin's Minuet in G.

872s Minuetto [B major]
     Str.
     Ricordi, Milan [n.d.]
     Score 5 p.

1040s Quies [Peace] Op. 137
     Str.
     Ricordi, Milan, ^c1907
     Score 6 p.

869s Son gaia, volubile, amorosa [I am happy,
     I fly, I am in love, romance without words]
     Str.(without Cb.)
     Ricordi, Milan, ^c1917
     Score 7 p.

551s L'ultimo canto [The last song, romance
     without words]
     Str.(without Cb.)
     Ricordi, Milan, ^c1917
     Score 7 p.

BONDEVILLE, EMMANUEL DE.
                b. Rouen, France 29 October 1898

2493 Bal des pendus [Ball of those   6'
     condemned to be hanged, scherzo for orchestra]
     3*,2,2,2-4,3,3,1-Timp.,Perc.-Str.
     Durand, Paris, ^c1933
     Score 32 p.
     *Based on the poem by Arthur Rimbaud. First
     performance Paris, 6 December 1930, Concerts
     Lamoureux, Albert Wolff conductor.*

5492 L'école des maris [School for   14'
     husbands. Suite for orchestra]
     1.Sganarelle et Ariste 2.Prelude to Act II
     (Valère et Isabelle) 3.La retraite
     4.Divertissement
     2,2,2,2-4,3,3-Timp.,Perc.-Cel.,Hp.-Str.
     Choudens, Paris, ^c1935
     Score 63 p.
     *From the comic opera in three acts. First
     performance Opéra-Comique, Paris, 19 June
     1935.*

BONELLI, AURELIO.   b. Bologna 1569

4337 Toccata [for brass instruments]   3'
     Edited by Robert D. King
     Double Brass Choirs: Cornets, Horns, Trombones,
     Baritones and Tubas
     Music for Brass, North Easton, Massachusetts,
     [1947]
     Score 8 p.
     *Originally published in Il Primo Libro de
     Ricercari et Canzoni a 4 voce con 2 Tocate e
     doi Dialoghi a 8, Venice, 1602.*

BONINCONTRO, G.

1542s Cantilène nostalgique [for violoncello
     solo and string orchestra. Orchestrated by
     Ciro Urbini]
     Solo Vc.-Str.
     Score: Ms. 5 p.
     Parts: [Evette & Schaeffer, Paris, ^c1925]

941s Je veux oublier [I wish to forget]
     Fl.,Cl.-Str.
     Score: Ms. 4 p.
     Parts: Bornemann, Paris, ^c1920

1187s Sogno! [Dream]
     Solo Vn.-Str.
     Score: Ms. 7 p.
     Parts: Decourcelle, Nice, ^c1919

BONIS, MÉLANIE (MME. ALBERT DOMANGE).
                    Paris 21 January 1858
     Sarcelles, Seine-et-Oise 18 March 1937

1319 [Suite, in the form of waltzes]
     1.Ballabile 2.Interlude et valse lente 3.
     Scherzo-valse
     1,1,2,1-2Hn.-Timp.-Str.
     Leduc, Paris, ^c1898
     Score 23 p.

BONNAUD, FRÉDÉRICK.

401s Dans la serre [In the greenhouse] inter-
     mezzo
     Str.
     Decourcelle, Nice [n.d.]
     Score 3 p.

751s Sérénade enfantine [Serenade for a child]
     2Ob.-Chimes-Str.
     Decourcelle, Nice [n.d.]
     Score 3 p.

BONNER, EUGENE MACDONALD.
           b. Washington, North Carolina 1889

3519 White nights, a prelude for orchestra, 10'
     Op. 17
     3*,3*,3*,3*-4,3,3,1-Timp.,Perc.-Cel.,2Hp.-Str.
     Ms.
     Score 50 p.
     *Composed 1925. First performance New York, 2
     April 1939, New York Philharmonic, John
     Barbirolli conductor.*

BONONCINI, GIOVANNI MARIA.   Montecorone, near
           Modena, Italy baptized 23 September 1642
                    Modena 18 November 1678

7186 Canon for 12 brass. Arranged by Michael
     Moore
     5Tpt.,5Tbn.,2Tuba
     Arco Music Publishers, North Hollywood,
     California, ^c1967
     Score 8 p.

Bonporti, Francesco Antonio

*First published in the composer's Varii Fiori,
Bologna, 1669.*

BONPORTI, FRANCESCO ANTONIO.
          Trento, Italy baptized 11 June 1672
          Padua 19 December 1748

Also known as Buonporti

2237s [Concerto, string orchestra and   *11'*
    cembalo, Op. 11 no. 5, F major. Revised by
    Guglielmo Barblan]
    1.Andantino grazioso 2.Recitativo: Adagio
    assai 3.Allegro deciso
    Solo Vn.(in 2nd movement only)-Cemb.-Str.
    Carisch, Milan, c1944
    Score 20 p.
    *Composed ca.1720. First performance of this
    modern edition Bolzano, Italy, 21 December 1938,
    Gruppo Universitario Musicale, Carlo Maria Giu-
    lini conductor, Renzo Ferraguzzi soloist.*

2356s [Concerto, string orchestra and   *14'*
    cembalo, Op. 11 no. 8, D major. Revised by
    Guglielmo Barblan]
    1.Allegro 2.Largo 3.Allegro vivace
    Cemb.-Str.
    Carisch, Milan, c1949
    Score 23 p.
    *Composed ca.1720. First performance of this
    modern edition Teatro alla Scala, Milan, 1951,
    Teatro alla Scala Orchestra, Carlo Maria Gui-
    lini conductor.*

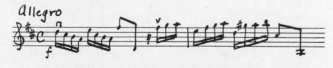

326v [Concerto, violin, strings and   *11'*
    cembalo, Op. 11 no. 3, B-flat major. Revision
    and realization of figured bass by Guglielmo
    Barblan]
    1.Allegro 2.Siciliana cromatica 3.Allegro
    Solo Vn.-Cemb.-Str.
    Ricordi, Milan, c1961
    Score 35 p.
    *Composed ca.1720. First performance of this
    modern edition, Milan, 15 February 1954,
    Angelicum Orchestra, Aladar Janes conductor.*

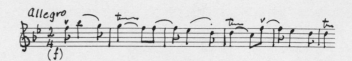

336v [Concerto, violin, strings and cem-   *13'*
    balo, Op. 11 no. 9, E major. Revised by
    Guglielmo Barblan]
    1.Allegro 2.Larghetto 3.Allegro (giusto)
    Solo Vn.-Cemb.-Str.
    Carisch, Milan, c1960
    Score 26 p.
    Composed ca.1720.

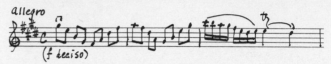

334v [Concerto, violin, strings and organ,   *12'*
    Op. 11 no. 4, B-flat major. Revision and re-
    alization of figured bass by Alceo Toni]
    1.Vivace, ma larghetto 2.Siciliana 3.Allegro
    Solo Vn.-Org.-Str.
    Carisch, Milan, c1942
    Score 24 p.

358v [Concerto, violin, violoncello obbli-   *10'*
    gato, strings and cembalo, Op. 11 no. 6, F
    major. Revised by Guglielmo Barblan]
    1.Comodo 2.Andante assai 3.Allegro (Minuetto
    variato)
    Solo Vn.-Cemb.-Str.
    Carisch, Milan, c1959
    Score 22 p.
    *Composed ca.1720. First performance of this
    modern edition Siena, 5 September 1941, Orches-
    tra dell'Accademia Chigiana, F. Previtali con-
    ductor.*

2364s [Invenzioni, violin and cembalo, Op. 10.
    Fantasia, Andamento and Bizzarria. Transcribed
    for string orchestra by Emily Daymond]
    Pno.(optional)-Str.
    Oxford University Press, London, c1947
    Score 9 p.
    *Excerpts from Four Inventions [BWV Anh. 173-
    176]. Mistakenly attributed to J. S. Bach.
    Originally composed for violin and cembalo by
    Bonporti as Invenzioni a Violino Solo, Op. 10,
    Bologna 1712.*

BONVIN, LUDWIG.   Siders, Canton Valais,
                    Switzerland 17 February 1850
                    Buffalo, New York 18 February 1939

1002 Ballade, Op. 25   5'
   2(2nd alt. Picc.),2,2,2-4,2,3,1-Timp.,Perc.-Str.
   Breitkopf & Härtel, Leipzig, c1897
   Score 29 p.

218s Christnachtstraum [Christmas night's dream]
   Op. 10
   Str.
   Siegel's, Leipzig [n.d.]
   Score 5 p.

4516 [Festival procession, Op. 27]
   2,2,2,2-4,2,3,1-Timp.,Cym.,B.Dr.(ad lib.)-Hp.
   (ad lib.)-Str.
   Breitkopf & Härtel, Leipzig, c1896
   Score 31 p.

2449 Melodie, Op. 56b
   1,2,2,2-2Hn.
   Ms.[n.d.] Breitkopf & Härtel, Leipzig
   Score 8 p.
   Originally for violin and piano.

2471 Romanze [for wind orchestra,   5'30"
   Op. 19a]
   1,2,2,2-2Hn.
   Ms.
   Score 15 p.
   *Originally composed for violin (or flute) and
   piano, then arranged for violin and orchestra.
   Arranged for wind instruments ca.1893. First
   performance Buffalo, New York, ca.1895, Canis-
   ius College Orchestra, the composer conducting.*

1073 [Three tone pictures, Op. 12]   16'
   1.[Elevation] 2.[Desire] 3.[Suppressed
   sadness at the joyous feast]
   2(2nd alt. Picc.),2,2,2-4,2,3,Bombardon-Timp.,
   Cym.-Str.
   Breitkopf & Härtel, Leipzig, c1893
   Score 39 p.

BORCH, GASTON LOUIS CHRISTOPHER.
        Guines, Pas de Calais, France 8 March 1871
                    Stockholm 14 February 1926

1016s Elégie, Op. 56 no. 1
   Str.
   Score: Ms. 5 p.
   Parts: Augener, London, c1899

870v Elégie, Op. 101
   Solo Vn.-2,2,2,2-2,2-Timp.-Hp.-Str.
   Augener, London, c1907
   Score 15 p.

BORCHARD, ADOLPHE.   Le Havre, France 30 June 1882
                        Paris 13 December 1967

514p Eskual herria (patrie Basque) [for piano
   and orchestra]
   Solo Pno.-3*,3*,2,2-4,2,3,1-Timp.,Perc.-Str.
   Evette & Schaeffer, Paris, c1922
   Score 134 p.

*Completed September 1921. First performance
Paris, 22 January 1922, Concerts Colonne,
Gabriel Pierné conductor, the composer as
soloist.*

BORCK, EDMUND VON.
              Breslau, Germany 22 February 1906
              killed in action near Nettuno, Italy
                             16 February 1944

3931 [Concerto for orchestra, Op. 14]   15'
   1.Allegro ma un poco maestoso 2.Adagio 3.
   Allegro vivo e robusto
   3*,2,3*,3*-4,3,2,1-Timp.,Perc.-Str.
   Universal Edition, Vienna, c1936
   Score 50 p.

BORDES, CHARLES.
         Le Roche-Corbon, near Vouvray-sur-Loire
                                12 May 1863
                        Toulon 8 November 1909

512p Rapsodie basque pour piano et orchestre,
   Op. 9 [revised edition]
   Solo Pno.-2*,1,2,2-2,2,3-Timp.,Perc.-2Hp.-Str.
   Rouart Lerolle, Paris, c1921
   Score 79 p.
   Composed 1888.

BORDIER, JULES.   Angers 23 August 1846
                         Paris 29 January 1896

690m Berceuse [for flute or oboe and string
   orchestra]
   Fl.(or Ob.)-Str.
   Score: Ms. 6 p.
   Parts: Durand, Paris [n.d.]

804v Canzonetta [for violin solo and orchestra]
   Solo Vn.-2,2,2,2-2,2-Timp.-Str.
   Score: Ms. 15 p.
   Parts: Costallat [n.p., n.d.]

689m Habanera [for oboe solo and orchestra]
   Solo Ob.-Fl.,Cl.-2Hn.-Str.
   Score: Ms. 31 p.
   Parts: Durand, Paris [n.d.]

702v Suite fantaisiste [Whimsical suite] Op. 40
   1.Air d'église [Sacred air] 2.Menuet-polonaise
   Solo Vn.-2(2nd alt. Picc.),2,2,2-4,2,3-Timp.,
   Tamb.-Hp.-Str.
   Richault, Paris, c1892
   Score 59 p.

BORGHINI, LOUIS-JEAN.   Vichy, France 1874

569m Clartés et ombres [Lights and shades   3'
   for oboe or violin solo and orchestra]
   Solo Ob.(or Vn.)-Fl.,Cl.-2Hn.-Str.
   Score: Ms. 7 p.
   Parts: Decourcelle, Nice, c1924
   *Composed 1923. First performance Monte Carlo,
   26 June 1924, the composer conducting.*

1213s L'eau qui dort [Sleeping waters] intermezzo
   Str.

Borghini, Louis-Jean

Score: Ms. 12 p.
Parts: Decourcelle, Nice, c1926

981s Petite suite
1.Petit prelude 2.Andante 3.Scherzo
Str.
Score: Ms. 20 p.
Parts: Decourcelle, Nice, c1925

917v Romance sans paroles [Romance without
words]
Solo Vn.-1,1,2,1-Hn.-Str.
Score: Ms. 20 p.
Parts: Decourcelle, Nice [n.d.]

BORGSTRØM, HJALMAR.   Christiania 23 March 1864
                             Oslo 5 July 1925

657p Hamlet [symphonic poem] Op. 13
Solo Pno.-2(2nd alt. Picc.),2,2,2-4,2,3,1-
Timp.,Perc.-Hp.-Str.
Norsk Musikforlag, Christiania, c1919
Score 59 p.

684v Romanze, Op. 12 [E major]
Solo Vn.-2,2,2,2-2,2-Timp.-Hp.-Str.
Kistner, Leipzig, c1901
Score 35 p.

6054 [Thoughts, symphonic poem]   44'
1.Allegro moderato 2.Non troppo allegro 3.An-
dante 4.Presto 5.Allegro molto
3*,2(1st alt. E.H.),2(2nd alt. B.Cl.),2-4,2,3,1
-Timp.,Perc.-Hp.-Str.
Norsk Musikforlag, Christiania, c1917
Score 127 p.
*Composed 1917. First performance Stockholm,
1918.*

BOŘKOVEC, PAVEL.   Prague 10 June 1894
                          Prague 22 July 1972

439m [Concerto grosso, 2 violins, violon-   25'
cello, orchestra and piano obbligato]
1.Largo - Poco allegro 2.Quasi adagio
3.Allegro
2 Solo Vn., Solo Vc.-2(2nd alt. Picc.),2,2,2-
2,2-Timp.,Perc.-Pno.-Str.
Melantrich, Prague, 1947
Score 111 p.
*Composed 1941-42. First performance Prague, 8
May 1943, Czech Philharmonic, Václav Talich
conductor. Awarded the Melantrich Prize, 1943.*

BORNE, FERNAND LE.
See: LEBORNE, FERNAND.

BORNSCHEIN, FRANZ CARL. Baltimore 10 February 1879
                         Baltimore 8 June 1948

654s Five early classics. Transcribed by Franz
C. Bornschein
1.Old French gavotte (Campra) 2.Prelude in C
(J.S. Bach) 3.Rose and Colas (Monsigny) 4.Ro-
mance in E-flat (from Haydn, Symphony 85, La
Reine) 5.Rondo in G (from Mozart, Symphony 12)
Pno.(ad lib.)-Str.
Ditson, Boston, c1921
Score 12 p.

655s Five later classics. Transcribed by Franz
C. Bornschein
1.Minuet in G (J.L. Dussek) 2.Theme in G (from
Beethoven, Sonatina no. 5) 3.Hark, hark, the
lark (Schubert, Cymbeline, serenade) 4.Char-
acter piece in G (Mendelssohn, Kinderstücke, no.
1) 5.Bourrée in A (L. Ries)
Pno.(ad lib.)-Str.
Ditson, Boston, c1922
Score 13 p.

678s Four modern classics. Transcribed by Franz
C. Bornschein
1.Consolation no. 5 (Liszt) 2.Prelude, Op. 28,
no. 7 (Chopin) 3.Evening song, Op. 85 no. 12
(R. Schumann) 4.Erotikon, Op. 43 no. 5 (Grieg)
Pno.(ad lib.)-Str.
Ditson, Boston, c1928
Score 12 p.

657s Four Russian numbers. Arranged by Franz
C. Bornschein
1.Nocturne (Borodin, Petite suite) 2.Dreaming
(Kopylov) 3.Canzonetta (Cui) 4.Petite valse,
Op. 10 no. 2 (Karganov)
Pno.(ad lib.)-Str.
Ditson, Boston, c1927
Score 16 p.

3014 Leif Ericson, symphonic poem   10'
3*,3*,3*,3*-4,3,3,1-Timp.,Perc.-Pno.,Cel.,Hp.-
Str.
Ms.
Score 115 p.
*Composed 1935. First performance Baltimore,
23 February 1936, Ernest Schelling conductor.*

2603 [Persian festivals. No. 1. Festival   9'
of Mithras told by the potter]
3*,2,2,2-4,3,3,1-Timp.-Str.
Ms.
Score 41 p.
*Composed 1922 as Three Persian Tone Poems.
First performance of that version, Baltimore,
10 December 1922, the composer conducting.
Rewritten in present form, 1940.*

2604 [Persian festivals. No. 2. Feast of   10'
roses told by the temple dancer (In the palace
garden)]
3*,2,2,2-4,3,3,1-Timp.,Perc.-Hp.-Str.
Ms.
Score 48 p.

2605 [Persian festivals. No. 3. Persian   6'
pageant told by the weaver (The triumph of
Nadir Shah)]
3*,2,2,2-4,3,3,1-Timp.,Perc.-Hp.-Str.
Ms.
Score 26 p.

2607 [The phantom canoe. Part 1. The lovers] 5'
3*,3*,2,2-4,3,3,1-Timp.-Hp.-Str.
Ms.
Score 17 p.
*The Phantom Canoe, Indian Suite for Symphony
Orchestra, was composed in 1916. First perform-
ance Baltimore, 24 November 1916, Baltimore
Symphony Orchestra, Gustav Strube conductor.*

2608 [The phantom canoe. Part 2. The stake] 5'
3*,3*,2,2-4,3,3,1-Timp.-Str.(2Solo Vn.)
Ms.
Score 12 p.

2609 [The phantom canoe. Part 3. The phan- 7'
tom canoe]
3*,2,2,2-4,3,3,1-Timp.-Hp.-Str.
Ms.
Score 12 p.

2610 [The phantom canoe. Part 4. The death 6'
song]
3*,3*,2,2-4,3,3,1-Timp.-Str.
Ms.
Score 11 p.

2611 [The phantom canoe. Part 5. The ghost 4'
fires]
3*,3*,2,2-4,3,3,1-Timp.,Indian Dr.,S.Dr.-Str.
Ms.
Score 22 p.

2606 The sea god's daughter, symphonic 11'
scherzo
3*,3*,3*,2-4,2,3,1-Timp.,Perc.-Str.
Ms.
Score 48 p.
Composed 1924; rewritten 1940. Received honorable mention in the Balaban & Katz competition, 1924. First performance Chicago, 10 February 1924, Chicago Theatre Symphony Orchestra, Nathaniel Finston conductor.

2909 Southern nights 12'
3*,2,2,2-4,3,3,1-Timp.,Perc.-Hp.-Str.
Ms.
Score 51 p.
Composed 1936. First performance Washington, D.C., 1 March 1936, National Symphony Orchestra, the composer conducting.

BORODIN, ALEXANDER PORFIRIEVICH.
                St. Petersburg 12 November 1833
                St. Petersburg 27 February 1887

553 [Mlada, opera-ballet. Finale. 5'
Orchestrated by N. Rimsky-Korsakov]
3*,2,2,2-4,2,3,1-Timp.,Perc.-Hp.-Str.
Belaieff, Leipzig, 1892
Score 42 p.
From the unfinished opera, composed 1872.

362 [On the steppes of Central Asia] 7'
2,2*,2,2-4,2,3-Timp.-Str.
Kalmus, New York [n.d.]
Score 23 p.
Composed 1880 for the silver jubilee of Alexander II.

39 Petite suite. Orchestrated by 24'
Alexander Glazunov
1.Au convent 2.Intermezzo 3.Mazurka
4.Mazurka 5.Rêverie 6.Serenade 7.Finale
3*(2nd Fl. alt. 2nd Picc.),2,2,2-4,2,3-Timp.,
Perc.-Str.
Bessel, St. Petersburg, 1889
Score 95 p.
Composed 1885 for piano; orchestrated 1889.

372 [Prince Igor. Overture. Orchestrated 10'
by Alexander Glazunov]
3*,2,2,2-4,2,3,1-Timp.-Str.
Kalmus, New York [n.d.]
Score 44 p.
From the opera, left unfinished. First performance St. Petersburg, 25 October 1890, Kutschera conductor.

492 [Prince Igor. March. Orchestrated by 5'
N. Rimsky-Korsakov]
3*,2,2,2-4,2,3,1-Timp.,Perc.-Str.
Backstage band(ad lib. in concert performance):
6Hn.,2Cnt.,Tuba-Drums
Belaieff, Leipzig, 1889
Score 37 p.

413 [Prince Igor. Polovetsian dances. 13'
Orchestrated by N. Rimsky-Korsakov]
No. 8. Dance of the Polovetsian maidens
3*,2,2,2-4Hn.-Timp.,Perc.-Str.
No. 17. Polovetsian dance with chorus
3*,3*,2,2-4,2,3,1-Timp.,Perc.-Hp.-Chorus(SATB,
optional in concert performance)-Str.
Kalmus, New York [n.d.]
Score 91 p.

413v [Quartet, strings, no. 2, D major. 9'
Nocturne. Transcribed for violin solo and
orchestrated by N. Rimsky-Korsakov]
Solo Vn.-2,2,2,2-2,2-Timp.-Str.
Belaieff, Leipzig, 1913
Score 16 p.

2918 [Quartet, strings, no. 2, D major. 9'
Nocturne. Transcribed by Nikolai Tcherepnin]
3,2,3,2-4,3,3,1-Timp.-Hp.-Str.
Universal Edition, Vienna, c1935
Score 35 p.

274 [Symphony no. 1, E-flat major] 31'
1.Adagio - Allegro 2.Scherzo 3.Andante 4.Allegro molto vivo
2,3*,2,2-4,2,3-Timp.-Str.
Bessel, St. Petersburg [n.d.]
Score 161 p.
Composed 1862-66. First performance St. Petersburg, 4 January 1869, Mili Balakirev conductor.

462 [Symphony no. 2, B minor. Revised by 28'
N. Rimsky-Korsakov and A. Glazunov]
1.Allegro 2.Scherzo: Prestissimo 3.Andante
4.Finale: Allegro
3*,2,2,2-4,2,3,1-Timp.,Perc.-Hp.-Str.
Kalmus, New York [n.d.]
Score 152 p.
Composed 1869-75. First performance 1876, Russian Musical Society of St. Petersburg, Eduard Napravnik conductor.

363 [Symphony no. 3, Unfinished, A minor 17'
Movements 1 and 2. Completed and orchestrated
by Alexander Glazunov]
1.Moderato assai 2.Scherzo: Vivo
2,2,2,2-4,2,3-Timp.-Str.
Belaieff, Leipzig [n.d.]
Score 75 p.
Published 26 January 1889. This is a posthumous work.

Borowski, Felix

BOROWSKI, FELIX.
    Burton, Westmoreland, England 10 March 1872
                Chicago 6 September 1956

842s Deux pièces [for string orchestra]
  1.Crépuscule [Twilight] 2.Serenade
  Str.
  Joseph Williams, London, c1905
  Score 11 p.

2691 Fantasie-overture, Youth   *12'*
  3(3rd alt. Picc.),3*,3*,3*-4,3,3,1-Timp.,Perc.-
  Str.
  Ms.
  Score 82 p.
  Composed 1922. First concert performance
  Chicago North Shore Festival, Evanston,
  30 May 1923, Chicago Symphony Orchestra, the
  composer conducting. Awarded a prize by the
  Chicago North Shore Festival Association,
  Evanston, Illinois, 1923.

5327 The mirror
  2,2,2,2-4,3,3,1-Timp.,Cym.,Gong-Hp.-Str.
  Ms.
  Score 40 p. Large folio
  Composed 1953. First performance Louisville,
  27 November 1954, Louisville Orchestra,
  Robert Whitney conductor.

2581 Peintures [Paintings for orchestra] *18'*
  1.[Portrait of a young girl] 2.[The garden
  of night] 3.[The festival]
  3(3rd alt. Picc.),3*,3*,3*-4,3,3,1-Timp.,Perc.
  -Hp.-Str.
  Ms.
  Score 49 p.
  Composed 1917. First performance Chicago, 25
  January 1918, Chicago Symphony Orchestra,
  Frederick Stock conductor.

5428 Le printemps passioné [Impassioned *11'*
  spring] poème pour orchestre
  3*(2nd alt. Picc.II),2,2,2-4,2,3,1-Timp.,Perc.
  -Hp.-Str.
  Ms.
  Score 56 p.
  Suggested in part by La Bonne Chanson of Paul
  Verlaine. Composed 1920. First performance
  Chicago North Shore Festival, Evanston,
  25 May 1920, Festival Orchestra, the composer
  conducting.

2773 Semiramis, tone poem for orchestra *15'*
  3(2nd and 3rd alt. Picc.),3*,3*,3*-4,4,3,1-
  Timp.,Perc.-2Hp.-Str.
  Ms.
  Score 89 p.
  Composed 1924. First performance Chicago, 13
  November 1925, Chicago Symphony Orchestra, Fred-
  erick Stock conductor.

658s Suite rococo, for string orchestra
  1.Caprice pompadour 2.Air à danser 3.Passepied
  Str.
  Score: Ms. 25 p.
  Parts: Laudy, London, c1900

2678 Symphony no. 1   *18'*
  1.Andante maestoso - Allegro 2.Andante tranquillo 3.Allegro spiritoso
  2,3*,3*,3*-4,3,3,1-Timp.,Perc.-Cel.,Hp.-Str.
  Ms.
  Score 139 p.
  Composed 1931-32. First performance Chicago,
  16 March 1933, Chicago Symphony Orchestra,
  Frederick Stock conductor.

5357 Symphony no. 2, E minor   *26'*
  1.Allegro con spirito 2.Andante molto tran-
  quillo 3.Vivace - Moderato - Vivace - Andante
  molto sostenuto - Allegro
  3(3rd alt. Picc.),3*,3*,3*-4,3,3,1-Timp.,Perc.
  -Hp.-Str.
  Ms.
  Score 147 p.
  Composed 1933. First performance Trinity
  Auditorium, Los Angeles, 22 July 1936, Jacques
  Samossoud conductor.

BØRRESEN, HAKON.   Copenhagen 2 June 1876
                Copenhagen 6 October 1954

610v [Concerto, violin, Op. 11, G major]
  1.Introduction 2.Adagio 3.Molto vivace
  Solo Vn.-2,2,2,2-4,2-Timp.-Str.
  Hansen, Copenhagen, c1908
  Score 84 p.
  Composed 1901-02. First performance Copenhagen,
  1905, Johan Svendsen conductor, Julius Thorn-
  berg soloist.

2148s [Nearing death, for string orchestra] *11'*
  Str.
  Edition Dania, Copenhagen, c1936 by Samfundet
  til Udgivelse af dansk Musik
  Score 6 p.
  Composed 1932. This is the prelude to the last
  act of the play Knud Lavard by Axel Juel.

5938 [Norsemen overture, Op. 16]
  3(3rd alt. Picc.),2,2,2-4,3,3,1-Timp.,Perc.-
  Str.
  Edition Dania, Copenhagen, c1939
  Score 52 p.
  Composed 1912.

5942 [Olympic hymn, after a Pythian hymn by
  Pindar, 520 B.C.]
  3*,2,2,2-4,3,3,1-Timp.,Perc.-Str.
  Edition Dania, Copenhagen, c1940
  Score 16 p.
  Composed 1940.

BORTKIEVICH, SERGEI EDUARDOVICH.
          Kharkov, Russia 28 February 1877
                Vienna 25 October 1952

1797s [Austrian suite for string   *14'*
  orchestra, Op. 51]
  1.[In St. Stephen's Cathedral] 2.[Walk in the
  Vienna woods] 3.[Vienna waltz] 4.[In the
  Wurstel Park]
  Pno.(or Hp.; ad lib.)-Str.
  Universal Edition, Vienna, c1939
  Score 25 p.

Originally composed for piano, 1935; arranged for string orchestra, 1935. First performance Vienna, 24 December 1935, Radio-Wien-Orchestra, Max Schönherr conductor.

436p [Concerto, piano, Op. 16, B-flat   *24'* major]
1.Lento 2.Andante sostenuto 3.Molto vivace e con brio
Solo Pno.-3(3rd alt. Picc.),2,2,2-4,2,3,1-Timp.,Perc.-Str.
Kistner, Leipzig, c1913
Score 108 p.
Composed 1912. First performance Berlin, 1912.

905v [Concerto, violin, Op. 22, D major]
1.Allegro deciso 2.Poème: Largo
3.Introduzione: Andantino – Alla marcia
Solo Vn.-2,3*,3*,3*-4,3,3,1-Timp.-Hp.-Str.
Rahter, Leipzig, c1923
Score 118 p.

608c [Concerto, violoncello, Op. 20, C minor]
In one movement
Solo Vc.-2,2,2,2-4,2,3,1-Timp.,Cym.,Tamb.-Hp.-Str.
Rahter, Leipzig, c1923
Score 91 p.

2447 Five Russian dances, Op. 18
1.Un poco maestoso 2.Andantino 3.Allegro
4.Valse 4.Presto
3*,2,2,2-4,2,3,1-Timp.,Perc.-Str.
Ms.
Score 56 p.
Originally composed for piano 4-hands.

2059 [Othello, symphonic poem after   *35'* Shakespeare's play, Op. 19]
3(3rd alt. Picc.),3*,3*,3*-4,3,3,1-Timp.,Perc.-2Hp.-Str.
Kistner, Leipzig, c1914
Score 114 p.
Composed 1912. First performance Berlin, 1913, the composer conducting.

4860 [Symphony no. 1, From my native land, Op. 52, D minor]
1.Un poco sostenuto – Allegro 2.Scherzo
3.Adagio 4.Finale: Allegro vivace
3(3rd alt. Picc.),2,2,2-4,2,3,1-Timp.,Perc.-Hp.-Str.
Ms.
Score 128 p.

4875 [Symphony no. 2, Op. 55, E-flat major]
1.Allegro ma non troppo 2.Vivace 3.Andante sostenuto 4.Vivace
2,2,2,2-4,3,3,1-Timp.-Str.
Ms.
Score 100 p.

BORTZ, ALFRED.   Berlin 12 September 1882
              Salzburg 15 November 1969

Full name Eduard Julius Alfred Bortz

4599 Sinfonietta pastorale, Op. 15   *30'*
1.[A spring morning] 2.[Forest idyll]
3.[A festival day in the village]
2,2,2,2-2,2,2-Timp.,Trgl.,Cym.-Str.
Simrock, Berlin, c1913
Score 86 p.

BORUP-JØRGENSEN, JENS AXEL.
        b. Hjørring, Jylland (Jutland),
             Denmark 22 November 1924

275v [Music for percussion and viola,   *11'* Op. 18]
Adagio non troppo – Lento – Un poco adagio – Andante – Un poco adagio
Solo Va.-Timp.,Perc.-Pno.,Marimba
Samfundet til Udgivelse af Dansk Musik [Copenhagen] c1960
Score 34 p.
Composed 1955-56.

BOSMANS, ARTHUR.   Brussels 13 October 1908

2199s Jakiana suite, for string orchestra   *6'* or string quartet [original version]
1.Prelude 2.Aria 3.Bourree
Str.
Henri Elkan, Philadelphia, Pa., c1960
Score 16 p.
Composed 1959. First performance Belo Horizonte, Brazil, 8 August 1961, Symphony Orchestra of the State Military Police, Sebastião Vianna conductor. A later edition includes flute, oboe, two clarinets, bassoon and horn.

384c Romance, for solo violoncello and   *5'* chamber orchestra
Solo Vc.-1,1,1,1-2,2,1-Hp.-Str.
Ms. c1976 by Arthur Bosmans
Score 17 p.

6439 [The street, symphonic rhapsody. *13'30"* Revised version]
3(3rd alt. Picc.),3*,2,2-4,3(3rd ad lib.),3,1-Timp.,Perc.-Pno.,Cel.(ad lib.),Hp.(ad lib.)-Str.
Éditions Metropolis, Antwerp, c1960
Score 67 p.
Composed 1932. First performance Royal Conservatory of Music, Liège, Belgium, 20 January 1934, Royal Conservatory of Music Orchestra, François Rasse conductor. Revised 1951. Awarded the César Franck Prize, 1933, by the Belgian government.

4411 La vie en bleu   *7'30"*
1.Fable 2.Jeu 3.Valse 4.Marche
2(2nd alt. Picc.),1,2,1-2,2,2-Timp.,Perc.-Pno.Cel.-Str.
Maurice Senart, Paris, c1938
Score 24 p.

BOSSI, MARCO ENRICO.
      Salò, Brescia, Italy 25 April 1861
  At sea (en route from America to Europe)
              20 February 1925

Bossi, Marco Enrico

447m [Concert piece, organ, brass, timpani *20'*
and strings, Op. 130, C minor]
Allegro sostenuto - Allegro - Maestosamente
Solo Org.-2,1,2Cnt.,3,1-Timp.,Deep Bell in C
(or Tam-tam)-Str.
C.F. Peters, Leipzig, ᶜ1908 by J. Rieter-
Biedermann, Leipzig
Score 55 p.

449m [Concerto, organ, Op. 100, A minor] *23'*
1.Allegro moderato 2.Adagio, ma non troppo
3.Allegro
Solo Org.-4Hn.-Timp.-Str.
C.F. Peters, Leipzig, ᶜ1900 by J. Rieter-
Biedermann, Leipzig
Score 71 p.

220 Hochzeits-Marsch [Wedding march, for organ,
Op. 110 no. 4. Transcribed for orchestra by
Karl Müller-Berghaus]
3*,2,2,2-4,3,3,1-Timp.,Perc.-Hp.-Str.
Senff, Leipzig, ᶜ1897
Score 19 p.

89s Intermezzi goldoniani, Op. 127 no. 1
1.Prelude and minuet 2.Gagliarda 3.Coprifuoco
[Curfew] 4.Minuet and musette 5.Serenatina
6.Burlesque
Str.
Rieter-Biedermann, Leipzig [n.d.]
Score 51 p.

1923 Siciliana e giga (stile antico), *6'*
Op. 73
2*,1,1,1-2Hn.-Timp.-Str.
Ricordi, Milan [n.d.]
Score 21 p.
*Composed 1895. First performance Rome, 1896,
the composer conducting.*

3764 Ultimo canto, pensée musicale [from] Op.
109
3,2,3*,2-4,0,3,1-Timp.-Hp.-Str.
Rieter-Biedermann, Leipzig, ᶜ1904
Score 19 p.

BÖTTCHER, E.

764s Kosestündchen! [Happy moments!] Ländler
Op. 79
Str.
Score: Ms. 7 p.
Parts: Oertel, Hannover [n.d.]

BOTTESINI, GIOVANNI.
Crema, Lombardy 22 December 1821
Parma 7 July 1889

1078s Rêverie
Solo Vc.-Str.
Score: Ms. 4 p.
Parts: Decourcelle, Nice [n.d.]

BOTTJE, WILL GAY.
b. Grand Rapids, Michigan 30 June 1925

441m Concertino for piccolo and orchestra *11'*
1.Very moderate - Energico 2.Intermezzo

3.Toccata: Presto
Solo Picc.-2,2*,2,2-3,2,2-Timp.,Perc.-Hp.-Str.
Ms.
Score 39 p.
*Composed 1956. First performance Akron, Ohio,
19 March 1957, Akron Symphony, Laszlo Krausz
conductor, William Hebert soloist.*

420m Concerto for flute and trumpet, with *21'*
strings, harp and percussion
1.Moderato 2.Ritmico giocoso 3.Very slowly -
Allegro moderato
Solo Fl., Solo Tpt.-Timp.,Perc.-Cel.,Hp.-Str.
Ms.
Score 94 p.
Composed 1955.

5747 Symphony no. 4, for band *24'*
1.Poco adagio - Piu mosso 2.Scherzo 3.Calmo
4.Allegro con brio
3(2nd&3rd alt. Picc.),2(2nd alt. E.H.),6*(1Cl.
in E-flat;1Alto Cl.),2-5Sax.(AATBar.B)-4,
3Cnt.,3,2Bar.Hn.,Tuba-Timp.,Perc.
Ms.
Score 88 p.
*Composed 1956. First performance Rochester,
May 1956, Eastman Wind Ensemble, Frederick
Fennell conductor.*

5746 Theme and variations for band *13'30"*
3*,2(2nd alt. E.H.),6*(1Cl. in E-flat;Alto Cl.),
2-5Sax.(AATBar.B)-4,3Cnt.,3,2Bar.Hn.,Tuba-
Timp.,Perc.-Cb.
Ms.
Score 40 p. Large folio
*Composed 1957. First performance Rochester,
New York, May 1958, Eastman Wind Ensemble,
Frederick Fennell conductor.*

BOUGHTON, RUTLAND.
Aylesbury, England 23 January 1878
London 25 January 1960

948m Concerto, flute and strings *15'*
1.Allegro 2.Adagio 3.Allegro molto
Solo Fl.-Str.
Hawkes & Son, London, ᶜ1938
Score 31 p.
*Composed 1937. First performance London, 25
March 1938, New Chamber Orchestra of London,
Peter Burges conductor, John Francis soloist.*

949m Concerto, oboe and strings *21'*
1.Allegro 2.Adagio espressivo 3.Allegro
moderato
Solo Ob.-Str.
Hawkes & Son, London, ᶜ1937
Score 38 p.
*Composed 1935 or 1936. First performance Ox-
ford, England, 6 May 1937, Boyd Neel String
Orchestra, Boyd Neel conductor, the composer's
daughter, Joy Boughton, soloist.*

441s Three folk dances for string orchestra,
Op. 23d
1.Hornpipe 2.The weary wave o'Tyne 3.Culloden,
a country dance
Soli(in no. 2 only): 2Vn.,Vc.-Str.

Curwen, London, c1913
Score 11 p.

BOURGAULT-DUCOUDRAY, LOUIS ALBERT.
Nantes 2 February 1840
Vernouillet, Seine et Oise 4 July 1910

1242 Le carnaval d'Athènes, danses grecques
1.Allegro un poco maestoso 2.Tempo di marcia
molto moderato 3.Tempo di valza 4.Moderato
3*,2*,2,4-4Hn.,Bugle in E-flat,2Tpt.,2Cnt.,3,1
-Timp.,Perc.-Hp.-Str.
Choudens, Paris, c1900
Score 66 p.
*Originally composed for piano duet, orchestra-
ted by the composer.*

BOURGUIGNON, FRANCIS DE.   Brussels 28 May 1890
Brussels 11 April 1961

5560 [Two South American sketches, Op. 26] *10'*
1.O luar do Sertão (Moonlight in the brush)
2.Tango
3(3rd alt. Picc.),2,3,2-4,4,3,1-Timp.,Perc.-
Cel.,Hp.-Str.
A. Cranz, Brussels, c1932
Score 31 p.
Composed 1928.

BOVÉ, HENRY.   Philadelphia 1897

3352 Three impressions
1.Andante 2.Allegretto 3.Allegro ma non
troppo
2,2(2nd alt. E.H.),2,2-2,2,1-Timp.-Hp.-Str.
Ms.
Score 55 p.
Composed 1939-40.

BOWLES, PAUL FREDERIC.
b. New York City 30 December 1910

3151 Yankee clipper, ballet   *40'*
Complete in 16 movements
3(2nd&3rd alt. Picc.),3(1st alt. E.H.),4*(B.Cl.
ad lib.),3*-0,3,3,1-Timp.,Perc.-Pno.,Hp.-
Voices(backstage)-Str.
Ms.
Score 243 p.
*Commissioned by the Ballet Caravan, 1936.
Composed 1936. First performance by the Ballet
Caravan, Robin Hood Dell, Philadelphia, 19
July 1937, Philadelphia Orchestra, Alexander
Smallens conductor.*

BOYCE, WILLIAM.   London ca.1710
Kensington, London 7 February 1779

6830 Overture in D minor, The Cambridge ode.
Transcribed and edited by Constant Lambert
Larghetto - Allegro assai
2Ob.,Bn.(optional)-Str.
Oxford University Press, London, c1939
Score 7 p.
*Originally composed for chorus, 1749, to a
text by William Mason. First performance
Senate House at Cambridge, 1 July 1749, at the
installation of the Duke of Newcastle as
chancellor of the University.*

Pan and Syrinx
See: STANLEY, JOHN.
[Pan and Syrinx. Overture]

221s [Sonatas nos. 1 and 2, two violins with
figured bass. Arranged for string orchestra
and piano by James Brown]
Sonata 1 in A minor: Prelude - Fugue - Balletto
grazioso
Sonata 2 in F major: Sinfonia - Interlude -
Bourree - Jig
Pno.-Str.
Stainer & Bell, London, c1924
Score 20 p.

1953s [Sonatas nos. 10 and 12, two   *14'*
violins with figured bass. Excerpts. Transcribed for small orchestra by C.M. Campbell
and Hubert Parry] Edited by Sydney Robjohns
Sonata 10: 1.Adagio - Allegro 2.Lento
3.Tempo di minuetto
Sonata 12: Tempo di gavotta
1,1,1,1-Timp.-Str.
Joseph Williams, London, c1892
Score 13 p.
First published in 1747.

704s [Symphony no. 1, B-flat major] Edited by
Constant Lambert
1.Allegro 2.Andante dolce 3.Vivace
Fl.(optional),2Ob.-Str.
Oxford University Press, London, c1928
Score 8 p.

727s [Symphony no. 2, A major] Edited by
Constant Lambert
1.Allegro assai 2.Vivace 3.Presto
2Ob.-Str.
Oxford University Press, London, c1928
Score 8 p.

774s [Symphony no. 3, C major] Edited by
Constant Lambert
1.Allegro 2.Vivace 3.Menuetto
2Ob.,Bn.(optional)-Str.
Oxford University Press, London, c1928
Score 10 p.

761s [Symphony no. 4, F major] Edited by
Constant Lambert
1.Allegro 2.Vivace ma non troppo 3.Gavot
2Ob.-2Hn.-Str.
Oxford University Press, London, c1928
Score 8 p.

848s [Symphony no. 5, D major] Edited by
Constant Lambert
1.Allegro ma non troppo 2.Tempo di gavotta
3.Menuetto
2Ob.(optional)-2Tpt.-Str.
Oxford University Press, London, c1928
Score 16 p.

753s [Symphony no. 6, F major] Edited by
Constant Lambert
1.Largo e sostenuto 2.Larghetto
2Ob.-Str.
Oxford University Press, London, c1928
Score 8 p.

Boyce, William

775s [Symphony no. 7, B-flat major] Edited by
Constant Lambert
1.Andante 2.Andante moderato 3.Jigg
2Fl.(optional),2Ob.-Str.
Oxford University Press, London, ᶜ1928
Score 10 p.

849s [Symphony no. 8, D minor] Edited by
Constant Lambert
1.Pomposo 2.Andante 3.Gavotta: Risoluto
2Fl.,2Ob.-Str.
Oxford University Press, London, ᶜ1928
Score 16 p.

BOYD, JEANNE.
        b. Mt. Carroll, Illinois 25 February 1890

5917 Eleventurous dances, suite for   21'
orchestra
1.Preludicrous: Fast and facetiously 2.Alle-
mandarin: With good manners 3.Courantics:
Friskily 4.Sarabandon: Forlornly 5.Haba-
nearly: Almost in the spirit of (♩=63-69)
6.Minuetiquette: Politely 7.Polkaleidoscope:
Galumphingly 8.Pavanille: With sweet state-
liness 9.Valsetting: With life, but with lim-
itations 10.Marchness: With merry cunning
11.Giguerilla: With skirmish
3*,2,3(3rd alt. B.Cl.),3*-4,2,3,1-Timp.,Perc.
Pno.-Str.
Ms.
Score 82 p.
*Commissioned by the Sigma Alpha Iota music
fraternity. Originally composed for string
quartet, two flutes, clarinet and piano, 1943.
This transcription for full orchestra, 1951.
Four movements of the orchestral version first
performed Chicago, 10 March 1959, American
Conservatory Symphony Orchestra, Russell Harvey conductor.*

5908 Introduction and fugue   7'
2,2,2,2-4,2,3,1-Timp.,Cym.,Bells-Str.
Ms.
Score 34 p.
*Composed 1949. First performance Rochester,
27 April 1960, Eastman-Rochester Symphony,
Howard Hanson conductor.*

5923 Song against ease, symphonic poem   17'
1.Lento - Moderato 2.Allegretto 3.Moderato
4.Alla marcia
3*,3*,3*,2-4,2,3,1-Timp.,Perc.-Hp.-Str.
Ms.
Score 66 p.
*Based on a poem, Song Against Ease, by Schar-
mel Iris, from his book Bread Out of Stone.
Composed 1940. First performance Rochester,
22 October 1946, Eastman-Rochester Symphony,
Howard Hanson conductor.*

3041 Symphonic suite. Andante lamentabile   5'
[original version]
2,3*,2,3*-4,1,3,1-Timp.-Hp.-Str.
Ms.
Score 16 p.

*From the suite composed 1922. First perform-
ance of this excerpt, Rochester, 25 November
1925, Rochester Philharmonic Orchestra, Howard
Hanson conductor. In a revision of this work
made in 1938, the composer added a 2nd trumpet,
cymbals and gong.*

BOYLE, GEORGE FREDERICK.
            Sydney, Australia 29 June 1886
            Philadelphia 20 June 1948

2876 Aubade, for orchestra   6'
3*,2,2,2-4Hn.-Timp.,Trgl.-Hp.-Str.
Ms.
Score 39 p.
*Composed 1915. First performance St. Louis,
Missouri, 5 March 1916, St. Louis Symphony
Orchestra, Max Zach conductor.*

708p Concertino, for piano and chamber   13'
orchestra
1.Carnival 2.Pastorale 3.March
Solo Pno.-1,1,1,1-Hn.-Str.
Ms.
Score 87 p.
*Originally composed as Suite for 2 Pianos, 1932.
Arranged 1935. First performance Philadelphia,
11 March 1936, Chamber Orchestra of Philadelphia and Composers' Laboratory, Isadore Freed
conductor, Josef Wissow soloist.*

720p [Concerto, piano, D minor]   25'
1.Moderato 2.Tranquillo, ma non troppo lento
3.Allegro energico, ma non troppo vivace
Solo Pno.-2,2(2nd alt. E.H.),2,2-4,2,3-Timp.,
Trgl.-Str.
Ms.
Score 152 p.
*Composed 1911. First performance Worcester
Music Festival, Worcester, Massachusetts, 28
September 1911, Gustav Strube conductor, Ernest
Hutcheson soloist.*

738c Concerto, violoncello and orchestra   22'
Solo Vc.-2,2,2,2-4,2-Timp.-Hp.-Str.
Ms.
Score 105 p.
*Composed 1917. First performance Washington,
D.C., 7 February 1918, Philadelphia Orchestra,
Leopold Stokowski conductor, Hans Kindler
soloist.*

2850 Slumber song   7'
2,2,2,2-4Hn.-Timp.,Trgl.-Hp.-Str.
Ms.
Score 18 p.
*Composed 1915. First performance Chicago, 9
November 1915, American Symphony Orchestra,
Glenn Dillard Gunn conductor.*

2903 Symphonic fantasie   13'
3*,3*,3*,3*-4,3,3,1-Timp.,Trgl.-Hp.-Str.
Ms.
Score 65 p.
*Composed 1915. First performance St. Louis,
Missouri, 15 December 1916, St. Louis Symphony
Orchestra, Max Zach conductor.*

BOZI, HAROLD DE.

1212s Brin de brise [A gentle breeze, romance
without words]
Fl.,Cl.-Str.
Score: Ms. 10 p.
Parts: Ricordi, Milan, c1927

BOZZA, EUGÈNE.   Nice 4 April 1905

2095s [Sinfonietta for string orchestra,   22'
Op. 61]
1.Andante - Allegro 2.Andante 3.Allegro molto
Str.
Alphonse Leduc, Paris, c1946
Score 35 p.
Composed 1944.

BRAEIN, EDVARD.   Kristiansund, Norway 3 April 1887
                  Kristiansund 20 September 1957

2175s [Cradle song, for string orchestra] 2'30"
Str.
Norsk Musikforlag, Oslo, c1950
Score 5 p.
Composed 1909.

5234 [Religious folk tunes from Nordmør]   13'
1.[I see Thee standing, Lamb of God, from the
region of Aure] 2.[Father, here's a tainted
soul, from the region of Stemshaug] 3.[A
little child so pleasant, from the region of
Stangvik]
2,2,2,2-2Hn.-Timp.-Str.
Harald Lyche, Drammen, Norway, c1947
Score 26 p.
Composed 1947.

BRAGA, FRANCISCO.   Rio de Janeiro 15 April 1868
                        Rio de Janeiro 14 March 1945

206s Aubade [Morning serenade] Op. 10
Str.
Bock, Dresden, c1898
Score 5 p.

4235 [Landscape, symphonic prelude]
2,2,2,2-4,2,2,1-Timp.,Cym.,B.Dr.-Hp.-Str.
Ms.
Score 23 p.

4147 [Marabá, symphonic poem on Brazilian
themes]
2,3*,2,2-4,2,3,1-Timp.,Cym.-Hp.-Str.
Casa Bevilacqua, Rio de Janeiro [n.d.]
Score 42 p.

366s Marionettes, gavotte
Str.
Leduc, Paris, c1895
Score 4 p.

BRAHMS, JOHANNES.   Hamburg 7 May 1833
                            Vienna 3 April 1897

160 [Academic festival overture, Op. 80]   13'
3*,2,2,3*-4,3,3,1-Timp.,Perc.-Str.
Breitkopf & Härtel, Wiesbaden [n.d.]

Score 36 p.
*Composed 1880 in acknowledgment of the honorary
doctor's degree awarded Brahms by the University of Breslau. First performance Breslau, 4
January 1881, the composer conducting.*

405p [Concerto, piano, no. 1, Op. 15,   42'
D minor]
1.Maestoso 2.Adagio 3.Rondo: Allegro non
troppo
Solo Pno.-2,2,2,2-4,2-Timp.-Str.
Peters, Leipzig [n.d.]
Score 101 p.
*Completed 1858. First and second movements re-
written from a sonata for two pianos, originally
composed as a symphony in 1854 and left unfinished. First performance Hanover, 22 January
1859, Joseph Joachim conductor, the composer
as soloist.*

386p [Concerto, piano, no. 2, Op. 83,   49'
B-flat major]
1.Allegro non troppo 2.Allegro appassionato
3.Andante 4.Allegretto grazioso
Solo Pno.-2*,2,2,2-4,2-Timp.-Str.
Breitkopf & Härtel, Leipzig [n.d.]
Score 107 p.
*First performance Budapest, 9 November 1881,
Alexander Erkel conductor, the composer as
soloist.*

425v [Concerto, violin, Op. 77, D major]   39'
1.Allegro non troppo 2.Adagio 3.Allegro
giocoso, ma non troppo vivace
Solo Vn.-2,2,2,2-4,2-Timp.-Str.
Breitkopf & Härtel, Wiesbaden [n.d.]
Score 66 p.
*Composed 1878. First performance Gewandhaus,
Leipzig, 1 January 1879, the composer con-
ducting, Joseph Joachim soloist.*

745m [Concerto, violin and violoncello,   33'
Op. 102, A minor]
1.Allegro 2.Andante 3.Vivace non troppo
Solo Vn., Solo Vc.-2,2,2,2-4,2-Timp.-Str.
Breitkopf & Härtel, Leipzig [n.d.]
Score 68 p.
*First performance Cologne, 18 October 1887, the
composer conducting, Joseph Joachim and Robert
Hausmann soloists.*

2324s [Eleven chorale-preludes, Op. 122. Book
II, no. 8, Es ist ein Ros' entsprungen. Tran-
scribed for string orchestra by Reginald
Jacques]
Str.
Oxford University Press, London, c1949
Score 3 p.
Originally composed for organ, 1896.

57s [Eleven chorale-preludes, Op. 122.   3'
Book II, no. 8, Es ist ein Ros' entsprungen.
Transcribed for string orchestra by A. Walter
Kramer]
Str.
Associated Music Publishers, New York, c1933
Score 3 p.

Brahms, Johannes

Transcribed 1933. First performance New York, broadcast from Station WOR, Cesare Sodero conductor.

633 [Fantasias, piano, Op. 116. No. 4, *4'*
Intermezzo. Arranged by Paul Klengel]
2,1,2,2-2Hn.-Str.
Simrock, Berlin, c1893
Score 8 p.
First performance Leipzig, 1892, Paul Klengel conductor.

525 [Hungarian dances. Nos. 1, 3, and 10. *8'*
Arranged by Johannes Brahms]
3*,2,2,2-4,2-Timp.,Perc.-Str.
Broude Brothers, New York [n.d.]
Score 22 p.
Originally composed for piano 4-hands. Arranged 1873; published 1874. First performance, Gewandhaus, Leipzig, February 1874, the composer conducting.

528 [Hungarian dances. Nos. 2 and 7. *5'*
Orchestrated by Andreas Hallén]
2,2,2,2-4,2,3-Timp.,Small Dr.-Str.
[n.p., n.d.]
Score 34 p.
Orchestrated and first performed Stockholm, 1894.

526 [Hungarian dances. No. 4. Orchestrated *5'*
by Paul Juon]
3*,2,2,2-4,2,3-Timp.-Hp.(or Pno.)-Str.
Simrock, Berlin, c1908
Score 19 p.
Orchestrated 1908. First performance Berlin, 1908.

527 [Hungarian dances. Nos. 5, 6, and 7. *6'*
Arranged by Martin Schmeling]
3*,2,2,2-4,2,3-Timp.,Perc.-Str.
Breitkopf & Härtel, Leipzig, c1956
Score 32 p.

836 [Hungarian dances. Nos. 11 through *13'*
16. Orchestrated by A. Parlow]
3*,2,2,2-4,2,3-Timp.-Hp.-Str.
Simrock, Leipzig [n.d.]
Score 95 p.

837 [Hungarian dances. Nos. 17 through *10'*
21. Orchestrated by Antonín Dvořák]
3*,2,2,2-4,2,3-Timp.,Perc.-Hp.-Str.
Simrock, Leipzig [n.d.]
Score 80 p.

634 [Intermezzo, Op. 117 no. 1. Arranged *5'*
for orchestra by Paul Klengel]
1,0,2,2-2Hn.-Str.
Simrock, Berlin, c1893
Score 7 p.
An arrangement of no. 1 of Brahms' Three Intermezzi, for piano, Op. 117. First performance Leipzig, 1892, Paul Klengel conductor.

193s [Intermezzo, Op. 117 no. 1. Arranged
for string orchestra by Paul Klengel]
Str.
Simrock, Berlin [n.d.]
Score 7 p.

485s [Liebeslieder waltzes, Op. 52. Arranged
for string quintet or string orchestra by
Friedrich Hermann]
Str.
[n.p., n.d.]
Score 39 p.
Originally composed for piano 4-hands and four voices.

1301s Lullaby. Arranged for string *3'*
orchestra by Henri Elkan
Str.(with Vn.III and Pno. ad lib.)
Elkan-Vogel, Philadelphia, c1933
Score 4 p.
Originally Op. 49 no. 4, for voice and piano. Arranged 1933. First performance Ardmore, Pennsylvania, 21 May 1933, Main Line Orchestra, Adolph Vogel conductor.

441 [Serenade no. 1, large orchestra, *35'*
Op. 11, D major]
1.Allegro molto 2.Scherzo 3.Adagio non troppo
4.Menuetto I, Menuetto II 5.Scherzo 6.Rondo
2,2,2,2-4,2-Timp.-Str.
Kalmus, New York [n.d.]
Score 84 p.
Composed 1857-59 as Octet in three movements for strings and woodwinds; arranged for orchestra 1859. First performance Hamburg, 1859, Joseph Joachim conductor.

529 [Serenade no. 2, small orchestra, *32'*
Op. 16, A major]
1.Allegro moderato 2.Scherzo 3.Adagio non
troppo 4.Quasi menuetto 5.Rondo
2,2,2,2-2Hn.-Str.(without Vn.)
Breitkopf & Härtel, Wiesbaden [n.d.]
Score 58 p.
Composed 1859-60. First performance at a Philharmonic concert, Hamburg, 10 February 1860, the composer conducting. Revised by the composer, 1875.

6701 [Sonata, piano, no. 3, Op. 5, F minor.
Transcribed for orchestra by Elizabeth
Camerano]
1.Allegro maestoso 2.Andante espressivo
3.Scherzo 4.Intermezzo 5.Finale
3(3rd alt. Picc.),3*,3*,3*-4,3,3,1-Timp.,B.Dr.
-Hp.-Str.
Ms. c1965 by Elizabeth Camerano
Score 186 p. Large folio
Originally composed 1853.

416 [Symphony no. 1, Op. 68, C minor] *48'*
1.Un poco sostenuto - Allegro 2.Andante sostenuto 3.Un poco allegretto e grazioso
4.Adagio - Più andante - Allegro non troppo,
ma con brio
2,2,2,3*-4,2,3-Timp.-Str.
Breitkopf & Härtel, Wiesbaden [n.d.]
Score 86 p.
Begun 1862; completed 1876. First performance Karlsruhe, 4 November 1876, Otto Dessoff conductor.

373 [Symphony no. 2, Op. 73, D major]   *43'*
1.Allegro non troppo 2.Adagio non troppo
3.Allegretto grazioso (Quasi andantino)
4.Allegro con spirito
2,2,2,2-4,2,3,1-Timp.-Str.
Breitkopf & Härtel, Wiesbaden [n.d.]
Score 74 p.
*Composed 1877. First performance Vienna, 30
December 1877, Hans Richter conductor.*

530 [Symphony no. 3, Op. 90, F major]   *36'*
1.Allegro con brio 2.Andante 3.Poco
allegretto 4.Allegro
2,2,2,3*-4,2,3-Timp.-Str.
Score: Kalmus, New York [n.d.] 86 p.
Parts: Breitkopf & Härtel, Leipzig [n.d.]
*Composed 1882-83. First performance Vienna,
2 December 1883, Hans Richter conductor.*

154 [Symphony no. 4, Op. 98, E minor]   *43'*
1.Allegro non troppo 2.Andante moderato
3.Allegro giocoso 4.Allegro energico e
passionato
2,2,2,3-4,2,3-Timp.,Trgl.-Str.
Breitkopf & Härtel, Wiesbaden [n.d.]
Score 98 p.
*Composed 1884-85. First performance Meinin-
gen, 25 October 1885, the composer conducting.*

524 Tragic overture, Op. 81, D minor   *13'*
3*,2,2,2-4,2,3,1-Timp.-Str.
Breitkopf & Härtel [n.p., n.d.]
Score 26 p.
*Composed 1880. First performance Vienna, 26
December 1880, Hans Richter conductor.*

3249 Variations and fugue on a theme by   *26'*
Handel, Op. 24. Orchestrated by Edmund
Rubbra [as his Op. 47]
2*,2,2,2-4,2,3-Timp.-Hp.-Str.
Universal Edition, London, ͨ1938
Score 84 p.
*Originally composed for piano, 1861. Orches-
trated 1938. First performance London, 17
November 1938, Royal Philharmonic Society,
Adrian Boult conductor.*

377 [Variations on a theme by Joseph   *17'*
Haydn, Chorale St. Antoni, for orchestra,
Op. 56a]
3*,2,2,3*-4,2-Timp.,Trgl.-Str.
Breitkopf & Härtel, Wiesbaden [n.d.]
Score 38 p.
*Composed 1873. First performance at a Phil-
harmonic concert, Vienna, 2 November 1873, the
composer conducting.*

5099 Variations on a theme by Robert Schumann,
for piano, Op. 9. Transcribed for orchestra by
Gregor Fitelberg
2(2nd alt. Picc.),2,2(2nd alt. B.Cl.),2-4,2,3,
1-Timp.,Cym.,Trgl.-Cel.,Hp.-Str.
Ms.
Score 57 p. Large folio
*The theme is from Schumann's Bunte Blätter, Op.
99 no. 1. Originally composed for piano, 1854.*

5909 [Variations on a theme by Robert Schumann,
piano 4-hands, Op. 23. Transcribed for orchestra by Theodor Müller-Reuter]
2,2,2,2-4,2,3-Timp.-Str.
J. Rieter-Biedermann, Leipzig, ͨ1901
Score 42 p.
*The theme is Schumann's Letzter Gedanke, com-
posed 1854. Brahms' Variations composed for
piano 4-hands, 1861.*

1317 [Waltzes, Op. 39. Arranged for orchestra
by Reynaldo Hahn]
3*,2,2,2-4,2,2Cnt.-Timp.,Perc.-2Hp.-Str.
Heugel, Paris [n.d.]
Score 95 p.
*Originally composed for piano 4-hands.
Waltzes 6 and 13 not included in this arrange-
ment.*

424v [Waltzes, Op. 39. No. 15, A major.
Arranged for violin solo and small orchestra
by William F. Happich]
Solo Vn.-2,2,2,1-2Hn.-Hp.-Str.
Ms.
Score 10 p.
Orchestrated for the Symphony Club, 1920.

BRAMBACH, CASPAR JOSEPH.   Oberdollendorf
          near Königswinter, Germany 14 July 1833
                              Bonn 19 June 1902

5213 [Ariadne. Overture]
2,2,2,2-4,2,3,1-Timp.-Str.
Fr. Kistner, Leipzig [1886]
Score 34 p.
*From the opera in 3 acts with libretto by Otto
Freudenberg.*

BRANCACCIO, CARLO.

Not to be confused with his son Roland, born
1913, or with Antonio Brancaccio, 1813-1846.

916 [Prelude for orchestra, Op. 1]   *4'*
2,3*,3*,3-4,3,3,1-Timp.-Hp.-Str.
Breitkopf & Härtel, Leipzig, ͨ1903
Score 20 p.

BRANDMANN, ISRAEL.
    b. Kamenetz-Podolsk, Ukraine 1 December 1901

3820 [The pioneers (Hechalutz), symphonic   *20'*
poem, Op. 10]
In one movement: [An old wanderer's song -
Lamentation - Song of the stone-masons -
Working song - Song of the night watchman -
Hora]
3*,3*,2,2-4,3,3,1-Timp.,Perc.-Cel.,Hp.-Str.
Ms.
Score 143 p.
*The Hechalutz were the Zionist settlers in 20th
century Palestine. Composed 1930. First per-
formance Vienna, 1 February 1931, Vienna Sym-
phony Orchestra, the composer conducting.*

1824s [Variations on a Palestinian folk dance,
for string quartet or string orchestra]
Str.

Brandmann, Israel

Jibneh, Vienna, ^c1934
Score 16 p.
Theme is Hava Nagila.

752p [Variations on a theme of Joel Engel, *14'*
for piano and string orchestra]
Solo Pno.-Str.
Ms.
Score 34 p.
Composed ca.1934.

BRANDTS-BUYS, JAN.
Zutphen, Holland 12 September 1868
Salzburg, Austria 8 December 1933

1547 Bilder aus dem Kinderleben [Pictures *18'*
from childhood]
2,2,2,2-4,3,3,1-Timp.,Perc.-Hp.-Str.
Schott, Mainz, ^c1922
Score 53 p.
*Composed 1921. First performance Mainz, January
1923, Hans Rosbaud conductor.*

601p [Concert piece, piano and orchestra, Op. 3,
D-flat major]
Solo Pno.-2,2,2,2-4,2-Timp.-Str.
A. Cranz, Leipzig [189-?]
Score 27 p.

541p [Concerto, piano, Op. 15, F major]
1.Allegro maestoso 2.Adagio ma non troppo 3.
Allegro vivace
Solo Pno.-2,2,2,3*(C.Bn. or Cb.Sarrus.)-4,2-
Timp.-Str.
Schlesinger, Berlin [1900]
Score 98 p.
Awarded the Bösendörfer Prize, Vienna, 1897.

1495s [Dances and airs, Op. 17. No. 2, D minor,
for violin, violoncello and string orchestra]
Solo Vn.,Solo Vc.-Str.
A. Cranz, Leipzig, ^c1900
Score 3 p.

1496s [Dances and airs, Op. 17. No. 5, G major,
for solo violin, harp and string orchestra]
Solo Vn.-Hp.-Str.
A. Cranz, Leipzig, ^c1900
Score 4 p.

744s Leid [Sorrow]
Hp. or Pno.(ad lib.)-Str.
Score: Ms. 6 p.
Parts: A. Cranz, Leipzig [1898?]
Originally composed for full orchestra.

1463s [Suite, string orchestra with harp and
horn, Op. 7, G major]
1.Ode 2.Scherzo 3.Intermezzo 4.Finale
Hn.-Hp.-Str.
A. Cranz, Hamburg [1896]
Score 19 p.

647c [Tancred, concert piece for violoncello
and small orchestra, Op. 35]
Solo Vc.-2,2,2,2-3,2-Timp.-Str.
Josef Weinberger, Leipzig, ^c1917
Score 41 p.
Tancred (1076-1112) was a hero of the Crusades.

129s Tristesse [Sorrow. Transcribed for string
orchestra by William F. Happich]
Str.
Ms.
Score 3 p.
*Originally composed for full orchestra. This
transcription commissioned by Edwin A.
Fleisher for the Symphony Club, Philadelphia,
1917. Bound with Komzák's Folksong.*

781s Trost im Leid [Comfort in sorrow]
Str.
Score: Ms. 3 p.
Parts: A. Cranz, Leipzig [1898?]

BRANSCOMBE, GENA. Picton, Ontario 4 November 1881
New York 26 July 1977

152s [A memory, violin and piano, Op. 21 *2'30"*
no. 3. Transcribed for string orchestra and
harp by William F. Happich]
Hp.-Str.
Ms.
Score 7 p.
*Originally composed ca.1910. This transcrip-
tion commissioned by Edwin A. Fleisher for the
Symphony Club, Philadelphia, 1922.*

7302 Quebec, symphonic suite for *14'30"*
orchestra and tenor voice
1.Prologue, Quebec, great guardian-portal
2.Baladine 3.Procession
Tenor Voice Solo(1st movement only)-3*,2,2,2-
4,4,3,1-Timp.,Perc.-Hp.-Str.
Ms.
Score 68 p. Large folio
*Originally composed as part of an opera, The
Bells of Circumstance, which remained unfinished.
Text of the first movement by the composer.
The baladine is a medieval French dance brought
to Canada by the earliest settlers. The 3rd
movement depicts the relief of the Quebec
garrison by French troops, 30 June 1665.
First performance Chicago, 1928, Chicago
Women's Symphony Orchestra, the composer con-
ducting.*

BRANT, CYR DE. pseudonym.
See: HIGGINSON, JOSEPH VINCENT.

BRANT, HENRY DREYFUS. Montreal 15 September 1913

2855 Ballad, for orchestra *5'*
1(alt. Picc.),1,2,1-2,2,1-Perc.-Pno.-Str.
Ms.
Score 20 p.
*Composed 1935. First performance New York, 22
April 1938, Radio WOR Little Symphony, Fritz
Mahler conductor.*

1064m Concerto for alto saxophone with *20'*
wind instruments and percussion
1.Prelude 2.Idyll - Moderato sostenuto
3.Caprice
Solo Alto Sax.-1,0,6*(1Alto Cl.)-Tuba(or Cb.)-
Perc.
Ms.
Score 150 p.

Originally composed for saxophone and orchestra, 1941. This transcription for saxophone and band, 1950.

4726 Dedication, in memory of a great man   *10'*
2,2,2,2-4,3,3,1-Timp.,Perc.-Str.
Ms.
Score 21 p.
Composed 1945. In memory of President Franklin D. Roosevelt.

2839 Lyric piece, for orchestra   *5'*
1,1,1,1-1,1,1-Str.
Ms.
Score 11 p.
Composed 1933. First performance New School for Social Research, New York, 16 October 1933, American Chamber Orchestra, Bernard Herrmann conductor.

3035 Music for a five and ten cent store, for full orchestra, Op. 3
2,2,3*-0,3,2,1-Perc.-2Pno.-Str.
Ms.
Score 57 p.
Originally composed for piano, violin and percussion, 1932. This orchestration 1933.

2847 Prelude and fugue, for brass and   *5'*
strings
2Hn.,2Tpt.,2Tbn.,Tuba-Str.
Ms.
Score 33 p.
Composed 1935.

4947 A requiem in summer   *10'*
1.Intrada: Calmo 2.Ricercata: Serioso, sostenuto
2Fl.,2Ob.,2Cl.,2Bn.-Str.(without Cb.)
Ms.
Score 39 p.
Originally composed 1934 as Intrada and Ricercata. Revised 1938, 1948.

1739s Two choral preludes for string   *10'*
orchestra
[1]In D major: Expressively [2]In A major: Very sustained
Str.
Ms.
Score 14 p.
Originally composed for two pianos; this version made 1932.

7070 Verticals ascending, after the Rodia   *8'*
Towers, for two separated instrumental groups [2 conductors]
Group I: 2Ob.,2Bn.-Alto Sax.(optional)-2Tpt., Tbn.-Pno.
Group II: Picc.,Fl.,Cl.,Alto Cl.,B.Cl.-2Hn., Tuba-Perc.-Electric Org.(optional)
MCA Music, New York, c1969
Score 42 p.
Inspired by the Watts Towers built by Simon Rodia in Los Angeles. Composed 1967.

BRASE, FRITZ.   Egestorf, Germany 4 May 1884

4612 [Episodes. Suite in three   *I: 10'*
movements]   *II: 12'*
1.Fackeltanz (Torch dance)   *III: 8'*
2.Reminiszenzen 3.Karneval
2(2nd alt. Picc.),2,2,2-4,2,3-Timp.,Perc.-Hp.-Str.
Richard Birnbach, Berlin, c1939
Score in reduction 23 p.

BRASSIN, LOUIS.   Aix-la-Chapelle 24 June 1840
St. Petersburg 17 May 1884

Family name was originally de Brassine

428p [Concerto, piano, no. 1, Op. 22,   *22'*
F major]
1.Allegro con fuoco 2.Andante 3.Allegro vivace
Solo Pno.-2,2,2,2-3,2,3-Timp.,Trgl.(ad lib.)-Str.
Score: Ms. 173 p.
Parts and solo: Breitkopf & Härtel, Leipzig [1865]
Composed 1862. First performance Berlin, 1864.

BRAUER, MAX.   Mannheim, Germany 9 May 1855
Karlsruhe, Germany 2 January 1918

306s [Suite, string orchestra, Op. 14, E minor]
1.Praeludium 2.Bourrée 3.Andante 4.Menuett 5.Rondo
Str.
R. Forberg, Leipzig [n.d.]
Score 42 p.

BRAUN, ED.

771m Fantasy for oboe and orchestra, Op. 26
Solo Ob.-2,0,2,2-2,2,1-Str.
Score: Ms. 37 p.
Parts: C.F. Schmidt, Heilbronn [n.d.]

BRAUN, YEHEZKIEL. Breslau, Germany 18 January 1922

2254s Psalm for string orchestra (1959)   *16'*
Str.
Israeli Music Publications, Tel Aviv, c1960
Score 44 p.
Commissioned by the Ramat-Gan Chamber Orchestra, Israel. Composed 1959. First performance Ramat-Gan, Israel, January 1960, Ramat-Gan Chamber Orchestra, F. Choset conductor.

6487 Symphony of dances   *20'*
2(2nd alt. Picc.),2(2nd alt. E.H.),2(2nd alt. B.Cl.),2(2nd alt. C.Bn.)-4,2,3,1-Timp.,Perc.-Hp.-Str.
Israeli Music Publications, Tel Aviv, c1963
Score 54 p.
Commissioned by the Israeli Composers' Fund, Jerusalem. Composed 1963. First performance Tel Aviv, February 1964, Israeli Philharmonic Orchestra, Sergiu Commissiona conductor.

Braunfels, Walter

BRAUNFELS, WALTER.
                    Frankfurt, Germany 19 December 1882
                    Cologne 19 March 1954

1579 [The birds, Op. 30. Doves' wedding]   *10'*
  2,2,2,2-4,2,3-Timp.,Perc.-Hp.-Str.
  Universal Edition, Vienna, c1921
  Score 33 p.
  *From the opera with libretto by the composer,
  after Aristophanes' play. Composed 1919. First
  performance Munich, 4 December 1920, Bruno
  Walter conductor.*

976 [Carnival overture to E.T.A. Hoffmann's   *12'*
  Princess Brambilla, Op. 22]
  3(3rd alt. Picc.),3*,5*,4,Heckelphone(or: 3,3,
  4,3)-6,4(1 ad lib.),3,1-Timp.,Perc.-Hp.-Str.
  Ries & Erler, Berlin, c1912
  Score 51 p.
  *Inspired by E.T.A. Hoffmann's story; Braunfels
  also composed an opera based on this story.
  Composed 1910. First performance Dresden, 1912,
  Ernst Schuch conductor.*

580p [Concerto, piano, Op. 21, A major]
  1.Allegro, ma non troppo 2.Adagio 3.Allegro
  Solo Pno.-3(2nd & 3rd alt. Picc.I & II),3*,4*,
  3-4,3,3,1-Timp.,Trgl.-Hp.-Str.
  F.E.C. Leuckart, Leipzig [n.d.]
  Score 140 p.

1580 [Don Juan, a classic-romantic   *30'*
  phantasmagoria, Op. 34]
  3(3rd alt. Picc.),3(3rd alt. E.H.),4,4-4,3,3,1
  -Timp.,Perc.-Hp.-Str.
  Universal Edition, Vienna, c1925
  Score 147 p.
  *Composed 1924. First performance Leipzig,
  1924, Wilhelm Furtwängler conductor.*

1581 [Fantastic apparitions of a theme of   *46'*
  Hector Berlioz, Op. 25]
  3(3rd alt. Picc.),3,4,4-4,3,3,1-Timp.,Perc.-
  2Hp.-Str.
  Universal Edition, Vienna, c1919
  Score 208 p.
  *Composed 1915-16. First performance Zurich,
  1920, Volkmar Andreae conductor.*

2222 Der gläserne Berg [The glass   *24'*
  mountain. Orchestral suite from the opera,
  Op. 39b]
  1.[Prelude] 2.[Will-o'the-wisps] 3.[The
  princess rides on the white wolf's back]
  4.[At the mother of the winds] 5.[At mother
  sun] 6.[With the good moon] 7.[Petrus and
  the princess wander through the starry space]
  8.[In the glass mountain] 9.[Deliverance of
  the enchanted prince]
  1(alt. Picc.),1(alt. E.H.),2,1(alt. C.Bn.)-2,
  1,1-Timp.,Perc.-Pno.,Cel.,Hp.,Harm.-Str.
  Universal Edition, Vienna, c1929
  Score 84 p.
  *From the opera with libretto by Josefa Elstner-
  Oertel. Composed 1928. First performance of
  this suite Cologne, 30 April 1929, Hermann
  Abendroth conductor.*

1578 Präludium und Fuge, Op. 36   *20'*
  3*,3*,5*(1Cl. in D),4*-4,3,3,1-Timp.,Perc.-
  Hp.-Str.
  Universal Edition, Vienna, c1926
  Score 64 p.
  *Composed 1925. First performance Krefeld,
  1925, Rudolf Siegel conductor.*

1449 [Serenade for small orchestra, Op.   *20'*
  20, E-flat major]
  1.Leicht bewegt 2.Lebhaft, ausgelassen 3.
  Ruhig 4.[Twice as fast as Movement 3]
  3,2*,2,2-4,2-Timp.,B.Dr.,Trgl.-Hp.-Str.
  Ries & Erler, Berlin, c1911
  Score 62 p.
  *Composed 1911. First performance Munich, 1912,
  Ferdinand Löwe conductor.*

1793 [Symphonic variations on an old French
  children's song, Op. 15]
  2(2nd alt. Picc.),2,2,2-4,2,3,1-Timp.,Perc.-
  Str.
  D. Rahter, Leipzig, c1909
  Score 87 p.

BRAVNIČAR, MATIJA.   Tolmin near Gorica,
                            Yugoslavia 24 February 1897

5404 [King Mattias, symphonic overture]   *7'*
  3*,3*,2,2-4,2,3,1-Timp.,Perc.-Str.
  [State Publishing House of Slovenia, Ljubljana,
  1948. Copyright assigned 1954 to Københavns
  Musik Forlag]
  Miniature score 65 p.
  *Composed 1932. First performance Ljubljana,
  14 November 1932, Slovenian Philharmonic
  Society, Mirko Polič conductor.*

5896 [Slovene burlesque dance]   *5'*
  3*,2,2,2-4,2,3,1-Timp.,Perc.-Hp.-Str.
  [State Publishing House of Slovenia, Ljubljana,
  1949. c1932 by Hinrichsen Verlag]
  Miniature score 45 p.
  *Composed 1932. Original title: Plesna Bur-
  leska. First performance Ljubljana, 19 February 1932, Slovenska Filharmonija Ljubljana,
  Mirko Polič conductor.*

6078 [Symphonic antithesis]   *25'*
  1.Largo 2.Allegro vivo
  3*,2,2,2-4,2,3,1-Timp.,Perc.-Hp.-Str.
  [State Publishing House of Slovenia, Ljubljana,
  1949. c1944]
  Score 135 p.
  *Commissioned by Københavns Musikforlag. Com-
  posed 1944. First performance Ljubljana,
  2 September 1948, Slovene Philharmonic Society,
  Jakov Cipci conductor. Awarded a prize by
  the Yugoslav Composers Society in 1953.*

BREE, JEAN BERNARD VAN.   Amsterdam 29 January 1801
                          Amsterdam 14 February 1857

160s Allegro [for 4 string quartets]
  Str.
  Theune, Amsterdam [n.d.]
  Score 52 p.
  *Posthumous work. First performance Caecilia
  Concert, Amsterdam, 19 November 1846.*

BRENNER, LUDWIG, RITTER VON.
Leipzig 19 September 1833
Berlin 9 February 1902

40s Schlummerlied [Slumber song, pizzicato-
piece] Op. 61
Str.(without Cb.)
Schlesinger, Berlin [n.d.]
Score 7 p.

BRENTA, GASTON.
Schaerbeek near Brussels 10 June 1902
Brussels 30 May 1969

5187 [Tin soldiers]   3'
2(2nd alt. Picc.),2,2,2-2,2,3-Timp.,Perc.-Str.
Universal Edition, Vienna, c1937
Score 13 p.
Composed 1937.

5561 [Variations on a Congolese theme]
1.Prélude 2.Fileuse 3.Mazurka 4.Fugato 5.
Tempo di valse 6.Ragtime 7.Oriental 8.Finale
2(2nd alt. Picc.),2(2nd alt. E.H.),2,2-4,2,3,1
-Timp.,Perc.-Hp.-Str.
Les Éditions Buyst, Brussels [n.d.]
Score 28 p.
Composed 1926.

BREPSANT, ENGLEHARDT(?).

788m Air varié no. 6, fantaisie pour clarinette
Solo Cl.-2,2,2,2-2,2,3-Timp.,B.Dr.,Side Dr.-
Str.
Score: Ms. 36 p.
Parts: Lafleur, Paris [n.d.]

BRESCIA, DOMENICO.
Pitano, Pola, Italy 1866
Oakland, California 1939

5083 Joyful moment
3*,2,2,2-4,2,3,1-Timp.-Hp.-Str.
Ms.
Score 12 p.

4185 Medea. Preamble and 6 interludes
Fl.,Cl.-Tam-tam-Pno.(alt. Cel.),Hp.-Str.
Ms.
Score 81 p.
Incidental music to the play by Euripides.

4819 Ricercare (quasi fantasia) e fuga
1,1,2,1-2,2,1-Timp.-Hp.-Str.
Ms.
Score 50 p.
*Originally composed for organ. Transcribed
for orchestra in 1933.*

4231 [Symphonic fragment, for trombones and
tuba]
3Tbn.,Tuba
Ms.
Score 4 p.
Composed 1900.

BRESGEN, CESAR.   Florence, Italy 16 October 1913

4336 [Hollersbach dance suite]

1.Leicht bewegt 2.Ganztaktig, ruhig fliessend
3.Lebhaft 4.Ruhig schwingend 4a.Lebhaft be-
schwingt 5.Polka
2,0,2,1-2,1-Timp.,Trgl.-Str.
Ludwig Voggenreiter, Potsdam, 1941
Score 19 p.

BRETON Y HERNÁNDEZ, TOMÁS.
Salamanca 29 December 1850
Madrid 2 December 1923

2374 Escenas andaluzas [Andalusian scenes,
Spanish suite]
1.Bolero 2.Polo gitano [Andalusian gypsy song]
3.March - Saeta 4.Zapateado [Clog-dance]
3*,2(2nd alt. E.H.),2,2-2,2,3,1-Timp.,Perc.-
Hp.-Str.
Ms.
Score 103 p.
Composed 1894.

BRÉVAL, JEAN BAPTISTE.   Paris 6 November 1753
Chamouille near Laon 18 March 1823

234m [Sinfonia concertante, clarinet, horn,
bassoon & string orchestra, Op. 38, F major]
1.Allegro maestoso 2.Adagio 3.Rondo (Alle-
gretto)
Solo Cl.,Solo Hn.,Solo Bn.-Str.
Edition KaWe, Amsterdam, c1968
Score in reduction 25 p.
Composed ca.1795.

BRIAN, HAVERGAL.
Dresden, Staffordshire 29 January 1876
Shoreham, England 28 November 1972

5276 Doctor Merryheart, a comedy overture   16'
Allegro vivace e giocoso - Whimsies and sun-
shadows - Smiles and storms - Dreams: Asleep in
the arms of Venus - Merryheart as chivalrous
knight chases Bluebeard - Merryheart fights a
dragon - Merryheart leads a procession of heroes
- Merryheart awake - The dance of Merryheart
3(3rd alt. Picc.),3*,3*,3*-4,3,3,1-Timp.,Perc.-
Hp.-Str.
Breitkopf & Härtel, Leipzig, c1913 by Havergal
Brian
Score 81 p.
*Composed 1911-12. First performance Second
Musical League Festival, Birmingham, England,
3 January 1913, Musical League Festival Orchestra, Julius Harrison conductor.*

6838 Fantastic variations on an old rhyme   20'
3(3rd alt. Picc.),2*,2,2-4,3,3,1-Timp.,Perc.-
Org.(ad lib.),Hp.-Str.
Breitkopf & Härtel, Leipzig, c1914 by Havergal
Brian
Score 46 p.
The old rhyme is Three Blind Mice. Composed

Brian, Havergal

*1907. First performance Brighton, Sussex, 28
April 1921, West Pier Orchestra, Lyell Taylor
conductor.*

4381 In memoriam, tone poem for orchestra   *17'*
3(3rd alt. Picc.),3*,3*,3(3rd alt. C.Bn.)-4,4,
3,1-Timp.,Perc.-Org.,2Hp.-Str.
Breitkopf & Härtel, Leipzig, ᶜ1913 by Havergal
Brian
Score 51 p.
*Composed 1910. First performance Usher Hall,
Edinburgh, 26 December 1921, Scottish Orchestra,
Landon Ronald conductor.*

BRICKEN, CARL ERNEST.
          b. Shelbyville, Kentucky 28 December 1898

2794 Suite for orchestra   *15'*
1.Adagio 2.Allegretto 3.Andante 4.Allegro
5.Moderato
2,2,2,3*-4,2,3,1-Timp.,Dulcitone-Hp.-Str.
Ms.
Score 68 p.
*Composed 1930. First performance Chicago, 16
December 1932, University of Chicago Symphony
Orchestra, the composer conducting.*

BRIDGE, FRANK.   Brighton, England 26 February 1879
                 Eastbourne, England 10 January 1941

1841s A Christmas dance, Sir Roger de Coverley,
for strings
Str.
Augener, London, ᶜ1923
Score 15 p.
Originally composed for string quartet, 1922.

1842s An Irish melody, The Londonderry Air,
for strings
Str.(Cb. ad lib.)
Augener, London, ᶜ1915
Miniature score 11 p.
*Commissioned by the Hambourg family in 1908,
to form one movement of a quartet on The
Londonderry Air. Collaborating composers
(York Bowen, Eric Coates, J.D. Davis, Hamilton
Harty) were also each to write one movement.
Originally composed for string quartet, 1908.*

367s Lament for string orchestra   *7'*
Str.
Goodwin & Tabb, London, ᶜ1915
Score 8 p.
*Composed 1915 on the death of the composer's
daughter, who perished in the Lusitania
disaster.*

6202 Norse legend. Transcribed for   *4'*
orchestra
1,1,2,1-2,2,1-Timp.-Hp.-Str.
Boosey & Hawkes, London, ᶜ1939 by Winthrop
Rogers
Score 16 p.
Originally composed for violin and piano, 1905.

816s Sally in our alley; Cherry ripe. Two old
English songs arranged for string quartet or
string orchestra

Str.(Cb. ad lib.)
Rogers, London [ᶜ1916]
Score 23 p.

4430 The sea, suite for orchestra   *21'*
1.Seascape 2.Sea foam 3.Moonlight 4.Storm
3*,3*,3*,3*-4,3,3,1-Timp.,Perc.-Hp.-Str.
Stainer & Bell, London, ᶜ1920 by Frank Bridge
Score 109 p. Large folio
*Composed 1910-11. First performance London,
Promenade Concerts, 24 September 1912.*

211s Suite for string orchestra [E minor]
1.Prelude 2.Intermezzo 3.Nocturne 4.Finale
Str.
Curwen & Tabb, London, ᶜ1920
Score 28 p.
Composed January, 1910.

2029 Summer, tone poem for orchestra   *12'*
2(2nd alt. Picc.),2,2,2-2,2-Timp.,Cym.-Cel.,
Hp.-Str.
Augener, London, ᶜ1923
Score 29 p.
*Composed 1914. First performance London, 13
March 1916, Royal Philharmonic Society, the
composer conducting.*

4637 There is a willow grows aslant a   *10'*
brook, impression for small orchestra
1,1,2,1-Hn.-Hp.-Str.
Augener Ltd., London, ᶜ1928
Score 16 p.
*The title is a quotation from Shakespeare's
Hamlet. Composed 1928. Presented as a ballet
by the Camargo Society. Work is also known as
the Ophelia Impression.*

2028 Two poems for orchestra   *10'*
3*,2,2,2-4,2,3,1-Timp.,Perc.-Hp.-Str.
Augener, London, ᶜ1923
Score 36 p.
*Based upon words of Richard Jefferies. Composed
1915. First performance Queen's Hall, London,
1 January 1917, the composer conducting.*

BRINDEL, BERNARD.   Chicago 23 April 1912

727p Concerto for piano and orchestra   *20'*
Solo Pno.-4*,2,2,3*-4,2,3,1-Timp.,B.Dr.-Str.
Ms.
Score 75 p.
Composed 1933.

3046 Five tonal pictures   *15'*
[1.Tranquil night 2.Spring reverie 3.Revelry
4.Autumnal meditation 5.Snowflakes]
4*,2,2,3*-4,2,3,1-Timp.,Perc.-Pno.-Str.
Ms.
Score 85 p.
Composed 1934-38.

BRINK, JULES TEN.   Amsterdam 4 November 1838
                      Paris 9 February 1889

962v [Concerto caractéristique, violin, Op. 11,
B-flat major]
1.Allegro molto 2.Reverie 3.Gypsy dance

Solo Vn.-3*,2,2,2-2,2,3-Timp.,Perc.-Str.
Score: Ms. 71 p.
Parts: Enoch, Paris [n.d.]

BRISSON, FREDERICK.   Angoulême 25 December 1821
                                    Orleans 1900

442s Ronde de nuit. Arranged for string
      quintet by E. Jacque
      Str.
      Richault, Paris [n.d.]
      Score 15 p.

BRISTOW, GEORGE FREDERICK.
              Brooklyn, New York 19 December 1825
              New York 13 December 1898

5412 [The great republic, Op. 47. Overture] 19'
      3*,2,2,2-4,2,3,1-Timp.,Perc.-Str.
      Ms.
      Score 66 p.
      From the cantata. First performance by the
      Brooklyn Philharmonic Society, 10 May 1879.

5440 [Rip Van Winkle, Op. 22. Overture]
      3*,2,2,2-4,2,3-Timp.-Str.
      Ms.
      Score 24 p.
      From the opera with libretto by Jonathan Howard
      Wainwright, based on the story by Washington
      Irving. First performance Niblo's Astor Place
      Theatre, New York, 27 September 1855.

5388 [Rip Van Winkle, Op. 22. No. 4, Concerted
      piece]
      2,2,2,2-2,2,3-Timp.-Str.
      Ms.
      Score 15 p.

5389 Serenade waltz
      1,1,2,1-2,1,1-Timp.-Str.
      Ms.
      Score 9 p.
      Composed 1849. Written for the Columbia
      College commencement.

6061 [Symphony no. 1, Op. 10, E-flat major] 43'
      1.[Introduction] - Allegro vivace 2.Adagio
      3.Minuetto - Trio 4.Finale: Allegro vivace -
      Allegro
      2,2,2,2-4,2,1-Timp.-Str.
      Ms.
      Score 89 p. Large folio
      Composed 1848.

5445 [Symphony no. 2, Jullien, Op. 24, D minor]
      1.Allegro appassionato 2.Allegretto 3.Adagio
      4.Finale: Allegro agitato - Grandioso
      2,2,2,2-4,2,3-Timp.-Str.
      Ms.
      Score 90 p. Large folio
      Written for Louis Antoine Jullien. First per-
      formance New York, 1 March 1856, New York Phil-
      harmonic Society, Louis Jullien conductor.

5694 [Symphony no. 3, Op. 26, F-sharp minor]
      1.Allegro 2.Andante 3.Scherzo 4.Finale:
      Allegro con fuoco

2,2,2,2-4,2,3-Timp.-Hp.-Str.
Ms.
Score 96 p.
Composed 1858. First performance New York,
26 March 1859, New York Philharmonic Society.

5542 [Symphony no. 4, Arcadian, Op. 49,
      E minor]
      1.Allegro appassionato 2.Adagio (Motive:
      Tallis' Evening Hymn) 3.Allegro ma non troppo
      (Indian war dance) 4.Finale: Allegro con
      spirito - Presto
      3*,2,2,2-4,2,3,1-Timp.,Cym.,Trgl.-Str.
      Ms.
      Score 192 p.
      Original title: The Pioneer. Composed 1872.
      First performance New York, 14 February 1874,
      New York Philharmonic Society.

5669 Waltz (For Columbia College)
      1,1,2,1-2,1,1-Timp.-Str.
      Ms.
      Score 6 p.

5638 [Winter's tale, overture]
      2(2nd alt. Picc.),2,2,2-2,2,2-Timp.,S.Dr.-Str.
      Ms.
      Score 24 p.
      Composed 1886 for the play by Shakespeare.

BRITAIN, RADIE.   Amarillo, Texas 17 March 1903

6220 Cactus rhapsody   12'
      3(3rd alt. Picc.),3(3rd alt. E.H.),2,2-4,3,3,1
      -Timp.,Perc.-Hp.-Str.
      Ms.
      Score 83 p. Large folio
      Composed 1950. First performance Washington,
      D.C., 4 April 1960, United States Air Force
      Symphony, John F. Yesutaitis conductor.

6298 Cowboy rhapsody   10'
      3(3rd alt. Picc.),2,2,2-4,3,3,1-Timp.,Perc.-
      Hp.-Str.
      Ms.
      Score 63 p. Large folio
      Composed 1956. First performance Amarillo,
      Texas, 23 October 1956, Amarillo Symphony
      Orchestra, A. Clyde Roller conductor.

6222 Franciscan sketches   16'
      1.San Luis Rey 2.Saint Francis of Assisi
      3(3rd alt. Picc.),2,2,3*-4,3,3,1-Timp.,Perc.-
      Pno.(alt. Cel. ad lib.),Org.,Hp.-Str.
      Ms.
      Score 26 p. Large folio
      Composed 1941. First performance Los Angeles,
      California, 9 January 1944, Whittier Symphony,
      Ruth Haroldson conductor.

2818 Heroic poem. Dedicated to Col.   15'
      Lindbergh's flight to Paris
      3*,3*,3*,3*-4,3(also 4Tpt. in rear of hall),3,1
      -Timp.,Perc.-Cel.,Hp.-Str.
      Ms.
      Score 62 p.
      Composed 1930. Awarded 3rd prize in the Holly-
      wood Bowl International Contest, 1930. First

Britain, Radie

performance Rochester, 3 March 1932, Rochester Philharmonic Orchestra, Howard Hanson conductor.

2813 Infant suite, three movements for   5'
small orchestra
1.The infant 2.Berceuse 3.Toy parade
1,1,1,1-Hn.,Tpt.-Perc.-Cel.(ad lib.),Hp.(or Pno.)-Str.
Ms.
Score 36 p.
Originally composed for piano, 1934; arranged for orchestra, 1935. First performance Los Angeles, 19 February 1936, Los Angeles Symphony Orchestra of the WPA, Modest Altschuler conductor.

3641 Light   9'
3*,3*,3*,3*-4,3,3,1-Timp.,Perc.-Hp.-Str.
Ms.
Score 57 p.
Composed 1935. First performance Chicago, 29 November 1938, Woman's Symphony Orchestra, Gladys Welge conductor. Awarded first prize in the National Contest for Women Composers sponsored by the Boston Woman's Symphony Society, 1941.

5398 Ontonagan sketches   15'
1.Sunset on Lake Superior 2.Woods at dusk
3.Victoria Falls
3(3rd alt. Picc.),3*,3*,3*-4,3,3,1-Timp.,Perc.-Pno.,Cel.,Hp.-Str.
Ms.
Score 121 p. Large folio
Suggested by scenes in Ontonagon County, Michigan. Composed 1939-40. Awarded first prize by the San Antonio Music Club, 1942.

2797 Prelude to a drama   6'
3,3,3,3-4,3,3,1-Timp.,Cym.-Hp.-Str.
Ms.
Score 36 p.
Original title: Pygmalion Overture (after the Greek Legend). Composed 1930. First performance Chicago, 31 January 1937, Illinois Symphony Orchestra of the WPA, Albert Goldberg conductor.

5578 Saturnale   12'
3(3rd alt. Picc.),3*,3*,3*-4,3,3,1-Timp.,Perc.-Pno.,Hp.-Tenor Voice(ad lib.)-Str.
Ms.
Score 90 p. Large folio
Composed 1940. First performance Washington, D.C., 19 February 1957, United States Air Force Symphony, George Howard conductor.

6437 [Symphony, Cosmic mist]   24'
1.In the beginning 2.Nebula 3.Nuclear fission
3(3rd alt. Picc.),2,2,2-4,3,3,1-Timp.,Perc.-Pno.,Hp.-Str.
Ms.
Score 107 p. Large folio
Composed 1962. Received the first National Award for Women Composers sponsored by the

National Society of Pen Women, Washington, D.C., 1964.

3045 [Symphony, Southern, in four   25'
movements]
1.Maestoso - Allegro 2.Adagio 3.Rhumbando
4.Allegro moderato
3*,3*,3*,3*-4,3,3,1-Timp.,Perc.-Cel.,Hp.-Str.
Ms.
Score 190 p.
Composed 1936-37. First performance Chicago, 4 March 1940, Illinois Symphony Orchestra of the WPA, Izler Solomon conductor.

BRITTEN, BENJAMIN.
    Lowestoft, Suffolk, England 22 November 1913
        Aldeburgh, England 4 December 1976

Full name: Edward Benjamin Britten

765p [Concerto, piano, no. 1, Op. 13, D   33'
major]
1.Allegro molto e con brio 2.Allegretto alla valse 3.Recitative and aria 4.Allegro moderato, sempre alla marcia
Solo Pno.-2(both alt. Picc.),2(2nd alt. E.H.),2,2-4,2,3,1-Timp.,Perc.-Hp.-Str.
Ms.
Score 232 p.
Composed 1938. First performance at a Promenade Concert, Queen's Hall, London, 18 August 1938, BBC Symphony Orchestra, Henry Wood conductor, the composer as soloist.

1156v [Concerto, violin, no. 1, Op. 15,
D minor]
1.Moderato con moto 2.Vivace 3.Passacaglia
Solo Vn.-3(2nd&3rd alt. 2Picc.),2,2,2-4,3,3,1-Timp.,Perc.-Hp.-Str.
Ms.
Score 125 p.
Composed 1939. First performance New York, 28 March 1940, New York Philharmonic, John Barbirolli conductor, Antonio Brosa soloist.

780p Diversions on a theme, piano solo   20'
and orchestra, Op. 21
Solo Pno.-2(2nd alt. Picc.),2(2nd alt. E.H.),2(2nd alt. Cl. in E-flat),3*-Alto Sax.(ad lib.)-4,2,3,1-Timp.,Perc.-Hp.-Str.
Boosey & Hawkes, New York, c1941
Score 81 p.
Solo piano is written for left hand alone. Composed at the suggestion of Paul Wittgenstein in 1940. First performance Philadelphia, 16 January 1942, Philadelphia Orchestra, Eugene Ormandy conductor, Paul Wittgenstein soloist.

Mont Juic
    See: BERKELEY, LENNOX.
        Mont Juic, suite of Catalan dances

317p Scottish ballad, for two pianos   13'
and orchestra, Op. 26
Lento - Alla marcia funebre (Lento maestoso) - Allegro molto - Vivacissimo

2Solo Pno.-2(2nd alt. Picc.),2,2,3-4,2,3,1-
Timp.,Perc.-Hp.-Str.
Ms. Boosey & Hawkes, c1946
Score 59 p. Large folio
*Composed 1941. First performance Cincinnati,
28 November 1941, Cincinnati Symphony Orches-
tra, Eugene Goossens conductor, Ethel Bartlett
and Rae Robertson soloists.*

2161s Simple symphony for string orchestra *15'*
(or string quartet), Op. 4
1.Boisterous bourrée 2.Playful pizzicato
3.Sentimental saraband 4.Frolicsome finale
Str.
Oxford University Press, London, c1934
Score 22 p.
*Note from composer: "Entirely based on mate-
rial from works which the composer wrote
between the ages of nine and twelve. Although
the development of these themes is in many
places quite new, there are large stretches
of the work which are taken bodily from the
early pieces - save for the re-scoring for
strings." Composed 1934. First performance
Stuart Hall, Norwich, 6 March 1934, Norwich
String Orchestra, the composer conducting.*

4059 Sinfonia da requiem, Op. 20   *20'*
1.Lacrymosa 2.Dies Irae 3.Requiem Aeternum
3*(3rd also alt. B.Fl.),3*,3*(1Cl. in E-flat),
3*-Alto Sax.-6(5th&6th ad lib.),3,3,1-Timp.,
Perc.-Pno.,2Hp.(2nd ad lib.)-Str.
Boosey & Hawkes, New York, c1942
Score 66 p.
*Composed 1940. First performance New York,
19 March 1941, New York Philharmonic, John
Barbirolli conductor.*

3292 Sinfonietta, Op. 1   *15'*
1.Presto 2.Variations 3.Tarantella
1,1,1,1-Hn.-Str.
Boosey & Hawkes, London, c1935
Score 48 p.
*Composed 1932. First performance London, Feb-
ruary 1933, Lemare Orchestra, Iris Lemare conductor.*

3310 Soirées musicales, suite of five   *11'*
movements from Rossini, Op. 9
1.March 2.Canzonetta 3.Tirolese 4.Bolero
5.Tarantella
2(2nd alt. Picc.),2,2,2-4,2,3-Timp.,Perc.-Hp.
(or Pno.)-Str.
Hawkes & Son, London, c1938
Score 65 p.
*Originally composed for flute, oboe, clarinet,
percussion, boys' voices and piano, 1935; transcribed 1936. The score also includes a version for small orchestra. First performance
London, 16 January 1937, BBC Orchestra,
Joseph Lewis conductor.*

Variations and fugue on a theme of Purcell
See: The young person's guide to the
        orchestra

1768s Variations on a theme of Frank   *25'*
  Bridge, Op. 10

Str.
Augener, London, c1911
Score 58 p.
*Written as a tribute to the composer's teacher,
Frank Bridge. The theme is taken from one of
his Idylls for string quartet. Composed 1937.
First performance at a Salzburg Festival,
Salzburg, summer 1937, Boyd Neel String Orches-
tra, Boyd Neel conductor.*

5173 The young person's guide to the   *17-19'*
orchestra, variations and fugue on a theme of
Purcell, Op. 34
3*,2,2,2-4,2,3,1-Timp.,Perc.-Hp.-Str.
Hawkes & Son, London, c1947
Score 69 p.
*Originally composed 1946 to form the sound
track of an educational film entitled Instru-
ments of the Orchestra. First performance
Liverpool, 15 October 1946, Liverpool Philhar-
monic Orchestra, Malcolm Sargent conductor.
Performed as a modern classical ballet Oui ou
Non? (Ballet de la Paix), Paris, June 1949,
Association des Amis de la Danse.*

BROCKWAY, HOWARD A.
                Brooklyn, New York 22 November 1870
                New York 20 February 1951

704v Cavatina, Op. 13
Solo Vn.-Cl.-2Hn.-Str.
Schlesinger, Berlin, c1895
Score 7 p.

5925 Sylvan suite for orchestra, Op. 19
1.At midday 2.Will o' the wisps 3.Dance of
the sylphs (slow waltz) 4.At midnight 5.At
daybreak
2,2,2,2-4,2,3,1-Timp.-Hp.-Str.
G. Schirmer, New York, c1900
Score 63 p.
*Composed ca.1898-99. First performance Boston,
6 April 1901, Boston Symphony Orchestra, Wilhelm Gericke conductor.*

BROD, HENRI.   Paris 4 April 1801
                                Paris 6 April 1839

691m Morceau de salon [for solo oboe and
orchestra] Op. 54
Solo Ob.-2,0,2,2-2,2-Timp.-Str.
Score: Ms. 61 p.
Parts: [n.p., n.d.]

BROMAN, STEN.   Uppsala, Sweden 25 March 1902

6777 [Symphony no. 4]   *22'*
1.Fantasia: Andante - Vivace - Adagio
2.Finale: Andante - Presto - Vivace
4*(2Picc.),3*,3*,3*-4,3,3,1-Timp.,Perc.-Cel.,
2Hp.-Str.
Edition Suecia, Stockholm [n.d.]
Score 79 p. Large folio
*Commissioned by the Detroit Symphony Orchestra.
Composed 1965. First performance Detroit, 17
November 1966, Detroit Symphony Orchestra,
Sixten Ehrling conductor.*

Bronsart, Hans von

BRONSART, HANS VON.   Berlin 11 February 1830
                      Munich 3 November 1913

Born: Hans Bronsart von Schellendorf

564p [Concerto, piano, Op. 10, F-sharp   *25'*
minor]
1.Allegro maestoso 2.Adagio ma non troppo 3.
Allegro con fuoco
Solo Pno.-2,2,2,2-4,2-Timp.-Str.
Fritsch, Leipzig [n.d.]
Score 71 p.
Composed and first performed Hanover, 1876.

5072 [Spring fantasy, Op. 11]
1.[Winter boredom] 2.[The approach of spring]
3.Liebestraum 4.[Life's storms] 5.[Hymn to
Spring]
3*,2,2,2-4,2,3,1-Timp.,Trgl.,B.Dr.-Hp.-Str.
Breitkopf & Härtel, Leipzig [1880]
Score 108 p.

BROOKS, ERNEST.
      b. Springfield, Missouri 14 October 1903

757p Piano symphony, Op. 98 [revised   *18'*
version]
1.[No tempo indicated] 2.[No tempo indicated]
3.Very fast
Solo Pno.-3*,2,3*,2-4,3,3,1-Timp.,Perc.-Str.
Ms.
Score 130 p.
Composed 1929; revised 1939.

BROTT, ALEXANDER.   Montreal 14 March 1915

5880 Prelude to oblivion (Atomic style)
1,1,1,1-0,2,2-Timp.,Perc.-Pno.,Hp.-Str.
Ms.
Score 21 p. Large folio
Composed 1951.

BROUSTET, ÉDOUARD.   Toulouse, France 29 April 1836
                     Louchon December 1901

581m Badinerie [for solo flute and orchestra]
Solo Fl.-2Cl.-Str.
Score: Ms. 18 p.
Parts: Durand, Paris [n.d.]

1522s Berceuse [violin and string orchestra]
Op. 105
Solo Vn.-Str.
Score: Ms. 8 p.
Parts: Durand, Paris [n.d.]

538s Introduction and gavotte [Op. 46, B-flat
major]
Str.
Hamelle, Paris [n.d.]
Score 7 p.

5408 [Moroccan dance (Air de ballet), Op. 53]
2*,2,2,2-4,2,2Cnt.,3,1-Timp.,Perc.-
Str.
V. Durdilly & Cie., Paris [n.d.]
Score 39 p.

5154 [Polish songs, Op. 31. Orchestrated by
Jules Massenet]
1.Moderato rubato 2.Vivo
2(2nd alt. Picc.),2,2,2-4,2,3-Timp.-Hp.-Str.
E. Minier, Paris [n.d.]
Score 31 p.

BROWN, GERTRUDE M. Briarcliff Manor, New York 1907

3030 Prelude and allegro   *10'*
3*,3*,2,2-3,2,3-Timp.-Str.
Ms.
Score 19 p.
*Composed 1929. First performance Rochester,
New York, 20 February 1930, Rochester Philhar-
monic Orchestra, Howard Hanson conductor.*

BROWN, HAROLD.   New York 1909

6602 Divertimento for small orchestra   *9'*
1.Air 2.Dance
1(alt. Picc.),1(alt. E.H.),2(2nd alt. B.Cl.),1
-2,2,1,1-Timp.,Perc.-Pno.(alt. Cel.),Hp.-Str.
Composers Facsimile Edition, New York, ᶜ1952
by Harold Brown
Score 60 p. Large folio
Composed 1945.

3952 Introduction and allegro for large   *20'*
orchestra
3*,2*,3*,2-4,3,3,1-Timp.,Perc.-Str.
Ms.
Score 119 p. Large folio
*Composed 1938. First performance Rochester,
New York, 29 October 1941, Eastman-Rochester
Symphony Orchestra, Howard Hanson conductor.*

3719 Orchestral suite no. 1   *25'*
1.Prelude 2.Interlude 3.Dirge 4.Dance
3*,3*,3*,2-4,3,3,1-Timp.,Perc.-Pno.,Cel.,Hp.-
Str.
Ms.
Score 166 p. Large folio
*Composed 1940. First performance Rochester,
26 October 1943, Eastman-Rochester Symphony
Orchestra, Howard Hanson conductor.*

1853s Suite for string orchestra   *17'*
1.Prelude 2.Slowly, with flowing lines
3.Crisp and bright
Str.
Ms.
Score 32 p. Large folio
*Composed 1937. First performance broadcast
over the Mutual Broadcasting System (WOR), New
York, 14 June 1937, Symphonic Strings, Alfred
Wallenstein conductor.*

BROWN, JAMES.

42s The Edric album; eight pieces by various
composers, for string orchestra with piano.
Edited by James Brown
1.Alceste, March (Gluck) 2.Gavotte (Handel)
3.O mistress mine (Morley) 4.Minuet (Purcell)
5.Ballet (J.S. Bach) 6.Scipio, March (Handel)
7.Lottie is dead (Traditional Swedish dance)
8.Traditional Swedish folk dance

Pno.(optional)-Str.
Stainer & Bell, London, c1919
Score 16 p.

43s The Sheen album; seven pieces for string
orchestra with piano. Edited by James Brown
1.Atys, Gavotte (Lully) 2.March (J.S. Bach)
3.Polonaise (J.S. Bach) 4.Bourrée in G minor
(Handel) 5.Minuet (Arne) 6.Jig: The Irish
washerwoman 7.Old English dance tune
Pno.(optional)-Str.
Stainer & Bell, London, c1920
Score 12 p.

34s Swedish dances, for string orchestra with
piano. Edited by James Brown
1.Polska 2.Daldans 3.Swedish waltz 4.Var-
sovienne (Swedish) 5.Polka 6.Swedish
folk-dance 7.Swedish folk-dance
Pno.(optional)-Str.
Stainer & Bell, London, c1920
Score 16 p.

850s The Tilford album; two modern pieces for
string orchestra. Edited by James Brown
1.Elegy (Harry Farjeon) 2.Aubade (Helen Milne)
Pno.(optional)-Str.
Stainer & Bell, London, c1926
Score 20 p.

BROWN, JAMES E.
        b. Huntington, New York 29 December 1937

7204 Fixed ideas   11'
2,0,2,2-2,2,2-Perc.-Str.
Ms.
Score 35 p.
*Composed 1974. First performance Bethlehem,
Pennsylvania, 16 March 1975, Temple University
Orchestra, Jonathan Sternberg conductor. Selected for performance by the Orchestra Society
of Philadelphia as part of its Pennsylvania Composers Project 1976, made possible by a grant
from the Pennsylvania Council for the Arts with
performance materials prepared by The Fleisher
Collection of Orchestral Music and performed at
the Mandell Theater, Drexel University, Philadelphia, 30 May 1976, Orchestra Society of
Philadelphia, Sidney Rothstein conductor.*

BROWN, RAYNER. Des Moines, Iowa 23 February 1912

188m Concerto for organ and band   25'
1.Allegro 2.Andante 3.Scherzo 4.Fugue
Solo Org.-3*,2,6*(1Cl. in E-flat,1Alto Cl.),2-
4Sax.-4,3,3,2Bar.,1-Timp.,Perc.-Hp.-Cb.
Western International Music, Los Angeles, c1971
by Avant Music, Los Angeles
Score 89 p.
*Composed 1960. First performance Los Angeles,
University of Southern California Band, Irene
Robertson soloist.*

239p Concerto for two pianos, brass and   25'
percussion
1.Prelude 2.Allegro 3.Cadenza 4.Scherzo 5.
Chorale 6.Fugue
2Solo Pno.-0,0,0,0-4,6,6,1-Timp.,Perc.

Western International Music, Los Angeles, c1972
by Rayner Brown
Score 93 p.
*Composed 1971. First performance La Mirada,
California, Los Angeles Brass Society, Lester
Remsen conductor, Sharon Davis and Russell
Stepan soloists.*

7172 Fantasy-fugue, for brass and percussion 10'
4Hn.,6Tpt.,4Tbn.,Tuba-Timp.,Perc.
Western International Music, Los Angeles, c1973
by Rayner Brown
Score 89 p.
*Composed 1965. First performance Los Angeles,
Los Angeles Brass Society, Lester Remsen con-
ductor.*

187m Five pieces for organ, harp, brass,   20'
percussion
1.Toccata 2.Lento 3.Scherzo 4.Passacaglia
5.Fugue
Solo Org.-0,0,0,0-4,4,4,Bar.,1-Timp.,Perc.-Hp.
Western International Music, Los Angeles, c1970
by Avant Music, Los Angeles
Score 86 p.
*Composed 1963. First performance Los Angeles,
Los Angeles Brass Society, Lester Remsen conductor, Ladd Thomas soloist.*

7173 Prelude and fugue, for brass and   12'
percussion
4Hn.,4Tpt.,4Tbn.,Bar.,Tuba-Timp.,Perc.
Western International Music, Los Angeles, c1966
by Avant Music, Los Angeles
Score 27 p.
*Composed 1962. First performance Los Angeles,
Los Angeles Brass Society, Lester Remsen conductor.*

BROWNING, MORTIMER.   Baltimore 16 November 1891
                        Milford, Delaware 24 June 1953

995m [Concerto, theremin and orchestra,   11'
Op. 71, F major, in one movement]
Solo Theremin-3,3,3,2-4,3,3,1-Timp.,Perc.-Hp.-
Str.
Ms.
Score 56 p.
*Composed 1938. First performance Paris, 24
January 1939, l'Orchestre Symphonique de Paris,
Jean Manuel conductor, Lucie Bigelow Rosen
soloist.*

BRUCH, MAX.   Cologne 6 January 1838
                        Friedenau, near Berlin 2 October 1920

547v [Adagio appassionata for violin and   7'
orchestra, Op. 57]
Solo Vn.-2,2,2,2-4,2,3-Timp.-Str.
Simrock, Berlin, 1891
Score 42 p.
Composed 1890.

502c [Adagio on Celtic melodies, for   6'
violoncello and orchestra, Op. 56]
Solo Vc.-2,2,2,2-2,2-Str.
Simrock, Berlin, 1891
Score 31 p.
Composed 1890.

Bruch, Max

575c [Ave Maria, concert piece for violon-   *4'*
cello and orchestra, Op. 61]
Solo Vc.-2,2,2,2-4,2,3-Timp.-Str.
Simrock, Berlin, 1892
Score 26 p.
Composed 1891.

461c [Canzone, for violoncello and   *5'*
orchestra, Op. 55]
Solo Vc.-2,2,2,2-4,2-Timp.-Str.
Breitkopf & Härtel, Leipzig [1891]
Score 27 p.
Composed 1889. First performance Berlin, 1890.

519v [Concert piece, for violin and   *11'*
orchestra, Op. 84]
1.Allegro appassionato 2.Adagio, ma non
troppo lento
Solo Vn.-2,3*,2,3*-4,2,3-Timp.-Str.
Simrock, Berlin, c1911
Score 70 p.
Composed 1910.

418v [Concerto, violin, no. 1, Op. 26,   *27'*
G minor]
1.Prelude 2.Adagio 3.Finale
Solo Vn.-2,2,2,2-4,2-Timp.-Str.
Kalmus, New York [n.d.]
Score 120 p.
*Sketched 1857. Completed 1866. First per-
formance Coblenz, 24 April 1866, the composer
conducting, Otto von Königslöw soloist. Later
revised. First public performance of revised
version Bremen, 7 January 1868, Rheinthaler
conductor, Joseph Joachim soloist.*

428v [Concerto, violin, no. 2, Op. 44,   *24'*
D minor]
1.Adagio ma non troppo 2.Recitative: Allegro
moderato 3.Finale: Allegro molto
Solo Vn.-2,2,2,2-4,2,3-Timp.-Str.
Simrock, Berlin, 1878
Score 132 p.
*Composed 1877. First public performance Lon-
don, 3 November 1877, the composer conducting,
Pablo de Sarasate soloist.*

452v [Concerto, violin, no. 3, Op. 58,   *32'*
D minor]
1.Allegro energico 2.Adagio 3.Finale: Alle-
gro molto
Solo Vn.-2,2,2,2-4,2,3-Timp.-Str.
Simrock, Berlin, 1892
Score 152 p.
*Composed 1890-91. First performance Düsseldorf,
31 May 1891, the composer conducting, Joseph
Joachim soloist.*

450v [Fantasie on Scotch folk tunes,   *39'*
violin and orchestra, Op. 46, E-flat major]
1.Einleitung 2.Allegro 3.Andante sostenuto
4.Finale: Allegro guerriero
Solo Vn.-2,2,2,2-4,2,3,1-Timp.,Perc.-Hp.-Str.
Kalmus, New York [n.d.]
Score 109 p.
*Composed 1879. First performance Hamburg,
September 1880, Pablo de Sarasate soloist.*

520v [In memoriam, adagio for violin and   *9'*
orchestra, Op. 65]
Solo Vn.-2,2*,2,3*-4,2,3-Timp.,Cym.-Str.
Simrock, Berlin, c1893
Score 35 p.
Composed 1892.

1165v Kol nidrei, Op. 47. Transcribed for   *10'*
solo violin or violoncello with string
orchestra by Norman Black
Solo Vn. or Solo Vc.-Hp.-Str.
Score: Ms. 17 p.
Vc. Solo *and* Piano reduction: G. Schirmer,
New York, c1928, 1938

470c [Kol nidrei, adagio on Hebrew melodies   *6'*
for violoncello and orchestra, Op. 47]
Solo Vc.-2,2,2,2-4,2,3-Timp.-Hp.-Str.
Kalmus, New York [n.d.]
Score 29 p.
*Composed for the Jewish community in Liverpool,
1880. First performance Berlin, 1881, the
composer conducting.*

868 [The Loreley, Op. 16. Introduction]   *7'*
2,2,2,2-4,2,3-Timp.-Hp.-Str.
Siegel, Leipzig [1875 or 1876]
Score 15 p.
*From the opera in four acts with libretto by
Emanuel Geifel. Composed 1863. First per-
formance Mannheim, 14 June 1863, Vincenz
Lachner conductor.*

503v [Romanze, viola and orchestra, Op.   *5'*
85, F major]
Solo Va.-1,1,2,2-3,2-Timp.-Str.
Schott, Mainz, c1911 by Max Eschig
Score 30 p.
Composed 1909. First performance Berlin, 1910.

553v [Romanze, violin and orchestra,   *9'*
Op. 42, A minor]
Solo Vn.-2,2,2,2-4,2-Timp.-Str.
Simrock, Berlin [1874]
Score 49 p.
Composed 1873.

531v [Serenade, violin and orchestra,   *35'*
Op. 75, A minor]
1.Andante con moto 2.Alla marcia 3.Notturno
4.Allegro energico e vivace
Solo Vn.-2,2,2,2-4,2-Timp.-Str.
Simrock, Berlin, c1900
Score 143 p.
*Composed 1899. First performance Paris, 15
May 1901, Orchestre Lamoureux, the composer
conducting, Joseph Debroux soloist.*

374 [Suite on Russian folk melodies, Op. 79b]
1.Andante sostenuto 2.Adagio ma non troppo
lento 3.Dance: Vivace ma non troppo 4a.Ada-
gio sostenuto 4b.Funeral march: Andante sostenuto 5.Allegro energico ma non troppo
3*,3*,2,3*-4,4,3,1-Timp.,Perc.-Hp.-Str.
Simrock, Berlin, c1904
Score 84 p.

Bruckner, Anton

2166 [Swedish dances, Op. 63. Series 1]   10'
2(2nd alt. Picc.),2(2nd alt. E.H.),2,2-4,2,3,1
-Timp.,Trgl.-Str.
Simrock, Berlin, c1892
Score 43 p.
Op. 63 composed 1890. First performance Berlin, 1891.

445 [Swedish dances, Op. 63. Series 2]   9'
2,2(2nd alt. E.H.),2,2-4,2,3,1-Timp.,Trgl.-Str.
Simrock, Berlin, c1892
Score 47 p.

608 [Symphony no. 1, Op. 28, E-flat major]   35'
1.Allegro maestoso 2.Scherzo 3.Grave und
Finale
2,2,2,2-4,2,3-Timp.-Str.
Siegel, Leipzig [1877 or 1878]
Score 214 p.
Composed 1868. First performance Sondershausen, 26 July 1868, the composer conducting.

375 [Symphony no. 2, Op. 36, F minor]   30'
1.Allegro passionato, ma un poco maestoso
2.Adagio ma non troppo 3.Allegro molto
tranquillo
2,2,2,2-4,2,3-Timp.-Str.
Simrock, Berlin [ca.1870]
Score 228 p.
Composed 1870. First performance Leipzig, 24 November 1870, the composer conducting.

1275 [Symphony no. 3, Op. 51, E major]   36'
1.Andante sostenuto 2.Adagio 3.Scherzo
4.Finale: Allegro ma non troppo
2,2,2,2-4,3,3,1-Timp.-Str.
Breitkopf & Härtel, Leipzig [1887]
Score 161 p.
Composed 1885-86. First performance Breslau, 26 October 1886, the composer conducting.

BRUCKEN-FOCK, GERARD VON.   Koudekerke near
        Middleburg, Holland 28 December 1859
    Herdenhout near Haarlem, Holland 15 August 1935

5796 [Breton suite (Suite no. 5)]
1.[The sea in the distance] 2.Caprice
3.[Morning on the sea] 4.Hymne 5.[Breton
boat song] 6.[The storm]
3*,3*,3*,3*-4,3,3,1-Timp.,Perc.-Str.
Broekmans & Van Poppel, Amsterdam [n.d.]
Score 28 p.

BRUCKNER, ANTON.
        Ansfelden, Upper Austria 4 September 1824
            Vienna 11 October 1896

1246s [Quintet, strings, F major. Edited   24'
by Josef V. Wöss]
1.Gemässigt 2.Scherzo 3.Andante [4]Finale:
Lebhaft bewegt
Str.
Universal Edition, Vienna, 1922
Score 64 p.
Composed 1879. First performance Vienna, 8 January 1885, Joseph Hellmesberger's Quartet. This edition 1921.

2078 [Symphony no. 1, C minor. Revised   40'
version]
1.Allegro 2.Adagio - Andante 3.Scherzo:
Lebhaft - Trio: Langsam 4.Finale: Bewegt und
feurig
2,2,2,2-4,2,3-Timp.-Str.
Universal Edition, Vienna [n.d.]
Score 141 p.
Composed 1865-66. Revised 1890-91. First performance Vienna, 13 December 1891, Hans Richter conductor.

2153 [Symphony no. 2, C minor]   50'
1.Moderato 2.Andante 3.Scherzo 4.Finale
2,2,2,2-4,2,3-Timp.-Str.
Score: Kalmus, New York [n.d.]
Parts: Universal Edition, Vienna [n.d.]
Composed 1871-72. First performance 26 October 1873, the composer conducting.

1585 [Symphony no. 3, D minor]   60'
1.Mässig bewegt 2.Adagio (etwas bewegt) quasi
andante 3.Scherzo 4.Finale: Allegro
2,2,2,2-4,3,3-Timp.-Str.
Kalmus, New York [n.d.]
Score 171 p.
Composed 1872-73. Revised 1876-77; second revision 1889. First performance Vienna, 16 December 1877, the composer conducting. Also known as Bruckner's Wagner Symphony.

6533 [Symphony no. 4, Romantic, E-flat   60'
major. Original version. Edited by Robert
Haas]
1.Bewegt, nicht zu schnell 2.Andante - Andante
quasi allegretto 3.Scherzo 4.Finale: Bewegt,
doch nicht zu schnell
2,2,2,2-4,3,3,1-Timp.-Str.
Bruckner-Verlag, Leipzig, c1952
Score 152 p.
Composed 1873-74; not published during Bruckner's lifetime.

1582 [Symphony no. 4, Romantic, E-flat   60'
major. Revised version. Edited by Josef V.
Wöss]
1.Ruhig bewegt (Allegro molto moderato)
2.Andante 3.Scherzo: Bewegt - Trio: Gemächlich 4.Finale: Mässig bewegt
3(1st alt. Picc.),2,2,2-4,3,3,1-Timp.,Cym.-Str.
Universal Edition, Vienna [n.d.]
Score 99 p.
Revised 1878-80. First performance of this version Vienna, 20 February 1881, Hans Richter conductor.

2079 [Symphony no. 5, B-flat major]   60'
1.Adagio - Allegro - Langsamer 2.Adagio -
Langsamer 3.Scherzo: Molto vivace - Trio
4.Finale: Adagio - Allegro
3(3rd alt. Picc.),2,2,2-4,3,3,1-Timp.,Cym.,
Trgl.-Str.
Universal Edition, Vienna [n.d.]
Score 171 p.
Composed 1875-76. Revised 1881. First performance Graz, Austria, 8 April 1894, Franz Schalk conductor.

THE EDWIN A. FLEISHER

Bruckner, Anton

2080 [Symphony no. 6, A major]   60'
1.Maestoso 2.Adagio (Sehr feierlich)
3.Scherzo: Ruhig bewegt (Etwas gemessen) -
Trio 4.Finale: Bewegt, doch nicht zu schnell
2,2,2,2-4,3,3,1-Timp.-Str.
Universal Edition, Vienna [n.d.]
Score 135 p.
*Composed 1879-81. First complete performance
13 December 1901, Gustav Mahler conductor.*

6690 [Symphony no. 7, E major. Original   68'
version. Edited by Robert Haas]
1.Allegro moderato 2.Adagio: Sehr feierlich
und sehr langsam 3.Scherzo: Sehr schnell 4.
Finale: Bewegt, doch nicht schnell
2,2,2,2-4,3,3,5(Wagner-Tubas)-Timp.-Str.
Bruckner-Verlag, Leipzig, c1944
Score 135 p.
*Composed 1881-83. First performance Leipzig,
30 December 1884, Arthur Nikisch conductor.*

1583 [Symphony no. 7, E major. Revised   70'
version]
1.Allegro moderato - Sehr ruhig 2.Adagio -
Moderato 3.Scherzo: Sehr schnell - Trio:
Etwas langsamer 4.Finale: Bewegt, doch nicht
schnell
2,2,2,2-4,3,3,5(4Wagner Tubas)-Timp.,Cym.,
Trgl.-Str.
Universal Edition, Vienna [n.d.]
Score 99 p.

1584 [Symphony no. 8, C minor]   80'
1.Allegro moderato 2.Scherzo: Allegro
moderato - Trio: Langsam 3.Adagio - Langsam
4.Finale: Feierlich, nicht schnell
3,3,3,3(3rd alt. C.Bn.)-8(5-8 alt. 4Tuba),3,3,
1-Timp.,Cym.,Trgl.-Hp.-Str.
Haslinger, Vienna [n.d.]
Score 129 p.
*Composed 1885-86. Revised 1889-90. First
performance Vienna, 18 December 1892, Hans
Richter conductor.*

2081 [Symphony no. 9, D minor]   60'
1.Feierlich - Sehr ruhig 2.Scherzo: Bewegt,
lebhaft - Trio: Schnell 3.Adagio (Feierlich)
3(3rd alt. Picc.),3,3,3*-8(5-8 alt. 4Tuba),3,
3,1-Timp.-Str.
Universal Edition, Vienna [1903]
Score 143 p.
*Composed 1891-94 (Finale unfinished). First
performance Vienna, 11 February 1903,
Ferdinand Loewe conductor.*

BRÜCKNER, OSKAR.   Erfurt, Germany 2 January 1857
                       Wiesbaden(?) 8 June 1930

1599s [Romance, for violoncello solo and string
orchestra, Op. 2]
Solo Vc.-Str.(without Vc.)
Score: Ms. 7 p.
Parts: Seeling, Dresden [n.d.]

BRUHNS, GEORGE F. W. Bunzlau, Silesia 10 April 1874
                     Cranford, New Jersey 2 July 1963

1437 American rhapsody   12'
3*,3(1Alto Ob.),3*,3-7Sax.(1Sopranino,2Sop.,

3Alto,Ten.,all ad lib.)-4,5(1B.Tpt. ad lib.),
3,1-Timp.,Perc.-Cel.,2Hp.,Banjo(2 players, ad
lib.)-Str.
R. Jungnickel, New York, c1927
Score 69 p.
*Composed 1927. First performance University
of Illinois, October 1927, A. A. Harding conductor.*

BRÜLL, IGNAZ.   Prossnitz, Moravia 7 November 1846
                 Vienna 17 September 1907

573p Andante und allegro, Op. 88 [concert piece
for piano and orchestra]
Andante moderato, con moto - Allegro vivace
Solo Pno.-2,2,2,2-4,2-Timp.-Str.
Bote & Bock, Berlin [1901?]
Score 68 p.

569p [Concerto, piano, no. 1, Op. 10, F major]
1.Allegro moderato 2.Andante: Molto espressivo
3.Finale: Presto
Solo Pno.-2,2,2,2-4,2-Timp.-Str.
Bote & Bock, Berlin [1877?]
Score 117 p.
First performance Vienna, 1861.

572p [Concerto, piano, no. 2, Op. 24, C major]
1.Allegro moderato 2.Andante 3.Allegro
Solo Pno.-2,2,2,2-4,2-Timp.-Str.
Bote & Bock, Berlin [1876?]
Score 140 p.

60 [Overture to Macbeth, Op. 46]   7'
3*,2,2,2-4,2,3,1-Timp.,S.Dr.-Str.
Breitkopf & Härtel, Leipzig [1884?]
Score 70 p.
Composed 1884. First performance Vienna, 1885.

551p [Rhapsody, piano and orchestra, Op. 65, 15'
D minor]
Solo Pno.-2,2,2,2-4,2,3-Timp.,Cym.,Trgl.-Str.
Doblinger, Vienna [1892]
Score in reduction 27 p.

263 Serenade für Orchester, Op. 29 [F   29'
major]
1.Allegro 2.Intermezzo: Allegretto moderato
3.Scherzo: Presto 4.Andante ma non troppo
5.Intermezzo: Allegretto 6.Finale: Allegro
2,2,2,2-2,2-Timp.-Str.
Bote & Bock, Berlin [1877]
Score 119 p.
Composed 1876. First performance Vienna, 1877.

26 Serenade für grosses Orchester, Op. 36   30'
[E major]
1.Allegro vivace 2.Marcia: Allegro ma non
troppo 3.Allegro moderato
3,2,2,2-4,2-Timp.-Str.
Schott, Mainz [1879]
Score 109 p.

BRUN, GEORGES.

1435 Paysages d'Alsace [Alsatian landscapes]
suite, Op. 90
1.[Morning in the Vosges] 2.[The procession

130

from St. Odile to Obernai] 3.[Idyll at Luisen-
thal] 4.[Holiday at Strasbourg]
2(2nd alt. Picc.),1,2,2-4,2,3,1-Timp.,Perc.-Hp.
-Str.
Lemoine, Paris, c1925
Score 95 p.

BRUNEAU, ALFRED.　　　　　　　Paris 3 March 1857
　　　　　　　　　　　　　　　　Paris 15 June 1934

Full name: Louis-Charles-Bonaventure-Alfred
　　　Bruneau

1202　L'attaque du moulin [The attack on　　　7'
　the mill] Op. 22. [Suite from the opera]
　1.[Prelude and chanson] 2.[The war; the
　forest] 3.[The betrothal in the mill]
3*,2,2,2-4,2,3,1-Timp.,Perc.-Hp.-Str.
Choudens, Paris [1893]
Score 118 p.
From the opera in four acts with libretto by
Louis Gallet, based on Zola's Soirées de Médan.
Composed 1892. First performance Opéra-
Comique, Paris, 23 November 1893.

1147　Les Bacchantes, Op. 17 [Suite from　　17'
　the ballet]
　1.[Procession of the priestesses of Ceres and
　Bacchus' retinue] 2.[Religious scene]
　3.[Myrrhine's dance] 4.[Theban march]
3*,2,2,2-4,2,2Cnt.,3,1-Timp.,Perc.-Hp.-Str.
Choudens, Paris, c1912
Score 95 p.
From the ballet in two acts. Book by the composer and Felix Naquet, based on Euripides.
Composed ca.1886.

1220　La belle au bois dormant [Sleeping　　12'
　Beauty, symphonic poem, Op. 13]
3*,2,2,2-4,2,2Cnt.,3,1-Timp.,Perc.-Hp.-Str.
Choudens, Paris, c1902
Score 58 p.
Composed 1883. First performance Paris, 1884,
Concerts Pasdeloup.

1504　L'enfant roi [The child king, Op. 29.　8'
　Prelude to the opera]
3*,3*,3*,3*-4,2,2Cnt.,3,1-Timp.,Perc.-Hp.-Str.
Choudens, Paris, c1905
Score 23 p.
From the opera in five acts with libretto by
Émile Zola. First performance Paris, 3 March
1905.

　Le faute de l'abbé Mouret [The sin of Abbé
　Mouret, Op. 31. Suites nos. 1 and 2 from the
　incidental music to the play]
1643 Suite no. 1. Le Paradou dans la vie　　12'
1550 Suite no. 2. Le Paradou dans la mort　18'
2(2nd alt. Picc.),2,2,2-4,2,3,1-Timp.,Perc.-
Org.,Hp.-SATB Voices(wordless, backstage)-Str.
Choudens, Paris, c1907
Scores: 110 p., 108 p.
For the drama by the composer, based on Zola's
short story. First performance Théâtre Odéon,
Paris, 1 March 1907.

824　[Messidor, Op. 25. Symphonic interlude　7'
　from the opera]
3*,3*,3*,3*-4,2,2Cnt.,3,1-Timp.,Perc.-Hp.-Str.
Choudens, Paris, c1897
Score 13 p.
From the opera in 3 acts and prologue with
libretto by Émile Zola. Composed 1895. First
performance Opéra, Paris, 19 February 1897.

1341　[Naïs Micoulin. Prelude to the opera]　4'
3*,3*,3*,3*-4,2,2Cnt.,3,1-Timp.,Perc.-Hp.-Str.
Choudens, Paris, c1906
Score 13 p.
From the opera in 2 acts with libretto by the
composer, based on Émile Zola's short story
La Douleur de Toine. Composed 1906. First
performance Monte Carlo, 2 February 1907.

869　L'ouragan [The hurricane] Op. 26.　　　20'
　Préludes
　1.Goël 2.[Bay of Grace] 3.L'ouragan 4.Le
　départ
3*,3*,3*,3*-4,2,2Cnt.,3,1-Timp.,Perc.-Hp.-Str.
Choudens, Paris, c1901
Score 39 p.
From the opera in four acts with libretto by
Émile Zola. Composed 1900. First performance
Opéra-Comique, Paris, 29 April 1901.

541m　[Romance, horn or violoncello or viola,
　F major]
Solo Hn.(or Vc. or Va.)-2,2*,2,2-Timp.-Hp.-Str.
J. Hamelle, Paris [ca.1883]
Score 15 p.

BRUNETTI, T. A.

975v　Historiette [for violin and orchestra,
　G major]
Solo Vn.-Ob.,2Cl.,Bn.-2Hn.-Str.
Score: Ms. 13 p.
Parts: Decourcelle, Nice [n.d.]

1678s　Marionettes [pizzicato for string　　3'
　orchestra and harp]
Hp.-Str.
Score: Ms. 9 p.
Parts: Gaudet, Paris, c1922

BRUNNER, HANS.　　　　　　　　Basel 18 June 1898

1095m　[Concerto, flute and string　　　　16'
　orchestra, Op. 30]
　1.Allegro ma non troppo 2.Poco adagio 3.Alle-
　gro con brio
Solo Fl.-Str.
Ms.
Score 29 p.
Composed 1947.

1092m　[Fantasy for saxophone and string　　10'
　orchestra, Op. 29]
　1.Allegro 2.Lento 3.Allegro moderato
Solo Sax.-Str.
Ms.
Score 17 p.

Bruno, Fr.

BRUNO, FR.

    1085s [Petite serenade, string orchestra,
    Op. 42, G major]
    Str.
    Cranz, Hamburg [n.d.]
    Score 3 p.

BRUSSELMANS, MICHEL.   Paris 12 February 1886
                         Brussels 1960

    5587 [Scenes from Brueghel, symphonic   *14'*
    sketches]
    1.Rentrée de la procession 2.La danse 3.
    Scène des buveurs [Drinking scene] 4.Idylle
    5.Kermesse flamande [Flemish festival]
    3*,3*,3*,3-4,3,3,1-Timp.,Perc.-Hp.-Str.
    A. Cranz, Brussels, c1932
    Score 75 p.
    Composed 1911.

BRUSTAD, BJARNE.   Christiania 4 March 1895.

    6316 [Symphony no. 1]   *30'*
    1.Andante 2.Andante - Più allegro e agitato
    3.Scherzo capriccioso 4.Finale: Allegro ma
    non troppo
    3,2(2nd alt. E.H.),2,2-4,3,3-Timp.,Perc.-Cel.,
    Hp.-Sop.Voice(4th movement only)-Str.
    Ms. c1949 by Bjarne Brustad
    Score 150 p.
    First performance Oslo, 10 March 1949, Oslo
    Philharmonic Orchestra, Odd Grüner-Hegge con-
    ductor.

BRYSON, ROBERT ERNEST.   Liverpool 31 March 1867
       St. Briavels, Gloucestershire 20 April 1942

    1337s Vaila, fantasy for string orchestra
    Str.
    Boosey & Hawkes, London, c1909
    Score 35 p.

BÜCHNER, FERDINAND.   Pyrmont, Germany 1825

    637m [Concerto, flute, Op. 38, F minor]   *18'*
    Solo Fl.-2,2,2,2-2,2,3-Timp.-Str.
    Zimmermann, Leipzig, c1896
    Score in reduction 31 p.
    Composed 1893. First performance St. Peters-
    burg, 1895.

BUCHT, GUNNAR.
             Danderyd, near Stockholm 5 August 1927

    435c [Concerto, violoncello, Op. 12]   *18'*
    1.Allegro ma non troppo 2.Adagio molto es-
    pressivo
    Solo Vc.-2,2,2,2-4,3,3-Timp.-Str.
    Ms.
    Score 41 p.
    Composed 1954. First performance Stockholm, 27
    November 1955, Swedish Broadcasting Corporation
    Orchestra, Sten Frykberg conductor, Claude
    Genetay soloist.

    2386s Strängaspel (1965) [Play for   *4'40"*
    strings]
    Str.
    Edition Suecia, Stockholm, c1968
    Score 12 p.
    Commissioned by The Workers' Educational Asso-
    ciation, Stockholm, for its 50th anniversary,
    1966. Composed 1965. First performance Stock-
    holm, 21 January 1966, Chamber Orchestra of
    The Workers' Educational Association, Sven
    Verde conductor.

    5985 [Symphony no. 4, Op. 21]   *18'*
    1. ♩ = 60 2. ♩ = 56 3.Tempo giusto, pesante
    2,2,2,2-Alto Sax.-4,4,3,1-Timp.,Cym.,S.Dr.-Str.
    Ms.
    Score 44 p.
    Composed 1957-58. First performance Stockholm,
    4 March 1959, Philharmonic Orchestra of Stock-
    holm, Sixten Ehrling conductor.

    7051 [Symphony no. 7]   *19'*
    1.Malgré tout (In spite of everything) 2.Tant
    mieux (So much the better)
    2(2nd alt. Picc.),2,2,2-Alto Sax.-4,4,3,1-Timp.,
    Perc.-Cel.,Hp.-Str.
    Edition Suecia, Stockholm, c1971
    Score 46 p.
    Commissioned by the Norrköping Symphony Orches-
    tra. Composed 1970-71. First performance
    Norrköping, Sweden, 26 March 1972, Norrköping
    Symphony Orchestra, Everett Lee conductor.

BÜCHTGER, FRITZ.   Munich 14 February 1903

    2005s [Music for a holiday, for string   *6'*
    orchestra]
    1.Intrata 2.Sehr ruhig 3.Tanz 4.Feierlicher
    Aufzug
    Str.
    Musikverlag Willy Müller, Karlsruhe [1934]
    Score 14 p.

BUCK, DUDLEY.   Hartford, Connecticut 10 March 1839
            Orange, New Jersey 6 October 1909

    6819 Festival overture on the American national
    air, The Star-Spangled Banner
    3*,2,2,2-4,3,3,1-Timp.,Perc.-Voice-Str.
    Ms.
    Score 43 p.

BUDASHKIN, NICOLAI PAVLOVICH.
           b. Lubakhovka, Kaluga 6 August 1910

    3427 [Festival overture, for large orchestra, *8'*
    commemorating the 20th anniversary of the great
    October Revolution, Op. 3]
    4*,2,2,2-4,3,3,1-Timp.,Perc.-Pno.-Str.
    Mussektor, Moscow, 1940
    Score 68 p.
    Composed 1937. First performance Moscow,
    November 1937, Moscow State Orchestra, Abram
    Stasevich conductor.

BULL, JOHN.   Somersetshire, England 1562 or 1563
                              Antwerp 12 or 13 March 1628

4628 John Bull suite for small orchestra. *13'*
Selected from the works of John Bull and
orchestrated by Everett Helm
1.The king's hunt 2.My selfe 3.Air: Most
sweet and fayre 4.Dance: Courante alarme 5.
Dance: Alman 6.Bull's goodnighte
1,1,1,1-2,2,1-Str.
Ms. [now published by Carl Fischer, New York]
Score 39 p.
Originally composed for virginals.

BULL, OLE BORNEMANN. Bergen, Norway 5 February 1810
                              Lysø, near Bergen 17 August 1880

1186v [Adagio religioso for violin with orches-
tra, Op. 1]
Solo Vn.-2,2,2,2-4,2,3-Timp.-Str.
Schuberth, Hamburg [1843]
Score 16 p.

402s La mélancolie [D minor] Arranged for string
orchestra by Johan Halvorsen
Str.
Hansen, Copenhagen, c1914
Score 3 p.

351v [Solitude on the mountain. Harmonized   *3'*
and transcribed for violin solo and string
orchestra by Johan S. Svendsen]
Solo Vn.-Str.
Wilhelm Hansen, Copenhagen [n.d.]
Score 3 p.
*Originally composed as a Melody in D, Saeter-
jentens Søndag.*

BULLERIAN, HANS.
     b. Schwarzburg-Sondershausen 28 January 1885

594c [Concerto, violoncello, Op. 41]
Solo Vc.-2,2,2,2-4,2,3,1-Timp.,Perc.-Hp.-Str.
Simrock, Berlin, c1927
Score 72 p.

BÜLOW, HANS VON.   Dresden 8 January 1830
                              Cairo 12 February 1894

Full name: Hans Guido, Freiherr von Bülow

7010 [Julius Caesar, Op. 10. Heroic overture]
3*,2,2,2-4,3,3,Ophicl.-Timp.,Perc.-Str.
Schott, Mainz [1860]
Score 64 p.
*From the incidental music for the play by
Shakespeare.*

2394 Mazurka-Fantasie, for piano, Op. 13.
Orchestrated by Franz Liszt
3*,2,2,2-2,2,3-Timp.-Str.
Leuckart, Breslau [n.d.]
Score 48 p.

6924 [The minstrel's curse, ballad after
Uhland's poem, Op. 16]
3*,2,2,2-4,2,4-Timp.,Trgl.,Cym.-Str.
Schlesinger, Berlin [1863]
Score 52 p.

5764 [Nirvana, orchestral fantasy in the form
of an overture, Op. 20]
3*,2,3,2-4,2,3,1-Timp.,Cym.-Str.
Jos. Aibl, Munich [1881]
Score 95 p.

BUNGERT, AUGUST.
     Mülheim on the Ruhr, Germany 14 March 1845
          Leutesdorf on the Rhine 26 October 1915

5715 [At the Wartburg, symphonic poem, Op. 29]
3*,2,2-4,2,3,1-Timp.,Perc.-Hp.-Str.
Luckhardt's Musik-Verlag, Stuttgart [n.d.]
Score 51 p.
*The Wartburg is the setting of the Tannhäuser
legend.*

5718 [Torquato Tasso, symphonic overture to
Goethe's play, Op. 14]
3*,2,2,2-4,2,3,1-Timp.,Cym.(or Tam-tam)-Str.
Luckhardt's Musik-Verlag, Stuttgart [n.d.]
Score 61 p.

BUNIN, REVOL SAMUILOVICH.   USSR 6 April 1924

284p [Concerto, piano and chamber orchestra]
1.Allegro 2.Andante 3.Allegro
Solo Pno.-2Hn.,Tpt.,Tbn.-Timp.,Perc.-Str.
Ms.
Score 62 p.

BUNNING, HERBERT.   London 2 May 1863
                    Thundersley, Essex 26 November 1937

297s The shepherd's call, Op. 43
Hn.(ad lib.)-Str.
Oertel, London [n.d.]
Score 3 p.

BUONPORTI, FRANCESCO ANTONIO.
     See: BONPORTI, FRANCESCO ANTONIO.

BURANELLO, IL.
     See: GALUPPI, BALDASSARE.

BURGER, MAX.   Oberalting, Munich 1 July 1856
                                        Bamberg 1917

272s [Eight character pieces, string orchestra,
Op. 77]
Str.
Schwann, Düsseldorf, 1911
Score 13 p.

1231s Festklänge bei Schulfeierlichkeiten
[Festive tunes for school celebrations] Op. 73
Org.(or Harm.; ad lib.),Pno.(ad lib.)-Str.
Schwann, Düsseldorf [n.d.]
Score 7 p.

273s [Sinfonietta, Op. 65, B-flat major]
Str.
Vieweg, Berlin, c1909
Score 11 p.

188s Stimmungsbilder [Scenes, for school string
orchestra and harmonium or organ without
pedals, Op. 39]

Burgmein, J.

1.[Born in a stable in Bethlehem, pastorale]
2.[Died on the cross at Golgotha, elegy]
3.[Risen from the tomb in glory, alleluja]
Harm. (or Org.)-Str.
Rahter, Hamburg, c1903
Score 17 p.

BURGMEIN, J. pseudonym.   Milan 19 December 1840
                            Milan 6 June 1912

Real name: Giulio Ricordi

720s [Aquarelles. No. 1, Folle ivresse.
Orchestrated by Leopoldo Mugnone]
Solo Vn.-Str.
Ricordi, Milan, c1919
Score 6 p.
Aquarelles originally composed for piano solo.
Arrangements first performed Milan, 1920.

2106 [Aquarelles. No. 2, Jeux d'enfants.   5'
Orchestrated by Leopoldo Mugnone]
3Fl.(3rd alt. Picc.),2Ob.,2Cl.-Perc.-Str.
Ricordi, Milan, c1919
Score 29 p.

776s [Aquarelles. No. 3, En rêvant. Orchestra-
ted by Leopoldo Mugnone]
Solo Vn.-Str.
Ricordi, Milan, c1919
Score 6 p.

2107 [Aquarelles. No. 4, Aubade champêtre.   5'
Orchestrated by Leopoldo Mugnone]
3*,2,2,2-4,2,3,1-Timp.,Perc.-Hp.-Str.
Ricordi, Milan, c1919
Score 25 p.

1362s Impressions de route [Traveler's impressions. No. 1, Romance poudrée. Orchestrated
by Leopold Mugnone]
Solo Vn.-Str.
Ricordi, Milan, c1916
Score 4 p.
Impressions de Route was originally composed
for piano; orchestrated in memory of the com-
poser. First performance Milan, 1916.

2111 Impressions de route [Traveler's   3'
impressions. No. 2, In the mountains.
Orchestrated by Leopold Mugnone]
2,2,2,3*-2Hn.
Ricordi, Milan, c1916
Score 9 p.

1363s Impressions de route [Traveler's impres-
sions. No. 3, Far-off memory! Orchestrated by
Leopoldo Mugnone]
Solo Vn.-Hp.(or Pno.)-Str.
Ricordi, Milan, c1916
Score 5 p.

3575 Impressions de route [Traveler's   3'
impressions. No. 4, Promenade de jeunes vil-
lageoises. Orchestrated by Leopoldo Mugnone]
2*,2,2,3*-2Hn.,2Tpt.-Timp.,Perc.-Str.
Ricordi, Milan, c1916
Score 17 p.

2108 Mon carnet de jeunesse [Diary of my   3'
youth] No. 1, Noël! Noël! Transcribed for
woodwinds by Leopoldo Mugnone
2*,3*,2,2
Ricordi, Milan, c1917
Score 8 p.
Originally composed for piano solo. Orchestra-
ted and first performed Milan, 1917.

2100 Mon carnet de jeunesse [Diary of my   4'
youth] No. 2, Pourquoi? Orchestrated by
Leopoldo Mugnone
2,2,2,2-2Hn.-Str.
Ricordi, Milan, c1917
Score 13 p.

897s Mon carnet de jeunesse [Diary of my   3'
youth] No. 3, Enivrement! Orchestrated by
Leopoldo Mugnone
Str.
Ricordi, Milan, c1917
Score 4 p.

2109 Mon carnet de jeunesse [Diary of my   4'
youth] No. 4, Dors, dors, mon enfant!
Orchestrated by Leopoldo Mugnone
1,1*,2,1-Hn.-Hp.
Ricordi, Milan, c1917
Score 7 p.

2101 Mon carnet de jeunesse [Diary of my   3'
youth] No. 5, Chantons le mai! Orchestrated by
Leopoldo Mugnone
1,1,2,2-4,1-Hp.-Str.
Ricordi, Milan, c1917
Score 15 p.

497s Piccolo intermezzo quasi minuetto [G major]
Str.(Cb. ad lib.)
Ricordi, Milan [n.d.]
Score 10 p.

634s Il racconto della nonna [Grandmother's
story] No. 1, C'erà una volta [Once upon a
time, preamble] Orchestrated by Leopoldo
Mugnone
Solo Va.-Str.(without Cb.)
Ricordi, Milan, c1917
Score 4 p.

2102 Il racconto della nonna [Grandmother's   3'
story] No. 2, Il lago [The lake, barcarole]
Orchestrated by Leopoldo Mugnone
2*,1,2,1-2Hn.-Str.
Ricordi, Milan, c1917
Score 13 p.

2103 Il racconto della nonna [Grandmother's   2'
story] No. 3, Le ondine [The waves, fantastic
dance] Orchestrated by Leopoldo Mugnone
2,2*,2,1-Hp.(or Pno.)-Vc.,Cb.
Ricordi, Milan, c1917
Score 9 p.

2104 Il racconto della nonna [Grandmother's   5'
story] No. 4, Il drago [The dragon, tragedy]
Orchestrated by Leopoldo Mugnone

2(2nd alt. Picc.),2,2,2-2Hn.-Hp.-Str.
Ricordi, Milan, c1917
Score 28 p.

2110 Il racconto della nonna [Grandmother's *2'*
story] No. 5, O mamma cara [O precious mother,
prayer] Orchestrated by Leopoldo Mugnone
2,2*,2,1-Hn.-Hp.
Ricordi, Milan, c1917
Score 5 p.

812s Il racconto della nonna [Grandmother's
story] No. 6, Le lucciolette [Fireflies,
scherzo] Orchestrated by Leopoldo Mugnone
Str.
Ricordi, Milan, c1917
Score 7 p.

2105 Il racconto della nonna [Grandmother's *2'*
story] No. 7, Buona notte, piccini [Good
night, children, epilogue] Orchestrated by
Leopoldo Mugnone
2*,2,2,2-2Hn.-Hp.-Str.
Ricordi, Milan, c1917
Score 10 p.

1497s Rosaura [Venetian carnival]
Solo Fl.-Str.
Ricordi, Milan [n.d.]
Score 3 p.

1047s Sérénade française [for string orchestra,
E major] From Le Livre des Sérénades
Str.
Ricordi, Milan [n.d.]
Score 6 p.

BURGSTALLER, SIEGFRIED. Papenburg 24 September 1883

2216 Sommerabend [Summer evening, idyll *13'*
for large orchestra, Op. 9]
3(1st alt. Picc.),3*,3*,3*-4,3,3,1-Timp.,Trgl.
-2Hp.-Str.
Ries & Erler, Berlin, c1930
Score 27 p. Large folio

BURKHARD, PAUL.   Zurich 21 August 1911

4993 [The shot from the pulpit. Overture] *9'*
2(both alt. Picc.),2,2,2-2,2,2-Timp.,Perc.-Str.
Universal Edition, Vienna, c1947
Score 58 p.
*Overture to the operetta based on a novel by
Conrad Ferdinand Meyer. Composed 1944.*

BURKHARD, WILLY.
Evillard sur Bienne, Switzerland 17 April 1900
Zurich 18 June 1955

1796s Toccata, for string orchestra, Op. 55 *15'*
1.Praeludium 2.Aria 3.Finale
Str.
Universal Edition, London, c1939
Score 18 p.
*Commissioned by the Zurich Kammerorchester and
Alexander Schaichet, 1938. First performance
Zurich, Switzerland, March 1939, Zurich Kammer-
orchester, Alexander Schaichet conductor.*

BURLE MARX, WALTER.
See: MARX, BURLE.

BURLEIGH, CECIL.   Wyoming, New York 17 April 1885

2309 At sunset, from Four Rocky Mountain *4'*
Sketches, Op. 11 no. 1. Arranged for orchestra
by William F. Happich
1,1,1,1-Hn.-Hp.-Str.
Ms.
Score 11 p.
Originally composed for violin and piano.

428s At twilight, Op. 14 no. 1. Arranged by
William F. Happich
Hp.-Str.
Ms.
Score 4 p.
*Originally composed for violin and piano in
Five Reminiscences. Arranged 1923.*

1069v [Concerto, violin, no. 2, Op. 43] *14'*
1.Somberly, rather gruffly 2.Chant
3.Swiftly, savagely
Solo Vn.-2(2nd alt. Picc.),2,2,2-4,2,3-Timp.-
Str.
Ms.
Score 87 p.
*Composed 1916. First performance Cleveland,
13 March 1921, Cleveland Symphony Orchestra,
Nicolai Sokoloff conductor, the composer as
soloist.*

1080v [Concerto, violin, no. 3, Op. 60] *18'*
1.Heroically 2.Slowly, tranquilly
Solo Vn.-2(2nd alt. Picc.),2,2,2-4,2,3,1-Timp.
-Hp.-Str.
Ms.
Score 74 p.
*Composed 1925. First performance Minneapolis,
13 December 1925, Minneapolis Symphony Orches-
tra, Henri Verbrugghen conductor, Gilbert
Ross soloist.*

2892 Evangeline, after Longfellow, Op. 41 *12'*
3*,2(2nd alt. E.H.),2,3*-4,2,3,1-Timp.,B.Dr.,
Cym.-Hp.-Str.
Ms.
Score 40 p.
*Composed 1918; revised 1930. First performance
Madison, Wisconsin, 15 November 1927, Madison
Civic Symphony Orchestra, Sigfrid Prager con-
ductor.*

474s Eventide, Op. 16 no. 1. Arranged by
William F. Happich
Hp.-Str.
Ms.
Score in reduction 5 p.
*Composed for violin and piano in Six Winter
Evening Tales. Arranged 1923.*

473s The meadow lark, Op. 17 no. 2. Arranged
by William F. Happich
Hp.-Str.
G. Schirmer, New York, c1914
Score in reduction 5 p.
*Composed for violin and piano in Tone Poems.
Arranged 1923.*

Burleigh, Cecil

2587 Mountain pictures, suite for orches-   *13'*
tra, Op. 42
1.Crags and cascades 2.Shepherd's song 3.Dis-
tant haze 4.Avalanche
3(3rd alt. Picc.),2(2nd alt. E.H.),2,3*-4,2,3,
1-Timp.,Cym.-Hp.-Str.
Ms.
Score 42 p.
Composed 1917. First performance St. Louis,
Missouri, 5 January 1923, St. Louis Symphony
Orchestra, Rudolph Ganz conductor.

153s Summer idyll, Op. 21 no. 2. Arranged by
William F. Happich
Hp.-Str.
Ms.
Score 10 p.
Composed for violin and piano in Four Small
Concert Pieces. Arranged 1922.

BURMESTER, WILLY.   Hamburg 16 March 1869
                         Hamburg 16 January 1933

1516s [Serenade, string orchestra, D major]
Str.
H. Böhm, Graz [Austria, n.d.]
Score 4 p.

BURNHAM, CARDON.   Kewanee, Illinois 1927

5615 Mosaic for orchestra (a quiet piece   *7'*
for orchestra)
2,2,2,2-2,2-Trgl.,Cym.-Cel.-Str.
Ms. ᶜ1957 by Cardon Burnham
Score 12 p.
Composed 1956. First performance Rochester,
10 April 1957, Eastman-Rochester Symphony
Orchestra, Howard Hanson conductor.

458m Suite concertante for flute, oboe,   *19'*
bassoon and strings
1.Antiphon for flute and strings 2.Chanty for
bassoon and strings 3.Canticle for oboe and
strings 4.Concertino grosso for flute, oboe,
bassoon and strings
Solo Fl., Solo Ob., Solo Bn.-Str.
Ms. ᶜ1957 by Cardon Burnham
Score 47 p.
Composed 1956. First performance Rochester,
8 April 1957, Eastman-Rochester Symphony
Orchestra, Howard Hanson conductor, Joseph
Mariano flautist, Robert Sprenkle oboist,
Carl Van Hoesen bassoonist.

6187 Symphony no. 1 (Bharata)   *10'*
1.Introduction: Very slow and sustained
2.Kirtanam: Faster 3.Meditation: Mysteriously
4.Khyal: Moderately fast - Faster with vigor
2*,2*,2*,1-2,2,1-Timp.,Cym.,Gong-Pno.,Cel.,
Hp.-Str.
Ms.
Score 39 p. Large folio
Bharata is a sixth-century Hindu legendary
figure to whom the complex system of Hindu
musical scales is attributed. Composed 1960.
First performance Toledo, Ohio, 11 November
1961, Toledo Symphony Orchestra, Joseph
Hawthorne conductor.

BURT, NATHANIEL.   Moose, Wyoming 21 November 1913

7100 The elegy of Lycidas, Op. 4   *10'*
3*,3*,2,2-4.2,3-Timp.,Perc.-Hp.-Str.
Ms. ᶜ[n.d.] by Nathaniel Burt
Score 46 p. Large folio
The title is derived from the elegiac poem by
John Milton. Composed 1952. First perform-
ance Princeton, New Jersey, 16 January 1954,
Nicholas Harsányi conductor.

BUSCEMI, ANTHONY.   Delia, Sicily 13 June 1888

4479 Gavotte. Orchestration by Otto Mueller
2*,1,2,1-2Hn.-Timp.,Trgl.,Bells-Str.
Ms.
Score 9 p.

1040m Melodie in B minor, for horn and
orchestra. Orchestration by Otto Mueller
Solo Hn.-1,1,2,2-2Hn.-Timp.-Hp.-Str.
Ms.
Score 8 p.

BUSCH, ADOLF.
        Siegen, Westphalia, Prussia 8 August 1891
                Guilford, Vermont 9 June 1952

3972 [Capriccio for small orchestra,   *22'*
Op. 46]
2(2nd alt. Picc.),2,2,2-2,2-Timp.-Str.
Eulenburg, Leipzig, ᶜ1932
Miniature score 86 p.
First performance Second International Music
Festival, Venice, 14 September 1932.

1776 [Variations and fugue on a Mozart   *25'*
theme, Op. 19]
2,2,2,2-2,2-Timp.-Str.
Simrock, Berlin, ᶜ1920
Score 47 p.
Composed 1916. First performance Berne, 1917,
Fritz Brun conductor.

4679 [Variations on the Radetzky March, Op. 9]
3*,2,2,3*-4,2,3,1-Timp.,Perc.-Hp.-Str.
N. Simrock, Berlin, ᶜ1917
Score 119 p.
Composed 1914. After the Radetzky March,
Op. 228 of Johann Strauss, the elder.

BUSCH, CARL.
        Bjérre, Jutland (Denmark) 29 March 1862
                Kansas City, Missouri 19 December 1943

429s Elegie [for strings, Op. 30]
Str.
Breitkopf & Härtel, Leipzig, ᶜ1899
Score 5 p.

1316 In the woodlands, miniature suite   *10'*
1.To a columbine 2.Summer day 3.Dialogue
4.Valse "Springtime"
1,1,2,1-2,2,1-Timp.,Perc.-Pno.(ad lib.)-Str.
FitzSimons, Chicago, ᶜ1928
Score 48 p.
Composed 1924. First performance Kansas City,
1924, the composer conducting.

Indian tribal melodies, four North American
legends for string orchestra
48s 1. A Chippewa vision
49s 2. A Chippewa love song (Why should I be
   jealous)
50s 3. A Chippewa lullaby
51s 4. Omaha Indian love song
Str.
C. Fischer, New York, c1918
Scores: 9 p., 7 p., 5 p., 7 p.

1348 Lyric suite   10'
1.Adoration 2.Intermezzo (from the music to
King John) 3.Reverie 4.March joyeuse
1,1,2,1-2,2,1-Timp.,Perc.-Pno.(ad lib.)-Str.
FitzSimons, Chicago, c1928
Score 36 p.
*Composed 1924. First performance Kansas City,
1924, the composer conducting.*

278 [Minnehaha's vision, symphonic poem   9'
after Longfellow's Song of Hiawatha]
2(2nd alt. Picc.),2(2nd alt. E.H.),3*,2-4,3,3,
1-Timp.,Cym.,Indian Dr.-Hp.-Str.
Jost, Leipzig, c1914
Score 34 p.
*First performance Kansas City, 1916, the com-
poser conducting.*

219s My old Kentucky home [American folk-song
no. 2. Arranged for string orchestra by Carl
Busch]
Str.
Breitkopf & Härtel, Leipzig, c1907
Score 5 p.

430s Old folks at home [American folk-song.
Arranged by Carl Busch]
Str.
Breitkopf & Härtel, Leipzig, c1897
Score 5 p.

1295 Ozarka suite   10'
1.A morning pastorale 2.On the banks of the
White River 3.At sunset 4.The hill-billies'
dance
1,1,2,1-2,2,1-Timp.,Perc.-Pno.(ad lib.)-Str.
FitzSimons, Chicago, c1928
Score 32 p.
*Composed 1924. First performance Kansas City,
1924, the composer conducting.*

841 Prolog to Tennyson's The Passing of   10'
Arthur, Op. 25
2,2,2,2-4,2,3,1-Timp.,Cym.-Hp.-Str.
Breitkopf & Härtel, Leipzig, c1899
Score 33 p.
*Composed 1895. First performance Leipzig,
1902, the composer conducting.*

1355 The song of Chibiabos, symphonic   10'
poem after the Song of Hiawatha by Longfellow
3(3rd alt. Picc.),2*,3*,3*-4,3,3,1-Timp.,Cym.-
Hp.-Str.
Hansen, Copenhagen [n.d.]
Score 37 p.
*Composed 1916. First performance Kansas City,
1917, the composer conducting.*

BÜSCHEL, BEN-ZION.
   See: ORGAD, BEN-ZION.

BUSH, ALAN DUDLEY.   Dulwich 22 December 1900

3436 Dance overture, Op. 12   14'
3(3rd alt. Picc.),2,3,2-2Sax.(AT)-4,3,3,1-
Timp.,Perc.-Str.
Boosey & Hawkes, London [n.d.]
Score 68 p.
*Commissioned by the BBC, 1930. Composed for
military band; orchestrated 1930. First performance at a Promenade Concert, London, 1931,
the composer conducting.*

3780 [Symphony, Op. 21, C major]
Prologue 1.Allegro molto 2.Lento molto
3.Allegro moderato e deciso
2(2nd alt. Picc.),2,3,3*-4,3,3Cnt.(1Sop.),3,1-
Timp.,Perc.-Pno.,Hp.-Str.
Boosey & Hawkes, London [n.d.]
Score 75 p. Large folio
*Composed 1939-40. First performance at a Prom-
enade Concert, London, July 1942.*

BUSH, IRVING.

7182 Fanfare
     See: FANFARES 1969 FOR 8 TRUMPETS.
     No. VII

BUSONI, FERRUCCIO.
                 Empoli, near Florence 1 April 1866
                         Berlin 27 July 1924

1418 Berceuse élégiaque [Lullaby of a   10'
man at his mother's bier, Op. 42]
3,1,3*-4Hn.-Gong-Cel.,Hp.-Str.
Breitkopf & Härtel, Leipzig, c1910
Score 19 p.
*In memoriam Anna Busoni who died 3 October 1909.
First performance New York, 21 November 1911,
New York Philharmonic, Gustav Mahler conductor.*

501m [Concertino, clarinet and small   7'
orchestra, B-flat major]
Solo Cl.-2Ob.,2Bn.-2Hn.-Trgl.-Str.
Breitkopf & Härtel, Leipzig, c1918
Score 27 p.
Composed 1918.

529p [Concertino for piano and orchestra.   7'
II. Romanza e scherzoso, Op. 54]
Solo Pno.-3*,2,2,2-4,2,3-Timp.,Glock.-Str.
Breitkopf & Härtel, Leipzig, c1922
Score 33 p.
*Composed 1922. First and third movements of
the Concertino were composed 1890 and pub-
lished as Konzertstück, Op. 31a.*

543v [Concerto, violin, Op. 35a, D major] 20'
In one movement
Solo Vn.-3*,2,2,2-4,2,3,1-Timp.,Perc.-Str.
Breitkopf & Hartel, Leipzig, c1899
Score 71 p.
Composed 1898.

5168 [Dance waltzes for orchestra, Op. 53] 14'
Introduction, 4 Waltzes and Coda

Busoni, Ferruccio

3*,2,2,2-4,2,3,1-Timp.,Perc.-Str.
Breitkopf & Härtel, Leipzig, c1917
Score 39 p.
Composed 1920.

545m Divertimento for flute and orchestra,   *8'*
Op. 52
Solo Fl.-0,2,2,2-2,2-Timp.,Trgl.-Str.
Breitkopf & Härtel, Leipzig, c1922
Score 23 p.
*Composed 1921. First performance Zurich, 2
October 1924, Othmar Schoeck conductor.*

870 [Indian diary, Op. 47. Book 2. Gesang   *6'*
vom Reigen der Geister (Song of the spirits'
dance)]
1,1,1,1-Tpt.,Tbn.-Timp.-Str.
Breitkopf & Härtel, Leipzig, c1916
Score 15 p.
First performance Berlin, 1916.

349p [Indian fantasy, for piano and   *20'*
orchestra, Op. 44]
Solo Pno.-2(2nd alt. Picc.),2(2nd alt. E.H.),2,
2-3,2-Timp.,Perc.-Hp.-Str.
Breitkopf & Härtel, Leipzig, c1915
Score 59 p.
Composed 1913.

5160 [Symphonic nocturne, Op. 43]   *10'*
3(3rd alt. Picc.),2*,3*,3*-3Hn.-Timp.,Perc.-
Cel.,Hp.-Str.
Breitkopf & Härtel, Leipzig, c1914
Score 20 p.
Composed 1912.

BUSSER, HENRI-PAUL.   Toulouse 16 January 1872
                          Paris 30 December 1973

1187 À la villa Médicis [symphonic suite   *28'*
in 3 parts] Op. 4
1.[The villa and the gardens] 2.[A May
evening in the woods] 3.[At San Gaetano;
conclusion]
2,2(2nd alt. E.H.),2,2-4,2,3,1-Timp.,Cym.-2Hp.
-Str.
Lemoine, Paris, c1901
Score 127 p.
*Composed 1895. First performance Paris, 1896,
the composer conducting.*

607m [Ballade, for harp and strings, Op. 65,
A major]
Solo Hp.-Str.
Evette & Schaeffer, Paris, c1920
Score 17 p.
*Composed for the competition of the Conserva-
toire National of Paris, 1918.*

566v Catalane, sur des airs populaires, Op. 78
Solo Va.-1(alt. Picc.),1,2,1-Hn.-Hp.-Str.
Lemoine, Paris, c1926
Score 15 p.

1455 Columba. Prelude, Act I   *6'*
3(2Picc.),2,3*,3-4,2,3,1-Timp.,Perc.-2Hp.-Str.
Choudens, Paris, c1921
Score 37 p.
From the opera composed 1920. First concert

*performance of Prelude, Paris, 1926, Concerts
Lamoureux, Paul Paray conductor.*

1166 [Hercules in the garden of the   *12'*
Hesperides, symphonic poem, Op. 18]
3*,3*,3*,3*-4,2,3,1-Timp.,B.Dr.,Cym.-2Hp.-Str.
Lemoine, Paris, c1901
Score 63 p.
*Composed 1898. First performance Paris, 1902,
Concerts Lamoureux, Camille Chevillard con-
ductor.*

711m Impromptu on Japanese airs, for harp and
orchestra, Op. 58
Solo Hp.-1(alt. Picc.),1(alt. E.H.),1,1-Hn.-
Trgl.-Str.
Score: Ms. 36 p.
Parts: Evette & Schaeffer, Paris [n.d.]
*Composed for the competition of the Conserva-
toire National of Paris, 1915.*

1427 Marche de fête [Festive march, for   *12'*
organ, Op. 36]
3*,2,2,2-4,2,3,1-Timp.,Cym.-Str.
Durand, Paris, c1911
Score 21 p.
*Composed and orchestrated 1907. First perform-
ance Bordeaux, 1908, Rhené-Baton conductor.*

1221 Les noces corinthiennes [Corinthian   *7'*
nuptials. Prelude to Act III]
3*,3*,3*,3*-4,3,3,1-Timp.,Perc.-2Hp.-Str.
Choudens, Paris, c1922
Score 39 p.
*First concert performance of Prelude, Paris,
1923, Concerts Lamoureux, Camille Chevillard
conductor.*

695m Pastorale, Op. 46
Solo Cl.-Hp.-Str.
Score: Ms. 15 p.
Parts: Evette & Schaeffer, Paris [n.d.]
*Composed for the competition of the Conserva-
toire National of Paris, 1912.*

1280 Petite suite, Op. 12   *20'*
1.[Secretly] 2.[Slow waltz] 3.[An old
melody] 4.[Scherzetto]
1,1,1,1-Hn.-Timp.,Trgl.(ad lib.)-Hp.-Str.
Durand, Paris [n.d.]
Score 47 p.
*Composed 1897. First performance Monte Carlo,
1898, Léon Jéhin conductor.*

622m Pièce de concert [for pedal harp and small
orchestra] Op. 32
Solo Hp.-Fl.,Cl.-Hn.-Str.
Leduc, Paris, c1907
Score 23 p.

1396 Suite brève, Op. 26   *12'*
1.Canzone 2.Passegiata [Promenade]
3.Trottola [Humming-top] 4.Nocturne 5.Valse-
impromptu
2,2,2,2-2,1-Timp.,Trgl.(ad lib.)-Hp.-Str.
Lemoine, Paris, c1899, 1904 and 1908
Score 67 p.
*Composed 1901. First performance Monte Carlo,
1902, the composer conducting.*

1041 Suite funambulesque [from the   15'
pantomime Blanc et Noir] Op. 20
1.Introduction 2.[Ballet waltz] 3.[Andante
and Creolian dance] 4.Finale
2,2(2nd alt. E.H.),2,2-2Hn.-Timp.,Trgl.,Tamb.-
Hp.(or Pno.)-Str. (or: 1,1,1,1-Hn.-Tamb.-Hp. or
Pno.-Str.)
Lemoine, Paris, c1901
Score 111 p.
*Composed 1899. First performance Monte Carlo,
1899, the composer conducting.*

BUTLER, JOHN C.   Houston, Texas 5 July 1929

421m Concerto for oboe and chamber   25'
orchestra
1.Fantasia: Allegro risoluto 2.Elegy: Lento
3.Burlesque: Allegro moderato
Solo Ob.-2(2nd alt. Picc.),1*,2,1-2,2,1-
Timp.,Perc.-Pno.(alt. Cel.),Hp.-Str.
Ms.
Score 141 p. Large folio
*Composed 1958-59. First performance 29th An-
nual Festival of American Music, Eastman-
Rochester Symphony Orchestra, Howard Hanson
conductor, Robert Sprenkle soloist. Dedicated
to Robert Sprenkle.*

BÜTTNER, MAX.   Rodach, Koburg 29 January 1891

643m [Concerto, harp, Op. 10, E-flat major]
I.Allegro moderato 2.Andante 3.Allegro
Solo Hp.-2,2(1st alt. E.H.),2,2-2,2-Timp.-Str.
Himmelreich, Munich [n.d.]
Score 71 p.

BUXTEHUDE, DIETRICH.   Oldesloe, Holstein ca.1637
                            Lübeck, Germany 9 May 1707

Also spelled: Diderik Buxtehude

2716 Chaconne, toccata and fugue. Arranged 11'
by Harvey Goodstein
1,1,1,1-Hn.-Timp.-Str.
Ms.
Score 21 p.
Originally composed for organ; arranged 1936.

2721 [Prelude and fugue, organ, E minor.   5'
Transcribed by Leonid Leonardi]
2,3*,3*,3*-4,3,3,1-Timp.-Str.
Ms.
Score 29 p.
*Transcribed 1935. First performance Baltimore,
Maryland, 22 January 1939, Baltimore Symphony
Orchestra, Werner Janssen conductor.*

1570s [Three pieces for organ. Transcribed for
string orchestra by Franco Margola]
1.Corale: Von Gott Will Ich Nicht Lassen [From
God Shall Nought Divide Me] 2.Corale: Vater
Unser in Himmelreich [Our Father in Heaven]:
Andante con moto 3.Canzonetta: Andante con
moto
Str.
G. Zanibon, Padua, c1952
Score 8 p.

BYRD, WILLIAM.   probably in Lincolnshire 1543
                    Stondon Massey, Essex 4 July 1623

Also spelled: Bird and Byrde

819s The carman's whistle. Arranged for string
orchestra by Granville Bantock
Str.
Curwen, London, c1928
Score 7 p.

4686 The Earle of Salisbury's pavane *and*   5'
A gigg. Transcribed for orchestra by Richard
Bales
1,1,2,1-2,2,1-Timp.-Hp.or Pno.(optional)-Str.
Ms.
Score 15 p.
*Both originally composed for keyboard (harpsi-
chord or virginal). The Pavane composed ca.
1612 and published as no. 6 in the collection
Parthenia. The Gigg published as A Gigg F.
Tr[egian], no. 180 in the Fitzwilliam Virginal
Book, probably compiled after 1621.*

235s Fantazia, for string sextet or small
string orchestra. Edited by Edmund H. Fellowes
Str.(without Cb.)
Stainer & Bell, London, c1922
Score 12 p.
From Psalms, Songs and Sonnets, 1611.

705s Jhon come kisse me now. Transcribed for
string orchestra by J. Bernard Jackson
Str.
Oxford University Press, London, c1926
Score 5 p.
*Original contained in the Fitzwilliam Virginal
Book. Variations used are Nos. 1,2,3,5,7,10,
11,12,14, and 15 of the original.*

220s The leaves be greene, (Browning) for
string orchestra. Edited by Richard R. Terry
Str.
Curwen [London], c1923
Score 8 p.

3183 Suite, selected from the Fitzwilliam   13'
Virginal Book and freely transcribed for
orchestra by Gordon Jacob
1.The Earle of Oxford's marche 2.Pavana 3.The
bells
3(3rd alt. Picc.),2,2,2-4,2,3,1-Timp.,Perc.,
Gong(ad lib.)-Org.(ad lib.),Hp.-Str.
Universal Edition, London, c1939
Score 42 p.
*Originally composed for clavichord, 16th cen-
tury; transcribed 1938. First performance
Teatro da Trinidade, Lisbon, Portugal, 19
October 1939, Orquestra Sinfonica Nacional,
Pedro de Freitas Branco conductor.*

Cadman, Charles Wakefield

C

CADMAN, CHARLES WAKEFIELD.
Johnstown, Pennsylvania 24 December 1881
Los Angeles 30 December 1946

1772s American suite, for string orchestra *12'*
1.Indian 2.Negro 3.Old fiddler
Str.
Composers Press, New York, c1938
Score 16 p.
Commissioned by F. Charles Adler for the Saratoga Spa Music Festival, 1937. Composed 1937. Original title: Suite on American Folk Tunes. First performance Saratoga Spa Music Festival, Saratoga Springs, New York, 18 September 1937, string players from the New York Philharmonic, F. Charles Adler conductor.

356p Aurora borealis, impressionistic *17'*
fantasy for piano and orchestra
Solo Pno.-3*,2(2nd alt. E.H.),2,2-4,2,3,1-
Timp.,Perc.-Hp.-Str.
Ms.
Score 49 p. Large folio
Composed 1942.

719p Dark dancers of the Mardi Gras, *10'*
fantasy for piano and orchestra
Solo Pno.-3(3rd alt. Picc.),2,2,2-Alto Sax.,
Ten.Sax.(ad lib.)-4,3,3,1-Timp.,Perc.-Str.
Ms.
Score 51 p. Large folio
Composed 1933. Original title: Scarlet Sister Mary. First performance, under original title, Milwaukee, 12 March 1933, Milwaukee Philharmonic Orchestra, Frank L. Waller conductor, Henry Jackson soloist.

5347 Huckleberry Finn goes fishing, *12'25"*
characteristic overture
3*,3*,3*,3*-4,3,3,1-Timp.,Perc.-Pno.,Hp.-Str.
Ms.
Score 68 p. Large folio
Suggested by quotations from Mark Twain's novel. Composed 1945.

451c A mad empress remembers, tone drama *15'*
for violoncello with orchestra
Solo Vc.-3*,3*,2,2-4,3,3,1-Timp.,Perc.-Cel.,
Hp.-Str.
Ms.
Score 68 p. Large folio
Composed 1944.

2178 Oriental rhapsody from Omar Khayyam *5'*
3*,2,2,2-4,2,3,1-Timp.,Perc.-Hp.-Str.
Kalmus, New York, c1929
Score 39 p.
Enlarged from the Prelude of the music commissioned by Ferdinand Pinney Earle for a motion picture entitled The Rubaiyat of Omar Khayyam, 1918. This version, 1921. First performance Los Angeles, 6 January 1922, Los Angeles Philharmonic Orchestra, Walter Henry Rothwell conductor.

5348 [Ramala. Two selections from the opera.
1.Spring dance of the willow wands 2.Processional and dance of sacrifice]
3*,2,3*,3*-4,3,3,1-Timp.,Perc.-Pno.,Hp.-Str.
Ms.
Score 37 p. Large folio
First performance Hollywood Bowl, California, July 1946, Leopold Stokowski conductor.

3766 Symphony no. 1, Pennsylvania *23'*
1.Andante moderato 2.Allegro scherzando 3.
Allegro con fuoco
3*(3rd alt. Picc.),2(2nd alt. E.H.),3*,2-4,3,3,
1-Timp.,Perc.-Org.,Cel.,Hp.-Str.
Ms.
Score 143 p.
Composed 1939. First performance Hollywood, California, 7 March 1940, Los Angeles Philharmonic, Albert Coates conductor.

1406 Thunderbird, orchestral suite, Op. 63 *14'*
1.Before the sunrise 2.Nuwana's love song 3.
Wolf dance 4.Night song 5.The passing of
Nuwana
3*,3*,2,2-4,2,3,1-Timp.,Perc.-Hp.-Str.
White-Smith, Boston, c1920
Score 94 p.
Composed 1916. Suite drawn from the incidental music to Norman Bel-Geddes's drama of the same name. Nos. 2, 3 and 4 based on Blackfoot Indian tunes. First performance Los Angeles, 9 January 1917.

1706s To a vanishing race, for string *3'*
orchestra, Op. 47 no. 1
Str.
Score: Ms. 2 p.
Parts: John Church, Cincinnati, c1917
Originally composed for piano, 1908; arranged for strings, 1913. First performance Denver Music Festival, Colorado, 17 May 1914, Russian Symphony Orchestra, Modest Altschuler conductor.

CAETANI, ROFFREDO, PRINCE OF BASSIANO.
Rome 13 October 1871
Rome 11 April 1961

5172 [Intermezzo sinfonico for large orchestra,
Op. 2]
3*,3*,3*,2-4,3,3,1-Timp.,Cym.-Str.
Schott, Mainz [ca.1891]
Score 71 p.
Composed 1889-90.

618 [Suite, Op. 10, B minor] *40'*
1.Allegro moderato 2.Allegro vivace 3.Adagio
4.Allegro 5.Allegro assai con fuoco
2,2,2,2-4,2-Timp.-Str.
Schott, Mainz [n.d.]
Score 168 p.
Composed 1901. First performance Rome, 1902.

619 [Symphonic prelude no. 1, Op. 8 no. 1,
E-flat major]
2,3*,3*,2-4,2,3,1-Timp.,Hp.-Str.
Schott, Mainz [n.d.]
Score 23 p.
Composed 1898. First performance Rome, 1899.

620 [Symphonic prelude no. 2, Op. 8 no. 2,
C minor]
3*,3*,3*,2-4,3,3,1-Timp.,Hp.-Str.
Schott, Mainz [n.d.]
Score 45 p.
Composed 1898. First performance Rome, 1899.

621 [Symphonic prelude no. 4, Op. 11 no. 1,
E minor]
3*,3*,3*,2-4,3,3,1-Timp.,Trgl.,Cym.-Str.
Schott, Mainz [n.d.]
Score 61 p.
Composed 1900. First performance Rome, 1901.

622 [Symphonic prelude no. 5, Op. 11 no. 2,
A minor]
3(3rd alt. Picc.),3*,3*,2-4,3,3,1-Timp.-Str.
Schott, Mainz [n.d.]
Score 55 p.
Composed 1900. First performance Rome, 1901.

CAGE, JOHN.   Los Angeles 5 September 1912

1016m First construction, in metal   *9'*
6 players:
1st - Thundersheet; Orchestra Bells
2nd (requires an assistant) - Str.Pno.
3rd - 12 Graduated Sleigh or Oxen Bells; Suspended Sleigh Bells; Thundersheet
4th - 4 Brake Dr.; 8 Cow Bells; 3 Japanese
Temple Gongs
5th - Thundersheet; 4 Muted Gongs; Water Gong;
Tam-tam; Suspended Gong
Ms.
Score 28 p.
*Composed 1939. First performance Cornish
School, Seattle, 9 December 1939, under the
composer's direction.*

1035m Imaginary landscape no. 1 (1939)   *6'*
4 players:
1st - Variable-speed Phono-Turntable and
Frequency Recordings
2nd - Variable-speed Phono-Turntable and
Frequency Recordings
3rd - Large Chinese Cym.
4th - Str.Pno.
Ms.
Score 9 p.
*Composed 1939. First performance Cornish
Theater, Seattle, 9 December 1939, by the
composer and others.*

1007m Imaginary landscape no. 3 (1942)   *3'*
6 players:
1st - Oscillator; Constant Frequency Record
2nd - Tin Cans
3rd - Tin Cans
4th - Buzzer; Record of Continuously Variable
Frequency
5th - Balinese Gongs; Generator Whine
6th - Coil (Plucked); Marimba
Ms.
Score 12 p.
*Composed 1942. First performance Chicago Arts
Club, 1 March 1942, the composer conducting.*

1020m Second construction, for percussion   *6'*
orchestra
4 players;
1st - 7 Sleigh Bells; Wooden Indian Rattle;
Wind Glass; Small Maracas
2nd - S.Dr.; Large Maracas; Small Maracas;
5 Tom-Toms; 3 Temple Gongs
3rd - Tam-tam; Thundersheet; 5 Muted Gongs;
Water Gong
4th - Str.Pno.
Ms.
Score 20 p.
*Composed 1940. First performance Reed College,
Portland, Oregon, 14 February 1940, under the
composer's direction.*

CAHNBLEY, AUGUST.

860m [Concertino for trumpet and orchestra]
1.Allegro con fuoco 2.Andante 3.Adagio
4.Allegretto
Solo Tpt.-2,2,2,2-2,2,1-Timp.,Perc.-Str.
Score: Ms. 39 p.
Parts: A.E. Fischer, Bremen [n.d.]

CAILLIET, LUCIEN.   Dijon 22 May 1891

4863 [Variations on Pop! Goes the Weasel]   *7'*
3*,3*(E.H. ad lib.),2,2-3Sax.(ATBar.)-4,3,3,1-
Timp.,Perc.-Str.
Elkan-Vogel, Philadelphia, c1940
Score 32 p.
Composed 1938.

CAJA, ALFONSO.   Italy 1889

1486 [Two idylls from Syracuse]   *10'*
1.Novelletta di Natale 2.Villanella
2,3*,2,2-2Hn.-Cel.-Str.
Senart, Paris, c1929
Score 12 p.
Composed 1928.

CALCAGNO, ELSA.   Buenos Aires 19 October 1910

5580 [Orchestral variations]   *12'*
3*,3*,3*,2-4,3,3,1-Timp.,Perc.-Cel.,Hp.-Str.
Ms.
Score 63 p. Large folio
*Composed 1954. First performance Buenos Aires,
1955, Radio Nacional, Bruno Bandini conductor.*

5583 [Sinfonietta for two string orches-   *12'*
tras and wind instruments]
1.Andante expresivo 2.Andante coral 3.Allegro
ritmico
2,2,2,2-2,2-Timp.-Str.(in 2 groups)
Ms.
Score 61 p.
Composed 1952-53.

6875 Suite norteña [Northern suite]
1.Amanecer en el altiplano 2.Bailecito
3.Cueca norteña 4.Carnavalito
1,1,1-Tpt.-Timp.-3Accordions(optional)-Str.
Ms.
Score 36 p.

Caldara, Antonio

CALDARA, ANTONIO.   Venice 1670
                              Vienna 28 December 1736

1826s Divertimento in B minor. Adapted for
modern performance by Karl Geiringer
1.Allegretto 2.Allegro assai
Str.
Ms.
Score 8 p.

CALDER, HATTIE M.

7319 Arch Street polka. Arranged for small   3'
orchestra by Sam Dennison
1,1,2*,1-Hn.,Tbn.-Perc.-Str.
Ms.
Score 8 p.
*Arranged 1977. First performance The Free
Library of Philadelphia, 8 May 1977,
The Fleisher Ensemble, Sam Dennison conductor.*

CALDWELL, JON. Rochester, New York 31 October 1947

196m Romance for oboe and strings   8'
Solo Ob.-Str.
Ms.
Score 9 p. Large folio
*Originally composed for solo oboe and string
quartet, 1973-74 and first performed Philadel-
phia, 12 October 1975, National Association
for American Composers and Conductors, Dorothy
Stone soloist. Transcribed for solo oboe and
string orchestra and first performed Philadel-
phia, 26 January 1976, Mostovoy Soloists, Marc
Mostovoy conductor, John DeLancie soloist.*

CALLAERTS, JOSEPH.   Antwerp 22 August 1838
                              Antwerp 3 March 1901

936v Concertpiece for violin and orchestra,
E major
Solo Vn.-2,2,2,2-2,2,1-Timp.-Str.
Ms.
Score 29 p.

CALMON, THEO. pseudonym.
See: KOCHMANN, SPERO.

CALVELLO, MIGUEL.

3891 Momento español [Spanish moment]
2,2,2,2-2,2,2,1-Timp.,Perc.-Str.
Score: Ms. 18 p.
Parts: Casa Editora Miguel Calvello, Buenos
      Aires [n.d.]

CAMBERT, ROBERT.   Paris ca.1628
                          London ca.February 1677

1938s [Pomone. Overture]
Str: Dessus de Violon(Vn.I), Haute-contre de
Violon(Vn.II), Taille de Violon(Va.), Basse de
Violon(Vc. and Cb.)
Score: S. Richault, Paris [1859?] 3 p.
Parts: Ms. c1976 by The Fleisher Collection of
Orchestral Music, Free Library of Philadelphia
*From the pastoral opera in five acts with
libretto by Pierre Perrin. Composed 1671.*

*First performance at the inauguration of the
Paris Opéra in the Salle du Jeu de Paume, 3
March 1671.*

CAMBINI, GIOVANNI GIUSEPPE.
                    Leghorn, Italy 13 February 1746
              Bicêtre near Paris 29 December 1825

295p [Concerto, piano and strings, Op.   14'30"
15 no. 3, G major. Revised by Guglielmo
Barblan]
1.Allegro 2.Rondo: Allegretto
Solo Pno.-Str.
Ricordi, Milan, c1959
Score 50 p.
Composed ca.1782-4.

CAMERON, RICHARD.   Philadelphia 1907

2901 Comedy overture   9'
3(3rd alt. Picc.),3*,4*(1Cl. in E-flat),3*-4,3,
3,1-Timp.,Perc.-Cel.,Hp.-Str.
Ms.
Score 69 p.
Composed 1932.

2902 For the children, suite in 7 move-   13'
ments
1.Fantastic music box 2.Ballet of the marionettes 3.Little Spanish march 4.The little
trumpet players 5.Dance of the little Cuban
boys 6.Pastorale 7.Farandole
2(2nd alt. Picc.),3*,2,2-2,2-Timp.,Perc.-Cel.,
Hp.-Str.
Ms.
Score 89 p.
*Composed 1935. Movements 1 and 2 originally
for piano. First performance of first six
movements only, Mitten Hall, Temple University,
Philadelphia, 30 July 1940, Pennsylvania Symphony Orchestra of the WPA, Guglielmo Sabatini
conductor.*

CAMPA, GUSTAVO E.   Mexico City 8 September 1863
                       Mexico City 29 October 1934

591v [Melody, violin and orchestra, Op. 1,
F major]
Solo Vn.-2,2,2,2-2Hn.-Timp.-Str.
Breitkopf & Härtel, Leipzig, c1890 by
G. Schirmer, New York
Score 8 p.

CAMPAGNOLI, BARTOLOMMEO.
          Cento di Ferrara, Italy 10 September 1751
             Neustrelitz, Germany 6 November 1827

1025m [Romance, flute and string orchestra]
Solo Fl.-Str.
Score: Ms. 8 p.
Solo & Parts: C.F. Schmidt, Heilbronn [n.d.]

Largo
p dolce

987v [Same as above. Transcribed for viola and
string orchestra by Louis Pegels]
Solo Va.-Str.
Score: Ms. 4 p.
Parts: C.F. Schmidt, Heilbronn [n.d.]

CAMPO, FRANK.   New York 4 February 1927

7131 Alpine holiday overture, Op. 11   8'
3*,3*,3*,3*-4,3,3,1-Timp.,Perc.-Str.
Ms. c1959 by Frank Campo
Score 72 p. Large folio
*Composed 1955. First performance Redlands,
California, 30 March 1957, University of Red-
lands Community Symphony, Wayne R. Bohrnstedt
conductor.*

7148 Capriccio for symphonic wind   10'
ensemble, Op. 48
4*(2Picc.),2,7*(1Cl. in E-flat,Alto Cl.),2-
4Sax.(AATBar.)-4,3,3,Bar.Hn.,2-Perc.-Cb.
Ms. c1975 by Frank Campo
Score 41 p. Large folio
*Composed 1975. First performance Los Angeles,
10 May 1975, University of Southern California
Wind Orchestra, Robert Wojciak conductor.*

7182 Fanfare
See: FANFARES 1969 FOR 8 TRUMPETS. No. III

7133 Music for Agamemnon, for band, Op. 33   5'
3*,3*,7*(1Cl. in E-flat,Alto Cl.,Cb.Cl.),3*-
4Sax.(AATBar.)-4,3,3,Bar.Hn.,2-Timp.,Perc.
Ms.
Score 44 p. Large folio
*Inspired by Aeschylus' play. Composed 1966.
First performance Los Angeles, 11 May 1966,
University of Southern California Wind Orches-
tra, Robert Wojciak conductor.*

7132 Partita for 2 chamber orchestras,   13'30"
Op. 45
1.Intrada 2.Marcia 3.Arietta 4.Scherzo
5.Musica sospesa 6.Fantasia 7.Toccata
Orchestra I: 1,0,2*-Perc.-Str.
Orchestra II: 0,1,0,1-Perc.-Str.
Ms. c1974 by Frank Campo
Score 82 p. Large folio
*Commissioned by Neville Marriner and the Los
Angeles Chamber Orchestra under a grant from
the California Arts Commission. Composed 1973.
First performance Los Angeles, 7 April 1974,
Los Angeles Chamber Orchestra, Neville Marri-
ner conductor.*

7150 Tricarnia, Op. 40   13'
1.Allegro moderato 2.Adagio 3.Allegro
3(3rd alt. Picc.),3(3rd alt. E.H.),3,3*-4,4,3,
1-Timp.,Perc.-Hp.-Str.
Ms.

Score 67 p. Large folio
Composed 1971.

CAMPRA, ANDRÉ.   Aix-en-Provence 4 December 1660
                       Versailles 29 June 1744

880s [Tancrède. Sarabande from the opera.   2'
Arranged for string orchestra by Gustav Sandré]
Str.
Schott, Mainz [n.d.]
Score 3 p.

CANNABICH, CHRISTIAN.
     Mannheim, Germany baptized 28 December 1731
              Frankfurt, Germany 20 January 1798

Full name: Johann Innocenz Christian Bonaventura
     Cannabich

208m [Concerto, flute, oboe, bassoon and
orchestra, C major] Edited by Bernhard Päuler
In one movement: Allegro assai moderato -
Cadenza - Adagio
Solo Fl., Solo Ob., Solo Bn.-2Hn.,2Tpt.-Timp.-
Str.
Edition Eulenberg, Adliswil-Zurich, c1972
Score 27 p.
*Composed before 1778. This first publication
edited from Ms. in the Bavarian State Library,
Munich (Mus. Ms. 1829).*

Allegro assai moderato

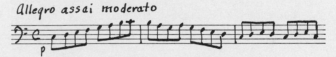

1985s [Divertimento, string orchestra, Op. 5,
D major. Adapted for modern performance by
Karl Geiringer]
1.Andante affetuoso 2.Allegro non tanto
Str.
Ms.
Score 12 p.

Andante affetuoso

6948 [Overture a 15, C major]
2,2,2,2-2Hn.-Str.
Score: Denkmäler der Tonkunst in Bayern,
VIII/2. Breitkopf & Härtel, Leipzig [1908].
Edited by Hugo Riemann. 19 p.
Parts: Ms. c1976 by The Fleisher Collection of
Orchestral Music, Free Library of Philadelphia

Allegro molto

Cannabich, Christian

7020 [Symphony no. 5, B-flat major]
1.Allegro 2.Andante 3.Allegro
2Cl.,2Bn.-2Hn.-Str.
Score: Denkmäler der Tonkunst in Bayern,
VIII/2. Breitkopf & Härtel, Leipzig, 1907.
Edited by Hugo Riemann. 41 p.
Parts: Ms. c1976 by The Fleisher Collection of
Orchestral Music, Free Library of Philadelphia

CANNING, THOMAS SCRIBNER.
b. Brookville, Pennsylvania 12 December 1911

3624 Overture to an illustrious American   7'
3*,2,2,2-4,3,3,1-Timp.,Perc.-Hp.-Str.
Ms.
Score 75 p.
*Composed 1940. Original title: To an
Illustrious American, signifying the char-
acter Charlie McCarthy. First performance
Rochester, New York, 18 April 1940, Rochester
Civic Orchestra, Howard Hanson conductor.*

6600 Rondo, for percussion and brass   8'30"
instruments
2Hn.,2Tpt.,3Tbn.,Tuba-Timp.,Perc.
Composers Facsimile Edition, New York, c1957
by Thomas Canning
Score 29 p.
Composed 1953. Revised 1964.

CANTU, CARLO ADOLFO.   Turin, Italy 21 January 1875
Turin, Italy 26 March 1942

657v Chanson suèdoise [Swedish song, for   4'
violin and orchestra, Op. 12]
Solo Vn.-1,1,2,1-2Hn.-Timp.-Hp.(ad lib.)-Str.
Score: Ms. 19 p.
Parts: Decourcelle, Nice, c1924
*Composed 1923. First performance Nice,
December 1924.*

CAPANNA, ROBERT.   Camden, New Jersey 7 July 1952

7292 Concerto for chamber orchestra
In one movement
1(alt. Alto Fl.),1(alt. E.H.),1,1-1,1,1-Perc.-
Pno.,Hp.-Str.
Ms.
Score 46 p. Large folio
Composed 1974.

268v Three songs, for solo violin, chorus,   15'
and orchestra
1.Last conquest of the eye 2.Ethereal
estuary 3.Bird of the sun
Solo Vn.-2,1,2,1-2,2,1-Chorus(SATB)-Str.
Ms.
Score 31 p. Large folio
*Texts by Henry David Thoreau. Composed for
advanced-level high school students. Commissioned by the Amherst Summer Music Center.*

*Composed 1976. First performance Amherst,
Massachusetts, 15 August 1976, Amherst Summer
Music Center, the composer conducting, Neil
Weintraub soloist.*

CAPLET, ANDRÉ.   Le Havre, France 23 November 1878
Paris 22 April 1925

522c [Epiphany (after an Ethiopian legend), 20'
fresco for violoncello and orchestra]
1.Cortège 2.Cadenza 3.Dance of the little
Moors
Solo Vc.-2(2nd alt. Picc.),2,2,2-4,2-Timp.,
Perc.-Cel.,Hp.-Str.
Durand, Paris, c1924
Score 110 p.
*Composed 1923. First performance Concerts
Colonne, Paris, 29 December 1923, Maurice
Maréchal soloist.*

6585 [Persian suite, for wind instruments]
1.Scharki 2.Nihavvend 3.Iskïa samaïsi
2,2,2,2-2Hn.
Ms.
Score 56 p.
Composed 1900.

CAPONSACCHI, JEAN.

465s Una carezza [A caress]   waltz
Str.
[n.p.,n.d.]
Score 13 p.

CAPPÉ, P.

1199s Gavotte
Str.
Score: Ms. 5 p.
Parts: Foetisch, Lausanne [n.d.]

CAPRI, ALFRED.

1308s Conte fleuri [Florid tale]   intermezzo
Fl.,Cl.-Str.
Score: Ms. 5 p.
Parts: Decourcelle, Nice, c1925

1409s Ton image [Thy image]   melody
Fl.,Cl.-Str.
Score: Ms. 7 p.
Parts: Decourcelle, Nice [n.d.]

CARABELLA, EZIO.   Rome 3 March 1891
Rome 19 April 1964

3918 Andante con variazioni   18'
3*,3*,2,2-4,3,4-Timp.,Perc.-Org.,Cel.,Hp.-Str.
Ricordi, Milan, c1923
Miniature score 75 p.
*First performance Augusteo, Rome, 20 February
1921, Bernardino Molinari conductor.*

4808 Aprilia   8'
3(3rd alt. Picc.),3*,2,3*-4,3,3,1-Timp.,Perc.-
Cel.,2Hp.-Str.
Ricordi, Milan, c1939
Score 42 p.
Composed 1929.

CARL, M.

783m [Concert-aria, clarinet solo and orchestra,
Op. 61, F major]
Solo Cl.-1,1,1,1-2,2,1-Timp.-Str.
Score: Ms. 31 p.
Parts: A.E. Fischer, Bremen [n.d.]

876m [Concerto, cornet à piston or trumpet,
Op. 84, E-flat major]
Solo Cnt.-2(2nd alt. Picc.),2,2,2-2,2,1-Timp.-
Str.
Score: Ms. 82 p.
Parts: A.E. Fischer [n.p., n.d.]

1065v [Concerto, violin, no. 3, D major]
Solo Vn.-1,1,2,1-2,2,1-Timp.-Str.
Score: Ms. 79 p.
Parts: Oertel, Hannover, 1886

814m In einsamen Stunden [trombone and
orchestra] Op. 72
Solo Tbn.-1,1,1,1-2,2-Timp.-Str.
Score: Ms. 7 p.
Parts: Engelmann & Mühlberg, Leipzig [n.d.]
*Bound with R. Bohne, Serenade for Horn and
Clarinet Soli, Op. 35.*

CARLI, ALBERTO. pseudonym.
See: PIZZINI, CARLO ALBERTO.

CARLSTEDT, JAN.
b. Orsa, Dalecarlia, Sweden 15 June 1926

2152s [Sonata for strings, Op. 7 no. 2]   *14'*
1.Preludio 2.Notturno 3.Finale
Str.
Ms.
Score 32 p.
*Originally composed as a sonata for two vio-
lins, Op. 7 no. 1, 1956. Arranged for strings
in 1956. First performance Stockholm, 10
October 1958, Swedish Radio Orchestra, Sten
Frykberg conductor.*

6804 [Symphony no. 1, Op. 1, E minor. Original
version]
1.Allegro 2.Largo 3.Vivo
3*,3*,3(2nd alt. Cl. in E-flat,3rd alt. B.Cl.),
3*-4,3,3,1-Timp.,Perc.-Str.
Edition Suecia, Stockholm [n.d.]
Score 163 p.
Composed 1952-54. Revised 1961.

7036 [Symphony no. 2, Op. 25, A symphony   *30'*
of brotherhood]
1.Moderato - Tranquillo 2.Allegro 3.Adagio -
Largo
3*,3*,3*,3*-4,3,3,1-Timp.,Perc.-Cel.-Str.
Edition Suecia, Stockholm, ᶜ1972
Score 161 p.
*Composed 1968-69. First performance Philhar-
monic Hall, Lincoln Center, New York City, 20
December 1970, Symphony of the New World, James
DePriest conductor. Dedicated to the memory
of Martin Luther King, Jr. This symphony
awarded a five year fellowship prize from the
Swedish State, 1970.*

CARNEVALE, LUIGI.   Philadelphia 1909
Washington, D.C. 16 April 1949

2800 Al tramónto [At sunset]   *5'*
2,3*,2,2-4Hn.-Timp.,Perc.-Hp.-Str.
Ms.
Score 12 p.
*Composed 1936-37. First performance Philadel-
phia, 10 February 1939, Italian Symphony
Orchestra, the composer conducting.*

2679 Capriccio orientale, tone poem   *9'*
3(2nd and 3rd alt. Picc.),2(2nd alt. E.H.),2,2
-4,4,3,1-Timp.,Perc.-2Hp.-Str.
Ms.
Score 48 p.
*Composed 1936; revised 1938. First performance
Philadelphia, 7 May 1938, Italian Symphony
Orchestra, the composer conducting.*

3060 Easter festival, chimes for orchestra   *7'*
4*,3*,4*,3*-4,3,3,1-Timp.,Perc.-Hp.-Str.
Ms.
Score 26 p. Large folio
*Composed 1938. First performance Philadelphia,
14 April 1939, Italian Symphony Orchestra, the
composer conducting.*

2642 Intermezzo, poemetto pastorale   *5'*
2,2,2,2-2Hn.-Hp.-Str.
Ms.
Score 18 p.
*Composed 1935. First performance on the com-
poser's wedding day, St. Nicholas Catholic
Church, Philadelphia, 8 September 1935, William
F. Happich conductor.*

3589 Symphonic ode   *5'*
2,2,2,2-4,2,1,1-Timp.-Hp.-Str.
Ms.
Score 23 p. Large folio
*Composed 1940. First performance Philadelphia,
27 February 1942, Pennsylvania Philharmonic
Orchestra Society, the composer conducting.*

3018 Villanella   *8'*
2,2,2,2-4,2,3-Timp.,Perc.-Hp.-Str.
Ms.
Score 36 p.
*Composed 1938. First performance Philadelphia,
10 February 1939, Italian Symphony Orchestra,
the composer conducting.*

CARPENTER, JOHN ALDEN.
Park Ridge, Chicago 28 February 1876
Chicago 26 April 1951

1216 Adventures in a perambulator   *26'*
1.En voiture! 2.The policeman 3.The hurdy-
gurdy 4.The lake 5.Dogs 6.Dreams
3(3rd alt. Picc.),3*,3*,2-4,2,3,1-Timp.,Perc.-
Pno.,Cel.,Hp.-Str.
G. Schirmer, ᶜ1917
Score 117 p.
*Completed 1914. First performance Chicago, 19
March 1915.*

Carr, Benjamin

CARR, BENJAMIN.   London 12 September 1768
                       Philadelphia 24 May 1831

7044 [The archers. Why, huntress, why.   *3'*
Arranged for voice and small orchestra by
Philip Weston]
High Voice-1,1,2,1-2Hn.-Str.
Concord Music Publishing, New York, c1941
Score 7 p.
*From the opera The Archers [or Mountaineers] of
Switzerland, with libretto by William Dunlap
based on Friedrich von Schiller's William Tell.
First performance New York, 18 April 1796, by
the Old American Company.*

7043 Ave Maria. Edited and arranged [for   *3'*
voice and small orchestra] by Philip Weston
High Voice-1,1,2,1-2Hn.-Hp.-Str.
Concord Music Publishing, New York, c1941
Score 11 p.
*Song with text by Sir Walter Scott. Originally
composed for voice and piano.*

7128 Federal overture (1794). Arranged   *8'*
for orchestra by Romulus Franceschini
[Introduction based on Yankee Doodle] - Mar-
seilles march - Ça ira - O dear what can the
matter be - The Irish washerwoman - Rose tree
- La carmagnole - President's march - Yankee
Doodle
2(2nd alt. Picc.),2,2,2-2,2,2-Timp.,Perc.-Str.
Ms. c1975 by Romulus Franceschini
Score 46 p. Large folio
*Composed 1794. First performance by the Old
American Company at the Cedar Street Theatre,
Philadelphia, 22 September 1794. Carr's
orchestral score and parts long lost. This
arrangement, adapted in 1975 from a piano ver-
sion published by Carr in Philadelphia, was
first performed at the National Gallery of
Art, Washington, D.C., 21 September 1975,
National Gallery Orchestra, Richard Bales
conductor.*

7139 Mélange. An easy selection of airs.   *9'*
Transcribed for small orchestra by Romulus
Franceschini
1.March 2.Waltz 3.Gavotte 4.Country dance
5.Slow air 6.Allegro moderato 7.Carillons
8.Cotillion 9.Pastorale 10.Hornpipe
11.Da Capo to No. 1, March
1,1,2,1-2,2-Timp.,Perc.-Str.
Ms. c1975 by Romulus Franceschini
Score 36 p.
*Originally composed for piano. First published
by Joseph Carr (father) in Baltimore (1815?)
as no. 25 in Benjamin Carr's Miscellany. Reissued in Philadelphia by George Willig ca.1832.
This transcription 1976, first performed Toms
River, New Jersey, 31 January 1976, Garden
State Philharmonic, Robert Fitzpatrick conductor.*

7320 Une petite ouverture. Arranged for   *3'*
wind octet by Sam Dennison
1,1,2*,1-1,1,1
Ms.
Score 5 p.

*Composed 1825. First performance of this
arrangement Brandywine River Museum, Chadd's
Ford, Pennsylvania, 20 June 1976, Fleisher
Ensemble, Sam Dennison conductor.*

CARRAUD, MICHEL-GASTON.
                 Mée, near Paris 20 July 1864
                    Paris 15 June 1920

798m Lied [for horn and orchestra]
Solo Hn.-2,2,2,2-Tpt.-Trgl.-Hp.-Str.
Ms.
Score 23 p.

CARSE, ADAM. Newcastle-on-Tyne, England 10 May 1878
        Great Missenden, England 2 November 1958

1130s Barbara Allen, variations for string
orchestra
Str.
Score: Ms. 26 p.
Parts: Novello, London, c1921

4675 Georgian tunes, six tunes popular in   *7'*
England in the middle of the 18th century.
Arranged for orchestra by Adam Carse
1.Admiral Vernon's march: Allegro marziale 2.O,
Mary, soft in feature: Andante sostenuto 3.Kick
him, Jenny: Vivace 4.Minuet by Mr. Stanley
5.Gavot by Mr. Humphries 6.Miss Baker's hornpipe: Allegro vivace
2(2nd alt. Picc.),2,2,2-2,2,3-Timp.,Perc.-Str.
Augener, London, c1935
Score 17 p.

1003 The merry milkmaids, Old English   *4'*
dance tune
2*,2,2,2-4,2,3,1-Timp.,Perc.-Str.
Augener, London, c1923
Score 20 p.
*Composed 1922. First performance Bournemouth,
1922, Dan Godfrey conductor.*

2026 The nursery, a dance-phantasy for   *13'*
orchestra
Introduction: The nursery at night (a)Dance
of the teddy bear (b)Dance of the fairy doll
(c)Dance of the wild nigger doll (d)Dance of
the top and the ball (e)Dance of the sailor
doll (f)Dance of the toy soldier - Finale:
The children's dance
2(2nd alt. Picc.),2,2,2-4,3,3,1-Timp.,Perc.-
Hp.-Str.
Augener, London, c1929
Score 50 p.
*Composed 1928. First performance Eastbourne,
1928, H. G. Amers conductor.*

Three dances, for string quartet or string
orchestra
818s 1.Dainty dance
506s 2.Languid dance
426s 3.Waltz
Pno.(ad lib.)-Str.
Augener, London, c1924
Scores: 4 p., 4 p., 7 p.

754s Two sketches
1.A northern song 2.A northern dance
Str.
Augener, London, ᶜ1924
Miniature score 15 p.
Composed 1923.

4634 Waltz-variations for orchestra
2(2nd alt. Picc.),2,2,2-4,2,3,1-Timp.,Perc.-
Str.
Augener, London, ᶜ1926
Score 25 p.

CARTER, ELLIOTT.   New York City 11 December 1908

280p Double concerto for harpsichord and   *23'*
piano with two chamber orchestras (1961)
Introduction - Cadenza for harpsichord - Alle-
gro scherzando - Adagio - Presto - Cadenzas
for piano - Coda
Orchestra I: Solo Hpscd.-Fl.(alt. Picc.)-Hn.,
Tpt.,Tbn.-Perc.-Va.,Cb.
Orchestra II: Solo Pno.-0,1,1,1-Hn.-Perc.-Vn.,
Vc.
Associated Music Publishers, New York, ᶜ1962,
1964
Score 168 p.
Commissioned by the Fromm Music Foundation.
Composed 1961. First performance at the Con-
cert of New American Music, presented by the
Fromm Music Foundation at the Grace Rainey
Rogers Auditorium, Metropolitan Museum of Art,
New York, for the 8th Congress of the Inter-
national Society for Musicology, 6 September
1961, Gustave Meier conductor, Ralph Kirk-
patrick harpsichord, Charles Rosen piano. Ded-
icated to Paul Fromm. Awarded the New York
Music Critics Circle Award, 1962.

6259 Holiday overture (1944/61) [revised   *10'*
version]
3*,3*,3*,3*-4,3,3,1-Timp.,Perc.-Pno.-Str.
Associated Music Publishers, New York, ᶜ1946,
1962
Score 70 p.
Composed 1944. First performance Frankfurt,
Germany, September 1946, Frankfurt Symphony,
Hans Blumer conductor. Revised 1961. Awarded
first prize, Independent Music Publishers Con-
test, 1945.

6247 [The Minotaur. Suite from the ballet] *24'*
Overture: Maestoso Scene I. a)Pasiphaë: Allegro misterioso b)Entrance of the bulls c)
Bull's dance with Pasiphaë: Allegro marcato
Scene II. a)Ariadne and Theseus: Allegretto
b)The labyrinth: Con moto e sostenuto c)
Theseus' farewell on entering the labyrinth:
Andante serioso d)Theseus fights and kills
the Minotaur: Allegro agitato e)Ariadne re-
winds her thread: Andante f)Theseus and the
Greeks emerge from the labyrinth: Allegro
agitato g)Theseus and the Greeks prepare to
leave Crete
2(2nd alt. Picc.),2(2nd alt. E.H.),2(2nd alt.
B.Cl.),2-4,2,2-Timp.,Perc.-Pno.-Str.
Associated Music Publishers, New York, ᶜ1956
Score 141 p.

Commissioned by the Ballet Society of New York.
Composed 1947. First performance of Suite,
Rochester, New York, 19 January 1956, Eastman-
Rochester Symphony Orchestra, Howard Hanson
conductor.

3073 Pocahontas, ballet-legend in one act   *40'*
Overture - Smith and Rolfe lost in the Virginia
forest - The Indians ambush John Smith - Prin-
cess Pocahontas and her ladies - Entrance of
Indian warriors - Torture of Smith - Pocahontas
saves Smith - Dance of Pocahontas and Smith:
Smith presents young Rolfe to Pocahontas -
Dance of Pocahontas and Rolfe - Pavane: Pocahontas and Rolfe sail for England, farewell of
Indians
3(3rd alt. Picc.),2,2,2-4,3,3,1-Timp.,Perc.-
Pno.,Hp.-Str.
Ms.
Score 127 p. Large folio
Commissioned by the Ballet Caravan, 1939. A
suite of four excerpts drawn from this ballet
received the Juilliard Publication Award, 1940.
First performance by the Ballet Caravan, in
conjunction with the American Lyric Theatre
and the League of Composers, New York, 24 May
1939, Fritz Kitzinger conductor.

6343 Symphony no. 1 [revised version]   *27'*
1.Moderately, wistfully 2.Slowly, gravely
3.Vivaciously
2(2nd alt. Picc.),2,2(1st alt. Cl. in E-flat),
2-2,2,1-Timp.-Str.
Associated Music Publishers, New York, ᶜ1961
Score 148 p.
Composed 1942. First performance Rochester,
New York, 1944, Eastman-Rochester Symphony
Orchestra, Howard Hanson conductor. Revised
1954.

6243 Variations for orchestra (1954-1955)   *24'*
2(2nd alt. Picc.),2,2,2-4,2,3,1-Timp.,Perc.-
Hp.-Str.
Associated Music Publishers, New York, ᶜ1957
Score 152 p.
Commissioned by The Louisville Philharmonic
Society. Composed 1954-55. First performance
Louisville, 21 April 1956, Louisville Orches-
tra, Robert Whitney conductor.

CASADESUS, FRANCIS.   Paris 2 December 1870
                  Suresnes near Paris 27 June 1954

Born: François Louis Casadesus

620m Hymne [for solo trumpet and orchestra]
Solo Tpt.-2,2*,2,2-4,0,2Cnt.,3,1-Timp.,Cym.-
Cel.,2Hp.-Str.
Choudens, Paris, ᶜ1923
Score 24 p.
First performance Concerts Lamoureux, Paris,
28 January 1923.

1222 Leis oulivettos, provincial dance from
the ballet Esterelle
2(2nd alt. Picc.),2,2,2-2,2,3,1-Timp.,Perc.-
Str.
Choudens, Paris [n.d.]
Score 32 p.

Casadesus, Francis

6995 [The reaper. Suite]
1.Cortège des moissonneurs [Procession of reapers]: Allegro moderato - Allegro vivace
2.Entr'acte du 2e acte: Adagio 3.Bourées et danses limousines: Allegro vivace - Allegretto - Allegro moderato - Allegro vivo
2(2nd alt. Picc.),2,2,2-4,2,3,1-Timp.,Perc.-Str.
Hayet, Paris, c1910
Score 81 p.
Incidental music for a play by Raoul Charbonnel. First performance Tulle, France, ca.1908.

6004 [Symphony, Scandinavian]   27'
1.Allegro moderato 2.Lento e sostenuto
3.Allegro energico
3*,3*,3*,3-4,2,2Cnt.,3,1-Timp.,Perc.-2Hp.-Str.
Deiss & Crépin, Paris, c1923
Score 158 p.
Composed 1906. First performance Moscow, 26 January 1908, Moscow Conservatory Orchestra, the composer conducting.

CASADESUS, MARIUS.   Paris 24 October 1892

5792 [Two pastoral sketches]
1.Grisaille [Study in grey]: Très lent 2.La trompette du boulanger [The baker's trumpet]: Allegro molto - Lent - Molto vivace - Presto
2,3*,2,2-4,2,3,1-Timp.,Perc.-Pno.-Str.
Choudens, Paris, c1930
Score 38 p.

CASADESUS, ROBERT.   Paris 7 April 1899
                            Paris 19 September 1972

241p Concerto for 2 pianos and orchestra,   19'
Op. 17
1.Allegro giocoso 2.Intermezzo: Allegretto
3.Vivo ma non troppo
2Solo Pno.-3(3rd alt. Picc.),3*,3*,3-4,3,3,1-Timp.,S.Dr.,Cym.-Str.
Ms.
Score 67 p.
Composed 1933. First performance Warsaw, April 1934, Walerian Bierdiajew conductor, Robert and Gaby Casadesus soloists.

427c [Concerto, violoncello and orchestra,   20'
Op. 43]
1.Allegro moderato 2.Allegretto vivace e spirituoso 3.Adagio mesto 4.Vivace
Solo Vc.-2,3*,3*,2-2,2,3,1-Timp.,S.Dr.,Trgl.-Str.
Ms.
Score 67 p.
Composed 1947-48. First performance Minneapolis, 30 December 1948, Minneapolis Symphony, Dimitri Mitropoulos conductor, Yves Chardon soloist.

7095 [Symphony no. 3, Op. 41]   20'
1.Vivo ma non troppo 2.Scherzando vivamente
3.Adagio mesto 4.Allegro ma non troppo
3(3rd alt. Picc.),3*,3*,4*-4,3,3,1-Timp.,Perc.-Str.
Ms.

Score 70 p. Large folio
Composed 1947. First performance Columbus, Ohio, 1968, Columbus Philharmonic, E. Whallon conductor.

CASALS, PABLO or PAU.
          Vendrell, Catalonia 29 December 1876
          Rio Piedras, Puerto Rico 22 October 1973

Baptized: Pablo Carlos Salvador Defilló de Casals

2395s Sardana, for 'cello orchestra   6'
32Vc. divided into 8 sections
c1967 by Tetra Music Corp. [Alexander Broude, New York]
Score 23 p.
One of six sardanas (the national dance of Catalonia) composed by Casals. This one composed 1930. First performance London, ca.1930, London Violoncello Club.

CASAVOLA, FRANCO.   Modugno 13 July 1891
                           Bari 7 July 1955

4007 Mattino di primavera [Spring morning] 12'
2,3*,3*,2-4,3,3,1-Timp.,Perc.-Cel.,Hp.-Str.
Ricordi, Milan, c1933
Miniature score 19 p.

CASCARINO, ROMEO.   Philadelphia 28 September 1922

1055m Blades of grass, for English horn,   7'
string orchestra and harp
Solo E.H.-Hp.-Str.
Lyra Music Edition, New York, c1961
Score 11 p.
Inspired by the poem Grass by Carl Sandburg. Composed 1945.

CASELLA, ALFREDO.   Turin, Italy 25 July 1883
                      Rome 5 March 1947

637p A notte alta [Late at night] poema   12'
musicale per pianoforte e orchestre
Solo Pno.-3(1st and 2nd alt.Picc.),3*,3*,2-4,3,3-Timp.,Perc.-Cel.,Hp.-Str.
Ricordi, Milan, c1922
Score 40 p. Large folio
Composed 1920. First performance Carnegie Hall, New York, 1 November 1921, Philadelphia Orchestra, Leopold Stokowski conductor, the composer as soloist.

1094s [Concerto. Arranged for string   24'
orchestra by Erwin Stein]
1.Sinfonia 2.Siciliana 3.Minuetto - Recitativo - Aria 4.Canzone
Str.
Universal Edition, Vienna, c1929
Score 65 p.
Originally composed as a string quartet in 1924.

1076m [Concerto, piano, violin, violon-   25'
cello and orchestra, Op. 56]
1.Largo, ampio, solenne - Allegro molto vivace
2.Adagio 3.Rondo: Tempo di giga

Casella, Alfredo

Solo Pno., Solo Vn., Solo Vc.-2(2nd alt.
Picc.),2*,3*,2-2,1,1,1-Timp.,Perc.-Str.
Ricordi, Milan, c1935
Score 128 p.
*Composed 1933. First performance Berlin, 17
November 1933.*

5218 [Concerto, strings, piano, timpani   *16'*
and percussion, Op. 69]
1.Primo tempo: Allegro alquanto pesante
2.Sarabanda: Grave, ampio 3.Finale: Allegro
molto vivace
Pno.-Timp.,Perc.-Str.
Universal Edition, Vienna, c1948
Score 74 p.
Composed 1943.

873v [Concerto, violin, A minor]   *30'*
Solo Vn.-2,3*,3*,2-4,2-Timp.,Perc.-Str.
Universal Edition, Vienna, c1929
Score 164 p.
*Composed 1928. First performance Moscow, 8
October 1928, the Moscow Conductorless Orches-
tra, Joseph Szigeti soloist.*

1915 Le couvent sur l'eau [The convent by   *18'*
the water, choreographic comedy on a subject
of J.L. Vaudoyer, symphonic fragments]
1.[Festive march] 2.[Children's round]
3.[Barcarole, sarabande] 4.[Walk of the aged
ladies] 5.[Nocturne, final dance]
4*,4*,4*,4*-4,4,3,1-Timp.,Perc.-Cel.,Mandolin,
2Hp.-Sop. Solo in no. 3-Str.
Ricordi, Milan, c1919
Score 93 p.
*Composed 1912. First performance Concerts
Monteux, Paris, 23 April 1914, the composer
conducting.*

1586 Elegia eroica [Heroic elegy]   *12'*
4,3*,4*(1Cl. in E-flat),3*-6,3,3,1-Timp.,Perc.-
Cel.,Hp.-Str.
Universal Edition, Vienna, c1922
Score 34 p.
*Composed 1916. First performance Augusteo,
Rome, 21 January 1917, Rhené-Baton conductor.*

1589 La giara-suite [The jar, symphonic   *18'*
suite from the choreographic comedy based upon
Pirandello's story of the same name]
1.(a)[Prelude] (b)[Sicilian dance] 2.(a)La
storia della fanciulla rapita dai pirati
(b)[Nela's dance] (c)[Entrance of the pea-
sants] (d)[Toast] (e)[General dance]
(f)Finale
2(2nd alt. Picc.),2,2*,2-4,2,1-Timp.,Perc.-
Ten. Solo in No. 2a-Str.
Universal Edition, Vienna, c1925
Score 105 p.
*Composed 1924. First performance New York,
October 1925, New York Philharmonic, Willem
Mengelberg conductor.*

3922 Introduzione, corale e marcia   *8'*
3*,3*,3*,3*-4,3,3,1-Timp.,Perc.-Pno.-Cb.
Universal Edition, Vienna, c1937
Score 38 p.
Composed 1931-35.

1588 Italia, rhapsody, Op. 11   *18'*
3(3rd alt. Picc.),3(1st alt. E.H.),4*(1Cl. in
E-flat),4*(1 ad lib.)-4,4,3,1-Timp.,Perc.-2Hp.
-Str.
Universal Edition, Vienna, c1912
Score 74 p.
*Composed 1909. First performance Paris, 23
April 1910, the composer conducting.*

5183 [Paganiniana, divertimento for   *19'*
orchestra on themes of Nicolò Paganini, Op. 65]
1.Allegro agitato 2.Polaccheta: Allegretto
moderato 3.Romanza: Larghetto cantabile,
amoroso 4.Tarantella: Presto molto
2(2nd alt. Picc.),2*,3*,2-4,2,1,1-Timp.,Perc.-
Str.
Universal Edition, Vienna, c1944
Miniature score 176 p.
*The first movement is based on themes from
Paganini's Violin Caprices, Op. 1 nos. 5, 12,
16 and 19. Theme of the second movement is
from the guitar quartet, Op. 4. Melody of the
Romanza is from The Spring, for violin and
orchestra, Op. 30. The Tarantella contains
another theme from the guitar quartet. Composed 1941-42. First performance Vienna, 1942,
Vienna Philharmonic Orchestra, Karl Böhm con-
ductor.*

615p Partita [for piano and orchestra]   *22'*
1.Sinfonia 2.Passacaglia 3.Burlesca
Solo Pno.-0,1,3*-3Tpt.-Timp.-Str.
Universal Edition, Vienna, c1926
Score 199 p.
*Composed 1925. First performance New York, 29
October 1925, Willem Mengelberg conductor.*

2210 Pupazzetti [Caricatures, 5 pieces   *22'*
for marionettes]
1.Marcietta 2.Berceuse 3.Serenata 4.Notturn-
ino 5.Polka
4*,3*,3*,2-Cnt.-Timp.,Perc.-Pno.-Str.
Chester, London, c1921
Miniature score 51 p.
*Composed 1915-18. First performance Paris,
October 1919, at a Concert Colonne, Gabriel
Pierné conductor.*

625p Scarlattiana [divertimento after   *25'*
music of Domenico Scarlatti, for piano and
small orchestra]
1.Sinfonia 2.Minuetto 3.Capriccio 4.Pas-
torale 5.Finale
Solo Pno.-2,2*,3,2-2,1,1-Timp.,Perc.-Str.
Universal Edition, Vienna, c1927
Score 137 p.
*Composed 1926. First performance New York, 22
January 1927, Otto Klemperer conductor, the
composer as soloist.*

4990 [Serenade for small orchestra,   *22'*
Op. 46b]
1.Marcia: Allegro vivace e ritmico 2.Notturno:
Lento, grave 3.Gavotta: Vivacissimo e spiritoso 4.Cavatina: Adagio molto e sentimentale
5.Finale: Vivacissimo, alla napoletana
2,1,2*,2-2,1,1-Timp.,Perc.-Str.
Universal Edition, Vienna, c1930

Casella, Alfredo

Score 88 p.
Originally composed as Serenade for Five (Wind)
Instruments, Op. 46, 1927. Transcribed for
small orchestra 1930.

1587 Suite, A Jean Huré [Op. 13, C major]   *20'*
1.Overture 2.Sarabande 3.Bourrée
3,2*,3,3-4,3-Timp.,Perc.-Cel.,Hp.-Str.
Universal Edition, Vienna, c1911
Score 99 p.
Composed 1909. First performance Paris, 23
April 1910, the composer conducting.

CASELLA, CÉSAR. the elder.   Lisbon 1819
                                     Lisbon 1886

1555s O belle nuit! [romantic serenade]
Solo Vc.-Str.
Score: Ms. 8 p.
Parts: Richault, Paris [n.d.]

CASELLA, CÉSAR. the younger.   Malaga (?)1848

1298s Sous l'ombrage [In the shade, musical
thought]
Solo Vc.-Str.
Score: Ms. 3 p.
Parts: Chaimbaud, Paris [n.d.]

CASELLATI, GINO.

368s Ninna-Nanna [lullaby for celesta and string
orchestra]
Cel.-Str.
Bongiovanni, Bologna [n.d.]
Score 4 p.

CASSADÓ, GASPAR.   Barcelona 30 September 1897
                         Madrid 24 December 1966

606c [Concerto, violoncello, D minor]   *19'*
1.Allegro 2.Andante con sentimento austero
Solo Vc.-2*,1,2,2-2,2-Timp.,Trgl.,Pandereta-
Hp.-Str.
Universal Edition, Vienna, c1926
Score 69 p.
Composed 1925. First performance Vienna, 15
December 1926, Leopold Reichwein conductor, the
composer as soloist.

CASSADÓ, JOAQUÍN.
         Mataro near Barcelona 30 September 1867
                         Madrid 25 May 1926

1638s Idylle
Solo Vc.-Str.
Score: Ms. 5 p.
Parts: Gaudet, Paris, c1912

CASTAGNONE, RICCARDO.
         b. Brunate, Como 10 September 1906

3324 Passacaglia   *10'*
2,3*,3*,3-4,3,3,1-Str.
Universal Edition, Vienna, c1939
Score 38 p.

4832 Preludio giocoso   *5'*
3*,3*,2,2-4,2,3-Timp.,Perc.-Cel.-Str.
Ricordi, Milan, c1936
Score 47 p.

CASTALDI, ALFONSO.   Maddalone, Italy 23 April 1874
                          Bucharest 6 August 1942

1167s Tarantella [D major]   *5'*
Str.
Ricordi, Milan, c1923
Miniature score 24 p.
First performance Bucharest, 1904, the com-
poser conducting.

CASTALDO, S. pseudonym.
See: KOCHMANN, SPERO.

CASTELNUOVO-TEDESCO, MARIO.   Florence 3 April 1895
              Los Angeles, California 16 March 1968

3318 Cipressi [Cypresses, remembering the   *8'*
cypresses of Usigliano di Lari]
3*,3*,4*,3-4,3,3,1-Timp.,Perc.-Cel.,2Hp.-Str.
Ms.
Score 26 p. Large folio
Composed for piano, 1920; first orchestrated
1921; newly orchestrated 1940. First perform-
ance (of original version) Florence, 1921,
Società Orchestrale Fiorentina, Ildebrando
Pizzetti conductor. First performance of 1940
version Symphony Hall, Boston, 25 October 1940,
Boston Symphony Orchestra, Serge Koussevitzky
conductor.

743p [Concerto, piano, no. 2, F major]   *28'*
1.Vivace e brillante 2.Romanza 3.Vivo e
impetuoso
Solo Pno.-2(2nd alt. Picc.),2,4*,2-4,3,3-Timp.,
Bells-Str.
Ms.
Score 271 p.
Composed 1936-37. First performance New York,
2 November 1939, New York Philharmonic, John
Barbirolli conductor, the composer as
soloist.

866v [Concerto, violin, Concerto Italiano,   *33'*
G minor]
1.Allegro moderato e maestoso 2.Arioso 3.
Vivo e impetuoso
Solo Vn.-2,2,2,2-2,2-Timp.-Org.-Str.
Ricordi, Milan, c1926
Score 123 p.
Composed 1924. First performance Rome,
January 1926, Bernardino Molinari conductor,
Mario Corti soloist.

4803 [Overture to Julius Caesar,   *11'30"*
Op. 78]
4*,3*,3*,3-4,3,3,1-Timp.,Perc.-Cel.,2Hp.-Str.
Ricordi, Milan, c1935
Score 54 p.
Composed 1934 as No. 4 of the composer's
Overtures to Shakespeare's plays. First per-
formance The Agosteo, Rome, ca.1935, Bernar-
dino Molinari conductor.

6224 [Overture to Much Ado About Nothing,   12'
Op. 164]
Introduction: Molto vivace I.Badinage: Alle-
gretto grazioso (quasi scherzo) - Molto vivace
- Meno mosso II.Funeral march: Moderato alla
marcia funebre - Agitato III.Love duet: An-
dantino tenero
2(1st alt. Picc.),2(2nd alt. E.H.),2(2nd alt.
B.Cl.),2-4,3,3,1-Timp.,Perc.-Pno.,Hp.-Str.
Ms.
Score 73 p. Large folio
*Commissioned by The Louisville Orchestra. Com-
posed 1953. First performance Louisville,
Kentucky, 8 May 1954, Louisville Orchestra,
Robert Whitney conductor.*

3933 [Overture to The Taming of the Shrew]
2(2nd alt. Picc.),2,2,2-4,2,1-Timp.,Perc.-
Pno.,Hp.-Str.
Ricordi, Milan, c1931
Miniature score 63 p.
*Composed 1930. First performance Florence, 21
March 1931, the Orchestra Stabile Fiorentina,
Vittorio Gui conductor.*

4870 [Overture to Twelfth Night, Op. 73]   9'
2,3*,3*,2-4,3,2-Timp.,Perc.-Cel.,Hp.-Str.
Ricordi, Milan, c1935
Score 61 p.
*Composed 1935 as no. 2 of the composer's Over-
tures to Shakespeare's plays. First performance Florence, 1935, Vittorio Gui conductor.*

CASTILLO, JESÚS.
Quezaltenango, Guatemala 9 September 1877
Quezaltenango, Guatemala 23 April 1946

3406 [Indigena, Mayan suite. Minuet no. 5.   2'
Arranged by Theodore Bingert]
3*,2,2,2-4,2,2-Timp.,Perc.-Str.
Ms.
Score 18 p.
*Composed 1925. First performance Washington,
D.C., 30 December 1929, the United Service
Orchestra, Lt. Charles Benter conductor.*

3293 [Quiché Vinák. Prelude and hymn to   8'
the sun]
3*,3*,0,2-4,2,3,1-Timp.,Perc.-Str.
Ms.
Score 46 p.
*From the native opera in three acts composed
1919-1924. First performance Guatemala City,
24 July 1924, Teatro Abril, Alberto Mendoza
conductor.*

4931 [Quiché Vinák. Savage dance]
2*,3*,2,2-4,2,3,1-Timp.,Perc.-Str.
Ms.
Score 38 p.

3586 Tecum overture   6'
3*,2,2,2-4,2,3-Timp.,Perc.-Pno.,Hp.-Str.
Ms.
Score 44 p.
*Composed 1898. First performance Washington,
D.C., 2 March 1931, the United Service Orches-
tra, Captain Stannard conductor.*

CASTILLO, RICARDO.
b. Quezaltenango, Guatemala 1 October 1891

3486 Guatemala, movimientos sinfónicos   10'
3*,2,2,2-2,2-Timp.-Str.
Ms.
Score 32 p.
*Composed 1934. First performance Guatemala
City, 10 November 1934, Orquesta del Conserva-
torio de Guatemala, Salvador Ley conductor.
See next entry for enlarged version.*

4915 Guatemala, movimientos sinfónicos   10'
[second version]
3*,2,2,2-4,2,2,1-Timp.-Str.
Ms.
Score 28 p.
This version composed 1943.

3967 [Guatemala suite. Procession]
2*,1,2,1-2,2,1-Timp.,Bell-Str.
Ms.
Score 7 p.
*Composed originally for piano; this arrangement
made 1932.*

6583 [Quiché Achí. Incidental music to   28'
a Guatemalan dance drama]
Prelude. Act I.Chamber of the princess:
Cadenza - Moderato Act II.War dance: Alle-
gretto, très rythmé Act III.Dance of the
princess: Andante mosso Act IVa.Quiché's
immolation: Moderato IVb.Finale: Agitato
3,2,2,2-4,2,3,1-Timp.,Perc.-Str.
Ms.
Score 55 p.
*Music for a Guatemalan dance drama written by
Carlos Giron Cerna. Composed 1946.*

CASTRO, JOSÉ MARÍA.   Buenos Aires 17 November 1892
Buenos Aires 10 August 1964

3631 Concerto grosso   16'
1.Allegro 2.Aria 3.Scena 4.Coral
5.Pastorale 6.Finale
2,2,2,2-2,1-Str.
Sociedad Internacional de Musica Contemporanea,
Buenos Aires, 1936
Score 46 p.
*Composed 1933. First performance Buenos Aires,
11 June 1933, Asociación del Profesorado
Orquestal, the composer conducting. Awarded
First Municipal Prize, Buenos Aires, 1933.*

3598 [Overture for a comic opera]   4'30"
2,2,2,2-3,2-Timp.-Str.
Ms.
Score 47 p.
*Composed 1934. First performance Buenos Aires,
9 November 1936, Orquesta Filarmónica de la
Asociación del Profesorado Orquestal, the com-
poser conducting.*

CASTRO, JUAN JOSÉ.
Avellaneda, province of Buenos Aires 7 March 1895
Buenos Aires 3 September 1968

3888 A una madre [To a mother] poema

Castro, Juan José

3(3rd alt. Picc.),3*,3*,3*-4,3,3,1-Timp.,Trgl.,
Cym.-Cel.,Hp.-Str.
Ms.
Score 72 p.
*Composed 1925. First performance Buenos Aires,
27 October 1925, Orquesta Colón, Gregor Fitel-
berg conductor.*

4233 Bodas de sangre [Blood wedding. No. 2.
Nana]
2,2*,2,1-2,1-Hp.-Str.
Ms.
Score 6 p.
*From the incidental music to the play by Fede-
rico García Lorca. Composed 1939. First performance Montevideo, Uruguay, 29 July 1939,
the composer conducting.*

Mêkhăno, ballet in 4 parts
3892 Part I. Preludio, Cuadro I
3893 Part II. Cuadro II
3894 Part III. Cuadro III
3895 Part IV. Cuadro IV
3*,3*,3*,3*-4,3,3,1-Timp.,Perc.-Cel.,Hp.-Str.
Ms.
Scores: 105 p., 119 p., 105 p., 65 p.
*Composed 1935. First performed Teatro Colón,
Buenos Aires, 17 July 1937.*

4917 Sinfonia Argentina   35'
1.Arrabal [Suburb]: Allegro marcato 2.Llanuras
[Plains]: Lento 3.Ritmos y danzas [Rhythms and
dances]: Vivo, ritmico - Allegretto comodo -
Allegretto tranquillo - Lento
3(3rd alt. Picc.),3*,3*,3*-4,3,3,1-Timp.,Perc.-
Cel.,Hp.-Str.
Ricordi, Milan, c1940
Score 156 p.
*Composed 1934. First performance Buenos Aires,
29 November 1936.*

3706 Suite breve [Short suite]
1.Allegro vivo 2.Marcial 3.Vivo 4.Lento
doloroso 5.Allegro vivo
2(2nd alt. Picc.),2(2nd alt. E.H.),2,2-2,2-
Trgl.,Tamb.-Str.
Ms.
Score 51 p.
*Composed 1929. First performance Buenos Aires,
11 May 1929, Orquesta Renacimiento, the composer conducting.*

3732 Suite infantil [Children's suite]
1.La historia de Mambrù [The story of Mambrù]
2.Ay! Ay! Ay! cuando veré a mi amor! [Ay! Ay!
Ay! when I see my love] 3.Sobre el puente de
Aviñón [On the bridge of Avignon] 4.Arroz con
leche [Rice with milk]
3*,2,2,2-4,3,3,1-Timp.,Perc.-Hp.-Str.
Ms.
Score 80 p.
Originally composed for piano.

CASTRO, RICARDO.   Durango, Mexico 7 February 1864
                      Mexico City 28 November 1907

597p [Concerto, piano, Op. 22, A major]
1.Allegro moderato 2.Andante 3.Polonaise

Solo Pno.-3*,2*,2,2-4,2,3,1-Timp.,Perc.-Str.
Hofmeister, Leipzig [n.d.]
Score 77 p.
*Composed before 1906. First performance Con-
certs de la Société Royale, Antwerp, the com-
poser as soloist.*

411c [Concerto, violoncello]
1.Allegro moderato - Cantabile - Allegro 2.
Thème varié. Andante - Allegretto con moto -
Moderato - Tempo di mazurka - Moderato 3.Vivo
- Allegro moderato
Solo Vc.-3*,2,2,2-4,2,3-Timp.,Perc.-Hp.-Str.
Ms.
Score 127 p.
*First performance Salle du Jardin Zoologique,
Amberes, Belgium, 4 December 1904, Edward
Keurvels conductor, Marix Loevensohn soloist.*

6711 [Oithona, symphonic poem, Op. 55]
3*,2*,2,2-2,2,4Cnt.,3,Ophicl.-Timp.,Perc.-Str.
Ms.
Score 49 p.
Composed 1885.

CASTRO, WASHINGTON.   Buenos Aires 13 July 1909

3676 Overtura festiva [Festival overture]   5'
2,1,2,1-2Hn.-Timp.,Trgl.-Str.
Ms.
Score 51 p.
*Composed 1941. First performance Buenos Aires,
24 September 1941, Orquesta Miguel Gianneo,
Bruno Bandini conductor.*

CASTRUCCI, PIETRO.   Rome 1679
                          Dublin 29 February 1752

731v [Concerto, violin, La cintola (The   8'
belt), G minor. Arranged by Alfred Moffat]
Solo Vn.-Str.
Score: Ms. 24 p.
Parts: Schott, London, c1926

CATALANI, ALFREDO.   Lucca 19 June 1854
                                Milan 7 August 1893

509s A sera [In the evening, andante mesto.
Fragment of a suite]
Str.(without Cb.)
Ricordi, Milan [n.d.]
Score 3 p.

CATEL, CHARLES SIMON.   L'Aigle, Orne 10 June 1773
                         Paris 29 November 1830

3047 [Les bayadères. Overture]
2,2,2,2-2,2,3-Timp.,Perc.-Str.
Ms.
Score 40 p.
From the opera composed 1810.

CATOIRE *or* KATUAR, GEORGY LVOVICH.
                          Moscow 27 April 1861
                          Moscow 21 May 1926

531p [Concerto, piano, Op. 21, A major]
Solo Pno.-3*,2(2nd alt. E.H.),2,2-2,2,3-Timp.,

Perc.-Str.
Russischer Musik-Verlag, Moscow, 1909
Score 115 p.

2322 [Symphony, Op. 7, C minor]
1.Allegro moderato e poco maestoso 2.Alle-
gretto con moto e capriccioso 3.Andante non
tanto 4.Allegro moderato, ma con spirito
3*,2,2,2-4,2,3,1-Timp.,Perc.-Hp.,Celesta
Mustel (may be replaced by Pno. or 2nd Hp.)-
Str.
Mussektor [n.p., n.d.]
Score 254 p.

CATURLA, ALEJANDRO GARCÍA.
                    Remedios, Cuba 7 March 1906
                    Remedios, Cuba 12 November 1940

2138 Bembé, mouvement Afro-Cubain   10'
1,1(alt. E.H.),2*,1-2,1,1-Perc.-Pno.
Senart, Paris, c1930
Score 48 p.
Composed 1928. First performance Paris, 21
December 1929, M.F. Gaillard conductor.

3814 Fanfarria, para despertar espiritus   1'
apolillados [Fanfare to waken moth-eaten
spirits]
1,0,2,1-2,2,1-Timp.,Perc.-Pno.
Ms.
Score 4 p.
Composed 1933. First performance Havana, 30
April 1933, Orquesta Filarmónica de la
Habana, Nicolas Slonimsky conductor. Also
performed under the title: Fanfare to Shake
Up an Old Fogey.

2795 Primera suite cubana [for eight wind   18'
instruments and piano]
1.Sonera 2.Comparsa 3.Danza
1(alt. Picc.),2,2,1-Hn.,Tpt.-Pno.
New Music Orchestra Series, San Francisco,
c1933
Score 32 p.
Composed 1932. First performance New York,
4 November 1932, Pan American Chamber Orchestra,
Nicolas Slonimsky conductor.

4063 [Suite, for orchestra]
1.Minstrels 2.Plantación 3.Berceuse 4.Vals
4*,3*,4*(1Cl. in E-flat),2-4,3,3,1-Timp.,Perc.
-Hp.-Str.
Ms.
Score 84 p.
Composed 1938. Awarded Honorable Mention in
the contest held by the Secretary of Education
in Cuba, 1938.

2137 [Three Cuban dances, for orchestra]   15'
1.Danza del tambor 2.Motivos de danzas 3.
Danza lucumi
3*,3*,3*,2-4,3,3,1-Timp.,Perc.-Pno.,Cel.,Hp.-
Str.
Senart, Paris, c1929
Score 52 p.
Composed 1928. First performance Havana, 9
December 1928, Orquesta Filarmónica.

4006 [Three Cuban dances. Arranged for   15'
12 players]
1.Danza del tambor 2.Motivos de danzas
3.Danza lucumi
1(alt. Picc.),1(alt. E.H.),2*,1-2,1,1,1-Perc.-
Pno.
Ms.
Score 65 p. Large folio
This arrangement 1930.

4148 Yamba-O, poema sinfónico
4*,3*,4*,3*-4,4,4,1-Timp.,Perc.,Cuban Perc.
Instruments(9 players)-Str.
Ms.
Score 67 p. Large folio
A symphonic movement from a larger (unfinished)
Negro liturgy, Liturgia, with poem by Alejo
Carpentier. Composed 1928-31. First perform-
ance Havana, 25 October 1931, Havana Philhar-
monic, Amadeo Roldan conductor.

CAUCHIE, F.

706s Bluette
Str.
Score: Ms. 3 p.
Parts: Decourcelle, Nice [n.d.]

827s En gondole [In the gondola, passing
thought]
Solo Ob.-Str.
Score: Ms. 6 p.
Parts: Cranz, Leipzig [n.d.]
Bound with Simple Histoire below.

827s Simple histoire, mélodie
Str.
Score: Ms. 7 p.
Parts: Cranz, Leipzig [n.d.]

CAVALLINI, ERNESTO.   Milan 30 August 1807
                             Milan 7 January 1874

734m [Adagio and variations for clarinet]   15'
Solo Cl.-Fl.-Str.
Score: Ms. 21 p.
Parts: Ricordi, Milan [n.d.]

CAZANEUVE, E.

1552s Lamento [for string orchestra, A major]
Str.
Score: Ms. 7 p.
Parts: Joubert, Paris [n.d.]

CAZDEN, NORMAN.   New York City 23 September 1914

3050 Concerto for 10 instruments, Op. 10   14'
1,1,1,1-2,1-Pno.-Va.,Vc.
Ms.
Score 40 p. Large folio
Composed 1937. First performance Juilliard
Graduate School, New York, 4 May 1937, Bernard
Wagenaar conductor.

3376 On the death of a Spanish child   4'
[original version for reduced band] Op. 20
3*,2,5*(1Cl. in E-flat),3*-2Alto Sax.,Ten.Sax.
-4,3,3,Baritone,2-Timp.,B.Dr.-Cb.

Cazden, Norman

Ms.
Score 16 p. Large folio
This version 1940.

3908 [On the death of a Spanish child,   4'
revised version for full band, Op. 20]
4(1Picc. in D-flat,1Picc. in C),2,6*(1Cl. in
E-flat,1Alto Cl.),3*-5Sax.(AATBar.B)-8(4Hn.
in E-flat),2,3Cnt.,3,Bar.,Euph.,2-Timp.,B.Dr.-
Cb.
Ms.
Score 14 p. Large folio
*This version 1941. Alternate titles: Spanish
Castle; Elegy Before Dawn.*

3087 Preamble, for orchestra, Op. 18   7'
3*,2,3*,3*-4,3,3,1-Timp.,B.Dr.,Cym.-Pno.-Str.
Ms.
Score 45 p. Large folio
Composed 1938.

4497 Songs from the Catskills, for symphonic
band, Op. 54. No. 1, The cordwood cutter
3*,2,6*(1Cl. in E-flat,Alto Cl. alt. 3rd Alto
Sax.),3*-5Sax.(AATBar.B)-4,2,3Cnt.,3,2,Bar.
Hn. or Euph.-Timp.,S.Dr.,B.Dr.-Cb.
Ms. ᶜ1949 by Norman Cazden
Score 16 p.
Composed 1949.

4739 Songs from the Catskills, for symphonic
band, Op. 54. No. 2, Betsy B.
2,2,4*,3*-4Sax.-4,2,3Cnt.,3,2-Bar.Hn.-Timp.,
S.Dr.,B.Dr.-Cb.
Ms. ᶜ1950 by Norman Cazden
Score 14 p.
Composed 1950.

4740 Songs from the Catskills, for symphonic
band, Op. 54. No. 3, A shantyman's life
3*,2,4*,Cl. in E-flat,Alto Cl.,3*-5Sax.(AAT
Bar.B)-4,2,3Cnt.,3,2-Bar.Hn.-Timp.,S.Dr.,B.Dr.
-Cb.
Ms. ᶜ1950 by Norman Cazden
Score 16 p.
Composed 1950.

4741 Songs from the Catskills, for symphonic
band, Op. 54. No. 4, The old tobacco box
3*,2,4*,Cl. in E-flat,Alto Cl.,3*-5Sax.(AAT
Bar.B)-4,2,3Cnt.,3,2-Bar.Hn.-Timp.,S.Dr.,B.Dr.
-Cb.
Ms. ᶜ1950 by Norman Cazden
Score 19 p.
*Composed 1950. First performance of all four
songs, Urbana, Illinois, 11 January 1951, University of Illinois Concert Band, Mark Hindsley
conductor.*

1046m Three ballads from the Catskills, for
small orchestra, Op. 52
1.The lass of Glenshee (viola solo) 2.The dens
of Yarrow ('cello solo) 3.The old spotted cow
(violin solo)
Solo Vn., Solo Va., Solo Vc.-1,1,2,1-2,2,2-
Timp.-Str.
Ms. ᶜ1949 by Norman Cazden
Score 66 p.

*Composed 1949. First performance Ann Arbor,
Michigan, 7 August 1950, University of Michigan Symphony Orchestra, Wayne Dunlap conductor.*

3398 Three dances, for orchestra, Op. 28   10'
1.Novelty number 2.Art dance 3.Whitewashed
stable
3*,2,4*,3*-4,4,3,1-Timp.,Perc.-Pno.-Str.
Ms.
Score 60 p. Large folio
Composed 1940.

CECCO, F. A.   Fara San Martino, Italy 1892

3484 Intermezzo, Rugiada sui prati [Dew on   7'
the meadow]
2,3*,3*,2-4Hn.,Tuba-Timp.-Hp.-Str.
Ms.
Score 19 p.
*Composed 1926. First performance Bologna,
Italy, 26 October 1926, Bolognese Orchestra,
G. Marinuzzi conductor.*

CECE, ANTONIO.   Saviano near Naples 12 March 1907
                                       Naples 1971

4829 [Concerto for chamber orchestra]   20'
1.Sostenuto - Allegro - Vivo 2.Largo - Poco
andante - Sostenuto 3.Allegro vivo
1,1,1,1-Hn.-Pno.-Str.
Ricordi, Milan, ᶜ1943
Score 110 p.

4805 [Nocturne for orchestra]   8'
2,3*,2,2-4Hn.-Timp.,Cym.,Tam-tam-Hp.-Str.
Ricordi, Milan, ᶜ1941
Score 40 p.

4804 Passacaglia   10'
3*,3*,3*,3*-4,3,3,1-Timp.,Cym.,Tam-tam-Hp.-
Str.
Ricordi, Milan, ᶜ1942
Score 52 p.

CELEGA, NICOLÒ.   Polesella 15 April 1844
                                       Milan July 1906

864s Minuetto, Op. 240
Str.
Ricordi, Milan [n.d.]
Score 7 p.

CENTOLA, ERNESTO.   Salerno 2 March 1862

1022s Impromptu [G major]
Str.
Score: Ms. 8 p.
Parts: Decourcelle, Nice, ᶜ1924

958v [Nocturne for violin solo and   4'
orchestra, Op. 18, G major]
Solo Vn.-2,2,2,2-2Hn.-Str.
Score: Ms. 12 p.
Parts: Decourcelle, Nice, ᶜ1923
*Composed 1923. First performance Constan-
tinople, December 1923.*

1132s Novelletta [for violin and string
orchestra] Op. 60
Solo Vn.-Str.
Score: Ms. 7 p.
Parts: Decourcelle, Nice, c1914

1073s Rêve [for violin solo and string
orchestra] Op. 73
Solo Vn.-Str.
Score: Ms. 6 p.
Parts: Decourcelle, Nice, c1926

1160s [Sweet remembrance, Op. 64]
Str.
Score: Ms. 7 p.
Parts: Decourcelle, Nice, c1923

CENTRAL PHILHARMONIC SOCIETY OF THE PEOPLE'S
REPUBLIC OF CHINA.

247p [Concerto for piano and orchestra,   18'50"
The Yellow River]
1.Prelude: The song of the Yellow River boat-
men 2.Ode to the Yellow River 3.The Yellow
River in wrath 4.Defend the Yellow River
Solo Pno.-2(2nd alt. Picc. and Zhúdí [Chinese
Fl.]),1,2,2-3,2,1-Timp.,Trgl.,Cym.-Pípá
[Chinese Mandolin],Hp.-Str.
[People's Republic of China, 1972]
Score 102 p.
*A Chinese popular song, East is Red, appears
in the last movement. Adapted by a committee
from the Yellow River Cantata composed
by Hsien Hsing-hai in 1939. The solo piano
part possibly composed by Yin Cheng-chung.
First performance outside China at the Saratoga
Festival, Saratoga Springs, New York, 25 August
1973, Philadelphia Orchestra, Eugene Ormandy
conductor, Daniel Epstein soloist.*

CERQUETTELLI, G.

1244s Minuetto
Str.
Carisch & Jänichen, Milan, c1908
Score 7 p.

CERRI, LUIGI.   Milan 28 December 1860

1098s Gavotta-pizzicato, Op. 79
Str.
Score: Ms. 8 p.
Parts: Ricordi, Milan [n.d.]

1100s Minuit, berceuse, Op. 155
Glock.,Bells-Str.
Score: Ms. 7 p.
Parts: Ricordi, Milan, c1914

1099s Notte stellata! [Starry night] idyl,
Op. 139
Str.
Score: Ms. 6 p.
Parts: Ricordi, Milan, c1921

CESANA, OTTO.   Brescia, Italy 7 July 1899

2857 [Concerto, 2 pianos, A minor]   17'
1.Serious 2.Wistful 3.Gay

2 Solo Pno.-2(alt. 2Picc.),2(2nd alt. E.H.),2
(2nd alt. Cl. in E-flat),2(2nd alt. C.Bn.)-4,
3,3,1-Timp.,Perc.-Hp.-Str.
Ms.
Score 98 p. Large folio
*Composed 1936. Original title: Concerto for
Two Pianos and Orchestra in Three Moods. First
performance New York, 22 April 1939, New York
Philharmonic, John Barbirolli conductor, Ignaz
Strasfogel and Boris Kogan soloists.*

754p [Concerto, 3 pianos, B-flat minor]   16'
1.Allegro con brio 2.Lento, tempo di notturno
3.Allegretto grazioso
3Solo Pno.-2(2nd alt. Picc.),2(2nd alt. E.H.),
2(2nd alt. B.Cl.),2-4,3,3,1-Timp.,Perc.-Hp.-
Str.
Ms.
Score 136 p. Large folio
*Composed 1933. First performance with only 2
soloists) New York, 1 March 1933, Radio City
Music Hall Symphony Orchestra, Erno Rapee conductor, Morton Gould and Bert Shefter soloists.*

2589 Negro heaven, symphonette   6'
Allegro con brio - Andantino - Allegro
2(2nd alt. Picc.),2(2nd alt. E.H.),4(1st alt.
Sop.Sax. in B-flat,2nd and 3rd alt. Alto Sax.
in E-flat,4th alt. Ten.Sax. in B-flat),2-4,3,3,
1-Timp.,Perc.-Pno.,Banjo-Str.
C. Fischer, New York, c1933
Score 57 p. Large folio
*Composed 1932. First performance broadcast
over WEAF, New York, 27 August 1932, NBC Symphony Orchestra, Erno Rapee conductor.*

3234 [Symphony, American, no. 1]   16'
1.Allegro con brio 2.Adagio solenne
3.Allegretto grazioso 4.Allegro con spirito
2(alt. 2Picc.),2(2nd alt. E.H.),2,2-4,3,3,1-
Timp.,Perc.-Hp.-Str.
Ms.
Score 178 p.
*Composed 1932. First performance broadcast
over NBC, New York, 22 January 1933, Radio City
Music Hall Orchestra, Erno Rapee conductor.
First concert performance New York, 25 April
1939, Brico Symphony Orchestra, Antonia Brico
conductor.*

2871 [Symphony, American, no. 2]   27'
1.Adagio 2.Lento con tenerezza 3.Lento non
troppo 4.Andante con moto
3(alt. 3Picc.),3(3rd alt. E.H.),3(alt. 3B.Cl.),
3(3rd alt. C.Bn.)-4,3,3,1-Timp.,Perc.-Cel.,Hp.
-Str.
Affiliated Music Corporation, New York, c1937
Miniature score 155 p.
*Composed 1934. First performance broadcast
from Radio City Music Hall, New York, 11
November 1934, Radio City Music Hall Symphony
Orchestra, Erno Rapee conductor.*

1867s [Symphony, miniature, for strings   12'
and guitar]
1.Allegro non troppo 2.Lento 3.Allegretto
4.Allegro vivace
Guit.(optional)-Str.

Cesti, Pietro

Ms.
Score 38 p.
*Composed 1942. First performance broadcast
over Station WOR, New York, 10 March 1942, Symphonic Strings, Alfred Wallenstein conductor.*

CESTI, PIETRO ANTONIO. Arezzo, Italy 5 August 1623
Florence 14 October 1669

Also known as Frate Antonio or Frat' Antonio
(Brother Antonio) and erroneously Marc' Antonio.

2043s Tu mancavi a tormentarmi crudelissima *6'*
speranza [Most cruel hope, you have ceased
tormenting me] Transcribed for string orches-
tra by Leopold Stokowski
Hp.-Str.
Broude Brothers, New York, ^c1949 by Leopold
Stokowski
Score 18 p.
Originally composed as a cantata.

CHABRIER, EMMANUEL.
Ambert, Puy-de-Dôme, France 18 January 1841
Paris 13 September 1894

Full name: Alexis-Emmanuel Chabrier

516 Bourrée fantasque. Transcribed for *5'*
orchestra by Felix Mottl
3*,3*,2,4-4,3,3,1-Timp.,Perc.-2Hp.-Str.
Enoch, Paris [n.d.]
Score 47 p.
*Originally composed for piano 1891. Orches-
trated by Felix Mottl 1897. First performance of transcription Karlsruhe, 1897, Felix
Mottl conductor.*

509 Cortège burlesque [Burlesque procession]
Transcribed for orchestra by P. Lacombe
2*,2,2,2-4,0,2Cnt.,3,1-Timp.,Perc.-Str.
Costallat, Paris, ^c1921
Score 46 p.
*Originally composed for piano. First published
posthumously, 1917.*

288 España [Spanish rhapsody] *7'*
3*,2,2,4-4,2,2Cnt.,3,1-Timp.,Perc.-2Hp.-Str.
Kalmus, New York [n.d.]
Score 61 p.
*Composed 1882. First performance Paris, Decem-
ber 1883, Charles Lamoureux conductor.*

819 [Gwendoline. Overture] *9'*
3*,2*,3*,4-4,2,2Cnt.,3,1-Timp.,Perc.-2Hp.-Str.
Enoch, Paris [n.d.]
Score 71 p.
*From the opera composed 1884. First perform-
ance Théâtre de la Monnaie, Brussels, 10
April 1886.*

820 [Gwendoline. Act II. Prelude] *5'*
3*,2*,2*,2-4,2,3,1-Timp.-2Hp.-Str.
Enoch, Paris [n.d.]
Score 20 p.
*First concert performance of Prelude, Paris,
22 November 1885, Charles Lamoureux conductor.*

517 Habanera. Transcribed for orchestra *3'*
2,1,2,1-2,0,2Cnt.-Timp.,Trgl.-Str.
Enoch, Paris [n.d.]
Score 17 p.
*Originally composed for piano; orchestrated
by the composer, 1885. First performance
Paris, 1885, Charles Lamoureux conductor.*

821 Joyeuse marche *4'*
3*,2,2,4-4,2,2Cnt.,3,1-Timp.,Perc.-2Hp.-Str.
Enoch, Paris [n.d.]
Score 31 p.
*Original title: Marche Française. Composed
1888. First performance Paris, 1889.*

516m [Larghetto for horn and orchestra]
Solo Hn.-2,2,2,2-Timp.-Str.
Costallat, Paris, ^c1913
Score 20 p.
Composed ca.1875. Published posthumously.

642 [Pastoral suite for orchestra] *16'*
1.Idylle 2.Danse villageoise [Rustic dance]
3.Sous bois [In the woods] 4.Scherzo - Valse
2(2nd alt. Picc.),1,2,2-2,0,2Cnt.,3-Timp.,Perc.
-Hp.-Str.
Enoch, Paris [n.d.]
Score 66 p.
*Originally composed for piano 1880 as part of
Dix Pièces Pittoresques. Orchestrated 1897.
First performance Paris, 1898.*

770 Le roi malgré lui [The king in *10'*
spite of himself. Polish festival]
2*,2,2,2-2,0,2Cnt.,3-Timp.,Perc.-Str.
Enoch, Paris [n.d.]
Score 63 p.
*From the opera in three acts based on a comedy
of F. Ancelot. Composed 1885-86. First performance Paris, 18 May 1887.*

1028 Le roi malgré lui [The king in *5'*
spite of himself. Slavic dance]
2*,2,2,2-2,0,2Cnt.,3-Timp.,Perc.-Str.
Enoch, Paris [n.d.]
Score 43 p.

706 [Three romantic waltzes. Transcribed *12'*
for orchestra by Felix Mottl]
1.Très vite et impétueusement 2.Mouvement
modéré de valse 3.Animé
3*,3*,3*,4-4,3,3,1-Timp.,Perc.-2Hp.-Str.
Enoch, Paris [n.d.]
Score 85 p.
*Originally composed for two pianos, 1883.
This orchestration 1899. First performance
Karlsruhe, 1900, Felix Mottl conductor.*

CHADWICK, GEORGE WHITEFIELD.
Lowell, Massachusetts 13 November 1854
Boston 4 April 1931

6394 Adonaïs, elegiac overture
3(3rd alt. Picc.),2,2,2-4,2,3,1-Timp.,B.Dr.-
Hp.-Str.
Ms.
Score 62 p.
Suggested by Shelley's poem, Adonaïs.

Composed 1899. First performance Boston, 3 February 1900, Boston Symphony Orchestra.

6447 Angel of death, symphonic poem
3*,3*,3*,2-4,2,3,1-Timp.,Perc.-2Hp.-Str.
Ms.
Score 59 p.
Composed 1917. First performance New York, 1919, New York Symphony Orchestra, in a memorial concert for Theodore Roosevelt.

5253 Aphrodite, symphonic fantasie for orchestra
3(3rd alt. Picc.),3*,3*,3*-4,4,3,1-Timp.,Perc.-Cel.,Hp.-Str.
A. P. Schmidt, Boston, c1912
Score 122 p.
Composed 1912. First performance Norfolk, Connecticut, 4 June 1912, at the Norfolk Festival.

6445 Cleopatra, symphonic poem
3(3rd alt. Picc.),3*,3*,2-4,3,3,1-Timp.,Perc.-Cel.(ad lib.),Hp.-Str.
Ms.
Score 91 p.
Composed 1904. First performance Worcester Festival, Massachusetts, October 1905.

6581 Elegy (In memoriam Horatio Parker)
3(3rd ad lib.),3*(E.H. ad lib.),2,2-4,2,3-Timp.-Org.(ad lib.),Hp.(ad lib.)-Str.
Ms.
Score 12 p.
Composed 1919.

1996 Euterpe, concert overture   *14'*
3*,2,2,2-4,2,3,1-Timp.-Hp.-Str.
G. Schirmer, New York, c1906
Score 47 p.
Composed 1903. First performance Boston, 23 April 1904, the composer conducting.

2280s Intermezzo, andantino semplice, for string orchestra
Str.
Ms.
Score 16 p.
This is 2nd movement from String Quartet, no. 4, E minor.

158 Melpomene, dramatic overture   *12'*
3*,2*,2,2-4,2,3,1-Timp.,Perc.-Str.
A. P. Schmidt, Boston, c1891
Score 55 p.
Composed 1886. First performance Boston, 24 December 1887, Wilhelm Gericke conductor.

6633 A pastoral prelude for orchestra
3*,3*,2,2-4,2-Timp.-Str.
Ms.
Score 52 p.
Score quotes a poem by William Wordsworth: The Gladness of the May. Composed 1890. First performance Boston, 30 January 1892, Boston Symphony.

2590 Rip Van Winkle overture   *12'*
3*,2,2,2-4,2,3,1-Timp.,Perc.-Str.
C.C. Birchard, Boston, c1931 by Eastman School

of Music
Score 86 p.
Composed 1879. First performance at the academic year-end concert at the Conservatory of Music, Leipzig, Germany, 20 June 1879, the composer conducting.

2240s Serenade in F for string orchestra
1.Allegro grazioso 2.Andantino 3.Tempo di menuetto 4.Finale: Presto non troppo
Str.
Ms.
Score 36 p.
Composed 1890.

1997 Sinfonietta, in four movements,   *18'*
D major
1.Risolutamente 2.Canzonetta 3.Scherzino 4. Finale
3(3rd alt. Picc.),2,2,2-4,2,3(ad lib.)-Timp.,Perc.-Hp.-Str.
G. Schirmer, New York, c1906
Score 83 p.
Composed 1904. First performance Boston, 21 November 1904, the composer conducting.

5260 Suite symphonique in E-flat   *30'*
1.Allegro molto animato - Molto maestoso 2. Romanza: Andantino espressivo 3.Intermezzo e humoreske: Poco allegretto 4.Finale: Allegro molto ed energico - Tranquillo - Largamente - Allegro molto energico - Molto vivace
3*,2,2,2-Alto Sax.(ad lib.)-4,3,3,1-Timp.,Perc.-Hp.-Str.
A.P. Schmidt, Boston, c1911
Score 153 p.
Composed 1910. First performance Chicago, 29 March 1911, Chicago Symphony Orchestra. Dedicated to Frederick A. Stock and the Theodore Thomas Orchestra of Chicago. Awarded first prize by the National Federation of Music Clubs, 1911.

123 [Symphonic sketches, suite for   *31'*
orchestra]
1.Jubilee 2.Noël 3.Hobgoblin 4.A vagrom ballad
3*,3*,3*,2-4,2,3-Timp.,Perc.-Hp.-Str.
G. Schirmer, New York, c1907
Score 151 p.
Composed 1895-96 and 1904. First performance 7 February 1908, Boston Symphony Orchestra, Karl Muck conductor.

7031 [Symphonic sketches, suite for   *8'*
orchestra. No. 1, Jubilee]
2(2nd alt. Picc.),2*,3*,2-4,2,3-Timp.,Perc.-Str.
G. Schirmer, New York, c1907
Score 41 p.

5511 [Symphony no. 2, Op. 21, B-flat major]
1.Andante non troppo - Allegro con brio 2. Allegretto scherzando 3.Largo e maestoso - Allegro non troppo 4.Allegro molto animato - Assai animato - Presto
2,2,2,2-4,2,3-Timp.-Str.
A.P. Schmidt, Boston, c1888

Chadwick, George Whitefield

Score 216 p.
Composed 1883-85. First performance of second movement only, Boston, 8 March 1884, Boston Symphony Orchestra. First performance of complete work Boston, 11 December 1886, Boston Symphony Orchestra, the composer conducting.

5262 [Symphony no. 3, F major]   35'
1. Allegro sostenuto 2.Andante cantabile
3.Vivace non troppo 4.Finale: Allegro molto energico - Animato - Presto
2,2,2,2-4,2,3,1-Timp.-Str.
A.P. Schmidt, Boston, ^c1896
Score 168 p.
Composed 1893-94. First performance Boston, 20 October 1894, Boston Symphony Orchestra, the composer conducting. Awarded the National Conservatory of Music Prize, 1893.

5304 Tam o'Shanter, symphonic ballade   18'
3(3rd alt. Picc.I,2nd alt. Picc.II),3*,4*,2-4,3,3,1-Timp.,Perc.-Hp.-Str.
Boston Music Co., Boston, ^c1917
Score 96 p.
Suggested by Robert Burns' poem, Tam o'Shanter. Composed 1914-15. First performance Norfolk Festival, Connecticut, 3 June 1915.

6461 [Three pieces for orchestra]   15'
1.Overture mignon: Allegro molto vivace
2.Canzone vecchia: Andantino e semplice
3.Fuga giocoso: Molto vivace
3(3rd alt. Picc.),3*,2,2-4,3,3,1-Timp.,Trgl., Xyl.-Hp.(ad lib.)-Str.
Ms.
Score 95 p.
Composed 1923.

CHAIKOVSKY, PETER ILICH.   Kamsko-Votinsk, district of Viatka, Russia 7 May 1840
St. Petersburg 6 November 1893

115s [Andante, from String Quartet, Op. 30. Arranged for string orchestra by Alexander Glazunov]
Str.
Jurgenson, Moscow, 1896
Score 13 p.

387p [Andante and finale, Op. 79. Orchestral accompaniment by Sergei Taneiev]
Solo Pno.-3*,2,2,2-4,2,3,1-Timp.,Perc.-Str.
Belaieff, Leipzig, 1897
Score 75 p.
Composed 1893. First performance of Op. 79, Moscow, 20 February 1896. See also Concerto No. 3, Catalog no. 581p.

75s [Andante cantabile, from String Quartet, Op. 11]
Str.
Kistner, Leipzig [n.d.]
Score 3 p.

116s [Barcarolle, Op. 37b no. 6. Arranged for string orchestra]
Str.
Score in reduction: 5 p.
Parts: C.F. Schmidt, Heilbronn [n.d.]

One of twelve pieces originally composed for piano, as The Seasons, Op. 37b.

2195 [Barcarolle, Op. 37b no. 6. Orchestrated by Rudolf Nováček]
2,2,2,2-3Hn.-Str.
Jurgenson, Moscow [n.d.]
Score 17 p.

194 Capriccio italien, Op. 45   15'
3*,3*,2,2-4,2,2Cnt.,3,1-Timp.,Perc.-Hp.-Str.
Breitkopf & Härtel, Leipzig [n.d.]
Score 62 p.
Composed 1880. First performance Moscow, 18 December 1880, Nikolai Rubinstein conductor.

384p [Concerto, piano, no. 1, Op. 23,   32'
B-flat minor. Revised version]
1.Allegro non troppo e molto maestoso
2.Andantino semplice 3.Allegro con fuoco
Solo Pno.-2,2,2,2-4,2,3-Timp.-Str.
Breitkopf & Härtel, Wiesbaden [n.d.]
Score 115 p.
Composed 1874-75. First performance Boston, 25 October 1875, Hans von Bülow soloist. Revised 1889.

400p [Concerto, piano, no. 2, Op. 44,   35'
G major. New edition, revised and abridged by A. Siloti, according to the composer's suggestions]
1.Allegro brillante e molto vivace 2.Andante non troppo 3.Allegro con fuoco
Solo Pno.-2,2,2,2-4,2-Timp.-Str.
Rahter, Leipzig [n.d.]
Score 155 p.
Composed 1879-80. First performance Moscow, 30 May 1882, Anton Rubinstein conductor, Sergei Taneiev soloist.

581p [Concerto, piano, no. 3, Op. 75,   12'
E-flat major. One movement only]
Solo Pno.-3*,2,2,2-4,2,3,1-Timp.-Str.
Novello, Ewer, London [n.d.]
Score 95 p.
Originally intended for a symphony. Chaikovsky rewrote this as the first movement of a piano concerto, 1893. Sergei Taneiev added his orchestration of the Andante and Finale, Op. 79 to form a complete concerto, 1895. First performance St. Petersburg, 19 January 1895.

411v [Concerto, violin, Op. 35, D major.   32'
New edition revised by the composer]
1.Allegro moderato 2.Canzonetta 3.Finale
Solo Vn.-2,2,2,2-4,2,1-Timp.-Str.
Breitkopf & Härtel, Wiesbaden [n.d.]
Score 97 p.
Composed 1878. First performance Vienna, 4 December 1881, Vienna Philharmonic, Hans Richter conductor, Adolf Brodsky soloist.

820s Douce rêverie et valse [Arranged for string orchestra by Heinrich Germer]
Str.
Bosworth, Leipzig [n.d.]
Score 7 p.
Numbers 21 and 8, respectively, from Album Pour les Enfants, Op. 39.

Chaikovsky, Peter Ilich

243 1812 ouverture solennelle, Op. 49   16'
3*,3*,2,2-4,2,2Cnt.,3,1-Timp.,Perc.-Banda
(Harmoniemusik, ad lib.)-Str.
Breitkopf & Härtel, Leipzig [n.d.]
Score 56 p.
Composed 1880. First performance Moscow, 20
August 1882, Ippolit Altani conductor.

295s [Elegy, for string orchestra, G major]
Str.
Rahter, Leipzig [n.d.]
Score 9 p.
Composed in 1884 on the death of J. V. Samarin;
later included in the music to Hamlet, as
Op. 67a.

1519 [Eugen Onegin, Op. 24. Overture]   2'
2,2,2,2-4Hn.-Str.
Jurgenson, Moscow [n.d.]
Score 6 p.
From the opera in 3 acts, inspired by Alexander
Pushkin's poem. Composed 1877-78.

294 [Eugen Onegin, Op. 24. Polonaise]   4'
2,2,2,2-4,2,3-Timp.-Str.
Luck's, Detroit [n.d.]
Score 27 p.

1027 [Eugen Onegin, Op. 24. Two ecossaises] 3'
2,2,2,2-4,2,3,1-Timp.-Str.
Jurgenson, Moscow [n.d.]
Score 17 p.

295 [Eugen Onegin, Op. 24. Waltz]   6'
3*,2,2,2-4,2,3-Timp.-Str.
Luck's, Detroit [n.d.]
Score 35 p.

414p Fantaisie de concert [piano, Op. 56,
G major]
1.Quasi rondo 2.Contrastes [3]Appendice
Solo Pno.-3,2,2,2-4,2,3-Timp.,Perc.-Str.
Jurgenson, Moscow [n.d.]
Score 145 p.
Composed 1884. First performance Moscow, 6
March 1885, Max Erdmannsdörfer conductor,
Sergei Taneiev soloist.

94 Fatum [Fate, symphonic poem, Op. 77]   10'
3*,3*,2,2-4,3,3,1-Timp.,Perc.-Hp.-Str.
Belaieff, Leipzig, 1896
Score 59 p.
Composed 1868. First performance Moscow, 27
February 1869. Withdrawn by composer; pub-
lished posthumously.

605 Francesca da Rimini, fantasy after   24'
Dante, Op. 32
3*,3*,2,2-4,2,2Cnt.,3,1-Timp.,Perc.-Hp.-Str.
Kalmus, New York [n.d.]
Score 119 p.
Composed 1876. First performance Moscow, 1877.

241 Hamlet, fantasy overture, Op. 67   19'
3*,3*,2,2-4,2,2Cnt.,3,1-Timp.,Perc.-Str.
Rahter, Hamburg [n.d.]
Score 99 p.

Composed 1888. First performance St. Peters-
burg, 24 November 1888, the composer con-
ducting.

6310 [Hamlet, Op. 67a. Overture, melodramas,
marches and interludes]
Act I.[Overture] No. 1: Mélodrame No. 1a:
Mélodrame No. 2: Fanfare No. 3: Mélodrame
No. 4: Mélodrame
Act II. No. 5: Entr'acte - Fanfare No. 6.
Fanfare
Act III. No. 7: Entr'acte No. 8: Mélodrame
Act IV. No. 9: Entr'acte (Elegie)
Act V. No. 12: Entr'acte: Marcia No. 14:
Marche funèbre [same as no. 12] No. 15: Fanfare
No. 16: Marche finale
2,2,2,2-2,2,1-Timp.,Perc.-Str.
Rahter, Hamburg [1888]
Score 121 p.
Composed 1891 as incidental music to Shake-
speare's play. First performance Mikhailovsky
Theatre, St. Petersburg, 21 February 1891.
Title misprinted as Op. 67b.

1017s [In autumn, tone picture, Op. 37a no. 10.
Arranged for string orchestra by Ludwig Sauer]
Str.
Score: Ms. 5 p.
Parts: C.F. Schmidt, Heilbronn [n.d.]
From Op. 37bis, The Seasons, 12 pieces for
piano solo. Original title: Octobre, Chant
d'Automne. Composed 1876.

4431 [Iolanthe, Op. 69. Introduction]   3'
3*,3*,2,2-4Hn.
Jurgenson, Moscow [1891]
Score 6 p.
From the opera in one act with libretto by
Modest Ilich Chaikovsky, based on Zvantzev's
translation of Henrik Hertz's play King Rene's
Daughter. Composed 1891.

242 Marche slave, Op. 31   8'
4*,2,2,2-4,2,2Cnt.,3,1-Timp.,Perc.-Str.
Kalmus, New York [n.d.]
Score 65 p.
Composed 1876. First performance Moscow, 17
November 1876, Nikolai Rubinstein conductor.

1232 Marche solennelle
3*,3*,2,2-4,2,3,1-Timp.,Perc.-2Hp.-Str.
Rahter, Hamburg [n.d.]
Score 29 p.

6629 Marche solenelle du couronnement
3*,3*,2,2-4,2,2Cnt.,3,1-Timp.,Perc.-Str.
Jurgenson, Moscow [1883]
Score 35 p.
Composed 1883 for the coronation of Tsar
Alexander III. First performance Moscow, 4
June 1883, Sergei Taneiev conductor.

1538 [Mazeppa. Introduction to the opera]   7'
3*,3*,2,2-4,2,2Cnt.,3,1-Timp.,Perc.-Str.
Kalmus, New York [n.d.]
Score 41 p.

Chaikovsky, Peter Ilich

652 [Mazeppa. Entr'acte, the battle of Poltava, symphonic picture]
3*,3*,2,2-4,2,2Cnt.,3,1-Timp.,Perc.-Str.
Jurgenson, Moscow [n.d.]
Score 31 p.

711 [Mazeppa. Gopak, Little Russian Cossack 5' dance]
3*,3*,2,2-4,2,2Cnt.,3,1-Timp.,Perc.-Str.
Jurgenson, Moscow [1883]
Score 45 p.

885s Mélancolie, chanson triste, Op. 40 no. 2 [Arranged for string orchestra]
Str.
Score: Ms. 7 p.
Parts: C.F. Schmidt, Heilbronn [n.d.]
Originally composed for piano.

2977 [Nutcracker, ballet, Op. 71. Complete in 2 acts]
3*,3*,3*,2-4,2,Toy Tpt.,3,1-Timp.,Perc.-Cel. (or Pno.),2Hp.-High Voices (one movement only)-Str.
Jurgenson, Moscow [n.d.]
Score 511 p.
Composed 1891-92. First performance Mary-insky Theatre, St. Petersburg, 18 December 1892, R. Drigo conductor.

136 [Nutcracker. Suite, Op. 71a]   25'
1.[Miniature overture] 2.[Characteristic dances: (a)March (b)Dance of the sugar-plum fairy (c)Russian dance, Trepak (d)Arabian dance (e)Chinese dance (f)Dance of the reed flutes] 3.[Waltz of the flowers]
4*,3*,3*,2-4,2,3,1-Timp.,Perc.-Cel.(or Pno.) Hp.-Str.
Breitkopf & Härtel, Wiesbaden [n.d.]
Score 109 p.

793 Oprichnik [The life guard. Introduction] 5'
3*,2,2,2-4,2,3,1-Timp.,Perc.-Str.
Breitkopf & Härtel, Leipzig [n.d.]
Score 17 p.
From the opera composed 1870-72. First performance St. Petersburg, 24 April 1874.

729 Oprichnik [The life guard. Dance]   6'
3*,2,2,2-4,2,3,1-Timp.,Perc.-Str.
Breitkopf & Härtel, Leipzig [n.d.]
Score 28 p.

418 L'orage [The storm, overture, Op. 76]   10'
3*,3*,2,2-4,2,3,1-Timp.,Perc.-Hp.-Str.
Belaieff, Leipzig, 1896
Score 78 p.
Inspired by A. Ostrovsky's play. Composed 1865. Published posthumously as Op. 76.

2483 [Oxana's caprices, Op. 14. Overture]
3*,2,2,2-4,2,3,1-Timp.,Perc.-Str.
Jurgenson, Moscow [n.d.]
Score 53 p.
Composed in 1874 as Kuznets Vakula [Vakula the Smith]; rewritten 1885. Alternate title: Tcherevichky (The Slippers). First performance of the overture Nobleman's Club, Moscow,

22 November 1874, Russian Musical Society, Nikolai Rubinstein conductor.

653 [Oxana's caprices, Op. 14. Suite] Edited by K. Saradiev
1.[Introduction, exorcism and snow storm]
2.[Minuet] 3.[Introduction to Act III]
4.[Russian dance] 5.[Cossack dance]
6.[Finale]
3*,2,2,2-4,2,3,1-Timp.,Perc.-Hp.-Str.
Jurgenson, Moscow [1879?]
Score 91 p.

497c Pezzo capriccioso [Capricious piece] Op. 62
Solo Vc.-2,2,2,2-4Hn.-Timp.-Str.
Jurgenson, Moscow [1887]
Score 17 p.
Composed 1887. First performance Moscow, 1889.

6843 [Pique dame *or* Queen of spades, Op. 68. Introduction]
3*,2,2,2-4,2,3,1-Timp.-Str.
Kalmus, New York [n.d.]
Score 12 p.
From the opera in three acts based on Push-kin's novel. Composed 1890. First performance St. Petersburg, 19 December 1890.

135 Romeo and Juliet overture-fantasy   19'
3*,3*,2,2-4,2,3,1-Timp.,Perc.-Hp.-Str.
Kalmus, New York [n.d.]
Score 78 p.
Composed 1870; revised 1879.

244s Serenade for strings, Op. 48 [C major]
1.Pezzo in forma di sonatina 2.Walzer
3.Élegie 4.Finale [Russian theme]
Str.
Kalmus, New York [n.d.]
Score 58 p.
Composed 1880.

834v Sérénade mélancolique, Op. 26   9'
[B-flat minor]
Solo Vn.-2,1,2,2-4Hn.-Str.
Jurgenson, Moscow [n.d.]
Score 29 p.
Composed January, 1875. First performance Moscow, 28 January 1876, Nikolai Rubinstein conductor, Adolf Brodsky soloist.

1340 [Six songs, voice and piano, Op. 6. No. 4, A tear trembles. Arranged for orchestra by A. Arends]
2,1,2,2-2,2-Str.
Jurgenson, Moscow [n.d.]
Score 7 p.

2978 [Sleeping Beauty, ballet, Op. 66. Complete in 3 acts]
3*,3*,2,2-4,2,2Cnt.,3,1-Timp.,Perc.-Pno.,Hp.-Str.
Ms.
Score 1239 p. in 3 volumes
Composed 1888-89. First performance Maryinsky Theatre, St. Petersburg, 15 January 1890, R. Drigo conductor.

Chaikovsky, Peter Ilich

114 [Sleeping Beauty. Suite, Op. 66a]   23'
1.Introduction: La fée des lilas 2.Adagio: Pas
d'action 3.Pas de caractère: Le chat botté et
la chatte blanche 4.Panorama 5.Valse
3*,3*,2,2-4,2,2Cnt.,3,1-Timp.,Perc.-Hp.-Str.
Rahter, Hamburg [n.d.]
Score 91 p.
*Also available in Kalmus edition, Catalog
no. 1748.*

1308 [Souvenir de Hapsal, three pieces,   3'
piano solo, Op. 2. No. 1, Ruins of a castle.
Transcribed for orchestra by M. Vladimirov]
3(3rd alt. Picc.),3*,2,2-4,4,3,1-Timp.,Perc.-
Hp.-Str.
Jurgenson, Moscow [n.d.]
Score 15 p.
Composed 1867.

117s [Souvenir de Hapsal, three pieces,   3'
piano solo, Op. 2. No. 3, Song without words.
Transcribed for string orchestra]
Str.
Score in reduction: 3 p.
Parts: C.F. Schmidt, Heilbronn [n.d.]
Composed 1867.

40 [Same as above. Transcribed for   3'
orchestra by Max Erdmannsdörfer]
2,2,2,2-2Hn.-Timp.-Hp.(or Pno.)-Str.
Jurgenson, Moscow [n.d.]
Score 11 p.

Souvenir d'un lieu cher; trois morceaux
[three pieces, for violin and piano, Op. 42.
Arranged for orchestra by Alexander Glazunov]
523v No. 1. Méditation
542v No. 2. Scherzo
550v No. 3. Mélodie
Solo Vn.-2,2,2,2-2Hn.-Hp.-Str.
Jurgenson, Moscow [n.d.]
Scores: 25 p., 25 p., 11 p.
*Composed 1878. Originally planned as the slow
movement for the Violin Concerto.*

2091s [Souvenir of Florence, sextet for   35'
strings, Op. 70, D minor]
1.Allegro con spirito 2.Adagio cantabile e
con moto 3.Allegro moderato 4.Allegro vivace
Str.(without Cb.)
State Music Publishers, Moscow, 1952
Score 108 p.
*Composed 1887-90. Revised 1891-92. First
performance St. Petersburg, 7 December 1892.*

650 [Suite no. 1, Op. 43, D minor]
1.Introduzione e fuga 2.Divertimento 3.Inter-
mezzo 4.[Miniature march] 5.Scherzo
6.Gavotte
3*,2,2,2-4,2-Timp.,Perc.-Str.
Kalmus, New York [n.d.]
Score 191 p.

1447 [Suite no. 2, Characteristic, Op. 53,
C major]
1.[Playing with sounds] 2.[Waltz] 3.[Bur-
lesque scherzo] 4.[Dreams of childhood]
5.[Baroque dance (In the style of Dargomyzhky)]

3*,3*,2,2-4,2,3,1-Timp.,Perc.-4Accordions (ad
lib. in No. 3),Hp.-Str.
Jurgenson, Moscow [n.d.]
Score 185 p.
*Composed 1883. First performance Moscow, 16
February 1884.*

1045 [Suite no. 3, Op. 55, G major]
1.[Elegy] 2.[Melancholic waltz] 3.[Scherzo]
4.[Theme and variations]
3(3rd alt. Picc.),3*,2,2-4,2,3,1-Timp.,Perc.-
Hp.-Str.
Bote & Bock, Berlin [n.d.]
Score 223 p.
*Composed 1884. First performance St. Peters-
burg, 24 January 1885.*

651 [Suite no. 4, Mozartiana, Op. 61]   25'
1.Gigue 2.Minuet 3.[Prayer, after a transcription by Liszt] 4.Thème et variations
2,2,2,2-4,2-Timp.,Perc.-Hp.-Str.
Kalmus, New York [n.d.]
Score 72 p.
*Composed 1886. First performance St. Peters-
burg, 1887, the composer conducting.*

2976 [Swan lake, Op. 20. Complete ballet in
4 acts]
3*,2,2,2-4,2,2Cnt.,3,1-Timp.,Perc.-Hp.-Str.
Jurgenson, Moscow, 1895
Score 635 p.
*Based on a scenario by Vladimir Begichev and
Vasily Geltzer with choreography by Julius
Reisinger. Commissioned by the directorate of
the Moscow Opera, 1875. Composed 1876. First
performance Bolshoi Theatre, Moscow, 4 March
1877, Stepan Ryabov conductor.*

7214 [Swan lake, Op. 20. Complete ballet in
4 acts]
3*,2,2,2-4,2,2Cnt.,3,1-Timp.,Perc.-Hp.-Str.
Kalmus, New York [n.d.]
Score 806 p. in 2 volumes

754 [Swan lake, Op. 20. Ballet suite]   19'
1.Scène 2.Valse 3.[Dances of the swans]
4.Scène 5.[Hungarian dance, czardas] 6.Scène
3*,2,2,2-4,2,2Cnt.,3,1-Timp.,Perc.-Hp.-Str.
Jurgenson, Moscow [n.d.]
Score 104 p.

6844 [Swan lake, Op. 20. Ballet suite]   25'
1.Scène 2.Valse 3.[Dance of the swans]
4.Scène 5.[Hungarian dance] 6.[Spanish dance]
7.[Neapolitan dance] 8.Mazurka
3*,2,2,2-4,3,2Cnt.,3,1-Timp.,Perc.-Hp.-Str.
Kalmus, New York [n.d.]
Score 127 p.

2979 Symphonie élégiaque. Transcribed for   41'
symphony orchestra by Erno Rapee from the Piano
Trio in A minor, Op. 50
1.Elegiac piece 2.Theme with variations
3.Final variation and coda
4,4,4,4-4,3,3,1-Timp.,Perc.-Pno.,Cel.,Hp.-Str.
Carl Fischer, New York, c1939
Score 174 p.
Piano Trio composed 1882. This transcription

Chaikovsky, Peter Ilich

1932. First performance broadcast over NBC, New York, 29 March 1936, Music Hall Symphony Orchestra, Erno Rapee conductor.

95 [Symphony no. 1, Winter dreams, Op. 13,   *30'*
G minor]
1.Allegro tranquillo 2.Adagio cantabile ma non tanto 3.Scherzo: Allegro scherzando giocoso 4.Finale: Andante lugubre
3*,2,2,2-4,2,3,1-Timp.,Perc.-Str.
Kalmus, New York [n.d.]
Score 139 p.
Composed 1866. First performance Moscow, 15 February 1868, Nikolai Rubinstein conductor.

273 [Symphony no. 2, Op. 17, C minor]
1.Andante sostenuto - Allegro vivo 2.Andantino marziale, quasi moderato 3.Scherzo 4.Finale: Moderato assai
3*,2,2,2-4,2,3,1-Timp.,Perc.-Str.
Kalmus, New York [n.d.]
Score 167 p.
Composed 1872. First performance Moscow, 7 February 1873, Nikolai Rubinstein conductor.

93 [Symphony no. 3, Op. 29, D major]   *47'*
1.Introduzione ed allegro - Moderato assai (Tempo di marcia funebre) 2.Alla tedesca - Allegro moderato e semplice 3.Andante elegiaco 4.Scherzo: Allegro vivo 5.Finale: Allegro con fuoco (tempo di polacca)
3*,2,2,2-4,2,3,1-Timp.-Str.
Breitkopf & Härtel, Leipzig, 1897
Score 162 p.
Composed 1875. First performance Moscow, 19 November 1875, Nikolai Rubinstein conductor.

116 [Symphony no. 4, Op. 36, F minor]   *42'*
1.Andante sostenuto 2.Andantino in modo di canzona 3.Scherzo 4.Finale
3*,2,2,2-4,2,3,1-Timp.,Perc.-Str.
Breitkopf & Härtel, Leipzig [n.d.]
Score 143 p.
Composed 1877. First performance Moscow, 22 February 1878, Nikolai Rubinstein conductor.

236 [Symphony no. 5, Op. 64, E minor]   *49'*
1.Andante - Allegro con anima 2.Andante cantabile con alcuna licenza 3.Valse: Allegro moderato 4.Finale: Andante maestoso
3(3rd alt. Picc.),2,2,2-4,2,3,1-Timp.-Str.
Breitkopf & Härtel, Leipzig [n.d.]
Score 162 p.
Composed 1888. First performance St. Petersburg, 17 November 1888, the composer conducting.

137 [Symphony no. 6, Pathetique, Op. 74,   *48'*
B minor]
1.Adagio - Allegro non troppo 2.Allegro con grazia 3.Allegro molto vivace 4.Finale: Adagio lamentoso
3(3rd alt. Picc.),2,2,2-4,2,3,1-Timp.,Perc.-Str.
Breitkopf & Härtel, Wiesbaden [n.d.]
Score 181 p.
Composed 1893. First performance St. Petersburg, 28 October 1893, the composer conducting.

654 [Symphony, Manfred, in 4 pictures   *57'*
after Byron's dramatic poem, Op. 58]
1.Lento lugubre 2.Vivace con spirito 3.Andante con moto 4.Allegro con fuoco
3(3rd alt. Picc.),3*,3*,3-4,2,2Cnt.,3,1-Timp.,Perc.-2Hp.,Harm.-Str.
Kalmus, New York [n.d.]
Score 316 p.
Composed 1885. First performance Moscow, 1886.

655 [The tempest, fantasy, Op. 18]   *18'*
3*,2,2,2-4,2,3,1-Timp.,Perc.-Str.
Jurgenson, Moscow [n.d.]
Score 102 p.
Based on Shakespeare's drama.

[Trio, piano, Op. 50, A minor. Transcribed for symphony orchestra by Erno Rapee]
See: Symphonie élégiaque...

1508 [Triumphal overture on the Danish   *15'*
national anthem, Op. 15]
3*,2,2,2-4,2,3,1-Timp.,Perc.-Str.
Jurgenson, Moscow [n.d.]
Score 63 p.

524v [Valse-scherzo, Op. 34, C major]
Solo Vn.-2,2,2,2-2Hn.-Str.
Jurgenson, Moscow [n.d.]
Score 39 p.
Composed 1877. First performance Paris, 21 October 1878.

496c [Variations on a rococo theme, Op. 33. New edition revised by the composer]
Solo Vc.-2,2,2,2-2Hn.-Str.
Kalmus, New York [n.d.]
Score 45 p.
Composed December, 1876.

755 [The voyevode, Op. 3. Overture]   *7'*
3*,3*,2,2-4,2,3,1-Timp.,Perc.-Str.
Jurgenson, Moscow [n.d.]
Score 37 p.
From the opera composed 1867-68. First performance Moscow, 11 February 1869.

1539 [The voyevode, Op. 3. Entr'acte et   *12'*
air de ballet]
3*,2,2,2-4,2,3,1-Timp.,Perc.-Hp.-Str.
Jurgenson, Moscow [n.d.]
Score 57 p.

419 [The voyevode, symphonic ballad. Op. 78] *10'*
3*,3*,3*,2-4,2,3,1-Timp.,Perc.-Cel.(or Pno.)-Hp.-Str.
Belaieff, Leipzig, 1897
Score 59 p.
Composed 1891; score destroyed by composer. Published from the parts posthumously as Op. 78.

CHAJES, JULIUS.   Lwów, Poland 21 December 1910

417c By the rivers of Babylon (137th   *6'*
Psalm)
High Voice Solo,Solo Vc.-2,2,2,2*-2,2,1-Timp.,Cym.-Str.

Ms. ^c1942 by Julius Chajes
Score 9 p. Large folio
*Composed 1942. First performance Cranbrook,
Michigan, 26 August 1942, Michigan Symphony
Orchestra, Walter Poole conductor, Marguerite
Kozenn soprano, Julius Sturm cellist.*

346p [Concerto, piano, in E. Revised   *26'*
version (1956)]
1.Allegro deciso 2.Andante cantabile 3.Allegro vivace e con fuoco - Tranquillo - Allegro
deciso
Solo Pno.-2,2,2,3*-4,3-Timp.,Trgl.,Cym.-Str.
Ms. ^c1955 by Julius Chajes
Score 104 p. Large folio
*Composed 1953. First performance Vienna, 25
November 1953, Vienna Radio Orchestra, Kurt
Richter conductor, composer as soloist. Revised 1956.*

443c [Concerto, violoncello, Op. 13, A   *21'*
minor]
1.Allegro moderato 2.Poco adagio 3.Allegro
molto
Solo Vc.-2,2,2,2-4,1-Timp.-Str.
Ms. ^c1932 by Transcontinental Music [n.p.]
Score 40 p.
*Composed 1930. First performance Karlsbad,
Czechoslovakia, 5 August 1932, Kurorchester,
Robert Manzer conductor, Franz Noli soloist.*

6105 Eros, symphonic poem   *10'*
2,2,2,3*-4,3,3,1-Timp.,Cym.-Str.
Ms.
Score 48 p. Large folio
*Composed 1960-61. First performance Detroit,
7 February 1961, Center Symphony Orchestra of
the Jewish Community Center, the composer conducting.*

2049s Four fugues in modo antico, for   *12'30"*
string orchestra, Op. 18
1.Allegro moderato 2.Andante sostenuto 3.
Scherzo: Allegretto 4.Vivo, ma non troppo
allegro
Str.(without Cb.)
Ms. ^c[n.d.] by Julius Chajes
Score 16 p.
*Originally composed for string quartet, 1933.
First performance Vienna, 3 May 1937, Kurt
Pahlen conductor. This work is also known as
Suite in D major, for strings.*

1965s Fugue no. 1, Op. 19, A minor   *7'*
Str.
Ms.
Score 10 p.
*Originally composed for organ, 1933. Transcribed for string orchestra, 1933. First
performance Jerusalem, 13 July 1935, Jerusalem
Chamber Orchestra, Karl Salomon conductor.*

761c Melodie, for violoncello and orchestra *2'*
Solo Vc.-2Cl.-2Hn.-Str.
Ms. ^c1929 by Julius Chajes
Score 3 p.
*Composed 1926. First performance Vienna, 20
February 1927.*

1947s Palestinian melodies, for string   *6'*
orchestra
1.Song of the well (Song and 4 variations)
2.Song of the pioneers (Canon): Allegro
3.Song of the night: Tranquillo 4.Song of the
desert: Allegro vivace - Vivo - Moderato -
Vivo 5.Song of Canaan: Allegro giocoso 6.Song
of Galilee (Song and 4 variations)
Str.
Ms. ^c1943 by Julius Chajes
Score 9 p.
*Originally composed for piano, 1942. Transcribed for strings by the composer, 1943.
Title changed later to Six Israeli Melodies.*

821p Romantic fantasy, for piano and   *10'*
orchestra
Moderato - Andante - Allegro
Solo Pno.-2,2,2,2-2,1-Timp.-Str.
Ms.
Score 31 p.
*Composed 1927. First performance Vienna, 8
October 1928, Radio Orchestra, Anton Konrath
conductor, the composer as soloist.*

2228s Theme and variations for string   *4'30"*
orchestra
Str.
Ms.
Score 10 p.
*Composed 1963. First performance Detroit, 7
January 1964, Center Symphony Orchestra of the
Jewish Community Center, the composer conducting.*

1185v Valse sentimentale, for violin or   *4'*
violoncello and orchestra
Solo Vn. or Solo Vc.-2Fl.-2Hn.-Str.
Ms.
Score 10 p.
*Originally composed for violoncello and piano,
1928, under the title Valse Triste.*

CHAMINADE, CÉCILE.   Paris 8 August 1857
                      Monte Carlo 18 April 1944

529m [Concertino, flute, Op. 107, D major]
Solo Fl.-1,2,2,2-4,0,3,1-Timp.-Hp.-Str.
Enoch, Paris, ^c1902, 1929
Score 46 p.

373p [Concertpiece, piano, Op. 40, C-sharp
minor]
Solo Pno.-3*,2*,2,2-4,2,2Cnt.,3,1-Timp.,Perc.-Str.
Enoch & Costallat, Paris [n.d.]
Score 67 p.
*First performance Paris, Concerts Lamoureux,
the composer as soloist.*

CHAMPION, MARGUERITE ROESGEN.
  See: ROESGEN-CHAMPION, MARGUERITE.

CHAPELLE, ED.

707m Fantasy, for trumpet and strings
Solo Tpt.-Str.
Ms.
Score 15 p.

Chapochnikov, Ilia

CHAPOCHNIKOV, ILIA.

3241 Les fragments des mélodies des montag-
nards [Fragments of mountain melodies]
1.Chanson balkare [Balkan song] 2.Chanson
tchetchène [Tchetchen song] 3.Chanson ossete
[Ossetian song] 4.Danse kabardienne [Kabardin
dance]
3*,3*,2,2-4,2,3,1-Timp.,Perc.-Hp.-Str.
Edition de Musique de l'État, Moscow, c1937
Score 28 p.

3100 Lezguinka du Daghestan
3*,3*,2,2-4,2,3,1-Timp.,Perc.-Hp.-Str.
Edition de Musique de l'État, Moscow, c1937
Score 38 p.

CHARPENTIER, GUSTAVE.
                        Dieuze, Lorraine 25 June 1860
                        Paris 18 February 1956

296 Impressions d'Italie   34'
1.Sérénade 2.[At the fountain] 3.[On mules]
4.[On the summit] 5.Naples
3(3rd alt. Picc.),3*,3*,4-Sax.-4,2,2Cnt.,3,1-
Timp.,Perc.-2Hp.-Str.
Heugel, Paris [n.d.]
Score 158 p.
*Composed in Italy, 1890. First performance
Paris, 1892.*

CHASINS, ABRAM.   New York City 17 August 1903

693p [Concerto, piano, no. 1, Op. 14,   20'
F minor]
1.Allegro vivace e molto energico 2.Andante
con grazia 3.Allegro assai
Solo Pno.-2(2nd alt. Picc.),2,2,2-4,2,3,1-
Timp.,Cym.-Str.
Ms.
Score 105 p.
*Composed 1928. First performance Philadelphia,
18 January 1929, Philadelphia Orchestra, Ossip
Gabrilovitch conductor, the composer as
soloist.*

694p [Concerto, piano, no. 2, Op. 17,   30'
F-sharp minor]
1.Allegro maestoso 2.Allegretto deciso
Solo Pno.-2,3*,3*,3*-4,3,3,1-Timp.,Perc.-Cel.-
Str.
Ms.
Score 111 p.
*Composed 1932. First performance Philadelphia,
3 March 1933, Philadelphia Orchestra, Leopold
Stokowski conductor, the composer as soloist.*

734p [Concerto, piano, no. 2, F-sharp   25'
minor. Revised, in one movement]
Solo Pno.-3(3rd alt. Picc.),3*,3*,3*-4,3,3,1-
Timp.,Perc.-Cel.-Str.
Ms.
Score 152 p.
*Revised 1937. First performance of revised
version New York, 7 April 1938, New York
Philharmonic, John Barbirolli conductor, the
composer as soloist.*

2463 Parade   8'
3*,3*,3*,3*-4,3,4,1-Timp.,Perc.-Hp.-Str.
J. Fischer, New York, c1931
Score 31 p.
*Composed 1930. First performance New York,
8 April 1931, New York Philharmonic, Arturo
Toscanini conductor.*

2462 Three Chinese pieces   9'
1.A Shanghai tragedy 2.Flirtation in a
Chinese garden 3.Rush hour in Hongkong
3*,2,2,2-4,2,3,1-Timp.,Perc.-Cel.,Hp.-Str.
Ms.
Score 46 p.
*Composed 1925. First performance New York,
8 April 1931, New York Philharmonic, Arturo
Toscanini conductor.*

CHAUSSON, ERNEST.   Paris 20 January 1855
                         Limay, Seine et Oise 10 June 1899

563 Air de danse *and* Danse rustique, Op. 18 7'
[incidental music to Shakespeare's The
Tempest]
3*,2,2,2-2,2,3-Timp.,Cym.,Trgl.-Hp.-Str.
Bornemann, Paris, c1902
Score 31 p.
*First performance Petit Théâtre des Mario-
nettes, Paris, 1888.*

433v Poème [violin and orchestra, Op. 25,
E-flat major]
Solo Vn.-2,2,2,2-4,2,3,1-Timp.-Hp.-Str.
Breitkopf & Härtel, Leipzig, c1898, 1907
Score 34 p.
*Composed 1896. First performance Concerts
Colonne, Paris, 4 April 1897, Eugène Ysaÿe
soloist.*

459 [Symphony, Op. 20, B-flat major]   35'
1.Lent 2.Très lent 3.Animé
3(3rd alt. Picc.),3*,3*,3-4,4,3,1-Timp.-2Hp.-
Str.
Rouart, Lerolle, Paris [n.d.]
Score 116 p.
*Composed ca.1890. First performance Société
Nationale, Paris, 18 April 1891, the composer
conducting.*

203 Viviane, poème symphonique, Op. 5   11'
3(3rd alt. Picc.),2,2,3-4,4(2 back scene),3,1-
Timp.,Perc.-2Hp.-Str.
Bornemann, Paris [n.d.]
Score 48 p.
*Composed 1882. First performance Société
Nationale, Paris, 1883.*

CHAVAGNAT, PIERRE EDOUARD.   Paris 17 October 1843
                             Paris 29 December 1913

1559s Grand'mère à ses enfants, air rustique
Str.
Score: Ms. 6 p.
Parts: Richault, Paris [n.d.]

CHAVARRI, EDUARDO LOPEZ.
                        Valencia, Spain 31 January 1871
                        Valencia, Spain 28 October 1970

431s Acuarelas valencianas
1.[Song] 2.[Summer] 3.[Dance]
Str.
Union Musical Española, Madrid, c1921
Score 21 p.

1562s Saluts et compliments [16th century
minuet]
Str.
Score: Ms. 5 p.
Parts: Richault, Paris [n.d.]

CHÁVEZ, CARLOS.   Calzada de Tacuba,
                    near Mexico City 13 June 1899
                    Mexico City 2 August 1978

5968 [Daughter of Colchis, symphonic suite] 23'
1.Preludio: Tranquillo - Moderato
2.Encantamiento [Enchantment]: Tempo giusto
3.Zarabanda [Saraband]: Poco andante 4.Peán
[Paean]: Lento 5.Postludio: Meno lento
3*,3*,4*(1Cl. in E-flat),3-4,3,3,1-Timp.,Perc.
-Hp.-Str.
Ediciones Mexicanas de Musica, Mexico City,
c1951
Score 49 p.
*Commissioned for Martha Graham by the Elizabeth
Sprague Coolidge Foundation. Composed 1943-44
as a ballet in 9 scenes. A shorter version of
this was performed by Martha Graham in New
York, 23 January 1946, under the title Dark
Meadow. This symphonic suite arranged for
large orchestra, 1947.*

3465 Energía
2Fl.(2nd alt. Picc.),Bn.-Hn.,Tpt.,B.Tbn.(alt.
Ten.Tbn.)-Va.,Vc.,Cb.
Ms.
Score 22 p.
*Composed 1925. First performance Paris, 11
June 1931, Orchestre Straram, Nicolas Slonimsky
conductor.*

3500 Soli for oboe, clarinet, trumpet and
bassoon
Ob.,Cl.,Bn.-Tpt.
Ms.
Score 14 p.
Composed 1933.

2146s [Symphony no. 5, for string   18'
orchestra]
1.Allegro molto moderato 2.Lento 3.Allegro
con brio
Str.
Affiliated Musicians, Inc., Los Angeles, c1954
Score 46 p.
*Commissioned by the Serge Koussevitzky Music
Foundation in the Library of Congress. Com-
posed 1953. First performance Los Angeles, 1
December 1953, Chamber Symphony Orchestra of
Los Angeles, the composer conducting. Dedi-
cated to the memory of Serge and Natalie
Koussevitzky.*

416m Toccata for percussion instruments   14'
1.Allegro, sempre giusto 2.Largo 3.Allegro
un poco marziale

Perc. I: Indian Dr.,Glock.,Small Indian Dr.
Perc. II: Side Dr.I, Xyl.,Indian Dr.,Ten.Dr.
Perc. III: Side Dr.II,Suspended Cym.
Perc. IV: Ten.Dr.,Chimes,Claves,Maraca,Suspend-
      ed Cym.
Perc. V: Timp.,Small Gong
Perc. VI: B.Dr.,Large Gong
Mills Music, Inc., New York, c1954
Score 26 p.
*Composed 1942. First performance Mexico City,
31 October 1947, National Conservatory of
Mexico Orchestra, Eduardo Hernandez Moncada
conductor.*

CHELARD, HIPPOLYTE ANDRÉ JEAN BAPTISTE.
                    Paris 1 February 1789
                    Weimar 12 February 1861

3075 [Macbeth. Overture to the opera]
3*,2,2,2-4,2,3,1-Timp.,B.Dr.,Cym.-Str.
Ms.
Score 58 p.
*First performance Opéra, Paris, 29 June 1827.
Revised 1828 and performed in Munich same year.*

CHEMBERDZHI, NIKOLAI KARPOVICH.
        Tsarskoye Selo (now Pushkin) 24 August 1903
                    Moscow 22 April 1948

Also transliterated as: Tchemberdjy

2984 Festival march   11'
3*,2,2,2-4,3,3,1-Timp.,Perc.-Str.
Mussektor, Moscow, 1933
Score 24 p.
*Composed 1932 for the 15th Jubilee of the Red
Army. First performance Moscow, 1933, Moscow
Orchestra of National Instruments, Peter
Alexeyev conductor.*

4241 [Solemn march]
3*,2,2,2-4,3,3,1-Timp.,Perc.-Str.
Moscow State, Moscow, 1933
Score 24 p.
*Composed on the occasion of the 15th anniver-
sary of the Red Army.*

945m Suite concertante, pour trompette,   35'
cor et trombone
1.Allegro 2.Andantino 3.Allegro inquieto 4.
Allegro sostenuto
Solo Hn.,Solo Tpt.,Solo Tbn.-3*,2,2,2-4,3,3,1-
Timp.,Perc.-Str.
Editions de Musique de l'URSS, Moscow, 1938
Score 159 p.
*First performance Moscow, 1935, Moscow Orches-
tra, Mikeladze conductor, Shukalov (horn), Orvid
(trumpet), and Rudnikov (trombone) soloists.*

CHEMIN-PETIT, HANS. Potsdam, Germany 24 July 1902

4658 [Little suite for nine solo instru-   20'
ments, from the puppet play Dr. Johannes
Faust]
1.Ouverture: Allegro 2.Melancholische Weise:
Langsam 3.Kasperles schnurriges Liedchen:
Allegretto 4.Nachtlied: Moderato 5.Erschein-
ung: Moderato 6.Kasperles Tanz mit seiner

Cherepnin, Aleksandr Nikolaevich

Gretl: Allegro molto
Ob.,Cl.,Bn.-Perc.-Str.
Robert Lienau, Berlin, c1940
Score 43 p.
Ein Kasperletheater is the German equivalent of the Punch and Judy show. Composed as incidental music for a puppet play, 1932. This suite 1939.

CHEREPNIN, ALEKSANDR NIKOLAEVICH.
See: TCHEREPNIN, ALEXANDER NIKOLAYEVICH.

CHEREPNIN, NIKOLAI NIKOLAEVICH.
See: TCHEREPNIN, NIKOLAI NIKOLAYEVICH.

CHERNETSKY, S. A.

4734 [Ukrainian march no. 2, for band]
1,0,4(1Cl. in E-flat)-2Sopranino Hn.,2Tpt.,2
Cnt.,2Alto Hn.,3Ten.Hn.,Bar.,2Tuba-Perc.
Moscow State, Moscow, 1936
Score 19 p.

CHERUBINI, LUIGI.   Florence 14 September 1760
                           Paris 15 March 1842

Full name: Maria Luigi Carlo Zenobio Salvatore
           Cherubini

1207 [Die Abenceragen. Overture]   7'
2,2,2,2-4,2,3-Timp.-Str.
Breitkopf & Härtel, Leipzig [n.d.]
Score 48 p.
From the opera first performed Paris, 6 April 1813.

953 [Ali Baba. Overture]   6'
2*,2,2,2-4,4,3,Ophicl.-Timp.,Perc.-Str.
Breitkopf & Härtel, Leipzig [n.d.]
Score 55 p.
From the opera in 4 acts composed 1833.

4401 [Ali Baba. Entr'acte and ballet music] 9'
Edited by Carl Reinecke
2,2,2,2-4,2,3-Timp.,Trgl.-Str.
Breitkopf & Härtel, Leipzig [1878]
Score 37 p.

600 [Anacreon. Overture]   9'
2(2nd alt. Picc.),2,2,2-4,2,3-Timp.-Str.
Breitkopf & Härtel, Leipzig [n.d.]
Score 76 p.
From the opera composed 1803.

1195 [Anacreon. Ballet music]   7'
2*,2,2,2-4,0,3-Timp.-Str.
Breitkopf & Härtel, Leipzig [n.d.]
Score 48 p.

558 [Concert overture. Revised by Friedrich 10'
Grützmacher]
1,2,2,2-4,2,3-Timp.-Str.
Kahnt, Leipzig [n.d.]
Score 50 p.
Composed for the London Philharmonic Society, 1815. First performance London, 1 May 1815, the composer conducting.

6957 [Contredanses, for orchestra] Edited by
Claudio Gallico and Sergio Albertini
1.La Florentine 2.La Théresita 3.La Joseph
4.La nouvelle Créole 5.Contredanse village-
ois 6.Pas sauté contredanse 7.Menuet village-
ois 8.Air de danse 9.La Melfort 10.La
bachanale 11.Contredanse 12.Contredanse
13.La bonne amitié
1(alt. Picc.),0,2,2-2,0,1-Timp.,Perc.-Str.
Litolff/C.F. Peters, Frankfurt, c1971
Score 51 p.
Nos. 1-8 composed 1808; nos. 9-11 composed 1809; nos. 12-13 composed 1810.

345 [Les deux journées (The water carrier). 6'
Overture]
2,2,2,2-3,0,1-Timp.-Str.
Breitkopf & Härtel, Leipzig [n.d.]
Score 51 p.
From the opera first performed Paris, 16 January 1800.

928 [Elisa. Overture]   6'
2,2,2,2-4Hn.-Timp.-Str.
Breitkopf & Härtel, Leipzig [n.d.]
Score 65 p.
From the opera composed 1794. First performance of opera Paris, 13 December 1794.

2128 [Faniska. Overture]   7'
2,2,2,2-2,2,1-Timp.-Str.
Breitkopf & Härtel, Leipzig [n.d.]
Score 59 p.
From the opera composed 1805. First performance of opera Vienna, 20 February 1806.

1048 [Lodoïska. Overture]   7'
2,2,2,2-2,2,1-Timp.-Str.
Breitkopf & Härtel, Leipzig [n.d.]
Score 54 p.
From the opera composed 1791. First performance of opera Paris, 18 July 1791.

996 [Medea. Overture]   9'
2,2,2,2-4Hn.-Timp.-Str.
Breitkopf & Härtel, Leipzig [n.d.]
Score 60 p.
From the opera composed 1797. First performance of opera Paris, 13 March 1797.

1086 [The Portuguese inn. Overture]   8'
2,2,2,2-2,2,1-Timp.-Str.
Breitkopf & Härtel, Leipzig [n.d.]
Score 63 p.
From the opera composed 1798. First performance of opera Paris, 25 July 1798.

2823 [The Portuguese inn. Overture.   8'30"
Rewritten and rescored by Quinto Maganini]
3*,2,3*,2-2,2,2,1-Timp.,S.Dr.,Cym.-Str.
Ms.
Score 41 p.
This version made 1934 and scored for both small and full orchestra. First performance New York, 23 April 1937, Federal Music Project Chamber Orchestra of the WPA, Quinto Maganini conductor.

199s [Quartet, strings, E-flat major. Scherzo]
Edited by Reinhold Jockisch
Str.
Kistner, Leipzig [n.d.]
Score 3 p.

292m [Two sonatas for horn or English horn
with string orchestra] Edited by Johannes
Wojciechowski
I.Larghetto II.Largo - Allegro moderato
Solo Hn. or E.H.-Str.
Hans Sikorski, Hamburg, c1954
Score 13 p.
Composed 1802.

CHESLOCK, LOUIS.   London 9 September 1899

4422 Cinderella, a ballet for children.   *45'*
Original version
1,1,1-1,1,1-Timp.,Perc.-Hp.-Str.
Ms.
Score 176 p.
*Composed 1945. First performance Baltimore,
Maryland, 11 May 1946, Peabody Ballet Company
and Senior Orchestra, the composer conducting.*

5787 Cinderella, a ballet for children   *60'*
[Enlarged version] Complete ballet in three
acts
1,1,1-1,1,1-Timp.,Perc.-Hp.-Str.
Ms.
Score 275 p. (176 plus XCIX)
*Enlarged 1958. First performance of enlarged
version Baltimore, 2 May 1958, Peabody Ballet
Company and Senior Orchestra, the composer
conducting.*

937m [Concerto, horn]   *20'*
1. ♩ = 108 2. ♩ = 63 3. ♩. = 63
Solo Hn.-1,1,1,1-2,1-Timp.-Str.
Ms.
Score 120 p.
Composed 1936.

1121v [Concerto, violin]   *22'*
1.Allegro moderato 2.Adagio lamento 3.Alle-
gretto scherzando
Solo Vn.-3*,2(2nd alt. E.H.),2,2-4,2,3,1-Timp.
-Str.
Ms.
Score 104 p.
*Composed 1921. First performance Baltimore,
Maryland, 25 February 1926, Peabody Conserva-
tory Senior Orchestra, Gustav Strube conductor,
Arthur Morgan soloist.*

3122 [The jewel merchants. Overture]   *12'*
2,2(2nd alt. E.H.),2,2-2,2,2-Timp.,Cym.-Hp.-
Str.
Ms.
Score 50 p.
*Composed 1930. Received honorable mention in
the Woman's Symphony Orchestra of New York
contest, 1938.*

3224 The legend of Sleepy Hollow   *15'*
3*,3*,3*,3*-Alto Sax.-4,2,3,1-Timp.,Perc.-Cel.,
Hp.-Str.

Ms.
Score 116 p.
Composed 1936.

4573 Rhapsody in red and white, an   *12'*
American divertissement
2(2nd alt. Picc.),2,2,2-4,3,3,1-Timp.,Perc.-
Pno.,Hp.-Str.
Ms.
Score 46 p. Large folio
*Commissioned by Reginald Stewart for the Bal-
timore Symphony Orchestra. Composed 1949.
First performance Baltimore, 8 February 1950,
Baltimore Symphony Orchestra, the composer
conducting.*

5758 Rhapsody in red and white, an   *12'*
American divertissement. Transcribed for band
by the composer
3*,2,6*(1Cl. in E-flat,1Alto Cl.),1-4Sax.(2
Alto,1Ten.,1Bar.)-4,2,3Cnt.,3,Bar.,2-Timp.,
Perc.-Vc.,Cb.
Ms.
Score 48 p. Large folio
*Transcription for band, 1955. First perform-
ance Fort Meade, Maryland, 21 September 1955,
the composer conducting.*

1765s Shire ami [Songs of my people]   *7'*
rhapsody for strings and harp
Hp.-Str.
Ms.
Score 13 p.
Composed 1932.

3605 Suite from David   *15'*
1.Prelude - Challenge of Goliath 2.Pastorale
- A Psalm of David 3.Dance - Praise ye the
Lord
3*,3*,3*,3*-4,2,3,1-Timp.,Perc.-Cel.,Hp.-Ten.
(or Bar.)Voice-Str.
Ms.
Score 80 p.
*Composed 1937. First performance Baltimore, 19
February 1939, Baltimore Symphony Orchestra,
Werner Janssen conductor.*

3099 Symphonic prelude   *15'*
3(3rd alt. Picc.),2,3*,3*-4,2,3,1-Timp.,B.Dr.,
Cym.-Hp.-Str.
Ms.
Score 52 p.
*Composed 1927. First performance Baltimore, 8
April 1928, Baltimore Symphony Orchestra, the
composer conducting.*

3243 [Symphony, D major]   *30'*
1.Molto moderato - Allegro 2.Largo 3.Allegro
vivace (Scherzo) 4.Andante comodo - Tempo di
marcia (Finale)
3*,3*,2,2-4,2,3,1-Timp.,Perc.-Hp.-Str.
Ms.
Score 225 p.
Composed 1932.

3607 Theme and variations, for chamber   *10'*
orchestra
Molto adagio - Vivace - Alla barcarola - Poco

Cheslock, Louis

maestoso - Con brio - Quasi fantasia - Allegro
- Alla marcia
Fl.-Hn.-2Pno.-Str.
Ms.
Score 44 p.
Composed 1934.

3190 Three tone poems, scenes   12'
1.Cathedral at sundown 2.'Neath Washington
Monument 3.At the railway station
3*,3*,2,2-4,2,3,1-Timp.,Perc.-Pno.,Cel.,Hp.-
Str.
Ms.
Score 53 p.
*Originally composed for string quartet and
piano, 1921; orchestrated 1922. Awarded prize
(in form of a performance) in the Chicago
Theatre Symphony Contest, 1923. First performance Chicago, 29 April 1923, Chicago Theatre Symphony Orchestra, Nathaniel Finston
conductor.*

3080 Two dances   6'
1.Polish dance 2.Spanish dance
Fl.,Cl.-2,2,2-Timp.,Perc.-Str.
Ms.
Score 24 p.
*Composed 1923. Both dances received awards
in the Chicago Daily News Contests, 1923-24;
the Spanish Dance received an additional
award as third Grand Prize. First performance
Baltimore, 18 April 1926, Baltimore Symphony
Orchestra, Gustav Strube conductor.*

1764s Two miniatures   6'
1.Slumber song 2.Serenade
Str.
Ms.
Score 9 p.
*Composed 1930. First performance Baltimore,
Maryland, 13 April 1930, Baltimore Symphony
Orchestra, Gustav Strube conductor.*

CHEVALLIER, ERNST AUGUST HEINRICH.
                        Hanover 12 May 1848
                        Hamburg 18 January 1908

274s Poëtische Skizzen [Poetic sketches]
1.An den Frühling [To spring] 2.Elfenscherz
[Elves' frolic] 3.Waldandacht [Woodland
prayer] 4.Im grünen Hag [In the green grove]
Str.
Leichssenring, Hamburg [n.d.]
Score 7 p.

CHEVILLARD, CAMILLE.   Paris 14 October 1859
                          Chatou 30 May 1923

386 Ballade symphonique, Op. 6   8'
3*,3*,3*,3*-4,2,3,1-Timp.,Cym.-Str.
Durand, Paris, c1913
Score 57 p.
*Composed 1889. First performance Concerts
Lamoureux, Paris, 23 February 1890, the com-
poser conducting.*

771 Le chêne et le roseau [The oak and   8'
the reeds, symphonic poem, Op. 7]

1.[The scenery] 2.[Dialogue] 3.[Drama]
3(3rd alt. Picc.),3*,3*,3-4,3,3,1-Timp.,Perc.
-2Hp.-Str.
Enoch, Paris [n.d.]
Score 48 p.
*Composed 1890; based on the fable by La Fon-
taine. First performance Concerts Lamoureux,
Paris, 8 March 1891, the composer conducting.*

346 Fantaisie symphonique, Op.10   15'
3*,2,2,3-4,2,3,1-Timp.,Cym.-2Hp.-Str.
Breitkopf & Härtel, Leipzig, c1901
Score 71 p.
*Composed 1893. First performance Concerts
Lamoureux, Paris, 21 October 1894, the composer
conducting.*

CHICHOV, IVAN PETROVICH.
                    b. Novocherkassk, Russia 1888

2921 [Symphony of the Steppes, Op. 12,   35'
D major]
1.Introduction and allegro 2.Andante non
troppo 3.Scherzo 4.Finale
3*,3*,4*,3*-4,2,3,1-Timp.,Perc.-Cel.,Hp.-Str.
Mussektor, Moscow, 1934
Score 189 p.
*Composed 1923-25. First performance at a con-
cert organized by the Committee of the T.S.F.
of the U.S.S.R., Moscow, 10 May 1933, A. I.
Orlov conductor.*

CHOPIN, FRÉDÉRIC.
          Żelazowa Wola near Warsaw, Poland 1 March 1810
                          (or 22 February 1810)
                          Paris 17 October 1849

378p [Concerto, piano, no. 1, Op. 11,   33'
E minor]
1.Allegro maestoso 2.Romanze 3.Rondo
Solo Pno.-2,2,2,2-4,2,1-Timp.-Str.
Kalmus, New York [n.d.]
Score 92 p.
*Completed August 1830. First performance
Warsaw, 11 October 1830, the composer as
soloist.*

766v [Concerto, piano, no. 1, Op. 11, E minor.
Romanze. Transcribed by August Wilhelmj]
Solo Vn.-2,0,2,2-2Hn.-Timp.-Str.
Kistner, Leipzig [n.d.]
Score 35 p.
*Transposed from original key of E major to D
major.*

298p [Concerto, piano, no. 2, Op. 21,   30'
F minor]
1.Maestoso 2.Larghetto 3.Allegro vivace
Solo Pno.-2,2,2,2-2,2,1-Timp.-Str.
Breitkopf & Härtel, Leipzig [n.d.]
Score 68 p.
*Composed 1829. First performance Warsaw, 17
March 1830, Karol Kurpiński conductor, the
composer as soloist.*

395p [Concerto, piano, no. 2, Op. 21,   24'
F minor. New orchestral accompaniment by Karl
Klindworth]

Solo Pno.-2,2,2,2-2,2,3-Timp.-Str.
Bote & Bock, Berlin [n.d.]
Score 163 p.

654c [Etude, piano, Op. 25 no. 7, C-sharp
minor. Transcribed in D minor for solo violon-
cello and orchestra by Jules de Swert]
Solo Vc.-2,1,2-2Hn.-Str.
Score: Ms. 8 p.
Parts: Schott, Mainz [n.d.]

Funeral march from the Sonata, Op. 35, in
B-flat minor
See: [Sonata, piano, Op. 35, B-flat minor.
    3rd movement, Funeral march. Transcribed
    for orchestra...]

455p [Grand fantasy on Polish tunes, Op.   *15'*
13, A major]
Solo Pno.-2,2,2,2-2,2-Timp.-Str.
Breitkopf & Härtel, Leipzig [n.d.]
Score 34 p.
*Composed before 1831. First performance
probably Warsaw, the composer as soloist.*

453p [Grand polonaise brilliant, Op. 22,   *15'*
E-flat major]
Solo Pno.-2,2,2,2-2Hn.-B.Tbn.-Timp.-Str.
Kalmus, New York [n.d.]
Score 27 p.
*Composed 1831-32. First performance Paris,
1834, F. A. Habeneck conductor.*

448p [Krakowiak, grand concert-rondo,   *14'*
Op. 14, F major]
Solo Pno.-2,2,2,2-2,2-Timp.-Str.
Breitkopf & Härtel, Leipzig [n.d.]
Score 38 p.
*Composed 1827. First performance probably
Warsaw, 1828, the composer as soloist.*

Là ci darem la mano, variations
See: [Variations on Là Ci Darem la Mano,
    Op. 2, B-flat major]

874s [Mazurka no. 7, piano, Op. 7 no. 3,
F minor. Arranged for string orchestra in F-
sharp minor by Mili Balakirev]
Str.
Zimmermann, Leipzig [n.d.]
Score 7 p.

5208 [Nocturne, piano, Op. 9 no. 2,   *4'30"*
E-flat major. Transcribed for orchestra by
Carl Müller-Berghaus]
2(2nd alt. Picc.),2,2,2-4,2,3-Timp.-Str.
Ries & Erler, Berlin [n.d.]
Score 14 p.

740v [Nocturne, piano, Op. 37 no. 1, G minor.
Arranged in E minor for violin and orchestra
by August Wilhelmj]
Solo Vn.-0,1,2,2-2Hn.-Str.
Breitkopf & Härtel, Leipzig [n.d.]
Score 8 p.

6938 [Preludes, piano, Op. 28. No. 6, B   *8'*
minor; No. 7, A major; No. 20, C minor. Transcribed for orchestra by Bernard Morgan]
1.No. 6, B minor   *2'45"*
  1,1,2,1-2Hn.-Cel.-Str.
2.No. 7, A major   *1'50"*
  1,1,2,1-2Hn.-Cel.-Str.
3.No. 20, C minor   *3'25"*
  2,2,2,2-4,0,3,1-Timp.,Perc.-Cel.-Str.
Ms. c1971 by Bernard Morgan
Score 26 p.
*This transcription 1938. First performance
Philadelphia, 28 December 1938, Philadelphia
Civic Symphony Orchestra, J.W.F. Leman conductor.*

Romanze. Transcribed by August Wilhelmj
See: [Concerto, piano, no. 1, Op. 11, E minor.
    Romanze. Transcribed...]

3076 [Sonata, piano, Op. 35, B-flat minor.   *9'*
3rd movement, Funeral march. Transcribed
anonymously for orchestra]
2,2,2,2-4,2,3-Timp.-Str.
Breitkopf & Härtel, Leipzig [1886]
Score 15 p.
*Apparently the same as the transcription below,
although transcriber is unnamed in this score.*

59 [Sonata, piano, Op. 35, B-flat minor.   *9'*
3rd movement, Funeral march. Transcribed for
orchestra by Gustav Schmidt]
2,2,2,2-4,2,3-Timp.-Str.
Breitkopf & Härtel, Leipzig [n.d.]
Score 15 p.
*This arrangement 1893; first performed Leipzig,
1894.*

2513 [Sonata, piano, Op. 35, B-flat minor.   *9'*
3rd movement, Funeral march. Transcribed for
orchestra by Henry J. Wood]
4*,4*,4*,4*(C.Bn. ad lib.)-6(5th&6th ad lib.),
3,4,1-Timp.(2players, 2nd ad lib.),Perc.-Org.
(ad lib.),2Hp.-Str.
Breitkopf & Härtel, Leipzig [n.d.]
Score 15 p.
*This arrangement first performed Queen's Hall,
London, Queen's Hall Orchestra, Henry J. Wood
conductor.*

1590 [Suite. Orchestrated by Mili Balakirev]
1.[Preamble/Etude, Op. 10 no. 6] 2.Mazurka,
Op. 41 no. 3 3.Intermezzo (Nocturne), Op. 15
no. 3 4.Finale (Scherzo), Op. 39 no. 3
3*,2*,2,2-4,2,3,1-Timp.,Perc.-Hp.-Str.
Zimmermann, Leipzig, c1909
Score 98 p.
Excerpted from various works for piano.

7064 [Suite. Transcribed for orchestra by
Rudolf Herfurth]
1.Präludium (Op. 28 no. 20 *and* Op. 45) 2.
Polonaise (Op. 26 no. 1, C-sharp minor) 3.
Etude (Op. 10 no. 7) 4.Valse (Op. 64 no. 1)
5.Scherzo (Op. 31)
3*,2(2nd alt. E.H.),2,3*-4,2,3,1-Timp.,Small
Bell,Trgl.-Hp.-Str.
Oertel, Hanover [n.d.]

Chopin, Frédéric

Score 122 p.
Excerpted from various works for piano.

495p [Variations on Là Ci Darem la Mano,   *14'*
Op. 2, B-flat major]
Solo Pno.-2,2,2,2-2Hn.-Timp.-Str.
Breitkopf & Härtel, Leipzig [n.d.]
Score 38 p.
*Composed 1827. First performance probably
Warsaw, 1828; subsequent performance Vienna,
11 August 1829, the composer as soloist.*

682m [Waltz, piano, Minute waltz, Op. 64 no. 1,
D-flat major. Transcribed in A-flat major for
flute and orchestra by Emil Prill]
Solo Fl.-2Cl.,Bn.-2Hn.-Str.
Score: Ms. 20 p.
Parts: Zimmermann, Leipzig, c1893

683m [Waltz, piano, Op. 64 no. 3, A-flat
major. Transcribed for flute and orchestra by
Emil Prill]
Solo Fl.-2Cl.,Bn.-2Hn.-Str.
Score: Ms. 26 p.
Parts: Zimmermann, Leipzig, c1893

CHOU WEN-CHUNG.   Chefoo, China 29 June 1923

5341 And the fallen petals, a triolet for   *9'*
orchestra
2(both alt. Picc.),2(2nd alt. E.H.),3*,2-4,2,
3,1-Timp.,Perc.-Cel.,Hp.-Str.
Ms. c1955 by C. F. Peters, New York
Score 47 p. Large folio
*The title is a line from a poem by Meng Hao-jan
(689-740). Commissioned by the Louisville
Orchestra. Composed 1954. First performance
Louisville, 9 February 1955, Robert Whitney
conductor.*

6724 Seven poems of T'ang Dynasty, for   *10'*
tenor voice, seven wind instruments, piano
and percussion
Solo Tenor Voice-1(alt. Picc.),1,1,1-1,1,1-
Perc.-Pno.
New Music Edition, New York, c1952
Score 36 p.
*Texts by Wang Wei (699-759), Liu Yü-hsi (772-
842), Chia Tao (788-843), Li Po (705-762),
Liu Tsung-yuan (773-819), and Liu Ch'ang-
ch'ing (710?-780?), translated by Louise Varèse
in collaboration with the composer. Composed
1951-52. First performance New York City, 16
March 1952.*

227m Soliloquy of a bhiksuni, for trumpet   *5'*
with brass and percussion ensemble
Solo Tpt.-4Hn.,3Tbn.,Tuba-Perc.
C. F. Peters, New York, 1961
Score 12 p.
*Based upon a scene from a 16th century Chinese
drama. A bhiksuni is a Buddhist nun. Composed
1958.*

6179 Two miniatures from T'ang, for chamber   *5'*
ensemble
2,0,1-Hn.-Perc.-Pno.,Hp.-Str.(no Cb.)
Composers Facsimile Edition, New York, c1957

by Chou Wen-chung
Score 20 p.
*Commissioned by Sarah Lawrence College. Com-
posed 1957.*

CHRISTIANSEN, CARL.   Amsterdam 1890
   1947

5144 [The toy box, suite for wind instru-   *11'*
ments]
1.Humoresque: Allegretto 2.Menuett: Andante
3.Pacific 123: Allegro 4.Pastoral: Andante
tranquillo 5.Tennsoldaternas marsch (Tin
soldiers march): Vivo allegro
2,1,2,2-2,1,1
Carl Gehrmans, Stockholm, c1938
Score 11 p.

CHVÁLA, EMANUEL.   Prague 1 January 1851
   Prague 28 October 1924

369s Sousedské [Folk-dances, in chamber style]
Str.(without Cb.)
F. A. Urbánek, Prague [n.d.]
Score 14 p.

CHWATAL, FRANZ XAVER. Rumburg, Bohemia 19 June 1808
   Soolbad, Elmen, Bohemia 24 June 1879

6180 [A merry sleigh ride, Op. 193. A musical
scherzo for piano 4-hands and various chil-
dren's instruments]
Tpt.-Schweinblasium(Hog's Bladder),2Comb Tpt.,
Dr.,Trgl.,Whip,2Sleighbells,Wineglasses,2Pop-
guns,Cast.,Sleigh(Sheet Iron)-Pno.
Litolff, Braunschweig [n.d.]
Score 24 p.

CIAJA, AZZOLINO BERNARDINO DELLA.
See: DELLA CIAJA, AZZOLINO BERNARDINO.

CIARDI, CESARE.   Florence 29 June 1818
   St. Petersburg 24 June 1877

576m Il carnevale di Venezia [Carnival of   *10'*
Venice], scherzo, Op. 22
Solo Fl.-Str.
Score: Ms. 18 p.
Parts: Ricordi, Milan [n.d.]

CIMAROSA, DOMENICO.
   Aversa, near Naples 17 December 1749
   Venice 11 January 1801

6423 Artemisia. Sinfonia dell'opera.   *7'*
Revised by Alceo Toni
0,2,2,2-2,2-Str.
Carisch, Milan, c1957
Score 22 p.
*From the unfinished opera, only 2 of 3 acts
completed with libretto by "Jamejo Cratisto,"
pseudonym for Count Giovanni Battista Colloredo.
Composed 1801.*

5731 Le astuzie femminili [Feminine wiles]
Ouverture. Elaborated by Alceo Toni
0,2,2,2-2Hn.-Str.
Carisch, Milan, c1957

Score 14 p.
From the two-act opera with libretto by Giovanni Palomba. Composed 1794.

1591 La Cimarosiana, 5 symphonic   15'
fragments. Arranged by G. Francesco Malipiero
3*,2,2,2-4,2-Timp.,Perc.-Str.
J.&W. Chester, London, c1927
Score 53 p.
Arranged 1921; reorchestrated 1921. First performance Paris, 1922, Ballet Russe.

5733 Giannina e Bernardone. Sinfonia.   6'
Revised by Alceo Toni
2Ob.-2Hn.-Timp.-Str.
Carisch, Milan, c1957
Score 28 p.
From the opera in 2 acts with libretto by Filippo Livigni. Composed 1781.

5725 Il giorno felice [The happy day]   4'
Ouverture. Elaborated by Alceo Toni
0,2,2,2-2,2-B.Dr.-Str.
Carisch, Milan, c1957
Score 16 p.
Overture to the cantata. Composed 1775.

3012 [Horace. Overture]
1,2,2,2-2,2-Str.
Ms.
Score 33 p.
Composed about 1794; probably the same work as Gli Orazii e Curiazii.

4663 L'impresario in angustie. Ouverture.
Arranged by Adam Carse
2,2,0,2-2,2-Timp.-Str.
Augener, London, c1946
Score 11 p.
From the opera in one act with libretto by Giuseppe Maria Diodati. Composed 1786.

4903 L'italiana in Londra [The Italian   4'
girl in London] Overture. Arranged and edited
by Robert Barclay
2,2,2,2-2,2-Timp.-Str.
Ms. c1952 by Robert Barclay
Score 30 p.
From the opera in 2 acts with libretto by Giuseppe Petrosellini. Composed 1778. First performance Rome, 1 January 1780.

6380 Il maestro di cappella. Ouverture.   4'
Edited by Alceo Toni
2,2,0,2-2Hn.-Timp.-Str.
Carisch, Milan, c1962
Score 12 p.

5751 Il matrimonio per raggiro [Marriage   6'
through trickery] Sinfonia. Edited by Alceo
Toni
0,2,0,2-2Hn.-Str.
Carisch, Milan, c1957
Score 28 p.
Opera originally titled L'Apprensivo Raggirato. Composed 1798. First performance Naples, 1798.

2288 Il matrimonio segreto [The secret   2'
marriage] Sinfonia
2,2,2,2-2,2-Timp.-Str.
Carisch, Milan, c1940
Score 25 p.
From the opera first performed Vienna, 7 February 1792.

5736 I nemici generosi [The gallant adversaries]
Sinfonia. Edited by Nino Negrotti
2,2,2,2-2,2-Timp.-Str.
Carisch, Milan, c1949
Score 12 p.
From the opera in two acts, composed 1795. First performance Rome, 26 December 1795. Revised 1797 as Il Duello Complimento.

6378 Penelope. Sinfonia dell'opera.   7'
Revised by Nino Negrotti
2,2,2,2-2,2-Timp.-Str.
Carisch, Milan, c1944
Score 42 p.
From the opera in 2 acts. Composed 1794.

6422 Le trame deluse [Frustrated plans] 3'30"
Sinfonia dell'opera. Edited by Alceo Toni
0,2,0,2-2Hn.-Str.
Carisch, Milan, c1957
Score 18 p.
From the opera in 2 acts. Composed 1786.

CIRRI, GIOVANNI BATTISTA.
                    Forlì, Italy 1 October 1724
                    Forlì, Italy 11 June 1808

413c [Concerto, violoncello and strings,   12'
Op. 14 no. 1, A major. Revised by Giorgio
Federico Ghedini]
1.Allegro maestoso 2.Adagio cantabile 3.Tempo
di minuetto
Solo Vc.-Str.
Ricordi, Milan, c1959
Score 40 p.
Composed as one of 6 concerti in Op. 14.

CLAASSEN, ARTHUR.
                    Stargard, Prussia 19 February 1859
                    San Francisco 16 March 1920

243s Sanssouci, minuet, Op. 1
Str.
Luckhardt, Berlin, c1890 by G. Schirmer
Score 5 p.
Based on a theme by Quantz.

758s Walzer-Idylle, Op. 11
1.Andante [Dusk] 2.Presto and andantino
[Rustic dance and parting]
Str.
G. Schirmer, New York, c1885
Score 15 p.

CLAFLIN, AVERY. Keene, New Hampshire 21 June 1898

3423 Chapter III, a symphony   48'
1.Maestoso e pòi allegro 2.Adagio 3.Allegro
vivace 4.Andante molto ritenuto
3(3rd alt. Picc.),3*,3(3rd alt. B.Cl.),3*-4,3,

Claflin, Avery

3,1-Timp.,Perc.-Hp.-Str.
Ms.
Score 310 p.
*Composed 1936-40. First performance (of
third movement only) Sioux City, Iowa, 17
January 1944, Sioux City Orchestra, Henri
Pensis conductor.*

6601 Fishhouse punch   5'
3(3rd alt. Picc.),3*,3*,3*-4,3,3,1-Timp.,Trgl.,
Cym.-Hp.-Str.
Composers Facsimile Edition, New York, c1956
by Avery Claflin
Score 65 p.
*Composed 1947-48. First performance Vienna,
1955, Vienna Orchestra, F. Charles Adler
conductor.*

CLAPP, PHILIP GREELEY.
                    Boston, Massachusetts 4 August 1888
                    Iowa City, Iowa 9 April 1954

354p [Concerto, 2 pianos and orchestra, B minor]
1.Lively 2.Very slow 3.Lively
2Solo Pno.-3(3rd alt. Picc.),2,2,2-4,3,3,1-
Timp.,Perc.-Str.
Ms.
Score 179 p. Large folio
*Originally composed as a concerto for one piano
1922. Revised 1936. Arranged for two pianos
in 1941. First performance of this version
Iowa City, Iowa, 20 December 1945, University
of Iowa Symphony Orchestra, the composer conducting, Norma Cross and Marshall Barnes
soloists.*

479m Dramatic poem for trombone and orchestra
1.Broad 2.Moderate 3.Not too fast
Solo Tbn.-3*,2(2nd alt. E.H.),2,3*-4,3,3,1-
Timp.,Perc.-Hp.-Str.
Ms.
Score 61 p.
*Composed in two movements 1912. First per-
formance Cambridge, Massachusetts, 1912,
Pierian Sodality Orchestra, the composer con-
ducting, Modeste Alloo soloist. Revised,
with a third movement added 1940.*

5377 A fanfare prelude   6'30"
4Hn.,3Tpt.,3Cnt.,2Fluegelhn.,4Tbn.,2Bar.,2Tuba
Ms.
Score 47 p. Large folio
*Commissioned by the State College Brass Choir
of Santa Barbara, California. Composed 1940.
First performance Santa Barbara, 1940, State
College Brass Choir, Maurice Faulkner con-
ductor.*

454c Fantasy on an old plain chant, for
violoncello and orchestra
1.Rhapsody 2.Dance
Solo Vc.-3*,2,2,2-4,2,3,1-Timp.,Perc.-Str.
Ms.
Score 92 p.
*Composed 1937-38; revised 1939. First per-
formance Iowa City, Iowa, 1940, University of
Iowa Symphony Orchestra, Hans Koelbel soloist.*

5417 A highly academic diversion on seven notes
1.Allegro 2.Variazione 3.Scherzo 4.Rondo:
Afternoon tea
1,1,2,1-2,2,1-Timp.,Perc.-Hp.-Str.
Ms.
Score 80 p.
*Composed 1931. First performance Iowa City,
Iowa, 1933, Chicago Little Symphony, George
Dasch conductor.*

5488 A hill rhapsody
3*,3*,3*,3*-4,2,3,1-Timp.,Perc.-Cel.,2Hp.-Str.
Ms.
Score 98 p. Large folio
Composed 1945; revised 1947.

5321 Overture to a comedy
3*,3*,3*,3*-4,3,3,1-Timp.,Perc.-Hp.-Str.
Ms.
Score 44 p. Large folio
*Composed 1937. First performance Cleveland,
Ohio, 1940, Cleveland Philharmonic Orchestra,
Karl Grossman conductor.*

5339 Prologue to a tragedy
3(3rd alt. Picc.),3*,3*,3*-4,3,3,1-Timp.,Perc.
-Hp.-Str.
Ms.
Score 63 p. Large folio
Composed 1939.

5370 A song of youth (after Hermann Hagedorn's
poem, A troop of the guard)
3(3rd alt. Picc.),3*,3*,3*-6,3,3,Euph.,Tuba-
Timp.,Perc.-Org.,2Hp.-Str.
Ms.
Score 137 p. Large folio
Composed 1909; revised 1950 and 1955.

6932 Summer, prelude for orchestra
3(3rd alt. Picc.),3*,4*(1Cl. in E-flat),3-4,3,
3,1-Timp.,Perc.-Hp.-Str.
Ms.
Score 69 p.
*Composed 1912. First performance Cambridge,
Massachusetts, 1912, Pierian Sodality Orchestra
of Harvard University. Revised 1917-18, and
1925. First performance of complete revised
version, Chicago, 1927, Chicago Symphony
Orchestra, Frederick Stock conductor.*

5337 Symphony no. 1, E major
1.Allegro 2.Adagio: Slow, broad 3.Scherzo:
Energetic, moderately quick 4.Finale: Majestic,
not slow
3*,3*,3*,2-4,4,3,1-Timp.,Perc.-Hp.-Str.
Ms.
Score 506 p. in 4 volumes
*Composed 1907-08; revised 1932. First perform-
ance Waterloo, Iowa, 27 April 1933, Waterloo
Symphony Orchestra, Edward Kurtz conductor.*

6933 [Symphony no. 3, E-flat major]
1.Allegro con spirito 2.Andante agitato quasi
allegro moderato 3.Allegretto grazioso
4*,4*,5*(1Cl. in E-flat),5*-8(4 alt. 4Small
Tuba),5,4,1-Timp.,Perc.-Org.,2Hp.-Str.
Ms.

Score 187 p. Large folio
*Composed 1916-17. First performance Boston, 6
April 1917, Boston Symphony Orchestra, the
composer conducting. Revised 1936, 1941, 1944.
This work is the 1944 version.*

5324 Symphony no. 5, D major
1.Moderate 2.Not too fast 3.Lively, energetic
3(3rd alt. Picc.),2,2,2-4,3,3,1-Timp.,Perc.-
Str.
Ms.
Score 84 p.
*Composed 1926; revised 1941. First performance
Iowa City, Iowa, 26 July 1944, University of
Iowa Orchestra, the composer conducting.*

3909 [Symphony no. 6, A Golden Gate   *40'*
symphony]
1.Sea and sky 2.Night 3.The city
4(3rd&4th alt. Picc.),3*,4*(1Cl. in E-flat),3*
-6,3,B.Tpt.,3,1,Euph.-Timp.,Perc.-Org.,Cel.,
2Hp.-Str.
Ms.
Score 148 p. Large folio
Composed 1927-28.

3901 [Symphony no. 7, A major]   *38'*
1.Slow but not dragging 2.Very lively
3.Quiet, not too slow
3(3rd alt. Picc.),2,3,3*-4,3,3,1-Timp.,Perc.-
2Hp.-Str.
Ms.
Score 211 p. Large folio
*Composed 1927-29. First performance Boston, 22
March 1931, People's Symphony Orchestra, the
composer conducting.*

5991 Symphony no. 8, C major   *22'*
1.Brisk, energetic 2.Quiet, slow without
dragging 3.Lively
4(3rd and 4th alt. Picc.),3*,4*,3*-4,4,3,Euph.,
Tuba-Timp.,Perc.-Org.(optional),Cel.,2Hp.-Str.
Ms.
Score 164 p. Large folio
*Composed 1929-30; revised 1934, 1937, 1947,
1950. First performance New York, 7 February
1952, New York Philharmonic Orchestra, Dimitri
Mitropoulos conductor.*

5383 [Symphony no. 9, The pioneers, E-flat
minor]
1.Lively 2.Moderate march time
4*,3(3rd alt. E.H.),4*,4*-4,4,3,Euph.,Tuba-
Timp.,Perc.-Hp.-Str.
Ms.
Score 108 p. Large folio
*Commissioned for the Chicago World's Fair,
1933. First performance Iowa City, Iowa, at
the Iowa City Centennial, 1939, University of
Iowa Symphony Orchestra, the composer conducting.*

5325 [Symphony no. 10, Heroic]
1.Introduction and allegro 2.Scherzo and trio
3.Finale and epilogue
4*(3rd alt. Picc.II),4*,4*,4*-6(5&6 optional),
4,3,Euph.,Tuba-Timp.,Perc.-2Hp.-Str.
Ms.

Score 197 p. Large folio
*Composed 1935-37; revised 1943. First perform-
ance Iowa City, Iowa, 23 May 1951, University
of Iowa Symphony Orchestra, the composer conducting. Written as a tribute to President
Theodore Roosevelt.*

CLARK, ELIZABETH.   Placerville, California 1917

990m [Concerto, flute, Little concerto]   *12'*
1.Allegro 2.Molto moderato 3.Vivace scher-
zando 4.Allegro moderato
Solo Fl.-1*,2(2nd alt. E.H.),2(2nd alt. B.Cl.),
2-4,2,2-Timp.,Perc.-Cel.,Hp.-Str.
Ms.
Score 93 p.
Composed 1938.

974m Larghetto, for English horn and   *7'*
orchestra
Solo E.H.-2,0,2,2-2,2,1-Timp.-Cel.,Hp.-Str.
Ms.
Score 25 p.
*Composed 1941. First performance Rochester,
New York, 3 February 1941, Eastman Little Sym-
phony Orchestra, Frederick Fennell conductor,
Ernest Harrison soloist.*

CLARKE, HENRY LELAND.
   b. Dover, New Hampshire 9 March 1907

6598 Monograph for orchestra   *9'*
In one movement: Adagio - Vivace - Tempo primo
2,2,2,2-2,2,3(Tuba may substitute for Tbn.III)
-Timp.,Perc.-Str.
Composers Facsimile Edition, New York, c1955
by Henry Leland Clarke
Score 36 p. Large folio
*Composed 1952. First performance Los Angeles,
27 May 1955, UCLA Symphony Orchestra, Lukas
Foss conductor.*

6599 Saraband for the golden goose   *4'*
1,1,1,1-1,1,1-Str.
Composers Facsimile Edition, New York, c1957
by Henry Leland Clarke
Score 20 p.
*Suggested by Jakob Grimm's fairy tale, The
Golden Goose. Commissioned by the Bohemians
of Los Angeles. Composed 1957. First performance Hollywood, 18 May 1957, Bohemians' Chamber Orchestra, Frank Hubbell conductor.*

CLARKE, JAMES HAMILTON SMEE.
   Birmingham, England 25 January 1840
   Banstead 9 July 1912

1083s Gavotte in F
Str.
Score: Ms. 8 p.
Parts: [n.p., n.d.]

CLARKE, JEREMIAH.   London ca.1673
   London 1 December 1707

4693 [The prince of Denmark's march, for   *2'*
harpsichord. Transcribed for orchestra by
Richard Bales]

Clausetti, Pietro

1,1,2,1-2,2,1-Timp.-Str.
Ms.
Score 12 p.
*This march, attributed to "Mr. Clarke", first
published in A Choice Collection of Ayres for
the Harpsichord or Spinnett, by John Young,
London, 1700. Listed as no. S125 in Henry
Purcell, 1659-1695: An Analytical Catalogue of
His Music, by Franklin B. Zimmerman.*

CLAUSETTI, PIETRO.　　　Naples 2 January 1904
　　　　　　　　　　　Rome 4 April 1963

4240　[Three dances and finale]　　　　　13'
1.Sarabanda: Andante grave 2.Minuetto I: Allegretto 3.Minuetto II: Andantino moderato 4.
Finale: Pomposo
2,2,2,2-2,2,2-Trgl.-Cel.,Hp.-Str.
G. Ricordi, Milan, c1936
Miniature score 30 p.

CLEMENT, FRANZ JOSEPH.　　　Vienna 1780
　　　　　　　　　　　　　Vienna 1842

Also known as: François Clement

1098v Concertine brillante [for violin and
string orchestra]
Solo Vn.-Str.
Ms.
Score 27 p.

1112v [Concerto, violin]
1.Allegro 2.Adagio 3.Rondo
Solo Vn.-1,2,2,2-2,2-Timp.-Str.
Ms.
Score 106 p.

1107v [Concerto, violin, D minor]
1.Moderato 2.Adagio 3.Rondo: Allegro
Solo Vn.-1,2,2,2-2,2-Timp.-Str.
Ms.
Score 82 p.

1110v Variations [for violin and orchestra,
Op. 1]
Solo Vn.-2Ob.-2Hn.(ad lib.)-Str.
Score: Ms. 24 p.
Parts: Vienna Bureau d'Arts et d'Industrie
[n.p., n.d.]

CLEMENTI, MUZIO.　　　Rome 23 January 1752
　　　　　　　　Evesham, England 10 March 1832

813p [Sonata, piano, Op. 34 no. 1, C major.
Freely arranged for piano and string orchestra
by Robert Barclay]
1.Allegro con spirito 2.Un poco andante quasi
allegretto 3.Finale: Allegro
Solo Pno.-Str.
Ms. c1952 by Robert Barclay

Score 57 p.
*Sonata first published 1795. This arrangement
1951.*

6501 [Symphony, chamber orchestra, Op. 44　15'
no. 1, B-flat major] Edited by Renato Fasano
1.Allegro assai 2.Un poco adagio 3.Minuetto:
Allegretto 4.Allegro assai
2,2,0,1-2Hn.-Str.
G. Ricordi, Milan, c1961
Score 55 p.
*Composed 1786. Originally published as Op. 18;
republished by André in Offenbach as Op. 44.*

6386 [Symphony, chamber orchestra, Op. 44　17'
no. 2, D major] Edited by Renato Fasano
1.Grave 2.Andante 3.Minuetto un poco allegro
2,2,0,1-2Hn.-Str.
G. Ricordi, Milan, c1959
Score 56 p.
*Composed 1786. Originally published as Op. 18;
republished by André in Offenbach as Op. 44.*

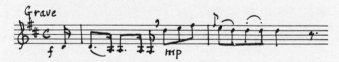

3925 [Symphony no. 1, C major. Tyson　　22'
WO 32. Reconstructed and completed by Alfredo
Casella]
1.Larghetto - Allegro vivace 2.Andante con
moto 3.Menuetto 4.Finale
2,2,2,2-2,2,3-Timp.-Str.
Ricordi, Milan, c1936
Miniature score 122 p.
*Originally composed between 1813 and 1825.
Completed by Alfredo Casella, 1935. First
performance Turin, Italy, 13 December 1935,
Alfredo Casella conductor.*

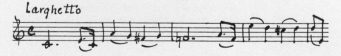

3921 [Symphony no. 4, D major. Tyson　　25'
WO 35. Revised by Alfredo Casella]
1.Introduzione e allegro vivace 2.Larghetto
cantabile 3.Minuetto pastorale 4.Finale

2,2,2,2-2,2,3-Timp.-Str.
Ricordi, Milan, c1936
Miniature score 130 p.
Originally composed 1819. This version, 1936.
First performance, the Augusteo, Rome, 5
January 1936, Alfredo Casella conductor.

CLEMUS, S. B. pseudonym.
See: SCHULTZE-BIESANTZ, CLEMENS.

CLEUVER, J.

275s [Suite, in 4 movements, G minor]
1.Praeludium 2.Andante sostenuto 3.Scherzo
4.Allegro energico
Str.
Oppenheimer, Hameln, c1904
Score 24 p.

CLEVE, HALFDAN.   Kongsberg, Norway 5 October 1879
                    Oslo 6 April 1951

509p [Concerto, piano, no. 1, Op. 3,   *29'*
A major]
1.Allegro risoluto energico 2.Andante tran-
quillo 3.Scherzo 4.Finale
Solo Pno.-2,2,2,2-4,2,3,1-Timp.,Trgl.-Str.
Breitkopf & Härtel, Leipzig, c1902
Score 152 p.
Composed 1898-1901. First performance Berlin,
21 March 1902.

570p [Concerto, piano, no. 2, Op. 6,   *25'*
B-flat minor]
1.Allegro moderato e maestoso 2.Adagio 3.
Finale: Allegro risoluto
Solo Pno.-2,2,2,2-4,2,3-Timp.-Str.
Breitkopf & Härtel, Leipzig, c1904
Score 97 p.
Composed 1903-04. First performance Chris-
tiania, 15 October 1904, Ivar Holter con-
ductor.

576p [Concerto, piano, no. 3, Op. 9,   *27'*
E-flat major]
1.Allegro energico 2.Andante tranquillo 3.
Scherzo 4.Finale: Allegro comodo
Solo Pno.-Str.
Breitkopf & Härtel, Leipzig, c1907
Score 75 p.
Completed 20 January 1906. First performance
Christiania, 6 October 1906, the composer con-
ducting.

6101 [Three pieces for orchestra, Op. 14]   *11'*
1.Preludium: Andante moderato 2.Elegie
(Traum): Lento 3.Humoreske: Allegretto
3(3rd alt. Picc.),2,2,2-4,2-Timp.,Trgl.,Cym.-
Hp.-Str.
Norsk Musikforlag, Oslo, Norway, c1953
Score 24 p.
First performance Oslo, 1915.

CLIFFORD, JULIAN.   London 28 September 1877
                      Hastings 27 December 1921

660s Midge, pizzicato pour orchestre à cordes
Str.
Score: Ms. 5 p.
Parts: Boosey, London, c1922

CLUZEAU-MORTET, LUIS.   Montevideo 16 November 1889
                         Montevideo 28 September 1957

3383 Llanuras [Plains] primera impresión   *9'*
sinfónica nativa
3*,2,2,2-4,4,3,1-Timp.-Cel.,Hp.-Str.
Marotti, Montevideo, c1934
Score 30 p.
Composed 1932. Awarded a performance in a
competition of symphonic works, sponsored by
the Servicio Oficial de Difusión Radio-
Eléctrica, Montevideo, 1932. First performance
Montevideo, 14 October 1933, Symphonic Orches-
tra of the SODRE, Lamberto Baldi conductor.

COATES, ERIC.
        Hucknall, Nottinghamshire 27 August 1886
                Chichester 21 December 1957

2034 Miniature suite   *13'*
1.Children's dance 2.Intermezzo 3.Scène du
bal
3*,2,2,2-2Hn.-Timp.,Perc.-Str.
Boosey, London, c1911
Score 67 p.
Composed 1910. First performance London, 1911,
the composer conducting.

1278 [Suite] From the country-side   *13'*
1.In the meadows, early morning 2.Among the
poppies, afternoon 3.At the fair, evening
2(2nd alt. Picc.),1,2,2-2,0,2Cnt.,-3-Timp.,Perc.
-Hp.-Str.
Hawkes, London, c1915
Score 76 p.
Composed 1915. First performance London, 1915,
the composer conducting.

CODA, CH.

1182s Exaltation [love-poem]
Str.
Score: Ms. 5 p.
Parts: Decourcelle, Nice, c1919

1079s Remembrance
Solo Vn.-Str.
Score: Ms. 5 p.
Parts: Decourcelle, Nice, c1924

CODIVILLA, FILIPPO.

3812 Ottetto
1.Allegro moderato 2.Andantino 3.Minuetto
4.Allegro moderato
1,1,1,1-2Hn.,Cnt.,Tbn.
Pizzi, Bologna, c1919
Miniature score 59 p.

Coedès-Mongin, A.

COEDÈS-MONGIN, A.

    5268 [Two pieces for orchestra]
      1.Nocturne, Op. 14 no. 1 2.Gigue, Op. 6b
      3*,2,2,2-4,2,3-Timp.-Hp.-Str.
      F. Durdilly/Ch. Hayet, Paris, c1913
      Score 40 p.

COENEN, JOHANNES MEINARDUS.
                    The Hague 28 January 1824
                    Amsterdam 9 January 1899

    755m [Concertino, clarinet, B-flat major]
      Solo Cl.-2,2,1,2-4,2,3-Timp.-Str.
      Score: Ms. 58 p.
      Parts: J. G. Seeling, Dresden [n.d.]

COERNE, LOUIS ADOLPHE.
              Newark, New Jersey 27 February 1870
                    Boston 11 September 1922

    6826 Excalibur, symphonic poem, Op. 180   10'
      3(3rd alt. Picc.),3*,3*,3*-4,3,3,1-Timp.,Perc.
      -Org.,2Hp.-Str.
      Ditson, Boston, c1931
      Score 59 p.
      *Suggested by an Arthurian legend as compiled
      by Thomas Malory and Alfred Tennyson. Com-
      posed 1921. First performance San Francisco,
      23 June 1931, San Francisco Symphony Orches-
      tra, Walter Damrosch conductor.*

COHN, ARTHUR.   Philadelphia 6 November 1910

    1899s Bet it's a boy, Op. 38. Music for   16'
      film slides made from the book of the same
      name by Betty Bacon Blunt
      Pno.-Str.(without Cb.)
      Ms.
      Score 134 p.
      *Commissioned by J. Gershon Cohen. Composed
      1941. According to the composer, the work
      may be performed with or without film slides.*

    999m [Concerto, flute, Op. 37]   45'
      1.Allegro con brio 2.Scherzo and 7 ostinati
      3.Interlude alla Kaddisch 4.Variations and
      codetta
      Solo Fl.-3*,3*,3*(2nd alt. Cl. in E-flat),3*-
      Alto Sax.-4,3,3,1-Timp.,Perc.-Cel.,Hp.-Str.
      Ms.
      Score 321 p. Large folio
      *Written at the suggestion of William Kincaid,
      1941.*

    1000m [Concerto, quintuple, for ancient   50'
      instruments, Op. 31]
      1.Non troppo allegro ed eroico 2.Pragmatic
      variations 3.Agitato e deciso
      Soli: Hpscd.,Descant Viol,Va. d'Amore,Va. da
      Gamba,Bass Viol-3*,3*,3*,3*-4,3,3,1-Timp.,
      Perc.-Cel.,Hp.-Str.
      Ms.
      Score 182 p. Large folio
      *Composed 1939-40, for the American Society of
      Ancient Instruments.*

    1737s Four preludes for string orchestra, 19'
      Op. 27

      1.Allegro giusto 2.Moderato 3.Lento assai
      4.Presto giojante
      Str.
      Ms.
      Score 63 p.
      *Composed 1936-37. First performance Federal
      Theatre of Music, New York, 26 May 1937,
      Greenwich Concert Orchestra of the WPA Federal
      Music Project of New York City, the composer
      conducting.*

    3520 Four symphonic documents, Op. 30   32'
      1.Oppression 2.Dictators 3.Exiles 4.----
      3*,3*,3*,3*-4,3,3,1-Timp.,Perc.-Cel.,Hp.-Str.
      Ms.
      Score 159 p. Large folio
      *Composed 1939. On the day the fourth movement
      was finished, Poland was invaded by the Nazis,
      impelling the composer to erase the title of
      that movement and to abandon thought of
      giving it a title. Won fifth place and a per-
      formance in a nationwide contest for American
      compositions instituted by the National Sym-
      phony Orchestra of Washington, D.C., 1941.*

    1859s Histrionics (A set of six pieces)   26'
      for large string orchestra, Op. 32
      1.Prattle 2.Oriental design 3.Dirge 4.Leaf
      flight 5.Execration 6.Dynamo
      Str.
      Ms.
      Score 136 p.
      *Originally composed as a string quartet
      titled Histrionics, Fourth String Quartet, Op.
      24 (1935). Arranged for large string orches-
      tra, 1939.*

    3413 Music for brass instruments, Op. 9 5'30"
      1.Andante 2.Moderato 3.Maestoso e mesto
      4.Allegro 5.Energico 6.Moderato e maestoso
      4Tpt.(or Hn.,3Tpt.),3Tbn.
      Ms.
      Score 39 p.
      *Composed 1934; revised 1939. First perform-
      ance Federal Music Theatre, New York, 26 May
      1937, members of the brass section of the
      Greenwich Concert Orchestra of the WPA Federal
      Music Project of New York City, the composer
      conducting.*

    1700s Retrospections for string orchestra, 20'
      Op. 11
      1.Night landscape 2.Drollery 3.Procession
      4.Profane chant
      Str.
      Ms.
      Score 41 p.
      *Composed 1933-34. First performance of first
      and third movements only, Philadelphia, 3
      April 1935, Chamber Orchestra of Philadelphia
      and Composers' Laboratory, Isadore Freed
      conductor.*

    1152v Suite, for viola and orchestra,   25'
      Op. 28
      1.Prelude 2.Hebrew ritual 3.Toil 4.Nocturne
      5.Burlesque dance
      Solo Va.-3*,3*,3*,3*-4,3,3-Timp.,Perc.-Cel.,

Hp.-Str.
Ms.
Score 171 p. Large folio
Composed 1938-39.

COHN, JAMES.   Newark, New Jersey 12 February 1928

235p Concertino in G-sharp for piano and   22'
orchestra [Op. 8]
1.Moderato - Allegro con brio 2.Molto allegro
- Andante - Molto allegro 3.Andante - Presto,
con anima - Meno mosso - Allegro con brio 4.
Moderato, ma con moto
Solo Pno.-2(both alt. Picc.),2,2,2-2Hn.-Timp.,
S.Dr.,Cym.-Str.
Ms. c1955 by James Cohn
Score 138 p. Large folio
Composed 1946.

172m Concerto in A, for concertina and   15'
string orchestra [Op. 44]
1.Capriccio: Allegretto 2.Romanza: Andante
espressivo 3.Rondo: Presto, con fuoco
Solo Concertina(or Vn.,or Xyl.,or Marimba)-Str.
Ms. c1966 by James Cohn
Score 40 p.
Commissioned by Alan Atlas. Composed 1966.

7254 Homage   6-7'
1(alt. Picc.),1,1,1-Alto Sax.-1,1,1-Timp.,
Perc.-Str.
Ms. c1959 by James Cohn
Score 12 p. Large folio
*Composed 1959. First performance Middletown,
Ohio, 13 November 1960, Middletown Civic Sym-
phony Orchestra, Valda Wilkerson conductor.
Contains quotations from The Star Spangled
Banner.*

2382s Israfel, a song, Op. 24   3'
Solo Tenor(or Sop.)Voice-Str.
Ms. c1954 by James Cohn
Score 10 p.
The poem by Edgar Allan Poe. Composed 1954.

2387s Music for strings [Op. 14-A]   15'
1.Adagio 2.Allegro 3.Adagio commodo - Allegro
marcato
Str.
Ms. c1950 by James Cohn
Score 13 p. Large folio
*Originally composed as String Quartet no. 2,
1950. Arranged for string orchestra 1955 and
first performed Provincetown, Massachusetts,
14 August 1955, Provincetown Symphony, Joseph
Hawthorne conductor.*

7256 Sinfonietta in F   13'30"
1.Allegro ma non troppo 2.Andante 3.Vivo
1(alt. Picc.),1,2,1-2Hn.-Timp.,Glock.-Str.
Ms. c1955 by James Cohn
Score 98 p. Large folio
Composed 1946.

7255 Symphony no. 1 in E-flat [Op. 11]   17'
1.Allegro 2.Andante con moto 3.Andante con
moto - Molto vivace - Allegretto moderato -
Allegretto vivace - Presto e con fuoco

4.Andante commodo - Allegretto, alla marcia
1(alt. Picc.),1,2,2*-Alto Sax.,Bar.Sax.-2,1,2,1
-Timp.,Perc.-Str.
Ms. c1954 by James Cohn
Score 92 p. Large folio
Composed 1947.

7257 Symphony no. 2 in F [Op. 13]   23'
1.Allegro 2.Presto 3.Andante con moto 4.Alle-
gro marcato
2*,2*,3*,2*-Alto Sax.-2,1,2,1-Timp.,Perc.-Str.
Ms. c1949 by James Cohn
Score 65 p. Large folio
*Composed 1949. First performance Palais des
Beaux Arts, Brussels, Belgian National Radio
Orchestra, Franz André conductor. Awarded a
Queen Elisabeth of Belgium Prize, December 1953.*

COLE, ROSSETTER GLEASON.
                Clyde, Michigan 5 February 1866
                Lake Bluff, Illinois 18 May 1952

626c Ballade, Op. 25
Solo Vc.-2,2,2,2-3,2-Timp.-Str.
G. Schirmer, New York, c1908
Score 18 p.

3633 Heroic piece, Op. 39   8'
3(3rd alt. Picc.),2,2,2-4,2,3,1-Timp.,Perc.-
Org.(ad lib.),Hp.-Str.
Ms.
Score 48 p.
*Originally composed for orchestra and organ,
1923; revised for orchestra alone, 1938. First
performance Chicago, 14 May 1939, Illinois
Symphony Orchestra of the WPA, Izler Solomon
conductor.*

3810 [The maypole lovers. Suite]   20'
1.Prelude and finale (Act I) 2.Roger's
monologue (Act I) 3.Dance (Act II)
3(3rd alt. Picc.),3*,3*,3*-4,2,3,1-Timp.,Perc.
-Hp.-Str.
Ms.
Score 135 p.
*This suite is a concert arrangement from the
opera in three acts. Composed 1919-27.
Orchestrated 1931. First performance Chicago,
9 January 1936, Chicago Symphony Orchestra,
Frederick Stock conductor.*

2592 Overture, Pioneer (1818-1918), dedi-   13'
cated to the memory of Abraham Lincoln, Op. 35
3(3rd alt. Picc.),3*,2,3*-4,3,3,1-Timp.,Perc.-
Org.,Hp.-Str.
Ms.
Score 88 p.
*Composed 1918, at the suggestion of Frederick
Stock, in commemoration of the Illinois State
Centennial. First performance Chicago, 14
March 1919, Chicago Symphony Orchestra, the
composer conducting.*

2591 Symphonic prelude, Op. 28   8'
3*,2,2,2-4,3,3,1-Timp.,Perc.-Org.(ad lib.),
Hp.-Str.
Ms.
Score 47 p.

Cole, Ulric

*Originally composed for organ under the title
Fantaisie Symphonique, 1911; orchestrated
1914. First performance Chicago, 11 March
1915, Chicago Symphony Orchestra, Glenn Dillard Gunn conductor.*

COLE, ULRIC.   New York City 9 September 1905

748p [Concerto, piano]   *23'*
1.Andante – Allegro con brio 2.Moderato
3.Andantino 4.Allegro deciso
Solo Pno.-3*,3*,2(2nd alt. B.Cl.),3*-4,2,3,1-
Timp.,Perc.-Str.
Ms.
Score 124 p.
Completed 1931.

1817s Two sketches   *7'*
Str.
Ms.
Score 18 p.
*Originally the last 2 movements of String
Quartet no. 1, composed 1932; transcribed 1938.
First performance in a broadcast, New York, 25
May 1938, String Symphony of the Mutual Broad-
casting System, Alfred Wallenstein conductor.*

COLERIDGE-TAYLOR, SAMUEL.   London 15 August 1875
                               Croydon 1 September 1912

1223 [Ballade, Op. 33, A minor]   *12'*
3*,2,2,2-4,2,3,1-Timp.,Cym.-Str.
Novello, London, c1899
Score 63 p.
*Composed for the Gloucester Musical Festival,
1898, and first performed there.*

147 The bamboula, rhapsodic dance, Op. 75   *9'*
3*,2,2,2-4,2,3,1-Timp.,Perc.-Str.
Hawkes & Son, London, c1911
Score 51 p.
*Composed 1909. First performance New York,
June 1910.*

3540 Danse nègre, Op. 35 no. 4
3*,2,2,2-4,2,3-Timp.,Perc.-Str.
Augener, London, c1901
Score 27 p.
*From his African Suite. Originally composed
as a quintet for strings, 1896; revised many
times and published 1898 in present form.*

1274 Four characteristic waltzes, Op. 22   *16'*
1.Valse bohémienne 2.Valse rustique 3.Valse
de la reine 4.Valse mauresque
3*,2,2,2-4,2,3,1-Timp.,Perc.-Str.
Novello, London, c1899
Score 50 p.
*Composed 1897. First performance at the
Promenade Concerts, London, 22 September 1898,
Henry Wood conductor.*

Four novelletten, Op. 52
521s No. 1, A major
539s No. 2, C major
540s No. 3, A minor
541s No. 4, D major

Perc.-Str.(Vn.Solo in No. 3)
Novello, London, c1903
Scores: 12 p., 10 p., 11 p., 14 p.

1765 Hemo dance, scherzo, Op. 47 no. 2   *7'*
3*,2,2,2-4,2,3-Timp.,Perc.-Str.
Ms.
Score 81 p.
Composed 1902.

1763 Hiawatha's wedding feast, orchestral *37'*
selection, Op. 30 no. 1. Arranged by W. G.
Ross
2,1,2,2-2,2,1-Timp.,Perc.-Hp.-Str.
Ms.
Score 81 p.
*Composed 1896. First performance Royal College
of Music, London, 11 November 1898.*

1764 Idyll, Op. 44   *5'*
2,2,2,2-4,2,3,1-Timp.-Hp.-Str.
Ms.
Score 37 p.
*Composed 1900. First performance Gloucester
Festival, 1901, the composer conducting.*

2010 Othello, orchestral suite, Op. 79
1.Dance 2.Children's intermezzo 3.Funeral
march 4.The willow song 5.Military march
3*,2,2,2-4,0,2Cnt.,3-Timp.,Perc.-Str.
Metzler, London, c1912
Score 56 p.
*First performance at His Majesty's Theatre,
London, 1911.*

3268 Petite suite de concert, Op. 77   *18'*
1.Le caprice de Nannette 2.Demande et response
3.Un sonnet d'amour 4.La tarantelle fretillante
3*,2,2,2-4,2,3-Timp.,Perc.-Str.
Boosey & Hawkes, London, c1911
Score 73 p.
Composed ca.1910.

831v [Romance, Op. 39, G major]
Solo Vn.-2,2,2,2-4,2,3,1-Timp.-Str.
Ms.
Score 35 p.

1774 Scenes from an everyday romance,   *12'*
Op. 41
1.Allegro 2.Andante 3.Tempo di valse, molto
moderato 4.Presto
3(3rd alt. Picc.),2,2,2-4,2,3-Timp.,Cym.,B.Dr.
-Hp.-Str.
Ms.
Score 151 p.
*First performance at the Philharmonic Society,
London, 24 May 1900.*

1766 Suite Nero, Op. 62. Incidental music   *24'*
to Stephen Phillips' drama
1.Prelude, Poppaea 2.Intermezzo 3.Eastern
dance 4.Finale
2,2,2,2-4,2,3,1-Timp.,Perc.-Hp.-Str.
Score: Ms. 154 p. in 4 volumes
Parts: Novello, London [n.d.]
*Composed 1905. First performance His Majesty's
Theatre, London, 1906.*

1762 Symphonic variations on an African   20'
air, Op. 63
3*,2(2nd alt. E.H.),2,2-4,2,3,1-Timp.,Perc.-
Hp.-Str.
Ms.
Score 107 p. Large folio
*Composed 1905. First performance London, 14
June 1906, Royal Philharmonic Society, the com-
poser conducting.*

COLIN, MARCEL.

685c Czardas [for violoncello and orchestra]
Solo Vc.-1,1,2,1(or Tbn.)-Tpt.-Timp.-Str.
Score: Ms. 26 p.
Parts: J. Yves, Paris, c1931

695v Danse serbe [by Marcel Colin and Hubert
Mouton]
Solo Vn.-1,1,2,1-2,2,3-Timp.,Perc.-Str.
Score: Ms. 22 p.
Parts: Heugel, Paris, c1917

1650s Rêverie, violoncelle et orchestre à
cordes
Solo Vc.-Str.
Score: Ms. 8 p.
Parts: J. Yves, Paris [n.d.]

1649s Sérénade des amours
Solo Vn.-Str.
Score: Ms. 5 p.
Parts: J. Yves, Paris [n.d.]

COLLINO, FEDERICO. Pinerolo, Italy 17 November 1869

882s Aria di ballo [Dance tune]
Str.
Decourcelle, Nice [n.d.]
Score 7 p.

1306s Berceuse
Fl.,Ob.-Str.
Decourcelle, Paris [n.d.]
Score 5 p.

COLLINS, WALTER R.

4608 Lilliputians, wooden shoe dance   5'
1(alt. Picc.),1,1-0,1,1-Timp.,Perc.-Str.
Schott, London, c1938
Score in reduction 5 p.

COLYNS, JEAN BAPTISTE.   Brussels 25 November 1834
Brussels 31 October 1902

795m [Fantasy, bassoon and string orchestra,
G minor]
Solo Bn.-Str.
Ms.
Score 19 p.

CONRADI, AUGUST.   Berlin 27 June 1821
Berlin 26 May 1873

713m Adagio and rondo [E minor]
Solo Fl.-Picc.,2,2,2-2,2,1-Timp.,Perc.-Str.
Score: Ms. 57 p.
Parts: C.F. Schmidt, Heilbronn [n.d.]

CONSOLO, FEDERIGO.   Ancona, Italy 8 April 1841
Florence 14 December 1906

4579 [On the banks of the Nile]
2,2,2,2-2Hn.-Tamb.-Str.
G. G. Guidi, Florence, 1882
Score 26 p.

CONSTANTINESCU, PAUL. Ploesti, Romania 30 June 1909
Bucharest 20 December 1963

2165s [Concerto for string orchestra]   21'
1.Allegro 2.Intermezzo: Andante appassionato
3.Rondo: Presto
Str.
Editura de Stăt Pentru Literatură si Artă,
Bucharest, 1956
Score 53 p.
*Commissioned by Uniunea Compozitorilor [Roman-
ian Composers' Union]. Originally composed for
string quartet, 1947. This version 1955. First
performance Bucharest, 16 February 1956, Radio
Orchestra Bucharest, Constantin Silvestri conductor.*

CONTRERAS, SALVADOR.   Cuerámaro, Guanajuato,
Mexico 10 November 1912

4143 [Music for symphony orchestra]   12'30"
3*,2,2,2-4,3,3,1-Timp.,Perc.-Str.
Ms.
Score 66 p.
*Composed 1940. First performance Mexico City,
16 August 1940, Orquesta Sinfónica de Mexico,
Carlos Chávez conductor.*

3694 Suite [for chamber orchestra]   16'
1.Allegro 2.Andante expressivo 3.Allegro
Cl.,Bn.-Tpt.-Pno.-Str.
Ms.
Score 43 p.
*Composed 1938. First performance Mexico City,
24 February 1941, Orquesta de Cámara de la
Sección de Radio de la Secreteria de Educación
Pública.*

CONUS, GEORG E.   Moscow 1 October 1862
Moscow September 1933

1646 Carmagnole, Op. 45, [Revolutionary song
and dance of the time of the French Revolution]
3*,2,2,2-4,2,3,1-Timp.,Perc.-Str.
Mussektor, Moscow, 1921
Score 13 p.

253 [The murmuring forest, Op. 30; symphonic
poem based on Korolenko's legend]
3(3rd alt. Picc.),2(1st alt. E.H.),2,2-4,2,3,
1-Timp.,Perc.-Hp.-Str.
Edition Russe de Musique, Berlin, c1909
Score 61 p.

CONUS, JULIUS.   Moscow 1 February 1869
Malenki 3 January 1942

475v [Concerto, violin, E minor]
In one movement
Solo Vn.-3,2,2,2-4,2,3-Timp.-Str.
Jurgenson, Moscow [1898]

Converse, Charles Crozat

Score 65 p.
*First performance Moscow, Ippolitov-Ivanov
conductor, the composer as soloist.*

CONVERSE, CHARLES CROZAT.
Warren, Massachusetts 7 October 1832
Englewood, New Jersey 18 October 1918

6808 [Hail Columbia, American concert overture]
3*,2,2,2-4,2,3,1(ad lib.)-Timp.,B.Dr. & Cym.-
Str.
P. Schott, Paris [n.d.]
Score 58 p.
Composed 1869.

5161 [In the springtime, festival overture]
2,2,2,2-4,2,3-Timp.-Str.
Schuberth, New York, c1913
Score 61 p.
Composed 1870.

CONVERSE, FREDERICK SHEPHERD.
Newton, Massachusetts 5 January 1871
Westwood, Massachusetts 8 June 1940

5820 Adagio for woodwinds and 2 horns
2,2,2,2-2Hn.
Ms.
Score 14 p.
Composed 1897.

2860 American sketches, symphonic suite   45'
for orchestra
1.Manhattan 2.The father of waters 3.Chicken
reel 4.Bright Angel Trail (A legend of the
Grand Canyon of Arizona)
3(3rd alt. Picc.),3*,3*,3*-4,3,3,1-Timp.,Perc.-
Org.,Cel.,2Hp.-Str.
Kalmus, New York, c1937
Miniature score 122 p.
*Composed 1929. First performance Boston, 8
February 1935, Boston Symphony Orchestra, Serge
Koussevitzky conductor.*

5776 Ave et vale [Hail and farewell]   13'
tone poem
3(3rd alt. Picc.),3*,3*,3*-4,3,3,1-Timp.,Perc.-
Hp.-Str.
Ms.
Score 64 p. Large folio
*Composed 1917. First performance St. Louis,
Missouri, 26 January 1917, St. Louis Symphony,
Max Zach conductor.*

5884 California, festival scenes for   13'
orchestra
Victory dance of the first inhabitants (Indian)
- Spanish padres and explorers - The march of
civilization, Coronado and the conquerors -
Land of poco tiempo - Midnight at El Pasco,
1927
3(3rd alt. Picc.),3*,4*(1Cl. in E-flat),3*-4,3,
3,1-Timp.,Perc.-Cel.,2Hp.-Str.
C.C. Birchard, Evanston, Illinois, c1929
Score 84 p. Large folio
*Suggested by scenes at the Fiesta in Santa
Barbara. Composed 1928. First performance
Boston, 6 April 1928, Boston Symphony Orchestra,
Serge Koussevitzky conductor.*

5485 Elegiac poem   18'
3(3rd alt. Picc.),3*,3*,3*-4,3,3,1-Timp.,Perc.
-2Hp.-Str.
Ms.
Score 55 p. Large folio
*Composed 1926. First performance Masonic Hall,
Cleveland, 2 December 1926, Cleveland Orchestra,
Nikolai Sokoloff conductor.*

5198 Endymion's narrative, romance for   15'
orchestra, Op. 10
3(3rd alt. Picc.),3*,2,3*-4,3,3,1-Timp.,Perc.-
Hp.-Str.
H.W. Gray Co., New York, c1909
Score 98 p. Large folio
*After episodes from Keats' Endymion. Composed
1901. First performance Boston, 11 April 1903,
Boston Symphony Orchestra, Wilhelm Gericke con-
ductor.*

5479 [Euphrosyne, overture, Op. 15]
2(2nd alt. Picc.),2,2,2-4,2,3,1-Timp.,Perc.-
Str.
Ms.
Score 64 p.
*Composed 1903. First performance Boston, 28
May 1903, Boston Pops Orchestra.*

323p Fantasy for piano and orchestra
Solo Pno.-3(3rd alt. Picc.),2,2,2-4,3,3,1-
Timp.,Glock.-Str.
Ms.
Score 96 p. Large folio
Composed 1922.

6238 Festival of Pan, romance for   18'
orchestra, Op. 9
3(3rd alt. Picc.),3*,3*,3*-4,3,3,1-Timp.,Perc.
-Hp.-Str.
G. Schirmer, Jr., Boston, c1903
Score 76 p.
*After episodes from Keats' Endymion. Composed
1900. First performance Boston, 22 December
1900, Boston Symphony Orchestra, Wilhelm Gericke conductor.*

1957 Flivver ten million, a joyous epic   12'
3(3rd alt. Picc.),3*,3*,3*-4,3,3,1-Timp.,Perc.
-Org.(or Factory Whistle offstage),Cel.,Hp.-
Str.
C.C. Birchard [n.p.] c1927
Score 63 p.
*Composed 1926. First performance Boston, 15
April 1927, Boston Symphony Orchestra, Serge
Koussevitzky conductor. Written in commemo-
ration of the ten-millionth Ford Model T pro-
duced.*

5833 Haul away, Jo! Variations for small
orchestra upon an American sailors' chantey,
Op. 91 [revised version]
1,1,2,1-2,2,1-Timp.,Glock.,Xyl.-Str.
Ms.
Score 21 p.
Composed for CBS 1939. Revised 1939.

5841   Indian serenade, for small orchestra,
Op. 14 no. 2
2,2,2,2-3Hn.-Hp.-Str.
Ms.
Score 10 p.
*First performance Boston, 8 May 1903, Boston
Pops Orchestra.   For another version see
below, Serenade for String Orchestra.*

5500   Jeanne d'Arc, dramatic scenes for
orchestra, Op. 23
1.Overture: In Domrémy 2.Pastorale reverie
3.Battle hymn 4.Night vision (Vision of St.
Michael) 5.The maid of God
2(2nd alt. Picc.),2(2nd alt. E.H.),2,3*-4,2,3,
1-Timp.,Perc.-Cel.,Hp.-Str.
Ms.
Score 128 p.
*Suite from the incidental music to Percy Mac-
kaye's play, Jeanne d'Arc.   Composed 1906.
First performance of this suite with enlarged
orchestration, Jordan Hall, Boston, 10 January
1907, Wallace Goodrich conductor.*

5494   [Masque of St. Louis, Cahókia. Prelude]
2(2nd alt. Picc.),3*,3*,3*-4,3,3,1-Timp.,Perc.
-Str.
Ms.
Score 63 p.
*The name Cahókia is that given to the mounds
built by the ancient race of the Mound Builders
in southwestern Illinois, near St. Louis,
Missouri.   Commissioned by the St. Louis Masque
and Pageant Society in commemoration of the
150th anniversary of the founding of St. Louis.
Composed 1914.   First performance on Art Hill
in Forest Park, St. Louis, 28 May 1914, by the
Pageant Drama Association.*

5495   [Masque of St. Louis, Cahókia. No. 20]
3*,2,3*,2-4,3,3,1-Timp.,Perc.-Str.
Ms.
Score 6 p.

5496   [Masque of St. Louis, Cahókia. No. 38:
Finale]
2,2,2,3*-4,3,3,1-Timp.,Perc.-Hp.-Str.
Ms.
Score 24 p.

1983   The mystic trumpeter, Op. 19, orchestral
fantasy on the poem by Walt Whitman
3(3rd alt. Picc.),3*,3*,3*-4,3,3,1-Timp.,Perc.
-Hp.-Str.
G. Schirmer, New York, c1907
Score 81 p.
*Composed 1903-04.   First performance Phila-
delphia, 4 March 1905, Fritz Scheel conductor.*

337p   Night *and* Day, two poems for piano and
orchestra, Op. 11
1.Night: Andante molto sostenuto e tranquillo
2.Day: Allegro con fuoco
Solo Pno.-2,3*,3*,3*-4,2,3,1-Timp.,Trgl.-Str.
Boston Music Co., Boston, c1906 by G. Schirmer,
Jr.
Score 89 p.
After two poems of Walt Whitman.   Composed

*1905.   First performance Boston, 21 January
1905, Boston Symphony Orchestra, Wilhelm
Gericke conductor, Heinrich Gebhard soloist.*

5795   Ormazd, symphonic poem for orchestra,   *10'*
Op. 30
3(3rd alt. Picc.),3*,3*,3*-6,3,3,1-Timp.,Perc.
-Pno.,Cel.,Hp.-Str.
H.W. Gray, New York, c1913
Score 92 p. Large folio
*Based on the Bundehesch of the ancient Persians,
as rendered by Percy Mackaye.   Composed 1911.
First performance at the Odeon, St. Louis,
Missouri, 26 January 1912, St. Louis Symphony,
Max Zach conductor.*

426m   Rhapsody for clarinet and orchestra, Op. 105
Solo Cl.-2(2nd alt. Picc.),2,0,2-2,2,1-Timp.-
Hp.-Str.
Ms.
Score 31 p.
Composed 1938.

2593   Scarecrow sketches   *20'*
1.Elegie 2.Romance 3.Witch dance
3(3rd alt. Picc.),2,3*,2-4,3,3,1-Timp.,Perc.-
Pno.,Hp.-Str.
Ms.
Score 47 p.
*Three excerpts from the photo-music-drama,
Puritan Passions, based on Percy Mackaye's
stage play, The Scarecrow.   Commissioned by
the Film Guild, Inc. of New York, 1923.   Com-
posed 1923.   First produced with orchestra in
New York, 14 October 1923, at the Cameo Thea-
ter.   First shown with full orchestra at
Jordan Hall, Boston, 18 December 1923, played
by the New England Conservatory Orchestra,
Wallace Goodrich conductor.*

2140s   Serenade for string orchestra
Str.
Ms.
Score 4 p.

5805   A song at evening
1(alt. Picc.),1,2,1-2,2,1-Cel.(or Pno.),Hp.-
Str.
Ms.
Score 14 p.
Composed 1937.

5504   Song of the sea, tone poem for orchestra
3(3rd alt. Picc.),3*,3*,3*-4,3,3,1-Timp.,Perc.
-Cel.,2Hp.-Str.
Ms.
Score 55 p. Large folio
*After the poem by Walt Whitman, On the Beach
at Night, from Sea-Drift.   Composed 1923.
First performance Boston, 19 April 1924, Boston
Symphony Orchestra, Pierre Monteux conductor.*

5911   [Symphony no. 1, Op. 7, D minor]   *33'*
1.Allegro 2.Andante 3.Scherzo: Allegro molto
e vivace 4.Finale: Allegro con fuoco - Presto
2,2,2,2-4,2,3-Timp.-Str.
Ms.
Score 131 p.

Converse, Frederick

*Composed 1898. First performance Munich, 14
July 1898.*

5406 Symphony no. 2, E minor   *35'*
1.Moderato e maestoso - Allegro con fuoco 2.
Andante espressivo - Allegro molto quasi presto
- Andante espressivo 3.Andante sostenuto molto
- Allegro molto e con fuoco
3(3rd alt. Picc.),3*,3*,3*-4,3,3,1-Timp.,Perc.
-Cel.,Hp.-Str.
Ms.
Score 200 p. Large folio
*Also known as Symphony no. 2, E major. Com-
posed 1922. First performance Boston, 22
April 1922, Boston Symphony Orchestra, Pierre
Monteux conductor.*

5309 Symphony no. 3, F major
1.Larghetto e sostenuto - Allegro appassionato
- Allegro molto e vivace - Largamente e sosten-
uto 2.Adagio espressivo - Adagio maestoso -
Largamente - Maestoso 3.Andante moderato e
sostenuto, poco maestoso - Allegro con fuoco e
giocoso - Misterioso
3(3rd alt. Picc.),3*,3*,3*-4,3,3,1-Timp.-Hp.-
Str.
Ms.
Score 136 p.
Composed 1934.

5419 Symphony no. 6, Op. 107, F minor
1.Andante sostenuto - Allegro con fuoco -
Adagio molto maestoso 2.Adagio sostenuto 3.
Allegretto vivace e marcato 4.Allegro con brio
3(3rd alt. Picc.),3*,3*,3*-4,3,3,1-Timp.,Glock.
-Cel.,Hp.-Str.
Ms.
Score 113 p.
*Composed 1940. First performance Indianapolis,
29 November 1940, Indianapolis Symphony Orches-
tra, Fabien Sevitzky conductor.*

5794 Three old-fashioned dances for chamber
orchestra, Op. 102
1.Minuet: Risoluto 2.Waltz: Molto cantabile
ed espressivo 3.Air de ballet: Allegretto
grazioso
1(alt. Picc.),1,1,1-2,2,1-Timp.,Trgl.-Hp.(or
Pno.)-Str.
Ms.
Score 35 p. Large folio
*Commissioned by the Converse Club. Composed
1938.*

5482 Youth, concert overture, Op. 6
2,2,2,2-2,2,3-Timp.-Str.
Ms.
Score 42 p.
Composed 1897. First performance Munich, 1897.

COOKE, GREVILLE.   London 14 July 1894

1952s Prelude for strings, an English   *9'*
pastoral (Evening over Bemerton, Salisbury)
Solo String Quartet-Str.
Joseph Williams, London, c1940
Score 8 p.
First performance Royal Academy of Music,

*London, the Royal Academy of Music Orchestra,
Herbert Withers conductor.*

COOLEY, CARLTON.   Milford, New Jersey 1898

1827s Eastbourne sketches for string   *10'*
orchestra
1.Promenade 2.The Downs 3.The Punch and Judy
show
Str.
Dimit, New York, c1941
Score 16 p.
*Originally composed for string quartet, 1926;
transcribed for string orchestra, 1941. First
performance broadcast over Station WOR, New
York, 8 March 1942, the Symphonic Strings, Alfred Wallenstein conductor.*

COOLS, EUGÈNE.   Paris 27 March 1877
                   Paris 5 August 1936

1514 La mort de Tintagiles. Prelude, Op. 92 *8'*
0,2*,2,2-2Hn.-Str.
Eschig, Paris, c1920
Score 11 p.
*Composed 1913. First performance Paris, 1913,
the composer conducting.*

1470 Musique pour Hamlet [symphonic   *35'*
fragments] Op. 85
1.Prélude, Act I. Le spectre 2.Prélude, Act
II. Hamlet 3.Prélude, Act III. To be or not
to be 4.Prélude, Act IV. Ophélie 5.Prélude,
Act V. Enterrement d'Ophélie 6.Marche funèbre
d'Hamlet
3,3*,3*,3-4,3,3-Timp.,Perc.-Str.
Eschig, Paris, c1920
Score 84 p.
*Composed 1914. First performance Paris, 1920,
Concerts Colonne, Gabriel Pierné conductor.*

1383 Nos filles reçoivent [Our daughters'   *20'*
reception, orchestral suite] Op. 93
1.[The welcome] 2.[The doll's funeral] 3.[A
marvelous story] 4.[Boys are noisy] 5.[The
rocking-chair] 6.[Let's dance] 7.[Leave-
taking]
2,2(2nd alt. E.H.),2,2-2,2-Timp.,Dr.-Hp.-Str.
Eschig, Paris, c1919
Score 56 p.
*Composed 1919. First performance Paris, 1920,
Concerts Colonne, Gabriel Pierné conductor;
later Ballet d'Enfants with scenario by M.
Frank-Choisy.*

COPLAND, AARON.   Brooklyn 14 November 1900

7248 Appalachian spring (Ballet for   *20'*
Martha). Suite [original version for 13
instruments]
1,0,1,1-Pno.-2Vn.I,2Vn.II,2Va.,1Cb.(composer
authorizes increase of string players to 8,
8,6,4,2)
Boosey & Hawkes, New York, c1945, 1958 by
Aaron Copland; first publication of original
version c1972 by Aaron Copland
Score 66 p.
From the ballet commissioned for Martha Graham

Copland, Aaron

by the Elizabeth Sprague Coolidge Foundation.
*Composed 1943-44 and first performed at the
Library of Congress, Washington, D.C., 30
October 1944, by Martha Graham and her company.
Received the Music Critics Circle of New York
Award for the outstanding theatrical work of
the 1944-45 season.*

6007 Appalachian spring (Ballet for   20'
Martha). Suite from the ballet
2(2nd alt. Picc.),2,2,2-2,2,2-Timp.,Perc.-Pno.,
Hp.-Str.
Boosey & Hawkes, New York, c1945
Score 82 p.
*This orchestral suite arranged 1945. First
performance New York, 4 October 1945, New York
Philharmonic, Artur Rodzinski conductor.
Awarded the Pulitzer Prize for Music, 1945.*

3069 Billy the Kid. Complete ballet   35'
3*(2nd alt. 2nd Picc.),2,2,2-4,3,3,1-Timp.,
Perc.-Pno.,Cel.,Hp.-Str.
Ms.
Score 169 p. Large folio
*Commissioned by the Ballet Caravan, 1938.
Composed 1938. First performance by the Ballet
Caravan, New York, 24 May 1939, Fritz Kit-
zinger conductor.*

4017 Billy the Kid. Suite from the ballet   20'
The open prairie - Street in a frontier town -
Card game at night - Running gun battle -
Celebration on Billy's capture - Billy's
death - The open prairie again
3*(2nd alt. 2nd Picc.),2,2,2-4,3,3,1-Timp.,
Perc.-Pno.,Cel.,Hp.-Str.
Boosey & Hawkes, New York, c1941
Score 94 p.
*Ballet composed 1938; suite arranged 1940.
First performance Boston, 30 January 1942,
Boston Symphony Orchestra, Richard Burgin con-
ductor.*

1068m Concerto, clarinet and string   16'30"
orchestra with harp and piano
In one movement
Solo Cl.-Pno.,Hp.-Str.
Ms.
Score 90 p. Large folio
*Commissioned by Benny Goodman. Composed 1948.
First performance New York, 6 November 1950,
NBC Symphony, Fritz Reiner conductor, Benny
Goodman soloist. In 1951 choreographed as The
Pied Piper by Jerome Robbins for the New York
City Ballet.*

738p [Concerto, piano and orchestra]   18'
1.Andante sostenuto 2.Molto moderato (molto
rubato) - Allegro assai
Solo Pno.-3*,3*,4*,3*-Alto Sax.(alt. Sop.Sax.)-
4,3,3,1-Timp.,Perc.-Cel.-Str.
Cos Cob Press, New York, c1929
Score 67 p.
*Composed 1926, at the suggestion of Serge
Koussevitzky. First performance Boston, 28
January 1927, Boston Symphony Orchestra, Serge
Koussevitzky conductor, the composer as
soloist.*

5037 Danzón cubano   6'
3(2nd alt. Picc.II),3*,3*,3*-4,3,3,1-Timp.,
Perc.-Pno.-Str.
Boosey & Hawkes, New York, c1949
Score 45 p.
*Composed to celebrate the 20th anniversary of
the League of Composers. Originally composed
for two pianos, 1942. Orchestral transcription
first performed Baltimore, 17 February 1946,
Baltimore Symphony Orchestra, Reginald Stewart
conductor.*

4271 Fanfare for the common man
See: TEN FANFARES BY TEN COMPOSERS FOR BRASS
AND PERCUSSION.

3450 John Henry   4'
1,1,2,1-2,2,1-Timp.,Perc.-Str.
Ms.
Score 24 p.
*Commissioned by CBS, 1940. Composed 1940.
First performance broadcast over CBS, New York,
5 March 1940, Columbia Concert Orchestra,
Howard Barlow conductor.*

4780 Letter from home. Arranged for   7'
large orchestra
3(3rd alt. Picc.),3*,3*,3*(C.Bn. ad lib.)-4,3,
3,1-Timp.,Perc.-Pno.(ad lib.),Cel.(ad lib.),
Hp.-Str.
Ms.
Score 38 p. Large folio
*Commissioned by Paul Whiteman and ABC. Ori-
ginally composed for small radio orchestra,
1944. First performance ABC Philco Radio Program, 17 October 1944, Paul Whiteman conductor.*

4056 Lincoln portrait, for speaker and   14'
orchestra
Speaker-2(alt. 2Picc.),3*,3*,3*-4,3,3,1-Timp.,
Perc.-Cel.(ad lib.),Hp.-Str.
Boosey & Hawkes, New York, c1943
Score 44 p.
*Commissioned by André Kostelanetz, 1942. Com-
posed 1942. First performance Cincinnati, 14
May 1942, Cincinnati Symphony Orchestra, André
Kostelanetz conductor, William Adams speaker.*

2995 Music for radio, a saga of the   13'
prairie
2*,2,2,1-3Sax.(AAT,2alt. 2Cl.,1 alt. B.Cl.)-2,
3,2,1-Timp.,Perc.-Pno.(alt. Cel.),Hp.-Str.
Ms.
Score 86 p.
*Commissioned by CBS, 1936. Composed 1937.
First performance in a broadcast by the CBS
Orchestra, New York, 25 July 1937, Howard
Barlow conductor.*

2856 Music for the theatre, suite in five 20'
parts for small orchestra
1.Prologue 2.Dance 3.Interlude 4.Burlesque
5.Epilogue
1(alt. Picc.),1(alt. E.H.),1(alt. Cl. in E-
flat),1-2Tpt.,1Tbn.-Perc.-Pno.-Str.
Cos Cob Press, New York, c1932
Score 71 p.
Commissioned by the League of Composers, 1925.

Copland, Aaron

Composed 1925. *First performance Boston, 20 November 1925, Boston Symphony Orchestra, Serge Koussevitzky conductor.*

3327 [Our Town, concert sequence]   11'
3(Alto Fl. alt. Picc.),3*,3*,3*,2(2nd alt. C.Bn.)
-3,3,2,1-Glock.-Hp.-Str.
Ms.
Score 64 p.
Composed 1940 for Sol Lesser's film production of Thornton Wilder's Our Town. First performance in a broadcast by the CBS Orchestra, New York, 9 June 1940, Howard Barlow conductor.

3090 An outdoor overture   10'
3*,2,2,2-4,2,3-Timp.,Perc.-Pno.(alt. Cel.)-Str.
Boosey & Hawkes, New York, ᶜ1940
Score 44 p.
Composed 1938. Commissioned and first performed by the High School of Music and Art, New York, 16 December 1938, Alexander Richter conductor.

959m Quiet city, for trumpet, English horn   8'
(or oboe) and string orchestra
E.H.(or Ob.)-Tpt.-Str.
Ms.
Score 18 p. Large folio
The thematic material is derived from incidental music composed for Irwin Shaw's stage play Quiet City, 1939. First performance Town Hall, New York, 28 January 1941, Saidenberg Little Symphony, Daniel Saidenberg conductor, Harry Glantz trumpet soloist.

6233 The red pony, film suite for   21'
orchestra
1.Morning on the ranch 2.The gift 3a.Dream march 3b.Circus music 4.Walk to the bunkhouse 5.Grandfather's story 6.Happy ending
2(both alt. Picc.),2(2nd alt. E.H. ad lib.),4 (3rd alt. B.Cl.,1Cl. in E-flat ad lib.),2-4(4th ad lib.),3,3,1-Timp.,Perc.-Pno.(alt. Cel.),Hp.-Str.
Boosey & Hawkes, New York, ᶜ1951
Score 119 p.
From the music for the Republic Pictures production of John Steinbeck's story. Composed 1948. This concert suite commissioned by Efrem Kurtz. First performance of suite Houston, 30 October 1948, Houston Symphony Orchestra, Efrem Kurtz conductor.

3978 [Rodeo, four dance episodes]   17'
1.Buckaroo holiday 2.Corral nocturne 3.Saturday night waltz 4.Hoe-down
3*,3*,3*,3*-4,3,3,1-Timp.,Perc.-Pno.,Hp.-Str.
Ms.
Score 179 p.
From the ballet composed 1942 and first performed New York, 16 October 1942, Ballet Russe de Monte Carlo, Franz Allers conducting. First performance of this suite at a Lewisohn Stadium Concert, New York, 22 June 1943, New York Philharmonic, Alexander Smallens conductor.

3528 El salón México   10'
3*,3*,4*,3*-4,3,3,1-Timp.,Perc.-Pno.-Str.
Boosey & Hawkes, London, ᶜ1939
Score 44 p.
Composed 1936. First performance Mexico City, 27 August 1937, Orquesta Sinfónica de México, Carlos Chávez conductor.

3602 Statements   17'
1.Militant 2.Cryptic 3.Dogmatic 4.Subjective 5.Jingo 6.Prophetic
3*,3*,3*,3*-4,3,3,1-Timp.,Perc.-Str.
Ms.
Score 86 p.
Composed 1933-35. Commissioned by the League of Composers, 1935. First performance (of fifth and sixth movements only) broadcast over NBC, Minneapolis, 9 January 1936, Minneapolis Symphony Orchestra, Eugene Ormandy conductor. First complete performance New York, 7 January 1942, New York Philharmonic, Dimitri Mitropoulos conductor.

2793 Symphonic ode   20'
4*,4*,4*,4*-8,5,3,2-Timp.,Perc.-Pno.,2Hp.-Str.
Ms.
Score 83 p. Large folio
Composed 1928-29. First performance Boston, 19 February 1932, Boston Symphony Orchestra, Serge Koussevitzky conductor. Dedicated to the Boston Symphony Orchestra on the occasion of its fiftieth anniversary.

2597 [Symphony, Dance]   20'
Introduction: Lento 1.Molto allegro 2.Andante moderato 3.Allegro vivo
3*,3*,4*,3*-4,3,2Cnt.,3,1-Timp.,Perc.-Pno.,Cel., 2Hp.-Str.
Cos Cob Press, New York, ᶜ1931
Score 87 p.
Composed 1922-25. Awarded prize in the Victor Talking Machine Co. Competition, 1929-30, as one of five outstanding works. First performance at a concert for the benefit of the unemployed musicians of Philadelphia, Academy of Music, Philadelphia, 15 April 1931, Philadelphia Orchestra, Leopold Stokowski conductor.

993m [Symphony, organ and orchestra]   24'
1.Prelude 2.Scherzo 3.Finale
Solo Org.-3*(2nd alt. 2nd Picc.),3*,2,3*-4,3, 3,1-Timp.,Perc.-Cel.,2Hp.(2nd ad lib.)-Str.
Ms.
Score 95 p. Large folio
Written at the request of Nadia Boulanger. Composed 1924. First performance New York, 9 January 1925, New York Symphony Society, Walter Damrosch conductor, Nadia Boulanger soloist. Rewritten for orchestra alone as Symphony no. 1.

2596 [Symphony no. 1] First symphony   24'
1.Prelude 2.Scherzo 3.Finale
3*(2nd alt. 2nd Picc.),3*,3*,3*-Alto Sax.(ad lib.)-8,5,3,1-Timp.,Perc.-Pno.,Cel.,2Hp.-Str.
Cos Cob Press, New York, ᶜ1931
Score 80 p.
Present version completed 1928. First

*performance Berlin, 10 December 1931, Berlin
Symphony Orchestra, Ernest Ansermet conductor.*

4708 [Symphony no. 2] Short symphony   *15'*
  1. ♩=144 2. ♩=44 3. ♩=144
  3*,3*,3*,3*-4,2-Pno.-Str.
  Ms.
  Score 74 p. Large folio
  *Composed 1932-33. First performance Mexico,
  23 November 1934, Orquesta Sinfónica de México,
  Carlos Chávez conductor. Later transcribed
  for string quartet, clarinet and piano under
  the title Sextet, 1937.*

6221 [Symphony no. 3]   *38'*
  1.Molto moderato, with simple expression
  2.Allegro molto 3.Andantino quasi allegretto
  4.Molto deliberato (freely, at first)
  4*(3rd alt. Picc.),3(3rd alt. E.H.),4(1Cl. in
  E-flat),3*-4,4,3,1-Timp.,Perc.-Pno.,Cel.,2Hp.-
  Str.
  Boosey & Hawkes, New York, c1947
  Score 153 p.
  *Commissioned by the Koussevitzky Music Founda-
  tion. Composed 1944-46. First performance
  Boston, 18 October 1946, Boston Symphony
  Orchestra, Serge Koussevitzky conductor.
  Awarded the New York Music Critics Circle
  Prize as the best orchestral work by an Ameri-
  can composer played during the season 1946-47.*

1799s Two pieces, for string orchestra   *11'*
  1.Lento molto 2.Rondino
  Str.
  Arrow, New York, c1940
  Score 13 p.
  *Originally composed for string quartet; tran-
  scribed 1928. First performance Boston, 14
  December 1928, Boston Symphony Orchestra, Serge
  Koussevitzky conductor.*

COPPOLA, PIERO.   Milan 11 October 1888
      Lausanne 17 March 1971

2121 Deux danses symphoniques   *8'*
  1.Habanera 2.Blues
  3,3,3*,2-4,3,3,1-Timp.,Perc.-Cel.,Hp.-Str.
  Leduc, Paris, c1930
  Score 33 p.
  *Composed 1930. First performance Concerts
  Lamoureux, Paris, 1930, M. Wolff conductor.*

3868 Fanfara di quattro soldatini di   *1'*
  piombo ubriachi [Fanfare for four tipsy toy
  soldiers]
  2Tpt.,Cnt.,Tbn.
  Ms.
  Score 1 p.
  Composed ca. 1921.

2135 Interlude dramatique   *10'*
  3*,3*,3*,4*-4,3,3,1-Timp.,Perc.-2Hp.-Str.
  Senart, Paris, c1930
  Score 55 p.
  *Composed 1928. First performance Paris, 1929,
  Orchestre Symphonique, Pierre Monteux con-
  ductor.*

2003 La ronde sous la cloche [The round   *13'*
  under the bell, symphonic poem, based on
  Louis Bertrand's Gaspard de la Nuit]
  3(3rd alt. Picc.),3*,3*,4*-4,4,3,1-Timp.,Perc.-
  Cel.,2Hp.-Str.
  Durand, Paris, c1928
  Score 49 p.
  *Composed 1924. First performance Concerts
  Pasdeloup, Paris, 1925, the composer conducting.*

1930 Scherzo fantasque   *10'*
  3*,2,2,2-4,2,3,1-Timp.,Perc.-Hp.-Str.
  Eschig, Paris, c1928
  Score 56 p.
  *Composed 1919. First performance Concerts du
  Conservatoire, Paris, 1919, Philippe Gaubert
  conductor.*

1931 Suite intima   *20'*
  1.[The tormented soul] 2.[The flute of the
  honey cup] 3.Burlesque
  3(3rd alt. Picc.),3*,3*,3*-4,3,3,1-Timp.,Perc.
  -Cel.,Hp.-Str.
  Eschig, Paris, c1927
  Score 87 p.
  *No. 1 composed for piano, and orchestrated
  1914; first performance Augusteo, Rome, Tullio
  Serafin conductor. Nos. 2 and 3 composed for
  piano, 1921, orchestrated 1923; first performance Paris, 1923, at a Pasdeloup Concert, the
  composer conducting.*

2342 [Symphony, A minor]   *35'*
  1.Allegro un poco agitato 2.Adagio molto
  3.Vivace
  3*,3*,3*,4*-4,3,3,1-Timp.,Perc.-Cel.,2Hp.-Str.
  Senart, Paris, c1925
  Score 122 p.
  *Composed 1923. First performance Concerts
  Pasdeloup, Paris, 13 November 1924, the composer conducting.*

COQUARD, ARTHUR.   Paris 26 May 1846
      Noirmontier 20 August 1910

445s À la bien-aimée, lied
  Vocal Recitation(ad lib.)-Str.(without Cb.)
  Costallat, Paris, c1909
  Score 5 p.

939v Légende [E minor]
  Solo Vn.-2,1,2,1-Hn.-Str.
  Score: Ms. 25 p.
  Parts: Grus, Paris [n.d.]

1060 En Norvège [In Norway, symphonic suite]
  1.[In the fjord] 2.[At Molde] 3.[North
  Cape] 4.[Final dance]
  3*,3*,3*,2-4,4,3,1-Timp.,Perc.-Cel.,Hp.-Str.
  Costallat, Paris [n.d.]
  Score 59 p.
  Composed 1907.

CORDERO, ROQUE.   Panama City 16 August 1917

4144 Capricho interiorano
  3*,2,3*,2-3,2,3-Timp.,Perc.-Str.
  Ms.

Cordero, Roque

Score 24 p.
Composed 1939. First performance Panama City, 1942, National Orchestra of Panama, Herbert de Castro conductor.

321v [Concerto, violin and orchestra]   *30'*
1.Largo - Allegro strepitoso - Allegro moderato
2.Lento 3.Allegro vigoroso
Solo Vn.-3*,2,3*,2-3,2,3,1-Timp.,Perc.-Str.
Ms. c1962 by Roque Cordero
Score 159 p. Large folio
Commissioned by the Serge Koussevitzky Music Foundation in the Library of Congress. Composed 1962. First performance Washington, D.C., 9 May 1965, at the 3rd Inter-American Music Festival, National Symphony Orchestra, Victor Tevah conductor, Alberto Lysy soloist. Dedicated to the memory of Serge and Natalie Koussevitzky.

5956 [Symphony no. 1, E-flat]   *30'*
1.Largo 2.Allegro vivace, ma non tanto
3.Adagio - Allegro energico
3(3rd alt. Picc.),2,3(1Cl. in E-flat),2-4,3,3,
1-Timp.,Perc.-Str.
Ms.
Score 126 p. Large folio
Composed 1945. First performance Panama City, 14 September 1955, National Orchestra of Panama, Roque Cordero conductor. Honorable mention: Reichhold Music Award, Detroit, 1947.

5980 [Symphony no. 2, in one movement]   *21'*
Lento - Presto e furioso - Allegro vivace -
Andante quasi adagio
3*,3*,3*,3*-4,2,3,1-Timp.,Perc.-Str.
Ms. c1957 by Roque Cordero
Score 99 p. Large folio
Composed 1956. First performance Caracas, Venezuela, 6 April 1957, Orquesta Sinfónica de Venezuela, Carlos Chávez conductor. Awarded the second prize at the Second Latin American Musical Festival, Caracas, 1957.

CORELLI, ARCANGELO.
    Fusignano, near Imola, Italy 17 February 1653
                        Rome 8 January 1713

Christmas concerto
    See: [Concerto grosso, Christmas concerto,
        Op. 6 no. 8, G minor]

1553s [Concerto grosso, Op. 6 no. 1, D major]
Edited by T.W. Werner
In one movement
2Solo Vn., Solo Vc.-Cemb.-Str.
Nagel, Hannover, c1929
Score 25 p.
Op. 6 consists of 12 Concerti Grossi, published Amsterdam ca.1713. Another edition was published Rome, 1714.

Largo

989s [Concerto grosso, Op. 6 no. 2,   *12'*
F major] Edited by Alceo Toni
In one movement
2Solo Vn., Solo Vc.-Pno.-Str.
Ricordi, Milan [n.d.]
Score 11 p.

Vivace

2376s [Concerto grosso, Op. 6 no. 3,   *13'*
C minor. Arranged by Rupert Erlebach]
1.Largo - Allegro - Adagio 2.Grave 3.Vivace
4.Allegro
2Solo Vn., Solo Va., Solo Vc.-Str.
Oxford University Press, London, c1928
Score 16 p.

Largo (♪=80)

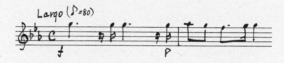

616s [Concerto grosso, Op. 6 no. 3,   *13'*
C minor. Arranged by Arnold Schering]
1.Largo - Allegro - Adagio 2.Grave 3.Vivace
4.Allegro
2Solo Vn., Solo Vc.-Pno.-Str.
Kahnt, Leipzig, c1921
Score 19 p.

1689s [Concerto grosso, Op. 6 no. 4, D major]
Edited by Joseph Joachim and Friedrich
Chrysander
In one movement
2Solo Vn., Solo Vc.-Str.
Augener, London [1888]
Score [20] p.

Adagio

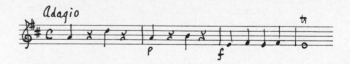

1690s [Concerto grosso, Op. 6 no. 5, B-flat
major] Edited by Joseph Joachim and Friedrich
Chrysander
In one movement
2Solo Vn., Solo Vc.-Str.
Augener, London [1888]
Score [23] p.

Adagio

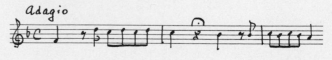

Corelli, Arcangelo

1691s [Concerto grosso, Op. 6 no. 6, F major]
Edited by Joseph Joachim and Friedrich
Chrysander
1.Adagio - Allegro 2.Largo 3.Vivace
4.Allegro
2Solo Vn., Solo Vc.-Str.
Augener, London [1888]
Score [24] p.

Adagio

650s [Concerto grosso, Op. 6 no. 7,   8'
D major. Revised by Alceo Toni]
1.Vivace - Allegro 2.Allegro 3.Andante largo
4.Allegro 5.Vivace
2Solo Vn., Solo Vc.-Org.-Str.
Ricordi, Milan, 1928
Score 20 p.

Vivace

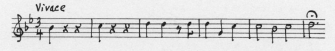

2329s [Concerto grosso, Christmas   15'
concerto, Op. 6 no. 8, G minor]
1.Vivace - Grave - Allegro 2.Adagio - Allegro
- Adagio 3.Vivace 4.Allegro 5.Pastorale
2Solo Vn., Solo Vc.-Cemb.-Str.
Kalmus, New York [n.d.]
Score 20 p.

Vivace

212s [Concerto grosso, Christmas concerto, 15'
Op. 6 no. 8, G minor. Revised by Rhené-Baton]
1.Vivace 2.Adagio 3.Vivace 4.Pastorale
2Solo Vn., Solo Vc.-Pno.-Str.
Durand, Paris, c1921
Score 25 p.

601s [Concerto grosso, Christmas concerto, 15'
Op. 6 no. 8, G minor. Arranged by Arnold
Schering]
1.Vivace - Allegro - Adagio - Allegro - Adagio
2.Vivace - Allegro 3.Pastorale
2Solo Vn., Solo Vc.-Pno.-Str.
Kahnt, Leipzig, c1913
Score 27 p.

2361s [Concerto grosso, Christmas concerto, 15'
Op. 6 no. 8, G minor] Edited by W. Whittaker
1.Vivace - Grave - Allegro 2.Adagio - Allegro
- Adagio 3.Vivace 4.Allegro 5.Pastorale
2Solo Vn., Solo Vc., Solo Hpscd. (or Pno.)-
Hpscd.(or Pno.)-Str.

Oxford University Press, c1936
Score in 2 parts: 9 p., 12 p.

1411s [Concerto grosso, Christmas concerto,
Op. 6 no. 8, G minor. Grave *and* Pastorale.
Arranged for string orchestra]
Str.
Score: Ms. 8 p.
Parts: Oppenheimer [n.p., n.d.]

1696s [Concerto grosso, Op. 6 no. 9, F major]
Edited by Joseph Joachim and Friedrich
Chrysander
1.Preludio 2.Allemanda 3.Corrente 4.Gavotta
5.Adagio 6.Minuetto
2Solo Vn., Solo Vc.-Str.
Augener, London [1888]
Score [13] p.

Largo

1697s [Concerto grosso, Op. 6 no. 10, C major]
Edited by Joseph Joachim and Friedrich
Chrysander
1.Preludio 2.Allemanda 3.Adagio 4.Corrente
5.Allegro 6.Minuetto
2Solo Vn., Solo Vc.-Str.
Augener, London [1888]
Score [19] p.

Andante largo

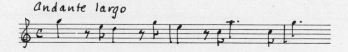

24s [Concerto grosso, Op. 6 no. 11, B-flat
major] Edited by Hjalmar von Dameck
1.Preludio 2.Allemanda 3.Adagio 4.Sarabanda
5.[Gigue]
2Solo Vn., Solo Vc.-Cemb.-Str.
Raabe & Plothow, Berlin, c1912
Score 8 p.

Andante largo

90s [Concerto grosso, Op. 6 no. 11, B-flat
major. Gigue. Arranged by Hjalmar von Dameck]
Str.
Score: Ms. 5 p.
Parts: Breitkopf & Härtel, Leipzig, c1904

913s [Concerto grosso, Op. 6 no. 12, F major]
Edited by Hjalmar von Dameck
1.Preludio 2.Allegro 3.Adagio 4.Sarabanda
5.Giga
2Solo Vn., Solo Vc.-Cemb.-Str.

Corelli, Arcangelo

Raabe & Plothow, Berlin, c1912
Score 16 p.

La follia
  See: [Sonata, violin and continuo, La
    follia, Op. 5 no. 12, D minor. Tran-
    scribed for violin and orchestra by
    Arthur Bosmans]

53s Four pieces. Arranged in the form of a
  suite for string orchestra by William F.
  Happich
  1.Preludio 2.Adagio 3.Gavotta 4.Giga
  Str.
  Ms.
  Score 17 p.
  *Pieces are arrangements of movements from
  Op. 5 no. 4; Op. 5 no. 10; Op. 5 no. 9;
  Op. 5 no. 5. Arranged 1918.*

1196s Praeludium *and* Gavotte [Arranged for
  string orchestra by J.B. Zerlett]
  Str.
  Lehne, Hannover [n.d.]
  Score 3 p.

495s Sarabanda, giga e badinerie   *8'*
  Str.
  Ricordi, Milan [n.d.]
  Score 10 p.

2410s [Same as above]
  Str.
  Broude Brothers, New York [n.d.]
  Score 10 p.

1268s Sarabande *and* Gavotte
  Str.
  Lehne, Hannover [n.d.]
  Score 3 p.

537c [Sonata, violin and continuo, Op. 5
  no. 5. Adagio. Transcribed by Paul Bazelaire]
  Solo Vc.-Str.
  Leduc, Paris, c1925
  Score 3 p.

896s [Sonata, violin and continuo, Op. 5   *15'*
  no. 8, E minor. Arranged for string orchestra
  by Guido Guerrini]
  1.Prelude 2.Allemande 3.Sarabande 4.Giga
  Str.
  Ricordi, Milan, c1927
  Miniature score 15 p.
  *Op. 5 consists of twelve sonatas for violin
  and continuo, first published in Rome, 1700.
  First performance of this transcription Augusteo, Rome, 2 May 1926, Bernardino Molinari
  conductor.*

272v [Sonata, violin and continuo, La follia,
  Op. 5 no. 12, D minor. Transcribed for violin
  and orchestra by Arthur Bosmans]

Solo Vn.-2,1,1,1-Timp.-Str.
Ms. c1976 by Arthur Bosmans
Score 15 p.
The folia or follia was a dance of Portuguese origin. This transcription, 1974.

879v [Sonata, violin and continuo, La   13'
follia, Op. 5 no. 12, D minor. Edited by
Issay Barmes and orchestrated by Max Reger]
Solo Vn.-2,2,0,2-Timp.-Str.
Schott, Brussels, c1914
Score 19 p.
This edition based on an arrangement by H. Leonard.

2345s [Sonata, 2 violins, violoncello and
figured bass, Op. 1 no. 2, E minor. Tran-
scribed for string orchestra by Paul Glass
and edited by Norman Black]
Grave - Allegro moderato - Adagio - Allegro
Pno. (optional)-Str.
Broadcast Music Incorporated, New York,
c1941 (not renewed)
Score 8 p.
One of twelve Sonatas a Tre first published in Rome, 1681.

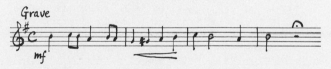

1127s [Suite. Selected and arranged for string
orchestra by Hermann Ritter]
1.Adagio 2.Moderato 3.Sarabande 4.Gavotte
Str.
C.F. Schmidt, Heilbronn [n.d.]
Score 4 p.

CORNELIUS, PETER.   Mainz 1824
                                     Mainz 1874

1361 [Der Barbier von Bagdad. Overture.   7'
Arranged by Felix Mottl]
3*,2,2,2-4,2,3,1-Timp.,Perc.-Hp.-Str.
Kahnt, Leipzig [n.d.]
Score 51 p.
Composed 1856. First performance Weimar, 1858.

2420 Der Cid. Overture   5'
3(3rd alt. Picc.),3*,3*,2-4,3,3,1-Timp.,Cym.-
Str.
Breitkopf & Härtel, Leipzig [n.d.]
Score 43 p.
From the opera in 3 acts. First performance Weimar, 1865. Score of overture dated Munich, 6 March 1865.

CORPUS, CONSTANTIN.

1392s Marsch, Op. 23
Str.
R. Schultz, Berlin [n.d.]
Score 3 p.

1393s Serenade, Op. 24
Str.
R. Schultz, Berlin [n.d.]
Score 3 p.

CORSANEGO, ARTHUR.

444s Galanterie, Op. 16
Str.
Richault, Paris, c1895
Score 7 p.

443s Scherzo, Op. 6 [A major]
Str.(without Cb.)
Richault, Paris, c1895
Score 5 p.

CORSEPPI, M.

805s Minuetto piccolo, Op. 7. Arranged by
Johannes Doebber
Str.
C. Simon, Berlin [n.d.]
Score 3 p.

COSMAN, BLAIR.   Rockford, Washington 1918

747p [Concertino, piano]   9'
2.Lento 3.Allegro vivace
Solo Pno.-2,2(2nd alt. E.H.),2,2-4,2,2-Timp.,
Perc.-Str.
Ms.
Score 53 p. Large folio
Composed 1940. First movement lacking from this version. First performance Eastman School of Music, Rochester, New York, during the symposium held 16-19 April 1940, Rochester Civic Orchestra, Howard Hanson conductor, Irene Gedney soloist.

COSME, LUIZ.   Porte Alegre, Brazil 1908

3701 Oração à Teiniaguá [Prayer to Teiniaguá]
3*,3*,3*,2-4,2,3,1-Trgl.-Cel.,Hp.-Str.
Ms.
Score 20 p.
Composed ca.1941.

COSSMANN, BERNHARD.   Dessau 17 May 1822
                     Frankfurt am Main 7 May 1910

661c Konzertstück [Concert piece, violoncello,
D major]
Solo Vc.-2,2,2,2-2,2,3-Timp.-Str.
Score: Ms. 81 p.
Parts: Breitkopf & Härtel, Leipzig [n.d.]

Couperin, François (Le Grand)

COUPERIN, FRANÇOIS (LE GRAND).
Paris 10 November 1668
Paris 12 September 1733

1935s Apothéose de Lulli [Arranged by Georges
Eugène Marty]
1.Lulli aux Champs Élysees concertant avec
les ombres lyriques 2.Rumeur souteraine
causée par les auteurs contemporains de Lulli
(Viste) 3.Plaintes de mêmes (Dolemment)
4.Enlévement de Lulli au Parnasse (Très
légérement)
Str.
[Durand, Paris, 191-?]
Score 4 p.
*Composed 1724-25 as a set of thirteen numbers
under this title for two treble and one bass
instrument and continuo. These excerpts are
Cauchie Thematic Index nos. 378, 381, 382, and
383. The title for the first number is misprinted and should be identified as [Air pour
les mêmes].*

1378s L'ausonienne, allemande. Cauchie no. 185.
Orchestrated by Michele Esposito
Str.
Oxford University Press, London, c1928
Score 4 p.
*This piece may be combined with Les Barri-
cades Mistérieuses (1377s), La Favorite
(1379s), and Les Moissonneurs (1376s) to
form a suite.*

1377s Les barricades mistérieuses, rondeau.
Cauchie no. 172. Orchestrated by Michele
Esposito
Fl.-Str.
Oxford University Press, London, c1929
Score 6 p.

2919 Concert dans le goût théatral   18'
[Concerto in theatrical style. Adapted for
chamber orchestra by Alfred Cortot]
1.Ouverture 2.Grand ritournelle 3.Air 4.Air
tendre (rondeau) 5.Air léger 6.Louré 7.Air
8.Sarabande 9.Air léger 10.Air tendre
11.Air de bacchantes
1,1,0,1-Cemb.(or Pno.)-Str.
Universal Edition, Vienna, c1933
Score 40 p.
*Cauchie nos. 328 through 338. First per-
formance at a concert of the École Normale
de Musique, Paris, 30 October 1930, Alfred
Cortot conductor.*

Dance suite
See: STRAUSS, RICHARD.
[Dance suite, from Couperin's piano
compositions collected and arranged
for small orchestra by Richard
Strauss]

1379s La favoite, chaconne à deux temps.
Cauchie no. 135. Orchestrated by Michele
Esposito
Fl.,Bn.-Str.

Oxford University Press, London, c1928
Score 6 p.

39s Four pieces in the form of a suite. Freely
arranged by James Brown
1.Prélude, les graces incomparables 2.Rondeau
3.Rondo passacaille 4.La gabrièle
Pno.-Str.
Stainer & Bell, London, c1919
Score 16 p.

1376s Les moissonneurs [The harvesters] Cauchie
no. 168. Orchestrated by Michele Esposito
Fl.,Bn.-Timp.-Str.
Oxford University Press, London, c1929
Score 6 p.

4137 Overture and allegro, from La Sultane   7'
suite [Free transcription by Darius Milhaud]
3*,3*,3*,2-3,3,3,1-Timp.,Perc.-Hp.-Str.
Elkan-Vogel, Philadelphia, c1944
Score 23 p.
*Commissioned by Vladimir Golschmann for the
St. Louis Symphony Orchestra, 1940. First
performance St. Louis, 17 January 1941, St.
Louis Symphony Orchestra, Vladimir Golschmann
conductor.*

2327s [Parnassus, or The apotheosis   13-14'30"
of Corelli. Cauchie nos. 370-376] Edited by
Jean-François Paillard
1.Corelli au pied de Parnasse [Corelli at the
foot of Parnassus]: Gravement 2.Corelli charmé
de la bonne réception [Corelli charmed by the
pleasant reception]: Gayment 3.Corelli buvant
à la source d'Hypocrène [Corelli drinking from
the spring of Hippocrene]: Modérément 4.En-
touziasme de Corelli [Corelli's ecstasy]: Vivement 5.Corelli après son entouziasme [Corelli
after his ecstasy]: Très doux 6.Les muses
reveillent Corelli [The muses awaken Corelli]:
Vivement 7.Remerciment de Corelli [Corelli's
thanks]: Gayment
Cemb.-Str.(without Va. and Vc.)
Editions Costallat, Paris, c1962
Score 24 p.
*First published in 1724 for two treble and one
bass instrument and continuo.*

536c Pièces en concert [Concert pieces] Compiled and edited by Paul Bazelaire
1.Prélude 2.Siciliana 3.[The trumpet]
4.Plaint 5.[Devil's air]
Solo Vc.-Str.(without Cb.)
Leduc, Paris, c1924
Score 7 p.

5973 [Suite in C minor. Selected and tran-
scribed for orchestra by Alexis Roland-Manuel]
1.Gravement 2.Bourrée: Gayement 3.Rondeau
4.Passacaille: Noblement et marquée
2,3*,2,2-4,2-Timp.,S.Dr.-Hp.-Str.
Éditions de L'Oiseau Lyre, Paris, c1936 by
Louise B.M. Dyer
Score 72 p.
*No. 1 originally composed 1692 as a Sonade in
E minor titled La Pucelle and later used as
La Française in the composer's The Nations*

(Premier Ordre), Cauchie catalog no. 390. Nos. 2 and 4 also from The Nations (Second Ordre) and composed somewhat later, ca.1724: No. 2 originally in G minor, Cauchie catalog no. 407; No. 4 originally in G minor, Cauchie catalog no. 408. The Nations first published 1726 as a set of 36 pieces for two treble and one bass instrument and continuo. No. 3 originally composed in D minor for harpsichord and first published 1722 as La Muse Plantine, Cauchie catalog no. 285, in the Dixneuvième Ordre of the composer's Third Book of Harpsichord Pieces.

COWELL, HENRY. Menlo Park, California 11 March 1897
Shady, New York 10 December 1965

3466 American melting pot set, for chamber   *18'*
orchestra
1.Chorale (Teutonic-American) 2.Air (Afro-American) 3.Satire (Franco-American) 4.Ala-pria (Oriental-American) 5.Slavic dance (Slavic-American) 6.Rhumba with added eighth (Latin-American) 7.Square dance (Celtic-American)
1,1,1,1-2,1,1,1-Perc.-Str.
Ms.
Score 76 p.
Composed 1940. First performance of 2nd, 5th and 6th movements at the Mountain State Forest Festival, Elkins, West Virginia, 2 October 1941, National Youth Administration Orchestra of Philadelphia, Louis Vyner conductor. First performance of 1st and 4th movements, including 2nd, 5th, and 6th also, at the tenth anniversary of the Orchestrette of New York, Carnegie Chamber Music Hall, New York, 3 May 1943, Frederique Petrides conductor.

4071 American pipers   *5'*
3*(2nd alt. Picc.),3*,3(3rd alt. B.Cl.),3*-4, 3,3,1-Timp.,Perc.-Str.
Ms.
Score 15 p. Large folio
Commissioned by the League of Composers, 1943.

4076 Ancient desert drone   *6'*
3,3*,3,3-4,3,3,1-Timp.,Perc.-Hp.-Str.
Associated Music Publishers, New York, c1943
Score 20 p.
Composed 1939-40. First performance South Bend, Indiana, 1940, South Bend Symphony Orchestra, Edwyn Hames conductor.

3161 Anthropos   *19'*
1.Repose 2.Activity 3.Repression 4.Liberation
2(2nd alt. Picc.),3*,3*,1-2,2,1,1-Timp.,Perc.-Str.
Ms.
Score 24 p. Large folio
Composed 1938. First performance of 4th movement only broadcast over the Mutual Broadcasting System, New York, March 1940, WOR Symphonietta, Alfred Wallenstein conductor.

4864 Celtic set   *10'*
1.Reel 2.Caoine [Keen - an Irish lament for

the dead] 3.Hornpipe
3*(2nd ad lib.),2*(2nd ad lib. or E.H.),6*(1 Cl. in E-flat),2(2nd ad lib.)-4Sax.(SATB)-4,2, 3Cnt.,3,Euph.,1-Timp.,Perc.-Cb.
G. Schirmer, New York, c1941
Score 36 p.
Composed 1938-39. First performance San Francisco, 1939, Goldman Band, Richard Franko Goldman conductor.

7291 Competitive sport
1(alt. Picc.),1,1,1-Str.
Ms.
Score 18 p. Large folio
Originally titled Dance of Sports. Commissioned by Charles Weidman for a dance performance.

758p [Concerto, piano]   *15'*
1.Polyharmony 2.Tone cluster 3.Counter rhythm
Solo Pno.-3(all alt. Picc.),4*,3,3-4,4,3,1-Timp.,Perc.-Str.
Ms.
Score 72 p.
Composed 1929. First complete performance Havana, 28 December 1930, Havana Philharmonic Orchestra, Pedro Sanjuan conductor, the composer as soloist.

273p [Concerto piccolo, piano]   *7'30"*
1.Larghetto 2.Andante 3.Allegretto
Solo Pno.-3(2nd alt. Picc.),3,3,3-4,3,3,1-Timp.,Perc.-Str.
Ms. c1951 by Associated Music Publishers, New York
Score 38 p.
Commissioned by Captain Francis Resta and the West Point Band. Originally composed for band, 1934.

264m Duo concertante for flute, harp   *13'30"*
and symphony orchestra
1.Andante 2.Allegro commodo
Solo Fl., Solo Hp.-3,3(3rd alt. E.H.),3(3rd alt. B.Cl.),3-4,3,3,1-Timp.,Perc.-Pno.(alt. Cel.)-Str.
Ms.
Score 36 p. Large folio
Written for Jackson Wiley and the Springfield, Illinois, Symphony Orchestra. Composed 1961.

1936s Ensemble, string quintet with   *15'*
thunder sticks
1.Larghetto 2.Prestissimo 3.Adagio legato 4.Allegro
3Thunder Sticks-Str.
Breitkopf Publications, New York, c1925
Score 22 p.
Composed 1924.

1707s Exultation, for string orchestra   *3'*
Str.
Adler, Berlin, c1931
Score 8 p.
Composed 1928.

4271 Fanfare for the forces of our Latin
American Allies

Cowell, Henry

See: TEN FANFARES BY TEN COMPOSERS FOR BRASS
AND PERCUSSION.

1708s Four continuations, for string   9'
orchestra, in multiples of nine
1.Inversion 2.Repetition 3.Interpolation
4.Addition
Str.
Ms.
Score 31 p.
Composed 1932. First performance Brooklyn,
New York, 1933, Knickerbocker Orchestra, J.
Edward Powers conductor.

4075 Gaelic symphony   18'
1.Maestoso 2.Andante cantabile 3.Allegretto
con moto 4.Allegro
3*,3*,4*,3(3rd ad lib.)-4Sax.(2Altos,Ten.,Bar.)
-4,3,3,1,Euph.-Timp.,Perc.-Str.
Ms.
Score 84 p. Large folio
Composed 1942. First performance of first
movement only broadcast over CBS, 1943, India-
napolis Symphony Orchestra, Fabien Sevitzky
conductor.

2692 Horn pipe   5'
2(alt. 2Picc.),2,2,2-2,2,2,1-Timp.,Perc.-Cel.,
Hp.-Str.
Ms.
Score 41 p.
Composed 1933. First performance Havana, 22
October 1933, Havana Philharmonic Orchestra,
Amadeo Roldan conductor.

2206s Hymn and fuguing tune no. 5   5'
1.Largo 2.Allegro
Str.
Ms.
Score 15 p.
Based on the fuguing tunes of William Billings.
Originally composed for five voices, 1945.
First performance with voices New York, 14
April 1946, Randolph Singers, David Randolph
conductor. First performance by string orches-
tra New York, 26 October 1952, Stokowski's
String Orchestra, Leopold Stokowski conductor.

2281s Hymn, chorale and fuguing tune no. 8,   8'
for string quartet or string orchestra
1.Hymn 2.Chorale - Fuguing tune
Str.(Cb. ad lib.)
Composers Facsimile Edition, New York, ᶜ1952
by Henry Cowell
Score 20 p.
Based on the fuguing tunes of William Billings.
Written for the Roth String Quartet. Composed
1947. First performance Florida State Univer-
sity School of Music Faculty Concert, Talla-
hassee, Florida, 11 May 1948.

299m Hymn and fuguing tune no. 10, oboe   7'
and strings
1.Hymn 2.Fuguing tune
Solo Ob.-Str.
Ms.
Score 25 p.
Based on the fuguing tunes of William Billings.
Composed 1955. First performance at Pacific

Coast Music Festival, Santa Barbara, California,
10 September 1955, Festival Orchestra, Leopold
Stokowski conductor.

3169 Old American country set   15'
1.Lilt (Blarneying lilt) 2.Chorale (Sunday
meeting house) 3.Ballade (Comallye) 4.Air
(Chirivari) 5.Hornpipe (Corn huskin' hornpipe)
2,2,2,1-2,2,1,1-Perc.-Banjo-Str.
Ms.
Score 38 p. Large folio
Composed 1939. First performance under title
Early American Country Set in a nationwide
broadcast over CBS, Indianapolis, Indiana, 28
February 1940, Indianapolis Symphony Orchestra,
Fabien Sevitzky conductor.

5877 Ongaku   14'
1.Grave 2.Allegretto
2,2(alt. E.H.),2,2-2,2-Timp.,Perc.-Cel.,Hp.-
Str.
Associated Music Publishers, New York [n.d.]
Score 24 p. Large folio
Commissioned by The Louisville Orchestra.
Composed 1957. First performance Louisville,
Kentucky, 26 March 1958, Louisville Orchestra,
Robert Whitney conductor.

1008m Ostinato pianissimo, for percussion   5'
band
1st - String Piano
2nd - String Piano
3rd - 8 Rice Bowls
4th - Xyl.
5th - 2 Bongos
6th - 2 Wood Blocks,Tamb.,Guiro
7th - 3 Low Drums(High,Med.,Low)
8th - 3 Gongs(High,Med.,Low)
New Music, New York, ᶜ1953
Miniature score 11 p.
Composed 1934. First performance Museum of
Modern Art, New York, 7 February 1943, League
of Composers percussion program, John Cage
conductor.

3746 Pastoral and fiddler's delight   10'
3(3rd alt. Picc.),3(3rd alt. E.H.),3(3rd alt.
B.Cl.),3-4,3,3,1-Timp.,Perc.-Hp.-Str.
Ms.
Score 35 p. Large folio
Composed upon commission by Leopold Stokowski
for the All-American Youth Orchestra of the
National Youth Administration, 1940. First
performance New York, 26 July 1940, All-
American Youth Orchestra, Leopold Stokowski
conductor.

3773 Polyphonica   6'
1,1,1,1-1,1,1-Str.
Ms.
Score 33 p.
Composed 1930. First performance Minneapolis,
25 May 1933, St. Paul Chamber Orchestra,
John J. Becker conductor.

1001m Pulse [5 players, 2 assistants]   5'
1st - 3 Korean Dragon's Mouths(Mouth Wood
     Block)(High,Med.,Low),3 Rectangular Wood

Blocks(High,Med.,Low)
2nd - 3 Chinese Tom Toms(High,Med.,Low),3
Different Size Dr.[no Snares](Sm.,Med.,
Large)(Indian Tom Toms may be used
instead)
3rd - 3 Rice Bowls(High,Med.,Low) or High
Tinkling Bowls with Small Metal or Hard
Wood Sticks,3 Japanese Temple Gongs(High,
Med.,Low) or 3 Bells
4th - 3 Cym.(Sm.,Med.,Large),3 Gongs(Sm.,Med.,
Large)
5th - 3 Pipe Lengths(High,Med.,Low),3 Brake
Dr.(High,Med.,Low)
Ms.
Miniature score 20 p.
*Composed 1939 for John Cage and his Percussion
Group. First performance the Cornish School,
Seattle, Washington, 19 May 1939, John Cage
conductor.*

2594 Reel   4'
2(2nd alt. Picc.),2,2,2-2,2,2-Timp.,Perc.-Str.
Ms.
Score 11 p.
*Originally composed for piano, 1928; orchestra-
ted 1932. First performance New School for
Social Research, New York, 17 May 1933, New
Chamber Orchestra, Bernard Herrmann conductor.*

1003m Return, for percussers and a   7'30"
       wailer
  1st - 3 Wood Blocks(High,Med.,Low)
  2nd - 3 Dragon's Mouths(High,Med.,Low),a
         Pane of Glass
  3rd - 3 Gongs(High,Med.,Low)
  4th - Sm. Bells,Japanese Wind Glasses,3 Tom
         Toms(High,Med.,Low)
  5th - 3 Japanese Cup Gongs(High,Med.,Low)
  6th - 3 Dr.(High,Med.,Low)
  (7th) - Wailer
Ms.
Miniature score 6 p.
*Composed 1938-39. First performance Seattle,
1939, John Cage's Percussion Orchestra, Lou
Harrison conductor.*

7074 Rhythmicana, for rhythmicon and   20'
      orchestra
1.Introduction 2.Scherzo 3.Passacaglia
4. ♩=120
Solo Rhythmicon-2*,2,2,2-4,3,3,1-Str.
Ms.
Score 61 p.
*Composed 1931. The rhythmicon is an electronic
instrument for the artificial production of
rhythms built by Lev Theremin to Cowell's
specifications.*

6377 Rondo for orchestra   5'30"
3,3(3rd alt. E.H.),3(3rd alt. B.Cl.),3-4,3,3,1
-Timp.,Cym.-Str.
Composers Facsimile Edition, New York, c1952
by Henry Cowell
Score 21 p.
*Composed 1952 for Fabien Sevitzky. First per-
formance Indianapolis, 6 December 1953,
Indianapolis Symphony Orchestra, Fabien
Sevitzky conductor.*

4865 Shipshape overture (for band)   8'
2*,2,7*(1Cl. in E-flat),1-4Sax.-4,Solo Cnt.,
Cnt.I(or Tpt.),2Tpt.(or Fluegelhn.),3Tbn.,
Euph.-Timp.,Perc.-Hp.(ad lib.)-Cb.
G. Schirmer, New York, c1942
Score 29 p.
*Written for the Pennsylvania Forensic and
Music League. Originally composed for band
1941; later transcribed for orchestra.*

3948 Some music for full orchestra   8'
5*,4*,4*,4*-5,3,3,1-Timp.,Perc.-Pno.-Str.
Ms.
Score 21 p. Large folio
*Composed ca.1920; one of a set of two orches-
tral works called Some Music and Some More
Music.*

7290 Steel and stone   5'
1,1,1,1-4Gongs-Str.
Ms.
Score 12 p. Large folio
*Commissioned by Charles Weidman for a dance
performance.*

2595 Suite, for small orchestra   6'
1(alt. Picc.),1,1,1-1,1,1-Perc.-Str.
Ms.
Score 16 p.
*Composed 1934. First performance Roerich Hall,
New York, 21 May 1934, Vrionides Sinfonietta,
Christos Vrionides conductor.*

3168 Symphonic opus 17, symphonic set in 14'
5 movements
1.Allegro quasi andante 2.Larghetto (Interlude) 3.Moderato maestoso 4.Andante con moto
(Interlude) 5.Allegro
2,2,3*,1-2,2,1-Timp.,Perc.-Str.
Ms.
Score 40 p. Large folio
*Originally composed for piano, voice, violon-
cello and flute, 1938, under the title Tocanta;
orchestrated 1939. First performance Chicago,
1 April 1940, Illinois Symphony Orchestra of
the WPA, Izler Solomon conductor.*

6396 Symphony no. 4, Short symphony   19'
1.Hymn 2.Ballad 3.Dance 4.Introduction and
fuguing tune
3(2nd alt. Picc.),3(3rd alt. E.H.),3(3rd alt.
B.Cl.),3-4,3,3,1-Timp.,Perc.-Hp.-Str.
Associated Music Publishers, New York, c1948
Miniature score 84 p.
*Last movement based on fuguing tunes of William
Billings. Written at the request of Serge
Koussevitzky. Composed 1946. First perform-
ance Boston, 24 October 1947, Boston Symphony
Orchestra, Richard Burgin conductor.*

6410 Symphony no. 5   28'
1.Con moto 2.Andante 3.Presto 4.Largo sostenuto
3(2nd alt. Picc.),3,3(3rd alt. B.Cl.),3-4,3,3,
1-Timp.,Perc.-Pno.-Str.
Associated Music Publishers, New York, c1948
Score 118 p.
Commissioned by Hans Kindler and the National

Cowell, Henry

Symphony Orchestra. Composed 1948. First performance Washington, D.C., 5 January 1949, National Symphony Orchestra, Hans Kindler conductor.

6323 Symphony no. 7 for small orchestra   *24'*
1.Maestoso – Allegro 2.Andante 3.Presto 4. Maestoso – Vigoroso
2,1(alt. E.H.),2(2nd alt. B.Cl.),1-2,1,1-Timp., Perc.-Pno.-Str.
Associated Music Publishers, New York [n.d.]
Score 53 p. Large folio
Composed 1952. First performance Baltimore, Candlelight Series, 25 November 1952, Baltimore Little Orchestra, Reginald Stewart conductor. Dedicated to Reginald Stewart.

6411 Symphony no. 9   *22'*
1.Largo 2.Allegro 3.Allegretto quasi andante 4.Presto 5.Allegro
2(2nd alt. Picc.,ad lib.),2(2nd alt. E.H.,ad lib.),2,2-2,2,2-Timp.,Perc.-Pno.(or Hp.)-Str.
Associated Music Publishers, New York [c1953]
Score 120 p.
Some parts of the symphony are based on the composer's Hymn and Fuguing Tune No. 9, for violoncello and piano, after William Billings. Commissioned by Otto Karp and the Green Bay Symphony. Composed 1950-53. First performance Green Bay, Wisconsin, 14 March 1954, Green Bay Symphony, Ralph Holder conductor. Dedicated to Otto Karp and the Green Bay Symphony.

6324 Symphony no. 10   *22'30"*
1.Hymn 2.Fuguing tune 3.Comeallye 4.Jig 5.Intermezzo 6.Fuguing tune
2,2(2nd alt. E.H.),2(2nd alt. B.Cl.),2-2,2-Timp.-Str.
Associated Music Publishers, New York [n.d.]
Score 38 p. Large folio
The first two movements are an expanded version of Cowell's Hymn and Fuguing Tune no. 5. Composed upon commission by F. Charles Adler and the Wiener Symphoniker for the 1953 Israeli tour; dedicated to them. First performance 1953, Wiener Symphoniker, F. Charles Adler conductor.

5356 [Symphony no. 11, Seven rituals of   *21'* music]
1.Andantino 2.Allegro 3.Lento 4.Presto 5.Adagio 6.Vivace 7.Andante
2(2nd alt. Picc.),2(2nd alt. E.H.),2,2-4,3,3, 1(ad lib.)-Timp.,Perc.-Pno.(alt. Cel.),Hp.(ad lib.)-Str.
Ms.
Score 98 p. Large folio
Commissioned by The Louisville Symphony Orchestra. Composed 1953. First performance Louisville, 29 May 1954, Louisville Symphony Orchestra, Robert Whitney conductor.

6654 Symphony no. 12   *15'*
1.Andante 2.Allegro 3.Presto 4.Maestoso
3(3rd alt. Picc.),2(2nd alt. E.H.),3(3rd alt. B.Cl.),2-4,3,2,1-Timp.,Perc.-Pno.,Cel.-Str.
Ms.
Score 70 p. Large folio

Composed 1955-56. First performance Houston, 28 March 1960, Houston Symphony, Leopold Stokowski conductor.

6655 Symphony no. 14   *24'30"*
1.Adagio – Allegro 2.Andante 3.Vivace 4.Allegro
3(3rd alt. Picc.),3(3rd alt. E.H.),3(3rd alt. B.Cl.),2-4,3,3,1-Timp.,Perc.-Pno.,Cel.-Str.
Ms.
Score 73 p. Large folio
Commissioned by the Serge Koussevitzky Foundation in the Library of Congress. Composed 1959-60. First performance at the Second Inter-American Music Festival, Cramton Auditorium, Washington, D.C., 27 April 1961, Eastman Philharmonic Orchestra, Howard Hanson conductor. Dedicated to the memory of Serge and Natalie Koussevitzky.

6657 Symphony no. 15, Thesis   *22'30"*
1.Largo 2.Andante 3.Presto 4.Allegretto 5. Allegro 6.Moderato
3(3rd alt. Picc.),3,3(3rd alt. B.Cl.),2-4,3,3 (3rd optional),1-Timp.,Perc.-Cel.-Str.
Associated Music Publishers, New York, c1962
Score 78 p.
Commissioned by Broadcast Music, Inc. Composed 1960. First performance Louisville, Kentucky, 7 October 1961, Louisville Orchestra, Robert Whitney conductor. Dedicated to Carl Haverlin and Broadcast Music, Inc.

3903 Synchrony   *12'*
3(alt. 3Picc.),3,3,3*-4,3,3,1-Timp.,Perc.-Pno. (optional)-Str.
Adler, Berlin, c1931
Score 34 p.
Composed 1930. Original title: Orchesterstück (Synchrony). First performance Paris, 6 June 1931, Orchestre Straram, Nicolas Slonimsky conductor.

787p Tales from our countryside   *12'*
1.Deep tides 2.Exultation 3.The harp of life 4.Lilt of the reel
Solo Pno.-3*,3,3,3-4,3,3,1-Timp.,Perc.-Str.
Ms.
Score 12 p. Large folio
Composed originally as four piano pieces, 1920-30; orchestrated 1941. First performance Atlantic City, New Jersey, May 1941, All-American Youth Orchestra, Leopold Stokowski conductor, the composer as soloist.

1876s Two appositions   *8'*
Str.
Ms.
Score 15 p.
Composed 1932 for dance performance by Doris Humphrey and her group. First performance Paris, 21 February 1932, l'Orchestre Symphonique de Paris, Nicolas Slonimsky conductor.

2601 Vestiges   *10'*
4*,3*,4*,3-4,3,3,1-Timp.,Cym.-Cel.-Str.
Ms.
Score 25 p.
Composed ca.1921.

3502   Vox humana   *10'*
3,3(3rd alt. E.H.),3,2-4,3,3,1-Timp.,Perc.-Hp.
-Str.
Ms.
Score 37 p.
Originally composed for French horn and piano,
1939; orchestrated 1939.

COWEN, FREDERIC H.
                Kingston, Jamaica 29 January 1852
                London 6 October 1935

1592   The butterfly's ball, concert   *10'*
overture
3(3rd alt. Picc.),2,2,2-4,2,3,1-Timp.,Bells-
Cel.(ad lib.),Hp.-Str.
Novello, London, c1901
Score 84 p.
Composed 1900.   First performance Queen's Hall,
London, 1901, Henry Wood conductor.

528p   Concertstück
Solo Pno.-2,2,2,2-4,2,3-Timp.,Trgl.-Hp.-Str.
J. Williams, London, c1900
Score 107 p.

2182   Deux morceaux [Two pieces]
1.Melodie   2.A l'espagnole
2,2,2,2-2Hn.,2Cnt.-Timp.-Hp.-Str.
A.J. Gutmann, Vienna, c1888
Score 33 p.

2040   Four English dances, in the olden   *25'*
style
1.Stately dance   2.Rustic dance   3.Graceful
dance   4.Country dance
2,2,2,2-4,2,3-Timp.,Cym.,Trgl.-Str.
Novello, London, c1901
Score 88 p.
Composed 1893-94 and 1896.   First performance
London, 1896, the composer conducting.

2035   Indian rhapsody   *15'*
3*,3*,2,2-4,2,3,1-Timp.,Perc.-Hp.-Str.
Boosey, London, c1903
Score 78 p.
Composed 1903.   First performance at the Here-
ford Festival, 1903, the composer conducting.

2041   A suite of old English dances,   *25'*
second set
1.Maypole dance   2.Peasants' dance   3.Minuet
d'amour   4.Old dance, with variations
3*,2,2,2-4,2,3,1-Timp.,Perc.-Str.
Novello, London, c1906
Score 115 p.
Composed 1905.   First performance London, 1905,
the composer conducting.

5381   [Symphony no. 3, Scandinavian, C   *37'*
minor]
1.Allegro moderato ma con moto   2.A summer
evening on the fiord   3.Scherzo   4.Finale:
Allegro ma non troppo
2,2,2,2-4,2,1-Timp.-Hp.-Str.
J. Gutmann, Vienna [n.d.]
Score 76 p.
Composed 1880.   First performance St. James's
Hall, London, 18 December 1880.

2044   [Symphony no. 4, The Welsh, B-flat   *37'*
minor]
1.Allegro vivace, non troppo   2.Lento tranquillo   3.Scherzo   4.Allegro moderato
2,2,2,2-4,2,3-Timp.-Hp.-Str.
Novello, London [n.d.]
Score 88 p.
Composed 1884.   First performance at the Phil-
harmonic concerts, London, 1884, the composer
conducting.

2043   [Symphony no. 5, F major]   *40'*
1.Molto sostenuto e maestoso   2.Allegretto,
quasi allegro   3.Adagio molto sostenuto   4.
Allegro con fuoco, ma deciso
2,2,2,2-4,2,3,1-Timp.-Hp.-Str.
Novello, London, c1906
Score 175 p.
Composed 1887.   First performance Cambridge,
June 1887, the composer conducting.

21   [Symphony no. 6, The Idyllic, E major]   *40'*
1.Allegro vivace   2.Allegro scherzando   3.Adagio
molto tranquillo   4.Finale: Molto vivace
3(3rd alt. Picc.),2(2nd alt. E.H.),3*,2-4,2,3,
1-Timp.,Perc.-Str.
Breitkopf & Härtel, Leipzig, c1898
Score 153 p.
Composed 1896-97.   First performance Richter
Concerts, London, 1897.

COX, RONALD B.   Mount Vernon, Ohio 28 February 1946

7282   American folk trilogy [for orchestra]
1.Fiddle dee dee: Tenderly, in a lilting two
2.Skip to my Lou: Majestically   3.Old MacDonald
had a farm: Allegro con spirito
2,1,2,2-4,2,2,1-Timp.,Glock.-Hp.-Str.
Ms.
Score 40 p.
An arrangement of three American folk melodies.
Originally composed for piano and double cho-
rus, 1974.   This transcription, 1975.

COYNER, LOU.   Pittsburgh 11 March 1931

383c   Dawnstone, for four 'cello soloists   *18'*
and chamber orchestra
In 2 groups: I. 4Solo Vc.,Bn.,Perc.,Cb.
              II. 1,1,1,1-2Hn.-Str.
Ms. c1974 by Lou Coyner
Score 55 p. Large folio
Dawnstone is the literal English translation
of eolith, the earliest tool from the Stone
Age.   Commissioned by the Pittsburgh Contem-
porary Music Symposium.   Composed 1974.

CRAS, JEAN EMILE PAUL.   Brest, France 22 May 1879
                          Brest, France 14 September 1932

4270   [Souls of children, for orchestra]   *15'*
1.Pures: Assez lent et calme   2.Naïves: Assez
animé - Modéré   3.Mystérieuses: Très lent -
Plus vite - Lent
2(2nd alt. Picc.),2(2nd ad lib.),2,2-3(3rd ad
lib.),2-Timp.,Trgl.-Hp.-Str.
Senart, Paris, c1924
Score 52 p.
Composed 1918.

Creston, Paul

CRESTON, PAUL.   New York 10 October 1906

Real name: Joseph Guttoveggio

7072 Anatolia (Turkish rhapsody) for band   *11'*
1.Slow 2.Moderately fast 3.Very slow
4.Moderately fast
3*,2,7(1Cl. in E-flat,2Cl. in B-flat,Alto Cl.,
Contralto Cl.,B.Cl.,Cb.Cl.),2-4Sax.(AATBar.)-
4,2,3Cnt.,3,Bar.,2-Timp.,Perc.-Cb.
Templeton Music Publ. Co. [Delaware Water
Gap, Pennsylvania] c1968
Score 52 p.
Based on Turkish folk songs and dances. Commissioned by Eastern Illinois University. Composed 1967. First performance Charleston, Illinois, 28 April 1968, Eastern Illinois University Band, the composer conducting.

4271 Fanfare for paratroopers
See: TEN FANFARES BY TEN COMPOSERS FOR BRASS
        AND PERCUSSION.

965s Gregorian chant for string   *6'30"*
orchestra (from String Quartet, Op. 8)
Str.
Alec Templeton, Inc., New Rochelle, New York,
c1957
Score 6 p.
String Quartet composed 1936. First performance of this version Oklahoma City, 17 November 1957, Oklahoma City Symphony Orchestra, Guy Fraser Harrison conductor.

2831 Out of the cradle endlessly rocking,   *15'*
Op. 5, for chamber orchestra (after the poem
by Walt Whitman)
2,1,2*,1-1,1,1,1-Timp.,Perc.-Org.(ad lib.),
Cel.,Hp.-Str.
Ms.
Score 34 p. Large folio
Composed 1934. First performance Rochester, New York, 19 October 1938, Rochester Civic Orchestra, Howard Hanson conductor.

922m [Partita, flute, violin, strings,   *16'*
Op. 12]
1.Preamble 2.Sarabande 3.Burlesk 4.Air
5.Tarantella
Solo Fl.,Solo Vn.-Str.
Ms.
Score 33 p. Large folio
Composed 1937. First performance at the Fourth Yaddo Music Period, Saratoga Springs, New York, 18 September 1937, Yaddo Orchestra, the composer conducting, Lois Porter violinist, Robert Silberberg flautist.

3025 Threnody, for orchestra, Op. 16   *12'*
3,2,2,2-4,2,3,1-Timp.,Perc.-Hp.-Str.
Ms.
Score 16 p. Large folio
Composed 1938 in memory of the composer's first child, Paul Julian Creston. First performance Pittsburgh, Pennsylvania, 2 December 1938, Pittsburgh Symphony Orchestra, Fritz Reiner conductor.

3019 Two choric dances, for full   *12'*
orchestra, Op. 17b
3(3rd alt. Picc.),2,2,2-4,2,3-Timp.,Perc.-Pno.
-Str.
Ms.
Score 53 p.
Originally composed for chamber orchestra, 1938, designed as Op. 17a; revised for full orchestra, probably 1938. First performance of revised version Cleveland, 20 February 1939, Cleveland Federal Symphony Orchestra of the WPA, Arthur Shepherd conductor.

4746 Zanoni, Op. 40, for band   *7'*
4*,2,6*(1 in E-flat),2-4Sax.-8(4 in F,4 in E-
flat),3Cnt.,2Tpt.,3Tbn.,Euph.,2Tubas-Timp.,
Perc.-Cb.
G. Schirmer, New York, c1949
Score 32 p.
Composed 1946. First performance New York, June 1947, Goldman Band, Edwin Franko Goldman conductor.

CRIST, BAINBRIDGE.   Lawrenceburg, Indiana 1883

3618 American epic: 1620, a tone poem   *13'*
3(3rd alt. Picc.),3*,3*,3*-4,3,3,1-Timp.,Perc.-
Hp.-Str.
Ms.
Score 44 p. Large folio
Composed 1941. First performance Washington, D.C., 28 February 1943, National Symphony Orchestra, Hans Kindler conductor.

2744 Chinese dance   *4'*
3(3rd alt. Picc.),3*,3*,3*-4,3,3,1-Timp.,Perc.
-Hp.-Str.
Ms.
Score 27 p.
Originally composed for piano, 1923; orchestrated 1923. First performance Boston, 23 May 1925, Boston Pops Orchestra, Agide Jacchia conductor.

2870 Chinese sketches   *9'*
3*,3*,3*,3*-4,3,3,1-Timp.,Perc.-Hp.-Str.
Ms.
Score 42 p.
Composed 1927.

2783 Egyptian impressions, Op. 1   *10'*
1.Caravan 2.To a mummy 3.Katabet 4.A desert
song
3*,3*,3*,3*-4,3,3,1-Timp.,Perc.-Cel.,Hp.-Str.
Ms.
Score 39 p.
Composed for large orchestra, 1913. First performance Boston, 22 June 1915, Boston Pops Orchestra, Ernst Schmidt conductor.

3259 Festival overture   *8'*
3(3rd alt. Picc.),3*,3*,3*-4,3,3,1-Timp.,
Perc.-Str.
Ms. c1940 by Bainbridge Crist
Score 74 p.
Composed 1939. First performance Washington, D.C., 3 January 1940, U. S. Marine Band Symphony Orchestra, Capt. W.F.H. Santelmann conductor.

3260 Hindu rhapsody   8'
   3(3rd alt. Picc.),3*,3*,3*-4,3,3,1-Timp.,
   Perc.-Cel.,Hp.-Str.
   Ms.
   Score 80 p.
   Composed 1939.

3570 Hymn to Nefertiti   15'
   3(3rd alt. Picc.),3*,3*,3*-4,3,3,1-Timp.,
   Perc.-Hp.-Str.
   Ms.
   Score 45 p.
   *Composed 1936. First performance Washington,
   D.C., 30 March 1937, U. S. Navy Band Symphony
   Orchestra, Lt. Charles Benter conductor.*

2827 La nuit revécue [The night remem-   9'
   bered]
   3*,3*,3*,3*-4,3,3,1-Timp.,Cym.-Hp.-Str.
   Ms.
   Score 31 p.
   *Composed 1931, after the poem, Senlin, by
   Conrad Aiken. First performance broadcast
   over NBC, New York, 8 March 1936, Radio City
   Music Hall Orchestra, Erno Rapee conductor.*

2778 Le pied de la momie [The mummy's   8'
   foot, Op. 2. Final dance]
   3(3rd alt. Picc.),3*,3*,3*-4,3,3,1-Timp.,Perc.
   -Hp.-Str.
   Ms.
   Score 99 p.
   *Composed 1914; based on the romance by Théo-
   phile Gautier. First performance Bournemouth,
   England, 3 December 1925, Bournemouth Municipal
   Orchestra, the composer conducting.*

3569 Place Pigalle, un souvenir de Mont-   6'
   martre
   1,1,2,1-2,2,1-Timp.,Perc.-Hp.-Str.
   Ms.
   Score 46 p.
   Originally composed 1929; this version 1939.

3795 Romance   6'
   1,1,2,1-2,2,1-Timp.(or B.Dr.),Perc.-Hp.(ad
   lib.)-Str.
   Ms.
   Score 26 p.
   Composed 1934.

CRISTOFARO, ALBERTO DE.

1000s Intermezzo religioso
   Hp.,Harm.(both ad lib.)-Str.
   Score: Ms. 7 p.
   Parts: Lemoine, Paris [n.d.]

CRUSELL, BERNHARD HENRIK.
                 Nystad, Finland 15 October 1775
                 Stockholm 28 July 1838

266m Concertante for clarinet, bassoon, horn
   and orchestra, Op. 3, B-flat major. Edited by
   Klaas Weelink
   1.Allegro 2.Andante sostenuto 3.Allegro ma
   non tanto
   Solo Cl., Solo Bn., Solo Hn.-1,2,0,2-2,2-

   Timp.-Str.
   KaWe, Amsterdam, c1961
   Score 67 p.
   First performance 1808.

CSONKA, PAUL.   Vienna 24 October 1905

276p Cuban concerto no. 1, concertino in   8'
   one movement for pianoforte and orchestra
   Andante moderato – Lento – Allegro
   Solo Pno.-2,2,2,2-4,2,3,1-Timp.,Perc.-Cel.,Hp.
   -Str.
   Ms.
   Score 49 p. Large folio
   *Composed 1946. First performance Havana, 1946,
   CMQ Radio Orchestra, the composer conducting,
   Francisco Godino soloist.*

2283s [Symphonietta for string orchestra]   12'
   Andante – Allegretto ma non troppo – Vivo –
   Andante – Allegro molto – Più lento
   Str.
   Ms.
   Score 39 p.
   *Composed 1957. First performance Havana,
   March 1958, Sociedad de Conciertos, the com-
   poser conducting.*

CUI, CÉSAR ANTONOVICH.   Vilna 18 January 1835
                      St. Petersburg 24 March 1918

2479 [Angelo. Introduction to the opera]
   3,2*,3*,2-4,2,3,1-Timp.,Perc.-Str.
   Bessel, St. Petersburg [n.d.]
   Score 13 p.
   *From the opera in four acts, based on Victor
   Hugo's drama. First performance of opera
   St. Petersburg, 13 February 1876.*

902v [Berceuse, violin and string orchestra,
   E-flat major]
   Solo Vn.-Str.
   Leduc, Paris [n.d.]
   Score 3 p.
   *Originally composed for violin and piano, as
   no. 8 of Douze Miniatures.*

901v [Cantabile, violin, B-flat major]
   Solo Vn.-2Fl.,2Cl.-2Hn.-Str.
   Leduc, Paris [n.d.]
   Score 5 p.
   *Originally composed for violin and piano, as
   no. 5 of Douze Miniatures.*

481c Deux morceaux [Two pieces] Op. 36
   1.Scherzando 2.Cantabile
   Solo Vc.-2,2,2,2-2Hn.-Str.
   Rahter, Leipzig [n.d.]
   Score 47 p.

1061 Le flibustier [The buccaneer] Prélude
   3(3rd alt. Picc.),2,2,2-4,2,3,1-Timp.,Perc.-
   Hp.-Str.
   Heugel, Paris, c1896
   Score 25 p.
   *From the opera composed 1888-89, based on the
   drama by Jean Richepin. First performance
   Opéra-Comique, Paris, 22 January 1894.*

Cui, César

1471 Le flibustier [The buccaneer] Entr'acte
3*,2,2,2-4,2,3,1-Timp.,Perc.-Hp.-Str.
Heugel, Paris, c1896
Score 18 p.

519 [The Mandarin's son. Overture]
2(2nd alt. Picc.),2,2,2-4,2,3(B.Tbn. alt.
Tuba)-Timp.,Perc.-Str.
Rahter, Hamburg [n.d.]
Score 34 p.
*From the operetta composed 1859. First public
performance St. Petersburg, 19 December 1878.*

2152 Marche solennelle, Op. 18
3(3rd alt. Picc.),2,2,2-4,2,2Cnt.,3,1-Timp.,
Perc.-Hp.-Str.
Rahter, Hamburg [n.d.]
Score 71 p.
Composed 1881.

100 Le prisonnier du Caucase. Danses
circassiennes
1.Danse des femmes 2.Danses des hommes (Lesghinka)
3*,2,2,2-4,2,3,1-Timp.,Perc.-Pno.,Hp.-Str.
Bessel, St. Petersburg [n.d.]
Score 55 p.
*From the opera in three acts composed 1857 and
1881-82, with libretto by Victor Alexandrovich Krilov, based on the poem by Pushkin.
First performance St. Petersburg, 16 February
1883.*

643 [Scherzo no. 1, Op. 1, F major]
3*,2,2,2-4,2,3,1-Timp.-Str.
Bessel, St. Petersburg [n.d.]
Score 37 p.
*Composed 1857, on the letters B,A,B,E,G and
C,C from Cui's wife's name and his own.*

644 [Scherzo no. 2, À la Schumann,   7'
Op. 2, G minor]
3(3rd alt. Picc.),2,2,2-4,2,3,1-Timp.-Str.
Bessel, St. Petersburg [n.d.]
Score 25 p.
Composed 1857.

1840 [Suite no. 1, Miniature, Op. 20]
1.[Little march] 2.[Impromptu à la Schumann]
3.[Cantabile] 4.[Grievous memory] 5.[Ber-
ceuse] 6.[Rustic scherzo]
2,2,2,2-4,2,1-Timp.-Hp.-Str.
Bessel, St. Petersburg [n.d.]
Score 32 p.

2311 [Suite, no. 1, Miniature, Op. 20.
Berceuse. Arranged by William F. Happich]
1,1,1,1-Hn.-Hp.-Str.
Ms.
Score 10 p.

187 [Suite no. 2, Op. 38, E major]
1.Tema con variazioni 2.Quasi ballata
3.Scherzo 4.Marcia
3*,2,2,2-4,2,3,1-Timp.,Cym.,Trgl.-Str.
Bessel, St. Petersburg [n.d.]
Score 123 p.
Composed 1887.

715 [Suite no. 3, À Argenteau, Op. 40]   29'
1.[The cedar] 2.[Serenade] 3.[Sham-battle]
4.[In the chapel] 5.[The rock]
3(3rd alt. Picc.),2,2,2-4,3,3,1-Timp.,Perc.-
Str.
Bessel, St. Petersburg [n.d.]
Score 69 p.
*Composed 1887. Published incorrectly as
Suite no. 4.*

357 [Suite no. 4, In modo populari,   19'
Op. 43]
1.Allegro moderato 2.Moderato 3.Vivace
4.Moderato 5.Allegretto 6.Vivace
2(2nd alt. Picc.),2,2,2-2Hn.-Timp.-Str.
Belaieff, Leipzig, c1891
Score 50 p.
*Composed 1890. First performance St. Peters-
burg, 1891. Published incorrectly as Suite
no. 3.*

557v Suite concertante, Op. 25
1.Intermezzo scherzando 2.Canzonetta
3.Cavatine 4.Finale-tarantella
Solo Vn.-3(1st&3rd alt. Picc.),2,2,2-4Hn.-
Timp.-Hp.-Str.
Belaieff, Leipzig, c1886
Score 141 p.
Composed 1883.

467 Tarantelle, Op. 12
3(3rd alt. Picc.),2,2,2-4,2,3,1-Timp.,Perc.-
Hp.-Str.
Durand, Paris [n.d.]
Score 36 p.

Trois scherzos, Op. 82
645 No. 1, C major
2,2,2,2-4,2,3,1-Timp.-Str.
646 No. 2, F major
3,2,2,2-4,0,3,1-Timp.,Trgl.-Hp.-Str.
647 No. 3, C minor
2,2,2,2-3,0,3,1-Timp.,Trgl.-Str.
Jurgenson, Moscow [n.d.]
Scores: 29 p., 35 p., 33 p.

833 Valse, Op. 65   6'
3(3rd alt. Picc.),2,2,2-4,2,3,1-Timp.,Bells-
Str.
Jurgenson, Moscow [n.d.]
Score 31 p.
*Composed 1903. First performance St. Peters-
burg, 1904.*

2920 [William Ratcliff. Overture to Act III]
2,2*,2,2-4,2,3,1-Timp.-Hp.-Str.
Bessel, St. Petersburg [n.d.]
Score 9 p.
*From the opera in three acts with libretto by
Alexei Nikolayevich Pleshcheyev, based on
Heine's drama. First performance St. Peters-
burg, 26 February 1869.*

CURSCH-BÜHREN, FRANZ THEODOR.
Troppau, Silesia 10 January 1859
Leipzig 11 March 1908

1239s Largo, Op. 157 no. 2

Harm.(or Org.; ad lib.)-Str.
Hug, Leipzig [n.d.]
Score 5 p.

838s La maggiolata [Florentine May serenade]
Op. 73 no. 1
Solo Vc.-Str.
F. Hofmeister, Leipzig, ᶜ1894
Score 7 p.

1403s Ungarische Weise [Hungarian tune]
Str.
Score: Ms. 11 p.
Parts: C.F. Kahnt, Leipzig [n.d.]
Based on battle song of the Kurucz warriors in 1672.

36s Valse mignonne [Favorite waltz] inter-
mezzo
Str.
A.E. Fischer, Bremen, ᶜ1900
Score 6 p.

CUSTER, ARTHUR.
                   Manchester, Connecticut 21 April 1923

6604 Concert piece for orchestra   10'
2(2nd alt. Picc.),2,2(2nd alt. B.Cl.),2-4,2,3,
1-Timp.,Perc.-Str.
Ms. [ᶜ1963 by Arthur Custer]
Score 66 p.
*Composed 1959. First performance Austin,
Texas, 26 April 1963, Inter-American Sympo-
sium Orchestra, Donald Johanos conductor.*

404c Five dialogues, for 'cello and   16'
orchestra
1.Moderato 2. ♪=152 3.Allegro moderato
4. ♩=92 5. ♩=132
Solo Vc.-2(2nd alt. Picc.),2,2(2nd alt. B.Cl.),
2(2nd alt. C.Bn.)-2,2,1-Timp.,Perc.-Pno.-Str.
Ms. [Composers Facsimile Edition, New York,
n.d.]
Score 111 p.
*Composed 1962. First performance Madrid, 3
August 1963, Madrid Philharmonic, Odón Alonso
conductor, Enrique Correa soloist.*

7029 Found objects II (Rhapsodality brass!) 15'
for orchestra
3*,2,3*,3*-Alto Sax.-4,3,3,1-Timp.,Perc.-Hp.-
Str.
Ms. ᶜ1969 by Arthur Custer
Score 51 p. Large folio
*Composed 1969. First performance New York
8 November 1969, Pro Arte Orchestra, Eleazar
de Carvalho conductor.*

6605 Passacaglia for small orchestra   10'
1(alt. Picc.),1(alt. E.H.),1(alt. B.Cl.),1(alt.
Alto Sax.)-2,1,1,1-Timp.,Perc.-Str.
Ms. [ᶜ1963 by Arthur Custer]
Score 47 p.
*Composed 1958; revised 1963. First performance
of revised version Chicago, 14 April 1963,
Chicago Chamber Orchestra, Dieter Kober conduc-
tor.*

6556 Songs of the seasons, for soprano   18'
and small orchestra
1.Now in the purple sunset (Primavera vieja,
poem by Luis Cernuda) 2.Autumn verses (Versos
de otoño, poem by Rubén Darío) 3.Blossoming
early mornings (Mañanicas floridas, poem by
Lope de Vega) 4.May song (Maya, poem by Lope
de Vega) 5.The air is glowing with heat (Can-
dente está la atmósfera, poem by Rosalia Castro)
Solo Sop. Voice-1(alt. Picc.),1,1(alt. Alto
Sax.),1-2,1-Timp.-Str.
Ms. [Composers Facsimile Edition, New York,
n.d.]
Score 116 p.
*Commissioned by Mrs. Faith B. Smeeth for the
Chicago Chamber Orchestra. Composed 1963-64.
First performance Chicago, 14 May 1965, Chicago
Chamber Orchestra, Dieter Kober conductor,
Salomej Valukas soprano.*

6603 Symphony no. 1 (Sinfonía de Madrid) 20'
1.Gran vía 2.Plaza mayor 3.Casa de campo
2(2nd alt. Picc.),2,2,2-4,2,3,1-Timp.,Perc.-
Str.
Ms. [ᶜ1963 by Arthur Custer]
Score 124 p.
*Composed 1960-61. First performance Madrid,
15 May 1961, Madrid Philharmonic, Odón Alonso
conductor.*

CZERNIK, WILLY.   Dresden 24 February 1901

4653 [Spook in the castle, night-time   7'30"
episode. Ballet music]
2(both alt. Picc.),2,2,2-4,2,3-Timp.,Perc.-Hp.-
3Ten. Voices(ad lib.)-Str.
Fr. Portius, Leipzig [n.d.]
Score 44 p.

CZERNY, CARL.   Vienna 20 February 1791
                       Vienna 15 July 1857

6923 [Symphony no. 2, Op. 781, D major]
1.Andante maestoso ma con moto - Allegro
vivace e con brio 2.Andantino grazioso un
poco moto 3.Scherzo: Molto vivace 4.Finale:
Allegro vivace
2,2,2,2-2,2,3(optional)-Timp.-Str.
C.A. Spina, Vienna [184-?]
Score 200 p.

CZERWONKY, RICHARD.   Birnbaum, Germany 23 May 1886

3210 Episode, symphonic rhapsody   9'
3(3rd alt. Picc.),2,2(2nd alt. B.Cl. ad lib.),
2-4,2,3,1-Timp.,Perc.-Pno.-Str.
Ms.
Score 44 p.
*Originally composed for violin and piano, 1922;
orchestrated 1929. First performance Berlin,
28 January 1931, Berlin Symphony Orchestra,
the composer conducting.*

3626 [Symphony no. 1, D minor]   30'30"
1.Adagio 2.Andante con moto 3.Allegretto
3*,2,2,2-4,2,3,1-Timp.,Perc.-Hp.-Str.
Ms.

Czerwonky, Richard

Score 133 p.
Composed 1936. First performance Chicago, 14 March 1937, Illinois Symphony Orchestra of the WPA, the composer conducting.

3085 Weltschmerz   8'
3*,3*,3*,2-4,3,3,1-Timp.,Perc.-Hp.-Str.
Ms.
Score 18 p.
Composed 1935. First performance Chicago, 7 August 1936, Chicago Philharmonic Orchestra, the composer conducting.

CZIBULKA, ALPHONS.
Szepes-Várallya, Hungary 14 May 1842
Vienna 27 October 1894

784s An Dich! [To you, waltz serenade, Op. 390]
Str.
C.F. Schmidt, Heilbronn, c1894
Score 11 p.

765s Barcarolle italienne, Op. 326
Str.
Cranz, Leipzig [n.d.]
Score 10 p.

1179s Fliegen-Menuett [from the comic operetta Der Bajazzo, Op. 380]
Str.
Kratochwill, Leipzig, c1893
Score 6 p.

732s Rendez-vous au bal, intermezzo, Op. 373
Str.
Cranz, Leipzig [n.d.]
Score 10 p.

659s Songe d'amour après le bal [Love's   4'
dream after the ball] intermezzo, Op. 356
Hp.(ad lib.)-Str.
Bosworth, London, c1898
Score 7 p.

D

Names beginning with d', da, or de are entered under the letter following the prefix: e.g., d'Albert; da Venezia; de Falla.

DAHL, INGOLF.   Hamburg 9 June 1912
Frutigen (Bern), Switzerland 7 August 1970

4862 Music for brass instruments   16'30"
1.Chorale fantasy on Christ Lay in the Bonds of Death: Sostenuto 2. Intermezzo: Allegro leggiero 3.Fugue: Moderato - Allegro giusto
1Hn.,2Tpt.,2Tbn.Tuba(ad lib.), in single or multiple instrumentation
M. Witmark, New York, c1949
Score 24 p.
The first movement is based on the original modal form of a Lutheran Easter chorale. Commissioned by Arthur Leslie Jacobs of the Church Federation of Los Angeles. First

performance Los Angeles, May 1944, at the Festival of Contemporary Music of Los Angeles.

2393s Variations for string orchestra   12'
on a theme by C.P.E. Bach
Str.
Tetra Music Co., New York, c1974
Score 22 p.
Theme based on the Larghetto Sostenuto section of Fantasia II, from the Sixth Book of C.P.E. Bach's Clavier-Sonaten und Freye Fantasien (1787) (Wotquenne catalog no. 61). Commissioned by the American Federation of Musicians' Congress of Strings, Western Section. Composed 1967. First performance University of Southern California, Los Angeles, 12 July 1967, American Federation of Musicians' Congress of Strings, Western Section, Walter Ducloux conductor. Revised for publication and Interlude added, 1968-69.

DALAYRAC, NICOLAS-MARIE. Muret, France 8 June 1753
Fonteney-aux-Roses, near Paris 26 November 1809

Also known as: d'Alayrac, Dallairac, Daleyrac, Dallerac

6582 [Leon, or the chateau of Monténéro. Overture]
1,2,2,2-2,2,1-Timp.-Str.
Pleyel, Paris [1798]
Score 46 p.
From the prose comedy in 3 acts by François Benoît Hoffmann.

DALCROZE, ÉMILE JAQUES.
See: JAQUES-DALCROZE, ÉMILE.

DALE, BENJAMIN JAMES.
Crouch Hill near London 17 July 1885
London 30 July 1943

4625 A holiday tune for small orchestra
1,1,2,1-2Hn.-Str.
Augener, London, c1922/1924/1925
Score 12 p.
Originally composed for violin and piano between 1916 and 1920. Orchestral version 1925.

4638 Prunella for small orchestra
1,1,2,1-2Hn.-Str.
Augener, London, c1923
Score 8 p.
Originally composed for violin and piano between 1916 and 1920. Orchestral version 1924.

DALL'ABACO, EVARISTO FELICE.   Verona 12 July 1675
Munich 12 July 1742

Also known as: Abaco, Evaristo Felice dall'
Dall'Abaco, E. Francesco

2102s [Concerto da chiesa, Op. 2 no. 4.   10'
Transcribed for string orchestra by Ettore Bonelli]
Aria: Allegro moderato - Largo 2.Presto
Str.
G. Zanibon, Padua, c1948

Score 11 p.
*Originally for two violins, viola and violon-
cello with basso continuo. First published in
Amsterdam, 1712-14 as one of the six concerti
in Op. 2.*

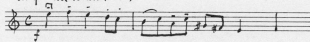

DALLIN, G. LEON.   Silver City, Utah 26 March 1918

4016 Chamber symphony   *12'*
    1.Allegro moderato 2.Andante 3.Allegro
    scherzando
    2,2,2,2-2Hn.-Str.
    Ms.
    Score 49 p. Large folio
    *Composed 1940-41. First performance Rochester,
    New York, during the symposium held 22-24
    April 1941, Rochester Civic Orchestra, Howard
    Hanson conductor.*

3712 Symphonic sketches   *10'*
    1.Caprice 2.Nocturne 3.Scherzo
    2(2nd alt. Picc.),2,2,2-4,2,3,1-Timp.,Perc.-
    Hp.-Str.
    Ms.
    Score 57 p.
    *Composed 1939. First performance Rochester,
    New York, 19 April 1940, Rochester Civic
    Orchestra, Howard Hanson conductor.*

DAL MONTE, EMILIO.

1201s Dors, ma brune! [Sleep, my brown darling,
    lullaby for string orchestra]
    Str.
    Score: Ms. 7 p.
    Parts: Foetisch Frères, Paris [n.d.]

1202s Doux serment [Sweet vows, intermezzo for
    string orchestra with flute]
    Fl.-Str.
    Score: Ms. 11 p.
    Parts: Foetisch Frères, Paris [n.d.]

1263s Musette, for solo violin and string
    orchestra
    Solo Vn.-Str.
    Score: Ms. 8 p.
    Parts: Foetisch Frères, Paris [n.d.]

1264s La patrouille liliputienne, fantaisie
    burlesque [for string orchestra]
    Str.
    Score: Ms. 10 p.
    Parts: Foetisch Frères, Paris [n.d.]

1265s Sérénade mignonne [for string orchestra]
    Str.
    Score: Ms. 10 p.
    Parts: Foetisch Frères, Paris [n.d.]

1203s Vieille histoire [for string orchestra]
    Str.
    Score: Ms. 8 p.
    Parts: Foetisch Frères, Paris [n.d.]

DANCLA, JEAN BAPTISTE CHARLES.
    Bagnères-de-Bigorre, France 19 December 1817
                        Tunis 9 November 1907

306 Menuet, for 2 violins. Transcribed for   *3'*
    various ensembles by W.F. Happich
    1.Woodwinds alone 2.Strings alone 3.Woodwinds
    and strings 4.Full orchestra
    2,2,2,2-4,2,3,1-Timp.,S.Dr.,Trgl.-Str.
    Ms.
    Score 9 p.
    *Each movement is a transcription of the minuet,
    originally composed for violin duet, ca.1850.
    These transcriptions commissioned for the
    Symphony Club by Edwin A. Fleisher, 1923.*

DANEAU, NICOLAS ADOLPHE GUSTAVE.
                    Binche, Belgium 17 June 1866
                        Brussels 12 July 1944

195s Petite suite [for string orchestra]
    1.Rêverie: Presque lent 2.Berceuse: Lent et
    sostenu 3.Sérénata: Très moderato
    Str.
    A. Cranz, Brussels [192-?]
    Score 10 p.

DANICAN-PHILIDOR, FRANÇOIS ANDRÉ.
    See: PHILIDOR, FRANÇOIS ANDRÉ DANICAN.

DANIELS, MABEL WHEELER.
    Swampscott, Massachusetts 27 November 1878
                        Boston 10 March 1971

2467 Deep forest [original version] prelude   *6'*
    for little symphony orchestra, Op. 34 no. 1
    1,1,1,1-1,1-Timp.,Bells,Cym.-Str.
    J. Fischer, New York, c1932
    Score 26 p.
    *Composed 1930. First performance Town Hall,
    New York, 3 June 1931, Barrère Little Symphony,
    Georges Barrère conductor.*

2680 Deep forest [transcription] for   *6'*
    symphony orchestra, Op. 34 no. 1
    2,2,2,2-4,2,3,1-Timp.,Perc.-Hp.-Str.
    Ms.
    Score 31 p.
    *Originally composed for chamber orchestra,
    1930. This transcription 1933. First perform-
    ance Weston, Connecticut, 7 August 1934, New
    York Orchestra, Nicolai Sokoloff conductor.*

3405 Pirates' island, Op. 34 no. 2   *6'30"*
    3(3rd alt. Picc.),2,2,2-4,2,3,1-Timp.,Perc.-
    Str.
    Ms.
    Score 66 p.
    *Composed 1934. First performance Harrisburg,
    Pennsylvania, 19 February 1935, Harrisburg
    Symphony Orchestra, George King Raudenbush
    conductor.*

Daniels, William Arthur

DANIELS, WILLIAM ARTHUR.
        b. Camden, New Jersey 4 September 1928

   7318 Woodwind quintet, based on   *20'*
     Afro-American folk music
     1.Blues 2.Spiritual, Mercy (adapted)
     3.Hambone variations
     1,1,2*,1-Traps-Cb.
     Ms.
     Score 25 p.
     First performance Philadelphia, 27 February
     1977, Arthur Daniels and members of the Jack
     Ebbert Jazz Band.

DANNING, SOPHUS CHRISTIAN.
        Odense, Denmark 16 June 1867
        Odense 7 November 1925

   403s [Prelude, string orchestra, A major]
     Str.
     Wilhelm Hansen, Copenhagen [n.d.]
     Score 7 p.

DANZI, FRANZ.   Schwetzingen, Germany 15 May 1763
                Karlsruhe 13 April 1826

   889m [Concerto, flute, Op. 30, G major]
     1.Allegro 2.Larghetto 3.Allegretto moderato
     Solo Fl.-2Ob.,2Bn.-2Hn.-Str.
     Score: Ms. 54 p.
     Parts: Breitkopf & Härtel, Leipzig [1806?]

   890m [Concerto, flute, Op. 31, D minor]
     1.Allegro 2.Larghetto 3.Polacca
     Solo Fl.-2Ob.,2Bn.-2,2-Timp.-Str.
     Score: Ms. 65 p.
     Parts: Breitkopf & Härtel, Leipzig [1806?]

  1047m [Sinfonia concertante for flute,   *25'*
     oboe, horn and bassoon with chamber orchestra,
     E-flat major] Edited by Heinz Zirnbauer
     1.Allegro 2.Adagio 3.Rondo allegretto
     Concertino: Fl.,Ob.,Bn.-Hn.
     Orchestra: 2Ob.(or 2Cl.)-2Hn.-Str.
     Schott, Mainz, ᶜ1939
     Score 48 p.
     Composed 1785.

   5803 [Symphony, Op. 25, C major] Edited by
     Thor Johnson and Donald M. McCorkle
     1.Larghetto - Allegro vivace 2.Andante modera-
     ato 3.Menuetto: Allegretto 4.Grave - Allegro
     1,2,0,2-2,2-Timp.-Str.
     Ms.
     Score 122 p. Large folio
     Originally published by Breitkopf & Härtel,
     Leipzig [n.d.]. First modern performance at
     the Fifth Early American Moravian Music Fes-
     tival and Seminar, Salem College, Winston-
     Salem, North Carolina, 25 June 1959, The
     Festival Orchestra, Thor Johnson conductor.

DARGOMYZHSKY, ALEXANDER SERGEIEVICH.
        Tula, Russia 14 February 1813
        St. Petersburg 17 January 1869

   323 [Cosatschoque, fantasy on a Cossack dance]
     2,2,2,2-2,2,2,Ophicl.-Timp.,B.Dr.-Str.
     Jurgenson, Moscow [1865?]
     Score 31 p.

  1537 [Fantasy on Finnish tunes]
     2(2nd alt. Picc.),2,2,2-4,0,2Cnt.,2,Ophicl.-
     Timp.,Cym.,B.Dr.-Str.
     B. Bessel, St. Petersburg [n.d.]
     Score 45 p.

  1593 [Fantasy-scherzo, Baba-Yaga, or From   *7'*
     the Volga to Riga, for orchestra]
     2,2,2,2-2,1,2Cnt.,3,1-Timp.,Cym.,B.Dr.-Str.
     Mussektor, Moscow, 1927
     Score 53 p.

DAUPRAT, LOUIS-FRANÇOIS.   Paris 24 May 1781
                   Paris 16 July 1868

   703m [Concerto, horn, no. 4, F major]
     1.Allegro moderato 2.Adagio, ma non troppo
     3.Rondo: Allegro
     Solo Hn.-2,2,0,2-2Hn.-Str.
     Score: Ms. 103 p.
     Parts: [Schoenenberger, Paris, n.d.]

   881m [Concerto, horn, no. 5, Op. 21, E major]
     1.Allegro risoluto 2.Poco adagio 3.Allegro
     moderato
     Solo Hn.-1,2,0,2-2Hn.-Str.
     Score: Ms. 64 p.
     Parts: [Schoenenberger, Paris, n.d.]

DAUS, ABRAHAM.   Berlin 22 June 1902
                   Tel Aviv 1974

  2245s Legend and scherzo for string   *16'*
     orchestra
     Legend: Molto lento- Scherzo: Molto vivace
     Str.
     Israeli Music Publications, Tel-Aviv, ᶜ[n.d.]
     by Abraham Daus

David, Ferdinand

Score 52 p.
Composed 1950.

DAVICO, VINCENZO.   Monaco 14 January 1889
                     Rome 8 December 1969

5315 Poemetti pastorali pour double   9'
quintette, harpe et piano
1.Egloga: Piuttosto adagio - Larghetto
2.Ditirambo: Allegretto, molto sostenuto
3.Elegia: Molto lento
1,1,1,1-Hn.-Pno.,Hp.-Str.
Max Eschig, Paris, c1924
Score 39 p.
Composed 1921.

645c Romance, for violoncello and orchestra
Solo Vc.-2,1,2,2-2Hn.-Timp.-Hp.-Str.
Score: Ms. 15 p.
Parts: Ricordi, Paris, c1919

DAVID, ADOLPHE-ISAAC.   Nantes, France 1842
                         Paris 24 June 1897

1579s La pluie [for piano, Op. 27. Transcribed
for string orchestra by H. Holzhaus]
Str.
Score: Ms. 6 p.
Parts: [Printed, n.p., n.d.]

DAVID, FÉLICIEN-CÉSAR.
        Cadenet, Vaucluse 13 April 1810
        St.-Germain-en-Laye, France 29 August 1876

4261 [Lalla-Roukh. Overture]
2*,2,2,2-4,2,3-Timp.,Perc.-Str.
E. Girod, Paris [n.d.]
Score 36 p.
*From the comic opera in 2 acts with libretto
by Hippolyte Lucas and Michel Carré, based on
Thomas Moore's poem, Lalla Rookh. Composed
1862.*

DAVID, FERDINAND.   Hamburg 19 January 1810
                     Klosters, Switzerland 18 July 1873

1192v [Andante and scherzo capriccioso for
violin and orchestra, Op. 16, D major]
Solo Vn.-2,2,2,2-2,2,1-Timp.-Str.
Breitkopf & Härtel, Leipzig [187-?]
Score in reduction 12 p.

594v [At the well, character piece for violin
and piano, Op. 39 no. 6. Transcribed for solo
violin and orchestra by Philipp Scharwenka]
Solo Vn.-2,0,2,2-2Hn.-Str.
Breitkopf & Härtel, Leipzig, c1895
Score 13 p.

538v [Concertino no. 1, violin and orchestra,
Op. 3, A major]
In one movement: Andante sostenuto - Allegro
con spirito - Andante sostenuto - Rondo vivace
Solo Vn.-2,2,2,2-2,2-Timp.-Str.
Score in reduction: Litolff, Brunswick [n.d.]
23 p.
Parts: Breitkopf & Härtel, Leipzig [1837]

749m [Concertino no. 4, trombone and   13'
orchestra, Op. 4, E-flat major]
1.Allegro maestoso 2.Andante marcia funebre
3.Allegro maestoso
Solo Tbn.-2,2,2,2-4,2,3-Timp.-Str.
Score: Ms. 74 p.
Parts: F. Kistner, Leipzig [183-?]
Composed and first performed Leipzig, 1837.

791m [Concertino, bassoon and orchestra,   8'
Op. 12, B-flat major]
1.Andante cantabile 2.Presto agitato 3.Più
moto
Solo Bn.-1,2,2,1-2(in B-flat),2-Timp.-Str.
Score: Ms. 95 p.
Parts: [F. Kistner, Leipzig, 1839]
Composed 1838. First performance Leipzig, 1839.

862v [Concerto, violin, no. 1, Op. 10, E minor]
1.Allegro con fuoco 2.Andante 3.Allegro gio-
coso
Solo Vn.-2(2nd alt. Picc.),2,2,2-2,2-Timp.-Str.
Score: Ms. 170 p.
Parts: Breitkopf & Härtel, Leipzig [1839]

994v [Concerto, violin, no. 2, Op. 14, D major]
1.Allegro molto moderato 2.Andante con moto,
attacca 3.Rondo capriccioso
Solo Vn.-2,2,2,2-2,2,B.Tbn.-Timp.-Str.
Score: Ms. 122 p.
Parts: F. Kistner, Leipzig [1842?]

992v [Concerto, violin, no. 3, Op. 17, A minor]
1.Allegro 2.Adagio 3.Rondo grazioso
Solo Vn.-2(2nd alt. Picc.),2,2,2-2,3-Timp.-
Str.
Score: Ms. 176 p.
Parts: F. Kistner, Leipzig [1844?]

718v [Concerto, violin, no. 4, Op. 23, E major]
1.Allegro 2.Adagio cantabile, non troppo
lento, attacca 3.Finale: Allegretto grazioso
Solo Vn.-2,2,2,2-2,2-Timp.-Str.
Score: Ms. 149 p.
Parts: Breitkopf & Härtel, Leipzig [1849]

499v [Concerto, violin, no. 5, Op. 35, D minor]
1.Allegro serioso 2.Adagio, attacca 3.Finale
vivace
Solo Vn.-2(2nd alt. Picc.),2,2,2-4,2,3-Timp.-
Str.
Score in reduction: C.F. Peters, Leipzig [190-?]
35 p.
Parts: Breitkopf & Härtel, Leipzig [1857?]

1172v [Introduction and variations on a song,
violin and orchestra, Op. 21, E major]
Solo Vn.-2,2,2,2-2,2,3-Str.
Breitkopf & Härtel, Leipzig [1846]
Score in reduction 16 p.

1026m [Introduction and variations on a theme
by Franz Schubert, clarinet and orchestra,
Op. 8, B-flat major]
Solo Cl.-1,2,0,2-2Hn.-Timp.-Str.
Breitkopf & Härtel, Leipzig [1838?]
Score in reduction 14 p.
The theme by Schubert is his Trauerwalz for

David, Ferdinand

piano, Op. 9 no. 2 (Deutsch catalog no. 365, no. 2).

1045v Introduction and variations on an original theme for violin and orchestra, Op. 13
Solo Vn.-2,2,2,2-2,2-Timp.-Str.
Score: Ms. 88 p.
Parts: F. Kistner, Leipzig [1840]

1020v Introduction and variations [on the theme] Je suis le petit tambour, for violin and orchestra, Op. 5
Solo Vn.-2,2,2,2-2,2-Timp.-Str.
Score: Ms. 70 p.
Parts: F. Kistner, Leipzig [187-?]

DAVID, JOHANN NEPOMUK.
b. Eferding, Upper Austria 30 November 1895

4298 [Dear Christians, let us now rejoice. Four pieces for brass instruments]
[1]Choral [2]Kanon [3]Ostinato [4]Schlusschoral
3Hn.,3Tpt.,2Fluegelhn.,Ten.Hn.,Bar.Hn.,Tbn,2Tuba-Timp.(2 players)
Score: Breitkopf & Härtel, Leipzig, c1937. 7 p.
Parts: Ms. c1976 by The Fleisher Collection of Orchestral Music, Free Library of Philadelphia
Based on Johann Sebastian Bach's chorale, BWV 388. Composed 1937.

4285 [Partita for orchestra, no. 1]   29'
1.Allegro moderato 2.Andante 3.Andante con moto 4.Allegretto con grazia 5.Vivace
2,3*,0,2-3,2,2-Timp.,Glock.-Str.
Score: Breitkopf & Härtel, Leipzig, c1936. 54 p.
Parts: Ms. c1976 by The Fleisher Collection of Orchestral Music, Free Library of Philadelphia
Composed 1935. First performance Leipzig, 22 October 1936 at a Gewandhaus Concert.

DAVIDOV, ALEXEI.   Moscow 5 April 1867
                          Berlin 7 March 1940

727c Fantaisie [violoncello and orchestra] Op. 11
Solo Vc.-3,3*,3,3*-4,2,3,1-Timp.,Cym.-Hp.-Str.
Jurgenson, Moscow [1904?]
Score 80 p.

DAVIDOV, KARL YULEVICH.
Goldingen, Kurland, Latvia 15 March 1838
Moscow 26 February 1889

Also known as: Charles Davidoff

587c Am Springbrunnen [At the fountain, violoncello and orchestra, Op. 20 no. 2]
Solo Vc.-2,2,2,2-2Hn.-Timp.-Str.
F. Kistner, Leipzig [190-?]
Score 28 p.
Orchestral accompaniment by Paul Gilson from Davidov's piano sketches.

555c [Ballade, violoncello and orchestra, Op. 25, G minor]
Solo Vc.-2,2,2,2-4,2,3-Timp.,Cym.-Str.

F. Kistner, Leipzig [1847?]
Score 21 p.
Solo revised by Julius Klengel.

564c [Concerto, violoncello, no. 1, Op. 5, B minor]
1.Allegro moderato 2.Kantilene, leading to 3.Allegretto
Solo Vc.-2,2,2,2-2,2,1-Timp.-Str.
F. Kistner, Leipzig [n.d.]
Score 82 p.

565c [Concerto, violoncello, no. 2, Op. 14, A major]
1.Allegro 2.Andante 3.Allegro con brio
Solo Vc.-2,2,2,2-2,2,3-Timp.-Str.
F. Kistner, Leipzig [n.d.]
Score 123 p.

554c [Concerto, violoncello, no. 3, Op. 18, D major]
1.Allegro moderato 2.Andante 3.Allegro vivace
Solo Vc.-2,2,2,2-2,2,3-Timp.-Str.
F. Kistner, Leipzig [n.d.]
Score 138 p.

616c [Concerto, violoncello, no. 4, Op. 31, E minor]
1.Allegro 2.Lento 3.Finale: Vivace
Solo Vc.-2(2nd alt. Picc.),2,2,2-4,2,3-Timp.-Str.
F. Kistner, Leipzig [n.d.]
Score 127 p.

445c [Fantasy on Russian songs, violoncello and orchestra, Op. 7]
Solo Vc.-2,2,2,2-2,2,1-Timp.-Str.
Kistner, Leipzig [n.d.]
Score 58 p.

DAVIDSON, HAROLD G.
Low Moor, Virginia 20 February 1893
Glendale, California 14 December 1959

216m Auto accident, for percussion   4'
Ten players: 3Timp.,Trap Dr.,B.Dr.,Siren,Ratchet,Chinese Wood Block,5Temple Bells,Tubular Chimes,Water-tuned Musical Tumblers,Xyl.,2Glass Plates-Pno.
Score: New Music Orchestra Series, San Francisco, c1936. 7 p.
Parts: Ms.
Composed 1935.

1709s Concert square dance, for string   1'30"
orchestra
Timp.(ad lib.)-Str.
Elkan-Vogel, Philadelphia, c1935
Score 7 p.
An original setting of old fiddler's tunes, featuring the Civil War song, Kingdom Coming. Was originally the 2nd number in a suite entitled Prelude, Square Dance and Fugue. Composed 1935. First performance Academy of Music, Philadelphia, 23 April 1935, Matinee Musical Club String Orchestra, Ben Stad conductor.

DAVIES, HENRY WALFORD.
                Oswestry, England 6 September 1869
        Wrington, Somerset, England 11 March 1941

1061s Solemn melody for strings and organ
    Org.-Str.
    Novello, London, c1909
    Score 4 p.

DAVIS, JOHN DAVID.
                Birmingham, England 22 October 1867
            Estoril, Portugal 20 November 1942

7195 The embroidered pannier, an old dance
    Tempo di gavotta - Musette
    1,0,1,1(all ad lib.)-Hn.(ad lib.)-Str.
    Augener, London, c1934
    Score 7 p.

542s Song of evening, for string orchestra,
    Op. 42
    Str.(Cb. ad lib.)
    Novello, London, c1908
    Score 9 p.

DAVISON, JOHN.   Istanbul, Turkey 31 May 1930

2359s Concerto grosso for three violas and
    string orchestra
    1.Adagio - Allegro giocoso 2.Adagio 3.Allegro
    deciso
    3Solo Va.-Str.(without Va.)
    Ms.
    Score 18 p.
    *Composed 1973. First performance Philadelphia,
    15 May 1974, Mostovoy Soloists, Marc Mostovoy
    conductor.*

7286 Liturgy for orchestra   9'
    3*,3*,2,2-2,3,3,1-Timp.,Perc.-Pno.-Str.
    Ms.
    Score 36 p.
    *Originally titled Rhapsody on a Gregorian Hymn.
    Based on the medieval plainchant hymn Pange
    Lingua. Composed 1974. Selected for perform-
    ance by the Orchestra Society of Philadelphia
    as part of its Pennsylvania Composers Project
    1977, made possible by grants from the National
    Endowment for the Arts and the Pennsylvania
    Council on the Arts with performance materials
    prepared by The Fleisher Collection of Orches-
    tral Music. Performed Main Hall, Drexel
    University, Philadelphia, 22 May 1977,
    Orchestra Society of Philadelphia, William
    Smith conductor.*

5742 Symphony no. 1 for small orchestra   18'
    1.Andante - Allegro 2.Andantino 3.Allegro
    2(2nd alt. Picc.),2,2,2-2,2,1-Timp.,Perc.-Str.
    Ms.
    Score 107 p.
    *The last movement is based on an English metri-
    cal psalm tune by an unknown composer, first
    published in Geneva, 1556, and associated with
    Sternhold's metrical version of Psalm 137.
    Composed 1957-58. First performance Rochester,
    New York, 16 April 1958, Eastman-Rochester Sym-
    phony Orchestra, Howard Hanson conductor.*

5851 Symphony no. 2   16'
    1.Moderato - Allegro 2.Andante - Presto -
    Andante 3.Vivace
    2(2nd alt. Picc.),2,2,2-4,2,3,1-Timp.-Pno.-Str.
    Ms.
    Score 109 p.
    *Composed 1958-59. First performance Rochester,
    New York, 29 April 1959, Eastman-Rochester Sym-
    phony Orchestra, Howard Hanson conductor.*

DAWSON, WILLIAM LEVI.
            b. Anniston, Alabama 26 September 1898

3407 Negro folk symphony   35'
    1.The bond of Africa: Adagio - Allegro con
    brio 2.Hope in the night: Andante 3.O lem-me
    shine: Allegro con brio
    3*,3*,4*(1Cl. in E-flat),3*-4,3,3,1-Timp.,
    Perc.-Hp.-Str.
    Ms.
    Score 145 p. Large folio
    *Composed 1930-31. First performance Phila-
    delphia, 16 November 1934, Philadelphia
    Orchestra, Leopold Stokowski conductor.*

DEBUSSY, CLAUDE.
            St.-Germain-en-Laye, France 22 August 1862
                        Paris 25 March 1918

L'après-midi d'un faune
    See: Prélude à l'après-midi d'un faune

379 Arabesque no. 1 [for piano. Transcribed   3'
    for small orchestra by H. Mouton]
    1,1,2,1-2Hn.-Str.
    Durand, Paris, c1904
    Score in reduction 4 p.
    *Composed for piano, 1888. This transcription
    1909. First performance Paris, 1910.*

380 Arabesque no. 2 [for piano. Transcribed   3'
    for small orchestra by H. Mouton]
    1,1,2,1-2Hn.-Trgl.-Str.
    Durand, Paris, c1904
    Score in reduction 5 p.
    See Catalog no. 379.

496 Berceuse héroique [in honor of His   4'
    Majesty King Albert I of Belgium and his
    soldiers]
    2,3*,3,3-4,2,3,1-Timp.-Hp.-Str.
    Durand, Paris, c1915
    Score 11 p.
    *Composed for piano 1914; orchestrated 1915.
    First performance Concerts Colonne-Lamoureux,
    Paris, 15 October 1915.*

561 Children's corner, suite for piano.   15'
    Transcribed for orchestra by André Caplet
    1.Doctor Gradus ad Parnassum 2.Jumbo's lullaby
    3.Serenade for the doll 4.The snow is dancing
    5.The little shepherd 6.Golliwogg's cake-walk
    2(2nd alt. Picc.),2,2,2-4,2-Perc.-Hp.-Str.
    Durand, Paris, c1908, c1911
    Score 80 p.
    *Composed for piano 1906-08. This transcription
    1910. First performance New York, 1910.*

Debussy, Claude

4823 Clair de lune. Transcribed for   4'30"
orchestra by Lucien Caillet
3,3*,3*,2-2,2,3,1-Timp.-2Hp.-Str.
Jobert, Paris, c1939
Score 16 p.
Originally composed for piano, 1892, as no. 3
of the Suite Bergamasque.

7118 Clair de lune. Transcribed for   4'30"
orchestra by Bernard Morgan
2,3*,2,2-4,3-Timp.,Cym.,Gong-Hp.-Str.
Ms. c1975 by Bernard Morgan
Score 20 p.
This arrangement 1938; first performed Irvine
Auditorium, University of Pennsylvania, Phila-
delphia, 28 December 1938, Civic Symphony
Orchestra, J. W. F. Leman conductor.

1738s Clair de lune. Transcribed for   4'
string orchestra by Joseph E. Barone
Str.
Ms.
Score 7 p.
This transcription 1937; first performance
Bryn Mawr, Pennsylvania, 6 October 1937, Bryn
Mawr String Sinfonietta, Joseph Barone con-
ductor.

411 Danse [for piano. Transcribed for   6'
orchestra by Maurice Ravel]
2,2,2,2-2,2-Timp.,Perc.-Hp.-Str.
Jobert, Paris, c1923
Score 37 p.
Originally composed for piano, 1890, as Taren-
telle Styrienne. This transcription 1922.
First performance Salle Gaveau, Paris, 18
March 1923, Orchestre Lamoureux, Paul Paray
conductor.

573m Danses [for harp or piano and string
orchestra]
1.Danse sacrée: Très modéré 2.Danse profane
[Secular dance]: Modéré
Pedal or Chromatic Hp.(or Pno.)-Str.
Durand, Paris, c1904, c1907, c1910
Score 28 p.
Commissioned by Pleyel et Cie. as a test piece
for the Brussels Conservatoire. Composed 1903,
for chromatic harp. Danse Sacrée was based on
one of Francisco de Lacerda's piano pieces.

Les danseuses de Delphes
See: [Preludes, piano. Book I, no. 1: Danseuses de Delphes...]

774 [L'enfant prodigue. Cortège et air de   5'
danse]
3(3rd alt. Picc.),3*,2,2-4,2-Timp.,Perc.-Hp.-
Str.
Durand, Paris, c1906
Score 20 p.
From the cantata composed 1884, awarded the
Prix de Rome. Re-orchestrated 1905; first
performance Théâtre Lyrique du Vaudeville,
Paris, December 1919.

507p Fantaisie pour piano et orchestre   22'
1.Andante ma non troppo 2.Lento e molto

espressivo - Allegro molto
Solo Pno.-3(3rd alt. Picc.),3*,3*,3-4,3,3-
Timp.,Cym.-2Hp.-Str.
E. Fromont, Paris, c1920
Score 148 p.
Composed 1889-90; performance forbidden by
the composer. Simultaneous first performances,
1919: Lyons, France, Marguerite Long soloist;
London, Alfred Cortot soloist.

Feuilles mortes
See: Suite. Transcribed for orchestra by
Hershy Kay

La fille aux cheveux de lin
See: [Preludes, piano. Book I, no. 8: La fille
aux cheveux de lin...]

Gigues
See: [Images pour orchestre. 1.Gigues]

Ibéria
See: [Images pour orchestre. 2.Ibéria]

560 [Images pour orchestre. 1.Gigues]   4'
4(2 are Picc.),4*(1Ob. d'Amore),4*,4*-4,4,3-
Timp.,Perc.-Cel.,2Hp.-Str.
Durand, Paris, c1918
Score 39 p.
Inspired by Paul Verlaine's poem, Streets.
Composed 1909-12; orchestration completed by
André Caplet under Debussy's guidance. First
performance Concerts Colonne, Paris, 26
January 1913.

559 [Images pour orchestre. 2.Ibéria]   17'
1.Par les rues et par les chemins [Through
streets and lanes]: Assez animé 2.Les parfums
de la nuit: Lent et rêveur 3.Le matin d'un
jour de fête [Morning of a feast-day]: Dans
un rythme de marche lointaine, alerte et
joyeuse
4*,3*,3,4*-4,3,3,1-Timp.,Perc.-Cel.,2Hp.-Str.
Durand, Paris, c1910
Score 110 p.
Composed 1906-08. First performance Concerts
Colonne, Paris, 20 February 1910, Gabriel
Pierné conductor.

799 [Images pour orchestre. 3.Rondes de   8'
printemps]
3(3rd alt. Picc.),3*,3,4*-4Hn.-Timp.,Perc.-
Cel.,2Hp.-Str.
Durand, Paris, c1910
Score 56 p.
Inspired by the Italian May-song, La Maggio-
lata. Composed 1908-09. First performance
Concerts Durand, Paris, 2 March 1910, the
composer conducting.

772 L'isle joyeuse [The prosperous island,   7'
for piano. Transcribed for orchestra by
Bernardino Molinari]
3(3rd alt. Picc.),3*,4*,3*-4,4,3,1-Timp.,Perc.-
Cel.,2Hp.-Str.
Durand, Paris, c1904
Score 69 p.
Composed for piano, 1904. First performance

*Paris, 18 February 1905, Ricardo Viñes soloist.
This transcription 1922. First performance
Augusteo, Rome, 1923, Bernardino Molinari con-
ductor.*

1286 Jeux, poème dansé   14'
4(2 are Picc.),4*,4*,3,Sarrus.-4,4,3,1-Timp.,
Perc.-Cel.,2Hp.-Str.
Durand, Paris, c1914
Score 118 p.
*Ballet commissioned by Sergei Diaghilev. Com-
posed 1912. First performance Théâtre des
Champs-Eleysées, Paris, 15 May 1913, choreog-
raphy by Vaslav Nijinsky.*

410 Marche ecossaise sur un thème populaire
[for orchestra]
3*,3*,2,2-4,2,3-Timp.,S.Dr.,Cym.-Hp.-Str.
Jobert, Paris [n.d.]
Score 33 p.
*Commissioned by Meredith Reid, a descendant of
the Earls of Ross; theme is The Earl of Ross
March, or Lords of the Isles. Originally
composed for piano 4-hands and orchestrated
by the composer, 1891.*

801 Le martyre de Saint Sébastien   25'
[symphonic fragments from the incidental music
to Gabriele d'Annunzio's mystery play]
1.La cour des Lys: Prélude, lent 2.Danse
extatique et Final du 1er acte: Assez animé
3.La passion: Lent 4.Le bon pasteur [The good
shepherd]: Sombre et lent
4(2 are Picc.),3*,4*,4*-6,4,3,1-Timp.,Perc.-
Cel.,3Hp.-Str.
Durand, Paris, c1912
Score 73 p.
*Commissioned by Gabriele d'Annunzio. Composed
1911; orchestrated by André Caplet under
Debussy's guidance. First performance Théâtre
du Châtelet, Paris, 22 May 1911, André Caplet
conductor.*

2973 Le martyre de Saint Sébastien. Fanfares 3'
1.Prélude: Le concile des faux dieux [Prelude:
Council of the false gods] 2.Toutes les voix,
Venge nos dieux! Venge nos temples!
0,0,0,0-6,4,3,1-Timp.
Durand, Paris, c1911
Score 5 p.

1125 Le martyre de Saint Sébastien. Prélude, 2'
Acte II: La chambre magique
4(2 are Picc.),2(2nd alt. E.H.),4*,4*-6,2,3,1-
Timp.,Tam-tam,Cym.-Cel.,3Hp.-Str.
Durand, Paris, c1912
Score 10 p.

800 La mer [three symphonic sketches]   18'
1.De l'aube à midi sur la mer [From dawn to
noon on the sea]: Très lent 2.Jeux de vagues
[Play of the waves]: Allegro 3.Dialogue du
vent et de la mer [Dialogue of wind and sea]:
Animé et tumultueux
3*,3*,2,4-4,3,2Cnt.,3,1-Timp.,Perc.-2Hp.-Str.
Kalmus, New York [n.d.]
Score 137 p.
Composed 1903-05. First performance at a

*Lamoureux Concert, Paris, 15 October 1905,
Camille Chevillard conductor.*

5995 Minstrels. Transcribed for orchestra   2'
by Charles O'Connell
3*,3*,4*,4*-4,3,3,1-Timp.,Perc.-2Hp.-Str.
Ms.
Score 15 p.
*Originally composed for piano, 1910, as No. 12
of Twelve Preludes, Book I.*

1411 [Music for King Lear]
1.Fanfare: Maestoso 2.Le sommeil de Lear
[Lear asleep]: Très lent et profondément expressif
2Fl.-4,3-Timp.,Dr.-2Hp.-Str.
Jobert, Paris, c1926
Score 7 p.
*Composed 1905 as incidental music to Shakes-
peare's play.*

409 Nocturnes [for orchestra and women's   14'
chorus]
1.Nuages [Clouds]: Modéré 2.Fêtes: Animé et
très rythmé 3.Sirènes: Modérément animé
3(3rd alt. Picc.),3*,2,3-4,3,3,1-Timp.,S.Dr.,
Cym.-2Hp.-8Soprano,8Mezzo-Soprano Voices
(without words)-Str.
E. Fromont, Paris, c1909
Score 111 p.
*Originally titled Trois Scènes au Crépuscule.
Inspired by the poetry of Henri de Régnier.
Composed 1892-99, with frequent later revisions.
First performance of Nuages and Fêtes, Concerts
Lamoureux, Paris, 9 December 1900, Camille
Chévillard conductor. First performance of
entire work, Paris, 27 October 1901.*

2350 Nocturnes [for orchestra and women's
chorus. Final version]
Jobert, Paris, c1930
Score 111 p.
*This version differs only slightly from Catalog
no. 409 above; instrumentation is identical.*

179 Petite suite [for piano 4-hands.   26'
Transcribed for orchestra by Henri Busser]
1.En bateau [On board]: Andantino 2.Cortège:
Moderato 3.Menuet: Moderato 4.Ballet: Allegro
giusto
2(2nd alt. Picc.),2(2nd alt. E.H.),2,2-2,2-
Timp.,Perc.-Hp.-Str.
Durand, Paris, c1907
Score 70 p.
*Composed 1889. This transcription 1905. First
performance Concerts Lamoureux, Paris, 1905,
Camille Chevillard conductor.*

497 La plus que lente, valse   3'
Fl.,Cl.-Pno.,Cemb.-Str.
Durand, Paris, c1912
Score 15 p.
*Composed for piano, 1910. Orchestrated by the
composer and first performed Paris, 1912.*

Poissons d'or
See: Suite. Transcribed for orchestra by
Hershy Kay

Debussy, Claude

341 Prélude à l'après-midi d'un faune   9'
3,3*,2,2-4Hn.-2Hp.-Antique Cym.-Str.
Kalmus, New York [n.d.]
Score 31 p.
*Inspired by Stéphane Mallarmé's poem Eglogue.
Composed 1892-94. First performance Société
Nationale, Paris, 22 December 1894, Gustave
Doret conductor.*

773 [Preludes, piano. Book I, no. 1: Dan-   2'
seuses de Delphes. Transcribed for orchestra
by H. Forterre]
2,2,2,2-2,2-Timp.,Cym.,Trgl.-Cel.,Hp.-Str.
Durand, Paris, c1923
Score 6 p.
*Originally composed for piano, 1909-10. This
transcription 1923. First performance Paris,
1924.*

183s [Preludes, piano. Book I, no. 8: La
fille aux cheveux de lin. Transcribed for
string orchestra by H. Mouton]
Str.
Score: Ms. 6 p.
Score in reduction and parts: Durand, Paris,
c1912
Originally composed for piano, 1909-10.

512m Première rhapsodie [for clarinet and
orchestra]
Solo Cl.-3,3*,2,3-4,2-Cym.,Trgl.-2Hp.-Str.
Durand, Paris, c1911
Score 45 p.
Composed 1909-10.

873 Printemps, suite symphonique   18'
In two movements
2(2nd alt. Picc.),2*,2,2-4,2,3-Timp.,Perc.-
Pno.(4-hands),Hp.-Str.
Durand, Paris, c1913
Score 98 p.
*Originally composed for orchestra and wordless
chorus, 1886-87; not performed; the full score
destroyed. Reorchestrated by Henri Büsser
from Debussy's score for piano 4-hands. First
performance Société Nationale, Paris, 18 April
1913, Rhené-Baton conductor.*

La puerta del vino
See: Suite. Transcribed for orchestra by
Hershy Kay

258m [Rhapsody for alto saxophone. Tran- 10'
scribed for orchestra by Jean-Jules Roger-
Ducasse]
Solo Sax.-3(3rd alt. Picc.),3*,2,2-4,2,3,1-
Timp.,Perc.-Hp.-Str.
Durand, Paris, c1919
Score 53 p.
*Originally composed for saxophone and piano,
1903-05. This orchestration 1919, with first
performance at the Société Nationale, Paris,
11 May 1919.*

Rondes de printemps
See: [Images pour orchestre. 3.Rondes de
printemps]

412 Sarabande [for piano. Transcribed for 6'
orchestra by Maurice Ravel]
2,2*,2,2-2,1-Tam-tam,Cym.-Hp.-Str.
Jobert, Paris, c1923
Score 11 p.
*From the collection Pour le Piano, composed
1896-1901. This transcription 1922. First
performance Salle Gaveau, Paris, 18 March
1923, Orchestre Lamoureux, Paul Paray conductor.*

3246 [Six épigraphes antiques, for piano 4-hands.
Transcribed for orchestra by Ernest Ansermet]
1.Pour invoquer Pan, dieu du vent d'été [To
invoke Pan, god of the summer wind] 2.Pour un
tombeau sans nom [For a nameless tomb] 3.Pour
que la nuit soit propice [That the night may
be propitious] 4.Pour la danseuse aux crotales
[For the dancing girl with castanets] 5.Pour
l'Égyptienne [For the Egyptian woman] 6.Pour
remercier la pluie au matin [Rendering thanks
for the morning rain]
3(3rd alt. Picc.),3*(E.H. alt. Ob. d'Amore ad
lib.),3(3rd alt. B.Cl.),3*-4,3,3-Timp.,Perc.-
Cel.,2Hp.-Str.
Durand, Paris, c1939
Score 96 p.
*Originally composed 1901 as incidental music
to Les Chansons de Bilitis, prose poems by
Pierre Louÿs. This transcription ca.1935.*

4727 Suite. Transcribed for orchestra by 13'
Hershy Kay
1.La terrasse des audiences du clair de lune:
Lent 2.La puerta del vino: Mouv't de Habanera
3.Feuilles mortes: Lent et mélancolique
4.Poissons d'or: Animé
3*,3*,3*,3*-4,3,3,1-Timp.,Perc.-Cel.,Hp.-Str.
Ms.
Score 47 p. Large folio
*Originally composed for piano. From Twelve
Preludes, Book II (1910-13): nos. 7, 3, and 2.
From Images for piano, Set II (1907): no. 3.
This arrangement 1946.*

Suite bergamasque. Movement no. 3. Clair de lune
See: Clair de lune

Tarentelle styrienne
See: Danse [for piano...]

La terrasse des audiences du clair de lune
See: Suite. Transcribed for orchestra by
Hershy Kay

1474 Le triomphe de Bacchus, divertissement
pour orchestre. Orchestrated by Marius François Gaillard
3*,3*,2,3-4,3,3,1-Timp.,B.Dr.,Cym.-2Hp.-Str.
Choudens, Paris, c1928
Score 24 p.
*The composer conceived this as an orchestral
work, but left only a version for piano 4-hands,
on which this orchestration is based. Inspired
by a poem by Théodore de Banville.*

DECOURCELLE, MAURICE HENRI. Paris 11 October 1815
died after 1880

162s Le couvre-feu, pensée musicale [Curfew,
a musical thought for string orchestra]
Str.
Paul Decourcelle, Nice [n.d.]
Score 3 p.

DÉDÉ, EUGÈNE.

1223s Abeilles et bourdons, Op. 562 [Bees and
bumble-bees, for string orchestra]
Str.
Score: Ms. 9 p.
Parts: Decourcelle, Nice, c1911

DEDECECK-DOSTAL, P.

1928 Mélodies slovaques
3*,2,2,2-4,2,3,1-Timp.,B.Dr.,Trgl.-Hp.-Str.
Ms.
Score 48 p.

DEDIEU-PETERS, MADELEINE.   France 1889

2231 Trois petits préludes   8'
1.De la neige [Snow]: Assez lent 2.Des fleurs
[Flowers]: Assez vif et léger 3.Du soleil
[Sun]: Rythmé et animé
3*,2,2,2-2,2,2,1-Timp.,Perc.-Hp.-Str.
Senart, Paris, c1927
Score 33 p.
*Composed 1917-23. First performance Paris,
May 1925, Th. Bériza conductor.*

DEERING, RICHARD.   Kent, England ca.1580
                London buried 22 March 1629 or 1630

Also spelled: Dering

696s Almaine, for string orchestra. Edited
by Richard R. Terry
Str.(Vn.I/II/III,Va.,Vc.)
Curwen, London, c1925 by Richard R. Terry
Score 3 p.
Originally for consort of viols.

DEFOSSEZ, RENÉ.   Spa, Belgium 4 October 1905

4971 [Aquarium, three impressions for   20'
orchestra]
1.Alcyonium palmatum 2.Evolutions des Mullus
barbatus 3.Repas des Calappa granulata [Meal
of the *Calappa granulata*]
1,1,1,1-2,1-Timp.,Perc.-Pno.(or Hp.)-Str.
Schott, Brussels, c1948
Score 68 p.
*Inspired by the aquarium at Monte Carlo. Move-
ment titles refer to species of fish. Composed
1927.*

DEGEN, HELMUT.   Aglasterhausen,
            near Heidelberg, Germany 14 January 1911

4979 [Capriccio for orchestra]   15'
2(2nd alt. Picc.),2,2,2-4,2,3,1-Timp.-Str.
Schott, Mainz, c1940
Score 70 p.
*Commissioned by The Friends of Music, Baden-
Baden. Composed 1939.*

4330 [Christmas music, for strings and wood-
winds]
Fl.,Ob.-Str.
P.J. Tonger, Cologne [n.d.]
Score 6 p.
Composed 1941.

DEGEYTER, PIERRE.   8 October 1849
        St. Denis, near Paris 27 September 1932

2496 Internationale. Transcribed for   3'
orchestra by Dmitri Rogal-Levitski
2,2,2,2-4,2,3,1-Timp.,Perc.-Hp.(ad lib.)-Str.
Mussektor, Moscow, 1928
Score 7 p.
*The international workers' song, composed
1888; the former Soviet national anthem.*

DEGNER, ERICH WOLF.
        Hohenstein-Ernstthal, Germany 8 April 1858
            Berka, near Weimar 18 November 1908

2300 Serenade [G minor]   14'
1.Mässig bewegt 2.Mässig bewegt
1,2*,2*,1-2Hn.-Str.
Kistner, Leipzig [1909]
Score 39 p.

DELAHAYE, L. L.

4395 [Colombine. Minuet no. 2]   4'
2,2,2,2-2Hn.-Timp.-Str.
Heugel, Paris [n.d.]
Score 7 p.

DELALANDE, MICHEL-RICHARD.
See: LALANDE, MICHEL-RICHARD DE.

DE LAMARTER, ERIC.
        Lansing, Michigan 18 February 1880
            Orlando, Florida 17 May 1953

1992 [The betrothal. Suite from the incidental
music to Maeterlinck's play]
1.Overture: Brightly 2.The veiled sweetheart:
Very moderately 3.Dance of the sweethearts:
Fast
3(3rd alt. Picc.),3*,2,2-4,3,3,1-Timp.,Perc.-
Str.
Society for the Publication of American Music
(G. Schirmer), New York, c1929 by Eric De
Lamarter
Score 46 p.
*Incidental music commissioned by Winthrop Ames
for his production of Maeterlinck's play. First
performance of this suite Chicago, 21 March
1919, Chicago Symphony Orchestra, the composer
conducting.*

3296 The black orchid, concert suite   15'
drawn from music for a highly stylized ballet-
satire
Prelude: Dawn stirrings - Dance of the unfold-
ing buds - Dance of the lovely morons - Dance
of the black orchid - Dance of the raucous
zealots - Dance of the bored optimist - Dance,
epilogue of the exasperated
3(3rd alt. Picc.),3*,3*,3*-4,4,3,1-Timp.,Perc.

De Lamarter, Eric

-Hp.-Str.
Edwards Brothers, Ann Arbor, Michigan, c1939
by Eric De Lamarter
Score 78 p.
Originally composed as a ballet, The Dance of Life; not performed. This suite extracted 1931, with title Suite from the Dance of Life. First performance Orchestra Hall, Chicago, 27 February 1931, Chicago Symphony Orchestra, the composer conducting. Revised and retitled, 1937.

4769 Huckleberry Finn overture   2'
2,2,2,2-4,3,3,1-Timp.,Perc.-Str.
M. Witmark, New York, c1948
Score 14 p.

4790 Ol' Kaintuck. Overture based on two   3'
Kentucky mountain tunes
2,2,3*,2-4,3,3,1-Timp.,Perc.-Str.
M. Witmark, New York, c1948
Score 17 p.

3247 Overture, "They, too, went t'town"   5'
[original version]
3*,3*,2,2-4,3,3,1-Timp.,Perc.-Hp.-Str.
Ms.
Score 35 p.
Based on two early New England hymn tunes. Composed 1921. First performance New York, 6 June 1938, Firestone Orchestra broadcast over NBC Radio, Alfred Wallenstein conductor. Later revised and retitled The Giddy Puritan.

2019s Serenade for string orchestra
1.Bend and weave: Moderate waltz tempo 2. Slow dance: Slowly 3.Jog trot: Moderately
Str.
M. Witmark, New York, c1949
Score 8 p.
Composed 1915.

1809s Serenade near Taos, for string   13'
orchestra
1.To the Lady: Andante con moto - Maestoso 2.Her caballero: Vivace - Trio: Poco meno comodo 3.Little folks' song: Semplice 4. Fiesta for Faquita: Allegro con spirito
Str.
Ricordi, Milan, c1939
Score 33 p.
First 3 movements composed 1930; 4th movement added 1938. First performance New York, 11 January 1938, Symphony Strings broadcast over Mutual Broadcasting System Radio Station WOR, Alfred Wallenstein conductor.

3112 Symphony no. 3, in E minor   45'
1.Very broadly 2.Very slowly 3.Brightly - but not too fast - Fast 4.Fast
3(3rd alt. Picc.),3*,3*,3*-4,4,3,1-Timp.,Perc. -Hp.-Str.
Ms. c1934 by Eric De Lamarter
Score 193 p. Large folio
Composed 1930-32. First performance Chicago, 16 February 1933, Chicago Symphony Orchestra, the composer conducting.

DELANEY, ROBERT MILLS.   Baltimore 24 July 1903
Santa Barbara, California 21 September 1956

1116v Adagio, for violin solo and string   9'
orchestra
Solo Vn.-Str.
Ms.
Score 14 p.
Originally composed for violin with piano accompaniment, 1934; transcribed 1935. First performance Concord, Massachusetts, 18 July 1935, Concord Summer School Orchestra, the composer conducting, Malcolm H. Holmes soloist.

3111 The constant couple, suite [from   20'
the incidental music to the play by George Farquhar]
1.Ouverture: Allegro assai 2.Romance 3. Scherzo: Allegro - Tempo di valse 4.Air: Molto adagio 5.Finale: Presto
1,1(alt. E.H.),1,1-2,1(alt. Small Tpt. in D),1 -Timp.,Perc.-Hp.-Str.
Ms.
Score 107 p.
Composed 1926. First performance Rochester, New York, 17 May 1928, Rochester Philharmonic, Howard Hanson conductor.

3373 Going to town, suite for orchestra   21'
1.Willow Creek, 5 A.M. 2.Mountain roads - The logging trucks 3.Archie Forson's cafe 4.The road to Eureka 5.Around town 6.Hauling home
2,2,2,2-4,3,3,1-Timp.,Perc.-Pno.,Cel.,Hp.-Str.
Ms.
Score 124 p.
Composed 1940. First performance at the Fall Symposium of American Music, Eastman School of Music, Rochester, New York, 25 October 1943, Eastman-Rochester Symphony Orchestra, Howard Hanson conductor.

3093 Pastoral movement   11'
2,2(2nd alt. E.H.),2,2-4Hn.-Str.
Ms.
Score 44 p.
Composed 1930.

3374 Symphonic piece no. 1   21'
1.Allegro molto 2.Andante ma non troppo 3. Presto assai 4.Allegro assai e ritmico
3(3rd alt. Picc.),3(3rd alt. E.H.),3,3-4,3,3,1 -Timp.,Perc.-Hp.-Str.
Ms.
Score 147 p.
Composed 1934-35. First performance Rochester, New York, 30 April 1936, Rochester Philharmonic Orchestra, Howard Hanson conductor.

3211 Work no. 22, scherzo for orchestra   5'30"
2,2,2,2-4,3,3,1-Timp.,Perc.-Pno.-Str.
Ms.
Score 40 p.
Commissioned by the Harvard University Orchestra, 1937. Composed 1937. First performance Paine Hall, Cambridge, 3 May 1939, Harvard University Orchestra, Malcolm H. Holmes conductor.

COLLECTION OF ORCHESTRAL MUSIC

DELAUNAY, RENÉ.   Tours, France 18 June 1880

  Also spelled: Delauney

  799s Amoureuse causerie [for violin, clarinet
    and string orchestra]
    Solo Vn.-Cl.-Str.
    Score: Ms. 9 p.
    Parts: Delrieu Frères, Nice, c1913

DELCROIX, LÉON CHARLES. Brussels 15 September 1880
                         Brussels 14 November 1938

  706m Lied élégiaque for English horn and
    orchestra
    Solo E.H.-2Cl.-2Hn.-Str.
    Ms.
    Score 15 p.

DELDEVEZ, ÉDOUARD MARIE ERNEST.   Paris 31 May 1817
                         Paris 6 (not 5) November 1897

  4297 [Concert overture, Op. 1, E-flat major]
    2,2,2,4-4,2,3-Timp.-Str.
    Richault, Paris [184-?]
    Score 51 p.
    Composed 1839.

  5881 [The magic violin, Op. 20. Overture]
    3*,2,2,2-4,2,2,2Cnt.,3,Ophicl.-Timp.,Perc.-
    2Hp.-Str.(with 2Va. d'Amore)
    S. Richault, Paris [1850]
    Score 49 p.
    From the opera in one act. Composed 1848.

  5777 [Robert Bruce overture, Op. 3]
    2(2nd alt. Picc.),2,2,2-4,2,2Cnt.,3,Ophicl.-
    Timp.,Perc.-Str.
    S. Richault, Paris [n.d.]
    Score 60 p.
    Composed 1854.

  5685 Suite de ballets, Op. 27
    1.La leçon de danse [The dancing lesson] (from
    the ballet Vert-Vert): a)Ouverture (La parade)
    b)Entrée c)Allemande, gigue et charivari
    général d)Valse allemande [German waltz]
    2.Galop des fous - La dansomanie à bedlam
    [Fools' gallop - Dance mania in Bedlam] (from
    the ballet Lady Henriette): Andantino - Alle-
    gro molto - La gigue - La valse - La cachucha
    [Andalusian dance] - Le menuet - Aux champs
    [In the field] - La tarentelle - La cracovienne
    3.Andante et intermezzo (from the ballet Euch-
    aris) 4.Bacchanale aux flambeaux [Bacchanal
    in torchlight] (from the ballet Eucharis) 5.
    Entr'acte (from the ballet Paquita): Contredan-
    ses françaises - Valse des Hussards 6.Pas des
    manteaux [Mantle-dance] (from the ballet Pa-
    quita): Gitanos
    3*,2,2,2-4,2,2Cnt.,3,Ophicl.-Timp.,Perc.-2Hp.-
    Str.
    S. Richault, Paris [186-?]
    Score 184 p.
    The ballet Vert-Vert, no. 1, composed with
    Auguste Tolbecque, 1851. Lady Henriette, no.
    2, composed with Friedrich von Flotow and
    Johann Friedrich Burgmüller, 1844. Eucharis,

nos. 3 and 4, composed 1844. Paquita, nos.
5 and 6, composed 1846.

DELGADILLO, LUIS ABRAHAM.   Managua 26 August 1887
                             Managua 1961

  4158 [Dance of the coca, Incan music,   4'
    Op. 110]
    2*,1,2,2-2,2,3-Timp.,Perc.-Str.
    Ms. c1932 by Foment Ministry [n.p.]
    Score 10 p.
    Composed 1928. First performance Managua,
    Nicaragua, 20 January 1929, the composer con-
    ducting.

  3784 La danza de flechas [The dance of   3'30"
    the arrows] música indigena nicaragüense -
    tema original del autor, Op. 150
    1,1,2,2-2,2,3-Timp.,Perc.-Str.
    Ms.
    Score 16 p.
    Composed 1937. First performance Managua,
    May 1938, Orquesta Filarmónica de Nicaragua,
    the composer conducting. Composer assigned
    Op. 150 to this work and to Catalog no. 3264.

  3194 En el Templo de Agat, danza indigena   6'
    nicaragüense, Op. 158
    1,1,2,2-2,1,2-Timp.,Perc.-Str.
    Ms.
    Score 11 p.
    Composed 1937. First performance Léon, Nicar-
    agua, 23 March 1938, Symphony Orchestra of Léon,
    the composer conducting.

  3264 [Inca symphony. Movement 3, Danza   6'
    salvaje (Savage dance), Op. 150]
    3*,2,2,2-4,2,3-Timp.,Perc.-Hp.-Str.
    Ms.
    Score 16 p.
    From the symphony composed 1926-27. First per-
    formance Municipal Theatre, Caracas, Venezuela,
    20 May 1927, Caracas Symphony Orchestra, the
    composer conducting.

  4157 Invocation to the moon, Incan music,   4'
    Op. 108
    3*,1,2,1-2,2,1-Timp.,Perc.-Str.
    Ms. c1930 by Foment Ministry [n.p.]
    Score 6 p.
    Composed 1928. First performance Ciudad
    Trujillo, Dominican Republic, 24 June 1946,
    Symphony Orchestra of Trujillo, the composer
    conducting.

  3789 Tramonto en la cumbre, oración del   5'
    Indio [Sunset on the mountain, prayer of the
    Indian]
    1,1,2,4-2,2,3-Timp.,Perc.-Str.
    Ms.
    Score 20 p.
    Composed 1938. First performance Managua,
    Nicaragua, 21 July 1941.

DELIBES, LÉO.
    Saint-Germaine du Val, Sarthe 21 February 1836
                           Paris 16 June 1891

  Full name: Clément Philibert Léo Delibes

Delibes, Léo

6747 [Coppélia, or The girl with the   *5'30"*
enamel eyes. Prelude *and* No.3. Mazurka]
2(2nd alt. Picc.),2,2,2-4,2,2Cnt.,3,1-Timp.,
Perc.-Hp.-Str.
Kalmus, New York [n.d.]
Score 81 p.
From the ballet in 2 acts with scenario by
Charles Louis Étienne Nuitter and Charles Vic-
tor Arthur Saint-Léon, based on E.T.A. Hoff-
mann's story Der Sandmann. First performance
Opéra, Paris, 25 May 1870.

6748 [Coppélia, or The girl with the   *9'*
enamel eyes. 5.Ballade 6.Slavic theme with
variations]
2(2nd alt. Picc.),2(2nd alt. E.H.),2,2-4,2,
2Cnt.,3,1-Timp.,B.Dr.,Cym.-Hp.-Str.
Kalmus, New York [n.d.]
Score 132 p.

1208 [Coppélia, or The girl with the   *23'*
enamel eyes. Orchestral suite from the ballet]
1.[Slavic folk melody with variations] 2.[Fes-
tive dance and waltz of the hours]: Allegro -
Tempo di valse - Allegretto 3.Notturno: Andante con moto 4.[Music of the automatons and
waltz]: Andante quasi allegretto - Tempo di
valse 5.Czardas: Allegro moderato marcato
2(2nd alt. Picc.),2,2,2-4,2,3-Timp.,Perc.-Hp.-
Str.
Fürstner, Berlin [n.d.]
Score 142 p.

403 [Kassya. Ballet from the opera]   *13'*
1.Obertas: Modéré 2.Danse ruthène: Lent 3.
Sumka: Andante 4.Trépak: Allegro non troppo
2(2nd alt. Picc.),2,2,2-4,0,2Cnt.,3,1-Timp.,
Perc.-Hp.-Str.
[Heugel, Paris, n.d.]
Score 51 p.
From the opera in 5 acts, with libretto based
on a story by Leopold von Sacher-Masoch. Com-
posed 1891; orchestration completed and reci-
tatives added by Jules Massenet after Delibes'
death. First performance Opéra-Comique, Paris,
21 March 1893.

406 [Kassya. Finale to Act I, Mazurka]   *3'*
2,2,2,2-4,2,3,1-Timp.,Perc.-Str.
Heugel, Paris, c1893?
Score 19 p.

404 [Kassya. Entr'acte-prelude to Act III,   *2'*
La neige]
0,2*,2,2-2,0,3-Timp.-Hp.-Str.
[Heugel, Paris, n.d.]
Score 8 p.

405 [Kassya. Polonaise]
2(2nd alt. Picc.),2,2,2-4,0,2Cnt.,3,1-Timp.,
Perc.-Hp.-Voices-Str.
[Heugel, Paris, n.d.]
Score 24 p.

1303 [Lakmé. Airs de danse]   *7'*
Introduction: Moderato - 1.Teràna: Andante
2.Rektah: Allegretto vivo 3.Persian: Allegretto - Andante 4.Coda: Allegretto marcato

2(2nd alt. Picc.),2,2,2-4,0,2Cnt.,3,1(or
Ophicl.)-Timp.,Perc.-Hp.-Str.
[Heugel, Paris, n.d.]
Score 37 p.
From the opera composed 1882.

1359 [Lakmé. Entr'acte, Act III]   *3'*
2*,2*,2,2-4,0,2Cnt.,3-Timp.-Hp.-Str.
[Heugel, Paris, n.d.]
Score 9 p.

Naila
See: La source

1407 [Le roi l'a dit. Overture]   *8'*
2(2nd alt. Picc.),2,2,2-4,2(both alt. Cnt.),3-
Timp.,Perc.-Str.
Heugel, Paris [n.d.]
Score 29 p.
From the comic opera composed 1872.

1133 Le roi s'amuse. Scène du bal: airs de *16'*
danse dans le style ancien
1.Gaillarde: Moderato ben marcato 2.Pavane:
Allegretto 3.Scène du bouquet: Andante 4.Les-
quercarde: Allegro 5.Madrigal: Andantino 6.
Passepied: Allegro 7.Final: Moderato 8.Chanson
(avec mandoline): Moderato
2,2,2,2-2,2-Timp.,Tamb.-Mandolin-Str.
Heugel, Paris [n.d.]
Score 52 p.
From the incidental music to Victor Hugo's
play composed for the revival of the work at
the Comédie Française, Paris, 22 November 1882.

1465 [La source. Intermezzo (Pas de fleurs).
Arranged by Franz Doppler]
2*,2,2,2-4,2,3,1-Timp.,B.Dr.,Bells-Hp.-Str.
Fürstner, Berlin [n.d.]
Score 17 p.
Composed in collaboration with Ludwig Minkus.
From the ballet La Source. First performance
Paris, 12 November 1866. Later performed in
Vienna under the title Naila.

287 [La source. Suite no. 3. Arranged by   *21'*
Ross Jungnickel]
1.Incantation: Lento - Allegro moderato, lead-
ing to 2.Romance: Allegro vivace - Andantino
3.Introduction and mazurka: Allegro moderato -
Tempo di mazurka 4.Finale: Allegro
3*,2,2,2-4,4,3,1-Timp.,Perc.-2Hp.-Str.
Ross Jungnickel, New York, c1920
Score 70 p.
First performance of this transcription Capitol
Theatre, New York, November 1920, Erno Rapee
conductor.

124 [Sylvia. Suite from the ballet]   *17'*
1.Prélude - Les chassereuses: Moderato maestoso
- Allegretto animato 2.Intermezzo et valse
lente: Moderato - Sostenuto 3.Pizzicati: Moderato 4.Cortège de Bacchus: Moderato ben marcato - Largo - Allegro vivace
2(2nd alt. Picc.),2,2,2-4,2,2Cnt.,3,Ophicl.-
Timp.,Perc.-Hp.-Str.
Kalmus, New York [n.d.]
Score 105 p.

From the ballet Sylvia, ou La Nymphe de Diane. Composed 1875. First performance Opéra, Paris, 14 June 1876.

DELIUS, FREDERICK.
                    Bradford, England 29 January 1862
                    Grez-sur-Loing, France 10 June 1934

1751s Air and dance for string orchestra *5'30"*
Str.
Winthrop Rogers/Hawkes & Son, London, c1931
Score 5 p.
Composed 1915.

1596 Brigg Fair, an English rhapsody   *16'*
3,3*,4*,4*-6,3,3,1-Timp.,Perc.-Hp.-Str.
Leuckart, Leipzig, c1910
Score 39 p.
Theme is the old English song Brigg Fair. Composed 1907. First performance Basel, January 1908, Hermann Suter conductor. First English performance Liverpool, February 1908, Granville Bantock conductor.

3042 La Calinda. Reorchestrated by   *3'30"*
Eric Fenby
2*,2,2,2-4,2,3,1(ad lib.)-Timp.,Perc.-Hp.,
Banjo(ad lib.)-Str.
Hawkes & Son, London, c1938
Score 22 p.
Originally composed as Dance of the Majorcans for the suite Florida, Catalog no. 2923. Retitled and used in the opera Koanga, composed 1895-97; first performance Elberfeld, Germany, 30 March 1904, Fritz Cassirer conductor. First performance of this version London, date unknown, London Philharmonic Orchestra, Malcolm Sargent conductor.

739c [Caprice and elegy for violon-   *6'30"*
cello and orchestra]
1.Caprice: Moderato 2.Elegy: Slow and sustained
Solo Vc.-1,2*,1,1-2Hn.-Hp.-Str.
Hawkes & Son, London, c1931
Score 19 p.
Composed 1930 with the assistance of Eric Fenby.

609p [Concerto for piano, C minor]   *30'*
In one movement
Solo Pno.-3(1st alt. Picc.),3*,2,3-4,2,3,1-
Timp.,B.Dr.,Cym.-Str.
Verlag Harmonie, Berlin, c1907
Score 61 p.
Composed 1897. First performance Elberfeld, 1904, Hans Haym conductor, Julius Buths soloist. Revised 1906. First performance London, October 1907, Henry Wood conductor, Theodor Szanto soloist.

820v [Concerto for violin and orchestra]   *27'*
In one movement
Solo Vn.-2,2*,2,2-4,2,3,1-Timp.-Hp.-Str.
Augener, London, c1921
Score 45 p.
Composed 1916.

722m Concerto for violin, violoncello   *21'*
and orchestra
In one movement
Solo Vn.,Solo Vc.-2,2*,2,2-4,2,3,1-Timp.-Hp.-Str.
Augener, London, c1922
Score 55 p.
Composed 1915-16. First performance Queen's Hall, London, January 1920, Henry Wood conductor, May and Beatrice Harrison soloists.

1597 [Dance rhapsody no. 1, for orchestra] *12'*
3(3rd alt. Picc.),3*(1B.Ob.),4*,4*(Sarrus. or C.Bn.)-6,3,3,1-Timp.,Perc.-2Hp.-Str.
Leuckart, Leipzig, c1910
Score 40 p.
Composed 1908. First performance Three Choirs Festival, Hereford, England, 1909, the composer conducting.

4624 A dance rhapsody, no. 2   *8'*
2(2nd alt. Picc.),3*,2,2-4,2,3,1-Timp.,Perc.-Cel.,Hp.-Str.
Augener, London, c1923
Score 33 p.
Composed 1916. First performance at Henry Wood's promenade season, London, 1923.

2923 Florida [tropical scenes for   *27'*
orchestra; original version]
1.Tages Anbruch [Daybreak]: Sehr mässig 2.Tanz der Majorkaner [Dance of the Majorcans]: Sehr zart, nicht schnell - Sehr stark und wild - Sehr zart 3.Am Fluss [At the river]: Mässig 4.Nachts [At night]: Zehr langsam und zart; mässig
3*,2,2,2-4,2,3,1-Timp.,Perc.-Hp.-Str.
Ms.
Score 101 p. Large folio
Composed 1886-87. First private performance Restaurant Rosenthal, Leipzig, 1888, Hans Sitt conductor. Revised and another movement added, 1890. First public performance Queen's Hall, London, 1 April 1937, London Philharmonic Orchestra, Thomas Beecham conductor. Delius used Movement 2 in his opera Koanga; see Catalog no. 3042.

2922 [Hassan. Scene-change and Serenade   *5'*
from the incidental music to the play]
1,2*,1,1-1,1,1,1-Timp.-Hp.-Str.
Ms.
Score 10 p. Large folio
Composed 1920 as incidental music to James Elroy Flecker's play. First performance His Majesty's Theatre, London, 23 September 1923, Eugene Goossens conductor.

1598 In a summer garden [original version] *13'*
3,3*,3*,3-4,2,3,1-Timp.,Glock.,Trgl.-Hp.-Str.
Leuckart, Leipzig, c1911
Score 34 p.
Composed 1908. First performance London, December 1909, Philharmonic Concert, the composer conducting. Revised 1913. First performance Edinburgh, 1913, Emil Mlynarski conductor.

Delius, Frederick

3043 Irmelin, prelude [for orchestra] 4'
2,2*,3*,2-2Hn.-Hp.-Str.
Hawkes & Son, London, c1938
Score 11 p.
*Composed 1931 or 1932, based on two themes
from the composer's opera Irmelin, composed
1890-92. First performance of this prelude
during a performance of the composer's opera
Koanga, Covent Garden, London, 23 September
1935, Thomas Beecham conductor.*

Koanga. La Calinda
See: La Calinda. Re-orchestrated by Eric
Fenby

348 Life's dance/Lebenstanz [final revised 12'
version]
4*,4*,4*,4*-4,3,3,1-Timp.,Perc.-Hp.(1 or
more)-Str.
Tischer & Jagenberg, Cologne, c1912
Score 63 p.
*Originally composed 1898 as La Danse Se Déroule.
First performance London, 30 May 1899, Alfred
Hertz conductor. Revised and retitled 1900.
First performance Düsseldorf, 1904, Julius
Buths conductor. Further revised 1911. First
performance Berlin, 1912, Oskar Fried conduc-
tor.*

2027 North Country sketches for orchestra 26'
1.Autumn - The wind soughs in the trees 2.
Winter landscape 3.Dance 4.The march of
spring - Woodland, meadows and silent moors
2(2nd alt. Picc.),3*,2,2-4,2,3,1-Timp.,Tamb.,
Trgl.-2Hp.-Str.
Augener, London, c1923
Score 76 p.
*Inspired by the composer's native Yorkshire.
Composed 1913-14. First performance London,
May 1915, London Symphony Orchestra, Thomas
Beecham conductor.*

On hearing the first cuckoo in spring
See: [Two pieces for small orchestra]

1599 [Paris, the song of a great city, 20'
for orchestra]
3(3rd alt. Picc.),4*,4*,4*-6,3,3,1-Timp.,Perc.
-2Hp.-Str.
Leuckart, Leipzig, c1909
Score 66 p.
*Composed 1899. First performance Elberfeld,
1901, Hans Haym conductor.*

4635 A song before sunrise, for small 5'
orchestra
2,1,2,2-2Hn.-Timp.-Str.
Augener, London, c1922
Score 18 p.
Composed 1918.

2997 A song of summer 9'30"
3(3rd alt. Picc.),3*,4*,4*-4,3,3,1-Timp.-Hp.-
Str.
Winthrop Rogers, London, c1931
Score 19 p.
*Begun as Poem of Love and Life, left unfinished
in 1918. Retitled and completed with the*

*assistance of Eric Fenby, 1930. First per-
formance Queen's Hall, London, 17 September
1931, BBC Orchestra, Henry Wood conductor.*

2537 The song of the high hills 35'
3(3rd alt. Picc.),3*,4*,4*(1Sarrus. or C.Bn.)-
6,3,3,1-Timp.(2 players),Perc.-Cel.,2Hp.-Word-
less Chorus(SATB)-Str.
Universal Edition, Vienna, c1923
Score 50 p.
*Composed 1911-12. First performance London,
26 February 1920, London Philharmonic Orchestra
with the Philharmonic Choir, Albert Coates
conductor.*

Summer-night on the river
See: [Two pieces for small orchestra]

1828s Two aquarelles. Transcribed for 4'
string orchestra by Eric Fenby
1.Lento, ma non troppo 2.Gaily, but not quick
Str.
Hawkes & Son, London, c1938
Score 10 p.
*Transcribed from To Be Sung of a Summer's
Night on the Water, a pair of part-songs with-
out words composed for unaccompanied mixed
chorus, 1917.*

192 [Two pieces for small orchestra] 11'
1.On hearing the first cuckoo in spring: Slow
- With easy flowing movement 2.Summer-night
on the river: Very quietly
2,1,2,2-2Hn.-Str.
Tischer & Jagenberg, Cologne, c1914
Score 14 p.
*Theme of Movement 1 is I Ola Dalom, from
Edvard Grieg's Norwegian Folk Songs, Op. 66.
Composed 1911-12. First performance London,
January 1914, London Philharmonic Orchestra,
Willem Mengelberg conductor.*

3346 The walk to the Paradise Garden, 8'
intermezzo from A Village Romeo and Juliet.
Reorchestrated by Thomas Beecham
2,2*,2,2-4,2,3-Timp.-Hp.-Str.
Hawkes & Son, London, c1940
Score 17 p.
*From the opera composed 1900-01. Originally
scored for a larger orchestra; this transcription 1939.*

DELLA CIAJA, AZZOLINO BERNARDINO.
Siena 21 March 1671
Pisa 15 January 1755

Variant spelling: Azzolino Bernardino Della Ciaia

1964s [Sonata, cembalo, G major. Toccata.
Transcribed for string orchestra by Hershy Kay]
Str.
Ms.
Score 5 p. Large folio
*Cembalo sonata composed 1727. This tran-
scription, 1941.*

Dello Joio, Norman

DELLER, FLORIAN JOHANN.
Drosendorf, Lower Austria baptized 2 May 1729
Munich 19 April 1773

Also known as: Döller, Teller, Töller

6314 Ballo polonois [Polish ball. Complete
ballet, sinfonia and 27 dances]
2,2,0,2-2Hn.-Cemb.-Str.
Score: Denkmäler Deutscher Tonkunst, XLIII/
XLIV. Breitkopf & Härtel, Leipzig, 1913.
Edited by Hermann Abert. 25 p.
Parts: Ms. ᶜ1976 by The Fleisher Collection of
Orchestral Music, Free Library of Philadelphia
Ballet composed between 1768 and 1770.

6315 La constance [Loyalty. Complete ballet,
sinfonia and 24 dances]
2Fl.-2Hn.-Cemb.-Str.
Score: Denkmäler Deutscher Tonkunst, XLIII/
XLIV. Breitkopf & Härtel, Leipzig, 1913.
Edited by Hermann Abert. 27 p.
Parts: Ms. ᶜ1976 by The Fleisher Collection of
Orchestral Music, Free Library of Philadelphia
Ballet composed between 1768 and 1770.

6318 [Orpheus and Eurydice. Complete ballet,
sinfonia and 30 dances]
2,2,0,2-2Hn.-Cemb.-Str.
Score: Denkmäler Deutscher Tonkunst, XLIII/
XLIV. Breitkopf & Härtel, Leipzig, 1913.
Edited by Hermann Abert. 64 p.
Parts: Ms. ᶜ1976 by The Fleisher Collection of
Orchestral Music, Free Library of Philadelphia
*Ballet composed 1763. First performance
Stuttgart, 11 February 1763, between the
second and third act of Niccolò Jommelli's
opera Didone Abbandonata.*

Allegro assai

6338 La schiava liberata [The freed slave girl.
Complete ballet, sinfonia and 17 dances]
2Fl.-2Hn.-Cemb.-Str.
Score: Denkmäler Deutscher Tonkunst, XLIII/
XLIV. Breitkopf & Härtel, Leipzig, 1913.
Edited by Hermann Abert. 27 p.
Parts: Ms. ᶜ1976 by The Fleisher Collection of
Orchestral Music, Free Library of Philadelphia
Ballet composed after 1768.

DELLO JOIO, NORMAN.   New York City 24 January 1913

6192 Concert music for orchestra   21'
3*,3*,3*,3*-4,3,3,1-Timp.,Perc.-Str.
Ms.
Score 69 p. Large folio
*Composed 1945. First performance Pittsburgh,
4 January 1946, Pittsburgh Symphony Orchestra,
Fritz Reiner conductor.*

360m Concertante for clarinet and   17'
orchestra
1.Adagio e con molto sentimento 2.Theme and
5 variations
Solo Cl.-2(2nd alt. Picc.),2(2nd alt. E.H.),2,
2-2,2-Timp.,Perc.-Cel.(optional)-Str.
Ms. ᶜ1955 by Norman Dello Joio
Score 53 p. Large folio
*Commissioned by Artie Shaw. Composed 1949.
First performance Chautauqua, New York, 22 May
1949, Chautauqua Symphony Orchestra, Franco
Autori conductor, Artie Shaw soloist.*

5125 Epigraph   7'
3*,2,3*,2-4,3,3,1-Timp.,Perc.-Cel.,Hp.-Str.
Ms.
Score 35 p. Large folio
*Composed 1951. First performance Denver, 29
January 1952, Denver Symphony Orchestra, Saul
Caston conductor.*

4792 New York profiles, a suite for   20'
orchestra
1.Prelude, The Cloisters 2.Caprice, The Park
3.Chorale fantasy, The Tomb: Adagio 4.Festal
dance, Little Italy – Chorale: Presto
2(2nd alt. Picc.),2(2nd alt. E.H.),2,2-2,2-
Timp.,Perc.-Str.
Ms.
Score 37 p. Large folio
*Composed 1949. First performance La Jolla,
California, 21 August 1949, Musical Arts
Society, Nicolai Sokoloff conductor.*

4800 Serenade for orchestra   16'
3*,3*,3*,2-4,3,3-Timp.,Perc.-Cel.(or Pno.),Hp.
-Str.
Ms.
Score 45 p. Large folio
*Composed 1948. First performance Cleveland,
20 October 1949, Cleveland Symphony Orchestra.
A version of Serenade was made into the ballet,
Diversion of Angels, 1955, for Martha Graham.*

5177 The triumph of St. Joan, a symphony   30'
in three movements
1.The maid: Adagio, molto espressivo 2.The
warrior: Molto appassionata 3.The saint:
Andante
2(2nd alt. Picc.),2(2nd alt. E.H.),2,2-4,2,3,
1-Timp.,Perc.-Str.

Dello Joio, Norman

Ms. c1952 by Carl Fischer
Score 77 p.
Composed 1951. Original title: Seraphic Dia-
logue. First performance Louisville, Kentucky,
5 December 1951, Louisville Symphony, Robert
Whitney conductor, dance solo by Martha Graham.

4785 Variations, chaconne, e finale   21'
1.Theme and 7 variations 2.Chaconne: Adagio
serioso 3.Finale: Allegro vivo, giocoso, e
ritmico
3*,3*,3*,3*-4,3,3,1-Timp.,Perc.-Str.
Ms.
Score 66 p. Large folio
Composed 1947. Original title: Three Symphonic
Dances. First performance Pittsburgh, 30
January 1948, Pittsburgh Symphony, Fritz Reiner
conductor.

DELUNE, LOUIS.   Charleroi, Belgium 15 March 1876
                              Paris 5 January 1940

583s [Variations and fugue in olden style on
a theme of G.F. Handel, Op. 7, D major]
Str.
Breitkopf & Härtel, Brussels, c1908
Score 20 p.
Theme from the final movement of Handel's
Concerto Grosso Op. 6 no. 10, Bell catalog
no. 123 no. 10.

DEL VALLE DE PAZ, EDGARDO SAMUEL.
                  Alexandria, Egypt 18 October 1861
                  Florence, Italy 5 April 1920

984s Arioso, Op. 26 no. 1 [for string orchestra]
Str.
Score: Ms. 7 p.
Parts: Augener, London [n.d.]

1480s [Ondina. Minuet, the fauns and the
dryads, Op. 21] *Published title:*
I fauni e le driadi, minuetto d'Ondina. 1re
suite d'orchestre, Op. 21. III: Le deità del
bosco
Solo Vn.-Str.
Augener, London [1889]
Score 8 p.

985s Preludio [for string orchestra]
Str.
Score: Ms. 3 p.
Parts: [Augener, London, n.d.]

DELVINCOURT, CLAUDE.   Paris 12 January 1888
Bivio di Albinia, Grosseto, Italy 5 April 1954

2492 Bal vénitien [Venetian ball, for   24'
orchestra]
1.Forlana: Allegretto 2.Passamezzo: Assez
animé 3.Burlesca: Allegro 4.Moresca: Allegro
non troppo 5.Tarantella: Vif et léger
2(both alt. Picc.),2,2,2-2,2,1,1-Timp.,Perc.-
Cel.,Hp.-Str.
Durand, Paris, c1934
Score 111 p.
First performance Paris, March 1930, Orchestre
Straram, Walter Straram conductor.

2924 Radio-sérénade [for orchestra]
1.Cortège [Procession]: Allegro moderato
2.Barcarolle: Andantino 3.Menuet: Allegretto
4.Pastorale: Andante 5.Retraite aux flambeaux
[Retreat by torchlight]: Tempo di marcia
2(2nd alt. Picc.),1,2,1-1,2,1(ad lib.),1(ad
lib.)-Timp.,Perc.-Hp.(or Pno.)-Str.
Durand, Paris, c1937
Score 87 p.
First performance in a radio broadcast, Paris,
August 1936, Désiré Émile Ingelbrecht con-
ductor.

DELYSSE, JEAN. pseudonym.
See: ROESGEN-CHAMPION, MARGUERITE.

DEMERSSEMAN, JULES AUGUSTE ÉDOUARD.
          Hondschoote, Belgium 9 January 1833
                  Paris 1 December 1866

898m [Concert piece no. 4, flute and
orchestra, Op. 80, A major]
1.Vivace 2.Adagio - Allegretto moderato -
Tempo adagio 3.Allegretto
Solo Fl.-1,1,2,1-2,2,1-Timp.-Str.
Score: Ms. 79 p.
Parts: Von Lehne, Hanover [n.d.]

866m [Concert piece no. 6, flute and
orchestra, Italian, Op. 82, F major]
1.Maestoso marciale 2.Chanson napolitaine:
Allegretto un poco più lento - Andante maestoso
3.Finale (Saltarello): Allegro vivace
Solo Fl.-1,1,2,1-2,2,1-Timp.,B.Dr.,Tamb.-Str.
Score: Ms. 68 p.
Parts: C.F. Schmidt, Heilbronn [n.d.]

768m Fantaisie originale [flute and orchestra,
Op. 43, A major]
Solo Fl.-2(2nd alt. Picc.),2,2,2-4,2,3-Timp.-
Str.
Score: Ms. 55 p.
Parts: C.F. Schmidt, Heilbronn [n.d.]

DENNISON, SAM.   Geary, Oklahoma 26 September 1926

155m Adagio, for horn and orchestra   6'
Solo Hn.-2,2,2,2-Timp.-Str.
Ms. c1978 by Sam Dennison
Score 11 p.
Composed 1977-78. First performance Philadel-
phia, 21 May 1978, Orchestra Society of
Philadelphia, Andrzej Jurkiewicz conductor,
Morris Goldman soloist.

179m Lyric piece for tuba and strings   8'
1.Calm 2.Rondo: Presto giocoso
Solo Tuba-Str.
Ms. c1977 by Sam Dennison
Score 36 p.
Commissioned by the Concerto Soloists of Phil-
adelphia. First movement composed 1976. First
performance Blair County Civic Music Associa-
tion, Altoona, Pennsylvania, 13 November 1976,
Concerto Soloists of Philadelphia, Marc
Mostovoy conductor, Carleton Green soloist.
Second movement composed 1977. Dedicated to
Beppi.

DENS, EMILE.   Marseilles 1866

   2236 Les lutins s'amusent [for orchestra]   *10'*
   3*,2,2,2-4,2,3-Timp.,Cym.,Trgl.-Str.
   Senart, Paris [1926]
   Score 48 p.
   Composed 1925. First performance Monte Carlo,
   1926, Léon Jéhin conductor.

DEPPE, LUDWIG. Alverdissen, Germany 7 November 1828
                      Bad Pyrmont 5 September 1890

   4558 [Overture to Theodor Körner's drama
   Zriny, Op. 4]
   2,2,2,3*-4,2,3-Timp.,Perc.-Str.
   Bote & Bock, Berlin [1878]
   Score 47 p.

DÉRÉ, JEAN.   Niort, France 23 June 1886
            Saint-Suzanne, Mayenne, France 6 December 1970

   3195 Quatre petites pièces pour orchestre
   1.Premières joies: Doux et calm (pas trop lent)
   2.La neige tombe [The snow is falling]: Lent
   3.Un drame à guignol [A puppet show]: Pas trop
   vite 4.Le cortège de rêves [The procession of
   dreams]: Solennel et mystérieux
   1,1,1,1-1,1,1-Timp.,Perc.-Hp.(or Pno.)-Str.
   Senart, Paris, c1937
   Score 29 p.

DERING, RICHARD.
   See: DEERING, RICHARD.

DESJOYEAUX, N.

   792s Andantino [G major]
   Solo Vn.(or Vc.)-Str.
   Decourcelle, Nice [n.d.]
   Score 3 p.

DESORMES, LOUIS CÉSAR.   Paris 1841
                           Paris October 1898

   Real name: Louis César Marchionne

   857s Mandolinen-Polka [for string orchestra]
   Str.
   Score: Ms. 5 p.
   Parts: Bote & Bock, Berlin [1878?]

   308s Sérénade de mandolines
   Str.
   Alphonse Leduc, Paris [n.d.]
   Score 4 p.

DESWERT, JULES.
   See: SWERT, JULES DE.

DETT, ROBERT NATHANIEL.
            Drummondville, Quebec 11 October 1882
            Battle Creek, Michigan 2 October 1943

   3627 Enchantment, a romantic suite   *15'*
   1.Incantation 2.Song of the shrine 3.Dance
   of desire 4.Beyond the dream
   3(3rd alt. Picc.),2,2,2-4,3,3,1-Timp.,Perc.-
   Hp.-Str.

Ms.
Score 136 p.
Originally composed for piano, 1921. First
performance of 3rd movement only by Percy Grain-
ger as pianist. This version 1922. Received
the Harmon Foundation Award.

DEVRIENT, F.

   856s Trois pièces, Op. 36. Transcribed for
   string orchestra by Hugo Willemsen
   1.Berceuse: Andante con moto 2.Dans la soli-
   tude: Lento, ma non troppo 3.Au printemps:
   Allegretto
   Str.(Cb. ad lib.)
   Score: Ms. 12 p.
   Parts: B. Schott's Söhne, Mainz [1899?]

DIAMOND, DAVID.   Rochester, New York 9 July 1915

   3036 Aria and hymn for orchestra (1937)   *13'*
   3(3rd alt. Picc.),3*,4*(1Cl. in E-flat),3*-4,
   3,3,1-Timp.,Perc.-Pno.,Hp.-Str.
   Ms.
   Score 35 p.
   Composed 1937. First performance 18 March 1941,
   NBC Symphony, Frank Black conductor.

   3181 Concert piece for orchestra (1939)   *11'*
   2,2,2,2-2,3,2-Timp.,Perc.-Pno.-Str.
   Ms. [Now published by Southern Music, New York]
   Score 73 p. Large folio
   Composed 1939. First performance Carnegie Hall,
   New York, 16 May 1940, Orchestra of the High
   School of Music and Art, Alexander Richter
   conductor.

   3414 Concerto for chamber orchestra, in   *15'*
   two parts (1940)
   1.Fanfare - Prelude and Fugue I 2.Prelude and
   Fugue II - Interlude - Transition - Fanfare
   (Coda)
   1,1,1,1-2Hn.,1Tpt.-Timp.-Str.
   Ms. [Now published by Southern Music, New York]
   Score 72 p. Large folio
   Composed 1940. First performance at the Sixth
   Yaddo Music Period, Saratoga Springs, New York,
   7 September 1940, Yaddo Chamber Orchestra, the
   composer conducting.

   806p Concerto for piano and orchestra   *22'*
   (1949-50)
   1.Andante - Allegretto - Allegro 2.Adagio,
   molto espressivo 3.Allegramente
   Solo Pno.-3*,3*,3*,2-4,2,3,1-Timp.,Perc.-Str.
   Ms.
   Score 84 p.
   Composed 1949-50. First performance New York,
   28 April 1966, New York Philharmonic, Leonard
   Bernstein conductor, Thomas Schumacher soloist.

   1082v Concerto for violin and orchestra   *25'*
   (1936)
   1.Moderato assai 2.Scherzo: Allegro vivace
   3.Largo - Presto - Epilogue
   Solo Vn.-3*,3*,4*(1Cl. in E-flat,2nd alt. Ten.
   Sax.),3*-4,2,2,1-Timp.,Perc.-Pno.,Hp.-Str.
   Ms. [Now published by Southern Music, New York]

Diamond, David

Score 87 p.
Composed 1936. First performance at a Composers' Forum Concert, New York, 24 March 1937, WPA Festival Symphony Orchestra of New York, the composer conducting, Nicolai Berezowsky soloist.

743c Concerto for violoncello and orchestra (1938)   *23'*
1.Moderato assai - Allegro 2.Elegy 3.Allegro veloce
Solo Vc.-3(3rd alt. Picc.),3*,3*,2-4,2,2,1-Timp.,Perc.-Pno.-Str.(without Vc.)
Ms. [Now published by Southern Music, New York]
Score 100 p.
Composed 1938. First performance at the Twelfth Annual Festival of American Music of the Eastman School of Music, Rochester, New York, 30 April 1942, Eastman-Rochester Symphony Orchestra, Howard Hanson conductor, Luigi Silva soloist.

3444 Elegy [first version] to the memory   *8'*
of Maurice Ravel, for brass instruments, harps and percussion (1938)
4Hn.,3Tpt.,3Tbn.,Tuba-Timp.,Perc.-2Hp.
Ms.
Score 25 p.
Composed 1938. First performance at the Eighth Annual Festival of American Music of the Eastman School of Music, Rochester, New York, 28 April 1938, Eastman-Rochester Symphony Orchestra, Howard Hanson conductor.

1782s Elegy [second version] in memory of   *8'*
Maurice Ravel, for string orchestra and percussion (1939)
Timp.,Perc.-Str.
Ms. [Now published by Southern Music, New York]
Score 14 p.
This version made 1939. First performance New York, 6 November 1939, Orchestrette Classique, Frederique Petrides conductor.

3442 Heroic piece, for small orchestra   *11'*
(1938)
1(alt. Picc.),2*,1,1-2,1,1,1-Cym.-Str.
Ms. [Now published by Southern Music, New York]
Score 29 p.
Composed 1938. First performance Zurich, 29 July 1938, Radio Orchestra of Zurich, Hermann Scherchen conductor.

2681 Hommage à Satie, à mémoire (1934)   *7'*
2,1,1,1-2Hn.-Timp.,Cym.-Hp.-Str.
Ms.
Score 23 p.
Composed 1934. First performance New School for Social Research, New York, 15 April 1934, Greenwich Sinfonietta, Gerald McGarrahan conductor.

3130 Music for double string orchestra,   *25'*
brass and timpani (1938-39)
1.Grave - Allegro vivace e ritmico - Lento assai - Allegro 2.Adagio - Allegro con brio
4Hn.,3Tpt.,3Tbn.,Tuba-Timp.-Str.
Ms.

Score 139 p. Large folio
Composed 1938-39. Revised 1968.

5151 Music for Shakespeare's Romeo and   *18'*
Juliet
1.Overture 2.Romeo and Juliet: Balcony scene 3.Romeo and Friar Lawrence 4.Juliet and her nurse 5.The death of Romeo and Juliet
2(2nd alt. Picc.),2(2nd alt. E.H.),2(2nd alt. B.Cl.),2-2,2,1-Timp.,Perc.-Hp.-Str.
Boosey & Hawkes, New York, c1948
Score 66 p.
Commissioned by Thomas Scherman. Composed 1947. First performance New York, 20 October 1947, Little Orchestra Society, Thomas Scherman conductor.

2904 Psalm for orchestra (1936)   *7'*
3*,3*,3*,3*-4,3,3,1-Timp.,Perc.-Pno.(alt. Cel.),2Hp.-Str.
Ms. [Now published by Southern Music, New York]
Score 35 p.
Composed 1936. First performance Rochester, New York, 10 December 1936, Rochester Philharmonic Orchestra, Howard Hanson conductor. Dedicated to André Gide. Received the Juilliard Publication Award, 1936.

1995s Rounds for string orchestra   *12'*
1.Allegro, molto vivace 2.Adagio, leading to 3.Allegro vigoroso
Str.
Elkan-Vogel, Philadelphia, Pa., c1946
Score 44 p.
Commissioned by Dimitri Mitropoulos. Composed 1944. First performance Minneapolis, 24 November 1944, Minneapolis Symphony Orchestra, Dimitri Mitropoulos conductor. Received the New York Music Critics Circle Award, 1945.

5631 Sinfonia concertante (1954-1956)   *23'30"*
1.Allegro aperto 2.Scherzo 3.Larghetto 4.Allegro deciso e ben ritmato
2*,2*,1,1-1,3,3,1-Timp.,Perc.-Pno.,Hp.-Str.
Ms.
Score 144 p. Large folio
Commissioned by the Rochester Friends of Music, 1953. Composed 1954-56. First performance Rochester, 7 March 1957, Rochester Philharmonic, Alfred Wallenstein conductor.

3564 Symphony no. 1 (1940-41)   *20'*
1.Allegro moderato con energia 2.Andante maestoso 3.Maestoso - Allegro vivo
3(3rd alt. Picc.),3*,3*,3*-4,3,3,1-Timp.,Perc.-Str.
Ms. [Now published by Southern Music, New York]
Score 104 p. Large folio
Composed 1940-41. First performance New York, 21 December 1941, New York Philharmonic, Dimitri Mitropoulos conductor.

6645 Symphony no. 2 (1942-43)   *33-35'*
1.Adagio funebre 2.Allegro vivo 3.Andante espressivo, quasi adagio 4.Allegro vigoroso
3(3rd alt. Picc.),3*,3*,3*-4,3,3,1-Timp.,Perc.-Str.
Ms. c1943 by David Diamond

Score 137 p.
Composed 1943. First performance Boston, 13
October 1944, Boston Symphony Orchestra, Serge
Koussevitzky conductor. The earlier, unrelated
work called Second Symphony has been withdrawn
at the composer's request.

4777 [Symphony no. 3 (1945)]   *35'*
1.Allegro deciso 2.Andante, leading to 3.
Allegro vivo 4.Adagio assai, leading to 5.
Allegro con impeto
3(3rd alt. Picc.),3*,3*,3*-4,3,3,1-Timp.,Perc.
-Pno.,Hp.-Str.
Ms.
Score 165 p. Large folio
Composed 1945. First performance Boston, 3
November 1950, Boston Symphony, Charles Munch
conductor.

6683 [Symphony no. 6 (1951-1954)]   *23'*
1.Introduzione: Adagio - Allegro fortemente
mosso 2.Adagio 3.Deciso: Poco allegro - Fuga
3*,3*,4*(1Cl. in E-flat),3*-4,3,3,1-Timp.,
Perc.-Pno.-Str.
Harms, Inc., New York, ᶜ1955
Score 88 p.
Composed 1951-54. First performance Boston,
8 March 1957, Boston Symphony, Charles Munch
conductor.

6271 Symphony no. 7 (1959)   *16'*
1.Andante - Allegro ma non troppo 2.Andante
3.Allegro moderato
3*,3*,4*(1Cl. in E-flat),3*-4,4 (1Tpt. in D),
3,1-Timp.,Perc.-Pno.,Hp.-Str.
Ms. [Now published by Southern Music, New York,
c1963]
Score 74 p. Large folio
Composed 1959. First performance Philadelphia,
26 January 1962, Philadelphia Orchestra, Eugene
Ormandy conductor.

6297 Symphony no. 8 (1960)   *28'*
1.Moderato - Adagio - Allegro vivo 2.Adagio
(tema), variations and double fugue
3*,3*,4*(1Cl. in E-flat),3-4,4(1 in C,1 in D,
2 in F),3,1-Timp.,Perc.-Pno.,Hp.-Str.
Ms. [Now published by Southern Music, New York,
c1963]
Score 108 p. Large folio
Composed 1960. First performance New York, 27
October 1961, New York Philharmonic, Leonard
Bernstein conductor.

3056 [Tom. Suite no. 1 for orchestra,   *12'*
from the ballet]
1.Fanfare 2.Prelude to Episode I 3.Intro-
duction and dance of the benevolent master and
mistress 4.Eliza's supplication (Pantomime)
5.The mortgage (Pantomime) 6.Dance of the
slave-traders and human bloodhounds 7.Dance
of thankfulness for freedom 8.Dance of New
England and New Orleans 9.Entrance of Eva
(Pantomime) 10.Tom's dance of revelation
through the Eternal Word 11.Music accompanying
Eva's departure and ascent into heaven accompanied by angels 12.Choral spiritual -
Conclusion

3*,3*,3*,3*-4,3,3,1-Timp.,Perc.-Pno.(alt. Cel.),
Hp.-Str.
Ms.
Score 100 p.
From the ballet with scenario by E. E. Cummings.
Composed 1936.

2879 Variations for small orchestra (1937) *15'*
2,2*,2*,1-2,1,1,1-Timp.,Perc.-Pno.-Str.
Ms.
Score 76 p.
Composed 1937. First performance at the Tenth
Annual Festival of American Music of the Eastman
School of Music, Rochester, New York, 23 April
1940, Eastman Little Symphony Orchestra, Fred-
erick Fennell conductor. Dedicated to Igor
Stravinsky.

6145 The world of Paul Klee   *12'*
1.Dance of the grieving child 2.The black
prince 3.Pastorale 4.The twittering machine
3*,3*,3*,2-4,3,3-Timp.,Perc.Pno.(alt. Cel.),
Hp.-Str.
Southern Music Publishing Co., New York, ᶜ1961
Score 56 p.
Inspired by the work of the artist Paul Klee
(1879-1940). Commissioned by the Rockefeller
Foundation for the Portland Junior Symphony.
Composed 1957. First performance Portland,
Oregon, 15 February 1958, Portland Junior Sym-
phony, Jacob Avshalomov conductor.

DIANDA, HILDA.   Córdoba, Argentina 13 April 1925

2112s [Music for strings]   *ca.14'*
1.Presto, molto ritmico e vivace 2.Adagio molto
tranquillo 3.Serenata: Andante
Str.
Ms. [Now published by Edición Heliográfica,
Buenos Aires]
Score 20 p. Large folio
Composed 1951. First performance 1953, by the
Orquesta Sinfónica de Tucumán, Carlos F.
Cillario conductor.

DIAZ, EUGENE.   Paris 27 February 1837
                Coleville, France 12 September 1901

Full name: Eugène-Émile Diaz de la Peña

404s Souvenir de Beaulieu, valse de concert
[for string orchestra]
Str.
Decourcelle, Paris [n.d.]
Score 3 p.

DIEM, BERT.

3393 Overture to the Willow Plate (based on
an old Chinese legend)
2,2*,2,2-2,3,2-Timp.,Perc.-Str.
Ms.
Score 32 p.
Written for the WPA of Pittsburgh, Pa.

DIEMER, EMMA LOU.   Kansas City 24 November 1927

6541 Symphonie antique (no. 3)   *10'*
1.Lively, accented 2.Flowing 3.With spirit

Diemer, Emma Lou

3*,2,2,2-4,3,3,1-Timp.,S.Dr.,B.Dr.-Str.
Ms. c1961 by Emma Lou Diemer [Now published
by Belwin-Mills, New York, c1966]
Score 55 p.
*Commissioned under the sponsorship of the Young
Composers Project for the senior high school
orchestras of Arlington, Virginia. Composed
1961. First performance Arlington, 20 May
1961, Washington-Lee High School Symphony
Orchestra, Dorothy Baumle conductor.*

5855 Symphony no. 2 on American Indian   18'
themes
1.Fast, spirited 2.Moderately slow, expressive
3.Fast, rhythmic
3*,3(3rd alt. E.H.),3(3rd alt. B.Cl.),3*-4,3,3,
1-Timp.,Perc.-Pno.,Cel.,Hp.-Str.
Ms.
Score 100 p. Large folio
*Composed 1959. First performance Rochester,
New York, 23 March 1959, Eastman-Rochester Symphony Orchestra, Howard Hanson conductor.
Second movement (under the title Night Song)
won the Edward B. Benjamin Award, second
place, 1959, for music of a quiet nature.*

DIÉMER, LOUIS.   Paris 14 February 1843
                           Paris 21 December 1919

578p Concert-Stück, pour piano et orchestre,
Op. 31
1.Prélude: Lento - Andantino 2.Final: Intro-
duction, Allegro molto - Allegro giocoso
Solo Pno.-2,2,2,2-4,2,3-Timp.-Str.
J. Hamelle, Paris [n.d.]
Score 72 p.

801v Concert-Stück, pour violon et orchestre,
Op. 33
1.Prélude et andantino: Moderato - Andantino
2.Introduction: Allegro - Saltarelle: Allegro
molto
Solo Vn.-2(1st alt. Picc.),2,2,2-4,2,3-Timp.,
Tamb.-Hp.-Str.
J. Hamelle, Paris [n.d.]
Score 55 p.

DIETRICH, ALBERT HERMANN.
       Forsthaus Golk near Meissen 28 August 1829
                           Berlin 20 November 1908

1064v [Concerto, violin, Op. 30]
1.Allegro 2.Adagio espressivo 3.Allegro molto
vivace
Solo Vn.-2,2,2,2-2,2-Timp.-Str.
Score: Ms. 92 p.
Parts: Hugo Pohle, Hamburg [n.d.]

712c Concertstück, Op. 32 [for violoncello
and orchestra]
1.Allegro 2.Romanze: Andante espressivo 3.
Finale: Allegro un poco maestoso
Solo Vc.-2,2,2,2-2,2-Timp.-Str.
Score: Ms. 134 p.
Parts: [Hugo Pohle, Hamburg, n.d.]

5720 [Overture for orchestra, Op. 35, C major]
2,2,2,2-4,2,3-Timp.,Trgl.-Str.

J. Rieter-Biedermann, Leipzig, 1882
Score 35 p.
*Composed for the opening celebration of the
Ducal Theater at Oldenburg and first performed
there, 8 October 1881.*

DIPPE, GUSTAV.
       Tilsit, East Prussia 19 September 1858
           Buckow, Germany 9 September 1914

276s Serenade, Op. 10, D major [for string
orchestra]
1.Tempo di marcia, poco maestoso 2.Andante
3.Presto 4.Allegro moderato
Str.
R. Schultz, Berlin [n.d.]
Score 23 p.

DITTERSDORF, KARL DITTERS VON.
                           Vienna 2 November 1739
           Castle Rothlhotta, Bohemia 24 October 1799

395c [Concerto, contrabass and orchestra,   10'
E-flat major. Krebs no. 171] Edited by Ludwig
and Franz Jaeger
1.Allegro 2.Adagio 3.Presto
Solo Cb.-2Fl.,2Ob.-2Hn.-Str.
Schott's Söhne, Mainz, c1937
Score in reduction 16 p.
*Originally composed as a concerto for violin
and chamber orchestra.*

398c [Concerto, contrabass and orchestra,   11'
E major. Krebs no. 172] Edited by Franz
Tischer-Zeitz
1.Allegro moderato 2.Adagio 3.Allegro
Solo Cb.-2Fl.-2Hn.-Cemb.-Str.
B. Schott's Söhne, Mainz, c1938
Score in reduction 16 p.

364m [Concerto, harp and orchestra,   20'
A major] Edited by Karl Hermann Pillney
1.Allegro molto 2.Larghetto 3.Rondeau
Solo Hp.-2Ob.-2Hn.-Str.
C.F. Peters, New York, c1958
Score 52 p.
*According to the editor, this work is a free
arrangement of a concerto for cembalo, composed 1779. Wind parts added; the cadenza in
the second movement is by the editor. This
composition is not listed in Krebs' thematic
catalog. First performance of this edition,
London, 18 May 1934, Sidonie Goossens soloist.*

943v [Concerto, violin and string orchestra,
G major. Krebs no. 160] Edited by Hans
Mlynarczyk and Ludwig Lürman
1.Allegro moderato 2.Adagio 3.Presto
Solo Vn.-Str.
Hofmeister, Leipzig, c1933
Score 35 p.
*Listed in The Breitkopf Thematic Catalog,
Supplement II, Leipzig, 1767.*

1606 [Divertimento, The struggle of the   15'
human passions, D major. Krebs no. 133]
Edited by Josef Liebeskind
1.Il superbo: Andante 2.L'umile [The humble]:

Andante 3.Il matto [The lunatic]: Menuetto
poco allegro 4.Il dolce [The pleasant]:
L'istesso tempo 5.Il contento: Andante 6.Il
costante: Menuetto 7.Il malinconico [The
melancholical]: Adagio 8.Il vivace: Allegro
assai
2Ob.-2Hn.(or 2Tpt.)-Str.
Reinecke, Leipzig, 1899
Score 19 p.

1605 [Esther. Overture to the oratorio.   12'
Krebs no. 318. *And* Ballet music. Krebs no. 135]
Edited by Josef Liebeskind
1.Ouverture zu dem Oratorium Esther: Grave e
maestoso 2.Musique pour un petit ballet en
forme d'une contre-danse
No. 1: 2Ob.,2Bn.-2Hn.-Str.
No. 2: 2,2,0,2-2,2-Timp.-Str.
Reinecke, Leipzig, 1899
Score 15 p.
No. 1 from the oratorio La Liberatrice del
Populo Giudaico nella Persia, o sia l'Esther.
First performance Vienna, 19 December 1773.

235m [Sinfonia concertante, viola and
contrabass with orchestra, D major. Krebs no.
127. Arranged by Klaas Weelink]
1.Allegro 2.Andantino 3.Menuetto 4.Allegro
ma non troppo
Solo Va., Solo Cb.-2Ob.-2Hn.-Hpscd.(ad lib.)-
Str.
Edition KaWe, Amsterdam, C1969
Score 12 p.

Symphonies are listed according to their order
in the Krebs thematic catalog.

4197 [Symphony in the style of five nations.
Krebs no. 18] Edited by Karl Geiringer
1.Tedesco: Andantino 2.Italiano: Allegro
3.Inglese: Allegretto 4.Francese: Menuett –
Turco: Trio 5.Rondo delle cinque nazioni
2Ob.(ad lib.)-2Hn.(ad lib.)-Str.
Ms. C[n.d.] by Karl Geiringer
Score 45 p.
This work announced as published in The
Breitkopf Thematic Catalog, Supplement III,
Leipzig, 1768. Original title is Sinfonia
Nazionale.

2200 [Symphony, E-flat major. Krebs no. 24] 14'
Edited by Josef Liebeskind
1.Allegro 2.Allegretto 3.Minuetto 4.Finale:
Vivace
2Ob.-2Hn.-Str.
Reinecke, Leipzig, 1899
Score 23 p.
Listed in The Breitkopf Thematic Catalog,
Supplement IV, Leipzig, 1769.

4676 [Symphony, C major. Krebs no. 32.
Arranged by Adam Carse]
1.Allegro assai 2.Andante 3.Allegro vivo
2Fl.(or 2Ob.; ad lib.)-2Hn.(ad lib.)-Str.
Augener, London, C1936
Score 15 p.
This work listed in The Breitkopf Thematic
Catalog, Supplement VI, Leipzig, 1771.

5545 [Symphony, The mail coach, B-flat   16-17'
major. Krebs no. 48] Revised by Eugen Bodart
1.Presto assai 2.Andante 3.Menuetto
4.Presto assai
2Ob.-2Hn.-Str.
Mannheimer Musik-Verlag, Mannheim, C1956
Score 32 p.
This work listed in The Breitkopf Thematic
Catalog, Supplement X, Leipzig, 1775.

2199 [Symphony, F major. Krebs no. 70]   13'
Edited by Josef Liebeskind
1.Allegro moderato 2.Rondo: Andante
3.Minuetto 4.Finale: Allegro
2Ob.-2Hn.-Str.
Reinecke, Leipzig, 1899
Score 21 p.
Listed in The Breitkopf Thematic Catalog,
Supplement XIV, Leipzig, 1781.

1600 [Symphony, The four ages of the world, 17'
C major. Krebs catalog no. 73] Edited by Josef
Liebeskind
1.Larghetto 2.Allegro e vivace 3.Minuetto con
garbo [Graceful minuet] 4.Finale: Presto
1,2,0,2-2,2-Timp.-Str.
Reinecke, Leipzig, 1899
Score 34 p.
First published 1786. This and the following
5 symphonies, Krebs catalog nos. 73 through 78,
were inspired by Ovid's Metamorphoses.

1601 [Symphony, The fall of Phaeton,   16'
D major. Krebs no. 74] Edited by Josef
Liebeskind
1.Adagio non molto – Allegro 2.Andante
3.Tempo di minuetto 4.Finale: Vivace ma non
troppo presto
1,2,0,2-2,2-Str.
Reinecke, Leipzig, 1899
Score 30 p.
First published 1786.

1602 [Symphony, Transformation of Actaeon   14'
into a deer, G major. Krebs no. 75] Edited by
Josef Liebeskind
1.Allegro 2.Adagio (più tosto andantino)
3.Tempo di minuetto 4.Finale: Vivace
Fl.,2Ob.-2Hn.-Str.
Reinecke, Leipzig, 1899
Score 26 p.
First published 1786.

2198 [Symphony, Andromeda's rescue by   17'
Perseus, F major. Krebs no. 76] Edited by
Josef Liebeskind
1.Adagio non molto 2.Presto (Vivace)
3.Larghetto 4.Finale: Vivace
2Ob.-2Hn.-Str.
Reinecke, Leipzig, 1899
Score 31 p.

1603 [Symphony, Transformation of Phineus   24'
and his friends into stone, D major. Krebs
no. 77] Edited by Josef Liebeskind
1.Andante più tosto allegretto 2.Allegro
assai 3.Andante molto 4.Finale: Vivace
1,2,0,2-2,2-Str.

Dittersdorf, Karl Ditters von

Reinecke, Leipzig, 1899
Score 39 p.

1604 [Symphony, Transformation of the   *20'*
Lycian peasants into frogs, A major. Krebs
no. 78] Edited by Josef Liebeskind
1.Allegretto non troppo presto 2.Adagio, ma
non molto 3.Minuetto: Moderato 4.Finale:
Adagio - Vivace, ma moderato
2,0,0,2-2Hn.-Str.
Reinecke, Leipzig, 1899
Score 30 p.

5233 [Symphony, C major. Krebs no. 93.
Arranged by Hermann Kretzschmar]
1.Allegro molto 2.Larghetto 3.Menuetto I:
Vivace - Menuetto II: Tranquillo 4.Finale:
Prestissimo
2Ob.,2Bn.-2,2-Timp.-Str.
Breitkopf & Härtel, Leipzig, c1896
Score 39 p.
Composed ca.1788.

DOHNÁNYI, ERNST VON. Poszony (now Bratislava)
               Czechoslovakia 27 July 1877
               New York City 9 February 1960

Born: Ernö Dohnányi

6161 American rhapsody for orchestra,   *10'*
Op. 47 (revised version)
3(3rd alt. Picc.),2(2nd alt. E.H.),2,2(2nd alt.
C.Bn.)-4,3,3,1-Timp.,Cym.,S.Dr.-Str.
Ms. c[n.d.] by Ernst von Dohnányi
Score 72 p. Large folio
*Composed in honor of the Sesquicentennial of
Ohio University, 1953. First performed in
this version Brevard, North Carolina, August
1961. Quotations: On Top of Old Smoky; I Am
a Poor Wayfaring Stranger; I Gave My Love a
Cherry; Turkey in the Straw; Two Country
Dances; Sweet Betsy from Pike.*

491c [Concert piece, violoncello and   *22'*
orchestra, Op. 12, D major]
In one movement
Solo Vc.-2,2,2,2-2,2-Timp.-Str.
Doblinger, Vienna, c1906
Score 59 p.
*Composed 1905. First performance Cologne, 4
December 1906, Hugo Becker soloist.*

408p [Concerto, piano, Op. 5, E minor]   *38'*
1.Adagio maestoso - Allegro - Adagio
2.Andante 3.Vivace
Solo Pno.-3*,2,2,3*-Timp.,Cym.,Trgl.-Str.
Doblinger, Vienna, c1904
Score 122 p.
Awarded the Bösendorfer Prize, 1899.

556v [Concerto, violin, Op. 27, D minor] *40'*
1.Molto moderato, maestoso e rubato 2.Andante
3.Molto vivace
Solo Vn.-2(2nd alt. Picc.),2(2nd alt. E.H.),2,
3*-4,2,3-Timp.,Trgl.-Hp.-Str.
Alberti, Berlin, c1920
Score 103 p.
Composed 1917. First performance Budapest,

*1919, the composer conducting, Emil Telmányi
soloist.*

315v [Concerto, violin, no. 2, Op. 43,   *30'*
C minor]
1.Allegro molto moderato 2.Intermezzo: Allegro
comodo e scherzando 3.Adagio molto sostenuto
4.Allegro risoluto e giocoso
Solo Vn.-3,2,2,2-4,2,3,1-Timp.,Perc.-Hp.-Str.
(without Violins)
Associated Music Publishers, New York, c1956
Score 90 p. Large folio
*Composed 1950. First performance San Antonio,
Texas, 26 January 1951, San Antonio Symphony,
Victor Alessandro conductor, Frances Magnes
soloist.*

892 Ruralia Hungarica, Op. 32b   *25'*
1.Andante poco moto, rubato 2.Presto, ma non
tanto 3.Allegro grazioso 4.Adagio non troppo
5.Molto vivace
3(3rd alt. Picc.),3*,3*,3*-4,3,3,1-Timp.,Perc.
-Cel.,Hp.-Str.
Rózsavölgyi, Budapest, c1925
Score 104 p.
*Composed 1924. First performance Budapest, 17
November 1924, the composer conducting. Transcribed for piano solo as Op. 33c.*

376 [Suite for orchestra in 4 movements,   *35'*
Op. 19]
1.Andante con variazioni: Andante con moto and
6 variations 2.Scherzo: Allegretto vivace
3.Romanza: Andante poco moto 4.Rondo: Allegro
vivace
3(3rd alt. Picc.),3*,3(3rd alt. B.Cl.),3*-4,2,
3-Timp.,Perc.-2Hp.-Str.
Doblinger, Leipzig, c1911
Score 142 p.
*Composed 1908-09. First performance Budapest,
21 February 1910, the composer conducting.*

2533 [Symphonic minutes, Op. 36]   *12'30"*
1.Capriccio: Vivacissimo possibile 2.Rapsodia:
Andante 3.Scherzo: Allegro vivace 4.Tema con
variazioni: Andante poco moto - Appassionato
5.Rondo: Presto
2(2nd alt. Picc.),2(2nd alt. E.H.),2(2nd alt.
B.Cl.),2-4,2,3-Timp.,Perc.-Cel.,Hp.-Str.
Rózsavölgyi, Budapest, c1935
Score 98 p.
*Composed 1933. First performance Budapest, 12
November 1934, Budapest Philharmonic, the com-
poser conducting.*

320 [Symphony, Op. 9, D minor]   *55'*
1.Allegro ma non troppo 2.Molto adagio 3.
Scherzo: Presto - Intermezzo: Andante poco
moto 4.Finale: Introduzione, Tema con variazioni e Fuga
4*(3rd alt. 2nd Picc.),3*,3(3rd alt. B.Cl.),4*
-6,3,3,1-Timp.,Perc.-2Hp.(2nd ad lib.)-Str.
B. Schott's Söhne, Mainz [190-?]
Score 181 p.
*Composed 1900-01. First performance Manches-
ter, 30 January 1902, Hans Richter conductor.*

845 [Variations on a nursery song for   *22'*
piano and orchestra, Op. 25]
Introduzione: Maestoso - Tema: Allegro - 11
Variations - Finale fugato: Allegro vivace
Solo Pno.-3*,2,2,3*-4,3,3,1-Timp.,Perc.-Cel.,
Hp.-Str.
Simrock, Berlin, c1922
Score 91 p.
Theme is Twinkle, Twinkle, Little Star. Com-
posed 1913. First performance Budapest, 17
February 1916, Blüthner Orchestra, Karl Panzner
conductor, the composer as soloist.

325 [The veil of Pierrette, Op. 18.   *70'*
Excerpts from the ballet]
1.[Pierrot's complaint of love]: Moderato 2.
[Waltz-round dance]: Molto allegro 3.[Jolly
funeral march]: Alla marcia 4.[Wedding waltz]
5.Menuett: Nicht zu langsam 6.[Pierrette's
dance of madness]: Allegro
2,2(2nd alt. E.H.),3,3*-4,2,3,1-Timp.,Perc.-Hp.
-Str.
Doblinger, Leipzig, c1911
Score 94 p.
From the ballet with book by Arthur Schnitzler.
Composed 1908-09. First performance Dresden,
22 January 1910, Ernst Schuch conductor.

DONATO, ANTHONY.   Prague, Nebraska 8 March 1909

2193s Elegy for strings   *10'30"*
Str.
Ms.
Score 20 p.
Composed 1938. First performance Lincoln,
Nebraska, 23 April 1939, Lincoln String
Orchestra, Dorothy Holcomb conductor.

6143 Episode   *10'30"*
3*(3rd alt. Picc.),3*,3*,3*-4,3,3,1-Timp.,Perc.
-Str.
Ms.
Score 41 p. Large folio
Composed 1954.

6144 Mission San José de Aguaya   *5'*
2,2,2,2-0,0,0-Str.
Ms.
Score 6 p.
Composed 1945. First performance Eureka Springs,
Arkansas, 30 August 1947, Ozark Workshop
Orchestra, Dorothy Holcomb conductor.

6217 Serenade for small orchestra   *13'*
1.Allegro 2.Molto andante 3.Allegro
moderato 4.Allegro
1(alt. Picc.),1,1,1-1,1,1-Timp.,Perc.-Hp.-Str.
Ms.
Score 81 p.
Commissioned by the Chicago Little Symphony,
1961. Composed 1961. First performance Tra-
verse City, Michigan, 3 March 1962, Chicago
Little Symphony Orchestra, Thor Johnson con-
ductor.

5889 Sinfonietta no. 2   *14'30"*
1.Allegro con brio 2.Andante 3.Molto allegro
2(2nd alt. Picc.),2,2,2-2,2,1-Timp.,Perc.-Hp.-

Str.
Ms. [Now published by Marks Music, New York]
Score 73 p.
Commissioned by the Peninsula Festival Associa-
tion, Fish Creek, Wisconsin, 1959. Composed
1959. First performance Fish Creek, 12 August
1959, Peninsula Festival Orchestra, Thor
Johnson conductor.

5916 Solitude in the city, a symphonic   *23'30"*
narration on a poem by John Gould Fletcher
1.Words at midnight: Slowly 2.The evening
rain: Quite fast 3.Street of sorrows: Moderately 4.Song in the darkness: Mod[erately]
slow
Narrator-3*(Picc. alt. Fl.3),3*,3*,3*(C.Bn.
alt. Bn.3)-4,3,3,1-Timp.,Perc.-Str.
Ms.
Score 79 p. Large folio
Commissioned for the Cincinnati Symphony
Orchestra by Thor Johnson, 1954. Composed 1954.
First performance Cincinnati, Ohio, 25 March
1955, Cincinnati Symphony Orchestra, Thor
Johnson conductor, Carl Jacobs narrator.

2194s Suite for strings   *10'*
1.Moderately fast 2.Slow 3.Fast and gay
Str.
Ms.
Score 21 p. Large folio
Composed 1948. First performance Seattle,
Washington, 9 August 1949, University of Wash-
ington Chamber Orchestra, Stanley Chapple
conductor.

5825 Two orchestral pieces   *1. 7'*
1.The plains 2.Prairie schooner   *2. 6'*
2,2,2,2-4,3,3,1-Timp.,Perc.-Hp.-
Str.
Composers Press, New York, c1957
Score 47 p.
The Plains composed 1952; Prairie Schooner,
1948. First performance of The Plains, Okla-
homa City, 31 October 1955, Oklahoma City
Symphony, Guy F. Harrison conductor. Prairie
Schooner first performed Rochester, New York,
19 October 1948, Eastman-Rochester Orchestra,
Howard Hanson conductor. Won the 1954 Sym-
phonic Award sponsored by The Composers Press.

DONATO, VINCENZO DI.   Rome 15 August 1887

755s Concerto grosso, on themes of F.A.   *6'*
Bonporti da Trento (1660)
1.Adagio - Presto 2.Andante 3.Presto (non
troppo)
Str.
De Santis, Rome, c1927
Score 8 p.
Composed 1921.

DONIZETTI, GAETANO.   Bergamo 29 November 1797
   Bergamo 8 April 1848

Baptized: Domenico Gaetano Maria Donizetti

2347s [Allegro, strings, C major] Edited   *6'*
by Bernhard Päuler

Donizetti, Gaetano

Str.
Henry Litolff/C.F. Peters, Frankfurt, ᶜ1971
Score 12 p.
Composed ca.1820. First published edition 1971.

4089 [Anna Bolena. Overture]
2,2,2,2-4,2,3-Timp.,B.Dr.,Cym.-Str.
Ms.
Score 60 p.
From the opera based on the story of Anne Boleyn. Composed 1830.

298m [Concertino, clarinet, B-flat major]
Edited by Bernhard Päuler
In one movement: Allegretto
Solo Cl.-2Ob.-2Hn.-Str.
Eulenburg, Zurich, ᶜ1972
Score 14 p.
Autograph in Museo Donizettiano, Bergamo.

4255 [Dom Sébastien, king of Portugal.
Introduction to Act I]
2,2,2,2-4,4,3,Ophicl.-Timp.,B.Dr.,S.Dr.-Str.
Bureau Central de Musique, Paris [184-?]
Score 6 p.
From the opera in five acts with libretto by Augustin-Eugène Scribe. Composed 1843.

4260 [Lucrezia Borgia. Prelude]
2*,2,2,2-4,2,3-Timp.,B.Dr.-Str.
Ms.
Score 14 p.
From the opera in 2 acts with libretto by Felice Romani after the drama by Victor Hugo. Composed 1833.

4291 [The martyrs. Overture]   7'
3*,2,2,4*-4,4(2nd alt. Cnt.),3,Ophicl.-Timp.,
Perc.-Hp.-Chorus(ad lib.)-Str.
Schonenberger, Paris [1840]
Score 45 p.
From the opera in 4 acts with libretto by Augustin-Eugène Scribe, in part derived directly from Corneille's Polyeucte and in part an adaptation of Salvatore Cammarano's Italian libretto Poliuto, itself derived from Polyeucte. Original title, Poliuto. Composed 1839. First performance Opéra, Paris, 10 April 1840.

5735 [Sinfonia concertata, chamber   6'
orchestra, D major] Revised by Giuseppe
Piccioli
Largo - Allegro
1,2,2,2-2Hn.,2Tpt.-Str.
Carisch, Milan, ᶜ1936
Score 28 p.
Composed 1816. First performance Bologna, 19 June 1817.

6867 Sinfonia for winds in G minor.   4'30"
Edited by Douglas Townsend
1,2,2,2-2Hn.
Tetra Music Corp. [n.p.] ᶜ1967
Score 16 p.
This edition based on a Ms. score dated 19 April 1817.

DONNER, MAX.   probably United States fl.1909

139s Canto religioso: air on the G string,
Op. 50 [for violin solo. Transcribed for string orchestra by William F. Happich]
Str.
Ms. [Original version published by C. Fischer, New York]
Score 4 p.
This transcription commissioned by Edwin A. Fleisher for the Symphony Club, 1919.

DONOVAN, RICHARD.
New Haven, Connecticut 29 November 1891
Middletown, Connecticut 22 August 1970

344m Fantasia for solo bassoon and seven 7'30"
instruments
Solo Bn.-Timp.,Perc.-Cel.-Vn.,Va.,Vc.,Cb.
Ms. ᶜ1961 by Richard Frank Donovan
Score 15 p. Large folio
Composed 1960; revised 1961. First performance Houston, Texas, 18 March 1960, Houston Symphony Orchestra, Leopold Stokowski conductor, Paul Tucci soloist.

6258 New England chronicle, an overture   10'
3*,3*,3*,3*-4,3,3,1-Timp.,Perc.-Str.
Ms. ᶜ1955 by Richard Donovan
Score 65 p. Large folio
Composed 1947. First performance New York City, 17 May 1947, NBC Symphony Orchestra, Alfred Wallenstein conductor.

6218 Passacaglia on Vermont folk tunes   12'30"
2(2nd alt. Picc.),2,2,2-4,2,3,1-Timp.,Perc.-Str.
Ms. ᶜ1952 by Richard Donovan
Score 43 p.
Composed 1949. First performance New Haven, Connecticut, 1 November 1949, New Haven Symphony Orchestra, the composer conducting.

980m Ricercare [for oboe and string   5'30"
orchestra, revised version]
Solo Ob.-Str.
Ms. [Now published by Boosey & Hawkes, New York]
Score 18 p.
Composed 1938 as Allegro-Fugato for Oboe and Strings. First performance at the 5th Yaddo Music Period, Saratoga Springs, New York, 11 September 1938, Yaddo Chamber Orchestra, the composer conducting, Arno Mariotti soloist. Revised and retitled 1939. First performance Rochester, New York, 25 April 1939, Eastman School Little Symphony Orchestra, Frederick Fennell conductor, Ezra Kotzin soloist.

2846 Smoke and steel, symphonic poem for   15'
orchestra
3(3rd alt. Picc.),3*,3(3rd alt. B.Cl.),3*-4,3,
3,1-Timp.,Perc.-Pno.-Str.
Ms.
Score 73 p.
Inspired by Carl Sandburg's poem. Composed 1932.

353m Suite for string orchestra and   *16'30"*
    oboe
    1.Allegro energico 2.Arietta: Adagio
    3.Rondo: Allegro con spirito
    Solo Ob.-Str.
    Ms. ^c1952 by Richard Donovan
    Score 45 p. Large folio
    Composed 1944-45. First performance Baltimore,
    Maryland, 11 March 1955, Baltimore Little Sym-
    phony, Reginald Stewart conductor, Alfred
    Genovese soloist.

2894 Symphony for chamber orchestra   *25'*
    1.Lento 2.Adagio 3.Allegro moderato
    1,1,1,1-Tpt.-Timp.,Perc.-Str.
    Ms.
    Score 77 p.
    Composed 1937. First performance (of 2nd move-
    ment only) at the Fourth Yaddo Music Period,
    Saratoga Springs, New York, 18 September 1937,
    Yaddo Chamber Orchestra, the composer con-
    ducting.

961m Wood notes for flute, harp and   *12'*
    string orchestra
    Solo Fl.-Hp.-Str.
    Ms.
    Score 34 p. Large folio
    Composed 1926 as Poem for Flute and String
    Orchestra. First performance at the 50th anni-
    versary celebration of Smith College, Northamp-
    ton, Massachusetts, 14 June 1925, Smith College
    Symphony Orchestra, the composer conducting,
    F. Kulovkis soloist. Revised and retitled,
    1939.

DOPPER, CORNELIS.
            Stadskanaal, Netherlands 7 February 1870
                    Amsterdam 18 September 1939

1123 Ciaconna gotica [Gothic chaconne]   *20'*
    3(3rd alt. Picc.),3*,3*,3*-4,3,3,1-Timp.,Perc.
    -Hp.-Str.
    Rahter, Leipzig, ^c1923
    Score 54 p.
    Originally titled Adagio Mesto. Composed 1920.
    First performance Concertgebouw, Amsterdam,
    24 October 1920, Concertgebouw Orchestra, the
    composer conducting.

DOPPLER, ALBERT FRANZ. Lwów, Poland 16 October 1821
                    Baden, near Vienna 27 July 1883

5754 Aus der Heimat [From the homeland, musical
    fragments in song and dance based partly on
    Austro-Hungarian folk melodies]
    Einleitung - Ober und Unter Oesterreich - Länd-
    ler - Steiermark - Tirol - Dalmatien - Kroaten
    Marsch - Bosnien - Kolo Tanz - Slovakischer
    Tanz - Böhmen - Ruthenischer Tanz (Kolomyika) -
    Polen - Ungarn (Csárdás)
    2(2nd alt. Picc.),2,2,2-4,2,3-Timp.,Perc.-Hp.-
    Str.
    J. Gutmann, Vienna [n.d.]
    Score 79 p.
    From the Festspiel of the same name. First
    performance Vienna, 24 April 1879. Choreography
    by K. Telle.

863m Fantaisie pastorale hongroise [for flute
    and orchestra, Op. 26] Edited by A. Klautzsch
    1.Molto andante 2.Andantino moderato - Allegro
    3.Allegro
    Solo Fl.-1,1,2,1-2,2,3,1-Timp.-Str.
    Score: Ms. 69 p.
    Parts: B. Schott's Söhne, Mainz [1887?]

DOPPLER, ÁRPÁD.   Budapest 5 June 1857
                    Stuttgart 13 August 1927

488s Schlummerlied [Lullaby, string orchestra,
    Op. 2, G major]
    Str.
    Breitkopf & Härtel, Leipzig [1890]
    Score 7 p.

DORET, GUSTAVE.
            Aigle, Switzerland 20 September 1866
                    Lausanne 19 April 1943

1486s Air [for violin or violoncello and
    string orchestra, F major]
    Solo Vn.(or Solo Vc.)-Str.
    Baudoux, Paris [n.d.]
    Score 11 p.

DÖRING, CARL HEINRICH. Dresden, Germany 4 July 1834
                    Dresden 26 March 1916

309s [Suite, string orchestra, Op. 16, A minor]
    1.Praeludium 2.Air: Andante molto 3.Gigue:
    Allegro vivo 4.Allemande: Larghetto 5.Fan-
    tasie und Fuge: Molto adagio
    Str.
    L. Hoffarth, Dresden [n.d.]
    Score 42 p.
    First performance Dresden, 14 April 1864,
    Dresdner Tonkünstlerverein.

1305s Waldrösleins Liebestraum, Op. 321 no. 2
    [for string orchestra]
    Str.
    Score: Ms. 4 p.
    Parts: L. Hoffarth, Dresden [n.d.]

DORN, HEINRICH LUDWIG EGMONT.
            Königsberg 14 November 1804
                    Berlin 10 January 1892

4510 [Die Nibelungen, Op. 73. Overture]
    3*,2,3,2-4,3,3,1-Timp.,Perc.-Hp.-Str.
    Bote & Bock, Berlin [185-?]
    Score 54 p.
    From the opera in 5 acts with libretto by E.
    Gerber.

DORN, OTTO.   Cologne 7 September 1848
                    Wiesbaden 8 November 1931

466s Abend-Musik, Op. 3 [for string orchestra]
    Str.(without Cb.)
    Challier, Berlin [n.d.]
    Score 3 p.

830s Preghiera, Op. 13 no. 3 [for violoncello
    and string orchestra] Edited by Oscar Brückner
    Solo Vc.-Str.

Dornaus, P.

J. André, Offenbach a.M. [1888?]
Score 4 p.
*Originally composed as a Bagatelle for violon-
cello and piano.*

DORNAUS, P.   Coblenz, Germany ca.1770

Two brothers: Philipp, b.1769, and Peter, b.1770

801m [Concerto, 2 horns, no. 1, Op. 14,
E major]
1.Allegro brioso 2.Romanza: Andantino 3.Rondo:
Tempo giusto - Alla polacca, moderato
Solo Hn.I,Solo Hn.II-2,0,0,2-2Hn.-Str.
Score: Ms. 51 p.
Parts: J. André, Offenbach a.M. [1802?]

DORNHECKTER, ROBERT.
            Franzburg, Pomerania 4 November 1839
            Stralsund, Pomerania 19 May 1890

993s Serenade, Op. 19 [for string orchestra,
piano and harmonium]
Pno.(or Hp.),Harm.(or Org.)-Str.(without Cb.)
L. Hoffarth, Dresden [n.d.]
Score 7 p.

DOSTAL, P. DEDECECK.
See: DEDECECK-DOSTAL, P.

DOTZAUER, JUSTUS JOHANN FRIEDRICH.
            Hässelrieth, Germany 20 June 1783
            Dresden 6 March 1860

682c Le carnaval de Venise, Op. 177 [for
violoncello and orchestra]
Solo Vc.-1,1,1,2-2Hn.-Str.
Score: Ms. 37 p.
Parts: W. Damköhler, Berlin [n.d.]

DOUGLAS, MARTHA ALTER. pseudonym.
See: ALTER, MARTHA.

DOWLAND, JOHN.   Ireland December 1562
                         London 21 January 1626

868s [Lachrimae, for lutes, viols, or violins.
5 excerpts. Transcribed for string orchestra
by Walther Pudelko]
1.Pavane, Lachrimae antiquae 2.Pavane, Lachrimae antiquae novae 3.Pavane, Semper Dowland
semper dolens 4.Galliarde, Dem König von
Dänemark 5.Allemande, George Whitehead
Str.(Vn.I/II,Va.I/II,Vc.)
Bärenreiter, Augsburg, 1926
Score 19 p.
*From Lachrimae, or Seven Teares Figured in
Seven Passionate Pavans, first published by
the composer, London, 1604.*

DRAESEKE, FELIX AUGUST BERNHARD.
                         Coburg 7 October 1835
                         Dresden 26 February 1913

556p [Concerto, piano, Op. 36, E-flat   33'
major]
1.Allegro moderato 2.Adagio 3.Allegro molto
vivace

Solo Pno.-2,2,2,2-2,2,3-Timp.-Str.
Kistner, Leipzig [1887]
Score 139 p.
*Composed 1885-86. First performance Sonders-
hausen, 4 June 1886, Karl Schroeder conductor.*

5098 [Jubilee overture, Op. 65]
3*,2,3,2-4,4,4,4-Timp.,Perc.-2Hp.-Str.
Breitkopf & Härtel, Leipzig, ᶜ1898
Score 55 p.
*Commissioned by the city of Dresden for the
70th birthday and the 25th year of reign of
His Majesty, King Albert of Saxony. Composed
1898.*

1779 Serenade für Orchester, Op. 49   23'
1.Marsch: Allegretto leggiero 2.Ständchen:
Andantino 3.Liebesscene: Andante con espres-
sione 4.Polonaise: Allegretto con brio 5.
Finale: Prestissimo leggiero
2,2,2,2-2,2,1-Timp.-Str.
Kistner, Leipzig [1889]
Score 54 p.
*Composed 1888. First performance Dresden, 21
October 1889, Dresdner Tonkünstlerverein,
Ernst Schuch conductor.*

1524 Symphonia tragica, Op. 40   49'
1.Andante - Allegro risoluto 2.Grave (Adagio
ma non troppo) 3.Scherzo: Allegro, molto
vivace 4.Finale: Allegro con brio
3*,2,2,2-4,3,3,1-Timp.,Gong-Str.
Kistner, Leipzig [1887]
Score 179 p.
*Composed 1886. First performance Dresden, 13
January 1888, Dresdner Tonkünstlerverein, Ernst
Schuch conductor.*

2060 [Symphony no. 2, Op. 25, F major]   37'
1.Allegro con moto 2.Allegretto marciale 3.
Allegro comodo 4.Presto leggiero
2,2,2,2-4,2,3-Timp.,Trgl.-Str.
Kistner, Leipzig [1884]
Score 177 p.
*Composed 1876. First performance Dresden, 15
February 1878, Ernst Schuch conductor.*

DRAGONETTI, DOMENICO.   Venice 7 April 1763
                             London 16 April 1846

436c [Concerto, contrabass and orchestra, A
major. Orchestration by Jesse Taynton and
William R. Smith]
1.Allegro moderato 2.Andante 3.Allegro ma
non troppo
Solo Cb.-2,2,0,2-2Hn.-Str.
Ms. ᶜ1977 by Jesse Taynton and William R. Smith
Score 68 p.

DRANGOSCH, ERNESTO.   Buenos Aires 22 January 1882
Buenos Aires 26 June 1925

3343 Obertura criolla, Op. 20 [Creole   7'
overture]
3(3rd alt. Picc.),2,2,2-4,2,3,1-Timp.,Perc.-Str.
Comisión Nacional de Cultura, Buenos Aires
[193-?]
Score 53 p.
*Composed 1920. First performance Teatro
Coliseo, Buenos Aires, 24 September 1920, Cos-
tanza Orchestra of Rome, Felix Weingartner
conductor. Received official recognition by
the Comisión Nacional de Cultura of Argentina.*

1883s Sogni d'un ballo, suite miniatura   *12'30"*
fantastica [Reveries of a ball, for string
orchestra]
1.Introduzione: Allegro appassionato 2.Invita-
zione alla danza: Allegretto grazioso 3.Danza
I: Tempo di valse lento 4.Danza II: Allegro
moderato giocoso 5.Dichiarazione [Declaration]:
Andante amoroso 6.Danza finale: Tempo di valse
appassionato
Str.
Ms.
Score 42 p.
*First performance Mar del Plata, Argentina,
February 1906.*

DREI, CLAUDIO GUIDI.
See: GUIDI, CLAUDIO.

DRESSEL, ERWIN.   Berlin 10 June 1909
Berlin December 1972

2131 [Symphony, D-flat major]   45'
1.Allegro moderato 2.Adagio sostenuto - Più
vivo 3.Presto - Andante - Presto come prima
4.Grave, lento e mesto - Molto vivace e presto
4(3rd and 4th alt. Picc.I & II),2,3(3rd alt.
B.Cl.),3*-4,3,3-Timp.,Perc.-Hp.-Str.
Hofmeister, Leipzig, C1928
Score 103 p.
*Composed 1927. First performance Hamburg, 19
January 1929, Gustav Brecher conductor.*

DREYSCHOCK, ALEXANDER.
Zack, Bohemia 15 October 1818
Venice 1 April 1869

110s Andante religioso, Op. 28 [for string
orchestra]
Str.
[Junne, Paris, n.d.]
Score 7 p.

479p Salut à Vienne, rondo brillant pour le
piano, Op. 32
Introduzione: Tempo di marcia - Rondo: Allegro
con moto
Solo Pno.-Trgl.-Str.
Score: Ms. 35 p.
Parts: B. Schott, Mainz [1846?]

DÜBEN, GUSTAF. the elder.   Stockholm 1624
Stockholm 19 December 1690

2059s [Three dances. Arranged by Sven E.   6'
Svensson]
1.Allemande 2.Courante 3.Sarabande
Cemb.-Str.
Firma Nottryck, Stockholm [n.d.]
Score 7 p.
Composed ca.1650.

DUBENSKY, ARCADY.   Viatka, Russia 15 October 1890
Tenafly, New Jersey 14 October 1966

795s Andante (Reminiscence) [for string   4'
orchestra]
Str.
Associated Music Publishers, New York, C1937
Score 3 p.
*First performance Philadelphia, 2 November
1932, Philadelphia Chamber String Sinfonietta,
Fabien Sevitzky conductor.*

1727s Andante russe [for string orchestra]   3'
Str.
Ms. [Now published by Ricordi, Milan]
Score 4 p.
*An excerpt from Suite Russe for orchestra,
composed 1925. Andante excerpted and transcribed 1925. First performance New York,
1925, radio broadcast over Station WOR, Alfred Wallenstein conductor.*

2756 Armenian dance   3'
1(alt. Picc.),1,2,1-2,1,1-Timp.,Perc.-Str.
Ms.
Score 11 p.
*Composed 1935. First performance New York,
1935, radio broadcast over Station WOR, Alfred
Wallenstein conductor.*

3462 Dance orientale   8'
3*,2(2nd alt. E.H.),2,2-4,2,3,1-Timp.,Perc.-
Str.
Ms.
Score 21 p.
Composed 1939.

3591 Fanfare and choral for 4 trumpets   3'
in B-flat
1.Allegro moderato 2.Andante con moto
4Tpt.
Ms. C1939 by Arcady Dubensky
Score 8 p.
*Commissioned by the Lotos Club of New York.
Composed 1939. First performance Lotos Club,
New York, 5 January 1940, New York Philhar-
monic trumpeters Harry Glantz, Nathan Prager,
William Vacchiano, and Sol Lubalin.*

1882s Fugue for 9 stands of first violin   4'
section
9Vn.I
Ricordi, Milan, C1932
Score 12 p.
*Composed 1932. First performance Philadelphia,
1 April 1932, Philadelphia Orchestra, Leopold
Stokowski conductor.*

Dubensky, Arcady

1710s Gossips [for string orchestra] 4'
Str.
C. Fischer, New York, c1935
Score 6 p.
Composed 1928. First performance Philadelphia, 24 November 1928, Philadelphia Chamber String Sinfonietta, Fabien Sevitzky conductor.

2755 Old Russian soldier's song 4'
3*,2,2,2-4,3,3,1-Timp.,Perc.-Str.
Ms. [Now published by Ricordi, Milan]
Score 21 p.
Originally composed for string orchestra, 1930. First performance New York, probably 1935, Station WOR radio broadcast, Alfred Wallenstein conductor.

2777 Political suite [for orchestra, 10'
original version]
1.Russian monarchy: Moderato maestoso 2.Nazi and Fascist: Allegro marciale 3.Communist: Allegretto
3*(1st alt. 2nd Picc.),2,3,2(1st alt. C.Bn.)-4,2,3,1-Timp.,Perc.-Str.
Ms.
Score 36 p.
Composed 1936. First performance New York, 17 September 1936, radio broadcast over Station WOR, Alfred Wallenstein conductor. A fourth movement was added later.

1816s Prelude (nocturne) [for string 3'30"
orchestra]
Str.
Ms. [Now published by Ricordi, Milan]
Score 7 p.
Composed 1936. First performance over an NBC radio broadcast from New York, 1937, Radio City Music Hall Orchestra, Erno Rapee conductor.

2770 Rajah (An old Arabian dance) 4'
3*,2,2,2-4,2,3,1-Timp.,Perc.-Pno.(or Cemb.)-Str.
Ms.
Score 12 p.
Composed 1930. First performance New York, 1931, in a broadcast by the NBC Symphony Orchestra, Walter Damrosch conductor.

Russian bells
2657 Movement 1: Allegro - Moderato 12'
2763 Movement 2: Andante - Allegretto - 8'
Andante
3*,3*,3,2-4,3,3,1-Timp.,Perc.-Pno.,Hp.-Str.
Ms. [Now published by Ricordi, Milan]
Scores: 79 p., 33 p.
First movement composed 1927. First performance New York, 29 December 1927, New York Symphony Society, the composer conducting. Second movement added 1937.

1858s Suite Anno 1600 [for string 14'
orchestra]
1.Allegretto 2.Fuga: Tempo giusto 3.Interludio (Angelus): Andantino 4.Minuetto: Allegretto 5.Sarabanda: Andante 6.Pastorale: Andantino con grazia - Allegro ma non troppo - Moderato

Str.
Ricordi, Milan, c1938
Score 23 p.
Composed 1937. First performance New York, 23 April 1939, New York Philharmonic, John Barbirolli conductor. A seventh movement was added later.

969m Suite for 9 flutes 15'
1.Prelude (Angelus) 2.Menuetto 3.Etude (Song of wind) 4.Angelus 5.Fughetta 6.Finale
Picc.,7Fl.,Alto Fl.
Ms.
Score 34 p.
Composed 1935. First performance New York, 26 January 1936, New York Flute Club, the composer conducting.

DUBOIS, CLÉMENT-FRANÇOIS THÉODORE.
Rosnay, Marne 24 August 1837
Paris 11 June 1924

738 Adonis, poème symphonique 17'
1.Mort d'Adonis [Death of Adonis] 2.Déploration des nymphes [The nymphs' lament] 3.Réveil d'Adonis [Revival of Adonis]
3(3rd alt. Picc.),3*,3*,3-4,3,3,1-Timp.,Perc.-Hp.-Str.
Heugel, Paris, c1907
Score 84 p.
Inspired by Charles Leconte de Lisle's Hymnes Orphiques. Composed 1906. First performance Concerts Colonne, Paris, 1907.

509c Andante cantabile [for violoncello and orchestra]
Solo Vc.-2,2,2,2-2Hn.-Timp.-Org.(ad lib.)-Str.
Heugel, Paris, c1899
Score 16 p.

530m Cavatine [for horn and small orchestra]
Solo Hn.-1,1,1,1-Str.
Heugel, Paris, c1911
Score 11 p.

565p [Concerto, piano, no. 2, F minor]
1.Allegro 2.Adagio 3.Allegro vivo, scherzando 4.Con molta fantasia - Allegro
Solo Pno.-2(2nd alt. Picc.),2,2,2-4,2,3-Timp.-Str.
Heugel, Paris, c1898
Score 120 p.

517v [Concerto, violin, D minor]
1.Allegro 2.Adagio 3.Allegro giocoso
Solo Vn.-2,2,2,2-4,2-Timp.,Trgl.-Str.
Heugel, Paris, c1898
Score 98 p.
First performance Paris, 28 November 1894, Henri Marteau soloist.

523p Concerto-capriccioso [for piano and orchestra]
Allegro - Adagio con fantasia
Solo Pno.-2(2nd alt. Picc.),2,2,2-4,2,3-Timp.-Str.
Heugel, Paris [n.d.]
Score 88 p.

Dubois, Théodore

371s Deux petites pièces [for string orchestra]
1.Prélude: Andantino molto espressivo 2.Es-
quisse [Sketch]: Allegretto quasi andante
Str.
Heugel, Paris, c1897
Score 7 p.

Deux pièces pour violon [and orchestra]
681v No. 1. Andante
      Solo Vn.-2,2,2,2-2Hn.-Timp.-Hp.-Str.
682v No. 2. Scherzo-valse
      Solo Vn.-2,2(2nd alt. E.H.),2,2-2,2-Timp.,
Trgl.-Str.
Heugel, Paris, c1905, c1906
Scores: 19 p., 27 p.

2459 Dixtuor [for wind quintet and string
quintet or string orchestra]
1.Larghetto - Allegro non troppo 2.Larghetto
3.Allegretto 4.Allegro
1,1,1,1-Hn.-Str.
Heugel, Paris, c1909
Score 135 p.

581c Esquisse [Sketch, for violoncello and
orchestra]
Solo Vc.-2,0,2,1-2Hn.-Str.
Heugel, Paris, c1901
Score 7 p.

557m Fantaisie [for harp and orchestra]
Solo Hp.-2,2,2,2-4,2-Timp.-Str.
Heugel, Paris, c1903
Score 70 p.

544c Fantaisie-Stück [Fantasy piece, for
violoncello and orchestra]
Allegro moderato - Andante très calme - Allegro
vivo, mouvement de saltarelle
Solo Vc.-2,2,2,2-3,2-Timp.-Hp.(or Pno.)-Str.
Heugel, Paris, c1912
Score 60 p.

1515 [La farandole. Suite no. 1]   17'
1.Les tambourinaires 2.Les âmes infidèles
3.La Provençale 4.Sylvine 5.La farandole
fantastique
3*(2nd alt. Picc.II),2(2nd alt. E.H.),2,4-4,2,
2Cnt.,3,1-Timp.,Perc.-Hp.-Str.
Heugel, Paris, 1885?
Score 81 p.
*The farandole is a Provençal dance. From the
ballet of the same name.*

1251 [La farandole. Suite no. 2]   12'
1.Adagio 2.Valse des olivettes 3.Cloches et
violoneux 4.Petit menuet 5.Valse des âmes
infidèles
3(3rd alt. Picc.),2,2,4-4,2,2Cnt.,3,1-Timp.,
Perc.-Hp.-Str.
Heugel, Paris, 1885
Score 81 p.

514c Nocturne [for violoncello and orchestra]
Solo Vc.-2,2,2,2-2Hn.-Hp.-Str.
Heugel, Paris, c1906
Score 20 p.

1395 [Notre Dame de la Mer, legendary   6'
poem. Symphonic interlude]
3,3*,3*,3*-4,3,3,1-Timp.-Org.,Hp.-Str.
Heugel, Paris, c1901
Score 30 p.
First performance Paris, 1897.

310s Petits rêves d'enfants [for string
orchestra]
Str.
Heugel, Paris, c1903
Score 5 p.

1608 Suite brève à l'aventure   9'
1.Petite danse gracieuse 2.En badinant 3.Duo
4.En valsant 5.Petite marche exotique
1(alt. Picc.),1,1,1-Hn.-Str.
Heugel, Paris, c1926
Score 33 p.

6937 [Suite for wind instruments, no. 1]
1.Petite mazurka 2.Canzonetta 3.Chaconne
2,1,2,2-Hn.
Heugel, Paris, c1898
Score 21 p.

6940 [Suite for wind instruments, no. 2]
1.Ronde des archers 2.Chanson lesbienne
3.Petite valse 4.Stella matutina 5.Menuet
2,1,2,2-Hn.
Leduc, Paris [n.d.]
Score 31 p.

1132 Suite villageoise   16'
1.Paysage 2.Intermède 3.Fête
3*,2,2,2-4,4,3,1-Timp.,Perc.-Str.
Heugel, Paris, c1894
Score 93 p.
*First performance Conservatoire, Paris, 1893,
the composer conducting.*

1036 Symphonie française [F major]   32'
1.Largo - Allegro 2.Andantino 3.Allegro vivo,
scherzando 4.Allegro con fuoco
3(3rd alt. Picc.),3*,3*,4(1Sarrus.)-4,3,3,1-
Timp.,Trgl.-Cel.,Hp.-Str.
Heugel, Paris, c1908
Score 193 p.
*First performance Paris, 1910, the composer
conducting.*

1336 [Symphony no. 2, D major]   28'
1.Allegro 2.Andante grave, quasi adagio 3.
Allegretto 4.Allegro con moto
3(3rd alt. Picc.),2,3*,2-Sarrus.-4,3,3,1-Timp.
-Str.
Heugel, Paris, c1913
Score 189 p.
First performance Paris, 1913.

1607 [Symphony no. 3, A major]   32'
1.Allegro 2.Andante molto espressivo 3.Alle-
gretto 4.Largo - Allegro maestoso sans lenteur
et chaleureux
2,2,3*,3*(Sarrus.or C.Bn.)-4,2,4(or 3Tbn.,Tuba)
-Timp.-Str.
Heugel, Paris, c1923
Score 116 p.

Dubois, Théodore

Composed 1921. First performance Conservatoire, Paris, 1923, the composer conducting.

1209 Trois airs de ballet   9'
    1.Tempo di valzo moderato 2.Allegretto 3.
    Saltarello: Allegro vivo
    2,2,2,2-2,2-Timp.,Trgl.-Str.
    Heugel, Paris [1892]
    Score 45 p.

311s [Xavière. Entr'acte-rigaudon. Transcribed
    for string orchestra]
    Str.
    Heugel, Paris, c1909
    Score 4 p.
    From the comic opera in 3 acts.

DUCASSE, JEAN-JULES-AIMABLE ROGER.
    See: ROGER-DUCASSE, JEAN-JULES AIMABLE.

DUCKWORTH, WILLIAM.
    b. Morganton, North Carolina 13 January 1943

7046 When in eternal lines to time thou   15'
    grow'st
    2,2,2,2-4,2,3,1-Perc.-Str.
    Ms. cby William Duckworth
    Score 26 p. Large folio
    *Based on the first phrase of the Gregorian
    chant Kyrie Orbis Factor. Selected for per-
    formance by the Orchestra Society of Philadel-
    phia as part of its Pennsylvania Composers
    Project 1974, made possible by a grant from
    the Pennsylvania Council for the Arts with per-
    formance materials prepared by The Fleisher
    Collection. First performance Mandell Theater,
    Drexel University, Philadelphia, 22 June 1974,
    Orchestra Society of Philadelphia, Sidney
    Rothstein conductor.*

DUCOUDRAY, LOUIS ALBERT BOURGAULT.
    See: BOURGAULT-DUCOUDRAY, LOUIS ALBERT.

DUKAS, PAUL.   Paris 1 October 1865
                          Paris 17 May 1935

182 L'apprenti sorcier [The sorcerer's   12'
    apprentice] scherzo
    3*,2,3*,4*-4,2,2Cnt.,3-Timp.,Perc.-Hp.-Str.
    Durand, Paris [1897]
    Score 74 p.
    *Inspired by Goethe's poem. First performance
    Société Nationale de Musique, Paris, 18 May
    1897, the composer conducting.*

477 [Ariane and Bluebeard. Introduction   8'
    to Act III]
    3(3rd alt. Picc.),3*,3*,4*-4,3,3-Timp.,Trgl.-
    Hp.-Str.
    Durand, Paris, c1907
    Score 13 p.
    *From the opera based on the story by Maurice
    Maeterlinck. Composed 1906. First performance
    Opéra Comique, Paris, 10 May 1907, Frans
    Rühlmann conductor.*

476 [Overture to Polyeucte]   15'
    2,3*,3*,3-4,2,3,1-Timp.-Hp.-Str.

Durand, Paris, c1910
Score 47 p.
*For the play by Pierre Corneille, based on
Greek myth. Composed 1891. First performance
Paris, January 1892, Charles Lamoureux con-
ductor.*

2303 La Péri. Fanfare pour précéder La Péri
    4Hn.,3Tpt.,3Tbn.,Tuba
    Durand, Paris, c1927
    Score 5 p.

847 La Péri, poème dansé   30'
    3(3rd alt. Picc.),3*,3*,3-4,3,3,1-Timp.,Perc.-
    Cel.,2Hp.-Str.
    Durand, Paris, c1911
    Score 137 p.
    *Ballet based on an Oriental legend. First
    performance Paris, 22 April 1912, the composer
    conducting.*

666 [Symphony in 3 parts, C major]   45'
    1.Allegro non troppo vivace, ma con fuoco 2.
    Andante espressivo e sostenuto 3.Allegro
    spiritoso
    3(3rd alt. Picc.),3*,2,4(2 ad lib.)-4,3,3,1-
    Timp.-Str.
    Rouart, Lerolle & Cie., Paris [n.d.]
    Score 215 p.
    *Composed 1896. First performance at the con-
    certs of the Opéra, Paris, 3 January 1897,
    Paul Vidal conductor.*

DUKE, JOHN WOODS. Cumberland, Maryland 30 July 1899

750p [Concerto, piano and string   20'
    orchestra, A major]
    1.Allegro marcato 2.Intermezzo 3.Rondo
    Solo Pno.-Str.
    Ms.
    Score 107 p.
    *Composed 1938. First performance Westfield,
    Massachusetts, 14 April 1939, Springfield
    Federal Orchestra of the WPA, Milton Aronson
    conductor, the composer as soloist.*

1813s Overture, in D minor, for string   10'
    orchestra
    Str.
    Ms.
    Score 21 p.
    *Composed 1928. First performance Northampton,
    Massachusetts, 9 December 1928, Smith College
    Symphony Orchestra, the composer conducting.*

DUKELSKY, VLADIMIR.
        Parfianovka, Russia 10 October 1903
        Santa Monica, California 17 January 1969

Also known as: Vernon Duke

791p Ballade for piano and strings with   12'
    timpani obbligato, revised version
    Solo Pno.-Timp.-Str.
    Ms.
    Score 52 p.
    Composed 1931; this new version 1943.

2993 [Symphony no. 2, D-flat major]   17'
1.Allegro molto 2.Minuetto 3.Allegro giocoso
4*,3(3rd alt. E.H.),4*(3rd alt. Cl. in E-flat),
3*-4,4,3,1-Timp.,Perc.-Pno.-Str.
Ms.
Score 130 p.
*Composed 1928. First performance Boston, 25
April 1930, Boston Symphony Orchestra, Serge
Koussevitzky conductor.*

DUMAS, LOUIS.   Paris 24 December 1877
              Dijon, France 9 May 1952

653p Fantaisie pour piano et orchestre
Solo Pno.-2,2,2,2-2,2,3-Timp.-Hp.-Str.
Score: Ms. 166 p.
Parts: Ricordi, Paris, c1918

DUMITRESCU, ION.
         Oteşani-Vîlcea, Romania 20 May 1913

6214 [Symphonic prelude]   8'25"
3*,3*,3*,3-4,4,3,1-Timp.,Perc.-Hp.-Str.
Editura de Stat Pentru Literatură şi Artă
[Bucharest, Romania, 1956]
Score 93 p.
*Composed 1952. First performance Bucharest,
Romania, 3 February 1952, State Philharmonic
Orchestra of Bucharest, Alfred Alessandrescu
conductor.*

DUNCAN, JOHN. Lee County, Alabama 25 November 1913

920m Pastoral poem [for flute and   6'
orchestra]
Solo Fl.-1,1,2,1-1,1,1-Timp.-Str.
Ms.
Score 34 p.
*Composed 1934. First performance Philadelphia,
28 December 1938, Anderson Memorial Orchestra,
Raymond L. Smith conductor, the composer as
soloist.*

DUNHILL, THOMAS FREDERICK.
              Hampstead 1 February 1877
      Scunthorpe, Lincolnshire 13 March 1946

532s The Chiddingfold suite for string orchestra,
Op. 60
1.March - Prelude 2.Dryads and fauns 3.The
mummers arrive 4.The vision of Richard Peyto,
glassmaker of Chiddingfold 5.Maypole dance
Str.
Novello, London, c1922
Score 30 p.
*Incorporates the English popular songs Venus
and Adonis and The Painful Plough. The village
of Chiddingfold was famous for its stained
glass.*

446s Dance suite for string orchestra, Op. 42
1.Balletto intrada 2.Rustic dance 3.Rigaudon
4.Reel
Str.
J. Curwen, London, c1924
Score 27 p.

1330s In rural England, suite, Op. 72 [for
string orchestra]
1.A pastoral 2.Playfellows 3.A country tune
4.Meadow-fairies 5.Festivity
Str.
Goodwin & Tabb, London, c1929
Score 16 p.

639s A sailor dance, Op. 46 no. 2 [for string
orchestra] Edited by Sydney Robjohns
Pno.(optional)-Str.(without Cb.)
J. Williams, London, c1928
Score 4 p.

1847s Suite of 4 pieces for string orchestra,
Op. 83 no. 1
1.Gavotte 2.Slow air 3.Elfin patrol
4.Country dance
Pno.(optional)-Str.(Vn.III optional, Cb.
optional)
J. Williams, London, c1936
Score 11 p.

973s Three pieces for string orchestra with
organ, Op. 67. Edited by James Brown
1.Venite adoremus 2.Canticum fidei 3.Hosanna
Org.-Str.
Stainer & Bell, London, c1928
Score 32 p.

DUNK, SUSAN SPAIN.
See: SPAIN-DUNK, SUSAN.

DUNKLER, EMILE.

447s Au bord de la mer, reverie [for string
orchestra]
Str.(without Cb.)
Richault, Paris [n.d.]
Score 8 p.

1657s [Berceuse, violin and piano, Op. 14.
Transcribed for solo violin and string
orchestra by Gustave Sandré]
Solo Vn.-Str.
Score: Ms. 7 p.
Parts: Jobert, Paris [n.d.]

DUNN, JAMES PHILIP.   New York 10 January 1884
        Jersey City, New Jersey 24 July 1936

2600 Overture on Negro themes   20'
3*(2nd alt. 2nd Picc. ad lib.),2(2nd alt. E.H.),
2,2-4,2,3,1-Timp.,Perc.-Hp.-Str.
J. Fischer, New York, c1925
Score 48 p.
*Originally composed for organ, 1921. This
transcription 1922. First performance Lewisohn
Stadium, New York, 22 July 1922, New York
Philharmonic, Henry Hadley conductor.*

DU PAGE, FLORENCE.
     Vandergrift, Pennsylvania 20 September 1910

Former name: Florence Anderson

1987s Two sketches for string orchestra   5'
1.Prelude to a lovely evening 2.Jumping Jack

Duparc, Henri

Str.
Ms. [c1946 by Florence Du Page]
Score 7 p. Large folio
Commissioned by F. Charles Adler for the Saratoga, New York, Festival, 1946. Composed 1946. First performance Saratoga Spa Music Festival, Saratoga, New York, 3 September 1946, New York Philharmonic, F. Charles Adler conductor.

DUPARC, HENRI.   Paris 21 January 1848
Mont-de-Marsan, Landes, France 12 February 1933

Full name: Marie-Eugène Henri Fouques Duparc

739 Aux étoiles, entr'acte   6'
2,2,2,2-2Hn.-Str.
Rouart, Lerolle & Cie., Paris, c1911
Score 19 p.
Composed 1910. First performance Concerts Lamoureux, Paris, 1911, Camille Chevillard conductor.

461 [Lenore, symphonic poem]   12'
3*,2,2,4(4th ad lib.)-4,2,3,1-Timp.,Perc.-Str.
A. Rouart, Paris [n.d.]
Score 50 p.
Inspired by Gottfried August Bürger's poem. Composed 1875. First performance Concerts Pasdeloup, Paris, 1877.

DUPÉRIER, JEAN.   Geneva 17 June 1886

5584 Concert pour Ninette ou Ninon
1.Pour Ninette ou Ninon 2.Pour que m'aime Ninon 3.Pour que danse Ninette 4.Pour Ninette, Ninon et toutes les autres
2(2nd alt. Picc.),2(2nd alt. E.H.),2,2-4,2,3-Timp.,Perc.-Pno.,Cel.-Str.
Edition Henn, Geneva, c1922
Score 94 p.
Composed 1922.

DUPORT, JEAN-LOUIS.   Paris 4 October 1749
Paris 7 September 1819

707c [Concerto, violoncello, no. 4, E minor]
1.[Allegro moderato] 2.Romance 3.Rondeau
Solo Vc.-2Ob.(ad lib.)-2Hn.(ad lib.)-Str.
Score: Ms. 66 p.
Parts: Imbault, Paris [n.d.]
The parts are inscribed "composé par M. L. DuPort", probably M(onsieur) [Jean] Louis Duport, the famous violoncellist.

DUPRATO, JULES-LAURENT.
Nîmes 20 August (not 26 March) 1827
Paris 20 May 1892

5200 [Les trovatelles. Overture]
2(2nd alt. Picc.),2,2,2-4,2,3-Timp.,Tamb.-Str.
Colombier, Paris [1854]
Score 44 p.
From the opéra-comique in one act with libretto by Michel Carré and Jules Lorin. First performance Paris, 28 June 1854.

DUPUIS, ALBERT.   Verviers, Belgium 1 March 1877
St. Josse-ten-Noodey, Belgium 19 September 1967

922v Fantaisie rapsodique [for solo violin and orchestra]
1.Allegretto tempo giusto 2.Lento très espressivo - Allegro scherzo 3.Allegretto
Solo Vn.-3(3rd alt. Picc.),2,2,2-4,2,4(1Cb. Tbn.)-Timp.,Perc.-Hp.-Str.
Schott Frères, Brussels, c1907
Score 84 p.

5590 [Jean Michel. Act 3, Entr'acte on popular airs from Liège]
3*,3*,2,2-4,3,3,1-Timp.,Perc.-Hp.-Str.
Éditions Buyst, Brussels [n.d.]
Score 41 p.
From the opera in four acts with libretto by Henry Vallier and George Garnir. First performance Théâtre de la Monnaie, Brussels, 4 March 1903.

5540 [Jean Michel. Act 4, Prelude]
3*,3*,3*,2-4,3,3-Timp.-Hp.-Str.
Éditions Buyst, Brussels [n.d.]
Score 11 p.

5586 [Lucas and Lucette, suite for orchestra. Children's pastorale in 4 movements]
1.Escapade matinale 2.La toupie 3.Sommeil sous la feuillée 4.Ronde joyeuse
3*,2*,2,2-4,2,3,1-Timp.,Perc.-Hp.-Str.
Edition Cranz, Brussels, c1936
Score 70 p.

DUPUIS, SYLVAIN.   Liège 9 October 1856
Bruges 28 September 1931

5554 [For a drama...symphonic overture]
2,2,2,2-4,2,3,1-Timp.-Str.
Édition Buyst, Brussels [n.d.]
Score 40 p.

DU PUY, EDOUARD.
Corcelles, Neuchâtel, Switzerland 1770 or 1771
Stockholm 3 April 1822

Full name: Jean Baptiste Edouard Louis Camille Du Puy

888m [Concerto, flute, no. 1, D minor]
1.Allegro ma non troppo 2.Andante, attacca 3.Rondo
Solo Fl.-2,2,2-4,2-Timp.-Str.
Score: Ms. 152 p.
Parts: Breitkopf & Härtel, Leipzig [1812?]

DURAND DE FONTMAGNE, BARONESS.

1137s Barcarolle [for solo violin and string orchestra]
Solo Vn.-Str.
Score: Ms. 7 p.
Parts: Manus Music, New York, c1926

DURANTE, FRANCESCO.
Frattamaggiore, near Naples 31 March 1684
Naples 30 September (not 13 August) 1755

2153s [Concerto, string orchestra, no. 1,   *15'*
F minor] Edited by Adriano Lualdi
1.Un poco andante - Allegro 2.Andante
3.Amoroso 4.Allegro assai
Str.
Carisch, Milan, c1948
Score 14 p.
This and the following editions based on 18th
century parts published ca.1735.

2154s [Concerto, string orchestra, no. 2,   *14'*
G minor] Edited by Adriano Lualdi
1.Affettuoso - Presto 2.Largo affettuoso
3.Allegro affettuoso
Str.
Carisch, Milan, c1948
Score 15 p.

2155s [Concerto, string orchestra, no. 3,   *11'*
E-flat major] Edited by Adriano Lualdi
1.Presto 2.Largo e staccato - Allegro moderato
- Largo e staccato - Allegro moderato 3.Alle-
gro 4.Allegro assai 5.Finale: Allegro vivace
Str.
Carisch, Milan, c1948
Score 11 p.

2156s [Concerto, string orchestra, no. 4,   *12'*
E minor] Edited by Adriano Lualdi
1.Adagio 2.Ricercare: Andante mosso e vivo
3.Largo 4.Presto
Str.
Carisch, Milan, c1948
Score 12 p.

2157s [Concerto, string orchestra, no. 5,   *10'*
A major] Edited by Adriano Lualdi
1.Presto 2.Largo 3.Allegro molto
Str.

Carisch, Milan, c1948
Score 10 p.

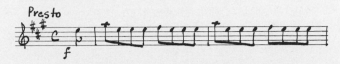

2158s [Concerto, string orchestra, no. 6,   *10'*
Study, A major] Edited by Adriano Lualdi
1.Allegro 2.Andante amoroso 3.Allegro
4.Minuè: Allegro 5.Canone a 3: Allegro
Str.
Carisch, Milan, c1948
Score 12 p.

2159s [Concerto, string orchestra, no. 7,   *12'*
C major] Edited by Adriano Lualdi
1.Moderato 2.Allegro 3.Larghetto 4.Presto
Str.
Carisch, Milan, c1948
Score 9 p.

2160s [Concerto, string orchestra, no. 8,   *16'*
Madness, A major] Edited by Adriano Lualdi
Allegro molto - Allegro non troppo - Affettuoso
- Allegro molto - Allegro - Affettuoso -
Allegro assai - Affettuoso - Allegro
Str.
Carisch, Milan, c1948
Score 17 p.

DURME, JEF VAN.
 See: VAN DURME, JEF.

DUTRÉZE, JEAN.

 1311s Air à danser
 Fl.,Cl.-Str.
 Score: Ms. 5 p.
 Parts: Decourcelle, Nice [n.d.]

DUTTON, FRED.

 7182 Fanfare
  See: FANFARES 1969 FOR 8 TRUMPETS. No. IV

Duvernoy, Victor-Alphonse

DUVERNOY, VICTOR-ALPHONSE.   Paris 30 August 1842
                             Paris 7 March 1907

524p Fantaisie symphonique [for piano and
      orchestra]
      1.Moderato poco maestoso 2.Adagio espressivo
      3.Presto
      Solo Pno.-3*,2,2,2-4,2,3-Timp.,Perc.-Str.
      Heugel, Paris, c1904, 1906
      Score 169 p.
      Dedicated to I. Philipp.

DUVOSEL, SERAPHIEN LIEVEN.   Ghent 14 December 1877
               St. Martens-Latem, near Ghent 20 April 1956

5854 [Christmas Eve, symphonic poem]   9'
      2,2(2nd alt. E.H.),2,2-4,2,3,1-Timp.-Cel.,Hp.-
      Str.
      Ms.
      Score 30 p. Large folio
      *No. 4 of the Leie cycle. Composed 1925. First
      performance Haarlem, Holland, 23 November 1938,
      Haarlem Orchestra Society, the composer con-
      ducting. Dedicated to the memory of Guido
      Gezelle.*

206   [The morning, symphonic poem]   8'
      3*,3*,3*,2-4,3,3,1-Timp.,Perc.-Hp.-Str.
      Breitkopf & Härtel, Leipzig, c1919
      Score 31 p.
      *No. 1 of the Leie cycle. Composed 1918. First
      performance Berlin, 1919, Rudolf Krasselt con-
      ductor. Dedication: In memoriam Jan Blockx.*

DVOŘÁK, ANTONÍN.
          Nelahozeves, Bohemia 8 September 1841
                             Prague 1 May 1904

47   [Carnival, overture, Op. 92]   9'
      3*,3*,2,2-4,2,3,1-Timp.,Perc.-Hp.-Str.
      Artia, Prague, 1955
      Score 82 p.
      *Originally Op. 91/2; see In Nature's Realm,
      catalog no. 378.*

407p [Concerto, piano, Op. 33, G minor]   28'
      1.Allegro agitato 2.Andante sostenuto 3.
      Finale: Allegro con fuoco
      Solo Pno.-2,2,2,2-2,2-Timp.-Str.
      Score: Ms. 159 p.
      Parts: Hainauer, Breslau [1883]
      *Composed 1876. First performance Prague, 24
      March 1878, Slavonic Concerts, Adolf Čech con-
      ductor, K. Slavkovskich soloist.*

427v [Concerto, violin, Op. 53, A minor]   32'
      1.Allegro ma non troppo 2.Adagio ma non
      troppo 3.Finale: Allegro giocoso, ma non
      troppo
      Solo Vn.-2,2,2,2-4,2-Timp.-Str.
      Artia, Prague, c1955
      Score 135 p.
      *Composed 1879; rewritten 1880-82. First per-
      formance Prague, 14 October 1883, National
      Theatre Orchestra, Mořic Anger conductor,
      František Ondřicek soloist. Originally dedi-
      cated to Joseph Joachim.*

410c [Concerto, violoncello, A major.   34'
      Edited and scored for orchestra by Günter
      Raphael]
      1.Andante 2.Andante cantabile 3.Allegro riso-
      luto
      Solo Vc.-2,2,2,2-4,2-Timp.-Str.
      Breitkopf & Härtel, Leipzig, c1930
      Score 66 p.
      *Originally composed for violoncello and piano,
      completed 1865; no orchestration by composer.
      This edition 1929. First known performance
      German Theatre, Prague, 28 March 1930, George
      Szell conductor, Hans Münch-Holland soloist.
      Dedicated to Ludevít Peer.*

469c [Concerto, violoncello, Op. 104,   37'
      B minor]
      1.Allegro 2.Adagio ma non troppo 3.Finale:
      Allegro moderato
      Solo Vc.-2(2nd alt. Picc.),2,2,2-3,2,3,1-Timp.,
      Trgl.-Str.
      Simrock, London, c1930
      Score in reduction 47 p.
      *Composed 1895. First performance London, 19
      March 1896, London Philharmonic, the composer
      conducting, Leo Stern soloist. Dedicated to
      Hans Wihan.*

485   [Czech suite for orchestra, Op. 39,   21'
      D major]
      1.Praeludium (Pastorale) 2.Polka 3.Sousedská
      (Minuetto) 4.Romanza 5.Finale (Furiant)
      2,3*,2,2-2,2-Timp.-Str.
      Schlesinger, Berlin [1881]
      Score 69 p.
      *Composed 1879. First performance Prague, 16
      May 1879, Adolf Čech conductor.*

856   [Dramatic overture, Op. 1(?)]   10'
      3*,3*,2,2-4,2,3,1-Timp.,Perc.-Hp.-Str.
      Simrock, Berlin, c1912
      Score 75 p.
      *Also known as Tragic Overture. Composed
      1870 for the opera Alfred, not performed in the
      composer's lifetime. First performance of the
      overture Prague, 4 January 1905, Czech Phil-
      harmonic, Oskar Nedbal conductor.*

587   [Festival march, Op. 54a]   5'
      2,2,2,2-4,2,3,1-Timp.,Trgl.-Hp.(ad lib.)-Str.
      Starý, Prague [1879]
      Score 23 p.
      *Composed 1879 for the silver wedding celebration
      of Emperor Franz Josef I and Empress Elisabeth
      of Austria. First performance New Bohemian
      Theater, Prague, 23 April 1879.*

874   [From the Bohemian forest, Op. 68.   4'
      No. 1, In the spinning room. Transcribed for
      orchestra by C. Zimmer]
      2(2nd alt. Picc.),2,2,2-4,2,3-Timp.,Perc.-Hp.-
      Str.
      Simrock, Berlin, c1910
      Score 38 p.
      Originally composed for piano 4-hands, 1883-84.

Dvořák, Antonín

467c [From the Bohemian forest, Op. 68.   6'
No. 5, Waldesruhe, for violoncello and orches-
tra]
Solo Vc.-1,0,2,2-2-Hn.-Str.
Simrock, Berlin, c1894
Score 11 p.
*No. 5 transcribed for violoncello and piano,
1891. Transcribed for violoncello and orches-
tra, 1893.*

42 [The golden spinning wheel, symphonic   25'
poem, Op. 109]
2,3*,2,3*(C.Bn. ad lib.)-4,2,3,1-Timp.,Perc.-
Hp.-Str.
Simrock, Berlin, c1896
Score 86 p.
*Inspired by the Czech legend as told by Jaromir
Erben. Composed 1896. First performance Lon-
don, 26 October 1896, Hans Richter conductor.*

636 [Heroic song, symphonic poem, Op. 111]   21'
2,2,2,2-4,2,3,1-Timp.,Perc.-Str.
Simrock, Berlin, c1899
Score 87 p.
*Composed 1897. First performance Vienna, 4
December 1898, Vienna Philharmonic, Gustav
Mahler conductor.*

855 Husitská, Op. 67 [Dramatic overture]   14'
3*,2(1st alt. E.H.),2,2-4,2,3,1-Timp.,Perc.-
Hp.-Str.
Simrock, Berlin, 1884
Score 103 p.
*Incorporates the 10th century chorale St. Wen-
ceslaus and the 15th century Hussite Hymn.
Composed 1883, for the reopening of the Czech
National Theater after a fire. First perform-
ance Prague, 18 November 1883, Morič Anger
conductor.*

378 [In Nature's realm, overture, Op. 91]   12'
2,3*,3*,2-4,2,3,1-Timp.,Trgl.,Cym.-Str.
Kalmus, New York [n.d.]
Score 91 p.
*Originally composed 1891 as the first part of
the triptych Nature, Life and Love, which also
included the Carnival and Othello overtures.
First performance of the triptych Prague, 28
April 1892, National Theatre Orchestra, the
composer conducting. The three overtures were
given their present titles for the Simrock
publication of 1893.*

In the spinning room
  See: [From the Bohemian forest, Op. 68. No. 1,
       In the spinning room]

Josef Kajetán Tyl, overture
  See: [My homeland, overture to the play
       Josef Kajetán Tyl, Op. 125a]

829 [Legends, for orchestra, Op. 59.   22'
Nos. 1-5]
1.Allegretto 2.Molto moderato 3.Allegro
giusto 4.Molto maestoso 5.Allegro giusto
2,2,2,2-4,2-Timp.,Trgl.-Hp.-Str.

Kalmus, New York [n.d.]
Score 114 p.
*Originally composed for piano 4-hands, 1880-81;
transcribed for orchestra 1881. First performance of Nos. 1, 3, and 4 only, Conservatory
of Music, Prague, 7 May 1882, Antonín Bennewitz
conductor.*

830 [Legends, for orchestra, Op. 59.   22'
Nos. 6-10]
6.Allegro con moto 7.Allegretto grazioso 8.
Un poco allegretto e grazioso 9.Andante con
moto 10.Andante
2,2,2,2-4Hn.-Timp.-Hp.-Str.
Simrock, Berlin, 1882
Score 101 p.

551v [Mazurka, violin and orchestra, Op.   5'
49, E minor]
Solo Vn.-0,0,2,2-2Hn.-Timp.-Str.
Simrock, Berlin, 1879
Score 27 p.
*Originally composed for violin and piano, 1879.
Transcribed for violin and orchestra, 1879.
Dedicated to Pablo de Sarasate.*

542 [My homeland, overture to the play   10'
Josef Kajetán Tyl, Op. 62a]
2,2,2,2-4,2,3-Timp.,Trgl.-Str.
Simrock, Berlin, 1882
Score 69 p.
*From the incidental music to the play by F. F.
Šamberk. Composed 1881-82. First performance
Prozatimni Theater, Prague, 3 February 1882,
Adolf Čech conductor.*

Nature, life and love
  See: [Carnival, overture, Op. 92]
       [In Nature's realm, overture, Op. 91]
       [Othello, overture, Op. 93]

233s [Nocturne for string orchestra, Op. 40,
B major]
Str.
Bote & Bock, Berlin [1883]
Score 7 p.
*Composed 1875; revised 1882-83. First perform-
ance Prague, 6 January 1883, the composer con-
ducting. The composer later transcribed this
work for violin and piano.*

541 [The noon witch, symphonic poem,   16'
Op. 108]
3*,2,3*,2-4,2,3,1-Timp.,Perc.-Str.
Simrock, Berlin, c1896
Score 38 p.
*Inspired by the Czech legend as told by Jaromir
Erben. Composed 1896. First public rehearsal
Conservatory of Music, Prague, 3 June 1896,
Antonín Bennewitz conductor. First performance
London, 21 November 1896, Henry Wood conductor.*

677 [Othello, overture, Op. 93]   14'
2,3*,2,2-4,2,3,1-Timp.-Hp.-Str.
Simrock, Berlin, c1894
Score 75 p.
*Inspired by Shakespeare's play. Originally
Op. 91/3; see In Nature's Realm, Catalog no.
378.*

Dvořák, Antonín

The peasant a rogue
See: [Šelma Sedlák, Op. 37. Overture]

605c Polonaise [for violoncello and piano,   *7'*
E-flat major. Transcribed for orchestra by
Anton Modr]
Solo Vc.-2,2,2,2-3,2-Timp.-Hp.-Str.
Score: Ms. 54 p.
Parts: Universal Edition, Vienna, c1925
*Composed 1879. First performance at the Ball
of the Academic Readers' Society, Prague, 6
January 1880, Orchestra of the 36th Infantry
Regiment, F. Sommer conductor.*

838 [Rhapsody for orchestra, Op. 14,   *19'*
A minor]
3*,3*,2,2-4,2,3,1-Timp.,Perc.-Hp.-Str.
Simrock, Berlin, c1912
Score 95 p.
*Composed 1874. First performance Prague, 3
September 1904, Czech Philharmonic, Oskar
Nedbal conductor.*

521v [Romance, violin and orchestra,   *8'*
Op. 11, F minor]
Solo Vn.-2,2,2,2-2Hn.-Str.
Simrock, Berlin, 1879
Score 55 p.
*Originally the slow movement of the String
Quartet in F minor, Op. 9, composed 1873.
Romanze transcribed simultaneously for violin
and piano and for violin and orchestra, 1877.
First performance Prague, 9 December 1877,
Adolf Čech conductor, Josef Markus soloist.*

466c [Rondo, violoncello and orchestra,   *5'*
Op. 94, G minor]
Solo Vc.-0,2,0,2-Timp.-Str.
Simrock, Berlin, c1894
Score 27 p.
*Originally composed for violoncello and piano,
1891. This version 1893.*

609 Scherzo capriccioso, Op. 66   *13'*
3*,3*,3*,2-4,2,3,1-Timp.,Perc.-Hp.-Str.
Bote & Bock, Berlin [1884]
Score 102 p.
*Composed 1883. First performance at the St.
John's Day Concert of the Society of Czech
Journalists, Prague, 16 May 1883, Adolf Čech
conductor.*

1400 [Šelma Sedlák, Op. 37. Overture]   *11'*
2(2nd alt. Picc.),2,2,2-4,2,3-Timp.,Trgl.-Str.
Simrock, Berlin [1879]
Score 71 p.
From the comic opera in 2 acts, composed 1877.

88s [Serenade for string orchestra, Op. 22,
E major]
1.Moderato 2.Tempo di valse 3.Scherzo:
Vivace 4.Larghetto 5.Finale: Allegro vivace
Str.
Kalmus, New York [n.d.]
Score 48 p.
*Composed 1875; revised 1878. First performance
Prague, 10 December 1876, Czech Philharmonic,
Adolf Čech conductor.*

520 Serenade [for wind instruments, Op. 44] *24'*
1.Moderato quasi marcia 2.Menuetto – Trio:
Presto 3.Andante con moto 4.Finale: Allegro
molto
0,2,2,3*(C.Bn. ad lib.)-3Hn.-Str.(Vc.,Cb.only)
Artia, Prague, 1956
Score 71 p.
*Composed 1878. First performance Prozatimni
Theater, Prague, 17 November 1878, the composer
conducting. Dedicated to Louis Ehlert.*

[Slavonic dances, for orchestra, Series I,
Op. 46]
543 Nos. 1-4: 1.Presto 2.Allegretto scher- *18'*
zando 3.Poco allegro 4.Tempo di minuetto
546 Nos. 5-8: 5.Allegro vivace 6.Alle-   *15'*
gretto scherzando 7.Allegro assai 8.Presto
3*,2,2,2-4,2,3-Timp.,Perc.-Str.
Kalmus, New York [n.d.]
Scores: 139 p., 136 p.
*Originally composed for piano 4-hands, 1878.
This transcription 1878. First performance of
Nos. 1, 3, and 4, Academy of the Society of
Czech Journalists, Prague, 16 May 1878, Adolf
Čech conductor. First performance of entire
series Crystal Palace, London, 15 February 1879.*

[Slavonic dances, for orchestra, Series II,
Op. 72]
544 Nos. 1-4: 1.Molto vivace 2.Allegretto *16'*
grazioso 3.Allegro 4.Allegretto grazioso
545 Nos. 5-8: 5.Poco adagio - Vivace   *18'*
6.Moderato, quasi menuetto 7.Allegro vivace
8.Grazioso e lento, quasi tempo di valse
2,2,2,2-4,2,3-Timp.,Perc.-Str.
Scores: 544 - Kalmus, New York [n.d.] 114 p.
       545 - Simrock, New York [1887] 110 p.
*Originally composed for piano 4-hands, 1886.
This transcription 1887. First performance of
nos. 1, 2, and 7 only, Prague, 6 January 1887,
the composer conducting.*

38 [Slavonic rhapsodies, Op. 45. No. 1,   *7'*
D major]
3*,2,2,2-4,2,3-Timp.,Perc.-Str.
[Simrock, Berlin, 1879]
Score 65 p.
*Composed 1878. First performance Prague, 17
November 1878, the composer conducting. Dedi-
cated to Baron Paul von Dervies.*

174 [Slavonic rhapsodies, Op. 45. No. 2,   *13'*
G minor]
2,2,2,2-4,2,3-Timp.,Perc.-Hp.-Str.
Simrock, Berlin, 1879
Score 73 p.

1349 [Slavonic rhapsodies, Op. 45. No. 3,   *14'*
A-flat major]
2,2,2,2-4,2,3-Timp.,Perc.-2Hp.(2nd ad lib.)-
Str.
Kalmus, New York [n.d.]
Score 63 p.
*Composed 1878. First performance Berlin, 24
September 1879, Symphonic Soirée of the Prussian
Royal Orchestra, Wilhelm Taubert conductor.*

Dvořák, Antonín

854 [Suite, orchestra, Op. 98b, A major]   14'
1.Andante con moto 2.Allegro 3.Moderato
(alla pollacca) 4.Andante 5.Allegro
3*,2,2,3*-4,2,3,1-Timp.,Perc.-Str.
Simrock, Berlin, c1911
Score 54 p.
Originally composed as Op. 98 for piano, 1894.
Transcribed for orchestra 1895. First perform-
ance Prague, 1 March 1910, Bohemian Orchestra
Society, Karel Kovařovic conductor.

197 [Symphonic variations, Op. 78]   23'
Theme, 27 Variations, and Finale
2(2nd alt. Picc.),2,2,2-4,2,3-Timp.,Trgl.-Str.
Simrock, Berlin [1888]
Score 53 p.
Composed 1877. First performance Prague, 2
December 1877, Prozatimni Theater Orchestra,
Ludevit Procházka conductor.

536 [Symphony no. 3 (old no. 1), Op. 10,   25'
E-flat major]
1.Allegro moderato 2.Adagio molto, tempo di
marcia 3.Finale: Allegro vivace
3*,3*,2,2-4,2,3,1-Timp.,Trgl.-Hp.-Str.
Simrock, Berlin, c1911
Score 146 p.
Composed 1873. First performance Prague, 30
March 1874, Bedřich Smetana conductor.

538 [Symphony no. 4 (old no. 2), Op. 13,   32'
D minor]
1.Allegro 2.Andante sostenuto e molto cantabile 3.Allegro feroce 4.Allegro con brio -
Poco meno mosso
2,2,2,2-4,2,3-Timp.,Perc.-Hp.-Str.
Simrock, Berlin, c1912
Score 146 p.
Composed 1874. First performance of entire
symphony, Prague, 6 April 1892, the composer
conducting.

262 [Symphony no. 5 (old no. 3), Op. 76,   45'
F major]
1.Allegro ma non troppo 2.Andante con moto
3.Scherzo: Allegro scherzando - Trio 4.Finale:
Allegro molto
2,2,2,2-4,2,3-Timp.,Trgl.-Str.
Kalmus, New York [n.d.]
Score 82 p.
Originally composed 1875 as Op. 24. First
performance Prague, 25 March 1879, Adolf Čech
conductor. Revised and renumbered, 1887.
First performance Crystal Palace, London, 7
April 1888, August Manns conductor.

539 [Symphony no. 6 (old no. 1), Op. 60,   43'
D major]
1.Allegro non tanto 2.Adagio 3.Scherzo
(Furiant): Presto - Trio: Poco meno mosso
4.Finale: Allegro con spirito
2,2,2,2-4,2,3,1-Timp.-Str.
Kalmus, New York [n.d.]
Score 140 p.
Completed 1880. First performance Slavonic
Concerts of Žofin, Prague, 25 March 1881, Adolf
Čech conductor.

537 [Symphony no. 7 (old no. 2), Op. 70,   30'
D minor]
1.Allegro maestoso 2.Poco adagio 3.Scherzo:
Vivace 4.Finale: Allegro
2,2,2,2-4,2,3-Timp.-Str.
Kalmus, New York [n.d.]
Score 139 p.
Originally published by Simrock, Berlin, as
Symphony no. 2. Commissioned by the London
Philharmonic Society. Composed 1884-85. First
performance London, 22 April 1885, the composer
conducting.

1365 [Symphony no. 8 (old no. 4), Op. 88,   35'
G major]
1.Allegro con brio 2.Adagio 3.Allegretto
grazioso 4.Allegro ma non troppo
2(2nd alt. Picc.),2(2nd alt. E.H.),2,2-4,2,3,1
-Timp.-Str.
Kalmus, New York [n.d.]
Score 178 p.
Composed 1889. First performance Prague, 2
February 1890, the composer conducting.

76 [Symphony no. 9 (old no. 5), From the   50'
New World, Op. 95, E minor]
1.Adagio - Allegro molto 2.Largo 3.Molto
vivace - Poco sostenuto 4.Allegro con fuoco
2(2nd alt. Picc.),2(2nd alt. E.H.),2,2-4,2,3,1
-Timp.,Trgl.,Cym.-Str.
Kalmus, New York [n.d.]
Score 79 p.
Composed 1893 during the composer's tour of
the U.S.A. First performance New York, 15
December 1893, New York Philharmonic, Anton
Seidl conductor.

Tragic overture
   See: [Dramatic overture, Op. 1 (?)]

1836 [Two waltzes, from Op. 54, for   5'
string orchestra. Transcribed for orchestra
by Rudolf Karel]
1.Moderato 2.Allegro vivace
3*,2,2,2-4,2,3-Timp.,Perc.-Hp.-Str.
Simrock, Berlin [c1913]
Score 27 p.
Op. 54, 8 Waltzes, composed for piano 1879-80.
Nos. 1 and 4 transcribed for string orchestra
by the composer, 1880. This transcription
ca.1913. First performance Prague, 1914.

Waldesruhe
   See: [From the Bohemian forest, Op. 68. No. 5,
   Waldesruhe]

700 [Wanda, Op. 25. Overture]
2,2,2,2-4,2,3-Timp.-Str.
A. Cranz, Leipzig [n.d.]
Score 41 p.
From the opera composed 1875.

540 [The water sprite, symphonic poem,   18'
Op. 107]
3*,3*,3*,2-4,2,3,2(2nd ad lib.)-Timp.,Perc.-
Str.

Dvořák, Antonín

Simrock, Berlin, c1896
Score 59 p.
*Inspired by the Czech legend as told by Jaromir
Erben. Composed 1896. First public rehearsal
Conservatory of Music, Prague, 3 June 1896,
Antonín Bennewitz conductor. First performance
London, 14 November 1896, Henry Wood conductor.*

217 [The wild dove, symphonic poem,   20'
Op. 110]
2(1st alt. Picc.),3*,3*,2-4,3,3,1-Timp.,Perc.-
Hp.-Str.
Simrock, Berlin, c1899
Score 59 p.
*Inspired by Jaromir Erben's ballad. Composed
1896. First performance Brno, 20 March 1898,
Leoš Janáček conductor.*

DYCK, VLADIMIR (?).

707s Au temple d'Apollon, invocation [for
string orchestra]
Str.
Score: Ms. 5 p.
Parts: Leduc, Paris [n.d.]

1256s Chant de douleur et d'amour [for string
orchestra]
Str.
Score: Ms. 8 p.
Parts: Hawkes & Son, London [n.d.]

731s Douleur apaisée, elegiac song [for string
orchestra]
Str.
Score: Ms. 4 p.
Parts: Leduc, Paris, c1919 by Vladimir Dyck

DZEGELENOK, ALEXANDER MIKHAILOVICH.
                              Moscow 24 August 1891
                              Moscow 31 January 1969

2452 [Egypt, orchestral suite, Op. 6.   7'
No. 1, In the temple of Amon Rha]
2,3*,2,2-4,2,3,1-Timp.,Perc.-Hp.-Str.
Universal Edition, Vienna/Mussektor, Moscow,
c1928
Score 17 p.
*Composed 1920. First performance of entire
suite Moscow, 13 December 1925, Moscow Symphony
Company, Konstantin Saradiev conductor. Dedi-
cated to Gordietta Berkholtz.*

2453 [Egypt, orchestral suite, Op. 6.   15'
No. 2, Procession]
3*,3*,3*,3*-4,4,3,1-Timp.,Perc.-Pno.,Cel.,Hp.-
Str.
Universal Edition, Vienna/Mussektor, Moscow,
c1929
Score 55 p.

2925 [Egypt, orchestral suite, Op. 6.   10'
No. 3, Morning]
3*,3*,3*,3*-4,2,3,1-Timp.,B.Dr.,Cym.-Pno.,Cel.,
Hp.-Str.
Universal Edition, Vienna/Mussektor, Moscow,
c1930

Score 33 p.

E

EARLS, PAUL HURLEN.
                    b. Springfield, Missouri 9 June 1934

5722 And on the seventh day...   7'
1,1,1,1-Hn.-Str.
Ms. c1958 by Paul H. Earls
Score 18 p.
*After the passage in Genesis. Composed 1958.
First performance Rochester, New York, 5 May
1958, Eastman School of Music Symphony,
Howard Hanson conductor. Received the Edward
Benjamin Award for music of a quiet, restful
nature, 1958.*

338p Concerto for piano and orchestra   25'
1.Moderato - Allegro 2.Andantino - Adagio
3.Allegro vivace
Solo Pno.-2(2nd alt. Picc.),2,2,2-4,2,2,1-
Timp.,Perc.-Str.
Ms.
Score 60 p. Large folio
*Composed 1958-59. First performance Rochester,
New York, 23 March 1959, Eastman-Rochester
Symphony, Howard Hanson conductor, Robert
Hopkins soloist.*

5768 68th Psalm   6'30"
2(2nd alt. Picc.),2,2,1-2,2,1-Timp.,S.Dr.,
Cym.-Pno.-Str.
Ms. c1959 by Paul Earls
Score 36 p.
*Commissioned by Anthony Kooiker and Hope
College, Holland, Michigan, 1958. A set of
variations on a Huguenot melody of the 16th-
17th centuries used for the 68th Psalm. Com-
posed 1958. First performance Rochester, New
York, 26 April 1958, Eastman-Rochester Sym-
phony, Howard Hanson conductor.*

EBEL, ARNOLD.   Heide, Holstein 15 August 1883
                              Berlin 4 March 1963

2088 Sinfonietta giocosa, Op. 39   35'
3*,3*,3*,3*-4,3,3,1-Timp.,Perc.-Hp.-Str.
Ries & Erler, Berlin, c1929
Score 156 p.
*Composed 1927. First performance Halle,
1929.*

EBERHARDT, E. GOBY.   Hattersheim 29 March 1852
                              Lübeck 13 September 1926

919v Nocturno [for violin or violoncello and
orchestra, Op. 43. Transcribed by J.W.A.
Gaspary]
Solo Vn.-2,2,2,2-2Hn.-Timp.-Str.
Böhme, Hamburg [n.d.]
Score 12 p.

918v Schlummerlied [for violin or violoncello
and orchestra, Op. 42. Transcribed by J.W.A.
Gaspary]
Solo Vn.-2,2,2,2-2Hn.-Timp.-Str.
Böhme, Hamburg [n.d.]
Score 5 p.

EBERHART, ERNEST.

105s Scène de ballet
Str.
Bosworth, Leipzig, c1893
Score 5 p.

EBERWEIN, CARL.   Weimar 10 November 1786
                         Weimar 2 March 1868

868m [Concerto, flute, E-flat major]
1.Allegro 2.Adagio 3.Rondo
Solo Fl.-0,2,2,2-2,2-Timp.-Str.
Ms.
Score 141 p.

ECKERBERG, SIXTEN.   Hjältevad,
              Ingatorp, Sweden 5 September 1909

5016 [Symphony no. 2]   41'
1.Allegro 2.Andante tranquillo 3.Allegro
moderato 4.Allegro
3*,2,2,2-4,3,3,1-Timp.,Perc.-Hp.-Str.
Ms.
Score 166 p.
Composed 1944. First performance Gothenburg,
15 November 1945, Orchestra Society of Gothenburg, the composer conducting.

ECKERT, CARL ANTON FLORIAN. Potsdam 7 December 1820
                            Berlin 14 October 1879

670c [Concerto, violoncello, Op. 26] New
edition by Hugo Becker
1.Allegro moderato 2.Andante 3.Allegro non
troppo
Solo Vc.-2*,2,2,2-4,2,3-Timp.,Perc.-Str.
Score: Ms. 91 p.
Parts: Bote & Bock, Berlin, c1908

ECKHOLD, HERMANN RICHARD.   Schandau, Saxony 1855

1086v Concertstück [for violin and orchestra,
Op. 5]
Solo Vn.-1,2,2,2-2,2-Timp.-Hp.(or Pno.; ad
lib.)-Str.
Breitkopf & Härtel, Leipzig [1883]
Score 119 p.

EEDEN, JEAN-BAPTISTE VAN DEN.
                    Ghent 26 December 1842
                    Mons 4 April 1917

575m Le matin
Solo Fl.-1,2,2,2-4,2,3-Timp.,Trgl.-Hp.-Str.
Ms.
Score 21 p.

EFFINGER, CECIL.   Colorado Springs 22 July 1914

5822 Little symphony no. 1, Op. 31   13'
1.Moderato 2.Presto 3.Adagio 4.Allegro
vivace
2(2nd alt. Picc.),1,2,1-2,1-Str.
Ms. c[n.d.] by Cecil Effinger
Score 32 p. Large folio
Commissioned by St. Louis Little Symphony,
1945. Composed 1945. First performance St.
Louis, Missouri, 29 June 1959, St. Louis Little
Symphony, Stanley Chapple conductor. Received
the Walter W. Naumburg Award, 1959.

EGGE, KLAUS.   Gransherad, Norway 19 July 1906

6934 [Symphony no. 1, Op. 17]   42'
1.Andante espressivo - Allegro assai e deciso
2.Adagio 3.Finale: Rondo e fuga - Allegro
molto e rigoroso
2,2,2,2-4,3,3,1-Timp.,Perc.-Str.
Harald Lyche & Co., Oslo, c1946
Score 148 p.
Composed 1941-42. First performance 4 October
1945. Dedicated to the Norwegian sailors, who
served in the Second Great War, in Memory of
Harald Nergaard, the Friend of my Childhood.

EGK, WERNER.   Auchsesheim, Bavaria 17 May 1901

4973 [Georgica, three pastoral pieces for   15'
orchestra]
1.Allegro 2.Tranquillo 3.Allegretto
2(2nd alt. Picc.),2(2nd alt. E.H.),2,2-4,3,3,1
-Timp.,Perc.-Str.
B. Schott's Söhne, Mainz, c1934
Score 49 p.
Inspired by the Georgics of Virgil. Composed
1934. First performance New York, November
1934.

EGÓN, RODRIGUE.   Berlin, Germany 1927

5658 [Three Romanian dances]   12'
1.Moderato - Andante tranquillo 2.Molto lento
- Vivo 3.Allegretto giocoso
3*,3*,2,2-2,3,2,1-Timp.,Perc.-Pno.,Cel.,Hp.-
Str.
Ms.
Score 42 p. Large folio
Originally composed for violin and piano, 1948.
For orchestra, 1950. First performance Belo
Horizonte, Brazil, 30 April 1956, Sociedade
Mineira de Concertos Sinfónicos, Guido Santor-
sola conductor.

EGRESSY, BÉNI.   Lászlófalva, Hungary 1814
                        Budapest 19 July 1851

1607s [Klapka march. Transcribed for string
orchestra by Géza Allaga]
Str.
Rozsnyai, Budapest [n.d.]
Score 5 p.

Egressy, Béni

1611s Szózat [Song. Transcribed for string
orchestra by Joseph Bloch]
Str.
Rozsnyai, Budapest [n.d.]
Score 3 p.

1421 [Szózat *and* Hymnus. Two patriotic songs
of Vörösmarty and Kölcsey, by Béni Egressy and
Franz Erkel. Transcribed for orchestra by
Franz Liszt]
2,2,2,2-4,2,3,1-Timp.,Perc.-Hp.-Str.
Rozsavölgyi, Budapest, 1878
Score 48 p.
*Arranged 1870-73. First performance Budapest,
19 March 1873, Franz Liszt conductor.*

EGVILLE, L. H. D'.

652s Romance, Op. 23 [B-flat major]
Str.
Score: Ms. 7 p.
Parts: International Music [n.p., n.d.]

EHLERT, LOUIS. Königsberg, Germany 13 January 1825
Wiesbaden 4 January 1884

6002 [Hafis, overture for orchestra, Op. 21]
2,2,2,2-4,2-Timp.-Str.
F.E.C. Leuckart, Breslau [1857]
Score 56 p.

EHRENBERG, CARL EMIL THEODOR. Dresden 6 April 1878
Munich 26 February 1962

772v Nachtlied [after Friedrich Nietzsche,
Op. 14]
Solo Vn.-2,2,2,2-4Hn.-Timp.-Hp.-Str.
Leuckart, Leipzig, c1911
Score 22 p.

2151 Sinfonische Suite, Op. 22   40'
1.[Prelude: At sunset] 2.[Scherzo: Twilight]
3.[In the darkness of night] 4.[At daylight]
3(3rd alt. Picc.),3*,2,2-4,2,3,1-Timp.,Perc.-
Cel.,Hp.-Str.
Ries & Erler, Berlin, c1925
Score 111 p.
*Composed 1924. First performance Cologne,
1925, the composer conducting.*

Zwei Stücke für Streichinstrumente, Op. 15
312s No. 1. Repos
313s No. 2. Scherzo
Str.(Solo Vn. in Repos)
Rahter, Leipzig, c1912
Scores: 10 p., 11 p.

EHRLICH, ABEL.
b. Cranz near Königsberg 3 September 1915

350v Bashrav, for violin solo and choir of
violins
Solo Vn.-Vn.Choir
Israeli Music Publications, Tel Aviv, c1958
Score 16 p.
*Originally composed for solo violin, 1953.
This arrangement 1956 by the composer.*

EIBENSCHÜTZ, JOSÉ.   Frankfurt 8 January 1872
Sülzhayn, Harz, Germany 27 November 1952

2093s [Finnish melody. Transcribed for
string orchestra by José Eibenschütz]
Str.
C.F. Schmidt, Heilbronn [n.d.]
Score 1 p.

EICHBERGER, WALTHER.

676m O sag' nicht nein [for voice or cornet
à pistons and orchestra]
Solo Voice-2,2,2,2-2,2,2-Hp.-Str.
L. Hoffarth, Dresden [n.d.]
Score 7 p.

EICHBORN, HERMANN LUDWIG.   Breslau 30 October 1847
Gries 15 April 1918

778m [Concertino pastorale, oboe, Op. 69,
D minor]
Solo Ob.-1,0,2,1-2,2-Timp.-Str.
C.F. Schmidt, Heilbronn a.N. [n.d.]
Score 55 p.

888s Die Glocken von Gries, Op. 48
Str.
Score: Ms. 7 p.
Parts: C.F. Schmidt, Heilbronn a.N. [n.d.]

EICHHEIM, HENRY.   Chicago, Illinois 3 January 1870
Montecito, California 22 August 1942

6139 Oriental impressions
1.Korean sketch 2.Japanese sketch 3.Japanese
nocturne 4.Entenraku 5.Siamese sketch 6.Noc-
turnal impressions of Peking 7.Chinese sketch
1(alt. Picc.),3*(2nd in lieu of Voice)-Perc.
(including Oriental instruments; 10 players)-
Pno.,Hp.-Female Voice-Str.
G. Schirmer, New York, c1929 by Henry Eichheim
Score 63 p.
*Movement 4 based on an elegy attributed to a
Chinese emperor of the 8th century. Written
for the Elizabeth Sprague Coolidge Berkshire
Festival in a shorter form under the title
Oriental Sketches, 1921. Enlarged in 1922 and
first performed Boston, 24 March 1922, the
composer conducting.*

EICHNER, ERNST.   Mannheim, Germany 9 February 1740
Potsdam, Germany 1777

6944 [Symphony, Op. 7 no. 5 (Op. 8 no. 4),
D major]
1.Allegro maestoso 2.Andante poco allegro 3.
Allegro
2Fl.(or 2Ob.)-2Hn.-Cemb.-Str.
Score: Denkmäler der Tonkunst in Bayern, Vol.
VIII/2. Breitkopf & Härtel, Leipzig
[1908] Edited by Hugo Riemann. 33 p.
Parts: Ms. c1976 by The Fleisher Collection of
Orchestral Music, Free Library of Philadelphia
Composed 1771.

EIGER, WALTER.

4776 Fantasy-overture on Canadian 7'
folktunes
3*,2,2,2-4,3,3,1-Timp.,Perc.-Str.
Ms.
Score 46 p. Large folio

EILENBERG, RICHARD.   Merseberg 13 January 1848
                          Berlin 6 December 1925

983s Ich engagiere Sie zum Walzer [May I have
this waltz, Op. 143]
Str.
Score: Ms. 16 p.
Parts: [O.B. Boise, New York, n.d.]

889s Naschkätzchen [Little sweet-tooth]
Intermezzo, Op. 136
Str.
Score: Ms. 13 p.
Parts: [n.p., n.d.]

808s Rêve du bal [waltz-intermezzo] Op. 155
Str.
Score: Ms. 12 p.
Parts: Hawkes, London [n.d.]

771s Sandmännchen [Lullaby] Op. 120
Bells-Str.
Score: Ms. 10 p.
Parts: O.B. Boise, New York, c1890

1019s Spanish serenade, Op. 117
Str.
Score: Ms. 11 p.
Parts: Hawkes [London, n.d.]

EINEM, GOTTFRIED VON.
          b. Bern, Switzerland 24 January 1918

6033 Capriccio, Op. 2   9'
3(3rd alt. Picc.),2,2,2-4,3,3,1-Timp.-Str.
Bote & Bock, Berlin, c1943
Score 50 p. Large folio
*Composed 1942-43. First performance Berlin,
February 1943, Berlin Philharmonic Orchestra,
Leo Borchard conductor.*

6274 Philadelphia symphony, Op. 28   16'
1.Allegro giusto 2.Andante 3.Allegro vivace
3*,2,2,2-4,3,3,1-Timp.-Str.
Hawkes & Son, London, c1961
Score 71 p.
*Commissioned by the Philadelphia Orchestra.
Composed 1960. United States premiere Philadelphia, 9 November 1962, Philadelphia Orchestra, Eugene Ormandy conductor.*

EISENMANN, WILL.   Stuttgart, Germany 3 March 1906

1115m Concerto da camera for alto   15'
saxophone and string orchestra
1.Andante amoroso 2.Molto vivace ed energico
3.Allegro scherzando
Solo Alto Sax.-Str.
Universal, Vienna, c1948
Score 28 p.

EISLER, HANNS.   Leipzig 6 July 1898
                          Berlin 6 September 1962

3059 [Symphony no. 1, Kleine Symphonie,   20'
Op. 29]
1.Theme and variations 2.Allegro assai
3.Invention
Fl.(alt. Picc.),3Cl.(1st alt. Alto Sax.,2nd
alt. Ten.Sax.)-0,2,1,1-Timp.,Perc.-Str.
Ms.
Score 42 p.
*Composed 1932. First performance London, March
1935, BBC Orchestra, Ernest Ansermet conductor.*

EITLER, ESTEBAN.   Bolzano, Tyrol 25 June 1913
                        São Paulo 25 June 1960

4713 [Divertimento 1950, for chamber orchestra]
1.Alegre 2.Lento y expresivo 3.Alegre, ligero
2,2,2,2-2,2,1-Str.
Ediciones Musicales Politonía, Buenos Aires,
c1950 by Esteban Eitler
Miniature score 32 p.
Composed 1950.

1971s Policromía 1950, for string orchestra
Lento - Energico - Allegro
Str.
Ediciones Musicales Politonía, Buenos Aires,
c1950 by Esteban Eitler
Miniature score 16 p.
Composed 1950.

EK, GUNNAR.   Åsarum, Blekinge, Sweden 21 June 1900

818p [Concerto, piano and orchestra,   25'
B minor]
Adagio - Allegro marcato - Adagio - Allegro
Solo Pno.-2(2nd alt. Picc.),2,2,2-4,2,3,1-
Timp.,Cym.-Str.
Ms.
Score 105 p.
*Composed 1944-45. First performance Malmö,
Sweden, 1946, Konserthusstiftelse, Georg
Schnéevoigt conductor, Brita Hjort-Karström
soloist.*

1206v [Fantasia, for violin and   ca.7'
orchestra]
Solo Vn.-2,2,2,2-2,2,1-Timp.-Str.
Carl Gehrmans, Stockholm, c1939
Score 19 p.
Composed 1937.

4349 [Scherzo for orchestra]   5'30"
2(2nd alt. Picc.),2,2,2-4(or 2),3(or 2),3(or 1),
1-Timp.,Perc.-Cel.-Str.
Carl Gehrmans, Stockholm, c1937, c1944
Score 22 p.
*Excerpt from Symphony no. 1, composed 1926 and
reorchestrated.*

6935 [Symphony no. 2. Finale: Rondo fugato] 9'
2,2,2,2-2,1,1,1-Timp.,Perc.-Str.
Carl Gehrmans Musikförlag, Stockholm, c1944
Score 39 p.
Composed 1930.

Eklund, Hans

EKLUND, HANS.   Sandviken, Sweden 1 July 1927

   5988 Musica da camera (1956) Op. 10 no. 2   *20'*
     1.Andante sostenuto 2.Mesto: Marcia funebre
     3.Allegro con brio
     Tpt.-Timp.,Military Dr.,Xyl.-Pno.-Str.
     Ms. [^c1963 by Föreningen Svenska Tonsättare,
     Stockholm]
     Score 55 p.
     Composed 1956 in memory of the American jazz
     pianist Art Tatum. First performance Stock-
     holm, 9 March 1956, Swedish Radio Symphony
     Orchestra, Sten Fryberg conductor.

EKMAN, KARL.   Kaarina, Finland 18 December 1869
                            Helsinki 4 February 1947

   467s Det gingo två flickor i rosendelund [Two
     maidens went to the rosary, West Finnish
     folk-song. Transcribed for string orchestra
     by Karl Ekman]
     Str.
     Apostol, Helsinki [n.d.]
     Score 3 p.

ELGAR, EDWARD.   Broadheath, England 2 June 1857
                          Worcester 23 February 1934

   897 Chanson de matin, Op. 15 no. 2   *4'*
     [G major]
     1,1,2,1-2Hn.-Hp.(or Pno.; ad lib.)-Str.
     Novello, London, ^c1901
     Score 16 p.
     This and the following entry were originally
     composed for violin and piano. Orchestrated
     by the composer 1901; first performed at a
     Queen's Hall Promenade Concert, London, 14
     September 1901.

   898 Chanson de nuit, Op. 15 no. 1   *4'*
     [G major]
     1,1,2,1-2Hn.-Hp.(or Pno.; ad lib.)-Str.
     Novello, London, ^c1901
     Score 11 p.

   283 Cockaigne (In London town), concert   *13'*
     overture, Op. 40
     2(2nd alt. Picc.),2,2,3*-4,2,2Cnt.,5(2 option-
     al),1-Timp.,Perc.-Org.-Str.
     Boosey, London, ^c1901
     Score 70 p.
     Composed 1900. First performance Royal Phil-
     harmonic Society Concert, London, 20 June 1901.

   544v [Concerto, violin, Op. 61, B minor]   *43'*
     1.Allegro 2.Andante 3.Allegro molto
     Solo Vn.-2,2,2,3*-4,2,3,1-Timp.-Str.
     Novello, London, ^c1910
     Score 99 p.
     Composed 1910. First performance London, 10
     November 1910, the composer conducting,
     Fritz Kreisler soloist.

   612c [Concerto, violoncello, Op. 85,   *28'*
     E minor]
     1.Adagio 2.Lento 3.Adagio 4.Allegro
     Solo Vc.-2(2nd alt. Picc.),2,2,2-4,2,3,1(ad
     lib.)-Timp.-Str.

Novello, London, ^c1921
Score 104 p.
Composed 1919. First performance Queen's Hall,
London, 26 October 1919, the composer con-
ducting, Felix Salmond soloist.

   1552 Contrasts (The gavotte AD 1700 and   *4'*
     1900), Op. 10 no. 3
     2*,2,2,2-4,2,3,1-Timp.,Perc.-Str.
     Novello, London, c1899
     Score 25 p.
     Composed 1899. First performance New Brighton
     Town Concerts, 16 July 1899.

   1113 The crown of India, orchestral   *16'30"*
     suite, Op. 66 [from the masque]
     1.Dance of the Nautch girls 2.Menuetto 3.
     Warrior's dance 4.Intermezzo 5.March of the
     Mogul emperors
     3*,2,3*,3*(or: 3*,2,2,2)-4,3(3rd ad lib.),3,1-
     Timp.,Perc.-Hp.-Str.
     Hawkes, London, ^c1913
     Score 53 p.
     First performance London, 11 March 1912.

   205 [Dream children, Op. 43]   *6'*
     1.Andante 2.Allegretto piacevole
     2,2,2,2-4Hn.-Timp.-Hp.-Str.
     Schott's Söhne, Mainz, ^c1913
     Score 29 p.
     Inspired by Charles Lamb's verses. Composed
     1902. First performance London, 4 September
     1902.

   1420 [The dream of Gerontius, oratorio,   *18'*
     Op. 38. Prelude *and* Angel's farewell]
     2(2nd alt. Picc.),3*,3*,3*-4,3,3,1-Timp.,Perc.-
     Org.,2Hp.(2nd ad lib.)-Mezzo-sop.Voice(ad lib.)
     -Str.
     Novello, London, ^c1902
     Score 26 p.
     Composed 1898. First performance Birmingham
     Triennial Festival, 3 October 1900.

   543s Elegy, adagio, Op. 58
     Str.
     Novello, London, ^c1910
     Score 4 p.

   282 Enigma variations; variations on an   *28'*
     original theme, Op. 36
     2(2nd alt. Picc.),2,2,3*-4,3,3,1-Timp.,Perc.-
     Org.(ad lib.)-Str.
     Kalmus, New York [n.d.]
     Score 128 p.
     Composed 1898. First performance St. James
     Hall, London, 19 June 1899, Hans Richter con-
     ductor.

   1610 [Falstaff, symphonic study, Op. 68,   *31'*
     C minor, with two interludes in A minor]
     3*,3*,3*,3*-4,3,3,1-Timp.,Perc.-2Hp.(2nd ad
     lib.)-Str.
     Novello, London, ^c1913
     Score 147 p.
     Composed 1912. First performance Leeds Musi-
     cal Festival, 1 October 1913, the composer
     conducting.

Elgar, Edward

716 [Falstaff. Two interludes, A minor.   4'
Transcribed for small orchestra by the
composer]
1.Jack Falstaff, page to the Duke of Norfolk
2.Gloucestershire; Shallow's orchard
3*,1,2,2-2Hn.-Timp.,Perc.-Hp.-Str.
Novello, London, c1914
Score 19 p.

5375 Froissart, concert overture, Op. 19   12'
2(2nd alt. Picc.),2,2,3*(C.Bn. ad lib.)-4,2,3-
Timp.,Cym.(ad lib.)-Str.
Novello, London, c1901
Score 64 p.
*Suggested by a scene from Sir Walter Scott's
Old Mortality which alludes to the medieval
chronicler Jean Froissart (1333?-ca.1400).
Composed 1890. First performance Worcester,
England, 9 September 1890, Three Choirs Fes-
tival, the composer conducting.*

2246 Gavotte. Transcribed for orchestra   5'
by Adolf Schmid
2(2nd alt. Picc.),2,2,2-4,2,3-Timp.,Perc.-Hp.
(ad lib.)-Str.
Schott's Söhne, Mainz [n.d.]
Score 16 p.
*Composed for violin and piano; orchestrated
1902.*

929 In the South (Alassio), concert   20'
overture, Op. 50
3(3rd alt. Picc.),3*,3*,3*-4,3,3,1-Timp.,Perc.
-2Hp.-Str.
Novello, London, c1904
Score 98 p.
*Composed 1903. First performance Elgar Festi-
val, London, 1904, the composer conducting.*

533s Introduction and allegro, Op. 47   8'
Solo Str. Quartet-Str.
Novello, London, c1905
Score 56 p.

1203 May-song, for small orchestra   4'
1,1,2,1-2,2(ad lib.),1(ad lib.)-Timp.,Trgl.
(both ad lib.)-Hp.(or Pno.)-Str.
Elkin, London [n.d.]
Score 9 p.

1309 Mazurka, Op. 10 no. 1   4'
2(2nd alt. Picc.),2,2,2-4,2,3,1-Timp.,Cym.,B.Dr.
-Str.
Novello, London, c1899
Score 23 p.
*First performance New Brighton Town Concerts,
1900.*

1070 Meditation from The Light of Life   6'
(Lux Christi), oratorio, Op. 29
2,2,2,3*-4,2,3,1-Timp.-Org.,Hp.-Str.
Novello, London, c1903
Score 15 p.
*Oratorio composed for and first performed at
the Worcester Musical Festival, September 1896,
the composer conducting.*

1385 Minuet, Op. 21
1,1,2,1-2Hn.-Timp.-Str.
J. Williams, London [n.d.]
Score 11 p.

24 Polonia, symphonic prelude, Op. 76   13'30"
3*,3*,3*,3*-4,3,3,1-Timp.,Perc.-Org.,2Hp.-Str.
Elkin, New York, c1915
Score 47 p.
*First performance Queen's Hall, London, 6 July
1915, the composer conducting.*

227 Pomp and circumstance, Op. 39. Military   5'
march no. 1, D major
4*(Picc.II ad lib.),2,3*,3*-4,2,2Cnt.,3,1-Timp.,
Perc.-Org.,2Hp.-Str.
Kalmus, New York [n.d.]
Score 26 p.
*First performance Liverpool, 19 October 1901,
Liverpool Orchestral Society, A. E. Rodewald
conductor.*

228 Pomp and circumstance, Op. 39. Military   5'
march no. 2, A minor
3*,2,3*,3*-4,2,2Cnt.,3,1-Timp.,Perc.-Str.
Boosey, London, c1902
Score 16 p.
First performance Liverpool, 19 October 1901.

7039 Pomp and circumstance, Op. 39.   5'
Military march no. 4. Arranged by Adolf Schmid
2(2nd alt. Picc.),2,2,2-4,2Cnt.,3-Timp.,Perc.-
Hp.-Str.
Boosey & Co., London, c1908
Score in reduction 7 p.
*Composed 1907. First performance Queen's Hall,
London, 24 August 1907.*

544m Romance, bassoon and orchestra,   8'
Op. 62
Solo Bn.-2,2,2,2(2nd ad lib.)-3,0,3(ad lib.)-
Timp.-Str.
Novello, London, c1912
Score 14 p.
*Composed 1910. First performance Hereford, 16
February 1911, the composer conducting, E. F.
James soloist.*

46 Salut d'amour, Op. 12   4'
2,2,2,2-2Hn.-Str.
Schott's Söhne, Mainz [n.d.]
Score 11 p.
Composed 1889. First performance London, 1889.

84s Serenade, for strings, Op. 20, E minor
Str.
Kalmus, New York [n.d.]
Score 13 p.

1198 Sérénade lyrique   3'
2,2,2,2-2Hn.-Timp.-Hp.-Str.
Chappell, London, c1900
Score 19 p.

55s Sospiri [Sighs] Adagio, Op. 70
Hp.(or Pno.),Harm.(or Org.)all ad lib.-Str.
Breitkopf & Härtel, Leipzig, c1914
Score 7 p.

Elgar, Edward

*First performance at a Promenade Concert,
London, 15 August 1914.*

1611 [Symphony no. 1, Op. 55, A-flat   51'
major]
1.Andante, nobilmente e semplice 2.Allegro
molto 3.Adagio 4.Lento
3(3rd alt. Picc.),3*,3*,3*-4,3,3,1-Timp.,Perc.
-2Hp.-Str.
Novello, London, c1908
Score 170 p.
*Composed 1907-08. First performance at a
Hallé Concert, Manchester, 3 December 1908,
Hans Richter conductor.*

1612 [Symphony no. 2, Op. 63, E-flat   50'
major]
1.Allegro vivace e nobilmente 2.Larghetto
3.Rondo 4.Moderato e maestoso
3(3rd alt. Picc.),3*,4*,3*-4,3,3,1-Timp.,Perc.
-2Hp.-Str.
Novello, London, c1911
Score 184 p.
*Composed 1910-11. First performance London
Music Festival, 24 May 1911, the composer conducting.*

1252 Three Bavarian dances, Op. 27   11'
1.Allegretto giocoso 2.Moderato 3.Allegro
vivace
2(2nd alt. Picc.),2,2,2-4,2,3,1-Timp.,Perc.-
Str.
J. Williams, London, c1901
Score 90 p.
*Dances are nos. 1, 3, and 5 of the choral
suite The Bavarian Highlands, composed 1894.
This version 1896. First performance London,
23 October 1897, August Manns conductor.*

1844 Triumphal march from Caractacus,   9'
cantata, Op. 35
2(2nd alt. Picc.),2,3*,3*-4,4,3,1-Timp.,Perc.-
Org.,Hp.-Str.
Novello, London, c1905
Score 28 p.
*From the cantata composed 1897. First per-
formance Leeds Festival, 5 October 1898, the
composer conducting.*

The wand of youth; music to a child's play,
Op. 1a and 1b
1081 First suite   18'
1.Overture 2.Serenade 3.Minuet 4.Sun dance
5.Fairy pipers 6.Slumber scene 7.Fairies
and giants
2(2nd alt. Picc.),2,2,3(C.Bn. ad lib.)-4,2,3,1
-Timp.,Perc.-Hp.-Str.
1277 Second suite   18'
1.March 2.The little bells 3.Moths and
butterflies 4.Fountain dance 5.The tame
bear 6.The wild bears
2(2nd alt. Picc.),2,2,2-4,2,3,1-Timp.,Perc.-
Hp.-Str.
Novello, London, c1908
Scores: 82 p., 104 p.
*Suites composed 1869; revised several times.
First Suite first performed London, 14 December 1907, at a Queen's Hall Symphony Concert.*

*Second Suite first performed Worcester Music
Festival, 9 September 1908.*

ELGÉ, LUCIEN GAUBERT.
See: GAUBERT-ELGÉ, LUCIEN.

ELÍAS, ALFONSO DE.   Mexico City 30 August 1902

4154 [The enchanted garden, symphonic triptych.
No. 1, In the garden]
2,2,2,2-2Hn.-Timp.-Str.
Ms.
Score 25 p.
*Composed 1924. First performance of entire
work Mexico City, 9 October 1927, Orchestra of
the Conservatory of Mexico, José Rocabruna
conductor.*

4155 [The enchanted garden, symphonic triptych.
No. 2, Contemplation]
2,2,2,2-2Hn.-Timp.-Str.
Ms.
Score 13 p.

4156 [The enchanted garden, symphonic triptych.
No. 3, The marvelous fountain]
2,2,2,2-2Hn.-Timp.-Str.
Ms.
Score 38 p.

3886 [Suite, for chamber orchestra]
1.[Prelude] 2.[Moonlight in Tlalmanalco]
3.Allegretto vivace
Cl.,Bn.-Tpt.-Pno.-Str.
Ms.
Score 45 p.

4824 [Variations on a Mexican theme, Las
Mañanitas]
2,2,2,2-2Hn.-Timp.-Hp.-Str.
Ms.
Score 47 p.
*First performance Mexico City, 4 March 1928,
Orchestra of the Conservatory of Mexico, José
Rocabruna conductor.*

ELKAN, HENRI.   Antwerp 23 November 1897

1729s Londonderry air; traditional   3'30"
English melody. Arranged for string orchestra
by Henri Elkan
Pno.(ad lib.)-Str.
Elkan-Vogel, Philadelphia, c1937
Score 4 p.
*Arranged 1937. First performance Ardmore,
Pennsylvania, 10 February 1937, Main Line
Orchestra, Adolph Vogel conductor.*

ELKUS, ALBERT ISRAEL.   Sacramento 30 April 1884
    Oakland 19 February 1962

2728 Impressions from a Greek tragedy   17'
1.Prelude: Sostenuto 2.Allegretto grazioso
3.Finale: Andante maestoso
3(3rd alt. Picc.),3*,3(3rd alt. B.Cl.),3(3rd
alt. C.Bn.)-4,3,3,1-Timp.,Perc.-2Hp.-Str.
Kalmus, New York, c1936
Score 83 p.

Composed 1920. First performance San Francisco, 27 February 1920, San Francisco Symphony Orchestra, Alfred Hertz conductor. Received the Juilliard Publication Award, 1935.

2602 On a merry folk tune, for small   3'
orchestra
2(alt. 2Picc.),2,2,2-3Hn.,2Tpt.-Timp.,Cym.-Str.
Ms.
Score 21 p.
Composed 1922. First performance San Francisco, 9 February 1923, San Francisco Symphony Orchestra, Alfred Hertz conductor.

ELMORE, ROBERT HALL.
                 b. Ramapatnam, India 2 January 1913

2852 Valley Forge 1777, a tone poem for   20'
full orchestra
1.Valley Forge 1777 2.Retreat of the American
army 3.General Washington seeks divine aid
4.Defeat of the enemy - Conclusion
3(3rd alt. Picc.),3*,4*,3*-4,4,3,1-Timp.,Perc.
-Cel.,Hp.-Str.
Ms.
Score 51 p.
Composed 1935. First performance Philadelphia, 9 April 1937, Philadelphia Orchestra, Leopold Stokowski conductor.

ELSENHEIMER, NICHOLAS J.   Wiesbaden 17 June 1866
                              Germany 2 July 1935

118s Scherz und Ernst [Playfulness and serious-
ness, humoresque; a conversation between Mr.
Pizzicato and Miss Sordina]
Str.
J. Church, New York, ᶜ1894
Score 4 p.

ELWELL, HERBERT. Minneapolis, Minnesota 10 May 1898

1994 The happy hypocrite, suite for   22'
orchestra from the pantomime ballet after the
story by Max Beerbohm
3*,3*,3*,3*-4,3,3,1-Timp.,Perc.-Cel.,Hp.-Str.
C. C. Birchard, Boston, ᶜ1928 by Eastman School
of Music
Score 108 p. Large folio
Composed 1927. First performance Rome, 21 May 1927, Augusteo Orchestra, the composer conducting.

EMBORG, JENS LAURSØN.
           Ringe (Funen), Denmark 22 December 1876
           Vordingborg 18 April 1957

415m [Chamber concerto for violin, flute,   15'
and piano with strings, Op. 57]
1.Allegretto giocoso 2.Adagio espressivo -
Vivace - Adagio 3.Allegro moderato
Solo Vn.,Fl.,& Pno.-Str.(without Vn.)
Samfundet til Udgivelse af Dansk Musik, Copen-
hagen, ᶜ1945
Score 62 p.
Composed 1945.

361m [Concerto for organ with strings and   15'
piano, Op. 49]
1.Maestoso 2.Andante espressivo 3.Allegro
Solo Org.-Pno.-Str.
Samfundet til Udgivelse af Dansk Musik, Copen-
hagen, ᶜ1926
Score 44 p.
Composed 1921.

2342s [Concerto for strings and piano,   12'
Op. 72]
1.Moderato con moto 2.Andante 3.Allegro
Pno.-Str.
Samfundet til Udgivelse af Dansk Musik, Copen-
hagen, ᶜ1934
Score 31 p.
Composed 1930.

551m [Concerto grosso, Op. 51, G minor]   17'
1.Andante - Allegro moderato con moto 2.Adagio
non troppo 3.Allegretto - Allegro molto
Solo Ob., Solo Vn., Solo Vc.-Pno.-Str.
F. Kistner & C.F.W. Siegel, Leipzig [n.d.]
Score 43 p.
Composed 1922. First performance Vordingborg, 1923.

5941 [Four Nordic dances for small orchestra,
Op. 88]
1.Marciale, con moto 2.Alla mazurka 3.Alla
polka, tranquillo 4.Allegretto con fuoco
2*,1,2,1-2,2,1-Timp.-Str.
Edition Dania, Copenhagen, ᶜ1939
Score 33 p.

5940 [The twelve masks, theme with 12   24'
variations and a gigue for orchestra, Op. 50]
3(3rd alt. Picc.),2,3*,2-4,2,2-Timp.,Tam-tam-
Cel.,Hp.-Str.
Samfundet til Udgivelse af Dansk Musik, Copen-
hagen, ᶜ1948
Score 107 p.
Inspired by twelve carvings in the medieval church of Vordingborg, Denmark. Composed 1921.

EMERSCHITZ, PHILIPP.

1289s Alpen-Poesie, Salon-Ländler
Solo Vn.,Solo Vc.-Str.
Score: Ms. 11 p.
Parts: Bosworth, Leipzig, ᶜ1913

EMMANUEL, MAURICE. Bar-sur-Aube, France 2 May 1862
                    Paris 14 December 1938

Real name: Marie François Emmanuel

5570 [Salamine. Overture]
4*,3(3rd alt. E.H.),3*,4*-4,4,4,1-Timp.,Perc.-
2Hp.-Str.
Editions Choudens, Paris, ᶜ1931
Score 44 p.
From the opera in 3 acts with libretto by Théodore Reinach, based on The Persians by Aeschylus. Composed 1921-23.

End, Jack

END, JACK.   Rochester, New York 31 October 1918

5918 Floor show, for band   15'
1.Line number 2.Skating act 3.Toe dance
4.Comics 5.Grand finale
3,3,5*,3-4Sax.-4,3,3,2Bar.,2-Timp.,Perc.
Ms.
Score 48 p. Large folio
*Composed 1941. First performance Rochester,
11 May 1943, Eastman School Symphony Band,
Frederick Fennell conductor.*

5786 Portrait by a wind ensemble   17'
1.Recitative 2.March 3.Finale
3*,3*,11*(1Cl. in E-flat,1Cb.Cl.),4-4Sax.-4,
5,5,2-Timp.,Perc.-Cb.
Ms.
Score 59 p. Large folio
*Composed 1958. First performance at the 27th
Annual Festival of American Music, Rochester,
New York, 17 April 1958, Eastman School Wind
Ensemble, Frederick Fennell conductor.*

ENESCO, GEORGES.
        Liveni-Vîrnav, Romania 19 August 1881
                        Paris 4 May 1955

5797 Dixtuor, Op. 14
1.Doucement mouvementé 2.Tempo di menuet lent
3.Allègrement
2,2*,2,2-2Hn.
Ms.
Score 95 p.
Composed 1906.

2046 Poème roumain [symphonic suite, Op. 1]
3(3rd alt. Picc.),3*,2,4(2 ad lib.)-4,2,2Cnt.,
3,1-Timp.,Perc.-2Hp.-Men's Chorus(wordless,
offstage)-Str.
Enoch, Paris, c1899
Score 140 p.
*First performance at a Châtelet Concert, Paris,
6 February 1898, Edouard Colonne conductor.*

1282 Rumanian rhapsody, Op. 11 no. 1,   11'
A major
3(3rd alt. Picc.),3*,2,2-4,2,2Cnt.,3,1-Timp.,
Perc.-2Hp.-Str.
Kalmus, New York [n.d.]
Score 89 p.
*First performance at a concert given by Pablo
Casals, Paris, February 1908, the composer
conducting.*

507 Rumanian rhapsody, Op. 11 no. 2,   7'
D major
3,3*,2,2-4,2,3-Timp.,Cym.-2Hp.-Str.
Enoch, Paris [n.d.]
Score 30 p.

1155v Scherzino
Solo Vn.-Pno.-Str.
Monde Musical [n.p., n.d.]
Score 7 p.

1761 Suite d'orchestre, Op. 9   31'
1.[Prelude in unison] 2.[Slow minuet]
3.[Interlude] 4.Final
3*,2(2nd alt. E.H.),2,2-4,2,3-Timp.,Cym.-Hp.-
Str.
Enoch, Paris [n.d.]
Score 111 p.

769c Symphonie concertante [violoncello
and orchestra, Op. 8]
Assez lent - Majestueux - Plus vite
Solo Vc.-2,2*,2,2-4,2,3-Timp.-Str.
Enoch, Paris, c1938
Score 97 p.
*Composed 1901. First performance 14 March
1909.*

2045 [Symphony, Op. 13, E-flat major]   33'
1.Assez vif et rythmé 2.Lent 3.Vif et
vigoureux
3(3rd alt. Picc.),3*,3(1Cl. in E-flat),4*-4,2,
2Cnt.,3,1-Timp.,Perc.-2Hp.-Str.
Enoch, Paris [n.d.]
Score 157 p.
*First performance at a Châtelet Concert, Paris,
21 January 1906, Edouard Colonne conductor.*

ENGEL, JOEL (JULIUS) DIMITRIEVICH.
                Berdjansk, Russia 16 April 1868
                        Tel Aviv 11 February 1927

927m [Suite no. 1 for orchestra. Transcribed
for string quintet and clarinet by S. Beileson]
1.Leitmotiv 2.Wiegenlied 3.Zockl [Dance]
4.Chassunohnigun [Wedding song] 5.Skotschne
(Tanz) 6.Festive dance
Solo Cl.-Str.
Mussektor, Moscow, 1930
Score 17 p.

ENGEL, LEHMAN.
        b. Jackson, Mississippi 14 September 1910

6668 The creation, for narrator and   30'
orchestra
1.Introduction: Religioso 2.Chaos: Misterioso
3.The first day, light 4.The second day, heaven 5.The third day, earth and sea, green of
earth 6.The fourth day, moon, stars, and sun
7.The fifth day, whales and the lesser fish,
the birds, fish and fowl: Be fruitful! 8.The
sixth day, cattle and creeping things, recitative, man, blessing, recitative, chorale
Narrator(ad lib.)-3*,3*,3(3rd alt. B.Cl.),3*-
4,3,3,1-Timp.,Perc.-Pno.(alt. Cel.),Hp.-Str.
Associated Music Publishers, New York, c1949
Miniature score 93 p.
*Composed 1946. First performance New York,
20 June 1948, CBS radio broadcast, the composer conducting, Michael Redgrave narrator.*

ENGLISH, GRANVILLE.
        Louisville, Kentucky 27 January 1895
                        New York 1 September 1968

2999 Ballet fantasy   20'
1.Prelude - On an eastern isle 2.Scherzo -
Down the cliff the island virgin came 3.Inter-
mezzo - ...a moon roll'd on 4.Finale - The
island festival
3(3rd alt. Picc.),2,2,2-4,2,3,1-Timp.,Perc.-

Hp.-Str.
Ms.
Score [97] p. Large folio
*Composed 1936-37. Inspired by Lord Byron's
Don Juan. First performance Brooklyn, New
York, 25 June 1939, Federal Symphony Orchestra
of the WPA, Eugene Plotnikoff conductor.*

4477 Evening by the sea (tone picture)   10'
2,2(2nd alt. E.H.),2,2-4,3,3,1-Timp.,Perc.-
Str.
Ms.
Score 30 p.
*Composed 1951. First performance Babylon, Long
Island, 17 May 1951, Babylon Symphony, Christos
Vrionides conductor. Revised 1954; first per-
formance Port Washington, Long Island, 20
January 1956.*

4667 Scherzo, Among the hills   6'30"
2,2,2,2-4,3,3,1-Timp.,Perc.-Hp.-Str.
Ms.
Score 32 p. Large folio
*Composed 1948. First performance Rochester,
Eastman-Rochester Symphony Orchestra,
Howard Hanson conductor.*

ENNA, AUGUST.   Nakskov, Denmark 13 May 1860
                     Copenhagen 3 August 1939

5093 [Fairy tales, symphonic pictures]   22'
1.Lento maestoso - Allegro con brio 2.Andante
lento 3.Allegro vivace 4.Allegro - Lento
espressivo - Adagio espressivo - Allegro moderato
3*(1st alt. Picc.),2,2,2-4,2,2,1-Timp.,Trgl.,
Tamb.-Hp.-Str.
Breitkopf & Härtel, Leipzig, ᶜ1905
Score 126 p.

5006 [Flaming love. Overture]
3,3*,3*,2-4,2,3,1-Timp.,Trgl.-Hp.-Str.
Breitkopf & Härtel, Leipzig, ᶜ1903
Score 32 p.
*From the opera in 2 acts with libretto by Peter
Andreas Rosenberg from a story by Kálmán Miks-
záth. First performance Weimar, 2 December
1904.*

4276 [Hans Christian Andersen overture]   8'
3(3rd alt. Picc.),2,2,2-4,2,2,1-Timp.-Str.
Breitkopf & Härtel, Leipzig, ᶜ1905
Score 47 p.
Composed 1905.

ENRICHI, ARMINIO.

1943s Lento mistico
Str.
Edizioni Ditta R. Maurri, Florence, ᶜ1936
Score 2 p.

ENSOR, SAMUEL. New Windsor, Maryland 27 August 1917

6122 Verses from a children's book, for   20'
narrator and orchestra
Introduction 1.Rain 2.The seashore 3.The
clown 4.The sky 5.Spring romance 6.Music

7.Play-time 8.Lullaby 9.Snow 10.Marbles -
Conclusion
Narrator-2(2nd alt. Picc.),2(2nd alt. E.H.),2
(2nd alt. B.Cl.),2(2nd alt. C.Bn.)-3,2,2,2-
Timp.,Perc.-Pno.,Cel.,Hp.-Str.
Ms. ᶜ1952 by Samuel S. Ensor
Score 96 p. Large folio
*Verses by David A. Loscalzo, Jr. Composed 1952.
First performance Cincinnati, 12 February 1960,
Cincinnati Symphony, Max Rudolf conductor,
Charlotte Shockley narrator.*

ENTHOVEN, HENRI EMILE.   Amsterdam 18 October 1903
                         New York 26 December 1950

1609 Ichnaton suite, Op. 15a   9'
1.Prelude to the hymn of sun 2.The ambassadors
3.Ichnaton 4.Epilogue
3(3rd alt. Picc.),3,3,3*-4,4,3,1-Timp.,Gong-
Pno.,Cel.,2Hp.-Str.
Universal Edition, Vienna, ᶜ1927
Score 22 p.
*Composed 1926, for the play about the Egyptian
king. First performance Utrecht, 1926.*

EPHROS, GERSHON.
b. Serotzk, near Warsaw, Poland 15 January 1890

2204s Aeolian for strings   13'30"
1.Allegro con spirito 2.Pastorale hebraique
3.Finale
Str.(without Cb.)
Ms.
Score 36 p.
*First movement is transcribed from Part I of
the Piano Sonata, 1944. Composed 1961. This
is also known as String Quartet no. 2.*

6821 [Hebrew suite]
1.Meditation 2.Ritual dances 3.Pastorale
4.Festive dance
2(2nd alt. Picc.),2,2(2nd alt. B.Cl.),2-4,3,3,
1-Timp.,Perc.-Str.
Ms.
Score 87 p.

2203s Introduction, andante and fugue   9'
Str.(without Cb.)
Ms.
Score 20 p.
*Composed 1957. First performance Carnegie
Recital Hall, New York, 15 September 1957,
Kohon String Quartet.*

EPPERT, CARL.   Carbon, Indiana 5 November 1882
                 Milwaukee 1 October 1961

2753 The argonauts of forty-nine, symphonic 20'
epic, Op. 35
The great wagon train starts its journey (determination) - Forward, heads up, courage,
hope - Memories of home, sacrifices - Steady,
determination, forward - Nearing the goal -
Triumph, success, gold, sacrifices - Was it
really worth while? - Song of sadness, cry of
the lost souls left behind
3*,2,4*,4*-4,3,3,1-Timp.,Large Cym.-Hp.-Str.
Ms.

Eppert, Carl

Score 95 p.
*Composed 1920; revised 1933. First perform-
ance Milwaukee, 25 February 1938, Wisconsin
Symphony Orchestra of the WPA, Sigfrid Prager
conductor.*

3777 [Ballet of the vitamins. Suite no. 1, *18'*
Op. 69a]
1.Introduction: Discovery of vitamins - Part I:
Vitamin A 2.Part IV: Vitamin D - Strength,
exuberance, pride, sturdiness - Peace,
serenity, contentment (In the Chopin manner)
3.Part III: Vitamin C (Finale to Suite no. 1)
4(3rd&4th alt. Picc.),3*,4*(2nd alt. Cl. in
E-flat),4(4th alt. C.Bn.)-4,3,3,1-Timp.,Perc.-
Hp.-Str.
Ms.
Score 80 p. Large folio
*This suite is part I, IV, III respectively of
the ballet. Introduction, Parts I and IV composed 1937; Part III composed 1940. First
and second movements (Parts I and IV) awarded
first prize in the Chicago Symphony Orchestra
Golden Jubilee contest for American composers,
season 1940-41. First performance of first 2
movements, under the title Two Symphonic Impressions, Chicago, 13 February 1941, Chicago
Symphony Orchestra, Frederick Stock conductor.*

3778 [Ballet of the vitamins. Suite no. 2, *15'*
Op. 69b]
1.Passacaglia: Vitamin E 2.Interlude: Vitamin
B - Chromatic fugue
3(3rd alt. Picc.),3(3rd alt. E.H.),4*,4*-4,3,3,
1-Timp.,Perc.-Hp.-Str.
Ms.
Score 84 p. Large folio
*This suite is parts V and II, respectively, of
the ballet. First performance Detroit, 21
February 1942, Detroit Symphony Orchestra,
Victor Kolar conductor.*

972m [Concerto grosso, woodwinds and *24'*
string orchestra, Op. 73, C minor]
1.Andante sostenuto - Allegro energico
2.Andante cantabile 3.Scherzo 4.Finale
1,1,1,1-Str.
Ms.
Score 79 p.
*Originally composed as Op. 66 for woodwind
quartet, 1936-37; transcribed 1940. First performance Milwaukee, 26 November 1941,
Milwaukee Sinfonietta of the Milwaukee Friends
of Music, Julius Ehrlich conductor.*

2865 Escapade, a musical satire for *11'*
orchestra (Satirical portrait) Op. 68
3*,3*,4*,4*-4,3,3,1-Timp.,Perc.-Hp.-Str.
Ms.
Score 83 p.
*Composed 1937. First performance Indianapolis,
Indiana, 3 January 1941, Indianapolis Symphony
Orchestra, Fabien Sevitzky conductor.*

2749 [A symphony of the city. No. 1, *10'*
Traffic, symphonic fantasy for orchestra,
Op. 50]
4(3rd&4th alt. 2Picc. & Alto Fl.),2(2nd alt.

E.H.),5*(1Cl. in E-flat),4*-8,4,4,1-Timp.(2
players),Perc.-2Hp.-Str.
Ms.
Score 81 p.
*Composed 1931; the first of a four-part sym-
phonic cycle. First performance in a broadcast, New York, 8 May 1932, NBC Symphony
Orchestra, Eugene Goossens conductor. Awarded
third prize in an NBC competition, 1932.*

2750 [A symphony of the city. No. 2, *21'*
City shadows, symphonic tone poem, Op. 51]
4(alt. 2Picc.),3*,4*(1Cl. in E-flat),4*-4,3,
4,1-Timp.,Perc.-Hp.-Str.
Ms.
Score 89 p.
*Composed 1934. Parts two and three of the
cycle, City Shadows and Speed, were first per-
formed at the Fifth Annual Festival of Ameri-
can Music of the Eastman School of Music,
Rochester, 4 April 1935, Rochester Philharmonic
Orchestra, Howard Hanson conductor.*

2751 [A symphony of the city. No. 3, Speed, *8'*
Op. 53]
3*,2(2nd alt. E.H.),4*,4*-4,3,4,1-Timp.,Perc.-
Hp.-Str.
Ms.
Score 78 p.
Composed 1933.

2752 [A symphony of the city. No. 4, City *14'*
nights, symphonic romance, Op. 55]
4*(3rd alt. 2nd Picc.),3*,4*,4*-4,5,4,1-Timp.(2
players),Perc.-Hp.-Str.
Ms.
Score 80 p.
*Composed 1932. First performance Rochester,
New York, 30 October 1935, Rochester Philharmonic Orchestra, Howard Hanson conductor.*

2845 [Symphony no. 2, A little symphony, *18'*
Op. 65. Transcribed for chamber orchestra]
1.Allegro maestoso - Allegro moderato 2.Scher-
zando 3.Finale
2(2nd alt. Picc.),1,2,2-2Hn.,2Tpt.-Timp.,Perc.
-Hp.-Str.
Ms.
Score 99 p.
*Originally composed as Op. 52 for woodwind
quintet, 1933. Transcribed 1935. First per-
formance of transcription Composers' Forum
Concert, Milwaukee, Wisconsin, 21 May 1936,
Milwaukee Concert Orchestra of the WPA, the
composer conducting.*

2853 [Symphony no. 3, Symphony of the *35'*
land, Op. 67, C minor]
1.Tillage 2.Earth-born 3.Slow winter 4.The
yield
3(3rd alt. Picc.),3*,4*,4*-4,3,4,1-Timp.,Perc.
-Hp.-Str.
Ms.
Score 149 p. Large folio
Composed 1936.

3191 [Symphony no. 4, Timber, Op. 70, *30'*
F major]

1.The birth and growth of the great forests of Northwest America 2.The tranquility and peacefulness of the forests before the advent of man 3.Death of the great trees by man and their final glorification
3(alt. 2Picc.),3(3rd alt. E.H.),4*,4*-4,4,4,1-Timp.,Perc.-Org.(ad lib.),Hp.-Str.
Ms.
Score 88 p. Large folio
Composed 1938.

3285 [Symphony no. 5, A cameo symphony   *19'* for chamber orchestra, Op. 71, C major]
1.Allegro energico 2.Adagio 3.Finale (Andante - Allegro vivo)
1,1,1,1-2,1,1-Timp.,Cym.-Str.
Ms.
Score 73 p.
Composed 1939.

1791s [Symphony no. 6, for string   *24'* orchestra, Op. 72, G minor]
1.Allegro energico 2.Andante con moto (Canzonetta) 3.Scherzo (Vivace) 4.Finale (Andante - Allegro)
Str.
Ms.
Score 62 p.
Originally composed as String Quartet, Op. 62, 1935; transcribed 1939. First performance Hollywood, 3 December 1940, Hollywood Symphonic Players, Ellis Levy conductor.

ERB, MARIE JOSEPH.   Strasbourg 23 October 1858
                    Andlau 9 July 1944

2219 [Suite, Op. 29, D minor]   *27'*
1.Prelude 2.Gavotte 3.Canzone 4.March
2,2,2,2-4,2,3-Timp.-Str.
Reinecke, Leipzig [n.d.]
Score 43 p.
Composed 1893. First performance Strasbourg, 1893, Franz Stockhausen conductor.

ERICHS, H.

745s Elfengesang, Op. 74
Str.
Score: Ms. 3 p.
Parts: Oertel, Hannover [n.d.]

779s Elfenreigen [Dance of the elves] Intermezzo, Op. 175
Str.
Score: Ms. 7 p.
Parts: Oertel, Hannover [n.d.]

450s Le moulin [The mill] Op. 85
Timp.-Str.
Oertel, Hannover [n.d.]
Score 4 p.

666s Pizzicato, Op. 174
Str.
Score: Ms. 5 p.
Parts: Oertel, Hannover [n.d.]
From the opera Der Vagabond.

708s [Reminiscence, Op. 112]
Str.
Score: Ms. 6 p.
Parts: Oertel, Hannover [n.d.]

807s Stiefmütterchen [Pansy] Op. 98
Fl.-Str.
Score: Ms. 10 p.
Parts: Oertel, Hannover [n.d.]

691s [Suite in D. Intermezzo, Op. 78]
2Fl.-Str.
Score: Ms. 10 p.
Parts: Oertel, Hannover [n.d.]

1193s Tändelei [Frolic] Op. 183
Str.
Lehne, Hannover [n.d.]
Score 1 p.

ERIKSSON, NILS. Norrköping, Sweden 3 September 1902

1086m [Concerto, bassoon, B minor]   *23'*
1.Allegro con moto 2.Adagio espressivo 3.Allegro con fuoco e burlesco
Solo Bn.-2,2,2,2-2,2,3-Timp.-Str.
Ms.
Score 114 p.
First performance Norrköping, Sweden, 20 February 1944, Orchestra Society of Norrköping, Heinz Freudenthal conductor, Harry Axelsson soloist.

ERLANGER, CAMILLE.   Paris 25 May 1863
                  Paris 24 April 1919

1290 [Le juif polonais. Prelude to Act III]
3,2*,2,2-4,3,3,1-Timp.,Perc.-Str.
Paul Dupont, Paris [n.d.]
Score 10 p.
From the opera first performed Opéra Comique, Paris, 9 April 1900.

ERLANGER, FRÉDÉRIC D', BARON.   Paris 29 May 1868
                      London 23 April 1943

Also known as: Frédéric Regnal

964v [Concerto, violin, Op. 17, D major]   *32'*
1.Allegro moderato e maestoso 2.Andante 3.Allegro molto
Solo Vn.-2,2,2,2-4,2,3,1-Timp.,Trgl.-Hp.-Str.
Rahter, Leipzig, ᶜ1903
Score 96 p.
First performance at a London Philharmonic concert, 12 March 1903, Fritz Kreisler soloist.

ERLEBACH, PHILIPP HEINRICH.   Esens 25 July 1657
                   Rudolstadt 17 April 1714

1442s Ouverturen-Suite für Streicher, no. 3. Transcribed by Max Seiffert
1.Ouverture 2.Air 3.Air bourrée 4.Air 5.Air menuet [played alternatively with] 6.Air courante 7.Air trio 8.Air ballet 9.Air gavotte 10.Air la plainte 11.Air le sommeil 12.Air la réjouissance
Cemb.-Str.

Erlebach, Philipp Heinrich

Kistner & Siegel, Leipzig [n.d.]
Score 28 p.
No. 3 from VI Ouvertures, published 1693.

1443s Ouverturen-Suite für Streicher, no. 4.
Transcribed by Max Seiffert
1.Ouverture 2.Air gavotte 3.Air menuet I
4.Air menuet II 5.Air bourrée 6.Air
courante 7.Air entrée 8.Air gavotte 9.Air
traquenard 10.Air
Cemb.-Str.
Kistner & Siegel, Leipzig [n.d.]
Score 27 p.
No. 4 from VI Ouvertures, published 1693.

ERLER, HERMANN. Radeberg, near Dresden 3 June 1844
Berlin 13 December 1918

Also published under the pseudonyms: Charles
Morley, Ernst Scherz

714s Da capo polka [by] Ernst Scherz
Str.
Score: Ms. 4 p.
Parts: Ries & Erler, Berlin [n.d.]

267s Geburtstags-Musik [by] Ernst Scherz
Str.
Erler, Berlin [n.d.]
Score 15 p.

ERNST, HEINRICH WILHELM. Brünn 6 May 1814
Nice 8 October 1865

633v Le carnaval de Venise, Op. 18 [burlesque
variations on the canzonetta Cara Mamma Mia]
Solo Vn.-Str.
Score: Ms. 34 p.
Parts: Kistner, Leipzig [n.d.]

404v [Concerto, violin, Allegro pathétique,
Op. 23, F-sharp minor]
Solo Vn.-2,2,2,2-3,2,3-Timp.-Str.
Score in reduction: Peters [Leipzig, n.d.]
27 p.
Parts: Breitkopf & Härtel, Leipzig [n.d.]

569c Elegie, Op. 10. Transcribed by Joseph
Strebinger
Solo Vc.-Fl.,2Cl.-Str.
Joh. André, Offenbach a.M. [n.d.]
Score 11 p.
Originally for violin and piano.

507v Fantaisie brillante, on the March   7'
and Romance from Rossini's Othello, Op. 11.
New edition revised and marked by Edmund
Singer
Solo Vn.-2,2,2,2-2,2,3-Timp.-Str.
H. Litolff, Braunschweig [n.d.]
Score in reduction 15 p.

892v [Nocturne no. 1, Op. 8 no. 1, A   2'
major. Transcribed by Hugo Heermann]
Solo Vn.-Str.
Schott's Söhne, Mainz [n.d.]
Score 5 p.

893v [Nocturne no. 2, Op. 8 no. 2, E   4'
major. Transcribed by Hugo Heermann]
Solo Vn.-Str.
Schott's Söhne, Mainz [n.d.]
Score 8 p.

1063v Polonaise de concert, Op. 17
Solo Vn.-1,1,2,1-2Hn.-Str.
Ms.
Score 45 p.

405v Ungarische Melodien, Op. 22
Solo Vn.-3*,0,2,2-2,2-Timp.,Trgl.-Str.
Universal Edition, Vienna [n.d.]
Score in reduction 15 p.

ERSFELD, CHR.

1189s Schlummerlied, Op. 11
2 Solo Vn.-Str.
C. Simon, Berlin [n.d.]
Score 3 p.

981v Ständchen [Serenade, Op. 10, G major]
Solo Va.-Str.
Score: Ms. 7 p.
Parts: C. Simon, Berlin [n.d.]

ERTEL, PAUL.   Posen, Germany 22 January 1865
Berlin 11 February 1933

4571 [The nightly military review, sym-   15'
phonic poem for orchestra, Op. 16]
3*,3*,3*,3(3rd alt. C.Bn.)-4,3,3,1-Timp.,Perc.
-Hp.-Str.
Bote & Bock, Berlin, c1907
Score 48 p.
After the poem by Joseph Christian von Zedlitz.

ESCOBAR, AMEDEO.   Pergola, Italy 14 August 1888

3860 Sonata-jazz, per orchestra-jazz [Jazz   12'
sonata for jazz orchestra]
2Alto Sax.(alt. 1st and 3rd Cl.),Ten.Sax(alt.
2nd Cl.),Bar.Sax.,B.Cl.-0,3,2,1-Timp.,Traps,
Vib.-Pno.,Hp.,Guit.-Str.
Ricordi, Milan, c1940
Score 77 p.

ESCOT, POZZI.   Lima, Peru 1 October 1931

6372 Cristos   13'
1.The seven words 2.Martyrdom 3.Apotheosis
Alto Fl.,C.Bn.-Perc.-3Vn.
Ms.
Score 15 p.
*Inspired by Gospel accounts of Jesus' life.
Composed 1963. First performance Donnell
Library, New York City, 14 December 1963, Com-
posers' Forum, Arthur Weisburg conductor.*

6381 Lamentos   14'
1.Sema elariís 2.Los gritos oh dios 3.Él es
un niño 4.Quién 5.Neám amén
Sop. Voice Solo-Perc.-Pno.-2Vn.,2Vc.
Ms.
Score 28 p.
Text based primarily on words from James

Joyce's Silents in Finnegans Wake and on all possible permutations of the Spanish word for God, Dios; as well as isolated words from James Baldwin's Giovanni's Room and André Schwarz-Bart's The Last of the Just. Commissioned by the Inter-American Council of Music. Composed 1962.

6758 Sands   10'
5Sax.(SAATB)-4B.Dr.-Elec.Guit.-17Vn.,9Cb.
Ms.
Score 30 p.
Commissioned for the Third Festival of Music, Caracas, Venezuela, 1966. Composed 1965. First performance at the Third Festival of Music, 6 May 1966, National Symphony Orchestra of Venezuela, Gonzalo Castellanos conductor.

6496 Visione   10'
Female Narrator-Sop. Voice Solo-Fl.(alt. Alto Fl.&Picc.)-Perc.-Cb.
Ms.
Score 22 p.
The text is taken from Rimbaud, Kandinsky, Gertrude Stein, Gunther Grass, Howard Griffin, and the Bhagavad-Gita. Commissioned by Bertram Turetzky. Composed 1964. First performance New York, 20 November 1964, Hartt Chamber Players.

ESCRICHE, ERNESTO HALFFTER.
See: HALFFTER, ERNESTO.

ESPÉJO, CÉSAR.

1178v [Gypsy airs. Arranged for orchestra by L. Gaubert-Elgé]
Solo Vn.-1,1,2,1-2,2,1-Timp.-Str.
Henry Lemoine, Paris, c1926
Score 20 p.

ESPOILE, RAÚL H.   Mercedes, Buenos Aires 1889

3745 Frenos, Op. 64. Dance and Finale of   8'
the first set
3*,3*,3*,Basset Hn.,3*-4,2,3,1-Timp.,Perc.-Cel.,2Hp.-Str.
Privately published [n.p., n.d.]
Score 24 p.
From the opera in 4 acts. Composed 1919. First performance of opera Colón Theatre, Buenos Aires, 19 June 1928, Tullio Serafin conductor.

ESPOSITO, MICHELE.
        Castellamare, Naples 29 September 1855
                Florence 23 November 1929

2031 Irish suite, Op. 55   15'
1.Allegro maestoso ed energico 2.Allegretto vivace 3.Lento 4.Tempo di minuetto 5.Molto vivo
2(2nd alt. Picc.),2,2,2-4,2,3,1-Timp.,Perc.-Str.
C.E. Edition, Dublin, c1915 by M. Esposito
Score 99 p.

602s Neapolitan suite, Op. 69 [A major]   18'
1.Allegro con brio 2.Notturno 3.Intermezzo
4.Serenata 5.Tarantella
Str.(no. 2 has Solo Vn.; no. 4, Solo Vc.)
C.E. Edition, Dublin [n.d.]
Score 47 p.

DE L'ESTALEUX, PAUL JEAN-JACQUES LACOME.
See: LACOME DE L'ESTALEUX, PAUL JEAN-JACQUES.

ESTRADA, JUAN AGUSTÍN GARCÍA.
See: GARCÍA ESTRADA, JUAN AGUSTÍN.

ETCHECOPAR, M.

1429s Chanson tendre
Solo Vn.-Str.
Leduc, Paris, c1910
Score 17 p.

ETLER, ALVIN DERALD.
        Battle Creek, Iowa 19 February 1913
        Northampton, Massachusetts 13 June 1973

268m Concerto for string quartet and   18'30"
string orchestra
1. ♪ = 72-76 2. ♩ = 144 3. ♪ = 76
Solo Str. Quartet-Str.
Ms.
Score 51 p. Large folio
Composed 1948. First performance Urbana, Illinois, 1949, Walden String Quartet with the University of Illinois Sinfonietta, John Kuypers conductor.

301m Concerto for wind quintet and   18'
orchestra. Revised version
1.Maestoso - Allegro moderato 2.Lento 3.Allegro energico
Wind Quintet (Fl.,Ob.,Cl.,Hn.,Bn.)-4Hn.,4Tpt.,4Tbn.-Timp.,Perc.-2Hp.-Str.
Ms.
Score 97 p. Large folio
Composed 1960; revised 1962. First performance Tokyo, 18 October 1962, New York Woodwind Quintet with the Japan Philharmonic, Akeo Watanabe conductor. First performance of revised version Boston, 23 November 1962, Boston Symphony Orchestra, Erich Leinsdorf conductor.

6397 Concerto in one movement   14'30"
4*(1Alto Fl. in G),4*(2 are E.H.),4*(1Cl. in E-flat),4*-4,3,3,1-Timp.,Perc.-Str.
Ms.
Score 102 p. Large folio
Commissioned by the Cleveland Orchestra for its Fortieth Anniversary Season. Composed 1957. First performance Cleveland, Ohio, 12 October 1957, the Cleveland Orchestra, George Szell conductor.

6589 Dramatic overture for orchestra   9'
2,2,2,2-4,3,3,1-Timp.-Str.
Associated Music Publishers, Inc., New York, c1961
Score 59 p.
Composed 1956.

Etler, Alvin Derald

6597 Elegy for small orchestra (1959) *4'20"*
1,1,2,2-2Hn.-Str.
Associated Music Publishers, New York, ᶜ1961
Score 11 p.
*Composed 1959. First performance Northampton,
Massachusetts, December 1959, Smith-Amherst
Orchestra.*

3439 Music for chamber orchestra *15'*
1,1,1,1-2,1,1-Timp.,S.Dr.-Str.
Ms.
Score 83 p.
*Composed 1938. First performance at the Fifth
Yaddo Music Period, Saratoga Springs, New York,
10 September 1938, Yaddo Chamber Orchestra,
Arthur Shepherd conductor.*

6749 Triptych for orchestra (1961) *16'*
1. ♩ = 56 2. ♩ = 138 3. ♩ = 60
2(both alt. Picc.),2(2nd alt. E.H.),2(2nd alt.
B.Cl.),2(2nd alt. C.Bn.)-2,2,2-Timp.,Perc.-
Str.
Associated Music Publishers, New York, ᶜ1965
Score 66 p.
*Composed 1961. First performance Northampton,
Massachusetts, April 1962, Smith-Amherst
Orchestra, Edwin London conductor.*

ETTINGER, MAX.   Lemberg 27 December 1874
                         Basel 19 July 1951

3939 An den Wassern Babylons, Gesänge *15'*
babylonischer Juden, für kleines Orchester
1,1,1-0,2,1-Timp.,Perc.-Str.
Ms. ᶜ1940 by Jibneh [Vienna]
Score 76 p.

EVANS, DAVID.
        b. Resolve, Glamorganshire 6 February 1874

1327s [Concerto, string orchestra, Op. 7, D
major]
Str.
Stainer & Bell, London, ᶜ1928 by David Evans
Score 39 p.

EVETT, ROBERT. Loveland, Colorado 30 November 1922

309p Concerto for piano and orchestra *18'*
1.Allegro grazioso 2.Andante con moto 3.Rondo
Solo Pno.-1,1,1,1-1,1-Timp.(ad lib.)-Str.
Composers Facsimile Edition [n.p.] ᶜ1958 by
Robert Evett
Score 93 p. Large folio
*Composed 1956. First performance Washington,
D.C., 18 April 1958, National Gallery Orchestra,
Richard Bales conductor, Harry McClure pianist.*

6548 Symphony no. 2, Billy ascends *14'*
In one movement
Solo Baritone Voice-3(1 Alto Fl.),3*,3*,3*-4,3,
3,1-Timp.,Perc.-Cel.,Hpscd.-Str.
Ms.
Score 70 p. Large folio
*Text by Herman Melville, from his Billy Budd.
Commissioned by the Third Inter-American Music
Festival. Composed 1965. First performance
Washington, D.C., 7 May 1965, National*

*Symphony Orchestra, Howard Mitchell conductor,
John Langstaff baritone soloist.*

6616 Symphony no. 3 *25'*
1.Allegro ma non troppo 2.Vivace 3.Adagio
4.Variations on a theme by Sarah Warnock Evett
(1881-1959): Allegro vivace
2,2(2nd alt. E.H.),2,2-4,3,3,1-Timp.,Perc.-Str.
Ms.
Score 114 p. Large folio
*Commissioned by the National Gallery of Art,
Washington, D.C. Composed 1965. First performance Washington, D.C., 6 June 1965,
National Gallery Orchestra, Richard Bales
conductor.*

EVSTAFIEV, P.

3541 Poëme mélancolique, fantaisie pour
l'orchestre
3(3rd alt. Picc.),2,2,2-4,2,3,1-Timp.,Trgl.,
Cym.-Hp.-Str.
Bessel, St. Petersburg [n.d.]
Score 29 p.

EYMIEU, HENRY.   Saillans, France 7 May 1860
                        Paris 21 March 1931

1523s Air à danser, Op. 125
Str.
Score: Ms. 7 p.
Parts: Lemoine, Paris [n.d.]

F

FABINI, EDUARDO F.
                Solis del Mataojo, Uruguay 8 May 1883
                        Montevideo 17 May 1950

3703 Campo [The country] poema sinfónico
3*,3*,3*,2-4,2,3,1-Timp.-Hp.-Str.
Ricordi [n.p., n.d.]
Score 45 p.
*First performance Montevideo, Uruguay, 11
October 1931, Orquesta del Servicio Oficial
de Difusión Radio Eléctrica (SODRE), the com-
poser conducting.*

3877 Mburucuyá, quadro sinfónico del *10'*
balletto omonimo [Symphonic scene from the
ballet of the same name]
4(2 are Picc.),3*,2,2-4,2,3,1-Timp.,Perc.-Cel.,
Hp.-Str.
Ricordi, Milan, ᶜ1937
Miniature score 50 p.

FACCIO, FRANCO.   Verona 8 March 1840
                         near Monza 21 July 1891

1457s Ad un bambino [To a baby, lullaby for
flute and strings]
Solo Fl.-Str.
Ricordi, Milan [n.d.]
Score 8 p.

FAIRCHILD, BLAIR.
Belmont, Massachusetts 23 June 1877
Paris 23 April 1933

718m Concerto de chambre pour violon, piano et
quatuor à cordes, Op. 26
1.Allegro 2.Andante 3.Allegro
Solo Pno.,Solo Vn.-Str.(Cb. ad lib.)
Augener, London, c1912
Score 57 p.

618v Étude symphonique pour violon et orchestre,
Op. 45
Solo Vn.-3(3rd alt. Picc.),3*,2,2-4,2-Timp.-
Str.
Durand, Paris, c1922
Score 44 p.

773v Légende [for violin and orchestra, Op. 31]
Solo Vn.-2,2*,2,2-4,2,3,1-Timp.-Str.
Demets, Paris, c1911
Score 65 p.

668v Rhapsodie [for violin and orchestra]   12'
Solo Vn.-2,2,2,2-2,2-Timp.,Perc.-Str.
Schott, Mainz, c1924
Score 19 p.
Composed on religious and secular themes of
ancient times and the Middle Ages, collected
by the composer in different villages of Yemen
and of Galicia, inhabited by Hebrew sects.

2022 Shah Féridoûn, musical picture after a
Persian legend, Op. 39
3*,3*,3*,2-4,3,3,1-Timp.,Cym.,Side Dr.-Str.
Augener, London, c1915
Score 47 p.

2023 Tamineh [sketch for orchestra after a
Persian legend]
1.Songe d'amour - Les jardins de Tamineh 2.
Paysage - La jeunesse de Sohrab
2,2*,2,2-4,2,3,1-Timp.-Hp.-Str.
Augener, London, c1913
Score 52 p.

FALK, GEORG PAUL.   died 26 May 1778

6953 [Partita, D major]
1.Allegro 2.Andante 3.Minuet 4.Allegro
assai
2Fl.,2Ob.-2Hn.,2Tpt.-Cemb.-Str.
Score: Österreichischer Bundesverlag, Vienna,
c1949. Edited by Walter Senn. 27 p.
Parts: Ms.

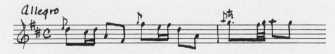

FALL, MORITZ.
Vienna 5 August 1848
Vienna 22 July 1922

785s Menuett, Op. 230 [G major]
Str.

Score: Ms. 3 p.
Parts: Apollo, Berlin, c1920
Bound with Krüger, An der Wiege des Kindes.

FALLA, MANUEL DE.
Cádiz 23 November 1876
Alta Gracia,
Córdoba, Argentina 14 November 1946

1594 El amor brujo   19'
1.Introduction and scene 2.At the gypsies
(The evening) 3.Song of love's sorrow 4.The
ghost 5.Dance of terror 6.The magic circle
(The fisherman's story) 7.Midnight (The magic
spell) 8.Ritual dance of the fire 9.Scene
10.Song of the will-o'-the-wisp 11.Pantomime
12.Dance of the game of love 13.Final (The
morning bells)
2(2nd alt. Picc.),1(alt. E.H.),2,1-2,2-Timp.,
Small Bells-Pno.-Voice in nos.3,10&12-Str.
J. & W. Chester, London, c1924
Score 108 p.
Composed 1913-14. First performance Teatro de
Lara, Madrid, 1915.

1072 El amor brujo. Le cercle magique   5'
(Récit du pêcheur) *and* Pantomime
2(2nd alt. Picc.),1,2,1-2,2-Timp.-Pno.-Str.
J. & W. Chester, London [n.d.]
Score 13 p.

4383 Aragonesa, pièce espagnole. Tran-   3'30"
scribed for orchestra by Hubert Mouton
1,1,2,1-2,2,1-Timp.,Cast.,Tamb.-Str.
Durand, Paris, c1923
Score in reduction 7 p.
Originally composed for piano as no. 1 of
Quatre Pièces Espagnoles, 1908.

579p [Concerto, harpsichord or piano,   10'
D major]
1.Allegro 2.Lento 3.Vivace
Solo Hpscd.-Fl.,Ob.,Cl.-Vn.,Vc.
Max Eschig, Paris, c1928
Score 42 p.
Composed 1926. First performance Barcelona,
5 November 1926, the composer conducting,
Wanda Landowska soloist.

3667 Fanfare pour une fête   30"
2Tpt.-Timp.,S.Dr.
Ms.
Score 4 p.
Composed ca.1921.

564 Noches en los jardines de España   25'
[Nights in the gardens of Spain, symphonic
impressions for piano and orchestra]
1.En el generalife 2.Danza lejana 3.En los
jardines de la Sierra de Córdoba
3*,3*,2,2-4,2,3,1-Timp.,Trgl.,Cym.-Pno.,Cel.,
Hp.-Str.
Max Eschig, Paris, c1923
Score 82 p.
Finished 1916. First performance London, 1921,
Edward Clark conductor, the composer as soloist.

1595 El sombrero de tres picos [The three-   12'
cornered hat. Three dances]

Falla, Manuel de

1.[The neighbors] 2.[The miller's dance (Far-
ruca)] 3.[Finale dance]
2(2nd alt. Picc.),3*,2,2-4,3,3,1-Timp.,Perc.-
Pno.,Cel.,Hp.-Str.
J.& W. Chester, London, c1925
Score 92 p.

1287 [La vida breve. Interlude *and* Dance] *7'*
3*,3*,3*,2-4,2,3,1-Timp.,Perc.-Cel.,2Hp.-Str.
Max Eschig, Paris, c1925
Score 44 p.
*From the opera in two acts, composed 1904-05.
First performance Casino Municipal, Nice, 1
April 1913. Awarded a prize by the Madrid
Real Academia de Bellas Artes.*

FANCHETTI, G.

778s J'y pense, air de ballet [for string
orchestra, Op. 5]
Str.
Score: Ms. 6 p.
Parts: Otto Wernthal, Berlin [n.d.]

112s Pizzicato-Arabeske [for string orchestra,
Op. 6]
Str.
Otto Wernthal, Magdeburg [n.d.]
Score 7 p.

FANELLI, ERNEST.   Paris 29 June 1860
                           Paris 24 November 1917

5592 Tableaux symphoniques. No. 1, Thèbes
1.Thèbes, devant le palais de Tahoser [Thebes,
before the palace of Tahoser]: Lento molto e
misterioso 2.Sur le Nil [On the Nile]: Allegro
moderato - Andante 3.Rentrée triomphale du
Pharaon [Triumphal return of the Pharaoh]: Allegro moderato
4*,3*,3*,4*-4,4,3-2Saxhorn(B.& Cb.)-Timp.,Perc.
-2Hp.-Mezzo-sop.-Str.
Max Eschig, Paris, c1912 by Le Monde Musicale
Score 91 p.
*Suggested by Théophile Gautier's novel, Roman
de la Momie. Composed 1883.*

FANFARES 1969 FOR 8 TRUMPETS.

7182   I. Reynolds, Jeffrey. ♩=60-72.   *7'*
       II. Bush, Irving. Maestoso.
      III. Campo, Frank. ♩=80.
       IV. Dutton, Fred. Medium slow.
        V. Kraft, William. ♩=70.
       VI. Schmidt, William. ♩.=76.
      VII. Rosenman, Leonard. ♩=120.
8Tpt.(2 in D,2 in C,2 in B-flat,2Bass Tpt.)
Avant Music, Los Angeles, c1970
Score 59 p.
*Commissioned by Thomas Stevens and Miles Ander-
son of the Los Angeles Brass Quintet. First
performance San Fernando Valley State College,
Northridge, California, 1 June 1969, William
Kraft conductor.*

FARAGO, MARCEL.   Timisoara, Romania 17 April 1924

7077 Children's march, Op. 35   *2'*
3*,2,2,2-4(3rd and 4th optional),4(3rd and 4th

optional),4(3rd&4th optional),1-Timp.,Perc.-
Hp.(optional)-Str.
Ms.
Score 21 p.
*Composed 1970. First performance Philadelphia,
4 December 1971, Philadelphia Orchestra,
William Smith conductor.*

430c [Concert fantasy for violoncello   *11'*
and orchestra, Op. 8]
Solo Vc.-2(2nd alt. Picc.),2,2,2-4,3,3-Timp.,
Perc.-Hp.-Str.
Ms.
Score 55 p.
Composed 1953.

363v [Concerto, violin and orchestra,   *35-38'*
Op. 11]
1.Quasi una cadenza 2.Intermezzo 3.Recita-
tivo 4.Lento 5.Finale
Solo Vn.-2,2,2,2-4,2,3-Timp.,Perc.-Hp.-Str.
Ms.
Score 45 p. Large folio
Composed 1955-56.

6409 Divertimento, Op. 17   *10'*
1.Overture: Allegro 2.Allegretto grazioso
3.Allegretto grazioso 4.Allegretto grazioso
5.Tempo di marcia: Molto allegro 6.Presto
7.Adagio 8.Finale: Allegro
1(alt. Picc.),1,1,1-1,1,1-Timp.,Perc.-Hp.-Str.
Ms.
Score 103 p. Large folio
Composed 1964.

6291 Prelude, interlude and postlude for *9'*
orchestra, Op. 10
[1]Prelude: Maestoso [2]Interlude: Andantino
quasi allegretto [3]Postlude
2(2nd alt. Picc.),2(2nd alt. E.H.),2,2-4,2,3,
1-Timp.,Perc.-Hp.-Str.
Ms.
Score 91 p. Large folio
Composed 1954.

210m Scherzo for 3 flutes, Op. 19b   *4'*
3Solo Fl.-B.Cl.-4Hn.,4Tpt.-Timp.,Perc.-Hp.-Str.
Ms.
Score 10 p.
*First performance Philadelphia, 3 April 1965,
Philadelphia Orchestra, William Smith con-
ductor.*

2141s Suite for strings, Op. 13   *12'*
1.Allegro 2.Lento 3.Allegretto grazioso
4.Allegro
Str.
Ms.
Score 35 p.
*Commissioned by Joseph Primavera. Composed
1958. First performance at the University of
Pennsylvania Museum, Philadelphia, 20 December
1958, Joseph Primavera conductor.*

FARINA, CARLO.   16th-17th century

1024s Die Torgauer Gagliarde und zwanzig
Brandi a 4. Edited by Hermann Diener

Str.
Kistner & Siegel, Leipzig, c1932
Score 8 p.
Die Torgauer Gagliarde was composed for the
wedding of Princess Sophie of Saxony and Georg
II of Hesse-Darmstadt in 1627.

FARKAS, EDMUND.   Puszta-Monostor, Hungary 1851
                         Klausenburg 1 September 1912

796s Szerenâd [Serenade for string orchestra,
D major]
1.Vonós-zenekarra 2.Romancz 3.Andante con
moto 4.Allegro
Str.(Solo Vn. in 2nd movement)
C.F. Schmidt, Heilbronn, c1904
Score 28 p.

FARNABY, GILES.   Truro, Cornwall, England ca.1560
                     buried London 25 November 1640

2370s Eight pieces for string orchestra.
Book I. Transcribed from keyboard pieces of
Farnaby and Byrd by Leslie Russell
1.Earle of Salisbury pavane (Byrd) 2.His
conceit (Farnaby) 3.His dreame (Farnaby) 4.
His humour (Farnaby)
Pno.(optional)-Str.
Oxford University Press, London, c1935
Score 4 p.
Transcribed from the Fitzwilliam Virginal
Book, compiled after 1621.

2371s Eight pieces for string orchestra.
Book II. Transcribed from keyboard pieces of
Farnaby and Byrd [sic] by Leslie Russell
1.Fantasia 2.A toye 3.His rest 4.Tower hill
[All by Farnaby]
Pno.(optional)-Str.
Oxford University Press, London, c1935
Score 35 p.

FARRAR, ERNEST BRISTOW.   Blackheath 7 July 1885
                      in action, France 18 September 1918

544s Three spiritual studies [for string
orchestra] Op. 33
1.Angelus 2.Introit 3.Credo
Str.
Stainer & Bell, London, c1925
Score 18 p.

FARWELL, ARTHUR. St. Paul, Minnesota 23 April 1872
                  New York 20 January 1952

702p Dawn, fantasy on Indian themes.   7'
Arranged for piano and small orchestra, Op. 12
Solo Pno.-1,1,2,1-2,1,1-Timp.-Str.
Ms.
Score 21 p.
Originally composed for piano, 1901; this
arrangement made 1926. First performance Pasa-
dena, California, Pasadena Community Playhouse,
21 February 1926, the Adolf Tandler Little
Symphony Orchestra, Adolf Tandler conductor,
Olive Heiss soloist.

2598 The gods of the mountain, suite for   15'
orchestra, Op. 52
1.The beggar's dreams 2.Maya of the moon 3.
Pinnacle of pleasure 4.The stone gods come
3(3rd alt. Picc.),3*,3*,3*-4,3,3,1-Timp.,Perc.
-2Hp.-Str.
Ms.
Score 73 p.
Commissioned by Stuart Walker for his Port-
manteau Theatre, 1917. Originally composed for
harp, violin and cello as preludes to the four
acts of Lord Dunsany's play. Orchestrated
1929; first performance Minneapolis, 13 Decem-
ber 1929, the Minneapolis Symphony Orchestra,
Henri Verbrugghen conductor.

2686 Pageant scene, Op. 39   10'
1.Processional entrance 2.Dance of idleness
3.Rustic dance 4.Recessional
1(alt. Picc.),1,2,1-2,2,1-Timp.,Small Dr.-Str.
Ms.
Score 76 p.
Commissioned by Kimball Union Academy, Meriden,
New Hampshire, 1913. Composed 1913. First
performance Meriden, New Hampshire, 24 June
1913, by an orchestra especially organized for
the Pageant of Meriden, the composer conducting.
This is a condensed version of that work.

2706 Rudolph Gott symphony, Op. 95   45'
1.Slowly 2.Slowly 3.Somewhat slowly 4.Fast
3(3rd alt. Picc.),3*,3*,3*-4,4,3,2-Timp.,Perc.
-Str.
Ms.
Score 312 p.
Completed 1934. Rudolph Rheinwald Gott (1872-
1911) died in the Philippine Islands; composer,
pianist and oboist, he was an intimate friend
of Arthur Farwell. The first movement is
based on an opening of 118 measures written
by Rudolph Gott about 1897 in a piano sketch
and intended for a symphony. The second and
third movements contain other of his themes.

2707 Symbolistic study no. 3, Once I passed
through a populous city, for orchestra, Op. 18
3(3rd alt. Picc.),3*,3*,3*-4,3,3,1-Timp.,Perc.
-Hp.-Str.
Ms.
Score 108 p.
Composed 1905, after the poem by Walt Whitman.
Orchestrated 1908, revised 1922. First per-
formance Philadelphia, 30 March 1928, Philadel-
phia Orchestra, Pierre Monteux conductor.

762p Symbolistic study no. 6, Mountain   15'
vision, concerto in one movement for two
pianos and string orchestra, Op. 37
2 Solo Pno.-Str.
Ms.
Score 63 p.
Originally composed for two pianos, 1912; this
version 1931. First performance in a broad-
cast, New York, 28 May 1939, CBS Orchestra,
Howard Barlow conductor, Karl Ulrich Schnabel
and Helen Fogel soloists. Won first prize and

Fasano, Renato

was awarded a nationwide broadcast in the
National Federation of Music Clubs Competition, 1939.

FASANO, RENATO.   Naples 21 August 1902

4874 [Heroic island, symphonic poem]   18'
3(3rd alt. Picc.),3*,2,2-4,3,3,1-Timp.,Perc.-
Pno.,Cel.,Hp.-Str.
Ricordi, Milan, c1942
Score 60 p.
Composed 1940.

FASCH, JOHANN FRIEDRICH.
             Buttelstedt, near Weimar 15 April 1688
             Zerbst, Germany 5 December 1758

6281 [Orchestra suite in B-flat major.   41'
Arranged by Hugo Riemann]
1.Ouverture: Grave - Presto - Grave 2.Air:
Andante sostenuto 3.Plaisanterie: Allegro
vivace 4.Air: Un poco allegro 5.Alla breve
6.Menuet I - Menuet II (Trio)
2Ob.,Bn.-Cemb.-Str.
Breitkopf & Härtel, Leipzig, [1950?]
Score 33 p.
Announced in the Breitkopf Thematic Catalog as
first published in 1765 under the title, Overture, Collection IV, no. 5.

(Grave)

5974 [Overture-suite for orchestra, E   25'
minor. Arranged by Günter Hausswald]
1.Ouvertüre: Largo - Allegro - Largo 2.Aria:
Andante 3.Bourrée 4.Aria: Largo 5.Gavotte
6.Menuet I - Menuet II
2,2,0,1-Str.-Cemb.
Breitkopf & Härtel, Leipzig, c1951
Score 24 p.

Largo

6510 [Symphony, G major] Edited by Max
Schneider
1.Allegro 2.Cantabile 3.Allegro
2Ob.,Bn.-2Hn.-Cemb.-Str.
Breitkopf & Härtel, Leipzig [1956]
Score 23 p.
Composed ca.1743.

FAURÉ, GABRIEL.   Pamiers, Ariège 12 May 1845
                       Paris 4 November 1924

525p Ballade, Op. 19 [F-sharp major]   13'
Solo Pno.-2,2,2,2-2Hn.-Str.
Hamelle, Paris [n.d.]
Score 59 p.
Originally composed for piano solo; orchestral
arrangement, 1881.

592v Berceuse [for solo violin and   4'30"
orchestra] Op. 16
Solo Vn.(or Vc.)-Fl.,Cl.-Str.
Hamelle, Paris [n.d.]
Score 11 p.
Originally composed for violin and piano, 1880.

875 [Dolly suite, 6 pieces for piano
duet, Op. 56. Transcribed for orchestra by
Henri Rabaud]
1.Berceuse 2.Mi-a-ou 3.Le jardin de Dolly
4.Kitty-valse 5.Tendresse 6.Le pas
espagnol
2(2nd alt.Picc.),2,2,2-4,2,3-Timp.,Perc.-Hp.-
Str.
Hamelle, Paris [n.d.]
Score 71 p.
Composed 1893-96. Orchestrated 1906. First
performance Paris, 1906, Rabaud conductor.

498c Élégie [violoncello and orchestra,   7'
Op. 24]
Solo Vc.-2,2,2,2-4Hn.-Str.
Hamelle, Paris [n.d.]
Score 19 p.
Originally composed for violoncello and piano,
1883.

458p Fantaisie [piano and orchestra,   18'
Op. 111, G major]
Solo Pno.-2,2,2,2-4,1-Timp.-Hp.-Str.
Durand, Paris, c1919
Score 80 p.
Composed 1919.

763 [Masques et bergamasques, Op. 112.   14'
Orchestral suite]
1.Overture 2.Minuet 3.Gavotte 4.Pastorale
2,2,2,2-2,2-Timp.-Hp.-Str.
Durand, Paris, c1919
Score 63 p.
From the stage work composed 1919 and first
performed Monte Carlo 10 April 1919. This
suite, 1920.

926 Pavane for orchestra and chorus (ad   5'
lib.), Op. 50
2,2,2,2-2Hn.-Vocal Quartet(ad lib.)-Str.
Broude Brothers, New York, c1952
Score 23 p.
Composed 1887. First performance Paris, 1888.

279 [Pelléas et Mélisande, Op. 80.   16'
Orchestral suite]
1.Prelude 2.Entr'acte - The spinner
3.Sicilienne 4.The passing of Mélisande
2,2,2,2-4,2-Timp.-Hp.-Str.
Kalmus, New York [n.d.]

Score 69 p.
*From the incidental music for the drama by
Maurice Maeterlinck. Composed 1898. First
performance London, 21 June 1898.*

585c [Pelléas et Mélisande, Op. 80. Entr'acte
no. 2, The spinner. Transcribed for violon-
cello and orchestra by F. Ronchini]
Solo Vc.-2,1,2,2-2,2-Hp.-Str.
Hamelle, Paris [n.d.]
Score [23 p.]

463 [Pelléas et Mélisande, Op. 80.   *3'*
Sicilienne]
2,1,1,1-2Hn.-Timp.-Hp.-Str.
Hamelle, Paris [n.d.]
Score 18 p.
*Originally composed as Op. 78, for violoncello
and piano; subsequently arranged for orchestra
and included in Pelléas et Mélisande.*

563c [Same as above. Arranged for violoncello
and orchestra]
Solo Vc.-2,0,2,1-2Hn.-Timp.-Str.
Hamelle, Paris [n.d.]
Score 18 p.

1058 [Pénélope, lyric poem in 3 acts.   *5'*
Prelude]
2,3*,3*,2-4,2,3,1-Timp.,Perc.-Str.
Heugel, Paris, c1913
Score 19 p.
*Composed 1913. First performance Monte Carlo,
4 March 1913.*

578v [Romance for violin, Op. 28, B-flat
major. Orchestrated by Ph. Gaubert]
Solo Vn.-2,1,2,2-Hn.-Hp.-Str.
Hamelle, Paris [n.d.]
Score 36 p.

515c Romance sans paroles, Op. 17 no. 3.
Transcribed for violoncello or violin solo and
small orchestra
Solo Vc.-1,1,1,1-Hp.-Str.
Hamelle, Paris [n.d.]
Score 15 p.
Originally composed for piano solo, 1883.

6003 Shylock, Op. 57   *21'30"*
1.Chanson: Allegro moderato 2.Entr'acte:
Andante moderato 3.Madrigal: Allegretto
4.Epithalame: Adagio 5.Nocturne: Andante
molto moderato 6.Final: Allegretto vivo
2,2,2,2-4,2-Timp.,Trgl.-2Hp.-Tenor Voice-Str.
J. Hamelle, Paris [189-?]
Score 87 p.
*Incidental music for Shakespeare's play, The
Merchant of Venice, as adapted by Edmond
Haraucourt. Composed 1889. First performance
Odéon, Paris, 17 December 1889.*

FAUST, GEORGE.
        b. New Brunswick, New Jersey 6 June 1937

6704 Adagio for small orchestra   *5'30"*
2,2,2,2-2Hn.-Hp.-Str.
Ms.

Score 17 p.
*Composed 1966. First performance Rochester,
New York, 5 May 1966, Eastman-Rochester Sym-
phony Orchestra, Howard Hanson conductor.
Received the Edward B. Benjamin Award for Quiet
Music, given May 1966 by the Eastman School of
Music.*

FEINBERG, SAMUEL EUGENIEVICH.   Odessa 26 May 1890
                                Moscow 23 October 1962

705p [Concerto, piano, Op. 20]   *26'*
In one movement
Solo Pno.-3(3rd alt. Picc.),2,3*,3*-4,2,3,1-
Timp.,Perc.-Str.
Mussektor, Moscow, 1934
Score 131 p.
*Composed 1931. First performance Voronezh,
1932, Konstantin Saradiev conductor, the com-
poser as soloist.*

FELLOWES, EDMUND HORACE.   London 11 November 1870
                           Windsor 20 December 1951

895s Eight short Elizabethan dance tunes by
un-named composers for string orchestra or
quintet. Edited by Edmund H. Fellowes
1.James his galliard 2.A toy 3.My robbin
4.Hollie berrie 5.Daphne 6.The wychie 7.
Tickle my toe 8.Strawberry leaves
Str.(without Cb.)
Stainer & Bell, London, c1924
Score 10 p.

FELTON, JAMES.   Philadelphia 9 October 1927

7287 Homage to Les Six   *ca.15'*
1.Moderate 2.Slow 3.Deliberate - Moderately
fast
4(4th alt. Picc.),4*,4*,4*-4,4,4,1-Timp.,Perc.
-Pno.,Cel.,2Hp.-Str.
Ms.
Score 51 p.
*Originally composed for piano 4-hands, 1973.
Arranged 1974. First performance (two movements only), Senior Student Concert, Academy
of Music, Philadelphia, 23 April 1975, Philadelphia Orchestra, William Smith conductor.
First performance of entire work Drexel University, Philadelphia, 22 May 1977, Orchestra
Society of Philadelphia, William Smith conductor.*

FENNER, BURT.   New York City 12 August 1929

7050 Symphony no. 2 in three movements, 1961
1. ♩ = 60 2. ♪ = 76 3. ♩ = 120
2,2,2(2nd alt. B.Cl.),2-4,3,3,1-Perc.-Str.
Ms.
Score 72 p. Large folio
*Composed 1961. Selected for performance by
the Orchestra Society of Philadelphia as part
of its Pennsylvania Composers Project 1974,
made possible by a grant from the Pennsylvania
Council for the Arts with performance materials
prepared by The Fleisher Collection of Orchestral Music. First performance Mandell Theatre,
Drexel University, Philadelphia, 22 June 1974,*

Fenner, Burt

*Orchestra Society of Philadelphia, Sidney
Rothstein conductor.*

7260   Symphony no. 3
1. ♩=120   2. ♩=60   3. ♩=160 – ♩=120 –
♩=160
2,2,2,2-4,3,3,1-Timp.,Perc.-Pno.-Str.
Ms. c1975 by Burt Fenner
Score 85 p.
*Composed 1975.   First performance University
Park, Pennsylvania, 15 May 1976, Pennsylvania
State University Symphony Orchestra, Douglas
Miller conductor.*

7300   Variations for string quartet and   12'
orchestra (1961)
Solo Str. Quartet-2,2,2,2-2,2,1-Timp.-Str.
Ms.
Score 42 p. Large folio
*Commissioned by the Mannes Orchestra.   Composed
1961.   First performance New York, February
1962, Mannes Orchestra, Carl Bamberger conduc-
tor.   Selected for performance by the Orchestra
Society of Philadelphia as part of its Pennsyl-
vania Composers Project 1977, made possible by
grants from the National Endowment for the Arts
and the Pennsylvania Council on the Arts with
performance materials prepared by the Fleisher
Collection of Orchestral Music.   Performed
Main Hall, Drexel University, Philadelphia, 24
April 1977, Orchestra Society of Philadelphia,
William Smith conductor.*

FENNEY, WILLIAM J.   Birmingham, England 21 May 1891
                                      Epsom July 1957

1597s   In the woods [for string orchestra with
solo violin]
Solo Vn.-Str.
J.&W. Chester, London, c1930
Score 4 p.

1605s   Prelude, aria and tarantella, for string
orchestra
Str.
Ms.
Score 39 p.

2347   Romance in early spring   5'
2,2,2,2-2Hn.-Timp.-Str.
Ms.
Score 12 p.
*Composed 1915.   First performance Birmingham,
30 March 1916, Granville Bantock conductor.*

FERGUSON, HOWARD.   Belfast 21 October 1908

3657   Partita, for orchestra   21'
1.Grave 2.Allegro un poco agitato 3.Andante
un poco mosso 4.Allegro con spirito
2(2nd alt. Picc.),3*,2,3*-4,3,3,1-Timp.,Perc.-
Hp.-Str.
Hawkes & Son, London, c1937
Score 101 p.
*Composed 1935-36.   First performance in a BBC
broadcast, London, 29 June 1937, BBC Orchestra, Adrian Boult conductor.*

FERLING.

705m   Andante de concert [clarinet and string
orchestra. Orchestrated by Paul Jeanjean]
Solo Cl.-Str.
Score: Ms. 5 p.
Parts: Evette & Schaeffer, Paris, c1924

FERNÂNDEZ, OSCAR LORENZO.
                      Rio de Janeiro 4 November 1897
                      Rio de Janeiro 26 August 1948

3330   Batuque, Negro dance from the opera   4'
Malazarte
3*,3*,3*,3*-4,3,3,1-Timp.,Perc.-Str.
New Music, Hollywood, c1939
Score 19 p.
*From the opera written on a poem by Graca
Oranha.   First performance Rio de Janeiro, 21
October 1933, Orchestra of the Instituto
Nacional de Musica, the composer conducting.*

1148v   [Concerto, violin, no. 1, A major]
In one movement
Solo Vn.-2,2(1st alt. E.H.),2(1st alt. B.Cl.),
2-2Hn.,2Tpt.-Timp.-Str.
Ms.
Score 59 p.

4162   [Hymn of the race]   10'
3*,3*,3*,3*-4,3,3,1-Timp.,Perc.-Str.
Ms.
Score 9 p.
*Commissioned by the government of Colombia.
Originally composed for chorus and orchestra,
1939, with a text by Guillermo Valencia.*

3765   Imbapâra (O suppliciado) [The   16'
sacrificed, Indian poem for large orchestra,
Op. 61]
3*,3*,3*,2,Sarrus.-2Sax.(AT)-4,4,3,1-Timp.,
Perc.-2Hp.-Str.
Ms.
Score 107 p.
*Composed 1929; a revised version is extant.
First performance Rio de Janeiro, 2 September
1929, Orchestra of the Escola Nacional de
Musica, Francisco Braga conductor.*

1022m   Nocturno, for alto saxophone and
chamber orchestra
Solo Alto Sax.-1,0,2-2Hn.-Pno.-Str.
Ms.
Score 6 p.
*Originally composed for voice and chamber
orchestra with a text by Eduardo Tauriulo, 1936.*

1060m   [The smooth shadow, Op. 59. Tran-   2'
scribed for alto saxophone and string
orchestra]
Solo Alto Sax.-Str.
Casa Vieira Machado, Rio de Janeiro [n.d.]
Score in reduction 3 p.
*Originally composed for voice and piano with
a text by Tasso da Silveira.*

FERNSTRÖM, JOHN.
　　　　I-Ch'ang, Hupei, China 6 December 1897
　　　　Hälsingborg, Sweden 19 October 1961

1087m [Concertino for flute with chamber　9'
orchestra and women's chorus, Op. 52]
Solo Fl.-2Cl.-Timp.,Cym.,Trgl.-Women's Chorus-
Str.
Ms.
Score 50 p.
Text from Carl Sandburg's poem, Early Moon.
Composed 1941. First performance Lund, Sweden,
1942, Orchestra Society of Lund, the composer
conducting, Carl Möller soloist.

1090m [Concerto, clarinet, Op. 30]　12'
1.Allegro moderato　2.Rondo
Solo Cl.-Timp.,Cym.-Str.
Ms.
Score 39 p.
First performance Hälsingborg, Sweden, 1937,
Orchestra Society of Northwest Scania, the
composer conducting, Nils Otteryd soloist.

2151s [Intimate miniatures for string　17'30"
orchestra, Op. 2]
1.Preludium　2.Intermezzo　3.Lamento (Adagietto)
4.Rondino
Str.
Edition Suecia, Stockholm, c1945 by Föreningen
Svenska Tonsättare
Score 14 p.
First performance Hälsingborg, Sweden, 1920,
Orchestra Society of Northwest Scania, Olof
Lidner conductor.

5021 [Symphony no. 6, Op. 12]　34'
1.Adagio - Moderato - Allegro vivo molto ener-
gico　2.Adagio cantabile - Andante　3.Scherzo:
Vivace　4.Finale: Maestoso e festivo - Presto
2(2nd alt. Picc.),3*,3*,2-4,3,3,1-Timp.,Cym.,
S.Dr.-Hp.-Str.
Ms.
Score 157 p.
First performance Malmö, 1941, Orchestra of
Malmö, the composer conducting.

5987 [Symphony no. 12, Op. 92]　33'
1.Introduktion: Långsamt - Allegro - Adagio
2.Giga fantastica　3.Finale: Grave - Allegro -
Grave
3*,3*,3*,2-2,2,3,1-Timp.,Perc.-Cel.-Str.
Ms.
Score 139 p.
Composed 1951. First performance over Sveriges
Radio, Stockholm, 22 August 1952, Stockholm
Radioorchester, Carl Garaguly conductor.

FERRABOSCO, ALFONSO (II).
　　　　Greenwich, England ca.1572(?) or ca.1575
　　　　buried Greenwich 11 March 1628

2015s The four note pavan. Scored from the
original version for viols by Arnold Dolmetsch.
Version for modern string instruments by
Percy A. Grainger
Str.
G. Schirmer, New York, c1944

Score 3 p.
Composed ca.1610.

FERRARIS, A.

1218s Serenade [piano and string orchestra,
F major]
Pno.-Str.
Score: Ms. 7 p.
Parts: Kuhl, Cologne, c1929

FERROUD, PIERRE-OCTAVE.
　　　　Chasselay, near Lyons, France 6 January 1900
　　　　Debrecen, Hungary 17 August 1936

4935 [Crowds, symphonic poem]　13'
3*,3*,3*,3*-Alto Sax.-4,4(1st alt. Tpt. in D),
3,1-Timp.,Perc.-Pno.,Cel.,2Hp.(2nd ad lib.)-
Str.
Durand, Paris, c1926
Score 81 p.
Composed 1922-24. First performance Paris,
21 March 1926.

4311 Sérénade　9'
1.Berceuse: Moderato assai　2.Pavane: Lento
3.Spiritual: Molto vivo
2,2(2nd alt. E.H.),2(2nd alt. B.Cl.),2-2,2,1-
Timp.(2 players),Perc.-Cel.(or Pno.),Hp.-Str.
Durand, Paris, c1928
Score 35 p.
Composed 1927.

4881 [Surgery, orchestral suite]　23'
1.Prélude: Lento　2.Mélodrame　3.Allegro
ritmico
3*,2*,3*,2*-4,3,3,1-Timp.,Perc.-Cel.,2Hp.(2nd
ad lib.)-Str.
Durand, Paris, c1928
Score 26 p.
Suite from the comic opera in one act with
libretto by Denis Roche and André G. Block,
after a story by Anton Chekhov. Opera composed
1927-28 and first performed Monte Carlo, 20
March 1928, Vincent Scotto conductor.

4880 [Symphony in A]　25'
1.Vivace　2.Andante: Espressivo assai　3.Alle-
gro con brio
3(3rd alt. Picc.),3*,3(3rd alt. B.Cl.),3*-4,3,
3,1-Timp.-Str.
Durand, Paris, c1931
Score 122 p.
Composed 1930. First performance at the Festi-
val of the International Society for Contem-
porary Music, Prague, 6 September 1935.

4936 [Youth. Orchestra suite from the　14'
ballet, no. 1]
3(3rd alt. Picc.),3*,4*(1Cl. in E-flat),3*-4,4,
3,1-Timp.,Perc.-Pno.,Cel.,2Hp.-Str.

Ferroud, Pierre-Octave

Durand, Paris, ᶜ1933
Score 92 p.
From the ballet in two scenes with scenario by
André Coeuroy and choreography by Serge Lifar.
Composed 1928-31. Ballet first performed
Paris, 29 April 1933.

4937 [Youth. Orchestra suite from the   *14'*
ballet, no. 2]
3(3rd alt. Picc.),3*,4*(1Cl. in E-flat),3*-4,
4,3,1-Timp.,Perc.-Pno.,Cel.,2Hp.-Str.
Durand, Paris, ᶜ1933
Score 151 p.

FESCA, FRIEDRICH ERNST. Magdeburg 15 February 1789
                         Karlsruhe 24 May 1826

4088 [Symphony no. 2, Op. 10, D major]
1.Poco adagio - Allegro molto assai 2.Andante
con moto 3.Scherzo presto 4.Allegro molto
assai
2,2,2,2-2Hn.,2Tpt.-Timp.-Str.
Ms.
Score 192 p.
Composed ca.1813.

FESTING, MICHAEL CHRISTIAN.   London ca.1680
                                   London 24 July 1752

178m [Concerto, 2 solo flutes, strings and
continuo, Op. 3 no. 11, E minor] Edited by
Richard Platt
1.Largo - Allegro - Largo 2.Allegro 3.Adagio
4.Allegro
2 Solo Fl.-Hpscd. or Org.-Str.
Oxford University Press, London, ᶜ1973
Score 24 p.
This edition based on parts first published by
William Smith, London, 1734.

FÉTIS, FRANÇOIS-JOSEPH. Mons, Belgium 25 March 1784
                         Brussels 26 March 1871

4247 L'amant et le mari [The lover and the
husband, Op. 9. Overture]
2,2,2,2-2Hn.-Str.
A la Lyre Moderne, Chez Mme. Benoist, Paris
[1820]
Score 19 p.
From the opéra-comique in two acts with
libretto by Victor Joseph Étienne and Jean
François Roger. First performance Théâtre
Royal de l'Opéra-Comique, Paris, 8 June 1820.

FETLER, PAUL.   Philadelphia 17 February 1920

6008 Contrasts for orchestra, a symphony   *20'*
in four movements
1.Allegro con forza 2.Adagio 3.Scherzo: Allegro ma non troppo 4.Allegro marciale - Presto
3*,3*,3*,3*-4,3,3,1-Timp.,Perc.-Pno.-Str.

Ms.
Score 112 p. Large folio
Commissioned by the American Music Center
under a grant from the Ford Foundation. Com-
posed 1958. First performance Minneapolis,
7 November 1958, Minneapolis Symphony, Antal
Dorati conductor.

FETRÁS, OSKAR.   Hamburg 16 February 1854
                         Hamburg 11 January 1931

Real name: Otto Faster

314s Schäfertanz [Shepherd's dance] Op. 132
Str.
Rahter, Leipzig, ᶜ1905
Score 5 p.

FÉVRIER, HENRI.   Paris 2 October 1875
                           Paris 6 July 1957

480s Gismonda. Interlude, Act III, La colline
des nymphes
2Hp.(or Pno.)-Str.
Heugel, Paris [n.d.]
Score 4 p.
From the opera first performed Paris, 15
October 1919.

1239 [Monna Vanna. Prelude to Act III,   *6'*
L'angoisse de Guido]
3*,3*,3*,3*-4,3,3,1-Timp.,Cym.,B.Dr.-Hp.-Str.
Heugel, Paris [n.d.]
Score 37 p.
From the opera based on the drama by Maurice
Maeterlinck, and first performed Paris, 13
January 1909.

596c La mort de Chrysis, no. 11 of the Suite
from the incidental music to Aphrodite
Solo Vc.-2,1,2,1-Timp.-Hp.-Str.
Heugel, Paris, ᶜ1915
Score 109 p.

FIAMINGO, CHARLES.

1062v Danse infernale, caprice fantastique
[for violin and orchestra, Op. 13]
Solo Vn.-3*,2,2,2-4Hn.-Trgl.-Str.
Forlivesi, Florence [n.d.]
Score 58 p.

FIBICH, ZDENKO.   Šeboršitz 21 December 1850
                         Prague 15 October 1900

1051s Bagatelles, Op. 19 [Transcribed by
Julius Rauscher]
1.[Waltz] 2.[From 1001 Nights]
Str.
F.A. Urbánek, Prague [n.d.]
Score 7 p.

285 [In the evening, idyl for orchestra,   *8'*
Op. 39]
3,3*,3*,2-4Hn.-Timp.,Cym.,Trgl.-Hp.-Str.
F.A. Urbánek, Prague [n.d.]
Score 47 p.
Composed 1893. First performance Prague, 8
April 1895, Adolf Čech conductor.

1613 [A night at Karlstein, Op. 26. Over-   7'
ture]
2,2,2,2-4,2,3-Timp.,Trgl.-Str.
Státní Nakladatelství Krásné Literatury, Hudby
a Umění, Prague, c1954
Score 59 p.
*Composed 1886. First performance Prague, 25
March 1886, Adolf Čech conductor.*

1883 [Othello, symphonic poem, Op. 6]   10'
3*,2,3,2-4,4,3,1-Timp.,Cym.,Trgl.-Hp.-Str.
F.A. Urbánek, Prague [n.d.]
Score 55 p.
*Composed and first performed Prague, 1873,
Bedřich Smetana conductor.*

808v [Poem. Arranged for violin solo by   3'
Jan Kubelik. Orchestrated by Jan Janota]
Solo Vn.-1,1,2,1-2,2,1-Str.
F.A. Urbánek, Prague, c1911
Score in reduction 7 p.
*Fragment from In the Evening, Op. 39.
Arranged by Kubelik 1908, by Janota 1911.*

1844s Poem. [Transcribed for string   4'
orchestra by Arcady Dubensky]
Str.
Ms.
Score 5 p.
*Originally composed for violin and piano.
First performance broadcast over Station WQXR,
New York, 1938, Eddy Brown conductor.*

1507 [Symphony no. 2, Op. 38, E-flat   25'
major]
1.Allegro moderato 2.Adagio 3.Scherzo 4.
Finale: Allegro energico
3,3*,3*,2-4,2,3,1-Timp.-Str.
F.A. Urbánek, Prague, c1911
Score 175 p.
*Composed 1892. First performance Prague, 9
April 1893, the composer conducting.*

1884 Veseloherni ouvertura [Comedy over-   6'
ture, Op. 35]
2,2,2,2-2,2-Timp.-Str.
Ms.
Score 53 p.
*Composed 1873. First public performance
Prague, 29 April 1883, Kopecki conductor.*

FIBY, HEINRICH.   Vienna 15 May 1834
                           Znaim 23 October 1917

[Two fantasy pieces for string orchestra,
Op. 32]
1358s No. 1. Wiegenlied
1361s No. 2. Mignon
Str.
A. Robitschek, Leipzig [n.d.]
Scores: 5 p., 7 p.

FICHER, JACOBO.   Odessa, Ukraine 14 January 1896

1145v Concerto [violin, Op. 46]   20'
1.Allegro 2.Lento 3.Allegro maestoso
Solo Vn.-2,2,2,2-4,2,3,1-Timp.-Str.
Ms.

Score 57 p. Large folio
*Composed 1942. Awarded Honorable Mention in
the invitation contest for a violin concerto
by Latin American composers, anonymously sponsored and supervised by the Edwin A. Fleisher
Music Collection of the Free Library of Philadelphia, 1942. First performance Buenos Aires,
17 July 1944, Orquesta Sinfónica de la Asociación de Músicos de la Argentina, the composer
conducting, Anita Sujovolsky soloist.*

3797 Los invitados [The guests. Complete   17'
ballet in 7 scenes, Op. 26]
Fl.,Cl.-2Sax.(AT)-0,2,1,1-Perc.-Pno.
Ms.
Score 167 p.
Composed 1933. Libretto by Boris Romanoff.

2298s Serenata, string orchestra, Op. 61   22'
1.Sonatina 2.Elegía 3.Danza 4.Rondo final
Str.
Editorial Argentina de Música, Buenos Aires,
c1964
Score 95 p.
*Composed 1947. First performance Buenos Aires,
1948, Orquesta Juvenil Argentina, Luis Gianneo
conductor.*

6757 [Shulamite, poem of love, Op. 8.   18'
Revised version 1960]
3*,3*,3*,3*-4,3,3,1-Timp.,Perc.-Cel.,Hp.-Str.
Ms.
Score 85 p.
*Suggested by Alexander Ivanovich Kuprin's
romantic novel, Shulamite. Composed 1927;
revised 1960. First performance (original
version), Buenos Aires, 20 June 1929, Asociación
del Profesorado Orquestal, Nikolai Malko conductor. Awarded first prize by the municipality
of Buenos Aires in 1931.*

3739 Sinfonia de cámara no. 1, Op. 20   15'
1.Lento - Allegro moderato 2.Lento - Allegro
assai 3.Scherzo - Allegro scherzando
4.Allegro
1,1(alt. E.H.),1,1-2Hn.,Tpt.-Timp.-Str.
Ms.
Score 80 p.
*Composed 1932. First performance Buenos Aires,
2 December 1932, Asociación del Profesorado
Orquestal, the composer conducting.*

3874 Suite symphonique no. 2, Op. 6   23'
1.Preludio 2.Scherzo 3.Andante 4.Allegro
final
3*,3*,3*,3*-4,3,3,1-Timp.,Perc.-Hp.-Str.
Ms.
Score 105 p.
*Composed 1926. First performance (of 2nd move-
ment only) Buenos Aires, 26 August 1926,
Asociación del Profesorado Orquestal, Ernest
Ansermet conductor. First performance (of 1st
and 3rd movements only) Buenos Aires, 9 July
1927, Asociación del Profesorado Orquestal,
Henry Hadley conductor.*

3826 [Symphony no. 2, Op. 24]   24'
1.Andante 2.Lento 3.Allegro molto

Ficher, Jacobo

3*,3*,3*,3*-4,3,3,1-Timp.-Hp.-Str.
Ms.
Score 122 p.
*Composed 1933. First performance Buenos Aires,
23 October 1939, Orchestra AGMA (Asociación
General de Músicos Argentinos), the composer
conducting.*

3880 [Symphony no. 3, Op. 36]   *32'*
1.Allegro moderato 2.Lento 3.Scherzo 4.
Allegro
3*,3*,3*,3*-4,3,3,1-Timp.-Hp.-Str.
Ms.
Score 244 p.
*Composed 1938-40. Awarded 1st prize by the
Comisión Nacional de Cultura, 1940.*

5783 [Symphony no. 4, Op. 60]   *31'*
1.Andante 2.Allegro agitato 3.Scherzo
4.Lento
3*,3*,3*,2-4,2,3,1-Timp.-Str.
Ms.
Score 111 p. Large folio
Composed 1946.

6680 [Symphony no. 5, Thus spake Isaiah,   *30'*
Op. 63]
1.Destruction 2.Consolation 3.Reconstruction
3*,3*,3*,3*-4,3,3,1-Timp.,Perc.-Str.
Ms. ᶜ1950 by Edition Argentina de Musica
Score 112 p.
*Prompted by the Second World War. Commis-
sioned by and dedicated to the Hebrew Society
of Argentina, Buenos Aires, 1947. Composed
1947. First performance Colón Theater, Buenos
Aires, 15 August 1954, Philharmonic Orchestra
of the City of Buenos Aires, the composer
conducting.*

6666 [Symphony no. 6, Op. 86]   *32'*
1.Allegro moderato 2.Andante 3.Scherzo:
Allegro scherzando 4.Allegro
3*,3*,3*,3*-4,3,3,1-Timp.,Perc.-Str.
Ms. ᶜ1956
Score 138 p. Large folio
Composed 1956.

3850 Tres bocetos sinfónicos, Op. 17 [Three
symphonic sketches, inspired by the Talmud]
1.Andante: Mesichta (Tema) 2.Allegro molto:
Plugta (Discusión) 3.Allegro moderato:
Mascana (Conclusión)
3*,3*,3*,2-4,3,3,1-Timp.-Str.
Ms.
Score 147 p.
*Composed 1930. Awarded 1st prize in the com-
petition sponsored by the Asociación del
Profesorado Orquestal, Buenos Aires, 1934.*

3730 [Two poems for chamber orchestra,   *8'*
Op. 10; nos. 16 and 42 from The Gardener of
Rabindranath Tagore]
1,1,1,1-2Hn.-Str.
Ms.
Score 30 p.
*Composed 1928. First performance Buenos Aires,
23 December 1928, Orquesta Renacimiento, Juan
José Castro conductor.*

FICKENSCHER, ARTHUR. Aurora, Illinois 9 March 1871
                      San Francisco 15 April 1954

3032 Day of judgment   *15'*
3(3rd alt. Picc.),3*,3*,3*-4,2,3,1-Timp.,Perc.
-Hp.-Str.
Ms.
Score 25 p. Large folio
*Composed 1927. First performance Grand Rapids,
Michigan, 10 February 1934, Grand Rapids Sym-
phony Orchestra, Karl Wecker conductor.*

3033 Out of the Gay Nineties   *9'*
3(3rd alt. Picc.),3*,2,2-4,2,3,1-Timp.,Perc.-
Hp.-Str.
Ms.
Score 25 p. Large folio
*Completed 1934. First performance Richmond,
Virginia, 4 December 1934, Richmond Symphony
Orchestra, the composer conducting.*

FIEDLER, MAX.   Zittau 31 December 1859
                   Stockholm 1 December 1939

1794 Lustspiel-Ouverture, Op. 11   *12'*
2,2,2,2-4,2,3-Timp.-Hp.-Str.
Ries & Erler, Berlin [n.d.]
Score 49 p.
*Composed 1913. First performance Essen, 1915,
the composer conducting.*

2436 Serenade, Op. 15 [G major]   *25'*
2,2,2,2-2,2-Timp.,Trgl.,Small Dr.-Str.
Ries & Erler, Berlin, ᶜ1932
Score 46 p.

FIELD, JOHN.   Dublin 26 July 1782
                   Moscow 23 January 1837

487p [Concerto, piano, no. 1, E-flat major]
1.[No tempo indicated] 2.Air ecossaise 3.
Rondo
Solo Pno.-1,2,0,2-2,2-Timp.-Str.
Ms.
Score 95 p.

503p [Concerto, piano, no. 3, E-flat major] *28'*
[1]Allegro moderato [2]Rondo
Solo Pno.-2,2,2,2-2,2-Timp.-Str.
Ms.
Score 240 p.

481p [Concerto, piano, no. 4, E-flat major] *25'*
[1]Allegro moderato [2]Adagio [3]Rondo
Solo Pno.-1,0,2,2-2,2-Timp.-Str.
Ms.
Score 272 p.
First published 1819.

504p [Concerto, piano, no. 6, C major]
In one movement: Allegro moderato - Larghetto
- Rondo
Solo Pno.-1,2,2,2-2,2,1-Timp.-Str.
Ms.
Score 198 p.

547p [Concerto, piano, no. 7, C minor]
[1]Allegro moderato [2]Rondo

Solo Pno.-2,2,2,2-2,2,1-Timp.-Str.
Ms.
Score 173 p.

FIELITZ, ALEXANDER VON.   Leipzig 28 December 1860
                          Bad Salzungen 29 July 1930

265 Vier Stimmungsbilder [Four character-   8'
     istic pieces, Op. 37]
     1.Idylle: Andantino con moto 2.Entr'acte:
     Andante 3.Hymnus: Andante religioso
     4.Scherzo capriccioso: Allegro giusto
     3*,3*,2,2-4,2,3-Timp.-Hp.-Str.
     Breitkopf & Härtel, Leipzig, c1904
     Score 41 p.
     *Composed 1900. First performance Berlin, 1901,
     the composer conducting.*

FILIPPI, AMEDEO DE. Ariano, Italy 20 February 1900

     Also known as: Philip Weston

7033 Blow the man down, sea chanty for   2'40"
      orchestra
      1,1,2,1-2,2,1-Timp.,Perc.-Pno.,Hp.-Str.
      Ms.
      Score 26 p. Large folio
      *Based on the traditional American sea chanty.
      Commissioned by CBS, 1941. Composed 1941.
      First performance New York City, 26 March
      1941, Columbia Symphony Orchestra on CBS
      Radio, Howard Barlow conductor.*

4150 Concerto for orchestra   15'
      1.Allegro 2.Adagio 3.Allegro non troppo,
      vigoroso
      3(3rd alt. Picc.),3*,3*,3*-4,3,3,1-Timp.-Str.
      Concord Music Publishing Co., New York, c1940
      Score 60 p.
      *Originally composed for flute, oboe, bassoon,
      horn, trumpet and strings, 1928; re-orchestra-
      ted by the composer 1940.*

1807s Diversions   14'
       1.Mock march 2.Waltz ostinato 3.The rival
       serenaders 4.Barn dance
       Str.
       Ms.
       Score 18 p. Large folio
       *Composed 1931. First performance Boston, 28
       April 1940, Woman's Symphony Society, Alexander
       Thiede conductor.*

7035 Down in the valley, American tune   2'40"
      1,1,2,1-2,2,1-Perc.-Pno.-Str.
      Ms.
      Score 14 p. Large folio
      *Commissioned by CBS, 1940. Composed 1940.
      First performance New York City, 12 March 1940,
      Columbia Symphony Orchestra on CBS Radio,
      Howard Barlow conductor.*

3350 Medieval court dances, based on   18'
      dance tunes from 13th century manuscripts
      1.Estampie 2.Trotto 3.Danse royale 4.Bal-
      letto (Lamento di Tristano) 5.Saltarello
      3(3rd alt. Picc.),3(3rd alt. E.H.),0,3(3rd alt.
      C.Bn.)-4,3,3,1-Timp.,Perc.-Hp.-Str.

Ms. c1940 by Amedeo de Filippi
Score 122 p.
*Composed 1938. First performance Chicago, 16
January 1940, Woman's Symphony Orchestra of
Chicago, Izler Solomon conductor.*

1798s Music for recreation   10'
       1.Intrada 2.Wistful air 3.Pizzicato 4.Pas-
       tel 5.Bergamask
       Str.
       E. Ascher, New York, c1940
       Score 14 p.
       Composed 1927.

7034 On Springfield mountain, for   2'50"
      orchestra
      1,1,2,1-2,2,1-Timp.,Perc.-Pno.-Str.
      Ms.
      Score 21 p. Large folio
      *Commissioned by CBS, 1939. Composed 1939.
      First performance New York City, 12 December
      1939, Columbia Symphony Orchestra on CBS Radio,
      Howard Barlow conductor.*

3351 Overture to Shakespeare's Twelfth   9'
      Night
      3(3rd alt. Picc.),2,2,2-4,2,3,1-Timp.-Str.
      Ms.
      Score 46 p. Large folio
      *Composed 1935. First performance Chelsea,
      Massachusetts, 20 May 1940, Chelsea Federal
      Symphony Orchestra of the WPA, Alexander
      Thiede conductor.*

7037 Raftsman's dance. Version for small   3'15"
      orchestra
      1,1,2,1-2,2,1-Timp.,Perc.-Pno.-Str.
      Ms.
      Score 20 p. Large folio
      *Commissioned by CBS, 1939. Composed 1939.
      First performance New York City, 5 December
      1939, Columbia Symphony Orchestra on CBS Radio,
      Howard Barlow conductor.*

2357s Two American sketches for string   4'
       orchestra
       1.Georgia boy 2.The boll weevil
       Pno.(optional)-Str.
       Ms.
       Score 16 p.
       *Commissioned by CBS, 1940. Composed 1940.
       First performance New York City, 7 April 1940,
       Columbia Symphony Orchestra on CBS Radio,
       Howard Barlow conductor.*

FILIPPUCCI, EDMUND.

586c Le chant du souvenir [The song of
      remembrance]
      Solo Vc.-1,1,2,2-2,0,2Cnt.,3-Timp.-Hp.-Str.
      Enoch, Paris, c1911
      Score 20 p.

1461s Élégie, Op. 45 [D minor]
       Solo Ob.(or Vn.)-Str.
       Enoch, Paris [n.d.]
       Score 4 p.

Filtz, Anton

FILTZ, ANTON.   (?)Bohemia ca.1730
                buried Mannheim, Germany 14 March 1760

   Also published as: Anton Fils, Anton Filz and
   Anton Fieltz

   4673 Symphony in E-flat. Arranged by Adam
      Carse
      1.Allegro 2.Andante 3.Presto
      2Fl.(optional)-2Hn.(optional)-Str.
      Augener, London, ᶜ1937
      Score 13 p.
      Listed in the Breitkopf Thematic Catalog,
      Supplement II, 1776, as one of Six Sympho-
      nies, Group II, no. 1.

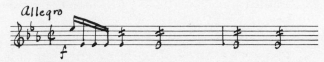

   6790 [Symphony no. 8, E-flat major]
      1.Allegro 2.Larghetto 3.Minuetto 4.Presto
      2 Ob.-2Hn.-Cemb.-Str.
      Ms. ᶜ1976 by The Fleisher Collection of
      Orchestral Music, Free Library of Philadelphia
      Score 24 p. Large folio

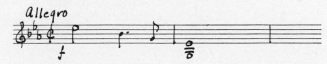

   4500 [Symphony in A major, Bohemian.   *5'30"*
      Arranged and edited by Robert Sondheimer]
      1.Allegro molto 2.Allegretto 3.Vivace
      Ob.,Bn.-2Hn.-Hpscd.(or Pno.)-Str.
      Edition Bernoulli, Berlin, ᶜ1932 by Robert
      Sondheimer
      Score 18 p.
      Listed in the Breitkopf Thematic Catalog,
      Supplement II, 1767, as one of Four Sympho-
      nies, Group V, no. 1.

FINE, IRVING.   Boston 3 December 1914
                                 Boston 23 August 1962

   2099s Serious song, a lament for string   *9'30"*
      orchestra
      Str.
      Ms.
      Score 17 p.
      Commissioned by the Louisville Orchestra,
      Robert Whitney, music director. Composed 1955.
      First performance Louisville, 16 November 1955,
      Louisville Orchestra, Robert Whitney conductor.

   4398 Toccata concertante   *10'*
      3*,3*,3*,3*-4,2,3,1-Timp.,Perc.-Pno.-Str.
      Ms.
      Score 75 p. Large folio
      Composed 1947. First performance Boston, 22
      October 1948, Boston Symphony Orchestra,
      Serge Koussevitzky conductor.

FINE, VIVIAN.   Chicago, Illinois 28 September 1913

   267p Concertante for piano and orchestra   *15'*
      1.Andante con moto 2.Allegro risoluto
      Solo Pno.-2(2nd alt. Picc.),2,2,2-2,2-Timp.-
      Str.
      Ms. ᶜ1957 by Vivian Fine
      Score 83 p.
      Composed 1943-44. First performance (first
      movement only) New York, 14 March 1948, radio
      performance by WOR Symphony, Sylvan Levin con-
      ductor, the composer as soloist.

   393c Divertimento for violoncello and   *5'*
      percussion
      Solo Vc.-Timp.,Cym.,Tamb.,W.Block,S.Dr.
      Ms. ᶜ1952 by Vivian Fine
      Score 11 p.
      Composed 1951. First performance Storm King
      Art Center, Mountainville, New York, 19 August
      1962, Hudson Valley Philharmonic Society,
      Sterling Hunkins violoncellist, James Coover
      percussionist.

FINNEY, ROSS LEE. Wells, Minnesota 23 December 1906

   3695 Barber shop ballad, the dark-eyed   *4'30"*
      canaler
      1,1,2(1st alt. Alto Sax.),1-2,2,2,1-Timp.,Perc.
      -Pno.-Str.
      Ms.
      Score 17 p.
      Commissioned by CBS for the American School of
      the Air, 1940. Composed 1939. First perform-
      ance New York, 6 February 1940, CBS Orchestra,
      Bernard Herrmann conductor.

   770p Concerto, piano   *20'*
      1.Grave - Allegro moderato 2.Maestoso con
      variazioni 3.Rondo
      Solo Pno.-2,2,2,2-4,2,3,1-Timp.-Str.
      Ms.
      Score 91 p.
      Originally composed as a piano sonata, 1934;
      transcribed 1935.

   6651 Hymn, fuguing, and holiday [revised   *10'*
      version]
      Hymn - 8 Variations - Fuguing I - Fuguing II -
      Holiday - Hymn
      3*,3*,3*,3*-4,3,3,1-Timp.,Perc.-Cel.(ad lib.),
      2Hp.(2nd ad lib.)-Str.
      Ms. [ᶜ1965 by Carl Fischer]
      Score 60 p. Large folio
      The hymn is William Billings' Berlin. Com-
      posed 1943. First performance at the Ditson
      Festival, New York, 17 May 1947, Alfred Wallen-
      stein conductor. Revised 1956. First perform-
      ance of revised version, 15 January 1966, Miami
      Philharmonic Orchestra, Fabien Sevitzky con-
      ductor.

3603 Overture for a drama, F minor   15'
3*,3*,3*,3*-4,3,3,1-Timp.,Perc.-Str.
Ms.
Score 77 p.
*Composed 1938. First performance Rochester,
New York, 28 October 1941, at a symposium by
the Eastman-Rochester Symphony Orchestra,
Howard Hanson conductor.*

3690 Prelude   7'
3*,3*,2,3*-3Sax.(Sop.,Alto,Bar.)-4,3,3,1-Timp.,
Perc.-Str.
Ms.
Score 57 p.
Composed 1937.

1805s Slow piece for string orchestra   5'
Str.
Ms.
Score 7 p.
*Originally composed as the slow movement of
Sonata for Cello and Piano; transcribed for
string orchestra, 1940, at the request of
Dimitri Mitropoulos. First performance
Minneapolis, 4 April 1941, Minneapolis Symphony
Orchestra, Dimitri Mitropoulos conductor.*

7076 Summer in Valley City, for band   16'30"
1.Fanfare 2.Interlude 3.Parade 4.Games 5.
Fireworks 6.Night
5(2Picc.),3*,7*(Cl. in E-flat,4Cl. in B-flat,
E-flat Cb.Cl. ad lib.),3*-4Sax.-4,4,4,2Bar.,2-
Timp.,Perc.
Henmar Press Inc., New York, c1971
Score 76 p.

FINZI, ALDO.   Milan 1897

5194 [The infinite, symphonic poem for
orchestra]
3(3rd alt. Picc.),3*,3*,3*-4,3,3,1-Timp.,Perc.
-Pno.,Cel.,2Hp.-Str.
Ricordi, Milan, c1935
Miniature score 41 p.

FINZI, GERALD.   London 14 July 1901
                           Oxford 27 September 1956

1892 A Severn rhapsody for chamber orchestra
1,1(alt. E.H.),1(alt. B.Cl.)-Hn.-Str.
Stainer & Bell, London, c1924 by Gerald Finzi
Score 11 p.
First performance London, 1 December 1925.

FIOCCO, JOSEPH-HECTOR.   Brussels 20 January 1703
                             Brussels 22 June 1741

452c [Concerto, violoncello and orchestra,
G major] Edited by Paul Bazelaire
1.Allègre 2.Modéré et gracieux 3.Lent et très
expressif 4.Très animé
Solo Vc.-Str.
Schott Frères, Brussels, c1937
Score 23 p.
*This work misattributed to Fiocco; actual
composer unknown.*

FIORILLO, DANTE.   New York 4 July 1905

3537 Concerto [for wind instruments and   30'
orchestra]
1.Largo 2.Courante 3.Hymnus 4.Finale
Concertino: Fl.,Cl.,Tpt.,Tbn.,Bn.
Orchestra: Timp.,Perc.-Str.
Ms.
Score 81 p.

2908 Introduction and passacaglia   11'
2*,2*,3*,2*-4,3,2,1-Timp.,Perc.-Str.
Ms.
Score 60 p.

3001 Partita on themes by an 18th century   23'
Fiorillo (Ignazio Fiorillo)
1.Invenzione 2.Chaconne 3.Furiant 4.Finale
2,2,2,2-3,2,3,1-Timp.-Str.
Ms.
Score 119 p.

1744s Preludio e fuga [for string orchestra, 7'
Op. 86]
Str.
Ms.
Score 19 p.
*Composed 1926. First performance of Prelude
only, Philadelphia, 28 March 1934, Chamber
Orchestra of Philadelphia and Composers' Labora-
tory, Isadore Freed conductor. First complete
performance New York, 1935, New York Civic
Orchestra.*

FISCHER, ADOLF.   Brussels 20 November 1847
                          Brussels 18 March 1891

687c Romance, Op. 5
Solo Vc.-2,2,2,2-2Hn.-Str.
Score: Ms. 10 p.
Parts: Leuckart, Leipzig [n.d.]

FISCHER, IRWIN.   Iowa City, Iowa 5 July 1903

6632 Overture on an exuberant tone row   8'
3*,2,2,2-4,3,3,1-Timp.,Perc.-Str.
Composers Facsimile Edition, New York, c1965
by Irwin Fischer
Score 48 p.
*Composed 1965. First performance Shreveport,
Louisiana, 30 November 1965, John Shenaut
conductor.*

FISCHER, JOHANN KASPAR FERDINAND.   ca.1650
                             Rastatt 27 March 1746

1225s Festmusik [Arranged for trumpets and
strings by Hilmar Höckner]
1.Ouverture 2.Entrée 3.Canaries 4.Gavotte
en rondeau 5.Passepied 6.Echo 7.Menuet
2Tpt.(ad lib.)-Str.
Kallmeyer, Berlin, 1929
Score 27 p.
From the Journal du Printemps (1695).

Fisher, John Abraham

FISHER, JOHN ABRAHAM.   London 1744
                           probably London May 1806

6150 [The syrens. Overture]
2Ob.-2Hn-Str.
Score: Ms. ᶜ1976 by The Fleisher Collection of
Orchestra Music, Free Library of Philadelphia.
23 p. Large folio
Parts: Printed for Ab Portal opposite the New
Church, Strand, London [ca.1777]
*Overture to the masque by Captain Edward
Thompson. Composed 1775. First performance
of the masque, London, 17 November 1775.*

FITELBERG, GREGOR.   Dvìnsk, Latvia 18 October 1879
                           Katowice 10 June 1953

1614 [Polish rhapsody, Op. 25]   *24'*
4*,4*,4*,4*-6,3,3,1-Timp.,Perc.-Hp.-Str.
Universal Edition, Vienna, ᶜ1914
Score 67 p.
Composed 1913. First performance Cracow, 1917.

284 [Symphony, Op. 16, E minor]   *20'*
1.Andante – Allegro agitato 2.Andante 3.
Scherzo 4.Finale: Allegro agitato
3*,3*,3*,2-4,2,3,1-Timp.,Perc.-Hp.-Str.
Breitkopf & Härtel, Leipzig, ᶜ1904
Score 140 p.
Composed 1903. First performance Warsaw, 1905.

1615 W głębi morza [At the bottom of the   *30'*
sea, tone picture in the form of an overture,
Op. 26]
4*,4*,4*,4*-6,3,3,1-Timp.,Perc.-Hp.-Str.
Universal Edition, Vienna, ᶜ1914
Score 72 p.
Composed 1915. First performance Cracow, 1917.

FITELBERG, JERZY.   Warsaw, Poland 20 May 1903
                              New York 25 April 1951

1617s [Concerto for string orchestra]   *18'*
In one movement
Str.
Universal Edition, Vienna, ᶜ1931
Score 36 p.
*Originally his String Quartet no. 2, composed
1928.*

1904s The golden horn, variations on a
Polish folksong for string orchestra
Str.
Dimit Edition, New York, ᶜ1943
Score 72 p.

6650 Nocturne for orchestra   *15'*
3(3rd alt. Picc.),3*,3*,3(3rd alt. C.Bn.)-4,
3,3,1-Timp.,Perc.-Hp.-Str.

Ms. ᶜ1945 by Associated Music Publishers, New
York
Score 65 p. Large folio
*Composed 1944. First performance New York, 28
March 1946, New York Philharmonic, Arthur
Rodzinski conductor.*

2376 Der schlecht gefesselte Prometheus   *35'*
[Loosely bound Prometheus, concert suite from
the ballet]
1.Overture 2.Ballad 3.The death of Damocles
4.Berceuse 5.Tango 6.Final
3*,2(2nd alt. E.H.),3(1Cl. in E-flat),3*-4,3,3,
1-Timp.,Perc.-Pno.-Str.
Ms.
Score 145 p.
Composed 1929.

FITZENHAGEN, WILHELM KARL FRIEDRICH.
                  Seesen, Brunswick 15 September 1848
                        Moscow 14 February 1890

678c Ballade for violoncello and orchestra,
Op. 10, F-sharp minor
Solo Vc.-2(2nd alt. Picc.),2,2,2-2,2,3-Timp.-
Str.
Ms.
Score 105 p.

669c [Concerto, violoncello, no. 1, Op. 2,
B minor]
In one movement
Solo Vc.-2,2,2,2-2,2,3-Timp.-Str.
Score: Ms. 85 p.
Parts: Breitkopf & Härtel, Leipzig [n.d.]

649c [Concerto, violoncello, no. 2, Op. 4,
A minor]
In one movement
Solo Vc.-2,2,2,2-2,2,1-Timp.-Hp.-Str.
Score: Ms. 119 p.
Parts: Breitkopf & Härtel, Leipzig [n.d.]

574c Resignation, [violoncello and orchestra,
sacred song without words, Op. 8]
Solo Vc.-1,1,2,1-2Hn.-Vc.,Cb.
Breitkopf & Härtel, Leipzig [n.d.]
Score 7 p.

FLAGNY, LUCIEN DE.   d. Paris May 1927

Real name: Lucien Grou

709s Pavane (Ancient air). Transcribed by
Lucien de Flagny. Arranged for string orchestra
by M. Laistner
Str.
Score: Ms. 5 p.
Parts: Schott, Mainz, ᶜ1912

FLAMENT, ÉDOUARD.   Douai 27 August 1880
                      Bois-Colombes 27 December 1958

1543s Langueur d'amour [for string orchestra,
Op. 99 no. 1]
Str.
Score: Ms. 4 p.
Parts: Ricordi, Paris, ᶜ1929

FLÉGIER, ANGE.   Marseilles 25 February 1846
                      Marseilles 8 October 1927

  982s Stances [Stanzas, for string orchestra]
    Str.
    Score: Ms. 6 p.
    Parts: Gallet, Paris [n.d.]

FLEISCHER, E.

  806s Nachtgesang *and* Pizzicato Gavotte [for
  string orchestra]
    Str.
    Score: Ms. 10 p.
    Parts: Oertel, Hannover [n.d.]

FLEISCHMANN, FRIEDRICH.
      Markleidenfeld near Würzburg 18 July 1766
             Meiningen 30 November 1798

  4099 [Symphony, Op. 5, A major]
    1.Allegro 2.Andante 3.Allegro 4.Presto
    1,2,0,2-2Hn.-Str.
    Ms.
    Score 113 p.
    Copied from printed edition of 1799.

FLEISCHMANN, OTTO.   Hamburg 15 December 1867
                  Hamburg 29 July 1924

  842m [Concertino, trombone and orchestra,
  Op. 35, B-flat major]
    In one movement: Allegro moderato - Adagio -
    Rondo: Allegretto
    Solo Tbn.-2,2,2,2-4,2,1-Timp.-Str.
    Score: Ms. 68 p.
    Parts: Benjamin, Leipzig [n.d.]

FLETCHER, GRANT.
      b. Hartsburg, Illinois 25 October 1913

  5466 Nocturne, Op. 4 no. 8, for orchestra   *5'*
    3(3rd alt. Picc.),2*,2,2-4,2,3,1-Timp.,Perc.-
    Hp.-Str.
    Ms.
    Score 35 p.
    Originally composed as no. 8 of 10 Nocturnes
    for piano solo, 1934. Orchestrated 1938.
    First performance of this version Abilene,
    Texas, 15 February 1954, Abilene Symphony,
    Julius Hegyi conductor.

  5460 The pocket encyclopedia of orchestral   *6'*
  instruments
    Speaker-2,2,2,2-2,2,2-Timp.-Str.
    (May be performed with only one each of the
    wind instruments, and Tbns. & Timp. may be
    omitted)
    Ms.
    Score 34 p.
    Commissioned by Carl A. Baumann. Composed
    1953. First performance Chicago, 18 April
    1953, Chicago Symphonietta, the composer con-
    ducting.

  468m Rhapsody for flute and strings   *12'*
    Solo Fl.-Str.
    Ms.
    Score 43 p.
    Composed 1935. First performance Rochester,
    New York, 19 October 1944, Rochester Symphony,
    Howard Hanson conductor, Joseph Mariano solo-
    ist.

  5465 A rhapsody of dances for orchestra   *9'*
    2,2,2,2-2,2,2-Timp.,Cym.-Str.
    (Fl.II, Ob.II, & Bn.II are optional)
    Ms.
    Score 45 p.
    Composed 1935, for the Phi Mu Alpha Little Sym-
    phony of Illinois Wesleyan University. First
    performance Ann Arbor, Michigan, 25 July 1938,
    University of Michigan Symphony, the composer
    conducting.

  6815 Seven cities of Cibola   *14'*
    The power of Spain - Conquest - Envy - Lust -
    Anger - Avarice - Gluttony - Pride - Recuerdos
    - Sloth - The power of Spain shall wax and wane
    2(2nd alt. Picc.),2,2,2-4,2,3,1-Timp.,Perc.-Pno.
    -Str.
    Ms.
    Score 101 p. Large folio

  5461 Symphony no. 1   *25'*
    1.Fast 2.Slow but with movement 3.Fast
    2,2,2,2-2,2-Timp.-Str.
    Ms.
    Score 181 p.
    Composed 1950. First performance Rochester,
    New York, 26 April 1951, Rochester Symphony,
    Howard Hanson conductor.

  6764 Two orchestral pieces   *13'*
    1.Sumare: Very slow - Very passionately 2.
    Wintare: Gravely
    2,2,2,2-2,2,1-Timp.-Str.
    Ms.
    Score 53 p.
    Sumare, after the poem Heat by Hilda Doolittle;
    Wintare, from a tune entitled The Gonesome Days
    of Summer. Commissioned for and dedicated to
    Thor Johnson. Composed 1956. First perform-
    ance Fish Creek, Door County, Wisconsin, Door
    County Festival Symphony, Thor Johnson conductor.

FLETCHER, PERCY E.   Derby 12 December 1879
                 London 10 September 1932

  1685s Balade *and* Bergomask [for string   *9'*
  orchestra]
    Str.(Cb. ad lib.)
    Boosey & Hawkes, London, c1931
    Score 12 p.

  1324s Folk tune *and* Fiddle dance, suite   *8'*
  for strings
    Str.
    Score: Ms. 26 p.
    Parts: Hawkes & Son, London, c1914

Fletcher, Percy E.

974s Two bagatelles for string orchestra   5'
1.Valsette   2.Pizzicato
Str.
Score: Ms. 14 p.
Parts: Novello, London, c1911

FLICK-STEGER, CHARLES.
b. Saylesville, Rhode Island 13 December 1899

3335 Slawisches Intermezzo, Op. 19   7'
1(alt. Picc.),1,2,1-2,2,1-Timp.,Perc.-Str.
Ms.
Score 65 p.
*Composed 1929. First performance Munich, 5
May 1929, Orchestra of the Munich Radio Sta-
tion, Franz Haupt conductor.*

FLIEGE, HERMANN. Stendal, Germany 9 September 1829
St. Petersburg November 1907

5897 [Chinese serenade, Op. 132 no. 2]
2(2nd alt. Picc.),2,2,2-4,2-Timp.,Perc.-Str.
[H. Erler, Berlin, n.d.]
Score 11 p.

FLIEGNER, H.

1195s Märchen [for string orchestra] Op. 22
Str.
Lehne, Hannover [n.d.]
Score 1 p.
Bound with Robert Lehmann, Abendruhe, Op. 33.

FLIES, BERNHARD.   Berlin ca.1770

1452s Wiegenlied. Arranged by C. Walther
Solo Hn.-Str.
Breitkopf & Härtel, Leipzig [n.d.]
Score 5 p.
Bound with Schubert, Wiegenlied.

FLOERSHEIM, OTTO. Aix-la-Chapelle 2 March 1853
Geneva 30 November 1917

5719 [Consolation, symphonic movement]
2,2,2,2-4Hn.-Str.
Breitkopf & Härtel, Leipzig, c1901
Score 16 p.

FLORES, BERNAL. San José, Costa Rica 28 July 1937

2266s Symphony no. 1 [for strings]   14'
In one movement
Str.
Ms.
Score 73 p.
*Commissioned by the Esso Oil Co. for the Third
Inter-American Music Festival of Washington,
D.C., 1965. Composed 1965. First performance
Washington, D.C., 8 May 1965, Festival Orches-
tra, Guillermo Espinosa conductor.*

FLORIDIA, PIETRO. Modica, Sicily 5 May 1860
New York 16 August 1932

7015 [Vittoria. Madrigal from the opera]
Bass-Bar. Voice Solo-2,2,2,2-4,2,2,1-Hp.-Str.
Ms.
Score 12 p.

FLORIO, CARYL. Tavistock, England 3 November 1843
Morgantown, South Carolina 21 November 1920

Real name: William James Robjohn

6466 Bolero for small orchestra
Fl.,Cl.-2Cnt.,Tbn.-Str.
Ms.
Score 67 p.

258p [Concerto, piano, A-flat major]
1.Allegro moderato 2.Rhapsodie (Es war ein
Traum): Largo 3.Finale: Moderato - Allegro
con maesta
Solo Pno.-3*,2,2,2-4,2Cnt.,2,1-Timp.,Cym.-Str.
Ms.
Score 142 p.
*Composed 1875. Re-orchestrated 1886. Revised
1915.*

6451 Marche triomphale
2*,2,2,2-4,2,2Cnt.,3,1-Timp.,Perc.-Str.
Ms.
Score 16 p.
Composed 1878.

290m Reverie, for solo violin, solo violoncello,
2 clarinetti and string orchestra
Solo Vn.,Solo Vc.-2Cl.-Str.
Ms.
Score 9 p.
Composed 1872.

6448 Scherzo for solo violin, solo violoncello,
2 clarinetti and string orchestra
Solo Vn.,Solo Vc.-2Cl.-Str.
Ms.
Score 22 p.
Composed 1872.

6468 Symphony no. 1, G major
1.Allegro moderato 2.Scherzo: Allegro leggiero
3.Finale: Allegro con moto
3*,2,2,2-4,2Cnt.,3,1-Timp.,Trgl.-Str.
Ms.
Score 116 p.
*Composed 1887. First performance Steinway
Hall, New York, 27 March 1888, Theodore Thomas
Orchestra, Theodore Thomas conductor.*

6472 [Symphony no. 2, C minor]
1.Largo - Allegro molto 2.Romanza 3.Scherzo
4.Episode and finale
3*,2,2,2-4,0,2Cnt.,3,1-Timp.-Str.
Ms.
Score 148 p.
*Composed 1887. First performance Steinway
Hall, New York, 27 March 1888, Theodore Thomas
Orchestra, Theodore Thomas conductor.*

FLOTOW, FRIEDRICH VON.
Teutendorf 27 (not 26) April 1812
Darmstadt 24 January 1883

4275 [Alessandro Stradella. Overture]   7'
2(2nd alt. Picc.),2,2,2-4,2,3-Timp.,Trgl.,B.Dr.
Str.
Cranz, Hamburg [n.d.]

Score 24 p.
*Originally composed as incidental music to the
play Stradella by Paul Duport and Philippe
Auguste Pittaud de Forges, based on the life
of composer Alessandro Stradella (1642-82).
First performance Palais-Royal, Paris, 4 Feb-
ruary 1837. Rewritten for the opera in 3 acts
with libretto by Friedrich Wilhelm Reise.
First performance in this form, Hamburg, 30
December 1844.*

1253 Martha. Overture   9'
2*,2,2,2-4,2,3,1-Timp.,Perc.-Str.
Choudens, Paris [n.d.]
Score 35 p.
Composed 1847.

4396 [Rübezahl. Overture]
2*,2,2,2-4,2,3,Ophicl.-Timp.,Trgl.,B.Dr.-Str.
Johann André, Offenbach am Main [1875]
Score 40 p.
*From the opera in three acts with libretto by
Gustav Heinrich Gans zu Putlitz. Composed
1853. First performance Frankfurt, 26 Novem-
ber 1853.*

FOCHEUX, JULIEN.

665s Dormez, mignonne [lullaby for string
orchestra]
Str.
Score: Ms. 5 p.
Parts: Durand, Paris [n.d.]

710s Espièglerie [Frolic, pizzicato polka for
string orchestra]
Str.
Score: Ms. 6 p.
Parts: Durand, Paris [n.d.]

372s Rêverie [for string orchestra]
Str.
Leduc, Paris [n.d.]
Score 4 p.

FOCK, A.

1521s Aubade [for string orchestra, G major]
Str.
Score: Ms. 10 p.
Parts: Lemoine, Paris [n.d.]

FOCK, GERARD VON BRUCKEN.
See: BRUCKEN-FOCK, GERARD VON.

FOERSTER, ADOLPH MARTIN.
Pittsburgh 2 February 1854
Pittsburgh 10 August 1927

6452 The falconer, Op. 31
2(2nd alt. Picc.),2,2,2-4,2,3-Timp.,Tamb.-Str.
Ms.
Score 59 p.
*After the poem by Karl Schäfer. Composed 1893.
First performance Scranton, Pennsylvania, 29
December 1893, the composer conducting.*

6369 [Thusnelda, after Karl Schäfer's poem,
Op. 10]
3*,2,2,2-4,2,3,1-Timp.-Str.
Ms.
Score 16 p.

FOERSTER, JOSEF BOHUSLAV.   Prague 30 December 1859
Nový Vestec, near Stará Boleslav 29 May 1951

373s [Andante cantabile and Allegretto (Viola
and Rosa), Op. 3]
Str.
F.A. Urbánek, Prague, ᶜ1914
Score 5 p.

821v [Concerto, violin, Op. 88, C minor]   35'
1.Allegro moderato 2.Andante sostenuto
Solo Vn.-2(2nd alt. Picc.),2(2nd alt. E.H.),2,
2-4,2,3-Timp.,Trgl.-Cel.,Hp.-Str.
Universal Edition, Vienna, ᶜ1913
Score 76 p.
*Composed 1911. First performance New York,
1911, Jan Kubelik soloist.*

2373 In den Bergen [symphonic poem, Op. 7]   30'
1.[Melancholy] 2.[Sunny day] 3.[Reverie in
the evening] 4.[Village festival]
2,2,2,2-4Hn.-Timp.,Trgl.-Str.
Universal Edition, Vienna [n.d.]
Score 109 p.
*Composed 1884. First performance Prague,
January 1886, the composer conducting.*

1616 Meine Jugend [symphonic poem, Op. 44]   25'
3*,2,3*,2-4,2,3,1-Timp.,Trgl.,B.Dr.-Hp.-Str.
Universal Edition, Vienna, ᶜ1910
Score 49 p.

FOGG, ERIC.   Manchester 21 February 1903
London 19 December 1939

3863 Fanfare   25"
4Tpt.
Ms.
Score 1 p.
Composed ca.1921.

FONSECA, JULIO.   San José, Costa Rica 22 May 1885
San José, Costa Rica 22 June 1950

Suite tropical
3801 No. 1. Fiesta campestre [Country   12'
festival]
3,2,2,2-2,2,1-Timp.,Perc.-Hp.-Str.
3802 No. 2. Idilio   8'
2,2,2,2-2,2,2,1-Str.
Ms.
Scores: 58 p., 18 p.
*Composed 1933. First performance San José,
Costa Rica, 4 December 1934, Orquesta de San
José, the composer conducting.*

FONTBONNE, L.

577m Harpe éolienne [for flute and   3'
orchestra]
Solo Fl.-1,2,2,2-Pno.-Str.

Fontmagne, Baroness Durand de

Score: Ms. 22 p.
Parts: Lemoine, Paris [n.d.]

FONTMAGNE, BARONESS DURAND DE.
See: DURAND DE FONTMAGNE, BARONESS.

FONTYN, JACQUELINE.
b. Antwerp, Belgium 27 December 1930

2275s Divertimento for string orchestra   *13'*
1.Introduzione: Lento - Allegro molto 2.Adagio
assai 3.Prestissimo
Str.
Editions Metropolis, Antwerp, c1959
Score 48 p.
*Composed 1957. First performance on BRT Radio,
Brussels, November or December 1957, Grand
Orchestre Symphonique de la Radio-Télévision
Belge, Daniel Sternefeld conductor. Awarded
honorable mention, Festival International de
Mannheim, 1961.*

256p Mouvements concertants [2 pianos   *ca.11'*
and strings]
1.Lento 2.Allegro
2Pno.-Str.
CeBeDeM, Brussels, c1967
Score 38 p.
Composed 1957.

6663 [Piedigrotta. Suite for orchestra,   *12'*
from the ballet]
1.Pantomime: Allegretto 2.Notturno: Lento
3.Danses: Vivo
2(2nd alt. Picc.),2(2nd alt. E.H.),3(B.Cl. ad
lib.),2-Alto Sax.in E-flat(ad lib.)-2,2,1-
Timp.,Perc.-Pno.,Hp.-Str.
CeBeDeM, Brussels, c1962
Score 111 p.
*Piedigrotta is a Neapolitan religious feast.
Commissioned by the Chapelle Musicale de la
Reine Elisabeth, Waterloo. Original version of
suite composed 1958. This suite arranged 1960;
first performed Brussels, December 1962, Radio
BRT Orchestra, Léonce Gras conductor.*

FOOTE, ARTHUR.   Salem, Massachusetts 5 March 1853
Boston 8 April 1937

432c [Concerto, violoncello, Op. 33]
1.Allegro ma non troppo 2.Andante con moto
3.Allegro comodo
Solo Vc.-2,2,2,2-4,0,3-Timp.-Str.
Ms.
Score 111 p.
*Composed 1894. First performance Chicago, 30
November 1894, Theodore Thomas Orchestra, Theo-
dore Thomas conductor, Bruno Steindel soloist.*

5865 Four character pieces after the Rubáiyát
of Omar Khayyám, Op. 48
1.Andante comodo 2.Allegro deciso 3.Comodo
4.Molto allegro
2,2,2,2-4,2,3,1-Timp.,Perc.-Hp.-Str.
Arthur P. Schmidt, Leipzig, c1912
Score 73 p.
*Inspired by the following verses from the
Rubáiyát: 1.Iram indeed is gone with all his*

*Rose. 2.They say the lion and the lizard keep;
Yet ah, that spring should vanish with the
rose! 3.A book of verses underneath the bough.
4.Yon rising moon that looks for us again;
Waste not your hour, nor in the vain pursuit.
Composed 1912.*

159 [Francesca da Rimini, Op. 24. Symphonic
prelude]
2,2,2,2-4,2,3,1-Timp.-Str.
A.P. Schmidt, Boston, c1892
Score 79 p.
First performance Boston, 1893.

466m A night piece   *6'30"*
Solo Fl.-Str.
Arthur P. Schmidt, Co., New York, c1934
Score 12 p.
*Originally composed for flute and string
quartet, 1918; later transcribed for flute
with string orchestra. First performance Bos-
ton, 13 April 1923, Boston Symphony Orchestra,
Pierre Monteux conductor.*

4302 Overture: In the mountains, Op. 14
2,2,2,2-4,2,3,1-Timp.,Cym.-Str.
Ms.
Score 67 p.
*Composed 1886. First performance Boston, 5
February 1887, Boston Symphony Orchestra,
Wilhelm Gericke conductor.*

2087s [Serenade for string orchestra, Op. 25,
E major]
1.Praeludium: Allegro comodo 2.Air: Adagio,
ma non troppo 3.Intermezzo: Allegretto grazi-
oso 4.Romanze: Andante con moto 5.Gavotte:
Allegro deciso
Str.
Arthur P. Schmidt, Leipzig, c1892
Score 28 p.
*Composed 1886. First performance Breslau, 9
March 1893, Breslau Orchestra, Georg Riemen-
schneider conductor.*

5288 [Suite for orchestra, Op. 36, D minor]
1.Allegro energico, con brio 2.Espressivo,
non troppo adagio 3.Andante espressivo, con
moto 4.Presto assai
2(2nd alt. Picc.),2(2nd alt. E.H.),2,2-4,2,3,1
-Timp.,Cym.-Str.
Arthur P. Schmidt, Leipzig, c1896
Score 168 p.
*Composed 1896. First performance Boston, 7
March 1896, Boston Symphony Orchestra.*

142s Suite [for string orchestra, Op. 63,
E major]
1.Prelude 2.Pizzicato and adagietto 3.Fugue
Str.
A.P. Schmidt [n.p.] c1909
Score 30 p.
*Composed 1907-08. First performance 7 April
1909, Boston Symphony Orchestra.*

2398s Theme and variations for string orchestra
Str.
Ms.

COLLECTION OF ORCHESTRAL MUSIC

Score 21 p. Large folio
*Composed 1907 as the second movement of the
Suite in E major, Op. 63 above. Now a separate
composition.*

FORCHHEIM, JOHANN WILHELM.　　　　　　ca.1635
　　　　　　　　　　　　　　　　22 November 1682

Also spelled: Furchheim

1670s　Suite für 5 Streicher. Arranged by Max
　　Seiffert
　　1.Prelude　2.Allemande　3.Courante　4.Sara-
　　bande　5.Gigue
　　Cemb.-Str.
　　Kistner & Siegel, Leipzig, ᶜ1930
　　Score 7 p.

FORNI, ORESTE.

763s　Valse des chasseurs
　　Str.
　　Score: Ms. 15 p.
　　Parts: Bote & Bock, Berlin [n.d.]

FORST, RUDOLF.　　　　　New York 20 October 1900
　　　　　　　　　Valhalla, New York 19 December 1973

3308　Aubade mexicaine　　　　　　　　　　　　2'
　　1.El queléle [The white hawk]　2.La primavera
　　[Springtime]
　　2,1,2,1-2,2,1-Timp.,Perc.-Hp.-Str.
　　Ms.
　　Score 20 p.
　　*Composed 1938. Based on two folk songs in
　　C.F. Lummis' collection, Spanish Songs of Old
　　California. First performance Greenwich,
　　Connecticut, 22 June 1938, Greenwich Orchestra,
　　Quinto Maganini conductor.*

746c　[Concerto, violoncello]　　　　　　　　23'
　　1.Allegro moderato e deciso　2.Larghetto
　　3.Allegro moderato
　　Solo Vc.-2,1,2,2-2Hn.-Str.
　　Ms.
　　Score 122 p.
　　Composed 1939.

3438　Divertimento, for chamber orchestra　　16'
　　1.Vocalise　2.Tempo di valse　3.Pastorale　4.
　　Toccata
　　1(alt. Picc.),1(alt. E.H.),2,1-Hn.,Tpt.-Str.
　　Ms.
　　Score 45 p.
　　*Composed 1937. First performance (of Toccata
　　only) in a broadcast, New York, 24 February
　　1938, the WOR Symphonietta, Alfred Wallenstein
　　conductor. Pastorale and Tempo di Valse first
　　performed Saratoga Springs, New York, 11 Sep-
　　tember 1938, at the Fifth Yaddo Music Period,
　　Yaddo Chamber Orchestra, Richard Donovan con-
　　ductor. Composer's note: The order of the
　　movements should be reversed. Rewritten 1940
　　as Three Pieces for flute, viola and harp.*

1819s　Music, for strings　　　　　　　　　　18'
　　Str.
　　Ms.

Score 23 p.
*Originally composed as Quartet for Strings,
1936; arranged for string orchestra, 1940. As
a string quartet it was awarded 3rd prize in
the NBC Music Guild contest, 1936.*

1792s　Symphonietta, for string orchestra　　15'
　　Str.
　　Ms.
　　Score 32 p.
　　*Composed 1936. First performance in a broad-
　　cast, New York, 15 December 1936, the WOR Sym-
　　phonietta, Alfred Wallenstein conductor.*

FÖRSTER, CHRISTOPH.
　　　　　　Bibra, Thuringia 30 November 1693
　　　　　　Rudolstadt, Germany 6 December 1745

450m　[Concerto, horn and string orchestra,
　　E-flat] Edited by Kurt Janetzky
　　1.Con discretione　2.Adagio　3.Allegro
　　Solo Hn.-Cemb.-Str.
　　VEB Friedrich Hofmeister, Leipzig, ᶜ1956
　　Score 24 p.
　　*First publication, edited from a Ms. in the
　　Sächsischen Landesbibliothek, Dresden.*

374s　[Suite, string orchestra, G major] Edited
　　by Hugo Riemann
　　1.Ouverture à la française　2.Caprice　3.Air
　　en sarabande　4.Menuet　5.Polonaise　6.Fanfare
　　7.Gigue
　　Str.
　　Breitkopf & Härtel, Leipzig [n.d.]
　　Score 15 p.

6530　[Symphony, E-flat major]
　　1.Allegro assai　2.Andante　3.Allegro
　　2Hn.-Cemb.-Str.
　　Breitkopf & Härtel, Leipzig [n.d.]
　　Score 8 p.
　　Composed ca.1740.

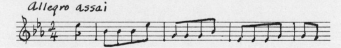

Förster, Rudolf

FÖRSTER, RUDOLF.   b. 1864
                          Berlin 23 December 1894

    1319s Arlequin [Harlequin] Intermezzo, Op. 350
       Str.
       Score: Ms. 12 p.
       Parts: L. Oertel, Hannover [n.d.]

FORSYTH, CECIL.   Greenwich 30 November 1870
                          New York 7 December 1941

    719v [Concerto, violin, G minor]   14'
       1.Appassionato - Moderato 2.Andante un poco
       sostenuto 3.Allegro con fuoco
       Solo Vn.-2,2*,2,2-4,2,3,1-Timp.,Cym.-Str.
       Schott's Söhne, Mainz, 1904
       Score 128 p.

FORT, ROBERT.

    976v Chanson andalouse [violin solo and   4'
       orchestra, B minor]
       Solo Vn.-2,2,2,1-Hn.-Timp.,Perc.-Hp.-Str.
       Score: Ms. 16 p.
       Parts: Decourcelle, Nice, c1928
       Composed 1928. First performance Monte Carlo,
       October 1928.

FORTERRE, H.

    1651s Sérénade [for violin and string orchestra]
       Solo Vn.-Str.
       Score: Ms. 7 p.
       Parts: E.Gaudet, Paris, c1923

FORTNER, WOLFGANG.   Leipzig 12 October 1907

    6048 [Capriccio and finale for orchestra]   15'
       1.Capriccio: Allegro, ma non troppo 2.Finale:
       Molto allegro
       3(3rd alt. Picc.),3*,3*,3*-4,3,3,1-Timp.,S.Dr.,
       Cym.-Str.
       B. Schott's Söhne, Mainz, c1940
       Score 54 p.
       Composed 1939.

    438m [Concerto for string orchestra]   13'
       1.Allegro vigoroso 2.Lied: Andante 3.Inter-
       mezzo: Andante con moto 4.Fuga: Allegro
       energico
       2Solo Vn.,Solo Vc.-Str.
       B. Schott's Söhne, Leipzig, c1933
       Score 26 p.
       Composed 1933. First performance Basel, 8
       December 1933, Basel Chamber Orchestra, Paul
       Sacher conductor.

    4402 Sinfonia concertante for orchestra   25'
       1.Andante 2.Andante: Ziemlich fliessend 3.
       Finale: Allegro
       2(both alt. Picc.),2,2,2-3,2,3-Timp.,Perc.-
       Str.
       B. Schott's Söhne, Mainz, c1937
       Score 68 p.
       Composed 1937.

    4966 [Swabian folk dances for orchestra]   8'
       2(2nd alt. Picc.),2,2,2-3,2,1-Timp.,Perc.-Str.

B. Schott's Söhne, Mainz, c1937
       Score 16 p.
       Composed 1937.

FOSS, LUKAS.   Berlin, Germany 15 August 1922

    Real name: Lukas Fuchs

    1079m [Concerto, oboe and orchestra]   14'30"
       1.Moderato - Allegro 2.Andante, on a Sicilian
       folk song 3.Moderato - Allegro - Andantino -
       Allegro
       Solo Ob.-1,0,1,1-1,1,1-Str.
       Ms.
       Score 81 p.
       Commissioned by Whitney Tustin. Composed 1948.
       First performance on a radio broadcast, 6 Feb-
       ruary 1950.

    828p [Concerto no. 2 for piano and   39'
       orchestra]
       1.Allegro sostenuto 2.Allegretto 3.Allegro
       vivace
       Solo Pno.-3*,2,3*(B.Cl. alt. Ten.Sax.)-4,3,1,1
       -Timp.,Perc.-Str.
       Ms.
       Score 148 p. Large folio
       Composed 1950-52. First performance Venice
       Festival, Venice, 7 October 1953. Awarded the
       Horblit-Boston Symphony Award.

    6219 Ode for orchestra (new version)   10'
       3*,3*,3*,3*-4,3,3,1-Timp.,Perc.-Pno.,2Hp.(2nd
       optional)-Str.
       Ms.
       Score 44 p. Large folio
       Composed 1944 as Ode to Those Who Will Not
       Return. Revised 1958. First performance of
       new version Philadelphia, 17 October 1958,
       Philadelphia Orchestra, Eugene Ormandy con-
       ductor.

    4818 Recordare, second tragic ode for   10'30"
       orchestra
       3*,3*,4*(1Cl. in E-flat),3*-4,3,3,1-Timp.,
       Perc.-Pno.,Cel.,Hp.-Str.
       Ms.
       Score 34 p. Large folio
       Composed 1948. First performance Boston, 31
       December 1948, Boston Symphony Orchestra, the
       composer conducting.

    6329 Song of anguish, Biblical cantata   19'
       for baritone and orchestra (Text from Isaiah)
       Bar. Voice Solo-3*,2,3*,3*-4,3,3,1-Timp.,Perc.
       -Pno.(alt. Cel.),Hp.-Str.
       Ms.
       Score 95 p. Large folio
       Commissioned by the Kulas Foundation in Cleve-
       land. Composed 1945 as the first of two
       Biblical Cantatas. First heard as background
       music for a dance performed by Pauline Kohner
       at Jacob's Pillow, Massachusetts, 1948. First
       concert performance Boston, 10 March 1950,
       Boston Symphony Orchestra, the composer con-
       ducting, Marco Rothmüller soloist.

6299 The song of songs, four settings for
voice and orchestra [2nd Biblical cantata]
1.Awake, O north wind 2.Come, my beloved
3.By night on my bed 4.Set me as a seal
Solo Voice-3*,3*,3*,3*-4(3rd&4th optional),3,
2-Timp.,Perc.-Hp.-Str.
Carl Fischer, New York, ᶜ1950
Score 96 p. Large folio
*Text from the Song of Solomon. Commissioned
by the League of Composers for Ellabelle Davis.
Composed 1946. First performance Boston, 7
March 1947, Boston Symphony Orchestra, Serge
Koussevitzky conductor, Ellabelle Davis
soprano. Awarded the Naumburg Prize.*

6330 Symphony of chorales for orchestra 31'
1.Toccata (Bach chorale no. 90, Hilf, Gott,
Lass Mir's Gelingen. BWV 343) 2.Andante
sostenuto (Bach chorales nos. 77 & 78, Herr,
Ich Habe Misgehandelt. BWV 330 & 331) - Contra-
punctus: B-A-C-H 3.Allegretto tranquillo
(Bach chorale no. 139, Nun Ruhen Alle Wälder.
BWV 392) 4.Introduzione - Vivace - Allegro
(Bach chorale no. 133, Nun Danket Alle Gott.
BWV 386)
3(3rd alt. Picc.),3*,3*(B.Cl. alt. Ten.Sax.),
3*-4,3,3,1-Timp.,Perc.-Mandolin(optional),
Pno.,Hp.-Str.
Ms.
Score 155 p. Large folio
*Composed for Albert Schweitzer at the request
of The Friends of Albert Schweitzer Founda-
tion, Boston, and commissioned by the Kousse-
vitzky Music Foundation. Composed 1955-58.
First performance Pittsburgh, 24 October 1958,
Pittsburgh Symphony Orchestra, William Stein-
berg conductor.*

FOSTER, ARNOLD WILFRED ALLEN.
b. Sheffield 6 December 1898

1334s Suite on English folk airs [for string
orchestra]
1.Prelude (Wheatley Morris Processional)
2.Toccata (Princess Royal, Gloucestershire)
3.Interlude (Searching for Lambs, Somerset)
4.Pastoral fantasy (Old Heddon of Fawsley,
Gloucestershire) 5.Finale (Radstock Jig and
Wyresdale Greensleeves dance)
Str.
Novello, London, ᶜ1930
Score 34 p.

FOSTER, GERÓNIMO BAQUEIRO.
See: BAQUEIRO FOSTER, GERÓNIMO.

FOSTER, STEPHEN COLLINS.
Lawrenceville, Pennsylvania 4 July 1826
New York 13 January 1864

7162 [The social orchestra. Anadolia 5'
and Jennie's own schottische. Transcribed for
orchestra by Richard Bales
1.Anadolia: Andante cantabile 2.Jennie's own
schottisch: Allegro non troppo
Solo Fl.(Anadolia only)-1(alt. Picc.),1,1,1-2,
2-Timp.,Cym.,Trgl.-Str.
Ms.

Score 22 p.
*Anadolia originally composed for solo flute or
solo violin. Jennie's Own Schottisch originally
composed for 1st violin or flute, 2nd violin,
and bass. Both first published in Foster's
The Social Orchestra, Firth, Pond and Company,
New York, 1854. This transcription 1954. First
performance in this version Washington, D.C.,
National Gallery Orchestra, Richard Bales conductor.*

190m [The social orchestra. Eulalie. Edited 2'
and arranged for solo flute by Richard Bales]
Solo Fl.
Ms.
Solo flute part 2 p.
*Foster's transcription for solo violin or solo
flute first published in Part I of his The
Social Orchestra by Firth, Pond, and Company,
1854. This arrangement 1966, first performed
Washington, D.C., 3 April 1966, National Gallery
Orchestra, Richard Bales conductor, William
Montgomery soloist.*

2390s [The social orchestra. Old folks 6'
quadrilles. Edited and transcribed for string
orchestra by Richard Bales]
1.Old Folks at Home: Allegro 2.Oh, Boys, Carry
Me 'Long: Allegro 3.Nelly Bly: Allegro 4.Fare-
well, My Lilly Dear 5.Plantation Jig [6]Coda:
Old Folks at Home
Str.
Ms.
Score 20 p.
*Originally composed for piano, first published
1853. Foster's transcription for flute, 2 violins, and bass first published in Part IV of
his The Social Orchestra, Firth, Pond, and
Company, New York, 1854. This transcription
with coda added by transcriber, 1966; first
performance Alexandria, Virginia, 21 April
1966, string section of National Gallery
Orchestra, Richard Bales conductor.*

2391s [The social orchestra. Village 6'
festival (a set of quadrilles). Edited and
transcribed for string orchestra by Richard
Bales]
Str.
Ms.
Score 26 p.
*Originally composed for flute, 2 violins, and
bass. First published in Part IV of Foster's
The Social Orchestra, by Firth, Pond, and
Company, New York, 1854. This transcription
1966; first performance Washington, D.C., 3
April 1966, National Gallery Orchestra,
Richard Bales conductor.*

7336 Stephen Foster medley. Arranged by Sam
Dennison
1.Old Uncle Ned 2.Camptown Races
2Cl.-Hn.,2Tpt.,Tbn.-Perc.-Accordion-Cb.
Ms. ᶜ1977 by The Fleisher Collection of Orchestral Music, Free Library of Philadelphia
Score 12 p.
*Arranged 1977. First performance Philadelphia,
16 February 1977, Fleisher Ensemble, Sam Dennison conductor.*

Fourdrain, Félix

FOURDRAIN, FÉLIX.   Nice 3 February 1880
                               Paris 23 October 1923

    944v Pensée musicale [solo violin and orchestra]
       Solo Vn.-1,1,1-Hn.-Timp.-Hp.-Str.
       Score: Ms. 11 p.
       Parts: L. Grus, Paris, c1919

FOURNIER, JEAN.

    5489 [Concert overture for orchestra, Op. 20]
       2,2,2,2-4,2,3,1-Timp.(2 players),S.Dr.&B.Dr.-
       Str.
       A. La Flûte de Pan, Paris, c[1937] by Jean
       Fournier
       Score 40 p.

FOURNIER, PAUL.

    4347 [Toccata, symphonic étude, Op. 20]   5'
       3(3rd alt. Picc.),2,2,2-4,2,Cnt.,3,1-Timp.,
       Perc.-2Hp.-Str.
       Durand, Paris [1899?]
       Score 39 p.

FOX, FRED.   Detroit 17 January 1931

    6213 Passacaglia for orchestra   10'
       3*,2,2,2-4,3,3,1-Timp.,Perc.-Str.
       Ms.
       Score 30 p. Large folio
       *Composed 1960. First performance San Antonio,
       January 1962, San Antonio Symphony Orchestra,
       Raphael de Castro conductor.*

    6212 Variations for orchestra   20'
       3*,2(2nd alt. E.H.),2,2-4,3,3,1-Timp.,Perc.-
       Str.
       Ms.
       Score 72 p. Large folio
       *Composed 1959. First performance Bloomington,
       Indiana, February 1960, Indiana University
       Philharmonic, Tibor Kozma conductor.*

FRACKENPOHL, ARTHUR.
        b. Irvington, New Jersey 23 April 1924

    5452 Allegro giocoso for band   4'30"
       3*,3*,5*(1 Cb.Cl.),2-4Sax.-4,3,3,Bar.,1-Timp.,
       Perc.-Cb.
       Ms.
       Score 23 p. Large folio
       *Written for Frederick Fennell and the Eastman
       Wind Ensemble. Composed 1955. First perform-
       ance Rochester, New York, October 1955, East-
       man Symphonic Wind Ensemble, Frederick Fennell
       conductor.*

    469m Arioso for flute and strings   3'30"
       Solo Fl.-Str.
       Ms.
       Score 8 p.
       *Originally composed as the slow movement of a
       sonatina for flute and piano, 1953. This
       version 1954. First performance Potsdam, New
       York, July 1955, Chamber Orchestra of the
       State University of New York at Potsdam,
       Maurice Baritaud conductor, Donald MacDonald
       soloist.*

    470m Concertino for clarinet and   7-8'
       orchestra
       1.Not too fast 2.Very slowly 3.Fast
       Solo Cl.-2,2,0,2-2,2,1-Timp.,S.Dr.-Hp.(or Pno.)
       -Str.
       Ms.
       Score 56 p. Large folio
       *Originally composed as a sonatina for clarinet
       and piano, 1948.*

    5443 Divertimento in F for chamber   13-14'
       orchestra: A little evening music
       1.Moderately: A kind of march with a canon and
       combined themes 2.Slowly: A passacaglia on a
       bass (somewhat altered) of Beethoven 3.Very
       fast: A polka in the form of a scherzo with
       coda 4.Fast: A rondo of sorts, mirrored in
       form, and with a fugal middle
       1,0,1-1,1,1-Str.
       Ms.
       Score 34 p. Large folio
       *Originally composed for 9 instruments, 1952;
       arranged for chamber orchestra same year. First
       performance Lake Placid, New York, October 1952,
       by a faculty ensemble from the State University
       of New York at Potsdam, Brock McElheran conduc-
       tor.*

    5437 A jubilant overture for orchestra   7'30"
       2,2,2,2-4,3,3,1-Timp.,Perc.-Str.
       Ms.
       Score 48 p. Large folio
       *Commissioned by the Springfield, Ohio, Symphony
       Orchestra. Composed 1955-56. First perform-
       ance Springfield, March 1956, Springfield
       Symphony Orchestra, Evan Whallon conductor.*

    5444 Processional 1951 for orchestra   4-5'
       2,2,2,2-4,3,3,1-Timp.(3 players),Perc.-Str.
       Ms.
       Score 21 p. Large folio
       *Written for the 1951 commencement exercises at
       the State University of New York at Potsdam.
       Composed 1951. First performance Potsdam, New
       York, June 1951, State University of New York
       Symphony Orchestra, Samuel Spurbeck conductor.*

    5454 Recessional 1952 for orchestra   3-4'
       2,2,2,2-4,3,3,1-Timp.,Perc.-Str.
       Ms.
       Score 26 p. Large folio
       *Written for the June 1952 commencement exer-
       cises at the State University of New York at
       Potsdam. Composed 1952. First performance
       Potsdam, New York, June 1952, State University
       of New York Symphony Orchestra, Samuel Spurbeck
       conductor.*

FRAIPONT, GEORGES.

    1511s Marivaudage, style ancien [for oboe
       and string orchestra]
       Solo Ob.-Str.
       Score: Ms. 6 p.
       Parts: Costallat, Paris [n.d.]

FRANÇAIX, JEAN.   Le Mans, France 23 May 1912

822p [Concertino for piano and orchestra]   *10'*
1.Presto leggiero 2.Lent 3.Allegretto 4.
Rondo: Allegretto vivo
Solo Pno.-2,2,2,2-2,2,2-Str.
B. Schott's Söhne, Mainz, c1935
Score 26 p.
*Composed 1932. First performance Paris, 15
December 1934, Lamoureux Orchestra, Jean Morel
conductor, the composer as soloist.*

5474 [Serenade for chamber orchestra]   *10'*
1.Vif 2.Andantino con moto 3.Un poco allegretto 4.Vivace
1,1,1,1-1,1,1-Str.
B. Schott's Söhne, Mainz [n.d.]
Score 55 p.
*Composed 1934. Later incorporated into a
ballet score called À la Françaix, with choreography by George Balanchine.*

FRANCESCHINI, ROMULUS.
                 b. Brooklyn, New York 5 January 1929

7127 Canticle for band (1964)   *4'30"*
1.Prelude 2.Celebration 3.Hymn
3*,2,6*(1 in E-flat;1Alto),2-4Sax.(2Alto,Ten.,
Bar.)-4,2,3Cnt.,3,Euph.,2-Timp.,Perc.-Cb.
Ms. c1967 by Elkan-Vogel, Philadelphia
Score 20 p.
*Composed 1964. Movements 1 and 2 published
under the title Prelude and Celebration.*

6911 De profundis (1969) for trumpet,   *10'*
bass clarinet, winds and percussion
Solo Tpt.,Solo B.Cl.-3*,2,10(1Cl. in E-flat,1
Alto Cl.),2-4Sax.-4,4,4Cnt.,3,Bar.,2-Timp.,
Perc.(4 players)
Ms.
Score 26 p. Large folio
*Commissioned by Robert Fitzpatrick and the St.
Joseph's Preparatory School Concert Band,
Philadelphia. Composed 1969. First performance
Philadelphia, 1 May 1970, St. Joseph's Prep
Concert Band, Robert Fitzpatrick conductor,
Theodore Anderer trumpet soloist, Ronald Kline
bass clarinet soloist.*

6936 Five paintings for orchestra   *15'*
1.Sky 2.Deluge 3.Paeans 4.Premonitions
5.Calm
2(2nd alt. Picc.),2(2nd alt. E.H.),2(2nd alt.
B.Cl.),2-4,2,3,1-Timp.,Perc.-Str.
Ms.
Score 41 p. Large folio
*Composed 1971. First performance Academy of
Music, Philadelphia, 30 April 1972, Youth
Orchestra of Greater Philadelphia, Joseph
Primavera conductor.*

3420 "I lift mine eyes...", chorale varia- *4'*
tions on a theme from Heinrich Schütz, for
brass instruments
Hn.,3Tpt.,2Tbn.,Euph.(or Bass Tbn.),Tuba
Ms.
Score 7 p.

*This is Heinrich Schütz's Psalmen David No.
CXXI, Ich Heb Mein Augen Sehnlich Auf. Composed 1972.*

6810 Metamusic 1: In memoriam Edgar   *8'*
Varèse
Ob.(or Sop.Sax.),Alto Sax.-Tpt.,Tbn.-Pno.,Cel.-
Gong,2Tam tams-Vn.,Vc.
Ms.
Score 30 p.
*Composed 1966. First performance Chicago, 8
December 1967, Contemporary Chamber Players of
the University of Chicago, Ralph Shapey con-
ductor.*

7218 Metamusic 2 (1970), for 4 instrumental
groups and 4-track magnetic tape (ring modula-
tion optional)
4Instrumental Groups(each group consisting of
at least 4 high, med. and low wind or string
instruments, or voices),4-Track Magnetic Tape,
4Ring Modulators(optional),4Voltage-Controlled
Filters(optional)
Ms.
Score of 9 sheets
*Composed 1970. First performance Glassboro,
New Jersey, 27 October 1976, Glassboro State
College Lab Band, John Thyhsen conductor.
Duration variable.*

6628 Montage: 25 for 6 (1965-1967) for flute,
clarinet, horn, piano, violin & 'cello and
optional whispering chorus
1,0,1-1Hn.-Pno.-Whispering Chorus(optional)-
Vn.,Vc.
Ms.
Score 25 p.
*Composed 1965. First performance Bennington,
Vermont, 17 August 1966, Bennington Composers'
Conference.*

7222 Omaggio a Kurt Weill (Waltzes and   *8'30"*
interludes) for orchestra
1(alt. Picc. and Alto Fl. in G [optional]),1,
2(2nd alt. B.Cl.),2(2nd Bn. only if B.Cl. not
available)-Alto Sax.(or E.H.)-2,2,2,1-Timp.,
Perc.-Hp.-Str.
Ms.
Score 28 p. Large folio
*Originally composed for solo accordion, 1975.
This transcription 1976.*

254m Piccola musica concertata, for   *4'30"*
strings and harpsichord
Solo Va.,Solo Vc.,Solo Hpscd.-Str.
Ms.
Score 10 p. Large folio
*Commissioned by the Sixteen Concerto Soloists.
Composed 1966 (based on a work for clarinet
and piano, 1952). First performance Univer-
sity Museum, University of Pennsylvania, Phil-
adelphia, 15 March 1967, the Sixteen Concerto
Soloists, the composer conducting, Susan Win-
terbottom violist, Earl Williams violoncellist,
Temple Painter harpsichordist.*

7206 Pilgrim psalm tunes (from the   *25'*
Ainsworth Psalter, 1612)

Franceschini, Romulus

39 tunes set for various ensembles
1(alt. Picc.),1,2*,1-Hn.,Cnt.,Euph.
Ms.
Score 30 p.
Based on Henry Ainsworth's collection first published in Amsterdam, 1612, under the title The Book of Psalms. The psalter was especially prepared for the congregations of Separatists and brought to America in 1620. Composed 1976. First performance Brandywine River Museum, Brandywine, Pennsylvania, 20 June 1976, The Fleisher Wind Ensemble, the composer conducting.

2339s Sinfonia (1970) for double strings,   8'
percussion, piano and celesta
1.Tempo rubato 2.Tempo giusto 3.Josquin
Perc.-Pno.& Cel.-Str. A & B Choirs
Ms.
Score 33 p.
Composed 1970. First performance Lawrence, Kansas, 4 May 1971, the University of Kansas Thirteenth Annual Symposium of Contemporary American Music, The University Orchestra, George Lawner conductor. Quotations: The chorale quotations in the second movement are J.S. Bach harmonizations. The music by Josquin Després in the third movement is the Benedictus from Missa l'Homme Armé.

2268s Sonatina for string orchestra   6'30"
1.Molto moderato 2.Allegro, sempre giusto
3.Lento 4.Allegretto
Str.
Ms.
Score 10 p. Large folio
Composed 1965. First performance Philadelphia, 2 April 1966, broadcast on Radio WFLN, Little Orchestra Society of Philadelphia, Sidney Rothstein conductor.

7337 Summer album (Seven bagatelles)   7'30"
for band
2*,1,5*(1Cl. in E-flat),1-4Sax.-2,2Cnt.,2,
Euph.,1-Perc.
Ms.
Score 45 p.
Composed 1978.

170m White spirituals for soprano and 12   20'
instruments
1.Green Fields 2.Invitation 3.Royal Proclamation 4.New Britain (Amazing Grace)
5.Dunlap's Creek 6.Davisson's Retirement
7.Sawyer's Exit 8.Missionary's Farewell
9.We'll Shout and Give Him Glory (Revival song)
Sop. Voice Solo-1,1,2(2nd alt. B.Cl.),1-1,0,
1-Str. Quintet(2Vns.,Va.,Vc.&Cb.)
Ms.
Score 77 p.
Settings of spiritual folksongs from the following collections: Southern Harmony [New Haven, Connecticut, 1835] (Nos. 1,3,4,5); Olive Leaf [Philadelphia, 1878] (Nos. 2,8,9); Knoxville Harmony [Madisonville, Tennessee, 1838] (No. 6); Original Sacred Harp [Atlanta, 1911] (No. 7). Composed 1977. First performance

Free Library of Philadelphia, 8 May 1977, The Fleisher Ensemble, the composer conducting, Johanna Albrecht soloist.

7217 The world of Thomas Eakins (1971)   10'30"
1.The Gross Clinic 2.Salutat 3.The Artist and his Father Hunting Reed-Birds 4.Sailing
2(2nd alt. Picc.),2(2nd alt. E.H.),2(2nd alt. B.Cl.),1-2,2,1-Timp.,Perc.-Pno.-Str.
Ms.
Score 24 p. Large folio
Composed 1971.

FRANCHETTI, ALBERTO.   Turin 18 September 1860
                           Viareggio 4 August 1942

64 Nella Foresta Nera [In the Black Forest, 9'
symphonic impressions]
3*,3*,3*,3-4,3,3,1-Timp.,Cym.,Trgl.-Hp.-Str.
Ricordi, Milan, c1900
Score 27 p.
Composed 1900. First performance Rome, 1901.

FRANCHOMME, AUGUSTE JOSEPH.   Lille 10 April 1808
                             Paris 21 January 1884

699c [Concerto, violoncello, no. 1, Op. 33,
C minor]
1.Allegro 2.Polacca
Solo Vc.-2,2,2,2-2,2-Str.
Score: Ms. 118 p.
Parts: Lemoine, Paris [n.d.]

686c Fantaisie [violoncello and orchestra,
Op. 36, on a theme by Handel]
Solo Vc.-2,0,2,2-2Hn.-Str.
Score: Ms. 22 p.
Parts: B. Schott, Mainz [n.d.]

634c [Romance, violoncello and string orchestra,
Op. 10, C major]
Solo Vc.-Str.
Score: Ms. 8 p.
Parts: F. Hofmeister, Leipzig [n.d.]

FRANCK, CÉSAR.   Liège 10 December 1822
                         Paris 8 (not 9) November 1890

814 Le chasseur maudit [The accursed   15'
hunter, symphonic poem]
3*,2,2,4-4,2,2Cnt.,3,1-Timp.,Perc.-Str.
Kalmus, New York [n.d.]
Score 83 p.
Composed 1882. First performance Société Nationale, Paris, 31 March 1883.

393p Des djinns [The spirits, symphonic poem]
Solo Pno.-2,2,2,4-4,2,3,1-Timp.-Str.
Enoch, Paris [n.d.]
Score 95 p.
Composed 1884; first performed Paris 15 March 1885.

122 Les Éolides [symphonic poem]   11'
2,2,2,2-4,2-Timp.,Perc.-Hp.-Str.
Enoch & Costallat, Paris [n.d.]
Score 67 p.
Inspired by the poem by Leconte de Lisle.

Composed and first performed 1876, at a concert at the Porte Saint Martin, Paris, Lamoureux conductor.

6005 [Grande pièce symphonique, Op. 17
no. 2. Andante. Transcribed for orchestra by
Charles O'Connell]
1,3*,3*,3*-4,3,3,1-Timp.,Chimes-Str.
Ms.
Score 12 p.
From no. 2 of the Six Pièces pour Grand Orgue,
Op. 17 (1860-62).

503 [Hulda. Ballet allégorique]   20'
1.Allegro maestoso   2.Danse de l'hiver
3.Danse des elfes   4.Danse et choeur des
ondines   5.Ronde générale
2*,2*,3*,4-4,2,2Cnt.,3,1-Timp.,Perc.-Str.
Choudens, Paris [n.d.]
Score 110 p.
From the opera in four acts composed 1882-84
with libretto by Charles Grandmougin after the
drama by Bjørnson.   First performance of opera
Paris, 4 March 1894.

1617 [Nocturne no. 2a, E-flat minor.   3'
Text by L. de Fourcaud; orchestration by
J. Guy Ropartz]
Solo Voice-2,1(alt. E.H.),2,2-Hn.-Hp.-Str.
Enoch, Paris, c1900
Score 15 p.
Composed 1884.

1284 [L'organiste. Eight short excerpts.   10'
Series I, nos.1-4. Arranged for orchestra by
Henri Busser]
1.Très lent   2.Andantino poco allegretto
3.Poco lento   4.Molto moderato
1,1,1,1-1,1-Timp.-Str.
Enoch, Paris [n.d.]
Score 47 p.
Composed 1889; arranged 1904.   First perform-
ance Paris, 1904, Henri Busser conductor.

1517 [L'organiste. Eight short excerpts.   9'
Series II, nos. 5-8. Arranged for orchestra by
Henri Busser]
1.Quasi lento   2.Andante   3.Andantino   4.Alle-
gretto (quasi allegro)
1,1(alt. E.H.),1,1-1,1-Timp.-Hp.-Str.
Enoch, Paris [n.d.]
Score 45 p.

508 Prélude, choral et fugue. Orchestrated   12'
by Gabriel Pierné
3*,3*,3*,4-Sarrus.-4,3,3,1-Timp.,Perc.-2Hp.-
Str.
Enoch, Paris [n.d.]
Score 69 p.
Composed 1884 for piano; orchestrated 1903.
First performance Concerts Colonne, Paris, 1903.

1254 Psyché, poème symphonique   21'
1.[Psyché asleep]   2.[Psyché carried away by
the Zephyrs]   3.[The gardens of Eros]
4.[Psyché and Eros]
3*,3*,3*,4-4,2,2Cnt.,3,1-Timp.-2Hp.-Str.
Bornemann, Paris, c1900

Score 62 p.
Composed 1887-88 for orchestra and chorus.
First performance Société Nationale, Paris, 10
March 1888.

184 [Rédemption. Part 2, no. 5, symphonic   7'
fragment for orchestra]
2,2,2,2-4,2,3,1-Timp.-Str.
Heugel, Paris, c1895
Score 38 p.
Rédemption, symphonic poem for orchestra and
chorus, composed 1872.   First performance at a
Concert Spirituel at the Odéon, Paris, 10
April 1873, Edouard Colonne conductor.

280 Symphony, D minor   37'
1.Lento - Allegro non troppo   2.Allegretto
3.Allegro non troppo
2,3*,3*,2-4,2,2Cnt.,3,1-Timp.-Hp.-Str.
Kalmus, New York [n.d.]
Score 151 p.
Completed 1888; first performance Paris, 17
February 1889, by the Société des Concerts du
Conservatoire.

394p Variations symphoniques [for piano   15'
and orchestra]
Solo Pno.-2,2,2,2-4,2-Timp.-Str.
Luck's, Detroit [n.d.]
Score 87 p.
Composed 1885.   First performance Paris, 1 May
1885, at the Société Nationale de Musique,
Louis Diémer soloist.

FRANCK, EDUARD.   Breslau, Germany 5 October 1817
                    Berlin 1 December 1893

4554 [Concert overture for orchestra, Op. 12,
E-flat major]
2,2,2,2-4,2,3-Timp.-Str.
Bote & Bock, Berlin [184-?]
Score 30 p.

FRANCK, MELCHIOR.   Zittau, Saxony ca.1579-80
                    Coburg, Bavaria 1 June 1639

1192s Two 6-part intradas. Arranged by A.
Schering
Str.
C.F. Kahnt, Leipzig, c1917
Score 5 p.

FRANCKENSTEIN, CLEMENS VON.
                     Wiesentheid 14 July 1875
                     Herchendorf 19 August 1942

1950 Rhapsodie, Op. 47   30'
3(3rd alt. Picc.),3(3rd alt. E.H.),3*,3*-4,3,
3,1-Timp.,Perc.-Cel.,2Hp.-Str.
Universal Edition, Vienna, c1926
Score 51 p.
Composed 1926.   First performance Munich, 1926,
the composer conducting.

1834 [Variations on a theme by Giacomo
Meyerbeer, Op. 45]
3,3*,3*,3-4,2,3,1-Timp.,Perc.-Hp.-Str.
Simrock, Berlin, c1924
Score 48 p.

Franco, Johan

FRANCO, JOHAN.
        b. Zaandam, The Netherlands 12 July 1908

4195 Baconiana, symphonic poem   *8'*
     3*,2,3*,2-3,3,2-Timp.,Perc.-Str.
     Ms. ^c1943 by Johan Franco
     Score 29 p. Large folio
     Suggested by the life of Francis Bacon (1561-
     1626). Composed 1941.

1138v Concerto, for violin and chamber   *15'*
     orchestra
     1.Allegro energico 2.Adagio 3.Finale (Alle-
     gro giocoso)
     Solo Vn.-1(alt. Picc.),1,2(2nd alt. B.Cl.),1-
     1,1-Timp.,Perc.-Pno.-Str.
     Ms.
     Score 74 p.
     Composed 1937, originally for violin and piano
     (or chamber orchestra). First performance of
     orchestral version under its original title,
     Concertino Lirico, Brussels, 6 December 1939,
     I.N.R. Orchestra, Franz Andre conductor, Carlo
     Van Neste soloist.

396c Concerto lirico no. 2, for violon-   *20'*
     cello and orchestra
     1.Maestoso espressivo 2.Adagio cantabile 3.
     Allegretto scherzando 4.Energico
     Solo Vc.-2,2(2nd alt. E.H.),2(2nd alt. B.Cl.),
     2-2,3,1,1-Timp.,Perc.-Hp.-Str.
     Ms. ^c1966 by Johan Franco
     Score 81 p.
     Composed 1962.

399c Fantasy for violoncello and orchestra *10'*
     (1951)
     Solo Vc.-2(2nd alt. Picc.),2(2nd alt. E.H.),3*,
     2-3,3,3-Timp.,Perc.-Str.
     Composers Facsimile Edition, New York, ^c1957
     by Johan Franco
     Score 44 p. Large folio
     Composed 1951. First performance Rotterdam,
     11 March 1958, Rotterdam Philharmonic Orches-
     tra, Eduard Flipse conductor, Samuel Brill
     soloist.

1773s In memoriam [for string orchestra]   *5'*
     Str.
     The Composers Press, New York, ^c1939
     Score 5 p.
     Originally composed 1932; this version 1936.
     First performance New York, 16 November 1941,
     National Youth Administration Orchestra of
     New York, Dean Dixon conductor.

977m Introduzione e scherzo [for clarinet *5'*
     and chamber orchestra]
     Solo Cl.-2Fl.-1,1,1-Timp.,Military Dr.-Pno.-
     Str.
     Ms.
     Score 33 p.
     Composed 1937. This work was later used as the
     last movement of the composer's Symphony II.

3902 Peripetie, symphonic poem   *10'*
     4*,4*,4*,4*-2,3,2,1-Timp.,Military Dr.-Cel.,
     2Hp.(2nd ad lib.)-Str.

Ms.
Score 52 p.
Composed 1935-36.

761p Serenata concertante [for piano and *12'*
     chamber orchestra]
     Solo Pno.-1,1,1,1-1,1,1-Timp.,Cym.,Military Dr.
     -Str.
     Ms.
     Score 49 p.
     Composed 1938. First performance Carnegie
     Chamber Music Hall, New York, 11 March 1940,
     Orchestrette Classique, Frederique Petrides
     conductor, William Masselos soloist.

3635 Sinfonia [for chamber orchestra]   *8'*
     1,1,1,1-Alto Sax.-1,1,1-Timp.,Military Dr.-Str.
     Ms.
     Score 24 p.
     Composed 1932. First performance Utrecht,
     Holland, 6 March 1933, Utrecht Municipal
     Orchestra, Henri Van Goudoever conductor.

2284s Suite for string orchestra   *15'*
     1.Prelude 2.Pastoral 3.Barcarolle 4.Pro-
     cessional 5.Scherzo with trio 6.Chorale
     Str.
     Composers Facsimile Edition, New York, ^c1945
     by Johan Franco
     Score 36 p.
     Composed 1945. First performance Town Hall,
     New York, 26 January 1946, American Chamber
     Music Ensemble, Harold Kohon conductor.

3580 Symphonie I   *25'*
     1. ♪ = +144 or -144 2. ♩ = +42 or -42 3.
     ♩ = 112
     3,2(1st alt. E.H.),2,2-Alto Sax.-2,2,2,1-Timp.,
     Perc.-Pno.,Cel.-Str.
     Ms.
     Score 90 p.
     Composed 1933. First performance Rotterdam,
     6 October 1934, Rotterdam Philharmonic Orches-
     tra, Eduard Flipse conductor.

760p Symphony concertante [for piano and *15'*
     orchestra]
     1.Allegretto elastico 2.Adagio pesante 3.
     Finale
     Solo Pno.-3*,2,3*,2-3,3,3-Timp.,Military Dr.,
     Cym.-Str.
     Ms.
     Score 56 p. Large folio
     Composed 1940. First performance Carnegie Hall,
     New York, 17 March 1941, National Orchestral
     Association, Leon Barzin conductor, William
     Masselos soloist.

FRANK, MARCEL.

1999s Symphony miniature in four move- *6'20"*
     ments for string choir
     1.Allegro 2.Very slow, rubato 3.Allegro 4.
     Lively
     Cel.,Hp.-Str.
     Ms.
     Score 14 p. Large folio

FRANKE, HERMANN.　　Neusalz am Oder 9 February 1834
　　　　　　　　　　　　　　　　　　　　Sorau 1919

　899m [Concerto, clarinet, no. 1, Op. 18]
　In one movement
　Solo Cl.-2,2,1,2-4,2,2-Timp.-Hp.-Str.
　Score: Ms. 63 p.
　Parts: Oertel, Hannover [n.d.]

　316s Zwiegesang [Duet, love song] Op. 29, no. 3
　Str.
　Hientzsch, Breslau [n.d.]
　Score 7 p.

FRANKENBURGER, PAUL.
　See: BEN-HAIM, PAUL. pseudonym.

FRANKO, SAM.　　New Orleans 20 January 1857
　　　　　　　　　　　　　New York 6 May 1937

　1313s Lullaby, Op. 3 no. 1
　Str.
　Tretbar, New York, c1901
　Score 7 p.

　1312s Valse gracieuse, Op. 5
　Str.
　Tretbar, New York, c1901
　Score 11 p.

FRANZ, J. H. pseudonym.
　See: HOCHBERG, HANS HEINRICH BOLKO, GRAF VON.

FRANZ, OSCAR.　　Pulsnitz 30 December 1843
　　　　　　　　　　　25 September 1889

　740m Concertstück [2 horns and orchestra, Op. 4]
　2Solo Hn.-1,1,2,1-0,2,1-Timp.-Str.
　Score: Ms. 18 p.
　Parts: J.G. Seeling, Dresden [n.d.]

FRANZ, ROBERT.　　Halle 28 June 1815
　　　　　　　　　　Halle 24 October 1892

　1353 Hebräische Melodie: Beweinet, Die　　　3'
　Geweint an Babels Strand [Arranged for
　orchestra by Johann N. Cavallo]
　3*,3*,2,2-4,2,3,1-Timp.,Trgl.-Hp.-Str.
　Leuckart, Leipzig [n.d.]
　Score 19 p.

FRANZE, JUAN PEDRO.　　Buenos Aires 10 July 1922

　6555 Berceuse trágica [Litany on the death　14'
　of Adolfine Henriette Vogel, Op. 7]
　Solo Soprano Voice-Bells-Str.
　Ms.
　Score 20 p.
　Poem by Heinrich von Kleist, translated into
　Spanish by Y.M. Coco Ferraris. Composed 1964.
　First performance Buenos Aires, 24 January
　1965, Chamber Orchestra of the Radio Nacional,
　Bruno Bandini conductor, Greta Cicerchia
　soprano.

　5832 [Dance of death from Kio Fong,　　　8'
　choreographic poem for orchestra, Op. 2]
　3*,2,2,3*-4,3,2,1-Timp.,Perc.-Cel.,Hp.-Str.

Ms.
Score 20 p. Large folio
Originally composed in 1942; new version 1948.
First performance of this version Buenos Aires,
13 December 1951, Orquesta Sinfónica de Radio
del Estado, Bruno Bandini conductor.

　5607 Lamento quechua, Op. 6　　　　　　　4'
　1,1,0,1-2Hn.-Perc.-Hp.-Str.
　Ms.
　Score 10 p.
　Composed 1952. First performance Buenos Aires,
　25 June 1953, Orquesta Sinfónica de Radio del
　Estado, Bruno Bandini conductor.

FRANZOT, EGIDIO.

　1283s Serenata for solo violin and string
　orchestra
　Solo Vn.-Str.
　Ms.
　Score 7 p.

FRASER, MARJORY KENNEDY.
　See: KENNEDY-FRASER, MARJORY.

FREDERICK II (THE GREAT).　　Berlin 24 January 1712
　　　　　　　　　　　　　　Potsdam 17 August 1786

　820m [Concerto, flute, no. 1, G major]
　1.Allegro 2.Cantabile 3.Allegro assai
　Solo Fl.-Str.(with Basso Continuo)
　Breitkopf & Härtel, Leipzig [n.d.]
　Score 32 p.

　821m [Concerto, flute, no. 2, G major]
　1.Allegro 2.Grave cantabile 3.Allegro assai
　Solo Fl.-Str.(with Basso Continuo)
　Breitkopf & Härtel, Leipzig [n.d.]
　Score 20 p.

　714m [Concerto, flute, no. 3, C major]　14'
　Edited by Gustav Lenzewski, Sr.
　1.Allegro 2.Grave 3.Allegro assai
　Solo Fl.-Cemb.-Str.
　Vieweg, Berlin, 1925
　Score 27 p.

　715m [Concerto, flute, no. 4, D major]　15'
　Edited by Gustav Lenzewski, Sr.
　1.Allegro 2.Adagio 3.Allegro
　Solo Fl.-Cemb.-Str.
　Vieweg, Berlin [n.d.]
　Score 31 p.

　943s [Symphony no. 1, G major] Edited by
　Gustav Lenzewski, Sr.
　1.Allegro 2.Andante 3.Presto
　Cemb.-Str.
　Vieweg, Berlin [1925]
　Score 18 p.

　944s [Symphony no. 2, G major] Edited by
　Gustav Lenzewski, Sr.
　1.Allegro 2.Andante 3.Presto
　Cemb.-Str.
　Vieweg, Berlin [1925]
　Score 14 p.

Frederick II

1619 [Symphony no. 3, D major] Edited by
Gustav Lenzewski, Sr.
1.Allegro 2.Andante 3.Allegro scherzando
2,2,0,1-2Hn.-Cemb.-Str.
Vieweg, Berlin [1925]
Score 27 p.

945s [Symphony no. 4, A major] Edited by
Gustav Lenzewski, Sr.
1.Allegro 2.Andante e poco piano 3.Presto
Cemb.-Str.
Vieweg, Berlin [n.d.]
Score 15 p.

FREDERIKSEN, SIGURD.   Denmark 28 February 1881
                              Los Angeles 22 February 1965

1093m Concerto for flute
1.Moderato 2.Andante tranquillo 3.Andante -
Allegro moderato - Andante moderato - Allegro
moderato
Solo Fl.-1,2,2,2-4,2,3,1-Timp.,Perc.-Pno.,Cel.,
Hp.-Str.
Ms.
Score 51 p.

5067 Five frescoes, variations for orchestra
1.Infantia (Childhood) 2.Pueritia (Boyhood)
3.Juventus (Youth) 4.Virilitas (Manhood) 5.
Senectus (Old age)
3*,3*,4*(1 in E-flat),2-4,2,3,1-Timp.,Perc.-
Cel.,Hp.-Str.
Ms.
Score 56 p.
*Inspired by Danish church paintings of the
14th century. Variations on a four-note theme.
Originally titled The Frescoes of the Five
Ages. First performance Los Angeles, 18 March
1934, Philharmonic Orchestra of Los Angeles,
Otto Klemperer conductor.*

1091m Noël, fantasy for two harps with
orchestra
1.Allegro maestoso 2.Andante tranquillo 3.
[Alla breve]
2Solo Hp.-1,1,2,1-2Hn.-Perc.-Str.
Ms.
Score 49 p.

FREDRICI, GUSTAF.   Stockholm 1770 or 1771
                           Vienna 1801

5114 [Symphony, unfinished, D minor.   7'
Adagio. Reconstructed by Sven E. Svensson]
2,1,2,1-2Hn.-Str.
Radiotjänst [Stockholm, 1941?]
Score 8 p.
*The orchestration made from a piano reduction
in a manuscript found in Vienna.*

FREED, ISADORE. Brest-Litovsk, Russia 26 March 1900
                Rockville Center, New York 10 November 1960

1136v Concerto for violin   25'
1.Andante come recitativo 2.Molto andante e
sostenuto 3.Allegro ben ritmato
Solo Vn.-2,2(2nd alt. E.H.),2,2-4,2,3-Timp.,
Trgl.-Str.
Ms.
Score 93 p. Large folio
Composed 1939.

1726s Music for strings   20'
Str.
Ms.
Score 38 p.
*Originally composed as Third String Quartet,
1937.*

2765 Pastorales, nine short pieces for   12'
orchestra
1.The bells 2.The mill 3.The hidden brook
4.The country cart 5.The shepherd's pipe 6.
At the fair 7.Grey skies 8.The village band
9.Country revel
2(2nd alt. Picc.),2(2nd alt. E.H.),2(2nd alt.
Cl. in E-flat),2-4,2,3,1-Timp.,Perc.-Cel.-Str.
Ms.
Score 74 p.
*Originally composed as a children's suite for
piano, 1933; transcribed for orchestra, 1936.
First performance (of first 8 movements) Mitten
Hall, Philadelphia, 12 June 1938, Philadelphia
Civic Symphony Orchestra of the WPA, the com-
poser conducting. First complete performance
Washington, D.C., 18 December 1938, National
Symphony Orchestra, Hans Kindler conductor.*

3709 Symphony no. 1   22'
1.Allegro risoluto 2.Andante quasi chorale
3.Vivo scherzando ma ben ritmato 4.Allegro
ardente
3*,3*,3*,3*-4,3,3,1-Timp.,Perc.-Hp.-Str.
Ms.
Score 159 p. Large folio
Composed 1941-42.

1880s Triptyque [for string orchestra]   10'
1.Energico 2.Molto sostenuto 3.Allegro,
molto deciso
Str.
La Sirène Musicale, Paris, ᶜ1933
Miniature score 32 p.
Composed 1932.

FRENKEL, STEFAN.   Warsaw 21 November 1902

864v [Concerto, violin and string   25'
orchestra, Op. 9]
1.Andante 2.Andante 3.Moderato
Solo Vn.-Str.
Ries & Erler, Berlin, ᶜ1929
Score 54 p.
*Composed 1927. First performance Dresden,
1929, Paul Scheinpflug conductor, the composer as soloist.*

FRESCOBALDI, GIROLAMO.
                Ferrara baptized 9 or 15 September 1583
                                Rome 1 March 1643

2384s [Aria, cembalo or organ,   6'
    La Frescobalda. Transcribed for string
    orchestra by Bernard Morgan]
    Str.
    Ms. c1975 by Bernard Morgan
    Score 7 p.
    *First published in Il Secondo Libro di Toccate,
    Canzone, Versi d'Hinni, Magnificat, Gagliarde,
    Correnti et Altre Partite d'Intavolatura di
    Cembalo et Organo, Rome, 1627.*

2385s Aria in C minor. Transcribed for string
    orchestra by Bernard Morgan
    Str.
    Ms. c1975 by Bernard Morgan
    Score 4 p. Large folio

2388s Fugue in G minor. Transcribed for string
    orchestra by Bernard Morgan
    Str.
    Ms. c1975 by Bernard Morgan
    Score 6 p.
    *Originally composed for harpsichord. Tran-
    scribed 1938. First performance of this
    arrangement Philadelphia, 16 November 1938,
    Philadelphia Civic Symphony Orchestra, J.W.F.
    Leman conductor.*

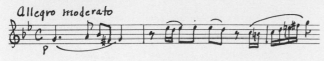

1373s Passacaglia. Orchestrated by Michele   4'
    Esposito
    Fl.,Bn.-Timp.(ad lib.)-Str.
    Oxford University Press, London, c1927
    Score 5 p.

3953 Passacaglia and fugue [Transcribed   9'
    for orchestra by Harold Brown]
    3,3*,3*,2-4,2,0,1-Timp.(ad lib.)-Str.
    Ms.
    Score 27 p.
    *Transcribed 1933. First performance New York,
    April 1937, Columbia University Orchestra,
    Harold Brown conductor.*

1786s Suite in D. Arranged for string   4'
    orchestra by Henri Elkan
    1.Canzona 2.Andante con moto 3.Toccata
    Pno.(ad lib.)-Str.
    Elkan-Vogel, Philadelphia, c1940
    Score 8 p.

3638 Toccata, organ. Freely transcribed   6'
    for orchestra by Hans Kindler
    3,2,3*,2-4,3,3,1-Timp.,B.Dr.-Str.
    Mills, New York, c1942
    Score 24 p.
    *Originally composed for organ; transcribed
    1937. First performance Washington, D.C., 31
    October 1937, National Symphony Orchestra,
    Hans Kindler conductor.*

FRIEBERT, JOSEPH.   born 1723
                                    Passau 6 August 1799

7164 [Christmas symphony from Passau   10'30"
    1774] Edited by Karlheinz Schultz-Hauser
    1.Allegro 2.Pastorale: Adagio 3.Presto
    2Tpt.(ad lib.)-Timp.(ad lib.)-Org.or Cemb.-
    Str.(Vn.III may substitute for Va.)
    Chr. Friedrich Vieweg, Berlin-Lichterfelde,
    c1965
    Score 20 p.
    First performance Passau, Christmas 1774.

FRIED, OSKAR.   Berlin 10 August 1871
                                Moscow 5 July 1941

2299 [Adagio and scherzo for wind instruments,
    2 harps and timpani, Op. 2]
    3(3rd alt. Picc.),3*,3*,3*-3Hn.-2Hp.-Timp.
    Breitkopf & Härtel, Leipzig, c1904
    Score 58 p.

3422 [Fantasy on themes from Engelbert
    Humperdinck's Hansel and Gretel]
    3*,2*(E.H. alt. 2nd Ob.),2,2-4,2,3,1(ad lib.)-
    Timp.,Perc.-Hp.(ad lib.)-Str.
    Schott's Söhne, Mainz, c1895
    Score 59 p.

281s Praeludium *und* Doppelfuge für grosses
    Streichorchester, Op. 10
    Str.
    Hainauer, Breslau [n.d.]
    Score 12 p.

Friedemann, Karl

FRIEDEMANN, KARL.   Mücheln, Germany 29 April 1862

    1054s Heimkehr vom Ball [Intermezzo for string
       orchestra] Op. 138
       Str.
       Score: Ms. 12 p.
       Parts: Wernthal, Berlin, ᶜ1903

    688s Liebessehnsucht [Italian guitar sere-
       nade for string orchestra, Op. 121]
       Str.
       Score: Ms. 15 p.
       Parts: Wernthal, Berlin, ᶜ1902

FRIEDMAN, IGNAZ.
              Podgorze near Cracow 14 February 1882
              Sydney, Australia 26 January 1948

    1421s Les révérences [minuet for string   *3'*
       orchestra]
       Str.(Cb. ad lib.)
       Wilhelm Hansen, Copenhagen, ᶜ1918
       Score 5 p.

FRISCHEN, JOSEF. Garzweiler, Palatinate 6 July 1863

    1618 Ein rheinisches Scherzo, Op. 14   *8'*
       3*,3*,3*,2-4,2,3-Timp.,Perc.-Hp.-Str.
       Universal Edition, Vienna [n.d.]
       Score 59 p.
       Composed 1902. First performance Cologne, 1904,
       at the Gürzenich Concerts, the composer con-
       ducting.

FRITZSCH, EMIL.

    1280s Paroles tendres, valse gracieuse, pour
       orchestre à cordes, Op. 50
       Hp.-Str.
       Score: Ms. 16 p.
       Parts: Gries & Schornagel, Hannover [n.d.]

FROHNE, VINCENT. La Porte, Indiana 26 October 1936

    5846 Night thoughts   *5'15"*
       2,3*,2,2-4,3,3-Timp.,Cym.,Trgl.-Hp.-Str.
       Ms.
       Score 11 p. Large folio
       Composed 1958 after a BBC literary production
       of the same name; the first of Two Pieces for
       Orchestra. First performance Rochester, 3
       May 1959, Eastman Philharmonic, Howard Hanson
       conductor. Received the Edward Benjamin Award
       for Quiet Music, 1959.

    5876 Rondo for orchestra   *5'15"*
       3*,2,3*,2-4,3,3,1-Timp.,Perc.-Str.
       Ms.
       Score 34 p. Large folio
       Composed 1959. First performance Rochester,
       23 March 1959, Eastman-Rochester Orchestra,
       Howard Hanson conductor.

FRONTINI, FRANCESCO PAOLO.   Catania 6 August 1860
                      Catania 28 July 1939

    1584s Confidence amoureuse, pour orchestre à
       cordes

       Str.
       Score: Ms. 4 p.
       Parts: Carisch & Jänichen, Milan, ᶜ1906

    194s Minuetto [for string orchestra]
       Str.
       Carisch & Jänichen, Milan, ᶜ1906
       Score 7 p.

FRUGATTA, GIUSEPPE.   Bergamo 26 May 1860
                      Milan 30 May 1933

    168s Tre pezzi all'antica, Op. 34. No. 1,
       Minuetto [Arranged for string orchestra by
       Ettore Panizza]
       Str.
       Score: Ms. 8 p.
       Parts: Ricordi, Milan [n.d.]

    986s Tre pezzi all'antica, Op. 34. No. 2,
       Sarabanda [Arranged for string orchestra by
       Ettore Panizza]
       Str.
       Score: Ms. 4 p.
       Parts: Ricordi, Milan [n.d.]

    987s Tre pezzi all'antica, Op. 34. No. 3,
       Gavotta [Arranged for string orchestra by
       Ettore Panizza]
       Str.
       Score: Ms. 7 p.
       Parts: Ricordi, Milan [n.d.]

FRUMERIE, GUNNAR DE.
           b. Nacka, near Stockholm 20 July 1908

Full name: Per Gunnar Fredrick de Frumerie

    5984 [Divertimento for orchestra]   *24'*
       1.Overture: Allegro 2.Aria: Andante elegiaco
       3.Dance: Allegro 4.Finale: Allegro vivace
       3*,2,2,2-4,2,3,1-Timp.,Perc.-Cel.,Hp.-Str.
       Ms.
       Score 135 p.
       Composed 1951.

    1098m [Pastoral suite for flute and   *15'*
       string orchestra]
       1.Preludium: Andante grazioso 2.Gavott: Alle-
       gro moderato (molto ritmico) 3.Saraband:
       Andante tranquillo 4.Siciliano: Andante
       grazioso 5.Final: Allegro vivace
       Solo Fl.-Hp.-Str.
       Nordiska Musikförlaget, Stockholm, ᶜ1944
       Score 16 p.
       Composed 1933.

    7250 [Suite in ancient style for small   *15'*
       orchestra, Op. 5b]
       1.Praeludium 2.Sarabande 3.Gavotte - Musette
       4.Sicilienne 5.Gigue
       2,2,2,2-2,1-Str.
       Edition Suecia, Stockholm, ᶜ1931 by Föreningen
       Svenska Tonsättare
       Score 19 p.
       Composed 1930. Originally composed as Suite
       for Piano, Op. 5a.

817p [Symphonic ballad for piano and   29'
  orchestra]
  1.Allegro moderato 2.Andante molto tranquillo
  3.Presto
  Solo Pno.-3*,2(2nd alt. E.H.),2,2-4,2,2-Timp.,
  Perc.-Cel.,Hp.-Str.
  Ms.
  Score 175 p.
  *Composed 1944. First performance Gothenburg,
  Sweden, 4 January 1945, Orchestra Society of
  Gothenburg, Issay Dobrowen conductor, the com-
  poser as soloist.*

5013 [Symphonic variations for orchestra]   20'
  3*,2(2nd alt. E.H.),2,2-4,2,3,1-Timp.,Perc.-
  Cel.,Hp.-Str.
  Ms.
  Score 100 p.
  *Composed 1941. First performance Stockholm,
  17 September 1941, Concert Society of Stock-
  holm, Carl Garaguly conductor.*

324p [Variations and fugue for piano   22-25'
  and orchestra]
  Solo Pno.-2(2nd alt. Picc.),2,2,2-4,2,3-Timp.,
  Perc.-Hp.-Str.
  Nordiska Musikförlaget, Stockholm, ᶜ1942
  Score 157 p.
  Composed 1932.

FRY, WILLIAM HENRY.   Philadelphia 10 August 1813
                                  Santa Cruz,
              Virgin Islands(?) 21 September 1864

6798 Adagio sostenuto
  2,2,2,2-4,2,3,1-Timp.-Str.
  Ms.
  Score 26 p.

6797 [Aurelia the vestal. Overture]
  2,2,2,2-4,2,3,1(Ophicl.)-Timp.-Str.
  Ms.
  Score 56 p.
  *From the opera in 3 acts with libretto by
  Joseph R. Fry. Composed 1841. This overture
  is originally from the opera Cristiani e
  Pagani and was transferred to Aurelia the
  Vestal without changes.*

5384 Hagar in the wilderness (Sacred symphony
  no. 3)
  3*,2,2,2-Sop.Sax.,Bass Sax.-4,3(and/or Cnt.),
  3,1-Timp.-Str.
  Ms.
  Score 68 p.
  Composed 1854.

5364 Overture to Evangeline
  1,1,2,1-2,2,1-Timp.,Small Dr.,Trgl.-Str.
  Ms.
  Score 49 p.
  *Composed for Mrs. H. L. Bateman's (née Sidney
  Frances Cowell) play Evangeline, first per-
  formed 19 March 1860.*

4204 Overture to Macbeth
  2(2nd alt. Picc.),2,2,2-4,2,3,Bombarde-Timp.,
  Perc.-Str.

Ms.
Score 33 p.
Overture to Shakespeare's play. Composed 1862.

5420 Santa Claus, Christmas symphony
  4*(1 is Flageolet),2,2,2-Sop.Sax.-4,4,2Cnt.,
  3,1-Timp.,Perc.-Str.
  Ms.
  Score 94 p. Large folio
  *Written for Jullien's Orchestra. Composed
  1853. First performance New York, 24 December
  1853, Jullien's Orchestra, Louis Antoine
  Jullien conductor.*

FUCHS, ALBERT.   Basel 6 August 1858
                         Dresden 15 February 1910

629v [Concerto, violin, Op. 25, G minor]
  1.Grave - Allegro assai 2.Adagio 3.Rondo:
  Allegro assai
  Solo Vn.-2,2,2,2-2,2-Timp.,Perc.-Str.
  Score: Ms. 177 p.
  Parts: Siegel, Leipzig, ᶜ1904

181s Golgatha [A passion prelude for string
  quartet or string orchestra, Op. 49]
  Str.(Cb. ad lib.)
  Oppenheimer, Hameln, ᶜ1909
  Score 7 p.

FUCHS, H.

857m [Concertino, horn, no. 1, E major]
  In one movement
  Solo Hn.-1,0,2,2-2Hn.-Timp.-Str.
  Score: Ms. 52 p.
  Parts: Hofmeister, Leipzig [n.d.]

882m [Concertino, horn, no. 2, F major]
  1.Adagio - Allegro moderato non troppo - Largo
  - (Allegro moderato non troppo) 2.Alla polacca
  Solo Hn.-1,2,0,2-2,2-Timp.-Str.
  Score: Ms. 66 p.
  Parts: Hofmeister, Leipzig [n.d.]

FUCHS, ROBERT. Frauenthal, Styria 15 February 1847
                         Vienna 19 February 1927

85s [Andante grazioso and capriccio for string
  orchestra, Op. 63]
  Str.
  Robitschek, Vienna [n.d.]
  Score 41 p.

122s Serenade [no. 1, for string orchestra,
  Op. 9, D major]
  1.Andante 2.Tempo di menuetto 3.Allegro
  scherzando 4.Adagio con molto espressione
  5.Finale: Allegro
  Str.
  Kistner, Leipzig [n.d.]
  Score 45 p.

284s Serenade no. 2 [for string orchestra,
  Op. 14, C major]
  1.Allegretto 2.Larghetto 3.Allegro risoluto
  4.Finale: Presto
  Str.

Fuchs, Robert

Kistner, Leipzig [n.d.]
Score 40 p.

285s Serenade no. 3 [for string orchestra,
Op. 21, E minor]
1.Romanze: Andante sostenuto 2.Menuetto 3.
Allegretto grazioso 4.Finale alla zingarese
Str.
Kistner, Leipzig [n.d.]
Score 39 p.

962s Serenade no. 4 [for string orchestra,
Op. 51, G minor]
1.Andante sostenuto 2.Allegretto grazioso
3.Menuett: Moderato amabile 4.Adagio 5.
Finale: Allegro con fuoco
2Hn.-Str.
Weinberger, Leipzig, c1892
Score 27 p.

6962 [Symphony, Op. 37, C major]
1.Allegro molto moderato 2.Intermezzo: Presto
3.Grazioso, ma molto lento, quasi adagio 4.
Finale: Allegro giusto
2,2,2,2-4,2-Timp.-Str.
Simrock, Berlin, 1885
Score 67 p.

443 [Symphony no. 2, Op. 45, E-flat major] 28'
1.Allegro moderato, ma energico 2.Andante
3.Menuetto: Allegretto grazioso 4.Finale:
Allegro giusto
2,2,2,3*-4,2,3-Timp.-Str.
Simrock, Berlin, 1888
Score 67 p.
Composed 1887. First performance Vienna, 18
December 1887, Philharmonic Orchestra, Hans
Richter conductor.

6930 [Waltzes, piano 4-hands, Op. 25. Book I,
nos. 1-12. Transcribed for orchestra by
Richard Heuberger]
2,2,2,2-2,2-Timp.-Str.
Kistner, Leipzig [1886]
Score 65 p.

6931 [Waltzes, piano 4-hands, Op. 25. Book II,
nos. 1-12. Transcribed for orchestra by
Richard Heuberger]
2,2,2,2-2,2-Timp.,Trgl.-Str.
Kistner, Leipzig [1886]
Score 74 p.

FUERSTNER, CARL.   Strasbourg, Alsace 16 June 1912

407c Concerto rapsodico for violoncello   22'
and orchestra, Op. 22
Allegro moderato ma con passione - Tempo giusto
- Quieto - Deciso - Adagio - Allegro vivo -
Allegro vivacissimo - Presto
Solo Vc.-2(2nd alt. Picc.),2(2nd alt. E.H.),2
(2nd alt. B.Cl.),2(2nd alt. C.Bn.)-2,2,1-Timp.,
Perc.-Hp.-Str.
Ms.
Score 108 p. Large folio
Composed 1947. First performance Rochester,
New York, 11 May 1947, Eastman School Little
Symphony, Frederick Fennell conductor, Luigi
Silva soloist.

5003 Metamorphoses on a chorale for brass
choir, Op. 25a (revised version)
4Hn.,8Tpt.,8Tbn.,4Baritones,2Tubas-Timp.,
Perc.
Ms.
Score 71 p.
Composed 1949 in a version for 20 trombones,
tubas and percussion and first performed
Rochester, New York, 5 April 1949. Revised
August 1949.

4489 [A Netherlands suite]
1.Allegro molto - Allegro vivace 2.Allegro
alla marcia 3.Allegro vivace
1,1,1,1-2,1,1-Timp.,Perc.-Str.
[n.p., n.d.]
Score 55 p.

FULEIHAN, ANIS.   Kyrenia, Cyprus 2 April 1900
                       Stanford, California 11 October 1970

716p [Concerto, piano and string
orchestra, no. 1]
1.Allegro moderato 2.Andantino con moto -
Allegro
Solo Pno.-Str.
Ms.
Score 55 p. Large folio
Commissioned by F. Charles Adler for the Sara-
toga Spa Music Festival, 1937. Composed 1937.
First performance Saratoga Spa Music Festival,
Saratoga Springs, New York, 11 September 1937,
string players from the New York Philharmonic,
F. Charles Adler conductor, the composer as
soloist.

744p [Concerto, 2 pianos]   22'
1.Allegro moderato 2.Slowly 3.Lively
2Solo Pno.-2(2nd alt. Picc.),2(2nd alt. E.H.),
2,3*-4,2,3,1-Timp.,Cym.-Str.
Ms.
Score 58 p. Large folio
Commissioned by the Nassau Philharmonic Society,
1940. Composed 1940. First performance
Hofstra College Auditorium, Hempstead, Long
Island, New York, 10 January 1941, Nassau Phil-
harmonic Society, Porter Smith conductor,
Ethel Bartlett and Rae Robertson soloists.

4922 Divertimento no. 2
1.Prelude: Moderato 2.Aria: Slowly 3.Fugue:
Fast and rhythmic
0,1,0,1-1,1-Str.
Ms.
Score 14 p. Large folio
Composed 1941.

745p Epithalamium, variations for piano   12'
and string orchestra
Solo Pno.-Str.
Ms.
Score 32 p. Large folio
Commissioned by and composed for the Philadelphia Chamber String Simfonietta, 1940.
First performance Philadelphia, 6 February
1941, by the Philadelphia Chamber String Simfonietta, Fabien Sevitsky conductor, the composer as soloist. Theme is a traditional

Lebanese epithalamium. Original title: Ritual,
later changed to Ceremonial, and lastly to
Epithalamium.

4908 Etude for orchestra   4'30"
3 (3rd Fl. optional & alt. Picc.),2,3*(B.Cl.
optional),3*(C.Bn. optional)-4,2,3,1-Timp.-
Pno.(ad lib.)-Str.
Ms.
Score 9 p. Large folio
Composed 1942.

4053 Etude no. 1, Melody for winds   4'30"
2(2nd ad lib.),2(2nd ad lib.),2,2(or Euphonium)
(2nd ad lib.)-3Sax.(2Alto,Ten.)(ad lib.)-4,3(or
Cnt.)(3rd ad lib.),3(2nd ad lib.),1-Timp.,Perc.
-Str.
G. Schirmer, New York, c1943
Score 19 p.
Composed 1941, no. 1 of 6 Concert Etudes.
First performance Camp Lee, Virginia, 25
October 1943, Camp Lee Symphony Orchestra,
George Hoyen conductor.

4054 Etude no. 2, Staccato and legato   4'30"
2,2(2nd ad lib.),2,2(or Euphonium)(2nd ad lib.)
-3Sax.(2Alto,Ten.)(ad lib.)-4,3(or Cnt.)(3rd ad
lib.),3,1-Timp.,Perc.-Str.
G. Schirmer, New York, c1943
Score 23 p.
Composed 1942.

1030m Fantasy for theremin and orchestra   12'
1.Moderato 2.Andantino 3.Allegro
Solo Theremin-2,2,2,2-4,3,3,1-Timp.-Str.
Ms.
Score 57 p.
Composed 1944. First performance New York, 26
February 1945, New York City Symphony Orchestra,
Leopold Stokowski conductor, Clara Rockmore
soloist.

3273 Fiesta, a sketch for orchestra   8'
3(3rd alt. Picc.),3*,3(3rd alt. B.Cl.),2-4,3,
3,1-Timp.,Trgl.,Cym.-Str.
Ms.
Score 36 p. Large folio
Commissioned by and composed for the Indian-
apolis Symphony Orchestra, 1939. First
performance Indianapolis, 1 December 1939,
Indianapolis Symphony Orchestra, Fabien
Sevitzky conductor.

3489 Invocation to Isis   7'
3(3rd alt. Picc.),3*,3*,3*-4,2,3,1-Timp.,Perc.
-Str.
Ms.
Score 22 p. Large folio
Commissioned by and composed for the Indian-
apolis Symphony Orchestra, 1941. First per-
formance Indianapolis, 28 February 1941,
Indianapolis Symphony Orchestra, Fabien
Sevitzky conductor.

2893 Mediterranean   14'
1.Shepherds 2.Peasants 3.Priests and priestesses 4.Musicians 5.Dancers
4*(3rd alt. 1st Picc.),4*,4*,4*-4,3,3,1-Timp.,

Perc.-Hp.-Str.
G. Schirmer, New York, c1935
Score 56 p.
Composed 1922. First performance Cincinnati,
15 March 1935, Cincinnati Symphony Orchestra,
Eugene Goossens conductor.

4930 Preface to a child's story book   8'
Moderato - ♩ = 104 - Andantino - Presto
3(2nd & 3rd alt. Picc.),3*,3*,3*-4,2,3,1-
Timp.,Cym.,Trgl.-Hp.-Str.
Ms.
Score 58 p.
Composed 1932. First performance New York,
1936, National Orchestral Association, Leon
Barzin conductor.

1794s Quartet, for string instruments   22'
(for solo quartet or string chamber orchestra
without bass)
Str.(without Cb.)
Ms.
Score 30 p. Large folio
Composed 1940. Original title: Quartet for
String Orchestra.

765c Rhapsody for violoncello and   18'
string orchestra
Calme - Allegro agitato - Calme
Solo Vc.-Str.
Ms.
Score 32 p. Large folio
Composed 1946.

939m Symphonie concertante, for string   25'
quartet and orchestra
1.Molto moderato 2.Andante con moto 3.Allegro
Solo Str. Quartet-3(3rd alt. Picc.),3*,3(3rd
alt. B.Cl.),2-4,2,3,1-Timp.-Str.
Ms.
Score 125 p. Large folio
Composed 1939. First performance New York, 25
April 1940, New York Philharmonic, John Bar-
birolli conductor, the Philharmonic String
Quartet: Mishel Piastro, Imre Pogany, Zoltan
Kurthy, Joseph Schuster soloists.

2766 Symphony no. 1   22'
1.Moderato 2.Cantabile 3.Misurato 4.Energico
3(2nd&3rd alt. Picc.),3*,3(2nd alt. Cl. in
E-flat,3rd alt. B.Cl.),3*-4,4(4th ad lib.),3,
1-Timp.,Cym.,B.Dr.-Str.
Ms.
Score 121 p. Large folio
Composed 1936. First performance New York, 31
December 1936, New York Philharmonic, John
Barbirolli conductor.

3576 Three serenades   12'
1.With zest 2.Slow 3.Very fast
3(3rd alt. Picc.),3*,3*,3*-4,3,3,1-Timp.,Perc.
-Cel.-Str.
Ms.
Score 62 p. Large folio
Composed 1941 with the original title: Diver-
timento.

Füllekruss, Emil

FÜLLEKRUSS, EMIL.
Stettin, Pomerania 2 September 1856
d. 1913

315s Ein Abend in Bellaggio [An evening in
Bellaggio] Waltz-Idyl, Op. 95
Str.
A.E. Fischer, Bremen, c1902
Score 5 p.

FUMAGALLI, BENITO.

1262s Bei giorni [Beautiful days] gavotte,
Op. 6. Freely arranged for string orchestra
by F. Th...t
Str.
J. Rieter-Biedermann, Leipzig, c1893
Score 3 p.

FUNCK, EDUARD.
Teterow, Mecklenburg 6 September 1861
Flensburg, Germany 1927

1640s Légende [solo violin and strings]
Solo Vn.-Str.
Score: Ms. 10 p.
Parts: [n.p., n.d.]

FURCHHEIM, JOHANN WILHELM.
See: FORCHHEIM, JOHANN WILHELM.

FÜRSTENAU, ANTON BERNHARD.
Münster, Germany 20 October 1792
Dresden 18 November 1852

726m [Concertino, flute and orchestra, Op. 119,
G major]
Allegro moderato - Adagio sostenuto - Rondo:
Allegretto - Meno mosso
Solo Fl.-1,2,2,2-2,2-Timp.-Str.
Score: Ms. 85 p.
Parts: Bote & Bock, Berlin [n.d.]

370m [Concertino, 2 flutes and orchestra,
Op. 41, F major]
1.Allegro non troppo, leading to 2.Adagio
sostenuto 3.Allegretto: Theme and 3 variations
4.Allegro
2Solo Fl.-0,2,2,2-2,2-Timp.-Str.
Breitkopf & Härtel, Leipzig [n.d.]
Score 75 p. Large folio
The theme in the third movement is from C.M.
von Weber's opera Der Freischütz.

765m [Concerto, flute, no. 7, Concertino,
Op. 77, E minor. New edition]
Allegro moderato - Adagio - Alla polacca
Solo Fl.-1,2,2,2-2,2-Timp.-Str.
Score: Ms. 104 p.
Parts: J. André, Offenbach am Main [n.d.]

901m [Concerto, flute, no. 8, Op. 84, D major]
Allegretto non tanto - Andante - Allegro
Solo Fl.-1,2,2,2-2,2-Str.
Score: Ms. 80 p.
Parts: Challier, Berlin [n.d.]

766m [Concerto, flute, no. 9, Concertino, Op. 100,
B minor]
Allegro moderato - Adagio cantabile - Rondo
Solo Fl.-2,2,2,2-2,2,1-Timp.-Str.
Score: Ms. 99 p.
Parts: J. André, Offenbach am Main [n.d.]

FUSSAN, WERNER.   Plauen, Germany 25 December 1912

6085 [Capriccio for orchestra, Op. 15]   8'
2(2nd alt. Picc.),2,2,2-4,2,3,1-Timp.-Str.
Ms.
Score 45 p.
Composed 1949.

2307s [Suite for strings (1950)]   12'
1.Marsch 2.Frisch bewegt 3.Aria 4.Capriccio
Str.
Breitkopf & Härtel, Leipzig, c1956
Score 18 p.
Composed 1950.

FUX, JOHANN JOSEPH.
Hirtenfeld, near St. Marein, Styria 1660
Vienna 13 (not 14) February 1741

5647 [Overture (Suite), D minor]
1.Ouverture 2.Menuet 3.Aria: Adagio 4.Fuga:
Presto 5.Lentement 6.Gigue 7.Aria
2Ob.,2Bn.-Str.-Basso Continuo
Score: Denkmäler der Tonkunst in Österreich,
IX, 2. Artaria, Vienna [1902] Edited by Guido
Adler. 20 p.
Parts: Ms. c1976 by The Fleisher Collection of
Orchestral Music, Free Library of Philadelphia

5649 [Overture (Suite), B-flat major]
1.Ouverture 2.Aria 3.Menuet I 4.Menuet II
5.Gavotte 6.Passepied, Der Schmidt 7.Gigue
2Ob.,2Bn.-Str.-Basso Continuo
Score: Denkmäler der Tonkunst in Österreich,
IX, 2. Artaria, Vienna [1902] Edited by Guido
Adler. 17 p.
Parts: Ms. c1976 by The Fleisher Collection of
Orchestral Music, Free Library of Philadelphia

1672s [Overture (Suite) for student orchestra]
Edited by H. Lemacher and P. Mies
1.Overture 2.Aria 3.Minuet I 4.Minuet II
5.Gavotte 6.Passepied: The Blacksmith
7.Gigue
Cemb.-Str.
P.J. Tonger, Cologne, c1929
Score 12 p.

5664   Sonata a quattro [B-flat major]
1.[Introduction] 2.Allegro 3.Adagio
4.Allegro
Bn.-Cnt.,Tbn.-Org.-Str.
Score: Denkmäler der Tonkunst in Österreich,
IX, 2. Artaria, Vienna [1902] Edited by Guido
Adler. 10 p.
Parts: Ms. c1976 by The Fleisher Collection of
Orchestral Music, Free Library of Philadelphia

4339   [Sacrae symphoniae, Book I. Sonata octavi
toni] Edited by R.D. King
Choir I: 2Cnt.,2Tbn.,Bar.,Tuba
Choir II: 2Cnt.,2Tbn.,Bar.,Tuba
(Hns. in F or E-flat may substitute for Tbns.)
[Music for Brass, Wakefield, Massachusetts,
1940]
Score 16 p.
First published in Venice, 1597.

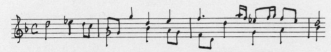

5663   Sonata a tre [F major]
Allegro - Grave - Presto - Grave - Presto
Bn.-Vn.I & II-Basso Continuo
Score: Denkmäler der Tonkunst in Österreich,
IX, 2. Artaria, Vienna [1902] Edited by Guido
Adler. 5 p.
Parts: Ms. c1976 by The Fleisher Collection of
Orchestral Music, Free Library of Philadelphia

GABRIEL-MARIE.
See: MARIE, GABRIEL.

GADE, JACOB.   Vejle, Jutland 29 November 1879
                     Copenhagen 21 February 1963

3557   The last viking, epic tone poem
3(3rd alt. Picc.),2(2nd alt. E.H.),2,2-4,3,3,1
-Timp.,Perc.-Str.
Ms.
Score 36 p.
Composed ca.1940.

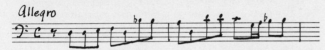

GADE, NIELS WILHELM.   Copenhagen 22 February 1817
                         Copenhagen 21 December 1890

286s   Aquarellen, Op. 19. Transcribed by Richard
Hofmann
1.Elegie 2.Scherzo 3.Canzonette 4.Humoreske
5.Novellette
Str.
F. Kistner, Leipzig [n.d.]
Score 15 p.
Originally composed for piano solo, 1850.

G

GAAL, FRANÇOIS.

1583s Sérénade (Amour d'artiste), Op. 51
Solo Vn.-Str.
Score: Ms. 6 p.
Parts: A. Cranz, Leipzig [n.d.]

GABRIELI, GIOVANNI.   Venice between 1554-1557
                           Venice 12 August 1612

4340   [Sacrae symphoniae, Book I. Canzon quarti
toni] Edited by R.D. King
Choir I: 2Cnt.,Tbn.,Bar.,Tuba
Choir II: 4Tbn.,Tuba
Choir III: 2Cnt.,2Bar.,Tuba
(Hns. in F or E-flat may substitute for Tbns.)
[Music for Brass, Wakefield, Massachusetts,
1941]
Score 15 p.
First published in Venice, 1597.

693v   Capriccio. Orchestrated by Carl   10'
Reinecke
Solo Vn.-2,2,2,2-2,2-Timp.-Str.
Ries & Erler, Berlin [n.d.]
Score 33 p.
Composed 1878; orchestrated 1891.

925v   [Concerto, violin, Op. 56, D minor]
1.Allegro con fuoco 2.Romanze 3.Rondo
scherzando
Solo Vn.-2,2,2,2-2,2-Timp.-Str.
Breitkopf & Härtel, Leipzig [n.d.]
Score 171 p.
Composed 1880.

Gade, Niels Wilhelm

4556 [Echoes from Ossian, overture, Op. 1] *10'*
2(2nd alt. Picc.),2,2,2-4,2,2,1(or C.Bn.)-
Timp.-Hp.-Str.
Breitkopf & Härtel, Leipzig [1841]
Score 60 p.
Suggested by James MacPherson's The Works of
Ossian, ostensibly translated from the 3rd-
century Irish bard. Composed 1840. First
performance Copenhagen, 19 November 1841.
Awarded a prize by the Copenhagen Musical
Society, 1840.

5008 [Hamlet, concert overture, Op. 37]   *10'*
3(3rd alt. Picc.),2,2,2-4,2,3,1-Timp.-Str.
Breitkopf & Härtel, Leipzig [1862]
Score 64 p.
Composed 1860-61.

3995 Holbergiana, suite for orchestra, Op. 61
1.Tempo di minuetto (Henrik und Pernille)
2.Allegro scherzando (Der Geschwätzige -
Jacob von Thybo) 3.Andantino (Die vielge-
launte Dame) 4.Finale: Allegro festivo (Der
masken Ball)
2(2nd alt. Picc.),2,2,2-4,2,3,1-Timp.,Trgl.-
Chorus(ad lib.)-Str.
Breitkopf & Härtel, Leipzig [n.d.]
Score 88 p.
Written for the 200th year Jubilee of the
Danish poet, Ludwig Holberg (1684-1754). Com-
posed 1884.

491s Der Kinder Christabend, Op. 36. Transcribed by Richard Hofmann
1.[Christmas bells] 2.[Child Jesus is born]
3.[The Christmas tree] 4.[Dance of the little
girls] 5.[Good night]
Str.
F. Kistner, Leipzig [n.d.]
Score 13 p.
Originally composed for piano solo.

5903 [Michelangelo, concert overture for
orchestra, Op. 39]
3(3rd alt. Picc.),2,2,2-4,2,3,1-Timp.-Str.
Fr. Kistner, Leipzig [1862?]
Score 53 p.
Composed 1861.

60s Novelletten, Op. 53 [F major]
Str.
Breitkopf & Härtel, Leipzig [n.d.]
Score 27 p.
Composed 1874.

564s Novelletten, no. 2, Op. 58 [E major]
Str.
Breitkopf & Härtel, Leipzig [n.d.]
Score 31 p.

5053 Sommertag auf dem Lande, Op. 55
1.Früh [Early]: Allegro vivo e grazioso 2.
Stürmisch [Stormy]: Allegro molto 3.Waldein-
samkeit [Sylvan solitude]: Larghetto con moto
4.Humoreske: Allegro comodo e scherzoso 5.
Abends, lustiges Volksleben [At evening, merry
folk life]: Andantino - Allegro vivace
2,2,2,2-3,2-Timp.-Str.

Breitkopf & Härtel, Leipzig [1880 or 1881]
Score 134 p.
Composed 1879.

5302 [Symphony no. 2, Op. 10, E major]
1.Andantino quasi allegretto 2.Andante con
moto 3.Scherzo: Molto allegro 4.Finale:
Allegro energico
2,2,2,2-4,2,3-Timp.(2 players)-Str.
Breitkopf & Härtel, Leipzig [1854 or 1855]
Score 195 p.
Composed 1843.

5064 [Symphony no. 3, Op. 15, A minor]
1.Presto 2.Andante sostenuto 3.Allegretto,
assai moderato 4.Finale: Allegro molto e con
fuoco 5.Andante sostenuto
2,2,2,2-4,2,1-Timp.-Str.
Breitkopf & Härtel, Leipzig [n.d.]
Score 196 p.
Composed 1846-47.

168 [Symphony no. 4, Op. 20, B-flat major] *20'*
1.Andantino - Allegro vivace e grazioso 2.
Andante con moto 3.Finale: Allegro molto
vivace
2,2,2,2-4,2-Timp.-Str.
F. Kistner, Leipzig [n.d.]
Score 120 p.
Composed 1849. First performance Copenhagen,
1850, the composer conducting.

5081 [Symphony no. 5, Op. 25, D minor]
1.Allegro con fuoco 2.Andante sostenuto 3.
Scherzo: Allegro molto vivace 4.Finale: An-
dante con moto - Allegro vivace
3*,2,2,2-4,2,3-Timp.-Pno.-Str.
Breitkopf & Härtel, Leipzig [1853 or 1854]
Score 199 p.
Composed 1852.

5056 [Symphony no. 7, Op. 45, F major]
1.Allegro risoluto 2.Andante 3.Scherzo:
Allegro vivace 4.Finale: Allegro vivace
2,2,2,2-4,2,3-Timp.-Str.
Breitkopf & Härtel, Leipzig [1865 or 1866]
Score 251 p.
Composed 1864-65.

5472 [Symphony no. 8, Op. 47, B minor]
1.Allegro molto e con fuoco 2.Allegro moderato
3.Andantino 4.Finale: Allegro non troppo e
marcato
3,2,2,2-4,2,3-Timp.-Str.
Fr. Kistner, Leipzig [1872]
Score 170 p.
Composed 1869-71.

GAEL, HENRI VAN.

1407s Gentil cotillon, intermezzo, Op. 152
Str.
Score: Ms. 10 p.
Parts: B. Schott's Söhne, Mainz [n.d.]

750s Petite marquise, menuet, Op. 166
Str.
Score: Ms. 8 p.
Parts: B. Schott's Söhne, Mainz [n.d.]

563s Sérénade, Op. 147 [F major]
Str.
Score: Ms. 7 p.
Parts: B. Schott's Söhne, Mainz [n.d.]

GAILLARD, MARIUS-FRANÇOIS.   Paris 13 October 1900
                                Paris 23 July 1973

181m [For Alexis, for violin, violoncello and
      percussion]
Solo Vn.,Vc.-Perc.
Max Eschig, Paris, c1931
Score 8 p.
Composed 1929.

GAITO, CONSTANTINO.   Buenos Aires 3 August 1878
                         Buenos Aires 14 December 1945

3394 Poema sinfónico, El ombú, Op. 31
4*,4*,4*(1Cl. in E-flat),4*-6,4,4,1-Timp.,Perc.
-Cel.,Hp.-Str.
Ms.
Score 58 p. Large folio
*Ombú refers to a South American tree. Com-
posed 1924. First performance Buenos Aires,
29 October 1925. Awarded first Municipal
Prize, Buenos Aires, 1924.*

GÁL, HANS.   Brunn, near Vienna 5 August 1890

4602 Sinfonietta, Op. 30   32'
1.Idylle: Molto tranquillo, quasi andante
2.Burleske: Allegretto con umore 3.Elegie:
Largo 4.Rondo: Vivace
2(2nd alt. Picc.),2(2nd alt. E.H.),2(2nd alt.
B.Cl.),2(2nd alt. C.Bn.)-3,2,2,1-Timp.,Perc.-
Hp.-Str.
N. Simrock, Berlin, c1929
Score 96 p.
*Also known as Symphony no. 1, Op. 30. Composed
1928.*

GALAJIKIAN, FLORENCE GRANDLAND.
            b. Maywood, Illinois 29 July 1900

2676 Symphonic intermezzo   11'
3(3rd alt. Picc.),3*,3(1st alt. Cl. in E-flat),
3*-4,3,3,1-Timp.,Perc.-Hp.-Str.
Ms.
Score 40 p.
*Composed 1931. First performance in a broad-
cast, New York, 1 May 1932, NBC Symphony
Orchestra, Eugene Goossens conductor. Awarded
fourth prize in the NBC Competition, 1932.*

2677 Tragic overture (Thruout the world   12'
the grim figure of tragedy moves and strikes)
3(3rd alt. Picc.),3*,3*,3*-4,3,3,1-Timp.,Trgl.,
Cym.-Cel.,Hp.-Str.
Ms.
Score 53 p.
*Composed 1934. First performance Chicago, 24
January 1937, Illinois Symphony Orchestra of
the WPA, Albert Goldberg conductor.*

GALEANO, IGNACIO VILLANUEVA.
               b. La Esperanza, Honduras 1885

4450 [Mr. Edwin A. Fleisher, military march]
1,1,2,1-Alto Sax.-2,2,2-B.Dr.,S.Dr.-Str.
Ms.
Score in reduction 2 p.
Composed 1946.

3769 Pan American Union march   3'
1*(in D),1,4(1Cl. in E-flat),1-3Sax.(Alto,
Ten.,Bar.)-2,2,3-Perc.-Pno.-Str.
Ms.
Score 20 p.
*Composed 1927. First performance Tegucigalpa,
Honduras, 15 December 1927, Banda de los
Supremos Poderes, José Benigno Cohello con-
ductor.*

4907 [Peace and reconciliation, march]
1,1,2,1-2,2,1-B.Dr.,S.Dr.-Str.
Ms.
Score in reduction 2 p.
Composed 1949.

2030s [Sinfonia patética, for strings, Op. 2]
Str.
Ms.
Score 10 p.
Composed 1949.

GALIMANY, ALBERTO.
               b. Villafranca, Spain 30 December 1889

4350 Panamá, capricho típico panameño [Char-
acteristic Panamanian caprice, for band]
Solo Cl.,Solo Cnt.-1,1,3(1 in E-flat),1-Alto
Sax.,Ten.Sax.,Bar.Sax.-2,3Cnt.,Flis-corno,3,
2Bar.,1-Timp.,Perc.
Música de Joaquín Mora, Barcelona [n.d.]
Score in reduction 6 p.

GALINDO, BLAS.   San Gabriel,
               Jalisco, Mexico 3 February 1910

4050 Danza de las fuerzas nuevas; Mexican
dance suite
1(alt. Picc.),1,1,1-1,2,2,1-Timp.,Perc.-Pno.-
Str.
Ms.
Score 87 p.

3876 Preludios
1.Introducción - Primer preludio - Interludio
- Segundo preludio 2.Tercer preludio - Cuarto
preludio
3*,3*,3(1 in E-flat),2-4,3,3,1-Timp.,Perc.-Hp.
-Str.
Ms.
Score 119 p.
Completed 1940.

2195s [Short symphony for strings.   16'30"
Revised version]
1.Allegro moderato 2.Largo 3.Allegro con
brio

Gallini, L.

Str.
Pan American Union, Washington, D.C., c1956
by Blas Galindo
Score 71 p.
Composed 1952. First performance Mexico City,
22 August 1952, Orquesta Sinfónica Nacional,
José Pablo Moncayo conductor. Revised 1953.

GALLINI, L.

952v Improvvisata [Impromptu, A-flat major.
Orchestrated by F. Seigle]
Solo Vn.-Fl.,Cl.-Str.
Score: Ms. 13 p.
Parts: Ricordi, Paris, c1928

GALUPPI, BALDASSARE.
Burano Island, near Venice 18 October 1706
Venice 3 January 1785

Called: Il Buranello

1037s Adagio e giga, D major. Orchestrated   *6'*
by Michele Esposito
Fl.,Bn.-Timp.(all ad lib.)-Str.
Oxford University Press, London, c1927
Score 9 p.

911m Aria, for clarinet and string orchestra
Solo Cl.-Str.
Ms.
Score 10 p.

2260s [Concerto, strings, no. 6, C   *10'*
minor] Edited by Virgilio Mortari
1.Grave 2.Allegro 3.Andante
Str.
G. Ricordi, Milan, c1959
Score 13 p.
Original title, Concerto a Quattro.

Grave

6348 [Olimpiade. Sinfonia from the opera]   *7'*
Edited by Roberto Lupi
1.Allegro 2.Andante 3.Minuetto
2Ob.-2Hn.-Str.
Carisch, Milan, c1956
Score 10 p.
From the opera in 3 acts with libretto by
Pietro Metastasio. First performance Milan,
26 December 1747.

6405 [Symphony no. 1, D major] Edited by
Giuseppe Piccioli
1.Allegro 2.Andantino 3.Allegro molto
1,2,0,1-2Hn.-Timp.-Str.
Carisch, Milan, c1959
Score 33 p.

Allegro

6417 [Symphony no. 2, D major] Edited by
Giuseppe Piccioli
1.Allegro 2.Allegretto 3.Allegro molto, quasi
presto
2,2,0,2-2,2-Timp.-Str.
Carisch, Milan, c1959
Score 29 p.

Allegro

6325 [Symphony no. 3, D major] Edited by
Giuseppe Piccioli
1.Allegro assai 2.Andantino 3.Allegro vivace
2,2,0,2-2,2-Timp.-Str.
Carisch, Milan, c1959
Score 24 p.

Allegro assai

GAMARRA, FRANCISCO GONZÁLEZ.
See: GONZÁLEZ GAMARRA, FRANCISCO.

GAMERO, M. DE ADALID.
See: ADALID Y GAMERO, M. DE.

GANDOLFO, EUGEN.   Genoa 1865

317s Marche héroique de Don Quichotte!
Str.
Decourcelle, Nice, c1892
Score 3 p.

467v Romance [for orchestra]   *4'*
Solo Vn.-1,1,2,1-2,2,1-Timp.-Hp.-Str.
Score: Ms. 17 p.
Parts: Decourcelle, Nice, c1930
Composed 1929. First performance Nice, Decem-
ber 1929.

GANNE, LOUIS GASTON.
Buxières-les-Mines 5 April 1862
Paris 13 July 1923

570s Arlequinade, pizzicati [D major]
Str.
Score: Ms. 10 p.
Parts: Enoch, Paris [n.d.]

García Estrada, Juan Agustín

2324 Extase, rêverie   3'
      2,2,2,2-2,0,3,1(ad lib.)-Timp.,Trgl.-Hp.(or
      Pno.),Org.(ad lib.)-Str.(with Soli Vn. and Vc.)
      Enoch, Paris [n.d.]
      Score 19 p.
      *Composed 1888. First performance Paris, 1889,
      the composer conducting.*

1307 Illys, suite byzantin, sur le   14'
      ballet La Princesse au Sabbat
      1.Cortège byzantin 2.Orientale 3.Nocturne
      4.Bacchanale
      2,1,2,1-2,0,2Cnt.,3-Timp.,Perc.-Hp.-Str.
      Costallat, Paris [n.d.]
      Score 61 p.

1488s Invocation
      Solo Vn.-Hp.(or Pno.)-Str.
      Costallat, Paris, c1903
      Score in reduction 5 p.

GANZ, RUDOLPH. Zurich, Switzerland 24 February 1877
                            Chicago 2 August 1972

5146 Laughter... yet love, a symphonic   7'
      overture to an unwritten comedy, Op. 34
      3*,2,2,2-4,2,3,1-Timp.,Perc.-Str.
      Ms.
      Score 61 p. Large folio
      *Commissioned in honor of the National Associa-
      tion of Schools of Music. Composed 1950.
      First performance Cincinnati, Ohio, 24 November
      1950, Cincinnati Symphony Orchestra, Thor
      Johnson conductor.*

1077m Percussional mêlée, Op. 33 no. 4   2'30"
      For 5 players:
      1st - Xylophone (also Bells,Cel.and Tubular
            Bells)
      2nd - Tubular Bells (Also Slapstick,Tamb.,
            Trgl.,Tam-tam and Birdcall)
      3rd - Snare Drum (Also Cuckoo,Lion's Roar,
            Temple Blocks and Slapstick or Shot)
      4th - Bass Drum (Also Cym.,Sandpaper,Rattle
            and Wind Whistle)
      5th - Timpani
      Mills Music, New York, c1944
      Score 7 p.

2732 Twenty animal pictures   22'
      1.The donkey 2.Capering kittens 3.Alligator's
      promenade 4.Galloping horses 5.Bumblebees
      6.Chipmunks 7.Elephants out for a walk 8.The
      polar bear swings along 9.A squirrel 10.The
      lion 11.Monkey-shines around the organ-grinder
      12.Fleas 13.Crickets 14.Two bears behind
      bars 15.Young eagles' pow-wow 16.There goes
      the big snake 17.Birds 18.Chickens 19.Lis-
      tening to the cuckoo 20.The grand parade
      3,3,3,3*(1st alt. Cl. in E-flat),3-4,3,3,1-Timp.,
      Perc.-Hp.-Str.
      Ms.
      Score 107 p.
      *Originally composed for piano, 1930; orchestra-
      ted 1932. First performance Detroit, 19
      January 1933, Detroit Symphony Orchestra, the
      composer conducting.*

GARCÍA-CATURLA, ALEJANDRO.
    See: CATURLA, ALEJANDRO GARCÍA.

GARCÍA ESTRADA, JUAN AGUSTÍN.
                        Buenos Aires 8 November 1895
                        Buenos Aires 27 September 1961

6124 [Aconcagua. The dream of the condor,
      symphonic poem]
      3*,3*,3*,3*-4,3,3,1-Timp.,Perc.-Cel.,Hp.-Str.
      Ms. [c1949 by Juan Agustín García Estrada]
      Score 84 p. Large folio
      *After the poem Le Sommeil du Condor, by Charles
      Marie Leconte de Lisle. Aconcagua is an
      Argentine Indian place name. Its original
      meaning is high place. Composed 1942. First
      reading, 1942, All-American Youth Orchestra,
      Leopold Stokowski conductor, on a South Amer-
      ican tour.*

2144s [Eighteenth-century bourrée]   3'
      Str.
      Ms. [c1943 by Juan Agustín García Estrada]
      Score 7 p.
      *Originally composed for string quartet, 1937.
      First performance of version for string
      orchestra Buenos Aires, 1943, Orquesta Radio
      del Estado, Bruno Bandini conductor.*

5639 [Introduction and waltz]   4'
      3*,3*,2,2-4Hn.-Trgl.,S.Dr.-Cel.,Hp.-Str.
      Ms. [c by Juan Agustín García Estrada]
      Score 18 p. Large folio
      *Composed 1950. First performance Buenos Aires,
      8 May 1949, Orquesta Radio del Estado, Bruno
      Bandini conductor.*

445m Pastoral (Arrullo), for clarinet and
      strings
      Solo Cl.-Str.
      Ms. [c1949 by Juan Agustín García Estrada]
      Score 7 p.
      *Original title Arrullo (Lullaby). Composed
      1949. First performance Buenos Aires (no date
      available), Orquesta Radio del Estado, Bruno
      Bandini conductor, Mr. Spatola soloist.*

5860 Ruralia Argentina. No. 1. Vidalita
      3*,3*,2,2-3Hn.-Perc.-Cel.,Hp.-High Voice-
      Str.
      Ricordi Americana, Buenos Aires, c1955
      Score 26 p. Large folio
      *The Vidala Santiagueña theme is of Quichuan
      (Precolumbian) origin. First performance of
      Ruralia Argentina, nos. 1, 2, and 5, Buenos
      Aires, 24 April 1952, Orquesta Radio del Estado,
      M. Drago conductor.*

5861 Ruralia Argentina. No. 2. Bailecito
      3*,2,2,2-3,2-2Alto Sax.-Timp.,Perc.-Cel.,Hp.,
      Guit.-Str.
      Ricordi Americana, Buenos Aires, c1955
      Score 58 p. Large folio
      A dance form derived from Gaucho motives.

3808 Ruralia Argentina. No. 3. Salteña [sym-
      phonic poem]
      3*,3*,3*,3*-4,3,3,1-Timp.,Perc.-Cel.,Hp.-Str.

García Estrada, Juan Agustín

Ortelli, Buenos Aires, ᶜ1940
Score 57 p.

5862 Ruralia Argentina. No. 4. Triste
2,3*,2,2-3Hn.-Timp.,S.Dr.-Hp.-Str.
Ricordi Americana, Buenos Aires, ᶜ1955
Score 11 p. Large folio
*First performance Coliseo Theatre, Buenos Aires,
2 July 1926, Concerts Asociación del Profesorado Orquestal, Henry Hadley conductor.*

5863 Ruralia Argentina. No. 5. Ranchera
3*,3*,2,2-4,3,3,1-Timp.,Perc.-Cel.,Hp.-Str.
Ricordi Americana, Buenos Aires, ᶜ1955
Score 48 p. Large folio

3337 Ruralia Argentina. No. 6. Huella   *4'*
3*,3*,2,2-4,3,3,1-Timp.,Perc.-Hp.-Str.
Ortelli, Buenos Aires, ᶜ1939
Score 14 p.
*Original title: Danza. First performance
Buenos Aires, 13 July 1929, Asociación del
Profesorado Orquestal, Nikolai Malko conductor.*

5864 Ruralia Argentina. No. 7. Estilo
2,3*,2,2-3Hn.-Timp.,Trgl.-Hp.-Str.
Ricordi Americana, Buenos Aires, ᶜ1955
Score 14 p. Large folio
*The estilo is based on the rhythms of the
tango.*

3455 Ruralia Argentina. No. 8. Pericón y gato
3*,3*,2,2-4,3,3,1-Timp.,Perc.-Cel.,Hp.-Str.
Ortelli, Buenos Aires, ᶜ1940
Score 53 p.

3715 Ruralia Argentina. No. 9. A la oración
2,3*,2,2-4Hn.-Perc.-Cel.,Hp.-Str.
Ortelli, Buenos Aires, ᶜ1940
Score 14 p.
Original title: Elegia.

444m [Song of Santos Vega, for clarinet   *2'30"*
and string orchestra]
Solo Cl.-Str.
Ms. [ᶜ1951 by Juan Agustín García Estrada]
Score 7 p.
*From the opera, The Death of Santos Vega, based
on Luis Bayón Herrera's play, Santos Vega (the
legendary Argentine minstrel). Composed 1930.
First performance of this arrangement Buenos
Aires (no date available), Orquesta Radio del
Estado, Bruno Bandini conductor.*

GARCÍA MORILLO, ROBERTO.   Buenos Aires 1911

3738 Poema   *4'*
1,2*,2,1-2,1,1-Timp.-Cel.,Hp.-Str.
Ms.
Score 34 p.
*Composed 1932. First performance Buenos Aires,
30 October 1936, School of Orchestra Ensemble,
Bruno Bandini conductor.*

GARDINER, HENRY BALFOUR.   London 7 November 1877
                            Salisbury 28 June 1950

1620 Overture to a comedy   *7'*
2,2,2,2-4,2,3,1-Timp.,Perc.-Hp.-Str.

Novello, London, ᶜ1913
Score 55 p.
*An early composition, revised in 1911. First
performance Queen's Hall, London, 1 May 1911,
New Symphony Orchestra.*

1076 Shepherd Fennel's dance
3*,3*,2,3*-4,2,3,1-Timp.,Perc.-2Hp.-Str.
Hawkes, London, ᶜ1912
Score 35 p.
*Based upon the story of The Three Strangers
from Thomas Hardy's Wessex Tales. First performance at a Promenade Concert, London, 1911.*

GARDNER, SAMUEL.   Elizabethgrad
          (now Kirovograd) Ukraine 25 August 1891

2833 Broadway, an orchestral tone poem for *16'*
full orchestra, organ, saxophones and banjo
3(3rd alt. Picc.),3*,4*(1Cl. in E-flat),3*-
3Alto Sax.-4,4,3,1-Timp.,Perc.-Org.,Cel.,2Hp.,
Ten.Banjo-Str.
Ms.
Score 114 p.
*Composed 1924. Received honorable mention in
the Musical America contest, 1928. First performance Boston, 18 April 1930, Boston Symphony
Orchestra, the composer conducting.*

GARRETA, JULI.
          San Feliu de Guixols, Catalonia 12 March 1875
                        San Feliu 2 December 1925

5798 [June, a sardana. Transcribed for orchestra
by Enric Casals]
3*,3*,2,2-4,3,3,1-Timp.,Tamb.-Str.
La Sardana Popular, Barcelona [n.d.]
Score 14 p.
*A Catalonian national dance. Originally com-
posed for cobla, the Catalonian sardana band.
Awarded 1st prize by Eusebi Patxot and Llagos-
tera, 1920.*

GARRIDO, PABLO.   Valparaiso 26 March 1905

1878s Fantasia submarina   *8'*
Pno.-Str.
Ms.
Score 32 p.
*The second from the composer's suite, Three
Fantasias; No. 1, Fantasia Militar, and No. 3,
Fantasia Aerea. Composed 1932. First perform-
ance Santiago, Chile, 3 August 1938, Orquesta
Sinfónica Nacional, the composer conducting,
Julio Oyague pianist.*

3792 Rapsodia chilena   *18'*
Fl.,4Cl.(2nd and 3rd alt. 2Alto Sax.;4th alt.
Ten.Sax.)-2Tpt.,Tbn.-Timp.,Perc.-Pno.,Guit.-
Str.
Ms.
Score 72 p.
*Commissioned by the Chilean magazine, Ercilla,
1937. Composed 1937. The principal theme is
the popular Chilean melody Rio, Rio. First
performance Santiago, Chile, July 1937, Orques-
ta Sinfónica Nacional, the composer conducting.*

GARRIDO-LECCA, CELSO.   Piura, Peru 9 March 1926

   6016 [Symphony in 3 parts]
   1.Lento – Allegro agitato 2.Calmo 3.Allegro
   molto
   3(3rd alt. Picc.),3*,3*,3*–4,3,3,1–Timp.,Perc.
   –Pno.,Hp.–Str.
   Ms.
   Score 109 p. Large folio
   Commissioned by the Edwin A. Fleisher Collec-
   tion of Orchestral Music. Composed 1960.
   First performance at the 2nd Inter-American
   Music Festival, Cramton Auditorium, Howard
   University, 22 April 1961, National Symphony
   Orchestra, Howard Mitchell conductor.

GASCO, ALBERTO.   Naples 3 October 1879
                              Rome 11 July 1938

   3930 Buffalmacco (Preludio giocoso)   4'
   3*,3*,3*,3–4,3,3,1–Timp.,Perc.–Cel.,Hp.–Str.
   Ricordi, Milan, c1921
   Miniature score 48 p.
   First performance Augusteo, Rome, December 1917,
   Bernardino Molinari conductor.

GASPARINI, JOLA.   Genoa 4 March 1882

   First name also spelled: Jole

   954s Pizzicato [for string orchestra, E major]
   Str.
   Score: Ms. 4 p.
   Parts: Carisch & Jänichen, Milan, c1910

GASSMANN, FLORIAN LEOPOLD. Brüx, Bohemia 3 May 1729
                            Vienna 20 January 1774

   1822s [Symphony, B minor. Arranged by   17'
   Karl Geiringer]
   1.Allegro moderato 2.Andante 3.Menuetto
   4.Allegro assai
   2Ob.–Str.
   Ms.
   Score 26 p.
   Arranged ca.1933.

GASTYNE, SERGE DE.   Paris 27 July 1930

   5661 Hollin Hall, ode for orchestra   20'
   3(3rd alt. Picc.),3*,3*,3*–4,4,3,1–Timp.,B.Dr.,
   Tam-tam–Pno.,Hp.–Str.
   Ms. c1958 by Elkan-Vogel [Philadelphia]
   Score 56 p. Large folio
   Commissioned by the Cincinnati Symphony
   Orchestra Society, 1956. Composed 1957.
   First performance Cincinnati, 12 April 1957,
   Cincinnati Symphony Orchestra, Thor Johnson
   conductor.

   5775 L'île Lumière [The Isle of Light,   30'
   symphonic suite in 5 movements]
   1.Arcane marine [Maritime arcanum]: Energico
   2.Mirage matinal [Morning mirage]: Calmo 3.
   Vendanges [Grape harvest]: Allegretto scherzando 4.Oceano noc [Nocturne]: Largo 5.Feu
   d'artifice [Fireworks]: Allegro con brio
   4(2nd alt. Fl. in G;4th alt. Picc.),4*,4*(3rd

alt. Cl. in E-flat),4*–4,4(1 in D),3,1–Timp.,
Perc.–Pno.,Cel.,Hp.–Str.
Ms. c1955 by Serge de Gastyne
Score 127 p. Large folio
Commissioned by the Cincinnati Symphony Orches-
tra. Composed 1955. First performance Cincin-
nati, 7 January 1956, Cincinnati Symphony
Orchestra, Thor Johnson conductor. L'île
Lumière is the nickname of the Ile de Ré, off
the coast of Brittany.

GATES, CRAWFORD.   San Francisco 29 December 1921

   6644 Symphony no. 3, in one movement,   15'
   Op. 38
   Part I. Introduction: Allegro Part II. Più
   mosso Part III. Adagio Part IV. Moderato
   3(3rd alt. Picc.),2,2,2–4,3,3,1–Timp.,Perc.–
   Pno.(alt. Cel.),Hp.–Str.
   Ms.
   Score 89 p. Large folio
   Commissioned by the Brigham Young University
   Research Grant, 1964. Composed 1962-64. First
   performance Dallas, Texas, 7 February 1965,
   Dallas Symphony Orchestra, George Trautwein
   conductor.

GATTY, NICHOLAS COMYN.
                Bradfield, England 13 September 1874
                       London 10 November 1946

   1326s The Haslemere suite. Edited by James
   Brown
   1.Prelude (Divisions on a ground) 2.Sarabande
   3.Air 4.Fugue 5.Finale alla giga
   Str.
   Stainer & Bell, London, c1928
   Score 22 p.

GAUBERT, PHILIPPE.   Cahors 3 July 1879
                             Paris 8 July 1941

   620v Fantaisie [for violin and orchestra]
   Solo Vn.–3,2,2,2–4,3,3,1–Timp.,Trgl.–Hp.–Str.
   Durand, Paris, c1922
   Score 43 p.
   Composed 1921.

   2052 Poème pastoral [symphonic suite]
   1a.Allègrement 1b.Idylle 2.Crépuscule 3.
   Danse
   3*,3*,3*,2–4,3,3,1–Timp.,Perc.–Hp.–Str.
   Carl Selva, Paris, c1912
   Score 69 p.
   First performance Concerts Lamoureux, Paris,
   February 1911, Camille Chevillard conductor.

   1434 Rhapsodie sur des thèmes populaires
   [for symphonic orchestra. Arranged for small
   orchestra by L. Gaubert-Elgé]
   1.Dans la montagne 2.Fête
   1,1,2,1–2,2,1–Timp.,Perc.–Hp.–Str.
   H. Lemoine, Paris, c1925
   Score 68 p.

GAUBERT-ELGÉ, LUCIEN.

   1018v Automne
   Solo Vn.–2Fl.,2Cl.–Str.

Gauby, Josef

Score: Ms. 11 p.
Parts: Evette & Schaeffer, Paris, c1922

GAUBY, JOSEF.   Lankowitz, Styria 17 March 1851
                       Graz, Austria 10 November 1932

2006s [Rosegger-Ländler, six Styrian dances 7'
for string orchestra and harp. Arranged by
Max Schönherr]
Introduction: Vivace 1.Behäbig 2.Sehr ruhig
und zart 3.Mässig bewegt 4.Anmutig bewegt
5.Ruhig, ausdrucksvoll 6.Bewegt Coda: Vivace
Hp.-Str.
Universal Edition, Vienna, c1939
Score 17 p.

GAUDIOSI, MARIO.

824p [Capriccio for piano and orchestra]
Solo Pno.-3*,3*,3*,3*-4,3,3,1-4Sax.-Str.
Edizioni Curci S.A., Milan, c1941
Score 74 p. Large folio

GAUL, HARVEY BARTLETT.   New York 11 April 1881
                                Pittsburgh 1 December 1945

1711s Fosteriana, two impressions based on 10'
Foster songs for string orchestra
1.Stephen Foster hums 'round his attic 2.
Stephen Foster often laughed
Str.
J. Fischer, New York, c1935
Score 26 p.
Composed 1935. First performance on a Foster
Memorial program, under the auspices of the
Tuesday Musical Club and the Carnegie Institute,
Pittsburgh, Pennsylvania, 11 January 1936,
Fillion Ensemble, Ferdinand Fillion conductor.

1836s From an Indian long house 12'
a.Seneca condolence dirge b.Tuscarora string
bean dance
Fl.-Indian Rattle,Indian Dr.(or Timp.)-Str.
C.C. Birchard, Boston, c1936 by Harvey Gaul
Score [17] p.
Composed 1931. First performance Carnegie
Music Hall, Pittsburgh, 12 April 1935, String
Symphony Ensemble of Pittsburgh, Oscar Del-
Bianco conductor.

1702s Three Palestinian pastels
1.Crepuscule on Mount Carmel 2.Palestinian
mother's song 3.Purim at Tel Aviv
Str.(with Solo Vc.,Solo Vn.)
J. Fischer, New York, c[n.d.]
Score 41 p.
Composed 1935. First performance Pittsburgh,
13 October 1935, Pittsburgh Symphony Orchestra,
Antonio Modarelli conductor.

GAULDIN, ROBERT.   Vernon, Texas 1931

5621 Diverse dances for chamber orchestra 14'
1.Contradance: Poco pesante 2.Minuet: Allegretto 3.Pavane: Adagio 4.Estampie: Allegro
2*,1,1,1-2,1,1-Timp.-Hp.-Str.
Ms.
Score 56 p. Large folio
Composed 1957. First performance Rochester,

16 April 1957, Eastman-Rochester Orchestra,
Howard Hanson conductor. The third movement
won second prize of the Edward B. Benjamin
Award for Quiet Music, 1957.

GAVEAUX, PIERRE.
Béziers, France 9 October 1760 (not August 1761)
   Charenton-le-Pont, near Paris 5 February 1825

4262 [La rose blanche et la rose rouge.
Overture, Op. 27]
2,2,2,2-2,2,1-Timp.-Str.
Frères Gaveaux, Paris [1809]
Score 27 p.
From the lyric drama in three acts with text
by René Charles Guilbert de Pixérécourt.

GEBER, E.

597s Oster-, Pfingst- und Weihnachtsklänge
[Tunes for Easter, Whitsuntide and Christmas]
Op. 10
Str.(without Cb.)
L. Oertel, Hannover [n.d.]
Score 3 p.

GEBHARD, HANS. Dinkelsbühl, Germany 18 August 1897
                Augsburg, Germany 2 October 1974

There is also a composer Hans Gebhard born 26
September 1882 in Mühlhausen.

5589 [Suite of country dances for small 18'
orchestra, Op. 23]
1.Auftakt: Lebendig und frisch 2.Marsch: Im
Marsch-tempo 3.Zwischenspiel: Ruhig fliessend
4.Kirchweihtanz: Nicht zu rasch 5.Zwischen-
spiel: Sehr getragen 6.Kehraus: Sehr lebendig
1,1,1-0,2,1-Timp.,Perc.-Str.
B. Schott's Söhne, Mainz, c1935
Score 52 p.

GEDALGE, ANDRÉ.   Paris 27 December 1856
                         Chessy 5 February 1926

520p [Concerto, piano, Op. 16]
1.Moderato maestoso 2.Andante 3.Allegro poco
a poco accelerando
Solo Pno.-2,3*,2,2-4,2,3-Timp.-Str.
Enoch, Paris, c1899
Score 149 p.

GEDIKE, ALEXANDER FEODOROVICH.
See: GOEDICKE, ALEXANDER FEODOROVICH.

GEEHL, HENRY ERNEST.   London 28 September 1881

2190 Suite espagnole 18'
1.Andalusian waltz 2.Little serenade 3.Moorish
intermezzo 4.Bolero - Finale
2(2nd alt. Picc.),2,2,2-2,0,2Cnt.,3-Timp.,Perc.
-Str.
Ms. cNovello, London [n.d.]
Score 93 p.
Composed 1900. First performance Guildhall
School of Music, London, 11 December 1901.

GEHRA, AUGUST HEINRICH.
    Langenwiese, near Ilmenau, Germany ca.1715
        20 September 1785

Also called (erroneously): Johann Heinrich Gehra

378v [Concerto, viola and orchestra, C major]
    Edited by Thor Johnson and Donald M. McCorkle
    1.Moderato 2.Andante 3.Allegro
    Solo Va.-Str.
    Ms.
    Score 34 p. Large folio
    Edited from a Johann Peter manuscript in the
    Moravian Music Foundation Archives. First
    modern performance at the Fourth Early American
    Moravian Music Festival, Moravian College,
    Bethlehem, Pennsylvania, 27 June 1957, The
    Festival Orchestra, Thor Johnson conductor,
    William Preucil soloist.

GEIRINGER, KARL.   Vienna 26 April 1899

1977s [Baroque suite no. 1, for string
    orchestra] Edited by Karl Geiringer
    1.Padouan 2.Intrada 3.Galliarda 4.Tanz
    5.Canzon 6.Chorea polonia 7.Volte
    8.Almande 9.Spagnoletta
    Str.
    Ms.
    Score 22 p.

1982s [Baroque suite no. 2, for string
    orchestra] Edited by Karl Geiringer
    1.Suite: a)Padouan b)Intrada c)Dantz
    d)Galliarda 2.[Intrada à 4] 3.Echo
    4.Suite: a)Ouverture b)Bourrée c)Air
    d)Passepied e)Gavotte
    Str.
    Ms.
    Score 29 p.

1983s [Baroque suite no. 3, for string
    orchestra] Edited by Karl Geiringer
    1.[Suite no. 1] a)Paduana b)Intrada c)Dantz
    d)Gogliarda 2.Pavana 3.Intrada 4.Tanz
    5.Nachtanz 6.Intrada 7.Padovana 8.Chorea
    polonia
    Str.
    Ms.
    Score 12 p.

1981s [Prelude and fugue from Musicalische
    Gemuthslust] Adapted by Karl Geiringer
    Andante maestoso - Allegro
    Str.
    Ms.
    Score 9 p.
    Composed ca.1712. This version edited ca.1935
    from a possibly unique copy of the collection
    Musicalische Gemuthslust in the library of the
    Musikfreunde Gesellschaft, Vienna.

GEISER, WALTHER.   Zofingen,
    Canton Aargau, Switzerland 16 May 1897

185m [Fantasy for string orchestra,   *17'*
    timpani and piano, Op. 31]
    Timp.-Pno.-Str.
    Bärenreiter, Basel, ᶜ1948
    Score 47 p.
    Also known as Fantasy no. 1. Composed 1942.

2053s [Fantasy no. 3 for string orchestra, *15'*
    Op. 39]
    1.Andante sostenuto (Theme and 2 variations)
    2.Allegro amabile e leggiero (Variations 3-8)
    3.Andante sostenuto (Variations 9-10)
    Str.
    Bärenreiter, Kassel and Basel [n.d.]
    Score 14 p.
    Composed 1949.

GEISLER, PAUL.   Stolp, Pomerania
    (now Poland) 10 August 1856
    Posen, Poland 3 April 1919

4359 [The pied piper of Hamelin, symphonic *10'*
    poem]
    3*(2nd alt. Picc.II),2,2,2-4,2,3,1-Timp.,Cast.,
    Glock.-Hp.-Str.
    Bote & Bock, Berlin [1881]
    Score 35 p.
    Alternate title: Die Marianer. First per-
    formance Magdeburg, 1880, under the auspices
    of the Allgemeiner Deutscher Musikverein.

4445 [Till Eulenspiegel, symphonic poem] *12'*
    3(3rd alt. Picc.),2,2,2-4,2,3,1-Timp.,Cym.,
    Trgl.-Hp.-Str.
    Bote & Bock, Berlin [1881]
    Score 55 p.

GELDER, MARTINUS VAN.
    See: VAN GELDER, MARTINUS.

GEMINIANI, FRANCESCO.   Lucca, Italy 1679 or 1680
    (baptized 5 December 1687)
    Dublin 17 September 1762

903s Andante, D major. Revision and   *5'*
    harmonization by Gino Marinuzzi
    Org.,Hp.-Str.
    Ricordi, Milan, ᶜ1925
    Miniature score 5 p.
    First performance Augusteo, Rome, March 1924,
    Marinuzzi conductor.

Geminiani, Francesco

1045s [Concerto grosso, Op. 2 no. 2, C minor]
Edited by Michele Esposito
Adagio - Allegro - Adagio - Allegro
Str.
Oxford University Press, London, c1927
Score 8 p.
Opus 2 comprises 12 Concerti Grossi, published in parts, London, 1732, and in score, Paris, 1755.

1241s [Same as above] Edited by Paul Mies
Adagio - Allegro - Adagio - Allegro
2 Solo Vn., Solo Vc.-Cemb.-Str. (without Cb.)
Filser, Augsburg [n.d.]
Score 19 p.

1494s [Concerto grosso, Op. 2 no. 3, D minor]
Edited by Walter Upmeyer
1.Presto 2.Adagio 3.Allegro
Cemb.-Str.
F. Vieweg, Berlin [1930?]
Score 7 p.

171s [Concerto grosso, Op. 3 no. 5, B-flat major] Arranged by Arnold Schering
Andante - Allegro - Andante - Allegro
Concertato: 2Vn.,Va.,Vc.
Ripieno: Pno.-Str.
C.F. Kahnt, Leipzig, c1918
Score 18 p.
Opus 3 comprises 6 Concerti Grossi composed ca.1735.

2242s [Concerto grosso (no. 1), D major.   10'
Transcribed from Arcangelo Corelli's Sonata
Op. 5 no. 1. Revised by Virgilio Mortari]
Grave - Allegro - Allegro - Allegro - Adagio - Allegro
Soli: 2Vn.,Va.,Vc.-Str.-Cemb.
Carisch, Milan, c1937
Score 14 p.
This is based on Corelli's Op. 5 no. 1, published in Rome, 1700 as XII Suonate a Violino e Violone o Cembalo. Geminiani's transcription as a concerto grosso published in London 1735.

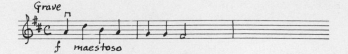

2238s [Concerto grosso (no. 9), A major.   13'
Transcribed from Arcangelo Corelli's Sonata
Op. 5 no. 9. Revised by Virgilio Mortari]
Preludio: Largo - Giga: Allegro - Gavotta: Allegro
Solo Vn.-Cemb.-Str.
Carisch, Milan, c1937
Score 12 p.
Geminiani's transcription published ca.1735.

321m [Concerto grosso (no. 12), La   13'30"
follia, D minor. Transcribed from Arcangelo
Corelli's Sonata Op. 5 no. 12. Revised by
Virgilio Mortari]
Follia - 23 Variations
Solo Vn.-Cemb.,Org.-Str.
Carisch, Milan, c1937
Geminiani's transcription published ca.1735.

GEMITO, ALESSANDRO DE CRISTOFARO.

4566 Allegro appassionato per orchestra
2(2nd alt. Picc.),3*,2,2-4,2,3,1-Timp.-Hp.-Str.
De Luigi Editore, Rome [n.d.]
Score 28 p.

4564 [Funeral march for orchestra]
2,3*,2,2-4,2,3,1-Timp.,B.Dr.-Str.
De Luigi Editore, Rome [n.d.]
Score 18 p.

4565 Sovra un'antica tomba [Over an ancient tomb]
2,3*,2,2-4Hn.-Timp.-Hp.-Str.
De Luigi Editore, Rome [n.d.]
Score 11 p.

GENDT, W. MERKES, VAN.
See: MERKES VAN GENDT, W.

GENÉE, FRANZ FRIEDRICH RICHARD.
Danzig 7 February 1823
Baden 15 June 1895

1572s Miranda-gavotte
Str.
Score: Ms. 4 p.
Parts: Cranz, Leipzig [n.d.]

GENG, CHARLES.

594s Menuet, [B-flat major]
Str.
Costallat, Paris [n.d.]
Score 11 p.

627v Notre Dâme des flots, meditation
Solo Vn.-2,2,2,2-4,2,3,1-Timp.-Hp.-Str.
Score: Ms. 11 p.
Parts: Costallat, Paris [n.d.]

GENZMER, HARALD.
        b. Blumenthal near Bremen 9 February 1909

236p [Concertino no. 2 for piano solo   21'
and strings]
1.Andante tranquillo - Allegro 2.Largo 3.
Burleske: Vivace 4.Finale: Adagio - Presto
Solo Pno.-Str.
Henry Litolff, Frankfurt/C.F. Peters, New York,
c1969
Score 64 p.
*Commissioned by the Frankfurt Adult Education
League. Composed 1963. First performance
Frankfurt, Living Music Week (Musica Viva-
Woche), 1964, Collegium Musicum der Frankfur-
ter Volkshochschule, Rudolf Lück conductor.*

2405s [Sonatina for strings]   12'
1.Adagio 2.Allegro moderato e energico 3.
(Pizzicato) Commodo 4.Tranquillo 5.Finale:
Allegro
Str.
Henry Litolff, Frankfurt/C.F. Peters, New York,
c1969
Score 19 p.
Composed 1968.

2373s Sonatina seconda, for strings [in F] 13'
1.Adagio, ma non troppo 2.Vivace 3.Largo
4.(Finale) Molto allegro
Str.
Henry Litolff, Frankfurt/C.F. Peters, New York,
c1972
Score 3 p.

GEORGE, THOM RITTER. Detroit, Michigan 23 June 1942

6470 In memoriam, CN 177 (1964)   6'
2,1,2,2-4Hn.-B.Dr.,Tam-tam-Hp.-Str.
Ms. c1964 by Thom Ritter George
Score 13 p.
*Composed 1964. First performance at the 34th
Annual Festival of American Music, Eastman
School of Music, Rochester, New York, 29 April
1964, Eastman-Rochester Symphony Orchestra,
Howard Hanson conductor. Won the Edward B.
Benjamin Award for Quiet Music, 1964.*

6678 Scènes de ballet, CN 212 (1965)   17'
1.Ouverture et danse générale: Allegro con brio
2.Quatre études: a)Andante ma non troppo b)
Allegro moderato c)Andante misterioso d)Viva-
ce pizzicato 3.Pas de deux: Adagio molto 4.
Finale: Allegro vivace

3*,2,2,2-4,2,3,1-Timp.,Perc.-Str.
Ms. c1965 by Thom Ritter George
Score 90 p. Large folio
*Composed 1964-65. Awarded the Howard Hanson
Prize at the Festival of American Music,
Eastman School of Music, Rochester, New York,
1965.*

GERBER, STEPHEN.   Middletown, Ohio 11 April 1948

154m Celebration suite for timpani and   13'
orchestra
1.Celebration 2.Soliloquy 3.Elan
Solo Timp.-3*,2,2,3*-4,4,3,1-Perc.-Str.
Ms. c1975 by Stephen Gerber
Score 104 p.
*Composed 1975. First performance Cincinnati,
5 April 1975, Cincinnati Symphony Orchestra,
Erich Kunzel conductor, Eugene Espino soloist.*

GERDES, FEDERICO.   Tacna, Peru 1873

3742 El rotario, marcha festiva, Op. 42   6'
2,2,2,2-2,2,2,1-Timp.,Perc.-Str.
Ms.
Score 19 p.
*Commissioned by the Rotary Club. First per-
formance Lima, Peru, 30 July 1922, Banda
Nacional, the composer conducting.*

GERHARD, FRITZ CHRISTIAN.   Germany 2 November 1911

2331s [Concertino for string orchestra, 1954] 8'
1.Schnelle Viertel, recht straff 2.Ruhig
3.Schnell, recht rhythmisch 4.Frisch
Str.
Breitkopf & Härtel, Wiesbaden, c1956
Score 11 p.
*Composed 1954. First performance Wuppertal,
Germany, 1956, Wuppertal Jugendorchester,
Lutz Goebel conductor.*

GERIN, CH.

1219s Rêverie champêtre [Rustic reverie]
Solo Vn.-Str.
Score: Ms. 8 p.
Parts: Decourcelle, Nice [n.d.]

GERKE, AUGUSTE.   Poland ca.1790
                                     Poland ca.1848

376v [Overture no. 2, violin and orchestra,
Op. 10]
Allegro assai - Recitativo - Adagio - Allegro
vivace - Larghetto - Allegro vivace
Solo Vn.-2(2nd alt. Picc.),2,2,2-2,2-Timp.-
Str.
Breitkopf & Härtel, Leipzig [n.d.]
Score 80 p. Large folio
*First modern performance at the Seventh Early
American Moravian Music Festival and Seminar,
Nazareth, Pennsylvania, 1964, The Festival
Orchestra, Thor Johson conductor.*

Gerlach, Theodor

GERLACH, THEODOR.   Dresden 25 June 1861
                                  Kiel 11 December 1940

92s Serenade, Op. 3 [B-flat major]
     1.Tempo di marcia 2.Andante leggiero
     3.Adagio 4.Duetto: Andante con moto
     5.Intermezzo 6.Finale: Moderato molto
     Str.
     Breitkopf & Härtel, Leipzig [n.d.]
     Score 24 p.

GERMAN, EDWARD.   Whitchurch,
            Shropshire, England 17 February 1862
                       London 11 November 1936

Real name: Edward German Jones

5201 Coronation march for full orchestra   5'
      2,2,2,2-2,2,3-Timp.,Perc.-Str.
      Novello & Co., London [n.d.]
      Score 23 p.
      *Composed 1911 for the coronation of King
      George V. Also known as Coronation March
      and Hymn.*

1520 Gipsy suite, four characteristic   12'
      dances
      1.Valse (Lonely life) 2.Allegro di bravura
      (The dance) 3.Menuetto (Love duet)
      4.Tarantella (The revel)
      2(2nd alt. Picc.),2,2,2-4,2,3-Timp.,Perc.-Hp.-
      Str.
      Novello, London, c1902
      Score 86 p.
      *First performance Crystal Palace, London,
      1892.*

3256 Nell Gwyn, three dances   10'
      1.Country dance 2.Pastoral dance 3.Merry-
      makers' dance
      2(2nd alt. Picc.),1,2,2-2,2(or Cnt.),3-Timp.,
      Perc.-Hp.-Str.
      Chappell, London, c1900
      Score 57 p.
      *Composed as incidental music to the play
      English Nell, 1900. First performance Prince
      of Wales Theatre, London, 1900.*

5191 [Orchestral suite in D minor. Valse   9'
      gracieuse]
      3*,2,2,2-4,2Cnt.,3,1-Timp.,Trgl.-Hp.-Str.
      Novello & Co., London, c1902
      Score 41 p.
      Composed for the Leeds Music Festival, 1895.

4284 [Romeo and Juliet. Pavane]
      2,1,2,2-2,2,3-Timp.,Perc.-Hp.-Str.
      Novello & Co., London, c1902
      Score 16 p.

*From the incidental music composed for Shake-
speare's play. Composed 1895. First performance Lyceum Theatre, London, 21 September 1895.*

4397 [Romeo and Juliet. Prelude]   5'30"
      2(2nd alt. Picc.),1,2,2-2,2,3-Timp.,Perc.-Hp.-
      Str.
      Novello & Co., London, c1902
      Score 33 p.

1518 Three dances, from the music to Shake-   9'
      speare's Henry VIII
      1.Morris dance 2.Shepherd's dance 3.Torch
      dance
      2(2nd alt. Picc.),2,2,2-2,2,3-Timp.,Perc.-Str.
      Novello, London, c1901
      Score 51 p.
      *Composed for the performance of the play at
      the Lyceum Theatre, London, January 1892.*

6974 Welsh rhapsody   18'
      1.Loudly proclaim: Allegro moderato (quasi
      Andante) 2.Hunting the hare - Bells of Aberdovy
      3.David of the white rock: Tranquillo 4.Men of
      Harlech: Allegro (Alla marcia)
      3*,2,2,2-4,2,3,1-Timp.,Perc.-Hp.-Str.
      Novello, London, c1905
      Score 86 p.
      *Based on Welsh folk melodies. Composed for and
      first performed at the Cardiff Musical Festival,
      1904.*

GERMANO, C.

1152s Pax [for solo oboe and string orchestra]
       Solo Ob.-Str.
       Score: Ms. 4 p.
       Parts: Decourcelle, Nice [n.d.]

1134s Pro patria
       Solo Va.-Str.
       Score: Ms. 8 p.
       Parts: Decourcelle, Nice [n.d.]

GERNSHEIM, FRIEDRICH.   Worms, Germany 17 July 1839
                        Berlin 10/11 September 1916

764v [Concerto, violin, Op. 42, D major]   26'
      1.Allegro non troppo 2.Andante affettuoso
      3.Finale: Allegro energico e con brio
      Solo Vn.-2,2,2,2-4,2-Timp.-Str.
      J. Rieter-Biedermann, Leipzig, 1880
      Score 47 p.
      *Composed 1879. First performance Rotterdam,
      22 January 1880, the composer conducting, Isidor
      Schnitzler soloist.*

595v [Concerto, violin, no. 2, Op. 86, F major]
      Allegro risoluto - Andante cantabile - Adagio -
      Allegro giocoso
      Solo Vn.-2(2nd alt. Picc.),3*,3*,2-4,2-Timp.,
      Glock.-Str.
      J. H. Zimmermann, Leipzig, c1914
      Score 80 p.
      Composed 1912.

582c [Concerto, violoncello, Op. 78, E   *17'*
minor]
In one movement
Solo Vc.-2,2,2,2-4,2,3-Timp.-Hp.-Str.
R. Forberg, Leipzig, ᶜ1907
Score 39 p.
Composed 1906. First performance Eisenach, 16
February 1907, the composer conducting, Karl
Piening soloist.

574m Divertimento, Op. 53 [E major]   *16'*
Solo Fl.-Str.
F. Luckhardt, Berlin, ᶜ1888 by G. Schirmer
Score 35 p.
Composed 1887. First performance Philharmonic
Club, New York, winter 1888-89.

652c Elohenu [God, Hebrew melody]
Solo Vc.-1,0,2,2-2Hn.-Str.
[n.p.] Leipzig [n.d.]
Score 5 p.

672v Fantasiestück, Op. 33 [D major]
Solo Vn.-2,2,2,2-2Hn.-Str.
Simrock, Berlin [n.d.]
Score 38 p.

937s [In memoriam, funeral song, Op. 91]
Org.-Str.
Oppenheimer, Hameln, ᶜ1915
Score 9 p.

1338 [Symphony no. 1, Op. 32, G minor]   *36'*
1.Allegro moderato 2.Larghetto 3.Scherzo
4.Finale: Allegro moderato assai
2,2,2,2-4,2,3-Timp.-Str.
Simrock, Berlin, ᶜ1911
Score 214 p.
Composed 1874-75. First performance Rotter-
dam, February 1875, the composer conducting.

4601 [Symphony no. 4, Op. 62, B-flat major]
1.Allegro 2.Andante sostenuto 3.Vivace
scherzando e con grazia 4.Allegro con spirito
e giocoso
2,3*,3*,2-4,2,3,1-Timp.,Cym.-Str.
N. Simrock, Berlin, ᶜ1896
Score 124 p.
Composed 1895.

4606 [Tone poem to a drama, Op. 82]
3(3rd alt. Picc.),3*,3*,3*-4,3,3,1-Timp.,Perc.
-Hp.-Str.
N. Simrock, Berlin, ᶜ1910
Score 80 p.
Composed 1910.

GERSCHEFSKI, EDWIN.
        b. Meriden, Connecticut 10 June 1909

3348 Septet, for brasses   *8'*
2Hn.,2Tpt.,2Tbn.,Tuba
Ms.
Score 35 p. Large folio
Commissioned by the League of Composers, and
composed 1938. First performance broadcast
over CBS, New York, 17 January 1939, brass

players from the Juilliard Graduate School,
Nicolai Berezowsky conductor.

2872 Test tubes, three pieces for full   *7'*
orchestra
1.Con moto 2.Andante sostenuto 3.Animato
3*,2,4*(1Cl. in E-flat),3*-Timp.,Perc.-Pno.
(alt. Cel.),2Hp.-Str.
Ms.
Score 35 p.
Composed 1936. First performance Bridgeport,
Connecticut, 6 May 1937, Bridgeport Orchestra
of the WPA, Frank Foti conductor.

GERSHWIN, GEORGE.
        Brooklyn, New York 26 September 1898
        Beverly Hills, California 11 July 1937

6664 An American in Paris. Revised by   *16'*
Frank Campbell-Watson
3(3rd alt. Picc.),3*,3*,2-3Sax.(1Alto,1Ten.,1
Bar.)-4,3,3,1-Timp.,Perc.-Cel.-Str.
New World Music Corp., New York, ᶜ1930
Score 94 p.
Composed 1928. First performance Carnegie
Hall, New York, 13 December 1928, New York
Philharmonic, Walter Damrosch conductor.

244p [Concerto, piano, in F] Edited by   *30'*
Frank Campbell-Watson
1.Allegro 2.Andante con moto 3.Allegro
agitato
Solo Pno.-3*,3*,3*,2-4,3,3,1-Timp.,Perc.-Str.
New World Music Corporation, New York, ᶜ1928,
1947
Score 116 p.
Commissioned by the Symphony Society of New
York. Composed 1925. First performance
Carnegie Hall, New York, 3 December 1925, New
York Symphony Orchestra, Walter Damrosch con-
ductor, the composer as soloist.

2377s Lullaby. Arranged for string orchestra
Str.
New World Music Corporation [New York] ᶜ1968
Score 12 p.
Originally composed for string quartet in 1919
or 1920. The opening theme incorporated into
an aria of the one-act opera, Blue Monday,
1922. First performance of quartet version at
Library of Congress, Washington, D.C., 29
October 1967, by the Juilliard String Quartet.
First performance in a transcription by Larry
Adler for harmonica and string quartet at the
Edinburgh Festival, 29 August 1963, by the
Edinburgh String Quartet and Larry Adler.

559p Rhapsody in blue, for jazz band and   *12'*
piano. Orchestrated by Ferde Grofé
Solo Pno.-1,1,2,1-3Sax.-2,2,1-Timp.,Perc.-
Banjo-Str.
Harms, New York, ᶜ1925
Score 81 p.
Completed 1923.

Gerstberger, Karl

GERSTBERGER, KARL.　　　Neisse 12 February 1892
　　　　　　　　　　　　Bremen 30 October 1955

　1564s [Concerto, string orchestra, Op. 19,
　G major]
　1.Andante con moto　2.Andantino　3.Allegro con
　brio
　Str.
　Bärenreiter, Kassel, 1930
　Score 42 p.
　Score dated Berlin, 19 September 1929.

GERSTER, OTTMAR.　　Braunfels, Germany 29 June 1897
　　　　　　　　　　　　Leipzig 31 August 1969

　1103m [Capricietto for four timpani and　　　*7'*
　string orchestra]
　Solo Timp.-Str.
　B. Schott's Söhne, Mainz and Leipzig, c1936
　Score 16 p.
　Composed 1932.

　915v [Concertino, viola, Op. 16]　　　*12'*
　1.Mässig bewegt　2.Ruhig, gehende Viertel
　3.Rondo
　Solo Va.-Ob.-Hn.-Timp.-Str.
　Benno Filser, Augsburg [n.d.]
　Score 28 p.

　5728 [Enoch Arden (The sea-gull's cry).　　*8'*
　Overture]
　2,2,2,2-4,3,3,1-Timp.,Perc.-Str.
　B. Schott's Söhne, Mainz, c1936
　Score 20 p.
　From the opera in 4 acts with libretto by K. M.
　von Levetzow, after the poem by Tennyson.　Com-
　posed 1936.　First performance Düsseldorf, 1936.

　5727 [Festive music for orchestra]　　　*7'*
　2,2,2,2-4,2,2-Timp.,Perc.-Str.
　B. Schott's Söhne, Mainz, c1937
　Score 24 p.
　Composed 1935.

　5122 [Upper Hessian peasant dances for　　　*12'*
　orchestra]
　1.Ziemlich langsam　2.Etwas plumpes Walzer-
　tempo　3.Etwas gemessen　4.Der Wetzlarer Och-
　senfestmarsch [The Wetzlar Oxen Festival march]:
　Etwas behäbiges Marschtempo
　1,1,2,1-2,2,1-Timp.,Perc.-Str.
　B. Schott's Söhne, Mainz, c1937
　Score 24 p.
　Composed 1938.

GERVAISE, CLAUDE.　　　　　16th century

　3231 Danses françaises de la Renaissance,　*5'*
　six danses, de Claude Gervaise, musicien de la
　chambre de François I et d'Henri II. Recueillies
　par Henry Expert, instrumentées par Rhené-
　Baton
　1.Branle de Bourgogne (Burgundy)　2.Branle de
　Poitou　3.Branle de Champagne　4.Branle gay
　5.Branle double　6.Gaillarde
　Fl.(alt. Picc.),Ob.,E.H.,2Bn.-Perc.-Str.
　M. Senart, Paris, c1937
　Score 24 p.

GERVASIO, N.　　　　　　　Savona, Italy 1847

　1021s Andantino religieux [D major]
　Str.
　Score: Ms. 5 p.
　Parts: Decourcelle, Nice, c1919

　361s Bice! Berceuse
　2Hn.(ad lib.)-Str.
　Decourcelle, Nice [n.d.]
　Score 3 p.

　536m Dans l'Oberland [little reverie]　　　*5'*
　Solo Ob.-1,0,2,1-2Hn.-Trgl.-Str.
　Decourcelle, Nice [n.d.]
　Score 7 p.
　Composed and first performed Nice, 1912, the
　composer conducting.

　799m Écoute-moi! [Listen to me, melody　　　*3'*
　for horn and small orchestra]
　Solo Hn.-1,1,2,1-Str.
　Score: Ms. 5 p.
　Parts: Decourcelle, Nice [n.d.]
　Composed and first performed Nice, May 1925,
　the composer conducting.

　752s En rêvant [Dreaming]
　Str.
　Decourcelle, Nice [n.d.]
　Score 3 p.

　1184s Feuille d'album, berceuse
　Str.
　Score: Ms. 4 p.
　Parts: Decourcelle, Nice, c1923

　496v Feuilles de printemps [bluette for　　　*4'*
　violin or viola with small orchestra]
　Solo Vn. or Va.-1,1,1,1-Str.
　Decourcelle, Nice [n.d.]
　Score 10 p.
　Composed 1897.　First performance Nice, Feb-
　ruary 1898, the composer conducting.

　1136s Le hautbois soupire [melody in the
　ancient style]
　Solo Ob.-Str.
　Score: Ms. 5 p.
　Parts: Decourcelle, Nice, c1923

　1561s Joyeux échos, petite valse-bluette
　Solo Fl.-Str.
　Score: Ms. 9 p.
　Parts: Decourcelle, Nice [n.d.]

　675s Menuet, D major
　2Hn.-Str.
　Decourcelle, Nice [n.d.]
　Score 4 p.

　1034s Page oubliée
　Solo Vc.-2Fl.-Str.
　Decourcelle, Nice [n.d.]
　Score 10 p.

Giannini, Vittorio

1458s Près du berceau, pensée fugitive
Solo Vn.-Fl.(obligato)-Str.
Decourcelle, Nice [n.d.]
Score 3 p.

1151s Souvenir de Naples
Solo Vn.-Str.
Score: Ms. 8 p.
Parts: Decourcelle, Nice, ᶜ1922

1074s Vers le ciel, prélude
Solo Vn.-Str.
Score: Ms. 6 p.
Parts: Decourcelle, Nice, ᶜ1928

GERWIN, G. pseudonym.
See: WINKLER, GERHARD.

GESUALDO, DON CARLO, PRINCE OF VENOSA.
Naples ca.1560
Naples 8 September 1613

1760s Dulcissima mia vita [She is the   7'
sweetness of my life, madrigal] Transcribed
for string orchestra by Tibor Serly
Str.
Edition Musicus, New York, ᶜ1939
Score 3 p.
Transcribed 1935.

GHEDIKE, ALEXANDER FEODOROVICH.
See: GOEDICKE, ALEXANDER FEODOROVICH.

GHEDINI, GIORGIO FEDERICO.
Cuneo, Piedmont, Italy 11 July 1892
Nervi, near Genoa, Italy 25 March 1965

768c [Inventions, concerto for violoncello, 19'
strings, timpani and cymbals]
1.Andante calmo e misterioso 2.Allegro espressivo 3.Allegretto 4.Andante 5.Allegro
moderato 6.Allegretto 7.Andante tranquillo
8.Allegro moderato e marcato 9.Vivace (all
continuous)
Solo Vc.-Timp.,Cym.-Str.
Ricordi & Co., Milan, ᶜ1941
Score 68 p.
*Composed 1940-41. First performance Venice,
10 September 1948. Dedicated to Alfredo
Casella.*

GHEVONDIAN, A. TER.
See: TER-GHEVONDIAN, A.

GHIONE, FRANCO.   Acqui, Italy 26 August 1886
Rome 19 January 1964

3929 Suol d'Aleramo [Small suite, for   15'
chamber orchestra]
1.Per i sentieri di Valoria [On the way to
Valoria] 2.Montanine [Girls of the mountains]
3.La leggenda del viandante [The story of the
hiker] 4.Sul prato (Giochi di bimbi ed echi
di canti, a sera) [In the park (The games of
the children and echoes of song, in the evening)]

1,1,1,1-Hn.-Pno.,Hp.-Str.
Ricordi, Milan, ᶜ1937
Miniature score 54 p.

GIALDINI, GIALDINO.   Pescia 10 November 1843
Pescia 6 March 1919

1422s Minuetto [A major]
Str.
Ricordi, Milan [n.d.]
Score 5 p.

GIANNEO, LUIS.
Buenos Aires, Argentina 9 January 1897
Buenos Aires 15 August 1968

1144v [Concerto, violin, Concierto Aymará]
1.Sostenuto 2.Lento 3.Non troppo vivo
Solo Vn.-2,2,2,2-4,2,3,1-Timp.-Str.
Ms.
Score 138 p. Large folio
*Composed 1942. Awarded 2nd Prize in the invi-
tation contest for a violin concerto by Latin
American composers, anonymously sponsored and
supervised by the Edwin A. Fleisher Music
Collection of the Free Library of Philadelphia,
1942. First performance Buenos Aires, 13 April
1944, orchestra of the Teatro Colón, Albert
Wolff conductor, Pessino soloist.*

3796 Obertura para una comedia infantil   6'
[for wind and percussion instruments]
2(1st alt. Picc.),2,2,2-2Hn.,1Tpt.-Trgl.,
Tambor(Dr.)-Cel.
Ms.
Score 25 p.
*Composed 1937. First performance in a broad-
cast, New York, 2 December 1941, NBC Symphony
Orchestra, Juan José Castro conductor.*

5640 Pericón, danza argentina [Argentine   6'
fan dance]
2(2nd alt. Picc.),2,2,2-4,3,3,1-Timp.,Perc.-
Hp.-Str.
Editorial Argentina de Música, Buenos Aires,
ᶜ1952
Score 34 p. Large folio
Composed 1948.

5643 [Variations on a tango theme]   22'
1.Preludio 2.Tema 3.Tango 4.In memoriam
5.1900 6.Intermezzo 7.Allegro vivo 8.Post-
ludio
2,2,2,2-2,2-Timp.,Perc.-Str.
Editorial Argentina de Música, Buenos Aires,
ᶜ1955
Score 95 p. Large folio
Composed 1954-55.

GIANNINI, VITTORIO.   Philadelphia 19 October 1903
New York 28 November 1966

1990s Concerto grosso for string orchestra 13'
1.Allegro 2.Introduction: Moderato - Aria:
Adagio 3.Allegro con brio
Str.

301

Giannini, Vittorio

Ms.
Score 19 p. Large folio
Composed 1946.

2897 Suite for orchestra   *15'*
1.On the lake 2.Siciliana 3.Sunset 4.Carnival
3(3rd alt. Picc.),3*,3(3rd alt. B.Cl.),3*-4,3,
3,1-Timp.,Perc.-Cel.(alt. Pno.),Hp.-Str.
Ms.
Score 109 p. Large folio
*Composed 1931. First performance New York, 23
June 1940, National Youth Administration Symphony Orchestra, the composer conducting.*

3115 Symphony, in memoriam Theodore   *30'*
Roosevelt
1.Grave 2.Andante sostenuto 3.Allegro vivo
4.Allegro appassionato
3*,3(3rd alt. E.H.),3(3rd alt. B.Cl.),3*-8,4,4,
1-Timp.,Perc.-Pno.,Cel.,Hp.-Str.
Ms.
Score 222 p.
*Commissioned by the trustees of the New York
State Theodore Roosevelt Memorial, 1934. Com-
posed 1935. First performance at the dedica-
tion of the New York State Theodore Roosevelt
Memorial, at the American Museum of Natural
History, broadcast from New York, 19 January
1936, NBC Symphony Orchestra, the composer
conducting. First concert performance at the
Sixth Annual Festival of American Music of the
Eastman School of Music, Rochester, New York,
30 April 1936, Rochester Philharmonic Orchestra,
Howard Hanson conductor.*

GIARDINI, FELICE DE.   Turin 12 April 1716
                              Moscow 8 June 1796

Also published as: Degiardino and Deiardino

2108s [Rondo. Transcribed for string   *5'*
orchestra by Ettore Bonelli]
Str.
Zanibon, Padua, c1937
Score 7 p.
*Originally composed for violin and figured
bass. This transcription 1936.*

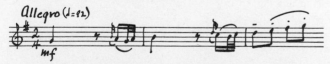

GIBBONS, ORLANDO.   Oxford (not Cambridge),
           England baptized 25 December 1583
                       Canterbury 5 June 1625

Fantazia (F major) for string quartet or
small string orchestra. Transcribed by Edmund
H. Fellowes
283s No. 1
637s No. 2
Str.
Stainer & Bell, London, c1925
Scores: 8 p., 8 p.

2349s In nomine [Consort of 5 parts, G minor] *2'*
Str.
Score: Musica Britannica, IX. Stainer & Bell,
London, c1962. Edited by Thurston Dart and
William Coates. 3 p.
Parts: Ms. c1976 by The Fleisher Collection of
Orchestral Music, Free Library of Philadelphia
Originally composed for viols.

4664 Suite. Transcribed for orchestra by   *9'*
Hershy Kay
1.A cornet voluntary: Andante 2.Madrigal -
Dainty fine bird: Slow 3.Fantasia: Maestoso
3*,3*,3*,3*-4,3,3,1-Timp.-Str.
Ms. c1948 by Hershy Kay
Score 37 p. Large folio
*Second movement is transcribed from Dainty
Fine Bird, No. 9 of Gibbons' First Set of
Madrigals and Mottets [sic] of 5 Parts: Apt
for Viols and Voyces, first published London,
1612. This transcription 1948. First per-
formance New York, 11 December 1948, New York
Philharmonic, Walter Hendl conductor.*

GIBBS, CECIL ARMSTRONG.   Great Baddow, near
          Chelmsford, England 10 August 1889
                        Chelmsford 12 May 1960

6855 Six British traditional tunes, freely   *13'*
arranged for small orchestra, Op. 132
1.The ballad of Yarrow 2.Have you seen but a
whyte lillie grow? 3.Dear harp of my country
4.Drink to me only with thine eyes 5.Waly,
Waly 6.The sentry box
2*,2,2-Timp.,Perc.-Pno.or Hp.-Str.
Oxford University Press, London, c1954
Score in reduction 22 p.

GIDEON, MIRIAM.   Greeley, Colorado 23 October 1906

3391 Allegro and andante, for orchestra   *12'*
2,2,2,2-2,1,1-Timp.-Str.
Ms.
Score 55 p.
Composed 1939.

6642 Symphonia brevis   *8'*
1.Allegro energico 2.Andante lirico - Chorale
2,2,2,2-4,2,2-Timp.-Str.
Composers Facsimile Edition, c1957 by Miriam
Gideon
Score 34 p.
*Commissioned by the Orchestra of the City
College of New York. Composed 1953. First
performance New York, 16 May 1953, Orchestra
of the City College of New York, Fritz Jahoda
conductor.*

GIGOUT, EUGÈNE.   Nancy 23 March 1844
                        Paris 9 December 1925

953v Méditation [C major]
Solo Vn.-2,2,2,2-2Hn.-Timp.-Str.
Score: Ms. 30 p.
Parts: Hamelle [n.p., n.d.]

GILARDI, GILARDO.   San Fernando 25 May 1889
                            Buenos Aires 16 January 1963

3805 Evocación Quichua   *8'*
      1,1,1,1-2,2,1-Timp.,Perc.-Str.
      Ms.
      Score 43 p. Large folio
      Originally composed for lute quartet, 1929;
      transcribed 1929. First performance Buenos
      Aires, 9 July 1941, Orquesta Sinfónica del
      Radio, Raúl Spivak conductor.

3369 Noviando, serie Argentina no. 2
      2,2,2,2-4,3,3,1-Timp.,Perc.-Hp.-Str.
      Ms.
      Score 33 p.
      First performance Buenos Aires, 13 April 1929,
      Orquesta Renacimiento, Juan José Castro con-
      ductor.

GILBERT, HENRY FRANKLIN BELKNAP.
        Somerville, Massachusetts 26 September 1868
        Cambridge, Massachusetts 19 May 1928

2613 Comedy overture on Negro themes   *9'*
      3(3rd alt. Picc.),2,2,2-4,2,3,1-Timp.,Bells-
      Str.
      H.W. Gray, New York, c1912
      Score 51 p.
      Composed ca.1906; revised 1909. Originally
      intended as the prelude to an opera, based
      upon the Uncle Remus stories of Joel Chandler
      Harris. The opera plan was abandoned and the
      overture was rewritten. First performance
      at an open-air Municipal Symphony Concert,
      Central Park Mall, New York, 17 August 1910,
      Franz Kaltenborn conductor.

2615 The dance in Place Congo, symphonic   *20'*
      poem, Op. 15
      3(3rd alt. Picc.),2,3*,3*-4,3,3,1-Timp.,Perc.-
      Hp.-Str.
      H.W. Gray, New York, c1922 by H. Gilbert
      Score 113 p.
      Composed ca.1906; inspired by writings of
      George W. Cable. First performance (as pan-
      tomime ballet), Metropolitan Opera House, New
      York, 23 March 1918, Metropolitan Opera Co.,
      Pierre Monteux conductor.

5650 Humoresque on Negro-minstrel tunes
      Allegro moderate e marcato - Andante espressivo
      2(2nd alt. Picc.),2,2,2-4,2,3,1-Timp.,Perc.-
      Hp.-Str.
      H.W. Gray Company, New York, c1913
      Score 54 p.
      Original title: Americanesque. Based on 3
      minstrel tunes: Turkey in the Straw (Zip Coon);
      Dearest May; Don't Be Foolish, Joe. Composed
      1903. First performance Boston, 24 May 1911,
      Boston Pops.

6841 Indian sketches, for orchestra
      1.Prelude: Andante con moto 2.Invocation:
      Andante: Posato 3.Song of the wolf: Andante

4.Camp dance: Allegretto 5.Nocturne: Larghetto
6.Snake dance: Moderato ma ruvidamente
3(3rd alt. Picc.),2,2,2-4,2,3,1-Timp.,Perc.-
Cel.,Hp.-Str.
Ms.
Score 92 p.
First performance 4 March 1921, Boston Sym-
phony Orchestra.

3457 The island of the fay, symphonic   *22'*
      poem after Edgar A. Poe
      3(3rd alt. Picc.),2,3*,3*-4,2,3,1-Timp.,Glock.
      -Cel.,2Hp.-Str.
      Ms.
      Score 82 p.
      Originally composed for piano, ca.1909.

3508 Nocturne, symphonic mood (after Walt   *12'*
      Whitman)
      3*,3*,3*,2-4,3,3,1-Timp.,Glock.-Cel.,2Hp.-Str.
      Ms.
      Score 48 p.
      Composed 1926. First performance Philadelphia,
      16 March 1928, Philadelphia Orchestra, Pierre
      Monteux conductor.

3509 Suite, for chamber orchestra   *16'*
      1.Prelude 2.Spiritual 3.Fantasy
      1(alt. Picc.),1,1,1(ad lib.)-Hn.-Timp.,Glock.-
      Hp.-Str.
      Ms.
      Score 102 p.
      Commissioned by Elizabeth Sprague Coolidge,
      1926. Composed 1927. First performance Boston,
      28 April 1928, Chamber Orchestra of Boston,
      Nicolas Slonimsky conductor.

6854 Symphonic piece
      3(3rd alt. Picc.),3*,3*,3*-4,3,3,1-Timp.,Perc.-
      Hp.-Str.
      Ms.
      Score 76 p.
      First performance 26 February 1926, Boston
      Symphony Orchestra.

5655 Symphonic prologue to J.M. Synge's   *5'*
      drama Riders to the Sea (revised version)
      3*,2,3*,3*-4,2,3,1-Timp.,Perc.-Hp.-Str.
      G. Schirmer, New York, c1919
      Score 31 p.
      Originally composed as Prelude for Small
      Orchestra, 1904; rescored and retitled, 1914.
      First performance of revised version New York,
      11 November 1917, New York Philharmonic.

2614 Two episodes for orchestra, Op. 2   *6'*
      1.Legend 2.Negro episode
      3*,2,2,2-4,0,3,1-Timp.-Str.(2Solo Vc. in no. 1)
      H.F. Gilbert, Boston, c1897
      Score 12 p.
      First performance Boston, 13 January 1896,
      Boston Ladies' Symphony Orchestra, Arthur W.
      Thayer conductor.

Gilchrist, William Wallace

GILCHRIST, WILLIAM WALLACE.
Jersey City 8 January 1846
Easton, Pennsylvania 20 December 1916

695p Suite for piano and orchestra
1.Scherzo 2.Idyll 3.Rondo grandioso
Solo Pno.-2,2,2,2-4,0,3,1-Timp.-Str.
Ms.
Score 109 p.

2465 Symphonic poem, G major   20'
2,2,2,2-4,2,3,1-Timp.-Hp.-Str.
Ms.
Score 87 p.
*Composed about 1910. First performance at the
unveiling of a bas-relief tablet, erected in
memory of the composer, in the corridor of the
Academy of Music, Philadelphia, Philadelphia
Orchestra, Leopold Stokowski conductor.*

2464 [Symphony no. 1, C major]   40'
1.Introduction: Vivace - Impetuoso 2.Adagio
3.Scherzo: Vivace 4.Finale: Molto allegro
3*,2,2,2-4,2,3,1-Timp.-Str.
Ms.
Score 253 p.
*Composed 1891. First performance Philadelphia,
1892, Manuscript Society and the Philadelphia
Symphony Society, the composer conducting.*

2470 [Symphony no. 2, D major. Edited and   40'
completed by William F. Happich]
1.Allegro moderato 2.Contemplation 3.Finale
- Allegro
2,2,2,2-4,2,3,1-Timp.,Perc.-Hp.-Str.
Ms.
Score 153 p.
*First performance Philadelphia, 9 April 1937,
Symphony Club Orchestra, William F. Happich
conductor.*

GILLARDINI, S.

1183s Minuetto [Ancient style, G minor]
Str.
Score: Ms. 7 p.
Parts: Decourcelle, Nice [n.d.]

GILLET, ERNEST.   Paris 13 September 1856
Paris 6 May 1940

2352s Au moulin [At the mill]   3'
Tic-tac(Drumstick on Music Stand)-Str.
Decourcelle, Nice [n.d.]
Score 3 p.

1866s Babillage (Plauderei)   3'30"
Str.
Paul Decourcelle, Nice [n.d.]
Score 3 p.

1413s Coeur brisé
Solo Vn.,Solo Vc.-Str.
Score: Ms. 6 p.
Parts: Decourcelle, Nice [n.d.]

318s Dans la forêt   3'30"
Str.
Decourcelle, Nice [1890]
Score 3 p.

320s Douce caresse
Str.
Decourcelle, Nice, c1893
Score 3 p.

511s Doux murmure
Str.(without Cb.)
Decourcelle, Nice [n.d.]
Score 3 p.

319s En chevauchant [On horseback]
Str.
Decourcelle, Nice [1890]
Score 3 p.

133s Entr'acte, gavotte   4'
Str.
Decourcelle, Nice [n.d.]
Score 4 p.

126s Gracieuse, gavotte
Str.
Ricordi, Milan, c1899
Score 5 p.

947v Idylle [violin solo and orchestra,   5'
E major. Orchestrated by R. Ziroldi]
Solo Vn.-1,1,2,2-2Hn.-Str.
Score: Ms. 14 p.
Parts: Decourcelle, Nice [n.d.]

708m Lamento [for trumpet and orchestra]   4'
Solo Tpt.-2,0,2,2-2Hn.-Str.
Score: Ms. 18 p.
Parts: Decourcelle, Nice, c1890 by C. Ugo
*Composed 1898. First performance Monte Carlo,
March 1890, Arthur Steck conductor.*

67s Loin du bal   3'
Str.
Decourcelle, Nice [n.d.]
Score 3 p.

1013s Madrigal pour violoncelle
Solo Vc.-Str.
Pitt & Hatzfeld, London [n.d.]
Score 7 p.

977v [Mélodie, no. 3, violin and orchestra,   2'
E major. Orchestrated by R. Ziroldi]
Solo Vn.-Fl.,Ob.,Cl.-Str.
Score: Ms. 3 p.
Parts: Decourcelle, Nice [n.d.]
*Composed 1894. First performance Paris, Jan-
uary 1895.*

127s Mes chers souvenirs
Str.
Ricordi, Milan, c1899
Score 10 p.

1472s Passe-pied [Air in the ancient   3'30"
  style]
  Solo Vc.(or Vn.)-Str.
  Decourcelle, Nice, c1890 by C. Ugo
  Score 3 p.

321s Patrouille enfantine
  Str.
  Decourcelle, Nice, c1890 by C. Ugo
  Score 3 p.

843s Petite câline, intermezzo
  Str.
  Ricordi, Milan [n.d.]
  Score 9 p.

972v Précieuse [E minor]   4'
  Solo Vn.-1,0,1-0,2,1-Dr.-Str.
  Score: Ms. 10 p.
  Parts: Decourcelle, Nice [n.d.]
  *Composed 1912. First performance Paris, April
  1912.*

140s Précieuse *and* Serenade-impromptu.
  Arranged for string orchestra by Theo. Moses-
  Tobani
  Solo Vn.-Str.
  C. Fischer, New York, c1890
  Score in reduction 11 p.

1082s La réponse du berger à la bergère,
  gavotte
  Str.
  Ricordi, Milan [n.d.]
  Score 7 p.

323s Sommeil d'enfant, berceuse
  Str.
  Decourcelle, Nice, c1892
  Score 3 p.

128s Sous l'ombrage
  Str.
  Decourcelle, Nice [n.d.]
  Score 3 p.

322s La toupie   2'30"
  Str.
  Decourcelle, Nice, c1890 by C. Ugo
  Score 3 p.

GILSE, JAN VAN.   Rotterdam 11 May 1881
                          Leyden 8 September 1944

2098 Variaties over een St. Nicolaasliedje
  [Variations on a Santa Claus song]
  2(2nd alt. Picc.),2(2nd alt. E.H.),2,2-4,2,3-
  Timp.-Str.
  A.A. Noske, Middelburg [1910]
  Score 81 p.

GILSE VAN DER PALS, LEOPOLD VAN.
  See: PALS, LEOPOLD VAN GILSE VAN DER.

GILSON, PAUL.   Brussels 15 June 1865
                          Brussels 3 April 1942

2325s Alla marcia [rhapsody for strings]
  Str.
  Maison Beethoven, Bruxelles [n.d.]
  Score 11 p.

5220 [Binche. Fantasy on popular airs from
  the Terror. Arranged for band by Jules
  Blangenois]
  2,2,5(1Cl. in E-flat),2-4Sax.-4,2E-flat Alto
  Hn.,2Tpt.,2Cnt.,5Bugles(1 in E-flat),3Tbn.,2
  Bar.,3Tubas(1Cb. Tuba)-Perc.
  Editions J. Buyst, Brussels [n.d.]
  Score 50 p
  *Also known as Fantaisie Carnavalesque. Com-
  posed 1906.*

1625s Elegie [C minor]
  Str.
  Ms.
  Score 24 p.

4542 [Inaugural fanfare for orchestra]
  3(3rd alt. Picc.),2,2,2-6,3,3,1-Timp.,Perc.-
  Str.
  May also be performed with additional instru-
  ments: 6Tpt.,6Tbn.,4Tubas,Hp.
  Breitkopf & Härtel, Leipzig, c1896
  Score 37 p.
  Composed 1887.

380s Mélodies écossaises
  1.The flowers of the forest 2.Sweet May
  morning 3.Jig and song (The general gathering
  1749)
  Str.
  Breitkopf & Härtel, Leipzig, c1895
  Score 17 p.

6975 Richard III overture
  2,2,2,2-4,2,3,1-Timp.,Perc.-Str.
  Ms.
  Score 60 p.
  Suggested by Shakespeare's play.

1235s Suite à la manière ancienne [E major]
  1.Moderato maestoso 2.Rapido 3.Andante
  ritenuto 4.Giga
  Str.
  A. Cranz, Leipzig [n.d.]
  Score 28 p.
  Composed 1913-14.

1624s Two Flemish folk-songs
  1.Slaet op den trommele van dirre don deine
  2.Van twee Koningskinderen
  Str.
  Ms.
  Score 28 p.

Ginastera, Alberto Evaristo

GINASTERA ALBERTO EVARISTO.
                    b. Buenos Aires 11 April 1916

777p Concierto argentino, para piano y
      orquesta
      1.Allegretto cantabile 2.Adagietto poético
      3.Allegro rustico
      Solo Pno.-2*,2*,3*,2-2,2,1-Timp.,Perc.-Cel.,Hp.
      -Str.
      Ms.
      Score 115 p. Large folio
      *First performance Montevideo, Uruguay, 18 July
      1941, Orquesta del Servicio Oficial de Difusión
      Radio Eléctrica (SODRE), Lamberto Baldi con-
      ductor, Hugo Balzo (to whom the work is dedi-
      cated) soloist.*

GIORDANI, TOMMASO.   Naples ca.1730
                     Dublin late February 1806

291p [Concerto, harpsichord and strings,   *13'*
      no. 3, C major] Edited by Riccardo Castagnone
      1.Allegro spiritoso 2.Larghetto 3.Presto
      Solo Hpscd.-Str.
      Ricordi, Milan, c1962
      Score 45 p.

294p [Concerto, harpsichord and strings,   *10'*
      no. 5, D major] Edited by Riccardo Castagnone
      1.Allegro 2.Rondò: Spiritoso
      Solo Hpscd.-Str.
      Ricordi, Milan, c1962
      Score 42 p.

GIORNI, AURELIO.   Perugia, Italy 15 September 1895
          Pittsfield, Massachusetts 23 September 1938

2737 Orlando Furioso, symphonic poem for   *15'*
      full orchestra
      3*,3*,3*,3*-4,3,3,1-Timp.,Perc.-Hp.-Str.
      Ms.
      Score 111 p.
      *Composed 1926. Freely based on episodes in
      Ludovico Ariosto's epic poem.*

GIOVANELLI, FRANCESCO.

1102s Annotta [sketch]
       Pno.,Harm.-Str.
       Ricordi, Milan, c1919
       Score 14 p.

1104s Elegia
       Pno.-Harm.-Str.
       Ricordi, Milan, c1919
       Score 11 p.

1103s Meditazione
       Pno.,Harm.-Str.
       Ricordi, Milan, c1919
       Score 9 p.

617s Nubi, [Clouds]
      Str.
      Ricordi, Milan, c1919
      Score 6 p.

GIPPS, RUTH.   Bexhill-on-Sea,
                    Sussex, England 20 February 1921

2313s Cringlemire Garden, an impression   *7'*
       for string orchestra
       Str.
       Ms.
       Score 6 p.
       *Composed 1951. First performance Birmingham,
       England, 20 February 1952, New Midland Orches-
       tra, the composer conducting.*

224m Leviathan, for solo double bassoon   *5'*
      and chamber orchestra, Op. 59
      Solo C.Bn.-1,2*,2,1-2Hn.-Str.
      Ms.
      Score 11 p.
      *Commissioned by Val Kennedy. Composed 1969.
      First performance London, 13 February 1971,
      Goldsmith's Repertoire Orchestra, Bryan Gipps
      conductor, Val Kennedy soloist.*

6874 Song for orchestra, Op. 33   *5'*
      2,2,3*,2-4,2,3,1-Timp.-Str.
      Ms.
      Score 11 p.
      Composed 1948.

6856 [Symphony no. 2, in one movement, Op. 30]
      2(both alt. Picc.),2(2nd alt. E.H.),2,2-4,2,3,
      1-Timp.,Perc.-Hp.-Str.
      Ms.
      Score 83 p.

6672 Symphony no. 3, Op. 57   *34'*
      1.Moderato - Allegro moderato 2.Theme: Con
      moto - 6 Variations - Coda: Moderato 3.Alle-
      gretto - Trio: Andante sostenuto - Coda 4.
      Andante: Allegro ritmico
      3(3rd alt. Picc.),3*,3*,3*-4,3,3,1-Timp.,Perc.
      -Cel.,Hp.-Str.
      Ms.
      Score 136 p. Large folio
      *Composed 1965. First performance London, 19
      March 1966, London Repertoire Orchestra, the
      composer conducting.*

7030 Symphony no. 4, Op. 61   *34'*
      1.Moderato - Allegro molto 2.Adagio 3.Scherzo:
      Allegretto 4.Finale: Andante

3(3rd alt. Picc.),3*,4*(1Cl. in E-flat),3*-4,
3,3,1-Timp.,Perc.-Cel.,Hp.-Str.
Ms.
Score 118 p. Large folio
*Composed 1972. First performance London, 28
May 1973, London Repertoire Orchestra, the
composer conducting. Dedicated to Sir Arthur
Bliss.*

GIRNATIS, WALTER.
   b. Posen, Germany (Poznań, Poland) 16 June 1894

4852 [Garden music for small orchestra]   *12'*
1.Polka: Con moto 2.Ländler: Lento 3.Kleines
Konzert: Allegro vivace
2(2nd alt. Picc. ad lib.),1,2,1-2,2,1-Timp.,
Trgl.,Cym.-Str.
B. Schott's Söhne, Mainz, c1940
Score 68 p.

GIULIANI, MAURO.   Barletta, Italy 1781
   Naples 8 May 1829 (not 1828)

411m [Concerto, guitar and strings, no. 2, *25'*
Op. 36, A major] Edited by Bruno Henze
1.Maestoso 2.Andantino 3.Rondo: Allegretto
Solo Guit.-Str.
VEB Friedrich Hofmeister, Leipzig [1960?]
Score 69 p.

GLANVILLE-HICKS, PEGGY.
   b. Melbourne, Australia 29 December 1912

314v Concerto romantico for viola and   *20'*
chamber orchestra
1.Maestoso 2.Lento moderato e molto espressivo
3.Molto spiritoso
Solo Va.-1,2*,2*,1-4,0,1-Hp.-Str.(w/o Va.)
American Composers Alliance, New York, c1957
by Peggy Glanville-Hicks
Score 106 p.
*Composed 1956. First performance Rainey
Auditorium, Metropolitan Museum of Art, New
York, February 1957, Carlos Surinach conduc-
tor, Walter Trampler soloist. Dedicated to
Walter Trampler.*

275p Etruscan concerto for piano and   *16'*
chamber orchestra
1.Promenade 2.Meditation 3.Scherzo
Solo Pno.-1,1,1,1-1,1-Timp.,Perc.-
Str.
Ms. c1955 by Peggy Glanville-Hicks
Score 82 p.
*Inspired by D. H. Lawrence's Etruscan Places
and The Painted Tombs of Tarquinia. Composed
1954. First performance New York, 25 January
1956.*

6638 Letters from Morocco for tenor and   *18'*
chamber orchestra
1.[No tempo indicated] 2.Presto 3.[No tempo
indicated] 4.Alla tarantella 5.Recitativo:
Andante tranquillo 6.Recitativo alla Muezzin
Solo Tenor-1,1,0,1-Tpt.-Timp.,Perc.-Hp.-Str.

American Composers Alliance, New York, c1953
by Peggy Glanville-Hicks
Score 63 p.
*Text by Paul Bowles (excerpts from his letters).
Composed 1952. First performance Museum of
Modern Art, New York, 22 February 1953, Contem-
porary Music Society, Leopold Stokowski con-
ductor, William Hess soloist.*

5308 Sinfonía da Pacifica   *15'*
1.Allegro energico 2.Recitativo: Lento tranquillo 3.Allegro giocoso
1,1,1,1-1,1,1-Timp.,Perc.-Str.
Ms. American Composers Alliance, New York,
c1953 by Peggy Glanville-Hicks
Score 50 p.
*Composed 1952-53. First performance Melbourne,
Australia, 25 June 1954, Bernard Heinze conductor.*

GLASER, SIGMUND.   Rokycan, Bohemia 1862

617c [Concerto, violoncello, Op. 8, A minor]
Allegro moderato - Andante - Allegro con fuoco
Solo Vc.-2,2,2,2-2,2-Timp.-Str.
Jurgenson, Moscow [n.d.]
Score 55 p.

GLASS, LOUIS CHRISTIAN AUGUST.
   Copenhagen 23 March 1864
   Copenhagen 22 January 1936

665p Fantasi, Op. 47 [D minor]
Solo Pno.-2,2,2,2-4,2,4-Timp.,Perc.-Str.
W. Hansen, Copenhagen [n.d.]
Score 51 p.

523c Frühlingslied, chant du printemps, Op. 31
Solo Vc.-2,1,2,2-2Hn.-Str.
W. Hansen, Copenhagen, c1903
Score 11 p.

GLAZUNOV, ALEXANDER KONSTANTINOVICH.
   St. Petersburg 10 August 1865
   Neuilly-sur-Seine, near Paris 21 March 1936

90 À la mémoire de Gogol, prologue sym-   *8'*
phonique, Op. 87
3*,2*,2,2-4,3,3,1-Timp.,Perc.-Hp.-Str.
Belaieff, Leipzig, 1912
Score 31 p.
*Nikolai Gogol (1809-52) was a Russian novelist
and playwright. Composed 1909. First performance St. Petersburg, 1909, the composer conducting.*

430 [À la mémoire de N. Rimsky-Korsakov,   *7'*
prélude pour grand orchestre, Op. 85 no. 2]
3(3rd alt. Picc.),3*,3*,3*-4,3,3,2-Timp.,Perc.
-Hp.-Str.
Belaieff, Leipzig, 1911
Score 30 p.
Composed 1908.

Glazunov, Alexander Konstantinovich

429 [À la mémoire de Vladimir Stasov, 4'
prélude pour grand orchestre, Op. 85 no. 1]
3*,3*,3,3*-4,3,3,1-Timp.,Perc.-Pno.,Hp.-Str.
Belaieff, Leipzig, 1911
Score 11 p.
*Composed 1906, in memory of the Russian music
critic and librarian.*

426 À la mémoire d'un héros, élégie pour 10'
grand orchestre, Op. 8
2,2*,2,2-4,2,3,1-Timp.-Str.
Belaieff, Leipzig, 1886
Score 45 p.
*Composed 1885. First performance St. Peters-
burg, 1886, George Dütch conductor.*

1134 Ballade pour grand orchestre, Op. 78 7'
3(3rd alt. Picc.),2,2,2-4,2,3,1-Timp.,Perc.-
Hp.-Str.
Belaieff, Leipzig, 1903
Score 38 p.
*Composed 1902. First performance St. Peters-
burg, 1902, the composer conducting.*

303 Carnaval, ouverture, Op. 45 [for 9'
orchestra]
3(3rd alt. Picc.),2,3,2-4,3,3,1-Timp.,Perc.-
Org.(ad lib.)-Str.
[Belaieff, Leipzig, 1894]
Score 59 p.
*Composed 1893. First performance St. Peters-
burg, 1893, the composer conducting.*

462c Chant du ménestrel, Op. 71 [for violon-
cello and orchestra]
Solo Vc.-3*,2,2,2-2Hn.-Str.
Belaieff, Leipzig, 1901
Score 13 p.
*Composed 1901. Later transcribed for violon-
cello and piano.*

434 [Chopiniana, Op. 46] Edited by J. 14'
Fortunatov
1.Polonaise, Op. 40 no. 1 2.Nocturne, Op. 15
no. 1 3.Mazurka, Op. 50 no. 3 4.Tarantelle,
Op. 43
3*,2,2,2-4,2,3-Timp.,Perc.-Str.
Score: Editions d'État Musique, Moscow, 1964.
105 p., and appendix of 55 p.
Parts: Belaieff, Leipzig [1894]
*Four of Chopin's piano works, transcribed for
orchestra by Glazunov in 1892. First perform-
ance St. Petersburg, 18 December 1893, Russian
Symphonic Concerts, Rimsky-Korsakov conductor.
Dedicated to the memory of Frédéric Chopin.*

411p [Concerto, piano, no. 1, Op. 92, 27'
F minor]
1.Allegro moderato 2.Tema con variazioni: An-
dantino tranquillo - 9 variations
Solo Pno.-3(3rd alt. Picc.),2,2,2-4,2,3,1-
Timp.,Perc.-Str.
Belaieff, Leipzig, 1912
Score 103 p.
*Composed 1911. First performance St. Peters-
burg, 1911, the composer as soloist.*

412p [Concerto, piano, no. 2, Op. 100, B major]
In one movement
Solo Pno.-3*,2,2,2-4,2,3,1-Timp.,Trgl.,Cym.-Str.
Belaieff, Leipzig, 1922
Score 71 p.
Composed 1917.

420v [Concerto, violin, Op. 82, A minor] 21'
In one movement: Moderato - Andante - Allegro
Solo Vn.-3*,2,2,2-4,2,3-Timp.,Perc.-Hp.-Str.
[Belaieff, Leipzig, 1905]
Score 66 p.
*Composed 1904. First performance St. Peters-
burg, 4 March 1905, Leopold Auer soloist. First
performance outside Russia, London, 17 October
1905, Henry Wood conductor, Mischa Elman solo-
ist.*

89 [Cortège solennel no. 1, for orchestra, 6'
Op. 50]
3*,2,3,2-4,3,3,1-Timp.,Perc.-Hp.-Str.
Belaieff, Leipzig, 1895
Score 31 p.
*Composed 1894. First performance St. Peters-
burg, the composer conducting. Dedicated to
Vladimir Stasov.*

1300 [Cortège solennel no. 2, for orchestra, 7'
Op. 91]
3*,2,3,2-4,3,3,1-Timp.,Perc.-Str.
Belaieff, Leipzig, 1912
Score 17 p.
*Composed 1909. First performance at the
twenty-fifth anniversary of the Russian Symphonic Concerts, St. Petersburg, 23 November
1909, the composer conducting.*

371 La danse de Salomée, Op. 90 no. 2 7'
[for orchestra]
3*,2*,2,2-4,2,3,1-Timp.,Perc.-Hp.-Str.
Belaieff, Leipzig, 1912
Score 41 p.
*Inspired by Oscar Wilde's poem Salome. Com-
posed 1909. First performance Paris, 13 June
1912.*

Deux préludes, Op. 85
See: [À la mémoire de Vladimir Stasov...]
[À la mémoire de N. Rimsky-Korsakov...]

2302 Les fanfares 2'
0,0,0,0-4,3,3,1-Timp.,S.Dr.,Cym.
Belaieff, Leipzig, 1891
Score 7 p.
*5 Fanfares nos. 3 and 5 by Glazunov, nos. 1, 2,
and 4 by Anatol Liadov. Also known as Slavlania.
Composed 1890. First performance St. Petersburg, 22 December 1890, Rimsky-Korsakov's
jubilee.*

289 Fantaisie, Op. 53 [for orchestra] 15'
3(3rd alt. Picc.),2(2nd alt. E.H.),3,2-4,3,3,1
-Timp.,Perc.-Hp.-Str.
Belaieff, Leipzig, 1896
Score 51 p.
*Composed 1894. First performance St. Peters-
burg, 1894, the composer conducting.*

333 Une fête slave, Op. 26 no. 4 [sym-   10'
phonic sketch for orchestra]
3*,2,2,2-4,2,3,1-Timp.,Perc.-Str.
Belaieff, Leipzig, 1890
Score 71 p.
*Originally composed 1888 as the finale of the
composer's String Quartet no. 3, Quatuor Slave.
Transcribed for orchestra 1888; first performance St. Petersburg, 1890, the composer conducting.*

433 [Finnish fantasy for orchestra, Op. 88]   15'
3*,3(3rd alt. E.H.),3(3rd alt. B.Cl.),3*-4,3,3,
2-Timp.,Perc.-Hp.-Str.
Belaieff, Leipzig, 1912
Score 51 p.
*Composed 1909. First performance Helsingfors,
7 November 1910, Philharmonic Society, the
composer conducting.*

432 [Finnish sketches for orchestra,   10'
Op. 89]
1.From Kalevala 2.Cortège solennel
3*,2(2nd alt. E.H.),2,2-4,2,3,1-Timp.,Perc.-
Hp.-Str.
Belaieff, Leipzig, 1914
Score 36 p.
*Kalevala is the Finnish national epic. Com-
posed 1912. First performance St. Petersburg,
1912, the composer conducting. Dedicated to
Robert Kajanus.*

1083 [The forest, fantasy for orchestra,   18'
Op. 19]
3*,2*,2,2-4,2,3,1-Timp.,Perc.-Hp.-Str.
Belaieff, Leipzig, 1889
Score 96 p.
*Composed 1887. First performance St. Peters-
burg, 1888, Rimsky-Korsakov conductor. Dedi-
cated to Vladimir Stasov.*

987 [From the Middle Ages, suite for   20'
orchestra, Op. 79]
1.Prélude 2.Scherzo 3.Sérénade du troubadour
4.Finale
3*,2(2nd alt. E.H.),2,2-4,3,3,1-Timp.,Perc.-
Pno.(ad lib.),Hp.-Str.
Belaieff, Leipzig, 1903
Score 97 p.
*Composed 1902. First performance St. Peters-
burg, 1904, the composer conducting. Dedicated to Véra Siloti.*

431 Intermezzo romantico, Op. 69   5'
3,2,2,2-4,2,3,1-Timp.-Str.
Belaieff, Leipzig, 1901
Score 34 p.
*Composed 1901. First performance St. Peters-
burg, 1902, the composer conducting.*

397 Le Kremlin, tableau symphonique,   16'
Op. 30
1.National holiday 2.In the monastery 3.
Meeting with the high prince
3(3rd alt. Picc.),3*,3*,3*-8,3,3Cnt.,3,6-
Timp.,Perc.-Hp.-Str.
Belaieff, Leipzig, 1892
Score 117 p.

*Composed 1890. First performance St. Peters-
burg, 1890, the composer conducting. Dedicated to the memory of Modeste Mussorgsky.*

1521 Légende carélienne pour orchestre,   10'
Op. 99
3(3rd alt. Picc.),3*,3,3*-6,3,3,2-Timp.,Perc.-
Cel.,2Hp.-Str.
Belaieff, Petrograd, 1918
Score 80 p.
*Inspired by a Finnish legend. Composed 1914.
Dedicated to Joseph Wihtol.*

1168 [March on a Russian theme, Op. 76]   6'
3*,2,3,2-4,3,3,1-Timp.,Perc.-Str.
Belaieff, Leipzig, 1902
Score 35 p.
Composed 1901.

422 Mazurka pour orchestre, Op. 18   8'
3*,2,2,2-4,2,3-Timp.,Perc.-Str.
Belaieff, Leipzig, 1889
Score 51 p.
*Composed 1888. First performance St. Peters-
burg, 1888, the composer conducting. Dedicated to Nicolas Antipov.*

1066v Méditation pour violon, Op. 32 [revised
edition]
Solo Vn.-2,2,2,2-2Hn.-Hp.-Str.
Belaieff, Leipzig, 1932
Score 6 p.
Dedicated to Paul Kochanski.

292 Ouverture solennelle pour grand   11'
orchestre, Op. 73
3*,2,2,2-4,2,3,1-Timp.,Perc.-Str.
Belaieff, Leipzig, 1901
Score 74 p.
*Composed 1897. First performance St. Peters-
burg, 1898, the composer conducting. Dedicated to the Russian Imperial Court Orchestra.*

308 [Overture no. 1 on Greek themes,   15'
Op. 3]
3*,2,2,2-4,2,3,1-Timp.,Perc.-Hp.(ad lib.)-Str.
Belaieff, Leipzig, 1896
Score 91 p.
*Composed 1881. First performance St. Peters-
burg, 1882, Anton Rubinstein conductor. Re-
vised 1884. Dedicated to L. A. Bourgault-
Ducoudray, who collected the Greek melodies on
which the overture is based.*

309 [Overture no. 2 on Greek themes,   15'
Op. 6]
3(3rd alt. Picc.),2,2,2-4,2,3,1-Timp.,Perc.-
Hp.-Str.
Belaieff, Leipzig, 1886
Score 119 p.
*Composed 1882. First performance St. Peters-
burg, 1883, Balakirev conductor. Dedicated
to M. A. Balakirev.*

Glazunov, Alexander Konstantinovich

2926 Paraphrase sur les hymnes des nations
alliées, pour orchestre, Op. 96
3*,3*,3,3*-4,3,3,2-Timp.,Perc.-Pno.4-hands,2Hp.
-Str.
Belaieff, Petrograd, 1915
Score 55 p.
*Based on the national hymns of Russia, Serbia,
Montenegro, France, England, Belgium, and Japan.*

1487 Pas de caractère (genre slave-hongrois) *3'*
pour orchestre, Op. 68
3*,2,2,2-4,2,3,1-Timp.,Cym.,Trgl.-Str.
Belaieff, Leipzig, 1900
Score 15 p.
*Composed 1900. First performance St. Peters-
burg, 1900, the composer conducting. Dedicated to Adelina Giuri.*

1224 Poème lyrique, andantino pour grand   *11'*
orchestre, Op. 12
2,2,2,2-4,2,3,1-Timp.-Hp.-Str.
Belaieff, Leipzig, 1888
Score 84 p.
*Composed 1882. First performance St. Peters-
burg, 1885, George Dütch conductor. Revised
1887.*

915 Le printemps, tableau musical pour   *12'*
orchestre, Op. 34
3(3rd alt. Picc.),3*,3*,2-4,0,3,1-Timp.,Small
Bells-Hp.-Str.
Belaieff, Leipzig, 1892
Score 43 p.
*Composed 1891. First performance St. Peters-
burg, 1893, the composer conducting. Dedicated to Nikolai Sokolov. Glazunov composed
different music for the tableau Spring in his
ballet The Seasons.*

3458 [Raymonda, Op. 57. Act I: Grande valse]
1.Grande valse 2.Pizzicato 3.Reprise de la
valse
3*,2,3,2-4,3,3,1-Timp.,Perc.-Hp.-Str.
Belaieff, Leipzig, 1898
Score 25 p.
*From the ballet composed 1896. First perform-
ance Maryinsky Theatre, St. Petersburg, 7 January 1898.*

91 [Raymonda, Op. 57. Act I: Introduction   *8'*
and Scene I]
3(3rd alt. Picc.),2,3,2-4,3,3,1-Timp.-Hp.-Str.
Belaieff, Leipzig, 1898
Score 21 p.

3459 [Raymonda, Op. 57. Act I: Valse fantastique]
3*,2,3,2-4,2-Timp.,Trgl.-Str.
Belaieff, Leipzig, 1898
Score 11 p.

3460 [Raymonda, Op. 57. Act I: Variations 1-3
and Waltz]
3*,2,3,2-4,2-Timp.,Perc.-Cel.,Hp.-Str.
Belaieff, Leipzig, 1898
Score 21 p.

92 [Raymonda, Op. 57. Act II: Grand coda]
3*,2,3,2-4,3,3,1-Timp.,Perc.-Str.
Belaieff, Leipzig, 1898
Score 21 p.

3461 [Raymonda, Op. 57. Act III: Coda]
3*,2,3,2-4,3,3,1-Timp.,Perc.-Str.
Belaieff, Leipzig, 1898
Score 18 p.

668 [Raymonda. Suite from the ballet, Op.   *40'*
57a]
3(3rd alt. Picc.),2(2nd alt. E.H.),3,2-4,3,3,
1-Timp.,Perc.-Cel.,Hp.-Str.
Belaieff, Leipzig, 1899
Score 108 p.

539m Rêverie, Op. 24 [for horn and orchestra]
Solo Hn.-2,1,2,2-Timp.-Hp.(or Pno.)-Str.
[Belaieff, Leipzig, 1922]
Score 13 p.
*Transcribed by the composer from his original
version for horn and piano, composed ca.1890.*

218m [Reverie, Op. 24. Transcribed for   *3'*
horn and orchestra by B. Jivoff]
Solo Hn.-2,2,2,2-Str.
Ms.
Score 13 p.
*Originally composed for horn and piano, ca.
1890.*

401 Rhapsodie orientale pour grand   *22'*
orchestre, Op. 29
1.Andante 2.Presto 3.Andante 4.Moderato
alla marcia 5.Finale: Allegro
3(3rd alt. Picc.),3*,4*(3rd alt. Picc.Cl.),2-
4,3,3,1-Timp.,Perc.-Hp.-Str.
Belaieff, Leipzig, 1891
Score 122 p.
*Composed 1889. First performance St. Peters-
burg, 1890, the composer conducting. Dedicated to Elie Répine.*

3472 [Ruses d'amour, Op. 61. No. 3: Ballabile
des paysans et des paysannes]
3*,2,2,2-4,2,3,1-Timp.,Perc.-Str.
Belaieff, Leipzig, 1900
Score 19 p.
*From the ballet, originally titled The Test of
Ladies or The Lady Domestic. Composed 1898.
First performance St. Petersburg, 30 January
1900.*

3473 [Ruses d'amour, Op. 61. No. 4: Grand pas
des fiancés]
3*,2,2,2-4,2,3,1-Timp.,Trgl.-Hp.-Str.
Belaieff, Leipzig, 1898
Score 17 p.

3474 [Ruses d'amour, Op. 61. No. 5: La
fricassée]
3*,2,2,2-4,2,3,1-Timp.,Perc.-Str.
Belaieff, Leipzig, 1898
Score 17 p.

966 Scène dansante, Op. 81   *12'*
3*,2,2,2-4,2,3,1-Timp.,Perc.-Hp.-Str.
Belaieff, Leipzig, 1905
Score 43 p.
*Composed 1904 as music to a ballet scene. First
performance St. Petersburg, 1904, the composer
conducting.*

3467 [Scènes de ballet, concert suite,   *4'*
Op. 52. No. 1: Préambule]
3*,2,3,2-4,3,3,1-Timp.,Perc.-Str.
Belaieff, Leipzig, 1896
Score 21 p.
*Composed 1894. First performance St. Peters-
burg, 1895, Russian Imperial Music Society
concert, the composer conducting. Dedicated
to the orchestra of the Opéra Russe, St. Petersburg.*

3468 Scènes de ballet... Op. 52. No. 2:   *7'*
Marionnettes
3*,2,3,2-2Hn.-Trgl.,Bells-Hp.-Str.(without Cb.)
Belaieff, Leipzig, 1896
Score 17 p.

3469 Scènes de ballet... Op. 52. No. 4:   *1'30"*
Scherzino
3*,2,3,2-4Hn.-Timp.,Trgl.-Str.
Belaieff, Leipzig, 1896
Score 11 p.

3470 Scènes de ballet... Op. 52. No. 5:   *8'*
Pas d'action
3*,2,3,2-4,0,3,1-Timp.-Hp.-Str.
Belaieff, Leipzig, 1896
Score 13 p.

3471 Scènes de ballet... Op. 52. No. 7:   *4'30"*
Valse
3*,2,3,2-4,2-Timp.,Trgl.,Bells-Hp.-Str.
Belaieff, Leipzig, 1896
Score 23 p.

246 Scènes de ballet... Op. 52. No. 8: Polonaise
3*,2,3,2-4,3,3,1-Timp.,Perc.-Str.
Belaieff, Leipzig, 1896
Score 29 p.

1005 [The sea, fantasy for orchestra,   *20'*
Op. 28]
3(3rd alt. Picc.),3*,3*,3-6,4,3,1-Timp.,Perc.-
2Hp.(2nd ad lib.)-Str.
Belaieff, Leipzig, 1890
Score 90 p.
*Composed 1889. First performance St. Peters-
burg, 1889, the composer conducting. Dedicated to the memory of Richard Wagner.*

1392 [The seasons. Autumn, Op. 67b]   *10'*
1.Bacchanal 2.Petit adagio 3.Variation, Le
satyre
3*,2(2nd alt. E.H.),2,2-4,2,3,1-Timp.,Perc.-
Cel.,Hp.-Str.
Belaieff, Leipzig, 1910
Score 62 p.

1378 [The seasons. Winter, Op. 67a]   *8'*
Introduction - 4 Variations: 1.Frost 2.Ice
3.Hail 4.Snow
3*,2,2,2-4,2,3,1-Timp.,Perc.-Cel.,Hp.-Str.
Belaieff, Leipzig, 1901
Score 37 p.
*From the ballet composed 1899. First perform-
ance St. Petersburg, 21 February 1900.*

247 [Serenade no. 1 for orchestra, Op. 7]   *6'*
2,2*,2,2-4,2(or 2Cnt.)-Timp.,Trgl.,Tamb.-Str.
Belaieff, Leipzig, 1886
Score 26 p.
*Composed 1883. First performance St. Peters-
burg, 1885, Mili Balakirev conductor.*

1186 [Serenade no. 2 for small orchestra,   *6'*
Op. 11]
2,1,2,2-2Hn.-Str.
Belaieff, Leipzig, 1888
Score 19 p.
*Composed 1884. First performance St. Peters-
burg, 1885, N. A. Rimsky-Korsakov conductor.*

930 [The song of destiny, dramatic over-   *12'*
ture, Op. 84]
3(3rd alt. Picc.),3*,3*,3*-4,3,3,1-Timp.-Hp.-
Str.
Belaieff, Leipzig, 1909
Score 55 p.
*Composed 1907. First performance St. Peters-
burg, 1907, the composer conducting. Dedicated to Maximilian Steinberg.*

1347 [Song of the Volga boatmen, arranged   *4'*
for orchestra and mixed chorus, Op. 97]
3*,2,2,2-4,2,3,1-Timp.,Perc.-Chorus(SATB)-Str.
Belaieff, Leipzig, 1915
Score 5 p.
*The traditional Russian song. This orchestra-
tion 1905. First performance St. Petersburg,
1906, Alexander Siloti conductor. Dedicated
to Alexander Siloti.*

427 Stenka Razine, Op. 13 [symphonic poem   *16'*
for orchestra]
3(3rd alt. Picc.),2,2,2-4,2,3,1-Timp.,Perc.-
Hp.-Str.
Belaieff, Leipzig, 1888
Score 98 p.
*Stenka Razin was executed in 1670 for leading
a Cossack rebellion against the Czarist government. Composed 1884. First performance St.
Petersburg, 1885, George Dütch conductor. Dedicated to the memory of Alexander Borodin.*

428 Suite caractéristique, Op. 9 [for   *40'*
orchestra]
1.Introduction - Danse rustique 2.Intermezzo
scherzando 3.Carneval 4.Pastorale 5.Danse
orientale 6.Elégie 7.Cortège
3*,2,2,2-4,2,3,1-Timp.,Perc.-Str.
Belaieff, Leipzig, 1887
Score 196 p.
*Composed 1884. First performance St. Peters-
burg, 1885, Rimsky-Korsakov conductor.*

Glazunov, Alexander Konstantinovich

423 [Symphony no. 1, Op. 5, E major] *42'*
1.Allegro 2.Scherzo: Allegro 3.Adagio 4.
Finale: Allegro
2,2,2,2-4,2,3-Timp.,Cym.,Trgl.-Str.
Belaieff, Leipzig, 1886
Score 231 p.
Originally composed 1881. First performance
St. Petersburg, 29 March 1882, Mili Balakirev
conductor. Dedicated to Nikolai Rimsky-
Korsakov.

424 [Symphony no. 2, Op. 16, F-sharp minor] *45'*
1.Andante maestoso - Allegro 2.Andante 3.Alle-
gro vivace 4.Intrada: Andantino sostenuto -
Finale: Allegro
3(3rd alt. Picc.),2(1st alt. E.H.),2,2-4,2,3,1
-Timp.,Cym.,Dr.-Str.
Belaieff, Leipzig, 1889
Score 221 p.
Composed 1886. First performance St. Peters-
burg, 1886, George Dutch conductor. Dedica-
ted to the memory of Franz Liszt.

291 [Symphony no. 3, Op. 33, D major] *40'*
1.Allegro 2.Scherzo: Vivace 3.Andante 4.
Finale: Allegro moderato
3(3rd alt. Picc.),2(1st alt. E.H.),2,2-4,3,3,1
-Timp.,Small Bells-Str.
Belaieff, Leipzig, 1892
Score 145 p.
Composed 1890. First performance St. Peters-
burg, 1891, Anatol Liadov conductor. Dedica-
ted to Peter Chaikovsky.

425 [Symphony no. 4, Op. 48, E-flat major] *32'*
1.Andante - Allegro moderato 2.Scherzo: Allegro vivace 3.Andante - Allegro
3(1st & 2nd alt. Picc.I & II),2(2nd alt. E.H.),
3,2-4,3,3,1-Timp.-Str.
Belaieff, Leipzig, 1894
Score 120 p.
Composed 1893. First performance St. Peters-
burg, 3 February 1894, the composer conducting.
Dedicated to Anton Rubinstein.

402 [Symphony no. 5, Op. 55, B-flat major] *36'*
1.Moderato maestoso 2.Scherzo: Moderato 3.
Andante 4.Allegro maestoso
3(3rd alt. Picc.),2,3(3rd alt. B.Cl.),2-4,3,3,
1-Timp.,Perc.-Hp.-Str.
Belaieff, Leipzig, 1896
Score 145 p.
Composed 1895. First performance St. Peters-
burg, 1896, the composer conducting. Dedica-
ted to Sergei Taneiev.

395 [Symphony no. 6, Op. 58, C minor] *38'*
1.Adagio - Allegro passionato 2.Tema con
variazioni: Theme and 7 variations 3.Inter-
mezzo: Allegretto 4.Finale: Andante maestoso
- Allegro pesante
3(3rd alt. Picc.),2,3,2-4,3,3,1-Timp.,Perc.-
Str.
Belaieff, Leipzig [1896]
Score 121 p.
Composed 1895. First performance St. Peters-
burg, 1896, the composer conducting.

1101 [Symphony no. 7, Op. 77, F major] *30'*
1.Allegro moderato 2.Andante 3.Scherzo: Allegro giocoso 4.Finale: Allegro maestoso
3*,2,2,2-4,2,3,1-Timp.,Perc.-Hp.-Str.
Belaieff, Leipzig, 1902
Score 143 p.
Composed 1900. First performance St. Peters-
burg, 3 January 1903, the composer conducting.
Dedicated to M. P. Belaiev.

1201 [Symphony no. 8, Op. 83, E-flat major] *40'*
1.Allegro moderato 2.Mesto 3.Allegro 4.
Finale: Moderato sostenuto - Allegro moderato
5(3rd alt. Picc.,1Alto Fl.,1C.Alto Fl.),3*,3
(3rd alt. B.Cl.),3*-4,3,3,1-Timp.,Perc.-Str.
Belaieff, Leipzig, 1907
Score 179 p.
Composed 1906. First performance St. Peters-
burg, 1906, the composer conducting.

6568 Theme and variations [Op. 72, F-sharp *18'*
minor] Transcribed for orchestra by Elizabeth
Camerano
3(3rd alt. Picc.),3*,3*,3*-4,3,3,1-Timp.,Perc.
-Hp.-Str.
Ms. c1962 by Elizabeth Camerano
Score 69 p.
Originally composed for piano solo, 1901.

1535 Triumphal march, for a grand *16'*
orchestra with chorus, Op. 40
4*(3rd alt. Picc.II),3(1C.Alto Ob.),4*,3*-4,3,
3,1-Timp.,Perc.-Chorus(SATB, ad lib.)-Str.
Belaieff, Leipzig, 1893
Score 35 p.
Composed for the World's Columbian Exposition
in Chicago, 1893.

435 [Two pieces for orchestra, Op. 14] *10'*
1.Idylle 2.Rêverie orientale
2,2,2,2-4Hn.-Hp.(ad lib.)-Str.
Belaieff, Leipzig, 1888
Score 31 p.
Composed 1886.

463c [Two pieces for violoncello and orchestra,
Op. 20]
1.Mélodie 2.Sérénade espagnole
Solo Vc.-2,2,2,2-4Hn.-Hp.-Str.
Belaieff, Leipzig, 1890
Score 51 p.
Composed 1888.

297 [Waltz no. 1, for orchestra, Op. 47] *13'*
3(3rd alt. Picc.),2,3,2-4,2,3-Timp.,Perc.-Hp.-
Str.
Belaieff, Leipzig, 1894
Score 46 p.
Composed 1893. First performance St. Peters-
burg, 1894, N. A. Rimsky-Korsakov conductor.
Dedicated to the composer's mother.

1255 [Waltz no. 2, for orchestra, Op. 51] *10'*
3*,2,2,2-4,2,3-Timp.,Perc.-Hp.-Str.
Belaieff, Leipzig, 1896
Score 55 p.

Composed 1894. First performance St. Peters-burg, 1894, the composer conducting. Dedica-ted to Nicolas Galkine.

1351 [Wedding march, for orchestra, Op. 21] *6'*
3*,2,2,2-4,2,3,1-Timp.,Perc.-Hp.-Str.
Belaieff, Leipzig, 1890
Score 28 p.
Composed 1888. First performance St. Peters-burg, 1889, the composer conducting. Dedica-ted to the composer's parents on their 25th wedding anniversary.

GLEBOV, IGOR. pseudonym.
See: ASAFIEV, BORIS VLADIMIROVICH.

GLEISSNER, FRANZ. Neustadt-am-Waldnab, Bavaria 1760
Vienna ca.1815

4103 Sinfonie, Op. 1
1,2,0,2-2Hn.-Str.
Ms.
Score 69 p.

GLIÈRE, REINHOLD MORITZOVICH. Kiev 11 January 1875
Moscow 23 June 1956

2123 [The Cossacks of Zaporozhe, symphonic *16'*
poem, Op. 64]
In one movement
3*,3*,3*,3-4,3,3,1-Timp.,Perc.-Str.
Universal Edition, Vienna/Mussektor, Moscow,
1929
Score 109 p.
Composed 1921. First performance Odessa, 23 December 1925.

3323 [Gulsara. Overture]
4*,4*(2 are E.H.),4*,4*-6,3,3,1-Timp.(2 play-ers),Perc.-2Hp.-Str.
Editions de l'Art de l'URSS, Moscow, 1938
Score 95 p.
From the opera inspired by an Uzbek theme, composed 1936. First performance Tashkent, USSR, 25 December 1949.

3577 [Heroic march of the Buriat-Mongolian *12'*
Autonomous Soviet Socialist Republic, Op. 71]
4*(3rd alt. Picc.II),4*,5*(1Cl. in E-flat),4*
-6,5,3,2-Timp.,Perc.-2Hp.-Str.
Editions de Musique de l'URSS, Moscow, 1940
Score 63 p. Large folio
Composed 1936. First performance Moscow, 1938, Moscow Philharmonic Orchestra, the composer conducting.

Ilia Murometz, symphony no. 3
See: [Symphony no. 3, Ilia Murometz, Op. 42,
B minor]

28s Mélodie. Transcribed for string orchestra
by William F. Happich
Str.
Ms.
Score 5 p.
This transcription commissioned by Edwin A. Fleisher for the Symphony Club, Philadelphia.

2927 [The red poppy, Op. 70. Complete ballet,
original version]
Complete in 3 acts
3(2nd & 3rd alt. Picc.I & II),3*,3(3rd alt.
B.Cl. & Cl. in E-flat),3(3rd alt. C.Bn.)-Alto
Sax.,Ten.Sax.-4,3,3,1-Timp.,Perc.-Pno.,Cel.,2
Hp.-Str.
Ms.
Score in 3 parts: 387 p., 538., 373 p.
Ballet in 3 acts with scenario by M. T. Kurilko. Composed 1926-27. First performance Bolshoi Theater, Moscow, 14 June 1927. Ballet was re-vised 1949 and is now known in the Soviet Union as The Red Flower. For excerpts from the ballet, see following 10 entries.

2499 [The red poppy, Op. 70. Act I: Dance in
the restaurant]
3,3*,3,3-4,3,3-Timp.,Perc.-2Hp.-Str.
Ms.
Score 15 p.

2575 [The red poppy, Op. 70. Act I: Girls]
3,3*,2,3*-Ten.Sax.-4,3,3-Timp.,Perc.-Pno.-Str.
Ms.
Score 23 p.

2398 [The red poppy, Op. 70. Act I: Russian *8'*
sailors' dance (Yablochko)]
3,3*,3*,3*-4,3,3,1-Timp.,Perc.-Str.
Luck's Music Library, Detroit [n.d.]
Score 31 p.

4215 [The red poppy, Op. 70. Act II: Cortège.
Orchestration by Arthur Cohn]
2,2,2,2-2Alto Sax.,Ten.Sax.-4,2,3,1-Timp.,
Perc.-Str.
Elkan-Vogel, Philadelphia, c1946
Score 27 p.

2502 [The red poppy, Op. 70. Act II: Dance of
the Chinese girls]
3*,3*,3(1Cl. in E-flat),3*-4,3-Timp.,Perc.-Cel.,
2Hp.-Str.
Ms.
Score 17 p.

2579 [The red poppy, Op. 70. Act II: Grand
adagio]
3(3rd alt. Picc.),3*,3*,3-4,3,3,1-Timp.,Perc.-
2Hp.-Str.
Ms.
Score 26 p.

2928 [The red poppy, Op. 70. Act III: Eccentric
dance]
3,3*,3*(B.Cl. alt. Alto Sax.),3-4,3,3-Timp.,
Perc.-Str.
Ms.
Score 22 p.

2500 [The red poppy, Op. 70. Act III: First
valse Boston]
3,3*,3*,3*-4,3,1,1-Timp.,Perc.-2Hp.-Str.
Ms.
Score 20 p.

Glière, Reinhold Moritzovich

2929 [The red poppy, Op. 70. Act III: Scene
of the Revolution]
3,3*,3*,3*-4,3,3,1-Timp.,Perc.-Str.
Ms.
Score 16 p.

6399 [The red poppy, Op. 70. Suite from the   20'
ballet, for large orchestra]
[1.Victorious dance of the coolies 2.Scene and
dance with the golden fingers 3.Coolie dance
4.The phoenix 5.Waltz 6.Dance of the Soviet
sailors (Russian sailors' dance)]
3(3rd alt. Picc.),3*,3(3rd alt. B.Cl. & Cl. in
E-flat),3(3rd alt. C.Bn.)-4,3,3,1-Timp.,Perc.
Cel.-2Hp.-Str.
Moscow State Publishers, Moscow, 1950
Score 147 p.

Russian sailor's dance from The Red Poppy, Op. 70
See: [The red poppy, Op. 70. Act I: Russian
sailor's dance (Yablochko)]
[The red poppy, Op. 70. Suite...]

1865 [Shah-Senem. Overture]   13'
3(3rd alt. Picc.),3*,3*,3-4,3,3,1-Timp.,Perc.-
2Hp.-Str.
Universal Edition, Vienna/Mussektor, Moscow,
1929
Score 67 p.
*From the opera composed 1925; revised 1933-34.
First performance Baku, U.S.S.R., 4 May 1934.
Dedicated to Mme. Chewkett-Khanoum Mamédova.*

396 [The Sirens, symphonic poem, Op. 33]   15'
4*,3*,4*,3*-6,3,3,1-Timp.,Perc.-Cel.,2Hp.-Str.
Belaieff, Leipzig, 1912
Score 90 p.
*Composed 1908. First performance Moscow, 30
January 1909, Emil Cooper conductor. Dedica-
ted to Marie Glière.*

556 [Symphony no. 1, Op. 8, E-flat major]   35'
1.Andante - Allegro moderato 2.Allegro molto
vivace 3.Andante 4.Allegro
3(3rd alt. Picc.),2,2,2-4,2,3,1-Timp.,B.Dr.,
Cym.-Str.
Belaieff, Leipzig, 1905
Score 153 p.
*Composed 1899-1900. First performance Moscow,
3 January 1903.*

557 [Symphony no. 2, Op. 25, C minor]   45'
1.Allegro pesante 2.Allegro giocoso 3.Andante
con variazioni 4.Allegro vivace
3(3rd alt. Picc.),3*,3(3rd alt. B.Cl.),3-4,3,3,
1-Timp.,Perc.-Hp.-Str.
Belaieff, Leipzig, 1912
Score 273 p.
*Composed 1907. First performance Berlin, 23
January 1908, Serge Koussevitzky conductor.
Dedicated to Serge Koussevitzky.*

984 [Symphony no. 3, Ilia Murometz,   ca.67'
Op. 42, B minor]
1.[Wandering pilgrims, Ilia of Murom, and
Sviatogor] (15'30") 2.[Solovei the brigand]
(25') 3.[At the court of Vladimir the Sun

Prince] (6') 4.[The exploits and petrification
of Ilia of Murom] (20')
4*(3rd alt. Picc.II),4*,4*,4*-8,4,4,1-Timp.,Perc.
-Cel.,2Hp.-Str.
Jurgenson, Moscow [n.d.]
Score 418 p. in 4 parts
*Ilia of Murom is a legendary Russian hero. Com-
posed 1909-11. First performance Moscow, 23
March 1912, Emil Cooper conductor. Dedicated
to Alexander Glazunov.*

GLINKA, MIKHAIL IVANOVICH.
Novosspaskoye, Russia 1 June 1804
Berlin 15 February 1857

310 [Capriccio brillante on the theme, Jota   9'
Aragonesa, for orchestra. Revised by N. Rimsky-
Korsakov and A. Glazunov]
2,2,2,2-4,2,3,Ophicl.-Timp.,Perc.-Hp.-Str.
Belaieff, Leipzig, 1901
Score 61 p.
*Also known as Spanish Overture No. 1. Theme
is a traditional Spanish dance melody. Com-
posed 1845.*

381 [Ivan Susanin. Overture]   10'
2,2,2,2-4,2,3-Timp.-Str.
B. Schott's Söhne, Mainz [1860?]
Score 66 p.
*From the opera composed 1835, inspired by the
Polish invasion of Russia in 1613. Title
changed to A Life for the Tsar for the first
performance, St. Petersburg, 9 December 1836.
Since 1917, known in the Soviet Union as Ivan
Susanin.*

1006 [Ivan Susanin. Dances]   10'
2,2,2,2-4,2,3-Timp.-Str.
Jurgenson, Moscow [1904?]
Score 13 p.

1135 [Ivan Susanin. Krakoviak]
2,2,2,2-4,2,3-Timp.-Str.
Jurgenson, Moscow [1904?]
Score 29 p.

1031 [Ivan Susanin. Mazurka]
2,2,2,2-4,2,3-Timp.-Str.
Jurgenson, Moscow [1904?]
Score 23 p.

Jota aragonesa
See: [Capriccio brillante on the theme, Jota
Aragonesa, for orchestra]

229 Kamarinskaia [fantasy on two Russian   7'
themes, for orchestra]. Revised by N. Rimsky-
Korsakov and A. Glazunov
2,2,2,2-2,2,1-Timp.-Str.
Belaieff, Leipzig, 1902
Score 33 p.
Composed 1848.

A life for the Tsar
See: [Ivan Susanin...]

1098 La première polka [for piano 4-hands.
Transcribed for orchestra by Mili Balakirev]
3*,2,2,2-4,2,3,1-Timp.,Perc.-Hp.-Str.
Jurgenson, Moscow [1904?]
Score 29 p.

670 [Prince Kholmsky. Incidental music to   21'
the play]
1.Ouverture: Maestoso e moderato assai - Agitato vivace 2.[Prelude to Act II]: Moderato
3.[Hebrew song]: Allegro moderato 4.[Ilyini-
shna's song]: Allegretto 5.[Prelude to Act
III]: Allegretto 6.[Rachel's dream]: Moderato
assai 7.[Prelude to Act IV]: Marcia, allegro
con spirito, maestoso 8.[Prelude to Act V]:
Allegro con spirito
2,2,2,2-2,2,1-Timp.-2Sop.Voices,Chorus(SATB)-
Str.
Jurgenson, Moscow [1904?]
Score 133 p.
*Composed 1840 for the play by Nestor Kukolnik,
to whom the music is dedicated.*

203s [Quartet, strings, no. 2, F major. Minuet
and trio]
Str.(without Cb.)
Kistner, Leipzig [190-?]
Score 1 p.
Composed 1830.

230 Ruslan and Ludmila. Overture   4'
2,2,2,3*-4,2,3-Timp.-Str.
Russian-American Music Publishers, New York,
1943
Score 62 p.
*From the opera based on Pushkin's poem. Com-
posed 1838-41. First performance Bolshoi
Theatre, St. Petersburg, 9 December 1842.*

4929 [Ruslan and Ludmila. Dances from   10'
Acts 3 and 4. Arranged by Mili Balakirev and
Sergei Liapunov]
3*,2,2,2-4,2,3-Timp.,Perc.-Str.
[Moscow State Publishers, Moscow, 1949]
Score 67 p.

1454 [Ruslan and Ludmila. March and Oriental
dances]
1.[March]: Tempo di marcia 2.[Oriental dances]:
Turkish, Arabic - Lesginka
3*,2,2,3*-4,2,3-Timp.,Perc.-Str.
Jurgenson, Moscow [1904?]
Score 45 p.

256 [Souvenir of a summer night in Madrid,   10'
fantasy on Spanish themes, for orchestra]
2,2,2,2-4,2,1-Timp.,Perc.-Str.
Kalmus, New York [n.d.]
Score 36 p.
*Also known as Spanish Overture No. 2. Com-
posed 1848.*

Spanish overtures
See: [Capriccio brillante on the theme, Jota
Aragonesa, for orchestra]
[Souvenir of a summer night in Madrid,
fantasy on Spanish themes]

632 Valse-fantaisie [for orchestra]   5'
2,2,2,2-2,2,1-Timp.,Trgl.-Str.
Kalmus, New York [n.d.]
Score 42 p.
Composed 1839; revised 1856.

GLUCK, CHRISTOPH WILLIBALD.
Erasbach, Bavaria 2 July 1714
Vienna 15 November 1787

1021 [Airs de ballet, suite no. 1. Arranged 18'
by F. A. Gevaert]
1.[Dance of the athletes] 2.Menuet 3.Passa-
caglia (all from Iphigenia at Aulis)
2,2,2,2-2,2-Timp.-Str.
Durand, Paris [n.d.]
Score 27 p.
Arranged 1876. First performance Paris, 1878.

490 [Airs de ballet, suite no. 2. Arranged   22'
by F. A. Gevaert]
1.Air 2.[Dance of the slaves] 3.Tambourin (all
from Iphigenia at Aulis) 4.Gavotte (Armide)
5.Grande chaconne (Iphigenia at Aulis, and
Orpheus)
2*,2,2,2-2,2-Timp.,Tamb.-Str.
Durand, Paris [n.d.]
Score 42 p.
Arranged 1878. First performance Paris, 1879.

902 [Alceste. Overture. Wotquenne no. 44.   9'
Revisions by Felix Weingartner]
2,2,2,3*-2,0,3-Str.
Breitkopf & Härtel, Leipzig, c1898
Score 27 p.
*From the opera composed 1767. First perform-
ance Vienna, 26 December 1767.*

674s [Alceste. Act I: Marche réligieuse.
Wotquenne no. 44. Transcribed for solo flute
and strings by J. Ollivier]
Solo Fl.-Str.
Score: Ms. 3 p.
Parts: Durand, Paris [n.d.]

4406 [Armide. Overture. Wotquenne no. 45]   5'
0,2,0,1-2,2-Timp.-Str.
Schlesinger, Berlin [184-?]
Score 14 p.
*From the opera in 5 acts with libretto by
Philippe Quinault. Composed 1777. First performance Académie Royale de Musique, Paris,
23 September 1777. This overture is the same
as that used for the opera Telemacco, first
performance in 1765.*

1468s [Armide. Act IV: Musette (Gavotte).
Wotquenne no. 45. Transcribed for bassoons
and string orchestra]
2Bn.-Str.
A. Durand, Paris [n.d.]
Score [4] p.

Gluck, Christoph Willibald

334 Ballet suite no. 1. Arranged by Felix   18'
Mottl
1.Introduction (Don Juan) - Air gai, Lento, Air
gai repeated (Iphigenia at Aulis) 2.Dance of
the blest (Orpheus) 3.Musette (Armide) 4.Air
gai (Iphigenia at Aulis) - Sicilienne (Armide),
Air gai repeated
3*,2(1st alt. E.H.),2,2-4,2-Timp.,Trgl.,Tamb.-
Str.
Peters, Leipzig [n.d.]
Score 43 p.
*Arranged 1896. First performance Karlsruhe,
1896, Mottl conductor.*

997 Ballet suite no. 2. Arranged by Felix   15'
Mottl
1.March (Alceste) - Minuet (Iphigenia at Aulis)
- March (repeated) 2.Grazioso (Paris and
Helena) 3.Dance of the slaves (Iphigenia at
Aulis)
2(2nd alt. Picc.),2,2,2-2,2,3-Timp.,Trgl.,Tamb.
-Str.
Peters, Leipzig [n.d.]
Score 33 p.
*Arranged 1899. First performance Karlsruhe,
1900, Mottl conductor.*

7016 [The dance. Sinfonia, G major. Wotquenne
no. 19]
1.Allegro 2.Andante 3.Allegro très énergique
2Ob.-2Hn.-Str.
Ms.
Score 23 p.
*From the dramatic pastorale in one act to the
poem by Pietro Metastasio. First performance
Teatro della Favorita, Laxenburg, near Vienna,
5 May 1755.*

1167 [Don Juan. Wotquenne no. II.2. Four
movements from the ballet. Arranged by Hermann
Kretzschmar]
1.Overture and Andante grazioso 2.Brillante,
Allegretto risoluto, Allegretto tranquillo
3.Allegro molto, grazioso 4.Finale
2,2,0,2-2,0,1-Str.
Breitkopf & Härtel, Leipzig, c1895
Score 31 p.
*Ballet composed 1761. This arrangement 1894.
First performance Leipzig, 1895, Kretzschmar
conductor.*

10 [Iphigénie en Aulide. Overture. Wot-   10'
quenne no. 40. Revised by Richard Wagner]
2,2,2,3-4,3-Timp.-Str.
Breitkopf & Härtel, Leipzig [n.d.]
Score 36 p.
*From the opera first performed at the Grand
Opéra, Paris, 19 April 1774.*

138s [Iphigénie en Aulide. Overture. Wotquenne
no. 40. Transcribed anonymously]
Pno.-Str.
Ms.
Score 25 p.
*Bound with Bach, Overture (Suite) No. 3, Two
Gavottes; Mozart, Don Giovanni, Canzonetta;
and Schubert, March, Op. 51 no. 1 (Marche
Militaire).*

7086 [Orphée et Eurydice. Overture and complete
dance music. French version. Wotquenne no. 41]
Edited by Mlle. F. Pelletan, Camille Saint-
Saëns and J. Tiersot
Overture: Allegro molto. Act I, Scene I: Pan-
tomime: Dolce Act II, Scene 1: Danse d'une
Furie: Vif - Air de Furies: Vivement. Act II,
Scene 2: Ballet des ombres heureuses: Lent;
très doux - Solo de flûte - Air [de ballet]:
Dolce con espressione Act II, Scene 3: Ballet:
Assez lent Act II, Scene 4: Ballet général des
ombres heureuses Act III, Scene 3: Ballet:
Gracieux - Gavotte: Allegro - Air vif - Menuet:
Gracieux ballet: Maestoso - Très lentement.
Chacone
2,2,2,2-2,2,3-Timp.-Str.
Score: Durand, Paris edition of 1898. 92 p.
Parts: Ms. c1975 by The Fleisher Collection of
Orchestral Music, Free Library of Philadelphia
*From the opera in three acts with text by
Ranieri da Calzabigi. First performance of
Italian version, Burgtheater, Vienna, 5 Octo-
ber 1762. This French version, with new
libretto by Pierre-Louis Moline and added bal-
let music first performed in Paris, 2 August
1774.*

1349s [Orphée et Eurydice. Overture. Wotquenne
no. 41. Transcribed for string orchestra by
W.G. Whittaker]
Str.
Oxford University Press, London, c1928
Score 6 p.

1350s [Orphée et Eurydice. Act I: Pantomime
(Lento); Act II: Lento dolcissimo; Act II:
Lento. Wotquenne no. 41] Transcribed by
W.G. Whittaker
Fl.(ad lib.)-Str.
Oxford University Press, London, c1928
Score 8 p.
*Title on score: Ballet Music from Orpheus,
Book I.*

1351s [Orphée et Eurydice. Act II: Allegretto
dolce; Act II: Lento. Wotquenne no. 41]
Transcribed by W.G. Whittaker
Fl.(ad lib.)-Str.
Oxford University Press, London, c1928
Score 7 p.
*Title on score: Ballet Music from Orpheus,
Book II.*

721s [Orphée et Eurydice. Act II: Air de ballet.
(Melody in F). Wotquenne no. 41. Arranged by
Sydney Robjohns]
Pno.-Str.
J. Williams, London, c1927
Score 3 p.

684s [Orphée et Eurydice. Act II: Air de   6'
ballet (Menuet). Wotquenne no. 41. Orchestrated by J. Ollivier]
2Fl.-Str.
Score: Ms. 5 p.
Parts: Durand, Paris [n.d.]

4413   Paride ed Elena [Paris and Helena. Overture. Wotquenne no. 39   Edited by Hans von
Bülow]
2,2,2,2-4,2,1-Timp.-Str.
C.F. Peters, Leipzig [186-?]
Score 28 p.
*From the opera in 5 acts, Paride ed Elena with
libretto by Ranieri di Calzabigi.   Composed
1769.*

942   Paride ed Elena [Paris and Helena.   10'
Act III, Ballettmusik: Aria per gli atleti
and Chaconne and gavotte. Wotquenne no. 39.
Arranged by Carl Reinecke]
0,2,2,2-2,2,3-Timp.-Str.
Breitkopf & Härtel, Leipzig [n.d.]
Score 21 p.
*Not the complete ballet music from the opera.
This arrangement 1874; first performance Leip-
zig, 1875, Reinecke conductor.*

653s   Paride ed Elena [Paris and Helena. Act
III: Gavotte. Wotquenne no. 39. Arranged by
Henry Lawson]
Str.
Score: Ms. 3 p.
Parts: B. Schott's Söhne, Mainz [n.d.]
Bound with Schubert, Serenade, D.957.

7090   [Semiramide riconosciuta. Act II: Tempo
di minuetto. Wotquenne no. 13. *And* Armide. Act
IV: Musette. Wotquenne no. 45. Transcribed for
brass ensemble by Norman Black]
1.Menuetto from Semiramide 2.Musette from
Armide
Hn.,2Tpt.,2Tbn.
Ms.
Score 11 p.

1747s   Sinfonia, G major. Edited by Hans   8'
Gál
2Hn.-Str.
Universal Edition, Vienna, c1934
Score 14 p.
*Original version, the overture to the opera
Ipermnestra, composed 1744. First performance
of this version in a broadcast, Copenhagen,
2 October 1934.*

5679   [Symphony for 2 horns and string   6'
orchestra, F major] Edited by Rudolf Gerber
1.Allegro 2.Andante affettuoso 3.Tempo di
menuetto with Trio
2Hn.-Cemb.-Str.
Bärenreiter, Kassel [1953]
Score 14 p.
Not listed in Wotquenne thematic catalog.

3726   Il Telemacco ossia l'Isola di Circe
[Telemachus or the Isle of Circe. Overture.
Wotquenne no. 34]
0,2,0,1-2,2-Timp.-Str.
Ms.
Score 26 p.
*Gluck later used this work as the overture to
his opera, Armide.*

3727   Il Telemacco ossia l'Isola di Circe
[Act I: Ballet music. Wotquenne no. 34]
Bn.-Str.
Ms.
Score 4 p.

6133   [Three festive marches for small orchestra.
Wotquenne no. II.B and II.A.3. Edited by Hans
Fischer]
1.March in G major 2.March from Allessandro
3.March from Allessandro
0,2,0,1-2,2-Timp.-Str.
Chr. Friedrich Vieweg, Berlin, c1937
Score 11 p.

GNAGA, ANDREA.

1180s   Frasi galanti [Courteous phrases,
minuet. Arranged for strings and flute by the
composer]
Fl.-Str.
Score: Ms. 5 p.
Parts: Ricordi, Milan [n.d.]

GNECCHI, VITTORIO.   Milan 17 July 1876
                             Milan 1 February 1954

2573   Cassandra. Overture
3*,3*,3*,2-4,2,2Cnt.,3,1-Timp.,Perc.-Cel.,Hp.-
Str.
Edition Adler, Berlin, c1933
Score 35 p.
Opera composed 1905; revised probably 1908.

2571   Danza campestre [Rustic dance] from the
opera, La Rosiera, Act II
3(3rd alt. Picc.),3*,3*,2-4,2,2Cnt.,3,1-Timp.,
Perc.-Pno.,Cel.,Hp.-Str.
Edition Adler, Berlin, c1933
Score 24 p. Large folio
Opera composed 1910.

2578   Tempo di sinfonia [D-flat major]
3(3rd alt. Picc.),3*,3*,2-4,2,Cnt.,3,1-Timp.,
Perc.-Cel.,2Hp.-Str.
Edition Adler, Berlin, c1933
Score 49 p. Large folio

GNESSIN, MIKHAIL FABIANOVICH.
            Rostov on the Don 2 February 1883
                           Moscow 5 May 1957

648   [D'après Shelley, symphonic fragment,
Op. 4, D major]
3*,3*,3,3*-4,2,3,1-Timp.-2Hp.-Str.
Jurgenson, Moscow [n.d.]
Score 27 p.

1624   [Jewish orchestra at the Burgomaster's   15'
ball, Op. 41, from the music to Gogol's Revisor]
1.Felicitation, fantasy 2.Quadrille
1,1,2,1-1,1-Cym.,Trgl.,Dr.-Pno.,Cemb.(ad lib.)
-Str.
Universal Edition, Vienna, c1929
Score 62 p.
*Composed 1928. First performance Meyerhold
Theater, Moscow, 1929.*

Gock, Emil

GOCK, EMIL.

859m Concert-fantasie [for trumpet and
orchestra, Op. 25]
Solo Tpt.-1,1,2,1-2,1,1-Timp.-Str.
Score: Ms. 19 p.
Parts: L. Oertel, Hannover [1886?]

1323s Waldesfrieden, Charakterstück
Str.
Score: Ms. 17 p.
Parts: L. Oertel, Hannover [n.d.]

GODARD, BENJAMIN LOUIS PAUL.   Paris 18 August 1849
Cannes 10 January 1895

658c Aubade for cello solo and orchestra, Op. 61
Solo Vc.-2,2,2,2-2Hn.-Str.
Score: Ms. 23 p.
Parts: Durand, Paris [n.d.]

682p [Concerto, piano, Op. 31, A minor]
1.Andante - Allegro vivace 2.Allegretto non
troppo 3.Andante quasi adagio 4.Vivace ma
non troppo
Solo Pno.-2,2,2,4-2,2,3-Timp.-Str.
Score: Ms. 240 p.
Parts: B. & Cie [n.p.] [n.d.]

631p [Concerto, piano, no. 2, Op. 148, G minor]
1.Con moto 2.Andante 3.Scherzo: Allegretto
4.Andante maestoso
Solo Pno.-2,2,2,2-2,2,1-Timp.-Str.
Score: Ms. 146 p.
Parts: Hamelle, Paris [n.d.]

515v [Concerto, violin, Concerto romantic, *24'*
Op. 35, A minor]
1.Allegro moderato 2.Adagio non troppo 3.
Canzonetta: Allegro moderato 4.Allegro molto
Solo Vn.-2,2,2,2-2,2-Timp.-Str.
Heugel, Paris [n.d.]
Score 94 p.
*First performance Paris, 1876, Mlle. Tayau
soloist.*

1128s [Concerto, violin, Concerto romantic, *4'*
Op. 35, A minor. Canzonetta. Arranged by
Heinrich Dessauer]
Solo Vn.-Str.
Bote & Bock, Berlin [n.d.]
Score in reduction 7 p.

676v [Concerto, violin, Op. 131, G minor]
1.Allegro moderato 2.Adagio quasi andante 3.
Allegro non troppo
Solo Vn.-2,2,2,2-2,2,1-Timp.,Perc.-Str.
Fürstner, Berlin, c1892
Score 51 p.

4299 [Dances for orchestra, Op. 51. No. 1,
Brésilienne]
2*,2,2,4*-2,2,3-Timp.,Perc.-Str.
Léon Grus, Paris [187-?]
Score 45 p.

5282 [Dances for orchestra, Op. 51. No. 2,
Kermis]
2*,2,2,4-4,2,2Cnt.,3,1-Timp.,Perc.-
Str.
Léon Grus, Paris [187-?]
Score 41 p.
Kermis is a country fair in the Netherlands.

5686 [Dances for orchestra, Op. 51. No. 3,
Funeral march]
2,2,2,4-2,2,3,1-Timp.,Perc.-Str.
Léon Grus, Paris [187-?]
Score 15 p.

738v En plein air, Op. 145. No. 1, À l'ombre
[for violin solo and orchestra]
Solo Vn.-Cl.,Bn.-Hn.-Str.
Simrock, Berlin, c1893
Score 7 p.

555v En plein air, Op. 145. No. 2, Sous la
charmille [for violin solo and orchestra]
Solo Vn.-2Cl.,2Bn.-2Hn.-Timp.-Str.
Simrock, Berlin, c1893
Score 11 p.

739v En plein air, Op. 145. No. 4, Danse rus-
tique [for violin solo and orchestra]
Solo Vn.-2,2,2,2-2Hn.-Timp.-Str.
Simrock, Berlin, c1893
Score 23 p.

560v En plein air, Op. 145. No. 5, La fée du
hallier [for violin solo and orchestra]
Solo Vn.-1,0,1,1-2Hn.-Timp.,Perc.-Str.
Simrock, Berlin, c1893
Score 23 p.

482p Fantaisie persane [Persian fantasy] Op.
152
Solo Pno.-2,2,2,2-2,2-Timp.,Perc.-Str.
Hamelle, Paris [n.d.]
Score 54 p.

661p Introduction et allegro pour piano et
orchestre, Op. 49
Solo Pno.-2,2,2,2-2,2,3-Timp.,Perc.-Str.
Score: Ms. 65 p.
Parts: Durand, Paris [n.d.]

43 Jocelyn suite no. 1
1.Prélude 2.Dans la montagne 3.Gavotte 4.
Carillon
3*,2(2nd alt. E.H.),2,2-4,2,2Cnt.,3,1-Timp.,
Perc.-Hp.-Str.
Choudens, Paris, c1894
Score 38 p.

44 Jocelyn suite no. 2
1.La grotte des aigles 2.Berceuse 3.Scène du
bal
3*,2(2nd alt. E.H.),2,2-4,2,3,1-Timp.,Perc.-
Hp.-Str.
Choudens, Paris, c1894
Score 40 p.

1329 Menuet pompadour, Op. 119   3'
1,1,1,1-Hn.-Str.
Hamelle, Paris, c1903
Score 7 p.
Composed and first performed Paris, 1892.

5569 [Oriental symphony, Arabia, China, Greece,
Persia, Turkey, Op. 84]
1.Les éléphants: Andante con moto 2.Chinoi-
serie: Allegro moderato 3.Sara la baigneuse
[Sara the bather]: Andantino con moto 4.Le
rêve de la Nikia [The dream of the Nikia]:
Quasi adagio 5.Marche turque [Turkish march]:
Tempo di marcia
3*,2,2,2-4,2,2Cnt.,3,1-Timp.,Perc.-
Hp.-Str.
Adolphe Fürstner, Leipzig [1884?]
Score 118 p.
*Suggested by poems of 1) Charles Marie Leconte
de Lisle; 2) Auguste de Châtillon; 3) Victor
Hugo; 4 & 5) Benjamin Godard. Composed 1884.
Dedicated to Carolus Duran.*

533m Scènes écossaises, Op. 138. No. 1,
Légende pastorale [for oboe solo and orchestra]
Solo Ob.-1,0,1,2-2,2-Timp.,B.Dr.-Str.
Hamelle, Paris [n.d.]
Score 12 p.

534m Scènes écossaises, Op. 138. No. 2, Séré-
nade à Mabel [for oboe solo and orchestra]
Solo Ob.-1,0,2,2-2Hn.-Str.
Hamelle, Paris [n.d.]
Score 8 p.

535m Scènes écossaises, Op. 138. No. 3, Marche
des Highlanders [for oboe solo and orchestra]
Solo Ob.-2*,0,2,2-2,2,1-Timp.,Perc.-Hp.-Str.
Hamelle, Paris [n.d.]
Score 24 p.

1279 Scènes italiennes, Op. 126. No. 1,   5'
Sérénade florentine
3*,2,2,2-2,2,3,1-Timp.,Perc.-Str.
Durand, Paris [n.d.]
Score 35 p.
Composed and first performed Paris, 1892.

1561 Scènes italiennes, Op. 126. No. 2,   3'
Sicilienne
2*,1,1,1-Hn.-Timp.-Str.
Durand, Paris [n.d.]
Score 17 p.

495 Scènes italiennes, Op. 126. No. 3,   3'
Tarentelle
3*,2,2,2-4,2,2Cnt.,3,1-Str.
Durand, Paris [n.d.]
Score 38 p.

231 Scènes poétiques, Op. 46. No. 1, Dans le
bois
2,2,2,4-4Hn.-Timp.-Str.
Bote & Bock, Berlin [n.d.]
Score 12 p.

232 Scènes poétiques, Op. 46. No. 2, Dans les
champs
2*,2,2,4-4Hn.-Str.
Bote & Bock, Berlin [n.d.]
Score 20 p.

233 Scènes poétiques, Op. 46. No. 3, Sur la
montagne
2*,2,2,4-4,2,3,1-Timp.,B.Dr.-Str.
Bote & Bock, Berlin [n.d.]
Score 27 p.

234 Scènes poétiques, Op. 46. No. 4, Au village
2*,2,2,4-4,2,3,1-Timp.,Perc.-Str.
Bote & Bock, Berlin [n.d.]
Score 43 p.

494 Scherzetto no. 2, Op. 108   2'
2*,1,1,2-2Hn.-Str.
Durand, Paris [n.d.]
Score 11 p.
Composed 1891. First performance Paris, 1892.

599m Suite [for flute and orchestra,   10'
Op. 116]
1.Allegretto 2.Idyll 3.Valse
Solo Fl.-Ob.,Cl.-2Hn.-Str.
Score: Ms. 33 p.
Parts: Durand & Schoenewerk, Paris [n.d.]

5199 [Symphony, Gothic, Op. 23]
1.Maestoso 2.Andantino quasi allegretto 3.
Grave ma non troppo lento 4.Presto 5.Allegro
non troppo
2,2,2,3*-2,2,3,1-Str.
B. Schott, Mainz [1885?]
Score 45 p.
*Composed 1883. Dedicated to Camille Saint-
Saëns.*

4436 [Tasso, dramatic symphony. Bohemian dance]
3*,2,2,2-2,2,3-Timp.,Perc.-Str.
C. Hartmann, Paris [1878]
Score 19 p.
*From the dramatic symphony Le Tasse, for solo
voices, chorus and orchestra. Composed 1878.
First performance at the Concerts du Châtelet,
Paris, 18 December 1878. Awarded prize by the
municipality of Paris.*

GOEB, ROGER.   Cherokee, Iowa 9 October 1914

2286s American dance no. 1 for string   3'
orchestra
Str.
American Composers Alliance, New York, c1952
by Roger Goeb
Score 5 p.
*Composed 1952 as 5 American dances. First per-
formance of nos. 1, 2 and 3 over CBS radio
network.*

2287s American dance no. 2 for string   3'
orchestra
Str.
American Composers Alliance, New York, c1952
by Roger Goeb
Score 5 p.

Goeb, Roger

2288s American dance no. 3 for string   *3'*
 orchestra
 Str.
 American Composers Alliance, New York, c1952
 by Roger Goeb
 Score 5 p.

6639 American dance no. 4, for orchestra   *3'*
 2,1,2,2-2,2,2-Timp.-Str.
 American Composers Alliance, New York, c1952
 by Roger Goeb
 Score 11 p. Large folio

6641 American dance no. 5, for orchestra   *3'*
 2,1,2,2-2,2,2-Timp.-Str.
 American Composers Alliance, New York, c1952
 by Roger Goeb
 Score 13 p. Large folio

6658 Concertant I for flute, oboe, clar-   *14'*
 inet and string orchestra
 Adagio - Grazioso
 Fl.,Ob.,Cl.-Str.
 American Composers Alliance, New York, c1952
 by Roger Goeb
 Score 37 p. Large folio
 Composed 1949. First performance at Yaddo,
 Saratoga Springs, New York.

1084m Concertant II for bassoon (or violon-   *12'*
 cello) and string orchestra
 1.Adagio 2.Grazioso
 Solo Bn.(or Vc.)-Str.
 Ms.
 Score 18 p.
 Composed 1951.

313v Concertant IIIa for solo viola,   *14'*
 woodwinds and brass
 1.Lento 2.Grazioso
 Solo Va.-3*,3*,3*,2-4,3,3,1
 American Composers Alliance, New York, c1952
 by Roger Goeb
 Score 37 p.
 Composed 1951.

312v Concertant IIIb for solo viola and   *14'*
 double wind quintet
 1.Lento 2.Grazioso
 Solo Va.-1,1,1,1-2,2,1,1
 American Composers Alliance, New York, c1952
 by Roger Goeb
 Score 27 p. Large folio
 Composed 1951.

260m Concertant IVa for clarinet, strings   *16'*
 and percussion
 1.Lento ma non troppo 2.Andante tranquillo
 Solo Cl.-Timp.,Perc.-Pno.(alt. Cel.)-Str.
 American Composers Alliance, New York, c1952
 by Roger Goeb
 Score 28 p. Large folio
 Composed 1951. Also arranged for clarinet,
 string quartet and piano.

6699 Concertino for orchestra
 1.Moderato 2.Lento 3.Vivace
 2(2nd alt. Picc.),2,3*,2-4,3,3,1-Timp.-Str.
 Composers Facsimile Edition, c1952 by Roger
 Goeb
 Score 83 p. Large folio
 Composed 1946.

6700 Concertino II for orchestra   *15'*
 2*,2,2,2-4,2,3,1-Timp.,Perc.-Pno.-Str.
 Composers Facsimile Edition, c1957 by Roger
 Goeb
 Score 61 p. Large folio
 Commissioned by the Louisville Orchestra. Com-
 posed 1956. First performance Columbia Audi-
 torium, Louisville, Kentucky, 28 November 1956,
 Louisville Orchestra, Robert Whitney conductor.

269p Concerto for piano and orchestra
 1.Allegro molto 2.Lento 3.Allegro
 Solo Pno.-2,1,2,1-2,2-Timp.,Perc.-Str.
 Composers Facsimile Edition, c1954 by Roger
 Goeb
 Score 87 p.

310v Concerto for violin and orchestra   *19'*
 1.Lento 2.Allegro molto 3.Moderato - Presto
 Solo Vn.-2,2,2,2-3,2,1-Timp.,Perc.-Pno.-Str.
 Composers Facsimile Edition, c1953 by Roger
 Goeb
 Score 59 p. Large folio
 Composed 1953.

4794 Prairie songs   *11'30"*
 1.Evening 2.Dance 3.Morning
 2,2,2,2-2,2,1-Timp.,Perc.-Str.
 Ms.
 Score 34 p. Large folio
 Composed 1947. Also arranged for woodwind
 quintet.

2294s Romanza for string orchestra
 Str.
 Composers Facsimile Edition, c1952 by Roger
 Goeb
 Score 19 p.

6706 [Symphony no. 3]
 1.Allegro moderato 2.Andante 3.Vivace
 3*,3*,3*,2-4,3,3,1-Timp.,Perc.-Cel.
 -Str.
 Composers Facsimile Edition, c1952 by Roger
 Goeb
 Score 87 p. Large folio

6707 [Symphony no. 4]   *25'*
 1.Allegro 2.Andante 3.Moderato
 3*,3*,3*,2-4,3,3,1-Timp.,Perc.-Str.
 Composers Facsimile Edition, c1955 by Roger
 Goeb
 Score 61 p. Large folio
 Composed 1954.

GOEDICKE, ALEXANDER FEODOROVICH.
Moscow 4 (not 3) March 1877
Moscow 9 July 1957

Also spelled: Ghedike and Gedike

673m [Concerto, French horn, Op. 40, F minor]
1.Allegro maestoso 2.Adagio non troppo 3.
Allegro
Solo Hn.-2,2,2,2-2Hn.-Timp.-Str.
Universal Edition, Vienna, 1931
Score 51 p.

1094m [Concerto, organ and string   30'
orchestra, Op. 35, D major]
1.Allegro moderato 2.Andante sostenuto 3.
Toccata: Presto con brio
Solo Org.-Str.
Muzsektor Gosizdata, Moscow [1927]
Score 82 p.
Composed 1926.

886m [Concerto, trumpet, Op. 41, B-flat minor]
In one movement
Solo Tpt.-2,2,2,2-4Hn.-Timp.,Perc.-Str.
Universal Edition, Vienna, 1931
Score 46 p.

589p [Concertstück, piano and orchestra, Op. 11,
B minor]
Solo Pno.-2,2,2,2-2,2,3-Timp.,Cym.-Str.
Jurgenson, Moscow [n.d.]
Score 73 p.
Awarded the Rubinstein Prize, Vienna, 1900.

2930 [Heat lightning, symphonic poem,   17'
Op. 39]
3(3rd alt. Picc.),3,3*,3*-4,3,3,1-Timp.,Perc.-
Hp.-Str.
Mussektor, Moscow, 1934
Score 109 p.
Composed 1929. First performance Moscow, 1932,
Boris Khaikin conductor.

2397 [In the war; six improvisations from   20'
the diary of a soldier killed in action,
Op. 26]
[Introduction] 1.[In the trenches]
2.[Attack] 3.[Calm] 4.[Funeral march]
5.[Battle] 6.[Finale]
3*,2,2,2-4,2,3,1-Timp.,Perc.-Str.
Universal Edition, Vienna, 1930
Score 59 p.
Composed 1926. First performance Moscow, 1928,
Boris Khaikin conductor.

The invasion of the Gauls, Op. 25
See: Virinea. The invasion of the Gauls...

1409 Ouverture dramatique, Op. 7   20'
3(3rd alt. Picc.),2,2,2-4,3,3,1-Timp.,Perc.-
Hp.-Str.
Jurgenson, Moscow [n.d.]
Score 70 p.
Composed 1898. First performance Moscow, 1900,
A. Litvinov conductor.

4203 [Prelude for organ, trumpet, harp   8'
and string orchestra, Op. 24]
Moderato - Agitato
Tpt.-Org.,Hp.-Str.
Muzsektor Gosizdata, Moscow [1928]
Score 45 p.

1322 [Symphony no. 1, Op. 15, F minor]   30'
1.Sostenuto 2.Larghetto con moto 3.Scherzo
4.Finale: Sostenuto
3(3rd alt. Picc.),2,3*,2-4,3,3,1-Timp.,Cym.-
Str.
Jurgenson, Moscow [n.d.]
Score 221 p.
Composed 1902. First performance at the
Siloti concerts, St. Petersburg, 1903, the
composer conducting.

2144 [Symphony no. 2, Op. 16, A major]   30'
1.Allegro non troppo, ma molto animato 2.An-
dante misterioso 3.Scherzo: Presto 4.Finale:
Allegro molto e vigoroso
3(3rd alt. Picc.),3(3rd alt. E.H.),3*,3*-4,3,3,
1-Timp.,Perc.-Str.
Edition Russe de Musique, Berlin [n.d.]
Score 140 p.
Composed 1907. First performance Moscow, 1907,
Serge Koussevitzky conductor.

1625 [Symphony no. 3, Op. 30, C minor]   35'
1.Moderato molto sostenuto 2.Moderato assai
3.Finale: Allegro appassionato
3(3rd alt. Picc.),3(3rd alt. E.H.),3*,3*-4,3,3,
1-Timp.,Perc.-Cel.,Hp.-Str.
Mussektor, Moscow, 1925
Score 251 p.
Composed 1922. First performance Moscow, 1923,
the composer conducting.

1626 [Virinea. The invasion of the Gauls,   8'
introduction to the opera, Op. 25]
3(3rd alt. Picc.),3(3rd alt. E.H.),3*,3*-4,3,
3,1-Timp.,Perc.-2Hp.-Str.
Universal Edition, Vienna, 1928
Score 41 p.
From the opera composed 1925. First perform-
ance Moscow, 1926, the Moscow Conductorless
Orchestra.

GOEHR, RUDOLPH.

4074 Suite on Greek tunes and dances
1.Lento 2.Andantino 3.Andante 4.Andante
2,2,2,2-4,2,3-Timp.,Perc.-Pno.,Hp.-Str.
Ms.
Score 42 p.

GOENS, DANIEL VAN.   d. Paris 10 May 1904

627c Cantabile, Op. 34
Solo Vc.-2,1,2,2-2Hn.-Str.
D. Rahter, Leipzig [n.d.]
Score 11 p.

501c [Concerto, violoncello, Op. 7, A minor]
In one movement
Solo Vc.-2,2*,2,2-2Hn.-Timp.-Str.

Goens, Daniel van

Score: Ms. 82 p.
Parts: Hamelle, Paris [n.d.]

512c [Concerto, violoncello, no. 2, Op. 30,
D minor]
1.Introduction: Lento - Allegro non troppo,
ma un poco agitato 2.Cantilène 3.Finale:
Allegro vivace
Solo Vc.-2,1,2,2-2,2,3-Timp.-Hp.-Str.
Decourcelle, Nice [n.d.]
Score 83 p.

1515s Élégie, Op. 10
Solo Vc.(or Vn.)-Str.
Hamelle, Paris [n.d.]
Score 3 p.

661s Gavotte-irda, Op. 13
Str.
Score: Ms. 6 p.
Parts: Durand, Paris [n.d.]

1247s Gavotte no. 3, Op. 29 [D major]
Str.
Score: Ms. 8 p.
Parts: Foetisch Frères, Lausanne [n.d.]

840s Invocation, Op. 36
Solo Vc.(or Vn.)-Str.
Score: Ms. 7 p.
Parts: Paris, J. Hamelle, c1900

1525 Romance sans paroles, Op. 12 no. 1   4'
2,0,2,2-2Hn.-Str.
Hamelle, Paris [n.d.]
Score 11 p.

500c Scherzo, Op. 12 no. 2
Solo Vc.-2,1,2,2-2Hn.-Timp.-Str.
Hamelle, Paris [n.d.]
Score 46 p.

GOETINCK, JULES.

529v Andante capriccioso [solo violin and
orchestra]
Solo Vn.-1,1,2,2-Timp.-Hp.-Str.
Score: Ms. 15 p.
Parts: Decourcelle, Nice [n.d.]

GOETZ, HERMANN.   Königsberg, Prussia
(now Kaliningrad, USSR) 7 December 1840
Hottingen, near Zurich 3 December 1876

552p [Concerto, piano, Op. 18, B-flat major] 26'
1.Mässig bewegt 2.Mässig langsam 3.Langsam
Solo Pno.-2,2,2,2-2,2-Timp.-Str.
Kistner, Leipzig [n.d.]
Score 230 p.
*Composed 1867. No. 5 of his posthumously pub-
lished works. First performance Basel, 1
December 1867, the composer as soloist.*

666v [Concerto, violin, Op. 22, G major]
Solo Vn.-2,2,2,2-2Hn.-Timp.,Trgl.-Str.
Kistner, Leipzig [n.d.]
Score 98 p.

*Composed 1868. Published 1880, No. 9 of his
posthumously published works. First performance Basel, 17 October 1880, Ernst Rentsch
soloist.*

5300 [Symphony, Op. 9, F major]   33'
1.Allegro moderato 2.Intermezzo: Allegretto
3.Adagio ma non troppo lento 4.Finale: Allegro con fuoco
2,2,2,2-4,2,3-Timp.-Str.
Fr. Kistner, Leipzig [187-?]
Score 220 p.
Composed 1873.

5665 [The taming of the shrew. Overture]   6'
2,2,2,2-4,2,3-Timp.-Str.
Fr. Kistner, Leipzig [1874?]
Score 15 p.
*From the opera in 4 acts with libretto by
Joseph Viktor Widmann, after Shakespeare's play.
Composed 1868-72. First performance Mannheim,
11 October 1874.*

GOETZE, HEINRICH.   Wartha, Silesia 7 April 1836
Breslau 14 December 1906

1420s [Serenade no. 1, Op. 22, D minor]
Str.
Breitkopf & Härtel, Leipzig [n.d.]
Score 9 p.

224s Serenade no. 2, Op. 23 [G major]
Str.
Breitkopf & Härtel, Leipzig [n.d.]
Score 13 p.

223s Skizzen [Sketches, six pieces for string
orchestra, Op. 24]
1.Mesto 2.Allegro maestoso 3.Andante 4.Alle-
gretto 5.Allegro moderato 6.Adagio
Str.
Breitkopf & Härtel, Leipzig [n.d.]
Score 13 p.

Zwanzig kleine Stücke [for string orchestra,
Op. 60, from original compositions for piano
and organ arranged by the composer 1904]
1274s Vol. I. 1.Andantino (Op. 3 no. 1) 2.
Adagio (Op. 42 no. 3) 3.Langsam und einfach
(Op. 17 no. 3) 4.Andante quasi adagio (Op.
39 no. 14) 5.Einfach und innig (Op. 4 no. 1)
6.Andante (Op. 58 no. 8) 7.Stilles Sehnen
(Op. 4 no. 7) 8.Andante (Op. 42 no. 28) 9.
Langsam, sehr zart (Op. 17 no. 1) 10.Adagio
(Op. 59 no. 7) 11.Innig, nicht zu langsam
(Op. 17 no. 6) 12.Largo (Op. 40 no. 6)
1275s Vol. II. 13.Etwas bewegt und leicht (Op.
17 no. 5) 14.Maestoso (Op. 39 no. 4) 15.
Nicht zu langsam (Op. 17 no. 4) 16.Bewegt
(Op. 1 no. 10) 17.Scherzo (Op. 4 no. 8) 18.
Moderato (Op. 20 no. 3) 19.Getrübtes Glück
(Op. 4 no. 6) 20.Maestoso (Op. 20 no. 5)
Str.
C.F. Vieweg, Berlin [1904?]
Score 12 p.

1343s Zwei Abendlieder, Op. 9
Str.
Raabe & Plothow, Berlin [n.d.]
Score 3 p.

448s Zwei Elegien, Op. 26
No. 1: A major. Arrangement of no. 7 of Op. 20,
Ten Organ Pieces. No. 2: B-flat major. Arrange-
ment of Organ Prelude no. 6, from the Ritter
Album
Str.
R. Sulzer, Berlin [n.d.]
Score 7 p.

GOEYENS, FERNAND.   Brussels 15 August 1892

5582 [Little suite in the style of the 18th *15'*
century]
1.Air vif 2.Air gracieux: Moderato cantabile
3.Air guerrier
2,2,2,1-2,2-Timp.-Str.
Buyst, Brussels [n.d.]
Score 15 p.
Dedicated to Jean Kumps.

GOHLISCH, WILHELM FERDINAND.
                    b. Hanover 28 September 1889

876v Scherzo [for violin and orchestra] Op. 8
Solo Vn.-1,2,2,2-2Hn.-Timp.-Str.
Gries & Schornagel, Hannover [n.d.]
Score 11 p.

GOHR, P.

1637s Old Netherland folk-songs
1.Menuet 2.Boufon 3.Rondedans 4.Charmoes
Str.
Ms.
Score 7 p.

GOLDBERG, THEO.   Chemnitz, Germany (now Karl-
        Marx-Stadt, East Germany) 29 September 1921

418m [Concerto for oboe, bassoon and   *12'*
orchestra, Op. 11]
1.Allegro con brio 2.Lento 3.Rondeau: Molto
allegro
Solo Ob.,Solo Bn.-4Hn.,2Tpt.,2Tbn.-Timp.,Perc.-
Str.
Ms.
Score 36 p.
Commissioned by the Berlin Symphony Orchestra.
Composed 1952. First performance West Berlin,
summer 1953, Berlin Symphony Orchestra, C. A.
Bünte conductor, B. Fest oboist, O. Steinkopf
bassoonist.

5873 Divertissement for orchestra, no. 3,   *12'*
Op. 16, G major
1.Allegro ma non troppo 2.Scherzo: Vivace
3.Variations 4.Finale: Allegro
2,2,2,2-2,2-Timp.,Perc.-Str.
Ms.
Score 53 p.
Theme for variations is a German (Silesian)

song from the 15th century, Ich Sah Einmal den
Lichten Morgensterne (I Once Saw the Bright
Morning Star). Composed 1957. First perform-
ance Vancouver, Canada, August 1958, CBC Con-
cert Orchestra, John Avison conductor. Dedi-
cated to Ursula.

GOLDMARK, CARL.   Keszthely, Hungary 18 May 1830
                    Vienna 2 January 1915

118 [Aus Jugendtagen, overture, Op. 53]   *14'*
3*,3*,3*,3*-6,3,4,1-Timp.,Perc.-Hp.-Str.
Doblinger, Leipzig, c1913
Score 56 p.
Composed 1911. First performance Vienna, 10
November 1912, Felix von Weingartner conductor.

469v [Concerto, violin, Op. 28, A minor]   *33'*
1.Allegro moderato 2.Air: Andante 3.Moderato
Solo Vn.-2(2nd alt. Picc.),2,2,2-4,2,3,1-Timp.
-Str.
Kalmus, New York [n.d.]
Score 105 p.
First performance at the Privat Musikverein,
Nuremberg, 28 October 1878, Johann C. Lauter-
bach soloist; first public performance at a
Vienna Gesellschafts-Konzert, 1 November 1878,
same soloist.

948 Gefesselten Prometheus des Aeschylos,   *16'*
Ouvertüre, Op. 38
3(3rd alt. Picc.),2,2,2-4,3,4,1-Timp.-Str.
Simrock, Berlin [n.d.]
Score 64 p.
Composed 1888-89. First performance Berlin,
25 November 1889.

3242 Das Heimchen am Herd [The cricket on the
hearth: Prelude to Act III]
3*,3*,3*,2-4,3,3,1-Timp.,Perc.-Str.
Berté, Leipzig [n.d.]
Score 24 p.
From the opera in three acts with libretto by
Alfred Maria Wilner based on Dickens' The
Cricket on the Hearth. Composed 1894-96.

502 [Im Frühling, overture, Op. 36]   *10'*
2,2,2,2-4,3,3,1-Timp.-Str.
Schott, Mainz [n.d.]
Score 25 p.
Composed 1889. First performance Vienna, 1
December 1889, Hans Richter conductor.

1148 [In Italien, overture, Op. 49]   *12'*
3*,3*,3*,2-4,3,3,1-Timp.,Perc.-Hp.-Str.
Schott, Mainz, c1904
Score 70 p.
Composed 1903. First performance Vienna,
January 1904, Ernst von Schuch conductor.

6899 Die Königin von Saba, Op. 27. Vorspiel
3,3*,3*,2-4,3,3,1-Timp.-Hp.-Str.
Hugo Pohle, Hamburg [n.d.]
Score 15 p.
From the opera in 4 acts with libretto by
Salomon Hermann Mosenthal. First performance
Court Opera, Vienna, 10 March 1875.

Goldmark, Carl

1419 [Die Königin von Saba, Op. 27. Intro- 6'
   duction to Act II. Night piece and festival
   music]
   3*,3*,3*,2-4,3,3,1-Timp.,Perc.-Hp.-Str.
   Schweers & Haake, Bremen [n.d.]
   Score 22 p.

127 [Die Königin von Saba, Op. 27. Ballet 11'
   music, Act III]
   3*,3*,3*,2-4,3,3,1-Timp.,Perc.-Hp.-Str.
   Schweers & Haake, Bremen [n.d.]
   Score 43 p.

1225 [Die Kriegsgefangene. Introduction to 7'
   Act II]
   2,3*,3*,2-4,3,3,1-Timp.,Perc.-Hp.-Str.
   Schuberth, Leipzig [n.d.]
   Score 18 p.
   From the opera composed 1897.

161 Penthesilea Ouvertüre, Op. 31 18'
   2(2nd alt. Picc.),2,2,2-4,2,3,1-Timp.-Str.
   Schott, Mainz [n.d.]
   Score 83 p.
   *Composed 1880. First performance Vienna, 5
   December 1880, Hans Richter conductor.*

Prometheus bound overture, Op. 38
   See: Gefesselten Prometheus des Aeschylos,
      Ouvertüre, Op. 38

37 [Sakuntala, overture, Op. 13] 19'
   2,3*,2,2-4,2,3,1-Timp.-Hp.-Str.
   Schott, London [n.d.]
   Score 81 p.
   *Composed 1864. First performance Vienna,
   December 1865, Otto Dessoff conductor.*

839 [Sappho overture, Op. 44] 13'
   3*,3*,3*,2-4,3,4,1-Timp.-Hp.-Str.
   Simrock, Berlin, c1894
   Score 95 p.
   *Composed 1892. First performance at a Phil-
   harmonic Concert, Vienna, 26 November 1893.*

2047 Scherzo, Op. 19 [E minor] 8'
   2,2,2,2-2,2-Timp.-Str.
   Gotthard, Vienna [n.d.]
   Score 54 p.
   *Composed 1870. First performance Vienna,
   March 1871, Otto Dessoff conductor.*

1424 Scherzo, Op. 45 [A major] 8'
   2,2,2,2-4,2,3-Timp.-Str.
   Peters, Leipzig, c1894
   Score 31 p.
   *Composed 1893. First performance Vienna,
   March 1894, J. N. Fuchs conductor.*

153 [Symphony no. 1, Rustic wedding, 45'
   Op. 26]
   1.Hochzeitsmarsch, Variationen 2.Brautlied,
   Intermezzo 3.Serenade: Scherzo 4.Im Garten:
   Andante 5.Tanz
   2,2,2,2-4,2,3-Timp.,Perc.-Str.
   Schott, Mainz [n.d.]
   Score 180 p.

*Composed 1875. First performance Vienna, 5
March 1876, Hans Richter conductor.*

3855 [Symphony no. 2, Op. 35, E-flat major]
   1.Allegro 2.Andante 3.Allegro quasi presto
   4.Andante assai: Allegro alla breve
   2,2,2,2-4,2,3,1-Timp.,Perc.-Str.
   Schott, Mainz [1888?]
   Score 64 p.
   First performance Dresden, 2 December 1887.

GOLDMARK, RUBIN.   New York 15 August 1872
                             New York 6 March 1936

1948 The call of the plains
   3(3rd alt. Picc.),3*,3*,3*-4,2,3,1-Timp.,
   Perc.-Hp.-Str.
   Carl Fischer, New York, c1925
   Score 19 p.
   *Composed ca.1915 for violin and piano,
   for Mischa Elman. Orchestrated 1922. First
   performance ca.1923, New York Symphony Orchestra, Walter Damrosch conductor.*

1621 A Negro rhapsody 14'
   3*,3*,3*,3*-4,3,3,1-Timp.,Perc.-Cel.,Hp.-Str.
   Universal Edition, Vienna, c1923
   Score 71 p.
   *Composed 1923. First performance San Francisco,
   1923, Alfred Hertz conductor.*

5902 Requiem, suggested by Lincoln's Gettys- 25'
   burg Address, for symphony orchestra
   3(3rd alt. Picc.),3*,3*,3*-8(4 ad lib.),4,3,1-
   Timp.,Perc.-Hp.-Str.
   G. Schirmer, New York, c1921
   Score 97 p.
   *Composed 1918. First performance New York, 30
   January 1919, New York Philharmonic Orchestra.*

1980 Samson, tone poem 24'
   1.Samson 2.Delilah 3.The betrayal 4.In the
   temple
   3*,3*,3*,3*-4,4,3,1-Timp.,Perc.-Hp.-Str.
   G. Schirmer, New York, c1916
   Score 103 p.

GOLDSCHMIDT, ADALBERT VON.   Vienna 5 May 1848
                                 Vienna 21 December 1906

5223 [The seven deadly sins. Prelude to Part
   III *and* Love scene]
   1.Lento 2.Largo e marcato
   Solo Soprano & Tenor-3,3*,3*,3-4,2,3,1-Timp.
   (2 players)-2Hp.-Str.
   Breitkopf & Härtel, Leipzig [1883 or 1884]
   Score 46 p.
   *From the cantata with text by Robert Hamerling.
   Composed 1870. First performance Berlin, 1876.*

GOLDSCHMIDT, OTTO.   Hamburg 21 August 1829
                             London 24 February 1907

655p [Concerto, piano, Op. 10, E-flat 17'
   major]
   In one movement

Solo Pno.-2,2,2,2-2,2,1-Timp.-Str.
Score: Ms. 134 p.
Parts: Breitkopf & Härtel, Leipzig [n.d.]

GOLESTAN, STAN.   Vaslui, Romania 26 May 1872
                     Paris 22 April 1956

2348 [Romanian rhapsody no. 1]   *11'*
3*,3*,2,3-4,2,3-Timp.,Perc.-2Hp.-Str.
Durand, Paris, c1930
Score 62 p.
*If no English horn is available, voice may be
substituted.*

GÖLLRICH, JOSEF.

776m Ein Märchen [for oboe and orchestra] Op. 4
Solo Ob.-2(2nd alt. Picc.),0,2,2-2,2,B.Tbn.-
Timp.,Perc.-Str.
Score: Ms. 32 p.
Parts: A.E. Fischer, Bremen [n.d.]

GOLTERMANN, GEORG EDUARD.   Hanover 19 August 1824
                            Frankfurt 29 December 1898

629c Adagio, Op. 83   *4'*
Solo Vc.-2,0,2,2-2Hn.-Str.
B. Schott's Söhne, Mainz [n.d.]
Score 12 p.

607c Ballade, Op. 81
Solo Vc.-2,0,2,2-2Hn.-Str.
Joh. André, Offenbach a.M. [n.d.]
Score 11 p.

475c [Concerto, violoncello, no. 1, Op. 14, *17'*
A minor]
1.Allegro moderato 2.Andante 3.Un poco piu
lento
Solo Vc.-2,2,2,2-2,2-Timp.-Str.
Score: Ms. 96 p.
Parts: Breitkopf & Härtel, Leipzig [n.d.]

717c [Concerto, violoncello, no. 2, Op. 30,
D minor]
In one movement
Solo Vc.-2,2,2,2-2,2-Timp.-Str.
Score: Ms. 95 p.
Parts: Joh. André, Offenbach am Main [n.d.]

718c [Concerto, violoncello, no. 3, Op. 51,
B minor]
1.Allegretto molto moderato 2.Andante espres-
sivo 3.Finale: Allegro
Solo Vc.-2,2,2,2-2,2-Timp.-Str.
Score: Ms. 129 p.
Parts: Joh. André, Offenbach am Main [n.d.]

697c [Concerto, violoncello, no. 4, Concert-
stück, Op. 65, G major]
Allegro - Andantino - Allegro molto
Solo Vc.-2,2,2,2-2,2-Timp.-Str.
Score: Ms. 107 p.
Parts: Joh. André, Offenbach a. Main, c1912

723c [Concerto, violoncello, no. 5, Concert-
stück, Op. 76, D minor]
1.Allegro moderato 2.Andante 3.Finale: Allegro
Solo Vc.-2,2,2,2-2,2-Timp.-Str.
Score: Ms. 129 p.
Parts: Joh. André, Offenbach a. M. [n.d.]

710c [Concerto, violoncello, no. 7, Op. 103,
C major]
Allegro moderato - Adagio - Finale: Allegro
comodo
Solo Vc.-2,2,2,2-2,2-Timp.-Str.
Score: Ms. 68 p.
Parts: Joh. André, Offenbach a. M. [n.d.]

711c [Concerto, violoncello, no. 8, Op. 130,
A major]
1.Allegro moderato - Andante sostenuto 2.Alle-
gro moderato
Solo Vc.-2,1,2,2-2Hn.-Str.
Score: Ms. 48 p.
Parts: Joh. André, Offenbach am Main [n.d.]

505c Élégie, Op. 88
Solo Vc.-1,0,2,2-2Hn.-Str.
Joh. André, Offenbach sur Main [n.d.]
Score 28 p.

762c [Nocturne for violoncello and orchestra,
Op. 108, F major]
Solo Vc.-2,0,2,2-2Hn.-Str.
Johann André, Offenbach [1886?]
Score in reduction 7 p.
Dedicated to Hugo Becker.

490c Romance, Op. 17 [E minor]
Solo Vc.-1,0,1,2-2Hn.-Str.
Joh. André, Offenbach s. M. [n.d.]
Score in reduction 7 p.

GOMES, ANTONIO CARLOS.
                Campinas, Brazil 11 July 1836
                Pará (Belém) 16 September 1896

3943 Côndor. Act I: Prelude
2*,3*,4(2B.Cl.),2-4,2,2Cnt.,3,1-Timp.,Perc.-
Hp.-Str.
Ms.
Score 23 p.

3944 Côndor. Act III: Nocturno
0,2,2,2-4Hn.-Hp.-Str.
Ms.
Score 10 p.

3946 Lo schiavo [The slave. Act I: Prelude]
3(3rd alt. Picc.),2,2,2-4,2,2Cnt.,3,1-Timp.,
Trgl.,B.Dr.-Hp.-Str.
Ms.
Score 12 p.
From the opera in four acts, composed 1888.

3945 Lo schiavo. Act IV: Preludio intermezzo
(Alvorada [Dawn])
2(2nd alt. Picc.),2,2,2-4,2,Cnt.(also 2 back-
stage),3,1-Timp.,Perc.-Hp.-Str.
Ms.
Score 21 p.

Gomes, Antonio Carlos

1118v Lo schiavo. Act IV: Romanza ilara, come
serenamente
2(2nd alt. Picc.),2,2,2-4,2,2Cnt.,3,1-Timp.-
Hp.-Solo Voice(or Solo Vn.)-Str.
Ms.
Score 29 p.

GOMES DE ARAÚJO, JOÃO.
Pindamonhangaba, Brazil 5 August 1846
São Paulo 8 September 1942

3790 Carmosina. Act I: Prelude
2,2,2,2-4,2,3,1-Str.
Ms.
Score 17 p.
*Composed 1880. First performance Teatro dal
Verne, Milan, Italy, 1888.*

1975s [Gavotte no. 1]
Str.
Ms.
Score 7 p.

1976s [Gavotte no. 2]
Str.
Ms.
Score 6 p.
Composed 1940.

3947 Haknor. Prelude [to the opera]
2,2,2,2-4,2,3,1-Str.
Ms.
Score 15 p.

1974s Minuetto
Str.
Ms.
Score 5 p.
Composed 1940.

GOMNAES, FREDRIK WILHELM.
Ringerike, Norway 4 April 1868
Oslo 28 August 1925

6088 [Symphony in A minor]   25'
1.Andante molto 2.Andante con moto 3.Humor-
eske: Allegro ma non troppo 4.Finale: Poco
andante - Allegro energico
2(2nd alt. Picc.),2,2.2-4,2,3,1-Timp.,Cym.-Str.
Norsk Musikforlag, Kristiania [n.d.]
Score 163 p.

GONZÁLEZ GAMARRA, FRANCISCO.   Cuzco, Peru 1890

3725 Preludio Incaico [Inca prelude,   4'30"
homage to Garcilaso Inca de la Vega, Op. 4]
1(alt. Picc.),1,2,2-4,2-Str.
Ms.
Score 20 p.
*Garcilaso de la Vega, called El Inca (born in
Cuzco, Peru, ca.1539, died in Spain, 1616),
was a Peruvian historian. Preludio composed
for piano, 1937; transcribed 1937. This composition is the second movement of the composer's Suite Cuzquena. Won First Prize of*

*the Committee for the Celebration of the
Fourth Centenary of the birth of Garcilaso de
la Vega, Peru, 1939.*

GOODSTEIN, HARVEY.   Belmar, New Jersey 1920

2822 Prelude, for orchestra   18'
2(2nd alt. Picc.),2,2,2-4,4,2,1-Timp.,Cym.,
Wood Block-Str.
Ms.
Score 34 p.
Composed 1937.

GOOSSENS, EUGENE.   London 26 May 1893
London 13 June 1962

845s By the tarn, a sketch for string orchestra
and clarinet, Op. 15 no. 1
Cl.(ad lib.)-Str.
J. & W. Chester, London, c1929
Score 7 p.
Composed 1916.

1618s Concertino for string octet or string
orchestra
Str.
J. & W. Chester, London, c1930
Miniature score 39 p.
Composed 1928.

947m [Concerto, oboe, Op. 45]   16'
1.Moderato 2.Andante con moto 3.Allegro
giocoso
Solo Ob.-2(2nd alt. Picc.),0,2(2nd alt. B.Cl.),
1-2,1-Perc.-Cel.,Hp.(ad lib.)-Str.
Ms.
Score 60 p.
*Composed 1927. First performance London, 2
October 1930, Leon Goossens soloist.*

3410 Fanfare for a ceremony   1'
4Tpt.
Ms.
Score 2 p.
*Composed 1921. First performance at a Goos-
sens' Concert (one of a series of concerts of
contemporary orchestral music), London, 27
October 1921, the composer conducting.*

3411 Fanfare for the artists   80"
4Tpt.,4Tbn.-Timp.,Side Dr.,Cym.
Ms.
Score 3 p.
*Also known as Fanfare for the Regiment. Writ-
ten for the Musicians' Benevolent Fund and
first performed London, 8 May 1930, by students
from the Military Academy for Bandsmen of
Kneller Hall, Captain Adkins conductor.*

4271 Fanfare for the Merchant Marine
See: TEN FANFARES BY TEN COMPOSERS FOR BRASS
AND PERCUSSION.

2120 Fantasy for nine wind instruments, Op. 40
1,1,2,2-2,1
J. Curwen, London, c1926
Score 27 p.
Composed 1924.

Gossec, François-Joseph

2217 Four conceits, Op. 20   *7'*
1.The gargoyle   2.Dance memories   3.A walking
tune   4.The marionette show
2(2nd alt. Picc.),2,2,2-4,2,3,1-Timp.,Perc.-
Cel.,Hp.-Str.
J. & W. Chester, London, C1921
Score 39 p.
Composed 1918. First performance Liverpool,
13 November 1918, the composer conducting.

982v Lyric poem   *13'*
Solo Vn.-2,2*,2,2-2,1-Timp.,Perc.-Str.
Ms.
Score 55 p.
Composed 1926. First performance Rochester,
New York, 11 September 1929.

405s Miniature fantasy, Op. 2
Str.
Goodwin & Tabb, C1915
Score 16 p.
Composed 1911.

2531 Prelude to Phillip II, for small   *9'*
orchestra, Op. 23
1,1,1,1-2,1-Timp.,Perc.-Hp.-Str.
J. & W. Chester, London, C1921
Score 27 p.
Commissioned by the Plough Society of London.
First performance at the Plough Society's
private performance of Emile Verhaeren's drama
Philip II, 1917, the composer conducting.
First concert performance at a Promenade Con-
cert, Queen's Hall, London, 27 August 1919,
the composer conducting.

2532 Rhythmic dance, for orchestra, Op. 30   *4'*
4*,3,3,3*-4,3,3,1-Timp.,Perc.-Str.
J. Curwen, London, C1928 by E. Goossens
Score 20 p.
Commissioned by the Aeolian Co. as a pianola
piece, 1920. Composed 1920; orchestrated
1920. First performance Rochester, New York,
12 May 1927, Rochester Philharmonic Orchestra,
the composer conducting.

2536 Sinfonietta, Op. 34   *15'*
Allegro - Andante molto - Scherzo
3(3rd alt. Picc.),3*,3*,2-4,3,3,1-Timp.,Perc.-
Cel.,Hp.-Str.
J. & W. Chester, London, C1928
Score 85 p.
Composed 1922. First performance London, 19
February 1923, the London Symphony Orchestra,
the composer conducting.

4193 Symphony no. 1, Op. 58   *38'*
1.Andante - Allegro con anima   2.Andante espressivo ma con moto   3.Divertimento: Allegro
vivo   4.Finale: Andante moderato
3(3rd alt. Picc.),3(3rd alt. E.H.),3(3rd alt.
B.Cl.),3(3rd alt. C.Bn.)-4,6,3,1-Timp.,Perc.-
Org.,Cel.,Hp.-Str.
Ms.
Score 171 p. Large folio
Composed 1938-40. First performance Cincinnati,
12 April 1940, Cincinnati Symphony Orchestra,
the composer conducting.

385 Tam o'Shanter, scherzo, Op. 17a   *3'*
3(3rd alt. Picc.),3*,3,3*-4,3,3,1-Timp.,Perc.-
Pno.,Hp.-Str.
J. & W. Chester, London, C1922
Score 31 p.
Composed 1918-19. First performance London,
29 April 1919, Royal Philharmonic Society, the
composer conducting.

3566 Three Greek dances, for small   *14'*
orchestra, Op. 44
1.Moderato   2.Andante languido   3.Vivo
1,1,1,1-1,1-Timp.,Perc.-Pno.,Cel.,Hp.-Str.
J. Curwen, London, C1930
Score 50 p.
Composed 1926. Original title: Three Pagan
Poems. First performance, under original title,
International Composers' Guild concert, Aeolian
Hall, New York, 28 November 1926, the composer
conducting.

1027m Three pictures for solo flute, string *15'*
orchestra and percussion, Op. 25
1.From the belfry of Bruges: Moderato con moto
2.From Bredon in the Cotswolds   3.From a balcony
in Montparnasse: Moderato
Solo Fl.-Timp.,Perc.-Pno.,Cel.,Hp.-
Str.
Ms. C[n.d.] by J. & W. Chester, Ltd., London
Score 72 p. Large folio
Composed 1935.

2529 Variations on Cadet Rousselle   *4'30"*
(French folk song), Op. 40. Arranged by Arnold
Bax, Frank Bridge, John Ireland and Eugene
Goossens. Orchestrated by Eugene Goossens
2,2,2,1-2,1-Timp.,Perc.-Hp.-Str.
J. & W. Chester, London [n.d.]
Score 28 p.
Dedicated to Edwin Evans, who suggested the
collaboration. Arranged, 1920; orchestrated,
1930. First performance Bournemouth, England,
5 November 1931, the Pavilion Orchestra, Dan
Godfrey conductor.

GOSSEC, FRANÇOIS-JOSEPH.
           Vergnies, Belgium 17 January 1734
           Passy (Paris) 16 February 1829

Also published as Gosseck, Gossei and Francesco
Gossek

32s Gavotte. Arranged by Emil Kross. Orchestra-
ted by Adolf Ischpold
Str.
Score: Ms. 4 p.
Parts: Bosworth, Leipzig, C1910

Gossec, François-Joseph

5441 [Symphony, Du répertoire de MM. Les
Amateurs, no. 2, C major]
1.Allegro maestoso 2.Larghetto 3.Presto
2Ob.,2Bn.-2,2,3-Timp.-Str.
Ms.
Score 119 p.
*Composed for the Concerts of Gentlemen Amateurs,
Paris, before 1770-73. Announced in the Breit-
kopf Thematic Catalog, Supplement XIV, 1781, p.7.*

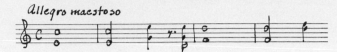

4672 [Symphony in D major. Edited by   *12'*
Adam Carse]
1.Allegro 2.Andante un poco allegretto 3.
Presto
2Ob.-2Hn.-Str.
Augener [London] c1938
Score 19 p.
*Composed 1776. First performed at a Concert
Spirituel, Paris, by the Gentlemen Amateurs.
First published as no. 3 in Trois Symphonies à
Huit Parties Composées par Messieurs Leduc
l'Aîné, Clo. Stamitz et Gossec.*

4386 [Symphony, Op. 5 no. 2, E-flat major]
1.Allegro moderato 2.Romanza: Andante 3.Min-
uet and Trio 4.Presto
2Fl.,2Cl.-2Hn.-Str.
[n.p., n.d.]
Score 24 p.
*Composed ca.1761-62. First published as no. 2
in Sei Sinfonie a piu Stromenti, by Bailleux,
Paris, probably 1773.*

1425s Tambourin. Arranged for string orchestra
in D major by Alfred Moffat
Str.
Schott's Söhne, Mainz, c1910
Score in reduction 6 p.

1441s Tambourin. Arranged for string orchestra
in E major by Cedric Sharpe
Str.
Score: Ms. 7 p.
Parts: J. & W. Chester, London [n.d.]
Same melody as previous entry.

GOTOVAC, JAKOV.
b. Split, Dalmatia, Yugoslavia 11 October 1895

6594 [Symphonic kolo, for orchestra, Op. 12] *8'*
3(3rd alt. Picc.),3*,3(3rd alt. B.Cl.),2-4,3,3,
1-Timp.,Perc.-Hp.-Str.
B. Schott's Söhne, Mainz, c1935
Score 52 p.
*Composed 1927. First performance Zagreb, Yugo-
slavia, 6 February 1927.*

GOTTHARD, JOHANN PETER.
Drahanovice, Moravia 19 January 1839
Vöslau 17 May 1919

Real name: Bohumil Pazdírek

581s [Suite, for string orchestra, Op. 152,
A minor]
1.Introduction 2.Sarabande 3.Larghetto 4.
Postludium
Str.
Simrock, Berlin, 1892
Score 22 p.

GOTTHELF, FELIX.   Gladbach, Germany 3 October 1857
Dresden 21 April 1930

1932 Ein Frühlingsfest [symphonic fantasy,   *13'*
Op. 7]
3*,2(2nd alt. E.H.),2,2-4,2,3-Timp.,Perc.-Str.
Ries & Erler, Berlin [n.d.]
Score 71 p.
*Composed 1892. First performance Cologne, 1893,
the composer conducting.*

GOTTLIEB-NOREN, HEINRICH.
See: NOREN, HEINRICH GOTTLIEB.

GOTTSCHALK, LOUIS MOREAU.   New Orleans 8 May 1829
Rio de Janeiro 18 December 1869

283p [Grande tarantelle, piano and orchestra,
Op. 67. Offergeld no. 259. Reconstructed
and transcribed for orchestra by Hershy Kay.
Solo piano part edited by Eugene List]
Solo Pno.-2,2,2,2-2,2-Timp.,Perc.-Str.
Boosey & Hawkes, New York, c1963
Score 66 p.
*This reconstruction commissioned by Eugene
List. Also known as Célèbre Tarantelle.
Composed 1869.*

5258 [Night in the tropics. Offergeld   *19'*
no. 255. Arranged by Howard Shanet]
1.Andante 2.Allegro moderato
3*,2,5(1Cl. in E-flat),2-4,3,4Cnt.,3,1-Ophicl.,
3Euph.-Timp., Perc.-Str.
Ms. c1958 by Howard Shanet
Score 61 p.

This is also known as Symphony no. 1. The 1st movement originally called Nuit dans les Tropiques, Symphonie pour Orchestre. Composed 1858-59. First performance of complete work at the Festival Gigantesca, Havana, 17 April 1861, the composer conducting.

2759 [Night in the tropics. Andante.   *8'*
Reconstructed by Quinto Maganini]
2(2nd alt. Picc.),2(2nd alt. E.H.),2,2-Alto
Sax.-2,2,2-Timp.,Perc.-Hp.-Str.
Edition Musicus, New York, c1937
Miniature score 23 p.
Reconstructed about 1932; first performance New York, 30 January 1933, Sinfonietta of New York, Quinto Maganini conductor.

GOTTSCHEER, WERNER.

870s Ein bosnisches Volksliedchen [A Bosnian folk-song]
Hp.(ad lib.)-Str.
Bosworth, Leipzig, c1913
Score 3 p.

GÖTZ, HERMANN.
See: GOETZ, HERMANN.

GOUDIMEL, CLAUDE BESANÇON.   1510
                    Lyons 27 August 1572

2645 Huguenot Psalm LXII. Transcribed by   *4'*
Isadore Freed
1,1,0,1-Hn.-Str.
Ms.
Score 8 p.
This and the following psalm originally composed as a choral motet; transcribed 1936. First performance Philadelphia, 11 March 1936, Chamber Orchestra of Philadelphia and Composers' Laboratory, Isadore Freed conductor.

2646 Huguenot Psalm CXXXIII. Transcribed   *4'*
by Isadore Freed
1,1,0,1-Hn.-Str.
Ms.
Score 8 p.

GOULD, MORTON.
      b. Richmond Hill, New York 10 December 1913

4770 American salute   *4'*
3(3rd alt. Picc.),2(2nd alt. E.H.),3*,2-4,3,
3,1-Timp.,Perc.-Pno.(optional),Hp.,Guit.(optional)-Str.
Mills Music Inc., New York, c1943
Miniature score 31 p.
Based on the American marching tune When Johnny Comes Marching Home, which Patrick S. Gilmore claimed he composed in 1863 under the pseudonym Louis Lambert. Composed 1942.

2757 Chorale and fugue in jazz   *14'*
3(3rd alt. Picc.),2(E.H. ad lib.),4*,3*-2Alto
Sax.(1st alt. Sop.),1Ten.Sax.-4,3,3,1-Timp.,
Perc.-2Pno.,Cel.-Str.

Ms.
Score 113 p.
Composed 1934. First performance at a concert for youth, Philadelphia, 2 January 1936, Philadelphia Orchestra, Leopold Stokowski conductor.

GOUND, ROBERT.   Seckenheim, near Heidelberg 1865
                              Vienna 1927

202s [Suite, for string orchestra, Op. 20,
A major]
Str.
Kistner, Leipzig [n.d.]
Score 51 p.

GOUNOD, CHARLES FRANÇOIS.   Paris 17 June 1818
                              Paris 18 October 1893

4405 [Cinq-Mars. Sarabande. Arranged by Florian
Pascal]
2,2,2,2-4Hn.-Str.
Léon Grus, Paris [1877]
Score 11 p.
From the opera in 4 acts with libretto by Louis Gallet and Paul Poirson, after Alfred de Vigny's novel. Composed 1876-77.

1517s Clos ta paupière [Close your eyes]
berceuse
Solo Vn.-Str.
Score: Ms. 6 p.
Parts: [Lemoine, n.p., n.d.]

4417 La colombe. Entr'acte   *4'*
2,2,2,2-4Hn.-Trgl.-Hp.-Str.
Choudens, Paris [187-?]
Score 7 p.
From the opéra-comique in 2 acts with libretto by Jules Barbier and Michel Carré, after La Fontaine. Composed 1859.

66s Dodelinette, berceuse
Str.
Lemoine [n.p., n.d.]
Score 4 p.

36 Faust ballet music   *16'*
2(2nd alt. Picc.),2,2,2-4,2,2Cnt.,3,1(Ophicl.)
-Timp.,Perc.-Hp.-Str.
Chappell, London [n.d.]
Score 81 p.
Composed for and added to the performances of the opera at the Académie Imperiale de Musique, Paris. First performance Paris, 3 March 1869.

1180v [Hymn to Saint Cecilia, for solo   *6'*
violin and orchestra]
Solo Vn.-2,1,2,2-4,2-Timp.-Hp.-Cb.
Lebeau, Paris [187-?]
Score 11 p.
Composed 1864.

235 Marionetten-Trauermarsch [Funeral   *6'*
march of the marionettes]
2,2,2,2-2,2,3,1-Timp.,Perc.-Str.
Luck's Music Library, Detroit [n.d.]
Score 19 p.
Composed and first performed Paris, 1873.

Gounod, Charles François

751v Méditation
Solo Vn.-1,2*,2,2-4Hn.-Hp.-Str.
Choudens, Paris [n.d.]
Score 9 p.

2378 Petite symphonie
1.Adagio et Allegretto 2.Andante cantabile
3.Scherzo 4.Finale
1,2,2,2-2Hn.
Éditions Costallat, Paris [c1934]
Score 48 p.
*Written for the Société de Musique de Chambre
pour Instruments à Vent. First performance
Salle Pleyel, Paris, 30 April 1885.*

5491 [Philémon et Baucis. Interlude: Entr'acte
and dance of the bacchantes]
2,2,2,2-4,2,3-Timp.,Perc.-Hp.-Str.
[Choudens, Paris, 186-?]
Score 16 p.
*From the opera in 3 acts with libretto by Jules
Barbier and Michel Carré. Composed 1859.*

6998 [The queen of Sheba. March and cortège]
3*,2,2,2-4,2,2Cnt.,3,Ophicl.-Timp.(2 players),
Perc.-Str.
Schott, Mainz [1870?]
Score in reduction 9 p.
*From the opera in 5 acts with libretto by Jules
Barbier and Michel Carré.*

4377 [Romeo and Juliet. Suite from the opera,
with instrumentation by Andrew Luck]
Introduction - Tempo di valse - Andante
1,1,1,1-2,1,1-Timp.,Perc.-Str.
Ms.
Score 15 p.
*From the opera in 5 acts with libretto by Jules
Barbier and Michel Carré, after Shakespeare's
play. Composed 1864. This orchestration 1915.*

4414 Saltarello   5'
3*,2,2,2-4,2,3,1-Timp.,Perc.-Str.
Novello, Ewer & Co., London [187-?]
Score 43 p.
Composed 1871.

1446s Souvenir d'un bal, air de ballet, oeuvre
posthume
2Fl.-Str.
Choudens, Paris [n.d.]
Score in reduction 5 p.

5340 [Symphony, no. 1, D major]   25'
1.Allegro molto 2.Allegretto moderato 3.
Scherzo: Non troppo presto 4.Finale: Adagio -
Allegro vivace
2,2,2,2-2,2-Timp.-Str.
Colombier, Paris [1855]
Score 136 p.
Composed 1855.

GOUVY, LOUIS THÉODORE.
Goffontaine, Germany 5 (not 2) July 1819
Leipzig 21 April 1898

1778 Petite suite gauloise, Op. 90   12'
1.[Introduction and menuet] 2.[Morning sere-
nade] 3.[Nocturnal round] 4.Tambourin
1,2,2,2-2Hn.
Jos. Aibl, Munich, c1900
Score 19 p.

573s Schwedischer Tanz [for string orchestra,
from the Octett, Op. 71 for wind instruments,
E-flat major. Arranged by August Horn]
Str.
Kistner, Leipzig [n.d.]
Score 11 p.

449s Sérénade, Op. 11 [E-flat major]
Str.
Costallat, Paris [n.d.]
Score 15 p.
*Performance in the Concerts Populaires and
Concerts du Châtelet, Paris.*

590m Sérénade, Op. 82   21'
Solo Fl.-Str.
Kistner, Leipzig [n.d.]
Score 37 p.

5062 [Symphonic paraphrases, for orchestra,
Op. 89]
Andante, non troppo - Largo, lento assai - Vivo
- Adagio maestoso - Allegro con brio - Tempo di
marcia - Alla breve - Tempo del tema
2(2nd alt. Picc.),2,2,2-4,2,3-Timp.-Str.
Breitkopf & Härtel, Leipzig, c1899
Score 51 p.

5094 [Symphony, Op. 87, G minor]
1.Poco adagio - Allegro - Tranquillo 2.Scherzo:
Allegro con brio 3.Andante con moto 4.Finale:
Allegro risoluto
2,2,2,2-4,2,3-Timp.-Str.
Breitkopf & Härtel, Leipzig [n.d.]
Score 206 p.

GRABNER, HERMANN.   Graz, Austria 12 May 1886
Bolzano, Italy 3 July 1969

4332 [Divertimento for small orchestra, Op.   22'
56. Edited by Walter Lott]
1.Bewegt 2.Gemächlich 3.Bewegt, in gestampften
Rhythmus 4.Rasch und frisch
1,1,2,1-2,2,1-Timp.-Str.
Fr. Kistner & C.F.W. Siegel, Leipzig, c1941
Score 68 p.

2220 Perkeo [suite for wind orchestra, Op. 15]
1.Introduction 2.Valse 3.Villanella 4.
Tarantella [Illumination of the castle]
2(2nd alt. Picc.),2,2,3*-4Hn.-Small Dr.
C.F. Kahnt, Leipzig, c1925
Score 31 p.

GRÄDENER, CARL GEORG PETER.
Rostock, Germany 14 January 1812
Hamburg 10 June 1883

5267 [Fiesco, overture after Schiller's
tragedy, Op. 30]
3(2nd & 3rd alt. Picc.),2(1st alt. E.H.),2,2-
2,2,3,1-Timp.,B.Dr.,Cym.-Str.
Hugo Pohle, Hamburg [n.d.]
Score 104 p.
*Full title of Schiller's play is The Conspiracy
of Fiesco at Genoa. Dedicated to the Philharmonic Concert Committee in Hamburg.*

GRÄDENER, HERMANN THEODOR OTTO.
Kiel, Germany 8 May 1844
Vienna 18 September 1929

5427 [Capriccio for orchestra, Op. 4]
2,2,2,2-2,2-Timp.-Str.
Hugo Pohle, Hamburg [n.d.]
Score 88 p.
*Dedicated to the Philharmonic Concert Committee
in Hamburg.*

613p [Concerto, piano, Op. 20, D minor] *23'*
1.Allegro moderato 2.Adagio non troppo 3.
Finale: Rondo
Solo Pno.-3*,2,2,3*-4,2-Timp.-Str.
Universal Edition, Vienna, c1914
Score 106 p.
*Composed 1915. First performance Vienna,
November 1916, Grete Hinterhofer soloist.*

830v [Concerto, violin, no. 2, Op. 41, *30'*
D minor]
1.Allegro non troppo 2.Andante 3.Finale:
Rondo capricioso
Solo Vn.-2,2,2,2-4,2-Timp.-Str.
Universal Edition, Vienna, c1914
Score 90 p.
*Composed 1903. First performance Vienna, 14
November 1905, Gustav Gutheil conductor,
Ondriček soloist.*

604c [Concerto, violoncello, no. 2, Op. *20'*
47, B minor]
1.Allegro moderato 2.Adagio 3.Finale: Rondo
Solo Vc.-2,2,2,2-4,2,3,1-Timp.-Str.
Universal Edition, Vienna, c1914
Score 87 p.
*Composed 1912. First performance Vienna, 4
November 1913, Ferdinand Löwe conductor, Paul
Grümmer soloist.*

2058 Sinfonietta, Op. 14 [C major] *25'*
1.Allegro 2.Scherzo 3.Andante 4.Finale:
Molto vivo
3*,2,2,2-4,2-Timp.-Str.
Eduard Wedl, Wiener-Neustadt [n.d.]
Score 226 p.
*Composed 1908. First performance Vienna, 20
March 1909, the composer conducting.*

1781 [Symphony no. 2, C minor] *56'*
1.Allegro un poco maestoso 2.Adagio non
troppo 3.Scherzo 4.Finale

3(3rd alt. Picc.),2,2,2-4,3,3,4-Timp.,Cym.,
Trgl.-Str.
Universal Edition, Vienna, c1912
Score 207 p.
*Composed 1903. First performance Vienna,
February 1903, Hellmesberger conductor.*

GRAENER, PAUL. Berlin 11 January 1872
Salzburg 13 November 1944

692s Au printemps
Str.
Score: Ms. 4 p.
Parts: Schott's Söhne, Mainz [n.d.]
Composed 1904.

1475 Aus dem Reiche des Pan, Suite, Op. 22 *15'*
1.Pan dreams in the moonlight 2.Pan sings of
love and longing 3.Pan dances 4.Pan sings the
world a lullaby
3*,3*,3*,3*-4,2,3-Timp.,Perc.-Hp.-Str.
Kistner, Leipzig, c1920
Score 39 p.
Composed and first performed Berlin, 1920.

1428s Chant du soir
Str.
Score: Ms. 6 p.
Parts: Schott's Söhne, Mainz [n.d.]

5071 [Comedietta, Op. 82] *11'*
3(3rd alt. Picc.),3(3rd alt. E.H.),3,2-4,1,1-
Timp.,Perc.-Pno.,Hp.-Str.
Ernst Eulenburg, Leipzig [1928]
Score 46 p.

630p [Concerto, piano, Op. 72, A minor]
1.Allegro moderato 2.Adagio 3.Allegro
Solo Pno.-2,2,2,2-4Hn.-Timp.-Str.
Simrock, Berlin, c1925
Score 67 p.

593c [Concerto, violoncello, Op. 78, A minor]
1.Allegro 2.Adagio 3.Vivace
Solo Vc.-1(alt. Picc.),1,2*,1-1,1-Timp.,Small
Dr.,Glock.-Pno.-Str.
Simrock, Berlin, c1927
Score 43 p.

1822 [Divertimento, for small orchestra, *18'*
Op. 67]
1.Allegro vivace 2.Allegretto scherzando 3.
Larghetto 4.Un poco allegretto 5.Allegro
2(2nd alt. Picc.),2,2,2-2,1-Timp.-Str.
Bote & Bock, Berlin, c1924
Score 59 p.
Composed 1923. First performance Berlin, 1924.

749s En route
Str.
Score: Ms. 7 p.
Parts: Schott's Söhne, Mainz [n.d.]
Composed 1904.

4698 [Evening song. Edited by Ludwig Kletsch] *3'*
1,1(E.H. ad lib.),1-Tpt.,Tbn.-Timp.-Pno.,Harm.
-Str.
B. Schott's Söhne, Mainz, c1938
Score in reduction 3 p.

Graener, Paul

3753 Die Flöte von Sanssouci, Suite für   12'
Kammerorchester, Op. 88
1.Introduction and sarabande 2.Gavotte 3.Air
4.Rigodon
2,2,0,2-2Hn.,2Tpt.-Timp.,Small Dr.-Cemb.-Str.
Eulenburg, Leipzig, c1930
Miniature score 38 p.
*First performance Berlin, 1931-32 season, Wil-
helm Furtwängler conductor.*

978 Musik am Abend, drei Sätze für kleines   15'
Orchester, Op. 44
1.Andantino 2.Larghetto 3.Allegretto
2,2(2nd alt. E.H.),2,2-2,2-Trgl.-Hp.-Str.
Simrock, Berlin, c1915
Score 30 p.
Composed 1913. First performance Leipzig, 1915.

4965 [Prince Eugene, the noble knight.   17'
Variations for orchestra, Op. 108]
3(3rd alt. Picc.),3(3rd alt. E.H.),3(3rd alt.
B.Cl.),3(3rd alt. C.Bn.)-4,3,3,1-Timp.,Perc.-
Hp.-Str.
B. Schott's Söhne, Mainz, c1939
Score 60 p.
Dedicated to Heinz Drewes.

2233 Romantische Phantasie, Op. 41   18'
3(3rd alt. Picc.),3(3rd alt. E.H.),3*,3*-4,3,
3,1-Timp.,Perc.-Hp.-Str.
W. Hansen, Copenhagen, c1923
Score 60 p.
*Composed 1921. First performance Copenhagen,
1922.*

6154 [Salzburg serenades for orchestra,   22'
Op. 115]
1.Andantino 2.Andante semplice - Allegretto -
Andante 3.Un poco allegretto 4.Tempo di
menuetto 5.Marche grotesque: Moderato - Vivace
3(3rd alt. Picc.),2(2nd alt. E.H.),2,2-3,1,2-
Timp.,Perc.-Hp.-Str.
Horst Sander, Leipzig, c1943
Score 74 p.
*Composed 1943. First performance Leipzig,
1943, Hermann Abendroth conductor. Dedicated
to Hans Luxenburger.*

2538 [Sinfonia breve, for orchestra, Op. 96] 20'
1.Allegro moderato 2.Adagio 3.Moderato un
poco maestoso
2,2,3*,3*-4,2,3-Timp.-Str.
Eulenburg, Leipzig, c1932
Score 54 p.

916s Symphonietta, Op. 27   25'
Hp.-Str.
Universal Edition, Vienna, c1910
Score 22 p.
Composed 1908.

1622 [Symphony, Op. 39, D minor]   30'
1.Larghetto - Allegro 2.Adagio 3.Allegro
energico
3*,3*,3*,3*-6,3,3,1-Timp.,Perc.-Hp.-Str.
Universal Edition, Vienna, c1912
Score 90 p.
Composed 1910. First performance Salzburg, 1912.

5126 [Three Swedish dances, Op. 98]   8'
1.Lappland: Moderato 2.Östergöth: Allegretto
3.Dalekarlien: Allegro non troppo ma marcato
2(2nd alt. Picc.),2,2,2-2,2-Timp.,Perc.-Str.
Bote & Bock, Berlin, c1932
Score 22 p.

3910 Turmwächterlied, Op. 107, Orchester-   16'
Variationen über ein Gedicht von Goethe [Ballad
of the tower watchman]
3(3rd alt. Picc.),3*,3(3rd alt. B.Cl.),3(3rd
alt. C.Bn.)-4,3,3-Timp.,Perc.-Hp.-Str.
Eulenburg, Leipzig, c1938
Miniature score 50 p.
*Based on a poem from the 2nd Book of Goethe's
Faust. First performance International Music
Festival, Baden-Baden, Germany, 23 April 1938,
G. E. Lessing conductor.*

1823 Variationen über ein russisches   19'
Volkslied (Ej uchnem-Dubinushka)
3(3rd alt. Picc.),3(3rd alt. E.H.),3*,3*-4,4,3,
1-Timp.,Perc.-Hp.-Str.
Bote & Bock, Berlin, c1922
Score 67 p.
Composed 1920. First performance Leipzig, 1921.

6156 [Viennese symphony, Op. 110]   25'
1.Allegro moderato 2.Andante sostenuto - Larghetto 3.Con moto - Andante
2,2,2,2-4,2,3-Timp.,Glock.-Str.
Eulenburg - Horst Sander, Leipzig, c1942
Score 79 p.
*First performance Berlin, 1941, Hans Knapperts-
busch conductor.*

1478 Waldmusik [Forest music] Op. 60   15'
3(3rd alt. Picc.),3,3*,3*-6,4,3,1-Timp.,Perc.-
Hp.-Str.
Kistner, Leipzig [n.d.]
Score 40 p.
Composed 1922. First performance Berlin, 1923.

GRÄFE, FRIEDEBALD.

852m Concerto for trombone and orchestra
In one movement
Solo Tbn.-1,1,2,1-2,2-Timp.,Perc.-Str.
Score: Ms. 60 p.
Parts: Benjamin, Leipzig, c1931

GRÄGER, RUDOLF.

1233s Ball-flirt, intermezzo
Str.
A.E. Fischer, Bremen [n.d.]
Score 3 p.

GRAINGER, PERCY ALDRIDGE.
                Melbourne, Australia 8 July 1882
                White Plains, New York 20 February 1961

1645 Hill-song no. 1, for room-music   15'
22-some (23-some at will)
2*,2*,2*,2*-Sopranino Sarrus.(or Ob.II),Ten.
Sarrus.(or Heckelphone, or Ten.Sax., or B.Cl.),
Sop.Sax.(or Cl.),Alto Sax.(or Alto Cl., or Hn.
in E-flat)-Hn.(ad lib.),Tpt.,Euph.-Timp.,Perc.-

Pno.,Harm.-Str.
Universal Edition, Vienna, ᶜ1924
Score 61 p.

1436 In a nutshell, suite for orchestra,   *18'*
piano and Deagan percussion instruments
1.Arrival platform humlet 2.Gay but wistful
3.Pastoral 4.The gum-suckers march
3*,3*,3*,3*-4,3,3,1-Timp.,Perc.,Deagan Steel
Marimba, Deagan Wooden Marimbaphone, Deagan
Swiss Staff Bells, Deagan Nabimba(4 to 8 players)-Pno.,Cel.,Hp.-Str.
G. Schirmer, New York, ᶜ1916 by Percy Grainger
Score 113 p.

287s Irish tune from County Derry, British
folk-music setting no. 15
2Hn.(ad lib.)-Str.
Schott, London, ᶜ1913
Score 8 p.

134s Mock Morris, dance for string   *3'30"*
orchestra
Str.(Cb. ad lib.)
Schott, London, ᶜ1911
Score 11 p.

906s Molly on the shore, British folk-   *3'*
music setting no. 1
Str.
Schott, London, ᶜ1911
Score 10 p.

313 Shepherd's hey, British folk-music   *2'*
setting no. 3
Fl.,Cl.-Hn.(ad lib.)-Baritone English (Chro-
matic) Concertina-Str.
Schott, London, ᶜ1911
Score 10 p.

4788 Spoon River, American folk-music   *4'30"*
settings no. 2, an American folk-dance set
for elastic scoring
Five different instrumental combinations possible, selected from following: 2*,1,1,1-1(or
E-flat Alto Hn.,or Alto Sax.),1(or Sop.Sax.),
3,1(ad lib.)-Timp.,Perc.-2Pno.(2nd ad lib.),
Harm.(or Org.),Hp.-Str.
G. Schirmer, New York, ᶜ1930
Score 30 p.
*Based on a fiddle-tune, Spoon River, as heard
at a dance at Bradford, Illinois in 1857 and
notated by Captain Charles H. Robinson. Composed 1919-29. Dedication: For Edgar Lee
Masters, poet of Pioneers.*

1387 The warriors, music to an imaginary   *18'*
ballet for orchestra and three pianos
3*,3*,Heckelphone(ad lib.),3*,3*-6,4,3,1-Timp.,
Perc.-3Pno.,Cel.,2Hp.-Str.
Schott, Mainz, ᶜ1926 by Percy Grainger
Score 112 p.

4752 Ye banks and braes o' Bonnie Doon, British
folk-music setting no. 32, Scottish folk-song
set for wind band (military band) with or without organ (or harmonium) or for wind choirs
with or without organ (or harmonium)

Six different instrumental combinations pos-
sible, selected from the following: 5*(3rd Fl.
ad lib.),3*(E.H. ad lib.),8*(1Cl. in E-flat ad
lib.; 1Alto Cl.; B.Cl.I ad lib.),4*(3rd Bn. &
C.Bn. ad lib.)-Sop.Sax.(ad lib.),2Alto Sax.,2
Ten.Sax.(2nd ad lib.),2Bar.Sax.(1st ad lib.),
Bass Sax.(ad lib.)-8Hn.(4 in E-flat),2Tpt.(ad
lib.),3Cnt.,2Fluegelhorn(ad lib.),3Tbn.,Bar.,
Euph.,2Tubas-Org.or Harm.-Cb.
G. Schirmer, New York, ᶜ1949
Score 5 p.

GRAM, PEDER.   Copenhagen 25 November 1881
                       Copenhagen 4 February 1956

869v [Concerto, violin, Op. 20, D minor]
1.Allegro moderato 2.Andante pastorale 3.
L'istesso tempo
Solo Vn.-2*,2*,2,2-4,2,3,1-Timp.-Str.
Wilhelm Hansen, Copenhagen [n.d.]
Score 56 p.

5943 [Overture, Op. 21, C major]   *9'*
3(3rd alt. Picc.),3*,2,3*-4,2,3,1-Timp.,Trgl.-
Str.
Samfundet til Udgivelse af Dansk Musik, Copen-
hagen, ᶜ1935
Score 55 p.
Composed 1921.

5944 [Prologue to a Shakespearean drama,   *8'*
Op. 27]
2,2,2,2-2,2,3-Timp.,Perc.-Str.
Edition Dania, Copenhagen, ᶜ1939 by Samfundet
til Udgivelse af Dansk Musik
Score 36 p.
Composed 1928.

880v Romance, violin and orchestra, Op. 5
Solo Vn.-2,1,2,2-2Hn.-Hp.-Str.
Wilhelm Hansen, Copenhagen [n.d.]
Score 15 p.

6062 Symphony no. 1, Op. 12   *30'*
1.Moderato ma risoluto 2.Sostenuto e risen-
tito 3.Vigoroso ma con grandezza
3(3rd alt. Picc.),3*,3*,3*-4,3,3,1-Timp.,Cym.
-Cel.,Hp.-Str.
Dansk Musikforlag, Copenhagen [1914]
Score 144 p.
*Composed 1910. First performance Copenhagen,
Dansk Koncert-forening.*

GRAMATGES, HAROLD. Santiago, Cuba 26 September 1918

5486 [Two Cuban dances for orchestra]   *7'*
1.Montuna: Allegro moderato 2.Sonera: Allegro
moderato
3*,3*,3*,3*-4,3,3,1-Timp.,B.Dr.,Cym.-Pno.,Cel.,
Hp.-Str.
Ms.
Score 33 p. Large folio
Composed 1950.

Granados, Enrique

GRANADOS, ENRIQUE.   Lérida, Spain 27 July 1867
                          At sea 24 March 1916

1979 Dante, symphonic poem, Op. 21
1.Dante e Virgilio 2.Paolo e Francesca
3*,3*,3*,4*-4,3,4,6-Timp.,Perc.-2Hp.-Str.
(Female voice solo in No. 2)
G. Schirmer, New York, c1915
Score 73 p.

6876 [Five pieces on popular Spanish melodies.
Transcribed for orchestra by Rafael Ferrer]
1.Añoranza: Allegretto con moto - Andante 2.
Ecos de la Parranda: Allegretto moderato 3.Za-
pateado: Allegro 4.Zambra: Andante - Vivo
5.Miel de la Alcarria: Allegro
3(3rd alt. Picc.),3*,3*,2-4,3,3,1-Timp.,Perc.-
Cel.,Hp.-Str.
Unión Musical Español, Madrid, c1960
Score 115 p.
*Nos. 1-4 are transcribed from Piezas Sobre
Cantos Populares Españoles, for piano. No. 5
is from the incidental music for a play by
Apeles Mestre.*

6779 [Goyescas. Intermezzo]   *4'*
3,2(2nd alt. E.H.),2,3-4,1,3-Timp.,Tamb.,Cast.
-2Hp.-Str.
Ms.
Score 11 p. Large folio
*From the opera, based mainly on the piano
pieces Goyescas, in 3 scenes with libretto by
Fernando Periquet y Zuaznabar. First performance Metropolitan Opera, New York, 28 January
1916.*

740 Tres danzas españolas. Orchestrated   *13'*
by J. Lamote de Grignon
1.Oriental 2.Andaluza 3.Rondalla
3*,3*,3,2-4,2,3,1-Timp.,Perc.-Hp.-Str.
Unión Musical Española, Madrid [n.d.]
Score 66 p.

GRANDJEAN, ANDRÉ.

1153s Aubade
Solo Vn.-Str.
Score: Ms. 8 p.
Parts: Decourcelle, Nice, c1923

1056s Canzonetta
Solo Vn.-Str.
Score: Ms. 10 p.
Parts: Decourcelle, Nice, c1928

1224s Chanson napolitaine
Solo Vn.-Str.
Score: Ms. 5 p.
Parts: Decourcelle, Nice, c1928

GRANT, WILLIAM PARKS.
                Cleveland, Ohio 4 January 1910

1932s Autumn woodland poem, Op. 16   *8'*
Str.
Ms. [Whitney Blake, New York, c1949]
Score 18 p.

*Original title: Poem for String Orchestra. Com-
posed 1945. First performance Rochester, New
York, October 1946, Eastman-Rochester Symphony
Orchestra, Howard Hanson conductor. Dedicated
to Grant Fletcher.*

412m Concerto for clarinet and orchestra, *20'*
Op. 14
1.Allegretto 2.Lento 3.Finale: Lento (Cadenza)
- Allegro moderato
Solo Cl.-2(2nd alt. Picc.),2(2nd alt. E.H.),2*,
2-4,2,3,1-Timp.,Perc.-Hp.-Str.
Ms.
Score 92 p.
Composed 1942-45.

302m Concerto for French horn and orchestra, *18'*
Op. 11
1.Largo - Allegro molto 2.Molto adagio 3.Fina-
le: Vivace
Solo Hn.-2(2nd alt. Picc.),2,2,2-3,2,3,1-Timp.-
Hp.-Str.
Ms.
Score 80 p.
*Composed 1940. First performance Rochester,
New York, 10 April 1941, broadcast over the Blue
Network, Rochester Civic Orchestra, Howard Han-
son conductor, Harold Meek soloist. Dedicated
to Harold Meek.*

4934 Dramatic overture (Orchestral   *9'30"*
overture no. 2), Op. 26
3*,3*,3*,3*(C.Bn. ad lib.)-4,3,3,1-Timp.,Perc.
-Pno.(alt. Cel. ad lib.)-Str.
Ms. [c1952 by American Composers Alliance, New
York]
Score 30 p. Large folio
Composed 1948.

4459 Homage ode (Orchestral overture no.   *8'*
3), Op. 30
2(2nd alt. Picc.),2(2nd alt. E.H.),2,2-4,2,3,1-
Timp.,Perc.-Str.
Ms. [c1950 by Associated Music Publishers,
New York]
Score 33 p. Large folio
*Composed 1949. First performance Oxford, Miss-
issippi, 30 April 1959, University of Mississippi Orchestra, Arthur Kreutz conductor. Dedicated to Edwin A. Fleisher and thematically
based on his initials: E.A.F.*

3333 Minuet, Op. 1 no. 5, D major   *2'*
2,1,2,2-2Hn.-Str.
Ms.
Score 13 p.
*Originally composed for piano, 1928; arranged
1928. First performance Columbus, Ohio, 7
April 1929, Columbus Symphony Orchestra, Earl
Hopkins conductor.*

6390 A musical tribute (Orchestral over- *14'*
ture no. 6) Op. 50 no. 2
3*,2(2nd alt. E.H.),3*,2-4,2,3,1-Timp.,Perc.-
Str.
Ms.

Score 43 p.
Composed 1955; revised 1959. Dedicated to Mr.
Henry S. Drinker and thematically based on his
initials: H. S. D.

3332 Overture to Shakespeare's Macbeth   *12'*
3(3rd alt. Picc.),2(2nd alt. E.H.),3*,2-4,3,3,
1-Timp.,Perc.-Hp.-Str.
Ms.
Score 65 p.
Composed 1929-30.

3331 Poème élégiaque, Op. 3   *15'*
3,2,2,2-4,2,3,1-Timp.,Perc.-Str.
Ms.
Score 45 p.
Composed 1928. First performance Columbus,
Ohio, 7 April 1929, Columbus Symphony Orchestra,
Earl Hopkins conductor.

4954 Rhythmic overture (Orchestral over-   *6'*
ture no. 1), Op. 23
2(2nd alt. Picc.),2(2nd alt. E.H.),2(2nd alt.
B.Cl.),2(2nd alt. C.Bn.)-4,2,3,1-Timp.,Perc.-
Str.
Ms. [American Composers Alliance, New York,
c1952]
Score 36 p. Large folio
Composed 1947. First performance Rochester,
New York, November 1951, Eastman-Rochester Sym-
phony Orchestra, Howard Hanson conductor.
Awarded 1st prize, Pennsylvania Federation of
Music Clubs, 1952.

1082m Scherzo for flute and small orchestra, *6'*
Op. 33
Solo Fl.-1(ad lib.),1,2(2nd alt. B.Cl.),1-2,1-
Tamb.-Cel.(or Pno.)-Str.
Ms. [American Composers Alliance, New York,
c1952]
Score 31 p. Large folio
Composed 1949. First performance Long Island,
May 1953, Town of Babylon Orchestra, Christos
Vrionides conductor, Milton G. Bergey soloist.

1926s Suite no. 1 for string orchestra,   *12'*
Op. 21
1.Prelude: Moderato ed animato 2.Slow move-
ment: Adagio 3.Fugue: Allegretto
Str.
Ms. [American Composers Alliance, New York,
c1952]
Score 14 p.
Commissioned by the Northwestern Louisiana
State College at Natchitoches. Composed 1946.
First performance Rochester, New York, Eastman-
Rochester Symphony Orchestra, Howard Hanson
conductor.

2289s Suite no. 2 for string orchestra,   *12'*
Op. 43
1.Prelude: Allegro moderato 2.Aria: Lento, ma
non troppo 3.Fugue: Allegretto
Str.
Ms. c1954 by Parks Grant
Score 16 p.

Composed 1952. First performance Austin, Texas,
7 April 1954, University of Texas Orchestra,
Alexander von Kreisler conductor.

2168s Suite no. 3 for string orchestra,   *24'*
Op. 53
1.Overture: Andante declamando - Allegro non
troppo 2.Dance: Allegretto 3.Scherzo and
epilogue: Allegro scherzando - Adagio tragico
Str.
Ms. c1959 by Parks Grant
Score 36 p.
Composed 1959. First performance Dallas, Texas,
11 December 1960, Dallas Symphony Orchestra,
Donald Johanos conductor.

3339 Symphonic fantasia, Op. 8   *12'*
3(3rd alt. Picc.),2*,2*,2-4,3,3,1-Timp.,Perc.-
Pno.-Str.
Ms.
Score 74 p.
Composed 1931. First performance Columbus,
Ohio, June 1932, Ohio State University Symphony
Orchestra, Eugene J. Weigel conductor.

3490 Symphony no. 1, Op. 6, D minor   *48'*
1.Lento - Allegro appassionato 2.Adagio ma non
troppo 3.Scherzo 4.Finale
3(3rd alt. Picc.),3*,3*(2nd alt. Cl. in E-flat,
B.Cl. alt. Cl.3),3*-5,3,3,1-Timp.,Perc.-Pno.
(alt. Cel.),2Hp.-Str.
Ms.
Score 206 p. Large folio
Composed 1930-38 as Op. 15. Renumbered 1959.

GRAUBART, MICHAEL HERBERT. Vienna 26 November 1930

7298 Aria for orchestra   *4-5'*
3(3rd alt. Picc.),3*,4*(2nd alt. Cl. in E-flat,
2B.Cl.),3*-4,3,3,1-Timp.,Perc.-Str.
Ms. c1974 by Michael Graubart
Score 27 p. Large folio
Composed in honor of the opening of a new
building at Morley College, London. Composed
1973. First performance London, 5 December
1973, Morley College Symphony Orchestra, Guy
Woolfenden conductor. Revised 1974.

GRAUN, CARL HEINRICH.
                    Wahrenbrück, near Dresden 7 May 1704
                                  Berlin 8 August 1759

409m [Concerto, flute, strings and con-   *20'*
tinuo, E minor] Edited by Johannes Brinckmann
1.Andante 2.Siciliano 3.Vivace
Solo Fl.-Cemb.-Str.(without Violas)
Willy Müller, Süddeutscher Musikverlag,
Heidelberg, c1958
Score 31 p.
Composed for Frederick the Great.

Graun, Carl Heinrich

328p [Concerto for harpsichord or organ and
string orchestra, F major] Edited by Hugo Ruf
1.Allegro non tanto 2.Largo 3.Allegretto
Solo Hpscd.or Org.-Str.
Willy Müller, Süddeutscher Musikverlag, Heidelberg, c1959
Score 35 p.

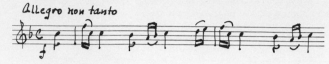

GRAUN, JOHANN GOTTLIEB.
                        Wahrenbrück, near Dresden 1703
                        Berlin 27 October 1771

305m [Concerto for bassoon, strings and continuo,
B-flat major] Edited by Hermann Töttcher
1.Allegro moderato 2.Grazioso 3.Allegro
Solo Bn.-Cemb.-Str.
Hans Sikorski, Hamburg, c1955
Score 42 p.

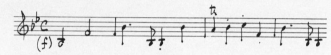

304m [Concerto for oboe, string orchestra and
continuo, C minor] Edited by Hermann Töttcher
1.(Allegro) 2.Affettuoso 3.Allegro molto
Solo Ob.-Cemb.-Str.
Hans Sikorski, Hamburg, c1953
Score 53 p.

283m [Concerto for violin and viola with   23'
string orchestra and continuo, C minor] Edited
by Kurt Janetzky. Cembalo realization by
Werner Richter
1.Allegro 2.Adagio, con sordini 3.Allegro
Solo Vn. & Solo Va.-Cemb.-Str.
Breitkopf & Härtel, Leipzig [1956]
Score 71 p.

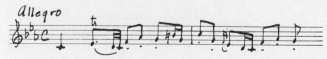

6534 [Symphony in D major] Edited by Max
Schneider
1.Allegro maestoso 2.Arietta: Grazioso 3.Alle-
gro moderato

2,0,0,2-2,3-Timp.-Cemb.-Str.
Breitkopf & Härtel, Leipzig [1957?]
Score 27 p.
Composed 1768.

GRAUPNER, CL.

1556s Das Schneeglöckchen, pour orchestre à
cordes
Glock.-Str.
Score: Ms. 3 p.
Parts: International, New York [n.d.]

1388s Ein Traum, pour orchestre à cordes
Str.
Score: Ms. 7 p.
Parts: International, New York [n.d.]

GRAZIANI-WALTER, CARLO.   Brussels 1 August 1851
                            Florence 30 August 1927

1565s Mirto e cipresso, elegia for string
orchestra, Op. 180
Hp.-Str.(Va. ad lib.)
Score: Ms. 9 p.
Parts: Carisch e Jänichen, Milan [n.d.]

GRAZIOLI, GIOVANNI BATTISTA.   Venice ca.1755
                                 Venice ca.1820

1390s [Minuetto. Orchestrated by Michele
Esposito]
Fl.,Bn.-Timp.(all ad lib.)-Str.
Oxford University Press, London, c1928
Score 7 p.

GRECHANINOV, ALEXANDER TIKHONOVICH.
                        Moscow 25 October 1864
                        New York 3 January 1956

1787s [Berceuse. Arranged for string   4'
orchestra by Henri Elkan]
Pno.(ad lib.)-Str.
Elkan-Vogel, Philadelphia, c1940
Score 6 p.
Originally composed for voice and piano;
arranged 1939. First performance at a Robin
Hood Dell Concert, Philadelphia, 26 July 1939,
Philadelphia Orchestra, Henri Elkan conductor.

851 [Elegiac poem, Op. 175]   9'30"
3*,3*,3*,3*-4,3(1Alto Tpt.),3,1-Timp.,Perc.-
Str.
Ms.
Score 24 p. Large folio
Composed 1944. First performance 29 March 1946,
Boston Symphony Orchestra, Serge Koussevitzky
conductor.

2118 [Symphony no. 1, Op. 6, B minor]   30'
1.Allegro non troppo 2.Andante sostenuto assai
3.Molto vivace (quasi presto) 4.Finale: Allegro spirituoso
3*,2(2nd alt. E.H.),2,2-4,2,3,1-Timp.,Perc.-
Hp.-Str.
Gutheil, Moscow [n.d.]
Score 140 p.
*Composed 1894. First performance St. Peters-
burg, 1895, Rimsky-Korsakov conductor.*

1623 [Symphony no. 2, Op. 27, A minor]   32'
1.Pastorale 2.Andante 3.Scherzo 4.Finale
3*,2,2,2-4,2,3,1-Timp.,Perc.-Str.
Gutheil, Moscow [n.d.]
Score 191 p.
*Composed 1908-09. First performance Moscow,
14 March 1909, Russian Music Society, the composer conducting.*

2209 [Symphony no. 3, Op. 100, E major]   35'
1.Moderato e poi poco a poco accelerando all'
allegro 2.Scherzo 3.Tema con variazioni 4.
Finale: Allegro vivace
3*,2,2,2-4,2,3,1-Timp.,Perc.-Str.
Ms.
Score 282 p.
*Composed 1920-23. First performance Kiev, 29
May 1924, the composer conducting.*

3656 [Symphony no. 4, Op. 102, À la   44'
mémoire de Chaikovsky, C major]
1.Largo - Allegro 2.Scherzo 3.Andante elegiaco 4.Finale
3(3rd alt. Picc.),3*,3*,3*-4,3,3,1-Timp.,Perc.
-Str.
Ms.
Score 274 p.
*Begun 1925 in Russia, completed 1927 in France,
and revised 1942 in New York. First performance New York, 9 April 1942, New York Philharmonic, John Barbirolli conductor.*

1896s Triptique, Op. 163   15'
1.En plein air 2.Meditation 3.Kermesse
Pno.,Hp.-Str.
Ms.
Score 40 p.
*Composer indicates that this is Op. 163
although all material bears the designation
Op. 161.*

GREEF, ARTHUR DE.   Louvain 10 October 1862
                      Brussels 29 August 1940

247s [Ballade, in the form of variations on
a Flemish folk song, Op. 1]
Str.
Peters, Leipzig [n.d.]
Score 15 p.

1105 Four old Flemish folk songs. Tran-   16'
scribed for orchestra by Arthur de Greef
1.The solitary rose 2.Hoepsasa 3.Wounded is
my heart 4.The Duke of Alva's statue
2(2nd alt. Picc.),2(1st alt. E.H.),2,2-2,2,3,1
-Timp.,Perc.-Hp.-Str.

Chester, London, c1915
Score 60 p.
*Composed 1894. First performance Queen's Hall,
London, 4 October 1896, A. de Greef conductor.*

566s [Same as above] No. 3, Wounded is my heart
Str.
Chester, London, c1915
Score 4 p.

488p Menuet varié [for piano and strings]
Pno.-Str.
Score: Ms. 25 p.
Parts: Heugel, Paris, c1913

1533 Suite d'orchestre [G major]
1.Largo 2.Rigodon 3.Orientale 4.Springdands
norvégien
2*,2,2,2-2,2,3-Timp.,Perc.-Hp.-Str.
Cranz, Leipzig [n.d.]
Score 47 p.

GREEN, RAY. Cavendish, Missouri 13 September 1909

4749 Kentucky mountain running set [for   7'
band]
2,1,3,1-Alto,Ten.& Bar.Sax.-8(4 in E-flat),2,
4Cnt.,Fluegelhorn,3Tbn.,Bar.,Euph.,Tuba-Timp.,
Perc.-Cb.
G. Schirmer, New York, c1948
Score 27 p.

217m Three inventories of Casey Jones, for 6'
percussion
Introduction - One, Two, Three - Repeat of
Introduction for Finale
Five players:
1st - 5 Pop Bottles, Large Bottle
2nd - High & Low Dr.
3rd - High & Low Cym.
4th - 4 Gongs
5th - Pno.
New Music Orchestra Series, San Francisco,
c1936
Score 3 p.
*Composed 1936. First performance Repertory
Playhouse, Seattle, 1938, sponsored by the
Cornish School, John Cage conductor.*

GREGH, LOUIS. Philippeville, Algeria 16 March 1843
          St. Mesme (Seine-et-Oise) 21 January 1915

815s [Ballroom whispers, Op. 66]
Str.(with Pno. or Hp.; ad lib.)
Bosworth, Leipzig, c1891
Score 9 p.

GREGOIR, EDOUARD GEORGES JACQUES.
          Turnhout, near Antwerp 7 November 1822
          Wyneghem 28 June 1890

4316 [Homage to Felix Mendelssohn Bartholdy,
concert overture no. 3, Op. 52]
Andante - Allegro ma non troppo
2,2,2,2-4,2,3,Ophicl.-Timp.,Trgl.-Str.

Grell, Eduard August

Marchand de Musique, Brussels; Wygant, The
Hague [185-?]
Score 14 p.

GRELL, EDUARD AUGUST.   Berlin 6 November 1800
                            Steglitz 10 August 1886

534c Terzett, for 3 violoncelli and string   6'
orchestra
3 Soli Vc.-Str.
[n.p., n.d.]
Score in reduction 4 p.
Composed 1876. First performance Berlin, 1878.

GRENZEBACH, ERNST.   b. Germany 1812

4668 [Waltzes for piano and 8 toy instruments,
Op. 5]
Cuckoo, Nightingale,Quail,Toy Tpt.,Dr.,Cym.,
Trgl.,Rattle-Pno.
Breitkopf & Härtel, Leipzig [188-?]
Score 16 p.

GRESS, RICHARD.   Endersbach 3 December 1893

1106s [Variations on a theme by Mozart, for
string orchestra, Op. 40]
Str.
Ries & Erler, Berlin, c1929
Score 28 p.

GRÉTRY, ANDRÉ ERNEST MODESTE.
                Liège, France February 1741
        Montmorency, near Paris 24 September 1813

788s Air de danse *and* Tambourin. Arranged for
string orchestra by Gustave Sandré
Str.
Schott, Mainz [n.d.]
Score 4 p.

1927s [Anacréon chez Polycrate. No. 2,
Graceful dance]
Bn.-Pno.(optional)-Str.
Breitkopf & Härtel, Leipzig [188-?]
Score 3 p.
*From the opera in three acts with libretto by
Jean Henri Guy. First performance Opéra,
Paris, 17 January 1797.*

3831 [Anacréon chez Polycrate. No. 4,
Divertissement, Act II, Air de caractère]
0,2,2,2-2Hn.,2Tpt.-Str.
Breitkopf & Härtel, Leipzig [n.d.]
Score 8 p.

4720 [Anacréon chez Polycrate. No. 5, Graceful
gavotte]
Fl.,Bn.-Pno.(optional)-Str.
Breitkopf & Härtel, Leipzig [188-?]
Score 10 p.

1894s [Anacréon chez Polycrate. No. 6, Gay
dance]
Str.(without Va.)
Breitkopf & Härtel, Leipzig [188-?]
Score 8 p.

4718 [Anacréon chez Polycrate. No. 7, Final
divertissement: Expressive dance]
2,2,2,2-Pno.(optional)-Str.
Breitkopf & Härtel, Leipzig [188-?]
Score 3 p.

4719 [Anacréon chez Polycrate. No. 8, Dance
of the fawns]
1,2,2,2-3Tbn.-Pno.(optional)-Str.
Breitkopf & Härtel, Leipzig [188-?]
Score 6 p.

4721 [Anacréon chez Polycrate. No. 9, Dance
of the three nations, France, Poland, Spain]
4*(2 are Picc.),2,2,2-2,2-Timp.-Pno.(optional)
-Str.
Breitkopf & Härtel, Leipzig [188-?]
Score 11 p.

4722 [Anacréon chez Polycrate. No. 10, Air for
the bacchantes]
2Picc.,2,2,2-3Tbn.-Pno.(optional)-Str.
Breitkopf & Härtel, Leipzig [188-?]
Score 9 p.

4723 [Anacréon chez Polycrate. No. 11,
Apollo's dance for Vestris]
Andante sostenuto - Theme - 5 Variations -
Coda
Solo Hn.-3*,2,2,2-2,2-Timp.-Hp.-Str.
Breitkopf & Härtel, Leipzig [188-?]
Score 42 p.

1978s [Anacréon chez Polycrate. No. 12,
Graceful dance]
Solo Fl.-Str.
Breitkopf & Härtel, Leipzig [188-?]
Score 5 p.

3832 [Anacréon chez Polycrate. No. 13,
Chaconne]
1,2,2,2-2Hn.,2Tpt.-Timp.-Str.(without Va.)
Breitkopf & Härtel, Leipzig [n.d.]
Score 14 p.

4724 [Anacréon chez Polycrate. No. 14, Air
for the Graces and Love]
1,Galoubet(Recorder),2,2,2-2,2-Timp.-Str.
Breitkopf & Härtel, Leipzig [188-?]
Score 24 p.

1372s [La caravane du Caire. Marche de la
caravane. Arranged by Gustave Sandré]
Str.
Schott, Leipzig [n.d.]
Score 3 p.
From the opera first performed 1783.

343 [Céphale et Procris. Three dances.   15'
Arranged by Felix Mottl]
1.Tambourin 2.Menuetto (Les nymphes de Diane)
3.Gigue
2*,2,2,2-2,2-Timp.,Perc.-Str.
Peters, Leipzig [n.d.]
Score 56 p.
*From the opera with libretto by Marmontel,
first performed Versailles, 30 December 1773.*

First performance of this arrangement Karls-ruhe, 1901, Felix Mottl conductor.

318m [Concerto, flute, 2 horns and   *16'*
strings, C major] Edited by Dieter Sonntag
1.Allegro 2.Larghetto 3.Allegro
Solo Fl.-2Hn.-Str.
Otto Heinrich Noetzel Verlag, Wilhelmshaven,
c1961
Score 24 p.
Commissioned by Lord Abingdon. Composed 1765.

756s Denys le tyran. Tambourin [Arranged for
string orchestra by Gustav Sandré]
Str.
Schott, Mainz [n.d.]
Score 3 p.
From the opera first performed Paris, 1794.

1473 L'épreuve villageoise. Overture.   *3'*
Arranged by Gustav F. Kogel
2*,2,0,2-2,2-Timp.-Str.
Breitkopf & Härtel, Leipzig, c1909
Score 15 p.
*From the comic opera first performed Paris,
1784.*

1317s L'épreuve villageoise. Rustic idyll
Str.
Score: Ms. 3 p.
Parts: Oertel, Hannover [n.d.]

6862 [The judgment of Midas. Overture]   *5'*
Edited by Antonio de Almeida
2Picc.(1st alt. Fl.),2,0,2-2Hn.-Str.
Heugel, Paris, c1961
Score 20 p.
*From the opera in 3 acts with libretto by
Thomas d'Hèle (versification partly by Louis
Anseaume). Composed 1778. First performance
privately at Mme. de Montesson's, Paris, 28
March 1778. First public performance Comédie-
Italienne, Paris, 27 June 1778.*

1938 Kleine Ballett-Musik [Arranged by   *12'*
Sam Franko]
1.Danse grave 2.Danse légère 3.Gavotte 4.
Marche des Janissaires
1(alt. Picc.),2,2,2-2,2-Timp.,Perc.-Str.
Ries & Erler, Berlin, c1930
Score 34 p.
Arranged 1930; first performance Berlin, 1930.

4631 [Lucile. Overture. Arranged by   *4'30"*
Adam Carse]
Vivace - Andante - Vivace, come prima
2Ob.(or 2Fl.),2Bn.-2,2-Timp.-Str.
Augener Ltd., London, c1941
Score 11 p.
*From the opera in 1 act with libretto by Jean
François Marmontel. First performance Théâtre
Comédie-Italienne, Paris, 5 January 1769.*

6863 Le magnifique. Overture. Edited by   *11'*
Antonio de Almeida
1,2,0,2-2,2-Timp.,Dr.-Str.
Heugel & Cie, Paris, c1962
Score 35 p.

*From the opera in three acts with libretto by
Jean Michel Sedaine, based on a tale by La
Fontaine. First performance Comédie-Italienne,
Paris, 4 March 1773.*

453c [Suite rococo for violoncello and
orchestra. Edited by Paul Bazelaire]
1.Chasse: Allegro 2.Ariette: Andantino
3.Gavotte: Allegretto 4.Tambourin: Presto
Solo Vc.-Str.
Schott Frères, Brussels, c1942
Score 16 p.
*This is a pasticcio from various works of
Grétry. No. 4, Tambourin, for example, is from
his opera, Céphale et Procris.*

GRIEG, EDVARD HAGERUP.
    Bergen, Norway 15 June 1843
    Bergen 4 September 1907

596 Altnorwegische Romanze, Op. 51   *20'*
3*,2,2,2-4,2,3,1-Timp.,Perc.-Hp.-Str.
Peters, Leipzig [n.d.]
Score 86 p.
*Composed 1892. First performance Bergen, 1893,
the composer conducting.*

87s Aus Holberg's Zeit (Holberg suite), Op. 40
1.Prelude 2.Sarabande 3.Gavotte und Musette
4.Air 5.Rigaudon
Str.
Peters [n.p.] [n.d.]
Score 19 p.
*Composed 1884 in commemoration of Ludwig Hol-
berg's bicentennial.*

376p [Concerto, piano, Op. 16, A minor]   *30'*
1.Allegro molto moderato 2.Adagio 3.Allegro
moderato molto e marcato
Solo Pno.-2(2nd alt. Picc.),2,2,2-4,2,3-Timp.-
Str.
C.F. Peters, Frankfurt [n.d.]
Score 82 p.
*Composed 1868. First performance Copenhagen,
1869, Edmund Neupert soloist.*

100s [Elegiac melodies, Op. 34]
1.[Wounded heart] 2.[Springtide]
Str.
Peters, Leipzig [n.d.]
Score 6 p.

4281 [Funeral march in memory of Rikard   *3'*
Nordraak, A minor. Transcribed for orchestra
by Johan Halvorsen]
3*,2,2,2-4,2,3,1-Timp.,Perc.-Str.
C.F. Peters, Leipzig [n.d.]
Score 8 p.
*Originally composed for solo piano, 1866, in
memory of the Norwegian composer Rikard Nordraak, 1843-1866.*

Huldigungsmarsch
    See: [Sigurd Jorsalfar. Three orchestral
        pieces, Op. 56. No. 3, Huldigungsmarsch]

Grieg, Edvard

248 Im Herbst [In autumn, concert   *11'*
     overture, Op. 11]
     3*,2,2,2-4,2,3,1-Timp.,Perc.-Str.
     Peters, Leipzig [n.d.]
     Score 59 p.
     Composed 1865. First performance Christiania,
     1867. Rescored 1888.

     Lyric pieces. Three suites arranged for
     string orchestra by Ross Jungnickel
12s No. 1
     1.Gade (Op. 57 no. 2) 2.Elegie (Op. 38 no. 6)
     3.Gratitude (Op. 62 no. 2) 4.Grandmother's
     minuet (Op. 68 no. 2) 5.At the cradle (Op. 68
     no. 5)
13s No. 2
     1.Albumleaf (Op. 47 no. 2) 2.Canon (Op. 38
     no. 8) 3.Little bird (Op. 43 no. 4)
     4.Scherzo (Op. 54 no. 5)
14s No. 3
     1.In my native country (Op. 43 no. 3)
     2.Secret (Op. 57 no. 3) 3.Peasant's song
     (Op. 65 no. 2) 4.Shepherd boy (Op. 54 no. 1)
     5.Homeward (Op. 62 no. 6)
     Str.
     Jungnickel, New York, c1919
     Score: 14 p., 16 p., 17 p.

232s [Lyric pieces, from Op. 68. Arranged   *6'*
     by the composer]
     1.[Evening in the mountains] 2.[At the cradle]
     Ob.-Hn.-Str.
     Peters, Leipzig [n.d.]
     Score 10 p.
     Originally composed for piano.

595 [Lyric suite, Op. 54. Orchestrated   *16'*
     by the composer]
     1.Shepherd boy 2.Norwegian rustic march 3.
     Nocturne 4.March of the dwarfs
     3*,2,2,2-4,2,3,1-Timp.,Perc.-Hp.-Str.
     Kalmus, New York [n.d.]
     Score 58 p.
     Originally composed for piano.

598 Norwegian dances, Op. 35. Orchestrated   *17'*
     by Hans Sitt
     1.Allegro marcato 2.Allegretto tranquillo
     grazioso 3.Allegro moderato alla marcia 4.
     Allegro molto
     3*,2,2,2-4,2,3,1-Timp.,Perc.-Hp.-Str.
     Kalmus, Scarsdale [n.d.]
     Score 71 p.
     Composed for piano. Orchestrated 1890; first
     performance Leipzig, 1890, Hans Sitt conductor.

69s [Norwegian melodies, Op. 63]
     1.[Popular song] (Melody by F. Due) 2.[Cow
     keeper's tune and country dance]
     Str.
     Peters, Leipzig [n.d.]
     Score 15 p.

597 Norwegischer Brautzug im Vorüberziehen   *4'*
     (Bridal procession) Op. 19 no. 2.
     Orchestrated by Johan Halvorsen
     2(2nd alt. Picc.),2,2,2-4,2,3-Timp.,Perc.-Str.
     Peters, Leipzig [n.d.]

Score 25 p.
Composed for piano; orchestrated and first per-
formed Christiania, 1903, Johan Halvorsen con-
ductor.

593 Peer Gynt suite, no. 1, Op. 46   *15'*
     1.Morning mood 2.Åse's death 3.Anitra's
     dance 4.In the hall of the mountain king
     3,2,2,2-4,2,3,1-Timp.,Perc.-Str.
     Kalmus, New York [n.d.]
     Score 39 p.
     Originally composed as incidental music to Hen-
     rik Ibsen's drama, 1875. First performance
     Christiania, 24 February 1876. Arranged as
     Suite, 1888.

48   Peer Gynt suite, no. 2, Op. 55   *14'*
     1.[The rape of the bride] (Ingrid's lamenta-
     tion) 2.[Arabian dance] 3.[Peer Gynt's home-
     coming] 4.[Solveijg's song]
     3*,2,2,2-4,2,3,1-Timp.,Perc.-Hp.-Str.
     Peters, Leipzig [n.d.]
     Score 57 p.
     Arranged as Suite, 1891.

128 [Sigurd Jorsalfar. Three orchestral   *20'*
     pieces, Op. 56]
     1.Introduction (In the king's hall) 2.Inter-
     mezzo (Borghild's dream) 3.Huldigungsmarsch
     2(2nd alt. Picc.),2,2,2-4,3,3,1-Timp.,Perc.-
     Hp.-Str.
     Kalmus, New York [n.d.]
     Score 35 p.
     Composed 1870. First performance Christiania,
     10 April 1872.

594 [Sigurd Jorsalfar. Three orchestral   *8'*
     pieces, Op. 56. No. 3, Huldigungsmarsch]
     2,2,2,2-4,3,3,1-Timp.,Perc.-Hp.-Str.
     Peters, Leipzig [n.d.]
     Score 23 p.

4343 [Sonata, piano, Op. 7, E minor. Minuet.
     Transcribed for orchestra by Robert Henriques]
     2(2nd alt. Picc.),2,2,2-4,2,3,1-Timp.-Str.
     Breitkopf & Härtel, Leipzig [188-?]
     Score 12 p.
     Originally composed for piano, 1865.

599 [Symphonic dances on Norwegian themes, *35'*
     Op. 64]
     1.Allegro moderato e marcato 2.Allegretto
     grazioso 3.Allegro giocoso 4.Andante - Alle-
     gro molto e risoluto
     3*,2,2,2-4,2,3,1-Timp.,Perc.-Hp.-Str.
     Peters, Leipzig [n.d.]
     Score 119 p.
     Composed 1898. First performance Bergen, 1898,
     the composer conducting.

6543 [Symphony, Unfinished, Op. 14. Transcribed
     for orchestra by Elizabeth Camerano]
     1.Adagio cantabile 2.Allegro energico
     3(3rd alt. Picc.),3*,3*,3*-4,3,3,1-Timp.,Trgl.,
     Cym.-Hp.(alt. Cel.)-Str.
     Ms. c1962 by Elizabeth Camerano
     Score 70 p.
     Based on Grieg's Two Symphonic Movements, for
     piano four-hands, Op. 14.

143s [Two melodies after original songs, for
string orchestra, Op. 53]
1.Norsk [Norwegian] 2.Det förste Möde [The
first meeting]
Str.
Peters, Leipzig [n.d.]
Score 11 p.

GRIFFES, CHARLES TOMLINSON.
Elmira, New York 17 September 1884
New York 8 April 1920

5772 Bacchanale   5'
3*,3*,3*,4*-4,3,3,1-Timp.,Perc.-Cel.,2(or 1)Hp.
-Str.
Ms.
Score 52 p.
*Originally composed for piano as No. 3 (Scherzo)
of Fantasy Pieces, Op. 6, 1913. First performance Philadelphia, 19 December 1919, Philadelphia Orchestra, Leopold Stokowski conductor.*

5770 Clouds   5'
4*,3(3rd alt. E.H.),3*,3*-4Hn.-Tam-tam-Cel.,
2Hp.-Str.
Ms.
Score 16 p.
*Originally composed for piano 1916 as No. 4 of
Roman Sketches, Op. 7. Later transcribed for
orchestra. First performance of orchestral
version Philadelphia, 19 December 1919, Philadelphia Orchestra, Leopold Stokowski conductor.*

6939 The kairn of Koridwen
Fl.,2Cl.-2Hn.-Pno.,Cel.,Hp.
Ms. c1976 by The Fleisher Collection of
Orchestral Music, Free Library of
Philadelphia
Score 162 p. Large folio
*Pantomime-ballet in 2 scenes. Text by Edouard
Schuré (1841-1929), adapted from Les Grandes
Légendes de France. Composed 1916 for The
Neighborhood Playhouse, New York City, as a
pantomime-ballet. First performance at The
Neighborhood Playhouse, 10 February 1917,
members of the Barrère Ensemble, Nikolai Soko-
loff conductor, the composer as pianist.*

6096 Overture [for orchestra]
3*,3*,3*,3-4,3,3,1-Timp.-Hp.-Str.
Ms.
Score 72 p. Large folio
An early work composed in Berlin, ca.1905.

1978 The pleasure dome of Kubla Khan,   13'
symphonic poem. Edited by Frederick Stock
3*,3*,3*,3-4,3,3,1-Timp.,Perc.-Pno.,Cel.,2Hp.-
Str.
G. Schirmer, New York, c1929
Score 46 p.
*First performance (original version) Boston,
28 November 1919, Pierre Monteux conductor.*

313m Poem for flute and orchestra   9'
Solo Fl.-2Hn.-Perc.-Hp.-Str.
G. Schirmer, Inc., New York, c1951
Score 32 p.

*Composed for Georges Barrère, 1918. First per-
formance New York, 16 November 1919, New York
Symphony Society, Walter Damrosch conductor,
Georges Barrère soloist.*

6827 [Sho-Jo, Japanese pantomime in one scene]
2(1st alt. Picc.),2(2nd alt. E.H.),2,2-2Hn.-
Timp.,Tam-tam,Chinese Dr.-Cel.,Hp.-Str.
Ms.
Score 31 p.
*Composed 1917. First performance Atlantic
City, New Jersey, 5 August 1917, Adolf Bolm's
Ballet Intime, Tulle Lindahl and Michio Ito
dancers.*

5780 [Symphonic fantasy]
3*,3*,3*,3-4,2,3-Timp.-2Hp.-Str.
Ms.
Score 80 p.
Composed 1907 in Berlin.

4840 The white peacock   6'
2(2nd alt. Picc.),2,2,2-2,3,2-Timp.,Tam-tam,
Cym.-Cel.,2Hp.-Str.
G. Schirmer, Inc., New York, c1917 (renewed
1945)
Score 21 p.
*Originally composed for piano 1915 as No. 1 of
Roman Sketches, Op. 7. Later transcribed for
orchestra. First performance of orchestral
version Philadelphia, 19 December 1919, Philadelphia Orchestra, Leopold Stokowski conductor.*

GRIFFIN, GEORGE EUGENE.   London 8 January 1781
London 28 May 1863

262p [Concerto, piano, Op. 1, A major]
1.Largo maestoso - Allegro moderato 2.Aria
con variazioni: Larghetto con espressione
3.Rondo: Allegretto scherzo
Solo Pno.-1,2,0,2-2Hn.-Tpt.-Timp.-Str.
Ms.
Score 88 p. Large folio
*The second movement is based on The Blue Bells
of Scotland, which the London actress
Dorothea Jordan claimed to have composed ca.
1800.*

GRIFFIS, ELLIOT.   Boston 28 January 1893
Los Angeles 8 June 1967

2910 Colossus (Paul Bunyan) symphonic poem   17'
3(3rd alt. Picc.),3*,4*,4*-4,3,4,1-Timp.,Perc.
-Cel.,Hp.-Str.
Ms.
Score 99 p.
*Composed 1925-26. Rewritten 1931; revised
1934.*

1806s Fantastic pursuit, symphony for   20'
string orchestra
1.Venturous youth - elusive beauty - struggle
- brief rapture 2.Separation - delay - vigil
- duress 3.Dark flight and escape - doubtful
victory 4.Pursuit - disclosure - surprise -
reconciliation
Str.

Griffis, Elliot

Ms.
Score 30 p.
*Composed 1936-37. First performance Philadel-
phia, 3 April 1941, Philadelphia Chamber Simfonietta, Fabien Sevitzky conductor.*

975m Montevallo, concerto for strings,   17'
piano and organ, based on southern mountain
tunes
1.Moderato con moto, ma sostenuto 2.Adagio
3.Allegretto 4.Allegro
Solo Pno.,Solo Org.-Str.
Ms.
Score 47 p.
*Composed 1937. First performance Ithaca, 2 May
1939, Cornell University Orchestra, George
Louis Coleman conductor, Ida Deck Haigh pianist,
Luther Noss organist.*

3180 Montevallo, symphonic suite for   17'
orchestra, based on southern white folks' tunes
3(3rd alt. Picc.),3*,2,2-4,3,3,1-Timp.,Perc.-
Str.
Ms.
Score 71 p.
*Originally composed as a concerto for strings,
piano and organ (see above). This version 1938.*

3581 A Persian fable, ballade for   5'30"
orchestra [revised version]
3(3rd alt. Picc.),2(2nd alt. E.H.),2,2-2,2,2-
Timp.,Perc.-Pno.(or Hp.)-Str.
Ms.
Score 38 p.
*Composed 1925. Revised 1940. First perform-
ance broadcast over Station WNYC, New York, 28
January 1940, WNYC Concert Orchestra of the
WPA, Macklin Marrow conductor.*

GRIGNON BOCQUET, JUAN LAMOTE DE.
  See: LAMOTE DE GRIGNON BOCQUET, JUAN.

GRIMM, CARL HUGO. Zanesville, Ohio 31 October 1890

5852 Pennsylvania, an overture for   12'
orchestra, Op. 56
2,2,2,2-4,2,3,1-Timp.,S.Dr.,Cym.-Str.
Ms.
Score 74 p. Large folio
*Composed 1955. First performance University
Park, Pennsylvania, 20 May 1956, Pennsylvania
University Symphony Orchestra, Theodore Karhan
conductor. Commissioned by and dedicated to
the Orchestra of the Pennsylvania State University, Theodore Karhan conductor.*

GRIMM, JULIUS OTTO.   Pernau 6 March 1827
                       Münster 7 December 1903

1120s [Suite in canonform, Op. 10, C major, for
string orchestra]
1.Allegro con brio 2.Andante lento 3.Tempo
di minuetto, ben moderato 4.Allegro risoluto
Str.
Rieter-Biedermann, Leipzig [n.d.]
Score 31 p.

54s [Suite no. 3, Op. 25, G minor, for string
orchestra]
1.[Introduction and fuga] 2.Canon 3.Intermezzo
4.Ländler 5.[Final fugue]
Str.
Breitkopf & Härtel, Leipzig, ^c1895
Score 19 p.
Composed 1895.

489s Träumerei für Streichorchester, Op. 2
no. 3
Str.
Breitkopf & Härtel, Leipzig, ^c1901
Score 5 p.
Originally composed for piano solo.

GROFÉ, FERDE.   New York 27 March 1892
                              3 April 1972

Born: Ferdinand Rudolph von Grofé

2616 Grand Canyon suite   34'
1.Sunrise 2.Painted Desert 3.On the trail
4.Sunset 5.Cloudburst
3(3rd alt. Picc.),3*,3*,3*-Alto Sax.-4,3,3,1-
Timp.,Perc.-Pno.,Cel.,Hp.-Str.
Ms.
Score 168 p.
*Composed 1931. First performance Chicago, 22
November 1931, Paul Whiteman and His Orchestra,
Paul Whiteman conductor.*

2748 Symphony in steel   9'
In one movement
3(3rd alt. Picc.),2(2nd alt. E.H.),3*,2-4Sax.-
4,3,3,1-Timp.,Perc.-2Pno.,Hp.-Str.
Ms.
Score 46 p.
*Commissioned 1935 by The American Rolling Mills
Co. Originally composed for symphonic band,
1935; transcribed 1935. First performance New
York, 1 February 1936, in an NBC broadcast,
Frank Black conductor.*

2805 Tabloid no. 1. Run of the news   3'
3(1st & 2nd alt. Picc.),2(2nd alt. E.H.),3(3rd
alt. B.Cl.),2-Alto Sax.(alt. Bar.Sax.),Ten.Sax.,
Bar.Sax.-4,3,3,1-Timp.,Perc.-2Pno.,Banjo-Str.
Ms.
Score 56 p.
*Composed 1933. First performance Carnegie Hall,
New York, 25 January 1933, Paul Whiteman and
His Orchestra, Paul Whiteman conductor.*

2806 Tabloid no. 2. Sob sister   5'
2(2nd alt. Picc.),2(2nd alt. E.H.),2,2-Ten.Sax.,
2Bar.Sax.(both alt. Alto Sax.)-4,3,3,1-Timp.,
Perc.-2Pno.(1st alt. Cel.),Banjo-Str.
Ms.
Score 32 p.

2807 Tabloid no. 3. Comic strips   3'
2(2nd alt. Picc.),2(2nd alt. E.H.),2,2-Ten.Sax.
(alt. 3rd Fl. and 5th Cl.),2Bar.Sax.(1st alt.
3rd Cl.,B.Cl.and 1st Alto Sax.; 2nd alt. 4th
Cl. and 2nd Alto Sax.)-4,4,3,1-Timp.,Perc.-
2Pno.(1st alt. Cel.),Banjo-Str.

Ms.
Score 33 p.

2808 Tabloid no. 4. Going to press   6'
2(both alt. Picc.),2*,2,2-Alto Sax.(alt. 5th
Cl. and B.Cl.),Ten.Sax.(alt. 3rd Fl.,3rd Picc.
and 4th Cl.),Bar.Sax.(alt. 3rd Cl. and 2nd
Alto Sax.)-4,4,3,1-Timp.,Perc.-2Pno.,Banjo-
Speaker-Str.
Ms.
Score 49 p.

GROLNIC, SIDNEY.   Philadelphia 15 March 1946

295v Overture for solo violin and   6'30"
string orchestra
Solo Vn.-Str.
Ms. ᶜ1970 by Sidney Grolnic
Score 27 p.
*Composed 1968-70. First performance Philadel-
phia, 7 May 1970, 16 Concerto Soloists, Marc
Mostovoy conductor, Romuald Teco soloist.
Dedication: For Marc Mostovoy and the 16 Con-
certo Soloists.*

GROOM, JOÁN.   Cameron, Missouri 4 February 1941

6471 Variations for orchestra   12'30"
2(2nd alt. Picc.),2(2nd alt. E.H.),2(2nd alt.
B.Cl.),2-4,2,2,1-Timp.,Perc.-Str.
Ms.
Score 62 p. Large folio
Composed 1963-64.

GROSS, CHARLES.   Boston 13 May 1934

7067 Irish suite (for band)   7'30"
1.Brian Boru 2.Nora 3.The paycock
3(3rd alt. Picc.),3*,8(Cl. in E-flat,3Cl. in
B-flat,Alto Cl.,Contralto Cl.,B.Cl.,Cb.Cl.),3*
-4Sax.(2Alto,Ten.,Bar.)-4,2,3Cnt.,Bar.,3,2-
Timp.,Perc.-Cb.
Templeton Publishing Co. [n.p.] ᶜ1971
Score 44 p.
*From the incidental music for two plays by
Sean O'Casey, The Plough and the Stars and
Juno and the Paycock. Brian Boru (926-1014)
was a king of Ireland. Composed 1968. First
performance Houston, Texas, 1970, University
of Houston Wind Ensemble, James T. Matthews
conductor. Dedication: To Sean O'Casey and
the Irish spirit.*

GROSSE, M.

375s Nachtstück für Streichorchester
Str.
C.F. Schmidt, Heilbronn [n.d.]
Score 4 p.

GROSSMANN, ERNST.

902m Fantasia in E-flat minor for trumpet in
B and orchestra
Solo Tpt.-1,1,2,1-2,2,1-Timp.-Str.
Score: Ms. 35 p.
Parts: Rühle & Wendling, Leipzig, ᶜ1923

GROSSMANN, LUDWIG.   Turka, Russia 6 March 1835
Warsaw 15 July 1915

1627 [Ukrainian overture to Anton Mal-   20'
czewski's poem, Maria]
2(2nd alt. Picc.),2,2,2-4,2,3,1-Timp.,Perc.-
Str.
Zimmermann, Leipzig [n.d.]
Score 85 p.
*Composed 1897. First performance Warsaw, 1898,
the composer conducting.*

GROSZ, WILHELM.   Vienna 11 August 1894
New York 10 December 1939

454p [Concerto, piano, symphonic dance,   20'
Op. 24]
In one movement
Solo Pno.-2(2nd alt. Picc.),2,2(1st alt. Alto
Sax. and Sop.Sax.; 2nd alt. Alto Sax. and Ten.
Sax.),2-3,2,1-Timp.,Perc.-Banjo-Str.
Universal Edition, Vienna, ᶜ1930
Score 154 p.
*Composed 1928. First performance Amsterdam,
21 February 1929, Mengelberg conductor.*

1628 [Overture to an opera buffa, Op. 14]   10'
2(2nd alt. Picc.),2,2,2-3,2,1-Timp.,Perc.-Pno.,
Cel.,Hp.-Str.
Universal Edition, Vienna, ᶜ1923
Score 72 p.
*Composed 1921. First performance Vienna, 1922,
Rudolf Nilius conductor.*

GROTE, A. R.

1394s Novellette [for solo violin and string
orchestra, Op. 45]
Solo Vn.-Str.
Score: Ms. 5 p.
Parts: A.E. Fischer, Bremen [n.d.]

GROVEN, EIVIND.
Lårdal, Telemark, Norway 8 October 1901

6223 [The wedding in the wood]   10'
1.Bruredans [Bridal dance] 2.Klokkelåten [The
bells sing] 3.Springar [Old dance]
2(2nd alt. Picc.),2(2nd alt. E.H.),2,2-2,2,2-
Timp.,S.Dr.-Str.
Ms. [ᶜ1949 by Eivind Groven]
Score 40 p.
*Based on Norwegian folk melodies from the col-
lection by Anders Heyerdal, Dances and Slåtts
from Aurskog. Composed 1939. First performance Bergen, Norway, January 1946, Harmonien
Orchestra, the composer conducting.*

GRUENBERG, LOUIS.
Brest Litovsk, Poland 3 August 1884
Los Angeles 9 June 1964

5467 Americana, suite for orchestra, Op. 48 20'
1.Morning song 2.Song of the plains 3.Song
at dusk 4.Variations on a whistling tune

Gruenberg, Louis

3(3rd alt. Picc.),3*,3*,3*-4,3,3,1-Timp.,Perc.
Pno.,Cel.,Hp.-Str.
Ms.
Score 114 p. Large folio
Composed 1945.

263p Concerto for piano and orchestra,   *33'*
no. 2, Op. 41
1.Slowly, gently and flowingly 2.Slow, sus-
tained, mysteriously 3.Somewhat faster 4.
Broad and expressively
Solo Pno.-3*,3*,3*,3*-4,3,3,1-Timp.,Perc.-Cel.,
Hp.-Str.
Ms.
Score 130 p. Large folio
Composed 1938. Revised 1963.

307v Concerto for violin and orchestra,   *37'*
Op. 47
1.Rhapsodic 2.With simplicity and warmth 3.
Lively, and with good humor
Solo Vn.-3(3rd alt. Picc.),3*,3*,3*-4,3,3,1-
Timp.,Perc.-Pno.(alt. Cel.),Hp.-Str.
Ms. c1959 by Louis Gruenberg
Score 163 p. Large folio
Commissioned by Jascha Heifetz. Composed 1944.
First performance Philadelphia, 1 December
1944, Philadelphia Orchestra, Eugene Ormandy
conductor, Jascha Heifetz soloist.

7002 The Daniel jazz (Vachel Lindsay) for   *16'*
a voice and eight instruments
Voice-Cl.,Tpt.-Perc.-Pno.-Str.(1,1,1,1,0)
Universal, Vienna, c1925
Score in reduction 60 p.
Text from Vachel Lindsay's book of poems, The
Daniel Jazz. Composed 1924. First perform-
ance New York, 22 February 1925.

2612 The enchanted isle, symphonic poem,   *16'*
Op. 11
3*,3*,3*,2-4,3,3,1-Timp.,Perc.-Cel.,Hp.-Str.
C.C. Birchard, Boston, c1930 by The Juilliard
Musical Foundation
Score 109 p.
Composed 1927; revised 1933. Awarded 2nd Amer-
ican prize in the International Schubert Cen-
tennial Contest sponsored by the Columbia
Phonograph Co., 1928. First performance Wor-
cester, Massachusetts, 3 October 1929, at the
Worcester Music Festival, Albert Stoessel
conductor.

2177 Jazz suite, Op. 28   *18'*
1.Fox trot tempo 2.Boston waltz tempo 3.
Blues tempo: Slow drag 4.Onestep tempo
3*,3*,3*,3*-4,3,3,1-Timp.,Perc.-Cel.,Hp.-Str.
Cos-Cob Press, New York, c1929.
Score 120 p.
Composed 1929. First performance Cincinnati,
1930, Fritz Reiner conductor.

6606 [Symphony no. 2, Op. 43]   *30'*
1.A broad expansive movement 2.Langsam und
aushaltend 3.Fantasievoll
3(3rd alt. Picc.),3*,3*,3*-4,3,3,1-Timp.,Perc.
-Pno.(alt. Cel.),Hp.-Str.

Ms.
Score 204 p.
Composed 1941; revised 1959 and 1963. First
performance Bamberg, Germany, 1 October 1965,
broadcast by the Bayerische Rundfunk, Jan
Koetsier conductor.

6783 Symphony no. 3, Op. 44
1.Genially 2.Slow & sustained 3.Broad & tran-
quilly - Somewhat faster
3(3rd alt. Picc.),3*,3*,3*-4,3,3,1-Timp.,Perc.
-Pno.(alt. Cel.),Hp.-Str.
Ms.
Score 184 p.
Composed 1941. Revised 1964.

GRUENTHAL, JOSEF.

3827 Trois novellettes pour grand orchestre
1.Battuto di quarti - con slancio 2.Lento
3.Moderato
2,2,2,2-4,2,3-Timp.,Tamb.-Str.
Ms.
Score 76 p.

GRUND, EDUARD.   Hamburg ca.1802

1005v [Concertino, violin and orchestra, Op.
4, C major]
In one movement
Solo Vn.-1,2,2,2-2,2-Timp.-Str.
Ms.
Score 118 p.

GRUNDMAN, CLARE.   Cleveland, Ohio 11 May 1913

195m Nocturne for harp and wind ensemble   *6'*
Solo Hp.-3,2,6*(1 in E-flat,B.Cl.,Cb.Cl.),2-
4Sax.(2Alto,Ten.,Bar.)-4,0,3Cnt.,3,Bar.,Tuba-
Timp.,Bells,Trgl.-Cb.
Boosey & Hawkes, New York, c1975
Score 17 p.
Composed 1974. Dedicated to the American Harp
Society.

7066 The spirit of '76 (for band). Based   *9'*
on songs of the time of George Washington and
the American Revolution
Washington's march at Trenton - Yankee Doodle
- Norah, dear Norah - Girls and boys - Chester
4*(2Picc.),2,7(Cl. in E-flat,3Cl. in B-flat,
Alto Cl.,B.Cl.,Cb.Cl.),2-4Sax.(2Alto,Ten.,Bar.)
-4,2,3Cnt.,Bar.,3,2-Timp.,Perc.
Boosey & Hawkes, New York, 1964
Score 52 p.
Composed 1963. First performance New York,
August 1964, The Goldman Band, Richard Franko
Goldman conductor. Dedicated to Richard Franko
Goldman and The Goldman Band.

GRÜNER-HEGGE, ODD.   Oslo, Norway 23 September 1899
Oslo 11 May 1973

2174s [Elegiac melody for string   *6'30"*
orchestra, Op. 3 no. 4]
Str.
Norsk Musikforlag, Oslo [c1952]

Score 5 p.
Originally composed for piano, 1918. Transcribed for orchestra, 1942. First performance Oslo, Norway, 28 March 1943, the Philharmonic Orchestra, Norwegian State Radio, the composer conducting.

GRUNEWALD, GOTTFRIED.   Quenstedt 20 January 1857
                               Magdeburg 25 April 1929

225s [Vineta, for string instruments with
  bells ad lib.]
  Bells(ad lib.)-Str.
  Heinrichshofen, Magdeburg [n.d.]
  Score 4 p.

GRÜTZMACHER, FRIEDRICH WILHELM LUDWIG.
                    Dessau, Germany 1 March 1832
                    Dresden 23 February 1903

756c [Concert fantasy for violoncello and
  orchestra on themes from the opera Santa
  Chiara, Op. 33]
  Solo Vc.-2,2,2,2-2,2,2-Timp.-Str.
  Litolff, Braunschweig [n.d.]
  Score in reduction 19 p.
  Santa Chiara is an opera by Ernst II, Duke of Saxe-Coburg-Gotha.

668c [Concerto, violoncello, no. 3, Op. 46,
  E minor]
  1.Allegro appassionato 2.Romanze: Andante
  cantabile, leading to [3]Allegro
  Solo Vc.-2(2nd alt. Picc.),2,2,2-2,2-Timp.-
  Str.
  Score: Ms. 134 p.
  Parts: Kahnt, Leipzig [n.d.]

684c [Concertstück, violoncello and orchestra,
  Op. 37, D minor]
  Solo Vc.-2(2nd alt. Picc.),2,2,2-2,2-Timp.-
  Str.
  Score: Ms. 108 p.
  Parts: Peters, Leipzig [n.d.]

677c Fantaisie hongroise [for violoncello and
  orchestra, Op. 7]
  Solo Vc.-1(alt. Picc.),2,2,2-2Hn.-Timp.-Str.
  Score: Ms. 68 p.
  Parts: Litolff, Braunschweig [n.d.]

631v [Romance, viola and orchestra, Op. 19
  no. 2]
  Solo Va.-Fl.,2Cl.,Bn.-Timp.-Str.
  Score: Ms. 13 p.
  Parts: Kahnt, Leipzig [n.d.]

946v [Romance, violin and orchestra, Op. 19
  no. 1, B-flat major]
  Solo Vn.-1,0,2,1-2Hn.-Timp.-Str.
  Score: Ms. 16 p.
  Parts: Kahnt, Leipzig [n.d.]

643c [Romance, violoncello and orchestra, Op.
  19 no. 3]
  Solo Vc.-1,0,2,1-2Hn.-Timp.-Str.
  Score: Ms. 13 p.
  Parts: Kahnt, Leipzig [n.d.]

646c [Variations on an original theme, for
  violoncello and string orchestra, Op. 31]
  Solo Vc.-Str.
  Score: Ms. 20 p.
  Parts: Breitkopf & Härtel, Leipzig [n.d.]

GRÜTZMACHER, LEOPOLD.
              Dessau, Germany 4 September 1835
              Weimar 26 February 1900

426c [Concerto, violoncello and orchestra,
  no. 2, Op. 9, A minor]
  1.Allegro risoluto 2.Andante cantabile 3.
  Finale: Allegro con fuoco
  Solo Vc.-2(2nd alt. Picc.),2,2,2-2,2-Timp.-Str.
  Friedrich Hofmeister, Leipzig [n.d.]
  Score 96 p. Large folio

GUARNIERI, ANTONIO DE.   Venice 2 February 1883

1918 [Impressioni di Spagna. No. 2, Una   4'
  noche a l'oriente, habanera]
  4(3rd & 4th alt. Picc.),4*,4*,4*-4,4,3,1-Timp.,
  Perc.-Cel.,Hp.-Str.
  Ricordi, Milan, ᶜ1919
  Score 13 p.
  Composed 1903. First performance La Scala, Milan, 1903, Arturo Toscanini conductor.

GUARNIERI, CAMARGO.
          Tiété, State of São Paulo 1 February 1907

Full name: Mozart Camargo Guarnieri

274p [Concerto, piano and orchestra,   22'30"
  no. 2]
  1.Decidido 2.Afetuoso 3.Vivo (Rondó)
  Solo Pno.-3*,3*,3*,3*-4,2,3,1-Timp.,Perc.-Hp.-
  Str.
  Ms. Associated Music Publishers, New York,
  ᶜ1947 by M. Camargo Guarnieri
  Score 87 p. Large folio
  Composed 1946. First performance CBS broadcast, 16 April 1947. Dedicated to Lidia Simões. Awarded the Alexandre Levi prize (Brazil).

1153v [Concerto, violin and orchestra]   17'
  In one movement
  Solo Vn.-3*,3*,3*,3*-4,2,3,1-Timp.,Perc.-Str.
  Ms.
  Score 84 p.
  Awarded first prize in an invitational contest for a violin concerto by Latin American composers, anonymously sponsored by the Edwin A. Fleisher Collection of Orchestral Music, Free Library of Philadelphia, 1942. First performance Rio de Janeiro, 20 September 1942, Orchestra of the Teatro Municipal.

3955 Dansa brasileira   3'
  3*,2,2,2-4,2,3,1-Timp.,Perc.-Str.
  Ms. ᶜ1943 by Camargo Guarnieri
  Score 15 p.
  First performance 7 March 1941, São Paulo Orchestra, the composer conducting.

Guarnieri, Camargo

6647 Dansa negra, for orchestra 4'
3*,3*,3*,3*-4,2,3,1-Timp.-Hp.-Str.
Ms. c1949 by Associated Music Publishers, New
York
Score 21 p. Large folio
*Originally composed for piano solo. This
transcription 1947.*

3956 Dansa selvagem [Savage dance] 4'
3*,3*,3*,3*-4,2,3,1-Timp.,Perc.-Hp.-Str.
Ms. c1943 by Camargo Guarnieri
Score 12 p.
*First performance 22 July 1941, São Paulo
Orchestra, the composer conducting.*

3957 Flôr de Tremembé 7'
1,0,1,1-Bar.Sax.-1,1,1-Perc.-Pno.,Hp.-Str.
Ms. c1943 by Camargo Guarnieri
Score 30 p.
*Composed 1937. First performance Rio de
Janeiro, ensemble of the Escola Nacional de
Musica, the composer conducting.*

6698 [Incantation for orchestra] 6'
3*,3*,3*,3*-4,2,3,1-Timp.-Pno.,Cel.-Str.
Ms.
Score 23 p. Large folio

3958 [Overture concertante] 12'
2,2,2,2-2,2-Timp.-Str.
Ms. c1943 by Camargo Guarnieri
Score 59 p.
*First performance 2 June 1943, São Paulo
Orchestra, the composer conducting.*

4035 Ponteio no. 1
Fl.,Cl.-2Hn.,Tpt.-Str.
Ms.
Score 4 p.
Composed 1931.

4036 Ponteio no. 3
2,0,2,1-2Hn.-Hp.-Str.
Ms.
Score 4 p.
Composed 1931.

1897s Ponteio no. 5
Str.
Ms.
Score 4 p.

6646 [Prologue and fugue] 8'
Prologue: Vigoroso - Grandioso. Fugue: Deciso
3(3rd alt. Picc.),3*,3*,3*-4,2,3,1-Timp.,Perc.
-Str.
Ms. [c1948 by Associated Music Publishers, New
York]
Score 57 p. Large folio
*Composed 1947. First performance Boston, 26
December 1947, Boston Symphony Orchestra,
Eleazar de Carvalho conductor. Dedicated to
Eleazar de Carvalho.*

6649 [Symphony no. 2, Uirapuru, The 25'
magic bird]
1.Enérgico 2.Terno 3.Festivo
3*,3*,3*,3*-4,3,3,1-Timp.,Perc.-Pno.-Str.

Ms. [Associated Music Publishers, New York]
Score 184 p. Large folio
*Composed 1946. Dedicated to Heitor Villa-Lobos.
Awarded 2nd prize in an international contest
sponsored by the Detroit Symphony.*

GUENTHER, FELIX. Trautenau 5 December 1886
New York 6 May 1951

2196 Deutsches rokoko, suite for small 20'
orchestra, after old masters
1.Overture (Adagio by Josef Meck) 2.Siciliano
(J. Ph. Kirnberger) 3.Andante grazioso (Fr.
L. Benda) 4.Halb-Steyrischer (Michael Haydn)
5.Aria (Emperor Joseph I) 6.Presto (Georg
Böhm) 7.Finale (Vivace by J. Ph. Kirnberger)
1,1,2,1-2Hn.-Str.
Ries & Erler, Berlin, c1931
Score 38 p.
*Composed 1929. First performance Berlin, 1930,
Kunwald conductor.*

GUERRI, M.

1644s Âme errante [for violin solo and string
orchestra]
Solo Vn.-Str.
Score: Ms. 5 p.
Parts: Gaudet, Paris [n.d.]

GUERRINI, GUIDO. Faenza, Italy 12 September 1890
Rome 13 June 1965

2004s [Seven variations on a saraband of 20'
Arcangelo Corelli]
Pno.-Str.
G. Ricordi, Milan, c1941
Score 69 p.
*Composed 1940. First performance Florence, 9
February 1941.*

1913 L'ultimo viaggio di Odisseo 20'
[Odysseus' last journey, symphonic poem]
4*(3rd alt. 2nd Picc.),3*,4,4-4,4,3,1-Timp.
Perc.-Cel.,2Hp.-Str.
Ricordi, Milan, c1928
Score 109 p.
*Composed 1921. First performance Augusteo,
Rome, 20 January 1924, Molinari conductor.*

GUIDI, CLAUDIO. Buenos Aires 17 August 1927

Also known as Claudio Guidi Drei

371v [Concertino bizzarro, for viola and 9'
orchestra]
1.Allegro 2.Lento 3.Allegro
Solo Va.-Fl.(alt. Picc.),C.Bn.-Tpt.,Tbn.-Timp.,
Perc.-Str.(without Va.)
Ms.
Score 79 p.
Composed 1957.

GUILMANT, ALEXANDRE. Boulogne-sur-Mer 12 March 1837
Meudon, near Paris 29 March 1911

Full name: Félix Alexandre Guilmant

4146 [March-fantasy on 2 religious chants,
Op. 44]
2,2,2,2-2,3,3-Timp.(2 players),Perc.
-Org.,4Hp.-Str.
Schott, Paris [1886?]
Score 40 p.
*Composed 1875. Dedicated to Eugène Henry,
organist in Rennes.*

1067m [Symphony for organ and orchestra,   *25'*
no. 1, Op. 42]
1.Introduction et allegro: Largo e maestoso
2.Pastorale: Andante quasi allegretto 3.Final:
Allegro assai
Solo Org.-2,2,2,2-4,2,3,1-Timp.,Cym.,B.Dr.-Str.
Schott, London/Durand, Paris [n.d.]
Score 97 p.
*First performance Paris, 22 August 1878, at the
Concerts du Palais du Trocadéro. Dedicated to
Leopold II, King of the Belgians.*

GUIMET, ÉMILE.   Lyons 1836

1305 [Taï-Tsoung. Grand ballet from Act III]
1.[The poetries - Play of the flowers] 2.[Im-
provised painting] 3.[The pudding-sleeves step]
4.[Dance with the fans] 5.[Martial dance]
2,2,2,2-4,2,3,1-Timp.,Perc.-Pno.,Hp.-Str.
Choudens, Paris [n.d.]
Score 129 p.

GUIRAUD, ERNEST.   New Orleans 23 June 1837
Paris 6 May 1892

527v [Caprice, for violin and orchestra]
1.Andante 2.Allegro appassionato
Solo Vn.-2,2,2,2-4,2-Timp.-Str.
Durand, Paris [n.d.]
Score 57 p.
*First performance at a Concert du Châtelet,
Paris, 6 April 1884, Sarasate soloist.*

861 [Chasse fantastique, symphonic poem]   *8'*
3*,2,2,2-4,4,3,1-Timp.,Perc.-Str.
Durand, Paris [n.d.]
Score 71 p.
*Inspired by a passage in Victor Hugo's Beau
Pécopin. Composed 1886. First performance
Paris, 1887.*

483 Danse persane, air de ballet   *5'*
4*,2,2,2-4,2,2Cnt.,3,1-Timp.,Perc.-2Hp.-Str.
Durand, Paris [n.d.]
Score 39 p.
Composed 1880. First performance Paris, 1880.

1845 [Gretna-Green, ballet. Overture]   *6'*
2(2nd alt. Picc.),2,2,2-4,2,2Cnt.,3,1-Timp.,
Perc.-Str.
Durand, Paris [n.d.]
Score 38 p.
*From the ballet composed 1872; first performed
Grand Opéra, Paris, 1873.*

1281 [Gretna-Green, ballet. Scène et valse] *5'*
2(2nd alt. Picc.),2,2,2-4,2Cnt.,3,1-Timp.,Perc.
-Str.
Durand, Paris [n.d.]
Score 40 p.

1020 Overture d'Arteveld, Op. 10   *8'*
3*,2,2,2-4,2,2Cnt.,3,1-Timp.,Perc.-Hp.-Str.
Durand, Paris [n.d.]
Score 59 p.
Composed 1882. First performance Paris, 1882.

1074 [Piccolino, comic opera. Overture]   *7'*
2,2,2,2-4,0,2Cnt.3-Timp.,Perc.-Str.
Durand, Paris [n.d.]
Score 37 p.
Composed 1876.

1479s [Piccolino, comic opera. Melodrama for
violin solo and string orchestra]
Solo Vn.-Str.
Durand, Paris [n.d.]
Score 4 p.

810 [Suite no. 1, for orchestra]   *16'*
1.Prelude 2.Intermezzo 3.Andante 4.Carnaval
2,2,2,2-4,2,2Cnt.,3,Ophicl.-Timp.,Perc.-Str.
Durand, Paris [n.d.]
Score 121 p.
*Composed 1891. First performance Paris, 1892,
the composer conducting.*

1112 [Suite no. 2, for orchestra]   *18'*
1.Petite marche 2.Divertissement 3.Rêverie
4.Final
2(2nd alt. Picc.),2,2,2-4,2,2Cnt.,3,1-Timp.,
Perc.-Str.
Durand, Paris [n.d.]
Score 96 p.
*Composed 1885. First performance Paris, 1887,
the composer conducting.*

GUND, ROBERT.
See: GOUND, ROBERT.

GUNGL, JOSEPH.   Zsámbék 1 December 1810
Weimar 31 January 1889

1095s Am Königssee [Ländler in the Upper
Bavarian style, for violin solo and string
orchestra]
Solo Vn.-Str.
Score: Ms. 15 p.
Parts: Bote & Bock, Berlin [n.d.]

GURIDI, JESÚS.   Vitoria, Basque province of
Alava 25 September 1886
Madrid 7 April 1961

6870 [An adventure of Don Quixote, symphonic
poem]
3*,3*,3(1Cl. in E-flat),3*-4,3,3,1-Timp.,Perc.
-Hp.-Str.
Unión Musical Española, Madrid, c1967
Score 96 p.
Suggested by Cervantes' novel.

Guridi, Jesús

6021 [Ten Basque melodies]   15'30"
1.Narrativa: Presto non troppo 2.Amorosa:
Lento 3.Religiosa: Andantino 4.Epitalamica:
Allegretto molto tranquillo 5.De ronda: Alle-
gretto non troppo 6.Amorosa: Andante con moto
7.De ronda: Allegretto risoluto 8.Danza:
Tempo de zortziko (Allegretto) 9.Elegiaca:
Andante sostenuto 10.Festiva: Allegro moderato
3(3rd alt. Picc.),2,2,2-4,2,3,1-Timp.,Perc.-
Cel.,Hp.-Str.
Unión Musical Española, Madrid, c1954
Score 77 p.
*Composed 1940-41. First performance Madrid,
12 December 1941, Orquesta Sinfónica de Madrid
(Orquesta Arbós), Enrique Jordá conductor.*

GURLITT, CORNELIUS.
                    Altona, Germany 10 February 1820
                    Altona, Germany 17 June 1901

885m [Concertstück, clarinet and orchestra,
Op. 70, F minor]
Solo Cl.-2,2,2,2-2,2-Timp.-Str.
Score: Ms. 89 p.
Parts: Engelmann & Mühlberg, Leipzig [n.d.]

GUTCHË, GENE.   Berlin 3 July 1907

Real name: Romeo Eugene Gutschë

6773 Aesop Fabler suite   18'
Enter Aesop - 1.The jay in peacock's feathers
2.The swan and the stork 3.The mice in council
4.The dog and his shadow 5.The fly 6.The
lion in love - Exit Aesop
3(3rd alt. Picc.),3(3rd alt. E.H.),3(3rd alt.
B.Cl.),3*-4,4,3,1-Timp.,Perc.-Str.
Ms.
Score 67 p. Large folio
*Commissioned by the Fargo-Moorhead (North
Dakota-Minnesota) Symphony Orchestra for its
35th anniversary in 1968. Composed 1966.*

7142 Bi-centurion, Op. 49   12'
3(3rd alt. Picc.I,2nd alt. Picc.II),3(3rd alt.
E.H.),3(2nd alt. Cl. in E-flat,3rd alt. B.Cl.),
3*-4,4,3,1-Timp.,Perc.-Str.
Regus Publisher [White Bear Lake, Minnesota]
c1975 by Gene Gutschë
Score 47 p.
*Commissioned by and dedicated to David Zinman
and the Rochester Philharmonic, 1974. Composed under a grant from the National Endowment of the Arts, 1975. First performance
Rochester, New York, 8 January 1976, Rochester
Philharmonic, David Zinman conductor.*

345m Bongo divertimento, Op. 35   12'
Entrada 1.Perpetuo 2.Pettifoggery 3.Blue-
bottle fly 4.Pasticcio 5.Magpie ritornello
Solo: Bongo,Timp.,Conga(1 player)-1,1,1,1-1,1-
Str.
Ms.
Score 66 p. Large folio
*Commissioned by the St. Paul Philharmonic
Society, 1962. Composed 1962. First perform-
ance St. Paul, Minnesota, 4 December 1962,*

*St. Paul Chamber Orchestra, Leopold Sipe con-
ductor, Marvin Dahlgren percussion soloist.*

6765 Classic concerto, for chamber   12'
orchestra, Op. 44
1.Scherzo 2.Minuet 3.Presto
1,1,1,1-Hn.-Str.
Ms. c1967 by Gene Gutschë
Score 54 p.
*Commissioned by the St. Paul Philharmonic
Society, 1967. Composed 1967. First perform-
ance St. Paul, Minnesota, 11 November 1967, St.
Paul Philharmonic Society, Leopold Sipe con-
ductor. Dedicated to the St. Paul Chamber
Orchestra, its president, board and Leopold
Sipe, the conductor.*

6037 Concertino for orchestra, Op. 28   18'
1.Elegy 2.Allegro con brio
1,1,1,1-2,1,1,1-Timp.,Perc.-Str.
Ms.
Score 48 p. Large folio
*Composed 1959. First performance University
of Minnesota, Minneapolis, 20 July 1965, Summer
Session Sinfonietta, Leopold Sipe conductor.*

345v [Concerto for violin and orchestra,   20'
Op. 36]
In one movement
Solo Vn.-2(2nd alt. Picc.),2(2nd alt. E.H.),2,
3*-2,2,2-Timp.,Perc.-Hp.-Str.
Ms.
Score 58 p.
*Composed 1962. Received the 8th International
Competition of Symphonic Composition Award and
the XVI Premio Citta di Trieste, 1969.*

834 Cybernetics XX, Op. 47   12'
1.Panorama 2.Kaleidoscope
3*,3(3rd alt. E.H.),3*,3*-4,4,3,1-Timp.,Perc.
-Str.
Ms. c1972 [by Gene Gutschë]
Score 35 p. Large folio
*Composed 1972. Won honorable mention in the
XIX Premio Citta di Trieste, 1972.*

6833 Epimetheus USA, Op. 46   8'
3(3rd alt. Picc.),3(3rd alt. E.H.),3(1Cl. in
E-flat),3*-Alto Sax.-4,4,3,1-Timp.,Perc.-
Str.
Ms.
Score 39 p. Large folio
*Commissioned by the Detroit Symphony Orchestra.
Composed 1968-69. First performance Detroit,
Michigan, 13 November 1969, Detroit Symphony
Orchestra, Sixten Ehrling conductor.*

272p Gemini, concerto for piano four-   20'
hands and orchestra, Op. 41
1.9...8...7...6...5...4...3...2...1...ZERO 2.
Walk into space 3.Earthbound
Solo Pno.4-hands-3(3rd alt. Picc.),3(3rd alt.
E.H.),3(3rd alt. B.Cl.),3*-4,3,3,1-Timp.,Perc.
-Str.
Ms. [c1966 by Gene Gutschë]
Score 58 p. Large folio

Inspired by the American space explorations of the 1960s. Commissioned by the University of Minnesota. Composed 1965. First performance Minneapolis, 26 July 1966, University of Minnesota Orchestra, Leopold Sipe conductor, Victoria Markowski and Franc Cedrone pianists.

6352 Genghis Khan, Op. 37   *9'*
3(2nd and 3rd alt. Picc.),3(3rd alt. E.H.),3
(3rd alt. B.Cl.),3*-4,4,2,1-Timp.,Perc.-Cb.
Ms. [c1963 by Gene Gutché]
Score 44 p.
Composed 1963. First performance Minneapolis, Minnesota, 6 December 1963, Minneapolis Symphony Orchestra, Stanislaw Skrowaczewski conductor.

6098 Holofernes overture, Op. 27 no. 1   *7'*
3*(2nd alt. Alto Fl.),3(3rd alt. E.H.),3(3rd
alt. B.Cl.),3*-Alto Sax.-4,4,3,1-Timp.,Perc.
-Str.
Ms.
Score 36 p. Large folio
Suggested by the Apocryphal Book of Judith. Composed 1958 as the overture to an unfinished opera, Holofernes, or Judith. First performance Minneapolis, Minnesota, 27 November 1959, Minneapolis Symphony Orchestra, Antal Dorati conductor. Received first honorable mention: Luria Award, 1958.

6692 Hsiang Fei, Op. 40   *14'*
1.Ch'ien Lung 2.Hsiang Fei 3.Tzu Hsi 4.A
faithful eunuch
0,0,0,0-4,4,3,1-Timp.,Perc.-Hp.-Str.
Ms. [c1965 by Gene Gutché]
Score 45 p. Large folio
Composed 1965. First performance Cincinnati, Ohio, 21 October 1966, Cincinnati Symphony Orchestra, Max Rudolf conductor.

7124 Icarus, programmatic suite in four   *30'*
movements, Op. 48
1.Cristóbal Colón [Columbus] 2.The sea 3.In-
surrection 4.Isthmus
3(2nd alt. Alto Fl.,3rd alt. Picc.),3(3rd alt.
E.H.),3(2nd alt. Cl. in E-flat,3rd alt. B.Cl.),
3*-4,4,3,1-Timp.,Perc.-Str.
Regus Publisher [White Bear Lake, Minnesota]
c1975 by Gene Gutché
Score 103 p.
Commissioned by the National Symphony Orchestra, Washington, D.C., as part of its Bicentennial Commission 1976. Composed 1974. First performance Washington, D.C., John F. Kennedy Center for the Performing Arts, 26 October 1976, The National Symphony Orchestra, Antal Dorati conductor. Dedicated to the American people. Includes a paraphrase of America the Beautiful in the 4th movement.

7238 Perseus and Andromeda XX, asymmetric   *22'*
dance suite in 3 movements, Op. 50
1.Immolation 2.Enter Perseus 3.Festival
3(3rd alt. Picc.),3(3rd alt. E.H.),3(1Cl. in
E-flat,3rd alt. B.Cl.),3*-Alto Sax.-4,4,3,1-
Timp.,Perc.-Str.

Bicentennial Edition c1977 by Gene Gutché
Score 79 p.
Inspired by the classical myth. Commissioned by the Cincinnati Symphony Orchestra. Composed 1976. First performance Cincinnati, 25 February 1977, Cincinnati Symphony Orchestra, Thomas Schippers conductor. Dedicated to Thomas Schippers and the Cincinnati Symphony Orchestra.

6354 Raquel, Op. 38   *8'*
3(3rd alt. Picc.),3(3rd alt. E.H.),3(3rd alt.
B.Cl.),3*-4,4,3,1-Timp.,Cym.,Suspended Cym.-
Str. OR: 2(2nd alt. Picc.),2(2nd alt. E.H.),
2(2nd alt. B.Cl.),2-4,2,2,1-Timp.,Cym.,Sus-
pended Cym.-Str.
Ms. [c1963 by Gene Gutché]
Score 20 p. Large folio
Composed 1963. First performance Tulsa, Oklahoma, 2 December 1963, Tulsa Philharmonic Orchestra, Franco Autori conductor.

285m Rites in Tenochtitlán, Op. 39, for   *18-20'*
organ or piano and chamber orchestra [original
version]
1.Sacrifice 2.Festival
Solo Org.(or Pno.)-1(alt. Picc.),1(alt. E.H.),
1,1(alt. C.Bn.)-2,1-Timp.,Perc.-Str.
Ms. [c1964 by Gene Gutché]
Score 62 p. Large folio
Tenochtitlán was the ancient Aztec capital, now Mexico City. Commissioned by the St. Paul Council of Arts and Sciences for the dedication of their new Arts and Science Center. Composed 1963. First performance St. Paul, Minnesota, 26 January 1965, St. Paul Chamber Orchestra, Leopold Sipe conductor, Eva Knardahl pianist. For later version for piano and full orchestra see next entry.

278p Rites in Tenochtitlán, Op. 39 no. 1,   *18'*
for piano and full orchestra [revised version]
1.Sacrifice 2.Incantation 3.Festival
Solo Pno.-3(2nd & 3rd alt. Picc.),3(3rd alt.
E.H.),3(1 in E-flat,3rd alt. B.Cl.),3*-4,4,3,1
-Timp.,Perc.-Str.
Ms. [c1964 by Gene Gutché]
Score 65 p. Large folio
Rescored and one movement added 1965. First performance of revised version New Orleans, 24 April 1967, New Orleans Philharmonic, Werner Torkanowsky conductor, Peretin soloist.

6159 Rondo capriccioso, Op. 21   *7'*
2,2,2,0(Woodwinds are divided into 2 sets, one
pitched at A-440 and one pitched at A-425)-2Hn.
-Cym.,Xyl.-Va.,Cb.
Ms.
Score 26 p. Large folio
Composed 1953. First performance New York City, 19 February 1960, New York Chamber Orchestra, Howard Shanet conductor.

6148 Symphony no. 4 in one movement,   *13'*
Op. 30
3*,3(3rd alt. E.H.),3,3*-4,3,3,1-Timp.,Perc.-
Cel.,Hp.-Str.

349

Gutchë, Gene

Ms.
Score 58 p. Large folio
Composed 1960. First performance Albuquerque, 8 March 1962, Albuquerque Symphony Orchestra, Maurice Bonney conductor. Winner of the Albuquerque Civic Symphony's National Composition Competition.

2205s [Symphony no. 5 for strings, Op. 34] 20'
1.Perpetuo 2.Burletta 3.Mesto 4.Lesto
Str.
Ms.
Score 53 p. Large folio
Composed 1962. First performance Chautauqua, New York, 29 July 1962, Walter Hendl conductor. Received the Oscar Espala honorable mention at the 1962 International Composition Competition.

6928 Symphony no. 6, Op. 45 25-28'
1.[Brass and Percussion] 2.[Strings, Celeste, Harp] 3.[Woodwinds, Xylophone] 4.[Tutti]
3(3rd alt. Picc.),3(3rd alt. E.H.),3(3rd alt. B.Cl.),3*-4,4,3,1-Timp.,Perc.-Cel.,Hp.-Str.
Ms.
Score 75 p. Large folio
Composed 1970. First performance Detroit, 7 October 1971, Detroit Symphony Orchestra, Sixten Ehrling conductor.

375m Timpani concertante, Op. 31 6-8'
Solo Timp.-3(3rd alt. Picc.),3(Cl. in E-flat optional,3rd alt. B.Cl.),3*-4,3,3,1-Perc.-Str.
Ms.
Score 32 p. Large folio
Composed 1961. First performance Oakland, California, 16 February 1962, Oakland Symphony Orchestra, Gerhard Samuel conductor, Harry Bartlett soloist.

GUTMAN, ARTHUR H.

2351s [Suite, strings, no. 1] 15'
1.Prelude: Adagio maestoso 2.Pastoral: Andante cantabile 3.Burlesque: Allegretto scherzando 4.Variations 5.Finale: Allegro con fuoco
Str.
Ms. c1938 by Arthur H. Gutman
Score 29 p.
Composed 1938.

GUY-ROPARTZ, JOSEPH.
See: ROPARTZ, JOSEPH GUY MARIE.

GYRING, ELIZABETH. Vienna 21 July 1906

1124v [Concerto, violin and orchestra] 20'
1.Moderato e molto espressivo 2.Rondo: Allegro
Solo Vn.-3*,2,3*,2-2Hn.,Tpt.-Timp.,Perc.-Str.
Ms.
Score 60 p.
Composed 1939.

3389 Orchesterstück no. 1 8'
4*,3*,4*,2-3,1,3,1-Str.
Ms.
Score 20 p.
Composed 1939.

3390 Orchesterstück no. 2 7'
4*,3(3rd alt. E.H.),4*,2-4,1,3,1-Timp.,Perc.-Str.
Ms.
Score 31 p.
Composed 1939.

3425 Orchesterstück no. 3 7'
4*,3*,3*,2-3,1,3,1-Timp.-Str.
Ms.
Score 28 p.
Composed 1939.

3426 Orchesterstück no. 4 7'
3*,3*,4*,3-3,1,3,1-Timp.-Str.
Ms.
Score 38 p.
Composed 1939.

5790 Scherzo no. 2 for orchestra 9'
Fl.,Cl.-Tpt.,Tbn.-Str.
Ms.
Score 10 p.
Composed 1948. First performance Eureka Springs, Arkansas, 28 August 1948, Ozark Symphony Orchestra, William Hanker conductor.

GYROWETZ, ADALBERT.
Budějovice, Bohemia 19 (or 20) February 1763
Vienna 19 March 1850

Also known as: Vojtěch Jírovec

6820 Serenade in F major
1.Adagio 2.Allegretto 3.Cantabile - Recitativo - Allegro 4.Rondo 5.Cantabile 6.Menuetto 7.Adagio 8.Rondo
2Fl.-2Hn.-Str.
Ms. c1976 by The Fleisher Collection of Orchestral Music, Free Library of Philadelphia
Score 63 p. Large folio
Edited from Ms. 597, Donaueschingen, West Germany, Fürstliche Fürstenberg Hofbibliothek.

5611 [Symphony in D major] Edited by Thor Johnson and Donald McCorkle
1.Adagio - Allegro 2.Andante poco adagio 3.Minuetto and Trio: Allegro 4.Presto
2,2-2Hn.-Timp.-Org.-Str.
Ms.
Score 100 p. Large folio
First modern performance, Third Early American Moravian Music Festival and Seminar, Winston-Salem, North Carolina, 25 June 1955, The Festival Orchestra, Thor Johnson conductor.

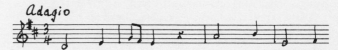

6968 Symphony in D major
1.Allegro 2.Andante 3.Rondo: Allegro
2Ob.-2,2-Timp.-Str.
Ms. c1976 by The Fleisher Collection of Orchestral Music, Free Library of Philadelphia
Score 41 p. Large folio

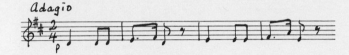

7006 [Symphony in D major]
1.Adagio - Allegro 2.Adagio 3.Allegro 4.Andante poco adagio 5.Finale: Prestissimo
2,2-2,2-Timp.-Str.
Ms. c1976 by The Fleisher Collection of Orchestral Music, Free Library of Philadelphia
Score 131 p.

6198 [Symphony in E-flat major]
1.Allegro 2.Andante 3.Minuetto and Trio
4.Presto ma non troppo
2Ob.-2Hn.-Str.
Ms. c1976 by The Fleisher Collection of Orchestral Music, Free Library of Philadelphia
Score 47 p. Large folio

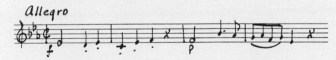

6250 [Symphony in E-flat major]
1.Adagio - Allegro 2.Adagio 3.Menuetto and Trio: Allegro 4.Rondo: Allegro
0,2,2,2-2,2-Timp.-Str.
Ms. c1976 by The Fleisher Collection of Orchestral Music, Free Library of Philadelphia
Score 123 p. Large folio

4102 [Symphony, Op. 23 no. 1]
1.Larghetto - Allegro 2.Adagio 3.Allegro
4.Allegretto
2,2,0,2-2Hn.-Str.
Ms.
Score 115 p.

4101 [Symphony, Op. 23 no. 2]
1.Largo - Allegro con spirito 2.Larghetto
3.Allegretto 4.Allegretto
2,2,2,2-2Hn.-Str.
Ms.
Score 102 p.

4100 [Symphony, Op. 47]
1.Allegro 2.Andante 3.Presto
2Ob.-2Hn.-Str.
Ms.
Score 49 p.

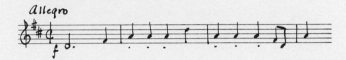

H

HAAN, WILLEM DE.   Rotterdam 24 September 1849
                         Berlin 27 September 1930

4520 [Two symphonic movements for orchestra, Op. 14]
1.Fahrt zum Hades: Larghetto - Allegro
2.Elysium: Maestoso
2,2,2,2-2,2,3-Timp.-Str.
B. Schott's Söhne, Mainz [188-?]
Score 27 p.

HAARKLOU, JOHANNES.
     Söndfjord, near Bergen, Norway 13 May 1847
                         Oslo 26 November 1925

647p [Concerto, piano, Op. 47, D minor]
1.Allegro 2.Largo 3.Finale: Allegro
Solo Pno.-2,2,2,2-4,2,3-Timp.-Str.
Reinecke, Leipzig [1922]
Score 79 p.

Haarklou, Johannes

897v [Concerto, violin, Op. 50, A major]
1.Poco allegro 2.In memoriam: Largo 3.Finale:
Andante
Solo Vn.-2(2nd alt. Picc.), 2,2,2-4,2-Timp.-
Str.
Score: Ms. 190 p.
Parts: Reinecke, Leipzig [1922?]
Dedicated to Willy Hess.

2063 [Funeral march for Mathias   *5'*
Skeibrok, Op. 14 no. 2]
2,2,2,2-4,2,3-Timp.-Str.
Reinecke, Leipzig [1921]
Score 11 p.

1849 [Marisagnet. Overture, Op. 42]   *18'*
2,2*2,2-4,2,3-Timp.-Str.
Reinecke, Leipzig [1922]
Score 35 p.
From the opera based on the life of St. Mary.
Dedicated to Johan Halvorsen.

2064 [Norwegian wedding march, Op. 15]   *6'*
2,2,2,2-2,2,3-Timp.-Str.
Reinecke, Leipzig [1921]
Score 19 p.

2065 [Requiem without words, in memory   *10'*
of Johan Svendsen, Op. 46]
2,2,2,2-4,2,3-Timp.-Str.
Reinecke, Leipzig [1922]
Score 19 p.

1149 Springdans, Op. 14 no. 1   *4'*
2,2,2,2-4,2,3-Timp.,Perc.-Str.
Reinecke, Leipzig [1921]
Score 19 p.
Dedicated to Jver Holter.

1091 St. Olaf-Legende, Op. 44   *5'*
2,2,2,2-4,2,3-Timp.-Str.
Reinecke, Leipzig [1922]
Score 11 p.
Dedicated to Harald Heide.

2066 [Symphony no. 3, Op. 49, C major]   *31'*
1.Allegro 2.De Faldne 1914-18 [To the memory
of the fallen, 1914-18]: Largo funebre 3.
Springdans med intermezzi: Allegro molto 4.
Finale: Andante sostenuto - Allegro - Andante
2(2nd alt. Picc.),2,2,2-4,2,3,1-Timp.-Str.
Reinecke, Leipzig [1922]
Score 99 p.
First performance Leipzig, 1922, Hermann
Scherchen conductor. Dedicated to Herman von
Tangen.

994 Westminster Abbey [suite for   *17'*
orchestra, Op. 45]
1.Praeludium: Maestoso 2.Dódstimen [Hour of
death]: Adagio 3.Ved Handels grav [At Handel's
tomb]: Adagio
2,2,2,2-4,2,3-Timp.-Str.
Reinecke, Leipzig [1922]
Score 31 p.

HAAS, JOSEPH.   Maihingen, Germany 19 March 1879
                    Munich 31 March 1960

5563 [A happy serenade for orchestra,   *22'*
Op. 41]
2,2,2,2-4,2-Timp.-Str.
Wunderhorn-Verlag, Cologne [1914]
Score 85 p.
Dedicated to the composer's wife.

4696 [Lyric intermezzo] Arranged by   *6'30"*
Leopold Weninger
1,1,1-0,1,1-Timp.-Harm.-Str.
B. Schott's Söhne, Mainz, ᶜ1938
Score in reduction 6 p.
Composed ca.1937.

1817 Variationen und Rondo über ein altdeutsches
Volkslied, Op. 45
2,2,2,2-4,2-Timp.-Hp.-Str.
Leuckart, Leipzig [n.d.]
Score 126 p.
Dedicated to Max von Schillings.

HABERT, JOHANNES EVANGELISTA.
          Oberplan, Bohemia 18 October 1833
          Gmunden, Austria 1 September 1896

3584 Menuett, Op. 112
2,0,2-2Hn.-Str.
Breitkopf & Härtel, Leipzig [n.d.]
Score 6 p.

1829s [Miniatures, 4 characteristic pieces for
piano. Transcribed for string orchestra,
Op. 38b]
1.Andante cantabile 2.Moderato con moto
3.Sostenuto 4.Allegro vivace
Str.
Breitkopf & Härtel, Leipzig [n.d.]
Score 11 p.

2390 Scherzo [for wind ensemble]
1,1,1,2-2Hn.
Score: Ms. 9 p.
Parts: Breitkopf & Härtel, Leipzig [n.d.]

1162s [Suite for string orchestra, harp and
timpani, Op. 98]
1.Präludium: Allegro con fuoco 2.Allemande
3.Sarabande 4.Gavotte 5.Gigue
Timp.-Hp.-Str.
Breitkopf & Härtel, Leipzig [n.d.]
Score 35 p.

HADLEY, HENRY KIMBALL.
          Somerville, Massachusetts 20 December 1871
          New York 6 September 1937

1976 The culprit fay, a rhapsody for   *15'*
grand orchestra after Joseph Rodman Drake's
poem, Op. 62
3(3rd alt. Picc.),3*,3*,2-4,2,3,1-Timp. Perc.
-Hp.-Str.
G.Schirmer, New York, ᶜ1910
Score 59 p.

Hadley, Henry Kimball

740c [Elegie and gavotte, violoncello and   8'
piano, Op. 36. Transcribed for violoncello
and orchestra by Samuel L. Laciar]
Solo Vc.-3(3rd alt. Picc.),2,2,2-2Hn.-Hp.-Str.
Ms.
Score 32 p.
Elegie commissioned by Richard Mansfield as
part of the incidental music to his play Herod,
never performed. Composed ca. 1910. First
performance of this version, Philadelphia,
21 July 1923, Fairmount Symphony Orchestra's
Lemon Hill concerts, the composer conducting,
Benjamin Gusikoff soloist.

2618 The enchanted castle, overture,   8'
Op. 117
2(2nd alt.Picc.),2,2,2-Alto Sax.,Ten.Sax.-4,3,
3,1-Timp.,S.Dr.,Cym.-Hp.-Str.
C. Fischer, New York, c1933
Score 35 p.

3226 In Bohemia, a concert overture, Op. 28
3*,2,2,2-4,3,3,1-Timp.,Perc.-Str.
G. Schirmer, New York, c1912
Score 35 p.
Commissioned by the Bohemian Club of San
Francisco. First performance in the United
States, Pittsburgh, 1902, Victor Herbert con-
ductor. Dedicated to Victor Herbert and the
Bohemian Club.

1960 The ocean, tone poem for orchestra, Op. 99
3(3rd alt. Picc.),3*,3*,3*-6(5th&6th ad lib.),
4,3,1-Timp.,Perc.-2Hp.-Str.
C.C. Birchard, Boston, c1924
Score 69 p.
Dedicated to the composer's wife.

2617 Salome, Op. 55 [inspired by Oscar   24'
Wilde's poem]
3(3rd alt. Picc.),3*,3*,3*-4,4,3,1-Timp.,
Perc.-2Hp.-Str.
Ries & Erler, Berlin, c1906
Score 86 p.
Composed 1905. First performance Boston, 12
April 1907, Karl Muck conductor.

2619 San Francisco, suite for orchestra,   12'
Op. 121
1.The harbor: Moderato e tranquillo - Allegro
con brio 2.Chinese quarter: Allegretto
moderato 3.Mardi Gras: Allegro non troppo
3(3rd alt. Picc.),3*(1st alt. Ob. d'Amore),
3*,2-4,3,3,1-Timp.,Perc.-Hp.-Str.
C.C. Birchard [Boston] c1932
Score 98 p. Large folio
Composed 1931. First performance Robin Hood
Dell, Philadelphia, 17 July 1932, Philadelphia
Orchestra, the composer conducting.

2620 Scherzo diabolique, Op. 135   6'
3(3rd alt. Picc.),3*,3*,3*-4,3,3,1-Timp.,
Perc.-Hp.-Str.
C. Fischer, New York, c1934
Score 61 p.
Composed 1934. First performance at the Cen-
tury of Progress Exposition, Chicago, Chicago

Symphony Orchestra, August 1934, the composer
conducting. Dedicated to Mrs. T. Mitchell
Hastings.

2834 Streets of Pekin, suite for orchestra   13'
1.Great Stone Man's Street: Poco lento 2.
Sweet Rain Street: Allegretto scherzando 3.
Ricksha boy (Ma Ben): Allegro 4.Jade Street
(Moonlight): Moderato e tranquillo 5.Shoe-
maker's Street: Allegretto giocoso 6.Sleeping
lotuses: Slowly and dreamily 7.The Forbidden
City: Molto moderato e maestoso
3(3rd alt. Picc.),3*,3*,3*-4,3,3,1-Timp.,Perc.-
Str.
Ms.
Score 69 p.
Composed 1930. First performance Tokyo, 24
September 1930, New Symphony Orchestra, the
composer conducting.

6216 A summer idyl, for small orchestra   10'
(posthumous). Completed from composer's sketches
and orchestrated by Philip James
1,1(alt. E.H.),2,1-2 Hn.-Timp.-Hp.-Str.
Ms.
Score 36 p.
Commissioned by Mrs. Henry Hadley for comple-
tion, 1938. Composed 1937-38. First per-
formance Carnegie Hall, New York, 6 April 1938,
New York Philharmonic, Philip James conductor.

1977 Symphonic fantasia for orchestra,   16'
Op. 46
3(3rd alt. Picc.),3*,3*,3*-4,4,3,1-Timp.,Perc.-
Hp.-Str.
G. Schirmer, New York, c1907
Score 59 p.
Dedicated to Léon Jehin.

6093 [Symphony no. 2, Op. 30, The four seasons,
F minor]
1.Winter: Moderato maestoso 2.Spring: Alle-
gretto con moto 3.Summer: Andante 4.Autumn:
Andante con moto - Allegro molto
3*,2(2nd alt. E.H.),2,2-4,2,3,1-Timp.,Perc.-
Hp.-Str.
Arthur P. Schmidt, Leipzig, c1902
Score 207 p.
Composed 1901. First performance New York, 20
December 1901, New York Philharmonic Orchestra,
Emil Paur conductor. Dedicated to John A. Stow.
Awarded the Paderewski and New England Conser-
vatory Prizes.

3705 [Symphony no. 3, Op. 60, B minor]   40'
1.Moderato e maestoso 2.Andante (Angelus) 3.
Scherzo: Allegro con leggerezza 4.Finale:
Allegro con giubilio
3(3rd alt. Picc.),2,2,2-4,2,3,1-Timp.,Perc.-
Hp.-Str.
Ms.
Score 224 p.
Composed 1906. First performance Berlin, 27
December 1907, Berlin Philharmonic, the com-
poser conducting.

Hadley, Henry Kimball

5673 [Symphony no. 4, Op. 64, North, East,   *40'*
South and West, D minor]
1.North: Lento, grave - Allegro energico 2.
East: Andante dolorosamente - Allegro non
troppo 3.South: Allegretto giocoso 4.West:
Allegro brillante
3*,3*,2,2-4,2,3,1-Timp.,Perc.-Hp.-Str.
G. Schirmer, New York, ^c1912
Score 152 p. Large folio
*Written for the Norfolk, Connecticut Festival.
Composed 1911. First performance Norfolk, 5
June 1911, the composer conducting.*

HAESER, GEORG.   Danzig, Poland 17 August 1865

197s Intermezzo für Streichquartett, Op. 24
Str.(Cb. ad lib.)
Hug, Basel, c1913
Score 6 p.

376s Zwei Bagatellen, Op. 16
1.Träumerei [Reverie]: Adagio 2.Ausblick
[View]: Allegro comodo
Str.
Hug, Basel [n.d.]
Score 5 p.

HAGELBAUER, C. A.

324s Heinzelmännchen's Brautfahrt [The goblin's
wedding journey]
Str.
Otto Wernthal, Berlin, ^c1902
Score 4 p.

HAGEN, FRANCIS FLORENTINE.
        Salem, North Carolina 30 October 1815
        Lititz, Pennsylvania 7 July 1907

6682 Overture in F major. Edited by Thor *6-7'*
Johnson and Ewald V. Nolte
2,2,2,2-2,1,1-Timp.-Str.
Ms.
Score 60 p.
*Original version composed between 1835-44.
This version 1966. First performance Winston-
Salem, North Carolina, 18 June 1966, Moravian
Music Festival Orchestra, Thor Johnson con-
ductor.*

HAHN, ALWIN.

832s Die Fliege [The fly] Intermezzo, Op. 7
[for string orchestra]
Str.
F. Schuberth, Jr., Leipzig [n.d.]
Score 3 p.

HAHN, GUNNAR.   Stockholm 1908

2187s [Gothic suite for string   *13'30"*
orchestra]
1.Polonäs [Polonaise] 2.Visa [Song] 3.Polska
med synkop [Syncopated Polish reel] 4.Visa
utan ord [Song without words] 5.Polska med
orgelpunkt [Polish reel with pedal point]

Str.
Nordiska Musikförlaget, Stockholm, ^c1949
Score 22 p.
*Based on 18th century tunes mainly taken from
Åhlström's Traditions of Swedish Folk Dances,
1814; the theme of the second movement is taken
from one of the Swedish Folk Ballads of Geijer-
Afzelius, They Were Two Royal Children. Dedi-
cated to the National Federation of Swedish
Orchestra Societies.*

HAHN, REYNALDO.   Caracas, Venezuela 9 August 1875
                     Paris 28 January 1947

2341 Le bal de Béatrice d'Este, suite   *12'*
[from the ballet]
1.Entrée pour Ludovic le More: Maestoso 2.Les-
quercade: Andantino 3.Romanesque: Lento 4.
Ibérienne: Marcato 5.Léda et l'oiseau [Leda
and the swan]: Modéré 6.Courante: Gai, sans
vitesse 7.Salut final au Duc de Milan:
Maestoso
2,1,2,2-2,1-Timp.,Cym.,Trgl.-Pno.,2Hp.
Heugel, Paris [n.d.]
Score 54 p.
*From the ballet of the same name about the
Renaissance Duchess of Milan. Composed 1906.
First performance Paris, 1909. Dedicated to
Camille Saint-Saëns.*

1629 [La fête chez Thérèse. Suite no. 1   *10'*
from the ballet]
1.La contredanse des grisettes 2.Valse de Mimi-
Pinson 3.Danse violente: Modéré sans lenteur,
martelé, farouche
4*,2(2nd alt. E.H.),2,3*-Alto Sax.-4,2,2Cnt.,
3-Timp.,Perc.-Pno.,Hp.-Str.
Heugel, Paris, ^c1910
Score 73 p.
*From the ballet composed 1908. First perform-
ance Opéra, Paris, February 1910.*

1630 [La fête chez Thérèse. Suite no. 2   *14'*
from the ballet]
1.Danse galante: Allegretto moderato 2.Scène
de l'essayage [Trying on costumes]: Allegro
grazioso 3.Danse triste: Mouv't de valse lente
4.Duo mimé: Andantino appassionato 5.Menuet
pompeux: Modéré
3(3rd alt. Picc.),2,2,3*-Alto Sax.-4,2,2Cnt.,
3-Timp.,Perc.-Pno.,2Hp.-Str.
Heugel, Paris, ^c1910
Score 76 p.

452m [Saraband and variations for bass clarinet
and orchestra. Transcribed for orchestra by
Lucien Cailliet]
Solo B.Cl.-2,3*,0,2-4,2,3,1-Timp.-Hp.-Str.
Ms.
Score 22 p.
Originally composed for clarinet and piano.

HAIEFF, ALEXEI.
       b. Blagovestchensk, Siberia 25 August 1914

277p Concerto for piano and orchestra   *24'30"*
(revised version)
1.Moderato 2.Lento libero 3.Andante - Allegro

Solo Pno.-3*,2,2,2-4,2,2-Timp.,Perc.-Str.
Ms. [c1954 by Boosey & Hawkes, New York]
Score 162 p. Large folio
*Composed 1949-50. First performance of revised
version Boston, 31 October 1952, Boston Sym-
phony Orchestra, Charles Munch conductor, Leo
Smit soloist. Dedicated to Janice Newman for
Leo Smit. Received the New York Music Critics
Award for 1952.*

6635   Divertimento   *11'30"*
1.Prelude: Allegro moderato   2.Aria: Andantino
3.Scherzo: Vivace   4.Lullaby: Lento   5.Finale:
Allegretto
2(2nd alt. Picc.),1(alt. E.H.),1-0,2,2-Str.
Boosey & Hawkes, New York, c1953
Score 40 p.
*Three movements were originally written for
piano, ca. 1940-42. Composed 1944. First performance Boston, 1 November 1946, Boston Symphony Orchestra, Richard Burgin conductor.
Choreographed in 1946 by George Balanchine for
the Ballet Society, New York.*

HAIGH, RICHARD.

1124s   Vertige, valse lente
Pno.-Str.
Stainer & Bell, London, c1911
Score 11 p.

HAINDL, FRANZ SEBASTIAN.
         Upper Bavaria, Germany 11 January 1727
         Passau, Bavaria 23 April 1812

6853   [Symphony, G major]
1.Allegro assai   2.Andante   3.Presto
2Hn.-Cemb.-Str.
Score: Denkmäler der Tonkunst in Österreich,
86. Österreichischer Bundesverlag, Vienna,
c1949. Edited by Walter Senn. 13 p.
Parts: Ms.

HAINES, EDMUND.   Ottumwa, Iowa 1914

4568   Informal overture   *7-8'*
3*,2(2nd alt. E.H.),2,3(C.Bn. optional)-4,3,3,
1-Timp.,Perc.-Pno.-Str.
Ms.
Score 50 p. Large folio
Composed 1948.

935m   Pastoral for flute and strings,   *4'30"*
Op. 6
Solo Fl.-Str.
Ms.
Score 5 p. Large folio
*Composed 1939. First performance on an NBC
radio broadcast from Rochester, New York,
March 1939, Rochester Civic Orchestra, Guy
Fraser Harrison conductor, Joseph Mariano
soloist. Used as the middle movement of Sym-
phony in Miniature no. 1, Catalog no. 3437.*

1114v   Poem for viola and chamber   *6'30"*
orchestra, Op. 3
Solo Va.-2,2*,0,1-Hn.-Hp.-Str.
Ms.

Score 13 p. Large folio
*Composed 1938-39. First performance Rochester,
New York, April 1939, Rochester Civic Orchestra, Howard Hanson conductor, Julia Wilkinson
soloist.*

3437   Symphony in miniature no. 1, for   *10'*
chamber orchestra, Op. 7
1.Fast   2.Pastoral: Slow   3.Fast (savagely)
2(2nd alt. Picc.),1,2,1-2,2-Str.
Ms.
Score 64 p.
*Composed 1940. First performance 10th Annual
Festival of American Music, Eastman School of
Music, Rochester, New York, 23 April 1940,
Eastman Little Symphony, Frederick Fennell
conductor.*

3674   Symphony no. 1, Op. 8   *25'*
1.Allegro molto   2.Andante   3.Poco allegretto
e grazioso   4.Presto
2(2nd alt. Picc.),2(2nd alt. E.H.),2,2-4,2,3-
Timp.,Perc.-Str.
Ms.
Score 160 p. Large folio
*Composed 1941. First performance 11th Annual
Festival of American Music at Eastman School
of Music, Rochester, New York, 28 April 1941,
Rochester Civic Orchestra, Howard Hanson conductor. Dedicated to Howard Hanson. Received
the Pulitzer Prize, 1941.*

3377   Three dances for orchestra, Op. 4   *10'*
1.Presto   2.Andante   3.Vivace
2(2nd alt. Picc.),2(2nd alt. E.H.),2,2-4,2,3-
Timp.,Perc.-Hp.-Str.
Ms.
Score 96 p.
*Composed 1939. First performance Rochester,
New York, 12 February 1940, Rochester Civic
Orchestra, Guy Fraser Harrison conductor.*

HALETZKI, PAUL.
      b. Koblenz-Metternich, Germany 12 May 1911

5471   [Merry overture, a joyful prelude   *5'*
for orchestra]
2(2nd alt. Picc.),1,3*,2-2,2,2-Timp.,Perc.
-Pno.,Hp.-Str.
B. Schott's Söhne, Mainz, c1939
Score 27 p.
Composed 1938.

HALÉVY, JACQUES-FRANÇOIS-FROMENTAL-ÉLIE.
                    Paris 27 May 1799
                    Nice 17 March 1862

Real name: Lévy

4300   Le Juif errant [The wandering Jew. No. 1,
Dance of the slaves. No. 2, Dance of the veils]
2*,2,2,2-4,2,2Cnt.,3-Timp.,Perc.-Str.
Brandus, Paris [1852]
Score 28 p.
*From the opera in five acts with libretto by
Eugène Scribe and Vernoy de Saint-Georges.
First performance Opéra, Paris, 23 April 1852.*

Halévy, Jacques

6978 La Juive [The Jewess. Overture]
3*,2,2,2-4,4,3,Ophicl.-Timp.,Perc.-Str.
A. Cranz, Brussels [n.d.]
Score 82 p.
*From the opera in five acts with libretto by
Eugène Scribe. First performance Opéra, Paris,
23 February 1835.*

4451 La reine de Chypre [The queen of Cyprus.
New overture]
2(2nd alt. Picc.),2,2,2-4,4(3rd&4th alt. Cnt.),
3,Ophicl.-Timp.,Perc.-Str.
Maurice Schlesinger, Paris [185-?]
Score 36 p.
*From the opera in five acts with libretto by
Vernoy de Saint-Georges. First performance
Opéra, Paris, 22 December 1841.*

HALFFTER, CRISTÓBAL.   Madrid 24 March 1930

6895 [Ducal mass, mixed chorus and   20'
orchestra]
1.Kyrie 2.Gloria 3.Sanctus 4.Benedictus
5.Agnus Dei
Chorus(SATB)-3(3rd alt. Picc.),3*,3*-Str.
(without Vn.)
c1959 by C. Halffter, Madrid
Score 104 p.
*Commissioned by Don Luis Martínez de Irujo and
Doña Cayetana Fitz James Stuart, Silva, Duke
and Duchess of Alba. First performance for
chorus and organ: Capilla del Palacio de
Liria, 15 June 1956, the chorus of the Radio
Nacional, the composer conducting, Maria
Josefa Valverde organist. First performance
for chorus and orchestra: Palacio de la
Música, 26 October 1956, the chorus of the
Radio Nacional, Cantores de Madrid and Orques-
ta Nacional, Ataúlfo Argenta conductor.*

HALFFTER, ERNESTO.   Madrid 16 January 1905

Full name: Ernesto Halffter Escriche

1523 Sinfonietta [D major]   35'
1.Pastorela: Allegro 2.Adagio 3.Allegretto
vivace (Minuetto) 4.Allegro giocoso
1,1,1,1-2,1,1-Timp.,B.Dr.,S.Dr.-Str.
Eschig, Paris, c1928
Score 151 p.
*Composed 1923-27. First performance Madrid,
April 1927, the composer conducting.*

HALFFTER, RODOLFO.   Madrid 30 October 1900

5784 [The baker's early awakening. Suite   13'
from the ballet, Op. 12a]
1.Entrada 2.Escena y danza primera (Habanera)
3.Danza segunda 4.Danza tercera 5.Danza
cuarta 6.Nocturno 7.Danza final
2(2nd alt. Picc.),2,2,2-2,2-Timp.,Perc.-Pno.-
Str.
Ediciones Mexicanas de Música, Mexico City,
c1952
Score 69 p.
*Composed 1940. First performance as ballet
choreographed by Anna Sokolow, Palace of Fine
Arts, Mexico City, 20 September 1940. First
performance of Suite, Xalapa, Mexico, 21 May
1948, Orquesta Sinfónica de Xalapa, José Ives
Limantour conductor. Dedicated to José Ives
Limantour.*

2136s [Don Lindo de Almeria. Suite from   20'
the ballet, Op. 7b]
1.Introducción y danza primera: Allegretto
vivace 2.Escena y danza segunda: Andante calmo
3.Danza tercera: Allegro, ma non troppo 4.
Danza cuarta: Allegro deciso ed energico 5.
Ceremonia nupcial: (Tres versillos de Fran-
cesc Llussá): Andante affettuoso 6.Danza
quinta y escena: Allegretto moderato 7.
Danza final: Tempo di marcia
Timp.,Perc.-Str.
Ediciones Mexicanas de Música, Mexico City,
c1956 by Rodolfo Halffter
Score 53 p.
*Composed 1935. First performance of Suite,
Collège d'Espagne, Paris, 13 March 1936, Cité
Universitaire Orchestre, Gustavo Pittaluga
conductor. First performance of ballet Teatro
Fabregas, Mexico City, 9 January 1940, Anna
Sokolow choreographer. Dedicated to José
Durand.*

773p Obertura concertante para piano   7'30"
y orquesta
Solo Pno.-1,2*,1,2-0,1,1-Timp.-Str.
Ministerio de Instrucción Pública, Barcelona,
c1938 by Rodolfo Halffter
Score 72 p.
*Composed 1932. First performance Madrid, 1933,
Orquesta Sinfónica de Madrid, the composer
conducting, José Cubiles soloist. Dedicated to
Leopoldo Querol. Received an award from the
Unión Radio de Madrid.*

3222 Suite para orquesta   12'30"
1.Nana: Tranquillo ed amabile 2.Scherzo: Allegro vivace 3.Elegia: Andantino, un poco lamentoso 4.Final: Allegro giusto
2(2nd alt. Picc.),2(2nd alt. E.H.),2,2-2,2-
Timp.-Pno.-Str.
Ministerio de Instrucción Pública, Barcelona,
c1938 by Rodolfo Halffter
Score 70 p.
*Composed 1924. First performance Madrid, 1928,
Orquesta Sinfónica de Madrid, Pérez Casas conductor.*

2143s [Three pieces for string   11'
orchestra, Op. 23]
1.Sonata 2.Arioso 3.Rondo
Str.
Ediciones Mexicanas de Música, Mexico City,
c1956 by Rodolfo Halffter
Score 26 p.
*Composed 1954. First performance Mexico City,
10 August 1955, Orquesta de Camara del Instituto Nacional de Bellas Artes, Salvador Ochoa
conductor.*

COLLECTION OF ORCHESTRAL MUSIC

6204   Tripartita, Op. 25   *13'*
1.Scherzo   2.Romanza sin palabras   3.Sonata
3*,2,2,3*-4,2,3,1-Timp.,Perc.-Pno.-
Str.
Ediciones Mexicanas de Música, Mexico City,
c1961 by Rodolfo Halffter
Score 61 p.
*Composed 1959.   First performance Mexico City,
15 July 1960, Orquesta Sinfónica Nacional,
Carlos Chavez conductor.   Dedicated to the composer's nephew, Cristobál Halffter.   Awarded
1st prize for a symphonic work, 1959, by the
Society of Authors and Composers of Mexico
and the National Institute of Fine Arts.*

HALLÉN, ANDRÉAS. Göteborg, Sweden 22 December 1846
                         Stockholm 11 March 1925

6099   [Autumn, 2 lyric tone pictures   *11'30"*
for small orchestra, Op. 38]
1.Mondeszauber [Moon magic - Dance of the
elves by moonlight]: Allegro   2.Traumbilder
in Dämmerungsschein [Dream pictures in the
twilight]: Andante espressivo
2,1,2,2-2Hn.-Timp.-Str.
A.B. Nordiska Musikförlaget, Stockholm, c1918
Score 35 p.

4604   [Gustaf Vasa's saga, suite for   *35'*
orchestra]
1.Das Morgenroth der Freiheit (Vorspiel) [The
dawn of freedom (Prelude)]: Un poco adagio
2.Die Vision: Andante poco sostenuto   3.
Aufruf zur Wehr [Call to arms]: Andante   4.
Der Einzug [Entrance] (Wasamarsch): Allegro
moderato   5.Per aspera ad astra: Andante
2,2,2,2-4,3,3,1-Timp.,Perc.-Hp.-
Str.
Raabe & Plothow, Berlin [1897]
Score 78 p.
*Composed 1897.   Dedicated to Her Majesty,
Queen Carol of Saxony, to commemorate the
400th birthday of Gustaf Vasa (1496-1560),
King of Sweden.*

5066   [Isle of the dead, symphonic poem   *15'*
for orchestra, Op. 45]
2,2,2,2-4,0,2,1-Timp.-Hp.-Str.
Raabe & Plothow, Berlin [1899]
Score 35 p.
*After the painting of the same name by Arnold
Böcklin.   Composed 1899.*

HALLER, EDWIN. pseudonym.
See: LAUTENSCHLÄGER, WILLI.

HALLNÄS, JOHAN HILDING.
              b. Halmstad, Sweden 24 May 1903

399m   [Concerto for flute, strings,   *17'*
timpani and percussion]
1.Sonatina: Lento - Allegro   2.Leggenda: Lar-
ghetto   3.Rondo: Allegro vivace
Solo Fl.-Timp.,Perc.-Str.
Ms.
Score 53 p.
*Composed 1958.   First performance Göteborg
Broadcasting Co., Göteborg, 7 May 1959,*

*Göteborgs Orkesterförening, Stig Westerberg
conductor, Håkan Edlén flutist.   Dedicated to
Håkan Edlén.*

7198   [Concerto for string orchestra,   *14'*
timpani and percussion]
1.Entrata: Allegro   2.Canzona: Andante espressivo   3.Serenata con intermezzo: Poco allegretto, grazioso   4.Final: Allegro vivace
Timp.,Perc.-Str.
Ms.
Score 46 p.
*Commissioned by Sven-Erik Bäck.   Conceived as
a ballet with scenes from Rostand's drama
Cyrano de Bergerac.   Composed 1959.   First
performance Stockholm, 15 August 1960, Ungdoms-
orkestern of Sveriges Radio, Sven-Erik Bäck
conductor.*

302v   [Concerto, violin, no. 2]   *16'*
1.Lento, espressivo - Allegro ma non troppo,
risoluto   2.Allegro
Solo Vn.-2,2,2,2-2,2,2-Timp.,Perc.-Pno.,Cel.-
Str.
Edition Suecia, Stockholm, c1966
Score 103 p.
Composed 1965.

2048s   [Little symphony for string   *20'*
orchestra, Op. 31]
1.Lento   2.Allegro molto   3.Andante   4.Finale:
Allegro espressivo
Str.
Ms.
Score 39 p.
*Composed 1948.   First performance Göteborg,
Sweden, 3 October 1948, Orchestra Society of
Göteborg, Sixten Eckerberg conductor.*

HALM, AUGUST.
         Gross-Altdorf, Württemberg, Germany
                            26 October 1869
              Saalfeld, Thuringia, Germany
                            1 February 1929

991s   Praeludium und Fuge [for string orchestra,
F minor]
Langsam - Ruhig
Str.
Bärenreiter, Augsburg [n.d.]
Score 7 p.

180s   [Symphony, string orchestra, D minor]
1.Allegro   2.Andante   3.Finale: Nicht schnell
Str.
Zumsteeg, Stuttgart, 1910
Score 27 p.

HALPHEN, FERNAND.   b.1872
                                             d.1917

2367   Sicilienne pour orchestre   *4'*
1,1-Hn.-Hp.(or Pno.)-Str.
Enoch, Paris [n.d.]
Score 15 p.
*Originally composed for flute or violin and
piano, 1895.   First performance Paris, 1897.*

Halvorsen, Johan

HALVORSEN, JOHAN.   Drammen, Norway 15 March 1864
Oslo 4 December 1935

1002v Air norvégien pour violon et orchestre,
Op. 7
Solo Vn.-2(2nd alt. Picc.),2,2,2-2Hn.-Timp.,
Trgl.-Str.
W. Hansen, Copenhagen [n.d.]
Score 39 p.
Dedicated to Johannes Wollf.

742v Andante religioso [violin and   *5'*
orchestra]
Solo Vn.-2,2,2,2-2Hn.-Timp.-Str.
W. Hansen, Copenhagen [n.d.]
Score 15 p.

2377 Bergensiana [Rococo variations on an   *6'*
old Bergen melody]
2(2nd alt. Picc.), 2,2,2-2,2,B.Tbn.-Timp.,
Perc.-Mand.-Str.
W. Hansen, Copenhagen, c1930
Score 25 p.
*Composed 1928. First performance Oslo, 1929.
Dedicated to the Copenhagen Philharmonic
Orchestra.*

903v Danses norvégiennes pour violon   *4'*
avec orchestre
1.Allegro con brio 2.Allegretto - Allegro con
fuoco - Presto
Solo Vn.-2,2,2,2-2,2-Timp.,Trgl.-Str.
W. Hansen, Copenhagen [n.d.]
Score 23 p.

1136 Fossegrimen, Op. 21. Dramatische   *22'*
Suiten für Orchester, Nr. 4
1.Allegro moderato 2.[Fairy dance]: Allegretto
grazioso 3.[Wedding march]: Allegretto mar-
ciale 4.[Melodrama and Aud's song]: Allegro -
Andante con moto 5.Fanitullen [Devil-dance]:
Allegro con fuoco
2(2nd alt. Picc.),2(2nd alt. E.H.),2,2-4,2,3-
Timp.,Perc.-Hp.-Str.
W. Hansen, Copenhagen [190-?]
Score 97 p.
*From the incidental music to Sigurd Eldegard's
gnome-play. Composed 1906. First performance
National Theater, Christiania, 1906. Dedicated
to King Hakon VII and Queen Maud.*

1093 [Gurre, Op. 17. No. 1, Evening   *4'*
landscape]
2(2nd alt. Picc.),2,2,2-4,2,3-Timp.,Trgl.-Hp.-
Str.
W. Hansen, Copenhagen [190-?]
Score 31 p.
*From the incidental music to Holger Drach-
mann's play. Composed 1900. First performance National Theater, Christiania, 1900.*

1119 [Gurre, Op. 17. No. 2b,   *3'*
Introduction and serenade]
2*,2,2,2-2Hn.-Trgl.-Hp.-Str.
W. Hansen, Copenhagen [190-?]
Score 23 p.

1169 [The king, Op. 19. No. 1,   *5'*
Symphonic intermezzo]
2(2nd. alt. Picc.),2,2,2-4,2,3,1-Timp.,S.Dr.,
Cym.-Hp.-Str.
W. Hansen, Copenhagen [190-?]
Score 41 p.
*From the incidental music to Bjørnstjerne
Bjørnson's play. Composed 1904. First per-
formance National Theater, Christiania, 1904.
Dedicated to Christian Sinding.*

1273s [The maiden's song, mosaic no. 4, violin
and string orchestra]
Solo Vn.-Str.
W. Hansen, Copenhagen [n.d.]
Score 3 p.
Dedicated to Kathleen Parlow.

1482s Norwegian song, the old fisherman's
song, Op. 31
Solo Vn.-Str.
W. Hansen, Leipzig, c1913
Score 5 p.

981 [Queen Tamara, Oriental character
piece. Dance scene]
2(2nd alt. Picc.),3*(2nd ad lib.),2,2-4,2,3-
Timp.,Perc.-Str.
W. Hansen, Copenhagen [190-?]
Score 31 p.
*Composed 1903. First performance National
Theater, Christiania, 1903. Dedicated to
Joachim Andersen.*

377s [Raven wedding in Crow's Bay. Arranged for
string orchestra]
Str.
C. Warmuth, Christiania [n.d.]
Score 5 p.
*An arrangement of the traditional Norwegian
song, Rabnabryllaup uti Kraakjalund.*

1051 Rhapsodie norvégienne no. 1
2(both alt. Picc.),2,2,2-4,2,3,1-Timp.,Perc.-
Str.
W. Hansen, Copenhagen, c1921
Score 67 p.
*Composed 1921. First performance Christiania,
1921. Dedicated to Crown Prince Frederik of
Denmark.*

1150 Rhapsodie norvégienne no. 2   *11'*
3*,2,2,2-4,2,3,1-Timp.,Perc.-Str.
W. Hansen, Copenhagen, c1921
Score 71 p.
*Composed 1921. First performance Christiania,
1921.*

682 Sérénade pour orchestre, Op. 33
2,1,2,2-Hp.-Str.
Norsk Musik-Forlag, Christiania, c1913
Score 13 p.
*Composed 1912. First performance Christiania,
1914.*

775 Suite ancienne à la memoire de   *25'*
Ludvig Holberg, Op. 31
1.Intrata: Allegretto moderato 2.Air con

variazioni: Andantino - 7 Variations 3.
Gigue: Allegro 4.Sarabande: Andante sos-
tenuto 5.Bourrée: Allegro con spirito
2(2nd alt. Picc.), 2,2,2-2,2-Timp.,Trgl.-Str.
W. Hansen, Leipzig, ᶜ1916
Score 68 p.
*Composed 1916. First performance Christiania,
1916, at a memorial concert for Holberg.
Dedicated to the orchestra of the National
Theater, Christiania.*

6045 [Symphony no. 1, C minor]   *41'*
1.Allegro non troppo 2.Andante 3.Scherzo:
Lento - Allegro con spirito - Allegretto -
Lento - Allegro molto 4.Finale (Rondo),
Introduction: Andante - Allegro deciso
3(2nd alt. Picc.),2,2,2-4,3,3,1-Timp.,Perc.-
Hp.(ad lib.)-Str.
Norsk Musikforlag, Oslo, ᶜ1926
Score 191 p.
*Composed 1923. First performance Oslo, Nor-
way, 30 April 1923, Christiania Musik-
forening, the composer conducting. Dedicated
to Hjalmar Borgstrøm.*

6681 [Triumphant entry of the Boyars]   *4'*
2*,2,2,2-4,2,3,1-Perc.-Str.
Luck's Music Library, Detroit [n.d.]
Score 27 p.
First published 1895.

200 Vasantasena [suite from the inci-   *20'*
dental music to the Hindu play]
1.Vorspiel: Moderato 2.Bajaderentanz [Hindu
dancing girls]: Allegro con spirito 3.Hymne
an Brahma: Largamente 4.Stilleben, Tanz und
Bacchanale: Andante con moto - Allegro vivace -
Presto
2(2nd alt. Picc.),2,2,2-4,2,3,1-Timp.,Perc.-
Str.
C.F. Peters, Leipzig, ᶜ1897
Score 60 p.
*Composed 1896. First performance National
Theater, Christiania, 1901. Dedicated to
Edvard Grieg.*

HAMBRAEUS, BENGT.   Stockholm 29 January 1928

2358s Pianissimo in due tempi per   *12'*
20 archi
1.Molto adagio, leading to 2.Molto allegro
Str.
Edition Suecia, Stockholm [n.d.]
Score 36 p.
*Commissioned by the Uppsala Chamber Orchestra,
1970. Composed 1970-72. First performance
Uppsala, 18 May 1972, Uppsala Chamber Orches-
tra, Carl Rune Larsson conductor.*

HAMERIK, ASGER.   Copenhagen 8 April 1843
              Frederiksborg, Denmark 13 July 1923

Born: Asger Hammerich

580c Concert-Romanze [violoncello and
orchestra, Op. 27]
Solo Vc.-2,2,2,2-2Hn.-Timp.-Str.
André, Offenbach a. M. [1879]

Score 28 p.
Dedicated to Friedrich Grützmacher.

62 [Hebrew trilogy for orchestra, Op. 19]   *13'*
1.Ouverture: Grave - Allegro 2.Lamento:
Andante 3.Sinfonia trionfale: Grave - Allegro
moderato e maestoso - Allegro
2,2,2,2-4,2,3-Timp.,B.Dr.,Gong-Hp.-Str.
Breitkopf & Härtel, Leipzig [1879]
Score 86 p.
Composed 1878.

266 [Nordic suite no. 1, Op. 22, C major]   *12'*
1.Im Walde: Adagio - Allegro molto 2.Volkslied:
Andante sostenuto 3.Springtanz: Allegro vivace
4.Menuet: Andante 5.Brautmarsch: Allegro
maestoso
2,2,2,2-4,2,3-Timp.,B.Dr.-Hp.-Str.
Breitkopf & Härtel, Leipzig [1893]
Score 102 p.
Composed 1871.

1196 [Nordic suite no. 2, Op. 23, G minor]   *16'*
1.Andante sostenuto 2.Allegro molto
3.Moderato 4.Moderato
2,2,2,2-4,2,3-Timp.,B.Dr.-Hp.-Str.
André, Offenbach a. M. [1875]
Score 123 p.
*Composed 1873. First performance Baltimore,
1874, the composer conducting.*

1288 [Nordic suite no. 3, Op. 24, A minor]   *18'*
1.Andante con moto - Allegro vivace 2.Allegro
vivace 3.Andante 4.Allegro
2,2,2,2-4,2,3-Timp.,B.Dr.,Trgl.-Hp.-Str.
André, Offenbach a. M. [1876]
Score 120 p.
*Composed 1874. First performance Baltimore,
1875, the composer conducting.*

1151 [Nordic suite no. 4, Op. 25, D major]   *24'*
1.Andante tranquillo - Allegro molto vivace
2.Andante sostenuto 3.Allegro molto vivace
4.Andante 5.Allegro maestoso
2,2,2,2-4,2,3,1-Timp.,B.Dr.,Trgl.-Hp.-Str.
Breitkopf & Härtel, Leipzig [1877]
Score 212 p.
*Composed 1876. First performance Baltimore,
1877, the composer conducting.*

1846 [Nordic suite no. 5, Op. 26, A major]   *20'*
1.Allegro 2.Andante con moto 3.Allegro
4.Andantino con moto 5.Allegro
3(3rd alt. Picc.),2,2,2-4,2,3,1-Timp.,B.Dr.-
Hp.-Str.
André, Offenbach a. M. [1880]
Score 152 p.
*Composed 1878. First performance Baltimore,
1879, the composer conducting. Dedicated to
Niels Gade.*

1848 Opera without words, Op. 30   *33'*
9 scenes in 3 movements
2,2,2,2-2,2,3-Timp.,Perc.-Str.
André, Offenbach a. M. [1883]
Score 181 p.

Hamerik, Asger

Composed 1881. First performance Baltimore, 1883, the composer conducting. Dedicated to Fernanda Henriques.

1632 [Symphony no. 1, Poétique, Op. 29,   21'
F major]
1.Allegro moderato ed espressivo 2.Allegro marcato 3.Andante con moto 4.Allegro giusto
2,2,2,2-2,2,3-Timp.,Cym.-Str.
André, Offenbach a. M. [1882]
Score 160 p.
Composed 1879. First performance Baltimore, 1881, the composer conducting. Dedicated to Anton Rubinstein.

1847 [Symphony no. 2, Tragique, Op. 32,   38'
C minor]
1.Grave - Allegro non troppo e patetico 2.
Andante penitente 3.Allegro marcato 4.Adagio
- Allegro passionato
3*,2,2,2-4,2,3,1-Timp.,B.Dr.,Cym.-Str.
André, Offenbach a. M. [1884]
Score 207 p.
Composed 1881. First performance Baltimore, 1882, the composer conducting. Dedicated to Ludwig II of Bavaria.

1182 [Symphony no. 3, Lyrique, Op. 33,   31'
E major]
1.Largo - Allegro molto vivace 2.Allegro grazioso 3.Andante sostenuto 4.Allegro con spirito
2,2,2,2-4,2,3-Timp.,Cym.-Str.
André, Offenbach a. M. [1885?]
Score 190 p.
Composed 1885. First performance Baltimore, 1886, the composer conducting. Dedicated to King Oscar II of Sweden and Norway.

1312 [Symphony no. 4, Majestueuse,   40'
Op. 35, C major]
1.Largo - Allegro impetuoso 2.Adagio espressivo 3.Allegro moderato 4.Maestoso e solenne
2,2,2,2-4,2,3,1-Timp.,B.Dr.,Trgl.-Hp.-Str.
André, Offenbach a. M. [1891]
Score 183 p.
Composed 1888. First performance Baltimore, 1889, the composer conducting. Dedicated to King Christian IX of Denmark.

34 [Symphony no. 5, Sérieuse, Op. 36,   25'
G minor]
1.Largo - Allegro con fuoco 2.Adagio non troppo 3.Scherzo allegro vivace 4.Grave - Allegro
3(3rd alt. Picc.),2,2,2-4,2,3,1-Timp.-Str.
Breitkopf & Härtel, Leipzig, c1893
Score 163 p.
Composed 1892. First performance Baltimore, 1893, the composer conducting.

93s [Symphony no. 6, Spirituelle, Op. 38,
G major]
1.Allegro moderato 2.Allegro molto vivace 3.
Andante sostenuto 4.Allegro con spirito
Str.
Breitkopf & Härtel, Leipzig, c1897
Score 35 p.

1256 [Tovelille, Op. 12. Prelude to Act IV] 12'
2,2,2,2-4Hn.-Str.
Andre, Offenbach a. M. [1875]
Score 12 p.
From the opera composed 1868.

HANDEL, DARRELL.   Lodi, California 23 August 1933

6715 Chamber suite for orchestra   9'
1.Lyric 2.Scherzo 3.Passacaglia
3*,3*,3*,2-4,2,3,1-Timp.,Perc.-Hp.-
Str.
Ms.
Score 68 p.
Composed 1966. First performance Rochester, April 1966, Eastman-Rochester Orchestra, Walter Hendl conductor.

HANDEL, GEORGE FRIDERIC.
Halle, Germany 23 February 1685
London 14 April 1759

5924 [Acis and Galatea. Overture. Bell   3'30"
no. 57] With additional accompaniments
by Wolfgang Amadeus Mozart. Edited by
Berthold Tours
0,2,2,2-2Hn.-Str.
Novello, Ewer & Co., London [1881]
Score 12 p.
Sinfonia from the serenata or masque. Libretto by John Gay with additions by John Dryden, Alexander Pope and John Hughes. Mozart's additions were made in 1788.

858s [Agrippina. Overture (Sinfonia). Bell no. 34]
Ob.-Str.
Score: Ms. 14 p.
Parts: Breitkopf & Härtel, Leipzig [n.d.]
From the opera composed 1709.

3989 [Alceste. Bell no. 148. Suite.   17'30"
Excerpted and transcribed by Zoltan Fekete]
1.Largo - Allegro - Largo 2.Lento - Larghetto
- Lento 3.Allegretto 4.Vivace 5.Larghetto pastorale
2,2(2nd alt. E.H.),2,2-2Hn.-Str.
Ms. c1943 by Zoltan Fekete
Score 22 p.
Most material is from Handel's incidental music composed 1750 for Tobias Smollett's play Alcestis, not produced. This transcription 1943. First performance Town Hall, New York, 5 February 1944, NBC Symphony Orchestra, Fekete conductor.

2341s [Alcina. Overture, musette and   6'
menuet. Bell no.102. Transcribed for string orchestra by Reginald Jacques]
Str.
Oxford University Press, London, c1947
Score 11 p.
From the opera composed 1735.

7197 [Alcina. Il ballo. Bell no. 102] Edited by
W.G. Whittaker
1.Gavotta 2.Sarabanda: Adagio 3.Menuet
4.[Bourrée]

2Fl.(optional),2Ob.(optional),Bn.(optional)-
Pno.(optional)-Str.
Oxford University Press, London,^c1927, ^c1955
Score 6 p.

1145s [Alcina. Dances. Bell no. 102] Edited by
W.G. Whittaker
1.Musette: Un peu lentement 2.Menuet: Allegro,
ma non troppo 3.Tamburino: [Presto] 4.Ballet
scene [Entrée des songes...]
1(or Picc. or Vn.),1(ad lib.)-Pno.(optional)-
Str.
Oxford University Press, London, ^c1927
Score 14 p.

1325s [Alcina. Dream music, Largo e piano. Bell
no. 102] Edited by Georg Göhler
Cemb.-Str.
[n.p., n.d.]
Score 8 p.

1436s [Alessandro. Overture. Bell no. 75 *and*
Admeto. Overture. Bell no. 76]
0,2,0,1-Str.
Hofmeister, Leipzig [1846]
Score 31 p.
*From the operas Alessandro, composed 1726; and
Admeto, based on Euripides' Alkestis, composed
1726-27.*

6881 [Almira. Overture and dances. Bell no. 9]
Edited by Gotthold Frotscher
Ouverture: (Adagio) - (Presto allegro) - Cha-
conne - Sarabande - Menuett - Rondeau -
Gavotte - Gigue
0,2,0,1-Cemb.-Str.(Vn.III ad lib.)
O.H. Noetzel, Wilhelmshaven, ^c1966
Score 31 p.
*Handel's first opera, composed 1704 at age 19.
First performance Theater beim Gänsmarkt,
Hamburg, 8 January 1705.*

4851 [Ariodante. Dances and pieces. Bell no.
101]
1.Sinfonia: Allegro 2.Ballo: Gavotte 3.Lar-
ghetto: Pastorale 4.Rondo 5.Rondo 6.Andante
allegro 7.Einzog der Mohren 8.Rondo 9.Sin-
fonia: Grave 10.Musette I: Lentement
11.Musette II: Andante 12.Allegro
2,2,0,1-2Hn.-Cemb.-Str.
G. Kallmeyer, Wolfenbüttel and Berlin, ^c1942
Score 35 p.
*From the opera in 3 acts with libretto by
Antonio Salvi, from Lodovico Ariosto's
Orlando Furioso. Composed 1734.*

7196 [Berenice. Minuet. Bell no. 111]   *4'*
Edited by W.G. Whittaker
1,1,1,1(all optional)-Pno.-Str.
Oxford University Press, London,^c1929
Score 4 p.
*From the opera in 3 acts with libretto by
Antonio Salvi. Completed January 1737.*

626s [Same as above] Transcribed for string
orchestra by W.T. Best
Str.
B. Schott's Söhne, Mainz [1889?]
Score 5 p.

1962s [Chandos anthems. No. 2: Sonata,   *5'*
D minor. Bell no. 54/2. Arranged for string
orchestra by Richard Horner Bales]
[Maestoso] - Allegro
Str.
Ms.
Score 15 p.
*An excerpt from the Chandos Anthems composed
1716-20 for the Chapel Royal at Cannons. This
numbering for identification (no. 2) follows
Chrysander's edition.*

548m [Concerto, oboe, continuo and string   *6'*
orchestra, no. 1, B-flat major. Bell no. 5/1]
Edited by Max Seiffert
1.Adagio, attacca 2.Allegro 3.Siciliana:
Largo 4.Vivace
Solo Ob.-2Cemb.-Str.
Breitkopf & Härtel, Leipzig [n.d.]
Score 13 p.
Composed ca.1703-05.

549m [Concerto, oboe, continuo and string   *6'*
orchestra, no. 2, B-flat major. Bell no. 5/2]
Edited by Max Seiffert
1.Vivace 2.[Bell: Fuga]: Allegro 3.Andante
4.Allegro
Solo Ob.-2Cemb.-Str.
Breitkopf & Härtel, Leipzig [n.d.]
Score 16 p.
Composed ca.1703-05.

546m [Concerto, oboe, continuo and string   *6'*
orchestra, no. 3, G minor. Bell no. 5/3]
1.Grave 2.Allegro 3.Sarabande: Largo
4.Allegro
Solo Ob.-Cemb.-Str.
[n.p., n.d.]
Score 9 p.
Composed 1703-05.

550m [Same as above] Edited by Max Seiffert
Breitkopf & Härtel, Leipzig [n.d.]
Score 17 p.

578c [Same as above] Transcribed for   *11'*
violoncello and string orchestra by W. H.
Squire
1.Grave 2.Andante 3.Allegro 4.Allegro
Solo Vc.-Str.
Score: Ms. 21 p.
Parts: B. Schott's Söhne, Mainz, ^c1926
*In the Bell catalog the second and third
movements are reversed. This transcription
1923. First performance London, 1924.*

174m [Concerto, oboe, continuo and   *10'*
string orchestra, E-flat major. Bell no. 51]
Edited by Fritz Stein
1.Largo 2.Allegro 3.Largo 4.Vivace
Solo Ob.-Cemb.-Str.
H. Litolff/C.F. Peters, Frankfurt, ^c1935, ^c1963
Score 18 p.
*Composed ca.1716. This is the first edition
of this work, based on a Ms. copy in the
Uppsala University Library.*

Handel, George Frideric

1108m [Concerto, organ, oboes and string   *14'*
orchestra, Op. 4 no. 1, G minor. Bell
no. 103/1] Edited by Fridrich Chrysander
1.Larghetto e staccato   2.Allegro   3.Adagio
4.Andante
Solo Org.-2Ob.-Str.
[Ausgabe der Deutschen Händelgesellschaft,
Leipzig, 1868]
Score 18 p.

1109m [Concerto, organ, oboes and string   *10'*
orchestra, Op. 4 no. 2, B-flat major. Bell
no. 103/2] Edited by Friedrich Chrysander
1.A tempo ordinario, e staccato   2.Allegro
3.Adagio, e staccato   4.Allegro, ma non
presto
Solo Org.-2Ob.-Str.
[Ausgabe der Deutschen Händelgesellschaft,
Leipzig, 1868]
Score 10 p.
Composed ca.1736.

1110m [Concerto, organ, oboes and string
orchestra, Op. 4 no. 3, G minor. Bell
no. 103/3] Edited by Friedrich Chrysander
1.Adagio   2.Allegro   3.Adagio   4.Allegro
Solo Org.-2Ob.-Str.(with Solo Vn. and Solo
Vc.)
[Ausgabe der Deutschen Händelgesellschaft,
Leipzig, 1868]
Score 10 p.

1111m [Concerto, organ, oboes and string   *16'*
orchestra, Op. 4 no. 4, F major. Bell
no. 103/4] Edited by Friedrich Chrysander
1.Allegro   2.Andante   3.Adagio   4.Allegro
Solo Org.-2Ob.-Str.
[Ausgabe der Deutschen Händelgesellschaft,
Leipzig, 1868]
Score 15 p.

1112m [Concerto, organ, oboes and string   *10'*
orchestra, Op. 4 no. 5, F major. Bell
no. 103/5] Edited by Friedrich Chrysander
1.Larghetto   2.Allegro   3.Alla siciliana
4.Presto
Solo Org.-2Ob.-Str.
[Ausgabe der Deutschen Händelgesellschaft,
Leipzig, 1868]
Score 5 p.

408m [Concerto, organ, oboes and string   *14'*
orchestra, Op. 7 no. 1, B-flat major. Bell
no. 128/1] Edited by Helmuth Walcha
1.Andante   2.Andante   3.Largo e piano
4.Bourrée: Allegro
Solo Org.-2Ob.,Bn.(optional)-Str.
B. Schott's Söhne, Mainz, c1943
Score 34 p.
Composed 1740; first published 1761.

407m [Concerto, organ, oboes and string
orchestra, Op. 7 no. 2, A major. Bell
no. 128/2] Edited by Helmuth Walcha
1.Ouverture: Grave   2.A tempo ordinario
(Allegro)   3.Organo ad libitum: Adagio
4.Allegro

Solo Org.-2Ob.,Bn.(optional)-Cemb.-Str.
B. Schott's Söhne, Mainz, c1942
Score 24 p.
Composed 1743; first published 1761.

406m [Concerto, organ, oboes and string   *17'30"*
orchestra, Op. 7 no. 3, B-flat major.
Bell no. 128/3] Edited by Helmuth Walcha
1.Allegro   2.Spiritoso   3.Menuet (A)
[4.Menuet (B) is lacking in this edition]
Solo Org.-2Ob.,Bn.(optional)-Str.
B. Schott's Söhne, Mainz, c1942
Score 32 p.
First published 1761.

405m [Concerto, organ, oboes and string   *18'*
orchestra, Op. 7 no. 4, D minor. Bell
no. 128/4] Edited by Helmuth Walcha
1.Adagio   2.Allegro   3.Allegro
Solo Org.-2Ob.,Bn.(optional)-Str.
B. Schott's Söhne, Mainz, c1940
Score 26 p.
First published 1761.

404m [Concerto, organ, oboes and string   *15'*
orchestra, Op. 7 no. 5, G minor. Bell no.
128/5] Edited by Helmuth Walcha
1.Allegro ma non troppo, e staccato   2.Andante
larghetto, e staccato - Adagio   3.Menuett
4.Gavotte
Solo Org.-2Ob.,Bn.(optional)-Str.
B. Schott's Söhne, Mainz, c1942
Score 26 p.
Composed 1750; first published 1761.

403m [Concerto, organ, oboes and string
orchestra, Op. 7 no. 6, B-flat major. Bell
no. 128/6] Edited by Helmuth Walcha
1.Pomposo   2.Adagio, quasi una fantasia
3.A tempo ordinario
Solo Org.-2Ob.,Bn.(optional)-Str.
B. Schott's Söhne, Mainz, c1942
Score 18 p.
First published 1761.

1113m [Concerto, organ or harp, flutes   *12'*
and strings, Op. 4 no. 6, B-flat major. Bell
no. 103/6] Edited by Friedrich Chrysander
1.Andante allegro   2.Larghetto   3.Allegro
moderato
Solo Org.(or Hp.)-2Fl.-Str.
[Ausgabe der Deutschen Händelgesellschaft,
Leipzig, 1868]
Score 7 p.
*Composed 1736 to be played during the first
act of the composer's Alexander's Feast, first
performed Covent Garden, London, 19 February
1736.*

744m [Same as above] Edited by Gustav Lenzewski
Chr. Fr. Vieweg, Berlin [n.d.]
Score 14 p.

435m [Concerto, organ or harpsichord,   *16'*
oboes and string orchestra, F major. Bell
no. 120/1] Edited by Friedrich Chrysander
1.Larghetto   2.Allegro   3.Larghetto   4.Allegro
Solo Org. or Solo Hpscd.-2Ob.-Str.

Handel, George Frideric

[Ausgabe der Deutschen Händelgesellschaft,
Leipzig, 1894]
Score 12 p.
*This is Handel's arrangement of his Concerto
Grosso, Op. 6 no. 1, of 1739. Popular title
is Cuckoo and Nightingale.*

730v [Concerto, viola, B minor. Arranged by
Henri Casadesus. Bell Appendix I no. 16]
1.Allegro moderato 2.Andante ma non troppo
3.Allegro molto
Solo Va.-2,0,0,2-Str.
Eschig, Paris, ᶜ1925
Score 35 p.
*Excerpts from various Handel compositions,
transcribed for viola and orchestra by
Casadesus.*

446c [Concerto, violoncello and strings.   13'
Transcribed from the Sonata in C major, for
viola da gamba and cembalo, Bell no. 7, by
Paul Bazelaire]
1.Andantino grazioso [Bell: Adagio] 2.Allegro
3.Adagio 4.Allegro vivace [Bell: Allegro]
Solo Vc.-Str.
Alphonse Leduc, Paris, ᶜ1946
Score 16 p.
*The transcriber's and publisher's title is mis-
leading as Handel did not compose a violon-
cello concerto. Handel's title is Sonata in
C major for Viola da Gamba and Cembalo,
composed ca.1703-05.*

2319 [Concerto, 2 wind choirs, string   12'
orchestra and continuo, B-flat major. Bell no.
162] Edited by Max Seiffert
1.Ouverture: Grave - Allegro ma non troppo
2.Allegro 3.Lento 4.A tempo ordinario - Alla
breve. Moderato 5.Menuet: Allegro
Choir I: 2Ob.,2Bn. - Choir II: 2Ob.,2Bn.-
2Cemb.-Str.
Breitkopf & Härtel, Leipzig, ᶜ1926
Score 23 p.
*Composed ca.1747. This edition dedicated to
Richard Strauss.*

2320 [Concerto, 2 wind choirs, string orches-
tra and continuo, F major. Bell no. 163]
Edited by Max Seiffert
1.Pomposo - Allegro 2.A tempo giusto 3.Largo
4.Allegro ma non troppo - A tempo ordinario
Choir I: 2Ob.,2Bn.,2Hn. - Choir II: 2Ob.,2Bn.,
2Hn.-Cemb.,Org.-Str.
Breitkopf & Härtel, Leipzig [n.d.]
Score 58 p.
*Composed ca.1750. This edition dedicated to
Karl Muck.*

2321 [Concerto, 2 wind choirs, string   16'
orchestra and continuo, F major. Bell no. 164]
Edited by Max Seiffert
1.Grave [Bell: Ouverture] - Allegro 2.Allegro
ma non troppo 3.Adagio - Andante larghetto
4.Allegro
Choir I: 2Ob.,2Bn.,2Hn. - Choir II: 2Ob.,2Bn.,
2Hn.-Cemb.,Org.-Str.
Breitkopf & Härtel, Leipzig [190-?]

Score 49 p.
Composed between 1740 and 1750.

2441 [Concerto for orchestra, F major. Bell no.
49] Edited by Max Seiffert
1.(Andante) 2.Alla hornpipe: (Allegro)
0,2,0,1-2Hn.-Cemb.,Org.-Str.
Breitkopf & Härtel, Leipzig, ᶜ1926
Score 12 p.
*Composed ca.1715. Used in the second version of
the Water Music, and possibly in the first as
well.*

6685 [Concerto for orchestra, D major.   10'
Bell no. 144B] Edited by Friedrich Chrysander
1.Largo 2.Allegro 3.Allegro ma non troppo
0,2,0,2-4,2-Timp.-Org.[Cemb.]-Str.
[Ausgabe der Deutschen Händelgesellschaft,
Leipzig, 1886]
Score 19 p.
*Composed ca.1748. This concerto was later
developed into the overture of the Fireworks
Music.*

2312 [Concerto grosso, orchestra and   8'
continuo, Op. 3 no. 1, B-flat major. Bell
no. 53/1] Edited by Max Seiffert
1.Allegro moderato 2.Largo, attacca 3.Allegro
2,2,0,2-2Cemb.-Str.
Breitkopf & Härtel, Leipzig, ᶜ1907
Score 17 p.
Composed ca.1716; first published 1734.

2313 [Concerto grosso, orchestra and   12'
continuo, Op. 3 no. 2, B-flat major. Bell
no. 53/2] Edited by Max Seiffert
1.Vivace - Largo - Allegro 2.Andante allegro
3.Andante - 2 Variations
Soli: Vn.I, Vn.II, Vc.-0,2,0,1-2Cemb.-Str.
Breitkopf & Härtel, Leipzig [n.d.]
Score 23 p.
Composed 1716; first published 1734.

1032m [Concerto grosso, orchestra and continuo,
Op. 3 no. 2, B-flat major. Bell no. 53/2.
Largo from Movement 1]
Solo Ob.-Str.
Durand, Schoenewerk et Cie., Paris [187-?]
Score 5 p.

2314 [Concerto grosso, orchestra and   8'
continuo, Op. 3 no. 3, G major. Bell no.
53/3] Edited by Max Seiffert
1.Largo, e staccato - Allegro 2.Adagio
3.Allegro
Soli: Vn.,Fl.(or Ob.),Cemb.-Cemb.-Str.
Breitkopf & Härtel, Leipzig [n.d.]
Score 18 p.
Composed ca. 1716; first published 1734.

2315 [Concerto grosso, orchestra and con-   12'
tinuo, Op. 3 no. 4, F major. Bell no. 53/4]
Edited by Max Seiffert
1.Grave - Allegro - Grave 2.Andante - Allegro
3.Allegro
0,2,0,1-2Cemb.-Str.
Breitkopf & Härtel, Leipzig [n.d.]
Score 20 p.

Handel, George Frideric

Composed 1716. First performance during the composer's opera Amadigi, 20 June 1716. First published 1734.

1091s [Same as above] Excerpts transcribed for oboe or bassoon and string orchestra by F.A. Gevaert
1.Andante 2.Menuet: Allegretto [Bell: Allegro]
Solo Ob.(Andante),Solo Bn.(Menuet)-Str.
Durand, Paris [n.d.]
Score 11 p.

2316 [Concerto grosso, orchestra and con- *10'*
tinuo, Op. 3 no. 5, D minor. Bell no. 53/5]
Edited by Max Seiffert
1.Andante - [Bell: Fuga] Allegro 2.Adagio - Allegro, ma non troppo 3.Allegro
0,2,0,1-2Cemb.-Str.
Breitkopf & Härtel, Leipzig [n.d.]
Score 24 p.
Composed ca. 1716; first published 1734.

2317 [Concerto grosso, orchestra and con- *7'*
tinuo, Op. 3 no. 6, D major. Bell no. 53/6]
Edited by Max Seiffert
1.Allegro moderato 2.Allegro
0,2,0,1-2Cemb.-Str.
Breitkopf & Härtel, Leipzig [n.d.]
Score 19 p.
Composed ca. 1716; first published 1734.

1585s [Concerto grosso, string orchestra and continuo, Op. 6 no. 1, G major. Bell no. 123/1] Edited by Max Seiffert
1.A tempo giusto 2.Allegro 3.Adagio
4.Allegro 5.Allegro
Soli: Vn.I,VnII,Vc.-2Cemb.-Str.
Breitkopf & Härtel, Leipzig [n.d.]
Score 22 p.
Composed 1739.

545s [Concerto grosso, string orchestra and continuo, Op. 6 no. 2, F major. Bell no. 123/2. Transcribed for string orchestra by S. Bachrich]
1.Andante larghetto 2.Allegro - Menuetto: Moderato, non troppo 3.Largo 4.Allegro, ma non troppo
Str.
Doblinger, Vienna [n.d.]
Score 15 p.
The Menuetto does not appear in most editions of this work. Composed 1739.

922s [Same as above] Edited by Gustav Kogel
1.Andante larghetto - Allegro 2.Largo
3.Allegro, ma non troppo
Soli: Vn.I,Vn.II,Vc.-Str.
C.F. Peters, Leipzig [n.d.]
Score 23 p.

1586s [Same as above] Edited by Max Seiffert
1.Andante larghetto 2.Allegro 3.Largo
4.Allegro, ma non troppo
Soli: Vn.I,Vn.II,Vc.-2Cemb.-Str.
Breitkopf & Härtel, Leipzig [n.d.]
Score 16 p.

1587s [Concerto grosso, string orchestra and continuo, Op. 6 no. 3, E minor. Bell no. 123/3] Edited by Max Seiffert
1.Larghetto - Andante 2.Allegro 3.Polonoise [*sic*]: Andante 4.Allegro, ma non troppo
Soli: Vn.I,Vn.II,Vc.-2Cemb.-Str.
Breitkopf & Härtel, Leipzig [n.d.]
Score 21 p.
Composed 1739.

1588s [Concerto grosso, string orchestra and continuo, Op. 6 no. 4, A minor. Bell no. 123/4] Edited by Max Seiffert
1.Larghetto affettuoso - Allegro 2.Largo [Bell: Largo e piano], attacca 3.Allegro
Soli: Vn.I,Vn.II,Vc.-2Cemb.-Str.
Breitkopf & Härtel, Leipzig [n.d.]
Score 20 p.
Composed 1920.

923s [Concerto grosso, string orchestra and continuo, Op. 6 no. 5, D major. Bell no. 123/5] Edited by Gustav Kogel
1.(Maestoso) 2.Allegro 3.Presto 4.Largo
5.Menuet: Un poco larghetto 6.Finale: Allegro
Soli: Vn.I,Vn.II,Vc.-Str.
C.F. Peters, Leipzig [n.d.]
Score 31 p.
In the Bell catalog the Menuet follows the second Allegro. Composed 1739.

1589s [Same as above] Edited by W. Weismann *15'*
1.[------] - Allegro 2.Presto 3.Largo
4.Allegro 5.Menuet: Un poco larghetto
Soli: Vn.I,Vn.II,Vc.-Cemb.(2nd optional)-Str.
Broude Bros., New York [n.d.]
Score 26 p.

1146s [Concerto grosso, string orchestra and continuo, Op. 6 no. 6, G minor. Bell no. 123/6] Edited by Ferdinand David
1.Larghetto affettuoso 2.Allegro ma non troppo 3.Musette: Allegretto [Bell: Larghetto]
4.Allegro molto vivace 5.Finale: Allegro con fuoco
Soli: Vn.I,Vn.II,Vc.-Str.
Simrock, Berlin [n.d.]
Score 23 p.
In the Bell catalog movements 4 and 5 are reversed. Composed 1739.

1590s [Same as above] Edited by Max Seiffert
1.Largo affettuoso - Allegro ma non troppo
3.Musette: Larghetto 3.Allegro 4.Allegro
Soli: Vn.I,Vn.II,Vc.-2Cemb.-Str.
Breitkopf & Härtel, Leipzig, c1907
Score 29 p.

1591s [Concerto grosso, string orchestra and continuo, Op. 6 no. 7, B-flat major. Bell no. 123/7] Edited by Max Seiffert
1.Largo - Allegro 2.Largo e piano - Andante, attacca 3.Hornpipe: Spiritoso
Soli: Vn.I,Vn.II,Vc.-2Cemb.-Str.
Breitkopf & Härtel, Leipzig [n.d.]
Score 22 p.
Composed ca. 1739.

Handel, George Frideric

1592s [Concerto grosso, string orchestra and
continuo, Op. 6 no. 8, C minor. Bell no.
123/8] Edited by Max Seiffert
1.Allemande: Andante 2.Grave - Andante allegro 3.Adagio - Siciliana: Andante 4.Allegro
Soli: Vn.I,Vn.II,Vc.-2Cemb.-Str.
Breitkopf & Härtel, Leipzig [n.d.]
Score 20 p.
Composed 1739.

1593s [Concerto grosso, string orchestra and
continuo, Op. 6 no. 9, F major. Bell no.
123/9] Edited by Max Seiffert
1.Largo - Allegro 2.Larghetto - Allegro
3.Menuet: Andante 4.Gigue: Allegro
Soli: Vn.I,Vn.II,Vc.-2Cemb.-Str.
Breitkopf & Härtel, Leipzig [n.d.]
Score 26 p.
Composed 1739.

1113s [Concerto grosso, string orchestra and
continuo, Op. 6 no. 10, D minor. Bell no.
123/10] Edited by Gustav Kogel
1.Ouvertüre: [Maestoso] 2.Allegro 3.Air:
Lento 4.Allegro moderato 5.Finale: Allegro [con fuoco]
Soli: Vn.I,Vn.II,Vc.-Str.
C.F. Peters, Leipzig [n.d.]
Score 23 p.
*In the Bell catalog another Allegro follows
the Air, and the last 2 movements are
reversed. Composed 1739.*

1594s [Same as above] Edited by Max   18'
Seiffert
1.Ouverture: Grave - Allegro 2.Air: Lente-
ment [Bell: Lento] 3.Allegro 4.Allegro
moderato
Soli: Vn.I,Vn.II,Vc.-2Cemb.-Str.
Breitkopf & Härtel, Leipzig [n.d.]
Score 29 p.

1090s [Concerto grosso, string orchestra and
continuo, Op. 6 no. 10, D minor. Bell no.
123/10. Allegro moderato] Edited by A. Samm
Str.
A. Durand, Paris [n.d.]
Score 2 p.
*Published as Gavotte du Concerto en Ré
Mineur.*

1595s [Concerto grosso, string orchestra and
continuo, Op. 6 no. 11, A major. Bell no.
123/11] Edited by Max Seiffert
1.Andante larghetto, e staccato - Allegro
2.Largo, e staccato - Andante 3.Allegro
Soli: Vn.I,Vn.II,Vc.-2Cemb.-Str.
Breitkopf & Härtel, Leipzig [1906?]
Score 41 p.
Composed 1739.

1596s [Concerto grosso, string orchestra and
continuo, Op. 6 no. 12, B minor. Bell no.
123/12] Edited by Max Seiffert
1.Largo - Allegro 2.Aria: Larghetto
3.Largo - Allegro

Soli: Vn.I,Vn.II,Vc.-2Cemb.-Str.
Breitkopf & Härtel, Leipzig, c1906
Score 25 p.
*Composed 1739. This edition dedicated to
Joseph Joachim.*

1381s [Concerto grosso, string orchestra and
continuo, Op. 6 no. 12, B minor. Bell no.
123/12. Movement 2, Larghetto e piano]
Edited by Michele Esposito
Str.
Oxford University Press, London, c1927
Score 3 p.

2318 [Concerto grosso, string orchestra,   18'
oboes and continuo, C major. Bell no. 105]
Edited by Max Seiffert
1.Allegro 2.Largo 3.Allegro 4.(Gavotte):
Andante non presto
Soli: Vn.I,Vn.II,Vc.-0,2,0,1-2Cemb.-Str.
Breitkopf & Härtel, Leipzig, c1906
Score 27 p.
*Composed 1736. First performance as an inter-
lude in the dramatic ode Alexander's Feast,
Covent Garden, London, 19 February 1736.
Authenticity has been questioned. This edi-
tion dedicated to D. F. Scheurleer.*

2325 [Same as above] Transcribed for   11'
orchestra by Felix Mottl
1.Allegro 2.Largo 3.Allegro
Soli: Vn.I,Vn.II,Vc.-2,2,2,2-2,2,0-Timp.-Str.
C.F. Peters, Leipzig [n.d.]
Score 50 p.
*This version lacks the Andante Non Presto
indicated in the Bell catalog.*

409v [Concerto grosso, violin, violon-   5'
cello and orchestra, B-flat major. Bell no.
35] Edited by Max Seiffert
1.Andante 2.Adagio 3.Allegro
Soli: Vn.,Vc.-0,2,0,2-2Cemb.-Str.
Breitkopf & Härtel, Leipzig [n.d.]
Score 16 p.
Composed ca.1710 as Sonata à 5.

1380s [Same as above] Transcribed for   5'
string quartet and string orchestra by Michele
Esposito
1.Andante 2.Adagio 3.Allegro
Soli: Vn.I,Vn.II,Va.,Vc.-Str.
Oxford University Press, London, c1929
Score 20 p.

7084 [Coronation anthems for George II.   5'30"
No. 1, Zadok the priest. Bell no. 78/1]
Edited by Friedrich Chrysander
Andante maestoso - A tempo ordinario
Mixed Chorus (7-part:SSAATBB)-2Ob.,2Bn.-3Tpt.-
Timp.-Org.-Str.
Score: [Ausgabe der Deutschen Händelgesell-
schaft, Breitkopf & Härtel, Leipzig, 1863]
26 p.
Parts: J. Walsh, London [n.d.]
*Text is an interpolation from the biblical
book of I Kings, 1:38-39. The first of four*

Handel, George Frideric

Coronation Anthems composed 1727. First per-
formance Westminster Abbey, London, 11 October
1727, the composer conducting.

Cuckoo and nightingale
    See: [Concerto, organ or harpsichord, oboes
        and string orchestra, F major. Bell no.
        120/1]

Dance of the sailors from Rodrigo
    See: [Rodrigo. Dance of the sailors (Matelot).
        Bell no. 23]

7082 [Deborah. Overture. Bell no. 94]
    Edited by Friedrich Chrysander
    Allegro - Grave - Poco allegro - Allegro
    2Ob.,Bn.-Cemb.-Str.
    Score: [Ausgabe der Deutschen Händelgesell-
    schaft, Leipzig, 1869] 7 p.
    Parts: J. Walsh, London [n.d.]
    From the oratorio with libretto by Samuel
    Humphreys. Composed 1732-33. First perform-
    ance King's Theatre, London, 17 March 1733,
    the composer conducting.

4661 [Esther. Overture. Bell no. 61]   8'
    Edited by Adam Carse
    Largo [Bell: Andante] - Larghetto - Allegro
    0,2,0,1-Str.
    Augener, London, ^c1939
    Score 12 p.
    From the original version of the oratorio,
    composed 1720. First performance at the Duke
    of Chandos' home, Cannons, probably 29 August
    1720. Oratorio revised, 1732. First per-
    formance London, 23 February 1732.

1227s [Same as above] Edited by Otto Sommer
    0,2,0,1-Cemb.-Str.
    Chr. Fr. Vieweg, Berlin [n.d.]
    Score 19 p.

1437s [Ezio. Overture. Bell no. 88]
    0,2,0,1-Str.
    [Hofmeister, Leipzig, 1844?]
    Score 4 p.
    From the opera composed 1731. First perform-
    ance King's Theatre, London, 15 January 1732.
    Title also spelled Aëtius or Oetius.

Fireworks music. An early version of the
overture
    See: [Concerto for orchestra, D major.
        Bell no. 144B]

7032 [Fireworks music. Bell no. 145]   16'
    Edited by Wilhelm Pfannkuch
    1.Ouverture: Adagio 2.Allegro 3.Lentement
    4.Bourrée 5.La paix: Largo alla Siciliana
    6.La réjouissance: Allegro 7.Menuet [I]
    8.Menuet [II]
    0,3,0,2*-3,3-Timp.-Str.
    Breitkopf & Härtel, Wiesbaden, ^c1969
    Score 67 p.
    Composed 1749 to celebrate the Peace of Aix-
    la-Chapelle. First performance Green Park,
    London, 27 April 1749.

2443 [Same as above] Edited by Max Seiffert
    Breitkopf & Härtel, Leipzig [n.d.]
    Score 47 p.

900 [Fireworks music. Bell no. 145. Suite   8'
    excerpted and edited for orchestra by Hamilton
    Harty]
    1.Overture: Maestoso - Allegro 2.Alla sicili-
    ana: Molto tranquillo con moto 3.Bourrée:
    Vivace, attacca 4.Menuetto [Bell: Menuet II]:
    Moderato con molto ritmo
    0,2,0,2-4,3-Timp.,S.Dr.-Str.
    Murdoch, Murdoch, London, ^c1924
    Score 22 p.
    First performance of this suite, Manchester,
    1923, Hallé Concerts, Harty conductor.

647s Five short pieces from a rare work.
    Selected and transcribed for string orchestra
    by Thomas F. Dunhill
    1.March: Allegro marziale 2.Andante pastorale:
    Andante con moto, ma tranquillo 3.Minuet I
    4.Minuet II 5.Gavotte: Allegro vigoroso
    Str.(Vn.III may substitute for Va.;Cb.
    optional)
    Oxford University Press, London, ^c1927
    Score 5 p.
    The score does not indicate the source of these
    excerpts, which may be spurious.

1014s [Giustino. Overture. Bell no. 108]
    2Ob.-Str.
    Score: Ms. 12 p.
    Parts: Novello, Ewer, London [n.d.]
    From the opera composed 1736. First perform-
    ance Covent Garden, London, 16 February 1737.

1545s [Hercules. Overture. Bell no. 136]
    Edited by Arnold Schering
    2Ob.-Pno.-Str.
    C.F. Kahnt, Leipzig, ^c1930
    Score 11 p.
    From the musical drama composed 1744. First
    performance King's Theatre, London, 5 Janu-
    ary 1745.

7081 [Jephtha. Overture. Bell no. 152]   5'
    Edited by Friedrich Chrysander
    Maestoso [Handel: Grave] - Allegro - Menuet
    2Ob.-Cemb.-Str.
    Score: [Ausgabe der Deutschen Händelgesell-
    schaft, Leipzig, 1886] 6 p.
    Parts: J. Walsh, London [1752]
    From the oratorio in three acts with libretto
    by Thomas Morell. Composed 1751. First per-
    formance Covent Garden, London, 26 February
    1752, the composer conducting.

536s [Jephtha. Overture. Bell no. 152] With
    additional accompaniments by Arthur Sullivan
    Str.
    Score: Ms. 9 p.
    Parts: Novello, London [n.d.]

6885 [Joseph and his brethren. Overture. Bell
    no. 135] Edited by Friedrich Chrysander
    Andante - Larghetto - Allegro - Menuet [Parts

to the Menuet not included]
20b.-Cemb.-Str.
[Ausgabe der Deutschen Händelgesellschaft,
Leipzig, ca.1883]
Score 7 p.
*From the oratorio in three acts with libretto
by James Miller. Composed 1743. First per-
formance Covent Garden, London, 2 March 1744,
the composer conducting. First published by
J. Walsh, London, 1744.*

3743 [Joshua. Suite no. 1 from the   *18'*
oratorio. Bell no. 141. Excerpted and transcribed for orchestra by Zoltan Fekete]
1.Introduction: Andante maestoso 2.Allegro
3.Larghetto 4.Allegretto scherzando 5.Andan-
tino 6.Grave 7.Grandioso
3*,2,2,2-4,3,3-Timp.-Str.
Ms. ᶜ1941 by Zoltan Fekete
Score 36 p.
*Most material is from the oratorio composed
1747. This transcription 1941. First performance New York, 5 December 1941, Midtown
Symphony Orchestra, Fekete conductor.*

3744 [Joshua. Suite no. 2 from the   *18'*
oratorio. Bell no. 141. Excerpted and transcribed for orchestra by Zoltan Fekete]
1.Ouverture: Allegro 2.Allegro con brio 3.
Largo 4.Scherzando 5.Allegro deciso
6.Grandioso
2,3*(E.H. ad lib.),2,2-4,3,3-Timp.-Str.
Ms. ᶜ1942 by Zoltan Fekete
Score 20 p. Large folio
*This transcription 1942; first performance
New York, 28 April 1942, Midtown Symphony
Orchestra, Fekete conductor. Transcription
later retitled Triumphal Suite.*

3760 Lamentation suite. Excerpted and   *18'*
transcribed for orchestra by Zoltan Fekete
1.Adagio - Allegro moderato 2.Allegro
moderato e molto deciso 3.Adagio (Pastorale)
4.Allegro energico
2,2,2,2-4,3,3-Timp.,B.Dr.-Str.
Ms. ᶜ1942 by Zoltan Fekete
Score 28 p.
*From an unidentified cantata. This tran-
scription 1942.*

851v Larghetto [for violin and string   *3'*
orchestra] Edited by Jenö Hubay
Solo Vn.-Str.
Zimmermann, Leipzig, ᶜ1908
Score 5 p.
*First performance of this edition Budapest,
1908, Hubay soloist.*

Largo from Xerxes
See: [Xerxes (Serse)...]

1438s [Lotario. Overture. Bell no. 84]
0,2,0,1-Str.
[Hofmeister, Leipzig, 1846?]
Score 8 p.
*From the opera composed 1729. First perform-
ance King's Theatre, London, 2 December 1729.*

711s Masque-suite...from the full score of a
rare and unknown work. Transcribed for string
orchestra by Thomas F. Dunhill
1.Prelude & Pastorale: Poco adagio - Con moto
2.Rigaudon: Allegro marcato 3.Sarabande:
Largo assai 4.Gavotte: Allegro 5.Minuet:
Grazioso 6.Gigue: Presto
Str.
Curwen, London, ᶜ1925
Score 11 p.
*The score does not indicate the source of
these dances; probably spurious.*

1273 [Messiah. Pastoral symphony. Bell   *4'*
no. 130]
2*,2,2,2-2Hn.-Str.
Novello, London [n.d.]
Score 3 p.
*From the oratorio composed 1741. First per-
formance Music Hall, Fishamble Street,
Dublin, 13 April 1742.*

5600 [Mirtillo suite. Arranged by   *19'30"*
Arnold Schering]
1.Ouverture: Maestoso 2.Sarabande [Largo
assai] 3.Musette: Amabile 4.Pastorale 5.
La gelosia: (Grave) 6.Entrée 7.Duetto:
(Grazioso) 8.Gigue
1Fl.,2Ob.-Cemb.-Str.
C.F. Kahnt, Leipzig, ᶜ1937
Score 19 p.
*The main title is the arranger's. No. 1 is
from the serenata, Il Parnasso in Festa (Bell
no. 98). No. 4 is from the oratorio, The
Triumph of Time and Truth (Bell no. 112). No. 7
is from the ballet suite, Terpsicore (Bell no.
100a). Nos. 2, 3, 5, 6 and 8 are from the opera
Il Pastor Fido (Bell no. 100b).*

1686s [Ottone. Overture. Bell no. 66]   *4'*
Edited by H.W. Hunt
1,2,0,1(all woodwinds optional)-Str.
Deane & Sons, London, ᶜ1926
Score 6 p.
*From the opera composed 1722. First perform-
ance King's Theatre, London, 12 January 1723.*

6921 [Same as above] Edited by Reginald Jacques
Maestoso - Allegro - Gavotte - Allegro
0,2,0,1-Str.
Oxford University Press, London, ᶜ1943
Score 11 p.

1636 Overture in D minor. Transcribed   *6'*
for full orchestra by Edward Elgar
3*,3*,3*,3*-4,3,3,1-Timp.,Perc.-Org.(ad lib.)-
Str.
Novello, London, ᶜ1923
Score 19 p.
*Score does not identify the original overture.
This transcription 1923. First performance
Worcester Festival, England, September 1923.*

7083 [Overture in B-flat major, for oboes,
strings and continuo. Bell no. 165] Edited by
Friedrich Chrysander
2Ob.,Bn.-Cemb.-Str.
Score: [Ausgabe der Deutschen Händelgesellschaft, Leipzig, 1894] 4 p.

Handel, George Frideric

Parts: J. Walsh, London [1758]
Composed ca. 1708.

Il parnasso in festa. Overture. Bell no. 98
See: [Mirtillo suite. Arranged by Arnold
Schering] 1.Ouvertüre

1440s [Partenope. Overture. Bell no. 85]
2Ob.-Str.
[Hofmeister, Leipzig, 1844?]
Score 9 p.
*From the opera composed 1730. First perform-
ance King's Theatre, London, 24 February 1730.*

Il pastor fido. Excerpts. Bell no. 100b.
See: [Mirtillo suite. Arranged by Arnold
Schering]

3522 [Il pastor fido. Suite from the   *24'*
opera. Bell no. 100. Excerpted and transcribed
for orchestra by Thomas Beecham]
1.Introduction and fugue - 5 Dances -
7.Finale: Allegro vivace
2,2,2,2-4,2-Timp.,S.Dr.,Trgl.-Str.
Boosey & Hawkes, London, ᶜ1941
Score 75 p.
*From the opera originally composed 1712.
Revised and enlarged 1734. First performance
of revised version King's Theatre, London,
18 May 1734. This transcription 1940. First
performance London, 31 May 1940, London Philharmonic, Thomas Beecham conductor.*

3051 Polonaise, arietta and passa-   *10'30"*
caglia. Transcribed for orchestra by Hamilton
Harty
1.Polonaise: Moderato e ben ritmato 2.Ari-
etta: Lento ma non troppo, attacca 3.Passa-
caglia: Allegro non troppo, deciso
3(3rd alt. Picc.),2,2,3*(C.Bn. ad lib.)-2,3-
Timp.-Str.
Boosey & Co., London, ᶜ1932
Score 24 p.
*Arietta and Passacaglia transcribed from Han-
del's opera Rodrigo, composed 1707 or 1708.
This transcription 1926. First performance
Manchester, England, 5 November 1926, Hallé
Concerts, Hamilton Harty conductor.*

1439s [Poro. Overture. Bell no. 86]
2Ob.-Org.-Str.(without Cb.)
[Hofmeister, Leipzig, 1844?]
Score 6 p.
*From the opera composed 1730-31. First per-
formance King's Theatre, London, 2 February
1731.*

1635s [Rodrigo. Overture. Bell no. 23]
Edited by H. Lemacher and P. Mies
Grave - Lentement - Gigue - Sarabande - Mate-
lot - Menuet - Bourrée - Menuet - Passacaille
0,2,0,1(all optional,Bn. ad lib.)-Cemb.-Str.
Tonger, Cologne [n.d.]
Score 20 p.
From the opera composed 1707 or 1708.

7080 [Rodrigo. Overture and dances. Bell   *8'*
no. 23] Edited and arranged [in 2 suites] by
Anthony Lewis and Philip Cranmer
Suite 1: Overture - Gigue - Sarabande -
Bourée - Menuet (1) - Matelot
Suite 2: Air - Menuet (2) - Passacaille
[The sequence of these dances is not Handel's]
2Ob.,Bn.-Cemb.-Str.
Oxford University Press, London, ᶜ1956
Score 36 p.

4211 [Rodrigo. Dance of the sailors (Matelot).
Bell no. 23] Orchestrated by Frederic H. Cowen
2,2,2,2-4,2-Timp.-Str.
Ms.
Score 28 p.

3759 [Samson. Suite from the oratorio.   *16'*
Bell no. 131. Excerpted and transcribed for
orchestra by Zoltan Fekete]
1.Andante pomposo - Allegro 2.Adagio 3.Andan-
tino scherzando 4.Allegro deciso - Moderato
2,3*(E.H. ad lib.),2,2-4,3,3-Timp.-Str.
Ms. ᶜ1942 by Zoltan Fekete
Score 25 p.
*Most material is from the oratorio composed
1741-42. First performance Covent Garden,
London, 18 February 1743. This transcription
1942.*

4688 Sarabande and bourrée. Adapted by Richard
Horner Bales
1.Largo 2.Allegro
1,1,1,1-1Hn.-Str.
Ms.
Score 7 p.
Sources for the 2 dances not identified.

2435 [Siroe. Overture. Bell no. 80] Edited by
F.H. Cowen
0,2,0,2(2nd ad lib.)-Str.
Goodwin & Tabb, London [n.d.]
Score 11 p.
*From the opera composed 1728. First perform-
ance King's Theatre, London, 17 February 1728.*

1450s [Sonata, violin and continuo, Op. 1
no. 14, A major. Bell no. 67/14. Transcribed
for string orchestra by Artur Willner]
1.Maestoso [Bell: Adagio] 2.Allegro 3.Largo
espressivo 4.Allegro
Str.
Ms. [Universal Edition, Vienna, n.d.]
Score 11 p.
Title on score: Concerto nach dem 5. Sonate.

1753s [Sonata, violin and continuo, Op. 1   *20'*
no. 15, E major. Bell no. 67/15. Transcribed
for string orchestra by Maxwell Weaner]
1.Adagio 2.Allegro 3.Largo 4.Allegro
Str.
Pro-Art Publications, New York, ᶜ1938
Score 16 p.
*First published by Jeanne Roger, Amsterdam,
ca.1722.*

2369s [Sonata, 2 violins, or 2 oboes,   *13'*
or 2 flutes, and continuo, Op. 2 no. 7,

G minor. Bell no. 68. Transcribed for string
orchestra by Ralph Nicholson]
1.Andante 2.Allegro 3.Arioso 4.Allegro
Str.
Oxford University Press, London, ᶜ1947
Score 16 p.
This work is also known as Sonata a Tre,
Op. 2, no.7. This edition has title:
Concerto in G Minor for Strings.

1634s [Sonata, 2 violins and continuo, Op. 5
no. 5, G minor. Bell no. 119/5. Transcribed
for string orchestra with cembalo by Eduard
Martini]
1.Largo 2.Come alla breve 3.Larghetto 4.
Bourrée 5.A tempo giusto - [Air]
Cemb.(or Pno.)-Str.(Va. ad lib.)
Chr. Fr. Vieweg, Berlin [n.d.]
Score 19 p.
Handel assembled the trio sonatas of Op. 5
from movements of other works. In the first
edition (J. Walsh, London, 1739) the
Bourrée is the final movement. This edition
dedicated to H. Abendroth.

1536s [Sonata, 2 violins and continuo,   *10'*
Op. 5 no. 6, F major. Bell no. 119/6. Tran-
scribed for string orchestra with cembalo by
Eduard Martini]
1.Largo 2.Allegro 3.Adagio 4.Allegro
5.[Menuett]: Andante 6.Allegro
Cemb.-Str.
Chr. Fr. Vieweg, Berlin [n.d.]
Score 19 p.
In the Bell catalog a different minuet pre-
cedes the 5th movement, and movement 6 is not
found.

107s [Suite de pièces, harpsichord, D minor.
Bell no. 60/11. Air. Transcribed for string
orchestra by Edmund Singer]
Str.(without Cb.)
W. Hansen, Copenhagen [190-?]
Score 3 p.
Composed ca.1719. First published by J. Walsh,
London, 1727, in the Second Collection of
Handel's keyboard music. Republished by
Walsh in 1733.

3900 [Suite de pièces, harpsichord,   *9'*
E minor. Bell no. 60/4 and 60/13. Excerpted
and transcribed for orchestra by Charles
Sanford Skilton]
1.Gigue 2.Sarabande 3.Fugue: Allegro
3(3rd alt. Picc.),3*,3*,3*-4,3,3,1-Timp.,B.Dr.,
Cym.-Str.
Ms.
Score 37 p.
All material composed ca.1719. Gigue from
Bell no. 60/13, first published by J. Walsh,
London, 1727. Sarabande and Fugue, Bell no.
60/4, first published by J. Cluer, London,
1720. This transcription 1938. First per-
formance Kansas City, Missouri, 4 January
1940, Kansas City Philharmonic, Karl Krueger
conductor.

41s Suite of five pieces for string orchestra
with piano. Freely arranged by James Brown
1.Chaconne: Giusto e vivace [from Almira,
Bell no. 9] 2.Sarabande: Theme and 2 Varia-
tions 3.Ritornello: Grazioso 4.Bourrée:
Allegro 5.Hornpipe: Molto vivace
Pno.(optional)-Str.
Stainer & Bell, London, ᶜ1919
Score 12 p.

Terpsicore. Duetto. Bell no. 100a
See: [Mirtillo suite. Arranged by Arnold
      Schering] 7.Duetto

7088 [Theodora. Overture. Bell no. 147]   *12'*
Edited by Friedrich Chrysander
Maestoso - Allegro - Trio: Larghetto e piano -
Courante
2Ob.-Cemb.-Str.
Score: [Ausgabe der Deutschen Händelgesellschaft, Breitkopf & Härtel, Leipzig, 1860] 7 p.
Parts: J. Walsh, London [1751]
From the oratorio in three acts with libretto
by Thomas Morell. Composed 1749. First per-
formance Covent Garden, London, 16 March 1750,
the composer conducting. Complete oratorio
first published by James Harrison, London,
ca.1785.

1226s [Same as above] Edited by Arnold Schering
Pno.-Str.
C.F. Kahnt, Leipzig, ᶜ1927
Score 11 p.

1205s [Three pieces. Transcribed for string
orchestra by Giuseppe Martucci]
1.Minuetto, G major: Moderato 2.Musetta,
E major: Andante 3.Gavotta, E minor: Allegro
Str.
Carisch & Jänichen, Milan, ᶜ1901
Score 7 p.
Excerpted from various Handel compositions.

586s [Three pieces. Transcribed for string
orchestra by Alois Schmitt]
1.Maestoso - Andante con moto [G minor] 2.
Largo [D minor] 3.Larghetto [D major]
Org.-Str.
Ries & Erler, Berlin [n.d.]
Score 15 p.
The score does not indicate the sources of
these pieces.

7087 [Triumph of time and truth. Overture.
Bell no. 153] Edited by Friedrich Chrysander
Maestoso - Allegro ma non troppo
2Ob.,2Bn.-Cemb.-Str.
Score: [Ausgabe der Deutschen Händelgesellschaft, Leipzig, 1865] 7 p.
Parts: J. Walsh, London [1757]
From the oratorio in 3 acts, with English
adaptation by Thomas Morell of an Italian
libretto by Benedetto Pamfili. This is Han-
del's last composition, a thorough reworking
of his Il Trionfo del Tempo e del Disinganno,
composed 1708, and his Il Trionfo del Tempo e
della Verità, of 1737. This English version

Handel, George Frideric

1757. First performance Covent Garden, London, 11 March 1757, the composer conducting.

3988 [Triumph of time and truth. Bell 33'
no. 153. Suite from the oratorio, excerpted
and freely arranged by Zoltan Fekete]
1.Grave - Allegro - Fugue 2.Largo - Larghetto 3.Pastorale - Moderato 4.Allegro
grandioso
3*(Picc. ad lib.), 3*,2,2-4,3,3-Timp.,B.Dr.(ad lib.)-Str.
Ms. c1943 by Zoltan Fekete
Score 55 p.

The triumph of time and truth. Pastorale.
Bell no. 112
See: [Mirtillo suite. Arranged by Arnold
Schering] 4.Pastorale

866 [Water music, 1st version. Bell no. 16'
50. Suite excerpted and transcribed for
orchestra by Hamilton Harty]
1.Allegro 2.Air: Andante un poco allegretto
3.Bourrée: Vivace, attacca 4.Horn-pipe:
Delicato, ma con molto brio 5.Andante
espressivo, attacca 6.Allegro deciso
2(2nd alt. Picc.),2,2,2-4,2-Timp.-Str.
Chappell, London, c1922
Score 28 p.
*For complete Water Music see entry below.
First performance of this suite Manchester,
1918, Hallé Concerts, Harty conductor.*

2442 [Water music, 2nd version. Bell no. 45'
55] Edited by Max Seiffert
Complete in 20 movements (Order differs from
that of Bell)
1(alt. Picc.),2,0,1-2,2-2Cemb.-Str.
Breitkopf & Härtel, Leipzig, c1922
Score 64 p.
*Originally composed for an entertainment given
by English King George I on the Thames, 22
August 1715. First published in this expanded
version by J. Walsh, London, ca.1732.*

63s [Xerxes (Serse). Larghetto (Largo), Ombra
mai fù. Bell no. 115. Transcribed for string
orchestra by Otto Wellmann]
Str.(Cb. ad lib.)
Carl Simon, Berlin [n.d.]
No score
From the opera composed 1737-38. First performance King's Theatre, London, 15 April 1738.

Zadok the priest
See: [Coronation anthems for George II. No. 1,
Zadok the priest. Bell no. 78/1]

HANDTKE, ROBERT ERNST. Reichenau, 22 December 1867

Also spelled: Handke

325s Serenade in F dur für Streichinstrumente,
Op. 25
Str.
Steingräber, Leipzig, c1912
Score 15 p.

HANFF, JOHANN NIKOLAUS.
Wechmar, near Mühlhausen, Germany 1630
Schleswig 1711

1723s [Two chorale preludes for organ. 5'
Transcribed by Leonid Leonardi]
1.Auf meinen lieben Gott 2. Ein' feste Burg
Str.
Ms.
Score 8 p.
*Originally for organ; transcribed 1935. First
performance Beverly Hills, 15 March 1940, the
Robert Pollack String Sextet, Leonid Leonardi
conductor.*

HANN, LEWIS ROBERT. London 1865

734s Sérénade angélique [for string orchestra]
Str.
Score: Ms. 5 p.
Parts: Laudy, London [n.d.]

HANSEN, EMIL ROBERT. Copenhagen 25 February 1860
Aarhus, Denmark 18 July 1926

1029m Melodie for flute and string orchestra,
Op. 12
Solo Fl.-Str.
Score: Ms. 5 p.
Parts: Carl Merseburger, Leipzig [n.d.]

700s [Symphonic suite for string orchestra and
horns, Op. 6]
1.Allegro 2.Andante 3.Allegro scherzando
4.Adagio - Maestoso e molto marcato
2Hn.-Str.
Wilhelm Hansen, Copenhagen [n.d.]
Score 59 p.

HANSON, C. J. GUNNAR. Sweden

4782 [Festivo, for large orchestra]
2(2nd alt. Picc.),2,2,2-4,3,3,1-Timp.,Perc.-Str.
Ms.
Score 30 p.
Composed 1946.

4817 Suite no. 1 for orchestra
1.Gavotte - Musette 2.Sarabande 3.Tempo di
menuetto
2,2,2,2-2Hn.-Timp.-Str.
Ms.
Score 16 p.
Composed 1949.

HANSON, HOWARD. Wahoo, Nebraska 28 October 1896

6231 Bold island suite, Op. 46 24'
1.Birds at the sea 2.Summer seascape
3.God in nature
3(3rd alt. Picc.),3*,2,2-4,3,3,1-Timp.,Perc.-
Pno.(alt. Cel.), Hp.-Str.
Ms. [Movements 1 & 3 c1962; movement 2 c1959
by Eastman School of Music, Rochester, New
York]
Score 114 p. Large folio
Commissioned by the Cleveland Symphony

Orchestra. Second movement composed 1959; 1st & 3rd movements composed 1961. First performance Cleveland, 25 January 1962, Cleveland Symphony Orchestra, George Szell conductor.

1071m Concerto for organ, strings and   *18'*
harp, Op. 22 no.3
In one movement
Solo Org.-Hp.-Str.
Ms.
Score 58 p.

352p Concerto for piano and orchestra,   *20'*
Op. 36, G major
1.Lento molto e molto tranquillo - Allegro deciso 2.Allegro feroce, molto ritmico 3. Andante molto espressivo 4.Allegro giocoso
Solo Pno.-3*,2,2,2-4,3,3,1-Timp.,S.Dr.,Xyl.-Str.
Ms.
Score 112 p. Large folio
Commissioned by the Koussevitzky Foundation. Composed 1948. First performance Boston, 31 December 1948, Boston Symphony Orchestra, the composer conducting, Rudolf Firkušny soloist.

6211 Elegy [In memory of Serge   *14'*
Koussevitzky, Op. 44]
2(2nd alt. Picc.),2(2nd alt. E.H.),2,2-4,3,3,
1-Timp.-Hp.-Str.
Eastman School of Music, Rochester, New York, c1956
Score 28 p.
Commissioned by the Boston Symphony Orchestra for its 75th anniversary. Composed 1955. First performance Boston, 20 December 1956, Boston Symphony Orchestra, Charles Munch conductor.

3628 Fanfare   *30"*
4Hn.,4Tpt.,3Tbn.,Tuba-Timp.
Ms.
Score 5 p.
Composed 1937-38. First performance Eighth Annual Festival of American Music of the Eastman School of Music, Rochester, New York, 28 April 1938, the composer conducting.

4271 Fanfare for the Signal Corps
See: TEN FANFARES BY TEN COMPOSERS FOR
        BRASS AND PERCUSSION.

351p Fantasy variations on a theme of   *12'*
youth, Op. 40
Solo Pno.-Str.
Ms.
Score 25 p.
Written for the centennial of the composer's alma mater, Northwestern University, Chicago, Illinois. Composed 1951. First performance Northwestern University, 18 February 1951.

1991 Lux aeterna, symphonic poem with   *18'*
viola obligato, Op. 24
Solo Va.-3*,2,2,3*-4,3,3,1-Timp.,Perc.-Pno.,
Cel.,2Hp.-Str.
G. Schirmer, New York, c1927 by Howard Hanson
Score 48 p.

6261 Mosaics   *10'*
3(3rd alt. Picc.),3*,3*,3*-4,3,3,1-Timp.,Perc.-
Cel.,Hp.-Str.
Ms. c1958 by Eastman School of Music, Rochester, New York
Score 48 p. Large folio
Commissioned by the Cleveland Orchestra to celebrate its 40th anniversary. Composed 1961. First performance Cleveland, 23 January 1962, Cleveland Orchestra, George Szell conductor.

1959 Pan and the priest, symphonic poem,   *10'*
Op. 26
3*,2(2nd alt. E.H.)2,3*-4,3,3,1-Timp.,Perc.-
Pno.-Str.
Birchard, Boston, c1927
Score 72 p.
Completed 1926. First performance Queen's Hall, London, October 1926, Henry Wood conductor.

473m Pastorale for solo oboe, strings   *6'*
and harp, Op. 38
Solo Ob.-Hp.-Str.
Ms.
Score 28 p.
Composed for the Chopin centennial, UNESCO, Paris 1949.

1012m Serenade for solo flute, harp and   *6'*
string orchestra, Op. 35
Solo Fl.-Hp.-Str.
Carl Fischer, New York, c1948
Score 14 p.
Commissioned by Radio Station WHAM, Rochester, New York. Composed 1945. First performance Boston, 25 October 1946, Serge Koussevitzky conductor, Georges Laurent flautist, Bernard Zighera harpist.

2621 [Symphony no. 1, Nordic, Op. 21,   *28'*
E minor]
1.Andante solenne - Allegro con fuoco 2. Andante teneramente con semplicita 3.Allegro con fuoco - Finale
3*,2,2,3*-4,3,3,1-Timp.,Perc.-Hp.-Str.
American Academy in Rome, 1929
Score 99 p.
Composed 1922. First performance Rome, 30 May 1923, the Augusteo Symphony Orchestra, the composer conducting.

4194 Symphony no. 2, Romantic, Op. 30   *24'*
1.Adagio - Allegro moderato, leading to 2. Andante con tenerezza 3.Allegro con brio
3*,3*,2,3*-4,3,3,1-Timp.,Perc.-Hp.-Str.
Eastman School of Music, Rochester, New York, c1932
Score 132 p.
Commissioned by Serge Koussevitzky for the 50th anniversary of the Boston Symphony Orchestra. Composed 1930. First performance Boston, 28 November 1930, Boston Symphony Orchestra, Serge Koussevitzky conductor.

3578 Symphony no. 3, Op. 33   *36'*
1.Andante lamentando 2.Andante tranquillo

Hanson, Howard

3.Tempo scherzando 4.Largamente e pesante
3*,3*,3*,3*-4,3,3,1-Timp.-Str.
Birchard, Boston, ᶜ1941 by Eastman School of
Music
Score 168 p.
*Composed 1936-37. First complete performance
in an NBC broadcast, 26 March 1938, NBC
Symphony, the composer conducting.*

4052 Symphony no. 4, Op. 34   20'
1.Andante inquieto 2.Elegy: Largo 3.Presto
4.Largo pastorale
3*,2,2(2nd alt. B.Cl.),3*-4,3,3,1-Timp.,Perc.-
Str.
Ms.
Score 81 p.
*Composed 1940-43. Awarded Pulitzer Prize
1944. First performance Boston, 3 December
1943, Boston Symphony Orchestra, the composer
conducting.*

5528 [Symphony no. 5, Sinfonia sacra,   13'
Op. 43]
In one movement: Adagio - Calmo - Allegretto -
Largamente - Largo
3*,2(2nd alt. E.H.),2,2-4,3,3,1-Timp.,Perc.-
Hp.-Str.
Eastman School of Music, Rochester, New York,
ᶜ1955
Score 47 p.
*Composed 1954. First performance Philadelphia,
18 February 1955, Philadelphia Orchestra,
Eugene Ormandy conductor.*

1968s Vermeland [from Scandinavian Suite, 2'30"
Op. 30] Transcribed for string orchestra by
Richard Bales
Str.
Ms.
Score 3 p.
*Originally composed for piano as no. 1 of the
Scandinavian Suite, Op. 13, 1918-1919. This
transcription 1944.*

HANSSEN, JOHANNES.
                Ullensaker, Norway 2 December 1874
                                          d.1967

6052 [Valdres march, Op. 1]   4'
2*,2,2,2-4,2,2,1-Timp.,Perc.-Str.
Norsk Musikforlag, Oslo, ᶜ1947
Score 20 p.
*Originally composed for military band, 1904.
First performance of this version Oslo, 7
December 1936, Philharmonic Orchestra
Society, Olav Kielland conductor.*

HAPPICH, WILLIAM F.

47s [Three pieces. Arranged for string
orchestra by William F. Happich]
1.At twilight, by Chanaud 2.Mazurka, by Bohm
3.Toy soldiers' march, by Kreisler
Str.
Ms.
Score 20 p.
Arranged June 1918, for the Symphony Club.

HARCOURT, EUGÈNE D'.   Paris 2 May 1859
                Locarno, Switzerland 4 March 1918

5598 [Tasso. Overture]
3(3rd alt. Picc.),3*,3(3rd alt. Basset Hn.),3*
-4,4,3,1-Timp.,B.Dr.,Cym.-2Hp.-Str.
Chez l'Auteur, Paris, ᶜ1903 by Choudens
Score 49 p.
*From the opera in 4 acts with libretto by
Jules and Pierre Barbier, based on the life of
the Italian poet Torquato Tasso (1544-95).
Composed 1903. First performance Monte Carlo,
14 February 1903.*

HARDER, KNUD.   Copenhagen 31 March 1885

1107 Japanisches Fest [scherzo for   12'
orchestra]
2(2nd alt. Picc.),2,2,2-4,2,3,1-Timp.,Perc.-
Hp.-Str.
Ries & Erler, Berlin [n.d.]
Score 26 p.
Composed 1911. First performance Berlin, 1912.

289s Schwarzwälder Zwischenklänge [Black Forest
interludes]
Str.
Süddeutscher Musikverlag, Strassburg, ᶜ1910
Score 15 p.
*Composed 1909. First performance Stuttgart-
Canstatt, 12 June 1909, the composer con-
ducting.*

HARMATI, SANDOR.   Budapest 9 July 1892
                Flemington, New Jersey 4 April 1936

3839 Prelude to a melodrama   14'
2(2nd alt. Picc.),3*,3*,3*-4,2,2-Timp.,Perc.
-Hp.-Str.
Birchard, Boston, ᶜ1934 by The Juilliard
Musical Foundation
Score 55 p.
*A study to a one act play on a Chinese-Cali-
fornian story, composed 1925.*

HARRIS, ARTHUR.   Philadelphia 3 April 1927

7163 Christmas, a medley of well-known carols.
Arranged for orchestra
Includes: Good King Wenceslas - Silent Night -
Joy to the World - First Noël - Deck the
Halls - What Child is This - We Wish You a
Merry Christmas
3*,2,2,2-2,2,2,1-Timp.,Perc.-Hp.-Str.
Continuo Music Press [n.p.] ᶜ1973
Score 59 p.

HARRIS, ROY.
        b. Lincoln County, Oklahoma 12 February 1898

2861 Andante   14'
3*,3*,2,2-4,3,3,1-Timp.,Perc.-Hp.-Str.
Ms.
Score 29 p.
*Composed 1925. First performance Rochester,
23 April 1926, Rochester Philharmonic Orchestra, Howard Hanson conductor.*

1766s Chorale for strings, Op. 3   9'
Str.
Flammer, New York, c1934
Score 18 p.
Composed 1932. First performance Los Angeles,
23 February 1933, Los Angeles Philharmonic
Orchestra, Artur Rodzinski conductor.

4491 Cimarron, symphonic overture [for band]
4*(2Picc.),2*,9*(1Cl. in E-flat;1Alto Cl.),
2-5Sax.-2,3,3Cnt.,3,2Bar.,2Tuba-Timp.,Perc.-Cb.
Mills Music Inc., New York, c1941
Score in reduction 12 p.
Cimarron Territory is now the Oklahoma Pan-
handle. Composed 1941. First performance
Tri-State Festival, Enid, Oklahoma, 18 April
1941, the composer conducting. Dedicated to
the State of Oklahoma.

912m [Concerto, piano, clarinet and string   24'
quartet, Op. 2] Edited by Harry Cumpson
1.Fantasia 2.Vivace 3.Andante 4.Finale
Solo Cl., Solo Pno.-Str.
Cos Cob Press, New York, c1932
Score 57 p.
Composed 1926. First performance Paris, 6 May
1927, Société Musicale Indépendente, Roth
Quartet, Nadia Boulanger pianist.

4944 Evening piece   6'
Solo Vn.-2,1,3*-2,1,1-Str.
Mills Music, Inc., New York, c1941
Score 4 p.
Composed 1941. First performance New York,
9 March 1941.

986m 4 minutes - 20 seconds
Solo Fl.-Str.(without Cb.)
Mills, New York, c1942
Score 10 p.
Composed 1934. First performance Pro Musica
Concert of American Music, Denver, Colorado,
11 June 1935, Nicolas Slonimsky conductor.

4791 Kentucky spring   10'
3(3rd alt. Picc.),3*,3*,3*-4,3,3,1-Timp.,
Perc.-Hp.-Str.
Ms.
Score 84 p. Large folio
Commissioned by the Louisville Orchestra.
Composed 1949. First performance Louisville,
Kentucky, 5 April 1949, Louisville Orchestra,
Robert Whitney conductor.

2002s Prelude and fugue for string   14'
orchestra
Str.
G. Schirmer, New York, c1936
Score 25 p.
Composed 1936. First performance Philadelphia,
28 February 1936, Philadelphia Orchestra, Wer-
ner Janssen, conductor.

HARRISON, AARON.   Taylor, Texas 12 January 1893

5414 The Philippines - Bolero   14'
2,2,3*,3*-4,4,3,1-Timp.,Perc.-Str.

Ms.
Score 61 p. Large folio
Commissioned for the Philippine Army. Com-
posed 1940.

HARRISON, JULIUS ALLEN GREENWAY.
                         Stourport, Worcestershire,
                             England 26 March 1885
                         London 5 April 1963

1785s Autumn landscape, for string   8'
orchestra
Str.
Hawkes, London c1938
Score 12 p.
Composed 1937.

1762s Cornish holiday sketches, for   14'
string orchestra
Theme 1.B & Q 2.Roland 3.J & P 4.Kynance
surf 5.The Lady Angela 6.Saturday night
7.Sunday morning 10/8/1935 8.Grey day reverie
11/8/1935 9.Family squabble 10.The Cardi-
nal's procession, Porthcurno 12/8/1935 11.The
camp fire at night 12.Maggie and the policeman - A Penzance romance (13.)Finale -
Mousehole hornpipe
Str.
Hawkes, London c1938
Score 23 p.
Composed 1935.

3973 Fanfare for a masked ball
4Tpt.-Cym.
Ms.
Score 1 p.
Composed especially for and published in Vol.
I, no. 5 (1 December 1921) of the magazine
Fanfare, a Musical Causerie, edited by Leigh
Henry and published by Goodwin & Tabb, London.

454s Prelude-music, for string orchestra and
piano (or harp)
Pno.(or Hp.)-Str.
Curwen, London c1922
Score 19 p.
Composed 1912.

HARRISON, LOU.   Portland, Oregon 14 May 1917

991m Bomba, for twenty instruments, five
players
1st - 2 Maracas, 3 Flower Pots;
2nd - 2 Metal Rattles, 3 Large Bells;
3rd - 3 Dragon's Mouths, Thundersheet;
4th - Rasp, 3 Chinese Woodblocks;
5th - Low Tam-tam, Bass Drum.
Ms.
Score 6 p.
Composed 1939.

1011m Canticle, for five players
1st - Sistrum, 3 Wood Blocks, 3 High Bells;
2nd - Gourd Rattle, 3 Dragon's Mouths,
       3 Large Glass Bells;
3rd - Wooden Rattle, 3 Clay Bells, 3 Large
       Cow Bells, Morache (Indian Wooden Rasp);
4th - Glass Wind Bells, Triangle, Suspended

Harrison, Lou

Turkish Cym., Large Bell, Tam-tam (very
large), Large Thundersheet;
5th - 3 High Drums, 3 Muted Gongs, 3 Low Drums.
Ms.
Score 8 p.
*Composed 1940. First performance Oakland,
California, 18 July 1940.*

983m Fifth simfony, for four players   *15'*
1st - Small Suspended Cym., Small Gong, Small
Triangle, Small Bell, Small Chinese
Block, Small Rattle, Small Sistrum,
Small Drum, Small Muted Gong, S.Dr;
2nd - Suspended Turkish Cym., High Medium Gong,
Large Triangle, High Medium Bell,
High Tortoise Shell, Low Rattle, Low
Sistrum, High Medium Drum, High Medium
Muted Gong;
3rd - Low Suspended Cym., Low Medium Gong, Low
Medium Bell, Low Tortoise Shell, Low
Medium Drum, Low Medium Muted Gong;
4th - Thundersheet, Low Gong, Low Bell, B.Dr.,
Low Muted Gong.
Ms.
Score 29 p.
*Composed 1939. First performance at the Cor-
nish School, Seattle, Washington, 19 May 1939,
John Cage conductor.*

1009m First concerto, for flute with ostinati
for percussion
1.Earnest and fresh 2.Slow and poignant
3.Strong and swinging
Solo Fl.-Perc.(2 players):1st-Tortoise Shell,
Tin Can Rattle, Rasp, 3 Gongs; 2nd-Inverted
Large Brass Bowl, Large Bell, 3 Drums.
Ms.
Score 7 p.
Composed 1939.

1006m Labrynth no. 3, five movements, for
percussion orchestra [11 players]
1.Ode 2.Passage through dreams 3.Seed
5.Image in the soil (Score does not indicate a
4th movement)
1st - 5 Wood Blocks, 3 Small Bells, Claves,
Sistrum, Triangle;
2nd - 5 Dragon's Mouths, 5 Flower Pots, 5 Cup
Bells, Maracas;
3rd - 5 Porcelain Bowls, 2 Gongs, Sistrum,
Flexatone;
4th - 5 Glasses, Wood Rattle, Rasp, Elephant
Bell;
5th - 5 Cow Bells, 5 Brake Drums, Guiro, Saw;
6th - 3 Muted Gongs, Javanese Button Gong,
Japanese Wind Glasses, Large Thundersheet;
7th - Teponazli, Large Temple Bell, Flexatone;
8th - 5 High Drums, Bongos, Guiro, Water Gong;
9th - Tom Toms, Maracas;
10th - 2 BDr., Tam-tam (very large and deep);
11th - Contrabass Viol, 2 Cym., Saw, Contrabass Dr.
Ms.
Score 84 p.
Composed 1940-41.

338m Suite for solo violin and solo   *16'*
piano with orchestra
1.Overture: Allegro 2.Elegy: Adagio 3.First
gamelan: Allegro 4.Aria: Lento espressivo
5.Second gamelan: Allegro moderato 6.Chorale
Solo Vn.,Solo Pno.-2Fl.,Ob.-Tam-tam-Cel., Tack-
piano,Hp.-2Vc.,Cb.
Associated Music Publishers, New York, c1955
by Lou Harrison
Score 45 p.
*Composed 1951. First performance Carnegie
Hall, New York, 11 January 1952, the composer
conducting, Anahid Ajemian violin, Maro
Ajemian piano.*

2297s Suite for strings
1.Allegro moderato 2.Adagio cantabile 3.
Molto moderato 4.Poco lento, affettuoso
5.Allegro
Str.
Ms.
Score 10 p. Large folio
Composed 1948.

HARSÁNYI, TIBOR.   Magyarkanizsa, Hungary
(now Kanjiza, Yugoslavia) 27 June 1898
Paris 19 September 1954

696p [Concertino, piano and string quartet]
1.Allegro deciso 2.Adagio 3.Presto
Solo Pno.-Str.(without Cb.)
Deiss, Paris, c1932
Score 46 p.
*Composed 1931. First performance Paris, 24
April 1932, Société Musicale Indépendante,
the composer as soloist.*

779p [Concertpiece, piano and orchestra]   *15'*
Solo Pno.-3(3rd alt. Picc.),3*,3*,2-4,2-Timp.,
Perc.-Str.
Senart, Paris, c1931
Miniature score 62 p.

3858 Ouverture symphonique   *7'*
3(3rd alt. Picc.),3*,3(2nd alt. Cl. in E-flat),
3(3rd alt. C.Bn.)-4,3,3,1-Timp.,Perc.-Cel.,Hp.
-Str.
Senart, Paris, c1931
Miniature score 36 p.

5082 [Three pieces for orchestra]
1.Sérénade: Allegro 2.Air: Sostenuto cantabile
3.Danse: Allegro
4*,3*,3*,2-4,3,3,1-Timp.,Perc.-Cel.,
Hp.-Str.
R. Deiss, Paris, c1928
Score 57 p.
*An adaptation from Four Pieces for Piano.
Composed 1926.*

HARTKE, STEPHEN PAUL.   b. Orange, New Jersey
6 July 1952

7219 Symphony no. one   *21'*
1.Maestoso - Allegro vivace - Maestoso 2.Con
brio - Largo - Leggiero
3*(1 Alto Fl.,2nd alt. Picc.),3*,3*,2-2Alto
Sax.-4,4(1Piccolo Tpt.),3,1-Perc.-

Str.
Ms. ^c1976 by Stephen Paul Hartke
Score 74 p. Large folio
*Composed 1974-76. Awarded the Hilda K.
Nitzsche Prize, University of Pennsylvania,
1976.*

HARTLEY, WALTER SINCLAIR.
            b. Washington, D.C. 21 February 1927

5393 Ballet music for orchestra (1949)   *16'*
[Concert version]
1.Prologue: Adagio 2.March: Allegro 3.
Scherzo: Allegro vivace 4.Nocturne: Andante
molto 5.Finale: Allegro molto 6.Epilogue:
Adagio
2(2nd alt. Picc.),2(2nd alt. E.H.),2,2-4,2,3,1
-Timp.,Perc.-Hp.-Str.
Ms.
Score 43 p. Large folio
*Composed 1949. First performance of concert
version Rochester, New York, 7 May 1950,
Eastman-Rochester Symphony Orchestra, Howard
Hanson conductor.*

5544 [Blood wedding, scenes from Lorca's   *15'*
drama, for orchestra]
1.Prelude and lullaby: Lento e sostenuto 2.
Dance: Allegretto (Ritmo de jota) 3.Soliloquy
and celebration: Andante sostenuto, ma con
moto - Allegro moderato (Ritmo de bolero)
2,2(2nd alt. E.H.),2,2-4,2,3,1-Timp.,Perc.
-Hp.-Str.
Ms.
Score 79 p. Large folio
*Originally composed for piano, 1956, for a
stage performance of Federico García Lorca's
play at Longwood College, Farmville, Virginia, March 1956.*

5366 Chamber symphony for woodwind and   *13'30"*
brass quartet, harp and string orchestra
1.Allegro robusto 2.Lento 3.Vivace, con fuoco
1(alt. Picc.),1,1,1-2,1,1-Hp.-Str.
Ms.
Score 88 p. Large folio
*Commissioned by the Koussevitzky Music Founda-
tion, 1954. Composed 1954. First performance Rochester, New York, May 1955, Eastman-
Rochester Symphony Orchestra, Howard Hanson
conductor.*

5320 Concert overture 1954   *7'*
2(2nd alt. Picc.),2,2,2-4,2,3,1-Timp.,Perc.
-Str.
Ms.
Score 48 p. Large folio
*Composed 1954. First performance Washington,
D.C., 30 November 1955, National Symphony
Orchestra, Howard Mitchell conductor. Winner
of the National Symphony Orchestra Prize for
an overture, 25th anniversary contest, 1955.*

5503 Concertino for chamber ensemble,   *14'30"*
1950-52
1.Andante - Allegro 2.Molto lento, liberamente 3.Scherzo: Vivace 4.Chaconne: Andante
molto

Cl.-Tbn.-Perc.-Pno.-4Vn.,4Vc.
Ms.
Score 54 p.
*Composed 1950; revised 1952. First perform-
ance of original version, Rochester, New
York, spring 1951, Eastman School of Music
Student Chamber Group, Donald Johanos con-
ductor.*

357p Concerto for piano and orchestra,   *19'*
1951-1952
1.Allegro con brio 2.Adagio 3.Allegro
grazioso
Solo Pno.-3(3rd alt. Picc.),2,2,2-4,3,3,1-
Timp.,Perc.-Str.
Ms.
Score 68 p. Large folio
*Composed 1951-52. First performance Rochester,
New York, May 1953, Eastman-Rochester Symphony
Orchestra, Howard Hanson conductor, Armand
Basile soloist.*

5738 Concerto for 23 wind instruments   *14'30"*
(1957)
1.Andante - Allegro non troppo 2.Vivace
3.Lento 4.Allegro molto
3(2nd & 3rd alt. Picc.),3(3rd alt. E.H.),3(3rd
alt. B.Cl.),3(3rd alt. C.Bn.)-4,3,3,1
Ms.
Score 66 p. Large folio
*Composed 1957. First performance Rochester,
New York, 3 May 1958, Eastman Symphonic Wind
Ensemble, Frederick Fennell conductor.*

2132s Elegy for strings   *5'*
Str.
Ms. [Interlochen Press, Interlochen, Michigan,
^c1958]
Score 3 p.
Composed 1952.

6552 Elizabethan dances for orchestra   *3'*
(1962)
1.Pavane: Andante 2.Fancy: Allegro con brio
3.Galliard: Vivace
2,2,2,2-2,2,2-Timp.,Perc.(optional,1-2 players)
-Str.
Ms. [Interlochen Press, Interlochen, Michigan,
^c1964]
Score 18 p.
*Originally composed for recorder ensemble,
1962. Transcribed for orchestra, 1962. First
performance Interlochen, Michigan, 24 July
1964, National Music Camp Intermediate Symphony Orchestra, Hermon Dilmore conductor.*

6544 Festive music for orchestra   *4'*
2,2,2,2-4,2,3,1-Timp.,Perc.-Str.
Ms. [Interlochen Press, Interlochen, Michigan,
^c1963]
Score 22 p. Large folio
*Commissioned by the Charleston Symphony Orches-
tra for the West Virginia Centennial program,
1963. Composed 1963. First performance
Charleston, West Virginia, 2 April 1963,
Charleston Symphony Orchestra, Geoffrey Hobday
conductor.*

Hartley, Walter S.

2269s Psalm for strings (1964)   6'
Str.
Ms. c1964 by Walter S. Hartley
Score 6 p.
*Composed 1964. First performance Rochester,
New York, 29 April 1964, Eastman-Rochester Sym-
phony Orchestra, Howard Hanson conductor.*

6677 Sinfonia no. 3 for brass choir   10'30"
(1963)
1.Lento 2.Adagio 3.Allegretto pesante
4Hn.,5Tpt.,3Tbn.,Bar.(or Euph.),Tuba
Tritone Press, Hattiesburg, Mississippi, c1966
by Walter S. Hartley
Score 58 p.
*Composed 1963. First performance Atlanta,
Georgia, 13 November 1964, Georgia State College Brass Ensemble, William Hill conductor.
Chosen as the outstanding work of the Symposium of Contemporary Music for Brass, Atlanta,
1964 (C. G. Conn Corporation Commission Award).*

5360 Sinfonietta for orchestra   12'
1.Allegro 2.Lento 3.Vivace
3(3rd alt. Picc.),2(2nd alt. E.H.),2,2-4,3,3,1
-Timp.,Perc.-Pno.,Hp.-Str.
Ms.
Score 45 p. Large folio
*Composed 1950. First performance Rochester,
New York, May 1951, Eastman-Rochester Sym-
phony Orchestra, Howard Hanson conductor.*

5312 Three patterns for small orchestra   5'
1.Adagio 2.Molto vivace 3.Andante mesto
2(2nd alt. Picc.),2(2nd alt. E.H.),2,2-2,2,1-
Timp.,Perc.-Hp.-Str.
Ms.
Score 7 p.
Composed 1951.

5361 Triptych for orchestra, 1951   15'
1.Adagio 2.Allegro con fuoco 3.Andante
sostenuto, ma con moto
2(2nd alt. Picc.),2,2,2-2,2,1-Timp.,Perc.-Str.
Ms.
Score 46 p. Large folio
*Commissioned by the Eastman School Little Sym-
phony, 1951. Composed 1951. First performance
Rochester, New York, May 1952, Eastman School
Little Symphony, Frederick Fennell conductor.*

HARTMANN, ARTHUR MARTINUS.
                    Maté Szalka, Hungary 23 July 1881
                    New York 30 March 1956

504m A Negro croon, arranged for French horn
solo and orchestra by William F. Happich
Solo Hn.-2,2,2,2-2Hn.-Hp.-Str.
Ms.
Score 9 p.
*Originally composed for violin and piano; this
arrangement 1920.*

HARTMANN, EMIL.   Copenhagen 21 February 1836
                         Copenhagen 18 July 1898

Born: Wilhelm Emilius Zinn Hartmann

408s [Berceuse, for string orchestra and harp
ad lib.]
Hp.(ad lib.)-Str.
Wilhelm Hansen, Copenhagen [n.d.]
Score 8 p.

1025v [Concerto, violin, Op. 19, G minor]
Allegro - Andante - Allegro molto vivace
Solo Vn.-2,2,2,2-2Tpt.-Timp.-Str.
Ms.
Score 51 p.

549c [Concerto, violoncello, Op. 26, D minor]
1.Allegro moderato 2.Canzonetta: Andante
3.Rondo pastorale: Allegretto
Solo Vc.-2,2,2,2-2-Timp.,Trgl.-Str.
Kistner, Leipzig [n.d.]
Score 76 p.

6591 [Nordic folk dances. No. 1, Scherzo,
Op. 18]
2,2,2,2-4,2,1-Timp.-Str.
Carl Simon, Berlin [1878]
Score 27 p.

6592 [Nordic folk dances. No. 2, Old
remembrances (Minuet), Op. 6a]
2,2,2,2-2,2,3-Timp.-Str.
Carl Simon, Berlin [1878]
Score 22 p.

6687 [Nordic folk dances. No. 3, The elf-
maidens and the huntsmen (Scherzo), Op. 6b]
3*(Picc. ad lib.),2,2,2-4,2,1-Timp.,Trgl.-Str.
Carl Simon, Berlin [1878]
Score 25 p.

6799 [Nordic folk dances. No. 4, Wedding
music, Op. 2]
3*(Picc. ad lib.),2,2,2-4(3rd & 4th ad lib.),
2,3,1(ad lib.)-Timp.,S.Dr.,B.Dr.-Str.
Carl Simon, Berlin [1878]
Score 29 p.

6800 [Nordic folk dances. No. 5, Spring dance,
Op. 3]
3*(Picc. ad lib.),2,2,2-4(3rd & 4th ad lib.),
2,2Cnt.(ad lib.),3,1(ad lib.)-Timp.,Perc.
-Str.
Carl Simon, Berlin [1878]
Score 25 p.

961 Runenzauber [Magic runes] Ouverture
2,2,2,2-4,2,3,1-Timp.-Hp.(ad lib.)-Str.
J. Schuberth & Co., Leipzig, c1896
Score 48 p.
*From the opera in one act with librettos by
E. Klingenfeld (German) and J. Lehmann (Danish),
based on Henrik Hertz's play Svend Dyrings Hus,
after a folktale. First performance in German
under the title Runenzauber, Hamburg, 15 October 1896. First performance in Danish, under
the title Ragnhild, Copenhagen, 27 December
1896.*

326s [Runenzauber. Mimic scene, for string
quintet]
Str.

Schuberth, Leipzig [n.d.]
Score 3 p.

2340 Serenade, Op. 43, B-flat major 25'
1.Andante 2.Scherzo: Allegro vivace con fuoco
3.Intermezzo: Andante 4.Finale: Andante –
Rondo: Allegro moderato
1,1,2,2-2Hn.-Vc.,Cb.
Ries & Erler, Berlin [n.d.]
Score 56 p.
*Composed 1888. First performance 1890, the
composer conducting.*

HARTMANN, THOMAS DE.
Khoruzhevka, Ukraine 21 September 1885
Princeton, New Jersey 26 March 1956

5509 [Esther, Op. 76. Four dances from 13'
Act III of the opera-oratorio]
1.Scythe (Arabesques de mouvements masculins):
Allegro feroce 2.Héllenique (Guirlandes de
jeunes filles en marche): Allegretto 3.Assy-
rienne (La jeune fille): Larghetto 4.Danse
parthe: Lento
3(3rd alt. Picc.),2(2nd alt. E.H.),2,2-4,3,3,
1-Timp.,Perc.-Pno.,Cel.,Hp.-Str.
Ms. C[n.d.] by Thomas de Hartmann
Score 35 p.
*From the opera-oratorio after Jean Racine's
play. Composed 1941. First performance of
these dances Chicago, June 1951, Nikolay
Malko conductor.*

6095 [Symphony no. 2, The legend of the 32'
sun, Op. 68]
Largo – Allegro molto – Andante con moto –
Larghetto – Allegro giocoso – Vivace con brio –
Moderato – Larghetto – Andante maestoso
3(2nd & 3rd alt. Picc.),3*,3(3rd alt. B.Cl.),
3*-4,3,3,1-Timp.,Perc.-Pno,Org.
(ad lib.),Cel.,2Hp.-Str.
Ms.
Score 117 p.
*Composed 1944. Written in memory of M. P.
Belaieff.*

5508 [Twelve Russian fairy tales, Op. 58] 18'
Introduction: Andante con moto 1.Verlióka
the monster: Lento 2.The little peasant: Lento assai – Scherzando 3.Ivan Tzarevitch: Largo cantabile 4.The witches' house: Misterioso
5.The wonderful Goussli: Largo 6.Baba-Yaga:
Moderato 7.Alenouchka's lullaby: Larghetto
8.The seven league boots: Con moto 9.The
princess: Larghetto 10.Katschei the dead:
Lento 11.The ride: Presto 12.The kingdom of
wonders: Solemne
3*,2(2nd alt. E.H.),2,2*-4,2,3,1-Timp.,Perc.
-Pno.,Org.,Hp.-Str.
Ms.
Score 59 p. Large folio
*Originally composed for piano, 1936; orches-
trated, 1938. First performance of this version Houston, Texas, 5 April 1956, Houston
Symphony Orchestra, Leopold Stokowski conductor.*

HARTOG, EDOUARD DE. Amsterdam 15 August 1829
The Hague 8 November 1909

4701 [Fairy tale, a character sketch for
orchestra, Op. 62]
2,2,2,2-4,2,3-Timp.-Str.
Schott Frères, Brussels [188-?]
Score 27 p.

4279 [Rigaudon for chamber orchestra, Op. 73]
2,2,2,2-2Hn.-Trgl.-Str.
Steyl & Thomas, Frankfurt [188-?]
Score 19 p.
*Inspired by the Provençal dance of the 17th
century.*

HARTOG, HENRI.

618s Bonheur, gavotte-serenade
Str.(without Cb.)
Schott, Mainz [n.d.]
Score 5 p.

738s Un petit rien
Str.(without Cb.)
Schott, Mainz [n.d.]
Score 3 p.

HARTY, HAMILTON. Hillsborough, County Down,
Ireland 4 December 1879
Brighton, England 19 February 1941

3294 The children of Lir, poem for 30'
orchestra
3(3rd alt. Picc.),3*,3*,3*-4,3,3,1-Timp.,Perc.-
Hp.-Sop. Voice-Str.
Universal Edition, London, C1939
Score 127 p.
*First performance London, 1 March 1939, the
BBC Orchestra, the composer conducting.*

5068 A comedy overture for orchestra, 10'
Op. 15
2(2nd alt. Picc.),2(2nd alt. E.H.),2,2-4,2,3,
1-Timp.,Trgl.-Str.
B. Schott's Söhne, Mainz, C1909
Score 51 p.
*Composed 1907. First performance Queen's
Hall Promenades, London, 1907.*

3662 Fanfare 45"
4Tpt.-Side Dr.
Ms.
Score 1 p.

952m In Ireland, fantasy for flute, harp 7'
and orchestra
Solo Fl., Solo Hp.-1,2*,2,1-2Hn.-Timp.,Perc.-
Str.
Ms.
Score 57 p.

2032 An Irish symphony (revised version) 36'
1.On the shores of Lough Neagh 2.The fair day
3.In the Antrim Hills 4.The 12th of July
3(3rd alt. Picc.),3*,2,2-4,2,3,1-Timp.,Perc.-
Hp.-Str.
Boosey, London, C1927

Harty, Hamilton

Score 132 p.
*Composed 1906; revised 1924 and first per-
formed at the Hallé Concerts, same year, the
composer conducting.*

3322 A John Field suite [Transcribed by   *18'*
Hamilton Harty]
1.Polka 2.Nocturne 3.Slow waltz (Remembrance)
4.Rondo (Midi)
1(alt. Picc.),1,1,1-Hn.,Tpt.-Timp.,Perc.-Hp.-
Str.
Universal Edition, London, ᶜ1939
Score 76 p.

453s The Londonderry air. Arranged for string
orchestra and harp by Hamilton Harty
Solo Vn.-Hp.-Str.
Curwen, London, ᶜ1924 by Hamilton Harty
Score 6 p.

1637 With the wild geese, poem for   *18'*
orchestra
3(3rd alt. Picc.)3*,3*,2-4,2,3,1-Timp.,Perc.-
Hp.-Str.
Novello, London, ᶜ1912
Score 75 p.
*Composed 1911. First performance at the Car-
diff Festival same year, the composer conducting. Based on Emily Lawless' epic poem of
the same name.*

HASSE, JOHANN ADOLF.   Bergedorf near Hamburg
                         baptized 25 March 1699
                         Venice 16 December 1783

684m [Concerto, flute and string   *11'*
orchestra, B minor]
1.Allegro non molto 2.Largo e moderato
3.Allegro
Solo Fl.-2Cemb.-Str.
Breitkopf & Härtel, Leipzig [n.d.]
Score 29 p.

15s [Euristeo. Overture. Arranged by Arnold
Schering]
Pno.-Str.
Kahnt, Leipzig, ᶜ1921
Score 9 p.

6912 [Sinfonia a 5, G major] Edited by Herbert
Kölbel
1.(Allegro) 2.Siciliano 3.Menuett 4.Polo-
naise 5.Plaisanterie
2Fl.-Cemb.-Str.(without Va.)
Hug, Zürich, ᶜ1966
Score 24 p.

HASSE, KARL.   Dohna, near Dresden 20 March 1883
                  Dresden 31 July 1960

580s [Serenade for string orchestra,   *25'*
Op. 5, C minor]
1.Allegro moderato 2.Adagio 3.Fuga: Allegro
moderato e grazioso
Str.
Rieter-Biedermann, Leipzig, ᶜ1909
Score 34 p.

HASSELMANS, LOUIS.   Paris 25 July 1878
             San Juan, Puerto Rico 27 December 1957

1035s Petite valse, Op. 13
Str.
Decourcelle, Nice [n.d.]
Score 7 p.

HÄSSLER, LOUIS.

813m [Concerto, tuba (or contrabass, bassoon or
trombone) Op. 14]
Allegro moderato - Andante - Rondo: Allegretto
Solo Tuba-2,2,2,2-2,4,3-Timp.-Str.
Score: Ms. 74 p.
Parts: Oertel, Hannover [n.d.]

HATIKVAH (national anthem of Israel)

4560 Israeli national anthem. Arranged for
orchestra by Julius Chajes
2,2,2,2-4,2,3-Timp.,B.Dr.-Str.
Ms. ᶜ1949 by Julius Chajes
Score 4 p.
*Arranged 1949. First performance New York,
4 May 1949, New York Philharmonic, Izler
Solomon conductor. Dedicated to Chaim Weizman,
first president of the State of Israel.*

HAUBIEL, CHARLES.   Delta, Ohio 30 January 1892

4480 1865 A.D., for symphony orchestra   *14'*
[Mississippi story, 1st version]
The plantation - In the cotton fields - In the
church - Battlefield - Vision - Home again -
Gay time in the home town
3(3rd alt. Picc.),3*,2-4,3,3,1-Timp.,Perc.
-Hp.-Str.
Ms.
Score 66 p.
*Originally composed for solo piano, 1939.
Expanded orchestral version 1943; first per-
formance under the title Mississippi Story,
Los Angeles, 24 April 1959, Highland Park
Symphony Orchestra, William Van Den Burg con-
ductor. Two later versions date from 1958
and 1962.*

384v Gothic variations for violin and   *17'*
orchestra
Solo Vn.-2(2nd alt. Picc.),2,2,2-2,2,2-Timp.,
Perc.-Hp.-Str.
Ms. [ᶜ1944 by the Composers Press, New York]
Score 79 p. Large folio
*Originally written for solo violin and piano,
1919; orchestral version, 1968. First per-
formance Wilshire Ebell Theater, Los Angeles,
9 June 1970, West Side Symphony Orchestra,
Bogidar Avramov conductor, Michael Foxman
soloist.*

6684 Heroic elegy for symphony orchestra   *12'*
3(3rd alt. Picc.),3*,3*,2-4,3,3,1-Timp.,Perc.
-Hp.-Str.
Ms. ᶜ1965 by Charles Haubiel
Score 43 p.
*Commissioned by Fabien Sevitzky. Composed
1965. First performance Warren Auditoriur,*

Downey, California, 21 February 1970, Louis S. Palange conductor.

2715 Karma, symphonic variations on a   30'
theme by Handel, in four cycles
1.The soul ascending 2.Toward the abyss
3.Resurrection 4.In retrospect
4*,3*,3*,3*-4,3,3,1-Timp.,Perc.-Pno.,Cel.-2Hp.-Str.
Ms.
Score 163 p.
Originally composed for piano, orchestrated 1928 and revised 1933. Awarded first American prize in the International Schubert Centennial Contest, 1928.

2900 Mars ascending   10'
3(3rd alt. Picc.),3*,3*,3*-4,4,3,1-Timp.,Perc.-Cel.,2Hp.-Str.
Ms.
Score 62 p.
Originally composed for piano, 1917; orchestrated 1923. Won honorable mention in the Paderewski Fund Prize Competition, 1934.

3326 Miniatures [for orchestra]   10'
1.A mystery 2.Madonna 3.Gayety 4.Shadows
5.Snow flakes 6.Festival
4*,3,3,2-4,3,4,1-Timp.,Perc.-Cel.,Hp.(or Pno.)-Str.
Ms.
Score 55 p.
Originally composed for piano 1937; this orchestration 1939.

1778s Miniatures, for string orchestra   10'
1.A mystery 2.Madonna 3.Gaiety 4.Shadows
5.Snowflakes 6.Festival
Str.
Composers Press, New York, c1939
Score 20 p.
First performance Brooklyn Museum, New York City, 23 April 1939, Federal Civic Orchestra of New York City of the WPA, Edgar Schenkman conductor.

1041m Nuances, suite for flute and strings   9'
1.Still: Lento ma non troppo 2.Fear: Molto allegro 3.Gentle: Andantino dolce 4.Plaintive: Lento e doloroso 5.Jocose: Allegrissimo
Solo Fl.-Str.
Ms. c1943 by The Composers Press, New York
Score 13 p. Large folio
Originally composed for solo flute and piano, 1938; for flute and strings, 1943. First performance of this version Eastman School of Music, Rochester, New York, 24 October 1945, Eastman-Rochester Symphony Orchestra, Howard Hanson conductor, Joseph Mariano soloist.

Passacaglia triptych
3650 No. 1. Chorale prelude   11'
3651 No. 2. Air and variations   17'
3652 No. 3. Fugue   10'
4*,4*,4*,3*-4,3,3,1-Timp.,Perc.-Cel.,Hp.-Str.
Ms.
Scores: 49 p., 74 p., 64 p.
No. 2 does not require celeste.

6824 Pioneers, symphonic saga   17'30"
1.Introduction - The watch of those who have gone before (The mound builders) 2.The Conestoga 3.Scalp dance 4.Father Marquette (The first missionary to Ohio) 5.The peace pipe 6. The first harvest 7.Barn dance 8. The lover's tryst - Interlude 9.Chorale
3(3rd alt. Picc.),3*,2,2-4,3,3,1-Timp.,Perc.-Hp.-Str.
Ms.
Score 122 p. Large folio
Movements 2 through 9 are based on American Indian and folk motives. Composed 1947. First performance Franklin High School Auditorium, Los Angeles, 19 February 1960, Highland Park Symphony Orchestra, Leon Arnaud conductor.

3192 Rittrati (Portraits)   16'
1.Capriccio 2.Idillio 3.Scherzo
4*,3*,3*,3*-4,2,3,1-Timp.,Perc.-Hp.-Str.
Ms.
Score 125 p.
Originally composed for piano, 1919; orchestrated 1934. Awarded second prize Swift & Co. Symphony Prize Competition, 1934. First performance Chicago, 12 December 1935, Chicago Symphony Orchestra, Frederick Stock conductor.

Solari, symphonic suite in 3 parts
3544 Part I. Dawn mists   9'
3545 Part II. Meridian (Toccata - fugue)   11'
3546 Part III. The plane beyond   15'
(Passacaglia)
4*,4*,4*,3*-4,3,3,1-Timp.,Perc.-Cel.,Hp.-Str.
Ms.
Scores: 43 p., 59 p. Large folio, 50 p.
Celeste not required in Part II. Originally composed for piano; orchestration completed 1936.

2690 Suite passecaille   23'
1.Allemande 2.Menuet 3.Sarabande (In the Phrygian mode) 4.Gavotte
Solo Str. Quartet-1,1,1,1-2,1,1-Timp.,Perc.-Pno.-Str.
Ms.
Score 89 p.
Originally composed for piano 1916; orchestrated 1930. First performance Los Angeles, 31 January 1936, Los Angeles Federal Symphony Orchestra of the WPA, Modest Altschuler conductor.

3174 Symphony no. 1, in form of   22'
variations
4*,3*,3*,3*-4,2,3,1-Timp.,Perc.-Str.
Ms.
Score 121 p. Large folio
Composed 1937.

2663 Vox cathedralis, chorale variations   16'
and fugue in classic style
3*,3*,3*,3*-4,4,3-Timp.-Org.(ad lib.)-Str.
Ms.
Score 56 p.
Originally composed for organ; transcribed for orchestra 1934. First performance New York,

Hauck, Emile

6 May 1938, Greenwich Symphony Orchestra of the WPA, Eugene Plotnikoff conductor.

HAUCK, EMILE.

1656s Imploration, melody for violin and string orchestra
Solo Vn.-Str.
Score: Ms. 2 p.
Parts: Delrieu, Paris [n.d.]

HAUER, JOSEF MATTHIAS.
Wiener-Neustadt, near Vienna 19 March 1883
Vienna 22 September 1959

4522 [Sinfonietta in three movements,   *25'*
Op. 50]
1.Langsam 2.Ländler 3.Die Viertel im Schritt
2*,2*,2*,2*-2,2-Timp.,Perc.-Pno.-
Str.
Universal Edition, Leipzig, c1929
Score 124 p.
Composed 1927.

4703 [Suite no. 7 for orchestra, Op. 48]   *17'*
1.Molto ritmico e marcato, alla marcia 2.
Lento, molto tranquillo 3.Allegro, alla marcia
veloce 4.Largo espressivo 5.Ländler
1,1,2*,1-2,1-Timp.,Perc.-Pno.-Str.
Universal Edition, Leipzig, c1927
Score 89 p.
Composed 1926.

HAUFRECHT, HERBERT. New York City 3 November 1909

3754 Overture for an American mural   *11'*
3*,2,3*,2-4,3,3,1-Timp.,Perc.-Pno.(ad lib.)-
Str.
Ms.
Score 34 p. Large folio
Composed for dedication ceremonies of the murals at Station WNYC. First performance under the title, Overture for an Abstract Mural, in a broadcast by the WNYC Concert Orchestra, 2 August 1939, the composer conducting.

7078 Prelude to a tragedy, an epic for   *7'*
band
3(3rd alt. Picc.),2,7(Cl. in E-flat, 3Cl. in
B-flat, Alto Cl.,B.Cl.,Cb.Cl.),2-4,3,3,Bar.,1-
Timp.,Perc.-Cb.
Murbo Music Publishing, New York,c1969
Score 32 p.
Inspired by Stephen Vincent Benet's poem, John Brown's Body. Composed 1967-68. First performance Mannes College of Music, New York, 1968, Mannes College Wind Ensemble, Simon Karasick conductor.

1910s Square set for string orchestra   *10'*
1.Reel 2.Clog dance 3.Jig tune
Str.
Broadcast Music, New York, c1942
Score 24 p.

1743s Suite for string orchestra   *18'*
1.Marcia 2.Arietta 3.Scherzino 4.Corteggio
5.Moto perpetuo (Fuga)

Pno.(ad lib.)-Str.
Ms.
Score 35 p.
Composed 1934. First performance New York, 27 April 1934, the Juilliard Graduate School String Orchestra, Edgar Schenkman conductor.

3221 Three fantastic marches   *7'30"*
1.Poco sostenuto 2.Andantino 3.Allegro
marcato
2(2nd alt. Picc.),2,2,2-2,1,1-Timp.,Perc.-Str.
Ms.
Score 33 p.
Composed 1939.

HAUSEGGER, SIEGMUND VON.
Graz, Austria 16 August 1872
Munich 10 October 1948

1638 Aufklänge [Symphonic variations on a   *30'*
children's song]
3*,3*,3*,3*-6,3-Timp.,Perc.-Cel.,2Hp.-Str.
Ries & Erler, Berlin, c1919
Score 124 p.
Composed 1917. First performance at the Allgemeiner Deutscher Musikverein Berlin festival, 1918, Philharmonic Orchestra, the composer conducting.

2192 Barbarossa, symphonic poem in three   *50'*
movements
1.The people's distress 2.The magic mountain
3.The awakening
3*,3*,3*,3-4,4,3,1-Timp.,Perc.-2Hp.-Str.
Ries & Erler, Berlin, c1901
Score 185 p.
Composed 1899. First performance Munich, 1900, Kaim Orchestra, the composer conducting.

2084 Dionysische Phantasie [symphonic   *18'*
poem]
4*,4*,4*,3(3rd alt. C.Bn.)-4,4,3,1-Timp.,
Perc.-2Hp.-Str.
Ries & Erler, Berlin, c1902
Score 102 p.
First performance Munich, February 1899, Kaim Orchestra, the composer conducting.

HAUSER, MISKA.   Pressburg
(now Bratislava, Czechoslovakia) 1822
Vienna 8 December 1887

1012v [Concerto, violin, no. 1, Op. 49, E minor]
In one movement
Solo Vn.-2,2,2,2-2,2,1-Timp.-Str.
Score: Ms. 119 p.
Parts: Siegel, Leipzig [n.d.]

476v [Hungarian rhapsody, violin and orchestra,
Op. 43]
Solo Vn.-2,0,2,2-2Hn.-Str.
Peters, Leipzig [n.d.]
Score in reduction 11 p.

HAUSSERMANN, JOHN, JR.   Manila 21 August 1909

3149 The after-Christmas suite, six   *22'*
sketches for orchestra, Op. 10
1.March of the toys 2.Song of the broken doll

3.A page of a story book 4.Serenade of the lost teddy bear 5.The music box that could not play 6.Epilogue
2(2nd alt. Picc.),2(2nd alt. E.H.),2,2-2,2,2-Timp.,Perc.-Pno.,Cel.,Hp.-Str.
Boosey, Hawkes, Belwin, New York [n.d.]
Score 63 p.
Composed 1933-34. First performance Cincinnati, 22 March 1938, Cincinnati Symphony Orchestra, Eugene Goossens conductor.

3175 Nocturne and danse for orchestra,   19'
Op. 8
2*,2,2,2-3,2,2,1-Timp.,Perc.-Cel.,Hp.-Str.
Boosey, Hawkes, Belwin, New York [n.d.]
Score 45 p.
Composed 1933. First performance Manila, 23 January 1934, Manila Symphony Orchestra, Alexander Lippay conductor.

3306 Symphony no. 1, Op. 16   35'
1.Allegro moderato 2.Scherzo (Vivace) 3.Lento e lamentoso 4.Allegro
2(2nd alt. Picc.),2(2nd alt. E.H.),2,2-4,2,3,1-Timp.,Perc.-Str.
Ms.
Score 176 p.
Composed 1938. First performance Cincinnati, 21 February 1941, Cincinnati Symphony Orchestra, Eugene Goossens conductor.

HAVE, WILLEM TEN.

1014v [Allegro brillant for violin and string orchestra, Op. 19]
Solo Vn.-Str.
Ms.
Score 12 p.

HAYDN, JOSEPH. Rohrau, Lower Austria 31 March 1732
                Vienna 31 May 1809

Full name: Franz Joseph (or Josef) Haydn

5998 [Acis and Galatea. Sinfonia. Ho.   7'30"
Ia: 5] Edited by H.C. Robbins Landon
1.Allegro molto 2.Andante grazioso 3.Finale: Presto
2Ob.(or 2Fl.),Bn.-2Hn.-Cemb.-Str.
Doblinger, Vienna, c1959
Score 20 p.
From the opera seria or festa teatrale with libretto by Giovanni Battista Migliavacca, composed for the wedding of Anton Esterhazy, son of Haydn's employer Prince Nicolaus I, and Marie Therese, daughter of Count Nicolaus Erdödy. First performance Eisenstadt, Hungary, 11 January 1763, the composer conducting. First modern performance in the courtyard of Haydn's house in Vienna, 31 May 1959, Kammerorchester der Wiener Konzerthausgesellschaft, Paul Angerer conductor.

863s [Adagio, violoncello and string orchestra, G major] Edited by Paul Bazelaire
Solo Vc.-Str.
Senart, Paris, c1922
Score 4 p.
Not traceable in Hoboken thematic catalog.

3683 [L'anima del filosofo. The thunderstorm. Ho. XXVIII: 13] Edited by Karl Geiringer
2,2,0,2-2,2,2-Timp.-Str.
Ms.
Score 35 p.
From the opera composed 1791; also called Orfeo ed Euridice.

5997 [The apothecary. Sinfonia. Ho.   7'
Ia: 10] Edited by H.C. Robbins Landon
1.Presto 2.Andante 3.Presto
1,2,0,1-2Hn.-Cemb.-Str.
Doblinger, Vienna, c1959
Score 24 p.
From the opera in three acts with libretto by Carlo Goldoni, based on his play. First performance Esterháza, Hungary, autumn 1768, the composer conducting. First modern performance Berlin, 22 March 1959, Hans von Benda conductor.

1838 [Armida. Overture. Ho. Ia: 14]   5'
1.Vivace, attacca 2.Andante, attacca 3.Vivace
1,2,0,2-2Hn.-Str.
Score: Ms. 36 p.
Parts: Breitkopf & Härtel, Leipzig [n.d.]
From the opera composed 1783. First performance Esterháza, 26 February 1784, the composer conducting. Parts in this edition erroneously titled Symphonie B-dur, Nr. 77.

6036 [Cassation, 4 horns, violin, viola and bass, D major. Hoboken deest] Edited by H.C. Robbins Landon
1.Allegro moderato 2.Menuet 3.Adagio 4.Menuet - Trio 5.Finale: Allegro
4Hn.-Str.(without Vn.II)
Doblinger, Vienna, c1960
Score 16 p.
Not in Hoboken thematic catalog, but undoubtedly genuine. Composed ca.1761-65.

Haydn, Joseph

670p [Concerto, clavier, F major. Ho.   *12'*
XVIII: F1] Edited by Gustav Lenzewski, Sr.
1.Allegro moderato 2.Andante 3.Presto
Solo Cemb.-2F1.-Str.
Chr. Friedrich Vieweg, Berlin [c1927]
Score 39 p.
Composed between 1763 and 1774.

331p [Concerto, clavier and orchestra,   *20'*
G major. Ho. XVIII: 4] Edited by Bruno Hinze-
Reinhold
1.Allegro moderato 2.Adagio cantabile 3.
Rondo: Presto
Solo Pno.(or Solo Cemb.)-2Ob.-2Hn.-Str.
Edition Peters, Leipzig, c1958
Score 44 p.
Composed before 1782, perhaps in the early
1770s. First published by Boyer, Paris, 1784,
in the version revised by Haydn for the
Viennese pianist Maria Theresia Paradis, who
performed it at the Concerts Spirituel, Paris,
April 1784.

312p [Concerto, clavier, 2 violins and contra-
bass, F major. Ho. XVIII: 7] Edited by Klaas
Weelinck
1.Moderato 2.Adagio 3.Allegro
Solo Cemb.(or Solo Pno.)-Str.(Va. ad lib.)
Edition KaWe, Amsterdam, 1962
Score 14 p.
Composed before 1766. Originally published
by G. Gardom, London, 1772. The work also
exists as a piano trio, Hoboken catalog no.
XV: 40, which has a different middle movement.

942m [Concerto, horn, D major. Ho. VIId: *16'*
4] Edited by Karl Geiringer
1.Allegro moderato 2.Adagio 3.Allegro
Solo Hn.-Str.
Ms.
Score 40 p.

343m [Concerto, 2 liras, 2 horns and   *15'30"*
strings, no. 1, C major. Ho. VIIh: 1] Edited
by H.C. Robbins Landon
1.Allegro con spirito 2.Andante 3.Finale:
Allegro con brio - Adagio - Tempo I^mo
Solo Lira I, Solo Lira II(or Solo Fl.I, Solo
Fl.II)-2Hn.-Str.(Vn.I,Vn.II,Va.I,Va.II,Vc.,Cb.)
Doblinger, Vienna, c1960
Score 40 p.
The lira organizzata is similar to the hurdy-
gurdy. Commissioned by the Austrian minister
to Naples, Norbert Hadrava, for King Ferdi-
nand IV of Naples and the Two Sicilies. Com-
posed 1786. First performance Naples, 1786,
Hadrava and Ferdinand IV soloists.

342m [Concerto, 2 liras, 2 horns and   *14'*
strings, no. 2, G major. Ho. VIIh: 2] Edited
by H.C. Robbins Landon
1.Vivace assai 2.Adagio ma non troppo
3.Rondo: Presto
Solo Lira I, Solo Lira II(or Solo Fl., Solo
Ob.)-2Hn.-Str.
Doblinger, Vienna, c1960
Score 44 p.

978m [Concerto, 2 liras, 2 horns and   *14'*
strings, no. 3, G major. Ho. VIIh: 3. Movement
1] Edited by Karl Geiringer with revisions by
Arthur Cohn
1.Allegro con spirito
Solo Lira I(Fl. & Ob. may substitute)-Fl.,Ob.-
2Hn.-Str.
Ms.
Score 39 p.

341m [Concerto, 2 liras, 2 horns and   *14'*
strings, no. 3, G major. Ho. VIIh: 3] Edited
by H.C. Robbins Landon
1.Allegro con spirito 2.Romance: Allegretto
3.Finale: Allegro [Haydn: Tempo di menuetto]
Solo Lira I,Solo Lira II(or Solo Fl.,Solo Ob.)
-2Hn.-Str.
Doblinger, Vienna, c1960
Score 40 p.
Haydn used the middle movement of this con-
certo in his Military Symphony, Ho. no. I: 100.

340m [Concerto, 2 liras, 2 horns and   *16'*
strings, no. 4, F major. Ho. VIIh: 4] Edited
by H.C. Robbins Landon
1.Allegro 2.Andante 3.Finale: Presto
Solo Lira I,Solo Lira II(or Solo Fl.,Solo Ob.)
-2Hn.-Str.
Doblinger, Vienna, c1959
Score 52 p.

339m [Concerto, 2 liras, 2 horns and   *12'30"*
strings, no. 5, F major. Ho. VIIh: 5] Edited
by H.C. Robbins Landon
1.[Allegro] 2.Andante 3.Finale: [Vivace]
Solo Lira I,Solo Lira II(or Solo Fl.,Solo Ob.)
-2Hn.-Str.
Doblinger, Vienna, c1960
Score 32 p.
Haydn used the second and third movements of
this concerto in his symphony, Ho. no. I: 89.

448m [Concerto, oboe and orchestra,   *22'*
C major. Ho. VIIg: C1] Edited by Alexander
Wunderer
1.Allegro spiritoso 2.Andante 3.Rondo:
Allegretto
Solo Ob.-2Ob.-2,2,-Timp.-Str.
Breitkopf & Härtel, Wiesbaden, 1954
Score 59 p.
Probably not composed by Haydn.

671p [Concerto, piano, D major.   *20'*
Ho. XVIII: 11]
1.Vivace 2.Un poco adagio 3.Rondo all'
ungherese: Allegro assai
Solo Pno.-2Ob.-2Hn.-Str.
Kalmus, New York [n.d.]
Score 44 p.
Composed before 1782.

1024m [Concerto, trumpet and   *ca.15'*
orchestra, E-flat major. Ho. VIIe: 1] Solo
transcribed for modern trumpet by A. Goeyens
1.Allegro 2.Andante 3.Finale: Allegro
Solo Tpt.-1,2,0,2-2,2-Timp.-Str.
Score: Ms. 107 p.
Parts: Albert J. Andraud Wind Instrument Music

Library, Cincinnati, ^c1944
Composed 1796 and dedicated to Antoine Wei-
dinger, inventor of the keyed trumpet.

156m [Same as above] Kalmus, New York [n.d.]
Score 35 p.

512v [Concerto, violin, C major. Ho. VIIa: *15'*
1] Edited by H.C. Robbins Landon
1.Allegro moderato 2.Adagio 3.Finale: Presto
Solo Vn.-Cemb.-Str.
Eulenburg, London [^c1952]
Score 63 p.
Composed before 1765. First performance
Eisenstadt, the composer conducting, Tomasini
soloist.

513v [Concerto, violin, G major. Ho. VIIa: *20'*
4]
1.Allegro moderato 2.Adagio 3.Allegro
Solo Vn.-Cemb.-Str.
Breitkopf & Härtel, Leipzig, ^c1909
Score 27 p.
Listed in The Breitkopf Thematic Catalog,
Supplement IV, Leipzig, 1769.

514v [Concerto, violin, B-flat major. *23'*
Ho. VIIa: B2]
1.Allegro con giusto 2.Adagio 3.Tempo di
menuetto
Solo Vn.-Cemb.-Str.
Breitkopf & Härtel, Leipzig, ^c1915
Score 28 p.
Listed in The Breitkopf Thematic Catalog,
Supplement II, Leipzig, 1767, as a concerto
by Christian Cannabich.

463m [Concerto, violin, clavier and *21'30"*
strings, F major. Ho. XVIII: 6] Score edited
by Paul Bormann [Parts edited by Helmut
Schultz]
1.Allegro moderato 2.Largo 3.Allegro
Solo Vn., Solo Pno.(or Solo Cemb.)-Str.
Score: Hawkes & Son, London, ^c1954. 38 p.
Parts: Musikwissenschaftlicher Verlag,
Leipzig [1937]
Composed before 1766.

482c [Concerto, violoncello and orchestra, *27'*
D major. Ho. VIIb: 2] Edited, cadenzas sup-
plied and woodwind parts added by F.A. Gevaert
1.Allegro moderato 2.Adagio 3.Allegro
[Haydn: Rondo. Allegro]
Solo Vc.-2,2,2,2-2Hn.-Str.
Breitkopf & Härtel, Leipzig [1893]
Score 41 p.
Composed 1783. First performance at one of
the Esterházy estates, probably 1783, the
composer conducting, Anton Kraft soloist.

408c [Concerto, violoncello and orchestra, *27'*
D major. Ho. VIIb: 2] Cadenzas supplied by
F.A. Gevaert and Gerhard Silwedel. Edited by
François Auguste Gevaert, revised by Heinz
Reinhart Zilcher
1.Allegro moderato 2.Adagio 3.Rondo: Allegro
Solo Vc.-2Ob.-2Hn.-Str.

Breitkopf & Härtel, Leipzig, ^c1956
Score 31 p.

503c [Concerto, violoncello, C major. *17'*
Ho. VIIb: 5. Developed by David Popper]
1.Allegro moderato 2.Andante 3.Allegretto
vivace
Solo Vc.-2,2,2,2-2Hn.-Str.
Ries & Erler, Berlin, ^c1899
Score 34 p.
Sketched by Haydn, ca.1769. Orchestrated by
Popper, 1898. Haydn's original sketch is now
lost.

Derbyshire marches
See: [Marches, military band. Ho. VIII:
1,2,3] Nos. 1 & 2
and
[Marches, wind ensemble. Ho. VIII:
1 and 2]

3963 [Divertimento, G major, Ho. X: 12. Transcribed for flute, 2 horns and string orchestra by Karl Geiringer]
1.Moderato 2.Adagio 3.Presto
Fl.-2Hn.-Str.
Ms.
Score 12 p.
Original instrumentation uncertain; may have
included baritone.

3232 [Divertimento, 8 instruments, F major.
Ho. II: 16] Edited by Karl Geiringer
1.Allegro 2.Minuet: Moderato - Trio 3.Adagio
4.Minuet: Poco vivace - Trio 5.Finale: Presto
0,2,0,2-2Hn.-Vn.I,Vn.II
Ms.
Score 26 p.

356m [Divertimento, flute and strings, *12'*
D major. Ho. II: D8] Edited by Hermann
Scherchen
1.Introduzione: Allegro moderato 2.Menuetto
3.Andante 4.Presto
Solo Fl.-Str.
Hug, Zürich [1940]
Score 8 p.
First modern performance Winterthur, Switzer-
land, 1941, Hermann Scherchen conductor.

6981 [Divertimento, flute, violine concertante,
viola and bass (with cembalo), D major. Ho. II:
D6] Edited by Frank Nagel
1.Tempo giusto 2.Allegro 3.Menuet 4.
Finale (Allegro)
Fl.-Cemb.-Str.(without Cb.)
Litolff's/C.F. Peters, Frankfurt, ^c1971
Score 20 p.
Edited from a manuscript in the library of the
Gesellschaft der Musikfreunde, Vienna,
inscribed: Al uso di Antonio Schaarschmidt
1767.

5959 [Divertimento, 2 oboes, 2 bassoons, *10'*
and 2 horns, C major. Ho. II: 7] Edited by
Karl Haas
1.Allegro 2.Menuett - Trio 3.Adagio
4.Menuett - Trio 5.Presto

Haydn, Joseph

0,2,0,2-2Hn.
Musica Rara, London, c1958
Score 7 p.
Composed ca.1761.

5957 [Divertimento, 2 oboes, 2 bassoons, *9'30"*
and 2 horns, F major. Ho. II: 23] Edited by
Alan Lumsden
1.Allegro 2.Menuet and trio 3.Andante
4.Menuet and trio 5.Allegro 6.Presto
0,2,0,2-2Hn.
Musica Rara, London, c1959
Score 10 p.
*Published as Parthia in F(G). Composed after
1775. First modern performance probably
Leipzig, February 1959, Leipzig Radio Orchestra, Kurt Janetzky conductor.*

1913s [Divertimento, strings, D major] Edited
by Karl Geiringer
1.Molto allegro - 4 Variations 2.Menuetto:
Allegretto 3.Presto
Str.
Ms.
Score 4 p.
Not traceable in Hoboken thematic catalog.

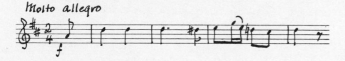

1789s [Divertimento, strings, E-flat major.
Ho. II: 6] Edited by Karl Geiringer
1.Allegro 2.Menuet 3.Adagio cantabile
4.Menuet 5.Finale: Presto
Str.(Cb. ad lib.)
Nagel, Hannover, c1931
Score 8 p.

1911s [Divertimento, strings, G major] Edited
by Karl Geiringer
1.Moderato 2.Menuetto: Allegretto 3.Presto
Str.
Ms.
Score 4 p.
Not traceable in Hoboken thematic catalog.

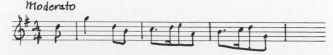

4392 [Divertimento, wind ensemble, B-flat *9'30"*
major. Ho. II: 46] Edited by Karl Geiringer
1.Allegro con spirito 2.Chorale St. Antoni:
Andante quasi allegretto 3.Menuetto - Trio
4.Rondo: Allegretto
0,2,0,4*-2Hn.
F. Schuberth, Leipzig, c1932
Score 7 p.
*Contrabassoon part originally for serpent.
Composed 1780; authenticity disputed; possibly by Ignaz Pleyel. Second movement based*

*on Chorale St. Antoni, an Austrian pilgrims'
song. This is the theme of Johannes Brahms'
Op. 56, Variations On a Theme by Joseph Haydn.*

English military marches
See: [Marches, military band. Ho. VIII:
1,2,3]

Feldpartie in C
See: [Divertimento, 2 oboes, 2 bassoons, and
2 horns, C major. Ho. II: 7]

Feldpartita in B-flat major
See: [Divertimento, wind ensemble, B-flat
major. Ho. II: 46]

Gott erhalte Franz den Kaiser
See: [Quartet, strings, Kaiser-Quartett,
Op. 76 no. 3, C major. Ho. III: 77.
Movement 2. Transcribed for string
orchestra by Erwin Stein]

939 [L'isola disabitata (The desert island). *7'*
Overture. Ho. Ia: 13. Edited for modern large
orchestra by Josef Liebeskind]
1.Largo 2.Vivace assai 3.Allegretto
4.Vivace assai
2,2,2,2-2,2-Timp.-Str.
Reinecke, Leipzig [1900]
Score 17 p.
*From the opera composed 1779. First perform-
ance Esterháza, 6 December 1779.*

March for the Prince of Wales
See: [Marches, wind ensemble. Ho. VIII:
1,2,3...] No. 3

5958 [March, 2 oboes, 2 bassoons, and 2 horns,
G major] Edited by Alan Lumsden
0,2,0,2-2Hn.
Musica Rara, London, c1959
Score 3 p.
*Not traceable in Hoboken thematic catalog.
Composed 1772(?). First modern performance
probably Leipzig, February 1959, Leipzig Radio
Orchestra, Kurt Janetzky conductor.*

5960 [Marches, wind ensemble. Ho. VIII: 1,2,3.
Edited and percussion parts added by Karl
Haas]
1.Derbyshire march no. 1 [E-flat major.
Ho. VIII: 1] 2.Derbyshire march no. 2 [C
major. Ho. VIII: 2] 3.March for the Prince of
Wales [Ho. VIII: 3]
0,0,2,2-2,1,Serpent-Timp.,Perc.
Musica Rara, London, c1960
Score 8 p.
*March for the Prince of Wales composed 1792.
The March for the Royal Society of Musicians,
Ho. no. VIII: 3bis, is the same music with*

added flute, 2nd trumpet, and strings.
Derbyshire Marches commissioned by Sir Henry
Harpur for the Volunteer Cavalry of Derby-
shire. Composed 1795.

3485 [Marches, wind ensemble. Ho. VIII: *3'*
1 and 2]
1.E-flat major, Ho. VIII: 1 2.C major,
Ho. VIII: 2
0,0,2,2-2,2,Serpent
Ms.
Score 9 p.
Commissioned by Sir Henry Harpur for the
Volunteer Cavalry of Derbyshire. Composed
1795. Popular title: Derbyshire Marches.

3499 [Notturno, orchestra, no. 4,   *11'30"*
F major. Ho. II: 28] Edited by Karl Geiringer
1.Allegro moderato 2.Adagio cantabile
3.Finale: Presto
1,0,1-2Hn.-Str.(with Va.II)
Ms. [ᶜ1932 by Karl Geiringer]
Score 34 p.
Composed ca.1792.

5999 [Orlando Paladino. Sinfonia. Ho. Ia: 16]
Edited by H.C. Robbins Landon
0,2,0,2-2Hn.-Str.
Doblinger, Vienna, ᶜ1960
Score 20 p.
From the opera in 3 acts with libretto by
Nunziato Porta after Lodovico Ariosto's
Orlando Furioso. First performance Ester-
háza, Hungary, 6 December 1782. First modern
performance Budapest, February 1960, Hun-
garian Radio Symphony Orchestra, Ervin Lukács
conductor.

2418 [Overture, D major. Ho. Ia: 4] Edited   *4'*
by H. Lemacher and P. Mies
1,2,0,2-2Hn.-Str.
P.J. Tonger, Cologne, ᶜ1931
Score 15 p.
Composed ca.1785, possibly as the finale of a
symphony. First published by Franz Anton
Hoffmeister, ca.1786.

4530 [Overture, D major. Ho. Ia: 4]   *4'*
Revised by Franz Wüllner
1,2,0,2-2Hn.-Str.
J. Rieter-Biedermann, Leipzig [1871]
Score 19 p.

Parthia in F(G)
See: [Divertimento, 2 oboes, 2 bassoons, and
        2 horns, F major. Ho. II: 23]

94s [Quartet, strings, Op. 3 no. 5,   *3'30"*
F major. Ho. III: 17. Movement 2, Serenade.
Transcribed for string orchestra]
Str.
G. Schirmer, New York, ᶜ1909
Score in reduction 5 p.

147s [Quartet, strings, Op. 3 no. 5,   *3'30"*
F major. Ho. III: 17. Movement 2, Serenade.
Transcribed for string orchestra]
Str.(without Cb.)

Leuckart, Leipzig [n.d.]
Score 4 p.

1208s [Quartet, strings, Kaiser-Quartett,   *8'*
Op. 76 no. 3, C major. Ho. III: 77. Movement
2, Variationen über das Deutschland-Lied.
Transcribed for string orchestra by Erwin Stein]
Str.
Universal Edition, Vienna, ᶜ1928
Score 8 p.

694s [Quartet, strings, Op. 76 no. 5, D major.
Ho. III: 79. Movement 2, Cantabile e mesto]
Str.(without Cb.)
C. Simon, Berlin [n.d.]
Score 3 p.
Published as Célèbre Largo.

3286 [The seven last words of Our   *70'*
Savior on the Cross. Ho. XX. Orchestral
version] Edited by Karl Geiringer
Introduction, 7 Sonatas, and Earthquake
2,2,0,2-2,2-Timp.-Str.
Ms.
Score 168 p.
Composed for Lenten services at Cadiz Cathe-
dral, 1785, to accompany the bishop's reading
of the seven words. Haydn later set the
music for string quartet and as an oratorio.

Lo speziale
See: [The apothecary. Sinfonia. Ho. Ia: 10]

SYMPHONIES

Symphonies are listed according to their
numbers in Anthony van Hoboken's Joseph Haydn:
Thematisch-bibliographisches Werkver-
zeichnis (Mainz: B. Schott's Sohne, 1957).

Symphonies marked "B&H ed." are from:
Joseph Haydns Werke. Erste Kritische Durch-
gesehene Gesamtausgabe. Edited by Eusebius
Mandyszewski and others. Breitkopf & Härtel,
Leipzig, 1907-1933.

Symphonies marked "Einstein ed." were edited
by Alfred Einstein for the Fleisher Collection from mss. in various European libraries.
All materials in manuscript.

Consult Hoboken for further information about
each symphony.

Symphonies which have popular titles are
listed below for ease of reference:

 30 Alleluja
 31 Ambush/Auf dem Anstand
 73 La chasse
101 The clock
105 Concertante
 60 Il distratto
104 Dudelsack
 45 Farewell
 59 Fire
 53 L'imperiale
103 Kettledrum roll

Haydn, Joseph

94 Kettledrum stroke
26 Lamentatione
69 Laudon
93 to 104 London symphonies
48 Maria Theresia
6 Le matin
43 Mercury
7 Le midi
100 Military
96 The miracle
31 Mit dem Hornsignal
94 Mit dem Paukenschlag
82 L'ours
92 Oxford
82 to 87 Paris symphonies
49 La Passione
103 Paukenwirbel
22 Der Philosoph
83 La poule
85 La reine
63 La Roxelane
104 Salomon
55 Der Schulmeister
8 Le soir
94 Surprise
8 La tempesta
64 Tempora mutantur
-- Toy *See:* MOZART, LEOPOLD. Toy symphony
44 Trauer-Symphonie
101 Die Uhr

2127 [Symphony no. 1, D major. Ho. I: 1.   *8'*
B&H ed.]
1.Presto 2.Andante 3.Finale: Presto
2Ob.-2Hn.-Str.

2249 [Symphony no. 2, C major. Ho. I: 2.   *10'*
B&H ed.]
1.Allegro 2.Andante 3.Finale: Presto
2Hn.-Str.

2250 [Symphony no. 3, G major. Ho. I: 3.   *12'*
B&H ed.]
1.Allegro 2.Andante moderato 3.Menuetto -
Trio 4.Finale: Presto
2Ob.-2Hn.-Str.

2251 [Symphony no. 4, D major. Ho. I: 4.   *12'*
B&H ed.]
1.Presto 2.Andante 3.Finale: Tempo di
menuetto
2Ob.-2Hn.-Str.

2252 [Symphony no. 5, A major. Ho. I: 5.   *12'*
B&H ed.]
1.Allegro 2.Adagio non troppo 3.Menuetto -
Trio 4.Finale: Presto
2Ob.-2Hn.-Str.
*The order of the movements differs from that
of Hoboken.*

2253 [Symphony no. 6, Le matin, D major.   *18'*
Ho. I: 6. B&H ed.]
1.Adagio - Allegro 2.Adagio - Andante
3.Menuetto - Trio 4.Finale: Allegro
1,2,0,1-2Hn.-Str.

635 [Symphony no. 7, Le midi, C major.   *22'*
Ho. I: 7. B&H ed.]
1.Adagio - Allegro 2.Recitativo: Adagio
3.Adagio 4.Menuetto - Trio 5.Finale: Allegro
2,2,0,1-2Hn.-Str.

1007 [Symphony no. 8, Le soir *or* La   *15'*
tempèsta, G major. Ho. I: 8. B&H ed.]
1.Allegro molto 2.Andante 3.Menuetto - Trio
4.La tempèsta: Presto
1,2,0,1-2Hn.-Str.

2141 [Symphony no. 9, C major. Ho. I: 9.   *9'*
B&H ed.]
1.Allegro molto 2.Andante 3.Finale: Menuetto,
Allegretto - Trio
2Ob.-2Hn.-Str.

2254 [Symphony no. 10, D major. Ho. I: 10.   *9'*
B&H ed.]
1.Allegro 2.Andante 3.Finale: Vivace
2Ob.-2Hn.-Str.

2255 [Symphony no. 11, E-flat major.   *13'*
Ho. I: 11. B&H ed.]
1.Adagio cantabile 2.Allegro 3.Menuetto -
Trio 4.Finale: Presto
2Ob.-2Hn.-Str.

2256 [Symphony no. 12, E major. Ho. I: 12.   *9'*
B&H ed.]
1.Allegro 2.Adagio 3.Finale: Presto
2Ob.-2Hn.-Str.

2413 [Symphony no. 13, D major. Ho. I: 13.   *14'*
B&H ed.]
1.Allegro molto 2.Adagio cantabile 3.Menuett
- Trio 4.Finale: Allegro molto
1,2-4Hn.-Timp.-Str.

2257 [Symphony no. 14, A major. Ho. I: 14.   *10'*
B&H ed.]
1.Allegro molto 2.Andante 3.Menuetto:
Allegretto - Trio 4.Finale: Allegro
2Ob.-2Hn.-Str.

2304 [Symphony no. 15, D major. Ho. I: 15.   *17'*
B&H ed.]
1.Adagio - Presto 2.Menuetto - Trio
3.Andante 4.Presto
2Ob.-2Hn.-Str.

2414 [Symphony no. 16, B-flat major.   *10'*
Ho. I: 16]
1.Allegro 2.Andante 3.Finale: Presto
2Ob.-Str.
Score: Ms. 15 p.
Parts: [n.p., n.d.]

2283 [Symphony no. 17, F major. Ho. I: 17.   *12'*
B&H ed.]
1.Allegro 2.Andante 3.Finale: Allegro molto
2Ob.-2Hn.-Str.

2258 [Symphony no. 18, G major. Ho. I: 18.   *10'*
B&H ed.]
1.Allegro molto 2.Andante molto 3.Tempo di
menuetto
2Ob.-2Hn.-Str.

Haydn, Joseph

2305 [Symphony no. 19, D major. Ho. I: 19. *8'*
B&H ed.]
1.Allegro molto 2.Andante 3.Presto
2Ob.-2Hn.-Str.

2306 [Symphony no. 20, C major. Ho. I: 20. *11'*
B&H ed.]
1.Allegro molto 2.Andante 3.Menuetto - Trio
4.Presto
2Ob.-2,2-Timp.-Str.

2354 [Symphony no. 21, A major. *13'30"*
Ho. I: 21. B&H ed.]
1.Adagio 2.Presto 3.Menuetto - Trio
4.Finale: Allegro molto
2Ob.-2Hn.-Str.

2284 [Symphony no. 22, Der Philosoph, *15'*
E-flat major. Ho. I: 22. B&H ed.]
1.Adagio 2.Presto 3.Menuetto - Trio
4.Finale: Presto
2E.H.-2Hn.-Str.

2355 [Symphony no. 23, G major. Ho. I: 23. *14'*
B&H ed.]
1.Allegro 2.Andante 3.Menuetto - Trio
4.Finale: Presto assai
2Ob.-2Hn.-Str.

2356 [Symphony no. 24, D major. Ho. I: 24. *15'*
B&H ed.]
1.Allegro 2.Adagio cantabile 3.Menuetto -
Trio 4.Finale: Allegro
1,2-2Hn.-Str.

2259 [Symphony no. 25, C major. Ho. I: 25. *11'*
B&H ed.]
1.Adagio - Allegro 2.Menuett - Trio 3.Presto
2Fl.-2Hn.-Str.

2357 [Symphony no. 26, Lamentatione, *14'*
D minor. Ho. I: 26. B&H ed.]
1.Allegro assai con spirito 2.Adagio
3.Menuetto - Trio
2Ob.-2Hn.-Str.
Erroneously published as a Weihnachtssymphonie
(Christmas symphony). Movements 1 and 2 are
based on Gregorian chants sung during Holy
Week.

2260 [Symphony no. 27, G major. Ho. I: 27. *9'*
B&H ed.]
1.Allegro molto 2.Andante [Siciliano]
3.Finale: Presto
2Ob.-Str.

1870 [Symphony no. 28, A major. Ho. I: 28. *11'*
B&H ed.]
1.Allegro di molto 2.Poco adagio 3.Menuetto:
Allegro molto - Trio 4.Presto assai
2Ob.-2Hn.-Str.

2261 [Symphony no. 29, E major. Ho. I: 29. *17'*
B&H ed.]
1.Allegro di molto 2.Andante 3.Menuetto:
Allegretto - Trio 4.Finale: Presto
2Ob.-2Hn.-Str.

2262 [Symphony no. 30, Alleluja, *11'*
C major. Ho. I: 30. B&H ed.]
1.Allegro 2.Andante 3.Tempo di menuetto
più tosto allegretto
2Ob.-2Hn.-Str.

1102 [Symphony no. 31, Mit dem Hornsignal *20'*
or Auf dem Anstand, D major. Ho. I: 31. B&H ed.]
1.Allegro 2.Adagio 3.Menuet - Trio
4.Finale: Moderato molto - 7 Variations -
Presto
1,2-4Hn.-Str.

2263 [Symphony no. 32, C major. Ho. I: 32. *13'*
B&H ed.]
1.Allegro molto 2.Menuetto - Trio 3.Adagio
ma non troppo 4.Presto
2Ob.-2,2-Timp.-Str.

2264 [Symphony no. 33, C major. Ho. I: 33. *16'*
B&H ed.]
1.Vivace 2.Andante 3.Menuetto - Trio
4.Finale: Allegro
2Ob.-2Hn.-Str.

2358 [Symphony no. 34, D. Ho. I: 34. *15'*
B&H ed.]
1.Adagio 2.Allegro 3.Menuetto moderato -
Trio 4.Presto assai
2Ob.-2Hn.-Str.

2359 [Symphony no. 35, B-flat major. *18'*
Ho. I: 35. B&H ed.]
1.Allegro di molto 2.Andante 3.Menuetto: Un
poco allegretto - Trio 4.Finale: Presto
2Ob.-2Hn.-Str.

2415 [Symphony no. 36, E-flat major. *15'*
Ho I: 36. B&H ed.]
1.Vivace 2.Adagio 3.Menuetto - Trio
4.Allegro
2Ob.-2Hn.-Str.

2265 [Symphony no. 37, C major. Ho. I: 37. *13'*
B&H ed.]
1.Presto 2.Andante 3.Menuetto - Trio
4.Presto
2Ob.-2Hn.-Str.

2360 [Symphony no. 38, C major. Ho. I: 38. *16'*
B&H ed.]
1.Allegro molto 2.Andante molto 3.Menuetto -
Trio 4.Allegro
2Ob.-2,2-Timp.-Str.

2361 [Symphony no. 39, G minor. Ho. I: 39. *15'*
B&H ed.]
1.Allegro assai 2.Andante 3.Menuetto - Trio
4.Finale: Allegro molto
2Ob.-4Hn.-Str.

2416 [Symphony no. 40, F major. Ho. I: 40. *12'*
B&H ed.]
1.Allegro 2.Andante più tosto allegretto
3.Menuet - Trio 4.Finale: Allegro
2Ob.-2Hn.-Str.

Haydn, Joseph

3212 [Symphony no. 41, C major. Ho. I: 41. *19'*
B&H ed.]
1.Allegro con spirito 2.Poco andante
3.Menuetto - Trio 4.Presto
1,2-2,2-Timp.-Str.

3205 [Symphony no. 42, D major. Ho. I: 42. *24'*
B&H ed.]
1.Moderato e maestoso 2.Andantino e cantabile
3.Menuet 4.Finale: Scherzando e presto
20b.-2Hn.-Str.

3206 [Symphony no. 43, Mercury, E-flat *25'*
major. Ho. I: 43. B&H ed.]
1.Allegro 2.Adagio 3.Menuetto - Trio
4.Finale: Allegro
20b.-2Hn.-Str.

1527 [Symphony no. 44, Trauer-Symphonie, *15'*
E minor. Ho. I: 44]
1.Allegro con brio 2.Menuetto: Allegretto -
Trio 3.Adagio 4.Finale: Presto
1,2-2Hn.-Str.
Score: Ms. 55 p.
Parts: B&H ed.

579 [Symphony no. 45, Farewell, F-sharp *22'*
minor. Ho. I: 45. B&H ed.]
1.Allegro assai 2.Adagio 3.Menuet: Allegretto
- Trio 4.Finale: Presto - Adagio
0,2,0,1-2Hn.-Str.

3207 [Symphony no. 46, B major. Ho. I: 46. *19'*
B&H ed.]
1.Vivace 2.Poco adagio 3.Menuet: Allegretto
- Trio 4.Finale: Presto e scherzando
20b.-2Hn.-Str.

3197 [Symphony no. 47, G major. Ho. I: 47. *20'*
B&H ed.]
1.Allegro 2.Un poco adagio, cantabile
3.Menuet al roverso - Trio al roverso
4.Finale: Presto assai
20b.-2Hn.-Str.

2140 [Symphony no. 48, Maria Theresia, *15'*
C major. Ho. I: 48]
1.Allegro 2.Adagio 3.Menuetto: Allegretto -
Trio 4.Finale: Allegro
20b.-2,2-Timp.-Str.
Score: Ms. 120 p.
Parts: B&H ed.

2445 [Symphony no. 49, La Passione, *22'*
F minor. Ho. I: 49. B&H ed.]
1.Adagio 2.Allegro di molto 3.Menuet - Trio
4.Finale: Presto
20b.-2Hn.-Str.

5773 [Symphony no. 50, C major. Ho. I: 50] *18'30"*
1.Adagio e maestoso - Allegro di molto
2.Andante moderato 3.Menuet - Trio 4.Finale:
Presto
0,2,0,1-2,2-Timp.-Str.
Haydn Society, Boston, c1951
Score 25 p.

286 [Symphony no. 51, B-flat major. *23'*
Ho. I: 51] Edited by Helmut Schultz
1.Vivace 2.Adagio 3.Menuetto - Trio I - Trio
II 4.Finale: Allegro
0,2,0,1-2Hn.-Str.
Haydn-Mozart Presse, Salzburg, c1951 by
Haydn Society Inc., Boston
Score 24 p.

4217 [Symphony no. 52, C minor. *ca.23'*
Ho. I: 52] Edited by Helmut Schultz
1.Allegro assai con brio 2.Andante 3.Menu-
etto: Allegretto - Trio 4.Finale: Presto
0,2,0,1-2Hn.-Str.
Haydn-Mozart Presse, Salzburg, c1951 by Haydn
Society Inc., Boston
Score 38 p.

3208 [Symphony no. 53, L'impériale, *19'30"*
D major. Ho. I: 53. Einstein ed.]
1.Maestoso largo - Allegro vivace 2.Andante
3.Presto
1,2,0,2-2Hn.-Str.
This symphony exists in several different ver-
sions. This edition is based on parts pub-
lished by Siéber, Paris, 1786, which lack the
minuet and trio listed in Hoboken.

6901 [Symphony no. 53, L'impériale, *24'*
D major. Ho. I: 53] Edited by Helmut Schultz
1.Largo maestoso - Vivace 2.Andante 3.Menu-
etto and Trio 4.Version A: Finale. Capriccio:
Moderato. Version B: Presto
1,2,0,1(2 in Version B)-2Hn.-Timp.-Str.
Haydn-Mozart Presse, Salzburg, c1951 by the
Haydn Society, Boston
Score 52 p.
This edition includes all movements appearing
in any early version.

850 [Symphony no. 54, G major. Ho. I: 54] *27'*
Edited by Carl Banck
1.Adagio maestoso - Allegro quasi presto 2.
Adagio assai 3.Menuetto: Allegro con moto -
Trio 4.Finale: Presto
0,2,0,2-2Hn.-Timp.-Str.(without Vc.)
Kistner, Leipzig [1880?]
Score 53 p.

6902 [Symphony no. 54, G major. *34'*
Ho. I: 54] Edited by Helmut Schultz
1.Adagio maestoso - Presto (In nomine domini)
2.Adagio assai 3.Menuet: Allegretto - Trio
4.Finale: Presto
2,2,0,2-2,2-Timp.-Str.
Haydn-Mozart Presse, Salzburg, c1951 by the
Haydn Society, Boston
Score 35 p.

1526 [Symphony no. 55, Der Schulmeister, *15'*
E-flat major. Ho. I: 55]
1.Allegro molto 2.Adagio 3.Menuetto - Trio
4.Finale: Presto
0,2,0,1-2Hn.-Str.
Score: Ms. 52 p.
Parts: B&H ed.

6903 [Symphony no. 55, Der Schulmeister,   *18'*
E-flat major. Ho. I: 55] Edited by Helmut
Schultz
1.Allegro di molto 2.Adagio, ma semplicemente
3.Menuetto and Trio 4.Finale: Presto
0,2,0,2-2Hn.-Str.
Haydn-Mozart Presse, Salzburg, ^c1951 by the
Haydn Society, Boston
Score 26 p.

899 [Symphony no. 56, C major. Ho. I: 56]   *18'*
Edited by Carl Banck
1.Allegro 2.Adagio 3.Menuetto: Allegretto -
Trio 4.Presto [Hoboken: Finale. Prestissimo]
0,2,0,1-2,2-Timp.-Str.
Kistner, Leipzig [1881]
Score 55 p.

6904 [Symphony no. 56, C major. Ho. I: 56] *28'*
Edited by Helmut Schultz
1.Allegro di molto 2.Adagio 3.Menuet and
Trio 4.Finale: Prestissimo
0,2,0,1-2,2-Timp.-Str.
Haydn-Mozart Presse, Salzburg, ^c1951 by the
Haydn Society, Boston
Score 39 p.

3262 [Symphony no. 57, D major. Ho. I: 57]
1.Adagio - Allegro di molto 2.Adagio
3.Menuet: Allegretto - Trio 4.Finale:
Prestissimo
2Ob.-2Hn.-Str.
Ms.
Score 42 p.

6905 [Symphony no. 57, D major. Ho. I: 57] *24'*
Edited by Helmut Schultz
1.Adagio - Allegro 2.Adagio 3.Menuet:
Allegretto and Trio 4.Prestissimo
0,2,0,1-2Hn.-Timp.-Str.
Haydn-Mozart Presse, Salzburg, ^c1951 by the
Haydn Society, Boston
Score 28 p.

3198 [Symphony no. 58, F major. Ho. I: 58. *15'*
Einstein ed.]
1.Allegro [Hoboken: Allegro moderato] 2.
Andante 3.Minuet alla zoppa: Un poco allegretto - Trio 4.Finale: Presto
2Ob.-2Hn.-Str.

5828 [Symphony no. 58, F major. Ho. I: *ca.22'*
58] Edited by H.C. Robbins Landon
1.Allegro 2.Andante 3.Menuet alla zoppa:
Un poco allegretto - Trio 4.Finale: Presto
0,2,0,1(ad lib.)-2Hn.-Cemb.-Str.
Haydn-Mozart Presse, Salzburg, ^c1958
Score 16 p.

5799 [Symphony no. 59, Fire, A major.   *ca.22'*
Ho. I: 59] Edited by H.C. Robbins Landon
1.Presto 2.Andante o più tosto allegretto
3.Menuetto 4.Allegro assai
0,2,0,1(ad lib.)-2Hn.-Cemb.-Str.
Haydn-Mozart Presse, Salzburg, ^c1958
Score 19 p.

931 [Symphony no. 60, Il distratto,   *17'*
C major. Ho. I: 60] Edited by Carl Banck
1.Adagio - Allegro di molto 2.Andante con
moto [Hoboken: Adagio] 3.Menuetto - Trio
4.Presto
2Ob.-2,2-Timp.-Str.
Kistner, Leipzig [1881]
Score 65 p.

5829 [Symphony no. 60, Il distratto,   *25'*
C major. Ho. I: 60] Edited by H.C. Robbins
Landon
1.Adagio - Allegro di molto 2.Andante
3.Menuetto - Trio 4.Presto 5.Adagio (di
lamentatione) 6.Finale: Prestissimo
0,2,0,1(ad lib.)-2,2-Timp.-Str.
Haydn-Mozart Presse, Salzburg, ^c1959
Score 29 p.

3199 [Symphony no. 61, D major. Ho. I: 61] *27'*
1.Vivace 2.Adagio 3.Menuetto: Allegretto -
Trio 4.Finale: Prestissimo
1,2,0,2-2Hn.-Timp.-Str.
Ms.
Score 63 p.

5830 [Symphony no. 61, D major. Ho. I: 61] *23'*
Edited by H.C. Robbins Landon
1.Vivace 2.Adagio 3.Menuet: Allegretto -
Trio 4.Prestissimo
1,2,0,2-2Hn.-Timp.-Str.
Haydn-Mozart Presse, Salzburg, ^c1959
Score 50 p.

6055 [Symphony no. 62, D major. Ho. I: 62] *20'*
1.Allegro 2.Allegretto 3.Menuett: Allegretto
- Trio 4.Finale: Allegro
1,2,0,2-2Hn.-Str.
Joseph Haydn-Institut, Cologne [n.d.]
Score 62 p.

6906 [Symphony no. 62, D major. Ho. I: 62] *22'*
Edited by Karl Heinz Füssl
1.Allegro 2.Allegretto 3.Menuet: Allegretto
and Trio 4.Finale: Allegro
1,2,0,2-2Hn.-Str.
Haydn-Mozart Presse, Salzburg, ^c1965
Score 35 p.

6907 [Symphony no. 63, La Roxelane,   *23'*
C major. First and second versions. Ho. I: 63]
Edited by H.C. Robbins Landon
First version: 1.Allegro 2. La Roxelane:
Allegretto (o più tosto allegro) 3.Menuet:
Allegretto and Trio 4.Finale: Prestissimo
Second version: 1.Allegro 2. La Roxelane:
Allegretto (o più tosto allegro) 3.Menuet and
Trio 4.Finale: Presto
First version: 1,2,0,2-2,2-Timp.-Str.
Second version: 1,2,0,1-2Hn.-Str.
Haydn-Mozart Presse, Salzburg, ^c1964
Score for first version 33 p.
Score for second version 30 p.
*First version composed 1777. Second version
composed ca.1777-1780.*

Haydn, Joseph

3209 [Symphony no. 63, La Roxelane, *21'*
C major. Ho. I: 63. Second version. Einstein
ed.]
1.Vivace 2.Roxelane: Allegretto più sosto.
[*sic*] 3.Minuet - Trio 4.Finale: Presto
1,2,0,2-2Hn.-Str.
Ms.
Score 44 p.

6908 [Symphony no. 64, Tempora mutantur, *20'*
A major. Ho. I: 64] Edited by H.C. Robbins
Landon
1.Allegro con spirito 2.Largo 3.Menuet:
Allegretto and Trio 4.Finale: Presto
0,2,0,1-2Hn.-Str.
Haydn-Mozart Presse, Salzburg, ᶜ1965
Score 22 p.

2417 [Symphony no. 64, Tempora mutantur, *16'*
A major. Ho. I: 64] Edited by Ludwig Landshoff
1.Allegro con spirito 2.Largo 3.Minuetto:
Allegretto - Trio 4.Finale: Presto
0,2,0,2-2Hn.-Str.
C.F. Peters, Leipzig, ᶜ1931
Score 32 p.

3213 [Symphony no. 65, A major. Ho. I: 65. *20'*
Einstein ed.]
1.Vivace con spirito 2.Andante 3.Menuetto -
Trio 4.Finale: Presto
2Ob.-2Hn.-Str.

5831 [Symphony no. 65, A major. Ho. I: 65] *23'*
Edited by H.C. Robbins Landon
1.Vivace e con spirito 2.Andante 3.Menuetto
4.Finale: Presto
0,2,0,1(ad lib.)-2Hn.-Str.
Haydn-Mozart Presse, Salzburg, ᶜ1958
Score 20 p.

3200 [Symphony no. 66, B-flat major. *30'*
Ho. I: 66]
1.Allegro con brio 2.Adagio 3.Minuetto -
Trio 4.Finale: Scherzando presto [Hoboken:
Finale. Presto]
0,2,0,2-2Hn.-Str.
Ms.
Score 53 p.

3201 [Symphony no. 67, F major. Ho. I: 67. *27'*
Einstein ed.]
1.Presto 2.Adagio 3.Minuet - Trio 4.Finale:
Allegro molto
0,2,0,2-2Hn.-Str.

3214 [Symphony no. 68, B-flat major. *33'*
Ho. I: 68. Einstein ed.]
1.Vivace 2.Menuetto: Allegretto - Trio
3.Adagio cantabile 4.Presto
0,2,0,2-2Hn.-Str.
In Hoboken the Adagio precedes the Menuetto.

3202 [Symphony no. 69, Laudon, C major. *18'*
Ho.I: 69. Einstein ed.]
1.Vivace [Hoboken: Allegro vivace] 2.Adagio
[Hoboken: Un poco adagio, più tosto] 3.Menu-
etto - Trio 4.Finale: Presto
0,2,0,2-2Hn.-Str.

3271 [Symphony no. 70, D major. Ho. I: *18'30"*
70]
1.Vivace con brio 2.Andante 3.Allegro con
brio - [Fugato]
1,2-2Hn.-Str.
Ms.
Score 28 p.
This edition lacks the Menuetto and Trio; the
instrumentation differs from Hoboken's.

3219 [Symphony no. 71, B-flat major. *35'30"*
Ho. I: 71. Einstein ed.]
1.Adagio - Allegro con brio 2.Adagio [with 3
variations and coda] 3.Minuet - Trio
4.Finale: Vivace
1,2,0,1-2Hn.-Str.

3275 [Symphony no. 72, D major. Ho. I: 72] *26'*
1.Allegro 2.Andante 3.Minuetto - Trio
4.Finale: Andante - 6 variations - Presto
1,2,0,1-2Hn.-Str.
Ms.
Score 31 p.

6909 [Symphony no. 72, D major. Ho. I: 72] *26'*
Edited by H.C. Robbins Landon
1.Allegro 2.Andante 3.Menuet and Trio
4.Finale: Andante with six variations - Presto
1,2,0,1-4Hn.-Timp.(optional)-Str.
Haydn-Mozart Presse, Salzburg, ᶜ1964
Score 24 p.

1808 [Symphony no. 73, La chasse, *25'*
D major. Ho. I: 73]
1.Adagio - Allegro 2.Andante 3.Menuetto:
Allegretto - Trio 4.La chasse [Hoboken: Presto]
1,2,0,2-2Hn.-Str.
Score: Eulenburg, Leipzig [n.d.]
Parts: B&H ed.
Some early editions showed trumpets and tim-
pani in the fourth movement.

3276 [Symphony no. 74, E-flat major. *26'*
Ho I: 74]
1.Vivace assai [Hoboken: Allegro] 2.Adagio
cantabile 3.Minuetto: Allegretto - Trio
4.Finale: Allegro assai
1,2,0,1-2Hn.-Str.
Ms.
Score 39 p.

2139 [Symphony no. 75, D major. Ho. I: 75] *14'*
1.Grave - Presto 2.Andante con variazioni
3.Menuetto: Allegretto - [Trio] 4.Finale:
Vivace
1,2,0,1-2,2-Timp.-Str.
Score: Ms. 96 p.
Parts: B&H ed.

3203 [Symphony no. 75, D major. Ho. I: *18'*
75. Einstein ed.]
1.Grave - Presto 2.Adagio [Hoboken: Andante
con variazioni] 3.Menuetto - Trio 4.Finale:
Vivace
1,2,0,1-2,2-Timp.-Str.

1809 [Symphony no. 76, E-flat major. *14'*
Ho. I: 76]

Haydn, Joseph

1.Allegro 2.Adagio 3.Menuetto: Allegretto
[Trio] 4.Finale: Allegro ma non troppo
1,2,0,2-2Hn.-Str.
Score: Ms. 120 p.
Parts: B&H ed.

3220 [Symphony no. 77, B-flat major.   23'30"
Ho. I: 77. Einstein ed.]
1.Vivace 2.Andante sostenuto 3.Minuet: Allegretto - Trio 4.Finale: Allegro spiritoso
1,2,0,1-Str.

1257 [Symphony no. 78, C minor. Ho. I: 78] 14'
1.Vivace 2.Adagio 3.Menuetto: Allegretto -
Trio 4.Finale: Presto
1,2,0,2-2Hn.-Str.
J. André, Offenbach a.M. [1895]
Score 43 p.

3272 [Symphony no. 79, F major. Ho. I: 79] 25'
1.Allegro con spirito 2.Adagio cantabile -
Un poco allegro 3.Menuetto: Allegretto - Trio
4.Finale: Vivace
1,2,0,2-2Hn.-Str.
Ms.
Score 46 p.

3277 [Symphony no. 80, D minor. Ho. I: 80. 17'
Einstein ed.]
1.Allegro spiritoso 2.Adagio 3.Minuetto -
Trio 4.Finale: Presto
1,2,0,2-2Hn.-Str.

1839 [Symphony no. 81, G major. Ho. I: 81] 16'
1.Vivace 2.Andante 3.Menuetto: Allegretto -
Trio 4.Finale: Allegro ma non troppo
1,2,0,2-2Hn.-Str.
Score: Ms. 96 p.
Parts: B&H ed.

649 [Symphony no. 82, L'ours, C major. 17'
Ho. I: 82]
1.Vivace assai 2.Allegretto 3.Menuetto: Un
poco allegretto - Trio 4.Finale: Vivace assai
1,2,0,2-2,2-Timp.-Str.
Kalmus, New York [n.d.]
Score 60 p.

1970 [Symphony no. 83, La poule, G minor. 15'
Ho. I: 83]
1.Allegro spiritoso 2.Andante 3.Menuetto:
Allegretto - Trio 4.Finale: Vivace
1,2,0,2-2Hn.-Str.
Score: Ms. 97 p.
Parts: B&H ed.

1226 [Symphony no. 84, E-flat major. 17'
Ho. I: 84]
1.Largo - Allegro 2.Andante 3.Menuetto:
Allegretto - Trio 4.Finale: Vivace
1,2,0,2-2Hn.-Str.
J. André, Offenbach a.M. [1871]
Score 51 p.

580 [Symphony no. 85, La reine, B-flat 24'
major. Ho. I: 85. B&H ed.]
1.Adagio - Vivace 2.Romanze: Allegretto
3.Menuetto: Allegretto - Trio 4.Finale: Presto
1,2,0,2-2Hn.-Str.

943 [Symphony no. 86, D major. Ho. I: 16'
86. B&H ed.]
1.Adagio - Allegro spiritoso 2.Capriccio:
Largo 3.Menuetto: Allegretto - Trio 4.Finale:
Allegro con spirito
1,2,0,2-2,2-Timp.-Str.

3204 [Symphony no. 87, A major. Ho. I: 29'
87. Einstein ed.]
1.Vivace 2.Adagio 3.Minuet - Trio 4.Vivace
1,2,0,2-2Hn.-Str.

518 [Symphony no. 88, G major. Ho. I: 22'
88. B&H ed.]
1.Adagio - Allegro 2.Largo 3.Menuetto:
Allegretto - Trio 4.Finale: Allegro con
spirito
1,2,0,2-2,2-Timp.-Str.

1871 [Symphony no. 89, F major. Ho. I: 89] 16'
1.Vivace 2.Andante con moto 3.Menuetto: Allegretto - [Trio] 4.Finale: Vivace assai
1,2,0,2-2Hn.-Str.
Score: Ms. 100 p.
Parts: B&H ed.

1301 [Symphony no. 90, C major. Ho. I: 90] 16'
1.Adagio - Allegro assai 2.Andante 3.Menuetto
- Trio 4.Finale: Allegro assai
1,2,0,2-2Hn.-Str.
Score: J. André, Offenbach a/Main [1870?] 59 p.
Parts: B&H ed.

1311 [Symphony no. 91, E-flat major. 15'
Ho. I: 91]
1.Largo - Allegro assai 2.Andante 3.Menuetto:
Un poco allegretto - Trio 4.Finale: Vivace
1,2,0,2-2Hn.-Str.
Score: J. André, Offenbach a/Main [1865] 60 p.
Parts: B&H ed.

581 [Symphony no. 92, Oxford, G major. 28'
Ho. I: 92. B&H ed.]
1.Adagio - Allegro spiritoso 2.Adagio 3.Menu-
etto: Allegretto - [Trio] 4.Presto
1,2,0,2-2,2-Timp.-Str.

992 [Symphony no. 93, D major. Ho. I: 93] 16'
1.Adagio - Allegro assai 2.Largo cantabile
3.Menuetto: Allegretto - Trio 4.Finale:
Presto ma non troppo
2,2,0,2-2,2-Timp.-Str.
Kalmus, New York [n.d.]
Score 19 p.

578 [Symphony no. 94, Mit dem Pauken- 20'
schlag or Surprise, G major. Ho. I: 94.
B&H ed.]
1.Adagio cantabile - Vivace assai 2.Andante
3.Menuetto: Allegro molto - Trio 4.Allegro
di molto
2,2,0,2-2,2-Timp.-Str.

1137 [Symphony no. 95, C minor. Ho. I: 22'
95. B&H ed.]
1.Allegro moderato 2.Andante 3.Menuetto -
Trio 4.Finale: Vivace
1,2,0,2-2,2-Timp.-Str.

Haydn, Joseph

1089 [Symphony no. 96, The miracle,   26'
D major. Ho. I: 96]
1.Adagio - Allegro 2.Andante 3.Menuetto:
Allegretto - Trio 4.Finale: Vivace assai
2,2,0,2-2,2-Timp.-Str.
Score: Eulenburg, London [1935?] Edited by
Ernst Praetorius. 56 p.
Parts: Kalmus, New York [n.d.]

1210 [Symphony no. 97, C major. Ho. I: 97. 25'
B&H ed.]
1.Adagio - Vivace 2.Adagio ma non troppo 3.
Menuetto: Allegretto - Trio 4.Finale: Presto
assai [Hoboken: Spiritoso]
2,2,0,2-2,2-Timp.-Str.

1152 [Symphony no. 98, B-flat major.   27'
Ho. I: 98. B&H ed.]
1.Adagio - Allegro 2.Adagio cantabile 3.
Menuetto: Allegro - Trio 4.Finale: Presto
1,2,0,2-2,2-Timp.-Str.

1176 [Symphony no. 99, E-flat major.   27'
Ho. I: 99]
1.Adagio - Vivace assai 2.Adagio 3.Menuetto:
Allegretto - Trio 4.Vivace
2,2,2,2-2,2-Timp.-Str.
Score: B&H ed.
Parts: Kalmus, New York [n.d.]

592 [Symphony no. 100, Military,   22'
G major. Ho. I: 100]
1.Adagio - Allegro 2.Allegretto 3.Menuetto:
Moderato - Trio 4.Finale: Presto
1,2,2,2-2,2-Timp.,Perc.-Str.
Luck's Music Library, Detroit [n.d.]
Score 53 p.

576 [Symphony no. 101, Die Uhr (The   25'
clock), D minor. Ho. I: 101. B&H ed.]
1.Adagio - Presto 2.Andante 3.Menuetto:
Allegretto - Trio 4.Finale: Vivace
2,2,2,2-2,2-Timp.-Str.

1334 [Symphony no. 102, B-flat major.   26'
Ho. I: 102. B&H ed.]
1.Largo - Vivace 2.Adagio 3.Menuetto:
Allegro - Trio 4.Finale: Presto
2,2,0,2-2,2-Timp.-Str.

577 [Symphony no. 103, Paukenwirbel,   25'
E-flat major. Ho. I: 103]
1.Adagio - Allegro con spirito 2.Andante
3.Menuetto - Trio 4.Allegro con spirito
2,2,2,2-2,2-Timp.-Str.
Score: Eulenburg, Zurich [n.d.] Edited by
Ernst Praetorius. 57 p.
Parts: B&H ed.

77 [Symphony no. 104, Salomon or   27'30"
Dudelsack, D major. Ho. I: 104. B&H ed.]
1.Adagio - Allegro 2.Andante 3.Menuetto:
Allegretto - Trio 4.Finale: Spiritoso
2,2,2,2-2,2-Timp.-Str.

594m [Symphony no. 105, Concertante,   22'
B-flat major. Ho. I: 105] Edited by Karl
Marguerre

1.Allegro 2.Andante 3.Allegro con spirito
Soli: Ob.,Bn.,Vn.,Vc.-1,2,0,1-2,2-Timp.-Str.
Breitkopf & Härtel, Wiesbaden, c1968
Score 95 p.

7231 [Symphony no. 107, B-flat major.   15'
Ho. I: 107] Edited by Ewald Lassen
1.Allegro 2.Andante 3.Allegro molto
2Ob.-2Hn.-Str.
C.F. Peters, Frankfurt, c1958
Score 17 p.

3990 [Symphony, C major. Ho. I: C27]   20'
Edited by Zoltan Fekete
1.Adagio - Allegro assai 2.Andante cantabile
3.Finale: Allegro moderato
2,2,0,2-2,2-Timp.-Str.
Ms. c1944 by Zoltan Fekete
Score 27 p.

Symphony, E-flat major
See: SWIETEN, GOTTFRIED VAN.
[Symphony, E-flat major]

[Symphony, Op. 10 no. 2, B-flat major. Ho. I: B2]
See: HAYDN, MICHAEL.
[Symphony, Op. 10 no. 2, B-flat major.
Ho. I: B2]

6366 [Ten minuets for orchestra. Ho. IX: Anhang]
Edited by Bernhard Paumgartner
1,2,2,2-2Hn.-Str.(Vn.I,Vn.II,Cb.)
Bärenreiter, Kassel, 1950
Score 12 p.
*Haydn excerpted these minuets from ten of his
symphonies and string quartets (no. 3 was
originally composed as a minuet for two violins
and bass) and transcribed them for use as dance
music.*

Toy symphony
See: MOZART, LEOPOLD.
Toy symphony

1861s [Trio, baryton, viola and bass,   12'
no. 82, C major. Ho. XI: 82. Transcribed for
string orchestra by Karl Geiringer]
1.Adagio 2.Allegro 3.Menuett: Allegretto -
Trio: Das alte Weib
Str.
Ms.
Score 11 p.
Title on score: Divertimento no. 82.

2421 [12 German dances, for orchestra.   7'
Ho. IX: 12] Edited by Otto Erich Deutsch
2(2nd alt. Picc.),2,2,2-2,2-Timp.-Str.(without
Va.)
Kistner & Siegel, Leipzig, c1931
Score 20 p.
*First performance Imperial Redoutensäle,
Vienna, 25 November 1792, at the masked ball
of the Artists' Pension Society.*

Zittau divertimenti, no. 6
See: [Divertimento, wind ensemble, B-flat
major. Ho. II: 46]

Healey, Derek Edward

HAYDN, MICHAEL.
    Rohrau, Lower Austria 14 September 1737
    Salzburg 10 August 1806

Full name: Johann Michael Haydn

4702 [Divertimento for 5 instruments,   *12'*
G major]
1.Marcia 2.Allegro spiritoso 3.Menuetto -
Trio 4.Andante 5.Menuetto 6.Polonese
7.Allegretto 8.Presto
Fl.,Bn.-Hn.-Vn.,Va.
Score: Denkmäler der Tonkunst in Österreich,
XIV/2. Artaria, Vienna, 1907. Edited by
L.H. Perger. 9 p.
Parts: Ms. A Fleisher Collection Edition.
c1977 by The Fleisher Collection of Orches-
tral Music, Free Library of Philadelphia
Composed 1785.

1970s [Divertimento for string orchestra,
B-flat major]
1.Allegro con garbo 2.Menuetto 3.Largo
4.Allegretto - 6 Variations 5.Menuetto
6.Rondeau, presto - Marcia, andantino
grazioso
Str.(without Cb.)
Score: Denkmäler der Tonkunst in Österreich,
XIV/2. Artaria, Vienna, 1907. Edited by
L.H. Perger. 26 p.
Parts: Ms. A Fleisher Collection Edition.
c1977 by The Fleisher Collection of Orchestral Music, Free Library of Philadelphia

4705 [Six minuets for orchestra]   *11'*
1,2,0,1-2Hn.-Str.
Score: Denkmäler der Tonkunst in Österreich,
XIV/2. Artaria, Vienna, 1907. Edited by
L.H. Perger. 6 p.
Parts: Ms. A Fleisher Collection Edition.
c1977 by The Fleisher Collection of Orches-
tral Music, Free Library of Philadelphia
Composed 1784.

4700 [Symphony, C major]
1.Allegro con spirito 2.Andante 3.Fugato
molto vivace
0,2,0,2-2,2-Timp.-Str.
Score: Denkmäler der Tonkunst in Österreich,
XIV/2. Artaria, Vienna, 1907. Edited by
L.H. Perger. 33 p.
Parts: Ms. A Fleisher Collection Edition.
c1977 by The Fleisher Collection of Orchestral Music, Free Library of Philadelphia
Composed 1788.

4283 [Symphony, C major]   *20'*
1.Allegro spiritoso 2.Rondo: Un poco adagio
3.Fugato, vivace assai
0,2,0,2-2,2-Timp.-Str.
Breitkopf & Härtel, Leipzig [1895?]
Score 51 p.
*Composed 1784. First published as Op. 1 no. 3
by Artaria, Vienna, and announced as published
in The Breitkopf Thematic Catalogue,*

*Supplement XVI, 1787. First modern perform-
ance Leipzig, 14 November 1894, Hans Sitt
conductor.*

4707 [Symphony, E-flat major]
1.Allegro spiritoso 2.Adagietto affettuoso
3.Finale: Presto
0,2,0,2-2Hn.-Str.
Score: Denkmäler der Tonkunst in Österreich,
XIV/2. Artaria, Vienna, 1907. Edited by
L.H. Perger. 22 p.
Parts: Ms. A Fleisher Collection Edition.
c1977 by The Fleisher Collection of Orchestral Music, Free Library of Philadelphia
Composed 1783.

1366 [Symphony, G major]   *15'*
Adagio maestoso - Allegro con spirito -
Andante sostenuto - Allegro molto
Fl.,2Ob.-2Hn.-Str.
Breitkopf & Härtel, Leipzig [n.d.]
Score 16 p.
*Composed 1783. Mistakenly published as Sym-
phonie Nr. 37, G dur, von W. A. Mozart,
K.425a(444). Mozart in fact composed only
the introductory Adagio Maestoso.*

3263 [Symphony, Op. 10 no. 2, B-flat   *10'*
major. Ho. I: B2. Adapted and edited by
Hans Gál]
1.Allegro assai 2.Andantino, sempre piano
3.Presto
2Ob.-2Hn.-Cemb.(ad lib.)-Str.
Universal Edition, London, c1939
Score 15 p.
*Movements 1 and 2 composed by Michael Haydn;
Movement 3 by Joseph Haydn. First published
by Bremner, Amsterdam, 1774.*

Toy symphony
  See: MOZART, LEOPOLD.
      Toy symphony

4709 [Turkish march for band]   *6'*
2,2,2,2-2,2-Cym.,Turkish Dr.
Score: Denkmäler der Tonkunst in Österreich,
XIV/2. Artaria, Vienna, 1907. Edited by
L.H. Perger. 6 p.
Parts: Ms. A Fleisher Collection Edition.
c1977 by The Fleisher Collection of Orches-
tral Music, Free Library of Philadelphia
Composed 1795.

3536 [Turkish suite, from the music to   *17'*
Voltaire's Zaire. Edited by Karl Geiringer]
1.Allegro assai 2.Andante 3.Maestoso
4.Allegro molto
1,2,0,2-2Hn.,Tpt.-Perc.-Str.
Ms.
Score 40 p.

HAZA, ULISES LANAO DE LA.
  See: LANAO DE LA HAZA, ULISES.

HEALEY, DEREK EDWARD.
    Wargrave, Berkshire, England 2 May 1936

Healey, Derek Edward

7144 Arctic images, a suite for orchestra *20'*
1.Bear hunter - Pitseolak (Pesante) 2.Caribou,
winter light - Niviaksiak (Triste) 3.Mosquito
dream - Kalvak (Scherzando) 4.Cliff dwellers
- Lyola (Misterioso) 5.The arrival of the sun
- Kenojuak (Giubilante)
2*,2,2(2nd alt. B.Cl.)-2,2,2-Timp.,Perc.-
Prepared Pno.&Cel.(1player)-Str.
Ms. ᶜ1971 by Derek Healey
Score 61 p. Large folio
*Inspired by Eskimo prints. Commissioned by
the Canadian Broadcasting Co. for the Vancouver Autumn Fair. Composed 1971. First performance Vancouver, Canada, 21 September 1971,
CBC Vancouver Chamber Orchestra, John Avison
conductor.*

162m Concerto for organ, string *12'30"*
orchestra and timpani [Op. 8]
1.Lento - Allegro furioso 2.Intermezzo:
Andantino - Vivace (non troppo)
Solo Org.-Timp.-Str.
Ms. ᶜ1960 by Derek Healey
Score 31 p. Large folio
*Commissioned by Gordon Jeffery. Composed
1960. First performance London, Ontario, win-
ter 1961, London (Ontario) Symphony, Gordon
Jeffery conductor, Barrie Cabena soloist.*

HEBERLEIN, HERMANN.   Markneukirchen, Saxony 1859

726c [Concertpiece, violoncello, Op. 8, D minor]
Allegro molto - Andante - Allegro molto
Solo Vc.-2,2,2,2-2,2,1-Timp.-Str.
Score: Ms. 63 p.
Parts: Joh. André, Offenbach a.M. [n.d.]

533c Fantaisie hongroise, pour violoncelle...
Op. 27
Solo Vc.-2*,1,2-2,2,1-Timp.,Trgl.-Hp.(ad lib.)
-Str.
Joh. André, Offenbach a.M. [n.d.]
Score 35 p.

HECHT, GUSTAV.   Quechlinburg 23 May 1851
                   Köslin 8 July 1932

1695s Old French gavotte, for string orchestra.
Arranged by Gustav Hecht
Timp.,Trgl.(ad lib.)-Str.
Vieweg, Berlin [n.d.]
Score 3 p.

HECK, J. ARMAND.

946s Ballade, A major
Solo Vn.-Str.
Score: Ms. 7 p.
Parts: Decourcelle, Nice [n.d.]

1571s Cavatine, A major
Solo Vn.-Str.
Score: Ms. 7 p.
Parts: Decourcelle, Nice, ᶜ1928

HECKSCHER, CÉLESTE.   Philadelphia 23 February 1860
                        Philadelphia 18 February 1928

Born: Céleste de Longpré Massey

2722 Fantasie, To the forest. Arranged *15'*
and orchestrated by J.W.F. Leman
1.The ride 2.Rest 3.Dance of the wood nymphs
4.The return
3*,2,2,2-4,2,3,1-Timp.,Perc.-Str.
Ms.
Score 91 p.
*Originally composed for violin and piano, ca.
1902. Orchestrated 1934.*

HEDDENHAUSEN, FRIEDEL-HEINZ.
        b. Langenhagen, near Hannover 8 August 1910

4976 [Peasant dances for orchestra]   *12'*
2(1st alt. Picc.),2,2,2-4,3,3,1-Timp.,Perc.-
Str.
B. Schott's Söhne, Mainz, ᶜ1934
Score 32 p.
*Composed 1933. First performance Berlin, 2
October 1933, radio performance by The Berlin
Symphony Orchestra, Heinrich Steiner conductor.*

HEDWALL, LENNART.
        Göteborg, Sweden 16 September 1932

2164s [Music no. 2 for string orchestra]   *13'*
1.Lento e malinconico 2.Poco allegretto -
Andante 3.Intermezzo: Allegro moderato quasi
valse 4.Sostenuto - Allegro vivace
Str.
Ms.
Score 27 p.
*Composed 1958. First performance Huddinge,
Sweden, 27 April 1958, Huddinge Orchestra
Society, the composer conducting.*

HEGAR, FRIEDRICH.   Basel 11 October 1841
                      Zurich 2 June 1927

675v Ballade, Op. 45
Solo Vn.-2,2,2,2-2Hn.-Str.
Simrock, Berlin,ᶜ1922
Score 23 p.

887v [Concerto, violin, Op. 3, D major]
1.Allegro ma non troppo 2.Intermezzo: Andante
con moto 3.Allegro ma non troppo
Solo Vn.-2,2,2,2-2,2-Timp.-Str.
Joh. André, Offenbach a.M. [n.d.]
Score 80 p.
Composed and first performed Zurich, March 1873.

591c [Concerto, violoncello, Op. 44, C minor]
1.Allegro deciso 2.Andante sostenuto
3.Allegro non troppo
Solo Vc.-2,2,2,2-4,2,3-Timp.,Trgl.-Hp.-Str.
Simrock, Berlin, ᶜ1919
Score 58 p.

HEIDEN, BERNHARD.   Frankfurt 24 August 1910

1044m Concerto for small orchestra [Oboe, *18'*
bassoon and trumpet solos]
1.Lento, con moto 2.Vivace 3.Adagio
4.Allegro molto
1,1,2,1-2,2-Str.
Ms.
Score 46 p. Large folio
Composed 1949. First performance Art Institute

394

Auditorium, Detroit, 7 December 1949, Little Symphony of Detroit, the composer conducting.

4492 Euphorion, scene for orchestra   *11'30"*
3(3rd alt. Picc.),2,2,2-4,3,3,1-Timp.,Perc.-Str.
Ms.
Score 49 p. Large folio
Commissioned by Indiana University, 1949, for the bicentennial celebration of Goethe's birthday. Euphorion is a character in Faust, Part II. Composed 1949. First performance Bloomington, Indiana, 9 November 1949, Indiana University Symphony Orchestra, Ernst Hoffman conductor.

5435 Memorial for orchestra   *15'*
2(2nd alt. Picc.),2,2,2-4,2,3,1-Timp.,Perc.-Str.
Ms.
Score 57 p. Large folio
Commissioned by the Fromm Music Foundation, 1955. Composed 1955. First performance New York, 4 October 1956, Symphony of the Air, Leopold Stokowski conductor.

3392 Symphony   *17'*
1.Allegro con spirito 2.Andante 3.Jouyssance vous donneray [You shall give rejoicing]
3*,2(2nd alt. E.H.),2,2-4,3,3,1-Timp.,Perc.-Str.
Ms.
Score 140 p.
Composed 1938. First performance Detroit, 16 April 1941, Michigan Symphony Orchestra of the WPA, Valter Poole conductor.

5369 Symphony no. 2   *24'*
1.Allegro con spirito 2.Andante molto sostenuto 3.Allegro - Poco adagio
3(3rd alt. Picc.),2,2,2-4,3,3,1-Timp.,Perc.-Str.
Ms.
Score 100 p. Large folio
Commissioned by Indiana University, 1954. Composed 1954. First performance, Bloomington, Indiana, March 1955, Indiana University Philharmonic Orchestra, Ernst Hoffman conductor.

6242 Variations for orchestra (1960)   *16'*
3(3rd alt. Picc.),3*,3*,3*-4,3,3,1-Timp.,Perc.-Hp.-Str.
Ms.
Score 65 p. Large folio
Commissioned by Indiana University for the dedication ceremonies of the Music School Auditorium. Composed 1960. First performance Bloomington, Indiana, 5 November 1961, Indiana University Philharmonic Orchestra, Tibor Kozma conductor.

HEIDINGSFELD, LUDWIG. Jauer, Germany 24 March 1854
Danzig 14 September 1920

5588 [Two gypsy dances, Op. 3. No. 1, B major. No. 2, G minor]
1.Sehr bewegt 2.Ziemlich bewegt

2,2,2,2-4,2,2-Timp.,S.Dr.,Tamb.-Str.
Breitkopf & Härtel, Leipzig [1893?]
Score 43 p.

HEILNER, IRWIN.   New York 14 May 1908

3539 Swing symphony   *30'*
In one movement
3(3rd alt. Picc.),2(2nd alt. E.H.),2,2-4,3,3,1-Timp.,Perc.-Cel.-Str.
Ms.
Score 170 p.
Composed 1937-39.

HEINICHEN, JOHANN DAVID.   Krössuln, near
Weissenfels, Germany 17 April 1683
Dresden 15 July 1729

5332 [Pastoral for Christmas Eve] Edited   *6'*
by J. Bachmair
2 Solo Ob.(or Fl.)-0,2,0,1-Cemb.(or Pno. or Org.)-Str.
Breitkopf & Härtel, Leipzig, c1929
Score 7 p.

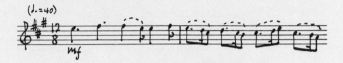

1398s [Pastoral for Christmas Eve. Arranged by Richard Fricke]
Cemb.-Str.
Score: Ms. 5 p.
Parts: Oppenheimer [n.p.] [n.d.]

HEINLEIN, FEDERICO.   Berlin 25 January 1912

3838 Variazioni, Op. 9   *14'*
3(3rd alt. Picc.),3*,3*,3*-4,3,3,1-Timp.,Trgl., Cym.-Str.
Ms.
Score 64 p.
Composed 1936.

HEINRICH, ANTHONY PHILIP.
Schönbüchel, Bohemia 11 March 1781
New York 3 May 1861

5947 Manitou mysteries, or The voice of the great spirit. Gran sinfonia misteriosa-indiana
1.Adagio assai - Allegretto moderato 2.Allegro giusto 3.Adagio 4.Finale: Allegro assai, quasi presto
3*,2,2,2-4,4,3,2(Ophicl. & Serpent)-Timp., Perc.-Str.
Ms.
Score 100 p. Large folio
Composed ca.1845.

HEINRICH XXIV, PRINCE REUSS.
See: REUSS, HEINRICH XXIV, Prince of Reuss-Köstritz

Heintze, Gustaf Hjalmar

HEINTZE, GUSTAF HJALMAR.
                    Jönköping, Sweden 22 July 1879
                    Saltsjöbaden, Sweden 4 March 1946

775m Elegie [for oboe and string orchestra]
Solo Ob.-Str.
Score: Ms. 12 p.
Parts: C.F. Schmidt, Heilbronn, c1897

HEISS, HERMANN. Darmstadt, Germany 29 December 1897
                    Darmstadt 6 December 1966

4356 [Heath, moor and seaside, a German
landscape for band]
2*(or 2Fl.),2,4(1 in E-flat),2-4Sax.-4,4,2Flü-
gelhorn,3,5(2Ten.,1Bar.,2Bass)-Timp.,Perc.
Chr. Friedrich Vieweg, Berlin, c1941
Score 32 p.
Composed 1938.

927s Sieben Stücke
Str.
C.F. Vieweg, Berlin [n.d.]
Score 8 p.

HELD, PAUL.   Warsaw 1888

936m [Concerto, oboe, Op. 80]   21'
1.Sonata form 2.Song form 3.Scherzo
Solo Ob.-Hp.-Str.
Ms.
Score 65 p.
*Originally composed as Quintet, for Oboe and
Strings, 1935. Arranged 1936.*

3086 Moses, symphonic poem, Op. 26   16'
3*,3*,3*,3*-4,3,3,1-Timp.,Perc.-Hp.-Str.
Ms.
Score 58 p.
Composed 1915.

3433 Tel Aviv, symphonic overture   10'30"
2,2,2,2-4,2,3,1-Timp.,Perc.-Pno.,Org.,Hp.-Str.
Ms.
Score 81 p.
*Composed 1928. First performance Chicago, 3
August 1938, Chicago Philharmonic Orchestra,
Richard Czerwonky conductor.*

HELFER, WALTER.
            Lawrence, Massachusetts 30 September 1896
            New Rochelle, New York 16 April 1959

3440 A fantasy on children's tunes   12'
1(alt.Picc.),1,1,1-2,1-Timp.,Perc.-Pno.,Cel.-
Str.
Ms.
Score 102 p.
*Composed 1936. First performance Rochester,
New York, 26 October 1937, Rochester Civic
Orchestra, Howard Hanson conductor.*

3215 Prelude to A Midsummer Night's   12'30"
Dream
1,1,1,2-1,1-Pno.-Str.
Ms.
Score 95 p.
Composed 1938. First performance Chicago,

*5 March 1940, Lange Little Symphony, Hans
Lange conductor. Awarded prize in the Paderewski Fund Prize Competition, 1938.*

2819 A water idyll, a barcarolle   8'
1,1,1,1-Hn.-Pno.-Str.
Ms.
Score 34 p.
*Composed 1936. Commissioned and first per-
formed New York, 2 March 1936, New York Phil-
harmonic Symphony Chamber Orchestra, Hans
Lange conductor.*

HELLER, JAMES G.   New Orleans 4 January 1892

1712s Elegie and pastorale, for string 24'
orchestra
Str.
Ms.
Score 19 p.
*Originally composed for voice and string quar-
tet, 1931. Transcribed for string orchestra,
1935.*

HELLER, STEPHEN.   Budapest 15 May 1813
                             Paris 14 January 1888

Spaziergänge eines Einsamen [Solitary walks]
Op. 78. Arranged for string orchestra by
Richard Hofmann
227s No. 2 in F major
451s No. 3 in B minor
604s No. 4 in B-flat major
Str.
Kistner, Leipzig [1891]
Scores: 7 p., 9 p., 5 p.
Originally composed for piano solo.

HELLMESBERGER, JOSEPH, SR. Vienna 23 November 1828
                           Vienna 24 October 1893

1242s Ball-scene, after a violin etude by
Mayseder
Timp.,Trgl.-2Hp.-Str. (2Fl.,2Ob.,2Bn. may
substitute for 2nd Hp.)
Universal Edition, Vienna [n.d.]
Score 19 p.

827 Gewitter-Scene [Storm scene, after an   8'
etude by Mayseder]
2,2,0,2-2Tpt.-Timp.-Hp.-Str.
Universal Edition, Leipzig [n.d.]
Score 19 p.

HELM, EVERETT.   Minneapolis 17 July 1913

4580 Brasiliana, suite for orchestra   12'
based on Brazilian folk melodies
1.Vem cà, meu anjo (Come here, my angel) 2.
Quero fugir-te (I would fly from you) 3.Per-
dão, Emilia (Forgive me, Emilia) 4.Easy four
3*,2,3*(B.Cl. optional),3*(C.Bn. optional)-4,
3,3,1-Timp.,Gong,Cym.-Hp.(ad lib.)-Str.
Ms.
Score 47 p. Large folio
Composed 1946.

4466 Cambridge suite for orchestra   16'
1.Overture 2.Aria 3.Dirge 4.Finale
3(3rd alt. Picc.),2,2,2-4,3,3,1(optional with
3rd Tbn.)-Timp.,Cym.,Trgl.-Pno.,Hp.-Str.
Ms.
Score 47 p. Large folio

325p [Concerto for piano and orchestra,   24'
no. 1, in G]
1.Allegro non troppo 2.Molto adagio - Adagi-
etto 3.Allegro moderato con brio
Solo Pno.-3,2,2,2-4,3,2,1-Timp.,Perc.-
Str.
Ms. [Schott & Co., London, c1951]
Score 91 p. Large folio
Composed 1950. First performance Berlin,
January 1951, Berlin Philharmonic Orchestra,
Joseph Keilberth conductor. First American
performance Carnegie Hall, New York, 24 April
1954, New York Philharmonic, Dimitri Mitro-
poulos conductor, Leonid Hambro soloist.

358p [Concerto for piano and orchestra,   15'
no. 2]
1.Moderato assai - Allegro moderato, leading
to 2.Adagio, leading to 3.Allegro
Solo Pno.-2,2,2,1-2,2,1-Perc.-Str.
Ms.
Score 43 p. Large folio
Commissioned by the Louisville Symphony Orches-
tra. Composed 1956. First performance Louis-
ville, Kentucky, 25 February 1956, Louisville
Symphony Orchestra, Robert Whitney conductor,
Benjamin Owen soloist.

1939s Concerto for string orchestra
1.Allegro energico 2.Adagio 3.Andante
Str.
Ms.
Score 49 p. Large folio
Composed 1950. First performance December
1952, Südwestfunk Orchestra, Paul Sacher
conductor.

1038m Five movements, for flute and strings
1.Adagio - Allegro 2.Trio: Moderato 3.
Vivace 4.Molto adagio 5.Alla marcia
Solo Fl.-Str.
Ms.
Score 12 p. Large folio

4467 Italian suite for small orchestra
1.Overture 2.Aria 3.Grottesco 4.Echo
5.March
2*,1,1,1-2,2,2-Str.
Ms.
Score 47 p.

1181v Kentucky sonata, for violin and orchestra
1.Andante - Allegro moderato - Cadenza 2.
Lento, ma non troppo 3.Gay, quick
Solo Vn.-2,2,2,2-4,2,2-Timp.-Str.
Ms.
Score 54 p. Large folio

4475 Three American songs for orchestra
1.Sailor song 2.Negro song 3.Religious song
3*,2,2,2-2,3,3,1-Timp.-Str.

Ms.
Score 24 p. Large folio

4476 Three gospel hymns for orchestra   15'
[original version]
1.Come and taste: Briskly 2.Jacob's ladder:
Tranquil 3.When the roll is called: Moderato
- March-like
3*,2,2,2-4,3,2-Timp.,Perc.-Str.
Ms.
Score 57 p. Large folio
Composed 1943.

6350 Three gospel hymns for orchestra   16'
[Revised version, 1953]
1.Come and taste: Con moto 2.Jacob's ladder:
Tranquillo 3.When the roll is called: Moderato,
alla marcia - Allegro molto
3*,2,2,2-4,3,2-Timp.,Perc.-Str.
Associated Music Publishers, New York, c1955
Score 54 p.
Originally composed 1943; revised 1953. First
performance of this version Cleveland, 12
April 1956, Cleveland Orchestra, George Szell
conductor.

HELMBURG, O.

196s Heimatlos [Homeless, elegy for piano,
Op. 63. Arranged by Holmes]
Hp.(or Pno.)ad lib.-Str.
Westphal, Berlin, c1919
Score in reduction 3 p.

HELYER, JACK.

4622 Rhythm and reason (Intermezzo   4'30"
in rhythm)
1,1,1-3Sax.-1Tpt.,1Tbn.-Perc.-Str.
B. Schott's Söhne, London, c1939
Score in reduction 4 p.

HENIOT, HANS LEVY.   Berlin 25 May 1902

3434 A mountain legend (Fortitude)   15'
3*,3*,3*,2-4,3,3,1-Timp.,Perc.-Hp.-Str.
Ms.
Score 63 p.
Composed 1926. First performance Detroit, 28
November 1929, Detroit Symphony Orchestra,
Ossip Gabrilovisch conductor. Awarded prize
in the Paderewski Fund Prize Competition, 1928.

HENLEY, WILLIAM.   West Bromwich, England 1876

Not William Ernest Henley (1849-1903).

835s Pizzicato-caprice, Op. 13
Str.
Jos. Williams, London, c1896
Score 11 p.

HENNEBERG, CARL ALBERT THEODOR.
                    b. Stockholm 27 March 1901

5034 [Bolla and Badin, Op. 40. Overture]   4'
3*,2,3,2-4,3,3,1-Timp.,Perc.-Str.
Ms.

Henneberg, Albert

Score 32 p.
From the opera composed in 1944.

1088m [Concertino for flute and string   *13'*
orchestra, Op. 39]
1.Moderato 2.Andante sostenuto 3.Allegro
leggiero
Solo Fl.-Str.
Ms.
Score 23 p.

6010 [In the shadow of the madonna,   *6'*
Op. 40. Prelude and tenor aria from the opera]
Tenor Voice Solo-3,3*,3*,3*-3,2-Trgl.,Tam-tam-
Cel.,Hp.-Str.
Ms.
Score 19 p.
*Commissioned by Föreningen Svenska Tonsättare.
From the opera in 3 acts with libretto by Ella
Byström-Baechström, after the novel In Trast-
evere by Oscar Levertin. Composed 1946-47.
First performance Stockholm, 30 December 1948,
the Swedish Broadcasting Orchestra, Ivar Hell-
man conductor.*

2170s [Serenade for string orchestra,   *20'*
Op. 20]
Andantino - Allegro scherzando - Meno mosso,
deciso - Andante cantabile - Con moto energico
Str.
Edition Suecia, Stockholm [n.d.]
Score 25 p.

5044 [Symphony no. 5, Op. 26]   *38'*
1.Largo - Allegro giusto 2.Andante cantabile
3.Allegro con brio
2(2nd alt. Picc.),2,2,2-4,2,3,1-Timp.-Str.
Ms.
Score 50 p. Large folio
*Composed 1932. First performance Stockholm,
1 December 1947, Swedish Radio Symphony Orchestra.*

HENRI, JACQUES.

179s Air de ballet [C major]
Fl.,Cl.-Str.
Score: Ms. 10 p.
Parts: B. Schott's Söhne, Mainz [n.d.]

1487s Rêve d'enfant, berceuse
Solo Vn.-Str.
Score: Ms. 4 p.
Parts: B. Schott's Söhne, Mainz [n.d.]

859s Valse intermezzo
Str.
Score: Ms. 8 p.
Parts: B. Schott's Sohne, Mainz [n.d.]

HENRIQUES, FINI VALDEMAR.
                    Copenhagen 20 December 1867
                    Copenhagen 27 October 1940

1491s Romanze, Op. 12 [G major]
Solo Vn.-Str.
Hansen, Copenhagen [n.d.]
Score 17 p.

592m [Suite, oboe and strings, Op. 13, F major]
1.Prelude 2.Intermezzo 3.Finale
Ob.-Str.
Hansen, Copenhagen [n.d.]
Score 17 p.
Score erroneously marked Op. 12.

HENRIQUES, ROBERT.   Copenhagen 14 December 1858
                          Copenhagen 29 December 1914

557c Tarantelle, Op. 10
Solo Vc.-2,0,2,2-2Hn.-Str.
Eulenburg, Leipzig [n.d.]
Score 29 p.

HENRY, LEIGH VAUGHAN.   Liverpool 23 September 1889
                         London 8 March 1958

3649 Fanfare, for wind and percussion   *48"*
(for a proclamation)
3*,1,2,0-2,2,3-Timp.,Side Dr.
Ms.
Score 6 p.

HENSCHEL, GEORGE. Breslau, Germany 18 February 1850
                  Aviemore, Scotland 10 September 1934

Born: Isador Georg Henschel. Knighted 1914.

95s Serenade in canonform, Op. 23, D major
1.Marcia 2.Andante 3.Scherzo 4.Finale
Str.
Breitkopf & Härtel, Leipzig [n.d.]
Score 38 p.

HENSELT, ADOLPH VON. Schwabach, Bavaria 9 May 1814
                      Warmbrunn, Silesia 10 October 1889

2124s Ave Maria, Op. 5 no. 4. Arranged   *2'30"*
by L. von Brenner
Str.(without Cb.)
Breitkopf & Härtel, Leipzig [1893?]
Score 2 p.

660p [Concerto, piano, Op. 16, F minor]   *38'*
1.Allegro patetico 2.Larghetto 3.Allegro
agitato
Solo Pno.-2,2,2,2-2,2,3-Timp.-Str.
Score: Ms. 221 p.
Parts: Breitkopf & Härtel, Leipzig [n.d.]
*Composed before 1845. First performance at a
Gewandhaus Concert, Leipzig, 5 October 1845,
Clara Schumann soloist.*

1039s Zwei kleine Walzer, Op. 28. Arranged by
Ludwig von Brenner
Str.
Kistner, Leipzig [n.d.]
Score 3 p.

HEPWORTH, WILLIAM.   Hamburg 16 December 1846
                          Chemnitz, Germany 12 April 1916

5203 [Suite in four movements for orchestra,
Op. 18]
1.Introduction und Fuge 2.Minuet 3.Intermezzo
4.Finale
2,2,2,2-4,2,2-Timp.-Str.

N. Simrock, Berlin, c1900
Score 43 p.

HERBERT, VICTOR.   Dublin 1 February 1859
                                    New York 26 May 1924

4227 Al fresco, intermezzo   3'
1,1,2,1-2,2,1-Timp.,Perc.-Pno.-Str.
Witmark & Sons, New York, c1904
Score in reduction 4 p.
*Originally composed for piano and published
under the pseudonym of Frank Roland. Arranged
for piano and orchestra by the composer. Later
included in Herbert's operetta, It Happened
in Nordland.*

397c [Concerto, violoncello, no. 1,   23'
Op. 8, D major]
1.Allegro con spirito 2.Andante - Scherzo
(Vivace) 3.Allegro fantastico
Solo Vc.-2(2nd alt. Picc.),2,2,2-4,2,3-Timp.-
Hp.-Str.
Ms.
Score 119 p.
*Composed 1884-85. First performance Stutt-
gart, 8 December 1885, the composer as soloist.*

630c [Concerto, violoncello, no. 2, Op. 30,
E minor]
Allegro impetuoso - Andante tranquillo -
Allegro
Solo Vc.-2,2,2,2-4,2,2-Timp.,Trgl.-Str.
Schuberth, Leipzig [n.d.]
Score 63 p.
*First performance March 1894, New York Phil-
harmonic, the composer as soloist.*

5707 Hero and Leander, a symphonic   *ca.30'*
poem, Op. 33
3(3rd alt. Picc.),3*,3*,3-4,3,3,1-Timp.,Perc.-
Hp.-Str.
Ms.
Score 120 p.
*First performance Pittsburgh, 18 January 1901,
Pittsburgh Symphony Orchestra, the composer
conducting.*

1217 Irish rhapsody   17'
3*,2,2,2-4,2,3,1-Timp.,Perc.-Hp.-Str.
G. Schirmer, New York, c1910
Score 54 p.

4371 Natoma. Prelude to Act III   4'
3*,3*,3*,3*-4,3,3,1-Timp.,B.Dr.,Cym.-Hp.-Str.
G. Schirmer, New York, c1911
Score 19 p.
*From the opera in 3 acts with libretto by
Joseph Deighn Redding. Composed 1909-10.
First performance Philadelphia, 25 February
1911, Philadelphia-Chicago Opera Company,
Cleofonte Campanini conductor.*

7013 Natoma. Grand fantasia on the opera.   20'
Arranged by Otto Langey
3*,3*,3*,3*-4,3,3,1-Timp.,Perc.-
Hp.-Str.
G. Schirmer, New York, c1911
Score 51 p.

582s Serenade, Op. 12, F major   *22'*
1.Entrance 2.Polonaise 3.Love scene
4.Canzonetta 5.Finale
Str.
G. Schirmer, New York, c1889
Score 49 p.

1170 Suite romantique, Op. 31
1.Visions 2.Morning serenade 3.Love's triumph 4.Wedding feast
3(3rd alt. Picc.),2,3*,2-4,3,3,1-Timp.,Perc.-
Hp.-Str.
Simrock, Berlin, c1901
Score 90 p.

Three compositions for string orchestra
102s No. 1 Air de ballet
103s No. 2 Forget-me-not
104s No. 3 Sunset
Str.(Trgl. and Hp. in No. 1)
G. Schirmer, New York, c1912
Scores: 7 p., 5 p., 3 p.

HERFURTH, W.   Gera, Germany 1825
                                    Gera 25 November 1906

877m [Concertino, trumpet and orchestra]
In one movement
Solo Tpt.-2,2,2,2-4,2,3-Timp.-Str.
Score: Ms. 81 p.
Parts: A.E. Fischer, Bremen [n.d.]

HERMANN, E. HANS G.   Leipzig 17 August 1870
                             Berlin 18 May 1931

696m Adagio pour clarinette et orchestre
Solo Cl.-Ob.-2Hn.-Str.
Ms.
Score 13 p.

692m Gavotte-intermezzo [clarinet and orchestra]
Solo Cl.-1,1,1,2-2Hn.-Str.
Ms.
Score 27 p.

HERMANN, ROBERT.   Bern, Switzerland 29 April 1869
                     Ambach, Bavaria 22 October 1912

822m Berceuse [horn and string orchestra, Op.
10]
Solo Hn.-Str.
Hofmeister, Leipzig [n.d.]
Score 11 p.
Originally composed for violoncello and piano.

HERMANN, RODOLPHE.

535c Lassitude [for violoncello solo   3'
and orchestra]
Solo Vc.-1,1,1,1-2,1,1-Timp.-Str.
Score: Ms. 7 p.
Parts: Choudens, Paris, c1927

542c Lied [for violoncello solo and orchestra]
Solo Vc.-1,1,1,1-2,1,1-Timp.,Trgl.-Str.
Score: Ms. 13 p.
Parts: Choudens, Paris, c1927

Hernández-Lizaso, Antonino

HERNÁNDEZ-LIZASO, ANTONINO.

7295 Oda romantica, Ignacio Agramonte [for
orchestra]
3*,3*,3*,3*-4,3,3,1-Timp.,Perc.-Str.
Ms.
Score 65 p.
*Agramonte was a hero of the first Cuban revolt
against Spanish rule. Composed 1963. First
performance Miami, 30 June 1976, Miami Philharmonic, the composer conducting.*

7294 Perichoresis [for orchestra]   *16'30"*
1.Allegretto - Allegro 2.Tema y variaciones
3.Allegro molto
2(2nd alt. Picc.),2,2,2-2,2-Str.
Ms.
Score 56 p. Large folio
*Perichoresis originally was a Greek dance
form. It became an early Christian theologi-
cal term referring to the Incarnation. The
movements of this work were inspired by the
following Biblical verses: Genesis 1:3;
Psalms 2:7; Acts 2:2-4. Composed 1969-70.*

HEROLD, LOUIS-JOSEPH-FERDINAND.
                         Paris 28 January 1791
                Thernes, near Paris 19 January 1833

4278 [Les rosières. Overture]
2,2,2,2-2Hn.-Timp.-Str.
Boieldieu Jeune, Paris [1817]
Score 16 p.
*From the opéra-comique in 3 acts with libretto
by Théaulon de Lambert. First performance
Opéra-Comique, Paris, 27 January 1817.*

4296 [Symphony no. 1, C major]
1.Allegro maestoso 2.Andante 3.Minuetto
4.Rondo: Vivace
2,2,2,2-2Hn.-Timp.-Str.
[Privately printed, 189-?]
Score 63 p.
Composed 1813.

5676 [Symphony no. 2, D major]
1.Introduzione: Largo - Allegro molto 2.
Andante 3.Rondo
2,2,2,2-2Hn.-Str.
[Privately printed, 189-?]
Score 67 p.
Composed 1814.

7097 [Zampa, ou La fiancée de marbre.   *8'*
Overture]
2*,2,2,2-4,2,3,Ophicl.-Timp.,Perc.-Str.
Luck's Music Library, Detroit [n.d.]
Score 36 p.
*From the opéra-comique in 3 acts with libretto
by Anne Honoré Joseph Mélesville. First per-
formance Opéra-Comique, Paris, 3 May 1831.*

HERRMANN, BERNARD.   New York 29 January 1911

1732s Sinfonietta, for string orchestra   *15'*
1.Prelude 2.Scherzo 3.Adagio 4.Interlude
5.Variations
Str.

New Music Orchestra Series, San Francisco,
c1936 by Bernard Herrmann
Score 12 p.
Composed 1935.

HERRMANN, EDUARD.
                 Oberrotweil, Germany 18 December 1850
                      Miami, Florida 24 April 1937

791v [Concerto, violin and orchestra, Op. 25]
1.Allegro maestoso 2.Andante 3.Allegro
giucante
Solo Vn.-2,2,2,2-2,2,1-Timp.-Str.
Wilhelm Schmid, Nürnberg [n.d.]
Score 59 p.
*Composed 1904. First performance New York, 17
February 1905, Franz X. Arens conductor, H. von
Dameck soloist.*

HERTEL, JOHANN WILHELM.
                 Eisenach, Germany 9 October 1727
                         Schwerin 14 June 1789

6531 [Symphony, G major]
1.Allegro 2.Larghetto 3.Presto
2,2,0,2-2Hn.-Cemb.-Str.
Breitkopf & Härtel, Leipzig [n.d.]
Score 20 p.
Composed ca.1765.

HERTZMAN, FRITHIOF.

1418s Romance [violoncello and string orchestra,
Op. 24, D major]
Solo Vc.-Str.
Wilhelm Hansen, Leipzig [n.d.]
Score 5 p.
*Solo can also be played by violin, flute,
clarinet, oboe or bassoon.*

HERVEY, ARTHUR.   Paris 26 January 1855
                         London 10 March 1922

1276 Life moods, variations for orchestra
3(3rd alt. Picc.),2(2nd alt. E.H.),2,2-4,3,3,1
-Timp.,Perc.-Org.(ad lib.),Hp.-Str.
Hawkes, London, c1911
Score 100 p.

HESELTINE, PHILIP.   London 30 October 1894
                         London 17 December 1930

Also published under the pseudonym: Peter Warlock

821s Capriol, suite for string orchestra
1.Basse-dance 2.Pavane 3.Tordion 4.Bransles
5.Pieds-en-l'air 6.Mattachins
Str.
Curwen, London, c1927
Score 20 p.

2082 An old song, for small orchestra   *3'*
1,1,1-Hn.-Str.
Chester, London, c1923
Score 7 p.
*First performance Birmingham, 16 November 1924,
Adrian Boult conductor.*

560s Serenade for strings
Str.
Oxford University Press, London, ^c1925
Score 6 p.
Composed 1923 in honor of Frederick Delius'
60th birthday.

HESSE, FÉLIX.

1177s Gavotte régence, pour orchestre à cordes
Str.
Score: Ms. 8 p.
Parts: Decourcelle, Nice, ^c1925

HEUBERGER, RICHARD FRANZ JOSEPH.
                    Graz, Austria 18 June 1850
                    Vienna 27 October 1914

201s Nachtmusik für Streichorchester,   *20'*
Op. 7
1.Allegretto 2.Allegro vivace 3.Andante
4.Presto
Str.
Kistner, Leipzig [n.d.]
Score 36 p.

447 [Variations on a theme by Franz Schu- *30'*
bert, Op. 11]
2,2,2,2-2,2-Timp.-Str.
Kistner, Leipzig [n.d.]
Score 43 p.
Composed 1878. First performance Vienna,
1879, the composer conducting.

HEUER, GUSTAV.   Weimar, Germany 16 November 1875

760m Praeludium, for flute and orchestra,
Op. 13a
Solo Fl.-0,2,2,2-4,2,3-Str.
Score: Ms. 22 p.
Parts: Filser, Augsburg [n.d.]

769m Scherzo, for flute and orchestra,
Op. 13b
Solo Fl.-0,2,2,2-2Hn.-Str.
Score: Ms. 37 p.
Parts: Filser, Augsburg [n.d.]

HEURTEUR, F.   d. Paris 1930

1217s Berceuse, pour orchestre à cordes
Solo Vn.-Str.
Score: Ms. 6 p.
Parts: Ricordi, Paris, ^c1922

979v Canzonetta, violin solo and orchestra   *2'*
Solo Vn.-1,1,1,1(all optional)-Str.
Score: Ms. 8 p.
Parts: Decourcelle, Nice, ^c1924
Composed 1923. First performance Paris,
September 1924, the composer conducting.

1016v Hyhra, melody for violin and   *1'*
orchestra
Solo Vn.-1,1,1,1-2Hn.-Str.
Score: 6 p.

Parts: Decourcelle, Nice, ^c1924
Composed 1924. First performance Paris,
September 1924, the composer conducting.

HEWITT, HARRY.   Detroit, Michigan 4 March 1921

4758 Dwellers in the mirage [Op. 37 no. 2]   *5'*
2(both alt. Picc.),2,2,2-4,2,2-Timp.,Cym.-Str.
Ms. [Now published by American Composers Alliance, New York, ^c1953 by Harry Hewitt]
Score 15 p.
Inspired by the novella by Abraham Merritt
(1882-1943). Composed 1942. This and Sha-
dow out of Time are two parts of a larger
work, Music for the Neocronomicon.

4725 A good-natured overture [Op. 57 no. 1] *6'*
2,2(2nd optional),2,2-4,2,2-Timp.-Str.
Ms. [Now published by American Composers Alli-
ance, New York, ^c1953 by Harry Hewitt]
Score 16 p.
Composed 1948.

7138 Haven, Op. 426 no. 3   *6-12'(optional)*
6,6,6,6(all optional)-6,7,7,7-Timp.,Perc.-
Pno.-Str. Divisi in 30 parts
Ms. ^c1975 by Harry Hewitt
Score 71 p. Elephant folio
Composed 1974. This is no. 4 of a group of
compositions delineating Zen states. Haven,
from the Japanese, means "the very eye of God."

4786 Prelude to Spoon River [Op. 53 no. 3] *4'*
2,E.H.,2,2-2Hn.-Str.
Ms. [Now published by American Composers Alliance, New York, ^c1953 by Harry Hewitt]
Score 4 p.
Originally composed 1938 in a longer version
to underscore the reading of a radio drama
entitled The Hill. Readings selected from the
poems in Edgar Lee Masters' Spoon River
Anthology. This version for chamber orchestra
first performed at Carnegie Recital Hall, New
York, 1 December 1944, New York Little Sym-
phony, Joseph Barone conductor.

2414s Quiet music no. 3, Op. 136 no. 3   *6'*
Str.
Ms.
Score 8 p.
Composed 1977.

4757 Shadow out of time, a nightmare for   *4'*
orchestra [Op. 37 no. 1]
2*(1st alt. Picc.),2(2nd alt. E.H.),2,3*-4,2,
2-Timp.,Perc.-Pno.,Hp.-Str.
Ms. [Now published by American Composers Alliance, New York, ^c1953 by Harry Hewitt]
Score 21 p.
Inspired by the short horror tales of Howard
Phillips Lovecraft (1890-1937). Composed
1942. This and Dwellers in the Mirage are
two parts of a larger work, Music for the
Neocronomicon.

Hewitt, Harry

4843 Sinfonia no. 1 [Op. 40 no. 1]   *16'*
1.Largo - Moderato - Lento 2.Lento - Allegro
- Lento 3.Lento
2,2,2,2-4,2-Timp.,S.Dr.,Cym.-Str.
Ms. [Now published by American Composers Alli-
ance, New York, c1953 by Harry Hewitt]
Score 28 p. Large folio
Composed 1943.

4849 Symphony no. 3 [Op. 43]   *27'*
In 5 movements (variable tempos within movements)
3(all alt. Picc.),3(3rd alt. E.H.),3,3*-4,3,3,
1-Timp.,Perc.-Str.
Ms. [Now published by American Composers Alliance, New York, c1953 by Harry Hewitt]
Score 88 p. Large folio
Composed 1941; revised 1951.

4793 Symphony no. 8 [Op. 103] C major   *ca.27'*
In 4 movements (variable tempos within move-
ments)
2(2nd alt. Picc.),2,2,2-4,2,2-Timp.,B.Dr.,
Cym.-Str.
Ms. [Now published by American Composers Alli-
ance, New York, c1953 by Harry Hewitt]
Score 109 p. Large folio
Composed 1944; revised 1948.

7247 Symphony no. 22, Op. 446   *20-25'*
In 4 movements with constantly varying tempi
3*(1st alt. Picc.II),3*(2nd alt. optional E.H.
II),3(3rd optional),3*-4,3,2,1-Timp.,Perc.-
Str.
Ms. c1975 by Harry Hewitt
Score 77 p. Large folio
Composed 1974-75.

4737 Taming of the Shrew. Overture   *6'*
[Op. 53 no. 6]
1,1,1,1-1,1-Timp.-Str.
Ms. [Now published by American Composers Alliance, New York, c1953 by Harry Hewitt]
Score 25 p.
From the incidental music to Shakespeare's
play. First performance Wynnewood, Pennsyl-
vania, 12 June 1948, the composer conducting.

2016s Twenty-four preludes for string   *ca.60'*
orchestra [Op. 19]
Str.
Ms. [Now published by American Composers Alli-
ance, New York, c1953 by Harry Hewitt]
Score 80 p. Large folio
Composed 1936-46. First performance of nos.
1-6 Chicago, November 1948, Egerinsky Sym-
phonietta, Egerinsky conductor. Awarded the
Leopold Egerinsky Prize, 1948.

7154 Yugen, Op. 426 no. 1   *variable duration*
4Fl.(1st and 3rd alt. Picc.) or 4Shō,2Ob.(2nd
alt. E.H.) or 2Hichiriki,2Cl.,2Bn.-4(3rd and
4th optional),2,2,1-Timp.,Perc.-Pno.-Str.
Ms. c1967 by Harry Hewitt
Score 14 p.
Yugen: A Chinese term of the Han period ap-
plied to the mysterious and sublime aspects of
Buddhism. Composed 1967 as no. 1 of four com-
positions delineating Zen states.

HEWITT, JAMES.   Dartmoor, England 4 June 1770
                          Boston 1 August 1827

4918 The battle of Trenton, a favorite   *9'*
historical military sonata. Transcribed for
orchestra by Richard Bales
Introduction - The army in motion - General
orders - Acclamation of the Americans - Drums
beat To Arms - Washington's march at the battle
of Trenton - The army crossing the Delaware -
Ardor of the Americans at landing - Trumpets
sound the charge - The attack - The Hessians
begging quarter - The fight renewed - General
confusion. The Hessians surrender themselves
prisoners of war - Grief of the Americans for
the loss of their comrades killed in the engage-
ment. Yankee Doodle - Quickstep - Trumpets of
victory - General rejoicing
1,1,2,1-2,2,1-Timp.,Perc.-Str.
Ms. c1955 by Richard Bales
Score 69 p. Large folio
Originally composed for piano and privately
published in 1797. This orchestration, 1950-
51, first performed Washington, D.C., National
Gallery of Art, 22 April 1951, National Gallery
Orchestra, Richard Bales conductor. Hewitt's
dedication is to George Washington.

7220 The federal constitution and liberty   *4'*
forever. Transcribed for voices and small
orchestra by R.D. Ward
1(alt. Picc.),2,0,2-2Hn.-SATB Voices(Chorus or
Solo)-Str.
Ms. c1975 by R.D. Ward
Score 18 p.
Hewitt's song, with text by William Milns, is
actually an arrangement for voice and keyboard
instrument of Yankee Doodle and an anonymous
Washington's March. First published by J.
Hewitt's Musical Repository, New York, 1798.
This version commissioned by the Richmond Sin-
fonia. Transcribed 1975. First performance
St. John's United Church of Christ, Richmond,
Virginia, 15 December 1975, Richmond Sinfonia,
Jacques Houtmann conductor.

7045 In a far distant clime. Edited and   *3'*
transcribed [for voice and small orchestra] by
Philip Weston
High Voice Solo-1,1,2,1-2Hn.-Str.
Concord Music Publishing, New York, c1941
Score 7 p.
Song with text by R. T. Spence. Originally
composed for voice and piano.

7303 The new federal overture. Tran-   *11'*
scribed for small orchestra by R.D. Ward
1(alt. Picc.),2,0,2-2Hn.-Pno.(optional)-Str.
Ms. c1975 by R.D. Ward
Score 46 p.
Originally composed 1797 as a potpourri over-
ture, quoting popular melodies of the period.
This transcription commissioned by the Rich-
mond Sinfonia. Transcribed 1975. First per-
formance St. John's United Church of Christ,
Richmond, Virginia, 15 December 1975, Richmond
Sinfonia, Jacques Houtmann conductor.

HICKS, PEGGY GLANVILLE.
  See: GLANVILLE-HICKS, PEGGY.

HIER, ETHEL GLENN.   Cincinnati, Ohio 25 June 1889
                Winter Park, Florida 14 January 1971

  3562 Campane d'Asolo [Bells of Asolo]   *6'30"*
  3,2,3*,3*-4,2,3,1-Timp.,Perc.-Pno.,Cel.,Hp.-
  Str.
  Ms.
  Score 20 p.
  *Originally composed for piano, 1938; arranged
  1938. First performance Rochester, New York,
  25 October 1939, Rochester Civic Orchestra,
  Howard Hanson conductor.*

  3329 Carolina Christmas, suite for   *12'*
  chamber orchestra
  1.Cousin Callie's garden 2.Tramp to Holly
  Hedge 3.Mocking birds at Johnson's Pond
  4.Twilight on the plantation
  2,2,2,2-4Hns.-Str.
  Ms.
  Score 74 p.
  *Originally composed for string quartet, 1926;
  transcribed for chamber orchestra, 1939.
  First performance at a concert of the National
  Association of American Composers and Conductors, New York, 28 January 1940, broadcast
  over Station WNYC, New York Civic Orchestra
  of the WPA, Macklin Marrow conductor. Title
  later changed to Carolina, Suite for Chamber
  Orchestra.*

  5275 Three pieces for orchestra   *12'*
  1.Foreboding 2.Asolo bells 3.Badinage
  3(2nd alt. Picc.),2,3*,2-4,3,3,1-Timp.,Perc.-
  Pno.,Cel.,Hp.-Str.
  Composers Press, New York, ᶜ1954
  Score 63 p.
  *No. 2 originally composed for piano, 1938.
  Transcribed for orchestra, 1938. No. 2, Asolo
  Bells, first performed in Rochester, New York,
  25 October 1939, Eastman-Rochester Symphony
  Orchestra, Howard Hanson conductor. Received
  the 1953 Symphonic Award sponsored by Com-
  posers Press.*

HIGGINSON, JOSEPH VINCENT.
        b. Irvington, New Jersey 17 May 1896

  Also known under the pseudonym: Cyr de Brant

  3072 Magdalen [for orchestra]   *8'*
  1,1(alt. E.H.),2,1-2,2,1-Timp.,Perc.-Pno.,Cel.-
  Str.
  Ms.
  Score 22 p.
  *Commissioned by Margaret Anglin as background
  music for her poem, Magdalen; never performed
  as such. Composed 1931. First performance
  New York, 7 April 1937, Greenwich Concert
  Orchestra of the WPA, Henry Aaron conductor.*

  3074 Rondo serieuse [for orchestra]   *5'*
  2(2nd alt. Picc.),1,2,1-2,2,1-Timp.-Pno.-Str.
  Ms.
  Score 24 p.

  *Originally composed as the 3rd movement of a
  sonata for organ, 1928. Transcribed for
  orchestra, 1930. First performance New York,
  7 April 1937, Greenwich Concert Orchestra of
  the WPA, Henry Aaron conductor.*

  3071 A song of yesteryear, sarabande   *2'*
  [wind quintet and string orchestra]
  1,1,1,1-Hn.-Str.
  Ms.
  Score 8 p.
  *Originally composed as part of a suite for
  piano, 1928. Transcribed for orchestra 1929.
  First performance New York, 20 May 1930, Bam-
  berger Symphony Orchestra broadcast over Radio
  Station WOR, Philip James conductor.*

HIJMAN, JULIUS.   Almelo, Holland 25 January 1901
                New York 6 January 1969

  4486 [Symphonic suite for orchestra, 1938]
  1.Allegro deciso 2.Intermezzo 3.Finale
  3*,2,2,2-4,3,3,1-Timp.,S.Dr.,Cym.-Str.
  Ms.
  Score 118 p.

HILL, EDWARD BURLINGAME.
        Cambridge, Massachusetts 9 September 1872
        Francestown, New Hampshire 9 July 1960

  712p Concertino in one movement, piano   *12'*
  and orchestra, Op. 36
  Solo Pno.-3(3rd alt. Picc.),3*,2,3*-4,3,3,1-
  Timp.,Perc.-Str.
  Ms.
  Score 68 p.
  *Composed 1931. First performance Boston, 25
  April 1932, Boston Symphony Orchestra, Serge
  Koussevitzky conductor, Jesús María Sanromá
  soloist.*

  2622 Lilacs, poem for orchestra, Op. 33   *14'*
  3(3rd alt. Picc.),3*,3*,3*-6,3,3,1-Timp.,Perc.
  -Pno.,Cel.,Hp.-Str.
  Cos Cob, New York, ᶜ1931
  Score 47 p.
  *Suggested by Amy Lowell's poem. Composed 1926.
  First performance Cambridge, Massachusetts,
  31 March 1927, Boston Symphony Orchestra, Serge
  Koussevitzky conductor.*

  2772 Stevensoniana, suite no. 1, Op. 24,   *15'*
  after poems from Robert Louis Stevenson's A
  Child's Garden of Verses
  1.March 2.Lullaby, The land of Nod 3.Scherzo
  4.The unseen playmate
  3*,3*,2,2-4,2,3,1-Timp.,Perc.-Cel.,Hp.-Str.
  Ms.
  Score 126 p.
  *Composed 1916-17. First performance New York,
  17 February 1918, New York Symphony Society,
  Walter Damrosch conductor.*

  1991s Suite for string orchestra
  1.Toccata 2.Quasi gavotta 3.Air 4.Giga
  Str.
  Ms.
  Score 18 p.

Hill, Edward Burlingame

2789 [Symphony, Op. 34, B-flat major]   21'
1.Allegro moderato, ma risoluto 2.Moderato
maestoso 3.Allegro brioso
4(3rd and 4th alt. Picc.),3*,4*,3*-6,4,3,1-
Timp.,Perc.-Str.
Ms.
Score 157 p.
Composed 1927. First performance Boston, 30
March 1928, Boston Symphony Orchestra, Serge
Koussevitzky conductor.

HILL, JACKSON.   Birmingham, Alabama 23 May 1941

7047 Mosaics   15'
1.Invocation 2.Fanfare 3.Nocturne 4.Scherzo
5.Epilogue
2,2,2,2-4,3,3,1-Timp.,Perc.-Pno.-Str.
Ms.
Score 37 p.
Composed 1965. Selected for performance by the
Orchestra Society of Philadelphia as part of
its Pennsylvania Composers Project 1974, made
possible by a grant from the Pennsylvania Coun-
cil for the Arts with performance materials
prepared by Fleisher Collection. First per-
formance Mandell Theater, Drexel University,
Philadelphia, 22 June 1974, Orchestra Society
of Philadelphia, Sidney Rothstein conductor.

HILL, MABEL WOOD.
    See: WOOD-HILL, MABEL.

HILLE, GUSTAV.   Jericho-on-Elbe 31 May 1851

327s Berceuse, Op. 46
Solo Vn.-Str.(without Cb.)
C.F.W. Siegel, Leipzig [n.d.]
Score 7 p.

HILLEMACHER, PAUL.   Paris 29 November 1852
                             Versailles 13 August 1933

663c [Suite in the olden style]   14'
1.Aria 2.Gaillarde 3.[Tender gavotte]
4.Tambourin
Solo Vc.-1,1(or Cl.),0,1-Timp.(or Tamb.)-Str.
Société Anonyme des Éditions Ricordi, Paris,
c1921
Score 42 p.

HILLER, FERDINAND.
          Frankfurt, Germany 24 October 1811
                    Cologne 10 May 1885

5263 Auf der Wacht. Nach dem Clavierstück aus
Op. 146, Aus dem Soldatenleben
2,2,2,2-4,2-Timp.,S.Dr.-Str.
B.Schott's Söhne, Mainz [1878?]
Score 16 p.
Originally composed for piano.

662p [Concert piece, piano, Op. 113, C major]
Alla marcia: Allegro energico con fuoco -
Andante religioso ma con moto - Allegro
Solo Pno.-2,2,2,2-2,2,3-Timp.-Str.
Score: Ms. 190 p.
Parts: [n.p., n.d]

679c [Concert piece, violoncello, Op. 104,
A minor]
Allegro moderato - Intermezzo: Allegretto ma
non troppo - Finale: Allegro con brio
Solo Vc.-2,2,2,2-2,2-Timp.-Str.
Score: Ms. 87 p.
Parts: G. Heinze, Leipzig [n.d.]

546p [Concerto, piano, Op. 69, F-sharp minor]
1.Moderato, ma con energia e con fuoco 2.
Andante 3.Allegro con fuoco
Solo Pno.-2(2nd alt. Picc.),2,2,2-2,2-Timp.-
Str.
Cranz, Leipzig [n.d.]
Score 80 p.

447v Fantasiestück [violin and orchestra,
Op. 152b]
Solo Vn.-2,2,2,2-2,2-Timp.-Str.
R. Forberg, Leipzig [n.d.]
Score 59 p.

1501s Friede [Peace, Op. 190. Arranged by
Harry Schloming]
Str.
[Cranz, n.p., n.d.]
Score 3 p.

HILLIER, LOUIS H.

978s Rêverie, Op. 31
Str.
Score: Ms. 11 p.
Parts: [n.p., n.d.]

HILLMANN, E.

1310s Am Sprudel [The bubbling fountain]
Str.
Score: Ms. 8 p.
Parts: Louis Oertel, Hannover [n.d.]

HILLMANN, KARL.   Frankfurt am Main 2 October 1867

635v [Elegie, violin and orchestra, Op. 35]
Solo Vn.-2,1,2,2-2Hn.-Timp.-Str.
Joh. André, Offenbach a.M. [n.d.]
Score 16 p.

2s Wiegenlied [Lullaby, Op. 21, G major]
Fl.(ad lib.)-Str.
Joh. André, Offenbach a/Main, c1901
Score 3 p.

HINDEMITH, PAUL.   Hanau
     near Frankfurt, Germany 16 November 1895
                    Frankfurt 28 December 1963

3928 [Chamber music no. 1, for small   30'
orchestra, Op. 24 no. 1]
1.Sehr schnell und wild 2.Mässig schnelle
Halbe 3.Quartett 4.Finale: 1921
1(alt. Picc.),0,1,1-Tpt.-Perc.-Pno.,Harm.-Str.
B. Schott's Söhne, Mainz, c1922
Miniature score 112 p.
Composed 1921. First performance Donau-
eschingen, 31 July 1922, Gesellschaft der Musik-
freunde concert, Hermann Scherchen conductor.

COLLECTION OF ORCHESTRAL MUSIC

342p [Chamber music no. 2 for piano and   20'
12 solo instruments (piano concerto), Op. 36
no. 1]
1.Sehr lebhafte Achtel 2.Sehr langsame Achtel
3.Kleines potpourri [Little potpourri]
4.Finale: Schnelle Viertel
Solo Pno.-1,1,2*,1-1,1,1-Str.(no Vn.II)
B. Schott's Söhne, Mainz, c1924
Score 96 p.
*Composed 1924. First performance Frankfurt,
1924, Emma Lübbecke-Job pianist.*

1151v [Chamber music no. 5, for solo   17'
viola and orchestra, Op. 36 no. 4]
1.Schnell Halbe 2.Langsam 3.Mässig schnelle
4.Variante eines Militärmarsches
Solo Va.-1(alt. Picc.),1,3*(1Cl. in E-flat),
3*-1,2,2,1-Vc.,Cb.
B. Schott's Söhne, Mainz, c1927
Miniature score 115 p.
*Composed 1927. First performance Berlin, 1927,
the State Opera Orchestra, Otto Klemperer conductor, the composer as soloist.*

5110 [Concert music for string orchestra   18'
and brass instruments, Op. 50 (1930)]
Part I: Mässig schnell, mit Kraft - Sehr
       breit, aber stets fliessend
Part II: Lebhaft - Langsam - Lebhaft
0,0,0,0-4,4,3,1-Str.
B. Schott's Söhne, Mainz, c1931
Score 79 p.
*Written for the 50th anniversary of the Boston
Symphony Orchestra. Composed 1930. First
performance Boston, 3 April 1931, Boston Sym-
phony Orchestra, Serge Koussevitzky conductor.*

1544 [Concert music for wind orchestra,   15'
Op. 41]
1.[Concertante overture] 2.[Six variations on
the song, Prince Eugene, the Glorious Knight]
3.[March]
1(alt. Picc.),1,4(1Cl. in E-flat)-2Hn.,3Tpt.,
2Flügelhorn(or Sop. Sax.),2Ten. Hn.(or Ten.
Sax. or Ten. Tuba),Baritone(or B.Cl.),3Tbn.,
3Tubas-Perc.
B. Schott's Söhne, Mainz, c1927
Score 49 p.
*Composed 1924. First performance Donau-
eschingen 1926, Hermann Scherchen conductor.*

1339 [Concerto for orchestra, Op. 38]   17'
1.Mit Kraft, mässig schnelle 2.Sehr schnelle
Halbe 3.Marsch für Holzbläser 4.Basso osti-
nato
2(2nd alt. Picc.),2,3*(1Cl. in E-flat),3*-3,
2,1,1-Timp.,Perc.-Str.
B. Schott's Söhne, Mainz, c1925
Score 41 p.
*Composed 1924. First performance Duisburg,
July 1925, Paul Scheinpflug conductor.*

4070 Cupid and Psyche, ballet overture   6'
2*,2,2,2-2,2,2-Timp.,Perc.-Str.
Associated Music Pub., New York, c1944
Score 19 p.
*From a ballet based on the Apuleius story
painted at the Villa Farnesina, Rome.*

*Composed 1943. First performance Philadelphia,
29 October 1943, Philadelphia Orchestra,
Eugene Ormandy conductor.*

1850 Der Dämon [dance pantomime in two   25'
parts, Op. 28]
14 dance movements
Fl.(alt. Picc.),Cl.-Hn.,Tpt.-Pno.-Str.
B. Schott's Söhne, Mainz, c1924
Score 72 p.
*Composed 1923. First performance Frankfurt am
Main, 1924. Composer notes that work is composed for stage only and not to be performed
in concert as a whole. Parts of it, however,
are suitable for concert performance.*

935s [Five pieces, in the first position for
advanced students, Op. 44 no. 4]
Str.
B. Schott's Söhne, Mainz, c1927
Score 30 p.

1903s [Four temperaments, theme with four
variations]
Pno.-Str.
Ms. c1940 by Associated Music Publishers, N.Y.
Score 61 p.
Composed 1941.

2307 Ein Jäger aus Kurpfalz, der reitet   5'
durch den grünen Wald, Op. 45 no. 3 [A Kurpfalz
huntsman riding through the greenwood]
1.Breit. Majestätisch 2.Munter
Variable Woodwinds and Strings
B. Schott's Söhne, Mainz, c1928
Score 11 p.
*Composed 1927. First performance Chamber
Music Festival, Baden-Baden 1928.*

5609 [Mathis der Maler, symphony]   26'
1.Engelkonzert [Angelic concert] 2.Grablegung
[Entombment] 3.Versuchung des heiligen Anton-
ius [Temptation of St. Anthony]
2(2nd alt. Picc.),2,2,2-4,2,3,1-Timp.,Perc.-
Str.
B. Schott's Söhne, Mainz, c1934
Score 65 p. Large folio
*Adapted from the opera in 7 scenes, composed
1934-35. Symphony in 3 movements first per-
formed Berlin, 12 March 1934, Berlin Phil-
harmonic, Wilhelm Furtwängler conductor.
First performance of the opera, Zurich, 28
May 1938.*

4322 [Neues vom Tage. Overture with   8'
concert ending]
2*(Fl. alt. 2nd Picc.),2*,3*(1Cl. in E-flat),
3*-Alto Sax.-1,2,2,1-Perc.-Str.
B. Schott's Söhne, Mainz, c1929, c1930
Score 55 p.
*From the comic opera in 3 parts with text by
M. Schiffer. Composed 1928-29. First performance Berlin, 8 June 1929, Otto Klemperer
conductor.*

1325 Nusch-Nuschi-Tänze [dances from the   12'
play for Burmese marionettes, Op. 20]
2*,3*,4*,3*-2,2,3,1-Timp.,Perc.-Cel.,Hp.-Str.

Hindemith, Paul

B. Schott's Söhne, Mainz, c1921
Score 38 p.
*Composed 1920; first performance Stuttgart,
1921, Fritz Busch conductor.*

3979 Plöner Musiktag. A. Morgenmusik   10'
[for brass instruments]
1.Mässig bewegt 2.Lied: Langsame Viertel
3.Bewegt
Variable Brasses
B. Schott's Söhne, Mainz, c1932
Score 6 p.
*Composed in 1932, as the first number of a
series of pieces which were written for a small
Music Festival at the State School in Plön,
Hollstein, Germany. The cycle, A Day of Music
at Plön, comprises four sections, providing
music for four different occasions during the
day. The other works in the cycle are: B.
Tafelmusik: 4 Pieces (March, Intermezzo, Trio
for Strings, Waltz) to be played during a meal;
C. Kantate: a cantata with German words after
Martin Agricola, 'Admonishing Young People to
Study Music'; D. Abendkonzert: 6 Pieces for
an Evening Concert (Introduction for Orches-
tra, Flute Solo with Strings, Two Duets for
Violin and Clarinet, Variations for Clarinet
and Strings, Trio for Recorders, Quodlibet for
Orchestra). First performance Plön, Germany,
June 1932.*

5251 Plöner Musiktag. B. Tafelmusik   9'30"
1.Marsch 2.Intermezzo 3.Trio für Streich-
instrumente 4.Walzer
Fl.-Tpt.(or Cl.)-Str: Any combination
B. Schott's Söhne, Mainz, c1932
Score 17 p.

5228 Plöner Musiktag. D. Abendkonzert.   5'30"
No. 1: Einleitungsstück für Orchester
Any combination of winds and strings
B. Schott's Söhne, Mainz, c1932
Score 9 p.

500m Plöner Musiktag. D. Abendkonzert.   3'
No. 2: Flötensolo mit Streichern
Solo Fl.-Str.: Any combination
B. Schott's Söhne, Mainz, c1932
Score 6 p.

499m Plöner Musiktag. D. Abendkonzert.   3'30"
No. 4: Variationen für Klarinette und Streicher
Theme and 4 variations
Solo Cl.-Str: Any combination
B. Schott's Söhne, Mainz, c1932
Score 6 p.

5252 Plöner Musiktag. D. Abendkonzert.   4'30"
No. 6: Quodlibet für Orchester
Any combination of winds and strings
B. Schott's Söhne, Mainz, c1932
Score 9 p.

2308 Spielmusik [for strings, flutes and   7'
oboes] Op. 43 no. 1
2Fl.,2Ob.-Str.
B. Schott's Sohne, Mainz, c1927
Miniature score 27 p.

*Composed 1926. First performance Chamber Music
Festival, Baden-Baden 1927.*

5979 [Suite of French dances. Dances by   8'
Claude Gervaise and Estienne Du Tertre from
Pierre Attaignant's collections, Livres de
Danceries (1547-1557). Arranged for small
orchestra]
1.Pavane und Gaillarde (Estienne Du Tertre)
2.Tourdion, C'est grand plaisir 3.Bransle simple 4.Bransle de Bourgongne (Claude Gervaise)
5.Bransle simple (Claude Gervaise) 6.Bransle
d'Escosse (Estienne Du Tertre) - Pavane, wie am
Anfang
2,2*,0,1-Tpt.-Lute-Str(without Cb.)
B. Schott's Söhne, Mainz, c1958
Score 32 p.

6074 [Symphonic dances (1937)]   ca.27'
1.Langsam 2.Lebhaft 3.Sehr langsam 4.Mässig
bewegt, mit Kraft
2(2nd alt. Picc.),2,2,2-4,2,3,1-Timp.,Perc.
-Str.
B. Schott's Söhne, Mainz, c1938
Score 125 p.
*Composed 1937. First performance London, 5
December 1937, the composer conducting.*

4080 Symphonic metamorphosis, of themes   18'
by Carl Maria von Weber
1.Allegro 2.Turandot: Scherzo 3.Andantino
4.March
3*,3*,3*,3*-4,2,3,1-Timp.,Perc.-Str.
B. Schott's Söhne, Mainz, c1945(by AMP)
Score 88 p.
*Theme of second movement from Turandot.
Other themes from Weber's music for piano four-
hands. Completed 1943. First performance New
York, 20 January 1944, New York Philharmonic,
Artur Rodzinski conductor.*

6024 Symphony in B-flat for concert band   19'
1.Moderately fast, with vigor - Molto agitato
2.Andante grazioso - Fast and gay 3.Fugue:
Rather broad
3*,2,7*,2-4Sax.-4,2,4Cnt.,3,Bar.,2Tubas-Timp.,
Perc.
B. Schott, London, c1951
Score 94 p.
*Composed 1951. First performance Washington,
D.C., 5 April 1951, United States Army Band,
the composer conducting.*

4067 Symphony in E-flat   30'
1.Sehr lebhaft 2.Sehr langsam 3.Lebhaft
4.Mässig schnelle Halbe
3*,3*,3*,3*-4,3,3,1-Timp.,Perc.-Str.
Ms.
Score 107 p. Large folio
*First performance Minneapolis, 21 November 1941,
Minneapolis Symphony Orchestra, Dimitri Mitropoulos conductor.*

HOAG, CHARLES K.   Chicago 14 November 1931

6927 Encounter for orchestra   11'
2,2,2,2-4,2,3,1-Timp.,S.Dr.-Str.
Ms.

Score 53 p.
Composed 1967. First performance Tulsa, Oklahoma, 14 February 1968, Tulsa Philharmonic, Franco Autori conductor.

6945 Fantasy on a Bach chorale   10'
3*,2,3*,2-4,3,3,1-Timp.,Perc.-Str.
Ms.
Score 54 p.
Based on two Johann Sebastian Bach harmonizations of the chorale Christus, Der ist Mein Leben, BWV 281, 282. Composed 1962. First performance Oklahoma City, Oklahoma, 13 March 1966, Oklahoma City Symphony, Guy Frazer Harrison conductor.

HOCHBERG, HANS HEINRICH BOLKO, GRAF VON.
        Fürstenstein Castle, Silesia 23 January 1843
                Bad Salzbrunn, Germany 1 December 1926

Pseudonym is J. H. Franz.

486p [Concerto, piano, Op. 42, C minor]
1.Sostenuto - Allegro non troppo, attacca
2.Larghetto 3.Vivace
Solo Pno.-2,3*,2,2-4,2,4-Timp.-Str.
Simrock, Berlin, C1906
Score 97 p.

4557 [Symphony, Op. 26, C major] By J.H. Franz
1.Moderato - Allegro giusto ed allerto 2.
Andante affabile 3.Non troppo mosso e smorfioso 4.Rondo - Finale: Largo - Allegro
2,2,2,2-4,2-Timp.-Str.
Bote & Bock, Berlin [1878?]
Score 175 p.
Composed 1879. Dedicated to King Albert of Saxony.

HÖFER, FRANZ.
        Griesbach im Rottal, Bavaria 27 August 1880
                Garmisch-Partenkirchen 13 November 1953

956s Sinfonietta no. 1, Op. 63, C major
1.Langsam - Allegro 2.Romanze
2,0,1(all ad lib.)-1,1(both ad lib.)-Timp.(ad lib.)-Pno.,Harm.-Str.
Chr. Fr. Vieweg, Berlin [n.d.]
Score 39 p.

HØFFDING, FINN.   Copenhagen 10 March 1899

5945 [Evolution, fantasy for orchestra,   9'
Op. 31]
3*,2,2,2-4,3,3,1-Timp.-Str.
Samfundet til Udgivelse af Dansk Musik, Copenhagen, C1947
Score 47 p.
Composed 1939. First performance Copenhagen, 4 September 1940, Tivoli Concert Hall Orchestra, Thomas Jensen conductor.

5946 [It's perfectly true, Op. 37, sym   9'
phonic fantasy for orchestra after Hans Christian Andersen's fairy tale]
3*,2,2,2-4,3,3,1-Timp.,Perc.-Str.
Samfundet til Udgivelse af Dansk Musik, Copenhagen, C1952

Score 58 p.
Composed 1943. First performance Copenhagen, 7 March 1944, the orchestra of the International Society for Contemporary Music, Lavard Früsholm conductor. Dedicated to Vera and Carl Johan Michaelsen.

HOFFER, BERNARD.   Zurich 14 October 1934

5743 Music for orchestra   20'
1.Adagio 2.Andante con moto 3.Scherzo: Allegro vivace 4.Sostenuto 5.Allegro molto
3(3rd alt. Picc.),3,3(3rd alt. B.Cl.),3-4,3,3,
1-Timp.,Perc.-Pno.-Str.
Ms.
Score 97 p. Large folio
Composed 1958. First performance Rochester, New York, 2 April 1958, Eastman-Rochester Symphony Orchestra, Howard Hanson conductor.

HÖFFER, PAUL.   Barmen, Germany 21 December 1895
                        Berlin 31 August 1949

4355 [A happy overture]   4'30"
2Cl.-2,2,2Flügelhorn,2Ten.Hn.,2Tbn.,Bar.,Tuba-
Perc.
Chr. Friedrich Vieweg, Berlin, C1942
Score 40 p.
Composed 1941.

4649 [A happy wind symphony] Edited by Walter Lott
1.Allegro moderato 2.Andante 3.Der Kuckuck und der Esel (The cuckoo and the donkey): Variations
2,2,3(1Cl. in E-flat),2-2,2,2Flügelhorn,2Ten.
Hn.,2Tbn.,Bar.,2Tuba-Perc.
Fr. Kistner & C.F.W. Siegel, Leipzig [n.d.]
Score 68 p.

1632s [Partita, 2 string orchestras, Op. 24]
1.Echo: Andante con moto 2.Fugato und Choral: Allegro 3.Marsch: Allegretto
Str.(in 2 orchestras)
Benno Balan, Berlin, C1930
Score 30 p.
First performance Pyrmont, 1930.

HOFFMANN, RICHARD.   Vienna 20 April 1925

1998s Prelude and double fugue for string   5'
orchestra
Str.
Ms. C1949 by Richard Hoffmann
Score 10 p.

HOFFMEISTER, FRANZ ANTON.
                Rothenburg on the Neckar 12 May 1754
                        Vienna 9 February 1812

236m [Concerto, clarinet, B-flat major]
1.Allegro 2.Adagio 3.Rondo
Solo Cl.-2Ob.-2Hn.-Str.
Ms. C1976 by The Fleisher Collection of Orchestral Music, Free Library of Philadelphia
Score 60 p. Large folio

Hoffmeister, Franz Anton

Edited from a Ms. in the Oesterreichische Nationalbibliothek, Vienna.

331m [Concerto, flute and orchestra,   22'
D major] Edited by Dieter Sonntag
1.Allegro 2.Adagio 3.Rondeau: Allegro
Solo Fl.-2Ob.-2Hn.-Str.
Hans Sikorski, Hamburg, 1954
Score 38 p.
This edition adapted from a Ms. in the Thurn and Taxis court library in Regensburg.

270p [Concerto, piano or harpsichord,   29'
Op. 24, D major] Edited by Ernst Hess
1.Allegro brioso 2.Adagio 3.Allegretto
Solo Pno.-2Ob.-2Hn.-Str.
Edition Kneusslin, Basel, ᶜ1964
Score in reduction 52 p.

276v [Concerto, viola, D major] Edited   16'
by Hans Mlynarczyk and Albert Kranz
1.Allegro 2.Adagio 3.Rondo
Solo Va.-2Ob.-2Hn.-Str.
H.L. Grahl, Frankfurt [196-?]
Score in reduction 19 p.

4205 [Serenade for wind instruments, E-flat
major] Edited by Ernst Hess
1.Adagio 2.Allegro 3.Menuettino 4.Alle-
gretto 5.Allegro moderato 6.Poco adagio
7.Rondo: Allegretto
2Ob.(or Fl.),2Cl.,2Bn.,C.Bn.(or Cb.)-2Hn.
Edition Kneusslin, Basel, ᶜ1962
Score 26 p.

HOFMANN, HEINRICH KARL JOHANN.
               Berlin 13 January 1842
      Gross-Tabarz, Thuringia 16 July 1902

558c [Concerto, violoncello, Op. 31, D minor]

1.Allegro ma non troppo 2.Adagio 3.Vivace
Solo Vc.-2,2,2,2-2,2-Timp.-Str.
Erler, Berlin [n.d.]
Score 43 p.
Dedicated to Friedrich Grützmacher.

552m Concertstück, Op. 98 [Concert   9'
piece for flute and orchestra]
Solo Fl.-2,2,2,2-4,2-Timp.-Str.
Breitkopf & Härtel, Leipzig [1889]
Score 36 p.
*Composed 1887. First performance Berlin, 1888.
Dedicated to Eugene Weiner.*

712s [Hungarian song, for string orchestra]
Str.
Score: Ms. 4 p.
Parts: [Ries & Erler, Berlin, n.d.]

2083 [Hungarian suite, Op. 16]   20'
1.[In the coronation hall] 2.[Romance]
3.[In the Hungarian steppes]
2(2nd alt. Picc.),2,2,2-4,2,3-Timp.,Perc.-Str.
Ries & Erler, Berlin [n.d.]
Score 47 p.
*Composed 1872. First performance Berlin, 1873,
Benjamin Bilse conductor.*

105 Irrlichter und Kobolde, Scherzo   7'
für Orchester [Will-o'-the wisps and
gnomes] Op. 94
2(2nd alt. Picc.),2,2,2-4,2,3-Timp.-Str.
Breitkopf & Härtel, Leipzig [1888]
Score 31 p.

5660 [Italian love story, Op. 19. Two scenes:
Dialogue *and* Carnival scene]
1.Dialogue: Andante sostenuto 2.Carnival
scene: Vivace
3*,2,2,2-4,2,3-Timp.-Str.
Breitkopf & Härtel, Leipzig [187-?]
Score 27 p.

5202 [Overture to a drama, Op. 28]
2(2nd alt. Picc.),2,2,2-4,2,3-Timp.-Hp.(ad
lib.)-Str.
Hermann Erler, Berlin [187-?]
Score 31 p.

824m [Serenade, flute and string orchestra,
Op. 65]
1.Allegro con moto 2.Andante tranquillo
3.Allegro vivace 4.Allegro vivo
Solo Fl.-Str.
Breitkopf & Härtel, Leipzig [1884?]
Score 35 p.

492s [Serenade, string orchestra, no. 1, Op. 72,
D major]
1.Allegro 2.Gavotte: Allegro non troppo -
Trio 3.[Slumber-song]: Moderato 4.Humoreske:
Allegro
Str.
Breitkopf & Härtel, Leipzig [1893?]
Score 27 p.

123s [Serenade, string orchestra, no. 2, Op. 93,
E minor]
1.Allegro con moto 2.Ländler-Menuett

3.Duett: Allegro
Str.
Challier, Berlin [n.d.]
Score 26 p.

4519 [Three character pieces, Op. 15]   21'
1.Peace in the shadow of a ruin (Vision):
Adagio assai 2.Ballad: Adagio 3.In the sunshine: Allegro
2(2nd alt. Picc.),2,2,2-2,2,3-Timp.,Perc.-Str.
Bote & Bock, Berlin [187-?]
Score 48 p.

HOFMANN, KARL.   Vienna 3 April 1835
                        Vienna 12 December 1909

840v [Concerto, 2 violins and orchestra, Op. 55,
D minor]
1.Allegro maestoso e molto moderato 2.Adagio
molto espressivo 3.Tarantella: Allegro con
fuoco
Solo Vn.I, Solo Vn.II-1,2,2,2-Timp.,Perc.-Hp.-
Str.
Score: Ms. 229 p.
Parts: [Schlesinger, Berlin, 188-?]

HOFMANN, RICHARD. Delitzsch, Germany 30 April 1844
                   Leipzig 13 November 1918

288s Aus der Jugendzeit, Suite, Op. 60 [From
childhood, for string orchestra]
1.[What the mother says] 2.[An obstinate little thing] 3.[Under close escort] 4.[The
parade ground] 5.[Little story] 6.[On
falling asleep]
Str.
Siegel, Leipzig [1886?]
Score 9 p.

HOFREITER, PAUL.   Miami Beach 9 September 1952

7102 Symphony no. 3, Op. 47   14'
Lento - Allegro con brio - Andante espressivo
- Moderato - Andante con moto - Allegro con
brio - Vivace
3*,3*,3*,3*-4,3,3,1-Timp.,Perc.-
Str.
Ms. c1975 by Paul Hofreiter
Score 82 p. Large folio
*Composed 1972-73. Selected for performance
by the Orchestra Society of Philadelphia as
part of its Pennsylvania Composers Project
1975, made possible by a grant from the Pennsylvania Council on the Arts with performance
materials prepared by the Fleisher Collection
of Orchestral Music. First performance Mandell Theater, Drexel University, Philadelphia,
4 May 1975, Orchestra Society of Philadelphia,
Sidney Rothstein, conductor.*

HOLBROOKE, JOSEF.   Croydon, England 5 July 1878
                      London 5 August 1958

2380 Dreamland suite, Op. 38   25'
1.[Ensemble] 2.[The dance] 3.[Dreaming]
4.[Hilarité]
3(3rd alt. Picc.),2,2,2-4,2,3,1-Timp.,Perc.-
Hp.-Str.

Ms. [Weekes, London, 1910?]
Score 80 p.
*Composed 1890. First performance Hereford
Festival, 1906, London Symphony Orchestra,
the composer conducting.*

3864 Fanfare of war, from Bronwen.   23"
Transcribed for brass and percussion by Arthur
Cohn
0,0,0,0-4,3,3,1-Timp.,B.Dr.,S.Dr.,Cym.(2
players)
Ms.
Score 4 p.
*Originally composed 1921 as part of the music
drama, Bronwen. This transcription 1943.*

1444s Les hommages, grande suite no. 3 [for
string orchestra]
1.Festiva, marche héroique (Hommage à Wagner)
2.Serenata (Hommage à Grieg) 3.Elégie (Hommage à Dvořák) 4.Finale: Introduction et
danse russe (Hommage à Tschaikovsky)
Str.
Ms.
Score 79 p.
*Originally composed for string orchestra, 1900.
Later transcribed for orchestra as the composer's Symphony no. 1.*

1633 Les hommages, symphony no. 1, Op. 40   25'
[for orchestra]
1.Festiva (Marcia héroique) (Hommage à Wagner)
2.Serenata (Hommage à Grieg) 3.Elegiae poeme
(Hommage à Dvořák) 4.Introduction and Russian
dance (Hommage à Tschaikowsky)
4*(Picc. alt. B.Fl.),4*(1Ob.d'Amore),6*(1Cl.
in E-flat,1Alto Cl. or Basset Hn.),4*-4Sax.
(SATB)-4(or 8),5,4,1-Timp.,Perc.-Hp.-Str.
Chester, London [n.d.]
Score 91 p.
*Transcribed 1907 from the suite Les Hommages
for string orchestra. First performance London, 1908, Promenade Concerts, Henry Wood conductor.*

964s [Pierrot and Pierrette, Op. 36. Ballet
music]
1.Harlequin 2.Columbine 3.Pantaloon 4.Clown
Str.
Ms.
Score 41 p.
*First performance His Majesty's Theatre, Lon-
don, 1909.*

2050 Pontorewyn, Op. 17 no. 8, music to   8'
the Welsh play by T.E. Ellis
1.Act I, March 2.Scene II: Evening 3.Finale
1,1,1,1-2,2,3-Timp.,Perc.,Str.
Novello, London [n.d.]
Score 14 p.
*Composed 1911. First performance Cardiff,
1914, Basil Cameron conductor.*

2051 The Raven, poem no. 1, for   25'
orchestra, Op. 25
4(4th alt. Picc.),4*,3*,4*-4,4,3,1-Timp.,Perc.
-Hp.-Str.
Novello, London [n.d.]

Holbrooke, Josef

Score 74 p.
*Inspired by Edgar Allan Poe's poem. Composed
1903. First performance Crystal Palace, London, 5 March 1905, August Manns conductor.
Revised for publication.*

2213 Three Blind Mice, symphonic   20'
variations, Op. 37 no. 1
3*,3(3rd alt. E.H.),2,3*-4(or 8),2,3,1-Timp.,
Perc.-Hp.-Str.
Novello, London [n.d.]
Score 51 p.
*First performance Queen's Hall, London, 9
November 1900, Promenade Concerts, Henry Wood
conductor.*

2212 Variations no. 2: The Girl I Left   15'
Behind Me, Op. 40 no. 2
3*,3*,3*,3*-4(or 8),2,2Cnt.,3,1-Timp.,Perc.-
2Hp.-Str.
Chester, London [n.d.]
Score 69 p.
*Composed 1908. First performance at the Bel-
gian Festival, London, 1908[?] Ostend Orchestra, the composer conducting.*

2388 Variations no. 3: Auld Lang Syne,   20'
Scotch, Op. 60
3(3rd alt. Picc.),3*,4*(1Cl. in E-flat),Basset
Hn.,3*-4(or 8),4,3,1,Euph.(ad lib.)-Timp.,Perc.
-Cel.,Hp.-Str.
Chester, London [c1906?]
Score 72 p.
*Composed 1906. First performance London,
August 1918, Queen's Hall Orchestra, Basil
Cameron conductor.*

2349 The Viking, poem no. 2, for grand   26'
orchestra, Op. 32 [revised version]
3*,3*,4*(1Cl. in E-flat),3*-4,2,2Cnt.,3,1-
Timp.,Perc.-2Hp.-Str.
Novello, London, c[n.d.] by Josef Holbrooke
Score 99 p.
*Inspired by Longfellow's poem The Skeleton in
Armour. Originally composed 1903. First
performance Liverpool, 1903, the composer con-
ducting. Revised 1904. First performance
Antwerp, 19 March 1904, Antwerp Symphony
Orchestra, Granville Bantock conductor.*

HOLDEN, DAVID JUSTIN.
     b. White Plains, New York 16 December 1911

746p Music for piano and strings   18'
1. ♩=80 2. ♪=52 3.Boisterously
Solo Pno.-Str.(Cb. optional)
Society for the Publication of American Music,
Published for the Society by G. Schirmer, New
York, c1940 by David Holden
Score 52 p.
*Composed 1936-37. First performance Cleveland,
27 May 1937, faculty members of Cleveland
Music School Settlement, Margaret Harold solo-
ist. Received the George Arthur Knight Prize
of Harvard University and the Society for the
Publication of American Music Award, 1939.*

HOLGUÍN, GUILLERMO URIBE.
     See: URIBE-HOLGUÍN, GUILLERMO.

HOLLAENDER, ALEXIS.   Ratibor, Silesia
     (now Raciborz, Poland) 25 February 1840
                            Berlin 5 February 1924

603s Notturno, Op. 44 [for string orchestra,
G major]
Str.
Oertel, Hanover [n.d.]
Score 11 p.

HOLLAENDER, GUSTAV.   Leobschütz, Silesia
     (now Glubczyce, Poland) 15 February 1855
                            Berlin 4 December 1915

554m Andante cantabile, Op. 60 [for   4'
flute and orchestra]
Solo Fl.-2,2,2,2-2,2-Timp.-Str.
Zimmermann, Leipzig, c1903
Score 18 p.
Composed 1900. First performance Berlin, 1902.

1031v Concert-polonaise, Op. 14 [for violin and
orchestra]
Solo Vn.-2(2nd alt. Picc.),2,2,2-2,2-Timp.-Str.
Score: Ms. 55 p.
Parts: Leuckart, Leipzig [1883]

586v [Concerto, violin, no. 1, Op. 52, G minor]
In one movement
Solo Vn.-2,2,2,2-4,2-Timp.-Str.
Ries & Erler, Berlin, c1893
Score 100 p.

611v [Concerto, violin, no. 3, Op. 66, D minor]
1.Allegro moderato 2.Andante 3.Allegro
risoluto
Solo Vn.-2,2,2,2-4,2-Timp.-Str.
Zimmermann, Leipzig, c1911
Score 162 p.

841v Elegie, Op. 33 [for violin and orchestra]
Solo Vn.-2,2,2,2-2Hn.-Timp.-Str.
Ms.
Score 27 p.

448v Romanze, Op. 10 [for violin and orchestra]
Solo Vn.-2,2,2,2-2,2-Timp.-Str.
Forberg, Leipzig [n.d.]
Score 35 p.

990s Spinnerlied, Op. 3 [Spinning song, for
string orchestra]
Str.
Score: Ms. 12 p.
Parts: Forberg, Leipzig [n.d.]

493s [Three pieces for string orchestra,
Op. 38a]
1.[Dream vision] 2.Berceuse 3.Walzer
Str.
Schlesinger, Berlin [1890]
Score 12 p.

HOLLANDER, BENOIT (BENNO).   Amsterdam 8 June 1853
London 27 December 1942

967s Christmas fantasia (Fantaisie de Noël)
1.Christmas eve 2.Santa Claus' ride through
space 3.Christmas day 4.Vesper vale 5.Fro-
lic - Dawn of a new year
Str.
Score: Ms. 60 p.
Parts: Hawkes & Son, London, ᶜ1924

908v Concerto for violin and orchestra,   30'
Op. 15 [D minor]
1.Allegro moderato 2.Lento 3.Allegro moderato
Solo Vn.-3(3rd alt. Picc.),2,2,2-4,2-Timp.-Str.
Chester, London, ᶜ1922
Score 63 p.
Composed ca.1896.

HOLMBOE, VAGN.   Horsens, Denmark 20 December 1909

414m [Chamber concerto no. 2, for flute,   17'
violin, percussion and string orchestra, Op.
20]
1.Allegro con brio 2.Intermezzo I: Vivace
3.Intermezzo II: Adagio 4.Finale: Allegro
molto
Solo Fl., Solo Vn.-Timp.,Perc.-Cel.-Str.
Edition Dania, Copenhagen, ᶜ1952
Score 49 p.
*Composed 1940. First performance Copenhagen,
21 April 1942, Young Musicians' Orchestra of
Copenhagen (Danish section of International
Society for Contemporary Music), Lavard
Friisholm conductor, Johan Bentzon flautist,
Else Marie Bruun violinist.*

257m [Concerto for violin, viola and   18'
orchestra, no. 9, Op. 39]
1.Allegro molto 2.Andante tranquillo
3.Allegro
Solo Vn., Solo Va.-2(2nd alt. Picc.),2,2,2-3,
3-Timp.,S.Dr.,Cym.-Str.
Viking Musikforlag, Copenhagen [ᶜ1956]
Score 76 p.
*Commissioned by Else Marie and Julius Koppel.
Composed 1945-46. First performance Copenhagen, 26 July 1947, Tivoli Symphony Concert,
Thomas Jensen conductor, Else Marie Koppel
violin, and Julius Koppel viola.*

HOLMÈS, AUGUSTA MARY ANNE.   Paris 16 December 1847
Paris 28 January 1903

281 [Andromeda, symphonic poem. Excerpt: 9'
Andromeda and the storm king. Re-orchestrated
by Ross Jungnickel]
3*,3*,3*,2-4,4,3,1-Timp.,Perc.-Pno.,Org.(both
optional),4Hp.-Str.
Ross Jungnickel, New York, ᶜ1921
Score 48 p.
*This orchestration 1921. First performance
Strand Theater, New York, September 1921,
Carlo Eduardo conductor.*

4219 [Ireland, symphonic poem]   13'
3*,3*,2,4-4,4,3,1-2Hp.-Timp.,Perc.
Str.

L. Grus [Paris, 1885]
Score 63 p.
*First performance Concerts Pasdeloup, Paris,
2 March 1882.*

HOLST, GUSTAV THEODORE.
Cheltenham, England 21 September 1874
London 25 May 1934

Born: Gustavus Theodore von Holst

1227 Beni Mora, oriental suite for   16'
orchestra, Op. 29 no. 1
1.First dance 2.Second dance 3.Finale: In
the Street of the Ouled Naïls
3(3rd alt. Picc.),3*,2,2-4,3,3,1-Timp.,Perc.-
2Hp.(2nd ad lib.)-Str.
Curwen, London, ᶜ1921 by Gustav Holst
Score 48 p.
*Composed 1910. First performance Queen's
Hall, London, 1 May 1912, the composer conducting.*

630 Egdon Heath, for orchestra, Op. 47   15'
2,3*,2,3*-4,3,3,1-Str.
Novello, London, ᶜ1928
Score 25 p.
*Inspired by Thomas Hardy's novel, The Return
of the Native. Commissioned by the New York
Symphony Orchestra. Composed 1927. First
performance New York, 12 February 1928, New
York Symphony Orchestra, Walter Damrosch con-
ductor.*

596m A fugal concerto for flute and oboe   10'
(or 2 solo violins) with string orchestra,
Op. 40 no. 2
1.Moderato 2.Adagio, segue 3.Allegro
Solo Fl., Solo Ob.(or Solo Vn.I & II)-Str.
Novello, London, ᶜ1923
Score 22 p.
*Composed 1923. First performance Queen's Hall,
London, 1923.*

1775 A fugal overture, Op. 40 no. 1   6'
3*,3*,3*,3*-4,3,3,1-Timp.,Perc.-Str.
(May be performed by smaller orchestra)
Novello, London, ᶜ1923
Score 29 p.
*Composed 1922. First performance Queen's
Hall, London, 11 October 1923, the composer
conducting.*

1090 Japanese suite, Op. 33   13'
In 6 movements
2(2nd alt. Picc.),3*,2,2-4,2,3,1-Timp.,Perc.-
Org.(optional),Hp.-Str.
Hawkes & Son, London, ᶜ1925
Score 40 p.
*Commissioned by Michio Ito. Composed 1915.
First performance Coliseum, London, 1916.*

1770 [The perfect fool, Op. 39. Ballet   14'
music]
3*,3*,3*,3*-4,4,3,1-Timp.,Perc.-Cel.,Hp.-Str.
Novello, London, ᶜ1923
Score 43 p.
From the opera with libretto by the composer.

Holst, Gustav Theodore

Composed 1921. First performance Covent Garden, London, 14 May 1923.

2036 The planets, suite for large   *55'*
orchestra, Op. 32
1.Mars 2.Venus 3.Mercury 4.Jupiter 5.Saturn
6.Uranus 7.Neptune
4(3rd alt. Picc. I, 4th alt. Picc. II & B.Fl.),
3(3rd alt. B.Ob.),4*,4*-6,4,3,2-Timp.(2 players),Perc.-Cel.,2Hp.,Org.-Women's Voices
(backstage)-Str.
Curwen, London, C1921 by Goodwin & Tabb, Ltd.
Score 187 p.
*Composed 1914-16. First performance of five
movements only, London, 1919. First complete
performance Queen's Hall, London, 15 November
1920, Albert Coates conductor.*

360s St. Paul's suite, for string   *12'*
orchestra
1.Jig 2.Ostinato 3.Intermezzo 4.Finale (The
Dargason)
Str.
F.&B. Goodwin, London, C1922 by Goodwin & Tabb,
Ltd.
Score 23 p.

2245 A Somerset rhapsody, Op. 21   *13'*
2(2nd alt. Picc.),2(1Ob. d'Amore),2,2-4,2,3,1-
Timp.,Perc.-Str.
Hawkes & Son, London, C1927
Score 27 p.
*Based on Somerset melodies collected by Cecil
Sharp and composed at his request, 1906-07.
First performance Queen's Hall, London, 6
April 1910, Edward Mason conductor.*

1501 Suite de ballet in E-flat,   *12'*
full orchestra, Op. 10
1.Danse rustique 2.Valse 3.Scène de nuit
4.Carnival
3(3rd alt. Picc.),2,2,2-4,2,3,1-Timp.,Perc.-
Hp.-Str.
Published for the Royal College of Music
Patron's Fund by Novello, London [n.d.]
Score 94 p.
*Composed 1900. First performance Queen's Hall,
London, 29 June 1904.*

1121 [Two songs without words for small   *8'*
orchestra, Op. 22. No. 1, Country song]
2(2nd alt. Picc.),1,2,2-2Hn.-Str.
Novello, London, C1922
Score 16 p.
*Two Songs Without Words composed 1906. First
performance London, 19 July 1906, the composer
conducting.*

2042 [Two songs without words for small   *8'*
orchestra, Op. 22. No. 2, Marching song]
2,1,2,2-2,2,1-Timp.,B.Dr.,S.Dr.-Str.
Novello, London, C1922
Score 21 p.

HOLSTEIN, FRANZ VON.   Braunschweig
(Brunswick), Germany 16 February 1826
Leipzig 22 May 1878

5217 [Frau Aventiure, an overture. Op. 41]
Orchestration by Albert Dietrich
2,2,2,2-4,2-Timp.-Str.
J. Rieter-Biedermann, Leipzig and Winterthur,
1879
Score 31 p.
*Composed 1877. Orchestrated from the com-
poser's sketches, 1879. First performance
Leipzig, 13 November 1879.*

HOLTER, IVER PAUL FREDRIK.
Gausdal, Norway 13 December 1850
Oslo 25 January 1941

784v [Concerto, violin, Op. 22, A minor]
1.Allegro molto moderato 2.Romance: Lento
3.Vigoroso e vivace
Solo Vn.-2,2,2,2-4,2,3-Timp.-Str.
Norsk Musikforlag, Kristiania, C1922
Score 123 p.
First performance Oslo, 1920.

2234 [Götz von Berlichingen. Suite from   *22'*
the incidental music to Goethe's play, Op. 10]
1.[March of homage] 2.[Still life] 3.[Scene
in the woods] 4.[Erotic] 5.[Secret court]
6.[Festive procession]
3*,2,2,2-4,2,3,1-Timp.,Perc.-Str.
W. Hansen, Copenhagen [n.d.]
Score 93 p.
Composed 1897; first performance Oslo 1898.

279s St. Hans Kveld [St. John's Eve, Norwegian
midsummer night, for string orchestra, Op. 4]
Str.
C. Warmuth, Christiania [n.d.]
Score 23 p.

HOLZBAUER, IGNAZ.   Vienna 17 September 1711
Mannheim, Germany 7 April 1783

3338 [Symphony, Op. 4 no. 3, E-flat   *15'*
major] Edited by Adam Carse
1.Allegro non troppo 2.Adagio grazioso 3.
Minuetto 4.La tempesta del mare (The storm at
sea)
0,2,0,2-2Hn.-Str.
Augener, London, C1939
Score 23 p.
Composed between 1750 and 1760.

1688s [Symphony, string orchestra, E major]
Edited by Edgar Rabsch
1.Andantino amoroso sempre piano 2.Allegro
molto e forte 3.Menuetto grazioso 4.Allegro
spirituoso
Str.
D. Rahter, Leipzig, C1932
Score 8 p.

Composed after 1753.

HOLZHAUS, HENRY.

1654s Élégie, Op. 2 [for violoncello and string orchestra]
Solo Vc.-Str.
Score: Ms. 10 p.
Parts: C.F. Schmidt, Heilbronn [n.d.]

HOLZMANN, RUDOLPH (*now* RODOLFO).
               Breslau, Germany 27 November 1910

5097 Passage perpétuel, for band   *3'*
2(2nd alt. Picc.),0,2(1Cl. in E-flat),1-3Sax.
(2Alto,1Ten.)-0,2,3,1-Timp.,Perc.-Cb.
Ms.
Score 12 p.
Composed 1935.

4164 [Two movements for orchestra. 1. In   *12'*
the style of a pavan]
3(3rd alt. Picc.),2,3(3rd alt. B.Cl.),3*-3,3,
2,1-Timp.,Perc.-Cel.-Str.
Ms.
Score 32 p. Large folio
Both movements composed 1934.

4165 [Two movements for orchestra. 2. In   *5'*
the style of a saltarello]
3*,2,3(3rd alt. B.Cl.),3*-3,3,2,1-Timp.,Perc.-
Cel.-Str.
Ms.
Score 43 p. Large folio

HOMMANN, CHARLES.

Born in U.S.; active in Philadelphia until 1857.

6438 [Overture in D] Edited and reconstructed
by Donald M. McCorkle
2,0,2,2-2,2,1-Timp.-Str.
Ms.
Score 50 p. Large folio
*Composed ca.1840. Reconstructed from parts
discovered in the Bethlehem Moravian Archives,
1961. Dedicated to Jedidiah Weiss, clockmaker in Bethlehem, Pennsylvania.*

5763 [Overture in D major]
3*,2*,2,2-2,2,1-Timp.-Str.
Ms. ᶜ1976 by The Fleisher Collection of
Orchestral Music, Free Library of Philadelphia

Score 76 p. Large folio

5624 [Symphony, E-flat major]   *25'*
1.Adagio - Allegro con brio 2.Andante sostenuto 3.Minuetto with Trio: Allegro 4.Finale:
Allegro assai
1,2,2,1-2Hn.-Str.
Ms. ᶜ1950 by the Board of Elders of the Northern Diocese of the Church of the United Brethren in the United States of America [Bethlehem,
Pennsylvania]
Score 220 p.
*This may be the earliest American symphony by
a native composer. Composed in the 1830's or
early 1840's. Composed for and dedicated to
the Philharmonic Society of Bethlehem, Pennsylvania.*

HONEGGER, ARTHUR.   Le Havre 10 March 1892
                   Paris 27 November 1955

840 Chant de joie [Song of joy]   *7'*
3*,3*,3*,3*-4,3,3,1-Cym.,B.Dr.-Cel.-Hp.-Str.
Senart, Paris, ᶜ1924
Score 27 p.
*Composed 1923. First performance Geneva,
April 1923, Schweitzer Tonkünstlerfest,
Ernest Ansermet conductor.*

5402 Le chant de Nigamon   *11'*
3*,2*,2,3*-4,2,3,1-Timp.,Perc.-Str.
Maurice Senart, Paris, ᶜ1927
Score 67 p.
*Composed 1917. First performance by the stu-
dent orchestra of the Paris Conservatoire, 3
April 1917, the composer conducting. First
professional performance Paris, Cirque d'Hiver,
3 January 1920, Orchestre Pasdeloup, Rhené-
Baton conductor.*

424p Concertino pour piano et orchestre   *13'*
In one movement: Allegro molto moderato -
Larghetto sostenuto - Allegro
Solo Pno.-2(2nd alt. Picc.),2(2nd alt. E.H.),
2,2-2,2,1-Str.
Senart, Paris, ᶜ1925, ᶜ1926
Score 46 p.
*Composed 1925. First performance Paris, 23
May 1925, Serge Koussevitzky conductor.*

2913 J.S. Bach suite. [Movements] from the   *12'*
French suites of Bach. Arranged for orchestra
by Arthur Honegger
1.Anglaise 2.Sarabande 3.Gavotte 4.Menuet

Honegger, Arthur

5.Gigue
2,2*,2(1st alt. Sop. Sax., 2nd alt. B.Cl.),2-
4,3-Cel.,Hp.-Str.
Universal Edition, Vienna, c1933
Score 26 p.
*Part of the ballet, Les Noces d'Amour et
Psyche, arranged especially for Ida Rubenstein.
First concert performance at the Concerts Pou-
let, Paris, 5 February 1933, Cloez conductor.*

5103 [The march on the Bastille (for Romain
Rolland's "14th of July")]
4*(2Picc.),2,3,3*-3Sax.-5,3,4,2-Perc.-
Unison Chorus(ad lib.)-Cb.
Le Chant du Monde, c[n.p., n.d.]
Score 22 p.
*Part of the incidental music for the drama by
Romain Rolland, Le Quatorze Juillet. Other
sections composed by Georges Auric, Jacques
Ibert, Charles Koechlin, Daniel Lazarus,
Darius Milhaud, and Albert Roussel. Composed
1936. First performance La Maison de la Cul-
ture, Paris, 14 July 1936, Roger Désormière
conductor.*

4201 [Napoleon. Chaconne of the empress]   4'
1(ad lib.),1,2(ad lib.),1-2,2(ad lib.),3(ad
lib.)-Timp.,Trgl.-Str.
Score: Ms. 9 p.
Parts: Salabert, Paris, c1927
*A tableau from the film, Napoléon, written and
directed by Abel Gance. Composed 1927.*

4712 [Napoleon. Children's dance]   1'30"
Fl.,Cl.,Bn.-Str.(without Cb.)
Score: Ms. 12 p.
Parts: Salabert, Paris, c1927

4199 [Napoleon. Romance of Violine]   2'30"
Fl.,Ob.,Cl.-Str.
Salabert, Paris, c1927
Score in reduction 2 p.

4200 [Napoleon. Scene with Napoleon]   1'30"
2,1,2,2-2,3,3,1-B.Dr.,Cym.-Str.
Salabert, Paris, c1927
Score in reduction 2 p.

4198 [Napoleon. The shadows]   2'30"
1,1,2,1(all ad lib.)-2(ad lib.),2,3(ad lib.)-
B.Dr.,Cym.-Str.
Salabert, Paris, c1927
Score in reduction 4 p.

3176 Nocturne   9'
3*,3*,3*,3-Sax(in E-flat)-4,3,0,1-Perc.-Hp.-
Str.
Universal Edition, London, c1939
Score 27 p.
*Composed 1936. First performance Venice
Festival, 1938.*

863 Pacific 231, mouvement symphonique   7'
3*,3*,3*,3*-4,3,3,1-Timp.,Perc.-Str.
Senart, Paris, c1924
Score 39 p.
*Pacific 231 is a locomotive. Composed 1923.
First performance Paris, 8 May 1924, Serge
Koussevitzky conductor.*

460 Pastorale d'été [A summer pastoral,   7'
symphonic poem]
1,1,1,1-Hn.-Str.
Senart, Paris, c1922
Score 16 p.
*Composed 1920. First performance Paris 1921.
Awarded the Prix Verley, 1921.*

5084 [Phaedra]   18'
1.Prélude: Largo 2.Cortège des suppliantes:
Andante moderato 3.Prélude: Andante molto
moderato 4.Imprécation de Thésée [Theseus'
curse]: Allegro 5.Prélude: Adagio 6.Mort de
Phaedre: Adagio non troppo
2(2nd alt. Picc.),2(2nd alt. E.H.),2,2-2,2,3,1
-Timp.,2Cym.-Str.
Senart, Paris, c1930
Score 48 p.
*Incidental music for the tragedy in 3 acts by
Gabriele d'Annunzio. Composed 1926. First
performance Teatro Costanzi, Rome, 19 April
1926, the composer conducting.*

852 Prélude pour La Tempête de Shakespeare   8'
2*,2*,2*,2*-4,2,3,1-Timp.,Perc.-Str.
Senart, Paris, c1924
Score 38 p.
*Composed 1922. First performance Théâtre des
Champs Elysées, Paris, 1 May 1923, Straram
conductor.*

HOPKINSON, FRANCIS. Philadelphia 21 September 1737
                     Philadelphia 9 May 1791

7042 My days have been so wondrous free.   3'
Edited and transcribed by Philip Weston
High Voice-1,1,2,1-Str.
Concord Music Publishing, New York, c1941
Score in reduction 5 p.
*Song with text by the composer. Composed 1759,
for voice and piano.*

HÖSER, OTTO.   Wiesbaden, Germany 13 April 1877

767s Rokoko, Op. 15 [for string orchestra]
1.Gavotte 2.Menuett
Str.
Score: Ms. 8 p.
Parts: Louis Oertel, Hannover [n.d.]

HOTH, GEORGE.

790v Nocturne, Op. 3 [violin and orchestra]
Solo Vn.-1,0,2,2-2Hn.-Hp.-Str.
Jurgenson, Moscow [1898?]
Score 15 p.

198s [Suite in olden style, Op. 6a, E minor]
1.Prelude 2.Minuet 3.Sarabande 4.Gavotte
Str.
Score: Ms. 24 p.
Parts: Rahter, Leipzig [n.d.]

HOVANESS, ALAN.
See: HOVHANESS, ALAN.

HOVEY, SERGE.   New York 10 March 1920

5890 Sholem Aleichem suite, for chorus,   *32'*
narrator and orchestra
Overture: ♩=97 - ♩=144 1.Adagio - Allegro
2. ♩=66 - ♩=85 - ♩=120 3.Adagio -
Allegro
Narrator - Ten. Voice Solo, Contralto Voice
Solo-3(3rd alt. Picc.),3*,3*,3*-4,2,1,1-Timp.,
Perc.-Pno.(alt. Cel.),Hp.-Chorus
(SATB)-Str.
Ms. ᶜ1957 by Serge Hovey
Score 155 p.
Based on stories by Sholem Aleichem (pseudonym for Shalom Rabinowitz, 1859-1916). Composed 1954. First performance Cincinnati, Ohio, 21 February 1958, Cincinnati Symphony Orchestra, Chorus of the College Conservatory of Music of Cincinnati, Children's Chorus from the Bureau of Jewish Education of Cincinnati, Thor Johnson conductor, Robert Bennett and Lucille Rinsky soloists.

HOVHANESS, ALAN.
b. Somerville, Massachusetts 8 March 1911

Born: Alan Hovhaness Chakmakjian

2025s Armenian rhapsody no. 1 [Op. 45]   *5'*
Ten.Dr.,Tamb.-Str.
Ms.
Score 19 p.
Based on Armenian mountain village tunes. Composed 1944. First performance Boston, 4 June 1944, the composer conducting.

Arevakal
See: [Concerto no. 1, for orchestra,
Arevakal (the Sun approaches), Op. 88]

Artik, concerto for horn in F and string
orchestra
See: [Concerto, horn and string orchestra,
Artik, Op. 78]

6296 [Concerto no. 1, for orchestra,   *22'*
Arevakal (the Sun approaches), Op. 88]
1.Incantation 2.Canzona 3.Estampie 4.Bar
(Dance) 5.Sharagan (Hymn) 6.Ballata
2,2,2,2-2,2-2,2-2,2-Timp.,S.Dr.-Hp.-Str.
Associated Music Publishers, New York, ᶜ1951
Miniature score 60 p.
Commissioned by the National Institute of Arts and Letters, New York. Composed 1951. First performance New York, February 1952, Little Orchestra Society, Thomas Scherman conductor.

306p [Concerto no. 5, for piano and string *14'*
orchestra, Op. 108]
1.Andante 2.Allegretto 3.Allegro 4.Allegro
5.Andante
Solo Pno.-Str.
Associated Music Publishers, N.Y. [n.d.]
Score 34 p.
Composed 1953. First performance Carnegie Hall, New York, 1954, National Orchestral Society, Leon Barzin conductor, Lillian Kallir soloist.

6342 [Concerto no. 7, for orchestra,   *20'*
Op. 116]
1.Allegretto 2.Allegro 3.Double fugue:
Allegretto
2,2,2,2-4,2,3,1-Timp.,Perc.-Cel.,Hp.-Str.
Associated Music Publishers, N.Y., ᶜ1955, 1961
Score 100 p.
Commissioned by The Louisville Symphony 1954. Composed 1953-54. First performance Louisville, Kentucky, 20 February 1954, Louisville Symphony, Robert Whitney conductor.

1080m [Concerto, flute and string   *10'*
orchestra, Elibris (Dawn god of Urardu),
Op. 50]
Solo Fl.-Str.
Ms. ᶜ1948 by Alan Hovhaness
Score 39 p.
Urardu or Urartu is now Armenia. Composed 1944. First performance Jordan Hall, Boston, 4 February 1945, in a concert of original compositions of creative Armenian music, the composer conducting, Philip Kaplan soloist. Revised 1948.

483m [Concerto, horn and string   *15'*
orchestra, Artik, Op. 78]
1.Alleluia 2.Ballata 3.Laude 4.Canzona (to
a mountain range) 5.Processional 6.Canon in
5 voices and 3 keys 7.Aria 8.Intonazione
Solo Hn.-Str.
Ms. ᶜ1950 by Alan Hovhaness
Score 33 p.
Artik is the name of a 7th century church. Composed 1950. First performance Eastman Theatre, Rochester, New York, 7 May 1954, Rochester Philharmonic Orchestra, Herman Genhart conductor, Morris Secon soloist.

240p [Concerto, piano and chamber   *15'*
orchestra, Zartik parkim (Awake, my glory!),
Op. 77]
1.Zankag [Gong]: Moderato 2.Tmpoug: Allegretto
(Dance-like) 3.Srynk [Flute]: Andante - Allegro
Solo Pno.-1,0,1-2,1-Timp.,Giant Tam-tam,Cym.-
Str.
Ms. ᶜ1949 by Alan Hovhaness
Score 71 p.
Composed 1949. First performance Albany, New York, 1 May 1949, Albany Symphony Orchestra, Edgar Curtis conductor, the composer as soloist.

355p [Concerto, piano and string   *18'*
orchestra, Lousadzak, Op. 48]
Solo Pno.-Str.
Ms. ᶜ1944 by Alan Hovhaness
Score 69 p.
Imitates instruments of the Middle East. Composed 1944. First performance Jordan Hall, Boston, 4 February 1945, in a concert of original compositions of creative Armenian music, the composer as conductor and soloist.

344v [Concerto, viola and string   *12'*
orchestra, Talin, Op. 93]
1.Chant 2.Estampie 3.Canzona
Solo Va.-Str.
Associated Music Publishers, N.Y. ᶜ1956, 1960

Hovhaness, Alan

Score 41 p.
Talin is the site of a 7th century Armenian church ruin. Commissioned by and dedicated to Ferenc Molnár. Composed 1952. First performance Colorado Springs, Colorado, 1952, Ferenc Molnár soloist.

Elibris (Dawn god of Urardu)
See: [Concerto, flute and string orchestra, Elibris (Dawn god of Urardu), Op. 50]

1081m [Etchmiadzin. Scene 6: Prayer of   4'
Saint Gregory, Op. 62b]
Solo Tpt.-Str.
Ms.
Score 4 p.
Etchmiadzin is an ancient Armenian city. From the oratorio in six scenes, with libretto by Zabelle Boyajian. Composed 1946. First performance Carnegie Hall, New York, 7 February 1947, the composer conducting, James Smith soloist.

Five hymns of serenity for [solo] trumpet, violin, piano, and string orchestra
See: Janabar (Journey) Five hymns of serenity...

221m Haroutiun (Resurrection), aria   10'
and fugue for trumpet and string orchestra, Op. 71
Solo Tpt.-Str.
C.F. Peters, New York, ᶜ1968
Score 18 p.
First performance Town Hall, New York, 6 March 1949, the composer conducting, William Vacchiano soloist.

478m Janabar (Journey), five hymns of   35'
serenity for trumpet, violin, piano and strings [Op. 81]
1.Fantasy 2.Yerk (Song) 3.Prayer 4.Sharagan (Hymn) 5.Tapor (Processional)
Solo Tpt., Solo Pno., Solo Vn.-Str.
Ms. ᶜ1951 by Alan Hovhaness
Score 55 p.
Composed 1950. First performance Carnegie Hall, New York, 11 March 1951, members of the New York Philharmonic, the composer conducting, Maro Ajemian piano, and Anahid Ajemian violin. Also entitled Concerto for Trumpet, Piano, Violin and Strings.

Lousadzak
See: [Concerto, piano and string orchestra, Lousadzak, Op. 48]

6341 Prelude and quadruple fugue, for   6'
orchestra, Op. 128
2,2,2,2-4,2,3-Timp.-Str.
Associated Music Publishers, N.Y., ᶜ1956, 1957
Score 47 p.
Composed 1955. First performance, Rochester, New York, 8 May 1955, Eastman-Rochester Symphony, Howard Hanson conductor.

238m Processional and fugue for trumpet (or clarinet) in B-flat and string orchestra,

Op. 76 no. 5
Solo Tpt.(Cl.)-Str.
Peters, New York, ᶜ1967
Score 10 p.

Resurrection
See: Haroutiun...Op. 71

Saint Vartan symphony
See: [Symphony no. 9, Saint Vartan, Op. 180]

1194v Sosi (Forest of prophetic sounds)   10'
1.Andante 2.Allegro moderato 3.Allegro
Solo Vn.-Hn.-Timp.,Giant Tam-tam-Pno.-Str.
Ms. ᶜ1949 by Alan Hovhaness
Score 36 p. Large folio
Composed 1948. First performance Town Hall, New York, 6 March 1949, the composer conducting, Anahid Ajemian soloist.

3587 Symphony no. 2, Op. 62   27'
1.Andante lamentoso 2.Allegro 3.Finale: Andante largamente
2,2,2,2-4,3,3,0-Timp.-Hp.-Str.
Ms.
Score 64 p. Large folio
Composed 1941. Symphony no. 2, Op. 132 is a different work.

5365 [Symphony no. 2, Mysterious   17'
mountain, Op. 132]
1. ♩=ca.88 2.Double fugue: ♩=ca.100 - Presto 3. ♩=ca.92 - ♩=ca.60
3,3*,3*,3*-5,3,3,1-Timp.-Cel.,Hp.-Str.
Ms. [Now published by Associated Music Publishers, New York, ᶜ1958]
Score 70 p. Large folio
Composed 1955. First performance Houston, Texas, 31 October 1955, Houston Symphony Orchestra, Leopold Stokowski conductor.

5358 [Symphony no. 9, Saint Vartan,   36'
Op. 180]
In 24 movements
0,0,0,0-Alto Sax.-1,4,1-Timp.,Perc.-Pno.-Str.
Ms. ᶜ1950 by Alan Hovhaness [Now published by Peer International]
Score 112 p. Large folio
Written for the 1500th anniversary of the Holy Wars of St. Vartan, an Armenian folk hero martyred in 451 A.D. Composed 1950. First performance Carnegie Hall, New York, 11 March 1951, members of the New York Philharmonic, the composer conducting.

Talin
See: [Concerto, viola and string orchestra, Talin, Op. 93]

390v Tzaikerk (Evening song) [Op. 53]   10'
Solo Vn.-Fl.-Timp.-Str.
Ms. ᶜ1945 by Alan Hovhaness
Score 46 p.
Composed 1945. First performance Symphony Hall, Boston, 10 March 1956, the composer conducting.

Zartik parkim
See: [Concerto, piano and chamber orchestra,
Zartik parkim (Awake, my glory!), Op. 77]

HOWE, MARY.   Richmond, Virginia 4 April 1882
                     Washington, D.C. 14 September 1964

3311 American piece, What price glory   15'
2(2nd alt. Picc.),2,2,2-4,3,3,1-Timp.,Perc.-
Hp.-Str.
Ms.
Score 96 p.
*Originally composed 1933. First performance
Chautauqua, New York, 26 July 1933, Chautauqua
Symphony Orchestra, Albert Stoessel conductor.
Revised 1940. First performance of this ver-
sion Washington, D.C., 10 July 1941, National
Symphony Orchestra, Antonia Brico conductor.*

742p Castellana, romanesco on Spanish   14'
themes, for two pianos and orchestra
Solo Pno.I, Solo Pno.II-2(2nd alt. Picc.),2,
2,2-4,3,3,1-Timp.,Perc.-Str.
Ms.
Score 91 p.
*Originally composed for two pianos, 1930.
Orchestrated 1935. First performance Washing-
ton, D.C., 13 January 1935, National Symphony
Orchestra, Hans Kindler conductor, Ethel
Bartlett and Rae Robertson soloists.*

3284 Coulennes, tableau de genre   10'
[period piece]
1,1,1,1-1,1-Timp.,Gong-Str.
Ms.
Score 30 p.
Composed 1936.

6769 Paean for orchestra   11'
3(3rd alt. Picc.),2,2,2-1Alto Sax.-4,3,3,1-
Timp.,Perc.-Hp.-Str.
Ms.
Score 40 p.

6770 Potomac, suite for orchestra.   21'
Prelude and three sketches
Prelude - river: Moderato 1.Mt. Vernon: Lento
2.Arlington: Allegro 3.Watergate: Moderato
2(2nd alt. Picc.),2,2,2-4,3,3,1-Timp.,S.Dr.,
Cym.-Hp.-Str.
Ms.
Score 69 p.
Composed 1940.

3302 Stars/Whimsy [2 pieces for   4'30"
orchestra]
1.Stars: Lento sonoro (3'30") 2.Whimsy:
Allegretto (1')
2*,1,1,1-2,1-Timp.,S.Dr.,Cym.-Hp.-Str.
Composers Press, New York, ᶜ1939
Score 13 p.
*Stars originally composed for piano, 1934.
Whimsy originally composed as Air Gai of Suite
Mélancolique for piano trio, 1931. Both works
transcribed for orchestra, 1937. First per-
formance of both works, Greenwich, Connecti-
cut, 6 July 1938, Maganini Chamber Orchestra,
Quinto Maganini conductor.*

HOWE, WALTER EDWARD.   Boston 1889

3065 Outside the tent   17'30"
3*,3*,2,3*-4,2,3,1-Timp.,Perc.-Cel.,Hp.-Str.
Ms.
Score 80 p.
*Composed ca.1924. First performance Rochester,
New York, 25 November 1925, Rochester Philhar-
monic, Howard Hanson conductor.*

HOWELL, DOROTHY.
              Handsworth, England 25 February 1898

2185 Lamia, symphonic poem   13'
3*,3*,3*,3*-4,3,3,1-Timp.,Perc.-Hp.-Str.
Novello, London, ᶜ1921
Score 79 p.
*Inspired by Keats' poem. Composed 1918.
First performance Queen's Hall, London,
1919.*

HOWELLS, HERBERT NORMAN.
       b. Lydney, Gloucestershire 17 October 1892

1095v Elegy for viola, string quartet   10'
and string orchestra
Solo Va.-String Quartet-Str.
Hawkes & Son, London, ᶜ1938
Score 9 p.
*Composed 1917. First performance Royal Albert
Hall, London, 17 December 1917, London Sym-
phony Orchestra, Hugh Allen conductor.*

3225 Puck's minuet, for orchestra, Op. 20
no. 1
2,0,3*(Bn. may substitute for B.Cl.)-Timp.,
Perc.-Pno.-Str.
Goodwin & Tabb, London, ᶜ1919
Score 23 p.
Composed 1917.

HRUBY, FRANK, JR.   Emporia, Kansas 1918

782p Concertino for piano and small   19'
orchestra
1.Allegro 2.Andante con moto, attacca
3.Allegro
Solo Pno.-2,2,2,2-2Hn.-Timp.-Str.
Ms.
Score 57 p.
*Composed 1941. First performance Seventh
Spring Symposium of American Music at Eastman
School of Music, Rochester, New York, 23-24
April 1941, Rochester Civic Orchestra, Howard
Hanson conductor, Thomas Nichols soloist.*

3177 Satirical suite, subjects for   6'
American lore
1.Traveling salesman 2.Hired workman 3.Hitch-
hiker
2(2nd alt. Picc.),2,2,2-2,2,1-Timp.,Perc.-Str.
Ms.
Score 27 p.
*Composed for piano 1939. Transcribed 1939.
First performance at the Ninth Annual Festival
of American Music at Eastman School of Music,
Rochester, New York, 25 April 1939, Eastman
School Little Symphony Orchestra, Frederick
Fennell conductor.*

Hruby, Frank, Jr.

3367 Tituba, ballet music   14'
2(2nd alt. Picc.),2,3*,3*-4,3,3-Timp.,Perc.-
Hp.-Str.
Ms.
Score 75 p.
*Composed 1940. First performance Sixth Spring
Symposium of American Music at Eastman School
of Music, Rochester, New York, 16-19 April
1940, Rochester Civic Orchestra, Howard Hanson
conductor.*

HRUBY, VIKTOR.   Vienna 9 May 1894

3935 Fantastisches Scherzo   12'
3(3rd alt. Picc.),2,2,2-4,3,3,1-Timp.,Perc.-
Hp.-Str.
Universal Edition, Vienna, c1939
Score 91 p.

HSIEN HSING-HAI.
See: CENTRAL PHILHARMONIC SOCIETY OF THE
PEOPLE'S REPUBLIC OF CHINA.
[Concerto for piano and orchestra, The
Yellow River]

HUBANS, CHARLES.   France ca.1820

1558s Gavotte Louis XIV
1,0,1-Str.
Score: Ms. 4 p.
Parts: Joubert, Paris [n.d.]

HUBAY, JENÖ.   Budapest 15 September 1858
                       Budapest 12 March 1937

Originally known as Eugen Huber.

665v Arioso, Op. 10 no. 1 [for violin and
orchestra]
Solo Vn.-2,2,2,2-2Hn.-Timp.-Str.
Bosworth, London, c1900
Score 7 p.

516v [Concerto, violin, no. 2, Op. 90,   30'
E major]
1.Allegro con fuoco 2.Larghetto 3.Allegro
non troppo
Solo Vn.-2,2,2,2-4,2,3-Timp.-Str.
J. Hamelle, Paris, c1904
Score 76 p.
*Composed 1899. First performance Gewandhaus,
Leipzig, 1900, Artur Nikisch conductor, the
composer as soloist.*

571v [Concerto, violin, no. 3, Op. 99,   32'
G minor]
1.Introduction quasi fantasia 2.Scherzo 3.
Adagio - Allegro 4.Finale: Allegro con fuoco
Solo Vn.-2(2nd alt. Picc.),2,2,2-4,2,3-Timp.,
Perc.-Hp.-Str.
Zimmermann, Leipzig, c1908
Score 124 p.
*Composed 1906. First performance Budapest,
1907, Stephan Kerner conductor, Franz von
Vecsey soloist.*

583v [Concerto, violin, no. 4, All'   28'
antica, Op. 101, C major]

1.Preludio 2.Corrente e musetto 3.Larghetto
4.Finale à capriccio
Solo Vn.-2(2nd alt. Picc.),2,2,2-3,2-Timp.,
Trgl.-Str.
Zimmermann, Leipzig, c1908
Score 66 p.
*Composed 1908. First performance Budapest,
1910, the composer conducting, Stefi Geyer
soloist.*

980v Concerto dramatique pour violon   30'
et orchestre, Op. 21 [A minor]
1.Allegro appassionato 2.Andante ma non tanto
3.Allegro con brio
Solo Vn.-2,2,2,2-4,2,3-Timp.-2Hp.-Str.
Score: Ms. 169 p.
Parts: [Lemoine, Paris, n.d.]
*Composed 1881. First performance Brussels,
1886, Joseph Dupont conductor, the composer as
soloist.*

744v Les fileuses, [from] Impressions   8'
de la Puszta [The spinning maidens, from
Impressions of Deep Hungary, Op. 44
no. 3]
Solo Vn.-2,2,2,2-3Hn.-Timp.,Trgl.-Hp.-Str.
Ries & Erler, Berlin [n.d.]
Score 22 p.
*Composed 1886. First performance Paris, 1887,
Hugo Hermann soloist.*

619v Poèmes hongrois, Op. 27 no. 1   6'
Solo Vn.-2,2,2,2-3,2,2-Timp.,Trgl.-Hp.-Str.
J. Hamelle, Paris [n.d.]
Score 16 p.
*Composed 1884. First performance Ostend,
1887, Leo Rinskopf conductor, the composer as
soloist.*

605v Poèmes hongrois, Op. 27 no. 6   6'
Solo Vn.-2(2nd alt. Picc.),2,2,2-3,2,2-Timp.,
Trgl.-Hp.-Str.
J. Hamelle, Paris [n.d.]
Score 18 p.

587v [Scènes de la Csárda, violin and   10'
orchestra. No. 2, Op. 13]
Solo Vn.-Dulcimer(or Hp., or both)-Str.
A. Cranz, Hamburg [n.d.]
Score 29 p.
*Composed 1875. First performance Concerts
Pasdeloup, Paris, 1884, Benjamin Godard con-
ductor, the composer as soloist.*

850v [Scènes de la Csárda, violin and   10'
orchestra. No. 3, Op. 18]
Solo Vn.-2,2,2,2-2,2,2-Timp.,Trgl.-Hp.-Str.
Hamelle, Paris [n.d.]
Score 36 p.
*Composed 1876. First performance Brussels,
1883, Joseph Dupont conductor, the composer as
soloist.*

589v [Scènes de la Csárda, violin and   10'
orchestra. No. 4, Hejre Kati (Heigh-ho
Kitty) Op. 32]
Solo Vn.-2,2,2,2-3,2,2-Timp.,Perc.-Hp.-Str.
Score: Ms. 39 p.

Parts: Hainauer, Breslau [n.d.]
Composed 1886. First performance Gewandhaus, Leipzig, 1888, Hugo Hermann soloist.

690v [Scènes de la Csárda, violin and   10'
orchestra. No. 5, Hullámzó Balaton (The
waves of Lake Balaton) Op. 33]
Solo Vn.-2(2nd alt. Picc.),2,2,2-4,2,1-Timp.-
Str.
Score: Ms. 40 p.
Parts: Hainauer, Breslau [n.d.]
Composed 1886. First performance Budapest, 1887, Alexander Erkel conductor, the composer as soloist.

580v [Scènes de la Csárda, violin and   12'
orchestra. No. 8, Azt mondják...(The story
goes...) Op. 60]
Solo Vn.-2,2,2,2-4,2,3-Timp.,B.Dr.,Cym.-Hp.
-Str.
W. Hansen, Leipzig, ^c1896
Score 42 p.
Composed 1886.

728v [Scènes de la Csárda, violin and   12'
orchestra. No. 12, Piczi tubiczám (My sweet
love) Op. 83]
Solo Vn.-2,2,2,2-3Hn.-Timp.,Trgl.-Cemb.(ad
lib.)-Hp.-Str.
Kistner, Leipzig [1900]
Score 23 p.
Composed 1898. First performance at a Museum Concert, Frankfurt, 1899, the composer as soloist.

907v [Scènes de la Csárda, violin and   12'
orchestra. No. 13, Op. 102]
Solo Vn.-3*,2,2,2-3,2,3-Timp.,Perc.-Hp.- Str.
Simrock, Berlin, ^c1929
Score 44 p.
Composed 1909. First performance Amsterdam, 1928, Eduard Zathureczky soloist.

817v [Scènes de la Csárda, violin and   12'
orchestra. No. 14, On themes by Lavotta,
Op. 117]
Solo Vn.-3*,2,2,2-4,2,3-Timp.,Perc.-Cel.,Hp.-
Str.
Universal Edition, Vienna, ^c1924
Score 59 p.
Composed 1922. First performance Budapest, 1926, the composer conducting, Ladislaus Szentgyörgyi soloist.

726v [Variations on a Hungarian theme,   15'
Op. 72]
Solo Vn.-2,2,2,2-3Hn.-Timp.,Trgl.-Str.
Simrock, Berlin, ^c1927
Score 21 p.
Composed 1887. First performance Music Academy, Budapest, 1907, Stefan Kerner conductor, the composer as soloist.

6155 [The village vagabond, Op. 50. Overture]
3*,3*,3*,2-4,3,3,1-Timp.,Perc.-Cimbalom,Hp.-
Str.
Harmonia, Budapest [n.d.]
Score 40 p.

From the opera in three acts with libretto by A. Váradi, based on a play by Ede Tóth, A Falu Rossza. First performance Budapest, 20 March 1896.

5490 [The violin-maker of Cremona,   4'30"
Op. 40. Overture]
3(3rd alt. Picc.),3*,3*,2-4,3,3,1-Timp.,Perc.-
Hp.(or Pno.)-Str.
Louis Oertel, Hannover [1897]
Score 19 p.
From the opera in one act with French libretto by Henri Beauclair, based on the play, Le Luthier de Crémone, by François Coppée. First performance Budapest, 10 November 1894.

846v Walzer-Paraphrase, Op. 105   10'
[violin and orchestra]
Solo Vn.-3*,2,2,2-4,2,3-Timp.,Perc.-Hp.-Str.
Zimmermann, Leipzig, ^c1913
Score 44 p.
Composed 1910. First performance Budapest, 1922, the composer conducting.

HUBER, GEORG WALTER.   Leipzig 9 April 1874

553m Fantasie für Harfe mit Orchester,   20'
Op. 9
Solo Hp.-2,2,2,2-4,2,3-Timp.-Str.
C. Giessel, Bayreuth, ^c1902
Score 47 p.
Composed 1899. First performance Frankfurt, 1901, Max Kaempfert conductor.

610m Meditation, Op. 10 [for violin,   10'
harp and orchestra]
Solo Vn., Solo Hp.-2,2,2,2-4,2,3-Timp.-Str.
C. Giessel, Bayreuth, ^c1902
Score 22 p.
Composed 1900. First performance Frankfurt, 1901, Max Kaempfert conductor.

HUBER, HANS.   Eppenberg, Switzerland 28 June 1852
                    Locarno, Switzerland 25 December 1921

5102 [A comedy overture, Op. 50]   11'
2,2,2,2-4,2,3-Timp.,Perc.-Str.
Breitkopf & Härtel, Leipzig [1879]
Score 62 p.

574p [Concerto, piano, Op. 36, C minor]   30'
1.[Prelude]: Langsam 2.Langsam 3.[As fast
as possible] 4.[With fire and swing]
Solo Pno.-2,2,2,2-2,2,3-Timp.,Trgl.-Str.
Breitkopf & Härtel, Leipzig [1878]
Score 140 p.
First performance Basel, 3 February 1878, the composer as soloist.

429p [Concerto, piano, Op. 113, D major]   22'
1.Introduction (Passacaglia) 2.Scherzo 3.
Intermezzo 4.Finale
Solo Pno.-2,2,2,2-4,2-Timp.,Trgl.-Str.
Score: Ms. 219 p.
Parts: Kistner, Leipzig [1899]
First performance Basel, 26 February 1899, Robert Freund soloist.

Huber, Hans

1812 [Symphony no. 6, Op. 134, A major]   25'
1.Allegro con spirito 2.Allegretto grazioso
3.Adagio, ma non troppo 4.Finale: Adagio, ma
non troppo – Allegretto grazioso – Allegro con
fuoco
3(3rd alt. Picc.),2,3*,3*–4,3,3,1–Timp.,Perc.–
Hp.–Str.
F.E.C. Leuckart, Leipzig [n.d.]
Score 155 p.

HUBER, JOSEPH.   Sigmaringen, Germany 17 April 1837
Stuttgart, Germany 23 April 1886

6013 [Symphony no. 3, Through darkness to the
light, Op. 10, E major]
In one movement
2,2,2,2–4,2,1–Timp.–Str.
Theodor Stürmer, Stuttgart [186–?]
Score 25 p.
*Suggested by a play, Through Darkness to the
Light, by Peter Lohmann.*

4273 [Symphony no. 4, Against the current, Op. 12,
C major]
In one movement
2,2,2,2–2,2,3–Timp.–Str.
Theodor Stürmer, Stuttgart [186–?]
Score 21 p.
*Suggested by a play, Against the Current, by
Peter Lohmann.*

HÜBLER, HEINRICH.

325m [Concert piece for four horns and orches-
tra]
4 Solo Hn.–2(2nd alt. Picc.),2,2,2–0,2,3–Timp.–
Str.
C.A. Klemm, Leipzig, 1888
Score in reduction 25 p.
Composed 1856.

HÜE, GEORGES-ADOLPHE.   Versailles 6 May 1858
Paris 7 June 1948

1283 Émotions, poème symphonique   15'
3*,3*,3*,3*–4,4,3,1–Timp.,Perc.–2Hp.–Str.
Rouart Lerolle, Paris, c1919
Score 81 p.
*Composed 1918. First performance Paris, 1919,
Gabriel Pierné conductor.*

562m Fantaisie pour flûte et orchestre   7'
Solo Fl.–Picc.,2(2nd alt. E.H.),2,2–2Hn.–Timp.,
Trgl.–Hp.(or Pno.)–Str.
Ms. Costallat, Paris, c1923
Score 49 p.
*Composed for the competition of the Conserva-
toire de Musique of Paris, 1913. First per-
formance at the Casino, Dieppe, 1913, Ferté
conductor.*

916v Fantaisie pour violon et orchestre   12'
Solo Vn.–3*,2,2,2–4,2,3–Timp.,Trgl.–Hp.–Str.
Ms.
Score 67 p.
*First performance at the Concerts Colonne,
Paris 1893, Pannequin soloist.*

685m Gigue [for flute and orchestra]   6'
Solo Fl.–0,2,2,2–Hn.–Trgl.–Cel.,Hp.–Str.
Ms.
Score 62 p.
*Composed with Nocturne (below), 1920. First
performance of both, Concerts Colonne, Paris,
1921.*

1966 [Le miracle. Ballet music from   15'
the opera]
1.Escholiers et ribaudes 2.[Bear dance and
4 variations] 3.[Round dance]
3*,3*,2,3–4,2,2Cnt.,3,1–Timp.,Perc.–Cel.,Hp.–
Str.
Choudens, Paris, c1910
Score 114 p.
*Opera composed 1909. First performance Opéra,
Paris, 1910. First concert performance of
ballet music, Paris, 1912, Camille Chevillard
conductor.*

686m Nocturne [for flute and orchestra]   7'
Solo Fl.–0,2*,2,1–Hn.–Hp.–Str.
Ms.
Score 47 p.

2369 Rêverie [for small orchestra]   3'
1,1,1,1–Str.
Leduc, Paris [1911?]
Score 7 p.
Composed 1911.

615v Romance [for violin and orchestra]   7'
Solo Vn.–2,1,2,2–Hn.–Str.
Baudoux, Paris [n.d.]
Score 16 p.
Composed 1905.

2368 Sérénade [for small orchestra]   4'
1,1,1,1–Str.
Leduc, Paris [n.d.]
Score 7 p.
Composed 1911.

1852 Titania [symphonic suite from the   23'
musical drama]
1.[The magic paradise – Dance of Philida] 2.
[Prelude – Hunt – Apparition]
3(3rd alt. Picc.),3*,3*,3*–4,3,3,1–Timp.,Perc.
–Cel.,Hp.–Str.
Choudens, Paris, c1903
Score 75 p.
*From the musical drama composed 1903. First
performance of this suite, Paris 1905, Edouard
Colonne conductor.*

HUFF, TRAVERS.   Coeur d'Alene, Idaho 1 June 1943

7203 Slow dance for orchestra   3'
2,2*,3*,2–2,0,2,1–Timp.,B.Dr.,Vibraphone–Str.
Ms. c1976 by Travers Huff
Score 14 p. Large folio
*Composed 1968. First performance Rochester,
New York, March 1968, Eastman-Rochester Sym-
phony Orchestra, Walter Hendl conductor.*

6836 Theme and variations for orchestra   14'
3*(Picc. alt. Alto Fl.), 2(2nd alt. E.H.),3*,

3*-4,3,3,1-Timp.,Perc.-Pno.,Hp.-Str.
Ms.
Score 52 p. Large folio
*Composed 1966. First performance Rochester,
New York, June 1966, Eastman-Rochester Symphony
Orchestra, Walter Hendl conductor.*

HUIZAR, CANDELARIO.
                    Jerez (now known as Garcia),
                    Zacatecas, Mexico 2 February 1883
                    Mexico City 3 May 1970

5407 [Images, symphonic poem]
3(3rd alt. Picc.),3*,3*,2-4,2,3,1-Timp.,Perc.
-Cel.,Hp.-Str.
Ms.
Score 137 p.
*Composed 1929. First performance Mexico City,
13 December 1929, Orquesta Sinfonica de Mexico,
Carlos Chavez conductor.*

3819 Pueblerinas [Village maidens]   *20'30"*
a.Moderato - Allegro b.Lento c.Allegro vivo
3(3rd alt. Picc.),3(E.H. alt. Ob. d'Amore &
B.Ob.),4(3rd alt. B.Cl.,4th alt. Requinto or
Cl. in E-flat),2-4,2,3-Timp.,Perc.-2Hp.-Str.
Ms.
Score 77 p.
*Composed 1931. First performance Mexico City,
6 November 1931, Orquesta Sinfónica de México,
Carlos Chavez conductor.*

HÜLLWECK, FERDINAND. Dessau, Germany 8 October 1824
                     Blasewitz, near Dresden 24 July 1887

4313 [Partita. Four pieces for orchestra,
Op. 22]
1.Capriccio 2.Intermezzo 3.Scherzoso
4.Alla polacca
3*(Picc. optional),2,2,2-4(3rd and 4th
optional),2,3(all optional)-Timp.-Str.
L. Hoffarth, Dresden [1879?]
Score 43 p.
*First performance Dresden, 28 April 1879,
Musicians' Society of Dresden, Ernst Schuch
conductor.*

HUMAN, ADOLPH.   Strehla, Saxony 1794

482m [Concerto, bassoon, F major]
Solo Bn.-1,2,2,2-2,2-Timp.-Str.
Ms.
Score 64 p.

HUMISTON, WILLIAM HENRY.
                    Marietta, Ohio 27 April 1869
                    New York 5 December 1923

22 A Southern fantasie [Melodies from the   *8'*
American South]
2(2nd alt. Picc.),2(2nd alt. E.H.),2,2-4,2,3,
1-Timp.-Str.
Breitkopf & Härtel, New York, c1911
Score 34 p.

HUMMEL, FERDINAND.   Berlin 6 September 1855
                             Berlin 24 April 1928

570m Grosse Fantasie, Op. 30 [for harp and
orchestra]
Solo Hp.-2,2,2,2-2Hn.-Timp.-Str.
Ms.
Score 26 p.

HUMMEL, JOHANN NEPOMUK. Pozsony, Hungary (now
            Bratislava, Czechoslavakia) 14 November 1778
                    Weimar, Germany 17 October 1837

270m [Concerto, mandolin and chamber   *20'*
orchestra, G major] Edited by Vinzenz
Hladky
1.Allegro moderato e grazioso 2.Andante con
  ariazioni (3 variations) 3.Rondo: Allegro
Solo Mandolin-2Fl.-2Hn.-Str.
V. Hladky, Vienna, c1957
Score 55 p.
Composed 1799. Authenticity in doubt.

622p [Concerto, piano, Op. 85, A minor]   *28'*
1.Allegro moderato 2.Larghetto, attacca
3.Rondo: Allegro moderato
Solo Pno.-1,2,2,2-2,2-Timp.-Str.
Score: Ms. 212 p.
Parts: [T. Haslinger, Vienna, 1827?]

518p [Concerto, piano, Op. 89, B minor.   *32'*
Movement 1: Allegro moderato. Newly
orchestrated by Xaver Scharwenka]
Solo Pno.-2,2,2,2-2,2-Timp.-Str.
Breitkopf & Härtel, Leipzig, c1903
Score 43 p.

237m [Concerto, piano and violin, Op. 17,
G major]
1.Allegro con brio 2.Andante con variazioni
3.Rondo
Solo Vn., Solo Pno.-1,2,0,2-2Hn.-Str.
Score: Ms. c1976 by The Fleisher Collection of
Orchestral Music, Free Library of Philadelphia.
88p. Large folio
Parts: Jean Traeg et Fils [n.p., n.d.]

989v Fantasie
Solo Va.-2Cl.-Str.
Score: Ms. 23 p.
Parts: [n.p., n.d.]

HUMMEL, JOSEPH FRIEDRICH.
                    Innsbruck, Austria 14 August 1841
                    Salzburg 29 August 1919

378s Mandolinata, Austria no. 10, Op. 61
Str.
Anton Aubitsch, Innsbruck, c1909
Score 7 p.

HUMPERDINCK, ENGELBERT.
                    Siegburg, near Bonn 1 September 1854
                    Neustrelitz 27 September 1921

1037 [Gaudeamus. Prelude]
3*,3*,3*,2-4,2,3,1-Timp.,Cym.,B.Dr.-Hp.-Str.
A. Fürstner, Berlin, c1919, c1920
Score 17 p.
*From the comic opera. First performance
Darmstadt, 18 March 1919.*

Humperdinck, Engelbert

2931 [Hansel and Gretel. Evening prayer   *8'*
and dream pantomime] Edited by Adolf Schmid
3*,2*,2,2-4,2,3,1-Timp.,Cym.,Trgl.-Hp.-Str.
C. Fischer, New York, ᶜ1937
Score 30 p.
From the opera in three acts with libretto
by Adelheid Wette, based on a fairy tale by
the brothers Grimm. First performance Weimar,
Hoftheater, 23 December 1893.

1426 [Hansel and Gretel. Knusperwalzer.   *5'*
Transcribed for small orchestra by Hans
Steiner]
2*,2,2,2-4(2ad lib.),3(ad lib.)-Timp.,Trgl.
-Glock.-Str.
B. Schott's Söhne, Mainz, ᶜ1895
Score 17 p.

11 [Hansel and Gretel. Prelude]   *8'*
3*,2,2,2-4,2,3,1-Timp.,Perc.-Str.
Kalmus, New York [n.d.]
Score 28 p.

7120 [Hansel and Gretel. Sandman's song,   *9'*
Evening prayer, and Dream pantomime]
3*,2(2nd alt. E.H.),2,2-4,2,3,1-Timp.,Cym.,
Trgl.-Voice parts optional-Str.
B. Schott's Söhne, Mainz [1894]
Score 22 p.

1370 Die Heirat wider Willen [Wed against their
will. Wedding in the Bastille]
2(2nd alt. Picc.),2(2nd alt. E.H.),2,2-4,2,3,
1-Timp.,Cym.,Glock.-Hp.-Str. Backstage: Signal-
trumpet,Gong,S.Dr.-Org.(or Harm.)
Brockhaus, Leipzig, ᶜ1905
Score 31 p.
From the opera first performed Berlin, 1905.

901 Humoreske [in E major]   *5'*
2,2,2,2-2,2-Timp.-Str.
O. Wernthal, Berlin [n.d.]
Score 27 p.

1211 [Königskinder. Prelude]   *7'*
3*,2,3*,3*-4,3,3,1-Timp.,Cym.,Trgl.-Str.
Brockhaus, Leipzig, ᶜ1897
Score 54 p.
From the fairy opera in three acts. First
performance Metropolitan Opera, New York, 28
December 1910.

6984 [Königskinder. Introduction to Act II]
2,2,2,2-4,2,3,1-Timp.,Perc.-Str.
Max Brockhaus, Leipzig, ᶜ1896
Score 24 p.

6985 [Königskinder. Introduction to Act III]
3*,2*,3*,3*-4,3,3,1-Timp.-Hp.-Str.
Max Brockhaus, Leipzig, ᶜ1896
Score 20 p.

1228 [Königskinder. Introductions to Acts
II and III]
3(3rd alt. Picc.),3*,3*,3*-4,3,3,1-Timp.,Cym.,
Trgl.-Hp.-Str.
Brockhaus, Leipzig, ᶜ1910
Score 36 p.

1138 [Die Marketenderin (The canteen woman).
Prelude]
3*,3*,2,2-4,3,3-Timp.,Perc.-Str.
A. Fürstner, Paris, ᶜ1914
Score 24 p.
From the ballad-opera. First performance
Cologne, 10 May 1914.

1188 [The Merchant of Venice. Love scene, from
the incidental music to Shakespeare's play]
2,1,2,2-2Hn.-Timp.-Hp.-Str.
Brockhaus, Leipzig [190-?]
Score 29 p.
First performance Berlin, 9 November 1905.

302 [Moorish rhapsody]   *28'*
1.Tarifa [Elegy at sunset] 2.Tanger [A night
in the Moorish coffee-house] 3.Tetuan [A
ride in the desert]
3*,2*,3*,3*-4,2,3,1-Timp.,Perc.-Str.
Brockhaus, Leipzig, ᶜ1899
Score 127 p.

6723 [Sleeping Beauty. Tone pictures]
1.Vorspiel [Prelude] 2.Ballade 3.Irrfahrten
[Wanderings] 4.Das Dornenschloss [The thorn
castle] 5.Festklänge [Festival sounds]
3*,2,2,2-4,3,3,1-Timp.,Cym.,Trgl.-Hp.-Str.
Max Brockhaus, Leipzig, ᶜ1902
Score 54 p.
From the fairy tale in three acts with libretto
by E. B. Ebeling-Filhès, after Charles Per-
rault.

959 [Same as above] Prelude alone

19s [Twelfth Night, incidental music to
Shakespeare's play. No. 7, Intermezzo]
S.Dr.(offstage)-Str.
Brockhaus, Leipzig, 1908
Score 2 p.
First performance Berlin, 17 October 1907.

18s [Twelfth Night, incidental music to
Shakespeare's play. Appendix: No. 11, Scene-
change after Scene I]
Hp.-Str.
Brockhaus, Leipzig [1908]
Score 2 p.
This appendix added after the first performance
of the incidental music.

HUMPHREY, DORIS. Oak Park, Illinois 17 October 1895
             New York City 29 December 1958

215m Dance rhythms, for percussion. Notated   *5'*
by Wallingford Riegger
Two players:
  I. 2Dr.,Tamb.,2Gongs,Cym.,Small Dr.,Large Dr.,
    B.Dr.,Tom Tom
  II. Gong,Cym.,3Blocks,Tom Tom,B.Dr.,Tamb.
New Music Orchestra Series, San Francisco,
ᶜ1936
Score 1 p.
Commissioned by the Bennington School of the
Dance, 1936. Composed 1936 as Part Three of a

ballet, New Dance. First performance Benning-
ton, Vermont, August 1936, by the Bennington
School of the Dance, Pauline Lawrence con-
ductor.

HUMPHRIES, JOHN.   England ca.1707
                                              1730

1050s Concerto for strings, Op. 2 no. 9
[E-flat major] Edited by Ludwig Lebell
1.Adagio 2.Allegro 3.Adagio 4.Allegro
Soli: Vn.I, Vn.II-Str.
Oxford University Press, London, ᶜ1927
Score 14 p.
First published by Benjamin Cooke, London, ca.
1730.

HUNRATH, AUGUST.   Bremen, Germany 19 May 1881

638m [Scherzo, flute and orchestra,   *3'*
Op. 2, E minor]
Solo Fl.-1,0,2,2-2Hn.-Timp.-Str.
Zimmermann, Leipzig, ᶜ1921
Score 11 p.

HUNT, FREDERICK.   Carmel, Indiana 3 December 1906
                      Rochester, New York 11 June 1967

4621 Air [for orchestra]   *5'*
2,3*,2,2-3Hn.-Timp.-Hp.-Str.
Carl Fischer, New York [n.d.]
Score 10 p.

6760 Canzona for chamber orchestra
1,2*,2,2-2,1-Str.
Ms.
Score 31 p.
Composed 1967. First performance Rochester
Community College, Rochester, New York, 16
April 1967, Rochester Chamber Orchestra,
David Fetler conductor.

182m Chaconne [for alto saxophone and   *19'*
orchestra]
Solo Alto Sax.-2,1,2,2-2Hn.-Hp.-Str.
Ms.
Score 84 p.

282p Deepdene [for harpsichord and chamber
orchestra]
Solo Hpscd.-1,1,1,1-Hn.-Str.
Ms.
Score 65 p.
Dedicated to the composer's friend John
Celentano.

261m Doric concerto, for [2] saxophones and
orchestra
1.Allegretto 2.Andante 3.Vivace
Solo Soprano Sax. & Solo Alto Sax.-1,1,1,1-
2Hn.-Hp.-Str.
Ms.
Score 68 p.
Composed 1965.

275m Fantasia, for solo clarinet and   *10'*
orchestra
Solo Cl.-2,2,2,2-4Hn.-Str.

Ms.
Score 28 p.

1188v Fantasy, for solo violin and   *5'30"*
orchestra
Solo Vn.-2,2,2,2-4Hn.-Timp.-Str.
Ms.
Score 24 p.
Composed 1943. First performance Rochester,
New York, 17 October 1944, Eastman-Rochester
Symphony Orchestra, Howard Hanson conductor,
Millard Taylor soloist.

6549 A summer symphony   *13'30"*
1.Allegretto 2.Andante 3.Allegro
2,2,2,2-4,2,3-Timp.-Str.
Ms.
Score 62 p.

6550 Symphony in E-flat major   *29'30"*
1.Allegretto 2.Andante 3.Vivace 4.Allegro
2,2,2,2-4,2,3-Timp.-Str.
Ms.
Score 88 p. Large folio
First performance Rochester, New York, 1940-
41 season, Eastman-Rochester Symphony Orches-
tra, Howard Hanson conductor.

6546 Symphony in G minor   *23'30"*
1.Moderato 2.Allegro 3.Andante 4.Allegro
2,2*,2,2-4,2,3-Timp.-Str.
Ms.
Score 80 p.
Composed 1964. First performance Rochester,
New York, 28 April 1965, Eastman-Rochester
Symphony Orchestra, Howard Hanson conductor.

HURÉ, JEAN. Gien, Loiret, France 17 September 1877
                            Paris 27 January 1930

238p [Nocturne, for orchestra with solo piano]
Solo Pno.-3(3rd alt. Picc.),3*,3*,2-4,3,3,1-
Timp.,Perc.-Cel.,Hp.-Str.
A. Zunz Mathot, Paris, ᶜ1908
Score 49 p.
Composed 1903. First performed by Marie
Louise Ritter. First American performance St.
Louis, Missouri, 7 January 1910, St. Louis
Symphony Orchestra, Max Zach conductor, Tina
Lerner, soloist.

HURLEBUSCH, CONRAD FRIEDRICH.
             Brunswick, Germany, probably 1696
             Amsterdam 17 December 1765

299v [Concerto, violin, A minor]
1.[Allegro] - Adagio - Alla breve 2.Adagio
3.Allegro
Solo Vn.-2Ob.,Bn.-2Cemb.-Str.
Score: Denkmäler Deutscher Tonkunst, XXIX.
Breitkopf & Härtel, Leipzig, 1907. Edited
by Arnold Schering. 28 p.
Parts: Ms. ᶜ1976 by The Fleischer Collection of
Orchestral Music, Free Library of Philadelphia

Hurlebusch, Conrad Friedrich

300v [Concerto, violin, B-flat major] Edited by
Marc Mostovoy
1.[Allegro] 2.Adagio 3.[Allegro]
Solo Vn.-2Ob.,Bn.-Cemb.-Str.
Ms. c1976 by The Fleisher Collection of Orches-
tral Music, Free Library of Philadelphia
Score 39 p.

HURLSTONE, WILLIAM YEATES.   London 7 January 1876
                                  London 30 May 1906

1639 Fantasie-variations on a Swedish air   *17'*
Andante maestoso - Swedish air - 18 variations
2(2nd alt. Picc.),2,2,3*-4,2,3-Timp.,Cym.,S.Dr.
-Str.
Novello, London [190-?]
Score 67 p.
Composed 1904. First performance London, May
1904.

HUSA, KAREL.   Prague 7 August 1921

6375 Divertimento for brass and   *15'*
percussion
1.Ouverture 2.Scherzo 3.Song 4.Slovak dance
0,0,0,0-4,3,3,1-Timp.,Perc.
Ms. c1958 by Karel Husa
Score 16 p. Large folio
Originally composed for piano 4-hands as part
of the Eight Czech Duets, 1955. This tran-
scription 1958. First performance Ann Arbor,
Michigan, August 1959, University of Michigan
Band, Henry Romersa conductor.

2328s [Four little pieces for strings]   *14'30"*
1.Variazioni 2.Notturno 3.Furiant (Czech
danza) 4.Coda
Str.
B. Schott's Söhne, Mainz, c1958
Score 16 p.
Composed 1955.

6754 [Fresco] Fresque for orchestra   *10'*
3,3,3,3-4,3,3,1-Timp.,Perc.-Pno.,
Hp.(2 if possible)-Str.
Ms. c1966 by Karel Husa
Score 67 p.
Part of Three Fresques. Composed 1946-47.
First performance of Three Fresques, Prague,
27 April 1949, concert of the Czech section
of the International Society for Contemporary
Music, Prague Radio Orchestra, Václav Smetá-
cek conductor.

HUSS, HENRY HOLDEN. Newark, New Jersey 21 June 1862
                          New York 17 September 1953

3475 La nuit [The night, poem for   *4'30"*
orchestra, Op. 21]
3*,2(2nd alt. E.H.),2,2-4,2,3,1-Timp.-Hp.-Str.
Ms.
Score 21 p.
Composed for piano, 1902. Transcribed 1939.
First performance Washington, D.C., 15 March
1942, National Symphony Orchestra, Francis
Garziglia conductor.

HUSSLA, VIKTOR.   St. Petersburg 16 October 1857
                          Lisbon 14 November 1899

1646s Schlummerlied, Op.3 [Slumber song, violin
and string orchestra]
Solo Vn.-Str.
Score: Ms. 4 p.
Parts: Rühle, Berlin [n.d.]

HUSSONMOREL, V.

1043s Gavotte [string orchestra, G major]
Str.
Enoch, Paris [n.d.]
Score 7 p.

HUSTON, SCOTT, JR.
            b. Tacoma, Washington 10 October 1916

3843 Columbia (Saga of a river), tone   *11'*
poem for orchestra, Op. 7
2(2nd alt. Picc.),2,2(2nd alt. B.Cl.),2-4,3,3,
1-Timp.,Perc.-Hp.-Str.
Ms.
Score 75 p.
Composed 1941. First performance Rochester,
New York, April 1941, Rochester Civic Orches-
tra, Howard Hanson conductor.

HUTCHESON, ERNEST.   Melbourne 20 July 1871
                          New York 9 February 1951

560p March for 2 pianos and orchestra of strings
Solo Pno.I, Solo Pno.II-Str.
Score: Ms. 33 p.
Parts: [C. Fischer, New York, n.d.]

HUTSCHENRUYTER, WOUTER.   Rotterdam 15 August 1859
                          The Hague 24 November 1943

191m [Nocturne, horn (Andante poco lento)
Op. 13]
Solo Hn.-3(3rd ad lib.),0,2,2-Hp.-Str.
Jos. Aibl, Munchen, c1898
Score 15 p.
Composed ca.1890-92.

HÜTTEL, JOSEPH.   Czechoslovakia 1893

2351 L'Arlequinade [for 13 musicians]   *6'*
1,1,1,1-1,1-Timp.,Perc.-Str.
Senart, Paris, c1931
Score 36 p.
Composed 1930. First performance Guild Theatre,
New York, 6 April 1930, Georges Barrère con-
ductor.

HUYBRECHTS, ALBERT.
               Dinant, Belgium 12 February 1899
Woluwé-St.Pierre, near Brussels 21 February 1938

5127 [Divertissement for brass and   *25'*
percussion]
1.Fanfares 2.Nocturne 3.Finale
0,0,0,0-4,4(1 small Tpt. in D),3,1-Timp.,Perc.
Ms. [Now published by CeBeDeM, Brussels, 1966]
Score 42 p.
Composed 1931.

HYATT, NATHANIEL IRVING.
North Troy, New York 23 April 1865
Ithaca, New York 19 October 1959

5526 Overture to Enoch Arden   12'
1,1,2,1-2,2,1-Timp.-Str.
Ms.
Score 45 p.
*Suggested by Alfred Tennyson's poem, Enoch
Arden. This work is the composer's graduation
thesis from the Leipzig Conservatory, composed
1892. First performance Leipzig, June 1892,
Leipzig Conservatory Orchestra, Hans Sitt
conductor.*

I

IBERT, JACQUES.   Paris 15 August 1890
                                 Paris 5 February 1962

5507 [The ballad of Reading Gaol]   25'
3(3rd alt. Picc.),3*,3*,2,Sarrus.-4,3,3,1-
Timp.,Perc.-Cel.,2Hp.-Str.
Leduc, Paris, c1924
Score 97 p.
*Inspired by Oscar Wilde's poem. Completed ca.
1920. First performance at the Concerts
Colonne, Paris, 22 October 1922, Gabriel
Pierné conductor.*

5901 Capriccio pour 10 instruments, 1938   10'
1,1,1,1-Tpt.-Hp.-Str.(without Cb.)
Or: Str. only(without Cb.)
Leduc, Paris, c1939
Score 41 p.
*Commissioned for the Venice Festival. Com-
posed 1937-38. First performance Venice, sum-
mer 1938, Venice Festival Orchestra, Nino
Sonzogno conductor.*

508c [Concerto, violoncello and winds]   11'
1.Pastorale 2.Romance 3.Gigue
Solo Vc.-2(2nd alt. Picc.),2,2(2nd alt. B.Cl.),
2-1,1
Heugel, Paris, c1926
Score 55 p.
*Composed 1925. First performance Paris, 28
February 1926, Paul Paray conductor, Madeleine
Monnier soloist.*

4879 Divertissement   16'
Played without pause: 1.Introduction 2.Cor-
tège 3.Nocturne 4.Valse 5.Parade 6.Finale
1(alt. Picc.),0,1,1(alt. C.Bn.)-1,1,1-Timp.,
Perc.-Pno.(alt. Cel.)-Str.
Durand, Paris, c1931
Score 62 p.
*From the incidental music to Eugene Labiche's
stage comedy Le Chapeau de Paille d'Italie.
First concert performance of this excerpt,
Paris, 30 November 1930, Vladimir Gol-
schmann conductor.*

604 Escales [Ports of call]
1.Calme 2.Modéré très rythmé 3.Animé

3*,3*,2,3-4,3,3,1-Timp.,Perc.-Cel.,2Hp.-Str.
Leduc, Paris, c1925
Score 91 p.
*First performance at the Concerts Lamoureux,
Paris, 6 January 1924, Paul Paray conductor.*

4308 Féerique   9'
3*,3*,3*,3-4,3,3,1-Timp.,Perc.
-2Hp.-Str.
Leduc, Paris, c1925
Score 39 p.
*Composed 1924. First performance at the Con-
certs Colonne, Paris, 6 December 1925, Gabriel
Pierné conductor.*

4882 [Perseus and Andromeda. Symphonic   15'
suite. Part I]
3(3rd alt. Picc.),3*,2,3,Sarrus. or C.Bn.-4,
3,2Cnt.,3,1-Timp.,Perc.-Cel.,2Hp.-
Str.
Durand, Paris, c1930
Score 65 p.
*From the opera Persée et Andromède, ou Le Plus
Heureux des Trois, in two acts with libretto
by Nino after Jules Laforgue's Moralités
Légendaires. Composed 1922.*

4883 [Perseus and Andromeda. Symphonic   12'
suite. Part II]
3(3rd alt. Picc.),3*,2,3,Sarrus. or C.Bn.-4,
3,2Cnt.,3,1-Timp.,Perc.,-Cel.,2Hp.-
Str.
Durand, Paris, c1930
Score 60 p.

IDE, CHESTER EDWARD.
Springfield, Illinois 13 June 1878
Greenwich, Connecticut 18 March 1944

7284 The merry-makers, quick-step [for
orchestra]
1,1,2,1-2,2,1,1-Timp.,Perc.-Str.
Ms.
Score 12 p.
Composed 1932.

4677 Symphony in A minor   25'
1.Allegro agitato ma non troppo 2.Adagio
pesante 3.Scherzo: Vivace 4.Finale: Con
energico
3*,2*,2,2-4,2,3,1-Timp.,Perc.-Str.
Privately published, Greenwich, Connecticut,
c1945 by Mrs. Chester Ide [Now published by
Edition Musicus, New York, 1947]
Score 124 p.
*Composed 1932. First reading 5 June 1946,
National Orchestral Association, Leon Barzin
conductor.*

IFUKUBE, AKIRA.
b. Kushiro, Hokkaido, Japan 7 March 1914

6249 [Aboriginal triptych, three pic-   11'30"
tures for chamber orchestra (14 solo
instruments)]
1.Payses: Tempo di jimkuu 2.Timbe (nom
régional) [a regional name] 3.Pakkai (chant
d'Aino)

Iliffe, Frederick

1,1,1,1-2,1-Timp.-Pno.-Str.
Ryuginsha, Tokyo, ^c1939 by Alexander
Tcherepnin
Score 52 p.
Composed 1938. First performance in an Italy-
Japan International Exchange Radio Broadcast,
Tokyo, March 1938, Nippon Kokyo Kangengaku-Dan
(now the N.H.K. Symphony Orchestra), Kojiro
Kobune conductor.

ILIFFE, FREDERICK.   Smeeton-Westerby,
            Leicestershire 21 February 1847
            Oxford 2 February 1928

332s Pizzicato serenade, Vergiss mein nicht
Str.
Augener, London [n.d.]
Score 4 p.

ILYNSKI, ALEXANDER ALEXANDROVICH.
        Tsarskoe Selo, Russia 24 January 1859
            Moscow 23 February 1920

968 Noure and Anitra, orchestral suite,   22'
Op. 13
Fairy tale in 8 movements
3*,3*,3*,2-4,2,2Cnt.,3,1-Timp.,Perc.-Pno.,Hp.-
Str.
Jurgenson, Moscow [n.d.]
Score 141 p.

656 Psyche, symphonic fragment, Op. 14   4'
2,2,2,2-4Hn.-Timp.-Hp.(or Pno.)-Str.
Jurgenson, Moscow [n.d.]
Score 19 p.

1229 Suite no. 1, Op. 4   20'
1.Introduzione - Corale - Fuga 2.Minuetto
3.Andante 4.Gavotta 5.Scherzo
3*,2,2,2-4,3,3,1-Timp.-Str.
Jurgenson, Moscow [n.d.]
Score 113 p.

IMELMANN, H.

1397s Wiegenlied [Lullaby] Op. 6
Solo Vn.-Str.
Lehne, Hannover [n.d.]
Score 8 p.

INCH, HERBERT REYNOLDS.
        b. Missoula, Montana 25 November 1904

5065 Answers to a questionnaire   16'
(variations)
2,2,2,2-4,3,3,1-Timp.,Perc.-Hp.-Str.
Ms.
Score 77 p.
Composed 1942. First performance Rochester,
New York, 28 October 1943, Eastman-Rochester
Symphony Orchestra, Howard Hanson conductor.

1300s Concertino for string orchestra   10'
[with piano]
1.Allegro moderato 2.Andante 3.Molto
allegro 4.Allegro
Pno.-Str.
Ms.

Score 13 p. Large folio
Composed 1953. First performance Rochester,
New York, 6 May 1955, Eastman-Rochester Sym-
phony Orchestra, Howard Hanson conductor.

2843 Serenade   20'
1.Allegro vivace 2.Andante con moto 3.Allegro
moderato 4.Andante mesto 5.Allegro con brio
1,1,2,1-2,1,1-Str.
Ms.
Score 74 p. Large folio
Composed 1936. First performance of first
three movements, Rochester, New York, 24
October 1939, Rochester Civic Orchestra,
Howard Hanson conductor.

2858 Suite for small orchestra   19'
1.Barcarolle 2.Nocturne 3.Finale
2(2nd alt. Picc.),1,2,1-2,1-Timp.,Perc.-Hp.-
Str.
Ms.
Score 123 p.
Composed 1929. First performance Rochester,
New York, 24 October 1930, Rochester Philhar-
monic Orchestra, Howard Hanson conductor.
Title later changed to Three Pieces for Small
Orchestra.

3002 Symphony   25'
1.Vivace 2.Allegro giusto 3.Andante sostenuto
4.Allegro feroce
3*,3*,3*,3*-4,3,3,1-Timp.,Perc.-Hp.-Str.
Ms.
Score 132 p. Large folio
Composed 1932; revised 1937-38.

2817 Variations on a modal theme   14'
3*,3*,2,3*-4,3,3,1-Timp.,Perc.-Str.
Ms.
Score 67 p.
Composed 1927. First performance Rochester,
New York, 29 April 1927, Rochester Philhar-
monic Orchestra, Howard Hanson conductor.

INDY, VINCENT D'.   Paris 27 March 1851
                    Paris 2 December 1931

Full name: Paul Marie Théodore Vincent d'Indy

2339 Chanson et danses, divertissement,   8'
Op. 50
1,1,2,2-Hn.
Durand, Paris [n.d.]
Score 43 p.
Composed 1898. First performance Paris, 1900.

[Chorale with variations, saxophone (or viola
or violoncello) and orchestra, Op. 55]
1037m Solo Alto Sax.-2,2,2,2-4,1,3-Timp.-Hp.-
        Str.
567v Solo Va.-2,2,2,2-4,1,3-Timp.-Hp.-Str.
Durand, Paris, ^c1903
Scores: 27 p. each
Composed 1903. First performance Boston, 5
January 1904.

563m [Concerto, piano, flute and violoncello
and string orchestra, Op. 89]

Indy, Vincent d'

1.Modéré, mais bien décidé 2.Lent et expres-
sif 3.Mouvement de ronde française
Solo Pno., Solo Fl., Solo Vc.-Str.
Rouart, Lerolle, Paris, c1927
Score 55 p.

802 [L'étranger, Op. 53. Introduction to   6'
Act II]
3*,3*,3*,3*-4,3,4-Timp.,Perc.-Hp.-Str.
Durand, Paris [n.d.]
Score 17 p.

511m [Fantaisie, oboe and orchestra, Op. 31]
Solo Ob.-3*,0,2,2-4,2,3-Timp.,Trgl.-Str.
Durand, Paris, c1908
Score 35 p.
*Composed 1888. First performance Concerts
Lamoureux, Paris, 23 December 1888, Albert
Weiss soloist.*

102 [Fervaal, Op. 40. Introduction to   7'
Act I]
2,2,2,2-4,1,3-Str.
Durand, Paris [n.d.]
Score 6 p.

498 [Fervaal, Op. 40. Prelude to Act III]
4*,3*,4*,4-4,4,2Bugle, Alto and Bar. Saxhorn,
4,1-Timp.,Perc.-Str.
Durand, Paris, c1895, 1906, 1908
Score 39 p.

1236 La forêt enchantée, après Uhland,   11'
Op. 8
3*,2,2,3-4,2,Cnt.,3,1-Timp.,Perc.-8Hp.-Str.
Heugel, Paris, c1892
Score 86 p.
*Composed 1878. First performance Paris, 1878,
Concerts Pasdeloup.*

475 Istar, symphonic variations, Op. 42   17'
3*,3*,3*,3*-4,3,3,1-Timp.,Perc.-2Hp.-Str.
Durand, Paris, c1897, 1909
Score 48 p.
*Composed 1896. First performance Brussels,
1897, Concerts Ysaÿe.*

803 Jour d'été à la montagne [Summer   33'
day in the mountains] Op. 61
1.[Daybreak] 2.[Day (Afternoon under the
pines)] 3.[Evening]
3*,3*,3*,3-4,3,4-Timp.,Perc.-Pno.,2Hp.-Str.
Durand, Paris, c1906
Score 111 p.
*Composed 1905. First performance Paris, 1906,
Concerts Colonne.*

1634 Karadec, suite from the incidental   10'
music to the play by André Alexandre, Op. 34
1.[Prelude] 2.[Song] 3.[Wedding in Brit-
tany]
2,2,2,2-2Hn.-Timp.,Trgl.-Str.
Heugel, Paris, c1893
Score 47 p.

472c Lied, Op. 19
Solo Vc.(or Va.)-2,0,2,2-2Hn.-Timp.-Str.
Hamelle, Paris [n.d.]

Score 35 p.
Composed 1884.

570 Médée [orchestral suite to the tra-   24'
gedy by Catulle Mendès, Op. 47]
1.Prélude 2.Pantomime 3.[Awaiting Medea]
4.Médée et Jason 5.Le triomphe auroral
2*,2*,2,2-3,2,3-Timp.,Cym.-Hp.-Str.
Durand, Paris, c1899
Score 77 p.
Composed 1898. First performance Paris, 1898.

872 Poème des rivages [symphonic suite]   45'
Op. 77
1.Calme et lumière 2.La joie du bleu profond
3.Horizons verts 4.Le mystère de l'océan
3*,3*,3*,3-4Sax.(ATTB)-4,4,4-Timp.,Perc.-Pno.,
Cel.,2Hp.-Str.
Rouart Lerolle, Paris, c1922
Score 160 p.
*Composed 1919-21. First performance Paris,
26 February 1922, Concerts Colonne, Gabriel
Pierné conductor.*

1190 La queste de Dieu, symphonie   12'
descriptive de La Légende de Saint-Christophe
(Op. 67)
3*,3*,3*,3-6,3,3Bugles,4-Timp.,Perc.-Pno.,2Hp.
-Str.
Rouart Lerolle, Paris, c1917
Score 46 p.

909 [Saugefleurie, legend for orchestra,   15'
after a fairy tale by Robert de Bonnières,
Op. 21]
3*,2,3,4-4,2,2Cnt.,3,1-Timp.,Perc.-2Hp.-Str.
Hamelle, Paris [n.d.]
Score 77 p.

1294 Serenade, Op. 16 no. 1 *and* Valse,   5'
Op. 17 no. 1
1(alt. Picc.),1,1,1-Cnt.-Timp.-Str.
Hamelle, Paris [n.d.]
Score 39 p.
*Originally composed for piano; orchestrated
1887. First performance Paris, 1892.*

571 Souvenirs, poème pour orchestre,   12'
Op. 62
3(3rd alt. Picc.),3*,3*,3-4,3,4-Timp.-2Hp.-Str.
Durand, Paris, c1907
Score 85 p.

6138 [Suite, In ancient style, Op. 24]   12'
1.Prélude 2.Entrée 3.Sarabande 4.Menuet
5.Ronde française
2Fl.-Tpt.-Str.(without Cb.)
J. Hamelle, Paris [1887?]
Score 55 p.
*Composed 1886. First performance Paris, 5
March 1887, Société Nationale de Musique.*

925s [Suite, In ancient style, Op. 24.
Nos. 3 and 4: Sarabande and Menuet. Tran-
scribed for string orchestra and piano]
Pno.-Str.
Score: Ms. 17 p.
Parts: Hamelle, Paris [n.d.]

Indy, Vicent d'

667 [Symphony, Cevenole, on a French   *32'*
mountain song]
1.Assez lent - Modérément animé 2.Assez
modéré, mais sans lenteur 3.Animé
Solo Pno.-3*,2*,3*,3-4,2,2Cnt.,3,1-Timp.,Perc.
-Hp.-Str.
Hamelle, Paris [n.d.]
Score 111 p.

569 [Symphony no. 2, Op. 57, B-flat major] *36'*
1.Extrêmement lent - Très vif 2.Modérément
lent 3.Modéré 4.Lent
3*,3*,3*,3-4,3,4-Timp.,Perc.-2Hp.-Str.
Durand, Paris, ᶜ1904
Score 192 p.

737 [Symphony no. 3, De Bello Gallico,   *30'*
Op. 70, D major]
1.Lent et calme - Animé 2.Assez vite 3.Lent
4.Très animé
3*,3*,4*,3-4,4(1 alt. Cnt.),4-Timp.,Perc.-
Cel.,2Hp.-Str.
Rouart Lerolle, Paris, ᶜ1919
Score 143 p.

2094 Tableaux de voyage [six pieces for
orchestra] Op. 36
2*,2,2,2-4,2,3-Timp.,Perc.-Hp.-Str.
Leduc, Paris, ᶜ1926
Score 51 p.
Originally composed for piano 1889; tran-
scribed 1891.

[Wallenstein trilogy, three symphonic
overtures after Schiller, Op. 12]
572 No. 1 Le camp de Wallenstein   *8'*
499 No. 2 Max et Thécla (The   *10'*
     Piccolomini)
573 No. 3 La mort de Wallenstein   *15'*
3(3rd alt. Picc.),2,3*,4-4,2,2Cnt.,3,1-Timp.,
Perc.-8Hp.-Str.
Durand, Paris [n.d.]
Scores: 74 p., 45 p., 73 p.
No. 1 composed 1879. No. 2 composed 1873.
No. 3 composed 1874. First complete perform-
ance Paris, 26 February 1888, Concerts
Lamoureux.

INGENHOVEN, JAN.   Breda, Netherlands 19 May 1876
                      Hoenderlo, Netherlands 20 May 1951

5800 [Symphonic composition no. 1, Lyric]
3(3rd alt. Picc.),3*,2,2-4,2-Timp.,Tamb.,
Trgl.-Hp.-Str.
A.A. Noske, Middelburg, Netherlands, 1909
Score 71 p.
Composed 1905.

5801 [Symphonic composition no. 2, Dramatic]
3(3rd alt. Picc.),3*,3*,3-4,3,3,1-Timp.,Cym.,
Trgl.-Hp.-Str.
A.A. Noske, Middelburg, Netherlands, 1909
Score 156 p.
Composed 1907.

5802 [Symphonic composition no. 3, Romantic]
2,2(2nd alt. E.H.),2,2-4,3-Timp.-2Hp.-Str.
A.A. Noske, Middelburg, Netherlands, 1910

Score 141 p.
Composed 1908.

INGHELBRECHT, DÉSIRÉ ÉMILE. Paris 17 September 1880
                            Paris 14 February 1965

4236 [El Greco, symphonic evocations]   *15'*
1.[Storm] 2.[The heathen] 3.Cortège funèbre
4.[The Christian girl] 5.Assomption
3*,3*,3*,3*-4,3,3,1-Timp.,Perc.-2Hp.-Str.
Maurice Senart, Paris, ᶜ1921
Score 58 p.
Composed 1920 for the Swedish Ballet. First
performance Paris, 18 November 1920, Swedish
Ballet Orchestra, the composer conducting.

2974 [Four fanfares for wind   *4'30"*
instruments]
1.Pour une fête 2.Pour le Président
3.Funèbre 4.Dédicatoire
4Hn.,3Tpt.,3Tbn.,Tuba-Timp.,Perc.
Senart, Paris, ᶜ1936
Score 16 p.

2232 La métamorphose d'Ève [for small   *10'*
orchestra]
1,1,2,1-2,1,1-Timp.,Perc.-Hp.(or Pno.)-Str.
Senart, Paris, ᶜ1928
Score 41 p.
Composed 1928.

532c Nocturne   *5'*
Solo Vc.(or Va. or Vn.)-2,2*,2,2-2,2,3-Timp.,
Trgl.-Hp.-Str.
Mathot, Paris, 1911
Score 19 p.
Composed 1905. First performance Paris, 1907,
the composer conducting.

1234 La nursery [Six children's pieces]   *14'*
1(alt. Picc.),1,2,1-2,1(alt. Cnt.),1-Timp.,
Perc.-Hp.-Str.
Leduc, Paris, ᶜ1920
Score 55 p.
Composed 1911. First performance Paris, 1912,
the composer conducting.

INGRAM, JOHN.
See: MORGAN, ROBERT ORLANDO.

IPPISCH, FRANZ.   Vienna 18 July 1883
                            Guatemala City 20 February 1958

3791 [A merry overture]   *4'30"*
2(2nd alt. Picc.),2,2,2-4,2,3-Timp.,Perc.-Str.
Ms.
Score 49 p.
Composed 1933. First performance Vienna, 6
September 1933, Konzert-Verein Orchester, Mar-
tin Sporr conductor.

3879 Sinfonia guatemalteca   *47'*
1.Allegro 2.Andante sostenuto 3.Scherzo
4.Finale
3(3rd alt. Picc.),2,2,2-4,3,3-Timp.-Str.
Ms.
Score 154 p.

Composed 1941. First performance Guatemala City, 13 September 1941, Orquesta Progresista, the composer conducting.

IPPOLITOV-IVANOV, MIKHAIL MIKHAILOVICH.
Gatchina, Russia 19 November 1859
Moscow 28 January 1935

1029 [Armenian rhapsody on national   *12'*
themes, Op. 48]
2,2,2,2-3,2-Timp.,Perc.-Str.
Jurgenson, Moscow [n.d.]
Score 24 p.
Composed 1909. First performance Moscow, 1909, Armenian Music Society, the composer conducting.

27 Caucasian sketches, Op. 10   *20'*
1.[In the mountain pass] 2.[In the village]
3.[In the mosque] 4.[Procession of the Sardar]
3*,3*,2,2-4,2,2Cnt.,2,2-Timp.,Perc.-Hp.-Str.
Kalmus, New York [n.d.]
Score 74 p.
Composed 1894. First performance Moscow, February 1895, Russian Music Society, Vassily Safonov conductor.

1008 [Caucasian sketches, series 2.   *30'*
Iveria, Op. 42]
1.[Introduction: Lamentation of the princess Ketevana] 2.Berceuse 3.[Lesghine dance]
4.[Georgian march]
3*,3*,2,2-4,2,3,1-Timp.,Perc.-Hp.-Str.
Jurgenson, Moscow [1905?]
Score 127 p.
Composed 1905. First performance Moscow, 1906, Russian Music Society, the composer conducting.

1914 [An episode from the life of   *15'*
Schubert, symphonic picture for orchestra and tenor]
Solo Tenor Voice(ad lib.)-2,2,2,2-4,2,3,1-Timp.,Perc.-Str.
Ms.
Score 78 p.
Composed 1929.

1872 [From Ossian, three musical   *25'*
tableaux, Op. 56]
1.[Lake Ljano] 2.[Kolmja's lamentation] 3.
[Ossian's monologue on contemporary heroes]
3(3rd alt. Picc.),3*,3*,3*-4,2,3,1-Timp.,Perc.
-Cel.,Hp.-Str.
Ms.
Score 91 p.
Composed 1925. First performance Moscow, 1927, Nikolai Golovanov conductor.

3280 [Jubilee march]   *4'*
3*,2,2,2-4,2,2Cnt.,3,1-Timp.,Perc.-Str.
Mussektor, Moscow, 1938
Score 54 p.
Composed 1931. First performance 1932, Sergei Chernetsky conductor.

1965 [Mtzyri, symphonic poem, after   *18'*
Lermontov, Op. 54]

3*,3*,3*,2-4,2,3,1-Timp.,Perc.-Cel.,Hp.-Voice
(ad lib.)-Str.
Mussektor, Moscow, 1929
Score 64 p.
Composed 1922. First performance Moscow, 1922, Russian Music Society, the composer conducting.

2080s [Quartet, strings, Op. 13, A minor.   *4'*
Excerpt, intermezzo, transcribed for string orchestra]
Str.
Ms.
Score 5 p.
Composed 1894. Transcriber unknown.

1549 [Sur le Volga, musical tableau,   *4'*
Op. 50]
1,1,0,1-1,1-Str.
Score: Ms. 12 p.
Parts: Jurgenson, Moscow [n.d.]
Composed 1910. First performance Moscow, 1910.

1868 [Symphonic scherzo, Op. 2]   *12'*
2,2,2,2-4,2,3-Timp.-Hp.-Str.
Ms.
Score 55 p.
Composed 1882. First performance St. Petersburg, 20 May 1882, the composer conducting.

717 [Symphony no. 1, Op. 46, E minor]   *32'*
1.Adagio - Allegro risoluto 2.Scherzo
3.Elegia 4.Finale: Allegro moderato
2,2,2,2-4,2,3,1-Timp.,Perc.-Str.
Jurgenson, Moscow [n.d.]
Score 172 p.
Composed 1907. First performance Moscow, 1908, Russian Music Society, the composer conducting.

2477 [Turkish fragments, Op. 62]   *14'*
1.[The caravan] 2.[At rest] 3.[At night]
4.[At the festival]
3*,3*,2,2-3,2,3,1-Timp.,Perc.-Hp.-Str.
Mussektor, Moscow, 1931
Score 86 p.

1635 [Turkish march, Op. 55]   *5'*
3*,2,2,2-4,2,3,1-Timp.,Perc.-Str.
Mussektor, Moscow, 1926
Score 29 p.
Composed 1928. First performance Baku, 1929, Vasa Suk conductor.

1866 [Yar-Khmel, spring overture, Op. 1]   *12'*
2,2,2,2-4,2,3-Timp.,Perc.-Str.
Ms.
Score 59 p.
Composed 1881. First performance St. Petersburg, 23 January 1883, at the Rubinstein concerts, the composer conducting.

IRADIER, SEBASTIAN DE.
See: YRADIER, SEBASTIAN.

IRELAND, JOHN.   Inglewood, Bowdon,
Cheshire 13 August 1879
Washington, England 12 June 1962

1783s Concertino pastorale for string   *20'*
orchestra

Ireland, John

1.Eclogue 2.Threnody 3.Toccata
Str.
Boosey & Hawkes, London, c1939
Score 28 p.
Commissioned by the Canterbury Festival. First performance Canterbury, June 1939, Boyd Neel String Orchestra, Boyd Neel conductor.

1009 The forgotten rite, prelude   *8'*
3(3rd alt. Picc.),3*,3*,2-4,2,3-Timp.-Cel.,Hp.
-Str.
Augener, London, c1918
Score 20 p.

2021 Symphonic rhapsody, Mai-Dun   *13'*
3(3rd alt. Picc.),3*,3*,2-4,3,3,1-Timp.,Perc.-
Str.
Augener, London, c1923
Score 48 p.
Composed 1912. First performance London, 1921.

ISENMANN, KARL. Gengenbach, Germany 29 April 1839
                 Illenau, Germany 1878

409s Im Traum [Dreaming] Adagietto, Op. 69
Str.
Ries & Erler, Berlin [n.d.]
Score 3 p.

ITASSE, LÉON.

4323 [Spanish rhapsody for orchestra, Op. 27]
2(1st alt. Picc.),2*,2,2-4,2,2Cnt.,3-Timp.,
Perc.-Str.
Mackar & Noël, Paris [188-]
Score 52 p.

IVANOV, MIKHAIL MIKHAILOVICH.
                Moscow 23 September 1849
                Rome 20 October 1927

1382 [The insects' ball, scherzo from The
cricket musician]
3*,3*,2,2-4,2,3,1-Timp.,Perc.-Hp.-Str.
Bessel, St. Petersburg [n.d.]
Score 65 p.

741 Suite orientale, Op. 20
1.[March] 2.[On the Bosporus] 3.Rêverie
4.[Oriental dance] 5.[In the harem]
3*,2,2,2-4,2,3,1-Timp.,Perc.-Hp.-Str.
Bessel, St. Petersburg [n.d.]
Score 150 p.

IVANOV-RADKEVICH, NIKOLAI PAVLOVICH.
          Krasnoyarsk, Siberia 10 February 1904
          Moscow 4 February 1962

4731 [Solemn march on Turkmenistan national
themes]
3*,2(2nd alt. E.H.),2,2-4,2,3,1-Timp.,Perc.-
Str.
State Music Publishers, Moscow, 1935
Score 40 p.
Composed 1934, for the tenth anniversary of the Soviet Socialist Republic of Turkmenistan.

2932 [Symphony no. 2]   *27'*
1.Lento con sordità - Allegro impetuoso
2.Pesante
3(3rd alt. Picc.),3*,4*,3*-4,3,3,1-Timp.,Perc.-
Pno.,Cel.,2Hp.-Str.
Mussektor, Moscow, 1935
Score 133 p.
Composed 1931-32. First performance in a U.S.S.R. Radio broadcast, Alexander Orlov conductor.

IVERSEN, BERNHARD.
          b. Munkbraruy, Germany 26 January 1881

1285s Gavotte, Op. 2. Arranged by Bernhard
Iversen
Solo Fl.-Pno.(ad lib.)-Str.
L. Schwann, Dusseldorf [n.d.]
Score 3 p.

IVES, CHARLES EDWARD.
          Danbury, Connecticut 20 October 1874
          New York City 19 May 1954

All summer long
See: The circus band

199m Allegretto sombreoso   *3'*
Solo E.H. or Voice(or Tpt. or Basset Hn.)-Fl.
-Pno.-3Vn.
Peer International, New York, c1958
Score 6 p.
Text is from George Gordon Byron's poem Manfred (lines 192-201). This version ca.1909. Arranged for voice and piano, 1921, as Incantation.

3970 Andante con moto; The last reader,   *2'30"*
Oliver Wendell Holmes
2Fl.,E.H. or Cnt.-Voice(if desired)-Str.
Ms.
Score 6 p.
Composed 1911.

3196 Calcium light night, for six   *2'30"*
winds, two drums and two pianos. Arranged and
edited by Henry Cowell in collaboration with
the composer
1(Picc.),1,1,1-Tpt.(Cnt.),Tbn.-S.Dr.,B.Dr.-
2Pno.(or Pno. 4-hands)
Merion Music [Theodore Presser, Bryn Mawr, Pa.]
c1964
Score 16 p.
Originally composed for piano, later (1907?) for winds, percussion and two pianos. Cowell's simplified arrangement made at Ives' request, 1936.

The camp meeting
See: Symphony no. 3, The camp meeting

6435 Central Park in the dark (In   *7'30"*
the good ole summer time)
2*,1,1,1(or Bar.Sax.)-Tpt.,Tbn.(or Ten.Sax.)-
S.Dr.,B.Dr.-2Pno.-Str.
Ms. [Boelke-Bomart, Hillsdale, N.Y., c1949]
Score 33 p.
Composed 1906. This work was first paired

with another work and entitled: I. A Contemplation of a Serious Matter or The Unanswered Perennial Question II. A Contemplation of Nothing Serious or Central Park in the Dark in 'The Good Old Summer Time'.

7280 The circus band. Edited by George   3'
F. Roberts
2*,0,2-1,1(Tpt. or Cnt.),3,1-Perc.-Chorus
(SSATTBB)-Str.(without Va.)
Peer International, New York, ᶜ1953, ᶜ1969
Score 16 p.
Not in John Kirkpatrick's catalog of Ives' works. Lyrics compiled by the composer from fragments and parodies of college songs. Composed 1894. The composer transcribed this work for the following media: orchestra; piano; voice and piano; voice and orchestra. The version for voice and piano is also known as All Summer Long.

A contemplation of nothing serious
See: Central Park in the dark...

6453 December   2'
Picc.,2Cl.-2,3,3,1-Unison Men's Chorus
Peer International, N.Y., ᶜ1963
Score 14 p.
Text is by Folgore da San Geminiano (fl. 1309-1317) from his Sonetti de Mesi, in the translation by Dante Gabriel Rossetti. Composed 1912-13. First performance, New York, 15 April 1934, Pan-American Association, Albert Stoessel conductor. Ives arranged this work for voice and piano in 1920(?) and published it as no. 37 of 114 Songs.

Four New England holidays
See: [Holidays symphony]

3723 From the steeples and the mountains   4'
Tpt.(2nd ad lib.),Tbn.-Bells(Chimes)[4 players, 4 sets of 8 bells each] or 2 Pno.
Peer International, N.Y., ᶜ1965
Score 9 p.
Original title: From the Steeples. Composed 1901. First performance New York, 30 July 1965, New York Philharmonic, Lukas Foss conductor.

6674 General William Booth enters   4'30"
into heaven. Arranged by John J. Becker
1,1,1,1-1,1,1-Timp. or B.Dr.-Pno.-Solo Voice
or Chorus-Str.
Merion Music [n.p.] ᶜ1935; 1964
Score 32 p. Large folio
Poem by Vachel Lindsay. Composed 1914 for 1) Voice and piano, 2) Mixed voices and orchestra. This arrangement, 1934, in collaboration with the composer. First performance of this arrangement San Jose State College, California, 14 May 1965, W. Gibson Walters conductor.

3966 The gong on the hook and ladder; or,   2'
Firemen's parade on Main Street
1,0,1,1-0,2,1-Perc.-Pno.-Str.
Peer International, New York, ᶜ1960

Score 14 p.
Composed 1909. First performance New York, 27 April 1934, Pan American Chamber Orchestra, Albert Stoessel conductor.

1893s Hallowe'en   3'
Pno.-Str.(without Cb.)
Ms.
Score 5 p.
Composed 1911. First performance San Francisco, 28 May 1933, New Music Society.

He is there!
See: They are there! ...

[Holidays symphony]   39'
Also available separately:
3022 I.   Washington's Birthday (Winter)   9'
Very slowly - Allegro - Andante
Fl.(alt. Picc.)-Hn.-Bells(optional)-Jew's
Harp(optional)-Str.
New Music, San Francisco, ᶜ1937
Score 20 p.
Composed originally for chamber orchestra; rescored 1913. First performance by the New Music Society of California, San Francisco, 3 September 1931, Nicolas Slonimsky conductor.
5150 II. Decoration Day (Spring)   9'
Very slowly - Allegro
3*,3*,3(1Cl. in E-flat),2-4,2,3,1-Timp.,Perc.-
Cel.-Str.
Ms.
Score 28 p.
Composed 1912.
2685 III. The Fourth of July (Summer)   6'
Adagio molto - Andante - Allegretto
3*,2,2,3*-4,4,1Cnt.,3,1-Timp.,Perc.-Pno.-Str.
New Music, San Francisco, ᶜ1932
Score 36 p. Large folio
Composed 1912-13. First performance Paris, 21 February 1932, L'Orchestre Symphonique de Paris, Nicolas Slonimsky conductor.
5075 IV. Thanksgiving and Forefather's   15'
Day (Autumn)
Adagio con moto - Andante con moto sed
maestoso
3*,2,2,3*-4,3,3,1-Timp.,Bells & Chimes(or Cel.
or Pno.)-Pno.,Cel.-SATB Chorus (16 measures)-
Str.
Ms.
Score 61 p.
Composed 1904.

2372s Hymn (Largo cantabile) [Olivet]
Str.
Peer International, New York, ᶜ1966
Score 5 p.
This is no. 1 of A Set of Three Short Pieces. Composed 1904.

In the good ole summer time
See: Central Park in the dark...

Incantation
See: Allegretto sombreoso...

431

Ives, Charles

Largo cantabile
See: Hymn (Largo cantabile)

6671 Lincoln the great commoner   5'
2(2nd may be Picc.),2,2,2-0,2,2,1(or 2)-Timp.,
Low Bell-Pno.-Chorus-Str.
Merion Music (Theodore Presser), Bryn Mawr,
Pennsylvania [c1959]
Score 16 p.
The poem by Edwin Markham. Composed 1912.
Arranged for voice and piano, 1921.

Lord of the harvest
See: Three harvest home chorales

7160 [March III. Third version] Edited by
Kenneth Singleton
1,0,1-0,0,Cnt.,1,1-Perc.-Vn.1,Vn.2
Merion Music, Bryn Mawr, Pennsylvania, c1975
Score 11 p.
Composed ca.1892, originally for piano (Ms.
now lost).

New England holidays
See: [Holidays symphony]

7157 The new river   3'
Picc.,2Cl.-Bar.Sax.-2 Cnt.(or 2Tpt.),Tbn.-
Timp.(or Long Drum)-Pno.-2-part Chorus-Str.
Ms. [Now published by Peer International]
Score 8 p.
Words by Charles Ives. Alternate title: The
Ruined River. Originally composed for chorus,
1911.

6455 The rainbow   1'30"
Fl.,Basset or E.H.-Pno.-Str.
Peer International, New York, c1959
Score 8 p.
Inspired by William Wordsworth's poem, My
Heart Leaps Up When I Behold. Composed 1914,
with the subtitle So May It Be! Arranged
1921 for voice and piano.

6731 Robert Browning overture   24'
3*,3*,2,3*-4,2,3,1-Timp.,Perc.-Str.
Peer International, New York, c1959
Score 87 p.
No. 2 of Men of Literature overtures. Com-
posed 1908-1912. Four missing pages of the
score were "recomposed" by Lou Harrison or
Henry Cowell. Salient features of this made
into the song, Paracelsus, 1921.

The ruined river
See: The new river

3969 Scherzo, All the way around and   1'30"
back
Cl.(or Fl.)-Bugle(or Tpt.)-Middle Bells(or Hn.)
-2Pno.-1Vn.(or Fl.)
Ms.
Score 4 p.
Composed 1907.

2811 Second orchestral set   20'
1.Very slowly 2.Allegro 3.Very slowly
3*,0,3,2-1,4,4,1-Timp.,Perc.-2Pno.,Org.,Cel.(or

Bells),Hp.,Zither,Melodia, Accordion-Str.
Ms.
Score 50 p.
Composed 1916.

2712 A set of pieces for theater or   9'
chamber orchestra
1.In the cage 2.In the inn (Potpourri)
3.In the night
1(ad lib.),2,2(2nd ad lib.),1(or Bar.Sax.)-
Hn.,Tbn.(ad lib.)-Timp.,Bells-2Pno.(3 players)
-Str.
Composed 1906-11. First performance of Move-
ment I, Paris, 21 February 1932, l'Orchestre
Symphonique de Paris, Nicolas Slonimsky con-
ductor. First performance of Movement III,
Minneapolis, at the Biennial Convention of the
National Federation of Music Clubs, 25 May
1933, St. Paul Chamber Orchestra, John Becker
conductor.

A set of three short pieces, no. 1
See: Hymn (Largo cantabile) [Olivet]

So may it be!
See: The rainbow

7096 A son of a gambolier. Transcribed for band
by Jonathan Elkus
3*,2,8*(Cl. in E-flat,Alto Cl.,Cb.Cl. in E-
flat,Cb.Cl. in B-flat),2-4Sax.-4,2,3Cnt.,3,
2Bar.,2-Timp.,Perc.-Cb.
Peer International, New York, c1956, c1962
Score 16 p.
Ives wrote three compositions incorporating the
Irish air, Son of a Gambolier. This tran-
scription is based on the arrangement of 1895
for voice and piano.

A symphony: New England holidays
See: [Holidays symphony]

3806 Symphony no. 1   40'
1.Allegro 2.Adagio molto 3.Scherzo
4.Allegro molto
2,2*,2,3*-4,2,3,1-Timp.-Str.
Peer International, New York, c1971
Score 82 p.
Composed 1896-98.

4773 Symphony no. 2   35'
1.Andante moderato 2.Allegro 3.Adagio can-
tabile 4.Lento maestoso 5.Allegro molto
vivace
3*,2,2,3*-4,2,3,1-Timp.,S.Dr.,B.Dr.-Str.
Southern Music Co., New York, c1951
Score 194 p.
Composed 1897-1901. First performance New
York, 22 February 1951, New York Philharmonic
Symphony, Leonard Bernstein, conductor.

6611 Symphony no. 3, The camp meeting   17'
1.Old folks gatherin 2.Children's day
3.Communion
1,1,1,1-2Hn.,Tbn.-Bells(ad lib.)-Str.
Associated Music Publishers, New York, c1947,
1964
Score 33 p.

Composed 1904-1911. Quotes many gospel hymns. First performance New York, League of Composers Concert, 6 April 1946, New York Little Symphony Orchestra, Lou Harrison conductor. Awarded Pulitzer Prize for music 1947.

6722　Symphony no. 4　　　　　　　　　30'
1.Prelude　2.Allegretto - Adagio - Allegro etc.
3.Fugue　4.Very slowly
5*(2Picc.),2,3,3-3Sax.(1 player, optional)-4,
6,2Cnt.,4,1-Timp.(2 players),Perc.-3Pno.(1Solo;
1Orch. 4-hands; 1Quartertone ad lib.),Cel.,Org.,
2Hp.,Ether Org.(optional)-Chorus(SATB)-Str.
Distant Choir: I: 2Solo Vn., Solo Va.(and/or Cl.
ad lib.),Hp.　IV: 5Solo Vn.,2Hp.
Associated Music Publishers, New York, ᶜ1965
Score 183 p.
Composed 1910-16.　First performance of second movement only Pro Musica Society, New York, 29 January 1927, Eugene Goossens, conductor.　First complete performance New York, 26 April 1965, American Symphony Orchestra, Leopold Stokowski conductor.　Scores of movements I and III are facsimiles of material reconstructed and edited by Romulus Franceschini and Nicholas Falcone, members of the Fleisher Collection staff.　Movement II prepared by Mr. Franceschini from published and manuscript sources.　Movement IV transcribed and edited from original sources by Theodore A. Seder, a former Curator of the Fleisher Collection.

7134　[Symphony no. 4. Movement no. 3,　8'30"
Fugue. Arranged for chamber orchestra by
Bernard Herrmann]
1,1,1,1-1,1,1-Timp.-Str.
Ms.
Score 18 p.
First performance of this arrangement New York, 27 May 1933, New Chamber Orchestra, Bernard Herrmann conductor.

6477　They are there! A war song march.　　3'
For unison chorus and orchestra
4*(2Picc.),2,2,2-4,2,2,1-Perc.-Pno.-Unison
Chorus-Str.
Peer International, New York, ᶜ1961
Score 19 p.
Words by Charles Ives.　Early version 1917 under the title He is There! Words revised 1942.　Full score completed by Lou Harrison.

6720　Three harvest home chorales　　　7'30"
1.Harvest home　2.Lord of the harvest
3.Harvest home
Chorus(SATB)-4Tpt.,3Tbn.,Tuba-Org.-Cb.
Ms. [ᶜ1949 by Mercury Music, New York]
Score 18 p.
Texts by Rev. George Burgess, John Hampton Gurney and Rev. Henry Alford.　No. 1 composed 1898; nos. 2 and 3 before 1902.　First performance Central Presbyterian Church, New York, ca.1900, when Ives was organist there. Second performance New York, 1948, Collegiate Chorale, Robert Shaw conductor.

2731　Three places in New England, an　　16'
orchestral set
1.The St. Gaudens' in Boston Common (Col. Shaw

and his colored regiment)　2.Putnam's Camp,
Redding, Connecticut　3.From the Housatonic at
Stockbridge, Robert Underwood Johnson
2*,2*,1,1-2,2,2,1-Perc.-Pno.,Org.(ad lib.)-
Str.
Birchard, Boston, ᶜ1935 by Charles E. Ives
Score 87 p.
Composed 1903-14.　First performance New York, 10 January 1931, Chamber Orchestra of Boston, Nicolas Slonimsky conductor.

4613　Tone roads, no. 1　　　　　　　　8'
1,0,1,1-Str.
Peer International, New York, ᶜ1949
Score 8 p.
Composed 1911.

6456　Tone roads, no. 3　　　　　　　　9'
Fl.,Cl.-Tpt.,Tbn.-Chimes
Peer International, New York, ᶜ1952
Score 12 p.
Composed 1915.

6454　The unanswered question　　　　　8'
4Fl.(or Ob. for Fl. 3; or Cl. for Fl. 4)-Tpt.
(or Ob. or E.H. or Cl.)-Str.
Southern Music Publishing, New York, ᶜ1953
Score 8 p.
Composed 1908.　Subtitled A Cosmic Landscape and originally paired with Central Park in the Dark.　First published in Montevideo, 1941, in Boletin Latino-Americano de Música under the title La Pregunta Incontestada.

6676　Variations on America. Arranged for　8'
orchestra by William Schuman
3(2nd & 3rd alt. Picc.),2,2,2-4,3,3,1-Timp.,
Perc.-Str.
Mercury Music [New York] ᶜ1949. Merion Music
[New York] ᶜ1964
Score 40 p. Large folio
Originally composed for organ, 1891 or 1892. This arrangement 1963, first performed New York City, 20 May 1964, New York Philharmonic, André Kostelanetz conductor.

War march, for chorus and orchestra
See: They are there!...

J

JACHINO, CARLO.　　San Remo, Italy 3 February 1887
　　　　　　　　　　　Rome 23 December 1971

4872　[Fantasy from The Red and the Black]　15'
3*,3*,3*,3*-Alto Sax.-4,3,3,1-Timp.,Perc.-
Cel.,2Hp.,Hawaiian Guit.-Str.
Ricordi, Milan, ᶜ1936
Score 59 p.
Suggested by Stendhal's novel.　Composed 1935. First performance Naples, April 1936.　Winner of a prize from the Società degli Artisti di Napoli, 1936.

Jacob, Gordon

JACOB, DOM CLÉMENT.
See: JACOB, MAXIME.

JACOB, GORDON PERCIVAL SEPTIMUS.
b. London 5 July 1895

1052m [Concerto, oboe and string   22'30"
orchestra, no. 1]
1.Allegro moderato 2.Andante con moto - Poco
più mosso 3.Allegro vivace - Andante con moto
- Molto allegro
Solo Ob.-Str.
Joseph Williams, London, ᶜ1945
Score 48 p.
*Composed 1933. First performance London, 1935,
Royal Philharmonic Orchestra, Thomas Beecham
conductor, Leon Goossens soloist.*

1370s Denbigh suite [for string orchestra]   11'
1.Praeludium 2.Pavane 3.Gavotte 4.Jig
Str.
Oxford University Press, London, ᶜ1929
Score 10 p.

3233 Divertimento for small orchestra   12'
1.Rondino 2.Interlude 3.Variations 4.Jig
1(alt. Picc.),1,2,1-2,2,1-Timp.,Perc.-Hp.-Str.
Universal Edition, London, ᶜ1939
Score 44 p.
*Originally composed as a wind quintet, 1932;
orchestrated, 1938. First performance London,
March 1939, London Symphony Orchestra, the
composer conducting.*

4615 Passacaglia on a well-known theme   6'
2(2nd alt. Picc.),2,2,2-4,2,3,1-Timp.,Perc.-
2Hp.(2nd ad lib.)-Str.
Joseph Williams, London, ᶜ1938
Score 30 p.
*The theme is Oranges and Lemons. Composed
1931. First performance London, 24 August
1935, BBC Symphony Orchestra, the composer
conducting.*

4617 [Sinfonietta, orchestra, no. 1]   12'30"
1.Allegro molto 2.Allegretto semplice
3.Allegro molto e con brio
2(2nd alt. Picc.),2,2,2-2,2,1-Timp.,Perc.-Str.
Joseph Williams, London, ᶜ1944
Score 96 p.
*Commissioned by the BBC. Composed 1943.
First performance BBC broadcast, 20 March 1943,
BBC Orchestra, Clarence Raybould conductor.*

4614 [Suite, orchestra, no. 1, in F]   13'30"
1.Overture 2.Air 3.Gavotte and musette
4.March
1(alt. Picc.),1,2,1-2,2,1-Timp.,Perc.-Hp.-Str.
Joseph Williams, London, ᶜ1943
Score 64 p.
*First performance on a BBC Empire Programme,
30 August 1939, BBC Empire Orchestra, Eric
Fogg conductor.*

JACOB, J.

690c Aubade
Solo Vc.-2,2,2,2-Hp.-Str.

Ms.
Score 11 p.

691c Danse tzigane [Gypsy dance]
Solo Vc.-2(2nd alt. Picc.),2,2,2-2Hn.-Trgl.-
Hp.-Str.
Ms.
Score 8 p.

665c Nocturne for violoncello and orchestra
Solo Vc.-2,2,2,2-2Hn.-Timp.-Hp.-Str.
Ms.
Score 14 p.

664c Rêverie for violoncello and orchestra
Solo Vc.-0,0,2,2-2Hn.-Timp.-Str.
Ms.
Score 4 p.

692c Ronde liègeoise
Solo Vc.-2(2nd alt. Picc.),2,2,2-2,2-Timp.,
Trgl.-Str.
Ms.
Score 26 p.

JACOB, MAXIME.   Bordeaux, France 13 January 1906

6034 Sérénade [Op. 3]   5'
2*,1,1,1-1,1,1-Timp.,S.Dr.-Str.
Jobert, Paris, ᶜ1928
Score 15 p.
*Composed 1923. First performance Paris, 25
October 1923, Orchestre des Ballets Suédois,
Roger Désormière conductor.*

JACOBI, FREDERICK.   San Francisco 4 May 1891
New York 24 October 1952

296p Ave rota [Hail to the wheel!]   14'
1.La balançoire [The swing] 2.The merman
[after Ethel Merman] 3.May dance
Solo Pno.-3*,2,2,2-4,3,3,1-Timp.,Perc.
-Str.
Ms.
Score 93 p. Large folio
*Written for the Juilliard Alumni. Composed
1939. First performance New York, 1939,
Juilliard Alumni Association, Charles Lichter
conductor, Adele Marcuse soloist.*

807p Concertino for piano and string   17'
orchestra
1.Allegro con spirito 2.Andante sostenuto
3.Tarantella
Solo Pno.-Str.
Elkan-Vogel, Philadelphia, ᶜ1947
Score 74 p.
*Composed 1946. First performance Saratoga
Springs, New York, 3 September 1946, New York
Philharmonic Orchestra, F. Charles Adler
conductor, Irene Jacobi soloist.*

330v Concerto, violin and orchestra   24'
[Cadenza by André Gertler]
1.Allegro con spirito - Allegro moderato 2.
Andante - Tranquillo ed espressivo - A tempo:
Doppio movimento 3.Rondo
Solo Vn.-3*,2,2,2-4,3,3,1-Timp.,Perc.-Hp.(ad

lib.)-Str.
Ms. [Leeds Music, New York, n.d.]
Score 140 p.
*Composed 1936-37. First performance Chicago,
14 March 1939, Chicago Symphony Orchestra,
Frederick Stock conductor, Albert Spalding
soloist.*

2434 Indian dances   16'30"
1.Buffalo dance 2.Butterfly dance 3.War
dance 4.Corn dance
3*,3(3rd alt. E.H.),3*,3*-4,3,3,1-Timp.,Perc.-
Cel.,Hp.-Str.
Universal Edition, Vienna, ᶜ1931
Score 108 p.
*Composed 1927-28. First performance Cambridge,
Massachusetts, 8 November 1928, Boston Symphony Orchestra, Serge Koussevitzky conductor.*

979m Night piece, for flute and small   5'
orchestra
Solo Fl.-0,2,2,2-2Hn.-Timp.,Perc.-Hp.-Str.
Boosey & Hawkes, New York, ᶜ1911
Score 12 p.
*Originally composed 1922 as part of the Assy-
rian Symphony. First separate performance
under the title Nocturne, Rochester, New
York, 30 December 1926, Rochester Little Sym-
phony, Howard Hanson conductor. Revised and
retitled 1941. First performance San Diego,
California, 22 July 1941, San Diego Symphony
Orchestra, Nikolai Sokoloff conductor, Alene
Benner soloist.*

1070m Rhapsody for harp and strings   9'
Solo Hp.-Str.
Ms.
Score 34 p. Large folio
*Composed 1940. First performance Oakland,
California, 1 August 1940, Mills College
Orchestra, Antonia Brico conductor, Marcel
Grandjany soloist.*

6408 Symphony in C   21'
1.Introduction and allegro 2.Andante
3.Scherzo and postlude
3(3rd alt. Picc.),3*,3(3rd alt. B.Cl.),3*-4,
3,3,1-Timp.,Perc.-Cel.,Hp.-Str.
Ms.
Score 151 p.
*Composed 1947. First performance San Fran-
cisco, 1 April 1948, San Francisco Symphony,
Pierre Monteux conductor.*

748c Three psalms (concerto), for   18'
violoncello and orchestra
1.Allegro cantabile, attacca 2.Allegretto
3.Allegro ritmico
Solo Vc.-2,2,2,2-2-Timp.,Perc.-Str.
Ms.
Score 100 p.
*Composed 1932. First performance Paris, 30
May 1933, École Normale Orchestra, Alfred
Cortot conductor, Diran Alexanian soloist.*

6407 Two pieces in Sabbath mood [large   10'
orchestra]

1.Kaddish 2.Oneg Shabat
1,2*,2*,1-2,2,1-Timp.,Cym.,Trgl.-Str.
Ms.
Score 44 p.
*Originally composed as two separate works for
organ: Kaddish and Toccata. This version
first performed Indianapolis, 13 February 1948,
Indianapolis Symphony, Fabien Sevitzky conductor.*

JACOBI, K.   If Karl: Coburg, Bavaria ca.1790
                  Coburg, Bavaria 12 May 1852

366m [Concertino, bassoon and orchestra,
Op. 7, B-flat]
1.Allegro 2.Adagio 3.Allegretto scherzando
Solo Bn.-1,0,2,2-2Hn.-Str.
Score: Ms. ᶜ1976 by the Fleisher Collection
of Orchestral Music, Free Library of Philadel-
phia. 87 p. Large folio
Parts: [Breitkopf & Härtel, Leipzig, 1828]

382m [Divertissement, bassoon and orchestra,
Op. 11]
Solo Bn.-1,0,2,2-2,2-Timp.-Str.
Score: Ms. ᶜ1976 by the Fleisher Collection
of Orchestral Music, Free Library of Philadel-
phia. 60 p. Large folio
Parts: [Breitkopf & Härtel, Leipzig, 1831]

481m [Introduction, theme and variations   10'
for bassoon and orchestra]
Solo Bn.-1,0,2,2-2Hn.-Str.
Score: Ms. 80 p.
Parts: [Breitkopf & Härtel, Leipzig, 1830]

346m [Potpourri, bassoon and orchestra, The
Berlin woman in Vienna, Op. 14]
Solo Bn.-1,2,0,2-2Hn.-Str.
Score: Ms. ᶜ1976 by the Fleisher Collection
of Orchestral Music, Free Library of Philadel-
phia. 77 p. Large folio
Parts: [Breitkopf & Härtel, Leipzig, 1835]

JACOBY, HANOCH.   Königsberg, E. Prussia
                  (now Kaliningrad, Russia) 2 March 1909

Born: Heinrich Jacoby

6490 Sinfonietta for orchestra   10'
3(3rd alt. Picc.),3*,3*,3*-4,3,3,1-Timp.,Perc.
-Str.
Israeli Music Publications, Tel Aviv, ᶜ1960
Score 46 p.
*Commissioned by the Israel Philharmonic
Orchestra, Tel Aviv. Composed 1960. First
performance Jerusalem, 10 October 1962, Kol-
Yisrael Symphony Orchestra, Harold Byrnes con-
ductor. Awarded a prize on the occasion of
the 25th anniversary of the Israel Philhar-
monic Orchestra, 15 July 1960.*

JADASSOHN, SALOMON.   Breslau, Prussia
                  (now Wroclaw, Poland) 13 August 1831
                  Leipzig 1 February 1902

735v Cavatine für Violine, Op. 69
Solo Vn.-0,0,2,2-2Hn.-Str.

Jadassohn, Salomon

Kistner, Leipzig [1882]
Score 11 p.

521c Cavatine für Violoncell und Orchester,
Op. 120
Solo Vc.-2,0,2,2-2Hn.-Str.
Breitkopf & Härtel, Leipzig, c1894
Score 13 p.

644p [Concerto, piano, no. 1, Op. 89, C minor]
In one movement: Introduction quasi recita-
tivo - Adagio sostenuto - Ballade
Solo Pno.-2,2,2,2-2,2-Timp.-Str.
Kahnt, Leipzig [1887?]
Score 83 p.

484p [Concerto, piano, no. 2, Op. 90,   25'
F minor]
1.Allegro energico e passionato 2.Andantino
quasi allegretto 3.Allegro appassionato
Solo Pno.-2,2,2,2-2,2-Timp.-Str.
Score: Ms. 161 p.
Parts: Breitkopf & Härtel, Leipzig [1888?]

5446 [Serenade, orchestra, no. 2, Op. 46,
D major]
1.Intrada e notturno 2.Menuetto 3.Finale
2,2,2,2-4,2-Timp.-Str.
Fr. Kistner, Leipzig [1875]
Score 45 p.

1456s [Serenade, strings and flute, Op. 80,
D major]
1.Intrata 2.Notturno 3.Menuetto 4.Tarantella
Fl.-Str.
Kistner, Leipzig [1886]
Score 45 p.

6012 [Serenade, wind orchestra, Op. 104c]
Edited by Philip Hale
1.Marsch 2.Notturno 3.Scherzo 4.Tempo di
bolero
2,2,2,2-2Hn.
Arthur P. Schmidt, Boston, c1890
Score 50 p.
Originally composed for piano, Op. 104.

5468 [Symphony no. 1, Op. 24, in C]
1.Allegro con brio 2.Scherzo 3.Largo e
mesto 4.Finale: Allegro molto e vivace
2,2,2,2-4,2-Timp.-Str.
C.F.W. Siegel, Leipzig [1861/62]
Score 76 p.

JÁMBOR, EUGEN VON.   Budapest 14 May 1853
                            Budapest 18 March 1914

277s [Serenade no. 2, string orchestra, Op. 65,
D major]
Str.
Rózsavölgyi, Budapest [1905?]
Score 19 p.

JAMES, DOROTHY.   Chicago 1 December 1901

946m Pastorals   7'
1.Brioso 2.Doloroso 3.Giocoso
Cl.-Hp.(or Cel.)-Str.

Ms.
Score 22 p.
*Composed 1932. First performance Hartland
(Michigan) Area Music Festival, 4 April 1934,
University of Michigan Symphony Orchestra,
E. William Doty conductor.*

3432 Three symphonic fragments   10'
1.Proem 2.Threnody 3.Persiflage
3*,3*,3*,3*-4,2,3,1-Timp.,Perc.-Cel.,Hp.-Str.
Ms.
Score 53 p.
*Composed 1931. First performance Rochester,
New York, 24 March 1932, Rochester Philhar-
monic Orchestra, Howard Hanson conductor.*

JAMES, PHILIP. Jersey City, New Jersey 17 May 1890
               Southampton, Long Island 1 November 1975

6864 Brennan on the moor, for large   4'
orchestra
3*,2,2,2-4,3,3,1-Timp.,Perc.-Str.
Southern, New York, c1966
Score 25 p.
*Theme is the Irish ballad. Commissioned by
CBS. Composed 1939.*

2626 Bret Harte, overture no. 3   13'
3(3rd alt. Picc.),2,2,2-4,3,3,1-Timp.,Perc.-
Hp.,Tenor Banjo(ad lib.)-Str.
Ms.
Score 85 p.
*Composed 1934. First performance New York, 20
December 1936, New York Philharmonic, John
Barbirolli conductor. Awarded honorable men-
tion in the American Composers' Contest spon-
sored by the New York Philharmonic, 1936.*

5376 Chaumont, symphonic poem for   10'
small orchestra
2(2nd alt. Picc.),2(2nd alt. E.H.),2,2-2,2-
Timp.,Tabor-Hp.-Str.
Ms.
Score 43 p.
*Inspired by the hills outside the town of
Chaumont, Haute-Marne, France. Composed 1948.
First performance New York, 2 May 1951, Wash-
ington Square College Orchestra, Frederic
Kurzweil conductor.*

2849 Gwalia [Wales], a Welsh rhapsody   17'
for orchestra
3(3rd alt. Picc.),2(2nd alt. E.H.),2,2-4,2,3,
1-Timp.,Perc.-Hp.-Voices(ad lib.)-Str.
Ms.
Score 94 p. Large folio
*Composed 1937. First performance New York, 18
February 1940, New York City Symphony Orchestra
of the WPA, the composer conducting.*

2624 Overture in olden style on French   12'
Noëls
3(3rd alt. Picc.),2,2,2-4,2,3,1-Timp.,Perc.-Str.
C.C. Birchard, Boston, c1931
Score 54 p.
*Composed 1926. First performance Montclair,
New Jersey, 14 December 1926, New Jersey
Orchestra, the composer conducting.*

5380 Overture to a Greek play   12'
3(3rd alt. Picc.),2,2,3*-4,3,3,1-Timp.,Perc.
-Pno.,Hp.-Str.
Ms.
Score 62 p. Large folio
*Composed 1952. First performance Rochester,
New York, 6 May 1967, Eastman-Rochester Sym-
phony Orchestra, Howard Hanson conductor.*

5668 Passacaglia (on an old Cambrian   7'
ground bass) [for band]
3*,2,6*(1 in E-flat,1Alto Cl.),3*(C.Bn. ad lib.)
-5Sax.-4,2,3Cnt.,3,Bar.,2-Timp.,Perc.
Ms.
Score 18 p. Large folio
*Originally composed for organ 1951. This
transcription 1957.*

5573 Passacaglia (on an old Cambrian   7'
ground bass) [for orchestra]
3*,2,2,3*(C.Bn. ad lib.)-4,3,3,1-Timp.,Perc.-
Hp.-Str.
Ms.
Score 13 p. Large folio
This transcription 1956.

5431 Il riposo (suite for small   7'
orchestra)
1.Maestoso [March] 2.Adagio [Chorale] 3.
Allegro scherzando - Alla marcia maestoso
[Fugue]
1(alt. Picc.),1(alt. E.H.),2,1-2,2,1-Timp.,
Perc.-Hp.-Str.
Ms.
Score 27 p.
*The name Il Riposo is taken from a 16th cen-
tury religious painting style. Movement 1
suggested by Jan van Eyck's altarpiece, The
March of the Magi; Movement II after a Byzantine mosaic in the basilica of Saint Apolli-
nare-Nuovo at Ravenna; Movement III suggested
by a painting in the Riposo style by Anthony
Van Dyck. Movement II based on an old Roman
tune, Urbs Beata Jerusalem. Originally composed 1921, as part of the composer's choral
setting of Stabat Mater Speciosa with text
by Jacopone da Todi (1230-1306). First performance of this suite, New York, Radio Station WOR, 7 May 1934, Bamberger Symphony,
the composer conducting.*

4847 Sinfonietta [revised version]   21'
1.Allegro scherzando 2.Allegro scherzando
3.Allegro con fuoco
1(alt. Picc.),1,2,1-2,2,1-Timp.,Perc.-Hp.-Str.
Ms.
Score 128 p. Large folio
*Originally composed for smaller orchestra,
1938. This revised version 1943. First performance Town Hall, New York, 30 January 1950,
Little Orchestra Society, Thomas Scherman
conductor.*

2625 Song of the night, symphonic poem   12'30"
3(3rd alt.Picc.),3*,2,3*-4,3,3,1-Timp.,Perc.-
Cel.(alt. Pno.),2Hp.-Str.
Ms.
Score 59 p.

*Composed 1931. First performance Carnegie
Hall, New York, 15 March 1938, Woman's Symphony Orchestra, Antonia Brico conductor.*

2745 Station WGZBX, a satirical suite   15'
1.In the lobby 2.Interference 3.A slumber
hour 4.Mike-struck
3(3rd alt. Picc.),2(2nd alt. E.H.),3*,3*-
3Sax.-4,3,3,1-Pno.(alt. Cel.),Hp.-Speaking
Voice(ad lib.)-Str.
Ms.
Score 129 p.
*Composed 1931. First performance in a broad-
cast from New York, 8 May 1932, NBC Symphony
Orchestra, Eugene Goossens conductor.*

1767s Suite for string orchestra   16'
1.Preamble 2.Musette 3.Interlude 4.Fugue
Str.
Kalmus, New York, c1938 (Juilliard Edition)
Score 40 p.
*Composed 1933. First performance New York
University, 28 April 1934, Washington Square
College String Orchestra, Martin Bernstein
conductor. Received the Juilliard Publica-
tion Award, 1937.*

4855 [Symphony no. 1]   39'
1.Andante solenne 2.Allegro con brio 3.
Tempo di marcia 4.Allegro con spirotoso [sic]
3*,3*,2,3*-4,3,4,1-Timp.(2 players),Perc.-
Hp.-Str.
Ms.
Score 189 p. Large folio
*Composed 1943. First performance in a
recording for the Society of Participating
Artists, Vienna, December 1952, the Vienna
Philharmonia, F. Charles Adler conductor.*

4856 [Symphony no. 2, in one movement]   20'
4(3rd & 4th alt. Picc.I & II),2,2,3-4,3,3,1-
Timp.,Perc.-Hp.-Str.
Ms.
Score 117 p. Large folio
Composed 1949.

2623 [Wir glauben all' an einen Gott.   7'
Transcribed for orchestra by Philip James]
1.Maestoso 2.Allegro
3*,2,2,3*-4,2,3,1-Timp.,Perc.-Org.-Str.
Ms.
Score 26 p.
*The chorale preceding the fugal section is
based on an old German Lutheran hymn. The
fugal portion is a setting of J.S. Bach's
chorale-prelude, the Giant Fugue, BWV 680.
First performance Brooklyn, 18 February 1929,
Brooklyn Orchestral Society, Philip James
conducting.*

JANÁČEK, LEOŠ.   Hukvaldy, Moravia
     (now Sklenov, Czechoslovakia) 3 July 1854
           Ostrava, Moravia 12 August 1928

2489 [Lachian dances. Nos. 1 & 2]   8'
1.[Old-fashioned] 2.[Blessed]
2(2nd alt. Picc.),3*,3*,2-4,2,3-Timp.,Perc.-
Org.(ad lib.),Hp.-Str.

Janáček, Leoš

Hudební Matice, Prague, ᶜ1928
Score 43 p.

2490 [Lachian dances. Nos. 3 & 4]   6'
3.[Town piper] 4.[Old-fashioned]
2,2,2,2-3,2,2-Timp.-Hp.-Str.
Hudebni Matice, Prague, ᶜ1928
Score 39 p.

2491 [Lachian dances. Nos. 5 & 6]   4'
5.[Country bumpkins' dance] 6.[Handsaw dance]
2,2,2,2-3,2,3-Timp.,Lyra-Hp.-Str.
Hudebni Matice, Prague, ᶜ1928
Score 31 p.

1640 Sinfonietta (1926)   25'
1.Allegretto 2.Andante - Allegretto 3.Modera-
to 4.Allegretto
4(4th alt. Picc.),2(2nd alt. E.H.),4*(1Cl. in
E-flat),2-4,14,4,3-Timp.,Bells-Hp.-Str.
Universal Edition, Vienna, ᶜ1927
Score 72 p.
Composed 1926. First performance Brno, 1926.

2391 Suite, Op. 3 [for orchestra]   14'
1.Con moto 2.Adagio 3.Allegretto 4.Con moto
2,2,2,2-3,2-Timp.,Trgl.-Hp.-Str.
Ms.
Score 108 p.
*First performance a radio broadcast, Frankfurt,
July 1930, Hans Rosbaud conductor.*

3750 [The village fiddler's child,   11'30"
ballad]
2,2,3*,2-3,2,3,1-Timp.,Perc.-Hp.-Str.
Hudebni Matice, Prague, 1924
Score 43 p.
Composed 1913.

JANSSEN, WERNER.   New York 1 June 1899

3836 Foster suite
1(alt. Picc.),1,2,1-2,2,1-Timp.,Perc.-Str.
C.C. Birchard, Boston, ᶜ1937
Score 43 p.
*Quotations: Jeanie with the Light Brown Hair,
Camptown Races, Old Black Joe, The Glendy
Burke, Old Folks at Home, Oh Susannah.*

2628 Fugue on the American folk song   8'
Dixie, from Louisiana Suite
3(3rd alt.Picc.),2,2,2-4,3,3,1-Timp.,Perc.-Str.
Eulenburg, Leipzig, ᶜ1934
Score 38 p.
*Composed 1930. First performance Rome,
Augusteo, 27 November 1932, Bernardino Moli-
nari conductor.*

2627 New Year's Eve in New York   20'
4*,3(3rd alt. E.H.),4*,3(3rd alt. C.Bn.)-3Sax.
(ATA, 1st & 2nd alt. Sop.Sax)-4,5,3,1-Timp.,
Perc.-Pno.,2Hp.,Tenor Banjo-Str.
C.C. Birchard, Boston, ᶜ1929
Score 91 p.
*First performance Rochester, New York, 8 May
1929, Rochester Philharmonic, Howard Hanson
conductor. Awarded American Prix de Rome.*

JAQUES-DALCROZE, ÉMILE.   Vienna 6 July 1865
                              Geneva 1 July 1950

741v [Concerto, violin, no. 1, Op. 50, C minor]
1.Allegro con ritmo 2.Largo 3.Finale quasi
fantasia: Allegro appassionato
Solo Vn.-3*,2(2nd alt. E.H.),2,2-4,2,3,1-Timp.,
Perc.-Hp.-Str.
Süddeutscher Musikverlag, Strassburg, ᶜ1902
Score 98 p.
*First performance at the Schweizer Tonkünstler-
fest 1901.*

652v [Concerto, violin, no. 2, Poème]
In two movements
Solo Vn.-2(2nd alt. Picc.),2,2,2-4,2,3,1-Timp.,
Perc.-Hp.-Str.
Simrock, Berlin, ᶜ1911
Score 101 p.

535 [Dance suite in 4 movements]
1.Moderato 2.Allegretto 3.Andante 4.Allegro
con brio
2(2nd alt. Picc.),2,2,2-4,2,3,1-Timp.,Perc.-
Hp.-Str.
Simrock, Berlin, ᶜ1911
Score 59 p.

475s Seven dances for string quartet or string
orchestra
Str.(without Cb.)
J. Williams, London, ᶜ1927
Score 24 p.

5148 [The twins of Bergamo. Act 2. Symphonic
entr'acte]
2(2nd alt. Picc.),2,2,2-4,2,3,1-Timp.,Perc.-
Pno.-Str.
Heugel, Paris [1908]
Score 44 p.
*From the opera based on a play by Florian.
First performance Brussels, 30 March 1908,
Sylvain Dupuis conductor.*

JARECKI, TADEUSZ.   Lvov, Poland 31 December 1888
                        New York 29 April 1955

2933 Chimère, poème symphonique, Op. 26   5'
3(2nd alt. Picc.,1Alto Fl.),3*,3*,2-4,2,3,1,
Euph.-Perc.-Pno.(ad lib.),Cel.,Hp.-Str.
C. Fischer, New York, ᶜ1928
Score 22 p.
*Composed 1911-25. First performance Philadel-
phia, 4 December 1925, Philadelphia Orchestra,
Leopold Stokowski conductor.*

JARNACH, PHILIPP.
        b. Noisy-le-Sec, near Paris 26 July 1892

280v [Concertino, after old published   14'30"
works of Giovanni Platti, for 2 solo violins
and string orchestra, Op. 31, E minor]
1.Ouvertüre 2.Arietta 3.Menuetto 4.Giga
2Solo Vn.-Str.
B. Schott's Söhne, Mainz, ᶜ1944
Score 36 p.
*Based on Platti works published ca.1759.
First performance Cologne, ca.1943.*

1545 [Morning sounds, romance no. 2, Op. 19] *15'*
3(3rd alt. Picc.),3*,3*,3(3rd alt. C.Bn.)-4,
3,3-Timp.,Perc.-Hp.-Str.
B. Schott's Söhne, Mainz, ᶜ1926
Score 28 p.
Composed 1925. First performance Gewandhaus,
Leipzig, November 1926.

5739 [Music with Mozart, symphonic *24'*
variations for orchestra, Op. 25]
1.Thema (Canzone) 2.Menuetto 3.Siciliano
4.Rondo
3(3rd alt. Picc.),2(2nd alt. E.H.),2,3(3rd
alt. C.Bn.)-3,2,3-Timp.,Perc.-Str.
B. Schott's Söhne, Mainz, ᶜ1935
Score 67 p.
Theme is from the Andante Grazioso of Mozart's
Piano Trio no. 6, K.542, composed 1788.

5281 Sinfonia brevis, für grosses *22'*
Orchester, Op. 11
4*(Picc. ad lib.),3*,3*,4*(C.Bn. ad lib.)-4,
3,3,1-Timp.,Perc.-Cel.(ad lib.),Hp.-Str.
B. Schott's Söhne, Mainz, ᶜ1925
Score 50 p.
Composed 1923. First performance Weimar, 1925.

JÄRNEFELT, ARMAS.   Viborg (Viipuri), Finland
                     (now in U.S.S.R.) 14 August 1869
                     Stockholm 23 June 1958

271 Berceuse   *4'*
0,0,2,1-2Hn.-Str.
Breitkopf & Härtel, Leipzig, ᶜ1905
Score 7 p.
Composed 1903. First performance Viborg, 1903,
the composer conducting.

1430s Berceuse. Transcribed for string
orchestra by Cedric Sharpe
Str.
Score: Ms. 7 p.
Parts: Chester, London, ᶜ1929
Originally for orchestra.

842 Korsholm [symphonic poem]   *18'*
3(3rd alt. Picc.),2,2,2-4,3,3,1-Timp.,Perc.-
Hp.-Str.
Breitkopf & Härtel, Leipzig, ᶜ1902
Score 60 p.

522 Praeludium [for small orchestra]   *3'*
1*,1,2,1-2,2-Timp.,Perc.-Str.
Breitkopf & Härtel, Leipzig [n.d.]
Score 15 p.
Composed 1900. First performance Viborg 1901,
the composer conducting.

Suite för Orkester. Edited by Julia A. Burt
1050 No. 1. [Introduction - Israel's   *6'*
      captivity]
803s No. 2. [Elizabeth's lament]   *6'*
1494 No. 3. Danse   *6'*
2(both alt. Picc.),3*,3*,2-4,2,3,1-Timp.,
Perc.-Str.
W. Hansen, Copenhagen, ᶜ1919
Scores: 10 p., 5 p., 29 p.

JARRETT, JACK.
        b. Asheville, North Carolina 17 March 1934

2115s Serenade [for string orchestra,   *7'*
Op. 10]
Str.
Ms.
Score 10 p. Large folio
Originally composed for string quartet 1957.
Transcribed same year. First performance
Rochester, New York, 3 May 1957, Eastman-
Rochester Symphony Orchestra, Howard Hanson
conductor. Awarded Third Prize in the Edward
Benjamin Contest for Quiet Music at Eastman
School of Music, 3 May 1957.

JEANJEAN, PAUL.

547m Air à danser [Dance tune, oboe and
orchestra]
Solo Ob.-2,0,2,2-2Hn.-Str.
Score: Ms. 12 p.
Parts: Evette & Schaeffer, Paris [n.d.]

1568s Airs vieillots [Old fashioned airs]
Solo Vc.-Str.
Score: Ms. 5 p.
Parts: Decourcelle, Nice, ᶜ1913

736m Andantino [for clarinet in B and orchestra]
Solo Cl.-2,2,0,2-2Hn.-Hp.-Str.
Score: Ms. 27 p.
Parts: Evette & Schaeffer, Paris [n.d.]

674c Conte d'amour [Love story]
Solo Vc.-1,0,2,1-2Hn.-Hp.-Str.
Score: Ms. 11 p.
Parts: Decourcelle, Paris, ᶜ1913

1076s Méditation
Str.
Score: Ms. 5 p.
Parts: Decourcelle, Nice, ᶜ1914

702m Nocturne [horn and chamber orchestra]
Solo Hn.-1,1*,2,1-Str.
Score: Ms. 12 p.
Parts: Evette & Schaeffer, Paris [n.d.]

738m Romance [for horn in F and orchestra]
Solo Hn.-1,1,2,2-Str.
Score: Ms. 18 p.
Parts: Evette & Schaeffer, Paris [n.d.]

1493s Romance pour violon
Solo Vn.-Str.
Score: Ms. 10 p.
Parts: Decourcelle, Nice, ᶜ1914

1159s Les sabots de Noël [The Christmas shoes]
Str.
Score: Ms. 7 p.
Parts: Decourcelle, Nice, ᶜ1921

733m Scherzo brillante
Solo Cl.-2Bn.-2Hn.-Timp.-Str.
Score: Ms. 20 p.
Parts: Evette & Schaeffer, Paris [n.d.]

Jeanjean, Paul

1176s Un soir dans la vallée
Str.
Score: Ms. 8 p.
Parts: Decourcelle, Nice, ᶜ1922

1636s Sommeil [Slumber]
Solo Vc.-Str.
Score: Ms. 4 p.
Parts: Gaudet, Paris, ᶜ1921

JEHIN, FERNAND.

841s Pensiero d'amore [Loving thought] habanera
Solo Vc.-Str.
Score: Ms. 7 p.
Parts: Delrieu, Nice, ᶜ1927

JEHIN, LÉON.   Spa, Belgium 17 July 1853
                Monte Carlo 14 February 1928

420s Souvenirs! Elégie
Soli: Vn.I,Vn.II,Va.,Vc.-Str.
Decourcelle, Nice [n.d.]
Score 7 p.

JEHMLICH, ROBERT.

851m [Concertino on the Russian national
hymn, Op. 3]
Solo Tbn.-2,2,2,2-2,2-Timp.-Str.
Score: Ms. 89 p.
Parts: A.E. Fischer, Bremen [n.d.]

JENKINS, CYRIL.
    b. Dunvant, near Swansea, Wales 9 October 1885

455s Welsh fantasia for strings, Op. 27
Str.
Curwen, London, ᶜ1913
Score 21 p.

JENKINS, JOHN.   Maidstone, Kent, England 1592
            Kimberley, Norfolk, England 27 October 1678

2020s [Fantasy, 5 viols, no. 1, D major]
Scored by Arnold Dolmetsch. Modern scoring by
Percy Aldridge Grainger
Original: 5 Viols; Modern: Str.
G. Schirmer, New York, ᶜ1944
Score 4 p.
*First modern performance in a Music for the
Viols concert, London, 19 March 1892, Arnold
Dolmetsch conductor.*

JENSEN, ADOLF. Königsberg, Germany 12 January 1837
            Baden-Baden, Germany 23 January 1879

4443 [Etudes, piano, Op. 32. No. 9, Serenade.
Transcribed for orchestra by Reinhold Becker]
2,1,2,1-4Hn.-Str.
C.F. Peters, Leipzig [188-?]
Score 7 p.

5551 [Wedding music, Op. 45. Transcribed for
orchestra by Reinhold Becker]
1.[Festive processional] 2.[Bridal song]
3.[Round dance] 4.Notturno
3*,2,2,2-4,3,3,1-Timp.,Cym.,Trgl.-Str.

Julius Hainauer, Breslau [n.d.]
Score 49 p.
Originally composed for piano 4-hands, ca.1873.

JENSEN, GUSTAV.   Königsberg, Prussia
(now Kaliningrad, U.S.S.R.) 25 December 1843
                Cologne 26 November 1895

1400s Grablied [Dirge. Transcribed for string
orchestra by Ewald Strässer]
Str.
Score: Ms. 3 p.
Parts: Ende, Cologne [n.d.]

132s Ländliche Serenade, Op. 37 [Rustic
serenade, for string orchestra]
In one movement
Str.
Forberg, Leipzig [n.d.]
Score 28 p.

737v Romanze für Violine, Op. 15   *10'*
Solo Vn.-2,2,2,2-2,2-Timp.-Str.
Ries & Erler, Berlin [n.d.]
Score 22 p.
Composed 1881. First performance Cologne 1883.

114s Sinfonietta, Op. 22 [for string orchestra]
1.Allegro un poco agitato 2.Intermezzo: Allegretto con delicatezza 3.Larghetto 4.Allegro
energico
Str.
Wernthal, Berlin [n.d.]
Score 35 p.

JENSEN, LUDVIG IRGENS.   Oslo, Norway 13 April 1894
                Enna, Sicily 11 April 1969

6091 [Partita sinfonica, symphonic suite] *18'*
1.Allegro marcato 2.Lento 3.Allegro 4.Grave
2(2nd alt. Picc.),2(2nd alt. E.H.),2,2-4,3,3,
1-Timp.,Perc.-Pno.,Cel.,Hp.-Str.
Norsk Musikforlag, Oslo, ᶜ1950
Score 71 p.
*Originally composed 1938 as incidental music
to H. E. Kinck's dramatic poem, Driftekaren.
First performance Oslo, 20 January 1939, Oslo
Philharmonic Orchestra, Odd Grüner-Hegge conductor.*

6087 Passacaglia [revised edition]   *21'*
Introduzione - Passacaglia - Fuga - Passacaglia
- Coda
3(3rd alt. Picc.),2,3*(or 2-2nd alt. B.Cl.),
3*(or 2-2nd alt. C.Bn.)-4,3,3,1-Timp.,Perc.-
Org.(ad lib.),Hp.-Str.
Norsk Musikforlag, Oslo, ᶜ1952
Score 78 p.
*Composed 1926-27. First performance Oslo, 19
January 1929, Oslo Philharmonic Orchestra, Odd
Grüner-Hegge conductor. Awarded second prize
in the Scandinavian section of the Schubert
Competition, 1928.*

6090 [Theme and variations, for orchestra] *22'*
2(2nd alt. Picc.),1,2(2nd alt. B.Cl.),2-4,3,
3,1-Timp.,Perc.-Pno.,Cel.,Hp.-Str.
Norsk Musikforlag, Oslo, ᶜ1948

Score 103 p.
*Originally composed 1925, under the title:
Variations and Fugue. Revised 1934. First
performance Oslo, 3 December 1934, Oslo Philharmonic Orchestra, Issay Dobrowen conductor.*

JERAL, WILHELM.   Prague 2 October 1861

602c [Concerto, violoncello, Op. 10, A major]
1.Allegro moderato 2.Adagio 3.Tarantella:
Presto
Solo Vc.-2,2,2,2-4,2-Timp.-Hp.-Str.
Rahter, Leipzig [n.d.]
Score 58 p.

601c Zigeunertanz, Op. 6 no. 2 [Gypsy dance]
Solo Vc.-2,2,2,2-2Hn.-Cym.,Trgl.-Str.
Rahter, Leipzig [n.d.]
Score 15 p.
Originally composed for violoncello and piano.

JIMÉNEZ, MIGUEL BERNAL.
See: BERNAL JIMENEZ, MIGUEL.

JIMÉNEZ-MABARAK, CARLOS.
                b. Tacuba, Mexico 31 January 1916

4251 [The little tailor and the elf,
symphonic suite for children's theater]
[Overture] - [The little tailor's song] -
[The clock's dance] - [The wizard of sloth] -
[The elf dances] - [The spinners' round] -
[The Spanish spinner] - [The Cuban spinner] -
[The Chinese spinner] - Coda
1,1,1,1-Tpt.-Perc.-Pno.-Str.
Ms.
Score 72 p.
Suggested by a play of Graciela Amador.

JIRÁK, KAREL BOLESLAV.
        Prague, Czechoslovakia 28 January 1891
                Chicago 30 January 1972

2353 [Overture to a Shakespeare comedy,   18'
Op. 22]
3*,3*,4*(1Cl. in E-flat),3*-4,3,3,1-Timp.,Perc.
-Cel.,Hp.-Str.
Universal Edition, Vienna, c1929
Score 74 p.
*Composed 1926. First performance Prague, 24
February 1927, the composer conducting.*

6780 Serenade for small orchestra, Op. 69 20'
1.Andante quasi allegretto 2.Scherzo: Vivace
3.Largo cantabile 4.Allegro vigoroso
2,2,2,2-4,2-Timp.-Str.
Ms.
Score 76 p. Large folio
Composed 1951-54.

6634 [Youth, symphonic overture, Op. 43]   10'
3*,3*,4*(1Cl. in E-flat),3*-4,3,3,1-Timp.,
Perc.-Hp.-Str.
Melantrich, Prague, 1946
Score 70 p.
*Composed 1940-41. First performance Prague,
8 May 1943, Czech Philharmonic Orchestra,
Václav Talich conductor. Awarded first*

*prize in the Melantrich Publishing House
Contest, 1942.*

JÍROVEC, VOJTĚCH.
See: GYROWETZ, ADALBERT.

JITOMIRSKY, ALEXANDER MATVEJEVICH.
See: ZHITOMIRSKI, ALEXANDER MATVEIEVICH.

JOACHIM, JOSEPH.
        Kitsee, Czechoslovakia 28 June 1831
                Berlin 15 August 1907

998v Andantino and allegro scherzoso, Op. 1
Solo Vn.-2,2,2,2-2,2-Timp.-Str.
Score: Ms. 100 p.
Parts: [Kistner, Berlin, 1849]

606v [Concerto, violin, G major]   30'
1.Allegro non troppo 2.Andante 3.Allegro
giocoso
Solo Vn.-2,2,2,2-4,2-Timp.-Str.
Bote & Bock, Berlin [1889]
Score 146 p.
*Composed 1864; revised 1889. First performance
Hanover, 5 November 1864, the composer as
soloist.*

783v [Concerto, violin, Op. 3, G minor]   12'
In one movement
Solo Vn.-2,2,2,2-4,2,2-Timp.-Str.
Score: Ms. 108 p.
Parts: Breitkopf & Härtel, Leipzig [1854]
*Composed 1844. First performance December
1853, the composer as soloist.*

536v [Concerto, violin, In Hungarian   28'
style, Op. 11, D minor]
1.Allegro 2.Romanze 3.Finale alla zingara
Solo Vn.-2,2,2,2-4,2-Timp.-Str.
Breitkopf & Härtel, Leipzig [1893]
Score 134 p.
*Composed 1857. First performance Hanover, 24
March 1860, the composer as soloist.*

554v Notturno für Violine mit Orchester, Op. 12
Solo Vn.-2,2,2,2-2Hn.-Str.
Simrock, Berlin, 1874
Score 23 p.

5287 [Overture to a comedy by Gozzi, Op. 8]
2,2,2,2-4,2-Timp.-Str.
N. Simrock, Berlin, c1902
Score 47 p.
*Suggested by Carlo Gozzi's tragicomedies Il
Re Cervo and La Donna Serpente. Composed 1853
or 1854.*

5095 [Overture to Hamlet, Op. 4]
2,2,2,2-4,2,3-Timp.-Str.
Breitkopf & Härtel, Leipzig [1909]
Score 67 p.
Composed 1853.

584v Variationen [violin and orchestra]   22'
Theme, 18 Variations and Finale
Solo Vn.-3*,2,2,2-2,2-Timp.-Str.
Bote & Bock, Berlin [1882]

Joan

Score 83 p.
*Composed 1880. First performance Berlin,
15 February 1881, the composer as soloist.*

JOAN.

The composer's name is probably a nom de plume.

1108v [Concerto, violin, Op. 4, F major]
1.Allegro 2.Adagio 3.Rondo: Andante
Solo Vn.-2Ob.-2Hn.-Str.
Score: Ms. 102 p.
Parts: Gombart, Augsbourg, 1799

JOHANSON, SVEN-ERIC.
b. Västervik, Småland, Sweden 1919

390c Concerto da camera per violoncello ed
orchestra 1958
1. ♩=60 2. ♩=104 3. ♩=72
Solo Vc.-1,1,1,1-2,1,1-Str.
Edition Suecia, Stockholm [n.d.]
Score 89 p.
Composed 1958.

6822 [Photos for orchestra, 1966]   *12'*
2,2,2,2-2,2,2-Timp.,Perc.-Cel.,Hp.-
Str.
Ms.
Score 38 p.
Composed 1966.

5986 [Symphony no. 3]   *30'*
1. ♩=80-♩=100 2. ♩=52 3. ♩ or ♪.=144
4. ♩=100
2(1st alt. Picc.),2,2,2-4,2,3,1-Timp.-Hp.-Str.
Ms.
Score 118 p.
*Composed 1956. First performance Göteborg,
Sweden, 23 September 1959, Göteborg Symphony
Orchestra, Dean Dixon conductor.*

JOHANSSEN, V.

379s Elegie
Str.
[n.p., n.d.]
Score 7 p.

JOHNS, LOUIS EDGAR.   Pittsburgh 27 September 1886

1775s Medieval suite, Op. 46   *11'*
1.Early Gothic 2.Revolt 3.Minnelied 4.Dance
of the May
Str.
Composers Press, New York, ᶜ1939
Score 24 p.
*Composed 1938. First performance Ithaca, New
York, 11 August 1939, Cornell String Sym-
phonietta, Ronald Ingalls conductor.*

JOHNSON, BERNARD.

1125s Elfentanz, for string orchestra
Str.
Stainer & Bell, London, ᶜ1912
Score 7 p.
Originally composed for organ.

JOHNSON, HORACE.
Waltham, Massachusetts 5 October 1893
Tucson, Arizona 30 May 1964

3625 Astarte   *20'*
3*,3*,2,2-4,2,3-Timp.,Perc.-Hp.-Str.
Ms.
Score 81 p.
*Inspired by Helen Redington's poem. Composed
1929. First performance New York, 2 January
1936, Richmond Symphony Orchestra of the WPA,
Eugene Plotnikoff conductor.*

3526 In the American manner [for   *5'*
orchestra]
1,1,2,1-2,2,1-Timp.,Cym.-Pno.-Str.
Ms.
Score 26 p.
*Originally composed for piano, 1926. Tran-
scribed 1933. First performance on an NBC
broadcast from New York, 23 April 1934, Radio
City Music Hall Orchestra, Erno Rapee conductor.*

2003s Music for strings   *11'*
Timp.-Pno.,Hp.-Str.
Ms.
Score 51 p. Large folio
Composed 1945.

3317 Streets of Florence   *12'*
1.Piazza Santo Spirito 2.Erta Canina 3.Borgo
San Jacopo
2(2nd alt. Picc.),3*,2,2-4,2,3-Timp.,Perc.-
Pno.,Cel.,Hp.(ad lib.)-Str.
Ms.
Score 31 p. Large folio
*Composed 1930. First performance Mexico City,
9 July 1937, Orquesta Sinfónica de México,
Carlos Chávez conductor.*

4801 Three four [symphonic waltz]   *5'*
3*,3*,2,3*-2,3,2-Timp.,Perc.-Hp.-Str.
Ms.
Score 24 p. Large folio
Composed 1942.

JOHNSON, HUNTER.
b. Benson, North Carolina 14 April 1906

2771 Concerto for small orchestra   *20'*
2,0,2-Pno.-Str.
Ms.
Score 63 p.
*Composed 1936. First performance New York, 5
May 1937, Greenwich Concert Orchestra, Lehman
Engel conductor.*

1083m For an unknown soldier   *8'*
Solo Fl.-Str.

Valley Music Press, South Hadley, Mass.,
C1944 by Hunter Johnson
Score 7 p.
*Suggested by Walt Whitman's poem, By the
Bivouac's Fitful Flame. Composed 1938. First
performance New York, February 1939, WPA
Orchestra, Chalmers Clifton conductor, Carle-
ton Sprague Smith soloist. Revised 1944.*

JOHNSON, LOCKREM.   Davenport, Iowa 15 March 1924

2400s Chaconne, Op. 29a   6'
Soli: Vn.I, Vn.II, Va.I, Va.II, Vc.-Str.
Ms.
Score 16 p.
*Originally composed for piano 1948. Won first
place in the piano section of the National
Federation of Music Clubs Contest, 1949.
Transcribed for strings 1949.*

5134 Lyric prelude, Op. 30   7'
3(3rd alt. Picc.),3*(E.H. optional),3(3rd
optional),2-4,3(3rd optional),3,1(optional)-
Timp.,Perc.-Hp.(optional)-Str.
Composers Facsimile Edition, New York, C1953
by Lockrem Johnson
Score 18 p. Large folio
*Composed 1948. Revised 1949. First per-
formance 16 August 1949, University of Washington Orchestra, Stanley Chapple conductor.*

JOHNSON, THOMAS F.
        b. Greeley, Colorado 18 November 1939

6750 The river   7'
2*,2,2,2-4,2,3-S.Dr.,Chimes-Str.
Ms.
Score 19 p.
*Inspired by Hermann Hesse's novel Siddhartha.
Composed 1966. First performance Rochester,
New York, 4 May 1967, 37th Annual Festival of
American Music, Eastman-Rochester Symphony
Orchestra, Howard Hanson conductor.*

JOHNSTON, DONALD O.
        b. Tracy, Minnesota 6 February 1929

5856 [Symphony no. 2, Three symphonias]   19'
1.Moderate - Rapid 2.Moderately slow -
Moderate 3.Rapid
2(2nd alt. Picc.),2,2(2nd alt. B.Cl.),2(2nd
alt. C.Bn.)-4,3,3,1-Timp.,Perc.-Hp.-Str.
Ms.
Score 74 p. Large folio
*Composed 1958-59. First performance Missoula,
Montana, 2 December 1962, Missoula Symphony
Orchestra, the composer conducting.*

6160 Symphony no. 3   21'
1.Moderate 2.Slow 3.Fast
2(2nd alt. Picc.),2,2,2(2nd alt. C.Bn.)-4,3,3,
1-Timp.,Perc.-Str.
Rochester Music Publishers, Fairport, New York,
C1961
Score 95 p. Large folio
Composed 1960.

6702 [Symphony no. 4]   25-30'
1.Slow - Fast 2.Fast 3.Moderate, heavily
2(2nd alt. Picc.),2,2,2-4,3,3,1-Timp.,Perc.-Hp.
-Str.
Ms. C1963 by Donald O. Johnston
Score 111 p. Large folio
*Commissioned by the University of Montana Band.
Scored for orchestra, 1961-62.*

JOKL, GEORG.   Vienna 31 July 1896

1415s Nachtmusik [Night music]
Hp.-Str.
Tischer & Jagenberg, Cologne, C1925
Score 25 p.

JOMMELLI, NICCOLÒ.
        Aversa, near Naples 10 September 1714
                Naples 25 August 1774

909m Aria for clarinet and string orchestra
Solo Cl.-Str.
Ms.
Score 13 p.

6420 [Chaconne for orchestra] Edited   5'
by Giuseppe Piccioli
2Ob.-2Hn.-Timp.-Str.
Carisch, S.A., Milan, C1937
Score 15 p.
Composed ca.1753.

JONAS, ERNST.

891s Liebeslied, Op. 58 [Love song]
Str.
Score: Ms. 4 p.
Parts: A. Cranz, Leipzig [189-?]

JONCIÈRES, VICTORIN DE.   Paris 12 April 1839
                              Paris 26 October 1903

Real name: Félix Ludger Rossignol

4503 [Hungarian serenade, for orchestra]   5'
2(2nd alt. Picc.),2,2,2-4,2,2Cnt.,3,1-Timp.,
S.Dr.,Trgl.-Str.
[Léon Grus, Paris, 1879]
Score 12 p.

JONES, CHARLES.
        b. Tamworth, Ontario, Canada 21 June 1910

4239 Five melodies for orchestra
1.March 2.Barcarole 3.Tarantella 4.Waltz
5.Finale: Allegro con spirito
3*,3*,3*,3*(C.Bn. ad lib.)-4,3,3,1-Timp.,Perc.
-Str.
Ms.
Score 104 p. Large folio
*Composed 1945. First performance Brussels
Film Festival, June 1947.*

6669 Little symphony for the new year   4'
1.Allegro 2.Andante 3.Vivo
1(alt. Picc.),1,1,1-0,3,2-Timp.,Cym.,S.Dr.-
Pno.-Str.
Mercury, New York, C1956 by Beekman Music

Jones, Charles

Score 28 p.
Commissioned by the Canadian Broadcasting Corporation. Composed 1953. First performance CBC broadcast 4 January 1954, CBC Orchestra, John Adaskin conductor.

3251 Suite, for small orchestra
1.Allegro 2.Allegretto 3.Larghetto 4.Allegro
1,1,1,1-2,1-Str.
Ms.
Score 116 p.

1790s Suite for string orchestra
1.Allegro moderato 2.Largo 3.Molto moderato
Str.
Ms.
Score 30 p.

JONES, EDWARD GERMAN.
See: GERMAN, EDWARD.

JONES, SAM LEANDER, JR.
b. Inverness, Mississippi 2 June 1935

5769 Meditation and scherzo, for   12'
orchestra
3*,3*,3*,3*-4,3,3,1-Timp.,Perc.-Pno.,Hp.-Str.
Ms.
Score 92 p. Large folio
Composed 1958. First performance Rochester, New York, 15 April 1958, Eastman-Rochester Symphony Orchestra, Howard Hanson conductor.

JONGEN, JOSEPH MARIE-ALPHONSE NICOLAS.
Liège, Belgium 14 December 1873
Sart-lez-Spa, near Liège 12 July 1953

617v [Concerto, violin, Op. 17, B minor]
1.Allegro poco maestoso 2.Adagio 3.Animé
Solo Vn.-2,2,2,2-4,2,3-Timp.-Str.
Durand, Paris, ᶜ1914
Score 132 p.
Composed ca.1900.

540c [Concerto, violoncello, Op. 18, D major]
1.Large 2.Assez lent 3.Modéré
Solo Vc.-3*,3*,2,2-4,2,3-Timp.,Cym.,Trgl.-Str.
Durand, Paris, ᶜ1911
Score 125 p.
Composed ca.1900.

1557 [Fantasy on two popular Walloon   15'
Noëls, Op. 24]
3*,3*,2,3*-4,3,3,1-Timp.,Perc.-Hp.-Str.
Durand, Paris, ᶜ1911
Score 117 p.
Composed 1909. First performance Brussels 1911.

5793 [Passacaglia and gigue, Op. 90]   16'
3*,3*,2,2-4,3,3,1-Timp.,Perc.-Cel.,
Hp.-Str.
A. Cranz, Brussels, ᶜ1932
Score 75 p.
Composed 1929.

JONSSON, JOSEF PETRUS.
Enköping, Sweden 21 June 1887
Norrköping, Sweden 9 May 1969

5036 [Fantasy overture, Op. 43]   5'
2,2,2,2-2,2-Timp.,Cym.-Str.
Ms.
Score 41 p.
Composed 1939.

6015 [Symphony no. 1, Nordland, Op. 23]   55'
1.Allegro energico, poco agitato 2.Andante poco tranquillo, quasi adagio 3.Allegretto pastorale 4.Molto adagio - Allegro vivace
2,3*,2,3*-4,2,3-Timp.,Trgl.,Tam-tam-Hp.-Str.
Ms. [ᶜ1949 by STIM, Stockholm]
Score 257 p.
Composed 1919-21. First performance Göteborg, Sweden, 10 October 1923, Orchestra Society of Göteborg, Ture Rangström conductor.

5046 [Symphony no. 3, Op. 50, C minor]   27'
1.Allegro risoluto 2.Adagio espressivo
3.Allegro vivace
2,2,2,2-2,2,3-Timp.-Str.
Ms.
Score 147 p.
Composed 1947. First performance Norrköping, Sweden, 26 October 1947, Orchestra Society of Norrköping, Heinz Freudenthal conductor.

JOPLIN, SCOTT.
See: ADLER, JAMES.
The classic rag-time suite

JORA, MIHAIL. Jassy (Iasi), Romania 14 August 1891
Bucharest 10 May 1971

6215 [Moldavian landscapes, suite, Op. 5]   26'
1.[On the bank of the Tazlau] 2.[Country dance] 3.[Wheatfields in the sunshine]
4.[Gypsy procession]
3*(Picc. alt. Fl.3),3*,3*,3*-4,3,3,1-Timp.,
Perc.-Cel.,Hp.-Str.
Score: Editura de Stat Pentru Literatură şi Artă [Bucharest, 1954] 182 p.
Parts: Editura Muzicala, Bucharest, 1958
Composed 1924. First performance Bucharest, 5 May 1924, State Philharmonic, Georges Enesco conductor.

JØRGENSEN, ERIK.   Birkerød, Denmark 10 May 1912

7054 Notturno per orchestra   10'
2(1Alto Fl.),2*,2*,2-2,1,1-Str.
Samfundet til Udgivelse af Dansk Musik, ᶜ1973
Score 17 p.
Composed 1965-66. First performance on Radio Denmark, Copenhagen, 10 June 1969, Aarhus Orkester, Aksel Wellejus conductor.

JOSTEN, WERNER.   Elberfeld, Germany 12 June 1885
New York 6 February 1963

3899 Batouala, poème chorégraphique   60'
[in 2 tableaux]
3*,3*,3*,3*-3Sax.(SAT)-4,3,3,1-Timp.,Perc.-
Pno.,Hp.-Voices(SATB)-Str. Backstage: Perc.-
2Pno.-Voices(SATB)
Ms.
Score 278 p.
Ballet based on René Maran's novel. Composed 1930-31.

1848s Canzona seria, for low strings   10'
Va.I/II,Vc.I/II,Cb.
Associated, New York, c1940 by composer
Score 20 p.
Composed 1937.

792p Concerto sacro I-II, for strings   I:20'
and piano   II:16'
I: 1.Annunciation 2.The miracle
II:1.Lament 2.Sepulchre and Resurrection
Solo Pno.-Str.
C.C. Birchard, Boston, c1931 by the Juilliard
Musical Foundation
Score 36 p.
*Suggested by the Isenheim votive altar triptych
at Colmar, Alsace, by Matthias Grünewald. Com-
posed 1925. Revised 1927. First performance
New York, 27 March 1929, Orchestra of the Juil-
liard Foundation, Albert Stoessel conductor.
Parts I and II may be performed separately.*

4003 Jungle, symphonic movement for full   14'
orchestra
4*,3,4(3rd alt. Cl. in E-flat, 4th alt. B.Cl.),
4*-6,5,3,1-Timp.,Perc.-Pno.,Cel.,2Hp.-Str.
Ms.
Score 78 p. Large folio
*Inspired by Henri Rousseau's painting, Forêt
Exotique. Composed 1928. First performance
Boston, 25 October 1929, Boston Symphony
Orchestra, Serge Koussevitzky conductor.*

1993s Symphony for strings   17'
1.Allegro vivace 2.Lento 3.Presto
Str.
Ms. [Now published by Henri Elkan, Phila.,Pa.]
Score 30 p.
*Composed 1935. First performance at the Sara-
toga Spa Music Festival, September 1946,
String Orchestra of the New York Philharmonic
Society, F. Charles Adler conductor.*

2890 Symphony in F   17'
Allegro vivace - Andante - Allegro moderato
3(2nd & 3rd alt. Picc.),3*,3(3rd alt. B.Cl.),
3*-4,3,3,1-Timp.,Perc.-Str.
Ms.
Score 82 p.
*Composed 1936. First performance Boston, 13
November 1936, Boston Symphony Orchestra, the
composer conducting.*

JOUBERT, JOHN PIERRE HERMAN.
         b. Cape Town, South Africa 20 March 1927

289p [Concerto, piano, Op. 25]   30-35'
1.Allegro 2.Lento 3.Lento - Allegro vivace -
Lento
Solo Pno.-2,2,2,2-4,2,3,1-Timp.,Perc.-Str.
Novello, London [c1964]
Score 234 p.
*Commissioned by Iso Elinson. Composed 1956-58.
First performance Manchester, England, 11 Jan-
uary 1959, Hallé Orchestra, George Weldon con-
ductor, Iso Elinson soloist.*

325v [Concerto, violin, Op. 13]   25-27'
1.Moderato con moto 2.Scherzo - Trio -

Scherzo 3.Lento - Allegro vivace - Molto
allegro
Solo Vn.-2(2nd alt. Picc.),2(2nd alt. E.H.),
2(2nd alt. B.Cl.),2-4,2,3,1-Timp.,Perc.-Str.
Novello, London [c1960]
Score 174 p.
*Commissioned by the York Festival. Composed
1954. First performance York Minster, York,
England, 17 June 1954, BBC Northern Orchestra,
John Hopkins conductor, Maria Lidka soloist.*

6498 In memoriam 1820, for orchestra,   16-18'
Op. 39
3(3rd alt. Picc.),3*,3*(1 in E-flat),3*-4,3,
3,1-Timp.,Perc.-Hp.-Str.
Novello, London [n.d.]
Score 75 p.
*Commissioned by the South African Broadcasting
Corporation for Settlers' Day, 1962, commemo-
rating the first British settlers in 1819-20.
Composed 1962. First performance Johannesburg,
South Africa, 7 September 1962, South African
Broadcasting Corporation Orchestra, Edgar
Cree conductor.*

6485 Sinfonietta [for chamber   18-19'
orchestra, Op. 38]
1.Allegro con spirito 2.Moderato - Allegro
0,2,0,2-2Hn.-Str.
Novello, London [1966]
Score 77 p.
*Commissioned by the Orchestra da Camera, Bir-
mingham. Composed 1962. First performance
Birmingham, England, 8 April 1962, Orchestra
da Camera, Brian Priestman conductor.*

6499 Symphony no. 1, Op. 20   26-32'
1.Allegro energico 2.Lento ma non troppo 3.
Presto 4.Adagio - Allegro vivace
2,2(2nd alt. E.H.),2,2-4,2,3,1-Timp.,Perc.-
Pno.-Str.
Novello, London [n.d.]
Score 249 p.
*Commissioned by the Hull Philharmonic Society.
Composed 1955. First performance Hull, Eng-
land, 12 April 1956, Hull Philharmonic
Orchestra, Vilem Tavsky conductor.*

JULIEN, PAUL.   Brest, France 12 February 1841
                              United States 1866

1544s Sérénade (Habanera)
Str.
Score: Ms. 4 p.
Parts: [Grus, Paris, n.d.]

JUNGMANN, ALBERT.
          Langensalza, Prussia 14 November 1824
          Pandorf, near Vienna 7 November 1892

575s Im Frühling, Intermezzo, Op. 335 [In
spring]
Hp.(ad lib.)-Str.
Joh. André, Offenbach a.M. [1875]
Score 12 p.

4665 [In the elves' grove, scherzo, Op. 334
no. 2]

Jungmann, Albert

2,2,2,2-4,2,3-Timp.,Cym.,B.Dr.-Hp.(ad lib.)-
Str.
Joh. André, Offenbach a.M. [186-?]
Score 27 p.

596s [Will-o'-the-wisp, Op. 217 no. 3]
Hp.-Str.
Joh. André, Offenbach a.M. [186-?]
Score 9 p.

JUON, PAUL.   Moscow 6 March 1872
                        Vevey, Switzerland 21 August 1940

802v Berceuse, Op. 28 no. 3
Solo Vn.-2,1,2,2-2Hn.-Trgl.,Glock.(ad lib.)-
Hp.(ad lib.)-Str.
Schlesinger, Berlin, c1904
Score in reduction 5 p.

2379 [Chamber symphony, Op. 27, B-flat   35'
major]
1.Allegro non troppo 2.Andante elegiaco
3.Allegro non troppo quasi moderato 4.Moderato
0,1,1,1-Hn.-Pno.-Str.(without Vn.II)
Schlesinger, Berlin, c1905
Score 80 p.
Composed 1904. First performance Gothenburg,
1907, Tor Aulin conductor, the composer as
pianist.

727v [Concerto, violin, no. 1, Op. 42, B minor]
1.Moderato 2.Romanze 3.Rondo
Solo Vn.-3(3rd alt. Picc.),2,2,3*-4,2-Timp.,
Trgl.,Glock.-Hp.-Str.
Schlesinger, Berlin, c1909
Score 79 p.

813v [Concerto, violin, no. 2, Op. 49, A major]
1.Allegro moderato 2.Elegie 3.Allegro
Solo Vn.-2(2nd alt. Picc.),2(2nd alt. E.H.),
2,2-4,2,3-Timp.,Trgl.-Str.
Schlesinger, Berlin, c1913
Score 97 p.

1209v [Concerto, violin, no. 3, Op. 88,   25'
A minor]
1.Risoluto 2.L'istesso tempo - Andante sem-
plice - Allegretto 3.Allegro giocoso
Solo Vn.-2,2,2,2-2,2-Timp.,Perc.-Str.
Richard Birnbach, Berlin, c1939
Score 86 p.

719m [Concerto, violin, violoncello and piano,
Op. 45]
1.Allegro moderato 2.Lento 3.Allegro non
troppo
Solo Vn., Solo Vc., Solo Pno.-2,2,2,3*-4,2,
3,1-Timp.,Trgl.,Glock.-Str.
Schlesinger, Berlin, c1912
Score 111 p.

37s [Five pieces for string orchestra,   15'
Op. 16]
Str.
Schlesinger, Berlin, c1901
Score 27 p.

1384s [Serenade, string orchestra,   13'
Op. 85, G major]
1.Allegro moderato 2.Adagietto 3.Tempo di
marcia
Pno.(ad lib.)-Str.(Cb. ad lib.)
Schlesinger, Berlin, c1929
Score 23 p.

342 Eine Serenadenmusik, Op. 40   30'
1.Moderato 2.Andante 3.Allegro non troppo
2,1,2,2-2Hn.-Timp.,Trgl.-Str.
Schlesinger, Berlin [190-?]
Score 58 p.
Composed 1908. First performance Berlin,
1910, Fritz Steinbach conductor.

1067 [Symphony, Op. 23, A major]   40'
1.Come passacaglia 2.Scherzo: Presto 3.
Romanze: Adagio 4.Finale: Allegro con fuoco
3*,3*,2,3*-4,2,3,1-Timp.-Hp.-Str.
Schlesinger, Berlin, c1903
Score 144 p.
Composed 1900. First performance Berlin 1901,
Fritz Steinbach conductor.

470 Vaegtervise, Op. 31 [Song of the town 35'
hall clock, fantasy on Danish folk melodies]
3(3rd alt. Picc.),3*,2,3*-6,2,3,1-Timp.,Perc.-
Hp.-Str.
Schlesinger, Berlin, c1906
Score 51 p.
Composed 1906. First performance Cologne,
1907, Fritz Steinbach conductor.

JURASSOVSKY, ALEXANDER.

1505 Les fantômes, poème symphonique, Op. 8
3*,3*,3*,3-6,3,3,1-Timp.,Perc.-2Hp.-Str.
Jurgenson, Moscow, 1912
Score 59 p.
Composed 1912.

JÜTTNER, OSKAR WILHELM.   Liegnitz, Silesia
              (now Legnica, Poland) 24 November 1863
                        Basel 19 August 1931

1547s Elégie, Op. 20
Solo Vn.-Str.
Score: Ms. 8 p.
Parts: A.E. Fischer, Bremen [n.d.]

988v Mazurka, Op. 26 no. 2
Solo Va.-Str.
Score: Ms. 4 p.
Parts: C.F. Schmidt, Heilbronn [n.d.]

K

KAAN-ALBEST, HEINRICH.   Tarnopol, Poland
              (now Ternopol, Ukraine) 29 May 1852
                        Roudná, Bohemia 7 March 1926

522s Adagio a scherzo
Str.
Fr. A. Urbánek, Prague [n.d.]
Score 7 p.

918s Sousedská [and] Serenáda
Fl.,Cl.-Str.
Fr. A. Urbánek, Prague [n.d.]
Score 10 p.

KABALEVSKY, DMITRI BORISOVICH.
          b. St. Petersburg 30 December 1904

4812 [Colas Breugnon (The master of   18'
Clamecy), Op. 24. Suite from the opera]
1.[Overture] 2.[National holiday]
3.[National disater, the plague] 4.[National
uprising]
3(3rd alt. Picc.),3(3rd alt. E.H.),3,3(3rd
alt. C.Bn.)-4,3,3,1-Timp.,Perc.-Hp.-Str.
Editions de Musique de l'URSS, Moscow, 1941
Score 168 p.
*From the opera composed 1937. First perform-
ance Leningrad, 22 February 1938, State Opera
of Leningrad.*

7331 [Same as above]
Kalmus, New York [n.d.]
Score 143 p.

6761 The comedians, suite, Op. 26   15-17'
In 10 movements
1(alt. Picc.),1(alt. E.H.),2,1-2,2,1,1-Timp.,
Perc.-Pno.-Str.
Kalmus, New York [1963?]
Score 99 p.
*Suite from music for the play Inventor and
Comedian by M. Daniel. Suite extracted 1940.
First concert performance Leningrad, 1940,
Leningrad State Philharmonic, Cyril Kondra-
shin conductor.*

369v [Concerto, violin and orchestra,   16-18'
Op. 48]
1.Allegro molto e con brio 2.Andantino canta-
bile 3.Vivace
Solo Vn.-1,1,2,1-2,1,1-Timp.,Perc.-
Str.
C.F. Peters, Leipzig [195-?]
Score 96 p.
*Commissioned by the Committee for Art of the
Soviet Ministry. Composed 1948. First per-
formances simultaneously on 29 October 1948:
Moscow Orchestra of the State Conservatory of
Music, M. Teryan conductor, Igor Bezrodny
soloist; Leningrad, I. Sherman conductor, Duma
Schneiderman soloist. Awarded the Stalin
Prize, 1949.*

4014 Poem of struggle, Op. 12   12'
3(3rd alt. Picc.),3*,3*,3*-4,3,3,1-Timp.,
Perc.-Chorus(SATB)-Str.
Mussektor, Moscow [n.d.]
Score 56 p.
*Composed 1930. First performance Moscow,
U.S.S.R. Radio Committee broadcast, Boris
Khaikin conductor.*

2934 Symphony no. 1, Op. 18   25'
1.Andante molto sostenuto 2.Allegro agitato
3(3rd alt. Picc.),3*,3*,3*-4,3,3,1-Timp.,Perc.
-Str.
Mussektor, Moscow [n.d.]

Score 127 p.
*Composed 1932. First performance Moscow
State Conservatory, 1932, Moscow Orchestra,
Boris Khaikin conductor.*

2935 Symphony no. 2, Op. 19   24'
1.Allegro quasi presto 2.Andante 3.Pres-
tissimo scherzando
3(3rd alt. Picc.),3*,3*,3*-4,3,3,1-Timp.,Perc.
-Str.
Ms.
Score 192 p.
*Composed 1934. First performance Moscow, 25
December 1934, Moscow Philharmonic, Albert
Coates conductor.*

2936 [Symphony no. 3, Requiem, Op. 22,   20'
for large orchestra and chorus. Text by N.
Asseiev]
1.Allegro, impetuoso 2.Andante marciale,
lugubre
3(3rd alt. Picc.),3*,3*,3*-4,3,3,1-Timp.,Perc.
-Pno.-Chorus(SATB)-Str.
Mussektor, Moscow, 1935
Score 95 p.
*Composed 1933. First performance Moscow,
January 1934, Moscow Orchestra and Chorus,
state radio broadcast, Boris Khaikin conductor.*

KAČINSKAS, JERONIMAS.
          b. Vidukle, Lithuania 17 April 1907

3547 Lento, for symphony orchestra   12-14'
3*,3*,3*,2-4,3,3,1-Timp.,B.Dr.,Cym.-Hp.-Str.
Ms.
Score 31 p.
*Composed 1957. First performance Boston, 16
November 1958, Boston University Orchestra,
the composer conducting.*

6983 [Song to light]
2,2,2,2-2,2-Timp.-Str.
Ms.
Score 17 p.
Composed 1947.

KADERAVEK, MILAN. Oak Park, Illinois 5 August 1924

5963 Sinfonietta   15'
1.Playfully 2.Tranquilly 3.Quickly, with
vigor
2(2nd alt. Picc.),2,2,2-4,3,3,1-Timp.,Perc.-Str.
Ms.
Score 115 p. Large folio
*Composed 1957-58. First performance Albuquer-
que, 13 January 1960, Albuquerque Civic Symphony, Maurice Bonney conductor. Received the
Albuquerque Civic Symphony's First Annual
Composition Award.*

5878 Three poems for orchestra   10'
1.Immortal autumn 2.Jack Frost 3.Evening
1,1,1,1-1,1,1-Timp.,Perc.-Pno.-Str.
Ms.
Score 32 p.
*Suggested by the poems Immortal Autumn by
Archibald MacLeish; Jack Frost, and Evening
by Emily Dickinson. Composed 1950. First*

Kaempfert, Max

performance Chicago, 8 November 1950, American Conservatory Symphonic Ensemble, Russell Harvey conductor.

KAEMPFERT, MAX.   Berlin 3 January 1871
             Solothurn, Switzerland 2 June 1941

   4778 [Rhapsody no. 9, A miners' festival.
   Transcribed for brass band]
   5Hn.,4Tpt.,Cnt.,2Flglhn.,3Ten.Hn.,Bar.,3Tbn.,
   Tuba-Timp.
   H. Bohne, Constance, ^c1939
   Score in reduction 12 p.
   Quotes four German miners' songs.

   1006s Spanisch, Op. 9
   Cast.,Tamb.-Hp.-Str.
   Score: Ms. 20 p.
   Parts: Ries & Erler, Berlin [n.d.]

   1007s Steckenpferdchen [Hobby-horse] Op. 8
   Str.(Cb. ad lib.)
   Score: Ms. 10 p.
   Parts: Ries & Erler, Berlin [n.d.]

KÄHLER, WILLIBALD.   Berlin 2 January 1866
           Klein-Machow, Berlin 17 October 1938

   653v Elegie   *7'*
   Solo Vn.-2,1,2,2-2Hn.-Str.
   Ries & Erler, Berlin, ^c1910
   Score 14 p.
   Composed 1907. First performance Schwerin 1909.

KAHN, ERICH ITOR.   Rimbach, Germany 23 July 1905
            New York 5 March 1956

   6766 Actus tragicus   *15'*
   1,1,1,1-Hn.-Str.(1,1,1,1,1)
   Composers Facsimile Edition, New York, ^c1955;
   ^c1960 by Erich Itor Kahn
   Score 56 p.
   Composed 1946. First performance Paris, 1947, Orchestre de la Radio, René Leibowitz conductor.

   6767 Music for 10 instruments and   *24'*
   soprano, Op. 3 (new version, 1953)
   1.Six bagatelles 2.Three scherzi 3.Choral
   prelude and aria
   Soprano Voice Solo-2,2,3*-Hn.-Vc.,Cb.
   Composers Facsimile Edition, New York, ^c1955;
   ^c1960 by Erich Itor Kahn
   Score 44 p.
   Texts by the composer. Text of Movement 1 is based on the poetry of Walther von der Vogelweide, also known as Spervogel (ca.1160-ca. 1230). Text of Movement 2 is adapted from the Chinese poet Li Po (701-62). Composed 1927-53. First performance Paris, 1953 or 1954, Radio Diffusion Française Orchestra, René Leibowitz conductor, Bethany Beardsley soloist.

   3443 Petite suite bretonne, pour petit   *12'*
   orchestre
   1.Matin 2.Première 3.Hymne 4.Chanson

   5.Berceuse 6.Deuxième danse 7.[The engulfed city]
   1,1,1,1-Hn.-Hp. (or Pno.)-Str.(without Cb.)
   Editions Pro Musica, Paris, ^c1936
   Score 19 p.

   6768 [Les symphonies bretonnes,   *14-15'*
   Op. 6a]
   1.Andante sostenuto e solenne 2.Allegretto
   grazioso 3.Non troppo lento 4.Allegretto
   ritenuto 5.Legierissimo, non allegro 6.
   Tempo di marcia
   3*,3*,3*,3*-4,3,3,1-Timp.-Hp.-Str.
   Composers Facsimile Edition, New York, ^c1955,
   ^c1960 by Erich Itor Kahn
   Score 72 p. Large folio
   Originally composed as Suite Bretonne for piano 4-hands, 1940-42, in the alien detention camp at Gurs, France. First performance of this orchestral version Baden-Baden, Germany, 1949 or 1950, Südwestfunk Orchester, Hans Rosbaud conductor.

KAHN, ROBERT.   Mannheim, Germany 21 July 1865
        Biddenden, Kent, England 29 May 1951

   598p [Concert piece, piano, Op. 74, E-flat]
   In one movement
   Solo Pno.-2,2,2,2-4,2-Timp.,Trgl.-Str.
   N. Simrock, Berlin, ^c1923
   Score 50 p.

KAISER, E.

     If Emil: Coburg, Germany 7 February 1853
         Munich 15 October 1929

   811m Adagio
   Solo Tbn.-2,2,2,2-2-2,2-Timp.-Str.
   Score: Ms. 22 p.
   Parts: A.E. Fischer, Bremen [n.d.]

KAJANUS, ROBERT.   Helsinki 2 December 1856
         Helsinki 6 July 1933

   4378 [Finnish rhapsody no. 1, Op. 5,   *8'*
   D minor]
   2(2nd alt. Picc.),2,2,2-4,2,3-Timp.-Str.
   Fr. Kistner, Leipzig [1890]
   Score 41 p.
   Composed 1882.

   1647 [Rhapsodie no. 2, Op. 8, F major]   *10'*
   2(2nd alt. Picc.),2,2,2-4,2,3-Timp.-Str.
   F. Kistner, Leipzig [n.d.]
   Score 63 p.
   Composed 1885. First performance Helsingfors, 1886, the composer conducting.

   2530 Sinfonietta, Op. 16
   1.Grave 2.Intermezzo 3.Adagio di molto
   4.Allegro con fuoco
   2,2,2,2-3Hn.-Timp.,Trgl.-Str.
   Breitkopf & Härtel, Leipzig, ^c1924
   Score 59 p.

KALAFATI, VASSILI PAVLOVICH.
        Eupatoria, Crimea 10 February 1869
        Leningrad 30 January 1942

549 Ouverture-Fantaisie, Op. 8
3(3rd alt. Picc.),3*,3,3*-4,3,3,1-Timp.,Perc.-
Hp.-Str.
M.P. Belaieff, Leipzig, 1906
Score 93 p.

548 Polonaise, Op. 14
3(3rd alt. Picc.),2,2,2-4,2,3,1-Timp.,Perc.-
Str.
M.P. Belaieff, Leipzig, c1913
Score 43 p.

967 [Symphony, Op. 12, A minor]
1.Allegro moderato 2.Allegro 3.Adagio
4.Finale
3,2*,2,2-4,2,3,1-Timp.-Str.
M.P. Belaieff, Leipzig, c1912
Score 151 p.

KALINNIKOV, VASSILI SERGEIEVICH.
Voin, near Mtzensk, Russia 13 January 1866
Yalta, Crimea 11 January 1901

742 Le cèdre et le palmier   7'
2,2,2,2-4,2,3-Timp.-Hp.-Str.
P. Jurgenson, Leipzig [n.d.]
Score 35 p.

483s Chanson triste. Transcribed for string
orchestra by M. Köhler
Str.
P. Jurgenson, Moscow [n.d.]
Score 3 p.
Originally composed for piano solo.

321 Intermezzo no. 1 [F-sharp minor]   4'
2,2,2,2-2,2,1-Timp.-Str.
P. Jurgenson, Leipzig [1901?]
Score 26 p.

322 Intermezzo no. 2 [G major]   5'
2,2,2,2-2,2,1-Timp.,Trgl.-Str.
P. Jurgenson, Leipzig [1901?]
Score 25 p.

660 Suite [D major]   17'
1.Andante 2.Allegro scherzando 3.Adagio
4.Allegro moderato
2(2nd alt. Picc.),2,2,2-4,2,3-Timp.,Perc.-
Hp.-Str.
P. Jurgenson, Leipzig [1902?]
Score 115 p.

858 [Symphony no. 1, G minor]   35'
1.Allegro moderato 2.Andante commodamente
3.Scherzo: Allegro non troppo 4.Finale:
Allegro moderato
3*,3*,2,2-4,2,3,1-Timp.,Perc.-Hp.-Str.
Jurgenson, Moscow [n.d.]
Score 209 p.

661 [Symphony no. 2, A major]
1.Moderato 2.Andante cantabile 3.Allegro
scherzando 4.Andante cantabile
3*,2(2nd alt. E.H.),2,2-4,2,3,1-Timp.-Hp.-Str.
P. Jurgenson, Leipzig [n.d.]
Score 211 p.

1412 [Tsar Boris. Overture *and*   20'
Entr'actes to the drama by Count Alexei
Tolstoi]
2(2nd alt. Picc.),2,2,2-4,2,3,1(ad lib.)-Timp.,
Perc.-Hp.(ad lib.)-Str.
P. Jurgenson, Leipzig [n.d.]
Score 153 p.
Composed and first performed Moscow 1899.

KALKBRENNER, FRIEDRICH WILHELM MICHAEL.
Kassel ca.8 November 1785
Deuil, Seine-et-Oise, France 10 June 1849

248p [Concerto, piano, no. 4, Op. 127, A-flat
major]
1.Maestoso brillante 2.Adagio 3.Rondo
Solo Pno.-1,2,2,2-2,2,3-Timp.-Str.
Ms. c1976 by The Fleisher Collection of
Orchestral Music, Free Library of Philadelphia
Score 183 p.
Originally for piano and string quintet, 1835.

KALLIWODA, JOHANN BAPTIST WENZEL.
Prague 21 February 1801
Karlsruhe 3 December 1866

1038 Concert-ouverture no. 17, Op. 242
2,2,2,2-4,2,3-Timp.-Str.
C.F.W. Siegel, Leipzig [n.d.]
Score 56 p.
*Composed 1863. First performance Donaues-
chingen 1864, the composer conducting.*

655m Concert rondo, Op. 80. Edited by   13'
W. Barge
Solo Fl.-1,0,2,1-2Hn.-Str.
J.H. Zimmermann, Leipzig [n.d.]
Score in reduction 25 p.

904m Concertino, oboe and orchestra, Op. 110
1.Allegro con fuoco 2.Romanze: Adagio
Solo Ob.-2,0,2,2-2,2,1-Timp.-Str.
Score: Ms. 106 p.
Parts: [n.d., n.d.]

357v [Introduction and grand polka in rondo
form, for two violins with orchestra, Op. 196]
Solo Vn.I, Solo Vn.II-2,0,2,2-2Hn.-Str.
Score: Ms. c1976 by The Fleisher Collection of
Orchestral Music, Free Library of Philadelphia.
71 p. Large folio
Parts: C.F. Peters, Leipzig [n.d.]

KALLSTENIUS, EDVIN.
Filipstad, Sweden 29 August 1881
Stockholm 22 November 1967

2046s [Musica gioconda, serenade for   16'30"
string orchestra, Op. 27]
1.Quasi marcia 2.Serenata, quasi sarabanda a
voce bassa 3.Piccolo rondo
Str.
Ms.[Gehrman's Musikförlag, Stockholm, 1953]
Score 30 p.
*Composed 1941-42. First performance Stockholm,
1942, Chamber Orchestra of Stockholm, Tobias
Wilhelmi conductor.*

Kallstenius, Edvin

2188s [Ostinato lirico]   7'
Str.
Nordiska Musikförlaget, Stockholm, ᶜ1956
Score 6 p.
*Originally composed as the second movement of
the composer's String Quartet no. 5, 1945.
First performance Sveriges Radio, Stockholm, 1
December 1949, Radiojänsts Kammerorkester, Lars-
Erik Larsson conductor.*

5042 [Passacaglia and variations on a   12'
Swedish rococo theme, Op. 25]
2,2,2,2-2,2-Timp.,Perc.-Str.
Ms.
Score 41 p.
*Theme is the Swedish popular Rococo melody Gub-
ben Noak [Old Man Noah]. Composed 1939. First
performance Stockholm, 1939, Smaller Broad-
casting Orchestra of Stockholm, Lars-Erik
Larsson conductor.*

5041 [Romantico, symphonic overture,   14'
Op. 24]
2,2,2,2-4,2,3,1-Timp.,Perc.-Str.
Ms.
Score 67 p.
*Composed 1938. First performance Gothenburg,
Sweden, 1941, Orchestra Society of Gothenburg,
Sixten Eckerberg conductor.*

5174 [Scherzo fugato, a merry piece in   6'
fuguing style, Op. 4b]
2,2(2nd ad lib.),2,2(2nd ad lib.)-4Hn.(3rd
& 4th ad lib.),2Tpt.-Timp.,Perc.-Str.
Universal Edition, Vienna, ᶜ1936
Score 33 p.
*Originally composed 1907 for string quartet,
Op. 4. This version 1923.*

820p [Sinfonia concertata, Op. 12, C   30'
major]
1.Moderato cantabile 2.Andante lento 3.Alle-
gro comodo
Solo Pno.-2(2nd alt. Picc.),2,2,2-4,2,3,1-
Timp.-Str.
Ms.
Score 182 p.
*Composed 1922. First performance Stockholm,
1930, Broadcasting Orchestra of Stockholm,
Ivar Hellman conductor, Fritjof Kjellberg
soloist.*

6011 [Sinfonietta no. 1, Op. 13, B minor] 17'
1.Scherzo serioso 2.Hymn: Adagio (quasi
corale) 3.Final: Allegro brioso
2(2nd alt. Picc.),2,2(2nd alt. B.Cl.),
2-4,2,3,1-Timp.-Str.
Ms.
Score 68 p.
*Composed 1923. First performance Gothenburg,
Sweden, 21 December 1927, Gothenburg Orchestra
Society, Tor Mann conductor.*

6040 [Suite for 9 solo instruments,   12'
Op. 23b]
1.Alla marcia gioiosa 2.Alla polacca svedese
3.Intermezzo funebre 4.Fugato doppio alla
danza rustica

1,1,1,1-Hn.-Str.(without Cb.)
Ms.
Score 52 p.
*Originally composed 1938 as Suite for 14 Wind
Instruments and Timpani, Op. 23a. This tran-
scription, 1949, written for the České Noneto
[Czech Nonet]. Another transcription below.*

5029 [Suite for 14-part orchestra,   12'
Op. 23c]
1.Alla marcia gioiosa 2.Alla polacca svedese
3.Intermezzo funebre 4.Fugato doppio alla
danza rustica
1,1,2,1-2,1-Timp.-Str.
Ms.
Score 67 p.
This transcription 1949.

5117 [Swedish rhapsody no. 2, Dalsland,   7'30"
Op. 22]
2,2,2,2-4(3rd & 4th ad lib.),2,2(2nd ad lib.)-
Timp.,S.Dr.,Trgl.-Str.
Universal Edition, Vienna ᶜ1938
Score 30 p.
*Dalsland is a province in western Sweden.
Composed 1936.*

6014 [Symphony no. 2, Op. 20, F minor]   31'
1.Allegro 2.Adagio 3.Allegro, ben ritmico
2(both alt. Picc.),3*,3*,2(2nd alt. C.Bn.)-
4,3,3,1-Timp.,Perc.-Hp.-Str.
Ms.
Score 157 p.
*Composed 1934-35. First performance Stockholm,
9 September 1943, Swedish Broadcasting Orchestra, Lars-Erik Larsson conductor.*

KALNINS, JĀNIS.   Pernava, Latvia 3 November 1904

5116 [Two Latvian peasant dances]   6'
1.Giocoso 2.Rustico
2,2(2nd alt. E.H.),2,2(2nd alt. C.Bn.)-4,2,3,
1-B.Dr.,S.Dr.-Str.
Universal Edition, Vienna, ᶜ1936
Score 15 p.

KALOMIRIS, MANOLIS.
                    Smyrna, Turkey 26 December 1883
                         Athens 3 April 1962

5858 L'anneau de la mère [The mother's   16'
ring. Suite from the opera]
1.Preludio 2.[Entrance of the lady] 3.[The
Christmas Eve revel]
3*,3*,3*,2-4,3,3,1-Timp.,Perc.-
Cel.,Hp.-Str.
Athens [Privately published by composer]
Score 59 p.
*From the opera in three acts, after the play
by Giannis Kambyssis. Opera composed 1916-17.
First performance of suite Athens, 12 October
1953, National Broadcasting Orchestra of
Athens, the composer conducting.*

368v [Concertino, violin and orchestra]   18'
1.Allegro vigoroso 2.Intermezzo 3.Giocoso
Solo Vn.-2(2nd alt. Picc.),2,2,2-4,2-Timp.-
Str.

Ms.
Score 62 p. Large folio
Composed 1955. First performance Athens, 20 January 1957, Athens State Orchestra, Andreas Paridis conductor, Viron Kolassis soloist.

6440 [Minas the rebel, corsair of the   *18'*
Aegean]
3*,3*,4*(1Cl. in E-flat, ad lib.),3*-6,4,4,1
-Timp.,Perc.-Cel.,2Hp.-Str.
Athens, C1952 by Manolis Kalomiris
Score 77 p.
Suggested by Costi Bastia's novel of the same name. Composed 1939. First performance Athens, 28 October 1940, Orchestra of the Athens Conservatoire, Leonidas Zoras conductor. Alternate title: Le Corsair.

5848 La mort de la vaillante, poème sym-   *13'*
phonique en forme de ballet
3*,3*,3*,3*-4,3,3,1-Timp.,Perc.-Hp.-Str.
Institut Français d'Athènes, Athens, 1948,
Cby Union des Compositeurs Hellènes, Athens
Score 60 p.
Composed 1944. First concert performance Athens, 26 October 1945, National State Orchestra, the composer conducting.

6441 [Rhapsody, Op. 22. Transcribed for   *8'*
orchestra by Gabriel Pierné]
3(3rd alt. Picc.),2(2nd alt. E.H.),2,2-4,3,3-
Timp.,Perc.-2Hp.-Str.
[Friends of Greek Music] Athens, 1957
Score 48 p.
Composed 1921 for piano. First performance of transcription, Athens, 12 December 1925, Orchestra of the Concert Society, Dimitri Mitropoulos conductor.

5906 Suite de la nouvelle Hellade, Op. 5   *25'*
[1.][From the old woman's stories] 2.[From the story of Erotocritos and Aretousa] 3. [Like a humorous dance] 4.Finale [The palace]
3(3rd alt. Picc.),3*,3*,3*-4,3,3,1-Timp.,Perc.-Cel.,2Hp.-Str.
Athens, C1958 by Manolis Kalomiris
Score 175 p.
Composed 1906-08. First performance of orchestral version Athens, 20 December 1910, Orchestra of the Conservatoire, the composer conducting. Revised 1936. Also known as Suite Grècque.

5939 [Symphony no. 1, La levendia,   *40'*
Op. 21, C minor]
1.Maestoso patetico - Molto vivace 2.[Cemetery on the mountainside] 3.Scherzo 4. (Finale) [Byzantine hymn to the Virgin victorious]
3(3rd alt. Picc.),3(3rd alt. E.H.),5*(1Cl. in E-flat),3(3rd alt. C.Bn.)-Alto Sax.-6,4,4,1-Timp.,Perc.-Pno.,Cel.,2Hp.-Chorus(SATB)-Str.
Union des Compositeurs Hellènes, Athens, C1956
Score 226 p.
Composed 1918-20. First performance Athens, 15 September 1920, Military Orchestra, Chorus of the Greek Conservatoire, the composer conducting. Also known as Valour Symphony.

5907 [Symphony no. 3, Palamas, in D]   *32'*
1.Moderato 2.Scherzo: Vivo 3.Lento ma non troppo 4.Finale: Calmo - Vivo
3*,3*,3*,3(3rd alt. C.Bn.)-4,3,3,1-Timp.,Perc.-Cel.,Hp.-Narrator-Str.
Athens, C1956 by Manolis Kalomiris
Score 171 p. Large folio
Text is four poems by Costi Palamas. Composed 1954-55. First performance Athens, 22 January 1956, Hellenic State Orchestra, Andreas Paridis conductor, Thanos Kotsopoulos narrator.

KAMINSKI, HEINRICH.
   Tiengen, Baden, Germany 4 July 1886
   Ried, Bavaria 21 June 1946

1648 Concerto grosso für Doppelorchester   *30'*
1.Breit mit grossem Ausdruck 2.Allegro più moto 3.Fuga
2Soli: Vn.,Va.,Vc. 2Orchestra: 1,1,0,1-1,1-Timp.,Perc.-Pno.(I)-Str.
Universal-Edition, Vienna, C1923
Score 96 p. Large folio
Composed 1922-23. First performance Kassel, June 1923.

932s Werk für Streichorchester [from the   *60'*
string quartet, F-sharp minor. Arranged by Reinhard Schwarz]
Solo Vn.-Str.
Universal-Edition, Vienna, C1928
Score 64 p.

KÄMPF, KARL.   Berlin 31 August 1874
   Munich 14 November 1950

208s [Two melodies, Op. 26]
1.Liebeslied 2.Wanderlied
Str.
O. Jonasson Eckermann, Berlin, C1905
Score 7 p.

KAPLAN, SOL.   b. 1919

772p Concerto [piano and orchestra]
1.Moderato 2.Adagio cantabile 3.Allegro con fuoco
Solo Pno.-0,1,0,1-1,1-Timp.,Xyl.-Str.
Ms.
Score 128 p.
Composed 1939.

5033 Overture to a three-minute egg
Fl.,Bn.-3Tpt.-S.Dr.,Cym.-Cel.-Str.
Ms.
Score 24 p.

KARASTOYANOFF, ASSEN PAVLOV.
   b. Samokov, Bulgaria 3 June 1893

5559 [Balkan suite]   *19'*
1.[On the shore of Iskar] 2.La danse de fête 3.[The shepherd and the quiet star-covered night] 4.[At the fair (dance)]
2(2nd alt. Picc.),2(2nd alt. E.H.),2,2-4,2,3,1-Timp.,Perc.-Cel.,Hp.-Str.
Choudens, Paris, C1931

Karastoyanoff, Assen Pavlov

Score 78 p.
*Composed 1923. First performance Assenovgrad,
Bulgaria, October 1923, Symphonic Orchestra of
Assenovgrad, the composer conducting.*

5547 [Oriental dance poem]   *7'*
2,2(2nd alt. E.H.),2,2-4,2,3,1-Timp.,Perc.-Str.
Choudens, Paris, ᶜ1931
Score 18 p.
*Composed 1924. First performance Assenovgrad,
Bulgaria, May 1924, Symphonic Orchestra of
Assenovgrad, the composer conducting.*

KAREL, RUDOLF.   Pilsen, Bohemia 9 November 1880
Terezin (Theresienstadt)
concentration camp, Bohemia 5 March 1945

1814 Démon [symphonic poem] Op. 23   *12'*
4*,3*,4*(1Cl. in E-flat),3*-4,4,3,1-Timp.,Perc.
-Pno.(alt. Cel.),Hp.-Str.
N. Simrock, Berlin, ᶜ1922
Score 100 p.
*Composed 1918-19. First performance Prague
1921, Vaclav Talich conductor.*

Slavische Tanzweisen [Slavic dance tunes]
Op. 16
1059 No. 1. C major   *4'*
1127 No. 2. G major   *3'*
3*,2,2,2-4,2,3,1-Timp.Perc.-Str.(Hp. in no. 2)
N. Simrock, Berlin, ᶜ1921
Scores: 50 p., 50 p.
*Composed 1912; first performance Prague, 1912,
Karl Nebdal conductor.*

832 Slavisches Scherzo-Capriccio, Op. 6   *8'*
3(3rd alt. Picc.),2,2,2-4,3(3rd ad lib.),3-
Timp.,Perc.-Hp.-Str.
N. Simrock, Berlin, ᶜ1912
Score 47 p.
Composed 1904. First performance Prague, 1904.

KARKOFF, MAURICE INGVAR.   Stockholm 17 March 1927

402m [Concerto, trombone and orchestra,   *15'*
Op. 35]
1.Moderato 2.Lento mesto ed elegiaco
3.Finale: Allegro vivace
Solo Tbn.-2(2nd alt. Picc.),2,2,2-3,2-Timp.,
Perc.-Str.
Ms.
Score 64 p.
*Composed 1958. First performance Norrköping,
Sweden, 4 December 1959, Orchestra of Norr-
köping, Herbert Blomstedt conductor, Magnus
Björklund soloist.*

434c [Concerto, violoncello and orchestra, *18'*
Op. 31]
1.Allegro 2.Lento espressivo 3.Finale
Solo Vc.-2(2nd alt. Picc.),2,2,2-2,1,1-Timp.,
Perc.-Str.
Ms.
Score 89 p.
*Composed 1958. First performance Örebro, Swe-
den, 20 October 1958, Örebro Orkesterförening,
Rune Larsson conductor, Guido Vecchi soloist.*

2316s [Short variations for string quartet *14'*
or string orchestra, Op. 9]
Str.
Edition Suecia, Stockholm, ᶜ1963
Score 17 p.
Composed 1953-56.

KARLOWICZ, MIECZYSLAW.
Wiszniewo, Poland 11 December 1876
Zakopane, Poland 8 February 1909

489v [Concerto, violin, Op. 8, A major]
1.Allegro moderato 2.Andante 3.Finale:
Vivace assai
Solo Vn.-2,2,2,2-4,2,3,1-Timp.-Str.
Schlesinger, Berlin, ᶜ1906
Score 99 p.

710 [Lithuanian rhapsody] Op. 11
3(3rd alt. Picc.),3*,3*,2-4,2,3-Timp.,Cym.,
Trgl.-Str.
Gebethner & Wolff, Warsaw, 1909
Score 47 p.

1649 [Primeval melodies, Op. 10]
1.[The song of the eternal yearning] 2.[The
song of love and death] 3.[The song of the
universe]
3(3rd alt. Picc.),3*,3*,3*-4,3,3,1-Timp.,Perc.
-Str.
Gebethner & Wolff, Warsaw [n.d.]
Score 81 p.

129 [Returning waves, tone poem, Op. 9]
3(3rd alt. Picc.),3*,3*,3*-4,3,3,1-Timp.,Perc.
-Hp.-Str.
Schlesinger, Berlin [n.d.]
Score 67 p.

709 [A sad tale, Op. 13]
4(1Alto Fl.,3rd alt. Picc.),4,4*(1Cl. in E-
flat),4*-6,3,3,1-Timp.,Gong.,Trgl.-Str.
Gebethner & Wolff, Warsaw [n.d.]
Score 31 p.

565s [Serenade, Op. 2, C major]
1.[March] 2.[Romance] 3.[Waltz] 4.[Finale]
Str.
Polskie Wydawnictwo Muzyczne, Cracow, 1954
Score 48 p.

708 [Stanislaus and Anna of Oswiecim, symphonic
poem, Op. 12]
4(4th alt. Picc.),4*,4*(1Cl. in E-flat),4*-6,
3,3,1-Timp.,Perc.-2Hp.-Str.
Gebethner & Wolff, Warsaw [n.d.]
Score 75 p.

KASHPEROV, LÉOCADIE.

4537 [Symphony, Op. 4, B minor]
1.Andante - Allegro risoluto - Andante 2.Alle-
gretto scherzando - Presto 3.Andante 4.
Finale: Andante sostenuto - Molto allegro -
Largo
3*,2(2nd alt. E.H.),2,2-4,2,3,1-Timp.-Str.
Bessel, St. Petersburg [n.d.]
Score 147 p.

KASSERN, TADEUSZ ZYGFRYD.
Lwów, Poland 19 March 1904
New York 2 May 1957

436m Concertino, oboe and string   6'
orchestra [Op. 29]
1.Allegro grazioso 2.Lento 3.Vivace assai
Solo Ob.-Str.
Ms.
Score 19 p.
*Composed 1946. First performance Chautauqua,
New York, 29 July 1950, Chautauqua Symphony
Orchestra, Franco Autori conductor, Arno
Mariotti soloist.*

2137s [Concerto, string orchestra, no. 1,   18'
Op. 15]
1.Allegro deciso e moltoritmico 2.Minuetto
3.Adagio 4.Rondo
Str.
Polskie Wydawnictwo Muzyczne, Cracow, ^c1945
Miniature score 58 p.
*Composed 1936; original version lost. Rewrit-
ten 1943. First performance Cracow, September 1945, Cracow Philharmonic, Walerjan Bierdiajew conductor.*

KÄSSMAYER, MORITZ.   Vienna 20 March 1831
Vienna 9 November 1884

[Folksongs for string orchestra. Arranged
by Moritz Kässmayer]
644s [Austrian songs, vol. VII, nos. 25-28,
Op. 30]
477s [Austrian songs, vol. VIII, nos. 29-32,
Op. 31]
593s [Viennese songs, vol. X, nos. 37-40,
Op. 34]
725s [Viennese songs, vol. XI, nos. 41-44,
Op. 36]
213s [German songs, vol. XIII, nos. 49-52,
Op. 41]
Str.
Schlesinger, Berlin [n.d.]
Scores: 21 p., 21 p., 19 p., 19 p., 21 p.

KATTNIGG, RUDOLF.
Oberdorf bei Treffen, Austria 9 April 1895
Klagenfurt, Austria 2 September 1955

1651 Burleske Suite, Op. 5   32'
1.Praeludium 2.Allegretto scherzando
3.Intermezzo 4.Rondo giocoso
3*,3*,2,3-4,3,3,1-Timp.,Perc.-Hp.-Str.
Wiener Philharmonischer Verlag, ^c1924
Score 123 p.
*Composed 1922. First performance Vienna,
February 1924, Leopold Reichwein conductor.*

KAUF, FRANZ.   Liegnitz, Germany 6 March 1883

31s Abendmusik
Str.(Cb. ad lib.)
Score: Ms. 6 p.
Parts: Cieplik, Beuthen [n.d.]

KAUFFMANN, FRITZ.   Berlin 17 June 1855
Magdeburg 29 September 1934

577p [Concerto, piano, Op. 25, C minor]
1.Allegro 2.Andante 3.Allegro giocoso
Solo Pno.-2,2,2,2-4,2-Timp.-Str.
Heinrichshofen, Magdeburg [n.d.]
Score 131 p.

720v [Concerto, violin, Op. 27, D minor]
1.Allegro moderato 2.Romanze: Andante
3.Vivace
Solo Vn.-2,2,2,2-4,2,3-Timp.,Trgl.-Str.
Heinrichshofen, Magdeburg [n.d.]
Score 82 p.
*Composed 1892. First performance Magdeburg,
8 November 1893, the composer conducting,
Felix Berber soloist.*

706v [Concerto, violin, no. 2, Op. 50, B minor]
1.Allegro, molto moderato 2.Intermezzo:
Andante 3.Finale: Allegro non troppo, ma con
brio
Solo Vn.-2,2,2,2-4,2,3,1-Timp.-Str.
Heinrichshofen, Magdeburg, ^c1909
Score 73 p.
*Composed 1907. First performance Berlin, 14
November 1908, Felix Berber soloist.*

583c [Concerto, violoncello, Op. 29, G minor]
1.Lebhaft 2.Feierlich langsam 3.Im Zeitmass
einer Tarantella
Solo Vc.-2(2nd alt. Picc.),2,2,2-4,2,3,1-
Timp.,Perc.-Str.
Heinrichshofen, Magdeburg, ^c1899
Score 51 p.

5632 [Dramatic overture for orchestra, Op. 23]
2(2nd alt. Picc.),2(2nd alt. E.H.),2,2-4,2,3,
1-Timp.,Cym.-Str.
Carl Paez, Berlin, ^c1893
Score 43 p.

KAUN, BERNHARD.   Milwaukee 5 April 1899

957m Sinfonia concertante for horn and   28'
orchestra
1.Moderato 2.Lento 3.Allegro con moto e
capriccioso 4.Allegro
Solo Hn.-3*,3*,3*,2-0,2,2-Timp.,Perc.-Cel.,Hp.-
Str.
Jupiter, Hollywood, ^c1940 by Bernhard Kaun
Score 110 p.
*Composed 1939. First performance Rochester,
New York, 11th Annual Festival of American
Music, 1 May 1941, Rochester Philharmonic
Orchestra, Howard Hanson conductor, Wendell
Hoss soloist.*

2841 Sketches, suite for orchestra   20'
1.Moderato (Scherzando) 2.Vivace (Grotesque)
3.Adagio 4.Allegro molto 5.Humoresque
6.Molto moderato 7.Allegro molto
3*,2,3(3rd alt. B.Cl.),3*-4,3,3,1-Timp.,Perc.-
Hp.-Str.
Ms.
Score 134 p.
Composed 1925. First performance Rochester,

Kaun, Hugo Wilhelm Ludwig

*New York, 29 April 1927, Rochester Philhar-
monic Orchestra, the composer conducting.*

KAUN, HUGO WILHELM LUDWIG.   Berlin 21 March 1863
                              Berlin 2 April 1932

1084 Am Rhein [overture, Op. 90]   *12'*
      3*,2,2,2-4,2,3,1-Timp.,Trgl.-Hp.-Str.
      Zimmermann, Leipzig, ᶜ1912
      Score 58 p.
      *Composed 1912. First performance Berlin,
      1912, Theodore Spiering conductor.*

627p [Concerto, piano, Op. 50,   *40'*
      E-flat minor]
      1.Nicht zu schnell, markig 2.Ruhig, mit
      innigster Empfindung 3.Sehr lebhaft, freudig
      erregt
      Solo Pno.-2,2,2,2-3,2,3-Timp.-Str.
      Rahter, Hamburg, ᶜ1903
      Score 125 p.

664p [Concerto, piano, no. 2, Op. 115, C minor]
      1.Energisch, nicht zu schnell 2.Sehr ruhig
      und innig 3.Etwas bewegt
      Solo Pno.-2(2nd alt. Picc.),2,2,2-4,2,3-Timp.-
      Str.
      André, Offenbach a.M. [n.d.]
      Score 158 p.
      Composed 1924.

890v Es war einmal [fantasy piece for violin
      and orchestra, Op. 66]
      Solo Vn.-3(3rd alt. Picc.),2*,2,2-4,2,3,1-
      Timp.,Trgl.-Hp.-Str.
      R. Kaun, Berlin, ᶜ1906
      Score 59 p.

5231 Festival march and hymn to liberty, sym-
      phonic poem, Op. 29
      3*,2,2,2-4,3,3,1-Timp.,Perc.-Org.(ad lib.)-
      Chorus(SATB, ad lib.)-Str.
      William Kaun, Milwaukee/Richard Kaun, Berlin,
      ᶜ1898 by Hugo Kaun
      Score 39 p.
      *The hymn to liberty is the Star-Spangled Ban-
      ner. Composed 1897 for the inauguration of
      the seventh season of the Chicago Symphony
      Orchestra. First performance Chicago, 22
      October 1897, Chicago Symphony Orchestra,
      Theodore Thomas conductor.*

2164 [Festive entrance march, Op. 99]   *10'*
      3*,2,2,3*-4,3,3,1-3Cnt.,3Tpt. backstage-Timp.,
      Perc.-Chorus(ad lib.)-Str.
      Zimmermann, Leipzig, ᶜ1915
      Score 31 p.
      *Composed 1915. First performance Berlin, 1915,
      Albert Thierfelder conductor.*

611c Gesangscene, Op. 35 [Vocal scene]
      Solo Vc.-2,2,2,2(2nd ad lib.)-3Hn.(3rd ad lib.)
      -Timp.-Hp.(ad lib.)-Str.
      Rahter, Hamburg, ᶜ1902
      Score 23 p.

2194 Hanne Nüte [A story of birds and men] *12'*
      Op. 107

3*,2,2,2-4,3,3-Timp.-Hp.-Str.
Zimmermann, Leipzig, ᶜ1918
Score 50 p.
*Composed 1917. First performance Rostock,
1918, Heinrich Schulz conductor.*

1171 Maria Magdalena [symphonic prologue   *12'*
      to Hebbel's drama, Op. 44]
      3(3rd alt. Picc.),3*,3*,2-4,3,3,1-Timp.,Perc.-
      Hp.-Str.
      Kahnt, Leipzig, ᶜ1904
      Score 40 p.
      *Composed 1895. First performance Chicago,
      1897, Theodore Thomas conductor.*

Originalkompositionen, Op. 70 [small or string
orchestra]
1653 No. 1. Fröhliches Wandern   *8'*
1654 No. 2. Idyll   *6'*
547s No. 3. Albumblatt (Str. only)   *5'*
1655 No. 4. Variationen   *12'*
1656 No. 5. Elegie   *6'*
1657 No. 6. Rondo   *8'*
      2,1,2,1-2,2,1-Timp.(ad lib.)-Str.
      Vieweg, Berlin, ᶜ1906, 1907
      Scores: 15 p., 13 p., 3 p., 20 p., 7 p., 13 p.
      *Composed 1906. First performance Berlin, 1907,
      Felix Weingartner conductor.*

1652 Sir John Falstaff [symphonic poem,   *20'*
      Op. 60]
      3*,2,3*,3*-4,3,3,1-Timp.,Perc.-Hp.-Str.
      Ries & Erler, Berlin, ᶜ1905 by Hugo Kaun
      Score 75 p.
      *Completed and first performed Berlin, 1905,
      Felix Weingartner conductor.*

1139 [Suite no. 1, From the March of   *35'*
      Brandenburg, Op. 92]
      1.[The heath of the March] 2.[Evening] 3.
      [Minuet] 4.[Nocturnal song] 5.[Of memorable
      times]
      3(3rd alt. Picc.),2(2nd alt. E.H.),3*,3*-4,3,
      3,1-Timp.,Perc.-Hp.-Str.
      Zimmermann, Leipzig, ᶜ1913
      Score 160 p.
      Composed 1912. First performance Berlin 1913.

5625 [Symphony no. 1, To my fatherland,
      Op. 22, D minor]
      1.Grave - Allegro 2.Andante moderato, quasi
      Adagio 3.Maestoso - Allegro agitato -
      Maestoso
      3(3rd alt. Picc.),2(2nd alt. E.H.),2,2-4,2,3,
      1-Timp.,Cym.-Str.
      Breitkopf & Härtel, Leipzig, ᶜ1898 by composer
      Score 143 p.
      Composed 1893.

1660 [Symphony no. 3, Op. 96, E minor]   *45'*
      1.Ruhig, ausdrucksvoll 2.Scherzo, Lebhaft
      3.Adagio, sehr ruhig 4.Finale: Etwas bewegt
      3*,3*,3*,3*-4,3,3,1-Timp.,B.Dr.-Cel.,Hp.-Str.
      Zimmermann, Leipzig, ᶜ1914
      Score 148 p.
      *Composed 1913. First performance Cassel, 1913,
      Robert Laugs conductor.*

[Three bagatelles, string orchestra, Op. 88]
185s No. 1. Liebeslied
186s No. 2. Mondnacht [Moonlit night]
187s No. 3. Menuett
Str.
Vieweg, Berlin, c1911
Scores: 5 p., 5 p., 7 p.

[Three simple pieces, Op. 76]
1658 No. 1. Scherzo   8'
2,2,2,2-4,2,-Timp.-Str.
1085 No. 2. Notturno   8'
2,2,2,2-2Hn.-Hp.(ad lib.)-Str.
1659 No. 3. Intermezzo   6'
2,2,2,2-4,2-Timp.-Str.
Vieweg, Berlin, c1907, 1908
Scores: 23 p., 15 p., 19 p.
Composed 1907. First performance Berlin,
1908, Leo Blech conductor.

Two symphonic poems composed to Longfellow's
Song of Hiawatha, Op. 43
109 No. 1. Minnehaha   12'
110 No. 2. Hiawatha   15'
3(3rd alt. Picc.),3*,3*,3-6,3,3,2-Timp.,Perc.-
2Hp.-Str.
Rahter, Hamburg, c1902
Scores: 47 p., 70 p.
Composed 1900. First performance Chicago,
1901, Theodore Thomas conductor.

KAY, HERSHY.   Philadelphia 17 November 1919

6557 Western symphony   26'
1.Andante 2.Slowly 3.Allegro 4.Saturday
night
2(both alt. Picc.),2,3*(2nd alt. Cl. in E-
flat),2-4,3(1st & 2nd alt. Cnt.),3(2nd alt.
Euph.),1-Timp.,Perc.-Pno.(alt. Cel.),Hp.-Str.
Boosey & Hawkes, New York, c1957
Score 265 p.
Commissioned by the New York City Ballet.
Composed 1954, on western themes. First performance New York, 7 September 1954, New York
City Ballet and Orchestra, Leon Barzin conductor, George Balanchine choreographer.

KAY, ULYSSES.   Tucson, Arizona 7 January 1917

1973s Ancient saga, a design for modern   8'
dance
Pno.-Str.
Ms.
Score 17 p.
Composed 1947.

1059m Brief elegy   5'
Solo Ob.-Str.
Ms.
Score 5 p.
Composed 1946. First performance Washington,
D.C., 9 May 1948, National Gallery Orchestra,
Richard Bales conductor, Leonard Shifrin
soloist.

953m Concerto for oboe   15'
1.Allegro 2.Lento 3.Allegro
Solo Ob.-2(2nd alt. Picc.),1(alt. E.H.),2,2-

4,2,1-Timp.-Str.
Ms.
Score 48 p. Large folio
Composed 1940. First performance Rochester,
16 April 1940, Rochester Civic Orchestra,
Howard Hanson conductor, Robert Sprenkle
soloist.

6269 Concerto for orchestra   18'
1.Allegro moderato 2.Adagio 3.Andante
2(2nd alt. Picc.),2,2,2-4,3,3,1-Timp.,Perc.-
Str.
Composer's Facsimile Edition, New York, c1952
by Ulysses Kay
Score 80 p. Large folio
Composed 1948. First public performance
broadcast on Music in the Making, New York,
22 May 1954, David Broekman conductor.

3851 [Danse Calinda, ballet in two   25'
scenes. Scene 1]
2(2nd alt. Picc.),1(alt. E.H.),2,1-2,2,2-Timp.,
Perc.-Pno.-Str.
Ms.
Score 62 p. Large folio
From the ballet based on a story by Ridgely
Torrence. Composed 1941. First performance
Rochester, 23 April 1941, Rochester Civic
Orchestra, Howard Hanson conductor.

4230 [Danse Calinda, ballet in two   14'
scenes. Suite from Scene 2]
2(2nd alt. Picc.),1(alt. E.H.),2,1-2,2,2-Timp.,
Perc.-Pno.-Str.
Ms.
Score 57 p. Large folio
Composed 1947. First performance New York,
23 May 1947, National Orchestral Association,
Leon Barzin conductor. Winner of the Anna
Babbit Gardner Award, Boston, 1947.

3898 Five mosaics   8'
1.Allegro 2.Lento 3.Allegretto 4.Andante
5.Allegro
1,1,1,1-2,1,1-Timp.,Perc.-Cel.-Str.
Ms.
Score 20 p. Large folio
Composed 1940.

6301 Portrait suite (after recent   18'
sculpture)
1.Prologue 2.Asymetric [sic] 3.Reclining
figure 4.Blossoming 5.Epilogue
2(2nd alt. Picc.),2,2,2-4,3,3,1-Timp.,Perc.-
Hp.-Str.
Ms. [c1952 by Ulysses Kay]
Score 128 p. Large folio
Movement 2 suggested by two sculptures by
Wilhelm Lehmbruch: Kneeling Woman, and
Rising Youth. Movement 3 suggested by Henry
Moore's Reclining Figure. Movement 4 sug-
gested by the sculpture Blossoming by
Jacques Lipchitz. Composed 1948. First
performance Erie, Pennsylvania, 22 April
1964, Erie Philharmonic Orchestra, James
Sample conductor. Awarded the Phoenix
Symphony Orchestra award, 1948, by the Arizona
Musicians Club.

Kay, Ulysses

5344 Serenade for orchestra   18'
1.Andante amabile 2.Presto 3.Elegy 4.Allegro
2(2nd alt. Picc.),2,2,2-4,2,3,1-Timp.-Str.
Ms.
Score 66 p. Large folio
Commissioned by the Louisville Orchestra. Composed 1954. First performance Louisville, Kentucky, 18 September 1954, Louisville Orchestra, Robert Whitney conductor.

4715 A short overture   7'
2(2nd alt. Picc.),2,2,2-2,2,2-Timp.,Perc.-Str.
Ms.
Score 36 p. Large folio
Composed 1946. First performance Brooklyn, 31 March 1947, New York City Symphony, Leonard Bernstein conductor. Won the Third Annual George Gershwin Memorial Award, 1947.

6266 Sinfonia in E   20'
1.Larghetto 2.Allegro pesante 3.Adagio
4.Allegro
2(2nd alt. Picc.),2,2,2-4,3,3,1-Timp.-Str.
Composers Facsimile Edition, New York, c1953
by Ulysses Kay
Score 105 p. Large folio
Composed 1950. First performance Rochester, New York, 2 May 1951, Eastman-Rochester Symphony Orchestra, Howard Hanson conductor.

3642 Sinfonietta for orchestra   10'
1.Allegro 2.Andante 3.Finale: Allegro
2,2,2,2-4,2-Timp.-Hp.-Str.
Ms.
Score 52 p. Large folio
Composed 1939.

4714 Suite for brass choir   9'
1.Fanfare and lyric 2.Chorale 3.Toccata
0,0,0,0-4,4,3,1
Ms.
Score 17 p.
Composed 1943. First performance Cincinnati, Ohio, spring 1947, Cincinnati Conservatory Brass Choir, Ernest N. Glover conductor.

6716 Suite for orchestra   19'
1.Fanfare 2.Three-four 3.Scherzo 4.Olden
tune 5.Finale
3*,3*,3*,3*-4,3,3,1-Timp.,Perc.-Pno.-Str.
Ms.
Score 91 p. Large folio
Composed 1945. First performance New York, American Youth Orchestra, Dean Dixon conductor. Awarded the Broadcast Music, Inc. Prize, 1947.

KAZANLY, NIKOLAI IVANOVICH.
                Tiraspol, Russia 17 December 1869
                St. Petersburg 5 August 1916

1851 [Carnival night, fantasy for orchestra]
3,3*,3*,3*-4,2,3,1-Timp.,Perc.-Hp.-Str.
Belaieff [n.p.] 1916
Score 57 p.
Composed 1914.

1498 Glinkiana [Suite of piano compositions of
M. Glinka. Orchestrated by N. Kazanly]
1.Fugue 2.Parting - Nocturne 3.Scottish
theme with variations
2,2*,2,2-4,2,3,1-Timp.-Hp.-Str.
Jurgenson, Moscow [n.d.]
Score 59 p.

1650 [Miranda. Overture]   8'
3*,3*,3*,3*-4,3,3,1-Timp.,Perc.-Hp.-Str.
Zimmermann, Leipzig [1911]
Score 35 p.
From the three act opera.

1460 [Villa by the sea, fantasy after the
painting by Arnold Böcklin]
3(3rd alt. Picc.),3*,3*,3*-4,2,3,1-Timp.,Perc.-
Pno.,Cel.,2Hp.-Str.
Belaieff, Leipzig, 1914
Score 50 p.
Composed 1913.

KAZDIN, ANDREW.

7191 Marche baroque, concert piece for band
2*,2*,6*(1 Alto Cl.,1Cb.Cl.),2*-5Sax.(SATBB)-
2,3,Cnt.,2,Bar.,1-Timp.,Cym.,S.Dr.-Cb.
Far West Music (Western International Music),
Los Angeles, c1954 by Andrew Kazdin
Score in reduction 12 p.

KECHLEY, GERALD. Seattle, Washington 18 March 1919

5626 [Symphony no. 1]   25'
1.Adagio con espresione 2.Allegretto scherzando 3.Adagio
2(2nd alt. Picc.),2,2,2-2,2,1-Timp.,Perc.-Str.
Ms.
Score 97 p. Large folio
Commissioned by the Seattle Women's Symphony. Composed 1956. First performance Seattle, Washington, 2 October 1956, Seattle Women's Symphony, Rachel Swarner Welke conductor.

KEENAN, GERALD.   Hornell, New York 21 June 1906

180m An elegy, for solo horn and strings   9'
Solo Hn.-Timp.-Str.
Ms.
Score 19 p.
Originally composed as Andante for Horn and Strings, 1934. Expanded to present version 1941. First performance West Chester, Pennsylvania, 1941, College Sinfonietta, the composer conducting.

KEGEL, C. VON.

1546s Des Geigers Heimweh, Ländler, Op. 65
Str.
Score: Ms. 13 p.
Parts: [n.p., n.d.]

986v Nocturne for viola and orchestra, Op. 78
Solo Va.-1,1,2,1-2Hn.-Str.
Score: Ms. 29 p.
Parts: [n.p., n.d.]

KÉLER-BÉLA.   Bártfeld, Hungary 13 February 1820
Wiesbaden, Germany 20 November 1882

Real name: Adalbert Paul von Kéler
Also published as Albert von Kéler.

4595 [Romantic overture, Op. 75]   8'
Edited by Max Villinger
1,1,1-0,1,1-Timp.,Perc.-Harm.-Str.
B. Schott's Söhne, Mainz, c1939
Score in reduction 11 p.

KELLER, GEORG.

1033s Erinnerung and Valse caprice, Op. 15
nos. 1 and 2
Bells(ad lib.)-Str.
Leuckart [n.p., n.d.]
Score 7 p.

992s Liebesgeständnis [Love's avowal] Op. 17
Str.
Leuckart [n.p., n.d.]
Score 6 p.

KELLER, HOMER.   1915

808p Concerto for piano and orchestra   15'
1.Allegro 2.Andante con moto 3.Allegro
Solo Pno.-2(2nd alt. Picc.),2,2,2-2,1,1-Timp.,
Perc.-Str.
Ms.
Score 94 p. Large folio
Commissioned by the Ojai Festival. Composed
1949. First performance Ojai, California, 29
May 1949, Ojai Festival Chamber Orchestra,
Thor Johnson conductor, Shura Cherkassky
soloist.

4802 Overture 1947   3'
3*,2,2,2-4,3,3,1-Timp.,S.Dr.-Str.
Ms.
Score 23 p. Large folio
Composed 1947.

1074m Serenade for clarinet and strings   6'
Solo Cl.-Str.
Ms.
Score 6 p.
Composed 1937. First performance Rochester,
New York, 1937, Eastman-Rochester Philharmonic
Orchestra, Howard Hanson conductor.

KELLER, WALTER.   Chicago 23 February 1873
Chicago 7 July 1940

[Synchronous prelude and fugue in F, Op. 10]
3156 Prelude   5'
3157 Fugue   5'
3158 Synchronous prelude and fugue   5'
1,2,2,1-4,2,3,1-Timp.-Org.-Str.
Ms.
Scores: 26 p. each
Originally composed for two pianos, 1919.
First performance Chicago, 11 February 1924,
Chicago Symphony, Frederick Stock conductor,
Stanley Martin organist.

KELLEY, EDGAR STILLMAN.
Sparta, Wisconsin 14 April 1857
New York 12 November 1944

1958 Aladdin, a Chinese suite, Op. 10
1.At the wedding of Aladdin and the princess
2.In the palace garden 3.[The flight of the
genie with the palace] 4.The return - Feast
of lanterns
3*,2,2,2-4,2,3,1-Timp.,Perc.-Hp.,Mand.-Str.
G. Schirmer, New York, c1915 by the composer
Score 103 p.
First performance, April 1894, The San Francisco Symphony, the composer conducting.

1302s Confluentia [for strings] Op. 2 no. 2
Str.
G. Schirmer, New York, c1912
Score 7 p.

1989 The pit and the pendulum, after Edgar Allan
Poe
3(3rd alt. Picc.),3*,3*,3-4,3,3,1-Timp.,Perc.-
Hp.-Str.
G. Schirmer, New York, c1930 by the composer
Score 62 p.
First performance Cincinnati May Festival,
1925, the composer conducting. Awarded prize
by National Federation of Music Clubs.

2780 [Symphony no. 1, Gulliver, F major]   28'
1.Lento - Allegretto tranquillo 2.Lento
rubato 3.Allegro agitato 4.[Allegro]
3(3rd alt. Picc.),2,2,2-4,2,3,1-Timp.,Perc.-
Str.
Affiliated Music [n.p.] c1936
Score 161 p.
Completed 1936. First performance Cincinnati,
9 April 1937, Cincinnati Symphony Orchestra,
Eugene Goossens conductor.

3217 [Symphony no. 2, New England, Op. 33,   46'
B-flat minor]
1.Lento maestoso 2.Larghetto misterioso 3.
Lento ma non troppo 4.New England hymn
5.Allegro
3*,3*,2(2nd alt. B.Cl.),2-4,2,3,1-Timp.,Perc.-
Hp.-Str.
The Edgar Stillman-Kelley Society, c1915
Score 151 p.
Written for and first performed at Norfolk
Music Festival, Norfolk, Connecticut, 3 June
1913, Philharmonic Society of New York, the
composer conducting.

KELLY, FREDERICK SEPTIMUS.
Sydney, Australia 29 May 1881
in battle, Beaucort, France 13 November 1916

869m [Serenade, flute, Op. 7, E minor]
1.Prelude 2.Idyl 3.Minuet 4.Air and
variations 5.Jig
Solo Fl.-Hn.-Hp.-Str.
Schott, London, c1914
Score 48 p.

KEMPTER, LOTHAR. Lauingen, Bavaria 5 February 1844
Vitznau, Switzerland 14 July 1918

Kempter, Lothar

664m [Capriccio, flute, Op. 32]   *11'*
Solo Fl.-1,2,2,2-4,2,3-Timp.-Str.
Score: Ms. 70 p.
Parts: Zimmermann, Leipzig, ᶜ1902
Composed 1900. First performance Zurich, 1901.

657m [Fantaisie pastorale, Op. 71]   *10'*
Solo Fl.-1,2,2,2-4,2,3,1-Timp.,Perc.-Hp.-Str.
Zimmermann, Leipzig, ᶜ1911
Score in reduction 15 p.
Composed 1910. First performance Zurich, 1911.

656m [Wedding music, Op. 39. No. 3, Vow   *10'*
taking *and* No. 4, Festive polonaise]
Solo Fl.-1,2(2nd alt. E.H.),2,2-4,2,3-Timp.,
Trgl.-Hp.-Str.
Zimmermann, Leipzig, ᶜ1904
Score in reduction 9 p.
Composed 1902. First performance Zurich, 1903.

KENNAN, KENT WHEELER.   Milwaukee 18 April 1913

3415 Air de ballet   *2'*
2(2nd alt. Picc.),2,2,2-2Hn.2Tpt.-Timp.,Perc.-
Pno.-Str.
Ms.
Score 17 p. Large folio
Composed 1939. First performance Detroit, 1 February 1941, Detroit Symphony Orchestra, Victor Kolar conductor.

955m Andante   *5'*
Solo Ob.-2,0,2,2-3Hn.-Str.
Ms.
Score 21 p. Large folio
Composed 1939. First performance Rochester, 21 January 1941, Rochester Civic Orchestra, Howard Hanson conductor, Robert Sprenkle soloist.

954m Il Campo di Fiori   *2'30"*
Solo Tpt.-2(2nd alt. Picc.),2,2,2-2Hn.-Timp.,
Perc.-Pno.-Str.
Ms.
Score 26 p. Large folio
Refers to the flea market in Rome. Composed 1938. First performance Rochester, 5 January 1939, Rochester Civic Orchestra, Howard Hanson conductor.

781p [Concertino, piano, For an American   *13'*
going to war]
Solo Pno.-2(2nd alt. Picc.),1,2,2-4,3,3,1-
Timp.,Perc.-Str.
Ms.
Score 91 p.
Completed 1941.

Dance divertimento
See: Air de ballet; Lament; Promenade

3417 Lament   *3'30"*
2,2,2,2-2,2-Perc.-Pno.-Str.
Ms.
Score 14 p.
Originally part of a piano quintet, 1935. Orchestrated 1939. First performance New York, 8 July 1941, NBC Symphony Orchestra, Frank Black conductor.

1127v Nocturne, viola and small orchestra   *4'*
Solo Va.-2,2,2,2-2Hn.-Timp.,Perc.-Pno.-Str.
Ms.
Score 12 p.
Composed 1938. First performance Rochester, 5 January 1939, Rochester Civic Orchestra, Howard Hanson conductor, Mordecai Lurie soloist.

3416 Promenade   *2'*
2,2,2,2-2-2,2-Timp.,Perc.-Pno.-Str.
Ms.
Score 15 p. Large folio
Composed 1938. First performance Rome, 8 June 1938, Orchestra da Santa Cecilia, Roberto Caggiano conductor.

KENNEDY-FRASER, MARJORY.
        Perth, Scotland 1 October 1857
        Edinburgh 21 November 1930

977s From the Hebrides. Arranged by Mary E.
Waddell from Songs of the Hebrides
1.Legende 2.Sea laughter 3.Sea longing
Str.
Score: Ms. 33 p.
Parts: Boosey, London, ᶜ1926

KERLL, JOHANN CASPAR VON.
        Adorf, Saxony, Germany 9 April 1627
        Munich 13 February 1693

4977 [Canzona no. 5, for organ or   *8'*
harpsichord, C major. Transcribed for orchestra by Hans F. Redlich]
3*,3*,B.Cl.,3*-2,3,3-Timp.,Perc.-Str.
Bote & Bock, Berlin, ᶜ1930
Score 24 p.
The original Canzona is published in Denkmäler der Tonkunst in Bayern, II/2, edited by Adolf Sandberger.

KERR, HARRISON.   Cleveland, Ohio 13 October 1897

305v Concerto for violin and orchestra   *21'30"*
[reduced orchestra version]
1.Andante quasi largo - Allegro 2.Lento
3.Allegro moderato
Solo Vn.-2(2nd alt. Picc.),2*,2*,2-2,2,1-Timp.,
Perc.-Str.
Composers Facsimile Edition, New York, ᶜ1958
by Harrison Kerr
Score 113 p.
Composed 1950-51. First performance New York, 12 December 1954, Symphony of the Air, David Brockman conductor, Oscar Ravina soloist. Revised 1956.

3363 Dance suite   *15'*
1.Maestoso 2.Grazioso 3.Andante moderato
4.Allegro vivace
3(3rd alt. Picc.),3*,3,3-4,3,3,1-Timp.,Perc.-
Pno.-Str.(Or: Timp.,Perc.-2Pno.-Str.)
Ms.
Score 69 p.
Composed 1938 as Dance Sonata for two pianos, timpani and percussion; first performed at Bennington College Festival, August 1938.

Orchestrated 1940 as Dance Suite; first performed Rochester, 27 October 1942, Eastman-Rochester Symphony Orchestra, Howard Hanson conductor.

7240 Episodes from The Tower of Kel   25'
  3(3rd alt. Picc.),3*,3*,3*-4,3,3,1-Timp.(2 players),Perc.-Pno.,Hp.-Str.
  Ms. c1972 by Harrison Kerr
  Score 155 p.
  Material derived from the opera The Tower of Kel, composed 1961.

7242 Sinfonietta [In one movement]   18'
  2*,2(2nd alt. E.H.),2(2nd alt. B.Cl.),2-2,2,
  2-Timp.,Perc.-Pno.-Str.
  Ms.
  Score 85 p.
  Commissioned by the University of Oklahoma Chamber Orchestra. Composed 1968. First performance Norman, Oklahoma, 25 April 1968, University of Oklahoma Chamber Orchestra, Donn Mills conductor.

6791 Symphony no. 1, in one movement   14'
  3(3rd alt. Picc.),3*,3*,3*-4,3,3,1-Timp.,Perc.
  -Pno.-Str.
  Arrow Music Press, New York, c1946
  Score 72 p.
  Composed 1927-29. Revised 1938. First performance Rochester, New York, 24 October 1945, Eastman-Rochester Symphony Orchestra, Howard Hanson conductor.

2874 [Symphony no. 2, D minor]   32'
  1.Allegro molto 2.Andantino 3.Allegro
  3(2nd & 3rd alt. Picc.),3*,3*,3*-4,3,3,1-Timp.,
  Perc.-Str.
  Ms.
  Score 197 p.
  Completed 1937.

KERVÉGUEN, G. DE.

735s Aubade [G major]
  Str.
  Score: Ms. 8 p.
  Parts: Leduc, Paris [n.d.]

1659s [Two minuets for flute, horn and strings]
  1.Menuet tendre 2.Menuet pompeux
  Fl.-Hn.(both optional)-Str.
  Le Beau, Paris [n.d.]
  Score 25 p.

KES, WILLEM.   Dordrecht, Holland 16 February 1856
                Munich 21 February 1934

970v Romance, violin and orchestra
  Solo Vn.-2,2,2,2-2Hn.-Str.
  Ms.
  Score 11 p.

KHACHATURIAN, ARAM ILICH.   Tiflis 6 June 1903
                             Moscow 2 May 1978

7117 [Gayne. Three dances from the   8'30"
  ballet]

1.Dance of young maidens 2.Lullaby 3.Sabre dance
  3*,3*,3*,2-Alto Sax.-4,3,3,1-Timp.,Perc.-Pno.,
  Cel.,Hp.-Str.
  Luck's Music Library, Detroit [n.d.]
  Score 53 p.
  Composed 1941-42; revised 1952. First performance Perm, U.S.S.R., 9 December 1942, by the Lenigrad Kirov Opera and Ballet Theatre.

6752 [Masquerade. Suite]   16'
  1.Waltz 2.Nocturne 3.Mazurka 4.Romance
  5.Galop
  2(2nd alt. Picc.),2,2,2-4,2,3,1-Timp.,Perc.-
  Str.
  Kalmus, New York [n.d.]
  Score 106 p.
  From the incidental music for M. I. Lermontov's play. First performance 1944.

3940 [Poem of Stalin]   23'
  3*,3*,2,2-4,3,3,1-Timp.,Perc.-Hp.-Chorus(SATB)
  -Str.
  Mussektor, Moscow [n.d.]
  Score 139 p.
  Composed 1938. First performance Moscow, 29 November 1938, Moscow State Orchestra and Choir, Alexander Gauck conductor.

3553 [Symphony no. 1]   25'
  1.Andante maestoso, con passione 2.Adagio
  sostenuto 3.Allegro risoluto
  3*,3*,3,2-4,3,3,1-Timp.,Perc.-Pno.,Hp.-Str.
  Mussektor, Moscow, 1939
  Score 268 p.
  Composed 1933-34. First performance Moscow, 1935, Moscow Philharmonic Orchestra, Eugen Szenkar conductor.

KHRENNIKOV, TIKHON NIKOLAIEVICH.
                b. Elets, Russia 10 June 1913

285v [Concerto for violin and orchestra, Op. 14]
  1.Allegro con fuoco 2.Andante espressivo
  3.Allegro agitato
  Solo Vn.-3(3rd alt. Picc.),2,3*,3*-4,3-Timp.,
  Perc.-Pno.,Cel.,Hp.-Str.
  State Publisher, Moscow, 1965
  Score 143 p.
  Composed 1959.

2941 [Symphony no. 1]   22'
  1.Allegro 2.Adagio 3.Allegro molto
  3*,2,2,2-4,2,3,1-Timp.,Perc.-Cel.-Str.
  Mussektor, Moscow, 1961
  Score 136 p.
  Completed 1935. First performance 10 October 1935, Moscow Radio Orchestra, Georg Sebastian conductor.

KIENZL, WILHELM.
        Waizenkirchen, Upper Austria 17 January 1857
                        Vienna 3 October 1941

Abendstimmungen [Evening moods, for strings
  and harp, Op. 53]
150s No. 1 [Harpist's evening song]   6'30"
111s No. 2 [Angelus in the convent]   6'30"

Kienzl, Wilhelm

151s No. 3 Serenade   8'
Hp.-Str.
C. Giessel, Bayreuth; Zimmermann, Leipzig
[n.d.]
Scores: 9 p. each

4659 [From old fairy tales, nine little tone
poems for piano, Op. 12. Nos. 7, 8, and 9
transcribed for orchestra]
1.[No. 7, How Sleeping Beauty comes to the old
spinning woman and pricks herself on the spin-
dle] 2.[No. 8, How Sleeping Beauty and the
whole Royal Court fall asleep] 3.[No. 9, How
Sleeping Beauty marries the prince]
2*,2,2,2-4,2,1-Timp.,Trgl.,Cym.-Hp.(ad lib.)-
Str.
Paul Voight, Kassel & Leipzig [188-?]
Score 17 p.
*These three excerpts are based on the Brothers
Grimm version of Sleeping Beauty.*

KIESSIG, GEORG.   Leipzig 17 September 1885
                         Nevers, France 20 September 1945

4362 [Festive music, for band, Op. 66   5'
no. 1]
2*,1,4(1 in E-flat),2-4Hn.,3Ten.Hn.,2Flugel-
horn,4Tpt.,3Herald Tpt.,Cnt. in E-flat,4Tbn.,
Bar.,2Tuba-Timp.,Perc.
Fr. Portius, Leipzig, C1938
Score in reduction 7 p.

4364 [Holiday music, for band, Op. 66   5'
no. 2]
2*,1,4(1 in E-flat),2-4Hn.,3Ten.Hn.,2Flugel-
horn,4Tpt.(3rd & 4th in E-flat),Cnt. in E-flat,
4Tbn.,Bar.,2Tuba-Timp.,Perc.
Fr. Portius, Leipzig, C1939
Score in reduction 4 p.

4528 [Three preludes, for band, Op. 72   9'
no. 1]
1.Im Marschtempo 2.Sehr ruhig (molto legato)
3.Froh bewegt
1,1,2-4,2Ten.Hn.,2Flugelhorn,3,1-B.Dr.-Cb.
Fr. Portius, Leipzig [n.d.]
Score 27 p.

KIETZER, ROBERT.

665m Für dich allein [For you alone]   3'
Op. 76
Solo Tpt.-2*,2,2,2-2,1,1-Dr.-Str.
Score in reduction: Ms. 8 p.
Parts: Zimmermann [n.p., 1899?]

KILPATRICK, JACK FREDERICK.
           Stilwell, Oklahoma 23 September 1915
           Muskogee, Oklahoma 22 February 1967

2314s Festival piece for string orchestra,
Op. 80
Str.
Ms. C1966 by Jack Kilpatrick
Score 8 p. Large folio
Composed 1946.

253m Romanza for oboe and strings, Op. 7   4'
Solo Ob.-Str.
Ms.
Score 5 p.
*Composed 1939. First performance Muskogee,
Oklahoma, 19 February 1941, Oklahoma State
Symphony, Victor Alessandro conductor, Walter
Kessler soloist.*

KINAPENNE, F.   b. Liège 1869

941v Petit conte [Little story]   3'
Solo Vn.-2,2,2-Str.
Score: Ms. 19 p.
Parts: P. Decourcelle, Nice, C1912
*Composed 1910. First performance Monte Carlo,
26 March 1911.*

KIRCHBACH, MAX. d. Darmstadt, Germany 10 March 1927

723m Traumbild [Vision]
Soli: Vn.,Va.,Vc.-2,2,2,2-2Hn.-Hp.-Str.
Hug, Zurich [n.d.]
Score 9 p.

KIRCHNER, LEON. Brooklyn, New York 24 January 1919

266p [Concerto, piano, no. 1]   30'
1.Allegro 2. ♩ =72-76 3. ♩ =66-72
Solo Pno.-3*,3*,2(1st alt. Cl. in E-flat),3*-
4,3,3,1-Timp.,Perc.-Cel.-Str.
Associated Music Publishers, New York, C1957
Score 102 p. Large folio
*Commissioned by the Koussevitzky Music Founda-
tion. Composed 1953. First performance New
York, 23 February 1956, New York Philharmonic,
Dimitri Mitropoulos conductor, the composer
as soloist.*

319m Concerto for violin, 'cello,   19'
10 winds and percussion
1.Allegro ma non troppo - Andante grazioso
2.Adagio - Andante
Solo Vn., Solo Vc.-1(alt. optional Picc.),1,
1,2*-1,2,2-Timp.,Perc.-Cel.
Associated Music Publishers, New York [n.d.]
Score 42 p. Large folio
*Commissioned by the Chamber Music Society of
Baltimore, Maryland. Composed 1960.*

6728 Toccata for strings, solo winds   14'
and percussion
0,1,1,1-1,1,1-Perc.-Cel.-Str.
Associated Music Publishers, New York, C1962
Score 45 p.
*Composed 1956. First performance San Francis-
co, California, 16 February 1956, San Francisco Symphony, Enrique Jordá conductor.*

KIRK, THERON.   Alamo, Texas 28 September 1919

5749 Adagietto   5'30"
1,1*,1,1-2Hn.-Timp.-Cel.-Str.
Ms.
Score 24 p. Large folio
*Composed 1953. First performance Greensboro,
North Carolina, 10 May 1955, North Carolina
Symphony, Benjamin Swalin conductor. Won the
Benjamin Award of 1954.*

COLLECTION OF ORCHESTRAL MUSIC

5895 Ballet music   *12'*
1.Overture 2.Pas de deux 3.Mazurka
4.Intermezzo 5.Finale
2(2nd alt. Picc.),2,2,2-4,3,3,1-Timp.,Perc.-
Str.
Ms.
Score 78 p. Large folio
Alternate title: Suite in Five Movements.
Composed 1958. First performance Galesburg,
Illinois, 17 May 1959, Knox-Galesburg Sym-
phony, Donn Mills conductor. Received the
Knox-Galesburg award for 1959.

5962 Concerto for orchestra (in one   *12'*
movement)
2(2nd alt. Picc.),2,2,2-4,3,3,1-Timp.,Perc.-
Pno.-Str.
Ms.
Score 66 p. Large folio
Commissioned by the West Virginia Creative
Arts Festival. Composed 1959. First per-
formance Charleston, West Virginia, 14 April
1960, Charleston Symphony Orchestra, Geoffrey
Hobday conductor.

341p Fantasy and frolic, for piano and   *10'*
orchestra
2(2nd alt. Picc.),2,2,2-4,3,3,1-Timp.,Perc.-
Pno.-Str.
Ms.
Score 50 p. Large folio
Alternate title: Dialogues. Composed 1958.
First performance Fort Wayne, Indiana, 18
February 1969, Fort Wayne Philharmonic Orches-
tra, James Sample conductor.

5750 Intrada   *4'30"*
3*,2,2,2-4,2,3-Timp.,Perc.-Str.
Ms.
Score 32 p. Large folio
Alternate title: An Opening Piece. Commis-
sioned by the San Antonio Symphony. Composed
1954. First performance Brownsville, Texas,
13 December 1954, San Antonio Symphony, Vic-
tor Alessandro conductor.

5891 An orchestra primer   *12'30"*
2(2nd alt. Picc.),2,2,2-4,3,3,1-Timp.,Perc.-
Narrator-Str.
Ms.
Score 28 p.
Can be played by a smaller orchestra. Com-
missioned by the Jacksonville Symphony Orches-
tra. Composed 1959. First performance Jack-
sonville, Florida, 29 March 1960, Jacksonville
Symphony Orchestra, James C. Pfohl conductor.

6104 [Symphony no. 2, Saga of the   *19'*
plains, D major]
2(2nd alt. Picc.),2,2(2nd alt. B.Cl.),2-4,3,
3,1-Timp.,Perc.-Hp.-Str.
Ms.
Score 76 p. Large folio
Commissioned for the Kansas Centennial Cele-
bration by the Topeka Civic Symphony. Com-
posed 1960. First performance Topeka, 25
January 1961, Topeka Civic Symphony, Everett
Fetter conductor.

KISTLER, CYRILL.   Gross-Aitingen,
              near Augsburg 12 March 1848
         Kissingen, Germany 1 January 1907

636v Serenade, Op. 72 [D minor]
Solo Vn.(or Va., or Vc.)-1,2,2,2-2Hn.-Timp.-
Str.
C. Simon, Berlin, C1903
Score 17 p.

514 Valse-Serenade, Op. 68
1,1,1,1-Hn.-Hp.(or Pno., ad lib.)-Str.
Bosworth, Leipzig, C1896
Score 11 p.

KITTL, JAN BEDRICH.
          Castle Vorlík, Bohemia 8 May 1806
               Lissa, Poland 20 July 1868

6929 [Symphony, Hunt symphony, no. 2,   *22'*
Op. 9, E-flat major] Edited by Jarmil
Burghauser
1.[Calling up - The chase begins] 2.[The chase
rests] 3.[The chase ends]
2,2,2,2-4,2,1-Timp.-Str.
[State Music Publishers] Prague, C1960
Score 140 p.
Composed 1837. First performance Prague, 7
April 1838.

KJERULF, HALFDAN.
     Christiania (now Oslo) 15 September 1815
        Grefsen, near Christiania 11 August 1868

192s [Five tone-pieces. Arranged by Karl
Wyrott]
1.Lullaby 2.Intermezzo 3.Berceuse 4.Scherzo
5.Caprice
Str.
Joh. André, Offenbach a.M. [n.d.]
Score 22 p.
Originally composed for piano solo.

1038s Wiegenlied [Cradle song]
Str.
Score: Ms. 3 p.
Parts: Ries & Erler [n.p., n.d.]

KLAAS, JULIUS.   Bochum, Germany 29 February 1888

1600s Aus galanter Zeit [From gallant   *35'*
times] Op. 10
1.Entrées 2.Sarabande 3.Gavotte 4.Menuett
5.Rigaudon
Fl.(alt. Picc.),Ob.-Str.
Ries & Erler, Berlin, C1931
Score 27 p.

KLAMI, UUNO KALERVO.
          Virolahti, Finland 20 September 1900
                    Helsinki 29 May 1961

243p [Four Finnish songs, piano and   *11'*
strings, Op. 12]
1.Lento 2.Lento molto tranquillo 3.Non
troppo adagio 4.Andante leggiero
Pno.-Str.
Fazerin Musiikkikauppa, Helsinki [n.d.]

Klami, Uuno Kalervo

Score 8 p.
*Erroneously published as Suite for Piano and
Strings. Composed 1930.*

5815 [Karelian rhapsody, Op. 15]   *13'*
4*,3*,3,3(3rd alt. C.Bn.)-4,4,3,1-Timp.,Perc.-
Cel.,2Hp.-Str.
Suomen Säveltaiteilijain Liito, Helsinki, c1936
Score 55 p.
*Composed 1927. First performance Helsinki,
1932.*

5810 [Overture to Alexis Kivi's comedy,   *9'*
The cobblers on the heath, Op. 26]
2(2nd alt. Picc.),2,2,2-2,2-Timp.-Str.
Suomen Säveltaiteilijain Liito, Helsinki, c1940
Score 67 p.
*Composed 1936. First performance Helsinki,
1937.*

4962 [3 Bf, impression at sea, Op. 11]   *6'*
Fl.,Cl.-Pno.-Str.
R.E. Westerlund, Helsinki [ca.1940]
Score 11 p.
*"Bf" is an abbreviation for Beaufort. Ori-
ginally composed as the finale of Merikuvia
[Sea pictures] Op. 7, 1928-30.*

KLAMMER, GEORGE.

825s Walzer-Intermezzo, Op. 4
Str.
[n.p., n.d.]
Score 3 p.

KLANERT, KARL.   Thale am Harz,
Germany 23 November 1873
Halle, Germany 25 January 1941

1178s Passions-Präludium, Op. 30
Solo Ob.(or Cl.)-Str.
H. Oppenheimer, Hameln [n.d.]
Score 5 p.

KLASSERT, MARTIN.

793s Frohe Laune [Good humor, gavotte, Op. 39]
Solo Vn.-Str.
B. Schott's Söhne, Mainz [n.d.]
Score 8 p.

KLAUWELL, OTTO.   Langensalza, Saxony 7 April 1851
Cologne 11 May 1917

410s Traumbild [Dream vision] Op. 19
Str.
Ries & Erler, Berlin [n.d.]
Score 3 p.

KLEBE, GISELHER WOLFGANG.
b. Mannheim, Germany 28 June 1925

4974 Con moto [Op. 2]   *8'30"*
2,2,2,2-4,2,3,1-Str.
Bote & Bock, Berlin, c1948
Score 28 p.
*Composed 1948. First performance Radio Bremen,
22 February 1953, Staatsorchester Oldenburg,
Hans Georg Ratjen conductor.*

KLECKI, PAWEŁ.
See: KLETZKI, PAUL.

KLEFFEL, ARNO.   Pössneck, Germany 4 September 1840
Nikolassee, near Berlin 15 July 1913

411s Wiegenliedchen [Cradle song]
Str.
Hermann Erler, Berlin [n.d.]
Score 5 p.

KLEIN, BRUNO OSCAR.   Osnabrück, Germany 6 June 1858
New York 22 June 1911

6979 [Kenilworth. Act II. March (Entrance of
the queen)]
3*,2,2,2-4,3,3,1-Timp.,Perc.-Str.
Hofmeister, Leipzig, c1894
Score 36 p.
*From the opera with libretto by Wilhelm Müller,
based on Sir Walter Scott's novel. First
performance Hamburg, 13 February 1895.*

551c Suite für Violoncell, Op. 28
1.Larghetto 2.Minuetto 3.Intermezzo 4.Finale
Solo Vc.-2,2,2,2-2,2-Timp.,Trgl.-Hp.-Str.
N. Simrock, Berlin, c1904
Score 46 p.

KLEIN, JOHN M. Rahns, Pennsylvania 21 February 1915

7297 African suite [for orchestra]   *ca.20'*
1.African litany 2.The rain forest 3.Moun-
tains of the Moon 4.The prayer plant 5.Spir-
its of sweet water 6.African nocturne
2(2nd alt. Picc.),1(alt. E.H.),2,1-2,3,3-
Timp.,Perc.(amplified)-Pno.(alt. Cel.),Hp.,
Guit.-Voices-Str.
Ms.
Score 163 p. Large folio
*Composed 1975. Selected for performance by
the Orchestra Society of Philadelphia as part
of its Pennsylvania Composers Project 1977,
made possible by grants from the National
Endowment for the Arts and the Pennsylvania
Council on the Arts with performance materials prepared by the Fleisher Collection of
Orchestral Music. First performance Main
Hall, Drexel University, Philadelphia, 22 May
1977, Orchestra Society of Philadelphia, Wil-
liam Smith conductor.*

1187v [Concerto, violin, in E]   *13'*
1.Lento - Allegro assai 2.Adagio ma non troppo
3.Allegro con fuoco
Solo Vn.-2(2nd alt. Picc.),2,2,2-4,3,3,1-Timp.,
Perc.-Hp.-Str.
Associated Music Publishers, New York, c1946
Score 72 p. Large folio
*Composed 1943. First performance New York,
ca.1945, CBS Symphony Orchestra, Mark Warnow
conductor, Arnold Polliekoff soloist.*

4766 Horace the bear   *7'*
Narrator-1(alt. Picc.),1,1,1-2,1,1-Timp.,Perc.
-Pno.(alt. Cel.),Hp.-Str.
Associated Music Publishers, New York [c1946]
Score 42 p. Large folio

Text from The Story of Horace, by Alice Coates.
Composed 1944. First performance New York,
1945, CBS Symphony Orchestra, Bernard Herrmann
conductor, Ogden Nash narrator.

KLEINMICHEL, RICHARD.   Posen, Germany
                    (now Poznań, Poland) 31 December 1846
                    Charlottenburg, Germany 18 August 1901

5295 [Fantasy-overture, Op. 25, A major]
2,2,2,2-4,2,3-Timp.-Str.
Breitkopf & Härtel, Leipzig [1888]
Score 69 p.

KLEMM, O.K.

823s Joie et douleur, célèbre romance russe.
Orchestrated by N. Gervasio
Solo Vn.(or Ob.)-2Cl.-Str.
P. Decourcelle, Nice [n.d.]
Score 4 p.

KLENAU, PAUL AUGUST VON.
                    Copenhagen 11 February 1883
                    Copenhagen 31 August 1946

1662 Jahrmarkt bei London (Bankholiday -   *18'*
Souvenir of Hampstead Heath, fantasy)
3*,2,2,3*-4,3,3,1-Timp.,Perc.-Pno.,Hp.,Mand.-
Solo Voice(Alto)-Str.
Universal-Edition, Vienna, c1922
Score 58 p.
Composed 1921. First performance Vienna, 1921,
Nils Grevillius conductor.

2282 Klein Ida's Blumen [Little Ida's   *12'*
flowers] Ballet overture, from the fairy tale
by H. C. Andersen
3(3rd alt. Picc.),2,2,2-4,3,3,1-Timp.,Perc.-
Pno.,Cel.,2Hp.(or 1).-Mand.-Str.
Universal-Edition, Vienna, c1916
Score 40 p. Large folio
Composed 1914. First performance Stuttgart,
28 January 1916.

1661 Paolo und Francesca [symphonic   *17'*
fantasy, on Dante's Inferno, Canto V]
5*,2,3,3*-6,4,3,1-Timp.,Perc.-Pno.,Cel.,2Hp.-
Str.
Universal-Edition, Vienna, c1919
Score 80 p.

KLENGEL, JULIUS.   Leipzig 24 September 1859
                    Leipzig 27 October 1933

717m [Concerto, violin and violoncello,   *25'*
Op. 61]
1.Allegro moderato 2.Andante 3.Allegro non
troppo
Solo Vn., Solo Vc.-2(2nd alt. Picc.),2,2,2-
4,2,3-Timp.,Trgl.-Str.
Breitkopf & Härtel, Leipzig, c1926
Score 77 p.
Composed 1924, for the composer's fiftieth
anniversary with the Leipzig Gewandhaus
Orchestra. First performance 9 October 1924,
Wilhelm Furtwängler conductor.

516c [Concerto, violoncello, no. 1, Op. 4,
A minor]
1.Allegro 2.Andante con moto 3.Allegro
vivace
Solo Vc.-2,2,2,2-2,2-Timp.-Str.
Breitkopf & Härtel, Leipzig [n.d.]
Score 170 p.

520c [Concerto, violoncello, no. 2, Op. 20,
D minor]
1.Allegro non troppo 2.Andante 3.Scherzo
4.Finale
Solo Vc.-2,2,2,2-2,2-Timp.-Str.
Breitkopf & Härtel, Leipzig [n.d.]
Score 185 p.

550c [Concerto, violoncello, no. 3, Op. 31,
A minor]
1.Allegro non troppo 2.Intermezzo 3.Finale
Solo Vc.-2,2,2,2-4,2,3-Timp.-Str.
Breitkopf & Härtel, Leipzig, c1895
Score 137 p.

359s Serenade, Op. 24 [F major]
1.Allegro con spirito 2.Arioso 3.Scherzo
4.Finale
Str.
Breitkopf & Härtel, Leipzig [n.d.]
Score 31 p.

KLEPPER, LEON.   Jassy, Romania 24 April 1900

293m Concertino, flute, piano and   *14'*
strings
1.Allegro comodo 2.Andante mesto 3.Allegro
moderato ma vehemente
Solo Fl., Solo Pno.-Str.
Israeli Music Publications, Tel-Aviv, c1962
Score 40 p.
Commissioned by the Israel Composers' Fund.
Composed 1960. First performance Kol-Israel
(Israel Broadcast Authority), Jerusalem, 1961,
Sergiu Comissiona conductor, Tel-Oren flau-
tist, Hadasa Shwimer pianist.

KLETSCH, LUDWIG.   Munich 13 June 1908
                    d. 14 December 1961

4618 [A Slavic tale, capriccio for   *8'*
orchestra]
1,1,1-4Sax.(2 Alto both alt. Cl.)-0,1,1-Timp.,
Perc.-Harm.-Str.
B. Schott's Söhne, Mainz, c1940
Score in reduction 6 p.

KLETZKI, PAUL (PAWEŁ KLECKI).
                    Łódź, Poland 21 March 1900
                    Liverpool 5 March 1973

1182v [Concerto, violin, Op. 19,   *35'*
G major]
1.Allegro moderato 2.Andante espressivo
3.Allegro giocoso
Solo Vn.-2(2nd alt. Picc.),2,2,3*-4,2-Timp.,
Perc.-Str.
N. Simrock, Berlin, c1928
Score 106 p.

Kletzki, Paul

4507 [Prelude to a tragedy, Op. 14, C minor]
3(3rd alt. Picc.),3*,3*,3*-4,3,3,1-Timp.,Perc.-
Org.(ad lib.)-Str.
N. Simrock, Berlin, c1926
Score 81 p.

231s [Sinfonietta, string orchestra, Op. 7,
E minor]
1.Allegro appassionato 2.Andante 3.Allegro
Str.
N. Simrock, Berlin, c1923
Score 66 p.

4506 [Symphony no. 1, Op. 17, D minor]   40'
1.Andante poco sostenuto - Allegro appassionato
2.Adagio 3.Allegro non troppo
4(all alt. Picc.),3*,3*,3*-4,3,3,1-Timp.,Perc.
-Hp.-Str.
N. Simrock, Berlin, c1927
Score 134 p.

4527 [Symphony no. 2, Op. 18, G minor]   50'
1.Allegro con fuoco 2.Andante sostenuto
3.Scherzo 4.Finale
4(3rd&4th alt. Picc.),3*,3,3(3rd alt. B.Cl.),3*-
6,3-Timp.,Perc.-Hp.-Voice(Finale only)-Str.
N. Simrock, Berlin, c1928
Score 181 p.

4543 [Variations, orchestra, Op. 20,   18'
E major]
3(3rd alt. Picc.),3*,3*,3*-4,3,3,1-Timp.,Trgl.,
Chimes-Cel.,Hp.-Str.
N. Simrock, Berlin, c1929
Score 63 p.

KLEVEN, ARVID PARLY.
                Drontheim, Norway 29 November 1899
                       Oslo 23 November 1929

6053 [Lotusland, symphonic poem, Op. 5]   18'
2(2nd alt. Picc.),2,2,2-4Hn.-Timp.,Cym.-Pno.,
Hp.-Str.
Norsk Musikverlag, Kristiania, c1923
Score 51 p.
Composed 1921. First performance Oslo, 1922,
Filharmonisk Selskaps Orkester.

KLING, HENRI.   Paris 15 February 1842
                         Geneva 2 May 1918

1663s Romanze [D major]
Solo Vn.-Str.
Score: Ms. 8 p.
Parts: Louis Oertel, Hannover [n.d.]

1309s [Scenes from childhood] Op. 529
In seven scenes
Str.
Score: Ms. 14 p.
Parts: Louis Oertel, Hannover [n.d.]

KLOSE, FRIEDRICH.   Karlsruhe 29 November 1862
              Ruvigliana, Lugano 24 December 1942

4502 [Andante religioso, interlude, Op. 9]
2,1,2,2-2Hn.-Str.
Luckhardt's Musik-Verlag, Leipzig [1894]

Score 7 p.
Composed 1894 as an addition to the composer's
Mass in D Minor, Op. 6, composed 1889.

1820 Elfenreigen [Dance of the elves]
2,2,2,2-4,2-Timp.,Cym.,Trgl.-2Hp.-Str.
F.E.C. Leuckart, Leipzig [n.d.]
Score 39 p.

KLUCEVSEK, GUY.   New York 26 February 1947

198m Chromatrope   12'
Solo Accordion-Alto Fl.,0,2,2-1,2,2-2Vn.,2Va.,
Vc.
Ms. c1975 by Guy Klucevsek
Scores: 12 p. each. Large folio
Composed 1975.

197m Coruscation for solo keyboard or   12-20'
multiple identical keyboards in unison
Suggested instruments: Accordion, Organ, Piano
(electric preferred), Harmonium, Harpsichord
Ms. c1974 by Guy Klucevsek
Score 5 p.
Composed 1973-74. First performance Glassboro
State College, New Jersey, February 1974, Guy
Klucevsek, accordion.

7149 Pentacle   8-12'
Accordion-Vn.I,Vn.II,Vc.
Ms. c1975 by Guy Klucevsek
Parts are scores, 2 p.
Commissioned by Patricia Tregellas, 1975, for
the Festival Quartet. Originally composed for
solo accordion, 1974.

7135 Spheres   20-60'
Cb.(drones)-Any No. of Melody Instruments
Ms. c1974 by Guy Klucevsek
Scores: 2 p. each
Originally composed for string bass, bass
accordion, and nine accordions, 1971-72. This
version 1974.

2383s Stationary movements   25'
3Vn.,2Va.,2Vc.
Ms.
Score 7 p. Large folio
Originally composed for seven accordions, 1971.

KLUGHARDT, AUGUST FRIEDRICH MARTIN.
                Köthen, Germany 30 November 1847
              Rosslau, near Dresden 3 August 1902

4555 [Concert overture, Op. 45, G major]
2,2,2,2-2,2-Timp.-Str.
Bote & Bock, Berlin [1884]
Score 27 p.

677v [Concerto, violin, Op. 68, D major]
In one movement
Solo Vn.-2,2,2,2-2,2-Timp.-Str.
E.W. Fritzsch, Leipzig, c1895
Score 58 p.

573c [Concerto, violoncello, Op. 59, A minor]
In one movement
Solo Vc.-2,2,2,2-2,2,3-Timp.-Str.

Siegel, Leipzig [n.d.]
Score 26 p.

532m Concertstück [oboe, Op. 18]   6'
Solo Ob.-2,0,2,2-2,2-Timp.-Str.
C.F.W. Siegel, Leipzig, c1874
Score 23 p.
Composed and first performed Neustrelitz 1873.

328s Drei Stücke, Op. 74
1.[Squire Joyous] 2.[The old song] 3.[With
dignity and grace]
Str.
Carl Giessel, Bayreuth [n.d.]
Score 15 p.

1664 Drei Stücke für Orchester, Op. 87
1.Capriccio 2.Gavotte 3.Tarantelle
2(2nd alt. Picc.),2,2,2-4,2,3-Timp.,Cym.,
Trgl.-Hp.-Str.
Carl Giessel, Bayreuth, c1901
Score 67 p.

1663 [On a walking tour, suite, Op. 67]
2,2,2,2-3,2,1-Timp.,Trgl.-Str.
Carl Giessel, Bayreuth, c1904
Score 42 p.

619c [Romance, Op. 83. Edited by Jacques van
Lier]
Solo Vc.-0,0,2,2-Str.
Carl Giessel, Bayreuth, c1902
Score in reduction 7 p.

792m [Romance, bassoon and orchestra]
Solo Bn.-1,1,2,1-2,2-Timp.-Str.
Score: Ms. 11 p.
Parts: C.F. Schmidt, Heilbronn [n.d.]

5612 [Symphony no. 1, Lenore, Op. 27, D minor]
1.Heftig bewegt 2.Marsch 3.Langsam 4.Mässig
2(2nd alt. Picc.),2,2,2-4,2,3-Timp.,Perc.-Str.
E. Eulenberg, Leipzig [1875]
Score 102 p.
*Suggested by Gottfried Bürger's dramatic bal-
lad, Lenore. First performance Weimar, 6
January 1873.*

5677 [Symphony no. 3, Op. 37, D major]   25'
1.Lebhaft 2.Langsam 3.Mässig 4.Munter
2,2,2,2-2,2-Timp.-Str.
Score: Ms. 78 p.
Parts: [Bote & Bock, Berlin, 1883]
First performance Neustrelitz, 3 November 1879.

191 [Symphony no. 5, Op. 71, C minor]
[1.]Allegro non troppo [2.]Adagio [3.]
Allegro vivace [4.]Andante [5.]Allegro molto
2(2nd alt. Picc.),2,2,2-4,2,2-Timp.,Trgl.-Str.
Carl Giessel, Bayreuth, c1900
Score 79 p.

KNAUTH, R. F. pseudonym.
See: FRANZ, ROBERT.

KNIPPER, LEV KONSTANTINOVICH.
        Tiflis, Georgia, Russia 16 December 1898
                      Moscow 30 July 1974

1666 Präludium-Scherzo, Op. 12b no. 1   4'
2(1st alt. Picc.),2(2nd alt. E.H.),2,1-4,1,1,1
-Timp.,Perc.-Hp.-Str.
Mussektor, Moscow, c1928
Score 19 p.
Composed 1925. First performance Moscow, 1926.

2122 Präludium, Op. 12b no. 2   3'
1,1,1,1-2,1-Timp.,Perc.-Str.
Mussektor, Moscow, c1929
Score 11 p.
Composed 1926. First performance Moscow, 1926.

2457 [Small lyric suite, Op. 18]   9'
2(2nd alt. Picc.),1,1,1-2Hn.-Timp.-Hp.-Str.
Mussektor, Moscow, c1930
Score 21 p.
Composed 1928.

1665 [Stories of an idol, Op. 1]   11'
[1.Introduction 2.Dance 3.The man's lament
and the god's dance 4.The man's curse 5.
The overthrow of the god 6.Epilogue]
3(3rd alt. Picc.),3(3rd alt. E.H.),3*,3*-4,2,
3,1-Timp.,Perc.-Str.
Mussektor, Moscow, c1927
Score 55 p.
*Composed 1923-24. First performance, Moscow,
8 March 1925, Konstantin Saradiev conductor.*

3159 [Vantch, third book of Tadzhik   22'
notations, Op. 29]
1.[My beloved] 2.[Song of the pathways] 3.
[The beautiful one] 4.Allegro molto 5.[In
the garden] 6.[Dear Khisrau]
1(alt. Picc.),1,1,1-Tenor Sax.-2,1,1-Timp.,
Perc.-2Guit.-Str.
Mussektor, Moscow, 1933
Score 61 p.
*Composed 1932. First performance Leningrad,
1933, Kjostov conductor.*

KNORR, IWAN.   Mewe, Germany 3 January 1853
                      Frankfurt 22 January 1916

108 [Variations on an Ukrainian folk-   16'
song, Op. 7]
2(2nd alt. Picc.),2,2,2-2,2-Timp.-Str.
Breitkopf & Härtel, Leipzig, 1891
Score 27 p.
*Composed 1891. First performance Frankfurt,
1892.*

KOC, MARCELO.   Vitebsk, USSR 4 June 1918

2103s Preludio, intermezzo y fuga   15'
Str.
Ms.
Score 29 p. Large folio
*Composed 1951. First performance Teatro Broad-
way, [Argentina?], 24 June 1952, Orquesta de
Amigos de la Música, Felix Prohaska conductor.
Won First Prize in Composition in Asociación
de Amigos de la Música competition, 1951.*

KOCH, ERLAND VON.   Stockholm 26 April 1910

Full name: Sigurd Christian Erland von Koch.

Koch, Erland von

1199v [Concerto, viola, Op. 33, F major.   17'
Original version]
1.Andante con moto 2.Presto 3.Allegro
Solo Va.-2(2nd alt. Picc.),1,2,2(2nd ad lib.)-
2,1-Timp.-Str.
Ms.
Score 112 p.
*Composed 1946. First performance Göteborg,
Sweden, 8 April 1948, Orchestra Society of
Göteborg, Sixten Eckerberg conductor, Henry
Stenström soloist. Later revised.*

6775 [Impulses for orchestra]   12'
3*,3*,3*,3*-4,3,3,1-Timp.,Perc.-Str.
Edition Suecia, Stockholm [n.d.]
Score 100 p.
Composed 1964.

5129 [Nordic capriccio, Op. 26]   6'
2(2nd alt. Picc.),2,2,2-2,2,1-Timp.-Str.
Edition Suecia, Stockholm, c1945 by Society of
Swedish Composers
Score 19 p.
Composed 1943.

2139s [Rural suite for strings, Op. 32]   14'
1.[Walking tune] 2.[Elegiac melody]
3.[Dance]
Str.
Carl Gehrmans, Stockholm, c1949
Score 27 p.
*No. 2 composed 1945. Nos. 1 and 3 added 1946.
First performance of suite Stockholm, 1946,
Swedish Radio Orchestra, Tor Mann conductor.*

5052 [Symphony no. 3, Op. 38, A minor]   23'
1.Allegro moderato 2.Adagio 3.Allegro
agitato
2(2nd alt. Picc.),2,2,2-4,3,3,1-Timp.,Perc.-
Hp.-Str.
Ms.
Score 114 p.
*Composed 1948. First performance Göteborg,
Sweden, 3 February 1949, Orchestra Society of
Göteborg, Sixten Eckerberg conductor.*

6018 [Symphony no. 4, Sinfonia seria,   25'
Op. 51. Original version]
1.Andante 2.Allegretto 3.Allegro moderato
2(2nd alt. Picc.),2(2nd alt. E.H.),2(2nd alt.
B.Cl.),2-4,2,3,1-Timp.,Perc.-Str.
STIM, Stockholm [n.d.]
Score 125 p.
Composed 1952-53. Revised 1966.

KOCH, FRIEDRICH ERNST.   Berlin 3 July 1862
Berlin 30 January 1927

871v [Concerto, violin, Deutsche
Rhapsodie, Op. 31, D major]
In one movement
Solo Vn.-2,2,2,2-4,2-Timp.-Hp.-Str.
C.F. Kahnt, Leipzig, c1907
Score 67 p.
*First performance Berlin, November 1907, Felix
Berber soloist.*

5675 [Symphonic fugue, Op. 8, C minor]   9'
[Introduction] - Fuge
2,2,2,2-4,2,3-Timp.-Str.
Breitkopf & Härtel, Leipzig, 1891
Score 21 p.

4505 [Symphony no. 2, Op. 10, G major]   42'
1.Lebhaft und frisch 2.Ruhig und gemessen
3.Rasch und derb 4.Ziemlich bewegt
3*,2,2,2-4,3,3-Timp.-Str.
Bote & Bock, Berlin [1891]
Score 219 p.

KOCHETOV, NIKOLAI RAZUMNIKOVICH.
b. Oranienbaum
(now Lomonosov), Russia 8 July 1864

1315 À la balalaïka, from Suite no. 2, Op. 7
2,2,2,2-4Hn.-Str.
P. Jurgenson, Leipzig [n.d.]
Score 15 p.

KOCHMANN, SPERO.   b. Berlin 31 March 1889

Also published as: Theo Calmon; S. Castaldo

4607 [Dance suite no. 2]   15'
1.[Gypsy mazurka] 2.Pizzicato - Polka 3.
Rokoko - Menuett 4.[Happy serenade]
5.[Viennese waltz]
1,1,1-0,1,1-Timp.,Perc.-Harm.-Str.(w/o Va.)
B. Schott's Söhne, Mainz, c1939
Score in reduction 15 p.

KOCKERT, OTTO.   Berlin 28 June 1865

1284s [Slumber song, Op. 60. Orchestrated
by Alfred Pagel]
Str.
Score: Ms. 6 p.
Parts: R. Birnbach, Berlin, c1922

KODÁLY, ZOLTÁN. Kecskemét, Hungary 16 December 1882
Budapest 6 March 1967

4325 [Ballet music]   5'
3*,2,2,2*-Alto Sax.-4,3,3Cnt.,3,1-Timp.,Perc.-
Cimbalom,Cel.-Str.
Universal Edition, Vienna, c1936
Score 28 p.
*Originally composed 1925 as part of the comic
folk opera Háry János, Op. 15, but not inclu-
ded in the published version.*

1667 Háry János-Suite   30'
1.Prelude 2.Viennese musical clock 3.Song
4.The battle and defeat of Napoleon 5.Inter-
mezzo 6.Entrance of the emperor and his court
3(all alt. Picc.),2,2(2nd alt. Alto Sax),2-
4,3,3Cnt.,3,1-Timp.,Perc.-Pno.,Cel.,Cimbalom
(or Cemb.)-Str.
Universal Edition, Vienna, c1927
Score 80 p.
*Composed 1925-26. First performance of this
suite New York, 15 December 1927, Willem Mengelberg conductor.*

2168 Marosszéki Táncok [Dances of   12'
Marosszék]

2(2nd alt. Picc.),2,2,2*-4,2-Timp.,Perc.-Str.
Universal-Edition, Vienna, ᶜ1930
Score 75 p.
*Composed 1929. First performance Dresden, 28
November 1930, Fritz Busch conductor.*

2167 Nyári este [Summer evening]   5'
1,2*,2,2-2Hn.-Str.
Universal-Edition, Vienna, ᶜ1930
Score 66 p.
*Composed 1906. Revised 1930. First perform-
ance 3 April 1930, New York Philharmonic
Orchestra, Arturo Toscanini conductor.*

KOECHLIN, CHARLES.   Paris 27 November 1867
          Le Canadel, Var, France 31 December 1950

5915 [Bandar-Log (Scherzo of the   15'
monkeys), Op. 176]
4*(3rd alt. Picc.),3*,4*(1 in E-flat),3*-2Sax.
(Sop.,Ten.)-4,4,Bugle,4,1-Timp.,Perc.-Pno.,
Cel.,2Hp.-Str.
Ms. [now published by Eschig, Paris]
Score 96 p.
*Based on an episode from Rudyard Kipling's
Jungle Book. Composed 1939. Orchestrated
1940. First performance Brussels, 13 Decem-
ber 1946, Orchestra of the Institut National
Belge de Radiodiffusion, Franz André conductor.*

5153 Cinq chorals dans les modes du   10'
moyen-âge, Op. 117b
3(2nd & 3rd alt. Picc.),3(2nd alt. Ob. d'Amore,
3rd alt. E.H.),3*,3*-4,4,3-Timp.,Cym.-Pno.,Hp.
-Str.
Editions Maurice Senart, Paris, ᶜ1933
Score 27 p.
*Composed 1931. Orchestrated 1932. First per-
formance Paris, 29 November 1932, Orchestre
Symphonique de Paris, Roger Désormière conductor.*

5512 La cité nouvelle, rêve d'avenir   32'
(poème symphonique), Op. 170
4(3rd & 4th alt. Picc.),3(3rd alt. E.H.),4*(1
in E-flat),3*-Alto Sax.-4,4,3,1-Timp.,Perc.-
Pno.,Cel.,2Hp.-Str.
Ms. [now published by Eschig, Paris]
Score 174 p.
*Composed 1938. First performance Paris, 16
January 1962, Orchestra of the Radiodiffusion-
Télévision Française, Maurice Le Roux con-
ductor.*

5972 La course de printemps, poème   25-28'
symphonique [Op. 95] d'après Le Livre de
la Jungle de R. Kipling
4(all alt. Picc.),3(2nd alt. Ob. d'Amore,3rd
alt. E.H.),3*,3*-4(5&6 ad lib.),4,4,2-Timp.,
Perc.-Pno.,Org.,2Hp.-Str.
Ms. [now published by Eschig, Paris]
Score 201 p.
*Composed 1911. Orchestrated 1925-27. First
performance Paris, 29 November 1932, Orchestre Symphonique de Paris, Roger Désormière
conductor.*

4438 [Fugue for orchestra, Op. 112   6'30"
no. 2, F minor]

3(2nd & 3rd alt. Picc.),3*(2nd alt. Ob. d'
Amore),3*,3*-4,4,3,1-Timp.-Pno.,2Hp.-Str.
Editions Maurice Senart, Paris, ᶜ1933
Score 22 p.
*Originally composed as no. 2 of Three Fugues
1929-1931. No. 2 orchestrated 1932. First
performance Paris, 29 November 1932, Orchestre
Symphonique de Paris, Roger Désormière con-
ductor.*

5642 La loi de la jungle, poème sym-   5'
phonique [Op. 175] d'après Le Livre de la
Jungle de R. Kipling
4*,3*,4*(1 in E-flat),4*(3rd ad lib.)-2Sax.
(Sop.,Ten.)-4,4,Bugle,4,1-Timp.,Perc.-Str.
Ms. [now published by Eschig, Paris]
Score 32 p.
*Composed 1939. First performance Brussels,
13 December 1946, Orchestra of the Institut
National Belge de Radiodiffusion, Franz André
conductor.*

5637 La méditation de Purun Baghât,   13'
poème symphonique [Op. 159] d'après Le Livre
de la Jungle de R. Kipling
4*(2nd & 3rd alt. Picc.),3*(3rd alt. E.H.),4*,
4*-6,4,4,1-Timp.,Perc.-Pno.,Org.,2Hp.-Str.
Ms. [now published by Eschig, Paris]
Score 51 p.
*Composed 1936. First performance Brussels,
13 December 1946, Orchestra of the Institut
National Belge de Radiodiffusion, Franz André
conductor.*

5888 Nuit de Walpurgis classique, poème   14'
symphonique d'après [Paul] Verlaine, Op. 38
Version définitive (avril 1916)
4*,3*(1 Ob. d'Amore),3*,5*(4th ad lib.)-5,4
(4th ad lib.),3,1-Timp.,Perc.-Pno.,Hpscd.,Cel.,
2Hp.,Harp Lute-Str.
Ms. [now published by Eschig, Paris]
Score 68 p.
*Composed 1901 to 1908. Orchestrated 1916.
First performance Paris, 15 June 1919, Orchestre Felix Delgrange, Felix Delgrange conductor.*

456m [Poem for horn and orchestra,   15'
Op. 70b]
1.Moderato 2.Andante 3.Final: Assez animé
Solo Hn.-3*,3*(2nd alt. Ob. d'Amore),3*,3*-
3,3,3,1-Timp.,Cym.,B.Dr.-Hp.-Str.
Ms. [now published by Eschig, Paris]
Score 93 p.
*Originally composed as Sonata for Horn and
Piano, Op. 70, 1918-25. Transcribed for
orchestra 1927. First performance Paris, 24
March 1927, Concerts Straram Orchestra, Wal-
ther Straram conductor, Edouard Vuillermoz
soloist.*

6102 [Symphony of hymns (in 5   Total 40'
sections)]
I. Hymne au soleil, Op. 127a   9'
4*,3(1st alt. E.H.),3*,4*(3rd optional)-5(5th
optional),4,4,1-Timp.,Cym.-Pno.,Cel.,2Hp.-Str.
*Alternate title: Choral Fugué en Ut. Com-
posed 1933. First performance Paris, 16 June
1938, Chant du Monde Orchestra, Roger*

Koechlin, Charles

Désormière conductor.

II. Hymne au jour, Op. 110   4'
Solo Ondes Martenot(optional)-3*,3*(1 Ob. d'
Amore),3*,3*-4,3,3,1-Timp.-Pno.,2Hp.(2nd
optional)-Str.
*Alternate title: Hymne pour Ondes Martenot
et Orchestre. Composed 1929. Orchestrated
1932. First performance Paris, 14 June 1938,
Chant du Monde Orchestra, Roger Désormière
conductor, Ginette Martenot soloist.*

III. Hymne à la nuit, Op. 48 no.1   4'
3,2*,3*,2-4,2,3,1-Timp.,B.Dr.-2Hp.(2nd
optional)-Str.
*Originally composed 1908 as Nuit de Juin, ou
Hymne à la Nuit, Part I of the symphonic poem,
L'Eté [Summer]. This version 1911. First
performance Paris, 14 June 1938, Chant du
Monde Orchestra, Roger Désormière conductor.*

IV. Hymne à la jeunesse, Op. 148   8'
4(1st & 2nd alt. Picc.),3,4*(1 in A),3*-6Sax.
(3 Alto,Ten.,Bar.,Bass)-4,4,4,1-Timp.,Perc.-
Pno.,Cel.,2Hp.-Str.
*Suggested by Le Voyage d'Urien by André Gide.
Composed 1934. Orchestrated 1935. First
performance Paris, 14 June 1938, Chant du
Monde Orchestra, Roger Désormière conductor.*

V. Hymne à la vie, Op. 69   15'
4*,4*,4*(1 in E-flat),4*-6,4,5,2-Timp.,B.Dr.-
Pno.,Org.,2Hp.-Double Chorus(SATB)-Str.
*Text by the composer. Composed 1918-19.
First performance Paris, 14 June 1938, Chant
du Monde Orchestra, Yvonne Gouverné Chorus,
Roger Désormière conductor.*

Entire Score and Parts for 6102 in Ms. 263 p.

6193 [Symphony no. 2, Op. 196]   44'
1.Fugue 2.Scherzo 3.Andante 4.Fugue modale
5.Finale
4(2nd, 3rd & 4th alt. Picc.),4*(2nd alt. Ob.
d'Amore),4*(3rd alt. Cl. in E-flat),4*-3Sax.
(Sop.,Alto,Ten.)-6,4(1st alt. Small Tpt. in
D),4,1-Timp.,Perc.-Pno.,Org.,Cel.,2Hp.-2
Ondes Martenot(or 1 & 1Org.)-Str.
Ms. [now published by Eschig, Paris]
Score 306 p.
*"Commissioned by the state." Composed 1943.
Orchestrated 1943-44. First performance
Mexico, 28 August 1952, Orquesta Sinfónica
Nacional, José Pablo Moncayo conductor.*

KOELLREUTTER, HANS JOACHIM.
        b. Freiburg im Breisgau 2 September 1915

6072 [Chamber symphony for 12 solo   16'
instruments]
1.Intrata 2.Musica de câmera
1,1,1,1-Hn.-Timp.-Cel.(or Pno.)-Str.
Ms.
Score 43 p.
*Composed 1949. First performance Zurich,
1951, Societé Suisse de Radiodiffusion, the
composer conducting.*

6200 [Mutations]   11'
2(2nd alt. Picc.),1,2,2-2,2-Timp.,Perc.-Pno.,
Cel.,Hp.-Str.
Ms.
Score 18 p. Large folio
*Composed 1953. First performance Jerusalem,
March 1961, Kol Israel Symphony Orchestra, the
composer conducting.*

KOESSLER, HANS.   Waldeck, Germany 1 January 1853
                   Ansbach, Germany 23 May 1926

1668 Symphonische Variationen   16'
3,2,2,3*-4,3,3,1-Timp.,Perc.-Str.
Universal-Edition, Vienna [n.d.]
Score 87 p.

KÖHLER, BERNHARD.

4549 Scherzo
3*,2,2,2-2,2-Timp.-Str.
Schott, London [1896]
Score 19 p.

KÖHLER, ERNESTO.   Modena, Italy 4 December 1849
                    St. Petersburg 17 May 1907

635m La capricieuse [concert piece]   5'
Op. 94
Solo Fl.-1,2,2,2-2,2,1,1-Timp.,Perc.-Str.
J.H. Zimmermann, Leipzig, c1905
Score in reduction 11 p.
*Composed and first performed St. Petersburg
1903.*

630m [Concert-fantasy for flute, Op. 62,   4'
on the Russian song Moskwa]
Allegro maestoso - Andantino - Allegretto
Solo Fl.-2*,1,2,1-2,2,1-Timp.,Perc.-Str.
Zimmermann, Leipzig, c1893
Score in reduction 9 p.
*Composed and first performed St. Petersburg
1892.*

663m [Concert-fantasy for flute, Op. 64,   4'
on motives from the opera The Governor of
Tours by Carl Reinecke]
Solo Fl.-1(alt. Picc.),1,2,1-2,2,1-Timp.,Perc.
-Str.
Zimmermann, Leipzig, c1894
Score in reduction 9 p.
*Composed and first performed St. Petersburg
1893.*

636m [Concerto, flute, Op. 97, G minor]   10'
Allegro giusto - Andante molto sostenuto -
Allegretto moderato
Solo Fl.-2*,2,2,2-4,2,3,1-Timp.,Perc.-Str.
Zimmermann, Leipzig, c1906
Score in reduction 25 p.
*Composed 1904. First performance St. Peters-
burg 1906.*

634m Fantasca [for flute, Op. 91]   4'
Solo Fl.-1(alt. Picc.),1(or 2),2,1(or 2)-2,2,
1-Timp.,Perc.-Str.
Zimmermann, Leipzig, c1904

Score in reduction 9 p.
*Composed and first performed St. Petersburg
1902.*

629m Hirten-Idylle [Shepherd's idyl]   5'
Op. 58
Solo Fl.-1,2,2,1-2,2,1-Timp.,Perc.-Str.
Zimmermann, Leipzig, ^c1891
Score in reduction 9 p.
*Composed 1889. First performance St. Peters-
burg 1891.*

646m Italienische Serenade [for cornet,   2'
Op. 74]
Solo Tpt.-1,1,2,1-2,1,1-Str.
Zimmermann, Leipzig, ^c1899
Score in reduction 3 p.
*Composed 1897. First performance St. Peters-
burg 1898.*

628m Papillon, Concert-étude, Op. 30   3'
no. 4
Solo Fl.-1(alt. Picc.),1,2,1-Timp.,Bells-Str.
Zimmermann, Leipzig [n.d.]
Score in reduction 7 p.
*Composed 1884. First performance St. Peters-
burg 1885.*

632m La romantique [concert fantasy,   6'
Op. 80]
Solo Fl.-1,1,2,1-2,2,1-Timp.,Perc.-Str.
Zimmermann, Leipzig, ^c1899
Score in reduction 14 p.
*Composed and first performed St. Petersburg
1897.*

631m [Swallows' flight, concert etude,   4'
Op. 72]
Solo Fl.-2Cl.,Bn.-2Hn.-Bells-Str.
Zimmermann, Leipzig, ^c1899
Score in reduction 9 p.
*Composed 1895. First performance St. Peters-
burg 1896.*

633m Zephyr [concert waltz for flute,   5'
Op. 81]
Solo Fl.-1,1,2,1-2Hn.-Timp.,Bells-Str.
Zimmermann, Leipzig, ^c1900
Score in reduction 13 p.
*Composed 1898. First performance St. Peters-
burg 1899.*

KOHLER, FRANZ.   Clinton, Iowa 20 February 1877
                      Erie, Pennsylvania 22 December 1918

527c Am Abend [violoncello and orchestra,
Op. 12b]
Solo Vc.-2,2,2,2-2Hn.-Str.
André, Offenbach a.M. [n.d.]
Score 44 p.

KÖHLER, OSKAR.   Schkeuditz, Saxony 19 May 1851
                      Erfurt, Germany 6 December 1917

887s [Autumnal mood, Op. 78 *and* Slumber
song, Op. 103]
Str.
Score: Ms. 7 p.
Parts: C.F. Schmidt, Heilbronn [n.d.]

746s Baladine [Buffoon, pizzicato piece]
Str.
Score: Ms. 6 p.
Parts: Oertel, Hannover [n.d.]

774m Notturno [oboe and string orchestra]
Solo Ob.-Str.
Score: Ms. 11 p.
Parts: Oertel, Hannover [n.d.]

1404s [Return of the harvesters]
Str.
Score: Ms. 8 p.
Parts: Kahnt, Leipzig [n.d.]

611s Seliger Kindertraum, Op. 143
Glock.-Str.
Oertel, Hannover [n.d.]
Score 4 p.

782s [Summer evening in Norway]
Glock.-Str.
Score: Ms. 7 p.
Parts: Oertel, Hannover [n.d.]

879s [Twilight hour, Op. 149 *and* Norwegian
cradle song, Op. 150]
Glock.-Str.
Bosworth, Leipzig, ^c1899
Score 7 p.

824s [Vespers in the Hermitage]
Glock.-Str.
C.F. Schmidt, Heilbronn [n.d.]
Score 3 p.

826s [With the elves and goblins, Op. 120]
Str.
Score: Ms. 4 p.
Parts: [n.p., n.d.]

KOHS, ELLIS BONOFF.   Chicago 12 May 1916

6311 Concerto for orchestra in one   16'
movement
3*,3*,3*,3*-4,3,3,1-Timp.,Perc.-Str.
Ms.
Score 79 p.
*Composed 1940-41. First performance at the
Festival of the International Society for
Contemporary Music, Berkeley, California, 9
August 1942, Werner Janssen Symphony, Werner
Janssen conductor.*

423c [Concerto, violoncello, in one   12'
movement, C major]
Solo Vc.-2,2,2,2-2Hn.-Str.
Ms.
Score 19 p. Large folio
*Composed 1947. First performance Los Angeles,
25 November 1952, University of Southern California Symphony Orchestra, John Barnett conductor, Marie Manahan soloist.*

6328 Four orchestral songs   11'30"
1.The rose 2.The mountain 3.The mermaid
4.Epitaph
Contralto Voice Solo; Tenor Voice Solo-2(2nd

Kohs, Ellis B.

alt. Picc.),3*,2,2-2,2,3,1-Perc.-Hp.-Str.
Ms.
Score 27 p.
*Text to nos. 1-3 by Anne Hill Lotterhos; to
no. 4 by George Santayana (from his tombstone).
Originally composed for voice and piano.
Orchestrated 1959.*

6326 Symphony no. 1, for small orchestra   *16'*
[A minor]
1.Allegro energico 2.Moderato, molto cantando
ed espressivo 3.Allegro non troppo
1,1,1,1-1,1,1-Timp.-Str.
Ms. C1955 by Ellis B. Kohs
Score 90 p.
*Composed 1950. First performance San Fran-
cisco, 3 January 1952, San Francisco Symphony,
Pierre Monteux conductor.*

6327 Symphony no. 2 for chorus and   *25'*
orchestra
1.Largo - Allegro ma non troppo 2.Mesto
3.Scherzo 4.Lento
2(2nd alt. Picc.),2(2nd alt. E.H.),2(2nd alt.
B.Cl.),2(2nd alt. C.Bn.)-2,2,2,1-Timp.,Perc.-
Hp.-Chorus(SATB)-Str.
Ms.
Score 58 p. Large folio
*Commissioned by the University of Illinois and
the Paul Fromm Foundation. Composed 1956.
First performance Urbana, Illinois, 13 April
1957, University of Illinois Symphony Orchestra with the University Oratorio Society,
Robert Shaw conductor.*

KOLB, BARBARA.
        b. Hartford, Connecticut 10 February 1939

7233 Crosswinds, for wind ensemble and   *13'*
percussion
Solo Alto Sax.-2,3*,3*,2-2,2,2-Perc.
Boosey & Hawkes, New York, C1974
Score 30 p.
Composed 1968-69.

KÖLLE, KONRAD.   b. Nienburg an der Weser,
                Germany 11 November 1882

1032v [Concerto, viola, Op. 38, A major]
1.Largo maestoso - Allegro 2.Tranquillo
3.Leggiero 4.A tempo molto
Solo Va.-1,2,1,2-Hn.-Str.
Ms.
Score 69 p.

KOMZÁK, KARL (*or* KAREL), SR. Prague 8 November 1850
                Baden, near Vienna 23 April 1905

Not to be confused with his son Karl Komzák Jr.
(1878-1924) or with the unrelated composer Karel
Komzák (1823-93).

129s [Folksong. Arranged for strings by
William Happich]
Str.
Ms.
Score 6 p.
Arranged 1917.

1252s Liebchen träumt, Op. 211 *and* Ueberselig,
Op. 212 [Darling sleeps *and* Overjoyed]
Hp.-Str.
Score: Ms. 5 p.
Parts: Blaha, Vienna [n.d.]

595s Volksliedchen *and* Märchen, Op. 135
Hp.(ad lib.)-Str.
Cranz, Brussels [n.d.]
Score 5 p.

KÖNIG-BOLLAND.

833m [Dramatic fantasy, clarinet and orchestra]
Solo Cl.-2,2,2,2-2,2,3-Timp.-Str.
Score: Ms. 72 p.
Parts: Lehne, Hannover [n.d.]

KOPP, LEO L.

3563 Rhapsody no. 2, Op. 13   *12'*
3,3*,3*,2-4,3,3,1-Timp.,Perc.-Hp.-Str.
Ms.
Score 107 p.
Composed 1940.

KOPPEL, HERMAN DAVID.   Copenhagen 1 October 1908

211m [Concerto for oboe and orchestra,   *20'*
Op. 82]
1.Pastorale 2.Rondo 3.Notturno 4.Rondo
Solo Ob.-2,0,2,2-2Hn.-Perc.-Cel.,Hp.-Str.
Samfundet til Udgivelse af Dansk Musik,
Copenhagen, C1973
Score 93 p.
*Commissioned by Danish State Radio, Copenhagen.
Composed 1970. First performance Danish State
Radio, Copenhagen, 18 February 1971, Leif
Segerstam conductor, Jørgen Hammergaard soloist.*

5952 [Festival overture, Op. 33]   *7'30"*
2(2nd alt. Picc.),2,2,2-4,3,3,1-Timp.,Trgl.,
Xyl.-Cel.-Str.
Samfundet til Udgivelse af Dansk Musik,
Copenhagen, C1947
Score 48 p.
*Composed 1939. First performance Copenhagen,
14 December 1939, Det Unge Tonekünstner Sels-
kabs Orkester, Martellius Lündquist conductor.*

KOPTIAIEV, ALEXANDER PETROVICH.
                St. Petersburg 12 October 1868
                Leningrad 27 January 1941

1816 Elegie, Op. 21
2,2,2,3*-4,2,3,1-Timp.,Perc.-Hp.-Str.
Zimmermann, Leipzig, C1911
Score 27 p.

664 Poème élégiaque, Op. 11   *15'*
2,2,2,2-4,2,3,1-Timp.-Str.
Jurgenson, Moscow [n.d.]
Score 48 p.

KOPYLOV, ALEXANDER ALEXANDROVICH.
                St. Petersburg 14 July 1854
        Strelna, near St. Petersburg 20 February 1911

1373 [Concert overture, Op. 31, D minor]   16'
3*,2,2,2-4,2,3,1-Timp.,Perc.-Str.
Zimmermann, Leipzig [n.d.]
Score 78 p.
*Composed 1910. First performance St. Peters-
burg, 1910.*

743 Scherzo, Op. 10 [A major]   9'
3*,2,2,2-4,2,3-Timp.-Str.
Belaieff, Leipzig [n.d.]
Score 71 p.
*Composed 1888. First performance St. Peters-
burg, 1889.*

415 [Symphony, Op. 14, C minor]   28'
1.Andante 2.Scherzo 3.Andante 4.Allegro
3*,2,2,2-4,2,3,1-Timp.-Str.
Belaieff, Leipzig, 1890
Score 185 p.
*Composed 1889. First performance St. Peters-
burg, 1890.*

KORESHCHENKO, ARSENYI NIKOLAIEVICH.
                    Moscow 18 December 1870
                    Kharkov 3 January 1921

1746 [Armenian suite, Op. 20]
1.[At the brook] 2.Scherzo 3.Tempo di valse
4.[Armenian dance] 5.Finale
3*,2(2nd alt. E.H.),2,2-4,2,3-Timp.,Perc.-
Pno.,Hp.,Mand.-Str.
Bessel, St. Petersburg [n.d.]
Score 74 p.

KORGANOV, GENARI OSSIPOVICH.
          Kvareli, Georgia, Russia 12 May 1858
          Rostov on the Don, Russia 12 April 1890

2310 In the gondola, Op. 6 no. 20. Arranged
by William F. Happich
1,1,1,1-Hn.-Hp.-Str.
Ms.
Score 14 p.

154s Mazurka, B minor. Arranged for string
orchestra and harp by William F. Happich
Hp.-Str.
Ms.
Score 14 p.
*From Arthur Hartmann's transcriptions for
violin and piano.*

KORN, PETER JONA.   Berlin 30 March 1922

5395 Adagietto, Op. 23   8'
1,1,1,1-2,1,1(optional)-Timp.-Str.
Ms.
Score 8 p. Large folio
*Composed 1954. First performance Austin,
Texas, 30 March 1955, University of Texas
Symphony, A. von Kreisler conductor.*

486m Concertino for horn and double   14'
string orchestra, Op. 15
Allegretto - Adagio - Rondino
Solo Hn.-Str.
Ms. [C1959 by Boosey & Hawkes, New York]
Score 20 p. Large folio
Composed 1952. First performance Ojai,

*California, 22 May 1953, Ojai Festival Orches-
tra, Thor Johnson conductor, Joseph Eger
soloist.*

465m Concerto for alto saxophone, Op. 31   20'
1.Allegro con spirito 2.Andante sostenuto -
Cadenza - Allegretto
Solo Sax.-2,2,2,2-4Hn.-Timp.-Str.
Ms.
Score 42 p. Large folio
*Commissioned by Sigurd Rascher. Composed 1956.
First performance Elkhart, Indiana, 6 January
1957, Elkhart Symphony, Zigmont Gaska con-
ductor, Sigurd Rascher soloist.*

5572 Idyllwild, overture to a music   4'30"
camp, Op. 4 [revised version, 1957]
2(2nd alt. Picc.),2*,2(2nd alt. B.Cl.),2-4,
2,3,1-Timp.,Perc.-Str.
Ms. [C by N. Simrock, Berlin]
Score 21 p. Large folio
Composed 1947. Revised 1957.

5394 In medias res overture, Op. 21   3'30"
2(2nd alt. Picc.),2*,2,2-4,2,3,1-Timp.,Perc.-
Hp.(ad lib.)-Str.
Ms. [C1963 by Boosey & Hawkes, New York]
Score 22 p.
*Composed 1953. First performance Los Angeles,
9 August 1955, Los Angeles Philharmonic
Orchestra, Izler Solomon conductor.*

475m Rhapsody for oboe and strings, Op. 14   8'
Solo Ob.-Str.
Ms. [C by N. Simrock, Berlin]
Score 9 p. Large folio
*Composed 1951. First performance Los Angeles,
14 March 1964, Los Angeles Philharmonic, Henry
Lewis conductor, Bert Gassman soloist.*

5791 [Symphony no. 1, Op. 3, C major.   22'
Revised version, 1957]
In one movement
3*,3*,3*(2nd alt. Cl. in E-flat),3*-4,3,3,1-
Timp.-Str.
Ms.
Score 50 p. Large folio
*Composed 1943-46. First performance University
of Southern California, Los Angeles, 1950, New
Orchestra of Los Angeles, the composer con-
ducting. Revised version, 1957.*

5330 [Symphony no. 2, Op. 13]   40'
1.Allegro con brio 2.Adagio 3.Allegretto
4.Allegro ma non troppo
4*,2(2nd alt. E.H.),4*,2-6,3,3,1-Timp.,Perc.-
Str.
Ms.
Score 163 p. Large folio
Composed 1950-52.

5535 [Symphony no. 3, Op. 30]   30'
In one movement
3(3rd alt. Picc.),3*,3*,3*-4,3,3,1-Timp.,Perc.
-Cel.,Hp.-Str.
Ms.
Score 82 p. Large folio
Composed 1956. First performance Los Angeles,

Korn, Peter Jona

21 November 1957, Los Angeles Philharmonic, Eduard van Beinum conductor.

5399 [Tom Paine, a symphonic portrait, *13'*
Op. 9]
3*,2(2nd alt. E.H.),2(2nd alt. B.Cl.),2-4,2,
3,1-Timp.,Perc.-Str.
Ms.
Score 73 p.
Composed 1949-50. First performance Malmö, Sweden, 8 December 1959, Malmö Symphony Orchestra, the composer conducting.

5310 Variations, on a tune from The *27'*
Beggar's Opera, Op. 26
1(alt. Picc.),1(alt. E.H.),2(2nd alt. B.Cl.),
1-2,1,1-Timp.,Perc.-Cel.,Hp.-Str.
Ms.
Score 44 p. Large folio
The theme is Air 16: Over the Hills and Far Away, from Act I. Commissioned by the Louisville Orchestra. Composed 1954-55. First performance Louisville, Kentucky, 1 October 1955, Louisville Orchestra, Robert Whitney conductor.

KORNAUTH, EGON. Olmütz, Moravia
(now Olomouc, Czechoslovakia) 14 May 1891
Vienna 28 October 1959

513c Ballade [violoncello and *13'*
orchestra, Op. 17]
Solo Vc.-3*,2*,3*,2-4,2,3-Timp.,Perc.-Hp.-Str.
Zimmermann, Leipzig [n.d.]
Score 50 p.

KORNGOLD, ERICH WOLFGANG. Brünn, Moravia
(now Brno, Czechoslovakia) 29 May 1897
Hollywood 29 November 1957

454 [Much ado about nothing, suite, Op. 11] *22'*
[1.Overture 2.Maidens in the bridal chamber
3.Dogberry and verges - March of the constables 4.Intermezzo 5.Mummery]
1(alt. Picc.),1,1,1-2,1,1-Timp.,Perc.-Pno.,
Hp.,Harm.-Str.
B. Schott's Söhne, Mainz, C1921
Score 81 p.
Composed 1918. First performance Vienna, 1919.

1402 Schauspiel-Ouverture, Op. 4 *16'*
3*,2,3*,3*-4,3,3,1-Timp.,Perc.-Hp.-Str.
Schott, Mainz, C1912
Score 62 p.
Composed 1911. First performance Gewandhaus, Leipzig, 1911, Arthur Nikisch conductor.

2169 [Der Schneemann. Overture] *5'*
2(2nd alt. Picc.),2,2,2-4,2,3-Timp.,Perc.-Hp.-
Str.
Universal Edition, Vienna, C1910
Score 23 p.
Composed 1909. First performance Vienna Staatsoper, 1910, Franz Schalk conductor.

1337 Sinfonietta, Op. 5 *45'*
1.Fliessend 2.Scherzo 3.Molto andante
4.Finale

3*,2(2nd alt. E.H.),3*,3*-4,3,3,1-Timp.,Perc.-
Pno.,Cel.,2Hp.-Str.
Schott, Mainz, C1914
Score 192 p.
Composed 1912. First performance Vienna, 1912, Felix Weingartner conductor.

455 [Sursum Corda, symphonic overture, *18'*
Op. 13]
3(3rd alt. Picc.),3*,4*,3*-4,4,3,1-Timp.,Perc.-
Pno.,2Hp.-Str.
Schott, Mainz, C1921
Score 78 p.
Composed and first performed 1919, the composer conducting.

KORNSAND, EMIL. Colmar, Alsace 12 February 1894
Cape Cod 15 June 1973

1190v Concerto for viola and orchestra *23'30"*
[Op. 38]
1.Sonata 2.Romance 3.Passacaglia 4.Scherzo:
a)Fugue - b)Reminiscences
Solo Va.-2,2*,2(2nd alt. B.Cl.),2-2,3,1
(optional)-Timp.,Perc.-Str.
Ms.
Score 91 p.
First performance Boston, 8 February 1945, Civic Symphony Orchestra, Paul Cherkassky conductor, the composer as soloist.

1075m Fantasia for organ and strings *11'*
Solo Org.-Str.
Ms.
Score 29 p. Large folio
Composed 1944.

2008s Polyphonia for string orchestra
1.Boldly and angularly 2.Lamentingly 3.Exuberantly - Dreamily 4.Flowingly - Coquettishly - Ponderously
Str.
Ms.
Score 47 p.
Composed in the 1950's.

KORTE, KARL. Ossining, New York 23 June 1928

6304 Ceremonial prelude and passa- *12'*
caglia for symphonic band
3*,3*,5*(1 in E-flat)-4Sax.-4,2,3Cnt.,3,Bar.,
2-Timp.,Perc.-Cb.
Ms.
Score 45 p. Large folio
Composed 1962. First performance Brevard Music Center, Brevard, North Carolina, 3 July 1962, Brevard Concert Band, James C. Pfohl conductor.

5948 For a young audience [first *12'*
orchestral version]
Prelude - Dance - Song - Fanfare and hymn
1,1,1,1-2,2,1-Timp.,S.Dr.-Str.
Ms.
Score 47 p.
Commissioned by the Greenwich Village Civic Symphony. Originally composed as a piano suite, 1958. Orchestrated 1959. First performance New York, 18 November 1960, Greenwich

Village Civic Symphony, Norman Masonson conductor. Later revised as Music for a Young Audience.

6309 Southwest (a dance overture). *10'*
Revised version
3*,2,2,2-4,3,3,1-Timp.,Perc.-Pno.,Hp.-Str.
Ms.
Score 51 p. Large folio
Composed 1962. First performance Mutual Broadcasting Network, Oklahoma City, 17 March 1963, Oklahoma City Symphony, Guy Fraser Harrison conductor. Revised 1963.

6225 Symphony no. 2, in one movement *20'*
3(3rd alt. Picc.),3*,3*,3*-4,3,3,1-Timp.,Perc.-Hp.-Str.
Ms.
Score 89 p. Large folio
Composed 1961. First performance Mutual Broadcasting Network, Oklahoma City, 28 November 1961, Oklahoma City Symphony Orchestra, Guy Fraser Harrison conductor.

KÓSA, GYÖRGY. Budapest 24 April 1897

2346 [Six pieces for orchestra] *10'*
[1.Loneliness 2.Reckless merriment 3.The sceptic's prayer 4.Timid yearning 5.Nevertheless 6.Hopeless]
3*,3*,3*,3*-4,3,3,1-Timp.,Perc.-Cel.,Hp.-Str.
Universal Edition, Vienna, c1926
Score 27 p.
Composed 1919. First performance Budapest, 1922, Philharmonic Orchestra, Ernst Dohnanyi conductor.

KOSAKOFF, REUVEN. New Haven 8 January 1898

2210s Three moods, based on Hebrew *8'*
cantillations
1.Aslo geresh, Dargo Tvir 2.Munach zorkoh, Munach segal 3.Fugue
Str.(without Cb.)
Ms.
Score 13 p.
Commissioned by the Workmen's Circle of New York. Composed 1952. First performance, New York, 1952, Lazar Weiner conductor.

KOSITZKY, PH.

3524 [Cossack Holota, suite, Op. 14]
1.[The song of Cossack Holota] 2.Hala 3.[Captain Puso] 4.[The battle]
3*,2,3*,2-4,2,3,1-Timp.,Perc.-Str.
Mussektor [n.p., n.d.]
Score 64 p.

KOSPOTH, OTTO KARL ERDMANN.
b. Muhltroff, Saxony 17--?
Berlin 23 June 1817

3055 [Symphony no. 7, Op. 23]
1.Allegro con brio 2.Andante un poco allegretto 3.Menuetto 4.Presto
2ob.-2Hn.-Str.
Ms.
Score 76 p.

KOSTAKOWSKY, JACOBO. Odessa, Russia 24 March 1893
Mexico City 17 August 1953

4919 [Chamber music no. 5, Street *10'*
sketches]
2*(Picc. optional),1,1-Tpt.-Pno.-Str.
Ms.
Score 24 p.
First performance Mexico City, 22 January 1937, Orquesta de Cámara de Mexico, Silvestre Revueltas conductor.

1202v [Concerto, violin, no. 1, C major]
Allegro non troppo - Andante espressivo - (Maestoso) poco animato - Allegro fuocoso
Solo Vn.-2(2nd alt. Picc.),2,3*,2-2,2,1,1-Timp.,Perc.-Hp.-Str.
Ms.
Score 56 p.
Composed 1942.

3889 Lascas [Fragments], symphonic poem
3*,2,4*,2-4,2,3,1-Timp.,Perc.-Hp.-Str.
Ms. c1940 by the composer
Score 156 p.
Composed 1939.

3882 El romancero gitano [The gypsy romancer, suite]
1.Moderato non troppo 2.Allegretto 3.Mosso 4.Allegro marcato
3*,2,4*,1-4,2,3,1-Timp.,Perc.-Cel.,Hp.-Str.
Ms.
Score 123 p.

KÖSZEGI, ALEXANDER. Hungary 1880
New York 15 December 1937

1619s Air [for string orchestra]
Str.
Ms.
Score 5 p.

1621s Gavotte [for string orchestra]
Str.
Ms.
Score 4 p.

1616s Menuet [for string orchestra]
Str.
Ms.
Score 5 p.

1620s Sicilienne [for string orchestra]
Str.
Ms.
Score 5 p.

KÖTSCHER, HANS. Weimar 12 November 1877
Düsseldorf 2 July 1925

278s Serenade, Op. 2 [G major]
1.Allegro scherzando 2.Menuetto 3.Andante, mit Variationen 4.Rondo
Str.
Hug, Leipzig [n.d.]
Score 23 p.

Koundourov, Aristote G.

KOUNDOUROV, ARISTOTE G.

1867   Conte no. 2 [Tale]
3*,2,2,2-4,2,3,1-Timp.,Perc.-Hp.-Str.
Ms.
Score 32 p.
Composed 1925; orchestrated 1929.

1952   Ikar [Icarus] symphonic poem
4(2 are Picc.),2,3,3*-6,3,3,1-Timp.,Perc.-2Hp.
-Str.
Ms.
Score 49 p.

2937   Suite grecque [Greek suite]
Part I. Andante maestoso - Con moto
Part II. Largo - Sirtos
3*,3*,3*,2-4,2,3,1-Timp.,Perc.-Hp.-Str.
Ms.
Score 128 p.
Composed 1930.

2938   Symphoniette
2,2,2,2-4,2,3,1-Timp.,Perc.-Cel.,Hp.-Str.
Ms.
Score 42 p.
Composed 1934.   Awarded the Academy of Athens Prize, 1934.

KOUSSEVITZKY, SERGE ALEXANDROVICH.
Vyshny Volochek, Russia 26 July 1874
Boston 4 June 1951

441c   [Concerto, contrabass, Op. 3,   20'
F-sharp minor]
1.Allegro 2.Andante 3.Allegro
Solo Cb.-2,2,2,2-4Hn.-Hp.-Str.
Ms.
Score 100 p.
Composed 1902.   First performance Moscow, 25 February 1905, Moscow Philharmonic Society, the composer as soloist.

KOUTZEN, BORIS.   Uman, near Kiev 1 April 1901
Mt. Kisco, New York 10 December 1966

763c   Concert piece for violoncello and   12'
strings
Andante sostenuto - Allegro - Adagio ma non
troppo - Rondo: Allegro giocoso
Solo Vc.-Str.
Elkan-Vogel, Philadelphia, c1946
Score 40 p.
Composed 1940.   First performance of this version, Saratoga Springs, New York, 7 September 1947, New York Philharmonic, F. Charles Adler conductor, Carl Stern soloist.

941m   Concerto, five solo instruments and   13'
strings
Recitativo - Passacaglia - Finale
Soli: Fl.,Cl.,Bn.,Hn.,Vc.-Str.
Ms.
Score 27 p.
Composed 1934.   First performance New York, 12 March 1935, National Orchestra Association, Leon Barzin conductor.

374v   Concerto for violin and orchestra   25'
1.Lento - Allegro 2.Lento 3.Allegro vivo
Solo Vn.-3(3rd alt. Picc.),2,2,2-4,2,3-Timp.,
Perc.-Hp.-Str.
Ms.
Score 146 p. Large folio
Composed 1946.   First performance Philadelphia, 22 February 1952, Philadelphia Orchestra, Eugene Ormandy conductor, Nadia Koutzen soloist.

5867   Divertimento for orchestra
1.Pop concert 2.At the ballet 3.Holiday mood
2(2nd alt. Picc.),2,2,2-2,2,1-Timp.,Perc.-Hp.
-Str.
Ms.
Score 114 p.
Composed 1956.   First performance Vassar College, Poughkeepsie, New York, 6 March 1966, Vassar College Orchestra, the composer conducting.

5387   From the American folklore, concert   8'
overture
3(3rd alt. Picc.),3*,3*,3*-4,3,3,1-Timp.,Perc.
-Hp.-Str.
Ms.
Score 34 p. Large folio
Based on American folksongs.   Composed 1943. First performance Pittsburgh, 5 April 1957, Pittsburgh Symphony, William Steinberg conductor.

2863   Poème-nocturne, Solitude   11'
3*,3*,3*,3*-4,2,3,1-Timp.,Perc.-2Hp.-Str.
Ms.
Score 56 p.
Composed 1927.   First performance Philadelphia, 1 April 1927, Philadelphia Orchestra, the composer conducting.

1130v   [Symphonic movement, violin and   12'
orchestra]
Solo Vn.-3(3rd alt. Picc.),3*,2,2-4,2,3,1-
Timp.,Perc.-Hp.-Str.
Ms.
Score 75 p.
Composed 1929.

3123   Symphony in C   27'
1.Allegro moderato 2.Adagio 3.[No tempo
indicated] 4.Allegro risoluto
3*,3*,3*,3*-4,3,3,1-Timp.,Perc.-Hp.-Str.
Ms.
Score 170 p. Large folio
Composed 1939.

3734   Valley Forge, symphonic poem   13'
3(2nd alt. Alto Fl.,3rd alt. Picc.),3*,3(2nd
alt. E-flat Cl.),3*-4,3,3,1-Timp.,Perc.-Hp.-
Str.
Ms.
Score 66 p.
Composed 1931.   First performance New York, 19 February 1940, National Orchestra Association, Leon Barzin conductor.   Received Juilliard Publication Award 1944.

KOVACH, K.V.

2939 [Abkhaz, 13 songs for orchestra]
2,2,2,2-2,2,2-Timp.,Perc.-Str.
Mussektor, Moscow, 1930
Score 54 p.

4012 [Abkhazian suite]
1.[Song of the lake] 2.[Shepherd's tale]
2,2,2,2-2,2,2-Timp.,Perc.-Str.
Mussektor, Moscow, 1930
Score 20 p.

1785 [In a Bombay hut, Abkhazian poem]
1,1,2,1-2,2,1-Timp.,Perc.-Pno.,Harm.-Str.
Mussektor, Moscow, 1929
Score 37 p.
Composed 1928.

3937 [Sharatyn, song of the Caucasus]
1,1,2-0,2,2-Timp.,Perc.-Pno.,Harm.-Str.
Mussektor, Moscow, 1931
Score 15 p.

4011 [Thy way, Abkhazian poem]
1,2,2,2-2,2,1-Timp.,Perc.-Pno.,Harm.-Str.
Mussektor, Moscow, 1929
Score 26 p.
Composed 1928.

3021 [Tkvarchely, Abkhazian symphonic poem]
2,2,2,2-2,2,2-Timp.,Perc.-Str.
Mussektor, Moscow,1930
Score 19 p.
Composed 1929.

KOVAŘOVIC, KAREL.   Prague 9 December 1862
                          Prague 6 December 1920

878s [Gavotta, for string orchestra, Op. 3]
Str.
Urbánek, Prague, 1884
Score 6 p.
First performance Budweis, 25 March 1884.

1669 [Waltz]   4'
1,1,1,1-2,1-Str.
Urbánek, Prague [n.d.]
Score 9 p.
Composed 1890. First performance Prague, 1891.

KOWALSKI, HENRI.   Paris 1841
                          Bordeaux 8 July 1916

690s Il était une fois, conte, Op. 64
Str.
Score: Ms. 8 p.
Parts: Schott, Mainz [n.d.]

1677s La malmaison, caprice, Op. 16 no. 12
Str.
Score: Ms. 4 p.
Parts: Schott, Mainz [n.d.]

KRAFT, LEO.   New York 24 July 1922

2274s Larghetto, in memory of Karol   5'
Rathaus

Timp.-Str.
Ms.
Score 8 p.
Composed 1954. First performance at a Karol Rathaus Memorial Concert, Queens College, New York, November 1955, Queens College Orchestra, John Castellini conductor.

6675 [Overture for orchestra, in G]   8'
Allegro con spirito - Andante - Allegro
2,1,2,2-2,2,2-Timp.,Cym.-Str.
Ms.
Score 43 p.
Composed 1947. First performance Jamaica, New York, 19 March 1949, Queens College Orchestral Society, Boris Schwarz conductor. Awarded the Queens Golden Jubilee Prize, 1949.

KRAFT, WILLIAM.   Chicago 6 September 1923

7182 Fanfare
See: FANFARES 1969 FOR 8 TRUMPETS. No. V

7181 Nonet for brass and percussion   25'
6 movements
0,0,0,0-1,2,1,1-Timp.,Perc.
Avant Music, Los Angeles, c1969
Score 90 p.
First performance Monday Evening Concerts, Los Angeles, 13 October 1958, the composer conducting.

KRAMER, A. WALTER.   New York 23 September 1890
                          New York 8 April 1969

1070v [Symphonic rhapsody, violin and   17'
orchestra, Op. 35, F minor]
Solo Vn.-2(2nd alt. Picc.),3*,2,2-4,2,3,1-
Timp.-Hp.-Str.
Ms.
Score 76 p.
Composed 1912. First performance Lewisohn Stadium, New York, 7 August 1919, Lewisohn Symphony Orchestra, Arnold Volpe conductor, Ilya Schkolnik soloist.

KRAMER, MARTIN.

3143 [Symphony no. 1, American, E-flat   47'
major]
1.Allegro 2.Rumbolero 3.Slow 4.Allegro molto
2(2nd alt. Picc.)1,2,1-4Sax.(all alt. Cl.)-
4,3,2-Timp.,Perc.-Str.
Ms.
Score 236 p.
Composed 1939.

KRAMM, GEORG.   Kassel, Germany 21 December 1856
                          Düsseldorf October 1910

4434 [Herod's feast - Salome dances, Op. 23]
3(3rd alt. Picc.),3*,2,2-4,3,3,1-Timp.,Perc.-
Hp.-Str.
C.F. Schmidt, Heilbronn, c1902
Score 39 p.

Krancher, Willy

KRANCHER, WILLY.   Basel, Switzerland 27 May 1900

319v [Rhapsody for viola and   *24'*
orchestra]
Solo Va.-2(2nd alt. Picc.),2,2,2-2,2,1-Timp.-
Hp.-Str.
Editions Metropolis, Belgium, c1959
Score 89 p.
Composed 1957. First performance Lugano,
Switzerland, 28 September 1958, Orchestra Radio
-Svizzera-Italiana, the composer conducting,
Renato Carenzio soloist.

KRANICH, ALWIN.

25s Märchen [Fairy tale] Op. 20
Str.
F.E.C. Leuckart, Leipzig, c1901
Score 6 p.

KRASUSKI, SL.

1141s Je vous adore, valse mignonne, Op. 51
Str.
Ms.
Score 12 p.

KRATZ, ROBERT.

961s Suite, Op. 20 [F major]
Andante - Scherzo - Finale
Str.
A.P. Küpper, Elberfeld [n.d.]
Score 15 p.

KRAUSE, EMIL.   Hamburg 30 July 1840
                           Hamburg 5 September 1916

1519s Abendlied [Evening song] Op. 56 no. 1a
Str.
[A. Cranz, n.p., n.d.]
Score 3 p.

KREIN, ALEXANDER ABRAMOVICH.   Nizhni-Novgorod
            (now Gorki), Russia 20 October 1883
                   Moscow 21 April 1951

893s Elégie, Op. 21
Str.
Mussektor, Moscow, c1927
Score 7 p.
Composed 1914.

929s [Hebrew sketches no. 1, Op. 12]
Cl.-Str.(without Cb.)
Mussektor, Moscow, c1928
Score 21 p.
Composed 1909.

1784s [Hebrew sketches no. 2, Op. 13]   *10'*
Cl.-Str.(without Cb.)
Mussektor, Moscow [n.d.]
Score 23 p.
First performance Moscow, 1910.

2020 [Mourning ode, to the memory of Lenin,
Op. 40]
3(3rd alt. Picc.),3,3*,3*-6,3,3,1-Timp.,Perc.-

2Hp.-Chorus(SATB)-Str.
Mussektor, Moscow, c1927
Score 35 p.
Composed 1925-26.

2940 [Night in the old market place,   *20'*
Op. 38]
In 16 scenes
1(alt. Picc),1(alt. E.H.),1,1-2,2,1,1-Timp.,
Perc.-Str.
Mussektor, Moscow, 1934
Score 105 p.
Composed 1924; from the incidental music to
the play by L. Perez. First performance Mos-
cow, 1934, Moscow Orchestra, USSR Radio Com-
mittee, Leo Binsburg conductor.

1671 La rose et la croix [symphonic   *20'*
fragments] Op. 26
1.[The chateau of Artchimbault. Twilight] 2.
[The lodgings of Isore] 3.[At the seaside]
4.[The song of Gaetan] 5.[The death of
Bertrand]
3*,3*,3*,3*-4,3,3,1-Timp.,Cym.,Gong-2Hp.-Str.
Mussektor, Moscow, c1927
Score 56 p.
Composed 1917-21; inspired by a poem of
Alexander Blok.

1670 [Symphony no. 1, Op. 35]   *35'*
1.Allegro con fuoco 2.Lento 3.Allegro
risoluto
3(3rd alt. Picc.),3*,3*,3*-4,3,3,1-Timp.,Cym.,
Dr.-Cel.,2Hp.-Str.
Mussektor, Moscow, 1926
Score 167 p.
Composed 1922-25.

3216 [Zagmuk. Suite from the opera]   *26'*
1.[Introduction to the 5th tableau] 2.[Dance
of the odalisques]
3*,3*,3*,3*-4,3,3,1-Timp.,Perc.-2Hp.-Chorus
(ad lib.)-Str.
Mussektor, Moscow, 1937
Score 43 p.
Composed 1929-30. First performance of suite
Moscow, 14 March 1937, Moscow Philharmonic
Orchestra, Nicolai Golovanov conductor.

KREISLER, FRITZ.   Vienna 2 February 1875
                         New York 29 January 1962

157s Andantino [violin and piano. Transcribed
for string orchestra by William Happich]
Str.
B. Schott's Söhne, Mainz, c1910
Score in reduction 3 p.
Attributed to Padre Martini when first pub-
lished. Kreisler acknowledged this as his
own composition in 1935.

712v [Concerto, violin, strings and   *11'*
organ, C major]
1.Allegro moderato e maestoso 2.Andante doloroso 3.Allegro assai
Solo Vn.-Org.-Str.
B. Schott's Söhne, Mainz/C. Fischer, New York,
c1928

Score 20 p.
Attributed to Vivaldi when first published.
Kreisler acknowledged this as his own composition in 1935.

4226 Liebesfreud. Transcribed for   *3'*
orchestra by Charles J. Roberts
Solo Vn.-1,1,2,1-3Sax.(optional)-2,2Cnt.,1-
Timp.,Trgl.,Bells-Str.
Carl Fischer, New York, ^C1914
Score in reduction 7 p.
Originally composed for violin and piano.

423v Praeludium and allegro [in the   *4'*
style of Gaetano Pugnani. Transcribed for
solo violin and small orchestra by W.F.
Happich]
Solo Vn.-2,2,2,2-2Hn.-Timp.-Str.
Ms.
Score 28 p.
Originally composed for violin and piano.
Attributed by Kreisler to Pugnani when first published by Carl Fischer in 1910. This transcription 1919.

3660 [Same as above. Transcribed for   *6'*
orchestra by Herman Rudin]
2,2,2,2-4,2,3,1-Timp.,Perc.-Hp.-Str.
Ms. ^C1940 by Charles Foley
Score 41 p.
Originally composed for violin and piano, and attributed by Kreisler to Pugnani. This transcription 1939. First performance Rochester, New York, 21 January 1940, Rochester Civic Orchestra, Guy Fraser Harrison conductor.

6514 [Same as above. Transcribed for   *5'30"*
orchestra by Fabien Sevitzky]
3*,3*,3*,3*-4,3,3,1-Timp.,Cym.,Bells-Cel.-Str.
Charles Foley, New York [^Cn.d. by Carl Fischer, New York]
Score 26 p.
Originally composed for violin and piano.
Attributed by Kreisler to Pugnani when first published by Schott in 1910. This transcription 1941; first performance Indianapolis, 3 November 1945, Indianapolis Symphony Orchestra, Fabien Sevitzky conductor.

4225 Schön Rosmarin. Transcribed for   *3'*
orchestra by Charles J. Roberts
Solo Vn.-1,1,2,1-2,2,1-Timp.,Trgl.-Str.
Carl Fischer, New York, ^C1914
Score in reduction 4 p.
Originally composed for violin and piano.

4224 Tambourin chinois, Op. 3. Transcribed   *4'*
for orchestra by Erno Rapee
2(both alt. Picc.),2,2,2-4,2(or 2Cnt.),3,1-
Timp.,Perc.-Hp.-Str.
Carl Fischer Inc., New York, ^C1927
Score in reduction 7 p.
Originally composed for violin and piano.

KREMENLIEV, BORIS ANGELOFF.
            ^{b.} Razlog, Bulgaria 23 May 1911

Also published as Boris Angeloff.

5371 Bulgarian rhapsody   *14'*
3(2nd & 3rd alt. Picc.),3(3rd alt. E.H.),2,2-
4,3,3,1-Timp.,Perc.-Hp.-Str.
Ms.
Score 91 p. Large folio
Composed 1952-53.

5372 Crucifixion, after the cycle of   *15'*
paintings by Rico Lebrun
1.Massacre of innocents   2.Workmen of death
3.Deposition
3(2nd alt. Picc. & Alto Fl.,3rd alt. Picc.),
2(2nd alt. E.H.),2(2nd alt. Cl. in E-flat),2-
3,4,4,Bar.,2-Timp.,Perc.-Pno.,Org.-Cb.
Ms.
Score 45 p. Large folio
Commissioned by the Theatre Arts Department, University of California at Los Angeles for a documentary film. First performance Los Angeles, 24 May 1952, the composer conducting.

5367 [Straight dance]   *3'45"*
3*,3*,2,2-4,2,3,1-Timp.,Perc.-Hp.-Str.
Ms.
Score 43 p. Large folio
Composed 1940. First performance NBC Radio, 18 April 1940, Rochester Civic Orchestra, Howard Hanson conductor.

5373 Study for orchestra   *5'*
1(alt. Alto Fl.),2*,3*,2*-2,2,1-Timp.,Perc.-
Hp.-Str.
Ms.
Score 15 p. Large folio
Composed 1947. First performance Los Angeles, 18 November 1952, UCLA Symphony Orchestra, Carl Bowman conductor.

5374 Wilderness road, for symphonic band   *10'*
1.The Great Smoky Mountains   2.Cherokee fire
dance   3.Daniel Boone
3*,2(2nd alt. E.H.),5*(1 Alto Cl.,),2-3Sax.
(Alto,Ten.,Bar.)-4,2,2Cnt.,3,Bar.,2-Timp.,
Perc.-Cb.
Ms.
Score 49 p. Large folio
Composed 1953. First performance Los Angeles, 25 May 1954, UCLA Symphonic Band, Clarence Sawhill conductor.

KREMSER, EDUARD.   Vienna 10 April 1838
                   Vienna 27 November 1914

994s Albumblatt [Albumleaf no. 1]
Timp.(ad lib.)-Hp.-Str.
Wiener Musik Verlagshaus, Vienna [n.d.]
Score 7 p.

5779 [Old French Christmas carol. Transcribed
for orchestra by Eduard Kremser]
2,2,2,2-4,2,3-Timp.,Perc.-Hp.-Str.
C. Hofbauer, Vienna [n.d.]
Score 14 p.

5697 [Thanksgiving prayer, We Gather Together,
no. 6 from the cycle, Six Old Dutch Folksongs]
2,2,2,2-4,2,3-Timp.,Trgl.,Tam-tam-Pno.,Org.,
Hp.-Chorus(TTBB&SATB ad lib.)-Str.

Krenek, Ernst

Leuckart, Leipzig [1879]
Score 9 p.
Melody is "1620," first published by Adrianus Valerius, 1626. German text by Joseph Weyl.

KŘENEK, ERNST.   Vienna 23 August 1900

368m [Concerto, harp, Op. 126] Harp part   *17'*
edited by Edna Phillips
1.Andante con moto 2.Allegretto 3.Adagio
Solo Hp.-1,1,1,1-2,1-Str.
Universal Edition [Vienna, c1961]
Score 33 p. Large folio
Composed for Edna Phillips, 1951. First performance Philadelphia, 12 December 1952, Philadelphia Orchestra, Eugene Ormandy conductor, Edna Phillips soloist.

812v [Concerto, violin, Op. 29]   *18'*
In one movement
Solo Vn.-2(2nd alt. Picc.),0,2,2-2,2-Str.
Universal Edition, Vienna, c1925
Score 44 p.
Composed 1923. First performance Dessau, 5 January 1924, Franz von Hösslin conductor, Alma Moodie soloist.

1673 [Concerto grosso no. 2, Op. 25]   *35'*
1.Allegro molto moderato e pesante 2.Adagio
3.Allegretto comodo 4.Andante quasi adagio
5.Allegro
Soli: Vn.,Va.,Vc.-2,2,2,2-1-Str.
Universal Edition, Vienna, c1925
Score 49 p.
Composed 1924. First performance Dresden 1925, Fritz Busch conductor.

5343 Eleven transparencies [Op. 142]   *20'*
1.Design from darkness 2.Flashes 3.Waves
4.Images and spooks 5.Rays of warmth 6.
Sparks cascading 7.Light and shade 8.Knocks
and dashes 9.Volcano of anguish 10.Upon
hearing the call from far away 11.The rest is
silence
2(1st alt. Picc.),2,2,2-4,2,2,1-Timp.,Perc.-
Hp.-Str.
Ms. [now published by B. Schott and Universal
Edition, Vienna, c1959]
Score 38 p. Large folio
Commissioned by The Louisville Orchestra. Composed 1954. First performance Louisville, Kentucky, 12 February 1955, The Louisville Orchestra, Robert Whitney conductor.

4207 [Jonny spielt auf, Op. 45. Fantasie.
Arranged for small orchestra by Emil Bauer]
1,1,2,1-3Sax.(1Sop.,2Alto,all ad lib.)-3(3rd
ad lib.),2,3(2nd & 3rd ad lib.)-Perc.-Flexa-
ton-Banjo(ad lib.),Harm.-Str.
Universal Edition, Vienna, c1928
Score in reduction 18 p.
Medley from the opera in two parts with libretto by the composer. Opera composed 1925-26. First performance Leipzig, 10 February 1927.

1674 Kleine Symphonie, Op. 58   *15'*
1.Andante sostenuto 2.Andantino 3.Allegretto,

poco grave
2,0,3(2nd alt. B.Cl.),2(2nd alt. C.Bn.)-0,3,
2,1-Timp.,Perc.-Hp.,2Mand.,Guit.,2Banjo-Str.
(Vn.I/II,Cb.I/II)
Universal Edition, Vienna, c1929
Score 50 p.
Composed 1928. First performance Berlin, 1 November 1928, Otto Klemperer conductor.

1888 Potpourri [for large orchestra,   *18'*
Op. 54]
Allegro vivace - Allegro con brio
2(2nd alt. Picc.),2(2nd alt. E.H.),3(3rd alt.
Cl. in E-flat & B.Cl.),2(2nd alt. C.Bn.)-0,3,
1-Timp.,Perc.-Pno.-Str.
Universal-Edition, Vienna, c1928
Score 70 p.
Composed 1927. First performance Cologne, 15 November 1927, Hermann Abendroth conductor.

1994s Symphonic elegy [Op. 105]   *10'*
Str.
Elkan-Vogel, Philadelphia, c1947
Score 14 p.
Composed 1946. First performance Saratoga Springs, New York, September 1946, Yaddo Festival Orchestra, Charles F. Adler conductor.

1777 [Symphonic music for 9 solo   *35'*
instruments, Op. 11]
1.Allegro deciso, ma non troppo 2.Adagio
1,1,1,1-Str.
Universal Edition, Vienna, c1923
Score 59 p.
Composed 1922. First performance Frankfurt, 18 December 1922, Hermann Scherchen conductor.

1776s Symphonic piece, for string   *16'*
orchestra, Op. 86
Str.
Ms.
Score 22 p.
Commissioned by the Kammerorchester, Basel, 1938. Composed 1939. First performance Ann Arbor, Michigan, 1 August 1939, University of Michigan Musical Society, Summer Session Symphony Orchestra, the composer conducting.

1672 [Three lively marches, Op. 44]   *10'*
1,1,4(1Cl. in E-flat)-2,2,1,1-Timp.,Perc.
Universal Edition, Vienna, c1929
Score 16 p.
Composed and first performed Baden-Baden, 1926.

4837 [The triumph of sensitivity.   *2'*
Suite, Op. 43a. No. 1, Overture]
2,2,2,2-0,2,3-Timp.-Str.
Universal Edition, Vienna
Score 10 p.
Commissioned by the Staatstheater, Kassel, Germany. Extracted, 1927, from incidental music to Goethe's play. First performance Hamburg, 28 November 1927, Gustav Brecher conductor.

KRENZ, JAN.   Włocławek, Poland 14 July 1926

6282 [Rhapsody, percussion and string   *8'*
orchestra]

Timp.,Xyl.,Tam-tam-Cel.-Str.
Polskie Wydawnictwo Muzyczne, Cracow, ^c1954
Score 25 p.
*Composed 1952. First performance Warsaw, 1952,
the National Philharmonic Orchestra, the com-
poser conducting.*

KRETER, LEO.   Rochester, Minnesota 29 August 1933

6588 Vortex, for brass   10'
4Hn.,3Tpt.,3Tbn.,Tuba-Timp.,Perc.
Ms.
Score 14 p. Large folio
*Composed 1962. First performance Wichita,
Kansas, 27 February 1962, University of
Wichita Brass Ensemble, Irving Sarin conductor.*

KRETSCHMER, EDMUND. Ostritz, Saxony 31 August 1830
                     Dresden 13 September 1908

412s Abendruhe [Peaceful evening] from Musi-
kalische Dorfgeschichten [Musical village
stories] Op. 26 no. 6
Str.
Ries & Erler, Berlin [n.d.]
Score 3 p.

6999 [Die Folkunger. Preludes to   9'
Acts 3 and 4]
2,2,2,2-4,2,3,1-Timp.-Org.-Str.
Kistner, Leipzig [1875]
Score 11 p.
*From the opera composed 1872. First perform-
ance Dresden, 21 March 1874.*

251   [Die Folkunger. Royal procession   4'
and Coronation march]
2(2nd alt. Picc.),2,2,2-4,3,3,1-Timp.,Perc.-
(4 Solo Voices, Chorus in first selection)-Str.
Fr. Kistner, Leipzig [n.d.]
Score 17 p.

5883 [Henry the Lion. Overture]
2,2,2,2-4,3,3,1-Timp.,Cym.,B.Dr.-Str.
Fr. Kistner, Leipzig [1877?]
Score 20 p.
*From the opera with libretto by the composer.
First performance Leipzig, 8 December 1877.*

KRETSCHMER, PAUL.

1573s Romanze [F major]
Soli Vn.,Vc.-Str.
Score: Ms. 7 p.
Parts: J.G. Seeling, Dresden [n.d.]

1575s Scherzo [C major]
Soli Vn.,Vc.-Str.
Score: Ms. 11 p.
Parts: J.G. Seeling, Dresden [n.d.]

KREUTZ, ARTHUR.   La Crosse, Wisconsin 25 July 1906

4027 American dances, for chamber   18'
orchestra
Jig time - Blues no. I - Blues no. II -
Boogie woogie
2(2nd alt. Picc.),2,2,2-Str.

Ms.
Score 96 p. Large folio
*Composed 1941. First performance New York,
30 December 1941, the WOR Sinfonietta, Milton
Katims conductor.*

1160v [Concerto, violin]   15'
1.Moderately 2.Moderately 3.Moderately fast
Solo Vn.-2,2,2,2-2,2,1-Str.
Ms.
Score 130 p.
*Composer won a Guggenheim Fellowship for this
and other works.*

4031 Dance music, Land be bright   12'
1(alt. Picc.),1,1,1-Hn.-Pno.-Str.
Ms.
Score 84 p.
*Commissioned by and originally composed 1942
as piano music for Martha Graham's modern
dance, Long May Our Land Be Bright. Transcribed 1942; first performance Austin, Texas,
26 April 1944, the University Symphony Orchestra, the composer conducting.*

4026 Music for symphony orchestra   21'
1.Flowing, rhythmic 2.Quietly, but with
intensity 3.Fast, furiously
2,3*,2,2-4,2,3-Timp.,Cym.-Str.
Ms.
Score 120 p. Large folio
*Composed 1940. First performance New York,
16 June 1940, NBC Symphony Orchestra broadcast,
Frank Black conductor. Awarded Prix de Rome,
1940.*

4032 Paul Bunyan, dance poem   12'
1.The kingdom of Kansas 2.Winter of the blue
snow 3.Paul Bunyan's dinner horn
2,2,3,2-0,3,3-Timp.,Cym.,S.Dr.-Pno.-Str.(without Vc.)
Ms.
Score 102 p. Large folio
Composed 1939.

4033 Symphonic sketch, on three   6'30"
American folk tunes
Kentucky moonshiner - The little brown jug -
Suckin' cider thru a straw
2(2nd alt. Picc.),2,2,2-2,2,3-Cym.-Pno.-Str.
Ms.
Score 50 p.
*Composed 1941. First performance 19th Festi-
val of the International Society for Contem-
porary Music, Berkeley, California, 1 August
1942, Northern California Symphony Orchestra
of the WPA, Nathan Abas conductor.*

KREUTZER, CHARLES-LÉON FRANÇOIS.
See: KREUTZER, LÉON-CHARLES FRANÇOIS.

KREUTZER, CONRADIN.
       Messkirch, Baden, Germany 22 November 1780
                Riga, Estonia 14 December 1849

4293 [Stopover in Granada. Overture]   9'
3*,2,2,2-8(4 offstage),2,3-Timp.-Str.
Joh. André, Offenbach a.M. [1875]

Kreutzer, Léon

Score 54 p.
*From the opera after the play by J. F. Kind.
Composed 1833. First performance Vienna, 13
January 1834.*

KREUTZER, LÉON-CHARLES FRANÇOIS.
Paris 23 September 1817
Vichy 6 October 1868

4447 [Symphony, B-flat major]
1.Andante - Allegro 2.Andante 3.Scherzo:
Presto 4.Finale: Vivace
2(2nd alt. Picc.),2,2,2-4,2,3-Timp.-Str.
[Salme, Paris, 186-?]
Score 80 p.

KREUTZER, RODOLPHE.   Versailles 16 November 1766
Geneva 6 January 1831

1111v [Concerto, violin, Grand, Op. 12, A major]
1.Allegro moderato 2.Adagio 3.Rondo
Solo Vn.-1,2-2Hn.-Str.
Score: Ms. 71 p.
Parts: Breitkopf & Härtel, Leipzig [n.d.]

1087v [Concerto, violin, no. 4, C major]
1.Allegro moderato 2.Siciliano 3.Rondo
Solo Vn.-2Ob.-2Hn.-Str.
Ms.
Score 99 p.

1096v [Concerto, violin, no. 6, E minor]
1.Allegro maestoso 2.Siciliano 3.Rondo
Solo Vn.-2Ob.-2Hn.-Str.
Ms.
Score 71 p.

1088v [Concerto, violin, no. 7, A major]
1.Maestoso 2.Adagio 3.Rondo
Solo Vn.-2Ob.-2Hn.-Str.
Ms.
Score 67 p.

1027v [Concerto, violin, no. 8, D minor]
Edited by Hans Sitt
1.Maestoso non troppo 2.Adagio 3.Rondo
Solo Vn.-1,2-2Hn.-Str.
Score: Ms. 59 p.
Parts: Joh. André, Offenbach a/M, c1907

1046v [Concerto, violin, no. 16, E minor]
1.Allegro moderato 2.Adagio 3.Rondo
Solo Vn.-1,2,0,1-2Hn.-Timp.-Str.
Score: Ms. 83 p.
Parts: Breitkopf & Härtel, Leipzig [n.d.]

1097v [Concerto, violin, no. 17, G major]
1.Maestoso 2.Adagio 3.Rondo
Solo Vn.-2,2-2Hn.-Timp.-Str.
Ms.
Score 45 p.

KREUZ, EMIL.   Elberfeld, Germany 25 May 1867
London 3 December 1932

940s [Suite, Op. 38, G major]
1.Prelude 2.Allemande 3.Gigue 4.Intermezzo
5.Scherzo 6.Finale

Str.
Score: Ms. 42 p.
Parts: [n.p., n.d.]

KŘIČKA, JAROSLAV.   Kelč, Moravia 27 August 1882
Prague 23 January 1969

1829 [Overture to The Blue Bird, Op. 16, after
Maeterlinck's drama]
2(2nd alt. Picc.),2(2nd alt. E.H.),2,2-4,2,3,
1-Timp.,Perc.-Hp.-Str.
N. Simrock, Berlin, c1913
Score 46 p.

1802 Scherzo idyllique, Op. 12
3(3rd alt. Picc.),3,3,3-4,3,3,1-Timp.,Perc.-
Str.
N. Simrock, Berlin, c1929
Score 60 p.

KRIEGER, JOHANN PHILIPP. Nürnberg 25 February 1649
Weissenfels 7 February 1725

1669s [Partie, F major (Feldmusik, 1704, no. 3).
Arranged by Max Seiffert]
Cemb.-Str.(or 0,3*,0,1-Cemb.-Str.)
Kistner & Siegel, Leipzig [n.d.]
Score 18 p.

456s Suite aus Lustige Feldmusic. Arranged by
Arnold Schering
1.Overture 2.Air-Minuet 3.Air-Fantasy
4.March 5.Chaconne 6.Minuet
Str.
C.F. Kahnt, Leipzig, c1912
Score 9 p.
*Originally published 1704 for winds and
string instruments.*

KRIENS, CHRISTIAN PIETER WILHELM.
Brussels 29 April 1881
Hartford, Connecticut 17 December 1934

2844 En Hollande, suite
1.Morning on the Zuider Zee 2.The Dutch mill
3.Evening sounds 4.Wooden shoe dance
2(2nd alt. Picc.),1,2,1-2,2,1-Timp.,Perc.-Str.
Score: Ms. 40 p.
Parts: C. Fischer, New York [n.d.]

KRIUKOV, VLADIMIR NIKOLAIEVICH.
b. Moscow 22 July 1902

2942 [Suite for grand orchestra, Op. 19]   17'
1.[Romantic dance] 2.[Voices of the night]
3.[City dance] 4.[Landscape]
3*,3*,3*,3*-4,3,3,1-Timp.,Perc.-Cel.,2Hp.-Str.
[State Music Publisher, Moscow, n.d.]
Score 93 p.
*Composed 1929. First performance, on a radio
broadcast, June 1929, Moscow Orchestra,
Sheidler conductor.*

2126 [The unknown woman, symphonic   8'
prologue to A. Block's drama, Op. 11]
3*,3*,3*,3*-4,3,3,1-Timp.,Perc.-Hp.-Str.
Universal Edition, Vienna, c1927
Score 41 p.
Composed 1923. First performance Moscow 1924.

KRÖBER, G. O.

595m Andante für Oboe   4'
  Solo Ob.-Str.
  Breitkopf & Härtel, Leipzig [1875]
  No score. Solo Ob. 3 p.

KROEGER, ALFRED C.   Hamburg 14 March 1890

3155 S.P.D.S.   20'
  3(3rd alt. Picc.),3*,3*,3*-4,3,3,1-Timp.,Perc.
  -Pno.,Cel.,2Hp.-Str.
  Ms.
  Score 95 p.
  *Composer desires meaning of title to remain
  unknown. Composed 1924. First performance
  Rochester, New York, 25 November 1925,
  Rochester Philharmonic Orchestra, Howard Han-
  son conductor. Received the Lillian Fair-
  child Award, 1925.*

KROMMER, FRANZ VINZENZ.
                 Kamenitz, Moravia 27 November 1759
                 Vienna 8 January 1831

4123 [Symphony, Op. 12, F major]
  1.Adagio - Vivace 2.Andante 3.Allegretto
  4.Allegro assai
  1,2,0,1-2Hn.-Str.
  Ms.
  Score 150 p.

4124 [Symphony, Op. 40, D major]
  1.Adagio - Allegro 2.Adagio 3.Menuetto
  4.Allegro
  1,2,2,1-2Hn.-Str.
  Ms.
  Score 148 p.

5565 [Symphony, Op. 102, C minor. Two
  movements edited by Thor Johnson and Donald
  M. McCorkle]
  1.Largo - Allegro vivace 2.Menuetto alle-
  gretto - Trio
  1,2,2,2-4,2,3-Timp.-Str.
  Ms.
  Score 81 p. Large folio
  *Score edited from a Ms. in the Bethlehem
  Archives of the Moravian Church in America.
  First modern performance at the Fourth Early
  American Moravian Music Festival and Seminar,
  Moravian College, Bethlehem, Pennsylvania,
  29 June 1957, Thor Johnson conductor.*

KRONKE, EMIL.   Danzig 29 November 1865
                           Dresden 16 December 1938

609m Kammer-Konzert [flute] im alten Stil,   15'
  Op. 112, G major
  1.Allemande 2.Gavotte 3.Air 4.Menuett
  Solo Fl.-Hp.-Str.
  J.H. Zimmermann, Leipzig, c1921
  Score 18 p.
  Composed 1918. First performance Leipzig 1920.

607p [Symphonic variations on a Nordic theme,
  Op. 14]
  Solo Pno.-2*,1,2,2-4,2,3,1-Timp.-Org.(or

Harm.),Hp.-Str.
  Steingräber, Leipzig, c1907
  Score 53 p.

KRUG, ARNOLD.   Hamburg 16 October 1849
                          Hamburg 4 August 1904

623v [Italian travel sketches, Op. 12]
  1.Serenade 2.Roman 3.Tarantella
  Solo Vn.-Str.
  R. Forberg, Leipzig [n.d.]
  No score. Solo Vn. 5 p.

62s Liebesnovelle [Love story] Op. 14
  [1.First meeting 2.Avowal 3.Love 4.Epilogue]
  Hp.(ad lib.)-Str.
  R. Forberg, Leipzig [n.d.]
  Score 35 p.

792v [Romance, violin, Op. 73]
  Solo Vn.-2,2,2,2-4Hn.-Timp.-Str.
  F.E.C. Leuckart, Leipzig [n.d.]
  Score 11 p.

570c [Romance, violoncello, Op. 60]
  Solo Vc.-2,2,2,2-4,2-Timp.-Str.
  F.E.C. Leuckart, Leipzig [n.d.]
  Score 10 p.

      Romanische Tänze [Romanesque dances] Op. 22
448   No. 1 F major   4'
449   No. 2 A major   5'
450   No. 3 D minor   5'
451   No. 4 A major   4'
452   No. 5 D major   5'
  3*,3*,2,2-4,2,3,1-Timp.,Perc.-Str.
  F. Kistner, Leipzig [n.d.]
  Scores: 33 p., 31 p., 33 p., 21 p., 31 p.
  *Composed 1879. First performance Hamburg,
  1880, the composer conducting.*

1598s Serenade, Op. 34 D major   26'
  1.Allegro vivace 2.Andante 3.Intermezzo
  4.Allegro molto e burlesco
  Fl.-Str.
  F. Luckhardt, Berlin, c1887 by G. Schirmer
  Score 43 p.

KRUG-WALDSEE, JOSEPH.
                 Waldsee, Germany 8 November 1858
                 Magdeburg 8 October 1915

      Zwei Stücke, Op. 41
229s No. 1 Andantino [G major]
228s No. 2 Serenade [C major]
  Str.
  F. Kistner, Leipzig, c1907
  Scores: 5 p., 5 p.

KRÜGER, ROBERT.   Berlin 27 March 1872

785s An der Wiege des Kindes [At the cradle]
  Str.
  Score: Ms. 3 p.
  Parts: Apollo, Berlin, c1920
  Bound with Moritz Fall, Menuett.

Krull, Fritz

KRULL, FRITZ.

1921s [Suite, string orchestra, Op. 5]
1.Intrada 2.Tanz 3.Air 4.Fuga
Str.
Georg Kallmeyer, Wolfenbüttel, 1943
Score 11 p.

KRYZHANOVSKI, IVAN IVANOVICH.   Kiev 8 March 1867
                                 Leningrad 9 December 1924

599v Ballade, Op. 11   11'30"
Solo Vn.-2,1,2,2-3Hn.-Timp.-Str.
Zimmermann, Leipzig [n.d.]
Score 44 p.

582v [Concerto, violin, Op. 10, A minor]   32'
1.Allegro 2.Adagio 3.Finale
Solo Vn.-2,2,2,2-4,2-Timp.-Str.
Zimmermann, Leipzig [n.d.]
Score 103 p.

KRZYWICKI, JAN.   Philadelphia 15 April 1948

161m Fantasy for tuba and strings (1964) 7'30"
1.Andante 2.Allegro
Solo Tuba - Str.
Ms.
Score 19 p. Large folio
Composed 1964. First performance Philadelphia,
4 December 1965, Philadelphia Orchestra, Wil-
liam Smith conductor, Paul Krzywicki soloist.

KUBIK, GAIL THOMPSON.   South Coffeyville,
                             Oklahoma 5 September 1914

717p American caprice, piano and chamber   3'
orchestra
Solo Pno.-1,1,2,1-2,2,1-Timp.,Perc.-Str.
Ms.
Score 49 p.
Originally composed for piano and string quartet, 1932; rewritten for piano and orchestra,
1936. First performance Monmouth, Illinois,
5 May 1936, Monmouth College Orchestra, the
composer conducting, Jeanne McIntyre soloist.

4774 Bachata (Alternate title: Cuban   5'
dance piece)
2(2nd alt. Picc.),2(2nd alt. E.H.),2(2nd alt.
B.Cl.),2-3,3,3-Perc.-Pno.-Str.
Ms.
Score 49 p.
Composed 1947, under the title Concert Rhumba.

1078v Concerto, violin and orchestra   16'
[revised version]
In one movement
Solo Vn.-2(2nd alt. Picc.),2,2,2-4,2,3-Timp.,
Perc.-Str.
Composed 1934; revised 1936. First perform-
ance of revised version Chicago, 2 January
1938, Illinois Symphony Orchestra of the WPA,
Izler Solomon conductor.

1174v [Concerto, violin, Op. 12, in D]   23'
1.Fast, with firmness 2.Slowly, smoothly
3.Rondo

Solo Vn.-2(2nd alt. Picc.),2,2,2-4,2,3-Timp.,
Perc.-Cel.-Str.
Ms.
Score 95 p. Large folio
Composed 1940. Revised 1951. Won the Heifetz
Prize given by Carl Fischer Inc., 1941.

7252 Folk song suite   10'
1.Whoopee-ti-yi-yo (Sketch for chamber orches-
tra) 2.Two hymn tunes (William Billings)
3.Camptown Races
1(alt. Picc.),1,2,1-2,2,1-Timp.,Perc.-Pno.(alt.
Cel.)-Str.
Ms.
Score 86 p. Large folio
Each movement also available separately.
No. 1 commissioned by CBS for its American
School of the Air series. Composed 1941.
First performance over the CBS Network, New
York, 8 April 1941, Columbia Concert Orches-
tra, Bernard Herrmann conductor. In no. 2 the
hymn tunes are When Jesus Wept and Chester,
both by William Billings. Composed 1945.
No. 3 commissioned by the BBC. Composed 1944.
First performance on the BBC Network (I.T.M.A.
program), 30 March 1944.

1860s Gavotte for string orchestra   3'30"
Str.
Ms.
Score 10 p.
Composed 1940.

4221 Puck, a legend of Bethlehem   8'
Narrator(optional)-1,1,1,1-1,1,1-Str.(without
Cb.)
Ms.
Score 21 p. Large folio
Poem by Mary B. Duryee. Composed 1940. First
performance over NBC's Blue Network, 29 Dec-
ember 1940.

4222 [Scherzo, for large orchestra,   10'
Op. 13]
4*,3*,3*,3*-4,3,3,1-Timp.,Perc.-Pno.,Cel.-Str.
Ms.
Score 46 p. Large folio
Composed 1940.

2835 Suite [revised version]   28'
1.Prelude 2.Scherzo 3.Theme song 4.Varia-
tions on a 13th century troubadour song
3(3rd alt. Picc.),3*,3*,3*-4,3,3,1-Timp.,Perc.-
Cel.-Str.
Ms.
Score 140 p. Large folio
Composed 1935; rewritten 1937.

KÜCKEN, FRIEDRICH WILHELM.
                    Bleckede, Hanover 16 November 1810
                    Schwerin, Germany 3 April 1882

4446 [Moorish serenade, Op. 95]
2(2nd alt. Picc.),2,2,2-2,0,2Cnt.,-3-Timp.,Perc.

-Str.
C.A. Challier, Berlin [187-?]
Score 31 p.

5667 [Prayer: Forsake us not, Op. 62 no. 3]
2,2,2,2-4,2,3,1-Timp.,Perc.-Str.
Fr. Kistner, Leipzig [1872?]
Score 11 p.

5216 [Russian fantasy, for orchestra, Op. 108]
3*(2nd ad lib.),2,2,2-4,0,2Cnt.,3,1-Timp.,Perc.
-Str.
Fr. Kistner, Leipzig [1879]
Score 49 p.

KUDELSKI, KARL MATTHIAS.   Berlin 17 November 1805
                    Baden-Baden 3 October 1877

797m [Concertino for horn and orchestra,
major]
Solo Hn.-1,1,2,2-3,2,3-Timp.-Str.
Score: Ms. 67 p.
Parts: C.F. Schmidt, Heilbronn [n.d.]

655c [Concerto, violoncello, Op. 29, F major]
In one movement
Solo Vc.-1,1,2,2-2,2,3-Timp.-Str.
Score: Ms. 149 p.
Parts: Bote & Bock, Berlin [n.d.]

KUHLAU, FRIEDRICH DANIEL RUDOLPH.
              Ülzen, Hanover 11 September 1786
                    Copenhagen 12 March 1832

432m [Concertino, 2 horns, Op. 45, F minor]
2 Solo Hn.-2,2,2,2-2,2,1-Timp.-Str.
Ms.
Score 111 p.

286p [Concerto, piano, Op. 7]   30'
1.Allegro 2.Adagio 3.Rondo: Allegro
Solo Pno.-1,2,2,2-2,2-Timp.-Str.
Samfundet til Udgivelse af Dansk Musik,
Copenhagen, c1958
Score 202 p.
Composed 1810.

6879 [The fairies' mound, Op. 100. Overture] *11'*
3*,2,2,2-4,2,1-Timp.,Perc.-Str.
Samfundet til Udgivelse af Dansk Musik,
Copenhagen, c1955
Score 59 p.
*From the incidental music to the romantic
drama by Johan Ludvig Heiberg. Composed 1828.
First performance Copenhagen, 6 November 1828.*

7056 [The fairies' mound, Op. 100.   *4'30"*
Act IV, Agnete's dream]
3*,2,2,2-4,2,1-Timp.,Perc.-Str.
Samfundet til Udgivelse af Dansk Musik,
Copenhagen, c1973
Score 37 p.

5953 [Overture to William Shakespeare,   *11'*
Op. 74]
2(2nd alt. Picc.),2,2,2-4,2,1-Timp.,Perc.-Str.
Edition Dania, Samfundet til Udgivelse af
Dansk Musik, Copenhagen, c1936

Score 55 p.
*Incidental music to the play, William Shake-
speare, by C. J. Boye. Composed 1826. First
performance Copenhagen, 28 March 1826.*

KUHN, SIEGFRIED.   Eisenach, Germany 15 April 1893
                killed in battle, Saluske Pathory,
                            Poland 15 July 1915

860s [Suite, string orchestra, C major]   *20'*
1.Overture 2.Gavotte 3.Sarabande 4.Gigue
Str.
Ries & Erler, Berlin [n.d.]
Score 19 p.

KÜHNE, J.C.

846m [Concertino, trombone and orchestra,
E-flat major. Arranged by Carl Gerlach]
Solo Tbn.-2,2,2,2-2,2,B.Tbn.-Timp.-Str.
Score: Ms. 48 p.
Parts: C.F. Schmidt, Heilbronn [n.d.]

KÜHNEL, EMIL.   Kratzoin, Bohemia 3 June 1881

249 [Tempests, from the life of an artist,
overture, Op. 13]
3*,2,2,2-4,2,3-Timp.,Perc.-Str.
Breitkopf & Härtel, New York [n.d.]
Score 55 p.

KÜHNEL, REINHOLD.

1288s Ergebung [Devotion] Andante religioso,
Op. 9
Harm.(or Org.)-Str.
Hoffarth, Dresden [n.d.]
Score 5 p.

KULLAK, THEODOR.   Krotoschin, Prussia
            (now Krotoszyn, Poland) 12 September 1818
                            Berlin 1 March 1882

673p [Concerto, piano, Op. 55, C minor]
1.Allegro 2.Adagio 3.Allegro moderato ma
con fuoco
Solo Pno.-2,2,2,2-4,2,3-Timp.-Str.
Score: Ms. 295 p.
Parts: Breitkopf & Härtel, Leipzig [n.d.]
Composed 1849. First performance Berlin, 1850.

KUMMER, FRIEDRICH AUGUST.
            Meiningen, Germany 5 August 1797
                    Dresden 22 May 1879

807m Divertissement [2 trumpets and orchestra]
2 Solo Tpt.-1,1,2,1-2,0,1-Timp.,Perc.-Str.
Score: Ms. 64 p.
Parts: Seeling, Dresden [n.d.]

639c [Fantasy, violoncello and strings, on I
Tuoi Frequenti Palpiti from Pacini's opera
Niobe, Op. 51]
Solo Vc.-Str.
Score: Ms. 23 p.
Parts: Mechetti, Vienna [n.d.]

Kummer, Friedrich August

709c Pièce fantastique, Op. 36
Solo Vc.-2,2,2,2-2,2-Timp.-Str.
Score: Ms. 79 p.
Parts: Hofmeister, Leipzig [n.d.]

KUNC, AYMÉ.   Toulouse, France 1877

763v [Romance for violin and orchestra]   *4'*
Solo Vn.-1,1,1,1-Hn.-Timp.-Str.
Lemoine, Paris, c1927
Score 10 p.

KUNC, BOŽIDAR.   Zagreb, Yugoslavia 18 July 1903
                   Detroit, Michigan 1 April 1964

6679 [Prelude to a funeral play, Op. 25]
3(3rd alt. Picc.),3*,3*,3*-4,3,3,1-Timp.,Perc.
-Pno.,Hp.-Str.
Ms.
Score 42 p.
*Composed 1935. First performance Zagreb, 3
February 1937, Zagreb Philharmonic, Lovro
Mataćić conductor.*

KUNITS, LUIGI VON.   Vienna 20 July 1870
                                 Toronto 8 October 1931

148s Romance. Arranged for string orchestra by
William F. Happich
Str.
Score: Ms. 7 p.
Parts: C. Fischer, New York, c1905

27s Scotch lullaby. Arranged for string
orchestra by William F. Happich
Str.
Score: Ms. 4 p.
Parts: C. Fischer, New York, c1905

KUNKEL, MAX JOSEPH.   Germany 26 August 1875

809m [Concertino, trombone or bassoon, E-flat
major]
Solo Tbn.-2,2,2,2-2,2,1-Timp.-Str.
Score: Ms. 23 p.
Parts: C.F. Schmidt, Heilbronn [n.d.]

KÜNNEKE, EDUARD. Emmerich, Germany 27 January 1885
                  Berlin 27 October 1953

4657 [Italian comedy overture after plays   *6'*
of Carlo Goldoni, Op. 46]
2(2nd alt. Picc.),2,2,2-2,2,3-Timp.,Perc.-Hp.
-Str.
Otto Wrede (Regina-Verlag), Berlin, c1939
Miniature score 47 p.

KUNOTH, GEORG.   1863
                                9 September 1927

4563 Hipp, hipp, hipp, hurra! (Kaiser-Marsch)
(Op. 24, Anno 1892)
1,1,1-Alto Sax.,Ten.Sax.-0,1,1-Perc.-Harm.,
Ten. Banjo-Str.(without Va.)
Georg Kunoth, Erben in Bremen [n.d.]
Score in reduction 3 p.
Composed 1892.

KUNTZEN, ADOLF KARL.
          Wittenberg, Germany 22 September 1720
          Lübeck, Germany ca.11 July 1781

6516 [Symphony, D minor] Edited by Max Schneider
2Ob.-Cemb.-Str.
Breitkopf & Härtel, Leipzig [n.d.]
Score 7 p.
Composed ca.1750.

KURKA, ROBERT.   Cicero, Illinois 22 December 1921
                  New York 12 December 1957

6872 The good soldier Schweik suite, for   *20'*
16 players, Op. 22
1.Overture 2.Lament 3.March 4.War dance
5.Pastoral 6.Finale
2*,2*,2*,2*-3,2,1-Timp.,S.Dr.
Weintraub Music Co., New York, c1956
Score 44 p.
*Adapted from the opera in two acts with
libretto by Lewis Allan, based on the novel by
Jaroslav Hasek. First performance New York
City Center, 23 April 1958, New York City
Opera Company.*

KURTHY, ZOLTAN.   b. Szászváros, Hungary 1902

3644 Overture [for orchestra]   *4'*
2,2,2,2-4,2,3-Timp.,Cym.,B.Dr.-Str.
Ms.
Score 30 p. Large folio
*Commissioned by John Barbirolli, 1939. Com-
posed 1939. First performance New York 12
August 1940, New York Philharmonic, the com-
poser conducting.*

3447 Scherzo   *8'*
2(2nd alt. Picc.),2,2,2-4,2,3-Timp.,Dr.-Str.
Ms.
Score 76 p.
Composed 1940.

KURTZ, EDWARD FRAMPTON.
          New Castle, Pennsylvania 31 July 1881
          Waterloo, Iowa 8 June 1965

3665 The daemon lover, tone poem   *16'*
for orchestra
3(3rd alt. Picc.),3(3rd alt. E.H.),3(2nd alt.
Cl. in E-flat, 3rd alt. B.Cl.),3(3rd alt.
C.Bn.)-4,4,3,1-Timp.,Perc.-2Hp.-Str.
Ms.
Score 109 p.
*Based on a Scottish ballad of Sir Walter Scott.
Composed 1932. First performance Cedar Falls,
Iowa, 15 February 1942, Iowa State Teachers
College Symphony Orchestra, the composer con-
ducting.*

3298 March in D   *6'*
3(3rd alt. Picc.),3*,3*,3*-4,4,3,1-Timp.,Perc.
-Hp.-Str.
Ms.
Score 57 p.
*Composed 1918. First performance Cincinnati,
12 July 1920, Cincinnati Symphony Orchestra,
the composer conducting.*

3498 Symphony [no. 1] A minor [original   30'
version]
1.Lento - Allegro molto 2.Andante sostenuto
3.Allegro un poco vivace 4.Finale
3(3rd alt. Picc.),3(3rd alt. E.H.),3(3rd alt.
B.Cl.),3*-4,4,3,1-Timp.,Perc.-Hp.-Str.
Ms.
Score 291 p.
*Composed 1927; subtitled Impressions from
Youth. First complete performance Waterloo,
Iowa, 15 December 1932, Waterloo Symphony
Orchestra, the composer conducting. Withdrawn
from circulation. See revised version below.*

4736 Symphony no. 1, A minor [revised version]
1.Lento - Allegro 2.Andante sostenuto 3.
Un poco allegro 4.Finale: Allegro giusto
3(3rd alt. Picc.),3*,3(3rd alt. B.Cl.),3(3rd
alt. C.Bn.)-4,4,3,1-Timp.,Perc.-Hp.-Str.
Ms.
Score 218 p.
This revision ca.1949.

3399 Symphony no. 2, C major   29'
1.Allegro moderato 2.Scherzo 3.Andante molto
espressivo 4.Allegro moderato
2,2,2,2-4,2,3-Timp.-Str.
Ms.
Score 140 p.
*First performance Cedar Falls, Iowa, 12
February 1939, Iowa State Teachers College
Symphony Orchestra, the composer conducting.*

3904 Symphony no. 3, C minor   30'
1.Adagio - Allegro 2.Adagio 3.Scherzo
4.Vivace
3(3rd alt. Picc.),2,2,2-4,3,3,1-Timp.-Str.
Ms.
Score 242 p.
*Composed 1939. First performance Cedar Falls,
Iowa, 7 May 1940, Iowa State Teachers College
Symphony Orchestra, the composer conducting.*

4493 Symphony no. 4, D major
1.Molto adagio - Allegro agitato - Vivace
2.Adagio lamentoso 3.Allegretto grazioso
4.Vivace
2,2,2,2-4,2,3,1-Timp.-Str.
Ms.
Score 129 p.
Composed 1942.

4772 Symphony no. 5, G major
1.Allegro 2.Larghetto 3.Vivace 4.Allegro
moderato
3(3rd alt. Picc.),2,2,2-4,2,3,1-Timp.-Str.
Ms.
Score 176 p.
*Composed 1943-49. First performance 28
September 1949.*

KUULA, TOIVO.   Vasa, Finland 7 July 1883
            Viborg (Viipuri), Finland 18 May 1918

2157 The devil's dance, Op. 9 no. 4   3'
[Edited and revised by Julia A. Burt]
1,1,2,1-2,2,1-Timp.-Str.
Wilhelm Hansen, Copenhagen, ᶜ1924
Score 21 p.

290s Kansanlaulu [Popular song] Op. 9 no. 2
Str.
Wilhelm Hansen, Copenhagen, ᶜ1929
Score 5 p.

L

LABEY, MARCEL.   Le Vesinet,
              Seine-et-Oise, France 6 August 1875
              Nancy, France 25 November 1968

511c Lied pour violoncelle et orchestre, Op. 19
Solo Vc.-2,2,2,2-4Hn.-Str.
Durand, Paris, ᶜ1921
Score 17 p.
Composed 1920.

LABORDE, ERNEST.

651s Intermezzo-caprice
Str.
Score: Ms. 15 p.
Parts: Joanin, Paris [n.d.]

LABROCA, MARIO.   Rome 22 November 1896
            Rome 1 July 1973

3924 Sonata per orchestra (pianoforte   8'
concertante)
3(3rd alt. Picc.),2,2,2-4,2,2-Timp.-Pno.-Str.
Ricordi, Milan, ᶜ1936
Score 50 p.
*Composed 1927-33. First performance Turin, 21
February 1936, Mario Rossi conductor.*

LABUNSKI, WIKTOR.   St. Petersburg 14 April 1895
            Lenexa, Kansas 26 January 1974

766p [Concerto, piano, Op. 16, C major]   18'
1.Krakowiak 2.Nocturne 3.Mazurek
Solo Pno.-2(2nd alt. Picc.),2,2,2-4,2,3,1-Timp.,
Trgl.-Str.
Ms.
Score 164 p.
*Composed 1937. First performance Kansas City,
Missouri, 16 February 1939, Kansas City Phil-
harmonic, Karl Krueger conductor, the com-
poser as soloist.*

3713 Symphony no. 1, Op. 14   30'
1.Andante - Allegro con spirito 2.Canzone
3.Scherzo 4.Poco andante - Allegro
3(2nd & 3rd alt. Picc.),3*,3*,3*-4,3,3,1-Timp.,
Cym.,B.Dr-Hp.-Str.
Ms.
Score 247 p.
*Composed 1936. First performance of second
movement only, Kansas City, Missouri, 18
August 1940, Kansas City Concert Orchestra,
the composer conducting.*

THE EDWIN A. FLEISHER

Lachner, Franz

LACHNER, FRANZ.
Rain-on-Lech, Upper Bavaria 2 April 1803
Munich 20 January 1890

6382 [Suite in four movements for   22'
orchestra, Op. 113, D minor]
1.Praeludium 2.Menuetto - Trio 3.Variationen
und Marsch 4.Introduzione und Fuge
3*,2,2,2-4,2,3-Timp.-Str.
B. Schott's Söhne, Mainz [1863]
Score 175 p.
Composed 1861.

186 [Suite no. 7, orchestra, Op. 190,   30'
D minor]
1.Ouverture 2.Scherzo 3.Intermezzo
4.Chaconne e fuga
2,2,2,2-4,2,3-Timp.-Str.
B. Schott's Söhne, Mainz [1883]
Score 151 p.
*Composed 1874. First performance Munich 1875,
the composer conducting.*

6241 [Symphony no. 5, Passionata, Op. 52,
C minor]
1.Andante - Allegro 2.Andante 3.Menuetto -
Trio 4.Finale
3*,2,2,2-4,2,3-Timp.-Str.
Tobias Haslinger, Vienna [1836]
Score 304 p.
*Also known as the Preis-Sinfonie [Prize-
winning Symphony]. Composed 1835. First per-
formance Vienna, 18 February 1836, Concerts
Spirituels, Ignaz von Seyfried conductor.
Awarded first prize at the Concert Spirituel.*

6185 [Symphony no. 8, Op. 100, G minor]
1.Andante - Allegro maestoso 2.Andante
3.Scherzo 4.Finale
3(3rd alt. Picc.),2,2,2-4,2,3-Timp.-Str.
B. Schott's Söhne, Mainz [1854/55]
Score 211 p.

LACHNER, VINCENZ.
Rain-on-Lech, Upper Bavaria 19 July 1811
Karlsruhe 22 January 1893

707v [Parting mood, romance, Op. 50]   5'
Solo Vn.-2Bn.-2Hn.-Str.
Leuckart, Leipzig [187-?]
Score 15 p.

LACIAR, SAMUEL LINE.
Mauch Chunk, Pennsylvania 26 July 1874
Philadelphia 14 January 1943

[Little suite for string orchestra]
1166v Movement 2. Romance
1912s Movement 4. Andante
Str.
Ms.
Scores: 5 p., 3 p.

4138 Symphony no. 1, B-flat major   14'
1.Andante - Allegro vivace 2.Scherzo
3(3rd alt. Picc.),2,3*,3*-4,2,3,1-Timp.-Hp.-
Str.
Ms.
Score 100 p.

LACOMBE, LOUIS TROUILLON.
Bourges, France 26 November 1818
Saint-Vaast-la-Hougue 30 September 1884

519c L'amour for 'cello and orchestra, Op. 77.
Edited by Paul Grümmer
Solo Vc.-0,0,2,1-2Hn.-Str.
Score: Ms. 14 p.
Parts: Costallat, Paris [n.d.]

674v Au tombeau d'un héros, élégie
Solo Vn.-2,2,2,2-4,2,3-Timp.-Str.
Richault, Paris, c1896
Score 36 p.

LACOMBE, PAUL.
Carcassonne, Aude, France 11 July 1837
Carcassonne 5 June 1927

1478s Aubade à Ninon
Solo Vn.-Str.
Enoch, Paris [n.d.]
Score 12 p.

6986 Aubade printanière [Spring aubade]   3'
Op. 37
2*,2,2,2-2,2Cnt.,3-Timp.,Trgl.-Str.
G. Hartmann, Paris [187-?]
Score 22 p.

256s Berceuse gasconne, Op. 102 no.1
Str.(without Cb.)
Leduc, Paris, c1902
Score 4 p.

5666 Chanson gasconne [Gascon song] Op. 60
2*,2,2,2-2,0,2Cnt.,3-Timp.-Str.
Ries & Erler, Berlin, c1893
Score 14 p.

261s Intermède, Op. 74
Str.(Cb. ad lib.)
Leduc, Paris, c1895
Score 4 p.

1388 Parade hongroise, Op. 53 [for   4'
orchestra]
2*,2,2,2-2,0,2Cnt.,3-Timp.,Trgl.-Str.
Heugel, Paris, c1892
Score 17 p.
*Originally composed for piano. Transcribed
for orchestra, 1890. First performance Carcassonne, 1891.*

884s Printemps joyeux [Joyous springtime] Op. 67
Str.
Score: Ms. 9 p.
Parts: Fromont, Paris [n.d.]

1040 Rapsodie [on Provençal tunes]   7'
Op. 128
2*,2,2,2-4,0,2Cnt.,3-Timp.,Trgl.-Str.
Enoch, Paris, c1907 by Raoul Chandon de
Briailles
Score 27 p.
Composed 1920. First performance Paris, 1921.

486

571m Sérénade d'automne, Op. 47 [original version]
Solo Fl., Solo Ob.-Hn.-Str.(without Cb.)
J. Hamelle, Paris [n.d.]
Score 6 p.

259s Sérénade d'automne, Op. 47 [transcribed for string orchestra]
Str.
Score: Ms. 11 p.
Parts: J. Hamelle, Paris [n.d.]

3679 Sous le balcon [Under the balcony] Op. 62
1,1,1,1-Hn.-Str.
Ries & Erler, Berlin, c1893
Score 7 p.

1095 Suite pastorale pour orchestre,   18'
Op. 31
1.[Morning in the woods] 2.Aubade 3.Idylle
4.Marche rustique
2(1st alt. Picc.),2,2,2-4,2,3-Timp.,Trgl.-Hp.-
Str.
Heugel, Paris [190-?]
Score 139 p.
Composed 1901.

1010 [Symphony no. 2, Op. 34, D major]   22'
1.Allegro 2.Adagio 3.Allegro vivo
4.Allegro con moto
2(2nd alt. Picc.),2,2,2-4,2,3-Timp.-Str.
J. Hamelle, Paris [n.d.]
Score 172 p.
Composed 1885.

LACOME DE L'ESTALENX, PAUL JEAN-JACQUES.
                    Houga, France 4 March 1838
                    Houga 12 December 1920

1120 Clair de lune, suite d'orchestre
[Moonlight]
1.Marche nocturne 2.Invocation 3.[Elves, scherzo] 4.Menuet bleu et Final
2(2nd alt. Picc.),1,2,1-2,2,3-Timp.,Perc.-Str.
Lemoine, Paris, c1901
Score 87 p.

LACOSTE, LOUIS DE.   France ca.1675
                                 Paris after 1757

329s Sarabande de Philomèle
Str.(without Va.)
Durand, Paris [n.d.]
Score 2 p.
From the opera Philomèle. First performance 1705.

LACROIX, EUGÈNE.   Eshen, England 13 April 1858
                      Paris after 1914

1535s Premières tendresses
Str.
Score: Ms. 4 p.
Parts: Costallat, Paris [n.d.]

LADUKHIN, NIKOLAI MIKHAILOVICH.
               b. St. Petersburg 3 October 1860

672s [Dusk, musical tableau, Op. 2]
Str.
Jurgenson, Moscow [1889?]
Score 11 p.

LAFITTE, JACQUES.

1215s Passepied, danse ancienne
Str.
Score: Ms. 7 p.
Parts: Decourcelle, Nice [n.d.]

LA GYE, PAUL.
          Saint-Gilles, near Brussels 8 June 1883
          Saint-Gilles 18 February 1965

5552 Le chevalier maudit [The   7'30"
accursed knight, Op. 20. Act I. Prelude]
2,2(2nd alt. E.H.),3*,3*-4,2,3,1-Timp.,Cym.-
Cel.,Hp.-Str.
J. Buyst, Brussels [n.d.]
Score 12 p.
From the opera composed 1908.

LAIGRE, PAUL.

1662s Prière du soir [Evening prayer] Op. 18
Hp.-Str.
Score: Ms. 7 p.
Parts: E. Gaudet, Paris [n.d.]

LAJTHA, LÁSZLÓ (*or* LESLIE).   Budapest 30 June 1891
                                Budapest 16 February 1963

2100s [Sinfonietta for string orchestra,   16'
Op. 43]
1.Molto allegro 2.Pas trop lent 3.Vivo e grazioso
Str.
Alphonse Leduc, Paris, c1948
Score 39 p.
Composed 1946.

LALANDE, MICHEL-RICHARD DE. Paris 15 December 1657
                             Versailles 18 June 1726

6891 [Symphonies for the king's suppers. 1st
caprice or the Villers-Cotterêts caprice]
Edited by Jean-François Paillard
1.Fièrement et détaché 2.Augmentation première air neuf 3.Trio 4.Augmentation 2ème
air neuf 5.Suitte [*sic*] de l'ancien
0,2,0,1-3Tpt.-Timp.-Cemb.-Str.
Costallat, Paris, c1965
Score 46 p.

6892 [Symphonies for the king's suppers. 2nd
fantasy or caprice which the king frequently
requested] Edited by Jean-François Paillard
In one movement
0,2,0,1-Cemb.-Str.
Costallat, Paris, c1965
Score 24 p.

6857 [Symphonies for the king's suppers. 3rd
caprice (8th set)] Edited by Jean-François
Paillard
In six movements

Lalande, Michel-Richard de

2,2,0,2-Cemb.-Str.
Costallat, Paris, c1965
Score 32 p.
Composed ca.1715-20.

4972 [Symphonies for the king's suppers.   *12'*
Suite I] Realization by Roger Désormière
1.Chaconne en écho 2.Muzette de Cardenio [from
the ballet] 3.Aria 4.Muzette pour les hautbois 5.Fanfare 6.Sinfonie du Te Deum
2Picc.,2,0,1-0,3,3-Timp.-Str.
Editions de l'Oiseau-Lyre, Paris, c1946 by
Louise B. M. Dyer
Score 29 p.

LALO, ÉDOUARD.   Lille, France 27 January 1823
                       Paris 22 April 1892

Full name: Victor-Antoine-Édouard Lalo

744 Allegro appassionato, Op. 27   *6'*
2,2,2,2-4,2,3-Timp.-Str.
J. Hamelle, Paris [n.d.]
Score 60 p.
Composed 1875. First performance Paris, 1875.

908 Arlequin, musique de carnaval
3*,2,2,2-2,2,3-Timp.,Cym.,Trgl.-Str.
O. Bornemann, Paris, c1900-1902
Score 21 p.

391p [Concerto, piano, F minor]
1.Lento - Allegro 2.Lento 3.Allegro
Solo Pno.-2,2,2,2-4,2,2Cnt.,3-Timp.-Str.
Hartmann, Paris [n.d.]
Score 136 p.

421v [Concerto, violin, Op. 20, F minor]   *31'*
Revised edition
1.Andante - Allegro 2.Andantino - Allegro con
fuoco
Solo Vn.-3*,2,2,2-2,2,3-Timp.,Trgl.-Str.
Durand, Paris, c1912
Score 114 p.
*First performance Paris, 18 January 1874, Pablo
de Sarasate soloist.*

449v [Concerto, violin, Russe, Op. 29,   *30'*
G minor]
1.Prélude - Allegro 2.Chants russes 3.Inter-
mezzo 4.Introduction - Chants russes
Solo Vn.-2,2,2,2-4,2,3-Timp.,Tamb.-Str.
Score in reduction: Peters [New York,
n.d.] 35 p.
Parts: [B. Schott's Söhne, Mainz, 1884?]
*Composed 1883. First performance Concerts
Populaires, Paris, M. P. J. Marsick soloist.*

478c [Concerto, violoncello, D minor]   *23'*
1.Prélude 2.Intermezzo 3.Allegro vivace
Solo Vc.-2,2,2,2-4,2,3-Timp.-Str.
Kalmus, New York [n.d.]
Score 153 p.
*Composed 1876. First performance Paris, 9
December 1877, Adolphe Fischer soloist.*

500 Divertissement pour orchestre   *14'*
1.Andante - Allegretto 2.Vivace 3.Andantino

4.Allegro con fuoco
3*,2,2,2-4,2,3,1-Timp.,Trgl.-Str.
Hartmann, Paris [n.d.]
Score 92 p.
*Composed 1870. First performance Concerts
Populaires, Paris, 8 December 1872.*

852v Fantaisie-ballet
Solo Vn.-2,2,2,2-2,0,3-Timp.-Str.
Score: Ms. 56 p.
Parts: J. Hamelle, Paris [n.d.]

460v Fantaisie norvégienne [violin and
orchestra]
1.Allegretto 2.Andante 3.Allegro - Presto
Solo Vn.-3*,2,2,2-2Hn.-Timp.,Trgl.-Str.
Bote & Bock, Berlin [1879]
No score

854v Guitare, Op. 28 [violin and orchestra]
Solo Vn.-2,2,2,2-2Hn.-Timp.,Tamb.-Hp.-Str.
Score: Ms. 24 p.
Parts: J. Hamelle, Paris [n.d.]
Originally composed for violin and piano, 1882.

853v [Namouna. Introduction and scherzo]
Solo Vn.-2,2,2,2-4,2,2Cnt.,3,Ophicl.-Timp.-Str.
J. Hamelle, Paris [n.d.]
Score 38 p.
*From the ballet composed 1881. First perform-
ance Paris, 6 March 1882.*

641 [Namouna. Suite no. 1 from the ballet]   *21'*
1.Prélude 2.Sérénade 3.Thème varié 4.[Shows
at the fair - The feast]
2,2,2,4-4,2,2Cnt.,3,Ophicl.-Timp.,Perc.-2Hp.-
Str.
J. Hamelle, Paris [n.d.]
Score 105 p.

457 [Namouna. Suite no. 2, Rapsodie, from   *14'*
the ballet]
1.Danses marocaines 2.Mazurka 3.[Siesta]
4.[Cymbal dance] 5.Presto
2(2nd alt. Picc.),2(both alt. E.H.),2,4-4,2,
2Cnt.,3,Ophicl.-Timp.,Perc.-2Hp.-Str.
J. Hamelle, Paris [n.d.]
Score 80 p.

1331 Namouna. Valse de la cigarette   *6'*
[from the ballet]
2,2,2,2-4Hn.-Timp.-Str.
J. Hamelle, Paris [n.d.]
Score 43 p.

612 Rapsodie   *10'*
3*,2,2,2-4,4,3,Ophicl.-Timp.,Perc.-Hp.-Str.
Bote & Bock, Berlin [1889]
Score 57 p.
Composed 1880. First performance Paris, 1880.

488 Le roi d'Ys. Overture   *11'*
2,2,2,2-4,4,3,1-Timp.,B.Dr.,S.Dr.-Str.
Kalmus, New York [n.d.]
Score 52 p.
*From the opera composed 1875-76. First per-
formance of the overture alone, Paris 1876.*

705v Romance-sérénade   5'
   Solo Vn.-2,2,2,2-2Hn.-Timp.-Str.
   Bote & Bock, Berlin [1879]
   Score 39 p.
   Composed 1880.

482 Scherzo, pour orchestre   5'
   3*,2,2,4-4,2,2Cnt.-,3,Ophicl.-Timp.-Str.
   Durand, Paris, c1907
   Score 32 p.
   Composed 1883. First performance Paris 1885.

422v Symphonie espagnole, Op. 21   28'
   1.Allegro non troppo 2.Scherzando 3.Inter-
   mezzo 4.Andante 5.Rondo
   Solo Vn.-3*,2,2,2-4,2,3-Timp.,Trgl.,Dr.-Hp.-
   Str.
   Kalmus, New York [n.d.]
   Score 79 p.
   *Composed 1874. First performance Paris, 7
   February 1875, Concerts Populaires, Pablo de
   Sarasate soloist.*

446 [Symphony, G minor]   34'
   1.Allegro non troppo 2.Vivace 3.Adagio
   4.Allegro
   3*,2,2,2-4,2,2Cnt.-,3,1-Timp.-Str.
   Heugel, Paris [n.d.]
   Score 149 p.
   Composed 1885. First performance Paris 1887.

1467 [Two aubades for 10 instruments]   9'
   1.Allegretto 2.Andantino
   1,1,1,1-Hn.-Str.
   Heugel, Paris [n.d.]
   Score 24 p.
   Composed 1871. First performance Paris, 1872.

LAMARTER, ERIC DE.
   See: DE LAMARTER, ERIC.

LAMBELET, VIVIEN.

689s Spanish intermezzo, to the memory of a
   toreador
   Str.
   Score: Ms. 9 p.
   Parts: Augener, London, c1926

LAMBERT, CONSTANT.   London 23 August 1905
                           London 21 August 1951

3289 Horoscope, orchestral suite from   25'
   the ballet
   1.Dance for the followers of Leo 2.Saraband
   for the followers of Virgo 3.Valse for the
   Gemini 4.Bacchanale 5.Invocation to the
   Moon and Finale
   3(3rd alt. Picc.),2(2nd alt. E.H.),2,2-4,3,3,
   1-Timp.,Perc.-Hp.-Str.
   Oxford University Press, London, c1939
   Score 118 p.
   *Composed 1938. First performance of this
   suite London, 8 August 1938, the composer
   conducting.*

3167 Music for orchestra   12'30"
   3(2nd & 3rd alt. Picc.),3*,3,3*-4,3,3,1-Timp.,

Perc.-Str.
   Oxford University Press, London, c1930
   Score 33 p.
   *Composed 1927. First performance in a radio
   broadcast, June 1929, BBC Orchestra.*

LAMOND, FREDERIC ARCHIBALD.
                        Glasgow 28 January 1868
               Stirling, Scotland 21 February 1948

4301 [From the Scottish highlands, concert
   overture, Op. 4]
   3(3rd alt. Picc.),3*,3*,3*-4,2,3,1-Timp.,Perc.-
   Str.
   Steyl & Thomas, Frankfurt a/M. [189-?]
   Score 39 p.
   *First performance London, 7 March 1895, London
   Philharmonic Society.*

LAMOTE DE GRIGNON BOCQUET, JUAN.
                           Barcelona 7 July 1872
                          Barcelona 11 March 1949

2242 Hispánicas [symphonic trilogy] 1.Anda-
   lousie
   3(3rd alt. Picc.),3(3rd alt. E.H.),3*,3-4,3,
   3,1-Timp.,Perc.-2Hp.-Str.
   Unión Musical Española, Barcelona, c1924
   Score 54 p.

LAMPE, WALTHER.   Leipzig 28 April 1872
                        Munich 23 January 1964

2301 [Serenade for 15 wind instruments, Op. 7]
   1.Allegro con grazia 2.Allegro scherzando
   3.Adagio 4.Molto vivace
   2,3*,3*,3*-4Hn.
   Simrock, Berlin, c1904
   Score 79 p.

LAMURAGLIA, NICOLÁS J.
               b. Buenos Aires 19 February 1896

1886s [Suite for string orchestra with piano]
   1.[Shadows of Chañar] 2.Leyenda 3.Fiesta
   Pno.-Str.
   Ms.
   Score 52 p. Large folio
   *Composed 1939. Received an Argentine govern-
   ment award, 1939.*

LAMY, ERNEST RICHARD.

4594 Passacaglia in E minor
   2,2,3*,3*-4,2,3,1-Timp.-Str.
   Ms.
   Score 24 p. Large folio
   Composed 1949.

LANAO DE LA HAZA, ULISES.
                    b. Callao, Peru 30 October 1913

3830 Anda, caminante, anda, Op. 27 [for   2'
   violin and piano. Transcribed for orchestra by
   Rudolph Holzmann]
   Tr.: Go on, wayfarer, go on
   2,2,2,2-2Hn.-Timp.-Str.
   Ms.

Lanao de la Haza, Ulises

Score 10 p.
*Composed 1939; transcribed 1941, as part of
the work, Two Impressions of Cuzco. First
performance Lima, 19 April 1942, Orquesta Sinfónica Nacional de Peru, Theo Buchwald conductor.*

3890 Recuerdos del Cuzco (Souvenir of Cuzco).
Orchestrated by Rudolph Holzmann
2,1,1,1-2Hn.-S.Dr.-Hp.-Str.
Ms.
Score 22 p.
*Cuzco was the Inca imperial capital. Composed
1941.*

LANDEAU, C.

1135s Cornemuse, dance from Brittany
Solo Vn.-Str.
Score: Ms. 6 p.
Parts: Decourcelle, Nice, ᶜ1922

LANDRÉ, GUILLAUME LOUIS FRÉDÉRIC.
The Hague 24 February 1905
Amsterdam 6 November 1968

6147 Quatre mouvements symphoniques   *17'*
(1949)
1.Lento e dolce 2.Vivo e leggiero 3.Notturno
4.Vivace e gioioso
3*,3*,3*,3*-4,3,3,1-Timp.,Perc.-Str.
Donemus, Amsterdam [n.d.]
Score 80 p.
*Composed 1949. First performance The Hague,
19 January 1950, Residentie Orchestra, Willem
van Otterloo conductor. Won a Dutch Ministry
of Education and Arts award.*

2041s Suite pour orchestre à cordes et   *13'*
piano (1936)
1.Allegro giocoso 2.Elégie 3.Vivace
Pno.-Str.
Editions de l'Oiseau Lyre, Paris, ᶜ1939 by
Louise B. M. Dyer
Score 35 p.
Composed 1936.

LANG, JOHANN GEORG.
Bohemia ca.1724
Coblenz ca.1794

2113s Sinfonia pastorale, G-dur. Edited by
Walter Höckner
1.Allegro 2.Allegretto 3.Presto
2Hn.(or Hn. & Tpt.)(ad lib.)-Str.
Fr. Portius, Leipzig [1940]
Score 21 p.

6209 [Symphony, G major]
1.Allegro molto 2.Andante 3.Presto
2Ob.(or 2Fl., or 2Vn.)-2Hn.-Pno.(all ad lib.)
-Str.
Robert Lienau, Berlin-Lichterfelde, ᶜ1941
Score 18 p.
Bound with Boccherini's Op. 15 no. 6.

LANGE, ARTHUR.
Philadelphia 16 April 1889
Washington, D.C. 7 December 1956

6068 American pastorale. No. 1, Antelope   *12'*
Valley
3*,3*,3*,2-4,3,3,1-Timp.,Perc.-Cel.,Hp.-Str.
Ms.
Score 52 p. Large folio
*Composed 1947. First performance New York, 20
July 1947, NBC Symphony Orchestra, Frank Black
conductor.*

6069 American pastorale. No. 2, Big trees   *14'*
3*,3*,3*,2-4,3,3,1-Timp.,Cym.,B.Dr.-Cel.,Hp.-
Str.
Ms.
Score 44 p. Large folio
*Composed 1947. First performance Santa Monica,
California, 1 February 1953, Santa Monica
Symphony Orchestra, the composer conducting.*

6058 American pastorale. No. 3, Mount   *13'*
Whitney
2,2*,2,2-4,3,3,1-Timp.,Perc.-Cel.,Hp.-Str.
Ms.
Score 41 p. Large folio
*Composed 1951. First performance Santa Monica,
California, 27 May 1951, Santa Monica Symphony
Orchestra, the composer conducting.*

392m Arabesque   *12'30"*
Solo Hp.-1,1,2,1-2,2-Timp.,Bells-Str.
Ms.
Score 45 p.
*Composed 1953. First performance Santa Monica,
California, 3 May 1953, Santa Monica Symphony
Orchestra, the composer conducting, Maryjane
Barton soloist. Awarded the Northern Califor-
nia Harpists' Association Composition Prize,
1954.*

6073 Atoms for peace, overture   *9'30"*
2(2nd alt. Picc.),2(2nd alt. E.H.),3*,2-4,3,
3,1-Timp.,Perc.-Str.
Ms.
Score 42 p. Large folio
*Composed 1955. First performance Santa Monica,
California, 19 June 1955, Santa Monica Symphony
Orchestra, the composer conducting.*

2176s Divertimento for string orchestra   *8'*
Str.
Ms. ᶜ1956 by Arthur Lange
Score 23 p.
*Composed 1956. First performance Santa Monica,
California, 13 May 1956, Santa Monica Symphony
Orchestra, the composer conducting.*

6084 The fisherman and his soul,   *25-40'*
symphonic suite
3(1 Alto Fl.),2(2nd alt. E.H.),3*,2-2Hn.-Timp.,
Perc.-Cel.,Hp.-Narrator(optional)-Str.
Ms.
Score 120 p. Large folio
*Based on the fairy tale by Oscar Wilde. Ori-
ginally composed for nonette as Four Symphonic
Murals 1939. This version for orchestra 1950.
First performance Santa Monica, California, 29
January 1950, Santa Monica Symphony Orchestra,
the composer conducting. Shorter duration is
for tone poem without narrator.*

6057 Symphony no. 1, Lyric-American   23'
  1.Allegro 2.Adagio cantabile 3.Allegro
  3*,2(2nd alt. E.H.),2,2-4,3,3,1-Timp.,Perc.-
  Cel.,Hp.-Str.
  Ms.
  Score 112 p. Large folio
  *Composed 1948. First performance Santa Monica,
  California, 22 May 1949, Santa Monica Symphony
  Orchestra, the composer conducting.*

LANGE, GUSTAV.   Schwerstedt,
            near Erfurt, Germany 13 August 1830
            Wernigerode, Germany 19 July 1889

  861s Albumblatt, Op. 293 [Album leaf]
    Str.
    Score: Ms. 4 p.
    Parts: Ries & Erler, Berlin [n.d.]

LANGE-MÜLLER, PETER ERASMUS.   Frederiksborg,
            near Copenhagen 1 December 1850
            Copenhagen 25 February 1926

  799v Romance, Op. 63
    Solo Vn.-2,1,2,2-2Hn.-Timp.-Str.
    Nordisk Musikforlag, Copenhagen [n.d.]
    Score 17 p.

LANGER, FERDINAND.
            Leimen, near Heidelberg 21 January 1839
            Kirneck, Black Forest 25 August 1905

  564m [Concerto, flute and orchestra, G minor]
    1.Allegro ma non troppo 2.Andante 3.Allegro
    Solo Fl.-1,2,2,2-2,2-Timp.-Str.
    Heckel, Mannheim [n.d.]
    Score 104 p.

LANGEY, OTTO.   Leichholz, Germany 20 October 1851
                 New York 16 March 1922

  1032s Mandolina, mexikanische Serenade, Op. 37
    Str.
    Score: Ms. 7 p.
    Parts: Oertel, Hanover [n.d.]

  601m Romance for oboe and orchestra
    Solo Ob.-1,0,2-2Hn.-Str.
    Score: Ms. 25 p.
    Parts: [Seeling, Dresden, n.d.]

  854s Serenata neapolitana, Op. 80
    Fl.-Str.
    Score: Ms. 13 p.
    Parts: Hawkes, London [n.d.]

  1002s Two little comrades, landler, Op. 62
    Solo Vn.I, Solo Vn.II-Str.
    Score: Ms. 11 p.
    Parts: Hawkes, London [n.d.]

LANGGAARD, RUED IMMANUEL.   Copenhagen 28 July 1893
                 Ribe, Denmark 10 July 1952

  4265 [Sphinx, musical tableau for   9-10'
    orchestra]
    3(3rd alt. Picc.),3*,3*,3-4,3,4,1-Timp.-Str.
    Wilhelm Hansen, Copenhagen [1914]

Score 23 p.
*Suggested by a poem by Viktor Rydberg. Com-
posed 1910.*

7055 [Symphony no. 4, Leaf-fall, in   23'
  one movement]
  2,2(2nd alt. E.H.),2,2(2nd alt. C.Bn.)-4,3,-
  Timp.-Str.
  Samfundet til Udgivelse af Dansk Musik [n.p.]
  c1973
  Score 117 p.
  Composed 1916; revised 1924.

6163 [Symphony no. 6, The heaven-   23-30'
  rending]
  In one movement
  3(3rd alt. Picc.),3(3rd alt. E.H.),3,3(3rd
  alt. C.Bn.)-4,8,3,1-Timp.,Perc.-Org.(ad lib.),
  Cel.,2Hp.-Str.
  Edition Dania, Copenhagen, c1946 by Samfundet
  til Udgivelse af Dansk Musik
  Score 72 p.
  Composed 1919; revised 1930.

LANGGAARD, SIEGFRIED.   Copenhagen 13 July 1852
                 Copenhagen 5 January 1914

  672p [Concerto, piano, E minor]
    1.Allegro maestoso 2.Adagio tranquillo
    3.Maestoso - Allegro
    Solo Pno.-2,2,2,2-4,2,3,1-Timp.-Str.
    W. Hansen, Copenhagen [n.d.]
    Score 105 p.

LANNER, JOSEPH FRANZ KARL.   Vienna 12 April 1801
            Oberdöbling, near Vienna 14 April 1843

  4441 [Baden ringlets, Op. 64]
    1,1,2(1Cl. in E-flat),1-2,4,1-Timp.,S.Dr.,B.Dr.
    -Str.
    Score: D.T.Ö., XXXIII/2. Universal Edition,
    Vienna, 1926. Edited by Alfred Orel. 10 p.
    Parts: Ms. c1976 by The Fleisher Collection of
    Orchestral Music, Free Library of Philadelphia
    Composed ca.1832.

  1937s [Dornbach ländler, Op. 9]   6'30"
    Str.(Vn.I,Vn.II,Vn.III,Cb.)
    Score: D.T.Ö., XXXIII/2. Universal Edition,
    Vienna, 1926. Edited by Alfred Orel. 2 p.
    Parts: Ms. c1976 by The Fleisher Collection of
    Orchestral Music, Free Library of Philadelphia
    Composed before 1825.

  4448 [Katherine-dances, Op. 26]
    1,0,2,1-2,3,1-Timp.-Str.(Vn.I-III,Cb.)
    Score: D.T.Ö., XXXIII/2. Universal Edition,
    Vienna, 1926. Edited by Alfred Orel. 9 p.
    Parts: Ms. c1976 by The Fleisher Collection of
    Orchestral Music, Free Library of Philadelphia
    Composed ca.1828.

  4455 [Pest-waltzes, Op. 93] [i.e., Budapest]
    2(2nd alt. Picc.),1,2,1-2,4,1-Timp.,Perc.-Str.
    Score: D.T.Ö., XXXIII/2. Universal Edition,
    Vienna, 1926. Edited by Alfred Orel. 12 p.
    Parts: Ms. c1976 by The Fleisher Collection of
    Orchestral Music, Free Library of Philadelphia
    Composed 1834.

Lanner, Joseph

4454 [The romantics, Op. 167]
2*,1,2,1-3,4,1,Bombardon-Timp.,Perc.-Str.
Score: D.T.Ö., XXXIII/2. Universal Edition,
Vienna, 1926. Edited by Alfred Orel. 20 p.
Parts: Ms. C1976 by The Fleisher Collection of
Orchestral Music, Free Library of Philadelphia
Composed 1841.

4453 [Schönbrunn waltzes, Op. 200]
2*,1,3,1-2,4,1,Ophicl.-Timp.,Perc.-Str.
Score: D.T.Ö., XXXIII/2. Universal Edition,
Vienna, 1926. Edited by Alfred Orel. 35 p.
Parts: Ms. C1976 by The Fleisher Collection of
Orchestral Music, Free Library of Philadelphia
Composed 1842; commemorates Vienna's palace.

4456 [Styrian dances, Op. 165]   5'30"
2,0,2,2-4,2,1-Timp.-Str.
Score: D.T.Ö., XXXIII/2. Universal Edition,
Vienna, 1926. Edited by Alfred Orel. 8 p.
Parts: Ms. C1976 by The Fleisher Collection of
Orchestral Music, Free Library of Philadelphia
Composed 1840.

4449 [Terpsichore waltzes, Op. 12]
1,0,2-2,3,1-Timp.,Anvils-Str.(w/o Va.,Vc.)
Score: D.T.Ö., XXXIII/2. Universal Edition,
Vienna, 1926. Edited by Alfred Orel. 11 p.
Parts: Ms. C1976 by The Fleisher Collection of
Orchestral Music, Free Library of Philadelphia
Composed before 1825.

2010s [Viennese ländler and waltzes] Edited by
Adolf Hoffmann
Pno.(ad lib.)-Str.(without Va.)
Georg Kallmayer, Wolfenbüttel & Berlin, C1939
Score 24 p.

4465 Die Werber [The suitors] Op. 103   7'
2(2nd alt. Picc.),1,2,1-2,4,1-Timp.,Perc.-Str.
Score: D.T.Ö., XXXIII/2. Universal Edition,
Vienna, 1926. Edited by Alfred Orel. 31 p.
Parts: Ms. C1976 by The Fleisher Collection of
Orchestral Music, Free Library of Philadelphia
Composed ca.1835.

LANTEIRÈS, ANDRÉ.

942v Méditation religieuse
Solo Vn.-1,1,1,1-Str.
Fromont, Paris [n.d.]
Score 12 p.

LÁNYI, ERNÖ.   Budapest 1861

1401s Danse phantastique
Trgl.-Str.
Score: Ms. 5 p.
Parts: [n.p., n.d.]

1175s [Hungary's mourning, Op. 170]
Str.
Eduard Klökner, Budapest, C1907
Score 7 p.

882v Romance hongroise, Op. 89
Solo Vn.-2,2,2,2-4Hn.-Timp.-Str.

[E. Klökner, Budapest, 189-?]
Score 9 p.

LAPARRA, RAOUL.   Bordeaux 13 May 1876
                      Suresnes, near Paris 4 April 1943

6170 [A Basque Sunday, poem in 4 parts]
1.[Toward the church] 2.[Pelota] 3.[In
front of a white house] 4.[At the feast]
3*,2(2nd alt. E.H.),2,2-4,2,2Cnt.,3,1-Timp.,
Perc.-Pno.,Org.,2Hp.-Str.
Choudens, Paris, C1922
Score 115 p.
*Composed 1908-18. First performance Boston,
18 April 1919, Boston Symphony Orchestra,
Henri Rabaud conductor, the composer as soloist.*

2384 [La habanera. Prelude]   5'
3*(1st & 2nd alt. Picc.),2(2nd alt. E.H.),3*,
3*-4,2,2Cnt.,3,1-Timp.,Perc.-2Hp.-Str.
Enoch, Paris [1908?]
Score 42 p.
*From the opera composed 1907. First perform-
ance Opéra Comique, Paris, 1908.*

2383 [La habanera. 3 entr'actes]
1.Doloroso e appassionato 2.Tempo di habanera
3.[A bad night]: Andantino
2,3*,3*,3*-4,2,3,1-Timp.,B.Dr.,Cym.-2Hp.-Str.
Enoch, Paris [1908?]
Score 24 p.

5156 [Spanish rhythms, suite for orchestra]
1.Paseo 2.Petenera 3.Tientos 4.Rueda
5.Calesera
2(2nd alt. Picc.),2(2nd alt. E.H.),2,2-4,2,
2Cnt.,3,1-Timp.,Perc.-2Hp.-Str.
Enoch, Paris, C1913, 1932
Score 70 p.

671m Suite italienne en forme de ballet   9'
[for trumpet and orchestra]
1.Préambule 2.Le lac tranquille (Nemi)
3.[Buffoonery]
Solo Tpt.-3*,2(2nd alt. E.H.),2,2-2Hn.-Timp.,
Perc.-Cel.,2Hp.-Str.
Ricordi, Milan, C1929
Score 34 p.

LAPHAM, CLAUDE.   Ft. Scott, Kansas 1890

728p [Concerto japonesa, piano, Op. 35,   18'
C minor]
1.Allegro con brio 2.Andante doloroso 3.Alle-
gro con spirito ma moderato
Solo Pno.-2,2,2,2-4,3,3,1-Perc.-Banjo-Str.
Ms.
Score 102 p.
*Commissioned by Victor Record Co. of Japan,
1935. Composed 1935. First performance
Tokyo, 30 April 1935, Tokyo Symphony Orchestra,
Klaus Pringsheim conductor, the composer as
soloist. Awarded silver medal by Takarazuka
Film Co., 1935.*

3053 Miharayama, Japanese tone poem,   6'
Op. 34
3(3rd alt. Picc.),3*,3*,3*-4,3,3,1-Timp.,Perc.-

2Hp.-Str.
Ms.
Score 55 p.
Miharayama is the Japanese suicide volcano.
Composed 1935. First performance Tokyo, 8
January 1935, Tokyo Symphony Orchestra, Klaus
Pringsheim conductor.

LAPORTE, LOUIS.

1507s [Gavotte in the olden style]
Solo Vn.-Str.
Score: Ms. 5 p.
Parts: O. Bornemann, Paris [1892]

798s Intermède-pizzicato
Str.
Score: Ms. 7 p.
Parts: O. Bornemann, Paris, c1892

LARMANJAT, JACQUES.   Paris 19 October 1878
                       Paris 7 November 1952

4939 [Serenade for orchestra, Op. 34]   *10'*
1.Allegro 2.Andante 3.Allegretto
2(2nd alt. Picc.),2(2nd alt. E.H.),2,2-Alto
Sax.(ad lib.)-4,2-Timp.,Perc.-Pno.,Hp.-Str.
A. Durand, Paris, c1928
Score 35 p.

LAROCHE, HERMANN AUGUSTOVICH.
                 St. Petersburg 25 May 1845
                 St. Petersburg 18 October 1904

550 [Festive march. Orchestrated by   *3'*
A. Glazunov]
3(3rd alt. Picc.),3*,3*,3*-4,2,3,1-Timp.,Perc.
-Str.
Belaieff, Leipzig, 1913
Score 27 p.

LA ROTELLA, PASQUALE.
          Bitonto, Italy 26 February 1880
            Bari, Italy 20 March 1963

381s Intermezzo d'archi
Str.
Bongiovanni, Bologna, c1921
Score 11 p.

LARSON, SIGVARD.   Fageräs, Sweden 13 March 1908

376m [Concert divertimento for clarinet   *7'30"*
and chamber orchestra]
1.Allegro - Andante 2.Andante espressivo
3.Allegro con brio
Solo Cl.-1(alt. Picc.),1,0,1-Hn.-Str.
Ms.
Score 39 p.
Composed 1953. First performance Stockholm,
20 June 1961, Stockholms Radioorkester, Stig
Westerberg conductor, Tore Westlund soloist.

374m [Concertino for oboe and   *11'30"*
orchestra]
1.Allegro 2.Andante cantabile 3.Allegro
moderato
Solo Ob.-3*,2,2,2-2,2,2-Timp.-Str.
Ms.

Score 48 p. Large folio
Composed 1952.

2179s [Little suite for string orchestra and
piano]
1.Preludium 2.Andante cantabile 3.Marciale
Pno.-Str.
Nordiska Musikförlaget, Stockholm, c1946
Score 6 p.
Composed 1944. First performance Viggbyholm,
Sweden, August 1945, Arbetarnas Bildningsför-
bunds Orkester, the composer conducting.

LARSSON, LARS-ERIK VILNER.
        b. Åkarp, near Lund, Sweden 15 May 1908

5106 [Concert overture no. 2, Op. 13]   *5'30"*
2,2,2,2-2,3,1-Timp.-Str.
Universal Edition, Vienna, c1936
Score 49 p.
Composed 1934. First performance Göteborg,
Sweden, 27 January 1935, Orchestra Society of
Göteborg, Tor Mann conductor.

1089m [Concerto for saxophone and   *20'*
strings, Op. 14]
1.Allegro 2.Adagio 3.Allegro scherzando
Solo Sax.-Str.
Ms.
Score 64 p.
Composed 1934. First performance Norrköping,
Sweden, 27 November 1934, Orchestra Society
of Norrköping, Tord Benner conductor, Sigurd
Rascher soloist.

772c [Concerto for violoncello, Op. 37]   *17'*
1.Allegro risoluto 2.Largo 3.Allegro
moderato
Solo Vc.-1,1,1,1-2,1-Timp.-Str.
Ms.
Score 80 p.
Composed 1947. First performance Stockholm,
29 April 1948, Symphony Orchestra of the Swe-
dish Broadcasting Corporation, Tor Mann con-
ductor, Gunnar Norrby soloist.

5180 [Divertimento no. 2, small   *13'*
orchestra, Op. 15]
1.Allegro con spirito 2.Adagio 3.Presto
1,1,1,1-Hn.-Str.
Universal Edition, Vienna, c1937
Score 48 p.
Composed 1935. First performance Göteborg,
Sweden, 18 October 1936, Orchestra Society of
Göteborg, Tor Mann conductor.

6063 [Little march for orchestra]   *2'30"*
2(2nd alt. Picc.),2,2,2-2,2,1-Timp.,S.Dr.-Str.
Nordiska Musikförlaget, Stockholm, c1942
Score 9 p.
Originally composed 1936 as part of Serenade
and Little March for two violins, violoncello
and piano.

6117 [Pastoral for chamber orchestra]   *4'*
Fl.,Cl.-Pno.(optional),Hp.-Str.
Carl Gehrmans, Stockholm, c1941
Score 12 p.
Commissioned by the Royal Dramatic Theatre of

Larsson, Lars-Erik

*Stockholm as incidental music to Vilhelm
Moberg's play, Kyskhet [Chastity] 1937. First
performance Stockholm, 9 March 1939.*

4996 [Pastoral suite for orchestra,   *12-13'*
Op. 19]
1.Overture 2.Romance 3.Scherzo
2,2,2,2-2,2-Timp.-Str.
Carl Gehrmans, Stockholm, ᶜ1942
Score 24 p.
*Commissioned by Sveriges Radio. Composed
1938 as movements 1, 3, and 4 of the composer's
Dagens Stunder [The Hours of the Day]. First
performance Stockholm, 11 October 1938, Swedish Radio Orchestra, the composer conducting.*

1931s [Pastoral suite for orchestra, Op. 19.
No. 2, Romance. Transcribed for string
orchestra]
Str.
Carl Gehrmans, Stockholm, ᶜ1942
Score 4 p.

5050 [The princess of Cyprus, Op. 9. Act II:
Passacaglia]
Allegro moderato - Maestoso - Allegro vivace
2,2,3*,3*-Alto Sax.-4,3,3,1-Timp.,Glock.-Hp.-
Tenor Voice-Str.
Ms.
Score 30 p. Large folio
*From the opera based on the Kalevala, Fin-
land's national epic. Composed 1930-36.
First performance Stockholm, 29 April 1937,
Royal Opera Orchestra, Herbert Sandberg con-
ductor.*

2085s [Serenade for string orchestra]   *3'*
2 Solo Vn., Solo Vc.-Str.
Nordiska Musikförlaget, Stockholm, ᶜ1942
Score 10 p.
*Originally composed 1936, as part of Serenade
and Little March, for two violins, violoncello
and piano. First performance Stockholm, 31
March 1937. For an orchestral version of the
Little March, see Catalog no. 6063.*

LASSEN, EDUARD.   Copenhagen 13 April 1830
                         Weimar 15 January 1904

4629 [Beethoven overture]   *13'*
2,2,2,2-4,2,3-Timp.-Str.
Julius Hainauer, Breslau, ᶜ1925
Score in reduction 14 p.
Composed for the Beethovenfeier, 1870.

671v [Concerto, violin, Op. 87, D major]
1.Allegro moderato 2.Andante cantabile
3.Allegro risoluto e capriccioso
Solo Vn.-3*,2,2,2-4,2,3-Timp.-Str.
Hainauer, Breslau [n.d.]
Score 118 p.

4387 [Festival overture, orchestra, Op. 51]
3*,2,2,2-4,2,3,1-Timp.,Perc.-Hp.-Str.
Julius Hainauer, Breslau [1873]
Score 65 p.

4439 [Music to Goethe's Faust. No. 3, Polo-
naise]

3*,2,2,2-4,2,3,1-Timp.,Perc.-Str.
Julius Hainauer, Breslau [187-?]
Score 23 p.
Composed 1876.

4600 [Symphony no. 1, D major]
1.Allegro con brio 2.Andante 3.Presto
4.Allegro con fuoco
2,2,2,2-4,2,3-Timp.-Str.
Julius Hainauer, Breslau [187-?]
Score 155 p.

4605 [Symphony no. 2, Op. 78, C major]
1.Allegro molto vivace 2.Larghetto 3.Presto
4.Allegro non troppo, ma con spirito
3*,2,2,2-4,2,3-Timp.-Str.
Julius Hainauer, Breslau [187-?]
Score 182 p.

597m [Two fantasies, bass trombone and   *10'*
orchestra, Op. 48]
1.[Devotion] 2.[Dance in the evening]
Solo B.Tbn.(or Bn. or Vc.)-2,2,2,2-2Hn.-Str.
Seitz, Leipzig [n.d.]
Score 15 p.
*Composed 1872. First performance Weimar, 1873,
the composer conducting.*

LASSUS, ROLAND DE.   Mons, Belgium 1532
                           Munich 14 June 1594

Also spelled: Orland(e) de Lassus, Orlando di
Lasso

4982 [Laudate Dominum omnes gentes, motet for
12 voices. Transcribed for small orchestra by
René Leibowitz]
1(alt. Picc.),1,2*,1-1,1,1-Str.(w/o Vn.II)
Ms.
Score 18 p.
Composed ca.1580; published Munich, 1604.

LÁSZLÓ, ÁKOS.   Nagyenyed, Hungary 1871

559v [Hungarian melodies, Op. 5]
Solo Vn.-2,2,2,2-2Hn.-Timp.,S.Dr.,Cym.-Str.
Score: Ms. 57 p.
Parts: Bote & Bock, Berlin, ᶜ1902

LÁSZLÓ, ALEXANDER.   Budapest 22 November 1895

759p 4D-122, a symphonic journey for   *20'*
piano and orchestra, Op. 17
Solo Pno.-3*,2,2,2-4,2,3,1-Timp.,Perc.-Str.
Ms.
Score 150 p. Large folio
Composed 1940-41.

3659 Improvisations on Oh Susannah   *11'*
(Stephen Foster), in the styles of Bach,
Mozart, Schubert, Brahms, Liszt, Debussy and
Gershwin, Op. 16
2(2nd alt. Picc.),2,2,2-4,2,3,1-Timp.,Perc.-Hp.
-Str.
Guild Publications of Art and Music, New York,
ᶜ1940
Score 61 p.
Composed 1940. First performance Washington,

D.C., 10 July 1940, National Symphony Orchestra, Hans Kindler conductor.

3658 Mechanized forces, march-fantasy on   *4'*
You're in the Army Now, Op. 18
3*,2,2,2-4,2,3,1-Timp.,Perc.-Str.
Guild Publications of Art and Music, New York,
^c1941
Score 30 p.
First performance Boston, 16 December 1941, Boston University Orchestra, Arthur Fiedler conductor.

LATANN, KARL.
    Kleine Leinungen, Germany 28 July 1840
    Bad Freienwalde, Germany 15 October 1888

1652s Am Kamin, Romanze, Op. 244 [By the fireplace]
Solo Vc.-Str.
Score: Ms. 4 p.
Parts: Benjamin, Leipzig [n.d.]

768s [Heart to heart, pizzicato-gavotte,   *4'*
Op. 222]
Str.
Score: Ms. 7 p.
Parts: Hawkes, London [n.d.]

LATHAM, WILLIAM PETERS.
    b. Shreveport, Louisiana 4 January 1917

1183v Fantasy for violin and orchestra   *11'*
Solo Vn.-3*,2,3*,3*,-4,3,3,1-Timp.,Trgl.,Cym.-Cel.-Str.
Ms.
Score 29 p. Large folio
Composed 1946. First performance Minneapolis, 23 May 1948, University of Minnesota Composers Forum Orchestra, Paul Oberg conductor, Emil Bock soloist.

467m Suite for trumpet and strings   *6'*
1.Prelude 2.Air 3.Dance
Solo Tpt.-Str.
Ms.
Score 30 p.
Composed 1951. First performance at the 21st Annual Festival of American Music, Rochester, New York, 4 May 1951, Eastman-Rochester Symphony Orchestra, Howard Hanson conductor, Sydney Mear soloist. Won first prize, Graduate Division of the Phi Mu Alpha Sinfonia National Composition Contest, 1952.

LA TOMBELLE, FERNAND DE.   Paris 3 August 1854
    Château de Fayrac, Dordogne 13 August 1928

496m [Ego sum resurrectio et vita,   *ca.8'*
Op. 34]
Solo Org.-2Ob.-Str.
Richault, Paris, ^c1894
Score 8 p.
Title from John 2:25.

LAUB, VÁŠA.

149s [Slavic tale, Op. 16. No. 1, Love song]
Str.

Hainauer, Breslau, ^c1893
Score 3 p.
Originally composed for piano 4-hands.

719s Valse noble, Op. 30
Str.
Hainauer, Breslau, ^c1893
Score 6 p.

LAUBER, JOSEPH.
    Ruswil, near Lucerne 27 December 1864
    Geneva 28 May 1952

658v Fantaisie, Op. 10
Solo Vn.-Orchestra of Violins: I,II,III,IV
Sandoz, Jobin, Paris, ^c1905
Score 23 p.

LAURENCE, FREDERICK.   London 25 May 1884

413s Tristis, for string orchestra
Str.
Curwen, London, ^c1919 by Goodwin & Tabb
Score 3 p.

LAUTENSCHLÄGER, WILLI.   Bonn 27 February 1880

Also published under several pseudonyms including
José Armándola; Edwin Haller.

1945s [Two pieces for string   *I: 4'*
orchestra]   *II: 4'*
1.Alter Reim/Old rhyme 2.Madrigal
2Cl.(ad lib.)-Str.
Richard Birnbach, Berlin, ^c1939
Score 12 p.

LAUWERYNS, GEORGES.   Brussels 9 August 1884

1026s [Gavotte in the olden style]
Str.
Decourcelle, Nice, ^c1922
Score 2 p.

LAVIGNAC, ALBERT.   Paris 21 January 1846
    Paris 28 May 1916

1001s Jour de fête, carillon, Op. 16. Transcribed for string orchestra by Leon Lemoine
Str.
Score: Ms. 8 p.
Parts: Lemoine, Paris [n.d.]

LAVÍN, CARLOS.   Santiago, Chile 10 August 1883
    Barcelona 27 August 1962

3237 Lamentationes huilliches.   *8'*
Orchestrated by Fritz Mueller
1.Kontenan 2.Kayfu mapu 3.Tayu tripayal
2,2(2nd alt. E.H.),2,2-3,3,3-Timp.,Perc.-Str.
Ms.
Score 16 p.
The Huilliche are a South American Indian tribe. Composed 1933. First performance Washington, D.C., 12 December 1934, US Marine Band Symphony Orchestra, Taylor Branson conductor.

La Violette, Wesley

LA VIOLETTE, WESLEY.
   b. St. James, Minnesota 4 January 1894

2718 Chorale   *4'*
2,3*,2,2-4,2,3,1-Timp.,Cym.-Hp.-Str.
Ms.
Score 5 p. Large folio
*Composed 1936. First performance Chicago, 31
July 1936, American Concert Orchestra, the
composer conducting.*

2649 Collegiana, festival rhapsody *10'*
4*,4*,3,4*-4,3,3,1-Timp.,Perc.-Str.
Ms.
Score 94 p.
*Based on eleven American university songs.
Composed 1934. First performance Chicago, 21
July 1936, Chicago Philharmonic, Richard
Czerwonky conductor.*

723p Concert piece   *20'*
Solo Pno.-3*,3*,2,4*-4,2,3,1-Timp.,Perc.-Cel.,
Hp.-Str.
Ms.
Score 55 p. Large folio
Composed 1937.

984m Concerto for string quartet with *23'*
orchestra
1.Allegro 2.Largo 3.Allegro
Soli: Vn.I&II,Va.,Vc.-3(3rd alt. Picc.),3*,2,
4*-4,2,3,1-Timp.,Perc.-Hp.-Str.
Ms.
Score 56 p. Large folio
*Commissioned by the Roth String Quartet. Com-
posed 1938-39.*

1885s Largo lyrico   *5'*
Timp.-Hp.-Str.
Ms.
Score 22 p.
*Commissioned by the Roth String Quartet. Com-
posed for string quartet, 1942. First per-
formance 1942. This transcription 1942.*

2633 Nocturne   *9'*
1(alt. Picc. ad lib.),2,2,1-2,1,1-Timp.,B.Dr.,
Cym.-Str.
Ms.
Score 27 p.
*Composed 1933. First performance Aurora, Illi-
nois, 17 April 1933, National Chamber Orches-
tra, Rudolph Ganz conductor.*

2631 Ode to an immortal   *12'*
3(3rd alt. Picc.),2,2,4*-4,3,3,1-Timp.,Perc.-
Org.,Hp.-Str.
Ms.
Score 55 p.
Composed 1934.

2632 Osiris, an Egyptian legend for *19'*
orchestra
In one movement
3*(1st alt. B.Fl.),3*,3*,3*-4,3,3,1-Timp.,
Perc.-Pno.,Org.,Cel.,2Hp.-Str.
Ms.
Score 86 p.
Composed 1934.

1715s Penetrella [Inner life]   *8'*
Str.
Ms.
Score 39 p.
*Composed 1928 at the request of Frederick
Stock. First performance Chicago, 30 November
1928, Chicago Symphony Orchestra, Frederick
Stock conductor.*

2899 Prelude and aria   *12'*
3*,3*,2,4*-5,3,3,1-Timp.,Perc.-Cel.,2Hp.-Str.
Ms.
Score 25 p. Large folio
Composed 1937.

3779 San Francisco overture   *14'*
3*,2,2,4*-4,2,3,1-Timp.,Perc.-Cel.,Hp.-Str.
Ms.
Score 67 p. Large folio
*Commissioned by Pierre Monteux. Composed 1939.
First performance San Francisco, 4 March 1941,
San Francisco Symphony Orchestra, the composer
conducting.*

2630 The spook hour, scherzino *5'*
1,2*,1,1-2,1,1-Timp.,Perc.-Hp.-Str.
Ms.
Score 48 p.
*Composed 1931. First performance New York, 25
October 1931, National Chamber Orchestra,
Rudolph Ganz conductor.*

2740 Symphony no. 1   *35'*
1.Lento - Allegro 2.Andante 3.Quasi presto
3(3rd alt. Picc.),3*,2,4*-Ten.Sax.-4,3,3,1-
Timp.,Perc.-Cel.,Hp.-Str.
Ms.
Score 141 p. Large folio
*First performance Rochester, New York, 19
October 1938, Rochester Civic Orchestra,
Howard Hanson conductor.*

3688 [Symphony no. 2, Tom Thumb, *8'*
B-flat major]
1.Lively 2.Very song-like 3.Fast, gaily and
brilliantly
2,0,2,2-4Sax.-2,Bar.Hn.,2,3-Timp.-Str.
Ms.
Score 26 p. Large folio
*Composed 1940. First performance Chicago, 25
May 1942, Illinois Symphony Orchestra of the
WPA, Rudolph Ganz conductor.*

LAVOTTA, RODOLPHE.

1615s Petite fantaisie hongroise no. 1
1,0,1(both optional, ad lib.)-Str.(Cb. ad lib.)
[Rozsnyai, Budapest, n.d.]
Score in reduction 4 p.

LAVRY, MARC.   Riga, Latvia 22 December 1903
        Haifa, Israel 20 March 1967

Born: Marc Levins

3763 Emek [symphonic poem]   *15'*
In one movement
2(both alt. Picc.),2(2nd alt. E.H.),2,2-4,3,3,
1-Timp.,Perc.-Hp.-Str.

Jibneh, Vienna, ^c1937
Score 48 p.

3453 [Hassidic dance, Op. 22]   6'
2(2nd alt. Picc.),2,2,2-4,2,3,1-Timp.,Perc.-
Hp.-Str.
Ms.
Score 29 p.
*Composed 1928. First performance Riga, Latvia,
20 August 1932, Riga Symphony Orchestra, the
composer conducting.*

1888s On the banks of Babylon, Op. 33
Str.
Ms.
Score 19 p.

LAWES, WILLIAM.
            Salisbury, England baptized 1 May 1602
                        Chester, England 1645

2022s [Fantasy and air, no. 1, G minor]   12'
Scored by Arnold Dometsch. Modern string
scoring by Percy Aldridge Grainger
Original: 5 Viols; Modern: Str.
G. Schirmer, New York, ^c1944
Score 7 p.
*Composed ca.1640. First modern performance Lon-
don, 2 April 1924, Arnold Dolmetsch conductor.*

LAWNER, MARK.   New York 8 April 1910

1988s Rhythmic overture for strings   9'30"–11'
Str.
Ms.
Score 32 p.
*Composed 1947. First performance Saratoga
Springs Music Festival, New York, October
1949, New York Philharmonic, F. Charles Adler
conductor. Won third prize in a contest for
orchestral works sponsored by The Musical
Leader of Chicago, 1949.*

LAZAR, FILIP.   Craiova, Romania 18 May 1894
                        Paris 4 November 1936

4884 [Concerto no. 4, Concerto di   20'
camera, Op. 24]
1.Lento 2.Moderato
1(alt. Picc.),1,1,1-1,1,1-Timp.,Perc.-Pno.-Str.
Durand, Paris, ^c1935
Score 46 p.
*Composed 1934. First performance Paris, 11
December 1935, Chamber Orchestra of the Paris
Philharmonic, Charles Münch conductor.*

2211 Concerto grosso no. 1, Op. 17   22'
Largo – 1.Allegro 2.Largo 3.Allegretto
4.Allegro
0,2,0,2-2,1-Timp.-Str.
Durand, Paris, ^c1930
Score 60 p.
*Composed 1929. First performance Boston,
March 1930, Serge Koussevitzky conductor.*

1890 Divertissement pour orchestre   12'
3(3rd alt. Picc.),3*,3*,3*-4,3,3,1-Timp.,Perc.
-Hp.-Str.

Durand, Paris, ^c1927
Score 32 p.
*Composed 1924. First performance Concerts
Colonne, Paris, March 1926, Georges Georgesco
conductor.*

2218 Le ring, musique pour orchestre   4'
no. 2
3(3rd alt. Picc.),3*,3*,3(3rd may be C.Bn.)-
4,3,3,1-Timp.,B.Dr.,Cym.-Str.
Durand, Paris, ^c1930
Score 29 p.
*A round, composed 1928. First performance
Paris, 1929, Georges Georgesco conductor.*

2352 Suite valaque [Wallachian suite   12'
for orchestra]
1.Berceuse 2.[The drinkers] 3.[Dance] 4.[Ox-
wagon] 5.[Water-sprites] 6.[Gypsy dance]
2,2(2nd alt. E.H.),2,2-2,2-Timp.-Cel.,Hp.-Str.
Ms.
Score 31 p.
*Composed 1927. First performance Paris 1929,
Walter Straram conductor.*

2004 Tziganes [Gypsies] scherzo   15'
3(2nd & 3rd alt. Picc.),3*,2,4*-3Sax.(SAT)-4,
3,3,1-Timp.,Perc.-Pno.,Cel.,Hp.-Str.
Durand, Paris [1927?]
Score 92 p.
*Composed 1925. First performance Boston,
November 1927, Serge Koussevitzky conductor.*

LAZZARI, SYLVIO.   Bozen (now Bolzano, Italy)
                              31 December 1857
                            Paris 18 June 1944

1644 Armor [prelude to the lyric drama]
3(3rd alt. Picc.),3*,3*,3-4,3,3,1-Timp.,Cym.-
2Hp.-Str.
La Sirène Musicale, Paris [n.d.]
Score 27 p.

2092 Effet de nuit, tableau symphonique
3(3rd alt. Picc.),3*,3*,3*-4,3,3,1-Timp.,Perc.
-Hp.-Str.
Leduc, Paris [n.d.]
Score 39 p.
Inspired by Paul Verlaine's poem.

1453 Tableaux maritimes, suite   32'
d'orchestre
1.[Sunset at sea] 2.[Waves] 3.[Shepherd on
the waste land] 4.[Ship fleeing the gale]
3,3*,3*,3-4,3,3,1-Timp.,Perc.-Hp.-Str.
Eschig, Paris, ^c1925
Score 134 p.
*Composed 1920. First performance Concerts
Pasdeloup, Paris, 1921, Rhené-Baton conductor.*

LEACH, JAMES.   Wardle, near Rochdale,
                              Lancashire 1762
            Blackley, near Manchester 8 February 1798

4620 Neptune's holiday, hornpipe   3'
1(alt. Picc.),1,1-0,1,1-Perc.-Str.
Schott, London, ^c1938
Score in reduction 4 p.

Lebede, Willibald

LEBEDE, WILLIBALD.
        b. Frankfurt an der Oder(?) 19 April 1872

  1240s [Two pieces for string orchestra, Op. 19]
    1.Melodie 2.Intermezzo fantastique
    Str.
    Bratfisch, Frankfurt/Oder [n.d.]
    Score 7 p.

LEBERT, A.

  1667s Cadeau mignon, pizzicato, Op. 349
    [Small gift]
    Str.
    Score: Ms. 4 p.
    Parts: Privately published [n.p., n.d.]

  1680s Galanterie royale, menuet, Op. 303
    Str.
    Score: Ms. 5 p.
    Parts: Éditions Margueritat, Paris [n.d.]

  1645s Le gué d'amour, Op. 189 [The trial of
    love]
    Solo Vn.-Str.
    Score: Ms. 5 p.
    Parts: Éditions Margueritat, Paris [n.d.]

LEBLANC, NESTOR.

  1249s Monts bleus (Estérel) [Provençal Alps]
    rêverie
    Str.
    Score: Ms. 7 p.
    Parts: Decourcelle, Nice, c1923

  1133s Rêverie. Orchestrated by H. Mouton
    Solo Vn.-Str.
    Score: Ms. 5 p.
    Parts: Decourcelle, Nice, c1926

LEBORNE, FERNAND. Charleroi, Belgium 10 March 1862
                    Paris 15 January 1929

  648v L'absent, Op. 50. No. 4, Nocturne [from
    incidental music to a play]
    Solo Vn.-2,2*,2,2-2,2,3-Timp.-Cel.,Hp.-Str.
    Joanin, Paris, c1904
    Score 16 p.

  921v Poème légendaire, Op. 67
    Solo Vn.-3(3rd alt. Picc.),2,2,2-4,2,3,1-Timp.,
    Perc.-Cel.,Hp.-Str.
    Ricordi, Paris, c1922
    Score 81 p.

  634v Rêverie, Op. 55
    Solo Va.(or Vn. or Vc.)-1,1,2,1-Hn.-Timp.-Hp.
    (or Pno.)-Str.
    Score: Ms. 24 p.
    Parts: Grus, Paris, c1910

  721m [Symphony-concerto, violin, piano and
    orchestra, Op. 37, E major]
    1.Maestoso 2.Adagio 3.Vivace
    Solo Vn., Solo Pno.-2(2nd alt. Picc.),2(2nd
    alt. E.H.),2,2-2,2,3-Timp.,Trgl.-Str.
    Joanin, Paris, c1903

    Score 174 p.
    Composed 1888.

LEBRECHT, VITTORIO.

  1067s Simplicitas, Op. 7
    Solo Vc.-Str.
    Score: Ms. 6 p.
    Parts: Decourcelle, Nice, c1923

LECLAIR, JEAN MARIE, "L'AÎNÉ".
               Lyons, France 10 May 1697
               Paris 22 October 1764

  Also published as: Leclerc and Claire

  298v [Concerto, violin, Op. 7 no. 2,
    D major] Edited by Jean-François
    Paillard
    1.Allegro non troppo 2.Adagio 3.Allegro
    Solo Vn.-Org. or Cemb.-Str.
    Éditions Costallat, Paris, c1962
    Score 35 p.
    Composed ca.1737.

  296v [Concerto, violin, Op. 10 no. 2,   15'
    A major] Edited by J. F. Paillard
    1.Allegro ma non troppo 2.Adagio 3.Allegro
    ma non troppo
    Solo Vn.-Org.(or Cemb.)-Str.
    Éditions Costallat, Paris, c1963
    Score 32 p.
    Composed 1743 or 1744.

  311v [Concerto, violin, Op. 10   18'30"
    no. 6, G minor] Edited by Jean-François
    Paillard
    1.Allegro ma poco 2.Aria grazioso: Andante
    3.Allegro
    Solo Vn.-Org.(or Cemb.)-Str.
    Éditions Costallat, Paris, c1963
    Score 47 p.
    Composed 1743 or 1744.

  1713s Sarabande and Tambourin. Edited   3'
    by Arcady Dubensky
    Str.
    Ms.
    Score 11 p.
    First performance of this edition Philadelphia,
    20 November 1935, Philadelphia Chamber String
    Sinfonietta, Fabien Sevitzky conductor.

LECOCQ, ALEXANDRE CHARLES.   Paris 3 June 1832
                   Paris 24 October 1918

  928v Andante nuptial
    Solo Vn.-2,2,2,2-2,2-Timp.-Str.
    Choudens, Paris [n.d.]
    Score 19 p.

  927v Offertoire
    Solo Vn.-2,2,2,2-2Hn.-Str.
    Score: Ms. 23 p.
    Parts: Choudens, Paris [n.d.]

  926v Romance
    Solo Vn.-1,1,2,1-2Hn.-Timp.-Str.

Score: Ms. 11 p.
Parts: Joubert, Paris [n.d.]

LEDERER, DEZSÖ.   Bekecsaba, Hungary 1858

966v All'ongharese
Solo Vn.-2,2,2,1-2Hn.-Timp.-Str.
Score: Ms. 16 p.
Parts: Bote & Bock, Berlin, C1907

1510s La dernière sérénade [The last serenade]
Solo Vn.-Str.
Score: Ms. 7 p.
Parts: Grus, Paris [n.d.]

1023s Minuetto. Orchestrated by Victor
Charmettes
Str.
Score: Ms. 8 p.
Parts: Enoch, Paris, C1908

865s [Two pieces for violin and string
orchestra]
1.Sarabande 2.Tempo di bourrée
Str.
Enoch, Paris, C1901
Score 8 p.

LEDUC, PAUL.   Paris 1871

959v Barcarolle   3'
Solo Vn.-1,1,2,1-2Hn.-Hp.-Str.
Score: Ms. 18 p.
Parts: Decourcelle, Paris, C1899
*Composed 1898. First performance Paris,
January 1899.*

884v Romance   4'
Solo Vn.-1,1,2,1-2Hn.-Str.
Score: Ms. 12 p.
Parts: Decourcelle, Paris, C1899
*Composed 1898. First performance Paris,
December 1898.*

LEE, DAI-KEONG.   Honolulu 2 September 1915

853s Gavotte Louis XV, Op. 54
Str.
Score: Ms. 10 p.
Parts: Augener, London [n.d.]

2014s Introduction and allegro   7'30"
Str.
Sprague-Coleman, New York, C1942
Score 16 p.
*Composed for CBS's American Festival, 1941.
First performance CBS network, 15 November
1941, CBS Symphony Orchestra, Howard Barlow
conductor.*

3835 Symphony no. 1   16'
In one movement
3*(2nd alt. Picc.II),2,2,2-4,3,3,1-Timp.,Cym.-
Str.
Ms.
Score 85 p. Large folio
Composed 1941-42.

LEE, ERNEST MARKHAM. Cambridge, England 8 June 1874
                      Eastbourne, England 13 November 1956

21s Light heart, a merry suite
1.Gavotte 2.Scherzetto 3.Sérénade napoli-
taine 4.Country dance
Str.
Lengnick, London, C1925
Score 12 p.

LEE, MAURICE.   Hamburg February 1821
                                  London 23 June 1895

645s Sylvana. Menuet d'Exaudet. Arranged by
Louis Lee
Str.
Score: Ms. 8 p.
Parts: [Augener, London, n.d.]
*From the ballet. Joseph Exaudet (1710-63)
was a violinist.*

LEFÉBURE, JOSEPH.   Gand, Belgium 1877

951v [Concerto, violin, G major]
1.Allegro con fuoco 2.Andante 3.Allegro
giocoso
Solo Vn.-2,2,2,2-4,2,3,1-Timp.-Str.
Privately published [n.p., n.d.]
Score 35 p.

LEFEBVRE, CHARLES ÉDOUARD.   Paris 19 June 1843
                       Aix-les-Bains, France 8 September 1917

298 Dalila, Op. 40 [Orchestral scenes   23'
after the drama by Octave Feuillet]
1.Prélude 2.Air de danse 3.Notturno appassionato 4.[Song of the calvary] 5.Final
2,2,2,2-4,2,3-Timp.,Trgl.-Hp.-Str.
J. Hamelle, Paris [n.d.]
Score 43 p.
Composed 1893. First performance Paris, 1894.

LEFÈVRE, ERNEST.

1344s Berceuse
Solo Vc.-Hp.-Str.
Score: Ms. 9 p.
Parts: [n.p., n.d.]

LEFTWICH, VERNON.   London 19 June 1881

7184 Elegy for orchestra
2,2,2,2-2Sax.(Alto & Ten.,both optional)-4,3,
3,1-Bells-Hp. or Pno.(optional)-Str.
Avant Music, Los Angeles, C1963
Score 12 p.

LEGLEY, VICTOR.   Hazebrouck, France 18 June 1915

4952 [The golden river, symphonic   6'
sketch, Op. 30]
2,2,2,2-2,1-Timp.-Str.
Ms.
Score 18 p.
*Composed 1948. First performance Brussels,
1948, Belgian Radio and Television Symphony
Orchestra, J. Verelst conductor.*

Legley, Victor

6119 [Little carnival overture] 4'
2(2nd alt. Picc.),2,2,2-4,3,3,1-Timp.,Perc.-
Str.
CeBeDeM, Brussels, C1958
Score 32 p.
*Commissioned by the Symphonic Orchestra of
Maastricht. Composed 1954. First performance
Maastricht, Holland, 1954, Limburg Symphony
Orchestra, André Rieu conductor.*

4916 [Music for a Greek tragedy, Op. 24] 18'
1.Adagio - Allegro 2.Adagio - Allegro
3(3rd alt. Picc.),3*,3*,3*-4,3,3,1-Timp.,Perc.
-2Hp.-Str.
Ms.
Score 106 p.
*Composed 1946. First performance Brussels,
1947, Belgian Radio and Television Symphony
Orchestra, Nino Sanzogno conductor.*

4923 Suite pour orchestre, Op. 18 24'
1.Prelude 2.Sarabande 3.Menuet 4.Gigue
3*,3*,4*(1Cl. in E-flat),3*-Alto Sax.-4,3,3,1-
Timp.,Perc.-Pno.,Cel.(alt. Glock.),2Hp.-Str.
Ms.
Score 123 p.
*Composed 1944. First performance Brussels,
1945, Belgian Radio and Television Symphony
Orchestra, Leonce Gras conductor. Won the
Irène Fuerison prize given by the Belgian
Royal Academy, 1945.*

4951 [Symphonic variations on an old 13'
Flemish song, Op. 6]
2,2,2,2-4,2,2,1-Timp.,Perc.-Hp.-Str.
Ms.
Score 86 p.
*Composed 1941. First performance Brussels,
1941, Belgian Radio and Television Symphony
Orchestra, Franz André conductor.*

LE-GRAND, ROBERT.

957v Conte romanesque, Op. 5 [Roman tale]
Solo Vn.-1,1,1,1-Hn.-Str.
Score: Ms. 11 p.
Parts: Durdilly, Paris, C1924

1554s Promenade sentimentale, rêverie, Op. 1
Str.
Score: Ms. 6 p.
Parts: Durdilly, Paris, C1924

LEHÁR, FRANZ.
Komorn (now Komarom), Hungary 30 April 1870
Bad Ischl, Austria 24 October 1948

955v [Hungarian fantasy, Op. 45] Edited by
P. A. Tirindelli
Solo Vn.-1,0,2-Str.
Schmidl, Trieste [n.d.]
Score 12 p.

2049 Eine Vision, Meine Jugend, Ouverture 8'
3*,2,2,2-4,2,3,1-Timp.,Cym.,Trgl.-Org.(ad
lib.),Hp.-Str.
Doblinger, Leipzig, C1907
Score 42 p.

LEHMANN, ROBERT.
Schweidnitz, Silesia 26 November 1841
Stettin, Pomerania 12 June 1912

1195s Abendruhe, Op. 33 [Evening calm]
Str.(without Cb.)
Von Lehne, Hanover [n.d.]
Score 1 p.
Published with H. Fliegner's Märchen, Op. 22.

LEICHTENTRITT, HUGO.
Pleszow, Poznań, Poland 1 January 1874
Cambridge, Massachusetts 13 November 1951

4360 Symphonic variations and gamelan on a
Siamese dance tune, Op. 30
3*,3*,3*,2-4,3,3,1-Timp.,Perc.-Pno.,Hp.-Str.
Ms.
Score 93 p.

LEIFS, JÓN. Sólheimar, Iceland 1 May 1899
Reykjavik, Iceland 20 July 1968

4209 [Icelandic dances, Op. 11 nos. 1-4. 10'
Transcribed for small orchestra by Jón Leifs
and Leopold Weninger]
1.Allegretto 2.Tempo giusto 3.Allegro
moderato ed energico 4.Allegro vivace
1,1,1-2Sax.(Alto, Ten.)-0,1,1-Timp.,Perc.-
Harm.-Str.
Kistner & Siegel, Leipzig, C1931
Score in reduction 9 p.
Originally composed for piano.

6955 [Icelandic overture, Op. 9]
2*,2(2nd alt. E.H.),2,2-2,2-Timp.,Perc.-Child-
ren's Chorus(ad lib.),Mixed Chorus(ad lib.)-
Str.
Score: Kistner & Siegel, Leipzig, C1933. 63 p.
Parts: Islandia Edition, Reykjavik, C1950
Composed 1926. First performance Oslo, 1926.

LEKEU, GUILLAUME. Heusy, Belgium 20 January 1870
Angers, France 21 January 1894

204s Adagio, Op. 3 10'
Soli: Vn.,Va.,Vc.-Str.
Rouart Lerolle, Paris [n.d.]
Score 15 p.

809 Fantaisie contrapuntique sur un 8'
cramignon liégeois
0,1,1,1-Hn.-Str.
Rouart Lerolle, Paris, C1925
Score 12 p.
*Composed 1890 for the Cercle Musical d'Ama-
teurs. First performance Concerts Privés,
Brussels 1925, Marcel Prévost conductor.*

504 Fantaisie sur deux airs 15'
populaires angevins
2,2,2,2-4,2,3-Timp.,Cym.,Trgl.-Str.
Rouart Lerolle, Paris, C1909
Score 51 p.
*Composed 1892. First performance Brussels,
June 1893, Eugène Ysaÿe conductor.*

LELEU, JEANNE.
          b. Saint-Mihiel, France 29 December 1898

  2458 Suite symphonique [wind instruments and
        piano]
        1.Prelude 2.[The tree of songs] 3.[Mass
        movements] 4.[Sacred grove] 5.Joie populaire
        2Fl.(2nd alt. Picc.),2*,1,1-1,2,1-Perc.-Pno.
        Leduc, Paris, C1926
        Score 62 p.

LEMACHER, HEINRICH.   Solingen 26 June 1891

  1661s [Easy dances and character pieces for
         strings] Edited by H. Lemacher and Paul Mies
         10 excerpts from works of Joseph Haydn,
         Florian Deller (1729-1773), Reinhard Keiser
         (1674-1739), Karl Ditters von Dittersdorf,
         Christoph Willibald Gluck, and Joseph Lanner
         Str.
         Tonger, Cologne, C1931
         Score 15 p.

LEMAIRE, JEAN EUGÈNE GASTON.
               Château d'Amblainvilliers,
                     France 9 September 1854
                     Paris 9 January 1928

  331s Minuetto
        Str.
        Leduc, Paris [n.d.]
        Score 7 p.

  1148s Pizzicati
         Str.
         Score: Ms. 5 p.
         Parts: A. Cranz, Leipzig [n.d.]

LEMAÎTRE, LÉON.

  1101s Aubade
         Str.
         Score: Ms. 8 p.
         Parts: Joanin, Paris [n.d.]

  1069s Gouttelettes diamantées [Sparkling
         little drops] intermezzo
         Str.
         Score: Ms. 4 p.
         Parts: Decourcelle, Nice, C1910

  1191s Mystérieuse, valse
         Str.
         Score: Ms. 11 p.
         Parts: Decourcelle, Nice [n.d.]

  1190s Petite gavotte, valse
         Str.
         Score: Ms. 7 p.
         Parts: Decourcelle, Nice [n.d.]

LEMATTE, F. E.

  1490s La poupée mécanique [The mechanical
         doll]
         Str.
         Score: Ms. 7 p.
         Parts: [n.p., n.d.]

LEMBA, ARTUR.
     Reval (now Tallinn), Estonia 24 September 1885
                     Tallinn 21 November 1963

  330s Berceuse
        Hp.(or Pno.)-Str.(without Cb.)
        Zimmermann, Leipzig, C1910
        Score 5 p.

LENDVAI, ERWIN.   Budapest 4 June 1882
                         London 31 March 1949

  1179 Archaische Tänze, Op. 30
        9 dance movements
        1(alt. Picc.),1(alt. E.H.),1,1-1,1,1-Timp.,
        Perc.-Hp.-Str.
        Simrock, Berlin, C1922
        Score 157 p.
        Composed 1921.

  2175 [Chamber suite, Op. 32]
        1.Tranquillo 2.Mosso 3.Alla marcia 4.Alle-
        gro con spirito 5.Adagio 6.Andantino mesto
        7.Largo rubato
        1,1,1,1-Hn.-Hp.-Str.
        Rahter, Leipzig, C1923
        Score 57 p.

  2498 [Dinner music for chamber orchestra,
        Op. 48b]
        2Ob.-2Hn.-Str.
        Kistner & Siegel, Leipzig, 1932
        Score 8 p.

  5264 [Festival march, for orchestra]
        2*,2,2,2-4,3,3,1-Timp.,Perc.-Str.
        N. Simrock, Berlin, C1912
        Score 24 p.

  1821 Scherzo, Op. 7
        3(3rd alt. Picc.),3*,4*,3*-4,3,3,1-Timp.,Perc.
        -Hp.-Str.
        Simrock, Berlin, C1911
        Score 55 p.

  1313 [Symphony, Op. 10, D major]
        1.Andante religioso 2.Con moto 3.Mesto ed
        assai tranquillo 4.Vivace
        3*,3(3rd alt. E.H.),4*(1Cl. in E-flat),3*-4,4,
        3,1-Timp.,Perc.-Org.(ad lib.),1 or 2Hp.-Str.
        Simrock, Berlin, C1912
        Score 131 p.

LENEPVEU, CHARLES FERDINAND.   Rouen 4 October 1840
                                 Paris 16 August 1910

  616v Romance sans paroles, Dormeuse
        Solo Vn.-2,0,2,2-4Hn.-Hp.-Str.
        Lemoine, Paris [n.d.]
        Score 16 p.

LENOM, CL.

  1660s Berceuse
         Solo Ob.-Str.
         Score: Ms. 6 p.
         Parts: Gaudet, Paris [n.d.]

Lenom, Cl.

1647s Ronde villageoise [A village dance]
Solo Ob.-Str.
Score: Ms. 5 p.
Parts: Gaudet, Paris [n.d.]

LENTZ, NICOLAAS.   1720?
                                          1782

287p [Concerto I for six instruments: cembalo
obbligato, 3 violins, viola and violoncello]
Edited by Willem Noske
1.Allegro 2.Andante 3.Vivace
Solo Cemb.-Str.
Edition Heuwekemeyer, Amsterdam, ^c1961
Score 31 p.
Composed before 1750.

LENZEWSKI, GUSTAV, SR.
        Schöneberg, near Berlin 17 August 1857
        Berlin-Charlottenburg 21 December 1928

[Dances of the 16th and 17th centuries. Transcribed for string orchestra by G. Lenzewski]
995s v.1 Melchior Franck, Valerius Otto
996s v.2 William Brade
997s v.3 Antony Holborn, Thomas Simpson, Valentin Hausmann
998s v.4 Hans Leo Hassler, Johann H. Schein
Str.
Chr. Friedrich Vieweg, Berlin [n.d.]
Scores: 12 p., 10 p., 12 p., 11 p.

LEO, LEONARDO ORTENSIO SALVATORE DE.
            San Vito degli Schiavi,
            near Brindisi, Italy 5 August 1694
            Naples 31 October 1744

387c [Concerto, violoncello, A major]   12'
Arranged and edited by Eugen Rapp
1.Andantino grazioso 2.Allegro 3.Larghetto
4.Allegro (assai)
Solo Vc.-Cemb.-Str.
Schott, London, ^c1955
Score 24 p.
Composed 1737. This edition 1937.

6404 [Emira. Sinfonia from the opera]   4'
Edited by Giuseppe Alfredo Pastore
2Hn.-Cemb.-Str.
Carisch, Milan, ^c1957
Score 8 p.
*From the opera composed 1735. First perform-
ance Naples, 12 July 1735.*

6400 La morte di Abel, sinfonia dell'   5'
oratorio. Edited by Giuseppe Alfredo Pastore
2Hn.-Cemb.-Str.
Carisch, Milan, ^c1957
Score 12 p.
From the oratorio composed 1732.

6356 [Saint Genevieve, sacred melodrama.
Sinfonia] Edited by Giuseppe Alfredo Pastore
2Ob.-2Hn.-Str.
Carisch, Milan, ^c1957
Score 16 p.
*Attributed to Leo; possibly composed by Giu-
seppe Sellitto (1700-1777).*

3238 [St. Helen at Calvary. Sinfonia]   5'
Edited by Hermann Kretzschmar
1.Maestoso 2.Larghetto 3.Allegro andante -
Maestoso
2,2,2,2-2Hn.-Str.
Breitkopf & Härtel, Leipzig, ^c1896
Score 11 p.
From the oratorio composed 1732.

910m Vocalise for bassoon and string orchestra
Solo Bn.-Str.
Ms.
Score 10 p.

LEONARD, CLAIR.   Newton, Massachusetts 1901

740p Concerto for piano and orchestra   22'
1.Ponderoso e presto 2.Adagio - Allegro
Solo Pno.-3*,2(2nd alt. E.H.),3*,3*-4,3,3,1-
Timp.,Perc.-Str.
Ms.
Score 87 p.
*Originally composed for piano solo, 1926. This
version 1938.*

3079 Rhumba and dead march   10'
3*,2(2nd alt. E.H.),2,3*-4,3,3,1-Timp.,Perc.-
Pno.-Str.
Ms.
Score 60 p.
*Composed 1935 for small orchestra and chorus.
Transcribed 1936. First performance of
Rhumba only, Boston, 15 May 1939, Boston Pops,
Malcolm Holmes conductor.*

LÉONARD, HUBERT. Bellaire, near Liège 7 April 1819
                                  Paris 6 May 1890

1021v Cavatine, Op. 50
Solo Vn.-Str.
Score: Ms. 7 p.
Parts: B. Schott's Söhne, Mainz [1878]

1044v [Concerto, violin, no. 2, Op. 14, D major]
1.Allegro moderato 2.Andante con récitativo
3.Rondo: Allegretto
Solo Vn.-2,2,2,2-2,2,3-Timp.-Str.
Score: Ms. 210 p.
Parts: B. Schott's Söhne, Mainz [1850?]

356v [Concerto, violin, no. 3, Op. 16]
1.Allegro moderato 2.Andante 3.Rondo (alla
spagnola) - Più vivo
Solo Vn.-1,2,2,2-2,2,3-Timp.-Str.
Score: Ms. ^c1976 by The Fleisher Collection of
Orchestral Music, Free Library of Philadelphia.
81 p. Large folio
Parts: B. Schott's Söhne, Mainz [1853]

1054v [Concerto, violin, no. 5, Op. 28, D major]
1.Allegro moderato 2.Andante 3.Allegretto
Solo Vn.-2,2,2,2-2,2-Timp.-Str.
Score: Ms. 94 p.
Parts: B. Schott's Söhne, Mainz [1867]

1168v Souvenir de Haydn, fantaisie sur l'hymne
nationale autrichienne, Op. 2
Solo Vn.-Str.

Score in reduction: G. Schirmer, New York,
c1901. 10 p.
Parts: Richault, Paris [n.d.]
*Theme is Haydn's Kaiserlied composed 1797 as
Austria's first national anthem, now the
national anthem of West Germany.*

LEONBRO, LEO.

1567s Pensée mystique [Mystical thought]
Solo Vn.-Str.
Score: Ms. 5 p.
Parts: Decourcelle, Nice, c1916

LEONCAVALLO, RUGGERO (*not Ruggiero*).
Naples 8 March 1858
Montecatini, near Florence 9 August 1919

622s Romanesca. Arranged by A. Ischpold   *4'*
1,0,1(both ad lib.)-Hp.(or Pno.)-Str.
Bosworth, Leipzig, c1898
Score 11 p.

5159 Tarentella, pour orchestre
3*,2,2,2-4,2Cnt.,3,1-Timp.,Trgl.,B.Dr.-Hp.-
Str.
Choudens, Paris, c1899
Score 31 p.

349 Valse coquette
2,2,2,2-4,2,3-Timp.-Str.
Brockhaus, Leipzig, c1896
No score published. Violin I part 4 p.

LEPLIN, EMANUEL.   San Francisco 3 October 1917
Martinez, California 1 December 1972

6344 Birdland, children's suite for   *10-12'*
orchestra
Overture - The dove - Interlude A 1.Bird's
lullaby - Interlude B 2.The bobolink -
Interlude C 3.The oriole 4.The crow
3*,3*,3*,2-4,3,3,1-Timp.,Trgl.-Hp.-Str.
Ms.
Score 43 p.
*Based on piano melodies by Leonora Armsby.
Composed 1948. First performance San Fran-
cisco, March 1948, San Francisco Symphony, the
composer conducting.*

6070 [Comedy, for orchestra]   *11'30"*
3*,3*,3*,3*-4,3,3,1-Timp.,Perc.-Hp.-Str.
Ms.
Score 102 p. Large folio
*Originally intended as Part II of an unfin-
ished work, The Drama. Composed 1946. First
performance Fresno, California, 20 October
1960, Fresno Philharmonic Orchestra, Paul
Vermel conductor.*

219m Meditation for horn and string   *7'*
orchestra
Solo Hn.-Str.
Ms.
Score 10 p.
Composed 1947.

6056 Prologue [for full orchestra,   *11'*
1960]
3*,3*,2,3*-4,3,3,1-Timp.,Perc.-Str.
Ms.
Score 58 p. Large folio
*Intended as part of an unfinished larger work,
The Drama. Commissioned by the Fresno Philharmonic Association. Composed 1960. First
performance Fresno, California, 20 October
1960, Fresno Philharmonic Orchestra, Paul Vermel conductor.*

239m Prologue for string orchestra and   *10'*
solo trio
Solo Ob., Solo Hn., Solo Va.-Str.
Ms.
Score 14 p.
*Composed 1945. First performance Frankfurt,
December 1945, Strings of the GI Symphony
Orchestra of the United States Army, the com-
poser conducting.*

314p Rustic dance   *7'*
2 Solo Pno.-Hn.-Str.
Ms.
Score 10 p.
*Composed 1941. First performance Oakland,
California, March 1941, Mills College Orches-
tra, the composer conducting.*

6208 Symphony no. 1, Of the twentieth   *42'30"*
century
1.Illumination 2.Consternation 3.Contem-
plation 4.Adaptation
3*,3*,3*,3*-4,4,3,1-Timp.,Perc.-Pno.,2Hp.-Str.
Ms.
Score 249 p. Large folio
*Commissioned by the Friends of the San Fran-
cisco Symphony Orchestra for its 50th anniversary. Composed 1961. First performance
San Francisco, 3 January 1962, San Francisco
Symphony Orchestra, Enrique Jorda conductor.*

6667 Symphony no. 2   *44'*
1.Poco vivace - Poco tranquillo 2.Poco adagio
- Andante moderato 3.Allegro molto vivace
4.Poco lento - Moderato con moto - Allegro con
brio - Vivace assai
3*,3*,3*,3*-4,4,3,1-Timp.,Perc.-2Hp.-Str.
Ms.
Score 238 p. Large folio
*Composed 1965. First performance San Fran-
cisco, 19 January 1966, San Francisco Symphony
Orchestra, Josef Krips conductor.*

6255 Three dances for small orchestra   *14'*
1.Menuetto con brio 2.Sarabande 3.Gigue
2,2,2,2-2,2-Timp.-Str.(without Vc. or Cb.)
Ms.
Score 33 p.
*Composed 1942. First performance San Fran-
cisco, 24 March 1958, San Francisco Symphony,
Enrique Jorda conductor.*

6046 Two pieces: Landscapes and   *23'*
skyscrapers
3(3rd alt. Picc.),3*,3*,3*-4,4,3,1-Timp.,Perc.
-Hp.-Str.

Le Rey, Frédéric

Ms.
Score 118 p. Large folio
Composed 1958-59. First performance San Francisco, 4 May 1960, San Francisco Symphony, Enrique Jorda conductor.

LE REY, FRÉDÉRIC.
See: REY, FRÉDÉRIC LE.

LEROUX, XAVIER.   Velletri, Italy 11 October 1863
Paris 2 February 1919

6989 [Harald, overture for orchestra]   *13'*
3*,2,3*,4-4,2,2Cnt.,3,1-Timp.-Hp.-Str.
Leduc, Paris, ᶜ1895
Score 79 p.

LESCHETIZKY, THEODOR.   Łańcut, Poland 22 June 1830
Dresden 14 November 1915

2212s [Berceuse, Op. 46 no. 1. Transcribed for string orchestra by Poul Kroman]
Str.
Ms.
Score 6 p.
Originally composed for piano.

LESSARD, JOHN AYRES.   San Francisco 3 July 1920

6353 Box Hill overture   *8'*
3*,2,2,2-4,2,2,1-Timp.-Str.
Composers Facsimile Edition, New York, ᶜ1952
by John Lessard
Score 64 p. Large folio
Composed at the Stanford White estate, Box Hill, 1946. First performance New York, 19 November 1946, New York City Symphony, Leonard Bernstein conductor.

324m Cantilena for oboe and string   *6'*
orchestra
Solo Ob.-Str.
Composers Facsimile Edition, New York, ᶜ1952
by John Lessard
Score 14 p.
Composed 1946. First performance New York, 12 November 1947, New York City Ballet Society Orchestra, Leon Barzin conductor, Harry Shulman soloist.

315m Concerto for flute, clarinet,   *14'*
bassoon, and string orchestra [1953 version]
1.Allegretto moderato 2.Andante con moto
3.Presto
Solo Fl., Solo Cl., Solo Bn.-Str.
Composers Facsimile Edition, New York, ᶜ1952
by John Lessard
Score 71 p.
Composed 1952, in acknowledgement of the National Academy of Arts and Letters Award received by the composer. First performance New York, 1953, Little Orchestra Society, Thomas Scherman conductor. Revised 1963.

6673 Concerto for [12] wind instruments   *14'*
1.Allegro 2.Adagio 3.Allegretto
2(both alt. Picc.),1,2,2-2,2,1
Ms. ᶜ1950 by Merrymount Press

Score 38 p.
Composed 1949. First performance New York, 29 January 1951, Little Orchestra Society, Thomas Scherman conductor.

LESUEUR, JEAN FRANÇOIS.
Drucat-Plessiel, France 15 February 1760
Paris 6 October 1837

5462 [Telemachus on Calypso's island, or The triumph of wisdom. Overture]
2,2,2,2-4,0,1-Timp.-Str.
[Chez H. Naderman, Paris, 1798]
Score 30 p.
From the tragic opera. First performance Paris, 11 May 1796.

LEUSCHNER, THEODORE ROBERT.
b. Morgenroth, Germany 8 April 1878

647m [Fantasy on the German traditional   *7'*
song May Breeze, for trumpet and orchestra]
Solo Tpt.-2,1,2,1-Timp.-Str.
Zimmermann, Leipzig, ᶜ1909
Score in reduction 13 p.

LEUTWILER, TONI.   Zurich 31 October 1923

383m [Concertino, horn and orchestra,   *4'*
Op. 105]
Solo Hn.-2,2,2,2-3,3,3-Timp.,Perc.-Cel.(ad lib.),Hp.-Str.
Otto Heinrich Noetzel, Wilhelmshaven, ᶜ1960
Score 20 p.
Commissioned by the Westdeutscher Rundfunk, Cologne, Germany. Composed 1957. First performance Cologne, 1 July 1958, Rundfunkorchester des Westdeutschen Rundfunks, Hermann Hagestedt conductor, Alfred Adamczyk soloist.

LEVADÉ, CHARLES GASTON.   Paris 3 January 1869
Paris 27 October 1948

255s Prelude religieux
Str.
Baudoux, Paris, 1896
Score 5 p.

LEVANT, OSCAR.   Pittsburgh 27 December 1906
Beverly Hills 14 August 1972

3592 Nocturne [original version]   *14'*
3(3rd alt. Picc.),3*,3*,3-4,3,3,1-Timp.,Perc.-Cel.,Hp.-Str.
New Music Society, Los Angeles, ᶜ1938 by Oscar Levant
Score 48 p.
Composed 1937. First performance Los Angeles, 14 April 1937, Federal Symphony Orchestra of the WPA, Gerald Strang conductor. Revised after this publication.

LEVIN, SYLVAN.   Baltimore, Maryland 2 May 1903

4498 Babe Ruth suite   *40'*
1.Youth (Variations on Take Me Out to the Ball Game) 2.The 60th home run 3.Waltz (Success)
4.The called home run 5.In memorium [*sic*]

2(both alt. Picc.),2(2nd alt. E.H.),2,2-2,3,
2-Timp.,Perc.-Hp.-Narrator-Str.
Ms.
Score 78 p.
*Commissioned by the Mutual Broadcasting Com-
pany. Composed 1948. First performance on
MBC, 3 October 1948, WOR Symphony, the com-
poser conducting, Stan Lomas narrator.*

LÉVY, CHARLES ÉMILE.
   See: WALDTEUFEL, ÉMILE.

LÉVY, ERNST.   Basel 18 November 1895

   4452 [Symphony no. 2, D major]
     In one movement
     3*,2(2nd alt. E.H.),2(2nd alt. B.Cl.),3*-4,3,
     3-Timp.-Str.
     Ms.
     Score 97 p.
     Composed 1922.

LEWINGER, MAX.   Sulkow,
       near Cracow, Poland 17 March 1870
             Dresden 31 August 1908

   843v Legende, Op. 9
     Solo Vn.-1,2,2,2-2Hn.-Timp.,Trgl.-Str.
     Zimmermann, Leipzig, c1904
     Score 31 p.

LEWIS, ALFRED.   Boston 1925

   751p Classical concerto for piano, Op. 13   *20'*
     1.Allegro 2.Andantino cantabile 3.Allegro
     Solo Pno.-2,2,2,2-2,2-Timp.-Str.
     Ms.
     Score 106 p.
     Composed 1939.

LEWIS, H. MERRILLS.   Meriden, Connecticut 1908

   958m Concertino for oboe and viola   *9'30"*
     1.Slowly 2.Fast, very rhythmically
     Solo Ob., Solo Va.-Str.
     Ms.
     Score 11 p.
     *Composed 1939. First performance Boston, 9
     February 1940, Composers' Forum Laboratory of
     the WPA.*

   3139 King of Elfland's daughter   *40'*
     1.Prelude: The valley of Erl - Forging of the
     magic sword 2.Song of Lirazel 3.The trolls
     4.The return of Elfland
     2(2nd alt. Picc.),2(2nd alt. E.H.),2,2-4,2,3,
     1-Timp.,Perc.-Hp.-Str.
     Ms.
     Score 175 p.
     *Inspired by E. J. M. Dunsany's fairy tale.
     Composed 1931-33. First performance of
     third movement only, Yale University com-
     mencement concert, New Haven, Connecticut, 29
     May 1931, Yale music students with the New
     Haven Symphony Orchestra, David Stanley Smith
     conductor. Awarded Yale's Steinert Prize.*

   3418 Two miniatures, for orchestra   *5'*
     1.The fairy tale of the echo glen 2.The magi-
     cian
     2(2nd alt. Picc.),2,2,2-4,2,3,1-Timp.-Pno.-Str.
     Ms.
     Score 12 p. Large folio
     *Originally composed for piano 4-hands, 1939.
     Transcribed 1939. First performance Rochester,
     New York, 22 January 1941, Rochester Civic
     Orchestra, Howard Hanson conductor.*

   3109 Two preludes on Southern folk   *9'*
     hymn tunes
     1.O wondrous love 2.The babe of Bethlehem
     1,1,1,1-2Hn.-Timp.-Str.
     Ms.
     Score 23 p.
     *Composed 1938. First performance of first
     movement only, Saratoga Springs, New York, 10
     September 1938, Yaddo Chamber Orchestra,
     Richard Donovan conductor.*

LEWIS, JOHN AARON.   La Grange, Illinois 3 May 1920

   318p Excerpts from The Comedy   *21'30"*
     1.Fanfare I 2.Spanish Steps 3.Polchinella
     4.La cantatrice 5.Piazza Navona 6.Fanfare II
     Solo Pno.-0,0,0,0-4,4,2,1-Perc.-Cb.
     MJQ Music, New York, c1960, 1961
     Score 41 p.
     *Inspired by the Italian Commedia dell'Arte.
     Suite composed 1957-59. First performance
     Monterey, California, October 1959, Monterey
     Festival Orchestra, Gunther Schuller con-
     ductor, the composer as soloist. Performed
     as a ballet, 1960.*

LEWIS, LEO RICH.
      South Woodstock, Vermont 11 February 1865
      Cambridge, Massachusetts 8 September 1945

   1851s Remembrance, for string orchestra   *8'*
     Str.
     Tufts [College] Music, Mass., c1933 by L. Lewis
     Score 15 p.
     *Composed 1932 as a movement of String Quartet
     no. 2. First performance Boston, 12 February
     1933, People's Symphony Orchestra, Thompson
     Stone conductor.*

   3648 Symphonic prelude, to Robert   *13'30"*
     Browning's tragedy A Blot in the Scutcheon,
     Op. 7
     3*,3*,2,3*-4,2,3,1-Timp.,Cym.-Hp.-Str.
     Tufts [College] Music, Mass., c1928 by L. Lewis
     Score 54 p.
     *Composed 1907. First performance Boston, 8
     March 1925, People's Symphony Orchestra,
     Stuart Mason conductor.*

LEY, SALVADOR.   Guatemala City 2 January 1907

   5405 Obertura jocosa   *6'*
     3*,2,2,2-2,2,3-Timp.,Trgl.,Cym.-Str.
     Ms.
     Score 41 p.
     *Composed 1950. First performance Guatemala
     City, 21 October 1952, Orquesta Sinfónica
     Nacional de Guatemala, the composer conducting.*

Ley, Salvador

5411 [Two fragments for modern dance]   *14'*
1.Andante 2.Allegro
3*,2,2,2-4,3,3-Timp.,Perc.-Str.
Ms. ^C1950 by Salvador Ley
Score 56 p.
Commissioned for the dancer Helga Norman.
Originally composed for piano 1932. First
performance of orchestral version Guadalajara,
Mexico, 18 September 1950, Guadalajara Sym-
phony and Ballet Ana Mérida, Carlos Jimenez
Mabarak conductor.

LIADOV, ANATOL KONSTANTINOVICH.
          St. Petersburg 11 May 1855
          Polynovka, Novgorod 28 August 1914

369 [Baba-Yaga, Russian fairy tale,   *4'*
Op. 56]
3*,3*,3*,3*-4,2,3,1-Timp.,Perc.-Str.
Belaieff, Leipzig, 1905
Score 34 p.

368 [Ballade, From olden times, Op. 21b]
3*,2,2,2-4,2,3,1-Timp.,Perc.-Pno.,Hp.-Str.
Belaieff, Leipzig, 1906
Score 22 p.

718 Danse de l'Amazone, Op. 65   *4'*
3*,3*,3,2-4,3,3,1-Timp.,Perc.-Str.
Jurgenson, Moscow [1909?]
Score 20 p.
Composed 1906. First performance St. Peters-
burg, 1906.

370 [Eight Russian folk songs, Op. 58]   *23'*
3*,3*,2,2-4,2-Timp.,Trgl.,Tamb.-Str.
Broude Brothers, New York [n.d.]
Score 39 p.

293 [The enchanted lake, Op. 62]   *6'*
3,2,3,2-4Hn.-Timp.,B.Dr.-Cel.,Hp.-Str.
Belaieff, Leipzig, 1909
Score 22 p.

2302 Les fanfares
See: GLAZUNOV, ALEXANDER KONSTANTINOVICH
    Les fanfares

311 [Fragment from the Apocalypse, Op. 66]
3(3rd alt. Picc.),3*,3,3*-4,3,3,2-Timp.,Perc.-
Cel.,Hp.-Str.
Belaieff, Leipzig, 1913
Score 30 p.
Inspired by Chapter 10 of the Apocalypse.

745 Intermezzo, Op. 8   *3'*
3*,2,2,2-4,2,3,1-Timp.,S.Dr.,Bells-Str.
Bessel, St. Petersburg [n.d.]
Score 29 p.

367 Kikimora, Op. 63
3*,3*,3*,2-4,2-Timp.,Xyl.-Cel.-Str.
Kalmus, New York [n.d.]
Score 32 p.

639 [Mazurka, rustic scene near the   *9'*
village tavern, Op. 19]
3*,2,2,2-4,2,3-Timp.,Perc.-Str.

Belaieff, Leipzig, 1888
Score 52 p.

1499 [A musical snuffbox, Op. 32]   *6'*
Picc.,2Fl.,3Cl.-Bells-Hp.
Belaieff, Leipzig, 1897
Score 10 p.
Originally composed for piano, 1893.

329 Nänie, Op. 67
3,1,2,2-4Hn.-Str.
Belaieff, Leipzig, 1914
Score 11 p.

1066 Polonaise, Op. 55   *5'*
3*,2,2,2-4,2,3,1-Timp.,Perc.-Str.
Belaieff, Leipzig, 1903
Score 23 p.
First performance 14 November 1902.

547 [Polonaise in memory of Pushkin,   *6'*
Op. 49]
3*,2,2,2-4,2,3,1-Timp.,Perc.-Str.
Belaieff, Leipzig, 1900
Score 26 p.
Composed 1899. First performance St. Peters-
burg, 1899.

746 Premier scherzo, Op. 16   *6'*
3*,2,2,2-4,2,3-Timp.-Str.
Bessel, St. Petersburg [n.d.]
Score 48 p.
Composed ca.1890.

2378s Two preludes. 1. E major 2. B-flat   *10'*
minor. Transcribed for string orchestra by
Bernard Morgan
Str.
Ms. ^C1975 by Bernard Morgan
Score 7 p.
Originally composed for piano. This tran-
scription 1939. First performance Philadel-
phia, 25 June 1939, Philadelphia Federal Sym-
phony Orchestra, J. W. F. Leman conductor.

LIAPUNOV, SERGEI MIKHAILOVICH.
        Yaroslavl, Russia 30 November 1859
                Paris 8 November 1924

611 Ballade, Op. 2   *12'*
3(3rd alt. Picc.),2*,2,2-4,2,3,1-Timp.,B.Dr.,
Cym.-Hp.-Str.
Bote & Bock, Berlin [1898]
Score 55 p.

463p [Concerto, piano, no. 1, Op. 4,   *25'*
E-flat minor]
1.Allegro con brio 2.Adagio 3.Allegro con
brio
Solo Pno.-3(3rd alt. Picc.),2,2,2-4,2,3,1-
Timp.,Cym.,Trgl.-Str.
Bote & Bock, Berlin [1892]
Score 75 p.
Composed 1890. First performance St. Peters-
burg, 1891, Mili Balakirev conductor.

515p [Concerto, piano, no. 2, Op. 38,   *18'*
E major]

In one movement
Solo Pno.-3,2*,2,2-4,2,3,1-Timp.,Perc.-Str.
Zimmermann, Leipzig, ^c1910
Score 71 p.
First performance St. Petersburg, April 1910.

1803 Hachisch, poème symphonique   24'
oriental, Op. 53
3(3rd alt. Picc.),3*,3*,3*-4,3,3,1-Timp.,Perc.
-2Hp.-Str.
Zimmermann, Leipzig [n.d.]
Score 103 p.
*Composed 1914. First performance St. Peters-
burg, 1914, the composer conducting.*

3724 Lesghinka. Transcribed for orchestra   8'
by Josef Alexander
3*,3*,2,3*-4,3,3,1-Timp.,Perc.-2Hp.-Str.
Ms.
Score 52 p.
*Originally composed for piano as no. 10 of
Twelve Transcendental Etudes, Op. 11. This
arrangement, 1938.*

1263 Polonaise, Op. 16   7'
3*,2*,3,2-4,2,3,1-Timp.,Perc.-Hp.-Str.
Zimmermann, Leipzig [n.d.]
Score 32 p.
*Composed 1905. First performance St. Peters-
burg, 1905, the composer conducting.*

443p [Rhapsody on Ukrainian themes,   15'
Op. 28]
Solo Pno.-3(3rd alt. Picc.),2*,2,2-4,2,3,1-
Timp.,Perc.-Str.
Zimmermann, Leipzig, ^c1908
Score 71 p.

1376 [Solemn overture on Russian themes,   20'
Op. 7]
3(3rd alt. Picc.),3*,3*,3*-4,3,3,1-Timp.,Perc.
-2Hp.-Str.
Jurgenson, Moscow [1899?]
Score 81 p.
*Composed 1895. First performance St. Peters-
burg, 24 April 1896.*

1191 [Symphony, Op. 12, B minor]   38'
1.Andantino - Allegro con spirito 2.Andante
sostenuto 3.Scherzo 4.Allegro molto
3(3rd alt. Picc.),2*,3*,2-4,2,3,1-Timp.-Str.
Zimmermann, Leipzig [n.d.]
Score 191 p.
*Composed 1901. First performance St. Peters-
burg 1902, the composer conducting.*

1122 Zelazova Vola [Chopin's birthplace,   15'
symphonic poem] Op. 37
3,2,2,2-4,2,3,1-Timp.,Perc.-Hp.-Str.
Zimmermann, Leipzig, ^c1910
Score 47 p.
*Composed 1909. First performance St. Peters-
burg, 1910, the composer conducting.*

LIDHOLM, INGVAR NATANAEL.
                b. Jönköping, Sweden 24 February 1921

2045s [Concerto for string orchestra]   14'

1.Largo 2.Allegro 3.Molto tranquillo -
Allegro commodo
Str.
Ms.
Score 28 p.
*Composed 1945. First performance Gävle, Swe-
den, 19 December 1948, Orchestra Society of
Gävle, the composer conducting.*

6100 [Toccata and canto for chamber   13-15'
orchestra]
1.Toccata 2.Canto
1(alt. Picc.),1,1,1-Str.
Carl Gehrmans, Stockholm, ^c1948
Score 23 p.
*Composed 1944. First performance Göteborg,
Sweden, 1945, Orchestra Society of Göteborg,
Isay Dobrowen conductor.*

LIE, SIGURD.   Drammen, Norway 23 May 1871
                      Drammen 29 September 1904

414s [Two songs. Transcribed for string
orchestra by Johan Halvorsen]
1.[Lament] 2.[Melody]
Str.
Brödrene Hals, Kristiania [n.d.]
Score 6 p.

LIEBERMANN, ROLF.   Zurich 14 September 1910

4970 Furioso für Orchester   8'30"
2(both alt. Picc.),2(1st alt. E.H.),2,2-4,3,
3,1-Timp.(2 players),Perc.-Pno.-Str.
Universal Edition, Vienna, ^c1948
Score 56 p.
*Composed 1947. First performance Kranich-
stein Castle, near Darmstadt, Germany, 1947,
Hessian State Orchestra, Hermann Scherchen
conductor.*

5189 [Suite on six Swiss folksongs,   11'
for small orchestra]
2,2(2nd alt. E.H.),2,2-2Hn.-Hp.-Str.
Universal Edition, Vienna, ^c1947
Score 26 p.

LIEBERSON, GODDARD.
                b. Hanley, Staffordshire 5 April 1911

1740s Homage to Handel, suite for strings   22'
1.Overture 2.Sarabande 3.Courante 4.Air
5.Menuetto
Str.
Ms.
Score 27 p.
*Composed 1936. First performance New York,
7 February 1937, Mozart String Sinfonietta,
Wesley Sontag conductor.*

LIEBERSON, SAMUEL A.   Odessa, Russia 29 July 1881

2729 In a winter garden, suite for   25'
grand orchestra
1.Backstage 2.The musical clown 3.The prima
ballerina 4.The juggler
4*(3rd alt. Picc.II),3*,3*,3*-4,3,3,1-Timp.,
Perc.-Pno.,Cel.,2Hp.-Str.

Liesering, Ludwig

Ms.
Score 107 p. Large folio
*Composed 1932. First performance Chicago, 14
March 1935, Chicago Symphony Orchestra, Fre-
derick Stock conductor. Won the Hollywood Bowl
Competition, 1934.*

LIESERING, LUDWIG.　Haintchen, Germany 15 May 1861

841m　[Concertino, cornet, D major]
Solo Cnt.-1,1,2,1-2,0,1-Timp.-Str.
Score: Ms. 53 p.
Parts: A.E. Fischer, Bremen, c1904

LIFTL, FRANZ.　　Allensteig, Austria 26 March 1864
Vienna 10 September 1932

680s　[Sleep well, my darling! Waltz-rondo,
Op. 75]
Str.
Joh. André, Offenbach a.M., c1897
Score 7 p.

LILJEFORS, INGEMAR KRISTIAN.
b. Göteborg, Sweden 13 December 1906

816p　[Concerto, piano, Op. 11]　　　　22'
1.Allegro moderato　2.Allegretto　3.Vivace
Solo Pno.-2,2,2,2-2,2,1-Timp.-Str.
Ms.
Score 187 p.
*Composed 1940. First performance Gävle, Swe-
den, 15 December 1940, Orchestra Society of
Gävle, the composer conducting, Eric Bengts-
son soloist.*

365v　[Concerto, violin and small orchestra]　19'
1.Introduzione - Allegro　2.Andante
3.Allegro giocoso
Solo Vn.-1,1,2,2-2,1-Timp.-Str.
Ms.
Score 117 p.
Composed 1956.

327p　[Rhapsody for piano and orchestra,　　17'
Op. 5]
Solo Pno.-2,2,2,2-2,2-Timp.-Str.
Ms.
Score 151 p.
Composed 1936.

LIMA SIQUEIRA, JOSÉ DE.
See: SIQUEIRA, JOSÉ DE LIMA.

LIMBERT, FRANK L.　　　New York 15 November 1866
Hanau, Germany 19 November 1938

651p　[Concert piece, piano, Op. 3, C minor]
Solo Pno.-2,2,2,2-2,2-Timp.-Str.
Steyl & Thomas, Frankfurt a.M. [n.d.]
Score 38 p.

5009　[Variations for orchestra on a theme of
Handel, Op. 16]
2,2,2,2-2,2,3-Timp.-Str.
Breitkopf & Härtel, Leipzig, c1904
Score 73 p.
*Theme is the Sarabande from Handel's seventh
Suite de Pièces pour le Clavecin, in G minor.*

LINCKE, PAUL.　　　　Berlin 7 November 1866
Clausthal-Zellerfeld,
near Göttingen, Germany 3 September 1946

1042s　Frische Blumen [Fresh flowers] Intermezzo
Str.
Apollo, Berlin, c1908
Score 9 p.

4690　Hanako, Japanese intermezzo　　　　　3'
1,1,1-0,1,1-Timp.,Perc.-Harm.-Str.
B. Schott's Söhne, Mainz, c1939
Score in reduction 4 p.

4689　Träume vom Lido [Dreams of Lido]　　　4'
1,1,1-0,1,1-Timp.,Perc.-Harm.-Str.
B. Schott's Söhne, Mainz, c1939
Score in reduction 4 p.
Suggested by the resort near Venice.

LINDBERG, OSKAR FREDRIK.
Gagnef, Sweden 23 February 1887
Stockholm 10 April 1955

2189s　[Adagio (Whitsuntide) for string　　4'30"
orchestra]
Str.
Nordiska Musikförlaget, Stockholm, c1945
Score 2 p.

2191s　[Leksand suite, Op. 41. Version　　　13'
for strings]
1.[Walking tune]　2.[Air]　3.[Polka and tune]
Str.
Nordiska Musikförlaget, Stockholm, c1948
Score 34 p.
*Leksand is a resort village in Dalecarlia,
Sweden. Originally composed for full orches-
tra, 1935.*

5118　[An old war song from Dalarna　　　　5'
ca.1500, Op. 42]
2,2(2nd ad lib.),2,2(2nd ad lib.)-4(3rd & 4th
ad lib.),2,3(2nd & 3rd ad lib.)-Timp.-Str.
Nordiska Musikförlaget, Stockholm, c1945
Score 25 p.
*Dalarna or Dalecarlia is a province in central
Sweden on the Norwegian border. This setting,
1936.*

5017　[Requiem, for soloists, chorus,　　　50'
orchestra and organ, Op. 21]
1.Requiem och Kyrie　2.Dies Irae　3.Interludium
4.Domine Jesu　5.Sanctus　6.Agnus Dei
4 Voice Solos(SATB)-2(2nd alt. Picc.),2(2nd
alt. E.H.),2,2-4,3,3,1-Timp.-Org.-Chorus
(SATB)-Str.
Ms.
Score 109 p.
*Composed 1920-22. First performance 23 Nov-
ember 1923, the Swedish Royal Court Orchestra,
Victor Wiklund conductor.*

5039　[Three Dalecarlian pictures, for　　　15'
orchestra, Op. 1]
1.Preludium - [Walking tune]　2.[Nightfall in
the forest]　3.[Game]
2,1,2,1-2,2,1-Timp.,Trgl.,Cym.-Str.

Ms.
Score 77 p.
Composed 1907-08. First performance Stockholm, 1909, Stockholm Conservatory Orchestra, the composer conducting.

LINDNER, AUGUST.   Dessau, Germany 29 October 1820
                       Hanover 15 June 1878

680c [Concerto, violoncello, Op. 34, E minor]
1.Allegro 2.Serenade: Andante 3.Tarantelle
Solo Vc.-2,2,2,2-2,2,3-Timp.-Str.
Score: Ms. 134 p.
Parts: Kistner, Leipzig [n.d.]

LINDPAINTNER, PETER JOSEPH VON.
                       Coblenz 9 December 1791
             Nonnenhorn, Lake Constance 21 August 1856

360v [Concertino for violin, Op. 42]
1.Romanze 2.Allegretto con moto 3.Andantino
Solo Vn.-2,0,2,2-2,2-Timp.-Str.
Score: Ms. c1976 by The Fleisher Collection of
Orchestral Music, Free Library of Philadelphia.
74 p. Large folio
Parts: H.A. Probst, Leipzig [1824 or 1825]

300m [Concerto for 2 horns]
1.Allegro con spirito 2.Romance 3.Rondo
2 Solo Hn.-2,2,0,2-2,2-Timp.-Str.
Ms.
Score 107 p.

LINEK, JIŘÍ IGNÁC.   Bohemia 1725
                            ?   1791

6733 [Christmas symphony, symphonia   *12'*
pastoralis, D major] Edited by Felix Schroeder
1.Allegro 2.Andante 3.Allegro
2Hn.(ad lib.)-Org. or Cemb.-Str.
Chr. Friedrich Vieweg, Berlin, c1963
Score 19 p.

LINK, EMIL.

886s Chant d'amour, mélodie romantique.
Arranged by F. Rehfeld
Str.
Score: Ms. 7 p.
Parts: C.F. Schmidt, Heilbronn [n.d.]

LINLEY, THOMAS, JR.   Bath, England 5 May 1756
                Grimsthorpe, Lincolnshire 5 August 1778

4642 Overture to The Duenna, or The   *5'30"*
Double Elopement. Edited by Adam Carse
0,2,0,2-2,2-Timp.-Str.
Augener, London, c1941
Score 15 p.
*Overture to the pasticcio comic opera with
libretto by Richard Brinsley Sheridan. Com-
posed 1775. First performance London, 21
November 1775.*

LINNALA, EINO MAUNO ALEKSANTERI.
             Helsingfors (Helsinki) 19 August 1896
                       Helsinki 8 June 1973

Born: Eino Borgman

2040s [Elegy for string orchestra and   *6'*
timpani]
Timp.(or B.Dr.)-Str.
R.E. Westerlund, Helsinki, c1945
Score 7 p.
Composed 1945.

5812 [Finnish rhapsody]   *10'*
2(2nd alt. Picc.),2(2nd alt. E.H.),2,2-4(3rd
& 4th optional),2,3(2nd & 3rd optional),1
(optional)-Timp.,Perc.-Str.
Suomen Säveltaiteilijain Liito [n.p.] c1938
Score 53 p.
*Composed 1932. First performance Helsinki,
1932.*

LIPIŃSKI, KAROL JÓZEF.
             Radzyń, Poland 30 October 1790
             Urłów near Lwów 16 December 1861

1055v [Concerto, violin, no. 3, Military,
Op. 24, E minor]
1.Allegro 2.Brillante 3.Risoluto
Solo Vn.-1,2,2,2-2,2,B.Tbn.-Timp.-Str.
Score: Ms. 118 p.
Parts: Hofmeister, Leipzig [1836]

500v [Same as above] Allegro. Freely revised
by August Wilhelmj
Solo Vn.-2,2,2,2-4,2,3-Timp.-Str.
Breitkopf & Härtel, Leipzig [n.d.]
Score in reduction 21 p.

1056v [Concerto, violin, no. 4, Op 32, A major]
1.Allegro 2.Andantino 3.Allegro
Solo Vn.-2,2,2,2-4,2,3-Timp.-Str.
Score: Ms. 118 p.
Parts: Hofmeister, Leipzig [184-?]

355v [Fantasy and variations for violin on
themes from the opera Les Huguenots by
Giacomo Meyerbeer, Op. 26]
Solo Vn.-1,2,2,2-2,2,1-Timp.-Str.
Score: Ms. c1976 by The Fleisher Collection of
Orchestral Music, Free Library of Philadelphia
71 p. Large folio
Parts: A.M. Schlesinger, Berlin [1836 or 1837]

303v [Fantasy and variations on themes from the
opera La Sonnambula by Bellini, Op. 23]
Solo Vn.-Str.
Fr. Kistner, Leipzig [n.d.]
Score 26 p. Large folio

LIPSCOMB, HELEN.
             Georgetown, Kentucky 20 April 1921
                       5 January 1974

2399s Chorale, waltz and lullaby
Pno.(optional)-Str.
Avant Music, Los Angeles, c1965
Score 15 p.

LISZT, FRANZ.   Raiding, Hungary 22 October 1811
                    Bayreuth, Germany 31 July 1886

739s Angelus [Prayer to the guardian angels]
Edited by Walter Bache

Liszt, Franz

Str.
B. Schott's Söhne, Mainz, 1887
Score 11 p.
*Originally composed 1877 as no. 1 of Années de
Pèlerinage, 3rd year, for piano. Transcribed
for string quartet, 1880. This transcription
1884. First performance London, 8 April 1886,
Walter Bache conductor.*

1153 [Années de pèlerinage, 2nd year,   8'
for piano. Nos. 1 and 2. Transcribed for
orchestra by Nicolas Kasanli]
1.Sposalizio [Nuptials] 2.Il Penseroso
2(2nd alt. Picc.),2*,3*,2-4,2,3,1-Timp.,Cym.,
Gong-Hp.-Str.
B. Schott's Söhne, Mainz [190-?]
Score 15 p.
*Composed 1838-39. Transcribed 1900. First
performance St. Petersburg, 1901, Kasanli
conductor.*

911 Ce qu'on entend sur la montagne   38'
[What one hears on the mountain, symphonic
poem]
3*,2,3*,2-4,2,3,1-Timp.,Perc.-Hp.-Str.
Breitkopf & Härtel, Leipzig [1882?]
Score 146 p.
*Inspired by Victor Hugo's poem. Composed 1848-
49; revised 1850 and 1854. First performance
of this final version, Weimar, 7 January 1857,
the composer conducting.*

1360 [Christus. March, The three holy   12'
kings]
3*,2,2,2-4,3,3,1-Timp.-Hp.-Str.
Kahnt, Leipzig [n.d.]
Score 42 p.
*From the oratorio composed 1863. First per-
formance Rome, 6 July 1867, Giovanni Sgambati
conductor.*

380p [Concerto, piano, no. 1, E-flat   18'
major]
1.Allegro maestoso 2.Quasi adagio - Allegretto
vivace 3.Allegro marziale animato
Solo Pno.-3*,2,2,2-2,2,3-Timp.,Cym.,Trgl.-Str.
Breitkopf & Härtel, Leipzig [1959?]
Score 58 p.
*Composed 1830-53. First performance Weimar,
17 February 1855, Berlioz conductor, the
composer as soloist. Revised 1856.*

381p [Concerto, piano, no. 2, A major]   19'
In one movement
Solo Pno.-3(3rd alt. Picc.),2,2,2-2,2,3,1-
Timp.,Cym.-Str.
Breitkopf & Härtel, Leipzig [n.d.]
Score 76 p.
*Composed 1839-56. First performance Weimar,
7 January 1857, the composer conducting, Hans
von Bronsart soloist. Revised 1861.*

379p [Concerto pathétique, 2 pianos,   14'
E minor. Transcribed for piano and orchestra
by Eduard Reuss]
In one movement
Solo Pno.-3,2,2,2-2,2,3-Timp.,Cym.,Trgl.-Hp.-
Str.

Breitkopf & Härtel, Leipzig [1894?]
Score 60 p.
*Originally composed for piano 4-hands, 1849;
for two pianos, 1856-65. This transcription
1894.*

444p [Fantasy on Hungarian folk tunes]   15'
Solo Pno.-3*,2,2,2-2,2,3-Timp.,Perc.-Str.
C.F. Peters, Leipzig [n.d.]
Score 43 p.
*Originally composed ca.1847 as Hungarian Rhap-
sody no. 14 for piano. This version 1852.
First performance Budapest, 1 June 1853, Franz
Erkel conductor, Hans von Bülow soloist.*

440p [Fantasy on themes from Beethoven's   14'
Ruins of Athens]
Solo Pno.-3*,2,2,2-2,2,3-Timp.,Perc.-Str.
C.F.W. Siegel, Leipzig [1865]
Score 57 p.
*Composed ca.1850. First performance Budapest,
1 June 1853, Franz Erkel conductor, Hans von
Bülow soloist.*

1551 [A Faust symphony, after Goethe]   72'
1.Faust 2.Gretchen 3.Mephistopheles
3(3rd alt. Picc.),2,2,2-4,3,3,1-Timp.,Cym.,
Trgl.-Org.,Hp.-Men's Chorus, Tenor Voice Solo
-Str.
Breitkopf & Härtel, Leipzig, 1917
Score 204 p.
*Composed 1854-57. First performance Weimar,
5 September 1857, the composer conducting.*

6913 [Festival march for the Goethe jubilee, for
orchestra]
3*,2,2,2-4,2,3,1-Timp.,Cym.,B.Dr.-Str.
Breitkopf & Härtel, Leipzig [1870]
Score 34 p.
*Originally composed for piano, 1849, for the
centennial of Goethe's birth. Transcribed by
Liszt, 1857. First performance Weimar, 3
September 1857.*

4433 [Festival prelude for orchestra]
2,2,2,2-2,2,3,1-Timp.,Cym.,B.Dr.-Str.
Hallberger, Stuttgart, 1857
Score 23 p.
*Originally composed for piano as Preludio Pom-
poso 1856. Transcribed 1857. First performance Weimar, 4 September 1857, the composer
conducting.*

747 Festklänge [Festive sounds, symphonic   18'
poem]
2,2,2,2-4,3,3,1-Timp.,B.Dr.,Cym.-Str.
Breitkopf & Härtel, Leipzig [1856?]
Score 128 p.
*Composed 1853. First performance Weimar, 9
November 1854, the composer conducting.*

2520 Feux follets [Will-o'-the-wisps,   5'
for piano. Transcribed for orchestra by Leo
Weiner]
3*,2,2,2-4,2,3,1-Timp.-Hp.-Str.
Rózsavölgyi, Budapest, ᶜ1934
Score 43 p.
Composed 1851 as no. 5 of the Études d'Exécution

Transcendante for piano. First performance of this transcription Budapest, 22 October 1934, Budapest Philharmonic, Alexander von Zemlinsky conductor.

748 Hamlet, symphonic poem after   *10'*
Shakespeare
3*,2,2,2-4,2,3,1-Timp.-Str.
Breitkopf & Härtel, Leipzig [1861?]
Score 49 p.
Composed 1858. First performance Sondershausen, 2 July 1876, Max Erdmannsdörfer conductor.

4728 [Harmonies poétiques et   *8'30"*
religieuses. No. 7, Funérailles, Octobre 1849.
Transcribed for orchestra by Hershy Kay]
3*,3*,3*,3-4,3,3,1-Timp.,Perc.-Hp.-Str.
Ms.
Score 29 p. Large folio
Originally composed for piano, 1849, on the deaths of Prince Felix Lichnowsky, Count Ladislaus Teleky, and Count Lajos Batthyani. This transcription 1946.

1258 Héroïde funèbre [symphonic poem]   *20'*
3*,3*,2,2-4,2,3,1-Timp.,Perc.-Str.
Breitkopf & Härtel, Leipzig [n.d.]
Score 56 p.
Originally the first movement of Symphonie Révolutionnaire, sketched 1830. This version 1849-50. First performance Breslau, 10 November 1857, Moritz Schön conductor.

985 Hungaria, symphonic poem   *22'*
3*,3*,2,2-4,3,3,1-Timp.,Perc.-Str.
Breitkopf & Härtel, Leipzig [1880?]
Score 106 p.
Composed 1848-56. First performance Budapest, 8 September 1856, the composer conducting.

877 [Hungarian attack march, for orchestra]   *5'*
3*,2,2,2-4,2,3,1-Timp.,Perc.-Str.
Schlesinger, Berlin [1876?]
Score 50 p.
Originally composed for piano, 1843. Transcribed 1875. First performance Budapest, 1875, the composer conducting.

117 [Hungarian rhapsody no. 1, C-sharp   *15'*
minor] Arranged for orchestra in C minor by
Karl Müller-Berghaus
3*,2,2,2-4,2,3,1-Timp.,Perc.-Hp.-Str.
Simrock, Berlin [n.d.]
Score 76 p.
Originally composed for piano, 1846.

132 [Hungarian rhapsody no. 2(4), C-sharp   *9'*
minor] Arranged for orchestra in C minor by
Karl Müller-Berghaus
2,2,2,2-4,2,3-Timp.,Perc.-Hp.-Str.
Kalmus, New York [n.d.]
Score 64 p.
Originally composed for piano, 1847. Liszt published his own orchestral transcription in 1875 as Rhapsody no. 4.

2503 [Hungarian rhapsody no. 2(4), C-sharp   *12'*
minor] Arranged for orchestra in D minor by
Otto Mueller
3*,2,3*,3*-4,2,3,1-Timp.,Perc.-Hp.-Str.
Ms.
Score 55 p.
This transcription 1934. First performance Philadelphia, 19 May 1934, Thaddeus Rich conductor.

134 [Hungarian rhapsody no. 9(6),   *10'*
Carnival at Pest, E-flat major] Arranged for
orchestra as no. 6 in D major by the composer
and Franz Doppler
3*,2,2,2-4,2,3,Ophicl.-Timp.,Perc.-Hp.-Str.
J. Schuberth, Leipzig [1875]
Score 74 p.
Originally composed for piano, 1851-53.

1197 [Hungarian rhapsody no. 12(2), C-sharp   *11'*
minor] Arranged for orchestra as no. 2 in
D minor by the composer and Franz Doppler
3*,2,2,2-4,2,3,1-Timp.,Perc.-Hp.-Str.
J. Schuberth, Leipzig [1875]
Score 49 p.
Originally composed for piano, 1854. Transcribed ca.1860.

5636 [Hungarian rhapsody no. 13, A minor]   *11'*
Arranged for orchestra by Wouter Hutschenruyter
3(3rd alt. Picc.),2,2,2-4,4,3,1-Timp.,Perc.-
Hp.-Str.
A.M. Schlesinger(?), Berlin [1901?]
Score in reduction 4 p.
Originally composed for piano.

5553 [Hungarian rhapsody no. 14(1),   *11'*
F minor] Arranged for orchestra as no. 1 by
the composer and Franz Doppler
3*,2,2,3-4,3,3,1(Ophicl.)-Timp.,Trgl.,Cym.-
2Hp.-Str.
Kalmus, New York [n.d.]
Score 62 p.
Originally composed for piano, 1853.

267 Hunnenschlacht [Battle of the Huns,   *16'*
symphonic poem after Wilhelm von Kaulbach's
painting]
3*,2,2,2-4,3,3,1-Timp.,Cym.-Org.-Str.
Breitkopf & Härtel, Leipzig [1893?]
Score 96 p.
Composed 1857. First performance Weimar, 29 December, 1857, the composer conducting.

835 [The ideals, symphonic poem]   *30'*
2,2,2,2-4,2,3,1-Timp.,Cym.-Str.
Breitkopf & Härtel, Leipzig [1880?]
Score 121 p.
Inspired by Schiller's poem. Composed 1857. First performance Weimar, 5 September 1857, the composer conducting.

698 [Legend no. 1, St. Francis of Assisi's
sermon to the birds, for piano. Transcribed
for orchestra by Felix Mottl]
2,2,2,2-4,2,3,1-Timp.-2Hp.-Str.
Rózsavölgyi, Budapest [n.d.]
Score 37 p.
Composed 1863 or earlier.

Liszt, Franz

6256 [The legend of Saint Elizabeth.   10'
     Introduction]
     3,2,2,2-4,2,3,1-Timp.-Str.
     Kahnt, Leipzig, 1872
     Score 13 p.
     *From the oratorio with text by Otto Roquette.
     Planned 1855; composed 1857-62. First per-
     formance Budapest, 15 August 1865, the composer
     conducting.*

508p Malédiction [piano and string   12'
     orchestra]
     Solo Pno.-Str.
     Breitkopf & Härtel, New York, c1915
     Score 32 p.
     Composed ca.1830; revised 1840.

584 Mazeppa, symphonic poem   18'
     3*,3*,3*,3-4,3,3,1-Timp.,Perc.-Str.
     Breitkopf & Härtel, Leipzig [1865?]
     Score 98 p.
     *Inspired by Victor Hugo's poem about the
     Ukrainian hero. Originally composed for piano,
     1826. Transcribed 1850. First performance
     Weimar, 16 April 1854, the composer conducting.*

1425 Mazurka brillante [for piano.   5'
     Transcribed for orchestra by Karl Müller-
     Berghaus]
     3*,2,2,2,-4,2,3-Timp.,Perc.-Hp.-Str.
     Senff, Leipzig [1879]
     Score 33 p.
     Composed 1850.

Mephisto waltz no. 1
     See: [Two episodes from Lenau's Faust.
            No. 2, Dance in the village inn]

583 Orpheus [symphonic poem]   13'
     3*,3*,2,2-4,2,3,1-Timp.-2Hp.-Str.
     Breitkopf & Härtel, Leipzig [n.d.]
     Score 40 p.
     *Composed 1853-54. First performance Weimar,
     16 February 1854, the composer conducting.*

3421 [Polonaise no. 2, piano, E major.   8'
     Transcribed for orchestra by Karl Müller-
     Berghaus]
     3*,2,2,2-4,2,3,1-Timp.,Perc.-Hp.-Str.
     Bartholf Senff, Leipzig [1879]
     Score 71 p.
     Originally composed for piano, 1851.

181 Les préludes [symphonic poem]   17'
     3(3rd alt. Picc.),2,2,2-4,2,3,1-Timp.,Perc.-
     Hp.-Str.
     Breitkopf & Härtel, Leipzig [n.d.]
     Score 77 p.
     *Originally composed 1848 as the introduction
     to the choral work Les Quatre Élémens. This
     version ca.1850, inspired by Lamartine's
     Méditations Poétiques. First performance Wei-
     mar, 28 February 1854, the composer conducting.*

Preludio pomposo
     See: [Festival prelude for orchestra]

719 [Prometheus, symphonic poem]   12'
     3*,3*,2,2-4,2,3,1-Timp.-Str.
     Breitkopf & Härtel, Leipzig [1856?]
     Score 77 p.
     *Composed 1850; rescored 1855. First perform-
     ance Brunswick, 18 October 1855, the com-
     poser conducting.*

226 [Rákóczi march for orchestra]
     3*,2,2,2-4,2,3,1-Timp.,Perc.-Str.
     J. Schuberth, Leipzig [1871]
     Score 92 p.
     *The traditional Hungarian march; this version
     1865. First performance Budapest, 17 August
     1865.*

437p Rhapsodie espagnole, piano. Tran-   12'
     scribed for piano and orchestra by
     Ferruccio Busoni
     1.Folies d'Espagne 2.Jota aragonesa
     Solo Pno.-3(3rd alt. Picc.),2,2,2-4,2,3,1-
     Timp.,Perc.-Str.
     C.F.W. Siegel, Leipzig [1895]
     Score 63 p.
     Originally composed 1863. Transcribed 1882.

909v [Romance oubliée [Forgotten romance.
     Transcribed for viola alta and orchestra by
     Hermann Ritter]
     Solo Va.(or Va. Alta)-Cl.-3Hn.-Str.
     [Bachmann, Hanover, n.d.]
     Score 7 p.
     *Originally composed as a song, 1848. Ritter's
     transcription ca.1880.*

Schubert's Märsche. No. 2. Trauer-Marsch
     See: SCHUBERT, FRANZ
            [March, piano 4-hands, Op. 40 no. 5.
            D.819. Transcribed by Franz Liszt]

1421 [Song and hymn, two patriotic poems]
     2,2,2,2-4,2,3,1-Timp.,Perc.-Hp.-Str.
     Rózsavölgyi, Budapest [1878]
     Score 48 p.
     *Based on two songs by Béni Egressi and Franz
     Erkel. Liszt's version 1870-73. First per-
     formance Budapest, 19 March 1873, the com-
     poser conducting.*

1172 [A symphony to Dante's Divine   46'
     Comedy]
     1.Inferno 2.Purgatorio
     3(3rd alt. Picc.),3*,3*,2-4,2,3,1-Timp.,Perc.-
     Harm.,2Hp.-Women's Chorus-Str.
     Breitkopf & Härtel, Leipzig [1865?]
     Score 145 p.
     *Composed 1847-56. First performance Dresden,
     7 November 1867, the composer conducting.*

601 Tasso, lamento e trionfo, symphonic   19'
     poem
     3*,2,3*,2-4,4,3,1-Timp.,Perc.-Hp.-Str.
     Kalmus, New York [n.d.]
     Score 88 p.
     *Inspired by Byron's poem. Composed 1849-54.
     First performance of final version Weimar, 19
     April 1854, the composer conducting.*

1542 [Tasso's funeral triumph, epilogue to   13'
the symphonic poem Tasso]
3*,2,2,2-4,2,3,1-Timp.,Bell or Gong-Str.
Breitkopf & Härtel, Leipzig [1877]
Score 38 p.
*Composed 1866 as no. 3 of the Odes Funèbres.
First performance New York, March 1877, New
York Philharmonic, Leopold Damrosch conductor.*

396p Todtentanz/Danse macabre [Dance of   15'
death]
Solo Pno.-3*,2,2,2-2,2,3,1-Timp.,Perc.-Str.
C.F.W. Siegel, Leipzig [1865]
Score 68 p.
*Paraphrase of Dies Irae. Composed 1839-59.
First performance The Hague, 15 April 1865,
J. H. Verhulst conductor, Hans von Bülow
soloist.*

843 [Two episodes from Lenau's Faust.   15'
No. 1, Nocturnal procession]
3(3rd alt. Picc.),3*,2,2-4,2,3,1-Timp.,Bell or
Gong-Hp.-Str.
[J. Schuberth, Hamburg, 1866]
Score 45 p.
Composed 1858-60.

202 [Two episodes from Lenau's Faust.   10'
No. 2, Dance in the village inn]
3(3rd alt. Picc.),2,2,2-4,2,3,1-Timp.,Cym.,
Trgl.-Hp.-Str.
Breitkopf & Härtel, Leipzig [1916?]
Score 68 p.
*Also known as First Mephisto Waltz. Composed
1858-59. First performance Weimar, 8 March
1861, the composer conducting.*

131 [Venezia e Napoli. No. 3, Tarantella,   6'
for piano. Transcribed for orchestra by Karl
Müller-Berghaus]
3*,2,2,2-4,2,3-Timp.,Perc.-Hp.-Str.
B. Schott's Söhne, Mainz [1883]
Score 51 p.
*Originally composed for piano, ca.1840.
Revised 1859 as the supplement to Années de
Pèlerinage, 2nd year. This transcription 1882.*

7011 Vom Fels zum Meer [From cliff to sea,
German victory march for orchestra]
3*,2,2,2-4,2,3,1-Timp.,Perc.-Str.
Score: Breitkopf & Härtel, Leipzig [186-?]
22 p.
Parts: Schlesinger, Berlin, 1865
*Originally composed for piano, 1853-56.
Orchestrated 1860.*

6064 Von der Wiege bis zum Grabe [From   13'
the cradle to the grave, symphonic poem after
a drawing by Mihály Zichy]
1.[The cradle] 2.[The struggle for existence]
3.[To the grave: The cradle of the future life]
4*(2Picc.),2(2nd alt. E.H.),2,2-4,2,3,1-Timp.,
Cym.-Hp.(ad lib.)-Str.
Bote & Bock, Berlin, 1883
Score 29 p.
Composed 1881-82.

2519 [Weinen, Klagen, variations on a   15'
theme of J. S. Bach, for piano. Transcribed
for orchestra by Leo Weiner]
2(2nd alt. Picc.),2,2,2-4,2,3,1-Timp.,Cym.-Str.
Rózsavölgyi, Budapest, c1934
Score 55 p.
*Theme from Bach's cantata, BWV 12. Com-
posed for piano, 1862.*

LITOLFF, HENRY CHARLES.   London 6 February 1818
          Bois-le-Combes, near Paris 6 August 1891

1028v [Concerto, violin, no. 1, Eroica, Op. 42,
E minor]
1.Allegro maestoso 2.Andante funèbre, attacca
3.Rondo: Allegretto
Solo Vn.-2,2,2,2-4,2,3-Timp.-Str.
Score: Ms. 203 p.
Parts: Litolff, Braunschweig [1858]

485p [Concerto symphonique, piano, no. 3,
National hollandais, Op. 45, E-flat major]
1.Maestoso 2.Presto 3.Andante 4.Allegro
vivace
Solo Pno.-2(2nd alt. Picc.),2,2,2-4,2,3-Timp.-
Str.
Score: Ms. 205 p.
Parts: Litolff, Braunschweig [n.d.]
Incorporates the Dutch national anthem.

496p [Concerto symphonique, piano, no. 4,
Op. 102, D minor]
1.Allegro con fuoco 2.Scherzo 3.Allegro
impetuoso
Solo Pno.-2(2nd alt. Picc.),2,2,2-4,2,3-
Timp.,Trgl.-Str.
Score: Ms. 296 p.
Parts: Litolff, Braunschweig [n.d.]

125 [Overture to Maximilian Robespierre,   10'
drama by Robert Griepenkerl, Op. 55]
2(2nd alt. Picc.),2,2,2-4,2,3-Timp.,Perc.-Str.
Litolff, Braunschweig [n.d.]
Score 80 p.
Composed 1850.

LIVIABELLA, LINO.   Macerata, Italy 7 April 1902
          Parma 21 October 1964

4868 Monte Mario [symphonic poem]   15'
3(3rd alt. Picc.),3*,3*,3*-4,3,3,1-Timp.,Perc.
-Pno.,Cel.,2Hp.-Str.
G. Ricordi, Milan, c1939
Score 68 p.
*Composed 1938. First performance Turin, 29
December 1939. Won the Premio S. Remo, 1940.*

LIZASO, ANTONINO HERNÁNDEZ.
See: HERNÁNDEZ-LIZASO, ANTONINO.

LLOYD, GERALD.   Lebanon, Ohio 6 September 1938

6705 Associations I for orchestra   8'
2,2,2,2-2,2,2,1-Timp.,Perc.-Pno.,Hp.-Str.
Ms. c1966 by Gerald Lloyd
Score 24 p. Large folio
*Composed 1966. First performance Rochester,
New York, April 1966, Eastman-Rochester Sym-
phony Orchestra, Walter Hendl conductor.*

Locatelli, Pietro Antonio

LOCATELLI, PIETRO ANTONIO.
　　　　　　　　Bergamo, Italy 3 September 1695
　　　　　　　　Amsterdam 30 March 1764

2403s [Concerto da camera, string　　　*12'30"*
　orchestra and cembalo, Op. 4 no. 10, E-flat
　major] Edited by Giacomo Benvenuti
　1.Adagio molto　2.Allegro　3.Minuetto
　Cemb.-Concertino Vns. I&II,Va.,Vc.-Str.
　Carisch, Milan, c1952
　Score 24 p.
　Op. 4 first published in Amsterdam, 1735.

2220s Concerto grosso for string orchestra,
　Op. 1 no. 2 [C minor] Edited by Sam Franko
　1.Adagio - Allegro　2.Largo　3.Allegro
　4.Allegro molto
　Cemb.(or Pno.)-Str.
　G. Schirmer, New York, c1928
　Score 19 p.
　Op. 1 first published in Amsterdam 1721.

960s [Concerto grosso for string orchestra,
　Op. 1 no. 6, C minor] Edited by Arthur Egidi
　Adagio - Allegro - Largo - Allegro
　Pno.-Str.
　Chr. Friedrich Vieweg, Berlin [1927]
　Score 14 p.

590s [Concerto grosso for string orchestra,
　Op. 1 no. 8, F minor] Edited by Arnold Schering
　Largo - Vivace - Largo andante - Andante -
　Pastorale
　Soli: Vn.I,Vn.II,Va.I,Va.II,Vc.-Pno.-Str.
　Kahnt, Leipzig, c1919
　Score 21 p.

2402s [Concerto grosso for string orchestra, *12'*
　Op. 1 no. 9, D major] Edited by Ettore Bonelli
　1.Allegro　2.Largo　3.Allemanda　4.Sarabanda

5.Allegro
Soli: Vn.I,Vn.II-Str.
G. Zanibon, Padua, c1948
Score 20 p.

2374s [Concerto grosso for string orchestra,
　Op. 1 no. 11, C minor] Edited by Olga Géczy
　1.Largo　2.Allemanda　3.Sarabanda　4.Giga
　Cemb.-Str.
　Editio Musica, Budapest/Edition Eulenberg,
　Zurich, c1973
　Score 14 p.

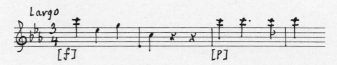

LOCKE, MATTHEW.　　　　　　Exeter, England 1622
　　　　　　　　　　　　　London ca.1677

2207s 'The tempest' music.　Suites I and II.
2208s [Harding catalog nos. 192 and 193]
　Arranged in two suites by W. Gillies Whittaker
　Cemb.(or Pno.)-Str.
　Oxford University Press, London, c1934
　Scores: 8 p., 8 p.
　From the opera in five acts with libretto and
　scenario by Thomas Shadwell after John Dryden
　and Sir William Davenant's alteration of
　Shakespeare's play The Tempest.　First per-
　formance Dorset Gardens, London, 30 April 1674.
　Instrumental music to the opera first pub-
　lished 1675.

LOEFFLER, CHARLES MARTIN.
　　　　　　Mulhouse, Alsace 30 January 1861
　　　　　　Medfield, Massachusetts 19 May 1935

4206 Canticum fratris solis [Canticle　　*18'*
　of Brother Sun] set for voice and chamber
　orchestra to the hymn by St. Francis of Assisi
　Voice Solo-3Fl.,E.H.-2Hn.-Pno.,Cel.,2Hp.-Str.
　Library of Congress, Elizabeth Sprague Coolidge
　Foundation, Washington, D.C.,c1929
　Score 95 p.
　Commissioned by The Coolidge Foundation to
　inaugurate the Library of Congress Chamber
　Music Auditorium.　Composed 1925.　First per-
　formance First Festival of Chamber Music,
　Library of Congress, Washington, D.C., 28 Octo-
　ber 1925, Frederick A. Stock conductor, Povla
　Frijsh soloist.

352v [Divertimento, violin and orchestra, *10'*
　A minor]
　1.Allegro　2.Andante　3.Moderato
　Solo Vn.-3(3rd alt. Picc.),3*,2,2-4,2,3,1-
　Timp.,Cym.-Hp.-Str.

Ms.
Score 124 p.
First performance Boston, 4 January 1895.

6828 Hora mystica, symphony in one movement
3(3rd alt. Picc.),4*,4*(1Cl. in E-flat),3-4,
4,3,1-Timp.,Bells-Pno.,Cel.,2Hp.-Men's Voices-
Str.
Ms.
Score 133 p. Large folio
*Composed 1915. First performance Boston, 2
March 1917, Boston Symphony, Carl Muck con-
ductor.*

1972 Memories of my childhood (Life in a   13'
Russian village), poem for modern orchestra
3(3rd alt. Picc.),3*,3*,3*-4.3,3,1-Timp.,Perc.-
4Mouth Org.-Pno.,Cel.,2Hp.-Str.
G.Schirmer, New York, ᶜ1925
Score 51 p.
*Awarded the Chicago North Shore Festival Asso-
ciation Prize, 1924. First public performance
Evanston, Illinois, 30 March 1924, Chicago
Symphony Orchestra, Frederick Stock conductor.*

1974 La mort de Tintagile, Op. 6   25'
In one movement
3(3rd alt. Picc.),3*,4*(1Cl. in E-flat),2-4,
2,2Cnt.,3,1-Timp.,Perc.-Hp.-Str.(including Va.
d'Amore)
G. Schirmer, New York, ᶜ1905
Score 97 p.
*Inspired by Maeterlinck's puppet play. Ori-
ginally composed for two viole d'amore and
orchestra, 1897. This version 1900. First
performance Boston, 16 February 1901, Boston
Symphony Orchestra.*

1975 A pagan poem (after Virgil), Op. 14   23'
In one movement
3(3rd alt. Picc.),3*,3*,2-4,6(3 backstage),3,
1-Timp.,Tam-tam,Glock.-Pno.-Hp.-Str.
G. Schirmer, New York, ᶜ1909
Score 107 p.
*Originally composed for chamber orchestra, 1901.
This version 1905-06. First performance Bos-
ton, 22 November 1907, Karl Muck conductor.*

1971 Poem for orchestra (inspired by Paul   16'
Verlaine)
3(3rd alt. Picc.),3*,3*,3-4,3,3,1-Timp.,
Glock.-Cel.,Hp.-Str.
G. Schirmer, New York, ᶜ1923
Score 60 p.
*Composed 1901. First performance Boston, 3
April 1902, Boston Symphony Orchestra, Wilhelm
Gericke conductor. Rescored; first perform-
ance Boston, 1 November 1918, Boston Symphony
Orchestra, Pierre Monteux conductor.*

377m [Spanish divertimento, saxophone and
orchestra]
1.Moderato 2.Andante 3.Allegro moderato
Solo Sax.-2(2nd alt. Picc.),2,2,2-2,2,3-Timp.,
Tamb.-Hp.-Str.
Ms.
Score 50 p.
Composed 1900.

349v Les veillées de l'Ukraine [Ukraine   10'
nights, for violin and orchestra]
1.Introduction and pastorale 2.[A night in
May] 3.[Russian songs] 4.[The young men make
merry]
Solo Vn.-3(3rd alt. Picc.),3*,2,2-4,2,3,1-
Timp.,Glock.-Hp.-Str.
Ms.
Score 159 p. Large folio
*Based on Nikolai Gogol's Evenings on a Farm
Near Dikanka. First performance Boston, 20
November 1891, Boston Symphony Orchestra.*

1973 La villanelle du Diable [Devil's   12'
round], Op. 9
3(3rd alt. Picc.),3*,3*,3-4,2,2Cnt.,3,1-Timp.,
Perc.-Org.,Hp.-Str.
G. Schirmer, New York, ᶜ1905
Score 84 p.
*Inspired by M. Rollinat's poem. Composed 1901.
First performance Boston, 2 April 1902, Wil-
helm Gericke conductor.*

LOEWENTHAL, G.

1277s Liebesglück [Happiness of love] Op. 60
Edited by Max Rhode
Solo Vn., Solo Vc.-Str.
Score: Ms. 13 p.
Parts: Apollo, Berlin [n.d.]

LÖHLEIN, GEORG SIMON.   Neustadt,
near Coburg, Bavaria baptized 16 July 1725
Danzig (Gdańsk), Poland 16 December 1781

261p [Concerto, harpsichord or piano, Op. 7
no. 1, F major]
1.Allegro moderato 2.Andantino grazioso
3.Rondo: Poco vivace
Solo Hpscd. or Pno.-Str.(without Va.)
Score: Ms. ᶜ1976 by The Fleisher Collection of
Orchestral Music, Free Library of Philadelphia.
47 p.
Parts: Chez Guera, Lyon [1781?]

260p [Concerto, harpsichord or piano, Op. 7
no. 2, E-flat major]
1.Allegro 2.Poco adagio 3.Rondo tempo di
gavotta
Solo Hpscd. or Pno.-Str.(without Va.)
Score: Ms. ᶜ1976 by The Fleisher Collection of
Orchestral Music, Free Library of Philadelphia.
44 p.
Parts: Chez Guera, Lyon [1781?]

Löhlein, Georg Simon

259p [Concerto, harpsichord or piano, Op. 7
no. 3, D major]
1.Allegro assai con brio 2.Andante grazioso
3.Rondo scherzante
Solo Hpscd. or Pno.-Str.(without Va.)
Score: Ms. c1976 by The Fleisher Collection of
Orchestral Music, Free Library of Philadelphia.
31 p. Large folio
Parts: Chez Guera, Lyon [1781?]

LOHSE, OTTO.   Dresden 21 September 1858
                                    Baden-Baden 5 May 1925

457s [The prince in spite of himself. Prelude
to Act III]
Hp.-Str.
Breitkopf & Härtel, Leipzig, c1919
Score 3 p.
*From the opera first performed Riga, Latvia,
1890.*

LOMBARD, LOUIS.   Lyons 15 December 1861
                                    Ithaca, New York November 1927

631s Cubana, caprice, Op. 36
Castanets(ad lib.)-Hp.(or Pno.)-Str.
Château de Trevano, Lugano [n.d.]
Score 21 p.

837s Élégie, Op. 31
Str.
Château de Trevano, Lugano [n.d.]
Score 8 p.

1578s The Lombard lakes, Op. 37
Hp.(ad lib.)-Str.
[n.p., n.d.]
Score 21 p.

LONGO, ACHILLE.   Naples 28 March 1900
                                    Naples 28 May 1954

3388 Notturno per orchestra   8'
2,2,2,2-2,2,1-Timp.,B.Dr.-Cel.,Hp.-Str.
Ricordi, Milan, c1940
Score 34 p.
Composed 1939.

LOPATNIKOFF, NIKOLAI LVOVICH.   Reval
          (now Tallin), Estonia 16 March 1903
                        Pittsburgh 7 October 1976

5305 Concertino for orchestra, Op. 30   11-13'
1.Toccata 2.Elegietta 3.Finale
2(2nd alt. Picc.),2(2nd alt. E.H.),2,2-2,2-
Timp.,Perc.-Pno.-Str.
Ms.
Score 69 p. Large folio
*Commissioned by the Koussevitzky Foundation.
Composed 1944. First performance Boston, 2
March 1945, Boston Symphony Orchestra, Serge
Koussevitzky conductor.*

804p Concerto for two pianos and   20-22'
orchestra, Op. 33
1.Allegro risoluto 2.Andante 3.Allegro molto
vivace
2 Solo Pno.-2(2nd alt. Picc.),2,2,2-2,2,2-
Timp.,Perc.-Str.
Ms.
Score 131 p. Large folio
*Composed 1950. First performance Pittsburgh, 7
December 1951, Pittsburgh Symphony Orchestra,
Vladimir Bakaleinikoff conductor, Vitya Vronsky
and Victor Babin soloists.*

1140v [Concerto, violin, Op. 26, D major]   23'
1.Allegro 2.Andante 3.Allegro con brio
Solo Vn.-2(2nd alt. Picc.),2,2,2-3,2-Timp.,
Perc.-Str.
Ms.
Score 156 p. Large folio
*Composed 1941. First performance Boston, 17
April 1942, Boston Symphony Orchestra, Serge
Koussevitzky conductor, Richard Burgin soloist.*

3761 Deux nocturnes, Op. 25   8'
1.Andante 2.Allegretto
2,2(2nd alt. E.H.),3*,2-4Hn.-Timp.,Perc.-Hp.-Str.
Ms.
Score 34 p. Large folio
*Originally the two middle movements of the first
version of Symphony no. 2; revised and retitled
1940.*

4857 Divertimento for orchestra, Op. 34   20'
1.Allegro risoluto - Molto vivace 2.Allegro
molto vivace 3.Andante
2(2nd alt. Picc.),2,2,2-2,2-Timp.,Perc.-Pno.-Str.
Ms.
Score 106 p. Large folio
*Commissioned by the Musical Arts Society of La
Jolla, California. Composed 1951. First per-
formance La Jolla, 19 August 1951, La Jolla
Festival Orchestra, Nikolai Sokoloff conductor.*

3614 Opus sinfonicum, Op. 21   11'
2,2(2nd alt. E.H.),2,2(2nd alt. C.Bn.)-3,3,2,1-
Timp.,Perc.-Str.
Ms.
Score 71 p.
*Composed 1933-41. First performance Cleveland,
9 December 1943, Cleveland Orchestra, Erich
Leinsdorf conductor. Won the Cleveland Orches-
tra's 25th Anniversary Competition.*

3756 Symphonietta, Op. 27   17'
1.Allegro 2.Andantino 3.Allegro molto
1(alt. Picc.),1,1,1-1,1-Timp.,Perc.-Pno.-Str.
Ms.
Score 110 p. Large folio
*Composed 1942. First performance on a CBS
radio broadcast, New York, 27 April 1942,
Columbia Concert Orchestra, Howard Barlow conductor. First concert performance at the 19th
Festival of the International Society for Contemporary Music, Berkeley, California, August
1942, California Youth Orchestra of Mills
College, Willem van den Burg conductor.*

3594 Symphony no. 2, Op. 24 [revised   25'
version]

1.Allegro moderato 2.Andante 3.Moderato
2(2nd alt. Picc.),2(2nd alt. E.H.),3*,2(2nd
alt. C.Bn.)-4,3,2,1-Timp.,Perc.-Hp.-Str.
Ms.
Score 132 p. Large folio
Composed 1939 in four movements. First per-
formance Boston, 22 December 1939, Boston
Symphony Orchestra, Serge Koussevitzky con-
ductor. 2nd and 3rd movements now Deux Noc-
turnes, Catalog no. 3761; present middle move-
ment added 1940.

5280 Symphony no. 3, Op. 35   *32-36'30"*
1.Allegro risoluto 2.Allegro molto 3.Andante
4.Allegro
2(2nd alt. Picc.),2(2nd alt. E.H.),2,2(2nd
alt. C.Bn.)-4,3,2,1-Timp.,Perc.-Pno.,Hp.-Str.
Ms.
Score 153 p. Large folio
Composed 1954. First performance Pittsburgh,
10 December 1954, Pittsburgh Symphony Orches-
tra, William Steinberg conductor.

LÓPEZ-BUCHARDO, CARLOS.
Buenos Aires 12 October 1881
Buenos Aires 21 April 1948

3505 [Argentine scenes, symphonic poem]   *20'*
1.[Holiday] 2.[The brook] 3.[Open country]
3(3rd alt. Picc.),3*,3*,3-4,3,3,1-Timp.,Perc.-
Cel.,Hp.-Str.
Ms. [Ricordi, Buenos Aires, ^c1927]
Score 104 p.
First performance Buenos Aires, 12 August 1922,
Felix Weingartner conductor.

LO PRESTI, RONALD.
b. Williamstown, Massachusetts 1933

5415 The masks   *5-8'*
1.Andante tranquillo 2.Allegro moderato
2(2nd alt. Picc.),2,2,2-4,3,3-Timp.-Str.
Ms.
Score 37 p. Large folio
Composed 1954. First performance at the 25th
Festival of American Music, Rochester, New
York, May 1955, Eastman-Rochester Philharmonic
Orchestra, Howard Hanson conductor. Won the
Koussevitzky Award, 1955.

LORA, ANTONIO.
Novale, Vicenza, Italy 2 December 1900
Santa Fe, New Mexico 19 October 1965

5967 Symphony no. 2   *20'*
1.Moderato assai 2.Allegretto vivace
3.Allegro deciso
3(3rd alt. Picc.),3*,3*,3*-4,3,3,1-Timp.,Perc.
-Hp.-Str.
Composers Facsimile Edition, New York, ^c1956
by Antonio Lora
Score 101 p. Large folio
Composed 1955. First performance Erie, Penn-
sylvania, 17 January 1961, Erie Philharmonic
Society, James Sample conductor.

LORENZ, JULIUS.   Hanover 1 October 1862
Glogau (now in Poland) 1 October 1924

724s [Quartet, strings, Op. 24, D minor. Adagio,
B-flat major]
Str.
Leuckart, Leipzig, ^c1901
Score 7 p.

LORTZING, GUSTAV ALBERT.   Berlin 23 October 1801
Berlin 21 January 1851

6593 [Andreas Hofer. Overture]
2,2,2,2-2,2,3-Timp.,Trgl.-Str.
Breitkopf & Härtel, Leipzig, ^c1940
Score 30 p.
From the Singspiel based on the story Das
Trauerspiel in Tyrol by Karl Immermann. Com-
posed 1832.

6532 [The armorer of Worms. Overture]   *8'*
Edited by Fritz Hoffmann
2,2,2,2-4,2,3-Timp.,B.Dr.,Trgl.-Str.
Breitkopf & Härtel, Leipzig [n.d.]
Score 44 p.
From the comic opera based on F. W. von Zieg-
ler's comedy Liebhaber und Nebenbuhler in
einer Person. Composed 1846. First perform-
ance Vienna, 31 May 1846.

4358 [Undine. Ballet music from the opera. *10'30"*
Transcribed for band by Hans Felix Husadel]
1.Allegro 2.Allegretto 3.Pas serieux
3*,2,8*(1Cl. in E-flat,1Alto Cl. in E-flat,1Cl.
in A-flat,1Cb.Cl.),2-5Sax.(Sop.,2Alto,Ten.,
Bar.)-4,2Sop. Cnt.,3,Sopranino Tpt. in E-flat,
3,Bar.,2Ten. Tubas,2-Timp.,Perc.
Richard Birnbach, Berlin, ^c1941
Score in reduction 8 p.
From the opera based on Friedrich de La Motte
Fouqué's version of the fairy tale. First
performance Magdeburg, 21 April 1845.

222 [Der Wildschütz. Overture]   *8'*
Tr: The marksman
2(2nd alt. Picc.),2,2,2-4,2,3-Timp.-Str.
Breitkopf & Härtel, Leipzig [n.d.]
No score published. Violin I part 5 p.
From the opera composed 1842. First perform-
ance Leipzig, 31 December 1842.

6515 Zar und Zimmermann [Czar and   *6-6'30"*
carpenter, *or* Peter the Shipwright] Edited by
Fritz Hoffmann
2(2nd alt. Picc.),2,2,2-4,2,3-Timp.,B.Dr.,
Trgl.-Str.
Breitkopf & Härtel, Leipzig [n.d.]
Score 31 p.
From the comic opera based on the play Le
Bourgmestre de Saardam ou Les Deux Pierres by
A. H. J. Mélesville, E. C. de Boirie and J. T.
Merle. Composed 1837. First performance
Leipzig, 22 December 1837.

LÖSCHHORN, CHARLES ALBERT.   Berlin 27 June 1819
Berlin 4 June 1905

572s [Evening calm, from the world of children]
Glock.-Hp.-Str.(without Cb.)
Challier, Berlin [n.d.]
Score 10 p.

Löschhorn, Charles Albert

7s Menuet, Op. 199 no. 1
Str.
Bote & Bock, Berlin, c1897
Score 3 p.

LOTH, LOUIS LESLIE.
      b. Richmond, Virginia 28 October 1888

737p [Concerto, piano, no. 1, In the form   20'
of variations, E major]
Solo Pno.-2,2,2,2-4,3,3-Timp.,Glock.-Str.
Ms.
Score 134 p.
Composed 1934.

LOTTO, IZYDOR.   Warsaw 22 December 1840
                Warsaw 13 July 1936

794v Fileuse, Op. 8 [The spinning girl] Edited
by Richard Hofmann
Solo Vn.-Str.
Score: Ms. 19 p.
Parts: Kistner, Leipzig [1861?]

LOUIS FERDINAND, PRINCE OF PRUSSIA.
                   Friedrichsfelde,
       near Berlin 18 November 1772
     Saalfeld, Germany 10 October 1806

Born: Friedrich Louis Christian

799p [Rondo for piano and chamber orchestra,
Op. 9, B-flat major]
Solo Pno.-Fl.,2Cl.-2Hn.-Str.
Breitkopf & Härtel, Leipzig [1808?]
Score 58 p.

LOVREGLIO, ELEUTERIO.

1653s Envolée matinale [Early riser] Intermezzo
Solo Vn.-Str.
Score: Ms. 3 p.
Parts: Decourcelle, Nice, c1923

1248s Serenatella
Str.
Score: Ms. 5 p.
Parts: Decourcelle, Nice, c1921

LUALDI, ADRIANO.
    Larino, Campobasso, Italy 22 March 1885
               Milan 8 January 1971

4811 [Adriatic suite]   16'30"
1.[Overture to a comedy] 2.[Sunset between
fields and shore] 3.[Kolo - Dalmatian
national dance]
3(3rd alt. Picc.),3*,3*,2-4,3,3-Timp.,Perc.-
Pno.,Cel.,Hp.-Str.
Ricordi, Milan, c1932
Score 64 p.
*Composed 1932. First performance Rome, 7
February 1932.*

LUBIN, ERNEST.   New York 2 May 1916

5085 A divertimento on American themes   8'30"
1.Entrata 2.Romanza 3.Finale: Allegro vivace

3*,3*,4*(1Cl. in E-flat),3*-3,2,3,1-Timp.,
Perc.-Str.
Ms.
Score 49 p. Large folio
*The themes are: Yankee Doodle, Jeanie With
the Light Brown Hair, Turkey in the Straw.
Composed 1940. First performance ca.1948,
Sidney Blackman conductor.*

5060 [Fifth Avenue. Two pieces from the   5'
ballet]
1.Street scene 2.Pick up
2*,1,3(1Cl. in E-flat),1-2,2,1-Timp.,Perc.-Str.
Ms.
Score 18 p. Large folio
*From the ballet composed 1944. First perform-
ance of Movement I in a version for two pianos,
over Station WNYC, New York, February 1952,
Blanche and Florence Zucker pianists. First
performance of Movement II, Manchester, Vermont, Middleburg Chamber Orchestra, Alan Carter conductor.*

497m Pavane for flute and strings [A minor]
Solo Fl.-Str.
Arthur P. Schmidt, Boston, c1954
Score 2 p.
*Composed 1945. First performance over Station
WQXR, New York, 20 February 1946, WQXR Chamber
Music Ensemble, Leon Barzin conductor.*

5058 A tragic overture   5-7'
3*,2,3(1Cl. in E-flat),3*-4,3,3,1-Timp.-Str.
Ms.
Score 40 p.
*Composed 1948. First performance over Station
WNYC, New York, 13 February 1957, National
Orchestral Association, Hugo Fiorato conductor.*

5059 Variations on a theme by   12-15'
Stephen Foster
3*,3*,3*,3*-4,2,3,1-Timp.,Trgl.-Str.
Ms.
Score 61 p. Large folio
*Themes are Oh, Susanna, by Stephen Foster,
1848, and Reuben, Reuben by William Gooch,
1871. Variations composed 1942. First
reading broadcast over Station WNYC, New York,
5 January 1945, National Orchestral Association, Leon Barzin conductor.*

LUBOMIRSKI, PRINCE LADISLAS.

1154 Poème symphonique [in three parts]   25'
2,3*,3*,2-4,2,3,1-Timp.,Cym.-2Hp.-Str.
Breitkopf & Härtel, Leipzig [1904]
Score 81 p.

LUBOMIRSKY, G.

1675 Danse orientale
2,2,2,2-2,2-Timp.,Tamb.-Hp.-Str.
Jurgenson, Moscow [1907?]
Score 12 p.

2478 Elégie [for small orchestra]
2,2,2,2-2,2-Timp.-Hp.-Str.
Jurgenson, Moscow [1914]
Score 19 p.

LUCA, A. DE.

558m Ballade [for bassoon and string orchestra]
Solo Bn.-Str.
Kahnt, Leipzig [1878]
Score 11 p.

LUCA, EDMOND DE.   Philadelphia 1909

726p Fantasia   18'
Solo Pno.-2(2nd alt. Picc.),2*,2,2-4,2,2-
Timp.,Perc.-Hp.-Str.
Ms.
Score 56 p.
Composed 1938.

2760 Robin Hood Dell suite   40'
1.Dell before concert 2.Scherzo 3.City of
the clouds 4.Imaginary rhumba
3(3rd alt. Picc.),3(3rd alt. E.H.),3,2-4,3,3,
1-Timp.,Perc.-Cel.,2Hp.-Str.
Ms.
Score 153 p.
*Composed 1935-36. Won the Robin Hood Dell
Composition Contest. First performance of
1st and 4th movements at a Robin Hood Dell
Concert, Philadelphia 4 July 1936, Philadelphia Orchestra, Saul Caston conductor.*

LUCAS, LEIGHTON.   London 5 January 1903

6123 Ballet de la reine, for orchestra   18'
1.Entrée et Pavan 2.Air de luth 3.Courante
4.Tordion 5.Sarabande 6.Bransles
2(2nd alt. Picc.),2,2,2-2,2,3-Timp.,Perc.-Hp.-
Str.
Ernst Eulenberg, London, c1960
Score 100 p.
*Sketched 1949 for the unfinished ballet Pavan
for Mary [Queen of Scots]. This suite 1959.
First performance BBC broadcast, London, 4
January 1960, Leighton Lucas Orchestra.*

LUCK, ANDREW J.   Schweinfurt, Bavaria 1861
                          Philadelphia 31 May 1937

2629 Grand march funèbre, Op. 2   5'
3*,2,3*,2-4,3,3,1-Timp.,Perc.-Str.
Ms.
Score 16 p.
Composed 1933.

LUENING, OTTO.   Milwaukee 15 June 1900

932m Concertino for flute, Op. 16   15'
Solo Fl.-Cel.,Hp.-Str.
Ms.
Score 43 p.
*Composed 1923. First performance Philadelphia,
30 January 1935, Chamber Orchestra of Phila-
delphia and Composers' Laboratory, Isadore
Freed conductor, the composer as soloist.*

2781 Prelude to a hymn tune by   10'
William Billings, Op. 37
1,1,1,1-Hn.-Pno.-Str.
American Composers Alliance, New York, c1943,
1954 by Otto Luening

Score 13 p.
*Composed 1937. First performance New York, 1
February 1937, New York Philharmonic Chamber
Orchestra, the composer conducting.*

973m Serenade, Op. 18   7'
3 Solo Hn.-Str.
Ms.
Score 22 p.
Composed 1927-28.

1902s Suite for string orchestra   10'
1.Overture 2.Song 3.Dance
Str.
Boosey & Hawkes, New York, c1942
Score 21 p.
*Composed 1937. First performance Saratoga
Springs, New York, 12 September 1937, F.
Charles Adler conductor.*

3634 Symphonic poem, Op. 15   15'
3(3rd alt. Picc.),3*,2,3*-4,3,3,1-Timp.,Perc.-
Pno.,Org.,Cel.,Hp.-Str.
Ms.
Score 44 p.
*Composed 1924. First performance New York,
16 October 1935, Brooklyn Symphony Orchestra
of the WPA, Franco Autori conductor.*

2782 Two symphonic interludes (sketches)   8'
3(3rd alt. Picc.),3(3rd alt. E.H.),3*,3*-4,3,
3,1-Timp.,Perc.-Pno.,Hp.-Str.
Ms.
Score 10 p. Large folio
*Composed 1935. First performance New York,
11 April 1936, New York Philharmonic, Hans
Lange conductor.*

LUFT, HEINRICH. Magdeburg, Germany 7 September 1813
                                    Magdeburg 1868

1078m [Concertino brillant, oboe, no. 1, Op. 5]
1.Allegro con spirito 2.Larghetto 3.Tempo
di polacca
Solo Ob.-1,0,2,2-4,2,1-Timp.-Str.
Score: Ms. c1976 by The Fleisher Collection of
Orchestral Music, Free Library of Philadelphia.
99 p.
Parts: Fr. Kistner, Leipzig [1839 or 1840]

LUIGINI, ALEXANDRE CLÉMENT LÉON JOSEPH.
                              Lyons 9 March 1850
                              Paris 29 July 1906

5157 Ballet russe, Op. 23   14'30"
1.Czardas 2.Valse lente 3.Scène 4.Mazurka
5.Marche russe
3*,2,2,2-4,3Cnt.,3,1-Timp.,Perc.-2Hp.-Str.
Léon Grus, Paris [n.d.]
Score 103 p.

1676 Carnaval turc [Turkish carnival]   7'
Op. 51
3*,2,2,2-4,2,3,1-Timp.,Perc.-2Hp.(2nd ad lib.)
-Str.
Enoch, Paris [n.d.]
Score 75 p.
Inspired by L. Leclair's poem. Composed 1900.

Luigini, Alexandre

First performance Paris, 1901, the composer conducting.

5162 Fête arabe, Yom el-id (Jour de fête),
Op. 49
1.Danse soudanaise 2.Chanson arabe 3.Danse
du ventre [Belly dance]
3(3rd alt. Picc.),2(1st alt. E.H.),2,2-4,4Cnt.,
3,1-Timp.,Perc.-Hp.-Str.
Léon Grus, Paris [n.d.]
Score 27 p.

3375 Le printemps, Op. 59 [Spring]
1,1,1,1-Hn.-Str.
Score: Ms. 19 p.
Parts: Andrieu, Paris [1904]

1296 Romance symphonique, Op. 65   7'
2,2*,2,2-4,2-Timp.-Str.
Enoch, Paris [n.d.]
Score 28 p.
Composed 1904. First performance Paris 1905.

LUKE, RAY.   Fort Worth, Texas 30 May 1928

5744 Suite for orchestra   9-10'
1.Allegro 2.Andante 3.Allegro
3*,2,2,2-4,3,3,1-Timp.,Perc.-Str.
Ms.
Score 78 p. Large folio
*Composed 1957. First reading Rochester, New
York, 15 April 1958, Eastman-Rochester Sym-
phony Orchestra, Howard Hanson conductor.*

5845 Symphony no. 1   23'
1.Presto 2.Adagio 3.Scherzo 4.Andante
3*,3*,3*,3*-4,3,3,1-Timp.,Perc.-Hp.-Str.
Ms.
Score 169 p.
*Composed 1958-59. First performance Oklahoma
City, 27 March 1960, Oklahoma City Symphony
Orchestra, Guy Fraser Harrison conductor.*

LULLY, JEAN-BAPTISTE.   Florence 28 November 1632
                          Paris 22 March 1687

Born: Giovanni Battista Lulli

4263 [Armide et Reynaud. Passacaille]
2Fl.,E.H.-Str.
Score: Fondation de l'Opéra en France, p.42-50.
Richault, Paris [1859?] Edited by Édouard
Deldevez. 9 p.
Parts: Ms.
*From the opera in five acts, with libretto by
Philippe Quinault after Torquato Tasso's Geru-
salemme Liberata. Composed 1686. First per-
formance Paris, 15 February 1686.*

99s [Armide et Reynaud. Suite for string
orchestra] Edited by Hilmar Höckner
8 excerpts
2,0,2,1(all optional)-Str.
Kallmeyer, Wolfenbüttel, c1930
Score 24 p.

2310s Le ballet des muses. I. Suite. Edited by
Karel Husa

In 8 excerpts
2Ob. or 2Fl.(ad lib.),Bn.(ad lib.)-Drum(ad lib.)
-Cemb.-Str.
Ms. c1966 by Karel Husa
Score 30 p.
*From the ballet with text by Isaac de Benserade.
First performance at Her Majesty's Château de
Saint-German en Laye, France, 2 December 1666.
This ballet was not published in Lully's life-
time and is not included in Henry Prunières'
edition of Lully's complete works (Paris,
1930-39). This edition based on a Ms. in the
Bibliothèque de Versailles.*

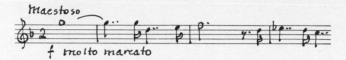

335 [Ballet pieces] Arranged by Felix   15'
Mottl
1.Introduction 2.Nocturne 3.Minuet 4.Prelude
- March
2,2,2,2-4,2-Timp.,Trgl.-Str.
Peters, Frankfurt [n.d.]
Score 37 p.
*Excerpts from the ballets, arranged 1901.
First performance Karlsruhe, 1902, Mottl con-
ductor.*

831s [Concerto for string orchestra. Arranged
by Felix Weingartner]
9 movements
Cemb.(or Pno.)-Str.
Breitkopf & Härtel, Leipzig, c1930
Score 23 p.
*Excerpted from various works of Lully, father
and/or son.*

1714s Gavotte. Arranged by Arcady   2'
Dubensky
Str.
Ms.
Score 7 p.
*This arrangement commissioned by Associated
Music Publishers, 1935. First performance
Philadelphia, 20 November 1935, Philadelphia
Chamber String Simfonietta, Fabien Sevitzky
conductor.*

3240 [Roland. Suite from the opera] Arranged by
William Lynen
1.Ouverture 2.Marsch 3.Air 4.Menuet
5.Gavotte 6.Gigue
1,2,0,1-2,2-Timp.-Str.
Sommermeyer, Baden-Baden, 1903
Score 23 p.
*From the opera first performed Versailles, 8
January 1685.*

399s Six pieces. Freely arranged by James
Brown
Pno.-Str.
Stainer & Bell, London, c1921
Score 12 p.

3639 Suite for orchestra. Excerpted from   *14'*
      several operas by Alfred Einstein
      1.Thesée, ouverture (1675) 2.Proserpine,
      menuet (1680) 3.Atys, air (1676) 4.Amadis,
      menuet (1684) 5.Thesée, 1a marche (1675)
      2,2,2,2-2,2,2-Timp.-Str.
      Music Press, New York, c1941
      Score 30 p.

3409 [Thesée. Overture] Edited by   *2'30"*
      Adam Carse
      1,1,1,1(all optional)-Str.
      Williams, London, c1922
      Score 4 p.
      From the opera first performed Saint Germain,
      near Paris, 12 January 1675.

LUMBYE, HANS CHRISTIAN.   Copenhagen 2 May 1810
                               Copenhagen 20 March 1874

7232 Champagner galop, Op. 14. Edited by Sven
      Lunn
      2*,1,2,1-0,4,1,1-Perc.-Str.
      Samfundet Til Udgivelse af Dansk Musik,
      Copenhagen, c1946
      Score 14 p.
      First performance Copenhagen, 22 August 1845,
      Tivoli Concert Hall Symphony Orchestra, the
      composer conducting.

6710 [The dream of the savoyard, fantasy]
      2(2nd alt. Picc.),1,2,1-2,4,1,1-Timp.,Perc.-
      Str.
      Breitkopf & Härtel, Leipzig [1853]
      Score 96 p.

5527 [Dream pictures, fantasy for   *8'30"*
      orchestra]
      3,Czakan,1,2,1-2,2,1,1-Perc.-Styrian
      Zither-Str.
      Breitkopf & Härtel, Leipzig [1875]
      Score 27 p.
      Composed 1846.

LUND, EMILIUS.

735m [Concert piece, oboe, Op. 10, D minor]
      Solo Ob.-2,0,2,2-2,2-Timp.-Str.
      Score: Ms. 58 p.
      Parts: Bote & Bock, Berlin [1870?]

LUND, JOHN REINHARD (*or* REINHOLD).
                      Hamburg 20 October 1859
                      ?Buffalo, New York after 1914

1011s Intermezzo, Op. 10
       Str.
       G. Schirmer, New York, c1890
       Score 5 p.

33s Liebeslied [Love song] Op. 7
     Str.
     Luckhardt, Berlin/G. Schirmer, New York, c1888
     Score 5 p.

LUNDQUIST, TORBJÖRN.   Stockholm 30 September 1920

6017 [Symphony no. 1, Chamber symphony,   *19'*
      Op. 11]

1.Serioso 2.Molto ritmico e frenetico
2(2nd alt. Picc.),2,2(2nd alt. B.Cl.),2(2nd
alt. C.Bn.)-2,2,2-Timp.-Str.
Ms.
Score 195 p.
Composed 1953-56. First performance Stockholm,
6 May 1956, Swedish Radio Orchestra, Sten Fryk-
berg conductor.

LUTOSɫAWSKI, WITOLD.   Warsaw 25 January 1913

5887 [Concerto for orchestra]   *29'*
      1.Intrada 2.Capriccio notturno e arioso
      3.Passacaglia, toccata e corale
      3(2nd&3rd alt. Picc.I&II),3(3rd alt. E.H.),
      3(3rd alt. B.Cl.),3(3rd alt. C.Bn.)-4,4,4,1-
      Timp.,Perc.-Pno.,Cel.,2Hp.-Str.
      Polskie Wydawnictwo Muzyczne, Cracow, c1956
      Score 152 p. Large folio
      Commissioned by the Polish Ministry of Culture
      and Art. Composed 1950-54. First performance
      Warsaw, 26 November 1954, Warsaw Philharmonic
      Orchestra, Witold Rowicki conductor.

362m [Dance preludes, solo clarinet and   *7'*
      orchestra]
      1.Allegro molto 2.Andantino 3.Allegro giocoso
      4.Andante 5.Allegro molto - Presto
      Solo Cl.-Timp.,Perc.-Pno.,Hp.-Str.
      Polskie Wydawnictwo Muzyczne, Cracow, c1957
      Score 48 p.
      Commissioned by the Polish Ministry of Culture
      and Art. Originally composed for clarinet and
      piano 1953-54. Rescored 1955. First perform-
      ance Katowice, Poland, 29 March 1956, Polish
      Radio Orchestra, Jan Krenz conductor, Alojzy
      Szulc soloist. Also transcribed for nonet,
      1959.

2185s [Funeral music for string   *13'30"*
       orchestra]
       Str.
       Polskie Wydawnictwo Muzyczne, Cracow, c1958
       Score 45 p.
       Commissioned by the Polish Ministry of Culture
       and Art. Composed 1956-58. First performance
       Katowice, Poland, 26 March 1958, Polish Radio
       Orchestra, Jan Krenz conductor.

6041 [Little suite]   *11'*
      1.[Fife] 2.Hurra polka 3.[Ditty] 4.[Dance]
      2(2nd alt. Picc.),2,2,2-4,3,3,1-Timp.,B.Dr.,
      S.Dr.-Str.
      Polskie Wydawnictwo Muzyczne, Cracow, 1951
      Score 63 p.
      Commissioned by Polish Radio. Originally com-
      posed for chamber orchestra 1950. This version
      1951. First performance Warsaw, 20 April 1951,
      Polish Radio Orchestra, Grzegorz Fitelberg
      conductor.

6131 [Silesian triptych, for soprano and   *9'*
      orchestra]
      1.Allegro non troppo 2.Andante quieto
      3.Allegro vivace
      Soprano Voice Solo-3*(2nd alt. Picc.II),2,
      3(3rd alt. B.Cl.),2-4,3,3,1-Timp.,Perc.-Cel.,
      Hp.-Str.

Lutosławski, Witold

Polskie Wydawnictwo Muzyczne, Cracow, ᶜ1955
Score 49 p.
*Commissioned by the Polish Ministry of Culture
and Art. Composed 1951. First performance
Warsaw, 2 December 1951, Polish Radio Orches-
tra, Grzegorz Fitelberg conductor, Maria
Drewniak soloist. Won First Prize at the
Polish Music Festival; Second State Prize of
Music, 1952.*

5436 [Symphonic variations, in one movement] *9'*
3*,3*,3(2nd alt. Cl. in E-flat, 3rd alt.
B.Cl.),3*-4,3,3,1-Timp.,Perc.-Pno.,Cel.,Hp.-
Str.
Polskie Wydawnictwo Muzyczne, Cracow [n.d.]
Score 45 p.
*Composed 1938. First performance Warsaw,
March 1939, Polish Radio Orchestra, Grzegorz
Fitelberg conductor.*

6006 [Symphony no. 1] *24'*
1.Allegro giusto 2.Poco adagio 3.Allegretto
misterioso 4.Allegro vivace
3*(2nd alt. Picc.II),3(3rd alt. E.H.),3(2nd
alt. Cl. in E-flat,3rd alt.B.Cl.),3*-4,3,3,1
-Timp.,Perc.-Pno.,Cel.,Hp.-Str.
Polskie Wydawnictwo Muzyczne, Cracow, ᶜ1957
Score 132 p. Large folio
*Composed 1947. First performance Katowice,
Poland, April 1948, Polish Radio Orchestra,
Grzegorz Fitelberg conductor.*

LUZZATI, ARTURO.   Turin, Italy 24 May 1875
Buenos Aires 25 June 1959

3793 Miramar, poema sinfónico, Op. 38 *16'*
3(3rd alt. Picc.),3*,2,2-4,3,3,1-Timp.-Hp.-
Str.
Ms.
Score 100 p.

LUZZI, G.

512s Contemplazione
Str.(without Cb.)
Ricordi, Milan [1888?]
Score 4 p.

662s Reihen [Round dance]
Str.(without Cb.)
Ricordi, Milan [1888?]
Score 4 p.

LVOV, ALEXEI FEDOROVICH.
Reval (now Tallinn), Estonia 5 June 1798
Romanovo, Lithuania 28 December 1870

5652 [Boris the village elder. Overture]
2,2,2,2-4,2,3,1-Timp.,Bells-Str.
Erchoff [St. Petersburg?, 185-?]
Score 42 p.
*From the comic opera in three acts, on the
subject of the War of 1812. Composed 1854.
First performance St. Petersburg, 1 May 1854.*

1448 [Ondine. Overture. Orchestrated by Mili
Balakirev]
2,2*,2,2-4,2,3,1-Timp.-Str.

Zimmermann, Leipzig [n.d.]
Score 52 p.
*From the opera first performed St. Petersburg,
20 September 1847.*

LYNN, GEORGE.
b. Edwardsville, Pennsylvania 5 October 1915

6389 Symphony no. 1 *22'*
1.Andante 2.Adagio 3.Frettoloso 4.Largo
frettoloso
2(2nd alt. Picc.),2,2,2-4,2,2,1-Timp.,Perc.-
Str.
Ms.
Score 112 p.
*Composed 1962-63. First performance Denver,
Colorado, 3 March 1964, Denver Symphony, Saul
Caston conductor. Won a grant from the Martha
Baird Rockefeller Foundation under the Com-
poser Assistance Program of the American Music
Center, 1963.*

LYON, JAMES.   Manchester, England 25 October 1872
Australia 25 August 1949

210s Idyl (reminiscences of Barmouth), *9'*
Op. 20
1.Allegretto scherzando 2.Larghetto 3.Adagio,
molto maestoso 4.Allegro giocoso
Str.
Breitkopf & Härtel, London [190-?]
Score 14 p.
Composed 1900.

M

MA SZŬ-TSUNG (MA SITSON).
b. Hai-Fung, Kwangtung, China 21 March 1912

306v [Concerto for violin and *30'*
orchestra, F major]
1.Allegro 2.Adagio 3.Allegro giocoso
Solo Vn.-3*,2,2,2-4,3,3,1-Timp.,Cym.,Trgl.-Str.
Moscow State Publishers, Moscow, 1959
Score 104 p.
*Composed 1943. First performance Shanghai,
May 1946, Shanghai Symphony Orchestra, the
composer conducting, Ma Si-hon soloist.*

MAAS, LOUIS PHILIPP OTTO.
Wiesbaden, Germany 21 June 1852
Boston, Massachusetts 17 September 1889

480p [Concerto, piano, Op. 12, C minor] *32'*
1.Allegro maestoso 2.Intermezzo 3.Presto
Solo Pno.-2.2,2,2-4,2-Timp.-Str.
Score: Ms. 300 p.
Parts: Breitkopf & Härtel, Leipzig [1887]

MAASZ, GERHARD.   Hamburg 9 February 1906

1601s Musik (Nr. 1) *14'*
1.Langsam 2.Nicht zu langsam 3.Schnelle
4.Kräftig und frisch
1,0,1-Str.

Ries & Erler, Berlin [n.d.]
Score 14 p.

4583 [Three Nordic dances]
1.[Maypole dance] 2.[Vine dresser's dance
(Sweden)] 3.Caro-As (Denmark)
2,1,2,1-1,2-Timp.,Perc.-Pno.(ad lib.)-Str.
P.J. Tonger, Cologne [n.d.]
Score 19 p.

MA'AYANI, AMI.   b. 1936

320v Concerto da camera for violin and strings
1.Prelude 2.Scherzo 3.Récitatif 4.Rondino
Solo Vn.-Str.
Israeli Music Publications, Tel Aviv, C1965
Score 58 p.
Composed 1964.

6615 Te'amim (Cantillation of the Bible)   10'
3*,2,2,2-4,3,3,1-Timp.,Perc.-Hp.-Str.
Israeli Music Publications, Tel Aviv, C1964
Score 59 p.
Te'amim are the notation symbols used in
Hebrew cantillation. Composed 1964.

MABARAK, CARLOS JIMÉNEZ.
See: JIMÉNEZ-MABARAK, CARLOS.

MCBRIDE, ROBERT GUYN.
          b. Tucson, Arizona 20 February 1911

3252 Fugato on a well-known theme   4'
1,1,2,2-2,2,1-Timp.,Trgl.,S.Dr.-Pno.-Str.
Ms.
Score 34 p.
Composed 1934. First performance Tucson 7 May
1935, University of Arizona Chamber Orchestra,
Henry Johnson, Jr. conductor.

4854 Mexican rhapsody   8'
3*,3*,4*(1Cl. in E-flat),3*-4,4,3,1-Timp.,
Perc.-Hp.-Str.
Eastman School of Music, Rochester, C1937
Score 52 p.
Based on three Mexican themes. Composed 1934.
First performance Rochester, New York, 1936,
Eastman-Rochester Symphony Orchestra, Howard
Hanson conductor.

3297 Prelude to a tragedy   10'
3*,3*,2,2-4Sax.(AATT)-4,4,3,1-Timp.,Perc.-Str.
Ms.
Score 43 p.
Composed 1935. First performance New York,
20 November 1935, New York Philharmonic, Hans
Lange conductor.

6816 Pumpkin-eater's little fugue   4'
2*,2,2,2-4,2,3(3rd optional),1-Timp.,Perc.-Str.
Associated Music Publishers, New York, C1955,
C1964
Score 32 p.
Based on two themes: Peter, Peter, Pumpkin
Eater and I Love Coffee, I Love Tea. Ori-
ginally composed for string orchestra 1955.
Full orchestra version 1964.

4787 [Sherlock Holmes suite for band.   3'
Baker Street]
3*,2,6*(1Cl. in E-flat,1Alto Cl. in E-flat),
2-4Sax.-4,0,3Cnt.,3,Bar.,Euph.,2-Timp.,Perc.
David Gornston, New York, C1946
Score in reduction 6 p.
Composed 1945.

3446 Show piece, ballet [in 12 scenes]   30'
3*,2,2(2nd alt. B.Cl.),3*-4,3,3,1-Timp.,Perc.-
Pno.,Hp.-Str.
Ms.
Score 185 p.
Commissioned by the Ballet Caravan, 1937.
Originally composed for piano, 1937; orchestra,
1937. First complete performance New York,
12 December 1937, Radio City Orchestra, Erno
Rapee conductor.

MCCARTY, PATRICK. Zanesville, Ohio 23 January 1928

5426 Ballata for band   6'
2(2nd alt. Picc.),3*,5*(1Alto Cl. in E-flat),
2-4Sax.-4,2,3Cnt.,3,Bar.,1-Timp.,Perc.
Ms.
Score 11 p. Large folio
Composed 1955. First performance Rochester,
New York, 12 December 1955, Eastman Wind
Ensemble, Frederick Fennell conductor. Won a
prize in the Southwestern Symposium of Con-
temporary American Music, Austin, Texas, 1956.

MCCAULEY, WILLIAM A.
     b. Tofield, Alberta, Canada 14 February 1917

424m Concerto for horn   16'30"
1.Allegro 2.Andante 3.Allegro scherzando
Solo Hn.-2(2nd alt. Picc.),2,2(2nd alt. B.Cl.),
2-3,3,3,1-Timp.,Perc.-Hp.-Str.
Ms.
Score 101 p. Large folio
Composed 1958-59.

423m Five miniatures for flute and strings   8'
1.Adventurous 2.Dolorous 3.Dextrous
4.Langorous 5.Capricious
Solo Fl.-Hp.(4th movement only)-Str.
Ms.
Score 15 p.
Composed 1958. First performance Rochester,
New York, 30 January 1959, Eastman-Rochester
Symphony Orchestra, Howard Hanson conductor,
Gerald Carey soloist.

MACCOLL, HUGH FREDERICK.
               Pawtucket, Rhode Island 1885
                                   d. 1953

3044 Arabs, symphonic illustration   8'
3*,3*,2,2-4,2,3,1-Timp.,Perc.-Hp.-Str.
Ms.
Score 37 p.
Originally composed for piano 4-hands, 1928;
orchestra, 1932. First performance Providence
Rhode Island, 13 November 1932, Providence
Symphony Orchestra, Wassili Leps conductor.

MacColl, Hugh Frederick

736p Ballad, Houris   20'
Solo Pno.-2,3*,2,2-4,2,3,1-Timp.,Perc.-Str.
Ms.
Score 133 p.
*Excerpted and adapted 1934 from Sahara Suite
(Houris) for two pianos, composed 1930. First
performance Providence, Rhode Island, 9 April
1935, Providence Symphony Orchestra, Wassili
Leps conductor, Lorette Gagnon soloist.*

3559 Noël - 8 pedal points and variations   20'
3*,2,2,2-4,2,3,1-Timp.,Perc.-Cel.,Hp.(ad lib.)
-8 Female Voices,Chorus(ad lib.)-Str.
Ms.
Score 66 p.
*Composed for piano, 1940. Transcribed 1940.
First performance Providence, 15 December 1940,
Rhode Island Symphony Orchestra of the WPA
with the St. Dunstan Boy Choristers and Catholic Choral Club of Providence, Edouard Caf-
fier conductor.*

3179 Romantic suite, in the form of   20'
variations on the Greek letters MAPθA
3*,2,2,2-4,2,3,1-Timp.,Perc.-Hp.-Str.
Ms.
Score 125 p.
*Composed for two pianos, 1935, for Arthur
and Martha Baird Allen. Transcribed 1935.
First performance Rochester, New York, 27
October 1936, Rochester Civic Orchestra,
Howard Hanson conductor.*

MCCOLLIN, FRANCES.   Philadelphia 24 October 1892
                        Philadelphia 25 February 1960

1742s Chorale prelude, All Glory, Laud   4'
and Honor
Str.
Ms.
Score 10 p.
*Originally composed for organ, 1936; tran-
scription commissioned by the Philadelphia
Chamber String Simfonietta, 1936; trans-
scription, 1937. First performance Philadel-
phia, 20 April 1938, Philadelphia Chamber
String Simfonietta, Fabien Sevitzky conductor.*

1741s Chorale prelude, Now All the Woods   3'
Are Sleeping
Str.
Ms.
Score 7 p.
*Composed for organ, 1935. Transcribed 1936;
intended as part of a larger work, Suburban
Sketches. First performance with Catalog no.
1742s.*

2308s Heavenly children at play, scherzo   7'
Str.
Ms.
Score 32 p.
*First performance Philadelphia, 9 January 1929,
Philadelphia Chamber String Simfonietta, Fabien
Sevitzky conductor.*

1734s A prayer   3'
Str.

Ms.
Score 5 p.
*Originally composed as an a capella chorus,
1930; transcription commissioned by the Philadelphia Chamber String Simfonietta, 1930;
transcription, 1930. First performance Philadelphia, 13 March 1933, Philadelphia Chamber
String Simfonietta, Fabien Sevitzky conductor.*

2076s Suite for strings   15'
1.Overture 2.Sarabande 3.Chaconne in F minor
Str.
Ms.
Score 45 p.
*Movements 1 and 2 transcribed from Suite in F,
1940.*

       Suite in F   22'30"
3104   1. Overture
3105   2. Pavane
3106   3. Minuet
3107   4. Sarabande
3108   5. Fugue
2(2nd alt. Picc.),2(2nd alt. E.H.),2,2-2,2-
Timp.,Glock.-Cel.,Hp.-Str.
Ms.
Scores: 38p., 16p., 57 p., 19 p., 55 p.
*Composed for string sextet, 1931-32. This ver-
sion 1933-34. First performance of 1, 4, and
5, Philadelphia, 24 May 1940, Pennsylvania
Symphony Orchestra of the WPA, Thaddeus Rich
conductor. First performance of 2, Philadelphia, 19 March 1943, Philadelphia Orchestra,
Eugene Ormandy conductor.*

MCCULLOH, BYRON.   Oklahoma City 1 March 1927

160m Concertino for large trombone   14'30"
and small orchestra (1974)
1.Prologos 2.Parodos 3.Arioso (quasi duo)
4.Katharsis
Solo Tbn.(or B.Tbn.), Solo Hpscd. (amplified)-
1(alt. Picc.),1,1,1-1,1-Perc.-Hp.-Str.
Score: Ms. ^{C}1975 by Byron McCulloh. 85 p.
Large folio
Score in reduction: C. Fischer, New York, ^{C}1976
*Commissioned by the First Annual Colloquium
for Contemporary Music in Pittsburgh. Composed 1974. First performance Pittsburgh, 16
October 1974, Pittsburgh Symphony Chamber
Orchestra, Donald Johanos conductor, the composer as trombone soloist, Don Franklin harp-
sichordist.*

159m Concerto for trombone and orchestra   8'
1.Slowly 2.Presto
Solo Tbn.-2,2,2,2-2,2,0,1-Timp.,Perc.-Pno.-Str.
Ms. ^{C}1973 by Byron McCulloh
Score 38 p.
*Composed for trombone and piano, 1949. Tran-
scribed 1949. First performance Rochester,
New York, January 1950, Eastman-Rochester Sym-
phony Orchestra, Howard Hanson conductor, the
composer as soloist.*

173m Symphony concertante, timpani and   25'
orchestra
1.Introduction and allegro moderato 2.Elegy

COLLECTION OF ORCHESTRAL MUSIC

McDonald, Harl

(E.B.R. via Mozart) 3.Vivo insectile
4.Proclamation and finale
Solo Timp.: 5 Pedal Timp.,4 Roto Toms,8Tom Toms
-3(3rd alt. Picc.),3(3rd alt. E.H.),3*,3*-4,3,
3,1-Perc.-Pno./Cel.,Hp.-Pre-Recorded Tape-Str.
Ms. c1973 by Byron McCulloh
Score 71 p. Large folio
*Commissioned by the Pittsburgh Symphony
Orchestra. Composed 1973. First performance
Pittsburgh, 19 December 1973, Pittsburgh Sym-
phony Orchestra, Donald Johanos conductor,
Stanley Leonard timpanist.*

7296   Symphony no. 1   22'
1.Foreword, fanfares, flourishes 2.Traceries
3.Lament 4.Coda
3*,3*,3*,3*-4,3,3,1-Timp.,Perc.-Cel.,Hp.-Str.
Ms.
Score 95 p. Large folio
*Commissioned by the Pittsburgh Symphony
Orchestra for its 50th anniversary. Composed
1975. First performance Pittsburgh, 7 October 1976, Pittsburgh Symphony Orchestra, André
Previn conductor. Lament originally composed
for flute, marimba, and harp, 1975, in memory
of Bernard Rogers. Orchestral version selected
for performance by the Orchestra Society of
Philadelphia as part of its Pennsylvania Composers Project 1977, made possible by grants
from the National Endowment for the Arts and
the Pennsylvania Council on the Arts with performance materials prepared by The Fleisher
Collection of Orchestral Music. Performed
Main Hall, Drexel University, Philadelphia,
27 March 1977, Orchestra Society of Philadelphia, William Smith conductor. Lament quotes
Dido's Lament from Henry Purcell's opera Dido
and Aeneas.*

MACCUNN, HAMISH.
         Greenock, Renfrew, Scotland 22 March 1868
                      London 2 August 1916

4632   Dowie dens o' Yarrow, ballad-   10'
overture, Op. 6
2,2,2,2-3,2,3,1-Timp.,Perc.-Str.
Augener, London [n.d.]
Score 47 p.
*Based on the Scottish ballad. First perform-
ance London, 13 October 1888, Crystal Palace
Orchestra, August Manns conductor.*

4645   Highland memories, 3 Scottish   12'
scenes, Op. 30
1.By the burnside 2.On the loch 3.Harvest
dance
2,2,2,2-2,2-Timp.-Str.
Augener, London, c1897
Score 34 p.
*First performance London, 13 March 1897, Crys-
tal Palace Orchestra, August Manns conductor.*

4633   The ship o' the fiend, ballad, Op. 5   9'
2,2,2,3*-2,2,3-Timp.,Cym.,B.Dr.-Str.
Augener, London [n.d.]
Score 44 p.
*Based on the Scottish ballad. First perform-
ance London, 21 February 1888.*

MCDONALD, HARL. near Boulder, Colorado 27 July 1899
                  Princeton, New Jersey 30 March 1955

4704   Chameleon variations [in the style   24'
of 10 composers]
4(2nd, 3rd & 4th alt. Picc.),4*,4,4,-3,3,3,1-
Timp.,B.Dr.,S.Dr.-Org.,Hp.-Str.
Elkan-Vogel, Philadelphia, c1941
Score 76 p.
*Composed 1940. First performance Philadel-
phia, 11 March 1941, Philadelphia Orchestra,
Eugene Ormandy conductor.*

4716   [Children's symphony (on   15'
familiar tunes)]
1.Allegro moderato 2.Andante patetico
3.Allegro scherzando 4.Allegro marziale
3(3rd alt. Picc.),3,3,3*-3,3,3,1-Timp.,Perc.-
Hp.-Str.
Elkan-Vogel, Philadelphia [n.d.]
Score 18 p.
*Themes are children's nursery rhymes. First
performance Philadelphia, 8 March 1950, Philadelphia Orchestra, Eugene Ormandy conductor.*

725p   Concerto for two pianos and   22'
orchestra
1.Molto moderato 2.Andante espressivo
3.Juarezca
2 Solo Pno.-3(3rd alt. Picc.),3*,4*,3*-4,4,3,1
-Timp.,Perc.-Str.
Ms.
Score 131 p.
*Composed 1936. First performance Philadelphia,
2 April 1937, Philadelphia Orchestra, Leopold
Stokowski conductor, Jeanne Behrend and
Alexander Kelberine, soloists.*

2768   Festival of the workers   14'
1.Procession of the workers 2.Dance 3.Exul-
tation of the workers
4*,3(3rd alt. E.H.),4*,3*-4,4,3,1-Timp.,Perc.-
2Hp.-Str.
Ms.
Score 81 p.
*Composed 1932. First complete performance
Philadelphia, 26 April 1934, Philadelphia
Orchestra, Leopold Stokowski conductor.*

3571   Legend of the Arkansas traveler,   4'30"
humoresque
3(3rd alt. Picc.),3*,3,3*-4,4,3-Timp.,Perc.-
Str.
Ms. c1939 by Elkan-Vogel, Philadelphia
Score 42 p.
*Composed 1939. First performance CBS Ford
Radio Hour broadcast from Detroit, 3 March
1940, Ford Orchestra, Eugene Ormandy con-
ductor.*

3066   Miniature suite   8'
1.Prelude 2.Air 3.Allemande
2,2,2,2-2Hn.-Str.
Ms. c1938 by Elkan-Vogel, Philadelphia
Score 14 p. Large folio
*Composed 1938. First performed as an ostensi-
ble composition of Handel's amanuensis John
Christopher Smith, Boston, 22 May 1939, Boston
Pops, Arthur Fiedler conductor.*

525

McDonald, Harl

4735 My country at war, symphonic suite *25-26'*
1.1941 2.Bataan 3.Elegy 4.Hymn of the people
3(3rd alt. Picc.),3(3rd alt. E.H.),4*,3*-4,4,
3,1-Timp.,Perc.-Hp.-Str.
Elkan-Vogel, Philadelphia, c1941
Score 118 p.
*First movement originally composed 1941 as
Overture 1941. Second movement composed as
separate tone poem 1942. Third and fourth
movements composed 1942. First performance of
complete suite Indianapolis, 8 January 1944,
Indianapolis Symphony Orchestra, Fabien
Sevitzky conductor.*

4685 Saga of the Mississippi *15'*
2 movements
3(3rd alt. Picc.),3*,3,3*-3,3,3-Timp.,Perc.-
Str.
Ms.
Score 82 p.
*Composed 1945-47. First performance Philadel-
phia, 9 April 1948, Philadelphia Orchestra,
Eugene Ormandy conductor.*

3572 San Juan Capistrano, two nocturnes *9'*
1.The mission 2.The fiesta
3(3rd alt. Picc.),3*,3,3*-4,4,3,1-Timp.,Perc.-
Hp.-Str.
Ms. c1938 by Elkan-Vogel, Philadelphia
Score 67 p.
*Composed 1938. First performance Boston, 30
October 1939, Boston Symphony Orchestra, Serge
Koussevitzky conductor.*

994m Suite for harp and orchestra *23'*
1.Allegro 2.Moderato 3.Allegro
Solo Hp.-2(2nd alt. Picc.),2,3,2-3,2-Timp.,
Perc.-Str.
Ms.
Score 135 p.
*Commissioned by Samuel R. Rosenbaum, 1940.
Composed 1940. First performance Philadelphia,
17 January 1941, Philadelphia Orchestra,
Eugene Ormandy conductor, Edna Phillips
soloist.*

2809 Symphony no. 1, The Santa Fé trail *22'*
1.The explorers (In the desert, In the mountains) 2.The Spanish settlements 3.The wagon
trains of the pioneers
3(3rd alt. Picc.),3(3rd alt. E.H.),4(4th alt.
B.Cl.),3(3rd alt. C.Bn.)-4,4,3,1-Timp.,Perc.-
2Hp.-Str.
Ms.
Score 147 p.
*Composed 1933. First performance Philadelphia,
16 November 1934, Philadelphia Orchestra,
Leopold Stokowski conductor.*

2868 Symphony no. 2, Reflections on an *32'*
era of turmoil [or Rhumba symphony]
1.Grave - Allegro 2.Andante moderato
3.Rhumba 4.Grave - Allegro brioso
3(3rd alt. Picc.),3(3rd alt. E.H.),3(3rd alt.
B.Cl.),3(3rd alt. C.Bn.)-4,4,3,1-Timp.,Perc.-
2Hp.-Str.
Ms.
Score 223 p.

*Composed 1934. First performance Philadelphia,
4 October 1935, Philadelphia Orchestra, Leopold Stokowski conductor.*

3307 Symphony no. 4 *25'30"*
1.Allegro moderato e risoluto 2.Largo e
lugubre 3.In the tempo of a cakewalk
4.Andante mosso e vigorosamente
3(3rd alt. Picc.),3*,4*,3(3rd alt. C.Bn.)-4,4,
3,1-Timp.,Perc.-Hp.-Str.
Ms.
Score 153 p.
*Composed 1937. First performance Philadelphia,
8 April 1938, Philadelphia Orchestra, Eugene
Ormandy conductor.*

2889 Three poems for orchestra, on *12'*
traditional Aramaic themes
3,3*(E.H. optional),3,3*-4,4,3,1-Timp.,Perc.-
Hp.(or Pno.)-Str.
Elkan-Vogel, Philadelphia, c1938
Score 35 p.
*Composed 1936. First performance Philadelphia,
18 December 1936, Philadelphia Orchestra,
Eugene Ormandy conductor.*

4589 Two concert pieces [From the *12'*
Damariscotta]
1.Nocturne 2.Waltz
3*,2,3,3*-3,3,2-Perc.-Hp.-Str.
Ms.
Score 27 p. Large folio
*The Damariscotta is a river in Maine. Com-
posed 1947. First performance Philadelphia,
8 January 1959, Philadelphia Orchestra, Eugene
Ormandy conductor.*

MACDOWELL, EDWARD ALEXANDER.
New York 18 December 1861
New York 23 January 1908

409p [Concerto, piano, no. 1, Op. 15, *30'*
A minor]
1.Maestoso - Allegro con fuoco 2.Andante
tranquillo 3.Presto
Solo Pno.-2,2,2,2-4,2-Timp.-Str.
Breitkopf & Härtel, Leipzig, c1911
Score 116 p.
*Composed 1882. First performance Vienna, 17
April 1898.*

365p [Concerto, piano, no. 2, Op. 23, *25'*
D minor]
1.Larghetto calmato 2.Presto giocoso 3.Largo
- Molto allegro
Solo Pno.-2,2,2,2-4,2,3-Timp.-Str.
Breitkopf & Härtel/AMP reprint, New York, n.d.
Score 98 p.
*Composed 1885. First performance New York, 5
March 1889, Theodore Thomas conductor, the
composer as soloist.*

337 [Hamlet *and* Ophelia, two poems, Op. 22] *15'*
3*,2,2,2-4,2,3-Timp.,Perc.-Str.
Hainauer, Breslau, 1885
Score 63 p.

903 Lamia, after Keats, Op. 29   35'
In one movement
3*,2,2,2-4,2,3,1-Timp.,Cym.,Gong-Str.
Arthur P. Schmidt, Boston, c1908
Score 57 p.
Composed 1888-89.

336 [Lancelot and Elaine, after   19'30"
Tennyson, Op. 25]
3*,2,2,2-4,2,3,1-Timp.,Perc.-Str.
Hainauer, Breslau, 1888
Score 73 p.
*Composed 1887-88. First performance Boston,
10 January 1890, Boston Symphony Orchestra,
Arthur Nikisch conductor.*

510c Romanze, Op. 35
Solo Vc.-2,2,2,2-2,2-Timp.-Str.
Hainauer, Breslau, c1888 by E.A. MacDowell
Score 14 p.
Composed 1880.

849 [The Saracens, after the Song of   3'
Roland, Op. 30]
1.[The Saracens] 2.[Lovely Aldâ]
3*,2,2,2-4,2,3,1-Timp.,Cym.,B.Dr.-Str.
Breitkopf & Härtel, Leipzig, c1891 by E.A.
MacDowell
Score 48 p.
*Composed 1887-88. First performance Boston,
November 1891, Boston Philharmonic, Bernhard
Listemann conductor.*

4228 [Sonata tragica, piano, Op. 45.   29'
Transcribed for orchestra as Sinfonia Tragica
by Modest Altschuler]
1.Largo maestoso 2.Molto allegro 3.Largo
con maesta 4.Allegro eroico
3(3rd alt. Picc.),3*,2,2-4,3,3,1-Timp.,Perc.-
Str.
Composers Press, New York, c1946
Score 137 p.
Composed 1892-93.

2510 [Sonata tragica, piano, Op. 45.   2'30"
Scherzo. Transcribed for orchestra by Adolf
Schmid]
2,2,2,3-4,2,3,1-Timp.,Perc.-Str.
G. Schirmer, New York, c1924
Score 27 p.
Composed 1892-93; transcribed 1924.

917 [Suite no. 1, Op. 42. New edition]   35'
1.In a haunted forest 2.Summer idyl 3.In
October 4.The shepherdess' song 5.Forest
spirits
3*,2,2,2-4,2,3,1-Timp.,B.Dr.,Cym.-Str.
Arthur P. Schmidt, Boston, c1891
Score 124 p.
*Composed 1890-91. First complete performance
Boston, 26 October 1895, Emil Paur conductor.*

934 [Suite no. 2, Indian, Op. 48]   31'
1.Legend 2.Love song 3.In wartime 4.Dirge
5.Village festival
3*,2,2,2-4,2,3,1-Timp.,B.Dr.,Cym.-Str.
Breitkopf & Härtel/AMP reprint, New York, n.d.
Score 120 p.

*Composed ca.1892. First performance New York,
23 January 1896, Boston Symphony Orchestra.*

6134 [Woodland sketches, piano, Op. 51.   2-3'
No. 1, To a wild rose. Transcribed for
orchestra]
0,0,0,0-2Hn.-Hp.-Str.
Ms. [copyright by Society of European Stage
Authors and Composers]
Score 7 p.
*Based on a simple melody of the Brothertown
Indians. First published 1896.*

503m [Woodland sketches, piano, Op. 51. No. 1,
To a wild rose. Transcribed for orchestra by
William Happich]
Solo Hn.-2,2,2,2-2Hn.-Hp.-Str.
Ms.
Score 6 p.
Composed 1896; transcribed 1920.

482s [Woodland sketches, piano, Op. 51.   2'
No. 3, At an old trysting-place. Transcribed
for strings by Edmund Tiersch]
Str.
Arthur P. Schmidt [Boston] c1923
Score 3 p.

4374 [Woodland sketches, piano, Op. 51.   2-3'
No. 5, From an Indian lodge. Transcribed for
chamber orchestra by Andrew Luck]
1,1,1,1-2,1,1-Timp.-Str.
Ms.
Score 4 p.

1036s [Woodland sketches, piano, Op. 51.   1'30"
No. 7, From Uncle Remus. Transcribed for string
orchestra by Edmund Tiersch]
Str.
Arthur P. Schmidt [Boston] c1923
Score 4 p.

MCEWEN, JOHN BLACKWOOD.
                        Hawick, Scotland 13 April 1868
                            London 14 June 1948

3172 Grey Galloway, a Border ballad   11'
3*,3*,3*,3*-6(5th & 6th ad lib.),3,3,1-Timp.,
Perc.-2Hp.(2nd ad lib.)-Str.
Novello, London, c1910 by J.B. McEwen
Score 63 p.
*Inspired by Thomas Cairncross' poem. Composed
1908. First performance London, 2 February
1909, Royal Philharmonic, Camille Chevillard
conductor.*

1369s The jocund dance [4 dance tunes]
Str.(Cb. ad lib.)
Oxford University Press, London, c1927
Score 10 p.

2337s Suite, for string orchestra
1.Prelude 2.What the cello said 3.[The
little master] 4.Orientale 5.Scherzo
Str.
Oxford University Press, London, c1936
Score 16 p.
*The second movement is an arrangement from
Four Lyrics by Moore Park.*

MACHTS, KARL.   Weimar, Germany 16 June 1846
                       Hanover February 1903

729s [Carinthian farewell and Tyrolean waltz]
Str.
Score: Ms. 9 p.
Parts: Oertel, Hanover [n.d.]

1402s Romanze
Solo E.H.-Str.
Score: Ms. 6 p.
Parts: Gründel, Leipzig [n.d.]

1399s Wiegenlied [Cradle song]
Solo Hn.-Str.
Score: Ms. 3 p.
Parts: Lehne, Hanover [n.d.]

MCKAY, GEORGE FREDERICK.
          Harrington, Washington 11 June 1899
          Stateline, Nevada 4 October 1970

4081 Bravura prelude, for brass ensemble   5'
4Hn.,4Tpt.,4Tbn.,2Bar.,Tuba
Associated Music Publishers, New York, ᶜ1943
Score 9 p.
*Composed 1936. First performance Rochester,
New York, 30 April 1939, Eastman School of
Music Symphonic Band, Frederick Fennell
conductor.*

2024s Buffalo and crow, songs and dances   8'
of the Oklahoma Indians, suite for strings
1.Song of the morning star 2.Lament 3.Ritual
dance
Str.
C.C. Birchard, Boston, ᶜ1951
Score 8 p.

3590 Fantasy on a Western folk song, O!   11'
Bury Me Not on the Lone Prairie, Op. 19
[revised version]
2,1*,2-Tpt.-Str.
Ms.
Score 35 p. Large folio
*Composed 1931; revised 1935. First perform-
ance Seattle, 11 November 1935, Seattle Symphony Orchestra, the composer conducting.*

2026s From the Maine woods, folk song   7'
suite for strings
1.The lumberman's life 2.The journey out
3.Shanty song
Str.
C.C. Birchard, Boston, ᶜ1951
Score 7 p.

2012s Halyard and capstan, a sea shanty   5'
suite for strings
1.Haul on the bowline 2.Shallow brown
3.Poor old man
Str.
C.C. Birchard, Boston, ᶜ1950
Score 7 p.

1823s Introspective poem, Op. 42   8'
Str.
Ms.

Score 9 p.
*Composed 1938. First performance Philadelphia,
3 April 1941, Philadelphia Chamber String
Simfonietta, Fabien Sevitzky conductor.*

3477 A Lanier pastorale, Op. 33 no. 2   10'
3,1,2,2-2Hn.-Women's Voices-Str.
Ms.
Score 14 p. Large folio
Composed 1935 in honor of Sidney Lanier.

4015 Pioneer epic (in one movement)   15'
3(2nd & 3rd alt. Picc.),3*,3*,3*-4,4,4-Timp.,
Perc.-Pno.-Str.
Ms.
Score 59 p. Large folio
*Originally composed as Act 3 of Epoch, choreo-
graphic drama, 1935. First performance of
this version Oakland, California, 17 February
1942, Oakland Symphony Orchestra, Orley See
conductor.*

1919s Port Royal, 1861, folksong suite   8'
for string orchestra, Op. 48
1.Hold your light on Canaan shore 2.Go down
in lonesome valley 3.Heaven shall be my home
Str.
C.C. Birchard, Boston, ᶜ1947
Score 8 p.
*Based on three Negro songs collected in the
Port Royal Islands, South Carolina in 1861.
Composed 1939.*

3871 A prairie portrait   11'
2,2(2nd alt. E.H.),2,2-4,2,3-Timp.-Hp.-Str.
Ms.
Score 23 p. Large folio
*Composed 1932. First performance Mutual radio
broadcast, San Francisco, 4 September 1941,
San Francisco Symphony Orchestra, Paul Lemay
conductor.*

2011s Rocky harbour and sandy cove, a   6'
Newfoundland suite for string orchestra
1.At the foot of the mountain brow 2.The
maiden who dwelt by the shore 3.Out upon the
ocean 4.Newfoundland dancers
Str.
C.C. Birchard, Boston, ᶜ1950
Score 8 p.

2815 A short symphony, From the Black   8'
Hills, Op. 5. Movement 1 only
2(2nd alt. Picc.),2(2nd alt. E.H.),2,1-4,2,2,1
-Timp.,Trgl.,Cym.-Hp.-Str.
Ms.
Score 30 p. Large folio
*Composed 1925. First performance Rochester,
New York, 1 May 1925, Rochester Philharmonic,
Howard Hanson conductor. Later used in Sin-
fonietta no. 1.*

2866 Sinfonietta no. 1, From a mountain   14'
town, Op. 5
1.Allegro energico 2.Andante espressivo
3.Allegretto scherzando
2(2nd alt. Picc.),2(2nd alt. E.H.),2,1-4,2,3,1
-Timp.,Perc.-Hp.-Str.

Ms.
Score 62 p.
*First movement taken from A Short Symphony.
Composed 1929. First performance Boston, 21
October 1934, People's Symphony Orchestra,
Fabien Sevitzky conductor.*

4711 Sinfonietta no. 2 [in one movement]   *12'*
Op. 22
2,2,2,3*-3,3,3-Timp.,Perc.-Str.
Ms.
Score 29 p. Large folio
*Composed 1933. First performance Rochester,
New York, January 1937, Eastman-Rochester Sym-
phony Orchestra, Howard Hanson conductor.*

2013s Sky-blue and meadow-green, suite for   *4'*
string orchestra in the spirit of Ohio folk
song
1.Good morning, pretty Molly 2.Beyond the
hillside 3.The keys to heaven
Str.
C.C. Birchard, Boston, ᶜ1950
Score 3 p.

964m Sonatine, Op. 15 [clarinet and   *8'*
strings]
1.Moderato espressivo 2.Giocoso
Solo Cl.-Str.
Ms. Senart, Paris, ᶜ1930
Score 26 p.
*Originally composed for clarinet and harmonium,
1929. Transcribed 1929. First performance
Seattle, 23 February 1932, University of
Washington Orchestra, the composer conducting,
Ronald Phillips soloist.*

4087 Symphonie miniature [Op. 40]   *11'*
1.March to tomorrow 2.Andante expressivo
[*sic*] (A prairie poem) 3.Allegretto giocoso
(Rondo on a jovial theme)
2(both alt. Picc.),2,2,2-3Sax.(2Alto,1Ten.)
(optional)-4,3,3-Timp.,Perc.-Str.
Score: Ms. 52 p.
Parts: C.C. Birchard, Boston, ᶜ1942

4755 Three street-corner sketches [for band]
1.A window shopper 2.Whistling newsboy
3.Daydream
Various instrumental groupings possible,
selected from among the following: 2*,2*,8*
(6Cl. in B-flat,1Alto Cl. in E-flat),1-7Sax.
(3Alto,2Ten.,Bar.,Bass)-4,4,3,Bar.,Euph.,1-
Timp.,Perc.-Pno.,Cel.(or Hp.)-Cb.
G. Schirmer, New York, ᶜ1949
Score 30 p.

3506 To a liberator, a Lincoln tribute,   *11'*
Op. 51
2,3*,3*,2-4,4,4-Timp.,S.Dr.-Mixed Chorus
(optional)-Str.
Ms.
Score 46 p. Large folio
*Commissioned by the Indianapolis Symphony
Orchestra, 1939. Composed 1940. First performance Indianapolis, 15 March 1940, Indianapolis Symphony Orchestra, Fabien Sevitzky
conductor.*

4710 Variants on a Texas tune   *11'*
(Mustang Grey) [Op. 39]
2,1,2,1-2Hn.-Str.
Ms.
Score 25 p. Large folio

MACKAY, HARPER.   Boston 13 October 1921

7190 Six minutes for six pieces   *6'*
[i.e. 6 instruments]
Fl.,Cl.,Bn.-Vn.,Va.,Vc.
Western International Music, Los Angeles,
ᶜ1970 by Holly-Pix Music Publishing, Sherman
Oaks, California
Score 24 p.

MACKENZIE, ALEXANDER CAMPBELL.
               Edinburgh 22 August 1847
               London 28 April 1935

3997 La belle dame sans merci, Op. 29
2,2,2,2-4,2,3,1-Timp.,Trgl.-Hp.-Str.
Novello, Ewer & Co., London [1884?]
Score 95 p.
*First performance London, 9 May 1883, London
Philharmonic, the composer conducting.*

5522 Benedictus, from Six pieces, Op. 37   *7'*
[No. 3. Transcribed for chamber orchestra]
2,0,2,2-2Hn.-Str.
Novello & Ewer, London, 1888
Score 8 p.
*Originally composed as no. 3 of Six Pieces for
Violin with Pianoforte Accompaniment, Op. 37,
1888.*

2183 Burns, second Scotch rhapsody, Op. 24 *17'*
2,2,2,2-4,0,2Cnt.,3,1-Timp.,Trgl.-Str.
Novello, London [n.d.]
Score 93 p.
*Composed 1879. First performance Glasgow 1881,
August Manns conductor.*

1853 Canadian rhapsody, Op. 67   *15'*
1.Allegro vivace 2.Andante 3.Allegretto
2(2nd alt. Picc.),2(1st alt. E.H. ad lib.),2,
2-4,2,3-Timp.,Perc.-Str.
Breitkopf & Härtel, Leipzig, ᶜ1905
Score 79 p.
*Composed 1904. First performance London, 1905,
the composer conducting.*

5211 [Colomba, Op. 28. Ballet music   *11'*
and Rustic march]
2(2nd alt. Picc.),2,2,2-4,2,3,1-Timp.,Perc.-Str.
Novello & Ewer, London [n.d.]
Score 62 p.
*From the opera in three acts with libretto by
Francis Hueffer based on the story by Prosper
Mérimée. First performance Drury Lane Theatre,
London, 9 April 1883. Libretto revised by
Claude Aveling, 1912.*

626p [Concerto, piano, Scottish, Op. 55,   *32'*
G major]
1.Allegro maestoso 2.Allegro vivace
Solo Pno.-2,2,2,2-4,2,3,1-Timp.,Perc.-Str.
Kistner, Leipzig, ᶜ1899

Mackenzie, Alexander Campbell

Score 90 p.
*First performance London, 1897, Ignace Pade-
rewski soloist.*

797v [Concerto, violin, Op. 32, C-sharp   32'
minor]
1.Allegro non troppo 2.Largo 3.Allegro vivace
Solo Vn.-2,2,2,2-4,2,3-Timp.,Trgl.-Str.
Novello, Ewer & Co., London [1886?]
Score 135 p.
*First performance Birmingham Music Festival,
England, 26 August 1885, Pablo de Sarasate
conductor.*

4575 Coronation march, Op. 63
3*,2,2,2-4,0,3Cnt.,3,1-Timp.,Perc.-Str.
Bosworth, London, c1902
Score 42 p.
*Composed for the coronation of King Edward
VII, 1902. First performance Westminster
Abbey, London, 9 August 1902.*

624c Larghetto and allegretto, Op. 10
Solo Vc.-2,2,2,2-2,2-Str.
Augener, London [n.d.]
Score 29 p.

2181 Rhapsodie ecossaise, Op. 21   25'
In one movement
2,2,2,2-4,2,3-Timp.-Str.
Neumeyer, London [n.d.]
Score 79 p.
*Composed 1878. First performance Glasgow,
January 1880, August Manns conductor.*

MCKINLEY, CARL.   Yarmouth, Maine 9 October 1895
Boston 24 July 1966

3257 Chorale, variations and fugue   18'
2(2nd alt. Picc.),2(2nd alt. E.H.),2,3*-4,3,
3,1-Timp.-Str.
Ms.
Score 72 p.
*Composed 1939. First performance Rochester,
New York, 29 October 1941, Eastman-Rochester
Symphony Orchestra, Howard Hanson conductor.*

2634 Masquerade, an American rhapsody   9'
4*,3*,4*,3-4,3,3,1-Timp.,Perc.-Pno.,Hp.-Str.
Ms.
Score 63 p. Large folio
*Composed 1924. First performance Evanston,
Illinois, 29 May 1926, Chicago Symphony
Orchestra, Frederick Stock conductor.*

MCMAHON, JOHN E.   Norwalk, Connecticut 1889

3478 Symphony in syncopation, Op. 6   20'
[B-flat minor]
1.Allegro 2.Andantino 3.Lento - Scherzo
4.Allegro vivace
3(2nd & 3rd alt. Picc.),3(3rd alt. E.H.),3,
3(2nd & 3rd alt. C.Bn.)-4,3,3,1-Timp.,Perc.-
Hp.-Str.
Ms.
Score 136 p.
*Composed 1939-40. First performance Bridge-
port, Connecticut, 10 December 1941, Bridge-*

*port Symphony Orchestra of the WPA, Frank
Foti conductor.*

MACMILLAN, ERNEST CAMPBELL.
Mimico, Ontario 18 August 1893
Toronto 6 May 1973

1779s Two sketches, based on French   7'
Canadian airs
1.[Our Lord in beggar's guise] 2.[À Saint
Malo]
Str.
Ms. c1928 by Oxford University Press, New York
Score 19 p.
*Originally composed for string quartet; tran-
scribed 1937. First performance Ravinia Park,
Illinois, 2 July 1937, Chicago Symphony
Orchestra, the composer conducting.*

MCPHEE, COLIN.   Montreal 15 March 1901
Los Angeles 7 January 1964

763p Concerto for piano with wind octet   15'
1.Allegretto 2.Chorale 3.Coda
Solo Pno.-2(2nd alt. Picc.),1,1,1-1,1,1
New Music, San Francisco, c1931 by composer
Score 51 p.
*Composed 1928. First performance Boston, 11
March 1929, Chamber Orchestra of Boston, Nico-
las Slonimsky conductor, the composer as solo-
ist.*

6302 Tabuh-Tabuhan, toccata for   17'
orchestra and 2 pianos
1.Ostinatos 2.Nocturne 3.Finale
4*,3*,3*,3*-4,3,3,1-Perc.-2Pno.,Cel.,Hp.-Str.
Associated, New York, c1956, 1960
Score 107 p.
*Composed 1936. First performance Mexico City,
1936, National Orchestra of Mexico, Carlos
Chavez conductor. Received an American Academy of Arts and Letters Award, 1954.*

6395 Transitions for orchestra   15'
3*,3*,2,2-4,3,3,1-Timp.,Perc.-Pno.-Str.
Associated, New York [n.d.]
Score 78 p.
*Commissioned by the Serge Koussevitzky Music
Foundation in the Library of Congress. Com-
posed 1954.*

MADETOJA, LEEVI ANTTI.
Uleåborg (now Oulu), Finland 17 February 1887
Helsinki 6 October 1947

2039s [Elegy for string orchestra,   5'
Op. 4 no. 1]
Str.
Oy Fazerin Musiikkikauppa Ab, Helsinki [n.d.]
Score 5 p.
*Originally composed as the first movement of
the composer's Symphonic Suite, Op. 4, 1910.
First performance Helsinki, 1910.*

5814 Kullervo, symphonic poem, Op. 15   16-18'
3(3rd alt. Picc.),2,3*,2-4,3,3,1-Timp.,Perc.-
Hp.-Str.
Suomen Säveltaiteilijain Liito, Helsinki, c1947

530

Score 75 p.
Kullervo is a tragic-heroic character from the Kalevala, the Finnish national epic. Composed 1913. First performance Helsinki, 1913.

5813 Okon Fuoko, Op. 58. Suite I   *14'*
[from the ballet]
1.[The dream juggler] 2.[Arrival of the guests] 3.[Dance of the puppets] 4.[Man's dance – Woman's dance – Danse grotesque]
3(3rd alt. Picc.),2,2,2-4,3,4,1-Timp.,Perc.-Cel.,Hp.-Str.
Suomen Säveltaiteilijain Liito, Helsinki, c1936
Score 41 p.
From the ballet in one act, with scenario in Danish by Poul Knudsen. Composed 1930. First performance Helsinki, 2 December 1930.

2042s [Song for string orchestra]
Str.
R.E. Westerlund, Helsinki [n.d.]
Score 4 p.

MADURO, CHARLES.

4429 España. Transcribed for orchestra by Adolf Schmid
3*,2(2nd alt. E.H.),2,2-4,3,3,1-Timp.,Perc.-Hp.-Str.
Editions Max Eschig, Paris, c1931 by composer
Score 56 p.

MAES, JEF.   Antwerp, Belgium 5 April 1905

6559 Ouverture concertante, for orchestra   *8'*
3*,2,2,2-4,3,3,1-Timp.,Perc.-Hp.-Str.
CeBeDeM, Brussels, c1963
Score 38 p.
Commissioned by the Philharmonie d'Anvers. Composed 1961. First performance Antwerp, 20 March 1961, Philharmonie d'Anvers, Eduard Flipse conductor.

MAESCH, LA VAHN.
        b. Appleton, Wisconsin 15 October 1904

2895 Passacaglia   *7'30"*
2,2(2nd alt. E.H.),2,2-4,3,3,1-Timp.,Perc.-Str.
Ms.
Score 32 p.
Composed 1937-38. First performance Rochester, New York, 30 March 1938, Rochester Civic Orchestra, Howard Hanson conductor.

2998 Suite on children's tunes   *10'30"*
1.Pantomime 2.Lullaby 3.Parade
2(2nd alt. Picc.),2(2nd alt. E.H.),2,2-4,2,2-Timp.,Perc.-Hp.-Str.
Ms.
Score 43 p. Large folio
Composed 1937. First performance NBC radio broadcast, Rochester, New York, 14 February 1938, Rochester Civic Orchestra, Guy Fraser Harrison conductor.

MAGANINI, QUINTO.
        Fairfield, California 30 November 1897
        Greenwich, Connecticut 10 March 1974

3870 Americanese, suite on 3 early   *11'*
American pieces
1.An old Connecticut tune (Archdale by Andrew Law) 2.A Village Festival (Stephen Foster) 3.A chant for Washington's funeral (Mt. Vernon, 1799 by Jenks)
1,1(alt. E.H.),2,1-2,2(alt. 2Cnt.),2-Timp.-Str.
Edition Musicus, New York, c1940 by composer
Score 18 p.

2684 The Cathedral at Sens, Op. 28   *22'*
In one movement
Solo Vc.-3,2,0,2-Pno.,Hp.-Chorus(SATB)-Str.
Ms. c1932 by J. Fischer, New York
Score 18 p.
Composed 1931. First performance Boston, 24 March 1940, Federal Music Project of the WPA, Earl Weidner conductor.

1728s Concerto for strings, Op. 31   *22'*
[D minor]
1.Fantasy 2.Nocturne 3.Fugue
Str.
J. Fischer, New York, c1934 by Quinto Maganini
Score 8 p.
Composed 1929-33. First performance New York, 6 January 1935, Maganini Chamber Symphony, the composer conducting. Nocturne available separately, Catalog no. 1722s.

2639 Even hours, a ballet suite, Op. 32   *22'*
1.IV A.M. 2.VI A.M. 3.Scherzo-intermezzo (Daylight hours) 4.VIII P.M. 5. X P.M.
2*,2,3*,2-2,2-Timp.,Perc.-Pno.,Hp.-Str.
Ms.
Score 55 p.
Composed 1928.

2641 Genevieve, Op. 35   *15'*
Theme (Sweet Genevieve), 10 Variations, Coda
3(3rd alt. Picc.),3*,3*,2-4,3,3,1-Timp.,Perc.-Hp.-Str.
Ms.
Score 42 p.
Composed 1935. First performance New York, 10 November 1935, Brooklyn Symphony Orchestra, the composer conducting.

2640 Napoleon I, an orchestral   *14'*
portrait, Op. 34
3(alt. 3Picc.),2,3*,2-4,4,3,1-Timp.,Perc.-Hp.-Str.
Ms.
Score 80 p.
Composed 1931. First performance New York, 10 November 1935, Brooklyn Symphony Orchestra of the WPA, the composer conducting.

2456 An ornithological suite
1.Humming birds 2.At dusk, a nightingale sings in the garden 3.Canonical cuckoos 4.Listen to the mocking-birds (Variations)
1(alt. Picc.),1,2(2nd ad lib.),1-2(2nd ad lib.),1-Perc.-Hp.-Str.
J. Fischer, New York, c1931
Score 28 p.

Maganini, Quinto

3162   The royal ladies, suite for   *17'*
orchestra
1.Fête champêtre 2.Threnody 3.Triumphal
march
3*(2nd alt. 2nd Picc.),2(2nd alt. E.H.),2,2-
3,3,3-Timp.,Perc.-Hp.-Str.
Edition Musicus, New York, c1940 by composer
Score 40 p.
Themes by Marie Antoinette, Anne Boleyn, and
Maria Antonia Walpurgis. Composed 1939.
First performance Greenwich, Connecticut, 3
February 1940, the composer conducting.

1438   La rumba, a Cuban rhapsody   *6'30"*
2*,2,2,2-2,2,2-Timp.,Perc.-Str.
J. Fischer, New York, c1928
Score 38 p.

2637   South wind, an orchestral fancy,   *16'*
Op. 36
4(3rd & 4th alt. Picc.),3*,3*,2-6,4,3,1-Timp.,
Perc.-Cel.,2Hp.-Str.
Ms.
Score 26 p.
Composed 1925 as Night on an Island of Phan-
tasy, Op. 10. Rewritten 1935.

2741   A suite of music by royalty,   *17'30"*
Op. 33. Transcribed for orchestra
1.Passetyme with goode company (Henry VIII)
2.Amaryllis (Louis XIII) 3.Madrigal (Gesualdo,
Prince of Venosa) 4.Military March (Fre-
derick the Great)
2(alt. 2Picc.),2,2,2-2,2,2-Timp.,Perc.-Hp.-
Str.
Edition Musicus, New York, c1936 by composer
Score 35 p.
Composed 1933. First complete performance
New York, 3 April 1937, Maganini Chamber Sym-
phony, Quinto Maganini conductor.

2638   [Symphony, Sylvan, Op. 29]   *17'*
1.Crags 2.Night 3.Daybreak 4.Frogs
1(alt. Picc.),1(alt. E.H.),1,1-2Hn.-Str.
Ms.
Score 18 p.
Composed 1932. First performance New York, 30
November 1932, New York Sinfonietta, the com-
poser conducting.

2788   Tuolumne, a Californian rhapsody,   *14'*
with trumpet obbligato, Op. 2
Solo Tpt.-3(3rd alt. Picc.),3*,2,2-4,3,3,1-
Timp.,Perc.-Hp.-Str.
J. Fischer, New York, c1930
Score 24 p.
Composed 1920. First performance New York,
9 August 1924. Revised 1926. First per-
formance Chautauqua, New York, 1929, Albert
Stoessel conductor. Maganini won the Pulitzer
Prize for this and other works, 1927.

MAGNARD, ALBÉRIC.   Paris 9 June 1865
Baron, Oise, France 3 September 1914

Full name: Lucien-Denis-Gabriel-Albéric Magnard

982   [Symphony no. 3, Op. 11, B minor]   *30'*

1.Introduction et ouverture 2.Danses
3.Pastorale 4.Vif
2,2,2,2-4,2,3-Timp.-Str.
Rouart Lerolle, Paris, c1902
Score 168 p.
Composed 1896. First performance Paris, 14
May 1899, the composer conducting.

1502   [Symphony no. 4, Op. 21, C-sharp   *35'*
minor]
1.Modéré 2.Vif 3.Sans lenteur et nuance
4.Animé
3*,3*,3*,2-4,3,3-Timp.-Hp.-Str.
Rouart Lerolle, Paris, c1921
Score 207 p.
Composed 1911-13. First performance Concerts
de l'Union des Femmes Professeurs et Composi-
teurs, Paris, 2 April 1914, the composer con-
ducting.

MAHAUT, ANTOINE.   Netherlands?   fl.1750

2230s [Symphony no. 4, strings, C minor]
1.Allegro 2.[No tempo] 3.Adagio 4.Presto
Cemb.(optional)-Str.
Edition Heuwekemeijer, Amsterdam, c1958
Score 15 p.
First published by Olofsen, Amsterdam 1751.

MAHLER, GUSTAV.   Kalištĕ, Bohemia 7 July 1860
Vienna 18 May 1911

6206   Kindertotenlieder [voice and
orchestra]
1.Nun will die Sonn' so hell aufgeh'n 2.Nun
seh' ich wohl, warum so dunkle Flammen 3.
Wenn dein Mütterlein 4.Oft denk' ich, sie
sind nur ausgegangen 5.In diesem Wetter
Voice Solo-3*,3*,3*,3*-4Hn.-Timp.,Glock.,Tam-
tam-Cel.,Hp.-Str.
C.F. Kahnt, Leipzig, c1905
Score 86 p.
Poems by Friedrich Rückert. Composed 1901-04.
First performance Vienna, 29 January 1905.

[Des Knaben Wunderhorn, songs for solo voice
and orchestra]
Suggested by poems from the folk lieder anthol-
ogy, Des Knaben Wunderhorn edited by Achim von
Arnim and Clemens Brentano.
6617   No. 1. Der Schildwache Nachtlied   *6'*
[The sentinel's night song]
Voice Solo-3*,3*,2,2-4,2-Timp.,Perc.-Hp.-Str.
Universal Edition, Vienna, c1941
Score 21 p.
Orchestrated by the composer as one of the Fünf
Humoresken, 1892. First performance Berlin,
12 December 1892, Berlin Philharmonic, Raphael
Maszkowski conductor, Amalie Joachim soloist.
6618   No. 2. Verlor'ne Müh' [Labor lost]   *2'15"*
Voice Solo-2,2,2,2-2Hn.-Trgl.-Str.
Universal Edition, Vienna, c1914
Score 7 p.
First performed with no. 1.
6619   No. 3. Trost im Unglück [Comfort   *2'25"*
in misfortune]
Voice Solo-3*,2,2,2-4,2-Timp.,Perc.-Str.
Universal Edition, Vienna, c1914

Mahler, Gustav

Score 17 p.
Composed as one of the Fünf Humoresken. First performance Hamburg, 27 October 1893, Laube Orchestra, the composer conducting, Paul Bulss soloist.

6620   No. 4. Wer hat dies Liedlein   2'30"
erdacht? [Who made up this little song?]
Voice Solo-2,2,2,2-2Hn.-Trgl.-Str.
Universal Edition, Vienna, c1940
Score 11 p.
Composed 1892 as one of the Fünf Humoresken. First performed with no. 3, Clementine Schuch-Prosska soloist.

6621   No. 5. Das irdische Leben [The   3'
earthly life]
Voice Solo-2,3*,2,2-3,1-Cym.-Str.
Universal Edition, Vienna, c1941
Score 17 p.
Composed 1893. First performance Vienna, 14 January 1900, Vienna Philharmonic, the composer conducting, Selma Kurz soloist.

6622   No. 6. Des Antonius von Padua   4'
Fischpredigt [Anthony of Padua's sermon to the fishes]
Voice Solo-2,2,2,3-4Hn.-Timp.,Perc.-Str.
Universal Edition, Vienna, c1941
Score 17 p.
Composed 1893. First performance Vienna, 29 January 1905, the composer conducting, Anton Moser soloist.

6623   No. 7. Rheinlegendchen   3'
Voice Solo-1,1,1,1-Hn.-Str.
Universal Edition, Vienna, c1941
Score 13 p.
First performed with no. 3.

6624   No. 8. Lied des Verfolgten im   3'40"
Turm [Song of the prisoner in the tower]
Voice Solo-2,2,2,2-4,2-Timp.-Str.
Universal Edition, Vienna [n.d.]
Score 17 p.
First performed with no. 6.

6625   No. 9. Wo die schönen Trompeten   5'35"
blasen [Where the proud trumpets blow]
Voice Solo-2,2,2-4,2-Str.
Universal Edition, Vienna [n.d.]
Score 9 p.
Composed ca.1895. First performed with no. 5.

6626   No. 10. Lob des hohen Verstandes   2'35"
[Praise of the lofty intellect]
Voice Solo-2,2,3,2-4,1,1,1-Timp.,Trgl.-Str.
Universal Edition, Vienna [n.d.]
Socre 9 p.
Composed 1896.

6576   Das Lied von der Erde, eine   60'
Symphonie für Stimmen und Orchester
1.Das Trinklied vom Jammer der Erde [The drinking song of earth's misery] 2.Der Einsame im Herbst [The lonely one in autumn]
3.Von der Jugend [Of youth] 4.Von der Schönheit [Of beauty] 5.Der Trunkene im Frühling [The drunk in spring] 6.Der Abschied [The parting]
Tenor & Contralto(or Bar.) Voice Solos-4*(3rd Fl. alt. Picc.II),3(3rd alt. E.H.),5*(1Cl. in E-flat),3(3rd alt. C.Bn.)-4,3,3,1-Timp.,Perc.-Cel.,2Hp.-Str.
Universal Edition, Vienna, c1964 by

Internationale Gustav Mahler Gesellschaft
Score 146 p.
Chinese poems translated in Hans Bethge's Die Chinesische Flöte. Composed 1908. First performance Munich, 20 November 1911, Bruno Walter conductor.

2076   [Symphony no. 1, The titan, D major]   60'
1.Langsam schleppend 2.Kräftig bewegt
3.Feierlich und gemessen, ohne zu schleppen
4.Stürmisch bewegt
4(3rd&4th alt. Picc.I&II),4(3rd alt. E.H.),4(1Cl. in E-flat, 3rd alt. B.Cl.),3(3rd alt. C.Bn.)-7,4,3,1-Timp.,Perc.-Hp.-Str.
Kalmus, New York [n.d.]
Score 265 p.
Composed 1883-88. First performance Budapest, 20 November 1889, the composer conducting.

6431   [Symphony no. 2, Resurrection, C minor] 80'
1.Allegro maestoso 2.Andante moderato 3.In ruhig fliessender Bewegung 4.Urlicht [Primeval light, from Des Knaben Wunderhorn] 5.Scherzo
4(all alt. Picc.),4(3rd&4th alt. E.H.),5(3rd alt. B.Cl.,2Cl. in E-flat,2nd Cl. in E-flat alt. 4th Cl. in B-flat),4(3rd&4th alt. C.Bn.)-10,10,4,1-Timp.(2 players),Perc.-Org.,2Hp.-Sop. & Alto Solo Voices,Chorus(SATB)-Str.
Universal Edition, Vienna, c1952
Score 209 p.
Text of final movement from Friedrich Klopstock's hymn, Die Auferstehung [The Ressurrection] with additional stanzas by the composer. First movement originally titled Totenfeier [Funeral Feast]. Composed 1888-94. First performance of first three movements only, Berlin, 4 March 1895, Berlin Philharmonic Orchestra, the composer conducting. First complete performance Berlin, 13 December 1895, Berlin Philharmonic Orchestra, Stern Singakademie Choir, Sängerbund des Lehrerverein, the composer conducting, Josephine von Artner and Hedwig Felden soloists.

6627   [Symphony no. 3, Ein Sommer-   90'
mittagstraum, D minor]
1.Kräftig, entschieden 2.Tempo di Menuetto 3.Comodo, scherzando, ohne Hast
4.Sehr langsam, misterioso 5.Lustig im Tempo und keck im Ausdruck 6.Langsam, ruhevoll, empfunden
4(all alt. Picc.),4(4th alt. E.H.),5(2Cl. in E-flat,3rd alt. B.Cl.,2nd Cl. in E-flat alt. Cl. in B-flat),4(4th alt. C.Bn.)-8,4,4,1-Timp.(2 players),Perc.-2Hp.-Contralto Solo, Women's Chorus,Boys' Chorus-Str.(Posthorn and Bells offstage)
Universal Edition, Vienna [1906]
Score 231 p.
Composed 1895-96. Revised 1899. First complete performance Krefeld, Germany, 9 June 1902.

6488   [Symphony no. 4, Humoreske, G major] 54'
New critical edition of the final version edited for the International Mahler Society by Erwin Ratz
1.Bedächtig 2.In gemächlicher Bewegung

Mahler, Gustav

3.Ruhevoll (Poco adagio) 4.Sehr behaglich
4(3rd & 4th alt. Picc.),3(3rd alt. E.H.),3(2nd
alt. Cl. in E-flat, 3rd alt. B.Cl.),3(3rd alt.
C.Bn.)-4,3-Timp.,Perc.-Hp.-Soprano Voice-Str.
Universal Edition, London, C1963
Score 125 p.
*Text of 4th movement from Des Knaben Wunder-
horn. Composed 1899-1901. First performance
Munich, 25 November 1901, Kaim Orchestra, the
composer conducting. First performance of
final version New York, 17 January 1911, New
York Philharmonic, the composer conducting.*

6839 [Same as above] Kalmus edition

1790 [Symphony no. 5, The giant,   65'
C-sharp minor]
I:1.Trauermarsch 2.Stürmisch bewegt II:3.
Scherzo III:4.Adagietto, attacca 5.Rondo -
Finale
4(3rd & 4th alt. 2Picc.),3(3rd alt. E.H.),3*,
3*-6,4,3,1-Timp.,Perc.-Hp.-Str.
Peters [n.p., n.d.]
Score 246 p.
*Composed 1901-02. First performance Cologne,
18 October 1904, the composer conducting.
Adagietto available separately, Catalog no.
226s.*

6961 [Symphony no. 6, Tragic, A minor]   75'
1.Allegro energico, ma non troppo 2.Andante
moderato 3.Scherzo 4.Finale
5*(3rd & 4th alt. Picc.),5*(3rd & 4th alt.
E.H.),5*(1Cl. in E-flat),5*-8,6,4,1-Timp.,
Perc.-Cel.,2Hp.-Str.
Kalmus, New York [n.d.]
Score 263 p.
*Composed 1903-04. First performance United
German Music Society festival at Essen, 17
May 1906, the composer conducting.*

1827 [Symphony no. 7, E minor]   80'
1.Langsam 2.Nachtmusik 3.Schattenhaft
4.Nachtmusik 5.Rondo finale
5(4th alt. Picc.II),4*,4*,4*-4,3,3,1,Tenor-
Horn-Timp.,Perc.-2Hp.,Mand.,Guit.-Str.
Bote & Bock, Berlin, C1909
Score 257 p.
*Composed 1904. First performance Prague,
1908, the composer conducting.*

6442 [Symphony no. 8, E-flat major]   90'
1.Hymnus: Veni, creator spiritus 2.[Final
scene from Faust]
6*(5th alt. Picc.I),5*,5*(1 in E-flat),5*-8,
8(4 offstage),7(3 offstage),1-Timp.,Perc.-
Pno.,Org.,Cel.,3Hp.,Harm.,Mand.-8 Solo Voices
(SSSAATBB),Choruses-Str.
Universal Edition, Vienna, C1911, 1938
Score 218 p. Large folio
*Composed 1906. First performance Munich, 12
September 1910, the composer conducting.*

2077 [Symphony no. 9, D major]   85'
1.Andante comodo 2.Im Tempo eines gemäch-
lichen Ländlers 3.Rondo-Burleske 4.Adagio
5*,4(4th alt. E.H.),5*,4*-4,3,3,1-Timp.,Perc.-
2Hp.-Str.

Universal Edition, Vienna, C1912
Score 182 p.
*Composed 1908. First performance Munich, June
1912, Bruno Walter conductor.*

6713 Symphony no. 10 in F-sharp.   65-70'
Performing version of the comprehensive full-
length sketch, prepared by Deryck Cooke
I:1.Adagio 2.Scherzo 1 (Schnelle Vierteln)
II:3.Allegretto moderato (Purgatorio)
4.Scherzo 2 (Allegro pesante) 5.Finale (Lento
non troppo - Allegro moderato - Tempo primo)
3(3rd alt. Picc.),3(3rd alt. E.H.),3(2nd alt.
Cl. in E-flat,3rd alt. Cl. in A & B.Cl.),3(2nd
& 3rd alt. C.Bn.)-4,4,4,1-Timp.(2 players),Perc.
-Hp.-Str.
Associated Music Publishers, New York, C1966
Score 293 p. Large folio
*Composed 1910; left unfinished at the compo-
ser's death. 1st and 3rd movements were
first performed, in a version completed by
Ernst Křenek, at the Opera House, Vienna, 12
October 1924, Vienna Philharmonic Orchestra,
Franz Schalk conductor. This version edited
and completed for performance by Deryck Cooke.
Final version first performed London, BBC
Henry Wood Promenade Concert, 13 August 1964,
London Symphony Orchestra, Berthold Gold-
schmidt conductor.*

MAHLER-KALKSTEIN.
See: AVIDOM, MENAHEM.

MAICHELBECK, FRANZ ANTON.
                    Reichenau, Germany 6 July 1702
          Freiburg-im-Breisgau, Germany 14 June 1750

914s Sonata a quattro. Arranged by Wilhelm
Weckbecker
1.Praeludium 2.Largo 3.Buffone 4.Giga
Str.
Universal Edition, Vienna, C1923
Score 11 p.
*Excerpted and transcribed from three clavier
sonatas, first published Augsburg, 1736.*

MAILMAN, MARTIN.   New York 30 June 1932

5458 Autumn landscape   7'30"
2,2,2,2-2,2,1-Timp.-Hp.-Str.
Ms.
Score 13 p. Large folio
*Composed 1954. First performance Rochester,
New York, May 1955, Eastman-Rochester Sym-
phony Orchestra, Howard Hanson conductor.
Won Edward Benjamin Award for Quiet Music, 1955.*

MAITLAND, S. MARGUERITE.   Philadelphia 1909

2739 The Snow Queen, seven scenes from   30'
the fairy tale by Hans Christian Andersen
2,3*,2,2-4,2,3,1-Timp.,Perc.-Cel.,2Hp.-Str.
Ms.
Score 167 p.
*Composed 1931-33. First performance Philadel-
phia, 23 March 1941, Pennsylvania Symphony of
the WPA, Guglielmo Sabatini conductor. Honorable mention, Carl F. Lauber Music Award, 1933.*

534

MAJOR, JAKAB GYULA.
　　　　　　　　Kosice, Hungary 13 December 1858
　　　　　　　　Budapest 30 January 1925

Real name: James Julius Mayer

567p Concert symphonique [piano, Op. 12, in D]
　　1.Allegro 2.Allegretto 3.Allegro
　　Solo Pno.-2,2,2,2-4,2,3-Timp.-Str.
　　F.E.C. Leuckart, Leipzig [n.d.]
　　Score 81 p.

333s Serenade, Op. 24, G major
　　1.Allegro 2.Andante 3.Gavotte 4.Allegro molto
　　Str.
　　F.E.C. Leuckart, Leipzig [n.d.]
　　Score 26 p.

MALÁT, JANI. Mlada Boleslav, Bohemia 16 June 1843
　　　　　　　　Prague 2 December 1915

1882 [Flowers from Bohemian meadows,　　　　10'
　　Czech songs arranged for orchestra]
　　3*,2,2,2-4,2,3-Timp.,Perc.-Str.
　　Urbánek, Prague [n.d.]
　　Score 63 p.
　　Arranged 1886.

1678 Furiant　　　　　　　　　　　　　　　　2'
　　1,1,1,1-2,2,1-Str.
　　F.A. Urbánek, Prague [n.d.]
　　Score 12 p.
　　Composed 1888.

1881 [Souvenir de Prague, 40 Czech　　　　　9'
　　songs arranged for orchestra. Nos. 1-20]
　　2,1,2,1-4,2,3-Timp.,Perc.-Str.
　　F.A. Urbánek, Prague [n.d.]
　　Score 63 p.
　　Arranged 1891.

MALDERE, PIERRE VAN.　　　Brussels 16 October 1729
　　　　　　　　　　　　　　Brussels 3 November 1768

4641 [Symphony, Op. 4 no. 3, B-flat major]
　　Edited by Adam Carse
　　1.Allegro assai 2.Andante un poco allegretto
　　3.Presto
　　2Ob.-2Hn.-Str.
　　Augener, London, ᶜ1938
　　Score 15 p.
　　First published by Venier, Paris, 1764.
　　English edition published by Longman & Luckey,
　　London, as VI Select Overtures, Op. IV.

MALER, WILHELM. Heidelberg, Germany 21 June 1902

2096s [Music for string orchestra]　　　　30'
　　1.Pastorale 2.Toccata, Fuge und Ostinato
　　3.Sonate (Allegro)
　　Str.
　　B. Schott's Söhne, Mainz, ᶜ1939
　　Score 35 p.
　　Composed 1937 for the Donaueschingen Music
　　Festival.

1959s [Three festive and playful pieces]
　　1.[Festive prelude to a song (Appeal, by Lorenz

Minderer)] 2.[Slow intermezzo] 3.Kleines
Rondo
　　Tpt.(or Voice)-Str.(Cb. ad lib.)
　　P.J. Tonger, Cologne [n.d.]
　　Score 11 p.

1957s [Three little festive pieces. Arranged
　　for string orchestra by Hilmar Höckner]
　　1.Energisches Marschtempo 2.Langsamer Satz
　　3.Ziemlich rasche
　　1,1,1(all optional)-Str.(Cb. ad lib.)
　　P.J. Tonger, Cologne [n.d.]
　　Score 7 p.

MALIPIERO, GIAN FRANCESCO.　　Venice 18 March 1882
　　　　　　　　　　　　　　　Treviso, Italy 1 August 1973

1264 Armenia [Armenian songs in　　　　　　12'
　　symphonic form]
　　3*,3*,3*,2-4,2-Timp.,Perc.-Cel.,Hp.-Str.
　　Senart, Paris, ᶜ1918
　　Score 20 p.
　　Composed 1917. First performance Paris, 1917,
　　Concerts Lamoureux, Gabriel Pierné conductor.

810p [Concerto, piano and orchestra, no. 1] 18'
　　1.Allegro moderato 2.Andante 3.Allegro
　　Solo Pno.-3*,2,2,2-4,2-Timp.,Perc.-Str.
　　G. Ricordi, Milan, ᶜ1934
　　Score 31 p. Large folio
　　Composed 1934. First performance Rome, 3
　　April 1935.

2205 Dalle tre commedie Goldoniane　　　　　25'
　　1.La Bottega da Caffé 2.Sior Todero Brontolon
　　3.Le Baruffe Chiozzotte
　　3(3rd alt. Picc.),3*,3*,3*-4,3,3,1-Timp.,Perc.-
　　Cel.,Hp.-Str.
　　Ricordi, Milan, ᶜ1923
　　Score 114 p.
　　From the operatic trilogy based on plays of
　　Goldoni. Composed 1919-21.

2363 L'esilio dell'eroe [The hero's　　　　15'
　　exile]
　　1.Andante 2.Allegro 3.Lento 4.Allegro, ben
　　ritmato 5.Maestoso
　　3(3rd alt. Picc.),3*,3*,3*-4,3,3,1-Timp.,Perc.
　　-Cel.,Hp.-Str.
　　Universal Edition, Vienna, ᶜ1927
　　Score 57 p.
　　Original title Sul Fiume del Tempo. Com-
　　posed 1926. First performance Philadelphia, 1
　　April 1927, Philadelphia Orchestra, Leopold
　　Stokowski conductor.

3982 Fanfare for an ominous declaration
　　0,0,0,0-1,2,1-B.Dr.-Str.
　　Ms.
　　Score 7 p.
　　First performance Hollywood, 23 July 1933,
　　Nicolas Slonimsky conductor.

2523 Il finto Arlecchino, symphonic fragments
　　1.Allegro 2.Largo 3.Allegro 4.Andante
　　2(2nd alt. Picc.),2,2,2-2,2-Timp.,Perc.-Cel.,
　　Hp.-Str.
　　Ms.

Malipiero, Gian Francesco

Score 45 p.
From the opera composed 1927 as part of the trilogy Il Mistero di Venezia.

458 Impressioni dal vero [of nature]   12'
1ª parte
1.[Tom-tit] 2.[Woodpecker] 3.[Eagle owl]
3(3rd alt. Picc.),3*,3*,2-4,2,-Timp.,Perc.-
Hp.-Str.
Senart, Paris, c1918
Score 38 p.
Composed 1910-11. First performance Milan, 15 May 1913, Alexander Birnbaum conductor.

244 Impressioni dal vero [of nature]   25'
2ª parte
1.Colloquio di campane 2.I cipressi e il vento 3.[Rustic festival]
4*(3rd alt. 2nd Picc.),3*,3*,3*-4,3,3,1-Timp.,
Perc.-Cel.,Hp.-Str.
Chester, London, c1920
Score 68 p.
Composed 1914. First performance Rome, 11 March 1917, Antonio Guarnieri conductor.

1683 Impressioni dal vero [of nature]   8'
3ª parte
1.Festa in Val d'Inferno 2.[The cocks]
3.La tarantella a Capri
3(3rd alt. Picc.),3*,3*,3*-4,3,3,1-Timp.,Perc.
-Cel.,Hp.-Str.
Universal Edition, Vienna, c1923
Score 31 p.
Composed 1921-22. First performance Amsterdam, 25 October 1923; performed Prague, 1923, Alfredo Casella conductor.

6039 Omaggio a Claude Debussy, piano. Transcribed for orchestra by Charles O'Connell
4*,3*,3*,4*-4,3,3,1-Timp.,Perc.-Cel.,2Hp.-Str.
Ms.
Score 7 p.
Originally composed 1920.

2393 Oriente immaginario   20'
1.Leggermente 2.Lento 3.Non troppo mosso
1(alt. Picc.),1,0,1-Perc.-Pno.,Cel.,Hp.-Str.
Chester, London, c1920
Score 27 p.
Composed 1920. First performance Paris, 23 December 1920.

2204 Per una favola cavalleresca [For a   30'
tale of chivalry, symphonic illustrations]
1.Calmo 2.Con molta gaiezza 3.Lento
4.Vivace
3(3rd alt. Picc.),3*,3*,3*-4,3,3,1-Timp.,
Perc.-Cel.,Hp.-Str.
Ricordi, Milan, c1921
Score 68 p.
Composed 1914. First performance Rome, 13 February 1921, Antonio Guarnieri conductor.

1271 Ricercari [for eleven instruments]   20'
1.Allegro 2.Andante 3.Allegro 4.Lento
5.Allegro
1(alt. Picc.),1,1,1-Hn.-4Va.,Vc.,Cb.
Score: Ms. 105 p.

Parts: Universal Edition, Vienna, c1925
Composed 1925. First performance Washington, 7 October 1926.

1677 Ritrovari [for eleven instruments]   18'
1.Allegro energico 2.Allegro mosso 3.Lento
e triste 4.Andante 5.Allegro vivace
1(alt. Picc.),1,1,1-Hn.-4Va.,Vc.,Cb.
Universal Edition, Vienna, c1928
Score 96 p.
Composed 1926. First performance Gardone, Italy, 26 October 1929.

Sinfonie del silenzio e della morte   20'
615 Part I. Danza tragica   8'
616 Part II. Sinfonia del silenzio   7'
617 Part III. Il molino della morte   5'
3(3rd alt. Picc.),3*,3*,3*-4,3,3,1-Timp.,Perc.
-Hp.-Str.
Rahter, Leipzig, 1910
Scores: 51 p., 29 p., 52 p.
Composed 1909. First performance Concerts Lamoureux, Paris 1917, Camille Chevillard conductor.

4833 [Symphony no. 1, In four tempi,   23'
like the four seasons]
1.Quasi andante 2.Allegro 3.Lento 4.Allegro
3*,3*,2,2-4,2,2,1-Timp.,Perc.-Cel.,Hp.-Str.
G. Ricordi, Milan, c1934
Score 50 p. Large folio
Composed 1933. First performance Florence, 2 April 1934.

3992 [Symphony no. 2, Elegiaca]   20'
1.Allegro 2.Lento 3.Mosso 4.Lento - Allegro
3*,2,2,2-4,3,3,1-Timp.,B.Dr.,Cym.-Hp.-Str.
Ricordi, Milan, c1936
Miniature score 53 p.
Composed 1936. First performance Seattle, 25 January 1937, Seattle Symphony Orchestra, Basil Cameron conductor.

634p Variazioni senza tema [7   18'
variations]
Solo Pno.-3(3rd alt. Picc.),3*,2,2-4,2-Timp.,
Perc.-Cel.,Hp.-Str.
Ricordi, Milan, c1924
Score 36 p.
Composed 1922. First performance Prague, 19 May 1925, Alfredo Casella conductor.

MALISZEWSKI, WITOLD.
          Mohylev-Podolsk, Poland 20 July 1873
          Warsaw 18 July 1939

638 Ouverture joyeuse, Op. 11   10'
3*,2,2,2-4,2,3,1-Timp.,Trgl.-Hp.-Str.
Belaieff, Leipzig, 1910
Score 62 p.
Composed 1909. First performance Odessa, 1910.

932 [Symphony no. 1, Op. 8, G minor]
1.Allegro sostenuto 2.Andante 3.Scherzo
4.Thème populaire [and variations]
3*,2,2,2-4,2,3,1-Timp.,Perc.-Str.
Belaieff, Leipzig, 1907
Score 123 p.

962 [Symphony no. 2, Op. 12, A major]
1.Allegro grazioso 2.Andante espressivo
3.Scherzo 4.Finale: Allegro con fuoco
3(3rd alt. Picc.),2,3,2-4,3,3,1-Timp.,S.Dr.,
Trgl.-Hp.-Str.
Belaieff, Leipzig, 1912
Score 145 p.

983 [Symphony no. 3, Op. 14, C minor]
1.Allegro non troppo 2.Adagio misterioso
3.Thème et (6) variations 4.Finale: Allegro
giocoso
3(3rd alt. Picc.),2,3,2-4,3,3,1-Timp.-Str.
Belaieff, Leipzig, 1912
Score 151 p.

MALLIA-PULVIRENTI, JOSIE.   b. Malta ?

3834 Espressionismo, poema sinfonico   12'
3(3rd alt. Picc.),3*,3*,3*-4,3,3,1-Timp.,Perc.
-Cel.,2Hp.-Str.
Chester, London, c1925
Score 51 p. Large folio
First performance Italy, November 1935.

MALLING, OTTO VALDEMAR.   Copenhagen 1 June 1848
                                 Copenhagen 5 October 1915

516p [Concerto, piano, Op. 43, C minor]
1.Allegro con fuoco 2.Notturno 3.Finale:
Presto
Solo Pno.-2,2,2,2-4,2-Timp.-Str.
W. Hansen, Copenhagen [n.d.]
Score 134 p.

MANASSE, OTTO.   ?Munich 10 June 1862

2143 [Introduction, variations and fugue   15'
on the chorale Jerusalem, Du Hochgebaute
Stadt]
3,3*,3*,3*-4,3,3,1-Timp.,Glock.-Org.(ad lib.)
-Str.
Ries & Erler, Berlin [n.d.]
Score 34 p.
Composed 1929. First performance Munich 1930.

MANCINELLI, LUIGI.   Orvieto, Italy 5 February 1848
                            Rome 2 February 1921

2203 Cleopatra, overtura [to Pietro   14'
Cossa's play]
3,2,2,2-4,4,3,1-Timp.,B.Dr.,Cym.-Hp.-Str.
Ricordi, Milan [1886?]
Miniature score 63 p.
*Composed 1875. First performance Rome, 25
November 1877.*

2202 [Venetian scenes, suite. No. 3,   4'
Flight of the lovers from Chioggia]
3(3rd alt. Picc.),3*,3*,3-4,3,3,1-Timp.,Perc.-
Hp.-Str.
Ricordi, Milan, c1922
Miniature score 41 p.
Composed 1889. First performance Madrid 1890.

MANDL, RICHARD.   Prossnitz, Moravia 9 May 1859
                         Vienna 1 April 1918

1053s [Hymn to the rising sun]
Org.,2Hp.-Str.
F.E.C. Leuckart, Leipzig, c1912
Score 9 p.

MANÉN, JUAN (*or* JOAN DE).   Barcelona 14 March 1883

838v Anyoransa, caprice catalan no. 1,   8'
Op. 13
Solo Vn.-2,2,2,2-2,2-Timp.,Perc.-Str.
Simrock, Berlin, 1898
Score 22 p.
*Composed 1896; withdrawn. Revised version is
Op. A-14.*

782v Aplech, caprice catalan no. 2,   7'
Op. 20
Solo Vn.-2,2,2,2-2,2-Timp.,Trgl.-Str.
Simrock, Berlin, 1898
Score 31 p.
*Withdrawn from circulation at composer's
request; replaced by Catalog no. 807v.*

807v [Caprice, violin, no. 2, Op. A-15,
D minor]
Solo Vn.-2,2,2,2-2,2-Timp.,Trgl.-Str.
Universal Edition, Vienna, c1926
Score 67 p.
*Composed 1897 as Aplech, Caprice Catalan no. 2,
Op. 20. Rewritten 1923. First performance
Plauen, 1923, Werner conductor, the composer
as soloist.*

827v Chanson et étude, Op. A-8   12'
Solo Vn.-Str.
Universal Edition, Vienna, c1925
Score 26 p.
*Composed 1909. First performance Barcelona
1910, the composer as soloist.*

811v Concerto espagnol no. 1 [violin,   35'
Op. A-7, D major]
1.Allegretto ben moderato 2.Lamento
3.Allegro molto
Solo Vn.-2(2nd alt. Picc.),2(2nd alt. E.H.),
2,2-4,2-Timp.,Perc.-Cel.,Hp.-Str.
Universal Edition, Vienna, c1927
Score 136 p.
*Composed 1897 as Op. 18. Rewritten 1919.
First performance Copenhagen, 1921, Paul von
Klenau conductor, the composer as soloist.*

4585 Divertimento [small orchestra]   14'
Op. A-32
2,2,2,2-2Hn.-Timp.,Tamb.-Str.
Editions Max Eschig, Paris, c1937
Score 36 p.

839v Plaintes et joies, caprice catalan no. 3,
Op. 23
Solo Vn.-2,2,2,2-2,2,3-Timp.,Perc.-Str.
Simrock, Berlin, 1899
Score 35 p.
*Withdrawn from circulation at composer's
request.*

1003v Scherzo fantastique, Op. 28
Solo Vn.-2,2,2,2-2,2-Timp.-Str.

Manén, Juan

Zimmermann, Leipzig, ᶜ1900
Score 56 p.
*Withdrawn from circulation at composer's
request.*

796v Strophes d'amour, caprice catalan no. 4,
Op. 24
Solo Vn.-3*,2,2,2-2,2,3-Timp.,Perc.-Str.
Simrock, Berlin, 1899
Score 46 p.
*Withdrawn from circulation at composer's
request.*

720m Suite, violon et piano concertantes, Op. 22
1.Preludio 2.Scherzo 3.Catalana 4.Finale
Solo Pno., Solo Vn.-2,2,2,2-2,2,3-Timp.,Trgl.-
Str.
Simrock, Berlin, 1899
Score 98 p.
*Composed 1898. Withdrawn from circulation at
composer's request.*

MANFREDINI, FRANCESCO MARIA. Pistoia, Italy ca.1680
Pistoia 1748

80s [Christmas symphony, pastorale for the
Blessed Nativity, C major] Edited by Arnold
Schering
In one movement
2 Solo Vn.-Pno.(or Org. or Harm.)-Str.
Kahnt, Leipzig, ᶜ1904
Score 7 p.
First published 1718.

316m [Concerto, 2 trumpets, string   8'
orchestra, cembalo and organ, D major]
Edited by Alceo Toni
1.Allegro 2.Largo 3.Allegro
2 Solo Tpt.-Cemb.,Org.-Str.
Carisch, Milan, ᶜ1938
Score 26 p.
Composed 1711.

MANFREDINI, VINCENZO.
Pistoia, Italy 22 October 1737
St. Petersburg 16 August 1799

301p [Concerto, harpsichord and   15'
orchestra, B-flat major] Edited by Alceo Toni
1.Allegro 2.Grave 3.Allegro
Solo Hpscd.-2Ob.-2Hn.-Str.
Carisch, Milan, ᶜ1957
Score 46 p.
First published by Evans, London, ca.1790.

MANIGOLD, JULIUS.
Masmünster, Alsace 23 November 1873
Meiningen, Germany 20 January 1935

660m [Concerto, flute, Op. 6, D minor]   15'
1.Allegro 2.Andante con moto 3.Allegro
energico
Solo Fl.-2(2nd alt. Picc.),2,2,2-4,2-Timp.,
Trgl.-Hp.-Str.
Score: Ms. 80 p.
Parts: Zimmermann, Leipzig, ᶜ1911
*Composed 1909. First performance Meiningen
1910, the composer as soloist.*

MANN, GEORG MATTHIAS.
See: MONN, GEORG MATTHIAS.

MANN, JOHANN CHRISTOPH.
See: MONN, JOHANN CHRISTOPH.

MANN, JOHANN GOTTFRIED HENDRIK.
The Hague 15 July 1858
Oudewater bij den Bosch,
Holland 10 February 1904

789m [Concerto, clarinet, Op. 90, C minor]
1.Allegro energico 2.Intermezzo: Andante
tranquillo 3.Finale: Tempo di polacca
Solo Cl.-2,2,2,2-2,2-Timp.-Str.
Score: Ms. 86 p.
Parts: Rühle & Wendling, Leipzig [n.d.]

MANNES, LEOPOLD DAMROSCH. New York 26 December 1899
Martha's Vineyard,
Massachusetts 11 August 1964

2682 Suite for orchestra, Breve ma   8'
grave
1.Preludio 2.Arie 3.Epilogo
2,2,2,3*-4,2-Timp.-Str.
Ms.
Score 24 p.
*Withdrawn from circulation at composer's
request. Composed 1924-26. First performance Rochester, New York, 23 January 1928,
Rochester Philharmonic, Howard Hanson conductor. Mannes won the Pulitzer Traveling
Scholarship, 1925, for this and other works.*

MANNFRED, HEINRICH.   Posen, Poland 27 July 1866

1012s Belauscht [Eavesdropper, intermezzo]
Op. 45
Hp.(ad lib.)-Str.
Friedländer, Berlin [n.d.]
Score 5 p.

1198s Prima ballerina, intermezzo, Op. 66
Hp.(ad lib.)-Str.

Ulbrich, Berlin, ᶜ1905
Score 6 p.

MANNHEIMER, JULIUS.

1405 [Serenade no. 2, Op. 6, D minor]
1.Allegro vivace 2.Allegretto scherzando
3.Langsam 4.Finale: Allegro
2,2,2,2-2,2(optional)-Timp.-Str.
Simrock, Berlin, 1889
Score 46 p.

MANNS, FERDINAND.   Witzenhausen,
          near Kassel, Germany 27 August 1844
          Oldenburg, Germany 1922

836m [Concerto, clarinet, Op. 29, B-flat major]
1.Allegro 2.Romanze 3.Rondo
Solo Cl.-1,1,2,1-2,2,1-Timp.-Str.
Score: Ms. 80 p.
Parts: A.E. Fischer, Bremen [n.d.]

759m [Concerto, flute, Op. 32, G major]
1.Allegro moderato 2.Più moto - Lento
3.Rondo
Solo Fl.-1,1,2,1-2,2,1-Timp.-Str.
Score: Ms. 145 p.
Parts: [n.p., n.d.]

MANNS, OTTO, JR.

643s A northern cradle song, Op. 11
Str.
Score: Ms. 7 p.
Parts: Novello, London, ᶜ1904

MANSCHINGER, KURT.   Vienna(?) 25 July 1902
          New York City 23 February 1968

Also known under the pseudonym: Ashley Vernon

1069m Rhapsody for oboe and string   6'
orchestra
Solo Ob.-Str.
Ms.
Score 17 p.
Composed 1946, under pseudonym Ashley Vernon.

MARAIS, MARIN.   Paris 31 May 1656
          Paris 15 August 1728

448c [La folia, violoncello and string   7'
orchestra, D minor] Edited by Paul Bazelaire
Solo Vc.-Str.
A. Leduc, Paris, ᶜ1941
Score 12 p.

MARCELLO, ALESSANDRO.   Venice 24 August 1669
          Padua 19 June 1747

Pseudonym: Eterico Stinfalico

464m [Concerto, oboe and string   10-11'
orchestra, C minor] Edited by Ettore Bonelli
1.Allegro moderato 2.Adagio 3.Allegro
Solo Ob.(or Solo Vn.)-Str.
G. Zanibon, Padua, ᶜ1948
Score 12 p.
*Formerly attributed to Benedetto Marcello or
Antonio Vivaldi.*

618m [Same as above] Edited by Richard   14'
Lauschmann
1.Allegro moderato 2.Adagio 3.Allegro
Solo Ob.-Cemb. or Pno.-Str.
Forberg, Leipzig, ᶜ1924
Score in reduction 8 p.

MARCELLO, BENEDETTO.   Venice 1 August 1686
          Brescia 25 July 1739

867v [Concerto, violin, D major] Edited   8'
by Tivadar Nachèz
1.Allegro 2.Adagio 3.Allegro moderato
Solo Vn.-Str.
B. Schott's Söhne, Mainz, ᶜ1928
Score 28 p.

380v [Concerto grosso, cembalo and   15'
string orchestra, Op. 1 no. 4, F major]
Edited by Ettore Bonelli
1.Largo 2.Presto vivace 3.Adagio
4.Prestissimo
Cemb.(ad lib.)-Str.
G. Zanibon, Padua, ᶜ1937
Score 20 p.
First published by G. Sala, Venice, 1708.

2343s [Toccata, harpsichord, C minor]
Transcribed by Bernard Morgan
Str.
Ms. ᶜ1971 by Bernard Morgan
Score 7 p.
*This transcription 1938. First performance
Philadelphia, 16 November 1938, Philadelphia
Civic Symphony Orchestra, J. W. F. Leman con-
ductor.*

Marchena, Enrique de

1335s [Same as above] Transcribed in D minor
by Michele Esposito
Str.
Chester, London [n.d.]
Score 8 p.

MARCHENA, ENRIQUE DE.   Santo Domingo,
          Dominican Republic 13 October 1908

4160 Suite de imagenes, Op. 54
1.[Dawn] 2.[Scherzo of light] 3.[Twilight]
3(3rd alt. Picc.),2,3*,2-4,3,3,1-Timp.,Perc.-
Hp.-Str.
Ms. ᶜ1942 by Enrique de Marchena
Score 70 p.
*Inspired by native Dominican folklore. Com-
posed 1942. First performance Ciudad Tru-
jillo, Dominican Republic, 29 April 1942,
Orquesta Sinfonica Nacional.*

MARCHIONNE, L. C.
     See: DESORMES, LOUIS CÉSAR.

MARCHISIO, GIACOMO.

30s Babillage [Babbling] caprice, Op. 453 no. 2.
Arranged by Paul Körke
Str.
Bosworth, London, ᶜ1911
Score in reduction 4 p.

MAREK, CZESLAW. Przemysl, Poland 16 September 1891

1679 Sinfonia à la mémoire de Franz   30'
Schubert
Introduction - Allegro - Epilogue
3*,3*,5*(1Cl. in E-flat,3rd alt. B.Cl.II),4*-
4,4,4,1-Timp.,Perc.-Cel.,2Hp.-Str.
Universal Edition, Vienna, ᶜ1928
Score 110 p.
*Composed 1928 for the centennial of Schubert's
death. First performance Zurich, October 1928,
Volkmar Andreae conductor.*

MARET, STANLEY.   Joplin, Missouri 25 June 1926

6092 Symphony no. 1   14'
1.Allegro vivace 2.Adagio 3.Allegro vigoroso
2,2(2nd alt. E.H.),2,2-2,3,2-Timp.,Perc.-Str.
Ms.
Score 89 p. Large folio
Composed 1956.

MARIE, GABRIEL.   Paris 8 January 1852
          Puigcerdá, Spain 29 August 1928

774v Berceuse
Solo Vn.-2,1,2,2-2Hn.-Str.
Enoch, Paris [n.d.]
Score 11 p.

1630s Doux sommeil, berceuse [Sweet slumber]
Str.
Margueritat, Paris [n.d.]
Score 3 p.

1320 En rêve [Dreaming]
2,2*,2,2-4,1-Timp.-Hp.-Str.
Costallat, Paris [n.d.]
Score 20 p.

874v Impressions. No. 2, Insouciance
Solo Vn.-1,1,2,2-2Hn.-Str.
Schott Frères, Brussels [1894]
Score 31 p.
Originally composed for violin and piano.

875v Impressions. No. 6, Allégresse [Gaiety]
Solo Vn.-2,1,2,2-2,2-Timp.-Str.
Schott Frères, Brussels [1894]
Score 31 p.
Originally composed for violin and piano.

1292 Kléis, symphonic suite   20'
1.Prologue 2.Danse des jeunes-filles
3.Kléis abandonnée 4.Epilogue
2,2(1st alt. E.H.),2,2-4,2,3,1-Timp.,Perc.-2Hp.
-Str.
Rouart Lerolle, Paris, ᶜ1913
Score 40 p.
*From the incidental music to Emile Sicard's
play. Composed 1913.*

MARINUZZI, GINO, SR.   Palermo, Italy 24 March 1882
          Milan 17 August 1945

1086s Andantino all'antica   4'
Fl.-Hp.(or Pno.)-Str.
Ricordi, Milan [n.d.]
Score 9 p.
*First performance Palermo, 1905, Circolo
Artistico, G. Zuelli conductor.*

4237 Elegia, per orchestra   10'
3(3rd alt. Picc.),3*,3*,3*-4,8(4 offstage),3,
1-Timp.,Perc.-Cel.,2Hp.-Str.
Ricordi, Milan, ᶜ1922
Miniature score 35 p.
*Composed 1920 under the title: Elegia in
Morte di un Eroe. First performance Chicago,
December 1920.*

1916 Suite siciliana   34'
1.[Christmas story] 2.[The emigrant's song]
3.[Rustic waltz] 4.[Popular festival]
3(2nd&3rd alt. 2Picc.),3*,4*(1Cl. in E-flat),3-
4Sax.(SATB ad lib.)-4,5(2 backstage),2Cnt.,3,2-
Timp.,Perc.-Cel.,2Hp.-Women's Chorus(ad lib.)-Str.
Ricordi, Milan, ᶜ1910
Score 116 p.
*Composed 1907. First performance Palermo,
March 1909, the composer conducting.*

4759 [Symphony in A]   35'
1.[Overture] 2.Georgica 3.Ditirambo and
Finale
3(3rd alt. Picc.),3*,4*(1Cl. in D),3*-4,3,3,1
-Timp.,Perc.-Pno.,Cel.,2Hp.-Str.
Ricordi, Milan, ᶜ1943

Score 214 p.
First performance Bologna, 18 May 1943.

MARIOTTE, ANTOINE.   Avignon 22 December 1875
          Izieux, Loire, France 30 November 1944

826m En montagne [In the mountains]
Soli: Ob.,Ob. d'Amore,E.H.(or 2Vn.,Vc. or Ob.,
Cl.,Bn.)-Str.
Score: Ms. 23 p.
Parts: Enoch, Paris, ᶜ1923

MARKEVITCH, IGOR.   Kiev 27 July 1912

3809 Concerto grosso   16'
1.Allegro con brio 2.Andante 3.Allegro
vivace e leggiero
2*,1,2*,1-Sop. Sax.-2,2,3,1-Timp.,Perc.-Str.
B. Schott's Söhne, Mainz [n.d.]
Score 52 p.
*Composed 1929. First performance Paris, 8
December 1930, Orchestre Symphonique de Paris,
Roger Desormière conductor.*

6293 [Icarus] In one movement   20-25'
3*,3*,3(1Cl. in E-flat),3*-4,3,3,1-Timp.,Perc.
-Pno.,Cel.-Str.
Boosey & Hawkes, London, ᶜ1952
Score 85 p.
*Originally intended as a ballet. Composed
1932. First concert performance, Paris, 25
June 1933. Revised 1943.*

4680 [Rebus. Suite from the ballet]   24'
In one movement
2(2nd alt. Picc.),2,2(1Cl. in E-flat),2-4,2,3,
1-Timp.,Perc.-Str.
B. Schott's Söhne, Mainz [n.d.]
Score 119 p.
*Originally intended as a ballet for Serge
Diaghilev. Composed 1931. First concert per-
formance Paris, 15 December 1931, the com-
poser conducting.*

MARKI, EUGENE.   New York 1917

1755s Yankee Doodle, theme and 5   10'
variations, Op. 3
Str.
Pro-Art, New York, ᶜ1938
Score 11 p.
*Composed 1937. First performance New York, 7
February 1937, Mozart String Sinfonietta,
Wesley Sontag conductor.*

MAROS, MIKLÓS.   Pécs, Hungary 14 November 1943

7001 Mutazioni [for wind instruments]   8'
3(1 Alto Fl.),3(3rd alt. E.H.),3(3rd alt. Cl.
in E-flat & B.Cl.),3(3rd alt. C.Bn.)-4,4,3,2
Ms.
Score 24 p. Large folio
*Commissioned by Swedish Radio, 1971. Com-
posed 1971. First performance Stockholm, 29
January 1972, Swedish Radio Orchestra, Stig
Westerberg conductor.*

MAROS, RUDOLF.   Stachy, Hungary 19 January 1917

6469 Sinfonietta no. 1, for chamber   5-6'
orchestra
1.Allegro 2.Moderato 3.Vivace
2Recorders(or 2Fl.)-2Tpt.(optional)-Timp.
Perc.(all optional)-Str.(Cb. optional)
Southern, New York, ᶜ1948
Score 14 p.
Composed 1947.

MARSCHALK, MAX.   Berlin 7 April 1863
     Poberow-on-the-Ostsee, Germany 24 August 1940

1680 Serenade, Op. 30
1.Alla tarantella 2.Intermezzo 3.Alla
mazurka
2(2nd alt. Picc.),2,2,2-4,3,3,1-Timp.,Perc.-
Str.
Dreililien, Berlin, ᶜ1906
Score 72 p.

MARSCHNER, HEINRICH AUGUST.
          Zittau, Germany 16 August 1795
          Hanover 14 December 1861

4814 [Hans Heiling. Overture, Op. 80]   9'
2,2,2,2-4,2,3-Timp.-Str.
Friedrich Hofmeister, Leipzig [1852]
Score 60 p.
*From the opera in three acts, with libretto by
Eduard Devrient. Composed 1831-32. First
performance Berlin, 24 May 1833.*

MARTEAU, HENRI.   Rheims, France 31 March 1874
          Lichtenberg, Germany 3 October 1934

568c [Concerto, violoncello, Op. 7, B-flat
major]
1.Allegro moderato 2.Lento 3.Rondo
Solo Vc.-2(2nd alt. Picc.),2(2nd alt. E.H.),2,
2-4,2,3-Timp.,Perc.-Hp.-Str.
Simrock, Berlin, ᶜ1905
Score 95 p.

660v [Suite, violin and orchestra, Op. 15,
A major]
1.Preludio, attacca 2.Tema con 5 variazioni
3.Menuetto 4.Finale - Rondo
Solo Vn.-2(2nd alt. Picc.),2(2nd alt. E.H.),2,
2-4,2-Timp.-Str.
C.F.W. Siegel, Leipzig [n.d.]
Score 123 p.
Composed 1912.

MARTÍ-LLORCA, JOSÉ. Valencia, Spain 8 October 1903

459m Concertino para oboe y orquesta,   12'
Op. 11
1.Allegretto con spirito 2.Lento 3.Allegro
quasi presto
Solo Ob.-1,0,1,1-2Hn.-Trgl.,S.Dr.-Cel.-Str.
Ms.
Score 59 p. Large folio
*Composed 1956. First performance Córdoba,
Argentina, 30 November 1957, Orquesta Sinfón-
ica de Córdoba, Olgerts Bistevins conductor,
José Russo soloist.*

Martin, E.

MARTIN, E.

    800m [Concerto, horn, F major]
      1.Allegro moderato 2.Andante 3.Allegretto
      Solo Hn.-2,2,2,2-2,2,1-Timp.-Str.
      Score: Ms. 100 p.
      Parts: [n.p., n.d.]

MARTÍN, EDGARDO.   Cienfuegos, Cuba 6 October 1915

    6801 Danzón para orquesta   *4'30"*
      3*,3*,3*,3*-4,3,3,1-Timp.,Perc.-Hp.-Str.
      Ms.
      Score 28 p.
      Composed 1954.

    2192s [Fugues for string orchestra,   *9'30"*
      Op. 14]
      4 Fugues
      Str.
      Pan American Union, Washington, D.C., ^c1954
      by Edgardo Martín
      Score 22 p.
      Composed 1947. First performance Havana, 20
      June 1947, Orquesta de Cámara de La Habana,
      José Ardévol conductor.

MARTIN, FRANK.   Geneva 15 September 1890
        Naarden, the Netherlands 21 November 1974

    6860 [Between the Rhone and the Rhine (Offi-
      cial festival march of the Swiss National
      Guard 1939 Zurich) for band]
      E-flat Cnt.,2Fluegelhorn,3Tpt.,4Alto Hn.,
      2Ten.Hn.,Bar.,3Tbn.,E-flat Bass,B-flat Bass-
      S.Dr.,B.Dr.,Cym.
      Hug & Co., Zurich [n.d.]
      Score in reduction 7 p.
      Composed 1939.

    3861 Fox trot
      1,1,1,1-1,1,1-Pno.-Str.
      Ms.
      Score 32 p.
      First performance Boston, 20 December 1927,
      Chamber Orchestra of Boston, Nicolas Slonim-
      sky conductor.

    5279 Petite symphonie concertante pour   *22'*
      harpe, clavecin, piano et deux orchestres à
      cordes
      1.Adagio - Allegro con moto 2.Adagio - Alle-
      gretto alla marcia - Vivace
      Pno.,Cel.,Hpscd.-Str.(in 2 groups)
      Universal Edition, Vienna, ^c1947
      Score 132 p.
      Composed 1944-45. First performance Zurich,
      17 May 1946.

MARTIN, RICCARDO. pseudonym.
      Hopkinsville, Kentucky 18 November 1874
      New York 11 August 1952

    Real name: Hugh Whitfield Martin

    6949 [Night at the oasis, picturesque   *5'30"*
      scene]
      3*,3*,3*,3*-4,4,3,1-Timp.,Perc.-Cel.,2Hp.-Str.

Ms. ^c1940
Score 16 p.
Composed 1941.

MARTINON, JEAN.   Lyons 10 January 1910
      Paris 1 March 1976

    5513 Musique d'exil, mouvement   *13-14'*
      symphonique, Op. 31
      2(both alt. Picc.),2(2nd alt. E.H.),2,2-Alto
      Sax.,Ten.Sax.-4,2,1-Timp.,Perc.-Pno.,Cel.,Hp.
      -Str.
      Choudens, Paris, ^c1947
      Score 75 p.
      Composed 1941, while the composer was a pri-
      soner of war in Germany, under the title:
      Stalag 9, ou Musique d'Exil.

MARTINU, BOHUSLAV.
      Policka, Czechoslovakia 8 December 1890
      Liestal, Switzerland 28 August 1959

    2028s Double concerto for 2 string   *20-24'*
      orchestras, piano and timpani
      1.Poco allegro 2.Largo 3.Allegro
      Timp.-Pno.-Str.(in 2 groups)
      Boosey & Hawkes, London, ^c1946
      Score 68 p.
      Composed 1938. First performance Basel, 9
      February 1940, Basel Chamber Orchestra, Paul
      Sacher conductor.

    6337 Estampes [impressions] for large   *20'*
      orchestra
      1.Andante 2.Adagio 3.Poco allegro
      2(2nd alt. Picc.),2(2nd alt. E.H.),2,2-4,2,3-
      Timp.,Perc.-Pno.,Hp.-Str.
      Southern, New York, ^c1962
      Score 58 p.
      Commissioned by The Louisville Orchestra.
      Composed 1958. First performance Louisville,
      Kentucky, 5 February 1959, Louisville
      Orchestra, Robert Whitney conductor.

    5455 Serenade pour orchestre de chambre   *12'*
      1.Allegro 2.Andantino moderato 3.Allegretto
      4.Allegro
      1,2,1,2-2,2,1-Str.
      B. Schott's Söhne, Mainz, ^c1931
      Score 36 p.
      Composed 1930.

    4058 Symphony no. 1   *40'*
      1.Moderato 2.Allegro 3.Largo 4.Allegro non
      troppo
      3*,3*,3,3*-4,3,3,1-Timp.,Perc.-Pno.,Hp.-Str.
      Ms.
      Score 160 p. Large folio
      Commissioned by the Koussevitzky Music Founda-
      tion. Composed 1942. First performance Bos-
      ton, 13 November 1942, Boston Symphony Orches-
      tra, Serge Koussevitzky conductor.

    4062 Symphony no. 2   *30'*
      1.Allegro moderato 2.Andante moderato
      3.Poco allegro 4.Allegro
      3(3rd alt. Picc.),3,3,2-4,3,3,1-Timp.,Perc.-
      Pno.,Hp.-Str.

Ms.
Score 97 p. Large folio
*Composed 1943. First performance Cleveland,
28 October 1943, Cleveland Orchestra, Erich
Leinsdorf conductor.*

5076 Symphony no. 4   *30-34'*
1.Poco moderato 2.Allegro vivo 3.Largo
4.Poco allegro
4*,4*,3,2-4,3,3,1-Timp.,Perc.-Pno.-Str.
Boosey & Hawkes, London, ᶜ1950
Score 166 p.
*Commissioned by Helene and William Ziegler.
Composed 1945. First performance Philadelphia,
30 November 1945, Philadelphia Orchestra,
Eugene Ormandy conductor.*

5259 Symphony no. 5   *27'*
1.Adagio - Allegro - Adagio 2.Larghetto
3.Lento - Allegro
3*,3,3,3-4,2,3,1-Timp.,Perc.-Pno.-Str.
Boosey & Hawkes, London, ᶜ1950
Score 136 p.
*Composed 1946. First performance New York,
24 January 1948.*

4781 Toccata e due canzoni   *18'*
1*,2,1,1-0,1-Timp.,Perc.-Pno.-Str.
Ms.
Score 56 p. Large folio
*Composed 1946. First performance Basel,
Switzerland, 21 January 1947.*

4045 Tre ricercare   *12'*
1(alt. Picc.),2,0,2-2Tpt.-2Pno.-Str.(without
Va. or Cb.)
Universal Edition, London, ᶜ1939
Score 82 p.
*First performance International Music Fes-
tival, Venice, 1938.*

MARTUCCI, GIUSEPPE.   Capua, Italy 6 January 1856
                         Naples 1 June 1909

1462 Andante, Op. 69 no. 2   *10'*
2,3*,2,2-4,2,3-Timp.-Hp.-Str.
Kistner, Leipzig, ᶜ1907
Score 30 p.
*Originally no. 2 of 3 Pieces for violoncello
and piano. This version 1888. First performance Turin, 1889, the composer conducting.*

542p [Concerto, piano, Op. 66, B-flat   *30'*
minor]
1.Allegro giusto 2.Larghetto 3.Allegro con
spirito
Solo Pno.-3*,2,2,2-4,2,3,Ophicl.-Timp.,Trgl.-
Str.
Kistner, Leipzig [1886]
Score 129 p.
*First performance Paris, 1878, Anton Rubin-
stein conductor, Beniamino Cesi soloist.*

[Four small pieces]
2114 No. 1. Canzonetta   *2'*
2115 No. 2. Tempo di gavotta   *6'*
2116 No. 3. Giga   *5'*
1919 No. 4. Notturno   *6'*

2,2,2,2-2,2-Timp.,Trgl.-Hp.-Str.
Ricordi, Milan [n.d.]
Scores: 8 p., 18 p., 10 p., 14 p.
*Composed 1900. First performance Turin, 25
November 1901, Luigi Mancinelli conductor.*

1920 Novelletta, Op. 82   *5'*
2,2*,2,2-4,2-Timp.,Cym.-Hp.-Str.
Ricordi, Milan [n.d.]
Score 22 p.
*Composed 1907. First performance Milan, 30
April 1908, the composer conducting.*

1035 [Symphony no. 1, Op. 75, D minor]   *27'*
1.Allegro 2.Andante 3.Allegretto 4.Mosso
3*,2,2,3*-4,2,3,1-Timp.-Str.
Kistner, Leipzig [1896]
Score 143 p.
*Composed 1895. First performance Turin 1896,
the composer conducting.*

812p [Theme and variations, Op. 58.   *15'*
Transcribed for piano and orchestra by Giu-
seppe Piccioli]
Solo Pno.-2(2nd alt. Picc.),2,2,2-2,2-Timp.-
Str.
G. Ricordi, Milan, ᶜ1940
Score 50 p.
*Originally composed for piano solo. This
transcription first performed Paris, 20
February 1938.*

MARTY, GEORGES-EUGÈNE.   Paris 16 May 1860
                              Paris 11 October 1908

731m Fantaisie no. 1. Orchestrated by Theodore
Dubois
Solo Cl.-2,2-2Hn.-Timp.-Str.
Score: Ms. 18 p.
Parts: Evette & Schaeffer, Paris [n.d.]
*Composed 1897 for clarinet and piano, for the
Concours du Conservatoire de Paris.*

MARVEL, ROBERT.   Webster City, Iowa 1918

3368 Sinfonietta. Movement no. 1,   *4'30"*
Allegro vivo
3*,3*,2,2-4,2,3,1-Timp.,Perc.-Pno.,Hp.-Str.
Ms.
Score 42 p.
*Composed 1940. First performance Rochester,
New York, 17 April 1940, Rochester Civic
Orchestra, Howard Hanson conductor.*

MARX, BURLE.   São Paulo, Brazil 23 July 1902

6825 Hallowe'en, a reveler's pageant   *15'*
in form of a passacaglia and fugue
3(2nd & 3rd alt. Picc.),3*,3*,3*-Alto Sax.-4,
3,3,1-Timp.,Perc.-Pno.(alt. Cel.),Hp.-Electric
Guit.(ad lib.)-Str.
Ms. ᶜ1967 by Burle Marx
Score 79 p. Large folio
*A symphonic homage to UNICEF. From the child-
ren's operetta, The Witch-Kids, composed 1963.
This version 1967.*

Marx, Burle

7109 Musica festiva, or Festive music   *7-8'*
3*,2,2,2-4,2,3-Timp.,Perc.-Str.
Ms. ^C1970 by Burle Marx
Score 39 p. Large folio
*Composed 1970. Original title Music for
Orchestra, conceived as the 3rd movement of
Symphony no. 4. This version first performed
in Porto Alegre, Brazil, 22 April 1975, Sym-
ph⌐ ⊣ Orchestra of Porto Alegre, John
Nⁱchling conductor.*

6345 [Symphony no. 3, Impressions of   *30'*
macúmba]
1.[Black magic - Waltz of the spirits]
2.[White magic]
3(3rd alt. Picc.),3*,4*(1Cl. in E-flat),3*-
Alto Sax.-4,4,3,1-Timp.,Perc.-Pno.(alt. Cel.),
2Hp.-Str.
Ms.
Score 128 p. Large folio
*Originally titled Sinfonia da Macúmba (Bra-
zilian voodoo). Composed 1954-56. First performance Rio de Janeiro, 30 June 1956, Orchestra Municipal, the composer conducting.*

7038 [Symphony no. 4 for chamber   *50'*
orchestra]
1.Allegro 2.Andante 3.Scherzo 4.Fuga
1(alt. Picc.),2Recorders(alt. SATB),1,1,1-2,1-
Timp.,Perc.-Hpscd.(alt. Cel.)-Str.
Ms. ^C1973 by Burle Marx
Score 121 p. Large folio
*Composed 1968-73. Selected for performance by
the Orchestra Society of Philadelphia as part
of its Pennsylvania Composers Project 1975,
made possible by a grant from the Pennsylvania
Council on the Arts with performance materials
prepared by the Fleisher Collection of Orches-
tral Music. First performance (of Allegro,
Andante, and Fugue) at Mandell Theater, Drexel
University, Philadelphia, 9 March 1975,
Orchestra Society of Philadelphia, Sidney
Rothstein conductor.*

MARX, JOSEPH.   Graz, Austria 11 May 1882
                   Graz 3 September 1964

616p Romantisches Klavierkonzert [E major] *40'*
1.Lebhaft 2.Nicht zu langsam 3.Sehr lebhaft
Solo Pno.-3(3rd alt. Picc.),2,2,2-4,2,3,1-
Timp.,Perc.-Str.
Universal Edition, Vienna, ^C1921
Score 159 p.
*Composed 1919. First performance Vienna,
December 1920, Ferdinand Löwe conductor.*

MARX, KARL.   Munich 12 November 1897

1201v [Concerto, viola, Op. 10, C minor] *30'*
1.Allegro moderato 2.Adagio (alla breve)
3.Allegro non troppo
Solo Va.-2(2nd alt. Picc.),2,2,2-2,2,2-Timp.,
Perc.-Str.
Bote & Bock, Berlin, ^C1930
Score 62 p.

MASCAGNI, PIETRO.   Leghorn, Italy 7 December 1863
                       Rome 2 August 1945

6835 Cavalleria rusticana. Intermezzo   *3'*
sinfonico
1*,1,2,2-Hn.-Org.,Hp.-Str.(Cb. ad lib.)
Kalmus, New York [n.d.]
Score 6 p.
*From the opera based on the play by Giovanni
Verga. First performance Rome, 17 May 1890.
Awarded first prize in the Sonzongo competi-
tion, 1889.*

4437 Cavalleria rusticana. Vorspiel *und*
Siciliana
3*,2,2,2-4,2,3,1-Timp.,Perc.-Hp.-Str.
Bote & Bock, Berlin [1893]
Score 19 p.

1188s [Gavotte of the dolls]   *2'30"*
Str.
Ricordi, Milan, ^C1903
Score in reduction 5 p.

MASCHERA, FIORENZO.   Brescia, Italy ca.1540
                         Brescia 1580 or 1584

Also spelled: Florentio Mascara

950s Canzone. Edited by Gustav   *2'*
Lenzewski, Sr.
Str.
Chr. Friedrich Vieweg, Berlin [n.d.]
Score 5 p.

MASETTI, ENZO.   Bologna 19 August 1893
                    Rome 11 February 1961

4244 [Contrasts, for orchestra]   *7'*
1.[Pierrot's night] 2.[Nénette and Rintintin]
3*,3*,3*,3*-4,3,3,1-Timp.,Perc.-Pno.,Cel.,2Hp.
-Str.
Ricordi, Milan, ^C1927
Miniature score 29 p.
*Pierrot is a stock character from the French
Comédie Italienne. Composed 1923. First per-
formance Rome, 15 March 1924.*

MASON, DANIEL GREGORY.
        Brookline, Massachusetts 20 November 1873
        Greenwich, Connecticut 4 December 1953

1995 Chanticleer, festival overture,   *11'*
Op. 27
3(3rd alt. Picc.),3*,3*,3*-4,3,3,1-Timp.,Perc.
-Hp.-Str.
Birchard, Boston, ^C1929 by The Juilliard
Musical Foundation
Score 78 p.
*First performance Cincinnati, 23 November 1928,
Fritz Reiner conductor.*

688p Prelude and fugue, Op. 20 [revised]   *14'*
Solo Pno.-3(3rd alt. Picc.),3*,3*,3*-4,3,3,1-

Timp.,Perc.-Hp.-Str.
Ms. c1933 by J. Fischer, New York
Score 63 p.
*Composed 1919-20. First performance Chicago,
4 March 1921, Frederick Stock conductor, John
Powell soloist.*

2888 Scherzo-caprice, Op. 14a   6'30"
1(alt. Picc.),1,2,1-Hn.-Pno.-Str.(Cb. ad lib.)
Ms.
Score 27 p.
*Originally the second movement of Sonata for
Clarinet and Piano, Op. 14. Composed 1912-15;
orchestrated 1915. First performance New
York, 2 January 1917, New York Chamber Music
Society, Carolyn Beebe conductor.*

1681 [Symphony no. 1, Op. 11, C minor]   38'
1.Largo sostenuto - Allegro moderato 2.Lar-
ghetto tranquillo 3.Allegro molto marcato
3(3rd alt. Picc.),3*,3*,3-4,3,3,1-Timp.,Perc.-
Hp.-Str.
Universal Edition, Vienna, c1926
Score 136 p.
*Composed 1913-14; revised 1922. First per-
formance New York, 1 December 1922, New York
Philharmonic, Josef Stransky conductor.*

3096 [Symphony no. 2, Op. 30, A major]   30'
1.Allegro un poco maestoso 2.Andante sostenuto 3.Vivace scherzando 4.Lento - Allegro
maestoso
3(3rd alt. Picc.),3*,3*,3*-4,3,3,1-Timp.,Perc.
-Cel.,Hp.-Str.
Ms.
Score 190 p.
*Composed 1928-30. First performance Cincin-
nati, 7 November 1930, Cincinnati Symphony
Orchestra, Fritz Reiner conductor.*

2885 [Symphony no. 3, Lincoln, Op. 35, in   30'
B-flat]
1.The candidate from Springfield (The young
Lincoln) 2.Massa Linkum 3.Old Abe's yarns
4.1865
3(3rd alt. Picc.),3*,3*,3*(C.Bn. ad lib.)-4,3,
3,1-Timp.,Perc.-Hp.-Str.
Ms.
Score 127 p.
*Composed 1935-36. First performance New York,
17 November 1937, New York Philharmonic, John
Barbirolli conductor.*

MASSA, JUAN BAUTISTA. Buenos Aires 29 October 1885
                        Rosario, Argentina 7 March 1938

3384 La muerte del Inca, poema sinfónico
3(3rd alt. Picc.),3*,3*,4*-4,0,3Cnt.,3,1-
Timp.,Perc.-Cel.,Hp.-Str.
Ricordi, Buenos Aires, c1939
Score 40 p.
*Composed 1932. First performance Buenos Aires,
15 October 1932, Colon Theatre Orchestra, the
composer conducting.*

3385 Primera suite argentina
1.Aire de Pericón 2.Tonada 3.Aire de gato
3*,3*,3*,4*-4,0,3Cnt.,3,1-Timp.,Perc.-Cel.,

Hp.-Str.
Ricordi, Buenos Aires [n.d.]
Score 40 p.
Composed 1929.

MASSARANI, RENZO.   Mantua, Italy 26 March 1898
                      Rio de Janeiro, Brazil 28 March 1975

4223 [Trumpet calls and dances for the   6'
play 18 BL]
3*,2,2,2-4,3,3,1-Timp.,Perc.-Str.
Ricordi, Milan, c1936
Miniature score 25 p.
*Composed as incidental music to the play 18 BL,
the Italian military lorry. First performance
Florence, 1934.*

MASSENET, JULES-ÉMILE FRÉDÉRIC.
                   Montaud, France 12 May 1842
                   Paris 13 August 1912

1304 Brumaire, ouverture pour le drame   12'
d'Edouard Noël
3*,3*,3(1Cl. in E-flat),3*-Cb.Sax.-4,3,3,1-
Timp.,Perc.-Org.(optional),Hp.-Str.
Heugel, Paris, c1900
Score 75 p.
Composed and first performed Paris 1899.

63 [Le Cid. Ballet music, 7 dances]   16'
2(2nd alt. Picc.),2(1st alt. E.H.),2,2-4,2,
2Cnt.,3,1-Timp.,Perc.-Hp.-Str.
Kalmus, New York [n.d.]
Score 249 p.
*From the opera composed 1884. First perform-
ance Paris, 30 November 1885.*

193 [Le Cid. Act III, Moorish rhapsody]
2*,2,2,2-4,2,2Cnt.,3,1-Timp.,Perc.-Hp.-Str.
Hartmann, Paris [n.d.]
Score 23 p.

1374 [Cigale. Suite from the ballet]   14'
Tr.: The grasshopper
1.[Waltz - Whirlwinds] 2.Cantabile 3.Variations
4.[Old-fashioned Christmas] - Dance of the grass-
hoppers]
3*,3*,2,2-4,3,3,1-Timp.,Perc.-Cel.,Hp.-Str.
Heugel, Paris, c1904
Score 81 p.
*Composed 1903. First performance Paris, 4
February 1904.*

554p [Concerto, piano, E-flat major]
1.Andante moderato - Allegro non troppo
2.Largo 3.Airs slovaques
Solo Pno.-3*,2,2,2-4,2,3-Timp.,Perc.-Cel.-Str.
Heugel, Paris, c1903
Score 172 p.
*Composed 1903. First performance Paris 8 Feb-
ruary 1903, Louis Diémer soloist.*

1447s Crépuscule [Twilight]   2'30"
Soli: Fl.,Vn.,Vc.-Str.
Heugel, Paris [n.d.]
Score 3 p.

Massenet, Jules

65s [Don César de Bazan. Berceuse, for   *5'*
strings]
Str.
Heugel, Paris, ^c1899
Score 5 p.
*Transcribed from the comic opera composed
1872. First performance Paris, 30 November
1872.*

4267 [Don César de Bazan. Sevillana   *2'30"*
entr'acte]
2(2nd alt. Picc.),2,2,2-4,0,2Cnt.,3-Timp.,
Perc.-Str.
G. Hartmann, Paris [1872?]
Score 12 p.

216 [Les Érinnyes, tragédie antique]   *20'*
1.Prélude 2.Scène religieuse 3.Entr'acte
4.Divertissement
2(2nd alt. Picc.),2,2,2-4,2,2Cnt.,3,Saxtuba-
Timp.,Perc.-Hp.-Str.
Heugel, Paris [n.d.]
Score 122 p.
*From the incidental music to Charles Leconte
de Lisle's tragedy. Composed 1871.*

1099 Esclarmonde, suite   *16'*
3(3rd alt. Picc.),3*,3*,2,Sarrus. or C.Bn.-
4,3,3,1-Timp.,Perc.-Org.,Hp.-Str.
Heugel, Paris [n.d.]
Score 135 p.
*From the opera composed 1888. First perform-
ance Paris, 14 May 1889.*

1212 [Espada. Suite from the ballet]   *12'*
1.Allegro - Madrilena 2.Panaderos 3.Boléro
4.Toréador et Andalouse 5.La danse de la
Mercédès
3*,2(2nd alt. E.H.),2,2-4,3,3,1-Timp.,Perc.-
Hp.-Str.
Heugel, Paris, ^c1908
Score 170 p.
*Composed 1907. First performance Monte Carlo,
15 February 1908.*

722s [Eve. Prelude] Transcribed for string   *4'*
orchestra by Guido Papini. Edited by Colin
MacLeod Campbell
Solo Vn.-Str.
J. Williams, London, ^c1925
Score 7 p.
From the sacred drama composed 1875.

553c Fantaisie
Solo Vc.-2,2,2,2-4,2,3-Timp.,Perc.-Str.
Heugel, Paris, ^c1897
Score 72 p.
Composed 1897.

4373 [Hérodiade. Act I: Promenade of the
slaves. Transcribed for chamber orchestra by
Andrew Luck]
1,1,1,1-1,1,1-Perc.-Hp.-Str.
Ms.
Score 8 p.
*From the opera based on a story by Gustave
Flaubert. Composed 1880. First performance
Brussels, 19 December 1881.*

183 [Hérodiade. Prelude to Act III]   *2'*
0,1,2,2-4,0,0,1-Timp.-Hp.-Str.
Heugel, Paris [n.d.]
Score 5 p.

1235 [Hérodiade. Act IV: Ballet music,   *9'*
5 dances]
3*(2nd alt. Picc.II),2,3(1Cl. in E-flat),2-
3Sax.-4,2,2Cnt.,4,1-Timp.,Perc.-Hp.-Str.
[Heugel, Paris, n.d.]
Score 41 p.

4376 [Hérodiade. Act IV: Ballet music. No. 5
Egyptian dance. Transcribed for chamber
orchestra by Andrew Luck]
1,1,1,1-2,1,1-Perc.-Hp.-Str.
Ms.
Score 7 p.

6993 Le jongleur de Notre-Dame. Acte III:
Pastorale mystique
2,3*,3,2-4Hn.-Timp.-Hp.-Str.
Heugel, Paris [n.d.]
Score 17 p.
*From the opera in three acts with libretto by
Maurice Léna. First performance Monte Carlo,
18 February 1902.*

Kassya
   See: DELIBES, LÉO
       [Kassya...]

5606 [Manon. Minuet, entr'acte, Acts II and III]
Cl.,Bn.(or Va. ad lib.)-Str.
Adolph Fürstner, Berlin [n.d.]
Score 3 p.
*From the opera based on the novel by Antoine
François Prévost. Composed 1882-83. First
performance Paris, 19 January 1884.*

7000 Marche héroique de Szabadi
4*(2Picc.),2,2,4-9Sax.(1Cb.Sax.)-4,4Cnt.,4,1-
Timp.(2 players),Perc.-4Hp.-Str.
G. Hartmann, Paris [n.d.]
Score 27 p.
*Composed 1879. First performance Paris, 1879,
Grand Festival de l'Opéra for the benefit of
the flood victims of Szeged, Hungary.*

156 [Phèdre. Overture to Racine's play]   *10'*
3*,2,2,2-4,2,2Cnt.,3,1-Timp.-Str.
Kalmus, New York [n.d.]
Score 54 p.
*From the incidental music to the tragedy, com-
posed 1875.*

1513 [Le roi de Lahore. Overture]   *5'*
2(2nd alt. Picc.),2,2,2-4,2,2Cnt.,3,Saxtuba-
Timp.,Perc.-Hp.-Str.
Heugel, Paris [n.d.]
Score 31 p.
*From the opera composed 1876. First perform-
ance Paris, 27 April 1877.*

1354 [The romance of Harlequin,   *9'*
pantomime]
2(2nd alt. Picc.),2,2,2-2,2-Timp.,Trgl.-Str.
Heugel, Paris [n.d.]

Score 43 p.
Originally composed for piano, 1870. First performance of orchestral version, Paris, 1875.

1259 [Rome. Overture]   *7'*
3*,3*,3,2-4,3,3,1,Sarrus.-Timp.,Perc.-2Hp.-Str.
Heugel, Paris, ᶜ1912
Score 58 p.
From the opera based on Alexandre Parodi's drama Rome Vainque. Composed 1911. First performance Monte Carlo, 17 February 1912.

1260 [Rome. Act III: The sacred grove]   *3'*
Fl.-Hn.-Timp.-2Hp.-Str.
Heugel, Paris [n.d.]
Score 185 p.

1335 Les Rosati, divertissement   *5'*
3*,2,2,2-4,2,3,1-Timp.,Perc.-Cel.,Hp.-Str.
Heugel, Paris, ᶜ1902
Score 67 p.
Composed and first performed Paris 1902.

255 Scènes pittoresques, suite no. 4   *25'*
1.Marche 2.Air de ballet 3.Angelus 4.Fête bohême
2(2nd alt. Picc.),2,2,2-4,4,3-Timp.,Perc.-Str.
B. Schott's Söhne, Mainz [n.d.]
Score 91 p.
Composed 1875. First performance Paris, 1876.

6275 [Spanish saraband from the 16th century. Transcribed for chamber orchestra by Jules Massenet]
1,1,0,1-2Tpt.-Tamb.-Str.
Heugel, Paris [n.d.]
Score 7 p.

207 [Suite no. 1, Op. 13]   *22'*
1.Pastorale et fugue 2.Variations 3.Nocturne 4.Marche et strette
3*,2,2,2-4,2,2Cnt.,3,1Saxtuba-Timp.,Perc.-Hp.-Str.
Durand, Paris [n.d.]
Score 108 p.
Composed 1866. First performance Paris, 24 March 1867, Concerts Pasdeloup.

290 [Suite no. 2, Scènes hongroises]   *25'*
1.Entrée en forme de danse 2.Intermède 3.Adieux à la fiancée 4.Cortège - Bénédiction nuptiale, etc.
3*,2,2,4(or 2)-4,2,2Cnt.,3,Saxtuba-Timp.,Perc.-Hp.-Str.
Heugel, Paris [n.d.]
Score 96 p.
Composed 1870. First performance Paris, 26 November 1871.

1180 [Suite no. 3, Scènes dramatiques]   *17'*
1.Prélude et divertissement (La Tempête) 2.Mélodrame (Othello) 3.Scène finale (Macbeth)
3*,2,2,4(or 2)-4,4,3,1-Timp.,Perc.-2Hp.-Str.
Hartmann, Paris [n.d.]
Score 108 p.
Composed 1873. First performance Paris, 1873.

417 [Suite no. 5, Scènes napolitaines]   *10'*
1.La danse 2.La procession et l'improvisateur 3.La fête
2(2nd alt. Picc.),2,2,2-4,0,3Cnt.,3,1Saxtuba-Timp.,Perc.-Str.
Heugel, Paris [n.d.]
Score 93 p.
Composed 1876.

1155 [Suite no. 6, Scènes de féerie]   *16'*
1.Cortège 2.Ballet 3.Apparition 4.Bacchanale
3*(3rd alt. Picc.II),2,3(1Cl. in E-flat),4-Alto Sax.-4,2,2Cnt.,4,1-Timp.,Perc.-Hp.-Str.
Heugel, Paris [n.d.]
Score 124 p.
Composed and first performed Paris 1879.

414 [Suite no. 7, Scènes alsaciennes,   *16'*
souvenirs]
1.[Sunday morning] 2.[In the tavern] 3.[Under the linden trees] 4.[Sunday evening]
2(2nd alt. Picc.),2,2,2-4,2(backstage),2Cnt.,3,1-Timp.,Perc.-Str.
Heugel, Paris [n.d.]
Score 122 p.
Composed 1881. First performance Paris 1882.

435v [Thaïs. Act II: Méditation]   *4'*
Solo Vn.-2,2*,2*,2*-4Hn.-Hp.-Chorus-Str.
Heugel, Paris, ᶜ1894
Score 13 p.
From the opera first performed Paris, 16 March 1894.

5539 Valse très lente
Fl.,Ob.,Cl.,Bn.-Str.
Heugel, Paris, ᶜ1901
Score 11 p.

76s [The Virgin. The last dream of the   *4'*
Virgin, prelude to Scene IV]
Solo Vc.-Str.
Heugel, Paris [n.d.]
Score 3 p.
From the oratorio composed 1880. First performance Paris, 22 May 1880.

MASSONEAU, LOUIS. Kassel, Germany 10 January 1766
Ludwigslust, Germany 4 October 1848

4125 Sinfonie, Op. 3 no. 1 [E-flat major]
1.Grave e sostenuto - Vivace assai 2.Andante 3.Allegretto 4.Presto
0,2,0,2-2Hn.-Str.
Ms.
Score 66 p.

4126 Sinfonie, Op. 3 no. 2 [D major]
1.Grave - Vivace assai 2.Andante - Allegretto 3.Allegretto scherzando
0,2,0,1-2Hn.-Str.

Maszynski, Piotr

Ms.
Score 73 p.

MASZYNSKI, PIOTR.   Warsaw 3 July 1855
                                     Warsaw 1 August 1934

   1027s Petite berceuse
   Str.
   Leuckart, Leipzig [n.d.]
   Score 6 p.

MATA, JULIO.   Cartago, Costa Rica 1899

   3875 Suite abstracta
   1.Ira 2.Amor 3.Pesar 4.Júbilo
   2,2,2,2-2,0,2Cnt.,2-Timp.,Perc.-Pno.-Str.
   Ms.
   Score 65 p.
   *First performance San José, Costa Rica, 23
   May 1941, Orchestra of San José, the composer
   conducting.*

MATHÉ, EDOUARD.   Versailles 1863

   1307s Nicette
   Fl.-Str.
   Score: Ms. 5 p.
   Parts: Decourcelle, Nice, ᶜ1923

   567c Reproches   3'
   Solo Vc.-1,1,2,1-Hn.-Timp.-Str.
   Score: Ms. 20 p.
   Parts: Decourcelle, Nice, ᶜ1925
   *Composed 1924. First performance Dieppe,
   August 1925, Paul Vizentini conductor.*

   678m Sérénade romantique   5'
   Solo Cl.-0,1,2(2nd ad lib.),1-2Hn.-Timp.-Str.
   Score: Ms. 11 p.
   Parts: [Decourcelle, Nice, n.d.]
   Composed and first performed Nice, June 1913.

   672c Vers le soir [Towards evening]   3'
   rêverie
   Solo Vc.-1,1,2,1-1,2-Timp.-Hp.-Str.
   Score: Ms. 8 p.
   Parts: [Decourcelle, Nice, n.d.]
   *Composed 1924. First performance Dieppe,
   August 1925, Paul Vizentini conductor.*

MATHIAS, WILLIAM.
   b. Whitland, Carmarthenshire, South Wales 1934

   7092 Serenade for small orchestra, Op. 18   8'
   1.Allegretto 2.Lento, ma con moto 3.Allegro
   con slancio
   2,2,2,1(optional)-2,2,2-Timp.,Perc.(optional)-
   Hp.-Str.
   Oxford University Press, London, ᶜ1963
   Score 45 p.
   *Commissioned by the Carmarthenshire Education
   Authority. Composed 1961.*

MATHIEU, ÉMILE-LOUIS-VICTOR.
                Lille, France 16 October 1844
                Ghent, Belgium 20 August 1932

   775v [Concerto, violin, D minor]
   1.Arch-angels of combat 2.Deep waters,
   dreaming swans 3.Morning walk
   Solo Vn.-2(2nd alt. Picc.),2(2nd alt. E.H.),2,
   2-2,2,3-Timp.,Perc.-Str.
   Score: Ms. 157 p.
   Parts: Breitkopf & Härtel, Leipzig, ᶜ1897

MATON, AD.

   704m Romance
   Solo Hn.-1,1,1,1-Str.
   Score: Ms. 18 p.
   Parts: Evette & Schaeffer, Paris [n.d.]

MATTHAEI, HEINRICH AUGUST. Dresden 30 October 1781
                         Leipzig 4 November 1835

   1051v [Concerto, violin, no. 2, Op. 9, B-flat
   major]
   1.Allegro 2.Adagio 3.Rondo
   Solo Vn.-1,2,0,2-2,2,1-Timp.-Str.
   Score: Ms. 172 p.
   Parts: [n.p., n.d.]

   1039v [Concerto, violin, no. 4, Op. 20, E minor]
   1.Allegro 2.Andante grazioso 3.Rondo
   Solo Vn.-1,2,2,2-2,0,B.Tbn.-Timp.-Str.
   Score: Ms. 177 p.
   Parts: [n.p., n.d.]

MATTHEY, JULIUS HERMANN.
        Weissenborn/Freiberg 27 November 1853
                   Leipzig 20 May 1923

   675c Concert-Stück [C minor]
   Solo Vc.-2,2,2,2-4,2,4-Timp.-Str.
   Score: Ms. 50 p.
   Parts: A.E. Fischer, Bremen [n.d.]

MAURER, LUDWIG WILHELM.   Potsdam 8 February 1789
                   St. Petersburg 6 November 1878

   362v [Concertante, 2 violins, Op. 56, F major]
   1.Allegro maestoso 2.Andante 3.Alla polacca
   2 Solo Vn.-1,2,2,2-2,2-Timp.-Str.
   Score: Ms. ᶜ1976 by The Fleisher Collection of
   Orchestral Music, Free Library of Philadelphia.
   122 p. Large folio
   Parts: Hofmeister, Leipzig [1830 or 31]

   1026v [Concertino, violin, no. 3, Op. 82,
   A minor]
   Concerto - Larghetto - Rondo
   Solo Vn.-1,2,2,2-2,2,3-Timp.-Str.
   Score: Ms. 88 p.
   Parts: Hofmeister, Leipzig [n.d.]

   900m [Concerto, clarinet, Op. 57, B-flat minor]
   1.Allegro moderato 2.Andante espressivo
   3.Allegretto vivo
   Solo Cl.-2,2,0,2-2,0,B.Tbn.-Timp.-Str.
   Score: Ms. 112 p.
   Parts: Hofmeister, Leipzig [n.d.]

1052v [Concerto, violin, no. 8, Op. 54,
F-sharp minor]
1.Allegro 2.Notturno 3.Alla polacca
Solo Vn.-1,0,2,2-2,2,1-Timp.-Str.
Score: Ms. 144 p.
Parts: Richault, Paris [n.d.]

MAURICE, ALPHONS.   Hamburg 14 April 1862
                            Dresden 27 January 1905

883v Sage [Legend] Op. 53
Solo Vn.-2,2,2,2,2-4,2-Timp.-Hp.-Str.
Eberle, Vienna [n.d.]
Score 19 p.

MAXWELL, CHARLES.   Leipzig 25 October 1892

6177 Congo spirituale, ballet for   18'
orchestra
3(3rd alt. Picc.),3*,3*,3*-4,3,3,1-Timp.,Perc.
-Hp.-Str.
Ms. [C1960 by Charles Maxwell]
Score 54 p. Large folio
*Suggested by Vachel Lindsay's poem The Congo.
Composed 1946 under the title Then I Had a
Vision, Toccata and Coda Religioso. First
performance Burbank, California, 2 March 1947,
Burbank Symphony Orchestra, Leo Damiani con-
ductor.*

6171 [Plymouth Rock overture]   8'30"-9'
2(2nd alt. Picc.),2,2,2-4,3,3,1-Timp.,Perc.-
Hp.-Str.
Ms. [C1960 by Charles Maxwell]
Score 55 p. Large folio
*Composed 1955. First performance Burbank,
California, 4 February 1956, Burbank Symphony
Orchestra, Leo Damiani conductor.*

6176 Punch and Judy overture   8-8'30"
2(2nd alt. Picc.),2,2,2-4,2,3,1-Timp.,Perc.-
Str.
Ms. [C1960 by Charles Maxwell]
Score 43 p. Large folio
*Composed 1959. First performance Redondo,
California, 7 October 1960, Beach Cities Sym-
phony, Louis Palange conductor.*

6175 [Stephen Foster overture]   8'30"
2(both alt. Picc.),2,2,2-4,3,3,1-Timp.,Perc.-
Hp.-Str.
Ms. [C1957 by Charles Maxwell]
Score 47 p. Large folio
*Quotes songs by Foster. Commissioned by the
Burbank Symphony. Composed 1956. First per-
formance Burbank, California, 26 August 1956,
Burbank Symphony, Leo Damiani conductor.*

MAYER, CHARLES.   Königsberg, Prussia
            (now Kaliningrad, USSR) 21 March 1799
                            Dresden 2 July 1862

686p [Concerto symphonique, piano, Op. 89,
D major]
1.Allegro 2.Andante quasi allegretto
3.Allegro
Solo Pno.-2,2,2,2-2,2,3-Timp.-Str.
Score: Ms. 194 p.
Parts: Richault, Paris [n.d.]

MAYER, WILLIAM.   New York 18 November 1925

2198s Andante for strings   6'
Str.
Ms.
Score 6 p.
*Originally composed as the slow movement of
the composer's String Quartet no. 1, 1952.
Transcribed 1956. First performance Ameri-
can Music Festival, New York, January 1958,
Mannes College Orchestra, Maurice Peress con-
ductor.*

367m Concert piece for trumpet and   9'
string orchestra
Solo Tpt.-Timp.,Perc.-Str.
Ms.
Score 48 p.
*Composed 1955. First performance New York, 21
January 1957, Little Orchestra Society, Thomas
Scherman conductor, Robert Nagel soloist.*

6164 Essay for brass and winds   11'
1,1,1,1-2,2,1,1-Timp.,S.Dr.
Ms. [C1961 by William Mayer]
Score 16 p. Large folio
*Commissioned by Robert Nagel's New York Brass
and Wind Ensemble. Composed 1953. First performance over WNYC at the American Music Festival, New York, February 1953, Mannes College
Orchestra, Franz Bibo conductor.*

6167 Hebraic portrait (in one movement) 11'30"
3(3rd alt. Picc.),3(3rd alt. E.H.),3(3rd alt.
B.Cl.),2-4,3,3,1-Timp.,Perc.-Pno.,Hp.-Str.
Ms.
Score 75 p. Large folio
*Composed 1955. First performance New York,
1958, Music in the Making Series, David
Broekman conductor.*

6201 Hello, world! (Around the world   25'
with music)
Voice Solo-2(2nd alt. Picc.),2(2nd alt. E.H.),
2(2nd alt. B.Cl.),2(2nd alt. C.Bn.)-3,2,2-
Timp.,Perc.-Pno.(alt. optional Cel.)-Dancers,
Audience participation-Str.
Ms. [Boosey & Hawkes, New York, C1956, 1957]
Score 200 p. Large folio
*Commissioned by the Little Orchestra Society.
Composed 1956. First performance New York,
10 November 1956, Little Orchestra Society,
Thomas Scherman conductor.*

6590 The snow queen, scenes from a suite   12'
[1964 version] based on the story by Hans
Christian Andersen
1.Abduction and escape 2.Reunion
3*,2(2nd alt. E.H.),2(2nd alt. B.Cl.),2(2nd
alt. optional C.Bn.)-4,3,3,1-Timp.,Perc.-Pno.,
Hp.(optional)-Str.
Ms.
Score 86 p. Large folio
*Commissioned by the Merry-Go-Rounders Ballet
Company. Originally composed as a full ballet,
scored for two pianos, 1963. These two move-
ments orchestrated 1964. First performance
New York World's Fair, 1 September 1964,*

Mayer, William

Ventnor Festival Orchestra, Russell Stanger conductor. Other movements later orchestrated but not included in this version.

6137 Two pastels for orchestra *11'*
3*,3*,3*,3*-4,3,3,1-Timp.,Perc.-Pno.(alt. Cel.),Hp.-Str.
Ms.
Score 74 p. Large folio
Suggested by two unidentified lines of poetry: "Fresh is the snow, and beautiful the footprints left there...", and "Of fireflies and a summer night..." Composed 1959. First performance New York, 12 February 1961, Orchestra of America, Richard Korn conductor.

MAYR, GIOVANNI SIMONE.
Mendorf, Bavaria 14 June 1763
Bergamo, Italy 2 December 1845

6368 Il segreto. Ouverture. Edited by Nino Negrotti
1,2,2,2-2,2-Timp.-Str.
Carisch, Milan, ᶜ1948
Score 14 p.
From the opera in one act. First performance Venice, 1797.

MC. *See MAC.*

MEDER, JOHANN GABRIEL (*or* JEAN G.).
Erfurt, Germany ca.1730
d. ca.1800

5608 Sinfonia in C. Edited by Thor Johnson and Donald McCorkle
1.Allegro con brio 2.Adagio 3.Rondo allegretto
0,2,0,1-2,2-Timp.-Org.-Str.
Ms.
Score 56 p. Large folio
First published probably as one of three symphonies comprising his Opus 3, 1782. This edition from a manuscript now owned by the Moravian Church. First modern performance at the Third Early American Moravian Music Festival and Seminar, Salem College, Winston-Salem, North Carolina, 22 June 1955, The Festival Orchestra, Thor Johnson conductor.

MEDTNER, NIKOLAI KARLOVICH.   Moscow 5 January 1880
London 13 November 1951

624p [Concerto, piano, no. 2, Op. 50, *38'*
C minor]
1.Toccata 2.Romanza 3.Divertimento
Solo Pno.-2,2,2,2-4,2,3,1-Timp.-Str.
Zimmermann, Leipzig [n.d.]
Score 242 p.

MEHLICH, ERNST.   Berlin 9 February 1888

38s Menuett, Op. 4 no. 1 [C major]
Str.
Reibenstein, Berlin, ᶜ1912
Score 5 p.

MÉHUL, ÉTIENNE-NICOLAS.
Givet, Ardennes 22 June 1763
Paris 18 October 1817

6577 [Bion. Overture]
2(2nd alt. Picc.),2,2,2-4,2,1-Str.
Ms. ᶜ1976 by The Fleisher Collection of Orchestral Music, Free Library of Philadelphia.
Score 62 p. Large folio
Edited from parts published by Pleyel, Paris, ca. 1804. From the opera in one act with libretto by François Benoît Hoffmann. First performance Paris, 27 December 1800.

4292 [Une folie. Overture]
2(2nd alt. Picc.),2,2,2-2Hn.-Str.
Ms.
Score 16 p. Large folio
From the opera in two acts with libretto by Jean Nicolas Bouilly. First performance Paris, 5 April 1802.

4252 [Héléna. Overture]
2Picc.,2,2,2-2,2-Timp.-Str.
Magazin de Musique de Cherubini, Méhul, Kreutzer, Rode, Isouard, et Boieldieu, Paris [ca.1803]
Score 27 p.
From the opera in three acts with libretto by Jean Nicolas Bouilly and Jacques Antoine Révéroni de Saint-Cyr. First performance Opéra-Comique, Paris, 1 March 1803.

3070 [Le jeune Henri. Overture, La chasse] *8'*
2,2,2,2-4Hn.-Timp.-Str.
Ms.
Score 94 p.
From the opera first performed Paris, 1 May 1797.

6971 [Joseph. Overture] *6'*
2,2,2,2-2,2-Timp.-Str.
Kalmus, New York [n.d.]
Score 11 p.
From the opera in three acts with libretto by Alexandre Duval. First performance Paris, 17 February 1807.

6172 Ouverture burlesque
Pno.-Vn.-3 Kazoos-Tpt.-Perc.
Durand, Paris [ca.1900]
Score 9 p.
Composed 1794.

7099 [Stratonice. Overture]
2,0,2,2-2,2(optional),1-Timp.-Str.
Ms. ᶜ1976 by The Fleisher Collection of Orchestral Music, Free Library of Philadelphia.
Score 42 p. [Parts first published by Cousineau, Paris, 1792]
From the opera in one act. Libretto by

*François Benoît Hoffman. First performance
Paris, 3 May 1792.*

4127 [Symphony no. 1, G minor]
1.Allegro 2.Andante 3.Menuetto 4.Allegro
agitato
2,2,2,2-2Hn.-Timp.-Str.
Ms.
Score 135 p.

7251 [Timoléon. Overture]
4*(2Picc.),2,2,2-2,2,3-Timp.-Str.
Score: Ms. ^C1977 by The Fleisher Collection
of Orchestral Music, Free Library of Phila-
delphia. 37 p. Large folio
Parts: N. Simrock, Bonn [ca.1833]
*From the incidental music to the tragedy by
Marie Joseph Chénier.*

6714 Le trésor supposé, ou Le danger   6'30"
d'écouter aux portes. Ouverture [The
imaginary treasure, or The danger of lis-
tening at doors. Overture]
2,2,2,2-2Hn.-Str.
Ms. ^C1976 by The Fleisher Collection of
Orchestral Music, Free Library of Philadelphia.
Score 21 p. Large folio
*From the opera in one act with libretto by
François Benoît Hoffman. First performance
Paris, 29 July 1802.*

MEINHARD, ADOLPHE.

731c [Concertino, violoncello, Op. 7, B minor]
1.Allegro moderato 2.Adagio 3.Valse assai
Solo Vc.-1,2,0,2-2Hn.-Str.
Score: Ms. 44 p.
Parts: Haslinger, Vienna [n.d.]

MEITUS, JULIUS SERGEIEVICH.   Elizabethgrad
       (now Kirovograd), Ukraine 28 January 1903

3235 [On the River Dnieper, suite no. 2]   27'
1.Andante 2.Andantino 3.Allegro 4.Allegro
energico
3(2nd & 3rd alt. Picc.),3*,3*,3*-4,6,4,1-Timp.,
Perc.-Pno.,Hp.-Str.
Mussektor, Moscow, 1935
Score 94 p.
Composed 1929-32.

MEJÍA, ESTANISLAO.   San Ildefonso Hueyotli,
          Tlaxcala, Mexico 13 November 1882
                          d. 15 June 1967

[Two Mexican pieces, from Suite Méxicana]
4151 Primero trozo méxicano
3849 Segundo trozo méxicano   11'
2,2,2,2-4,2,3,1-Timp.,Perc.-Hp.-Str.
Ms.
Scores: 31 p., 28 p.
*Composed 1919. First performance Mexico City,
1 May 1919, Orquesta del Sindicato de Filar-
mónicos, José Rocabruna conductor.*

MELCHERS, HENRIK MELCHER.   Stockholm 30 May 1882
                          d. 9 April 1961

2178s [Elegy for string orchestra.   8'
Transcribed from the String Quartet, Op. 17]
Str.
Edition Suecia, Stockholm, ^C1945 by STIM
Score 4 p.

MELKIKH, DMITRI MIKHEYEVICH.
               Moscow 11 February 1885
               Moscow 22 February 1943

1682 [Alladine and Palomides, Op. 2.   7'
Conclusion]
3(3rd alt. Picc.),3*,3(3rd alt. B.Cl.),3*-
4,2,3,1-Timp.,Perc.-Hp.-Str.
Musiksektion des Staatsverlages, Moscow, 1928
Score 16 p.
*From the incidental music to Maurice Maeter-
linck's play. First performance Moscow, 1923.*

1684 Epitaphe, Op. 7   8'
3(3rd alt. Picc.),3*,3*,3*-4,3,3,1-Timp.,Perc.
-Hp.-Str.
Section Musicale, Editions d'État, Moscow, 1927
Score 31 p.
*Composed 1916. First performance Moscow, 8
March 1925, Konstantin Saradiev conductor.*

MELLIN, G.

2461 Menuet badin [Playful minuet]
2,2,2,2-2Hn.
Score: Ms. 13 p.
Parts: Evette & Schaeffer, Paris [n.d.]

MENDELSSOHN, ARNOLD.   Ratibor, Silesia
       (now Raciborz, Poland) 26 December 1855
                 Darmstadt 19 February 1933

2295 Suite, Op. 62 [for band]   20'
8 movements
2(2nd alt. Picc.),2,2,2-2,2,3-Timp.,Trgl.,Tamb.
Leuckart, Leipzig, ^C1916
Score 35 p.

MENDELSSOHN, FELIX.   Hamburg 3 February 1809
                      Leipzig 4 November 1847

Full name: Jakob Ludwig Felix Mendelssohn-
           Bartholdy

993 [Athalie, Op. 74. Overture from the   8'
incidental music to Racine's tragedy]
2,2,2,2-2,2,3-Timp.-Hp.-Str.
Breitkopf & Härtel, Leipzig [n.d.]
Score 38 p.
*Composed 1845. First performance Charlotten-
burg, 1 December 1845, the composer conducting.*

50 [Athalie, Op. 74. War march of the   5'
priests]
2,2,2,2-2,2,3,Ophicl.-Timp.-Str.
Breitkopf & Härtel, Leipzig [n.d.]
Score 14 p.

196 [Calm sea and prosperous voyage,   12'
overture, Op. 27]
3*,2,2,3*-2,3-Timp.-Str.

Mendelssohn, Felix

Breitkopf & Härtel, Leipzig [n.d.]
Score 46 p.
*Inspired by two poems by Goethe. Composed
1828. First public performance Berlin, 1
December 1832.*

410p Capriccio brillant, Op. 22   12'
Solo Pno.-2,2,2,2-2,2-Timp.-Str.
Kalmus, New York [n.d.]
Score 26 p.
*Composed 1832. First performance London, 25
May 1832, the composer as soloist.*

370p [Concerto, piano, no. 1, Op. 25,   18'
G minor]
1.Molto allegro con fuoco 2.Andante 3.Presto
Solo Pno.-2,2,2,2-2,2-Timp.-Str.
Kalmus, New York [n.d.]
Score 48 p.
*Composed 1830-31. First performance Munich,
17 October 1831, the composer as soloist.*

364p [Concerto, piano, no. 2, Op. 40,   25'
D minor]
1.Allegro appassionato 2.Adagio 3.Presto
scherzando
Solo Pno.-2,2,2,2-2,2-Timp.-Str.
Breitkopf & Härtel, Leipzig [n.d.]
Score 52 p.
*Composed 1837. First performance Birmingham,
21 September 1837, George Smart conductor,
the composer as soloist.*

315p [Concerto, 2 pianos and orchestra,   30'
no. 1, E major] Edited by Karl-Heinz Köhler
1.Allegro vivace 2.Adagio non troppo - Più
mosso 3.Allegro
2 Solo Pno.-1,2,2,2-2,2-Timp.-Str.
Deutscher Verlag für Musik, Leipzig, ᶜ1967
Score 162 p.
*Composed 1823. First performance in Mendels-
sohn's home, Berlin, 14 November 1824, the
composer and his sister Fanny as soloists.
First public performance London, 13 July 1829,
the composer and Ignaz Moscheles soloists.*

431v [Concerto, violin, Op. 64, E minor] 29'
In one movement: Allegro molto appassionato -
Andante - Allegretto non troppo
Solo Vn.-2,2,2,2-2,2-Timp.-Str.
Breitkopf & Härtel, Wiesbaden [n.d.]
Score 55 p.
*Composed 1844. First performance Leipzig, 13
March 1845, Gewandhaus Orchester, Niels Gade
conductor, Ferdinand David soloist.*

Fingal's cave overture
  See: [The Hebrides, overture, Op. 26]

4521 [Funeral march for band, Op. 103] Edited
by Julius Rietz
1,2,4,2Basset Hn.,3*-4,2,3,Bass-Horn
Breitkopf & Härtel, Leipzig [1875?]
Score 6 p.
*Composed 1836, for the funeral of Norbert
Burgmüller.*

52 [The Hebrides, overture, Op. 26]   10'
2,2,2,2-2,2-Timp.-Str.
Breitkopf & Härtel, Wiesbaden [n.d.]
Score 42 p.
*Composed 1829-30. First performance London,
14 May 1832, Thomas Attwood conductor.*

954 [Heimkehr aus der Fremde, Op. 89.   6'
Overture] Tr.: Son and stranger
2,2,2,2-2,2-Str.
Breitkopf & Härtel, Leipzig [n.d.]
Score 18 p.
*From the singspiel composed 1829. First per-
formance in Mendelssohn's home, Berlin, 26
December 1829, the composer conducting. First
public performance Leipzig, 26 October 1848,
Julius Rietz conductor.*

1945 [Die Hochzeit des Camacho. Overture] 6'
Tr.: Camacho's wedding
2,2,2,2-4,2,3-Timp.-Str.
Breitkopf & Härtel, Leipzig [n.d.]
Score 40 p.
*From the opera composed 1825. First perform-
ance Berlin, 29 April 1827.*

Lobgesang. Symphony
  See: [Symphony no. 2, Op. 52a, B-flat major]

1854 Marsch für Orchester, Op. 108, D dur   6'
0,2,2,2-2,2,3-Timp.-Str.
Breitkopf & Härtel, Leipzig [n.d.]
Score 7 p.
*Composed 1841. First performance Dresden,
1841, to honor the painter Peter Cornelius.*

7137 [A midsummer night's dream, Op. 61. Com-
plete music to Shakespeare's play]
Overture: Allegro di molto 1.Scherzo (after
Act I) 2.Act II, Scene 1: Over hill, over
dale 3.Scene 3: Song with chorus 4.Andante
5.Intermezzo (after Act II) 6.Act III, Scene
1: Allegro 7.Nocturne 8.Act IV, Scene 1:
Andante 9.Wedding march (after Act IV) 10.
Act V, Scene 1: Marcia funebre 11.Advance of
clowns 12.Music between Scenes 1 & 2 13.
Finale: Allegro di molto
2,2,2,2-2,3,3,0,Ophicl.-Timp.,Trgl.,Cym.-2
Solo Sop. Voices, Women's Chorus-Str.
Kalmus, New York [n.d.]
Score 174 p.
*Overture originally composed 1826 as a piano
duet, then orchestrated as a concert overture,
Op. 21. First performance Stettin, Prussia,
20 February 1827, Carl Loewe conductor. Incidental music (nos. 1-13) to Shakespeare's play
commissioned by the King of Prussia and composed in 1843. First performance of complete
work, Neues Palais, Potsdam, Germany, 14 October 1843. Overture and nos. 1, 5, 7, and 9 are
also available individually as Catalog nos.
17, 720, 25, 18, and 1261 respectively.*

4533 [Overture, band, Op. 24, C major. Original
instrumentation]
2*,2,4,2 Basset Hn.,3*-4,2,3,Bass-Horn-Perc.
Breitkopf & Härtel, Leipzig [1893]

Score 32 p.
*Composed 1824. First performance Bad Doberan,
Germany, 1824.*

4753 [Overture, band, Op. 24, C major]
Arranged for contemporary band by Felix
Greissle
4*,2,6*(1Cl. in E-flat, 1 Alto Cl. in E-flat),
2-4Sax.-8,2,2Cnt.,2Fluegel Hn.,3,Bar.,Euph.,
Tuba-Perc.-Cb.
G. Schirmer, New York, ᶜ1948
Score 47 p.
*Composed 1824. First performance Bad Doberan,
Germany, 1824.*

878 [Overture, Trumpet, Op. 101, C major]   *8'*
2,2,2,2-2,2,3-Timp.-Str.
Breitkopf & Härtel, Leipzig [n.d.]
Score 49 p.
*Composed 1825. First performance Berlin, 18
April 1828, the composer conducting.*

224 [Overture to The tale of lovely   *10'*
Melusine, Op. 32]
2,2,2,2-2,2-Timp.-Str.
Breitkopf & Härtel, Leipzig [n.d.]
Score 50 p.
*Inspired by Franz Grillparzer's opera libretto.
Composed 1833. First performance London, 7
April 1834, Ignaz Moscheles conductor.*

371p Rondo brillant, Op. 29   *10'*
Solo Pno.-2,2,2,2-2,2-Timp.-Str.
Breitkopf & Härtel, Leipzig [n.d.]
Score 34 p.
*Composed 1834. First performance London, 8
May 1834, George Smart conductor, Ignaz
Moscheles soloist.*

75 Ruy Blas overture, Op. 95 [after   *8'*
Victor Hugo]
2,2,2,2-4,2,3-Timp.-Str.
Kalmus, New York [n.d.]
Score 38 p.
*Composed 1839. First performance Leipzig, 11
March 1839, the composer conducting.*

933 [St. Paul, Op. 36. Overture]   *7'*
2,2,2,2,Serpent-2,2,3-Timp.-Org.-Str.
Breitkopf & Härtel, Leipzig [n.d.]
Score 26 p.
From the oratorio composed 1834-36.

492p Serenade und Allegro giojoso, Op. 43 *11'*
Solo Pno.-1,2,2,2-2,2-Timp.-Str.
Breitkopf & Härtel, Leipzig [n.d.]
Score 35 p.
*Composed 1838. First performance Leipzig, 2
April 1838, the composer as soloist.*

1890s [Sinfonia no. 9, Swiss, C minor]
1.Grave - Allegro 2.Andante 3.Scherzo, La
Suisse 4.Allegro vivace
Str.
Möseler, Wolfenbüttel, ᶜ1962
Score 44 p.
Composed 1823.

2279s Suite for strings (originally   *21-23'*
Four Pieces for string quartet, Op. 81).
Transcribed for string orchestra by Norman
Black
1.Tema con variazioni 2.Scherzo 3.Capriccio
4.Fuga
Str.
Ms. ᶜ[n.d.] by Norman Black
Score 37 p.
*Nos. 1 and 2 composed 1847. No. 3 composed
1843; no. 4 composed 1827. This transcription
1965.*

2346s [Symphonic movement in C minor, for
string orchestra] Edited by Hellmuth Christian
Wolff
Str.
VEB Deutscher Verlag für Musik, Leipzig, ᶜ1967
Score 14 p.
Completed 29 December, probably 1823.

152 [Symphony no. 1, Op. 11, C minor]   *30'*
1.Allegro di molto 2.Andante 3.Menuetto
4.Allegro con fuoco
2,2,2,2-2,2-Timp.-Str.
Kalmus, New York [n.d.]
Score 60 p.
*Composed 1824. First performance Leipzig, 1
February 1827, J. Ph. Schulz conductor.*

167 [Symphony no. 2, Op. 52a, B-flat   *16'*
major]
1.Allegro 2.Allegretto un poco agitato
3.Adagio religioso
2,2,2,2-4,2,3-Timp.-Str.
Kalmus, New York [n.d.]
Score 71 p.
*From the Lobgesang (Hymn of Praise), symphony-
cantata composed 1840.*

6 [Symphony no. 3, Scotch, Op. 56,   *36'*
A minor]
Played continuously: 1.Andante con moto -
Allegro agitato 2.Scherzo assai vivace
3.Adagio cantabile 4.Allegro guerriero -
Finale maestoso
2,2,2,2-4,2-Timp.-Str.
Breitkopf & Härtel, Wiesbaden [n.d.]
Score 78 p.
*Composed 1829-42. First performance Leipzig,
3 March 1842, the composer conducting.*

133 [Symphony no. 4, Italian, Op. 90,   *25'*
A major]
1.Allegro vivace 2.Andante con moto 3.Con
moto moderato 4.Saltarello
2,2,2,2-2,2-Timp.-Str.
Breitkopf & Härtel, Wiesbaden [n.d.]
Score 66 p.
*Composed 1830-33. First performance London,
13 May 1833, the composer conducting.*

383 [Symphony no. 5, Reformation,   *25'*
Op. 107, D minor]
1.Andante - Allegro con fuoco 2.Allegro
vivace 3.Andante 4.Chorale: Andante con
moto - Allegro vivace
2,2,2,4(C.Bn. & Serpent)-2,2,3-Timp.-Str.

Mendoza, Vicente

Litolff, Braunschweig [n.d.]
Score 67 p.
*Composed 1829-30. First performance Berlin,
15 November 1832, the composer conducting.*

MENDOZA, VICENTE T.
Cholula, Puebla, Mexico 27 January 1894
Mexico City 27 October 1964

4169 Danza Tarahumara [from Chihuahua, Mexico]
3*,3*,3*(1Cl. in E-flat),1-Timp.,Perc.-Str.
Ms.
Score 23 p.
*Composed 1930. First performance Mexico City,
22 July 1930, Orquesta Sinfónica de Mexico,
Carlos Chavez conductor.*

Impresiones de estío [Impressions of summer]
4170 Movement 1. Allegro (Hispania fecunda)
4171 Movement 2. Lento
4172 Movement 3. Allegro moderato
4173 Movement 4. Allegro molto - Moderato
0,0,1,1-Tpt.-Perc.-Pno.-Str.
Ms.
Scores: 16 p., 5 p., 5 p., 14 p.
Composed 1937.

4136 Jalisco (Part I)   *3'30"*
1,1,1,1-0,1,1-S.Dr.,Trgl.-Pno.-Str.
Ms.
Score 8 p.

MENNICKE, KARL.   Reichenbach, Germany 12 May 1880
killed in battle, Galicia June 1917

1433 [Overture to a play]   *16'*
3*,3*,3*,3*-4,2,3,1-Timp.-Str.
Kistner, Leipzig [n.d.]
Score 54 p.

MENNIN, PETER.   Erie, Pennsylvania 17 May 1923

Born: Peter Mennini

5130 Canzona for band   *5'*
3*,2,6*(1Cl. in E-flat, 1 Alto Cl.),2-4Sax.-
4,2,3Cnt.,3,Bar.,1-Timp.,Perc.-Cb.
Ms. [Carl Fischer, New York, C1951]
Score 31 p. Large folio
*Commissioned by Edwin Franko Goldman through
the League of Composers, for the Goldman Band.
Composed 1951. First performance New York, 15
June 1951, Goldman Band, Richard Franko Gold-
man conductor.*

5131 Concertato for orchestra (Moby Dick)   *11'*
3*,3*,3*,2-4,3,3,1-Timp.,Perc.-Str.
Ms. [Carl Fischer, New York, C1952]
Score 66 p. Large folio
*Commissioned by the Erie Philharmonic. Com-
posed 1952. First performance Erie, 20 October 1952, Erie Philharmonic, Fritz Mahler conductor.*

332p [Concerto for piano]   *26'*
1.Maestoso - Allegro 2.Adagio religioso
3.Allegro vivace - Più mosso (Veloce)
Solo Pno.-3*,2,2,2-4,2,3,1-Timp.,Perc.-Str.

Ms. [C1958 by Carl Fischer, New York]
Score 148 p. Large folio
*Commissioned by the Cleveland Symphony in
celebration of its 40th anniversary. Composed 1957-58. First performance Cleveland,
27 February 1958, Cleveland Symphony, George
Szell conductor, Eunice Podis soloist.*

4815 [Symphony no. 5]   *21-24'*
1.Con sdegno 2.Canto 3.Allegro tempestuoso
3*,2,2,2-4,3,3,1-Timp.,Perc.-Str.
Ms. [Carl Fischer, New York, C1950]
Score 125 p. Large folio
*Commissioned by the Dallas Symphony League.
Composed 1949-50. First performance Dallas,
2 April 1950, Dallas Symphony Orchestra, Walter Hendl conductor.*

6260 Symphony no. 6   *26'*
1.Maestoso - Allegro 2.Grave 3.Allegro
vivace
3*,3*,3*,2-4,2.3,1-Timp.,Perc.-Str.
Ms. [Carl Fischer, New York, C1953]
Score 167 p. Large folio
*Commissioned by The Louisville Orchestra.
Composed 1952-53. First performance Louis-
ville, 18 November 1953, Louisville Orchestra,
Robert Whitney conductor.*

MENNINI, LOUIS.
b. Erie, Pennsylvania 18 November 1920

6567 Symphony no. 2, "da festa"   *18-22'*
1.Allegro con moto 2.Largo sostenuto 3.
Allegro robusto
3(3rd alt. Picc.),2,2,2-4,3,3,1-Timp.,Perc.-
Str.
Ms.
Score 91 p. Large folio
*Commissioned by the Erie Sesquicentennial Com-
mittee. Composed 1963. First performance
Erie, 7 September 1963, Erie Philharmonic
Orchestra, James Sample conductor.*

MENU, PIERRE.   Paris 1896
Paris 16 October 1919

526p Fantaisie dans l'ambiance espagnole.
Orchestrated by Roger-Ducasse
Solo Pno.-3*,3*,2,2-4,2,3,1-Timp.,Perc.-Hp.-
Str.
Durand, Paris, C1924
Score 113 p.
Composed 1917.

MERCADANTE, GIUSEPPE SAVERIO RAFFAELE.
Altamura, Italy baptized 17 September 1795
Naples 17 December 1870

7129 [Overture on motifs from Rossini's Stabat
Mater]
2,2,2,2-4,2,2,1-Timp.-Str.
Score: Ms. C1976 by The Fleisher Collection of
Orchestral Music, Free Library of Philadelphia.
70 p.
Parts: [Paris, Eugène Troupenas, n.d.]
*Composed for first performances at Naples,
3, 6, and 8 April 1843.*

MERIKANTO, AARRE.   Helsinki 29 June 1893
                    Helsinki 28 September 1958

5809 [The abduction of Kyllikki,   *15-17'*
ballet music]
1.Lemminkäinen 2.Kyllikki 3.Nocturne 4.Arrival of Lemminkäinen on the island and Kyllikki's abduction
3(3rd alt. Picc.),2,3,2-3,2,3-B.Dr.-Pno.-Str.
Suomen Säveltaiteilijain Liitto, Helsinki, ᶜ1937
Score 117 p.
Suggested by episodes from the Finnish epic, Kalevala. Composed 1935. First performance Helsinki, 1935.

505m [Concerto, clarinet, horn, violin   *18'*
and strings]
1.Largo - Allegro 2.Largo 3.Allegro vivace
Solo Cl., Solo Hn., Solo Vn.-Str.(w/o Cb.)
B. Schott's Söhne, Mainz, ᶜ1925
Score 78 p.
Composed 1923. First performance Donaueschingen, 1925.

MERKES VAN GENDT, W.

452s Albumblatt, Op. 42
Str.
Oertel, Hanover [n.d.]
Score 5 p.

MERRIMAN, THOMAS.

5413 Theme and four variations for   *6'30"*
brass choir
2Hn.,4Tpt.,3Tbn.,Bar.,Tuba
Associated Music Publishers, New York, ᶜ1951
Score 15 p.

MERTENS, JOSEPH.   Antwerp 17 February 1834
                    Brussels 30 June 1901

1435s [Two concert pieces]
1.Lento 2.Grazioso tempo non troppo allegro
Str.
J. Williams, London [n.d.]
Score 11 p.

382s [Two concert pieces, suite no. 3]
1.Contemplation 2.Impromptu
Str.
Choudens, Paris [n.d.]
Score 15 p.

MERZDORF, G. A.

780m [Concertino, clarinet, A-flat major]
Solo Cl.-1,0,1-2,4,Ten.Hn.,1-Timp.-Str.
Score: Ms. 25 p.
Parts: Seeling, Dresden [n.d.]

MESQUITA, CARLOS DE.

1503s Lola, pièce de genre, Op. 85
Str.
Lemoine, Paris [n.d.]
Score 7 p.

1448s Rêverie [In memory of Izeil] Op. 70
Solo Hn.-Hp.(or Pno.)-Str.
Lemoine, Paris [n.d.]
Score 4 p.

MESSAGER, ANDRÉ CHARLES PROSPER.
       Montluçon, France 30 December 1853
              Paris 24 February 1929

1503 Hélène, suite [music to Paul Delair's drama]
2,2,2,2-4,0,2Cnt.,3-Timp.-Str.
Choudens, Paris [n.d.]
Score 65 p.
First performance Paris, 15 September 1891, Albert Carrel conductor.

MESSIAEN, OLIVIER EUGÈNE PROSPER CHARLES.
              b. Avignon 10 December 1908

4889 [Forgotten offerings, symphonic   *11'*
meditation]
3,3*,3*,3-4,3,3,1-Timp.,Perc.-Str.
Durand, Paris, ᶜ1931
Score 30 p.
Composed 1930. First performance Paris, 19 February 1931, Orchestre des Concerts Straram, Walter Straram conductor.

MEUERER, JOH.

If Johannes Georg B., then born Würzburg 1871.

872m [Concertstück, clarinet, Op. 2, B-flat major]
Solo Cl.-2,2,0,2-2,2-Timp.-Str.
Score: Ms. 58 p.
Parts: A.E. Fischer, Bremen [n.d.]

MEULEMANS, ARTHUR.   Aarschot, Belgium 19 May 1884
                    Brussels 29 June 1966

6434 [Egmont. Overture to the final scene]   *6'*
3(3rd alt. Picc.),3*,3*,2-4,3,3,1-Timp.,Perc.-Hp.-Str.
Uitgave Arthur Meulemansfonds, Antwerp, ᶜ1961
Score 44 p.
From the opera composed 1944. First performance Antwerp, 27 September 1960, Royal Flemish Opera Orchestra, Frits Celis conductor.

6433 [Pliny's Fountain, symphonic   *19'*
sketches]
1.Summer morning at Pliny's Fountain [Limburg, Belgium] 2.At twilight 3.Night festival
4*,3*,3*,4*-4,3,3,1-Timp.,Perc.-Cel.,2Hp.-Str.
Uitgave Arthur Meulemansfonds, Antwerp, ᶜ1958
Score 111 p.
Composed 1913. First performance Antwerp, 28 April 1929, Vlaamse Concerten, the composer conducting.

6607 [Symphony no. 4, for winds and   *15'*
percussion]
1.Poco agitato 2.Allegretto scherzando
3.Adagio 4.Fanfare e rondo
3(2nd & 3rd alt. Picc.),3*(2nd alt. E.H.II),3*,3*-4,3,3,1-Timp.,Perc.-Cel.(alt. Keyboard

Meyer, Karl Clemens

Carillon)
Uitgave Arthur Meulemansfonds, Antwerp, ^c1964
Score 110 p.
Composed 1935.

MEYER, KARL CLEMENS.
    Oberplanitz, Saxony 25 February 1868
   Schwerin-Mecklenburg, Germany 4 August 1958

671s [Cradle song] Arranged for strings by
  L. Klemcke
  Str.
  Score: Ms. 3 p.
  Parts: C.F. Schmidt, Heilbronn [n.d.]

5074 [Mecklenburg march. Arranged for
  military band by Carlfr. Pistor-Rostock]
  2,2,4(1Cl. in E-flat),2-4,4,1Cnt.,2Fluegel
  Hn.,3,3Ten.Hn.,Bar.,2-Timp.,B.Dr.,S.Dr.
  Althen & Claussen, Schwerin [n.d.]
  Score 10 p.

MEYER, LEOPOLD DE.
    Baden, near Vienna 20 December 1816
       Dresden 5 March 1883

4289 [Moroccan march. Transcribed for orchestra
  by Hector Berlioz]
  4*,2,2,2-4,2,2Cnt.,3,Ophicl.-Timp.,Perc.-Str.
  A. Diabelli, Vienna [1846]
  Score 35 p.
  Originally composed for piano.

MEYERBEER, GIACOMO.   Berlin 5 September 1791
          Paris 2 May 1864

Born: Jakob Liebmann Beer

4268 L'Africaine [The African girl, or Vasco
  da Gama. Overture]
  4*,4*,3*,4-4,2,2Cnt.,3,Ophicl.-Timp.,Perc.-
  2Hp.-Str.
  Brandus, Paris [n.d.]
  Score 11 p.
  From the opera with libretto by Eugène Scribe.
  Composed 1838-64. First performance post-
  humously, Paris, 28 April 1865.

6130 L'étoile du nord [The North Star. Overture]
  2*,2,2,2-4,2(or 2Cnt.),3-Timp.,Perc.-2Hp.-Str.
  Brandus, Paris [n.d.]
  Score 52 p.
  From the opera with libretto by Eugène Scribe
  about Czar Peter the Great. Some of the music
  adapted from the composer's earlier opera,
  Ein Feldlager in Schlesien. First performance
  Paris, 16 February 1854.

4469 [Festival march for the Schiller Cen-
  tenary Celebration]
  3*,2,2,4-4,2,2Cnt.,3,Ophicl.-Timp.,Perc.-2Hp.-
  Str.
  Schlesinger, Berlin [1860]
  Score 43 p.
  Composed 1859.

4290 Ouverture en forme de marche pour l'Inauguration de l'Exposition Universelle de Londres
  1862

1.Marche triomphale 2.Marche religieuse
3.Pas redoublé [Quickstep]
4*,2,3*,4-4,4,3,Ophicl.-Timp.,Perc.-Str.
G. Brandus & S. Dufour, Paris [n.d.]
Score 68 p.

6173 [The prophet. Coronation march]   *4'*
  3*,2,2,4-4,4,3,Ophicl.-Timp.,Perc.-Str.
  Breitkopf & Härtel, Leipzig [1893 or 1894]
  Score 19 p.
  From the opera with libretto by Eugène Scribe,
  about the Anabaptist Uprising of 1534. Com-
  posed 1843. First performance Paris, 16 April
  1849.

4295 [Struensee, incidental music to the *12'*
  play by Michael Beer. Overture]
  3*,2,2,2-4,2,3,1-Timp.-Hp.-Str.
  Schlesinger, Berlin [1847]
  Score 60 p.
  First performance Berlin, 19 September 1846.

4312 [Struensee, incidental music to the play
  by Michael Beer. 2nd entr'acte: Polonaise]
  3*,2,2,2-4,2,3,1-Timp.-Str.
  G. Brandus et S. Dufour, Paris [n.d.]
  Score 37 p.

45 [Torch dance no. 1]   *6'*
  2*,2,2,2-4,2,3,Ophicl.-Timp.,Perc.-Str.
  Bote & Bock, Berlin [n.d.]
  Score 35 p.
  Composed 1842 for the wedding of the Crown
  Prince of Bavaria.

176 [Torch dance no. 2, military band. *6'*
  Transcribed for orchestra by W. Wieprecht]
  2,2,2,2-4,2,3,Ophicl.-Timp.,Perc.-Str.
  Brandus & Dufour, Paris [n.d.]
  Score 44 p.
  Composed 1850 for the wedding of Princess
  Charlotte of Prussia.

12 [Torch dance no. 3]   *9'*
  3*,2,2,2-4,2,3,Ophicl.-Timp.,Perc.-Str.
  Bote & Bock, Berlin [n.d.]
  Score 67 p.
  Composed 1853 for the wedding of Princess Anna
  of Prussia.

162 [Torch dance no. 4, military band. *8'*
  Transcribed for orchestra by W. Wieprecht]
  3*,2,2,2-4,3,3,Ophicl.-Timp.,Perc.-Str.
  Brandus & Dufour, Paris [n.d.]
  Score 47 p.
  Composed 1858.

MEYER-HELMUND, ERIK. St. Petersburg 25 April 1861
          Berlin 4 April 1932

1157v Fantaisie, Op. 44
  Solo Vn.-2(2nd alt. Picc.),2,2,2-2,2-Timp.,
  Perc.-Str.
  Rahter, Hamburg [n.d.]
  Score 48 p.

5702 Maschka. II. Mazurka. Arranged for
  orchestra by Karl Komzàk

COLLECTION OF ORCHESTRAL MUSIC

Miaskovsky, Nikolai

2,2(2nd optional),2,2(2nd optional)-4(3rd&
4th optional),2,2Cnt.(ad lib.),3(1st&2nd
optional)-Timp.(optional),Perc.-Hp.(optional)-
Str.
Bosworth, Leipzig, ᶜ1895
Vn.I part in lieu of score 2 p.

5603 Sérénade, Op. 62. Edited by H. W. Nicholl
3*,2,2,2-2,2,1-Timp.,Trgl.-Str.
Ries & Erler, Berlin, ᶜ1888 by Edward Schuberth & Co.
Score 30 p.

836s Sérénade roccoco, pizzicato
Glock.(ad lib.)-Str.
Bosworth, London, 1893
Score 7 p.

MEYER-OLBERSLEBEN, MAX.
Olbersleben, near Weimar 5 April 1850
Würzburg, Germany 31 December 1927

5449 [Hymn to the sun, tone poem, Op. 90]   18'
3(3rd alt. Picc.),2,2,2-4,2,3,1-Timp.,Trgl.,
Cym.-Hp.-Str.
C.F.W. Siegel, Leipzig [n.d.]
Score 58 p.
*Suggested by the poem Sonnenhymnus by Robert
Pilatz.*

MEYERS, EMERSON.   Washington, D.C. 27 October 1910

329p Concertino for piano and   22'30"
orchestra
1.Sonata 2.Variant similarities
Solo Pno.-2(2nd alt. Picc.),2,2,2-4,3,2-Timp.,
Perc.-Str.
Ms.
Score 130 p. Large folio
*Commissioned by Richard Bales. Composed 1949.
First performance Library of Congress, Washing-
ton, D.C., 9 December 1949, National Gallery
Orchestra, Richard Bales conductor, the com-
poser as soloist.*

MEZZACAPO, E.

1658s Le chant du gondolier, barcarolle
Solo Ob.-Str.
Score: Ms. 8 p.
Parts: Gaudet, Paris, ᶜ1915

1648s Tristesse [Sadness, romance without   4'
words]
Solo Ob.-Str.
Score: Ms. 8 p.
Parts: Gaudet, Paris, ᶜ1915

MIASKOVSKY, NIKOLAI IAKOVLEVICH.
Novogeorgievsk, near Warsaw 20 April 1881
Moscow 9 August 1950

1685 Alastor [Poem, after Shelley]   23'
Op. 14
3(3rd alt. Picc.),3(3rd alt. E.H.),3*,3*-6,3,
3,1-Timp.,Perc.-Cel.,2Hp.-Str.
Mussektor, Moscow, 1922
Score 84 p.

*Completed 1913. First performance Moscow, 5
November 1914, Serge Koussevitsky conductor.*

2396 Concertino lirico, G major, Op. 32   20'
no. 3
1.Allegretto 2.Andante monotono 3.Allegro
giocoso
1,0,1,1-Hn.-Hp.-Str.
Universal Edition, New York, 1930
Score 55 p.
*Composed 1929. First performance with Op. 32
no. 1.*

1162v [Concerto, violin, Op. 44]   36'
1.Allegro 2.Adagio molto cantabile 3.Allegro
molto
Solo Vn.-3*,2,2,2-4,3-Timp.,Perc.-Str.
Ms.
Score 117 p.
*Composed 1938. First performance Moscow, 10
January 1939, Moscow State Orchestra,
Alexander Gauck conductor, David Oistrakh
soloist.*

409c [Concerto, violoncello, Op. 66,   28'
C minor]
1.Lento ma non troppo 2.Allegro vivace -
Andante semplice e tranquillo
Solo Vc.-2,2,2,2-4,2-Timp.-Str.
State Music Publishers, Moscow, 1947
Score 60 p.
*Composed 1944-45. First performance Moscow,
17 March 1945, All-Union Radio Orchestra,
A. Orlov conductor, Sviatoslav Knushevitzky
soloist.*

2943 Fragment lyrique
2,3*,3*,2-4,3,3,1-B.Dr.-Str.
New Music Orchestra Series, San Francisco,
ᶜ1934
Score 15 p.
*Later used as fourth movement of Symphony no.
14, Op. 37.*

3534 Huldigungs Ouverture (Homage   10'
overture), Op. 48
3*,3*,3*,3*-4,3,3,1-Timp.,Perc.-Str.
Mussektor, Moscow, 1939
Score 61 p.
*Written 1939 for the 60th birthday of Josef
Stalin. First performance Moscow, 20 December
1939, Moscow Orchestra, Nikolai Golovanov conductor.*

2395 Serenata, Op. 32 no. 1, E-flat   20'
major
1.Allegro marcato 2.Andante 3.Allegro vivo
2(2nd alt. Picc.),2,2,2-2,1-Str.
Universal Edition, New York, 1930
Score 39 p.
*Completed 1929. First performance Moscow, 7
October 1929, Persimfans (orchestra without
conductor).*

1623s Sinfonietta, Op. 32 no. 2, B minor
1.Allegro pesante e serioso 2.Andante

557

Miaskovsky, Nikolai

3.Presto
Str.
Universal Edition, New York, 1931
Score 42 p.

1893 [Symphony no. 1, Op. 3, C minor]   40'
1.Lento ma non troppo 2.Larghetto 3.Allegro
assai e molto risoluto
3*,2,2,2-4,2,3,1-Timp.-Str.
Universal Edition, New York, 1929
Score 140 p.
*Composed 1908. Revised 1911 and 1922. First
performance Pavlovsk, 20 May 1914, A. Asfanov
conductor.*

1894 [Symphony no. 2, Op. 11, C-sharp   45'
minor]
1.Allegro 2.Molto sostenuto 3.Allegro con
fuoco
3(3rd alt. Picc.),3*,3*,3*-6,4,3,2-Timp.-Str.
Universal Edition, New York, 1928
Score 160 p.
*Completed 1911. First performance Moscow, 11
July 1912, Konstantin Saradiev conductor.*

1686 [Symphony no. 3, Op. 15, A minor]   45'
1.Non troppo vivo; vigoroso 2.Deciso e
sdegnoso
3(3rd alt. Picc.),3*,3*,3*-6,3,3,1-Timp.,
Perc.-Str.
Mussektor, Moscow, 1927
Score 156 p.
*Completed 1914. First performance Moscow, 14
February 1915, Emil Cooper conductor.*

1687 [Symphony no. 4, Op. 17, E minor]   35'
1.Andante 2.Largo 3.Allegro energico
3(3rd alt. Picc.),3*,3*,3*-6,3,3,1-Timp.,Perc.
-Str.
Mussektor, Moscow, 1926
Score 131 p.
*Completed 1918. First performance Moscow, 8
February 1925, Konstantin Saradiev conductor.*

1688 [Symphony no. 5, Op. 18, D major]   45'
In one movement
3(3rd alt. Picc.),3*,3*,3*-6,3,3,1-Timp.,Perc.
-Str.
Mussektor, Moscow, 1926
Score 127 p.
*Composed 1918. First performance Moscow, 18
July 1920, Nikolai Malko conductor.*

1689 [Symphony no. 6, Op. 23, E-flat]   75'
1.Poco largamente - Allegro feroce 2.Presto
tenebroso 3.Andante appassionato 4.Allegro
vivace
3(3rd alt. Picc.),3*,3*,3*-6,3,3,1-Timp.,Perc.
-Cel.,Hp.-SATB Chorus-Str.
Universal Edition, New York, ᶜ1925
Score 228 p.
*Completed 1923. First performance Moscow, 4
May 1925, Nikolai Golovanov conductor.*

1690 [Symphony no. 7, Op. 24, B minor]   25'
1.Andante sostenuto - Allegro minaccioso
2.Andante - Allegro precipitato
3(3rd alt. Picc.),3*,3*,3*-4,2,3,1-Timp.,Perc.

-Hp.-Str.
Universal Edition, New York, ᶜ1926
Score 124 p.
*Completed 1922. First performance Moscow, 8
February 1925, Konstantin Saradiev conductor.*

1691 [Symphony no. 8, Op. 26]   56'
1.Andante - Allegro 2.Allegro risoluto e
con spirito 3.Adagio 4.Allegro deciso
3(3rd alt. Picc.),3*,3*,3*-6,3,3,1-Timp.,Perc.
-Hp.-Str.
Universal Edition, New York [n.d.]
Score 200 p.
*Completed 1925. First performance Moscow, 23
May 1926, Konstantin Saradiev conductor.*

1887 [Symphony no. 9, Op. 28]   33'
1.Andante sostenuto 2.Presto 3.Lento molto
4.Allegro con grazia
3(3rd alt. Picc.),3*,3*,2-4,3,3,1-Timp.,Perc.-
Hp.-Str.
Universal Edition, New York [n.d.]
Score 180 p.
*Completed 1927. First performance Moscow, 29
April 1928, Konstantin Saradiev conductor.*

1895 [Symphony no. 10, Op. 30, F minor]   20'
In one movement
4(4th alt. Picc.),3*,3*,3*-8,4,3,1-Timp.,Perc.
-Str.
Mussektor, Moscow, 1930
Score 96 p.
First performance Moscow, 7 April 1928.

2944 [Symphony no. 11, Op. 34]   30'
1.Lento 2.Andante 3.Precipitato
3*,3*,3*,2-4,3,3,1-Timp.,Perc.-Str.
Mussektor, Moscow, 1934
Score 144 p.
*Completed 1932. First performance Moscow, 16
January 1933, Moscow Orchestra, Konstantin
Saradiev conductor.*

2468 [Symphony no. 12, Collective farm,   35'
Op. 35]
1.Andante 2.Presto 3.Allegro festivo
3*,3*,3*,2-4,3,3,1-Timp.,Perc.-Str.
Universal Edition, Vienna, 1932
Score 145 p.
*Composed 1932 for the 15th anniversary of the
October Revolution. First performance Moscow,
1 June 1932, Bolshoi Theatre Orchestra, Albert
Coates conductor.*

3479 [Symphony no. 14, Op. 37, C major]   40'
1.Allegro giocoso 2.Andantino, quasi allegretto
3.Quasi presto 4.Andante sostenuto 5.Allegro
con fuoco
3*,3*,3*,2-4,3,3,1-Timp.,Perc.-Str.
Mussektor, Moscow, 1936
Score 151 p.
*Composed 1933. First performance Moscow, 24
February 1935, Moscow Symphony Orchestra, V.
Kubatsky conductor. Fourth movement is
actually Fragment Lyrique.*

3480 [Symphony no. 15, Op. 38, D minor]   40'
1.Andante - Allegro appassionato 2.Moderato

assai 3.Allegro molto 4.Poco pesante -
Allegro
3*,3*,3*,2-4,3,3,1-Timp.,Perc.-Str.
Mussektor, Moscow, 1937
Score 175 p.
*Completed 1934. First performance Moscow, 28
October 1935, Radio Orchestra, Leo Ginsberg
conductor.*

3481 [Symphony no. 16, Op. 39, F major]   *33'*
1.Allegro vivace 2.Andantino semplice 3.
Sostenuto - Andante marciale, ma sostenuto
4.Tempo precedente - Allegro, ma non troppo
3*,3*,3*,2-4,3,3,1-Timp.,Perc.-Str.
Mussektor, Moscow, 1939
Score 179 p.
*Completed 1936. First performance Moscow, 24
October 1936, Philharmonic Orchestra, Eugen
Szenkar conductor.*

3857 [Symphony no. 18, Op. 42, C major]   *21'*
1.Allegro risoluto 2.Lento, ma non troppo -
Andante narrante 3.Allegro giocoso
3*,2(2nd alt. E.H.),2,2-4,3,3,1-Timp.,Perc.-
Str.
Mussektor, Moscow, 1940
Score 99 p.
*Composed 1937. First performance Moscow, 1
October 1937, Philharmonic Orchestra,
Alexander Gauck conductor.*

3482 [Symphony no. 21, Fantaisie, Op. 51]   *18'*
In one movement
3*,3*,3*,3*-4,3,3,1-Timp.-Str.
Mussektor, Moscow, 1941
Score 50 p.
*Composed for the 50th anniversary of the Chi-
cago Symphony Orchestra and awarded First
Stalin Prize, 1940. First performance Moscow,
18 November 1940, Moscow State Orchestra,
Alexander Gauck conductor.*

6432 [Symphony no. 27, Op. 85, C minor]   *34'*
1.Adagio - Allegro animato - Molto meno mosso
2.Adagio - Molto elevato 3.Presto ma non
troppo
3*,3*,3*,3*-4,3,3,1-Timp.,Perc.-Str.
State Music Publishers, Moscow, 1951
Score 149 p.
*Composed 1949. First performance Moscow, 9
December 1950. Posthumously awarded the Stalin Prize (First Place) 1950, for this symphony and the Quartet no. 13.*

MICHALSKY, DONAL.   Pasadena 13 July 1928

183m Concertino in Re for trombone and band
Andante maestoso (Tema) - Allegro non troppo
Part II (Variazioni)
Solo Ten. Tbn.-2(2nd alt. Picc.),3*,4*,2-
4Sax.-3,4,3,1-Timp.,Perc.-Cb.
Western International Music, Los Angeles,
C1974 by Pillin Music, Los Angeles
Score 68 p.
Composed 1953-54.

MICHELET, MICHEL.   Kiev 26 June 1894

Born: Mikhail Isaakovich Lewin

1808s [Elegy for string orchestra, Op. 4] *8'30"*
Str.
Ms.
Score 8 p.
*Composed 1918. First performance Kiev, 1918,
Kiev Symphony Orchestra, Reinhold Glière con-
ductor.*

MIELCK, ERNST.   Viborg, Finland 24 October 1877
                    Locarno, Italy 22 October 1899

240 Dramatische Ouverture, Op. 6
3(3rd alt. Picc.),2,2,3*-4,3,3,1-Timp.,Gong-
Hp.-Str.
Hofmeister, Leipzig [n.d.]
Score 55 p.

MIERSCH, PAUL FRIEDRICH THEODOR.
                    Dresden 18 January 1868
                    New York 1 March 1956

877s [Pleasant memories, strings, Op. 13]
Str.
Decourcelle, Nice, C1896
Score 3 p.

119s Two pieces for violin, Op. 27
1.Elegy 2.Cradle song
Str.
G. Schirmer, New York, C1900
Score 8 p.

MIGNAN, ÉDOUARD-CHARLES-OCTAVE. Paris 17 March 1884
                    Paris 17 September 1969

647v Andalouse [violin and orchestra]
Solo Vn.-3*,2,2,2-2,2,3,1-Timp.,Perc.-Hp.-Str.
Enoch, Paris, C1920
Score 45 p.

950v Sérénade nordique, D major
Solo Vn.-1,1,2,1-2Hn.(or 2Tpt.)-Timp.-Str.
Enoch, Paris, C1927
Score 14 p.

MIGNONE, FRANCISCO.
              b. São Paulo, Brazil 3 September 1897

3555 Ao anoitecer [At dusk] berceuse
2Fl.,2Ob.-Cel.,Hp.-Str.
Ms.
Score 29 p.
*Composed 1925. First performance São Paulo,
16 August 1925, São Paulo Orchestra, Torquato Amore conductor.*

3653 [Congada, Afro-Brazilian dance]   *4'30"*
3*,3*,3*,3*-4,3,3,1-Timp.,Perc.-Cel.,Hp.-Str.
Ricordi, Milan, 1937
Miniature score 38 p.
*Composed 1921. First performance (under title
Dansa) São Paulo, 10 September 1922, São
Paulo Symphony Orchestra, the composer con-
ducting.*

Mignone, Francisco

768p [Fantasia brasileira no. 1]   15'
Solo Pno.-2,2,2,2-4,2,3-Timp.,Perc.-Str.
Ricordi, Milan, c1938
Miniature score 73 p.
Composed 1929. First performance São Paulo,
20 March 1931, São Paulo Symphony Orchestra,
the composer conducting.

776p [Fantasia brasileira no. 3]
Solo Pno.-3*,2,2,2-4,3,3,1-Timp.,Perc.-Cel.,Hp.
-Str.
Ms.
Score 73 p.
Composed 1934. First performance São Paulo,
10 May 1934, São Paulo Symphony Orchestra,
the composer conducting.

3803 Festa das igrejas [Festival of the
churches]
1.S. Francisco da Baia (Baia) 2.Rosario, de
Ouro Prêto (Minas) 3.0 Outerinho da Gloria
(Rio de Janeiro) 4.Nossa Senhora da Brasil
(Aparecida)
3*,3*,3*,3*-4,3,3,1-Timp.,Perc.-Pno.,
Org.,Cel.,2Hp.-Str.
Ms.
Score 60 p. Large folio
Composed 1940. First performance São Paulo,
January 1942, the composer conducting.

3728 Plenilunio [Full moon]
2,3*,2,2-4Hn.-Pno.,Cel.,Hp.-Str.
Ms.
Score 21 p. Large folio
Composed 1936.

3153 Sonho de um menino travêsso (Desenho   9'
animado) [A mischievous boy's dream
(Animated sketch)]
3*,2,2,2-4,3,3,1-Timp.,Perc.-Cel.,Hp.-Str.
Escola Nacional de Musica, Rio de Janeiro, 1938
Score 37 p.
Composed 1935. First performance Rio de
Janeiro, 1936, Rio de Janeiro Municipal
Orchestra, Heitor Villa-Lobos conductor.

3325 Suite brasileira [in 3 movements]   7'
3*,2,3*,3*-4,3(1st alt. Cnt.),3,1-Timp.-Cel.,
Hp.-Str.
Ms.
Score 42 p.
Originally composed for piano, 1928; orches-
trated 1929. First performance Rio de
Janeiro, 9 December 1933, Philharmonic Orches-
tra of Rio de Janeiro, Burle Marx conductor.

MIGOT, GEORGES ELBERT.   Paris 27 February 1891

864 La fête de la bergère, suite   19'
1.Prelude-introduction 2.Pastoral 3.Finale
1,1,1,1-2,1-Perc.-Hp.-Str.
Senart, Paris c1926
Score 83 p.
Composed 1917. First performance Concerts
Lamoureux, Paris, 1924, Albert Wolff con-
ductor.

1237 Le paravent de laque aux cinq   12'
images [The lacquered screen with five
pictures]
2,2,2,2-2-Timp.,Perc.-Pno.,Cel.,Hp.-Str.
Senart, Paris, c1921
Score 28 p.
Composed 1909. First performance Concerts
Lamoureux, Paris, 1922, Paul Paray conductor.

2095 Prélude pour un poète   9'
1,1,2*,2*-2,1,1,1-Timp.-Cel.,Hp.-Str.
Leduc, Paris, c1930
Score 22 p.
Composed 1928. First performance Paris, 1928,
Symphonic Orchestra, Pierre Monteux con-
ductor.

MIGUEZ, LEOPOLDO.   Rio de Janeiro 9 September 1850
                    Rio de Janeiro 6 July 1902

3454 Parisina, d'après Lord Byron [symphonic
poem] Op. 15
3(3rd alt. Picc.),2(2nd alt. E.H.),2,2-4,2,4,
1-Timp.,Perc.-Pno.(ad lib.),Hp.-Str.
Ms.
Score 71 p.

MILANOLLO, TERESA. Savigliano, Italy 28 August 1827
                   Paris 25 October 1904

Full name: Domenica Maria Teresa Milanollo

632v Variations humouristiques [on the air
Malborough, violin and string orchestra, Op. 5]
Solo Vn.-Str.
Ms.
Score 17 p.

MILDE, LUDWIG.

698m Andante and rondo, bassoon and orchestra,
Op. 25
Solo Bn.-2,2,2,2-2,2,1-Timp.-Str.
Ms.
Score 46 p.

MILFORD, ROBIN.   Oxford, England 22 January 1903
                   Lyme Regis, England 29 December 1959

1540 Suite for chamber orchestra, Op. 5   12'
1.Prelude 2.Air 3.Minuet and trio 4.Quick
dance 5.Slow dance 6.Jig
2,1,2,2(or 1,1,1)-Hn.(or Cnt.)-Str.
Oxford University Press, London, c1925
Score 30 p.
Composed 1923. First performance Birmingham,
1927, City Orchestra, Adrian Boult conductor.

120s [Suite, oboe and strings, Op. 8, D minor]
1.Overture 2.Gavotte 3.Minuet and musette
4.Air
Solo Ob.-Str.
Oxford University Press, London, c1926
Score 12 p.

MILHAUD, DARIUS.   Aix-en-Provence 4 September 1892
                   Geneva 22 June 1974

Milhaud, Darius

1692 Actualités [film music for a newsreel] *3'*
1.[At the press exhibition] 2.[Official
reception of the aviators] 3.[The boxing
kangaroo] 4.[Water works] 5.[A railroad hold-
up] 6.[The derby]
2Cl.-2Tpt.,Tbn.-Timp.,Perc.-Str.
Universal Edition [n.p.] ^c1929
Score 7 p.
*Composed 1928. First performance Baden-Baden
Music Festival, 1928.*

306m [Concerto, clarinet and orchestra, *20'*
Op. 230]
1.Animé 2.Très décidé 3.Lent 4.Animé
Solo Cl.-2(2nd alt. Picc.),2,2,2-2,2,2,1-
Timp.,Perc.-Hp.-Str.
Elkan-Vogel, Philadelphia, ^c1942
Score 69 p.
*Commissioned by Benny Goodman, though not
performed by him. Composed 1941. First
performance Marine Barracks, Washington, D.C.,
30 January 1945.*

1019m [Concerto, percussion and small *7'*
orchestra]
In one movement
Solo Perc.-2Fl.(both alt. Picc.),2Cl.-Tpt.,
Tbn.-Str.
Universal Edition, Vienna [n.d.]
Score 31 p.
Composed 1929-30.

305p [Concerto, piano, no. 3, Op. 270] *18-20'*
1.Alerte et avec élégance 2.Lent 3.Avec
esprit et vivacité
Solo Pno.-2(2nd alt. Picc.),2,2,2-2,2,2,1-
Timp.,Perc.-Str.
Ms. ^c1947 by Associated Music Publishers,
New York
Score 68 p. Large folio
*Commissioned by Emile Baume. Composed 1945.
First performance at the Spring Festival in
Prague, Czechoslovakia, 25 May 1945, Emile
Baume soloist.*

801p [Concerto, 2 pianos and orchestra, *18'*
Op. 228]
1.Animé 2.Funèbre 3.Vif et précis
2 Solo Pno.-2(2nd alt. Picc.),2,2,2-2,2,2,1-
Timp.,Perc.-Str.
Ms.
Score 74 p. Large folio
*Commissioned by Vitya Vronsky and Victor Babin.
Composed 1941. First performance Pittsburgh,
13 November 1942, Pittsburgh Symphony Orches-
tra, Fritz Reiner conductor, Vitya Vronsky
and Victor Babin soloists.*

934v [Concerto, viola] *15'*
1.Animé 2.Lent 3.Souple et animé 4.Vif
Solo Va.-2(2nd alt. Picc.),2,3*,2-2,2,1,1-
Timp.,Perc.-Hp.-Str.
Universal Edition, Vienna, ^c1930
Score 42 p.
*Composed 1929. First performance Frankfurt,
19 January 1930, the composer conducting, Paul
Hindemith soloist.*

346v [Concerto, violin, no. 2, Op. 263] *20'*
1.Récitatif – Animé – Cadenza – Mouvement du
début 2.Lent et sombre 3.Emporté
Solo Vn.-2(2nd alt. Picc.),3*,3*,2-2,2,2,1-
Timp.,Perc.-Str.
[Associated Music Publishers, New York, ^c1948]
Score 145 p.
*Commissioned by Arthur LeBlanc. Composed 1946.
First performance Paris, 7 November 1948,
Orchestra of the Paris Conservatory, André
Cluytens conductor, Arthur LeBlanc soloist.*

424c [Concerto, violoncello, no. 2, *20'*
Op. 255]
1.Gai 2.Tendre 3.Alerte
Solo Vc.-2(2nd alt. Picc.),2,2,2-2,2,1-Timp.,
Perc.-Hp.-Str.
Associated Music Publishers, New York, ^c1947
Score 115 p.
*Commissioned by Edmond Kurtz. Composed 1945.
First performance New York, 28 November 1945,
New York Philharmonic, Artur Rodzinski con-
ductor, Edmond Kurtz soloist.*

3974 Fanfare
Tpt.-Timp.,Perc.-Va.,Vc.
Ms.
Score 5 p.
*First performance Havana, 23 April 1933,
Orquesta Filarmónica de la Habana, Nicolas
Slonimsky conductor.*

1801 [Five symphonies]
1. Le printemps
2*,1,1-Hp.-Str.(without Cb.)
*First performance, Rio de Janeiro, 1918,
Francisco Braga conductor.*
2. Pastorale
Fl.,E.H.,Bn.-Str.(no Vn.II)
*First performance Paris, 1919, Vladimir
Golschmann conductor.*
3. Sérénade
1,0,1,1-Str.(no Vn.II)
*First performance Pro Arte Concerts, Brussels,
1920, the composer conducting.*
4. Dixtuor à cordes
4Vn.,2Va.,2Vc.,2Cb.
*First performance Concerts à Art et Action,
Paris 1921, the composer conducting.*
5. Dixtuor d'instruments à vent
2*,2*,2*,2-2Hn.
*First performance Concerts of the Société des
Instruments à Vent, Paris, 1922, the composer
conducting.*
Universal Edition, Vienna, ^c1922
Scores in one volume. 80 p.

6303 [Funeral cortege, for orchestra, *11'*
Op. 202]
2,1,2(alt. 2Alto Sax.),1-0,2,2,1-Perc.-Hp.-Str.
Ms.
Score 28 p. Large folio
*Originally composed 1939 for André Malraux's
film Espoir, about the Spanish Civil War.*

Milhaud, Darius

*First performance New York, July or August
1940, CBS Symphony, the composer conducting.*

6573 The household Muse/La muse   *24'30"*
ménagère [for chamber orchestra, Op. 245]
1,1,1,1-Hn.-Str.
Elkan-Vogel, Philadelphia, c1965
Score 35 p.
*Originally composed 1944, for piano, as a sur-
prise for the composer's wife. First performance of this version 30 May 1945,
Orchestre de la Radiodiffusion Belge. Dedication: MMMM [Madeleine Milhaud, Muse
Ménagère].*

4593 [Kentuckiana, divertissement on   *9'*
20 Kentucky airs, Op. 287b]
2*,2,2,2-4,2,2-Timp.,Perc.-Str.
Ms.
Score 48 p. Large folio
*Commissioned by the Louisville Orchestra.
Originally composed for two pianos. First
performance of orchestral version Louisville,
4 January 1949, Louisville Orchestra, Robert
Whitney conductor.*

5019 [Madame Bovary. Album.   *13'30"*
Orchestrated by Stéphane Chapelier]
14 excerpts from the film music
2(2nd alt. Picc.),1(alt. E.H.),2,1-2,2,1-
Timp.,Perc.-Hp.(or Pno.)-Str.
Enoch, Paris, c1948
Score 49 p.
*From the music composed 1933 for Robert Aron's
film, based on Gustave Flaubert's novel.
Milhaud extracted and transcribed this and
the following work for piano, then commis-
sioned Chapelier to orchestrate them.*

5018 [Madame Bovary. Three waltzes.   *3'40"*
Orchestrated by Stéphane Chapelier]
1.Romanesque 2.Nostalgique 3.Ephémère
2(2nd alt. Picc.),1,2,1-2,2,1-Timp.,Trgl.-
Hp.-Str.
Enoch, Paris, c1949
Score 20 p.

5022 Opus Americanum, no. 2 [Moses,   *18'*
ballet suite in 9 movements, Op. 218]
2(2nd alt. Picc.),2,2(2nd alt. Alto Sax.),2-
2,2,2-Timp.,Perc.-Hp.-Str.
Elkan-Vogel, Philadelphia, c1947
Score 100 p.
*Commissioned by Richard Pleasant, director of
Ballet Theatre. Originally composed 1940 as
a ballet under the title The Man of Midian,
or Moses, but not performed as such. First
concert performance San Francisco, 6 December
1943, San Francisco Symphony Orchestra, Pierre
Monteux conductor.*

565 Saudades do Brazil   *40'*
2(2nd alt. Picc.),2,2,2-2,2,2-Timp.,Perc.-Str.
Eschig, Paris, c1923
Score 77 p.

1693 Sérénade   *15'*
1.Vif 2.Tranquille 3.Vif

2(1st alt. Picc.),2,2,2-2,2-Timp.,Perc.-Str.
Universal Edition, Vienna, c1923
Score 72 p.
*Composed 1920-21. First performance Con-
certs Colonne, Paris 1921, Gabriel Pierné
conductor.*

4940 [Symphonic suite no. 2, Op. 57,   *22'*
taken from Proteus, Op. 17]
1.Ouverture 2.Prélude et fugue 3.Pastorale
4.Nocturne 5.Final
3(3rd alt. Picc.),3*,3*,4-4,3,3,1-Timp.,Perc.-
Cel.,Hp.-Str.
Durand, Paris, c1921
Score 169 p.
*Some of the music originally composed 1913 for
Paul Claudel's satiric drama Protée [Proteus].
Expanded and orchestrated for full orchestra
1919. Second Symphonic Suite extracted from
this in 1919. First performance of Suite,
Concerts Colonne, Paris, 24 October 1920,
Gabriel Pierné conductor.*

1631 [Three rag caprices]   *5'*
1,1,1,1-2,1,1-Perc.-Str.
Universal Edition, Vienna, c1930
Score 26 p.
*Originally composed for piano 1921; orches-
trated 1926. First performance Paris, 1930,
M. F. Gaillard conductor.*

4751 Two marches [Band version,   *5'30"*
Op. 260b]
1.In memoriam 2.Gloria victoribus
3*,1,4(1Alto Cl. in E-flat),1-4Sax.-4,2,3Cnt.,
3,Bar.,1-Timp.,Perc.-Cb.
G. Schirmer, New York, c1947
Score 27 p.
*Originally composed for orchestra 1945; no. 1
in memory of Pearl Harbor. Transcribed for
symphonic band by the composer 1946. First
performance of band version New York, 1948,
Goldman Band.*

5922 West Point suite, for concert band   *8-10'*
[Op. 313]
1.Introduction 2.Recitative 3.Fanfare
3*,2,7*(1Cl. in E-flat,1Alto Cl.),2-4Sax.(SATB)
-4,4,4Cnt.,2Fluegel Hn.,3,2Bar.,2Euph.,2-Timp.,
Perc.-Cb.
Associated Music Publishers, New York, c1954
Score 40 p.
*Commissioned for the West Point Sesquicenten-
nial Celebration of 1952. Composed 1951.
First performance New York, 5 January 1952,
United States Military Academy Band, Francis
E. Resta conductor.*

200m [Winter concertino, for trombone   *18'*
and strings]
In one movement: Animé - Très modéré - Animé
Solo Tbn.-Str.
Associated Music Publishers, New York, c1955,
1957
Score 36 p.
*Composed 1953, as the final composition in the
cycle The Four Seasons. First performance*

*Brooklyn, 28 March 1954, Brooklyn Community
Symphony Orchestra, Davis Shuman soloist.*

MILLER, CHARLES.   Russia 1 January 1899

4779 Appalachian Mountains, an American   *12'*
folk rhapsody for orchestra
3(3rd alt. Picc.),3*,3*,2-4,2,3,1-Timp.,Perc.-
Cel.,Hp.-Str.
Max Eschig, Paris, [C]1939
Miniature score 51 p.
*Composed 1930. First performance Paris, 18
May 1938, Orchestre Colonne, the composer con-
ducting.*

MILLET, ALBERT.

1534s [Minuet, flute and strings, G major]
Solo Fl.(or Ob., or Cl.)-Str.
Costallat, Paris, 1887
Score 5 p.

MILLÖCKER, KARL.   Vienna 29 April 1842
                        Baden, near Vienna 31 December 1899

1433s Herzblättchen [Darling]
Str.
Ries & Erler, Berlin [n.d.]
Score 15 p.

MILLS, CHARLES.
        b. Asheville, North Carolina 8 January 1914

314m Concertino for oboe and strings   *12'*
1.Allegretto 2.Adagietta 3.Allegro con brio
Solo Ob.-Str.
Composer's Facsimile Edition, New York, [C]1968
by Charles Mills
Score 31 p.
Commissioned by Harold Gomberg. Composed 1956.

2239s Prologue and dithyramb for strings   *8'*
1.Larghetto con moto 2.Vivace
Str.
Composers Facsimile Edition, New York, [C]1955
by Charles Mills
Score 13 p. Large folio
*Commissioned by the Cleveland Chamber Music
Society. Composed originally for string
quartet. Transcribed for string orchestra
1954. First performance of this version New
York, 8 March 1955, Manhattan School Orchestra,
Jonel Perlea conductor.*

3714 [Symphony no. 1, E minor]   *24'*
1.Introduction and Allegro 2.Largo 3.Finale
3(3rd alt. Picc.),3*,4*,4*-4,3,2,2-Timp.,Perc.
-Pno.-Str.
Ms.
Score 111 p. Large folio
Composed 1940.

3823 [Symphony no. 2, C major]   *30'*
1.Allegro moderato 2.Aria, fugue and postlude
3.Vivace
3(3rd alt. Picc.),3*,4*,4*-4,3,3,2-Timp.,Perc.
-Pno.-Str.
Ms.

Score 101 p. Large folio
Composed 1941.

6362 [Symphony, Crazy Horse]   *17'30"*
1.The holy man 2.The warrior 3.The tragic
hero
3,3*,3*,3*-4,4,3-Timp.-Str.
Composers Facsimile Edition, New York, [C]1958
by Charles Mills
Score 76 p. Large folio
*Suggested by the life of the Sioux Indian
chief, Crazy Horse (1842?-77). Composed 1957.
First performance Cincinnati, 28 November 1958,
Cincinnati Symphony Orchestra, Max Rudolf
conductor.*

6763 Theme and variations, Op. 81   *12'*
3,3*,3*,3-4,4,3,3-Timp.-2Hp.-Str.
Ms.
Score 78 p. Large folio
Composed 1951.

MILOK, E.

1075s Ecoute! [Hark!, little serenade]
Str.
Decourcelle, Nice, [C]1906
Score 5 p.

MINDREAU, ERNESTO LOPEZ.
                b. Chiclayo, Peru 17 June 1890

3266 Marinera y tondero (danses   *3'30"*
péruviennes). Arranged by Fritz A. Mueller
2,2,2,2-4,2,3,1-Timp.,Perc.-Str.
Ms.
Score 23 p.
*Originally composed for piano. Arranged 1937.
First performance Washington, D.C., 7 April
1938, United Service Orchestra, Capt. William
F. H. Santelmann conductor.*

MING, JAMES   Brownwood, Texas 21 May 1918

3132 Dance suite   *13'*
1.Allegro 2.Andante 3.Allegro
3*,3*,3*,2-4,3,3-Timp.,Perc.-Pno.-Str.
Ms.
Score 43 p. Large folio
*Composed 1938-39. First performance Rochester,
at a symposium 18-21 April 1939, Rochester
Civic Orchestra, Howard Hanson conductor.*

3396 Music for a film   *14'*
1.An evening at the theatre 2.An afternoon in
Italy 3.An evening in the city
3*,3*,3*,2-4,3,3-Timp.,Perc.-Pno.-Str.
Ms.
Score 45 p. Large folio
*Composed 1939-40. First performance Rochester,
during a symposium 16-19 April 1940, Rochester
Civic Orchestra, Howard Hanson conductor.*

3126 Music for orchestra   *8'*
2,3*,3*,2-4,2,3,1-Timp.,Perc.-Pno.-Str.
Ms.
Score 32 p.

Minguzzi, Giovanni

Composed 1938. First performance Rochester, 19 October 1938, Rochester Civic Orchestra, Howard Hanson conductor.

MINGUZZI, GIOVANNI.   Forli, Italy 20 October 1870

191s Adagietto [for string orchestra] Op. 7
Str.
Carisch & Jänichen, Leipzig, ^C1908
Score 5 p.

190s Minuetto [for string orchestra] Op. 8
Str.
Carisch & Jänichen, Leipzig, ^C1908
Score 6 p.

MISKOW, SEXTUS.   Nyborg, Denmark 3 February 1857
Copenhagen 24 November 1928

415s Fader vor [The Lord's prayer]
Hp.(ad lib.)-Str.
W. Hansen, Copenhagen, ^C1903
Score 7 p.

MISTOWSKI, ALFRED.

917s Aria for string orchestra
Solo Vn.-Str.
Chester, London, ^C1923
Score 4 p.

MITCHELL, LYNDOL.
Itta Bena, Mississippi 16 February 1923
d. 1963

334m Concerto grosso for three trombones   *15'*
and [chamber] orchestra (in stile barocco)
1.Adagio maestoso - Allegro di molto
2.Larghetto affetuoso 3.Presto
3 Solo Tbn.-1,1,1,1-2,1-Str.
Ms.
Score 60 p.
Composed 1961.

6305 Kentucky mountain   *11'30"-13'30"*
portraits
1.Cindy 2.Ballad 3.Shivaree
2(2nd alt. Picc.),2,2,2-4,2,3-Timp.,Perc.-Str.
Eastman School of Music, Rochester, ^C1957
Score 75 p.
Completed 1956.

2226s Melody for strings   *8'*
Str.
Ms.
Score 5 p.
Composed 1951. First performance Rochester, New York, 1951-52, Eastman-Rochester Symphony Orchestra, Howard Hanson conductor.

6320 Overture for orchestra
2(2nd alt. Picc.),2,2,2-4,3,3,1-Timp.,Perc.-Str.
Ms.
Score 44 p. Large folio
Composed 1950.

347v Toccata for violin and orchestra   *8'*
Solo Vn.-2(2nd alt. Picc.),2,2,2-4,3,3,1-Timp.,
Perc.-Str.
Ms.
Score 46 p. Large folio
Composed 1952.

MŁYNARSKI, EMIL.   Kibarty, Poland 18 July 1870
Warsaw 5 April 1935

287v [Concerto, violin, no. 1, Op. 11, D minor]
1.Allegro moderato 2.Adagio 3.Allegro
Solo Vn.-3*,2,2,2-4,2,3-Timp.-Str.
M. Józefowicz, Leipzig [n.d.]
Score 87 p.
Awarded first prize at the Paderewski Competition in Leipzig, 1898.

1813 [Symphony, Op. 14, F major]   *40'*
1.Andante - Allegro 2.Adagio 3.Presto
4.Moderato
4*,4*,4*,4*-6,3,3,1-Timp.,Perc.-Hp.-Str.
Bote & Bock, Berlin, ^C1912
Score 211 p.
Composed 1909. First performance Glasgow, 1911, the composer conducting.

MODARELLI, ANTONIO.   Braddock, Pennsylvania 1894
Charleston, West Virginia 1 April 1954

5543 Legend of Ann Bailey
3*,2,2,2-4,3,3,1-Timp.,Perc.-Str.
Ms.
Score 50 p.
The pioneer Ann Bailey (1742-1825) helped lift the Indian siege of Fort Lee, West Virginia in 1791.

5518 Ode to Lincoln
3*,3*,2,2-4,3,3,1-Timp.,Perc.-Str.
Ms.
Score 53 p.

5555 River saga
3(3rd alt. Picc.),3*,2,2-4,3,3,1-Timp.,Perc.-
Hp.-Str.
Ms.
Score 83 p.
Suggested by the Kanawha River in West Virginia. Commissioned by Gustavus Capito. Composed 1949. First performance Charleston, West Virginia, November 1949, Charleston Symphony Orchestra, the composer conducting.

5176 [September, symphonic poem]
4*,3*,3*,3*-4,3,3,2-Timp.,Perc.-Hp.-Str.
State Music Publishers, Moscow, ^C1931
Score 93 p.

5520 Three miniatures
1.Marching song 2.Lullaby 3.Children's dance
2(2nd alt. Picc.),2,2,2-3,2,2-Perc.-Str.
Ms.
Score 17 p.

5516 Unto the hills, symphonic poem for
orchestra
3*,2,2,2-4,3,3,1-Timp.,Perc.-Hp.-Str.

Ms.
Score 32 p.
*Composed 1939. First performance Wheeling,
1939, Wheeling Symphony, the composer conducting.*

MOERAN, ERNEST JOHN.
Heston, Middlesex 31 December 1894
Kenmare, Ireland 1 December 1950

3299 Farrago, suite   14'
1.Prelude 2.Minuet 3.Rondino 4.Rigadon
2(2nd alt. Picc.),1,2,2-2,2,3-Timp.,Perc.-Str.
Ms.
Score 93 p.
*Composed 1932. First performance London, 1933,
BBC Orchestra, Julian Clifford conductor.*

3160 First rhapsody   15'
3(3rd alt. Picc.),3*,3*,2-4,3,3,1-Timp.,Perc.
-Str.
Hawkes, London, ᶜ1925
Score 40 p.
*Composed 1921-22. First performance Man-
chester, England 24 January 1924, Hallé
Orchestra, Hamilton Harty conductor.*

3125 In the mountain country, symphonic   7'
impression
3(3rd alt. Picc.),2,3*,2-4,2,3,1-Timp.,Perc.-
Str.
Oxford University Press, London, ᶜ1925
Score 22 p.
*Composed 1920. First performance London, 24
November 1921, Queen's Hall Orchestra, Adrian
Boult conductor.*

MOESCHINGER, ALBERT.   Basel 10 January 1897

5266 [Variations and finale on a theme   20'
by Clarke, Op. 32]
Timp.,S.Dr.-Str.
B. Schott's Söhne, Mainz, ᶜ1935
Score 49 p.
*Composed 1933. Theme is Jeremiah Clarke's
Trumpet Tune often misattributed to Purcell.*

MOEVS, ROBERT W.
b. La Crosse, Wisconsin 2 December 1920

5886 Symphony in three movements   26'30"
1.Introduzione 2.Presto 3.Rondò quasi una
fantasia
3(3rd alt. Picc.),3*,3*,3*-4,3,3,1-Timp.,Perc.
-Hp.-Str.
Ms.
Score 112 p. Large folio
*Commissioned by the League of Composers for the
fortieth anniversary of the Cleveland Orches-
tra. Composed 1954-56. First performance
Cleveland, 10 April 1958, Cleveland Orchestra,
George Szell conductor.*

MOHAUPT, RICHARD.
Breslau, Germany 14 September 1904
Reichenau, Lower Austria 3 July 1957

4768 Lysistrata. Suite from the dance   14'
comedy

1.The wives on strike, and Dance mondaine
2.Conspiracy of the husbands 3.Rondo of the
girls 4.Dance of the huntress
3(3rd alt. Picc.),2(2nd alt. E.H.),2,2(2nd
alt. C.Bn.)-4,3,3,1-Timp.,Perc.-Pno.-Str.
Associated Music Publishers, New York, ᶜ1946
by Richard Mohaupt
Score 60 p. Large folio
*Music for the dance-comedy, after Aristophanes,
composed 1941. This suite 1946. First performance under the alternate title Choreographic Episodes, Kansas City, Missouri, 1946,
Kansas City Symphony. Revised 1955 and
retitled Der Weiberstreik von Athen [The Wives
of Athens on Strike].*

4591 Max and Moritz, a musical story of   26'
two bad boys. Text by Theo Phil (adapted from
the book by Wilhelm Busch)
Narrator-2(2nd alt. Picc.),1,2,1-2,2,1-Timp.,
Perc.-Pno.(alt. Org.)-Str.
Associated Music Publishers, New York, ᶜ1947
Score 83 p. Large folio
*Originally composed as a dance-burlesque, 1945.
This version, 1946. First performance Karls-
ruhe, Germany, 18 December 1950.*

4789 Overture after Shakespeare's Much Ado About
Nothing
2,2,2,2-4,2,3,1-Timp.,Perc.-Hp.(alt. Pno.)-Str.
Remick Music Corporation, New York, ᶜ1941
Score 29 p.

4587 [Town piper music. Orchestral   14'
version]
3(3rd alt. Picc.),2(2nd alt. E.H.),3(2nd alt.
Cl. in E-flat,3rd alt. B.Cl.),2(2nd alt. C.Bn.)
-4,3,2Cnt.(ad lib.),3,1-Timp.,Perc.-Str.
Associated Music Publishers, New York, ᶜ1949
Score 67 p. Large folio
*Suggested by Albrecht Dürer's mural Nürn-
berger Stadtpfeifer. Composed 1939. First
performance New York, 1941, NBC Symphony.*

MOHR, HERMANN. Nienstedt, Germany 9 November 1830
Philadelphia 25 May 1896

362s Polacca, Op. 48, D major
2Pno.(8 hands)-Str.(or Str. alone)
Score: Ms. 12 p.
Parts: C. Simon, Berlin [n.d.]

MOLÉ, CH.

1524s Doux souvenirs [Sweet memories]
Solo Vn.-Str.
Score: Ms. 7 p.
Parts: Richault, Paris [n.d.]

1525s Soupirs du coeur [Deep sighs]
Solo Vn.-Str.
Score: Ms. 5 p.
Parts: Richault, Paris [n.d.]

MOLINA PINILLOS, JOSÉ.   Guatemala City 1889

4732 [Guatemalan rhapsody no. 2, National
pictures]

Molique, Wilhelm Bernhard

1,1,1-0,1,1-Str.
Ms.
Score in reduction 6 p.
*Composed 1939. First performance Guatemala,
30 May 1939, Guatemala Radio Orchestra, the
composer conducting.*

MOLIQUE, WILHELM BERNHARD. Nürnberg 7 October 1802
        Cannstadt, near Stuttgart 10 May 1869

537v [Concertante, two violins, F major]
In one movement
2Solo Vn.-Str.
Breitkopf & Härtel, New York, C1912
Score in reduction 16 p.
Composed 1827.

223m [Concerto, flute, Op. 69, D minor] Edited
by A.K. Kurth
1.Allegro 2.Andante 3.Rondo
Solo Fl.-1,2,0,2-2,2-Timp.-Str.
Score: Ms. 115 p.
Parts: Raabe & Plothow, Berlin [n.d.]

1036v [Concerto, violin, no. 5, Op. 21, A minor]
Allegro - Andante - Rondo
Solo Vn.-1,2,2,2-2,2-Timp.-Str.
Score: Ms. 169 p.
Parts: Hofmeister, Leipzig [n.d.]

659c [Concerto, violoncello, Op. 45, D major]
Allegro - Andante - Rondo
Solo Vc.-1,2,2,2-2,2-Timp.-Str.
Score: Ms. 216 p.
Parts: Kistner, Leipzig [n.d.]

MOLLEDA, JOSÉ MUÑOZ.
See: MUÑOZ MOLLEDA, JOSÉ.

MÖLLER, C. C.

334s Bagatellen, Op. 268
Str.
W. Hansen, Copenhagen [n.d.]
Score 9 p.

MOLTER, JOHANN MELCHIOR.
      Tiefenort, Germany 10 February 1696
      Durlach, Germany 12 January 1765

380m [Concerto, clarinet and string orchestra,
no. 1, A major] Edited by Heinz Becker
1.Concerto moderato 2.Largo 3.Allegro
Solo Cl.-Cemb.-Str.
Breitkopf & Härtel, Wiesbaden, C1957
Score 12 p.

400m [Concerto, clarinet and string orchestra,
no. 2, D major] Edited by Heinz Becker
1.Moderato 2.Largo 3.Allegro
Solo Cl.-Cemb.-Str.

Breitkopf & Härtel, Wiesbaden, C1957
Score 13 p.

379m [Concerto, clarinet and string orchestra,
no. 3, G major] Edited by Heinz Becker
1.Concerto moderato 2.Adagio 3.Allegro
Solo Cl.-Cemb.-Str.
Breitkopf & Härtel, Wiesbaden, C1957
Score 13 p.

378m [Concerto, clarinet and string orchestra,
no. 4, D major] Edited by Heinz Becker
1.Moderato 2.Adagio 3.Allegro
Solo Cl.-Cemb.-Str.
Breitkopf & Härtel, Wiesbaden, C1957
Score 14 p.

1416s [Concerto pastorale, for strings and harpsichord (piano or organ), G major] Urtext
edition by Karlheinz Schultz-Hauser
1.Larghetto - Allegro e forte 2.Aria 1
3.Aria 2 4.Aria 3 (Larghetto da capo)
Cemb.-Str.
Chr. Friedrich Vieweg, Berlin-Lichterfelde, C1961
Score 12 p.

MOMPOU, FEDERICO.   Barcelona 16 April 1893

4259 Scènes d'enfants. Transcribed for   8'
chamber orchestra by Alexandre Tansman
1.[Street calls] 2.[Game] 3.[Girls in the
garden] 4.[Games on the beach]
2,1,1-Perc.-Pno.,Cel.-Str.(without Va.)
Maurice Senart, Paris,C1936
Score 47 p.
Originally composed for piano, 1915-18.

2945 Suburbis, faubourgs. Transcribed for   13'
orchestra by Manuel Rosenthal
1.[The street, the guitar player and the old

horse] 2.[Gypsies, no. 1] 3.[Gypsies, no. 2]
4.[The little blind girl] 5.L'homme à
l'Ariston
2(alt. 2 Picc.),2(2nd alt. E.H.),2(2nd alt.
B.Cl.),2-2,2,1-Timp.,Perc.-Hp.-Str.
Maurice Senart, Paris, ᶜ1936
Score 64 p.
Originally composed for piano, 1916-17.

MONCAYO, JOSÉ PABLO.
          Guadalajara, Mexico 29 June 1912
          Mexico City 16 June 1958

1062m Amatzinac, for flute and string orchestra
Solo Fl.-Str.
Ms.
Score 23 p.
Suggested by an Aztec subject. Originally composed for flute and string quartet, 1935. First performance Mexico City, 25 November 1935.

4159 Hueyapán [symphonic dance]
3*,2,4*(1 Alto Cl. in E-flat),2-4,3,3,1-Timp.,
Perc.-Str.
Ms.
Score 92 p.

MONCORGÉ, RÉMY.

1270s Menuet, A minor
Str.
Score: Ms. 5 p.
Parts: Decourcelle, Nice [n.d.]

MONELLO, SPARTACO VINDICE.   Boston 29 June 1909

5514 Concerto for orchestra (1955)   *20'*
[Op. 26]
1.Allegro 2.Adagio 3.Allegro giocoso
2,2,2,2-2,2-Timp.,Perc.-Str.
Ms.
Score 71 p.
Composed 1955.

825p [Concerto grosso, piano and string   *19'*
orchestra, Op. 15]
1.Moderato 2.Adagio 3.Allegro con spirito
Solo Pno.-Str.
Ms.
Score 56 p.
Composed 1950.

5290 Country dance for orchestra [Op. 18]   *9'*
3*,2,2,2-3,2,2-Timp.,Perc.-Str.
Ms.
Score 46 p.
Composed 1951.

6542 Divertimento for orchestra [Op. 33]   *5'*
3*,1,4*(1Cl. in E-flat),1-2Sax.(Alto,Ten.)-2,
2,Cnt.,3,1-Timp.,Perc.-Str.
Ms.
Score 24 p.
Composed 1964.

5185 Symphony no. 1 [Op. 9]   *40'*
1.Lento - Allegro 2.Adagio 3.Scherzo

4.Allegro con moto
3*,2,2,2-4,3,3,1-Timp.,Perc.-Str.
Ms.
Score 171 p.
Composed 1946.

2061s Symphony no. 2, for string   *28'*
orchestra [Op. 11]
1.Adagio - Allegro 2.Adagio 3.Allegro
Str.
Ms.
Score 50 p.
Composed 1947. First complete performance White Plains, New York, 1 December 1950, Little Orchestra Society, Thomas Scherman conductor.

MONGE, F. DE.

743s Romance sans paroles
Hn.-Str.
Score: Ms. 5 p.
Parts: A. Leduc, Paris [n.d.]

MONIUSZKO, STANISLAW.
       Ubiel, near Minsk, Russia 5 May 1819
       Warsaw 4 June 1872

1787 [The countess. Overture] Edited by Gustav
Roguski
2(2nd alt. Picc.),2,2,2-4,2,3,1-Timp.,Perc.-
Str.
Gebethner, Warsaw [1898]
Score 43 p.
From the opera in four acts composed 1858-59. First performance Warsaw, 7 February 1860.

1434s [The countess. Polonaise-entr'acte]
Solo Vc.-Va.,Vc.I/II,Cb.
Score: Ms. 7 p.
Parts: Gebethner, Warsaw, ᶜ1894

797 [Halka. Mazurka] Edited by Gustav   *4'30"*
Roguski
2*,2,2,2-4,2,3,1-Timp.,Perc.-Str.
Gebethner, Warsaw [n.d.]
Score 25 p.
From the opera composed 1847.

MONN, GEORG MATTHIAS.   Vienna 9 April 1717
         Vienna 3 October 1750

Original family name: Mann

827p [Concerto, harpsichord, D major]
1.Allegro 2.Andante 3.Tempo di menuetto
Solo Hpscd.-Cemb.-Str.(without Va. and Vc.)
Score: Denkmäler der Tonkunst in Österreich,
XIX/2. Artaria, Vienna, 1912. Edited by
Wilhelm Fischer. 15 p.
Parts: Ms. ᶜ1976 by The Fleisher Collection of
Orchestral Music, Free Library of Philadelphia
Composed 1746.

Monn, Georg Matthias

618c [Concerto, violoncello or cembalo,   20'
G minor]
Allegro - Adagio - Allegro non tanto
Solo Vc.(or Cemb.)-Cemb.-Str.
Score: Denkmäler der Tonkunst in Österreich,
XIX/2. Artaria, Vienna, 1912. Edited by
Wilhelm Fischer. 39 p.
Parts: Universal Edition, Vienna, c1913
*Composed and performed at Vienna between 1740
and 1750.*

6786 [Symphony in D major]
1.Allegro 2.Aria 3.Menuetto 4.Allegro
2,0,0,1-2Hn.-Cemb.-Str.
Score: Denkmäler der Tonkunst in Österreich,
XV/2. Artaria, Vienna, and Breitkopf & Här-
tel, Leipzig, 1908. Edited by Karl Horwitz
and Karl Riedel. 14 p.
Parts: Ms. c1976 by The Fleisher Collection of
Orchestral Music, Free Library of Philadelphia
Composed 1740.

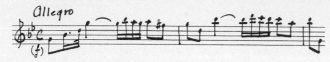

6787 [Symphony in E-flat major]
1.Allegro assai 2.Andante 3.Menuetto
4.Presto
2Ob.-2Hn.-Cemb.-Str.
Score: Denkmäler der Tonkunst in Österreich,
XV/2. Artaria, Vienna, and Breitkopf & Här-
tel, Leipzig, 1908. Edited by Karl Horwitz
and Karl Riedel. 18 p.
Parts: Ms. c1976 by The Fleisher Collection of
Orchestral Music, Free Library of Philadelphia
*This symphony may have been composed by Johann
Christoph Monn, nephew of Georg.*

5152 [Symphony, 2 horns, string orchestra and
cembalo, D major]
1.Allegro 2.Andante 3.Presto
2Hn.-Cemb.-Str.(without Va.)
Score: Denkmäler der Tonkunst in Österreich,
XIX/2. Artaria, Vienna, 1912. Edited by Wilhelm Fischer. 10 p.
Parts: Ms. c1976 by The Fleisher Collection of
Orchestral Music, Free Library of Philadelphia

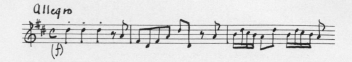

2065s [Symphony, string orchestra and cembalo,
D major]
1.Allegro 2.Larghetto 3.Allegro
Cemb.-Str.
Score: Denkmäler der Tonkunst in Österreich,
XIX/2. Artaria, Vienna, 1912. Edited by Wil-
helm Fischer. 12 p.
Parts: Ms. c1976 by The Fleisher Collection of
Orchestral Music, Free Library of Philadelphia

2063s [Symphony, string orchestra and cembalo,
G major]
1.Allegro 2.Andante 3.Presto
Cemb.-Str.
Score: Denkmäler der Tonkunst in Österreich,
XIX/2. Artaria, Vienna, 1912. Edited by Wil-
helm Fischer. 9 p.
Parts: Ms. c1976 by The Fleisher Collection of
Orchestral Music, Free Library of Philadelphia

2067s [Symphony, string orchestra and cembalo,
A major]
1.Larghetto 2.Allegro moderato 3.Andante
4.Presto
Cemb.-Str.
Score: Denkmäler der Tonkunst in Österreich,
XIX/2. Artaria, Vienna, 1912. Edited by Wil-
helm Fischer. 9 p.
Parts: Ms. c1976 by The Fleisher Collection of
Orchestral Music, Free Library of Philadelphia

2066s [Symphony, string orchestra and cembalo,
B-flat major]
1.Adagio 2.Allegro 3.Largo 4.Allegro assai
Cemb.-Str.
Score: Denkmäler der Tonkunst in Österreich,
XIX/2. Artaria, Vienna, 1912. Edited by Wil-
helm Fischer. 11 p.
Parts: Ms. c1976 by The Fleisher Collection of
Orchestral Music, Free Library of Philadelphia

2270s [Symphony, string orchestra and cembalo,
B major]
1.(Allegro) 2.Andante 3.Presto
Cemb.-Str.
Score: Denkmäler der Tonkunst in Österreich,
XV/2. Artaria, Vienna, 1908. Edited by Karl
Horwitz and Karl Riedel. 9 p.
Parts: Ms. C1976 by The Fleisher Collection of
Orchestral Music, Free Library of Philadelphia

MONN, JOHANN CHRISTOPH.   1726
                          Vienna 24 June 1782

Also spelled: Mann

2064s Divertimento [cembalo and strings,
D major]
1.Andante molto cantabile 2.Allegro
3.Menuet - Trio 4.Allegro molto
Cemb.-Str.
Score: Denkmäler der Tonkunst in Österreich,
XIX/2. Artaria, Vienna, 1912. Edited by Wil-
helm Fischer. 9 p.
Parts: Ms. C1976 by The Fleisher Collection of
Orchestral Music, Free Library of Philadelphia

MONSIGNY, PIERRE ALEXANDRE.
          Fauquembergues, France 17 October 1729
                     Paris 14 January 1817

1022 [Aline, queen of Golconda. Chaconne   5'
   and Rigodon. Transcribed by F.A. Gevaert]
   2,2,0,2-2Hn.-Str.
   A. Durand, Paris [n.d.]
   Score 31 p.
   From the opera. First performed Paris Opéra,
   15 April 1766. Transcription 1876; first
   performance Brussels 1877.

6358 [Le déserteur. Ouverture]
   2Ob.,2Bn.-2Hn.-Str.
   Ms. C1976 by The Fleisher Collection of Orchestral Music, Free Library of Philadelphia
   Score 19 p. Large folio
   From the opera in three acts. First performance Comédie-Italienne, Paris, 6 March 1769.

6858 On ne s'avise jamais de tout. Ouverture.
   Edited by Antonio de Almeida
   Tr.: You can never think of everything
   2Ob.-2Hn.-Str.
   Heugel, Paris, C1964
   Score 12 p.
   From the opera after a tale by Jean de La Fon-
   taine. First performance Paris, 14 September
   1761.

MONTAGNÉ, E.

748s Caressante [Caressing] scherzetto
   Str.(Cb. ad lib.)
   Score: Ms. 11 p.
   Parts: A. Leduc, Paris, c1904

1015s Fanfaretta
   Str.(Cb.ad lib.)
   Score: Ms. 8 p.
   Parts: A. Leduc, Paris, c1905

MONTEMEZZI, ITALO.
          Vigasio, near Verona 4 August 1875
                   Vigasio 15 May 1952

4246 Paolo e Virginia   25'
   3(3rd alt. Picc.),3*,3*,3(3rd alt. C.Bn.)-4,3,
   3,1-Timp.,Perc.-Cel.,2Hp.-Str.
   Ricordi, Milan, 1929
   Miniature score 63 p.
   Suggested by the novel by Jacques-Henri Bernar-
   din de Saint-Pierre. Composed 1930. First
   performance Rome, February 1930.

MONTEVERDI, CLAUDIO.
          Cremona, Italy baptized 15 May 1567
               Venice 29 November 1643

2319s [Il ballo delle ingrate. Ballo.   5'
   Realized by Raymond Leppard]
   Tr.: The dance of the heartless ladies
   Cemb.(or Pno.)-Str.
   Faber Music Ltd., London, C1967
   Score 9 p.
   From the opera-ballet. First performed Mantua,
   4 June 1608. First performance of this edition,
   1958, Aldeburgh Festival.

2372 Concerto. Settimo libro de   20'
   madrigali [Transcribed by G. F. Malipiero]
   2,2,2,2-2Hn.-Str.
   Ms.
   Score 44 p.
   Transcribed 1929, first performance Prague, 5
   September 1930.

2221s Orfeo [favola in musica].   8-10'
   Sinfonie e ritornelli. Transcribed for string
   orchestra by Gian Francesco Malipiero
   1.Allegro 2.Allegro energico 3.Lento
   4.Allegro 5.Moresca
   Str.
   G. Ricordi, Milan, 1930
   Score 13 p.
   From the opera based on the myth. First performance Mantua, 22 February 1607, under the
   title La Favola d'Orfeo.

Monti, Vittorio

MONTI, VITTORIO.   Naples 6 January 1868
                          Paris ca.1925

   Also published under the pseudonym: V. Timon

   1096s Coquetterie
          Solo Vn.-Str.
          Score: Ms. 9 p.
          Parts: Ricordi, Paris, ^c1913

MOÓR, EMANUEL. Kecskemét, Hungary 19 February 1863
               Mont-Pélerin, Switzerland 20 October 1931

   124s Barcarole, Op. 38 [D minor]
         Str.
         N. Simrock, Berlin, ^c1895
         Score 7 p.

   612p [Concerto, piano, D major]
         1.Allegro moderato 2.Molto andante 3.Finale
         Solo Pno.-2,2,2,2-4,2,3-Timp.-Str.
         N. Simrock, Berlin, ^c1894
         Score 99 p.

   642p [Concerto, piano, Op. 57, D-flat   20'
         major]
         Langsam - Adagio - Allegro
         Solo Pno.-2,2,2,2-4,3,3,1-Timp.-Str.
         C.F.W. Siegel, Leipzig [1906?]
         Score 87 p.

   816m [Concerto, piano, violin, violoncello 23'
         and orchestra, Op. 70]
         1.Allegro 2.Intermezzo 3.Adagio 4.Allegro
         con brio
         Solo Pno., Solo Vn., Solo Vc.-2,2,2,2-4,3,3,1
         -Timp.,Cym.,Trgl.-Str.
         Score: Ms. 168 p.
         Parts: C.F.W. Siegel, Leipzig [1908?]

   785v [Concerto, violin, Op. 62, G major]
         1.Mässig bewegt 2.Scherzo 3.Finale
         Solo Vn.-2,2,2,2-4,2,3-Timp.-Str.
         Simrock, Berlin, ^c1905
         Score 106 p.
         *First performance London, 1907, Eugène Ysaÿe
         soloist.*

   545c [Concerto, violoncello, no. 1, Op. 61,
         E minor]
         In one movement
         Solo Vc.-2,2,2,2-4,2,3-Timp.,Cym.,Trgl.-Str.
         C.F.W. Siegel, Leipzig [n.d.]
         Score 70 p.

   559c [Concerto, violoncello, no. 2, Op. 64,
         C-sharp minor]
         1.Largo 2.Presto 3.Adagio 4.Allegro
         Solo Vc.-2,2,2,2-4,2,3,1-Timp.-Str.
         C.F.W. Siegel, Leipzig [n.d.]
         Score 78 p.

   561c [Concerto, 2 violoncellos, Op. 69,
         D major]
         1.Molto moderato 2.Intermezzo 3.Adagio
         4.Finale
         2 Solo Vc.-2,2,2,2-4,2,3-Timp.,Trgl.-Str.
         C.W.F. Siegel, Leipzig [n.d.]
         Score 70 p.

   4524 [Improvisations on an original theme,
         Op. 63]
         In one movement
         2,2,2,2-4,3,3,1-Timp.,Trgl.,Cym.-Hp.-Str.
         C.F.W. Siegel, Leipzig [n.d.]
         Score 71 p.
         Composed 1906.

   593v Rhapsodie, Op. 84, A major   *14'30"*
         Solo Vn.-2,2,2,2-4,2,3-Timp.-Str.
         A. Zunz-Mathot, Paris, ^c1909
         Score 34 p.

   125s Serenade, Op. 16, F major
         Str.
         B. Schott's Söhne, Mainz [n.d.]
         Score 19 p.

   172s [Suite, Op. 73, C major. Transcribed for
         string orchestra by the composer]
         Solo Vn.-Str.
         C.F.W. Siegel, Leipzig [n.d.]
         Miniature score 30 p.
         Originally composed for violin and piano.

   2366 Suite for double quintet, Op. 103, A major
         1,1,1,1-Hn.-Str.
         A. Zunz-Mathot, Paris, ^c1913
         Miniature score 64 p.

   6952 [Symphonic thoughts, suite, Op. 75]
         1.Largo 2.Allegro 3.Adagio 4.Allegro
         2,2,2,2-4,3,3,1-Timp.-Hp.-Str.
         A. Zunz-Mathot, Paris, ^c1909
         Score 82 p.
         Composed 1908.

   6292 [Symphony no. 2, Kossuth, C major]
         1.Andante maestoso - Allegro con brio 2.
         Andante sostenuto 3.Scherzo 4.Allegro poco
         maestoso
         2,2,2,2-4,2,3,1-Timp.-Str.
         N. Simrock, Berlin, 1895
         Score 100 p.
         *Composed 1895. First performance Pest, Hun-
         gary, 20 November 1895, the composer conducting.*

   5788 [Symphony no. 3, Op. 45, D minor]
         1.Allegro un poco agitato 2.Andante sostenuto
         3.Scherzo 4.Finale
         3*,3*,3*,2-4,3,3,1-Timp.-Str.
         Rózsavölgyi, Budapest [189-?]
         Score 114 p.
         Composed 1895.

MOORE, DOUGLAS STUART.
               Cutchogue, New York 10 August 1893
               Greenport, Long Island 25 July 1969

   4842 Farm journal, suite for chamber   *13-16'*
         orchestra
         1.Up early 2.Sunday clothes 3.Lamplight
         4.Harvest song
         2(2nd alt. Picc.),2,2,2-2,1-Timp.,Perc.-Str.
         Carl Fischer, New York, ^c1950
         Score 94 p.
         *Much of the thematic material originally com-
         posed 1940 for a documentary film, Power and*

the Land. *This suite commissioned by The Little Orchestra Society. Composed 1947. First performance New York, January 1948, Little Orchestra Society, Thomas Scherman conductor.*

2821 Overture on an American tune   *6'*
3*,2,2,2-4,3,3,1-Timp.,Perc.-Hp.-Str.
Ms.
Score 58 p.
Composed 1931. First performance under original title Overture Babbitt, New York, 11 December 1932, Manhattan Symphony Orchestra, the composer conducting.

1953 Pageant of P. T. Barnum, suite for   *18'*
orchestra
1.Boyhood at Bethel 2.Joice Heth, 161-year-old
Negress 3.General and Mrs. Tom Thumb 4.Jenny
Lind 5.Circus parade
3*,3*,3*,3*-4,3,3,1-Timp.,Perc.-Cel.,Hp.-Str.
C.C. Birchard, Boston, [c]1929
Score 90 p.
Completed 1924; first performance Rochester, 21 November 1927, Rochester Philharmonic Orchestra.

3637 Village music, for small or full   *12'*
orchestra
1.Square dance 2.Procession 3.Nocturne 4.Jig
2*(Picc. ad lib.),1(ad lib.),2,1(ad lib.)-2(ad
lib.),2,1-Timp.,Perc.-Str.
Ms.
Score 59 p.
Commissioned by Music Press, 1941. Composed 1941. First performance New York, 18 December 1941, National Youth Administration Symphony Orchestra, Dean Dixon conductor.

MOORE, TIMOTHY.
         b. Cambridge, England 19 February 1922

202m Concerto for clarinet and strings   *14'30"*
1.Allegro 2.Adagio 3.Rondo: Allegro
Solo Cl.-Str.
Ms. [c]1975 by Timothy Moore
Score 44 p.
Composed 1956.

203m Concerto for trumpet and strings   *20'*
1.Allegro moderato 2.Adagio 3.Rondo
Solo Tpt.-Str.
Ms. [c]1975 by Timothy Moore
Score 51 p.
Composed 1948. First performance London, 21 May 1949, Hendon String Orchestra, Roy Budden conductor, David Mason soloist.

MORALES, OLALLO JUAN MAGNUS.
        Almeria, Spain 15 October 1874
        Tällberg, Sweden 29 April 1957

5035 [Overture to Abu Casem's slippers,   *10'30"*
Op. 16]
3*,3*,3*,3*-4,3,3,1-Timp.,Perc.-Cel.,Hp.-Tenor
Voice-Str.
Ms.
Score 80 p. Large folio

Composed 1926. First performance Barcelona, 7 October 1929, The Exhibition Orchestra, Adolf Wiklund conductor.

MORENO, SEGUNDO LUÍS.
    Cotacachi, Imbabura, Ecuador 3 August 1882
         Quito, Ecuador 18 December 1972

3740 La coronación, marcha triunfal [on a   *5'*
fragment of the national hymn of Ecuador]
2,2,2,2-2,2,2-Timp.-Str.
Ms.
Score 32 p.
Originally composed for military band to celebrate the New Year, 1918. Orchestrated 1920.

3884 Diez de Agosto [The tenth of August,   *10'*
overture]
2,2,2,2-0,3,3-Str.(without Va.)
Ms.
Score 59 p.
Composed 1911. First performance at a concert commemorating the first centenary of the independence of Venezuela, 4 July 1911, Domenico Brescia conductor. Awarded second prize at the Inter-Provincial Exposition of Ibarra, 1929.

4186 [Prelude for small orchestra]
2,2,2,1-0,2,3Cnt.,3-B.Dr.-Str.
Ms.
Score 8 p.
Composed 1910. First performance Quito, Ecuador, 20 July 1910.

[Suite ecuatoriana no. 1]
4249 Movement 1. Preludio sinfónico
5645 Movement 2. Danza ecuatoriana (Sanjuanito)
4250 Movement 3. Romanza sin palabras [without
                 words]
5646 Movement 4. Rondo
2,2,2,2-2,0,2Cnt.,2-Timp.,Perc.-Str.
Ms.
Scores: 15 p., 20 p. (large folio), 12 p.,
31 p. (large folio)
Composed 1922. First performance Cuenca, Ecuador, 24 July 1940.

MORET, ERNEST.

[Three pieces for violin and orchestra]
667v No. 1 Berceuse pour un soir d'automne
Solo Vn.-1,1,2,2-2Hn.-Hp.-Str.
809v No. 2 Chant et danse slaves
Solo Vn.-2,2(2nd alt. E.H.),2,2-2,2,3-Timp.,
Perc.-Hp.-Str.
691v No. 3 Airs bohémiens
Solo Vn.-3*,2,2,3*-4,2,3,1-Timp.,Perc.-Hp.-Str.
Heugel, Paris, [c]1909, [c]1909, [c]1912
Scores: 11 p., 45 p., 29 p.

MORGAN, BERNARD.   Bialystok, Poland 1 August 1910
                  Philadelphia 16 August 1976

7209 Divertimento for orchestra
1.Overture 2.Plaintive song 3.March 4.Malicious mischief 5.Sermon
3*,2,2,2-4,3,3,1-Timp.,Perc.-Pno.,Hp.-Str.
Ms. [c]1976 by Bernard Morgan
Score 199 p.

Morgan, Bernard

7126 Hebrew suite   16'
1.[Wedding dance] 2.[Lullaby] 3.[Banquet
music]
3*,3*,2,2-4,2,3,1-Timp.,Perc.-Cel.,Hp.-Str.
Ms. c1975 by Bernard Morgan
Score 78 p.
*Based on traditional Jewish melodies. Composed
1936. First performance Temple University,
Philadelphia, 4 August 1936.*

7103 Impressions of Mummers' Day
1.Fanfare 2.Parade 3.Fancy Dress Division
4.Eccentric waltzers 5.Struttin' high (minstrels)
3*,3*,3*,2-4,3,3,1-Timp.,Perc.-Pno.,Cel.,Hp.-
Str.
Ms. c1975 by Bernard Morgan
Score 94 p. Large folio
*Originally composed 1941, under the title Mum-
mers' Day Suite. First performance 8 March
1976, Philadelphia Orchestra, William Smith
conductor. Fanfare available separately as
Catalog no. 7112.*

7210 Mist on the riverside
2,3*,3*,2-4,2,3,1-Timp.,Perc.-Pno.,Cel.-Str.
Ms. c1976 by Bernard Morgan
Score 17 p.
Composed 1952.

2379s Music for strings
1.Allegro energico 2.Slow 3.Allegro 4.Vivo
Str.
Ms. c1975 by Bernard Morgan
Score 87 p.
*Composed 1948. First performance of move-
ments I and III, Philadelphia, 6 December
1976, Mostovoy Soloists, Marc Mostovoy conductor.*

7165 Palestinian fantasy
1(alt. Picc.),1,2,1-2,2,1-Timp.,Perc.-Str.
Ms. c1975 by Bernard Morgan
Score 26 p.

7211 Today's children, a ballet suite
1.Commencement 2.Competition 3.Frustration
4.Statement
3*,3*,3*,2-4,3,3,1-Timp.,Xyl.-Pno.-Str.
Ms. c1976 by Bernard Morgan
Score 65 p.
*Commissioned by the Philadelphia Dance Associ-
ation. Composed 1940. First performance in a
piano version, All-Philadelphia Dance Recital,
12 April 1940.*

MORGAN, ROBERT ORLANDO.
            b. Manchester, England 16 March 1865

Also published under the pseudonym: John Ingram

356 La mort de Melisande, by John Ingram
[pseudonym]
3*,2(2nd alt. E.H.),2,3-4,2,3,1-Timp.,Perc.-
Cel.,Hp.-Str.
Breitkopf & Härtel, New York, c1922
Score 16 p.

MORILLO, ROBERTO GARCÍA.
    See: GARCÍA MORILLO, ROBERTO.

MORITZ, EDVARD.   Hamburg 23 June 1891

3595 [Concerto, percussion and   24'
wind orchestra, Op. 55]
1.Allegro 2.Blues 3.Kleines Intermezzo
4.Finale
3*,2,3*,2-2,1,1,1-Timp.,Perc.
Ms.
Score 82 p.
*Composed 1927. First performance Wiesbaden,
16 April 1928, Wiesbaden Orchestra, Carl
Schuricht conductor.*

739p [Concerto, piano, Op. 46]   25'
1.Rasche Viertel 2.Kleines Intermezzo 3.Ruhig
4.Vivace
Solo Pno.-1(alt. Picc.),1,1,1-2,1-Perc.-Str.
Ms.
Score 109 p.
*Composed 1928. First performance Berlin, 1929,
Berlin Philharmonic Orchestra, the composer
conducting, Birger Hammer soloist.*

943m [Concerto, saxophone, Op. 97]   35'
1.Allegro molto 2.Molto andante 3.Vivace
Solo Sax.-3*,2,2,2-4,3,3,1-Timp.,Perc.-Hp.-Str.
Ms.
Score 179 p.
*Composed 1939-40. First performance Philadel-
phia, 26 May 1940, Pennsylvania Symphony Orches-
tra of the WPA, the composer conducting, Cecil
Leeson soloist.*

1123v [Concerto, viola, Op. 98]   35'
1.Molto moderato 2.Molto andante 3.Molto
vivace
Solo Va.-3*,2,2,3*-4,3,3,1-Timp.,Perc.-Hp.-Str.
Ms.
Score 120 p.
Composed 1939.

3316 Divertimento, Op. 63   15'
1.Allegro molto 2.Andante 3.Allegro moderato
3*,2,3*,3*-4Hn.,1Tpt.-Timp.,Perc.-Hp.
Ms.
Score 64 p.
Composed 1928.

MORLEY, CHARLES. pseudonym.
    See: BEHR, FRANZ FRANÇOIS.

MOROSS, JEROME.   Brooklyn 1 August 1913

2799 Biguine   5'
3*,2,3*,2-4,4,3,1-Timp.,Perc.-Pno.-Str.
New Music, San Francisco, c1935
Score 32 p.

2798 Paeans   5'
2*,1,1,1-2,2,1-Timp.,Perc.-Pno.-Str.
New Music, San Francisco, c1933
Score 16 p.
*Composed 1931. First performance New York, 13
February 1932, Chamber Symphony Orchestra,
Bernard Herrmann conductor.*

4040 Symphony   *22'*
1.Theme and variations 2.Sonata - Scherzo 3.
Invention (A ramble on a hobo tune) 4.Fugue
3(3rd alt. Picc.),3(3rd alt. E.H.),3(2nd alt.
Cl. in E-flat,3rd alt. B.Cl.),3(3rd alt. C.Bn.)
-4,3(1st alt. Tpt. in D &Cnt. in B-flat),3,1-
Timp.,Perc.-Cel.(alt. Pno.)-Str.
Ms.
Score 106 p. Large folio
*Composed 1940-42. First performance Seattle,
18 October 1943, Seattle Symphony Orchestra,
Sir Thomas Beecham conductor.*

3476 A tall story   *9'*
3(3rd alt. Picc.),2,3(3rd alt. B.Cl.),2-4,3,
3,1-Timp.,Perc.-Str.
Ms.
Score 63 p.
*Commissioned by CBS, 1938. Composed 1938.
First performance CBS broadcast, New York, 25
September 1938, Howard Barlow conductor.*

MORRIS, HAROLD.   San Antonio, Texas 17 March 1890
                                New York 6 May 1964

697p [Concerto, piano]   *27'*
1.Allegro moderato, marcato 2.Variations on
the American Negro Pilgrim song 3.Rondo
Solo Pno.-2,3*,2,2-4,3,3,1-Timp.,Perc.-Str.
C.C. Birchard, Boston, ^C1932
Score 154 p. Large folio
*Composed 1927; second movement from the Negro
song, I'm a Poor Wayfarin' Stranger. First
performance Boston, 23 October 1931, Boston
Symphony Orchestra, Serge Koussevitzky con-
ductor, the composer as soloist. Received the
Juilliard Publication Award, 1932.*

1119v [Concerto, violin]   *23'*
1.Very broadly 2.Slowly 3.With vivacity and
humor
Solo Vn.-2,2,2,2-4,2,2-Timp.,Perc.-Str.
Ms.
Score 126 p.
*Composed 1938. First performance NBC broad-
cast, New York, 25 May 1939, Frank Black conductor, Philip Frank soloist. Won first prize
in the National Federation of Music Clubs
Competition, 1939.*

5135 Dramatic overture [final version]   *14'*
3*,3*,4*(1Cl. in E-flat),3*-4,3,3,1-Timp.,
Perc.-Str.
Ms.
Score 25 p. Large folio
*Composed 1950. First performance Austin, 5
February 1950, Austin Symphony Orchestra.*

3616 Passacaglia   *10'*
2,3*,2,2-4,3,3,1-Timp.,Trgl.,Cym.-Str.
Ms.
Score 24 p.
Composed 1939.

2644 Poem, for orchestra, after Tagore's   *13'*
Gitanjali
4,3*,3*,3*-4,3,3,1-Timp.,Perc.-Cel.,Hp.-Str.
Ms.
Score 54 p.

*Composed 1916. First performance under origi-
nal title Symphonic Poem, Cincinnati, 29 November 1918, Cincinnati Symphony Orchestra, Eugène
Ysaÿe conductor.*

3781 Prelude and fugue   *11'*
2,3*,2,2-4,3,3,1-Timp.,Perc.-Str.
Ms.
Score 44 p.

3300 Suite, for small orchestra   *16'*
1.Fugal overture 2.Intermezzo 3.Humoreske
1,1,1,1-1,1,1-Timp.,Perc.-Pno.-Str.
Ms.
Score 12 p. Large folio
*Composed 1938. First performance in a CBS
broadcast, New York, 1 November 1941, Howard
Barlow conductor.*

2696 Symphony, Prospice, from the poem   *33'*
by Robert Browning
1.Elegy 2.Scherzo 3.Adagio recitativo
4.Allegro vigoroso
3(3rd alt. Picc.),3*,3*,3*-4,3,3,1-Timp.,Perc.-
Pno.,Cel.-Str.
Affiliated Music Corp., New York, ^C1938
Score 105 p.
Composed 1934.

2643 Variations on the American Negro   *14'*
spiritual, I Was Way Down a-Yonder (Dum-a-Lum),
for chamber orchestra
1,1,1,1-Hn.-Pno.-Str.
Ms.
Score 64 p.
*Composed 1929. First performance New York, 10
January 1932, New York Chamber Music Society,
Carolyn Beebe conductor.*

MORTARI, VIRGILIO.   Passirana di Lainate,
                         near Milan 6 December 1902

3911 Rapsodia   *16'*
3*,3*,3*,3*-4,3,3,1-Timp.,Perc.-Hp.-Str.
Ricordi, Milan, ^C1933
Miniature score 64 p.
*Composed 1929-30. First performance at the
Ninth Festival of the International Society for
Contemporary Music, London, 27 July 1931,
Alfredo Casella conductor.*

MORTELMANS, LODEWIJK.   Antwerp 5 February 1868
                          Antwerp 24 June 1952

1683s Three little elegies
1.Méditation triste 2.Résignation 3.Tré-
passés [The dead]
Str.
Ms.
Score 9 p.

MORTET, LUIS CLUZEAU.
See: CLUZEAU MORTET, LUIS.

MÓRY, JANOS VON.   Banska Bystrica, Hungary
                  (now Czechoslovakia) 10 July 1892

1796 [At the foot of Krivan mountain,   *12'*
Slovac dance suite, Op. 19]

Móry, Janos von

3(3rd alt. Picc.),2,2,2-4,2,3,1-Timp.,Perc.-
Hp.-Str.
Ries & Erler, Berlin, ^c1929
Score 55 p.
Composed 1928. First performance Breslau, 1929.

1795 [Slovac pastoral dances] Op. 18   *10'*
3(3rd alt. Picc.),3(3rd alt. E.H.),3,3-4,3,3,
1-Timp.,Perc.-Hp.-Str.
Ries & Erler, Berlin, ^c1928
Score 36 p.
*Composed 1928. First performance Magdeburg
1929.*

MOSCHELES, IGNAZ.   Prague 30 May 1794
                           Leipzig 10 March 1870

684p [Concerto, piano, no. 2, Op. 56, E-flat
major]
Allegro moderato - Adagio - Allegretto
Solo Pno.-2,2,2,2-4(2 ad lib.),2,B.Tbn.-Timp.
-Str.
Score: Ms. 151 p.
Parts: Haslinger, Vienna [n.d.]

446p [Concerto, piano, no. 3, Op. 58,   *28'*
G minor]
Allegro moderato - Adagio - Allegro agitato
Solo Pno.-2,2,2,2-2,2,3-Timp.-Str.
Score: Ms. 71 p.
Parts: [Schlesinger, Berlin, n.d.]
*Composed 1820-21. First performance Paris
ca.1821.*

691p [Concerto, piano, no. 5, Op. 87, C major]
Allegro moderato - Adagio - Allegro vivace
Solo Pno.-2,2,2,2-4(2 ad lib.),2,B.Tbn.-Timp.
-Str.
Score: Ms. 208 p.
Parts: Haslinger, Vienna [n.d.]
Composed after 1830.

692p [Concerto, piano, no. 6, Fantastique,
Op. 90, B-flat major]
Solo Pno.-2,2,2,2-2,2,B.Tbn.-Timp.-Str.
Score: Ms. 124 p.
Parts: Schlesinger, Berlin [n.d.]

MOSER, FRANZ JOSEPH.   Vienna 20 March 1880
                              Vienna 27 March 1939

1694 [Serenade for 15 wind instruments,   *30'*
Op. 35]
2(2nd alt. Picc.),3*,3*,3*-4Hn.
Universal Edition, Vienna, ^c1922
Score 80 p.
*Composed 1921. First performance Vienna, 7
March 1922, the composer conducting.*

MÖSER, L.

818m Stilles Sehnen [Secret longing]
Solo Ob.-1,0,2-2Hn.-Timp.-Str.
Ms.
Score 5 p.

MOSER, RUDOLF.
          Niederuzwil, Switzerland 7 January 1892
          Silvaplana, Switzerland 20 August 1960

477m [Concerto, oboe and string   *16'*
orchestra, Op. 86]
1.Allegro moderato 2.Andante 3.Vivace
Solo Ob.-Str.
Ms.
Score 13 p.
*Composed 1950. First performance Basel, 10
February 1952, Basel Conservatory Orchestra,
Walter Geiser conductor, Hubert Fauquex soloist.*

1116m [Concerto, organ and string   *20-25'*
orchestra, Op. 37]
1.Allegro moderato 2.Poco adagio 3.Allegro
Solo Org.-Pno.(ad lib.)-Str.
Ms.
Score 40 p.
*Composed 1927. First performance Basel, 1
February 1928, Basel Chamber Orchestra, Paul
Sacher conductor, Adolf Hamm soloist.*

389v [Concerto, viola and chamber   *18'*
orchestra, Op. 62]
1.Allegro 2.Andante 3.Presto
Solo Va.-1,0,1,1-Hpscd.(or Pno.)-Str.
Ms.
Score 42 p.
*Commissioned by Alexander Schaichet and the
Zurich Chamber Orchestra. Composed 1934.
First performance Zurich, 24 January 1935,
Zurich Chamber Orchestra, the composer con-
ducting, Alexander Schaichet soloist.*

1208v [Concerto, violin and string   *18'*
orchestra, Op. 39]
1.Allegro moderato 2.Larghetto 3.Allegro
vivace
Solo Vn.-Timp.-Hpscd.(or Pno.)-Str.
Ms.
Score 42 p.
*Composed 1928. First performance Basel, 17
November 1928, Basler Kammerorchester, Paul
Sacher conductor, Anna Hegner soloist.*

5418 [Overture to a church music   *10'*
recital, Op. 41]
2,1,1,1-2,1-Timp.-Str.
Ms.
Score 37 p.
*Composed 1928. First performance Basel, 28
February 1930, Basel Orchestra Union, the com-
poser conducting.*

775c [Passacaglia for violoncellos,   *10'*
Op. 72]
Violoncellos (divided into seven groups)
Ms.
Score 11 p.
*Commissioned by Julius Bächi and Heinrich Wag-
ner for the Concert to Honor Pablo Casals,
1941. Composed 1941. First performance
Zurich, 26 October 1941, the composer con-
ducting.*

MOSSOLOV, ALEXANDER VASSILIEVICH.
                              b. Kiev 10 August 1900

2124 [Iron foundry, engine music, Op. 19]   *10'*
3*,3*,3*,3*-4,3,3,1-Timp.,Perc.-Str.

Mussektor, Moscow, c1929
Score 38 p.
Composed 1928. First performance 1928.

MOSZKOWSKI, MORITZ (*or* MAURICE).
Breslau, Germany 23 August 1854
Paris 4 March 1925

637v Ballade, Op. 16 no. 1
Solo Vn.-2,2,2,2-2,2-Timp.-Hp.(ad lib.)-Str.
J. Hainauer [Breslau, n.d.]
Score 47 p.

[Boabdil, the last king of the Moors.
Excerpts]
4368 Prelude
3*,3*,2,3-4,2,3,1-Timp.-2Hp.-Str.
950 Ballet music I. Malaguena   5'
3*,2,2,2-4,2,3,1-Timp.,Perc.-2Hp.-Str.
629 Ballet music II. Scherzo-Valse   5'
3*,2,2,2-4Hn.-Timp.,Trgl.-Hp.-Str.
5682 Ballet music III. Moorish fantasy 5'
3*,2,2,3*-4,4,3,1-Timp.,Perc.-2Hp.-Str.
C.F. Peters, Leipzig [n.d.]
Scores: 12 p., 42 p., 30 p., 23 p.
*From the opera about Muḥammad XI, called Boab-
dil, the last Nasrid sultan of Granada. First
performance Berlin, 21 April 1892.*

449p [Concerto, piano, Op. 59, E major]   34'
1.Moderato 2.Andante 3.Scherzo 4.Allegro
deciso
Solo Pno.-2,2,2,2-4,2,3-Timp.,Trgl.-Hp.-Str.
C.F. Peters, Leipzig, c1898
Score 113 p.
Composed 1898. First performance Berlin 1899.

602v [Concerto, violin, Op. 30, C major]   30'
1.Allegro commodo 2.Andante 3.Vivace
Solo Vn.-2,2,2,2-4,2-Timp.-Str.
Bote & Bock, Berlin [n.d.]
Score 266 p.
*Composed 1881. First performance Leipzig,
Emile Sauret soloist.*

776 [Don Juan and Faust. Incidental music   10'
(Six Airs de Ballet, Op. 56) to the drama by
Christian Grabbe]
1.Entr'acte 2.Sarabande 3.Passepied 4.Inter-
mezzo 5.Fantasmagorie 6.Minuetto
2,2,2,2-2Hn.-Timp.,Trgl.Dr.-Hp.-Str.
Ries & Erler, Berlin, c1896
Score 40 p.
*Composed 1896. First performance Berlin, 1897,
the composer conducting. Nos. 2 and 3 available separately as Catalog no. 383s and 384s.*

13 [From other lands, Op. 23]
[1.Russian 2.Italian 3.German 4.Spanish
5.Polish 6.Hungarian]
3*,2,2,2-4,2,3-Timp.,Perc.-2Hp.(2nd ad lib.)-
Str.
J. Hainauer, Breslau [n.d.]
Score 155 p.

61 Habanera, Op. 65 no. 3   3'
3*,2,2,2-4,2-Timp.,Trgl.,Tamb.-Hp.-Str.
C.F. Peters, Leipzig, c1904

Score 26 p.
First performance Paris, 1901.

783s Intimité, Op. 77 no. 5. Arranged by Alfred
Kaiser
Pno.-Str.
Score: Ms. 9 p.
Parts: B. Schott's Söhne, Mainz [n.d.]
Originally composed for piano solo.

5537 [Joan of Arc, Op. 19, symphonic poem,   15'
after Schiller's drama, The Maid of Orleans]
1.[Joan's idyllic life - A vision convinces
her of her noble mission] 2.[Inner discord -
Reminiscences] 3.[Entrance of the victors to
the coronation at Rheims] 4.[Joan in prison;
her bonds are broken - Triumph, death and trans-
figuration]
3*,2,2,2-3-4,3,3-Timp.,Perc.-Hp.-Str.
Julius Hainauer, Breslau [n.d.]
Score 316 p.

Laurin, Op. 53 [ballet]
5533 Bacchanale
5595 No. 3 [Introduction and dance of the
rose-elves]
5681 No. 4 [March of the dwarfs]
5301 No. 7 [Valse coquette]
3*,2,2,3-4,4,3,1-Timp.,Perc.-Hp.-Str.
Bote & Bock, Berlin, c1895, c1896
Scores: 28 p., 19 p., 19 p., 20 p.
Composed 1895 or before, not 1896.

82s Prélude et fugue, Op. 85 [D minor]
Str.
C.F. Peters, Leipzig, c1911
Score 14 p.

798 Près du berceau [At the cradle]   2'
Op. 58 no. 3
2,1,2,1-2Hn.-Str.
Enoch, Paris, c1896
Score 8 p.
*Composed 1894. First performance Berlin, 1895,
the composer conducting.*

5538 Serenata, Op. 15. Transcribed   2'30"
for orchestra by Fabian Rehfeld
2*,2,2,2-4,2,3-Glock.-Hp.-Str.
Julius Hainauer, Breslau [n.d.]
Score 9 p.
Originally composed for piano.

675 [Spanish dance, Op. 21 no. 4. Arranged by
Ross Jungnickel]
3*,2,2,2-4,2,Cnt.,3,1-Timp.,Perc.-Hp.-Str.
R. Jungnickel, New York, c1925
Score 31 p.

589 [Spanish dances, Op. 12, pt. 1. No. 2   5'
in G minor *and* No. 5 in D major. Orchestrated
by P. Scharwenka]
3*,2,2,2-4,2,3-Timp.,Perc.-Str.
C.F. Peters, Leipzig [n.d.]
Score 33 p.
*Composed for piano solo. Orchestrated 1877;
first performance Berlin, 1888.*

Moszkowski, Moritz

590 [Spanish dances, Op. 12, pt. 2. No. 1   9'
in C major; No. 3 in A major; No. 4 in B-flat
major. Orchestrated by Valentine Frank]
3*,2,2,2-4,2,3-Timp.,Perc.-Str.
C.F. Peters, Leipzig [1884]
Score 39 p.
Composed for piano solo. Orchestrated 1876.

1804 [Suite no. 1, Op. 39, F major]   30'
1.Allegro molto e brioso 2.Allegretto giojoso
3.Tema con variazioni 4.Intermezzo 5.Per-
petuum mobile
3(2nd & 3rd alt. Picc.),2,2,3-4,2-Timp.,Trgl.,
Small Bells-Hp.-Str.
J. Hainauer, Breslau [n.d.]
Score 201 p.
Composed and first performed Berlin, 1885.

1818 [Suite no. 2, Op. 47, G minor]   30'
1.Prelude 2.Fugue 3.Scherzo 4.Larghetto
5.Intermezzo 6.March
3(3rd alt. Picc.),2,2,3*-4,2,3,1-Timp.,Perc.-
Org.,Hp.-Str.
J. Hainauer, Breslau [n.d.]
Score 159 p.
Composed and first performed Berlin, 1889.

MOULE-EVANS, DAVID.
        b. Ashford, Kent, England 21 November 1905

1950s The haunted place, miniature for   4'
string orchestra
Str.
Williams, London, C1949 by David Moule-Evans
and Joseph Williams, Ltd.
Score 8 p.
Composed 1949.

4616 The spirit of London, concert   14-15'
overture
2(2nd alt. Picc.),2,2,2-4,3(3rd optional),3,
1(optional)-Timp.,Perc.-Hp.-Str.
Williams, London, C1947 by David Moule-Evans
and Joseph Williams, Ltd.
Score 92 p. Large folio
Composed 1947.

4611 Vienna rhapsody   12-13'
2(2nd alt. Picc.),2,2,2-4,2,3,1-Timp.,Perc.-
Hp.-Str.
Williams, London, C1948 by David Moule-Evans
and Joseph Williams, Ltd.
Score 73 p. Large folio
Composed 1948.

MOUQUET, JULES.   Paris 10 July 1867
                       Paris 25 October 1946

137s Berceuse, flûte, Op. 22
Solo Fl.-Str.
H. Lemoine, Paris, C1908
Score 8 p.

234s Deux petites pièces, Op. 25
1.Au berceau 2.Sarabande
Str.
H. Lemoine, Paris, C1908
Score 8 p.

537m La flûte de Pan, sonata, Op. 15   14'
1.[Pan and the shepherds] 2.[Pan and the
birds] 3.[Pan and the nymphs]
Solo Fl.-0,1,1,1-Hn.-Timp.-Hp.(ad lib.)-Str.
H. Lemoine, Paris [n.d.]
Score 48 p.

732m Solo de concours. Orchestrated by Ciro
Urbini
Solo Cl.-1,1,2,1-2,2,3-Timp.-Str.
Score: Ms. 22 p.
Parts: Evette & Schaeffer, Paris, C1925
*Composed for the competition of the Conserva-
toire National de Paris, 1902.*

MOURANT, WALTER.   Chicago 29 August 1910

6755 Aria for orchestra (Harpers   16'30"
Ferry, W. Va.)
3*,3*,3*,3*-4,3,3,1-Timp.,Perc.-Hp.-Str.
Ms. C1960 by Walter Mourant
Score 31 p. Large folio
*Composed 1960. First performance Rochester,
6 May 1967, Eastman-Rochester Symphony Orches-
tra, Howard Hanson conductor.*

MOURET, JEAN JOSEPH.   Avignon 11 April 1682
                           Charenton 20 December 1738

6916 [Suite no. 1. Fanfares for trumpets, tim-
pani, violins and oboes] Realization by
Michel Sanvoisin
In four movements
0,2,0,2-2Tpt.-Timp.-Cemb.-2Vn.,Cb.
Heugel, Paris, C1970
Score 16 p.

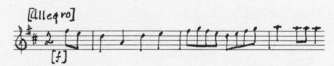

MOUSSORGSKY, MODEST PETROVICH.
    See: MUSSORGSKY, MODEST PETROVICH.

MOUTON, HUBERT.

713s Une toute petite pensée, intermezzo
Str.
Score: Ms. 12 p.
Parts: Durand, Paris, C1913

MOWREY, DENT.   New York 11 June 1889

2878 Danse americaine   7'
3,2,2,2-4,4,3,1-Timp.,Perc.-Hp.-Str.
Ms.
Score 27 p.
*Originally composed for piano, 1929; orches-
trated 1933. First performance Portland, Ore-
gon, 21 November 1933, Portland Symphony
Orchestra, Willem van Hoogstraten conductor.*

MOYSE, LOUIS.
b. Scheveningen, Netherlands 14 August 1912

422m Marlborian concerto no. 1, for   20'
2 horns soli and string orchestra
1.Allegro molto 2.Andante 3.Allegro (Tempo
di marcia) 4.Allegro molto vivo
2 Solo Hn.-Str.
Ms.
Score 70 p.
*Composed 1958 at Marlboro Music School, Ver-
mont. First performance Ninth Annual May Festival Concert at the Brattleboro Music Center,
Vermont, 17 May 1959, Brattleboro Festival
Orchestra, the composer conducting, Myron
Bloom and Richard Mackey soloists.*

MOYZES, ALEXANDER.   Klástor pod Znievom,
Slovakia 4 September 1906

5181 [Jánošík, overture to an   7'30"
adventure-play]
2(2nd alt. Picc.),1,2,1-2,2,1-Timp.,Perc.-
Pno.(or Hp.)-Str.
Universal Edition, Vienna, c1936
Score 58 p.
*Jánošík was the Slovak Robin Hood. Composed
1934. First performance Stuttgart, 1936.
Revised 1943.*

MOZART, LEOPOLD.   Augsburg 14 November 1719
Salzburg 28 May 1787

Full name: Johann Georg Leopold Mozart

757m [Concerto, trumpet, D major] Edited   9'
by Max Seiffert
1.Adagio 2.Allegro moderato
Solo Tpt.-2Hn.-Cemb.-Str.
Kistner & Siegel, Leipzig, 1931
Score 17 p.
Composed 1762.

2947 [Sinfonia di caccia, G major]   14'
Edited by Max Langer [Hunting symphony]
1.Vivace 2.Andante 3.Menuett
4Hn.-Rifle(or Perc.)-Str.
Universal Edition, Vienna, c1935
Score 21 p.
*First performance of this arrangement Vienna,
5 May 1934.*

267m [Sinfonia di camera, horn and string
orchestra, D major] Edited by Edmond Leloir
1.Allegro moderato 2.Andante 3.Allegro
Hn.-Cemb.-Str.
Edition KaWe, Amsterdam, c1965
Score 12 p.
Composed 1755.

4647 Toy symphony   12'
1.Allegro 2.Menuetto 3.Finale: Allegro
Tpt.-Dr.,Trgl.,Cuckoo,Quail,Nightingale,Rattle
-Pno.-Vn.I,Vn.II,Cb.
Augener Ltd. [London, n.d.]
Score 8 p.
*Formerly attributed to Joseph Haydn, sometimes
to Michael Haydn. Also known as Kindersinfonie
and Sinfonia Berchtoldsgadensis.*

MOZART, WOLFGANG AMADEUS. Salzburg 27 January 1756
Vienna 5 December 1791

741s Adagio und Allegro für eine Orgelwalze.
K.594. Transcribed by Alois Schmitt
Ob.,2Bn.(all ad lib.)-Org.-Str.
Ries & Erler, Berlin [n.d.]
Score 17 p.
Published as Fantasy in F minor.

2214s Adagio and fugue for string   8-9'
orchestra [C minor] K.546
1.Adagio 2.Fuga
Str.
Broude Brothers, New York, c1952
Score 6 p.
Composed 1788.

508v [Adagio for violin, E major. K.261]   5'
Solo Vn.-2Fl.-2Hn.-Str.
Breitkopf & Härtel, Leipzig [n.d.]
Score 6 p.

2542 Allegro, Schlusssatz einer   3'
Symphonie [Finale of a symphony] K.207a(121)
2Ob.-2Hn.-Str.
Breitkopf & Härtel, Leipzig, 1881
Score 7 p.

522m [Andante for flute, C major.   3'
K.285e(315)]
Solo Fl.-2Ob.-2Hn.-Str.
Breitkopf & Härtel, Leipzig [n.d.]
Score 6 p.

1054m [Same as above] Edited by H.   3'
Lemacher and P. Mies
Solo Fl.(or Vn.)-2Ob.(ad lib.)-2Hn.(ad lib.)-
Pno.(ad lib.)-Str.
[P.J. Tonger, Cologne, n.d.]
Score 8 p.

2412 [Apollo et Hyacinthus, or Hyacinthi   3'
Metamorphosis. Prologus. K.38]
2Ob.-2Hn.-Str.
Breitkopf & Härtel, Leipzig [n.d.]
Score 4 p.

2409 [Ascanio in Alba. Overture. K.111]   3'
2,2,2,2-Timp.-Str.
Breitkopf & Härtel, Leipzig [1879]
Score 8 p.

1011 [Bastien und Bastienne. Intrada.   2'
K.46b(50)]
2Ob.-2Hn.-Str.
Breitkopf & Härtel, Leipzig, 1879
Score 2 p.

2226 [Cassation no. 1 (Divertimento),   15'
G major. K.63]
1.[March] 2.Allegro 3.Andante 4.Menuet
5.Adagio 6.Menuet 7.Finale
2Ob.-2Hn.-Str.
Breitkopf & Härtel, Leipzig, 1878
Score 18 p.

2227 [Cassation no. 2, B-flat major.   14'
K.63a(99)]

Mozart, Wolfgang Amadeus

1.[March] 2.Allegro molto 3.Andante 4.Menuet
5.Andante 6.Menuet 7.Allegro
2Ob.-2Hn.-Str.
Breitkopf & Härtel, Leipzig [n.d.]
Score 14 p.

1891s [Church sonata, G major. K.241] Edited by
Alfred Einstein
Org.-Str.(without Va.)
Music & Letters [XXI:1 January 1940]
Score 7 p.
*Edited from photographs of the Ms. transmitted
by the USSR Society for Cultural Relations
with Foreign Countries.*

1892s [Church sonata, C major. K.263] Edited by
Alfred Einstein
2Tpt.-Org.-Str.(without Va.)
Music & Letters [XXI:1 January 1940]
Score 17 p.
Edited with the above.

254p [Church sonata, C major. K.336]   5'
Edited by Hans Fischer
Solo Org.(or Hpscd., or Pno.)-Str.(ad lib.; no
Va.)
Chr. Friedrich Vieweg, Berlin, c1937
Score 15 p.

2223s [Church sonatas: 1.E-flat major. *I: 1'30"*
K.41h(67) 2.B-flat major. K.41i(68) *II: 3'30"*
3.D major. K.41k(69) 4.D major.   *III: 3'*
K.124a(144) 5.F major. K.124b(145) *IV: 4'*
6.B-flat major. K.212 7.G major.   *V: 2'30"*
K.241 8.F major. K.241a(224)   *VI: 4'*
9.A major. K.241b(225)] Edited by   *VII: 3'*
Minos E. Dounias   *VIII: 5'*
Bn.(ad lib.)-Org.-Str.(w/o Va.)   *IX: 5'*
Bärenreiter, Kassel, c1959
Score 24 p.

999 [La clemenza di Tito (Titus). Overture.   5'
K.621]
2,2,2,2-2,2-Timp.-Str.
Breitkopf & Härtel, Wiesbaden [n.d.]
Score 11 p.

333m [Concert rondo, horn, E-flat major.   5'45"
K.371] Orchestration completed by Waldemar
Spiess
Solo Hn.-2Ob.-2Hn.-Str.
[Breitkopf & Härtel, Leipzig, c1940]
Score 12 p.

398p [Concert rondo, piano, D major.   8'
K.382]
Solo Pno.-1,2-2,2-Timp.-Str.
Breitkopf & Härtel, Leipzig [n.d.]
Score 13 p.

624m [Concerto, bassoon, B-flat major.   19'
K.186e(191)]
1.Allegro 2.Andante ma adagio 3.Rondo
Solo Bn.-2Ob.-2Hn.-Str.
Breitkopf & Härtel, Leipzig [n.d.]
Score 20 p.

525m [Concerto, clarinet, A major. K.622]   29'
1.Allegro 2.Adagio 3.Allegro

Solo Cl.-2Fl.,2Bn.-2Hn.-Str.
Breitkopf & Härtel, Leipzig [n.d.]
Score 58 p.

519m [Concerto, flute, no. 1, G major.   20'
K.285c(313)]
1.Allegro maestoso 2.Adagio non troppo
3.Rondo
Solo Fl.-2,2-2Hn.-Str.
Breitkopf & Härtel, Wiesbaden [n.d.]
Score 31 p.

520m [Concerto, flute, no. 2, D major.   13'
K.285d(314)]
1.Allegro aperto 2.Andante ma non troppo
3.Allegro
Solo Fl.-2Ob.-2Hn.-Str.
Breitkopf & Härtel, Leipzig [n.d.]
Score 26 p.
*Composed 1778. May have been intended for
oboe.*

524m [Concerto, flute and harp, C major.   26'
K.297c(299)]
1.Allegro 2.Andantino 3.Rondo: Allegro
Solo Fl., Solo Hp.-2Ob.-2Hn.-Str.
Breitkopf & Härtel, Wiesbaden [n.d.]
Score 52 p.

700m [Concerto, horn, no. 1, D major.   8'
K.386b(412)]
1.Allegro 2.Allegro
Solo Hn.-2Ob.,2Bn.-Str.
Breitkopf & Härtel, Leipzig [n.d.]
Score 14 p.

502m [Concerto, horn, no. 2, E-flat   10'
major. K.417]
1.Allegro maestoso 2.Andante 3.Rondo
Solo Hn.-2Ob.-2Hn.-Str.
Breitkopf & Härtel, Wiesbaden [n.d.]
Score 18 p.

672m [Concerto, horn, no. 3, E-flat   10'
major. K.447]
1.Allegro 2.Romance: Larghetto 3.Allegro
Solo Hn.-2Cl.,2Bn.-Str.
Breitkopf & Härtel, Wiesbaden [n.d.]
Score 20 p.

701m [Concerto, horn, no. 4, E-flat   15'
major. K.495]
1.Allegro moderato 2.Romanza 3.Rondo
Solo Hn.-2Ob.-2Hn.-Str.
Breitkopf & Härtel, Leipzig [n.d.]
Score 22 p.

674p [Concerto, piano, no. 1, F major.   15'
K.37]
1.Allegro 2.Andante 3.[Allegro]
Solo Pno.-2Ob.-2Hn.-Str.
Breitkopf & Härtel, Leipzig [n.d.]
Score 34 p.

675p [Concerto, piano, no. 2, B-flat   12'
major. K.39]
1.Allegro spiritoso 2.Andante 3.Molto
allegro
Solo Pno.-2Ob.-2Hn.-Str.

Mozart, Wolfgang Amadeus

Breitkopf & Härtel, Leipzig [n.d.]
Score 32 p.

676p [Concerto, piano, no. 3, D major.   *12'*
K.40]
1.Allegro maestoso 2.Andante 3.Presto
Solo Pno.-2Ob.-2Hn.,2Tpt.-Str.
Breitkopf & Härtel, Leipzig [n.d.]
Score 32 p.

385p [Concerto, piano, no. 4, G major.   *13'*
K.41]
1.Allegro 2.Andante 3.Molto allegro
Solo Pno.-2Fl.-2Hn.-Str.
Breitkopf & Härtel, Leipzig [n.d.]
Score 32 p.

476p [Concerto, piano, no. 5, D major.   *17'*
K.175]
1.Allegro 2.Andante ma un poco adagio
3.Allegro
Solo Pno.-2Ob.-2Hn.,2Tpt.-Str.
Breitkopf & Härtel, Leipzig [n.d.]
Score 34 p.

677p [Concerto, piano, no. 6, B-flat   *16'*
major. K.238]
1.Allegro aperto 2.[Andante un poco adagio]
3.Rondeau: Allegro
Solo Pno.-2Fl.,2Ob.-2Hn.-Str.
Breitkopf & Härtel, Leipzig [n.d.]
Score 30 p.

592p [Concerto, 3 pianos, no. 7, Lodron,   *23'*
F major. K.242]
1.Allegro 2.Adagio 3.Rondo: Tempo di
menuetto
3 Solo Pno.-2Ob.-2Hn.-Str.
Breitkopf & Härtel, Leipzig [n.d.]
Score 80 p.

679p [Concerto, piano, no. 8, Lützow,   *16'*
C major. K.246]
1.Allegro aperto 2.Andante 3.Tempo di
menuetto
Solo Pno.-2Ob.-2Hn.-Str.
Breitkopf & Härtel, Leipzig [n.d.]
Score 34 p.

418p [Concerto, piano, no. 9, Jeunehomme,   *31'*
E-flat major. K.271]
1.Allegro 2.Andantino 3.Rondo: Presto
Solo Pno.-2Ob.-2Hn.-Str.
Breitkopf & Härtel, Wiesbaden [n.d.]
Score 52 p.

421p [Concerto, 2 pianos, no. 10,   *23'*
E-flat major. K.316a(365)]
1.Allegro 2.Andante 3.Rondo: Allegro
2 Solo Pno.-2Ob.,2Bn.-2Hn.-Str.
Kalmus, New York [n.d.]
Score 48 p.

477p [Concerto, piano, no. 11, F major.   *14'*
K.387a(413)]
1.Allegro 2.Larghetto 3.Tempo di menuetto
Solo Pno.-2Ob.,2Bn.-2Hn.-Str.
Breitkopf & Härtel, Leipzig [n.d.]
Score 32 p.

641p [Concerto, piano, no. 12, A major.   *28'*
K.386a(414)]
1.Allegro 2.Andante 3.Allegretto
Solo Pno.-2Ob.-2Hn.-Str.
Breitkopf & Härtel, Leipzig [n.d.]
Score 30 p.

439p [Concerto, piano, no. 13, C major.   *18'*
K.387b(415)]
1.Allegro 2.Andante 3.Allegro
Solo Pno.-2Ob.,2Bn.-2,2-Timp.-Str.
Breitkopf & Härtel, Leipzig, 1878
Score 42 p.

447p [Concerto, piano, no. 14, E-flat   *16'*
major. K.449]
1.Allegro vivace 2.Andantino 3.Allegro ma
non troppo
Solo Pno.-2Ob.-2Hn.-Str.
Breitkopf & Härtel, Leipzig [1878]
Score 36 p.

416p [Concerto, piano, no. 15, B-flat   *29'*
major. K.450]
1.Allegro 2.Andante 3.Allegro
Solo Pno.-1,2,0,2-2Hn.-Str.
Breitkopf & Härtel, Leipzig [n.d.]
Score 44 p.

593p [Concerto, piano, no. 16, D major.   *18'*
K.451]
1.Allegro assai 2.Andante 3.Allegro di molto
Solo Pno.-1,2,0,2-2,2-Timp.-Str.
Breitkopf & Härtel, Leipzig, 1878
Score 52 p.

456p [Concerto, piano, no. 17, G major.   *31'*
K.453]
1.Allegro 2.Andante 3.Allegretto
Solo Pno.-1,2,0,2-2Hn.-Str.
Kalmus, New York [n.d.]
Score 54 p.

422p [Concerto, piano, no. 18, B-flat   *30'*
major. K.456]
1.Allegro vivace 2.Andante un poco sostenuto
3.Allegro vivace
Solo Pno.-1,2,0,2-2Hn.-Str.
Breitkopf & Härtel, Leipzig, 1878
Score 64 p.

413p [Concerto, piano, no. 19, F major.   *20'*
K.459]
1.Allegro 2.Allegretto 3.Allegro assai
Solo Pno.-1,2,0,2-2Hn.-Str.
Breitkopf & Härtel, Leipzig [n.d.]
Score 62 p.

417p [Concerto, piano, no. 20, D minor.   *31'*
K.466]
1.Allegro 2.Romance 3.Rondo: Allegro assai
Solo Pno.-1,2,0,2-2,2-Timp.-Str.
Breitkopf & Härtel, Leipzig [n.d.]
Score 56 p.

419p [Concerto, piano, no. 21, C major.   *29'*
K.467]
1.[Allegro maestoso] 2.Andante 3.Allegro

Mozart, Wolfgang Amadeus

vivace assai
Solo Pno.-1,2,0,2-2,2-Timp.-Str.
Breitkopf & Härtel, Wiesbaden [n.d.]
Score 56 p.

509v [Concerto, piano, no. 21, C major.   *4'*
K.467. Andante. Transcribed for violin and
orchestra by Camille Saint-Saëns]
Solo Vn.-1,2,0,2-Str.
Durand, Paris, c1906
Score 14 p.

420p [Concerto, piano, no. 22, E-flat   *32'*
major, K.482]
1.Allegro 2.Andante 3.Rondo: Allegro
Solo Pno.-1,2,0,2-2,2-Timp.-Str.
Breitkopf & Härtel, Leipzig [n.d.]
Score 66 p.

402p [Concerto, piano, no. 23, A major.   *24'*
K.488]
1.Allegro 2.Adagio 3.Allegro assai
Solo Pno.-1,0,2,2-2Hn.-Str.
Breitkopf & Härtel, Wiesbaden [n.d.]
Score 54 p.

403p [Concerto, piano, no. 24, C minor.   *28'*
K.491]
1.Allegro 2.Larghetto 3.Allegretto
Solo Pno.-1,2,2,2-2,2-Timp.-Str.
Breitkopf & Härtel, Leipzig [n.d.]
Score 64 p.

438p [Concerto, piano, no. 25, C major.   *22'*
K.503]
1.Allegro maestoso 2.Andante 3.Allegretto
Solo Pno.-1,2,0,2-2,2-Timp.-Str.
Breitkopf & Härtel, Leipzig [1879]
Score 68 p.

401p [Concerto, piano, no. 26, Corona-   *33'*
tion, D major. K.537]
1.Allegro 2.Larghetto 3.Allegretto
Solo Pno.-1,2,0,2-2,2-Timp.-Str.
Breitkopf & Härtel, Leipzig [n.d.]
Score 56 p.

451p [Concerto, piano, no. 27, B-flat   *21'*
major. K.595]
1.Allegro 2.Larghetto 3.Allegro
Solo Pno.-1,2,0,2-2Hn.-Str.
Breitkopf & Härtel, Leipzig [n.d.]
Score 50 p.

401v [Concerto, violin, no. 1, B-flat   *15'*
major. K.207]
1.Allegro moderato 2.Adagio 3.Presto
Solo Vn.-2Ob.-2Hn.-Str.
Breitkopf & Härtel, Leipzig, 1877
Score 26 p.

402v [Concerto, violin, no. 2, D major.   *12'*
K.211]
1.Allegro moderato 2.Andante 3.Rondo: Allegro
Solo Vn.-2Ob.-2Hn.-Str.
Breitkopf & Härtel, Wiesbaden [n.d.]
Score 22 p.

548v [Concerto, violin, no. 3, G major.   *27'*
K.216]
1.Allegro 2.Adagio 3.Rondo: Allegro
Solo Vn.-2Ob.(2Fl.)-2Hn.-Str.
Breitkopf & Härtel, Wiesbaden [n.d.]
Score 34 p.

483v [Concerto, violin, no. 4, D major.   *27'*
K.218]
1.Allegro 2.Andante cantabile 3.Rondo
Solo Vn.-2Ob.-2Hn.-Str.
Breitkopf & Härtel, Leipzig, 1878
Score 30 p.

486v [Concerto, violin, no. 5, A major.   *29'*
K.219]
1.Allegro aperto 2.Adagio 3.Rondo
Solo Vn.-2Ob.-2Hn.-Str.
Luck's, Detroit [1881]
Score 32 p.

432v [Concerto, violin, no. 6, E-flat   *26'*
major. K.365b(268)]
[1.Allegro?] 2.Un poco adagio 3.Rondo
Solo Vn.-1,2,0,2-2Hn.-Str.
Luck's, Detroit [n.d.]
Score 50 p.

403v [Concerto, violin, no. 7, D major.   *35'*
K.271i(271a)] Edited by Albert Kopfermann
1.Allegro maestoso 2.Andante 3.Allegro
Solo Vn.-2Ob.-2Hn.-Str.
Breitkopf & Härtel, Leipzig, c1907
Score 44 p.

872v [Concertone, for 2 solo violins,   *22'*
C major. K.166b(190)]
1.Allegro spiritoso 2.Andantino grazioso
3.Tempo di menuetto
2 Solo Vn.-2Ob.-2Hn.,2Tpt.-Str.
Breitkopf & Härtel, Leipzig [n.d.]
Score 44 p.

2555 [Contradance, B-flat major.   *2'*
K.73g(123)]
2Ob.-2Hn.-Str.(without Va.)
Breitkopf & Härtel, Leipzig, 1882
Score 3 p.

2559 [Contradance, La bataille, C major.   *2'*
K.535]
1*,0,2,1-1Tpt.-Perc.-Str.(without Va.)
Breitkopf & Härtel, Leipzig, 1882
Score 5 p.

2562 [Contradance, Les filles   *2'*
malicieuses, G major. K.610]
2Fl.-2Hn.-Str.(without Va.)
Breitkopf & Härtel, Leipzig, 1882
Score 1 p.

2560 [Contradance, Der Sieg vom Helden   *2'*
Coburg, C major. K.587]
1,1,0,1-1Tpt.-Str.(without Va.)
Breitkopf & Härtel, Leipzig, 1882
Score 4 p.

Mozart, Wolfgang Amadeus

Contradances
See Also: [Overture and 3 contradances,
            K.588a(106)]

2556 [Four contradances. K.271c(267)]   *7'*
1,2,0,1-2Hn.-Str.(without Va.)
Breitkopf & Härtel, Leipzig, 1882
Score 5 p.

2557 [Six contradances. K.448b(462)]   *6'*
2Ob.-2Hn.-Str.(without Va.)
Breitkopf & Härtel, Leipzig, 1882
Score 4 p.

2561 [Two contradances. K.603]   *3'*
1*,2,0,2-2Tpt.-Timp.-Str.(without Va.)
Breitkopf & Härtel, Leipzig, 1882
Score 3 p.

1705s [Five contradances. K.609]   *8'*
Fl.-Perc.-Str.(without Va.)
Breitkopf & Härtel, Leipzig, 1882
Score 7 p.

951s [Five contradances. K.609] Edited by   *8'*
Gustav Lenzewski, Sr.
Fl.-Perc.-Str.(without Va.)
Vieweg, Berlin [n.d.]
Score 7 p.

2558 [Nine contradances or quadrilles.   *13'*
K.Anh.293b(510)]
2*,2,2,1-2,2-Timp.,Perc.-Str.(without Va.)
Breitkopf & Härtel, Leipzig, 1882
Score 11 p.

880 Così fan tutte. Overture. K.588   *5'*
2,2,2,2-2,2-Timp.-Str.
Breitkopf & Härtel, Leipzig [n.d.]
Score 13 p.

2326 Six dances, strings and optional   *13'*
winds. Arranged by Cyril B. Rootham
2(1 alt. Picc.),2,0,2-2Hn.-Str.
Oxford University Press, London, c1927
Score 13 p.

2081s [Divertimento (String quartet   *12-13'*
no. 24), D major. K.125a(136)]
1.Allegro 2.Andante 3.Presto
Str.(without Cb.)
Breitkopf & Härtel, Leipzig, 1882
Score 10 p.

2082s [Divertimento (String quartet   *10'30"*
no. 25), B-flat major. K.125b(137)]
1.Andante 2.Allegro di molto 3.Allegro assai
Str.(without Cb.)
Breitkopf & Härtel, Leipzig, 1882
Score 7 p.

2083s [Divertimento (String quartet   *10-12'*
no. 26), F major. K.125c(138)]
1.(Allegro) 2.Andante 3.Presto
Str.(without Cb.)
Breitkopf & Härtel, Leipzig, 1882
Score 8 p.

1485 [Divertimento no. 1, E-flat major.   *10'*
K.113]
1.Allegro 2.Andante 3.Menuetto 4.Allegro
2Ob.,2E.H.,2Cl.,2Bn.-2Hn.-Str.
Breitkopf & Härtel, Leipzig [n.d.]
Score 14 p.

1968 [Divertimento no. 2, D major. K.131]   *19'*
1.[Allegro] 2.Adagio 3.Menuetto 4.Allegretto
5.Menuetto 6.Adagio 7.Allegro molto
1,1,0,1-4Hn.-Str.
Breitkopf & Härtel, Leipzig [n.d.]
Score 32 p.

2365 [Divertimento no. 3, E-flat major.   *11'*
K.159d(166)]
1.Allegro 2.Menuetto 3.Andante grazioso
4.Adagio 5.Allegro
2Ob.,2E.H.,2Cl.,2Bn.-2Hn.
Breitkopf & Härtel, Leipzig [n.d.]
Score 10 p.

2330 [Divertimento no. 4, B-flat major.   *11'*
K.159b(186)]
1.Allegro assai 2.Menuetto 3.Andante
4.Adagio 5.Allegro
2Ob.,2E.H.,2Cl.,2Bn.-2Hn.
Breitkopf & Härtel, Leipzig [n.d.]
Score 6 p.

2506 [Divertimento no. 5, eight movements,   *12'*
C major. K.159c(187)]
2Fl.-5Tpt.-4Timp.
Breitkopf & Härtel, Leipzig, 1880
Score 6 p.

2331 [Divertimento no. 6, C major.   *7'*
K.240b(188)]
1.Andante 2.Allegro 3.Menuetto 4.Andante
5.Menuetto 6.[Gavotte]
2Fl.-5Tpt.-4Timp.
Breitkopf & Härtel, Leipzig [n.d.]
Score 4 p.

2224 [Divertimento no. 7, D major.   *15'*
K.173a(205)]
1.Largo 2.Allegro 3.Menuetto 4.[Adagio]
5.Menuetto 6.Finale: Presto
Bn.-2Hn.-Str.
Breitkopf & Härtel, Leipzig [n.d.]
Score 10 p.

2332 [Divertimento no. 8, F major. K.213]   *6'*
1.Allegro spiritoso 2.Andante 3.Menuetto
4.Molto allegro
2Ob.,2Bn.-2Hn.
Breitkopf & Härtel, Leipzig [n.d.]
Score 6 p.

2333 [Divertimento no. 9, B-flat major.   *8'*
K.240]
1.Allegro 2.Andante grazioso 3.Menuetto
4.Allegro
2Ob.,2Bn.-2Hn.
Breitkopf & Härtel, Leipzig [n.d.]
Score 9 p.

Mozart, Wolfgang Amadeus

757s [Divertimento no. 10, F major. K.247]
1.Allegro 2.Andante grazioso 3.Menuetto
4.Adagio 5.Menuetto 6.Andante 7.Allegro
assai
2Hn.-Str.
Breitkopf & Härtel, Leipzig [n.d.]
Score 24 p.

2225 [Divertimento no. 11, D major. K.251]   16'
1.Allegro molto 2.Menuetto 3.Andantino
4.Menuetto 5.Allegro assai 6.Marcia alla
francese
Ob.-2Hn.-Str.
Breitkopf & Härtel, Leipzig [n.d.]
Score 26 p.

2439 [Divertimento no. 12, E-flat major.   8'
K.240a(252)]
1.Andante 2.Menuetto 3.Polonaise 4.Presto
assai
2Ob.,2Bn.-2Hn.
Breitkopf & Härtel, Leipzig [n.d.]
Score 5 p.

2334 [Divertimento no. 13, F major. K.253]   9'
1.Thema mit Variationen: Andante 2.Menuetto
3.Allegro assai
2Ob.,2Bn.-2Hn.
Breitkopf & Härtel, Leipzig [n.d.]
Score 8 p.

2335 [Divertimento no. 14, B-flat major.   9'
K.270]
1.Allegro molto 2.Andantino 3.Menuetto
4.Presto
2Ob.,2Bn.-2Hn.
Breitkopf & Härtel, Leipzig [n.d.]
Score 9 p.

682s [Divertimento no. 15, B-flat major.
K.271b(287)]
1.Allegro 2.Andante grazioso 3.Menuetto
4.Adagio 5.Menuetto 6.Andante 7.Molto
allegro
2Hn.-Str.
Breitkopf & Härtel, Leipzig [n.d.]
Score 31 p.

2336 [Divertimento no. 16, E-flat major.   9'
K.271g(289)]
1.Adagio 2.Allegro 3.Menuetto 4.Adagio
5.Presto
2Ob.,2Bn.-2Hn.
Breitkopf & Härtel, Leipzig, 1880
Score 11 p.

723s [Divertimento no. 17, D major.   15'30"
K.320b(334)]
1.Allegro 2.Andante 3.Menuetto 4.Adagio
5.Menuetto 6.Rondo: Allegro
2Hn.-Str.
Breitkopf & Härtel, Leipzig [n.d.]
Score 35 p.

692v [Divertimento no. 17, D major.   15'
K.320b(334). Arranged for solo violin and
orchestra by Willem Kes]
1.Allegro 2.Adagio 3.Menuetto 4.Rondo

Solo Vn.-2,2,2,2-2Hn.-Timp.,Perc.-Str.
Schott, Mainz, c1922
Score 52 p.

595c [Divertimento no. 17, D major.   5'
K.320b(334). Minuet. Transcribed for violon-
cello and string orchestra by Paul Bazelaire]
Solo Vc.-Str.
Senart, Paris [n.d.]
Score 5 p.

33 Don Giovanni. Overture. K.527   6'
2,2,2,2-2,2-Timp.-Str.
Breitkopf & Härtel/Associated, New York [n.d.]
Score 16 p.

138s [Don Giovanni. Canzonetta. K.527.
Arranged for string orchestra anonymously]
Str.
Ms.
Score 39 p.
*Bound with Gluck, Iphigénie en Aulide, Over-
ture; Bach, Overture (Suite) No. 3, Two
Gavottes; and Schubert, March, Op. 51 no. 1
(Marche Militaire).*

Dorfmusikanten-Sextette
See: [A musical joke. K.522]

904 Die Entführung aus dem Serail.   5'
Overture. K.384
1*,2,2,2-2,2-Timp.,Perc.-Str.
Breitkopf & Härtel, Leipzig [n.d.]
Score 32 p.

Fantasy for a musical clock. K.594
See: Adagio und Allegro für eine Orgelwalze.
K.594

2886 [Fantasy for a musical clock. K.608]   14'
Orchestrated by Tibor Serly
1.Allegro 2.Andante
2,2,2,2-4,2,2,1-Timp.-Str.
Ms.
Score 42 p.
*Orchestrated 1928. First performance Budapest,
13 May 1935, Budapest Philharmonic Orchestra,
Tibor Serly conductor.*

3504 Fantasy for a musical clock. K.608   11'
Transcribed for orchestra by Eric Werner
2(1st alt. Picc.),2,2,2-2,2,2-Timp.-Str.
Associated Music Publishers, New York, c1941
Score 52 p.
*Transcribed 1932. First performance Saar-
brucken, Germany, 1932, Saarbrucken Symphony
Orchestra, Felix Lederer conductor.*

1942 [La finta giardiniera. Overture.   3'
K.196]
2Ob.-2Hn.-Str.
Breitkopf & Härtel, Leipzig, 1881
Score 7 p.

2411 [La finta semplice. Sinfonia.   5'
K.46a(51)]
2,2,0,2-2Hn.-Str.

Breitkopf & Härtel, Leipzig, 1882
Score 11 p.

677s Four pieces for string orchestra.
Arranged by Franz C. Bornschein
Pno.(ad lib.)-Str.
O. Ditson, Boston, c1928
Score 12 p.

5670 Galimathias musicum [Quodlibet] K.32.
Completed and edited by Aldo Provenzano (1956)
2Ob.,Bn.-2Hn.-Cemb.-Str.
Ms.
Score 32 p.

2563 [Six German dances. K.509]   16'30"
3*,2,2,2-2,2-Timp.-Str.(without Va.)
Breitkopf & Härtel, Leipzig, 1881
Score 17 p.

2564 [Six German dances. K.536]   14'
3*,2,2,2-2,2-Timp.-Str.(without Va.)
Breitkopf & Härtel, Leipzig, 1881
Score 9 p.

2565 [Six German dances. K.567]   14'
3*,2,2,2-2,2-Timp.,Perc.-Str.(without Va.)
Breitkopf & Härtel, Leipzig, 1881
Score 13 p.

2566 [Six German dances. K.571]   15'
2(2nd alt. Picc.),2,2,2-2,2-Timp.,Perc.-Str.
(without Va.)
Breitkopf & Härtel, Leipzig, 1881
Score 15 p.

2567 [Twelve German dances. K.586]   26'
3*,2,2,2-2,2-Timp.,Tamb.-Str.(without Va.)
Breitkopf & Härtel, Leipzig, 1881
Score 22 p.

2568 [Six German dances. K.600]   15'
3*,2,2,2-2,2-Timp.-Str.(without Va.)
Breitkopf & Härtel, Leipzig, 1881
Score 12 p.

2569 [Four German dances. K.602]   10'
3*,2,2,2-2,2-Timp.-Hurdy-Gurdy-Str.(without
Va.)
Breitkopf & Härtel, Leipzig, 1881
Score 6 p.

2570 [Three German dances. K.605]   7'30"
3*,2,0,2-2,2,2Posthorn-Timp.,Bells-Str.
(without Va.)
Breitkopf & Härtel, Leipzig, 1881
Score 7 p.

2285 [Eight German dances. Compiled and 18'
arranged by Fritz Steinbach]
3*,2,2,2-2,2,2Posthorn-Timp.,Handbells-Str.
Simrock, Berlin, c1910
Score 23 p.

2539 [Idomeneo. Overture. K.366]   5'
2,2,2,2-2,2-Timp.-Str.
Breitkopf & Härtel, Leipzig, 1881
Score 11 p.

896 [Idomeneo. Concert suite. K.366.   15'
Arranged by Ferruccio Busoni]
2,2,2,2-2,2-Timp.,Perc.-Str.
Breitkopf & Härtel, Leipzig, c1919
Score 27 p.
Suite arranged 1918.

2540 [Idomeneo. Ballet music. K.367]   30'
2,2,2,2-2,2-Timp.-Str.
Breitkopf & Härtel, Leipzig, 1881
Score 45 p.

1375s [Idomeneo. Ballet music. Gavotte. K.367]
Edited by Michele Esposito
2Ob.(or 2Fl.),2Bn.-2Hn.-Timp.-Str.
Oxford University Press, London, c1929
Score 6 p.

113s [Idomeneo. Ballet music. K.367. Suite
selected and arranged by Florence A. Marshall]
Pno.-Str.
Goodwin & Tabb, London, c1908
Score 19 p.

71s [Eine kleine Nachtmusik, serenade for 15'
strings, G major. K.525]
1.Allegro 2.Romanze 3.Menuetto 4.Rondo
Str.
Breitkopf & Härtel, Wiesbaden [n.d.]
Score 12 p.
Composed 1787.

2410 [Lucio Silla. Overture. K.135]
2Ob.-2Hn.,2Tpt.-Timp.-Str.
Breitkopf & Härtel, Leipzig, 1880
Score 12 p.

2551 [March. K.189c(237)]   4'
2Ob.,2Bn.-2Hn.,2Tpt.-Str.(without Va.)
Breitkopf & Härtel, Leipzig, 1881
Score 4 p.

2550 [March. K.213b(215)]   3'30"
2Ob.-2Hn.,2Tpt.-Str.
Breitkopf & Härtel, Leipzig, 1881
Score 3 p.

2549 [March. K.214]   3'30"
2Ob.-2Hn.,2Tpt.-Str.
Breitkopf & Härtel, Leipzig, 1881
Score 4 p.

7323 [March. K.248]
2Hn.-Str.
Breitkopf & Härtel, Leipzig, 1881
Score 3 p.

2552 [March. K.249]   3'30"
0,2,0,2-2,2-Str.
Breitkopf & Härtel, Leipzig, 1881
Score 4 p.
*Composed 1776 as the introduction and finale
to the Haffner Serenade, K.248b(250).*

2553 [Two marches. K.320a(335)]   8'
2,2-2,2-Str.
Breitkopf & Härtel, Leipzig, 1881
Score 7 p.

Mozart, Wolfgang Amadeus

7324 [March. K.320c(445)]
2Hn.-Str.
Breitkopf & Härtel, Leipzig, 1883
Score 3 p.

2554 [Three marches. K.383e,385a,383F   13'
(408)]
2,2,0,2-2,2-Timp.-Str.
Breitkopf & Härtel, Leipzig, 1881
Score 15 p.

225 [The marriage of Figaro. Overture.   3'
K.492]
2,2,2,2-2,2-Timp.-Str.
Breitkopf & Härtel, Wiesbaden [n.d.]
Score 14 p.

1410 Maurerische Trauermusik. K.479a(477)   4'
2Ob.,Cl.,Bassethorn,C.Bn.-2Waldhorn(or 2Bas-
sethorn)-Str.
Breitkopf & Härtel, Leipzig, 1881
Score 5 p.

5245 [Minuet (without trio), E-flat major,
K.73t(122)]
2Ob.-2Hn.-Str.(Vn.I,Vn.II,Cb.)
Breitkopf & Härtel, Leipzig, 1886
Score 1 p.

2543 [Minuet (Sinfonie-Menuett).   6'
K.383f(409)]
2,2,0,2-2,2-Timp.-Str.
Breitkopf & Härtel, Leipzig, 1881
Score 6 p.

2544 [Five (Six) minuets. K.448a(461)]   10'
2,2,0,2-2Hn.-Str.(without Va.)
Breitkopf & Härtel, Leipzig, 1882
Score 8 p.

2545 [Two minuets with contradances.   5'
K.448c(463)]
2Ob.,Bn.-2Hn.-Str.(without Va.)
Breitkopf & Härtel, Leipzig, 1882
Score 4 p.

2546 [Twelve minuets. K.568]   29'
3*,2,2,2-2,2-Timp.-Str.(without Va.)
Breitkopf & Härtel, Leipzig, 1881
Score 18 p.

2547 [Twelve minuets. K.585]   29'
3*,2,2,2-2,2-Timp.-Str.(without Va.)
Breitkopf & Härtel, Leipzig, 1881
Score 18 p.

2516 [Six minuets. K.599]   14'
2(2nd alt. Picc.),2,2,2-2,2-Timp.-Str.(without
Va.)
Breitkopf & Härtel, Leipzig, 1881
Score 9 p.

2548 [Four minuets. K.601]   10'
3*,2,2,2-2,2-Timp.-Hurdy-Gurdy-Str.(without
Va.)
Breitkopf & Härtel, Leipzig, 1881
Score 8 p.

2517 [Two minuets. K.604]   5'
2,0,2,2-2,2-Timp.-Str.(without Va.)
Breitkopf & Härtel, Leipzig, 1881
Score 3 p.

2408 [Mitridate, Rè di Ponto. Overture.   5'
K.74a(87)]
2Fl.,2Ob.-2Hn.-Str.
Breitkopf & Härtel, Leipzig, 1881
Score 8 p.

1453s [A musical joke. K.522]   18'
1.Allegro 2.Menuetto 3.Adagio cantabile
4.Presto
2Hn.-Str.
Breitkopf & Härtel, Wiesbaden [n.d.]
Score 17 p.
*Also known as Dorfmusikanten (Village Musi-
cians).*

3661 [Ombra felice e Io ti lascio, e questo
addio, recitative and aria (rondo). K.255]
Edited by Fritz Kneusslin
Contralto Voice Solo-2Ob.-2Hn.-Str.
Edition Kneusslin, Basel, ᶜ1957
Score 11 p.

5239 [Overture and 3 contradances.   7'
K.588a(106)]
2Ob.,2Bn.-2Hn.-Str.(Vn.I,Vn.II,Cb.)
Breitkopf & Härtel, Leipzig, 1886
Score 6 p.

113 [Les petits riens. Ballet music.   16'
K.299b(Anh.10). Arranged by Georg Göhler]
2,2,2,2-2,2-Timp.-Str.
Score: Ms. 64 p.
Parts: Breitkopf & Härtel, Leipzig, ᶜ1907

1943 [Il re pastore. Overture. K.208]   2'
2Ob.-2Hn.,2Tpt.-Str.
Breitkopf & Härtel, Leipzig, 1879
Score 8 p.

881v [Rondo for violin. K.373]   4'
Solo Vn.-2Ob.-2Hn.-Str.
Breitkopf & Härtel, Leipzig, 1881
Score 8 p.

1184v [Same as above] Edited by   5'
H. Lemacher and P. Mies
P.J. Tonger, Cologne [n.d.]
Score 16 p.

1068v [Rondo concertant, violin.   6'
K.261a(269)]
Solo Vn.-2Ob.-2Hn.-Str.
Breitkopf & Härtel, Leipzig, 1881
Score 10 p.

879 [Der Schauspieldirektor. Ouverture.   5'
K.486]
2,2,2,2-2,2-Timp.-Str.
Breitkopf & Härtel, Leipzig [n.d.]
Score 16 p.

2541 Die Schuldigkeit des ersten Gebotes. *6'*
Sinfonia. K.35 [Tr.: The obligation of the
First Commandment]
2Ob.,2Bn.-2Hn.-Str.
Breitkopf & Härtel, Leipzig, 1880
Score 4 p.

760 [Serenade no. 1, D major. K.62a(100)] *21'*
2,2,-2,2-Str.
Breitkopf & Härtel, Leipzig, 1878
Score 24 p.

1092s [Serenade no. 1, D major. K.62a(100).
Menuett and Andante. Arranged by Gustav Hecht]
Str.(Cb. ad lib.)
Vieweg, Berlin [n.d.]
Score 4 p.

795 [Serenade no. 2, F major. K.250a(101)] *7'*
1,2,0,1-2Hn.-Str.(without Va.)
Breitkopf & Härtel, Leipzig [n.d.]
Score 4 p.

796 [Serenade no. 3, D major. K.167a(185)] *25'*
2,2-2,2-Str.
Breitkopf & Härtel, Leipzig, 1880
Score 36 p.

1093s [Serenade no. 3, D major. K.167a(185).
Finale. Arranged by Gustav Hecht]
Str.(Cb. ad lib.)
Vieweg, Berlin [n.d.]
Score 8 p.

761 [Serenade no. 4, D major. K.189b(203)] *23'*
2,2,0,1-2,2-Str.
Breitkopf & Härtel, Leipzig [n.d.]
Score 36 p.

777 [Serenade no. 5, D major. K.213a(204)] *24'*
2,2,0,1-2,2-Str.
Breitkopf & Härtel, Leipzig [n.d.]
Score 44 p.

52s [Serenade no. 6 (Serenata notturna), *9'*
D major, for two small orchestras. K.239]
Orchestra I: Str.; Orchestra II: Timp.-Str.
Breitkopf & Härtel, Wiesbaden [n.d.]
Score 16 p.

585 [Serenade no. 7, Haffner, D major. *23'*
K.248b(250)]
2,2,0,2-2,2-Str.
Breitkopf & Härtel, Leipzig [n.d.]
Score 100 p.

399v [Serenade no. 7, Haffner, D major.
K.248b(250). Rondo. Transcribed for solo
violin and string orchestra by Norman Black
from violin and piano transcription of Fritz
Kreisler]
Solo Vn.-Str.
Ms.
Score 16 p.

1244 [Serenade no. 8 (Notturno), D major, *15'*
for four orchestras. K.269a(286)]
Each orchestra: 2Hn.-Str.

Breitkopf & Härtel, Leipzig [n.d.]
Score 32 p.

778 [Serenade no. 9, Posthorn, D major. *25'*
K.320]
2,2,0,2-2Hn.,Posthorn,2Tpt.-Timp.-Str.
Breitkopf & Härtel, Leipzig [n.d.]
Score 74 p.

2297 [Serenade no. 10, B-flat major. *35'*
K.370a(361)]
0,2,2,2Bassethorn,3*-4Hn.-Cb.(if no C.Bn.)
Breitkopf & Härtel, Wiesbaden [n.d.]
Score 56 p.

2329 [Serenade no. 11, E-flat major. *20'*
K.375]
0,2,2,2-2Hn.
Breitkopf & Härtel, Leipzig [n.d.]
Score 28 p.

3722 [Serenade no. 11, E-flat major. *8'*
K.375. Adagio. Transcribed by Zoltan Fekete]
2,2,2,2-2Hn.-Str.
Ms.
Score 7 p.
Transcribed 1941.

2364 [Serenade no. 12, Nacht Musique, *14'*
C minor. K.384a(388)]
2Ob.,2Cl.,2Bn.-2Hn.
Breitkopf & Härtel, Leipzig [n.d.]
Score 22 p.

Serenade, Eine kleine Nachtmusik. K.525
See: [Eine kleine Nachtmusik, serenade for
strings, G major. K.525]

619m [Sinfonia concertante, oboe, clari- *25'*
net, horn, bassoon and orchestra, E-flat major.
K.297b(Anh.9)]
1.Allegro 2.Adagio 3.Andantino con variazioni
Soli: Ob.,Cl.,Bn.,Hn.-2Ob.-2Hn.-Str.
Breitkopf & Härtel, Wiesbaden [n.d.]
Score 59 p.

[Six three-part fugues for violin, viola and
violoncello/contrabass. K.404a]
1958s No. 1, D minor: Prelude - Fuga
1915s No. 2, G minor: Prelude - Fuga
1967s No. 6, F minor: Prelude - Fuga
Str.(Vn.,Va.,Vc.)
Ms. ^C1976 by The Fleisher Collection of Orches-
tral Music, Free Library of Philadelphia
Scores: 12 p., 11 p., 14 p.
The preludes are Mozart's original compositions.
The fugues are transcribed from J. S. Bach
(Nos. 1 and 2) and W. F. Bach (No. 6).

2407 [Il sogno di Scipione. Overture. *4'*
K.126]
2,2-2,2-Timp.-Str.
Breitkopf & Härtel, Leipzig, 1880
Score 8 p.

6987 [Sonata, piano, A major. Alla turca. *4'*
K.331. Transcribed for orchestra by Prosper
Pascal]

Mozart, Wolfgang Amadeus

3*,2,2,2-2,2-Perc.-Str.
J. Rieter-Biedermann, Leipzig [n.d.]
Score 23 p.

2277s [Sonata, piano 4-hands, D major.   8'
K.123a(381). Transcribed for string orchestra
by Leo Weiner]
1.Allegro 2.Andante 3.Allegro molto
Str.
Elkan-Vogel, Philadelphia, c1964
Score 16 p.
This transcription 1933.

4733 [Lo sposo deluso, ossia La rivalità   6'30"
di tre donne per un solo amante. Overtura.
K.424a(430)]
2,2,0,2-2,2-Timp.-Str.
Breitkopf & Härtel, Leipzig, 1882
Score 10 p.

5240 [Symphonic movement (Finale), D major.
K.111a(120)]
2,2-2,2-Timp.-Str.
Breitkopf & Härtel, Leipzig, 1886
Score 4 p.

5225 [Symphonic movement (Finale), C major.
K.213c(102)]
2Ob.-2Hn.,2Tpt.-Str.
Breitkopf & Härtel, Leipzig, 1886
Score 10 p.

716m [Symphonie concertante, violin and   35'
viola. K.320d(364)]
1.Allegro maestoso 2.Andante 3.Presto
Solo Vn., Solo Va.-2Ob.-2Hn.-Str.
Breitkopf & Härtel, Leipzig [n.d.]
Score 62 p.

1088 [Symphony no. 1, E-flat major. K.16]   8'
1.Molto allegro 2.Andante 3.Presto
2Ob.-2Hn.-Str.
Breitkopf & Härtel, Leipzig [n.d.]
Score 12 p.

2215 [Symphony no. 2, B-flat major.   12'
K.Anh.223a(17)]
1.Allegro 2.[Andante] 3.Menuetto 4.Presto
2Ob.-2Hn.-Str.
Breitkopf & Härtel, Leipzig [n.d.]
Score 10 p.
Probably spurious.

2267 [Symphony no. 3, E-flat major. K.Anh.109[I]
(18)]
See: ABEL, KARL FRIEDRICH.
       [Symphony no. 18, Op. 7 no. 6]

2268 [Symphony no. 4, D major. K.19]   9'
1.Allegro 2.Andante 3.Presto
2Ob.-2Hn.-Str.
Breitkopf & Härtel, Leipzig [n.d.]
Score 10 p.

2142 [Symphony no. 5, B-flat major. K.22]
1.Allegro 2.Andante 3.Allegro molto
2Ob.-2Hn.-Str.
Breitkopf & Härtel, Leipzig [n.d.]
Score 9 p.

1140 [Symphony no. 6, F major. K.43]   12'
1.Allegro 2.Andante 3.Menuetto 4.Allegro
2Fl.,2Ob.-2Hn.-Str.
Breitkopf & Härtel, Leipzig [n.d.]
Score 14 p.

2269 [Symphony no. 7, D major. K.45]   10'
1.Allegro 2.Andante 3.Menuetto 4.Finale
2Ob.-2,2-Timp.-Str.
Breitkopf & Härtel, Leipzig [n.d.]
Score 12 p.

2270 [Symphony no. 8, D major. K.48]   14'
1.[Allegro] 2.Andante 3.Menuetto 4.[Allegro]
2Ob.-2,2-Timp.-Str.
Breitkopf & Härtel, Leipzig [n.d.]
Score 16 p.

2271 [Symphony no. 9, C major.   12'
K.75a(73)]
1.Allegro 2.Andante 3.Menuetto 4.Allegro
molto
2,2-2,2-Timp.-Str.
Breitkopf & Härtel, Leipzig [n.d.]
Score 13 p.

2272 [Symphony no. 10, G major. K.74]   9'
1.[Allegro] 2.[Andante] 3.[Allegro]
2Ob.-2Hn.-Str.
Breitkopf & Härtel, Leipzig [n.d.]
Score 12 p.

2273 [Symphony no. 11, D major.   11'
K.73q(84)]
1.Allegro 2.Andante 3.Allegro
2Ob.-2Hn.-Str.
Breitkopf & Härtel, Leipzig [n.d.]
Score 14 p.

2274 [Symphony no. 12, G major.   13'
K.75b(110)]
1.Allegro 2.[Andante] 3.Menuetto 4.Allegro
2,2,0,2-2Hn.-Str.
Breitkopf & Härtel, Leipzig [n.d.]
Score 14 p.

2402 [Symphony no. 13, F major. K.112]   15'
1.Allegro 2.Andante 3.Menuetto 4.Molto
allegro
2Ob.-2Hn.-Str.
Breitkopf & Härtel, Leipzig, 1880
Score 12 p.

2275 [Symphony no. 14, A major. K.114]   12'
1.Allegro moderato 2.Andante 3.Menuetto
4.Molto allegro
2,2-2Hn.-Str.
Breitkopf & Härtel, Leipzig [n.d.]
Score 14 p.

2403 [Symphony no. 15, G major. K.124]   15'
1.Allegro 2.Andante 3.Menuetto 4.Presto
2Ob.-2Hn.-Str.
Breitkopf & Härtel, Leipzig, 1880
Score 12 p.

2404 [Symphony no. 16, C major. K.128]   14'
1.Allegro maestoso 2.Andantino grazioso

Mozart, Wolfgang Amadeus

3.Allegro
2Ob.-2Hn.-Str.
Breitkopf & Härtel, Leipzig [n.d.]
Score 12 p.

2323 [Symphony no. 17, G major. K.129]   10'
1.Allegro 2.Andante 3.Allegro
2Ob.-2Hn.-Str.
Breitkopf & Härtel, Leipzig, 1880
Score 16 p.

1046 [Symphony no. 18, F major. K.130]   11'
1.Allegro 2.Andantino grazioso 3.Menuetto
2Fl.-4Hn.-Str.
Breitkopf & Härtel, Leipzig [n.d.]
Score 18 p.

2405 [Symphony no. 19, E-flat major.   14'
K.132]
1.Allegro 2.Andante 3.Menuetto 4.Allegro
5.Andantino grazioso
2Ob.-4Hn.-Str.
Breitkopf & Härtel, Leipzig [n.d.]
Score 19 p.

2406 [Symphony no. 20, D major. K.133]   14'
1.Allegro 2.Andante 3.Menuetto 4.[Allegro]
1(obbligato),2-2,2-Str.
Breitkopf & Härtel, Leipzig, 1880
Score 20 p.

1245 [Symphony no. 21, A major. K.134]   13'
1.Allegro 2.Andante 3.Menuetto 4.Allegro
2Fl.-2Hn.-Str.
Breitkopf & Härtel, Leipzig [n.d.]
Score 18 p.

1126 [Symphony no. 22, C major. K.162]   7'
1.Allegro assai 2.Andantino grazioso
3.Presto assai
2Ob.-2,2-Str.
Breitkopf & Härtel, Leipzig [n.d.]
Score 12 p.

14 [Symphony no. 23, D major. K.162b(181)]   8'
1.Allegro spiritoso 2.Andantino grazioso
3.Presto assai
2Ob.-2,2-Str.
Breitkopf & Härtel, Leipzig [n.d.]
Score 14 p.

1156 [Symphony no. 24, B-flat major.   8'
K.166c(182)]
1.Allegro spiritoso 2.Andantino grazioso
3.Allegro
2Fl.,2Ob.-2Hn.-Str.
Breitkopf & Härtel, Leipzig [n.d.]
Score 12 p.

1189 [Symphony no. 25, G minor. K.183]   18'
1.Allegro con brio 2.Andante 3.Menuetto
4.Allegro
2Ob.,2Bn.-4Hn.-Str.
Breitkopf & Härtel, Wiesbaden [n.d.]
Score 19 p.

1302 [Symphony no. 26, E-flat major.   10'
K.166a(184)]

1.Molto presto 2.Andante 3.Allegro
2,2,0,2-2,2-Str.
Breitkopf & Härtel, Leipzig [n.d.]
Score 22 p.

1310 [Symphony no. 27, G major.   11'
K.162a(199)]
1.Allegro 2.Andantino grazioso 3.Presto
2Fl.-2Hn.-Str.
Breitkopf & Härtel, Leipzig [n.d.]
Score 16 p.

1262 [Symphony no. 28, C major.   16'
K.173e(200)]
1.Allegro spiritoso 2.Andante 3.Allegretto
4.Presto
2Ob.-2,2-Str.
Breitkopf & Härtel, Leipzig [n.d.]
Score 22 p.

1333 [Symphony no. 29, A major.   18'
K.186a(201)]
1.Allegro moderato 2.Andante 3.Menuetto
4.Allegro con spirito
2Ob.-2Hn.-Str.
Breitkopf & Härtel, Leipzig [n.d.]
Score 24 p.

1358 [Symphony no. 30, D major.   14'
K.186b(202)]
1.Molto allegro 2.Andantino con moto
3.Menuetto 4.Presto
2Ob.-2,2-Str.
Breitkopf & Härtel, Leipzig, 1880
Score 16 p.

1451 [Symphony no. 31, Parisian, D major.   19'
K.300a(297)]
1.Allegro assai 2.Andantino 3.Allegro
2,2,2,2-2,2-Timp.-Str.
Breitkopf & Härtel, Wiesbaden [n.d.]
Score 40 p.

3366 [Symphony no. 31, Parisian, D major.
K.300a(297). Andante]
1,1,0,1-2Hn.-Str.
Ms.
Score 7 p.
Written to replace original slow movement.

1377 [Symphony no. 32, G major. K.318]   10'
1.Allegro spiritoso 2.Andante
2,2,0,2-4,2-Timp.-Str.
Breitkopf & Härtel, Leipzig [n.d.]
Score 16 p.
*First performed as the overture to Francesco
Bianchi's opera La Villanella Rapita. Also
available as Catalog no. 4128.*

1213 [Symphony no. 33, B-flat major.   22'
K.319]
1.Allegro assai 2.Andante moderato 3.Menuetto
4.Allegro assai
2Ob.,2Bn.-2Hn.-Str.
Breitkopf & Härtel, Leipzig [n.d.]
Score 26 p.

Mozart, Wolfgang Amadeus

1390 [Symphony no. 34, C major. K.338]   22'
1.Allegro vivace 2.Andante di molto
3.Allegro vivace
2Ob.,2Bn.-2,2-Timp.-Str.
Kalmus, New York [n.d.]
Score 36 p.

2223 [Symphony no. 35, Haffner, D major.   17'
K.385]
1.Allegro con spirito 2.[Andante] 3.Menuetto
4.Presto
2,2,2,2-2,2-Timp.-Str.
Breitkopf & Härtel, Leipzig [n.d.]
Score 36 p.

1444 [Symphony no. 36, Linz, C major.   26'
K.425]
1.Adagio - Allegro spiritoso 2.Poco adagio
3.Menuetto - Trio 4.Presto
0,2,0,2-2,2-Timp.-Str.
Breitkopf & Härtel, Wiesbaden [n.d.]
Score 44 p.

1366 [Symphony no. 37, G major. K.425a(444)]
See: HAYDN, MICHAEL.
      [Symphony, G major]

1177 [Symphony no. 38, Prague, D major.   27'
K.504]
1.Adagio 2.Allegro 3.Andante 4.Presto
2,2,0,2-2,2-Timp.-Str.
Kalmus, New York [n.d.]
Score 40 p.

73 [Symphony no. 39, E-flat major. K.543]   29'
1.Adagio - Allegro 2.Andante con moto
3.Menuetto: Allegretto 4.Allegro
1,0,2,2-2,2-Timp.-Str.
Breitkopf & Härtel, Wiesbaden [n.d.]
Score 44 p.

8 [Symphony no. 40, G minor. K.550.   29'
First and second versions]
1.Allegro molto 2.Andante 3.Menuetto: Allegretto 4.Allegro assai
1,2,2,2-2Hn.-Str.
Breitkopf & Härtel, Wiesbaden [n.d.]
Score 49 p.

107 [Symphony no. 41, Jupiter, C major.   28'
K.551]
1.Allegro vivace 2.Andante cantabile 3.Alle-
gretto 4.Molto allegro
1,2,0,2-2,2-Timp.-Str.
Breitkopf & Härtel, Leipzig [n.d.]
Score 56 p.

2276 [Symphony 'no. 42', F major. K.75]   15'
1.Allegro 2.Menuetto 3.Andantino 4.Allegro
2Ob.-2Hn.-Str.
Breitkopf & Härtel, Leipzig [n.d.]
Score 11 p.

2277 [Symphony 'no. 43', F major.   13'
K.42a(76)]
1.Allegro maestoso 2.Andante 3.Menuetto
4.Allegro
2Ob.,2Bn.-2Hn.-Str.

Breitkopf & Härtel, Leipzig [n.d.]
Score 11 p.

2278 [Symphony 'no. 44', D major. K.73l   9'
(81)]
1.Allegro 2.Andante 3.Allegro molto
2Ob.-2Hn.-Str.
Breitkopf & Härtel, Leipzig, 1881
Score 11 p.

2279 [Symphony 'no. 45', D major. K.73n   12'
(95)]
1.Allegro 2.Andante 3.Menuetto 4.Allegro
2Fl.,2Ob.-2Tpt.-Str.
Breitkopf & Härtel, Leipzig, 1881
Score 11 p.

2280 [Symphony 'no. 46', C major. K.111b   11'
(96)]
1.Allegro 2.Andante 3.Menuetto 4.Allegro
molto
2Ob.-2Hn.,2Tpt.-Timp.-Str.
Breitkopf & Härtel, Leipzig [n.d.]
Score 11 p.

2281 [Symphony 'no. 47', D major. K.73m   11'
(97)]
1.Allegro 2.Andante 3.Menuetto 4.Presto
2Ob.-2Hn.,2Tpt.-Timp.-Str.
Breitkopf & Härtel, Leipzig [n.d.]
Score 12 p.

1493 [Symphony 'no. 54', B-flat major.   9'
K.74g(Anh.216)]
1.Allegro 2.Andante 3.Menuet 4.Allegro molto
2Ob.-2Hn.-Str.
Breitkopf & Härtel, Leipzig, c1910
Score 14 p.

6415 [Symphony, C major] Edited by Nino   27'
Negrotti
1.Allegro con brio 2.Andante grazioso
3.Allegro assai
0,2,0,2-2,2-Timp.-Str.
Carisch, Milan, c1944
Score 63 p.
Not listed in Köchel; authenticity doubtful.

3611 [Symphony, Lambach, G major.   14'
K.45a(Anh.221)] Edited by Zoltan Fekete
1.Allegro maestoso 2.Andante 3.Presto
2Ob.(Cl. in absence of Ob.II)-2Hn.-Str.
Ms.
Score 28 p.

6508 [Symphony, Cavalier, B-flat major.   14'
K.45b(Anh.214)] Edited by Alfred Einstein
1.Allegro 2.Andante 3.Menuetto 4.Trio
5.Allegro
2Ob.-2Hn.-Str.
C.F. Peters, New York, c1964
Score 24 p.

6365 [Symphony, D major. K.141a   9'
(126, 161/163)]
1.Allegro moderato 2.Andante 3.Presto
2,2-2,2-Timp.-Str.
Bärenreiter, Kassel, 1956
Score 18 p.

The Presto also available as Symphonic Movement, D major, K.141a(163), Catalog no. 5244.

6364 [Symphony, D major. K.196 and 207a   10'
(126)] Edited by Hermann Beck
1.Allegro molto 2.Andantino grazioso
3.Allegro
2Ob.-2Hn.-Str.
Bärenreiter, Kassel, 1958
Score 19 p.

5989 [Thamos, König in Ägypten.   19'30"
Entr'actes, from the incidental music, K.336a
(345), to the play by Tobias Phillip von
Gebler]
0,2,0,2-2,2-Timp.-Str.
Breitkopf & Härtel, Leipzig, 1881
Score 34 p.

Turkish march (from Piano Sonata K.331)
   See: [Sonata, piano, A major. Alla turca.
   K.331. Transcribed for orchestra by
   Prosper Pascal]

La villanella rapita
   See: [Symphony no. 32, G major. K.318]

382 [Die Zauberflöte. Overture. K.620]   6'
2,2,2,2-2,2,3-Timp.-Str.
Breitkopf & Härtel, Leipzig [n.d.]
Score 26 p.

MRACZEK, JOSEPH GUSTAV.   Brünn, Austria
   (now Brno, Czechoslovakia) 12 March 1878
   Dresden 24 December 1944

2371 Drei Stücke in Tanzform   13'
1.[Waltz] 2.[Minuet] 3.[Round dance]
2*,2(2nd alt. E.H.),2,2-4,2,3,1-Timp.,Perc.-
Hp.-Str.
Ms.
Score 37 p.
*Composed 1927. First performance in a radio
broadcast, Breslau, 1929.*

2572 Eva [symphonic poem]
3(3rd alt. Picc.),3*,3*,3*-4,4,3,1-Timp.,Perc.
-Cel.(ad lib.),2Hp.(2nd ad lib.)-Str.
Heinrichshofen, Magdeburg, C1920
Score 53 p.
Composed about 1921.

1408 Orientalische Skizzen [Oriental   17'
sketches]
1.Harem 2.[The Khalif] 3.[Going to the
mosque] 4.[Chess] 5.[In the divan] 6.[The
magician] 7.[Dance of the odalisk]
1(alt.Picc),2*,2*,1-1,1-Timp.,Perc.-Cel.(ad
lib.),Hp.-Str.
F.E.C. Leuckart, Leipzig [n.d.]
Score 54 p.

MRACZEK, KARL.   Brünn, Austria
   (now Brno, Czechoslovakia) 1 September 1902
   Brno 22 October 1928

1480 Slavische Tänze [Slavic dances]   10'
3(3rd alt. Picc.),3,3*,3*-4,3,3,1-Timp.,Perc.-

Hp.-Str.
Ries & Erler, Berlin, C1928
Score 34 p.
*Composed 1927. First performance Brünn, 1928,
Frotzler conductor.*

MUCZYNSKI, ROBERT.   Chicago 19 March 1929

7061 Charade for orchestra, Op. 28   7'30"
3*,2,2,2-4,3,3,1-Timp.,Perc.-Str.
G. Schirmer, Inc., New York, C1974
Score 43 p.
*Composed 1970-71. First performance Cincinnati,
29 October 1972, Cincinnati Symphony Orchestra,
Erich Kunzel conductor.*

MUELLER, OTTO.   Voehl, Kassel, Germany 1870

2635 Atlantis, symphonic poem   11'
3*,2,2,3*-4,3,3,1-Timp.,Perc.-Hp.-Str.
Ms.
Score 50 p.
*Composed 1911. First performance Philadelphia,
2 April 1913 at a Manuscript Music Society Concert, Philadelphia Orchestra, the composer
conducting.*

2501 La chasse, ouverture   9'
caractéristique
3*,2,2,2-4,2,3,1-Timp.,Perc.-Hp.-Str.
Ms.
Score 39 p.
*Composed 1930. First performance Cincinnati,
2 April 1933, Cincinnati Symphony Orchestra,
Vladimir Bakaleinikov conductor.*

1074v [Concerto, violin, no. 1, in D]   26'
1.Allegro moderato 2.Andante con moto
3.Allegro molto
Solo Vn.-2,2,2,2-2Hn.-Timp.-Str.
Ms.
Score 97 p.
*Composed 1898. First performance Frankfurt,
22 Feburary 1900, Frankfurt Music Society,
Max Kaempfert conductor, the composer as
soloist.*

1075v [Concerto, violin, no. 2, in G]   24'
1.Allegro maestoso 2.Romanza 3.Allegro con
fuoco
Solo Vn.-2,2,2,2-4,2,3,1-Timp.-Str.
Ms.
Score 114 p.
*Composed 1906. First performance Philadelphia,
21 May 1939, Philadelphia Federal Orchestra of
the WPA, the composer conducting, Isadore
Schwartz, soloist.*

2636 Scherzo grotesque   8'
3*,2,2,2-4,3,3,1-Timp.,Perc.-Str.
Ms.
Score 47 p.
*Composed 1925. First performance at a Robin
Hood Dell Concert, Philadelphia, 28 August
1930, Philadelphia Orchestra, Alexander
Smallens conductor.*

Mueller, Otto

2505 Schlaraffiada, carnival overture   10'
3(3rd alt. Picc.),3*,2,3*-4,3,3,1-Timp.,Perc.-
2Hp.-Str.
Ms.
Score 81 p.
*Composed 1921. First performance Philadelphia,
21 April 1922, Philadelphia Orchestra, the
composer conducting.*

MUELLER, PAUL.
    See: MÜLLER-ZÜRICH, PAUL.

MUFFAT, GEORG. Mégève, Savoy baptized 1 June 1653
                Passau, Bavaria 23 February 1704

490m [Concerto grosso no. 2, Cor vigilans,
A major]
1.Sonata 2.Corrente 3.Gavotta 4.Rondeau
Concertino: Vn.I(or Ob.I),Vn.II(or Ob.II),Vc.
& Cb.(or Bn.)
Ripieno: Cemb.-Str.
Score: Denkmäler der Tonkunst in Österreich,
XI/2. Artaria, Vienna, 1904. Edited by Erwin
Luntz. 12 p.
Parts: Ms. C1976 by The Fleisher Collection of
Orchestral Music, Free Library of Philadelphia
*This and the following concerti grossi first
published 1701, as part of 12 Concerti Grossi,
under the title Ausserlesene mit Ernst und
Lust Gemengte Instrumental-Musik [Selected
Instrumental Music, Mixed with Seriousness and
Mirth].*

488m [Concerto grosso no. 4, Dulce somnium,
G minor]
1.Sonata 2.Sarabanda 3.Aria 4.Borea
Concertino: Vn.I,Vn.II,Vc. & Cb.
Ripieno: Cemb.-Str.
Score: Denkmäler der Tonkunst in Österreich,
XI/2. Artaria, Vienna, 1904. Edited by Erwin
Luntz. 10 p.
Parts: Ms. C1976 by The Fleisher Collection of
Orchestral Music, Free Library of Philadelphia

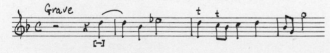

487m [Concerto grosso no. 5, Saeculum, D major]
1.Sonata 2.Allemanda 3.Gavotta 4.Menuet
Concertino: Vn.I,Vn.II,Vc. & Cb.
Ripieno: Cemb.-Str.
Score: Denkmäler der Tonkunst in Österreich,
XI/2. Artaria, Vienna, 1904. Edited by Erwin
Luntz. 10 p.
Parts: Ms. C1976 by The Fleisher Collection of
Orchestral Music, Free Library of Philadelphia

485m [Concerto grosso no. 10, Perseverentia,
G major]
1.Allemanda 2.Gavotta 3.Menuet
Concertino: Vn.I(or Ob.I),Vn.II(or Ob.II),
Vc. & Cb.(or Bn.)
Ripieno: Cemb.-Str.
Score: Denkmäler der Tonkunst in Österreich,
XI/2. Artaria, Vienna, 1904. Edited by Erwin
Luntz. 8 p.
Parts: Ms. C1976 by The Fleisher Collection of
Orchestral Music, Free Library of Philadelphia

484m [Concerto grosso no. 11, Delirium amoris,
E minor]
1.Sonata 2.Ballo 3.Menuet 4.Giga
Concertino: Vn.I,Vn.II,Vc. & Cb.
Ripieno: Cemb.-Str.
Score: Denkmäler der Tonkunst in Österreich,
XI/2. Artaria, Vienna, 1904. Edited by Erwin
Luntz. 12 p.
Parts: Ms. C1976 by The Fleisher Collection of
Orchestral Music, Free Library of Philadelphia

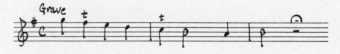

474m [Concerto grosso no. 12, Propitia   18'
sydera, G major]
1.Sonata 2.Aria 3.Gavotta 4.Ciaconna
5.Borea
Concertino: Vn.I,Vn.II,Vc. & Cb.
Ripieno: Cemb.-Str.
Score: Denkmäler der Tonkunst in Österreich,
XI/2. Artaria, Vienna, 1904. Edited by Erwin
Luntz. 30 p.
Parts: Ms. C1976 by The Fleisher Collection of
Orchestral Music, Free Library of Philadelphia

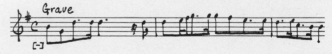

[Florilegium primum]
2117s Fasciculus I, Eusebia (Dances 1-7)

Muffat, Georg

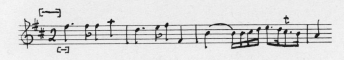

2118s Fasciculus II, Sperantis gaudia *12'*
(8-14)

2119s Fasciculus III, Gratitudo (15-21)

2120s Fasciculus IV, Impatientia (22-28)

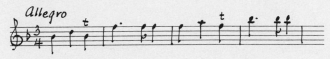

2121s Fasciculus V, Sollicitudo (29-35)

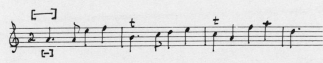

2122s Fasciculus VI, Blanditiae (36-42)

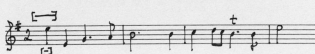

2123s Fasciculus VII, Constantia (43-50)

Cemb.-Str.
Scores: Denkmäler der Tonkunst in Österreich,
I/2. Artaria, Vienna, 1894. Edited by Heinrich
Rietsch. 18 p., 19 p., 16 p., 17 p., 15 p.,
16 p., 14 p.
Parts: Ms. [c]1976 by The Fleisher Collection of

Orchestral Music, Free Library of Philadelphia
First published 1695-96.

2033s [Florilegium primum] Fasciculus III,
Gratitudo. Edited by Carl August Rosenthal
Piano(optional)-Str.
Music Press, New York, [c]1946
Score 20 p.
*Order of the movements differs slightly from
the Denkmäler edition.*

[Florilegium secundum]
2213s Fasciculus I, Nobilis juventus *11'*
(Dances 1-7)

2231s Fasciculus II, Laeta Poesis (8-14)

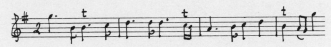

2247s Fasciculus III, Illustres primitiae
(15-23)

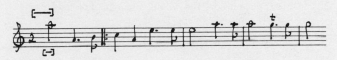

2278s Fasciculus IV, Splendidae nuptiae
(24-30)

2317s Fasciculus V, Colligati montes (31-38)

2320s Fasciculus VI, Grati hospites (39-45)

Muffat, Georg

2321s Fasciculus VII, Numae ancile (46-53)

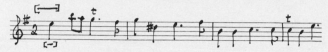

2318s Fasciculus VIII, Indissolubilis
amicitia (54-62)

Cemb.-Str.
Scores: Denkmäler der Tonkunst in Österreich,
II/2. Artaria, Vienna, C1895. Edited by Hein-
rich Rietsch. 22 p., 21 p., 22 p., 18 p.,
24 p., 19 p., 19 p., 24 p.
Parts: Ms. C1976 by The Fleisher Collection of
Orchestral Music, Free Library of Philadelphia
First published 1695-96.

910s [Florilegium secundum. Fasciculus IV,
Splendidae nuptiae] Arranged for string
orchestra by Arthur Egidi
1.[Overture] 2.[The peasants] 3.Canaries
4.[The cavaliers] 5.[Minuet I] 6.[Air]
7.[Rigaudon for the young peasant women from
Poitou] 8.[Minuet II]
Str.
C.F. Vieweg, Berlin [1927]
Score 11 p.
Arranged 1927. No. 6 is an Air from Flori-
legium Primum.

20s Passacaglia. Edited by L. Stollbrock   *4'*
Str.
Rieter-Biedermann, Leipzig, C1889
Score 13 p.
From his Chamber Sonata no. 5.

1814s Suite. Arranged by Karl Geiringer   *20'*
1.Ouverture 2.Bourrée 3.Air 4.Gigue
5.Chaconne
Str.
Ms.
Score 7 p.
Arranged 1938.

MÜHLFELD, WILHELM.

850m [Concertstück, trombone, Op. 7, B-flat
major]
Solo Tbn.-2,2,2,2-2,2-Timp.-Str.
Score: Ms. 37 p.
Parts: A.E. Fischer, Bremen [n.d.]

MULÈ, GIUSEPPE.
Termini Imerese, Sicily 28 June 1885
Rome 10 September 1951

2206 [Dafni, pastoral poem. Danza   *4'*
satiresca]
3*,3*,3*,3*-4,3,4,1-Timp.,Perc.-Hp.-Str.
G. Ricordi, Milan, C1930
Score 20 p.
First concert performance Rome, September 1929,
the composer conducting.

5112 [Largo]
Pno.,Hp.,Harm.-Str.
F. Bongiovanni, Bologna, C1931
Score 11 p.

1921 Sicilia canora [Tuneful Sicily. No. 2, *8'*
The orange trees are blossoming]
3*,3*,3*,2-4,3,3,1-Timp.,Perc.-Cel.,Hp.-Str.
G. Ricordi, Milan, C1920
Score 29 p. Large folio
Composed 1916. First performance Palermo,
April 1917, the composer conducting.

3551 [La Zolfara. Dance of the whip]   *10'*
3*,3*,4*(1 in E-flat),2-4,3,3,1-Timp.,Perc.-
Hp.-Str.
G. Ricordi, Milan, C1939
Score 39 p.
From the opera first performed Rome, 25 Febru-
ary 1939, Tullio Serafin conductor.

MÜLLER, BERNHARD.
Sonneberg, Germany 25 January 1824
Meiningen, Germany 5 December 1883

737m [Evening in the mountains, Op. 12]
Solo Ob.-1,0,2,2-2,2,B.Tbn.-Timp.-Str.
Score: Ms. 17 p.
Parts: C. Merseburger, Leipzig [n.d.]

598m [Serenade, flute and horn, Op. 15]
Solo Fl., Solo Hn.-0,2,2,2-2Hn.-Timp.-Hp.-Str.
Score: Ms. 27 p.
Parts: C. Merseburger, Leipzig [n.d.]

MÜLLER, IWAN.   Reval, Estonia 14 December 1786
Bückeburg, Germany 4 February 1854

831m [Concerto, clarinet, no. 4, A minor]
In one movement
Solo Cl.-1,2,0,2-2Hn.-Str.
Score: Ms. 43 p.
Parts: Dufaut & Dubois, Paris [n.d.]

697m [Concerto, clarinet, no. 5, E-flat major]
In one movement
Solo Cl.-2,2,0,2-2,2-Timp.-Str.
Score: Ms. 79 p.
Parts: Dufaut & Dubois, Paris [n.d.]

855m [Concerto, clarinet, no. 6, G minor]
Allegro moderato - Bolero
Solo Cl.-2,2,0,2-2,2-Timp.-Str.
Score: Ms. 83 p.
Parts: Dufaut & Dubois, Paris [n.d.]

MÜLLER, J.

[Three marches. Transcribed by Géza Allaga]
1610s [Batthyány march]
1609s [Damjanich march]
1608s [Kossuth march]
Str.(Cb. ad lib.)
Rozsnyai, Budapest [n.d.]
Scores: 5 p. each

MÜLLER, PAUL.
See: MÜLLER-ZÜRICH, PAUL.

MÜLLER, PETER ERASMUS LANGE.
See: LANGE-MÜLLER, PETER ERASMUS.

MÜLLER, SIGFRID WALTHER.
                    Plauen, Germany 11 January 1905
                    Mingechaur, USSR 2 November 1946

372m [Concerto, bassoon and chamber   18'
orchestra, Op. 56, F major]
Introduction, Theme, 8 Variations and Rondo
Solo Bn.-1,1,2-1,1-Timp.,Perc.-Str.
Ernst Eulenburg, Leipzig, C1938
Score 62 p.
First performance Baden-Baden, 1938, G. E.
Lessing conductor.

391m [Concerto grosso, trumpet and small   15'
orchestra, Op. 50, D major]
1.Maestoso 2.Allegro 3.Adagio 4.Rondo
Solo Tpt.-2,2,2,2-2Hn.-Timp.,Trgl.-Str.
Ernst Eulenberg, Leipzig, C1936
Score 88 p.

4229 [Happy music for orchestra, Op. 43]   25'
1.Ouverture 2.Intermezzo 3.Menuett
4.[Variations and finale on a children's song]
2(2nd alt. Picc.),2,2,2-3,2,2-Timp.,Perc.-Str.
Ernst Eulenberg, Leipzig, C1933
Miniature score 98 p.
First performance Leipzig, 7 March 1933, the
composer conducting.

MÜLLER-BERGHAUS, KARL.
                    Braunschweig, Germany 14 April 1829
                    Stuttgart, Germany 11 November 1907

Born: Karl Müller

880m Ballade [trombone and orchestra]
Solo Tbn.-2,2,2,2-4,2,2,1-Timp.,Perc.-Hp.-Str.
Score: Ms. 46 p.
Parts: Rühle & Wendling, Leipzig [n.d.]

715v [Concerto, violin, Hungarian, Op. 60,
D minor]
1.Allegro 2.Lento 3.Finale
Solo Vn.-2,2,2,2-2,2,3-Timp.,Perc.-Hp.-Str.
Louis Oertel, Hannover [n.d.]
Score 95 p.

1548s [Pizzicato-serenade, Beloved, forgotten]
Str.
Score: Ms. 7 p.
Parts: Rühle & Wendling, Leipzig [n.d.]

MÜLLER-OLDENBURG, KARL.

767m [Concerto, flute, D minor]
Allegro con gravita - Andante religioso -
Finale
Solo Fl.-1,2,2,2-2,2,B.Tbn.-Timp.-Str.
Score: Ms. 139 p.
Parts: Louis Oertel, Hannover [n.d.]

MÜLLER-ZÜRICH, PAUL.   ·   Zurich 19 June 1898

Also published as Paul Müller.

1033m [Concerto, organ and string   20'
orchestra, Op. 28]
1.Toccata 2.Aria variata 3.Allegro comodo
Solo Org.-Str.
B. Schott's Söhne, Mainz, C1939
Score 40 p.
Commissioned by Kammerorchester Zurich (Alexan-
der Schaichet). Composed 1938. First per-
formance Zurich, 27 November 1938, Kammer-
orchester Zurich, the composer conducting,
Kurt Wolfgang Senn soloist.

450c [Concerto, violoncello, Op. 55]   22-23'
1.Allegro energico 2.Andante sostenuto
3.Allegro vivace
Solo Vc.-2(2nd alt. Picc.),2,2,2-2,2,1-Timp.,
Perc.-Str.
Ms. [Now published by Ahn & Simrock]
Score 114 p.
Commissioned by The Louisville Orchestra. Com-
posed 1954. First performance Louisville,
Kentucky, 23 April 1955, Louisville Orchestra,
Robert Whitney conductor, Grace Whitney
soloist.

MUNCK, ERNEST DE.   Brussels 21 December 1840
                            London 6 February 1915

Born: Ernest Demunck

546c [Concerto, violoncello, Dramatique,
A minor]
1.Allegro risoluto 2.Andante 3.Finale
Solo Vc.-2,2,2,2-2,2-Timp.-Str.
Score: Ms. 109 p.
Parts: J. Hamelle, Paris [n.d.]

MUÑOZ MOLLEDA, JOSÉ.   La Línea
                    de la Concepción, Spain 16 February 1905

6897 [Circus suite. Orchestral version]
1.Preludio 2.[Pirouette] 3.[On the wire]
4.[The cage of death] 5.[Jugglers] 6.[Tamer]
2(2nd alt. Picc.),2*,2,2-2,2,1-Timp.,Perc.-
Pno.,Hp.-Str.
Unión Musical Española, Madrid, C1955
Score 83 p.
Originally composed for piano, 1954.

MURADELI, VANO ILICH.
                    Gori, Georgia, Russia 6 April 1908
                    Tomsk, Siberia 14 August 1970

3938 [Symphony, in memory of Sergei   46'
Mironovich Kirov]

Murley, Kenneth

1.Andante maestoso - Allegro risoluto
2.Andante 3.Vivo 4.Allegro maestoso
3(3rd alt. Picc.),3(3rd alt. E.H.),3*,2-4,3,3,
1-Timp.,Perc.-Str.
Mussektor, Moscow, 1940
Score 224 p.
Composed 1938. First performance Moscow, 28
November 1938, Moscow Philharmonic Orchestra,
the composer conducting.

MURLEY, KENNETH.
             b. Scranton, Pennsylvania 7 March 1931

6142 To autumn   6'30"
2(2nd alt. Picc.),2*,2,2-2,2,3-Timp.,Cym.,
Bells-Str.
Ms.
Score 16 p.
Composed 1960. First performance Rochester,
27 April 1960, Eastman-Rochester Symphony
Orchestra, Howard Hanson conductor. Winner of
the Edward B. Benjamin Award, 1960.

MURRAY, EDWARD.   New York 1890

3896 Chaconne   20'
3(3rd alt. Picc.),3*,3,3*-4,3,3,1-Timp.,Perc.-
Hp.-Str.
Ms.
Score 186 p.
Composed 1936-37.

5416 Fugue in G for orchestra   14-15'
3(3rd alt. Picc.),3*,3*,3*-4,3,3,1-Timp.-Hp.-
Str.
Ms.
Score 75 p. Large folio
Composed 1943.

2089s Rhapsody for six part strings
Str.(without Cb.)
Ms.
Score 65 p.

MURRILL, HERBERT HENRY JOHN.   London 11 May 1909
                             London 24 July 1952

7079 Three hornpipes   5'
2(2nd alt. Picc.),1,2,1-2,2,3-Timp.,Perc.-Str.
(or Pno.-Str. only)
Oxford University Press, London, ^c1952
Score in reduction 16 p.
Composed 1932.

MUSSORGSKY, MODEST PETROVICH.
              Karevo, Pskov, Russia 21 March 1839
                 St. Petersburg 28 March 1881

Also transliterated: Moussorgsky

465 [Boris Godunov. Introduction *and*   5'
Polonaise. Transcribed by N. Rimsky-Korsakov]
3(3rd alt. Picc.),3*,3,3-4,2,2Cnt.,3,1-Timp.,
Perc.-Hp.-Str.
Bessel, Petrograd [n.d.]
Score 45 p.

[The fair at Sorochinsk. Excerpts orchestrated
by Anatol Liadov]
315 Introduction   5'
301 Gopak   3'
3*,3*,2,2-4,2,3,1-Timp.,Perc.-Str.
Bessel, St. Petersburg [n.d.]
Scores: 24 p., 15 p.
Composed 1877.

2946 [Festive march] Orchestrated by N. Rim-
sky-Korsakov. Edited by Paul Lamm
3*,2,2,2-4,2,2Cnt.,3,1-Timp.,Perc.-Str.
Mussektor, Moscow, 1931
Score 29 p.
Posthumous work intended as part of the opera
Mlada.

1193 [Intermezzo, B minor. Orchestrated by 8'
N. Rimsky-Korsakov]
2,2,2,2-4,2,3,1-Timp.-Str.
Bessel, St. Petersburg [n.d.]
Score 41 p.
Composed 1867. Orchestrated 1882-84.

312 [Khovanshchina. Introduction]   3'
2,2,2,2-4Hn.-Timp.,Gong-Hp.-Str.
Bessel, St. Petersburg [n.d.]
Score 11 p.
From the opera in five acts about Prince Ivan
Khovansky (d. 1682). Composed 1872-80. Com-
pleted and orchestrated by N. Rimsky-Korsakov.
First performance St. Petersburg, 21 February
1886, the Musical Dramatic Club, E. Goldstein
conductor.

1782 [Khovanshchina. Entr'acte (Act IV,   3'
Scene 2)]
3,2,2,2-4,2,3,1-Timp.-Str.
Bessel, St. Petersburg [n.d.]
Score 11 p.

4948 [Khovanshchina. Entr'acte (Act IV,   4'
Scene 5). Arranged by Leopold Stokowski]
3,2,3*,3*-4,2,3,2-Timp.,Perc.-Str.
Broude Brothers, New York, ^c1950 by Leopold
Stokowski
Score 15 p.

436 [Khovanshchina. Persian dances]   6'
3*,2(2nd alt. E.H.),2,2-4,2,3,1-Timp.,Perc.-
Hp.-Str.
Bessel, St. Petersburg, ^c1910
Score 33 p.
Orchestrated by N. Rimsky-Korsakov about 1879.
First performance November 1879 at a Musical
Free School Concert, Mili Balakirev conductor.

399 [Night on the bald mountain, fantasy] 10'
3*,2,2,2-4,2,3,1-Timp.,Perc.-Hp.-Str.
E. Kalmus, New York [n.d.]
Score 64 p.
A posthumous work, completed and orchestrated
by N. Rimsky-Korsakov 1884-85. First perform-
ance St. Petersburg, 15 October 1886, N. Rim-
sky-Korsakov conductor.

1877 [Pictures at an exhibition, for   29'
piano] Transcribed for orchestra by Maurice

Ravel
3(3rd alt. Picc.),3(3rd alt. E.H.),3*,3*-Alto
Sax.-4,3,3,1-Timp.,Perc.-Cel.,2Hp.-Str.
Russischer Musikverlag, Berlin, ^C1929
Score 128 p.
Inspired by Victor Hartmann's paintings. Originally composed 1874. First performance of this transcription Paris, 19 October 1922, Serge Koussevitzky conductor.

663 [Same as above] Instrumentation   20'
by M. Touschmaloff, edited by N. Rimsky-
Korsakov
1.Promenade 2.Il vecchio castello [The old
castle] 3.[Ballet of the chicks in their
shells] 4.Samuel Goldenberg und Schmuyle
5a.Limoges, le marché 5b.Catacombae
6a.[The hut on hens' feet] 6b.[The great
gate at Kiev]
3*,3*,3*,2-4,2,3,1-Timp.,Perc.-Pno.,Hp.-Str.
Bessel, St. Petersburg [n.d.]
Score 81 p.

1695 [Scherzo, B-flat major. Orchestrated   6'
by N. Rimsky-Korsakov]
2,2,2,2-2,2,3-Timp.-Str.
Mussektor, Moscow, 1928
Score 17 p.
Composed 1858. Orchestrated 1882-84. First performance Moscow, 1885.

7004 [Songs and dances of death. No. 4,   5'
Field-Marshal Death. Transcribed for voice and
orchestra by J. Schwarzdorf]
Solo Voice-2,2,2,2-4,2,3,1-Timp.,Perc.-Str.
Ms.
Score 16 p.
Text in Russian by Count Arseny Golenishchev-Kutuzov (1848-1912). Originally composed for voice and piano, 1877.

314 [Turkish march, A-flat major]   5'
3*,2,2,2-4,2,2Cnt.,3,1-Timp.,Perc.-Str.
Bessel, St. Petersburg [n.d.]
Score 28 p.
Composed 1880. Orchestrated by N. Rimsky-Korsakov; first performance St. Petersburg, 1882.

MYDDLETON, W. H.

1003s Eventide
Fl.,Cl.-Harm.(ad lib.)-Str.
Score: Ms. 11 p.
Parts: Hawkes, London [n.d.]

N

NABOKOV, NICOLAS.
        b. Lubcha, Minsk, Russia 17 April 1903

3229 Les danses de Polichinelle
3(3rd alt. Picc.),3(3rd alt. E.H.),3*,3*-Sop.
Sax.,Ten. Sax.-4,3,3,1-Timp.,Perc.-Pno.,Hp.-
Str.

Ms.
Score 121 p.

5362 Symboli Chrestiani [baritone and   17'
orchestra]
Bar. Voice Solo-2,0,0,2-2,2-Timp.,Perc.-Pno.,
Cel.,Hp.-Str.
Ms. [Now published by Ricordi, Milan]
Score 51 p.
The text is in Greek and Latin, from early Christian sources. Commissioned by the Louisville Orchestra. Composed 1956. First performance Louisville, Kentucky, 15 February 1956, Louisville Orchestra, Robert Whitney conductor, William Pickett baritone soloist.

NACHÈZ, TIVADAR.   Budapest 1 May 1859
                           Lausanne 29 May 1930

Also known as: Theodor Naschitz

681s Abendlied [Evening song] Op. 18
Solo Vn.-Str.
Joh. André, Offenbach a.M. [n.d.]
Score 4 p.

767v [Concerto, violin, no. 2, Op. 36, B minor]
1.Allegro appassionato 2.Adagio 3.Allegro
appassionato
Solo Vn.-2,2,2,2-4,2,3-Timp.-Str.
Hofmeister, Leipzig, ^C1908
Score 75 p.
Composed 1904-07. First public performance London, 17 April 1907, Frederick Cowen conductor, the composer as soloist.

Danses tziganes, Op. 14 [Gypsy dances on
Hungarian airs]
696v Vol. I. Nos. 1 and 2
697v Vol. II. Nos. 3 and 4
Solo Vn.-2,2,2,2-4,2-Timp.,Perc.-Str.
Forberg, Leipzig [n.d.]
Scores: 54 p., 55 p.

NADELMANN, LEO.

2271s Mutations for string orchestra
1.Andante - Lento - Allegro 2.Misurato -
Animato - Misurato 3.Con brio - Lento - Molto
tranquillo - Andante
Str.
Israeli Music Publications, Tel Aviv, ^C1963
Score 17 p.
Commissioned by OMANUT, Zurich, and Israeli Music Publications, Tel Aviv. Composed 1963.

NAGAN, ZVI.

276m Music for two recorders, harpsichord and
orchestra
1.Allegro vivace 2.Adagio 3.Allegro con fuoco
Solo Descant Recorder, Solo Treble Recorder-
(0,2,0,2-2,1-Wood Block-Hpscd.-Str.(without
Vc.,Cb.)
Israeli Music Publications, Tel Aviv, ^C1962
Score 37 p.

Naginski, Charles

NAGINSKI, CHARLES.   Cairo, Egypt 29 May 1909
                    Lenox, Massachusetts 4 August 1940

    3017 Five pieces from a children's   20'
    suite, Op. 6
    1.The hobby horse 2.Waltz for the sad doll
    3.Wooden soldiers 4.Sandy 5.Travel
    3,2(2nd alt. E.H.),2(1st alt. Cl. in E-flat),2
    -4,2,3,1-Timp.,Perc.-Pno.,Hp.-Str.
    Ms.
    Score 82 p.
    *Composed 1938. First performance Boston 11
    June 1940, Boston Pops, Arthur Fiedler con-
    ductor.*

    3116 The Minotaur, ballet   30'
    11 scenes
    3*,2(2nd alt. E.H.),3*,2-4,2,3,1-Timp.,Perc.-
    Pno.,Hp.-Str.
    Ms.
    Score 190 p.
    Composed 1938 for Ballet Caravan.

    3010 "1936", Op. 2   6'
    3*,3*,3*,3*-4,3,3,1-Timp.,Perc.-Pno.-Str.
    Ms.
    Score 23 p. Large folio
    Composed 1936.

    3145 Nocturne and pantomime   10'
    3*,2(2nd alt. E.H.),2,2-4,2,3,1-Timp.,Perc.-
    Hp.-Str.
    Ms.
    Score 69 p.
    Composed 1938.

    2891 Sinfonietta, Op. 4   20'
    1.Allegro 2.Allegro scherzando 3.Andante
    4.Vivo
    3*,2,2,2-2,2,2-Timp.,Perc.-Pno.-Str.
    Ms.
    Score 89 p. Large folio
    *Composed 1937. First performance CBS broad-
    cast, New York, 19 May 1938, Columbia Concert
    Orchestra, Victor Bay conductor. Awarded
    American Prix de Rome, 1938.*

    3608 Suite, for small orchestra
    1.Menuet 2.Gavotte 3.Marche
    2(2nd alt. Picc.),2(2nd alt. E.H.),2,2-2,1,1
    -Timp.,Perc.-Hp.-Str.
    Ms.
    Score 63 p.
    *Composed 1931. First performance New York,
    7 April 1935, Greenwich Sinfonietta of the
    WPA, Charles Lichter conductor.*

    3230 Symphony no. 1, Op. 1   20'
    1.Allegro moderato 2.Allegretto vivace
    3.Adagio espressivo 4.Allegro con brio
    3(3rd alt. Picc.),3*,3*,3*-4,3,3,1-Timp.,Perc.
    -Hp.-Str.
    Ms.
    Score 106 p.
    Composed 1934-35.

NAGLER, FRANCISCUS.
            Prausitz bei Riesa, Germany 22 July 1873
            Leisnig, Germany 6 June 1957

    [Two Christmas pieces, Op. 93]
    1207s No. 1a [Shepherds' lullaby at the manger
    in Bethlehem]
    1387s No. 2a [Glory to God!]
    Solo Vn.I, Solo Vn.II-Str.(Cb. ad lib.)
    Oppenheimer, Hameln [n.d.]
    Scores: 7 p., 7 p.

    [Two lyric pieces, Op. 24]
    514s No. 1 [Devotion]
    515s No. 2 [Prayers]
    Org.-Str.
    Chr. Fr. Vieweg, Berlin [n.d.]
    Scores: 5 p., 7 p.

NAPOLI, JACOPO.   Naples 26 August 1911

    4738 Preludio di caccia [Hunt prelude]   7'
    3*,3*,3*,2-4,3,4-Timp.,Perc.-Pno.,Hp.-Str.
    G. Ricordi, Milan, c1941
    Score 52 p.
    *Composed 1935. First performance Naples, 4
    January 1940.*

NAPOLINO DI SAN SILVESTRO, BARON.
    See: FLORIDIA, PIETRO.

NÁPRAVNÍK, EDUARD FRANTSEVICH.
                    Býšt, Bohemia 24 August 1839
                    Petrograd 23 November 1916

    494p [Concerto symphonique, piano, Op. 27,
    A minor]
    1.Allegro energico 2.Larghetto 3.Allegro
    vivace
    Solo Pno.-2*,2,2,2-2,2,3-Timp.,Trgl.-Str.
    Rahter, Hamburg [n.d.]
    Score 234 p.

    Danses nationales, Op. 20
    2172 No. 2 [Cossack dance from Little Russia]
    2173 No. 5 Tarantelle
    2188 No. 6 Mazurka
    2(2nd alt. Picc.),2,2,2-4,2,3,1-Timp.,Perc.-Str.
    Rahter, Leipzig [n.d.]
    Scores: 100 p., 64 p., 55 p.
    *Composed 1876. First performance St. Peters-
    burg, 8 January 1877, the composer conducting.*

    1181 [Don Juan, Op. 54. Suite from the   15'
    incidental music to Alexei Tolstoy's dra-
    matic poem]
    1.[Overture] 2.[Song of the nightingale]
    3.[At the fountain] 4.[Melodrama] 5.[Fandango]
    3*,2(2nd alt. E.H.),2,2-4,2,3,1-Timp.,Perc.-
    2Hp.(2nd ad lib.)-Str.
    Jurgenson, Moscow [1901?]
    Score 142 p.

    921s [Dubrovsky, Op. 58. No. 21, Night-
    intermezzo]
    Str.
    [Mussektor, Moscow, 1928]
    Score 5 p.
    *From the opera based on Pushkin's work. First
    performance St. Petersburg, 15 January 1895.*

500p Fantaisie russe, Op. 39
Solo Pno.-2*,2,2,2-2,2,3-Timp.,Perc.-Str.
Rahter, Hamburg [n.d.]
Score 91 p.
Composed 1881.

408v Fantaisie sur des thèmes russes, Op. 30
Solo Vn.-2(2nd alt. Picc.),2,2,2-2,2,3-Timp.,
Perc.-Str.
Bote & Bock, Berlin [n.d.]
Score 70 p.

258 Marcia funebre, Op. 42b
2,2*,2,2-4,2,3,1-Timp.,Perc.-Hp.-Str.
Rahter, Hamburg [n.d.]
Score 31 p.

238s Mélancolie, Op. 48 [G minor]
Str.
Jurgenson, Moscow [1888?]
Score 6 p.

5585 [Serenata from String Quartet no. 1]
2,2,2,2-2Hn.-Trgl.-Hp.-Str.
Bessel, St. Petersburg [n.d.]
Score 63 p.
*Excerpted and transcribed from String Quartet
no. 1, Op. 16, composed 1873.*

532v [Suite, violin and orchestra, Op. 60]
1.Molto moderato - Allegro moderato 2.Scherzo
3.Elegie 4.Tarantella
Solo Vn.-2*,2,2,2-2,2,3-Timp.,Perc.-Str.
Simrock, Berlin, c1898
Score 62 p.

521 [Symphony no. 3, Demon, Op. 18, E minor]
Part I: 1.Allegro appassionato 2.Allegro
giocoso 3.Poco a poco accelerando 4.Lar-
ghetto lamentoso Part II: Lento con devozione
6.Allegro 7.Maestoso religioso
3*,2,2,2-4,2,3,1-Timp.,Perc.-Hp.-Str.
Rahter, Hamburg [n.d.]
Score 173 p.
Inspired by Mikhail Lermontov's poem.

[Two Russian pieces, Op. 74]
5594 No. 1 Fantaisie
2008 No. 2 Conte [Tale]
2(2nd alt. Picc.),2,2,2-4,2,3,1-Timp.,Perc.-
Str.
Jurgenson, Moscow [1905 or 1906]
Scores: 41 p., 39 p.

[Two Spanish pieces, Op. 51]
1461 [No. 1. Romance]   4'
1032 [No. 2. Fandango]   4'
3*,2,2,2-4,2,3,1-Timp.,Perc.-Hp.-Str.
Jurgenson, Moscow [1892?]
Scores: 19 p., 35 p.

NARDINI, PIETRO.   Leghorn, Italy 12 April 1722
                        Florence 7 May 1793

1140s Adagio [G major. Transcribed by Guglielmo
Zuelli]
Org.,Hp.-Str.
Bongiovanni, Bologna [n.d.]

Score 23 p.
*Excerpted and transcribed from a sonata for
violin and piano.*

745v Adagio, violin, E-flat major. Transcribed
by Gustav Jensen
Solo Vn.-2,0,0,2-Str.(without Vn.)
Augener, London [n.d.]
Score 5 p.

497v [Concerto, violin, E minor]   6'
Orchestrated by C. Angelelli. Revised by
Emilio Pente
1.Allegro moderato 2.Andante cantabile
3.Allegro giocoso
Solo Vn.-1,1,1,1-2Hn.-Str.
B. Schott's Söhne, Mainz, c1925
Score 20 p.

501v [Concerto, violin, A major] Edited   8'
by Tivadar Nachèz
1.Allegro moderato 2.Adagio 3.Allegro
gracioso
Solo Vn.-Org.-Str.
B. Schott's Söhne, Mainz, c1914
Score in reduction 11 p.

282v [Concerto, violin, Op. 1, G major]
Edited by Olivér Nagy and Tibor Ney
1.Allegro moderato 2.Adagio 3.Allegro con
brio
Solo Vn.-Hpscd.-Str.
Edition Eulenburg, Zurich, c1973 by Editio
Musica, Budapest
Score 30 p.
First published in Amsterdam before 1770.

NAUMANN, EMIL.   Berlin 8 September 1827
                           Dresden 23 June 1888

5331 [Loreley. Overture, Op. 25]
3*,2,2,2-4,2,3-Timp.-Str.
J. Schuberth, Leipzig [n.d.]
Score 56 p.
*From the opera in four acts with libretto by
Otto Raquette.*

NAUMANN, KARL ERNST.
                 Freiberg, Saxony 15 August 1832
                 Jena, Germany 15 December 1910

975 Pastorale in F dur, Op. 16   8'
1,2,2,2-2Hn.-Str.
Breitkopf & Härtel, Leipzig [1889?]
Score 31 p.
*Composed 1888. First performance Jena 1889,
the composer conducting.*

3757 Serenate (Nonett) Op. 10
1.Allegro con brio 2.Romanze 3.Menuetto
4.Finale
1,1,0,1-Hn.-Str.
Score: Ms. 84 p.
Parts: Simrock, Berlin [n.d.]

NAUMANN, OTTO.   Berthelsdorf, Saxony 5 May 1871
                     Mainz 6 August 1932

Naumann, Otto

5774 [Junker Übermut, scherzo, Op. 2]
3(2nd & 3rd alt. Picc.I & II),3(3rd alt. E.H.),
3(2nd alt. Cl. in E-flat, 3rd alt. B.Cl.),3*-
4,3,3,1-Timp.,Perc.-Hp.-Str.
Heinrichshofen, Magdeburg, ^C1902
Score 59 p.
The Junkers were the Prussian landed gentry.

NAVRÁTIL, KARL.   Prague 24 April 1867
                               Prague 23 December 1936

6994 [Symphony, Op. 4, G minor]
1.Allegro maestoso 2.Allegretto quasi scherzando 3.Allegro con anima
2,2,2,2-2,2,3-Timp.-Hp.-Str.
Ms.
Score 66 p.
Composed 1902.

NEDBAL, OSKAR.   Tábor, Bohemia 26 March 1874
                     Zagreb, Yugoslavia 24 December 1930

1178 Der faule Hans [Lazy Hans, ballet suite,
Op. 18]
6 dance movements
3*,3*,3*,2-4,2,3,1-Timp.,Perc.-Hp.-Str.
Bosworth, Leipzig, ^C1907
Score 120 p.

444 Scherzo-Caprice, Op. 5
3*,2,2,2-4,2,3,1-Timp.,Trgl.-Str.
Simrock, Berlin, ^C1896
Score 36 p.

1696 Suite mignonne, Op. 15 [From the cycle
From Childhood]
1.[Cradle song] 2.[First dance steps]
3.[March of the little soldiers]
2(2nd alt. Picc.),2,2,2-4,2-Timp.,Perc.-Hp.-
Str.
M. Urbánek, Prague [n.d.]
Score 27 p.

NEGLIA, FRANCESCO PAOLO.   Enna, Sicily 22 May 1874
                           Intra, Italy 31 July 1932

2276s [Arioso, for string orchestra,   4'30"
timpani, harp and harmonium, Op. 17p. Transcribed from the Sonata in Olden Style, violin
and piano]
Timp.-Hp.,Harm.-Str.
Augusta Edizioni Musicali, Turin, ^C1955 by
Giuseppe Neglia
Score 16 p.
Sonata in Olden Style composed 1901. Arioso
transcribed 1901. First performance Hamburg,
16 April 1902, the composer conducting.

2104s Due gavotte per orchestra d'archi.
Edited by R. Bossi
Str.
Augusta Edizioni Musicali, Turin [n.d.]
Score 9 p.

6560 Intermezzo breve per orchestra, Op. 3   4'
(5p)
2,2,3*,2-4,2,3,1-Timp.-Hp.-Str.
Augusta Edizioni Musicali, Turin, ^C1952 by

Giuseppe Neglia
Score 13 p.
Composed 1896. First performance Lugano,
Switzerland, 28 November 1952, Radio Svizzera
Italiana-Lugano, Otmar Nussio conductor.

2105s Minuetto in stile antico, Op. 14
Str.
G. & P. Mignani, Florence [n.d.]
Score 4 p.
Composed 1901.

NEGREA, MARŢIAN.
          Vorumloc, Transylvania 29 January 1893
          Bucharest, Romania 13 July 1973

5926 [Romanian rhapsody no. 1, Op. 14]   13-14'
2,2,2,2-4,2,3,1-Timp.,Perc.-Hp.-Str.
Editura de Stat, Bucharest, 1949
Score 60 p.
Composed 1935. First performance Bucharest,
17 November 1938, Bucharest Radio Orchestra,
the composer conducting. Awarded the George
Enescu First Prize in Composition by the
Romanian Ministry of Arts, 1938.

NEHL, WILHELM.   Düsseldorf 6 August 1847
                          Düsseldorf 4 February 1921

1316s Im trauten Heim [Cozy home] Ländler
Str.(with Vn.III)
Score: Ms. 11 p.
Parts: Oertel, Hanover [n.d.]

NEIBIG, ALBERT.   Braunschweig 30 July 1832
                         Braunschweig 7 March 1888

785m Concert-Arie, Op. 82
Solo Cl.-1,1,1,1-2,2,1-Dr.-Str.
Score: Ms. 47 p.
Parts: A.E. Fischer, Bremen [n.d.]

NEIDHARDT, KARL.   Dresden 7 October 1872

1287s Serenade [A major]
Str.
Otto Koch, Bückeburg [n.d.]
Score 8 p.

NEITZEL, OTTO.   Falkenburg, Pomerania
          (now Zlocieniec, Poland) 6 July 1852
                          Cologne 10 March 1920

510p [Concerto, piano, Op. 26, C minor]   38'
1.Allegro moderato 2.Allegretto moderato
3.Lento 4.Allegro marcato
Solo Pno.-2,2,2,2-4,2,3-Timp.,Trgl.-Str.
C. Giessel, Bayreuth, ^C1900
Score 190 p.
Composed 1897. First performance Cologne 1899.

NELHYBEL, VACLAV.
          b. Polanka, Czechoslovakia 24 September 1919

6969 Concerto antifonale for brass ensemble
1.Grave 2.Allegro con bravura 3.Molto sostenuto 4.Vivo
In 3 groups: 3Hn.,4Tpt.,5Tbn.,2Tuba

Franco Colombo, New York, c1966
Score 57 p.

NELSON, LARRY ALAN.
b. Broken Bow, Nebraska 27 January 1944

7049 Variations for orchestra   *18'*
3*,2,4*,2-4,3,2-Perc.-Str.
Ms. c1974 by Larry Alan Nelson
Score 86 p. Large folio
Commissioned by the National Endowment for the
Arts, 1974. Composed 1973-4. Revised 1975.
Selected for performance by the Orchestra Soci-
ety of Philadelphia as part of its Pennsyl-
vania Composers Project 1974, made possible by
a grant from the Pennsylvania Council for the
Arts with performance materials prepared by
the Fleisher Collection of Orchestral Music.
First performance Drexel University, Philadel-
phia, 22 June 1974, Orchestra Society of Phila-
delphia, Sidney Rothstein, conductor.

NELSON, RONALD JACK.
b. Joliet, Illinois 14 December 1929

5879 Sarabande: For Katharine in April   *6'*
2,2(2nd alt. E.H.),2,2-2,2-Glock.-Cel.
(optional), Hp.-Str.
Ms. [c1958 by Ron Nelson]
Score 13 p. Large folio
Composed 1954. First performance at the 24th
Annual Festival of American Music, Rochester,
May 1954, Eastman-Rochester Symphony Orchestra,
Howard Hanson conductor. Winner of the Edward
B. Benjamin Award, 1954.

6656 [Savannah River holiday overture]   *8'45"*
3,2,2,2-4,3,3,1-Timp.,Perc.-Pno.(alt. Cel.),
Hp.-Str.
Eastman School of Music, Rochester, c1957
Score 61 p.

NEPOMUCENO, ALBERTO. Fortaleza, Brazil 6 July 1864
Rio de Janeiro 16 October 1920

3941 O Garatuja. Preludio
3*,2,2,2-4,3,3,1-Timp.,Perc.-Hp.-Str.
Ms.
Score 89 p.
From an unfinished comic opera. First per-
formance Rio de Janeiro, 26 October 1904,
Artur Napoleão conductor.

5558 Suite brasileira
1.Madrugada na serra 2.Intermedio 3.La sesta
na rêde 4.Batuque
3*,2,2,2-4,3,3,1-Timp.,Perc.-Hp.-Str.
Ms.
Score 138 p.
Based on Brazilian Negro themes. Composed 1892.
Original title: Serie Brasileira.

3154 [Symphony, G minor]
1.Allegro com enthusiasmo 2.Andante quasi
adagio 3.Presto - Intermezzo 4.Con fuoco
3*,2,2,2-4,3,3,1-Timp.-Str.
Universidade do Brasil, Rio de Janeiro, 1938
Score 156 p.
Composed 1900.

NERUDA, FRANZ XAVER.   Brünn, Moravia
(now Brno, Czechoslovakia) 3 December 1843
Copenhagen 19 March 1915

1345s Berceuse slave, Op. 11. Arranged by
Alfred Oelschlegel
Hp.-Str.
Rahter, Leipzig, c1911
Score 7 p.

603c [Concerto, violoncello, Op. 59,   *20'*
D minor]
In one movement
Solo Vc.-2,2,2,2-2,2-Timp.-Str.
Solo: Urbánek, Prague [n.d.]
Score and parts: Ms. Score 85 p.
Composed 1887. First performance Copenhagen
1888.

NESVERA, JOSEF. Horovice, Bohemia 24 October 1842
Olmütz (now Olomouc), Moravia 12 April 1914

523s Idylla, Op. 42
Str.
Fr. Urbánek, Prague [n.d.]
Score 6 p.

NETTO, BARROZO.
See: BARROZO NETTO, JOACHIM ANTONIO.

NEUBAU(E)R, FRANZ CHRISTOPH.   Hořin, Bohemia 1760
Bückeburg, Germany 11 October 1975

4129 [Symphony, Op. 8, B-flat major]
1.Allegro 2.Adagio 3.Allegro
1,2,0,1-2Hn.-Str.
Ms.
Score 64 p.

4130 [Symphony, La bataille, Op. 11, D major]
In one movement
2,2,0,1-2Hn.-Str.
Ms.
Score 167 p.

NEUKIRCHNER, WENZEL.
b. Neustreischitz, Bohemia 8 April 1805

381m [Fantasy for bassoon]
Solo Bn.-2,2,2,2-2-2,2-Timp.-Str.
Ms. c1976 by The Fleisher Collection of Orches-
tral Music, Free Library of Philadelphia
Score 62 p. Large folio

NEUKOMM, SIGISMUND VON.   Salzburg 10 July 1778
Paris 3 April 1858

4131 [Symphony, Heroic, Op. 19, D major]
1.Allegro con spirito 2.Menuetto 3.Con poco
di moto 4.Allegro molto
1,2,2,2-2,2,3-Timp.-Str.
Ms.
Score 176 p.

NEUPERT, EDMUND.
Christiania (now Oslo) 1 April 1842
New York 22 June 1888

Neupert, Edmund

2235 Resignation [Arranged by Edvard   *5'*
Grieg]
2,2,2,2-2Hn.-Str.
W. Hansen, Copenhagen [1896?]
Score 9 p.

2129 Vor der Schlacht/Before the battle,   *4'*
piano. Transcribed for orchestra by Johan
Svendsen
3*,2,2,2-4,3,3,1-Timp.,Perc.-Str.
W. Hansen, Copenhagen [1896?]
Score 35 p.

NEVIN, ETHELBERT WOODBRIDGE.
            Edgeworth, Pennsylvania 25 November 1862
            New Haven, Connecticut 17 February 1901

109s La guitare (Pierrot et Pierrette).
Arranged for string orchestra by Paul Th.
Miersch
Str.
Boston Music, Boston, ᶜ1896 by G. Schirmer
Score 7 p.

NEWLANDSMITH, ERNEST.

780s Nocturne [F major]
Str.
Schott & Co., London [n.d.]
Score 5 p.

NEWMAN, JOEL.   b. 1918

7107 Sixteenth-century Italian dances. From
British Museum Royal Appendix Ms. 59-62.
Edited by Joel Newman
1.Paduana del re (The king's pavan) 2.El tutu
(Saltarello) 3.La monina (pavana) 4.[Salta-
rello] 5.La cornetta (pavana) 6.[Salta-
rello] 7.[Pavana] 8.El picardo (saltarello)
9.Passo e mezzo (pavana) 10.La gamba (saltarello) 11.El todescho (pavana) 12.Saltarello
4 parts (ATTB Recorders or modern Str.)
The Pennsylvania State University, University
Park, Pennsylvania, ᶜ1966
Score 24 p.

NEWMAN, THEODORE SPENCER.   New York 18 June 1933
                             Miami, Florida 16 February 1975

297m Concerto for organ and orchestra, 1963
1.Allegro brillante 2.Allegro giocoso
Solo Org.-1(alt. Picc.),1(alt. E.H.),1(alt.
B.Cl.)-1,2,2-Timp.,Perc.-Str.
Ms.
Score 105 p.
*Composed 1963. First performance in a concert
sponsored by the Musical Fund Society of Phil-
adelphia, Academy of Music, Philadelphia, 2
April 1964, members of the Philadelphia Orches-
tra, Vernon Hammond conductor, Robert Elmore
soloist. Awarded the McCollin Prize by The
Musical Fund Society of Philadelphia.*

6000 Divertimento for chamber orchestra,   *10'*
1959
1.Introduction 2.Capriccio 3.Pastoral, hunt,
storm and chorale 4.Little rondo

2(2nd alt. Picc.),2,2,2-2,2,2-Timp.,Perc.-
Hp.-Str.
Ms.
Score 91 p.
*Composed 1959. First reading Juilliard School
of Music, New York, May 1959, Juilliard Stu-
dent Orchestra, George Mester conductor.*

5994 Fanfare for orchestra, 1959   *4'30"*
3*,3,3(3rd alt. B.Cl.),3*-4,3,3,1-Timp.,Perc.
-Str.
Ms.
Score 23 p. Large folio
*Composed 1959. First reading Juilliard School
of Music, New York, December 1959, Julliard
Orchestra, Jean Morel conductor.*

2166s Hymn for string orchestra, 1959   *5-6'*
Str.
Ms.
Score 7 p.
*Composed 1959. First reading Juilliard School
of Music, New York, April 1959, Juilliard Stu-
dent Orchestra, George Mester conductor.
Received the Benjamin Award at Juilliard, 1959.*

323m Nocturne for clarinet and strings, 1963
Solo Cl.-Str.
Ms.
Score 9 p.
*Commissioned by The Juilliard School of Music.
Composed 1963.*

6370 Overture-fantasy for chamber   *15'*
orchestra, 1963
2(2nd alt. Picc.),2,2(2nd alt. B.Cl.),2-2,2,2
-Timp.,Perc.-Pno.(alt. Cel.)-Str.
Ms.
Score 80 p.
*Composed 1963. First performance Aspen, Colo-
rado, August 1963, Aspen School Orchestra,
James Levine conductor.*

2233s Song for strings and harp, 1962
Hp.-Str.
Ms.
Score 7 p.
*Originally composed for strings alone, 1960.
This version for strings and harp, 1962. Ori-
ginal version won the Benjamin Award at
Juilliard, 1960.*

6001 Toccata for orchestra, 1959   *10'*
3*,3*,3*,3*-4,3,3,1-Timp.,Perc.-Pno.-Str.
Ms.
Score 70 p. Large folio
*Composed 1959. First performance Manhattan
School of Music, New York, 7 May 1960, Orches-
tra of the Manhattan School of Music, Nicho-
las Flagello conductor.*

NICK, EDMUND JOSEF.
            Reichenberg, Bohemia 22 September 1891
            Geretsried, Bavaria 11 April 1974

679s Boston-Intermezzo   *5'*
Solo Vn.-Str.
Ries & Erler, Berlin [n.d.]
Score 11 p.

NICODÉ, JEAN LOUIS. Jerczig, Poland 12 August 1853
                Langebrück, near Dresden 5 October 1919

[Italian folk dances and songs, Op. 13]
5616 No. 1 Tarantella
      3*,2,2,2-4,2,3-Timp.,Perc.-Str.
5617 No. 2 Canzonetta
      2,2,2,2-2Hn.-Timp.-Str.
      Breitkopf & Härtel, Leipzig, C1894
      Scores: 51 p., 11 p.
      Originally composed for piano.

5614 Die Jagd nach dem Glück [The quest for   6'
      happiness] Op. 11
      3*,2,2,2-4,2,3-Timp.-Str.
      Breitkopf & Härtel, Leipzig [1878]
      Score 77 p.

1855 Maria Stuart, Op. 4 [Symphonic   16'
      poem]
      3*,2,2,2-4,2,3,1-Timp.,Perc.-Str.
      Breitkopf & Härtel, Leipzig [n.d.]
      Score 80 p.
      *Composed 1878. First performance Dresden 1879,
      the composer conducting.*

66 Das Meer [The sea] Symphonie-Ode, Op. 31.
    Nr. 1, Das Meer
    3,2,2,3*-4,3,4,5-Timp.,Cym.-Org.-Str.
    Breitkopf & Härtel, Leipzig, 1889
    Score 43 p.
    *Composed 1888. First performance of complete
    work, Dresden 1889, the composer conducting.*

[Scenes from the South, piano 4-hands, Op. 29.
Transcribed for orchestra by M. Pohle]
1429 No. 1 Bolero   6'
30   No. 2 [Moorish dance-song]   2'
1363 No. 4 Andalusienne   4'
1381 No. 5 Provincial story   4'
28   No. 6 In der Taberna   5'
      2(2nd alt. Picc.),2,2,2-4,2,3,1-Timp.,Perc.-
      Hp.-Str.
      Breitkopf & Härtel, Leipzig, C1904
      Scores: 33 p., 9 p., 23 p., 17 p., 27 p.

1184 Symphonische Variationen, Op. 27   20'
      Präludium - Thema -[12 Variations]- Finale
      2,2,2,3*(C.Bn. optional)-4,2,4(4th optional),
      1(optional)-Timp.,Cym.-Hp.(optional)-Str.
      Breitkopf & Härtel, Leipzig [n.d.]
      Score 111 p.
      *Composed 1884. First performance Dresden
      1885, the composer conducting.*

5729 [Two pieces, Op. 32]
      1.[A tale] 2.[In the country]
      20b.(2nd alt. E.H.)-2Hn.-Str.
      Breitkopf & Härtel, Leipzig [1890]
      Score 21 p.

NICOLAI, OTTO.   Königsberg, East Prussia
                        (now USSR) 9 June 1810
                        Berlin 11 May 1849

Full name: Carl Otto Ehrenfried Nicolai

6083 [Christmas overture, on the chorale Vom
      Himmel Hoch, Da Komm' Ich Her]

2,2,2,2-2,2,3,1-Timp.-Org.(ad lib.)-SATB Cho-
rus(ad lib.)-Str.
Bote & Bock, Berlin [1938]
Score 54 p.
*Chorale text by Martin Luther. Chorale melody
also attributed to Luther but probably of much
older origin.*

51 [The merry wives of Windsor. Overture]   8'
    2(2nd alt. Picc.),2,2,2-4,2,3-Timp.,Perc.-Str.
    Luck's Music Library, Detroit [n.d.]
    Score 44 p.
    *From the opera based on Shakespeare's play.
    Composed 1846. First performance of overture
    Vienna, 1 April 1847. First performance of
    opera Berlin, 9 March 1849.*

NIELSEN, CARL AUGUST.
                Nørre Lyndelse, Denmark 9 June 1865
                Copenhagen 3 October 1931

6511 [Aladdin. Seven pieces, Op. 34]   25'
      1.Orientalsk Festmarsch 2.[Aladdin's dream
      and Dance of the morning mist] 3.Hindu-Dans
      4.[Chinese dance] 5.[Market place in Ispa-
      han] 6.[Prisoners' dance] 7.[Negro dance]
      2(both alt. Picc.),2(2nd alt. E.H.),2,2-4,2,3,
      1-Timp.,Perc.-Cel.-Chorus(ad lib.)-Str.
      Skandinavisk og Borup, Copenhagen, C1940
      Score 89 p.
      *From the incidental music to the play by Adam
      Oehlenschlager based on the story from the
      Arabian Nights. Composed 1918. First perform-
      ance Copenhagen, 15 February 1919.*

2234s [Bohemian-Danish folksong, para-   8'
       phrase]
       Str.
       Skandinavisk og Borup, Copenhagen, C1942
       Score 11 p.
       *Composed 1928. First performance Copenhagen,
       1 November 1928, State Radio Orchestra, Jaro-
       slav Krupka conductor.*

849m [Concerto, clarinet, Op. 57]
      In one movement
      Solo Cl.-2Bn.-2Hn.-S.Dr.-Str.
      Kistner & Siegel, Leipzig, 1931
      Score 52 p.
      *Composed 1928. First performance Copenhagen,
      2 October 1928.*

329m [Concerto, flute and orchestra]   18'
      Edited by Emil Telmányi
      1.Allegro moderato 2.Allegretto
      Solo Fl.-0,2,2,2-2,0,1-Timp.-Str.
      Samfundet til Udgivelse af Dansk Musik,
      Copenhagen, C1952
      Score 64 p.
      *Composed 1926. First performance Paris, 21
      October 1926, Emil Telmányi conductor, Holger
      Gilbert-Jespersen soloist.*

868v [Concerto, violin, Op. 33]   36'
      1.Praeludium 2.Poco adagio - Rondo
      Solo Vn.-2(2nd alt. Picc.),2,2,2-4,2,3-Timp.-
      Str.
      W. Hansen, Leipzig, C1919

Nielsen, Carl

Score 102 p.
First performance Copenhagen, 28 February 1912.

1141 Helios overture, Op. 17   13'
3(3rd alt. Picc.),2,2,2-4,3,3,1-Timp.-Str.
Kalmus, New York [n.d.]
Score 35 p.
*Composed 1903. First performance Copenhagen,
8 October 1903, Royal Orchestra, Johan Svendsen conductor.*

335s [Little suite, string orchestra,   15'
Op. 1, A minor]
1.Präludium 2.Intermezzo 3.Finale
Str.
W. Hansen, Copenhagen [n.d.]
Score 33 p.
Composed 1888.

1265 [Maskarade. Dance of the cocks]   5'
3*,2,2,2-4,3,3,1-Timp.,Trgl.-Str.
W. Hansen, Leipzig, ^c1914
Score 27 p.
*From the opera based on Ludvig Holberg's
comedy. Composed 1904-06. First performance
Copenhagen, 11 November 1906.*

6513 [Rhapsodic overture, a fantasy journey 10'
to the Faroe Islands]
3(3rd alt. Picc.),2,2,2-4,2,3-Timp.,Perc.-Str.
Skandinavisk og Borup, Copenhagen, ^c1942
Score 33 p.
*Composed 1927. First performance Copenhagen,
27 November 1927, Royal Orchestra, the composer conducting.*

1458 Saga-Dröm [Saga-dream] Op. 39   8'
3,2,2,2-4,3,3,1-Timp.,Perc.-Str.
W. Hansen, Copenhagen, ^c1920
Score 17 p.
*Composed 1907. First performance Copenhagen,
6 April 1908, the composer conducting.*

1062 [Symphony no. 1, Op. 7, G minor]   28'
1.Allegro orgoglioso 2.Andante 3.Allegro
comodo 4.Finale: Allegro con fuoco
3*,2,2,2-4,2,3-Timp.-Str.
W. Hansen, Copenhagen [n.d.]
Score 163 p.
*Composed 1891-92. First performance Copen-
hagen 1905, the composer conducting.*

1080 [Symphony no. 2, The four tempera-   28'
ments, Op. 16]
1.Allegro collerico 2.Allegro comodo e
flemmatico 3.Andante malincolico 4.Allegro
sanguineo
3(3rd alt. Picc.),2(2nd alt. E.H.),2,2-4,3,3,
1-Timp.-Str.
W. Hansen, Copenhagen [n.d.]
Score 157 p.
*Composed 1900. First performance Copenhagen,
1 December 1902, the composer conducting.*

1230 [Symphony no. 3, Sinfonia espansiva,
Op. 27, D minor]
1.Allegro espansivo 2.Andante pastorale
3.Allegretto un poco 4.Finale: Allegro

3(3rd alt. Picc.),3(3rd alt. E.H.),3,3(3rd alt.
C.Bn.)-4,3,3,1-Timp.-Sop. Voice, Bar. Voice
(or Cl.,Tbn.)-Str.
Kahnt, Leipzig, ^c1913
Score 155 p.
First performance Copenhagen, 28 February 1912.

1384 [Symphony no. 4, The inextin-   35'
guishable, Op. 29]
In one movement
3(3rd alt. Picc.),3,3,3-4,3,3,1-Timp.-Str.
W. Hansen, Leipzig, ^c1916
Score 111 p.
*Composed 1914-16. First performance Copen-
hagen, 1 February 1916, the composer conducting.*

6509 [Symphony no. 5, Op. 50]   37-39'
Revised by Erik Tuxen
1.Tempo giusto - Adagio 2.Allegro - Andante
un poco tranquillo
3(3rd alt. Picc.),2,2,3*-4,3,3,1-Timp.,Perc.-
Cel.-Str.
Skandinavisk Musikforlag, Copenhagen, ^c1950
Score 172 p.
*Composed 1921-22. First performance Copen-
hagen, 24 January 1922, Musikforeningen, the
composer conducting.*

5951 [Symphony no. 6, Sinfonia semplice]   32'
Revised by Richard Dahl Eriksen
1.Tempo giusto - Allegro passionato 2.Humor-
eske 3.Proposta seria 4.Tema con [9] variazioni
3*,2,2,2-4,2,3,1-Timp.,Perc.-Str.
Samfundet til Udgivelse af Dansk Musik, Copenhagen, ^c1957 by Edition Dania
Score 162 p.
*Composed 1924-25. First performance Copen-
hagen, 11 December 1925, Royal Orchestra, the
composer conducting.*

NIELSEN, LUDOLF.
                Nørre-Tvede, Denmark 29 January 1876
                Copenhagen 11 May 1939

1484s Berceuse, Op. 9
Solo Vn.-Str.
W. Hansen, Copenhagen [n.d.]
Score 7 p.

5278 Nocturne lyrique, Op. 48
2,2*,2,1-Hn.-Cel.-Str.(without Cb.)
Edition Dania, Copenhagen, ^c1937
Score 7 p.

NIELSEN, RICCARDO.   Bologna, Italy 3 March 1908

2094s [Music for strings]
1.Andante 2.Presto 3.Adagio 4.Allegro
5.Adagio molto, quasi largo
Str.
F. Bongiovanni, Bologna, ^c1948
Score 46 p.
Composed 1946.

NIELSEN, TAGE.
        b. Frederiksberg, Denmark 16 January 1929

7053 Il giardino magico [The magic garden] *10'*
3(2nd & 3rd alt. Picc.),2(2nd alt. E.H.),3(2nd
alt. Cl. in E-flat, 3rd alt. B.Cl.),2-Alto
Sax.-4,2,1,1-Perc.-Pno.,Hpscd.,Hp.-Str.
Samfundet Til Udgivelse af Dansk Musik, Copen-
hagen, ^c1974
Score 31 p.
Commissioned by the Aarhus Municipal Orchestra.
Composed 1967-68. First performance Aarhus,
Denmark, 24 March 1969, the Aarhus Municipal
Orchestra, Per Dreier conductor.

NIEMANN, RUDOLF FRIEDRICH.
        Wesselburen, Holstein 4 December 1838
        Wiesbaden 3 May 1898

4444 Gavotte, piano, Op. 16. Transcribed for
orchestra by Karl Müller-Berghaus
2(2nd alt. Picc.),2,2,2-4,2,1,1-Timp.-Hp.(ad
lib.)-Str.
Hugo Pohle, Hamburg [n.d.]
Score 11 p.

NIEMANN, WALTER.   Hamburg 10 October 1876
        Leipzig 17 June 1953

242s Anakreon, Op. 50
1.[Springtime mood] 2.[Solemn temple dance]
Str.
Kahnt, Leipzig, ^c1918
Score 18 p.
Inspired by two poems of Anakreon (fl.521 B.C.).

834s [Four old dances, for string orchestra]
1.Entrée, Op. 59 no. 6 2.Sarabande, Op. 113
no. 4 3.Minuet, Op. 80 no. 4 4.Pavane, Op.
107 no. 6
Str.
C.F. Peters, Leipzig, ^c1931
Score 14 p.
All originally composed for piano.

1417s Rheinische Nachtmusik, Op. 35
2Hn.-Str.
Wunderhorn, Cologne, 1914
Score 15 p.

1230s [Two elegies for string orchestra]
1.Once upon a time, Op. 80 no. 1 2.Elegia,
Op. 102 no. 4
Str.
C.F. Peters, Leipzig, ^c1930
Score 7 p.
Originally composed for piano.

1173s [Two pieces for string orchestra]
1.Christmas pastorale, Op. 80 no. 10
2.Gavotte, Op. 108 no. 2
Str.
C.F. Peters, Leipzig, ^c1929
Score 11 p.
Originally composed for piano.

NIEUWENHOVE, E. VAN.
  See: AGRÈVES, ERNEST D'.

NIKISCH, ARTHUR.
  Lébényi Szent-Miklós, Hungary 12 October 1855
        Leipzig 23 January 1922

5457 [Fantasia on themes from Victor E. Nes-
sler's opera, The Trumpeter of Säckingen]
2,2,2,2-4,2,3-Timp.,Perc.-Hp.-Str.
J. Schuberth, Leipzig [n.d.]
Score 63 p.

NIVERD, LUCIEN. Vouziers, France 20 September 1879
        Paris 22 May 1967

Full name: Adolphe Lucien Niverd. Also published
under the pseudonym: Jacques d'Artoy

1018s Chacone [*sic*]
Str.
Score: Ms. 9 p.
Parts: Gallet, Paris [n.d.]

1009s Divertissement pompadour
Str.
Score: Ms. 6 p.
Parts: Gallet, Paris [n.d.]

NIVERD, U.

1532s Lucy-pavane
Str.
Richault, Paris [n.d.]
Score 4 p.

NIXON, ROGER.   Tulare, California 8 August 1921

7069 Fiesta del Pacifico (for band)   *8'*
3*,2,5*(1Cl. in E-flat, 1 Alto Cl.),2-4Sax.-
4,0,4Cnt.,3,Bar.,2-Timp.,Perc.-Hp.-Cb.
Boosey & Hawkes, New York, ^c1966
Score 74 p.
Fiesta del Pacifico is an annual festival held
in San Diego, California. Composed 1960.
First performance San Francisco, December 1960,
San Francisco State College Symphonic Band,
Edwin C. Kruth conductor.

NOELTE, A. ALBERT. Starnberg, Bavaria 10 March 1885
        Chicago 2 March 1946

3620 Four symphonic impressions, Op. 29 *29'*
1.Maestoso 2.De profundis 3.Allegro moderato
4.Grave - Allegro
3(3rd alt. Picc.),3*,3*,3*-4,3,3,1-Timp.,Perc.
-Hp.-Str.
Ms.
Score 129 p. Large folio
Composed 1934-36. First performance Chicago,
18 February 1937, Chicago Symphony Orchestra,
Frederick Stock conductor.

3445 Suite, Op. 27   *18'*
1.Humoreske 2.Intermezzo appassionato
3.Burleske
3(3rd alt. Picc.),3*,4*,3*-4,3,3,1-Timp.,Perc.
-Cel.,Hp.
Ms.
Score 104 p. Large folio
Commissioned by the Chicago Symphony Orchestra,
1931. Composed 1931. First performance Chi-
cago, 13 March 1931, Chicago Symphony Orches-
tra, Frederick Stock conductor.

Noelte, A. Albert

902s [Suite in one movement, Op. 22]
Grave - Allegro - Arie - Allegro
Timp.-Str.
O. Halbreiter, Munich, C1929
Score 16 p.

NÖLCK, AUGUST.   Lübeck, Germany 9 January 1862

721c [Concerto, violoncello, A minor]
1.Introduction: Lento - Allegro moderato 2.
Lento 3.Finale: Allegro con fuoco
Solo Vc.-2,2,2,2-2-Timp.-Str.
Score: Ms. 210 p.
Parts: Joh. André, Offenbach a.M., C1912

NORDEN, LEO.
See: ALETTER, WILHELM.

NORDEN, NORRIS LINDSAY. Philadelphia 24 April 1887
                        Philadelphia 3 November 1956

4914 Clouds of the north, for orchestra
2,2,2,2-4,2,3-Timp.-Hp.(or Pno.)-Str.
Ms. C1942 by N. Lindsay Norden
Score 17 p.
*Composed 1941. First performance Rochester,
1941, Rochester Philharmonic Orchestra, José
Iturbi conductor.*

4912 Fog, for orchestra
2,2,2,2-4,2,3-Timp.-Hp.-Str.
Ms.
Score 24 p.

5101 A garden
2,2,2,2-2Hn.-Hp.-Str.
Ms.
Score 17 p.

4958 Music for a tragedy
2,2,2,2-4,2,3-Timp.-Hp.-Str.
Ms.
Score 56 p. Large folio
Composed 1950.

5089 Music for children [20 movements]
2(2nd alt. Picc.),2,2,2-2,2,3-Timp.,Perc.-Hp.-
Str.
Ms.
Score 53 p. Large folio

5100 Reflections in the river
2,2,2,2-4,2,3-Timp.-Hp.-Str.
Ms.
Score 27 p.
*Composed 1943. Alternate title: Images in the
River. First performance Washington, National
Symphony Orchestra, Hans Kindler conductor.*

774c Romanza, in the style of Mendelssohn
Solo Vc.-2,2,2,2-2Hn.-Timp.-Str.
Ms.
Score 44 p.
*Composed ca.1945. First performance Phila-
delphia, WPA Symphony Orchestra, the composer
conducting, John Gray soloist.*

5087 The white swan
3(3rd alt. Picc. ad lib.),2,2,2-4,2,3,1-

Timp.,Trgl.-Hp.-Str.
Ms.
Score 24 p.
Composed 1936.

NORDGREN, ERIK.
    b. Sireköping, Skåne, Sweden 13 February 1913

401m [Concerto, clarinet, Op. 26]   *18'*
1.Allegro 2.Andante 3.Allegro furioso
Solo Cl.-2(2nd alt. Picc.),2,2,2-3(3rd ad lib.),
2,1-Timp.,Perc.-Hp.(Pno. ad lib.)-Str.
Ms.
Score 105 p.
*Composed 1950. First performance Stockholm,
7 October 1951, Swedish Radio Orchestra, Sten
Frykberg conductor, Thore Janson soloist.*

NORDOFF, PAUL.   Philadelphia 4 June 1909
                        Philadelphia 18 January 1977

753p [Concerto, piano, in D]   *18'*
1.Allegro 2.Lento 3.Allegro molto
Solo Pno.-2(2nd alt. Picc.),2(2nd alt. E.H.),
2,2-4,2,3-Timp.,Perc.-Cel.-Str.
Ms.
Score 109 p. Large folio
*Composed 1935. First performance Washington,
D.C., 12 February 1939, National Symphony
Orchestra, Hans Kindler conductor, the compo-
ser as soloist.*

1134v [Concerto, violin, G major]   *20'*
1.Largo - Allegro 2.Lento 3.Allegro
Solo Vn.-2(2nd alt. Picc.),2,2(1st alt. Cl. in
E-flat, 2nd alt. B.Cl.),2-4,2,3,1-Timp.,Perc.-
Cel.,Hp.-Str.
Ms.
Score 145 p. Large folio
Composed 1939-40.

3582 Prelude and three small fugues   *7'*
1(alt. Picc.),1(alt. E.H.),1,1-2,1-Timp.,Trgl.
-Pno.-Str.
Ms.
Score 47 p.
*Composed for two pianos, 1930. Orchestrated
1932. First complete performance Philadelphia,
9 June 1940, Pennsylvania Symphony Orchestra
of the WPA, Guglielmo Sabatini conductor.*

3146 Suite for orchestra   *17'*
1.March 2.Intermezzo 3.Toccata 4.Minuet
5.Fugue 6.Tango 7.Tarantella
3*,2(2nd alt. E.H.),2,2-4,2,2,1-Timp.,Perc.-
Cel.,Hp.-Str.
Ms.
Score 84 p.
*Composed 1938. First performance St. Louis, 6
December 1940, St. Louis Symphony Orchestra,
Vladimir Golschmann conductor.*

3558 Variations on a Bavarian dance theme   *5'*
2(2nd alt. Picc.),2(2nd alt. E.H.),2,2-4,2,1-
Timp.,Perc.-Cel.,2Hp.-Str.
Ms.
Score 40 p.
*Originally composed for piano, 1933. Orches-
trated 1933-35.*

NOREN, HEINRICH GOTTLIEB.   Graz 6 January 1861
                        Rottach, Bavaria 6 June 1928

Also published as: H. Gottlieb Noren

2154 Aria religiosa, Op. 9
      1,2,2,2-4,1,3-Timp.-Hp.-Str.(with Vn. Solo)
      Eos, Berlin, ^c1913
      Score 16 p.

860v [Concerto, violin, Op. 38, A minor]
      1.Allegro con spirito e poco agitato 2.Inter-
      mezzo melanconico 3.Finale rustico
      Solo Vn.-3(3rd alt. Picc.),3*,2,2-4,2,3-Timp.,
      Perc.-Hp.-Str.
      Eos, Berlin, ^c1912
      Score 233 p.
      *Composed 1911. First performance Danzig, 28
      May 1912, Alexander Petschnikov soloist.*

566c [Elegiac vocal scene, Op. 10]
      Solo Vc.-2,2,2,2-2Hn.-Timp.-Str.
      Kahnt, Leipzig, ^c1904
      Score 18 p.

1828 [Kaleidoscope, variations and double   *37'*
      fugue on an original theme, Op. 30]
      3(3rd alt. Picc.),3*,3*,3*-4,3,3,1-Timp.,Perc.
      -Hp.-Str.
      Lauterbach & Kuhn, Leipzig, ^c1908
      Score 224 p.
      Composed 1920. First performance Berlin 1922.

2155 Symphonische Serenade, Op. 48   *34'*
      1.Allegretto pastorale 2.Scherzo 3.Nächt-
      licher Reichen 4.Finale: Allegro giocoso
      3(3rd alt. Picc.),3*(2nd alt. E.H.II),3(3rd
      alt. B.Cl.),2-4,3,3,1-Timp.,Perc.-Hp.-Str.
      Eos, Berlin, ^c1915
      Score 228 p.

2290 [Symphony, Vita, Op. 36, D major]
      1.Prolog 2.Skepsis 3.Einst 4.Finale,
      Lebenslust [Love of life]
      3(3rd alt. Picc.),3*,3*,3*-8(5th alt. Ten.
      TubaI),3(3rd alt. B.Tpt.),3,Ten.TubaII,3B.
      Tuba(3rd alt. Cb.Tuba)-Timp.,Perc.-2Hp.-Str.
      Eos, Berlin, ^c1913
      Score 325 p.

NORMAN, LUDVIG.   Stockholm 28 August 1831
                       Stockholm 28 March 1885

Full name: Fredrik Vilhelm Ludvig Norman

1391 [Symphony no. 3, Op. 58, D minor]
      1.Allegro appassionato 2.Andante cantabile
      3.Allegretto molto commodo 4.Allegro molto
      2,2,2,2-4,2,3-Timp.,Trgl.-Str.
      Musikaliska Konstföreningen, Stockholm, 1885
      Score 144 p.

NOSKOWSKI, ZYGMUNT VON.   Warsaw 2 May 1846
                    Wiesbaden, Germany 23 July 1909

1173 [The deserted hut, Op. 16. Gypsy   *15'*
      dance *and* Ukrainian dance]
      2(2nd alt. Picc.),2,2,2-2,2,1-Timp.,Perc.-Str.

J. Hainauer, Breslau [n.d.]
Score 54 p.
*From the incidental music to the play, com-
posed 1883. First performance Warsaw, 1884.*

1697 [Echoes and recollections, fantasy on
      Polish national songs]
      7 sections played without pause
      3*,3*,3*,2-4,2,3,1-Timp.,Perc.-Hp.-Str.
      Gebethner & Wolff, Warsaw [n.d.]
      Score 47 p.

721 Das Meerauge/Morskie Oko, Op. 19   *10'*
     2(2nd alt. Picc.),2,2,2-4,2,3-Timp.-Str.
     J. Hainauer, Breslau [n.d.]
     Score 63 p.
     *Das Meerauge (The Eye of the Sea) is a lake
     in the Tatra Mountains. Composed 1885. First
     performance Warsaw, 1885.*

1495 Polonaise élégiaque, Op. 22 no. 3
      0,0,2,2-2Hn.-Str.
      J. Hainauer, Breslau [n.d.]
      Score 3 p.
      Composed 1886. First performance Warsaw, 1886.

1114 [The steppe, symphonic poem, Op. 66]   *18'*
      3*,2,2,2-4,2,3,1-Timp.,Perc.-Hp.-Str.
      Gebethner & Wolff, Warsaw [n.d.]
      Score 92 p.

NOVÁČEK, OTTOKAR EUGEN. Fehértemplom, Hungary
            (now Bela Crkva, Yugoslavia) 13 May 1866
                           New York 3 February 1900

553p [Concerto, piano, Eroico, Op. 8,   *25'*
      C minor]
      In one movement: Allegro - Adagio - Presto
      Solo Pno.-3*,2,2,2-4,3,3,1-Timp.,Perc.-Str.
      W. Hansen, Copenhagen [n.d.]
      Score 143 p.

717v Perpetuum mobile   *3'30"*
      Solo Vn.-2,2,2,2-2,2-Timp.,Perc.-Hp.-Str.
      C.F. Peters, Leipzig, ^c1895
      Score 19 p.

NOVÁČEK, RUDOLF. Fehértemplom, Hungary 7 April 1860
                           Prague 12 August 1929

1885 [Elegy, farewell at the lying-in-state,
      Op. 56]
      1,1,2,1-4,2,Fluegelhorn,3-Hp.-Str.
      H. Weiner (for the composer), Prague [n.d.]
      Score 12 p.

2387 [Sinfonietta, Op. 48, D minor]   *14'*
      1.Allegro molto 2.Presto 3.Adagio
      4.Allegro molto vivace
      1,1,2,2-2Hn.
      Breitkopf & Härtel, Leipzig, ^c1905
      Score 27 p.

NOVÁK, VÍTĚZSLAV.   Kamenice nad Lipou,
                      Bohemia 5 December 1870
            Skutec, Czechoslovakia 18 July 1949

1698 [In the Tatra Mountains, tone poem,   *18'*
      Op. 26]

Novák, Vitězslav

3*,3*,3*,3*-4,3,3,1-Timp.,Perc.-Hp.-Str.
Universal Edition, Vienna, ^c1910
Score 67 p.
*Composed 1902. First performance Prague, 25
November 1902, Czech Philharmonic, Oskar
Nedbal conductor.*

1702 Lady Godiva Ouverture, Op. 41   15'
3(3rd alt. Picc.),3*,3*,3*-4,3,3,1-Timp.,Perc.
-Hp.-Str.
Universal Edition, Vienna, ^c1919
Score 63 p.
*Composed 1907. First performance Prague, 24
November 1907, L. Celansky conductor.*

1879 Marysa, Op. 18 [Dramatic overture]   10'
2,3*,2,2-4,2,3,1-Timp.,Gong-Str.
Ms.
Score 73 p.
*Composed 1898. First performance Prague 1899,
Czech Philharmonic Orchestra, Oskar Nedbal
conductor.*

881 [Of eternal longing, tone poem, Op. 33] 25'
3,3*,3*,3*-4,2,3,1-Timp.,Perc.-2Hp.-Str.
Breitkopf & Härtel, Leipzig, ^c1906
Score 87 p.
*Composed 1904. First performance Prague, 8
February 1905, Czech Philharmonic, Oskar
Nedbal conductor.*

1700 Serenade, Op. 36   25'
1.Praeludium 2.Serenata 3.Notturno
4.Finale: Allegro capriccioso
2,2,2,2-4,2-Hp.-Str.
Universal Edition, Vienna, ^c1913
Score 49 p.
*Composed 1905. First performance Prague, 6
March 1906, Czech Philharmonic, Oskar Nedbal
conductor.*

1699 [Slovak suite, Op. 32]   25'
1.[In church] 2.[With children] 3.[Lovers]
4.[At the dance] 5.[At night]
2,2,2,2-3Hn.-Org.(ad lib.),Hp.-Str.
M. Urbánek, Prague, ^c1911
Score 63 p.
*Composed 1903. First performance Prague, 4
February 1906, Czech Philharmonic, V. Zemá-
nek conductor.*

1701 [Toman and the wood nymph, Op. 40]   25'
3(3rd alt. Picc.),3*,3*,3*-6,3,3,1-Timp.,Perc.
-2Hp.-Str.
Universal Edition, Vienna, ^c1919
Score 151 p.
*Composed 1907. First performance Prague, 5
April 1908, Karel Kovarovic conductor.*

NOVIKOFF, S.

1466s Prélude
Hn.-Hp.-Str.
Jurgenson, Moscow [1903?]
Score 6 p.

NOWAKOWSKI, JOSEPH.   Mniszck, Poland 1800
                             Warsaw 1865

861m [Concertino, trombone, A-flat major]
Solo Tbn.-2,2,2,2-2,2-Timp.-Str.
Score: Ms. 56 p.
Parts: A.E. Fischer, Bremen [n.d.]

NOWOWIEJSKI, FELIX.   Wartenburg
           (now Barczewo, Poland) 7 February 1877
                  Poznań, Poland 18 January 1946

410v Légende, Op. 32
Solo Vn.-2,2,2,2-2,2-Timp.,Perc.-Hp.-
Str.
W. Hansen, Leipzig, ^c1914
Score 19 p.

1780 [Polish courtship, overture]
2(2nd alt. Picc.),2,2,2-4,2,3-Timp.,Perc.-Str.
J. Schuberth, Leipzig, ^c1903
Score 62 p.

4536 Slawische Volksscene (Kujawiak),   8'
Op. 18
3*,2,2,2-4,2,3,1-Timp.,Perc.-Str.
Bote & Bock, Berlin, ^c1912
Score in reduction 4 p.
Title refers to Kujawy province, Poland.

NUSSIO, OTMAR.   Grosseto, Italy 23 October 1902

4933 Danza ticinese [from Ticino,   6'
Switzerland]
2(both alt. Picc.),2,2,2-4,2,3-Timp.,Perc.-
Pno.,Hp.-Str.
Universal Edition, Vienna, ^c1943
Score 30 p.

6075 Escapades musicales   11'
1.Introduzione e marcetta 2.Minuetto
3.Allegro finale
2*,2(2nd alt. E.H.),2,2-2,2,1-Timp.,Perc.-Str.
Ernst Eulenburg, London, ^c1956
Score 56 p.
Composed 1949.

NYMAN, UNO.   Linköping, Sweden 1879

1887s In memoriam   10'
Str.
Ms.
Score 14 p.
*Composed 1936. First performance Milwaukee,
1936, Young People's Orchestra, Milton Rush
conductor.*

3601 Mirage, a fantasy   15'
1,1,1,1-Hn.-Pno.-Str.
Ms.
Score 48 p.
*Composed 1926. First performance Milwaukee,
21 May 1936, Milwaukee Concert Orchestra of
the WPA, Carl Eppert conductor.*

NYSTROEM, GÖSTA. Silvberg, Sweden 13 October 1890
          Särö, near Göteborg, Sweden 9 August 1966

1196v [Concerto, viola and chamber   18-20'
orchestra, Homage à la France]
1.Allegro, très rythmé 2.Lento, molto tranquillo 3.Allegro scherzando

Solo Va.-1,1,1,1-2,1-Timp.-Hp.-Str.
Ms.
Score 99 p.
*Composed 1940. First performance Göteborg, 30
October 1941, Orkesterföreningen, Matti Rubin-
stein conductor, Tage Broström soloist.*

364v [Concerto for violin and   24-30'
  orchestra]
In one movement
Solo Vn.-2(2nd alt. Picc.),1,2,1-2,1,1-Timp.,
Perc.-Cel.,Hp.-Str.
Ms.
Score 115 p.
*Composed 1954. First performance Göteborg, 23
January 1957, Göteborgs Orkesterföreningen,
Sixten Eckerberg conductor, Tibor Varga
soloist.*

321p [Concerto ricercante for piano,   22-24'
  string orchestra, percussion, harp and celesta]
In one movement
Solo Pno.-Timp.,Perc.-Cel.,Hp.-Str.
Ms.
Score 118 p.
*Composed 1959. First performance Stockholm,
15 May 1960, Orchestra of the Swedish Radio,
Sten Frykberg conductor, Käbi Laretei soloist.*

4980 "1945", ouverture symphonique   12'
3*,2(2nd alt. E.H.),2,2-4,3,3,1-Timp.,Perc.-
Hp.-Str.
Ms.
Score 101 p.
*Composed 1945. First performance Göteborg,
Sweden, 11 October 1945, Orkesterföreningen,
Sixten Eckerberg conductor.*

390m [Partita for flute, string orchestra 16'
  and harp]
1.Lento 2.Allegro 3.Adagio - Tempo di valse
4.Canto semplice 5.Molto ritmico
Solo Fl.-Hp.-Str.
Edition Suecia, Stockholm [n.d.]
Score 42 p.
*Composed 1953. First performance on Sveriges
Radio Göteborg, 18 January 1954, Göteborg
Symphony Orchestra, Sixten Eckerberg con-
ductor, Håkan Edlen soloist.*

770c [Sinfonia concertante for violon-   36'
  cello and orchestra]
1.Grave 2.Allegro bucolico 3.Lento - Più
vivo
Solo Vc.-2,2,2,2(or 1,1,1,1)-4Hn.(or 2Hn.),
2Tpt.-Timp.-Pno.,Hp.-Str.
Ms.
Score 140 p.
*Composed 1944. First performance Göteborg, 12
April 1945, Göteborgs Orkesterföreningen,
Sixten Eckerberg conductor, Guido Vecchi
soloist.*

5023 Sinfonia espressiva [Symphony no. 2] 30'
1.Lento 2.Allegro scherzando 3.Adagio
4.Allegro risoluto - Lentando, Grave - Allegro
2(2nd alt. Picc.),2,3*,3*-4,3,3,1-Timp.,Perc.-
Str.

Ms.
Score 140 p.
*Composed 1935. First performance Göteborg, 18
February 1937, Göteborgs Orkesterföreningen,
Tor Mann conductor.*

5221 [Theater suite no. 2, from the   28'
incidental music to Shakespeare's The Tempest]
1.[Prelude] 2.[Ferdinand and Miranda] 3.
[Caliban and the sailors] 4.[Harvest dance]
2(2nd alt. Picc.),2(2nd alt. E.H.),2(2nd alt.
B.Cl.),2(2nd alt. C.Bn.)-4,2,3,1-Timp.,Perc.-
Pno.,Cel.,Hp.-Women's Chorus(ad lib.)-Str.
Ms.
Score 144 p. Large folio
*Composed 1934. First performance Göteborg, 6
March 1941, Göteborgs Orkesterföreningen,
Matti Rubinstein conductor.*

6060 [Theater suite no. 4, incidental   16'
music to Shakespeare's The Merchant of Venice]
1.[Prelude] 2.Burlesk 3.Nocturne (Fresco-
baldiana) 4.[Mask play]
1,1,1,1-Tpt.-Timp.,Perc.-Cemb.,Mand.,Guit.-Str.
Edition Suecia, Stockholm, ᶜ1947 by Föreningen
Svenska Tonsättare
Score 50 p.
*Commissioned by the Göteborgs Stadsteater.
Composed 1936. First performance in the Göteborgs Stadsteater, Göteborg, 21 April 1936,
Göteborg Symphony Orchestra, Matti Rubinstein
conductor.*

O

OBERTHÜR, KARL.   Munich 4 March 1819
                               London 8 November 1895

561m [Concertino, harp, Op. 175, G minor]
Solo Hp.-2,2,2,2-2,2-Str.
Score: Ms. 134 p.
Parts: Hofmeister, Leipzig [n.d.]

556m Loreley [a legend, for harp, Op. 180]
Solo Hp.-3*,2,2,2-2,2,3-Timp.-Str.
Louis Oertel, Hannover [n.d.]
Score 43 p.

OCKI-ALBI, G. N.

3923 Scènes pittoresques roumaines, première
  suite
1.March 2.Air de ballet 3.Doina [Shepherd's
song] 4.Fête roumaine
3(3rd alt. Picc.),3*,3*,3-4,3,3,1-Timp.,Perc.-
Hp.-Str.
Ms.
Score 60 p.

O'DONNELL, BERTRAM WALTON.
                      Madras, India 28 July 1887
                      Belfast, Ireland 20 August 1939

972s Miniature suite
1.Canzonetta 2.Pizzicato 3.Caprice

O'Donnell, Bertram Walton

Str.
Score: Ms. 27 p.
Parts: Hawkes & Son, London, ^c1925

5695 Two Irish tone sketches, Op. 20   12'
1.The mountain sprite 2.At the pattern
[Irish dance]
2*,1(alt. E.H.),2,1-2,3,3-Timp.,Perc.-Harm.-
Str.
Hawkes & Son, London, ^c1924
Score in reduction 12 p.

OEHME, ROBERT.   Dresden 20 May 1860

1071s Myrthe [Myrtle] Arranged by Gustave Sandré
Str.
Score: Ms. 4 p.
Parts: [n.p., n.d.]

1081s Rittersporn [Lark-spur] Arranged by
Gustave Sandré
Str.
Score: Ms. 4 p.
Parts: B. Schotts Söhne, Mainz [n.d.]

OELSCHLEGEL, ALFRED.   Auscha, Bohemia
(now Ustek, Czechoslovakia) 25 February 1847
                          Leipzig 19 June 1915

416s [Renaissance, humorous sketch, Op. 109]
Glock.-Str.(without Cb.)
Ries & Erler, Berlin [n.d.]
Score 13 p.

OERTEL, AUGUST.

1170s Am stillen, klaren See [At the clear and
quiet lakeside, fantasy piece]
Str.
Score: Ms. 6 p.
Parts: Oertel, Hannover [n.d.]

1278s Wiegenlied [Cradle song] Op. 5
Solo Vn.-Str.
Score: Ms. 10 p.
Parts: [n.p., n.d.]

OFFENBACH, JACQUES.   Cologne 20 June 1819
                          Paris 5 October 1880

Real name: Jakob Eberst

6922 [La Belle Hélène. Overture]   8'
2*,2,2,2-4,2,3-Timp.,Perc.-Hp.-Str.
Luck's Music Library, Detroit [n.d.]
Score 42 p.
From the operetta in three acts with libretto
by Henri Meilhac and Ludovic Halévy. First
performance Paris, 17 December 1864.

635c [Musette, air de ballet, violoncello
and piano, Op. 24. Transcribed by Norbert Sal-
ter]
Solo Vc.-Str.
Score: Ms. 8 p.
Parts: Schlesinger, Berlin, ^c1902

6785 Orpheus in the underworld. Overture.   9'
Arranged by C. Binder

2(2nd alt. Picc.),2,2,2-4,2,3,1-Timp.,Perc.-Hp.
(or Pno.)-Str.
Luck's Music Library, Detroit [n.d.]
Score 42 p.
From the operetta with libretto by Hector Cré-
mieux and Ludovic Halévy. Original version in
two acts first performed Paris, 21 October
1858. Revised to four acts. First performance
Paris, 7 February 1874.

7021 [Tales of Hoffmann. Intermezzo and   5'30"
Barcarole]
2,2,2,2-4,2Cnt.,3-Timp.,Perc.-Hp.-Str.
Luck's Music Library, Detroit [n.d.]
Score 12 p.
From the opera in three acts based on stories
by E.T.A. Hoffmann. Left unfinished at the
composer's death; recitatives and part of
scoring added by Ernest Guiraud. First performance Paris, 10 February 1881.

OGAREW, M. DE.

590c [Memento, prayer, Op. 13]
Solo Vc.-2,2,2,2-4,2,3-Perc.-Str.
Klemm, Dresden [n.d.]
Score 15 p.

OHLSEN, EMIL.
          Ahrensböck, near Lübeck, Germany 27 May 1860
                                      died after 1927

1087s Pierrette [love serenade, Op. 117]
Solo Vc.-Glock.-Hp.(ad lib.)-Str.
Julius Jäger, Berlin, ^c1905
Score 7 p.

OLDBERG, ARNE.   Youngstown, Ohio 12 July 1874
                    Evanston, Illinois 17 February 1862

711p [Concerto, piano, no. 2, Op. 43]   30'
1.Animato ed energico 2.Nocturne 3.Molto
moderato ed espressivo
Solo Pno.-2(2nd alt. Picc.),2(2nd alt. E.H.),2,
2-4,2,3-Timp.,Perc.-Str.
Ms.
Score 230 p.
Composed 1930. Awarded prize in the Hollywood
Competition, 1931. First performance Holly-
wood,16 August 1932, Los Angeles Philharmonic
Orchestra, Frederick Stock conductor, Hilda
Edwards soloist.

2803 Symphony no. 3, Op. 41   40'
1.Moderato e sostenuto 2.Canzone 3.Finale:
Introduzione e scherzo
3(3rd alt. Picc.),3*,3*,3*-4,4,3,1-Timp.,Perc.-
Hp.-Str.
Ms.
Score 261 p.
Composed 1925. First performance Chicago, 18
March 1927, Chicago Symphony Orchestra, Fre-
derick Stock conductor.

3593 Variations, for orchestra, Op. 49   15'
2,3*,3,2-4,2,3,1-Timp.,Perc.-Str.
Ms.
Score 69 p.

*Originally composed for string orchestra, 1938.
Transcribed 1939.*

OLDENBURG, CARL MÜLLER.
   See: MÜLLER-OLDENBURG, KARL.

OLIPHANT, LILIAN BLAIR.
   See: BLAIR-OLIPHANT, LILIAN.

OLLONE, MAX D'   Besançon, France 13 June 1875
                      Paris 15 May 1959

  536p Fantaisie [piano, E-flat major]
    Solo Pno.-2,2,2,2-4,2,3-Timp.,Perc.-Str.
    Enoch, Paris, c1900
    Score 97 p.

  693m Fantaisie orientale [clarinet and orchestra]
    Solo Cl.-2,2*,0,2-4,2-Timp.,Perc.-Hp.-Str.
    Score: Ms. 36 p.
    Parts: Evette & Schaeffer, Paris [n.d.]

  680v Le ménétrier [The village fiddler,
    symphonic poem]
    1.[In the native country] 2.[With the Bohe-
    mians] 3.[Returning home]
    Solo Vn.-3*,3*,2,2-4,2,3,1-Timp.,Perc.-Hp.-
    Str.
    Heugel, Paris, c1911
    Score 105 p.

OLSEN, OLE.   Hammerfest, Norway 4 July 1850
                 Oslo 10 November 1927

  543p Petite suite, Op. 50 [5 movements]
    Pno.-Str.
    A. Cranz, Brussels [n.d.]
    Score 29 p.

  417s [Suite, in 7 movements, Op. 60, from the
    music to Nordahl Rolfsen's fairy poem,
    Svein Uroed]
    Str.
    Norsk, Christiania [n.d.]
    Score 11 p.
    First performance Stockholm 1892.

  2165 [Symphony no. 1, Op. 5, G major]
    Allegro maestoso - Scherzo - Andante - Andante
    quasi adagio
    2,2,2,2-4,2,3-Timp.-Str.
    A.J. Gutmann, Vienna, c1884
    Score 69 p.

  101s Town and country/Aus Dorf und Stadt
    Str.
    Theo. Presser [n.p., n.d.]
    No score. Violin I part 7 p.

OLSEN, POUL ROVSING.   Copenhagen 4 November 1922

  6884 Schicksalslieder [Songs of destiny, after
    Hölderlin, Op. 28]
    1.[Half of life] 2.[Hyperion's song of des-
    tiny] 3.[To the Fates] 4.Abendlied
    Voice Solo-Fl.,Cl.-Str.
    Samfundet til Udgivelse af Dansk Musik, Copen-
    hagen, c1961

Score 26 p.
Composed 1953.

  6883 [Symphonic variations, Op. 27]
    2(2nd alt. Picc.),2,2,2-4,2,2-Timp.,Perc.-Hp.-
    Str.
    Samfundet til Udgivelse af Dansk Musik, Copen-
    hagen, c1958
    Score 70 p.
    Composed 1953.

OLSEN, SPARRE.   Stavanger, Norway 25 April 1903

Full name: Carl Gustav Sparre Olsen

  6203 [Music for orchestra, Op. 38]
    2(2nd alt. Picc.),2,2,2-4,2,2,1-Timp.,Perc.-
    Str.
    Ms. c1949 by Sparre Olsen
    Score 71 p.
    *Composed 1949. First performance Oslo, 3 Novem-
    ber 1948, Oslo Philharmonic Orchestra, Öivin
    Fjeldstad conductor.*

  5235 Nidarosdomen [The cathedral, fugue and *5'*
    chorale for orchestra, Op. 29]
    2,2,2,2-4,2,3,1-Timp.-Str.
    Norsk Musikforlag, Oslo, c1947
    Score 28 p.
    *Nidarosdomen is the cathedral of Trondheim
    (formerly Nidaros), where Norwegian kings are
    crowned. First performance New York, 1948.*

  388m Serenade for flute and string   *12-13'*
    orchestra, Op. 45
    1.Allegro ma non troppo 2.Andante con moto
    3.Allegro giocoso
    Solo Fl.-Str.
    Norsk Musikforlag, Oslo, c1957
    Score 38 p.
    *Composed 1955. First performance Oslo, 31
    October 1956, Oslo Philharmonic, Öivin Fjeld-
    stad conductor, Alf Andersen soloist.*

  6097 [Two old Norwegian hymns from   *5'*
    Gudbrandsdal. Transcribed for flute, clarinet
    and strings by Sparre Olsen]
    1.Moderato 2.Andantino
    1,0,1-Str.
    Norsk Musikforlag, Oslo, c1955
    Score 8 p.
    *Gudbrandsdal is the scene of much of the Peer
    Gynt legend. This arrangement 1939. First
    performance Oslo, 30 March 1940, Norwegian
    Broadcasting Orchestra, Hugo Kramm conductor.*

  6089 [Variations on a Norwegian folk tune, *7'*
    for orchestra, Op. 5]
    1,1,1,1-2,2,2-Str.
    Norsk Musikforlag, Oslo, c1947
    Score 26 p.
    *Originally composed for piano, 1931. Tran-
    scribed for orchestra, 1946. First performance
    Trondheim, Norway, 29 April 1948, Trondheim
    Symfoniorkester, Olav Kielland conductor.*

ONSLOW, GEORGE.
          Clermont-Ferrand, France 27 July 1784
          Clermont-Ferrand, France 3 October 1853

Onslow, George

6796 [Symphony no. 1, Op. 41, A major]
1.Largo - Allegro spirituoso 2.Adagio
espressivo 3.Minuetto 4.Vivace
2,2,2,2-4,2,3-Timp.-Str.
F. Kistner, Leipzig [n.d.]
Score 144 p.
*Composed for and dedicated to La Société des
Concerts du Conservatoire de Musique à Paris.*

6753 [Symphony no. 2, Op. 42, D minor]
1.Allegro vivace ed energico 2.Andante grazioso 3.Menuetto 4.Presto agitato
2,2,2,2-4,2,3-Timp.-Str.
F. Kistner, Leipzig [n.d.]
Score 144 p.

ORGAD, BEN-ZION.   Gelsenkirchen,
             near Essen, Germany 21 August 1926

Born: Ben-Zion Büschel

273m Music for orchestra with horn solo
1.Andante 2.Allegro
Solo Hn.-3*(2nd alt. Fl. in G),0,2*,3*-Tbn.-
Timp.,Perc.-Pno.,Cel.,Hp.-Str.
Israeli Music Publications, Tel Aviv, C1960
Score 73 p.
Composed 1960.

ORLAMÜNDER.

837m [Concerto, bassoon, B-flat major]
In one movement
Solo Bn.-1,2,2-2,2,1-Timp.-Str.
Ms.
Score 47 p.

ORNSTEIN, LEO. Kremenchug, Russia 11 December 1892

Nocturne and danse
2880 Nocturne   *ca.12'*
4*,4*,4*(3rd alt. Cl. in E-flat),4*-6,3,3,1-
Timp.,Perc.-Cel.,Hp.-Str.
2881 Danse (Also known as Dance of Fates)   *5'*
4*(3rd alt. Picc.II),4*,4*,4*-6,4,3,1-Timp.,
Perc.-Cel.,Hp.-Str.
Ms.
Scores: 76 p., 52 p.
*Commissioned by the League of Composers, 1935.
Composed 1936. First performance St. Louis,
12 February 1937, St. Louis Symphony Orchestra,
Vladimir Golschmann conductor.*

ORREGO SALAS, JUAN ANTONIO.
             b. Santiago, Chile 18 January 1919

6146 Sinfonia no. 3, Op. 50   *30'*
1.Allegro maestoso 2.Allegretto ben marcato
3.Recitativo lento 4.Andante cantabile
3*,3*,3*,3*-4,2,3,1-Timp.,Perc.-Hp.-Str.
Ms.
Score 198 p. Large folio
*Commissioned by Inocente Palacios. Composed
1961. First performance, Howard University,
Washington, D.C., Second Annual Inter-American Music Festival, 22 April 1961, National
Symphony Orchestra, Howard Mitchell conductor.*

OSBORNE, WILLSON.   4 April 1906

4706 Prelude for brass instruments
3Tpt.,3Tbn.,Tuba
Ms. [Now published by Music for Brass, C1951]
Score 12 p.

OSTROGLAZOV, M.

2948 Le crépuscule [Twilight, sketch for
orchestra] Op. 11
2,2*,2,2-4,2,3,1-Timp.,Perc.-Pno.,2Hp.-
Str.
P. Jurgenson, Leipzig [n.d.]
Score 38 p.

4366 [Illustration: Apocalypse 6:8 and 21:1,
Op. 12 no. 1]
Allegro - Adagio
3*,2*,2,2-4,2,3,1-Timp.,Perc.-2Hp.-Str.
Jurgenson, Moscow [n.d.]
Score 50 p.
*From the New Testament: 6:8 describes the
Horseman Death; Chapter 21, the New Jerusalem.*

OSWALD, HENRIQUE.   Rio de Janeiro 14 April 1852
                      Rio de Janeiro 9 June 1931

730p [Concerto, piano, Andante con variazioni]
Solo Pno.-1,2*,1,1-2,2-Timp.-Str.
Ms.
Score 80 p.

3942 Festa [Festival]
4*,3*,3*,3*-4,3,3,1-Timp.,Perc.-Cel.(or Glock.),
Hp.-Str.
Ms.
Score 72 p. Large folio

3261 Sinfonia
1.Allegro moderato 2.Adagio 3.Scherzo
4.Allegro deciso
4*,3*,3*,3*-4,4(3rd & 4th alt. 2Cnt.),3,1-
Timp.,Perc.-Hp.-Str.
Ms.
Score 249 p.

OTAKA, HISATADA.   Tokyo 26 September 1911
                        Tokyo 16 February 1951

4890 [Japanese suite no. 2 for small   *13'*
orchestra, Op. 12]
1.Allegretto moderato 2.Allegretto 3.Lento
cantabile 4.Allegro agitato
2(2nd alt. Picc.),2(2nd alt. E.H.),2(2nd alt.
B.Cl.),2-2,2-Timp.,Perc.-Cel.,Hp.-Str.
Universal Edition, Vienna, C1941
Score 87 p.

OTEY, ORLANDO.   Mexico City 1 February 1925

5767 Alacrán, sinfonía breve
1.A la marcia, con spirito 2.Andante
sostenuto 3.Presto
3*,2,2,2-4,2,3,1-Timp.,S.Dr.,Cym.-Str.
Ms. C1959 by Orlando Otey
Score 73 p. Large folio
Alacrán (scorpion) is an Aztec ritual dance.

Commissioned by the Lancaster Symphony Orchestra. Composed 1957. First performance Lancaster, Pa., 3 December 1957, Lancaster Symphony Orchestra, Louis Vyner conductor.

2162s Suite for strings
1.Allegro ma molto maestoso 2.Adagio
3.Allegro deciso - Alacrán
Str.
Ms.
Score 30 p.
Commissioned by Louis Vyner. Composed 1958. First performance Newtown Square, Pennsylvania, 19 April 1958, Marple-Newtown String Ensemble, Louis Vyner conductor.

OTTERLOO, JAN WILLEM VAN.
          b. Winterswijk, Holland 27 December 1907

6539 [Sinfonietta for wind instruments] *15'30"*
1.Molto sostenuto - Allegro 2.Tempo vivo
(scherzando) 3.Molto sostenuto 4.Molto
allegro
3*,3*,3*,3*-4Hn.
Donemus, Amsterdam, c1948
Score 53 p. Large folio
Composed 1943.

OTTO-OLSEN.

1034 Rhapsodie danoise, Op. 6   *15'*
2(2nd alt. Picc.),2,2,2-4,2,3,1-Timp.,Perc.-
Hp.-Str.
W. Hansen, Copenhagen, c1916
Score 61 p.

OUDSHOORN, ANTON M.   Leyden, Holland ca.1840

1470s Au berceau [At the cradle, A major]
Solo Vc.-Str.
P. Decourcelle, Nice [n.d.]
Score 5 p.

699s Conte d'enfant [Children's story]
Solo Vc.-Str.
P. Decourcelle, Nice [n.d.]
Score 3 p.

1655s Doloroso, melodie
Solo Vc.-Str.
Score: Ms. 3 p.
Parts: Decourcelle, Nice [n.d.]

871s Encore une [One more, little waltz]
Str.
P. Decourcelle, Nice [n.d.]
Score 5 p.

1489s Fanfaretta
Solo Vc.-Cl.-Str.
P. Decourcelle, Nice [n.d.]
Score 5 p.

1295s Heureux moment [Blissful moment, little waltz]
Str.
Score: Ms. 11 p.
Parts: Decourcelle, Nice [n.d.]

1471s Joyeux retour [Joyous return] scherzo
Solo Vc.-Str.(Vc. ad lib.)
P. Decourcelle, Nice [n.d.]
Score 5 p.

791s Méditation. Arranged by Germano
Solo Vc.-Str.
P. Decourcelle, Nice [n.d.]
Score 3 p.

1181s Mignonnette, waltz
Str.
Score: Ms. 11 p.
Parts: Decourcelle, Nice [n.d.]

1220s Plaisanterie [Frolic]
Str.
Score: Ms. 7 p.
Parts: Decourcelle, Nice [n.d.]

1469s Souvenir [G major]
Solo Vc.-Str.
P. Decourcelle, Nice [n.d.]
Score 3 p.

939s Villanelle. Arranged by Ziroldi
Solo Vc.-Str.
P. Decourcelle, Nice [n.d.]
Score 4 p.

OVANIN, NIKOLA LEONARD.
          b. Sisak, Yugoslavia 25 November 1911

6522 Dusk, Op. 78   *7'*
2,2(2nd alt. E.H.),3*,2-4Hn.-Hp.-Str.
Ms. c1952 by Nikola Leonard Ovanin
Score 26 p.
Composed 1948. First performance San Jose, California, 13 June 1950, San Jose State College Symphony Orchestra, the composer conducting.

6523 Elegy   *5-6'*
1,1,2,1-3Hn.-Str.
Ms. c1962 by Nikola Leonard Ovanin
Score 21 p.
Composed 1956. First performance Long Beach, California, 24 May 1961, Composers' Concert Symphony Orchestra of Long Beach State College, the composer conducting.

6524 Prélude moderne for orchestra,   *4'30"*
Op. 67-1
3*,3*,3*,3-4,3,3,1-Timp.,Perc.-Hp.-Str.
Ms. [C. Fischer, New York, c1947]
Score 23 p. Large folio
Original band version (1946) commissioned by Kenneth Bovee, president of the Michigan School Band and Orchestra Association. Transcribed for orchestra, 1947. First performance Spokane, Washington, 1948, Spokane Philharmonic Orchestra, Harold Whelan conductor.

6497 Suite for orchestra [Pleiades]   *32'*
7 movements
3*,3*,2,2-4,3,3-Timp.,Perc.-Cel.,Hp.-Str.
Ms. c1964 by Nikola Leonard Ovanin
Score 170 p. Large folio

Pache, Johannes.

Composed 1954. First performance of movements 1, 2, 3, 5 and 7 in a radio broadcast from Oklahoma City, 1965, Oklahoma City Symphony, Guy Fraser Harrison conductor. Subtitle "Pleiades" added, 1969. The seven stars correspond to the seven movements of the suite.

P

PACHE, JOHANNES.
                Bischofswerda, Saxony 9 December 1857
                Limbach, Germany 21 December 1897

1029s Es war ein Traum [It was a dream]
   Solo Vc.-Str.
   Hug [n.p.] ᶜ1892
   Score 5 p.

PACHELBEL, JOHANN.
                Nuremburg baptized 1 September 1653
                Nuremburg 3 March (buried 9 March) 1706

7283 [Chaconne, organ, E minor. Freely   *7'30"*
   transcribed for orchestra by Arthur Bosmans]
   2,2,2,2-2,1-Timp.-Str.
   Ms. ᶜ1976 by Arthur Bosmans
   Score 29 p.

1251s [Partita, G major. Arranged by Max
   Seiffert]
   1.Sonatina 2.Ballet 3.Sarabande 4.Aria
   5.Gigue 6.Finale
   Cemb.-Str.
   Kistner & Siegel, Leipzig [n.d.]
   Score 10 p.

2216s Praeludium, chorale and fugue [for organ].
   Transcribed by Eric De Lamarter
   Str.
   Ricordi, New York, ᶜ1939
   Score 8 p.
   Originally composed as three unrelated works.

PACHERNEGG, ALOIS.   Irdning im Ennstal,
                Styria, Austria 21 April 1892
                Vienna 13 October 1964

4619 Ländlerische Tänze [in 5 movements]   *9'*
   1,1,1-0,1,1-Perc.-Harm.-Str.
   B. Schott's Söhne, Mainz, ᶜ1939
   Score in reduction 8 p.

PACHULSKI, HEINRICH ALBERTOVICH.
                Lasa, Poland 16 October 1857
                                          ca.1917

1506 Marche solennelle, Op. 15   *15'*
   3*,2,2,2-4,2,3,1-Timp.,Perc.-Str.
   P. Jurgenson, Moscow [n.d.]
   Score 32 p.
   Composed 1898. First performance Moscow 1899.

933s [Moment musical, C minor, from Op. 22]
   Str.
   P. Jurgenson, Leipzig [n.d.]
   Score 7 p.

1832 Suite, Op. 13 [in 4 movements]   *40'*
   2,2,2,2-2Hn.-Timp.-Str.
   P. Jurgenson, Moscow [n.d.]
   Score 106 p.
   Composed and first performed Moscow 1897.

PACHULSKI, LADISLAUS.

4504 Andante
   2(2nd alt. Picc.),2,2,2-4,2,3-Timp.-Hp.-Str.
   Heinrich Wolff, Wiesbaden [189-?]
   Score 15 p.

PADEREWSKI, IGNACE JAN.
                Kuryłówka, Poland 18 November 1860
                New York 29 June 1941

540p [Concerto, piano, Op. 17, A minor]   *30'*
   1.Allegro 2.Romanza 3.Allegro molto vivace
   Solo Pno.-3*,2(1st alt. E.H.),2,2-4,2,3-Timp.-
   Str.
   Bote & Bock, Berlin [n.d.]
   Score 126 p.
   Composed 1888.

599p Fantaisie polonaise, Op. 19   *21'*
   Solo Pno.-3*,3*,2,2-4,2,3,1-Timp.,Perc.-Hp.-
   Str.
   Bote & Bock, Berlin, ᶜ1895 by G. Schirmer
   Score 95 p.
   Composed 1893.

PAER, FERDINANDO.   Parma 1 June 1771
                Paris 3 May 1839

4090 [La Camilla ossia Il Sotterraneo.
   Overture]
   2,2,2,2-2Hn.-Timp.,S.Dr.-Str.
   Ms.
   Score 41 p.
   From the opera composed 1799. First performance Vienna, 23 February 1799.

4091 [Poche, ma buone ossia Le donne cambiate.
   Overture]
   2,2,2,2-2Hn.-Str.
   Ms.
   Score 44 p.
   From the opera first performed Vienna, 18 December 1800. German version: Der Lustige Schuster.

4132 [Symphony no. 3, D major]
   1.Vivace 2.Andante sostenuto 3.Allegro con
   spirito
   1,2,0,2-2Hn.-Timp.-Str.
   Ms.
   Score 46 p.

PAGANINI, NICOLÒ.   Genoa 27 October 1782
                Nice 27 May 1840

2407s Caprice no. 24, Op. 1, A minor. Transcribed for string orchestra by David Saturen
   Str.
   Ms. ᶜ1975 by David Saturen
   Score 11 p.
   From the 24 Caprices for solo violin, composed 1801-07. This transcription 1974. First

performance Philadelphia, 11 November 1974,
The Mostovoy Soloists of Philadelphia, Marc
Mostovoy conductor.

412v [Concerto, violin, no. 1, Op. 6,   23'
  D major]
  1.Allegro maestoso 2.Adagio espressivo
  3.Rondo
  Solo Vn.-2,2,2,2*-2,2,3,1-Timp.,Perc.-Str.
  Score: Ms. Edited by Ferdinand David. 164 p.
  Parts: Kalmus, New York [n.d.]
  Composed ca.1818. First documented perform-
  ance Naples, 29 March 1819, the composer as
  soloist. First published 1851 as no. 1 of
  composer's posthumous works.

1117v [Same as above] Arranged by August   20'
  Wilhelmj
  In one movement
  Solo Vn.-2,2,2,2-4,2,1-Timp.-Str.
  N. Simrock, Berlin [188-?]
  Score 76 p.
  Transcribed 1883.

758s [Same as above] Arranged by August   20'
  Wilhelmj. Solo part transcribed for violon-
  cello by Mildred Wellerson
  Solo Vc.-2,2,2,2-4,2,1-Timp.-Str.
  Score: N. Simrock, Berlin [188-?] 76 p.
  Solo: N. Simrock, Berlin, c1924. 12 p.

1089v [Same as above] Movement no. 1.   14'
  Transcribed by Fritz Kreisler
  Solo Vn.-2,2,2,2-4,2-Timp.-Hp.-Str.
  C. Foley, New York, c1936
  Score 100 p.
  Transcription 1936. First performance, under
  title Koncertstück, Chicago, 29 October 1936,
  the Chicago Symphony Orchestra, Frederick
  Stock conductor, Fritz Kreisler soloist.

577v [Concerto, violin, no. 2, La clochette,
  Op. 7, B minor] Solo part edited by Massart
  1.Allegro maestoso 2.Adagio 3.Rondo
  Solo Vn.-1,2,2,1-2,2,3-Timp.,Perc.-Str.
  Kalmus, New York [n.d.]
  Score 170 p.
  Posthumous work no. 2.

889v Introduction, Thema und Variationen.   7'
  Arranged by August Wilhelmj
  Solo Vn.-2,2,2,2-2,2,2-Timp.-Str.
  B. Schott's Söhne, Mainz [1909?]
  Score 47 p.

480v [Moto perpetuo, violin, Op. 11,   4'
  C major]
  Solo Vn.-2Fl.-Str.
  H. Litolff, Braunschweig [1911?]
  Score in reduction 31 p.
  Also known as Allegro de Concerto, and Sonata
  Mouvement Perpétuel. Posthumous work no. 6.

277v [Same as above]   6'
  Solo Vn.-2(2nd alt. Picc.),2,2,2-2Hn.-Perc.-
  Str.
  Universal Edition, Vienna, c1942
  Score 22 p.

6174 [Same as above] Transcribed for   5'
  orchestra alone by Charles Maxwell
  1,1,1,1-1,1,1-Timp.-Str.
  Ms. [c1960 by Charles Maxwell]
  Score 40 p. Large folio
  Originally composed for solo violin and orches-
  tra. This transcription commissioned by the
  Posella Chamber Group, 1949. First performance
  of this transcription, Pepperdine College
  Auditorium, Los Angeles, 6 October 1949,
  Posella Chamber Symphony, Leonard Posella con-
  ductor.

4578 [Same as above] Transcribed for   5'
  orchestra alone by Victor Vaszy
  2,2,2,2-4,2,3,1-Timp.-Str.
  Rózsavölgyi, Budapest, c1937
  Score 22 p.
  In this transcription the solo part has been
  assigned to the first violins.

498v Non più mesta [introduction and variations]
  Op. 12. Solo part edited by Massart
  Solo Vn.-2,2,2,1-4,0,3-Timp.,B.Dr.-Str.
  Ms.
  Score 31 p.
  Posthumous work no. 7, based on a theme from
  Rossini's La Cenerentola.

753v [Octave study. Arranged from Caprices 23
  and 17, Op. 1, by Tivadar Nachèz]
  Solo Vn.-2,2,2,2-2Hn.-Timp.-Str.
  W. Hansen, Copenhagen [n.d.]
  Score 16 p.

1030v I palpiti [introduction and variations]
  Op. 13. Solo part edited by Massart
  Solo Vn.-2,2,2,1-2,2,B.Tbn.-Timp.,Turkish Band-
  Str.
  Ms.
  Score 51 p.
  Posthumous work no. 8, based on Di Tanti Pal-
  piti, from Rossini's Tancredi.

565v Le stregghe [Witches dance] Op. 8. Solo
  part edited by Massart
  Solo Vn.-2,2,2,1-2,2,3-Timp.,Perc.-Str.
  Lemoine [n.p., n.d.]
  Score 46 p.

PAHISSA, JAIME.   Barcelona 7 October 1880
                           Buenos Aires 27 October 1969

3824 El camí [The highway, symphonic poem]   16'
  3*(2nd alt. Picc.),3*,3*,3-4,3,3,2-Timp.-2Hp.-
  Str.
  [Unión Musical Española, Barcelona, c1929]
  Score 69 p.
  Composed 1908. First performance Barcelona,
  21 March 1909, Asociación Musical de Barce-
  lona, the composer conducting.

3787 Monodia, para orquesta   9'
  3*,2,2,3*-4,3,3,1-Timp.-Str.
  Ms.
  Score 11 p.
  Composed 1925. First performance Barcelona,
  12 October 1925, Orchestra Pau Casals, Pablo
  Casals conductor.

Pahissa, Jaime

3729 Suite intertonal para orquesta   20'
   1.Preludio 2.Andante agitato 3.Intermezzo
   4.Marcia funèbre
   2(alt. 2Picc.),1,2,1-2,2,2-Timp.,Perc.-Hp.-Str.
   Unión Musical Española, Barcelona [n.d.]
   Score 69 p.
   Composed 1926. First performance Barcelona,
   26 October 1926, Orchestra Pau Casals, Pablo
   Casals conductor.

1908s [Symphony no. 2 for string orchestra]
   1.Preludio intertonal 2.Andante 3.Final
   Str.
   Unión Musical Española, Barcelona, C1927
   Score 52 p.
   First performance Barcelona, 3 November 1921,
   Orchestra Pau Casals, Pablo Casals conductor.

PAINE, JOHN KNOWLES.
                     Portland, Maine 9 January 1839
                     Cambridge, Massachusetts 25 April 1906

5433 [Azara. Act II, Scene 1b: Orchestral scene
   and Act III, Scene 3: Ballet, three Moorish
   dances]
   3(3rd alt. Picc.),3*,3*,3*-8(4 onstage),3,3,1-
   Timp.,Perc.-Hp.-Str.
   [Breitkopf & Härtel, Leipzig, 1901?]
   Score 103 p.
   From the opera based on the legend of
   Aucassin and Nicolette. Composed ca.1900.
   Never staged. First concert performance of
   Moorish dances only, Boston, 9 March 1900,
   Boston Symphony Orchestra.

4517 [Overture to Shakespeare's As You Like It,
   Op. 28]
   3*,2,2,2-4,2,3-Timp.-Str.
   Breitkopf & Härtel, Leipzig, C1907 [C1936]
   Score 63 p.
   First performance 1876.

4546 [Poseidon and Amphitrite, Op. 44]
   3*,3*,2,2-4,2,3,1-Timp.-Hp.-Str.
   Breitkopf & Härtel, Leipzig, C1907
   Score 60 p.

5274 Prelude to Oedipus Tyrannus, Op. 35
   2,2,2,2-4,2,3-Timp.-Str.
   Kalmus, New York [n.d.]
   Score 32 p.
   From the incidental music to Sophocles' play.
   Composed 1881. First performance Harvard
   University, Cambridge, Massachusetts, 17 May
   1881, the composer conducting.

5541 [Symphony no. 1, Op. 23, C minor]
   1.Allegro con brio 2.Allegro vivace 3.Adagio
   4.Allegro vivace
   2,2,2,2-4,2,3-Timp.-Str.
   Breitkopf & Härtel, Leipzig, C1908 by Mary E.
   Paine
   Score 179 p.
   First performance Boston, January 1876, Theo-
   dore Thomas Orchestra, Theodore Thomas con-
   ductor.

5424 [Symphony no. 2, Spring, Op. 34, in A] 58'
   1.Introduction 2.Scherzo 3.Adagio 4.Allegro

giojoso
   2,2,2,2-4,2,3-Timp.-Str.
   A.P. Schmidt, Boston/Cranz, Hamburg, C1880
   Score 147 p.
   Composed 1880. First performance Cambridge,
   Massachusetts, 10 March 1880, Theodore Thomas
   conductor.

5061 [The tempest, Op. 31, D minor]   25'
   3*,2,2,2-4,2,3,1-Timp.-Hp.-Str.
   Breitkopf & Härtel, Leipzig, C1907 [C1936 by
   Mary E. Paine]
   Score 97 p.
   After Shakespeare. Composed 1876. First per-
   formance 1877, Theodore Thomas Orchestra,
   Theodore Thomas conductor.

PAINTER, PAUL.   Sumner, Missouri 1908

925m Petite pastorale, oboe and orchestra   6'
   Solo Ob.-2,1,2,2-4,2,3,1-Timp.,Bells-Str.
   Ms.
   Score 29 p.
   Composed 1934. First performance Winfield,
   Kansas, September 1935, Winfield High School
   Orchestra, the composer conducting, Mark Alt-
   vater soloist.

924m Sylvan colors, horn and orchestra   5'
   Solo Hn.-2,2,2,2-3,2,3,1-Timp.,Perc.-Str.
   Ms.
   Score 16 p.
   Composed 1934. First performance Winfield,
   Kansas, September 1935, the composer conducting,
   Tom Seymour soloist.

PAISIELLO, GIOVANNI.   Taranto, Italy 9 May 1740
                         Naples 5 June 1816

4321 [Le barbier de Seville. Overture]   6'
   2,2,0,2-2Hn.-Str.
   Le Duc, Paris [179-?]
   Score 10 p.
   Subtitle: La Precauzione Inutile. From the
   opera based on Beaumarchais' comedy of 1775.
   Composed 1782. First performance St. Peters-
   burg, 26 September 1782.

300p [Concerto, cembalo, C major] Edited   25'
   by Adriano Lualdi
   1.Allegro 2.Larghetto 3.Rondò: Allegro
   Solo Cemb.-2,0,0,1-2Hn.-Str.
   Carisch, Milan, C1948
   Score 59 p.
   Composed between 1776 and 1784.

6859 [Il duello comico. Overture] Edited by
   Antonio de Almeida
   2Fl.,2Ob.-2Tpt.-Str.
   Heugel, Paris, C1964
   Score 23 p.
   From the opera composed 1774.

3554 [La Frascatana. Overture]
0,2,0,1-2Hn.-Str.
Ms.
Score 17 p.
From the opera first performed Venice, November, 1774.

6424 [Funeral symphony for the death of   *10'*
Pope Pius VI, C minor] Reconstructed for
modern orchestra by Giuseppe Piccioli
In one movement
2,2,2,2-2,2-Timp.-Str.
Carisch, Milan, ^C1940
Score 18 p.
Composed 1799. First performance Naples, 7 September 1799.

6367 [Nina, or Mad for love. Sinfonia]   *6'30"*
Edited by Giuseppe Piccioli
0,2,2,2-2Hn.-Str.
Carisch, Milan, ^C1938
Score 18 p.
From the opera. First performance Caserta, near Naples, 25 June 1789.

4314 [Le philosophe imaginaire. Overture]
2Ob.-2Hn.-Str.
n.p. [178-?]
Score 9 p.
Original title: Gli Astrologi Immaginari. Also known as I Visionari. From the opera based on Jean François Marmontel's tale Le Connoisseur. First performance St. Petersburg, 14 February 1779. Not to be confused with the composer's opera Il Socrate Immaginario, composed 1775.

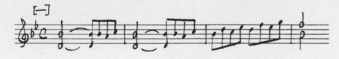

6398 La scuffiara (La modista raggiratrice).   *4'*
Sinfonia. Edited by Giuseppe Piccioli. Tr.:
The cheating milliner
2,2,0,2-2,2-Str.
Carisch, Milan, ^C1937
Score 16 p.
From the opera first performed Naples, 1787.

6418 [Symphony in 3 movements, D major]   *6'*
Edited by Giuseppe Piccioli
1.Allegro 2.Andantino 3.Allegro molto
2Ob.-2Hn.-Str.
Carisch, Milan, ^C1938
Score 29 p.
Edited from the autograph manuscript in the Library of the Royal Conservatory of Music, Naples.

PALADILHE, ÉMILE.   Montpellier, France 3 June 1844
Paris 8 January 1926

214s Mandolinata, souvenir de Rome. Arranged by
L. Grillet
Str.
Heugel, Paris [n.d.]
Score 8 p.

1343 Le passant [The wayfarer] Prelude   *3'*
2,2,2,2-2Hn.-Str.
Heugel, Paris [n.d.]
Score 19 p.
From the opera, composed 1870. First performance Paris, 1872.

5808 Patrie [Fatherland. Ballet music]
1.[Entrance of the ship] 2.[Parade of the nations] 3.Andante 4.Intermezzo 5.Valse
6.Ensemble
3*,2,2,2-4,2,2Cnt.,3,1-Timp.,Perc.-2Hp.-Str.
Choudens, Paris [1886]
Score 90 p.
From the opera adapted from Victorien Sardou's drama, Patrie! First performance Paris, 20 December 1886.

1332 [Suzanne. Overture]   *5'*
2(2nd alt. Picc.),2,2,2-4,2,3-Timp.,Perc.-Str.
Ch. Egrot, Paris [n.d.]
Score 41 p.
From the comic opera, composed 1878. First performance Paris, 1879.

PALANGE, LOUIS S.
b. Oakland, California 17 December 1917

237p [Concerto, piano, Romantic]   *30'*
1.Andante con moto - Allegro non troppo
2.Andante sostenuto 3.Allegro con brio
Solo Pno.-2,2,2,2-4,3,3,1-Timp.-Str.
Ms. ^C1950, 1976 by Louis S. Palange
Score 132 p.
Composed 1949. First performance Cleveland, 13 May 1954, The Cleveland Women's Symphony Orchestra, Hyman Schandler conductor, Robert Kitt pianist.

7243 Don Juan's coda, symphonic poem   *10'*
3*,3*,2,2-4,3,3,1-Timp.,Perc.-Hp.-Str.
Ms. ^C1972 by Louis S. Palange
Score 53 p.
After Byron's poem. Intended as an extension to Richard Strauss' Don Juan. Composed 1971. First performance Downey, California, 12 February 1972, Downey Symphony, the composer conducting.

Palaschko, Johannes

PALASCHKO, JOHANNES.   Berlin 13 July 1877
                             Berlin 21 October 1932

  913v Nordisches Volkslied, Op. 50 no. 2
    Solo Vn.-1,0,2,2-2Hn.-Hp.-Str.
    Score: Ms. 12 p.
    Parts: Zimmermann, Leipzig, C1912

  1064s Volkslied, Op. 10 no. 3
    Str.
    Score: Ms. 4 p.
    Parts: Bote & Bock, Berlin [n.d.]

PALESTER, ROMAN.   Sniatyn, Poland
                   (now Ukraine) 28 December 1907

  2252s Adagio for string orchestra   7'
    Str.
    Southern, New York, C1963
    Score 9 p.
    Composed 1960.

PALICOT, GEORGES.   France fl.1900

  733s Madrigal-pizzicati
    Str.
    Score: Ms. 8 p.
    Parts: [n.p., n.d.]

PALMER, ROBERT M.   Syracuse 2 June 1915

  1115v P⌣   for violin and small orchestra   4'
    Solo Vn.-1,2*,2,1-2Hn.-Str.
    Ms.
    Score 14 p.
    *Composed 1938. First performance Rochester,
    20 October 1938, Rochester Civic Orchestra,
    Howard Hanson conductor, John Celentano
    soloist.*

PALMGREN, SELIM.   Björneborg
               (now Pori), Finland 16 February 1878
                       Helsinki 13 December 1951

  307 Aus Finnland, Op. 24   20'
    1.[Dreams in springtime] 2.[Minuet in folk
    style] 3.[Dance of the falling leaves]
    4.[Sleigh-ride]
    3*,2,2,2-4,3,3,1-Timp.,Perc.-Hp.-Str.
    Schlesinger, Berlin [n.d.]
    Score 50 p.
    *Composed 1908-1909. First performance
    Helsingfors 1910, the composer conducting.*

  461p [Concerto, piano, no. 2, Der Fluss,   24'
    Op. 33, E major]
    In one movement
    Solo Pno.-2(2nd alt. Picc.),2(2nd alt. E.H.),2,
    2-4,2,3,1-Timp.,Perc.-Cel.-Str.
    Wilhelm Hansen, Copenhagen, C1913
    Score 102 p.

  497p [Concerto, piano, no. 3, Metamor-   18'
    phoses, Op. 41] Edited by Julia Burt
    In one movement
    Solo Pno.-2(2nd alt. Picc.),2(2nd alt. E.H.),2,
    2-4,2,3,1-Timp.,Perc.-Cel.-Str.

Wilhelm Hansen, Copenhagen, C1920
Score 87 p.

  828 A pastorale in 3 scenes, Op. 50.   16'
    Edited by Julia Burt
    1.[Morning] 2.[Elegy] 3.[Evening]
    2,2(2nd alt. E.H.),2,2-4,2-Timp.,Trgl.-Cel.,
    Hp.-Str.
    Wilhelm Hansen, Copenhagen, C1920
    Score 27 p.
    *Composed 1918. First performance Helsingfors,
    1919, the composer conducting.*

  1431s Refrain de berceau. Arranged by Cedric
  Sharpe
    Str.
    Score: Ms. 6 p.
    Parts: J. & W. Chester [n.p.] C1930

  418s Wiegenlied [Cradle song] Op. 17 no. 9
    Str.
    K.G. Fazer, Helsingfors, C1913
    Score 3 p.
    *Op. 17 originally composed for piano solo as
    24 Preludes.*

PALS, LEOPOLD VAN GILSE VAN DER.
                        St. Petersburg 5 July 1884
                 Dornach, Switzerland 7 February 1966

  894v [Concert piece, violin, Op. 10, B minor]
    In one movement
    Solo Vn.-2,2,2,2-4,2-Timp.-Str.
    Ernst Eulenburg [n.p.] C1912
    Score 39 p.

PALUMBO, COSTANTINO.   Torre Annunziata,
                   near Naples 30 November 1843
             Posillipo, near Naples 15 January 1928

  5212 Rama, poema sinfonico   13'
    3*,3*,2,2-4,4,3,Ophicl.-Timp.,Perc.-Hp.-Str.
    Società Musicale Napolitana, Naples [188-?]
    Score 51 p.
    Suggested by the Hindu epic, Ramayana.

PANNAIN, GUIDO.   Naples 17 November 1891

  4761 [Fountains beyond the seas]   5'
    3(3rd alt. Picc.),3*,3*,2-4,3,3,1-Timp.,Perc.-
    Pno.,Cel.,2Hp.-Str.
    Ricordi, Milan, C1942
    Score 73 p.
    Composed 1939.

PAPANDOPULO, BORIS.   Honnef-on-the-Rhine,
                       Germany 25 February 1906

  5227 Concerto da camera, Op. 11   20'
    1.Capriccio 2.Intermezzo 3.Fuga 4.Pas-
    torella 5.Finale
    2(2nd alt. Picc.),2(2nd alt. E.H.),2(2nd alt.
    B.Cl.),2-Pno.-Sop. Voice(without text)-Vn.
    Universal Edition, Vienna, C1941
    Score 68 p.
    Composed 1929.

PAPE, GUSTAVE.

576s Gavotte jouvence
  Str.
  Score: Ms. 6 p.
  Parts: André, Paris [n.d.]

PARFREY, RAYMOND.   Harrow, England 6 May 1928

7151 A leonine overture   3'30"
  2,2,2,1-2,1,1-Timp.,Perc.-Str.
  Ms. ᶜ1972 by Raymond Parfrey
  Score 16 p. Large folio

PARIBENI, GIULIO CESARE.   Rome 27 May 1881
                                  Milan 13 June 1960

1881s [Largo, from Quartet in F major]
  Str.
  A.& G. Carisch, Milan, ᶜ1934
  Score 8 p.
  First performance Philadelphia, 24 March 1935,
  Italo-American Philharmonic Orchestra, Gugli-
  elmo Sabatini conductor.

PARISH-ALVARS, ELIAS.
        Teignmouth, England 28 February 1808
                  Vienna 25 January 1849

710m [Concerto, harp, Op. 81,   20'
  G minor]
  1.Allegro moderato 2.Romanza 3.Rondo
  Solo Hp.-1,2,2,2-2,2,3-Timp.-Hp.-Str.
  Score: Ms. 150 p.
  Parts: Fr. Kistner, Leipzig [1892?]

659m [Concerto, harp, Op. 98, E-flat major]
  1.Allegro brillante 2.Andante 3.Rondo
  Solo Hp.-2,2,2,2-2,2,3-Timp.-Str.
  Score: Ms. 141 p.
  Parts: B. Schott's Söhne [n.d.]

658m Grand Marche. Arranged by Ludwig   6'
  Richter
  Solo Hp.-2,2,2,2-2,2,3-Timp.-Str.
  C. Giessel, Bayreuth, ᶜ1902
  Score 36 p.

PARKER, HORATIO WILLIAM.   Auburndale,
              near Boston 15 September 1863
          Cedarhurst, New York 18 December 1919

6569 The ballad of a knight and his daughter
  [for chorus and orchestra, Op. 6]
  2,2,2,2-2,2,3-Timp.-Chorus(SATB)-Str.
  Ms.
  Score 36 p.
  Text is the German poem by Count Friedrich
  Leopold Stolberg, translated into English by
  the composer's mother, Isabella Parker. Com-
  posed 1884. First performance Munich, 1884.

6476 Cáhal Mór of the wine-red hand, a   12'
  rhapsody, Op. 40
  Bar. Voice Solo-2(2nd alt. Picc.),2,2,2-4,2,3,
  1-Timp.,Perc.-Hp.-Str.
  Score and parts: Ms. 61 p.

Solo: H.W. Gray, New York, ᶜ1910. 23 p.
Text is James Clarence Mangan's poem. Com-
posed 1893. First performance Boston, 29
March 1895, Boston Symphony Orchestra, Max
Heinrich soloist.

6653 Concert overture, Op. 4 [E-flat major]
  2,2,2,2-2,2,3-Timp.-Str.
  Ms.
  Score 46 p.
  Composed 1884. First performance Munich, 7
  July 1884.

337m [Concerto, organ, Op. 55]   23'
  1.Allegro moderato - Andante 2.Allegretto
  3.Allegro moderato, molto risoluto
  Solo Org.-0,0,0,0-4,2,3,1-Timp.-Hp.-Str.
  Novello, London, ᶜ1903
  Score 67 p.
  Composed 1902. First performance Boston, 26
  December 1902, Boston Symphony Orchestra, Wil-
  helm Gericke conductor, the composer as
  soloist.

6813 [Fairyland, Op. 77. Prelude, inter-   30'
  mezzo and ballet from the opera]
  3(3rd alt. Picc.),2,2,2-4,3,3,1-Timp.,Perc.-
  Hp.-Str.
  Ms.
  Score 79 p.
  Composed 1915. First performance Los Angeles,
  1 July 1915. Awarded prize of the National
  Federation of Women's Clubs.

6373 A northern ballad, Op. 46   12'
  3(3rd alt. Picc.),2*,2,2-4,2,3,1-Timp.,Perc.-
  Hp.-Str.
  Ms.
  Score 59 p.
  Composed 1899. First performance Boston, 29
  December 1899, Boston Symphony Orchestra, Wil-
  helm Gericke conductor.

6332 [Overture to Count Robert of Paris]   10'
  2,2,2,2*-4,2,3,1-Timp.,B.Dr.,Cym.-Str.
  Ms.
  Score 48 p.
  Inspired by Walter Scott's novel. Composed
  1890. First performance New York, 10 December
  1890, Manuscript Society.

6688 Regulus, heroic overture, Op. 5
  2(2nd alt. Picc.),2,2,2-4,2,3-Timp.-Str.
  Ms.
  Score 43 p.
  Composed 1884.

2315s Scherzo in D minor
  Str.
  Ms.
  Score 15 p.

6789 Scherzo in G minor, Op. 13
  2,2,2,2-2Hn.-Timp.-Str.
  Ms.
  Score 32 p.
  Composed 1884. First performance Munich, 1884.

Parker, Horatio

6613 Symphony in C, Op. 7
1.Andante maestoso – Allegro molto 2.Andante
moderato 3.Allegro scherzo 4.Allegro molto
vivace
2,2,2,2-4,2,3-Timp.-Str.
Ms.
Score 140 p.
Composed 1884.

6579 [Twilight, aria, Op. 62]
Mezzo-Sop. Voice Solo-2,3*,2,2-4,2,3,1-Timp.-
Hp.-Str.
Score: Ms. 54 p.
Solo: G. Schirmer, New York, C1912. 19 p.
Text by J. de Beaufort, in French or English.
Composed 1907. Published erroneously as Op. 64.

6575 Vathek, symphonic poem, Op. 56   *15'*
3(3rd alt. Picc.),3*,3*,2-4,4,3,1-Timp.,Perc.-
Hp.-Str.
Ms.
Score 56 p.
After W. Beckford's novel. Composed 1903.
First performance in a recording session ca.
1967, The Royal Philharmonic Orchestra of Lon-
don, Karl Krueger conductor.

6788 Venetian overture, Op. 12
2,2,2,2-2Hn.-Timp.-Str.
Ms.
Score 29 p.
Composed 1884.

PARKER, PHYLLIS NORMAN.

1279s Ballet piquant
1.Minuet 2.Sleepy dance 3.[Dance piquant]
4.Dance of the fairies
Str.
Score: Ms. 20 p.
Parts: Hawkes & Son, London, C1918

PARODI, RENATO.   Naples 14 December 1900

4807 [Villanelle (Introduction and fugue)]   *7'*
In one movement: Andante – Allegro – Lento
4*(2 Picc.),3*,3*,3-4,4,3,3,1-Timp.,Perc.-Cel.,
Hp.-Str.
Ricordi, Milan, C1939
Score 38 p.
Composed 1936. First performance Naples, 4
June 1937.

PARRIS, HERMAN M.   Yekaterinoslav
     (now Dnepropetrovsk), Russia 30 October 1903

794p Concertino for piano and chamber   *14'*
orchestra
1.Moderato 2.Andante moderato e espressivo
3.Allegro vivace e giojante
Solo Pno.-1,1,1,1-1,1,1-Timp.-Str.
Ms.
Score 113 p. Large folio
Composed 1946. First performance Philadelphia,
March 1947, Symphony Club, Arthur Cohn con-
ductor, Claire Shapiro soloist.

335p Concerto no. 6, piano and orchestra   *26'*
1.Allegro comodo 2.Andante e grazioso

3.Allegro e molto energico
Solo Pno.-3*,2,2,2-4,2,3,1-Timp.,Perc.-Str.
Ms.
Score 143 p. Large folio
Composed 1949.

1191v [Concerto for violin]   *30'*
1.Allegro ma non troppo 2.Andante con moto
3.Allegro con brio
Solo Vn.-3*,2,2,2-4,2,3,1-Timp.,Perc.-Str.
Ms.
Score 158 p. Large folio
Composed 1946.

2134s Elegiac overture for strings   *7'*
Str.
Ms.
Score 17 p.
Composed 1948. First performance Philadelphia,
1949, String Orchestra of the Museum of the
University of Pennsylvania, Arthur Cohn con-
ductor.

350m Elegiac rhapsody   *14'*
Solo Tbn. or Solo Tuba-Str.
Ms.
Score 17 p. Large folio
Composed 1960.

5913 Four etchings, for orchestra   *14'*
1.Nocturne 2.Valse erotique 3.Lullaby
4.Gayety
2,2,2,2-2,2,1-Timp.,Perc.-Str.
Ms.
Score 43 p. Large folio

4925 Hospital suite [in 10 movements]   *22'*
2(2nd alt. Picc.),2(2nd alt. E.H.),2,2-4,3,3,1
-Timp.,Perc.-Hp.-Str.
Ms. C1948 by Herman M. Parris
Score 55 p. Large folio
Composed 1946. First performance New York, 13
May 1948, Doctors' Orchestral Society of New
York, I. Strassfogel conductor.

4924 In memoriam [Joshua Levitsky]   *10'*
2,3*,2,2-4,3,3,1-Timp.-Str.
Ms.
Score 12 p.

437c Invocation and lamentation   *18'*
In one movement
Solo Vc.-2,2,2,2-4,2,3,1-Timp.,Perc.-Str.
Ms.
Score 61 p. Large folio
Inspired by Jewish liturgical music. Composed
1946.

2135s Lament for string orchestra   *6'*
Str.
Ms.
Score 5 p. Large folio
Composed 1955. First performance Philadel-
phia, December 1955, String Orchestra of the
Museum of the University of Pennsylvania,
Arthur Cohn conductor.

385m Nocturne for bass clarinet and   *10'*
orchestra

Solo B.Cl.-2,2,2,2-4,3,3,1-Timp.-Str.
Ms.
Score 16 p.
Composed 1946.

417m Nocturne for clarinet and strings   *10'*
Solo Cl.-Str.
Ms.
Score 8 p.

2180s Nocturne for string orchestra   *8'*
Str.
Ms.
Score 10 p. Large folio
Composed 1958.

4920 Overture, America   *8'*
3*,3*,2,2-4,3,3,1-Timp.,Perc.-Str.
Ms.
Score 49 p. Large folio
Composed 1946.

5914 [Rhapsody no. 1, Hebrew rhapsody]   *16'*
4*,3*,3*,3*-4,3,3,1-Timp.,Perc.-Hp.-Str.
Ms.
Score 73 p. Large folio
Composed 1947.

5920 Rhapsody no. 2, Heart, for orchestra   *16'*
3*,3*,2,3*-4,3,3,1-Timp.,Perc.-Str.
Ms.
Score 71 p. Large folio
Composed 1947-48.

5771 Suite no. 1 for symphonic band in   *16'*
9 movements
3*,3*,6*(1Cl. in E-flat,1Alto Cl.),2-4Sax.-4,
2,3Cnt.,3,2Bar.,Tuba-Timp.,Perc.-Cb.
Ms.
Score in reduction 23 p.
*Composed 1947. First performance 1948,
Second United States Army Band.*

2145s Suite for strings [in 4 movements]   *22'*
Str.
Ms.
Score 42 p.
Composed 1948.

387m Suite for trumpet and strings [in   *17'*
6 movements]
Solo Tpt.-Str.
Ms.
Score 24 p.
Composed 1960.

5400 [Symphony no. 1, Akiba, in one   *25'*
movement]
3*,3*,3,2-4,3,3,1-Timp.,Perc.-Hp.-Str.
Ms.
Score 175 p. Large folio
Composed 1946.

5248 Symphony no. 2   *32'*
1.Poco sostenuto - Allegro 2.Andante
3.Scherzo 4.Allegro moderato
2,2,2,2-4,2,3,1-Timp.-Str.
Ms.

Score 138 p. Large folio
Composed 1947.

3998 Symphony no. 3 (1948)   *25'*
In one movement
3*,3*,3*,3*-4,3,3,1-Timp.,Perc.-Hp.-Str.
Ms.
Score 141 p. Large folio

5368 Symphony no. 4   *18'*
1.Largo e dolente 2.Allegro con fuoco
3*,3*,3*,3*-4,3,3,1-Timp.,Perc.-Pno.,Hp.-Str.
Ms.
Score 75 p. Large folio
Composed 1950.

5904 Three orchestral abstracts   *12'*
1.Crystal chandelier 2.Lavender forest
3.Spanish shawl
2,2(2nd alt. E.H.),2,2-4,3,3-Timp.,Perc.-Pno.,
Hp.-Str.
Ms.
Score 42 p. Large folio
Composed 1948.

PARRISH, CARL.
            Plymouth, Pennsylvania 9 October 1904
            Valhalla, New York 27 November 1965

6540 [Robin and Marion. Pageant music, a   *10'*
set of mediaeval dances]
1.Danse royale 2.Virelai 3.Ballade 4.Ron-
deau 5.Chanson 6.Estampie
3*,2,2,2-4,3,3,1-Timp.,Perc.-Cel.-Str.
Ms.
Score 32 p.
*From the incidental music to Adam de la Halle's
pastoral drama of 1285, Li Gieus (Le Jeu) de
Robin et de Marion. Based on songs by Adam
and other trouvères. Composed 1948. First
performance of this suite, Princeton, New
Jersey, 1948, Westminster Choir College, Sandor Salgo conductor.*

PARRY, CHARLES HUBERT HASTINGS.
            Bournemouth, England 27 February 1848
                        Knight's Croft,
            Rustington, England 7 October 1918

524s An English suite   *14'*
1.Prelude 2.In minuet style 3.Saraband
4.Caprice 5.Pastoral 6.Air 7.Frolic
Str.
Novello, London, ᶜ1921
Score 39 p.
First performance London, 10 May 1921.

525s Suite in F, Lady Radnor's suite   *12'*
1.Prelude 2.Allemande 3.Sarabande 4.Bourrée
5.Slow minuet 6.Gigue
Str.
Novello, London, ᶜ1902
Score 23 p.
*First performance 29 June 1894, by Lady Rad-
nor's String Band.*

2038 Symphonic variations   *12'*
2,2,2,2-4,2,3,1-Timp.-Str.

Parry, Charles

Novello, London [n.d.]
Score 76 p.
Composed 1896. First performance London, 3 June 1898, Philharmonic Society, the composer conducting.

2039 Symphony in C, The English   *38'*
1.Allegro energico 2.Andante sostenuto 3. Allegro molto scherzoso 4.Moderato
2,2,2,2-4,2,3(ad lib.)-Timp.-Str.
Novello, London, ^c1907
Score 146 p.
Composed 1888. First performance London, June 1889, Philharmonic Society, the composer conducting.

2189 Symphony in F, Cambridge   *40'*
1.Andante sostenuto - Allegro moderato 2. Scherzo 3.Andante 4.Allegro vivace
2,2,2,2-4,2,3-Timp.-Str.
Novello, London [n.d.]
Score 186 p.
Composed 1881. First performance Cambridge, 12 June 1883, Charles Villiers Stanford conductor.

PARTOS, OEDOEN   Budapest 1 October 1907

6252 Images for orchestra   *18'*
1.Tranquillo 2.Allegro molto - Più lento 3.Allegro molto vivace
3*,3*,3*,3(3rd alt. C.Bn.)-4,3,3,1-Timp.,Perc. -Pno.,Cel.,Hp.-Str.
Ms. ^c1961 by Israeli Music Publications, Tel Aviv
Score 90 p. Large folio
Commissioned by the Israel Philharmonic Orchestra. Composed 1960. First performance Tel Aviv, 20 December 1962, Israel Philharmonic Orchestra, Antal Dorati conductor. Awarded the First Prize of the Israel Philharmonic Orchestra, 1960.

416c Oriental ballad   *7'*
Solo Vc.(or Va.)-2(2nd alt. Picc.),2*,3*,2-4, 2,2,1-Timp.,Perc.-Cel.,Hp.-Str.
Ms. ^c1958 by Israeli Music Publications, Tel Aviv
Score 31 p.
Composed 1955. First performance of this version, Radio Tel Aviv broadcast, March 1958, Kol Yisrael Orchestra, Garry Bertini conductor, Usi Wiesel violoncello soloist.

295m Visions: Recitative, invocation and   *16'* dance
Solo Fl.-Pno.-Str.
Israeli Music Publications, Tel Aviv, ^c1957
Score 54 p.
Based on a Yemenite theme. Commissioned by Michael Taube and the Ramat Gan Chamber Orchestra. Composed 1957. First performance Beit HaEsrach, Ramat Gan, Israel, February 1957, Ramat Gan Chamber Orchestra, Michael Taube conductor, Hanoch Tel Oren soloist.

PARTRIDGE, BARRS.

1005s Thistledown, pizzicato

Str.
Score: Ms. 4 p.
Parts: W. Paxton, London, ^c1924

PARYS, GEORGES VAN.

641v Pensée musicale. Arranged by A. Chantrier
Solo Vn.-1,1,1,1-2Hn.-Str.
Score: Ms. 18 p.
Parts: Grus, Paris, ^c1924

PASHCHENKO, ANDREI FILIPPOVICH.
     Rostov-on-the-Don, Russia 15 August 1883
     Moscow 16 November 1972

3452 [Eagles in revolt. Cossack dance]
3*,2,2,2-4,3,3,1-Timp.,Perc.-Pno.-Str.
[Mussektor, Leningrad, 1934]
Score 31 p.
From the opera composed 1925. First performance Leningrad, 7 November 1925.

PASHLEY, NEWTON H.   Dividing Creek, New Jersey 1904

3013 Prelude
3*,3*,2,3*-4,3,3,1-Timp.,Perc.-Pno.-Str.
Ms.
Score 23 p.
Composed 1928. First performance Rochester, 8 June 1928, Rochester Philharmonic Orchestra, Howard Hanson conductor.

PASQUINI, ERCOLE.   Ferrara, Italy birthdate unknown
     Rome between 1608 and 1620

1371s [Canzona francese, cembalo. Transcribed for orchestra by Michele Esposito]
Fl.,Bn.(both ad lib.)-Str.
Oxford University Press, London, ^c1927
Score 4 p.

PATZKE, EDMUND.

876s Es war einmal [Once upon a time]
Str.
Bosworth, London, ^c1896
Score 3 p.

1580s Puie de fleurs [Shower of blossoms]
Str.
Score: Ms. 11 p.
Parts: Cranz, Vienna [n.d.]

PAUDERT, E.

853m Concertstück
Solo Tuba-2Cl.-2,2,1-Timp.-Str.
Score: Ms. 24 p.
Parts: A.E. Fischer, Bremen [n.d.]

819m [Renowned variations for clarinet, no. 1]
Solo Cl.-1,1,1-2,2,1-Timp.,Perc.-Str.
Score: Ms. 37 p.
Parts: Ehrler, Leipzig [n.d.]

794m [Variations for bassoon, no. 1]
Solo Bn.-1,0,2-2,2,1-Timp.-Str.
Score: Ms. 48 p.
Parts: Bellmann & Thümer, Dresden [n.d.]

PAUL, CARL.

879m Fantasiestück
Solo Bn.-1,2,2,2-4Hn.-Hp.-Str.
Score: Ms. 22 p.
Parts: M. Leichssening, Hamburg [n.d.]

PAULSON, GUSTAF.
Hälsingborg, Sweden 22 January 1898
Hälsingborg 17 December 1966

398m [Concerto, English horn, Op. 99]   *12-16'*
1.Moderato 2.Allegro molto 3.Andante
Solo E.H.-Timp.,Perc.-Str.
Ms.
Score 21 p.
*Composed 1958. First performance Hälsingborg,
Sweden, 23 March 1960, Nordvästa Skånes Orkes-
terförening, Carl Garaguly conductor, Curt
Jonasson soloist.*

773c [Concerto, violoncello, no. 1, Op. 39] *27'*
1.Più vivo 2.Adagio 3.Allegro vivace
Solo Vc.-2(2nd alt. Picc.),2(2nd alt. E.H.),
2(2nd alt. B.Cl.),2-2,2,2-Timp.,Perc.-Str.
Ms.
Score 119 p.
Composed 1944.

433c [Concerto, violoncello, no. 2, Op. 90] *23'*
1.Allegro moderato 2.Allegro molto 3.Adagio
Solo Vc.-2(both alt. Picc.),2(both alt. E.H.),
2,2-3,2,3-Timp.,Perc.-Pno.-Str.
Ms.
Score 59 p.
*Composed 1957. First performance Hälsingborg,
Sweden, 20 January 1958, Nordvästa Skånes
Orkesterförening, Håkan von Eichwald con-
ductor, Alexander Wittenberg soloist.*

PAUMGARTNER, BERNHARD.   Vienna 14 November 1887
Salzburg 26 July 1971

2362 [Suite in G minor]   *15'*
1.Gigue, attacca 2.Air 3.Menuett 4.Rigaudon
2(2nd alt. Picc.),2(2nd alt. E.H.),2,2-2,2-
Timp.,Perc.-Pno.,Cel.,Hp.-Str.
Ms. [Universal Edition, Vienna, n.d.]
Score 68 p.
*Gigue based on a theme by Lully; other move-
ments based on themes by Rameau. Composed
1924. First performance Salzburg, 1924, the
composer conducting.*

PAUR, EMIL.   Czernowitz, Bukovina
(now Ukrainian SSR) 29 August 1855
Mistek, Czechoslovakia 7 June 1932

6665 [Symphony, In nature, A major]
1.Allegro moderato 2.Poco adagio 3.Molto
vivace 4.Allegro moderato
3(3rd alt. Picc.),3*,3*,3*-4,3,3,1-Timp.,B.Dr.,
Trgl.-Org.-Str.
F.E.C. Leuckart, Leipzig, c1909
Score 128 p.
*Composed 1908. First performance Pittsburgh,
1 January 1909, Pittsburgh Symphony Orchestra,
the composer conducting.*

PAZ, EDGARDO SAMUEL DEL VALLE DE.
See: DEL VALLE DE PAZ, EDGARDO SAMUEL.

PAZ, JUAN CARLOS.   Buenos Aires 5 August 1901
Buenos Aires 26 August 1972

3887 Movimiento sinfónico, Op. 13
4(2Picc.),4*,4*,4*-6,4,3,1-Timp.-Str.
Ms.
Score 49 p. Large folio
Composed 1930. Reorchestrated 1933.

3961 Obertura para 12 instrumentos,   *5'30"*
Op. 19
1*,1,1,1-2,1,1-1Vn.,1Va.,1Vc.,1Cb.
Ms.
Score 49 p.
Composed 1931-36.

3691 Preludio para Juliano Emperador,   *12'*
Op. 12
3*,3*,2,2-4,2,3,1-Timp.-Str.
Ms.
Score 72 p.
*Prelude to Henrik Ibsen's play Emperor and
Galilean. Composed 1931. First performance
Buenos Aires, 2 July 1933, Asociación del
Profesorado Orquestal, José Maria Castro con-
ductor.*

PAZDIREK GOTTHARD, JOHANN PETER.
See: GOTTHARD, JOHANN PETER.

PEINIGER, OTTO.

619s Anne de Bretagne, menuet de la cour de
Louis XII
Str.
Kahnt, Leipzig [n.d.]
Score 6 p.

PEÑA, ANGEL.   Laoag,
Ilcos Norte, Philippines 22 April 1921

6812 Igorot rhapsody
3*,2,2,2-4,3,3,1-Timp.,Perc.-Str.
Ms.
Score 60 p. Large folio

2282s Prelude and fugue no. 2   *5'*
Str.
Ms. c1965 by Southern Music, New York
Score 10 p.
*Based on the Filipino song Bahay Kubo (My Nipa
Hut). Composed 1953. First performance St.
Joseph's College, Quezon City, Philippines, 2
February 1957, Manila Broadcasting Company
Theatre Orchestra, Maximino Isla conductor.*

Pente, Emilio

PENTE, EMILIO.   Padua 16 October 1860
                          Bad Sachsa, Germany 14 May 1929

770s Tendresse, Op. 11
Str.
Score: Ms. 9 p.
Parts: B. Schott's Söhne, Mainz [n.d.]

PEPPING, ERNST. Duisburg, Germany 12 September 1901

5469 [Invention for small orchestra]   4'
2,2,2,2-2,2-Str.
B. Schott's Söhne, Mainz, ᶜ1931
Score 14 p.

5470 [Variations on a theme by Ludwig   13'
Senfl (ca.1490-1543), Lust hab ich ghabt zur
Musika]
1,1,1,1-1,1-Str.
B. Schott's Söhne, Mainz, ᶜ1937
Score 33 p.

PERAGALLO, MARIO.   Rome 25 March 1910

740s Adagio
Hp.(or Pno.)-Str.
De Santis, Rome, ᶜ1927 by Dorica
Score 5 p.
Composed 1925.

4831 Concerto per orchestra   18'
1.Allegro 2.Andante sostenuto 3.Allegro
energico
3*,3*,3*,3*-4,3,3,1-Timp.,Perc.-Pno.,Hp.-Str.
Ricordi, Milan, ᶜ1939
Score 115 p.
*Composed 1939. First performance Rome, 25
March 1940.*

787s Lento
Str.
De Santis, Rome, ᶜ1927 by Dorica
Score 3 p.
Composed 1926.

PERGAMENT, MOSES.   Helsinki 21 September 1893

1198v [Dybbuk, fantasy for violin]   6'30"
Solo Vn.-2,2,2,2-4Hn.-Perc.-Cel.,Hp.-Str.
Ms.
Score 25 p.
*In Jewish folklore, a dybbuk is the spirit of
a dead person which possesses a living soul.
Composed 1935-36.*

6814 [Krelántems and Eldeling. Orchestral
suite from the ballet]
1.Tempo di marcia 2.Allegro festoso 3.Molto
adagio 4.Allegro giocoso
4(all alt. Picc.),4*,4*,4*-4,4,4,1-Timp.,Perc.
-Cel.,Hp.-Str.
Edition Suecia, Stockholm [n.d.]
Score 139 p.
First performance Stockholm, 16 March 1928.

6026 Rapsodia ebraica per grande orchestra 19'
In one movement
3*,2(2nd alt. E.H.),2,2-4,2,3,1-Timp.,Perc.-

Hp.-Str.
Bongiovanni, Bologna, ᶜ1948
Score 100 p.
Composed 1935.

PERGER, RICHARD VON.   Vienna 10 January 1854
                             Vienna 11 January 1911

688v [Concerto, violin, Op. 22, C minor]   25'
In one movement
Solo Vn.-2,2,2,2-3,2-Timp.-Str.
Ries & Erler, Berlin [n.d.]
Score 70 p.
*Composed 1892. First performance Rotterdam
1893, the composer conducting.*

633c [Serenade, violoncello and string   11'
orchestra, Op. 21, B-flat major]
1.Un poco allegro, ma tranquillo 2.Allegretto
moderato e grazioso 3.Vivace
Solo Vc.-Str.
Rieter-Biedermann, Leipzig [n.d.]
Score 29 p.
*Composed 1890. First performance Rotterdam
1891, the composer conducting.*

PERGOLESI, GIOVANNI BATTISTA.
                      Jesi, Italy 4 January 1710
            Pozzuoli, near Naples 16 March 1736

1914s [Concertino no. 2, strings and   11'30"
continuo, G major] Edited by F. Rikko
1.Largo 2.Da capella non presto 3.Andante
(Largo) 4.Allegro
Cemb.-Str.
Weaner-Levant, New York, ᶜ1945
Score 24 p.
*First published by Carlo Ricciotti as no. 4
of six Concerti Armonici, The Hague, 1740.
Walsh's edition (London, 1755), names Ricciotti
as the composer. Two extant 18th century manu-
scripts attribute the work to Pergolesi.*

121s [Concertino no. 4, strings, F minor.
Arranged for concert use by Sam Franko]
Largo - Allegro giusto - Andante - Allegro con
spirito
Str.
G. Schirmer, New York, ᶜ1916
Score 25 p.

2250s [Concertino no. 5, strings, E-flat   7'
major] Edited by Renato Fasano
1.Affettuoso 2.Presto 3.Largo 4.Vivace

Perkowski, Piotr

Str.
Ricordi, Milan, ^c1959
Score 26 p.

2375s [Concertino no. 6, strings and   *10'30"*
continuo, B-flat major. Parts revised by
Filippo Caffarelli]
1.Andante 2.Presto 3.Adagio affettuoso
4.Allegro moderato
Str.
Score: Gli Amici Musica da Camera, Rome, ^c1942.
13 p.
Parts: [no publisher] Rome, ^c1955 by Filippo
Caffarelli

303m [Concerto, flute, 2 violins and   *ca.13'*
continuo, G major] Edited by Johannes
Brinckmann
1.Spiritoso 2.Adagio 3.Allegro spiritoso
Solo Fl.-Cemb.-Str.(without Va. or Vc.)
Sikorski, Hamburg, ^c1955
Score 25 p.

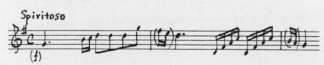

915m [Concerto, oboe. Excerpted and   *12'*
transcribed by John Barbirolli from various
works]
1.Largo [from Stabat Mater] 2.Allegro [from a
sonata for 2 violins and bass] 3.Andantino
[Se tu m'ami] 4.Allegro [from a sonata for
2 violins and bass]
Solo Ob.(or Solo Fl.)-Str.
Oxford, London, ^c1936
Score 9 p.
Arranged 1935. First performance Edinburgh,
16 December 1935, Scottish Orchestra, John
Barbirolli conductor, Evelyn Rothwell soloist.

372v [Concerto, violin and orchestra,   *18'*
B-flat major] Edited by Adriano Lualdi
1.Allegro 2.Largo 3.Allegro
Solo Vn.-2Ob.,Bn.-2Hn.-Str.
Carisch, Milan, ^c1948
Score 39 p.

1467s [Sinfonia, G major] Pergolesi Gesell-
schaft edition
Allegro - Andante - Presto
2Hn.-Cemb.-Str.
Wunderhorn, Cologne [n.d.]
Score 8 p.

PÉRILHOU, ALBERT.   Daumazan, Ariège, France 1846
               Tain, Drôme, France 1936

538m Ballade pour flûte
Solo Fl.-0,1,1,1-Hn.-Hp.-Str.
Heugel, Paris, ^c1914
Score 23 p.
Composed 1903 as Morceau de Concours for the
Paris Conservatory.

2292 Divertissement [for wind instruments]   *12'*
1.Conte [Tale] 2.Musette 3.La chasse
4.Bourrée
2,2,2-4Hn.
Heugel, Paris, ^c1906
Score 28 p.
Composed 1904. First performance Paris, 1905,
Concerts Colonne.

6276 [An evening in Bresse, ballad and dance]
1,1,1,1-2Hn.(2nd ad lib.)-Timp.-Str.
Heugel, Paris, ^c1910
Score 31 p.

522p [Fantasy, piano, no. 2, G major]
Solo Pno.-2,2,2,2-4,2,3,1-Timp.-Org.(optional)
-Str.
Heugel, Paris, ^c1895
Score 95 p.

801s Une fête patronale en Vélay. No. 2,
Bourrée et musette
Str.
Heugel, Paris, ^c1908
Score 7 p.

[Quartet, strings, D major]
478s Movement 1. Sérénade
479s Movement 3. Intermezzo
Str.(without Cb.)
Heugel, Paris, ^c1906, ^c1908
Scores: 7 p., 5 p.

PERKOWSKI, PIOTR. Oweczacz, Poland 17 November 1902

2949 Sinfonietta, Op. 17   *20'*
1.Allegro 2.Intermezzo 3.Vivo

Perle, George

2(alt. 2Picc.),2,2,2-4,2,2,1-Timp.,Perc.-Pno.
-Str.
Eschig, Paris, ^c1935
Score 51 p.
*First performance Lvov, Poland, 1932, Gregor
Fitelberg conductor.*

PERLE, GEORGE.   Bayonne, New Jersey 6 May 1915

332v Serenade, viola and solo instruments   *13'*
1.Rondo 2.Ostinato 3.Recitativo 4.Scherzo
5.Coda
Solo Va.-1,1,1,1-Alto Sax.-1,1,1-Perc.-Cb.
Ms.
Score 80 p.
*Commissioned by Walter Trampler. Composed
1962. First performance New York, 10 May
1962, Composers Showcase concert, Arthur Weisberg conductor, Walter Trampler soloist.*

6449 Three movements for orchestra   *16'*
1.Prelude 2.Contrasts 3.Ostinato
4*,3,3*,2-4,3,3,1-Timp.,Perc.-Pno.,Cel.,Hp.-
Str.
Merion Music, Bryn Mawr, Pennsylvania, ^c1963
Score 62 p. Large folio
*Composed 1960. First performance Amsterdam,
14 June 1963, Festival of the International
Society for Contemporary Music, Roelof Krol
conductor.*

PERONI, ALESSANDRO. Mondavio, Italy 13 October 1874
                     Milan 9 April 1964

562s Minuetto
Str.
Ricordi, Milan, ^c1911
Score 8 p.

PEROSI, LORENZO.   Tortona 20 December 1872
                          Rome 12 October 1956

6818 Tema variato per orchestra
2,2,2,2-4,3,3,1-Timp.-Str.
C.F. Kahnt, Leipzig, ^c1903
Score 41 p.
Composed 1903.

PERSICHETTI, VINCENT.   Philadelphia 6 June 1915

756p [Concertino, piano and orchestra,   *9'*
Op. 16]
Solo Pno.-2,2,2,2-2,2-Timp.-Str.
Ms.
Score 39 p. Large folio
*Composed 1940. First performance Rochester,
23 October 1945, Eastman-Rochester Symphony
Orchestra, Howard Hanson conductor.*

308p [Concerto, piano, Op. 90]   *27'*
1.Allegro non troppo 2.Andante sostenuto
3.Allegro vivace
Solo Pno.-3*,2,3*,2-4,3,3,1-Timp.,Perc.-Str.
Ms. ^c1963 by Elkan-Vogel, Philadelphia
Score 161 p. Large folio
*Commissioned by Anthony di Bonaventura. Com-
posed 1962. First performance Dartmouth College, Hanover, New Hampshire, 2 August 1964,*

*Dartmouth Symphony, Mario di Bonaventura con-
ductor, Anthony di Bonaventura soloist.*

5255 Dance overture [Op. 20]   *8'*
3*,3*,3*,3*-4,4,3,1-Timp.,Perc.-Pno.-Str.
American Music Center, New York, ^c1944 [for
Juilliard School of Music]
Score 36 p.
*Composed 1942. First performance Rochester,
1944, Eastman-Rochester Symphony Orchestra,
Howard Hanson conductor.*

4859 Divertimento for band, Op. 42   *10'*
1.Prologue 2.Song 3.Dance 4.Burlesque
5.Soliloquy 6.March
4*(2Picc.),2(2nd alt. E.H.),6*(1Cl. in E-flat,
Alto Cl.),2-4Sax.-4Hn. in F,4Hn. in E-flat,2,
3Cnt.,3,Bar.,Euph.,Tuba-Timp.,Perc.
Oliver Ditson/Presser, Bryn Mawr, Pa., ^c1951
Score 47 p.
*Composed 1950. First performance New York, 16
June 1950, Goldman Band, the composer conducting.*

5195 Fables for narrator and orchestra   *22'*
(1943) [Op. 23]
1.The fox and the grapes 2.The wolf and the
ass 3.The hare and the tortoise 4.The cat
and the fox 5.A raven and a swan 6.The mon-
key and the camel
Narrator-3*,3*,3*,2-4,3,3,1-Timp.,B.Dr.-Pno.-
Str.
Ms.
Score 108 p. Large folio
*Texts are six of Aesop's fables. Composed 1943.
First performance Philadelphia, 20 April 1945,
Philadelphia Orchestra, Eugene Ormandy con-
ductor, Robert Grooters narrator.*

6473 Fairy tale for orchestra [Op. 48]   *3'30"*
3*,3*,2,2-4,2,3,1-Timp.,B.Dr.-Str.
Ms.
Score 20 p. Large folio
*Composed 1950. First performance Philadelphia,
31 March 1951, Philadelphia Orchestra, Alexander Hilsberg conductor.*

1066m The hollow men [Op. 25]   *7'*
Solo Tpt.-Str.
Elkan-Vogel, Philadelphia, ^c1948
Score 14 p.
*After T. S. Eliot's poem. Composed 1944.
First performance Germantown, Pennsylvania, 12
December 1946, Germantown Symphony Orchestra,
Arthur Lipkin conductor.*

6108 Serenade no. 1, Op. 1 (1929)   *11'*
1.Prelude 2.Episode 3.Song 4.Interlude
5.Dance
1,1,1,1-2,2,1,1
Ms.
Score 42 p.
*Composed 1929. First performance San Angelo
College, San Angelo, Texas, 21 April 1952, New
York Wind Ensemble.*

5192 Serenade no. 5 for orchestra [Op. 43]   *9'*
1.Prelude 2.Poem 3.Interlude 4.Capriccio

5.Dialogue 6.Burla
2,2,2,2-4,2,3,1-Timp.-Str.
Ms.
Score 77 p. Large folio
*Commissioned by the Louisville Philharmonic
Society. Composed 1950. First performance
Louisville, Kentucky, 15 November 1950, The
Louisville Orchestra, Robert Whitney con-
ductor.*

5197 [Symphony no. 3, Op. 30]   30'
1.Somber 2.Spirited 3.Singing 4.Fast and
brilliant
3*,3*,3*,3*-4,3,3,1-Timp.,Perc.-Pno.-Str.
Ms.
Score 212 p. Large folio
*Composed 1946. First performance Philadel-
phia, 21 November 1947, Philadelphia Orchestra, Eugene Ormandy conductor.*

5179 [Symphony no. 4, Op. 51]   22'30"
1.Adagio - Allegro 2.Andante 3.Allegretto
4.Presto
3*,3*,3*,2-4,2,3,1-Timp.-Str.
Ms.
Score 155 p. Large folio
*Composed 1951. First performance Philadel-
phia, 17 December 1954, Philadelphia Orchestra, Eugene Ormandy conductor.*

2075s [Symphony no. 5, Op. 61]   18'
Str.
Ms.
Score 35 p. Large folio
*Commissioned by the Louisville Philharmonic
Society. Composed 1953. First performance
Louisville, Kentucky, 28 August 1954, The
Louisville Orchestra, Robert Whitney con-
ductor.*

5870 [Symphony no. 7, Liturgical, Op. 80] 23'
1.Lento 2.Allegro 3.Andante 4.Vivace
5.Adagio
4*(2Picc.),3*,4*(1Cl. in E-flat),3*-4,3,3,1-
Timp.,Perc.-Str.
Ms. c1959 by Elkan-Vogel, Philadelphia
Score 139 p. Large folio
*Commissioned by the St. Louis Symphony Society
on its 80th anniversary. Composed 1959.
First performance St. Louis, 24 October 1959,
St. Louis Symphony Orchestra, Edouard van
Remoortel conductor.*

PESCARA, AURELIO PATERAS.   f1.1945

4590 Commedia dell'arte, capriccio sinfonico
1.Preludio 2.Notturno 3.Burlesca e finale
3*,3*,3*,3*-4,3,3,1-Timp.(alt. Xyl.),Perc.-
Pno.-Str.
Ms.
Score 42 p. Large folio

PESSARD, ÉMILE-LOUIS-FORTUNÉ.   Paris 29 May 1843
                                  Paris 10 February 1917

385s [Le capitaine Fracasse. Menuet des petits
violins]
Str.(Vc. ad lib., no Cb.)

Leduc, Paris [n.d.]
Score 7 p.
From the comic opera.

699m Dans la forêt, solo de concours, Op. 130
Solo Hn.-2,2,2,2-0,2,3-Timp.-Str.
Score: Ms. 20 p.
Parts: Evette & Schaeffer, Paris [n.d.]

4691 [Piece for orchestra in A minor, Op. 18]
2,2,0,2-Hn.-Str.
Alphonse Leduc, Paris [186-?]
Score 8 p.
Originally composed for piano as Boutade.

PETERKA, RUDOLF.   Brünn, Moravia
          (now Brno, Czechoslovakia) 17 April 1894
                        Berlin 18 September 1933

1142 [Triumph of life, a rhapsodic prelude,
Op. 8]
3(3rd alt. Picc.),2,2,2-4,3,3,1-Timp.,Perc.-
Hp.-Str.
Simrock, Berlin, c1922
Score 37 p.

PETERS, GUIDO.   Graz, Austria 29 November 1866
                        Vienna 11 January 1937

1703 [Symphony no. 3, F-sharp minor]   45'
1.Sehr ruhig 2.Wild, möglichst rasch
3.Adagio 4.Ruhig bewegt
3(3rd alt. Picc.),3(3rd alt. E.H.),3(3rd alt.
B.Cl.),3(3rd alt. C.Bn.)-4,3,3,1-Timp.,Perc.-
Str.
Universal Edition, Vienna, c1920
Score 121 p.
*Composed 1914-18. First performance Vienna,
1919.*

PETERS, MADELEINE DEDIEU.
See: DEDIEU-PETERS, MADELEINE.

PETERS, MAX.   Arendsee, Germany 16 October 1849
          Charlottenburg, near Berlin 14 February 1927

1259s Passionsmusik, Op. 79
Timp.(optional)-Org.-Str.
H. Oppenheimer, Hamelin [n.d.]
Score 9 p.
*Based on the chorale Ein Lämmlein Geht und
Trägt die Schuld.*

PETERS, PAUL.

236s Andante, Op. 9
Solo Vn.-Str.
[Schlesinger, Berlin, n.d.]
Score 7 p.

PETERS, WILLIAM CUMMING.   England 1805
                              (?) Pittsburgh 1866

6199 Symphony in D. Edited by Frederick   10'
T. Wessel
1.Andante 2.Rondo
1,0,1,1-2,1-Str.(without Va.)
Ms.

Peterson-Berger, Olof Wilhelm

Score 38 p.
*Composed 1831. Probable first performance
Economy, Pennsylvania, Harmony Society Orchestra, Johann Christoph Mueller probable conductor. Economy, founded by the Harmony Society as a commune, was near the modern town of
Ambridge.*

PETERSON-BERGER, OLOF WILHELM.   Ullånger,
                    Ångermanland, Sweden 27 February 1867
                          Östersund, Sweden 3 December 1942

5978 [Symphony no. 3, Lapland]   *45'*
1.Allegro moderato 2.Moderato 3.Tranquillo
4.Moderato
3(3rd alt. Picc.),3*,3*,2-4,3,3,1-Timp.,Perc.-
Pno.,Hp.-Str.
Elkan & Schildknecht, Emil Carelius, Stockholm, ^C1922
Score 191 p.
*Incorporates Lapp melodies. Composed 1913-15.
First performance Stockholm, 11 December 1917.*

PETIT, ALEXANDRE S.

772m Gracieux babil [Pleasant chatter]
Solo Ob.-1,0,2,1-2Hn.-Str.
Score: Ms. 16 p.
Parts: E. Gaudet, Paris, ^C1915

773m Historiette
Solo Ob.-1,0,2,2-Str.
Score: Ms. 27 p.
Parts: E. Gaudet, Paris [n.d.]

PETRASSI, GOFFREDO.
                b. Zagarolo, near Rome 16 July 1904

1154v Introduzione e allegro, per violono   *7'*
concertante e 11 strumenti
Solo Vn.-1,1,1,1-2,1-Pno.-2Vc.,1Cb.
Ricordi, Milan, ^C1934
Miniature score 24 p.
*First performance Rome, February 1934, Mario
Rossi conductor.*

3917 Ouverture da concerto   *9'*
2*,2*,2*,2*-Ten.Sax.-2,2,1-Pno.-Str.
Ricordi, Milan, ^C1934
Miniature score 64 p.
*Composed 1931. First performance Rome, June
1931.*

PETRUSHKA, SHABTAI.   Leipzig 15 March 1903

5778 Hebrew suite. Four Israel songs   *9'*
arranged [for band] by Shabtai Petrushka
1.Prelude (based on the song, Open Ye Doors of
Righteousness by N.C. Melamed) 2.Fanfare and
march (based on a hora by Moshe Rapaport)
3.Air (Traditional) 4.Dance (based on The
Sheep Shearers' Song by Y. Admon)
A: 2*,0,4-4,2,2Cnt.,2Tbn.,2Ten.Hn.,Bar.,Tuba-
Perc.
B: 2*,2,6*(1Cl. in E-flat),2-4Sax.-4,2,2Cnt.,
3Tbn.,2Ten.Hn.,2Bar.,Tuba-Perc.
Ms. ^Cby Shabtai Petrushka [n.d.]
Score in reduction 5 p.

*Commissioned by the Jewish Soldiers' Welfare
Committee, Tel Aviv. Composed 1943. First
performance Tel Aviv, 1944, Band of the
Palestine Regiment, British Army, Middle East,
George Perry conductor.*

PETTERSSON, ALLAN.   Stockholm 19 September 1911

2167s [Concerto no. 1 for string orchestra] *21'*
1.Allegro 2.Andante 3.Largamente - Allegro -
Largo
Str.
Ms.
Score 44 p.
*Composed 1949-50. First performance Stockholm, 6 April 1952, Swedish Radio Symphony
Orchestra, Tor Mann conductor.*

6803 [Symphony no. 2, in one movement]   *42'*
2(both alt. Picc.),2,2(2nd alt. B.Cl.),2-2,2,
2-Timp.,Perc.-Cel.-Str.
Edition Suecia, Stockholm [n.d.]
Score 139 p.
Composed 1952-53.

6030 [Symphony no. 3 (1954-1955)]   *33'30"*
1.Andante con moto - Allegro con moto 2.Largo
con espressione 3.Allegro comodo 4.Allegro
con moto
3*,3*,3*,3*-4,3,3,1-Timp.,Perc.-Str.
Ms.
Score 159 p.
*Composed 1954-55. First performance Göteborg,
Sweden, 21 November 1956, Göteborg Symphony
Orchestra, Tor Mann conductor.*

6806 [Symphony no. 4, in one movement]   *35'*
3*,3*,3*,3*-4,3,3,1-Timp.,Perc.-Cel.-Str.
Edition Suecia, Stockholm [n.d.]
Score 151 p.
Composed 1958-59.

6776 [Symphony no. 5, in one movement]   *42'*
2(2nd alt. Picc.),2,2(2nd alt. B.Cl.),3*-4,3,
3,1-Timp.,Perc.-Str.
Edition Suecia, Stockholm [n.d.]
Score 147 p.
Composed 1960-62 for radio orchestras.

PETYREK, FELIX.   Brünn, Moravia
          (now Brno, Czechoslovakia) 14 May 1892
                          Vienna 1 December 1951

2239 Arabische Suite [in 6 movements]   *20'*
2(2nd alt. Picc.),1,2,2-2,0,1-Timp.,Perc.-Hp.-
Cb.
Ms. [Universal Edition, Vienna, n.d.]
Score 29 p.
*Composed 1924. First performance Lvov, Poland,
1928.*

2112 [Divertimento, winds, B-flat major]   *20'*
1.Grave, molto maestoso 2.Presto 3.Adagietto
arioso 4.Allegro molto, con brio
2(2nd alt. Picc.),1,1,2-2Hn.
Ms. [Universal Edition, Vienna, n.d.]
Score 54 p.
Composed 1923. First performance Berlin, 1925.

PEUERL, PAUL.   (?) Austria ca.1570
                                      ca.1624-25

Also known as: Peurl, Bäwerl, Bäurl, Beurlin

1668s [Newe Padouan, Intrada, Däntz und
   Galliarda. 5 suites for string orchestra.
   With Two canzones, for string orchestra]
   Edited by Karl Geiringer
   Str.
   Kallmeyer, Wolfenbüttel, ^C1931
   Score 29 p.
   First published 1611 and 1613.

PEZEL, JOHANN CHRISTOPH.
          (?) Calau, near Brandenburg 5 December 1639
               Bautzen, Germany 13 October 1694

Also known as: Bässel, Betzel(d)(ius),
Petzold(t), Pezelius, Pezelt, etc.

458s [Delitiae musicales oder Lust-Musik.
   Suite, arranged by Arnold Schering]
   1.Sonata 2.Bransle 3.Amener 4.Courante
   5.Bal 6.Sarabande 7.Gigue 8.Conclusio
   Pno.-Str.
   Kahnt, Leipzig, ^C1913
   Score 15 p.
   First published at Frankfurt a.M., 1678.

4623 [Fünffstimmigte blasende Musik. Vol. I,
   nos. 1-25] Edited by Alan Lumsden
   2Tpt.,3Tbn.(Hn. may substitute for Tbn.I)
   Musica Rara, London, ^C1960
   Score 28 p.
   First published Frankfurt, 1685.

PFITZNER, HANS ERICH.   Moscow 5 May 1869
                                 Salzburg 22 May 1949

1876 [The Christmas elf, Op. 20. Overture]   *10'*
   2(2nd alt. Picc.),2,2,2-2Hn.-Timp.,Perc.-Hp.-
   Str.
   Ries & Erler, Berlin, ^C1906
   Score 63 p.
   From the opera composed 1906. First perform-
   ance Munich, 11 December 1906.

1704 [Käthchen von Heilbronn, Op. 17.   *12'*
   Overture]
   3*,2,2,2-4,3,3,1-Timp.,Perc.-Hp.-Str.
   Ries & Erler, Berlin, ^C1905
   Score 52 p.
   From the incidental music to Heinrich von
   Kleist's play. Composed 1905. First per-
   formance Berlin, 19 October 1905.

990 [Palestrina. 3 preludes]   *25'*
   4(3rd & 4th alt. Picc.),3*,4*(3rd alt. Cl. in
   E-flat),4*-6,4,4,1-Timp.,Perc.-Hp.-Str.
   Fürstner, Berlin, ^C1916
   Separate scores: 11 p., 35 p., 11 p.
   From the musical legend composed 1912-15.
   First performance Munich, 12 June 1917.

1298 Scherzo   *12'*
   3*,2,2,2-2,2-Timp.-Str.
   Brockhaus, Leipzig [n.d.]

Score 19 p.
Composed 1888. First performance Berlin, 4
May 1893, Berlin Philharmonic Orchestra, the
composer conducting.

PHILE, PHILIP.   Germany ca.1734
                                 Philadelphia 1793

7119 [President's march. Transcribed for   *2'*
   orchestra by Romulus Franceschini]
   2,2,2,2-2,2,2-Timp.,Perc.-Str.
   Ms. ^C1975 by Romulus Franceschini
   Score 6 p. Long folio
   First published ca.1793. In 1798 Joseph Hop-
   kinson wrote the poem, Hail Columbia, for this
   march. This arrangement, 1975, extracted from
   Benjamin Carr's Federal Overture (1794).

PHILIDOR, FRANÇOIS ANDRÉ DANICAN.
            Dreux, France 7 September 1726
                 London 24 August 1795

4662 Les femmes vengées [Wives avenged, or   *6'*
   sham infidelities. Overture] Arranged and
   edited by Adam Carse
   2,2(or 2Fl. or 2Cl.),0,2-Timp.-Str.
   Augener, London, ^C1947
   Score 16 p.
   From the opera, originally titled Le Rémois.
   First performance Paris, 20 March 1775.

PHILLIPS, BURRILL.   Omaha 9 November 1907

950m Concert piece, American dance   *4'*
   Solo Bn.-Str.
   Ms.
   Score 16 p.
   Composed 1940. First performance Rochester,
   25 April 1940, Rochester Philharmonic Orches-
   tra, Howard Hanson conductor, Vincent Pezzi
   soloist.

1099m Concerto grosso for string quar-   *12-15'*
   tet and small orchestra
   1.Allegro con brio 2.Grave 3.Vivace
   Concertino: Vn.I,Vn.II,Va.,Vc.
   Ripieno: 1,1,1,1-Hn.-Str.
   Ms.
   Score 68 p. Large folio
   Composed 1950. First complete performance
   Ithaca, New York, 1951; Walden String Quartet
   and Cornell University Orchestra, Robert Hull
   conductor.

5136 Courthouse square, for orchestra   *14'*
   1.R.F.D. 2.Prairie idyll 3.Town, Saturday
   night
   3(3rd alt. Picc.),3*,3*,3*-4,3,3,1-Timp.,Perc.
   -Hp.-Str.
   Ms.
   Score 57 p. Large folio
   Composed 1936. First performance Rochester,
   April 1936, Eastman-Rochester Symphony Orches-
   tra, Howard Hanson conductor.

3533 Dance   *4'30"*
   3*,2,2,2-4,2,3,1-Timp.,Perc.-Hp.-Str.
   Ms.

Phillips, Burrill

Score 27 p.
*Composed 1940. First performance Rochester,
26 April 1940, Rochester Civic Orchestra,
Howard Hanson conductor.*

2060s Divertimento for strings   *12-15'*
1.Allegro moderato e giocevole 2.Lento
3.Allegro burlando
Str.
Ms.
Score 27 p. Large folio
*Composed 1950. First performance Rochester,
1951, Eastman-Rochester Symphony Orchestra,
Howard Hanson conductor.*

1804s Music for strings   *12'*
1.Reconnaissance 2.Concertino 3.American
Mercury, 1928
Str.
Ms.
Score 37 p.
*Composed 1938. First performance Rochester,
24 October 1939, Rochester Civic Orchestra,
Howard Hanson conductor.*

6850 La piñata
2Fl.(2nd alt. Picc.)-2Tpt.-Perc.-Hpscd.-Sop.
Voice-Vn.I,Vn.II,Cb.
Ms.
Score 115 p.
*Based on Mexican children's game-songs col-
lected by José Limón. Commissioned by The
Juilliard School. Composed 1968-69.*

3304 Play ball, a ballet in one act   *17'*
3*,2,2,2-4,3,3,1-Timp.,Perc.-Str.
Ms.
Score 140 p.
*Composed 1938. First performance Rochester,
29 April 1938, Rochester Civic Orchestra,
Howard Hanson conductor.*

4004 Selections from McGuffey's Reader,   *16'30"*
suite
1.The one-horse shay 2.John Alden and Priscilla 3.Midnight ride of Paul Revere
3*,2,2,2-4,3,3,1-Timp.,Perc.-Cel.,Hp.-Str.
Eastman, Rochester, C1937
Score 85 p.
*Composed 1933-34. First performance Rochester,
3 May 1934, Rochester Philharmonic Orchestra,
Howard Hanson conductor.*

3003 Symphony concertante   *13'*
1.Allegro 2.Adagio 3.Allegro scherzando
1,1,2(2nd alt. B.Cl.),1-2,1,1-Timp.,Perc.-
Pno.-Str.
Ms.
Score 94 p.
*Composed 1935. First performance Rochester,
3 April 1935, Eastman School Little Symphony
Orchestra, Karl Van Hoesen conductor.*

6751 Theater dances   *12-14'*
2,2,2,2-4,3,3,1-Timp.,Perc.-Str.
Ms.
Score 64 p. Large folio
Composed 1966-67. First performance Ithaca,

*New York, 21 April 1967, Ithaca High School
Orchestra, John Whitney conductor.*

3532 Three satiric fragments   *5'30"*
Greeting - Dance - Farewell
2,2,2,2-2,1,1-Timp.,Perc.-Str.
Ms.
Score 40 p.
*Composed 1941. First performance Rochester,
2 May 1941, Rochester Civic Orchestra, Howard
Hanson conductor.*

1097m Triple concerto, clarinet, viola,   *25'*
piano and orchestra
1.Lento - Allegro 2.Lento 3.Allegro vivo
Solo Cl., Solo Pno., Solo Va.-1(alt. Picc.),
1,1,1-2,1,1-Timp.,Perc.-Str.
Ms.
Score 100 p. Large folio
*Composed 1953. First performance Quincy,
Illinois, 1953, Quincy Society of Fine Arts
(which commissioned the work), George Irwin
conductor.*

PIAGGIO, CELESTINO.
          Concordia, Argentina 20 December 1886
          Buenos Aires 28 October 1931

3342 Obertura en Do menor [C minor]   *12'*
2,2,2,2-4,2,3,1-Timp.,Perc.-2Hp.-Str.
Comisión Nacional de Cultura, República
Argentina, Buenos Aires, C1939
Score 78 p.
*Composed 1914. First performance Buenos Aires,
9 September 1919, Sociedad Argentina de Conciertos Sinfónicos, Franco Paolantonio conductor.*

PIASTRO, JOSEF. Kerch, Crimea, Russia 1 March 1889
          Monrovia, California 14 May 1964

3005 Crimean rhapsody, Bachchissaray   *15'*
3*,2(2nd alt. E.H.),2,3*-4,2,4,1-Timp.,Perc.-
Hp.-Str.
Ms.
Score 67 p.
*Named for a Crimean village. Originally com-
posed for violin, 1920. Transcribed 1938.
First performance Standard Oil Hour radio
broadcast, San Francisco, 5 October 1938, San
Francisco Symphony Orchestra, Mishel Piastro
conductor.*

PIATIGORSKY, GREGOR.   Yekaterinoslav
(now Dnepropetrovsk), Russia 17 April 1903
          Brentwood, California 6 August 1976

757c Variations on a Paganini theme,   *10'*
violoncello and piano. Accompaniment tran-
scribed for orchestra by Arthur Cohn
Solo Vc.-2,2,2,2-4,3,3,1-Timp.,Perc.-Str.
Ms. [C1946 by Elkan-Vogel, Philadelphia]
Score 65 p. Large folio
This transcription 1946.

PIATTI, ALFREDO CARLO.
          Bergamo, Italy 8 January 1822
          Bergamo 19 July 1901

COLLECTION OF ORCHESTRAL MUSIC

653c Airs baskyrs, scherzo, Op. 8
Solo Vc.-Str.
Score: Ms. 20 p.
Parts: Ricordi, Milan [n.d.]
Composed ca.1845.

695c [Concertino, violoncello, Op. 18, C major]
1.Allegro appassionato 2.Adagio 3.Allegro
vivo agitato
Solo Vc.-1,2,2,2-2,2-Timp.-Str.
Score: Ms. 130 p.
Parts: Joh. André, Offenbach a.M. [n.d.]

631c [Concerto, violoncello, no. 2, Op. 26,
D minor]
1.Maestoso 2.Andante lento 3.Allegro vivo
Solo Vc.-2,2,2,2-2,2,1-Timp.,Perc.-Str.
Score: Ms. 147 p.
Parts: Hofmeister, Leipzig [n.d.]
First performance Leipzig, 1877.

636c Fantasia romantica
Solo Vc.-1,2,2,2-2,2,1-Timp.-Str.
Score: Ms. 111 p.
Parts: Schlesinger, Berlin [n.d.]
First performance Berlin, 1885.

PICCINNI, NICCOLÒ (*or* NICCOLA).
Bari, Italy 16 January 1728
Passy, near Paris 7 May 1800

5732 [Dido. Overture] Revised by Giuseppe   *10'*
Piccioli
2,2,2,2-2,2-Str.
Carisch, Milan, ^c1948
Score 30 p.
From the opera. First performance Fontaine-
bleau, 16 October 1783. First public perform-
ance, Paris, 1 December 1783.

5730 La molinarella [The little miller   *5'*
girl] Sinfonia. Revised by Nino Negrotti
2Ob.-2Tpt.-Str.
Carisch, Milan, ^c1949
Score 12 p.
Alternate title: Il Cavaliere Ergasto. From
the opera. First performance Naples, 1766.

PICK-MANGIAGALLI, RICCARDO.
Strakonice, Bohemia 10 July 1882
Milan 8 July 1949

3916 [Casanova in Venice. Carnival scene]   *8'*
3*,3*,3*,2-4,3,3,1-Timp.,Perc.-Cel.,Hp.-Str.
Ricordi, Milan, ^c1931
Miniature score 70 p.
From the ballet composed 1929. First perform-
ance of this excerpt Milan, 6 February 1931,
Alceo Toni conductor.

1907 Due preludi, Op. 42   *10'*
1.[Voices and shadows of evening] 2.[Surging
waves]
3(2nd & 3rd alt. Picc.I&II),3(3rd alt. E.H.),
4*(1Cl. in E-flat),3*-4,4,3,1-Timp.,Perc.-
Pno. 4-hands,Cel.,2Hp.-Str.
Ricordi, Milan, ^c1920
Score 58 p. Large folio

Composed 1918. First performance Rome, 1 March
1921, Victor de Sabata conductor.

1904 Notturno e rondò fantastico, Op. 28   *12'*
3*,4*(3rd Ob. ad lib.),4*(1Cl. in E-flat),3*-
4,3,3,1-Timp.,Perc.-Cel.,Hp.-Str.
Ricordi, Milan, ^c1931
Score 56 p.
Composed 1914. First performance Milan, 6 May
1919, Ettore Panizza conductor.

1905 Piccola suite [Little suite]   *9'*
1.I piccoli soldati 2.Berceuse 3.La danza
d' Olaf
3*,3*,3*,3*-4,3,3,1-Timp.,Perc.-Cel.,Hp.-Str.
Ricordi, Milan, ^c1927
Score 75 p.
Composed 1927. First performance Milan, 12
June 1927, Victor de Sabata conductor.

1903 Poemi per orchestra, Op. 45   *23'*
1.Elegia 2.[Strolling singers] 3.[A tuneful
cradle] 4.Ballata macabra
3*,3*,4*(1Cl. in E-flat),3*-4,3,3,1-Timp.,Perc.
-Pno.,Cel.,Hp.-Str.
Ricordi, Milan, ^c1926
Score 119 p.
Composed 1923. First performance Milan, 23
April 1925, Vittorio Gui conductor.

1906 Preludio e fuga, Op. 47   *9'*
3*,3*,3*,3*-4,3,3,1-Timp.,Perc.-Str.
Ricordi, Milan, ^c1927
Score 65 p.
Composed 1927. First performance Rome, 11
March 1928, Bernardino Molinari conductor.

635p Sortilegi, poema sinfonico, Op. 39   *12'*
Solo Pno.-3*,3*,3*,2-4,2,3,1-Timp.,Perc.-Hp.-
Str.
Ricordi, Milan, ^c1921
Score 57 p.
Composed 1917. First performance Milan, 13
December 1917, Arturo Toscanini conductor.

532p Trois miniatures, Op. 4   *7'*
1.À l'automne 2.Danse mignonne 3.[Goblin]
Solo Pno.-Str.
Universal Edition, Vienna, ^c1910
Score 23 p.
Composed 1908. First performance Milan, 1909,
the composer as soloist.

PICQUET, GEORGES.

1060s L'âme des roses [The soul of the roses]
Str.
Score: Ms. 12 p.
Parts: Decourcelle, Nice, ^c1921

1294s Une caresse, intermezzo valse
Str.
Score: Ms. 12 p.
Parts: Decourcelle, Nice [n.d.]

1551s C'est l'heure bleue, intermezzo valse
[Twilight hour]
Fl.,Cl.-Str.

Picquet, Georges

    Score: Ms. 8 p.
    Parts: Decourcelle, Nice [n.d.]

1174s [Naples by moonlight]
    Str.
    Score: Ms. 15 p.
    Parts: Decourcelle, Nice, [C]1921

1229s Ton souvenir [Thy memory]
    Str.
    Score: Ms. 8 p.
    Parts: Decourcelle, Nice, [C]1921

PIERCE, THEODORE.   Springfield, Massachusetts 1914

3516 Divertissements for orchestra   23'
    1.Overture 2.Pastorale 3.Pavane 4.Finale
    3(3rd alt. Picc.),2,2,2-4,2,3,1-Timp.,Perc.-
    Cel.,Hp.-Str.
    Ms.
    Score 106 p.
    Completed 1940.

PIERNÉ, GABRIEL.   Metz, France 16 August 1863
    Ploujean, near Morlaix, Finistère 17 July 1937

6268 [Album for my little friends, solo   2'
    piano, Op. 14. No. 4, Little gavotte. Tran-
    scribed for small orchestra]
    1,1,1-Hn.-Str.
    Leduc, Paris [1887, 1932 reprint]
    Score 5 p.
    Originally composed 1887.

71 Le bouton d'or. Suite d'orchestre   14'
    1.Introduction - Pas d'ensemble 2.Mouvement
    de valse 3.[The son of the Virgin] 4.[Morning
    brightness] 5.[The light]
    2,1,2,1-2,2,3-Timp.,Perc.-Str.
    Choudens, Paris [n.d.]
    Score 23 p.
    From the ballet composed 1893. First perform-
    ance Paris, 1893, the composer conducting.

528m Canzonetta   7'
    Solo Cl.-2,1,1,1-Hn.-Str.
    Leduc, Paris [n.d.]
    Score 8 p.

1000 Les cathédrales, prélude   6'
    2,2*,2*,2*-2,3,3-Timp.,Perc.-Harm.(optional),
    2Hp.-Chorus(SATB, optional)-Str.
    Rouart Lerolle, Paris, [C]1916
    Score 23 p.
    Composed 1914 for Eugène Morand's dramatic
    poem. First performance Paris, 6 November
    1915, the composer conducting.

337s Chanson d'autrefois, Op. 14 no. 5 [Song
    of olden times]
    Str.(without Cb.)
    Leduc, Paris [n.d.]
    Score 4 p.

339s Chanson de la grand-maman, Op. 3
    Str.(without Cb.)
    Leduc, Paris [n.d.]
    Score 3 p.

6795 Le collier de saphirs [The sapphire
    necklace] Suite
    1.Introduction 2.Sérénade de Gilles
    3.Entr'acte et 2[d] tableau
    2,2,2,2-2,0,2Cnt.,-3-Timp.,Perc.-2Hp.-Str.
    Alphonse Leduc, Paris [189-?]
    Score 55 p.
    From the pantomime-ballet composed 1891.

540m [Concert piece, harp, Op. 39, G-flat   13'
    major]
    Solo Hp.-2,2,2,2-4,2,3-Timp.,Trgl.-Str.
    J. Hamelle, Paris [n.d.]
    Score 79 p.
    First performance London, 1905.

544p [Concerto, piano, Op. 12, C minor]
    1.Allegro 2.Scherzando 3.Final
    Solo Pno.-2,2,2,2-4,2,3-Timp.,S.Dr.-Str.
    Leduc, Paris [n.d.]
    Score 111 p.
    Composed 1887.

387 [La Croisade des Enfants. Prelude to   5'
    Part II, La grand'route]
    3,3*,3*,3,Sarrus.-4,3,3,1-Timp.,Trgl.-2Hp.
    (2nd optional)-Str.
    Joanin, Paris, [C]1905
    Score 16 p.
    From the cantata based on Marcel Schwob's
    poem. Composed 1904. First performance Paris,
    18 January 1905, Eduard Colonne conductor.

Cydalise et le chèvre-pied
1079 [Suite no. 1]   20'
1393 [Suite no. 2]   15'
    6(alt. 6Picc.),4*,5*(1Cl. in E-flat),4*-4,3,3,
    1-Timp.,Perc.-Pno.(alt. Hpscd. in no. 1),Cel.,
    2Hp.-Chorus(no. 2 only)-Str.
    Heugel, Paris, [C]1923
    Scores: 154 p., 99 p.
    From the ballet composed 1919. First perform-
    ance Paris, 15 January 1923.

650v Fantaisie basque, Op. 49   16'
    Solo Vn.-2,2,2,2-3,2-Timp.,Perc.-Hp.-Str.
    Durand, Paris, [C]1928
    Score 48 p.

2093 Farandole, Op. 14 no. 2   2'
    1*,1,1,1-Hn.,Cnt.-Tamb.-Str.
    Leduc, Paris [n.d.]
    Score 7 p.
    Composed 1883. First performance Paris, 1903,
    the composer conducting.

846 [Franciscan landscapes, Op. 43]   17'
    1.[In the garden of St. Clare] 2.Les olivaies
    de la plaine d'Assise 3.Sur la route de
    Poggio-Bustone
    3(3rd alt. Picc.),3*,3,3*-4,2,2Cnt.,3,1-Timp.,
    Perc.-Cel.,2Hp.-Str.
    J. Hamelle, Paris, [C]1920
    Score 72 p.
    Composed 1920. First performance Paris, 1921,
    Concerts Colonne, the composer conducting.

6996 Giration, divertissement choré-   8'30"
     graphique
     1,0,1,1-0,1,1-Pno.-Str.(1,1,1,1,1)
     Senart, Paris, C1935
     Score 40 p.
     *Commissioned by the Thomson-Houston Company.
     From the ballet composed 1934. First perform-
     ance Paris, 22 March 1934.*

1479 Impressions de Music Hall   20'
     1.Chorus girls (French blues) 2.L'exentrique
     (Little Tich) 3.Les espagnols 4.Clowns
     musicaux
     3*(2nd alt. Picc.II),3,3,3(3rd alt. C.Bn.)-4,
     4,3,1-Timp.,Perc.-Pno.,Cel.,Hp.-Str.
     Eschig, Paris, C1927
     Score 104 p.
     *Composed 1927. First performance Paris, 6
     April 1927, Concerts Colonne, the composer
     conducting.*

1321 Intermezzo   4'
     2,2,2,2-4Hn.-Timp.-Str.
     Costallat, Paris [n.d.]
     Score 31 p.
     *Composed 1881. First performance Paris, 1894,
     the composer conducting.*

501 [Izeÿl. Suite from the incidental music 13'
     to Silvestre and Eugène Morand's play]
     2(2nd alt. Picc.),2*,2,2-4,2,2Cnt.,3,1-Timp.,
     Perc.-Cel.(or Pno.),Hp.-Str.
     Durand, Paris [n.d.]
     Score 46 p.
     *Composed 1893. First performance Paris, 24
     January 1894.*

527m Pièce pour hautbois   ca.4'
     Solo Ob.-2,0,2,2-4Hn.-Timp.-Str.
     Leduc, Paris [n.d.]
     Score in reduction 5 p.

511p Poème symphonique, Op. 37
     Solo Pno.-2(2nd alt. Picc.),2,2,2-4,2,3,1-
     Timp.,Perc.-Str.
     J. Hamelle, Paris [n.d.]
     Score 84 p.
     Composed 1901.

     Ramuntcho
669 [Overture, on Basque themes]   8'
780 Rapsodie basque [from Act II]   6'
     2(2nd alt. Picc.),2,2,2,Sarrus.-4,2,3-Timp.,
     Perc.-2Hp.-Str.
     Enoch, Paris, C1908
     Scores: 18 p., 21 p.
     *From the incidental music to Pierre Loti's
     play. Composed 1907. First performance Paris,
     29 February 1908.*

61s Sérénade, Op. 7
     Hp. or Pno.(optional)-Str.(Cb. ad lib.)
     Leduc, Paris [n.d.]
     Score 7 p.

779 Sérénade à Colombine, Op. 32   4'
     2,2,2,2-2Hn.-Trgl.-Hp.(optional)-Str.
     Enoch, Paris, C1895

     Score 27 p.
     *Composed for piano 1887; orchestrated 1887.
     First performance Paris, 1888, the composer
     conducting.*

621m Solo de concert pour basson, Op. 35
     Solo Bn.-2,2,2,1-2Hn.-Timp.-Str.
     Evette & Schaeffer, Paris, C1919
     Score 31 p.
     *Composed 1898 for the Paris Conservatoire
     competition.*

338s La veillée de l'ange gardien, Op. 14
     no. 3 [Vigil of the guardian angel]
     Str.
     Leduc, Paris [n.d.]
     Score 3 p.

PIERRE-PIERRE, H.   Nice 1878

1006v Chanson de Prairial
     Solo Vn.-1,1,2-2Hn.-Str.
     Score: Ms. 6 p.
     Parts: Decourcelle, Nice, C1928
     *Prairial is the ninth month of the French Revo-
     lutionary calendar. Composed 1928. First
     performance Monte Carlo, 20 April 1929, Fer-
     nand Seigle conductor.*

PIHIER, FRANCIS.

592s Menuet
     Str.
     Score: Ms. 7 p.
     Parts: André, Paris [n.d.]

PIKET, FREDERICK.   Constantinople 6 January 1903
                     Long Island 28 February 1974

1992s Concerto for string orchestra   13'30"
     1.Allegro 2.Andante quasi adagio 3.Allegro
     vivace
     Str.
     Ms.
     Score 47 p.

359m Concerto for symphonic band   14'
     1.Allegro moderato 2.Andante 3.Allegro vivo
     4.Commodo, quasi alla marcia 5.Allegro
     3*,2,6*(1Cl. in E-flat,1Alto Cl.),2-5Sax.-4,2,
     2Cnt.,2Fluegelhn.,3,Euph.,Tuba & Bass-Timp.,
     Perc.-Cb.
     Ms.
     Score 95 p. Large folio
     *Composed 1946. First performance Syracuse,
     New York, 1947, Syracuse University Band, G.
     Simmons conductor.*

4576 Curtain raiser to an American play   5'30"
     3(all alt. Picc.),2,3*,2-4,3,3,1-Timp.,Perc.-
     Str.
     Associated Music Publishers, New York, C1949
     Score 41 p. Large folio
     *First performance Minneapolis, 30 December
     1948, Minneapolis Symphony Orchestra, Dimitri
     Mitropoulos conductor.*

Piket, Frederick

6094 Essays in rhythm [revised version]   *14'*
1.Tango 2.Rumba 3.Slow foxtrot 4.Waltz –
Galop
2(both alt. Picc.),2,2(2nd alt. B.Cl.),2-2,3,
2-Timp.,Perc.-Str.
Ms. ^c[n.d.] by Frederick Piket
Score 78 p.
*Composed 1943. First performance Chautauqua,
New York, 29 July 1952, Chautauqua Symphony,
Franco Autori conductor. Revised 1960.*

6128 The funnies, for orchestra   *10'*
1.Superman 2.Blondie 3.Orphan Annie 4.Nancy
5.Gasoline Alley
2(2nd alt. Picc.),2(2nd alt. E.H.),3*,2-4,4,3,
1-Timp.,Perc.-Str.
Ms. ^c[n.d.] by Frederick Piket
Score 72 p. Large folio
*Composed 1942. First performance Chautauqua,
New York, 13 August 1950, Chautauqua Symphony,
Franco Autori conductor.*

6106 Variations and fugue for orchestra,   *18'*
on the Negro spiritual Go Down, Moses
[revised version]
2(2nd alt. Picc.),2,3*,2-4,3,3,1-Timp.,Perc.-
Str.
Ms. ^c[n.d.] by Frederick Piket
Score 79 p. Large folio
*Composed 1944. Revised 1952. First perform-
ance Fort Wayne, Indiana, 1952, Fort Wayne
Symphony Orchestra, Igor Buketoff conductor.*

PILATI, MARIO.   Naples 16 October 1903
                         Naples 10 December 1938

3408 Alla culla [The cradle, lullaby]   *5'*
1,1,1,1-Hn.-Cel.,Hp.-Str.
Ricordi, Milan, ^c1940
Score 15 p.
Composed 1938.

3919 Concerto in Do maggiore per orchestra *24'*
1.Allegro cantabile, un poco maestoso 2.Adagio
3.Rondo alla tirolese
2(2nd alt. Picc.),2,2,2-4,3,3-Timp.-Pno.-Str.
Ricordi, Milan, ^c1937
Miniature score 133 p.
Composed 1931-32.

639p [Suite for piano and strings]   *15'*
1.Introduzione 2.Sarabanda 3.Minuetto in
rondò 4.Finale
Solo Pno.-Str.
Ricordi, Milan, ^c1927
Score 32 p.
*Composed 1923. First performance Cagliari,
Sardinia, 30 May 1925, the composer con-
ducting.*

PIMSLEUR, SOLOMON.   Paris 19 September 1900
                         New York 22 April 1962

3141 First drama in a cycle of symphonies,   *30'*
Op. 40
3(3rd alt. Picc.),3*,3*,3*-4,3,3,1-Timp.-Str.
Ms.
Score 265 p.
Composed 1937.

1718s Partita for string orchestra,   *35'*
Op. 30
1.Toccata 2.Sarabande 3.Double 4.Fuga
Str.
Ms.
Score 96 p.
*Composed 1932 for violin, viola and piano.
This version 1934.*

2787 Symphonic ode and peroration, Op. 35 *15'*
4*,3*,4*(1Alto Cl. or Basset Hn.),3*-6,2,2Cnt.,
3,1-Timp.-Str.
Ms.
Score 110 p.
Composed 1935-36.

Symphonic suite, Op. 33   *24'*
2647 No. 1 Devout prelude   *8'*
2695 No. 2 Solemn interlude   *6'*
2804 No. 3 Impetuous toccata   *5'*
2814 No. 4 Fugal fantasia   *5'*
3(3rd alt. Picc.),3*,2,2-4,2,3,1-Timp.-Str.
Ms.
Scores: 64 p., 40 p., 35 p., 32 p.
*Transcribed 1930-32 from Op. 18 for piano,
composed 1922. Theme from Beethoven's Hammerklavier Sonata, Op. 106.*

2689 Symphony to disillusionment, Op. 25   *30'*
In one movement
3,3*,3*,2-4,3,3,1-Timp.-Hp.-Str.
Ms.
Score 184 p.
*Original title: Overture to Disillusionment.
Composed 1928-29.*

PINILLA, ENRIQUE.   Lima, Peru 3 August 1927

6977 Canto para orquesta no. 1   *9'*
2,2,2,2-Alto Sax.-4,2,3,1-Timp.,Perc.-Pno.,
Cel.,Hp.-Str.
Ms.
Score 12 p. Large folio
*Composed 1963. First performance Bad Godes-
berg, West Germany, 1964, Beethoven Hall
Orchestra, José Malsio conductor.*

242m [Three movements for percussion   *12'*
and piano]
1.Allegro 2.Largo 3.Allegro
Perc.(5 players)-Pno.
Ms.
Score 32 p.
*Composed 1960. First performance West Berlin,
6 July 1961, Hochschule für Musik Orchester,
Christian Süss conductor.*

PINILLOS, JOSÉ MOLINA.
See: MOLINA PINILLOS, JOSÉ.

PINTO, ALFREDO.   Mantua, Italy 22 October 1891
                      Buenos Aires 26 May 1968

3223 Eros, preludio   *6'30"*
3(3rd alt. Picc.),3*,3*,3*-4,3,3,1-Timp.,Cym.-
Cel.,2Hp.-Str.
Ms.
Score 42 p.

Composed 1930. First performance Buenos Aires, 31 May 1930, Asociación del Profesorado Orquestal, Juan José Castro conductor.

5687 El gualicho [The philter of love. *14-18'*
Argentine set from the opera]
3*,3*,3*,3*-4,3,3,1-Timp.,Perc.-Cel.,2Hp.-Str.
Ms. C1939 by Alfredo Pinto
Score 71 p.
From the opera based on Argentine folk themes, composed 1938. First performance Buenos Aires, 17 November 1940, Orquesta del Teatro Colón, Albert Wolff conductor. This set extracted 1953. Opera awarded first prize in the Concourse of the Teatro Colón, 1939.

343p [Italian folklore set] *15'*
1.[The awakening] 2.[Fishermen's rhythm]
3.[Impassioned singing] 4.[Merry dance]
Solo Pno.-2,2,2,2-2,2,2-Timp.,Perc.-Sop. Voice
-Str.
Ms.
Score 66 p.
Composed 1935. First performance Buenos Aires, 27 October 1935, Asociación Argentina de Música de Cámara, the composer conducting, Esther Gurrea soloist.

5689 Nostalgie, preludio sinfonico *5'*
2,3*,2,2-2,2,2-Timp.-Cel.,Hp.-Str.
Ms.
Score 26 p.
Composed 1928. First performance Buenos Aires, 3 August 1929, Orquesta Filarmónica de la Asociación del Profesorado Orquestal, Nikolai Malko conductor.

5672 Rebelión, poema sinfónico *12'*
3*,3*,4*(1Cl. in E-flat),2-4,3,3,1-Timp.,Perc.
-Pno.,Cel.-Str.
Ms.
Score 59 p. Large folio
Composed 1938. First performance Buenos Aires, 27 September 1943, Orquesta Filarmónica de la Asociación del Profesorado Orquestal, José F. Vásquez conductor. Awarded first prize for symphonic poems, Municipality of Buenos Aires Concourse of 1939.

847m Rhapsody no. 1, Irish rhapsody, Op. 62
Solo Hp.-Str.
Score: Ms. 30 p.
Parts: International Music, New York, C1917

5683 [Songs, symphonic poem]
1.[Song to your memory] 2.[Song to life]
3*,3*,2,2-4,3,3,1-Timp.,Perc.-Cel.,Hp.-Str.
Ms.
Score 59 p.
Composed 1934.

PIRANI, EUGENIO. Bologna 8 September 1852
Berlin 12 January 1939

1705 Ballade, Op. 47
3*,2,2,2-4,2,3-Timp.,Perc.-Str.
Schlesinger, Berlin [n.d.]
Score 27 p.

1474s Berceuse, Op. 31
Solo Vc. or Vn.-Str.
Joh. André, Offenbach a.M. [1888?]
Score 7 p.

703v Caprice, Op. 50
Solo Vn.-2,2,2,2-2,2-Timp.,Cym.-Str.
Schlesinger, Berlin [n.d.]
Score 22 p.

954 Fête au château de Heidelberg, Op. 43 *25'*
1.[Arrival of the guests] 2.[Moonlight on the terrace] 3.Danses 4.Bacchanale
3*,2,2,2-4,2,3,1-Timp.,Perc.-Hp.-Str.
Bote & Bock, Berlin [n.d.]
Score 115 p.
Composed and first performed Heidelberg, 1888.

571p Scene veneziane, Op. 44
1.Gondolata 2.In San Marco 3.[Last night of carnival]
Solo Pno.-3*,2,2,2-4,2,3-Timp.,Perc.-Str.
Schlesinger, Berlin [n.d.]
Score 51 p.

PISTER, LOUIS.

1531s Menuet
Str.
Score: Ms. 6 p.
Parts: Hartmann, Paris [n.d.]

PISTON, WALTER HAMOR.
Rockland, Maine 20 January 1894
Belmont, Massachusetts 12 November 1976

729p Concertino, pianoforte and chamber *14'*
orchestra
Solo Pno.-2,2,2,2-2Hn.-Str.
Arrow, New York, C1938
Score 65 p.
Commissioned by CBS, 1936. Composed 1937. First performance New York, 20 June 1937, CBS Orchestra broadcast, the composer conducting, Jesús María Sanromá soloist.

299p Concerto, two pianos and orchestra *23'*
1.Allegro non troppo 2.Adagio 3.Con spirito
Solo Pno.I, Solo Pno.II-3*,3*,3*,3*-4,2,3,1-
Timp.,Perc.-Str.
Associated Music Publishers, New York [C1959]
Score 80 p. Large folio
Composed 1959; not performed in this version.

337v Concerto, viola and orchestra *23'*
1.Con moto moderato e flessibile 2.Adagio con fantasia 3.Allegro vivo
Solo Va.-3*,3*,3*,3*-4,2,3,1-Timp.,Perc.-Hp.-
Str.
Associated Music Publishers, New York [C1957]
Score 88 p. Large folio
Composed 1957. First performance Boston, 7 March 1958, Boston Symphony Orchestra, Charles Munch conductor, Joseph de Pasquale soloist. Received the New York Music Critics' Circle Award, 1958.

Piston, Walter

323v [Concerto, violin, no. 2 (1960)]   22'
1.Moderato 2.Adagio 3.Allegro
Solo Vn.-3*,3*,3*,3*-4,2,3,1-Timp.,Perc.-Hp.-
Str.
Associated Music Publishers, New York, ᶜ1962
Score 89 p. Large folio
*Commissioned by Joseph Fuchs under a grant
from the Ford Foundation. Composed 1960.
First performance Pittsburgh, 28 October 1960,
Pittsburgh Symphony Orchestra, William Stein-
berg conductor, Joseph Fuchs soloist.*

2854 Concerto for orchestra   14'
1.Allegro moderato ma energico 2.Allegro
vivace 3.Adagio - Allegro moderato
3,3*,3*,3*-4,3,3,1-Timp.,Perc.-Pno.-Str.
Cos Cob Press, New York, ᶜ1934
Score 71 p.
*Composed 1933. First performance Cambridge,
Massachusetts, 6 March 1934, Boston Symphony
Orchestra, the composer conducting.*

4271 Fanfare for the Fighting French
See: TEN FANFARES BY TEN COMPOSERS FOR
       BRASS AND PERCUSSION

291m Fantasy for English horn, harp and   10'
strings
Solo E.H.-Hp.-Str.
Associated Music Publishers, New York, ᶜ1955
Score 14 p.
*Composed 1953. First performance Boston, 1
January 1954, Boston Symphony Orchestra,
Charles Munch conductor, Louis Speyer English
horn soloist, Bernard Zighera harpist.*

3552 [The incredible flutist. Suite]   18'
In one movement
3*,3*,3*,3*-4,3,3,1-Timp.,Perc.(4 players)-
Pno.-Str.
Associated, New York, ᶜ1938
Score 92 p.
*From the ballet composed 1938. First perform-
ance of the suite Pittsburgh, 22 November 1940,
Pittsburgh Symphony Orchestra, Fritz Reiner
conductor.*

326m Prelude and allegro   12'
Solo Org.-Str.
Arrow Music Press, New York, ᶜ1944
Score 25 p.
*Composed 1943. First performance Boston, 29
October 1943.*

2840 Prelude and fugue   13'
3,3*,3*,3*-4,3,3,1-Timp.-Hp.-Str.
Cos Cob Press, New York, ᶜ1937
Score 33 p.
*Commissioned by the League of Composers, 1933.
Composed 1934. First performance Cleveland,
12 March 1936, Cleveland Orchestra, Artur
Rodzinski conductor.*

5966 Serenata for orchestra (1956)   12'
1.Con allegrezza 2.Con sentimento 3.Con
spirito
2,2,2,2-4,2-Timp.-Hp.-Str.
Associated Music Publishers, New York, ᶜ1958

Score 68 p.
*Commissioned by The Louisville Philharmonic
Society. Composed 1956. First performance
Louisville, Kentucky, 24 October 1956, Louis-
ville Orchestra, Robert Whitney conductor.*

4060 Sinfonietta   17'
1.Allegro grazioso 2.Adagio 3.Allegro vivo
2,2,2,2-2Hn.-Str.
Boosey & Hawkes, New York, ᶜ1942
Score 49 p.
*Composed 1940-41. First performance Boston,
10 March 1941, Zighera Chamber Orchestra, Bernard Zighera conductor.*

2648 Suite for orchestra   15'
1.Allegro 2.Andante 3.Allegro
3(3rd alt. Picc.),3*,3*,3*-4,3,3,1-Timp.,Perc.
-Pno.-Str.
Cos Cob Press, New York, ᶜ1930
Score 66 p.
*Composed 1929. First performance Boston, 28
March 1930, Boston Symphony Orchestra, the
composer conducting.*

6335 [Suite, no. 2, for orchestra]   23'
1.Prelude 2.Sarabande 3.Intermezzo
4.Passacaglia and fugue
3*,3*,3*,3*-4,3,3,1-Timp.,Perc.-Str.
Associated Music Publishers, New York, ᶜ1953
Score 93 p. Large folio
*Commissioned by the Dallas Symphony Orchestra.
Composed 1947. First performance Dallas, 29
February 1948, Dallas Symphony Orchestra,
Antal Dorati conductor.*

6376 Symphonic prelude   10'
3*,3*,3*,3*-4,3,3,1-Timp.-2Hp.-Str.
Associated Music Publishers, New York [ᶜ1962]
Score 22 p. Large folio
*Commissioned by the Association of Women's
Committees for Symphony Orchestras. Composed
1961. First performance Cleveland, Ohio, 20
April 1961, Cleveland Orchestra, George Szell
conductor.*

6351 Symphony no. 2   26'
1.Moderato 2.Adagio 3.Allegro
3*,3*,3*,3*-4,3,3,1-Timp.,Perc.-Str.
Ms. [Associated, New York, ᶜ1944]
Score 129 p. Large folio
*Commissioned by the Alice M. Ditson Fund.
Composed 1943. First performance Washington,
D.C., 5 March 1944, National Symphony Orches-
tra, Hans Kindler conductor. Received the
New York Music Critics Circle Award, 1945.*

6246 Symphony no. 3   30'
1.Andantino 2.Allegro 3.Adagio 4.Allegro
3*,3*,3*,3*-4,3,3,1-Timp.,Perc.-2Hp.-Str.
Boosey & Hawkes, London, ᶜ1951
Score 116 p.
*Commissioned by the Koussevitzky Music Founda-
tion. Composed 1947. First performance Boston, 9 January 1948, Boston Symphony Orchestra, Serge Koussevitzky conductor. Awarded
the Pulitzer Prize for Music, 1948.*

6110   Symphony no. 4   23'
1.Piacevole 2.Ballando 3.Contemplativo
4.Energico
3*,3*,3*,3*-4,3,3,1-Timp.,Perc.-2Hp.-Str.
Associated Music Publishers, New York, ^C1953
Score 135 p.
*Commissioned by the University of Minnesota
for its Centennial Celebration, 1951. Composed 1950. First performance Minneapolis,
30 March 1951, Minneapolis Symphony Orchestra,
Antal Dorati conductor.*

5567   Symphony no. 5   23'
1.Lento - Allegro con spirito 2.Adagio
3.Allegro lieto
3*,3*,3*,3*-4,3,3,1-Timp.,Perc.-2Hp.-Str.
Associated Music Publishers, New York, ^C1956
Score 96 p.
*Commissioned by the Juilliard School of Music
for its 50th anniversary. Composed 1954.
First performance New York, 24 February 1956,
Juilliard Orchestra, Jean Morel conductor.*

5568   Symphony no. 6   25'
1.Fluendo espressivo 2.Leggerissimo vivace
3.Adagio sereno 4.Allegro energico
3*,3*,3*,3*-4,3,3,1-Timp.,Perc.-2Hp.-Str.
Associated Music Publishers, New York, ^C1957
Score 125 p.
*Commissioned in celebration of the 75th season
of the Boston Symphony Orchestra. Composed
1955. First performance Boston, 25 November 1955, Boston Symphony Orchestra, Charles
Munch conductor.*

6195   Symphony no. 7 (1960)   19'
1.Con moto 2.Adagio pastorale 3.Allegro
festevole
3*,3*,3*,3*-4,3,3,1-Timp.,Perc.-2Hp.-Str.
Associated Music Publishers, New York, ^C1961
Score 92 p.
*Commissioned by the Philadelphia Orchestra
Association. Composed 1960. First performance Philadelphia, 10 February 1961, Philadelphia Orchestra, Eugene Ormandy conductor.
Awarded the Pulitzer Prize for Music, 1961.*

6355   Three New England sketches   15'
1.Seaside 2.Summer evening 3.Mountains
3*,3*,3*,3*-4,3,3,1-Timp.,Perc.-2Hp.-Str.
Associated Music Publishers, New York [^C1959]
Score 81 p.
*Commissioned by the Worcester County Musical
Association. Composed 1959. First perform-
ance Worcester Music Festival, Worcester,
Massachusetts, 23 October 1959, Detroit Sym-
phony Orchestra, Paul Paray conductor.*

6387   Variations on a theme by Edward   11'
Burlingame Hill
3*,3*,3*,2-4,2,3,1-Timp.,Perc.-Str.
Associated Music Publishers, New York [^C1964]
Score 28 p. Large folio
*Commissioned by Isaac Kibrick for the Civic
Symphony Orchestra of Boston. Composed 1963.
First performance Boston, 30 April 1963, Civic
Symphony Orchestra of Boston, Kalman Novak
conductor.*

PITT, PERCY.   London 4 January 1870
                               London 23 November 1932

548s   Air de ballet, Op. 1 no. 1
Solo Vn.-Str.
Novello, London, ^C1899
Score 8 p.

644v   Ballade, Op. 17   15'
Solo Vn.-2,2,2,2-4,2,3-Timp.-Hp.-Str.
Novello, London, ^C1900
Score 40 p.
*Composed 1900. First performance London, 3
May 1900, Henry Wood conductor, Eugène Ysaÿe
soloist.*

PITTALUGA, GUSTAVO.   Madrid 8 February 1906

5063   [Little suite for ten instruments]
1.Habanera 2.Serenata 3.Pasodoble
1(alt. Picc),0,1,1-0,1,1-Hp.-Str.(without Va.)
A. Leduc, Paris, ^C1934
Score 24 p.
First performance Paris, 1935.

6880   La romeria de los cornudos [The cuckold's
fair, ballet (new version)]
10 excerpts
2(both alt. Picc.),1(alt. E.H.),2(both alt.
Cl. in E-flat),1-2,2-Timp.-Pno.-Voice-Str.
Union Musical Española, Madrid, ^C1963
Score 84 p.
*First symphonic performance Madrid, 1930,
Orquesta de Cámara de Madrid, Arturo Saco del
Valle conductor.*

PITTRICH, GEORGE WASHINGTON.
                               Dresden 22 February 1870
                               Nuremberg 28 April 1934

10s   Abendlied, Op. 42
Str.
Kistner, Leipzig, ^C1902
Score 7 p.

237s   Berceuse, Op. 52
Str.
Kistner, Leipzig, ^C1903
Score 7 p.

854m   [Concerto, clarinet, E-flat major]
In one movement
Solo Cl.-2,2,1,2-2,2,1-Timp.-Str.
Score: Ms. 75 p.
Parts: [n.p., n.d.]

4669   Engelreigen, Op. 35 [Angels' round dance]
2(2nd alt. Picc.),1,2,2-2Hn.-Perc.-Hp.(ad lib.)
-Str.
B. Schott's Söhne, Mainz [1899]
Score 8 p.

1772   Serenade, Op. 21   6'
2,2,2,2-2Hn.-Str.
B. Schott's Söhne, Mainz [n.d.]
Score 7 p.
*Composed 1890. First performance Dresden,
1891, the composer conducting.*

Pizzetti, Ildebrando

PIZZETTI, ILDEBRANDO.   Parma 20 September 1880
                                 Rome 13 February 1968

752c [Concerto, violoncello, in C]   30'
1.Concitato 2.Largo 3.Allegro energico
Solo Vc.-2(2nd alt. Picc.),2,2,2-4,2-Timp.,
Perc.-Hp.-Str.
Ricordi, Milan, C1935
Miniature score 115 p.
*Composed 1934. First performance Third Vene-
tian Music Festival, Venice, 11 September
1934, the composer conducting, Enrico
Mainardi, soloist.*

1910 Concerto dell'estate [Summer concert] 25'
1.[Morning] 2.Notturno 3.Gagliarda e finale
3(3rd alt. Picc.),3*,3*,3-4,3,3,1-Timp.,Perc.-
Pno.,Cel.,2Hp.-Str.
Ricordi, Milan, C1929
Score 120 p.
*Composed 1928. First performance New York,
28 February 1929, New York Philharmonic, Arturo
Toscanini conductor.*

1911 [Oedipus Rex, 3 symphonic preludes]   15'
1.Largo 2.Con impeto 3.Con molta espressione
di dolore
2,2,2,2-2,2-Timp.,Perc.-Str.
Ricordi, Milan, C1924
Score 79 p.
*Inspired by Sophocles' play. Composed 1902.
First performance Milan, March 1903, Cleofonte Campanini conductor.*

1157 [La Pisanella. Suite from the   25'
incidental music to Gabriele d'Annunzio's
play]
2(2nd alt. Picc.),2,2,2-4,2-Timp.,Perc.-Pno.,
Cel.,2Hp.-Str.
Forlivesi, Florence, C1922
Score 120 p.
*Composed 1913. First performance Paris, 11
June 1913.*

PIZZINI, CARLO ALBERTO.   Rome 22 March 1905

4764 Grotte di Postumia, divertimento in   16'
forma di tema con variazioni
3(3rd alt. Picc.),3*,3*,3*-Alto Sax.-4,4,3,1-
Timp.,Perc.-Pno.,Cel.,Hp.-Str.
Ricordi, Milan, C1942
Score 67 p.
*The village of Postumia or Postojna, now in
Yugoslavia, is noted for its limestone cave.
Composed 1941. First performance Rome, 28
December 1941.*

PLATTI, GIOVANNI BENEDETTO. (?) Venice 9 July 1697
                      Würzburg, Germany 11 January 1763

310p [Concerto, cembalo, strings and con- 16'
tinuo, no. 2, C minor] Revised by Fausto
Torrefranca
1.Andantino molto mosso 2.Adagio 3.Allegro
Solo Cemb.(or Solo Pno.)-Cemb.(or Pno.)-Str.
Carisch, Milan, C1953
Score 24 p.

304p [Concerto, string quartet and con-   16'
tinuo, no. 1, G major] Revised by Fausto
Torrefranca
1.Allegro assai 2.Largo 3.Allegro assai
Solo Cemb.-Str.(without Cb.)
Carisch, Milan, C1949
Score 24 p.
Probably composed between 1720 and 1725.

PLAZA, JUAN BAUTISTA.   Caracas 19 July 1898
                       Caracas 1 January 1964

1802s Fuga criolla, Venezolana   8'
Str.
Ms.
Score 14 p.
*Originally composed as a string quartet, 1932;
transcribed, 1935. First performance Santi-
ago, Chile, 1936, George Hoyen conductor.*

PLEYEL, IGNAZ JOSEPH.
         Ruppersthal, near Vienna 1 June 1757
                   Paris 14 November 1831

1200s Siciliano, serenade, from violin duet
Op. 59. Transcribed by Carl Pfleger
Str.
J. Eberle, Vienna [n.d.]
Score 3 p.

229m [Sinfonia concertante, piano and violin,
no. 3, A major]
1.Allegro 2.Adagio 3.Rondo moderato
Solo Vn., Solo Pno.-2Ob.,2Bn.-2Hn.-Str.
Score: Richomme, Paris [n.d.] 137 p.
Parts: Ms. C1976 by The Fleisher Collection of
Orchestral Music, Free Library of Philadelphia

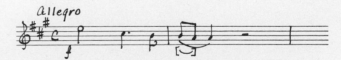

4133 [Symphony, Op. 66, C major]
1.Adagio - Allegro 2.Adagio 3.Allegretto
- Trio 4.Tempo giusto
1,2,0,2-2,2-Timp.-Str.
Ms. C1976 by The Fleisher Collection of Orches-
tral Music, Free Library of Philadelphia
Score 146 p.
*First published by Imbault, Paris, as Sinfonie
Périodique no. 27 (without trumpets or*

timpani), ca.1797. First published with this instrumentation by André, Paris, ca.1804.

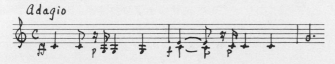

4134 [Symphony, Op. 68, G major]
1.Allegro vivace assai 2.Adagio 3.Menuetto
4.Rondo allegro
2,2,0,1-2Hn.-Str.
Ms.
Score 149 p.

6178 Symphony in C. Arranged by Adam   25'
Carse
1.Adagio - Allegro molto 2.Adagio 3.Minuetto
4.Presto
2,2,0,2-2,2-Timp.-Str.
Augener, London, c1949
Score 58 p.

POENITZ, FRANZ.
               Bischofswerda, Germany 17 August 1850
                              Berlin 19 March 1913

560m [Vineta, fantasy, Op. 74]   10'
Solo Hp.-3*,2,2,2-4,3,3,1-Timp.,Perc.-Str.
J.H. Zimmerman, Leipzig [n.d.]
Score 72 p.
Composed 1907. First performance Berlin, 1909, the composer as soloist.

POGOJEV, W.   Moscow 6 February 1872

407 [Ballet dances, Op. 8]
1.Sarabande 2.Pas d'action 3.Polka 4.Petite
valse
3*,2,2,2-4,2-Timp.,Perc.-Hp.-Str.
Belaïeff, Leipzig, 1911
Score 32 p.

551 Polonaise, Op. 11
3*,2,2,2-4,2,3,1-Timp.,Perc.-Str.
Belaïeff, Leipzig, 1912
Score 30 p.

1129s Prelude, G-sharp minor [Arranged by
Fabien Sevitzky]
Str.
Ms.
Score 4 p.
Arranged and first performed Philadelphia, 20 November 1929, Chamber String Simfonietta, Fabien Sevitzky conductor.

POHL, JOSEF.

786m Divertissement [clarinet, E-flat major]
Solo Cl.-2(2nd alt. Picc.),1,1,1-2,4,1-Timp.-
Str.
Score: Ms. 18 p.
Parts: Seeling, Dresden [n.d.]

POHL, RICHARD.   Leipzig 12 September 1826
                  Baden-Baden, Germany 17 December 1896

516s Abendlied [Evening song]
Str.
Fürstner, Berlin [n.d.]
Score 5 p.

POHLIG, KARL.   Teplitz, Bohemia 10 February 1858
                   Brunswick, Germany 17 June 1928

1510 Per aspera ad astra [symphonic poem] 55'
1.Dem Tode entgegen [Against death] 2.Rück-
blick ins Leben [Look back at life] 3.Ent-
schlafen [Dying] 4.Verklärung [Transfigura-
tion]
2,2,2,2-4,2,3,1-Timp.,Perc.-Hp.-Women's Chorus
(SA)-Str.
Ries & Erler, Berlin [n.d.]
Score 143 p.
Composed 1902. First performance Stuttgart, 1903, the composer conducting.

POKORNÝ, FRANZ XAVER.
          Königstadl, Bohemia 20 December 1728
          Regensburg, Germany 2 July 1794

428m [Concerto, clarinet, E-flat major]   18'
Edited by Heinz Becker
1.Allegro 2.Andante 3.Allegro
Solo Cl.-2Fl.-2Hn.-Str.
Breitkopf & Härtel, Wiesbaden, c1957
Score 26 p.

427m [Concerto, clarinet, B-flat major]   12'
Edited by Heinz Becker
1.Allegro moderato 2.Andante 3.Presto
Solo Cl.-2Hn.-Str.
Breitkopf & Härtel, Wiesbaden, c1957
Score 13 p.

POLACI.

1248 [Symphony, D major] Edited by Robert
Sondheimer
In one movement
4Hn.-Pno.-Str.
Bernoulli, Berlin [1923]
Score 10 p.

POLIN, CLAIRE.   Philadelphia 1 January 1926

212m Scenes from Gilgamesh, a ballet   16'30"
1.Arrival of Enkidu 2.Ishtar descending
3.Siduri
Solo Fl.-Str.
Ms. Seesaw Music Corporation, New York, c1974
Score 22 p.
Ballet commissioned by Joseph Barone and the Museum of the University of Pennsylvania

Pollarolo, Carlo Francesco

*Sinfonietta. Composed 1960. First perform-
ance Philadelphia, November 1960, Museum of
the University of Pennsylvania Sinfonietta,
Joseph Barone conductor, Sue Kahn flutist.*

POLLAROLO, CARLO FRANCESCO. Brescia, Italy ca.1653
Venice 1722

2389s Fugue in D minor. Transcribed by Bernard
Morgan
Str.
Ms. ᶜ1975 by Bernard Morgan
Score 6 p.
*Originally composed for organ. Transcribed
1938. First performance Philadelphia, 16
November 1938, Philadelphia Civic Symphony
Orchestra, J. W. F. Leman conductor.*

POLOVINKIN, LEONID ALEXEIEVICH.
Kurgan, Siberia 25 August 1894
Moscow 8 February 1949

2952 [Dances of the riddles]   15'
1.[The doll] 2.Marsch 3.[The ballerina]
4.[Moods] 5.Charlie Chaplin
1(alt. Picc.),1,1-2,2,1-Timp.,Perc.-Str.
Mussektor, Moscow, 1930
Score 25 p.
*Composed 1928. First performance Moscow,
1928, the composer conducting.*

2951 [I am little, we are mighty, ballet.   25'
Suite]
1.Introduction [The sea] 2.[Dance with
brushes] 3.Marche 4.Valse 5.[Meeting with
the enemy] 6.[Group dance]
2(2nd alt. Picc.),1,1,1-2,2,1-Timp.,Perc.-Hp.-
Str.
Mussektor, Moscow, 1933
Score 121 p.
*Composed 1931. First performance Moscow,
1932, Moscow Philharmonic Orchestra, the composer conducting.*

2950 [Overture for the First of May]   15'
4*(2nd alt. Picc.III), 2,2,3*-4,3,3,1-Timp.,
Perc.-2Hp.-Str.
Mussektor, Moscow, 1932
Score 54 p.
*Composed 1930. First performed in a radio
broadcast Moscow, 1930, the composer con-
ducting.*

3854 [Symphony no. 3, Romantic]   18'
In one movement
3(2nd & 3rd alt. Picc.),3*,3*,3*-4,3,3,1-Timp.,
Perc.-Hp.-Str.
Mussektor, Moscow, 1937
Score 91 p.
*Composed 1932. First performance Moscow, 1933,
Moscow Philharmonic Orchestra, Konstantin
Saradiev conductor.*

4370 [Telescope II for orchestra]   15'
3(2nd & 3rd alt. Picc.),2,2,2-4,3,3,1-Timp.,
Perc.-Hp.-Str.
Universal Edition, Vienna/Mussektor, Moscow,
ᶜ1930
Score 61 p.
Composed 1928, Part II of a four-part work.

POMAR, JOSÉ.   Mexico City 18 June 1880

3960 Huapango
2Picc.,2,2,3,2-2Sax.(Sop.,Alto)-4,3,2-Timp.,
Perc.-Hp.-Str.
Ms.
Score 28 p.
*Composed 1931. First performance Mexico City,
10 July 1932, Orquesta Sinfónica de México,
Carlos Chavez conductor.*

PONCE, MANUEL MARÍA.
Fresnillo, Mexico 8 December 1882
Mexico City 24 April 1948

790p Balada mexicana
Solo Pno.-2,2,2,2-4,2,3,1-Timp.,Cym.-Str.
Ms.
Score 51 p. Large folio
Composed 1918.

3818 Chapultepec [revised version]
1.Primavera 2.Nocturno 3.Canto y danza
3*,2,3*,2-4,3,3,1-Timp.,Perc.-Cel.-Str.
Ms.
Score 70 p. ᶜ1940 by the composer
*Composed 1929; revised 1934. First perform-
ance Mexico City, 24 August 1934, Orquesta
Sinfónica de México, Carlos Chavez conductor.*

4904 Danse des anciens mexicains   2'
3*,2,2,2-2Tpt.-Timp.,Perc.-Str.
Ms.
Score 12 p.
*Incorporates Mexican Indian musical material.
Composed 1930. First performance Mexico City,
13 October 1933, Orquesta Sinfónica Nacional,
Silvestre Revueltas conductor.*

3774 Gavota
2,1,1,1-2Hn.-Timp.-Str.
Ms.
Score 16 p.
Composed 1900.

1909s [Impressions of night, symphonic   18'
suite]
1.[Night] 2.[In the time of the Sun King]
3.[Lullaby] 4.Scherzo di Puck
Str.
Ms.
Score 40 p.
Composed 1923.

Instantáneas mexicanas [Mexican   9'
snapshots]
4174   No. 1. Canto de la malinche [male actor]
4175   No. 2. Música Yaqui [original version]
4176   No. 2. Música Yaqui [revised version]
4177   No. 3. Cielito lindo [original version]

4178 No. 3. Cielito lindo [revised version]
4179 No. 4. ["If someone..." Original version]
4180 No. 4. ["If someone..." Revised version]
4181 No. 5. [Dance]
4182 No. 6. [The children's early morning]
4183 No. 7. [Playing]
1,1,2,1-Timp.,Perc.-Guit.-Str.
Ms.
Scores: 3 p., 4 p., 8 p., 4 p., 9 p., 5 p.,
        2 p., 4 p., 4 p., 4 p.

3885 Poema elegiaco   *10'*
2,2(2nd alt. E.H.),2,2-4,2,3,1-Timp.,Perc.-
Str.
Ms.
Score 27 p.
Composed 1934.

4756 [The soldier's hymn to the flag]
3*,2,7*(2Cl. in E-flat,Alto Cl.),2-4Sax.(SATB)
-2,2Alto Hn.,2Bugles,3Cnt.,2Tbn.,2Bar.,Tuba,
Cb.Tuba-Timp.,Perc.-Cb.
Ms.
Score 13 p.

PONCHIELLI, AMILCARE.   Paderno Fasolaro,
                   Cremona, Italy 31 August 1834
                        Milan 16 January 1886

1266 [Gioconda. Dance of the hours]   *9'*
3*,2,2,2-4,2,2Cnt.,3,1-Timp.,Perc.-Hp.-Str.
Ricordi, Milan [n.d.]
Score 73 p.
Composed 1876.   First performance Milan 1876.

PONS, CHARLES.   Nice 7 December 1870
                         Paris 16 March 1957

698s Pizzicati [D major]
Str.
Decourcelle, Nice [n.d.]
Score 7 p.

POOT, MARCEL.   Vilvoorde, near Brussels 7 May 1901

1106m Ballade   *11'*
Solo Vn.I, Solo Vn.II, Solo Va., Solo Vc.-
2,2,2,2-4,2,2-Timp.-Str.
Eschig, Paris, ᶜ1939
Score 66 p.
*Composed 1937.   First performance Brussels, 5
May 1938, Orchestre National de Belgique with
the Quatuor Pro Arte, Franz André conductor.*

4333 [Impromptu in the form of a rondo]   *7'*
1,1,1,1-2,2,2-Timp.,Perc.-Pno.-Str.
Eulenburg, Leipzig, ᶜ1939
Score 36 p.
*Composed 1937.   First performance Brussels,
1937, Hermann Scherchen conductor.*

2953 Jazz-music   *4'*
3(3rd alt. Picc.),3*,3*,3*-Alto Sax.-4,3,3,1-
Perc.-Str.
Eschig, Paris, ᶜ1933
Score 40 p.
*Composed 1930.   First performance Brussels, 21
February 1932, Defauw Concerts, Désiré
Defauw conductor.*

4975 Musique légère/Lichte muziek   *9'*
1.Humoresque 2.Valse romantique 3.Marche
2,1,2,1-2,2,1-Timp.,Perc.-Str.
Universal Edition, Vienna, ᶜ1946
Score 85 p.
Composed 1946.

4964 [Rhapsody for orchestra]   *9'*
3*,3*,3*,3*-4,3,3,1-Timp.,Perc.-Str.
Universal Edition, Vienna, ᶜ1948
Score 70 p.
*Composed 1947.   First performance Dortmund,
West Germany, ca.1947.*

5546 [Variations in the form of dances,   *9'30"*
suite]
1.Thème (chanson popular) 2.Gavotte 3.Valse
viennoise 4.Danse cultuelle 5.Danse plé-
béienne
2,2,2,2-4,2,3,1-Timp.,Perc.-Hp.(ad lib.)-Str.
Éditions Buyst, Brussels [n.d.]
Score 45 p.
Composed 1923.

POPOV, GAVRIL NIKOLAIEVICH.
          Novocherkassk, Russia 12 September 1904
          Repino, near Leningrad 17 February 1972

3412 Septuor [Septet] Op. 2   *28'*
1.Moderato cantabile 2.Scherzo 3.Largo
4.Finale
1(alt. Picc.),0,1,1-Tpt.-1Vn.,1Vc.,1Cb.
Mussektor, Moscow, 1928
Miniature score 111 p.
*Composed 1926-27.   First performance Moscow,
13 December 1927.*

POPP, WILHELM.   Coburg, Germany 29 April 1828
                                    Hamburg 1903

639m Brillante dramatische Fantasie,   *8'*
Op. 492
Solo Fl.-0,2,2,1-2,2,B.Tbn.-Timp.-Str.
Zimmermann, Leipzig, ᶜ1898
No score published. Director's part 7 p.

763m Concert-Fantasie, Op. 382
Solo Fl.-0,2,2,2-2,2,B.Tbn.-Timp.-Str.
Score: Ms. 55 p.
Parts: Cranz, Hamburg [n.d.]

567m [Concerto, flute, Italian, Op. 392,
G major]
In one movement
Solo Fl.-0,2,2,2-2,2,B.Tbn.-Timp.,Perc.-Str.
Score: Ms. 67 p.
Parts: Cranz [n.p., n.d.]

867m [Concerto, flute, Little, Op. 438, D major]
In one movement
Solo Fl.-Str.
Score: Ms. 14 p.
Parts: Forberg, Leipzig [n.d.]

764m [Concerto, flute, Nightingale, Op. 361,
A major]
In one movement
Solo Fl.-0,1,2,1-2,2,1-Timp.,Perc.-Str.

Popp, Wilhelm

Score: Ms. 21 p.
Parts: Rühle & Wendling, Leipzig [n.d.]

579m [Concerto, flute, Spanish, Op. 420, in A]
In one movement
Solo Fl.-0,2,2,2-2,2,B.Tbn.-Timp.,Perc.-Str.
Score: Ms. 63 p.
Parts: Cranz, Leipzig [n.d.]

1395s Es war ein Traum [It was a dream] Op. 444
Str.
Score: Ms. 6 p.
Parts: A.E. Fischer, Bremen [n.d.]

589m [Greetings to Hungary, Op. 407]
Solo Fl.-Str.
Score: Ms. 18 p.
Parts: Cranz [n.p., n.d.]

568m [Hungarian rhapsody, Op. 385]
Solo Fl.-0,2,2,1-2,2,1-Timp.,Perc.-Str.
Score: Ms. 36 p.
Parts: Cranz, Leipzig [n.d.]

1576s [La Romanesca, 16th century melody
transcribed for strings, Op. 408]
Str.
Score: Ms. 6 p.
Parts: Cranz, Leipzig [n.d.]

587m Sérénade de concert, Op. 333
Solo Fl.-Str.
Score: Ms. 10 p.
Parts: Cranz, Leipzig [n.d.]

741m Das Vergissmeinnicht, Op. 422
Solo Tpt.-Str.
Score: Ms. 5 p.
Parts: Cranz, Hamburg [n.d.]
Based on Franz von Suppe's Forget-me-not.

POPPER, DAVID.   Prague 16 June 1843
                       Baden, near Vienna 7 August 1913

719c [Concerto, violoncello, no. 1, Op. 8,
D minor]
In one movement
Solo Vc.-2,2,2,2-2,2,3-Timp.-Str.
Score: Ms. 118 p.
Parts: André, Offenbach a.M. [n.d.]

524c [Concerto, violoncello, no. 2, Op. 24,
E minor]
1.Allegro moderato 2.Andante 3.Allegro molto
moderato
Solo Vc.-2,2,2,2-4,2,3,1-Timp.-Str.
Hofmeister, Leipzig [n.d.]
Score 119 p.

632c [Concerto, violoncello, no. 3, Op. 59,
G major]
In one movement
Solo Vc.-2,2,2,2-2,2-Timp.-Str.
Rahter, Hamburg [n.d.]
Score 46 p.

483c Elfentanz, Op. 39
Solo Vc.-2(2nd alt. Picc.),2,2,2-2Hn.-Trgl.-

Str.
Rahter, Leipzig [n.d.]
Score 23 p.

517c [Gavotte, violoncello, no. 2, Op. 23,
D major]
Solo Vc.-2,2,2,2-2Hn.-Perc.-Str.
Hofmeister, Leipzig [n.d.]
Score 14 p.

489c [Hungarian rhapsody, violoncello,   *7'*
Op. 68. Orchestrated by Max Schlegel]
Solo Vc.-2,2,2,2-4,2,3-Timp.,Perc.-Str.
Hofmeister, Leipzig, c1894
Score 25 p.

484c Im Walde, Suite, Op. 50
Solo Vc.-2,2,2,2-2-Timp.,Trgl.-Str.
Rahter, Leipzig [n.d.]
Score 69 p.

492c [Papillon, masquerade scene, Op. 3 no. 4]
Solo Vc.-2,2,2,2-2,2-Perc.-Str.
Senff, Leipzig [n.d.]
Score 23 p.

487c [Requiem, adagio, Op. 66]
3Solo Vc.-2,2,2,2-2Hn.-Timp.-Str.
Rahter, Leipzig, c1892
Score 23 p.

468c Sérénade orientale, Op. 18
Solo Vc.-1,1,2,1-2Hn.,Tbn.(or Bn.II)-Str.
Senff, Leipzig, c1904
Score 22 p.

485c Tarantelle, Op. 33. Orchestrated by Paul
Gilson
Solo Vc.-2,2,2,2-2Hn.-Timp.,Perc.-Str.
Rahter, Hamburg [n.d.]
Score 30 p.
Originally composed for violoncello and piano.

486c Vito [Spanish dance] Op. 54 no. 5.   *5'*
Orchestrated by I. H. Oushoorn
Solo Vc.-1,0,2,2-2Hn.-Str.
Rahter, Hamburg [n.d.]
Score 18 p.
Originally composed for violoncello and piano.

493c Widmung [Dedication] Op. 11 no. 1.
Orchestrated by Paul Gilson
Solo Vc.-1,2,2,2-2,2,3-Timp.-Str.
Simrock, Berlin, c1901
Score 19 p.

PORPORA, NICOLA ANTONIO.   Naples 17 August 1686
                              Naples 3 March 1768

625s [Sonata a tre, D major. Transcribed   *10'*
as a concerto grosso by Vittorio Gui]
Soli Vn.I/II, Vc.-Pno.,Org.-Str.
Ricordi, Milan [n.d.]
Score 24 p.
*First performance of transcription Milan, 25
May 1912, Vittorio Gui conductor.*

PORRINO, ENNIO. Cagliari, Sardinia 20 January 1910
                              Rome 25 September 1959

[Altaîr, ballet in three scenes]
4729 Scene 1. [The market place]   12'30"
3*,3*,3*,3*-Alto Sax. or E.H.(ad lib.)-4,3,3,1
-Timp.,Perc.-Pno.,Cel.,Hp.-Str.
Offstage: 2Tpt.,2Tbn.,Perc.(all optional)
4841 Scene 2. [The ship]   12'30"
3*,3*,3*,3*-4,3,3,1-Timp.,Perc.-Pno.,Cel.,Hp.-
Str.
4878 Scene 3. [The island]   13'
3*,3*,3*,3*-Alto Sax.(ad lib.)-4,3,3,1-Timp.,
Perc.-Pno.,Cel.,Hp.-Str.
Offstage: Indian Drums(or Timp.)
Ricordi, Milan, C1939
Scores: 92 p. (Large folio), 78 p., 103 p.

PORTER, WILLIAM QUINCY.
            New Haven, Connecticut 7 February 1897
            Bethany, near New Haven 12 November 1966

3028 Dance in three-time   9'
1,1,1,1-2,1,1-Timp.,Perc.-Str.
Ms.
Score 43 p. Large folio
*Commissioned by the Little Symphony Society of
St. Louis, 1937. Composed 1937. First per-
formance St. Louis, 2 July 1937, St. Louis
Little Symphony, Hans Lange conductor.*

6412 The desolate city   12'
Bar. Voice Solo-3*,2(2nd alt. E.H.),2,2-4,3,3,
1-Timp.,Perc.-Str.
Ms. Composers Facsimile Edition [New York]
C1953 by Quincy Porter
Score 20 p. Large folio
*Commissioned by Thor Johnson and the Cincin-
nati Symphony Orchestra. Composed 1950. First
performance Cincinnati, Ohio, 24 November 1950,
Cincinnati Symphony Orchestra, Thor Johnson
conductor, Mack Harrell soloist.*

418c Fantasy [after Boccherini]   10'
Lento - Allegro - Lento
Solo Vc.-2Ob.-2Hn.-Tamb.-Str.
Ms. Composers Facsimile Edition [New York]
C1950 by Quincy Porter
Score 27 p.
*Composed 1950. First performance New York,
30 March 1950, ensemble conducted by Eleazar
de Carvalho, Aldo Parisot soloist.*

296m Fantasy on a pastoral theme   8'
Solo Org.-Str.
Ms. Composers Facsimile Edition [New York]
C1946, C1952 by Quincy Porter
Score 14 p.
*Commissioned by E. Power Biggs. Composed 1943.
First performance Harvard University, Cam-
bridge, Massachusetts, 1943, members of the
Boston Symphony Orchestra, Arthur Fiedler
conductor, E. Power Biggs soloist.*

1840s Music for strings   10'
Str.
Music Press, New York, C1941
Score 19 p.
Composed 1941.

5704 New England episodes   20'
In one movement
3*,3*,2,2-4,2,3,1-Perc.-Str.
Ms. [Now published by Composers Facsimile
Edition, New York, C1958 by Quincy Porter]
Score 46 p. Large folio
*Commissioned by the Festival Committee of the
Inter-American Music Festival. Composed 1958.
First performance First Inter-American Music
Festival, George Washington University, Wash-
ington, D.C., 18 April 1958, National Sym-
phony Orchestra, Howard Mitchell conductor.*

3061 Poem and dance   10'
2(2nd alt. Picc.),3*,2,2-4,3,3,1-Timp.,Perc.-
Hp.-Str.
Ms.
Score 42 p. Large folio
*Commissioned by the Cleveland Orchestra. Com-
posed 1932. First performed Cleveland, 24
June 1932, Cleveland Orchestra, the composer
conducting.*

3103 Symphony no. 1   27'
1.Allegro moderato 2.Andante 3.Allegro
3*,3*,3,3*-4,3,3,1-Timp.,Perc.-Hp.-Str.
Ms.
Score 159 p. C1938 by the composer
*Composed 1934. First performance New York,
2 April 1938, New York Philharmonic, the composer conducting.*

[Two dances for radio]   11'
4983 No. 1 Dance in 4-time
5132 No. 2 Dance in 5-time
2(2nd alt. Picc in no. 1),2(2nd alt. E.H. in
no. 2),2,2-4,2,2-Timp.,Perc.-Hp.-Str.
Ms.
Scores: 16 p., 40 p.
*Commissioned by CBS. Composed 1938. First
performance over CBS Radio New York, 1938, CBS
Orchestra.*

1266s Ukrainian suite
1.Largo 2.Allegro moderato 3.Andante con
moto 4.Presto 5.Andante 6.Allegro
Str.
Birchard, Boston, for Eastman School of Music,
C1927
Score 11 p.
*First performance, Eastman School American
Composers' Series, Rochester, 1 May 1925.*

POTPESCHNIGG, HEINRICH. Graz, Austria 1 August 1847
                              Graz 1 September 1932

632s Aus der Steiermark [From Styria]
Pno.(ad lib.)-Str.(without Cb.)
Ries & Erler, Berlin [n.d.]
Score 10 p.

POTT, AUGUST.   Northeim,
            near Hanover, Germany 7 November 1806
                  Graz, Austria 27 August 1883

1000v Variations de concert [on a Dutch theme]
Op. 20
Solo Vn.-2,2,2,2-2,2,3-Timp.-Str.

Pottebaum, William G.

Score: Ms. 102 p.
Parts: Kistner, Leipzig [n.d.]

POTTEBAUM, WILLIAM G.
        b. Teutopolis, Illinois 30 December 1930

6401 Concerto for orchestra (1963)   *16'*
1.Largo misterioso 2.Allegro con spirito
3.Largo in distanza - Allegro determinato
3(2nd & 3rd alt. Picc.),3*,3*,3*-4,3,3,1-Timp.,
Perc.-Pno.,Cel.,Hp.-Str.
Ms.
Score 64 p. Large folio

POUGET, LÉO.

1577s Romance, C major
Solo Vn.-Hp.-Str.
Score: Ms. 11 p.
Parts: Costallat, Paris, c1915

POULENC, FRANCIS.   Paris 7 January 1899
                            Paris 30 January 1963

2954 Deux marches et un intermède   *6'*
1,1,1,1-Tpt.-Str.
Rouart, Lerolle, Paris, c1938
Score 20 p.
*Completed 1937. First performance London 6
June 1938, BBC Orchestra.*

3984 [Sketch for a fanfare] Arranged   *1'15"*
by Arthur Cohn
1(alt. Picc.),1,1,1-1,1,B.Tbn.-Str.(w/o Cb.)
Ms.
Score 7 p.
Arranged 1944.

POWELL, JOHN.   Richmond, Virginia 6 September 1882
            Charlottesville, Virginia 15 August 1963

1984 In old Virginia, overture, Op. 28
3(3rd alt. Picc.),3*,3*,2-4,2,3,1-Timp.,Perc.-
Hp.-Str.
G. Schirmer, New York, c1927
Score 62 p.

1988 Rhapsodie nègre
Solo Pno.-3*,3*,3*,2-4,3,3,1-Timp.,Perc.-Cel.,
Hp.-Str.
G. Schirmer, New York, c1921
Score 86 p. Large folio

3313 Symphony
1.Allegro non troppo 2.Allegretto sostenuto
3.Adagio 4.Grave
3(3rd alt. Picc.),2(2nd alt. E.H.),3*,3*-4,3,
3,1-Timp.,Perc.-Hp.-Str.
Ms.
Score in 2 volumes: 164 p., 156 p.
*Commissioned by the National Federation of
Music Clubs.*

POWELL, LAURENCE.
        b. Birmingham, England 13 January 1899

4216 The county fair, suite for orchestra *17'*
1.Ballyhoo spielers and vegetable judges

2.Merry-go-round 3.Romance on the Ferris wheel
4.Roller coaster 5.Horse race (the wrong horse
wins) 6.Snake charmer 7.Katzenjammer
2,2,2,2-2,2,3,1-Timp.,Perc.-Cel.-Str.
C.C. Birchard, Boston, c1936
Score 84 p.
Composed 1936.

3077 Deirdre of the sorrows, romantic   *10'*
prelude
2,3*,2,2-4,2,3,1-Timp.-Str.
Ms.
Score 43 p.

3064 Keltic legend, revised version   *12'*
3*,2,2,2-4,2,3,1-Timp.,Perc.-Hp.-Str.
Ms.
Score 85 p.
*Composed 1923; revised 1930. First performance
of revised version Madison, Wisconsin 20 May
1931, Madison Civic Symphony Orchestra, Sigfrid Prager conductor.*

1758s Picnic, Arkansas pastoral   *3'30"*
Str.
Ms.
Score 20 p.
*Commissioned by the Oklahoma Chamber Music
Society, 1935. Composed 1936. First perform-
ance Oklahoma City, 21 March 1936, Oklahoma
Chamber Music Society, Ben Bruce Blakeney
conductor.*

1771s Suite, for string orchestra   *35'*
1.Lento - Vivace 2.Lento 3.Presto
Str.
Ms.
Score 61 p.
*Composed 1931. First performance Grand Rapids,
9 May 1940, Grand Rapids Symphony Orchestra of
the WPA, the composer conducting.*

3135 Symphony no. 1   *35'*
In one movement
3*,3*,3*,3*-4,3,3,1-Timp.-Hp.-Str.
Ms.
Score 244 p.
Composed 1928-30.

4213 [Symphony no. 2]   *22'*
1.Allegro grazioso 2.Adagio 3.Presto molto
4.Allegro vivace
2(2nd alt. Picc.),2(2nd alt. E.H.),2,2-2,2,3,
1-Timp.,Perc.-Str.
Ms.
Score 133 p.
Composed 1943.

1916s Three little nothings, for strings
1.Moderato 2.Andante espressivo 3.Presto
Str.
Ms.
Score 12 p.
Composed 1923; revised 1947.

3119 Variations for orchestra   *38'*
3*,3*,4*(1Cl. in E-flat ad lib.),3*-4,2,3,1-
Timp., Perc.-Pno.,Cel.,Hp.-Str.

Ms.
Score 184 p.
*Composed 1939. First performance Rochester,
28 October 1941, Eastman-Rochester Symphony
Orchestra, Howard Hanson conductor.*

POZDRO, JOHN WALTER.   Chicago 14 August 1923

5753 [Symphony no. 2]   25'
1.Con espressione 2.Moderato 3.Allegro
3(3rd alt. Picc.),2,2(2nd alt. B.Cl.),2-4,3,
3,1-Timp.,Perc.-Hp.-Str.
Ms.
Score 120 p. Large folio
*Composed 1956-57. First performance Rochester,
4 May 1958, Eastman Symphony Orchestra, Howard
Hanson conductor.*

6564 [Symphony no. 3]   21'
1.Largo - Con spirito 2.Allegretto 3.Lar-
ghetto 4.Vivace
2(2nd alt. Picc.),2(2nd alt. E.H.),2,2-4,2,3,
1-Timp.,Perc.-Cel.-Str.
Ms.
Score 93 p. Large folio
*Commissioned by the Oklahoma City Symphony
Orchestra under a grant from the Ford Foundation. Composed 1959. First performance Oklahoma City, 19 December 1959, Oklahoma City
Symphony Orchestra, Guy Fraser Harrison conductor.*

PRADO, PROSPERO BISQUERTT.
   See: BISQUERTT PRADO, PROSPERO.

PRATELLA, FRANCESCO BALILLA.
                     Lugo, Italy 1 February 1880
                     Ravenna 18 May 1955

3866 Fanfara per la festa di Fanfare   23"
3Hn.,Tpt.
Ms.
Score 1 p.
*Composed 1921 for the magazine Fanfare, a
Musical Causerie.*

PRATT, SILAS GAMALIEL.
              Addison, Vermont 4 August 1846
              Pittsburgh 30 October 1916

1631s Serenade, B-flat major
Str.
C. Fischer, New York, ᶜ1891
Score 9 p.

PRAUS. ARNOŠT.

526s [Slavic dance]
Str.
Fr. Urbánek, Prague [n.d.]
Score 15 p.

PREYER, CARL ADOLPH.
              Pforzheim, Germany 28 July 1863
              Lawrence, Kansas 16 November 1947

713p [Concert piece, Op. 49] Orchestrated 20'
   by Carl Busch

Solo Pno.-2,2,2,2-4,2,3,1-Timp.-Str.
Ms.
Score 76 p.
*Composed 1907. First performance Lawrence,
Kansas, April 1908, Minneapolis Symphony
Orchestra, Emil Oberhoffer conductor, the com-
poser as soloist.*

PŘIBÍK, JOSEPH.   Bohemia 1853

549s [Furiant, strings, D major]
Str.
Fr. Urbánek, Prague [n.d.]
Score 9 p.

527s [Russian serenade]
Str.
Fr. Urbánek, Prague [n.d.]
Score 7 p.

PRIETO, MARÍA TERESA.
          b. Oviedo, Asturias, Spain 22 April 1900

421c [Adagio and fugue, Op. 9]   11'
Solo Vc.-3*,3*,3*,2-4,2,2-Str.
Ms. [Ediciones Mexicanas de Música, Mexico
City, ᶜ1953]
Score 51 p.
*Composed 1947-48. First performance Mexico
City, 2 April 1948, Orquesta Sinfónica de
México, Carlos Chavez conductor, Imre Hartman
soloist.*

6580 Chichén Itzá, for orchestra [Op. 3]   9'
3*,3*,3*,2-4,2,3,1-Timp.,Perc.-Hp.-Str.
Ms.
Score 52 p.
*Chichén Itzá is a Mayan archaeological site in
Yucatan. Composed 1944. First performance
Mexico City, 2 July 1944, Orquesta Sinfónica
de México, Carlos Chavez conductor.*

6406 La danza prima   20'
1.Fuga 2.Scherzo 3.Allegro
4*(2 are Picc.),3*,3*,2-4,2,3,1-Timp.,Perc.-
Str.
Ms.
Score 144 p.
*Inspired by a medieval dance from Asturias.
Composed 1951. First performance Mexico City,
6 April 1951, Orquesta Sinfónica de México,
Carlos Chavez conductor.*

6519 Sinfonia breve [Op. 3a]   16'
1.Allegro moderato 2.Andante expresivo
3.Allegro
3*,3*,3*,2-4,2,3,1-Trgl.-Cel.-Str.
Ms.
Score 91 p.
*Composed 1945. First performance Mexico City,
22 June 1945, Orquesta Sinfónica de México,
Carlos Chavez conductor.*

6388 Sinfonia cantabile   ca.18'
1.Adagio - Allegro 2.Andante 3.Tempo di
valse 4.Rondò: Allegro
3*,3*,3*,2-4,2,3,1-Timp.,Trgl.-Hp.-Str.
Ms.

Prieto, María Teresa

Score 99 p.
*Composed 1954. First performance Mexico City,
18 September 1955, Orquesta Sinfónica de
México, Erich Kleiber conductor.*

6536 Suite de ballet [Op. 18]   20'
1.Obertura 2.Fuga 3.Scherzino 4.Interludio
5.Final
3*,3*,3*,2-4,2,3,1-Timp.,Perc.-Hp.-Str.
Ms.
Score 130 p.
*Composed 1956. First performance Mexico City,
24 March 1961, Orquesta Sinfónica de México,
Luis Herrera de la Fuente conductor.*

PRILL, EMIL.   Stettin, Pomerania 10 May 1867
                   Berlin 28 February 1940

640m Tarantelle, from Etudes, Op. 6   2'
Solo Fl.-2,0,2,2-2,2-Timp.-Str.
Zimmerman, Leipzig, ^c1904
Score in reduction 5 p.
*Composed 1900. First performance Berlin, 1903,
the composer as soloist.*

PRIVANO, G.

5284 Rêverie pour orchestre, Op. 5
3*,3*,2,2-4,2,3-Timp.-Hp.-Str.
P. Jurgenson, Moscow [n.d.]
Score 17 p.

PROCHASKA, FR.

1396s Sérénade
Str.
Score: Ms. 5 p.
Parts: Bosworth, London [n.d.]

PROCHÁZKA, RUDOLF.   Prague 23 February 1864
                         Prague 23 March 1936

386s [Harpist's variations on a Mozart theme,
Op. 16]
Str.
Hoffmann, Prague, ^c1906
Score 24 p.
*Mozart's theme composed 1787 for the harpist
Joseph Häusler, of Prague.*

2241 [Two symphonic songs, Op. 24]   14'
1.[A midnight hour] 2.[The gods of Greece]
3*,2,3*,2-4,3,3,1-Timp.,Perc.-Pno.,Hp.-Str.
(with Viola d'amore)
Universal Edition, Vienna, ^c1913
Score 32 p.
Composed 1913. First performance Prague 1914.

PROHASKA, KARL. Mödling, near Vienna 25 April 1869
                           Vienna 27 March 1927

438 Serenade, Op. 20   33'
1.Moderato 2.Vivace 3.Adagio ma non troppo
4.Tempo di menuetto 5.Molto vivace
2,2,3*,2-4,2-Timp.,Perc.-Str.
Breitkopf & Härtel, Leipzig, ^c1924
Score 72 p.
*Completed 1917. First performance Vienna,
January 1918, Franz Schalk conductor.*

PROKOFIEV, SERGEI SERGEIEVICH.   Sontsovka,
    Ekaterinoslav Guberniya (now Krasnoe,
      Donbas region), Ukraine 23 April 1891
                    Moscow 5 March 1953

Ala et Lolli, Scythian suite, Op. 20
See: [Scythian suite (Ala et Lolli), Op. 20]

1934 [Chout, ballet suite in 12 movements,   35'
Op. 21a] Edited by F.H. Schneider
3*,3*,3*,3-4,3,3,1-Timp.,Perc.-Pno.,2Hp.-Str.
Gutheil, Moscow, ^c1924
Score 156 p.

6584 [Cinderella. Symphonic suite no. 1,   32'
Op. 107] Edited by Harold Sheldon
1.Introduction 2.Pas de chat [The cat's dance]
3.Quarrel 4.Fairy Grandmother and Fairy Winter 5.Mazurka 6.Cinderella goes to the ball
7.Cinderella's waltz 8.Midnight
3*,3*,3*,3*-4,3,3,1-Timp.,Perc.-Pno.,Hp.-Str.
Leeds Music, New York, ^c1949
Score 160 p.
*From the ballet, Op. 87. The symphonic suites
extracted, with substantial revisions, 1946.
First performance of Suite no. 1 Moscow, 12
November 1946. First performance of Suite no.
3 over a radio broadcast from Moscow, 3 September 1947, All-Union Radio Orchestra, Abram
Stassevich conductor.*

6425 [Cinderella. Symphonic suite no. 3,
Op. 109]
1.Pavana 2.[Cinderella and the prince] 3.[The
three oranges] 4.Southern borders (Temptation) 5.Orientaliia 6.[The prince has found
Cinderella] 7.[Waltz medley] 8.Amorozo
3*,3*,3*,3*-4,3,3,1-Timp.,Perc.-Pno.,Cel.,2(or
1)Hp.-Str.
[State Music Publishers] Moscow, 1954
Score 100 p.

428c [Concertino, violoncello and   18'
orchestra, Op. 132, G minor. Completed by
Mstislav Rostropovich and Dmitri Kabalevsky]
1.Andante mosso 2.Andante 3.Allegretto
Solo Vc.-2,3*,2,2-4,2,3,1-Timp.,Perc.-Str.
State Music Publishers, Moscow, 1960
Score 63 p.
*Composition begun 1952; only the second move-
ment and parts of the first and third were completed in piano score at the composer's death.
Piano sketch and solo part completed by Rostropovich, 1956. Orchestrated by Kabalevsky,
1959. First performance in this version Moscow, 18 March 1960, Moscow Philharmonic,
Abram Stassevich conductor, Mstislav Rostropovich soloist.*

588p [Concerto, piano, no. 1, Op. 10,   13'
D-flat major]
In one movement
Solo Pno.-3*,2,2,3*-4,2,3,1-Timp.,Perc.-Str.
Jurgenson, Moscow, 1911
Score 75 p.
*Awarded the Rubinstein Prize 1910. First per-
formance Moscow, July 1912, the composer as
soloist.*

Prokofiev, Sergei

633p [Concerto, piano, no. 3, Op. 26,   *26'*
C major] Edited by F.H. Schneider
1.Andante - Allegro 2.Andantino 3.Allegro ma
non troppo
Solo Pno.-2(2nd alt. Picc.),2,2,2-4,2,3-Timp.,
Perc.-Str.
Gutheil, Moscow, ^c1923
Score 211 p.
*Completed 1921. First performance Chicago, 16
December 1921, Frederick Stock conductor, the
composer as soloist.*

1023v [Concerto, violin, Op. 19, D major]   *22'*
Edited by F.H. Schneider
1.Andantino 2.Scherzo: Vivacissimo 3.Moderato
Solo Vn.-2(2nd alt. Picc.),2,2,2-4,2,0,1-
Timp.,Perc.-Hp.-Str.
Gutheil, Moscow, ^c1924
Score 115 p.
*Composed 1913. First performance Paris, 18
October 1913, Marcel Darrieux soloist.*

1158v [Concerto, violin, no. 2, Op. 63,   *24'30"*
G minor]
1.Allegro moderato 2.Andante assai 3.Alle-
gro, ben marcato
Solo Vn.-2,2,2,2-2,2-Perc.-Str.
Kalmus, New York [n.d.]
Score 87 p.
*Composed 1935. First performance Madrid, 1
December 1935, Madrid Symphony Orchestra,
Enrique Arbos conductor, Robert Soetens
soloist.*

Concerto, violoncello, Op. 58, E minor
  See: [Sinfonia concertante, violoncello and
    orchestra, Op. 125, E minor]

2400 Divertimento, Op. 43   *14'*
1.Moderato, molto ritmato 2.Larghetto 3.
Allegro energico 4.Allegro non troppo e
pesante
2,2,2,2-4,2,3,1-Timp.,Perc.-Str.
Edition Russe de Musique, Berlin [n.d.]
Score 84 p.
*Composed 1925-29. First performance Paris, 22
December 1929, the composer conducting.*

4028 Fanfare, pour une spectacle
3Tpt.
Ms.
Score 3 p.

5448 [Lieutenant Kijé. Symphonic suite,   *18'*
Op. 60]
1.The birth of Kijé 2.Romance 3.Kijé's
wedding 4.Troika 5.The burial of Kijé
3*,2,2,2-Ten.Sax.-4,2,Cnt.,3,1-Perc.-Pno.,Cel.,
Hp.-Str.
Kalmus, New York [n.d.]
Score 72 p.
*From the music to the film Lieutenant Kijé,
based on the story by Yuri Tynianov and
directed by A. Feinzimmer. Film music composed 1933. This suite extracted 1934. First
performance Paris, 20 February 1937, the composer conducting.*

1864 [Love of the three oranges,   *15'*
symphonic suite, Op. 33a] Edited by Albert
Spalding
1.Les ridicules 2.Le magicien Tchelio et Fata
Morgana jouent aux cartes 3.Marche 4.Scherzo
5.Le prince et la princesse 6.Le fuite
3*,3*,3*,3-4,3,3,1-Timp.,Perc.-2Hp.-Str.
Édition Russe de Musique, Berlin, ^c1926
Score 107 p.
*Composed 1919. Suite arranged 1924. First
performance Paris, 29 November 1925, Philippe
Gaubert conductor.*

5823 Ouverture [American] Op. 42   *8'*
[Original version]
1,1,2,1-0,2,1-Timp.,Perc.-2Pno.,Cel.,2Hp.-Vc.,
2Cb.
Édition Russe de Musique/Boosey & Hawkes,
London/New York, ^c1948
Score 59 p.
*Commissioned by the Aeolian Company of New
York for the opening of Aeolian Hall. This
version composed 1926. First performance Mos-
cow, 7 February 1927, Conductorless Orchestra.*

2170 Le pas d'acier [Age of steel]   *35'*
ballet, Op. 41
3*,3*,4*(1Cl. in E-flat),3*-4,4,3,1-Timp.,Perc.
-Pno.-Str.
Édition Russe de Musique, Berlin [n.d.]
Score 231 p.
*Composed 1925-26. First performance Paris, 7
June 1927, Ballet Diaghilev, Roger Desormière
conductor.*

5429 [Peter and the wolf, symphonic tale *26'*
for children, Op. 67]
Narrator-1,1,1,1-3,1,1-Timp.,Perc.-Str.
Edwin F. Kalmus, New York [n.d.]
Score 79 p.
*Text by the composer. Commissioned by the
Central Children's Theater of Moscow. Com-
posed 1936. First performance Moscow, 2 May
1936, the composer conducting.*

3494 [Romeo and Juliet. Suite no. 1, Op. 64bis]
1.Danse populaire 2.Scène 3.Madrigal 4.
Menuet 5.Masques 6.Romeo et Juliette
7.Fin de Tybalt
3*,3*,3*,3*-Ten.Sax.-4,2,Cnt.,3,1-Timp.,Perc.
-Pno.,Hp.-Str.
Mussektor, Moscow, 1938
Score 131 p.
*Symphonic Suites nos. 1 and 2 extracted from
the original ballet composed 1935. Suite no.
3 extracted from the final version, 1944.
Suite no. 1 first performed Moscow, 24 Novem-
ber 1936, Moscow Philharmonic Orchestra,
Nicolas Semjonovich Golovanov conductor.*

3495 [Romeo and Juliet. Suite no. 2,   *32'*
Op. 64ter]
1.[Montagues and Capulets] 2.[The young girl
Juliet] 3.[Friar Lawrence] 4.Danse 5.
[Romeo with Juliet before parting] 6.[Dance
of the Antillian girls] 7.[Romeo at the tomb
of Juliet]
3*,3*,3*,3*-Ten.Sax.-4,2,Cnt.,3,1-Timp.,Perc.-

Prokofiev, Sergei

Pno.(alt. Cel.),Hp.-Str.(Viola d'Amore ad lib.)
Mussektor, Moscow, 1938
Score 110 p.
*This suite first performed Leningrad, 15
April 1937.*

6486 [Romeo and Juliet. Suite no. 3,   *ca.20'*
Op. 101]
1.Romeo at the fountain 2.Morning dance 3.
Juliet 4.The nurse 5.Aubade 6.The death of
Juliet
3*,3*,3*,3*-4,3,3,1-Timp.,Perc.-Pno.,Cel.,
2Hp.-Str.
State Music Publishers, Moscow, 1963
Score 81 p.
*First performance of this suite Moscow, 8
March, 1946, V. Degtiarenko conductor.*

1933 [Scythian suite (Ala et Lolli),   *19'*
Op. 20] Edited by F.H. Schneider
1.[Adoration of Véless and Ala] 2.[The hos-
tile god and dance of the dark spirits] 3.
[Night] 4.[Glorious departure of Lolli and
cortege of the sun]
4*(3rd alt. Alto Fl.),4*,4*,4*-8,4(or 5),4,1-
Timp.,Perc.-Pno.,Cel.,2Hp.-Str.
Gutheil, Moscow, ᶜ1923
Score 108 p.
*Completed 1915. First performance St. Peters-
burg, 29 January 1916, the composer conducting.*

401c [Sinfonia concertante, violoncello   *38'*
and orchestra, Op. 125, E minor] Edited by M.
Rostropovich
1.Andante 2.Allegro giusto 3.Andante con
moto - Allegretto - Allegro marcato
Solo Vc.-2(2nd alt. Picc.),2,2,2-4,2,3,1-
Timp.,Perc.-Cel.-Str.
State Music Publishers, Moscow, 1959
Score 111 p.
*Originally composed 1933-38 as Concerto no. 1
for violoncello, Op. 58. Revised 1952-53, and
retitled Sinfonia Concertante, Op. 125. First
performance in this form Copenhagen, 9 December 1954, Danish Radio Orchestra, T. Jensen
conductor, Mstislav Rostropovich conductor.*

5207 A summer day, children's suite   *11'*
[Op. 65bis]
1.Morning 2.Tip and run 3.Waltz 4.Repen-
tance 5.March 6.Evening 7.The moon is over
the meadows
2,2,2,2-2,2-Timp.,Perc.-Str.
Edition Russe de Musique/Boosey & Hawkes,
London, ᶜ1936, ᶜ1948
Score 33 p.
*Excerpted and transcribed from piano suite
Music for Children, Op. 65, composed 1935.
This suite 1941. First performance over
radio Moscow, 1946.*

1878 Symphonie classique, Op. 25   *13'*
[D major]
1.Allegro con brio 2.Larghetto 3.Gavotte
4.Finale: Molto vivace
2,2,2,2-2,2-Timp.-Str.
Kalmus, New York [n.d.]

Score 96 p.
*Composed 1916-17. First performance Leningrad,
21 April 1918, the composer conducting.*

1863 [Symphony no. 2, Op. 40]   *34'*
1.Allegro ben articolato 2.Andante
3*,3*,3*,3*-4,3,3,1-Timp.,Perc.-Pno.-Str.
Edition Russe de Musique, Berlin [n.d.]
Score 217 p.
*Completed 1925. First performance Paris, 6
June 1925, Serge Koussevitsky conductor.*

6191 [Symphony no. 3, Op. 44, C minor]   *33'*
1.Moderato 2.Andante 3.Allegro agitato
4.Andante mosso
3*,3*,3*,3*-4,3,3,1-Timp.,Perc.-2Hp.-Str.
Édition Russe de Musique, Berlin, 1931
Score 204 p. Large folio
*Based on themes from the composer's opera The
Angel of Fire. Composed 1928. First performance Paris, 17 May 1929, Orchestre Symphonique de Paris, Pierre Monteux conductor.*

6538 [Symphony no. 4, Op. 47/112,   *36'*
C major. Revised version]
1.Andante - Allegro eroico 2.Andante tranquillo 3.Moderato, quasi allegretto 4.Alle-
gro risoluto
3*,3*,4*(1Cl. in E-flat),3*-4,3,3,1-Timp.,Perc.
-Pno.,Hp.-Str.
Sovietskii Kompozitor, Moscow, 1962
Score 252 p.
*First and fourth movements based on themes
from the composer's ballet of 1929, The Pro-
digal Son. Second and third movements
entirely excerpted from the ballet. Symphony
commissioned by the Boston Symphony Orchestra.
Composed 1930 as Op. 47. First performance
Boston, 14 November 1930, Boston Symphony
Orchestra, Serge Koussevitzky conductor.
Revised 1947 and renumbered Op. 112.*

6391 [Symphony no. 5, Op. 100, B-flat   *ca.40'*
major]
1.Andante 2.Allegro marcato 3.Adagio
4.Allegro giocoso
3*,3*,4*(1Cl. in E-flat),3*-4,3,3,1-Timp.,Perc.
-Pno.,Hp.-Str.
State Music Publishers, Moscow, 1947
Score 207 p.
*Incorporates material from the composer's
ballet Cinderella. Composed 1944. First performance Moscow, 13 January 1945, probably
Moscow Philharmonic, the composer conducting.*

6392 [Symphony no. 6, Op. 111,   *43-45'*
E-flat minor]
1.Allegro moderato 2.Largo 3.Vivace
3*,3*,4*(1Cl. in E-flat),3*-4,3,3,1-Timp.,Perc.
-Pno.,Cel.,Hp.-Str.
State Music Publishers, Moscow, 1960
Score 194 p.
*Composed 1945-47. First performance Lenin-
grad, 11 October 1947, Leningrad Philharmonic
Orchestra, Eugene Mravinsky conductor.*

6162 [Symphony no. 7, Op. 131,   *30'*
C-sharp minor] Edited by V. Levitskaia

1.Moderato 2.Allegretto 3.Andante espres-
sivo 4.Vivace
3*,3*,3*,2-4,3,3,1-Timp.,Perc.-Pno.,Hp.-Str.
State Music Publishers, Moscow, 1959
Score 172 p.
*Composed 1952. First performance Moscow, 11
October 1952, Samuil Samosud conductor.
Awarded the Lenin Prize, 1957.*

PROUT, EBENEZER.
           Oundle, Northamptonshire 1 March 1835
           London 5 December 1909

4644 Minuet and trio for orchestra, Op. 14
2(2nd alt. Picc.),2,2,2-4,2,3-Timp.-Str.
Augener, London [1880?]
Score 27 p.

PROVAZNÍK, ANATOL.
    Rychnov nad Kněžnou, Bohemia 10 March 1887
           Prague 24 September 1950

3934 Ländliche Suite [Rustic suite]   *16'*
Op. 53
1.Marcia 2.Dans la Moravie 3.Furiant
4.Danse
2(2nd alt. Picc.),1,2,1-2,2,1-Timp.,Perc.-Str.
Universal Edition, Vienna, c1936
Score 97 p.

PROVINCIALI, EMILIO.

790s Aubade
Solo Vn.-Str.
Decourcelle, Nice [n.d.]
Score 3 p.

419s Scherzo for strings
Str.
Decourcelle, Nice [n.d.]
Score 7 p.

PRUME, FRANÇOIS HUBERT.
           Stavelot, Belgium 3 June 1816
           Stavelot 14 July 1849

929v [Concerto, violin, no. 3, Op. 8, A major]
In one movement
Solo Vn.-2,2,2,2-4,2,3-Timp.,Perc.-Str.
Score: Ms. 59 p.
Parts: Breitkopf & Härtel, Leipzig [n.d.]

1022v La mélancolie, Op. 1
Solo Vn.-Str.
Score: Ms. 30 p.
Parts: A.E. Fischer, Bremen [n.d.]

PRÜMERS, ADOLF.
           Burgsteinfurt, Germany 1 September 1877
           Herne, Germany 25 September 1955

387s Zwei Concertstücke, Op. 15
1.[Forest mystery] 2.[Gnomes' round dance]
Str.
Ries & Erler, Berlin [n.d.]
Score 12 p.

PUCCINI, DOMENICO VINCENZO MARIA.
           Lucca, Italy 1771
           Lucca 25 May 1815

288p [Concerto, piano, B-flat major]   *19'*
Edited by Marcello Abbado
1.Allegretto 2.Adagio 3.Allegretto non presto
Solo Pno.-2Ob.-2Hn.-Str.
Ricordi, Milan, c1962
Score 48 p.

PUCCINI, GIACOMO.   Lucca 22 December 1858
           Brussels 29 November 1924

498s Crisantemi [Chrysanthemums]
Str.(without Cb.)
Ricordi, Milan [n.d.]
Score 7 p.

PUGNANI, GAETANO.   Turin 27 November 1731
           Turin 15 July 1798

[Favorite minuet of Pugnani]
  See: BAILLOT, PIERRE MARIE FRANÇOIS
    DE SALES.
    Menuet favori de Pugnani, variations

PUNTO, GIOVANNI. pseudonym.
      Žehušice, Bohemia 28 September 1746
           Prague 16 February 1803

Real name: Jan Václav Stich

233m [Concerto, horn, no. 5, F major]
Arranged by Klaas Weelink
1.Allegro moderato 2.Adagio 3.Rondeau "en
chasse"
Solo Hn.-2Ob.-2Hn.-Str.
Edition KaWe, Amsterdam, c1968
Score 24 p.

PURCELL, HENRY.   London 1659
           London 21 November 1695

2034s [Abdelazer. Incidental music to   *12'*
the play by Aphra Behn. Zimmerman no. 570]
Edited by Edvard Fendler
1.Overture 2.Rondeau 3.Air 4.Air 5.Minuet
6.Air 7.Jig 8.Hornpipe 9.Air
Cemb. or Pno.-Str.
Music Press, New York, c1947
Score 20 p.
*Composed 1695. First performance London, 4
April 1695.*

1245s [Same as above] Arranged by Hilmar Höckner
Str.
Kallmeyer, Wolfenbüttel, c1926
Score 28 p.

2098s [Amphitryon. Instrumental suite.
Zimmerman no. 572/1-8]
1.Overture 2.Saraband 3.Air 4.Hornpipe
5.Minuet 6.Bourrée 7.Scotch tune 8.Hornpipe
Str.
The Purcell Society/Novello, London, c1947 by
Gerald M. Cooper
Score 10 p.

Purcell, Henry

*From the incidental music to the play by John
Dryden, based in part on the plays by Molière
and Plautus. First performance London, April
1690.*

928s [Chacony, G minor. Zimmerman no. 730]
Transcribed and edited by Hannah Bryant
Str.(without Cb.)
Chester, London, c1925
Miniature score 7 p.

3431 [Dido and Aeneas. Dido's lament,   *5'*
When I am laid in earth. Zimmerman no. 626/
38a and 38b] Arranged by Charles O'Connell
Ob.,E.H.,Bn.-Str.
Ms.
Score 5 p.
*From the opera composed ca.1689. Transcribed
1936.*

3600 [Same as above] Arranged by Bernard   *4'*
Rogers
2,2,2,2-2,2-Str.
Rochester, Fairport, New York, c1960
Score 8 p.
*Arranged 1934. First performance Rochester,
30 April 1934, Eastman School Little Symphony
Orchestra, Karl Van Hoesen conductor.*

7158 [Same as above] Arranged by Paul Tanner *5'*
6Tbn.
Western International Music, Los Angeles,
c1965 by Holly-Pix Music Publishing Company,
North Hollywood, California
Score 7 p.

2335s Dido and Aeneas. Suite from the   *9'*
opera. Zimmerman nos. 626/1, 13, 22, 23, 29a,
30, 34a. Edited for strings and continuo by
E.J. Dent
1.Overture 2.The triumphing dance 3.Echo
dance of furies 4.Second act tune 5.Third
act tune 6.Sailors' dance 7.Dance of witches
and sailors
Cemb.-Str.
Oxford University Press, c1937
Score 12 p.

3430 [Dioclesian. Overture. Zimmerman   *5'*
no. 627/3a, 3b] Edited by Adam Carse
1,1,1,1(all optional)-Str.
Williams, London, c1922
Score 4 p.
*Composed as an opera with dialogue, entitled
The Prophetess or History of Dioclesian, 1690.
Arranged 1921.*

737s [The fairy queen. Zimmerman no. 629.
Dances. Arranged by Cyril Bradley Rootham]
1.Hornpipe 2.Rondeau 3.Air in D minor 4.Jig
5.Entry dance 6.Dance for the fairies 7.
Dance for the Green Men 8.Dance for the
Haymakers (1st and 2nd version) 9.Air in C
major 10.Monkey's dance
Str.(Cb. ad lib.)
Curwen, London, c1923
Score 17 p.
*From the opera after Shakespeare. First per-
formance London, April 1692.*

4055 [The fairy queen. Zimmerman no. 629.   *14'*
Suite selected and orchestrated by Harold
Byrns]
1.Ciaconna, for Chinese man and woman 2.Mon-
keys' dance 3. ...Next, Winter Comes Slowly
... 4.Danza giocosa 5.The plaint (...O Let
Me Weep Forever) 6.Sinfonia (Finale)
2,2(2nd alt. E.H.),0,2-2Hn.,2Tpt.-Timp.-Str.
Ms.
Score 39 p.
This version 1943.

2224s [Fantasias, strings. Zimmerman   *10'*
nos. 732, 743, 736, 737. Arranged by André
Souris]
Str.
CeBeDeM, Brussels, c1961
Score 26 p.
This transcription 1960.

The Gordian Knot untied. Zimmerman no. 597.
Two suites. Edited by Gustav Holst
528s Suite no. 1
1.Overture 2.Air 3.Rondeau minuet 4.Air
5.Jig
529s Suite no. 2
1.Chaconne 2.Air 3.Minuet
Str.
Novello, London, c1922
Scores: 22 p., 15 p.
*From the incidental music to the play (author
unknown), composed 1691.*

2348s In nomine [à 6 in G minor.   *2'30"*
Zimmerman no. 746]
Str.
Score: The Purcell Society/Novello, London,
c1959. 2 p.
Parts: Ms. c1973 by The Fleisher Collection of
Orchestral Music, Free Library of Philadelphia
*Originally composed for viols, probably before
1680.*

6967 [The Indian queen. Zimmerman no. 630.
Instrumental suite]
Act I: 1.First music 2.Second music 3.Over-
ture 4.Trumpet tune (Prologue in score)
Act II: 5.Symphony 9a.[Symphony] 10.Dance
Act III: 12.Dance 14.Symphony 16.Trumpet
overture 22.Air (Appendix in score) 17c.
Chorus tune 18.Third act tune Act IV: 20.
Fourth act tune Act V: 21a.[Introduction]
Additional act by Daniel Purcell: Symphony -
Trumpet air
20b.,Bn.-Tpt.-Timp.-Str.
Score (Complete opera): Novello, London [n.d.]
110 p.
Parts (Suite only): Ms. c1973 by The Fleisher
Collection of Orchestral Music, Free Library
of Philadelphia
*From the opera, in five acts with an additional
act by Daniel Purcell, with libretto by John
Dryden and Robert Howard, adapted from their
play of 1664. First performance of the opera
London, 1695.*

305s The married beau. Zimmerman no. 603.   *12'*
Edited by Gustav Holst

1.Overture 2.Hornpipe 3.Slow air 4.Trumpet
air 5.Jig 6.Hornpipe 7.March 8.Hornpipe
on a ground
2,2,2,1(all ad lib.)-2,2(all ad lib.)-Perc.
(ad lib.)-Str.
Novello, London, ᶜ1928
Score 35 p.
From the incidental music to John Crown's play,
composed 1694.

2368s [Overture and Suite fragment in   7'
G major. Zimmerman no. 770] Edited by W.
Gillies Whittaker
1.Adagio 2.Allegro 3.Menuet 4.Bourrée
5.Coranto 6.Hornpipe
Pno. or Hpscd.(ad lib.)-Str.
Oxford University Press, London, ᶜ1938
Score 7 p.

388s Set of act tunes and dances. Arranged by
Arthur Bliss
1.Overture (The Gordian knot) 2.Air (Dis-
tressed innocence) 3.Saraband (Amphitryon)
4.Minuet (Distressed innocence) 5.Hornpipe
(The married beau)
Str.
Goodwin, London, ᶜ1923
Score 7 p.

2366s [Sonata no. 6, G minor. Zimmerman   7'
no. 807] Arranged by W. Gillies Whittaker
Str.
Oxford University Press, London, ᶜ1930
Score 12 p.
Also known as the Great Chaconne in G minor.

1748s Sonata no. 9, The golden sonata,   8'
F major. Zimmerman no. 810. Arranged by Henri
Elkan
Pno.(ad lib.)-Str.
Elkan-Vogel, Philadelphia, ᶜ1938
Score 19 p.
Transcription commissioned by the American
Society of Ancient Instruments, 1938. First
performance Philadelphia, 5 April 1938, Ameri-
can Society of Ancient Instruments.

484s [Suite, C major. Transcribed for string
orchestra by William Y. Hurlstone]
1.Prelude 2.Saraband 3.Minuet 4.March
Str.
Curwen, London, ᶜ1910
Score 7 p.
Nos. 1 and 4 from Fifth Suite for Harpsichord;
no. 2 from Second Suite; no. 3 from First and
Eighth Suites.

4844 [Suite, harpsichord, D minor.   8'
Zimmerman no. 668. Transcribed for orchestra
by Ernest Lubin]
1.Almand 2.Courant I 3.Courant II
3*,2,2,2-2,2-Timp.,Glock.,Trgl.-Str.
Associated Music Publishers, New York, ᶜ1949
Score 40 p.
Composed 1689. This transcription 1948.
First performance New York, 9 January 1950,
National Orchestral Association, Leon Barzin
conductor.

517s Suite for strings, from the dramatic music
of Henry Purcell. Arranged and edited by
Albert Coates
1.Rondeau 2.Slow air 3.Air 4.Minuet
5.Allegro quasi presto
Str.
Novello, London, ᶜ1921
Score 9 p.

589s Three, four and five part fantasias for
strings. Transcribed by Peter Warlock, edited
by André Mangeot
Str.(without Cb.)
Curwen, London, 1927
Score 47 p.
Zimmerman nos. 732 through 743; 745. Composed
1680.

1336s [Three pieces] Arranged by Hugo Werle
1.Allemande, Zimmerman no. 666/2 2.Sarabande,
Zimmerman no. 665/4 3.Cebell, Zimmerman no.
T678
Str.
Breitkopf & Härtel, Leipzig [n.d.]
Score 7 p.

1105s The virtuous wife. Suite. Zimmerman no.
611. Edited by Gustav Holst
1.Overture 2.Slow air 3.Hornpipe 4.Minuet I
5.Minuet II 6.Allegro
2,2,2,1-2,2-Perc.-Str.(or Str. only)
Novello, London, ᶜ1925
Score 24 p.
Music to d'Urfey's play, performed at London
1680.

Trumpet voluntary [Zimmerman no. S125)
  See: CLARK, JEREMIAH.
     [The prince of Denmark's march...]

PURSELL, BILL (*or* WILLIAM). Tulare, California 1926

5996 Three Biblical scenes for orchestra
1.Christ looking over Jerusalem 2.Suffer
the little children to come unto me 3.Trial,
crucifixion and resurrection
3*,3*,3*,2-4,3,3,1-Timp.,Perc.-Pno.(alt. Cel.),
Hp.-Str.
Ms.
Score 91 p. Large folio
Composed 1953. First performance Eastman
School of Music, Rochester, May 1953, Eastman
School Broadcasting Orchestra, Howard Hanson
conductor. First movement received the first
Edward B. Benjamin Award for Quiet Music, 1953.

Q

QUANTZ, JOHANN JOACHIM.
       Oberscheden, Germany 30 January 1697
          Potsdam, Germany 12 July 1773

351m [Concerto, flute, For Potsdam,   17'30"
D major] Edited by Walter Upmeyer
1.Allegretto 2.Più tosto andantino 3.Presto

Quantz, Johann Joachim

Solo Fl.-Cemb.-Str.
Bärenreiter, Kassel and Basel, C1957
Score 31 p.

559m [Concerto, flute, G major] Arranged   *12'*
by Julius Weissenborn
1.Allegro 2.Mesto 3.Allegro vivace
Solo Fl.-Str.
Breitkopf & Härtel, Leipzig, 1884
Score 53 p.

QUESADA, JOSÉ.   San Rafael, Costa Rica 1884

3606 El son de la luna, Op. 6   *2'*
3*,2,3*,2-4,3,4-Timp.,Perc.-Pno.,Hp.-Str.
Ms.
Score 16 p.
Trombone I indicated as solo. Composed 1929.
First performance San José, Costa Rica, 20
December 1930, The Melodians Orchestra, the
composer conducting, Victor Guillen trombonist.

R

RAASTED, NIELS OTTO.   Copenhagen 26 November 1888
                         Copenhagen 31 December 1966

5949 Sinfonia da chiesa, Opus 76   *30'*
1.Moderato - Allegro, ma non troppo 2.Andante
tranquillo 3.Moderato
2Tpt.,2Tbn.-Timp.-Org.-Str.
Edition Dania, Copenhagen, C1947 by Samfundet
til Udgivelse af Dansk Musik
Score 64 p.
Quotes Luther's setting of Psalm 46, Ein'
Feste Burg Ist Unser Gott. Composed 1944.
First performance Copenhagen, 4 April 1946,
State Radio Symphony Orchestra, Launy Gron-
dahl conductor.

RÄÄTS, JAAN.   Tartu, Estonia 15 October 1932

2249s [Concerto for strings, Op. 16]
1.Allegro 2.Andante 3.Allegro 4.Grave
5.Allegro
Str.
Ms.
Score 45 p.

RABAUD, HENRI.   Paris 10 November 1873
                        Paris 11 September 1949

749 Divertissement sur des chansons   *15'*
russes, Op. 2
2,2,2,2-4,2,3-Timp.,Cym.-Hp.-Str.
Enoch, Paris, C1899
Score 90 p.
First performance Rome 1896, the composer
conducting.

493 Eglogue, poème virgilien, Op. 7   *5'*
2,2,2,2-2Hn.-Timp.-Hp.-Str.
Durand, Paris [n.d.]
Score 9 p.
Composed 1898. First performance Paris 1899,
the composer conducting.

1371 [Mârouf, the cobbler of Cairo.   *15'*
Dances]
3(3rd alt. Picc.),3(3rd alt. E.H.),3(1Cl. in
E-flat),2-4,3,3,1-Timp.,Perc.-Cel.,Hp.-Str.
Choudens, Paris, C1914
Score 92 p.
First performance Paris 1914, M. Ruhlmann con-
ductor.

[The Merchant of Venice. Three English suites]
671 [Suite no. 1]   *7'*
672 [Suite no. 2]   *7'*
673 [Suite no. 3]   *6'*
1,1,0,1-2Tpt.-Dr.-Hpscd.,Harm.,Hp.-Str.
Durand, Paris, C1924
Scores: 24 p., 14 p., 17 p.
From the incidental music to Lucien Nepoty's
adaptation of Shakespeare's play arranged
from works by Elizabethan composers.

487 La procession nocturne, Op. 6   *15'*
3,2,2,2-4,2,3,1-Timp.,B.Dr.-Hp.-Str.
Durand, Paris, C1910
Score 30 p.
Inspired by Nikolaus Lenau's poem Faust.
First performance Paris, 1899, Edouard Colonne
conductor.

730m Solo de concours, Op. 10
Solo Cl.-Str.
Score: Ms. 16 p.
Parts: Evette & Schaeffer, Paris [n.d.]
Composed for the Paris Conservatoire compe-
tition, 1901.

1285 [Symphony no. 2, Op. 5, E minor]   *50'*
1.Allegro moderato 2.Andante 3.Scherzo
4.Finale
2(2nd alt. Picc.),2,2,2-4,2,3,1-Timp.,Perc.-
Hp.-Str.
Enoch, Paris [n.d.]
Score 243 p.
First performance Paris 1899, Concerts Colonne,
the composer conducting.

RACHMANINOFF, SERGEY VASSILIEVICH.
          Oneg, Novgorod, Russia 1 April 1873
          Beverly Hills, California 28 March 1943

Andante cantabile
See: [Moments musicaux, Op. 16. No. 3...]

4294 [Capriccio bohémien, Op. 12]   *20'*
3*,2,2,2-4,2,3,1-Timp.,Perc.-Hp.-Str.
State Publishers Music, Moscow, 1966
Score 70 p.
Composed 1894. First performance Moscow, 22
November 1895.

389p [Concerto, piano, no. 1, Op. 1,   *26'*
F-sharp minor]
1.Vivace 2.Andante 3.Allegro vivace
Solo Pno.-2,2,2,2-4,2,3-Timp.,Perc.-Str.
Gutheil/Boosey & Hawkes, London, C1947
Score 94 p.
First performance Moscow 1891; revised 1917.

382p [Concerto, piano, no. 2, Op. 18,   *34'*
C minor]
1.Moderato 2.Adagio sostenuto 3.Allegro
scherzando
Solo Pno.-2,2,2,2-4,2,3,1-Timp.,Perc.-Str.
Gutheil/Boosey & Hawkes, London, ᶜ1947
Score 116 p.
*Composed 1900. First performance Moscow, 14
October 1901, Philharmonic Society, the com-
poser as soloist.*

367p [Concerto, piano, no. 3, Op. 30,   *40'*
D minor]
1.Allegro ma non tanto 2.Intermezzo 3.Finale
Solo Pno.-2,2,2,2-4,2,3,1-Timp.,Perc.-Str.
Kalmus, New York [n.d.]
Score 138 p.
*Composed 1909. First performance New York, 28
November 1909, Walter Damrosch conductor, the
composer as soloist.*

632p [Concerto, piano, no. 4, Op. 40,   *29'*
G minor]
1.Allegro vivace 2.Largo 3.Allegro vivace
Solo Pno.-3*,3*,2,2-4,2,3,1-Timp.,Perc.-Str.
Tair, Paris, ᶜ1928 by S. Rachmaninoff
Score 144 p.
*Composed 1926. First performance Philadelphia,
18 March 1927, Philadelphia Orchestra, Leopold
Stokowski conductor, the composer as soloist.*

269 [Fantasy, Op. 7]
3*,2,2,2-4,2,3,1-Timp.,Perc.-Hp.-Str.
Jurgenson, Moscow [1893?]
Score 69 p.
*Inspired by Mikhail Lermontov's poem The Rock.
Composed 1893. First performance Moscow, 20
March 1896.*

2396s [Moments musicaux, Op. 16. No. 3, Andante
cantabile. Transcribed for string orchestra by
Alexander Reisman]
Str.
Western International Music, Los Angeles, ᶜ1965
by Artransa Music, Los Angeles
Score 10 p.
Originally composed for piano 1896.

6278 Polka de W[assili] R[achmaninoff]   *3'30"*
1,1,2,1-2,1,1-Timp.,Perc.-Str.
Ms.
Score 15 p.
*Based on a theme by the composer's father.
Originally composed for piano 1911. This
transcription 1926; transcriber unknown.*

4380 [Prelude, piano, Op. 3 no. 2,   *4'*
C-sharp minor] Transcribed for orchestra by
Modest Altschuler
3(3rd alt. Picc.),2(2nd alt. E.H.),2,2-4,3,3,1
-Timp.,Perc.-Hp.-Str.
Ms.
Score 12 p.
Originally composed 1892.

1706 [Same as above] Transcribed for   *5'*
orchestra by Henry J. Wood
3,3*,3*,3*-4,3,3,2-Timp.,Perc.-Org.-Str.

Novello, London, ᶜ1914
Score 12 p.
*Composed for piano, 1892. This transcription,
1913. First performance London, 1915, Henry
Wood conductor.*

4394 [Prelude, piano, Op. 23 no. 5,   *4'*
G minor. Transcribed for orchestra by Modest
Altschuler]
3(3rd alt. Picc.),2(2nd alt. E.H.),2,2-4,3,3,1
-Timp.,Perc.-Hp.-Str.
Ms.
Score 16 p.
Originally composed 1903.

7244 [Prince Rostislav, poem for orchestra,
after Alexei Tolstoy] Edited by Pavel Lamm
3*,3*,2,2-4,2,2Cnt.,3,1-Timp.,Perc.-Hp.-Str.
State Music Publishers, Moscow, 1947
Score 85 p.
*Composed 1891. First performance Moscow, 2
November 1945, N. Anosov conductor.*

710p Rapsodie sur un thème de Paganini,   *24'*
Op. 43
Solo Pno.-3*,3*,2,2-4,2,3,1-Timp.,Perc.-Hp.-
Str.
C. Fischer, New York, ᶜ1934 by Charles Foley
Score 119 p.
*Composed 1934. First performance Baltimore,
7 November 1934, Philadelphia Orchestra, Leo-
pold Stokowski conductor, the composer as
soloist.*

6762 [Symphony no. 1, Op. 13, D minor]   *40'*
1.Grave - Allegro ma non troppo 2.Allegro
animato 3.Larghetto 4.Allegro con fuoco
3(3rd alt. Picc.),2,2,2-4,3,3,1-Timp.,Perc.-
Str.
State Music Publishers, Moscow, 1947
Score 245 p.
*Composed 1895. First performance St. Peters-
burg, 27 March 1897, Alexander Glazunov conductor.*

1530 [Symphony no. 2, Op. 27, E minor]   *46'*
1.Largo - Allegro moderato 2.Allegro molto
3.Adagio 4.Allegro vivace
3(3rd alt. Picc.),3(3rd alt. E.H.),3*,2-4,3,3,
1-Timp.,Perc.-Str.
Kalmus, New York [n.d.]
Score 230 p.
*Composed 1906-07. First performance Moscow,
1908, the composer conducting. Awarded the
Glinka Prize in December 1908.*

2955 [Symphony no. 3, Op. 44, A minor]   *42'*
1.Lento - Piu vivo 2.Adagio ma non troppo -
Allegro vivace 3.Allegro
3*,3*,3*,3*-4,3,3,1-Timp.,Perc.-Cel.,Hp.-Str.
Tair [Paris, n.d.]
Score 208 p.
*Composed 1935-36. First performance Philadel-
phia, 6 November 1936, Philadelphia Orchestra,
Leopold Stokowski conductor.*

355 Die Toteninsel, Op. 29 [Isle of death] *22'*
3(3rd alt. Picc.),3*,3*,3*-6,3,3,1-Timp.,Perc.

Rachmaninoff, Sergey

-Hp.-Str.
Gutheil, Moscow [n.d.]
Score 71 p.
Inspired by Arnold Böcklin's painting. Composed 1907. First performance Moscow, 1 May 1909, the composer conducting.

486 Vocalise, Op. 34 no. 14   *4'*
2,3*,2,2-2Hn.-Str.
S. Rachmaninoff, New York, ^c1919
Score 10 p.
Originally composed for piano, 1912.

RADECKE, ROBERT.
          Dittmannsdorf, Germany 31 October 1830
          Wernigerode am Harz, Germany 21 June 1911

4540 [Symphony, Op. 50, F major]   *35'*
1.Allegro non troppo 2.Allegro molto
3.Andante sostenuto 4.Allegro con spirito
2,2,2,2-4,2-Timp.-Str.
Bote & Bock, Berlin [1878]
Score 200 p.
Composed 1878.

RADKEVICH, NIKOLAI PAVLOVICH IVANOV.
     See: IVANOV-RADKEVICH, NIKOLAI PAVLOVICH.

RADOUX, JEAN-THÉODORE.
          Liège, Belgium 9 November 1835
          Liège 21 March 1911

693c Elegy for violoncello
Solo Vc.-2Bn.-Hn.-Timp.-Str.
Ms.
Score 16 p.

815m Lamento
Solo Va., Solo Vc.-1,1,2,2-2,2,3-Timp.-Hp.-Str.
Ms.
Score 20 p.

812m Nocturne, E major
Solo Tbn.-Pno.-Str.
Ms.
Score 15 p.

RAEBEL, MAX.   Bielefeld, Germany 8 January 1874
                                    d. ca.1919

35s Berceuse
Str.
Joh. André, Offenbach a.M., ^c1906
Score 4 p.

264 [Two Norwegian dances, Op. 12 no. 1]
Fl.,Cl.-Cnt.,Tbn.-Perc.-Str.
Gehrman, Stockholm, ^c1906
Score in reduction 7 p.

RAFF, JOSEPH JOACHIM.
          Lachen, Lake of Zurich 27 May 1822
          Frankfurt 25 June 1882

698v À la hongroise, Op. 203 no. 5
Solo Vn.-2,2,2,2-4,2-Timp.,Trgl.-Str.
C.F.W. Siegel, Leipzig [1876?]
Score 47 p.

Originally no. 5 of the cycle Volker, tone poems for violin and piano.

5557 [Bernhard of Weimar. Two marches]
1.Allegro vivace ed energico 2.Andante moderato
3*,2,2,2-4,2,3,1-Timp.-Str.
Jos. Aibl, Munich [187-?]
Score 56 p.
From the incidental music to Wilhelm Genast's play. Composed 1858.

746v Cavatina, Op. 85 no. 3
Solo Vn.-0,2,2,2-2Hn.-Timp.-Str.
Kistner, Leipzig [1874]
Score 13 p.
Originally composed for violin and piano.

623p [Concerto, piano, Op. 185, C minor]   *27'*
1.Allegro 2.Andante, quasi larghetto
3.Allegro
Solo Pno.-2,2,2,2-4,2,3-Timp.-Str.
C.F.W. Siegel, Leipzig [1873]
Score 140 p.
Composed 1870-73. First performance Wiesbaden, 30 March 1873, Karl Müller-Berghaus conductor, Hans von Bülow soloist.

656v [Concerto, violin, no. 1, Op. 161,   *29'*
B minor] Edited by August Wilhelmj
1.Allegro patetico 2.Andante non troppo
3.Allegro trionfale
Solo Vn.-2,2,2,2-4,2,3-Timp.-Str.
C.F.W. Siegel, Leipzig [1891?]
Score 107 p.
Composed 1870-71. First performance Wiesbaden, 24 August 1871, Wilhelm Jahn conductor, August Wilhelmj soloist.

663v [Concerto, violin, no. 2, Op. 206,   *32'*
A minor]
1.Allegro 2.Adagio 3.Allegro
Solo Vn.-2,2,2,2-4,2-Timp.-Str.
C.F.W. Siegel, Leipzig [1878]
Score 144 p.
Composed 1877. First performance Erfurt, 1 November 1877, Adolf Golde conductor, Hugo Heermann soloist.

562c [Concerto, violoncello, Op. 193,   *24'*
D minor]
1.Allegro 2.Larghetto 3.Vivace
Solo Vc.-2,2,2,2-2,2-Timp.-Str.
C.F.W. Siegel, Leipzig [1875]
Score 103 p.
Composed 1874. First performance Dresden, 4 November 1874, Julius Rietz conductor, Friedrich Grützmacher soloist.

388v La fée d'amour, Op. 67   *10'*
Solo Vn.-2,2,2,2-2Hn.-Timp.-Str.
B. Schott's Söhne, Mainz [1890?]
Score 119 p.
First performance Weimar, 20 April 1855, the composer conducting, Edmund Singer soloist.

5237 [The fisherwomen of Procida, suite for piano 4-hands, Op. 82. No. 12, Tarantella.

Transcribed by Karl Müller-Berghaus]
3*,2,2,2-4,2,3-Timp.,Perc.-Hp.-Str.
J. Schuberth, Leipzig [1882?]
Score 31 p.

2085 [From Thuringia, suite]   35'
1.Salus intrantibus 2.Elisabethenhymne
3.[Dance of the gnomes and sylphs] 4.Varia-
tionen über das Volkslied 5.Ländliches Fest
2,2,2,2-4,2,3-Timp.,Perc.-Str.
Ries & Erler, Berlin, C1893
Score 119 p.
*Composed 1875. First performance Sondershau-
sen, 27 March 1878, Max Erdmannsdörfer conductor.*

338 Italienische Suite   30'
1.Ouverture 2.Barcarole 3.Intermezzo
(Pulcinella) 4.Nocturne 5.Tarantelle
2,2,2,2-4,2,3-Timp.-Str.
Ries & Erler, Berlin [n.d.]
Score 107 p.
*Composed 1871. First performance Berlin, 26
November 1883, Franz Wüllner conductor.*

Macbeth overture
See: [Shakespeare overtures. No. 2, Macbeth]

5529 Mazurka, Op. 174 no. 8
2,2,2,2-2,2,3-Timp.-Str.
Robert Seitz, Leipzig [186-?]
Score 29 p.
*Transcribed from Fantasy Dances for piano
4-hands.*

621p [Ode to spring, Op. 76]   13'
Solo Pno.-3*,2,2,2-4,2-Timp.-Str.
B. Schott's Söhne, Mainz [1860?]
Score 85 p.
*Composed 1857. First performance Mainz, 6
February 1860, Friedrich Marpurg conductor,
Betty Schott soloist.*

739m Romance, Op. 182 no. 1   4'
Solo Hn.-2,2,2,2-2Hn.-Timp.-Str.
Ms.
Score 28 p.
*Composed 1873. First performance Wiesbaden,
5 December 1873, Karl Müller-Berghaus con-
ductor, Zschernek soloist.*

5378 [Shakespeare overtures. No. 2, Macbeth]
Edited by E.A. MacDowell
3*,2,2,2-4,2,3-Timp.,Mil.Dr.-Str.
Arthur P. Schmidt, Boston, C1891 by E.A.
MacDowell
Score 74 p.

2392 [Sinfonietta, winds, Op. 188,   21'
F major]
1.Allegro 2.Allegro molto 3.Larghetto
4.Vivace
2,2,2,2-2Hn.
Score: Ms. 83 p.
Parts: [Kistner, Leipzig, n.d.]
*Composed 1873. First performance St. Peters-
burg, 13 March 1875.*

563p [Suite, piano, Op. 200, E-flat   43'
major]
1.Introduction und Fuge 2.Menuett 3.Gavotte
und Musette 4.Cavatine 5.Finale
Solo Pno.-2,2,2,2-2,2-Timp.-Str.
C.F.W. Siegel, Leipzig [1876]
Score 157 p.
*Composed 1875. First performance Hamburg,
1875, G. Härtel conductor, Karl Faelten
soloist.*

5597 [Suite, piano, Op. 204, B-flat major.
No. 3, Rigaudon. Transcribed by Karl Müller-
Berghaus]
2(both alt. Picc.),2,2,2-4,2,3,1-Timp.,Perc.-
Hp.-Str.
C.A. Challier, Berlin [1877?]
Score 31 p.

689v [Suite, violin, Op. 180, G minor]   29'
1.Allegro 2.Minuetto 3.Corrente 4.Aria
5.Il moto perpetuo
Solo Vn.-2,2,2,2-2,2-Timp.-Str.
C.F.W. Siegel, Leipzig [1873]
Score 101 p.
*Composed 1873. First performance Hamburg, 9
December 1873, G. Härtel conductor, Hugo
Heermann soloist.*

7098 [Symphony no. 1, To the fatherland,   69'
Op. 96, D major]
1.Allegro 2.Scherzo 3.Larghetto 4.Allegro
dramatico 5.Larghetto sostenuto - Andante
moderato - Allegro deciso, trionfante
2,2,2,2-4,2,3-Timp.-Str.
J. Schuberth, Leipzig & New York [1863]
Score 271 p.
*Won the prize of the Vienna Gesellschaft der
Musikfreunde, 1863.*

169 [Symphony no. 3, In the forest,   31'
Op. 153, F major]
1.[Daytime] 2.[Twilight A.Dreaming B.Dryads'
dance] 3.[Night]
3*,2,2,2-4,2,3-Timp.,Trgl.-Str.
Kistner, Leipzig [1870?]
Score 323 p.
*Composed 1869. First performance Weimar, 17
April 1870, Karl Stör conductor.*

1 [Symphony no. 5, Lenore, Op. 177,   34'
E major]
1.[Happiness of love] 2.[Separation]
3.[Reunion in death]
2,2,2,2-4,2,3-Timp.,Perc.-Str.
Ries & Erler, Berlin [n.d.]
Score 226 p.
*Composed 1870-72. First performance Berlin,
29 October 1873, Benjamin Bilse conductor.*

6286 [Symphony no. 10, At autumn   33'30"
time, Op. 213, F minor]
1.[Impressions and sensations] 2.[Ghosts'
round dance] 3.Elegie 4.[The hunt]
3(3rd alt. Picc.),2,2,2-4,2,3-Timp.-Str.
C.F.W. Siegel, Leipzig [1882]
Score 123 p.

Raff, Joachim

177 [Symphony no. 11, Winter, Op. 214,   *34'*
A minor]
1.[The first snow] 2.Allegretto 3.[By the
fire] 4.Carneval
2,2,2,2-4,2,3-Timp.,Trgl.-Str.
C.F.W. Siegel, Leipzig [1883]
Score 163 p.
Composed 1876-77. First performance Wiesbaden,
21 February 1883, Louis Lüstner conductor.

RAGGHIANTI, IPPOLITO.   Viareggio, Italy 1866
                       Viareggio 21 November 1894

875s Pic-nic marche!
Str.(Cb. ad lib.)
Decourcelle, Nice, ᶜ1892
Score 7 p.

873s La valse des amoureux
Str.(Cb. ad lib.)
Decourcelle, Nice, ᶜ1892
Score 7 p.

RAIF, OSKAR.   Zwolle, Holland 31 July 1847
                      Berlin 29 July 1899

568p [Concerto, piano, Op. 1, G minor]   *22'*
1.Allegro moderato 2.Romanze 3.Vivace
Solo Pno.-2,2,2,2-2,2-Timp.-Str.
Breitkopf & Härtel, Leipzig [1878]
Score 91 p.
Composed 1875. First performance Berlin 1877.

RAIMANN, RUDOLF.   Veszprem, Hungary 7 May 1861
                  Vienna 26 September 1913

736s [Coffee klatch, Op. 10]
Str.
Score: Ms. 5 p.
Parts: A. Cranz, Leipzig [n.d.]

RAITIO, VÄINÖ EERIKKI.
            Sortavala, Finland 15 April 1891
            Helsinki 10 September 1945

5811 [The swans, Op. 15]   *8'*
3,3*,3*,3-4,3,3,1-Timp.,Perc.-Cel.-Str.
Suomen Säveltaiteilijain Liitto, Helsinki,
ᶜ1937
Score 34 p.
Inspired by Otto Manninen's poem Joutsenet.
Composed 1919. First performance Helsinki,
1920.

RAKOV, NIKOLAI PETROVICH.
           b. Kaluga, Russia 14 March 1908

5088 Danse tartare
1,1,1,1-2,1,1-Perc.-Harm.-Str.
Tsebrat, Moscow, 1935
Score in reduction 8 p.

2262s [Little symphony for string   *ca.12'*
orchestra (1962)]
1.Allegro moderato 2.Andante 3.Vivo 4.
Andante sostenuto - Allegro - Presto
Str.
[Musgiz], Moscow, 1963

Score 31 p.
Composed 1962. First performance Moscow,
1963.

3314 Mariische Suite, Op. 7   *14'*
1.Allegro moderato 2.Andante 3.Allegro
3(3rd alt. Picc.),2(2nd alt. E.H.),2,2-4,3,3,1
-Timp.,Perc.-Hp.-Str.
[Mussektor] Moscow, 1933
Score 70 p.
Composed 1932. First performance Moscow,
1932, Moscow Orchestra, Victor Smirnov con-
ductor.

2956 Scherzo, Op. 4   *6'*
3(3rd alt. Picc.),2,2,2-4,2,2,1-Timp.,Perc.-
Str.
[Mussektor] Moscow, 1936
Score 59 p.
Composed 1929. First performance USSR Radio
broadcast, 1927, Moscow Orchestra, Sheidler
conductor.

3098 Suite dansante, Op. 8   *14'*
1.Vivo 2.Andante 3.Allegro 4.Moderato
5.Presto
1,1(alt. E.H.),1,1-2,1,1-Timp.,Perc.-Pno.-Str.
[Mussektor] Moscow, 1938
Score 67 p.
Composed 1934. First performance Moscow, 30
March 1935, Moscow Philharmonic, Alexander
Melik-Pashaev conductor.

RAMEAU, JEAN-PHILIPPE.
       Dijon, France baptized 25 September 1683
                   Paris 12 September 1764

68 [Acante et Céphisse, ou La sympathie. *12'*
Suite arranged by Hermann Kretzschmar]
1.Muzette 2.Rigaudon and minuet 3.Gavotte
2,2,2,2-2Hn.-Str.
Rieter-Biedermann, Leipzig, 1895
Score 9 p.
From the pastoral first performed Paris, 18 or
19 November 1751. Arranged 1894. First per-
formance Leipzig 1895.

804 Castor et Pollux. Suite arranged by   *30'*
F.A. Gevaert
1.Overture 2.Gavotte 3.Tambourin 4.Air gai
5.Minuet 6.Passepied 7.Chaconne
2(alt. 2Picc.),2,0,2-2Hn.-Tamb.-Str.
Durand, Paris [n.d.]
Score 51 p.
From the tragedy first performed Paris, 24
October 1737.

Concertos for strings
  See: Six concerts en sextuor

Dardanus. Selections edited by Vincent d'Indy
1023 1ʳᵉ suite   *20'*
1.Introduction 2.Tambourin 3.[Solemn air]
4.[Lively air] 5.[Gay rondo]
1469 2ᵉ suite   *20'*
1.Introduction 2.[Slumber rondo] 3.[Graceful
gavotte] 4.Rigaudon
2,2,0,2-Str.

Durand, Paris [n.d.]
Scores: 25 p., 17 p.
*From the tragedy first performed Paris, 19
November 1739.*

4280 Les fêtes d'Hébé, ou Les talents lyriques.
Ouverture
2,2,0,2,-2,2-Timp.-Str.
Score: Fondation de l'Opéra en France,
p.73-79. Richault, Paris [1859?] Edited by
Édouard Deldevez. 7 p.
Parts: Ms.
*From the ballet first performed Paris, 21 May
1739.*

Les fêtes d'Hébé. Selections edited by
Alexandre Guilmant
1077 1ʳᵉ suite   22'
1.[Lively air (Dance of the Lacedaemonians)]
2.[Gavotte (Sailor's dance)] 3.Tambourins 4.
Rigaudons 5.Chaconne - Pas de cinq [Dance
of five]
1430 2ᵉ suite   20'
1.Introduction 2.Minuets 3.Bourrée 4.Passe-
pieds 5.[Country dance]
2(alt. 2Picc.),2,0,2-Str.
Durand, Paris [n.d.]
Scores: 27 p., 17 p.

1255s Gavotte. Arranged by Berthold Tours
Str.
Score: Ms. 8 p.
Parts: Novello, Ewer, London [n.d.]

Hippolyte et Aricie. Selections edited by
Vincent d'Indy
1118 1ʳᵉ suite   18'
1.March 2.Air en rondeau 3.Gavottes
4.Chaconne 5.Minuets
1386 2ᵉ suite   12'
1.1ᵉʳ & 2ᵉ airs des matelots 2.1ʳᵉ gavotte
3.1ᵉʳ & 2ᵉ rigaudons en tambourin
3*(Picc. or Flageolet in 2ᵉ only),2,0,2-Tamb.
(2ᵉ only)-Str.
Durand, Paris [n.d.]
Scores: 27 p., 11 p.
*From the tragedy first performed Paris, 1
October 1733.*

Les Indes galantes. Selections edited by
Paul Dukas
1158 1ʳᵉ suite   15'
1.March 2.Minuet 3.[Dance of the savages]
4.Chaconne
1185 2ᵉ suite   15'
1.[Entrance of the four nations] 2.Musette
(Rondo) 3.Rigaudons 4.Tambourins 5.Gavotte
en rondeau
2,2,0,2-2Tpt.(1ʳᵉ only)-Timp.(1ʳᵉ only)-Str.
Durand, Paris/Kalmus, New York [n.d.]
Scores: 35 p., 12 p.
*From the ballet first performed Paris, 23
August 1735. Revised 1736.*

70 [Platée. Suite arranged by Hermann   12'
Kretzschmar]
1.Overture 2.Loure 3.Minuet 4.Chaconne
2,2,2,2-2,2-Timp.-Str.

Rieter-Biedermann, Leipzig, 1895
Score 27 p.
*From the ballet first performed Versailles, 31
March 1745. Arranged 1894. First performance
Leipzig, 1895.*

1837 Rigodon. Arranged by Heinrich G. Noren
2,2,2,2-2Hn.-Str.
Eos, Berlin, ᶜ1913
Score 15 p.

248s Six concerts en sextuor. Edited by Camille
Saint-Saëns
6 concertos: C minor; G major; A major; B-flat
major; D minor; G minor
Str.
Durand, Paris [n.d.]
Score 86 p.

3347 Suite [from the harpsichord works]   12'
Arranged by Amedeo de Filippi
1.Les Niais de Sologne [The buffoons of
Sologne] 2.Musette en rondeau 3.Rigaudon
4.Menuet 5.Gigue en rondeau
2,2,2,2-2Hn.,2Tpt.-Timp.-Str.
Ms.
Score 25 p. Large folio
*Composed 1928. First performance in a broad-
cast, New York, 14 December 1937, CBS Orchestra,
Howard Barlow conductor.*

794s Tambourin. Arranged by Gustav Sandré
Str.
B. Schott's Söhne, Mainz [1899]
Score 3 p.

614 [Three ballet pieces. Arranged by   12'
Felix Mottl]
1.Menuett 2.Musette 3.Tambourin
2*,2(2nd alt. E.H.),2,2-2,2-Timp.,Perc.-Str.
C.F. Peters, Leipzig [n.d.]
Score 35 p.
*Arranged 1898 from Platée and Les Fêtes d'Hébé.
First performance of this version Carlsruhe,
1899, Felix Mottl conductor.*

484 Zaïs. Ouverture   5'
2Picc.,2,0,2-Muffled Dr.-Str.
Durand, Paris, ᶜ1911
Score 14 p.
*From the ballet first performed Paris, 29
February 1748.*

69 [Zoroaster. Suite arranged by Hermann   14'
Kretzschmar]
1.[Lively gavotte in rondo form] 2.[Air and
entrance of the Indians] 3.Sarabande 4.Minuet
2,2,2,2-2Hn.-Str.
Rieter-Biedermann, Leipzig, 1895
Score 15 p.
*From the tragedy first performed Paris, 5
December 1749. Arranged 1894. First perform-
ance Leipzig, 1895.*

RANGSTRÖM, TURE.   Stockholm 30 November 1884
                          Stockholm 11 May 1947

5043 Dityramb. Edited by Kurt Atterberg   19'
2,3*,2,2-4,3,3,1-Timp.,Cym.-Str.

Rangström, Ture

Ms.
Score 67 p.
*Inspired by August Strindberg's poem Sångare
(The Singer). Composed 1909. First perform-
ance Stockholm, 27 March 1910, Armas Järnefelt
conductor.*

1321s Divertimento elegiaco
1.Preludio visionario 2.Scherzo leggiero 3.
Canzonetta malinconica 4.Giga fantastica
Str.
Nordiska, Stockholm, ^c1921
Score 15 p.
Composed 1918.

1210v [Partita, violin and orchestra,   *18'*
B minor]
1.Préambule 2.Menuet 3.Air 4.Gaillarde
Solo Vn.-2,2,2,2-2,2-Timp.,Trgl.-Str.
Universal Edition, Vienna, ^c1935
Score 47 p.
*Composed 1933. First performance Stockholm, 5
December 1934, Stockholm Philharmonic Orches-
tra, Adolf Wiklund conductor, Charles Barkel
soloist.*

5525 [Symphony no. 2, My country, D minor] *38'*
1.[Fairy tales] 2.[Woods, waves, summer
nights] 3.[Dreams]
3(3rd alt. Picc.),2(2nd alt. E.H.),2(2nd alt.
B.Cl.),2-4,3,3,1-Timp.,Perc.-Str.
Wilhelm Hansen, Copenhagen, ^c1922
Score 167 p.
*Composed 1919. First performance Stockholm,
20 November 1919, Stockholm Philharmonic
Orchestra, Georg Schnéevoigt conductor.*

5012 [Symphony no. 4, Invocation]   *35'*
1.Preludio 2.Alla toccata 3.Intermezzo,
sotto voce 4.Recitativo ed arioso 5.Finale
3(3rd alt. Picc.),2(2nd alt. E.H.),2(2nd alt.
B.Cl.),2-4,3,3,1-Timp.,Perc.-Pno.,Org.-Str.
Ms.
Score 111 p.
*Composed 1936. First performance Stockholm,
20 November 1936, Stockholm Philharmonic
Orchestra, the composer conducting.*

6691 [Vauxhall, miniature suite in 7   *18'*
movements]
2(2nd alt. Picc.),2,2,2-2,2,2-Timp.,Perc.-
Hp.(or Pno.)-Str.
Ms. [^c1937 by Ture Rangström]
Score 62 p.
*Inspired by Anna Maria Lenngren's poem Gröna
Lund. Composed 1937. First performance
Stockholm, 26 September 1937, Concert Society,
the composer conducting.*

RANTA, SULHO VEIKKO JUHANI.
      Peräseinäjoki, Finland 15 August 1901
                Helsinki 5 May 1960

5816 [Northern images, suite, Op. 44]   *12'*
1.[Nocturnal landscape] 2.[Lullaby] 3.
[Popular dance - Reindeer bells]
2(2nd alt. Picc.),2,2,2-4(3rd & 4th ad lib.),
2,3(2nd & 3rd ad lib.)-Timp.,Perc.-Str.

Suomen Säveltaiteilijain Liitto, Helsinki,
^c1938
Score 43 p.
*Composed 1933. First performance Helsinki,
1933.*

RAPHLING, SAM.   Fort Worth, Texas 19 March 1910

252p [Concerto, piano, no. 3]   *19'*
1.Moderately lively 2.Lively and lightly
3.Slowly 4.Moderately
Solo Pno.-2,2(1st alt. E.H.),2,2-4,2,3,1-Timp.
-Str.
Ms. [^c1960 by Beekman, New York]
Score 130 p.

RAPOPORT, EDA.   Daugavpils, Latvia 9 December 1886
                   New York 9 May 1968

1801s Adagio   *7'*
Str.
Ms.
Score 7 p.
*Composed 1940. First performance New York,
December 1948, Dean Dixon conductor.*

749p [Concerto, piano]   *15'*
1.Allegro moderato 2.Allegro scherzando e
leggiero 3.Moderato con moto
Solo Pno.-2,2,2,2-2,2,2-Timp.,Perc.-Cel.,Hp.-
Str.
Ms.
Score 90 p. Large folio
Composed 1939.

1161v Fantasie for violin   *20'*
1.Moderato 2.Andante 3.Allegro energico
Solo Vn.-2,1,2,1-2,2,2-Timp.,Perc.-Str.
Ms.
Score 98 p. Large folio
*Composed 1942 as Concerto for Violin. First
performance New York, April 1948, National
Orchestra Society, Leon Barzin conductor.*

956m Israfel, after Edgar Allan Poe   *10'*
Fl.-Hp.-Str.
Ms.
Score 23 p.
*Composed 1936. First performance Philadel-
phia, 17 November 1957, Philadelphia Chamber
Orchestra, Herbert Fiss conductor.*

1900s Lament (Revolt in the Warsaw Ghetto)   *7'*
Str.
Ms.
Score 13 p.
*Composed 1943. First performance New York,
3 May 1944.*

Lamentations based on Hebrew themes
745c Original version: Solo Vc.-2,3*,2,2-2,3,
3,1-Timp.,Trgl.-Hp.-Str.
753c Second version (1940): Solo Vc.-1,1,1,1-
Hn.-Timp.-Pno.-Str.
Scores: 28 p., 30 p.
Solo: Cantor, Boston, ^c1933 by Eda Rapoport
Composed 1933.

3672 The mathmid, symphonic poem   15'
3*,3*,2,2-4,2,2-Timp.,Perc.-Hp.-Str.
Ms.
Score 40 p.
Inspired by Chaim Bialik Nachman's poem. Composed 1935. First performance Brooklyn, 31 January 1943, New York City Symphony Orchestra of the WPA, Emerson Buckley conductor.

4037 Suite for orchestra   10'
1.At the sea 2.A Starry Night (after Van Gogh) 3.Valse
2,3*,2,2-2,2-Timp.,Perc.-Hp.-Str.
Ms.
Score 34 p.
Composed for piano, 1942. Transcribed 1943.

1924s Three pastels for string orchestra   10'
1.A weeping willow 2.The boatman 3.In the garden
Str.
Ms.
Score 19 p.
Composed 1947. First performance New York, Norman Black conductor.

RASSE, FRANÇOIS. Helchin, Belgium 27 January 1873
Brussels 4 January 1955

748m [Concertino, trombone, D minor]
In one movement
Solo Tbn.-2,2,2,2-2,2,0,1-Timp.-Str.
Ms.
Score 35 p.

RATHAUS, KAROL. Tarnopol, Poland (now Ternopol, Ukraine) 16 September 1895
New York 21 November 1954

840m [Allegro concertante, Op. 30]
Solo Tpt.-Str.
Benno Balan, Berlin, c1932
Score 16 p.
Original title: Kleines Vorspiel. Composed 1930. First performance Berlin, 1930, Michael Taube conductor.

3187 [Le lion amoureux. Suite]   15'
1.Sarabande 2.The lion's dance 3.The queen and the lion 4.Dance of the flower girl 5.Finale
3*,2,3*,3*-4,3,3,1-Timp.,Perc.-Pno.,Hp.-Str.
Ms.
Score 90 p.
Based on a fable by Lafontaine. Composed 1937. First concert performance London, 13 May 1938, BBC Orchestra, Clarence Raybould conductor.

4592 Polonaise symphonique, Op. 52   6'
3*,2,2,2-4,3,3,1-Timp.,Perc.-Str.
Ms. [Associated Music Publishers, New York]
Score 25 p. Large folio
Commissioned by the New York Philharmonic. Composed 1943. First performance New York, 26 February 1944, New York Philharmonic, Artur Rodzinski conductor.

4816 Salisbury Cove, an overture, Op. 65   15'
3*,2,3(1Cl. in E-flat),3*-4,3,3,1-Timp.,Perc.-Pno.,Cel.,Hp.-Str.
Ms.
Score 31 p. Large folio
Salisbury Cove is near Bar Harbor, Maine. Composed 1949. First performance St. Louis, 21 January 1950, St. Louis Symphony Orchestra, Vladimir Golschmann conductor.

4588 Vision dramatique, Op. 55   12'
2(2nd alt. Picc.),2,3*,2-4,3,3,1-Timp.,Perc.-Pno.-Str.
Ms. c1946 by Associated Music Publishers, New York
Score 44 p. Large folio
Composed 1945. First performance Tel Aviv, 4 April 1948, Palestine Philharmonic Orchestra, Jascha Horenstein conductor. First U.S. performance New York, 18 November 1948, New York Philharmonic, Dimitri Mitropoulos conductor.

RATNER, LEONARD GILBERT. Minneapolis 30 July 1916

1989s Suite for string orchestra   14'
1.Concerto - Allegro 2.Molto lento 3.Introduction and fugue
Str.
Ms.
Score 37 p.

RAVANELLO, ORESTE. Venice 25 August 1871
Padua 1 July 1938

787m Meditazione, Op. 118 no. 3
Solo Cl.-Str.
Zanibon, Padua [n.d.]
Score 4 p.

890s Vision, Op. 11 no. 2
Str.
Zanibon, Padua, c1911
Score 4 p.

RAVEL, JOSEPH MAURICE. Ciboure, Basses-Pyrénées, France 7 March 1875
Paris 28 December 1937

566 Alborada del gracioso [Serenade of the clown]   10'
3*,3*,2,3*-4,2,3,1-Timp.,Perc.-2Hp.-Str.
Eschig, Paris, c1923
Score 42 p.
Originally no. 4 of Miroirs for piano, composed 1905. Transcribed 1918. First performance Paris, 17 May 1919, Pasdeloup Orchestra, Rhené-Baton conductor.

2208 Bolero   12'
3*(2nd alt. 2nd Picc.),3*(2nd alt. Ob. d'Amore),4*(1Cl. in E-flat),3*-3Sax.-4,4,3,1-Timp.,Perc.-Cel.,Hp.-Str.
Durand, Paris, c 1929
Score 66 p.
Composed as a ballet, 1928. First stage performance Paris, 22 November 1928, Walter Straram conductor. First concert performance Paris, 11 January 1930, Lamoureux Orchestra, the composer conducting.

Ravel, Maurice

683p [Concerto, piano, G major]   20'
    1.Allegramente 2.Adagio assai 3.Presto
    Solo Pno.-2*,2*,2,2-2,1,1-Timp.,Perc.-Hp.-Str.
    Durand, Paris, C1932
    Score 95 p.
    Composed 1929-31. First performance Paris,
    14 January 1932, Lamoureux Orchestra, the
    composer conducting, Marguerite Long soloist.

    Daphnis et Chloé. Fragments symphoniques
782 [Suite no. 1] Nocturne - Interlude -   10'
    Danse guerrière
783 [Suite no. 2] Lever du jour - Panto-   9'
    mine - Danse générale
    4(3rd alt. Picc., 1 in G; 2nd alt. Picc.II in
    Suite no. 2 only),3*,4*(1Cl. in E-flat),4*-
    4,4,3,1-Timp.,Perc.-Cel.,2Hp.-Chorus (SATB,
    ad lib.)-Str.
    Durand, Paris, C1911, C1913
    Scores: 66 p., 125 p.
    From the ballet composed 1909-11. First per-
    formance of Suite no. 1, Paris, 2 April 1911,
    Colonne Orchestra, Gabriel Pierné conductor.
    First performance of ballet Paris, 8 June 1912.

513m Introduction et allegro pour harpe   12'
    Solo Hp.-Fl.,Cl.-Str.(without Cb.)
    Durand, Paris, C1906
    Score 37 p.
    Composed 1905. First performance Paris, 22
    February 1907, Charles Domergue conductor,
    Micheline Kahn soloist.

781 [Ma mère l'Oye. (Mother Goose)   6'
    Prelude and spinning wheel dance]
    2(2nd alt. Picc.),2(2nd alt. E.H.),2,2-2Hn.-
    Timp.,Perc.-Cel.,Hp.-Str.
    Durand, Paris, C1912
    Score 28 p.
    Composed for piano 4-hands, 1908. Transcribed
    as a ballet and prelude added, 1911. First
    performance Paris, 28 January 1912, Gabriel
    Grovlez conductor.

408 [Ma mère l'Oye, 5 pieces for children]   14'
    1.[Pavan of Sleeping Beauty] 2.[Tom Thumb]
    3.[Laideronette] 4.[Discourse of the Beauty
    and the Beast] 5.[The enchanted garden]
    2(2nd alt. Picc.),2(2nd alt. E.H.),2,3*-2Hn.-
    Timp.,Perc.-Cel.,Hp.-Str.
    Durand, Paris, C1912
    Score 53 p.
    Orchestrated 1911.

4212 Menuet antique   ca.6'
    3*,3*,3*,3*-4,3,3,1-Timp.-Hp.-Str.
    Enoch, Paris, C1928, C1930
    Score 27 p.
    Originally composed for piano, 1895. Tran-
    scribed for orchestra, 1929. First perform-
    ance Paris, 11 January 1930, Lamoureux
    Orchestra, the composer conducting.

6205 La vallée des cloches/The valley   4'
    of bells, from Miroirs. Transcribed by Mario
    Castelnuovo-Tedesco
    3,2,3,2-4,2,3-Timp.,Perc.-Cel.,Hp.-Str.
    Associated Music Publishers, New York, C1955
    Score 16 p.

Miroirs composed for piano, 1904-05. This
transcription of the fifth movement made in
1950 at the request of Pierre Monteux for the
San Francisco Orchestra. First performance
Rome, 26 February 1956, Orchestra of the
National Academy of Saint Cecilia, Fernando
Previtali conductor.

567 Pavane pour une infante défunte   6'
    2,1,2,2-2Hn.-Hp.(or Pno.)-Str.
    Demets, Paris, C1910
    Score 7 p.
    Originally composed for piano, 1899. Tran-
    scribed 1910. First performance Paris, 25
    December 1911, Concerts Hasselmans, Alfredo
    Casella conductor.

268 Rapsodie espagnole   17'
    1.Prélude à la nuit, attacca 2.Malagueña
    3.Habanera 4.Feria
    4(2 are Picc.),3*,3*,3,Sarrus.-4,3,3,1-Timp.,
    Perc.-Cel.,2Hp.-Str.
    Durand, Paris, C1908
    Score 89 p.
    Rapsodie composed 1907. First performance
    Paris, 15 March 1908, Colonne Orchestra.

4955 [Sonatine for piano. Mouvement   4'
    de menuet. Transcribed for wind ensemble by
    Hershy Kay]
    2,2,2,2-2Hn.
    Ms.
    Score 4 p.
    Composed 1903-05. Transcribed 1946.

466 Le tombeau de Couperin, suite   14'
    d'orchestre
    1.Prélude 2.Forlane 3.Menuet 4.Rigaudon
    2(2nd alt. Picc.),2(2nd alt. E.H.),2,2-2,1-
    Hp.-Str.
    Durand, Paris, C1919
    Score 56 p.
    Excerpted and transcribed 1917 from the six
    movement piano suite, composed 1914-17.
    First performance Paris, 28 February 1920,
    Pasdeloup Orchestra, Rhené-Baton conductor.

453v Tzigane [Gypsy] rapsodie de concert
    Solo Vn.-2(2nd alt. Picc.),2,2,2-2,1-Perc.-
    Cel.,Hp.-Str.
    Durand, Paris, C1924
    Score 31 p.

456 La valse [Choreographic poem]   13'
    3(3rd alt. Picc.),3*,3*,3*-4,3,3,1-Timp.,Perc.
    -2Hp.-Str.
    Durand, Paris, C1921
    Score 132 p.
    Composed 1920. First performance Paris, 1922.

610 Valses nobles et sentimentales pour   15'
    orchestre
    8 movements
    2,3*,2,2-4,2,3,1-Timp.,Perc.-Cel.,2Hp.-Str.
    Durand, Paris [n.d.]
    Score 74 p.
    Composed for piano, 1910. Transcribed 1911.
    First performance Paris, 15 February 1914,
    Orchestre de Paris, Pierre Monteux conductor.

RAVINA, JEAN-HENRI.   Bordeaux 20 May 1818
                          Paris 30 September 1906

    1675s Andante, Op. 118 no. 2
    Org. or Harm.-Str.
    Zanibon, Padua [n.d.]
    Score 3 p.

    641s Andantino dans le style ancien, Op. 84
    Str.(without Cb.)
    Score: Ms. 7 p.
    Parts: B. Schott's Söhne, Mainz [n.d.]

    1674s Canto mistico, Op. 118 no. 1
    Org.-Str.
    Zanibon, Padua [n.d.]
    Score 4 p.

    894s Petit bolero, Op. 62
    Str.
    Score: Ms. 11 p.
    Parts: B. Schött's Sohne, Mainz [n.d.]
    Originally composed for piano.

    155s Scherzetto dans le style ancien, Op. 85
    Str.(without Cb.)
    Score: Ms. 5 p.
    Parts: B. Schott's Sohne, Mainz [n.d.]

RAYMOND, E. LANCELOT.

    209s Adagio
    Str.
    A. Lengnick, London [n.d.]
    Score 4 p.

RAZIGADE, GEORGES.

    1057s Amore estinto [Faded love] valse lente
    Str.
    Score: Ms. 11 p.
    Parts: Razigade, Bordeaux, ᶜ1912

    1055s Conte à la veillée [Bedtime story]
    Str.
    Score: Ms. 5 p.
    Parts: Razigade, Bordeaux, ᶜ1921

    1058s L'éternelle nuit, valse lente-intermezzo
    Str.
    Score: Ms. 9 p.
    Parts: Razigade, Bordeaux, ᶜ1927

    1062s Lontanetta [Music from a distance]
    Str.
    Score: Ms. 9 p.
    Parts: Razigade, Bordeaux, ᶜ1922

    1063s Papillons crépusculaires [Butterflies at
    twilight]
    Str.
    Score: Ms. 13 p.
    Parts: Razigade, Bordeaux, ᶜ1914

    728s [Puppets and jumping jacks, intermezzo]
    Str.
    Score: Ms. 8 p.
    Parts: Razigade, Bordeaux, ᶜ1912

    599s [Sylvia the rope-dancer]
    Str.
    Razigade, Bordeaux, ᶜ1925
    Score 6 p.

READ, GARDNER.   Evanston, Illinois 2 January 1913

    2086s Arioso elegiaca, Op. 91   *7'30"*
    Str.
    Ms. [ᶜ1971 by C.F. Peters, New York]
    Score 9 p.
    Composed 1950-51. Commissioned by the Zimbler
    String Sinfonietta and first performed by them,
    Boston, 8 April 1953.

    4496 A bell overture, Op. 72   *7'30"*
    3*,3*,3*,3*-4,3,3,1-Timp.,Perc.-Cel.,Hp.-Str.
    Ms. [Southern Music, New York, ᶜ1950]
    Score 29 p. Large folio
    Composed 1946. Commission and first perform-
    ance by the Cleveland Symphony Orchestra,
    Cleveland, 22 December 1946, Rudolph Ringwall
    conductor.

    5322 Chorale and fughetta, Op. 83a   *4'*
    4Hn.,4Cnt. or 4Tpt.,3Tbn.,2Bar.,Tuba
    Ms. [Robert D. King, North Easton, Mass.,ᶜ1957]
    Score 20 p.
    Originally composed for women's chorus and
    wind orchestra, 1949, as part of the composer's
    cantata In Grato Jubilo. This transcription
    1953. First performance Cincinnati, 1 Decem-
    ber 1954, Cincinnati Conservatory Brass Choir,
    Ernest Glover conductor.

    760c [Concerto, violoncello, Op. 55]   *25'*
    In one movement
    Solo Vc.-3*(2nd alt. Picc.II),3*,3*,2-4,3,3-
    Timp.,Perc.-Hp.-Str.
    Ms. [Associated Music Publishers, New York,
    ᶜ1946]
    Score 93 p. Large folio
    Composed 1939-45. First performance New Haven,
    14 October 1975, New Haven Symphony Orchestra,
    Erich Kunzel conductor, Barry Sills soloist.

    1100v [Fantasy, viola, Op. 38]   *10'*
    Solo Va.-3*,3*,2,2-4,3,3,1-Timp.,Perc.-Hp.-Str.
    Ms.
    Score 27 p. Large folio
    Composed 1935. First performance Rochester,
    22 April 1937, Rochester Civic Orchestra,
    Howard Hanson conductor, Julia Wilkinson
    soloist.

    4495 First overture, Op. 58   *8'*
    3*,3*,3*,3*-4,3,3,1-Timp.,Perc.-Pno.,Hp.-Str.
    Ms. [Composers Press, Philadelphia, ᶜ1949]
    Score 57 p. Large folio
    Commissioned by Fabien Sevitzky and Indianapo-
    lis Symphony Orchestra. Composed 1943. First
    performance Indianapolis, 6 November 1943,
    Indianapolis Symphony Orchestra, Fabien Sevit-
    zky conductor.

    797p Music for piano and strings, Op. 47a *24'*
    In one movement
    Solo Pno.-Str.

Read, Gardner

Ms.
Score 59 p.
Originally composed as Piano Quintet, Op. 47, 1937-45. Transcribed 1946. First performance New York, 12 February 1947, CBS Symphony Orchestra, Daniel Saidenburg conductor, Leonard Shure soloist.

4041 Night flight, tone poem, Op. 44   7'
3*,2,3*,3*-4,2,3,1-Timp.,Perc.-Hp.-Str.
Ms.
Score 22 p. Large folio
Inspired by Antoine de St.-Exupery's novel Night Flight. Composed 1936-42. First performance Rochester, 27 April 1944, Eastman-Rochester Symphony Orchestra, Howard Hanson conductor.

4858 Nine by six, suite for wind   15'30"
instruments, Op. 86
1.Fast and buoyant 2.Steadily and somberly
3.Lightly and carefree 4.Slowly and solemnly
- Spiritedly
1(alt. Picc.),1(alt. E.H.),1(alt. B.Cl.),1-Hn.,Tpt.
Ms. [c1973 by C.F. Peters, New York]
Score 38 p. Large folio
Composed 1950. First performance Boston, 27 April 1951, New England Conservatory of Music student ensemble, the composer conducting.

3382 Pan e Dafni, Op. 53   10'
4*(1Alto Fl. in G),3*,3*,3*-4,0,3,1-Timp.,
Perc.-Hp.-Str.
Ms.
Score 30 p. Large folio
Composed 1940.

4218 Partita, Op. 70   11'
1.Allegro giusto 2.Larghetto 3.Allegro molto energico
1,1,1,1-1,1,1-Timp.-Str.
Ms. [Southern Music, New York, c1950]
Score 32 p. Large folio
Composed 1946. First performance Eastman School of Music, Rochester, 4 May 1947.

2906 [Passacaglia and fugue, organ,   12'
Op. 34a, D minor. Transcribed for orchestra]
3*(2nd alt. 2nd Picc),3*,3*,3*-4,3,3,1-Timp.-Cel.,Hp.-Str.
Ms.
Score 60 p.
Originally composed 1935-36; transcribed upon commission by the Ravinia Festival Association. First performance Ravinia Park, Illinois, 30 June 1938, Chicago Symphony Orchestra, Artur Rodzinski conductor.

4548 Pennsylvaniana, Op. 67   16'
1.Dunlap's Creek 2.I'm a Beggar 3.John Riley
4*,3*,3*,3*(or 3*,2,2,2)-4,3,3,1-Timp.,Perc.-Pno.,Hp.(both optional)-Str.
Ms.
Score 81 p. Large folio
Based on three melodies of western Pennsylvania. Commissioned by the Pittsburgh Symphony Orchestra. Composed 1946-47. First

performance Pittsburgh, 21 November 1947, Pittsburgh Symphony Orchestra, Fritz Reiner conductor.

4478 Petite pastorale, Op. 40a   2'
1,1,2,2-2Hn.-Str.
Ms. [c1941 by Gardner Read]
Score 3 p. Large folio
Originally composed for piano, 1936, as Op. 40. This transcription, 1940. First performance Interlochen, 1 August 1940, Faculty Little Symphony of National Music Camp, Guy Fraser Harrison conductor.

1039m Poem, for horn in F or viola, Op. 31b 3'
Solo Hn. or Solo Va.-Hp.-Str.
Ms. [C. Fischer, New York, c1945]
Score 4 p. Large folio
Originally composed for French horn and piano, 1934, as Op. 31. Transcribed for viola and piano, 1940, as Op. 31a. This transcription, 1946.

2790 Prelude and toccata, Op. 43   7'
2*,2,2,2-2,2,2-Timp.-Str.
Ms.
Score 26 p. Large folio
Composed 1936-37. First performance Rochester, 29 April 1937, Rochester Philharmonic Orchestra, Howard Hanson conductor.

1941s Quiet music for strings, Op. 65   9'30"
Str.
Ms.
Score 13 p.
Composed 1946. First performance Washington, D.C., 9 May 1948, National Gallery Orchestra, Richard Bales conductor.

2824 Sketches of the city, symphonic   15'
suite, Op. 26, after poems of Carl Sandburg
1.Fog 2.Nocturne in a deserted brickyard
3.Prayers of steel
4*(3rd alt. Alto Fl.),3*,3*,3*-4,3,3,1-Timp.,
Perc.-Cel.,2Hp.-Str.
Ms.
Score 40 p. Large folio
Composed 1933. First performance Rochester, 18 April 1934, Rochester Civic Orchestra, Howard Hanson conductor.

4743 Sound piece for brass and   5'30"
percussion, Op. 82
4Hn.,4Tpt.,3Tbn.,Bar.,2Tuba-Timp.,Perc.
Music for Brass [Robert D. King] North Easton, Mass. c1950 by Gardner Read
Score 10 p.
Composed 1949. First performance Boston, 11 May 1949, Boston University Brass Ensemble, the composer conducting.

1745s Suite, Op. 33a   12'
1.Prelude 2.Scherzetto 3.Sarabande 4.Rondo
Str.
Ms.
Score 15 p. Large folio
Originally composed for string quartet, 1935; transcribed for string orchestra, 1937. First

concert performance at the Saratoga Spa Music
Festival, Saratoga Springs, New York, 14 September 1937, string players from the New York
Philharmonic, F. Charles Adler conductor.

2883 Symphony no. 1, Op. 30   40'
1.Lento mistico - Allegro molto deciso 2.Largo
e molto espressivo 3.Allegro vivace 4.Allegro
feroce
3(2nd alt. Alto Fl.,3rd alt. Picc.),3*,3*,3*
-4,3,3,1-Timp.,Perc.-Cel.,2Hp.-Str.
Ms.
Score 137 p.
Composed 1934-36. First performance New York,
4 November 1937, New York Philharmonic, John
Barbirolli conductor. Awarded first prize in
the American Composers' Contest sponsored by
the New York Philharmonic, 1937.

4051 Symphony no. 2, Op. 45   25'
1.Presto assai e molto feroce 2.Adagio
3.Largamente - Allegro risoluto e molto
energico
3*,3*,3*,3*-4,3,3,1-Timp.,Perc.-Hp.-Str.
Ms.
Score 110 p. Large folio
Composed 1940-42. First performance Boston,
26 November 1943, Boston Symphony Orchestra,
the composer conducting. Awarded first prize
in the Paderewski Fund Prize Competition,
1943.

5338 Symphony no. 3, Op. 75   23'
1.Introduction and passacaglia 2.Scherzo
3.Chorale and fugue
3*,3*,3*,3*-4,3,3,1-Timp.,Perc.-Pno.-Str.
Ms.
Score 84 p. Large folio
Composed 1946-48. First performance Pittsburgh, 2 March 1962, Pittsburgh Symphony
Orchestra, William Steinberg conductor.

6551 Symphony no. 4, Op. 92   27'
1.Largo, con intenzita - Appassionato molto
2.Lento sostenuto - Allegro scherzando
3*,3*,3*,3*-4,3,3,1-Timp.,Perc.-Str.
Ms.
Score 106 p. Large folio
Composed 1951-58. First performance Cincinnati, 30 January 1970, Cincinnati Symphony
Orchestra, Erich Kunzel conductor.

5531 The temptation of St. Anthony,   35'
a dance symphony in 4 scenes, Op. 56
3*,3*,3*,3*-4,3,3,1-Timp.,Perc.-Cel.,Hp.-Str.
Ms.
Score 110 p. Large folio
Suggested by Gustave Flaubert's novel. Composed 1940-47. First performance Chicago, 9
April 1953, Chicago Symphony Orchestra,
Rafael Kubelik conductor.

3762 Three satirical sarcasms, Op. 29a   7'
1.Ironical march 2.Is it a waltz? 3.Eccentric dance
3*,3*,3*,3*-3,3,3,1-Timp.,Perc.-Pno.-Str.
Ms.
Score 24 p. Large folio

Originally composed for piano, 1934-35;
transcribed, 1941. First performance Rochester,
27 October 1942, Eastman-Rochester Symphony
Orchestra, Howard Hanson conductor.

1045m Threnody, Op. 66a   5'
Solo Fl.-Hp.-Str.
Ms.
Score 13 p.
Originally composed for flute and piano, 1946.
This transcription 1946. First performance
Eastman School of Music, Rochester, 21 October 1946.

5336 Toccata giocosa, Op. 94   6'30"
2(2nd alt. Picc.),2,2,2-4,2,3,1-Timp.,Perc.-
Hp.-Str.
Ms. Alec Templeton, New York, C1954, C1964
Score 104 p. Large folio
Commissioned by the Louisville Orchestra.
Composed 1953. First performance Louisville,
13 March 1954, Louisville Orchestra, Robert
Whitney conductor.

5323 Vernal equinox, Op. 96 [tone poem]   10'
2,2*,2,2-4,3,3-Timp.,Perc.-Cel.,Hp.-Str.
Ms.
Score 27 p.
Commissioned by the Brockton Orchestral
Society. Composed 1955. First performance
Brockton, Massachusetts, 12 April 1955,
Brockton Orchestral Society, Moshe Paranov
conductor.

REBIKOV, VLADIMIR IVANOVICH.
                 Krasnoyarsk, Siberia 31 May 1866
                 Yalta 4 August 1920

930s [Autumn leaves, piano, Op. 29. Transcribed
for strings]
Str.
P. Jurgenson, Moscow [n.d.]
Score 15 p.

931s [The Christmas tree, Op. 21. Waltz]
Str.
P. Jurgenson, Moscow [n.d.]
Score 5 p.
From the ballet composed 1902. First performance Moscow, 30 October 1903.

1512 [The Christmas tree. Suite, Op. 21a]   14'
1.[Waltz] 2.[Procession of the gnomes]
3.[The harlequins' dance] 4.[Dance of the
Chinese dolls] 5.[Angels' ladder] 6.[Dark
night]
2,2*,2,2-4,3,3,1-Timp.,Perc.-Cel.,Hp.-Str.
P. Jurgenson, Moscow [n.d.]
Score 75 p.
From the ballet. Composed 1902. First performance Moscow, 1903.

176s Les feux du soir [suite for piano.
Transcribed for strings]
Str.
P. Jurgenson, Moscow [n.d.]
Score 14 p.

Rebikov, Vladimir

1110s [Hindustani night, from Autour du monde, for piano, Op. 9. Transcribed for strings]
Str.
P. Jurgenson, Moscow [n.d.]
Score 5 p.

251s [Mélomimiques, three scenes for piano, Op. 11, from the story, Mila et Nolli, by N. Wagner. Transcribed for strings]
1.[Mila's death] 2.[Mila's burial] 3.[Nolli's thoughts]
Str.
P. Jurgenson, Moscow [n.d.]
Score 9 p.

250s Rêveries d'automne, album de miniatures, piano, Op. 8 [Transcribed for strings]
1.Le dernier rendez-vous 2.Berceuse
3.Journée d'automne 4.Le repentir
5.Souvenir douloureux 6.Bouffonnerie
Str.
P. Jurgenson, Moscow [n.d.]
Score 19 p.

324 Suite miniature [no. 1]   10'
1.Berceuse 2.La rêvue 3.Moment triste
4.Tarentelle
2,1,2,2-2,2,1-Timp.,Perc.-Str.
P. Jurgenson, Moscow [n.d.]
Score 29 p.
Composed 1898. First performance Kischinev, 1898, the composer conducting.

657 Suite miniature no. 2   9'
1.[Dance of the odalisques] 2.[Characteristic dance] 3.[Oriental dance] 4.[Etude]
2,2(2nd alt. E.H.),2,2-4,2,1-Timp.,Perc.-Str.
P. Jurgenson, Moscow [n.d.]
Score 34 p.
Composed and first performed Moscow, 1903.

REBLING, GUSTAV.   Barby, Germany 10 July 1821
                         Magdeburg 9 January 1902

660c [Elegie, violoncello, Op. 32, F major]
Solo Vc.-2,2,2,2-2Hn.-Timp.-Str.
Score: Ms. 25 p.
Parts: Breitkopf & Härtel, Leipzig [n.d.]

Zwei Stücke, Op. 49
877v No. 1. Romanze [G major]
Solo Vn.-2,2,2,2-2Hn.-Str.
878v No. 2. Ballade [D minor]
Solo Vn.-2,2,2,2-2,0,3-Str.
Heinrichshofen, Magdeburg [n.d.]
Scores: 19 p., 19 p.

REED, ALFRED.   New York City 25 January 1921

7065 Passacaglia for concert band   11'
3*,3*(E.H. optional),7*(Cl. in E-flat, Alto Cl.,Cb.Cl.),3*(C.Bn. optional)-4Sax.-4,3, 2Cnt.,4,Bar.,2-Timp.,Perc.-Hp.(optional)-Cb.
Frank Music Corporation, New York, C1967
Score 39 p.
Composed 1966.

367v Rhapsody, viola and orchestra   15'
In one movement

Solo Va.-3(3rd alt. Picc.),3*,4*(1Cb.Cl. in B-flat or C.Bn.),2-4,3,3,1-Timp.,Perc.-Hp.-Str.
Ms. [C1966, Boosey & Hawkes, New York]
Score 67 p. Large folio
Composed 1954-56 at the request of Milton Katims. First performance Bloomington, Indiana, 6 May 1959, Indiana University Symphony Orchestra, Tibor Kozma conductor, David Dawson soloist. Awarded the Luria Prize, School of Music of Indiana University, 1959.

REED, HERBERT OWEN.   Odessa, Missouri 17 June 1910

766c Concerto, violoncello and orchestra   19'
In one movement
Solo Vc.-3*,2,2,3*-4,3,3,1-Timp.,Perc.-Str.
Composers Press, New York, C1951
Score 47 p.
Composed 1948-49. First performance East Lansing, 18 November 1956, Michigan State University Symphony Orchestra, the composer conducting, Louis Potter, Jr., soloist. Won the 1949 Symphonic Award sponsored by Composers Press.

3089 Evangeline [after Longfellow]   15'
1.The village of Grand Pré 2.Exile
3*,3*,2,2-4,3,3,1-Timp.,Perc.-Cel.,Hp.-Str.
Ms.
Score 70 p. Large folio
Composed 1938. First performance Rochester, 30 March 1938, Rochester Civic Orchestra, Howard Hanson conductor.

3488 Overture   6'
2,2,2,2-4,3,3,1-Timp.,Perc.-Str.
Ms.
Score 38 p. Large folio
Composed 1940. First performance as Overture: 1940, Rochester, 27 October 1941, Eastman-Rochester Symphony Orchestra, Howard Hanson conductor.

3088 Symphony no. 1   20'
1.Allegro 2. ♩=88 3.Largamente con moto
3*,3*,3*,2-4,3,3,1-Timp.,Perc.-Str.
Ms.
Score 119 p. Large folio
Composed 1939. First performance Rochester, 27 April 1939, Rochester Philharmonic Orchestra, Howard Hanson conductor.

REED, WILLIAM HENRY.   Frome, England 29 July 1876
                        Dumfries, Scotland 2 July 1942

1121s Suite for string orchestra
1.Idylle 2.Valse caractéristique 3.Finale
Str.
Score: Ms. 49 p.
Parts: Novello, London, C1908

REESEN, EMIL.   Copenhagen 30 May 1887
                       Copenhagen(?) 1964

2149s [Two Danish folksongs for strings]
1.[Agnete and the merman] 2.[I went out on a

summer day]
Str.
Edition Dania, Copenhagen, ^c1937
Score 6 p.
Composed 1936. First performance Copenhagen,
September 1936, Danish State Radio Orchestra.

REGAMEY, CONSTANTIN.   Kiev, Russia 28 January 1907

6270 [Five études]   17'
Sop. Voice Solo - 2(2nd alt. Picc.),1,1,1-
Alto Sax.-2,1-Perc.-Pno.,Hp.-Str.
Impero, Wiesbaden, ^c1959
Score 79 p.
Texts are poems of ancient India. Commissioned
by Südwestfunk, Baden Baden, West Germany.
Originally composed for soprano voice and
piano, 1955. Transcribed 1956. First per-
formance Zurich, June 1957, Festival of the
International Society for Contemporary Music,
Studio-Orchester Beromünster.

REGER, MAX.   Brand, Bavaria 19 March 1873
                         Leipzig 11 May 1916

750v [Aria, Op. 103a no. 3]
Solo Vn.-1,1,1,1-Hn.-Str.
Lauterbach & Kuhn, Leipzig, ^c1908
Score 6 p.
Originally composed 1907 as part of the Suite
in A minor for violin and piano, Op. 103.

1192 Eine Ballettsuite, Op. 130   11'
1.Entrée 2.Colombine 3.Harlequin 4.Pierrot
und Pierrette 5.Valse d'amour 6.Finale
2,2,2,2-4,2-Timp.,Trgl.-Str.
C.F. Peters, Leipzig, ^c1913
Score 119 p.
Composed 1913. First performance Bremen, Octo-
ber 1913, Ernst Wendel conductor.

1194s [Christmas, Op. 145 no. 3c] Edited by
Otto Meyer
Str.
H. Oppenheimer, Hameln [n.d.]
Score 5 p.
Originally composed for organ.

836v [Concerto, violin, Op. 101, A major]
1.Allegro moderato 2.Largo con gran espres-
sione 3.Allegro moderato
Solo Vn.-2,2,2,2-4,2-Timp-Str.
C.F. Peters, Leipzig, ^c1908
Score 175 p.

1811 [Four tone poems, Op. 128, after   19'
A. Böcklin]
1.[The fiddling hermit] 2.[Sport of the
waves] 3.[The Isle of the dead] 4.[Bacchanals]
3(3rd alt. Picc.),2(2nd alt. E.H.),2,3-4,3,3,1
-Timp.,Perc.-Hp.-Str.
Bote & Bock, Berlin, ^c1913
Score 93 p.
Composed 1913. First performance Essen,
November 1913, Ernst Schuch conductor.

859v Gavotte, Op. 103a no. 2. Transcribed   8'
by Wilhelm Tschinkel
Solo Vn.-2(2nd alt. Picc.),1,1,1-2Hn.-Str.

Bote & Bock, Berlin, ^c1921
Score 6 p.
From the composer's Suite in A minor, Op. 103,
composed 1907 for violin and piano.

1138s Romanze [harmonium, A minor. Transcribed
by Richard Lange]
Str.
Carl Simon, Berlin, ^c1908
Score 3 p.

956 [Suite, G minor. Transcribed by Max Reger
from several works by J.S. Bach]
1.Grave - Allegro 2.Sarabande 3.Courante
4.Bourrée 5.Gigue
2,2,0,2-2Tpt.-Timp.-Str.
Peters, Leipzig, ^c1916
Score 39 p.

1231 Variationen und Fuge über ein   25'
Thema von Mozart, Op. 132
3,2,2,2-4,2-Timp.-Hp.-Str.
N. Simrock, Berlin [n.d.]
Score 98 p.
Composed 1914. First performance Berlin, 5
February 1915, the composer conducting.

1833 Eine Vaterländische Ouverture,   8'
Op. 140
3(3rd alt. Picc.),2,2,3*-4,5,5,1-Timp.,Perc.-
Org.-Str.
N. Simrock, Berlin, ^c1914
Score 60 p.
Composed 1914. First performance Berlin, 5
February 1915, the composer conducting.

Zwei Romanzen, Op. 50
814v No. 1 [G major]   5'
815v No. 2 [D major]   6'
Solo Vn.-2,2,2,2-2Hn.-Timp.-Str.
Jos. Aibl, Munich, ^c1901
Scores: 31 p., 35 p.

REGNAL, FRÉDÉRIC. pseudonym.
See: ERLANGER, BARON FRÉDÉRIC D'.

REHBAUM, THEOBALD.   Berlin 7 August 1835
                                Berlin 2 February 1918

628s Aria, Op. 26 [F major]
Str.
Carl Simon, Berlin, ^c1895
Score 3 p.

REICH, SCOTT.   Philadelphia 24 September 1954

7281 Abysmal love (continued):   8'
The garden of optimistic fatalism
In one movement
2(alt. 2Picc.),2(2nd alt. E.H.),2*,1-Sop.Sax.
(alt. Alto & Ten.Sax.)-1,1,1-Perc.-Electric
Pno.(alt. Pno.),Electric Guit.(alt. Guit.),
B.Guit.-Str.
Ms. ^c1976 by Scott Reich
Score 20 p.
Composed 1976.

Reicha, Anton

REICHA, ANTON.　　　　　Prague 26 February 1770
　　　　　　　　　　　　　Paris 28 May 1836

4104　Sinfonie [Op. 41, E-flat major]
　　1.Largo - Allegro spiritoso　2.Un poco adagio
　　3.Allegro　4.Un poco vivo
　　1,2,0,2-2Hn.-Timp.-Str.
　　Ms.
　　Score 91 p.

4105　[Sinfonie, Op. 42, E-flat major]
　　1.Allegro assai　2.Adagio　3.Allegro
　　(Menuetto)　4.Allegro scherzando
　　1,2,2,2-2Hn.-Timp.-Str.
　　Ms.
　　Score 87 p.

REICHA, JOSEPH.　　　　　Klatovy, Bohemia 1746
　　　　　　　　　　　　　Bonn 1795

714c　[Concerto, violoncello, Op. 2 no. 1,
　　E-flat major]
　　1.Allegro　2.Romance　3.Rondo
　　Solo Vc.-2Ob.-2Hn.-Str.
　　Ms.
　　Score 79 p.

708c　[Concerto, violoncello, Op. 4 no. 1,
　　A major]
　　1.Allegro moderato　2.Largo　3.Rondo
　　Solo Vc.-2Ob.-2Hn.-Str.
　　Ms.
　　Score 61 p.

288v　[Concerto concertante, 2 violins, Op. 3,
　　D major] Edited by Bernhard Päuler
　　1.Allegro　2.Romanze　3.Rondo
　　2 Solo Vn.-2Ob.-2Hn.-Str.
　　Edition Eulenburg, Zurich, ᶜ1970
　　Score 72 p.
　　First published by Simrock, Bonn, ca.1795.

REICHARDT, OSSIAN.

1258s　Andante religioso, Op. 15
　　Solo Vn., Solo Vc.-Org.(or Harm.)-Str.
　　H. Oppenheimer, Hameln [n.d.]
　　Score 3 p.

REICHE, EUGEN.

652m　[Concerto, trombone, no. 2, A major]　*12'*
　　1.Allegro maestoso　2.Adagio　3.Rondo
　　Solo Tbn.-2,2,2,2-4,2,3(or 2 & Tuba)-Timp.-Str.
　　Zimmermann, Leipzig [1906?]
　　Score in reduction 15 p.

REICHEL, BERNARD.
　　　　　b. Neuchâtel, Switzerland 3 August 1901

5345　Suite symphonique (1954)　　　　*22'*
　　1.Molto moderato - Allegro　2.Adagio　3.Tempo
　　di siciliano　4.Finale
　　2(2nd alt. Picc.),2(2nd alt. E.H.),2,2-4,2,3,1
　　-Timp.,Perc.-Cel.,Hp.-Str.
　　Ms.
　　Score 114 p. Large folio
　　Commissioned by the Louisville Philharmonic
　　Society. Composed 1954-55. First performance

Louisville, 11 June 1955, Louisville Orchestra,
Robert Whitney conductor.

REICHERT, F.

906m　Fantasie [for clarinet and orchestra]
　　Solo Cl.-1(alt. Picc.),2,2,2-2,2,1-Timp.,Trgl.
　　-Str.
　　Score: Ms. 73 p.
　　Parts: A.E. Fischer, Bremen [n.d.]

REIFF, LILI SARTORIUS.
　　　　　　　b. Bamberg, Germany 21 June 1866

5141　Präludium und Walzer für Orchester
　　2(2nd alt. Picc.),2,2,2-4,3,3,1-Timp.,Perc.-
　　Cel.,Hp.-Str.
　　Ms.
　　Score 49 p.

5155　[Spanish procession]
　　2(2nd alt. Picc.),3*,2,2-4,2,3,1-Timp.,Perc.-
　　Org.,Hp.-Str.
　　Ms.
　　Score 30 p.

2062s　[Three round dances]
　　Hp.-Str.
　　Ms.
　　Score 17 p.

REINAGLE, ALEXANDER.　　　Portsmouth, England
　　　　　　　　　　　　　baptized 23 April 1756
　　　　　　　　　　　　　Baltimore 21 September 1809

7040　I have a silent sorrow here. Tran-　　*3'*
　　scribed by Philip Weston
　　High Voice-Fl.,Ob.,2Cl.,Bn.-Str.
　　Concord Music Publishing, New York, ᶜ1941
　　Score in reduction 5 p.
　　Song with text by Richard Brinsley Sheridan.
　　Originally composed for voice and piano.

7113　Federal march. As performed in the　　*3'*
　　grand procession in Philadelphia the 4th of
　　July 1788. Transcribed by Sam Dennison
　　2(2nd alt. Picc.),2,2,2-2,2,3(1B.Tbn.or Tuba)-
　　Timp.-Str.
　　Ms. ᶜ1975 by Sam Dennison
　　Score 6 p.
　　Composed 1788 (instrumentation unknown; score
　　and parts lost). Performed as part of the
　　celebration commemorating the ratification of
　　the Constitution of the U.S. by 10 of the 13
　　states. This transcription 1975 from the
　　first published edition for piano.

2381s　Madison's march *and* Mrs.　　　*4'*
　　Madison's minuet. Transcribed for strings
　　by Sam Dennison
　　Str.
　　Ms. ᶜ1975 by Sam Dennison
　　Score 6 p.
　　Madison's March composed 1809. Mrs. Madison's
　　Minuet composed 1796. Transcription from an
　　early published edition for piano.

REINECKE, CARL HEINRICH CARSTEN.
Altona, Germany 23 June 1824
Leipzig 10 March 1910

645m Ballade, Op. 288   9'
  Solo Fl.-2,2,2,2-2,2-Timp.,Perc.-Str.
  Zimmermann, Leipzig, ^C1911
  Score in reduction 13 p.

  [Biblical pictures, Op. 220]
6963 Part I: No. 1 Ruth and Boaz; no. 4, Jacob's
  dream; no. 5, Judas Maccabeus
6964 Part II: No. 8, The shepherds in the fields;
  no. 9, Journey to Bethlehem; no. 10, Repose of
  the holy family; no. 13, The marriage at Cana
  2,2,2,2-4,2,3-Timp.,Perc.-Str.
  Zimmermann, Leipzig, ^C1894
  Scores: 33 p., 40 p.
  Transcribed from a suite for piano.

762m [Concerto, flute, Op. 283, D major]   18'
  1.Allegro molto moderato 2.Lento 3.Finale
  Solo Fl.-2,2,2,2-4,2-Timp.,Trgl.-Str.
  Ms.
  Score 131 p.
  *Composed 1908. First performance London, 9
  September 1909, Henry Wood conductor.*

526m [Concerto, harp, Op. 182, E minor]   23'
  1.Allegro moderato 2.Adagio 3.Scherzo
  Solo Hp.-2,2,2,2-4,2-Timp.,Trgl.-Str.
  N. Simrock, Berlin [n.d.]
  Score 123 p.
  *Composed 1884. First performance Leipzig, 16
  October 1884, the composer conducting, Edmund
  Schuecker soloist.*

519p [Concerto, piano, Op. 72, F-sharp   32'
  minor]
  1.Allegro 2.Adagio 3.Allegro con brio
  Solo Pno.-2,2,2,2-2,2-Timp.-Str.
  Breitkopf & Härtel, Leipzig [n.d.]
  Score 80 p.
  *Composed 1860. First performance Leipzig, 24
  October 1861, Ferdinand David conductor, the
  composer as soloist.*

435p [Concerto, piano, no. 2, Op. 120,   22'
  E minor]
  1.Allegro 2.Andantino 3.Allegro brillante
  Solo Pno.-2,2,2,2-2,2-Timp.-Str.
  Score: Ms. 252 p.
  Parts: Fr. Kistner, Leipzig [n.d.]
  *Composed 1872. First performance Leipzig, 14
  November 1872, Ferdinand David conductor, the
  composer as soloist.*

643p [Concerto, piano, no. 3, Op. 144,   29'
  C major]
  1.Allegro 2.Largo 3.Allegro vivace e
  grazioso
  Solo Pno.-2,2,2,2-4,2-Timp.-Str.
  C.F.W. Siegel, Leipzig [n.d.]
  Score 196 p.
  *Composed 1877. First performance Leipzig, 11
  October 1877, Ferdinand David conductor, the
  composer as soloist.*

628p [Concerto, piano, Op. 254, B minor]   19'
  1.Allegro 2.Adagio 3.Allegretto
  Solo Pno.-1,2,2,2-2,2-Timp.-Str.
  Score: Ms. 103 p.
  Parts: Zimmermann, Leipzig, ^C1901
  *Composed 1901. First performance Leipzig,
  1902, Hans Sitt conductor, Charlotte Bresch
  soloist.*

780v [Concerto, violin, Op. 141, G minor]   28'
  1.Allegro moderato 2.Lento 3.Moderato con
  grazia
  Solo Vn.-2,2,2,2-2,2,3-Timp.-Str.
  Breitkopf & Härtel, Leipzig [n.d.]
  Score 133 p.
  *Composed 1876. First performance Leipzig, 21
  December 1876, Gewandhaus Orchestra, the com-
  poser conducting, Joseph Joachim soloist.*

687p [Concertstück, piano, Op. 33, G minor]
  1.[No tempo indicated] 2.Lento 3.Allegro
  Solo Pno.-2,2,2,2-2,2,3-Timp.-Str.
  Score: Ms. 109 p.
  Parts: J. Schuberth, Leipzig [n.d.]

5432 [Dame Kobold, overture to the play   8'
  by Calderón de la Barca, Op. 51]
  2,2,2,2-2,2-Timp.-Str.
  Breitkopf & Härtel, Leipzig [185-?]
  Score 64 p.

5601 [Five tone pictures for orchestra]
  2,2,2,2-4,3,3-Timp.,Trgl.-Str.
  Breitkopf & Härtel, Leipzig [1882]
  Score 31 p.
  *Movements 1 and 2 are excerpts from the opera
  König Manfred. Movement 3 is an excerpt from
  the incidental music to Schiller's play Wil-
  helm Tell, Op. 102. Movements 4 and 5 are
  excerpts from Sommertagsbilder, Op. 161.
  Movement 4 inspired by a poem by J. Altmann;
  Movement 5 by a poem by Heinrich Heine.*

5010 [Jubilee overture for orchestra, Op. 166]
  3*,2,2,Basset Hn.(ad lib.),2-4,2,3-Timp.-Str.
  Breitkopf & Härtel, Leipzig [1882]
  Score 72 p.
  *Composed 1881 for the 100th anniversary cele-
  bration of the Gewandhaus Concerts, Leipzig,
  of which Reinecke was music director.*

434v Kinderträume [Child's dreams]   5'
  Op. 202 no. 1, from the cycle Von der Wiege
  bis zum Grabe. Edited by H.W. Nicholl
  Solo Vn.-2,0,2-4Hn.-Timp.-Str.
  E. Schuberth, New York, ^C1888
  Score 15 p.
  *Composed 1888. First performance Leipzig, 9
  February 1890, the composer conducting. Also
  available for string orchestra as Catalog no.
  178s.*

  [King Manfred, Op. 93]
5382 [Overture]
  3*,2,2,2-4,2,3-Timp.-Hp.-Str.
5224 [Ballet music]
  3*,2,2,2-4,2,3,1-Timp.,Perc.-Hp.-4Women's Voices
  -Str.

Reinecke, Carl

778v Romanze (Introduction, Act IV)
Solo Vn.-2,0,2,2-Timp.-Str.
Breitkopf & Härtel, Leipzig [n.d.]
Scores: 80 p., 35 p., 5 p.
From the opera in five acts, composed 1866.
First performance Wiesbaden, 26 July 1867.

612m Notturno, Op. 112
Solo Hn.-2,1,2,2-2Hn.-Timp.-Str.
Fr. Kistner, Leipzig [n.d.]
Score 17 p.

779v Romanze, Op. 155 [A minor]
Solo Vn.-2,2,2,2-2Hn.-Timp.-Str.
Breitkopf & Härtel, Leipzig [n.d.]
Score 39 p.

637c [Romanzero, violoncello, Op. 263,   *16'*
A minor]
Solo Vc.-2(2nd alt. Picc.),2,2,2-4,2-Timp.-
Hp.(ad lib.)-Str.
Score: Ms. 86 p.
Parts: Reinecke, Leipzig [n.d.]
Composed 1902. First performance Leipzig, 20
January 1906, Winderstein conductor, Julius
Klengel soloist.

135s Serenade, Op. 242
1.Marcia 2.Arioso 3.Scherzo 4.Cavatine
5.Fughetta giojosa 6.Finale
Str.
Zimmermann, Leipzig, ^c1898
Score 27 p.

5007 [Solemn prologue in the form of an
overture, Op. 223]
2,2,2,2-4,3,3,1-Timp.-Str.
Breitkopf & Härtel, Leipzig, ^c1894
Score 57 p.
Composed 1893 for the 150th anniversary cele-
bration of the Leipzig Gewandhaus Concerts, of
which Reinecke was music director.

5054 [Symphony no. 1, Op. 79, A major]   *24'*
1.Lento - Allegro con brio 2.Andante
3.Scherzo 4.Finale
2,2,2,2-4,2,3-Timp.-Str.
Breitkopf & Härtel, Leipzig [1864]
Score 154 p.

5092 [Zenobia, overture, Op. 193]
2,2,2,2-4,2,3-Timp.-Str.
Breitkopf & Härtel, Leipzig and Brussels [1887]
Score 41 p.
Overture to Julius Leopold Klein's play
Zenobia.

486s Zwölf Tonbilder [12 tone pictures]
Str.
Breitkopf & Härtel, Leipzig [n.d.]
Score 27 p.
Collected from earlier works.

REINHARDT, C., JR.

1296s Klänge vom Gebirge [Mountain echoes]
2 Solo Vn.-Str.
Score: Ms. 13 p.
Parts: Louis Oertel, Hannover [n.d.]

REINHOLD, HUGO.   Vienna 3 March 1854
                         Vienna 4 September 1935

291s Praeludium, Menuett und Fuge, Op. 10
Str.
Kistner, Leipzig [n.d.]
Score 27 p.

550p Suite, Op. 7 [E-flat major]   *24'*
Pno.-Str.
Kistner, Leipzig [n.d.]
Score 59 p.
First performance Vienna, 9 December 1877, at
a Philharmonic Concert.

REINWARTH, R.

600s Sie tanzt im Traum
Str.
Bellman & Thümer, Dresden [n.d.]
Score 8 p.

REISE, JAY.   New York 9 February 1950

7200 Hieronymo is mad againe   *13'*
3*,3*,3*(1Cl. in E-flat alt. 2nd Cl. in A),3*-
4,3,3,1-Timp.,Perc.-Pno.,Cel.,Hp.-Str.
Ms. ^c1976 by Jay Reise
Score 53 p. Large folio
Title refers to Thomas Kyd's The Spanish Tra-
gedy. Composed 1975. Selected for performance
by the Orchestra Society of Philadelphia as
part of its Pennsylvania Composers Project
1976, made possible by a grant from the Penn-
sylvania Council for the Arts with performance
materials prepared by The Fleisher Collection
of Orchestral Music. First performance, Dre-
xel University, Philadelphia, 25 April 1976,
Orchestra Society of Philadelphia, Sidney
Rothstein conductor.

7143 Concerto for nine players   *15'*
In one movement with cadenzas
Alto Fl.,Cl.-Perc.-Pno.4-hands-Vn.,Cb.
Ms. ^c1975 by Jay Reise
Score 60 p.
Composed 1975. First performance Tanglewood-
Lenox, Massachusetts, 18 August 1975, Berk-
shire Music Center Chamber Players, David
Stahl conductor. Awarded the Koussevitzky
Tanglewood Prize in composition, 1975.

REISER, ALOIS.   Prague 4 April 1884

736c [Concerto, violoncello, Op. 14]   *35'*
1.Sostenuto 2.Andante molto sostenuto
3.Allegro con fuoco
Solo Vc.-3*,2,3*,2-4,2-Timp.,Trgl.-Hp.-Str.
Ms.
Score 162 p.
Composed 1919. First performance Los Angeles,
23 March 1933, Los Angeles Philharmonic Orches-
tra, Artur Rodzinski conductor, Ilya Bronson
soloist. Received honorable mention in the
Hollywood Bowl competition, 1932.

2719 Erewhon, Op. 19   *17'*
3*,3*,3*,3*-4,3,3,1-Timp.,Perc.-Hp.-Str.

Ms.
Score 51 p.
*Composed 1934. First performance Los Angeles,
24 January 1936, Los Angeles Federal Symphony
Orchestra of the WPA, the composer conducting.*

2699 Evening of summer, symphonic idyll,   *15'*
Op. 8
3*,3*,3*,2-4,0,2Cnt.(or 2Tpt.)3,1-Timp.,Bells,
Cym.-Str.
Ms.
Score 33 p.
*Composed 1910. First performance Prague,
August 1911, Prague Philharmonic Orchestra,
W. Zemanek conductor.*

2746 Slavic rhapsody, Op. 15   *30'*
3*,3*,3*,3*-4,3,3,1-Timp.,Perc.-Hp.-Str.
Ms.
Score 95 p.
*Composed 1915. First performance Los Angeles,
8 March 1931, Los Angeles Philharmonic Orchestra, the composer conducting.*

REISSIGER, KARL GOTTLIEB.   Belzig,
        near Wittenberg, Germany 31 January 1798
                    Dresden 7 November 1859

832m [Concertino, clarinet, Op. 63, E-flat
major]
1.Allegro moderato 2.Andante con espressione
3.Rondo: Allegretto
Solo Cl.-2,2,0,2(or 2,1,1,2)-2,2,3(ad lib.)-
Timp.-Str.
Score: Ms. 99 p.
Parts: C.F. Schmidt, Heilbronn [n.d.]

6280 Die Felsenmühle [The mill on the   *8'*
cliff at Estalières. Overture]
3*,2,2,2-4,2,3-Timp.,Perc.-Str.
Simrock, Berlin [1868]
Score 75 p.
*From the opera. First performance Dresden,
10 April 1831.*

REISSMANN, AUGUST.
        Frankenstein, Silesia 14 November 1825
                    Berlin 13 July 1903

1004v Suite, Op. 41 [A major]
1.Prelude 2.Nocturne 3.Scherzo 4.Adagio
5.Finale
Solo Vn.-2,2,2,2-2,2-Timp.-Str.
Score: Ms. 158 p.
Parts: Kistner, Leipzig [n.d.]

REITRAC, F.

591s Souvenir [E major]
Str.(Cb. ad lib.)
Score: Ms. 4 p.
Parts: A. Leduc, Paris [n.d.]

REIZENSTEIN, FRANZ.   Nuremberg 7 June 1911
                    London 15 October 1968

6076 Capriccio [for orchestra]   *5'*
1(alt. Picc.),1,2,1-2,2-Perc.-Str.
Ernst Eulenburg, London, ᶜ1957
Score 45 p.
*Originally composed for piano and string
orchestra, 1938. This version 1938. First
performance in a BBC broadcast, London, 1938,
Serge Krisch conductor.*

RENIÉ, HENRIETTE.   Paris 18 September 1875
                    Paris 1 March 1956

586m [Concerto, harp, C minor]
1.Allegro risoluto 2.Adagio 3.Scherzo
4.Allegro con fuoco
Solo Hp.-2,2,2,2-2Hn.-Timp.-Str.
Gay & Tenton, Paris [n.d.]
Score in reduction 64 p.
Composed 1901.

RENSBURG, JACQUES E.   Rotterdam 22 May 1846
                    Bonn December 1910

552c [Concerto, violoncello, Op. 3, A minor]
1.Allegro molto moderato 2.Adagio 3.Rondo
Solo Vc.-2,2,2,2-2,2-Timp.-Str.
Ries & Erler, Berlin [n.d.]
Score 80 p.

650c [Concertstück, violoncello, Op. 1,
B minor]
Recitativ - Adagio - Allegro moderato
Solo Vc.-2,2,2,2-2,2-Timp.-Str.
Score: Ms. 85 p.
Parts: Breitkopf & Härtel, Leipzig [n.d.]

RESPIGHI, OTTORINO.   Bologna 9 July 1879
                    Rome 18 April 1936

440c [Adagio with variations]   *11'*
Solo Vc.-3*,3*,2,2-2Hn.-Hp.-Str.
F. Bongiovanni, Bologna, ᶜ1932
Score 36 p.
*Originally composed for violoncello and piano,
1921. Transcribed and two new variations
added at the request of Antonio Certani.
First performance Bologna, 1921.*

[Ancient dances and airs for lute. Transcribed
for orchestra]
1896 Suite I   *15'*
2,3*,0,2-2,1-Cemb.,Hp.-Str.
1897 Suite II   *20'*
3(3rd alt. Picc.),3*,2,2-3,2,3-Timp.-Cemb.
4-hands,Cel.,Hp.-Str.
2074s Suite III   *16'*
Str.
G. Ricordi, Milan, ᶜ1920, ᶜ1924, ᶜ1932
Scores: 53 p., 82 p., 20 p.
*Suite I composed 1916. First performance Rome,
March 1917, Bernardino Molinari conductor.
Suite II composed 1923. First performance
Rome, February 1924, Molinari conductor.
Suite III composed 1931. First performance
Milan, January 1932.*

1898 Ballata delle gnomidi   *18'*
4(2Picc.,2Fl.),3*,4*(1Cl. in E-flat),3*-4,4,3,

Respighi, Ottorino

1-Timp.,Perc.-2Hp.-Str.
G. Ricordi, Milan, ^c1920
Score 66 p. Large folio
Composed 1919. First performance Rome, April 1929, Bernardino Molinari conductor.

3920 Belfagor. Overture   7'
3(3rd alt. Picc.),3*,4*(1Cl. in E-flat),3*-4,3,
3,1-Timp.,Perc.-Cel.,Hp.-Str.
G. Ricordi, Milan, ^c1925
Miniature score 60 p.
From the opera composed 1925. First performance Milan, 26 April 1923, Antonio Guarnieri conductor.

5027 [The birds, suite]   20'
1.Preludio [after Bernardo Pasquini, 1637-1710] 2.[The dove, after Jacques de Gallot, ca.1670] 3.[The hen, after Jean-Philippe Rameau, 1683-1764] 4.[The nightingale, after an unknown 17th-century English composer] 5.[The cuckoo, after Pasquini]
2(2nd alt. Picc.),1,2,2-2,2-Cel.,Hp.-Str.
Ricordi, Milan, ^c1928
Score 58 p.
Composed 1927. First performance Saõ Paulo, Brazil, June 1927, the composer conducting.

998m Concerto à cinque
Soli: Ob., Tpt., Pno., Vn., Cb.-Str.
G. Ricordi, Milan, ^c1934
Miniature score 54 p.
Composed 1933. First performance Rome, April 1933, the composer conducting.

586p [Concerto, piano, in the Mixolydian mode] 36'
1.Moderato 2.Lento 3.Passacaglia
Solo Pno.-3*,3*,2,2-4,2,3,1-Timp.,Gong-Str.
Bote & Bock, Berlin, ^c1926
Score 84 p.
Composed 1925.

837v [Concerto, violin, Gregoriano, A minor] 30'
1.Andante tranquillo - Allegro molto moderato
2.Andante espressivo 3.Allegro energico
Solo Vn.-2,3*,3*,2-4,2,3-Timp.-Cel.,Hp.-Str.
Universal Edition, Vienna, ^c1922
Score 63 p.
Composed 1920. First performance Rome, February 1922, Bernardino Molinari conductor, Mario Corti soloist.

1900 Feste romane   23'
1.[Circus games] 2.[The jubilee] 3.[Harvest festivals in October] 4.[Epiphany]
3(3rd alt. Picc.),3*,4*(1Cl. in E-flat),3*-4,4,3,1-3Sop. Buccine(or Tpt.)-Timp.,Perc.-Pno.,Org.,Mand.-Str.
G. Ricordi, Milan, ^c1929
Score 153 p.
Completed 1928. First performance New York, 21 February 1929, Arturo Toscanini conductor.

1899 Fontane di Roma   18'
1.[The fountain of Valle Giulia at dawn] 2.[The Triton fountain at morn] 3.[The fountain of Trevi at mid-day] 4.[The Villa Medici fountain at sunset]

3*,3*,3*,2-4,3,3,1-Timp.,Perc.-Pno.,Org.,Cel.,
2Hp.(ad lib.)-Str.
G. Ricordi, Milan, ^c1918
Score 64 p.
Composed 1916. First performance Rome, March 1916, Antonio Guarnieri conductor.

1901 Pini di Roma   20'
1.[The pines of the Villa Borghese] 2.[Pines near a catacomb] 3.[The pines of the Janiculum] 4.[The pines of the Appian Way]
3(3rd alt. Picc.),3*,3*,3*-4,3(3rd also backscene),3,1-6Buccine(SSTTBB)(or Hn.5 & 6 and Tpt.4)-Timp.,Perc.-Pno.,Org.,Cel.,Hp.-Str.
G. Ricordi, Milan, ^c1925
Score 81 p.
Composed 1924. First performance Rome, December 1924, Bernardino Molinari conductor.

725v Poema autunnale   13'
Solo Vn.-2(2nd alt. Picc.),3*,2,2-2,1-Cel.,Hp.-Str.
Bote & Bock, Berlin, ^c1926
Score 24 p.
Composed 1925.

1043 Rossiniani [suite for orchestra]   20'
1.Capri and Taormina 2.Lamento 3.Intermezzo 4.Tarantella
3(3rd alt. Picc.),3*,2,2-4,2,3,1-Timp.,Perc.-Cel.,Hp.-Str.
D. Rahter, Leipzig, ^c1927
Score 94 p.
Adapted from Rossini's Les Riens.

1707 Sinfonia drammatica   60'
1.Allegro energico 2.Andante sostenuto 3.Allegro impetuoso
3*,3*,4*(1Cl. in E-flat),3*-6,3,3,1-Timp.,Perc.-Pedal Org.,Hp.-Str.
Universal Edition, Vienna, ^c1923
Score 208 p.
Composed 1914. First performance Rome, 24 January 1915, Bernardino Molinari conductor.

1902 Vetrate di chiesa [Church windows,   27'
four symphonic impressions]
3(3rd alt. Picc.),3*,3*,3*-4,3,3,1(1Tpt. backstage)-Timp.,Perc.-Pno.,Org.,Cel.,Hp.-Str.
G. Ricordi, Milan, ^c1927
Score 98 p.
Composed 1926. First performance Boston, March 1927, Serge Koussevitzky conductor.

REUCHSEL, MAURICE.   Lyons 22 November 1880
                                Lyons 12 July 1968

340s Berceuse [B major]
Str.(without Cb.)
J. Hamelle, Paris [n.d.]
Score 5 p.

956v Leïlah rêve [Leïlah's dream]   5'
Solo Vn.-1,1,1,1-Hn.-Hp.(ad lib.)-Str.
Score: Ms. 12 p.
Parts: Decourcelle, Nice, ^c1927
Composed 1927. First performance Lyons, December 1927, the composer as soloist.

341s   Scherzo [A minor]
   Str.(without Cb.)
   J. Hamelle, Paris [n.d.]
   Score 5 p.

REUSS, HEINRICH XXIV, PRINCE OF REUSS-KÖSTRITZ.
   Trebschen, near Züllichau, Poland 8 December 1855
         Schloss Ernstrunn, Austria 2 October 1910

4603   [Symphony, Op. 10, C minor]
   1.Assai sostenuto - Allegro   2.Andante
   3.Allegro molto
   3,2,2,3*-4,2-Timp.,Perc.-Str.
   Senff, Leipzig [1892]
   Score 85 p.

1713   [Symphony no. 3, Op. 28, E minor]   30'
   1.Poco adagio   2.Andante un poco sostenuto
   3.Allegro vivace
   2,2,2,2-4,2,3-Timp.-Str.
   Carl Giessel, Bayreuth, C1907
   Score 111 p.

REUTTER, HERMANN.   Stuttgart 17 June 1900

545p   [Concerto, piano, Op. 19]
   1.Fliessend   2.[Theme and variations]
   Solo Pno.-2*,1,1,1-1,1-Timp.,Perc.-Str.
   B. Schott's Söhne, Mainz, C1926
   Score 36 p.

REUTTER, JOHANN ADAM KARL GEORG VON.
                  Vienna baptized 6 April 1708
                  Vienna 11 March 1772

6307   [Dinner music, C major]
   1.Intrada   2.Larghetto, cantabile   3.Menuetto
   4.Finale
   0,2,0,1-4Tpt.(2 are Clarini)-Timp.-Cemb.-Str.
   Score: Denkmäler der Tonkunst in Oesterreich,
   XV/2. Artaria, Vienna and Breitkopf & Härtel,
   Leipzig, 1908. Edited by Karl Horwitz and
   Karl Riedel. 15 p.
   Parts: Ms. C1976 by The Fleisher Collection of
   Orchestral Music, Free Library of Philadelphia
   Composed 1757 for the Imperial Court in Vienna.

REVUELTAS, SILVESTRE.   Santiago Papasquiaro,
                  Mexico 31 December 1899
                  Mexico City 5 October 1940

6712   Alcancías [Penny banks, 3 pieces]
   1.Allegro   2.Andantino   3.Allegro vivo
   1*,1,2(1Cl. in E-flat)-1,2,1-Timp.,Perc.-Str.
   Ms.
   Score 79 p.
   *Composed 1932. First performance Mexico City,
   August 1932, Orquesta del Conservatorio, the
   composer conducting.*

6493   La coronela [The girl colonel, ballet in
   four episodes based on the engravings of José
   Guadalupe Posada. Completed by Eduardo Hernandez Moncada and José Yves Limantour, 1961]
   4*,3*,3*(1st alt. Cl. in E-flat),3*-4,3,3,1-
   Timp.,Perc.-Pno.-Str.
   Ms. [C1962 by Southern Music, New York]
   Score 161 p. Large folio
   *Ballet with book by Waldeen, Gabriel Ledesma
   and Seki Sano. Revueltas sketched the first
   three episodes in 1940. After his death Blas
   Galindo composed the fourth episode using
   themes by Revueltas. The entire ballet was
   orchestrated by Candelario Huizar. First performance with Huizar's orchestration, Palacio
   de Bellas Artes, Mexico City, 23 November 1940,
   Ballet de Bellas Artes, Eduardo Hernandez
   Moncada conductor, choreography by Waldeen.
   First three episodes reorchestrated by Hernandez Moncada and fourth episode composed and
   orchestrated by José Yves Limantour using
   Revueltas' themes from La Coronela and the
   films Vámonos con Pancho Villa and Los de Abajo,
   1961.*

3968   Homenaje à Federico García Lorca
   1.Baile   2.Duelo [Sorrow]   3.Son
   Picc.,Cl. in E-flat-0,2,1,1-Perc.-Pno.-Str.
   (without Va.,Vc.)
   [n.p., n.d.]
   Score 79 p.
   *Composed 1937. First performance Madrid, 22
   September 1937, Madrid Symphony Orchestra,
   the composer conducting.*

6526   Itinerarios [in one movement]
   2,3*,3*,1-Bar.Sax.(alt. Sop.Sax.)-2,3,3,1-
   Timp.,Perc.-Pno.,Hp.-Voices-Str.
   Ms.
   Score 50 p.
   Suggested by the Spanish Civil War.

6492   Janitzio [in one movement]
   3*,2,2(1Cl. in E-flat),2-4,2,2,1-Perc.-Str.
   Ms. [C1966 by Southern Music, New York]
   Score 47 p.
   *Janitzio is a fishermen's island in Lake Pat-
   zucaro, central Mexico. First performance
   Mexico City, 13 October 1933, the composer
   conducting.*

5484   [Mayan night, suite for orchestra]   10'
   1.Lento, molto sostenuto   2.Lento - Allegro
   2(both alt. Picc.),1,2,1-4,1,1,1-Timp.,Perc.-
   Str.
   Ms.
   Score 55 p.
   *Originally composed 1939 for the film directed
   by C. Urueta.*

3776   Ocho por radio [8 musicians   6'
   broadcasting]
   0,0,1,1-Tpt.-Perc.-Str.(without Va.)
   Ms.
   Score 24 p.
   *Composed 1933. First performance Mexico City,
   13 October 1933, Orquesta da Cámara, the composer conducting.*

Revueltas, Silvestre

3699 Planos [Planes, a geometric dance]   *9'*
0,0,2*,1-Tpt.-Pno.-Str.(without Va.)
Ms.
Score 26 p.
Composed 1934. First performance Mexico City,
5 November 1934, Orquesta Sinfónica de México,
the composer conducting.

6495 El ranacuajo paseador [Polliwog   *10'*
takes a stroll, ballet]
1*,0,2(1Cl. in E-flat)-0,2,1-Perc.-Str.(without Va. or Vc.)
Ms.
Score 20 p.
Composed 1933. First performance Mexico City,
4 October 1940, Ballet de Bellas Artes, chor-
eography by Anna Sokolow.

6479 Redes [Nets, suite]   *18'* *16'*
1.The fishermen - The child's funeral -
Setting out to fish 2.The fight - The return
of the fishermen with their dead friend
2*,2,2,2-4,2,2,1-Timp.,Perc.-Str.
Ms.
Score 79 p.
Originally composed 1935 for the film Redes.
First performance of this suite Barcelona,
Spain, 7 October 1937.

4184 [Toccata without fugue]
1*,0,3*(1Cl. in E-flat)-1,1,-Timp.-2Vn.
Ms.
Score 17 p.
Composed 1933.

3987 Tres sonetos [Three sonnets]
0,0,3*,1-1,2,0,1-Low Tam-tam-Pno.
Ms.
Score 10 p.
Composed 1938.

6527 Ventanas [Windows]
3*,3*,4*(1Cl. in E-flat),2-4,4,3,1-Timp.,
Perc.-Str.
Ms.
Score 60 p.
Composed 1931. First performance Mexico City,
4 November 1932, Orquesta Sinfónica de México,
the composer conducting.

REY, FRÉDÉRIC LE.   Cherbourg, France 19 May 1858
Asnières, near Paris 6 June 1942

1679s Capriccietto
Str.
Score: Ms. 4 p.
Parts: Krier, Paris, C1929

REYER, LOUIS-ÉTIENNE-ERNEST.
Marseilles 1 December 1823
Le Lavandou, France 15 January 1909

1238 [War march and dances, from Sigurd]   *4'*
3*,2,2,4-4,2,3,1-Timp.,Perc.-2Hp.-Str.
Heugel, Paris [n.d.]
Score 26 p.
Composed 1882-83. First performance Brussels,
1884.

REYNAUD, LOUIS.

770m Pulcinello
Solo Picc.-0,2,1,1-2,2,3-Timp.,Perc.-Str.
Score: Ms. 19 p.
Parts: Gaudet, Paris [n.d.]

REYNOLDS, JEFFREY.

7182 Fanfare
See: FANFARES 1969 FOR 8 TRUMPETS. No. I

REZNIČEK, EMIL NIKOLAUS VON.   Vienna 4 May 1860
Berlin 2 August 1945

788v [Concerto, violin, E minor]
1.Allegro molto 2.Allegretto con comodo
Solo Vn.-2(2nd alt. Picc.),2(2nd alt. E.H.),
2,2-4,2-Timp.,Perc.-Str.
R. Birnbach, Berlin, C1924
Score 55 p.
Composed 1922. First performance Berlin, 26
February 1925, the composer conducting, Ignatz
Waghalter soloist.

6842 Donna Diana. Overture [original   *5'*
version]
3(3rd alt. Picc.),2,2,2-4,2-Timp.,Trgl.-Hp.-
Str.
Kalmus, New York [n.d.]
Score 32 p.
From the opera with libretto by the composer,
based on the comedy by Agustín Moreto y Cavana.
Composed 1894. First performance Prague, 16
December 1894.

5286 Donna Diana. Overture. Revised   *6'*
version
3(3rd alt. Picc.),2,2,2-4,2,3(all ad lib.)-
Timp.,Trgl.-Hp.(ad lib.)-Str.
Universal Edition, Vienna, C1938
Score 41 p.
First performance of this version with text
revised by Julius Kapp, Wuppertal, Germany,
15 November 1933.

4258 [Donna Diana. Waltz-intermezzo,   *3'*
original version]
2*,2,2,2-4,2-Timp.,Bells-Hp.-Str.
J. Schuberth, Leipzig [1896]
Score 16 p.

6346 [Donna Diana. Waltz-intermezzo,   *3'*
revised version]
2*,2,2,2-4,2-Timp.,Bells-Hp.(or Pno.)-Str.
[Universal Edition, Vienna, C1938]
Score 16 p.

1082 Eine Lustspiel-Ouverture   *12'*
3*,2,2,2-4,2-Timp.-Str.
Ries & Erler, Berlin, C1896
Score 50 p.
Composed 1895. First performance Berlin, 1896,
Felix Weingartner conductor.

900v Nachtstück
Solo Vn.(or Vc.)-4Hn.-Hp.-Str.
Dreililien, Berlin, C1905
Score 11 p.

2576 Raskolnikoff, Ouvertüre-Phantasie
3(3rd alt. Picc.),3,3(3rd alt. Cl. in E-flat),
3(3rd alt. C.Bn.)-4,3,3,1-Timp.,Perc.-Cel.,
Org.(ad lib.),Hp.-Str.
Edition Adler, Berlin, c1932
Score 64 p.
Inspired by Dostoevsky's Crime and Punishment.
First performance Berlin, 1931, Berlin Phil-
harmonic Orchestra, Wilhelm Furtwängler con-
ductor.

252s Serenade [G major]
Str.
Richard Birnbach, Berlin, c1923
Score 21 p.

319 Symphonische Suite [D major]   *35'*
1.Rondo 2.Andante 3.Finale
3*,2,2,3*-4,2,3-Timp.-Str.
Ries & Erler, Berlin, c1896
Score 85 p.
Composed 1895. First performance Berlin, 1896.

607 Symphonische Suite [E minor]   *25'*
1.Ouverture 2.Adagio 3.Scherzo Finale
3(3rd alt. Picc.),2,2,2-4,2,3,1-Timp.,Perc.-
Str.
E.W. Fritzsch, Leipzig, 1883
Score 141 p.
Composed 1883. First performance Berlin, 1885.

2375 Symphonische Variationen über Kol   *30'*
Nidrey
3(2nd & 3rd alt. 2Picc.),3(3rd alt. E.H.),3*,
3*-4,2,3,1-Timp.,Perc.-Cel.,2Hp.-Str.
Ms.
Score 103 p.

1710 [Symphony, D major]   *35'*
1.Andante - Poco agitato 2.Andante 3.Minuetto
4.Allegretto con anima
2,2,2,2-4,2-Timp.-Str.
Universal Edition, Vienna [n.d.]
Score 73 p.
Composed 1918. First performance Leipzig, 28
November 1918, Artur Nikisch conductor.

552 [Symphony, F minor]   *40'*
1.Moderato pesante 2.Trauermarsch auf den
Tod eines Komödianten 3.Allegro molto
4.Moderato un poco maestoso
2,2,2,3*-4,2,3-Timp.,Cym.,B.Dr.-Str.
N. Simrock, Berlin, c1919
Score 89 p.
First performance Munich, March 1924, Bruno
Walter conductor.

3254 [Symphony, Ironic, B-flat major]
1.Lustig 2.Rasch und leicht 3.Mit
abgeklärter Ruhe 4.Sehr lustig
3(3rd alt. Picc.),2,2,2-2,2-Timp.-Str.
N. Simrock, Berlin, c1905
Score 51 p.
First performance Berlin, 30 March 1905, under
original title Symphonietta, Berlin Philhar-
monic Orchestra, the composer conducting.

2294 Traumspiel-Suite [after Strindberg]   *25'*
1.[Fairhaven and Foulstrand] 2.[Fall and
spring] 3.[In Fingal's cave] 4.[Wind and
waves waltz] 5.[The lawyer] 6.[The daughter's
farewell]
1(alt. Picc.),1(alt. E.H.),2*,1-1,1-Timp.,
Perc.-Cel.(or Pno.),Hp.-Str.
N. Simrock, Berlin, c1921
Score 30 p.

RHEINBERGER, JOSEF VON.
                Vaduz, Liechtenstein 17 March 1839
                Munich 25 November 1901

1049m [Concerto, organ, Op. 137, F major]   *25'*
1.Maestoso 2.Andante 3.Finale: Con moto
Solo Org.-3Hn.-Str.
Fr. Kistner, Leipzig [1884]
Score 39 p.
First performance Munich, 1884, Horatio Parker
soloist.

220m [Concerto, organ, Op. 177, G minor]   *22'*
1.Grave 2.Andante 3.Con moto
Solo Org.-2Hn.,2Tpt.-Timp.-Str.
Rob. Forberg, Leipzig, c1894
Score 51 p.

5604 [Elegiac march, Op. 167b]   *8'*
3*,2,2,2-2,2,3-Timp.-Str.
Rob. Forberg, Leipzig [188-?]
Score 31 p.

6950 Passacaglia für Orchester, Op. 132b
3*,2,2,2-2,2,3-Timp.-Str.
Rob. Forberg, Leipzig [188-?]
Score 51 p.

335m [Suite, Op. 149]
1.Con moto 2.[Theme with variations]
3.Sarabande 4.Finale
Solo Org., Solo Vn., Solo Vc.-Str.
Fr. Kistner, Leipzig [1891]
Score 55 p.

108s [Vision, organ, Op. 156 no. 5. Transcribed
by A. Walter Kramer]
Str.
G. Schirmer, New York, c1911
Score 3 p.

5548 [Wallenstein, symphonic tone   *12'*
painting, Op. 10. No. 3, Wallenstein's camp]
3*,2,2,2-4,2,3-Timp.,Perc.-Str.
E.W. Fritzsch, Leipzig [1867]
Score 192 p.
Suggested by Friedrich von Schiller's trilogy
about the Thirty Years' War. First perform-
ance Munich, 1866.

RHENÉ-BATON.   Courseulles-sur-Mer,
            Calvados, France 5 September 1879
            Le Mans, France 23 September 1940

Real name: René Baton

563v Fantaisie orientale, Op. 34
Solo Vn.-2,2,2,2-4,1-Timp.,Perc.-Cel.,Hp.-Str.

Rhené-Baton

Durand, Paris, ^c1926
Score 40 p.

1554 [For the funeral of a Breton sailor, *8'*
Op. 33]
3*,2,2,2-4,4,3,1-Timp.,Perc.-Str.
Durand, Paris, ^c1924
Score 16 p.
Composed 1923. First performance Paris, 2
February 1925, the composer conducting.

1240 [Minuet for the king's brother, Op. 5] *6'*
3,2,2,2-4,2,3-Timp.,Perc.-Hp.-Str.
Durand, Paris, ^c1909
Score 37 p.
Composed 1901. First performance Paris, 1903,
the composer conducting.

499c Poème élégiaque, Op. 32
Solo Vc.-2,2,2,2-4,2,3,1-Timp.-Hp.-Str.
Durand, Paris, ^c1924
Score 30 p.
Composed 1923.

505p Variations sur un mode éolien, Op. 4
Solo Pno.-3(3rd alt. Picc.),2,3*,2-4,3,3,1-
Timp.,Perc.-Hp.-Str.
Durand, Paris, ^c1908
Score 87 p.
Composed 1902.

RHODEN, NATALIA NAANA. Sacramento, California 1922

Pseudonym: Natalie Claire Rhoden

3538 Intermezzo *2'*
Cl.,Bn.-Str.
Ms.
Score 6 p.
Composed 1939. First performance Rochester,
23 April 1941, Rochester Civic Orchestra,
Howard Hanson conductor.

3525 Scherzo no. 1 *2'30"*
3*,2,2,2-4,2,3,1-Timp.,Perc.-2Hp.-Str.
Ms.
Score 30 p.
Composed 1940. First performance Rochester,
23 April 1941, Rochester Civic Orchestra,
Howard Hanson conductor.

3840 Scherzo no. 3
3*,2,2,2-4,2,3,1-Timp.,Perc.-2Hp.-Str.
Ms.
Score 30 p.
First performance Rochester, 23 April 1941,
Rochester Civic Orchestra, Howard Hanson
conductor.

RIBIOLLET, EDMOND.

617m [Spring shower, violin and violoncello.
Orchestrated by N. Gervasio]
Solo Vn., Solo Vc.-1,1,2,1-Bells-Str.
Decourcelle, Nice, ^c1918
Score 7 p.

RICCI, POMPEO.

1581s Gavotta-rococò
Str.
Score: Ms. 4 p.
Parts: Ricordi, Milan [n.d.]

RICCIARDI, VINCENZO.

1520s Strimpellata [Strumming]
Str.
Score: Ms. 5 p.
Parts: Ricordi, Milan, ^c1930

RICCI-SIGNORINI, ANTONIO. Massalombarda,
near Ravenna, Italy 22 February 1867
Bologna 10 March 1965

268s Andantino e Tempo di minuetto
Str.(without Cb.)
Carisch, Milan, ^c1925
Score 8 p.

433s [Grandma Teresa's tales. Siren]
Trgl.,Bells-Hp.-Str.
Carisch, Milan, ^c1921
Score 19 p.
Originally composed for piano.

2327 [Landscapes, for small orchestra]
1.[At dawn] 2.[Cypresses] 3.[Evening in the
mountains]
2*,1,2-2Hn.-Perc.-Str.
Carisch, Milan, ^c1909
Score 23 p.

476s Larghetto e Tempo di furlana
Str.(without Cb.)
Carisch, Milan, ^c1925
Score 11 p.

436s [A Nervi. Two impressions]
1.[The sick child] 2.[Emigranti]
Str.
Carisch, Milan, ^c1922
Score 19 p.
Originally composed for piano.

435s [A Regoledo. Two impressions]
1.[The cascade] 2.[A little brook]
2Hp.-Str.
Carisch, Milan, ^c1922
Score 31 p.
Originally composed for piano.

2450 [Sketches, for small orchestra]
1.[Girls at the fountain] 2.[Devotees in
church] 3.[The lamplighter]
2*,0,2-2Hn.-Bell-Harm.-Str.
Carisch & Jänichen, Milan, ^c1914
Score 31 p.

470s Stati d'anima [Moods, suite no. 1]
1.Andantino 2.Molto lento 3.Largo
Str.
Carisch & Jänichen, Milan, ^c1914
Score 27 p.

432s Stati d'anima [Moods, suite no. 2]
1.Largo 2.Quasi lento 3.Andante animato
Str.
Carisch, Milan, ^c1920
Score 31 p.

434s [Three poetic pieces]
1.Arietta 2.Canzone 3.Melodia
Str.
Carisch, Milan, ^c1921
Score 27 p.
*Transcribed from three Poetic Suites for
piano.*

RICCIUS, KARL AUGUST.
                        Bernstadt, Germany 26 July 1830
                             Dresden 8 July 1893

806m [Concertino, 2 cornets, D major]
Maestoso - Andante - Allegro
2Soli Cnt.-1,1,2,1-2,2,1-Timp.-Str.
Score: Ms. 68 p.
Parts: Seeling, Dresden [n.d.]

RICE, N.H.

169s Serenade, Op. 3
1.Allegro moderato 2.Andante 3.Allegretto
4.Allegro con brio
Str.
Simrock, Berlin, ^c1899
Score 43 p.

RICE, WILLIAM E.   Houston, Texas 27 June 1921

7293 Concerto for winds and percussion   *18'*
1.Intrada 2.March, after Schubert 3.Intro-
duction and allegro
3(3rd alt. Picc.),3*,3*,3*-4,3,3,1-Timp.,Perc.
-Cel.
Ms.
Score 73 p. Large folio
*Second movement is based on the Marcia of
Schubert's Divertissement à la Hongroise,
Deutsch no. 818. Composed 1950. First per-
formance Houston, Texas, 30 October 1956,
Houston Symphony Society, Leopold Stokowski
conductor. Revised 1959. First movement
awarded Second Prize in the Thor Johnson
Brass Composition Competition, 1950.*

2415s Meditation on a gospel tune (1976)   *4'*
Str.
Ms. ^c1976 by William E. Rice
Score 12 p.
*Theme is the 19th century American hymn Shall
We Gather at the River?, text and music by
Robert Lowry. Originally composed for organ,
1976. This transcription 1976. First per-
formance New Hampshire Music Festival, 22 July
1976, Thomas Nee conductor.*

RICHTER, EDWARD CHRISTIAN GOTTFRIED.   Hamburg 1887
                             Philadelphia 1943

1730s Barcarole nocturne, Op. 25   *5'*
Str.
Ms.

Score 6 p.
Composed 1937.

2702 Joy in solitude, a meditation,   *5'*
Op. 23
1,1,2,2-2,2,3-Timp.,Perc.-Str.
Ms.
Score 26 p.
Composed 1935.

3039 Melodic fantasy, Op. 27   *8'*
1,1,2,2-3,2,1-Timp.,Perc.-Str.
Ms.
Score 38 p.
Composed 1937.

3696 [Old World suite, Op. 6. No. 2,   *6'*
Meditation]
1,1,2,2-2,2,1-Trgl.-Hp.(or Pno.)-Str.
Ms.
Score 27 p.
Composed 1922. Revised 1938.

3038 Valse nocturne, clouds in the   *2'30"*
night, Op. 24
1,1,2,1-2,2,1-Pno.(or Hp.)-Str.
Ms.
Score 17 p.
*Composed 1937. First performance Philadelphia,
27 December 1937, National Youth Administration Orchestra, the composer conducting.*

RICHTER, FRANZ XAVER.
              Holleschau, Moravia 1 December 1709
                   Strasbourg 12 September 1789

1673s [Sinfonia da camera, B-flat major]
Edited by Walter Upmeyer
1.Allegro moderato 2.Andante 3.Fuga
Cemb.-Str.
Nagel, Hanover, ^c1931
Score 12 p.

RICHTER, GUSTAV.   d. Vienna 8 June 1930

577s Poesie und Prosa, Op. 80
Hp.(ad lib.)-Str.
Joh. André, Offenbach a.M. [n.d.]
Score 7 p.

RICHTER, JOSEF.

651m [Song without words, waldhorn]   *3'*
Solo Hn.-1,1,2,2-2,0,3-Timp.-Hp.-Str.
C. Giessel, Bayreuth [n.d.]
Score in reduction 7 p.

RICHTER, WILLIBALD.

1084s Abendgesang [Evening song]
Str.

Ricordi, Giulio

Score: Ms. 4 p.
Parts: B. Schott's Söhne, Mainz [n.d.]

RICORDI, GIULIO
See: BURGMEIN, J. pseudonym.

RIEDE, FR.

[Six small pieces, string orchestra]
1385s No. 1 Am Bach [At the brook]
1386s No. 3 Tändelei [Trifling]
Str.
Scores: Ms. 3 p., 4 p.
Parts: International, New York [n.d.]

RIEDEL, KARL.   Kronenberg, Germany 6 October 1827
                 Leipzig 3 June 1888

697s [Night song]
Str.
Kahnt, Leipzig [n.d.]
Score 7 p.
Composed 1887.

RIEGGER, WALLINGFORD CONSTANTIN.
                Albany, Georgia 29 April 1885
                New York 2 April 1961

3530 The cry, Op. 22   6'
3*,3*,3(1Cl. in E-flat),3*-4,3,3,1-Timp.,Cym.-
Str.
Ms.
Score 30 p.
*Commissioned by Hanya Holm, 1935. Composed
for piano 4-hands, 1935. Transcribed 1935.*

2785 Dichotomy   12'
1(alt. Picc.),1,1,1-1,2-Timp.,Perc.-Pno.-Str.
New Music, San Francisco, ᶜ1932
Score 54 p.
*Composed 1931-32. First performance Berlin,
10 March 1932, Michael Taube Chamber Orchestra, Nicolas Slonimsky conductor.*

3529 Evocation, Op. 17a   4'
3*,3*,3(1Cl. in E-flat),3*-4,3,3,1-Timp.,Perc.
-Str.
Ms.
Score 29 p.
*Composed for piano 4-hands, 1932. Transcribed
1938.*

402c Introduction and fugue, Op. 74   8'
Solo Vc.-3*,2,3*,2-4,3,3,1-Timp.
Ms. [ᶜ1961 by Associated Music Publishers,
New York]
Score 40 p.
*Originally composed as Op. 69 for violoncel-
los. First performance in this form, East-
man School of Music, Rochester, 29 October
1960, Eastman Wind Ensemble, Frederick Fennell
conductor, Ronald Leonard soloist.*

3531 New dance, Op. 18b   5'30"
3*,3*,3(3rd alt. B.Cl.),3(3rd alt. C.Bn.)-
Alto Sax.-4,3,3,1-Timp.,Perc.-Hp.-Str.
Ms.
Score 40 p.

*Composed 1934 for piano 4-hands, as the finale
of a larger work, New Dance, commissioned by
Doris Humphrey. This version 1940. First
performance Pittsburgh, 30 January 1942, Pittsburgh Symphony Orchestra, Fritz Reiner conductor.*

3697 Rhapsody, Second April   12'
3(2nd & 3rd alt. Picc.),3*,3*,3*-6,4,4,1-Timp.,
Perc.-2Hp.-Str.
Ms.
Score 88 p.
*Composed 1925. First performance New York,
29 October 1931, New York Philharmonic, Erich
Kleiber conductor.*

2021s Study in sonority, Op. 7   9'
10(or any multiple of 10)Vn.
G. Schirmer, New York, ᶜ1930
Score 24 p.
*Composed 1927. First performance Ithaca, New
York, 11 August 1927, Ithaca Conservatory stu-
dent ensemble, the composer conducting.*

4748 Symphony no. 3 [Op. 42]   23'
1.Moderato - Allegro 2.Andante affettuoso
3.Moderato - Allegro molto 4.Beginning rather
slowly - Allegro - Allegro feroce
2(2nd alt. Picc.),2(2nd alt. E.H.),2,2(2nd alt.
C.Bn. optional)-4,3,3,1-Timp.,Perc.-Str.
Ms.
Score 166 p.
*Commissioned by the Alice M. Ditson Fund. Com-
posed 1947. First performance New York, 16
May 1948, CBS Symphony, Dean Dixon conductor.
Received the New York Music Critics' Circle
Award for the 1947-48 season and the Walter W.
Naumburg Recording Award.*

6562 Symphony no. 4, Op. 63   24'
1.Allegro moderato 2.Allegretto con moto -
Allegro 3.Sostenuto - Presto
3(3rd alt. Picc.),3*,3(3rd alt. B.Cl.),3*-4,3,
3,1-Timp.,Perc.-Str.
Associated Music Publishers, New York [ᶜ1958]
Score 131 p. Large folio
*Commissioned by the Fromm Music Foundation.
Second movement based on the composer's ballet
Chronicle. Composed 1956. First performance,
Festival of Contemporary Arts at the University
of Illinois, Urbana, 12 April 1957, University
of Illinois Orchestra, Bernard Goodman con-
ductor.*

336p Variations for piano and orchestra,   20'
Op. 54
Solo Pno.-2(2nd alt. Picc.),2,2,2-4,2,3,1-
Timp.,Perc.-Str.
Ms. ᶜ1955 by Associated Music Publishers, New
York
Score 58 p. Large folio
*Commissioned by The Louisville Philharmonic
Society. Composed 1952-53. First performance
Louisville, 13 February 1954, The Louisville
Orchestra, Robert Whitney conductor, Benjamin
Owen soloist.*

318v Variations for violin and orchestra,   *16'*
Op. 71
Solo Vn.-3*,2,2,3*-4,2,3,1-Timp.,Perc.-Hp.-Str.
Ms. [^C1960 by Associated Music Publishers, New
York]
Score 29 p.
*Commissioned by The Louisville Philharmonic
Society. First performance Louisville, 1
April 1959, Robert Whitney conductor, Sidney
Harth soloist.*

RIEMENSCHNEIDER, GEORG.
                Stralsund, Germany 1 April 1848
                Breslau, Germany 14 September 1913

342s [At the image of the Virgin]
Str.
E.W. Fritzsch, Leipzig [n.d.]
Score 3 p.

RIEPEL, JOSEPH.
        Hörschlag, Austria baptized 23 January 1709
            Regensburg, Bavaria 23 October 1782

5629 [Symphony, D major] Edited by Thor Johnson
and Donald M. McCorkle
1.Allegro molto 2.Allegretto 3.Prestissimo
2Fl.-2Hn.-Str.
Ms. Prepared by The Fleisher Collection of
Orchestral Music, from the Archives of the
Moravian Church in America (Bethlehem, Pennsylvania Collection)
Score 19 p.
*Edited from a manuscript copied by the Mora-
vian, Johann Friedrich Peter, in 1767 and
believed to be the only extant copy of this
work. First modern performance, Third Early
American Moravian Music Festival and Seminar,
Salem College, Winston-Salem, North Carolina,
21 June 1955, The Festival Orchestra, Thor
Johnson conductor.*

RIES, FERDINAND.
        Bad Godesberg, near Bonn 29 November 1784
                Frankfurt 13 January 1838

806v [Concerto, violin, E minor]   *25'*
1.Allegro 2.Andante, quasi larghetto 3.Rondo
vivace
Solo Vn.-2,2,2,2-2,2-Timp.-Str.
Ries & Erler, Berlin [n.d.]
Score in reduction 28 p.

4106 [Symphony, Op. 23 no. 1, D major]
1.Adagio - Allegro molto vivace 2.Marche
funebre 3.Menuetto moderato 4.Allegro
1,2,2,2-2,2-Timp.-Str.
Ms.
Score 232 p.

4107 [Symphony, Op. 23 no. 2, C minor]
1.Allegro ma non troppo 2.Andantino 3.Menu-
etto allegretto 4.Allegro ma non troppo
1,2,0,2-2,2,1-Timp.-Str.
Ms.
Score 148 p.

RIES, FRANZ.   Berlin 7 April 1846
                Naumburg, Germany 20 June 1932

175 Dramatische Ouverture, Op. 30   *18'*
2,2,2,2-4,2,3-Timp.-Str.
H. Erler, Berlin [n.d.]
Score 54 p.
*Composed 1878. First performance Leipzig,
1878, the composer conducting.*

161s Nachtstück [Nocturne] Op. 32
Str.(without Cb.)
Ries & Erler, Berlin [n.d.]
Score 1 p.

655v [Suite, violin, no. 2, F major.   *13'*
Romance and Scherzo, Op. 27]
Solo Vn.-2(2nd alt. Picc.),2,2,2-2,2,3-Timp.-
Str.
Ries, Dresden [n.d.]
Score 50 p.
Composed 1877. First performance Berlin, 1878.

670v [Suite, violin, no. 3, G minor.   *15'*
Bourrée, Adagio and Perpetuum mobile, Op. 34]
Solo Vn.-2(2nd alt. Picc.),2,2,2-2Hn.-Timp.-
Str.
Ries & Erler, Berlin [n.d.]
Score 33 p.
Composed 1882. First performance Berlin, 1883.

RIES, HUBERT.   Bonn 1 April 1802
                Berlin 14 September 1886

729v [Concerto, violin, no. 1, Op. 13, D major]
In one movement
Solo Vn.-1,2,2,2-2,2-Timp.-Str.
Score: Ms. 85 p.
Parts: Bote & Bock, Berlin [n.d.]

RIETHMÜLLER, HELMUT.   Cologne 16 May 1912

4969 [Hymnic music, Op. 17]   *18'*
In one movement
2,2,2,2-3,3,3,1(offstage 3,6,2,1)-Timp.,Perc.-
Org.-Str.
Universal Edition, Vienna, ^C1943
Score 67 p.
Composed 1940.

2055s [Romance for string orchestra,   *3'*
Op. 26]
Str.
Universal Edition, Vienna, ^C1944
Score 7 p.

RIETI, VITTORIO.
            b. Alexandria, Egypt 28 January 1898

767c [Concerto, violoncello and   *13'*
12 instruments]

Rieti, Vittorio

1.Cadenza - Allegretto moderato con grazia
2.Poco sostenuto - Allegro
Solo Vc.-1,1,2,2-2,1-Timp.,Perc.-Cb.
Ricordi, Milan, ᶜ1936
Score 94 p.
*Composed 1934. First performance Rome, April
1934.*

4846 [Hippolytus, symphonic suite] 20'
1.Prologue 2.Variation d'Hippolyte 3.Entrée
de la nourrice 4.Phèdre et Aphrodite 5.
Hippolyte et la nourrice 6.Le chant du départ
7.La mort d'Hippolyte
4(3rd & 4th alt. Picc.I&II),3*,4*(1Cl. in
E-flat),3*-4,4,3,1-Timp.,Perc.-Str.
Max Eschig, Paris, ᶜ1939
Score 113 p.
From the ballet composed 1937.

5326 [Introduction and game of the hours] 6'
2(2nd alt. Picc.),2(2nd alt. E.H.),2,2-4,2,3,
1-Timp.-Str.
Ms.
Score 45 p. Large folio
*Commissioned by The Louisville Philharmonic
Society under a grant from the Rockefeller
Foundation. Composed 1953. First perform-
ance Louisville, 16 October 1954, The Louis-
ville Orchestra, Robert Whitney conductor.*

6427 The night shadow, ballet suite on 25'
themes by V. Bellini [in 14 movements]
2(2nd alt. Picc.),2,2,2-4,2,3-Timp.,Perc.-Str.
Ms. ᶜ1946 by Vittorio Rieti
Score 176 p.
*Alternate titles: Sonnambula, Somnambule.
Commissioned by Ballet Russe de Monte Carlo.
Ballet composed 1941-42. First performance,
New York, 27 February 1946, Ballet Russe de
Monte Carlo, Emanuel Balaban conductor, chor-
eography by George Balanchine.*

4861 [Noah's Ark, suite from the ballet] 17'
1.[Prelude to Act I] 2.[The flood] 3.[Pre-
lude to Act II] 4.[March of the animals]
5.[The rainbow]
3(3rd alt. Picc.),3(3rd alt. E.H.),4(3rd alt.
B.Cl.,1Cl. in E-flat),3*-6,3,3,1-Timp.,Perc.-
Pno.,Cel.-Str.
Universal Edition, Vienna, ᶜ1926
Score 53 p.
*Ballet composed 1922. This suite 1923. First
performance Prague, 15 May 1925, Festival of
the International Society for Contemporary
Music, Alfredo Casella conductor.*

6446 Pasticcio (Chess serenade) for 20'
orchestra [revised version]
1.Overture 2.Serenade 3.Prelude 4.Gavotte
5.Interlude 6.Valse 7.Serenade 8.Clown
march
1(alt. Picc.),1,2,1-2,2,1-Timp.,Perc.-Pno.-
Str.
Ms.
Score 82 p. Large folio
*Originally composed as Chess Serenade, suite
for two pianos, 1945. This transcription commissioned by The Royal Winnipeg Ballet of*

*Canada. Transcribed and retitled, 1956.
First performance as a ballet, Winnipeg, 1956,
The Royal Winnipeg Ballet of Canada. Revised
after first performance.*

3755 Sinfonietta per piccola orchestra 15'
1.Allegro 2.Allegretto alla marcia 3.Allegro
deciso
1(alt. Picc.),1,1,2-2,2,2-Timp.,Perc.-Str.
Ricordi, Milan, ᶜ1934
Miniature score 68 p.
*Composed 1932. First performance Paris, May
1932, Roger Desormière conductor.*

6429 [Symphony no. 4, Tripartita] 15'
1.Poco sostenuto - Allegro moderato 2.Alle-
gretto vivace alla marcia 3.Poco sostenuto -
Allegro con brio
2(2nd alt. Picc.),1,1,2-2,2,2-Timp.,Perc.-Str.
Associated Music Publishers, New York, ᶜ1947
Score 80 p. Large folio
*Composed 1944. First performance St. Louis,
16 December 1944, St. Louis Symphony Orchestra, Vladimir Golschmann conductor.*

6462 [Symphony no. 5] 15'
1.Allegro giocoso 2.Andante tranquillo
3.Presto
2(2nd alt. Picc.),2,2,2-4,3,3-Timp.,Perc.-Str.
Associated Music Publishers, New York [ᶜ1946?]
Score 77 p. Large folio
*Composed 1945. First performance Venice, Sep-
tember 1945, Venice Festival Orchestra, Roger
Desormière conductor.*

6465 Trionfo di Bacco e Arianna [Ballet- 18'
cantata]
2(2nd alt. Picc.),2,2,2-4,2,3-Timp.,Perc.-
Chorus(SATB)-Str.
Ms. ᶜ1948 by Associated Music Publishers, New
York
Score 139 p. Large folio
*Text is a Florentine carnival song written by
Lorenzo de' Medici, The Magnificent. Com-
missioned by the Ballet Society, 1946. Com-
posed 1946-47. First performance New York, 9
February 1948, Leon Barzin conductor, chor-
eography by George Balanchine.*

6636 [Two pastorals for small orchestra] 14'
1.Adagio - Allegro moderato - Adagio 2.Alle-
gro non troppo
1,1,1,2-2,1-Str.
Ms. Universal Edition, Vienna [n.d.]
Score 56 p.
Composed 1925.

RIETZ, JULIUS.   Berlin 28 December 1812
                 Dresden 12 September 1877

4220 Concert-Ouverture für das
Niederrheinische Musikfest, Op. 7
2,2,2,2-4,2,3-Timp.-Str.
Kistner, Leipzig [1839 or 1840?]
Score 78 p.

677m Concertstück, Idyllische Scene, Op. 41
Soli: Fl.,Ob.,Cl.,Bn.,Hn.-1,1,1,1-3,2-Timp.-
Str.

R. Seitz, Leipzig [n.d.]
Score in reduction 39 p.
*Composed 1870. First performance Dresden,
1871, the composer conducting.*

730c Fantaisie pour violoncello, Op. 2
Solo Vc.-1,2,2,2-2,2-Timp.-Str.
Score: Ms. 137 p.
Parts: Kistner, Leipzig [1844?]

4932 [Overture for the golden wedding celebration of the king and queen of Saxony, Op. 53]
3*,2,2,2-4,2,3-Timp.-Str.
Robert Seitz, Leipzig [1872]
Score 89 p.

6851 [Overture to a comedy, Op. 18]
2,2,2,2-2,2-Timp.-Str.
Fr. Kistner, Leipzig [n.d.]
Score 68 p.

5442 [Symphony no. 3, Op. 31, E-flat major]
1.Allegro moderato ma con fuoco 2.Con moto
moderato 3.Andante sostenuto 4.Allegro di
molto
2,2,2,2-4,2-Timp.-Str.
Breitkopf & Härtel, Leipzig [1856?]
Score 185 p.

RIGEL, HENRI JOSEPH.
Wertheim, Franconia, Germany 9 February 1741
Paris 2 May 1799

6157 [Symphony, Op. 12 no. 1, D major]
1.Allegro 2.Andante 3.Presto
2Ob.-2Hn.-Str.
Score: Ms. Edited by Barry S. Brook. 27 p.
Large folio
Parts: Ms. C1976 by The Fleisher Collection of
Orchestral Music, Free Library of Philadelphia
*Listed in The Breitkopf Thematic Catalog, Sup-
plement II, 1767. Later published in Paris by
the composer as no. 1 of his Op. 12, Six
Sinfonies.*

6265 [Symphony, Op. 12 no. 3, C major]
1.Allegro 2.Andante 3.Allegro assai
2Ob.-2Hn.-Str.
Score: Ms. Edited by Barry S. Brook. 34 p.
Large folio
Parts: Ms. C1976 by The Fleisher Collection of
Orchestral Music, Free Library of Philadelphia
Composed ca.1767.

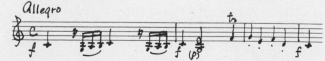

6444 [Symphony, Op. 12 no. 4, C minor]
1.Allegro 2.Largo non troppo 3.Allegro
spiritoso
2Ob.-2Hn.-Str.
Score: Ms. Edited by Barry S. Brook. 35 p.
Large folio
Parts: Ms. C1976 by The Fleisher Collection of
Orchestral Music, Free Library of Philadelphia
Composed ca.1769.

ŘIHOVSKÝ, ADALBERT VOJTĚCH.
Dub, Moravia 21 April 1871
Prague 15 September 1950

1708 [Bohemian dances, Op. 18]
1,0,2-2,2,1-Trgl.-Str.
M. Urbánek, Prague [n.d.]
Score 19 p.

RIISAGER, KNUDÅGE. Port Kunda, Estonia 6 March 1897
Copenhagen 26 December 1974

5954 [Primavera, concert overture, Op. 31]   5'
3*,2,2,2-4,2,3-Timp.,Perc.-Str.
Edition Dania, Copenhagen, C1947 by Samfundet
til Udgivelse af Dansk Musik
Score 32 p.
*Composed 1934. First performance Copenhagen,
31 January 1935, Danish Concert Society, Emil
Reesen conductor.*

5955 [Three Danish street carols]   8'
1.[Now let us dance and sing] 2.[In spring-
time] 3.[The birds' song]
3*,2(2nd alt. E.H.),2(1st alt. Cl. in E-flat),
2(2nd alt. C.Bn.)-4,3,3,1-Timp.,Perc.-Str.
Edition Dania, Copenhagen, C1939 by Samfundet
til Udgivelse af Dansk Musik
Score 24 p.
*Composed 1937. First performance Copenhagen,
12 April 1938, Copenhagen Symphony Orchestra,
Emil Reesen conductor.*

5107 [Variations on a theme of C.M.   10'
Bellman, Op. 45]
2(2nd alt. Picc.),1,2,1-2,2,1-Timp.,Perc.-Str.
Carl Gehrman, Stockholm, C1945
Score 76 p.
*Theme is Mother Dear, Slap Your Hand Now On
Your Skirt by the poet-composer Carl Michael
Bellman.*

RIMSKY-KORSAKOV, NIKOLAI ANDREIEVICH.
Tikhvin, near Novgorod, Russia 18 March 1844
Liubensk, near St. Petersburg 21 June 1908

359 [At the grave, Op. 61]
3(3rd alt. Picc.),2,2,2-4,2,3,1-Timp.,Perc.-
Hp.-Str.
Belaieff, Leipzig, 1905
Score 11 p.
Composed 1904 in memory of M. P. Belaieff.

677

Rimsky-Korsakov, Nikolai

1532 [Boyarina Vera Sheloga. Overture]
2,2,2,2-4,2,3-Timp.-Str.
Bessel, St. Petersburg [n.d.]
Score 17 p.
*From the opera composed 1877 as a prologue to
The Maid of Pskov. Revised 1898. First per-
formance Moscow, 27 December 1898.*

332 Capriccio espagnol, Op. 34   15'
1.Alborada 2.Variazioni 3.Alborada 4.Scena
e canto gitano 5.Fandango asturiano
3*,2(1st alt. E.H.),2,2-4,2,3,1-Timp.,Perc.-
Hp.-Str.
Kalmus, New York [n.d.]
Score 90 p.
*Composed 1887. First performance St. Peters-
burg, 1887, the composer conducting.*

358 [Christmas Eve. Suite]   26'
3(3rd alt. Picc.),2,3(3rd alt. Cl. in E-flat),
2-4,3,3,1-Timp.,Perc.-Cel.,Hp.-Str.
Score: Belaieff, Leipzig, 1904. 106 p.
Parts: Kalmus, New York [n.d.]
*From the opera based on Gogol's story. Com-
posed 1894-95. First performance St. Petersburg, 10 December 1895, the composer conducting.*

374p [Concerto, piano, Op. 30, C-sharp minor]
In one movement
Solo Pno.-2,2,2,2-2,2,3-Timp.-Str.
Belaieff, Leipzig, 1886
Score 82 p.
Composed 1882.

439 [Le coq d'or. Introduction *and*   8'
Bridal procession]
3*,3*,3*,3*-4,3,3,1-Timp.,Perc.-Cel.,2Hp.-Str.
Luck's, Detroit [n.d.]
Score 37 p.
*From the opera based on Pushkin's fairytale.
Composed 1906-07. First performance Moscow,
20 October 1909.*

662 Le coq d'or. Suite, 4 tableaux   27'
musicales. Arranged by A. Glazunov and
M. Steinberg
3*(2nd alt. Picc.II),3*,3*,3*-4,3,3,1-Timp.,
Perc.-Cel.,2Hp.-Str.
Jurgenson, Moscow [1909?]
Score 106 p.

364 Dubinushka, chanson russe, Op. 62
3*,2,3,2-4,3(3rd optional),3,1-Timp.,Perc.-
SATB Chorus(ad lib.)-Str.
Belaieff, Leipzig, 1907
Score 26 p.
The traditional song, arranged 1905-06.

204 [Fairytale, Op. 29]   13'
3*,2,2,2-4,2,3,1-Timp.,Perc.-Hp.-Str.
Belaieff, Leipzig [n.d.]
Score 79 p.
*Inspired by a poem by Alexander Pushkin. Com-
posed 1880. First performance St. Petersburg,
1881, the composer conducting.*

474v Fantaisie sur des thèmes russes, Op. 33
Solo Vn.-2,2,2,2-2,2-Timp.,Trgl.-Str.
Belaieff, Leipzig, 1887
Score 55 p.
Composed 1887.

328 Fantaisie sur des thèmes serbes, Op. 6   6'
3*,2,2,2-4,2,3-Timp.,Perc.-Str.
Belaieff, Leipzig, 1895
Score 47 p.
*Composed 1867. First performance St. Peters-
burg, 12 May 1867, Mili Balakirev conductor.
Revised 1888.*

Flight of the bumblebee
   See: [Tsar Saltan. Flight of the bumblebee]

2057 [Legend of the invisible city of Kitezh.
Four musical tableaux] Edited by Maximilian
Steinberg
3(3rd alt. Picc.),3*,3*,3*-4,3,3,1-Timp.,Perc.
-Cel.,2Hp.,Domras and Balalaikas (ad lib.)-Str.
Belaieff, Leipzig, 1926
Score 94 p.
*From the opera composed 1903-05. First per-
formance St. Petersburg, 20 February 1907.*

[The maid of Pskov (Pskovitianka)]
784 [Overture]   8'
275 [Intermezzo no. 1]
276 [Intermezzo no. 2]
277 [Act III, scene 1]
3(3rd alt. Picc.),3*,3*,3*-4,3,2Cnt.backstage
(Act III only),3,1-Timp.,Gong-Str.
Bessel, St. Petersburg [n.d.]
Scores: 28 p., 11 p., 5 p., 25 p.
*From the opera composed 1868-72; revised 1877
and 1891-92. First performance of final version St. Petersburg, 18 April 1895.*

101 [May night. Overture]   8'
2,2,2,2-4,2,3-Timp.-Str.
Belaieff, Leipzig, 1895
Score 22 p.
*From the opera based on Gogol's story. Com-
posed 1877-79. First performance St. Petersburg, 21 January 1880, Eduard Napravnik conductor.*

2009 [Mlada. Act III: Night on Mt.   25'
Triglav]
4(2nd & 3rd alt. 2Picc.,4th Alto Fl.),3(2nd &
3rd alt. 2E.H.),4*(2nd & 3rd alt. 2Cl. in E-
flat),3(3rd alt. C.Bn.)-6,3,3,1-Timp.,Perc.-
Org. backstage(ad lib.),3Hp.-Str.
Belaieff, Leipzig, 1902
Score 133 p.
*From the opera composed 1889-90. First per-
formance St. Petersburg, 1 November 1892.*

81 [Mlada. Suite]   15'
1.Introduction 2.Rédowa 3.Danse lithuanienne
4.Danse indienne 5.Cortège
4*(1Alto Fl.),3*(1Alto Ob.),4*,3(3rd alt. C.Bn.)
-6,3,3,1-Timp.,Perc.-3Hp.-Str.
Belaieff, Leipzig, 1895
Score 68 p.

1531 [Overture on Russian themes, Op. 28]   *12'*
2(2nd alt. Picc.),2,2,2-4,2,3-Timp.,Tamb.-Hp.
(optional)-Str.
Belaieff, Leipzig, 1886
Score 71 p.
Composed 1866. Revised 1880.

960 [Pan Voyevoda. Suite, Op. 59]   *21'*
1.Introduction 2.Krakoviak 3.Nocturne
4.Mazurka 5.Polonaise
3*,2(2nd alt. E.H.),2,2-4,2,3,1-Timp.,Perc.-Hp.
-Str.
Bessel, St. Petersburg [n.d.]
Score 90 p.
From the opera composed 1902-03.

360 [Russian Easter overture, Op. 36]   *13'*
3(3rd alt. Picc.),2,2,2-4,2,3,1-Timp.,Perc.-
Hp.-Str.
Belaieff, Leipzig [n.d.]
Score 97 p.
*Based on Russian liturgical themes. Composed
1888. First performance St. Petersburg, 1888,
the composer conducting.*

4379 [Sadko. Song of India. Transcribed   *3'*
by M. Altschuler]
3(3rd alt. Picc.),2*,2,2-4,2,3,1-Timp.,Perc.-
Hp.-Str.
Ms.
Score 8 p.
*From the opera composed 1894-96. First per-
formance Moscow, 7 January 1898, Michele
Esposito conductor.*

1481 Sadko, tableau musical, Op. 5   *13'*
3*,2,2,2-4,2,3,1-Timp.,Perc.-Hp.-Str.
Jurgenson, Moscow [n.d.]
Score 59 p.
Composed 1867. Revised 1891.

32 Scheherazade, Op. 35   *41'*
1.Largo e maestoso - Allegro non troppo 2.
Lento - Allegro molto 3.Andantino quasi allegretto 4.Allegro molto
3*,2(2nd alt. E.H.),2,2-4,2,3,1-Timp.,Perc.-
Hp.-Str.
Kalmus, New York [n.d.]
Score 227 p.
*Inspired by the Thousand and One Nights. Com-
posed 1888. First performance St. Petersburg,
3 November 1888, the composer conducting.*

437 [The snow maiden (Snegourochka).   *8'*
Suite]
1.Introduction 2.[Dance of the birds]
3.Cortège 4.Danse des bouffons
3*,2(2nd alt. E.H.),2,2-4,2,3,1-Timp.,Perc.-
Str.
Kalmus, New York [n.d.]
Score 73 p.
*From the opera composed 1880-81. First per-
formance St. Petersburg, 10 February 1882.*

316 Symphoniette sur des thèmes russes,   *18'*
Op. 31
1.Allegretto pastorale 2.Adagio 3.Scherzo-
Finale

2,2,2,2-4,2,3-Timp.-Str.
Belaieff, Leipzig, 1887
Score 124 p.
Composed 1879. Revised 1880-84.

722 [Symphony no. 1, Op. 1, E minor. Revised]
1.Largo assai - Allegro 2.Andante tranquillo
3.Scherzo 4.Allegro assai
2,2,2,2-4,2,3-Timp.-Hp.(ad lib.)-Str.
Bessel, St. Petersburg [n.d.]
Score 117 p.
Composed 1861-65. Revised 1884.

163 [Symphony no. 2, Antar, Op. 9,   *26'*
F-sharp minor]
1.Largo - Allegro giocoso 2.Allegro 3.
Allegro risoluto alla marcia 4.Allegretto
vivace
3(3rd alt. Picc.),2(2nd alt. E.H.),2,2-4,2,3,1
-Timp.,Perc.-Hp.-Str.
Kalmus, New York [n.d.]
Score 196 p.
*Based on an Arabian story by Sennkovsky. Com-
posed 1868. Revised 1875 and 1897.*

361 [Symphony no. 3, Op. 32, C major]   *30'*
1.Moderato assai - Allegro 2.Scherzo
3.Andante, attacca 4.Allegro con spirito
3*,2,2,2-4,2,3,1-Timp.-Str.
Belaieff, Leipzig, 1888
Score 151 p.
*Composed 1866-73. First performance St. Peters-
burg, 18 February 1874, the composer conducting.
Revised 1885-86.*

440 [Tsar Saltan. Flight of the   *2'*
bumblebee]
2,2,2,2-4,2,3,1-Timp.,Cym.-Str.
Kalmus, New York [n.d.]
Score 7 p.
*From the opera based on Pushkin's poem. Com-
posed 1898-1900. First performance Moscow, 3
November 1900.*

82 [Tsar Saltan. Suite, Op. 57]   *17'*
1.Allegretto alla marcia 2.Allegro
3.[The three wonders]
3*,3*,3*,3*-4,3,3,1-Timp.,Perc.-Cel.,Hp.-Str.
Bessel, St. Petersburg [n.d.]
Score 71 p.

80 [The Tsar's bride. Overture]   *6'*
3*,2,2,2-4,2,3,1-Timp.-Hp.-Str.
Belaieff, Leipzig, 1900
Score 31 p.
*From the opera composed 1898-99. First per-
formance Moscow, 3 November 1899.*

RISCHBIETER, WILHELM ALBERT.
Brunswick, Germany 20 July 1834
Dresden 11 February 1910

833s Souvenir du bal, Op. 47
Str.
Oertel, Hanover [n.d.]
Score 7 p.

Ritchie, John A.

RITCHIE, JOHN A.
    b. Wellington, New Zealand 29 September 1921

  284m Concertino, clarinet and strings   *17'*
    1.Allegro moderato 2.Andante piacevole
    3.Allegro scherzando - Adagio
    Solo Cl.-Str.
    Novello, London, C1963
    Score 39 p.
    Composed 1958. First performance Christchurch,
    New Zealand, 20 May 1960, New Zealand National
    Orchestra, the composer conducting, Frank Gurr
    soloist.

  2243s Suite for strings (1956)   *16'*
    1.Triptych 2.Air 3.Intrada 4.Fugue
    Str.
    Ms. C1956 by John A. Ritchie
    Score 40 p.
    Composed 1956. First performance Wellington,
    New Zealand, November 1956, Alex Lindsay
    String Orchestra, Alex Lindsay conductor.

RITTER, ALEXANDER.   Narva, Estonia 27 June 1833
                         Munich 12 April 1896

  1709 [Olaf's wedding dance, Op. 22]   *14'*
    3(3rd alt. Picc.),3*,3*,3*-4,4,3,1-Timp.,Perc.
    -2Hp.-Str.
    Aibl, Munich, C1896
    Score 40 p.

RITTER, REINHOLD.

  796m [Concert fantasy, clarinet, Op. 15]
    Solo Cl.-1,2,0,1-2,2,1-Timp.-Str.
    Score: Ms. 43 p.
    Parts: Oertel, Hanover [n.d.]

  907m [Titania, concert fantasy, Op. 26]
    Solo Cl.-1,2,0,2-2,2-Timp.-Str.
    Score: Ms. 34 p.
    Parts: A.E. Fischer, Bremen, C1906

RIVIER, JEAN.   Villemomble, France 21 July 1896

  1830s Adagio   *7'*
    Str.
    Senart, Paris, C1931
    Miniature score 6 p.
    Composed 1930. First performance Paris, 1
    March 1931, Orchestre Symphonique de Paris,
    Pierre Monteux conductor.

  2134 Chant funèbre   *7'*
    2,3*,3*,2-4,3,3,1-Timp.,Perc.-Cel.,Hp.-Str.
    Senart, Paris, C1929
    Score 15 p.
    Composed 1927. First performance Paris, 4
    February 1928, Concerts Pasdeloup, Albert
    Wolff conductor.

  2132 Danse [after Gide's Return from Chad]   *8'*
    3*,3*,3*,2-4,3,3,1-Timp.,Perc.-Hp.-Str.
    Senart, Paris, C1929
    Score 63 p.
    Composed 1928. First performance Paris 17
    February 1928, Concerts Lamoureux, Albert
    Wolff conductor.

  3630 Ouverture pour une opérette   *6'30"*
    imaginaire
    2,2,2,2-2,2,1-Timp.,Trgl.-Hp.-Str.
    Senart, Paris, c1931
    Miniature score 26 p.
    Composed 1930.

  4253 Paysage pour une Jeanne d'Arc   *9'*
    à Domrémy
    2,2,2,2-2,1-Bells,Trgl.-Cel.,Hp.-Str.
    Universal Edition, Vienna, C1936
    Score 22 p.
    Composed 1936. First performance Paris, 31
    January 1937.

  2078s [Symphony no. 2, strings, C major]   *19'*
    1.Allegro molto, deciso e marcato 2.Adagio
    3.Molto vivo e ritmico
    Str.
    B. Schott's Söhne, Mainz, C1938
    Score 21 p.
    Composed 1937.

  2133 Trois pastorales   *10'*
    1.Prélude 2.Glas [Death knell] 3.Chanson
    2,1,1,1-2,1,1-Timp.-Cel.,Hp.-Str.
    Senart, Paris, C1929
    Score 27 p.
    Composed 1928. First performance Paris, 7
    February 1929, Walther Straram conductor.

ROBBERECHTS, ANDRÉ.   Brussels 13 December 1797
                         Brussels 23 May 1860

  600m Pastorale. Orchestrated by Gaston Nardon
    Solo Ob.-Bn.-2Hn.-Str.
    Score: Ms. 6 p.
    Parts: Costallat, Paris [n.d.]

ROBERT-HANSEN.
  See: HANSEN, EMIL ROBERT.

ROBERT-LE-GRAND.
  See: LE-GRAND, ROBERT.

ROBERTS, CLIFFORD.

  1126s Pastorale
    Str.(Cb. ad lib.)
    Stainer & Bell, London, C1916 by composer
    Score 7 p.

ROBERTS, ROWLAND.
    b. Valparaiso, Indiana 2 September 1916

  5133 Caliban, overture for orchestra   *14'30"*
    2(2nd alt. Picc.),2(2nd alt. E.H.),2,2-4,3
    (3rd optional),3,1-Timp.,Perc.-Hp.-Str.
    Ms.
    Score 51 p. Large folio
    Composed 1952. First performance Oklahoma
    City, 16 December 1952, Oklahoma City Sym-
    phony Orchestra, Guy Fraser Harrison con-
    ductor.

ROBINSON, BERENICE.   New York City 1911

  3360 Overture in D [Op. 12]   *5'*
    2,2,2,2-4,2,3-Timp.-Str.

Ms.
Score 50 p.
Commissioned by the High School of Music and Art, New York, 1938. Composed 1940. First performance New York, 22 May 1941, High School of Music and Art Orchestra, Alexander Richter conductor.

ROBJOHN, WILLIAM JAMES.
See: FLORIO, CARYL. pseudonym.

ROBLES, DANIEL ALOMÍA.
Huánuco, Peru 3 January 1871
Chosica, near Lima 17 July 1942

4166 Himno al sol. Arranged for orchestra by Rudolph Holzmann
1,2*,2,1-2,2,3-Timp.,Perc.-Str.
Ms.
Score 18 p. Large folio
Theme is an Incan hymn. First performance New York, ca.1934. First Peruvian performance Lima, 16 October 1939, Orquesta Sinfónica Nacional, Theo Buchwald conductor.

ROBRECHT, CARL.   Immenhausen, Germany 25 June 1888

4609 Schwärmerei/Musical revelry   5'
1,0,1-0,2,1-Timp.-Harm.-Str.(without Va.)
B. Schott's Söhne, Mainz, ᶜ1939
Score in reduction 6 p.

ROCCA, LODOVICO.   Turin, Italy 29 November 1895

4242 [The dybbuk. Two symphonic pictures   8'
from the opera. Picture 2: Finale]
3(3rd alt. Picc.),3*,3*,2-4,3,3,1-Timp.,Perc.-Pno.,Cel.,Hp.-Str.
Ricordi, Milan, ᶜ1936
Score 37 p.
From the opera after Salomon Anski's play, based on the Jewish legend of a living person possessed by a dead person's spirit. First performance Milan, 24 March 1934.

ROCHBERG, GEORGE. Paterson, New Jersey 5 July 1918

6745 Black sounds (1965)   13'
2(both alt. Picc.),1,2(1st alt. Cl. in E-flat, 2nd alt. B.Cl.)-2,2,2,1-Timp.,Perc.-Pno.(alt. Cel.)
Ms.
Score 86 p. Large folio
Music for The Act, a ballet-mime choreographed by Anna Sokolow. Commissioned by the Lincoln Center Fund for NET Educational TV. Composed 1965. First performance New York, September 1965, NET telecast. Shared the Prix Italia.

5932 Chamber symphony for nine   17-18'
instruments (1953)
1.Allegro 2.Liberamente, quasi parlando - Quasi Tempo I (ma non tranquillo) 3.Marcia 4. ♪=ca.126
0,1,1,1-1,1,1-Vn.,Va.,Vc.
Ms.
Score 141 p. Large folio
Composed 1953. First performance Baltimore, 21 April 1954, Baltimore Chamber Society, Hugo

Weisgall conductor. Quotes the fratello motif of Luigi Dallapiccola's opera Il Prigioniero.

6609 Cheltenham concerto [in 7 movements]   15'
1,1,1,1-1,1,1-Str.
Suvini Zerboni, Milan, ᶜ1960
Score 40 p.
Commissioned by the Cheltenham Art Center, Pennsylvania. Composed 1958. First performance Philadelphia, 1958. Awarded first prize in the choral and orchestral category of the international competition of the Italian section of the International Society for Contemporary Music, 1959.

5970 David, the Psalmist, solo cantata   25'
[revised version, 1967]
1.Shema Yisroel (Prelude) 2.Psalm 6 3.Interlude 4.Psalm 29 5.Interlude 6.Psalm 57 7.Shema Yisroel (Postlude)
Ten. Voice Solo-3*,3*,3*,3*-4,3,3,1-Timp., Perc.-Str.
Ms.
Score 85 p. Large folio
Texts in Hebrew. Originally composed 1954. First performance of this version Philadelphia, 8 December 1966, University of Pennsylvania Orchestra, Melvin Strauss conductor.

5038 Night music for orchestra (1949)   12'
3*,3(3rd alt. E.H.),3(3rd alt. B.Cl.),3*-4,3, 3,1-Timp.,Perc.-Hp.-Str.
Ms.
Score 57 p. Large folio
Originally part of Symphony no. 1. Composed as a separate work, 1949. First performance New York, 23 April 1953, New York Philharmonic, Dimitri Mitropoulos conductor. Winner of the Eighth Annual George Gershwin Memorial Award, 1952.

5936 Symphony no. 1 (1957)   25'
1.Allegro risoluto 2.Tema e variazioni 3.Finale
3(3rd alt. Picc.),3(3rd alt. E.H.),3(3rd alt. B.Cl.),3*-4,3,3,1-Timp.,Perc.-Str.
Ms. [ᶜ1957 by Theodore Presser, Bryn Mawr, Pa.]
Score 150 p. Large folio
Originally planned in five movements, 1948. Two movements deleted, of which one became the composer's Night Music for Orchestra. Composed 1949-57. First performance Philadelphia, 28 March 1958, Philadelphia Orchestra, Eugene Ormandy conductor.

5930 Symphony no. 2 (1955-1956)   28'
In one movement
3*,3*,3*,3*-4,3,3,1-Timp.,Perc.-Str.
Ms. [ᶜ1958 by Theodore Presser, Bryn Mawr, Pa.]
Score 133 p. Large folio
Composed 1955-56. First performance Cleveland, 28 February 1959, Cleveland Orchestra, George Szell conductor. Received the Naumburg Recording Award, 1961.

6890 Symphony no. 3 (1969)   40'
In one movement
6(3rd & 4th alt. Picc.),6(4th alt. E.H.),7*

Rochberg, George

(4th&5th alt. Cl. in E-flat;1Cb.Cl.),6*-6,8,
7(1Cb.Tbn.),3(3rd alt. Cb.Tuba)-Timp.(2
players),Perc.-Pno.,Org.,Cel.-Electric Org.-
SATB Voices,Chamber Chorus,Double Chorus-Str.
Ms.
Score 176 p. Large folio
*Vocal texts used are 1) Saul, Was Verfolgst Du
Mich? from the cantata by Heinrich Schütz 2)
Durch Adams Fall Ist Ganz Verderbt, from the
Lutheran chorale and 3) Agnus Dei, from the
Roman Catholic liturgy. Commissioned by the
Juilliard School of Music, 1967. Composed
1966-69. First performance New York, 24
November 1970, Juilliard Theater Orchestra,
Juilliard Chorus and the Collegiate Chorale,
Abraham Kaplan conductor.*

6035   Time-span (II) for orchestra (1962)   *10'*
3,3*,3*,2-4,3,3,1-Perc.-Pno.,Cel.-Str.
Leeds Music, New York, ^C1965 by MCA
Score 46 p.
*Original version commissioned by the St. Louis
Symphony. Composed 1960. Revised 1962.
First performance Buffalo, New York, 19 January 1964, Buffalo Philharmonic Orchestra, the
composer conducting. Dedication: To the
memory of my son Paul whose time-span was so
brief.*

5931   Waltz serenade for orchestra (1957)   *9'30"*
3(3rd alt. Picc.),3*,3*(1st alt. Alto Sax.),
3*-4,3,3,1-Timp.,Perc.-Cel.,Hp.-Str.
Ms. [^C1958 by Theodore Presser, Bryn Mawr, Pa.]
Score 50 p. Large folio
*Originally composed for string orchestra, ca.
1955, under the title Ballet Music. This ver-
sion 1957. First performance Cincinnati, 14
February 1958, Cincinnati Symphony Orchestra,
Thor Johnson conductor.*

6729   Zodiac for orchestra (1964) [in   *14'*
12 movements]
3(3rd alt. Picc.),3*,4*(1Cl. in E-flat),3*-4,3,
3,1-Timp.,Perc.-Pno.,Cel.,Hp.-Str.
Ms.
Score 91 p. Large folio
*Originally composed as 12 Bagatelles for piano,
1952. This version 1964. First performance
Cincinnati, 8 May 1965, Cincinnati Symphony
Orchestra, Max Rudolf conductor.*

ROCHE, GUSTAVE.

1643s   Badinage
Solo Vn.-Str.
Score: Ms. 5 p.
Parts: Margueritat, Paris [n.d.]

1539s   Ballade
Solo Ob.(or Vn.)-Str.
Score: Ms. 5 p.
Parts: Enoch, Paris [n.d.]

1538s   Matinée florentine, romance
Solo Vn.-Str.
Score: Ms. 7 p.
Parts: Enoch & Costallat, Paris [n.d.]

1537s   Nuit vénitienne, barcarolle
Solo Vn.-Str.
Score: Ms. 6 p.
Parts: Enoch & Costallat, Paris [n.d.]

RODE, JACQUES-PIERRE-JOSEPH.
                           Bordeaux 26 February 1774
              Château-Bourbon, France 25 November 1830

1102v   Air varié, Op. 13
Solo Vn.-1,2,0,2-2Hn.-Str.
Score: Ms. 23 p.
Parts: Breitkopf & Härtel, Leipzig [n.d.]

1040v   [Concerto, violin, no. 7, Op. 9, A minor]
Revised by H.E. Kayser
1.Moderato 2.Adagio 3.Rondo con spirito
Solo Vn.-1,2,0,2-2Hn.-Timp.-Str.
Score: Ms. 83 p.
Parts: Jean André, Offenbach a.M. [n.d.]

1091v   [Thème varié, no. 4]
Solo Vn.-1,2,2,2-2Hn.-Timp.-Str.
Score: Ms. 30 p.
Parts: Breitkopf & Härtel, Leipzig [n.d.]

1092v   Variations, Op. 19
Solo Vn.-1,2,0,2-2,2-Timp.-Str.
Score: Ms. 24 p.
Parts: Breitkopf & Härtel, Leipzig [n.d.]

RODRIGO, JOAQUÍN.
              b. Sagunto, Valencia 22 November 1902

373v   Cançoneta   *4'*
Solo Vn.-Str.
Joaquín Rodrigo, Madrid, ^C1947
Score 4 p.
*Composed 1923. First performance Madrid, 1923,
Orquesta de Cámara, Angel Grande conductor.*

437m   [Concerto for guitar and   *21'30"*
orchestra, Aranjuez]
1.Allegro con spirito 2.Adagio 3.Allegro
gentile
Solo Guit.-2(2nd alt. Picc.),2(2nd alt. E.H.),
2,2-2,2-Str.
Sociedad de Estudios y Publicaciones, Madrid,
^C1949 by Joaquín Rodrigo
Score 91 p.
*Aranjuez, near Madrid, is the site of a Span-
ish royal palace. Composed 1939. First performance Barcelona, 9 November 1940, Mendoza
conductor, Regino Sainz de la Maza soloist.*

271p   [Concerto for piano and orchestra,   *30'*
Heroic]
1.Allegro con brio 2.Scherzo 3.Largo 4.Final
Solo Pno.-3(2nd & 3rd alt. Picc.I&II),2,2,2-
4,2,3-Timp.,Perc.-Str.
Ms. [^C1957 by Unión Musical Española, Madrid]
Score 206 p. Large folio
*Composed 1942. First performance Lisbon, 5
April 1943, Orquesta Nacional, Ernesto Halff-
ter conductor, Leopoldo Querol soloist.
Awarded the National Prize for Music by the
(Spanish) National Ministry of Education, 1942.*

438c [Concerto for violoncello and   20'
orchestra, In modo galante]
1.Allegretto grazioso 2.Adagietto 3.Rondo
giocoso
Solo Vc.-2(2nd alt. Picc.),2,2,2-2,2-Str.
Ms. [C1956 by Joaquín Rodrigo]
Score 101 p.
Commissioned by Gaspar Cassadó. Composed 1949.
First performance Madrid, 4 November 1949,
Orquesta Nacional, Ataulfo Argenta conductor,
Gaspar Cassadó soloist.

6132 Cuatro madrigales amatorios [in   8-9'
4 movements]
Voice Solo-2(2nd alt. Picc.),2,1-1,1-Trgl.-Str.
J. & W. Chester, London, C1960
Score 58 p.
Inspired by Spanish coplas of the 16th century.
Commissioned by The Louisville Orchestra.
Composed 1948. First performance Louisville,
9 November 1948, The Louisville Orchestra,
Robert Whitney conductor, Marimi del Pozo
soloist.

6865 [Music to a Salamancan codex on a text by
Miguel de Unamuno]
Solo Bass Voice, Chorus(SATB)-Picc.,Fl.,E.H.-
Hn.,Tpt.-Hp.-Str.
Unión Musical Española, Madrid, C1966
Score 40 p.
Text is Unamuno's poem Salamanca. Composed
1953 to commemorate the Seventh Centennial of
the University of Salamanca. First perform-
ance Salamanca, Spain, 12 October 1953.

6740 [Soleriana, suite for orchestra,   25'
after sonatas of Padre Soler]
1.Entrada 2.Fandango 3.Tourbillon 4.Pastoral
5.Passepied 6.Fandango a lo alto 7.Contra-
danza 8.Boleras
2*,1,1,1-1,1-Str.
Unión Musical Española, Madrid, C1967
Score 255 p.
From the dance music commissioned by the Span-
ish dancer Antonio (Antonio Ruiz Soler). Com-
posed 1953. First performance Festivales de
España, Granada, Spain, July 1953, Orquesta
de Cámara de Madrid, Angel Curras conductor,
Ballet de Antonio with Antonio choreographer
and soloist.

259m Sones en la Giralda (Fantasia   9'
sevillana)
In one movement
Solo Hp.-2(2nd alt. Picc.),1,1,1-1,1-Str.
Ms.
Score 68 p.
Composed 1963. First performance London, 13
March 1963, BBC Concert Orchestra, Vilem
Tausky conductor, Marisa Robles soloist.

5745 Tres viejos aires de danza   8'
1.Pastoral 2.[Minuet] 3.Jiga
1,1,1,1-2Hn.-Str.
Joaquín Rodrigo, Madrid, C1947
Score 26 p.
Composed 1927-30. First performance Valencia,
Spain, 1931, Orquesta Sinfónica de Valencia,
Señor Izquierdo conductor.

ROECKEL, JOSEPH LEOPOLD.   London 11 April 1838
                          Vittel, France 20 June 1923

1020s Air du dauphin
Str.
Score: Ms. 4 p.
Parts: [n.p., n.d.]

ROESGEN-CHAMPION, MARGUERITE.
                          b. Geneva 25 January 1894

796p Aquarelles pour clavecin et   12'
orchestre
1.Prisme 2.Harmonies 3.Sérénade
Solo Hpscd.-Fl.,Ob.-Str.
Senart, Paris, C1929
Score 28 p.
Composed 1927. First performance Paris, 26
November 1933.

ROGATIS, PASCUAL DE.   Teora, Italy 16 May 1880

3236 [Huemac. Danza]   8'
3*,3*,3*,2-4,3,3,1-Timp.,Perc.-Cel.,Hp.-Str.
Ms.
Score 39 p.
From the opera composed 1915. First perform-
ance, Buenos Aires, 28 August 1916, La Scala
Orchestra of Milan, the composer conducting.
Awarded a prize by the city of Buenos Aires,
1916.

ROGER-DUCASSE, JEAN-JULES AIMABLE.
                          Bordeaux 18 April 1873
            Le Taillan-Médoc, near Bordeaux 19 July 1954

815 [The ferret's merry play, scherzo]   5'
3(3rd alt. Picc.),3*,2,2,Sarrus.-4,3,3,1-Timp.,
Perc.-2Hp.-Str.
Durand, Paris, C1912
Score 49 p.
Composed 1911. First performance Paris, 1920.

817 [In Marguerite's garden. Interlude]   11'
3,3*,3*,2-4,2,3,1-Timp.,Perc.-Cel.,2Hp.-Str.
Durand, Paris, C1912
Score 64 p.
From the symphonic poem for double chorus and
orchestra, composed 1901-05. First perform-
ance Paris, 18 April 1913, Société Nationale.

816 Nocturne de printemps   12'
3(3rd alt. Picc.),3*,3*,2-4,2,3,1-Timp.,Perc.-
Cel.,2Hp.-Str.
Durand, Paris, C1920
Score 35 p.
Composed 1918. First performance Paris, 14
February 1920, Concerts Pasdeloup, Rhené-Baton
conductor.

254 Orphée, fragments symphoniques   8'
1.Évocation 2.Course du flambeau
4*,4*,4*,3,Sarrus.-4,3,3,1-Timp.,Perc.-2Hp.-Str.
Durand, Paris, C1914
Score 89 p.
From the mimodrama with libretto by the compo-
ser, composed 1912. First concert performance
St. Petersburg, 31 January 1914.

Roger-Ducasse, Jean-Jules

474   Petite suite   7'
1.[Recollections] 2.Berceuse 3.[Clarion call]
3(3rd alt. Picc.),3*,2,2-4,3,3,1-Timp.,Perc.-
Hp.-Str.
Durand, Paris, C1911
Score 26 p.
*Composed 1899. First performance Paris, March
1911.*

4008   Poème symphonique, sur le nom de
Gabriel Fauré
3*,3*,3*,2-4,3,3,1-Timp.,Perc.-Hp.-Str.
Durand, Paris, C1923
Miniature score 31 p.
Composed 1922.

510   Prélude d'un ballet   3'
3,3*,2,2-4,3-Timp.,Perc.-Hp.-Str.
Durand, Paris, C1911
Score 9 p.
*Composed 1910. First performance Paris, 1911,
Concerts Lamoureux, Camille Chevillard con-
ductor.*

473c   Romance
Solo Vc.-2,0,2,1-Hn.-Str.
Durand, Paris, C1919
Score 15 p.
Composed 1918.

5215   Sarabande, poème symphonique   19'
3(3rd alt. Picc.),3*,2,2-4,3,3,1-Timp.,Perc.-
2Hp.-Voices offstage(SAT or 3Cl.)-Str.
Durand, Paris, C1911
Score 32 p.
*Composed 1910. First performance Paris, 22
January 1911, Concerts Colonne.*

1024   Suite française en ré majeur   20'
1.Ouverture 2.Bourrée 3.Récitatif et air
4.Menuet vif
3(3rd alt. Picc.),3(E.H. alt. Ob. d'Amore),2,2-
4,2,3,1-Timp.,Perc.-Hp.-Str.
Durand, Paris, C1909
Score 109 p.
*Composed 1907. First performance Paris, March
1909.*

882   Suite pour petit orchestre   7'
1.Sans lenteur 2.Lent 3.Très vite et très
rythmé
2,2,2,2-2Hn.-Timp.-Str.
Durand, Paris, C1919
Score 27 p.
*Composed 1918. First performance Paris 1919,
Concerts Lamoureux, Camille Chevillard conductor.*

515m   Variations plaisantes sur un thème grave
Solo Hp.-3(3rd alt. Picc.),3*,2,2-4,3,3,1-
Timp.,Perc.-Str.
Durand, Paris, C1909
Score 72 p.
*Composed 1906. First performance Paris, 24
January 1909, Concerts Lamoureux, Camille
Chevillard conductor, Marcel Grandjany soloist.*

ROGERS, BERNARD.   New York 4 February 1893
Rochester, New York 24 May 1968

2825   Adonais, prelude and slow march   12'
3(3rd alt. Picc.),3*,3*,3*-4,3,3,1-Timp.,Perc.
-Cel.,Hp.-Str.
Ms.
Score 33 p.
*Composed 1926. First performance Rochester,
29 April 1927, Rochester Philharmonic Orches-
tra, Howard Hanson conductor.*

5289   Characters from Hans Christian   8'
Andersen, suite for orchestra
1.The shirt-collar 2.The rose tree 3.The snow
queen 4.The emperor's new clothes
2(2nd alt. Picc.),2,2,2-2,2,1-Timp.,Perc.-Pno.,
Hp.-Str.
Ms. [C1946 by Elkan-Vogel, Philadelphia]
Score 26 p.
*Commissioned by radio station WHAM, Rochester.
Composed 1944. First performance Rochester,
28 April 1945, Eastman-Rochester Symphony
Orchestra, Howard Hanson conductor.*

3687   The colours of war   6'
3*,2,2,2-4,2,3,1-Timp.,Perc.-Hp.-Str.
Ms.
Score 22 p. Large folio
*Composed 1939. First performance Rochester, 25
October 1939, Rochester Civic Orchestra, Howard
Hanson conductor.*

3684   The dance of Salome   10'
3*,3*,3*,3*-4,3,3,1-Timp.,Perc.-Cel.,Hp.-Str.
Ms.
Score 65 p. Large folio
*Composed 1940. First performance Eastman
School of Music, Rochester, 25 April 1940,
Rochester Philharmonic Orchestra, Howard Han-
son conductor.*

5480   Dance scenes, for orchestra
1.The rising moon 2.Fire flies 3.Samurai
2(2nd alt. Picc.),2,2,3*-4,2,3,1-Timp.,Perc.-
Pno.,Hp.-Str.
Ms.
Score 60 p. Large folio
*Commissioned by The Louisville Orchestra.
First performance Louisville, 28 October 1953,
The Louisville Orchestra, Robert Whitney con-
ductor.*

472m   Fantasia, horn, kettledrums and   11'
strings
Solo Hn.-Timp.-Str.
Ms. [C1955 by Theodore Presser, Bryn Mawr, Pa.]
Score 26 p. Large folio
*Composed 1954. First performance Rochester, 11
February 1955, Rochester Philharmonic, Erich
Leinsdorf conductor, Morris Secon soloist.*

938m   Fantasy, flute, viola and orchestra   7'
Solo Fl., Solo Va.-0,2,2,2-4,2,3,1-Timp.-Hp.-
Str.(without Va.)
Ms.
Score 27 p.

Composed 1938. First performance Rochester, 25 April 1938, Rochester Civic Orchestra, Guy Fraser Harrison conductor, Joseph Mariano flautist, Mordecai Lurie violist.

2736 Once upon a time, five fairy tales   *12'*
2(alt. 2Picc.),2,2,2-2,2,1-Timp.,Perc.-Clavi-
cemb.(Adapted Pno.),Hp.-Str.
Kalmus, New York, ^C1936 (for the Juilliard
Foundation)
Score 64 p.
Composed 1935. First performance Rochester, 4 April 1935, Rochester Philharmonic Orchestra, Howard Hanson conductor.

3621 The plains, landscapes for orchestra   *13'*
1.Nocturne 2.Storm 3.Daybreak
1(alt. Picc.),1(alt. E.H.),2,1-2,1,1-Timp.,
Perc.-Hp.-Str.
Ms.
Score 77 p.
Commissioned by the League of Composers. Composed 1940. First performance in a CBS radio broadcast, New York, 3 May 1941, Columbia Concert Orchestra, Howard Barlow conductor.

6457 The silver world   *16'*
1.The silver world 2.A hobby horse 3.Marche
chinoise 4.A princess 5.Tug of war
1(alt. Picc.),1-Str.
Southern Music, New York, ^C1953
Score 24 p.
Composed 1956. First performance Rochester, 25 July 1957, Eastman Chamber Orchestra, Frederick Fennell conductor.

675m Soliloquy [no. 1] flute and string   *6'*
orchestra
Solo Fl.-Str.
Birchard, Boston, ^C1926 by Eastman School of Music
Score 9 p.
Composed 1922. First performance Rochester, 1926, Rochester Philharmonic, Howard Hanson conductor.

934m Soliloquy no. 2, bassoon and string   *6'*
orchestra
Solo Bn.-Str.
Ms.
Score 10 p.
Composed 1938. First performance Rochester, 18 October 1938, Rochester Civic Orchestra, Howard Hanson conductor, Vincent Pezzi soloist.

3173 The song of the nightingale, suite   *19'*
1.Prelude 2.The gardens of the porcelain
palace 3.Expedition of the Chinese gentlemen
4.Berceuse 5.A court festival 6.The clock-
work nightingale 7.Death and the emperor
8.The song of the nightingale 9.Happy ending
2(2nd alt. Picc.),2(2nd alt. E.H.),3*,2-4,3,
3,1-Timp.,Perc.-Cel.,Hp.-Str.
Ms.
Score 122 p.
Inspired by Hans Christian Andersen's stories. Composed 1939. First performance Cincinnati, 21 March 1940, Cincinnati Symphony Orchestra, Eugene Goossens conductor.

3136 The supper at Emmaus   *6'*
3(3rd alt. Picc.),3*,3*,3*-4,3,3,1-Timp.,Perc.-
Cel.,Hp.-Str.
Ms.
Score 17 p. Large folio
Composed 1936. First performance Eastman School of Music, Rochester, 29 April 1937, Rochester Philharmonic Orchestra, Howard Hanson conductor.

2658 [Symphony no. 2, A-flat major]   *22'*
In one movement
3*,3*,4*(1Cl. in E-flat),3*-4,4,3,1-Timp.,
Perc.-Cel.,2Hp.-Str.
Ms.
Score 103 p.
Composed 1928. First performance Rochester, 24 October 1930, Rochester Philharmonic Orchestra, Howard Hanson conductor.

2859 [Symphony no. 3, C major]   *42'*
1.Allegro 2.Elegy 3.Andante maestoso -
Vivace fantastico 4.Andante calmo - Allegro
energico
3(3rd alt. Picc.),3*,3*,3*-4,4,3,1-Timp.,
Perc.-Hp.-Str.
Ms.
Score 167 p.
Composed 1936. First performance Rochester, 27 October 1937, Rochester Philharmonic Orchestra, Howard Hanson conductor.

4796 [Symphony no. 4, To soldiers]   *24'*
1.Battle fantasy 2.Eulogy 3.Fugue - Epilogue
3*,2,2(2nd alt. B.Cl.),2(2nd alt. C.Bn.)-4,3,
3,1-Timp.,Perc.-Str.
Ms.
Score 117 p. Large folio
Composed 1947. First performance Rochester, 6 May 1948, Eastman-Rochester Symphony Orchestra, Howard Hanson conductor.

2650 Three Eastern dances   *12'*
1.With pennons 2.Mourning 3.With swords
3*(1st*2nd alt. optional B.&Alto Fl.),3*,
3*,3*-4,2,3,1-Timp.,Perc.-Pno.,Cel.,Hp.-
Mezzo-sop. Voice (optional)-Str.
Ms.
Score 71 p.
Composed 1932. First performance Rochester, 3 May 1934, Rochester Philharmonic Orchestra, Howard Hanson conductor.

2828 Two American frescoes   *10'*
1.The Mississippi 2.Ojibway battle dance
3(3rd alt. Picc.),3*,3*,3*-4,3,3,1-Timp.,Perc.-
Pno.,Org.(ad lib.),Hp.-Str.
Ms.
Score 86 p.
Composed 1934. First performance Rochester, 16 January 1936, Rochester Philharmonic Orchestra, Howard Hanson conductor.

ROGISTER, JEAN.   Liège, Belgium 25 October 1879
                         Liège 20 March 1964

290v [Concerto, violin, in G]
1.Allegro commodo 2.Grave 3.Rondo
Solo Vn.-2,2,2,2-2Hn.-Timp.,Perc.-Str.

Rogister, Jean

Ms.
Score 80 p.
*Composed 1945. First performance Liège, 9
August 1947, René Defossez conductor, Henri
Koch soloist.*

6914 [Dramatic sketch, for orchestra]
2,2,2,2-4,3,3,1-Timp.,Perc.-Hp.-Str.
Ms.
Score 57 p.
*Originally composed for string quartet, 1935.
This transcription 1952. First performance
Liège, 2 February 1962, Grand Orchestre du
Conservatoire, Fernand Quinet conductor.*

6954 [Fantasy burlesque on a popular theme]
3*,2(2nd alt. E.H.),3(3rd alt. Cl. in E-flat),
2-4,3,3,1-Timp.,Perc.-Cel.-Str.
Ms.
Score 57 p.
*Theme is a Walloon song about the misadven-
tures of St. Aubin, Walloon patron of drunk-
ards. Composed 1928. First performance
Liège, 1 December 1928, orchestra conducted by
the composer.*

6886 Improvisation sur un thème
3(3rd alt. Picc.),3(3rd alt. E.H.),3,3-4,3,3,
1-Timp.,Perc.-Cel.,Hp.-Str.
Ms.
Score 45 p.
*Originally titled Métamorphose. Composed
1948. First performance Liège, 22 October
1949, Le Grand Orchestre du Conservatoire
Royal de Liège, Fernand Quinet conductor.*

ROHDE, FRIEDRICH WILHELM.
Altona, Germany 11 December 1856
Gentofte, near Copenhagen 6 April 1928

5s Serenade, Op. 14
1.Piacevole e con tenerezza 2.Andante
3.À la guitare 4.Rondo
Str.
Ries & Erler, Berlin [n.d.]
Score 23 p.

RÖHNER, J. C.   b. ca.1780
                                        d. ca.1830

5566 [Symphony, chamber orchestra, Op. 3,
D major] Edited by Thor Johnson and Donald M.
McCorkle
1.Adagio grave - Allegro assai 2.Andante
grazioso 3.Minuetto 4.Allegro
1,2-2,2-Timp.-Str.
Ms. Prepared by The Fleisher Collection of
Orchestral Music, from the Archives of the
Moravian Church in America (Bethlehem, Penn-
sylvania Collection) ^C1956? by The Moravian
Music Foundation, Inc., Winston-Salem, N.C.
Score 131 p. Large folio
*First published by Hummel, Amsterdam, ca.1803.
This edition based on a manuscript copied by
the Moravian, Johann Friedrich Peter. First
modern performance, Quincentennial Early
American Moravian Music Festival, Central
Moravian Church, Bethlehem, 27 June 1957, The
Festival Orchestra, Thor Johnson conductor.*

RÖHRICHT, PAUL. Grünberg, Silesia 13 November 1867
                 Schreiberhau, Silesia 17 October 1925

4485 O du mein Edelweiss! Walzer. Transcribed
for band by M. Busch
1,1,4(1Cl. in E-flat),1-4Sax.-4,2,Fluegelhn.,
3Ten.Hn.,2Tbn.,Bar.,2-Perc.
Fr. Portius, Leipzig [n.d.]
No score published. Clarinet I part 2 p.
*This work attributed to Paul Röhricht and
Adolf Friedrich Christian.*

ROLDÁN GARBES, AMADEO.   Paris 12 July 1900
                             Havana 2 March 1939

3813 [Call to awaken Papa-Montero]   60"
Cl.-2Hn.,2Tpt.,Tbn.-Cuban Timp.
Ms.
Score 2 p.

4163 Obertura sobre temas populares cubanos
3(3rd alt. Picc.),3*,4*,3*-4,3,3,1-Timp.,Perc.
-Cel.,Hp.-Str.
Ms.
Score 75 p.
*Composed 1925. First performance Havana, 29
November 1925, Orquesta Filarmónica de la
Habana, Pedro Sanjuan conductor.*

3567 [La Rebambaramba. Part II: Interludio]
3,3*,3*,2-4,3,3-Timp.,Cym.-Str.
Ms.
Score 23 p.
*From the ballet suite composed 1927-28. First
concert performance Havana, 12 August 1928,
Havana Philharmonic Orchestra, the composer
conducting.*

1010m Ritmica V [for percussion, 11 players]
1st-Clave I [Very High]
2nd-Clave IV [Very Low]
3rd-2 Cencerros [Cow Bells], Clave III [Low]
4th-Quijada, Clave II [High]
5th-Guiro
6th-2 Maracas
7th-2 Bongos
8th-Timbales
9th-Timp.
10th- B.Dr.
11th-Marimbula or Cb.
Ms.
Miniature score 15 p.
*Composed 1930. First performance Cornish
School, Seattle, John Cage conductor.*

992m Ritmica VI [for percussion, 11 players]
1st-2 Cencerros [2 Cow Bells (High & Low)]
2nd-2 Maracas [High & Low]
3rd-Clave [High]
4th-Clave [Low]
5th-Quijada

6th-Guiro
7th-2 Bongos [High & Low]
8th-2 Timbales
9th-Timp.
10th-B.Dr.
11th-Marimbula or Cb.
Ms.
Miniature score 14 p.
First performance Cornish School, Seattle.

ROLÓN, JOSÉ.
    Ciudad Gusmán, Jalisco, Mexico 22 June 1883
        Mexico City 3 February 1945

3315 Ballet de los gallos   *6'*
3(3rd alt. Picc.),3*,3*,2-4,3,3,1-Timp.,Perc.-
Pno.,Hp.-Str.
Ms.
Score 30 p.
*Composed 1931. First performance Mexico City,
25 March 1932, Orquesta Sinfónica de México,
Carlos Chavez conductor.*

322p [Concerto, piano and orchestra, Op. 42]
1.Allegro energico 2.Poco lento 3.Allegro
con fuoco
Solo Pno.-3*,3*,2,2-4,3,3,1-Timp.,Perc.-Str.
Ms.
Score 194 p.
*Composed 1935. First performance by a local
ensemble, Guadalajara, Mexico, 31 January 1936,
the composer conducting. Second performance,
Mexico City, 4 September 1942, Orquesta Sinfónica de México.*

3883 El festin de los enanos, Op. 30 [The feast
of the dwarfs]
3*,2,2,2-4,2,3,1-Timp.,Perc.-Cel.,Hp.-Str.
Ms.
Score 68 p.
*Inspired by Alfonso Gutierrez Hermosillo's
poem. Composed 1927. First performance
Mexico City, 4 March 1928, Orchestra of the
National Conservatory, José Rocabruna conductor. Awarded first prize by the First Congress of Music, Mexico, 1927.*

ROMAN, JOHAN HELMICH.   Stockholm 26 October 1694
       Haraldsmåla, Sweden 19 October 1758

1205v [Concerto, violin, D minor] Edited by
Hilding Rosenberg
1.Allegro 2.Andante 3.Allegro
Solo Vn.-Cemb.-Str.
Nordiska Musikförlaget, c1935
Score 22 p.

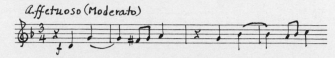

2071s [Concerto grosso, 2 violins, cembalo, *7'*
and string orchestra, G minor. After the
Sonata Op. 1 no. 6 by Francesco Geminiani]
Edited by Hilding Rosenberg
1.Affetuoso (Moderato) 2.Allegro

Concertino: Vn.I,Vn.II; Ripieno: Cemb.-Str.
Carl Gehrman, Stockholm, c1944
Score 9 p.

384m [Concerto grosso, 2 violins, cembalo and
string orchestra, B-flat major] Edited by
Valdemar Söderholm
1.Adagio e staccato - Allegro 2.Adagio
3.Allegro
Soli: Vn.I, Vn.II-Cemb.-Str.
Nordiska Musikförlaget, Stockholm, c1945
Score 23 p.

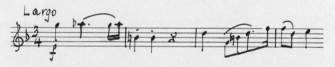

5105 [Partita, oboe, cembalo and string orches-
tra, C minor] Edited by Hilding Rosenberg
Sinfonia; 1.Allegro 2.Con spirito (Moderato
con fuoco) 3.Andante 4.Largo 5.Presto - Più
tranquillo - Presto 6.Menuetto 7.Presto
Ob.-Cemb.-Str.
Carl Gehrman, Stockholm, c1944
Score 30 p.

5807 [Sinfonia no. 16, D major] Edited   *8'30"*
by Claude Genetay
1.Allegro 2.Larghetto 3.Allegro
1,2-Cemb.-Str.
Carl Gehrman, Stockholm, c1950
Score 14 p.

2138s [Sinfonia no. 20, E minor] Edited   *9'30"*
by Claude Genetay
1.Allegro staccato 2.Larghetto 3.Allegro
assai 4.Allegro
Cemb.-2Fl.-Str.

Roman, Johan

Carl Gehrman, Stockholm, ^c1950
Score 15 p.

6116 Sinfonia per la chiesa. Edited by Hilding
Rosenberg
1.Andante 2.Grave 3.Fuga
0,1,0,1-Org.(ad lib.)-Str.
Nordiska Musikförlaget, Stockholm, ^c1935
Score 15 p.

ROMBERG, ANDREAS JACOB.
                    Vechta, Germany 27 April 1767
                    Gotha, Germany 10 November 1821

4108 Sinfonia alla turca, Op. 51 [C major]
1.Allegro 2.Vivace 3.Andante quasi allegretto 4.Vivace
2*,2,2,2-2,2-Timp.,Perc.-Str.
Ms.
Score 165 p.

ROMBERG, BERNHARD HEINRICH.
                    Dinklage, Germany 11 November 1767
                    Hamburg 13 August 1841

715c Concertino suisse, violoncelle, Op. 78
1.Allegro non troppo 2.Andante cantabile
3.Allegretto
Solo Vc.-0,0,2,2-2Hn.-Timp.-Str.
Score: Ms. 80 p.
Parts: Jean André, Offenbach a.M. [n.d.]

720c [Concerto, violoncello, no. 1, Op. 2,
B-flat major]
1.Allegro 2.Andante 3.Rondo
Solo Vc.-1,2,0,2-2Hn.-Str.
Score: Ms. 86 p.
Parts: Jean André, Offenbach a.M. [n.d.]

706c [Concerto, violoncello, no. 2, Op. 3,
D major]
1.Allegro maestoso 2.Andante grazioso
3.Rondo
Solo Vc.-1,2,0,1-2Hn.-Str.
Score: Ms. 108 p.
Parts: [Jean André, Offenbach a.M., n.d.]

722c [Concerto, violoncello, no. 4, Op. 7,
E minor]
1.Allegro 2.Andante poco lento 3.Rondo à la
polacca
Solo Vc.-1,2,0,2-2Hn.-Str.
Score: Ms. 92 p.
Parts: Costallat, Paris [n.d.]

648c [Concerto, violoncello, no. 8, Op. 48,
A major]
1.Allegro 2.Lento grazioso 3.Vivace
Solo Vc.-1,2,0,2-2Hn.-Str.
Score: Ms. 74 p.
Parts: Lemoine, Paris [n.d.]

724c [Concerto, violoncello, no. 10, Op. 75,
E major]
1.Allegro non troppo 2.Andante sostenuto
3.Rondo vivace
Solo Vc.-1,0,2,2-2Hp.-Timp.-Str.
Score: Ms. 83 p.
Parts: Jean André, Offenbach a.M. [n.d.]

3613 Kinder-Symphonie, Op. 62 [Children's
symphony, C major]
1.Allegro maestoso 2.Tempo di menuetto
3.Adagio lamentabile 4.Allegretto - Presto
Tpt.-Dr.,Trgl.,Quail,Cuckoo, Nightingale,Rattle
-Str.(without Va. or Vc.)
Breitkopf & Härtel, Leipzig [n.d.]
Score 16 p.

628c Souvenir de St. Petersbourg, fantaisie sur
des airs du Comte Michel Wielhorski, Op. 77
Solo Vc.-Str.
Score: Ms. 36 p.
Parts: Joh. André, Offenbach a.M. [n.d.]

4109 Trauer Symphonie, Op. 23 [C minor]
1.Andante lento maestoso - Allegro 2.Adagio
non troppo
1,2,2,2-2Hn.-Timp.-Str.
Ms.
Score 90 p.
Composed 1810 in memory of Louise of Prussia.

RONGÉ, JEAN-BAPTISTE. Liège, Belgium 1 April 1825
                        Liège 28 October 1882

709m Berceuse for trumpet and trombone
Soli Tpt.,Tbn.-1,1,1,2-4Hn.-Timp.-Str.
Ms.
Score 8 p.

RONSARD, JULES.

1405s Charme d'amour
Str.
Score: Ms. 12 p.
Parts: R. Dietrich, Leipzig [n.d.]

RÖNTGEN, JULIUS.   Leipzig 9 May 1855
                        Utrecht 13 September 1932

415p [Concerto, piano, Op. 18, D major]   *24'*
1.Allegro 2.Larghetto espressivo 3.Finale
Solo Pno.-2,2,2,2-2,2-Timp.-Str.
Score: Ms. 260 p.
Parts: Breitkopf & Härtel, Leipzig [n.d.]
*Composed 1880. First performance Amsterdam,
1882.*

2099 [Old Netherlandish dances, Op. 46]
1.Salterelle 2.Branle de Bourgogne 3.Ronde
4.Gaillarde la Brune 5.Bergerette, Les grands
douleurs 6.Pavane, Lesquercarde

2(1st alt. Picc.),2,2,2-4,2,3-Timp.,Trgl.-Hp.-
Str.
A.A. Noske, Middelburg, Netherlands [1904?]
Score 40 p.
*Arranged from a collection published Antwerp,
1551.*

ROOS, ROBERT DE.   The Hague 10 March 1907

3853 Ouverture voor een tragi-comedie   *6'*
3(3rd alt. Picc.),3*,3*,2-4,3,3,1-Timp.,Perc.
Str.
Universal Edition, London, ^c1938
Score 23 p.
*Commissioned by Willem Mengelberg. Composed
1937.*

ROOSEVELT, J. WILLARD.   Madrid 16 January 1918

6709 Amistad [Friendship, homage to Morel   *6'*
Campos]
2(2nd alt. Picc.),2,2,2-4,2,3,1-Timp.,Perc.-
Pno.-Str.
Ms.
Score 50 p. Large folio
*Commissioned by the Columbia University Orches-
tra. Composed 1965. First performance New
York, 26 February 1966, Columbia University
Orchestra, Howard Shanet conductor.*

405c Concerto for 'cello and orchestra   *14'*
in 3 movements
Solo Vc.-2(2nd alt. Picc.),2,2,2-4,2,3,1-Timp.
(alt. Xyl.),B.Dr.,S.Dr.-Str.
Ms. ^c1963 by J. Willard Roosevelt
Score 80 p. Large folio
*Commissioned by the Columbia University Orches-
tra. Composed 1963. First performance McMil-
lin Theatre, Columbia University, New York, 27
April 1963, Howard Shanet conductor, Jerome
Kessler soloist.*

ROOTHAM, CYRIL BRADLEY.
          Bristol, England 5 October 1875
          Cambridge, England 18 March 1938

1340s Miniature suite
1.Allegretto 2.Lento assai 3.Allegro
moderato e leggiero 4.Molto vivace
Str.
Curwen, London, ^c1925 by Cyril Bradley Rootham
Score 22 p.

534s Rhapsody on an old English tune (Lazarus)
Str.
Murdoch, London, ^c1924
Score 19 p.

ROPARTZ, JOSEPH GUY MARIE.
       Guingamp, Côtes du Nord, France 15 June 1864
         Lanloup, France 22 November 1955

644c Adagio
Solo Vc.-2,2,2,2-2Hn.-Str.
Dupont-Metzner, Nancy [n.d.]
Score 12 p.

568 Carnaval, impromptu symphonique
2,2,2,2-4,2,3,1-Timp.,Perc.-Str.

Bailly, Paris [n.d.]
Score 36 p.

1025 La chasse du Prince Arthur   *10'*
3(3rd alt. Picc.),3*,3,3-4,3,4-Timp.,Cym.-Hp.-
Str.
Durand, Paris, ^c1913
Score 68 p.
*Composed 1911-12. First performance Paris,
1912, Concerts Lamoureux, Camille Chevillard
conductor.*

384 Cinq pièces brèves [Five short pieces] *8'*
1,1,1,1-2Hn.-Timp.-Str.
Heugel, Paris [n.d.]
Score 61 p.
Composed 1889. First performance Paris, 1891.

1012 La cloche des morts [The death knell] *7'*
2,2,2,2-4,2,4-Timp.,Perc.-Hp.-Str.
Baudoux, Paris [n.d.]
Score 27 p.
*Composed 1887; revised 1902. First performance
Nancy, 1902, the composer conducting.*

250 Divertissement   *6'*
2,3*,2,2-4,2,3-Timp.,Dr.-Hp.-Str.
Durand, Paris, ^c1919
Score 46 p.
*Composed 1915. First performance Paris, 1920,
Concerts Lamoureux, Camille Chevillard con-
ductor.*

989 Fantaisie, en ré majeur   *15'*
3*,2,2,2-4,2,3-Timp.-Str.
Baudoux, Paris [n.d.]
Score 84 p.
*Composed 1897. First performance Paris, 6
March 1898, Concerts Colonne, Edouard Colonne
conductor.*

687m Lamento
Solo Ob.-2,0,2,2-2Hn.-Str.
Ms.
Score 27 p.

1856 Les Landes [The Breton heath]   *8'*
2,2,2,2-4,2,3,1-Timp.,Perc.-Hp.-Str.
Rouart, Lerolle, Paris, 1888
Score 43 p.
*Composed 1887. First performance Paris, 1889,
Société Nationale de Musique, Gabriel-Marie
conductor.*

1514s Méditation, Op. 17   *2'*
Solo Vc.-Str.
Score: Ms. 3 p.
Parts: Costallat, Paris [n.d.]

2957 Oedipe à Colone, musique pour la tragédie
de Sophocle
1.Prélude du 1er acte 2.Entrée de Thesée
3.Prélude du 2e acte 4.Lamento 5.Prélude du
3e acte
2(2nd alt. Picc.),2(2nd alt. E.H.),2,2-2-
Timp.-Hp.-Str.
Durand, Paris, ^c1925
Score 80 p.

Ropartz, Guy

531m Pastorale et danses
Solo Ob.-2,0,2,2-2,1-Timp.-Hp.-Str.
Enoch, Paris [n.d.]
Score 43 p.
Composed 1907 for the Paris Conservatoire competition.

1110 Pêcheur d'Islande [Iceland fisherman] *15'*
1.La mer d'Islande 2.Scène d'amour 3.Danses
2,2(2nd alt. E.H.),3*,2-4,2(alt. 2Cnt.),3,1-
Timp.-Hp.-Str.
Choudens, Paris, C1893
Score 110 p.
From the incidental music to Pierre Loti's play. Composed 1889-91. First performance Paris, 1899, Concerts Colonne, the composer conducting.

747m [Piece in E-flat minor, trombone]
Solo Tbn.-2,2,2,2-4,2,3-Timp.-Str.
Score: Ms. 29 p.
Parts: Evette & Schaeffer, Paris [n.d.]

572c Rhapsodie
Solo Vc.-2,2*,2,1-3,1-Timp.,Perc.-Hp.-Str.
Durand, Paris, C1928
Score 43 p.
Composed 1928.

645v Romanza e scherzino
Solo Vn.-1,2*,1,1-2Hn.-Timp.-Hp.-Str.
Durand, Paris, C1927
Score 26 p.

848 Scènes bretonnes, Op. 24 *10'*
1.Avant le pardon 2.Le Passe-pied 3.Par les
forières 4.La dérobée
2(2nd alt. Picc.)2,2,2-4,2,3-Timp.,B.Dr.-Str.
J. Hamelle, Paris [1884?]
Score 63 p.
Withdrawn from circulation at composer's request.

257s Sérénade
Str.
Rouart, Lerolle, Paris [n.d.]
Score 12 p.
Composed 1892.

1456 Soir sur les chaumes, étude *12'*
symphonique [Evening in the fields]
3*,3*,3*,2-4,3,4-Timp.-Hp.-Str.
Durand, Paris, C1914
Score 60 p.
Composed 1913. First performance Paris, 1914, Concerts Colonne, Gabriel Pierné conductor.

5605 [Symphony no. 1, on a Breton choral] *40'*
1.Lent et majestueux - Assez animé 2.Lent -
Vif 3.Pas très vite, mais joyeux
3,3(3rd alt. E.H.),3,3-4,3,4-Timp.-Str.
A. Ponscarme, Paris [1895]
Score 145 p.
Composed 1894-95.

5971 [Symphony no. 4, C major] *28'*
In one movement
2,2(2nd alt. Picc.),3*,2-4,2,4-Timp.-Hp.-Str.

The Boston Music Company, Boston, C1914
Score 107 p.
Composed 1910.

ROREM, NED.   Spring Grove, Indiana 23 October 1923

350p Concerto no. 2, piano and orchestra *18'*
(1950)
1.Somber and steady - Allegro 2.Quiet and sad
3.Real fast!
Solo Pno.-2(2nd alt. Picc.),2,2,2-2,1-Timp.,
Perc.-Hp.-Str.
Ms. [Now published by Southern, New York]
Score 167 p.
Composed 1950-51.

5434 Design for orchestra, 1953 *17'30"*
In one movement
2(2nd alt. Picc.),2,2,2-4,2,2-Timp.,Perc.-Pno.,
Cel.,Hp.-Str.
Ms.
Score 111 p.
Commissioned by The Louisville Orchestra. Composed 1953. First performance Louisville, 28 May 1955, The Louisville Orchestra, Robert Whitney conductor.

6107 Eagles, for orchestra *8'30"*
In one movement
3*,3*,4*(1Cl. in E-flat),3*-4,3,3,1-Timp.,Perc.
-Pno.(alt. Cel.),Hp.-Str.
Ms. [C1962 by Boosey & Hawkes, New York]
Score 46 p. Large folio
Suggested by Walt Whitman's poem The Dalliance of the Eagles. Composed 1958. First performance Philadelphia, 23 October 1959, Philadelphia Orchestra, Eugene Ormandy conductor.

2183s Pilgrims [for string orchestra] *6'*
Str.
Ms.
Score 8 p.
Suggested by Julien Green's novel Le Voyageur Sur La Terre and by Hebrews 11:13, "...they were strangers and pilgrims on the earth...". Composed 1958. First performance New York, 1959, Music in the Making, Howard Shanet conductor.

4893 Symphony no. 1 (1949) *27'*
1.Maestoso 2.Andantino 3.Largo 4.Allegro
2(2nd alt. Picc.),2,2,2-4,2,2-Timp.,Perc.-Hp.-
Str.
Ms.
Score 96 p. Large folio
Originally conceived as a Mass without words. Composed 1949. First performance Vienna, February 1951, Jonathan Sternberg conductor.

5826 [Symphony no. 2 (1956)] *18'*
1.Broad, moderate 2.Tranquillo 3.Allegro
2(2nd alt. Picc.),2(2nd alt. E.H.),2,2-2,1,1-
Timp.,Perc.-Hp.(alt. Pno.)-Str.
Ms.
Score 105 p.
Commissioned by Nicolai Sokoloff and the Musical Arts Society of La Jolla, California.

Composed 1945. First performance La Jolla, 5 August 1956, Nicolai Sokoloff conductor.

5837 [Symphony no. 3]   *23'30"*
1.Passacaglia 2.Allegro molto vivace 3.Largo
4.Andante 5.Allegro molto
3*,3*,3*,3*-4,3,3,1-Timp.,Perc.-Pno.,Cel.,Hp.-
Str.
Boosey & Hawkes, London, ᶜ1960
Score 106 p.
Composed 1957-58. First performance New York, 16 April 1959, New York Philharmonic, Leonard Bernstein conductor.

ROSEINGRAVE, THOMAS.   Winchester, England 1690
                    Dunleary, Ireland 23 June 1766

2312s [Three pieces. Transcribed for   *9'*
string orchestra by Humphrey Searle]
1.Fugue I 2.Voluntary IV 3.Fugue III
Str.
Faber Music Ltd., London, ᶜ1967
Score 10 p.
Transcribed from 15 Voluntarys and Fugues, for organ or harpsichord, published 1730.

ROSELLÓ, MANUEL BLANCAFORT DE.
See: BLANCAFORT DE ROSELLÓ, MANUEL.

ROSENBERG, HILDING CONSTANTIN.
            b. Bosjökloster, Sweden 21 June 1892

6109 Bergslagsbilder [Scenes from the   *16'*
Bergslag, suite, Op. 72]
1.[The people] 2.[The countryside] 3.[The
mill-race] 4.[Light summer nights] 5.[The
old manor] 6.[Bergslag industry]
2,1,2,1-2-2,2,1-Timp.,Perc.-Str.
Nordiska Musikförlaget, Stockholm, ᶜ1944
Score 76 p.
Originally composed in 1937 for the film Bergs-slagsfolk, directed by Gunnar Olsson.

2184s [Concerto no. 1, for string   *23'*
orchestra]
1.Allegro con fuoco - Cantabile tranquillo
2.Andantino ma tranquillo 3.Allegro assai
Str.
Nordiska Musikförlaget, Stockholm, ᶜ1947
Score 40 p.
Composed 1946.

397m [Concerto no. 3 for orchestra,   *20'*
Louisville (1954)]
1.Andante quieto - Allegro vivace 2.Poco
adagio - Presto - Poco adagio 3.Allegro
energico
Concertino Vn.,Va.,Vc.-2(2nd alt. Picc.),2(2nd
alt. E.H.),2,2-4,2,3,1-Timp.,Perc.-Cel.,Hp.-
Str.
Ms.
Score 79 p.
Commissioned by The Louisville Orchestra. Composed 1954. First performance Louisville, 12 March 1955, The Louisville Orchestra, Robert Whitney conductor, concertino section con-sisting of Sidney Harth, violin; Virginia Schneider, viola; and Grace Whitney, violon-cello.

4547 Los intereses creados. Suite from   *12'*
the music to Jacinto Benavente's play, Op. 31]
1.Tempo di galliarda 2.Sarabande 3.Musette
4.[Harlequin's song] 5.Fughetta
0,1,1,1-2Hn.-Perc.-Cel.,Hp.-Str.
Breitkopf & Härtel, Leipzig, ᶜ1930
Score 15 p.

5123 [Little overture, to a comedy   *3'30"*
by Calderón]
2,1,0,1-Alto Sax.,Ten.Sax.-2,2,1-Timp.,Perc.-
Pno.-Str.
Nordiska Musikförlaget, Stockholm, ᶜ1944
Score 24 p.
Composed 1936.

5045 Lycksalighetans Ö [The isle of   *18'*
felicity. Music of the winds, in 7 movements]
3(3rd alt. Picc.),2,2,2-4,3,3,1-Timp.,Perc.-
Cel.,2Hp.-Str.
Ms.
Score 63 p.
From the opera composed 1944. First perform-ance Stockholm, 1 February 1945, H. Sandberg conductor.

6115 [Marionettes. Overture]   *6'*
2,2,2,2-2-2,2-Timp.,Perc.-Str.
Nordiska Musikförlaget, Stockholm, ᶜ1944
Score 16 p.
From the opera buffa based on Jacinto Bena-vente's comedy Los Intereses Creados. Com-posed 1937. First performance Stockholm, 14 February 1939, H. Sandberg conductor.

6805 Metamorfosi sinfoniche nr. 1   *16'30"*
3*,3*,3*,3*-4,3,3,1-Timp.,Perc.-2Hp.(or Pno.,
Hp.)-Str.
Edition Suecia, Stockholm [n.d.]
Score 73 p.
Composed 1963.

6809 Metamorfosi sinfoniche nr. 3
1(alt. Picc.),1,1-Pno.-Str.
Edition Suecia, Stockholm [n.d.]
Score 41 p.
Composed 1964.

2182s Ouvertura bianca-nera (1946)   *10'*
Str.
Nordiska Musikförlaget, Stockholm, ᶜ1946
Score 16 p.
Composed 1946.

Resa till Amerika [Journey to America]
6112 1.[The harbor]   *11'*
2(both alt. Picc.),2,2(1st alt. Alto Sax.,2nd
alt. Ten.Sax.),2-4,3,3,1-Timp.,Perc.-Hp.-Str.
6113 2.[Intermezzo]   *4'*
2,2,2,2-4,2,3,1-Timp.,Perc.-Str.
6114 3.[Railway fugue]   *5'*
2,2,2(2nd alt. B.Cl.),2-4,3,3,1-Timp.,Perc.-
Hp.-Str.
Edition Suecia, Stockholm, ᶜ1939 by STIM
Scores: 47 p., 6 p., 28 p.
From the opera composed 1932. First perform-ance Stockholm, 24 November 1932, the composer conducting.

Rosenberg, Hilding

6111 Sinfonia da chiesa no. 2   22'
1.Allegro ma non troppo 2.Moderato 3.Lento
espressivo 4.Allegro moderato
2(2nd alt. Picc.),2,2,2-4,2-Timp.,S.Dr.-Str.
Nordiska Musikförlaget, Stockholm, c1947
Score 52 p.
Composed 1924.

1204v [Suite for violin and orchestra]   17'
1.Introduction 2.Tempo di valse 3.Melodi
4.Pastorale 5.Humoresk
Solo Vn.-2(both alt. Picc.),1,2,1-Str.
Nordiska Musikförlaget, Stockholm, c1942
Score 24 p.
Composed 1922.

1276s [Suite on Swedish folk tunes]
1.Allegro assai 2.Moderato 3.Poco allegro
4.Andante mesto 5.[Devil's polka]
Str.
Nordiska Musikförlaget, Stockholm [n.d.]
Score 28 p.
Composed 1927.

6028 [Symphony no. 2, Sinfonia grave]   21'
1.Allegro energico 2.Poco adagio - Allegro
assai - Poco adagio - Allegro assai 3.Allegro
risoluto
2(2nd alt. Picc.),2,2,2-4,2,3,1-Timp.,Perc.-
Str.
Ms.
Score 116 p.
Composed 1928-35.

5020 [Symphony no. 3, The four ages of man] 33'
1.Moderato - Allegro 2.Andante sostenuto
3.Allegro con fuoco, molto marcato 4.Andante
semplice
2,2,2,2-4,2,3,1-Timp.,Perc.-Hp.-Str.
Ms. [Nordiska Musikförlaget, Stockholm, c1940?]
Score 104 p.
*Suggested by Romain Rolland's novel Jean
Christophe. Composed 1939.*

5827 [Symphony no. 6, Sinfonia semplice   25'
(1951)]
1.Adagio 2.Allegro 3.Allegro recitativo
4.Allegro moderato
2(1st alt. Picc.),2(2nd alt. E.H.),2,2-3,2,3-
Timp.,Perc.-Str.
Ms.
Score 60 p.
*Commissioned by the Gävle (Sweden) Symphony
Orchestra. Composed 1951. First perform-
ance Gävle, 1951, Gävle Symphony Orchestra,
Stig Westerberg conductor.*

5025 Yttersta Domen [The Last Judgment.   8'
Overture, Op. 48]
2(2nd alt. Picc.),2,2,2-4,2,3,1-Timp.,Perc.-
Pno.-Str.
Edition Suecia, Stockholm [n.d.]
Score 45 p.
From the ballet-pantomime composed 1930.

ROSENFELD, JSIDOR.

4544 [Symphony, Op. 20, F major]
1.Allegro con brio 2.Andante 3.Menuetto

4.Finale
2,2,2,2-2,2-Timp.-Str.
Bote & Bock, Berlin [1870]
Score 251 p.

ROSENHAIN, JACOB JACQUES.
                 Mannheim, Germany 2 December 1813
                 Baden-Baden, Germany 21 March 1894

666p [Concerto, piano, Op. 73, D minor]   28'
1.Allegro non troppo 2.Andante 3.Presto
Solo Pno.-2,2,2,2-4,2-Timp.-Str.
Score: Ms. 185 p.
Parts: Breitkopf & Härtel, Leipzig [n.d.]
*Composed 1885. First performance Baden-Baden,
1886, the composer conducting.*

809s [In the evening, tone pictures, Op. 99]
Str.
Breitkopf & Härtel, Leipzig [n.d.]
Miniature score 24 p.

ROSENMAN, LEONARD.   Brooklyn 7 September 1924

7182 Fanfare
See: FANFARES 1969 FOR 8 TRUMPETS. No. VII

ROSENMÜLLER, JOHANN.   Ölsnitz, Germany ca.1620
                 Wolfenbüttel, Germany 10 September 1684

953s [Chamber sonata, string orchestra, D major]
Edited by Arthur Egidi
1.Sinfonia (seconda) 2.Allemanda 3.Correnta
4.Ballo 5.Sarabanda
Cemb.-Str.(with Vn.III)
Chr. Fr. Vieweg, Berlin [n.d.]
Score 11 p.
First published Venice, ca.1670.

207s [Studenten-Music. Suite arranged by
Arnold Schering]
1.Paduane 2.Allemande 3.Courante 4.Ballo
5.Sarabande
Pno.-Str.(with Va.II)
Kahnt, Leipzig, c1914
Score 11 p.
Composed 1654.

ROSENSTEEL, F. C.

343s Entr'acte-menuet
Str.
J. Hamelle, Paris [n.d.]
Score 5 p.

ROSENSTOCK, JOSEPH.   Cracow 27 January 1895

617p [Concerto, piano, Op. 4, C-sharp   25'
minor]
In one movement
Solo Pno.-3(1st alt. Picc.),3*,3*,3*-4,3,3,1-
Timp.,Perc.-Cel.,Hp.-Str.
Ms. Universal Edition [Vienna, n.d.]
Score 139 p.
*Composed 1919. First performance Vienna,
April 1920.*

1711 Overture for a merry play, Op. 5   14'
3*,3*,3*,3*-4,3,3,1-Timp.,Perc.-Pno.,Cel.,2Hp.

-Str.
Universal Edition, Vienna, [C]1921
Score 59 p.
Composed 1920. First performance Nuremberg, 1921, the composer conducting.

ROSETTI, FRANCESCO ANTONIO.
      Litomerice, North Bohemia 26 October 1746
      Ludwigslust, Germany 30 June 1792

Real name: Franz Anton Rössler

410m [Concerto, horn and orchestra,   *15'*
D minor] Edited by Bernhard Krol
1.Allegro molto 2.Romanze: Adagio 3.Rondo
Solo Hn.-2Ob.-2Hn.-Str.
N. Simrock, Hamburg, [C]1959
Score 76 p.
Unpublished in Rosetti's time. This first edition 1959. First modern performance Cap d'Ail, France, 20 July 1960, Haydn-Kammerorchester, Helmut Link conductor, Siefried Schergaut soloist.

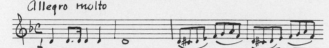

272m [Concerto, horn and orchestra,   *15'*
E-flat major]
1.Allegro moderato 2.Romanze 3.Rondeau
Solo Hn.-2Ob.-2Hn.-Str.
Score: Denkmäler der Tonkunst in Bayern, XII/1.
Breitkopf & Härtel, Leipzig, 1912. Edited by
Oscar Kaul. 36 p.
Parts: Ms. [C]1976 by The Fleisher Collection of
Orchestral Music, Free Library of Philadelphia

265m [Concerto, 2 horns in E-flat and   *18'*
orchestra, E-flat major] Edited by Klaas
Weelink
1.Allegro 2.Romance 3.Rondo
2 Solo Hn. in E-flat-2Fl.-2Hn.-Str.
Edition KaWe, Amsterdam, [C]1964
Score 40 p.

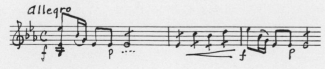

7062 [Partita, wind ensemble, D major]
1.Allegro assai 2.Larghetto 3.Menuetto
moderato - Trio 4.Rondeau
0,2,2,1-2Hn.
Score: Denkmäler der Tonkunst in Bayern,

XXXIII/2. Benno Filser Verlag, Augsburg, 1925.
Edited by Oscar Kaul. 14 p.
Parts: Ms. [C]1976 by The Fleisher Collection of
Orchestral Music, Free Library of Philadelphia

7289 [Partita, wind ensemble, B-flat major]
1.Marche 2.Minuetto 3.Allegretto 4.Andante
5.Tempo di minuetto moderato 6.Allegro
0,1,2,1-2Hn.
Score: Denkmäler der Tonkunst in Bayern,
XXXIII/2. Benno Filser Verlag, Augsburg, 1925.
Edited by Oscar Kaul. 7 p.
Parts: Ms. [C]1976 by The Fleisher Collection of
Orchestral Music, Free Library of Philadelphia

7063 [Partita, wind ensemble and contrabass,
F major]
1.Allegro molto 2.Andante grazioso 3.Minu-
etto fresco - Trio 4.Rondo
0,3,0,1-2Hn.-Cb.
Score: Denkmäler der Tonkunst in Bayern,
XXXIII/2. Benno Filser Verlag, Augsburg, 1925.
Edited by Oscar Kaul. 19 p.
Parts: Ms. [C]1976 by The Fleisher Collection of
Orchestral Music, Free Library of Philadelphia

7140 [Symphony, C major]
1.Vivace non presto 2.Menuetto fresco - Trio
3.Romanze 4.Capriccio
1,2,0,2-2Hn.-Str.
Score: Denkmäler der Tonkunst in Bayern,
XXIIa. Breitkopf & Härtel, Leipzig, 1912.
Edited by Oscar Kaul. 32 p.
Parts: Ms. [C]1977 by The Fleisher Collection of
Orchestral Music, Free Library of Philadelphia
Composed before 1784.

6956 [Symphony in C]
1.Adagio - Allegro molto 2.Adagio 3.Menuet
4.Presto

Rosetti, Francesco

2Ob.-2Hn.-Str.
Score: Denkmäler der Tonkunst in Bayern, XII/2.
Breitkopf & Härtel, Leipzig, 1912. Edited
by Oscar Kaul. 39 p.
Parts: Ms. C1976 by The Fleisher Collection of
Orchestral Music, Free Library of Philadelphia
Composed ca.1781. First published as no. 1 in
Trois Simphonies a Grand Orchestre. Oeuvre V.
Chès J. J. Hummel à Berlin et Amsterdam.

Adagio

7005 [Symphony in D]
1.Allegro moderato 2.Andantino 3.Menuett:
Moderato 4.Allegretto capriccio
2Ob.-2Hn.-Str.
Score: Denkmäler der Tonkunst in Bayern, XII/2.
Breitkopf & Härtel, Leipzig, 1912. Edited by
Oscar Kaul. 32 p.
Parts: Ms. C1976 by The Fleisher Collection of
Orchestral Music, Free Library of Philadelphia
Composed 1780. First published as no. 2 in
Six Simphonies...Dédiées A.S.A.S. Monseigneur
le Prince Regnant d'Oetting-Oetting et d'Oet-
ting-Wallerstein (Paris, Sieber).

Allegro moderato

7019 [Symphony in E-flat major]
1.Largo - Allegro assai 2.Menuetto 3.Andante
4.Allegro non molto
1,2,0,1-2Hn.-Str.
Score: Denkmäler der Tonkunst in Bayern,
XXIIa. Breitkopf & Härtel, Leipzig, 1912.
Edited by Oscar Kaul. 31 p.
Parts: Ms. C1976 by The Fleisher Collection of
Orchestral Music, Free Library of Philadelphia
Composed 1784. First published as no. 3 in
III Simphonies a Plusieurs Instruments, Op. 5,
by Artaria, Vienna.

Largo

4110 [Symphony, F major]
1.Presto 2.Andante 3.Fresco ma non troppo
allegro (Menuetto) 4.Allegro molto
1,2,0,1-2Hn.-Str.
Ms.
Score 75 p.
Published by André, Offenbach a.M., as Op. 13.

Presto

6670 [Symphony in G minor] Edited by Fritz
Kneusslin
1.Vivace 2.Menuet fresco 3.Andante ma alle-
gretto 4.Allegro scherzante
1,2,0,1-2Hn.-Str.
Edition Kneusslin, Basel, C1965
Score 33 p.
Composed 1787.

Vivace

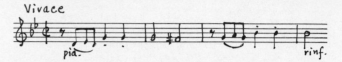

ROSOWSKY, SALOMO.   Riga, Latvia 15 March 1878
                          New York 30 July 1962

3994 [Chassidim, fantastic dance]
3(3rd alt. Picc.),3(3rd alt. E.H.),4*,3*-4,3,
3,1-Timp.,Perc.-Org.,Cel.,2Hp.-Str.
Ms.
Score 53 p. Large folio
Composed 1914.

ROSSELLINI, RENZO.   Rome 2 February 1908

4763 [Engravings of old Rome]   14'
1.[Christmas] 2.[The carts] 3.Saltarello
nella Villa Borghese
3(3rd alt. Picc.),3*,3*,3*-4,3,3,1-Timp.,Perc.
-2Pno.(or 1Pno. 4-hands)-Str.
Ricordi, Milan, C1938
Score 65 p.
Inspired by engravings of Roman scenes by
Bartolommeo Pinelli (1781-1835). Composed
1937. First performance Rome, January 1938.

3845 [Prelude to Tasso's Aminta]
4(3rd alt. Picc.,1B.Fl.),3*,3*,3*-4,3,2-Timp.,
Perc.-Pno.,Cel.,Hp.-Str.
Ricordi, Milan, C1934
Miniature score 18 p.
Composed 1932. First performance Turin, 10
March 1933, Willy Ferrero conductor.

1839s La sera fiesolana [Evening in   7'30"
Fiesole]
Str.
Ricordi, Milan, C1939
Score 6 p.
Originally composed 1939 as part of String
Quartet no. 1.

ROSSI, MARCELLO.   Vienna 16 October 1862
                         Bellagio, Italy 4 June 1897

[Two salon pieces, Op. 13]
578s No. 1 Pensée fugitive
363s No. 2 Bonbon musical

Str.
Joh. André, Offenbach a.M. [n.d.]
Scores: 7 p., 7 p.

ROSSI, MICHEL ANGELO.   Genoa ca.1602
                                 Rome 7 July 1656

636p [Toccata, cembalo, G major.   5'
Transcribed by Alceo Toni]
Solo Pno.-Org.-Str.
Ricordi, Milan [n.d.]
Miniature score 11 p.
Composed before 1657. Transcribed 1922.
First performance Milan, December 1923, Alceo
Toni conductor.

ROSSIGNOL, FÉLIX LUDGER.
    See: JONCIÈRES, VICTORIN DE.

ROSSINI, GIOACCHINO ANTONIO.
                Pesaro, Italy 29 February 1792
                Passy, near Paris 13 November 1868

1375 [The barber of Seville. Overture]   8'
2*,2,2,2-2,2,3-Timp.,Perc.-Str.
Breitkopf & Härtel, Leipzig [n.d.]
Score 36 p.
Originally composed as Overture to the opera
Elisabeth, 1815. First performance Rome, 20
February 1816.

3269 [La Cenerentola. Overture]
2(1st alt. Picc.),2,2,1-2,2-Timp.-Str.
Kalmus, New York [n.d.]
Score 26 p.
From the opera about Cinderella. Composed
1816-17. First performance Rome, 25 January
1817.

2424 La gazza ladra [The thieving magpie.   7'
Overture. Arranged by G. Kogel]
2*,2,2,2-4,2,3,1-Timp.,Perc.-Str.
Breitkopf & Härtel, Leipzig [n.d.]
Score 51 p.
From the opera first performed Milan, 31
May 1817.

3283 L'Italiana in Algieri. Ouverture
1,2,2,2-2,2-Timp.-Str.
Luck's Music Library, Detroit [n.d.]
Score 54 p.
From the opera first performed Venice, 22 May
1813.

6416 Preludio religioso durante l'offer-   6'
torio della messa solenne. Edited by Alceo Toni
2,3*,3*,3-4,2,3,1-Str.
Carisch, Milan, ᶜ1957
Score 25 p.

4304 Robert Bruce. Ouverture   7'
2(2nd alt. Picc.),2,2,2-4,4(3rd & 4th alt.
Cnt. I&II),3,Ophicl.-Timp.,Perc.-Str.
[Troupenas, Paris, 1846?]
Score 28 p.
From the pasticcio adapted by Louis-Abraham
Niedermeyer from Rossini's operas. First
performance Paris, 30 December 1846.

4490 La scala di seta [The silken   6'30"
staircase. Sinfonia] Revised by E. De Guarnieri
1,2,2,2,1-2Hn.-Str.
Carisch, Milan, ᶜ1937
Score 24 p.
From the opera composed 1812. First perform-
ance Venice, 9 May 1812.

4192 [Semiramis. Overture] Edited by   12'
Gustav Schmidt
2*,2,2,2-4,2,3-Timp.,B.Dr.-Str.
Breitkopf & Härtel, Leipzig [1911]
Score 59 p.
From the opera after Voltaire's play Semiramis.
Composed 1822-23. First performance Venice,
3 February 1823.

5806 Serenade [Rossini: Serenata per   7'30"
piccolo complesso] Edited by Eileen Swift
1,2*-Str.
Swift Musical Service [n.p.] ᶜ1959
Score 12 p.
Composed 1823 for Vincenzo (?) Bianchi.

5724 [The siege of Corinth. Sinfonia]   9'30"
3*,2,2,2-4,2,4-Timp.,Perc.-Str.
Carisch, Milan, ᶜ1939
Score 39 p.
From the opera composed 1820-23. First per-
formance in this form, Paris, 9 October 1826.

5734 Il signor Bruschino. Sinfonia.   5'
Revised by E. De Guarnieri
1,2,2,2,1-2Hn.-Str.
Carisch, Milan, ᶜ1937
Score 21 p.
From the opera after the comedy Le Fils Par
Hasard by Alissan de Chazet and E.-T. Maurice
Ourry. Composed 1812. First performance
Venice, January 1813.

4111 [Tancredi. Overture]   4'
2,2,2,2-2,2-Timp.-Str.
Ms.
Score 47 p.
From the opera after Tasso and Voltaire. Com-
posed 1813. First performance Venice, 6
February 1813.

230m Variations for clarinet and   8'30"
orchestra. Edited by Eileen Swift
Solo Cl.-1,0,2,1-2Hn.-Str.
Swift Musical Service [n.p.] ᶜ1959
Score 14 p.
Composed 1810.

5723 Il viaggio a Reims [The journey to   8'
Rheims, or The inn of the golden lily.
Sinfonia] Revised by Giuseppe Piccioli

Rossini, Gioacchino

2*,2,2,2-2,2,3-Timp.,B.Dr.,Trgl.-Str.
Carisch, Milan, ^c1938
Score 45 p.
From the stage cantata composed 1825 for the
coronation festivities of Charles X of France.
First performance Paris, 19 June 1825.

1324 [William Tell. Overture] Edited by   12'
Fritz Hoffmann
2*,2(1st alt. E.H.),2,2-4,2,3-Timp.,Perc.-Str.
Breitkopf & Härtel, Leipzig [n.d.]
Score 51 p.
From the opera composed 1829, based on Schil-
ler's play. First performance Paris, 3 August
1829.

6847 William Tell. [Act I] Pas de six   6'
3*,2,2,2-2,2-Str.
Kalmus, New York [n.d.]
Score 26 p.

RÖSSLER, FRANZ ANTON.
See: ROSETTI, FRANCESCO ANTONIO.

ROTELLA, PASQUALE LA.
See: LA ROTELLA, PASQUALE.

ROTERS, ERNST.   Oldenburg, Germany 6 July 1892

4968 Tanzsuite für Orchester oder   16'
Kammerorchester, Op. 23
1(alt. Picc.),1,1*(alt. B.Cl. ad lib.),1*
(alt. C.Bn. ad lib.)-Perc.-Pno.-Str. *or*
2(2nd alt. Picc.),2,2*(1st alt. B.Cl. ad lib.),
2*(1st alt. C.Bn. ad lib.)-2,2,1-Perc.-Hp.(ad
lib.)-Str.
Universal Edition, Vienna, ^c1936
Score 56 p.

ROTHMÜLLER, ARON MARKO.
            b. Trnjani, Croatia 31 December 1908

1874s Chaim Nachman Bialik, in memory   7'30"
Str.(without Vn.II or Cb.)
Omanut, Zagreb, ^c1936
Score 8 p.
Composed 1934 in memory of the Jewish poet.

ROUBAUD, ANDRÉ.

626v Romance en mi
Solo Vn.-1,1,1,1-2,0,2Cnt.,2-Timp.-Str.
Score: Ms. 14 p.
Parts: Ricordi, Paris, ^c1919

ROUSSEAU, JEAN-JACQUES.   Geneva 28 June 1712
            Ermenonville, near Paris 2 July 1778

6383 Le devin du village [The village   3'
seer. Overture] Edited by Heinrich Schwartz
2,2,0,2-2,2-Timp.-Str.
Breitkopf & Härtel, Leipzig [1905?]
Score 11 p.
From the opera with libretto by the composer.
First performance with this overture and
Rousseau's own recitatives, Paris, 1 March
1753.

2511 [Le devin du village. Songs and dances]
Edited by Heinrich Schwartz
1.Arie der Colette 2.[Entrance of the sooth-
sayer] 3.[Aria of the soothsayer] 4.Panto-
mime 5.Romanze des Colin 6.Pantomime
2,2,0,2-2,2-Timp.-Str.
Breitkopf & Härtel, Leipzig [n.d.]
Score 33 p.

ROUSSEAU, L. JULIEN.

1293s Les petits Moukjiks (Brollops marche)
Str.
Score: Ms. 7 p.
Parts: [Decourcelle, Nice, n.d.]

ROUSSEAU, MARCEL-AUGUSTE-LOUIS. Paris 18 August 1882
                        Paris 11 June 1955

    Known as: Marcel Samuel-Rousseau

865 Bérénice [Music to Racine's tragedy]
2,2(2nd alt. E.H.),2,2-4,4(2 backstage),3-
Timp.-Hp.-Str.
Choudens, Paris, ^c1920
Score 94 p.

973 Noël berrichon   12'
1.Danse et chanson sur la grand' place 2.
Veillée de minuit 3.Refrain de Noceux
4.Les promis 5.Assemblée
1(alt. Picc.),1,1,1-1,2,3-Timp.,Perc.-Cel.,Hp.
-Str.
J. Hamelle, Paris, ^c1910
Score 87 p.
Composed 1908. First performance Paris, 1910.

2146 [Scherzo on children's songs]
3(3rd alt. Picc.),2,2,2-4,2,Cnt.,3-Timp.,Perc.-
Cel.,2Hp.-Str.
Carl Selva, Paris, ^c1914
Score 43 p.

ROUSSEAU, SAMUEL-ALEXANDRE.
            Neuvemaison, Aisne, France 11 June 1853
                        Paris 1 October 1904

614m Fantaisie pour harpe chromatique
Solo Hp.-Str.
Heugel, Paris, ^c1904
Score 37 p.

ROUSSEL, ALBERT CHARLES PAUL MARIE. Tourcoing,
            Département du Nord, France 5 April 1869
                    Royan, France 23 August 1937

587p [Concerto, piano, Op. 36, C major]   17'
1.Allegro molto 2.Adagio 3.Allegro con
spirito
Solo Pno.-2(2nd alt. Picc.),2*,2,2-2,2-Timp.,
Perc.-Str.
Durand, Paris, ^c1928
Score 72 p.
Composed 1927. First performance Paris, 7
June 1928, Serge Koussevitzky conductor,
Alexander Borowsky soloist.

1562 [Concerto for small orchestra,   *14'*
Op. 34]
1.Allegro 2.Andante 3.Presto
2(2nd alt. Picc.),2,2,2-2,1-Timp.-Str.
Durand, Paris, ^c1927
Score 44 p.
Composed 1926-27. First performance Paris, 5
May 1927, Walther Straram conductor.

Évocations, Op. 15
366 No. 1 Les dieux dans l'ombre des   *15'*
cavernes [The gods in the darkness of the
caves]
304 No. 2 La ville rose   *15'*
305 No. 3 Aux bords du fleuve sacré   *20'*
[On the banks of the sacred river]
3(3rd alt. Picc.),3*,3*,3*-4,3,3,1-Timp.,Perc.
-Cel.(no. 3 only),2Hp.-Solo Voices & Chorus
(no. 3 only)-Str.
Durand, Paris, ^c1912
Scores: 61 p., 71 p., 96 p.
Composed 1910-11. First performance Paris,
18 May 1912, Société National, Rhené-Baton
conductor.

3976 [Fanfare for a pagan rite]
4Tpt.-Timp.
Ms.
Score 5 p.
Composed 1921.

812 Le festin d'araignée [The spider's   *20'*
banquet, symphonic excerpts, Op. 17]
In one movement
2(2nd alt. Picc.),2(2nd alt. E.H.),2,2-2,2-
Timp.,Perc.-Cel.,Hp.-Str.
Durand, Paris, ^c1914
Score 67 p.
From the ballet-pantomime composed 1912.
First performance Paris, 3 April 1913, Gabriel
Grovlez conductor.

4886 A glorious day, Op. 48, for band
2*,2,6*(1Cl. in E-flat,1Alto Cl.),2-4Sax.
(ATBB)-4,2,2Cnt.,4,Bar.,Tuba-Timp.,Perc.
Durand, Paris, ^c1933
Score in reduction 15 p.
Composed 1932.

1500 Le marchand de sable qui passe [The *16'*
sand vendor passing by]
Fl.,Cl.-Hn.-Hp.-Str.
Eschig, Paris, ^c1910
Score 29 p.
Composed 1908 for Jean Aubry's play. First
performance Le Havre, 16 December 1908.

1869 Petite suite, Op. 39   *12'*
1.Aubade 2.Pastorale 3.Mascarade
2(2nd alt. Picc.),2,2,2-2,2-Timp.,Perc.-Str.
Durand, Paris, ^c1929
Score 48 p.
Composed 1929. First performance Paris, 6
February 1930, Walther Straram conductor.

818 Pour une fête de printemps, Op. 22   *12'*
3*,3*,2,3-4,2,3,1-Timp.,Perc.-Hp.-Str.
Durand, Paris, ^c1921

Score 56 p.
Composed 1920. First performance Paris, 29
October 1921, Concerts Colonne, Gabriel Pierné
conductor.

2959 Rapsodie flamande, Op. 56   *9'30"*
3*,3*,3*,3*-4,3,3,1-Timp.,Perc.-Hp.-Str.
Durand, Paris, ^c1936
Score 65 p.
Composed 1935-36. First performance Brussels,
12 December 1936, Philharmonic Society of
Brussels, Erich Kleiber conductor.

1703s Sinfonietta, Op. 52   *9'30"*
1.Allegro molto 2.Andante 3.Allegro
Str.
Durand, Paris, ^c1934
Score 17 p.
Composed 1934. First performance Paris, 19
November 1934, Orchestre Féminin de Paris,
Jane Evrard conductor.

1553 [Suite, Op. 33, F major]   *15'*
1.Prélude 2.Sarabande 3.Gigue
3*(2nd alt. Picc.II),3*,3*,3-4,4,3,1-Timp.,
Perc.-Cel.,Hp.-Str.
Durand, Paris, ^c1927
Score 104 p.
Composed 1926. First performance Boston, 29
January 1927, Boston Symphony Orchestra, Serge
Koussevitzky conductor.

862 [Symphony no. 1, The poem of the   *35'*
forest, Op. 7, D minor]
1.[Winter forest] 2.[Renewal] 3.[Summer
evening] 4.Faunes et dryads
3(3rd alt. Picc.),3*,2,2-4,2,3,1-Timp.,Perc.-
2Hp.-Str.
Rouart, Lerolle, Paris, ^c1909
Score 181 p.
Composed 1904-06. First performance Brussels,
22 March 1908, Concerts Populaires, Sylvain
Dupuis conductor.

2448 [Symphony no. 3, G minor]   *45'*
1.Allegro vivo 2.Adagio 3.Vivace 4.Allegro
con spirito
3(2nd & 3rd alt. 2Picc.),3*,3*,3*-4,4,3,1-
Timp.,Perc.-Cel.,2Hp.-Str.
Durand, Paris, ^c1931
Score 140 p.
Commissioned by the Boston Symphony Orchestra.
Composed 1929-30. First performance Boston,
24 October 1930, Boston Symphony Orchestra,
Serge Koussevitzky conductor.

2958 [Symphony no. 4, Op. 53, A major] *22'30"*
1.Lento - Allegro con brio 2.Lento molto
3.Allegro scherzando 4.Allegro molto
3*,3*,3*,3*-4,4,3,1-Timp.,Perc.-Hp.-Str.
Durand, Paris, ^c1935
Score 119 p.
Composed 1930. First performance Paris, 19
October 1935, Pasdeloup Orchestra, Albert
Wolff conductor.

ROWLEY, ALEC.   London 13 March 1892
                     London 10 January 1958

Rowley, Alec

1845s Christmas suite, for strings
1.Prelude 2.Siciliana 3.Minuet 4.Sarabande
5.Bourrée 6.Fughetta 7.Finale
Pno.(optional)-Str.(Cb. optional)
Novello, London, ^c1930
Score 18 p.
Based on Christmas carols.

1832s Dream fantasy (Noël)   4'
Cel.(optional)-Str.
J. Williams, London, ^c1936
Score 7 p.

1843s Folk dance suite
1.With marjoram gentle 2.Sweet William
3.Shepherds' purse 4.Love lies bleeding
5.Lords and ladies
Str.
Stainer & Bell, London, ^c1929
Score 14 p.

222s Nautical suite
1.Ashore 2.In harbour 3.Outward bound
Pno.(optional)-Str.(Cb. optional)
Stainer & Bell, London, ^c1927
Score 13 p.

1332s Shepherd's delight, suite
1.Spring woodland 2.Hush song 3.Shepherd's
rondel
Str.
Goodwin & Tabb, London, ^c1929
Score 8 p.

ROYCE, EDWARD.
        Cambridge, Massachusetts 25 December 1886
        Stanford, Connecticut 7 July 1973

2651 Far ocean, tone poem   10'
3,3(3rd alt. E.H.),3,3-4,3,3,1-Timp.,Perc.-
Hp.-Str.
C.C. Birchard, Boston, ^c1931 (for Eastman
School of Music)
Score 61 p.
*Composed 1929. First performance Rochester,
3 June 1929, Rochester Philharmonic Orchestra,
the composer conducting.*

2842 The fire bringers, a tone poem   12'
3,3*,3,3-4,2,3,1-Timp.,Perc.-2Hp.-Str.
Ms.
Score 50 p.
*Composed 1926. First performance Rochester,
23 April 1926, Rochester Philharmonic Orchestra, Howard Hanson conductor.*

ROZKOŠNÝ, JOSEF RICHARD.   Prague 21 September 1833
                           Prague 3 June 1913

811s Zwei Novelletten
1.Andantino 2.Allegro moderato
Str.
Score: Ms. 16 p.
Parts: M. Urbánek, Prague [n.d.]

ROZSA, MIKLOS.   Budapest 18 April 1907

6047 Concert overture, Op. 26   10'
2(2nd alt. Picc.),2,2,2-4,3,3,1-Timp.,Perc.-

Hp.-Str.
Ernst Eulenburg, London, ^c1957
Score 100 p.
*Inspired by the Hungarian revolt of October
1956. Composed 1956. First performance
Düsseldorf, 26 September 1957, Düsseldorf City
Orchestra, the composer conducting.*

6565 Kaleidoscope, six short pieces,   10'
Op. 19a
1.March 2.Zingara 3.Musette 4.Berceuse
5.Chinese carillon 6.Burlesque
1(alt. Picc.),1,1,1-1,1,1-Timp.,Perc.-Hp.-Str.
Ms.
Score 50 p.
*Originally composed for piano, 1946. Tran-
scribed 1958. First performance Vienna, 1958,
State Orchestra of Vienna, the composer conducting.*

4068 Serenade, Op. 10   25'
1.Marcia 2.Serenata 3.Danza 4.Notturno
5.Marcia
1(alt. Picc.),1,1,1-1,1-Timp.,Perc.-Str.
Breitkopf & Härtel, Leipzig, ^c1933
Score 64 p.

6081 Thema, Variationen und Finale,   18'
Op. 13
2(2nd alt. Picc.),2,2,2(2nd alt. C.Bn.)-3,2,3-
Timp.,Perc.-Cel.,Hp.-Str.
Ernst Eulenburg, Leipzig, ^c1935
Score 114 p.
*Composed 1933. First performance Duisberg,
Germany, 8 October 1934, Duisberg City Symphony,
Otto Volkmann conductor.*

6049 Three Hungarian sketches, Op. 14   19'
1.Capriccio 2.Pastorale 3.Danza
2(2nd alt. Picc.),2,2,2-4,2,3-Timp.,Perc.-Cel.,
Hp.-Str.
Ernst Eulenburg, London, ^c1959
Score 125 p.
*Composed 1938. First performance International
Music Festival, Baden-Baden, Germany, June
1939, Festival Orchestra, G. E. Lessing con-
ductor. Revised 1959.*

RÓZYCKI, LUDOMIR.   Warsaw 6 November 1883
                        Katowice, Poland 1 January 1953

3543 Anhelli, d'après J. Słowacki, Op. 22
3(3rd alt. Picc.),3*,3*,3(3rd alt. C.Bn.)-4,3,
3,1-Timp.,Perc.-Hp.-Str.
Albert Stahl, Berlin [n.d.]
Score 77 p.
Composed 1909.

4013 Bolesław Smiały, Op. 8 [Boleslav the Bold]
3(3rd alt. Picc.),3*,4*(1Cl. in E-flat),3*-6,
3,3,2-Timp.,Perc.-2Hp.-Str.
Gebethner & Wolff, Warsaw [n.d.]
Score 38 p.
Inspired by Stanislas Wyspianski's poem.

658p [Concerto, piano, Op. 43, G minor]   30'
1.Andante - Allegro 2.Andante 3.Finale:
Allegro giocoso

Solo Pno.-3(3rd alt. Picc.),2(2nd alt. E.H.),
2,2-4,2,3-Timp.,Perc.-Str.
W. Hansen, Copenhagen, ^c1921
Score 119 p.

5821 [Pan Twardowski. Dances of the   *9'*
mountaineers, Op. 45]
3(3rd alt. Picc.),3*,3*,3*-4,3,3,1-Timp.(alt.
Xyl.),Perc.-Str.
Wilhelm Hansen, Copenhagen [^c1923]
Score 19 p.
From the ballet after the novel by Józef
Kraszewski. First performance Warsaw, 9 May
1921, Warsaw Opera Ballet.

RUBBRA, CHARLES EDMUND.
        b. Northampton, England 23 May 1901

2480 [Symphony no. 1, Op. 44]   *34'*
1.Allegro moderato e tempestoso 2.Perigour-
dine 3.Lento - Coda: Fuga
3*(1st alt. Picc.II),3*,3*,3*-4,3,3,1-Timp.,
Perc.-Hp.-Str.
Universal Edition, London, ^c1937
Score 159 p.
Completed 1937. First performance London, 30
April 1937, BBC Orchestra, Adrian Boult con-
ductor.

RUBINSTEIN, ANTON GRIGORIEVICH. Vykhvatintsy,
          Volhynia, Russia 28 November 1829
Peterhof near St. Petersburg 20 November 1894

165 Bal costumé [suite, in 6 movements,   *31'*
Op. 103. Orchestrated by Max Erdmannsdörfer]
3*,2,2,2-4,2,3,1-Timp.,Perc.-Hp.-Str.
Bote & Bock, Berlin [n.d.]
Score 92 p.
Originally composed for piano duet. Orches-
trated 1895. First performance Bremen, 1895,
Max Erdmannsdörfer conductor.

1348s Berceuse, G major
Str.
Score: Ms. 6 p.
Parts: Bessel, St. Petersburg [n.d.]

426p Caprice russe [Russian caprice] Op. 102
Solo Pno.-3*,2,2,2-2,2-Timp.-Str.
Senff, Leipzig [n.d.]
Score 100 p.

445p [Concerto, piano, no. 1, Op. 25, in E]
1.Moderato 2.Andante con moto 3.Con moto
Solo Pno.-2,2,2,2-2,2-Timp.-Str.
C.F. Peters, Leipzig [n.d.]
Score 111 p.

602p [Concerto, piano, no. 2, Op. 35, F major]
1.Allegro vivace assai 2.Adagio non troppo
3.Moderato
Solo Pno.-2,2,2,2-2,2(1 alt. Cnt.)-Timp.-Str.
Aug. Cranz, Hamburg [n.d.]
Score 104 p.

406p [Concerto, piano, no. 3, Op. 45,   *35'*
G major] Revised edition
1.Moderato assai 2.Moderato 3.Allegro non
troppo

Solo Pno.-2,2,2,2-2,2-Timp.-Str.
Bote & Bock, Berlin [n.d.]
Score 152 p.

383p [Concerto, piano, no. 4, Op. 70,   *31'*
D minor]
1.Moderato assai 2.Andante 3.Allegro
Solo Pno.-3*,2,2,2-2,2-Timp.-Str.
Simrock, Berlin [n.d.]
Score 145 p.

501p [Concerto, piano, no. 5, Op. 94,   *28'*
E-flat major]
1.Allegro moderato 2.Andante 3.Allegro
Solo Pno.-2,2,2,2-2,2-Timp.-Str.
Senff, Leipzig [n.d.]
Score 172 p.

904v [Concerto, violin, Op. 46, G major]
1.Moderato assai 2.Andante 3.Moderato assai
Solo Vn.-2,2,2,2-2,2-Timp.-Str.
C.F. Peters, Leipzig [n.d.]
Score 59 p.

577c [Concerto, violoncello, Op. 65, in A]
1.Moderato con moto 2.Adagio - Allegro non
troppo
Solo Vc.-2,2,2,2-2,2-Timp.-Str.
Simrock, Berlin [n.d.]
Score 122 p.

620c [Concerto, violoncello, no. 2, Op. 96,
D minor]
In one movement
Solo Vc.-2,2,2,2-2,2-Timp.-Str.
Senff, Leipzig [n.d.]
Score 83 p.
Completed 1874. Performance Moscow, 1877.

610p [Concertstück, piano, Op. 113, A-flat major]
Solo Pno.-3*,2,2,2-4,2-Timp.-Str.
Jurgenson, Moscow [n.d.]
Score 83 p.

1214 [Der Dämon. Balletmusik]   *14'*
3*,2,2,2-4,2,3-Timp.,Perc.-Str.
Simrock, Berlin [n.d.]
Score 88 p.
From the opera composed 1874.

4957 [Dmitri Donskoi, or The battle of   *11'*
Kulikovo. Overture]
3*,2,2,2-4,2,3-Timp.-Str.
Bote & Bock, Berlin [1865?]
Score 62 p.
From the opera first performed St. Petersburg,
30 April 1852.

1124 Don Quixote [humoresque, musical   *15'*
portrait, Op. 87. New edition]
3*,2,2,2-4,2,3-Timp.-Str.
Simrock, Berlin [n.d.]
Score 99 p.

831 Eroica, fantasy, Op. 110   *15'*
3*,2,2,2-4,2,2Cnt.,3,1-Timp.,Perc.-Str.
Senff, Leipzig [n.d.]
Score 88 p.

Rubinstein, Anton

431p [Fantaisie, piano, Op. 84, C major]   *30'*
Solo Pno.-2,2,2,2-2,2-Timp.-Str.
B. Senff, Leipzig [n.d.]
Score 170 p.

6915 [Faust, a musical portrait, Op. 68]
3*,2,2,2-4,2,3,1-Timp.-Str.
C.F.W. Siegel, Leipzig [1864]
Score 92 p.
Inspired by Goethe's poem. First performance
Leipzig, November 1864.

172 [Feramors. Ballet music and bridal   *15'*
procession]
3*,2,2,2-4,2,3,1-Timp.,Perc.-Hp.-Str.
Senff, Leipzig [n.d.]
Score 116 p.
From the opera composed 1861.

7057 [Ivan IV, The Terrible, musical
portrait, Op. 79]
In one movement
3*,2,2,2-4,2,3,1-Timp.-Str.
Score: Ms. 118 p. Large folio
Parts: Bote & Bock, Berlin [187-?]

460c Mélodie en fa, piano, Op. 3 no. 1.   *3'*
Transcribed by Vincent d'Indy
Solo Vc.-2,2,2,2-2Hn.-Timp.-Str.
J. Hamelle, Paris [n.d.]
Score 19 p.
Orchestrated 1877. First performance Paris,
1878, Concerts Colonne.

1712 Ouverture solennelle, Op. 120   *25'*
3*,2,2,2-4,2,3,1-Timp.,Perc.-Pno.,Org.,Hp.-Str.
Jurgenson, Leipzig [1900?]
Score 72 p.

4390 [Overture to Antony and Cleopatra, Op. 116]
3*,2,2,2-4,4,3,1-Timp.,Perc.-Hp.-Str.
B. Senff, Leipzig [1890]
Score 71 p.

5698 Overture triomphale, Op. 43   *12'*
3*,2,2,2-4,2,3,1-Timp.,Perc.-Hp.-Str.
B. Schott's Söhne, Mainz [1863]
Score 74 p.
First performance Weimar (?), 1854, Franz
Liszt conductor.

Die Rebe [The vine]
5353 [Dance of the children with Gaiety *and*
No. 20, Dance of the vines]
5352 [Love scene]
5349 [No. 4, Dance of the old *and* No. 5, Dance
of the young]
5350 [Nos. 8 and 9, The wine tasting *and* Nos.
10 through 15, Wines of the nations]
5354 [Nos. 22 and 24, Bacchanales *and* No. 26,
Dance of the vines]
5351 [The seduction (Dance of intoxication)]
3*,3*,2,2-4,2,3,1-Timp.,Perc.-Hp.,2Mand.,Guit.-
Str.
B. Senff, Leipzig [1884?]
Scores: 21 p., 15 p., 23 p., 84 p., 88 p., 9 p.
From the ballet composed 1882.

252 Rêve angélique [Heavenly dream] Op. 10   *5'*
no. 22. Transcribed by Leopold Schade
3*,2,2,2-4,2,3,1-Bell-Hp.-Str.
B. Schott's Söhne, Mainz [n.d.]
Score 21 p.
Originally composed for piano; orchestrated
1899.

468v Romance et caprice, Op. 86
Solo Vn.-3*,2,2,2-2,2,3-Timp.-Str.
J. Hamelle, Paris [n.d.]
Score in reduction 27 p.

1534 La Russie. morceau symphonique
4(2 are Picc.),3*,3*,2-4,2,3,1-Timp.,Perc.-Hp.-
Chorus(SATB)-Str.
Jurgenson, Moscow [n.d.]
Score 87 p.

218 Sérénade russe no. 1. Transcribed by   *7'*
Karl Müller-Berghaus
2(2nd alt. Picc.),2,2,2-4,2,3-Timp.,Perc.-Hp.-
Str.
B. Senff, Leipzig, ^c1899
Score 36 p.
From Op. 93 vol. 6 originally composed for
piano.

219 Suite, 5 miniatures, piano, Op. 93   *9'*
vol. 9. Transcribed for orchestra by Karl
Müller-Berghaus
1.Marche orientale 2.Sérénade 3.Chevalier et
payse [Knight and peasant woman] 4.Berceuse
5.Cortége
2(alt. 2Picc.),2,2,2-4,2,3,1-Timp.,Perc.-Hp.-
Str.
B. Senff, Leipzig, ^c1899
Score 74 p.

6482 Suite pour orchestre, Op. 119
1.Prélude 2.Elegie 3.Capriccio 4.Intermezzo
5.Scherzo 6.Finale
3*,2,2,2-4,2,3,1-Timp.-Str.
B. Senff, Leipzig, ^c1895
Score 88 p.

7014 [Symphony no. 2, Ocean, Op. 42,   *68'*
C major]
1.Moderato assai 2.Lento assai - Con moto
moderato 3.Andante 4.Allegro 5.Andante
6.Scherzo 7.Andante - Allegro con fuoco
3*,2,2,2-4,2,3,1-Timp.,B.Dr.-Hp.-Str.
B. Senff, Leipzig [n.d.]
Score 461 p. Large folio
Original version (Movements 1,5,4, and 7 of
this third and final version) composed 1854.
First performance Gewandhaus, Leipzig, 14
November 1854, Julius Rietz conductor. Move-
ments 3 and 6 added ca.1872. Movement 2, The
Storm, added ca.1877, available separately as
Catalog no. 442. First performance of complete
work, Berlin, 1884.

676 [Symphony no. 4, Dramatique, Op. 95,   *44'*
D minor]
1.Lento - Allegro moderato 2.Presto 3.Adagio
4.Largo - Allegro con fuoco
3*,2,2,2-2,2,3-Timp.-Str.

B. Senff, Leipzig [1875?]
Score 340 p.

944 [Symphony no. 5, Op. 107, G minor]   30'
1.Moderato assai 2.Andante 3.Allegro vivace
2,2,2,2-4,2-Timp.-Str.
B. Senff, Leipzig [1881?]
Score 262 p.

986 [Symphony no. 6, Op. 111, A minor]   34'
1.Moderato con moto 2.Moderato assai
3.Allegro vivace 4.Moderato assai
2,2,2,2-4,2,3-Timp.-Str.
B. Senff, Leipzig [1887?]
Score 250 p.

214 Valse-caprice [piano] Transcribed by   5'
Karl Müller-Berghaus
3*,2,2,2-4,2,3,1-Timp.,Perc.-Hp.-Str.
B. Senff, Leipzig [n.d.]
Score 47 p.

RUBINSTEIN, BERYL.   Athens, Georgia 26 October 1898
                     Cleveland 29 December 1952

732p Concerto in C for piano and   31'
orchestra
In one movement
Solo Pno.-3*,2,2,2-2,2,2-Timp.-Str.
Ms.
Score 187 p.
Composed 1935. First performance Cleveland, 12 November 1936, Cleveland Orchestra, Artur Rodzinski conductor, the composer as soloist.

3138 Scherzo   15'
3(3rd alt. Picc.),3*,3*,3*-4,3,3,1-Timp.,Perc.-Cel.,2Hp.(2nd optional)-Str.
Ms.
Score 126 p.
Composed 1925-26. First performance Cleveland, 17 March 1927, Cleveland Orchestra, the composer conducting.

RUDHYAR, DANE.   Paris 23 March 1895

Born: Daniel Chennevière

1763s Five stanzas, for strings   20'
Str.
New Music Orchestra Series, Hollywood, c1938 by the composer
Score 26 p.
Composed 1927.

3185 Ouranos, syntony in 3 movements   17'
1.Fashioner 2.Preserver 3.Regenerator
1(alt. Picc.),2*,1(alt. Cl. in E-flat),1-2,2,1,1-Timp.,Perc.-3Pno.-Str.
Ms.
Score 68 p.
Completed 1926.

2801 Sinfonietta
3(alt. 3Picc.),3*,3*,3*-6,4,3,2-Timp.,Perc.-Pno.-Str.
New Music Orchestra Series, San Francisco, c1934 by the composer

Score 39 p.
Composed 1927.

3492 The surge of fire, symphonic   19'
trilogy
1(alt. Picc.),1,1,1-1,1,1-Timp.-3Pno.-Str.
Ms.
Score 88 p. Large folio
Composed 1921-23. First performance Los Angeles, 22 October 1925, the New Music Society of California, Adolph Tandler conductor, Winifred Hooke, Wesley Kuhnle, Homer Simmons soloists.

7329 Threnody. Orchestrated by George   8'
W. Champion
2(2nd alt. Picc.),2,3*,2-4,4,2,1-Timp.,Perc.-Pno.-Str.
Ms. [American Composers' Alliance, New York, c1973]
Score 21 p. Large folio
Sketched during the 1920's. This orchestration 1974. First performance University of California at San Diego, La Jolla, March 1974, University and La Jolla Civic Orchestra, Thomas Nee conductor.

7330 Thresholds. Orchestrated by George   28'
Champion
1.Contemplative and serene 2.With elusive charm 3.With fiery intensity 4.Broad and lyrical
4*(1Alto Fl.),3*,3*,3*-4,4,3,1-Timp.,Perc..-Pno.,Hp.-Str.
Ms. [American Composers' Alliance, New York, c1975]
Score 82 p. Large folio
Originally composed 1954-55. This orchestration, 1974.

3491 To the Real, symphonic tryptych   14'
1.Passion 2.Struggles 3.Initiation
3(2nd & 3rd alt. Picc.),Alto Fl.(alt. 3rd Picc.),3*,3*(1st alt. Cl. in E-flat),3*-4,3,3,1-Timp.,Perc.-2Pno(2nd alt. Cel.)-Str.
Ms.
Score 64 p. Large folio
Completed 1922.

RUDIN, HERMAN.   Rochester, New York 1906

3599 Facets, scherzo for orchestra,   4'
Op. 3
3*(2nd alt. 2nd Picc.),2,2,2-4,2,1,1-Timp.,Perc.-Pno.,Hp.-Str.
Ms.
Score 49 p.
This is the third movement of the composer's suite, Symphonic Fragments, composed 1934. First performance (of entire suite) Rochester, 1 November 1934, Rochester Philharmonic Orchestra, Howard Hanson conductor.

963m Israfel, poem, Op. 10   7'
Solo Fl., Solo Hp.-Str.
Ms.
Score 30 p.
Inspired by Edgar Allan Poe's poem. Composed 1939. First performance Rochester, 3 March

Rudin, Herman

1940, Guy Fraser Harrison conductor, Joseph
Mariano soloist.

3026 Legend, tone poem, Op. 11   9'
[Revised version]
3*,3*,3*,3*-4,3,3,1-Timp.,Perc.-Pno.,Cel.,Hp.-
Str.
Ms.
Score 40 p.
Composed 1938; revised 1940. First perform-
ance Rochester, 7 March 1940, Rochester Phil-
harmonic Orchestra, José Iturbi conductor.

1733s Prelude and allegro in olden style,   8'
Op. 8
Str.
Ms.
Score 13 p.
Composed 1933. First performance Rochester,
1 May 1934, Eastman School Symphony Orches-
tra, Samuel Belov conductor.

RUDIN, RICHARD.

7307 First attack
In one movement
3*,2,3*,3*-4,3,3,1-Timp.,Perc.-Hp.-Str.
Ms.
Score 36 p. Large folio
Composed 1974.

RUDOLPH, OSKAR.   Lützen, Saxony 28 November 1856
                     Erfurt, Germany 28 April 1913

802s [A little dance in the spinning-room]
Intermezzo, Op. 22
Str.
C.F. Kahnt, Leipzig [n.d.]
Score 5 p.

623s Knecht Rupprecht [Santa Claus] Op. 21
Str.(without Cb.)
C.F. Kahnt, Leipzig [n.d.]
Score 7 p.

RUDORFF, ERNST FRIEDRICH KARL.
                     Berlin 18 January 1840
                     Berlin 31 December 1916

4630 [Overture to Ludwig Tieck's fairy tale
Blond Ekbert, Op. 8]
2,2,2,2-4,2,1-Timp.-Str.
N. Simrock, Berlin, 1882
Score 83 p.

599c Romanze, Op. 7
Solo Vc.-2,2,2,2-4,2-Timp.-Str.
Schlesinger, Berlin [n.d.]
Score 35 p.

759v Romanze, Op. 41
Solo Vn.-2,2,2,2-4,2-Timp.-Str.
Bote & Bock, Berlin [n.d.]
Score 35 p.

4514 [Symphony no. 1, Op. 31, B-flat   46'
major]
1.Allegro assez vivace 2.Adagio molto

sostenuto 3.Presto 4.Finale
2,2,2,3*-4,2-Timp.-Str.
Bote & Bock, Berlin [1883]
Score 306 p.

5005 [Symphony no. 3, Op. 50, B minor]
1.Allegro con brio 2.Adagio in modo di marcia
funebre 3.Un poco allegretto 4.Allegro
giocoso
2,2,2,2-4,2,3-Timp.,Perc.-Str.
N. Simrock, Berlin, C1910
Score 114 p.

RÜFER, PHILIPPE-BARTHÉLEMY.
                     Liège, Belgium 7 June 1844
                     Berlin 15 September 1919

1072v [Concerto, violin, Op. 33, in D]
1.Allegro maestoso 2.Adagio 3.Allegro
Solo Vn.-2,2,2,2-2,2-Timp.-Str.
Peters, Leipzig [n.d.]
Score 57 p.

RUFTY, HILTON.   Richmond, Virginia 1909

4694 Hobby-on-the-green. Transcribed   2'30"
by Richard Bales
3*,2,3*,2-4,3,3,1-Timp.,Perc.-Hp.-Str.
Ms.
Score 19 p.
Originally composed for piano solo, 1929.
This transcription 1941. First performance
Washington, D.C., 14 February 1943, National
Symphony Orchestra, Hans Kindler conductor.

RUGGLES, CARL. Marion, Massachusetts 11 March 1876
                Bennington, Vermont 24 October 1971

Born: Charles Sprague Ruggles

3718 Angels, for muted brass [revised   5'
version]
4Tpt.,2Tbn.
American Music Edition, New York, C1960
Score 5 p.
Originally from the symphonic suite Men and
Angels. Composed 1921. Revised 1938. First
performance Miami, Florida, 24 April 1939,
the composer conducting.

2802 Men and mountains, symphonic   10'
ensemble [revised version]
1.Men - Rhapsodic proclamation 2.Lilacs
3.Marching mountains
2*,2*,1,1-2,2,1-Cym.-Pno.-Str.
CR [i.e., Carl Ruggles], Arlington, Vermont,
C1927
Score 23 p.
Composed 1924. First performance of revised
version New York, 19 March 1936, New York
Philharmonic, Hans Lange conductor.

1731s Portals, for string orchestra   7'
Str.
New Music, San Francisco, C1930 by Carl Ruggles
Score 16 p.
Originally composed 1926; later rescored for
full string orchestra. First performance of

revised version New York, 26 October 1929, Conductorless Orchestra.

2826 Sun-treader   *15'*
5(4th & 5th alt. Picc.),5(2 are E.H.),5*(1Cl. in
E-flat),4*-6,5,5,2-Timp.,Perc.-2Hp.-Str.
New Music, San Francisco, ᶜ1934 by Carl Ruggles
Score 51 p.
*Composed 1932. First performance Paris, 25
February 1932, Orchestre Symphonique de Paris,
Nicolas Slonimsky conductor. Selected to
represent the U.S. at the Fourteenth Festival
of the International Society for Contemporary
Music, Barcelona, April 1936.*

RÜHLMANN, ADOLF JULIUS.   Dresden 28 February 1816
                                   Dresden 27 October 1877

878m [Fantasy, trombone and orchestra]
Solo Tbn.-1,1,2,1-2,2-Str.
Score: Ms. 24 p.
Parts: Leichssenring, Hamburg [n.d.]

RUSSELL, ARMAND.   Seattle 23 June 1932

5619 Balletic symphony   *25'*
1.Allegro ma scorrevole 2.Scherzo 3.Lento
e dolente - Con moto 4.Allegro agitato
3*,2,2,2-4,2,3,1-Timp.,Perc.-Str.
Ms.
Score 141 p. Large folio
*Composed 1957. First performance Rochester,
15 April 1957, Eastman-Rochester Symphony
Orchestra, Howard Hanson conductor.*

6244 Four tableaux for orchestra   *28'*
1.Moderately fast and flowing 2.Brisk and
animated 3.Slow and tranquil 4.Fast and
decisive
1,1,1,1-1,1,1-Timp.,Perc.-Str.
Ms.
Score 119 p. Large folio
*Commissioned by the University of Hawaii
Music Department. Composed 1962. First performance Honolulu, 27 May 1962, University of
Hawaii Chamber Orchestra, the composer conducting.*

RUSSELL, WILLIAM.   Canton, Missouri 1905

1013m Fugue, eight percussion instruments
1st-Timp.(Pedal)
2nd-Pno.
3rd-Bells(Glock.)
4th-Xyl.
5th-3Trgl.(4, 6, 10 inch)
6th-9Cym.(Suspended 14 inch Cym.,Chinese Crash
    Cym.,14 inch Turkish Cym.,2Finger Cym.,2
    16 inch Cym.,18 inch Cym.,Suspended Chi-
    nese Cym.)
7th-B.Dr.
8th-S.Dr.
New Music Edition [n.p.] ᶜ1933
Score 8 p.

1065m March suite for percussion orchestra
1.School march 2.Wedding march 3.Military
march 4.Hunger march 5.Funeral march

Cowbells,Cym.,Woodblock,Tam-tam,Slide Whistle,
Trgl.,S.Dr.,Flat Haitian Dr.,B.Dr.-Pno.
Ms.
Score 4 p.

1017m Percussion studies in Cuban rhythms
1.Havanera 2.Rhumba 3.Tiempo de son
4 players:
1st-Guiro,Cow Bell,Maracas
2nd-Claves,Quijadas
3rd-Marimbula
4th-Bongos,Cow Bell
Ms.
Score 6 p.
*First performance Seattle, 19 May 1939, John
Cage conductor.*

214m Three dance movements, for percussion *5'*
1.Waltz 2.March 3.Fox trot
4 players:
1st-Small Trgl.,Large Trgl.,Small Dinner Bell,
    Bottle,Steel Bar(or Anvil),Ginger Ale Bot-
    tle,Tom Tom
2nd-Finger Cym.,Suspended Turkish Cym.,Sus-
    pended Chinese Cym.,2Hand Cym.,Tom Tom
3rd-Small Wood Block,Large Wood Block,S.Dr.,
    B.Dr.
4th-Pno.,Slapstick
New Music, San Francisco, ᶜ1936
Score 7 p.
*Composed 1933. First performance San Fran-
cisco, 28 May 1934, New Music Society of
California, Henry Cowell conductor.*

RUSSO, WILLIAM JOSEPH.   Chicago 25 June 1928

5847 [Symphony no. 2, Titans, Op. 32,   *17'30"*
C major]
1.Slow, quasi recitativo - Allegro 2.Theme
and variations 3.[Scherzo] 4.[Finale]
4(4th alt. Picc.),4*,4*,4*(or 3*,3*,3*,3*)-4,
5,4(or 3),1-Timp.,Perc.-Pno.,Hp.-Str.
Ms.
Score 76 p. Large folio
*Commissioned by the Koussevitzky Foundation in
the Library of Congress. Composed 1958.
First performance New York, 16 April 1959,
Leonard Bernstein conductor, Maynard Ferguson
trumpet soloist.*

RUTTE, EUGEN MIROSLAV.   b. 1855
                                        Prague 1903

530s Menuett, Op. 17 [B-flat major]
Str.(Cb. ad lib.)
Fr. A. Urbánek, Prague [n.d.]
Score 5 p.

RYAN, DESMOND LUMLEY.   London 1851
                          London 29 November 1888

4529 Toy symphony in C major
1.Adagio - Allegro 2.Largo, quasi adagio
3.Minuet and trio 4.Medley finale
Cuckoo,Wachtel,Tpt.,Nachtigal,Turkish Bells,
Rattle,Trgl.,Cym.,Cast.,S.Dr.,Tamb.,Sop.Mirle-
ton,Bar.Mirleton-Pno.-Vn.I,Vn.II,Vc.
Metzler, London [1885]

Rybaltschenko, Vsevolod

Score 35 p.
Composed 1885.

RYBALTSCHENKO, VSEVOLOD.

3305 Ein Fest der Massen [Festival of the
masses, symphonic poem]
3(3rd alt. Picc.),3(3rd alt. E.H.),3,3(3rd alt.
C.Bn.)-4,4,3,1-Timp.,Perc.-Hp.-Str.
Mussektor [n.p.] 1933
Score 104 p.
Composed 1931.

RYBNER, CORNELIUS.   Copenhagen 26 October 1855
                           New York 21 January 1929

Born: Peter Martin Cornelius Rübner

678v [Concerto, violin, Op. 30, G minor]
1.Allegro moderato 2.Andante con espressione
3.Allegro con energico
Solo Vn.-2(2nd alt. Picc.),2,2,2-2,2-Timp.,
Perc.-Str.
Franquet, Greiz [n.d.]
Score 76 p.
*Composed 1887. First performance Karlsruhe,
1888, Felix Mottl conductor, Florian Zajic
soloist.*

RYBRANT, STIG.   Norrköping, Sweden 8 August 1916

4988 [Comedy overture]   *7'30"*
2(2nd alt. Picc.),2,2,2-2,2,1-Timp.,Perc.-Str.
Ms.
Score 56 p.
*Composed 1943. First performance Norrköping,
Sweden, 9 January 1944, Orchestra Society of
Norrköping, Heinz Freudenthal conductor.*

6031 [Happy strings! Scherzo for four   *4'*
trombones and tuba]
4Tbn.,Tuba
Ms. [Now published by Der Musikus, Sweden]
Score 12 p.
*The strings are silent, hence the title.
First performance in a radio broadcast, Sweden,
1953. Later retitled: Deep Brass Yoke.*

5015 [Symphony no. 1, E minor]   *37'*
1.Andante, ma molto sostenuto - Allegro
moderato 2.Andante sostenuto 3.Allegro vivace
con spirito
2(2nd alt. Picc.),2,2,2-4,3,3,1-Timp.,Perc.-
Hp.-Str.
Ms.
Score 254 p.
*First performance Stockholm, 9 November 1943,
Broadcasting Orchestra of Stockholm, Tor Mann
conductor.*

RYTEL, PIOTR.   Vilna, Poland 16 May 1884
                       Warsaw 2 January 1970

3936 Korsarz [The corsair, symphonic poem after
Byron] Op. 6
3(3rd alt. Picc.),3*,3*,3*-6,3,3,1-Timp.,Perc.
-Hp.-Str.
Polskie Wydawnictwo, Warsaw [n.d.]
Score 73 p.

3596 [Legend of St. George, symphonic poem,
Op. 9]
3(3rd alt. Picc.),3*,3*,3*-6,3,3,1-Timp.,Perc.
-Org.,Hp.-Str.
Privately published, Warsaw, ^C1926
Score 84 p. Large folio

S

SAAR, LOUIS VICTOR FRANZ.
                       Rotterdam 10 December 1868
             St. Louis, Missouri 23 November 1937

1477s Chanson d'amour, Op. 60 no. 2
Solo Vn.-Str.
C. Fischer, New York, ^C1911
Score 5 p.

1476s En berceau, Op. 86a [Cradle song]
Solo Vn.-Str.
J. Church, Cincinnati, ^C1917
Score 5 p.
Composed for Christmas, 1916.

1819 From the mountain kingdom of the Great
Northwest [Canada]
1.Pastorale 2.Lake Emerald 3.The glacier
4.Where the waters meet
3*,3*,3*,2-4,3,4,1-Timp.,Perc.-Hp.-Str.
F.E.C. Leuckart, Leipzig [n.d.]
Score 60 p.

1475s Gondoliera, Op. 52 no. 4
Solo Vn.-Str.
F.E.C. Leuckart, Leipzig, ^C1908
Score 6 p.

SABATA, VICTOR DE.   Trieste 10 April 1892
                     Santa Margherita Ligure,
                        Italy 11 December 1967

4871 [The night of Plato]   *21'*
3(2nd&3rd alt. Picc.),3(3rd alt. E.H.),3(3rd
alt. B.Cl.),3*-4,3,3,1-Timp.,Perc.-Cel.,2Hp.-
Str.
Ricordi, Milan, ^C1924
Score 127 p.
Composed 1924.

SABATHIL, FERDINAND.   Sangerberg,
             near Marienbad, Bohemia 12 November 1852

844m Divertissement, Op. 54
Solo Tbn.-2,2,2,2-4,2,3-Timp.-Str.
Score: Ms. 51 p.
Parts: A.E. Fischer, Bremen [n.d.]

SACCHINI, ANTONIO MARIA GASPARO GIOACCHINO.
                       Florence 14 June 1730
                       Paris 6 October 1786

6861 Oedipe à Colone. Ouverture. Edited by   *5'*
Antonio de Almeida
2Ob.-2Hn.-Timp.-Str.
Heugel, Paris, ^C1961

Score 23 p.
From the opera based on Sophocles' play. Composed 1785. First performance Versailles, 4 January 1786.

SACHS, JULIUS. Meiningen, Germany 12 December 1830
Frankfurt 28 December 1887

598c Ständchen [Serenade] Op. 31   5'
Solo Vc.-2,1,2,1-2Hn.-Timp.-Str.
R. Seitz, Leipzig [1874?]
Score 27 p.

SACHS, LÉO.   Frankfurt 3 April 1856
Paris 13 November 1930

1306 Babil d'oiseaux [Twittering birds]
2,2,2,2-2Hn.-Timp.,Cym.-Hp.-Str.
J. Hamelle, Paris [n.d.]
Score 28 p.

SACHSE, E.

810m [Concertino, trombone, B-flat major]
1.Allegro maestoso 2.Adagio 3.Allegro moderato
Solo Tbn.-1,2,2,2-2,2-Timp.-Str.
Score: Ms. 51 p.
Parts: C.F. Schmidt, Heilbronn [n.d.]

SADAI, YIZHAK.   Sofia, Bulgaria 13 May 1935

6460 Ricercar symphonique (1963)   9'30"
3*,3*,3*,3*-2Sax.(AT)-4,3,2,1-Timp.,Perc.-Hp.-Str.
Israeli Music Publications, Tel Aviv, c1963
Score 48 p.
Composed 1963. First performance Haifa, 27 February 1964, Israel Philharmonic Orchestra, Mendi Rohan conductor.

SADUN, ICILIO.
b. Viareggio, Italy 27 November 1872

1097s Le passant [The passerby]
Str.
Score: Ms. 3 p.
Parts: Ricordi, Milan, c1917

SAEVERUD, HARALD SIGURD JOHAN.
b. Bergen 17 April 1897

6697 [Ballad of revolt, Op. 22a no. 5]   5'30"
2(1st alt. Picc.),2,2,2-4,3,3,1-Timp.,Perc.-Hp.-Str.
Musikk-Huset A/S, Oslo, c1946
Score 23 p.
Composed 1943 for piano, Op. 22, and for orchestra, Op. 22a. First performance Oslo, 4 October 1945, Filharmonisk Selskap, the composer conducting.

6042 Canto ostinato, Op. 9   9'
3*,2(2nd alt. E.H.),2(2nd alt. B.Cl.),2-4,3,3,1-Timp.,Perc.-Cel.,Hp.-Str.
Norsk Musikforlag, Oslo, c1937
Score 52 p.
Composed 1934. First performance Oslo, 1934.

2173s Divertimento no. 1, Op. 13   13'
1.Marcia 2.Amoroso 3.Andante 4.Variazioni continue
Fl.-Str.
Norsk Musikforlag, Oslo, c1940
Score 22 p.
Composed 1939. First performance Bergen, 1941.

6694 [Variations on a shepherd's tune,   12'
Op. 15]
1,1,1(alt. B.Cl.),1-2,1-Str.
Musikk-Huset A.S., Oslo, c1948
Score 27 p.
Original title: Variazioni Innocente. Composed 1941. First performance Bergen, 6 March 1941, Bergen Harmonien, the composer conducting.

SAINT-GEORGE, GEORGE.   Leipzig 6 November 1841
London 5 January 1924

L'ancien régime, 2 petite suites
975s   I: 1.Preludio 2.Allemanda 3.Sarabanda
4.Menuetto I & II 5.Bourrée 6.Giga
976s   II: 1.Preludio 2.Allemanda 3.Sarabanda
4.Bourrée 5.Tambourin 6.Giga
Str.
Scores: Ms. 18 p., 27 p.
Parts: Augener, London [n.d.]

SAINT-QUENTIN, G. DE.

525c Première romance, Op. 19
Solo Vc.-2,2,2,2-2Hn.-Str.
J. Hamelle, Paris [n.d.]
Score 15 p.

SAINT-SAËNS, CHARLES-CAMILLE. Paris 9 October 1835
Algiers 16 December 1921

430p Africa, fantaisie, Op. 89   11'
Solo Pno.-2,2,2,2-2,0,2Cnt.,3-Timp.,Perc.-Str.
Durand, Paris [n.d.]
Score 94 p.
Composed 1891. First performance Paris, 25 October 1891, Concerts Colonne, Mme. Roger-Miclos soloist.

474c Allegro appassionato, Op. 43
Solo Vc.-2,2,2,2-2Hn.-Str.
Luck's, Detroit [n.d.]
Score 23 p.
Originally composed for violoncello and piano, 1875.

427p Allegro appassionato, Op. 70
Solo Pno.-2,2,2,2-2,2-Str.
Durand, Paris, c1905
Score 28 p.
Composed 1884.

Andromaque
998 Ouverture   8'
937 Prélude du 4e acte   5'
2(2nd alt. Picc.),2,2,2-2,2,3-Timp.,Cym.-Str.
Durand, Paris [n.d.]
Scores: 43 p., 9 p.
From the incidental music to Racine's play. Composed 1902. First performance Paris, 7 February 1903.

Saint-Saëns, Camille

1026 [Ascanio. Airs de ballet]   *24'*
    11 movements
    3(3rd alt. Picc.),2,2,3*-4,0,3Cnt.,3,1-Timp.,
    Perc.-Mouth Org.,2Hp.-Str.
    Durand, Paris [n.d.]
    Score 109 p.
    From the opera composed 1888. First perform-
    ance Paris, 21 March 1890. First concert per-
    formance Boulogne-sur-Mer, 26 August 1890.

582m [Ascanio. Airs de ballet. Movement 7,
    Poco adagio. Transcribed by P. Taffanel]
    Solo Fl.-1,2,2-2Hn.-Hp.-Str.
    Score: Ms. 8 p.
    Parts: Durand, Paris [n.d.]

894 Les barbares. Ouverture   *11'*
    3*,3*,3*,3*-4,4,3,1-Timp.,Perc.-Hp.-Str.
    Durand, Paris [n.d.]
    Score 67 p.
    From the opera composed 1901. First perform-
    ance Paris, 23 October 1901.

456v Caprice andalous, Op. 122
    Solo Vn.-2,2,2,2-2,2,3-Timp.-Hp.(ad lib.)-Str.
    Durand, Paris, ᶜ1904
    Score 50 p.
    Composed 1904.

420 Le carnaval des animaux, grande   *21'*
    fantaisie zoologique (Complete in 14
    movements)
    Picc.,Fl.,Cl.-Xyl.-2Pno.,Mouth Org.-Str.
    Durand, Paris, ᶜ1922
    Score 61 p.
    Composed 1886. First performance Paris, 1886,
    at Mardi Gras. Second performance Paris, 26
    February 1922. Quotes French popular songs
    and themes by Mendelssohn, Berlioz and Rossini.

388p [Concerto, piano, no. 1, Op. 17,   *28'*
    D major]
    1.Andante - Allegro assai 2.Andante sos-
    tenuto quasi adagio 3.Allegro con fuoco
    Solo Pno.-2,2,2,2-4,2-Timp.-Str.
    Durand, Paris [n.d.]
    Score 149 p.
    Composed 1858-59. First performance Leipzig,
    26 October 1865, Gewandhaus Orchestra, the
    composer as soloist.

360p [Concerto, piano, no. 2, Op. 22,   *22'*
    G minor]
    1.Andante sostenuto 2.Allegro scherzando
    3.Presto
    Solo Pno.-2,2,2,2-2,2-Timp.,Cym.-Str.
    Durand, Paris [n.d.]
    Score 111 p.
    Composed 1868. First performance Paris, May
    1868, Rubinstein conductor, the composer as
    soloist.

390p [Concerto, piano, no. 3, Op. 29,   *28'30"*
    E-flat major]
    1.Moderato assai 2.Andante 3.Allegro non
    troppo
    Solo Pno.-2,2,2,2-2,2,3-Timp.-Str.
    Durand, Paris [n.d.]

Score 146 p.
Composed 1869. First performance Leipzig, 25
November 1869, Gewandhaus Orchestra, the com-
poser as soloist.

361p [Concerto, piano, no. 4, Op. 44,   *24'*
    C minor]
    1.Allegro moderato - Andante 2.Allegro vivace
    Solo Pno.-2,2,2,2-2,2,3-Timp.-Str.
    Durand, Paris [n.d.]
    Score 155 p.
    Composed 1875. First performance Paris, 31
    October 1875, Edouard Colonne conductor, the
    composer as soloist.

362p [Concerto, piano, no. 5, Op. 103,   *30'*
    F major]
    1.Allegro animato 2.Andante 3.Molto allegro
    Solo Pno.-3*,2,2,2-4,2,3-Timp.,Gong-Str.
    Durand, Paris, ᶜ1896
    Score 151 p.
    Composed 1896. First performance Paris, 3
    June 1896, the composer as soloist.

457v [Concerto, violin, no. 1,   *10'*
    Concertstück, Op. 20, A major]
    1.Allegro 2.Andante espressivo 3.Tempo I
    Solo Vn.-2,2,2,2-2,2-Timp.-Str.
    J. Hamelle, Paris [n.d.]
    Score 64 p.
    Composed 1859. First performance Paris, 4
    April 1867, Pablo de Sarasate soloist.

535v [Concerto, violin, no. 2, Op. 58, C major]
    1.Allegro moderato e maestoso 2.Andante
    espressivo - Allegro scherzando
    Solo Vn.-2,2,2,2-2,2,3-Timp.-Hp.-Str.
    Durand, Paris [n.d.]
    Score in reduction 43 p.
    Composed 1858.

400v [Concerto, violin, no. 3, Op. 61,   *28'*
    B minor]
    1.Allegro non troppo 2.Andantino quasi alle-
    gretto 3.Molto moderato e maestoso
    Solo Vn.-2(2nd alt. Picc.),2,2,2-2,2,3-Timp.-
    Str.
    Kalmus, New York [n.d.]
    Score 125 p.
    Composed 1880. First performance Paris, 2 Jan-
    uary 1881, Pablo de Sarasate soloist.

507c [Concerto, violoncello, no. 1,   *19'*
    Op. 33, A minor]
    In one movement
    Solo Vc.-2,2,2,2-2,2-Timp.-Str.
    Kalmus, New York [n.d.]
    Score 72 p.
    Composed 1872. First performance Paris, 19
    January 1873, August Tolbecque soloist.

465c [Concerto, violoncello, no. 2, Op. 119,
    D minor]
    1.Allegro moderato e maestoso - Andante sos-
    tenuto 2.Allegro non troppo
    Solo Vc.-2,2,2,2-4,2-Timp.-Str.
    Durand, Paris, ᶜ1903
    Score 61 p.
    Composed 1902.

178 Danse macabre [symphonic poem, Op. 40]   7'
3*,2,2,2-4,2,3,1-Timp.,Perc.-Hp.-Str.
Kalmus, New York [n.d.]
Score 54 p.
Composed 1875. First performance Paris, Concerts Colonne, 24 January 1875.

805 [Déjanire. Act IV: Prélude and Cortège]   6'
3*,3(3rd alt. E.H.),3,3*-4,4,4-Timp.,Perc.-2Hp.-Str.
Durand, Paris, C1911
Score 42 p.
Originally composed 1898 for the incidental music to Louis Gallet's play. Rewritten as an opera, 1911. First performance Monte Carlo, 14 March 1911.

73s [Le Déluge, Op. 45. Prélude]   8'
Str.
Durand, Paris, C1913
Score 8 p.
From the oratorio composed 1874. First performance Paris, 5 March 1876.

919 [Étienne Marcel. Airs de ballet]   18'
A.[Entry of the students and ribalds] B.[Martial musette] C.Pavane D.Valse E.[Entry of the bohemians] F.Final
3*,2,2,2-4,2,3-Timp.,Perc.-Str.
Durand, Paris [n.d.]
Score 115 p.
From the opera composed 1877-78. First performance Lyons, 8 February 1879.

807 La foi [Faith. Three tableaux, Op. 130] 16'
1.Poco allegro 2.Andantino 3.Allegro moderato e maestoso
3*,2(2nd alt. E.H.),2,2-4,3,3-Timp.,Perc.-Harm.,Hp.-Str.
Durand, Paris, C1909
Score 90 p.
From the incidental music to Eugène Brieux's play. First performance Monte Carlo, 10 April 1909.

211 Gavotte, Op. 23 [C minor]   2'
2,2,2,2-2,0,3-Timp.-Str.
Durand & Schoenewerk, Paris [n.d.]
Score 16 p.
Composed for piano, 1871. Transcribed 1872. First performance Paris, 1872.

444v Havanaise, Op. 83   9'30"
Solo Vn.-2,2,2,2-2,2-Timp.-Str.
Durand, Paris [n.d.]
Score 37 p.
Composed 1887. First performance Paris, 7 January 1894, Martin-Pierre-Joseph Marsick soloist.

86 [Henry VIII. Ballet-divertissement]   18'
1.Introduction - Entrée des clans 2.Idylle écossaise 4.Danse de la gipsy 6.Gigue et final
3*,3,3*(2nd alt. Alto Cl.),2-4,2,2Cnt.,3,1-Timp.,Perc.-2Hp.-Str.
Durand, Paris [n.d.]
Score 79 p.

From the opera composed 1882. First performance Paris, 5 March 1883.

441v Introduction et rondo capriccioso,   10'
Op. 28
Solo Vn.-2,2,2,2-2,2(or 2Cnt.)-Timp.-Str.
Durand, Paris, C1909/Kalmus, New York, n.d.
Score 46 p.
Composed 1863. First performance Paris, 6 November 1913.

893 Javotte, fantaisie. Premier tableau: 8'
La fête au village
3*,2,2,2-4,0,4Cnt.,3,1-Timp.,Perc.-Hp.-Str.
Durand, Paris [n.d.]
Score 100 p.
From the ballet composed 1896. First performance Lyons, 3 December 1896.

180 La jeunesse d'Hercule [Hercules'   16'
youth] Op. 50
3*,2,2,2-4,2,2Cnt.,Bugle,3,1-Timp.,Perc.-Hp.-Str.
Durand & Schoenewerk, Paris [n.d.]
Score 73 p.
First performance Paris, 28 January 1877, Edouard Colonne conductor.

785 La jota aragonese, Op. 64   4'
3*,2,2,2-4,2,2Cnt.,3-Timp.,Perc.-Hp.-Str.
Durand, Paris [n.d.]
Score 41 p.
Composed 1880. First performance Paris, 6 February 1881.

1457 Marche du couronnement, Op. 117   8'
3*,2,2,3*-4,4,3,1-Timp.,Perc.-2Hp.-Str.
Durand, Paris, C1902
Score 40 p.
Composed for and first performed at the coronation of King Edward VII, London, 9 August 1902.

480 Marche héroïque, Op. 34   7'
3*,2,2,2-4,2,3,1-Timp.,Perc.-Hp.-Str.
Durand, Paris [n.d.]
Score 41 p.
Composed 1870. First performance Paris, 10 December 1871.

455v Morceau de concert, Op. 62 [E minor] 15'
Solo Vn.-2,2,2,2-2,2-Timp.-Str.
Durand, Paris [n.d.]
Score 58 p.
Composed 1880.

507m Morceau de concert, Op. 94
Solo Hn.-2,2,2,2-3Tbn.-Timp.-Str.
Durand, Paris [n.d.]
Score 22 p.
Originally composed for horn and piano, 1887.

514m Morceau de concert, Op. 154
Solo Hp.-2,2,2,2-2,2-Timp.-Str.
Durand, Paris, C1919
Score 54 p.
Composed 1918.

Saint-Saëns, Camille

724m La muse et le poète, Op. 132   *16'*
Solo Vn., Solo Vc.-2,2,2,2-2,2,3-Timp.-Hp.-Str.
Durand, Paris, ^c1910
Score 67 p.
*Composed 1909. First performance London, 7
June 1910, Eugène Ysaÿe and Joseph Hollmann
soloists.*

512 Une nuit à Lisbonne, barcarolle, Op. 63 *4'*
1,1,1,1-2Hn.-Hp.-Str.
Durand, Paris [n.d.]
Score 14 p.
*Composed 1880. First performance Paris, 23
January 1881.*

510m Odelette, Op. 162
Solo Fl.-0,2,0,2-Str.
Durand, Paris, ^c1920
Score 24 p.
Composed 1920.

87 [Omphale's spinning wheel, Op. 31]   *9'*
3*,2,2,3*-4,2,3-Timp.,Perc.-Hp.-Str.
Durand, Paris [n.d.]
Score 44 p.
*Composed 1869. First performance in this
form, Paris, 9 January 1872, Société Nationale.*

947 Orient et Occident, marche, Op. 25   *6'*
3*,3*,3*,3*-4,3,3,1-Timp.,Perc.-Str.
Durand, Paris, ^c1909
Score 44 p.
Composed 1869. First performance Paris, 1869.

1857 Ouverture de fête, Op. 133   *8'*
3*,3*,3*,3*-4,4,3,1-Timp.,Perc.-2Hp.-Str.
Durand, Paris, ^c1910
Score 53 p.
*Composed 1909 for the dedication of the Musée
Océanographique de Monaco.*

918 [Overture to an unfinished comic   *5'*
opera, Op. 140]
2,2,2,2-2,2,2-Str.
Durand, Paris, ^c1913
Score 24 p.
*Composed 1854. First performance London, 2
June 1913.*

936 [Parysatis. Airs de ballet]   *7'*
3(3rd alt. Picc.),3(3rd alt. E.H.),3*,4*-4,4,
3,1-Timp.,Perc.-2Hp.-Str.
Durand, Paris [n.d.]
Score 56 p.
*From the incidental music to Jane Dieulafoy's
play. Composed 1902. First performance
Béziers, 17 August 1902.*

209 Phaéton, poème symphonique, Op. 39   *9'*
3*,2,2,3*(C.Bn. ad lib.)-4,2,3,1-Timp.,Perc.-
2Hp.-Str.
Kalmus, New York [n.d.]
Score 43 p.
*Composed 1873. First performance Paris, 7
December 1873, Concerts Colonne.*

946 [Phryné. Introduction to Act II]   *4'*
2,2,2,2-2Hn.-Str.
Durand, Paris [n.d.]
Score 12 p.
*From the opera composed 1892-93. First per-
formance Paris, 24 May 1893.*

806 La princesse jaune [The yellow   *7'*
princess, Op. 30. Overture]
2(2nd alt. Picc.),2(1st alt. E.H.),2,2-4,2,3-
Timp.,Perc.-Hp.-Str.
[n.p., n.d.]
Score 41 p.
*From the comic opera composed 1872. First
performance Paris, 12 June 1872.*

883 [Proserpine. Entr'acte]   *3'*
3*,2*,2,2-4,0,2Cnt.,3,1-Timp.,Perc.-Str.
Durand, Paris, ^c1909
Score 31 p.
*From the opera based on Auguste Vacquerie's
play. Composed 1886-87. First performance
Paris, 16 March 1887.*

208 Rapsodie bretonne   *23'*
2,2*,2,2-4,2,3-Str.
Durand, Paris [n.d.]
Score 36 p.
*Originally composed for organ, 1866, in Three
Rhapsodies on Breton Themes, Op. 7. Tran-
scribed 1892. First performance 1893.*

460p Rhapsodie d'Auvergne, Op. 73
Solo Pno.-3*,2,2,2-4,2,3-Timp.,Perc.-Str.
Durand, Paris [n.d.]
Score 52 p.
*Composed 1884. First performance Marseilles,
December 1884, the composer as soloist.*

212 Rigaudon, Op. 93 no. 2   *3'*
2,2,2,2-2,2,2-Timp.-Str.
Durand, Paris [n.d.]
Score 25 p.
*Op. 93 composed 1892 to supplement Marc-
Antoine Charpentier's incidental music
(revised by Saint-Saëns) for Molière's play
Le Malade Imaginaire. First performance 28
November 1892.*

509m [Romance, flute, Op. 37]
Solo Fl.-0,2,2,2-4,2-Timp.-Str.
Durand, Paris [n.d.]
Score 18 p.
Composed 1874.

506m [Romance, horn, Op. 36]   *5'*
Solo Hn.-2,1,2,1-Str.
Durand, Paris [n.d.]
Score 8 p.
Composed 1874.

454v [Romance, violin, Op. 48]
Solo Vn.-1,1,1,1-2Hn.-Str.
Durand, Paris [n.d.]
Score 19 p.
*Originally composed for violin and piano, 1874.
Transcribed 1876.*

615c [Romance, violoncello, Op. 16 no. 4]
Solo Vc.-2,2,2,2-Str.
J. Hamelle, Paris [n.d.]
Score 9 p.
*From the Suite, Op. 16, originally composed
for violoncello and piano, 1862.*

511 [Samson et Dalila, Op. 47. Act III: *8'*
Danse bacchanale]
3*,3*,3*,3*-4,2,2Cnt.,3,1-Timp.,Perc.-2Hp.-Str.
Kalmus, New York [n.d.]
Score 45 p.
*From the opera first performed Weimar, 2
December 1877.*

210 [Samson et Dalila, Op. 47. Dance of *3'*
Dagon's priestesses]
2,2,2,2-4Hn.-Timp.,Perc.-Hp.-Str.
Durand [Paris, n.d.]
Score 11 p.

344s Sarabande, Op. 93 no. 1
Str.
Durand, Paris [n.d.]
Score 5 p.

723 Sérénade *5'*
2,1*,2-2Hn.-Hp.-Str.
Choudens, Paris [n.d.]
Score 15 p.
Composed 1866.

88 Suite algérienne, Op. 60 *20'*
1.Prélude: En vue d'Alger 2.Rhapsodie
mauresque 3.Rêverie du soir 4.Marche militaire française
3*,2,2,2-4,2,2Cnt.,3,1-Timp.,Perc.-Str.
Kalmus, New York [n.d.]
Score 101 p.
*Composed 1880. First performance Paris, 19
December 1880.*

513 Suite pour orchestre, Op. 49 *17'*
1.Prélude 2.Sarabande 3.Gavotte 4.Romance
5.Finale
2,2(2nd alt. E.H.),2,2-2,2-Timp.-Str.
Durand, Paris [n.d.]
Score 48 p.
Composed 1863. First performance Paris, 1865.

478 [Symphony no. 1, Op. 2, E-flat major] *31'*
1.Adagio - Allegro 2.Marche-scherzo 3.Adagio
4.Allegro maestoso
3*,2,3*,2(or 4)-4,2,2Cnt.,3,2Saxhn.(B.&Cb.)-
Timp.,Cym.-2Hp.-Str.
Durand, Paris [n.d.]
Score 156 p.
*Composed 1852. First performance Paris, 18
December 1853, François Seghers conductor.*

479 [Symphony no. 2, Op. 55, A minor] *23'*
1.Allegro marcato 2.Adagio 3.Scherzo presto
4.Prestissimo
3*,2(2nd alt. E.H.),2,2-2,2-Timp.-Str.
Durand, Paris, c1908
Score 98 p.
*Composed 1859. First performance Leipzig, 20
February 1859.*

699 [Symphony no. 3, Op. 78, C minor] *36'*
1.Adagio - Allegro moderato 2.Allegro
moderato - Presto - Maestoso
3(3rd alt. Picc.),3*,3*,3*-4,3,3,1-Timp.,Perc.
-Pno.,Org.-Str.
Kalmus, New York [n.d.]
Score 176 p.
*Composed 1886. First performance London, 19
May 1886.*

517m Tarantelle, Op. 6 *6'*
Soli Fl. & Cl.-1*,2,0,2-2,2,2-Timp.-Str.
Durand, Paris [n.d.]
Score 68 p.
Composed 1857.

Le timbre d'argent [The silver bell]
884 Ouverture *8'*
750 No. 6 Les abeilles [The bees]
938 No. 23 Valse vénitienne
3*,2,2,2-4,2,3,Cb.Tbn.(Valse only)-Timp.,Perc.-
Hp.(not in Les Abeilles)-Str.
Choudens, Paris [n.d.]
Scores: 60 p., 15 p., 39 p.
*From the opera composed 1875-77. First per-
formance Paris, 23 February 1877.*

537p Wedding cake, caprice-valse, Op. 76
Solo Pno.-Str.
Durand, Paris [n.d.]
Score 21 p.
Composed 1885, with English title.

SALAS, JUAN ANTONIO ORREGO.
See: ORREGO SALAS, JUAN ANTONIO.

SALIERI, ANTONIO.
Legnago, near Verona 18 August 1750
Vienna 7 May 1825

6402 [Axur, king of Ormus. Sinfonia] *4'*
Revised by Nino Negrotti
2,2,2,2-2,2-Timp.,Perc.-Str.
Carisch, Milan, c1947
Score 10 p.
*From the opera. First performance in French,
titled Tarare, Paris, 8 June 1787. This
Italian version first performed Vienna, 8 Jan-
uary 1788.*

6421 La grotta di Trofonio. Sinfonia. Revised
by Giuseppe Piccioli
2,2,2,2-2Tpt.-Timp.-Str.
Carisch, Milan, c1961
Score 48 p.
*From the opera buffa in two acts with libretto
by Giovanni Battista Casti. First performance
Vienna, 12 October 1785.*

6500 [Symphony, Giorno onomastico, *19'*
D major] Revised by Renzo Sabatini
1.Allegro, quasi presto 2.Larghetto
3.Minuetto 4.Allegretto
2,2,0,2(2nd optional)-2,2-Timp.-Str.
Ricordi, Milan, c1961
Score 69 p.

Salieri, Antonio

*Edited from the holograph in the Austrian
National Library in Vienna.*

6494 [Symphony, Veneziana, D major]   9'
Revised by Renzo Sabatini
1.Allegro assai 2.Andantino grazioso 3.Presto
2Ob.-2Hn.-Str.
Ricordi, Milan, ᶜ1961
Score 25 p.

SALMHOFER, FRANZ.   Vienna 22 January 1900
                           Vienna 22 September 1975

679m [Concerto, trumpet, C major]   15'
1.Maestoso - Allegro moderato 2.Andante,
feierlich 3.Scherzando
Solo Tpt.-3(2nd alt. Picc.),3*,3*,3*-4,3,3,1-
Timp.,Perc.-Hp.-Str.
Ms. [Universal Edition, Vienna, n.d.]
Score 50 p. Large folio
*Composed 1922. First performance Vienna, 1922,
Laborers' Symphony, the composer conducting,
Wendt soloist.*

2238 Kammersuite für 16 Instrumente, Op. 19
1.Sarabande 2.Scherzando 3.Menuett 4.Finale
1(alt. Picc.),2,2(2nd alt. B.Cl.),2-2Hn.-Hp.-
Str.
Universal Edition, Vienna, ᶜ1924
Score 71 p.
*First performance Vienna, 10 May 1923, Phil-
harmonisches Kammerorchester, Rudolf Nilius
conductor.*

SALVAYRE, GERVAIS-BERNARD-GASTON.
                Toulouse, France 24 June 1847
                St. Ague, near Toulouse 16 May 1916

390s Air de danse varié
Str.(Cb. ad lib.)
Choudens, Paris [n.d.]
Score 23 p.

1422 Suite espagnole
1.Alla zingara 2.Aragonaise lente 3.Sérénade
burlesque 4.Marche bohémienne
2(2nd alt. Picc.),2,2,2-4,2,2Cnt.,3,1-Timp.,
Perc.-Hp.-Str.
Choudens, Paris [n.d.]
Score 79 p.

SALVIUCCI, GIOVANNI.   Rome 26 October 1907
                              Rome 5 September 1937

4830 Introduzione, passacaglia e finale   13'
3(3rd alt. Picc.),3*,3*,3*-4,3,3,1-Timp.,Perc.
-Str.
Ricordi, Milan, ᶜ1936
Score 45 p.
*Composed 1934. First performance Rome, 29
December 1934. Awarded the prize of the Con-
corso Sinfonico Nazionale, 1934.*

4243 Sinfonia da camera per 17 strumenti   15'
1.Allegro 2.Adagio 3.Allegretto vivace
4.Allegro - Andante
1,1,1,1-1,1-Str.
Ricordi, Milan, ᶜ1936
Score 127 p.
*Composed 1933. First performance Rome, 25
April 1934.*

3915 Sinfonia italiana   10'
In one movement: Allegro - Largo - Presto
3(3rd alt. Picc.),3*,3*,3*-4,4,3,1-Timp.,Perc.
-Str.
Ricordi, Milan, ᶜ1934
Miniature score 49 p.
*Composed 1932. First performance Rome, 25
February 1934, Dimitri Mitropoulos conductor.*

SAMAZEUILH, GUSTAVE MARIE VICTOR FERNAND.
                     Bordeaux 2 June 1877
                     Paris 4 August 1967

254s Deux pièces dans le style ancien
Str.
Durand, Paris, ᶜ1912
Score 9 p.
Composed 1902.

4382 Divertissement et musette   15'
1,1,1,1-Hn.-Str.(without Cb.)
Durand, Paris, ᶜ1912
Score 18 p.
Composed 1902.

5409 Étude symphonique
3*,3*,3*,3-4,3,3,1-Timp.,Perc.-2Hp.-Str.
Durand, Paris, ᶜ1906-09
Score 63 p.
*Inspired by Elémir Bourges' dramatic poem La
Nef, on the subject of the Prometheus myth.
Composed 1905. First performance 1907.*

SAMET, ELIAS EMILE.   Tarnow, Poland 4 July 1862
                             Vienna 26 August 1926

282s Bagatellen, Op. 87 [5 movements]
Str.
Joh. André, Offenbach a.M. [1893?]
Score 11 p.

777s Serenade, Op. 142 [4 movements]
Hp.-Str.
Joh. André, Offenbach a.M. [1900?]
Score 15 p.

579s [What the brook tells, Op. 117]
Str.(Cb. ad lib.)
Joh. André, Offenbach a.M. [1899?]
Score 11 p.

SAMINSKY, LAZARE.
    Vale-Hotzulovo, near Odessa 8 November 1882
    Port Chester, New York 30 June 1959

1079v Hebrew rhapsody, Op. 3 no. 2   5'
Solo Vn.-2,2,2,2-2,2-Timp.,Perc.-Hp.-Str.
Ms.
Score 27 p.
Originally composed for violin and piano, 1911.
Transcribed 1923. First performance Paris,
24 June 1923, Colonne Orchestra, the composer
conducting, Helen Teschner Tas soloist.

3811 Pueblo, a moon epic, Op. 45   18'
1.Sick of the snow, the tent, the shia seed
2.Call the wind, Highward ho!
3(3rd alt. Picc.),3*,3*,3*-4,3,3,1-Timp.,
Perc.,Wind Machine-Pno.,Cel.,Hp.-Str.
Ms.
Score 72 p.
Commissioned by the League of Composers, 1936.
Composed 1936. First performance Washington,
D.C., 17 February 1937, National Symphony
Orchestra, the composer conducting.

3619 Stilled pageant (Fêtes passées),   10'
Op. 48
1.Ozymandias (after Shelley) 2.Venezia
3(3rd alt. Picc.),3*,3*,3*-4,2-Timp.,Perc.-
Pno.(alt. Cel.),Hp.-Str.
Senart, Paris, C1937
Score 33 p.
Composed 1927-35. First performance Zurich,
August 1938, Zurich Symphony Orchestra, Her-
mann Scherchen conductor.

2136 [Symphony no. 2, Of the summits,   18'
Op. 19, B major]
1.Maestoso, marcato 2.Tranquillo sognando -
In lontananza leggerissimo - Maestoso, con
forza
3(3rd alt. Picc.),3*,3*,3*-4,3,3,1-Timp.,Perc.
-Pno.,2Hp.-Str.
Senart, Paris, C1924
Score 71 p.
Composed 1918. First performance Amsterdam,
16 November 1922, Concertgebouw Orchestra,
Willem Mengelberg conductor.

4684 [Symphony no. 3, Des mers, Op. 30]   30'
1.Poco lento 2.Andantino tranquillo
3(3rd alt. Picc.),3*,3*,3*-4,3,3,1-Timp.,Perc.
-Pno.,Cel.,2Hp.-Str.
Universal Edition, Vienna, C1926
Score 78 p.
Composed 1919-1925. First performance Paris,
June 1925, Colonne Orchestra, the composer
conducting.

2960 Vigiliae, triade de poèmes, Op. 4   14'
1.Tranquillo - Calando 2.Lento mistico
3.Scintillante
3(3rd alt. Picc.),3*,3,3*-4,2,3,1-Timp.,Perc.
-Pno.,Hp.-Str.
[Mussektor, Moscow, 1926]
Score 71 p.
Composed 1910-11. First performance Moscow,
20 February 1913, Serge Koussevitzky Orchestra,
the composer conducting.

SAMMARTINI, GIOVANNI BATTISTA.   Milan 1700/01
    Milan 15 January 1775

1972s Andante for string orchestra
Str.
Ms.
Score 3 p.

6317 [Symphony, C major] Edited by   15'
Fausto Torrefranca and Roberto Lupi
1.Allegro assai 2.Andante 3.Allegrissimo
0,2,0,2-2Hn.-Timp.-Str.
Carisch, Milan, C1936
Score 12 p.
Composed between 1745 and 1760.

6419 [Symphony no. 3, G major] Edited by   9'
Fausto Torrefranca
1.Spiritoso (Allegro) 2.Andantino e grazioso
3.Rondò (Allegro vivo)
2(ad lib.),2(ad lib.)-2Hn.-Cemb.-Str.
Carisch, Milan, C1931
Score 22 p.

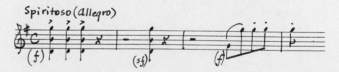

SAMMARTINI, GIUSEPPE, "IL LONDONESE".
    Milan ca.1693
    London before 24 June 1751

2302s [Concerto grosso, Christmas   15'
concerto, Op. 5 no. 6, G minor] Edited by
Karlheinz Schultz-Hauser
1.Spiritoso 2.Rondo 3.Pastorale
Org.(or Cemb.)-Str.
Chr. Friedrich Vieweg, Berlin, C1965
Score 28 p.
Appeared originally in 12 Trio Sonatas, Op. 3,
composed 1743. Six of these were expanded by
Sammartini into concerti grossi, Op. 5.

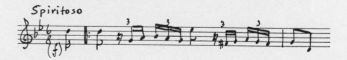

Sammartini, Giuseppe

2050s [Concerto grosso, strings and cembalo,
Op. 11 no. 4, D minor] Edited by Sydney Beck
1.Andante - Tempo giusto 2.Andante sostenuto
3.Allegro assai 4.Tempo di minuetto
Soli: 2Vn.,Vc.-Pno.(or Cemb.)-Str.
Music Press, New York [c1940]
Score 31 p.
First published 1738.

468s [Sonata à tre, Op. 3 no. 9. Adagio.
Transcribed by Vittorio Gui *as* Aria: Andante
cantabile]
Str.
Universal Edition, Vienna, c1926
Score 6 p.

SAMUEL, ADOLPHE ABRAHAM.   Liège 11 July 1824
                                 Ghent 11 September 1898

5506 [Symphony no. 6, Op. 44, D minor]
A.Genesis B.Eden C.Caïn D.Lux luceat! -
Laus et jubilatio
3*,3*,3*,3*-4,3,3,2-Timp.,Cym.-Str.
Schott Frères, Brussels [1890]
Score 170 p.
*First performance Royal Conservatory of Music
at Gand, Belgium, 30 November 1889, Conser-
vatory subscription concert, the composer
conducting.*

SANDBY, HERMAN.   Kundby, Denmark 21 March 1881
                         Copenhagen 14 December 1965

6371 Aftenstemning [At twilight]
4Hn.-Str.
Skandinavsk Musikforlag, Copenhagen, c1944
Score 7 p.
*Composed 1943. First performance Copenhagen,
ca.1943, Danish State Radio Orchestra, Launy
Gröndahl conductor.*

2150s Berceuse   6'
Hp.(ad lib.)-Str.
Skandinavsk og Borups Musikforlag, Copenhagen,
c1935
Score 7 p.
*Composed 1933. First performance Copenhagen,
ca.1933, Danish State Radio Orchestra, Launy
Gröndahl conductor.*

5574 Nordisk rapsodi   16'
In one movement
2,3*,2,2-4,2,3,1-Timp.-Str.
Skandinavsk Musikforlag, Copenhagen, c1955

Score 71 p.
*Composed 1940. First performance Copenhagen,
10 October 1942, Danish State Radio Orchestra,
Launy Gröndahl conductor.*

588s Norwegian bridal march   4'
Str.(Cb. ad lib.)
C. Fischer, New York, c1917
Score 7 p.
Composed 1917.

587s Song of Vermland (Swedish folksong)   3'
Str.(Cb. ad lib.)
C. Fischer, New York, c1917
Score 3 p.
Composed 1917.

307m [Two pieces, oboe and orchestra]
1.Andante 2.Allegro non troppo
Solo Ob.-Cl.,Bn.-2Hn.-Str.
Skandinavsk Musikforlag, Copenhagen, c1945
Score 12 p.
Composed 1941.

SANDERS, ROBERT L.   Chicago 2 July 1906
                            Delray Beach, Florida 26 December 1974

5871 [L'Ag'ya. Complete ballet]   21'
3*,2,2,2-Alto Sax.-4,2,3,1-Timp.,Perc.-Cel.,
Hp.-Str.
Ms. [c1944 by Robert L. Sanders]
Score 111 p. Large folio
*Commissioned by Katherine Dunham. Composed
1938 (the music lost). Recreated 1943-44.
First performance of new version, Hollywood,
California, 28 July 1944, Los Angeles Phil-
harmonic Orchestra, Antal Dorati conductor,
with Katherine Dunham & Co.*

2816 Scenes of poverty and toil   21'
1.Bread line 2.Sweat shop 3.Lame beggar
4.Wanton 5.Street gang
3(3rd alt. Picc.),2,2,2-4,3,3,1-Timp.,Perc.-
Org.(ad lib.),Cel.,Hp.-Str.
Ms.
Score 129 p.
*Alternate titles: The Tragic Muse; Olympia.
Composed 1934-35. First performance Chicago,
30 January 1936, Chicago Symphony Orchestra,
Eric De Lamarter conductor.*

2887 Suite, for large orchestra   20'
1.Prelude 2.Mississippi 3.Barn dance
4.Finale
3(3rd alt. Picc.),3*,4*(1Cl. in E-flat),3*-
3Sax.-4,3,3,1-Timp.,Perc.-Pno.,Cel.,Hp.-Str.
Ms.
Score 151 p.
*Composed 1926-29. First performance, Rochester,
22 November 1929, Rochester Philharmonic,
Howard Hanson conductor.*

5430 [Symphony for concert band,   20'
B-flat major]
1.Andante 2.Adagio 3.Allegro spirito
3*,1,6*(1Cl. in E-flat,1Alto),1-4Sax.-4,2,
4Cnt.-,3,Bar.,Tuba-Timp.,Perc.
Ms.

Score 103 p. Large folio
*Composed 1943. First performance Brooklyn,
27 June 1944, The Goldman Band, the composer
conducting.*

5905 Symphony in A   *27'*
1.Allegro 2.Adagio 3.Presto 4.Andante al
recitativo - Alla marcia vivace
3(3rd alt. Picc.),3*,2,2-4,2,3,1-Timp.,Perc.-
Str.
Ms. [^c1955 by Robert L. Sanders]
Score 115 p. Large folio
*Commissioned by the Knoxville Symphony Orches-
tra under a Ford Foundation grant. Composed
1954-55 under a Guggenheim Fellowship. First
performance Knoxville, Tennessee, 10 November
1959, Knoxville Symphony Orchestra, David Van
Vactor conductor.*

4234 [Symphony (Little), no. 1, G major]   *14'*
1.Allegro 2.Largo 3.Allegro moderato
2(2nd alt. Picc.),2,2,2-4,2,3-Timp.-Str.
Ms. [^c1936 by Robert L. Sanders]
Score 55 p. Large folio
*Composed 1935-36. First performance New York,
26 February 1939, New York Philharmonic
Orchestra, the composer conducting. Shared
New York Philharmonic award for shorter
works, 1938.*

5359 [Symphony (Little), no. 2, B-flat major] *15'*
1.Allegro cantabile 2.Molto lento 3.Vivace
2(2nd alt. Picc.),2(2nd alt. E.H.),2,2-4,2,3,
1-Timp.,Perc.-Hp.-Str.
Ms. [Now published by Ricordi]
Score 83 p. Large folio
*Commissioned by Louisville Philharmonic, 1953.
Composed 1953. First performance Louisville,
9 February 1954, Louisville Philharmonic
Orchestra, Robert Whitney conductor.*

SANDI, LUIS.   Mexico City 22 February 1905

6742 [Bonampak. Suite from the ballet]   *28'*
In five movements
3(3rd alt. Picc.),2(2nd alt. E.H.),1-3,3,2,1-
Timp.,Perc.-Str.(without Va.)
Peer International Corp., New York, ^c1958
Score 108 p.
*From the ballet on a Mayan subject. First
performance Mexico City, 2 November 1951.*

5464 Feria [A fair, symphonic poem]
1.Allegro moderato 2.Allegro 3.Lento
3*,3*,4(1Cl. in E-flat,1B.Cl.),2-4,3,3,1-Timp.,
Perc.-Pno.,Hp.-Str.
Ms.
Score 40 p.
Composed 1942.

5138 Las guarecitas [The girls]
2,1(alt. E.H.),2-0,2,1-Tamb.-Vihuela,Guit.-
Str.
Ms.
Score 30 p.
Composed 1941.

5752 Suite banal   *10'*
1.Allegro molto 2.Lento 3.Allegro vivo
4.Lento y fuerte
Cl.,Bn.-Tpt.-Perc.-Cel.-Str.
Ms. [Ediciones Mexicanas de Música, Mexico
City, ^c1935]
Score 19 p.
Composed 1937.

SANDOVAL, MIGUEL.   Guatemala City 22 November 1903
                              New York 24 August 1953

3654 Eres tú (Bolero). Arranged by R. Dermond
3*,2,2,2-2,2,2-Xyl.(or Bells)-Str.
Ms.
Score 15 p.

SANDRÉ, GUSTAVE.   France 17 May 1843
                       Paris 26 February 1916

789s Berceuse de Philis (17me siècle)
Str.
B. Schott's Söhne, Mainz [1900?]
Score 3 p.

546s Gavotte, Op. 37 no. 2
Str.
Score: Ms. 5 p.
Parts: Paul Dupont [Paris, n.d.]

239s Menuet, Op. 37 no. 1
Str.
Score: Ms. 5 p.
Parts: Paul Dupont [Paris, n.d.]

585m Pastorale, Op. 28
Solo Ob.-2,0,2,2-2Hn.-Str.
Score and parts: Ms. Score 17 p.
Solo: J. Hamelle, Paris [n.d.]

26s Serenade, Op. 24
1.Preludio 2.Scherzo 3.Romanza 4.Inter-
mezzo 5.Finale: Allegro molto animato
Str.
Breitkopf & Härtel, Paris [n.d.]
Score 37 p.

823m [Under the bower, aubade, Op. 48]
Solo Fl., Solo Cl.-Str.
Score: Ms. 12 p.
Parts: [Enoch, Paris, n.d.]

SANJUÁN, PEDRO.
            b. San Sebastián, Spain 15 November 1886

4082 Castilla   *25'*
1.Panorama 2.[On the plain] 3.[Threshing
songs]
3(3rd alt. Picc.),3*,3(3rd alt. B.Cl.),3*-
Alto Sax.-4,3,3,1-Timp.,Perc.-Cel.,2Hp.-Str.
Ms. ^c1941 by Eschig, Paris
Score 134 p. Large folio
*Composed 1925. First performance Havana, 12
June 1927, Havana Philharmonic Orchestra, the
composer conducting.*

Liturgia negra [based on Cuban themes]
4083 1.Chango (Invocación-Danza ritual)   *8'*

Sanjuán, Pedro

4084   2.Iniciación   4'
4085   3.Babaluayé [God of resurrection]   4'
4086   4.Canto à Oggun [Song to the moon god]   7'
6245   5.Comparsa lucumi [Masquerade of the   6'
       chieftains]
       3*,3*,3*,3*-4,3,3,1-Timp.,Perc.-Str.
       Eschig, Paris, C1939
       Scores: 41 p., 25 p., 29 p., 22 p., 42 p.
       Composed 1929. First performance Havana,
       1930, Havana Philharmonic Orchestra, the com-
       poser conducting. Awarded the National Music
       Prize of Spain, 1934.

3767   Rondo fantástico, Op. 3   5'
       4*(3rd alt. Picc.I),3*,2,2-4,3,3,1-Timp.,Perc.
       -Hp.-Str.
       Ms. C1941 by Eschig, Paris
       Score 40 p.
       Based on a Basque theme. Composed 1926.
       First performance Havana, 29 November 1926,
       Havana Philharmonic Orchestra, the composer
       conducting.

4065   Sones de Castilla [Sounds of Castile]   23'
       1.[Twilight on the plain] 2.[Tambourine dance]
       3.[Barren plain] 4.[Feast]
       2*,1,1,1-Tpt.-Perc.-Pno.-Str.
       Ms. C1941 by Eschig, Paris
       Score 125 p.

SANNEMANN, MAX.   Seehausen, Saxony 15 April 1867
                             Ballenstedt, Saxony ?1929

3s   Wiegenlied (Berceuse), Op. 24
     Hp.(ad lib.)-Str.
     Zimmermann, Leipzig [n.d.]
     Score 7 p.

SANSONI, LUIGI.

1582s Parrucche bianche [White wigs,   5'
       minuet]
       Str.
       Score: Ms. 5 p.
       Parts: Ricordi, Milan, C1928
       Originally composed for small orchestra.

SANTOLIQUIDO, FRANCESCO.
         San Giorgio a Cremano, Naples 6 August 1883
                             Naples 24 August 1971

1917   Acquarelli, suite sinfonica   14'
       1.[Morning in the woods] 2.[It's snowing]
       3.[Evening] 4.Festa notturna
       3*,3*,3*,3-4,2,3,1-Timp.,Perc.-Hp.-Str.
       Ricordi, Milan, C1922
       Score 67 p.
       Composed 1921. First performance Rome, 11
       April 1923, Albert Coates conductor.

3386   [Dawn of glory on the Uariéu Pass,   9'
       heroic prelude]
       3*,3*,2,3-4,3,4-Timp.,Perc.-Hp.-Str.
       Ricordi, Milan, C1939
       Score 36 p.
       First performance Rome, 13 November 1940,
       Hellmuth Thierfelder conductor.

2518   [The perfume of the Saharan oases]   8'
       3*,3*,2,4*-4,3,3,1-Timp.,Perc.-Hp.-Str.
       Chester, London, C1923
       Score 27 p.
       Composed 1913. First performance Tunis, 17
       April 1918, Dragoutine Pokorny conductor.

2430   La sagra dei morti, elegia sinfonica   8'
       2,3*,2,2-4,3,3,1-Timp.,Perc.-Hp.-Str.
       Chester, London [n.d.]
       Score 19 p.
       Composed 1920 in memory of Italian war heroes.
       First performance Rome, May 1929, Mario Rossi
       conductor.

4346   [Symphony no. 1, F major]
       1.Allegro moderato 2.Andante 3.Scherzo
       4.Finale
       3*,3*,2,4*-4,3,3,1-Timp.,Perc.-Hp.-Str.
       Grandi, Rome, C1921 by Francesco Santoliquido
       Score 178 p.
       Composed 1916.

2476   Twilight on the sea   10'
       2,3*,2,2-4,3,3,1-Timp.,Perc.-Hp.-Str.
       Grandi, Rome, C1920
       Score 40 p.
       Composed 1909. First performance Nuremberg,
       19 January 1909, the composer conducting.

SANTORO, CLAUDIO.   Manaos, Brazil 23 November 1919

2032s [Music for string orchestra]   8'
       Str.
       Ms. [Ricordi Brasileira, Saõ Paulo, n.d.]
       Score 12 p.
       Composed 1946. First performance Rio de
       Janeiro, 22 March 1947, Symphony Orchestra of
       Brazil, Oliviero de Fabritis conductor.

4985   [Symphony no. 3, C major]
       1.Andante 2.Allegretto 3.Adagio 4.Allegro
       moderato
       3*,2,3*,2-4,3,3,1-Timp.,Perc.-Pno.-Str.
       Ms.
       Score 81 p.
       Composed 1948. First performance Rio de
       Janeiro, 20 December 1949, Symphony Orchestra
       of Brazil, Eleazar de Carvalho conductor.
       Awarded first prize in the National Contest
       conducted by the Symphony Orchestra of Brazil
       in combination with the Berkshire Music Center.

SANTÓRSOLA, GUIDO.
             Canosa di Puglia, Italy 18 November 1904

457m   Concertino para guitarra y orquesta   18'
       1.Humorístico 2.Á manera de Vidalita
       3.Final: Movido
       Solo Guit.-3*,1,3*,1-1,1-Susp.Cym.-Cel.-Str.
       Ms. [Southern, New York, n.d.]
       Score 27 p. Large folio
       Commissioned by Servicio Oficial Difusión Radio
       Eléctrica (SODRE) of Uruguay. Composed 1942.
       First performance Montevideo, 4 September 1943,
       Orquesta Sinfónica del SODRE, the composer con-
       ducting, Abel Carlevaro soloist. Awarded first
       prize, SODRE competition, August 1942.

286m [Concerto, bassoon]   14'
1.Con humorismo 2.Aria, con basso ostinato
3.Finale
Solo Bn.-3*,2,3*-3,3,3-Timp.,Mil.Dr.,Trgl.-
Cel.,Hp.-Str.
Ms. [Southern, New York, n.d.]
Score 44 p. Large folio
Commissioned by Gerhart Haase. Composed 1959.

328v [Concerto, viola]   15'
1.Poco movido 2.Adagio 3.Allegro moderato
Solo Va.-1,3*,3*,1-4Hn.-Chorus(SATB, optional)
-Str.(with optional Va.d'Amore)
Ms. [Southern, New York, n.d.]
Score 31 p. Large folio
*Composed 1933. First performance Montevideo,
November 1944, Orquesta Sinfónica del Servicio
Oficial Difusión Radio Eléctrica, Erich Klei-
ber conductor, the composer as soloist.*

327v [Concerto, violin. Revised version] 18'30"
1.Allegro moderato 2.Andante 3.Allegretto
mosso
Solo Vn.-3*,2,2,2-4,3-Timp.,Perc.-Cel.-Str.
Ms. [Southern, New York, n.d.]
Score 58 p.
Composed 1962.

2128s Prelude y fuga a la manera clásica   12'
Str.(divided into 2 orchestras)
Ms. [Southern, New York, n.d.]
Score 50 p.
*Originally composed for two violas with contra-
bass, 1937. First performance of this version,
Buenos Aires, October 1955, Sinfónica de la
Radio del Estado, Bruno Bandini conductor.*

2126s Preludios (5 pequeños poemas   5'
psíquicos), no. 1
Str.
Ms. [Southern, New York, n.d.]
Score 27 p.
*Excerpted and transcribed from the piano suite
composed 1936. First performance Montevideo,
21 August 1956, Orquesta de Cámara de la Asociación Uruguaya de Cultura Artística, the
composer conducting.*

5710 Preludios, no. 3   3'
1,1,2,1-2Hn.-Hp.-Str.
Ms. [Southern, New York, n.d.]
Score 9 p.
*Excerpted and transcribed 1943 from the piano
suite composed 1936. First performance Estu-
dio Auditorio del SODRE, Montevideo, 22 May
1948, Orquesta Sinfónica del Servicio Oficial
Difusión Radio Eléctrica, Hermann Scherchen
conductor.*

5709 Saudade [Memory; longing]   5'
3*,3*,3*,2-3Hn.-Timp.,Trgl.-Cel.,Hp.-Str.
Ms. [AGADU, Montevideo, C1944]
Score 22 p.
*Originally composed for violin and piano, 1931.
First performance in this form, Montevideo,
17 June 1943, Orquesta Sinfónica del Servicio
Oficial Difusión Radio Eléctrica, Fritz Busch
conductor.*

5706 Semblanza de Artigas [Portrait of Artigas]
1.Calmo 2.Con heroismo 3.Amplio y tranquilo
4.Himno: Maestoso
3(3rd alt. Picc.),3*,3*,3*-4,4,3,1-Timp.,Perc.
-Cel.,2Hp.-Speaker,Chorus(SATB)-Str.
Ms. [Southern, New York, n.d.]
Score 58 p.
*José Gervasio Artigas led the Uruguayan War of
Independence from 1810 to 1820. Text is Barto-
lome Hidalgo's poem, Octavas Orientales. Com-
posed 1952. Awarded a prize in the Uruguayan
Ministry of Public Instruction and Social
Security competition, 1957.*

5712 [Two studies for symphony orchestra]   10'
1.Sonata monotemática 2.Mangangá
3*,2,2,2-4,3,3,1-Timp.-Str.
Ms. [AGADU, Montevideo, C1958]
Score 104 p.
Originally composed for solo viola, 1953.

5711 Vida de Artigas [Life of Artigas]   10'
1.Preludio 2.Tema heroico 3.Éxodo
3*,2,2,2-4,4,3,1-Timp.,Perc.-Hp.-Str.
Ms. C1952 by AGADU, Montevideo
Score 32 p. Large folio
*Commissioned by Servicio Oficial Difusión
Radio Eléctrica of Uruguay (SODRE). Composed
1951. First performance Montevideo, 12 November 1955, Orquesta Sinfónica del SODRE, the
composer conducting. Awarded first prize,
SODRE competition, 1951.*

SANTOS, DOMINGO.   San Esteban, El Salvador 1892

3707 Martita, overture no. 1   10'
3*,2,2,2-4,3,3,1-Timp.,Perc.-Str.
Ms.
Score 59 p.
*Composed 1924. First performance San Salvador,
7 December 1924, Paul Müller conductor.*

4167 La tarde, intermezzo [Afternoon]
2,2,2,2-2Hn.-Timp.-Hp.-Str.
Ms.
Score 16 p.
Composed 1929.

SAPELNIKOV, VASSILY LVOVICH.
                              Odessa 14 November 1867
                         San Remo, Italy 17 March 1941

4367 Polka caprice. Transcribed for orchestra
by Modest Altschuler
3(3rd alt. Picc.),2,2,2-4,2,3,1-Timp.,Perc.-
Hp.-Str.
Ms.
Score 11 p.
*Originally composed for piano. Transcribed
1916.*

SARACENI, FRANCO.

1942s Due piccole invenzioni
Str.
De Santis, Rome, C1934 by Dorica, Rome
Score 4 p.
Composed 1934.

Sarasate, Pablo de

SARASATE, PABLO DE.   Pamplona, Spain 10 March 1844
                      Biarritz, France 20 September 1908

451v Airs écossais, Op. 34
      Solo Vn.-2,2,2,2-2,2,3-Timp.-Str.
      Simrock, Berlin, 1892
      Score 19 p.

445v Airs espagnols
      Solo Vn.-2,2,2,2-2,0,3-Timp.-Str.
      Durand, Paris [n.d.]
      Score 55 p.

442v Carmen fantaisie, Op. 25 [on themes from
      Bizet's opera]
      Solo Vn.-2(2nd alt. Picc.),2,2,2-4,2,3-Timp.,
      S.Dr.-Hp.-Str.
      Choudens, Paris [n.d.]
      Score in reduction 21 p.

585v Chansons russes d'après Kaschine et
      Gurileff, transcrites et variées, Op. 49
      Solo Vn.-2,2,2,2-2,0,3-Timp.,Perc.-Str.
      Zimmermann, Leipzig, ^c1904
      Score 35 p.

588v La chasse, Op. 44 [The hunt]
      Solo Vn.-2,2,2,2-4,2,3-Timp.,Trgl.-Str.
      Zimmermann, Leipzig, ^c1901
      Score 59 p.

510v Danse espagnole, Adios Montañas   3'
      Mias, célèbre zortzico, Op. 37. Orchestrated
      by Leo Blech
      Solo Vn.-2,2,2,2-2Hn.-Timp.-Hp.-Str.
      B. Schott's Söhne, Mainz, ^c1895
      Score 12 p.
      *Note on score: Célèbre zortzico de Joaquin
      Larregla. Originally composed for violin and
      piano.*

581v L'esprit follet, Op. 48
      Solo Vn.-2,2,2,2-2Hn.-Timp.-Str.
      Zimmermann, Leipzig, ^c1905
      Score 27 p.

845v Fantaisie sur La Flûte Enchantée de Mozart,
      Op. 54
      Solo Vn.-2,2,2,2-2Hn.-Timp.-Hp.-Str.
      Zimmermann, Leipzig, ^c1908
      Score 35 p.

471v Faust fantaisie [on themes from Gounod's
      opera]
      Solo Vn.-2,2,2,2-2,2,3-Timp.-Str.
      Bote & Bock, Berlin [1885?]
      Score in reduction 15 p.

683v Jota de Pablo, Op. 52
      Solo Vn.-2,2,2,2-2,2-Timp.,Tamb.-Hp.-Str.
      Zimmermann, Leipzig, ^c1907
      Score 35 p.

600v Jota de Pamplona, Op. 50
      Solo Vn.-2,2,2,2-2,2,3-Timp.,Perc.-Str.
      Zimmermann, Leipzig, ^c1904
      Score 31 p.

758v Jota de San Fermin, Op. 36
      Solo Vn.-2(2nd alt. Picc.),2,2,2-2,2,3,1-Timp.,
      Perc.-Hp.-Str.
      Simrock, Berlin, ^c1894
      Score 36 p.

760v Muiñeira, thème montagnard varié, Op. 32
      Solo Vn.-2,2,2,2-2,0,3-Timp.,Perc.-Str.
      Senff, Leipzig [1887]
      Score 43 p.

430v Navarra, Op. 33
      2 Soli Vn.-2,2,2,2-2,2,3-Timp.,Perc.-Str.
      Simrock, Berlin, 1889
      Score 42 p.

596v Nocturne-sérénade, Op. 45
      Solo Vn.-2,2,2,2-2Hn.-Hp.-Str.
      Zimmermann, Leipzig, ^c1901
      Score 27 p.

985v Peteneras, caprice espagnol, Op. 35
      Solo Vn.-2,2,2,2-2,2,3-Timp.,Perc.-Str.
      Simrock, Berlin, ^c1894
      Score 44 p.
      Peteneras are Andalusian popular songs.

549v Rêve, Op. 53 [Dream. Orchestration com-
      pleted by T. Bretón]
      Solo Vn.-2,2,2,2-2Hn.-Timp.-Hp.-Str.
      Zimmermann, Leipzig, ^c1909
      Score 35 p.

      Spanische Tänze
685v Introduction et caprice-jota, Op. 41
914v Miramar, zortzico, Op. 42 (Score is Ms.)
570v Introduction et tarantelle, Op. 43
      Solo Vn.-2,2,2,2-2,2,3(Op. 41 only),0-Timp.,
      Perc.-Str.
      Zimmermann, Leipzig, ^c1899
      Scores: 35 p., 20 p., 43 p.

426v Zigeunerweisen [Gypsy airs] Op. 20   10'30"
      Solo Vn.-2,2,2,2-2,2-Timp.,Trgl.(ad lib.)-Str.
      Kalmus, New York [n.d.]
      Score 39 p.

SARMIENTOS, JORGE A.
                    b. Guatemala City 19 February 1931

309m [Concerto for 5 timpani and   10'
      orchestra, Op. 18]
      1.Moderato 2.Danza 3.Allegro moderato
      Solo Timp.-3(3rd alt. Picc.),3(3rd alt. E.H.),
      3(3rd alt. B.Cl.&E-flat Cl.),3*-4,4,3,1-Perc.-
      Str.
      Ms. [Southern, New York, n.d.]
      Score 44 p.
      *Commissioned by the Pan American Union. Com-
      posed 1962. First performance Washington, D.C.,
      7 May 1965, Third Inter-American Music Festi-
      val, National Symphony Orchestra, Howard
      Mitchell conductor, Fred Begun soloist.*

SARO, HANS.

786s [Children's dreams. Arranged by August
      Horn]

Str.
C.F. Schmidt, Heilbronn [n.d.]
Score 7 p.

SARÓN, PEDRO HUMBERTO ALLENDE.
  See: ALLENDE SARÓN, PEDRO HUMBERTO.

SARTORIO, ARNOLD.   Frankfurt 30 March 1853

  1342s [My darling, lullaby, Op. 372. Tran-
    scribed by Hermann Voigt]
    Str.(Cb. ad lib.)
    Raabe & Plothow, Berlin [n.d.]
    Score 5 p.
    Originally composed for piano.

SÁS, ANDRÉS.   Paris 6 April 1900
                                     Lima, Peru 26 July 1967

  3741 Himno y danza   *7'*
    3(3rd alt. Picc.),3*,3*,3*-4,3,3,1-Timp.,Perc.
    -Cel.,2Hp.-Str.
    Ms.
    Score 25 p.
    *No. 1 of Tres Estampas Peruanas. Originally
    composed for piano, 1938. This version 1941.
    First performance London, 11 February 1943,
    BBC Theatre Orchestra, Stanford Robinson con-
    ductor.*

  1147v Recuerdos [Memories]   *7'*
    Solo Vn.-2(2nd alt. Picc.),2,2,2-2,1,1,1-
    Timp.,Perc.-Cel.,Hp.-Str.
    Ms.
    Score 36 p.
    Composed 1941.

SATIE, ERIK ALFRED LESLIE.
        Honfleur, Calvados, France 17 May 1866
                                     Paris 1 July 1925

  2381 Les aventures de Mercure [Complete   *20'*
    ballet]
    2*,1,2,1-2,2,1,1-Perc.-Str.
    Ms. Universal Edition, Vienna [ᶜ1930]
    Score 92 p.
    *Composed 1924. First performance Paris, 15
    June 1924, Etienne de Beaumont conductor.*

  1714 Cinq grimaces pour Un Songe d'une   *15'*
    Nuit d'Été
    3(1st alt. Picc.),3*,2,3*-2,3,3,1-Timp.,Perc.-
    Str.
    Universal Edition, Vienna, ᶜ1929
    Score 20 p.
    Composed 1914.

  751 Gymnopédies. Transcribed for orchestra *8'*
    by Claude Debussy
    1.Lent et grave 2.Lent et douloureux
    2Fl.,Ob.-4Hn.-Cym.-2Hp.-Str.
    Baudoux, Paris [1897]
    Score 7 p.
    *Composed for piano, 1888. First performance
    of this transcription Paris, 20 February
    1897.*

  2370 Jack in the box. Orchestrated by   *6'30"*
    Darius Milhaud

1.Prélude 2.Entr'acte 3.Final
2(2nd alt. Picc.),2,2,2-2,2,2-Timp.,Perc.-Str.
Universal Edition, Vienna, ᶜ1929
Score 47 p.
*Originally composed for piano, 1900. Orches-
trated 1926. First performance Paris, 1926.*

  3867 Sonnerie [Fanfare to awaken the good *20"*
    fat king of the monkeys who always sleeps with
    only one eye shut]
    2Tpt.
    Ms.
    Score 1 p.
    Composed 1921.

  4248 Trois petites pièces montées   *5'*
    1.De l'enfance de Pantagruel: Rêverie 2.Marche
    de Cocagne: Démarche 3.Jeux de Gargantua: Coin
    de polka
    1,1,1,1-1,2,1-Perc.-Str.
    La Sirène, Paris, ᶜ1921
    Score 20 p.
    Composed 1919.

SATUREN, DAVID.   Philadelphia 11 March 1939

  2355s Dialogue between harpsichord and   *7'*
    strings
    Hpscd.-Str.
    Ms. ᶜ1973 by David Saturen
    Score 25 p.
    Composed 1972.

  2354s Largo for strings   *5'*
    Str.
    Ms.
    Score 15 p.
    *Composed 1965-66. First performance Philadel-
    phia, 17 May 1966, Concerto Soloists of Phila-
    delphia, Marc Mostovoy conductor.*

  2334s Ternaria [1st version] for organ,
    timpani and strings
    1.Fast and energetic 2.Slow and passionate
    3.And the house will rock, man!
    Org.-Timp.-Str.
    Ms. ᶜ1970 by the composer
    Score 60 p. Large folio
    *Commissioned by Robert Plimpton and Sixteen
    Concerto Soloists. Composed 1968. First per-
    formance Moorestown, New Jersey, 26 October
    1969, Sixteen Concerto Soloists, Marc Mostovoy
    conductor, Robert Plimpton organist.*

  6900 Ternaria [2nd version] for organ,
    timpani and orchestra
    2,2,2,2-4,3,3,1-Timp.,Perc.-Org.-Str.
    Ms. ᶜ1970 by the composer
    Score 60 p. Large folio
    *This version commissioned by the Trenton Sym-
    phony, 1970. First performance Trenton, 6
    December 1970, Trenton Symphony, William Smith
    conductor, Robert Plimpton organist.*

SATZ, ILIA.   Chernobyl, near Kiev 30 April 1875
                              St. Petersburg 12 December 1912

  971 [Dance of the satyrs] Edited by Reinhold
    Glière

717

Satz, Ilia

3(3rd alt. Picc.),3*,3*,3*-4,3,3,1-Timp.,Perc.
-Str.
Édition Russe de Musique, Berlin, 1913
Score 46 p.

1452 Miserere, valse. Orchestrated by Reinhold
Glière
2,2*,2,2-4,2,3,1-Timp.,Perc.-Str.
Jurgenson, Moscow [1913]
Score 26 p.

SAUER, EMIL VON.   Hamburg 8 October 1862
                         Vienna 28 April 1942

561p [Concerto, piano, no. 1, E minor.   30'
Second edition]
1.Allegro patetico 2.Scherzo 3.Cavatina
Solo Pno.-2(2nd alt. Picc.),2,2,2-3,2,3-Timp.
-Str.
B. Schott's Söhne, Mainz, c1900
Score 79 p.

575p [Concerto, piano, no. 2, C minor]   30'
1.Moderato lamentoso - Vivacissimo 2.Andante
3.Allegro deciso, assai moderato
Solo Pno.-2(2nd alt. Picc.),3*,2,2-4,2,3,1-
Timp.,Perc.-Str.
B. Schott's Söhne, Mainz [n.d.]
Score 70 p.
*Composed 1903. First performance Berlin,
November 1903, Richard Strauss conductor, the
composer as soloist.*

SAUNIER, E.

1222s Mignardises [Delicacies] Transcribed by
G. Bonincontro
Str.
Score: Ms. 5 p.
Parts: Decourcelle, Nice, c1919
Originally composed for piano.

SAURET, ÉMILE.   Dun-le-Roi, France 22 May 1852
                   London 12 February 1920

847v Andante et caprice de concert, Op. 67 17'
Solo Vn.-2,2,2,2-2,2-Timp.,Trgl.-Str.
Zimmermann, Leipzig, c1907
Score in reduction 31 p.

545v [Concerto, violin, Op. 26, D minor]
1.Moderato 2.Larghetto 3.Larghetto - Allegro
Solo Vn.-2,2,2,2-4,2,3-Timp.-Str.
Breitkopf & Härtel, Leipzig [1884]
Score 81 p.

818v Elegie et rondo, Op. 48
Solo Vn.-2,2,2,2-2Hn.-Timp.,Trgl.-Hp.(ad lib.)
-Str.
Score: Ms. 81 p.
Parts: Novello, Ewer, London, c1893

857v Farfalla, caprice
Solo Vn.-2,2,2,2-2Hn.-Timp.,Trgl.-Str.
O. Forberg, Leipzig, c1909
Score 27 p.

761v Rapsodie russe, Op. 32
Solo Vn.-2,2,2,2-2,2-Timp.-Str.

Kistner, Leipzig [n.d.]
Score 95 p.

723v Rhapsodie suédoise, Op. 59
Solo Vn.-2,2,2,2-4,2-Timp.,Trgl.-Str.
R. Forberg, Leipzig, c1898
Score 55 p.

SAVANT, VICTOR.   San Francisco 14 June 1944

6730 Movement for orchestra III, Op. 3   3'30"
2(2nd alt. Picc.),2,2,2-1,1,1-Perc.-Pno.-Str.
Ms.
Score 18 p. Large folio
*Composed March 1966. First performance Roches-
ter, 11 April 1966, Eastman-Rochester Symphony,
Walter Hendl conductor.*

SAVASTA, JEAN.

1566s Sérénade à Jacqueline
Solo Vn.-Str.
Score: Ms. 5 p.
Parts: Decourcelle, Nice, c1910

SCALERO, ROSARIO.
        Moncalieri, near Turin, Italy 24 December 1870
          Settimo Vittone, near Turin 25 December 1954

258s [Suite, string quartet and string
orchestra, Op. 20]
1.[Choral prelude] 2.[Variations on a theme
by Robert Schumann (Op. 68 no. 2)] 3.[Finale]
String Quartet - Str.
Breitkopf & Härtel, Leipzig, c1921
Score 35 p.

SCARLATTI, ALESSANDRO.   Palermo 2 May 1660
                                Naples 22 October 1725

Baptized: Pietro Alessandro Gaspare Scarlata

Concerti grossi, strings and continuo
1243s [No. 1] F minor (originally G minor).
Arranged by Arnold Schering
Grave - Allegro - Largo - Allemanda
Pno.-Str.
C.F. Kahnt, Leipzig [n.d.]
Score 11 p.

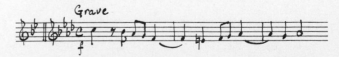

2306s [Same as above] Edited by Walter   7'30"
Upmeyer
C.F. Vieweg, Berlin [n.d.]
Score 12 p. Bound with no. 2 below

2306s No. 2 C minor (originally G minor).   7'
Edited by Walter Upmeyer
Allegro - Grave - Minuetto
Cemb. - Str.
C.F. Vieweg, Berlin [n.d.]
Score 12 p. Bound with no. 1 above

Scarlatti, Alessandro

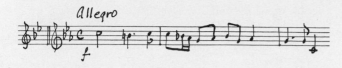

957s No. 3 F major. Edited by Gustav
Lenzewski
Allegro - Largo - Allegro
Cemb.-Str.
C.F. Vieweg, Berlin [n.d.]
Score 13 p.

2255s [Concerto, 2 violins and string 9'
orchestra, no. 6, E major] Revised by Renato
Fasano
1.Allegro 2.Allegro 3.Largo 4.Affettuoso
(Allegretto)
Solo Vn.I, Solo Vn.II-Cemb.-Str.(w/o Vn.)
Ricordi, Milan, c1959
Score 19 p.
*One of six concertos for two violins and
strings published by B. Cooke, London,
ca.1740.*

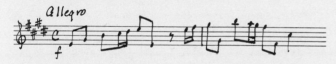

207m [Sinfonia no. 6, flute, strings and basso
continuo, A minor] Edited by Rolf-Julius Koch
1.Vivace 2.Adagio 3.Allegro 4.Adagio
5.Allegro
Solo Fl.-Cemb.-Str.
C.F. Peters, Frankfurt & New York, c1972
Score 23 p.

6357 [Symphony, chamber orchestra, no. 1, 11'
F major] Edited by Raymond Meylan
1.Allegro 2.Adagio 3.Allegro 4.Adagio
5.Allegro
2Fl.-Cemb.-Str.
Bärenreiter, Kassel, c1954 by Her Majesty
Queen Elizabeth II
Score 18 p.
*Composed ca.1715. This and the following
three symphonies taken from twelve symphonies
in a holograph Ms. found in the Music Library
of Buckingham Palace and now in the British
Museum.*

6359 [Symphony, chamber orchestra, no. 2, 7'
D major] Edited by Raymond Meylan
1.Spiritoso 2.Adagio 3.Allegro 4.Adagio
5.Presto
Fl.-Tpt.-Cemb.-Str.
Bärenreiter, Kassel, c1957 by Her Majesty
Queen Elizabeth II
Score 18 p.

6360 [Symphony, chamber orchestra, no. 4, 14'
E minor] Edited by Raymond Meylan
1.Vivace 2.Adagio 3.Allegro 4.Adagio
5.Allegro
Fl.,Ob.-Cemb.-Str.
Bärenreiter, Kassel, c1955 by His Majesty King
George VI [sic]
Score 19 p.

6361 [Symphony, chamber orchestra, no. 5,
D minor] Edited by Raymond Meylan
1.Spiritoso, e staccato 2.Adagio 3.Allegro
4.Adagio 5.Allegro assai
2Fl.-Cemb.-Str.
Bärenreiter, Kassel, c1954 by Her Majesty
Queen Elizabeth II
Score 19 p.

557s Toccata, aria, minuetto, giga. Arranged by
Michele Esposito
Fl.,Bn.-Timp.(all ad lib.)-Str.
Oxford University Press, London, c1925
Score 16 p.

4826 [Toccata, cembalo, no. 9, A minor.
Transcribed by Leon Stein]
3,2,3,2-4,3,3,1-Timp.-Str.
Ms. [C. Fischer, c1945?]
Score 25 p.
*This transcription, 1945. First performance
Chicago, 11 September 1945, Chicago Symphony
Orchestra, Désiré Defaw conductor.*

Scarlatti, Domenico

Ms. of the original toccata for harpsichord is in the Conservatorio di Musica Giuseppe Verdi, Milan.

SCARLATTI, DOMENICO.   Naples 26 October 1685
Madrid 23 July 1757

Domenico Scarlatti's works are identified by Kirkpatrick and Longo catalog numbers.

2337 [Allegro, B-flat major. K.249; L.39.   3'
Transcribed by Giacomo Setaccioli]
1,2,2,2-2Hn.
G. Ricordi, Milan, ^c1921
Score 7 p.
Transcribed from a keyboard sonata, 1921.
First performance Milan, 1921.

1692s Burlesca [from Sonata, clavier,   3'
G minor. K.450; L.338] Arranged by Henri Elkan
Str.
Elkan-Vogel, Philadelphia, ^c1934
Score 6 p.
Arranged 1934. First performance New York,
November 1934, broadcast by WOR Symphonietta,
Alfred Wallenstein conductor.

1687s [Concerto, organ and strings.   6'
Transcribed by G. Francesco Malipiero from
the keyboard sonata, K.91; L.176]
Org.-Str.
Ms.
Score 29 p.

574s Four pieces. Arranged by Michele Esposito
1.Moderato [K.69; L.382] 2.Siciliana [K.446;
L.433] 3.Pastorale [K.9; L.413] 4.Scherzo
[K.525; L.188]
Fl.,Bn.-Timp.(all ad lib.)-Str.
Oxford University Press, London, ^c1925
Score 19 p.
Excerpted from various keyboard sonatas.

1918s [Sonata, harpsichord, D minor.   3'
K.9; L.413. Transcribed for string orchestra
by Harold Byrns]
Str.
Ms.
Score 4 p.
First published in Essercizi per Gravicembalo,
Adamo Scola, London, 1738.

2472 [Same as above] Transcribed for winds by
Louis Hasselmans
2,2,2,2-2Hn.
B. Schott's Söhne, Mainz [n.d.]
Score 5 p.

1917s [Sonata, harpsichord, Gavotta,   2'
D minor. K.64; L.58. Transcribed for string
orchestra by Harold Byrns]
Str.
Ms.
Score 2 p.
First published 1742.

7130 [Sonata, harpsichord, G minor. K.450;
L.338. Transcribed for winds by Bernard Morgan]
2,2,2,2-2Hn.
Ms. ^c1975 by Bernard Morgan
Score 4 p.
First published ca.1755. This transcription
1939.

2488 [Sonatas, piano. Toccata, Bourrée   12'
and Gigue. K.279, 377 and 96; L.468, 263 and
465. Transcribed for orchestra by Alfredo
Casella]
2,1,1,2-2,1-Perc.-Str.
M. Senart, Paris, ^c1933
Score 29 p.
Orchestrated 1933. First performance Lyons,
6 November 1933, Amis due Trigentuor, Charles
Strong conductor.

1901s [Suite for string orchestra.   13'
Transcribed by Harold Byrns from various
keyboard sonatas]
1.Capriccio [K.20; L.375] 2.The echo [K.380;
L.23] 3.[The huntsman. K.96; L.465] 4.Sici-
liana [K.446; L.433] 5.Pizzicato [K.159;
L.104] 6.[Gossip. K.519; L.475]
Str.
Ms.
Score 24 p.
First performance Chicago, 10 December 1942,
Chicago Symphony Orchestra, Hans Lange con-
ductor.

269s [Suite for string orchestra. Transcribed
by Julius Harrison from various keyboard
sonatas]
1.Praeludium [K.430; L.463] 2.Sarabande
[K.8; L.488] 3.Capriccio [K.20; L.375]
Str.
Novello, London, ^c1925
Score 15 p.

724 Trois pièces. Transcribed for orchestra by
Roland-Manuel from various keyboard sonatas
1.Allegro [K.450; L.338] 2.Adagio [K.69;
L.382] 3.Allegrissimo (La chasse) [K.96;
L.465]
2,2(2nd alt. E.H.),2,2-2,2-Timp.-Hp.-Str.
A. Gutheil/Breitkopf & Härtel, Leipzig [n.d.]
Score 23 p.

SCARMOLIN, ANTHONY LOUIS. Schio, Italy 30 July 1890
Fairview, New Jersey 13 July 1969

4020 The ambassador overture
2(2nd alt. Picc.),2,2,2-2Sax.(AT ad lib.)-4,2,
3,1(ad lib.)-Timp.,Perc.-Str.
Ludwig Music, Cleveland, ^c1938
Score 16 p.

2097s Arioso for strings   6'
Str.
Ms. ^c1953? by A. Louis Scarmolin
Score 12 p.
Composed 1953.

5499 [The caliph. Dance]   5'
2(2nd alt. Picc.),2,2,2-2,2,3-Timp.,Perc.-Cel.,
Hp.-Str.

Ms.
Score 31 p. Large folio
From the opera composed 1948.

4039 The clockmaker, Op. 125   *4'*
2,2,2,2-3,3,3(or 1,1,1,1-2,2,1)-Timp.,Perc.-
Hp.-Str.
Ms.
Score 10 p. Large folio
Composed 1932. First performance in a WOR broadcast, New York, 25 March 1933, Bamberger Little Symphony Orchestra, Philip James conductor.

3362 Dramatic overture, Op. 162   *6'*
2,2,2,2-2Sax.-4,3,3,1-Timp.,Perc.-Str.
Ludwig Music, Cleveland, ^C1940
Score 32 p.
Commissioned by the Ludwig Music Publishing Company, 1938. Composed 1938. First performance Cleveland, 22 January 1941, Cleveland Heights High School Orchestra, Ralph E. Rush conductor.

3643 Dramatic tone poem   *15'*
2(2nd alt. Picc.),2,2,2-4,3,3,1-Timp.,Perc.-
Hp.-Str.
C. Fischer, New York, ^C1940
Score 44 p.
Composed 1924. First performance Chicago, 2 June 1939, American Symphony Orchestra of the WPA, Ralph Cissne conductor.

5476 Invocation, Op. 205   *16'*
2(2nd alt. Picc.),2,2,2-4,3,3,1-Timp.,Perc.-
Cel.,Hp.-Str.
Ms. ^C1947? by A. Louis Scarmolin
Score 41 p. Large folio
Composed 1947.

4022 Mercury overture, Op. 163
2(2nd alt. Picc.),2,2,2-2Sax.(AT ad lib.)-4,2,
3,1(ad lib.)-Timp.,Perc.-Str.
Ludwig Music, Cleveland, ^C1939
Score 18 p.

3647 Night, poem for orchestra, Op. 156   *10'*
2,2,2,2-4,3,3,1-Timp.-Str.
C. Fischer, New York, ^C1938
Score 25 p.
Composed 1937. First performance Teaneck, New Jersey, 8 December 1939, Teaneck Symphony Society, Otto Radl conductor. Received honorable mention in a Woman's Symphony Orchestra contest, New York, 1938.

4025 Nostalgic retrospect, Op. 140   *8'*
2,2,2,2-4,3,3,1-Timp.,Perc.-Cel.,Hp.-Str.
Ms.
Score 30 p. Large folio
Composed 1936.

5501 [The oath. Prelude]   *1'30"*
2,2,2,2-4,3,3,1-Timp.,Cym.-Cel.,Hp.-Str.
Ms. ^C1945? by A. Louis Scarmolin
Score 7 p. Large folio
From the opera composed 1945.

3950 Overture on a street vendor's   *8'*
ditty, Op. 160
2,2,2,2-4,3,3,1-Timp.,Cym.-Str.
C. Fischer, New York, ^C1943
Score 41 p.
Composed 1938.

4034 Pastorale, Op. 194   *10'*
2,2,2,2-4,3,3,1-Timp.,Cym.-Cel.,Hp.-Str.
Ms.
Score 47 p. Large folio
Composed 1943.

5493 Poème pathétique, Op. 196   *10'*
3,2,2,2-4,3,3,1-Timp.,Cym.-Str.
Ms. ^C1944? by A. Louis Scarmolin
Score 39 p.
Composed 1944.

1818s Sinfonietta, Op. 168, A major   *15'*
Str.
American Music Center, New York, ^C1944
Score 48 p.
Composed 1939.

5498 The sunlit pool   *4'*
2(2nd alt. Picc.),2,2,2-2,2,3,1-Timp.-Hp.-Str.
Ms. [^C1951? by A. Louis Scarmolin]
Score 16 p.
Composed 1951.

3340 [Symphony, miniature, Op. 171,   *15'*
C major]
1.Moderato con grazia 2.Andantino 3.Presto
2,2,2,2-2Sax.(AT ad lib.)-4,2,3,1-Timp.,Perc.-
Str.
Ludwig Music, Cleveland, ^C1940
Score 36 p.
Commissioned by the Ludwig Music Publishing Company, 1939. Composed 1939. First performance Cleveland, 27 February 1940, Cleveland Heights High School Orchestra, Ralph E. Rush conductor.

3821 [Symphony, Op. 154, E minor]   *30'*
In one movement
2(2nd alt. Picc.),2(2nd alt. E.H.),3*,3*-4,3,
3,1-Timp.,Perc.-Str.
Ms.
Score 158 p.
Composed 1937.

5477 Symphony no. 2, Op. 200   *20'*
1.Allegro moderato 2.Adagio espressivo
3.Con moto
2(2nd alt. Picc.),2,2,2-4,3,3,1-Timp.,Perc.-
Cel.,Hp.-Str.
Ms. ^C1946? by A. Louis Scarmolin
Score 140 p. Large folio
Composed 1946.

5475 [Symphony no. 3, Sinfonia breve]   *16'*
2,2,2,2-4,3,3,1-Perc.-Hp.-Str.
Ms. [^C1952? by A. Louis Scarmolin]
Score 43 p. Large folio
Composed 1952.

Scarmolin, Louis

5502 Three miniatures   *7'*
2(2nd alt. Picc.),2,2,2-4,2,3,1-Timp.,Perc.-
Str.
Ms. ^C1954? by A. Louis Scarmolin
Score 42 p.
Composed 1940.

4023 The tower prince, Op. 181
2,2,2,2-2Sax.(AT ad lib.)-4,2,3,1-Timp.,Perc.-
Str.
Ludwig Music, Cleveland, ^C1941
Score 24 p.

3435 Two symphonic fragments, Op. 78   *10'*
No. 1 in D minor   No. 2 in E-flat major
2,2(2nd alt. E.H.),2,2-4,3,3,1-Timp.,Perc.-
Cel.,Hp.-Str.
Sam Fox, New York, ^C1953 by the composer
Score 35 p.
Composed 1928.

4038 Upon looking at an old harpsichord,   *4'*
Op. 44
1,1,1,1-Pno.-Str.
Ms.
Score 11 p. Large folio
Composed 1927.

1898s Variations on a folk song, Op. 192   *9'*
Str.
Ms.
Score 16 p.
Composed 1942.

3597 Visions, a symphonic impression,   *10'*
Op. 173
2,2,2,2-4,3,3,1-Timp.,Perc.-Str.
Ms.
Score 43 p. Large folio
Composed 1939.

SCASSOLA, A.

1204s Romance, E major
Solo Vn.-Str.
Score: Ms. 7 p.
Parts: Foetisch, Lausanne [n.d.]

SCHAEFER, ALBERT.

2431 [Harp prelude on Mozart's Ave Verum   *3'*
Corpus]
2,2,2,3-2,0,3-Timp.-Hp.(or Pno.)-Str.
Carl Simon, Berlin [n.d.]
Score 15 p.
*Written 1891 for the centennial of Mozart's
death.*

SCHÄFER, DIRK.   Rotterdam 23 November 1873
                        Amsterdam 16 February 1931

270 Rhapsodie javanaise, Op. 7   *7'*
3*,3*,3*,2-4,2,3,1-Timp.,Perc.-Hp.-Str.
Breitkopf & Härtel, Leipzig, ^C1906
Score 43 p.
*Composed 1904. First performance Amsterdam,
1905, the composer conducting.*

2097 Suite pastorale, Op. 8
3*,3*,3*,2-4,2,3,1-Timp.,Trgl.-Hp.-Str.
A.A. Noske, Middelburg, ^C1908
Score 59 p.

SCHÄFER, KARL HEINZ.
                     Rosbach, Rhineland 29 July 1899
                                            d. 1970

2018s [Music for strings, Op. 50, in   *22'*
5 movements]
Str.
Willy Müller, Heidelberg [^C1942]
Score 37 p.
Composed 1941.

SCHAFFRATH, CHRISTOPH.
                     Hohestein-on-Elbe, Germany 1709
                             Berlin 17 February 1763

2267s [Symphony, strings, A major] Edited by
Max Schneider
1.Allegro 2.Andante 3.Allegro
Cemb.-Str.
Breitkopf & Härtel, Leipzig [^C1954]
Score 11 p.
Composed ca.1760.

SCHAPER, GUSTAV.
                Hohenwartsleben, Germany 17 October 1845
                        Magdeburg, Germany June 1906

260s [Musical memory book, Op. 12]
Str.
H. Litolff, Braunschweig [n.d.]
Score 7 p.

SCHARF, MORITZ.   Pirna, Saxony 13 January 1838
                         Dresden 13 August 1908

459s Träumerei [Reverie] Op. 25. Arranged for
string orchestra by H. Heinemann
Str.
Gustav Haushahn, Magdeburg [n.d.]
Score 3 p.

SCHARWENKA, (LUDWIG) PHILIPP.
               Samter, Posen, Poland 16 February 1847
               Bad Nauheim, Germany 16 July 1917

5693 [Dramatic fantasy, Op. 108]   *34'*
1.Allegro patetico 2.Andante tranquillo
3.Allegro
2,3*,3*,2-4,3,3,1-Timp.-Hp.-Str.
Breitkopf & Härtel, Leipzig, ^C1900
Score 157 p.
Awarded a prize by the German Music Association.

16s Für die Jugend, Op. 71 nos. 1, 3, 4.
Transcribed for strings by Max Burger
Str.
Breitkopf & Härtel, Leipzig, ^C1896
Score 11 p.

3751 Liebesnach, Fantasiestück, Op. 40
2,2,2,2-4,2,3-Timp.-Str.
Praeger & Meier, Bremen [n.d.]
Score 55 p.

213 [Polish dance tunes, piano 4-hands, Op. 38
    vol. 1. Transcribed for orchestra]
    1.Vivace 2.Comodo 3.Moderato
    3*,2,2,2-4,2,3-Timp.-Str.
    Praeger & Meier, Bremen [n.d.]
    Score 64 p.

3579 Serenade, Op. 19
    1.Marcia 2.Andante 3.Tempo di menuetto
    4.Rondo pastorale
    2,2,2,2-2,2,3-Timp.-Str.
    Praeger & Meier, Bremen [1881?]
    Score 99 p.

5684 [Spirits of forest and mountain,   7'
    Op. 37]
    3*,2,2,2-4,2-Timp.-Str.
    Breitkopf & Härtel, Leipzig [1881]
    Score 72 p.

1108 [Two Polish folk dances, Op. 20]   14'
    3*,2,2,2-2,2-Timp.-Str.
    Joh. André, Offenbach a.M. [n.d.]
    Score 26 p.
    Composed 1875. First performance Berlin, 1876.

6910 [Waves of Spring, symphonic poem, Op. 87]
    3*,2,2,2-4,2,3,1-Timp.-Hp.-Str.
    Carl Simon, Berlin, C1891 by the composer
    Score 95 p.

SCHARWENKA, (FRANZ) XAVER.
        Samter, Posen, Poland 6 January 1850
        Berlin 8 December 1924

633s Andante religioso
    Org.,Hp.-Str.
    Score: Ms. 14 p.
    Parts: Augener [n.p., n.d.]

618p [Concerto, piano, no.1, Op. 32, B-flat minor]
    1.Allegro patetico - Adagio 2.Allegro assai
    3.Allegro non tanto
    Solo Pno.-2(1st alt. Picc.),2,2,2-2,2,3-
    Timp.-Str.
    Praeger & Meier, Bremen [n.d.]
    Score 100 p.
    First performance Hanover, May 1877, the com-
    poser as soloist.

493p [Concerto, piano, no. 2, Op. 56,   30'
    C minor]
    1.Allegro 2.Adagio 3.Allegro non troppo
    Solo Pno.-2,2,2,2-4,2,3-Timp.-Str.
    Breitkopf & Härtel [n.p., n.d.]
    Score 124 p.
    First performance Vienna, 24 February 1881,
    the composer as soloist.

502p [Concerto, piano, no. 3, Op. 80,   30'
    C-sharp minor]
    1.Maestoso 2.Adagio - Allegro non troppo
    Solo Pno.-2,2,2,2-4,2,3-Timp.,Trgl.-Str.
    Breitkopf & Härtel, Leipzig, C1899
    Score 95 p.

595p [Concerto, piano, no. 4, Op. 82, F minor]
    1.Allegro patetico 2.Intermezzo 3.Lento

Solo Pno.-2,2,2,2-4,2,3-Timp.,Perc.-Str.
    F.E.C. Leuckart, Leipzig, C1908
    Score 106 p.
    Composed 1908.

7 [Polish national dance, Op. 3 no. 1]   4'
    Transcribed by H. Kling
    2*,2,2,2-4,2(or Cnt.),3-Timp.,Trgl.-Str.
    Breitkopf & Härtel, Leipzig, C1893
    Score 17 p.
    Originally composed for piano. First perform-
    ance Geneva, 1893.

SCHAUB, HANS FERDINAND. Frankfurt 22 September 1880
        Hanstedt, Germany 12 November 1965

    Born: Siegmund Schaub

5556 Abend-Musik für Orchester   10'
    2(2nd alt. Picc.),2,2,2-4,2,3-Timp.,Perc.-
    Cel.(ad lib.),Hp.(ad lib.)-Str.
    Schott, Mainz, C1935
    Score 19 p.
    Composed 1929.

1174 Drei Intermezzi, Op. 5
    2(1st alt. Picc.),2,2,2-2,2-Timp.,Trgl.-Str.
    N. Simrock, Berlin, C1913
    Score 46 p.

5450 Fest-Marsch, Op. 2
    3*,2,2,2-4,2,3,1-Timp.-Str.
    C.F. Schmidt, Heilbronn a/N., C1911
    Score 27 p.

1798 [Nutcracker and mouse-king, Op. 7.   35'
    Suite]
    1.Ouverture 2.Intermezzo 3.Balletmusik
    4.Grotesker Marsch
    3(3rd alt. Picc.),2,2,2-4,3-Timp.,Perc.-Hp.-
    Str.
    N. Simrock, Berlin, C1922
    Score 61 p.
    From the incidental music to the play after
    E. T. A. Hoffmann's story. Composed 1918.
    First performance Hamburg, 1918.

SCHEFTER, RICHARD.

397s Nachtgesang [Night song] Op. 7
    Solo Vc.-Str.
    Ries & Erler, Berlin [n.d.]
    Score 5 p.

SCHEIDT, SAMUEL.   Halle-on-Saale, Germany
                   baptized 4 November 1587
                   Halle-on-Saale 24 March 1654

2720 [Our Father in heaven, choral   2'
    prelude for orchestra] Transcribed by Leonid
    Leonardi
    2,3*,3*,3*-4,3,3,1-Str.
    Ms.
    Score 9 p.
    Originally composed for organ. Transcribed
    1935. First performance St. Louis, 4 December
    1936, St. Louis Symphony Orchestra, Vladimir
    Golschmann conductor.

Scheidt, Samuel

5166 Cantio sacra, Warum betrübst du   *17'*
dich, mein Herz. Transcribed for chamber
orchestra by George Rochberg
2Ob.(2nd alt. E.H.)-0,2,1-Str.
Ms. [^{c}n.d., Presser, Bryn Mawr, Pennsylvania]
Score 40 p. Large folio
Originally composed for organ, first pub-
lished in Scheidt's Tabulatura Nova, Hamburg,
1624. This transcription 1953. First per-
formance Philadelphia, ca.1953, Settlement
Music School Orchestra, Arthur Cohn con-
ductor.

SCHEIFFELHUT, JACOB. Augsburg baptized 19 May 1647
                     Augsburg 2 July 1709

909s [Lieblicher Frühlings-Anfang. Suite no. 7]
Arranged by Rudolf Moser
Praeludium - Allemande - Courante - Ballo -
Sarabande - Aria - Gigue
Cemb.(or Pno.)-Str.(without Cb.)
C.F. Vieweg, Berlin [n.d.]
Score 16 p.
Originally published at Augsburg, 1685.
First performance of arrangement at the Musi-
cal Science Congress, Basel 1924.

SCHEIN, JOHANN HERMANN.
                Grünhain, Saxony 20 January 1586
                Leipzig 19 November 1630

184s Canzon (5 stimmige Fuge), Corollarium,
1615. Edited by Arthur Prüfer
Str.
Breitkopf & Härtel, Leipzig [n.d.]
Score 8 p.

[Banchetto musicale (1617)] Edited by Arthur
Prüfer
460s   Suite no. 7
461s   Suite no. 8
2332s Suite no. 10
462s   Suite no. 14
2333s Suite no. 19
Each suite: 1.Padouana à 5   2.Gagliarda à 5
3.Courante à 5   4.Allemande à 4   5.Tripla
à 4
Str.
Breitkopf & Härtel, Leipzig [1903?]
Scores: 8 p. each
Banchetto Musicale, 20 Partitas (or Suites)
originally published at Leipzig in 1617.

Suite no. 7

Suite no. 8

Suite no. 10

Suite no. 14

Suite no. 19

SCHEINPFLUG, PAUL.
        Loschwitz, near Dresden 10 September 1875
        Memel (Klaipeda), Latvia 11 March 1937

5602 Ouverture zu einem Lustspiel von   *15'*
Shakespeare, Op. 15
3(3rd alt. Picc.),3*(2nd alt. E.H.),3(1 in D),
3(3rd alt. C.Bn.)-4,3,3,1-Timp.,Perc.-Str.
Heinrichshofen, Magdeburg, ^{c}1908
Score 67 p.

SCHELB, JOSEF.   Bad Krozingen,
                Breisgau, Germany 14 March 1894

4836 [Variations on an old Alsatian tune]   *8'*
2(1st alt. Picc.),1(or 2),1(or 2),1(ad lib.)-
2(ad lib.),1-Timp.,S.Dr.-Str.
Willy Müller, Heidelberg, ^{c}1939
Score 19 p.
Theme is the melody D'Zit Isch Do.

SCHELLENDORF, HANS BRONSART VON.
  See: BRONSART, HANS VON.

SCHELLING, ERNEST HENRY.
     Belvidere, New Jersey 26 July 1876
     New York 8 December 1939

640v [Concerto, violin, B major]
In one movement
Solo Vn.-3(3rd alt. Picc.),3*,3*,3*-4,3,3,1-
Timp.,Perc.-2Hp.-Str.
F.E.C. Leuckart, Leipzig, ᶜ1924
Score 91 p.
*Composed 1916. First performance Providence,
17 October 1916, Boston Symphony Orchestra,
Fritz Kreisler soloist.*

582p Impressions from an artist's life *36'*
Solo Pno.-3*,3*,3*,3(or 2)-4,3,3,1-Timp.,Perc.
-Org.,2Hp.-Str.
F.E.C. Leuckart, Leipzig [n.d.]
Score 145 p.
*First performance Boston, 31 December 1915,
the composer as soloist.*

1986 Légende symphonique [in 2 movements] *23'*
3*,3*,2,3*-4,2,3-Timp.-Hp.-Str.
G. Schirmer, New York, ᶜ1907
Score 85 p.
*First American performance Philadelphia, 31
October 1913, Leopold Stokowski conductor.*

2734 Morocco, symphonic tableau *20'*
In 4 movements
3*,3*,4*(Cl. in D alt. Cl. in E-flat),3*-4,4,
3,1-Timp.,Perc.-Pno.,Cel.,2Hp.-Str.
Carl Fischer, New York [n.d.]
Score 141 p.
*Composed 1927. First performance for the
benefit of the Pension Fund of the New York
Philharmonic, New York, 19 December 1927, New
York Philharmonic, the composer conducting.*

423p Suite fantastique, Op. 7 *28'*
1.Allegro marziale 2.Molto vivace 3.Inter-
mezzo 4.Molto vivace (Virginia reel)
Solo Pno.-3*,3*,3*,3*-4,2,3,1-Timp.,Tamb.-
2Hp.(2nd ad lib.)-Str.
D. Rahter [n.p.] ᶜ1908
Score 99 p.
*Composed 1905-06. First performance Amster-
dam, 10 October 1907, Willem Mengelberg conductor.*

2693 Tarantella, for chamber orchestra. *2'30"*
Arranged by Isadore Freed
1,1,0,1-Str.
Ms.
Score 16 p.
*Originally composed for string quartet.
Arranged for chamber orchestra, 1936. First
performance Philadelphia, 26 February 1936,
Chamber Orchestra of Philadelphia and Com-
posers' Laboratory, Isadore Freed conductor.*

1215 A victory ball, fantasy after the poem
by Alfred Noyes
3(3rd alt. Picc.),3*,3*,3*-4,4,3,1-Timp.,Perc.
-Org.,Cel.,2Hp.-Str.
F.E.C. Leuckart, Leipzig [n.d.]
Score 72 p.

*Composed 1922-23. First performance Philadel-
phia, 23 February 1923, Leopold Stokowski conductor.*

SCHENCK, ELLIOT.   Paris 4 April 1868
        New York 1939

2705 Five pastels *15'*
2,3(3rd alt. E.H.),3,4*-6,3,3,1-Timp.,Perc.-
Cel.,Hp.-Str.
Ms.
Score 97 p.
*Composed 1922. First(?) performance Minneapol-
is, 2 March 1924, Minneapolis Symphony Orches-
tra, Henri Verbrugghen conductor.*

2687 In a withered garden, tone poem *14'*
3,3(3rd alt. E.H.),4*,4*-6,3,3,1-Timp.,Perc.-
Cel.,Hp.-Str.
Ms.
Score 48 p.
*First public performance Chicago, 12 January
1923, Chicago Symphony Orchestra, Frederick
Stock conductor.*

2774 Indian overture, The Arrow Maker, *7'*
from the incidental music to the play by
Mary Austen
2,2(2nd alt. E.H.),2,2-4,3,3,1-Timp.,Perc.-
Hp.-Str.
Ms.
Score 51 p.
*Composed ca.1910. First performance New York,
1910, New Theatre Orchestra, the composer
conducting.*

2697 Suite, from music to Shakespeare's *15'*
Tempest
1.Ariel 2.Dance of nymphs and reapers
3.Intermezzo 4.The hunt
2,2(2nd alt. E.H.),2,2-4,3,3,1-Timp.,Perc.-
Cel.,Hp.-Str.
Ms.
Score 84 p.
*Composed ca.1916. First performance New York,
24 April 1916, the composer conducting.*

SCHENK, JOHANN BAPTIST.
  Wiener-Neustadt, Austria 30 November 1753
     Vienna 29 December 1836

4692 Der Dorfbarbier [The village barber]
Sinfonia
2,2,2,2-2,2-Str.
Score: Denkmäler der Tonkunst in Österreich,
XXXIV/66. Universal Edition, Vienna, ᶜ1927.
Edited by Robert Haas. 12 p.
Parts: Ms. ᶜ1975 by The Fleisher Collection of
Orchestral Music, Free Library of Philadelphia
*From the Singspiel based on Paul Weidmann's
play. First performance Vienna, 30 October
1796.*

Schiassi, Gaetano

SCHIASSI, GAETANO MARIA.   Bologna 10 March 1698
                                    Lisbon 1754

   1704s [Christmas symphony] Edited by Walter
   Upmeyer
   Cemb.(or Org.)-Str.
   C.F. Vieweg, Berlin [n.d.]
   Score 14 p.

SCHIBLER, ARMIN.
      b. Kreuzlingen, Switzerland 20 November 1920

   1193v [Fantasy, viola, Op. 15]   11'
   Solo Va.-1,0,1,1-2Hn.-Timp.-Str.
   Ms. [Ahn & Simrock, Berlin, ^c1945]
   Score 28 p.
   *Composed 1946. First performance Winterthur,
   1946 or 1947, Musikkollegium orchestra, Her-
   mann Scherchen conductor, Oskar Kromer
   soloist.*

SCHICKELE, PETER.   Ames, Iowa 17 July 1935

   5982 Invention for orchestra   8'
   Slow - Fast - Slow
   3*,3*,3*,3*-4,3,3,1-Timp.,Perc.-Pno.-Str.
   Ms.
   Score 41 p. Large folio
   *Composed 1958. Awarded Honorable Mention by
   Gershwin Memorial Foundation, March 1959.*

   7125 Maiden on the moor   8'
   Solo Countertenor or Contralto-Ob.-2Hn.-
   Finger Cym.-Str.
   Ms. ^c1975 by Theodore Presser, Bryn Mawr, Pa.
   Score 36 p.
   *Anonymous 14th-century English text, transla-
   ted by Brian Stone. Composed 1975. First
   performance Philadelphia, 5 May 1975, The
   Mostovoy Soloists, Peter Schickele conductor,
   John Ferrante countertenor.*

SCHIFFER, JOHANN.

   1320s Tändelei, Op. 89
   Str.
   Score: Ms. 6 p.
   Parts: J. Schiffer, Frankfurt a.M. [n.d.]

SCHILLINGER, JOSEPH. Kharkov, Russia 31 August 1895
                           New York 23 March 1943

   968m First airphonic suite, theremin and   8'
   orchestra, Op. 21
   1.Prelude 2.Song 3.Interlude 4.Dance
   5.Postlude 6.Dithyramb 7.Finale
   Solo Theremin-3*,3*,2,3*-4,2,3,1-Timp.,Perc.-
   Str.
   Ms.
   Score 43 p.

*Commissioned by the Cleveland Orchestra, 1929.
Composed 1929. First performance Cleveland,
28 November 1929, Cleveland Orchestra, Nikolai
Sokoloff conductor, Leon Theremin soloist.*

   3142 March of the Orient, Op. 11   3'30"
   3*,3*,3*,3*-6,3(3rd alt. Tpt. in F),3,1-Timp.,
   Perc.-2Hp.-Str.
   Ms.
   Score 28 p.
   *Composed 1924. First performance Leningrad,
   12 May 1926, State Philharmonic Orchestra,
   Nikolai Malko conductor.*

   3129 North Russian symphony, Op. 22   11'
   In one movement
   3*,3*,2,3(3rd alt. C.Bn.)-4,3,3,1-Timp.,Perc.-
   Accordion-Str.
   Ms.
   Score 93 p.
   Commissioned by RCA, 1930. Composed 1930.

   3290 Symphonic rhapsody, October, Op. 19   18'
   4(2 are Picc., 1st alt. Alto Fl.),3*,3*(B.Cl.
   alt. Ten.Sax.),3*-2Alto Sax.-4,4,3,1-Timp.,
   Perc.-Pno.-Str.
   Ms.
   Score 151 p.
   *Commissioned by The Moscow State Conductorless
   Orchestra, 1927. Composed 1927. First performance Moscow, 7 November 1927, Conductorless Orchestra. Chosen as the best symphonic
   work composed in the USSR in the first decade
   by the State Committee, 1927.*

SCHILLINGS, MAX VON.   Düren, Germany 19 April 1868
                              Berlin 24 July 1933

   590v [Concerto, violin, Op. 25, A minor]   40'
   1.Allegro energico 2.Andante con espressione
   3.Allegro con brio
   Solo Vn.-3,3*,2(2nd alt. B.Cl.),2-4,3,3,1-
   Timp.,Perc.-Hp.-Str.
   N. Simrock, Berlin, ^c1909
   Score 86 p.
   *Composed 1909. First performance Berlin, 1910,
   Philharmonic Orchestra, the composer con-
   ducting, Felix Berber soloist.*

   5549 [Ingwelde. Prelude to Act II]   6'
   3,3*,3*,2-4,3,3,1-Hp.-Str.
   Schuberth, Leipzig [1894?]
   Score 21 p.
   *From the opera composed 1893. First perform-
   ance Karlsruhe, 13 November 1894.*

   1094 [Moloch, musical tragedy. Harvest   10'
   festival]
   3(2nd alt. Picc.),3*,2,3*-4,3(3rd ad lib.),3,
   1-Timp.,Perc.-Hp.-Str.
   Bote & Bock, Berlin, ^c1907
   Score 30 p.
   *Composed 1905. First performance Dresden,
   1906.*

   1346 [Der Pfeifertag. Prelude to Act III,   11'
   Von Spielmanns Leid und Lust]
   3(3rd alt. Picc.),3*,2,3*-4,3,3,1(2Tpt.&2Tbn.

back-scene)-Timp.,Perc.-Str.(Violotta&Quintet)
Bote & Bock, Berlin, c1899
Score 23 p.
Composed 1897. First performance Schwerin, 1899.

1143 Symphonischer Prolog zu Sophokles'   *14'*
König Oedipus, Op. 11
3(3rd alt. Picc.),3*,2,3-4,3,3,1-Timp.,Perc.-
Hp.-Str.
Bote & Bock, Berlin, c1900
Score 27 p.
Composed 1899. First performance Berlin, 1900.

[Two symphonic fantasies, Op. 6]
5564 No. 1 Meergruss [Sea greeting]   *15'*
5581 No. 2 Seemorgen [Morning at sea]   *14'*
3(3rd alt. Picc. in no. 2),3*,3*,3-4,3,3,1-
Timp.,Perc.-Hp.-Str.
Fürstner, Berlin, c1896
Scores: 74 p., 61 p.

6029 [The witch-song, Op. 15]   *25'*
3(3rd alt. Picc.),3*,3*,3*-4,3,3,1-Timp.,Perc.
-Hp.-Narrator-Str.
Forberg, Leipzig, c1903
Score 45 p.
Musical recitation of the poem by Ernst von Wildenbruch, Das Hexenlied, with English translation by John Bernhoff.

995 Ein Zwiegespräch [A dialogue, tone   *20'*
poem, Op. 8]
2,2,2,2-4,2-Trgl.-Hp.(ad lib.)-Str.
Ries & Erler, Berlin [n.d.]
Score 62 p.
Composed 1897. First performance Berlin, 1898, Felix Weingartner conductor.

SCHINDLER, FRITZ.
           Bözingen, Switzerland 29 March 1871
                    Biel 6 March 1924

Also known under pseudonyms: Adolf Berry, Otto von Walden

1492s Aus seliger Zeit, Op. 61 [by Otto von
Walden]
2 Solo Vn.-Str.
J.H. Zimmermann, Leipzig, c1896
Score in reduction 5 p.

SCHIUMA, ALFREDO LUIGI.
           Spinazzola, Italy 25 June 1885
            Buenos Aires 24 July 1963

3710 Pitunga
3,3*,3*,3*-4,4,4-Timp.,Perc.-Cel.,2Hp.-Sop.
Voice(ad lib.)-Str.
Ms.
Score 70 p. Large folio
Composed 1928. First performance Buenos Aires, 31 March 1929, Asociación Sinfónica de Buenos Aires.

SCHJELDERUP, GERHARD ROSENKRONE.
       Christiansand, Norway 17 November 1859
         Benediktbeuren, Bavaria 29 July 1933

1048m Sommernacht auf dem Fjord   *11'*
Solo E.H.-3*,2,3*,2-4,2,3,1-Timp.,Perc.-Str.
Bote & Bock, Berlin, c1904
Score 14 p.

SCHLEGEL, C.

730s In der Spinnstube [intermezzo] Op. 76
Glock.-Str.
Score: Ms. 11 p.
Parts: L. Oertel, Hannover [n.d.]

SCHLEIN, IRVING.   New York 18 August 1905

1984s [Suite for string orchestra, Op. 2]   *8'*
1.Andante sostenuto 2.Andante cantabile
3.Air for strings
Str.
Ms.
Score 14 p.
Composed 1947.

SCHLESINGER, SEBASTIAN BENSON.
               Hamburg 24 September 1837
               Nice 8 January 1917

3678 [Etude, Op. 11, C-sharp minor]
1,1,2,1-2,2,3-Timp.,Trgl.-Hp.-Str.
A.P. Schmidt, Boston/G.Astruc, Paris, c1905
Score 15 p.

6152 [Little symphonic suite on 6 melodies.
Transcribed by N. Gervasio]
1,1,2,1-Bells-Pno.-Str.
Arthur P. Schmidt, Boston, c1917
Score 70 p.
Composed originally for voice and piano, 1883-1910.

5599 Marche nuptiale, Op. 50
3*,2,2,2-4,2,2Cnt.,3,1-Timp.,Perc.-Org.(ad
lib.),Hp.-Str.
Ditson, Boston/G. Astruc, Paris, c1905
Score 26 p.

7008 Six melodious studies [for piano]. No. 5,
Evening thought. Transcribed by Adolf
Neuendorff
1,1,2,2-2Hn.-Glock.-Str.
Ms.
Score 5 p.
This transcription 1885.

SCHLÖGER, MATTHÄUS.   1722
               Vienna 30 June 1766

2229s [Partita, string orchestra and harpsichord,
B-flat major]
1.Allegro 2.Largo 3.Menuetto 4.Finale
Cemb.-Str.(without Va.)
Score: Denkmäler der Tonkunst in Österreich,
XV/2. Artaria, Vienna; Breitkopf & Härtel,
Leipzig, 1908. Edited by Karl Horwitz and Karl
Riedel. 8 p.
Parts: Ms. c1976 by The Fleisher Collection of
Orchestral Music, Free Library of Philadelphia

Schlottmann, Louis

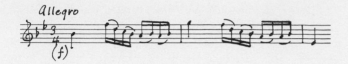

SCHLOTTMANN, LOUIS.   Berlin 12 November 1826
                      Berlin 13 June 1905

   4518 Ouverture zu Shakespeare's Romeo und   *10'*
      Julia, Op. 18
      2,2,2,2-2,2,3-Timp.-Hp.-Str.
      Bote & Bock, Berlin [1867]
      Score 72 p.

SCHMELZ, REINHARD.

   144s Träumerei [Reverie]
      Str.
      F. Luckhardt, Berlin, c1889 by G. Schirmer
      Score 7 p.
      Composed for the Ladies' Orchestra, New York.

SCHMIDT, C.   fl. ca.1790-ca.1810

   348m Introduction, theme and variations
      Solo Bn.-Str.
      Ms. c1976 by The Fleisher Collection of
      Orchestral Music, Free Library of Philadelphia
      Score 21 p. Large folio

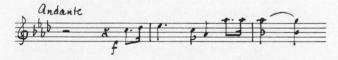

SCHMIDT, FRANZ.   Pressburg 22 December 1874
                  Perchtoldsdorf, near Vienna 11 February 1939

   302p [Concertante variations on a theme   *26'*
      of Beethoven for piano and orchestra] Solo
      set for piano 2-hands by Friedrich Wührer
      Solo Pno.-2,2,2,2-4,2,3-Timp.,Tamb.-Str.
      Universal Edition, Vienna, c1952
      Score 123 p.
      Commissioned by Paul Wittgenstein. Originally
      composed with piano solo for left hand, 1923.
      First performance of this version, Wuppertal-
      Barmen, 12 April 1940, Fritz Lehmann con-
      ductor.

   307p [Concerto, piano, no. 2, E-flat major] *38'*
      Solo set for piano 2-hands by Friedrich Wührer
      1.Allegro moderato 2.Andante 3.Vivace
      Solo Pno.-2,2,2,2-4,2-Timp.-Str.
      Universal Edition, Vienna, c1952
      Score 185 p.
      Commissioned by Paul Wittgenstein. Originally
      composed for left hand, 1934. First perform-
      ance of this version, 5 February 1940, Munich
      Philharmonic Orchestra, Oswald Kabasta con-
      ductor.

   5277 [Notre Dame. Act I: Intermezzo and   *16'*
      carnival music]
      3*,2,2,3*-4,3,3-Timp.,Perc.-2Hp.-Str.
      Drei Masken, Munich/Universal Edition, Vienna,
      c1914
      Score 98 p.
      From the opera composed 1904 after Victor
      Hugo's novel. First performance of this suite
      Vienna, 6 December 1903, Vienna Philharmonic
      Orchestra, Ernst von Schuch conductor.

   5175 [Symphony no. 1, E major]   *40'*
      1.Sehr langsam 2.Langsam 3.Schnell und
      leicht 4.Lebhaft
      3(3rd alt. Picc.),2(2nd alt. E.H.),2,3(3rd
      alt. C.Bn.)-4,3,3,1-Timp.-Str.
      Eberle, Vienna [1902]
      Score 122 p.
      Composed 1896-99. First performance Vienna,
      25 January 1902, the composer conducting.
      Awarded the Beethoven Prize of the Gesell-
      schaft der Musikfreunde, 1900.

   1726 [Symphony no. 2, E-flat major]   *56'*
      1.Lebhaft 2.Allegretto con variazioni
      3.Scherzo 4.Finale
      4*,3*,5*(1Cl. in E-flat),3*-8,4,3,1-Timp.,Perc.
      -Str.
      Universal Edition, Vienna, c1914
      Score 183 p.
      Composed 1912-13. First performance Vienna,
      1914, Franz Schalk conductor.

   1964 [Symphony no. 3, A major]   *50'*
      1.Allegro molto moderato 2.Adagio 3.Scherzo
      4.Lento - Allegro vivace
      2,2,2,2-4,2,3-Timp.-Str.
      Universal Edition, Vienna, c1928
      Score 147 p.
      Composed 1927-28. First performance Vienna,
      2 December 1929, Franz Schalk conductor.

   6239 [Symphony, no. 4, C major, in one   *46'*
      movement]
      2(2nd alt. Picc.),3*,3(1Cl. in E-flat),3*-
      4,3,3,1-Timp.,Perc.-2Hp.-Str.
      Universal Edition, Vienna, c1934
      Score 143 p.
      Composed 1932-33 as a requiem for the composer's
      daughter, Emma Schmidt Holzschuh. First per-
      formance Vienna, 10 January 1934, Vienna Sym-
      phony Orchestra, Oswald Kabasta conductor.

   1088s Wiegenlied [Cradle song] Op. 20
      Str.
      Score: Ms. 7 p.
      Parts: L. Oertel, Hannover [n.d.]

SCHMIDT, HERMANN.   Greiz, Germany 9 March 1885

   908m [Concerto for clarinet]   *10'*
      1.Allegro maestoso 2.Andante quasi lento
      3.Polacca
      Solo Cl.-1,1,2,1-2,2,1-Timp.-Str.
      Score: Ms. 53 p.
      Parts: Heinrichshofen, Magdeburg, c1931

SCHMIDT, WILLIAM.   Chicago 6 March 1926

186m Chamber concerto for organ and   *16'30"*
brass quintet
1.Sonata 2.Spiritual phantasy
Solo Org.-0,0,0,0-1,2,1,1
Western International, Los Angeles, ᶜ1970
Score 50 p.
Composed 1969. First performance Biola Col-
lege, La Mirada, California, 27 February 1970,
Fine Arts Brass Quintet, Rayner Brown soloist.

7177 Chorale, march and fugato for brass choir.
Nos. 3, 4, 5 of Variations on a Negro Folk
Song
0,0,0,0-4,3,3,Bar.,1-Timp.,Perc.
Western International, Los Angeles, ᶜ1966 by
Avant, Los Angeles
Score 15 p.

7182 Fanfare
See: FANFARES 1969 FOR 8 TRUMPETS. No. VI

7174 The Natchez Trace, concert march   *4'*
2,2,5*(1 Alto Cl.),2-4Sax.-4,3,3,2Bar.,1-
Timp.,Perc.-Cb.
Avant Music, Los Angeles, ᶜ1959
Score in reduction 9 p.
Composed 1957. First performance Colorado
State College, Greeley, 29 July 1958, Summer
Concert Band, Clarence E. Sawhill conductor.

7175 Sakura, variations on a Japanese   *8'*
folk song for band
3*,2,8*(1Cl. in E-flat,1 Alto Cl.,2Cb.Cl.),2-
5Sax.(2Alto, 2Ten.,Bar.)-4,3,3,2Bar.,1-Timp.,
Perc.-Hp.-Cb.
Western International, Los Angeles, ᶜ1968
Score 31 p.

7176 Short'nin' bread variations
0,0,0,0-4,4,4,Bar.,2-Timp.,Perc.-Hp.
Western International, Los Angeles, ᶜ1973
Score 62 p.

7178 Variations on a Negro folk song   *7'*
3*,3*,6*(1 Alto Cl.,1Cb.Cl.),2-4Sax.-4,3,3,
Bar.,1-Timp.,Perc.-Hp.-Cb.
Avant Music, Los Angeles, ᶜ1961
Score 66 p.
Theme is Goin' Home On A Cloud. Originally
composed for brass quintet, 1955. This ver-
sion, 1959. First performance University of
California, Los Angeles, 25 March 1959, The
University Concert Band, Clarence E. Sawhill
conductor. For variant instrumentation, see
Chorale, March and Fugato for brass choir.

SCHMIDT-BERKA.

1028s Paradies-Reigen, Intermezzo
Str.
Carl Paez, Berlin, ᶜ1894
Score 5 p.

SCHMITT, FLORENT.
         Blâmont, Lorraine, France 28 September 1870
         Neuilly, near Paris 17 August 1958

2975 Antoine et Cléopâtre, 1ʳᵉ suite
d'orchestre, Op. 69. No. 2, Fanfare, Le camp
de Pompée
0,0,0,0-4,3,3,1-Timp.,Perc.
Durand, Paris, ᶜ1921, ᶜ1929
Score 7 p.
Composed ca.1919-20, for André Gide's adapta-
tion of Shakespeare's Anthony and Cleopatra.

Çançunik [Without equal] suite, Op. 79
2005 No. 1 Lied-nocturne   *6'*
1(alt. Picc.),1,1,1-2,2,2-Timp.,Perc.-2Hp.(2nd
ad lib.)-Str.
2006 No. 2 Scherzo-tarantelle   *6'*
2*,2,2,3*(C.Bn. ad lib.)-4,2,3,1-Timp.,Perc.-
2Hp.(2nd ad lib.)-Str.
Durand, Paris, ᶜ1929
Scores: 26 p., 51 p.
Composed 1927. First performance Paris, 1929.

661v Chanson à bercer, Op. 19 no. 1   *8'*
Solo Vn.(or Vc.)-1,1,1,1-Str.
J. Hamelle, Paris, ᶜ1909
Score 7 p.
Composed 1901.

506c Chant élégiaque, violoncelle, Op. 24   *15'*
Solo Vc.-2(2nd alt. Picc.),2*,2,2,Sarrus.(ad
lib.)-4,2,3,1-Timp.,Perc.-Hp.-Str.
Durand, Paris, ᶜ1912
Score 23 p.
Originally composed for cello and piano, 1899-
1903. Orchestrated 1911. First performance
Paris, 1912, Concerts Lamoureux, Camille
Chevillard conductor.

4953 Dionysiaques, Op. 62   *10'*
4*(2Picc.),3*,Sarrus.,9*(2Cl. in E-flat,2B.Cl.,
2Cb.Cl.),2-7Sax.(2 Alto,2Ten.,2Bar.,Bass)-2Hn.,
3 Alto Hn. in E-flat,2Tpt.,2Cnt.,5 Bugles,
4Tbn.,2Bar.,4 Tuba(2Cb. Tuba)-Timp.,Perc.-Cel.
-Cb.
Durand, Paris, ᶜ1925
Score 57 p.
Composed 1914. First performance Paris, 9
June 1925, Musique de la Garde Républicaine,
Guillaume Balay conductor.

539c Final, violoncelle et orchestre,   *8'*
Op. 77
Solo Vc.-2*,2,2,3*(C.Bn. ad lib.)-4,2,3,1-
Timp.,Perc.-2Hp.(2nd ad lib.)-Str.
Durand, Paris, ᶜ1927
Score 80 p.
Composed 1927. First performance Paris, 1930,
Concerts Lamoureux, Albert Wolff conductor.

2027s [Janiana, Op. 101]   *20'*
1.Assez animé 2.Musette 3.Choral 4.Avec
entrain, sans précipitation
Str.
Durand, Paris, ᶜ1943
Score 43 p.
Commissioned by Jane Evrard. Composed 1941.
First performance March 1942, Orchestre Jane
Evrard, Jane Evrard conductor.

Schmitt, Florent

568v Légende for viola, Op. 66   8'
Solo Va.(or Alto Sax.)-3*,3*,3*,3*-4,3,3,1-
Timp.,Perc.-Cel.,2Hp.(2nd ad lib.)-Str.
Durand, Paris, ᶜ1920
Score 40 p.
Composed 1919. First performance Paris, 1921,
Concerts Pasdeloup, Rhené-Baton conductor.

508m Lied et scherzo, Op. 54   10'
Solo Hn.-2*,2*,2,2-Hn.
Durand, Paris, ᶜ1912
Score 39 p.
Composed 1910. First performance Paris, 1912,
Concerts Colonne, Gabriel Pierné conductor.

Mirages pour orchestre, Op. 70
3817 No. 1 Tristesse de Pan
3913 No. 2 La tragique chevauchée [The tragic
ride]
3*,3*,3*,3*-4,3,3,1-Timp.,Perc.-Cel.,2Hp.(2nd
ad lib.)-Str.
Durand, Paris, ᶜ1925
Miniature scores: 36 p., 79 p.
Composed 1921-23.

Pupazzi [Puppets] Op. 36
471s No. 2 Damis
472s No. 5 Clymène
Str.
A.Z. Mathot, Paris, ᶜ1911
Scores: 3 p., 5 p.

548c Rêve au bord de l'eau, Op. 19 no. 4   10'
Solo Vc.(or Vn.)-1,1,1,1-Hp.-Str.
Score: Ms. 20 p.
Parts: J. Hamelle, Paris, ᶜ1919
Composed 1898. Orchestrated 1913. First per-
formance Paris, 1913, Concerts Lamoureux,
Camille Chevillard conductor.

5536 Rêves [Dreams, Op. 65 no. 1]   8'
3(3rd alt. Picc.),3*,3*,3*-4,3,3,1-Timp.,Perc.
-Cel.,2Hp.-Str.
Durand, Paris, ᶜ1919
Score 39 p.
Composed 1913-15. First performance Paris,
1918, Lamoureux and Colonne Orchestras,
Camille Chevillard conductor.

4941 Salammbô, Op. 76. Suite II   15'
3*,3*,3*,3*-4,3,3,1-Timp.,Perc.-Cel.,2Hp.
(2nd ad lib.)-Str.
Durand, Paris, ᶜ1928
Score 62 p.
One of three orchestral suites from the music
to the film, Salammbô, based on Gustave Flau-
bert's novel. Composed 1925. First sym-
phonic performance Paris, 20 November 1927,
Concerts Colonne, Gabriel Pierné conductor.

5596 [The sandman, a week in dance.   40'
Complete ballet, Op. 73]
2(2nd alt. Picc.),2(2nd alt. E.H.),2,3*-4,2,3,
1-Timp.,Perc.-Pno.,Cel.,2Hp.(2nd ad lib.)-Str.
Durand, Paris, ᶜ1926
Score 245 p.
Ballet with scenario based on a story by Hans
Christian Andersen, Ole Lukoie. Originally

composed for piano 4-hands, 1912, under the
title A Week of the Little Elf the Sandman.
This transcription 1923; first performed, Paris,
February 1924, Albert Wolff conductor.

Soirs [Evenings, Op. 5]
844s No. 2 Spleen
345s No. 4 Après l'été [Indian summer]
Str.
Durand, Paris, ᶜ1921
Scores: 7 p., 4 p.

6648 [Stele for the tomb of Paul Dukas, Op. 87
no. 1. Transcribed for orchestra]
3*,3*,3*,3*-4,3,3,1-Timp.,Perc.-Cel.,2Hp.
(2nd ad lib.)-Str.
Ms.
Score 15 p. Large folio
First movement of the suite, Chaîne Brisée
[Broken Chain]. Originally composed for piano,
1935. First performance of orchestral version,
Paris, 18 December 1938, Société des Concerts,
Charles Munch conductor.

4942 Suite sans esprit de suite, Op. 89   15'
1.Majeza 2.Charmilles 3.Pécorée de Calabre
4.Thrène 5.Bronx
3(3rd alt. Picc.),3(3rd alt. E.H.),3*,3*-4,3,
3,1-Timp.,Perc.-Cel.(alt. Glock),2Hp.-Str.
Or 2(2nd alt. Picc.),2(2nd alt. E.H.),2,2-2,2,
2-Hp.-Str.
Durand, Paris, ᶜ1938
Score 102 p.
Originally composed for piano 4-hands;
orchestrated 1938. First performance Paris, 29
January 1938, Colonne Orchestra, Paul Paray
conductor.

393 La tragédie de Salomé, Op. 50   30'
1.Prelude 2.Lent
3*,3*,3*,3,Sarrus.-4,3,3,1-Timp.,Perc.-2Hp.-
Str.
Durand, Paris, ᶜ1912
Score 136 p.
Composed 1907. First performance Paris, 1909,
Concerts Colonne, Gabriel Pierné conductor.

Trois rapsodies, Op. 53
1558 No. 1 Viennoise   8'
3*,2,2,2,Sarrus.-4,2,3,1-Timp.,Perc.-Hp.-Str.
1559 No. 2 Polonaise   6'
3*,3*,2,3*(C.Bn. ad lib.)-4,2,3,1-Timp.,Perc.-
Cel.,2Hp.(2nd ad lib.)-Str.
1560 No. 3 Française   6'
3*,2,2,3*(C.Bn. ad lib.)-4,2,3,1-Timp.,Perc.-
2Hp.(2nd ad lib.)-Str.
Durand, Paris, ᶜ1928
Scores: 60 p., 56 p., 48 p.
Composed 1900-03. First performance Paris,
1911, Concerts Lamoureux, Camille Chevillard
conductor.

SCHMITT, GEORG ALOYS.   Hanover 2 February 1827
                            Dresden 15 October 1902

615m [Conzertstück, oboe, Op. 29, F major]
Solo Ob.-2,0,2,2-2,2-Timp.-Str.
Schlesinger, Berlin [n.d.]
Score 43 p.

SCHMITZ, ELIE ROBERT.   Paris 8 February 1889
                  San Francisco 5 September 1949

    811p [Concerto, piano, no. 1, Op. 7]   22'
      1.Lento 2.Adagio 3.Allegro giusto
      Solo Pno.-3*,3*,2,2-4,3,3,1-Timp.,Perc.-Hp.-
      Str.
      Ms.
      Score 96 p. Large folio
      First performance by the composer.

SCHMUTZER, JOHANN.

    1408s Walzer-Intermezzo, Op. 52
      Str.
      Score: Ms. 10 p.
      Parts: Joh. Schmutzer, Baden-Baden [n.d.]

SCHNÉGANS, JULES.

    421s Sérénade et rêverie
      Str.
      Choudens, Paris [n.d.]
      Score 13 p.

SCHNEIDER, GEORG ABRAHAM.
               Darmstadt, Germany 19 April 1770
                    Berlin 19 January 1839

    862m [Concertino, flute, Op. 82, E minor]
      Solo Fl.-2Hn.(ad lib.)-Str.
      Score: Ms. 37 p.
      Parts: Fr. Hofmeister, Leipzig [1818?]

    [Concerto, F major]
      1.Allegro moderato 2.Adagio 3.Polacca
    884m The same for flute, Op. 83
    856m The same for bassoon, Op. 85
    858m The same for horn, Op. 86
    870m The same for oboe, Op. 87
      Solo-2,2,0,2-2,2-Timp.-Str.
      Scores: Ms. 97 p., 92 p., 92 p., 94 p.
      Parts: Fr. Hofmeister, Leipzig [1818-19?]

SCHNEIDER, RICHARD.   Berlin 24 February 1884

    974v Romance, Op. 18   5'
      Solo Vn.-1,1,1,1-Hn.(or Tpt.)-Str.
      Score: Ms. 8 p.
      Parts: P. Decourcelle, Nice [n.d.]
      *Composed 1927. First performance Nice, March
      1928.*

SCHNÉKLÜD, AD.

    715s Aubade-pizzicato, Op. 47
      Str.
      Score: Ms. 6 p.
      Parts: A. Leduc, Paris [n.d.]

SCHNITTELBACH, NATHANAEL.
        Danzig (now Gdansk, Poland) 16 June 1633
           Lübeck, Germany 16 November 1667

    1250s Suite for strings and cembalo. Revised by
    Max Seiffert
      Cemb.-Str.
      Kistner & Siegel, Leipzig [n.d.]
      Score 14 p.

SCHOECK, OTHMAR.
      Brunnen, Switzerland 1 September 1886
               Zurich 8 March 1957

    789v [Concerto, violin, Op. 21, B-flat   20'
    major]
      1.Allegretto 2.Grave 3.Allegro con spirito
      Solo Vn.-2,2,2,2-2,2-Timp.-Str.
      Hug, Leipzig [n.d.]
      Score 71 p.

    278m [Don Ranudo de Colibrados, Op. 27.   5'
    Intermezzo: Serenade]
      Solo Ob., Solo E.H.-Str.
      Breitkopf & Härtel, Leipzig, c1948
      Score 8 p.
      *From the comic opera in four acts with libretto
      by Armin Rüeger after Ludwig Holberg's comedy.*

    1159 Serenade, Op. 1   10'
      1,1,1,1-Hn.-Str.
      Hug, Leipzig [n.d.]
      Score 43 p.

    2056s [Suite, strings, Op. 59, A-flat   25'
    major]
      1.Andante maestoso 2.Pastorale tranquillo
      3.Tempo di marcia allegro 4.Poco adagio
      5.Presto
      Str.
      Universal Edition, Vienna, c1947
      Score 41 p.
      *Composed 1945. First performance Winterthur,
      Switzerland, 14 September 1946, Musikkolle-
      giums Winterthur concert in honor of the com-
      poser's 60th birthday, Hermann Scherchen con-
      ductor.*

SCHOEMAKER, MAURICE.
      Anderlecht, near Brussels 27 December 1890
               Brussels 24 August 1964

    4245 Feu d'artifice [Fireworks]   11'
      3(3rd alt. Picc.),3*,4*(1Cl. in E-flat),3*-
      4,3,3,1-Timp.,Perc.-Str.
      Schott Frères, Brussels, c1932
      Score 86 p.
      Composed 1924.

    3815 [The three wise men from the East]   6'
      2,2,2,2-2,2,2-Timp.,Perc.-Str.

Schoenberg, Arnold

J. Buyst, Brussels [n.d.]
Score 12 p.
Composed 1934.

SCHOENBERG, ARNOLD.　　　Vienna 13 September 1874
　　　　　　　　　　　　　Los Angeles 13 July 1951

3011　Fünf Orchesterstücke, Op. 16　　　27'
[revised edition]
1.[Presentiments]　2.[The Past]　3.[Colors]
4.[Peripeteia]　5.[The Obbligato Recitative]
4*(3rd alt. 2nd Picc.),4*,5*(5th is Cb.Cl.),4-
6,3,4,1-Timp.,Perc.-Cel.,Hp.-Str.
C.F. Peters, Leipzig, ᶜ1912
Score 60 p.
*Composed 1909. Revised 1922. First perform-
ance of original version London, 3 September
1912, Queen's Hall Orchestra, Henry J. Wood
conductor.*

1716　Kammersymphonie für 15 Solo-　　　22'
Instrumente, Op. 9 [in one movement]
1,2*,3*(Cl. in D alt. Cl. in E-flat),2*-2Hn.-
Str.
Universal Edition, Vienna, ᶜ1912
Score 56 p.
*Composed 1906. First performance Vienna, 1907,
Rosé Quartet and the Vienna Philharmonic
Woodwind Ensemble.*

5219　Serenade, Op. 24　　　28'
Cl.,B.Cl.-Mand.,Guit.-Bar. or Bass Voice-Vn.,
Va.,Vc.
Wilhelm Hansen, Copenhagen, ᶜ1924
Score 63 p.
*First public performance Donaueschingen Music
Festival, 20 July 1924, the composer con-
ducting.*

4750　Theme and variations, Op. 43a for　　　14'
band
4*(2Picc.),2,6*(1Cl. in E-flat, 1 Alto Cl.),
2-4Sax.-4Hn. in E-flat,4Hn. in F,2Cnt.,2Tpt.,
2Fluegelhn.,3Tbn.,Bar.,Euph.-Bass,Tuba-Timp.,
Perc.-Cb.
Schirmer, New York, ᶜ1944, 1949
Score 63 p.
Composed 1943 at the request of Carl Engel.

905s　Verklärte Nacht, Op. 4. First　　　22'
transcription for string orchestra
Str.
Universal-Edition, Vienna, ᶜ1917
Score 36 p.
*After the poem Zwei Menschen, from Weib
und Welt by Richard Dehmel. Originally composed as a string sextet 1899, first performed Vienna, 18 March 1902, Tonkunst-
lerverein concerts, Rosé Quartet and members
of the Vienna Philharmonic Orchestra led by
Arnold Rosé. Transcribed 1917.*

2209s　[Same as above. Revised version,　　　22'
1943]
Str.
Associated, New York, ᶜ1917, ᶜ1943
Score 34 p.
Made into the ballet Pillar of Fire with

*choreography by Anthony Tudor, first perform-
ance New York, 8 April 1942, Ballet Theatre.*

SCHOENE, ADOLPH WALDEMAR.　　　Dresden 30 July 1877

5517　In memory of the unknown soldier,　　　9'
Op. 55
4Hn.,4Tpt.,3Tbn.,1Tuba-Timp.,Perc.
Ms. ᶜ1945 by A.W. Schoene
Score 20 p.
*Composed 1911 as Funeral March. First per-
formance Berlin, March 1911, Second Guard Regi-
ment Military Band, Max Graf conductor.
Retitled after World War I.*

SCHOENEFELD, HENRY.　　　Milwaukee 4 October 1857
　　　　　　　　　　　　Los Angeles 4 August 1936

346s　Characteristic suite, Op. 15
1.Allegretto con moto e grazioso　2.Marcio-
fantastico　3.Menuetto　4.Rondo
Str.-(Perc. in no. 2)
C.F. Summy, Chicago, ᶜ1893
Score 31 p.

SCHÖNHERR, MAX.
　　　Marburg a.d. Drau, Austria 23 September 1903

6652　Tänze aus Österreich, Op. 25　　　20'
2(2nd alt. Picc.),2,2,2-4,2,3-Timp.,Perc.-Hp.
-Str.
Ludwig Doblinger, Vienna, ᶜ1938
Score 84 p.
*First performance Vienna, November 1937, RAVAG
(Radio Vienna), Vienna Symphony Orchestra, the
composer conducting.*

SCHÖNWALD, ALBERT.
See: SIKLÓS, ALBERT.

SCHORNSTEIN, E. HERMANN.　　　b. ca.1811
　　　　　　　　　　　Elberfeld, Germany 20 April 1882

685p　[Concerto, piano, no. 1, Op. 1, F minor]
1.Allegro con moto　2.Andante　3.Rondo
Solo Pno.-1,2,2,2-2,2-Timp.-Str.
Ms.
Score 276 p.

SCHREKER, FRANZ.　　　Monaco 23 March 1878
　　　　　　　　　　　Berlin 21 March 1934

1717　Ekkehard [symphonic overture, Op. 12]　　8'
2,3*,3*,3*-4,3,3,1-Timp.,Perc.-Org.(ad lib.)-
Str.
Jos. Eberle, Vienna [n.d.]
Score 51 p.
*Composed 1902. First performance Vienna, Octo-
ber 1903, the composer conducting.*

1719　Der Geburtstag der Infantin, Suite　　　30'
[after Oscar Wilde's novel. Revised version]
3(3rd alt. Picc.),3*,3*,3*-4,3,3,1-Timp.,Perc.
-Cel.,2Hp.,4Mand.,4Guit.-Str.
Universal Edition, Vienna, ᶜ1923
Score 72 p.
*Composed 1908. First performance Vienna, 1908.
Revised 1923. First performance Amsterdam,
1923, Willem Mengelberg conductor.*

145s Intermezzo, Op. 8
Str.
Bosworth, Leipzig, ^c1902
Score 13 p.

1718 Kammersymphonie [in one movement]   30'
1,1,1,1-1,1,1-Timp.,Perc.-Pno.,Cel.,Hp.,Harm.-
Str.
Universal Edition, Vienna, ^c1917
Score 101 p.
First performance Vienna, 12 March 1917.

1723 Kleine Suite für Kammerorchester   20'
1.Praeludium 2.Marcia 3.Canon 4.Fughette
5.Intermezzo 6.Capriccio
1(alt. Picc.),2*,2*,2*-Alto Sax.-2,1,2,1-Timp.,
Perc.-Pno.,Cel.,Hp.-Str.
Universal Edition, Vienna, ^c1929
Score 48 p.
*Composed 1928. First performance Breslau, 17
January 1929, the composer conducting.*

1721 Der Schatzgräber [The treasure   14'
hunter. Act III, Symphonic interlude]
3(3rd alt. Picc.),3*,3*,3*-4,3,3,1-Timp.,Perc.
-Cel.,2Hp.-Str.
Universal Edition, Vienna, ^c1923
Score 46 p. Large folio
*Composed 1918. First performance Frankfurt-
on-Main, 1920.*

1720 Ein Tanzspiel   15'
1.Sarabande 2.Menuett 3.Madrigal 4.Gavotte
2,2,2,2-4,2,3-Timp.,Perc.-Hp.-Str.
Universal Edition, Vienna, ^c1921
Score 46 p.
*Composed 1909 for piano. Orchestrated 1919.
First performance Darmstadt, 1921.*

2527 Vier kleine Stücke   15'
1.Timoroso 2.Violente 3.Incalzando
4.Gradevole
3*,3(3rd alt. E.H.),3*,4*-Alto Sax.-4,3,3,1-
Timp.,Perc.-Pno.,2Hp.-Str.
Heinrichshofen, Magdeburg, ^c1930
Score 36 p. Large folio

1722 Vorspiel zu einem Drama   25'
4*,4*,5*,3*-6,4,3,1-Timp.,Perc.-Pno.,2Cel.,2(or
4)Hp.-Str.
Universal Edition, Vienna, ^c1914
Score 81 p. Large folio
*Composed 1913. First performance Vienna,
1914, the composer conducting.*

SCHROEDER, WILLIAM A.   Brooklyn 10 November 1888
                               Wilton, Connecticut 20 April 1960

3711 Rhapsody, Op. 9   14'
3(3rd alt. Picc.),4*,3*,2-4,3,3,1-Timp.,Perc.-
Hp.-Str.
Ms.
Score 87 p.
*Composed 1921-22. First performance New York,
30 December 1923, New York Philharmonic,
Henry Hadley conductor.*

SCHUBERT, FRANZ.
          Lichtenthal (Vienna) 31 January 1797
          Vienna 19 November 1828

Franz Schubert's works are identified by Deutsch
catalog numbers.

2427 [Claudine von Villa Bella. Overture.   8'
D.239]
2,2,2,2-2,2-Timp.-Str.
Breitkopf & Härtel, Leipzig [n.d.]
Score 22 p.
From the Singspiel composed 1815.

4442 [Divertissement à la hongroise,   4'
piano 4-hands, Op. 54, G minor. March and trio.
D.818] Transcribed by Jules Bordier
2,2,2,2-4,2,3-Perc.-Str.
Richault, Paris [1882?]
Score 15 p.
Composed ca.1824.

245 [Same as above] Transcribed by   4'
Franz Liszt
2,2,2,2-4,2,3,1-Timp.,Perc.-Str.
A. Fürstner, Berlin [n.d.]
Score 27 p.
Composed 1824; orchestrated 1870.

1789 Erlkönig [Song] Op. 1. D.328.   5'
Transcribed by Nikolai Kazanly
2,2*,2,2-4,2,3,1-Timp.,Cym.-Hp.-Str.
J.H. Zimmermann, Leipzig [n.d.]
Score 19 p.
*Originally composed for voice and piano, 1815.
Poetry by Goethe.*

584p [Fantasia, piano, Wanderer, Op. 15,   20'
C major. D.760. Transcribed for piano and
orchestra by Franz Liszt]
Solo Pno.-2,2,2,2-2,2,3-Timp.-Str.
Cranz, Leipzig [n.d.]
Score 86 p.
*Transcribed 1851. First performance Jena, 10
March 1856, Franz Liszt conductor, Julius von
Bronsart soloist.*

826 [Fantasia, piano 4-hands, Op. 103,   8'
F minor. D.940. Transcribed by Felix Mottl]
3*,2,2,2-4,2,3-Timp.,Trgl.-Hp.-Str.
B. Schott's Söhne, Mainz [n.d.]
Score 53 p.
*Composed 1828; orchestrated 1897. First per-
formance Carlsruhe, 1898, Felix Mottl con-
ductor.*

853 [Fierabras. Overture. D.796]   9'
2,2,2,2-4,2,3-Timp.-Str.
Breitkopf & Härtel, Leipzig [n.d.]
Score 40 p.
*From the opera composed 1823. First perform-
ance Vienna, 6 January 1829, Ignaz Schuppanzigh conductor.*

2426 [Die Freunde von Salamanka. Overture.   7'
D.326]
2,2,2,2-2,2-Timp.-Str.
Breitkopf & Härtel, Leipzig [n.d.]

Schubert, Franz

Score 25 p.
From the Singspiel composed 1815.

664s Fünf Deutsche [Tänze] mit Coda und
sieben Trios. D.90
Str.
Breitkopf & Härtel, Leipzig [n.d.]
Score 7 p.
Composed 1813.

1923s Fünf Menuette mit sechs Trios.   *15'*
D.89
Str.(without Cb.)
Score: Breitkopf & Härtel, Leipzig, 1886. 6 p.
Parts: Ms. C1976 by The Fleisher Collection of
Orchestral Music, Free Library of Philadelphia
*Composed 19 November 1813. First performance
Schubert's home, Vienna, ca.1813.*

[Hungarian march]
See: [Divertissement à la hongroise, piano
4-hands, Op. 54, G minor. March and trio.
D.818]

4331 [Eine kleine Trauermusik, E-flat   *7'*
minor. D.79]
2Cl.,2Bn.,C.Bn.-2Hn.,2Tbn.
Score: Breitkopf & Härtel, Leipzig, 1889. 2 p.
Parts: Ms. C1976 by The Fleisher Collection of
Orchestral Music, Free Library of Philadelphia
Composed 1813.

829v [Konzertstück, violin and orchestra,   *8'*
D major. D.345]
Solo Vn.-2Ob.-2Tpt.-Timp.-Str.
Breitkopf & Härtel, Leipzig, 1897
Score 28 p.
Composed 1816.

138s [March, piano 4-hands, Op. 51 no. 1.
D.733] Transcribed anonymously
Pno.-Str.
Ms.
Score 8 p.
*Opus 51 composed about 1822 as Trois Marches
Militaires. This work bound with Bach, Over-
ture (Suite) No. 3, Two Gavottes; Mozart, Don
Giovanni, Canzonetta; and Gluck, Iphigénie en
Aulide, Overture.*

1771 [Same as above] Transcribed by Gustav   *8'*
Brecher
4(3rd&4th alt. Picc.),4(2nd alt. E.H.),4*,3*-
4,4,4,1-Timp.,Perc.-Str.
J.H. Zimmermann, Leipzig [n.d.]
Score 30 p.
*Orchestrated 1914. First performance Cologne,
1915, Gustav Brecher conductor.*

1160 [Same as above] Transcribed by   *7'*
E. Guiraud
2*,2,2,2-4,2,3-Timp.,Trgl.-Str.
A. Durand, Paris [n.d.]
Score 14 p.
*Orchestrated 1887. First performance Paris,
1888, E. Guiraud conductor.*

1791 [March, piano 4-hands, Op. 40 no. 2.   *10'*
D.819. Transcribed by Rudolf Ochs]
2,2,2,2-2,2,3-Timp.,Perc.-Str.
Ries & Erler, Berlin, C1928
Score 18 p.
*Op. 40 originally composed ca.1824 as Six
Grand Marches and Trios. Orchestrated 1928
and here published as Heroischer Marsch, not
to be confused with D.602. First performance
Berlin, 1929.*

1054 [March, piano 4-hands, Op. 40 no. 3.   *10'*
D.819. Transcribed by Franz Liszt]
3*,2,2,2-4,2,3,1-Timp.,Cym.-Str.
A. Fürstner, Berlin [n.d.]
Score 42 p.
Orchestrated 1870.

4309 [March, piano 4-hands, Op. 40 no. 5.   *4'*
D.819. Transcribed by Franz Liszt]
2,2,2,2-4,2,3,1-Timp.-Str.
Fürstner, Berlin [1870?]
Score 41 p.
*Composed ca. 1824. Later known as Trauer-
marsch.*

1394 [March, piano 4-hands, Op. 121 no. 1.   *8'*
D.886. Transcribed by Franz Liszt]
3*,2,2,2-4,2,2,1-Timp.-Str.
A. Fürstner, Berlin [n.d.]
Score 26 p.
*Op. 121 composed 1824 as Deux Marches Carac-
téristiques; orchestrated 1870.*

1922s [Minuet, string quartet, D major.   *ca.2'*
D.86]
Str.(without Cb.)
Score: Breitkopf & Härtel, Leipzig, 1886. 1 p.
Parts: Ms. C1976 by The Fleisher Collection of
Orchestral Music, Free Library of Philadelphia
*Composed November 1813. First performance
Schubert's home, Vienna, ca.1813.*

2397s [Moment musicale, piano, Op. 94. No. 2,
Andantino. D.780. Transcribed by Alexander
Reisman]
Str.
Western International, Los Angeles, C1966
Score 17 p.
Originally composed 1823.

4697 [Moment musicale, piano, Op. 94   *2'*
no. 3. D.780] Transcribed by G. Rhode-Royer
1,1,1-0,1,1-Timp.,Trgl.-Harm.-Str.
Schott, Mainz, C1939
Score in reduction 2 p.
Composed 1823.

926s [Same as above] Transcribed by Charles
Woodhouse
Str.
Hawkes, London, C1929
Score 4 p.

2419 [Overture, B-flat major. D.11]   *7'*
2,2,2,2-2,2-Timp.-Str.
Breitkopf & Härtel, Leipzig [n.d.]
Score 22 p.

Composed for the operetta Der Spiegelritter about 1812. First performance of overture Vienna, 21 March 1830, Ferdinand Schubert conductor.

991 [Overture, D major. D.26]   *9'*
2,2,2,2-2,2,3-Timp.-Str.
Breitkopf & Härtel, Leipzig [n.d.]
Score 18 p.
Composed 1812. First public performance Vienna, 18 March 1838, Ferdinand Schubert conductor.

1489 [Overture, B-flat major. D.470]   *7'*
0,2,0,2-2,2-Timp.-Str.
Breitkopf & Härtel, Leipzig [n.d.]
Score 16 p.
Composed 1816. First public performance Vienna, 21 March 1830, Ferdinand Schubert conductor.

885 [Overture, D major. D.556]   *7'*
2,2,2,2-2Hn.-Timp.-Str.
Breitkopf & Härtel, Leipzig [n.d.]
Score 16 p.
Composed 1817. First public performance Vienna, 17 April 1836, Leopold Jansa conductor.

786 [Overture, In Italian style,   *8'*
D major. D.590]
2,2,2,2-2,2-Timp.-Str.
Breitkopf & Härtel, Leipzig [n.d.]
Score 20 p.
Composed 1817. First public performance Vienna, 1 March 1818.

920 [Overture, In Italian style,   *7'*
C major. D.591]
2,2,2,2-2,2-Timp.-Str.
Breitkopf & Härtel, Wiesbaden [n.d.]
Score 18 p.
Posthumous Op. 170. Composed 1817. First performance Vienna, 21 March 1830, Ferdinand Schubert conductor.

957 [Overture, E minor. D.648]   *8'*
2,2,2,2-4,2,3-Timp.-Str.
Breitkopf & Härtel, Leipzig [n.d.]
Score 40 p.
Composed 1819. First performance Vienna, 14 March 1819(?).

1344 [Overture, piano 4-hands, Op. 34. D.675]
Transcribed by Edgar Stillman-Kelley
3*,2,2,2-4,2,3-Timp.-Str.
O. Ditson, Boston, ᶜ1927
Score 50 p.
Composed 1819.

6982 [Overture, string quintet, C minor.   *10'*
D.8. Transcribed by Wolfgang Hofmann]
1,0,2,1-2Hn.-Str.
Henry Litolff/C.F. Peters, Frankfurt, ᶜ1970
Score 32 p.
Composed 1811. First public performance New York, 13 December 1948, Little Orchestra Society.

292v [Polonaise, violin, B-flat major. D.580]
Edited by Otto Erich Deutsch
Solo Vn.-0,2,0,2-2Hn.-Str.
Edition Strache, Vienna, ᶜ1928
Score 10 p.
Composed 1817. First performance Vienna, 29 September 1818, Ferdinand Schubert soloist.

2580 [Rondo, piano 4-hands, Op. 107, A major.
D.951. Transcribed by Leo Weiner]
2,2,2,2-2,2,3-Timp.-Str.
Rózsavölgyi, Budapest, ᶜ1935
Score 35 p.
Composed 1828; orchestrated 1934.

291v [Rondo, violin, A major. D.438]   *14'*
Solo Vn.-Str.(without Cb.)
Breitkopf & Härtel, Leipzig, 1897
Score 20 p.
Composed 1816.

223 [Rosamunde. Overture, C minor (from   *10'*
Die Zauberharfe). D.644]
2,2,2,2-4,2,3-Timp.-Str.
Breitkopf & Härtel, Leipzig [n.d.]
Score 60 p.
Originally composed 1820 for Georg von Hofmann's play Die Zauberharfe. First performance Vienna, 19 August 1820. Added to the incidental music to Helmina von Chézy's play Rosamunde, 1823 after its first performance. First published as Ouverture zum Rosamunde.

907 [Rosamunde. Overture, D minor (from   *7'*
Alfonso und Estrella). D.732]
2,2,2,2-2,2,3-Timp.-Str.
Breitkopf & Härtel, Leipzig [n.d.]
Score 32 p.
Composed 1821-22 for the opera Alfonso and Estrella, but first performed as Overture to Rosamunde, Vienna, 20 December 1823.

575 [Rosamunde. Entr'acte and ballet   *13'*
music, nos. 1, 2, 9. D.797]
2,2,2,2-2,2,3-Timp.-Str.
Luck's Music Library, Detroit [n.d.]
Score 23 p.

2512 [Rosamunde. Entr'acte and ballet music,
nos. 5, 9. D.797] Edited by Max Reger
2,2,2,2-2Hn.-Str.
Breitkopf & Härtel, Leipzig [n.d.]
Score 13 p.
Composed 1823 for the musical drama by Helmina von Chézy. This edition ca.1916.

2292s [Salve Regina, Op. 153, A major.   *12'30"*
D.676] Edited by Fritz Kneusslin
Sop. Voice Solo-Str.
Kneusslin, Basel, ᶜ1956
Score 10 p.
Composed November 1819.

653s Serenade [Ständchen, no. 4 of Schwanengesang, song cycle. D.957] Arranged by Henry Lawson
Str.
Score: Ms. 4 p.

Schubert, Franz

Parts: B. Schott's Söhne, Mainz [n.d.]
Composed 1828 for voice and piano. Bound with
Gluck, Paride ed Elena, Gavotte.

2244 [Sonata, 2 pianos, Grand duo,   35'
Op. 140, C major. Transcribed as Sinfonie by
Joseph Joachim. D.812]
1.Allegro moderato 2.Andante 3.Scherzo - Trio
4.Finale: Allegro moderato [Deutsch: Allegro
vivace]
3*,2,2,2-4,2,3-Timp.-Str.
Cranz, Leipzig [1873]
Score 215 p.
Composed 1824. Joachim believed the sonata
was a piano version of the lost Gmunden-Gas-
tein Symphony and "re-orchestrated" it, 1855.
First performance Hanover, 9 February 1856,
Joseph Joachim conductor.

678 [Symphony no. 1, D major. D.82]   26'
1.Adagio - Allegro vivace 2.Andante
3.Allegro 4.Allegro vivace
1,2,2,2-2,2-Timp.-Str.
Breitkopf & Härtel, Wiesbaden [n.d.]
Score 64 p.
Composed 1813. First public performance
London, 5 February 1881, August Manns con-
ductor.

687 [Symphony no. 2, B-flat major. D.125]   28'
1.Largo - Allegro vivace 2.Andante
3.Menuetto 4.Presto vivace
2,2,2,2-2,2-Timp.-Str.
Broude Bros., New York [n.d.]
Score 108 p.
Composed 1815. First public performance Lon-
don, 20 October 1877, August Manns conductor.

712 [Symphony no. 3, D major. D.200]   23'
1.Adagio maestoso - Allegro con brio
2.Allegretto 3.Menuetto 4.Presto vivace
2,2,2,2-2,2-Timp.-Str.
Breitkopf & Härtel, Wiesbaden [n.d.]
Score 48 p.
Composed 1815. First public performance Lon-
don, 19 February 1881, August Manns conductor.

637 [Symphony no. 4, Tragic, C minor.   30'
D.417]
1.Adagio molto - Allegro vivace 2.Andante
3.Menuetto 4.Allegro
2,2,2,2-4,2-Timp.-Str.
Breitkopf & Härtel, Leipzig [n.d.]
Score 60 p.
Composed 1816. First public performance Leip-
zig, 19 November 1849, A. F. Riccius con-
ductor.

679 [Symphony no. 5, B-flat major. D.485]   27'
1.Allegro 2.Andante con moto 4.Menuetto
4.Allegro vivace
1,2,0,2-2Hn.-Str.
Breitkopf & Härtel, Leipzig [n.d.]
Score 48 p.
Composed 1816. First private performance
Schottenhof, Vienna, 3 October 1816; first
public performance London, 1 February 1873,
August Manns conductor.

680 [Symphony no. 6, C major. D.589]   32'
1.Adagio - Allegro 2.Andante 3.Scherzo
4.Allegro moderato
2,2,2,2-2,2-Timp.-Str.
Breitkopf & Härtel, Wiesbaden [n.d.]
Score 68 p.
Composed 1818. First public performance Vienna,
14 December 1828, Johann Schmiedel conductor.

150 [Symphony no. 7, The great,   46'
C major. D.944]
1.Andante - Allegro 2.Andante con moto
3.Scherzo 4.Allegro vivace
2,2,2,2-2,2,3-Timp.-Str.
Breitkopf & Härtel, Wiesbaden [n.d.]
Score 122 p.
Composed 1828; posthumous work, discovered by
Robert Schumann. First performance Leipzig,
21 March 1839, Felix Mendelssohn conductor.

5 [Symphony no. 8, Unfinished, B minor.   23'
D.759]
1.Allegro moderato 2.Andante con moto
2,2,2,2-2,2,3-Timp.-Str.
Breitkopf & Härtel, Wiesbaden [n.d.]
Score 31 p.
Composed 1822. First performance Vienna, 17
December 1865, Johann Herbeck conductor.

2961 [Symphony, E major. D.729.   37'
Orchestrated by Felix Weingartner]
1.Adagio - Allegro 2.Andante 3.Scherzo
4.Allegro vivace
2,2,2,2-4,2,3-Timp.-Str.
Universal Edition, Vienna, C1934
Score 149 p.
Completed from a sketch composed 1821. First
performance Vienna, 9 December 1934, Vienna
Philharmonic Orchestra, Felix Weingartner
conductor.

1858 Der Teufel als Hydraulicus.   5'
Overture. D.4
2,0,2,1-2Hn.-Str.
Breitkopf & Härtel, Leipzig, 1886
Score 12 p.
Composed ca.1811.

886 [Des Teufels Lustschloss. Overture.   10'
D.84]
2,2,2,2-2,2,3-Timp.-Str.
Breitkopf & Härtel, Leipzig [n.d.]
Score 24 p.
For the opera composed 1814.

Trauermarsch
See: [March, piano 4-hands, Op. 40 no. 5.
       D.819. Transcribed by Franz Liszt]

2428 [Der vierjährige Posten. Overture.
D.190]
2,2,2,2-2,2-Timp.-Str.
Breitkopf & Härtel, Leipzig [n.d.]
Score 23 p.
For the Singspiel composed 1815. First per-
formance Vienna, 30 January 1897, at the
Schubert Centenary.

1452s [Wiegenlied (Cradle song), Op. 98 no. 2.
D.498. Transcribed by C. Walther]
Solo Hn., Solo Vn., Solo Vc.-Str.
Ms.
Score 5 p.
Originally composed for voice and piano, 1816.

6846 [Die Zwillingsbrüder. Overture.   4'
D.647]
2,2,2,2-2,2-Timp.-Str.
Breitkopf & Härtel, Leipzig, 1889
Score 14 p.
*From the Singspiel commissioned by the Kärnt-
nertor-Theater. Overture composed 1819.
First performance Vienna, 14 June 1820.*

SCHULE, BERNARD EMMANUEL.   Zurich 22 July 1909

2054s Sérénade, string orchestra   10'
1.Alla marcia 2.Andante 3.Tempo di minuetto
4.Giocoso
Str.
Rouart-Lerolle, Paris, c1949
Score 11 p.

SCHULER, CHARLES.

605s Berceuse from Suite Mignonne, Op. 12
no. 4
Str.
W. Hansen, Copenhagen [n.d.]
Score 4 p.

702c [Burleske, violoncello, Op. 24]
Solo Vc.-2,2,2,2-2,2-Timp.-Str.
Score: Ms. 50 p.
Parts: Joh. André, Offenbach a.M., c1906

SCHULLER, GUNTHER.   New York 22 November 1925

6703 Seven studies on themes of Paul Klee 23'
1.Antique harmonies 2.Abstract trio 3.Little
blue devil 4.The twittering-machine 5.Arab
village 6.An eerie moment 7.Pastorale
3(2nd&3rd alt. Picc.),3*,3*,3*-4,3,3,1-Timp.,
Perc.-Pno.,Hp.-Str.
Universal Edition, London, c1962
Score 62 p.
*Commissioned jointly by the Minneapolis Sym-
phony, The Ford Foundation and The American
Music Center, 1959. Composed 1959. First
performance Minneapolis, 27 November 1959,
Minneapolis Symphony, Antal Dorati conductor.*

6695 Symphonic study (reduced orchestra   9'
version)
4(3rd alt. Picc.,4th optional),3(3rd alt.
E.H.),3(3rd alt. B.Cl.),2-4,3,3,1-Timp.,Cym.-
Cel.,Hp.-Str.
Ms. Controlled by Associated, New York
Score 36 p. Large folio
*Composed for larger orchestra, November 1947-
October 1948. First performance Cincinnati,
1948, College of Music Orchestra, Roland
Johnson conductor. This version revised 1964.*

SCHULTHESS, WALTER.   Zurich 24 July 1894
                              Zurich 23 June 1971

673v [Concertino, violin, Op. 7]   9'
1.Moderato 2.Andante sostenuto 3.Allegro
giocoso
Solo Vn.-2,2,2,2-2Hn.-Hp.-Str.
B. Schott's Söhne, Mainz, c1921
Score 45 p.
*Composed 1918. First performance at the
Schweizer Tonkünstlerfest, 1920.*

1330 Serenade, Op. 9, B-flat major   30'
1.Allegro molto 2.Lento 3.Allegro non troppo
2,3*,2,2-2,2-Timp.-Str.
B. Schott's Söhne, Mainz, c1921
Score 39 p.
*Composed 1920. First performance Basel, Octo-
ber 1921.*

SCHULTZE-BIESANTZ, CLEMENS.
          Bückeburg, Germany 1 February 1876
          Braunschweig, Germany 3 June 1935

5243 [Humoristic march, symphonic poem]
3*,2,2,2-4,2,3,1-Timp.,Perc.-Hp.-Str.
Henry Litolff, Braunschweig, c1900
Score 23 p.

5241 [Knight-errant, symphonic poem]
3*,2(2nd alt. E.H.),2,2-4,2,3,1-Timp.,Perc.-
Hp.-Str.
Henry Litolff, Braunschweig, c1900
Score 31 p.

5242 Patheticon, symphonic poem
3*,2(1st alt. E.H.),2(1st alt. B.Cl.),2-4,2,
3,1-Timp.-Hp.-Str.
Henry Litolff, Braunschweig, c1900
Score 26 p.

SCHULZ-BEUTHEN, HEINRICH.   Beuthen 19 June 1838
                                    Dresden 12 March 1915

1359s Abschieds-Klänge [Parting tunes] Op. 28
1.Allegretto 2.Poco moderato
Str.
[n.p., n.d.]
Score 10 p.
Composed 1880.

6254 [The isle of the dead, symphonic poem]
2,2,2,2-4,2,3,1-Timp.,Perc.-Hp.-Str.
Louis Oertel, Hanover, c1909
Score 31 p.
*Suggested by Arnold Böcklin's painting. Dedi-
cated to the University of Leipzig on the
occasion of its 500-year jubilee, 1909.*

649p [Tarantella, piano and orchestra, from
Op. 40, A minor]
Solo Pno.-Fl.-Tpt.-Timp.,Perc.-Str.
Reinecke [n.p., n.d.]
Score 7 p.

789p Rhapsodie russe
Solo Pno.-2,2,2,2-2,2-Timp.-Str.
Jurgenson, Moscow [1895?]
Score 57 p.

Schulz-Schwerin, Karl

SCHULZ-SCHWERIN, KARL.
                Schwerin, Germany 3 January 1845
                Mannheim 24 May 1913

   1304s Geständnis [Confession] Op. 20
   Str.
   C.F.W. Siegel, Leipzig [n.d.]
   Score 5 p.

SCHUMAN, WILLIAM HOWARD.   New York 4 August 1910

   322v Concerto, violin and orchestra,   *26'*
   1958 revision
   Solo Vn.-3(3rd alt. Picc.),3*(2nd ad lib.),
   4*(3rd ad lib.),3*(2nd ad lib.)-4,3,3-Timp.,
   Perc.-Str.
   Ms. [C1960 by Theodore Presser, Bryn Mawr, Pa.]
   Score 104 p. Large folio
   Commissioned by Samuel Dushkin. Original version composed 1946-47. Revised 1954, 1957, and 1958. This version first performed Aspen, 9 August 1959, Aspen Festival Orchestra, Izler Solomon conductor, Roman Totenberg soloist.

   5438 Credendum   *18'*
   1.Declaration 2.Chorale 3.Finale
   4(2nd&3rd alt. Picc.,4th ad lib.),4*(3rd ad
   lib.),5*(1Cl. in E-flat,3rd ad lib.),4*(3rd
   ad lib.)-6,4,3,2-Timp.,Perc.-Pno.-Str.
   Ms. [Now Merion Music, Bryn Mawr, Pa., C1956]
   Score 103 p. Large folio
   Commissioned through the United States Department of State for the National Commission for UNESCO. Composed summer 1955. First performance, benefit for UNESCO, Cincinnati, 4 November 1955, Cincinnati Symphony Orchestra, Thor Johnson conductor.

   4745 George Washington Bridge, an   *10'*
   impression for band, in one movement
   3*,2,6*(1Cl. in E-flat,1Alto Cl.),2-5Sax.(2
   Alto,Ten.,Bar.,Bass)-4Hn. in F,4Hn. in E-flat,
   3Cnt.,2Tpt.,3Tbn.,Bar.,Euph.,Tubas-Timp.,Perc.
   -Cb.
   G. Schirmer, New York, C1951
   Score 47 p.
   Composed 1950.

   6643 New England triptych   *13'*
   1.Be glad then, America 2.When Jesus wept
   3.Chester
   3(3rd alt. Picc.),3*,4*(1Cl. in E-flat),2-4,3,
   3,1-Timp.,Perc.-Str.
   Ms. [Now Merion Music, Bryn Mawr, Pa., C1957]
   Score 70 p. Large folio
   After three hymns of William Billings (1746-1800). Commissioned by André Kostelanetz. Composed 1956. First performance Miami, 28 October 1956, University of Miami Symphony Orchestra, André Kostelanetz conductor.

   4838 Newsreel, in 5 shots, for orchestra   *8'*
   3(2nd alt. Picc.,3rd optional),3*(2nd Ob.
   optional),5*(Cl. in E-flat,3rdCl.,B.Cl. all
   optional),3*(2nd&C.Bn. optional)-3Sax.(2Alto,
   Ten.,all optional)-4(2nd&4th optional),3,3,1-
   Timp.,Perc.-Pno.(optional)-Str.
   G. Schirmer, New York, C1943

Score 44 p.
Originally composed for band, 1941.

6725 The orchestra song   *3'30"*
2*,1,2*(B.Cl. ad lib.),1-4,3(1Cnt.),3,1-
Timp.,Perc.-Str.
Theodore Presser, Bryn Mawr, Pa., C1964 by
Merion Music, Inc.
Score 21 p.
Based on traditional Austrian melodies. Originally composed for voices. First performance of this version, 11 April 1964, Minneapolis Symphony Orchestra, André Kostelanetz conductor.

6718 Philharmonic fanfare   *1'30"*
4(4th ad lib.),4*(3rd ad lib.),5*(1Cl. in E-
flat ad lib.,3rd ad lib.),4*(3rd ad lib.)-6(5th
&6th ad lib.),4(4th ad lib.),3,2(1Ten. Tuba ad
lib.,1Bass Tuba)-Timp.,Perc.(ad lib.)-Str.
Ms. [Theodore Presser, Bryn Mawr, Pa., C1962
by Merion Music, Inc.]
Score 13 p. Large folio
Commissioned by the New York Philharmonic Orchestra. Condensed from the composer's Symphony no. 7, 2nd movement. First performance of fanfare alone, North Meadow, Central Park, New York, June 1965, New York Philharmonic, William Steinberg conductor.

406c A song of Orpheus, fantasy   *20'*
Solo Vc.-3(3rd alt. Picc.),3*,3*,2-4Hn.-Hp.-
Str.
Ms. [C1963 by Theodore Presser, Bryn Mawr, Pa.]
Score 92 p. Large folio
Commissioned by the Ford Foundation for Leonard Rose. A fantasy based on Schuman's Orpheus With His Lute. This work composed 1960-61. First performance Indianapolis, 17 February 1962, Indianapolis Symphony Orchestra, Izler Solomon conductor, Leonard Rose soloist.

6717 Symphony no. 7, in one movement   *26'*
4(4th ad lib.,2nd&3rd alt. Picc.),4*(3rd ad
lib.),5*(1Cl. in E-flat ad lib.,3rd ad lib.),
4*(3rd ad lib.)-6(5th&6th ad lib.),4(4th ad
lib.),3,2(1Ten. Tuba ad lib.,Bass Tuba)-Timp.,
Perc.-Pno.-Str.
Theodore Presser, Bryn Mawr, Pa., C1962 by
Merion Music, Inc.
Score 96 p. Large folio
Commissioned by the Serge Koussevitzky Foundation in the Library of Congress and the Boston Symphony Orchestra in celebration of the 75th anniversary of the Orchestra and in memory of Serge and Natalie Koussevitzky. Composed 1960. First performance Boston, 21 October 1960, Boston Symphony Orchestra, Charles Munch conductor. The second movement is condensed as Philharmonic Fanfare, Catalog no. 6718.

6727 [Symphony no. 8]   *30'*
1.Lento sostenuto - Pressante vigoroso - Lento
2.Largo 3.Presto
4(3rd&4th alt. Picc.),4*(3rd ad lib.),4*
(3rd ad lib.),4*(3rd ad lib.)-6,4,4,1-Timp.,
Perc.-Pno.,2Hp.-Str.

Theodore Presser, Bryn Mawr, Pa., ^c1962 by
Merion Music, Inc.
Score 123 p. Large folio
Commissioned by the New York Philharmonic.
Composed 1962. First performance New York, 4
October 1962, New York Philharmonic, Leonard
Bernstein conductor.

SCHUMANN, CAMILLO.
                    Königstein, Germany 10 March 1872
                    Gottleuba, Germany 29 December 1946

829m [Andante and capriccio, Op. 36]
Solo Fl.-0,2,2,2-2Hn.-Str.
Score: Ms. 76 p.
Parts: C.F. Schmidt, Heilbronn a.N. [n.d.]

830m [Fantasy piece, Op. 31, D minor]
Solo Ob.-2,0,2,2-2Hn.-Str.
Score: Ms. 33 p.
Parts: C.F. Schmidt, Heilbronn a.N. [n.d.]

SCHUMANN, CLARA JOSEPHINE WIECK.
                    Leipzig 13 September 1819
                    Frankfurt a.M. 20 May 1896

690p [Concerto, piano, Op. 7, A minor]
1.Allegro maestoso 2.Romanze 3.Finale
Solo Pno.-2,2,2,2-2,2,1-Timp.-Str.
Score: Ms. 155 p.
Parts: Hofmeister [n.p., n.d.]

SCHUMANN, GEORG ALFRED.
                    Königstein, Germany 25 October 1866
                    Berlin 23 May 1952

1859 Im Ringen um ein Ideal [Struggle   30'
for an ideal, symphonic poem] Op. 66
4*,4*,3,3*-4,3,3,1-Timp.,Perc.-2Hp.-Str.
F.E.C. Leuckart, Leipzig, 1914
Score 88 p.
Composed 1914. First performance Berlin, 1915,
Arthur Nikisch conductor.

951 Lebensfreude [Joy of life, overture]   15'
Op. 54
4*,3,3,3*-4,3,3,1-Timp.,Perc.-Hp.-Str.
Ries & Erler, Berlin [n.d.]
Score 71 p.
Composed 1910. First performance Berlin, 1911,
Arthur Nikisch conductor.

1065 Liebesfrühling, Ouvertüre, Op. 28   15'
3*,2,2,3-4,2,Cnt.,3,1-Timp.,Perc.-Str.
Breitkopf & Härtel, Leipzig, ^c1901
Score 61 p.
Composed 1901. First performance Berlin, 1901,
the composer conducting.

1111 Eine Serenade, Op. 34, F major   25'
1.Auf dem Wege 2.Nächtlicher Spuk
3.Ständchen 4.Intermezzo 5.Finale
3*,2,2,3*-4,2,3,1-Timp.,Perc.-Hp.-Str.
Bote & Bock, Berlin, ^c1904
Score 132 p.
Composed 1904. First performance Meiningen,
1904, Fritz Steinbach conductor.

3842 Symphonische Variationen über den Choral:
Wer Nur den Lieben Gott Lässt Walten, Op. 24
2,3,2,3-4,3,3,1-Timp.-Org.(ad lib.),Hp.-Str.
Hofmeister, Leipzig [n.d.]
Score 70 p.
Chorale attributed to Georg Neumark (1621-1681).
First performance Bremen, 11 January 1899.

789 Tanz der Nymphen und Satyrn [from]   10'
Amor und Psyche, Op. 3
3*,2,2,2-4,2,3-Timp.,Perc.-Str.
Breitkopf & Härtel, Leipzig [n.d.]
Score 35 p.
Composed 1886. First performance Leipzig, 1887,
the composer conducting.

1826 Variationen und Doppelfuge über ein   25'
lustiges Thema, Op. 30
3*,2,2,4*-4,2,3,1-Timp.,Perc.-Hp.-Str.
Leuckart, Leipzig [n.d.]
Score 79 p.
Composed 1901. First performance Berlin, 1902,
Felix Weingartner conductor.

1725 Variationen und Fuge über ein Thema   35'
von Johann Sebastian Bach, Op. 59
3(3rd alt. Picc.),3*,3,3*-4,3,3,1-Timp.,Perc.-
Hp.-Str.
Ries & Erler, Berlin, ^c1914
Score 102 p.
Composed 1914. First performance Berlin, 1914,
Arthur Nikisch conductor.

1161 Variationen und Gigue über ein Thema   35'
von Händel, Op. 72
3*,2,3*,3*-4,3,3,1-Timp.,Perc.-2Hp.-Str.
Schlesinger, Berlin, ^c1925
Score 118 p.
Composed 1923. First performance Leipzig,
1924, Wilhelm Furtwängler conductor.

1314 Zur Carnevalszeit, Suite, Op. 22   20'
1.Allegro con fuoco 2.Andantino marcato
3.Presto
3*,2,2,3*-4,2,3,1-Timp.,Perc.-Hp.-Str.
Leuckart, Leipzig [n.d.]
Score 81 p.
Composed 1896. First performance Berlin, 1897,
the composer conducting.

SCHUMANN, ROBERT.   Zwickau, Saxony 8 June 1810
                    Endenich, near Bonn 29 July 1856

70s Abendlied, Op. 85 no. 12
Str.
Cranz, Leipzig [n.d.]
Score in reduction 1 p.
Op. 85 originally composed for piano 4-hands
as Zwölf Klavierstücke.

3523 [Same as above] Freely   3'45"
transcribed by Harl McDonald
2,2,3,2-3,2,2-Str.
Ms. [now Elkan-Vogel, Bryn Mawr, Pa.]
Score 13 p.
Transcribed on commission by the RCA Victor
Co., 1939. First performance, Boston Pops
Orchestra, Arthur Fiedler conductor.

Schumann, Robert

472v [Same as above] Arranged by August   2'
Wilhelmj
Solo Vn.-0,0,2,2-2Hn.-Str.
B. Schott's Söhne, Mainz [n.d.]
Score 5 p.

1059s Adagio (Canon) from Studien für den
Pedalflügel, Op. 56 no. 6. Arranged by Franz
Ries
Str.
Ries & Erler, Berlin [n.d.]
Score 3 p.

701s Bilder aus Osten, 6 impromptus, Op. 66.
Transcribed by Friedrich Hermann
Str.
Kistner, Leipzig [n.d.]
Score 23 p.
Originally composed for piano 4-hands, 1848.

6965 [Same as above. Transcribed by   22'
Carl Reinecke]
2,2,2,2-2,2-Timp.,Perc.-Str.
Fr. Kistner, Leipzig [1875]
Score 109 p.

716s A bower of roses. Arranged by Charles
Tourville
Str.
Joseph Williams, London, C1927
Score 4 p.
Originally composed for voice and piano.

2996 Carnival, piano, Op. 9 [Complete]   38'
Orchestrated by Rimsky-Korsakov, Glazunov,
Liadov, and Tcherepnin
3(3rd alt. Picc.),2,2,2-4,2,3,1-Timp.,B.Dr.-
Hp.-Str.
[n.p., n.d.]
Score 213 p.
*First performance (as a ballet) St. Peters-
burg, 1910.*

372p [Concerto, piano, Op. 54, A minor]   27'
1.Allegro affettuoso 2.Intermezzo 3.Allegro
vivace
Solo Pno.-2,2,2,2-2,2-Timp.-Str.
Kalmus, New York [n.d.]
Score 94 p.
*Original title Phantasie. Composed 1841-45.
First performance Dresden, 4 December 1845,
Ferdinand Hiller conductor, Clara Schumann
soloist.*

1203v [Concerto, violin, D minor] Edited   27'
by Georg Schünemann
1.In kräftigem, nicht zu schnellem Tempo
2.Langsam 3.Lebhaft, doch nicht schnell
Solo Vn.-2,2,2,2-2,2-Timp.-Str.
B. Schott's Söhne, Mainz, C1937
Score 54 p.
*Composed 1853 for Joseph Joachim, who never
performed it. First performance Berlin, 26
November 1937, Berlin Philharmonic Orchestra,
Georg Kulenkampff soloist.*

479c [Concerto, violoncello, Op. 129,   22'
A minor]

In one movement
Solo Vc.-2,2,2,2-2,2-Timp.-Str.
Breitkopf & Härtel, Wiesbaden [n.d.]
Score 40 p.
Composed 1850.

518m Concertstück, Op. 86 [F major]   21'
1.Lebhaft 2.Romanze 3.Sehr lebhaft
4Soli Hn.-3*,2,2,2-2,2,3-Timp.-Str.
KaWe, Amsterdam, C1964
Score 77 p.
*Composed 1849. First performance Leipzig, 25
February 1856, Julius Rietz conductor.*

1556 Esquisses [Sketches] piano, Op. 58.   14'
Transcribed by C. Chevillard
2,2,2,2-4,2,3,1-Timp.,Cym.-Str.
Durand, Paris [n.d.]
Score 41 p.
*Composed 1845; orchestrated 1905. First per-
formance Paris, 1905, C. Chevillard conductor.*

4269 [Etudes symphoniques in the form of
variations, Op. 13 nos. 1, 2, 3, 7, 9.
Transcribed by Willem Kes]
3*,3*,3*,3*-4,2,3,1-Timp.-Hp.-Str.
Simrock, Berlin [1897]
Score 39 p.
*Originally composed for piano in twelve varia-
tions on a theme by Baron August von Fricken,
1834.*

416v [Fantasy, violin, Op. 131, C major]   14'
Edited by Clara Schumann
Solo Vn.-2,2,2,2-2,2-Timp.-Str.
Breitkopf & Härtel, Leipzig [n.d.]
Score 28 p.
*Composed 1853. First performance Düsseldorf,
27 October 1853, the composer conducting,
Joseph Joachim soloist.*

1093v [Same as above] Transcribed by Fritz
Kreisler
Solo Vn.-2(2nd alt. Picc.),2,2,2-4,2,3-Timp.-
Str.
Foley, New York, C1936
Score 76 p.
*Transcribed 1936. First performance of this
version, Chicago, 29 October 1936, Chicago
Symphony Orchestra, Frederick Stock conductor,
Fritz Kreisler soloist.*

1450 [Faust. Overture]   6'
2,2,2,2-4,2,3-Timp.-Str.
Breitkopf & Härtel, Leipzig [n.d.]
Score 24 p.
*Overture composed 1853. First performance
posthumously, Cologne, 14 January 1862, Ferdinand Hiller conductor.*

5919 Fest-Ouverture mit Gesang, Op. 123.   8'
Edited by Clara Schumann
2,2,2,2-4,2,3-Timp.-Chorus(SATB)-Str.
Breitkopf & Härtel, Leipzig, 1887
Score 30 p.
*Based on the drinking song Bekränzt mit Laub.
Composed 1852-53. First performance Düssel-
dorf, 17 May 1853, Lower Rhine Festival,*

Schumann, Robert

Düsseldorf Musikverein and Gesangsverein, the composer conducting.

787 [Genoveva, Op. 81. Overture]   *10'*
2,2,2,2-4,2,3-Timp.-Str.
Kalmus, New York [n.d.]
Score 23 p.
Composed 1847 for the opera. First performance Leipzig, 25 February 1850, the composer conducting.

399p [Introduction and allegro, piano,   *13'*
Op. 134, in D]
Solo Pno.-2,2,2,2-2,2,1-Timp.-Str.
Breitkopf & Härtel, Leipzig [n.d.]
Score 31 p.
Composed 1853. First performance Utrecht, 26 November 1853, the composer conducting, Clara Schumann soloist.

530p Introduction and allegro appassionato, *15'*
Op. 92
Solo Pno.-2,2,2,2-2,2-Timp.-Str.
Kalmus, New York [n.d.]
Score 52 p.
Composed 1849. First performance Leipzig, 14 February 1850, Julius Rietz conductor, Clara Schumann soloist.

67 [Manfred, Op. 115. Overture]   *10'*
2,2,2,2-4,3,3-Timp.-Str.
Breitkopf & Härtel, Leipzig [n.d.]
Score 42 p.
From the incidental music composed 1848. First performance Leipzig, 14 March 1852, the composer conducting.

788 [Manfred, Op. 115. Suite]   *8'*
1.Entr'acte 2.Ranz des vaches 3.Apparition de la fée des Alpes
2,2(1 alt. E.H.),2,2-2,1-Hp.-Str.
Durand, Paris [n.d.]
Score 15 p.
Composed 1849; arranged 1878. First performance Paris, 1879.

1254s Northern song. Arranged by E.W. Ritter
Str.
Score: Ms. 2 p.
Parts: [n.p., n.d.]

188 Ouverture, Scherzo und Finale, Op. 52 *20'*
2,2,2,2-2,2,3-Timp.-Str.
Kalmus, Paris [n.d.]
Score 46 p.
Composed 1841; revised 1845. First performance Dresden, 4 December 1845, Ferdinand Hiller conductor.

921 [Overture to Goethe's Hermann und   *8'*
Dorothea, Op. 136, B minor]
3*,2,2,2-2,2-Side Dr.-Str.
Breitkopf & Härtel, Leipzig [n.d.]
Score 18 p.
Composed 1851. First performance Leipzig, 26 February 1857, Julius Rietz conductor.

906 [Overture to Schiller's Braut von   *9'*
Messina, Op. 100, C minor]
3*,2,2,2-2,2,3-Timp.-Str.
Breitkopf & Härtel, Leipzig [n.d.]
Score 35 p.
Composed 1850-51. First performance Düsseldorf, 13 March 1851, the composer conducting.

888 [Overture to Shakespeare's Julius   *9'*
Caesar, Op. 128]
2*,2,2,2-4,2,3,1-Timp.-Str.
Breitkopf & Härtel, Leipzig, 1883
Score 39 p.
Composed 1850-51. First performance Düsseldorf, 3 August 1852, the composer conducting.

463s Rêverie, Op. 15 no. 7
Bn.(ad lib.)-Str.
Durand, Paris [n.d.]
Score 3 p.
From Op. 15, Kinderscenen, originally composed for piano.

1253s Sailor's song. Arranged by E.W. Ritter
Str.
Score: Ms. 4 p.
Parts: Hawkes & Son, London [n.d.]
Originally composed for piano in Album für die Jugend, Op. 68.

166s Spanisches Liederspiel, Op. 75. Transcribed by Friedrich Hermann
1.[First meeting] 2. Intermezzo 3.[Amorous grief] 4.[At night] 5.[It is revealed]
6.[Melancholy] 7.[Avowal] 8.[Message]
9.[I am loved]
Str.
C.F. Kahnt, Leipzig [n.d.]
Score 43 p.
Originally composed for four voices and piano 1849.

106 [Symphony no. 1, Op. 38, B-flat   *33'*
major]
1.Andante - Allegro molto vivace 2.Larghetto
3.Scherzo 4.Allegro animato e grazioso
2,2,2,2-4,2,3-Timp.,Trgl.-Str.
Breitkopf & Härtel, Wiesbaden, ᶜ1965
Score 108 p.
Composed 1841. First performance Leipzig, 31 March 1841, Felix Mendelssohn conductor.

111 [Symphony no. 2, Op. 61, C major]   *39'*
1.Sostenuto assai - Allegro ma non troppo
2.Scherzo 3.Adagio espressivo 4.Allegro molto vivace
2,2,2,2-2,2,3-Timp.-Str.
Breitkopf & Härtel/AMP, New York [n.d.]
Score 134 p.
Composed 1845-46. First performance Leipzig, 5 November 1846, Felix Mendelssohn conductor.

221 [Symphony no. 3, Rhenish, Op. 97,   *30'*
E-flat major]
1.Lebhaft 2.Scherzo 3.Nicht schnell
4.Feierlich 5.Lebhaft
2,2,2,2-4,2,3-Timp.-Str.
Breitkopf & Härtel/AMP, New York [n.d.]
Score 67 p.

Schumann, Robert

Composed 1850. First performance Düsseldorf, 6 February 1851, the composer conducting.

2191 [Symphony no. 4, Op. 120, D minor]   25'
Edited by Gustav Mahler
1.Ziemlich langsam 2.Romanze 3.Scherzo
2,2,2,2(all doubled)-4,2,3-Timp.-Str.
Breitkopf & Härtel, Leipzig, 1882
Score 97 p.
Composed 1841 as Second Symphony. First performance Leipzig, 6 December 1841, Ferdinand David conductor. Revised 1851. First performance of the revision as Symphony no. 4, Op. 120, Düsseldorf, 3 March 1851, the composer conducting.

151 [Same as above] Edited by Clara   27'
Schumann
2,2,2,2-4,2,3-Timp.-Str.
Breitkopf & Härtel, Wiesbaden [n.d.]
Score 96 p.

SCHÜRMANN, GEORG CASPAR.   Idensen, Hanover ca.1672
Wolfenbüttel 25 February 1751

2326s Die getreue Alceste. Suite. Edited and arranged by Gustav Friedrich Schmidt
2Ob.(ad lib.),Bn.(ad lib.)-Cemb.-Str.
Musikalische Kultur und Wissenschaft, Wolfenbüttel, ᶜ1934
Score 18 p.
From the opera after Euripides; composed 1719. First performance Braunschweig, February 1719.

SCHUSTER, WENZEL.

988s Addio Napoli [Farewell to Naples] Op. 12
Solo Vn.-Str.
Score: Ms. 7 p.
Parts: F. Hofmeister, Leipzig [n.d.]

SCHÜTT, EDUARD.   St. Petersburg 22 October 1856
Obermias, Italy 26 July 1933

603p [Concerto, piano, Op. 7, G minor]
1.Allegro energico 2.Moderato assai
3.Allegro grazioso
Solo Pno.-2(2nd alt. Picc.),2,2,2-2,2-Timp.-Str.
E.W. Fritzsch, Leipzig [n.d.]
Score 69 p.
First performance St. Petersburg, January 1882, the composer as soloist.

539p [Concerto, piano, Op. 47, F minor]
1.Allegro risoluto 2.Andante tranquillo
3.Allegro vivace
Solo Pno.-2(2nd alt. Picc.),2,2,2-4,2,3-Timp.,Perc.-Str.
Kalmus, New York [n.d.]
Score 90 p.

165s Serenade, Op. 6, D major
Str.
Joh. André, Offenbach a.M. [n.d.]
Score 39 p.

SCHUYER, ARY.   The Hague 25 May 1881

518c [Concerto, violoncello, A minor]
In one movement
Solo Vc.-2,3*,3*,2-4,2,3,1-Timp.-Hp.-Str.
Joh. André, Offenbach a.M. [n.d.]
Score 126 p.

SCHWALM, ROBERT.   Erfurt, Germany 6 December 1845
Königsberg, Germany 6 March 1912

708v [Konzertstück, violin, Op. 51, G major]
Solo Vn.-2,2,2,2-4Hn.-Timp.-Str.
C.F.W. Siegel, Leipzig [n.d.]
Score 35 p.

163s Serenade, Op. 50, G major
Str.
C.F.W. Siegel, Leipzig [n.d.]
Score 25 p.

SCHWARZLOSE, OTTO.   Genthin, Saxony 23 January 1858

1238s Des Jünglings Leid und Freud', Op. 86
Str.
L. Frankenstein, Breslau, ᶜ1897
Score 11 p.

SCHWERIN, KARL SCHULZ.
See: SCHULZ-SCHWERIN, KARL.

SCHWINDEL, FRIEDRICH.   Amsterdam 3 May 1737
Carlsruhe 7 August 1786

4643 [Symphony, F major] Arranged by Adam Carse
1.Allegro 2.Andante 3.Presto
2Ob. or 2Fl.-2Hn.-Str.
Augener, London, ᶜ1937
Score 13 p.
First published by J. J. Hummel, Amsterdam, 1770, as no. 2 of its series Sinfonie Périodique. Listed in the Breitkopf Thematic Catalogue, Supplement V, 1770.

SCHYTTE, LUDVIG THEODOR.
Aarhus, Denmark 28 April 1848
Berlin 10 November 1909

6059 [Pantomimes, piano 4-hands, Op. 30.
Transcribed by Karl Müller-Berghaus]
3*,3*,3*,2-4,2,3,1-Timp.,Perc.-Hp.-Str.
Carl Simon, Berlin [1879]
Score 83 p.

SCIANNI, JOSEPH. Memphis, Tennessee 6 October 1928

5620 Batik   9'
2*,2*,3*,2-4,3,3,1-Timp.,Perc.-Hp.-Str.
Ms.
Score 47 p. Large folio

COLLECTION OF ORCHESTRAL MUSIC

Composed 1957. First performance Rochester, 1957, Eastman-Rochester Symphony Orchestra, Howard Hanson conductor.

5622 Shiloh overture   5'
3*,2,2,2-4,3,3-Timp.,Perc.-Str.
Ms.
Score 45 p.
Commemorates the Civil War battle of 1862. Composed 1956. First performance Rochester, 2 May 1956, Eastman-Rochester Symphony Orchestra, Howard Hanson conductor.

6535 Sinfonia breve   12'
1.Allegro con rigore 2.Adagio cantabile
3.Allegro con spirito
2(2nd alt. Picc.),2,2,2-2,2,1-Timp.,Perc.-Str.
Ms. [Presser, Bryn Mawr, Pennsylvania, ᶜ1959]
Score 69 p.
Composed 1958. First performance Rochester, April 1958, Eastman-Rochester Symphony Orchestra, Howard Hanson conductor. Second movement received the Edward Benjamin Award for Quiet Music, 1958.

SCONTRINO, ANTONIO.   Trapani, Italy 17 May 1850
                             Florence 7 January 1922

1969 Sinfonia marinaresca [Symphony of the sea]
1.Mare calmo 2.[The island of the monkeys]
3.Canto della Sirene 4.Tempesta
4*(3rd alt. 2nd Picc.),3*,3,2-4,2,2Cnt.,4,1-
Timp.,Perc.-Hp.-Str.
Carisch & Jänichen, Milan, ᶜ1897
Score 147 p.

SCOTT, CYRIL MEIR.
         Oxton, Cheshire, England 27 September 1879
                         Eastbourne 31 December 1970

4550 Aubade, Op. 77   18'
3(3rd alt. Picc.),3*,3*,2-4,2,3,1-Timp.,Perc.-
2Hp.-Str.
B. Schott's Söhne, Mainz, ᶜ1911
Score 35 p.
Composed 1911.

557p [Concerto, piano, C major]   22'
1.Allegro maestoso 2.Adagio 3.Allegro poco
moderato
Solo Pno.-2(2nd alt. Picc.),1,2,2-Timp.,Perc.-
Cel.,Hp.-Str.
B. Schott's Söhne, Mainz, ᶜ1922
Score 86 p.
Composed 1913-14. First performance London, 1915, Thomas Beecham conductor, the composer as soloist.

2287 Passacaglia nos. 1, 2   25'
4(4th alt. Picc.),4*,5*,5*-6,4,3,1-Timp.,Perc.
-Pno.,Org.,Cel.,2Hp.-Str.
B. Schott's Söhne, Mainz, ᶜ1922
Score 36 p.

2962 Souvenir de Vienne. Transcribed by   3'
Ernest Austin
2,0,2,2-2,0,2Cnt.,1-Timp.,Trgl.-Str.
Ms.
Score 10 p.

Originally composed as a piano solo, 1923; orchestrated, 1923.

97s [Suite no. 1, for strings]   9'
1.Silver threads among the gold 2.Long, long
ago 3.Oh, dear, what can the matter be...
Str.
Boosey & Hawkes, London, ᶜ1931
Score 8 p.

SCOTTOLINE, ANGELO.   Philadelphia 26 December 1908

2418s Nightmare for strings
Str.
Ms. ᶜ1974 by Angelo C. Scottoline
Score 31 p.
Composed 1958. First performance Stratford, New Jersey, 1959, Edward Bonnelly Orchestra, Edward Bonnelly conductor.

SCRIABIN(E), ALEXANDER.
See: SKRIABIN, ALEXANDER NIKOLAIEVICH.

SCULL, HAROLD T.   London 1898

1004m Solemn prelude, Op. 76   6'
Org.-Str.
Augener, London, ᶜ1940
Score 7 p.
Composed ca.1928. First performance London, 7 May 1938, Ernest Read Symphony Orchestra, the composer conducting.

SEARCH, FREDERICK PRESTON.
                   Pueblo, Colorado 22 July 1889
            Carmel Valley, California 1 November 1959

734c [Concerto, violoncello, A minor]   21'
1.Allegro 2.Andante con moto - Moderato
3.Allegro
Solo Vc.-2,2,2,2-4,2,3,1-Timp.,Cym.-Str.
Ms.
Score 115 p.
Commissioned by Michel Penha, 1932. Composed 1932. First performance Carmel-by-the-Sea, California, 22 August 1933, Monterey Peninsula Orchestra, Michel Penha conductor, the composer as soloist.

2775 The dream of McKorkle, overture   16'
3(3rd alt. Picc.),3*,3*,3*(C.Bn. ad lib.)-4,3,
3,1-Timp.,Perc.-Str.
Ms.
Score 74 p.
McKorkle was a legendary California '49er. Composed 1932. First performance Oakland, California, 4 August 1936, Oakland Symphony Orchestra of the WPA, Gastone Usigli conductor.

2832 Exhilaration   9'30"
1,1,1,1-1,1,1-Timp.,Perc.-Pno.(optional)-Str.
Ms.
Score 56 p.
Transcribed 1934 from Exhilaration Overture. First performance San Mateo, California, 30 October 1938, Federal Music Project Orchestra of the WPA, Arthur Gundersen conductor.

Search, Frederick

2701 Exhilaration overture   10'
3(3rd alt. Picc.),3*,3,3*-4,3,3,1-Timp.,Perc.-
1 or 2Hp.-Str.
Ms.
Score 67 p.
*Completed 1934. First performance San Fran-
cisco, 9 January 1936, Federal Symphony Orchestra of the WPA, the composer conducting.*

5868 Polly, a jolly suite   14'
1.Jollity 2.Minuet 3.Berceuse 4.Quicksilver
3(3rd alt. Picc.),3*,3*,3*(C.Bn. ad lib.)-4,3,
3,1-Timp.,Perc.-Str.
Ms. Composers Facsimile Edition, New York,
C1958 by Frederick Preston Search
Score 89 p. Large folio

2837 Rhapsody   19'30"
1.Allegro moderato 2.Allegretto 3.Moderato
4.Allegro
3(3rd alt. Picc.),3*,3*,3*-4,3,3,1-Timp.,Perc.
-Cel.(ad lib.),Hp.(ad lib.)-Str.
Ms.
Score 150 p.
*Composed 1934. First performance San Fran-
cisco, 30 April 1936, Federal Symphony Orchestra of the WPA, the composer conducting.*

735c Romanze   4'
Solo Vc. or Va.-Hp.(ad lib.)-Str.
Ms.
Score 14 p.
*Transcribed 1938 from String Quartet no. 6,
composed 1932.*

3698 Romanze for symphony orchestra   4'
2,2,2,2-4,3,3,1-Timp.,Perc.-Pno.(ad lib.)-Str.
Ms.
Score 26 p.
*Transcribed 1938 from String Quartet no. 6,
composed 1932. First performance Golden Gate
International Exposition, San Francisco, 20
September 1939, Jack Joy Concert Orchestra,
Jack Joy conductor.*

3704 Sinfonietta   20'
1.Allegro moderato 2.Scherzo 3.Larghetto
4.Allegro con spirito
1,1,1,1-1,1,1-Timp.,Perc.-Str.
Ms.
Score 155 p.
Composed 1938.

3057 [Symphony no. 2. No. 1, Allegro]   8'30"
3(3rd alt. Picc.),3*,3*,3*-4,3,3,1-Timp.,Perc.
-Str.
Ms.
Score 86 p.
*Original title: Overture. Composed 1938.
First performance Oakland, California, 23
February 1940, Northern California Symphony
Orchestra of the WPA, Nathan Abas conductor.*

5705 Symphony no. 4 in B-flat, Roan   27'
stallion, in two movements
3(3rd alt. Picc.),3*,3*,3*-4,3,3,1-Timp.,Perc.
-Str.
Ms.
Score 245 p.

SEARCH, SARA OPAL.   Fort Worth, Texas 1890

1875s [Symphony, string orchestra,   25'
C minor]
1.Allegro appassionato 2.Andante sostenuto
3.Scherzo 4.Finale
Str.
Ms.
Score 58 p.
*Composed 1940. First performance over Radio
WOR, New York, 1 November 1942, Symphonic
Strings, Alfred Wallenstein conductor.*

3951 [Symphony no. 1, C minor]   25'
1.Allegro appassionato 2.Andante sostenuto
3.Scherzo 4.Finale: Allegro
3(3rd alt. Picc.),3*,3*,3*-4,3,3,1-Timp.,Perc.
-Str.
Ms.
Score 174 p.
*Originally composed for string orchestra, 1940.
This version ca.1941.*

SEARLE, HUMPHREY.   Oxford, England 26 August 1915

4610 Night music, Op. 2   9'
1(alt. Picc.),1,1(alt. B.Cl.),1(alt. C.Bn.)-
1,1,1-Timp.(alt. S.Dr.)-Str.
Joseph Williams, London, C1947
Score 32 p.
Composed 1943.

ŠEBEK, GABRIEL.

1886 Danses bulgares, Op. 7 nos. 1 *and* 2   4'
2(2nd alt. Picc.),2,2,2-4,2,3-Timp.,Perc.-Str.
Fr. Urbánek, Prague [n.d.]
Score 33 p.
Composed 1886.

SEDIWY, J.

79s Doux réveil, valse lente [Sweet awakening]
Str.
Joh. André, Offenbach a.M., C1901
Score 6 p.

SEELING, HANS.   Prague 1828
                             Prague 26 May 1862

4598 [From an artist's memoirs, tone poems for
piano, Op. 13. Nos. 2, 7, 6, 9, 10. Tran-
scribed for orchestra by Karl Müller-Berghaus]
2,2,3*(B.Cl. ad lib.),2-4,2,3,1-Timp.,B.Dr.-
Hp.-Str.
Bartholf Senff, Leipzig [1875?]
Score 63 p.
Originally composed for piano ca.1861.

SEGER, HANS.

5078 Piccola ouverture dodecafonica   6'
2(2nd alt. Picc.),2,2,2-2,2,1-Timp.,Perc.-Hp.-
Str.
Ms.
Score 64 p.
Composed 1949.

5143 Rondó di Pinocchio   5'
2*,1,1,2-2,1-Timp.,Perc.-Cel.,Hp.-Str.
Ms.
Score 56 p.
*Probably from a ballet or suite, based on Carlo
Lorenzini's story. Composed 1948. First per-
formance Lugano, 6 June 1948.*

SEIGLE, FERNAND.   Marseilles 1879

978v Cavatine   7'
Solo Vn.-1,1,2,1-2Hn.-Timp.-Str.
Score: Ms. 20 p.
Parts: Decourcelle, Nice, c1926
*Composed 1926.   First performance Monte Carlo,
June 1926, the composer conducting.*

746m Légende
Solo Hn.-2(2nd alt. Picc.),2,2,1-2,2,3,1-Timp.,
Trgl.-Str.
Score: Ms. 36 p.
Parts: Evette, Paris, c1927

SEISS, ISIDOR WILHELM.   Dresden 23 December 1840
                          Cologne 25 September 1905

600c Adagio, Op. 13
Solo Vc.-2,1,1,2-2Hn.-Str.
Schlesinger, Berlin [n.d.]
Score 19 p.

SEITZ, FRIEDRICH.
          Günthersleben, Germany 12 June 1849
          Dessau, Germany 22 May 1918

736v [Concerto, violin, Op. 25, A minor]
In one movement
Solo Vn.-1,1,2,1-2,2-Timp.-Str.
A. Rathke, Madgeburg, c1902
Score 63 p.

SEKLES, BERNHARD.   Frankfurt 20 June 1872
                        Frankfurt 15 December 1934

1356 [The dwarf and the Infanta, suite]   22'
1.Pastorale und Marche miniature 2.[Entry
and dance of the bullfighters] 3.[Boy dancers'
Lady dance] 4.[Hunters' furioso - The dwarf's
dance]
3(3rd alt. Picc.),3(3rd alt. E.H.),3(3rd alt.
B.Cl.),3-4,5(2 backstage),3,1-Timp.,Perc.-Hp.
-Str.
Brockhaus, Leipzig, c1913
Score 83 p.
*From the ballet after Oscar Wilde. First
performance Frankfurt a.M., 1913.*

2174 [Little suite in memory of E.T.A.   20'
Hoffmann, Op. 21]
1.Scherzando, ma non troppo presto 2.Menuetto
3.Intermezzo 4.Allegretto
3(3rd alt. Picc.),3*,3,3-4,3,3,1-Timp.,Perc.-
Hp.-Str.
D. Rahter, Leipzig, c1912
Score 70 p.

2291 Serenade für 11 Soloinstrumente, Op. 14
1.Tema con 9 variazioni 2.Scherzino

3.Divertimento in forma di fuga 4.Intermezzo
5.Finale: Allegro comodo
1,1,1,1-Hn.-Hp.-Str.
D. Rahter, Leipzig, c1907
Score 67 p.

SELBY, WILLIAM.   England 1738
                          Boston December 1798

7041 The lovely lass. Edited by Philip   3'
Weston
High Voice Solo-1,1,2,1-Str.
Concord Music Publishing, New York, c1941
Score in reduction 5 p.
Originally composed for voice and piano.

SELDENECK AFFROSSIMOFF, JOAS VON.

298s Serenade, Op. 4
1.Marcia 2.Andante (Romanza) 3.Scherzo
4.Finale
Str.
Challier, Berlin [n.d.]
Score 39 p.

SELMER, JOHAN PETER.
          Christiania (now Oslo) 20 January 1844
                        Venice 22 July 1910

4277 [Finnish festival music, Op. 31]
3*,2,2,2-4,3,3,1-Timp.,Perc.-Str.
Haakon Zapffe, Christiania/Breitkopf & Härtel,
Leipzig [189-?]
Score 39 p.
Composed 1892.

1039 [In the mountains, Op. 35]   22'
1.[Melancholy and longing] 2.[Norwegian Alp-
horn] 3.[Song and dance]
3*,2,2,2-4,2,3,1-Timp.,Perc.-Str.
E.W. Fritzsch, Leipzig [n.d.]
Score 54 p.
Composed 1892.

6951 [Prometheus, symphonic poem, Op. 50]
3*,2(1st alt. E.H.),2,2-4,4,3,1-Timp.,Perc.-
Hp.-Str.
Constantin Wild's Verlag, Leipzig [1899?]
Score 147 p.
Composed 1898.

4523 Scène funèbre, L'année terrible
1870-1871, Op. 4
3*,2,2,2-4,2,2Cnt.,3,1-Timp.,Perc.-Hp.-Str.
Carl Warmuth, Christiania [1886?]
Score 27 p.
*Inspired by Victor Hugo's poem L'Année Terri-
ble, commemorating the Paris Commune of 1870-71.
Composed 1871. First performance Christiania,
30 September 1871.*

SENFL, LUDWIG.   Zurich(?) ca.1490
                                      Munich 1543

1863s Das Geläut zu Speier [canon,   3'
transcribed by Arcady Dubensky]
Str.
Ms.

Sepaniac, Walter J.

Score 10 p.
This transcription 1935.

SEPANIAC, WALTER J.   Philadelphia 30 April 1923

    7308   The seeker, Op. 38   *ca.12'*
    2(2nd alt. Picc.),3*,3*,3*-4,3,3,1-Timp.,Perc.
    -Hp.-Str.
    Ms. ᶜ1961 by W.J. Sepaniac
    Score 64 p. Large folio
    *Composed 1940. First performance Bucks
    County, Pennsylvania, 9 March 1963, Delaware
    Valley Philharmonic, Henry Kerr Williams
    conductor.*

SERAFINÉ-ALSCHAÚSKY, J. F.

    838m   Im Walde/In the forest
    Solo Hn.-2,2,2,2-4,2,3,1-Timp.,Perc.-Str.
    Score: Ms. 48 p.
    Parts: C.F. Schmidt, Heilbronn a.N., ᶜ1913

SEREBRIER, JOSÉ.
                b. Montevideo, Uruguay 3 December 1938

    2109s [Elegy for strings]   *8'*
    Str.
    Pan American Union, Washington, D.C., ᶜ1956
    by José Serebrier
    Score 14 p.
    *Composed 1954. First performance Montevideo,
    Uruguary, 22 November 1955, National Chamber
    Orchestra, Guido Santórsola conductor.*

    5623   [Symphony no. 1 in one movement]   *20'*
    3*,3*,3*,3*-4,3,3,1-Timp.,Perc.-Org.,Cel.,Hp.-
    Str.
    Ms. [ᶜ1957 by Southern, New York]
    Score 81 p. Large folio
    *Composed 1956-57. First performance Houston,
    4 November 1957, Houston Symphony, Leopold
    Stokowski conductor. Composer received the
    Young Composers Award of Broadcast Music, Inc.
    for this work and his Quartet for Saxophones.*

SERLY, TIBOR.   Losonc, Hungary 25 November 1900

    4894   American elegy   *6'*
    3(3rd alt. Picc.),2,2,2-4,3,3,1-Timp.,Perc.-
    Str.
    Ms. [Modus Associates, Ann Arbor, ᶜ1975]
    Score 21 p. Large folio
    *Based on Taps. Composed 1945. First perform-
    ance Chautauqua, 1948, Chautauqua Festival
    Orchestra, Franco Autori conductor.*

    3752   Colonial pageant, symphonic suite in two
    movements
    3(3rd alt. Picc.),2(2nd alt. E.H.),2(1st alt.
    Cl. in E-flat,2nd alt. B.Cl.),3*-4,3,3,1-
    Timp.,Perc.-Cel.,Hp.-Str.
    Ms.
    Score 81 p. Large folio

    1101m Concerto for trombone and orchestra   *16'*
    1.Allegro moderato 2.Più lento 3.Allegro
    Solo Tbn.-2(2nd alt. Picc.),1,2,1-Hn.-Timp.,
    Perc.-Str.

Ms. [Now published by Southern, New York]
Score 49 p.
*Composed 1952. First performance Chautauqua,
17 August 1952, Davis Shuman soloist.*

    2253s Lament in memory of Béla Bartók,   *8'*
    ML4
    Str.
    Southern Music, New York, ᶜ1963
    Score 12 p.
    *Serly's fourth composition based on his musi-
    cal system, Modus Lascivus. Also called
    Homage to Béla Bartók. Composed 1952. First
    performance Budapest, 1960, Budapest Radio
    Orchestra, the composer conducting.*

    Mischianza. Two suites from the ballet
    3560   First suite   *12'*
    3561   Second suite
    3(3rd alt. Picc.),2(2nd alt. E.H. in Second),
    2(1st alt. Cl. in E-flat&2nd alt. B.Cl. in
    Second),3*-4,3,3,1-Timp.,Perc.-Cel.,Hp.-Str.
    Ms.
    Scores: 60 p., 56 p.
    *From the ballet about the British occupation
    of Philadelphia during the Revolutionary War.
    Commissioned by Catherine Littlefield for the
    Philadelphia Ballet Company. Composed 1936.
    Suites extracted 1937.*

    1189v Rhapsody for viola and orchestra   *10'*
    Solo Va.-2(2nd alt. Picc.),2,2,2-2,2-Timp.,
    Perc.-Hp.-Str.
    Ms. [Now published by Southern, New York]
    Score 39 p.
    *Based on Hungarian folk melodies. Composed
    1947. First performance New York, 27 February
    1948, NBC Symphony Orchestra, the composer
    conducting, Emanuel Vardi soloist.*

    3015   Six dance designs   *13'*
    1.Promenade 2.Dance dialogue 3.Donkeys
    4.Doldrums (Fox trot 1920) 5.Tap dance (Fox
    trot 1934) 6.Dragons
    4*,3*,4*(3rd alt. Cl. in E-flat),3*-4,3,4(4th
    ad lib.),1-Timp.,Perc.-Cel.,Hp.-Str.
    Ms.
    Score 46 p. Large folio
    *Composed 1933. First performance Budapest, 13
    May 1935, Budapest Philharmonic Orchestra, the
    composer conducting.*

    2007s Sonata concertante   *15'*
    1.Moderato 2.Lento 3.Presto
    Str.
    Ms. [ᶜn.d. by Modus Associates, Ann Arbor]
    Score 27 p. Large folio
    *Composed 1935-36. First performance Budapest,
    1936, Budapest Radio Orchestra, the composer
    conducting.*

    3588   [Symphony no. 1, In three movements,   *18'*
    B minor]
    1.Lento - Allegretto 2.Adagio 3.Allegro
    moderato
    4*,3*,4*(3rd alt. Cl. in E-flat),3(3rd alt.
    C.Bn.)-4,3,3,1-Timp.,Perc.-Cel.,Hp.-Str.
    Ms.

Score 115 p.
Composed 1931. First performance Budapest, 13 May 1935, Budapest Philharmonic Orchestra, the composer conducting.

3164 Symphony in two movements [for   14'
band, C major]
1.Moderato 2.Allegretto con grazia
3(3rd alt. Picc.),3*,3*(2nd alt. Cl. in E-flat),3*-4,3,3,1-Timp.,Perc.
Ms.
Score 40 p.
Composed 1932.

4821 Transylvanian rhapsody [original   10'
version]
1.Moderato poco rubato 2.Allegretto grazioso
- Allegro giusto
2,0,1-2,1-Str.
Ms.
Score 26 p.
Composed 1926. First performance Philadelphia, 1932, members of The Philadelphia Orchestra, the composer conducting.

SEROCKI, KAZIMIERZ.   Toruń, Poland 3 March 1922

2219s Sinfonietta per due orchestre   14'
d'archi
1.Allegro 2.Adagio 3.Vivace
Str.(in two sections)
Polskie Wydawnictwo, Kraków, ᶜ1957
Score 75 p.
Composed 1956. First performance Kratowice, Poland, September 1956, string ensembles of the Polish Radio Symphony Orchestra, Jan Krenz conductor. Awarded First Prize in the Polish Radio's Fitelberg Competition for Composers.

SEROV, ALEXANDER NIKOLAIEVICH.
St. Petersburg 23 January 1820
St. Petersburg 1 February 1871

725 [Dance of the Zaporogne Cossacks]   4'
3*,3*,2,3-4,2,3,1-Timp.,Perc.-Str.
Bessel, St. Petersburg [n.d.]
Score 32 p.
Inspired by Nikolai Gogol's Taras Bulba. Composed 1867.

SERVAIS, ADRIEN FRANÇOIS.
Hal, near Brussels 6 June 1807
Hal 26 November 1866

725c [Concerto, violoncello, Op. 5, B minor]
Edited by Hugo Becker
1.Allegro 2.Andante cantabile 3.Allegro
Solo Vc.-2,2,2,2-2,2,3-Timp.-Str.
Score: Ms. 125 p.
Parts: B. Schott's Söhne, Mainz [n.d.]

704c [Concerto, violoncello, Militaire, Op. 18, C minor]
1.Allegro moderato 2.Andante religioso
3.Rondo
Solo Vc.-1,2,2,2-2,2,3-Timp.,Perc.-Str.
Score: Ms. 112 p.
Parts: B. Schott's Söhne, Mainz [n.d.]

429c Fantaisie burlesque (ou le carnaval de
Venise), Op. 9
Solo Vc.-3*,2,2,2-2,2,3-Timp.,Trgl.-Str.
Score: Ms. ᶜ1976 by The Fleisher Collection of Orchestral Music, Free Library of Philadelphia.
51 p. Large folio
Parts and solo: Les fils de B. Schott, Mayence [1850?]

641c Fantaisie sur deux airs russes, Op. 13 6'
Solo Vc.-Str.
Score: Ms. 20 p.
Parts: B. Schott's Söhne, Mainz [n.d.]

755c Morceau de concert, Op. 14
Solo Vc.-2,2,2,2-4,2,3-Timp.-Str.
Les Fils de B. Schott, Mayence [1854?]
Score in reduction 18 p.

1504s La romanesca [16th century dance]
Solo Vc.-Str.
Score: Ms. 8 p.
Parts: F.E.C. Leuckart, Leipzig [n.d.]

SESSIONS, ROGER HUNTINGTON.
b. Brooklyn 28 December 1896

2653 [The black maskers. Suite]   22'
1.Dance (Scene I) 2.Scene (Scene III) 3.
Dirge (Scene IV) 4.Finale (Scene V)
3(1st&2nd alt. Picc.,3rd alt. Fl. in G),3(3rd alt. E.H.),4*(1Cl. in E-flat),3*-4,4,3,1-Timp.,Perc.-Pno.,Org.-Str.
Cos Cob Press, New York, ᶜ1932
Score 109 p.
From the incidental music to Leonid Andreyev's play, composed 1923. First performance of this suite, Cincinnati, 5 December 1930, Cincinnati Symphony Orchestra, Fritz Reiner conductor.

316p Concerto, pianoforte and orchestra   18'
1.Tranquillo - Allegro 2.Adagio 3.Adagio
Solo Pno.-3*,3*,3*(1Cl. in E-flat),3*-4,2,3,1-Timp.,Perc.-Str.
Ms. [Edward B. Marks Music, New York, ᶜ1959]
Score 79 p. Large folio
Commissioned by the Juilliard Musical Foundation. Composed 1956. First performance at Juilliard Festival of American Music, New York, 10 February 1956, Juilliard Orchestra, Jean Morel conductor, Beveridge Webster soloist.

1077v [Concerto, violin, B minor]   29'
1.Largo e tranquillo 2.Scherzo 3.Romanza
4.Molto vivace
Solo Vn.-3(2nd alt. Picc.,3rd alt. Alto Fl.),3*(2nd alt. 2nd E.H.),4*(1Cl. in E-flat, Basset Hn. or Alto Cl.),3*-4,2,2-Timp.,Perc.-Str.(without Vn.)
Edgar Stillman-Kelley Society, ᶜ1937 by Affiliated, New York
Score 98 p.
Composed 1935. First performance Chicago, 8 January 1940, Illinois Symphony Orchestra of the WPA, Izler Solomon conductor, Robert Gross soloist.

Sessions, Roger

6253 Divertimento for orchestra   20'
1.Prelude 2.Aria 3.Toccata 4.Perpetuum
mobile 5.Epilogue
3*,2*,2*,2-2,2,2,1-Timp.,Perc.-Pno.-Str.
Ms. [c1960 by E.B. Marks, New York]
Score 137 p. Large folio
Commissioned by the Portland Symphony Orches-
tra in commemoration of the 100th anniversary
of the State of Oregon. Composed 1959. First
performance Honolulu, 9 January 1965.

6428 Idyll of Theocritus   42'
Sop. Voice Solo-2(2nd alt. Picc.),2*,2*,2-4,2,
3,1-Timp.,Perc.-Cel.,Hp.-Str.
Edward B. Marks Music, New York, c1957
Score 160 p.
Text is Theocritus' Idyll No. 2, The Sorceress,
translated from the Greek by R. C. Trevelyan.
Commissioned by The Louisville Orchestra.
Composed 1956. First performance Louisville,
14 January 1956, The Louisville Orchestra,
Robert Whitney conductor, Audrey Nossaman
soloist.

2652 Symphony for orchestra [E minor]   23'
1.Giusto 2.Largo 3.Allegro vivace
3(3rd alt. Picc.),3(3rd alt. E.H.),4*(1Cl. in
E-flat),3*-4,4,3,1-Timp.,Perc.-Pno.-Str.
Cos Cob Press, New York, c1929
Score 78 p.
Composed 1926-27. First performance Boston,
22 April 1927, Boston Symphony Orchestra,
Serge Koussevitzky conductor.

6430 Symphony no. 3   32'
1.Allegro grazioso 2.Allegro, un poco ruvido
3.Andante sostenuto 4.Allegro con fuoco
3*,3*,4*(1Cl. in E-flat),3*-4,2,3,1-Timp.,
Perc.-Cel.,Hp.-Str.
Edward B. Marks Music, New York, c1962
Score 159 p.
Commissioned by the Koussevitzky Music Founda-
tion and the Boston Symphony Orchestra for the
orchestra's 75th anniversary. Composed 1955-
57. First performance Boston, 6 December
1957, Boston Symphony Orchestra, Charles Munch
conductor.

SEVERN, EDMUND.
              Nottingham, England 10 December 1862
              Melrose, Massachusetts 14 May 1942

1076v [Concerto, violin]   25'
1.Allegro energico 2.Andante espressivo
3.Adagio non troppo - Allegro con fuoco
Solo Vn.-2(2nd alt. Picc.),2(2nd alt. E.H.),2,
2-2,2,3,1-Timp.,Perc.-Str.
Ms.
Score 164 p.
Composed 1908. First complete performance
New York, 7 January 1916, New York Philhar-
monic, Josef Stransky conductor, Maximilian
Pilzer soloist.

2867 Song celestial   10'
3(3rd alt. Picc.),2,2,2-4,3,3,1-Timp.,Perc.-
Hp.-Str.
Ms.

Score 26 p.
Originally composed for violin, piano and
organ, 1904; transcribed for orchestra, 1912.
First performance Blankenbergh, Belgium, 1912,
Théâtre de la Monnaie Orchestra, Edouard Blitz
conductor.

2738 Suite, from old New England   20'
1.Pastoral legend 2.Rustic humoresque
3.Lament 4.Kitchen dance
3*,2(2nd alt. E.H.),3*(B.Cl. ad lib.),3*(C.Bn.
ad lib.)-4,2,3,1-Timp.,Perc.-Hp.-Str.
Ms.
Score 127 p.
Originally composed for violin and piano, 1912.
Transcribed 1919 on commission from John J.
Bishop for the Springfield Music Festival.
First performance Springfield, Massachusetts,
17 May 1919, Metropolitan Opera House Orches-
tra, the composer conducting.

SEVITZKY, FABIEN.
              Vishny Volochok, Russia 29 September 1891
              Athens, Greece 3 February 1967

1171s Russian folk song, freely transcribed
Str.
Ms.
Score 5 p.

SEYBOLD, ARTUR.   Hamburg 6 January 1868
          Weissenfels, near Leipzig 15 December 1948

347s Neckteufelchen, bagatelle, Op. 109
Str.
Rahter, Leipzig, c1903
Score 3 p.

SEYFFARDT, ERNST HERMANN.
                      Krefeld, Germany 6 May 1859
       Garmisch-Partenkirchen, Germany December 1942

659v Phantasiestück, Op. 6
Solo Vn.-2,2,2,2-2Hn.-Timp.-Str.
Score: Ms. 50 p.
Parts: Cranz, Hamburg [n.d.]

SEYMER, JOHN WILLIAM.   Stockholm 21 August 1890
                          Stockholm 17 March 1964

4997 [Miniatures for orchestra]   11'
1.[Summer morning] 2.[At a forest pool]
3.[Everyone in passing]
2(2nd alt. Picc.),1,2,1-2,2,2-Timp.-Str.
Ms.
Score 29 p.

SGAMBATI, GIOVANNI.   Rome 28 May 1841
                              Rome 14 December 1914

389 Berceuse-rêverie, Op. 42 no. 2.   4'
Transcribed by Jules Massenet
2,1*,1,1-Hn.-Timp.-Hp.-Str.
B. Schott's Söhne, Mainz, c1910
Score 12 p.
Originally composed for piano. This version
1890.

534p [Concerto, piano, Op. 15, G minor]　　20'
1.Moderato maestoso　2.Romanza　3.Allegro
animato
Solo Pno.-2,2,2,2-4,2,3,1-Timp.-Str.
B. Schott's Söhne, Mainz [1883]
Score 117 p.

388 [Symphony, Op. 16, D major]　　40'
1.Allegro vivace　2.Andante mesto　3.Scherzo
4.Serenata　5.Finale: Allegro con fuoco
3*,2,2,2-4,2,3,1-Timp.-2Hp.-Str.
B. Schott's Söhne, Mainz [1883]
Score 99 p.
First performance Rome, 28 March 1881.

Te Deum laudamus, andante solenne, Op. 28
760s　Original version: Org. or Harm.-Str.
4342　Transcribed for orchestra: 2,3*,2,2-4,2,3,
1-Timp.-Org.(ad lib.)-Str.
B. Schott's Söhne, Mainz, ᶜ1908
Scores: 5 p., 12 p.
Originally composed 1893.

SHAFFER, SHERWOOD M.
　　　　　b. Beeville, Texas 15 November 1934

333p　Concertante for pianoforte and　　20'
string and woodwind quintets
1.Allegro　2.Adagio　3.Allegro non troppo ma
energico
Solo Pno.-1,1,1,1-Hn.-Str.
Ms.
Score 98 p. Large folio
Composed 1959-60. First performance Philadel-
phia, 29 April 1960, Curtis Wind and String
Quintets, the composer conducting, Michele
Levin soloist.

2147s　Concerto grosso for string orchestra　19'
1.Allegro ma non troppo　2.Adagio molto espressivo　3.Vivace
Str.
Ms.
Score 44 p.
Composed 1957. First performance Philadelphia,
20 February 1958, Curtis Institute of Music
string class, Tashiai Eto conductor.

SHAPERO, HAROLD.　Lynn, Massachusetts 29 April 1920

4142　Nine-minute overture　　9'
3*,3*,3(1Cl. in E-flat),2-4,3,3,1-Timp.,Perc.-
Pno.-Str.
Ms.
Score 47 p. Large folio
Composed 1940. First performance broadcast
from New York, 8 June 1941, CBS Orchestra,
Howard Barlow conductor.

SHAPEY, RALPH.　　Philadelphia 12 March 1921

327m　Concerto, clarinet and chamber group　9'
Solo Cl.-Hn.-B.Dr.,Tom-toms-Pno.-Vn.,Vc.
Ms. Composers Facsimile Edition, New York,
ᶜ1958 by Ralph Shapey
Score 39 p.
Composed 1954 under the Frank Huntington
Beebe Scholarship. First performance New York,

20 March 1955, New York Philharmonic Chamber
Society, the composer conducting, Stanley
Drucker soloist.

6334　Dimensions for soprano and 23　　18'
instruments
Sop. Voice Solo-Fl.(alt. Picc.),Ob.(alt. E.H.)
-Ten.Sax.-Hn.,Tpt.-Timp.,Perc.-Pno.-Cb.
Ms. Composers Facsimile Edition, New York,
ᶜ1961 by Ralph Shapey
Score 87 p. Large folio
Commissioned by the Paul Fromm Music Founda-
tion. Composed 1960. First performance New
York, 13 May 1961, the composer conducting,
Bethany Beardslee soloist.

6333　Incantations for soprano and 10　　22'
instruments
Sop. Voice Solo-Alto Sax.-Hn.,Tpt.-Timp.,Perc.
-Pno.-Vc.
Ms. Composers Facsimile Edition, New York,
ᶜ1963 by Ralph Shapey
Score 92 p. Large folio
Composed 1961. First performance New York,
22 April 1961, Composers' Forum, the composer
conducting, Bethany Beardslee soloist.

SHAPLEIGH, BERTRAM.　　　　Boston 15 January 1871
　　　　　　Washington, D.C. 4 July 1940

4515　Ramayana, suite for orchestra, Op. 45
1.Ayodhya　2.Rama and Sita in the forest
3.The monkey war　4.Mandodari's lament
5.The return to Ayodhya
2(2nd alt. Picc.),2,2,2-4,2,3-Timp.,Perc.-Hp.-
Str.
Breitkopf & Härtel, London, ᶜ1907 by composer
Score 101 p.
Inspired by the Hindu epic, Ramayana.

SHCHEDRIN, RODION KONSTANTINOVICH.
　　　　　b. Moscow 16 December 1932

6587　[Suite, accordion, harp, and strings]
1.Prelude　2.Intermezzo　3.Amoroso　4.Cadenza
e fuga　5.Finale
Accordion-Hp.-Str.(without Va.&Vc.)
Ms.
Score 23 p.
Composed 1961.

SHCHERBACHEV, NIKOLAI VLADIMIROVICH.
　　　　　b. St. Petersburg 24 August 1853

713　Deux idylles　　16'
1.[The shepherd's star, pastoral scene]
2.[Crossing the water, scherzino]
3*,2*,2,2-4Hn.-Timp.,Trgl.-Hp.-Str.
Belaieff, Leipzig, 1887
Score 54 p.

400　Sérénade, Op. 33　　4'30"
3*,2,2,2-4Hn.-Hp.-Str.
Belaieff, Leipzig, 1894
Score 23 p.

Shcherbachev, Vladimir

SHCHERBACHEV, VLADIMIR VLADIMIROVICH.
Warsaw 24 January 1889
Leningrad 5 March 1952

4009 [The storm. Suite from the music to the
film based on Alexander Ostrovsky's play]
7 movements
3(3rd alt. Picc.),3*,3(3rd alt. Cl. in E-flat&
B.Cl.),3(3rd alt. C.Bn.)-4,3,3,1-Timp.,Perc.-
Hp.-Str.
Mussektor, Moscow, 1937
Score 111 p.

2147 [Symphony no. 1, Op. 5, C minor]   30'
In one movement
4(1Alto Fl.,3rd alt. Picc.),3*,4*,3*-4,3,3,1-
Timp.,Perc.-2Hp.-Str.
[Mussektor] Moscow, 1929
Score 98 p.
*Composed 1914-15. First performance St.
Petersburg, 22 October 1916, Alexander Siloti
conductor.*

2966 [Symphony no. 3]
1.Moderato, alla breve - Animato 2.Lento 3.
Allegro molto 4.Lento 5.Allegro con moto
3(3rd alt. Picc.),3*,3(2nd alt. Cl. in E-flat,
3rd alt. B.Cl.&Cl. in E-flat),3*-4,3,3,1-
Timp.,Perc.-Pno.,Cel.,2Hp.-Str.
[Mussektor] Moscow, 1935
Score 129 p.
*Composed 1927-30. First performance Lenin-
grad, 2 February 1932, State Academic Philharmonic Orchestra, the composer conducting.*

SHEBALIN, VISSARION IAKOVLEVICH.
Omsk, Russia 11 June 1902
Moscow 29 May 1963

347m [Concertino for horn and small orchestra,
Op. 14 no. 2]
1.Andante cantabile - Allegro moderato
2.Andante 3.Vivo
Solo Hn.-2,2,2,2-0,2,1-Timp.,Perc.-Hp.-Str.
Sovetskii Kompositor, Moscow, 1960
Score 62 p.
Composed 1930.

3163 [Symphony no. 1, Op. 6, F minor]   50'
1.Moderato tranquillo - Allegro moderato
2.Andante, molto quieto 3.Allegro giusto
3(3rd alt. Picc.),3*,3*,3*-6,3,3,1-Timp.,Perc.
-Cel.-Str.
Mussektor, Moscow/Universal Edition, Vienna,
1932
Score 162 p.
*Composed 1925. First performance Leningrad,
13 November 1926, Leningrad Philharmonic
Orchestra, Konstantin Saradiev conductor.*

3171 [Symphony no. 2, Op. 11, C-sharp   35'
minor]
1.Andante - Allegro 2.Allegro assai - Andante
cantabile - Presto
3(3rd alt. Picc.),3*,3*,3-4,3,3,1-Timp.,Perc.-
Pno.-Str.
[Mussektor] Moscow, 1934
Score 99 p.

*Composed 1929. First performance over radio,
1931, Moscow Orchestra, Vasili Shirinsky conductor.*

SHEDRIN, RODION.
See: SHCHEDRIN, RODION KONSTANTINOVICH.

SHEKHTER, BORIS SEMIONOVICH. Odessa 20 January 1900
Moscow 16 December 1961

2507 [Turkmenia, suite]   15'
1.Allegro giocoso 2.Lento 3.Allegro marciale
3*,2(2nd alt. E.H.),2,2-4,2,3,1-Timp.,Perc.-
Str.
[Mussektor] Moscow, 1933
Score 55 p.
*Composed 1932. First performance Moscow,
1932, Moscow Philharmonic Orchestra, Boris
Khaikin conductor.*

SHENSHIN, ALEXANDER ALEXEIEVICH.
Moscow 18 November 1890
Moscow 18 February 1944

1459 [Gossamer, Op. 2, after K. Balmont's poem]
3,3*,3*,3-4,0,0,1-Cel.,Hp.-Str.
Jurgenson, Moscow [1913]
Score 12 p.

SHEPHERD, ARTHUR.   Paris, Idaho 19 February 1880
Cleveland 12 January 1958

731p Fantaisie [revised]   18'
Solo Pno.-3*,2,2,2-4,2,3,1-Timp.,Perc.-Str.
Ms.
Score 106 p.
*Original title: Fantaisie Humoresque. Com-
posed 1912; later revised. First performance
of this version Cleveland, 18 November 1920,
Cleveland Orchestra, the composer conducting,
Heinrich Gebhard soloist.*

1962 Horizons, four Western pieces   43'
3(3rd alt. Picc.),3*,3*,3*-Ten.Sax.-4,5,3,1-
Timp.,Perc.-Pno.,Org.,Cel.,2Hp.-Str.
C.C. Birchard [n.p.] 1929 by The Juilliard
Musical Foundation
Score 157 p.
*Completed 1927. First performance Cleveland,
19 December 1929, Cleveland Orchestra,
Nicolai Sokoloff conductor.*

1961 Overture to a drama   17'
3(3rd alt. Picc.),3*,3*,3-4,3,3,1-Timp.,Perc.-
2Hp.(2nd ad lib.)-Str.
C.C. Birchard, Boston, ᶜ1925
Score 67 p.
Completed 1919.

SHOSTAKOVICH, DMITRI DMITRIEVICH.
St. Petersburg 25 September 1906
Moscow 9 August 1975

2970 L'Age d'Or, Op. 22 [The Golden Age,   20'
ballet suite]
1.Introduction 2.Adagio 3.Polka 4.Danse
2*,2*,3*(1Cl. in E-flat),2*-Sop.Sax.-4,3,3,
Bar.,1-Timp.,Perc.-Harm.-Str.

Shostakovich, Dmitri

[Mussektor] Moscow, 1935
Score 66 p.
From the ballet composed 1929-30. First per-
formance Leningrad, 26 October 1930.

Babi Yar symphony
See: Symphony no. 13...

2969 [The bolt, Op. 27. Suite]
1.Introduction 2.Polka 3.Variation 4.Tango
5.Intermezzo 6.Finale
3*(2nd alt. Picc.II),3*,4*(1Cl. in E-flat),3*
-6,3,3,1-Timp.,Perc.-Str.-Band(ad lib.,Finale
only):2Tpt.,3Cnt.,2Alto Hn.,2Tbn.,2Bar.,2Tuba
Ms.
Score 86 p. Large folio
From the ballet composed 1930-31. First per-
formance Leningrad, 8 April 1931.

698p [Concerto, piano, no. 1, Op. 35,   22'
C minor]
1.Allegro moderato 2.Lento 3.Moderato
4.Allegro brio
Solo Pno.-Tpt.-Str.
[Mussektor] Moscow, 1934
Score 59 p.
Composed 1933. First performance Leningrad,
15 October 1933, Leningrad Philharmonic Orches-
tra, Fritz Stiedry conductor, the composer as
soloist.

290p [Concerto, piano, no. 2, Op. 102]   19'
1.Allegro 2.Andante 3.Allegro
Solo Pno.-3*,2,2,2-4Hn.-Timp.,Mil.Dr.-Str.
Sovetskii Kompozitor, Moscow, 1957
Score 102 p.
Composed 1957. First performance Moscow, 10
May 1957, Nikolai Anosov conductor, Maxim
Dmitrievich Shostakovich soloist.

335v [Concerto, violin, Op. 99]   35'
1.[Nocturne] 2.[Scherzo] 3.Passakalia
4.Burleska
Solo Vn.-3(3rd alt. Picc.),3(3rd alt. E.H.),3
(3rd alt. B.Cl.),3(3rd alt. C.Bn.)-4Hn.,Tuba-
Timp.,Perc.-Cel.,2Hp.-Str.
State Music Publishers, Moscow, 1957
Score 129 p.
Composed 1947-48. First performance Lenin-
grad, 29 October 1955, Leningrad Philharmonic,
Eugene Mravinsky conductor, David Oistrakh
soloist.

412c [Concerto, violoncello, Op. 107]   27'
1.Allegretto 2.Moderato 3.Cadenza 4.Allegro
con moto
Solo Vc.-2(2nd alt. Picc.),2,2,2(2nd alt.
C.Bn.)-Hn.-Timp.-Cel.-Str.
State Music Publishers, Moscow, 1960
Score 73 p.
Composed 1959. First performance Leningrad,
4 October 1959, Leningrad Philharmonic,
Eugene Mravinsky conductor, Mstislav Rostro-
povich soloist.

7249 [Festival overture, Op. 96]
3*,3,3,3*-8,6,6,1-Timp.,Perc.-Str.
Kalmus, New York [n.d.]

Score 55 p.
Composed 1954.

3702 Five preludes. Arranged by Lan   7'
Adomian
3(alt. 3Picc.),3(3rd alt. E.H.),3*,3*-4,3,3,1-
Timp.,Perc.-Pno.-Str.
Ms.
Score 54 p.
Nos. 20, 7, 21, 14 and 6 of 24 Preludes for
piano, Op. 34, composed 1932-33. Arranged
1936.

6347 [Hamlet. Suite from the music to   20'
Shakespeare's tragedy, Op. 32]
1.[Introduction and night watch] 2.[Funeral
march] 3.[Flourish and dancing music] 4.
[Desire] 5.[Actors' pantomime] 6.[Procession]
7.Muzykalnaia pantomima 8.[The banquet] 9.
[Ophelia's song] 10.[Cradle song] 11.[Requiem]
12.[Tournament] 13.Marsh Fortinbrasa
1,1,1,1-2,2,1,1-Timp.,Perc.-Str.
Sovetskii Kompozitor, Moscow, 1960
Score 104 p.
Composed 1931. First performance Moscow, 1931.
Shostakovich wrote other music for a film ver-
sion of Hamlet in 1963.

3748 Lady Macbeth of Mtsensk. Three   10'
fragments transcribed by Quinto Maganini
1.Burying the corpse in the cellar 2.The
ghost disappears 3.The drunks at the wedding
3*,2(2nd alt. E.H.),2,2-4,2,3,1-Timp.,Perc.-
Str.
Edition Musicus, New York, ᶜ1940 by composer
Score 15 p.
From the opera composed 1930-32, based on
Nicolai Leskov's short story. Transcribed
1940. Opera later retitled Katerina Ismailova.

2968 Les monts d'or [The golden mountains,
Op. 30. Suite from the music to the film]
1.Introduction 2.Valse 3.Fugue 4.Intermezzo
5.Marche funèbre 6.Finale
3*,3*,3*,3*-3Sax.(SAT)-8,4,4,2-Timp.,Perc.-
Org.,2Hp.,Hawaiian Guit.-Str.
[Mussektor] Moscow, 1935
Score 77 p.
Composed 1931.

2971 [The nose. Suite, Op. 15]
1.Ouverture 2.Intermezzo 3.Galop
1*,1,1(Cl. in E-flat),2*-1,1,1-Perc.-Pno.,2Hp.
-Str.
Ms.
Score 64 p.
From the opera based on Gogol's short story.
Composed 1927-28. First performance Lenin-
grad, 13 January 1930, Leningrad Philharmonic
Orchestra, Nikolai Malko conductor.

6349 Ovod [The gadfly. Suite]   22'30"
1.Overture 2.Contradance 3.Folk feast
4.Interlude 5.Waltz "Barrel-organ" 6.Galop
7.Introduction 8.Romance 9.Intermezzo 10.
Nocturne 11.Scene 12.Finale
3*,3,3(all alt. Alto Sax.),3*-4,4,3,1-Timp.,
Perc.-Pno.,Cel.,Hp.-Str.

Shostakovich, Dmitri

State Music Publishers, Moscow, 1960
Score 165 p.
*From the music to the film based on the novel
by Ethel L. Voynich. Composed 1955.*

4987 [Prelude, piano, Op. 34 no. 14,   2'30"
E-flat minor. Transcribed by Leopold Sto-
kowski]
3,3*,4*,4*-4,4,4,1-Timp.,Perc.-Hp.-Str.
Broude Brothers, New York, c1948 by Stokowski
Score 8 p.
From Twenty-four Preludes, composed 1932-33.

1743 [Symphony no. 1, Op. 10, F minor]   25'
1.Allegretto - Allegro non troppo 2.Allegro
3.Lento 4.Allegro molto
3*,2;2,2-4,3,3,1-Timp.,Perc.-Pno.-Str.
Kalmus, New York [n.d.]
Score 92 p.
*Composed 1926. First performance Leningrad,
12 May 1926, Leningrad Philharmonic Orchestra,
Nicolai Malko conductor.*

2497 [Symphony no. 2, October, Op. 14, B major]
In one movement
3*,2,2,2-4,3,3,1-Timp.,Perc.-Chorus(SATB)-Str.
[Mussektor] Moscow, 1927
Score 85 p.
*Text is a poem by A. Bezimensky. Composed
1927 for the Tenth Anniversary of the October
Revolution. First performance Leningrad, 6
November 1927, Leningrad Philharmonic Orches-
tra and Chorus, Nikolai Malko conductor.*

2469 [Symphony no. 3, The first of May,   28'
Op. 20, E-flat major]
1.Allegretto - Allegro 2.Andante 3.Allegro
molto 4.Moderato
3*,2,2-4,2,3,1-Timp.,Perc.-Chorus(SATB)-Str.
[Mussektor] Moscow, 1932
Score 102 p.
*Composed 1929. First performance Leningrad,
21 January 1930.*

6443 [Symphony no. 4, Op. 43]   50'
1.Allegretto poco moderato - Presto 2.Moderato
con moto 3.Largo - Allegro
6*(2 are Picc.),4(4th alt. E.H.),6*(1Cl. in
E-flat),4*-8,4,3,2-Timp.(2 players),Perc.-Cel.,
2Hp.-Str.
Score: Sovetskii Kompozitor, Moscow, 1962,
227 p.
Parts: Kalmus, New York [n.d.]
*Composed 1935-36. Rehearsed for performance
in December 1936 by the Leningrad Philharmonic,
Fritz Stiedry conductor, but withdrawn by the
composer before the premiere. First performance Moscow, 30 December 1961, Moscow Philharmonic, Kiril Kondrashin conductor.*

2482 [Symphony no. 5, Op. 47, D minor]   47'
1.Moderato 2.Allegretto 3.Largo 4.Allegro
non troppo
3*,2,3(1Cl. in E-flat),3*-4,3,3,1-Timp.,Perc.-
Pno.,Cel.,2Hp.-Str.
Kalmus, New York [n.d.]
Score 165 p.
Composed 1937. First performance Leningrad,

*21 November 1937, Leningrad Philharmonic
Orchestra, Eugene Mravinsky conductor.*

3999 [Symphony no. 6, Op. 54, B minor]
1.Largo 2.Allegro 3.Presto
3*,3*,4*(3rd alt. Cl. in E-flat),3(3rd alt.
C.Bn.)-4,3,3,1-Timp.,Perc.-Cel.,Hp.-Str.
[Mussektor] Leningrad, 1941
Score 150 p.
*Composed 1939. First performance Leningrad,
5 November 1939.*

4000 [Symphony no. 7, Leningrad, Op. 60,   86'
C major]
1.Allegretto 2.Moderato (poco allegretto)
3.Adagio 4.Allegro non troppo
3*2nd alt. Alto Fl. in G,3rd alt. Picc.),3*,4*
(3rd alt. Cl. in E-flat),3*-4,3,3,1-Timp.,Perc.
-Pno.,2Hp.-Str.
State Music Publishers, Moscow, 1942
Score 177 p.
*Composed 1941. First performance Kuibyshev,
5 March 1942, Bolshoi Theatre Orchestra,
Samuel Samosud conductor. Awarded the Stalin
Prize 1942.*

5843 [Symphony no. 8, Op. 65]   60'
1.Adagio - Allegro non troppo 2.Allegretto
3.Allegro non troppo 4.Largo 5.Allegretto
4(3rd&4th alt. Picc.I&II),3*,4*(1Cl. in E-flat),
3(3rd alt. C.Bn.)-4,3,3,1-Timp.,Perc.-Str.
State Music Publishers, Moscow, 1946
Score 181 p.
*Composed 1943. First performance Moscow, 4
November 1943, State Symphony Orchestra of the
USSR, Eugene Mravinsky conductor.*

5785 [Symphony no. 9, Op. 70]   24'
1.Allegro 2.Moderato 3.Presto 4.Largo
5.Allegretto
3*,2,2,2-4,2,3,1-Timp.,Perc.-Str.
Breitkopf & Härtel, Leipzig, c1947
Score 79 p.
*Composed 1944-45. First performance Leningrad,
3 November 1945, Leningrad Philharmonic,
Eugene Mravinsky conductor.*

6363 [Symphony no. 10, Op. 93]   50'
1.Moderato 2.Allegro 3.Allegretto 4.Andante
- Allegro
3*(2nd alt. Picc.II),3(3rd alt. E.H.),3(3rd
alt. Cl. in E-flat),3(3rd alt. C.Bn.)-4,3,3,1-
Timp.,Perc.-Str.
State Music Publishers, Moscow, 1954
Score 219 p.
*Composed 1953. First performance Leningrad,
17 December 1953, Leningrad Philharmonic
Orchestra, Eugene Mravinsky conductor.
Received the New York Music Critics Circle
Award, 1953.*

5935 [Symphony no. 11, The year of 1905,   60'
Op. 103]
Played without pause: 1.[The palace square]
2.[The 9th of January] 3.[In memoriam]
4.[The tocsin]
3(3rd alt. Picc.),3(3rd alt. E.H.),3(3rd alt.
B.Cl.),3(3rd alt. C.Bn.)-4,3,3,1-Timp.,Perc.-

Sibelius, Jean

Cel.,2 to 4Hp.-Str.
State Music Publishers, Moscow, 1958
Score 238 p.
*Inspired by the unsuccessful Russian revolt of
1905. Commissioned for the 40th anniversary
of the Russian Revolution of 1917. Composed
1956-57. First performance Moscow, 30 Octo-
ber 1957, State Symphony Orchestra of the
USSR, Nathan Rakhlin conductor. Awarded the
Lenin Prize.*

6518 [Symphony no. 12, The year 1917, *ca.40'*
Op. 112]
Played without pause: 1.Revolutionäres Petrograd 2.[The rising] 3.Aurora 4.[Dawn of
humanity]
3(3rd alt. Picc.),3,3,3(3rd alt. C.Bn.)-4,3,
3,1-Timp.,Perc.-Str.
Breitkopf & Härtel, Leipzig, 1962
Score 191 p.
*Commemorates the beginning of the Russian
Revolution. Aurora was the ship from which
the first shots of the Revolution were fired.
Composed 1961. Simultaneous first performances, Leningrad and Kuibyshev, 1 October
1961. Leningrad performance, Leningrad Philharmonic, Eugene Mravinsky conductor.*

6966 [Symphony no. 13, Babi Yar, Op. 113] *56'*
1.Babi Yar 2.Humor 3.In the store 4.Fears
5.Careers
Bass(Bar.) Voice Solo,Male Chorus-3*,3(3rd alt.
E.H.),3(3rd alt. Cl. in E-flat&B.Cl.),3*(C.Bn.
alt. 3rd)-4,3,3,1-Timp.,Perc.-Pno.,Cel.,2 to 4
Hp.-Str.
Ms. Leeds (Canada), Ontario, C1970
Score 223 p. Large folio
*Words by Yevgeny Yevtushenko. Composed 1961.
First performance Moscow, 18 December 1962.*

6980 [Symphony no. 14, Op. 135] *50'*
1.De profundis 2.Malagueña 3.Lorelei 4.The
suicide 5.On watch 6.Madam, look! 7.In
prison 8.The Zaporozhian cossacks' answer to
the Sultan of Constantinople 9.O Delvig,
Delvig 10.The death of the poet 11.Conclusion
Soprano&Bass Voice Solos-Perc.-Cel.-Str.(10Vn.,
4Va.,3Vc.,2Cb.)
Ms.
Score 153 p.
*Poems by Federico García Lorca (nos. 1, 2),
Guillaume Apollinaire (nos. 3-8), Wilhelm Kar-
lovich Küchelbecker (no. 9), Rainer Maria
Rilke (nos. 10, 11). Composed 1969. First
performance Leningrad, 29 September 1969,
Moscow Chamber Orchestra, Rudolph Barshai con-
ductor, Galina Vishnevskaya, soprano, Mark
Rezhetin, bass.*

1112s [Two pieces for string octet, Op. 11]
1.Prelude 2.Scherzo
Str.(without Cb.)
Mussektor, Moscow, 1928
Score 38 p.
Composed 1924-25.

SHULMAN, ALAN.   Baltimore, Maryland 4 June 1915

2392s Threnody for string orchestra   *5'30"*
Str.
Tetra Music Corp., New York, C1974
Score 8 p.
Originally composed for string quartet, 1950.

SIBELIUS, JEAN.
                 Tavastehus, Finland 8 December 1865
       Järvenpää, near Helsinki 20 September 1957

Born: Johan Julius Christian Sibelius

2077s Andante festivo   *5'*
Timp.(ad lib.)-Str.
Oy. R.E. Westerlund, Helsinki, C1941
Score 4 p.
*Originally composed for string quartet, 1922.
This version 1924.*

2177s Arioso, Op. 3
Voice Solo-Str.
Oy. R.E. Westerlund, Helsinki, C1951, C1960
Score 11 p.
*Text is J. L. Runeberg's poem The Maiden's
Seasons. Composed 1893. Revised 1911.*

1492 Autrefois, scène pastorale,   *4'*
Op. 96b. Edited by Julia A. Burt
2,0,2,2-2Hn.-Timp.-Str.
W. Hansen, Copenhagen, C1923
Score 10 p.
*Composed 1920. First performance Helsinki,
1921.*

753 Der Barde, Op. 64   *5'*
2,2,3*,2-4,2,3-Timp.,Perc.-Hp.-Str.
Breitkopf & Härtel, Leipzig, C1914
Score 19 p.
*Composed 1913. First performance Helsingfors,
1913.*

326 [Belshazzar's feast, Op. 51. Suite,   *15'*
Belsazar] Revised by Paul Juon
1.Oriental procession 2.Solitude 3.Night
music 4.Khadra's dance
2(2nd alt. Picc.),1,2-2Hn.-Perc.-Str.
Schlesinger, Berlin, C1907
Score 18 p.
*From the incidental music to Hjalmar Procopé's
play. Composed 1906.*

59s Canzonetta, Op. 62a
Str.
Breitkopf & Härtel, Leipzig, C1911
Score 7 p.
*Composed 1911. First performance Helsingfors,
3 April 1911.*

7141 Canzonetta, Op. 62a. Arranged by Igor
Stravinsky
Cl.,B.Cl.-4Hn.-Hp.-Cb.
Breitkopf & Härtel, Wiesbaden, C1964
Score 8 p.
*This arrangement made after Stravinsky was
awarded the Wihuri-Sibelius Prize in 1963.
First performance, 22 March 1964, Finnish
Broadcasting Company.*

Sibelius, Jean

470v [Concerto, violin, Op. 47, D minor]   30'
  1.Allegro moderato 2.Adagio di molto
  3.Allegro, ma non tanto
  Solo Vn.-2,2,2,2-4,2,3-Timp.-Str.
  Luck's, Detroit [n.d.]
  Score 67 p.
  Composed 1903-04; revised 1905. First per-
  formance of this version, Berlin, 19 October
  1905, Karl Halir soloist.

885v Devotion (Ab imo pectore), Op. 77   6'
  no. 2. Edited by Julia A. Burt
  Solo Vn.-2,0,2,2-4,0,3-Str.
  W. Hansen, Copenhagen, C1923
  Score 11 p.
  Composed 1913. First performance Helsingfors,
  1914.

198 Die Dryade, Op. 45 no. 1   6'
  3*,2,3*,2-4,3,3,1-Perc.-Str.
  Breitkopf & Härtel, Leipzig, C1910
  Score 23 p.
  Composed 1910. First performance Helsingfors,
  1910.

84 Finlandia, Op. 26 no. 7   8'
  2,2,2,2-4,3,3,1-Timp.,Perc.-Str.
  Breitkopf & Härtel, Wiesbaden [n.d.]
  Score 25 p.
  Composed 1899. First performance Helsingfors,
  2 July 1900, Helsingfors Philharmonic.

Four legends from the Kalevala, Op. 22
  See: [Lemminkäinen suite...]

396v [Humoresque no. 1, Op. 87 no. 1]   3'30"
  Solo Vn.-2,2,2,2-2Hn.-Timp.-Str.
  W. Hansen, Copenhagen, C1942
  Score 15 p.
  Composed 1917.

597v Humoresque no. 2, Op. 87 no. 2.   8'
  Edited by Julia A. Burt
  Solo Vn.-2Hn.-Timp.-Str.
  W. Hansen, Copenhagen, C1923
  Score 14 p.

679v Humoresque no. 3, Op. 89a. Edited   8'
  by Julia A. Burt
  Solo Vn.-Str.
  W. Hansen, Copenhagen, C1923
  Score 25 p.
  Op. 89 composed 1917.

607v Humoresque no. 4, Op. 89b. Edited   8'
  by Julia A. Burt
  Solo Vn.-Str.
  W. Hansen, Copenhagen, C1923
  Score 7 p.

394v [Humoresque no. 5, Op. 89 no. 3]   3'
  Edited by Julia A. Burt
  Solo Vn.-2,0,2,2-Str.
  W. Hansen, Copenhagen, C1922
  Score 11 p.

393v [Humoresque no. 6, Op. 89 no. 6]   2'30"
  Edited by Julia A. Burt

Solo Vn.-2Fl.,2Bn.-Str.
  W. Hansen, Copenhagen, C1923
  Score 11 p.

4318 [In memoriam, funeral march, Op. 59]   10'
  2,3*,3*,3*-4,3,3,1-Timp.,Perc.-Str.
  Breitkopf & Härtel, Leipzig, C1910
  Score 36 p.
  In memory of the Finnish patriot Eugen Schau-
  man, who assassinated the Russian Governor-
  General of Finland in 1904. Composed 1909.
  First performance Helsingfors, 3 April 1911,
  the composer conducting.

344 Karelia-Ouvertüre, Op. 10   8'
  3*,2,2,2-4,3,3,1-Timp.,Perc.-Str.
  Breitkopf & Härtel, Leipzig, C1906
  Score 33 p.

958 Karelia-Suite, Op. 11   14'
  1.Intermezzo 2.Ballade 3.Alla marcia
  3*,2(1st alt. E.H.),2,2-4,3,3,1-Timp.,Perc.-
  Str.
  Breitkopf & Härtel, Leipzig, C1906
  Score 43 p.
  Composed 1893. First performance Helsingfors,
  1893, the composer conducting.

1199 [King Christian II, Op. 27. Suite]   24'
  1.Nocturne 2.Élégie et musette 3.Serenade
  4.Ballade
  2,2,2,2-4,2,3-Timp.,Perc.-Str.
  Breitkopf & Härtel, Leipzig, C1899
  Score 64 p.
  From the incidental music to Adolf Paul's
  play, composed 1897. First performance
  Helsingfors, 1898.

734v Laetare anima mea [Rejoice, my soul]   7'
  Op. 77a. Edited by Julia A. Burt
  Solo Vn.-2,0,2-2Hn.-Timp.-Hp.-Str.
  W. Hansen, Copenhagen, C1922
  Score 13 p.
  Composed 1913. First performance Helsingfors,
  1914.

[Lemminkäinen suite (Four legends), Op. 22]
4998 No. 1 [Lemminkäinen and the maidens
  of the island]   15'30"
  2(both alt. Picc.),2,2,2-4,3,3-Timp.,Perc.-Str.
4999 No. 2 Lemminkäinen in Tuonela   14'30"
  2,2*,2*,2-4,3,3-Perc.-Str.
582 No. 3 The swan of Tuonela   9'
  Solo E.H.-0,1,1*,2-4,0,3-Timp.,B.Dr.-Hp.-Str.
726 No. 4 [Lemminkäinen's return]   7'
  2Picc.,2,2,2-4,3,3,1-Timp.,Perc.-Str.
  1 & 2: Breitkopf & Härtel, Wiesbaden, C1954
  3 & 4: Breitkopf & Härtel, Leipzig, C1901
  Scores: 69 p., 55 p., 16 p., 66 p.
  Lemminkäinen is a hero of the Finnish national
  epic, Kalevala. Composed 1895. First per-
  formance 13 April 1896, the composer con-
  ducting. Revised 1897; further revisions
  1900 and 1939.

1015 Night-ride and sunrise, Op. 55   15'
  3*,2,3*,3*-4,2,3,1-Timp.,Perc.-Str.
  Schlesinger, Berlin, C1909

Score 47 p.
Composed and first performed Helsingfors,
1907, the composer conducting.

103 Die Okeaniden/Aallottaret, Op. 73   *14'*
3*,3*,3*,3*-4,3,3-Timp.,Perc.-2Hp.-Str.
Breitkopf & Härtel, Leipzig, ^C1915
Score 35 p.
Commissioned by Carl Stoeckel for the 28th
Norfolk Festival. Composed 1913. First per-
formance Norfolk, Connecticut, 4 June 1914,
the composer conducting.

468 Pan und Echo, Tanz-Intermezzo,   *5'*
Op. 53a [revised version]
2(2nd alt. Picc.),2,2,2-4,2,3-Timp.,Perc.-Str.
Schlesinger, Berlin [n.d.]
Score 14 p.
Composed and first performed Helsingfors,
1906, the composer conducting. Revised 1909.

259 [Pelleas and Melisande, suite, Op. 46] *18'*
1.At the castle gate 2.Melisande 2a.At the
seashore 3.A spring in the park 4.The three
blind sisters 5.Pastorale 6.Melisande at the
spinning-wheel 7.Entr'acte
1(alt. Picc.),1(alt. E.H.),2,2-2Hn.-Timp.,
Perc.-Str.
Kalmus, New York [n.d.]
Score 33 p.
From the incidental music to Maurice Maeter-
linck's play. Composed 1905.

952 [Pohjola's daughter, Op. 49]   *12'*
3*,3*,3*,3*-4,2,2Cnt.,3,1-Timp.-Hp.-Str.
Schlesinger, Berlin, ^C1906
Score 46 p.
Inspired by the Finnish national epic Kalevala.
Composed 1904.

364s Rakastava [The lover, suite, Op. 14] *15'*
1.Rakastava [The lover] 2.[The lovers' path]
3.[Good evening - Farewell!]
Timp.,Trgl.-Str.
Breitkopf & Härtel, Leipzig, ^C1913
Score 15 p.

58s Romanze in C, Op. 42
Str.
Breitkopf & Härtel, Leipzig, ^C1909
Score 7 p.
Composed 1903.

752 [A saga, Op. 9]   *20'*
2(2nd alt. Picc.),2,2,2-4,3,3,1-Perc.-Str.
[Kalmus, New York, n.d.]
Score 85 p.
Composed 1891. First performance Helsingfors,
16 February 1893, the composer conducting.

5335 Scaramouche, Op. 71. Edited by   *56'*
Julia A. Burt
In 3 groups, 1 backstage: 2(2nd alt. Picc.),
2,2,2-4Hn.,Cnt.-Timp.,Perc.-Pno.-Str.
W. Hansen, Copenhagen, ^C1918
Score 230 p.
Complete music to the tragic pantomime in two
acts by Poul Knudsen and Mikael Trepka Bloch.

Commissioned by Wilhelm Hansen. Composed 1913.
First performance Copenhagen, 12 May 1922.

Scènes historiques I-III, Op. 25
1075 I.   All'overtura   *5'*
1103 II. Scena   *5'*
1144 III. Festivo   *5'*
2(both alt. Picc. in Nr.2),2,2,2-4,3,3-Timp.,
Perc.-Str.
Breitkopf & Härtel, Leipzig, ^C1912
Scores: 18 p., 39 p., 69 p.
Composed 1899. First performance Helsingfors,
1899, the composer conducting.

104 Scènes historiques IV-VI, Op. 66   *17'*
IV. The chase, overture V.Love-song
VI.At the drawbridge
3*,2,2,2-4Hn.-Timp.,Perc.-Hp.-Str.
Breitkopf & Härtel, Leipzig, ^C1913
Score 40 p.
Composed 1911. First performance Helsingfors,
1912, the composer conducting.

727 [Spring song, Op. 16]   *12'*
2(alt. 2Picc.),2,2,2-4,3,3,1-Timp.,Bells-Str.
Breitkopf & Härtel, Leipzig, ^C1903
Score 26 p.
Composed 1894.

270s Suite champêtre, Op. 98b [Rustic suite]
Edited by Julia A. Burt
1.Pièce caractéristique 2.Mélodie élégiaque
3.Danse
Str.
W. Hansen, Copenhagen, ^C1923
Score 11 p.
Composed 1921.

1455s Suite mignonne, Op. 98a
1.Petite scène 2.Polka 3.Epilogue
2Fl.-Str.
Score: Ms. 41 p.
Parts: Chappell, London, ^C1921
Composed 1921.

The swan of Tuonela
    See: [Lemminkäinen suite (Four legends),
        Op. 22. No. 3, The swan of Tuonela]

327 Swanehvit [Suite, Op. 54]   *30'*
1.The peacock 2.The harp 3.The maiden with
the roses 4.Listen, the robin sings 5.The
prince alone 6.Swanehvit and the prince
7.Song of praise
2,2,2,2-4Hn.-Timp.,Perc.-Hp.-Str.
Schlesinger, Berlin, ^C1909
Score 50 p.
From the incidental music to August Strind-
berg's play. Composed 1908.

688 [Symphony no. 1, Op. 39, E minor]   *45'*
1.Andante ma non troppo - Allegro energico
2.Andante 3.Scherzo 4.Finale (quasi una
fantasia)
2(alt. 2Picc.),2,2,2-4,3,3,1-Timp.,Perc.-Hp.-
Str.
Kalmus, New York [n.d.]
Score 160 p.

Sibelius, Jean

*Composed 1899. First performance Helsingfors,
26 April 1899.*

689 [Symphony no. 2, Op. 43, D major]   *46'*
1.Allegretto 2.Andante, ma rubato 3.Viva-
cissimo 4.Finale: Allegro moderato
2,2,2,2-4,3,3,1-Timp.-Str.
Breitkopf & Härtel, Leipzig, ^C1903, 1931
Score 145 p.
*Composed 1902. First performance Helsingfors,
8 March 1902, the composer conducting.*

980 [Symphony no. 3, Op. 52, C major]   *27'*
1.Allegro moderato 2.Andantino con moto,
quasi allegretto 3.Allegro (ma non tanto)
2,2,2,2-4,2,3-Timp.-Str.
[Schlesinger, Berlin, n.d.]
Score 70 p.
*Composed 1904-07. First performance Helsing-
fors, 25 September 1907, the composer conducting.*

83 [Symphony no. 4, Op. 63, A minor]   *33'*
1.Tempo molto moderato, quasi adagio 2.Alle-
gro molto vivace 3.Il tempo largo 4.Allegro
2,2,2,2-4,2,3-Timp.,Bells-Str.
Breitkopf & Härtel, Leipzig, ^C1912
Score 68 p.
*Composed 1909-10. First performance Helsing-
fors, 3 April 1911, the composer conducting.*

1939 [Symphony no. 5, Op. 82, E-flat   *27'*
major] Edited by Julia A. Burt
1.Tempo molto moderato - Allegro moderato -
Presto 2.Andante mosso, quasi allegretto
3.Allegro molto - Misterioso
2,2,2,2-4,3,3-Timp.-Str.
W. Hansen, Copenhagen, ^C1921
Score 136 p.
*Composed 1914. First performance Helsingfors,
8 December 1915, the composer conducting.*

1967 [Symphony no. 6, Op. 104, D minor]   *32'*
1.Allegro molto moderato 2.Allegretto
moderato 3.Poco vivace 4.Allegro molto
2,2,3*,2-4,3,3-Timp.-Hp.-Str.
Hirsch, Stockholm [n.d.]
Score 87 p.
*Composed 1923. First performance Helsinki,
19 February 1923, the composer conducting.*

1940 [Symphony no. 7, Op. 105, C major]   *22'*
Edited by Julia A. Burt
In one movement
2,2,2,2-4,3,3-Timp.-Str.
W. Hansen, Copenhagen, ^C1925
Score 76 p.
*Composed 1924. First performance Helsinki,
1925, the composer conducting.*

199 Tanz-Intermezzo, Op. 45 no. 2   *4'*
2,1,2,1(or 1,0,2)-4,2(or 2,2,1)-Timp.,Perc.-
Hp.-Str.
Breitkopf & Härtel, Leipzig, ^C1907
Score 23 p.
*Composed and first performed Helsingfors, 1909,
the composer conducting.*

5057 Tapiola, Op. 112   *16'*
3(3rd alt. Picc.),3*,3*,3*-4,3,3-Timp.-Str.
Ms. [Breitkopf & Härtel, Leipzig, ^C1926]
Score 58 p. Large folio
*Inspired by stories of Tapio, the forest god
in the Finnish national epic Kalevala. Com-
missioned by the New York Symphony Society.
Composed 1925. First performance New York,
26 December 1926, New York Symphony Orchestra,
Walter Damrosch conductor.*

2158 [The Tempest, Op. 109. No. 1,   *5'*
Prelude]
3*,2,3*(1Cl. in E-flat),2-4,3,3,1-Timp.,Perc.-
Str.
W. Hansen, Copenhagen, ^C1929
Score 25 p.
*From the incidental music to Shakespeare's
play. Commissioned by the Royal Theater,
Copenhagen. Composed 1926. First performance
Copenhagen, 16 March 1926.*

5333 [The Tempest. Suite no. 1, Op. 109b]   *20'*
1.[The oak tree] 2.Humoreske 3.Caliban's
Lied 4.[The harvesters] 5.Canon 6.Scène
7.Intrada - Berceuse 8.[Entr'acte - Ariel's
song] 9.Der Sturm
3(3rd alt. Picc.),2,3*(2nd alt. Cl. in E-flat),
2-4,3,3,1-Timp.,Perc.-Hp.-Str.
W. Hansen, Copenhagen, ^C1929
Score 77 p.

5316 [The Tempest. Suite no. 2, Op. 109c]   *16'*
1.Chor der Winde 2.Intermezzo 3.Tanz der
Nymphen 4.Prospero 5.Lied I 6.Lied II
7.Miranda 8.[The Naiads] 9.Tanz-Episode
2,2,2(2nd alt. B.Cl.),2-4Hn.-Timp.,Perc.-Hp.-
Str.
W. Hansen, Copenhagen, ^C1929
Score 50 p.

[Two serenatas, Op. 69]
642v Serenata I, Op. 69a [D major]   *10'*
643v Serenata II, Op. 69b [G minor]   *8'*
Solo Vn.-2,2,2,2-4Hn.-Timp.(&Trgl. in II)-Str.
Breitkopf & Härtel, Leipzig, ^C1913
Scores: 23 p., 35 p.
Composed 1912-13.

791 Valse chevaleresque, Op. 96c.   *4'*
Edited by Julia A. Burt
2,2,2,2-4,2,3-Timp.,S.Dr.-Str.
W. Hansen, Copenhagen, ^C1922
Score 35 p.

790 Valse lyrique, Op. 96a. Edited by   *5'*
Julia A. Burt
2,2,2,2-4,2,3-Timp.,Trgl.-Str.
W. Hansen, Copenhagen, ^C1922
Score 31 p.
*Composed 1920. First performance Helsinki,
1921.*

85 Valse romantique, Op. 62b   *5'*
2,0,2-2Hn.-Timp.-Str.
Breitkopf & Härtel, Leipzig, ^C1911
Score 27 p.
*Composed 1910. First performance Helsingfors,
1911.*

49 Valse triste, Op. 44, from the music   6'
to Arvid Järnefelt's drama Kuolema
1,0,1-2Hn.-Timp.-Str.
Breitkopf & Härtel, Leipzig, ^c1904
Score 11 p.
*Composed 1910. First performance Helsingfors,
1910, the composer conducting.*

SICCARDI, HONORIO.   Buenos Aires 13 September 1897
                       Buenos Aires 10 September 1963

3881 Buenos Aires, suite sinfónica
1.Plaza Constitución 2.Vals del café 3.Inter-
mezzo (Tempo di tango) 4.Calle Corrientes
5.Marcha de los atletas 6.Atardecer en
Parque Patricios 7.Mirajes 8.Invocación al
porvenir
3*,3*,3(3rd alt. B.Cl.),3(3rd alt. C.Bn.)-4,3,
2,1-Timp.,Perc.-Pno.,Cel.,Hp.-Contralto Voice-
Str.
Ms.
Score 119 p.
Composed 1935.

1150v [Concerto, violin, C major]
1.Optimismo 2.Saudades [Longing] 3.Joke
Solo Vn.-3(3rd alt. Picc.),3(3rd alt. E.H.),
3(3rd alt. B.Cl.),3(3rd alt. C.Bn.)-4,2,3,1-
Timp.,Perc.-Pno.,Cel.,Hp.-Str.
Ms.
Score 115 p. Large folio
Composed 1942.

5524 [Puppets, suite in 10 movements]   12'
2(1st alt. Picc.),1,2(2nd alt. B.Cl.),2(2nd
alt. C.Bn.)-1,1-Perc.
Ms.
Score 32 p. Large folio
*From the ballet composed 1936. First perform-
ance Buenos Aires, probably 1936, Asociación
General de Músicos de la Argentina, Jacobo
Ficher conductor. Awarded first prize from
the city of Buenos Aires.*

SIEGL, OTTO.   Graz, Austria 6 October 1896

1628s Kleine Unterhaltungsmusik [Music   22'
for entertainment] Op. 69
1.March 2.Adagio [Resignation] 3.[Round
dance] 4.Canzonetta 5.Rondo - Finale
Pno.-Str.(Cb. ad lib.)
Tonger, Cologne, ^c1930
Score 37 p.

4991 Lyrische Tanzmusik, Op. 82   17'
2,2,2,2-2,1-Timp.-Pno.(ad lib.)-Str.
Universal Edition, Vienna, ^c1936
Score 83 p.

1423s Sinfonietta, Op. 63   30'
1.Praeludium 2.Elegie 3.Marsch 4.Scherzo
5.Finale
Str.
Benno Filser, Augsburg, ^c1929
Score 41 p.
Composed 1928.

SIEGMEISTER, ELIE.   New York 15 January 1909

2708 American holiday [revised]   10'30"
1(alt. Picc.),1(alt. E.H.),1,1-1,1,1-Timp.,
Perc.-Pno.-Str.
Ms.
Score 80 p.
*Original title: May Day. Originally composed
for large orchestra, 1933. This version 1933.
First performance New York, 16 October 1933,
American Chamber Orchestra, Lan Adomian con-
ductor. Revised 1971.*

3137 Rhapsody   12'
2(2nd alt. Picc.),2(2nd alt. E.H.),2(2nd alt.
B.Cl.),2-4,2,3,1-Timp.,Perc.-Str.
Ms.
Score 61 p. Large folio
Composed 1937.

741c The strange funeral in Braddock   7'30"
Solo Bar. Voice(or Solo Vc.)-3*,3*,2,3*-4,3,3,
1-Timp.,Perc.-Pno.-Str.
Ms.
Score 40 p. Large folio
*Originally composed for voice and piano, 1933.
Transcribed 1938.*

3184 A Walt Whitman overture For You,   11'
O Democracy
2,2(2nd alt. E.H.),2,2-2,2,1-Timp.,Perc.-Hp.-
Str.
Ms.
Score 61 p. Large folio
*Composed 1939. First performance over radio,
New York, 31 March 1940, WNYC Concert Orches-
tra, the composer conducting. First concert
performance Rochester, 27 October 1943, East-
man-Rochester Symphony Orchestra, Howard
Hanson conductor.*

SIEMONN, GEORGE.   Baltimore 12 February 1874
                       New York 21 November 1952

5293 Aspirations   17'
3(3rd alt. Picc.),3*,3*,2-4,3,3,1-Timp.,Perc.-
Str.
Ms.
Score 48 p.
*Composed 1933. First performance Baltimore,
25 February 1934, Baltimore Symphony Orchestra,
the composer conducting.*

5294 Carnival time   14'
3*,2,3*,2-4,2,3,1-Timp.,Perc.-Str.
Ms.
Score 72 p.
*First performance Baltimore, 11 January 1925,
Baltimore Symphony Orchestra.*

456c Legend for 'cello and orchestra
Solo Vc.-3,2,3*,2-4,2,3,1-Timp.-Str.
Ms.
Score 35 p.
Composed 1910.

5386 Pioneers   23'
3*,3*,3*,3*-4,3,3,1-Timp.,Perc.-Str.

Siemonn, George

Ms.
Score 54 p.

5690 Three pictures for orchestra   24'
1.Mountains 2.The desert 3.The city
3(3rd alt. Picc.),3*,3*,2-4,2,3,1-Timp.,Perc.-
Hp.-Str.
Ms.
Score 70 p.
*Composed 1914. First performance Baltimore,
15 January 1933, Baltimore Symphony Orchestra.*

5691 Youth overture
2,2,2,2-4,2,3,1-Timp.-Str.
Ms.
Score 49 p.

SIEP, WILLEM FREDERIK.
                Arnhem, Netherlands 21 November 1866
                Nice(?), France 19 March 1926

1360s Impression de Mai
Str.
Alsbach, Amsterdam [n.d.]
Score 3 p.
*Transcribed from Op. 1, Four Bagatelles for
piano.*

SIGNORINI, ANTONIO RICCI.
See: RICCI-SIGNORINI, ANTONIO.

SIKLÓS, ALBERT.   Budapest 26 June 1878
                             Budapest 2 April 1942

Born: Albert Schönwald; changed name in 1910

1614s Csinom Palkó
Str.(Cb. ad lib.)
Rozsnyai, Budapest [n.d.]
Score 5 p.

1613s Hej, Rákóczi, Bercsényi!
Str.(Cb. ad lib.)
Rozsnyai, Budapest [n.d.]
Score 3 p.

1727 [Suite no. 3, Op. 37, F major]
1.Allegretto 2.Andante con moto 3.Alle-
gretto con grazia 4.Andante cantabile
5.Tempo di gavotto
2,2,2,2-2Hn.-Hp.-Str.
Rozsnyai, Budapest [n.d.]
Score 26 p.

SILIÉZAR, FELIPE.   Guatemala City 1 May 1903

3617 Hechizo Maya [Bewitching Maya]   6'
Op. 73
3*,2,2,2-4,2,3,1-Timp.,Perc.-Str.
Ms.
Score 19 p.
No. 2 of the suite Maya, composed 1935.

SILVA, JESÚS BERMÚDEZ.
See: BERMÚDEZ-SILVA, JESÚS.

SILVER, CHARLES.   Paris 16 April 1868
                           Paris 10 October 1949

5726 [Sleeping Beauty. Symphonic suite]
1.Rêverie de la princesse 2.Divertissement
3.Urgèle et ses gnomes 4.La chasse
3(3rd alt. Picc.),3*,3*,2-4,3,3-Timp.,Perc.-
Cel.,Hp.-Str.
Choudens, Paris, C1901 by L. Grus
Score 81 p.
*From the opera based on Charles Perrault's
fairy tale. First performance Marseilles,
1902.*

SILVER, MARK.   Pinsk, Russia 1892
                Newark, New Jersey 23 January 1965

6308 Funeral march (symphonic poem)   15'
3(3rd alt. Picc.),3*,3*,3*-4,2,3,1-Timp.,Perc.
-Str.
Ms.
Score 55 p.
*Also known as Marcia Funebre. Depicts a
Jewish funeral procession in a small Russian
town. Composed 1915-16. First performance
May 1920, New Symphony Orchestra, Artur
Bodanzky conductor.*

3121 Peace and war, symphonic poem   25'
3*,3*,3*,3*-4,4,3,1-Timp.,Perc.-Str.
Ms.
Score 129 p.
*Composed 1918. First performance Rochester,
1 May 1925, Rochester Philharmonic Orchestra,
Howard Hanson conductor.*

SIMON, ANTON IULIEVICH.   France 5 August 1850
                St. Petersburg 1 February 1916

46s Berceuse
Str.
Otto Junne, Leipzig [n.d.]
Score 11 p.

2007 Danse de bayadères, fantaisie, Op. 34
3*,2,2,2-4,2,3,1-Timp.,Perc.-Str.
Jurgenson, Moscow [1891]
Score 43 p.

1118s Plainte élégiaque, Op. 38 no. 1
Str.
Score: Ms. 5 p.
Parts: Jurgenson, Moscow [1915?]

1724 La revue de nuit, Op. 36
3*,2,2,3*-4,2,2Cnt.,3,1-Timp.,Perc.-Str.
Jurgenson, Moscow [1890]
Score 85 p.
Inspired by Shukovsky's ballad.

SIMONETTI, ACHILLE.   Turin, Italy 12 June 1857
                          London 19 November 1928

687s Minuetto
Str.
Score: Ms. 6 p.
Parts: B. Schott's Söhne, Mainz, C1904

646v Romanza   3'
Solo Vn.-0,0,2,2-2Hn.-Str.
Score: Ms. 4 p.

758

Parts: Ricordi, Milan, ^c1914
Composed 1890. Orchestrated 1913. First performance Dublin, 1914.

1557s Ronde joyeuse
Str.
Score: Ms. 9 p.
Parts: Ricordi, Milan, ^c1920

1156s Sérénade
Str.
Score: Ms. 7 p.
Parts: Decourcelle, Nice, ^c1906

SIMONINI, UGO.

1214s Oubliée [Forgotten] menuet
Str.
Score: Ms. 4 p.
Parts: Decourcelle, Nice, ^c1914

SINDING, CHRISTIAN.
           Kongsberg, Norway 11 January 1856
           Oslo 3 December 1941

530v Abendstimmung/Evening harmonies, Op. 120
Solo Vn.-2,2,2,2-4Hn.-Timp.-Hp.-Str.
Breitkopf & Härtel, Leipzig, ^c1915
Score 15 p.

457p [Concerto, piano, Op. 6, D-flat   *36'*
major] Revised edition
1.Allegro non troppo 2.Andante 3.Allegro non assai
Solo Pno.-2,2,2,2-4,2,3,1-Timp.-Str.
W. Hansen, Copenhagen [n.d.]
Score 148 p.
Composed 1887-88. First performance Berlin, 1890.

488v [Concerto, violin, no. 1, Op. 45,   *20'*
A major]
In one movement
Solo Vn.-2,2,2,2-4,2-Timp.-Str.
W. Hansen, Copenhagen [n.d.]
Score 53 p.

491v [Concerto, violin, no. 2, Op. 60, D major]
1.Allegro non troppo 2.Andante 3.Finale: Allegro
Solo Vn.-2,2,2,2-4,2-Timp.-Hp.-Str.
C.F. Peters, Leipzig [1897?]
Score 115 p.

5680 Episodes chevaleresques, Op. 35
1.Tempo di marcia 2.Andante funebre 3.Allegretto 4.Finale: Allegro moderato
4*(2 are Picc.),2,3,3*-4,3,3,1-Timp.,Perc.-Hp.-Str.
C.F. Peters, Leipzig [1899]
Score 103 p.
Composed 1888.

752v Legende, Op. 46   *8'*
Solo Vn.-2,2,2,2-4,2-Timp.-Hp.-Str.
W. Hansen, Copenhagen [n.d.]
Score 43 p.

406v Romanze, Op. 100
Solo Vn.-2,2,2,2-4,2-Timp.-Hp.-Str.
Breitkopf & Härtel, Leipzig, ^c1910
Score 23 p.

792 Rondo infinito, Op. 42   *7'*
3(3rd alt. Picc.),2,2,2-4,3,3,1-Timp.,Perc.-Str.
W. Hansen, Copenhagen, ^c1898
Score 65 p.
Inspired by Holger Drachmann's poem. Composed 1897. First performance Berlin, 1899.

603 [Rustle of spring, Op. 32 no. 3.   *3'*
Orchestrated by Hans Sitt]
2,2,2,2-4,2,3,1-Timp.,Glock.-Hp.-Str.
C.F. Peters, Leipzig [n.d.]
Score 31 p.
Originally composed for piano. This version 1905. First performance Berlin, 1906.

465v [Suite, violin, Op. 10, A minor]   *15'*
1.Presto 2.Adagio 3.Tempo giusto
Solo Vn.-2,2,2,2-2Hn.-Hp.-Str.
C.F. Peters, Leipzig [n.d.]
Score 38 p.
Composed 1887. First performance Berlin, 1888.

155 [Symphony no. 1, Op. 21, D minor.   *40'*
Revised version]
1.Allegro moderato 2.Andante 3.Vivace 4.Allegro
3*,2,2,2-4,3,3,1-Timp.-Str.
C.F. Peters, Leipzig [n.d.]
Score 164 p.
Composed 1889. Revised 1893.

602 [Symphony no. 2, Op. 83, D major]
1.Allegro moderato 2.Andante 3.Allegro 4.Andante - Tempo I
3(3rd alt. Picc.),2,2,2-4,3,3,1-Timp.,Perc.-Str.
Simrock, Berlin, ^c1907
Score 134 p.

1267 [Symphony no. 3, Op. 121, F major]   *35'*
1.Con fuoco 2.Andante 3.Allegro 4.Non troppo allegro
3(3rd alt. Picc.),2,2,2-4,3,3,1-Timp.,Perc.-Str.
C. F. Peters, Leipzig [n.d.]
Score 227 p.
Composed 1892. First performance Berlin, 1893.

SINGER, EDMUND.
           Totis (Tata), Hungary 14 October 1830
           Stuttgart 23 January 1912

945v Tarantella, Op. 6
Solo Vn.-3*,2,2,2-2,2-Timp.,Perc.-Str.
Score: Ms. 57 p.
Parts: Kistner, Leipzig [1856]

SINGER, OTTO, JR.   Dresden 14 September 1863
           Leipzig 8 January 1931

483p [Concerto, piano, Op. 8, A major]
In one movement

Singer, Otto Jr.

Solo Pno.-3*,2,2,2-4,2,3,1-Timp.,Perc.-Str.
F.E.C. Leuckart, Leipzig, ^c1905
Score: Ms. 165 p.

749v Concertstück, Op. 6 [D major]
Solo Vn.-2,2,2,2-2,2-Timp.-Str.
F.E.C. Leuckart, Leipzig [n.d.]
Score 31 p.

SINIGAGLIA, LEONE.   Turin, Italy 14 August 1868
                          Turin 16 May 1944

481v [Concerto, violin, Op. 20, A major]
1.Allegro risoluto 2.Adagio 3.Allegro vivo
e con grazia
Solo Vn.-2,2,2,2-4,2-Timp.-Str.
Breitkopf & Härtel, Leipzig, ^c1903
Score 83 p.
*Composed 1899. First performance Berlin, 1901,
Berlin Philharmonic, Arrigo Serato soloist.*

Danze piemontesi, sopra temi popolari, Op. 31
574   No. 1 Andantino mosso - Allegro   5'
giocoso
3*,2,2,2-4,2-Timp.-Hp.-Str.
1491 No. 2 Allegro con brio   9'
3*,2,2,2-4,2,3-Timp.,Perc.-Str.
Breitkopf & Härtel, Leipzig, ^c1907
Scores: 20 p., 49 p.
*Composed 1903. First performance Turin, 14
May 1905, Arturo Toscanini conductor.*

5171 [Lament in memory of a young artist
(Natale Canti), Op. 38]
2,3*,2,2-4,2-Timp.,Tam-tam-Org.(or C.Bn.),Hp.-
Str.
Breitkopf & Härtel, Leipzig, ^c1930
Score 23 p.
Composed 1928.

15   [Overture to Goldoni's comedy Le   7'
Baruffe Chiozzotte, Op. 32]
3*,2,2,2-4,2,3-Timp.,Perc.-Str.
Breitkopf & Härtel, Leipzig, ^c1908
Score 51 p.
*Composed 1905. First performance Utrecht, 21
December 1907, Wouter Hutschenruyter conductor.*

65   Piemonte, suite sopra temi popolari,   28'
Op. 36
1.Through fields and woods 2.A rustic dance
3.In montibus sanctis 4.Carnevale piemontese
3*,3*,2,2-4,2,3-Timp.,Perc.-Hp.-Str.
Breitkopf & Härtel, Leipzig, ^c1912
Score 155 p.
*Composed 1909. First performance Utrecht, 16
February 1910, Wouter Hutschenruyter conductor.*

609v Rapsodia piemontese, Op. 26
Solo Vn.-2,2,2,2-4,2-Timp.-Str.
Breitkopf & Härtel, Leipzig, ^c1905
Score 21 p.

561v Romanze, Op. 29
Solo Vn.-2,2,2,2-4Hn.-Timp.-Str.
Breitkopf & Härtel, Leipzig, ^c1906
Score 11 p.

Romanze and humoreske, Op. 16
488c No. 1 Romanze
Solo Vc.-2,1,2,2-4Hn.-Timp.-Str.
480c No. 2 Humoreske
Solo Vc.-3*,2,2,2-4,2-Timp.-Str.
Rahter, Leipzig [n.d.]
Scores: 14 p., 46 p.

550s Scherzo, Op. 8   3'30"
Str.(without Cb.)
Ricordi, Milan [n.d.]
Score 7 p.

141s Zwei Charakterstücke, Op. 35
1.[Rain song] 2.Étude-caprice
Str.
Breitkopf & Härtel, Leipzig, ^c1910
Score 13 p.

SIQUEIRA, JOSÉ DE LIMA.
              b. Conceição, Brazil 24 June 1907

5170 [The awakening of Ariel]   10'
3,3*,3*,2-4Hn.-Xyl.-2Hp.-Str.
Ms.
Score 40 p.
*Suggested by Shakespeare's play The Tempest.
Composed 1939.*

4835 [Brazilian dance no. 2]   3'
3*,3*,3*,2-4,3,3,1-Timp.,Perc.-Pno.-Str.
Ms.
Score 24 p.
*Based on Brazilian samba themes. Composed
1941.*

4877 [Brazilian dance no. 4]   4'
3*,3*,3*,2-Alto Sax.-4,3,3,1-Timp.,Perc.-Pno.,
Cel.-Str.
Ms.
Score 30 p.
*Composed 1940. First performance Rio de Ja-
neiro, ca.1940, Orquestra Sinfônica Brasileira,
the composer conducting.*

3872 [Brazilian dawn, symphonic poem]   8'
3*,2(2nd alt. E.H.),2,2-4,3,3,1-Timp.,Perc.-
Hp.-Str.
Ms.
Score 39 p.
Received an award from the city of São Paulo.

4168 Mêdo, [Fear, prelude for orchestra]   4'
3*,2,2,2-4,3,3,1-Timp.,Perc.-Str.
Ms.
Score 15 p.
*Composed 1934. First performance Rio de Janei-
ro, 1937, the composer conducting.*

5562 Os pescadores [The fishermen, sym-   18'
phonic poem]
3*,2,3*,2-4,3,3,1-Timp.,Perc.-Hp.-Str.
Ms.
Score 54 p.
*Inspired by the poem by Alvaro de Alencastre
(b.1875). Composed 1934.*

4161 [Scenes of the Brazilian northeast. 8'
Original version]
3*,3*,2,2-4,3,3,1-Timp.,Perc.-Cel.,Hp.-Str.
Ms.
Score 45 p.
This version composed 1941. Revised 1951.

SITT, HANS.   Prague 21 September 1850
       Leipzig 10 March 1922

858v [Concerto, viola, Op. 68, A minor]
In one movement
Solo Vn.-2,2,2,2-2,2,3-Timp.-Str.
Eulenburg, Leipzig, c1900
Score in reduction 25 p.

1139v [Concerto, violin, no. 1, Op. 11,
D minor] Edited by Adolf Brodsky
1.Allegro moderato 2.Andante 3.Finale
(Tarantella)
Solo Vn.-2(2nd alt. Picc.),2,2,2-4,2,3-Timp.-
Str.
Score: Ms. 224 p.
Parts: Breitkopf & Härtel, Leipzig [n.d.]

701v [Concerto, violin, no. 2, Op. 21, A minor]
1.Allegro moderato 2.Andante tranquillo
3.Moderato - Allegro con fuoco
Solo Vn.-2,2,2,2-4,2,3-Timp.-Str.
F.E.C. Leuckart, Leipzig [1884]
Score 71 p.

828v [Concerto, violin, no. 3, Op. 111, D minor]
1.Allegro moderato 2.Andante sostenuto
3.Allegro ma non troppo
Solo Vn.-2,2,2,2-4,2,3,1-Timp.-Str.
Eulenburg, Leipzig, c1912
Score 79 p.

701c [Concerto, violoncello, no. 2, Op. 38,
D minor]
1.Allegro un poco agitato 2.Andante 3.Allegro
Solo Vc.-2,2,2,2-4,2,3-Timp.-Str.
Score: Ms. 154 p.
Parts: Eulenburg, Leipzig [n.d.]

564v Concertstück, Op. 46 [G minor]
Solo Va.-2,2,2,2-2,2,3-Timp.-Str.
Eulenburg, Leipzig [n.d.]
Score 43 p.

1365s Gavotte, Op. 113 no. 3
Str.
Fazer, Berlin, c1912
Score 5 p.

539v Nocturne
Solo Vn.-2,0,2,2-2Hn.-Timp.-Str.
Score: Ms. 22 p.
Parts: Breitkopf & Härtel, Leipzig [n.d.]

1s Spinning song, Op. 95 no. 11
Str.
O. Forberg, Leipzig, c1908
Score 7 p.

Wiegenlied und Gavotte, Op. 48
64s No. 1 Wiegenlied [Cradle song]

797s No. 2 Gavotte
Str.
Bosworth, Leipzig, c1892
Scores: 5 p., 7 p.

SIVORI, ERNESTO CAMILLO.   Genoa 25 October 1815
      Genoa 19 February 1894

1271s Romance sans paroles, Op. 23 no. 1
Solo Vn.-Str.
Score: Ms. 6 p.
Parts: Joh. André, Offenbach a.M. [n.d.]

SKILTON, CHARLES SANFORD.
   Northampton, Massachusetts 16 August 1868
     Lawrence, Kansas 12 March 1941

732c American Indian fantasie 12'
Solo Vc.-3(3rd alt. Picc.),3*,3*,3*-4,3,3,1-
Timp.,Perc.-Hp.-Str.
Ms.
Score 41 p.
Originally composed for organ, 1920. Transcribed 1929. First performance Interlochen, Michigan, 14 August 1932, National High School Orchestra, Vladimir Bakaleinikov conductor, Philip Abbas soloist.

2654 Autumn night 5'
3(3rd alt. Picc.),3*,3*,3*-4Hn.-Timp.-Str.
Ms.
Score 14 p.
This and Shawnee Indian Hunting Dance (Catalog no. 2655) were originally composed 1922 as movements of Sonata no. 2 in G minor for violin and piano. This version 1930. First performance Detroit, 11 December 1930, Detroit Symphony Orchestra, Ossip Gabrilowich conductor.

2656 Overture in E major 8'
3(3rd alt. Picc.),3*,3*,3*-4,3,3,1-Timp.,Perc.
-Hp.-Str.
Ms.
Score 42 p.
Composed 1931. First performance Rochester, 28 March 1934, Rochester Philharmonic Orchestra, Howard Hanson conductor.

2655 Shawnee Indian hunting dance 4'
3(3rd alt. Picc.),3*,3*,3*-4,3,3,1-Timp.,Perc.
-Hp.-Str.
Ms.
Score 18 p.
See the composer's Autumn Night.

1946 [Suite primeval. Part I, Two 10'
Indian dances]
1.Deer dance (Rogue River, Oregon) 2.War
dance (Cheyenne)
3*,2(2nd alt. E.H.),2,2-4,3,3,1-Timp.,Perc.-
Hp.-Str.
C. Fischer, New York, c1917
Score 28 p.
Originally composed for string quartet, 1915. Transcribed 1916. First performance Minneapolis, 29 October 1916, Minneapolis Symphony Orchestra, Emil Oberhoffer conductor.

Skilton, Charles

1947 [Suite primeval. Part II]   25'
1.Sunrise song (Winnebago) 2.Gambling song
(Rogue River, Oregon) 3.Flute serenade
(Sioux) 4.Moccasin game (Winnebago)
3(3rd alt. Picc.),3*,3*,3*-4,3,3,1-Timp.,Perc.
-Str.
C. Fischer, New York, ^C1921
Score 84 p.
*Based on tribal Indian melodies. Composed
1920. First performance Minneapolis, 13
November 1921, Minneapolis Symphony Orchestra,
Emil Oberhoffer conductor.*

SKÖLD, KARL YNGVE.   Vallby, Sweden 29 April 1899

815p [Concerto, piano, no. 2, Op. 46]   30'
1.Moderato - Allegro non troppo 2.Andante
3.Allegro deciso
Solo Pno.-2,2,2,2-4,2,3,1-Timp.-Str.
Ms.
Score 129 p.
*Composed 1946. First performance Göteborg,
Sweden, 8 October 1947, Swedish Broadcasting
Orchestra, Tor Mann conductor, Greta Eriksson
soloist.*

1197v [Concerto, violin, Op. 40]   28'
1.Allegro moderato 2.Andante 3.Allegro
scherzando
Solo Vn.-2,2,2,2-2,2,1-Timp.,Perc.-Str.
Ms. [Edition Suecia, Stockholm, ^C1947]
Score 104 p.
*Composed 1941. First performance Bad Homburg,
West Germany, August 1948, Bad Homburg Kur-
orchester, Senta Bergman soloist.*

396m [Concerto, violin, violoncello and   28'
orchestra, Op. 52]
1.Moderato e deciso 2.Andantino 3.Allegro
moderato
Solo Vn., Solo Vc.-2(2nd alt. Picc.),2,2,2-2,2,
1-Timp.-Str.
Ms.
Score 84 p.
*Composed 1950. First performance Malmö, Swe-
den, 11 January 1955.*

5028 Sinfonia da chiesa, Op. 38, D major   24'
1.Fantasia 2.All' improvisato 3.Fughetta
4.Passacaglia
2(2nd alt. Picc.),2,2,2-2,2,1-Timp.-Org.-Str.
Ms.
Score 72 p.
*First performance Stockholm, 26 September
1937, Concert Society of Stockholm, Adolf Wiklund conductor, Lince Berglund organist.
Passacaglia available separately as Catalog
no. 7239.*

2172s [Suite no. 2, Op. 48]   24'
1.Largo - Allegro moderato 2.Lento 3.Giga
Str.
Ms.
Score 37 p.
*Composed 1947. First performance Hälsingborg,
Sweden, 3 October 1951.*

5014 [Symphony no. 3, Op. 50]   33'
1.Moderato, ma risoluto 2.Adagio 3.Allegro
scherzando 4.Allegro non troppo
2(2nd alt. Picc.),2(2nd alt. E.H.),2,2-4,2,3-
Timp.-Str.
Ms.
Score 124 p.
*Composed 1948. First performance Norrköping,
Sweden, 26 February 1949, Norrköping Orches-
tra Society, Heinz Freudenthal conductor.*

SKOP, V.F.

357s [Suite, strings, Op. 15, A major]
1.Praeludium 2.Ländler 3.[Slow waltz]
4.Andante con variazioni 5.Finale
Pno.,Harm.-Str.
Chr. Fr. Vieweg, Berlin [n.d.]
Score 52 p.

SKRIABIN, ALEXANDER NIKOLAIEVICH.
                              Moscow 6 January 1872
                              Moscow 27 April 1915

375p [Concerto, piano, Op. 20, F-sharp   27'
minor]
1.Allegro 2.Andante 3.Allegro moderato
Solo Pno.-3*,2,2,2-4,2,3-Timp.-Str.
Belaieff, Leipzig, 1898
Score 67 p.
Composed 1896.

1933s [Nuances, piano, Op. 56 no. 3. Tran-
scribed by Modest Altschuler]
Str.
Ms.
Score 1 p.
Composed for piano, 1906 or 1907.

330 Le poème de l'extase, Op. 54   24'
4*,4*,4*,4*-8,5,3,1-Timp.,Perc.-Org.,Cel.,2Hp.
-Str.
Belaieff, Leipzig, 1908
Score 101 p.
*Composed 1908. First performance New York, 10
December 1908, Russian Symphony Society,
Modest Altschuler conductor.*

398 Rêverie, Op. 24   3'
2,2,2,2-4,2,3,1-Timp.-Str.
Belaieff, Leipzig, 1899
Score 15 p.
*Composed 1898. First performance Moscow, 24
March 1899, Vassily Safonov conductor.*

859 [Symphony no. 1, Op. 26, E major]   45'
1.Lento 2.Allegro dramatico 3.Lento
4.Vivace 5.Allegro 6.Andante
3(3rd alt. Picc.),2,3,2-4,3,3,1-Timp.,Bells-
Hp.-Mezzo Sop., Ten. Voices, Chorus(SATB)-Str.
Belaieff, Leipzig, 1900
Score 129 p.
*Composed 1899. First performance Moscow, 29
March 1901, Vassily Safonov conductor.*

860 [Symphony no. 2, Op. 29, C minor]   50'
1.Andante - Allegro giocoso 2.Allegro
3.Andante - Più vivo, poco agitato 4.Tempes-
toso 5.Maestoso

3(3rd alt. Picc.),2,3,2-4,3,3,1-Timp.,Gong-Str.
Belaieff, Leipzig, 1903
Score 183 p.
*Composed 1901. First performance St. Peters-
burg, 25 January 1902, Anatol Liadov con-
ductor.*

394 [Symphony no. 3, The divine poem,   *38'*
Op. 43, in C]
Lento - Luttes [Struggles] - Voluptés - Jeu
divin [Divine game]
4*,4*,4*,4*-8,5,3,1-Timp.,Perc.-2Hp.-Str.
Belaieff, Leipzig, 1905
Score 207 p.
*Composed 1904. First performance Paris, 29
May 1905, Arthur Nikisch conductor.*

1108s Trois préludes. Transcribed by   *6'30"*
Th. Hartmann
1.Op. 11 no. 4: Lento   2.Op. 11 no. 5: Andante
3.Op. 11 no. 15: Lento
Solo Va. or Vc.(no. 1), Solo Vn.(no. 2)-Str.
Belaieff, Leipzig, 1928
Score in reduction 7 p.
*Op. 11, Twenty-four Preludes, originally com-
posed for piano.*

5899 Two etudes. Arranged by LaSalle Spier   *6'*
1.Op. 2 no. 1: Andante   2.Op. 8 no. 12:
Patetico
3*,2,2,2-4,3,3,1-Timp.,Perc.-Hp.-Str.
Ms. ᶜ1960 by LaSalle Spier
Score 21 p.
*Originally composed for piano, Op. 2 in 1886
or 1887, Op. 8 in 1894 or 1895. This transcription by the National Symphony Orchestra, 1940. First performance
Washington, 24 November 1940, National Symphony Orchestra, Hans Kindler conductor.*

SKROWACZEWSKI, STANISŁAW.
            b. Lwów, Poland 3 October 1923

2217s [Symphony for strings, Op. 25]   *22'*
1.Adagio - Allegro   2.Adagio un poco mosso
3.Presto
Str.
Polskie Wydawnictwo, Cracow, ᶜ1956
Score 37 p.
*Composed 1948. First performance Paris,
April 1949, Chamber Orchestra of the Radio-
Diffusion Française, André Girard conductor.
Awarded second prize in the International Com-
petition for Composition, Belgium, 1953.*

SLAVENSKI, JOSIP.   Cakovec, Yugoslavia 11 May 1896
                  Belgrade 30 November 1955

2521 Balkanophonia, Op. 10   *18'*
1.Danse serbe   2a. Chanson albanaise   2b.
Danse des derviches   3a.Chanson grecque   3b.
Danse roumaine   4.Ma chanson   5.Danse bulgare
2(2nd alt. Picc.),2(2nd alt. E.H.),2,2-4,2,3 -
Timp.,Perc.-Hp.-Str.
B. Schott's Söhne, Mainz, ᶜ1928
Score 51 p.
*First performance Berlin, 25 January 1929,
Prussian State Orchestra, Erich Kleiber con-
ductor.*

SLONIMSKY, NICOLAS.   St. Petersburg 27 April 1894

3693 Fanfare, for the WPA Music   *2'*
Copying Project of the Free Library of Phila-
delphia. Edited by Arthur Cohn
2,2,3(1Cl. in E-flat),3*-4,2-Perc.-Cel.-Str.
Ms.
Score 8 p.
Commissioned by Arthur Cohn. Composed 1942.

4030 Fanfarria habanera [to awaken those   *2'*
who have been out all night]
1*,0,2(1Cl. in E-flat)-Hn.-Perc.
Ms.
Score 7 p.
*Composed 1933. First performance Havana, 30
April 1933, Havana Philharmonic Orchestra, the
composer conducting.*

3419 Four simple pieces   *7'*
1.Little overture   2.Dreams and drums   3.Music
box   4.Automobile waltz
2(2nd alt. Picc.),0,2-2Tpt.-Timp.,Bells-Str.
Coleman-Ross, New York, ᶜ1955
Score 19 p.
*Originally composed for piano, 1930 as Four
Compositions for Young People. Transcribed
1931. First performance St. Paul's School,
Concord, New Hampshire, 16 November 1931, Chamber Orchestra of Boston, the composer conducting.*

3859 Little march for the Big Bowl   *2'*
(Marche grotesque). Edited by Arthur Cohn
Picc.-2,2,1-Perc.-Pno.-Str.
Ms.
Score 7 p.
*Originally composed 1928 as part of Studies in
Black and White for piano. Transcribed 1933.
First performance Hollywood Bowl, 23 July 1933,
the composer conducting.*

3804 My toy balloon, variations on a   *6'*
Brazilian tune
3*,2,2,2-2,2,3,1-Timp.,Perc.,Toy Balloons-Pno.,
Cel.,Hp.-Str.
[n.p., n.d.]
Score 30 p.
*Originally composed for piano 1942; orchestratd
1942. First performance Boston, 14 July 1942,
Boston Pops Orchestra, Arthur Fiedler con-
ductor.*

4018 Overture on an ancient Greek theme   *3'*
Tpt.-Perc.-Str.
Ms.
Score 7 p.
*Composed 1933. First performance Hollywood
Bowl, 13 July 1933, the composer conducting.*

3959 Pequeña suite [Little suite]
1.Jazzelette   2.A penny for your thoughts   3.
Happy farmer   4.Fugato   5. Anatomy of melancholy   6.Bitonal march   7.Valse très sentimentale   8.Typographical errors
1(alt. Picc.),1,1-Perc.
Ms.
Score 26 p.
Movements 1-6 and 8 originally composed 1928

Slunicko, Jan

*in Studies in Black and White for piano.
Transcribed and Valse added, 1941. First
performance Buenos Aires, 31 October 1941,
Grupo Renovación concert, the composer conducting.*

SLUNICKO, JAN.   Humpolec, Bohemia 23 March 1852
                       Augsburg 5 May 1923

77s Suite, Op. 71
1.Nocturne 2.Scherzo 3.Idyl 4.Pastorale
Str.(Cb. optional)
Anton Böhm, Augsburg, ^C1909
Score 16 p.

SLY, ALLAN B.   Reading, England 1907

3253 Holiday tune   *4'*
2(2nd alt. Picc.),2,2,2-3,2,2-Timp.,Perc.-Str.
Ms.
Score 24 p.
*Composed 1925. First performance London, 17
March 1926, London Symphony Orchestra, Adrian
Boult conductor.*

3118 Miniature symphony   *14'*
In one movement
3*,3*,2,3*-4,2,3,1-Timp.,Cym.-Str.
Ms.
Score 52 p.
*Completed 1935. First performance Rochester,
27 October 1937, Rochester Civic Orchestra,
Howard Hanson conductor.*

SMAREGLIA, ANTONIO. Pola, Istria, Italy 5 May 1854
                    Grado, near Trieste 15 April 1929

5091 La falena. Scena di seduzione e lamento
nella foresta
3(3rd alt. Picc.),3*,3*,3*-4,3,3,1-Timp.,Cym.
-Hp.-Str.
[n.p., n.d.]
Score 20 p.
*From the opera composed 1895. First perform-
ance Venice, 4 September 1897.*

2075 [The vassal of Szigeth. Hungarian   *8'*
ballet music]
3*,2,3*,2-4,2,2Cnt.,3,1-Timp.,Perc.-Str.
J. Weinberger, Leipzig [n.d.]
Score 31 p.
*From the opera composed 1888. First perform-
ance Vienna, 4 October 1889, Hans Richter conductor.*

SMETANA, BEDRICH.   Litomysl, Bohemia 2 March 1824
                    Prague 12 May 1884

613 The bartered bride. Overture   *6'*
3*,2,2,2-4,2,3-Timp.-Str.
Kalmus, New York [n.d.]
Score 37 p.
*From the opera composed 1863-66. First per-
formance Prague, 30 May 1866.*

6920 [The bartered bride. Three dances] *10'*
1.Polka 2.Furiant 3.Dance of the comedians
3*,2,2,2-4,2,3-Timp.,Perc.-Str.
Kalmus, New York [n.d.]

Score 90 p.
*Added 1869 to the opera composed 1863-66.
First performance with Polka, Prague, 29 January 1869. First performance with all three
dances, Prague, 1 June 1869.*

6234 [Same as above] Arranged by Hugo   *10'*
Riesenfeld
3*,2,2,2-4,2,3-Timp.,Perc.-Str.
G. Schirmer, New York, ^C1912, ^C1940
Score 71 p.

1786 [Bohemian song]   *14'*
2,2,2,2-4,2,3-Timp.,Trgl.-Chorus(SATB)-Str.
Em. Starý, Prague [n.d.]
Score 48 p.
*Composed 1868. First performance Prague, 29
March 1875, Karel Bendl conductor.*

1880 The carnival of Prague. Edited by   *10'*
Otakar Zich
1.Introduction: Throng of masks 2.Polonaise:
Opening of the ball
3*,2,2,2-4,4,3,1-Timp.,Perc.-Str.
Foerster, Prague, ^C1924
Score 29 p.
*Composed 1883. First performance Prague, 2
March 1884, Moric Anger conductor.*

4956 [Czech dances, nos. 2, 5, and 10.   *15'*
Transcribed by Harold Byrns]
1.The merry chicken yard, polka 2.The little
onion, minuetto 3.Circus
3(3rd alt. Picc.),3(3rd alt. E.H.),3(3rd alt.
B.Cl.),3(3rd alt. C.Bn.)-4,3,3,1-Timp.,Perc.-
Cel.,Hp.-Str.
Mercury Music, New York, ^C1942
Score 80 p.
*From the dance cycle composed 1878-79 for
piano.*

6339 [Doctor Faustus, overture to the   *3'*
puppet play by Matej Kopecký]
0,0,0,0-2,0,1-B.Dr.,Trgl.-Pno.-Str.
Hudebni Matice, Prague, 1945
Score 20 p.
*Kopecký's puppet play was based on the tragedy
by Christopher Marlowe. Composed 1862.
First performance Prague, 31 December 1862,
Moric Anger conductor.*

3632 [From my life, string quartet,   *25'*
E minor. Transcribed by George Szell]
1.Allegro vivo appassionato 2.Allegro
moderato alla polka 3.Largo sostenuto
4.Vivace
3*,2,2,2-4,2,3,1-Timp.,Perc.-Hp.-Str.
Boosey & Hawkes, New York, ^C1941
Score 109 p.
*Originally composed 1876. Transcribed 1940.
First performance New York, 8 March 1941, NBC
Symphony Orchestra, George Szell conductor.*

532 [Hakon Jarl, symphonic poem]   *10'*
3*,2,3*,2-4,2,3,1-Timp.,Perc.-Hp.-Str.
Simrock, Berlin, ^C1896
Score 83 p.

COLLECTION OF ORCHESTRAL MUSIC

Composed 1861. First performance Prague, 24 February 1864, the composer conducting.

702 [The kiss. Overture]   *3'*
3*,2,2,2-4,2,3-Timp.,Trgl.-Str.
J. Weinberger, Leipzig [n.d.]
Score 34 p.
From the opera composed 1876. First performance Prague, 7 November 1876.

704 [Libussa. Overture]   *9'*
3*,2,2,2-4,4,3,1-Timp.,Perc.-Str.
J. Weinberger, Leipzig [n.d.]
Score 30 p.
From the opera composed 1872. First performance Prague, 11 June 1881.

Má Vlast [My country, 6 symphonic poems]
623 No. 1. Višehrad   *10'*
624 No. 2. Vltava [Moldau]   *13'*
625 No. 3. Šárka   *9'*
626 No. 4. Z českých luhuv a hájuv
[In Bohemian meadows and forests]
627 No. 5. Tábor   *7'*
628 No. 6. Blaník   *15'*
3,2,2,2-4,2,3,1-Timp.,Perc.-Hp.-Str.
Urbánek, Prague [n.d.]
Scores: 40 p., 64 p., 84 p., 58 p., 70 p., 77 p.
Composed 1874-78.

6340 [Oldřich and Božena, overture to the
puppet play by Matěj Kopecký]
2Cl.-2,1-Timp.-Str.
Hudebni Matice, Prague, 1945
Score 32 p.
Kopecký's puppet play was based on a story by A. J. Zýma. Composed 1863. First performance Prague, 31 December 1863, Moric Anger conductor.

534 [Richard III, symphonic poem]   *9'*
3*,2,2,2-4,2,3,1-Timp.,Perc.-Hp.-Str.
Simrock, Berlin, ᶜ1896
Score 75 p.
Composed 1858. First performance Prague, 5 January 1862, the composer conducting.

900s Rybář, Op. 103 [The fisher]
Hp.,Harm.-Str.
Em. Starý, Prague [1867?]
Score 12 p.
Music to a living picture, after Goethe's poem. Composed 1866. First performance Žofin, 12 April 1869, the composer conducting.

703 [The secret. Overture]   *5'30"*
2,2,2,2-4,2,3-Timp.-Str.
J. Weinberger, Leipzig [n.d.]
Score 30 p.
From the opera composed 1876-77. First performance Prague, 18 September 1878.

1044 [Two widows. Ballet music]   *3'*
2,2,2,2-4,2,3-Timp.,Trgl.-Str.
Bote & Bock, Berlin [1882?]
Score 23 p.
From the comic opera composed 1873-74. First performance Prague, 27 March 1874, the composer conducting.

533 [Wallenstein's camp, symphonic poem]   *14'*
3*,2,2,2-4,4,3,1-Timp.,Perc.-Str.
Simrock, Berlin, ᶜ1896
Score 93 p.
Composed 1856. First performance Göteborg, Sweden, ca.1857, the composer conducting.

SMIT, LEO.   Philadelphia 12 January 1921

Not Leo Smit (1900-ca.1943).

5627 Symphony no. 1 in E-flat   *30'*
1.Adagio - Allegro moderato 2.Andante sostenuto 3.Allegretto scherzando 4.Allegro vivace
2(2nd alt. Picc.),2,2,2-4,2,2-Timp.-Str.
Ms.
Score 155 p.
Commissioned by the Koussevitzky Music Founda-tion for the 30th anniversary of the League of Composers. Composed 1955. First performance Boston, 1 February 1957, Boston Symphony Orches-tra, Charles Munch conductor.

SMITH, DAVID STANLEY.   Toledo, Ohio 6 July 1877
                New Haven, Connecticut 17 December 1949

917m Fête galante, Op. 48 [revised]   *10'*
Solo Ob.-0,2,2,2-4Hn.-Timp.-Hp.-Str.
Ms.
Score 42 p.
Composed 1921; revised 1930. First performance New Haven, 22 February 1931, New Haven Symphony Orchestra, the composer conducting, Georges Barrère soloist.

1985 Prince Hal, an overture, Op. 31   *13'*
3(3rd alt. Picc.),3*,3*,2-4,3,3,1-Timp.,Perc.-
Hp.-Str.
G. Schirmer, New York, ᶜ1915
Score 65 p.
Inspired by Shakespeare's play Henry V.

2779 [Symphony no. 3, Op. 60, C minor]   *30'*
1.Andante maestoso - Allegro molto 2.Allegro
molto 3.Andante con moto 4.Allegro moderato
3(3rd alt. Picc.),3*,3*,3*-4,3,3,1-Timp.,Perc.
-Cel.,Hp.-Str.
Ms.
Score 213 p.
Composed 1928. First performance Cleveland, 8 January 1931, The Cleveland Orchestra, the composer conducting.

SMITH, HALE.   Cleveland 29 June 1925

7073 Somersault, a twelve tone adventure *4'30"*
3*,2,6*(1Cl. in E-flat,Alto Cl.),3*(C.Bn.
optional)-4Sax.-4,3,3Cnt.,3,Bar.,2-Timp.,Perc.
-Cb.
Frank Music Corp., New York, ᶜ1964
Score 19 p.

SMITH, JULIA.   Denton, Texas 25 January 1911

6737 American dance suite [revised]   *10'*
1.Chicken reel (Country fiddler's tune) 2.
Negro lullaby (All the pretty little horses)
3.Lost my partner (Skip to my Lou) 4.One

Smith, Julia

morning in May (Appalachian mountain tune)
1(alt. Picc.),1(alt. E.H.),2,1-2,2,1-Timp.
(optional),Perc.-Pno.(or Hp.)-Str.
Oliver Ditson, Boston, c1938, 1957, 1963
Score 60 p.
*Commissioned by Frédérique Petrides and the
Orchestrette of New York. Composed 1935.
First performance New York, 10 February 1936,
Orchestrette of New York, Frédérique Petri-
des conductor. Revised 1962-63.*

5397 Episodic suite [revised version]   9'
1.Allegro ma non troppo 2.Homage to Griffes
3.Waltz for Little Lulu (The Saturday Evening
Post) 4.March 5.Toccata
3*,2,2,2-4,2,3,1-Timp.,Perc.-Hp.-Str.
Harold Flammer, New York, c1938
Score 30 p. Large folio
*Originally composed for piano, 1936. This
version 1938. First performance New York,
February 1940, Orchestrette Classique, Frédérique Petrides conductor.*

5391 Hellenic suite   15'
1.Sirtos 2.Berceuse 3.Saga
2(2nd alt. Picc.),2(2nd alt. E.H.),2,2-4,2,
3,1-Timp.,Perc.-Hp.-Str.
Ms. c1941 by Julia Smith [c1977 by Mowbray
Music Publishers, New York]
Score 54 p. Large folio
*Sirtos is a Greek folk dance. Commissioned by
Orchestrette Classique of New York. Composed
1940-41. First performance New York, 3 March
1941, Orchestrette Classique, Frédérique
Petrides conductor.*

6735 The stranger of Manzano. Overture   6'
1(alt. Picc.),1(alt. E.H.),2,1-2,2,1-Timp.,
Perc.-Pno.,Cel.,Hp.-Str.
Ms. c1946 by Julia Smith
Score 51 p. Large folio
*From the opera composed 1944-46. First per-
formance Southern Methodist University, Dal-
las, 6 May 1947, North Texas State University
Opera Workshop of Denton, Texas, Wilfred Bain
conductor.*

6736 The stranger of Manzano. Mexican   15'
dances (ballet from the opera)
1.El jarabe [Sweet talk] 2.Valse - La botel-
la 3.La virgen y las fieras
1(alt. Picc.),1(alt. E.H.),2(1st alt. Cl. in
E-flat),1-2,2,1-Timp.,Perc.-Pno.-Str.
Ms. c1946 by Julia Smith
Score 97 p. Large folio

SMYTH, ETHEL MARY.   Foots Gray, Kent 22 April 1858
                      Woking, Surrey 8 May 1944

3165 Two interlinked French folk   4'
melodies
1,1,1,1-2,1-Timp.,Perc.-Hp.(or Pno.)-Str.
Ms. [Oxford University Press, London, c1929]
Score 23 p.

SNOÈK, I.

1007v [Rêverie, violin, no. 2, Summer, Op. 128]
Solo Vn.-1,2,2,2-2Hn.-Timp.-Str.

Score: Ms. 35 p.
Parts: J. Yves Krier, c1916

1641s [The shepherdess of the Alps, tyrolienne,
Op. 129]
Solo Vn.-Str.
Score: Ms. 11 p.
Parts: J. Yves Krier, Paris [n.d.]

SOBANSKI, HANS JOACHIM.
                  Breslau, Silesia 19 July 1906
                                      d. 1959

5121 [Silesian heaven, a happy overture]   7'
3*,2,2,2-4,3,3,1-Timp.,Perc.-Str.
Universal Edition, Vienna, c1943
Score 46 p.

SOBECK, JOHANN.   Luditz, Bohemia 30 April 1831
                      Hanover 9 June 1914

848m [Concerto, clarinet, Op. 22, G minor]
In one movement
Solo Cl.-1,2,0,2-2,2,1-Timp.-Str.
Score: Ms. 75 p.
Parts: Nagel, Hannover [n.d.]

SÖDERLUNDH, LILLE BROR.
                Kristinehamn, Sweden 21 May 1912
                     Stockholm 23 August 1957

2186s Christina-musik för stråkorkester   11'
1.Polacca 2.Sarabanda 3.Gavotta 4.Musette
5.Giga
Str.
Nordiska, Stockholm, c1958
Score 19 p.

395m [Concertino, oboe and strings]   13'30"
1.Allegro 2.Andante sostenuto 3.Allegro
Solo Ob.-Str.
Ms.
Score 27 p.
Composed 1944.

2190s [Three popular waltzes]
Str.
Nordiska, Stockholm, c1956
Score 11 p.

SOKOLOV, NIKOLAI ALEXANDROVICH.
                  St. Petersburg 26 March 1859
                  St. Petersburg 27 March 1922

264s La caressante, polka, Op. 38
Str.(Cb. ad lib.)
Belaieff, Leipzig, 1899
Score 5 p.

1399 Divertissement, Op. 42
In 10 movements
3(3rd alt. Picc.),2(2nd alt. E.H.),2,2-4,2,3,1
-Timp.,Perc.-Pno.,Hp.-Str.
Belaieff, Leipzig, 1913
Score 134 p.

889 Élégie, Op. 4   8'
2,2,2,2-4,2-Timp.-Str.

Belaieff, Leipzig, 1888
Score 27 p.
Composed 1886. First performance St. Petersburg, 1888.

262s [Serenade on a children's song]
Str.
Belaieff, Leipzig, 1895
Score 11 p.
From the composer's Quintet, Op. 3.

263s [Serenade no. 2, Op. 23, G major]
Str.
Belaieff, Leipzig, 1895
Score 7 p.

365 Variations sur un thème russe
3*,2,2,2-4,2,3,1-Timp.,Perc.-Hp.-Str.
Belaieff, Leipzig, 1903
Score 62 p.
Six variations by Artsÿbushev, Wihtol, Liadov, Rimsky-Korsakov, Sokolov, and Glazunov.

189s Les vendredis, polka [The Fridays]
Str.
Belaieff, Leipzig, 1899
Score 9 p.
Composed by Sokolov with Glazunov and Liadov.

1413 [The wild swans. Suite from the ballet, Op. 40a]
1.Introduction 2.Polka 3.[Waltz caprice] 4.[Scene and dance of the witches] 5.Pastorale 6.Adagio 7.[Dance of the buffoons] 8.[Oriental dance] 9.Mazurka
3(3rd alt. Picc.),2,2,2-4,2,3,1-Timp.,Perc.-Hp.-Str.
Belaieff, Leipzig, 1902
Score 130 p.

1432 [The winter's tale. Complete music to Shakespeare's play, Op. 44]
3(3rd alt. Picc.),3*,3,2-4,3,3,1-Timp.,Perc.-Hp.-Str.
Belaieff, Leipzig, 1915
Score 111 p.

SOLHEIM, KARSTEN.   Bergen, Norway 1869
                                 Bergen 1953

2111s [Old minuet]   6'30"
Str.
Norsk Musikforlag A/S, Oslo, ᶜ1946
Score 6 p.

SOLNITZ, ANTON WILHELM.   Bohemia ca.1722
                                 Leiden, Netherlands 1758

2106s [Serenade (Sinfonia), string orchestra, F major] Edited by Eugen Bodart
1.Allegro molto 2.Adagio 3.Allegro, tempo di menuetto
Str.
Mannheimer Musik-Verlag, Mannheim [1954]
Score 8 p.
First modern performance over Süddeutscher Rundfunk.

SOMERS, HARRY STEWART.   Toronto 11 September 1925

2142s North country, four movements   12'
Str.
Ms. [Berandol Music, Scarborough, Ontario]
Score 21 p.
Composed 1948. First performance Toronto, 1948, CBS Symphony Orchestra, Geoffrey Waddington conductor.

5859 Passacaglia and fugue   12'
3*,3*,3*,3*-4,3,3,1-Perc.-Str.
Ms. [Berandol Music, Scarborough, Ontario]
Score 37 p. Large folio
Composed 1954. First performance Toronto, 1954, CBC Symphony Orchestra, Ettore Mazzoleni conductor.

2285s Scherzo for strings   5'
Str.
Associated Music Publishers, New York, ᶜ1948
Score 14 p.
Composed 1947. First performance Toronto, 1947, CBC Symphony Orchestra, Harold Sumberg conductor.

SOMERVELL, ARTHUR. Windermere, England 5 June 1863
                              London 2 May 1937

1414s Air in C major
Pno.(optional)-Str.
J. Williams, London, ᶜ1930
Score 4 p.

1137v [Concerto, violin, G minor]   30'
1.Allegro moderato e con grazia 2.Adagio 3.Allegro giocoso
Solo Vn.-2,2,2,2-3,1,3,1-Timp.-Str.
Boosey, London, ᶜ1933
Score 119 p.
Composed 1933. First performance Edinburgh, 20 October 1932, Reid Concerts, Mary Grierson conductor, Jelly d'Aranyi soloist.

SOMMA, BONAVENTURA. Chianciano, Italy 30 July 1893
                              Rome 23 October 1960

4651 Leggenda pastorale per orchestra
2,3*,3*,3*-4,3,3,1-Timp.,Perc.-Cel.,Hp.-Str.
Piccinelli, Rome, ᶜ1943
Score 15 p.

5149 Toccata
4*(2 are Picc.),3*,4*(1Cl. in E-flat),3*-4,4,3,2-Timp.,Perc.-2Pno.,2Hp.-Str.
Piccinelli, Rome, ᶜ1943
Score 57 p.

SOMMERLATT.

406s Engelsflüstern [Angel's whisper]
Str.

767

Soriano, Alberto

Oertel, Hannover [n.d.]
Score 4 p.

SORIANO, ALBERTO.   b. Santiago del Estero,
                        Argentina 5 February 1915

377v [Concerto, violin and strings]   18'
Solo Vn.-Str.
1.Lento - Allegretto 2.Canción 3.Allegro
Ms.
Score 38 p.
*Composed 1956. First broadcast performance
Montevideo, Uruguay, 26 August 1956, Sinfônia
Oficial del SODRE (Servicio Oficial Difusión
Radio Eléctrica), Victor Tevah conductor,
Miguel Pristsch soloist.*

454m [Divertimento, bassoon and strings]   12'
1.Lento 2.Allegro - Presto 3.Final
Solo Bn.-Str.
Ms.
Score 26 p.
*Composed 1954. First performance Montevideo,
Uruguay, 18 October 1955, Orquesta Juvenil
Anfión, Beatriz Tuset Collazo conductor,
Gerard Haase soloist.*

5872 Los rituales   22'
1.Anunciación 2.Allegro 3.Cortejo [Court-
ship] 4.Scherzo - Coral
3*,2,3*,3*-4,3,3,1-Timp.-Pno.,Hp.-Str.
Ms.
Score 64 p. Large folio
*Composed 1953. First complete performance
Bucharest, 6 May 1960, Bucharest Symphony
Orchestra, Josif Conta conductor.*

5688 [Suite for orchestra]   23'
1.Antifonas 2.Scherzino 3.Canto 4.Ronda
3*,2,3*,3*-4,3,3,1-Timp.-Hp.-Str.
Ms.
Score 93 p.
*Composed 1956. First performance Dresden, 23
November 1967, Dresden Philharmonic.*

SORO, ENRIQUE.   Concepción, Chile 15 July 1884
                    Santiago, Chile 2 December 1954

638p [Concerto, piano, D major]   30'
1.Andante ma non troppo 2.Scherzando 3.Alle-
gro ma non troppo
Solo Pno.-2,2,2,2-4,2,4-Timp.-Str.
Ricordi, Milan, C1923
Score 83 p.
*Composed 1921. First performance Santiago,
1922.*

1922 Suite sinfonica no. 2   27'
1.Nocturno 2.[Remote recollections] 3.
[Restlessness] 4.Meditación 5.[The mystic
hour]
2,2,2,2-4,2,4-Timp.,Bell-Org.,Hp.-Str.
Ricordi, Milan, C1923
Score 94 p.
*Composed 1920. First performance Santiago,
1921.*

SORRENTINO, CHARLES.   Sicily 13 August 1906

5521 Jolly whistler, scherzo   5'30"
2(2nd alt. Picc.),2,3*,2-2,2,2,1-Timp.,Perc.-
Str.
Ms.
Score 29 p.
Composed 1952.

453m Swans and the jackal. Complete ballet   5'
Soli: Fl.,Ob.,Cl.,Bn.,Hn.-2Tpt.,Tbn.-Timp.,
Perc.-Str.
Ms.
Score 21 p.
*First concert performance New York, ca.1949,
CBS Symphony Orchestra, Bernard Herrmann con-
ductor.*

SOSNIK, HARRY.   Chicago 13 July 1906

7071 Rock-o-rondo. A neo-classic/rock   5'
band piece
3*,2,7*(Cl. in E-flat,Alto Cl.,Cb.Cl.),2-4Sax.
-4,3,3,Bar.,2-Timp.,Perc.-Electric Guit.,Fender
Bass Guit.(both optional)-Cb.
Bourne Co., New York, C1972
Score in reduction 16 p.
Composed 1972.

SOUSA, JOHN PHILIP.
                Washington, D.C. 6 November 1854
                Reading, Pennsylvania 6 March 1932

7108 The stars and stripes forever.   4'30"
Orchestrated by Leopold Stokowski
3*,2,2,2-3Sax.(ATB)-2,4,3,1-Perc.-Pno.(or Hp.)
-Str.
A. Broude, New York, C1971 by Leopold Stokowski
Score 24 p.
*Composed 1896. First performance Philadelphia,
15 May 1897.*

SOWERBY, LEO.   Grand Rapids, Michigan 1 May 1895
                  Port Clinton, Ohio 7 July 1968

5318 All on a summer's day   10'
2(2nd alt. Picc.),2(2nd alt. E.H.),2,2-4,2,3,
1-Timp.,Perc.-Hp.-Str.
Ms.
Score 74 p.
*Commissioned by the Louisville Orchestra.
Composed 1954. First performance Louisville,
8 January 1955, Louisville Orchestra, Robert
Whitney conductor.*

778p Ballad, King Estmere   16'
2Soli Pno.-3*,3*,2,3(3rd alt. C.Bn.)-4,3,3,1-
Timp.,Perc.-Str.
Ms.
Score 158 p.
*Composed 1921-22. First performance Rome, 8
April 1923, Albert Coates conductor, the com-
poser and Carlo Zecchi soloists.*

3636 Concert overture   9'
3*,2,2,2-4,3,3,1-Timp.,Perc.-Hp.-Str.
Music Press, New York, C1941
Score 60 p.
Composed 1941.

1990 From the northland, impression of   *20'*
Lake Superior country, suite
1.Forest voices 2.Cascades 3.Burnt Rock pool
4.The shining big-sea water
3(3rd alt. Picc.),3*,4*(1Cl. in E-flat),3*-4,3,
3,1-Timp.,Perc.-Pno.,Cel.,Hp.-Str.
G. Schirmer, New York, ^c1927 by Leo Sowerby
Score 62 p.
Completed 1924.

967m Medieval poem   *17'*
Solo Org.-1,1(alt. E.H.),2(2nd alt. B.Cl.),1-
2,1-Timp.,Perc.-High Voice-Str.
Eastman School of Music, Rochester, ^c1927
Score 80 p.
*Commissioned by the Chicago Chapter of the
National Association of Organists, 1926.
Composed 1926. First performance Chicago, 20
April 1926, Eric De Lamarter conductor, Rollo
Maitland soloist.*

1954 Money musk, a country dance tune   *4'*
3(2nd&3rd alt. 2Picc.),2,3*,2-4,3,3,1-Timp.,
Perc.-Hp.-Str.
C.C. Birchard, Boston, ^c1925
Score 22 p.
Composed 1917 for piano. Transcribed 1924.

3062 Prairie, symphonic poem   *17'*
3(3rd alt. Picc.),3*,3*,3*-4,3,3,1-Timp.,Perc.
-Cel.-Str.
Ms.
Score 70 p.
*Inspired by Carl Sandburg's poem. Composed
1929. First performance Interlochen, Michigan,
11 August 1929, National High School Orchestra,
the composer conducting.*

2659 A set of four, suite of ironics   *18'*
1.Slowly, waywardly 2.Fairly fast, with
ginger 3.Quietly, wistfully 4.Lively, on the
jump
3(3rd alt. Picc.),3*,3*,2-4,3,3,1-Timp.,Perc.-
Pno.,Hp.,Mand.-Str.
C.C. Birchard, Boston, ^c1931 by Eastman School
of Music
Score 102 p.
*Composed 1917. First performance Chicago, 15
February 1918, Chicago Symphony Orchestra,
Frederick Stock conductor.*

4002 [Symphony no. 2, B minor]   *28'*
1.Sonatina 2.Recitative 3.Fugue
3(3rd alt. Picc.),3*,3*,3*-4,3,3,1-Timp.,Perc.
-Hp.-Str.
Ms.
Score 166 p.
*Composed 1926-27. First performance Chicago,
29 March 1929, Chicago Symphony Orchestra,
Frederick Stock conductor.*

SPAIN-DUNK, SUSAN.   London 1885

1427s [Suite, string orchestra, B minor]
1.[Prelude] 2.Interlude 3.Romance 4.Scherzo
5.Finale
Str.
Ms.
Score 17 p.

SPARY, JOSEF FRANZ.   Graz, Austria 28 April 1715
                     Kremsmünster, Austria 5 April 1767

1297s Ballgespräch, Intermezzo, Op. 45
Str.
Score: Ms. 8 p.
Parts: Oertel, Hannover [n.d.]

SPEAIGHT, JOSEPH.   London 24 October 1868
                           London 20 November 1947

Some Shakespeare fairy characters
22s Part I: 1.Cobweb, Moth and Mustardseed
2.The lonely shepherd 3.Puck
23s Part II: 4.Queen Mab sleeps 5.Titania
Str.(without Cb.)
Hawkes, London, ^c1916
Scores: 16 p., 12 p.

SPECTOR, IRWIN. Garwood, New Jersey 11 January 1916

442c Rhapso-concerto, violoncello and   *13'*
orchestra
In one movement
Solo Vc.-2,2,2,2-4,3,3-Timp.,Perc.-Hp.-Str.
Ms.
Score 32 p.
*Composed 1947. First performance Normal, Illi-
nois, 23 April 1950, Illinois State Normal
University Symphony Orchestra, the composer
conducting, Fritz Magg soloist.*

SPEER, WILLIAM HENRY.   London 9 November 1863
                          Sidmouth, England 21 May 1937

1123s Nocturne, Op. 17
Str.
Stainer & Bell, London, ^c1913
Score 4 p.

SPEIDEL, WILHELM.   Ulm, Germany 3 September 1826
                          Stuttgart 13 October 1899

König Helge, Op. 50
5269 Conzert-Ouverture, Op. 50a
3*,2,2,2-4,3,3-Timp.-Hp.-Str.
458c Intermezzo, Helge's Liebestraum, Op. 50b
Solo Vc.-2,2,2,2-4,0,3-Timp.-Hp.-Str.
H. Pohle, Hamburg [188-?]
Scores: 45 p., 13 p.
Composed for Adam Oehlenschläger's verse drama.

SPELMAN, TIMOTHY MATHER.   Brooklyn 21 January 1891
                          Florence, Italy 21 August 1970

1728 Barbaresques, a suite for orchestra   *17'*
1.Touggourt (In an Arab cafe) 2.El-Kantara
(The mouth of the desert) 3.El-Outaia
(Sirocco, the breath of the sand) 4.Biskra
(The gyrations of a camel) 5.Tunis (In the
Souk)
2(2nd alt. Picc.),2(2nd alt. E.H.),2,2-2,1,2-
Timp.,Perc.-Hp.-Str.
Chester, London, ^c1922
Score 78 p.
*Composed 1922. First performance Brooklyn,
1923.*

Spelman, Timothy

4825 Homesick Yankee in North Africa
2(2nd alt. Picc.),3*,3*(2nd alt. Alto Sax.),2
-4,3,2-Timp.,Perc.-Pno.,Cel.,Hp.-Str.
Ms.
Score 32 p. Large folio
Composed 1944.

3303 Symphony in G minor   *35'*
1.Largo e maestoso - Allegro non troppo 2.
Largo e sostenuto 3.Andantino ben ritmato e
scherzando – Allegretto 4.Allegro ben ritmato
2(2nd alt. Picc.),3*,3*,3,Sarrus.-4,2,2-Timp.,
Perc.-Cel.,2Hp.-Str.
Ms.
Score 142 p.
*Composed 1935. First performance Rochester,
29 October 1936, Rochester Civic Orchestra,
Howard Hanson conductor.*

SPENDIAROV, ALEXANDER AFANASIEVICH.
                    Kakhovka, Crimea 1 November 1871
                    Erivan, USSR 7 May 1928

1729 [Crimean sketches, series II, Op. 23] *18'*
1.Taksim (Preludio) - Péchraf (Intermezzo)
2.Chant d'amour 3.Danse Baglama 4.Lamenta-
tion de la fiancée 5.[The mouse] 6.Danses:
Oïnavà - Khaïtarma
3(3rd alt. Picc.),3*,2,3*-4,3,3,1-Timp.,Perc.-
Hp.-Str.
Mussektor, Moscow/Universal Edition, Vienna,
1927
Score 64 p.
*Composed 1912. First performance St. Peters-
burg, 1914.*

1482 Danse ancienne, Op. 12
2,2,2,2-3Hn.-Timp.,Trgl.-Str.
Jurgenson, Moscow [n.d.]
Score 15 p.
Composed 1896.

Deux morceaux, Op. 3
1730 No. 1 Menuet
1797 No. 2 Berceuse
2,2(1 only in no. 2),2,2-2Hn.-Hp.(no. 2 only)-
Str.
Bessel, St. Petersburg [n.d.]
Scores: 9 p., 9 p.
Menuet composed 1895. Berceuse composed 1897.

464 Esquisses de Crimée, suite   *10'30"*
orientale, Op. 9
1.Air de danse 2.Chanson élégiaque 3.Chanson
à boire 4.Air de danse Kaïtarma
3*,2(2nd alt. E.H.),2,2-4,2,3,1-Timp.,Perc.-
Hp.-Str.
Bessel, Petrograd [1915?]
Score 35 p.
Composed 1903.

1841 Études d'Erivan, Op. 30
1.Enseli 2.Hidjas
3*,2*,2,3*-4Hn.-Timp.,Perc.-Pno.-Str.
[Mussektor, Erivan, Armenian SSR] 1927
Score 30 p.
*Based on Arab-Armenian melodies. Composed
1925.*

2964 [March, Op. 26]
3*(3rd alt. 2nd Picc.),2,2,3*-4,3,3,1-Timp.,
Perc.-Str.
Jurgenson, Moscow [n.d.]
Score 21 p.
Based on Cossack war songs. Composed 1915.

1783 Ouverture de concert, Op. 4
3*,2,2,2-4,2,3,1-Timp.-Str.
Bessel, St. Petersburg [n.d.]
Score 48 p.
Composed 1900.

640 Prélude funèbre, Op. 20   *5'*
2,0,2,2-4Hn.-Perc.-Hp.-Str.
Belaïeff, Leipzig, 1911
Score 7 p.
Composed 1908.

421 [The three palms, Op. 10]   *18'*
3*,3*,3(3rd alt. B.Cl.),3*-4,2,3,1-Timp.,Perc.-
2Hp.-Str.
Belaïeff, Leipzig, 1907
Score 70 p.
*Inspired by Mikhail Lermontov's poem. Com-
posed 1905.*

1806 [Two Crimean Tartar songs, Op. 25]   *7'*
1.[Cradle song] 2.[Dance song]
Solo Voice or Vn.-1,1,1,2-Perc.-Hp.,2Mand.-Str.
[Mussektor, Erivan, Armenian SSR] 1929
Score 17 p.
*Composed 1915. First performance Moscow, 25
December 1927, the composer conducting.*

728 Valse de concert, Op. 18   *8'*
3(3rd alt. Picc.),2(2nd alt. E.H.),2,2-4,2,3,
1-Timp.,Perc.-Hp.-Str.
Jurgenson, Moscow [1908]
Score 45 p.
Composed 1907.

SPERANZA, GIOVANNI ANTONIO.   Mantua 1812
                                       Milan 1850

1046s Premier sommeil, berceuse. Arranged by
Camusat
Str.
Score: Ms. 10 p.
Parts: Gallet, Paris [n.d.]
Presumably by G. A. Speranza.

SPIALEK, HANS.   Vienna 17 April 1894

2714 Sinfonietta   *18'*
1.Prelude 2.Slow movement 3.Scherzo conven-
tionale 4.Finale
3(3rd alt. Picc.),2(2nd alt. E.H.),3*,2-4,3,3,
1-Timp.,Perc.-Cel.,Hp.-Str.
Chappell, New York, c1936
Score 92 p.
*Composed 1935. First performance New York, 15
November 1936, NBC Symphony Orchestra broadcast, Frank Black conductor.*

2710 The tall city [original version]   *20'*
1.General view 2.The avenue 3.A shanty
between two skyscrapers 4.Moon over the city
5.Holiday

3(alt. 3Picc.),3*,4*,3*-3Sax.(2A,1T)-4,4,3,1-
Timp.,Perc.-Pno.,Cel.,Hp.-Str.
Harms, New York, ᶜ1933
Score 122 p.
*Composed 1933 for the opening of NBC's new
studios. First performance of this version
New York, 1 December 1933, NBC Symphony Orches-
tra broadcast, Frank Black conductor.
Revised 1934.*

SPIER, LASALLE.   Washington, D.C. 19 November 1889

440m Concerto pastorale for carillon   22'
and orchestra
1.Andante - Allegro con spirito 2.Notturno
3.Allegro giocoso
Solo Carillon(tape recording)-1(alt. Picc.),1
(alt. E.H.),2,1-2,2,1-Timp.,Perc.-Str.
Ms. ᶜ1958 by LaSalle Spier
Score 32 p. Large folio
*Commissioned by Richard Bales. Composed 1957.
First performance, Festival of American Music,
Washington, D.C., 25 May 1958, National Gallery
Orchestra, Richard Bales conductor. Solo
carillon part was a tape recording by Charles
T. Chapman, carilloneur at Luray Singing
Tower, Luray, Virginia.*

6141 Concerto piccolo, A day in the   11'
country
1.Pastorale 2.Cornucopia (10 short episodes)
3.Contraddanze
1(alt. Picc.),1,1,1-1,2,1-Timp.,Perc.-Str.
Ms. ᶜ1962 by LaSalle Spier
Score 13 p. Large folio
*Composed 1959. First performance Washington,
D.C., 20 March 1960, American University
Orchestra, George Steiner conductor.*

6489 Impressions of the Bowery, N.Y.   6'30"
3*,2(2nd alt. E.H.),2,2-4,2,3,1-Timp.,Perc.-
Hp.-Str.
Ms. ᶜ1964 by LaSalle Spier
Score 28 p.
*Originally composed for piano 4-hands, 1919.
This transcription commissioned by Hans Kind-
ler, 1933. First performance Washington, D.C.,
28 January 1934, National Symphony Orchestra,
Hans Kindler conductor.*

430m Journey with a clarinet   13'
Solo Cl.-1(alt. Picc.),1,1,1-2,2,1-Timp.(alt.
Chimes),Perc.-Hp.-Str.
Ms. ᶜ1959 by LaSalle Spier
Score 52 p. Large folio
*Commissioned by Richard Bales. Composed 1949.
First performance Festival of American Music,
Washington, D.C., 8 May 1949, National Gal-
lery Orchestra, Richard Bales conductor, Ray
Hinshaw soloist.*

6426 Suite eulogistic   20'
1.Invocation 2.Dedication 3.Epilogue
4.Requiescat 5.Coda
2*,2,2,2-4,2,3,1-Timp.,Perc.-Hp.-Str.
Ms. ᶜ1964 by LaSalle Spier
Score 58 p.
Invocation and Epilogue commissioned by Richard

*Bales. Entire work commissioned by Howard
Mitchell. Last three movements originally
composed for piano, 1914. Suite composed
1950-51. First complete performance Washington, D.C., 19 March 1952, National Symphony
Orchestra, Howard Mitchell conductor.*

5928 Tone poem U.S.A.   11'
In 12 movements
1(alt. Picc.),1,2,1-2,2,1-Timp.,Perc.-Hp.-Str.
Ms. ᶜ1960 by LaSalle Spier
Score 20 p. Large folio
*Commissioned by Richard Bales. Composed 1952.
First performance Festival of American Music,
Washington, D.C., 17 May 1953, National Gal-
lery Orchestra, Richard Bales conductor.*

SPINDLER, FRITZ. Wurzbach, Germany 24 November 1817
        Lössnitz, near Dresden 26 December 1905

1412s Elfentanz, Op. 258 no. 3
Glock.-Str.
Score: Ms. 5 p.
Parts: Praeger & Meier, Bremen [n.d.]

SPINELLI, NICOLA.   Turin, Italy 29 July 1865
        Rome 17 October 1909

5717 [A basso porto. Prelude to Act III]
3,2,3*,2-4,3,3,1-Timp.,Perc.-Hp.-Str.
Martin Oberdörffer, Leipzig [1894]
Score 15 p.
*From the opera based on Goffredo Cognetti's
play. First performance Cologne, 18 April
1894.*

SPIRÉA, ANDRÉ.

6561 Divertimento for orchestra   12'
1.Introduction 2.Scherzo 3.Intermède
4.Finale
2,2,3*,2-4,3,3,1-Timp.,Perc.-Str.
Israeli Music Publications, Tel Aviv, ᶜ1961
Score 61 p.
*Commissioned by the Israeli Composers' Fund.
Composed 1960.*

274m Poème pour hautbois et orchestre   12'
Solo Ob.-1,0,1,2-2,1-Timp.-Str.
Israeli Music Publications, Tel Aviv, ᶜ1964
Score 38 p.
Composed 1964.

SPISAK, MICHAL.
        Dabrowa Górnicza, Poland 14 September 1914
        Paris 29 January 1965

1050m Concerto, bassoon and orchestra, 1944
1.Allegro moderato 2.Andante 3.Allegro
Solo Bn.-1,1,1-1,1,1,1-Str.
Ms. [Revised version now Ricordi, Milan]
Score 71 p.
*Composed 1944. First performance at the Fes-
tival of the International Society for Con-
temporary Music, Copenhagen, 2 June 1947.
Revised 1956.*

Spohr, Louis (Ludwig)

SPOHR, LOUIS (LUDWIG).
Brunswick, Germany 5 April 1784
Kassel 22 October 1859

948v Adagio, D-dur. Edited by Carl   5'
Rundnagel
Solo Vn.-Str.
Score: Ms. 12 p.
Parts: B. Schott's Söhne, Mainz [n.d.]

4196 [Concert overture in strict style, Op. 126,
D major]
2,2,2,2-4,2,3-Timp.-Str.
Siegel und Stoll, Leipzig [1846]
Score 50 p.
Composed 1842.

473v [Concertante, two violins, no. 2,   13'
Op. 88, B minor] Edited by Hans Sitt
1.Allegro 2.Andantino 3.Finale: Rondo
2Solo Vn.-2,0,2,2-2Hn.-Str.
Eulenburg, Leipzig [n.d.]
Score in reduction 41 p.

288m [Concerto, string quartet and   26'30"
orchestra, Op. 131, A minor] Edited by Klaus
Weelinck
1.Allegro moderato 2.Adagio 3.Rondo
Soli: Vn.I,Vn.II,Va.,Vc.-2,2,2,2-2,2,3-Timp.-
Str.
Edition KaWe, Amsterdam, c1963
Score 95 p.
Composed 1845.

865v [Concerto, violin, no. 1, Op. 1,   22'
A major]
1.Allegro vivace 2.Siciliano 3.Polonaise
Solo Vn.-2,0,0,2-2Hn.-Str.
Score: Ms. 137 p.
Parts: Breitkopf & Härtel, Leipzig [n.d.]
Composed 1802.

1043v [Concerto, violin, no. 3, Op. 7, C major]
1.Adagio - Allegro 2.Siciliano 3.Rondo alla
polacca
Solo Vn.-2,2,2,2-2,2-Timp.-Str.
Score: Ms. 163 p.
Parts: B. Schott, Mainz [n.d.]
Composed 1805.

832v [Concerto, violin, no. 7, Op. 38,   22'
E minor]
1.Allegro 2.Adagio 3.Rondo: Allegretto
Solo Vn.-2,2,2,2-2,2-Timp.-Str.
Score: Ms. 158 p.
Parts: Breitkopf & Härtel, Leipzig [n.d.]

502v [Concerto, violin, no. 8, In Form   18'
einer Gesangsszene, Op. 47, A minor]
1.Allegro molto 2.Adagio - Andante 3.Allegro
moderato
Solo Vn.-1,0,2,1-2Hn.-Timp.-Str.
Miniature score: Eulenburg, Leipzig [n.d.]
43 p.
Parts: Breitkopf & Härtel, Leipzig [n.d.]
*Composed 1816. First performance Milan, 27
September 1816, the composer as soloist.*

1060v [Concerto, violin, no. 9, Op. 55, D minor]
1.Allegro 2.Adagio 3.Rondo: Allegretto
Solo Vn.-2,2,2,2-2,2,3-Timp.-Str.
Score: Ms. 164 p.
Parts: Joh. André, Offenbach a.M. [n.d.]
*Composed 1820. First public performance
Quedlinburg, 14 October 1820, the composer
as soloist.*

1035v [Concerto, violin, no. 11, Op. 70,
G major] Edited by Hans Sitt
1.Adagio - Allegro vivace 2.Adagio 3.Rondo
Solo Vn.-2,2,2,2-2-Timp.-Str.
Score: Ms. 157 p.
Parts: Breitkopf & Härtel, Leipzig [n.d.]

800v [Concerto, violin, no. 13, Op. 92,   12'
E major]
In one movement
Solo Vn.-2,0,2,2-2,2-Timp.-Str.
Score: Ms. 88 p.
Parts: Breitkopf & Härtel, Leipzig [1836?]
First published as Second Concertino.

995v [Concerto, violin, no. 14, Then and now,
Op. 110, A minor]
In one movement
Solo Vn.-2(2nd alt. Picc.),2,2,2-2,2,3-Timp.,
S.Dr.-Str.
Score: Ms. 165 p.
Parts: Pietro Mechetti [Vienna, 1840]
*First published as Concertino. First per-
formance at the Norwich Festival 1839, the
composer as soloist.*

Fantasy on Raupach's Die Tochter der Luft in
form of a concert overture, Op. 99
See: [Symphony no. 5, Op. 102, C minor]
1.Andante - Allegro

126 [Faust, Op. 60. Overture]   5'
2,2,2,2-4,2,3-Timp.-Str.
Breitkopf & Härtel, Leipzig [1890?]
Score 15 p.
*From the opera composed 1815. First perform-
ance Prague, 1 September 1816, Carl Maria
von Weber conductor.*

4315 [Jessonda, Op. 63. Overture] Edited   7'
by Gustav F. Kogel
2(both alt. Picc.),2,2,2-4,2,3-Timp.-Str.
C.F. Peters, Leipzig [1881]
Score 17 p.
*From the opera based on Antoine-Marin
Lemierre's tragedy La Veuve de Malabar.
First performance Kassel, Germany, 28 July
1823.*

6734 [Nocturne for wind instruments and   35'
Turkish band, Op. 34] Edited by Eric Simon
1.Marcia 2.Menuetto 3.Andante con variazioni
4.Polacca 5.Adagio 6.Finale
2*(Fl. alt. Picc.,2nd Picc. optional),2,2,4*
(3rd optional)-2,2,Post Horn(or Cnt. or Tpt.),
1-Perc.
Tetra Music Corp. (Broude, New York), c1966
Score 112 p.
Composed ca.1812-13. First published 1815.

3700 [Symphony no. 2, Op. 49, D minor]   *23'30"*
1.Allegro 2.Larghetto 3.Scherzo - Trio 1 -
Trio 2 - Coda 4.Finale
2,2,2,2-2,2-Timp.-Str.
Ms.
Score 145 p. Large folio
First performance London, 10 April 1820, London Philharmonic Orchestra, the composer conducting.

7059 [Symphony no. 5, Op. 102, C minor]
1.Andante - Allegro 2.Larghetto 3.Scherzo
4.Presto
2,2,2,2-4,2,3-Timp.-Str.
Tobias Haslinger, Vienna [1839]
Score 156 p.
The first movement is the composer's Op. 99, Fantasy on Raupach's Die Tochter der Luft. First movement composed 1836. Last three movements added 1837.

5713 [Symphony no. 6, Historical, in the style and taste of 4 different periods, Op. 116, G major]
1.Bach-Händel'sche Periode, 1720 2.Haydn-Mozart'sche Periode, 1780 3.Beethoven'sche Periode, 1810 4.Allerneueste Periode, 1840
2(2nd alt. Picc.),2,2,2-4,2,3-Timp.,Perc.-Str.
Pietro Mechetti, Vienna [1842]
Score 100 p.
Composed 1839.

5671 [Symphony no. 9, The seasons, Op. 143]
I.[Winter - The transition to spring - Spring]
II.[Summer - Entry into autumn - Autumn]
2,2,2,2-4,2,3,B.Hn.-Timp.-Str.
Schuberth, Hamburg [1853]
Score 164 p.
Composed 1849-50.

SPONTINI, GASPARE LUIGI PACIFICO.
                    Majolati, Ancona, Italy 14 November 1774
                    Majolati 24 January 1851

4577 [The vestal. Overture]   *7'*
3*,2,2,2-4,2,3-Timp.-Str.
G.G. Guidi, Florence [1870?]
Score 32 p.
From the opera composed 1805. First performance Paris, 16 December 1807.

SPORCK, GEORGES.   Paris 9 April 1870
                          Paris 17 January 1943

1023m [Fantasy-caprice, harp and orchestra]
Solo Hp.-2,2*,2,2-4,2,2Cnt.,3,1-Timp.,Perc.-Cel.-Str.
E. Ploix, Paris, [C]1903 by Georges Sporck
Score 35 p.

STABILE, JAMES.   Brooklyn 28 May 1937

7189 Suite for brass choir   *10'*
1.Allegro 2.Andante 3.Allegro
6Tpt.,6Tbn.,Tuba-Timp.(optional)
WIM, Los Angeles, [C]1970 by James Stabile
Score 36 p.

Composed 1961. First performance Nyack, New York, 14 May 1962, Nyack College Brass Choir, the composer conducting.

STAHL, WILLY.   New York 1896
                          Hollywood 11 April 1963

5069 The perfume shop, suite for orchestra
1.Rose 2.Quelques Fleurs 3.Narcisse Noir
2(2nd alt. Picc.),1,2,1-2,2,1-Timp.,Perc.-Pno.,Hp.-Str.
Ms.
Score 37 p.

2051s A piece for strings and harp, 1936
Hp.-Str.
Ms.
Score 9 p.
Composed 1936.

3228 Symphony no. 1   *20'*
1.Vivace 2.Andante sostenuto 3.Scherzo
4.Andante moderato
3(1st&2nd alt. Picc.),2(2nd alt. E.H.),2(2nd alt. B.Cl.),3*-4,4,4,1-Timp.,Perc.-Pno.,Cel.,Hp.-Str.
Ms.
Score 122 p.
Composed 1934. First performance Hollywood, 18 October 1938, Los Angeles Federal Symphony Orchestra of the WPA, Gastone Usigli conductor.

STAHLKNECHT, JULIUS.
              Posen (now Poznan, Poland) 17 March 1817
                          Berlin 14 January 1892

696c [Concerto, violoncello, no. 1, Op. 14, in D]
In one movement
Solo Vc.-1,0,2,2-2Hn.-Str.
Score: Ms. 35 p.
Parts: Heinrichshofen, Magdeburg [n.d.]

728c [Concerto, violoncello, no. 2, Op. 15, D major]
1.Allegro maestoso 2.Adagio 3.Allegretto grazioso
Solo Vc.-2,2,2,2-2,2-Timp.-Str.
Score: Ms. 153 p.
Parts: Heinrichshofen, Magdeburg [1859?]

STAMITZ, CARL PHILIPP.
                    Mannheim, Germany 7 May 1745
                    Jena, Germany 9 November 1801

1759s [Andantinetta, strings] Edited by   *4'*
Quinto Maganini
Str.
Edition Musicus, New York, [C]1937
Score 4 p.
First performance New York, 30 January 1933, New York Sinfonietta, Quinto Maganini conductor.

Stamitz, Carl

250m [Concerto, bassoon, F major] Edited   *15'*
by Johannes Wojciechowski
1.Allegro maestoso 2.Molto adagio 3.Poco
presto
Solo Bn.-2Ob.-2Hn.-Str.
Sikorski, Hamburg, ^c1956
Score 30 p.

249m [Concerto, clarinet, E-flat major]   *13'*
Edited by Johannes Wojciechowski
1.Allegro 2.Aria 3.Rondo alla scherzo
Solo Cl.-2Fl.-2Hn.-Str.
Sikorski, Hamburg, ^c1953
Score 35 p.

251m [Concerto, clarinet, no. 3, B-flat   *18'*
major] Edited by Johannes Wojciechowski
1.Allegro moderato 2.Romanze 3.Rondo
Solo Cl.-2Ob.-2Hn.-Str.
C.F. Peters, Frankfurt, ^c1957
Score 47 p.
Composed ca.1785, probably for Josef Beer,
clarinetist of the Berlin Hofkapelle.

222m [Concerto, 2 clarinets, B-flat major]
Edited by Walter Lebermann
1.Allegro 2.Andante moderato 3.Tempo di
minuetto
2Solo Cl.-2Ob.(ad lib.)-2Hn.(ad lib.)-Str.
Litolff/Peters, Frankfurt, ^c1968
Score 58 p.

462m [Concerto, clarinet, bassoon, and
orchestra, B-flat major] Edited by Johannes
Wojciechowski
1.Allegro moderato 2.Andante moderato
3.Rondo
Solo Cl.,Solo Bn.-2Hn.-Str.
Sikorski, Hamburg, ^c1954
Score 38 p.

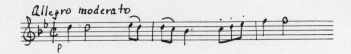

246m [Concerto, flute and strings,   *15'30"*
G major] Edited by Ingo Gronefeld
1.Allegro moderato 2.Andante un poco adagio
3.Allegro
Solo Fl.-Str.
F.E.C. Leuckart, Munich-Leipzig, ^c1957
Score 25 p.
From Ms. parts in the Court Library at Regens-
burg.

849v [Concerto, viola, Op. 1, D major]   *22'*
Edited by Kurt Soldan
1.Allegro 2.Andante moderato 3.Rondo
Solo Va.-2Cl.-2Hn.-Str.
Peters, Leipzig [1937]
Score 39 p.

308v [Concerto, violin, G major] Edited by Max
Hochkofler
1.Allegro maestoso 2.Andante moderato
3.Rondo
Solo Vn.-2Fl.-2Hn.-Str.
Edition Eulenburg, London, ^c1957
Score 52 p.
First published by Breitkopf, Leipzig, ca.
1776.

392c [Concerto, violoncello, no. 1,   *17'*
G major] Edited by Walter Upmeyer
1.Allegro con spirito 2.Romance 3.Rondo
Solo Vc.-2Fl.-2Hn.-Str.
Bärenreiter, Kassel, ^c1953
Score 51 p.

394c [Concerto, violoncello, no. 2,   *15'*
A major] Edited by Walter Upmeyer
1.Allegro con spirito   2.Romance   3.Rondo
Solo Vc.-2Fl.-2Hn.-Str.
Bärenreiter, Kassel, ^c1951
Score 46 p.

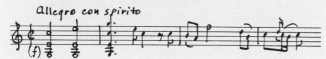

391c [Concerto, violoncello, no. 3,   *14'*
C major] Edited by Walter Upmeyer
1.Allegro con spirito   2.Andante poco moderato
3.Rondo: Allegro
Solo Vc.-2Ob.-2Hn.-Str.
Bärenreiter, Kassel, ^c1953
Score 44 p.
This and the two concerti above (Catalog nos.
392c, 394c, and 391c) written for King Fried-
rich Wilhelm II of Prussia.

2303s [Orchestra-quartet, string orchestra,
C major] Edited by Helmut Mönkemeyer
1.Allegro assai   2.Andante di molto   3.Poco
presto
Str.(without Cb.)
B. Schott's Söhne, Mainz, ^c1959
Score 19 p.
Originally published by the composer at
Strasbourg, ca.1770.

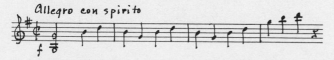

2305s [Orchestra-quartet, string orchestra,
G major] Edited by Adolf Hoffmann
1.Allegro con spirito   2.Andante grazioso
3.Presto
Str.
Möseler, Wolfenbüttel, ^c1961
Score 24 p.
Composed as a string quartet ca. 1770.
Listed in Supplement X(1775) of the Breitkopf
Thematic Catalog.

2304s [Orchestra-quartet, string orchestra,
A major] Edited by Adolf Hoffmann
1.Allegro poco moderato   2.Romanze   3.[Rondo]
Str.
Möseler, Wolfenbüttel, ^c1961
Score 18 p.
Originally published as a string quartet by
Breitkopf, Leipzig, 1775.

383v [Sinfonia concertante for 2 solo violins
and orchestra, C major] Edited by Fritz
Kneusslin
1.Allegro moderato   2.Andante   3.Menuett
2Solo Vn.-2Fl. or 2Ob.-2Hn.-Str.
Hug, Zurich, ^c1947
Score 48 p.

256m [Sinfonia concertante for violin,   *21'30"*
viola, and orchestra, D major] Edited by Fritz
Kneusslin
1.Allegro moderato   2.Romance   3.Rondeau
Solo Vn., Solo Va.-2Hn.-Str.
Edition Kneusslin, Basel, ^c1956
Score 26 p.

6959 [Symphony, Op. 13 no. 1 (London   *10'30"*
edition), *or* Op. 16 no. 1 (Paris edition),
E-flat major]
1.Allegro con spirito   2.Andante non moderato
3.Presto
2,2-2Hn.-Str.   Or: 2Fl.-2Hn.-Str.
Score: Denkmäler der Tonkunst in Bayern,
VIII/2. Breitkopf & Härtel, Leipzig, 1907.
Edited by Hugo Riemann. 25 p.
Parts: Ms. ^c1976 by The Fleisher Collection of
Orchestral Music, Free Library of Philadelphia
Published in 1778 by Breitkopf, Leipzig, as
Op. 13 no. 1. Also published in Paris as
Op. 16 no. 1.

Stamitz, Carl

2229 [Same as above] Edited by Gustav
Lenzewski, Sr.
2Fl.-2Hn.-Str.
Vieweg, Berlin [n.d.]
Score 23 p.

7017 [Symphony, Op. 13 no. 4, G major]
1.Presto 2.Andantino 3.Prestissimo
2Fl.-2Hn.-Str.
Score: Denkmäler der Tonkunst in Bayern,
VIII/2. Breitkopf & Härtel, Leipzig, 1907.
Eidted by Hugo Riemann. 23 p.
Parts: Ms. c1976 by The Fleisher Collection of
Orchestral Music, Free Library of Philadelphia
Listed in the Breitkopf Thematic Catalog, Sup-
plement XII, Leipzig, 1778. Also published
as Op. 16 no. 4.

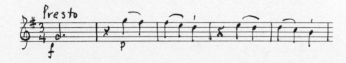

3364 [Symphony, Op. 13 no. 5, C major]
1.Grave - Allegro assai 2.Andante grazioso
3.Allegro
2Ob.-2Hn.-Str.
Ms.
Score 35 p.

3365 [Symphony, Op. 13 no. 6, F major]
1.Allegro con spirito 2.Andante moderato
3.Presto
2Ob.-2Hn.-Str.
Ms.
Score 31 p.

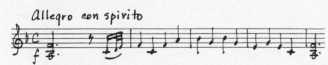

4272 [Symphony, D major]
1.Allegro maestoso 2.Andante 3.Allegro assai
2Ob.-2Hn.-Str.
Ms.
Score 31 p.
Listed in the Breitkopf Thematic Catalog, Sup-
plement VIII (1773).

STAMITZ, JOHANN WENZEL ANTON.   Německý Brod
(Deutschbrod), Bohemia 17 or 19 June 1717
Mannheim, Germany 27 March 1757

Christened: Jan Václav Antonín Stamic

245m [Concerto, flute, strings and cembalo,
C major] Edited by Herbert Kölbel
1.Allegro assai 2.Andante poco adagio
3.Prestissimo
Solo Fl.-Cemb.-Str.
Hug, Zurich, c1966
Score 46 p.
First modern performance Dresden, 17 August
1954, Immanuel Lucchesi soloist.

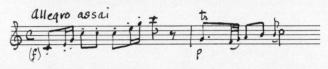

244m [Concerto, oboe, strings and   14'
cembalo, C major] Edited by H. Töttcher and
H.F. Hartig
1.Allegro 2.Adagio 3.Tempo di menuet
Solo Ob.-Cemb.-Str.
Sikorski, Hamburg, c1957
Score 24 p.
Probably composed for Alexandre Lebrun, solo
oboist of the Mannheim orchestra. As a violin
concerto, this work was listed in Part II of
the Breitkopf Thematic Catalog, Leipzig, 1762.

2301s [Symphonies, Mannheim, string   1. 11'
orchestra.1.G major   2.A major   2. 15'
3.B-flat major] Edited by Adolf   3. 11'
Hoffmann
No. 1: Allegro - Larghetto - Presto No. 2:
Allegro assai - Andante - Presto No. 3:Allegro
- Andante - Presto
Str.
Karl Heinrich Möseler, Wolfenbüttel, c1957
Score 23 p.
The symphony in A major was listed in Supple-
ment I to the Breitkopf Thematic Catalog,
Leipzig, 1766; the one in B-flat major was
listed in Part I, Leipzig, 1762.

1.G major

Stanford, Charles Villiers

2. A major

Allegro assai

3. B-flat major

Allegro

4210 [Symphony, Op. 3 no. 2, D major]
1. Presto 2. Andantino 3. Menuetto 4. Prestis-
simo
2Ob.(or 2Fl.)-2,2-Timp.-Str.
Score: Denkmäler der Tonkunst in Bayern, III/1.
Breitkopf & Härtel, Leipzig, 1902. Edited by
Hugo Riemann. 23 p.
Parts: Ms. c1976 by The Fleisher Collection of
Orchestral Music, Free Library of Philadelphia

Presto

1955s [Symphony, Op. 3 no. 3, G major]   12'
Arranged by Adam Carse
1. Allegro 2. Andantino 3. Presto
2Hn.(ad lib.)-Str.
Augener, London, c1936
Score 12 p.
First published by Huberty, Paris, ca.1757.

Allegro

2534 [Symphony, Pastorale, Op. 4 no. 2, D major]
Edited by Walter Upmeyer
1. Presto 2. Larghetto 3. Minuetto
2Ob.(or 2Fl.)-2Hn.-Str.
Vieweg, Berlin [1931]
Score 15 p.

Presto

4191 [Symphony, D major] Edited by Hans T.
David
1. Allegro 2. Andante 3. Menuetto 4. Presto
2Ob.-2,2-Timp.-Str.

New York Public Library, New York, 1937
Score 23 p.

Allegro

2228 [Symphony, E-flat major] Edited by
Gustav Lenzewski, Sr.
1. Allegro assai 2. Andante 3. Minuetto
2Ob.(or 2Fl.)-2Hn.-Str.
Vieweg, Berlin [n.d.]
Score 23 p.

Allegro assai

STANDFORD, PATRIC.
        b. Barnsley, Yorkshire 5 February 1939

7166 [Symphony no. 1, The seasons,   43'
Op. 40]
1. Allegro deciso, risoluto 2. Lento 3. Scherzo
4. Adagio - Allegro - Adagio (Variations)
3*,3*,4*(1Cl. in E-flat),3*-Alto Sax.-4,3,3,1-
Timp.,Perc.-Cel.,Hp.-Str.
Ms. c1973 by Novello, Kent, England
Score 98 p. Large folio
*Composed 1971-72. First performance Trieste,
Italy, 22 October 1972, Orchestra del Teatro
Communale, Bruno Rigacci, conductor. Awarded
the second prize at the Premio Citta di Trieste
International Competition, 1972.*

STANFORD, CHARLES VILLIERS.
                        Dublin 30 September 1852
                        London 29 March 1924

535p [Concerto, piano, no. 2, C minor]
1. Allegro moderato 2. Adagio molto 3. Allegro
molto
Solo Pno.-2,2,2,2-4,2,3-Timp.-Str.
Stainer and Bell, London, c1926
Score 161 p.
*First performance 3 June 1915, Music Festival
of Norfolk, Connecticut, Arthur Mees conductor,
Harold Bauer soloist.*

2025 Irish rhapsody no. 1, Op. 78,   13'
D minor
2(2nd alt. Picc.),2(2nd alt. E.H.),3*,3*-4,3,
3,1-Timp.,Perc.-Hp.-Str.
Stainer and Bell, London, c1902
Score 65 p.

4341 [Oedipus Rex. Prelude, Op. 29]   10'
2,2(2nd alt. E.H.),2,2-2,2,3-Timp.-Hp.-Str.
Novello, Ewer, London [1887]
Score 27 p.
*From the incidental music to Sophocles' play.
First performance Cambridge, England, 1887.*

Stanford, Charles Villiers

713v [Suite, violin, Op. 32, D major]   20'
1.Ouverture 2.Allemande 3.Ballade
4.Tambourin 5.Rondo finale
Solo Vn.-2,2,2,2-4,2-Timp.-Str.
Novello, Ewer, London [n.d.]
Score 154 p.
*First performance Berlin, 14 January 1889, the
composer conducting, Joseph Joachim soloist.*

2033 Suite of ancient dances (from Op. 58)
1.Morris dance 2.Sarabande 3.Branle 4.Minuet
5.Passepied
2,2,2,2-2,2-Timp.,Perc.-Str.
Boosey, London, ᶜ1895
Score 15 p.
*Op. 58, Ten Dances for piano; suite orches-
trated by the composer. First performance
London, 28 August 1895.*

1731 [Symphony, The Irish, Op. 28, F minor] *36'*
1.Allegro moderato 2.Allegro molto vivace
3.Andante con moto 4.Allegro moderato
2,2,2,2-4,3,3-Timp.-Hp.-Str.
Novello, Ewer, London [n.d.]
Score 183 p.
*Composed 1886. First performance London, 17
May 1887, Hans Richter conductor.*

2024 [Symphony no. 5, L'Allegro ed Il Pen- *32'*
sieroso, Op. 56, D major]
1.Allegro moderato 2.Allegretto grazioso
3.Andante molto tranquillo 4.Allegro molto
2,2,2,2-4,2,3-Timp.-Org.(ad lib.)-Str.
Stainer & Bell, London, ᶜ1923
Score 149 p.

157 [Symphony no. 7, Op. 124, D minor]
1.Allegro 2.Tempo di menuetto 3.Variations
and finale
2,2,2,2-4,2,3-Timp.-Str.
A.P. Schmidt, Boston, ᶜ1912
Score 109 p.

STANGE, MAX.   Ottensen, Germany 10 May 1856
                           Berlin 25 January 1932

622c [Adagio, violoncello, Op. 47, B major]
Solo Vc.-2,1,2,1-2Hn.-Str.
Raabe and Plothow, Berlin [n.d.]
Score 11 p.

451m [A good night, song for cornet]
Solo Cnt.-2,2,2,2-4Hn.-Str.
Raabe & Plothow, Berlin [1878?]
Score in reduction 1 p.
*Originally composed for voice and piano with
text by Siegfried August Mahlmann. Transcribed
1878.*

4596 [To the homeland, overture, Op. 40]
3*,3*,3*,2-4,2,3,1-Timp.,Perc.-Str.
Raabe & Plothow, Berlin [1888?]
Score 43 p.

[Zwei Romanzen, Op. 52]
422s No. 1. A major
423s No. 2. F major
Str.

Raabe and Plothow, Berlin [n.d.]
Scores: 5 p., 5 p.

[Zwei Stücke, Op. 48]
424s No. 1. Serenade
425s No. 2. Nachtgebet [Evening prayer]
Str.
Raabe & Plothow, Berlin [n.d.]
Scores: 5 p., 3 p.

STANISLAS, ADOLF.

867s Tentation [Temptation] Op. 22
Hp.(ad lib.)-Str.
Enoch, Paris, ᶜ1901
Score 15 p.

STANLEY, JOHN.   London 17 January 1713
                                London 19 May 1786

2401s [Concerto, strings and continuo, Op. 2
no. 4, D minor] Edited by Gerald Finzi
1.Adagio 2.Allegro 3.Andante 4.Allegro
Concertino: Solo Vn., Solo Vc.-Hpscd.-Str.
Or: Solo Hpscd.-Str. Or: Solo Vn., Solo Vc.-Str.
Hawkes & Son, London, ᶜ1954
Score 34 p.
*First published 1742 in a set of six concertos
for strings and continuo.*

2200s [Pan and Syrinx. Overture]   *3'30"*
Edited by Constant Lambert
2Ob.(ad lib.),Bn.(ad lib.)-Str.
Oxford University Press, London, ᶜ1937
Score 7 p.
*Attribution to William Boyce has been refuted.
Winds are obligatory in Stanley's original.*

STAR SPANGLED BANNER.

115 Arrangement in B-flat by William F.
Happich
2,2,2,2-4,0,2Cnt.,3,1-Timp.-Str.
Ms.
Score 6 p.

98s Arrangement in C by William F. Happich
Str.
Ms.
Score 3 p.

STARER, ROBERT.   Vienna 8 January 1924

7068 Dirge for band
3*,1,6*(1Cl. in E-flat, 1Alto Cl.),1-4Sax.-
4,2,3Cnt.,3,Bar.,1-Timp.,Perc.-Cb.
Music Corporation of America, New York, ᶜ1965
Score 15 p.
*Composed 1963-64. First performance Rochester,
30 April 1964, Eastman Wind Ensemble, Donald
Hundsberger conductor.*

2009s Fantasy for strings with solo trio   8'
Str.
Ms.
Score 21 p.
*Composed 1945. First performance Tel Aviv,
11 March 1947, Palestine Philharmonic Orches-
tra, Georg Singer conductor.*

5571 Prelude and rondo giocoso   10'
2(2nd alt. Picc.),2,2,2-4,2,3,1(or 2,2,1)-
Timp.,Perc.-Str.
Ms.
Score 41 p.
*Composed 1954. First performance New York, 27
October 1956, New York Philharmonic, Dimitri
Mitropoulos conductor.*

STARK, ROBERT.
          Klingenthal, Germany 19 September 1847
          Würzburg, Germany 29 October 1922

843m [Ballade, trombone and orchestra, Op. 20]
Solo Tbn.-2,2,2,2-4,2,1,1-Timp.-Str.
Score: Ms. 41 p.
Parts: Rühle & Wendling, Leipzig [n.d.]

782m [Canzone, clarinet and strings, Op. 41]
Solo Cl.-Str.
Score: Ms. 10 p.
Parts: A. E. Fischer, Bremen [n.d.]

790m [Concerto, clarinet, no. 1, Op. 4,
E-flat major]
In one movement
Solo Cl.-2,2,0,2-3,2-Timp.-Str.
Score: Ms. 118 p.
Parts: A.E. Fischer, Bremen, [c]1901

873m [Concerto, clarinet, no. 2, Op. 13,
F major]
In one movement
Solo Cl.-1,2,1,2-2,2-Timp.-Str.
Score: Ms. 115 p.
Parts: C.F. Schmidt, Heilbronn [n.d.]

835m [Concerto, clarinet, no. 3, Op. 50,
D minor]
1.Adagio – Allegro con brio 2.Adagio
3.Allegro vivace
Solo Cl.-2,2,2,2-2,2,3-Timp.-Str.
Score: Ms. 111 p.
Parts: C.F. Schmidt, Heilbronn, [c]1895

STAROKADOMSKI, MIKHAIL LEONIDOVICH.
          Brest-Litovsk, Russia 13 June 1901
          Moscow 24 April 1954

2965 [Concerto for orchestra, Op. 14]   22'
1.Sinfonia 2.Passacaglia 3.Toccata
3(3rd alt. Picc.),3*,3(1Cl. in E-flat),3*-4,3,
3,1-Timp.,Perc.-Str.
Mussektor, Moscow, 1936
Score 98 p.
*Composed 1933. First performance Moscow,
1934, Moscow Philharmonic Orchestra, Gregor
Fitelberg conductor.*

STARZER, JOSEF.   Vienna 1726
                      Vienna 22 April 1787

911s [Divertimento, strings, C major] Edited by
Gustav Lenzewski, Sr.
1.Allegro 2.Minuetto 3.Larghetto 4.Allegro
Str.
C.F. Vieweg, Berlin [n.d.]
Score 17 p.

2272s [Divertimento, strings, A minor]
1.Allegro 2.Menuetto 3.Alternativo 4.Allegro
Str.
Score: Denkmäler der Tonkunst in Oesterreich,
XV/2. Artaria, Vienna, 1908. Edited by Karl
Horwitz and Karl Riedel. 13 p.
Parts: Ms. [c]1976 by The Fleisher Collection of
Orchestral Music, Free Library of Philadelphia

STAVENHAGEN, BERNHARD.
          Greiz, Germany 24 November 1862
          Geneva 25 December 1914

604p [Concerto, piano, Op. 4, B minor]   13'
In one movement
Solo Pno.-3*,2,2,3*-4,2,3,1-Timp.,Perc.-Str.
Ries & Erler, Berlin, [c]1894
Score 87 p.

STEA, VICENTE.   Gioia del Colle, Italy 1884
                      Lima, Peru 1943

5178 Burlesca
3*,2,2,2-2,2-Timp.-Str.
Ms.
Score 43 p.
*First performance Lima, Peru, 13 November 1940,
Orquesta Sinfónica Nacional, the composer con-
ducting.*

4187 [Dance no. 1 for orchestra]
3(3rd alt. Picc.),3*,2,2-4,3,3,1-Timp.,Perc.-
Cel.-Str.
Ms.
Score 24 p.
*First performance Lima, Peru, 13 November 1940,
Orquesta Sinfónica Nacional, the composer con-
ducting.*

1207v [Meditation]
Solo Vn.-2,2,2,2-2Hn.-Hp.-Str.
Ms.
Score 27 p.
*First performance Lima, Peru, 1 December 1917,
Orquesta Sinfónica Nacional, A. Padovani con-
ductor.*

3768 [Nocturne for orchestra]   5'30"
2,2,2,2-2Hn.-Hp.-Str.
Ms.
Score 23 p.
*First performance Lima, Peru, 13 November 1940,
Orquesta Sinfónica, the composer conducting.*

STEARNS, THEODORE.   Berea, Ohio 10 June 1880
                      Los Angeles 1 November 1935

185 [Hiawatha's wedding. Suite: Before the door
of the wigwam]

Stearns, Theodore

3*,2,2,2-4,2,3,1-Timp.,Perc.-Str.
Ms.
Score 15 p.
Composed 1897.

2688 [Snow bird. Dream ballet]
3*,2(2nd alt. E.H.),3*,2-4,3,3,1-Timp.,Perc.-
Hp.-Str.
Ms.
Score 49 p.
*From the opera composed 1919. First perform-
ance Chicago, 13 January 1923, Chicago Civic
Opera Co., Giorgio Polacco conductor.*

STECK, PAUL.

1221s Berceuse, for string orchestra
Str.
Score: Ms. 4 p.
Parts: Decourcelle, Nice, C1913

642s Chanson de Mai, Op. 9
Solo Vn.-Str.
Decourcelle, Nice [n.d.]
Score 5 p.

427s Flirtation, for string orchestra
Str.
Decourcelle, Nice [n.d.]
Score 4 p.

1513s Joyeuse promenade, Op. 13
Str.
Bournemann, Paris [n.d.]
Score 7 p.

648s Nous deux! [We two] Op. 7
Solo Vn., Solo Vc.-Str.
Decourcelle, Nice [n.d.]
Score 3 p.

348s Pour éveiller Colombine,
Op. 12
Str.
Decourcelle, Nice, C1898
Score 3 p.

1485s Sérénade monégasque, Op. 10
Solo Vn.-Str.
Decourcelle, Nice [n.d.]
Score 3 p.

STEENEBRUGEN, J.

865m Morceau de concours
Solo Tbn.-Str.
Ms.
Score 11 p.

STEGER, CHARLES FLICK.
See: FLICK-STEGER, CHARLES.

STEHMAN, JACQUES.   Brussels 8 July 1912
                          Brussels May 1975

2202s [Suite for strings]   14'
1.Ouverture 2.Passepied 3.Menuet 4.Aria
5.Intermède 6.Badinerie

Str.
CeBeDeM, Brussels, C1956
Score 37 p.
*Composed 1953. First performance Wiesbaden,
West Germany, 14 December 1955, Städtisches
Sinfonie Orchester, Franz-Paul Decker con-
ductor.*

6120 Symphonie de poche, 1950   15'
1.Introduction 2.Vif 3.Lent 4.Allegre
2,2,2,2-4,2,3-Timp.,S.Dr.,Cym.-Str.
CeBeDeM, Brussels, C1958
Score 54 p.
*Composed 1950. First performance Brussels, 7
January 1951, Belgian National Orchestra,
Edouard van Remoortel conductor. Awarded the
Belgian Musical Critics Union prize 1952.*

STEIBELT, DANIEL.   Berlin 22 October 1765
                  St. Petersburg 2 October 1823

894m [Concerto, harp, E-flat major]
1.[No tempo indicated] 2.Adagio 3.Allegretto
Solo Hp.-2,2,0,2-2Hn.-Str.
Ms.
Score 82 p.

STEIGER, CH.

670s Consolation, for string orchestra
Str.
Score: Ms. 4 p.
Parts: Durand, Paris, C1906

685s Prière [Prayer] for string orchestra
Str.
Score: Ms. 4 p.
Parts: Durand, Paris, C1906

717s Rapsodie, for string orchestra
Str.
Score: Ms. 4 p.
Parts: Durand, Paris, C1906

STEIN, EGON.   Vienna 2 February 1903

2197s Sinfonietta for string orchestra   15'
1.Allegro ma non troppo 2.Un poco lento,
molto espressivo 3.Allegro giusto
Str.
Ernst Eulenburg, London, C1959
Score 47 p.
*Composed 1958-59. First performance London,
9 March 1958, Twentieth Century Ensemble,
Hans Hubert Schoenzeler conductor.*

STEIN, LEON.   Chicago 18 September 1910

5662 Adagio and rondo ebraico   11'
2(2nd alt. Picc.),2,2,2-2,2,1-Timp.,Perc.-Str.
Ms.
Score 70 p.
*Commissioned by Strauss Community Center
Orchestra. Composed 1957. First performance
Chicago, 25 May 1957, Strauss Community Cen-
ter Orchestra, Albert Freedman conductor.*

5090 A festive overture   9'30"
3(3rd alt. Picc.),2,2,2-4,3,3,1-Timp.-Str.
Ms.
Score 75 p.
*Composed 1950. First performance Oklahoma
City, 14 April 1951, Oklahoma Symphony, Victor
Alessandro conductor.*

5921 Great Lakes suite for orchestra   12'
1.Over the blue 2.At anchor 3.Waltz with a
wave 4.A gob on the go
1,1,2,1-2,2,1-Timp.-Str.
Ms.
Score 74 p.
*Composed 1944. First performance U.S. Naval
Training Station, Great Lakes, Illinois, 2
November 1944, Great Lakes Concert Orchestra,
the composer conducting.*

3097 Passacaglia, for orchestra   12'
3(3rd alt. Picc.),3*,3*,3*-4,2,3,1-Timp.,Cym.-
Str.
Ms.
Score 70 p.
*Composed 1936. First performance Chicago, 1
September 1942, Chicago Philharmonic Orches-
tra, Richard Czerwonky conductor.*

3101 Prelude and fugue   14'
3(3rd alt. Picc.),2,3*,2-4,2,3,1-Timp.,Cym.-
Str.
Ms.
Score 93 p.
*Composed 1934. First performance Chicago, 30
June 1936, Illinois Symphony Orchestra of the
WPA, the composer conducting.*

498m Rhapsody   24'
Solo Fl.-Hp.-Str.
Ms.
Score 109 p.
*Composed 1955. First performance University
of Chicago, 8 November 1955, Chicago Sin-
fonietta, the composer conducting, Walfrid
Kujala soloist.*

1864s Sinfonietta, for string orchestra   19'
1.Moderato - Allegro 2.Adagio 3.Allegro
molto 4.Molto moderato - Allegro energico
Str.
Ms.
Score 56 p.
*Composed 1938 under title Symphonic Suite for
string orchestra (Catalog no. 1774s); revised
1941. First performance Grand Rapids Symphony Orchestra of the WPA, Grand Rapids,
Michigan, 9 February 1941, Leo Krakow conductor.*

3250 Suite Hebraic   26'
1.Rhapsody 2.Scherzando Chassidic 3.Recita-
tive-dance
3(3rd alt. Picc.),2(2nd alt. E.H.),3*,2(2nd
alt. C.Bn.)-4,2,3,1-Timp.,Perc.-Hp.-Str.
Ms.
Score 177 p.
Composed 1933, on traditional Jewish themes.

1774s Symphonic suite, for string   20'
orchestra
1.Adagio - Allegro 2.Adagio 3.Allegro molto
4.Molto moderato - Allegro energico
Str.
Ms.
Score 70 p.
Composed 1938.

3906 Symphony in C   25'
1.Allegro molto energico 2.Andante 3.Alle-
gro molto 4.Allegro
3,3*,4*,2-4,3,3,1-Timp.-Str.
Ms.
Score 260 p.
Composed 1939.

4949 Symphony no. 3   40'
1.Andante - Allegro 2.Adagio 3.Allegro
4.Andante - Allegro
3(3rd alt. Picc.),2,4*,2-4,3,3,1-Timp.,Perc.-
Str.
Ms.
Score 291 p. Large folio
Composed 1950.

STEINBERG, MAXIMILIAN OSSEYEVICH.
                    Vilna, Lithuania 4 July 1883
                    Leningrad 6 December 1946

2056 Fantaisie dramatique, Op. 9   18'
3(3rd alt. Picc.),3*,3*,3*-4,3,3,1-Timp.,Perc.
-Cel.,Hp.-Str.
Belaieff, Leipzig, 1912
Score 42 p.
*Composed 1910. First performance Moscow, 29
December, 1910, Willem Mengelberg conductor.*

2054 [Les métamorphoses. Suite du ballet] 30'
1.[Introduction] 2.[Decoration of the statue
of Jupiter - Dance of the Phoenician slaves]
3.[Pan] 4.[Apollo - Dance of the Muses] 5.
[Transformation of Adonis - Vernal dances of
the sylvan deities]
4(2nd alt. Contralto Fl.,3rd alt. 2nd Picc.),3*,
4*,3-4,2,2Cnt.,3,1-Timp.,Perc.-Pno.(ad lib.),
Cel.,2Hp.-Str.
Belaieff, Leipzig, 1928
Score 96 p.
*Composed 1912. First performance St. Petersburg
10 November 1912, Alexander Siloti conductor.*

2055 Prélude symphonique, Op. 7   15'
3(3rd alt. Picc.),3*,3,3*-4,3,3,1-Timp.,Perc.-
Pno.,2Hp.-Str.
Belaieff, Leipzig, 1910
Score 27 p.
*Composed 1908. First performance St. Peters-
burg, 24 October 1908, Alexander Siloti con-
ductor.*

5002 [Princess Maleine. Overture to Maeter-
linck's play, Op. 11]
3*,3*,2,3*-4,3,3,1-Timp.,Perc.-Pno.,Hp.-Sop.
Voice, Alto Voice, Women's Chorus-Str.
[Mussektor] Moscow, 1926
Score 35 p.
Composed 1916.

Steinberg, Maximilian

1733 [Symphony no. 1, Op. 3, D major]   40'
1.Allegro non troppo 2.Allegro vivace
3.Andante molto sostenuto 4.Allegro moderato
3(3rd alt. Picc.),2,2,3*-4,3,3,1-Timp.,Perc.-
Str.
Belaieff, Leipzig, 1911
Score 159 p.
*Composed 1905-06. First performance St.
Petersburg, 21 March 1908, F. Blumenfeld
conductor.*

1792 [Symphony no. 2, Op. 8, B-flat minor] 40'
1.Moderato 2.Allegro non troppo 3.Lento
3(3rd alt. Picc.),3*,3,3*-6,3,3,2-Timp.,Perc.-
Pno.(ad lib.)-Str.
Belaieff, Leipzig, 1912
Score 170 p.
*Composed 1909. First performance St. Peters-
burg, 27 November 1909, Alexander Siloti
conductor.*

2487 [Symphony no. 3, Op. 18, in G]
1.Allegro molto 2.Allegro 3.Lento non
troppo 4.L'istesso tempo
3(3rd alt. Picc.),3*,3*(B.Cl. alt. Cl. in D),
3*-4,3,3,1-Timp.,Perc.-Cel.,Hp.-Str.
Mussektor/Universal Edition, Vienna, 1930
Score 159 p.
*Composed 1928. First performance Leningrad,
3 March 1929, the composer conducting.*

3424 [Symphony no. 4, Turksib, Op. 24]
1.[Across sands and mountains] 2.[Rhapsody
(Songs of the past and the present)] 3.
[Guiding the steel road; In an unceasing combat; Against the desert; Across rocky mountains; Across chasms; And sands], 4.[Devil's
cart]
3(3rd alt. Picc.),3*,3,3*-4,3,3,1-Timp.,Perc.-
2Hp.(2nd ad lib.)-Str.
Mussektor, Moscow, 1935
Score 205 p.
*Composed 1933 to commemorate the completion
of the Turkestan-Siberian railroad, 1 May 1931.*

1732 Variations, Op. 2   20'
3*,2,2,2-4,2,3,1-Timp.,Perc.-Str.
Belaieff, Leipzig, 1906
Score 74 p.
*Composed 1905. First performance St. Peters-
burg, 19 December 1906, Alexander Glazunov
conductor.*

STEINER, GITTA.   Prague, Czechoslovakia

6708 Movement for eleven   5'
1(alt. Picc.),0,2-1,2,1,1-Vn.,Va.,Vc.
Ms.
Score 41 p. Large folio
*Composed 1966. First performance New York, 24
May 1966, Juilliard School of Music Orchestra,
Arthur Weisberg conductor.*

2295s Tetrark for string orchestra   5'
Str.
Ms.
Score 12 p.
Composed 1965, originally as a string quartet.

*Received the Grechaninov Memorial Prize for a
string composition, June 1966.*

STEINERT, ALEXANDER LANG. Boston 21 September 1900

767p Concerto sinfonico [piano and   14'
orchestra]
In one movement
Solo Pno.-3(3rd alt. Picc.),3*,3*,3*-4,3,3,1-
Timp.,Perc.-Str.
Ms.
Score 111 p.
*Composed 1934. First performance Boston, 8
February 1935, Boston Symphony Orchestra,
Serge Koussevitzky conductor, the composer as
soloist.*

3067 Nuit méridionale [Southern night]   12'
2,3*,3*,2-4,2,3,1-Timp.,Perc.-Cel.,Hp.-Str.
Ms.
Score 51 p.
*Composed 1925-26. First performance Boston,
15 October 1926, Boston Symphony Orchestra,
Serge Koussevitzky conductor. Awarded Prix de
Rome, 1927.*

STENHAMMAR, KARL WILHELM EUGEN.
                         Stockholm 7 February 1871
                         Stockholm 20 November 1927

313p [Concerto, piano, no. 1, Op. 1,   45'
B-flat minor. Orchestrated by Kurt Atterberg]
1.Molto moderato e maestoso 2.Vivacissimo
3.Andante 4.Allegro commodo
Solo Pno.-2,2,2,2-4,2,3(or 2,2,1)-Timp.-Str.
Ms.
Score 272 p.
*Originally composed 1893. First published by
Julius Hainer, Breslau, 1894. Material
destroyed in World War II. This version
reconstructed from the piano reduction, 1945-
46.*

654p [Concerto, piano, no. 2, Op. 23, D minor]
In one movement
Solo Pno.-2,2,2,2-4,2,3,1-Timp.-Str.
Hansen, Christiania [n.d.]
Score 125 p.

1057 Midvinter, Op. 24   12'
3*,2,2,3-4,3,3,1-Timp.-Chorus(SATB)-Str.
Hansen, Christiania [n.d.]
Score 71 p.
*Based on several old dance tunes and the
Psalm Blessed Day sung on Christmas morn in
the church of Mora. Composed 1900. First
performance Stockholm, 1902, the composer conducting.*

6032 Serenade, Op. 31   33'
1.Overtura 2.Canzonetta 3.Scherzo 4.Not-
turno 5.Finale
2(2nd alt. Picc.),2(2nd alt. E.H.),2,2-4,2,3-
Timp.,Perc.-Str.
Edition Suecia, Stockholm, ᶜ1936 by STIM
Score 152 p.
*Composed 1918. First performance Göteborg,
Sweden, Göteborg Orchestra Society, the com-
poser conducting.*

6958 [Spring night, Op. 30 no. 2] Edited   6'
by Stig Rybrant
Mixed Chorus-2,2,2,2-4,2,3-Hp.-Str.
Ms. CEdition Suecia, Stockholm [n.d.]
Score 31 p. Large folio
*Text is Oscar Levertin's poem, Vårnatt. Score
reconstructed in 1965 by Stig Rybrant from
Stenhammar's pencil sketch.*

891v [Two sentimental romances, Op. 28]
Solo Vn.-1,1,2,2-2Hn.-Str.
W. Hansen, Christiania, C1916
Score 26 p.

STEPHAN, RUDI.   Worms, Germany 29 July 1887
                 Tarnopol, Galicia 29 September 1915

757v [Music for violin and orchestra]   19'
Solo Vn.-3(3rd alt. Picc.),3(3rd alt. E.H.),
3(B.Cl. alt. Cl.III),3*-4,3,2,1-Timp.,Perc.-
Hp.-Str.
B. Schott's Söhne, Mainz, C1924
Score 36 p.

2328 Musik für sieben Saiten-Instrumente.   25'
Edited by Karl Holl
1.Sehr ruhig 2.Sehr getragen
Pno.,Hp.-Str.
B. Schott's Söhne, Mainz, C1923
Score 62 p.
*Posthumous work. First performance Bochum,
1924.*

STERN, ROBERT. Paterson, New Jersey 1 February 1934

2092s In memoriam Abraham   7'
Str.
Ms.
Score 5 p.
*Composed 1955. First performance Redlands,
California, 21 April 1956, University-Com-
munity Orchestra of the University of Redlands
with the Vine Street Musical Workshop, Edward
C. Tritt conductor. Received the Edward B.
Benjamin Award for Quiet Music, 1956.*

5459 Ricordanza for chamber orchestra   8'
2(2nd alt. Picc.),1,3*,1-2,1-Str.
Ms.
Score 15 p.
Composed 1955.

STERNBERG, ERICH WALTER.   Berlin 31 May 1891
                          Tel Aviv 15 December 1974

2256s The story of Joseph, suite in   35'
10 movements
Str.
Novello, London, C1942
Score 84 p.
*Composed 1938. First performance Jerusalem,
15 November 1938, Palestine Broadcasting Ser-
vice Radio Orchestra, Karl Salomon conductor.*

STEUERMANN, EDWARD.
        Sambor, near Lwów, Poland 18 June 1892
                New York City 11 November 1964

7332 Auf der Galerie [cantata]
Chorus(SATBB)-2(1st alt. Picc.,2nd alt. Alto
Fl.),2(2nd alt. E.H.),3*,2(2nd alt. C.Bn.)-2,
2,2-Timp.,Perc.-Pno.,Hp.,Guit.-Str.
Ms. C1964 by Edward Steuermann
Score 33 p. Large folio
*Text from Franz Kafka's Ein Landarzt (A
Country Doctor). Composed 1964. First per-
formance New York, 11 November 1965, The Cam-
erata Singers with members of The Orchestra of
America, Abraham Kaplan conductor.*

7333 Drei Chöre
1.Die Nacht 2.Das Lied 3.Der Gott der Juden
Chorus(SATB)-1,1,1,1-1,0,1-Timp.,Perc.-Pno.,Hp.
-Vc.,Cb.
Ms.
Score 38 p.
*Die Nacht has text by Michelangelo; Das Lied
text by Berthold Viertel (1885-1953); Der
Gott der Juden adapted from a Psalm. Composed
1956. First performance in a radio broadcast,
Vienna, 1959, Michael Gielen conductor. First
performance in the United States, New York, 11
November 1965, The Camerata Singers with mem-
bers of The Orchestra of America, Abraham
Kaplan conductor.*

6612 Suite for chamber orchestra   12'
1.Con moto 2.Vivace 3.Poco largo - Con moto
- Sostenuto 4.Allegro agitato
1,1,2*,1-1,1,1-Timp.,Perc.-Pno.,Hp.,Mand.,Guit.
-Str.
Ms. C1964 by Edward Steuermann
Score 39 p.
*Composed 1964. First performance New York, 11
November 1965, members of The Orchestra of
America, Abraham Kaplan conductor.*

6781 Variations for orchestra
3*,3*,3*,3*-2,2,2-Timp.,Perc.-Pno.,Hp.,Mand.-
Str.
Ms.
Score 28 p.
Composed 1958.

STEVENS, BERNARD GEORGE.   London 2 March 1916

4995 Eclogue for small orchestra [Op. 8]   7'
1,1,1,1-2Hn.-Timp.-Str.
Alfred Lengnick, London, C1948
Score 12 p.
Composed 1946.

STEVENS, HALSEY.   Scott, New York 3 December 1908

2133s Adagio and allegro, 1955   14'30"
Str.
Composers Facsimile Edition, New York, C1955
by Halsey Stevens
Score 17 p. Large folio
*Originally composed as String Quartet no. 3,
1949. Transcribed 1955. First performance
San Francisco, 24 March 1957, members of The
San Francisco Symphony, Earl Murray conductor.*

5748 Five pieces for orchestra, 1958   11'
1.Rondino 2.Chaconne 3.Scherzando 4.Chorale

Stevens, Halsey

5.March
2(2nd alt. Picc.),2,2,2-4,3,3,1-Timp.,Perc.-
Str.
Composers Facsimile Edition, New York, ^C1958
by Halsey Stevens
Score 56 p. Large folio
*For orchestra and for band; the band version
was arranged by Donald Bryce Thompson from the
composer's sketches. Composed 1954-58. First
performance Redlands, California, 22 March
1958, University-Community Symphony, Edward C.
Tritt conductor.*

5311 Green Mountain overture (Revised,   6'
1953)
2(2nd alt. Picc.),2,2,2-4,3,3,1-Timp.,Perc.-
Pno.-Str.
Composers Facsimile Edition, New York, ^C1954
by Halsey Stevens
Score 39 p. Large folio
*Composed at the request of Alan Carter, 1947-
48. Revised 1953. First performance Talla-
hassee, Florida, 20 March 1954, Florida State
University Symphony, the composer conducting.*

5741 Sinfonia breve (1957)   14'30"
1.Allegro moderato 2.Adagio 3.Allegro ma
non troppo
2(both alt. Picc.),2,2,2-4,2,3,1-Timp.,Perc.-
Pno.(alt. Cel.),Hp.-Str.
Composers Facsimile Edition, New York, ^C1958
by Halsey Stevens
Score 87 p.
*Commissioned by The Louisville Orchestra.
Composed 1956-57. First performance Louis-
ville, 20 November 1957, The Louisville
Orchestra, Robert Whitney conductor.*

5844 Symphonic dances, 1958   14'45"
1.Allegro moderato 2.Adagio 3.Allegro
3(2nd alt. Alto Fl.,3rd alt. Picc.),3(3rd alt.
E.H.),3(3rd alt. B.Cl.),3(3rd alt. C.Bn.)-4,3,
3,1-Timp.,Perc.-Pno.(alt. Cel.),2Hp.-Str.
Ms. ^C1958 by Halsey Stevens
Score 97 p. Large folio
*Commissioned by the San Francisco Symphony
under a grant from the Ford Foundation. Composed 1958. First performance San Francisco,
10 December 1958, San Francisco Symphony
Orchestra, Enrique Jordá conductor.*

5740 Symphony no. 1 (Revised, 1950)   16'30"
In one movement
3(2nd alt. Alto Fl. optional,3rd alt. Picc.),
3(3rd alt. E.H.),3(3rd alt. B.Cl.),3*-4,3,3,1-
Timp.,Perc.-Pno.,Hp.-Str.
Composers Facsimile Edition, New York, ^C1952
by Halsey Stevens
Score 80 p. Large folio
*Composed 1941-45. First performance San
Francisco, 7 March 1946, San Francisco Sym-
phony Orchestra, the composer conducting.
Revised 1950. First performance Los Angeles,
2 March 1950, Los Angeles Philharmonic, the
composer conducting.*

5874 Triskelion, 1953   20'
1.Adagio - Allegro moderato 2.Poco adagio
3.Vivace, ben accentato
2(2nd alt. Picc.),2(2nd alt. E.H.),2(2nd alt.
B.Cl.),2-4,2,3,1-Timp.,Perc.-Pno.,Hp.-Str.
Ms. ^C1953 by Halsey Stevens
Score 106 p. Large folio
*Commissioned by The Louisville Orchestra.
Composed 1953. First performance Louisville,
Kentucky, 27 February 1954, The Louisville
Orchestra, Robert Whitney conductor.*

STEWART, FRANK GRAHAM.
          b. La Junta, Colorado 12 December 1920

971m Concertino, clarinet and small   14'
orchestra
1.Allegro grazioso 2.Moderato andantino
3.Allegro scherzando
Solo Cl.-1,1,0,1-2Hn.-Timp.-Str.
Ms.
Score 129 p.
*Composed 1941. First performance Rochester,
18 March 1942, Rochester Civic Orchestra,
Howard Hanson conductor, the composer as
soloist.*

STHAMER, HEINRICH.   Hamburg 11 January 1885

640p [Concerto, piano, Op. 9, B major]
In one movement
Solo Pno.-2,3*,2,2-4,2,3,1-Timp.,Perc.-Hp.-Str.
Schlesinger, Berlin, ^C1913
Score 78 p.

STICH, JAN VÁCLAV.
See: PUNTO, GIOVANNI. pseudonym.

STILL, WILLIAM GRANT.
          b. Woodville, Mississippi 11 May 1895

2660 Afro-American symphony   23'
1.Moderato assai 2.Adagio 3.Animato 4.Lento
3(3rd alt. Picc.),3*,4*,2-4,3,3,1-Timp.,Perc.-
Cel.,Hp.,Ten.Banjo-Str.
J. Fischer, New York, ^C1935
Score 88 p. Large folio
*Score quotes the poetry of Paul Laurence Dun-
bar. Composed 1930. First performance
Rochester, 29 October 1931, Rochester Philhar-
monic Orchestra, Howard Hanson conductor.*

1955 Darker America   17'
2,2*,2,2-1,1,1-Perc.-Pno.-Str.
C.C. Birchard, Boston, ^C1928 by Eastman School
of Music
Score 47 p.
*Composed 1924. First performance, Rochester,
21 November 1927, Rochester Philharmonic
Orchestra.*

2877 Dismal Swamp   15'
3(3rd alt. Picc.),3*,4*,3*-4,3,3,1-Timp.,Perc.
-Pno.-Str.
New Music, California, ^C1937 by W.G. Still
Score 32 p.
*Composed 1935. First performance Rochester,
30 October 1936, Rochester Philharmonic Orches-
tra, Howard Hanson conductor.*

2767   Ebon chronicle   *12'30"*
3(3rd alt. Picc.),3*,4*,3*-4,3,3,1-Timp.,Perc.
-Cel.,Hp.-Str.
Ms.
Score 42 p. Large folio
*Composed 1934. First performance Fort Worth,
3 November 1936, Fort Worth Symphony Orchestra
with Paul Whiteman and His Orchestra, Paul
Whiteman conductor.*

2830   From the journal of a wanderer   *20'*
1.Phantom trail 2.Mystic moon 3.Magic bells
4.The valley of echoes 5.Devils' hollow
3(alt. 3Picc.),4*,4*,3-4,3,3,1-Timp.,Perc.-Cel.,
Hp.-Str.
Ms.
Score 60 p. Large folio
*Composed 1925. First concert performance
Rochester, 8 May 1929, Rochester Philharmonic
Orchestra, Howard Hanson conductor.*

3487   La Guiablesse [The she-devil]   *4'30"*
Three dances
3(3rd alt. Picc.),3*,3*,2-4,3,3,1-Timp.,
Perc.-Hp.-Str.
Ms.
Score 34 p.
*Ballet composed 1932. First performance
Rochester, 5 May 1933, Rochester Civic Orches-
tra, Howard Hanson conductor.*

709p   Kaintuck' (Kentucky)   *15'*
Solo Pno.-3(3rd alt. Picc.),3*,4*,2-4,3,3,1-
Timp.,Perc.-Str.
Ms.
Score 30 p. Large folio
*Commissioned by the League of Composers, 1935.
Composed 1935. First performance Rochester,
16 January 1936, Rochester Philharmonic
Orchestra, Howard Hanson conductor, Harry
Watts soloist.*

2248s [Panamanian dances] Based on Pana-   *13'*
manian folk themes collected by Elisabeth Waldo
1.Tamborito 2.Mejorana y socavon 3.Punto
4.Cumbia y congo
Str.
Southern Music, New York, ᶜ1953
Score 32 p.
*Originally composed for string quartet, 1947.
Arranged for string orchestra, 1948. First
performance on NBC, 22 May 1955, John Barnett
conductor.*

STILLMAN KELLEY, EDGAR.
  See: KELLEY, EDGAR STILLMAN.

STIX, CARL.

624s   Flitterwochen [Honeymoon] Op. 147
Str.
Joh. André, Offenbach a.M., ᶜ1896
Score 4 p.

1460s Habanera, Spanish serenade, Op. 139
2Fl.-(Perc. ad lib.)-Hp.-Str.
Joh. André, Offenbach a. M., ᶜ1894
Score 4 p.

8s   Legende, Op. 141
Solo Vn.-Org.,Hp.(or Pno.)-Str.
Joh. André, Offenbach a.M., ᶜ1896
Score 8 p.

669s   Mein Blondchen, Op. 179
Glock.(ad lib.)-Hp.-Str.
Joh. André, Offenbach a.M. [n.d.]
Score 15 p.

230s   Spielerei (Coquetterie), Op. 140
Str.
Joh. André, Offenbach a.M. [n.d.]
Score 3 p.

1459s Traumgeister [Dream visions] Op. 138
2Fl.-Glock.(ad lib.)-Hp.-Str.
Joh. André, Offenbach a.M., ᶜ1894
Score 8 p.

629s   Waldnixlein tanzt [Dancing forest-nymph]
Op. 162
Glock.-Hp.-Str.
Bosworth, Leipzig [n.d.]
Score 4 p.

STIX, OTTO.   Vienna 14 November 1873

216s   Frühlingszauber [Spring magic] Op. 48
Hp. or Pno.(ad lib.)-Str.
Joh. André, Offenbach a.M., ᶜ1896
Score 9 p.

215s   Liebesglück [Happiness of love] Op. 51
Glock.-Hp.-Str.
Joh. André, Offenbach a.M., ᶜ1896
Score 7 p.

STOCK, DAVID FREDERICK.   Pittsburgh 3 June 1939

7285   Inner space [for orchestra]   *14'*
3*,2,2,2-4,3,3,1-Timp.,Perc.-Str.
Ms. ᶜ1973 by David Stock
Score 74 p. Large folio
*Composed 1971-73. First performance at World
Music Days of the International Society for
Contemporary Music, Boston, 30 October 1976,
New England Conservatory Symphony Orchestra,
Gunther Schuller conductor.*

STOCK, FREDERICK AUGUST.
              Jülich, Germany 11 November 1872
              Chicago 20 October 1942

823v   [Concerto, violin, D minor]   *28'*
1.Prelude 2.Adagio 3.Finale
Solo Vn.-3(3rd alt. Picc.),2(2nd alt. E.H.),2,
2-4,2,3-Timp.,Perc.-Cel.,Hp.-Str.
Universal Edition, Vienna, ᶜ1928
Score 129 p.
*Composed for the Litchfield County Choral
Union Festival in Norfolk, Connecticut and
first performed there 3 June 1915, the com-
poser conducting, Efrem Zimbalist soloist.*

5976   [Symphony no. 1, Op. 18, C minor]   *54'*
1.Einleitung, sehr langsam - Allegro, ma non
troppo 2.Scherzo 3.Andante cantabile

Stoerkel, E.

4.Adagio maestoso - Allegro moderato
4(3rd&4th alt. Picc.,4th ad lib.),3*(2nd alt.
E.H.II),3(3rd alt. B.Cl.),4*-4,4,3,2-Timp.,
Perc.-Hp.-Str.
Breitkopf & Härtel, Leipzig, ^c1912
Score 264 p.
*First performance Chicago, 31 December 1910,
Chicago Symphony Orchestra, the composer
conducting.*

STOERKEL, E.

1010s Norvedjana
Fl.-Str.
G. Ricordi, Milan [n.d.]
Score 6 p.

STOESSEL, ALBERT FREDERIC.
St. Louis 11 October 1894
New York 12 May 1943

3794 Early Americana, suite   12'
1.President's march 2.Minuet 3.Minuet
4.General Burgoyne's march
3*,3*,2,2-4,3,3,1-Timp.,Perc.-Hp.-Str.
C.C. Birchard, Boston, ^c1936
Score 18 p.
*First(?) performance Chautauqua, 27 July 1935,
Chautauqua Symphony Orchestra, the composer
conducting.*

STÖHR, RICHARD.   Vienna 11 June 1874
Montpelier, Vermont 11 December 1967

1835s Concert im alten Styl, Op. 68   40'
1.Intrata 2.Sarabande und Scherzo 3.Bur-
leske und Aria 4.Introduction und Finale
Timp.,Perc.-Pno.-Str.
Ms.
Score 123 p.
Composed 1937.

2343 Kammersymphonie, Op. 32   36'
1.Allegro 2.Andante quasi marcia 3.Allegro
4.Un poco grave - Allegro
0,1,1,1-Hn.-Hp.-Str.(without Cb.)
C.F. Kahnt, Leipzig, ^c1921
Score 109 p.
*Composed 1912. First performance Vienna, 12
December 1912.*

669v Konzert-Fantasie, Op. 50   15'
Solo Vn.-2,2,2,2-4,2,3-Timp.,Perc.-Hp.-Str.
C.F.W. Siegel, Leipzig [n.d.]
Score 59 p.
*Composed 1916. First performance Vienna, 15
April 1917, Hermann von Schmeidel conductor,
Nora Duesberg soloist.*

349s Suite, Op. 8 [C major]
1.[Prelude] 2.Andante 3.[Fugue]
Str.
Leuckart, Leipzig, ^c1909
Score 39 p.

STOJOWSKI, SIGISMUND. Strzelce, Poland 14 May 1869
New York 5 November 1946

Born: Zygmunt Denis Antoni Stojowski

605p [Concerto, piano, no. 1, Op. 3, F-sharp
minor]
1.Andante poco mosso 2.Andante sostenuto
3.Allegro con fuoco
Solo Pno.-2(2nd alt. Picc.),2(2nd alt. E.H.),
2,2-4,2,3-Timp.,Perc.-Str.
Augener, London [n.d.]
Score 102 p.

614p [Concerto, piano, no. 2, Op. 32, A-flat
major]
Prologue, Scherzo et Variations
Solo Pno.-3(3rd alt. Picc.),3*,2,2-4,2,3-
Timp.,Perc.-Hp.-Str.
Heugel, Paris, ^c1923
Score 197 p.
*First performance London, 23 June 1913,
Arthur Nikisch conductor, the composer as
soloist.*

359v [Concerto, violin, Op. 22, in G]
1.Allegro deciso 2.Andante non troppo
3.Allegro giocoso
Solo Vn.-2,2,2,2-4,2,3-Timp.-Hp.-Str.
Arthur P. Schmidt, Boston, ^c1908
Score 101 p. Large folio

1017v Romanze, Op. 20
Solo Vn.-2,2,2,2-4,2,3-Timp.,Cym.-Hp.-Str.
C.F. Peters, Leipzig, ^c1901
Score 23 p.

5210 [Suite, Op. 9, E-flat major]
1.Thème varié 2.Intermède polonais 3.Rêverie
et cracovienne
3(3rd alt. Picc.),3*,2,2-4,4,3,1-Timp.,Perc.-
Hp.-Str.
Stanley Lucas, Weber, Pitt & Hatzfeld, London,
^c1893 by H.B. Stevens Company
Score 79 p.

STÖLZEL, GOTTFRIED HEINRICH.
Grünstädtel, Germany 13 January 1690
Gotha, Germany 27 November 1749

308m [Concerto, oboe, strings and continuo,
D major] Edited by Hermann Töttcher
1.[Allegro] 2.Andante 3.Allegro
Solo Ob.-Cemb.-Str.
Sikorski, Hamburg, ^c1953
Score 18 p.

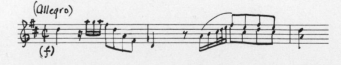

434m [Concerto grosso for four   20'
instrumental choirs]
1.--- 2.Adagio 3.Vivace
4 sections: I.3Tpt.,Timp. II.3Tpt.,Timp.
III.Fl.,3Ob.,Bn. IV. 2Cemb.(ad lib.)-Str.
Score: Denkmäler Deutscher Tonkunst, XXIX/XXX.
Breitkopf & Härtel, Leipzig, ^c1907. Edited by
Arnold Schering. 52 p. Large folio
Parts: Ms.
Composed after 1719.

STOLZENBERG, GEORG.   Berlin 11 July 1857

566m [Serenade, clarinet and strings,   *20'*
Op. 6, D minor]
1.Allegro 2.Scherzo 3.Etwas langsam und
schmachtend 4.Finale
Solo Cl.-Str.
Breitkopf & Härtel, Leipzig [n.d.]
Score 39 p.
Composed 1886.   First performance Berlin 1888.

STOPE, H.

769s Hand in hand, pizzicato gavotte
Str.
Score: Ms. 10 p.
Parts: P. Linke, Berlin [n.d.]

STÖR, KARL.   Stolberg, Germany 29 June 1814
                     Weimar 17 January 1889

910v [Concerto, violin, Op. 30, B minor]
1.Allegro vivace e deciso 2.Larghetto, ma
non lento 3.Allegro deciso
Solo Vn.-2,2,2,2-4,2,3,1-Timp.-Hp.-Str.
Richter & Hopf, Halle a.S. [n.d.]
Score 95 p.

579c Ständchen
Solo Vc.-2,2,2,2-2Hn.-Timp.-Str.
E.W. Fritsch, Leipzig, 1874
Score 25 p.

STORCH, E.

700c Konzertstück
Solo Cb.-2,2,2,2-2,2,3-Timp.-Str.
Score: Ms. 93 p.
Parts: B. Schott's Söhne, Mainz [n.d.]

STRADELLA, ALESSANDRO.   Montefestino, Italy 1642
                          Genoa 25 February 1682

386m Sonata for trumpet and strings.   *7'*
Edited by Owen Jander
1.[Allegro] 2.[Andante] Aria 3.[Allegro]
4.[Allegretto] Aria
Solo Tpt.-Cemb.-Str.(in 2 choirs)
Robert King Music, North Easton, Massachusetts,
c1960
Score 32 p.

STRANG, GERALD. Claresholm, Canada 13 February 1908

213m Percussion music for three players
1.Alla marcia - Trio 2.Moderato 3.Rondino
Three players:
  I. Suspended Cym.,5Temple Blocks,5Small Bells,
Anvil or Iron Pipe
  II. 2Wood Blocks,3Chinese Dr.
  III. Trgl.,2Maracas,2Gongs,B.Dr.
New Music Orchestra Series, San Francisco,
c1936
Score 8 p.
*Composed 1935. First performance Seattle,
ca.1938, John Cage conductor.*

3117 Symphony
1.Allegro moderato 2.Moderato 3.Scherzo
4.Adagio - Alla marcia
3(3rd alt. Picc.),3*,3(3rd alt. B.Cl.),3*-
4,3,3-Timp.,Perc.-Hp.-Str.
Ms.
Scores: 59 p., 20 p., 49 p.
Completed 1942.

STRÄSSER, EWALD. Burscheid, Rhineland 27 June 1867
                         Stuttgart 4 April 1933

4s Intermezzo, Op. 7
Str.
H. vom Ende, Köln a.Rh. [n.d.]
Score 10 p.
Originally composed for piano.

5714 [Symphony no. 1, Op. 22, G major]   *40'*
1.Alla breve e con anima 2.Andante sostenuto
3.Scherzo 4.Finale
3(3rd alt. Picc.),2(2nd alt. E.H.),2,3*-4,2,
3,1-Timp.,Cym.-Str.
Tischer & Jagenberg, Cologne, c1910
Score 164 p.

STRAUS, OSCAR.   Vienna 6 March 1870
                 Ischl, Austria 11 January 1954

726s Alt-Wiener Reigen, Op. 45
Str.
B. Schott's Söhne, Mainz [n.d.]
Score 8 p.

358s Serenade, Op. 35 [G minor]
1.Allegro commodo 2.Scherzino 3.Andantino
4.Walzer 5.Alla marcia (Finale)
Str.
B. Schott's Söhne, Mainz [n.d.]
Score 29 p.

STRAUSS, EDUARD.   Vienna 15 March 1835
                     Vienna 28 December 1916

4458 Abonnenten [Subscribers] Walzer, Op. 116
2*,2,2,2-4,2,3-Timp.,Perc.-Hp.-Str.
F. Schreiber, Vienna [1874]
No score published. Violin I part 3 p.

4420 Akademische Burger, Walzer, Op. 68
2*,2,2,2-4,2,3,1-Timp.,S.Dr.-Hp.-Str.
C. Spina, Vienna [1871?]
No score published. Violin I part 3 p.

Strauss, Eduard

4426 Aula-Lieder, Walzer, Op. 113
2*,1,2,2-4,2,3-Timp.,Perc.-Str.
F. Schreiber, Vienna [1874?]
No score published. Violin I part 3 p.

7028 Bahn frei Polka (schnell) Op. 45   *3'*
2*,2,2(1Cl. in E-flat),2-4,4,3,1-Perc.-Str.
Kalmus, New York [n.d.]
Score in reduction 3 p.

4464 [Consequences waltzes, Op. 143]
2*,2,2,2-4,2,3-Timp.,Perc.-Hp.-Str.
F. Schreiber, Vienna [1876]
No score published. Violin I part 3 p.

4415 Deutsche Herzen, Walzer, Op. 65
2*,2,2,2-4,2,3,1-Timp.,Perc.-Hp.-Str.
C. Spina, Vienna [1871]
No score published. Violin I part 4 p.

4427 [Fatinitza waltzes, Op. 147]
2*,1,2,2-4,2,3,1-Timp.,Perc.-Hp.-Str.
[n.p., n.d.]
No score published. Violin I part 5 p.
*Based on themes from Franz von Suppé's
operetta Fatinitza based on Eugène Scribe's
play La Circassienne.*

4474 Fesche Geister, Walzer, Op. 75   *6'*
2*,2,2,2-4,2,3-Timp.,S.Dr.-Hp.-Str.
C.A. Spina, Vienna [1871?]
No score published. Violin I part 3 p.

4473 [From student days, waltzes, Op. 141]
2*,2,2,2-4,2,3-Timp.,Perc.-Hp.-Str.
F. Schreiber, Vienna [1876]
No score published. Violin I part 3 p.

4424 [From the life of law, waltzes, Op. 126]
2*,2,2,2-4,2,3-Timp.,Perc.-Hp.-Str.
F. Schreiber, Vienna [1875]
No score published. Violin I part 3 p.

4410 Giroflé-Girofla, Walzer, Op. 123
2*,1,2,2-4,2,3,1-Timp.,Perc.-Str.
Henry Litolff, Braunschweig [1875?]
No score published. Violin I part 3 p.
*Based on themes from Alexandre Charles
Lecocq's opera Giroflé-Girofla.*

4472 [Homage waltzes, Op. 88]
2*,2,2,2-4,2,3,1-Timp.,Perc.-Hp.-Str.
C. Spina, Vienna [1872]
No score published. Violin I part 3 p.

4419 [Hypotheses, waltzes, Op. 72]
2*,2,2,2-4,2,3-Timp.,S.Dr.-Hp.-Str.
C. Spina, Vienna [1872?]
No score published. Violin I part 3 p.

4384 [Life is beautiful, waltzes, Op. 150]   *7'*
2*,1,2,2-4,2,3-Timp.,Perc.-Hp.-Str.
F. Schreiber, Vienna [1876?]
No score published. Violin I part 3 p.

4462 [Manuscripts, waltzes, Op. 90]
2*,2,2,2-4,2,3-Timp.,Perc.-Hp.-Str.
C. Spina, Vienna [1872]
No score published. Violin I part 3 p.

4407 Märchen aus der Heimat, Walzer, Op. 155
2*,2,2,2-4,2,3-Timp.,Perc.-Hp.-Str.
F. Schreiber, Vienna [1877]
No score published. Violin I part 3 p.

4409 Mit frohem Muth und heiterem Sinn,
Walzer, Op. 153
2*,1,2,2-4,2,3,1-Timp.,S.Dr.-Hp.-Str.
A. Cranz, Hamburg? [1877]
No score published. Violin I part 3 p.

4471 [Nosegays of myrtle, waltzes, Op. 87]
2*,2,2,2-4,2,3-Timp.,S.Dr.-Hp.-Str.
C. Spina, Vienna [1872]
No score published. Violin I part 3 p.

4463 [Public opinion waltzes, Op. 104]
2*,2,2,2-4,2,3-Timp.,Perc.-Hp.-Str.
F. Schreiber, Vienna [1874?]
No score published. Violin I part 3 p.

4408 Studentenball-Tänze, Walzer, Op. 101
2*,2,2,2-4,2,3-Timp.,S.Dr.-Hp.-Str.
F. Schreiber, Vienna [1873]
No score published. Violin I part 3 p.

4460 Theorien, Walzer, Op. 111
2*,2,2,2-4,2,3-Timp.,Perc.-Hp.-Str.
F. Schreiber, Vienna [1874]
No score published. Violin I part 3 p.

4425 Verdicte, Walzer, Op. 137
2*,2,2,2-4,2,3-Timp.,Perc.-Hp.-Str.
F. Schreiber, Vienna [1876?]
No score published. Violin I part 3 p.

STRAUSS, FRANZ. Parkstein, Bavaria 26 February 1822
Munich 31 May 1905

650m [Concerto, horn, no. 1, Op. 8,   *12'*
C minor]
In one movement
Solo Hn.-1,2,2,2-2,2,1-Timp.-Str.
Ms.
Score 58 p.
First performance Leipzig, 1917.

STRAUSS, JOHANN. the elder.   Vienna 14 March 1804
Vienna 25 September 1849

5250 Die Adepten, Op. 216
2(2nd alt. Picc.),1,2,1-2,4,1-Timp.,B.Dr.-Str.
Score: Denkmäler der Tonkunst in Oesterreich,
XXXV/2. Universal Edition, Vienna, 1928.
Edited by Hans Gál. 14 p.
Parts: Ms. [c]1976 by The Fleisher Collection of
Orchestral Music, Free Library of Philadelphia
*First performance Vienna, Fasching (Carnival)
1847, Technicians' Ball, composer conducting.*

Bridal wreaths, waltzes, Op. 118
See: Myrthenwalzer...

7052 Deutsche Lust, oder Donau-Lieder ohne
Text, Walzer, Op. 127
1,1,2,1-2,2,1-Timp.-Str.
Score: Ms. [c]1976 by The Fleisher Collection of
Orchestral Music, Free Library of Philadelphia

50 p.
Parts: Tobias Haslinger, Vienna [1841]
First performance Vienna, 17 February 1841.

5299 Elisabethen-Walzer, Op. 71
1(alt. Picc.),1,2,1-2,4,1-Timp.,B.Dr.-Str.
(without Va.,Vc.)
Score: Denkmäler der Tonkunst in Oesterreich,
XXXV/2. Universal Edition, Vienna, 1928.
Edited by Hans Gál. 14 p.
Parts: Ms. C1976 by The Fleisher Collection of
Orchestral Music, Free Library of Philadelphia
*First performance Hietzing, near Vienna, 26
June 1834, the composer conducting.*

5298 Masken-Lieder [waltzes] Op. 170
2*,1,2,1-2,4,1-Timp.,B.Dr.-Str.
Score: Denkmäler der Tonkunst in Oesterreich,
XXXV/2. Universal Edition, Vienna, 1928.
Edited by Hans Gál. 14 p.
Parts: Ms. C1976 by The Fleisher Collection of
Orchestral Music, Free Library of Philadelphia
*Title refers to Zur Maske, a pawnshop in
Vienna, known for renting masquerade cos-
tumes. First performance Vienna, 24 Novem-
ber 1844, the composer conducting.*

5303 Myrthenwalzer [Bridal wreaths] Op. 118   7'
1(alt. Picc.),1,2,1-2,4,1-Timp.,B.Dr.-Str.
Score: Denkmäler der Tonkunst in Oesterreich,
XXXV/2. Universal Edition, Vienna, 1928.
Edited by Hans Gál. 13 p.
Parts: Ms. C1976 by The Fleisher Collection of
Orchestral Music, Free Library of Philadelphia
*Commemorates Queen Victoria's wedding. First
performance Vienna, 11 February 1840, the
composer conducting.*

5297 Philomelen-Walzer, Op. 82
1(alt. Picc.),1,2,1-2,4,1-Timp.,B.Dr.-Str.
(without Va.,Vc.)
Score: Denkmäler der Tonkunst in Oesterreich,
XXXV/2. Universal Edition, Vienna, 1928.
Edited by Hans Gál. 12 p.
Parts: Ms. C1976 by The Fleisher Collection of
Orchestral Music, Free Library of Philadelphia
*First performance Vienna, 10 August 1835, the
composer conducting.*

7023 Radetzky march, Op. 228   2'30"
3*,2,2,2-4,2,3,1-Perc.-Str.
Luck's Music Library, Detroit, C1965
Score 9 p.
*First performance Wasser-Glacis, 31 August
1848, at a victory concert to aid wounded
soldiers of the Austrian Army in Italy.*

5283 Die Sorgenbrecher, Op. 230   8'
2*,1,2,2-4,1-Timp.,Perc.-Str.
Score: Denkmäler der Tonkunst in Oesterreich,
XXXV/2. Universal Edition, Vienna, 1928.
Edited by Hans Gál. 13 p.
Parts: Ms. C1976 by The Fleisher Collection of
Orchestral Music, Free Library of Philadelphia
*Sorgenbrecher refers to wine. First perform-
ance Vienna, 22 February 1848, the composer
conducting.*

5296 Täuberln-Walzer, Op. 1
1,0,3-2,3-Timp.-Str.(w/o Va.,Vc.)
Score: Denkmäler der Tonkunst in Österreich,
XXXV/2. Universal Edition, Vienna, 1928.
Edited by Hans Gál. 6 p.
Parts: Ms. C1976 by The Fleisher Collection of
Orchestral Music, Free Library of Philadelphia
*First performance at the Two Pigeons Inn,
Vienna, ca.May 1826, the composer conducting.*

5182 Wiener Karnevals-Walzer, Op. 3
1(alt. Picc.),0,2-2,3-Timp.,Perc.-Str.
Score: Denkmäler der Tonkunst in Oesterreich,
XXXV/2. Universal Edition, Vienna, 1928.
Edited by Hans Gál. 11 p.
Parts: Ms. C1976 by The Fleisher Collection of
Orchestral Music, Free Library of Philadelphia
Waltzes composed ca.1827.

STRAUSS, JOHANN. the younger.
Vienna 25 October 1825
Vienna 3 June 1899

7027 Accelerationen Walzer, Op. 234   6'
2*,2,2,2-4,2,1,1-Timp.,S.Dr.-Hp.-Str.
Kalmus, New York [n.d.]
Score in reduction 9 p.
Composed 1860.

2011 An der schönen blauen Donau   8'
[On the beautiful blue Danube] Walzer, Op. 314
2(2nd alt. Picc.),2,2,2-4,2,1,1-Timp.,Perc.-
Hp.-Str.
Breitkopf & Härtel, Leipzig [n.d.]
Score 35 p.
*Composed 1866. First performance Vienna, 15
February 1867, the composer conducting.*

6834 [Artist's life waltzes, Op. 316]   10'
2*,2,2,2-4,2,3-Timp.,Perc.-Str.
Kalmus, New York [n.d.]
Score 28 p.
First performance Vienna, 18 February 1867.

6849 [Cagliostro in Wien. Bitte schön,   3'
polka française, Op. 372]
2*,2,2,2-4,2,3-Timp.,Perc.-Str.
Score: Ms. C1976 by The Fleisher Collection of
Orchestral Music, The Free Library of Phila-
delphia. 20 p.
Parts: Friedrich Schreiber, Vienna [1875]
*From the operetta about Alessandro Caglios-
tro (1743-95). First performance Vienna, 27
February 1875.*

7024 [Egyptian march, Op. 335]   4'
2*,2,2,2-4,2,3,1-Perc.-Str.
Luck's Music Library, Detroit [n.d.]
Score 23 p.
First published in 1870.

4461 [Embrace, ye millions! waltzes,   9'
Op. 443] Edited by Arthur Luck
2(2nd alt. Picc.),2,2,2-4,2,3-Timp.,Perc.-Hp.-
Str.
Luck's Music Library, Detroit, C1960
Score 40 p.
Composed 1892.

Strauss, Johann

2018 [Emperor waltz] Op. 437   6'
2,2,2,2-4,2,3-Timp.,Perc.-Hp.-Str.
Breitkopf & Härtel/Associated, New York [n.d.]
Score 44 p.
Composed 1893.

6848 [Excursion train polka, Op. 281]   3'
2*,2,2,2(1Cl. in E-flat),2-4,2,1-Timp.,Perc.-Str.
Score: Ms. C1976 by The Fleisher Collection of
Orchestral Music, Free Library of Philadelphia.
21 p.
Parts: C.A. Spina, Vienna [1864]

1484 Die Fledermaus. Overture   7'
2(2nd alt. Picc.),2,2,2-4,2,3-Timp.,Perc.-Str.
Breitkopf & Härtel, Wiesbaden [n.d.]
Score 36 p.
*Composed 1873. First performance Vienna, 5
April 1874.*

2015 [Die Fledermaus. Du und du, Walzer,   5'
Op. 367]
2(2nd alt. Picc.),2,2,2-4,2,3-Timp.,Perc.-Str.
Breitkopf & Härtel, Leipzig [n.d.]
Score 30 p.

6852 Die Fledermaus. Polka française, Op. 362
2*,2,2,2-4,2,3-Timp.,Perc.-Str.
Score: Ms. C1976 by The Fleisher Collection of
Orchestral Music, Free Library of Philadelphia.
21 p.
Parts: Friedrich Schreiber, Vienna [1874]
*From the operetta. First performance Vienna,
5 April 1874.*

4317 [Die Fledermaus. Tick-tack polka,   3'
Op. 365]
2*,2,2,2-4,2,3,1-Timp.,Perc.-Str.
Luck's Music Library, Detroit [n.d.]
Score 15 p.

7025 Furioso polka (quasi galopp),   2'
Op. 260
2*,2,2,2-4,2,3-Timp.,Perc.-Str.
Luck's Music Library, Detroit [n.d.]
Score 15 p.
First published 1862.

7022 [The gypsy baron. Overture]   8'
2*,2,2,2-4,2,3-Timp.,Perc.-Hp.-Str.
Score: Southern, New York, C1956. 37 p.
Parts: Luck's Music Library [Detroit, n.d.]
*From the operetta. First performance Vienna,
24 October 1885.*

2967 [The gypsy baron. Overture. Arranged   7'
by Adam P. Lesinsky]
2(2nd alt. Picc.),2,2,2-4,2,3,1(optional)-
Timp.,Perc.-Hp.-Str.
Carl Fischer, New York, C1936
Score 35 p.

7026 [The gypsy baron. Treasure waltz,   7'30"
Op. 418]
2(2nd alt. Picc.),2,2,2-4,2,3-Timp.,Perc.-Hp.-
Str.
Luck's Music Library, Detroit [n.d.]
Score 34 p.

6610 Ins Centrum [Bull's eye!] Walzer, Op. 387
2*,2,2,2-4,2,3-Timp.,Perc.-Zither(or Hp.)-Str.
Score: Ms. 46 p. Large folio
Parts: A. Cranz, Hamburg/C.A. Spina, Vienna
[1880]

6878 Juristen-Ball-Polka (schnell), Op. 280
2*,2,2,2(1Cl. in D),2-4,2,1-Timp.,Perc.-Str.
Score: Ms. C1976 by The Fleisher Collection of
Orchestral Music, Free Library of Philadelphia.
21 p.
Parts: C.A. Spina, Vienna [1864]

4457 [Der Karneval in Rom. Carnevalsbilder,
Walzer, Op. 357]
2*,2,2,2-4,2,3-Timp.,Perc.-Str.
C.A. Spina's Nachfolger (Friedrich Schreiber),
Vienna [1873]
No score published. Violin I part 3 p.
*From the operetta based on Victorien Sardou's
play Piccolino. First performance Vienna, 1
March 1873, the composer conducting.*

6869 [Der Karneval in Rom. Nimm sie hin! Polka
française, Op. 358]
2*,2,2,2-4,2,3-Timp.,Perc.-Str.
Score: Ms. C1976 by The Fleisher Collection of
Orchestral Music, Free Library of Philadelphia.
16 p.
Parts: C.A. Spina, Vienna [1873]

4412 [The merry war. Italian waltzes, Op. 407]
2*,1,2,2-4,2,3-Timp.,S.Dr.-Str.
A. Cranz, Hamburg [1882]
No score published. Violin I part 3 p.
*First performance of the operetta Vienna, 25
November 1881.*

3078 Morgenblätter Walzer [Morning papers
waltz] Op. 279
2*,2,2,2-4,2,1,1-Timp.,Perc.-Str.
Score: Ms. 47 p.
Parts: Cranz [n.p., n.d.]
Composed 1864.

4385 [Eine Nacht in Venedig. Lagunen-Walzer,
Op. 411]
2(2nd alt. Picc.),1,2,2-4,2,3-Timp.,Perc.-Str.
A. Cranz, Hamburg [1883, 1884]
Score in reduction 11 p.
*First performance of the operetta Berlin, 3
October 1883, the composer conducting.*

7155 Nachtfalter Walzer, Op. 157
2*,2,2,2-4,2,1,1-Timp.-Str.
Score: Ms. C1976 by The Fleisher Collection of
Orchestral Music, The Free Library of Phila-
delphia. 61 p.
Parts: Carl Haslinger, Vienna [1855]
Composed 1854.

1048s Neue Pizzicato-Polka, Op. 449
Str.
Score: Ms. 6 p.
Parts: [n.p., n.d.]

5247 Neu-Wien, Walzer, Op. 342   9'
2(2nd alt. Fl.),2,2,2-4,2,3,1-Timp.,Perc.-Str.

Score: Denkmäler der Tonkunst in Oesterreich,
XXXII/2. Universal Edition, Vienna, 1925.
Edited by Hans Gál. 35 p.
Parts: Ms. ᶜ1976 by The Fleisher Collection of
Orchestral Music, Free Library of Philadelphia
Composed 1870.

4418 Nordseebilder, Walzer, Op. 390   *8'*
2*,1,2,2-4,2,3-Timp.,S.Dr.-Hp.-Str.
[A. Cranz, Hamburg, 1880]
Score in reduction 11 p.

491 Perpetuum mobile, Op. 257   *5'*
2(2nd alt. Picc.),2,3(1Cl. in E-flat),2-4,2,1-
Timp.,Perc.-Hp.-Str.
Ms.
Score 19 p.
Composed 1862.

6778 Pizzicato Polka   *3'*
2*,2,2,2-4,3,3,1-Timp.,Perc.-Str.
Luck's Music Library, Detroit [n.d.]
Score 7 p.
By Josef and Johann Strauss, the younger.

6478 [Prinz Methusalem. Methusalem-   *6'*
Quadrille, Op. 376]
2*,2,2,2-4,2,3-Timp.,Perc.-Str.
Score: Ms. ᶜ1976 by The Fleisher Collection of
Orchestral Music, Free Library of Phila-
delphia. 36 p.
Parts: C.A. Spina, Vienna [1877]
*First performance of the operetta Vienna, 3
January 1877.*

2016 Rosen aus dem Süden, Walzer, Op. 388   *7'*
2,2,2,2-4,2,3-Timp.,Perc.-Hp.-Str.
Breitkopf & Härtel, Leipzig [n.d.]
Score 39 p.
Composed 1878.

2012 [Tales from the Vienna Woods, waltz,   *9'*
Op. 325]
2(2nd alt. Picc.),2,2,2-4,3,3,1-Timp.,Perc.-
Hp.,Zither-Str.
Breitkopf & Härtel, Leipzig [n.d.]
Score 46 p.
*Composed 1868. First performance Vienna, 9
June 1868, the composer conducting.*

6726 [Thunder and lightning, polka   *3'*
schnell, Op. 324]
2*,2,2,2-4,3,3,1-Timp.,Perc.-Str.
Score: Luck's, Detroit, ᶜ1970. 12 p.
Parts: Kalmus, New York [n.d.]
First published 1868.

2017 [Voices of spring, waltz, Op. 410]   *6'*
2,2,2,2-4,2,3-Timp.,Perc.-Hp.-Str.
Breitkopf & Härtel, Leipzig [n.d.]
Score 33 p.
Composed 1881. First performance Vienna, 1881.

2013 Wein, Weib und Gesang [Wine, women   *6'*
and song] Walzer, Op. 333
2(2nd alt. Picc.),2,2,2-4,2,3-Timp.,Perc.-Hp.-
Str.
Breitkopf & Härtel, Leipzig [n.d.]

Score 33 p.
*Composed 1869. First performance Vienna, 2
February 1869, the composer conducting.*

2014 Wiener Blut [Viennese blood] Walzer,   *6'*
Op. 354
2(2nd alt. Picc.),2,2,2-4,2,3-Timp.,Perc.-Str.
Breitkopf & Härtel, Leipzig [n.d.]
Score 31 p.
Composed 1871.

STRAUSS, JOSEF.   Vienna 22 August 1827
                                Vienna 21 July 1870

4423 Hochzeits-Klänge, Walzer, Op. 242   *8'*
2*,2,2,2-4,4,3,1-Timp.,S.Dr.-Hp.-Str.
C.A. Spina, Vienna [1868]
No score published. Violin I part 3 p.

3063 [Village swallows of Austria, waltzes,
Op. 164]
2(2nd alt. Picc.),2,2,2-4,2,3,1-Timp.,Perc.-Hp.
-Str.
Luck's, Detroit [n.d.]
Score 34 p.

STRAUSS, RICHARD.   Munich 11 June 1864
                               Garmisch-Partenkirchen,
                               Germany 8 September 1949

1824 Eine Alpensinfonie, Op. 64   *50'*
In one movement
4(3rd&4th alt. 2Picc.),3(3rd alt. E.H.),Heckel-
phone, 4(1Cl. in E-flat; Cl. in C alt. B.Cl.),
4(4th alt. C.Bn.)-8(5th to 8th alt. 4Ten. Tuba),
4,4,2-Timp.,Perc.-Org.,Cel.,2Hp.-Str.
Leuckart, Leipzig, ᶜ1915
Score 159 p.
*Composed 1914. First performance Vienna, 28
October 1915, Philharmonic Orchestra, the composer conducting.*

1735 Also sprach Zarathustra, Op. 30   *35'*
4*(3rd alt. Picc.II),4*,4*(1Cl. in E-flat),
4*-6,4,3,2-Timp.,Perc.-Org.,2Hp.-Str.
J. Aibl, Leipzig, ᶜ1896/Universal Edition,
Vienna, ᶜ1924
Score 115 p.
*Inspired by Nietzsche's poem. Composed 1896.
First performance Frankfurt, 27 November 1896,
the composer conducting.*

1536 Aus Italien [symphonic fantasy]   *47'*
Op. 16
1.[In the Campagna] 2.[Amid the ruins of
Rome] 3.[At the shore of Sorrento] 4.[Nea-
politan folk life]
3*,2(2nd alt. E.H.),2,3*-4,2,3-Timp.,Perc.-
Hp.-Str.
Aibl, München [n.d.]
Score 265 p.
*Composed 1885-86. First performance Munich, 2
March 1887, the composer conducting.*

1087 [Le bourgeois gentilhomme] Der   *42'*
Bürger als Edelmann. Orchestersuite
In 9 movements
2(alt. 2Picc.),2(2nd alt. E.H.),2,2-2,1,1-Timp.,

Strauss, Richard

Perc.-Pno.,Hp.-Str.
Fürstner, Berlin, ^c1912, ^c1918
Score 112 p. Large folio
*From the incidental music to Molière's play
Le Bourgeois Gentilhomme, composed 1912. This
suite 1918. First performance Berlin, 26
January 1920.*

392p Burleske, D minor   17'
Solo Pno.-3*,2,2,2-4,2-Timp.-Str.
Steingräber, Leipzig, ^c1894
Score 75 p.
*Composed 1886. First performance Eisenach, 21
June 1890, the composer conducting, Eugen
d'Albert soloist.*

Concertino for clarinet and bassoon
See: Duet-concertino for clarinet and bassoon
with string orchestra

593m [Concerto, horn, Op. 11, E-flat major] *17'*
1.Allegro 2.Andante - Allegro
Solo Hn.-2,2,2,2-2,2-Timp.-Str.
Kalmus, New York [n.d.]
Score 60 p.
*Composed 1882-83. First performance Mein-
ingen, 4 March 1885, Hans von Bülow conductor,
Leinhos soloist.*

1114m [Concerto, oboe, D major]   23'
Allegro moderato - Andante - Vivace
Solo Ob.-2,E.H.,2,2-2Hn.-Str.
Hawkes & Son, London, ^c1948
Score 61 p.
*Written at the request of John de Lancy. Com-
posed 1945-46. First performance Zurich, 26
February 1946, Tonhalle Orchestra, Volkmar
Andreae conductor, Marcel Saillet soloist.*

805v [Concerto, violin, Op. 8, D minor]   30'
1.Allegro 2.Lento 3.Presto
Solo Vn.-2,2,2,2-4,2-Timp.-Str.
Universal Edition, Vienna, ^c1897
Score 95 p.
*Composed 1881-82. First performance Dresden,
1902, Hugo Heerman soloist.*

1104 [Dance suite, from Couperin's piano compositions collected and arranged for small
orchestra by Richard Strauss]
1.Einzug und feierlicher Reigen (Pavane)
2.Courante 3.Carillon 4.Sarabande 5.Gavotte
6.Wirbeltanz 7.Allemande 8.Marsch
2,2(2nd alt. E.H.),2,2-2,1,1-Perc.-Cemb.,Cel.,
Hp.-Str.
Fürstner, Paris, ^c1923
Score 55 p.
*Completed 1923. First performance as a ballet
Vienna, 17 February 1923, Redoutensaal Orchestra, Clemens Krauss conductor. First concert
performance Berlin, 18 January 1924.*

1736 Don Juan, tone poem after Nicolaus   17'
Lenau, Op. 20
3(3rd alt. Picc.),3*,2,3*-4,3,3,1-Timp.,Perc.-
Hp.-Str.
Universal Edition, Vienna, ^c1896
Score 96 p.

*Composed 1888. First performance Weimar, 11
November 1889, the composer conducting.*

1738 Don Quixote, Op. 35
3*,3*,3*,4*-6,3,3,2-Timp.,Perc.-Hp.-Str.
Universal Edition, Vienna, ^c1898
Score 94 p.
*Composed 1897. First performance Cologne, 8
March 1898, Franz Wüllner conductor.*

1117m Duet-concertino, clarinet and   20'
bassoon
1.Allegro moderato 2.Andante 3.Rondo
Solo Cl. & Bn.-Hp.-Str.
Hawkes & Son, London, ^c1949
Score 71 p.
*Commissioned by Radio Lugano. Composed 1947.
First performance Lugano (Radio Monte Ceneri),
4 April 1948, Orchestra della Radio Svizzera
Italiana, Otmar Nussio conductor, Armando
Basile and Bruno Bergamaschi, soloists.*

3717 Feierlicher Einzug der Ritter des
Johanniterordens
3 Solo Tpt.-0,0,0,0-4,12,4,2-Timp.
Ms. [Schlesinger, Berlin, ^c1909]
Score 12 p.

469 [Same as above] Edited by Paul Juon   10'
3*,2,2,3*-4,3,3,1-Timp.,Perc.-Org.(ad lib.)-
Str.
Schlesinger, Berlin, ^c1909
Score 11 p.

1875 Festliches Praeludium, Op. 61   12'
5*,4,Heckelphone, 5(1Cl. in E-flat),5*-8,4,
6Tpt. backstage, 4,1-Timp.,Perc.-Org.-Str.
A. Fürstner, Paris, c1913
Score 52 p.
*Composed for the inauguration of the Konzert-
haus of Vienna, 19 October 1913.*

6491 Festmarsch, Op. 1   12'
3*,2,2,2-4,2,3,1-Timp.-Str.
Breitkopf & Härtel, Leipzig [1881]
Score 25 p.
*Composed 1876. First performance Munich, 26
March 1881, Wilde Gungl, Franz Strauss con-
ductor.*

1873 [Feuersnot, Op. 50. Love scene]   10'
3(3rd alt. Picc.),3*,3(3rd alt. B.Cl.),3(3rd
alt. C.Bn.)-4,3,3,1-Timp.,Perc.-Harm. backstage, 3Hp.(3rd ad lib., backstage)-Str.
Fürstner, Berlin, ^c1901
Score 29 p.
*From the vocal poem in one act. Composed
1900-01. First performance Dresden, 21 November 1901.*

1825 Ein Heldenleben [A hero's life]   40'
Op. 40
4*,4*(4th alt. E.H.),4*(1Cl. in E-flat),4*-8,
5,3,2-Timp.,Perc.-2Hp.-Str.
Leuckart, Leipzig, ^c1899
Score 139 p.
*Composed 1898. First performance Frankfurt-am
Main, 3 March 1899, the composer conducting.*

Stravinsky, Igor

1927 [Intermezzo, Op. 72. Four symphonic   *30'*
interludes]
1.[Travel-fever and waltz scene]   2.[Medita-
tion by the fireside]   3.[At the card table]
4.[Joyous conclusion]
2(2nd alt. Picc.),2(2nd alt. E.H.),2,2-3,2,2-
Timp.,Perc.-Pno.,Hp.-Str.
Fürstner, Berlin, ᶜ1924
Score 80 p. Large folio
From the opera with libretto by the composer.
Composed 1923. First performance Dresden,
4 November 1924.

2526 Kampf und Sieg [Battle and victory]   *8'*
3*,2,2,2-4,3,3,1-Timp.,Perc.-Str.
Heinrichshofen, Magdeburg, ᶜ1930
Score 40 p.
Depicts the German-Swedish battle of Lützen
in 1632. Composed 1894. First performance
Weimar, 1894.

1737 Macbeth, Tondichtung, Op. 23   *20'*
[revised]
3(3rd alt. Picc.),3*,3*,3*-4,4,3,1-Timp.,Perc.-
Str.
Aibl, Munich, ᶜ1896
Score 83 p.
Composed 1886-87; revised 1890. First per-
formance Weimar, 13 October 1890, the com-
poser conducting.

2069s Metamorphosen, for 23 solo strings   *30'*
10Vn.,5Va.,5Vc.,3Cb.
Boosey & Hawkes, London, ᶜ1946
Score 94 p.
Commissioned by Paul Sacher. Composed 1944-45.
First performance Zurich, 25 January 1946,
Collegium Musicum, Paul Sacher, conductor.
Quotes Beethoven's Eroica Symphony.

1874 Der Rosenkavalier. Suite. Edited by   *20'*
N. Nambuat
1.Aufzug des Rosenkavaliers und Duett   2.Ochs-
Walzer   3.Arie des Tenors   4.[Breakfast scene]
5.Terzett   6.[Closing duet]
2,2,2,2-4,2,3,Euph.-Timp.,Perc.-Str.
Fürstner, Paris, ᶜ1911
Score in reduction 19 p.
From the opera composed 1909. First perform-
ance Dresden, 26 January 1911.

5401 [Royal march. Transcribed by Otto   *5'*
Singer]
6(2ad lib.,2Picc.),4(2ad lib.),6(2ad lib.,2Cl.
in E-flat),4(2ad lib.)-8,12,4,1-Timp.,Perc.(12
additional drums)-2Hp.-Str.
Fürstner, Berlin, ᶜ1906
Score 18 p.
Originally composed for piano, 1906. This
version first performed Berlin, 6 March 1907,
the composer conducting.

4369 [Salome, Op. 54. Fantasy. Arranged by
Johann Doebber]
2(2nd alt. Picc.),2(1st alt. E.H.),2,2(2nd alt.
C.Bn.)-4,3,3,1-Timp.,Perc.-Hp.-Str.
Fürstner, Berlin, ᶜ1909
Score 90 p.

1013 [Salome, Op. 54. Salome's dance]   *15'*
4*,3*,Heckelphone,6*(1Cl. in E-flat),4*-6,4,
4,1-Timp.,Perc.-Cel.,2Hp.-Str.
Fürstner, Berlin, ᶜ1905, ᶜ1906
Score 40 p.
From the opera after Oscar Wilde, composed
1903-05. First performance Dresden, 9 Decem-
ber 1905, Ernst von Schuch conductor.

2293 [Serenade for thirteen winds, Op. 7]   *10'*
2,2,2,3*(C.Bn. or B.Tuba)-4Hn.
J.Aibl, Leipzig/Kalmus, New York [n.d.]
Score 43 p./Score 22 p.
Composed 1881. First performance Dresden, 27
November 1882, Franz Willner conductor.

1347s [Same as above] Transcribed for   *10'*
string orchestra by Hermann Ley
Pno.,Harm.,Hp.(all ad lib.)-Str.
J. Aibl, Leipzig [n.d.]
Violin conductor 5 p.

1042 Symphonia domestica, Op. 53   *42'*
In one movement
4*,3*,Ob.d'Amore,5*,5*-4Sax.(SABB)-8,4,3,1-
Timp.,Perc.-2Hp.-Str.
Bote & Bock, Berlin, ᶜ1904
Score 123 p.
Composed 1903. First performance New York, 31
March 1904, the composer conducting.

350 [Symphony, Op. 12, F minor]   *45'*
1.Allegro ma non troppo   2.Scherzo   3.Andante
cantabile   4.Allegro assai, molto appassionato
2,2,2,2-4,2,3,1-Timp.-Str.
Universal Edition, Vienna [n.d.]
Score 248 p.
Composed 1882-83. First performance New York,
13 December 1884, Theodore Thomas conductor.

1734 [Till Eulenspiegel's merry pranks,   *18'*
Op. 28]
4*,4*,4*,4*-8(4ad lib.),6(3ad lib.),3,1-Timp.,
Perc.-Str.
Score: C.F. Peters, Leipzig, ᶜ1932. 60 p.
Parts: Kalmus, New York [n.d.]
Composed 1894-95. First performance Cologne,
5 November 1895, Franz Willner conductor.

351 Tod und Verklärung, Op. 24 [Death and   *25'*
transfiguration]
In one movement
3,3*,3*,3*-4,3,3,1-Timp.,Gong-2Hp.-Str.
Kalmus, New York [n.d.]
Score 90 p.
Composed 1888-89. First performance Eisenach,
21 June 1890, Allgemeiner Deutscher Musik
Verein, the composer conducting.

STRAVINSKY, IGOR FEDOROVICH.
    Oranienbaum, near St. Petersburg 17 June 1882
               New York City 6 April 1971

5818 Agon, ballet [Complete]   *23'*
3(3rd alt. Picc.),3*,3*,3*-4,4,3-Timp.,Perc.-
Pno.,Hp.,Mand.-Str.
Boosey & Hawkes, New York, ᶜ1957
Score 85 p.

Stravinsky, Igor

Commissioned by Lincoln Kirstein and George Balanchine on a grant from the Rockefeller Foundation. Ballet with choreography by George Balanchine. Composed 1953-57. First performance Los Angeles, 17 June 1957, Robert Craft conductor.

1150s Apollon Musagète. Complete ballet
[original version]
Str.
Édition Russe de Musique, Berlin, ᶜ1928
Score 67 p.
Composed 1927-28. First performance Library of Congress, Washington, D.C., 27 April 1928. Slightly revised 1947.

459p Capriccio, piano and orchestra, in   *12'*
3 parts
Solo Pno.-3(3rd alt. Picc.),3*,3*(2nd alt. Cl. in E-flat),2-4,2,3,1-Timp.-Str. Quartet-Str.
Édition Russe de Musique, Berlin [n.d.]
Score 109 p.
Composed 1929. First performance Paris, 6 December 1929, Ernest Ansermet conductor, the composer as soloist.

1935 Chant du rossignol [The nightingale's *20'*
song, symphonic poem] Edited by F.H. Schneider
2(2nd alt. Picc.),2(2nd alt. E.H.),2(1Cl. in E-flat),2-4,3,3,1-Timp.,Perc.-Pno.,Cel.,2Hp.-Str.
Édition Russe de Musique, Berlin, ᶜ1921
Score 83 p.
Based on themes from the composer's opera Le Rossignol, composed 1909-14. First performance of this work Geneva, 6 December 1919, Orchestre de la Suisse Romande, Ernest Ansermet conductor.

4078 Circus polka, composed for a young   *4'*
elephant
3*,2,2,2-4,2,3,1-Timp.,Perc.-Str.
Associated Music Publishers, New York, ᶜ1944
Score 32 p.
Originally composed for band, 1942, on commission from Ringling Bros. and Barnum and Bailey Circus. Transcribed 1942. First performance of this version Cambridge, Massachusetts, 13 January 1944, Boston Symphony Orchestra, the composer conducting. Performance repeated in Boston, next day.

652p Concerto, piano and wind instruments *20'*
1.Lento - Allegro 2.Largo 3.Allegro
Solo Pno.-3*,3*,2,2-4,4,3,1-Timp.-Cb.
Édition Russe de Musique, Berlin, ᶜ1924
Score 60 p.
Composed 1923-24. First performance Paris, 22 May 1924.

4079 Danses concertantes
1.Marche-introduction 2.Pas d'action 3.Thème varié 4.Pas de deux 5.Marche-conclusion
1,1,1,1-2,1,1-Timp.-Str.(without Vn.II)
Associated Music Publishers, New York, ᶜ1942
Score 111 p.
Composed 1941-42. First performance Los Angeles, 8 February 1942, Janssen Symphony Orchestra, the composer conducting.

6871 Eight instrumental miniatures   *8'*
1.Andantino 2.Vivace 3.Lento 4.Allegretto 5.Moderato: Alla breve 6.Tempo di marcia 7.Larghetto 8.Tempo di tango
2,2,2,2-1Hn.-2Vn.,2Va.,2Vc.
J.&W. Chester, Ltd., London, ᶜ1963
Score 16 p.
Originally composed as Les Cinq Doigts for piano in 1921. Revised and set for instruments 1962.

3983 Fanfare for a liturgy
4Tpt.-S.Dr.
Ms.
Score 1 p.
Composed for Leigh Henry.

6943 [Fanfare for a new theatre]   *34"*
2Tpt.
Ms.
Score 1 p.
Composed 1964. First performance Lincoln Center, New York, 19 April 1964.

4021 Fanfare from the Marche Royale
Cl.,Bn.-Tpt.,Tbn.-Perc.-Vn.,Cb.
Ms.
Score 9 p.

1463 [The firebird. First suite] Suite   *30'*
de l'oiseau de feu
1.[Introduction-Kastcheï's enchanted garden] 2.[Supplications of the firebird] 3.[The princesses play with the golden apples] 4. [Round dance of the princesses] 5.[Infernal dance of all the subjects of Kastcheï]
4*(3rd alt. 2nd Picc.),4*,4*(3rd alt. Cl. in D),4*-4,3,3,1-Timp.,Perc.-Pno.,Cel.,3Hp.-Str.
Jurgenson, Moscow [1912?]
Score 99 p.
From the ballet based on the Russian fairy tale. Commissioned by Sergei Diaghilev. Composed 1909-10. First performance Paris, 25 June 1910, Ballet Russe, Gabriel Pierné conductor. This suite, 1911.

4305 [The firebird. Second suite, 1919 version]
1.Introduction – The firebird and its dance 2.The princesses' khorovod (Round) 3.Infernal dance of King Kashchei 4.Lullaby 5.Finale: Lento maestoso
2(2nd alt. Picc.),2(2nd alt. E.H.),2,2-4,2,3, 1-Timp.,Perc.-Pno.,Hp.-Str.
Kalmus, New York [n.d.]
Score 77 p.
A revised version was made in 1945.

1327 [Fireworks, Op. 4]   *8'*
3*,2(2nd alt. E.H.),3(3rd alt. B.Cl.),2-6,3,3, 1-Timp.,Perc.-Cel.,2Hp.-Str.
B. Schott's Söhne, Mainz [1908?]
Score 31 p.
Composed 1908. First performance St. Petersburg, 6 February 1909, Alexander Siloti conductor.

4077 Four Norwegian moods   *9'*
1.Intrada 2.Song 3.Wedding dance 4.Cortège

2(2nd alt. Picc.),2(2nd alt. E.H.),2,2-4,2,2,1
-Timp.-Str.
Associated Music Publishers, New York, c1944
Miniature score 48 p.
Composed 1942. First performed with Circus Polka.

7075 L'histoire du soldat [Complete]   35'
Reader(Narrator),3Characters(The Soldier,The
Devil,The Princess)-Cl.,Bn.-Cnt.,Tbn.-Perc.-
Vn.,Cb.
Kalmus, New York [n.d.]
Score 68 p.
*To be read, played and danced. Libretto in
French by Charles Ferdinand Ramuz. English
and German translations included. Composed
1918. First performance Lausanne, 28 September 1918, Ernest Ansermet conductor.*

6207 Jeu de cartes [A card game, ballet   23'
in 3 deals]
2(2nd alt. Picc.),2(2nd alt. E.H.),2,2-4,2,3,1
-Timp.,B.Dr.-Str.
B. Schott's Söhne, Mainz, c1937
Score 101 p.
*Composed 1936. First performance New York, 27
April 1937, American Ballet, the composer
conducting.*

2113 Octuor. Edited by Albert Spalding   18'
[original version]
1.Sinfonia 2.Tema con variazione 3.Finale
1,0,1,2-2Tpt., 2Tbn.
Édition Russe de Musique, Berlin, c1924
Score 53 p.
*Composed 1922-23. First performance Paris,
18 October 1923. Revised 1952.*

4044 Ode in three parts
1.Eulogy 2.Eclogue 3.Epitaph
3(3rd alt. Picc.),2,2,2-4,2-Timp.-Str.
Ms. c1943 by Igor Stravinsky
Score 24 p.
Commissioned by the Koussevitzky Music Foundation. Composed 1943. First performance Boston, 8 October 1943, Boston Symphony Orchestra, Serge Koussevitzky conductor.

1951 Petrouchka [Burlesque scenes in 4   25'
pictures]
I.[Popular feast in Shrove-tide week] II.[In
Petrouchka's quarters] III.[In the Moor's
apartment] IV.[The carnival (toward evening)]
4(3rd&4th alt. 2Picc.),4(4th alt. E.H.),4(4th
alt. B.Cl.),4(4th alt. C.Bn.)-4,2,2Cnt.,3,1-
Timp.,Perc.-Pno.,Cel.,2Hp.-Str.
Édition Russe, Berlin [n.d.]
Score 156 p.
*Composed 1910-11. First performance Paris,
13 June 1911, Ballet Diaghilev.*

1936 [Pulcinella. Suite] Edited by Albert   22'
Spalding
1.Sinfonia 2.Serenata 3.Scherzino 4.Tarantella 5.Toccata 6.Gavotta 7.Vivo 8.Minuetto
- Finale
2(2nd alt. Picc.),2,0,2-2,1,1-Str.
Édition Russe de Musique, Berlin, c1924

Score 75 p.
*From the ballet composed 1919 on themes attributed to Pergolesi. First performance Paris,
15 May 1920.*

2401 Quatre études pour orchestre   8'
1.Danse 2.Excentrique 3.Cantique 4.Madrid
3(3rd alt. Picc.),3(3rd alt. E.H.),3*(B.Cl.
alt. Cl. in E-flat),2-4,4,4,1-Timp.-Pno.,Hp.-
Str.
Édition Russe de Musique, Berlin [n.d.]
Score 51 p.
*Nos. 1-3 originally composed 1914 as Three
Pieces for String Quartet; no. 4 originally
sketched for pianola. This version 1929.
First performance Berlin, 7 November 1930.*

1739 Rag-time   12'
1,0,1-1,0,Cnt.,1-Perc.-Str.(without Vc.)
Chester, London, c1920
Score 15 p.
*Composed 1918. First performance London, 27
April 1920, Arthur Bliss conductor.*

2117 Le sacre du printemps [The rite   25'
of spring] Complete. Edited by F.H. Schneider
5*(3rd alt. 2nd Picc.),5*(4th alt. 2nd E.H.),
5*,5*-8(7th&8th alt. 2Ten.Tuba),5,3,2-Timp.,
Perc.-Str.
Édition Russe de Musique, Berlin, c1921
Score 139 p.
*Composed 1912-13. First performance Paris,
29 May 1913, Ballet Diaghilev.*

1423 Scherzo fantastique, Op. 3   16'
4*(2nd alt. Alto Fl.,3rd alt. 2nd Picc.),3*,
4*(3rd alt. Cl. in D),3*-4,3-Cym.-Cel.,3Hp.-
Str.
Jurgenson, Moscow [1908?]
Score 69 p.
Composed 1907-08. First performance St. Petersburg, 9 February 1909, Alexander Siloti conductor.

2296 [Song of the Volga boatmen]   4'
2*,2,2,3-4,3,3,1-Timp.,Perc.
Chester, London, c1920
Score 4 p.
*The traditional Russian song, arranged 1919.
First performance London, 4 February 1923,
Eugene Goossens conductor.*

1740 Suite no. 1 pour petit orchestre   4'30"
1.Andante 2.Napolitana 3.Española 4.Balalaïka
2(2nd alt. Picc.),1,2,2-1,1,1,1-B.Dr.-Str.
Kalmus, New York [n.d.]
Score 30 p.
*Originally composed 1917 in 5 Easy Pieces for
piano 4-hands. Transcribed 1925. First performance Milan, 17 June 1926, Hermann
Scherchen conductor.*

1741 Suite no. 2 pour petit orchestre   6'30"
1.Marche 2.Valse 3.Polka 4.Galop
2(2nd alt. Picc.),1,2,2-1,2,1,1-Perc.-Pno.-Str.
Kalmus, New York [n.d.]
Score 28 p.

Stravinsky, Igor

Composed 1919. First performance London, 8
June 1922, Eugene Goossens conductor.

1464 [Symphony no. 1, E-flat major]   28'
1.Allegro moderato 2.Scherzo 3.Largo
4.Finale
3(3rd alt. Picc.),2,3,2-4,3,3,1-Timp.,Perc.-
Str.
Jurgenson, Moscow [1913?]
Score 164 p.
Composed 1905-07. First performance St.
Petersburg, 5 February 1908, Imperial Orches-
tra.

4043 [Symphony in C]   29'
1.Moderato alla breve 2.Larghetto concertante 3.Allegretto 4.Largo - Tempo giusto
3(3rd alt. Picc.),2,2,2-4,2,3,1-Timp.,Perc.-
Str.
Ms. ᶜ1940 by Schott, London
Score 209 p. Large folio
Composed 1938-40. First performance Chicago,
7 November 1940, Chicago Symphony Orchestra,
the composer conducting.

STREET, JOSEPH.

650p [Concerto, piano, no. 1, Op. 20,   19'
E-flat major]
1.Allegro 2.Larghetto espressivo 3.Rondo
Solo Pno.-2,2,2,2-2,2-Timp.-Str.
Breitkopf & Härtel, Leipzig [n.d.]
Score 256 p.

659p [Concerto, piano, no. 2, Op. 24,   28'
F minor]
1.Allegro moderato poco maestoso 2.Adagio
3.Finale
Solo Pno.-2,2,2,2-2,2-Timp.-Str.
Breitkopf & Härtel, Leipzig [n.d.]
Score 258 p.

STRIEGLER, KURT.   Dresden 7 January 1886
                 Wildthurn, Germany 4 August 1958

2473 [Chamber symphony, Op. 14, G major]   55'
1.Adagio - Allegro 2.Larghetto 3.Scherzo
4.Finale: Thema und Variationen
1,1,1,1-Hn.-Str.(Cb. optional)
Otto Junne, Leipzig, ᶜ1912
Score 85 p.
First performance Dresden, 8 March 1912,
Tonkünstler Verein, the composer conducting.

793v [Concerto, violin, Op. 15, D minor]
1.Allegro 2.Adagio 3.Finale: Capricioso
Solo Vn.-2,2(2nd alt. E.H.),2,2-4,2-Timp.-Str.
O. Junne, Leipzig, ᶜ1913
Score 69 p.

STRINGFIELD, LAMAR.
           Raleigh, North Carolina 10 October 1897
           Asheville, North Carolina 21 January 1959

3451 Dance of the frogs   3'30"
1,1,2,1-2,2-S.Dr.-Str.
Sprague-Coleman [n.p.] ᶜ1940
Score 33 p.

Commissioned by CBS for the American School
of the Air, 1939. Composed 1939. First performance under original title Frogs, in a
CBS broadcast, New York, 12 December 1939,
Columbia Concert Orchestra.

From the Southern mountains, suite, Op. 41
2661 No. 1 Mountain song   4'30"
2662 No. 4 Cripple Creek   3'
2(2nd alt. Picc.),2(1st alt. E.H. in no. 1),
2,2-2Sax.(AT)-4,2,3,1-Timp.,Perc.-Str.
Carl Fischer, New York, ᶜ1927, ᶜ1930
Scores: 22 p., 20 p.
Composed 1927. No. 1 first performed Nashville, 1 April 1927, Nashville Symphony
Orchestra, the composer conducting; no. 4
first performed New York, November 1927, the
composer conducting. Suite received the
Pulitzer Prize, 1928.

3016 Indian legend, Op. 23 no. 1   10'
3*,2,2,2-4,2,3,1-Timp.,Perc.-Hp.-Str.
Ms.
Score 68 p.
Originally composed for flute and string quar-
tet, 1924; orchestrated 1924. First perform-
ance New York, 6 March 1927, Sunday Symphonic
Society, Josiah Zuro conductor.

3604 Kidder Kole (from the Blue Ridge)   3'30"
3*,2,2,2-4,2,3,1-Timp.,Perc.-Str.
Ms.
Score 40 p.
Composed 1937. First performance New York,
1939, WOR Symphony Orchestra, Morton Gould
conductor.

1756s Mountain dew (from the Blue Ridge)   6'
Str.
Sprague-Coleman, New York, ᶜ1937
Score 11 p.
Commissioned by F. Charles Adler for the
Saratoga Spa Music Festival, 1937. Composed
1937. First performance Saratoga Springs,
New York, 11 September 1937, F. Charles Adler
conductor.

2784 The seventh queue, an imaginary   12'
ballet, Op. 38
3*,3*,2,2-4,2,3,1-Timp.,Perc.-Hp.-Str.
Ms.
Score 61 p.
Composed 1927. First performance Washington,
D.C., 14 February 1928, Washington National
Opera Association, the composer conducting.

STRINGHAM, EDWIN JOHN.
           Kenosha, Wisconsin 11 July 1890
           Chapel Hill, North Carolina 1 July 1974

2836 The ancient mariner, symphonic poem   14'
after the poem by Samuel Taylor Coleridge
3(3rd alt. Picc.),3(3rd alt. E.H.),3(3rd alt.
B.Cl.),3*-4,3,3,1-Timp.,Perc.-Cel.,2Hp.-Str.
Ms.
Score 51 p.
Composed 1927. First performance Denver, 16
March 1928, Civic Symphony Orchestra of Den-
ver, Horace E. Tureman conductor.

2727   Nocturne no. 1   13'30"
3(3rd alt. Picc.),3*,3*,2-4,3,3,1-Timp.,Perc.-
Cel.,2Hp.-Str.
Ms.
Score 43 p.
Composed 1931. First performance Rochester,
9 December 1932, Rochester Philharmonic
Orchestra, Howard Hanson conductor.

2810   Notturno   8'
2,2*,2,Alto Cl.(optional),2-2Hn.-Hp.
Ms.
Score 26 p.
Originally composed as a string quartet, 1935;
arranged, 1936.

2851   [Symphony no. 1, Italian, B-flat   27'
minor]
1.Allegro con spirito 2.Adagio - Scherzo
3.Finale
3(3rd alt. Picc.),3*,3(3rd alt. B.Cl.),3*-
4,3,3,1-Timp.,Perc.-Cel.,2Hp.-Str.
Ms.
Score 207 p.
Commissioned by the Minneapolis Symphony
Orchestra, 1929. Composed 1929. First per-
formance Minneapolis, 15 November 1929, the
Minneapolis Symphony Orchestra, Henri Ver-
brugghen conductor.

2820   Three pastels   6'
1.Nude 2.Dance rustic 3.Pastorale
1,2,2,2-2,0,2-Timp.,Perc.-Cel.-Str.
Ms.
Score 24 p.
Originally composed for piano, 1914; orches-
trated, 1915; this version, 1924. First per-
formance of this version Rochester, 17 May
1928, Rochester Philharmonic Orchestra,
Howard Hanson conductor.

STROHBACH, SIEGFRIED.   Hannover, Germany 1929

393m   [Concerto for 2 flutes, glockenspiel, and
string orchestra, G major (1959)]
1.Allegro comodo 2.Andante grazioso 3.Alle-
gro con brio
Solo Fl.I & II, Solo Glock.-Str.
Breitkopf & Härtel, Wiesbaden, ᶜ1960
Score 44 p.

STRONG, GEORGE TEMPLETON.   New York 26 May 1856
Geneva, Switzerland 27 June 1948

747v   Americana, deux petits poèmes
1.Andante 2.Animato
Solo Vn.-2,1,2,2-2,1-Timp.-Str.
Henn, Geneva, ᶜ1919, ᶜ1920
Score 15 p.
Composed 1904.

2225s   [Chorale on a theme of Leo Hassler   7'
(1601), Wenn Ich Einmal Scheiden Soll]
Str.
Edition Henn, Geneva [ᶜ1933]
Score 4 p.
This work originally composed for piano,
1927. Transcribed 1929. First performance

Geneva, 13 May 1933, Parish Orchestra of St.
Pierre-Fusterie, Louis Duret conductor.

526c   Élégie
Solo Vc.-2,3*,3*,2-4,2,3,1-Timp.-Hp.-Str.
Henn, Geneva, ᶜ1922
Score 18 p.
Composed 1916. First performance 1923,
Schweizer Tonkünstlerfest.

6741   [King Arthur, symphonic poem]
3(2nd&3rd alt. Picc.),3*,4*(1Cl. in C),3*-
4,3,2Cnt.,3,1-Timp.,Perc.-Str.
Edition Henn, Geneva, ᶜ1921
Score 142 p.
Composed 1916.

755v   Ein Märchen [A fairy tale] Gestrebt-
Gewonnen-Gescheitert, Op. 12
Solo Vn.-2,2,2,2-4,2-Timp.-Str.
Kistner, Leipzig [1883?]
Score 51 p.

5759   [Symphony no. 2, Sintram, Op. 50,   52'
G minor]
1.Ziemlich langsam-Rasch 2.Langsam 3.[The
two terrible companions] 4.[The victorious
struggle]
3(3rd alt. Picc.),3*,3*,3-4,3,3,1-Timp.,Cym.-
Str.
Franz Jost, Leipzig [1894]
Score 224 p.
Suggested by F. H. K. de la Motte Fouqué's
romance Sintram and Albrecht Dürer's copper
engraving Ritter, Tod und Teufel. Composed
1887-79. First performance Brooklyn, 12 April
1892, Anton Seidl conductor.

721v   Une vie d'artiste, poème symphonique
Solo Vn.-3*,2*,3*,2-4,2,3,1-Timp.-Str.
Henn, Geneva, ᶜ1920, ᶜ1921
Score 33 p.
Composed 1919. First performance Zurich,
June 1920, Twentieth Festival of the Associa-
tion of Swiss Musicians, Volkmar Andreae con-
ductor, Joseph Szigeti soloist.

STRUBE, GUSTAV.   Ballenstedt, Germany 3 March 1867
Baltimore, Maryland 2 February 1953

45s   Berceuse
Str.(Cb. ad lib.)
Boston Music Co./G. Schirmer, Boston, ᶜ1908
Score 3 p.

2704   Little symphony no. 1   20'
3(3rd alt. Picc.),3*,3*,2-4,3-Timp.,Cym.-Cel.,
Hp.-Str.
Ms.
Score 77 p.
Composed 1922.

5969   The Lorelei [symphonic poem]   8'
3(3rd alt. Picc.),4*,3*,3-4,4,3,1-Timp.,Perc.-
Hp.-Str.
Ms.
Score 50 p.
Suggested by Frederic A. Kummer's poem.

Strube, Gustav

Composed 1911-12. First performance Boston, 25 January 1913 (public rehearsal 24 January), Boston Symphony Orchestra, the composer conducting.

6294 Narcissus and Echo [symphonic poem]   8'
3,3*,2,2-4,4-Timp.-Hp.-Str.
Ms.
Score 25 p.
Suggested by Malfilâtre's poem of 1769, Narcisse Dans l'Île de Venus. Composed 1911-12. First performance Boston, 25 January 1913 (public rehearsal 24 January), Boston Symphony Orchestra, the composer conducting.

1998 Puck, a comedy overture   7'
3*,3*,3*,3-4,4,3,1-Timp.,Perc.-Str.
G. Schirmer, New York, ᶜ1910
Score 53 p.

2735 Symphonic prologue   12'
3(3rd alt. Picc.),3*,3*,2-4,2,3,1-Timp.,Perc.-Cel.,Hp.-Str.
Ms.
Score 70 p.
Composed 1925. First performance Baltimore, 24 April 1927, the composer conducting. Awarded prize by the Sesqui-Centennial International Exposition, Philadelphia, 1926.

2747 Symphony   33'
1.Allegro moderato 2.Un poco adagio 3.Scherzo 4.Allegro molto
3(3rd alt. Picc.),3*,3*,3*-4,4,3,1-Timp.,Perc.-Cel.,Hp.-Str.
Ms.
Score 197 p.
Composed 1921-22, in memory of Sidney Lanier, poet, musician and critic. First performance Washington, D.C., 17 March 1925, New York Symphony Orchestra, the composer conducting.

1987 [Symphony, B minor]   35'
1.Andante - Allegro comodo 2.Adagio 3.Scherzo 4.Finale
3(3rd alt. Picc.),3*,3*,3-4,4,3,1-Timp.,Perc.-Hp.-Str.
G. Schirmer, New York, ᶜ1910
Score 154 p.

STRUSS, FRITZ.   Hamburg 28 November 1847
                                    d. ca.1912

756v [Concerto, violin, no. 1, Op. 4, in A]
1.Allegro moderato 2.Andante 3.Finale
Solo Vn.-2,2,2,2-2,2-Timp.-Str.
Fr. Kistner, Leipzig [n.d.]
Score 163 p.

969v [Concerto, violin, no. 2, Op. 9, D major]
1.Allegro 2.Adagio 3.Rondo
Solo Vn.-2,2,2,2-2,2-Timp.-Str.
Score: Ms. 198 p.
Parts: Bote & Bock, Berlin, ᶜ1895

STRUTT, DOROTHY.
          b. Hornchurch, Essex, England 18 May 1941

7299 The folding of a paper, Op. 1   25'
no. 36
2Ten. Voices(Sprechstimme)-Bn.-1,3,3-Timp.,S.Dr.-Cel.-Str.
Ms.
Score 75 p. Large folio
Texts in French by Stéphane Mallarmé, Paul Valéry, and Charles Baudelaire. Composed 1962.

STUBBE, ARTUR.
          b. Köpenick, near Berlin 18 October 1866

609c Chant oublié [Forgotten song] Op. 23 no. 2
Solo Vc.-1,0,2,1-2Hn.-Str.
Score: Ms. 4 p.
Parts: Bote & Bock, Berlin, ᶜ1908

STUBBS DU PERRON, EDUARDO WALTER.
          b. Lima, Peru 31 December 1891

3675 [Atahualpa. Death of Atahualpa,   8'
Op. 17]
3*,2*,2,2-4,2,4,1-Timp.,Perc.-Hp.-Str.
Ms.
Score 22 p.
From the ballet composed 1915. First performance over Radio Paris, 1934.

STÜRMER, BRUNO. Freiburg, Germany 9 September 1892
                          Bad Homburg, Germany 19 May 1958

4928 [Dance suite for band]
1(ad lib.),0,3(1Cl. in E-flat ad lib.)-2Tpt.,2Ten. Hn.,2Fluegelhn.,2Waldhn.,2Tbn.(2nd ad lib.),Bar.,2Tuba(2nd ad lib.)-Perc.
Chr. Vieweg, Berlin [1940?]
Score 16 p.
Composed 1939.

1629s Feierliche Musik [Solemn music] Op. 65
1.Prelude 2.Choral 3.Fugue
2String Orchestras (or 2Quintets)
P.J. Tonger, Cologne, ᶜ1931
Score 24 p.

4328 [Suite for nine solo instruments,   20'
Op. 9, G minor]
1,1,1,1-Str.
B. Schott's Söhne, Mainz, ᶜ1923
Score 47 p.

STUTELY, GORDON E.

1368s Salt o' the sea, suite, Op. 26   10'
Str.
Oxford University Press, London, ᶜ1929
Score 20 p.

SUDESSI, POMPILIO. Treviso, Italy 4 September 1853
                          Treviso 28 April 1923

1560s Guitarada, capriccio pizzicato
Str.
Score: Ms. 7 p.
Parts: E. Kramer-Bangert, Kassel, ᶜ1902

866s Pavane des pages
Str.
P. Decourcelle, Nice [n.d.]
Score 5 p.

980s Propos galants, scène de ballet
Str.
Score: Ms. 7 p.
Parts: E. Fromont, Paris, ^c1894

SUK, JOSEF. the elder.
Křečovice, Bohemia 4 January 1874
Benešov, near Prague 29 May 1935

2289 Dramatická ouvertura, Op. 4   *10'*
2,3*,2,2-4,2,3,1-Timp.-Str.
Ms.
Score 55 p.
Composed 1891. First performance Prague, 9
July 1892.

5657 [A fairytale, suite for orchestra   *31'*
based on themes from the music to Julius
Zeyer's Radúz and Mahulena, Op. 16]
3*,3*,3*,2-4,2,3,1-Timp.,Perc.-Hp.-Str.
N. Simrock, Berlin, ^c1901
Score 86 p.
This suite composed 1900.

533v Fantasie, Violine und Orchester,   *30'*
Op. 24
Solo Vn.-2,2,2,2-4,2,3,1-Timp.,Perc.-Str.
N. Simrock, Berlin, ^c1905
Score 80 p.
Composed 1902-03. First performance Prague,
9 January 1904, Oskar Nedbal conductor, Karl
Hofmann soloist.

391s [Meditation on the old Bohemian carol *7'*
St. Wenceslas, Op. 35]
Str.
Fr. A. Urbánek, Prague, ^c1914
Miniature score 11 p.

5403 [New life, march, Op. 35c]   *6'*
3(3rd alt. Picc.),2,3,2-4,3,3,1-Timp.,Perc.-
Chorus(SATB)-Str.
Hudební Matice, Prague, ^c1948
Score 46 p.
Originally composed for piano 4-hands, 1919.
This transcription, 1920. Text added 1930.
Winner of the Sokol Community's contest for a
new festive march, 1919. Awarded first prize
in the music contest at the Olympic Games,
Los Angeles, 1932.

2444 Praga [symphonic poem, Op. 26]
3(3rd alt. Picc.),3*,3*,3*-4,3,3,1-Timp.,Perc.
-Org.,Hp.-Str.
Ms. [M. Urbánek, Prague, ^c1929]
Score 119 p.

1016 Scherzo fantastique, Op. 25   *18'*
3*,3*,3*,2-4,2,3,1-Timp.,Perc.-Hp.-Str.
Breitkopf & Härtel, Leipzig [n.d.]
Score 71 p.
Composed 1903. First performance Prague, 18
April 1905, J. Kàan conductor.

170s Serenade, Op. 6   *25'*
Str.
Kalmus, New York [n.d.]
Miniature score 55 p.

201 Ein Sommermärchen, Tondichtung, Op. 29 *55'*
3(3rd alt. Picc.),3*(2nd alt. 2nd E.H.),3*,3*-
6,3,3,1-Timp.,Perc.-Pno.,Org.,Cel.,2Hp.-Str.
Universal Edition, Vienna, ^c1910
Score 173 p.
Composed 1907-09. First performance Prague,
26 January 1909, Karel Kovařovic conductor.

979 [Symphony no. 1, Op. 14, E major]   *40'*
1.Allegro 2.Adagio 3.Allegro vivace
2(2nd alt. Picc.),2,2,2-4,2,3,1-Timp.-Str.
N. Simrock, Berlin, ^c1900
Score 103 p.
Composed 1897-99. First performance Prague,
25 November 1899, Oskar Nedbal conductor.

5073 [Symphony no. 2, Asrael, Op. 27,   *60'*
C minor]
1.Andante sostenuto 2.Andante 3.Vivace
4.Adagio 5.Adagio e maestoso - Allegro
appassionato - Adagio e mesto
3*,3*,3*,3*-4,3,3,1-Timp.,Perc.-Hp.-Str.
Breitkopf & Härtel, Leipzig [1907]
Score 252 p.
Asrael represents the angel of death. Com-
posed 1905-06. First performance Prague, 3
February 1907.

5757 Zrání [symphonic poem, Op. 34]   *40'*
3(1st&3rd alt. Picc.II&I),3(3rd alt. E.H.),3
(3rd alt. B.Cl.),3(3rd alt. C.Bn.)-6,9(6 offstage),3,1-Timp.,Perc.-Pno.,Cel.,Hp.-Women's
Chorus(offstage)-Str.
Hudební Matice, Prague, ^c1924
Score 183 p.
Inspired by a poem by Antonín Sova. Composed
1912-17. First performance Prague, 30 Octo-
ber 1918.

SULLIVAN, ARTHUR.   London 13 May 1842
London 22 November 1900

7003 Overture di ballo   *10'*
2*,2,2,2-4,2,3,2(or 1)-Timp.,Perc.-Str.
Novello, London, 1889
Score 80 p.
Composed 1870. First performance Birmingham
Festival, 31 August 1870.

7012 Overture in C (In memoriam)   *13'*
2,2,2,2-4,2,3,Ophicl.-Timp.,Perc.-Org.-Str.
Novello, Ewer & Co., London [191-?]
Score 74 p.
Composed 1866 on the death of the composer's
father. First performance Norwich Festival,
30 October 1866.

4393 [The tempest. Three dances]
2,2,2,2-2,2,3-Timp.,Perc.-Str.
Novello, London, ^c1904
Score 57 p.
From the incidental music to Shakespeare's
play. Composed ca.1860. First performance
London, 12 April 1862, August Manns conductor.

799

Sulzbach, Emil

SULZBACH, EMIL.   Frankfurt 7 May 1855
                    Bad Homburg, Germany 25 May 1932

  584s Vier kleine Stücke
    Str.
    B. Schott's Söhne, Mainz [n.d.]
    Score 19 p.

SUMERLIN, MACON.   Rotan, Texas 24 October 1919

  7188 Fanfare, andante and fugue
    3Hn.,4Tpt.,2Tbn.,Bar.Hn.,Tuba-S.Dr.,B.Dr.
    WIM, Los Angeles, c1963 and 1964 by Maxima
    Press (c1965 by Far West Music, Los Angeles)
    Score 16 p.

SUPPÉ, FRANZ VON.   Spalato, Dalmatia 18 April 1819
                           Vienna 21 May 1895

  4666 Banditenstreiche· Ouverture   7'30"
    2*,2,2,2-4,2,3-Timp.,Perc.-Guit.-Male Voice-
    Str.
    C.F.W. Siegel, Leipzig [1868]
    Score 55 p.
    From the operetta first performed Vienna, 27
    April 1867.

  4432 Die Irrfahrt um's Glück. Overture   6'
    2(2nd alt. Picc.),2,2,2-4,2,3,Bombardon-Timp.,
    Perc.-Str.
    C.F.W. Siegel, Leipzig [1869?]
    Score 44 p.
    For the magical folk play by Carl Elmar.

  6946 [Light cavalry. Overture]   8'
    2*,2,2,2-4,2,3-Timp.,S.Dr.,B.Dr.-Str.
    Luck's Music Library, Detroit [n.d.]
    Score 40 p.
    From the operetta first performed Vienna, 21
    March 1866.

  4906 [Morning, noon and night in Vienna.   7'
    Overture to the folk play]
    2(2nd alt. Picc.),2,2,2-4,2,3-Timp.,S.Dr.,
    B.Dr.-Str.
    Kalmus, New York [n.d.]
    Score 56 p.

  4400 Pique Dame. Overture   8'
    2(2nd alt. Picc.),2,2,2-4,2,3,Ophicl.-Timp.,
    Perc.-Str.
    C.F.W. Siegel, Leipzig [1867]
    Score 55 p.
    From the operetta. First performance Graz,
    Austria, 24 June 1864.

  4324 Poet and peasant overture   10'
    2(2nd alt. Picc.),2,2,2-4,2,3,Ophicl.-Timp.,
    Perc.-Hp.-Str.
    Luck's Music Library, Detroit [n.d.]
    Score 46 p.
    From the incidental music to Carl Elmar's
    comedy Dichter und Bauer. Composed 1846.
    First performance Vienna, 24 August 1846.

  7007 Des Wanderers Ziel. Overture
    2*,2,2,2-4,2,3,Ophicl.-Timp.,B.Dr.-Hp.-Str.
    C.F.W. Siegel, Leipzig [1871]

Score in reduction 13 p.
From Karl Meisl's allegorical festival play.

SURAK, RONALD MARTIN.
              b. Shamokin, Pennsylvania 1 August 1940

  301v Miniatures [6 movements]   10'
    Solo Vn.-Str.
    Ms.
    Score 24 p.
    Commissioned by the Sixteen Concerto Soloists
    of Philadelphia. Composed 1967-68. First
    performance Philadelphia, 20 November 1968,
    Sixteen Concerto Soloists, Marc Mostovoy con-
    ductor, Romulo Teco soloist.

  7202 Philokalia [for orchestra]   6'
    3*,3*,3*,3*-4,3,2,1-Timp.,Perc.-Hp.-Str.
    Ms.
    Score 19 p. Large folio
    Inspired by Philokalia of 1782, writings by
    the Hesychasts, Orthodox Christian mystics.
    Composed 1972. Selected for performance by
    the Orchestra Society of Philadelphia as part
    of its Pennsylvania Composers Project 1976,
    made possible by grants from the National
    Endowment for the Arts and the Pennsylvania
    Council on the Arts with performance materials
    prepared by the Fleisher Collection of Orches-
    tral Music. First performance Drexel Univer-
    sity, Philadelphia, 16 May 1976, Sidney Roth-
    stein conductor.

SURINACH, CARLOS.   Barcelona 4 March 1915

  6537 Acrobats of God, ballet   23'
    1(alt. Picc.),1(alt. E.H.),1,1-1,1,1,1(optional)
    -Timp.,Perc.-Hp.-Str.
    Ms.
    Score 112 p.
    Commissioned by Martha Graham. Composed 1960.
    First performance New York, 27 April 1960,
    Martha Graham and Company.

  6529 Apasionada, ballet   35'
    1(alt. Picc.),1(alt. E.H.),1(alt. B.Cl.),1-1,1,
    1-Timp.,Perc.-Pno.-Cb.
    Ms. [Associated Music Publishers, New York]
    Score 157 p.
    Commissioned by Pearl Lang. Composed 1960.
    First performance New York, 5 January 1962,
    Pearl Lang and Company, the composer con-
    ducting.

  340p Concertino for piano, strings and   16'
    cymbals
    1.Chacona 2.Andante 3.Vivace
    Solo Pno.-Cym.-Str.
    Ms. Associated Music Publishers, New York
    [c1956]
    Score 54 p. Large folio
    Commissioned by MGM Records. Composed 1956.
    First performance New York, 19 February 1957,
    the composer conducting, William Masselos
    soloist.

  6528 David and Bath-sheba, ballet   23'
    2(both alt. Picc.),2(both alt. E.H.)-2,2-

Svendsen, Johan

Timp.,Perc.-Pno.,Hp.-2Cb.
Ms. Associated, New York, ^c1959 by composer
Commissioned by CBS Television Network. Composed 1959. First performance over CBS-TV from New York, 15 May 1960, Alfredo Antonini conductor, choreography by John Butler.

5824 Embattled garden, ballet   21'
1(alt. Picc.),1(alt. E.H.),1,1-1,1,1-Timp.,
Perc.-Hp.-Str.
Ms. Associated, New York [c1958]
Score 88 p. Large folio
Title refers to the Garden of Eden. Commissioned for Martha Graham by the Bethsabée de Rothschild Foundation. Composed 1957-58. First performance New York, 3 April 1958, Martha Graham and Company.

5314 Fandango for orchestra   10'
3(2nd&3rd alt. Picc.),3*(2nd alt. E.H.),3*,2-
4,3,3,1-Timp.,Perc.-Hp.-Str.
Ms. [Associated, New York, ^c1954]
Score 47 p. Large folio
Composed 1954. First performance Utica, New York, 4 April 1961, Utica Symphony Orchestra, José Serebrier conductor.

5835 Feria magica, overture   6'
2(both alt. Picc.),2,2,2-4,2,3,1-Timp.,Perc.-
Hp.-Str.
Associated Music Publishers, New York, ^c1957
Score 66 p.
Suggested by the fairs of Spain. Commissioned by the Louisville Philharmonic Society. Composed 1956. First performance Louisville, 14 March 1956, The Louisville Orchestra, Robert Whitney conductor.

5396 Passacaglia symphony   19'
1.Allegro ma non tanto 2.Larghetto 3.Scherzando 4.Maestoso ma deciso
3(2nd&3rd alt. Picc.I&II),3*,3*,3*-4,3,3,1-
Timp.,Perc.-Str.
Ms. [Peer International, New York, ^c1959]
Score 86 p. Large folio
Composed 1945. First performance Barcelona, Spain, 8 April 1945, Barcelona Municipal Orchestra, Eduardo Toldrá conductor.

5313 Ritmo jondo [ballet]   20'
1.Tres jaleos 2.Danza chica 3.Bulerías
4.Rituales 5.Saeta 6.Danza grande
7.Garrotín
1(alt. Picc.),1(alt. E.H.),1,1-1,1,1-Timp.,
Perc.-3Handclappers-Str.
Ms. [Associated, New York, ^c1953, ^c1958]
Score 83 p. Large folio
Movements 2, 3, 6, 7 are flamenco dances. Saeta is a prayer sung during the Good Friday procession in Seville. Commissioned by the Bethsabée de Rothschild Foundation. Composed 1952. First performance as a ballet under the title Deep Rhythm, New York, 15 April 1953, José Limon and Company, the composer conducting, choreography by Doris Humphrey.

5836 Sinfonia chica (1957)   16'
1.Allegro 2.Adagio 3.Frenetico
2(both alt. Picc.),2(2nd alt. E.H.),2,2-2,1-
Timp.,Perc.-Str.
Associated Music Publishers, New York, ^c1958
Score 119 p.
Commissioned by the Advisory Board of the Musical Arts Society of La Jolla, California. Composed 1957. First performance La Jolla, 6 August 1957, Musical Arts Society Orchestra of La Jolla, the composer conducting.

5317 Sinfonietta flamenca   12'
1.Vivo grazioso 2.Andantino 3.Allegro ma
non troppo 4.Presto agitato
2(both alt. Picc.),2(2nd alt. E.H.),2,2-4,2,3,
1-Timp.,Perc.-Hp.-Str.
Associated Music Publishers, New York, ^c1955
Score 98 p.
Commissioned by the Louisville Philharmonic Society under a grant from the Rockefeller Foundation. Composed 1953. First performance Louisville, 9 January 1954, The Louisville Orchestra, Robert Whitney conductor.

SVENDSEN, JOHAN SEVERIN.
             Christiania (now Oslo) 30 September 1840
             Copenhagen 14 June 1911

2130 Andante funèbre   6'
2,2,2,2-4,2,3,1-Timp.-Str.
W. Hansen, Leipzig, ^c1895
Score 13 p.
Composed 1894. First performance Copenhagen, 1894.

606 Carneval in Paris, Op. 9   11'
3*,2,2,2-4,2,3,1-Timp.,Perc.-Str.
C.F.W. Siegel, Leipzig [n.d.]
Score 49 p.

482v [Concerto, violin, Op. 6, A major]
1.Allegro moderato ben risoluto 2.Andante
3.Allegro giusto
Solo Vn.-2,2,2,2-2,2-Timp.-Str.
E.W. Fritzsch, Leipzig [n.d.]
Score 148 p.
Composed 1869.

476c [Concerto, violoncello, Op. 7, D major]
In one movement
Solo Vc.-2,2,2,2-2,2-Timp.-Str.
C.F.W. Siegel, Leipzig, 1871
Score 75 p.
Composed 1871.

1404 Fest-Polonaise, Op. 12   13'
3*,2,2,2-4,3,3,1-Timp.,Perc.-Str.
W. Hansen, Copenhagen [n.d.]
Score 56 p.
Composed 1895.

351s I Fjol gjaett'e Gjeitinn [Norwegian
folk-song]
Str.
C.F.W. Siegel, Leipzig, 1877
Score 9 p.

Svendsen, Johan

890 Krönungs-Marsch [Coronation march]   7'
Op. 13
2,2,2,2-4,3,3,1-Timp.,Perc.-Str.
C.F.W. Siegel, Leipzig [n.d.]
Score 21 p.
For the coronation of Oscar II.

170 Norwegischer Künstlerkarneval, Op. 14   8'
3*,2,2,2-4,3,3,1-Timp.,Perc.-Str.
C.F. Peters, Leipzig [n.d.]
Score 37 p.
*Composed 1909. First performance Copenhagen,
1909, the composer conducting.*

Rapsodies norvégiennes
166   No. 1, Op. 17, B minor   8'
121   No. 2, Op. 19, A major   9'
120   No. 3, Op. 21, C major   12'
1030   No. 4, Op. 22, in D   12'
2(2nd alt. Picc. in no. 2 and 3),2,2,2-4,2,3-
Timp.-Str.
W. Hansen, Copenhagen [n.d.] (no. 1)
C. Warmuth, Christiania [n.d.] (nos. 2, 3, 4)
Scores: 41 p., 61 p., 54 p., 68 p.
*Composed 1897-99. First performance of all
four, Copenhagen, 1899, the composer conducting.*

490v Romance, violin and orchestra, Op. 26
Solo Vn.-1,1,2,2-2Hn.-Timp.-Str.
W. Hansen, Copenhagen [n.d.]
Score 13 p.

1163v [Same as above] Arranged by Samuel
L. Laciar
Solo Vn.-3(3rd alt. Picc.),2,2,2-4,2,3,1-Str.
Ms.
Score 17 p.

119 Romeo und Julia, Op. 18   11'
2,2,2,2-4,2,3,1-Timp.-Str.
Breitkopf & Härtel, Leipzig [n.d.]
Score 56 p.
*Composed 1879. First performance Christiania,
1880, the composer conducting.*

910 Sigurd Slembe [symphonic introduction,   7'
Op. 8]
2,2,2,2-4,2,3,1-Timp.-Str.
E.W. Fritzsch, Leipzig, 1872
Score 63 p.
*Composed 1871, for B. Björnson's drama. First
performance Christiania, 1872, the composer
conducting.*

393s Solitude sur la montagne [melody by Ole
Bull. Arranged by Johan Svendsen]
Str.
W. Hansen, Copenhagen [n.d.]
Score 3 p.

299 [Symphony no. 1, Op. 4, D major]   29'
1.Molto allegro 2.Andante 3.Allegretto
scherzando 4.Maestoso
2,2,2,2-4,2,3-Timp.-Str.
E.W. Fritzsch, Leipzig [n.d.]
Score 195 p.

684 [Symphony no. 2, Op. 15, B-flat   28'
major]
1.Allegro 2.Andante sostenuto 3.Intermezzo
4.Finale
2,2,2,2-4,2,3-Timp.-Str.
C.F.W. Siegel, Leipzig, 1877
Score 107 p.
*Composed 1875. First performance Christiania,
1876, the composer conducting.*

350s [Two Icelandic melodies]   7'
Str.
C.F.W. Siegel, Leipzig [n.d.]
Score 9 p.

1014 Zorahayda, Op. 11 (after Washington   11'
Irving's legend of the Rose of the Alhambra)
2,2,2,2-4,2,3-Timp.-Str.
W. Hansen, Copenhagen [n.d.]
Score 44 p.
Composed 1895.

392s Zwei schwedische Volksmelodien.   7'
Arranged by Johan S. Svendsen
1.[Everything under the firmament] 2.[Thou
old, breezy, mountain-covered North]
Str.
W. Hansen, Copenhagen [n.d.]
Score 9 p.

SWEPSTONE, EDITH.   b. England 19th c.

481s Minuet, C major
Str.
Score: Ms. 7 p.
Parts: B. Schott's Söhne [Mainz, n.d.]

649s Tarentelle, A minor
Str.
Score: Ms. 11 p.
Parts: B. Schott's Söhne, Mainz [n.d.]

SWERT, JULES DE.   Louvain, Belgium 15 August 1843
                    Ostend, Belgium 24 February 1891

Also spelled: Deswert, Jules

716c [Concerto, violoncello, no. 1, Op. 32,
D minor]
In one movement
Solo Vc.-2,2,2,2-2,2,3-Timp.-Str.
Score: Ms. 86 p.
Parts: B. Schott [n.p., n.d.]

638c [Concerto, violoncello, no. 2, Op. 38,
C minor]
In one movement
Solo Vc.-2,2,2,2-3,2,3-Timp.-Str.
Score: Ms. 65 p.
Parts: Cranz, Bruxelles [n.d.]

656c [Serenade, violoncello and orchestra,
Op. 36]
Solo Vc.-2,2,2,2-2Hn.-Str.
Score: Ms. 18 p.
Parts: A. Cranz, Leipzig [n.d.]

SWIETEN, GOTTFRIED VAN.   Leiden, Netherlands 1734
                                    Vienna 29 March 1803

876 [Symphony, E-flat major] Edited by Carl
Banck
1.Allegro assai e spiritoso 2.Andante
sostenuto e grazioso 3.Menuetto: Un poco
allegretto - Trio 4.Allegro assai
2Ob.-2Hn.-Str.
Kistner, Leipzig [1880?]
Score 42 p.
*Rediscovered ca.1880; long misattributed to
Joseph Haydn.*

SZABELSKI, BOLESŁAW.
                    b. Radoryż, Poland 3 December 1896

6283 Concerto grosso (1954)   *19'*
1.Allegro assai 2.Lento 3.Allegro
2(2nd alt. Picc.),2,2,2-4,3,3-Timp.,Perc.-
Pno.-Str.
Polskie Wydawnictwo, Cracow, ^C1958
Score 62 p.
*Composed 1954. First performance Katowice,
Poland, 12 May 1955, Great Symphonic Orchestra
of the Polish Radio, Henryk Czyż conductor.*

6288 [Suite, Op. 10. Toccata]   *5'*
2(2nd alt. Picc.),2,2,2-4,2,3,1-Timp.,Perc.-
Pno.,Hp.-Str.
Polskie Wydawnictwo, Cracow, ^C1950
Score 40 p. Large folio

SZABÓ, FERENC.   Budapest 27 December 1902
                             Budapest 4 November 1969

1815s Suite lyrique   *15'*
1.Allegro moderato 2.Recitativo 3.Aria
4.Rondo
Str.
Editions de Musique de l'URSS, Moscow, 1939
Score 30 p.
*Composed 1936. First performance Moscow, 1936,
Moscow Philharmonic Orchestra, Nikolai Snosov
conductor.*

SZELL, GEORGE.   Budapest 7 June 1897
                               Cleveland 30 July 1976

2237 Lyrische Ouverture, Op. 5   *20'*
4(3rd&4th alt. 2Picc.),3(3rd alt. E.H.),4
(3rd alt. B.Cl.),4*-3,4,3,1-Timp.,Perc.-Cel.,
2Hp.-Str.
Universal Edition, Vienna, ^C1922
Score 94 p.
*Composed 1920. First performance Vienna, 1922,
Philharmonic Orchestra, Felix Weingartner
conductor.*

1742 Variationen über ein eigenes Thema,   *16'*
Op. 4
3*,2(2nd alt. E.H.),2(2nd alt. B.Cl.),2-4,3,3,

1-Timp.,Perc.-Hp.-Str.
Universal Edition, Vienna, ^C1916
Score 84 p.
*Composed 1913. First performance Vienna, 1915,
Ferdinand Löwe conductor.*

2385 Wiener Carneval, Ouverture
4*,3*,4*,3*-4,3,3,1-Timp.,Perc.-Hp.-Str.
Ms.
Score 98 p. Large folio

SZENDY, ARPÁD.   Szarvas, Hungary 11 August 1863
                             Budapest 10 September 1922

1237s Air, Op. 16 no. 2b
Solo Vn.-Str.
Rozsnyai, Budapest [n.d.]
Score 3 p.
Op. 16 originally composed for piano solo.

SZERDAHELYI, J.

1161s A csikós-tanyán [The herdsman's camp]
Transcribed by József Bahnert
Solo Cl.(ad lib.)-Str.
Rozsnyai, Budapest [n.d.]
Score 8 p.

SZULC, JÓSEF ZYGMUNT.   Warsaw 4 April 1875
                                     Paris 10 April 1956

1508s Élégie, D minor
Solo Vn.-Str.
Score: Ms. 6 p.
Parts: Ricordi, Paris, ^C1924

651v Sérénade
Solo Vn.-Fl.,2Cl.-Str.
Score: Ms. 11 p.
Parts: L. Grus, Paris, ^C1924

SZYMANOWSKI, KAROL.
                 Timoshovka, Ukraine 6 October 1882
                         Lausanne 28 March 1937

825v [Concerto, violin, Op. 35]   *18'*
In one movement
Solo Vn.-3(3rd alt. Picc.),3(3rd alt. E.H.),4*,
3(3rd alt. C.Bn.)-4,3,3,1-Timp.,Perc.-Pno.,
Cel.,2Hp.-Str.
Universal Edition, Vienna, ^C1923
Score 76 p. Large folio
*Composed 1918. First performance Warsaw, 1922,
Gregor Fitelberg conductor, Emil Mlynarski
soloist.*

3847 Konzert Ouverture, Op. 12   *16'*
3(3rd alt. Picc.),3(3rd alt. E.H.),4*(3rd alt.
Cl. in E-flat),3(3rd alt. C.Bn.)-6,3,3,1-Timp.,
Perc.-Hp.-Str.
Universal Edition, Vienna, ^C1937
Score 82 p.
Composed ca.1905.

1744 [Symphony no. 3, Chant de la nuit,   *20'*
Op. 27]
In one movement
4*,4*,5*(1Cl. in E-flat),4*-6,4,4,1-Timp.,

Täglichsbeck, Thomas

Perc.-Pno.,Org.,Cel.,2Hp.-Ten. Solo,Mixed Chorus-Str.
Universal Edition, Vienna, ^c1925
Score 88 p. Large folio
Text from the second Divan of Mevlana Djelaleddin Rumi. Composed 1918. First performance Warsaw, 1920.

T

TÄGLICHSBECK, THOMAS.　　　　Ansbach 31 December 1799
　　　　　　　　　　　　　　　Baden-Baden 5 October 1867

1061v　Variations sur un air stirien, Op. 12
Solo Vn.-2,2,2,2-2,2,1(ad lib.)-Timp.(ad lib.)
-Str.
Score: Ms. 65 p.
Parts: Jules Wander, Leipzig [n.d.]

TAKÁCS, JENÖ.
　　　　b. Siegendorf, Austria 25 September 1902

6662　Eisenstädter divertimento, Op. 75　　　*12'*
1.Praeludium　2.Reigen　3.[Vinedresser's dance]　4.Aria　5.Soldaten-Tanz (A la hornpipe)
2(2nd alt. Picc.),2,2,2-4(3rd&4th ad lib.),2,1
-Timp.,Perc.-Hp.-Str.
Universal Edition, Vienna, ^c1964
Score 36 p.
Based on Baroque Hungarian themes. Composed 1961-62. First performance Stuttgart, 10 May 1964, South German Radio Light Orchestra, Fritz Mareczek conductor.

6660　[Folk dances from Burgenland,　　　*14'*
Austria, Op. 57]
1.[Marching up]　2.[Smuggler]　3.[Folksong]
4.[Pillow dance]　5.Kroatischer Tanz
2(2nd alt. Picc.),1,2,1-2,1,1-Timp.,Perc.-Str.
Ms. [Now Universal Edition, Vienna, ^c1963]
Score 29 p.
Composed 1952. First performance Nürnburg, June 1953, Radio Nürnburg.

6640　[From foreign lands and folks,　　　*17'30"*
Op. 37a]
1.Von den Britischen Inseln　2.Saltarello
(Italien)　3.Negro spiritual (USA)　4.
Spanische Strassenmusikanten　5.Lied der
spanischen Kolonisten (Philippinen)　6.[Medicine man's dance, South Seas]　7.(Japan)
[Cherry blossom song]　8.[Bagpipes, Hungary]
2(2nd alt. Picc.),2,2,2-2,1,1-Timp.,Perc.-
Hp.-Str.
Universal Edition, Vienna [^c1960?]
Score 45 p.
Orchestrated 1960 from two earlier works for piano. First performance Hilversum, Netherlands, 10 September 1964, Radio Hilversum Promenade Orchestra, Gijsbert Nieuwland conductor.

6732　Ländliches Barock, Orchester-Suite,　　　*18'*
Op. 48
1.Intrada　2.Aria　3.Steyrer Tanz

4.[Shepherd's dance]　5.Springtanz　6.[Prayer]
7.[Bagpipes - Hungarian dance]
2(2nd alt. Picc.),2,2,2-2,2,B.Tbn.(ad lib.)-
Timp.,Perc.-Hp.(or Pno.)-Str.
Universal Edition, London, ^c1953
Score 57 p.
Composed 1941. First performance Sopron, Hungary, 26 October 1941, Orchestra of the Franz Liszt Musical Society of Sopron, the composer conducting.

6637　Overtura semiseria, Op. 69　　　*8'*
2(2nd alt. Picc.),2,2,2-4,2,2-Timp.,Perc.-Hp.-
Str.
Universal Edition, Vienna [^c1960?]
Score 36 p.
Transcribed in part from Sonata Breve for trumpet and piano. Composed 1958-59. First performance Cincinnati, 23 October 1959, Cincinnati Symphony Orchestra, Max Rudolf conductor.

2273s　Passacaglia, Op. 73　　　*ca.13'*
Str.
Doblinger, Vienna, ^c1963
Score 28 p.
Composed 1960. First performance Zurich, 3 September 1961, Radio Zürich Symphony Orchestra, Jean-Marie Auberson conductor.

6586　Suite of old Hungarian dances,　　　*8'*
Op. 42 [in 5 movements]
1,1,0,1-1,1-Pno.(ad lib.)-Str.
SIDEM (Société Intercontinentale d'Éditions
Musicales), Geneva, ^c1949
Score 8 p.
Composed 1946. First performance Pécs, Hungary, 1946, Chamber Orchestra of the Pécs Conservatory of Music, Sirio Piovesan conductor.

TAL, JOSEF.　Posen, German Poland 18 September 1910

Born: Joseph Gruenthal

297p　Concerto no. 3, piano and　　　*17'30"*
orchestra with tenor voice
In one movement
Solo Pno., Ten. Voice Solo-2(2nd alt. Picc.),
2(2nd alt. E.H.),2(2nd alt. B.Cl.),1-2,2-
Timp.,Perc.-Cel.,Hp.-Str.
Ms. Israeli Music, Tel Aviv, ^c1959
Score 58 p.
Hebrew text by Eleazar HaKalir; with German and English translations. Composed 1956. First performance Jerusalem, 4 December 1956, Kol-Yisrael Symphony Orchestra, Michael Taube conductor, the composer as pianist, Haim Flaschner tenor.

6264　Symphony no. 2　　　*12'*
In one movement
3*,3*,3*,3*-4,3,3,1-Timp.,Perc.-Pno.,Cel.,Hp.
-Str.
Israeli Music Publications, Tel Aviv, ^c1960
Score 87 p. Large folio
Commissioned by the Israel Philharmonic Orchestra, 1960. Composed 1960. First performance Jerusalem, 5 December 1961.

Kol-Yisrael Symphony Orchestra, Shalom Ronli-Riklis conductor. Received an award from the Milo Artist Club of Tel Aviv.

TAMIANI, CORY.

7187 The White Sun-Lady, for band
3*,2,5*(1Alto Cl.),2-5Sax.(AATTB)-4,3,3,Bar.,
1-Timp.,Perc.-Cb.
Avant Music, Los Angeles, ᶜ1960
Score 18 p.
Based on the Seminole song for the dying.

TANEIEV, ALEXANDER SERGEIEVICH.
St. Petersburg 17 January 1850
St. Petersburg 7 February 1918

1415 Ballade, Op. 11 [after Alexei   *20'*
Tolstoy's poem Aliosha Popovich]
3(3rd alt. Picc.),3*,3*,3*-4,2,3,1-Timp.,Perc.
-Pno.,Hp.-Str.
Jurgenson, Moscow [1906?]
Score 49 p.

1063 Festlicher Marsch, Op. 12   *5'*
3*,2,2,2-4,3,3,1-Timp.,Perc.-Hp.-Str.
J.H. Zimmermann, Leipzig [1901?]
Score 25 p.

1362 Hamlet overture, Op. 31   *19'*
3(3rd alt. Picc.),3*,3*,2-4,3,3,1-Timp.,Perc.-
Hp.-Str.
J.H. Zimmermann, Leipzig [1906?]
Score 67 p.

569v Rêverie, Op. 23
Solo Vn.-2,2,2,2-2Hn.-Timp.,Perc.-Str.
J.H. Zimmermann, Leipzig [n.d.]
Score 27 p.

1092 [Suite no. 2, Op. 14, F major]   *20'*
1.Tema con variazioni 2.Menuetto 3.Andantino
4.Finale
3(3rd alt. Picc.),2(2nd alt. E.H.),2,2-4,2,3,1
-Timp.,Perc.-Hp.-Str.
J.H. Zimmermann, Leipzig [1901?]
Score 134 p.

1109 [Symphony no. 2, Op. 21, B-flat   *23'*
minor]
1.Andante - Allegro 2.Scherzo - Andantino
con moto 3.Adagio mosso 4.Allegro vivacissimo
3(3rd alt. Picc.),2(2nd alt. E.H.),2,2-4,2,3,1
-Timp.,Perc.-Hp.-Str.
J.H. Zimmermann [1903?]
Score 170 p.

1745 [Symphony no. 3, Op. 36, E major]
1.Andantino con moto - Allegro risoluto
2.Scherzo 3.Andante 4.Allegro
3(3rd alt. Picc.),3*,2,2-4,2,3,1-Timp.,Perc.-
Hp.-Str.
Jurgenson, Moscow [1908?]
Score 131 p.

Two mazurkas, Op. 15
2162 No. 1   *6'*
2163 No. 2   *6'*
3(3rd is Picc. in no. 1),2(2nd alt. E.H.),2,2-4,

2,3,1-Timp.,Perc.-Str.
Scores: Ms. 38 p., 28 p.
Parts: [Zimmerman, Leipzig, 1902?]

2161 Valse mélancolique   *4'*
2,1,2,2-2Hn.-Str.
J.H. Zimmermann, Leipzig [1906?]
Score 31 p.
Excerpted and transcribed from String Quartet no. 2.

TANEIEV, SERGEI IVANOVICH.
Vladimir 25 November 1856
Moscow 19 June 1915

440v [Concert suite in five movements, Op. 28]
Solo Vn.-2(2nd alt. Picc.),2(2nd alt. E.H.),2,
2-2,2-Timp.,Perc.-Hp.-Str.
Édition Russe de Musique, Berlin, 1910
Score 126 p.

[Oresteia, musical trilogy, Op. 6]
1268 Ouverture   *19'*
1204 Second tableau, entr'acte   *3'*
3*,2,2,2-4,2,3,1-Timp.,Perc.-Pno.(Ouverture),
2Hp.(2nd in Entr'acte only)-Str.
Belaieff, Leipzig, 1897, 1901
Scores: 60 p., 15 p.
Composed 1894. First performance St. Petersburg, 1895.

922 [Symphony no. 1, Op. 12, C minor]   *32'*
1.Allegro molto 2.Adagio 3.Scherzo 4.Finale
3(3rd alt. Picc.),2,3,3*-4,3,3,1-Timp.,Perc.-
Str.
Belaieff, Leipzig, 1901
Score 144 p.
Composed 1892.

TANNER, PAUL.
b. Skunk Hollow, Kentucky 15 October 1917

192m Aria for trombones [with concert   *5'*
band]
2Solo Tbn.(Ten.,Bass)-2,2,5*(1Alto Cl.),1-4Sax.
-4,4,3,Bar.,1-Timp.,Perc.-Cb.
WIM, Los Angeles, ᶜ1967
Score in reduction 12 p.
Composed 1962. First performance 1962, the composer as one of the soloists.

7159 El cangrejo (the crab)
6Tbn.-Perc.
WIM, Los Angeles, ᶜ1965
Score 15 p.
Composed and first performed 1961.

193m Concert duet for tenor and bass   *5'15"*
trombones [with concert band]
2Solo Tbn.-2,2,5*(1Alto),1-4Sax.-4,4,3,Bar.,1
-Timp.,Perc.-Cb.
WIM, Los Angeles, ᶜ1969
Score in reduction 16 p.
Composed 1964. First performance 1964, Clarence Sawhill, conductor, Ken Sawhill and the composer, soloists.

Tanner, Paul

194m Concerto for two trombones   *7'30"*
In one movement
2Solo Tbn.-2,2,6*(1Cl. in E-flat)-4Sax.-4,4,3,
Bar.,1-Timp.,Perc.-Cb.
WIM, Los Angeles, ^c1965
Score in reduction 15 p.
Composed 1960. First performance 1960, Don
Staples and the composer, soloists.

TANNER, PETER.   Rochester, New York 25 June 1936

425m Concerto for flute and orchestra   *18'*
1.Moderato - Andante con moto 2.Scherzo
3.Theme and variations
Solo Fl.-1,2,2,2-2,2,1-Timp.,Perc.-Hp.-Str.
Ms. ^c1959 by Peter Tanner
Score 80 p. Large folio
Composed 1958. First performance Rochester, 1
May 1959, Eastman-Rochester Symphony Orches-
tra, Howard Hanson conductor, Joanne L.
Dickinson soloist.

TANSMAN, ALEXANDRE.   Lódź, Poland 12 June 1897

774p [Concerto, piano, no. 2]   *24'*
1.Allegro risoluto 2.Scherzo 3.Lento e Finale
Solo Pno.-3*,3*,3*,2-4,3,3,1-Timp.,Perc.-Str.
Eschig, Paris, ^c1930
Score 141 p.
Composed 1927. First performance Boston, 29
December 1927, Boston Symphony Orchestra,
Serge Koussevitzky conductor, the composer
as soloist.

1509 Danse de la sorcière   *8'*
3*,2,3*,2-4,3,3,1-Timp.,Perc.-Pno.,Cel.,Hp.-
Str.
Eschig, Paris, ^c1926
Score 32 p.
Composed 1922. First performance Brussels, 5
May 1924, Concerts Populaires, Vladimir
Golschmann conductor.

4064 Rapsodie polonaise   *11'30"*
3*,3*,3*,2-Alto Sax.-4,3,3,1-Timp.,Perc.-Pno.,
Cel.-Str.
Associated Music Publishers, New York, ^c1942
Score 57 p.
Composed 1940. First performance St. Louis,
14 November 1941, St. Louis Symphony Orchestra,
Vladimir Golschmann conductor.

1747 Sinfonietta for chamber orchestra   *15'*
1.Allegro assai 2.Mazurka 3.Notturno
4.Fuga e toccata
1,1,1,1-1,1,2-Timp.,Perc.-Pno.(alt. Cel.)-Str.
Universal Edition, Vienna, ^c1926
Score 55 p.
Composed 1924. First performance Paris, 23
March 1925, Société de Musique de Chambre,
the composer conducting.

4069 Symphony no. 5, in D   *26'*
1.Lento - Allegro con moto 2.Intermezzo
3.Scherzo 4.Lento - Allegro con moto
3*,2,3*,2-4,3,3,1-Timp.,Perc.-Pno.-Str.
Ms. ^c1942 by Associated, New York
Score 38 p. Large folio

Composed 1942. First performance Washington,
D.C., 2 Feburary 1943, National Symphony
Orchestra, the composer conducting.

4845 Toccata   *8'*
3*,3*,3*,3*-4,4,3,1-Timp.,Perc.-Pno.,Cel.,
Hp.-Str.
Max Eschig, Paris, ^c1932
Score 48 p.
Composed 1929.

TARENGHI, MARIO.   Bergamo, Italy 10 July 1870
                                        Milan 1938

Andante and aria, Op. 59
438s No. 1 Andante elegiaco
437s No. 2 Aria all'antica
Str.
Carisch & Jänichen, Milan, ^c1912
Scores: 11 p., 11 p.

TARP, SVEND ERIK.
      b. Thisted, Jutland, Denmark 6 August 1908

5188 [The battle of Jericho, Op. 51]
2(2nd alt. Picc.),2,2,2-4,3,3,1-Timp.,Perc.-
Str.
Engström & Sødring, Copenhagen, ^c1949
Score 26 p.
Suggested by the American Negro spiritual
Joshua Fit de Battle of Jericho. Composed
1949.

5950 [Comedy overture no. 1, Op. 36]   *6'*
2,2,2,2-4,3,3-Timp.,Perc.-Str.
Samfundet til Udgivelse af Dansk Musik,
Copenhagen, ^c1943
Score 32 p.
Composed 1940. First performance Copenhagen,
1940, Danish State Radio Symphony Orchestra,
Emil Reesen conductor.

413m [Concertino, flute, Op. 30]   *10'*
1.Allegro vivace 2.Andantino 3.Rondo
giocoso
Solo Fl.-0,2,0,2-2Hn.-Perc.-Str.
Samfundet til Udgivelse af Dansk Musik,
Copenhagen, ^c1939
Score 28 p.
Composed 1938. First performance Copenhagen,
probably 1938, Symphony Orchestra of Tivoli
Concert Hall, Thomas Jensen conductor, Johan
Bentzon soloist.

6693 [Symphony, Op. 50, E-flat]   *24'*
1.Meditativo 2.Animato 3.Sereno
2(2nd alt. Picc.),2,2,2-4,3,3,1-Timp.,Perc.-
Str.
Samfundet til Udgivelse af Dansk Musik, Copen-
hagen, ^c1949
Score 60 p.
Composed 1948. First performance Copenhagen,
10 March 1948, Danish State Radio Symphony
Orchestra, Svend Christian Felumb conductor.

TARTANAC, H.

920v [Suite, violin, G major]
1.March 2.Berceuse 3.Scherzettino 4.
Andante, mazurka and finale
Solo Vn.-2(2nd alt. Picc.),1,2,1-2,2,1,1-
Timp.,Perc.-Str.
Score: Ms. 124 p.
Parts: Enoch, Paris [n.d.]

TARTINI, GIUSEPPE.   Pirano (Istria) 8 April 1692
                     Padua 26 February 1770

530c Adagio. Transcribed by Paul Bazelaire
Solo Vc.-Str.
Senart, Paris [n.d.]
Score 3 p.

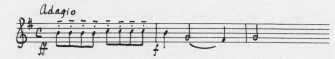

1299s Andante. Arranged by Henri Elkan   5'
Pno.(ad lib.)-Str.(Vn.III ad lib.)
Elkan-Vogel, Philadelphia, c1933
Score 7 p.
Originally composed for violin. This arrange-
ment, 1933. First performance Ardmore, Penn-
sylvania, 21 May 1933, Main Line Orchestra,
Adolph Vogel conductor.

310m [Concerto, flute, G major] Edited by   10'
Johannes Brinckmann
1.Allegro non molto 2.Andante 3.Allegro
Solo Fl.-Cemb.-Str.
Sikorski, Hamburg, c1954
Score 21 p.

5530 [Concerto, 2 oboes, 2 horns, and   12'
strings, no. 58, F major] Freely elaborated
by Ettore Bonelli
1.Allegro 2.Molto adagio 3.Minuetto
4.Allegro
2 Ob.-2Hn.-Str.
G. Zanibon, Padua, c1948
Score 12 p.
Edited from a manuscript in the Library of the
Most Venerable Ark of St. Anthony, Padua.

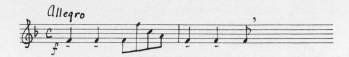

382v [Concerto, violin, D major]   20'
Revised by Ettore Bonelli
1.Allegro 2.Largo 3.Allegro assai
Solo Vn.-2Hn.,2Tpt.-Timp.-Str.
G. Zanibon, Padua, c1953
Score 24 p.

835v [Concerto, violin, D major]   22'
Revised by Mario Corti
1.Allegro 2.Largo 3.Allegro
Solo Vn.-Cemb.-Str.
Ricordi, Milan [n.d.]
Miniature score 41 p.
First performance of this edition Padua, 23
March 1924, Oreste Ravanello conductor.

906v [Concerto, violin, D minor] Edited by
Emilio Pente
1.Allegro 2.Grave 3.Presto
Solo Vn.-Str.
A. Benjamin, Leipzig, c1898 by H. Thiemer
Score in reduction 14 p.

258v [Same as above] Edited by Rudolf
Baumgartner
1.Allegro assai 2.Grave 3.Presto
Solo Vn.-Cemb.-Str.
Hug, Zurich, c1958
Score 20 p.
Edited from a Ms. in the Musical Archives of
the Cappella Musicale Antoniana, Padua.
First performance of this edition Lucerne,
Switzerland, 1957, Festival Strings Lucerne,
Wolfgang Schneiderhan soloist.

Tartini, Giuseppe

259v [Concerto, violin, E major] Edited by
Hermann Scherchen
1.Grandioso 2.Andante 3.Allegro grazioso
Solo Vn.-Str.
Hug, Zurich, C1947
Score 14 p.
Probably composed between 1735 and 1750.

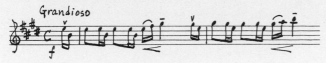

271v [Same as above]
Kalmus [n.p., n.d.]
Score 12 p.

260v [Concerto, violin, G major] Edited by
Jürgen Braun
1.Allegro non presto 2.Andante 3.Allegro
assai
Solo Vn.-Org. or Cemb.-Str.
Eulenburg, Zurich, C1972
Score 20 p.
*Probably composed between 1735 and 1750. This
edition based on sources at the University of
California, Berkeley; Bibliothèque Nationale,
Paris; and the Cappella Musicale Antoniana,
Padua. The Padua source includes a Grave
movement which is reproduced in an Appendix
to this edition.*

261v [Concerto, violin, G minor]   14'30"
Edited by Giovanni Guglielmo
1.Allegro 2.Fuga à la brève 3.Largo,
cantabile 4.Allegro assai
Solo Vn.-Org. or Cemb.-Str.
Zanibon, Padua, C1972
Score 48 p.
First published by Le Cène, Amsterdam, 1728.

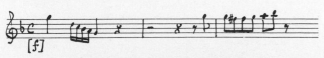

270v [Concerto, violin, A major]
1.Allegro ma non molto 2.Adagio 3.Allegro
assai
Solo Vn.-Str.
Kalmus, New York [n.d.]
Score 36 p.

855v [Concerto, violin, A major] Revised   20'
by Mario Corti
1.Allegro moderato 2.Largo 3.Allegro
(assai)
Solo Vn.-Cemb.-Str.
Ricordi, Milan [n.d.]
Miniature score 44 p.
*First performance of this edition Padua, 23
March 1924, Oreste Ravanello conductor.*

1122v [Concerto, violin, A major]   10'
Edited by Alfred Einstein
1.Allegro 2.Grave 3.Allegro
Solo Vn.-Str.
Ms.
Score 25 p.
Originally published 1734.

262v [Concerto, violin, B-flat major] Edited by
Jürgen Braun
1.Allegro 2.Largo andante 3.Allegro
Solo Vn.-Org. or Cemb.-Str.
Eulenburg Octavo Edition, Eulenburg, Zurich,
C1972
Score 16 p.
*Probably composed between 1750 and 1770.
This edition based on the autograph in the
Cappella Musicale Antoniana, Padua.*

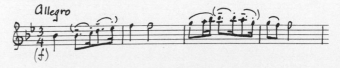

625c [Concerto, violoncello, D major]   12'
Arranged by Louis Delune
1.Poco largo, pomposo - Allegro moderato
2.Grave ed espressivo 3.Finale: Allegro
Solo Vc.-2Hn.-String Quartet, Str.
Breitkopf & Härtel, Leipzig [1910?]
Score 27 p.
Originally a viola da gamba concerto.

Poco largo, pomposo

449c [Concerto, violoncello, A major] *12'*
Elaboration by Oreste Ravanello
1.Allegro 2.Larghetto 3.Allegro assai
Solo Vc.-Org.(ad lib.)-Str.
G. Zanibon, Padua, ᶜ1938
Score 20 p.

Allegro

2222s [Quartet, strings, no. 125, D major. *6'*
Andante *and* Presto. Transcribed for string
orchestra by Ettore Bonelli]
Str.
G. Zanibon, Padua, ᶜ1948
Score 8 p.

Andante

630v [Pastorale, violin and continuo, *11'*
A major. Transcribed by Ottorino Respighi]
Solo Vn.-Str.
Ricordi, Milan, ᶜ1921
Score 12 p.
Transcribed 1920. First performance Rome,
1921, Ottorino Respighi conductor.

Grave

2417s Sinfonia in A [for string orchestra]
1.Allegro assai 2.Andante assai 3.Menuett:
Allegro assai
Str.
Kalmus, New York [n.d.]
Score 9 p.

Allegro assai

2360s Sinfonia pastorale, D major. Edited by
Arnold Schering
Allegro non troppo - Moderato - Adagio
cantabile - Allegro
Solo Vn.-Cemb.-Str.
C.F. Kahnt, Leipzig, ᶜ1926
Score 19 p.

Allegro ma non troppo

699v [Sonata, violin, The devil's trill, *5'*
G minor] Arranged by Albert Becker
1.Larghetto 2.Allegro assai 3.Adagio -
Allegro assai
Solo Vn.-0,2,2,2-2Hn.-Timp.-Str.
Breitkopf & Härtel, Leipzig [1889?]
Score 27 p.
Originally composed ca.1713.

Larghetto

826v [Same as above] Arranged by Hugo *5'*
Kauder
1.Larghetto affettuoso 2.Allegro moderato
3.Grave - Allegro assai
Solo Vn.-Str.
Universal Edition, Vienna, ᶜ1923
Score 34 p.
This arrangement 1921. First performance
Vienna, 1922, Hugo Kauder conductor, Hugo
Gottesmann soloist.

711v [Same as above] Arranged by Fritz *5'*
Kreisler
1.Larghetto - Allegro energico 2.Grave
3.Allegro assai
Solo Vn.-Org.-Str.
G. Schirmer, New York, ᶜ1905 by E. Eulenburg
Score in reduction 15 p.

TAUBERT, ERNST EDUARD.
Regenwalde 25 September 1838
Berlin 14 July 1934

175s [Suite in five movements, Op. 67, D
major]
Str.
Kahnt, Leipzig, ᶜ1903
Score 19 p.

Taubert, Wilhelm

TAUBERT, WILHELM.   Berlin 23 March 1811
                             Berlin 7 January 1891

   4538 [Birthday march, Op. 146]
     3*,2,2,2-2,2,3-Timp.,Perc.-Str.
     Bote & Bock, Berlin [1865]
     Score 50 p.
     Composed for the birthday of Prince Friedrich
     Wilhelm Victor Albert of Prussia.

   694c [Concerto, violoncello, Op. 173, D minor]
     1.Allegro 2.Andante con moto 3.Finale
     Solo Vc.-1,2,2,2-2,2-Timp.-Str.
     Score: Ms. 202 p.
     Parts: Simrock, Berlin [1870?]

   5447 [Overture to A Thousand and One Nights,
     Op. 139]
     2,2,2,2-4,2,3-Timp.-Str.
     Kistner, Leipzig [1862]
     Score 96 p.

   499s [The tempest, Op. 134. No. 16, Little
     love song]
     Str.(without Cb.)
     Breitkopf & Härtel, Leipzig [n.d.]
     Score 3 p.

   4535 [Victory and festival march, Op. 166]
     3*,2,2,2-4,6,3,1-Timp.,Perc.-Str.
     Bote & Bock, Berlin [1869]
     Score 55 p.

TAUSCH, JULIUS.   Dessau, Germany 15 April 1827
                        Bonn 11 November 1895

   5453 Fest-Ouvertüre, Op. 9
     2,2,2,2-4,2,3-Timp.-Str.
     Hugo Pohle, Hamburg [186-?]
     Score 48 p.

TAUSIG, CARL.   Warsaw 4 November 1841
                        Leipzig 17 July 1871

   596p [Hungarian gypsy melodies] Arranged by
     Albert Eibenschütz
     Solo Pno.-3*,2,2,2-2Hn.-Timp.,Trgl.-Str.
     Senff, Leipzig [1890?]
     Score 46 p.
     Originally composed for piano.

TAVAN, EMILE.

   1666s Grand'mère au rouet [Grandmother at
     the spinning wheel] caprice de genre
     Str.
     Score: Ms. 4 p.
     Parts: Tavan, Paris [n.d.]

TAVERNER, JOHN.   Tattershall, Lincolnshire ca.1495
                  Boston, Lincolnshire 25 October 1545

   2350s Missa Gloria tibi Trinitas. Benedictus:
     In nomine. Transcribed for string orchestra

Str.
Ms. ^c1976 by The Fleisher Collection of
Orchestral Music, Free Library of Philadelphia
Score 3 p.
Originally composed for viols.

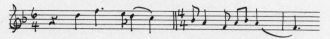

TAYBER, ANTON.
  See: TEYBER, ANTON.

TAYLOR, CLIFFORD.
                    b. Avalon, Pennsylvania 20 October 1923

   7110 Commencement suite for chorus and   *8'30"*
     orchestra. Balade de bon conseyl
     Chorus(SSA or TTB)-2,2,2,2-2,2,3-Timp.,Perc.-
     Hp.-Str.
     Ms. ^c1959 by Clifford Taylor
     Score 21 p. Large folio
     The poem by Geoffrey Chaucer. Commissioned
     by Chatham College, Pittsburgh. Composed
     1958. First performance Chatham College,
     June 1959, Mihail Stolarevsky, conductor.

   7115 Commencement suite. Processional,   *7'*
     Op. 20
     2,2,2,2-2(or 4),2,2,1-Timp.,Perc.-Hp.(optional)
     -Str.
     Ms. ^c1959 by Clifford Taylor
     Score 21 p. Large folio

   2380s Concerto grosso for strings, Op. 15   *13'*
     1.Slowly 2.Fast
     Str.
     Ms. ^c1957 by Clifford Taylor
     Score 33 p.
     Composed 1957. First performance Dallas, 1959,
     Dallas Symphony Orchestra, Samuel Adler, con-
     ductor.

   7116 Sinfonia seria   *11'30"*
     Solo Fl.,Solo Bar.-3*,3*,6*(1Cl. in E-flat,
     1Alto),3*-6Sax.-4,3,2Fluegelhn.,4,Bar.,6-
     Timp.,Perc.-Cb.
     Ms. ^c1965 by Clifford Taylor
     Score 51 p. Large folio
     Composed 1965. First performance Philadelphia,
     March 1971, Temple University Wind Ensemble,
     Keith Brown conductor, Carole Jordan flautist,
     Robert Hall baritone horn soloist.

   7114 Theme and variations, Op. 8   *14'*
     3*,3*,3*,3*-4,3,3,1-Timp.,Perc.-Pno.-Str.
     Ms. ^c1954 by Clifford Taylor
     Score 76 p. Large folio
     Composed 1954. First performance Washington,
     D.C., 1955, National Symphony Orchestra,

Howard Mitchell, conductor. Awarded first prize in The National Symphony Orchestra's 25th Anniversary Composer's Contest.

TAYLOR, COLIN.   Oxford, England 21 February 1881
                  Stellenbosch, South Africa 20 June 1973

1701s Prelude and sarabande
       Str.(Cb. optional)
       Oxford University Press, London, ^c1930
       Score 6 p.

TAYLOR, DEEMS.   New York 22 December 1885
                              New York 3 July 1966

2664 Circus day, Op. 18, eight pictures   *20'*
      from memory [revised version]
      1.Street parade 2.The big top 3.Bareback
      riders 4.Trained animals: a. The lion cage -
      b. The dog and monkey circus - c. The waltzing
      elephants 5.Tight-rope walker 6.Jugglers
      7.Clowns 8.Finale
      3(3rd alt. Picc.),3*,3(1Cl. in E-flat),2-3Sax.
      (ATB)-4,3,3,1-Timp.,Perc.-Str.
      J. Fischer, New York, ^c1934 by Deems Taylor
      Score 144 p. Large folio
      Commissioned by Paul Whiteman. Original ver-
      sion sketched 1925 and scored by Ferde Grofé.
      This version scored by composer, 1933. First
      performance of movements 1, 4a, 4b, 6, 7 and
      8, New York, 17 February 1934, New York Phil-
      harmonic, the composer conducting.

4271 Fanfare for Russia
      See: TEN FANFARES BY TEN COMPOSERS FOR BRASS
            AND PERCUSSION

2665 The portrait of a lady, rhapsody,   *12'*
      Op. 14
      1,1,1,1-Hn.-Pno.-Str.
      J. Fischer, New York, ^c1932
      Score 49 p.
      Commissioned by Carolyn Beebe for the New
      York Chamber Music Society, 1920. Originally
      composed 1920; completely rewritten 1923.
      First performance New York, 3 February 1925,
      New York Chamber Music Society, Carolyn Beebe,
      pianist-conductor.

3556 [Ramuntcho. Act III: Introduction   *8'30"*
      and ballet]
      3(3rd alt. Picc.),2(2nd alt. E.H.),3*,2-4,3,3,
      1-Timp.,Perc.-Hp.-Str.
      J. Fischer, New York, ^c1940 by Deems Taylor
      Score 68 p. Large folio
      From the opera based on Pierre Loti's novel,
      composed 1936-39. First performance of this
      excerpt New York, 24 March 1940, New York
      Philharmonic, Albert Stoessel conductor.

1272 Through the looking glass, five   *30'*
      pictures from Lewis Carroll, Op. 12
      1a.Dedication 1b.The garden of live flowers
      2.Jabberwocky 3.Looking-glass insects 4.The
      White Knight
      3(3rd alt. Picc.),3*,3*,3*-4,3,3,1-Timp.,Perc.
      -Pno.-Str.
      J. Fischer, New York, ^c1923
      Score 137 p.

TAYLOR, H. J.

394s Memories
      Str.
      Stainer & Bell, London, ^c1909
      Score 6 p.

TAYLOR, RAYNOR.   England ca.1747
                          Philadelphia 17 August 1825

7153 Philadelphia march. Transcribed   *4'30"*
      by Sam Dennison
      2(2nd alt. Picc.),2,2,2-2,2,3,1(optional)-
      Timp.-Str.
      Ms. ^c1975 by Sam Dennison
      Score 6 p.
      Originally published for piano, 1807. This
      transcription 1975.

TAYLOR, SAMUEL COLERIDGE.
      See: COLERIDGE-TAYLOR, SAMUEL.

TCHAIKOVSKY, PETER ILYICH.
      See: CHAIKOVSKY, PETER.

TCHEMBERDJY, NIKOLAI KARPOVICH.
      See: CHEMBERDZHI, NIKOLAI KARPOVICH.

TCHEREPNIN, ALEXANDER NIKOLAYEVICH.
                  b. St. Petersburg 21 January 1899

608m [Chamber concerto, flute and   *12'*
      violin with orchestra, Op. 33, D major]
      1.Allegro maestoso 2.Andantino 3.Vivace
      4.Allegro molto
      Solo Fl., Solo Vn.-2Hn.,2Cnt.-Timp.-Str.
      B. Schott's Söhne, Mainz, ^c1925
      Score 58 p.
      Composed 1924. First performance Donaues-
      chingen, 1925. Won a prize in Schott's
      contest, 1925.

471m [Concerto, harmonica, Op. 86]   *27'*
      1.Allegro 2.Lento 3.Presto 4.Poco soste-
      nuto - Allegretto
      Solo Harmonica-2,2,2,2-4,2,3,1-Timp.,Perc.-Hp.
      -Str.
      Ms. [Associated, New York, ^c1956]
      Score 88 p. Large folio
      Commissioned by John Sebastian. Composed 1953.
      First performance Venice, 11 September 1956,
      Orchestra di Teatro Fenice, Fabien Sevitzky
      conductor, John Sebastian soloist.

2980 Danses russes, Op. 50   *10'*
      1.Allegro moderato 2.Vivace 3.Allegretto
      4.Allegro 5.Allegro marciale
      2(2nd alt. Picc.),2(2nd alt. E.H.),2(2nd alt.
      Cl. in E-flat),2-4,2,3,1-Timp.,Perc.-Hp.-Str.
      Pro Musica, Paris [n.d.]
      Score 34 p.
      First performance Paris, 1935, Orchestra of
      the Philharmonic Society, Charles Munch con-
      ductor.

6525 La femme et son ombre [The woman   *15'*
      and her shadow. Suite, Op. 79b]
      1.In a shrine 2.Cortège 3.Pas de deux

Tcherepnin, Alexander

4.Tokyo onda
2(2nd alt. Picc.),1,2,1-2,1,1-Timp.,Perc.-Pno.,
Hp.(optional)-Str.
Associated Music Publishers, New York, ^c1948
Score 104 p.
*Sometimes called Japanese Suite. From the
ballet with book by Paul Claudel. Composed
1948. First performance Paris, 14 June 1948,
Les Ballets de Paris de Roland Petit.*

6050 Georgiana, suite for orchestra, Op. 92
1.Ceremonial 2.Veils and daggers 3.Chota and
Thamar 4.Kartsuli 5.Apotheosis
2,2,2,2-4,2,3,1-Timp.,Perc.-Str.
Eulenburg, London, ^c1959
Score 100 p.
Composed 1959. First performance London, 1960.

5109 [The marriage of Zobeide. Act II: 10'
Festive music, Op. 45b]
1.Ouverture 2.Einzug 3.Tanz 4.Finale
2(2nd alt. Picc.),2,2,2-4,2,3,1-Timp.,Perc.-
Hp.-Str.
Universal Edition, Vienna, ^c1932
Score 61 p.
*From the opera based on Hugo von Hofmannsthal's
play. Opera composed 1929-30. First perform-
ance Vienna, 17 March 1933. This suite 1930.
First performance Berlin, 1933.*

471c Rapsodie géorgienne
1.Andante 2.Vivace
Solo Vc.-2(1st alt. Picc.),2,2,2-2,2-Timp.,
Perc.-Str.
Durand, Paris, ^c1924
Score 56 p.

1854s Suite géorgienne   20'
1.Ouverture 2.Moderato tranquillo 3.Allah-
verdhî 4.Finale (Prière de Shamie)
Pno.-Str.
Ms.
Score 51 p.

1555 [Symphony, Op. 42, E major]
1.Maestoso - Allegro risoluto 2.Vivace
3.Andante 4.Allegretto con anima
2(2nd alt. Picc.),2,2,2-4,2,3,1-Timp.,Perc.-
Str.
Durand, Paris, ^c1929
Score 80 p.

5610 [Symphony no. 2, Op. 77, E-flat   25'
major]
1.Sostenuto - Allegro 2.Lento 3.Allegro
4.Poco sostenuto - Allegretto
3(3rd alt. Picc.),3*,3*,3*-4,3,3,1-Timp.(alt.
Xyl.),Perc.-Pno.,Cel.,Hp.-Str.
Ms. [Associated, New York, ^c1957]
Score 130 p. Large folio
*Commissioned by Associated Music Publishers.
Composed 1946-51. First performance Chicago,
20 March 1952, Chicago Symphony Orchestra,
Rafael Kubelik conductor.*

1773 [Three pieces for chamber   25'
orchestra, Op. 37]
1.Ouverture 2.Mystère 3.Pour un entraînement

de boxe (Prélude)
1,0,1-2Hn.,2Cnt.-Timp.,Perc.-Str.
Universal Edition, Vienna, ^c1927
Score 45 p.
*Composed 1924. First performance Riga, Lat-
via, 1926, the composer conducting.*

TCHEREPNIN, NIKOLAI NIKOLAYEVICH.
St. Petersburg 14 May 1873
Issy-les-Moulineaux, near Paris 26 June 1945

701 [Armida's pavilion. Suite, Op. 29]
In 9 movements
3(3rd alt. Picc.),3*,3,3*-4,3,3,1-Timp.,Perc.-
Cel.(or Pno.),2Hp.-Str.
Belaïeff, Leipzig, 1906
Score 157 p.
*From the ballet composed 1903. First perform-
ance of this suite St. Petersburg, 1903,
Alexander Siloti conductor.*

594p [Concerto, piano, Op. 30, C-sharp   26'
minor]
In one movement
Solo Pno.-3(3rd alt. Picc.),3*,2,2-4,2,3,1-
Timp.,Perc.-Str.
Jurgenson, Moscow [n.d.]
Score 138 p.
*Composed 1910. First performance St. Peters-
burg, 1910, Belaiev concerts, the composer
conducting.*

923 [Dramatic fantasy after a poem by Fyodor
Tuchev, Op. 17]
3(3rd alt. Picc.),3*,3,2-6,3,3,1-Timp.,Cym.-
Hp.-Str.
Belaïeff, Leipzig, 1904
Score 115 p.
Composed ca.1903.

1364 [The enchanted kingdom, Op. 39]
4(4th alt. Picc.),3*,3,2-4,3,3,1-Timp.,Perc.-
Pno.,Cel.,2Hp.-Str.
Jurgenson, Moscow [1910?]
Score 63 p.
*Inspired by the Russian story The Firebird.
Composed ca.1905.*

2187 [The fisherman and the tiny fish, Op. 41]
1.Andantino commodo 2.Moderato assai 3.
Moderato assai - Molto risoluto 4.Andantino
mosso 5.Allegro marciale 6.Andantino con
moto
3(3rd alt. Picc.),3*,3(3rd alt. Basset-Hn.),
3*-4,4,3,1-Timp.,Perc.-Pno.,Cel.,2Hp.-Str.
Mussektor, Moscow, 1921
Score 63 p.
Inspired by Pushkin's poem. Composed ca.1907.

1483 Gavotte
2,2,2,2-4,2-Str.
Jurgenson, Moscow [1908?]
Score 15 p.

1442 Narcisse et Echo, Op. 40
5*(3rd alt. 2nd Picc.,4th alt. Alto-Fl.&3rd
Picc.),3*,3,3*-6,3,3,1-Timp.,Perc.-Pno.,Cel.,
2Hp.-Chorus(SAT)-Str.

Telemann, Georg Philipp

Jurgenson, Moscow [1913?]
Score 211 p.
Composed ca.1906.

714 Prélude pour La Princesse Lointaine, Op. 4
3*,2,2,2-4,2,3,1-Timp.-Hp.-Str.
Belaïeff, Leipzig, 1899
Score 23 p.
Composed ca.1897 for Edmond Rostand's play.

1397 Scène dans la caverne des sorcières, de
la tragédie Macbeth, Op. 12
3(3rd alt. Picc.),3*,3*,3*-4,3,3,1-Timp.,Perc.
-Str.
Belaïeff, Leipzig, 1902
Score 135 p.
Composed ca.1902.

TELEMANN, GEORG PHILIPP.
    Magdeburg, Germany 14 March 1681
     Hamburg 25 June 1767

231m [Concerto, 2 horns and string orchestra,
D major] Reconstructed by Edmond Leloir
1.Spiritoso, ma non allegro 2.Adagio - Allegro
3.Largo 4.Allegro assai
2Solo Hn.-2Ob.(ad lib.)-Hpscd.-Str.
Edition KaWe, Amsterdam, C1967
Score 16 p.

280m [Concerto, 2 horns, strings, and cembalo,
Dinner music 1733, III no. 3, E-flat major]
Edited by Max Seiffert
1.Maestoso - Allegro 2.Grave 3.Vivace
2Solo Hn.-Cemb.-Str.
Breitkopf & Härtel, Leipzig, C1933
Score 16 p.

247m [Concerto, 3 horns, 2 oboes (ad lib.)
and strings, D major] Edited by Edmond Leloir
1.Vivace 2.Grave 3.Presto
3Solo Hn.-2Ob.(ad lib.)-Cemb.-Str.
Edition KaWe, Amsterdam, C1966
Score 19 p.
Probably composed between 1712 and 1721.

312m [Concerto, oboe, string orchestra and
continuo, D minor] Edited by Hermann Töttcher
1.Adagio 2.Allegro 3.Adagio 4.Allegro
Solo Ob.-Cemb.-Str.
Sikorski, Hamburg, C1953
Score 18 p.

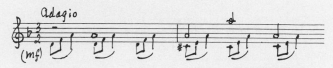

311m [Concerto, oboe, string orchestra, *13'*
and continuo, E minor] Edited by Hermann
Töttcher
1.Andante 2.Allegro molto 3.Largo 4.Allegro
Solo Ob.-Cemb.-Str.
Sikorski, Hamburg, C1954
Score 28 p.

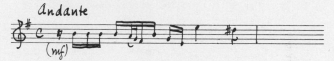

349m [Concerto, oboe, string orchestra, *10'*
and continuo, F minor] Revised by Felix
Schroeder
1.Allegro 2.Largo 3.Vivace
Solo Ob.-Cemb.-Str.
Eulenburg, London, C1958
Miniature score 31 p.
Composed between 1712 and 1721.

354m [Concerto, 3 oboes, 3 violins and *12'30"*
continuo, B-flat major] Edited by Hermann
Töttcher
1.Allegro 2.Largo 3.Allegro
3Ob.-Cemb.-3Vn.,Cb.
Sikorski, Hamburg, C1958
Score 27 p.

243m [Concerto, trumpet, 2 oboes, *15'*
strings and continuo, D major] Edited by
Hermann Töttcher
1.Allegro 2.Grave 3.Vivace
Solo Tpt.-2Ob.-Cemb.-Str.
Simrock, Hamburg, C1961
Score 32 p.

Telemann, Georg Philipp

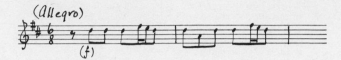

(Allegro)

398v [Concerto, viola and strings,   15'
G major] Edited by Hellmuth Christian Wolff
1.Largo 2.Allegro 3.Andante 4.Presto
Solo Va.-Str.
Bärenreiter, Kassel [c1949?]
Score 19 p.

Largo

1034v [Concerto, violin, strings and continuo,
A minor] Edited by Joh. Harder
1.Allegro 2.Andante 3.Presto
Solo Vn.-Cemb.-Str.
D. Rahter, Leipzig, c1932
Score 15 p.
Composed 1728.

Allegro

6121 Sinfonia melodica C-dur. Edited by   12'
Fritz Oberdörffer
1.Vivace assai 2.Sarabande 3.Bourrée
4.Menuet en rondeau 5.Loure 6.Chaconnette
7.Gigue ou Canarie
2Ob.(or 2Fl.)-Cemb.-Str.
Chr. Friedrich Vieweg, Berlin, c1936
Score 16 p.
*Composed for Count Ludwig VIII of Hesse-
Darmstadt.*

Vivace assai

1085m [Suite, flute, strings, and   31'
cembalo, A minor]
1.Ouverture 2.Les plaisirs 3.Air à
l'Italien 4.Menuets 1 and 2 5.Réjouissance
6.Passepied 1 and 2 7.Polonaise
Solo Fl.-Cemb.-Str.
Kalmus, New York [c1948]
Score 32 p.

(Lento)

269m [Suite, 2 horns, 2 violins and bass,
F major] Edited by Horst Büttner
1.Ouverture 2.Rondeau 3.Sarabande 4.Menuet
5.Bourrée
2Solo Hn.-Cemb.-Str.(without Va.)
Eulenburg, London [c1950]
Miniature score 16 p.

Lento

4361 [Suite, B-flat major. Transcribed for
band by R. Kröber]
1.Altdeutsch 2.Neudeutsch 3.Sarabande und
Bourrée 4.Menuet en rondo 5.Gigue
2(ad lib.),2(ad lib.),3(1Cl. in E-flat),1(ad
lib.)-2Wald Hn.,2Tpt.,2Fluegel Hn.,2Ten. Hn.,
2Tbn.(2nd ad lib.),Bar.,2Bass-Timp.,Lg.Dr.,
Sm.Dr.-Lyra(ad lib.)
Chr. Friedrich Vieweg, Berlin, c1941
Score 12 p.
*Movements 1 and 2 are from Telemann's Over-
ture for strings and cembalo, G major; 3, 4,
and 5, from Sinfonia Melodica for strings,
2 oboes, and cembalo, C major.*

Moderato 8va - - - - - - - - -

1234s [Suite, Tafelmusik 1733, III no. 1,
B-flat major] Edited by Max Seiffert
1.Ouverture 2.Bergerie 3.Allegresse 4.
Postillons 5.Flaterie 6.Badinage 7.Menuet
8.Conclusion
2Ob.-Cemb.-Str.
Breitkopf & Härtel, Leipzig [1933?]
Score 27 p.

Lentement

6194 [Suite (overture), D major] Edited   14'
by Friedrich Noack
1.Ouverture 2.Plainte 3.Réjouissance
4.Carillon 5.Tintamare [Seascape] 6.Loure
7.Menuet I 8.Menuet II
2Ob.,Bn.-2Hn.-Cemb.-Str.
Bärenreiter, Kassel, c1955
Score 15 p.
Composed and first performed Darmstadt, 1765.

(Maestoso)

959s [Suite (overture), Don Quixote, *15'30"*
G major] Edited by Gustav Lenzewski, Sr.
In 8 movements
Cemb.-Str.
Chr. Fr. Vieweg, Berlin [n.d.]
Score 20 p.

912s [Suite (overture), G major] Edited by
Gustav Lenzewski, Sr.
1.[Overture] 2.Menuett 3.Altdeutsch 4.
Neudeutsch (18. Jahrhundert) 5.Schwedisch
6.Dänisch 7.[Old wives' dance]
Cemb.-Str.
Chr. Fr. Vieweg, Berlin [n.d.]
Score 18 p.

630s [Suite (overture), G minor] Edited by
Arnold Schering
1.Ouverture 2.Napolitaine 3.Polonaise
4.Murky 5.Menuet 6.Musette 7.Harlequinade
Pno.-Str.
Kahnt, Leipzig, ᶜ1925
Score 17 p.

621s [Suite (overture), A minor] Edited by
Arnold Schering
1.Ouverture 2.Rondo 3.Gavotte 4.Courante
5.Rigaudon 6.Forlane 7.Menuett
Pno.-Str.
Kahnt, Leipzig [n.d.]
Score 17 p.

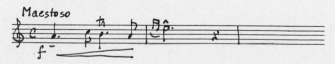

TELLAM, H.

1569s Sérénité, andante religioso
Solo Vn.-Str.
Score: Ms. 4 p.
Parts: Decourcelle, Nice, ᶜ1919

1185s Vie brisée! [Shattered life]
Str.
Score: Ms. 8 p.
Parts: Decourcelle, Nice, ᶜ1916

1406s [Your heart and mine, canzonetta on
E. Bernay's poem]
Solo Vn.-Str.
Score: Ms. 3 p.
Parts: Decourcelle, Nice, ᶜ1918

TELLO, RAFAEL J.   Mexico City 5 September 1872
                        Mexico City 17 December 1946

4153 Intermezzo   *15'*
2,1,2,2-2Hn.-Timp.-Str.
Ms.
Score 26 p. Large folio
*Composed 1915. First performance Mexico City,
1 August 1915, Orquesta Nacional de México,
Carlos J. Meneses conductor.*

4152 Minuetto humorístico   *6'*
3*,2,2,2-4Hn.-Trgl.-Hp.-Str.
Ms.
Score 7 p.
*Composed 1932. First performance Mexico City,
24 October 1933, Cuarteto Nacional de México,
Luis Saloma conductor.*

TEMPLETON, ALEC.   Cardiff, Wales 4 July 1909
                        Greenwich, Connecticut 28 March 1963

3964 Bach goes to town. Transcribed by   *3'*
Henry Brant
Solo Cl.-1,2(2nd alt. E.H.),2,1-2,2-Timp.,Perc.
-Str.
Ms.
Score 25 p.
*Originally composed for piano, 1936. Tran-
scribed 1936. First broadcast performance
Chicago, December 1938, Benny Goodman con-
ductor. First concert performance New York,
15 January 1939, members of the New York Phil-
harmonic, Henry Brant conductor, Benny Goodman
soloist.*

TEMPLETON STRONG, GEORGE.
See: STRONG, GEORGE TEMPLETON.

TEN BRINK, JULES.
See: BRINK, JULES TEN.

TEN FANFARES BY TEN COMPOSERS FOR BRASS AND
PERCUSSION

4271   I. Copland, Aaron. Fanfare for the
common man
0,0,0,0-4,3,3,1-Timp.,Perc.
     II. Cowell, Henry. Fanfare for the forces
of our Latin American Allies
0,0,0,0-4,3,3-Perc.
     III. Creston, Paul. Fanfare for Para-
troopers
4Hn.,3Tpt.,3Tbn.-S.Dr.,Cym.
     IV. Fuleihan, Anis. Fanfare for the
Medical Corps
4Hn.,3Tpt.,3Tbn.,Tuba

Ten Fanfares

          V. Goossens, Eugene. Fanfare for the
Merchant Marine
0,0,0,0-4,4(1 offstage),3,1-Timp.,Perc.
          VI. Hanson, Howard. Fanfare for the
Signal Corps. Orchestration by Godfrey Turner
4Hn.,3Tpt.,3Tbn.,Tuba-Timp.,Perc.
          VII. Piston, Walter. Fanfare for the
Fighting French
4Hn.,3Tpt.,3Tbn.,Tuba-Timp.,Perc.
          VIII. Taylor, Deems. Fanfare for Russia
4Hn.,3Tpt.,3Tbn.,Tuba-Timp.,Perc.
          IX. Thomson, Virgil. Fanfare for France
4Tpt.,3Tbn.-S.Dr.,Ten.Dr.
          X. Wagenaar, Bernard. Fanfare for
Airmen
4Hn.,3Tpt.,3Tbn.,Tuba-Timp.,S.Dr.
Boosey & Hawkes, New York, c1944 [No. IX
c1944 by Virgil Thomson]
Score 42 p.
*Commissioned by Eugene Goossens for the Cin-
cinnati Symphony. First performances
Cincinnati, 1942-43 season, Cincinnati Symphony Orchestra, Eugene Goossens conductor.*

TEN HAVE, WILLEM.
    See: HAVE, WILLEM TEN.

TER-GHEVONDIAN, A.

    2149 [Four Armenian songs, Op. 11]
    2,2(2nd alt. E.H.),2,2-4,2,3,1-Timp.,Perc.-
    Hp.-Str.
    [Mussektor, Armenian SSR] 1927
    Score 45 p.

    1807 [Seda. March from the opera, Op. 15]
    3*,3*,3*,2-4,2,3,1-Timp.,Perc.-Hp.-Str.
    [Mussektor, Armenian SSR] 1929
    Score 29 p.

TERSCHAK, ADOLF.
          Hermannstadt, Transylvania 6 April 1832
                    Breslau 3 October 1901

    728m Le babillard [The babbler] Op. 23   6'
    Solo Fl.-1,2,2,1-2,2,1-Timp.-Str.
    Score: Ms. 41 p.
    Parts: Kistner, Leipzig [1860?]

    752m Carnaval suisse, Op. 133
    Solo Fl.-2,2,2,2-2,2,1-Timp.-Str.
    Score: Ms. 69 p.
    Parts: Joh. André, Offenbach a.M. [1874?]

    751m Columbus, rapsodie américaine, Op. 132
    Solo Fl.-2(2nd alt. Picc.),2,2,2-2,2,2-Timp.-
    Str.
    Score: Ms. 77 p.
    Parts: Joh. André, Offenbach a.M. [1874]

    828m Concertstück, Op. 51 [E minor]
    Solo Fl.-2,2,2,2-2,2,1-Timp.-Str.
    Score: Ms. 81 p.
    Parts: [C.F. Peters, Leipzig, n.d.]

    753m Murillo, allegro de concert, Op. 138   8'
    Solo Fl.-2,2,2,2-2,2,1-Timp.-Str.
    Score: Ms. 73 p.
    Parts: Kistner, Leipzig [1874?]

    729m Le papillon en voyage, étude-   9'
    caprice, Op. 139
    Solo Fl.-1,2,2,2-2,2,1-Str.
    Score: Ms. 56 p.
    Parts: Kistner, Leipzig [1874]

TESCHNER, G.

    182s Lilla Heddi (La petite Heddi)
    Str.
    G. Teschner, Lódz, Russia [n.d.]
    Score 5 p.

TESORONE, A.

    1209s Enfin seuls! [Alone, at last!]
    Str.
    Score: Ms. 9 p.
    Parts: Decourcelle, Nice, c1896

TESSARINI, CARLO.   Rimini, Italy ca.1690
                    ca.15 December 1766

    284v [Concerto, violin and strings, Op. 1
    no. 4, D major] Edited by Hermann Müller
    1.Allegro 2.Largo 3.Allegro
    Solo Vn.-Cemb.-Str.
    Edition Eulenburg, Adliswil-Zurich, c1973
    Score 22 p.
    First published in Venice 1729.

TEYBER, ANTON.   Vienna 8 September 1754
                    Vienna 18 November 1822

    4112 [Symphony, Op. 1, C major]
    1.Adagio maestoso - Allegro assai spiritoso
    2.Andantino con moto 3.Menuet 4.Allegro assai
    1,2,0,2-2Hn.-Str.
    Ms.
    Score 140 p.
    Composed 1799.

THADEWALDT, HERMANN.   Bodenhagen 8 April 1827
                    Berlin 11 February 1909

    1357s Abendständchen [Evening serenade] Op. 20
    Solo Vc.-Str.
    Score: Ms. 11 p.
    Parts: C.F. Schmidt, Heilbronn a.N. [n.d.]

    620s Herbstlied [Autumn song] Op. 23
    Str.(without Cb.)
    C.F. Schmidt, Heilbronn a.N. [n.d.]
    Score 1 p.

    81s Najadengesang [Naiads' song] Op. 24
    Solo Vn.-Str.(Cb. optional)
    C.F. Schmidt, Heilbronn a.N. [n.d.]
    Score 2 p.

606s Traumgesang [Dream melody] Op. 25
Str.(Cb. optional)
C.F. Schmidt, Heilbronn a.N. [n.d.]
Score 1 p.

THALBERG, SIGISMOND.   Geneva 8 January 1812
                        Posilipo, Naples 27 April 1871

478p [Concerto, piano, Op. 5, F minor]   20'
1.Allegro maestoso 2.Adagio 3.Rondo
Solo Pno.-2,2,2,2-2,2,3-Timp.-Str.
Ms.
Score 185 p.

THALLON, ROBERT.   Liverpool 18 March 1852
                        Brooklyn 13 March 1910

2125s Evening song
Str.
[n.p., n.d., possibly Ditson, Boston]
Score 3 p.

THATCHER, HARRY, JR.   Ruthven, Iowa 6 July 1905
                                            d. 1937

5532 Symphony in E minor   30'
1.Slow 2.Moderately quick 3.Fast
3*,3*,3*,2-4,4,3,1-Timp.,Perc.-Cel.,2Hp.-Str.
Ms.
Score 152 p. Large folio
Composed 1933. First performance Iowa City,
6 May 1936, University of Iowa Symphony
Orchestra, Frank Estes Kendrie conductor.

THATCHER, HOWARD RUTLEDGE.
                    Baltimore 17 September 1878
                    Baltimore 21 February 1973

442m [Concerto, clarinet]   12'30"
1.Allegro con brio 2.Andantino con moto
3.Scherzo 4.Allegro con brio
Solo Cl.-1,1,1,1-2,2,1-Timp.-Hp.-Str.
Ms.
Score 51 p.
Composed 1954. First performance Brevard,
North Carolina, 20 August 1955, Transylvania
Orchestra, J. Christian Pfohl conductor,
Ignatius Gennusa soloist.

443m Concerto for horn   12'
1.Allegro con brio 2.Andante non stentando
3.Allegro non troppo
Solo Hn.-2,2,2,2-3,2,3-Timp.-Hp.-Str.
Ms.
Score 43 p. Large folio
Composed 1951. First performance Baltimore,
9 March 1952, Baltimore Symphony Orchestra,
the composer conducting, Leigh Martinet
soloist.

370v [Concerto, viola]   12'
1.Allegro 2.Andante espressivo 3.Vivace
Solo Va.-1,1,2,1-2,2,1-Timp.-Hp.-Str.
Ms.
Score 64 p.
Composed 1958.

366v [Concerto, violin, A major]   22'
1.Allegro con brio 2.Andante religioso ma con

moto 3.Allegro con fuoco
Solo Vn.-3*,2,2,2-4,3,3,1-Timp.,Cast.,Trgl.-
Hp.-Str.
Ms. [C1938 by J. Fischer, New York]
Score 114 p.
Composed 1931. First performance Baltimore,
20 March 1932, Baltimore Symphony Orchestra,
the composer conducting, Barbara Lull soloist.

5766 Lyric suite   18'
1.Marionettes 2.Kaddish 3.Procession
4.Berceuse 5.Tarantelle
3*,3*,3*,3*-4,3,3,1-Timp.,Perc.-Hp.-Str.
Ms.
Score 50 p. Large folio
Originally composed for piano, 1938-49.
Orchestrated 1949-50. First performance
Baltimore, 4 February 1951, Baltimore Sym-
phony Orchestra, the composer conducting.

THÈVE, ED.

1540s Sous les grands pins [Under tall pines]
Str.
Score: Ms. 3 p.
Parts: Durdilly, Paris, C1925

THIEME, KARL.   Niederschlema, Erzgebirge
                    (now East Germany) 23 June 1909

4584 [Cousin Michael, a merry suite]   12'
Michael's song - 4 variations
2Fl.(2nd optional, alt. Picc.),2Ob.(2nd
optional)-Str.(3Vn.,Vc.,Cb. ad lib.)
Georg Kallmeyer, Wolfenbüttel, C1939
Score 24 p.

THIERIOT, FERDINAND.   Hamburg 7 April 1838
                            Hamburg 4 August 1919

968s Serenade, Op. 44 [F major]
Str.
J. Rieter-Biedermann, Leipzig [n.d.]
Score 39 p.

136s Waltz, Op. 54 no. 1. Edited by Max
Vogrich
Str.
J. Rieter-Biedermann, Leipzig, C1891
Score 3 p.

THIMAN, ERIC HARDING.
                    b. Ashford, Kent 12 September 1900

1833s Variations on a theme of Elgar
Str.
Novello, London, C1940
Score 22 p.

THOMAS, AMBROISE.   Metz, France 5 August 1811
                            Paris 12 February 1896

4256 [Gille and Gillotin. Overture]
2,2,2,2-4,2,3-Timp.,Perc.-Str.
Paris, Colombier [1874]
Score 30 p.
From the comic opera composed 1861. First per-
formance Paris, 22 April 1874.

Thomas, Ambroise

215 [Mignon. Overture]   7'
2*,2,2,2-4,2,3-Timp.,Perc.-Hp.-Str.
Kalmus, New York [n.d.]
Score 36 p.
*From the opera based on Goethe's Wilhelm
Meister novels. Composed 1865. First perform-
ance Paris, 17 November 1866.*

4365 [Mignon. Gavotte]   2'30"
2,2,2,2-4,2,3-Timp.-Str.
Heugel, Paris [1867]
Score 5 p.

1432s [Mignon. Gavotte. Arranged by C. Sharpe]
Str.
Score: Ms. 6 p.
Parts: Chester, London, C1929

6917 [Mina, or The ménage à trois. Overture]
2(2nd alt. Picc.),2,2,2-4,0,2Cnt.,3-Timp.,
Perc.-Str.
Bureau Central de Musique, Paris [n.d.]
Score 38 p.
*From the comic opera. First performance Paris,
10 October 1843.*

THOMAS, ARTHUR GORING.
                Ratton Park, Sussex 20 November 1850
                        London 20 March 1892

979s Winds in the trees. Scored by Stanley
Hawley
Str.
Score: Ms. 5 p.
Parts: Boosey, London, C1908

THOMAS, KURT GEORG HUGO.   Tönning,
        Schleswig-Holstein, Germany 25 May 1904
        Bad Oeynhausen, West Germany 1 April 1973

4501 [Suite for student orchestra, no. 1,
Op. 18a]
1.Marsch 2.Kanon 3.Tanz 4.Duett
5.Variationen 6.Marsch
Fl.(ad lib.),Ob. or Cl.(ad lib.)-Hn. or Tpt.
(ad lib.)-Timp.,Trgl.(both ad lib.)-Pno. or
Cemb.-Str.(without Cb.;Va. ad lib.)
Breitkopf & Härtel, Leipzig, C1932
Score 23 p.

4534 [Suite for youth orchestra, no. 2, five
German dances, Op. 22]
Woodwinds-Brass-Timp.,Perc.(all ad lib.)-Pno.
or Cemb.-Str.
Breitkopf & Härtel, Leipzig, C1938
Score 31 p.

THOMASSIN, DÉSIRÉ.   Vienna 11 February 1858
                        Munich 24 March 1933

888v [Concerto, violin, Op. 75, B minor]
In one movement
Solo Vn.-2,2,2,2-4,2,3-Timp.-Str.
F. Zorn, Nuremberg [n.d.]
Score 91 p.

THOMÉ, FRANCIS.
        Port Louis, Mauritius 18 October 1850
                Paris 16 November 1909

Real name: Joseph François Luc Thomé

4440 Entr'acte pizzicato, Op. 39b
2,2,2,2-2Hn.-Tamb.-Str.
H. Lemoine, Paris [1881]
Score 25 p.

569s Gavotte madrigal
Str.
Score: E. Hatzfeld [n.d.] C1896. 3 p.
Parts: International, New York [n.d.]

523m Légende, Op. 122
Solo Hp.-2(2nd alt. Picc.),2(1st alt. E.H.),2,
2-2,2-Timp.,Perc.-Str.
J. Hamelle, Paris [n.d.]
Score in reduction 15 p.

646s Minuetto, Op. 68 [G minor]
Str.
B. Schott's Söhne, Mainz [n.d.]
Score 4 p.

1500s Scènes champêtres [Rustic scenes] angelus
Bells,Trgl.-Str.
A. Sporck, Paris, C1904
Score 3 p.

THOME, JOEL.   Detroit, Michigan 7 January 1939

7185 Homage to Varèse on a painting by Magritte
2(1Alto),0,3*(1Cl. in E-flat)-2,2,3,1-Perc.-
Str.
Ms. C1976 by Joel Thome
Score 16 p. Large folio
Composed 1969.

THOMPSON, RANDALL.   New York 21 April 1899

704p Jazz poem   14'
Solo Pno.-3(3rd alt. Picc.),2,3(1Cl. in D),3*-
4,3,3,1-Timp.,Perc.-Str.
Ms.
Score 84 p.
*Originally composed for piano, 1927; tran-
scribed for piano and orchestra, 1928. First
performance Rochester, 27 November 1928,
Rochester Philharmonic Orchestra, Howard Han-
son conductor, the composer as soloist.*

2683 Pierrot and Cothurnus   10'
2,3*,2,3*-4,2-Timp.,Perc.-Hp.-Str.
Ms.
Score 61 p. Large folio
*Composed 1922 as the prelude to Edna St. Vin-
cent Millay's play Aria da Capo. Awarded
Prix de Rome, 1922. First performance Rome,
17 May 1923, Accademia di Santa Cecilia
orchestra, the composer conducting.*

2667 The piper at the gates of dawn   12'
3*,3*,4*(1Cl. in D),3*-4,3,3,1-Timp.,Perc.-
Pno.,Cel.,2Hp.-Str.
Ms.

Score 55 p.
Composed 1924, after Kenneth Grahame's The Wind in the Willows. First performance Rome, 27 May 1924, Augusteo Orchestra, the composer conducting.

4214   Symphony no. 1   *24'*
1.Allegro brioso 2.Poco adagio 3.Allegro
3(3rd alt. Picc.),3*,3*,3*-4,2,3,1-Timp.,Perc.
-Org.,Hp.-Str.
Eastman School of Music, Rochester, ᶜ1931
Score 140 p.
First performance Rochester, 20 February 1930, Eastman-Rochester Symphony Orchestra, Howard Hanson conductor.

2666   Symphony no. 2   *28'*
1.Allegro 2.Largo 3.Vivace 4.Andante
moderato - Allegro con spirito
3(3rd alt. Picc.),3(3rd alt. E.H.),3,3-4,3,
3,1-Timp.,Cym.-Str.
C.C. Birchard, Boston, ᶜ1932 by Eastman School
of Music
Score 178 p. Large folio
Composed 1931. First performance Rochester, 24 March 1932, Rochester Philharmonic Orchestra, Howard Hanson conductor.

THOMSON, VIRGIL.
          b. Kansas City, Missouri 25 November 1896

4271   Fanfare for France
See: TEN FANFARES BY TEN COMPOSERS FOR BRASS
          AND PERCUSSION

3144   Filling station, ballet [complete]   *20'*
1.Introduction 2.Mac's dance 3.Scene - Motor-
ist and Mac 4.Truck driver's dance 5.Scene -
State trooper and truck drivers 6.Dance of
family life 7.Tango 8.Waltz 9.The Big
Apple 10.The hold-up 11.The chase 12.Finale
2(2nd alt. Picc.),2(2nd alt. E.H.),2,2-4,3,3,
1-Timp.,Perc.-Pno.-Str.
Ms.
Score 210 p.
Commissioned by Ballet Caravan, 1937. Composed 1937. First performance Hartford, Connecticut, 6 January 1938, Ballet Caravan.

6947   [Louisiana story. Acadian songs and   *14'*
dances]
1.Sadness 2.Papa's tune 3.A narrative 4.
The alligator and the 'coon 5.Super-sadness
6.Walking song 7.The squeeze box
2(2nd alt. Picc.),2(2nd alt. E.H.),2,2-2,2,
2-Perc.-Hp.(or Pno.),Accordion(or Pno.)-Str.
G. Schirmer, New York, ᶜ1948, 1951 by composer
Score 77 p.
Music for Robert Flaherty's film. Based on songs from Irene Thérèse Whitfield's Louisiana French Folk Songs and on John and Alan Lomax's collections of fiddle music. Composed 1948. Sound track recorded 1948 by the Philadelphia Orchestra, Eugene Ormandy conductor. Awarded the Pulitzer Prize for music in 1949.

3708   The plough that broke the plains
1.Prelude - Fugue 2.Pastorale (Grass) 3.
Cattle 4.The homesteader 5.Warning 6.War
and the tractor 7.Speculation (Blues) 8.
Drought 9.Wind and dust 10. Devastation
1(alt. Picc.),1(alt. E.H.),3*(2nd alt. Alto
Sax.,B.Cl. alt. Ten. Sax.),1-2,2,2-Timp.,Perc.
-Harm.,Guit.(alt. Banjo)-Str.
Ms. [ᶜ1942 by Music Press, New York]
Score 144 p.
Commissioned by the U.S. Farm Security Admin-istration for Pare Lorenz's documentary film. Composed 1936.

3731   The river. Complete film music
1(alt. Picc.),2(2nd alt. E.H.),2(2nd alt.
B.Cl.),1-2,2,2-Timp.,Perc.-Banjo-Str.
Ms.
Score 202 p.
Commissioned by the U.S. Farm Security Admin-istration for the documentary film. Composed 1937.

4754   A solemn music, for band   *ca.5'*
4*(2Picc.),2,6*(1Cl. in E-flat, 1Alto Cl.),2-
4Sax.-8(4Hn. in E-flat),2,3Cnt.,3,2Bar.,2Euph.,
2-Timp.,Perc.
Schirmer, New York, ᶜ1949
Score 20 p.
Commissioned by the League of Composers for the Goldman Band. Composed 1949. First per-formance, New York City, 17 June 1949, Gold-man Band, the composer conducting.

4892   [Symphony no. 1, On a hymn tune,   *20'*
A major]
1.Introduction and allegro 2.Andante canta-
bile 3.Andantino 4.Allegro alla breve
2(2nd alt. Picc.),2,2,3*-4,2,3,1-Timp.,Perc.-
Str.
Ms. [Southern Music, New York, ᶜ1954]
Score 112 p. Large folio
Hymn is How Firm a Foundation, words and music commonly ascribed to Robert Keene. The melody is also called Geard. Also quoted: Yes, Jesus Loves Me; For He's A Jolly Good Fellow. Com-posed 1926-28. First performance New York, 22 February 1945, New York Philharmonic, the com-poser conducting.

THONY, CH.

1498s Berceuse
Solo Vn.-Str.
Score: Ms. 6 p.
Parts: Richault, Paris [n.d.]

THUILLE, LUDWIG WILHELM ANDREAS MARIA.
                    Bozen, Tyrol 30 November 1861
                    Munich 5 February 1907

5692   [Theuerdank. Prelude to Act I, Op. 16] *9'*
3*,2,2,2-4,3,3,1-Timp.,Cym.,Trgl.-Str.
Kistner, Leipzig, ᶜ1899
Score 32 p.
From the opera in three acts composed 1893-95. First performance Munich, 12 March 1897.

Thul, Friedrich von

THUL, FRIEDRICH VON.   d.Vienna 29 November 1911

 759s Wiegenlied
       Solo Vn.-Str.
       Joh. André, Offenbach a.M. [n.d.]
       Score 10 p.

THURNER, FRIEDRICH EUGEN.
              Montbéliard, France 9 December 1785
                       Amsterdam 21 March 1827

 871m [Concerto, oboe, no. 2, Op. 39, C major]
       1.Grave - Allegro 2.Adagio 3.Allegretto con
       variazioni
       Solo Ob.-2,0,2,2-2,2-Timp.-Str.
       Ms.
       Score 164 p.

THYRESTAM, GUNNAR.   Gävle, Sweden 11 October 1900

 394m Concentus gravis   20'
       1.Sonata di forma 2.Ostinato grave e respon-
       sorium 3.Finale alla toccata
       Solo Org.-Timp.-Str.
       Ms.
       Score 55 p.
       *Composed 1957. First performance Hälsingborg,
       20 October 1960, Northern Skane Orchestra,
       Anton Heiller conductor, Alf Linder soloist.*

THYROLF, C.

 686s Zwei Stücke im nordischen Charakter
       1.Schwedisches Tanzlied 2.Halling
       Str.
       Score: Ms. 10 p.
       Parts: Louis Oertel, Hannover [n.d.]

TIEDEMANN, PAUL.

 500s Tanzweisen, Op. 1
       Str.
       Fr. Kistner, Leipzig, C1906
       Score 23 p.

 501s Tanzweisen, Op. 2 [Neue Folge]
       Str.
       Fr. Kistner, Leipzig, C1907
       Score 19 p.

TIESSEN, HEINZ.   Königsberg 10 April 1887
                         Berlin 29 November 1971

 694v Totentanz-Suite [Dance of Death] Op. 29
       Solo Vn.-2(2nd alt. Picc.),1,2,2-2,1-Timp.,
       Perc.-Str.
       Ries & Erler, Berlin, C1928
       Score 35 p.
       *From the music to Gerhart Hauptmann's Die
       Armseligen Besenbinder [The Poor Broom-makers].*

2089 Vorspiel zu einem Revolutionsdrama,   12'
       Op. 33
       2(2nd alt. Picc.),2,2,3*-4,2,3,1-Timp.,Perc.-
       Str.
       Ries & Erler, Berlin, C1927
       Score 29 p.
       *Composed 1921-23. First performance Berlin,
       9 March 1927, Emil Bohnke conductor.*

TILL, JACOB.

7288 [Waltzes for the pianoforte. Nos. 1 and 3.
       Transcribed by Sam Dennison]
       1,1,2*,1-1,1,Euph.
       Ms. C1977 by The Fleisher Collection of Orches-
       tral Music, Free Library of Philadelphia
       Score 6 p. Large folio
       *This transcription 1976. First performance
       Free Library of Philadelphia, 17 November
       1976, Fleisher Ensemble, Sam Dennison con-
       ductor.*

TILLMETZ, RUDOLF.   Munich 1 April 1847
                           Munich 25 January 1915

 644m [Concert-etude, flute, Op. 22,   3'
       D major]
       Solo Fl.-2,2,2,2-4,2,3,1-Timp.-Str.
       J.H. Zimmermann, Leipzig [n.d.]
       Score in reduction 9 p.
       Composed 1890. First performance Munich, 1892.

 584m Ungarische Phantasie, Op. 25   7'
       Solo Fl.-1,2,2,2-4,3,3-Timp.,Tamb.-Str.
       Score: Ms. 56 p.
       Parts: Fr. Kistner, Leipzig [n.d.]
       Composed 1894. First performance Munich, 1895.

TINEL, PIERRE-JOSEPH EDGAR.
              Sinay, East Flanders 27 March 1854
                     Brussels 28 October 1912

5080 [Katharina, Op. 44. Overture]   16'
       3*,3*,3*,2,Sarrus.-4,3,3,1-Timp.,Tam-tam-2Hp.
       -Str.
       Breitkopf & Härtel, Leipzig, C1909
       Score 47 p.
       *From the religious opera. First performance
       Brussels, 27 February 1909.*

4545 [Katharina, Op. 44. Dances,   ca.7'30"
       sacred and profane]
       3*,2,2,2,Sarrus.-4,3,3,1-Timp.,Perc.-2Hp.-Str.
       Breitkopf & Härtel, Leipzig, C1908
       Score 15 p.

TINIAKOV, ALEXANDRE.

1175 [Suite, Op. 8, F-sharp minor]   18'
       1.Elegie 2.Scherzo 3.Ballade 4.Tarantelle
       3(3rd alt. Picc.),2*,3,2-4,2,3,1-Timp.,Perc.-
       Hp.-Str.
       J.H. Zimmermann, Leipzig [n.d.]
       Score 114 p.

TOCCHI, GIANLUCA.   Perugia, Italy 10 January 1901

4775 [Three pieces for orchestra]   18'
       3(3rd alt. Picc.),3*,3*,3*-6,4,3,1-Timp.(2
       players),Perc.-Hp.-Str.
       Ricordi, Milan, C1939
       Score 104 p. Large folio
       *Composed 1938. First performance Venice, 8
       September 1938.*

TOCH, ERNST.   Vienna 7 December 1887
                      Los Angeles 1 October 1964

6480 Big Ben, variation-fantasy on the   20'
Westminster chimes, Op. 62
3*,3*,3(1Cl. in E-flat),2-4,4,3,1-Timp.,Perc.-
Cel.,Hp.-Str.
Associated, New York, ᶜ1935, 1956
Miniature score 54 p.
*Composed 1934. First performance Cambridge,
Massachusetts, 20 December 1934, Boston Sym-
phony Orchestra, Serge Koussevitzky con-
ductor. Revised 1956.*

4946 Bunte Suite, Op. 48   18'
1.Marschtempo 2.Intermezzo 3.Adagio espressivo 4.Marionetten-Tanz 5.Galante Passacaglia 6.Karussel
2(2nd alt. Picc.),2*,2,2-2,2,B.Tbn.-Timp.,
Perc.-Pno.-Str.
B. Schott's Söhne, Mainz, ᶜ1929
Score 83 p.
*Commissioned by Frankfurter Rundfunk. First
performance Frankfurt, 22 February 1929,
Frankfurter Rundfunk orchestra, Hans Flesch
conductor.*

548p [Concerto, piano, Op. 38]   22'
1.Molto pesante 2.Adagio 3.Rondo disturbato
Solo Pno.-3(2 alt. 2Picc.),2,4,3*-3,3,3,1-
Timp.,Perc.-Org.-Str.
B. Schott's Söhne, Mainz, ᶜ1926
Score 89 p.
*Composed 1925. First performance Düsseldorf,
8 October 1926, Hans Weisbach conductor,
Walter Gieseking soloist.*

4306 Fanal, Orchester und Orgel, Op. 45   8'
3*,2*,3(1Cl. in E-flat),3*-4,4,3,1-Timp.,Perc.
-Org.-Str.
B. Schott's Söhne, Mainz, ᶜ1928
Score 16 p.
Composed February 1928.

3775 Fünf Stücke für Kammerorchester,   20'
Op. 33
1.Langsam 2.Ruhig 3.Intermezzo 4.Heftig,
eigenwillig 5.Allegro assai
2,0,2*-Timp.,Perc.-Str.
B. Schott's Söhne, Mainz, ᶜ1924
Miniature score 55 p.
*Composed 1924. First performance at the
Third Festival of the International Society
for Contemporary Music, Prague, 15 May 1925,
Prague Philharmonic Orchestra, Erich Kleiber
conductor.*

4950 Kleine Theater-Suite, Op. 54   16'
1.Ouvertüre 2.[Shy courtship] 3.Tanz
4.Nachtstück 5.Finale
3*,2,3(1Cl. in E-flat),2-2,2,3,1-Timp.,Perc.-
Hp.-Str.
B. Schott's Söhne, Mainz, ᶜ1931
Score 42 p.
First performance Berlin, 9 February 1931.

4303 Komödie für Orchester, Opus 42   16'
3*,2*,3(1Cl. in E-flat),2-3,2,2,1-Timp.,Perc.-
Cel.,Hp.-Str.
B. Schott's Söhne, Mainz, ᶜ1927
Score 44 p.

*Composed 1927. First performance Berlin, 13
November 1927, Berlin Philharmonic Orchestra,
Wilhelm Furtwängler conductor.*

5249 Notturno   11'
2(2nd alt. Picc.),2,2,2-2,2,3-Xyl.-Hp.-Str.
(without Cb.)
Ms. [Now Mills Music, New York, ᶜ1957]
Score 23 p. Large folio
*Commissioned by the Louisville Orchestra.
Composed 1953. First performance Louisville,
2 January 1954, Louisville Orchestra, Robert
Whitney conductor.*

5363 Peter Pan, Op. 76   15'
1.Allegro giocoso 2.Andante semplice e
grazioso 3.Allegro vivo
3*,2,3(1Cl. in E-flat),2-4,2,2-Timp.,Perc.-Hp.
-Str.
Ms. [B. Schott's Söhne, Mainz, ᶜ1958]
Score 47 p.
*Commissioned by the Serge Koussevitzky Music
Foundation in the Library of Congress for the
Seattle Symphony. First performance Seattle,
13 February 1956, Seattle Symphony, Milton
Katims conductor.*

3345 Pinocchio, a merry overture   7'
3*,2,2,2-2,2,3-Timp.,Perc.-Str.
Associated Music Publishers, New York, ᶜ1937
Score 30 p.
*Composed 1936. First performance Los Angeles,
10 December 1936, Los Angeles Philharmonic
Orchestra, Otto Klemperer conductor.*

1468 Spiel für Blasorchester, Op. 39   10'
2(2nd alt. Picc.),1,5(1Cl. in E-flat optional),
1-4,4,3,1Ten. Hn.,Bar.2Flügelhn.-Timp.,Perc.
B. Schott Söhne, Mainz, ᶜ1926
Score 28 p.
*Composed for and first performed at the Donau-
eschingen Chamber Music Festival, 1926.*

6481 [Symphony no. 2, Op. 73]   30'30"
1.Allegro fanatico 2.Sehr leicht, huschend,
schattenhaft 3.Adagio 4.Allegro
3(2nd&3rd alt. Picc.),3(3rd alt. E.H.),3(3rd
alt. B.Cl.&Cl. in E-flat),2-3,3,3,1-Timp.(2
players)-Pno.4-hands,Org.,2Hp.-Str.
Associated Music Publishers, New York, ᶜ1953
Miniature score 140 p.
*Composed 1952. First performance Vienna, 11
January 1952, Vienna Symphony Orchestra, Herbert Häfner conductor.*

5329 [Symphony no. 3, Op. 75]   27'30"
1.Molto adagio 2.Andante tranquillo - Allegro
3.Allegro impetuoso
3(3rd alt. Picc.),3*,3(1Cl. in E-flat),3*-4,4,
3,1-Timp.,Perc.-Org.-Str.
Mills Music, New York, ᶜ1957
Miniature score 95 p.
*Commissioned by the American-Jewish Tercen-
tenary Committee of Chicago, 1954. Composed
1954-55. First performance Pittsburgh, 2
December 1955, Pittsburgh Symphony Orchestra,
William Steinberg conductor.*

Toeschi, Carlo Giuseppe

TOESCHI, CARLO GIUSEPPE.
          probably Padua 1722 or 1724
          Munich 12 April 1788

   4640 [Symphony, D major] Arranged by Adam Carse
     1.Allegro 2.Andante 3.Presto
     2Ob.(or 2Fl.)-2Hn.-Str.
     Augener, London, C1936
     Score 15 p.
     *Published by J. J. Hummel, Amsterdam, 1770, as
     no. 1 of its series Symphonie Périodique.
     Listed in the Breitkopf Thematic Catalogue,
     Supplement V, 1770.*

   4468 [Symphony, G major]
     1.Allegro 2.Andante 3.Presto
     2,0,0,2-2Hn.-Str.
     Score: Ms. 23 p.
     Parts: Ms. C1976 by The Fleisher Collection of
     Orchestral Music, Free Library of Philadelphia

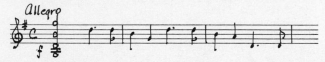

TOMA, ALBERTO.

   899s Lea, gavotta-pizzicata
     Str.
     P. Decourcelle, Nice [n.d.]
     Score 3 p.

TOMASI, HENRI.   Marseilles 17 August 1901
                 Paris 13 January 1971

   844v Chant hébraïque
     Solo Vn.-3(3rd alt. Picc.),2(2nd alt. E.H.),2,
     2-4,2-Timp.,Perc.-2Hp.-Str.
     Henry Lemoine, Paris, C1931
     Score 12 p.

   2266 Cyrnos [symphonic poem]
     3(3rd alt. Picc.),3*,2,3-4,3,3,1-Timp.,Perc.-
     Pno.,Cel.,Hp.-Str.
     Henry Lemoine, Paris, C1930
     Score 134 p.
     *Composed 1929. First performance Paris, 30
     November 1929, the composer conducting.*

   2983 Deux danses cambodgiennes   *8'30"*
     1.Offrande du lotus or et argent 2.Butsomali
     1,1,0,1-2,1-Timp.,Perc.-Hp.-Str.
     Henry Lemoine, Paris, C1937
     Score 32 p.
     *First performance Paris, 23 May 1935,
     l'Orchestre National, the composer conducting.*

   2981 Don Juan de Mañara, suite
     1.[The garden of Girolama] 2.[The last sere-
     nade of Don Juan] 3.Procession 4.[Easter
     Sunday in Seville]
     2(2nd alt. Picc.),2(2nd alt. E.H.),2,2-2,2,1-
     Timp.,Perc.-Cel.,Hp.,Harm.(ad lib.)-Str.
     Henry Lemoine, Paris, C1936
     Score 72 p.
     *First performance Paris, 20 March 1937,
     Lamoureux Orchestra, Eugene Bigot conductor.*

   2982 Petite suite médiévale
     1.Prélude 2.Pastorale 3.Prière et complainte
     4.Le tournoi
     2*,0,0,1-2,1,1-Hp.-Str.(without Cb.)
     Henry Lemoine, Paris, C1936
     Score 40 p.
     *First performance in a radio broadcast, Paris,
     March 1937, the composer conducting.*

TOMKINS, THOMAS.   St. David's, England 1572
                 Martin Hussingtree June 1656

   1812s Fantasia. Arranged by Edmund H. Fellowes
     Str.(without Cb.)
     Stainer & Bell, London, C1931
     Score 4 p.

TOMMASINI, VINCENZO.   Rome 17 September 1878
                 Rome 23 December 1950

   2207 Il beato regno [Blessed reign]   *13'*
     poema
     3*,3*,3*,2-4,3,3,1-Timp.,Perc.-Pno.,Cel.,Hp.-
     Str.
     G. Ricordi, Milan, C1922
     Score 64 p. Large folio
     *Composed 1920. First performance Rome, April
     1922, Albert Coates conductor.*

   1924 Il carnevale di Venezia [Variations *12'*
     in the style of Paganini]
     3(2nd&3rd alt. 2Picc.),3*,4*(1Cl. in E-flat),
     3*-4,3,4-Timp.,Perc.-Cel.,Hp.-Str.
     G. Ricordi, Milan, C1929
     Score 86 p.
     *Composed 1928. First performance New York,
     10 October 1929, Arturo Toscanini conductor.*

   1908 Chiari di luna   *14'*
     1.Chiese e ruine 2.Serenate
     3*,3*,3*,2-4,0,2Cnt.,3,1-Timp.,Perc.-Cel.-Hp.
     -Str.
     G. Ricordi, Milan, C1921
     Score 45 p.
     *Composed 1915. First performance Rome,
     November 1916, Arturo Toscanini conductor.*

   567s [Les femmes de bonne humeur. Andante]
     Str.
     J. & W. Chester, London, C1920
     Score 3 p.
     *From the ballet based on a comedy by Goldoni,
     accompanied by a series of sonatas by Domenico
     Scarlatti, and orchestrated by Tommasini.*

1715 [Les femmes de bonne humeur. Cinq   *12'*
sonates] Arranged by Vincenzo Tommasini
2,2,2,2-4,2-Timp.,Trgl.-Cemb.-Str.
J.&W. Chester, London, ᶜ1920
Score 25 p.
Arranged 1919. First performance London, 9
March 1921, Albert Coates conductor.

2577 Nápule, fantasia per orchestra   *20'*
3(3rd alt. Picc.),3*,4*(Cl. in E-flat alt. Cl.
in D),3*-6,4,3,1-Timp.,Perc.-Hp.-Str.
Edition Adler, Berlin, ᶜ1931
Score 131 p. Large folio
Composed 1930. First performance Freiburg,
Germany, 7 December 1931, Municipal Orches-
tra, Hugo Balzer conductor.

1909 Paesaggi toscani [Tuscan landscapes]   *14'*
rapsodia
3(3rd alt. Picc.),3*,2,2-4,2,3,1-Timp.,Perc.-
Hp.-Str.
G. Ricordi, Milan, ᶜ1924
Score 84 p.
Composed 1922. First performance Rome, Decem-
ber 1923, Bernardino Molinari conductor.

3914 Preludio, fanfara e fuga   *13'30"*
3*,3*,3*,3*-4,3,3,1-Timp.,Perc.-Cel.,Hp.-Str.
G. Ricordi, Milan, ᶜ1928
Miniature score 74 p.
Composed 1927. First performance Rome, Decem-
ber 1928, Augusteo Orchestra, Victor de Sabata
conductor.

TORELLI, GIUSEPPE.   Verona 22 April 1658
   Bologna 8 February 1709

1031s [Concerto grosso, strings and   *11'*
organ, Op. 8 no. 1, C major] Edited by Alceo
Toni
1.Vivace 2.Largo 3.Allegro
Soli: Vn.I,Vn.II,Vc.-Org.-Str.(without Vc.)
G. Ricordi, Milan, 1927
Score 27 p.
Op. 8 first published 1709 as 12 Concerti
Grossi.

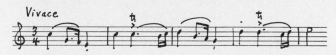

908s [Concerto grosso, strings and organ,
Christmas concerto, Op. 8 no. 6, G minor]
Arranged by Arnold Schering
1.Grave - Vivace 2.Largo 3.Vivace
Soli: Vn.I,Vn.II-Pno.(or Org.)-Str.
C.F. Kahnt, Leipzig, ᶜ1926
Score 11 p.

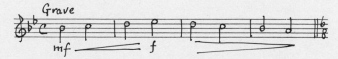

695s [Sinfonia, Op. 6 no. 6, E minor] Arranged
by Arnold Schering
1.Allegro moderato 2.Adagio 3.Presto
Pno.-Str.(without Cb.)
C.F. Kahnt, Leipzig, ᶜ1913
Score 11 p.
Op. 6 first published 1698 as Concerti
Musicali.

232m [Sinfonia, D major. Excerpt *and* Sonata a
5 with trumpet, D major. Excerpt] Arranged by
Jean-François Paillard
Solo Tpt.-Cemb.(or Org.)-Str.(2 choirs)
Costallat, Paris, ᶜ1962
Score 16 p.

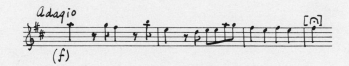

TORRÁ, CELIA.   Concepción del Uruguay,
   Argentina 18 September 1889

3677 Suite para orquesta   *19'*
1.En piragua [In the canoe] 2.Cortejo
3.Fiesta indígena
3*,2,2,2-2,2,2-Timp.,Perc.-Pno.,Cel.,Hp.-Str.
Ricordi Americana, Buenos Aires, 1944
Score 95 p.
Composed 1930-31. First performance of no. 2
Buenos Aires, 23 December 1930, Orquesta de
la Asociación Lago di Como, Bruno Bandini
conductor; no. 1 and no. 3 Buenos Aires, 28
November 1937, Orquesta Sinfónica Femenina,
the composer conducting. Awarded prize, 1938,
by the Salón Nacional de Música, Argentina.

TOSELLI, ENRICO.   Florence 13 March 1883
   Florence 15 January 1926

1603s Canzonetta, C major
Str.
Score: Ms. 8 p.
Parts: Delrieu, Nice, ᶜ1923

1604s Une chanson d'amour, serenatella
Str.
Score: Ms. 5 p.
Parts: Delrieu, Nice, ᶜ1923

Toselli, Enrico

1602s Dernière serenata, crépuscule d'automne.
Arranged by E. Gandolfo
Solo Vn.-Str.
Score: Ms. 4 p.
Parts: Delrieu, Nice, ^c1924

TOVEY, DONALD FRANCIS.   Eton 17 July 1875
                       Edinburgh 10 July 1940

311p [Concerto, piano, Op. 15, A major]   *30'*
1.Energico 2.Adagio ma non troppo 3.Alla
marcia
Solo Pno.-2,2,2,2-4,2-Timp.-Str.
B. Schott's Söhne, Mainz, ^c1906
Score 96 p.
Composed 1903. First performance London,
November 1903, Queen's Hall Orchestra, Henry
J. Wood conductor, composer as soloist.

750c [Concerto, violoncello, Op. 40,   *60'*
C major]
1.Allegro moderato 2.Andante maestoso
3.Intermezzo 4.Rondo
Solo Vc.-2(2nd alt. Picc.),2,2,2-4,2,3-Timp.-
Str.
Oxford University Press, London, ^c1937
Score 106 p.
First performance Edinburgh, 22 November 1934,
the composer conducting, Pablo Casals, soloist.

TOWNSEND, DOUGLAS.   New York 8 November 1921

4896 Divertimento
1,1,1,1-Str.
Ms.
Score 71 p.
Composed 1949.

4895 Fantasy
2,2,2,2-2,2-Timp.-Str.
Ms.
Score 80 p.
Composed 1949. First performance 1950.

TRAETTA, FILIPPO.   Venice 8 January 1777
                    Philadelphia 9 January 1854

7089 [Sinfonia concertata, D major]
1.Adagio - Allegro 2.Adagio 3.Minuetto
e trio all'ebraica 4.Fugato
1,2(or 2Cl.)-2Hn.-Timp.-Str.
Ms.
Score 29 p.
Composed 1803. From Ms. parts in the Histori-
cal Society of Pennsylvania, Philadelphia.

TRAPP, MAX.   Berlin 1 November 1887
                 Berlin 29 May 1971

856v [Concerto, violin, Op. 21, A minor]
1.Bewegt 2.Adagio 3.Ruhig
Solo Vn.-3(2nd&3rd alt. 2Picc.),3*,3*,3*-4,2,
3,1-Timp.,Perc.-Str.
F.E.C. Leuckart, Leipzig, ^c1901
Score 97 p.
First performance at the Tonkünstler festival,
Kiel, 1925.

2535 Divertimento für Kammerorchester, Op. 27
1.Intrada 2.Serenata 3.Scherzetto 4.Aria
5.Finale
1,1,1,1-1,1,1,1-Timp.-Str.
E. Eulenburg, Leipzig, ^c1931
Score 82 p.

TRAVERSARI, PEDRO P.   Quito, Ecuador 1874

1879s Triptico indoandino (Tocata serranera)
Op. 25 no. 1
1.Crepúsculo 2.Nocturnal 3.Auroral
Str.
Ms.
Score 17 p.

TREMBLAY, GEORGE AMEDÉE.   Ottawa 14 January 1911

6284 Symphony in one movement   *19'*
3*,3*,4*(1Cl. in E-flat),3*-4,3,3,1-Timp.,
Perc.-Hp.-Str.
Ms.
Score 93 p. Large folio
Composed 1949. First performance Hamburg,
1962, Hamburg Symphony Orchestra, Frederic
Balazs conductor.

TRIGGS, HAROLD.   Denver 25 December 1900

1857s The bright land   *10'30"*
Str.
Ms.
Score 14 p. Large folio
Incorporates traditional cowboy songs: Old
Paint (I'm Aleavin' Cheyenne) and The Dreary,
Dreary Life. Composed 1942. First perform-
ance broadcast over MBC, New York, 29 March
1942, Symphonic Strings, Alfred Wallenstein
conductor.

TRIMBLE, LESTER ALBERT.
          b. Bangor, Wisconsin 29 August 1923

6414 Closing piece (1957)   *10'*
3*,2(2nd alt. E.H.),2(2nd alt. B.Cl.),2-4,2,3,
1-Timp.,Perc.-Str.
Ms. [Now Duchess Music Corp.]
Score 61 p. Large folio
Also known as Music for Orchestra and A Night
View of Pittsburgh. Commissioned by Pitts-
burgh Symphony Orchestra, 1957. Composed
1957. First performance, in honor of the
tenth anniversary of the International Music
Fund, Pittsburgh, 7 February 1958, Pittsburgh
Symphony Orchestra, William Steinberg con-
ductor. Revised 1968 under the title Sonic
Landscape.

460m Concerto for winds and strings   *18'*
1.Adagio - Allegro 2.Adagio 3.Allegro
Soli: Fl.,Ob.,Cl.,Bn.-Str.
Ms. ^c1957 by Lester Trimble [Now C.F. Peters,
New York]
Score 49 p. Large folio
Original title: Concerto for Woodwinds and
Strings. Composed 1954. First performance
Copenhagen, 26 September 1956, Young Com-
posers League.

6413   Symphony in 2 movements [revised   14'
       version]
       1.Adagio quasi andante 2.Moderato
       3*,3*,3*,2-4,3,3,1-Timp.,Perc.-Cel.,Hp.-Str.
       Ms. [Now C.F. Peters, New York, ^c1964]
       Score 72 p. Large folio
       Composed 1950. First performance of this ver-
       sion, New York, 14 April 1964, National Orches-
       tra Association, John Barnett conductor.

TROGNÉE, EMILE.

667m   Fantaisie-Caprice   5'
       Solo Tpt.-2,2,2,2-4,2,3-Timp.-Str.
       J.H. Zimmermann, Leipzig [1907?]
       Score in reduction 9 p.

648m   Valse lente pour cornet à pistons   5'
       Solo Tpt.-1,0,2,2-2,2,1-Dr.-Str.
       J.H. Zimmermann, Leipzig [1907?]
       Score in reduction 7 p.

TROIANI, GAETANO.   Castiglione, Italy 1873
                             Buenos Aires 1942

1868s Due pezzi. Transcribed by   5'
       Bruno Bandini
       1.Estilo 2.Cueca
       Str.
       G. Ricordi, Milan, ^c1937
       Miniature score 12 p.
       Composed and transcribed 1937. First perform-
       ance Buenos Aires, 8 June 1937, Orquesta de
       Cámara del Profesorado Orquestal, Bruno
       Bandini conductor.

3878   Scene infantili, suite per orchestra 9'
       1.Serenità 2.[Lullaby] 3.[The rag doll]
       3*,3*,2,2-4,2-Perc.-Cel.,Hp.-Str.
       G. Ricordi, Milan, ^c1925
       Miniature score 37 p.

TRUNK, RICHARD.
           Tauberbischofsheim, Baden 10 February 1879
               Herrsching am Ammersee 2 June 1968

307s   Eine kleine Serenade, Op. 55   15'
       Str.
       F.E.C. Leuckart, Leipzig, ^c1927
       Score 11 p.
       Composed 1925.

TSCHAIKOWSKY, PETER ILYITCH.
       See: CHAIKOVSKY, PETER IL'ICH.

TUBIN, EDUARD.   Tartu, Estonia 18 June 1905

6807   [Kratt. Suite from the ballet]   25'
       2(both alt. Picc.),2*,2,1-2,2,2-Timp.,Perc.-
       Pno.,Hp.-Str.
       Edition Suecia, Stockholm [n.d.]
       Score 116 p.
       Composed 1961.

2296s Music for strings   14'
       1.Moderato 2.Allegro 3.Adagio
       Str.
       Ms.

Score 24 p.
Composed 1962-63. First performance Luzerne,
Switzerland, 22 June 1963, Kammerorchester,
Celia Aumere conductor.

6970   [Symphony no. 9, Sinfonia semplice]   25'
       1.Adagio - Allegro 2.Adagio, lento - Presto -
       Adagio, lento
       2,2,2,2-4,2,3-Timp.-Str.
       Ms.
       Score 79 p.
       Composed 1969-70. First performance Stockholm,
       20 November 1971, Symphony Orchestra of the
       Swedish Radio, Stig Westerberg conductor.

7199   Symphony no. 10   27'
       In one movement
       3,3*,2,2-4,2,3,1-Timp.-Str.
       Ms.
       Score 88 p.
       Composed 1973. First performance Göteborg,
       Sweden, 27 September 1973, Göteborgs Sym-
       foniker, William Byrd conductor.

TUCCI, TERIG.   Buenos Aires 23 June 1897

6512   [Chilean dance and song]   3'
       2,2,2,2-2,3,3-Timp.,Perc.-Cel.,Hp.-Str.
       C. Fischer, New York, ^c1938
       Score in reduction 7 p.
       Based on the Chilean dance, zamacueca. Com-
       missioned by NBC. Composed 1937. First per-
       formance broadcast from New York on the NBC
       Radio series, The Other Americas, 1937, NBC
       Concert Orchestra, Joseph Littau conductor.

TULL, FISHER.   Waco, Texas 1934

7193   Liturgical symphony, for brass choir
       1.Lento - Allegretto ritmico - Andante
       2.Pesante 3.Allegretto - Lento
       4Hn.,6Tpt.,4Tbn.,2Bar.,2Tuba-Timp.,Perc.
       WIM, Los Angeles, ^c1970 by Avant Music
       Score 77 p.

7194   Variations on an Advent hymn
       4Hn.,6Tpt.,4Tbn.,2Bar.,2Tuba-Timp.,Perc.
       WIM, Los Angeles, ^c1973 by Avant Music
       Score 41 p.
       The theme is the plainsong melody Veni, Emman-
       uel. Variations composed 1962. First per-
       formance Huntsville, Texas, 1962, Sam Houston
       Brass Choir, the composer conducting.

TULOU, JEAN LOUIS.   Paris 12 September 1786
                          Nantes 23 July 1865

827m   [Concerto, flute, no. 1, A major]
       1.Allegro moderato 2.Adagio 3.Rondo
       Solo Fl.-2,2,0,2-2Hn.-Timp.-Str.
       Score: Ms. 51 p.
       Parts: H. Lemoine [Paris, n.d.]

572m   [Concerto, flute, no. 3, Op. 10, D major]
       In one movement
       Solo Fl.-0,2,0,2-2Hn.-Timp.-Str.
       Score: Ms. 163 p.
       Parts: H. Lemoine [Paris, n.d.]

Tulou, Jean Louis

905m Grand solo concertante, pour deux
flutes, Op. 83
1.Allegro 2.Adagio sostenuto 3.Allegro
2Solo Fl.-0,2,0,2-2,0,3-Timp.-Str.
Score: Ms. 63 p.
Parts: B. Schott, Mainz [n.d.]

TUMA, FRANZ.   Kostelecz, Bohemia 2 October 1704
                            Vienna 4 February 1774

1143s Tanz-Suite. Arranged for string
orchestra by Otto Schmid
1.Gagliarda 2.Siciliana 3.Menuett 4.Presto
Str.
C.F. Vieweg, Berlin [n.d.]
Score 8 p.

TURINA, JOAQUÍN.   Seville 9 December 1882
                              Madrid 14 January 1949

756 Danzas fantásticas   15'
1.Exaltación 2.Ensueño [Fantasy] 3.Orgía
3(3rd alt. Picc.),3*,3*,3*-4,3,3,1-Timp.,Perc.
-Hp.-Str.
Unión Musical Española, Madrid, c1921
Score 83 p.

757 La Procession du Rocio   8'
1.Triana en fête 2.La procession
3*,3*,3*,3*-4,3,3,1-Timp.,Perc.-Hp.-Str.
Rouart, Lerolle, Paris, c1913
Score 41 p.
Refers to an annual religious procession in
June, at Triana, Spain. Composed 1912. First
performance Madrid, 1913, Enrique Fernández
Arbós conductor.

253p Rapsodia sinfónica   9'
Solo Pno.-Str.
Unión Musical Española, Madrid, c1931
Score 33 p.

940 Sinfonia sevillana
1.Panorama 2.Por el rio Guadalquivir
3.Fiesta en San Juan de Aznalfarache
3(3rd alt. Picc.),3*,3*,3*-4,3,3,1-Timp.,Perc.
-Hp.-Str.
Unión Musical Española, Madrid, c1925
Score 108 p.

6868 La venta de los gatos, leyenda bec-
queriana. Transcribed by M. Palau
2(2nd alt. Picc.),2,2,2-2,2,2-Timp.,Perc.-
Pno.-Str.
Unión Musical Española, Madrid, c1966
Score 99 p.
Inspired by the Leyendas of Gustavo Adolfo
Bécquer. Composed 1924, originally for piano.

TURKIN, MARSHALL W.   Chicago 1 April 1926

5634 Jubilation overture   5'
3*,3*,3*,3*-4,3,3,1-Timp.,B.Dr.,Cym.-Hp.-Str.
Ms.
Score 38 p. Large folio
Composed for the birth of the composer's first
son, 1954. First performance Valencia, Spain,
14 February 1957, Orquesta Municipal de
Valencia, José Iturbi conductor.

TUTHILL, BURNET CORWIN.   New York 16 November 1888

2730 Bethlehem, pastorale for orchestra,   8'
Op. 8
3,3*,2*,Basset Hn.(ad lib.),3*-4,3,3,1-Timp.,
Perc.-Hp.-Str.
Ms.
Score 14 p.
Composed 1934. First performance Interlochen,
Michigan, 22 July 1934, National High School
Orchestra, the composer conducting.

2742 Come seven, rhapsody, Op. 11   6'
3(3rd alt. Picc.),2,3*,2-4,3,3,1-Timp.,Perc.-
Cel.-Str.
Ms.
Score 24 p.
Composed 1935. First performance Rochester,
27 October 1937, Rochester Civic Orchestra,
Howard Hanson conductor.

1043m [Concerto, clarinet, Op. 28]   16'
1.Allegro moderato 2.Adagio 3.Finale
Solo Cl.-2,2,2,0,2-2Hn.-Str.
Ms. [Elkan-Vogel, Philadelphia, c1954]
Score 31 p. Large folio
Composed 1948-49. First performance Memphis,
March 1950, Southwestern College Orchestra,
the composer conducting, Richard Reynolds
soloist.

425c Concerto for string bass and wind   15'
orchestra, Op. 45
1.Allegro moderato 2.Molto vivace 3.Passa-
caglia
Solo Cb.-2(2nd alt. Picc.),2,2(2nd alt. B.Cl.),
2-4,2,3-Timp.
Ms.
Score 63 p.
Composed 1962, at Robert Zimmerman's request.
First performance Eastman School of Music,
Rochester, 12 December 1962, Eastman-Rochester
Symphony Orchestra, Howard Hanson conductor,
Robert Zimmerman soloist.

271m Concerto for 2 clarinets. Edited by   15'
Burnet Tuthill
1.Largo 2.Allegro
2Solo Cl.-2Hn.-Str.
Ms.
Score 19 p. Large folio
Composed ca.1800, composer unknown. Edited
from Ms. parts in the Library of Congress,
1955.

4561 Elegy, Op. 26a   7'
2,2,2,2-4,3,3,1-Timp.-Str.
Ms.
Score 7 p.
Originally the second movement of the compo-
ser's Suite for Band, Op. 26. This version

1948. First performance Memphis, 22 November 1949, Southwestern College Orchestra, the composer conducting.

446m Flute song, Op. 31 no. 2   6'
Solo Fl.-2Hn.-Str.
Ms.
Score 5 p.
Composed 1954-55. First performance Tuscaloosa, Alabama, April 1955, Composer's Forum Orchestra, the composer conducting.

4586 Intrada
1,1,1,1-1,1-Pno.-Str.
Ms.
Score 13 p.
Composed 1934.

2743 Laurentia, symphonic poem, Op. 16   14'
3*,3*,4*(Cb.Cl. ad lib.),3*-4,3,3,3Ten.Tuba (ad lib.),1-Timp.,Perc.-Hp.-Str.
Ms.
Score 28 p.
Composed 1929-36. Incorporates a French Canadian song Isabeau s'y Promene.

1042m Nocturne for flute and string   4'
quartet, Op. 4
Solo Fl.-Str.(Cb. ad lib.)
Ms. ᶜ1937 by Burnet Tuthill
Score 7 p.
Composed 1933. First performance National Music Camp, Interlochen, Michigan, 1934.

4482 Overture for symphonic band, Op. 19   9'
4*(2 are Picc.),3*,7*(1Cl. in E-flat,1Alto Cl.),2-5Sax.(2A,T.,Bar.,B)-4,2,2Cnt.,Fluegel-hn.,3,2Bar.,2-Timp.,Perc.-Cb.
Ms. ᶜ1938 by Burnet Tuthill [Now Elkan-Vogel, Philadelphia]
Score in reduction 14 p.
Composed 1937. First performance Interlochen, Michigan, August 1937, National Music Camp High School Band, the composer conducting.

5765 Processional for band, Op. 37   5'
3*,2,6*(1Cl. in E-flat, 1Alto Cl.),2-4Sax.-4,2,2Cnt.,3,Bar.,Tuba-Timp.,Perc.
Ms. [Now Interlochen Press, Michigan]
Score 12 p.
Composed 1957. First performance Berea, Ohio, 26 January 1958, Baldwin-Wallace College Band, Kenneth Snapp conductor.

336m Rhapsody, clarinet and orchestra,   9'
Op. 33
Solo Cl.-1(alt. Picc.),1,0,1-2,1,1-Timp.,B.Dr.,S.Dr.-Str.
Ms.
Score 17 p. Large folio
Composed 1954-56. First performance Tuscaloosa, Alabama, 20 April 1956, Orchestra of the Southeastern Composers' Forum, the composer conducting, Richard Reynolds soloist.

4483 Rowdy dance, Op. 27a   2'
3*,2,3,2-4,3,3,1-Timp.,Perc.-Str.
Ms. [Now Summy-Birchard, Evanston, Illinois,

ᶜ1955]
Score 12 p.
Composed 1948. First performance Memphis, January 1949, Indianapolis Symphony Orchestra, Fabien Sevitzky conductor.

4487 Suite for band, Op. 26   14'
1.Allegro giocoso 2.Adagio - Andante maestoso
3.Scherzo 4.Rondo a la polka
3*,2,7*(1Cl. in E-flat, 1Alto Cl.),2-4Sax.-4,2,2Cnt.,3,Bar.,2-Timp.,Perc.
Ms. [Summy-Birchard, Evanston, Illinois, ᶜ1955]
Score 53 p. Large folio
Composed 1946. First performance Rochester, 3 May 1947, Eastman School Band, Frederick Fennell conductor. Awarded a prize in the Columbia University Band Composition Contest, 1947.

4574 Symphony in C, Op. 21   22'
1.Lento - Allegro 2.Vivace 3.Adagio
4.Allegro à la rhumba
2(2nd alt. Picc.),3*,3*,2-4,3,3,1-Timp.,Cym.-Hp.-Str.
Ms.
Score 72 p. Large folio
Composed 1941. First performance Memphis, 10 March 1942, Memphis Symphony Orchestra, the composer conducting.

262m Trombone trouble, Op. 46   4'
3Solo Tbn.-2,2,2,2-4Hn.-Timp.,B.Dr.,Cym.-Str.
Ms.
Score 14 p.
Composed 1963. First performance Memphis, 2 May 1964, Memphis Symphony Orchestra, Vincent de Frank conductor, Jack Hale, Harry Day and Ralph Hale soloists.

TWEEDY, DONALD NICHOLS.
               Danbury, Connecticut 23 April 1890
               Danbury 21 July 1948

2838 L'allegro, symphonic study   17'
3(3rd alt. Picc.),3(1Alto Ob.),3*,3(3rd alt. C.Bn.)-4,3,3,1-Timp.,Perc.-2Hp.-Str.
Ms.
Score 45 p. Large folio
Composed 1925. First performance Rochester, 1 May 1925, Rochester Philharmonic Orchestra, Howard Hanson conductor.

TYRWHITT, GERALD HUGH.
See: BERNERS, LORD.

U

UGARTE, FLORO M.   Buenos Aires 15 September 1884

3493 La rebelión del agua, poema sinfónico
4(3rd&4th alt. Picc.),4*,4*,4*-4,3,3,1-Timp.,Perc.-Cel.,2Hp.-Str.
Ms.
Score 93 p. Large folio

Ugo, S.

UGO, S.

    1681s Arlequinade. Transcribed by A. Lebert
    Str.
    Score: Ms. 4 p.
    Parts: Editions Margueritat, Paris [n.d.]

UHL, ALFRED.   Vienna 5 June 1909

    2068s [Introduction and variations on a   *15'*
    16th century melody]
    Str.
    Universal Edition, Vienna, ᶜ1948
    Score 26 p.
    Based on the melody Es Geht Eine Dunkle
    Wolk' Herein. Composed 1947. First perform-
    ance Salzburg Festival, July 1948, Vienna
    Philharmonic Orchestra, Wilhelm Furtwängler
    conductor.

UHL, EDMUND.   Prague 25 October 1853
                   Wiesbaden March 1929

    1131v Romanze, für Violine mit Orchester, Op. 7
    Solo Vn.-2,2,2,2-2Hn.-Timp.-Hp.-Str.
    F.E.C. Leuckart, Leipzig [n.d.]
    Score 19 p.

    1269 Slavische Intermezzi, Op. 17
    3*,2,2,2-4,2,3,1-Timp.,Perc.-Hp.-Str.
    C.F. Kahnt, Leipzig, ᶜ1904
    Score 59 p.

UHLIG, A.

    947s Romanze, Violoncell, Op. 3
    Solo Vc.-Str.
    Score: Ms. 7 p.
    Parts: J.G. Seeling, Dresden [n.d.]

ULDALL, HANS.   Flensburg 18 November 1903

    3981 [Music, for brass and percussion]   *14'*
    1.[Hanseatic Tower music] 2.Tanzstück
    3.Kriegsmarsch
    2Hn.,2Flügelhn.,2Ten. Hn.,2Tpt.,2Tbn.,Tuba-
    Timp.,Sm.Dr.,Rühr Trommel[Ten. Dr.]
    F.E.C. Leuckart, Leipzig, ᶜ1935
    Score 39 p.

URAY, ERNST LUDWIG.
           b. Schladming, Styria 26 April 1906

    5120 Tanzstück   *8'*
    2(2nd alt. Picc.),2,2,2-4(4th ad lib.),2,3-
    Timp.,Perc.-Hp.-Str.
    Universal Edition, Vienna, ᶜ1938
    Score 40 p.

URBAN, HEINRICH.   Berlin 27 August 1837
                  Berlin 24 November 1901

    689c Barcarole [violoncello, Op. 18, G minor]
    Solo Vc.-Fl.,Ob.-Hn.-Str.
    Score: Ms. 15 p.
    Parts: F.E.C. Leuckart, Leipzig [n.d.]

    1037v [Concerto, violin, Op. 22, D minor]
    In one movement
    Solo Vn.-2,2,2,2-4,2-Timp.-Str.
    Score: Ms. 98 p.
    Parts: C.A. Challier, Berlin [n.d.]

    6774 [Overture to a carnival play, Op. 20]
    3*,2,2,2-4,2,3-Timp.,Perc.-Str.
    F.E.C. Leuckart, Leipzig [1877]
    Score 93 p.

    5641 Der Rattenfänger von Hameln, Fantasiestück,
    Op. 25
    3*,2,2,2-4,2,3-Timp.,Perc.-Str.
    C.A. Challier, Berlin [189-?]
    Score 35 p.
    Suggested by Julius Wolff's poem.

    1013v [Romance, violin, Op. 17]
    Solo Vn.-2Cl.-Hn.-Str.
    Score: Ms. 25 p.
    Parts: F.E.C. Leuckart, Leipzig [n.d.]

URIBE-HOLGUÍN, GUILLERMO.   Bogotá 17 March 1880
                               Bogotá 26 June 1971

    3381 Bajo su ventana, improvisación [Under her
    window]
    1,1,1,1-4,3-Cel.-Str.
    Ms.
    Score 24 p.
    Composed 1930. First performance Bogotá,
    Colombia, 20 October 1930, Sociedad de Con-
    ciertos Sinfónicos del Conservatorio, the
    composer conducting.

    3692 Bochica, Op. 73   *13'*
    [A.The flooded plain B.The arrival of Bochica
    C.The dialogue of Bochica with the people
    D.The cataract - hymn - dance]
    3*,3*,3*,3*-4,3,3,1-Timp.,Perc.-Hp.-Str.
    Ms.
    Score 98 p.
    Bochica is an Andean Indian sun god. Composed
    1939. First performance Bogotá, 12 April 1940,
    Orquesta Sinfónica Nacional, the composer con-
    ducting.

    3527 Cantares [Songs] Op. 33 [original   *12'*
    version]
    3*,2,2,2-4,2,3,1-Timp.-Hp.-Str.
    Ms.
    Score 46 p.
    Originally composed 1929. First performance
    Bogotá, 2 September 1929, Orquesta Sinfónica
    Nacional, the composer conducting. A revised
    version, 1939.

    3848 Carnavalesca [Carnival time] Op. 34
    3*,3*,3*,3-4,3,3,1-Timp.,Perc.-Cel.,Hp.-Str.
    Ms.
    Score 45 p. Large folio
    Composed 1929. First performance Bogotá, 8
    July 1929, Sociedad de Conciertos Sinfónicos
    del Conservatorio, the composer conducting.

    4681 [Creole ballet no. 1, Op. 78 no. 1]
    3*,2,2,2-4,2-Timp.,Perc.-Hp.-Str.

Ms.
Score 18 p.
Composed 1945.

4682 [Creole ballet no. 2, Op. 78 no. 2]
3*,3*,2,3*-4,3,3,1-Timp.,Tamb.-Hp.-Str.
Ms.
Score 28 p.

4683 [Creole ballet no. 3, Op. 78 no. 3]
3*,3*,2,2-4,2,3,1-Timp.,Perc.-Pno.,Cel.-Str.
Ms.
Score 29 p.

3622 Marcha festiva, Op. 26 no. 2 *10'*
3*,3*,3,3-4,3,3,1-Timp.,Perc.-Hp.-Str.
Ms.
Score 26 p.
*Composed 1928. First performance Bogotá, 20
August 1928, Orquesta Sinfónica Nacional, the
composer conducting.*

3985 Para levantar el telón [Curtain-raiser]
4Tpt.,3Tbn.,Tuba
Ms.
Score 2 p.
Composed 1938.

3548 Serenata, Op. 29 *12'*
3*,3*,3*,2-4,2,3,1-Timp.,Perc.-Cel.,Hp.-Str.
Ms.
Score 37 p.
*Composed 1928. First performance Bogotá, 29
October 1928, Sociedad de Conciertos Sin-
fónicos del Conservatorio, the composer con-
ducting.*

5929 [Symphony no. 7, Op. 102] *23'*
1.Allegro comodo 2.Vivace assai 3.Adagio
4.Allegro animato
3*,3*,3*,3*-4,3,3,1-Timp.,Perc.-Hp.-Str.
Ms.
Score 69 p.
*Composed 1957. First performance Bogotá, ca.5
April 1957, Orquesta Sinfónica de Colombia,
Olav Roots conductor.*

3568 Tres danzas, Op. 21 [original version] *15'*
1.Joropo 2.Pasillo 3.Bambuco
3*,3*,2,2-4,3,3,1-Timp.,Perc.-Hp.-Str.
Ms.
Score 55 p.
*Originally composed 1926. First performance
Bogotá, 27 May 1927, Sociedad de Conciertos
Sinfónicos del Conservatorio, the composer
conducting.*

URSPRUCH, ANTON.   Frankfurt a.M. 17 February 1850
                     Frankfurt a.M. 11 January 1907

663p [Concerto, piano, Op. 9, E-flat major]
1.Allegro ma non troppo 2.Andante lento e
mesto 3.Allegro
Solo Pno.-2,2,2,2-4,2-Timp.-Str.
A. Cranz, Hamburg [n.d.]
Score 121 p.

Zwei Stücke für Violine, Op. 11
923v No. 1 Notturno
924v No. 2 Romanze
Solo Vn.-2,2,2,2-2Hn.-Str.
A. Cranz, Hamburg [n.d.]
Scores: 7 p., 25 p.

USPENSKY, VICTOR ALEXANDROVICH.
                          Kaluga 31 August 1879
                     Tashkent 9 October 1949

2985 Four melodies of central Asian
nationalities
1.Akramchan (Afghanistan) 2.Siliycha (Cossack
3.Krasivie volosi (Cossack) 4.Zolotie kosi
(Uzbek)
3,3*,2,2-3,2,3-Bells,Oriental Dr.,Nagara-Hp.-
Str.
Mussektor, Moscow, c1934
Score 47 p.

V

VALCÁRCEL, THEODORO.   Puno, Peru 18 October 1900
                          Lima 20 March 1942

1855s Ayarache [Funeral song] Arranged by
Rudolph Holzmann. Edited by Arthur Cohn
Hp.-Str.
Ms.
Score 10 p.
*Composed 1939. First performance Lima, 9 Octo-
ber 1939, Orquesta Sinfónica Nacional, Theo-
dore Buchwald conductor.*

1146v Concierto indio, para violin i orquesta
1.Allegro festivo 2.Cantabile mesto 3.In
senso popolare 4.Allegro agitato
Solo Vn.-2,2,2,2-3,2-Timp.,Perc.-Str.
Ms.
Score 77 p.
Composed 1942.

VALEN, OLAV FARTEIN.
          Stavanger, Norway 25 August 1887
          Haugesund, Norway 14 December 1952

6051 Pastorale, Op. 11 *5'*
2,2,2,2-Hn.-Timp.-Str.
Norsk Musikforlag, Oslo, c1933
Score 11 p.
*Composed 1930. First performance Oslo, 1931,
Oslo Philharmonic Orchestra, Olav Kielland
conductor.*

VALENSIN, GEORGES.

547c Menuet [violoncello, F major, from
Symphony no. 1. Transcribed by Paul Bazelaire]
Solo Vc.-Str.
M. Senart, Paris, c1922
Score 5 p.

Valensin, Georges

656s Minuet, in G, from Symphony no. 1.
Edited by Karl Rissland
Pno.-Str.
O. Ditson, Boston, ^C1926
Score [6] p.
Bound with Giovanni Bolzoni, Minuetto in B-flat major.

VALENTINI, GIUSEPPE.   Florence or Rome ca.1680
                           Florence ca.1746

365m [Concerto, oboe and violin, no. 3,   10'
C major] Edited by Renato Fasano
1.Allegro 2.Largo 3.Presto - Affettuoso
Solo Ob.,Solo Vn.-Cemb.-Str.
Ricordi, Milan, ^C1959
Score 28 p.

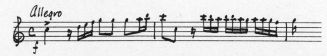

1049s [Concerto grosso, strings and   12'
organ, Op. 7 no. 2, D minor] Edited by Alceo
Toni
In one movement
Soli: Vn.I,Vn.II,Vc.-Org.-Str.(without Vc.)
G. Ricordi, Milan, 1927
Score 26 p.
Op. 7 published 1710 as Twelve Concerti Grossi.

2300s [Symphony, Christmas, Op. 1 no. 12,   15'
B-flat major] Edited by Felix Schroeder
1.Largo 2.Andante e forte 3.Allegro
4.Largo 5.Presto
Cemb.-Str.(without Va.)
Chr. Friedrich Vieweg, Berlin, ^C1961
Score 12 p.

VALLE DE PAZ, EDGARDO DEL.
See: DEL VALLE DE PAZ, EDGARDO SAMUEL.

VALLE-RIESTRA, JOSÉ MARÍA.
                  Lima, Peru 9 November 1859
                  Lima 25 January 1925

3645 Atahuallpa. Marcha de la coronación
3*,3*,3*,2-4,3,4,5-Timp.,Perc.-2Hp.-Str.
Editorial Musical Maldonado, Lima [n.d.]
Score 11 p. Large folio

3655 En Oriente [sketch for orchestra]
3*,3*,2,2-4,2,3,1-Timp.,Perc.-Hp.-Str.
Editorial Musical Maldonado, Lima, 1936
Score 22 p. Large folio
First performance Lima, 28 November 1917, A. Padovani conductor.

3265 Lament and glorification, elegia.   5'
Transcribed by R.M. Eckman
3(1Picc. in D-flat),3*,4*(1Alto Cl.),2-2,2,3,
1-Timp.,Perc.-Str.
Ms.
Score 20 p.
Originally composed for piano; arranged for orchestra, 1931. First performance Washington, D.C., 5 May 1931, Captain William J. Stannard conductor.

VALLS, JOSEP.   Barcelona 1904

1104m [Concerto, string quartet and   22'
orchestra]
2Solo Vn.,Solo Va.,Solo Vc.-2,2,2,2-2,2,1-
Timp.-Str.
Senart, Paris, ^C1933 by Josep Valls
Score 92 p.
Composed 1931. First performance Paris, 1933, Calvet String Quartet and Lamoureux Orchestra, Albert Wolff conductor. Awarded the Edward Garrett McCollin First Prize in the Musical Fund Society of Philadelphia competition, 1931.

Names beginning with Van which do not appear here may be located under the second part of the name:
e.g. Van Bree, see Bree.

VAN DAM, LOUIS.

846s Poésie musicale [from Op. 28]
Str.
Breitkopf & Härtel, Brussels [n.d.]
Score 10 p.

VAN DEN BEEMT, HEDDA.
              Dordrecht, Holland 31 October 1880
              Philadelphia 15 February 1925

6080 Aucassin and Nicolette. Introduction *and*
Shepherd scene
2,3*,3*,2-4,2,3,1-Timp.,Perc.-Hp.-Str.
Ms.
Score 43 p.
From an opera based on the 13th-century French legend. Composed 1905-13. First performance of this excerpt Philadelphia, 2 April 1913, Philadelphia Orchestra, Leopold Stokowski conductor.

VAN DER STUCKEN, FRANK VALENTIN.
              Fredericksburg, Texas 15 October 1858
              Hamburg, Germany 16 August 1929

4288 Rigaudon, Op. 25   4'
2,2,0,2-2,2-Timp.-Str.
Oertel, Hannover [1894?]
Score 19 p.

VAN DER VOORT, ?.

    5055 Sinfonietta [F major]
       1.Andante - Allegro moderato 2.Andantino
       3.Allegro scherzando 4.Allegro
       1,1,1,1-1,1-Hp.-Str.
       Ms.
       Score 54 p.

VAN DURME, JEF.
       b. Kemzeke-Waas, East Flanders 7 May 1907

    4813 Ballade no. 2, Op. 38
       2(2nd alt. Picc.),3*,3*,2-4,3,3-Timp.,Perc.-
       Str.
       Ms.
       Score 54 p. Large folio
       Composed 1948.

VAN GELDER, MARTINUS.   Amsterdam 31 July 1854
                        Philadelphia 1941

    3354 Concert Walzer (Volks Walzer), Op. 11
       2*,2,2,2-4,4,3,1-Timp.,Perc.-Str.
       Ms.
       Score 46 p.
       Composed 1874.

    788p [Concerto, piano, Op. 30]
       1.Allegro maestoso 2.Intermezzo 3.Intro-
       duzione - Allegro
       Solo Pno.-2(2nd alt. Picc.),2,2,2-2,2,3-Timp.
       -Str.
       Ms.
       Score 96 p.

    3353 Dramatisches Praeludium, Op. 35
       2(2nd alt. Picc.),2,2,2-4,4,3,1-Timp.,B.Dr.-
       Org.(ad lib.)-Str.
       Ms.
       Score 31 p.

    2963 Fantaisie concertante
       2(2nd alt. Picc.),2,2,2-2,2,3-Timp.,Perc.-Str.
       Ms.
       Score 34 p.
       Composed 1869.

    2588 Jubel Marsch, Op. 10
       2(2nd alt. Picc.),2,2,2-4,4,3-Timp.,Perc.-Str.
       Ms.
       Score 32 p.

    1905s The Lingac boat song
       Str.
       Ms.
       Score 3 p.

    3986 Peace (In memoriam), Op. 1
       2,2,2,2-2,2,3-Timp.-Str.
       Ms.
       Score 21 p.

    4140 [Symphony no. 1, Op. 6]
       1.Allegro con fuoco 2.Andante ma non troppo
       3.Scherzo 4.Finale
       2(2nd alt. Picc.),2,2,2-4,4,3-Timp.-Str.
       Ms.
       Score 192 p.
       Composed 1871.

    4141 [Symphony no. 2, Op. 24]
       1.Molto moderato 2.Larghetto con moto
       3.Lento - Scherzo 4.Finale
       2(2nd alt. Picc.),2,2,2-4,4,3,1-Timp.-Str.
       Ms.
       Score 139 p.
       Composed 1888. First performance, as Op. 30,
       Philadelphia, 29 January 1904, The Philadel-
       phia Orchestra, Fritz Scheel conductor.

    4139 Triomf Marsch
       2(2nd alt. Picc.),2,2,2-4,2,3-Timp.,Perc.-Str.
       Ms.
       Score 14 p.

VAŇHAL, JAN KŘTITEL.
        Nechanicz, Bohemia 12 May 1739
                     Vienna 20 August 1813

Also published as: Johann Baptist Wanhal *or*
Wanhall

    6079 [Overture, flute, oboes, horns, and
       strings, A major]
       1.Allegro 2.Cantabile 3.Minuetto 4.Allegro
       1,2-2Hn.-Str.
       Ms. ᶜ1976 by The Fleisher Collection of Orches-
       tral Music, Free Library of Philadelphia
       Score 35 p. Large folio
       Listed in The Breitkopf Thematic Catalogue,
       Supplement VI, 1771. Title page reproduced
       from an edition published by R. Bremner, Lon-
       don, probably 1777.

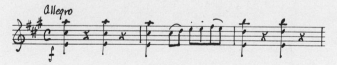

    4499 [Symphony, flutes, horns, and   *18'30"*
       strings, C major] Edited by Robert Sondheimer
       1.Allegro moderato 2.Andante 3.Menuetto
       (Vivace) 4.Presto
       2Fl.-2Hn.-Str.
       Edition Bernoulli [Leipzig?] ᶜ1933 by
       Robert Sondheimer
       Score 23 p.
       Composed 1765.

Vaňhal, Jan Křtitel

6547 [Symphony, flutes or oboes, horns, and
strings, D minor]
1.Allegro 2.Andante 3.Presto
2Fl. or 2Ob.-2Hn.-Str.
Ms.
Score 17 p.

VAN VACTOR, DAVID.   Plymouth, Indiana 8 May 1906

1736s Chaconne, for strings (after   8'30"
Bach)
Str.
Ms.
Score 22 p.
*Composed 1928. First performance Rochester,
17 May 1928, Rochester Philharmonic Orchestra,
Howard Hanson conductor.*

929m Concerto for flute   20'
1.Allegro 2.Lento tenerézza 3.Allegro
scherzando 4.Adagio - Allegro
Solo Fl.-0,1,1,1-2Hn.-Timp.,Perc.-Cel.,Hp.-
Str.(without Vn.)
Ms.
Score 63 p.
*Composed 1931-32. First performance Chicago,
26 February 1933, Civic Orchestra of Chicago,
Eric De Lamarter conductor, Caroline Sol-
fronck soloist.*

1125v Concerto for viola [In 1 movement]   18'
Solo Va.-2,2,2,2-2Hn.,2Tpt.-Timp.,Glock.-Hp.-
Str.
Ms.
Score 57 p. Large folio
*Composed 1940. First performance Ravinia Park,
Illinois, 13 July 1940, Chicago Symphony
Orchestra, the composer conducting, Milton
Preves soloist.*

926m Concerto grosso, 3 flutes, harp and   15'
orchestra
1.Andante sostenuto - Allegro 2.Adagio
3.Allegro giocoso
3Solo Fl., Solo Hp.-1(alto Fl.),2*,1,1-2Hn.-
Timp.-Str.
Ms.
Score 78 p.
*Commissioned by the Chicago Symphony Orchestra,
1934. Composed 1934-35. First performance
Chicago, 4 April 1935, Chicago Symphony
Orchestra, Frederick Stock conductor, Joseph
Vito harpist, Ernest Liegl, Emil Eck and the
composer soloists.*

3328 Divertimento for small orchestra   20'
1.Ouverture 2.Ballad 3.Waltz 4.Song and
dance
1(alt. Picc.),1,1,1-1,1,1-Perc.-Pno.-Str.
Ms.
Score 81 p. Large folio

*Commissioned by the Ravinia Festival Associa-
tion, 1939. Composed 1939. First performance Ravinia Park, Illinois, 8 July 1939, Chicago Symphony Orchestra, the composer conducting.*

5422 Fanfare for orchestra   4'
3*,3*,3*,3*-4,2,2Cnt.,3,1-Timp.,Perc.-Str.
Ms.
Score 22 p. Large folio
*Originally titled Fanfare: Salute to Russia.
Commissioned by Fabien Sevitzky, 1943. Com-
posed 1943. First performance Indianapolis,
23 January 1943, Indianapolis Symphony
Orchestra, Fabien Sevitzky conductor.*

1752s Five bagatelles, for strings   20'
Str.
Ms.
Score 31 p. Large folio
*Commissioned by the Saidenberg Symphonietta,
1937. Composed 1938. First performance Chi-
cago, 7 February 1938, Saidenberg Symphonietta,
Daniel Saidenberg conductor.*

2869 Five little pieces, for big   17'
orchestra
1.Miniature march 2.Waltz 3.Scherzo 4.Lento
5.Rondo
3(3rd alt. Picc.),2,2,3*-4,3,3,1-Timp.,Perc.-
Hp.-Str.
Ms.
Score 82 p.
*Composed 1930. First performance Ravinia
Park, Illinois, 5 July 1931, Chicago Symphony
Orchestra, Eric De Lamarter conductor.*

2873 The masque of the red death   4'30"
2,2,2,2-4,2,3,1-Perc.-Str.
Ms.
Score 27 p.
Composed 1932.

5421 Music for the Marines
3*(2nd alt. Picc.II),3*,4*(1Cl. in E-flat alt.
Cl. in A),3*-4,4,3,1-Timp.,Perc.-Hp.-Str.
Ms.
Score 159 p. Large folio
*Composed 1943. First performance Indianapolis,
27 March 1943, Indianapolis Symphony Orches-
tra, Fabien Sevitzky conductor.*

2907 Ouverture to a comedy   10'
3*,2,2,3*-4,2,3,1-Timp.,Perc.-Hp.-Str.
Ms.
Score 91 p.
*Composed 1934. First performance Chicago,
20 June 1937, Illinois Symphony Orchestra of
the WPA, the composer conducting.*

3344 Overture to The Taming of the Shrew   5'
3*,2,2,2-4,2,3-Timp.,Perc.-Hp.-Str.
Ms.
Score 84 p.
*Commissioned by the Indianapolis Symphony
Orchestra, 1940. Composed 1940. First per-
formance Indianapolis, 14 March 1941, Indiana-
polis Symphony Orchestra, Fabien Sevitzky*

*conductor. Title later changed to Overture
to a Comedy no. 2.*

2862 Passacaglia and fugue   10'
3(3rd alt. Picc.),3*,3*,3*-4,3,3,1-Timp.-Str.
Ms.
Score 33 p. Large folio
*Composed 1933. First performance Chicago, 28
January 1934, Chicago Civic Orchestra, the
composer conducting.*

3356 Symphonic suite   19'
1.March 2.Serenade 3.Waltz 4.Chorale and
Finale
3(3rd alt. Picc.),3*,3*,3*-4,3,3,1-Timp.,Perc.
-Org.,Hp.-Str.
Ms.
Score 80 p. Large folio
*Commissioned by the Ravinia Festival Associa-
tion, 1938. Composed 1938. First perform-
ance Ravinia Park, Illinois, 21 July 1938,
Chicago Symphony Orchestra, the composer con-
ducting.*

3355 Symphony [no. 1] in D   30'
1.Largo - Allegro vivace 2.Adagio 3.Alle-
gretto 4.Larghetto - Moderato assai
3(3rd alt. Picc.),2,3*,3*-4,3,3,1-Timp.,Perc.-
Pno.-Str.
Ms.
Score 132 p. Large folio
*Composed 1936-37. Won a prize in the New
York Philharmonic's American Composers' Con-
test, 1937-38. First performance New York, 19
January 1939, New York Philharmonic, the com-
poser conducting.*

5964 Symphony no. 2   31'
1.Allegro moderato 2.Adagio 3.Allegretto
4.Allegro giusto
3*,3*,3*,3*-4,3,3,2-Timp.,Perc.-Pno.-Str.
Ms. c1958 by David Van Vactor
Score 118 p. Large folio
*Composed 1955-58 (under a Guggenheim grant
for 1957-58). First performance, Pittsburgh,
3 April 1959, Pittsburgh Symphony Orchestra,
William Steinberg conductor.*

3783 Variazioni solénne   9'
3(2nd&3rd alt. Picc.),3*,3*,3*-4,3,3,1-Timp.,
Perc.-Str.
Ms.
Score 60 p. Large folio
*Composed 1941. First performance under the
title, Gothic Impressions, Chicago, 26 February 1942, Chicago Symphony Orchestra, the
composer conducting.*

VAN WESTERHOUT, NICCOLÒ.
                    Mola di Bari 17 December 1857
                    Naples 21 August 1898

519s Berceuse, G major
Str.
G. Ricordi, Milan, c1921
Score 3 p.

1089s Menuetto, G major   5'
Str.
G. Ricordi, Milan [n.d.]
Score 4 p.

810s Preludio, on the theme Quando Corpus, from
Pergolesi's Stabat Mater
Str.
G. Ricordi, Milan [n.d.]
Score 4 p.

494s Serenata, A major   5'
Str.
G. Ricordi, Milan [n.d.]
Score 3 p.

VARDELL, CHARLES GILDERSLEEVE, JR.
          Salisbury, North Carolina 19 August 1893
          Winston-Salem, North Carolina 19 October 1962

3841 Joe Clark steps out
3*,2,2,2-4,2,3,1-Timp.,Perc.-Str.
Eastman School of Music, Rochester, c1937
Score 24 p.
*First performance Rochester, 14 January 1937,
Rochester Philharmonic Orchestra, Howard Han-
son conductor.*

VARÈSE, EDGARD.   Paris 22 December 1885
                            New York 6 November 1965

3965 Intégrales, small orchestra   11'
and percussion
2Picc.,Ob.,2Cl.(1 in E-flat)-1,2,3-Perc.
J. Curwen, London, c1926 by the composer
Score 47 p.
*First performance Paris, ca.January 1931,
Marius François Gaillard conductor.*

1002m Ionisation [13 players]
  1st-Large Chinese Cym.,B.Dr.(very deep),
      Tam-tam(high)
  2nd-Gong,Tam-tam(high),Tam-tam(low)
  3rd-2Bongos(high & low),Side Dr.,B.Dr.(medium
      & large)
  4th-Mil.Dr.,Side Dr.
  5th-Siren(high),Str.Dr.
  6th-Siren(low),Slapstick,Guiro
  7th-3Chinese Blocks(high, medium, low),
      Claves,Trgl.
  8th-S.Dr.(with loosened snares),2Maracas(high
      & low)
  9th-Flat Mil.Dr. with snares, S.Dr.,Susp.Cym.
  10th-Sleigh Bells,Cym.,Tubular Chimes
  11th-Guiro,Cast.,Cel.
  12th-Tamb.,Anvil,Large Tam-tam(very deep)
  13th-Pno.,Slapstick,Trgl.,Sleigh Bells
G. Ricordi, New York, c1934
Score 23 p.
*Composed 1931. First performance New York, 6
March 1933, Pan American Association of Composers, Nicolas Slonimsky conductor.*

VARVOGLIS, MARIO.   Brussels 22 December 1885
                          Athens 30 July 1967

2769 [St. Barbara, symphonic prelude]   12'
3*,3*,2,2-4,2,3,1-Timp.,Perc.-Hp.-Str.

Varvoglis, Mario

Union des Compositeurs Hellènes, Athens, ^c1948
Score 36 p.
*Suggested by Sotiris Skipis' drama of the same
name. Composed 1912. First performance
Düsseldorf, 1912, Karl Panzner conductor.*

VÁSQUEZ, JOSÉ FRANCISCO.
b. Guadalajara, Mexico 4 October 1895

775p [Concerto, piano, no. 3]
1.Moderato 2.Andante melancólico 3.Moderato
Solo Pno.-3*,3*,2,2-4,2,3,1-Timp.,Perc.-Str.
Ms.
Score 172 p.
Composed 1936.

[Three aquarelles of travel]
4188 No. 1 [Untitled]
4189 No. 2 Lake Amatitlán
4190 No. 3 Return
3*,3*,2,2-4,2,3,1-Timp.,Perc.-Hp.(in no. 2
only)-Str.
Ms.
Scores: 11 p., 17 p., 25 p.
Composed 1929.

VASSILENKO, SERGEI NIKIFOROVICH.
Moscow 30 March 1872
Moscow 11 March 1956

731 Au soleil, suite, Op. 17   25'
1.Prélude 2.The cicadas 3.The driade 4.The
gnomes 5.La ronde aërienne
3(3rd alt. Picc.),2,2,2-4,3,3-Timp.,Perc.-Hp.-
Str.
P. Jurgenson, Moscow [n.d.]
Score 137 p.
*Composed 1910. First performance Moscow,
March 1911, the composer conducting.*

2019 Chinesische Suite, Op. 60   30'
1.[Procession to the temple of the ancestors]
2.[Evening in springtime] 3.[Obsequies] 4.
[Joyous dance] 5.[The princess' lamentation]
6.[a.Echo of the golden lakes b.Chinese
market]
3(3rd alt. Picc.),3*,2,2-4,3,3,1-Timp.,Perc.-
Pno.,Cel.,Hp.-Str.
Universal Edition, Vienna, 1930
Score 109 p.
*Composed 1927. First performance Leningrad,
30 October 1927, the composer conducting.*

2481 [Hindu suite, Op. 42b]   42'
In 10 movements
3(3rd alt. Picc.),3(3rd alt. E.H.),3(3rd alt.
B.Cl.,1Cl. in E-flat,ad lib.),3(C.Bn. ad lib.)-
4,6,2Cnt.(ad lib.),3,1-Timp.,Perc.-Org.(ad
lib.),Cel.,2Hp.-Chorus(SATB ad lib.)-Str.
Mussektor, Moscow, ^c1931
Score 197 p.
*Composed 1927. First performance Moscow, 1927,
Moscow Philharmonic Orchestra, the composer
conducting.*

1944 Hyrcus nocturnus - Polyot Vyedhme   16'
[Nocturnal goat - Witches' flight, symphonic
poem, Op. 15]

3(3rd alt. Picc.),3*,3,3*-4,3,3,1-Timp.,Perc.-
Hp.-Str.
P. Jurgenson, Moscow [n.d.]
Score 119 p.
*Composed 1908. First performance Moscow, 21
January 1909, Emil Cooper conductor.*

758 [The garden of death, symphonic   18'
poem] Op. 12
3(3rd alt. Picc.),2(2nd alt. E.H.),3*,3*-4,3,
3,1-Timp.,Perc.-Org.(ad lib.),Cel.,Hp.-Str.
P. Jurgenson, Moscow [n.d.]
Score 48 p.
*Composed 1907. First performance Moscow, 22
April 1908, the composer conducting.*

730 Poème épique, Op. 4   15'
3(3rd alt. Picc.),2,3,3*-4,3,3,1-Timp.,Perc.-
Hp.-Str.
P. Jurgenson, Moscow [n.d.]
Score 75 p.
*Composed 1900. First performance Moscow, 2
March 1903, the composer conducting.*

3193 [Rhapsody of the Red Army, Op. 77]   17'
3*,2,2,2-4,3,3,1-Timp.,Perc.-Str.
Mussektor, Moscow, 1935
Score 65 p.
*Composed 1932. First performance Moscow, 1932,
Moscow Philharmonic Orchestra, the composer
conducting.*

2088s [The son of the sun, Op. 63. Waltz.   3'
Transcribed by Grégor Fitelberg]
Str.
Russian-American Music Publishers, New York,
^c1946
Score 8 p.
*From the opera Syn Solnza, based on the Boxer
Rebellion of 1900 in China. First perform-
ance Moscow, 23 May 1929.*

3673 Soviet East, Op. 75 [First album]
1.Pamir 2.Armenia 3.Uzbehkistan 4.Kazak-
stan 5.Tadjekistan 6.Azerbaidjan 7.Dag-
hestan
3(3rd alt. Picc.),3(3rd alt. E.H.),2,2-4,3,3,
1-Timp.,Perc.,Daira,Timplipito-Str.
Mussektor, Moscow, 1933
Score 103 p.
*Composed 1932, for the 15th anniversary of
the Red Army.*

1299 [Symphony no. 1, Op. 10, G minor]   50'
1.Molto sostenuto 2.Vivace 3.Andante
misterioso 4.Finale
3(3rd alt. Picc.),2(2nd alt. E.H.),3*,2-4,3,
3,1-Timp.,Perc.-Hp.-Str.
P. Jurgenson, Leipzig [n.d.]
Score 274 p.
*Composed 1904-06. First performance Moscow,
17 February 1907, the composer conducting.*

2193 [Symphony no. 2, Op. 22, F major]   35'
1.Allegro appassionato 2.Adagio mosso
3.Allegro impetuoso e fantastico
3(3rd alt. Picc.),3,3,3-4,3,2Cnt.,3,1-Timp.,
Perc.-Hp.-Str.

Mussektor, Moscow, 1925
Score 170 p.
*Composed 1912. First performance Moscow, 7
January 1913, Emil Cooper conductor.*

3140 [Turkmenistan pictures on Turk-   25'
menistan folk themes, Op. 68]
1.[The steppe in bloom] 2.[The nomads] 3.[At
night] 4.[March]
3(3rd alt. Picc.),3*,3*,2-4,3,3,1-Timp.,Perc.-
Hp.-Str.
Mussektor, Moscow, 1933
Score 99 p.
*Composed 1931. First performance in a radio
broadcast, Moscow, 1931, the Moscow Orchestra,
the composer conducting.*

1352 Valse fantastique, Op. 18   10'
3(3rd alt. Picc.),3*,2,2-4Hn.-Trgl.-Hp.-Str.
P. Jurgenson, Moscow [n.d.]
Score 30 p.
*Composed 1912. First performance Moscow, 3
January 1915, the composer conducting.*

VAUCLAIN, ANDRÉ CONSTANT.
b. Philadelphia 5 August 1908

5699 Narrative   5'30"
2,2,2,2-2,2,2-Timp.-Hp.-Str.
Ms.
Score 36 p.
*Composed 1954. First performance Philadelphia,
4 May 1958, Philadelphia Little Symphony
Society, Robert Mandell conductor.*

4984 Prelude to Endymion   8'30"
3(3rd alt. Picc.),2,2,2-4,3,3-Timp.-Str.
Ms. [Now Southern Music, New York]
Score 27 p. Large folio
*Suggested by Keats' Endymion. Composed 1949.
First performance Festival of American Music,
Rochester, 4 May 1951, Eastman-Rochester
Symphony Orchestra, Howard Hanson conductor.*

5238 Serenade and dance   10'
3*,2,2,2-4,3,3-Timp.,Cym.-Str.
Ms. [Now Southern Music, New York]
Score 49 p.
Composed 1951.

2129s Suite for strings and piano
1.Molto moderato 2.Leggiero 3.Largo
4.Allegretto
Pno.-Str.
Ms.
Score 43 p. Large folio
Composed 1956.

1966s Symphony for strings and piano   20'
1.Allegro 2.Largo 3.Vivo - Andantino -
Allegro
Pno.-Str.
Ms.
Score 55 p. Large folio
*Composed 1948. First performance Philadel-
phia, 26 February 1950, New Chamber Orchestra
of Philadelphia, Ifor Jones conductor, Martha
Massena pianist.*

4960 Symphony in G minor   29'
1.Allegro 2.Largo 3.Presto
3(3rd alt. Picc.),3*,3*,3*-4,3,3,1-Timp.-Str.
Ms.
Score 201 p. Large folio
Composed 1947.

4820 Symphony in one movement   15'
3*,2,2,2-4,3,3-Timp.-Str.
Ms.
Score 96 p.
*Originally titled Symphony in E minor. Com-
posed 1940-46. First performance Philadel-
phia, 18 April 1947, Philadelphia Orchestra,
Eugene Ormandy conductor.*

5708 Symphony no. 4   20'
1.Vivo 2.Andante 3.Allegro
3(3rd alt. Picc.),3*,3*,3*-4,3,3,1-Timp.-Str.
Ms.
Score 94 p. Large folio
Composed 1954.

VAUGHAN, CLIFFORD.
b. Bridgeton, New Jersey 23 September 1893

7183 White jade, for orchestra   5'
2,2(1st alt. E.H.),2,2-2Sax.-Timp.,Perc.-Pno.,
Hp.(optional)-Str.
WIM, Los Angeles, [C]1964
Score 10 p.
*White Jade refers to Kwan Yin, Chinese goddess
of mercy and purity. Commissioned by Ruth
St. Denis and the Denishawn Dancers, 1928.
Composed 1928. First performance India, ca.
1928, by the Denishawn Dancers, Clifford
Vaughan conductor, Ruth St. Denis choreogra-
pher and dance soloist.*

VAUGHAN WILLIAMS, RALPH.   Down Ampney,
Gloucestershire 12 October 1872
London 26 August 1958

969s The Charterhouse suite. Edited by James
Brown
1.Prelude 2.Slow dance 3.Quick dance 4.Slow
air 5.Rondo 6.Pezzo ostinato
Pno.-Str.
Stainer & Bell, London, [C]1923
Score 31 p.
Originally composed for piano.

912v [Concerto, violin, Accademico,   20'
D minor]
1.Allegro pesante 2.Adagio 3.Presto
Solo Vn.-Str.
Oxford University Press, London, [C]1927
Score 30 p.
*Composed 1924. First performance 6 November
1925, London Chamber Orchestra, Anthony Ber-
nard conductor, Yelly d'Aranyi soloist.*

502s Fantasia on a theme by Thomas   14'
Tallis
Soli: Vn.I,Vn.II,Va.,Vc.-Str.
G. Schirmer, New York, [C]1921 by Goodwin & Tabb
Score 21 p.

Vaughan Williams, Ralph

1834s Five variants of Dives and Lazarus   12'
2Hp.-Str.
Oxford University Press, London, ᶜ1940
Score 19 p.
Commissioned by the British Council for the New York World's Fair. Composed ca.1938. First performance New York, 10 June 1939, New York Philharmonic, Adrian Boult conductor.

3278 Job, a masque for dancing, from   45'
Blake's Illustrations of the Book of Job
3(3rd alt. Picc.,B.Fl. in G),3*,3(3rd alt. B.Cl.),3*-Sax. in E-flat-4,3,3,1-Timp.,Perc.-Org.(ad lib.),2Hp.-Str.
Oxford University Press, London [n.d.]
Score 109 p.
Composed ca.1927. First concert performance Norwich, England 23 October 1930, the composer conducting.

1170v The lark ascending, romance   13'
Solo Vn.-2,1,2,2-2Hn.(or 1,1,1,1-Hn.)-Trgl.-Str.
Oxford University Press, London, ᶜ1925
Miniature score 24 p.
Inspired by George Meredith's poem. Composed 1914; revised 1920. First full performance London, 14 June 1921, Second Congress of the British Music Society, British Symphony Orchestra, Adrian Boult conductor, Marie Hall soloist.

914 A London symphony [no. 2]   43'
1.Lento - Allegro risoluto 2.Lento 3.Scherzo (nocturne) 4.Andante con moto - Maestoso alla marcia
3(3rd alt. Picc.),3*,3*,3*-4,2,2Cnt.,3,1-Timp.,Perc.-2Hp.-Str.
Stainer & Bell, London, ᶜ1920
Score 199 p.
Composed 1912. First performance London, 1914. Subsequently revised and first performed London, 4 May 1920, Albert Coates conductor.

1439 Norfolk rhapsody no. 1, E minor   10'
2(2nd alt. Picc.),3*,3(1Cl. in E-flat ad lib.),2-4,2,3,1-Timp.,Side Dr.-Hp.-Str.
Oxford University Press, London, ᶜ1925
Score 40 p.
Composed 1902. First performance London, 1906, Henry Wood conductor.

2037 Old King Cole, a ballet for   30'
orchestra
3(2nd alt. Picc.),2,2,2-4,2,3,1-Timp.,Perc.-Cel.(ad lib.),Hp.-Chorus(ad lib.)-Str.
(or: 2,1,2,2-2,2,3)
J. Curwen, London, ᶜ1925 by composer
Score 86 p.
Composed 1922. First performance Cambridge, 1922, Bernhard Ord conductor.

1019 Pastoral symphony [no. 3]   35'
1.Molto moderato 2.Lento moderato
3.Moderato pesante 4.Lento - Moderato maestoso
Sop. Solo,Ten.Solo(offstage),Solo Vn.-3(3rd alt. Picc.),3*,3,2(or 2,2,2,2)-4,3(or 2),3,1-

Timp.,Perc.-Cel.,Hp.-Str.
J. Curwen, London, ᶜ1924
Score 105 p.
Composed 1920. First performance London, 26 January 1922, Adrian Boult conductor.

2989 Symphony, in F minor   32'
1.Allegro 2.Andante moderato 3.Scherzo
4.Finale con epilogo fugato
3(2nd alt. Picc.),3(3rd alt. E.H.),3(B.Cl. ad lib.),3(C.Bn. ad lib.)-4,2,3,1-Timp.,Perc.-Str.
Oxford University Press, London, ᶜ1935
Score 118 p.
Composed 1930-34. First performance in a BBC broadcast, London, 10 April 1935, Adrian Boult conductor.

1205 The wasps, Aristophanic suite   20'
1.Overture 2.Entr'acte 3.March past of the kitchen utensils 4.Entr'acte 5.Ballet and final tableau
2(2nd alt. Picc.),2,2,2-4,2,3(or 2,1,2,1-2,1)-Timp.,Perc.-Hp.-Str.
Schott, London [n.d.]
Score 117 p.
Composed 1909. First performance Cambridge, 1909, Charles Wood conductor.

VEGA, AURELIO DE LA.   Havana 28 November 1925

6614 Cantata para dos sopranos, contralto   14'
y orquesta de cámara
2Sop. Voice Solos, Alto Voice Solo-2(2nd alt. Picc.),1,2(1Cl. in E-flat),1-Alto Sax.-2,2,1,1-Timp.,Perc.-Pno.-Str.
Ms. ᶜ1958 by Aurelio de la Vega
Score 79 p. Large folio
Texts in Spanish with English translations, from Roberto Fernández Retamar's Alabanzas, Conversaciones. Composed 1958. First performance Thirteenth Coolidge Festival, Washington, D.C., 1 November 1964, National Symphony Orchestra, Walter Hendl conductor, Karen Roewade, Nancy Williams, and June Genovese soloists.

369m Divertimiento   8'
Solo Vn., Solo Vc., Solo Pno.-Str.
Ms.
Score 66 p.
Composed 1956. First performance Redlands, California, 29 January 1958, University-Community Symphony Orchestra, Edward C. Tritt conductor, John Golz violinist, Frances Crane violoncellist, John Robertson pianist.

2196s Elegia para orquesta de cuerdas   9'
Str.
Ms.
Score 31 p.
Commissioned by the Sociedad de Conciertos, Havana. Composed 1954. First performance London, 16 November 1954, Royal Philharmonic Orchestra, Alberto Bolet conductor.

6169 Obertura a una farsa seria   ca.15'
2,2,2,2-4,3,3,1-Timp.,Perc.-Hp.-Str.
Ms.

Score 73 p. Large folio
*Inspired by Charles de Peyret-Chappuis' play,
Frenzy. Composed 1950. First performance
Havana, 28 April 1951, Orchestra of the
National Institute of Music, Enrique González
Mantici conductor. Awarded the National Sym-
phonic Prize by the Cuban Ministry of Educa-
tion, 1957.*

VENEZIA, FRANCO DA.   b. Venice 2 November 1876

2062 Venetianische Suite, Op. 24   *18'*
1.[Disembarkment at St. Mark's day] 2.[Idyl
on the lagoon] 3.[Scene at the Campiello]
4.Madrigal 5.[Carnival]
3*,3*,2,2-4,2,3,1-Timp.,Perc.-Cel.,2Hp.(2nd
ad lib.)-Str.
J. Rieter-Biedermann, Leipzig, ᶜ1913
Score 139 p.
*Composed 1912. First performance Turin, 1913,
the composer conducting.*

VEPRIK, ALEXANDER MOISEIEVICH.
                    Balta, Russia 23 June 1899
                    Moscow 13 October 1958

2125 [Dances and songs of the ghetto, Op. 12]
3*,3(3rd alt. E.H.),3(3rd alt. B.Cl.),3(3rd
alt. C.Bn.)-4,3,3,1-Timp.,Perc.-Pno.,Cel.,
Hp.-Str.
Mussektor/Universal Edition, Vienna, 1929
Score 39 p.
Composed 1927. First performance Moscow, 1928.

3291 Fünf kleine Orchesterstücke, Op. 17   *12'*
1,2*,2(2nd alt. B.Cl.),1-2,2,2-Timp.,Perc.-Str.
Mussektor, Moscow, 1934
Score 40 p.
*Composed 1930. First performance in a radio
broadcast, Moscow, 1932, the Moscow Orchestra,
Grigori Hamburg conductor.*

2988 [Mourning song, Op. 20 no. 2]   *7'*
0,3*,3*,3(3rd alt. C.Bn.)-5,3,4,1-Timp.,Perc.-
Pno.,Hp.-Str.
Mussektor, Moscow, 1934
Score 22 p.
*Composed 1933. First performance Moscow,
1933, Moscow Philharmonic Orchestra, Hermann
Scherchen conductor.*

VERACINI, FRANCESCO MARIA. Florence 1 February 1690
                              Pisa ca.1750

439s [Largo. Transcribed by Bernardino
Molinari]
Solo Vn.-Org.-Str.
Carisch, Milan, ᶜ1922
Score 11 p.

560c Menuet et gavotte. Transcribed by Paul
Bazelaire
Solo Vc.-Str.
Senart, Paris [n.d.]
Score 7 p.

VERDI, GIUSEPPE.   Le Roncole,
            near Busseto, Italy 10 October 1813
                    Milan 27 January 1901

4266 [Aida. Prelude]   *8'*
3,2,2,2-4,2,3,Ophicl.-Timp.-Str.
Leduc, Paris [n.d.]
Score 7 p.
*From the opera in four acts composed 1870.
First performance Cairo, 24 December 1871.*

6743 [Aida. Act II: Triumphal march   *12'*
and Ballet music]
3*,2,2,2-4,4,3,1-Timp.,Perc.-Str.
Score: Broude Bros., New York [n.d.] 162 p.
Parts: Luck's, Detroit [n.d.]

4345 [La forza del destino. Overture]   *7'*
2*,2,2,2-4,2,3,1-Timp.,Perc.-2Hp.-Str.
Ricordi, Milan [n.d.]
Miniature score 41 p.
*From the opera in four acts composed 1861.
First performance St. Petersburg, 10 November
1862.*

7018 [Sicilian vespers. Overture]   *9'*
2*,2,2,2-4,2,2Cnt.,3,1-Timp.,Perc.-Str.
Kalmus, New York [n.d.]
Score 70 p.
*Commissioned for the Great Exhibition in Paris,
1855. From the opera in five acts. First
performance Paris, 13 June 1855.*

6793 La Traviata. Prelude, Act I   *3'30"*
1,1,1,2-4Hn.-Str.
Luck's, Detroit [n.d.]
Score 6 p.
*From the opera in three acts composed 1853,
based on Alexandre Dumas' play. First performance Venice, 6 March 1853.*

6794 La Traviata. Prelude, Act III   *3'30"*
1,1,2,2-Hn.-Str.
Luck's, Detroit [n.d.]
Score 4 p.

VERETTI, ANTONIO.   Verona 20 February 1900

3844 Il favorito del re. Fuga e marcia   *5'*
3*,3*,3*,3*-4,3,3,1-Timp.,Perc.-Str.
Ricordi, Milan, ᶜ1934
Miniature score 34 p.
*First performance of this excerpt from the
opera, Rome, 19 January 1933, R. Santarelli
conductor.*

1168s Partita no. 1   *15'*
1.Preludio 2.Scherzo 3.Aria 4.Fugato
5.Finale
Str.
Ricordi, Milan, ᶜ1927
Score 22 p.
*First performance Milan, March 1928, Arrigo
Pedrollo conductor.*

4869 [Symphony no. 1, Italian: The people *12'*
and the prophet]
In one movement

Veretti, Antonio

3(3rd alt. Picc.),3*,3*,3*-4,4,3,1-Timp.,Perc.
-Pno.,2Hp.-Str.
Ricordi, Milan, ^c1932
Score 56 p.
Composed 1929. First performance Liège, 4
September 1930, Festival of the International
Society for Contemporary Music, Alfredo
Casella conductor.

4730 [Symphony no. 2, Epic]   35'
1.Andante grave - Allegro ben ritmico 2.
Andante lento 3.Tempo di marcia
3(3rd alt. Picc.),3*,4*(1Cl. in E-flat),3*-
4,3,3,1-Timp.,Perc.-Cel.,Hp.-Str.
Ricordi, Milan, ^c1939
Score 113 p.
Composed 1938.

VERHEY, THEODOR H.H.   Rotterdam 10 June 1848
                              Rotterdam 28 January 1929

661m [Concerto, clarinet, Op. 47, G minor] 16'
1.Allegro 2.Nocturne 3.Finale à l'hongroise
Solo Cl.-2,2,2,2-4,2,3-Timp.,Perc.-Str.
Score: Ms. 93 p.
Parts: J.H. Zimmermann, Leipzig [n.d.]
Composed 1900. First performance Rotterdam,
1901.

662m [Concerto, flute, no. 1, Op. 43,   12'
D minor]
In one movement
Solo Fl.-2,2,2,2-4,2,3-Timp.-Str.
Score: Ms. 95 p.
Parts: J.H. Zimmermann, Leipzig [n.d.]
Composed 1898. First performance Rotterdam,
1900.

670m [Concerto, flute, no. 2, Op. 57,   14'
A minor]
1.Allegro 2.Andantino 3.Vivace leggiero
Solo Fl.-2(2nd alt. Picc.),2,2,2-4,2,3,1-Timp.,
Perc.-Str.
Score: Ms. 112 p.
Parts: J.H. Zimmermann, Leipzig, ^c1907
Composed 1905. First performance Rotterdam,
1907.

603v [Concerto, violin, Op. 54, A minor]   25'
1.Allegro 2.Allegretto con moto 3.Allegro
Solo Vn.-2,2,2,2-4,2,3,1-Timp.,Perc.-Str.
J.H. Zimmermann, Leipzig [n.d.]
Score 128 p.

VERNEUIL, RAOUL DE.   Lima, Peru 9 April 1899

3716 [Las llamas. Danza peruana]   1'30"
2*,2*,1,1-2,2,1,1-Timp.,Perc.-Pno.,Hp.-Str.
Ms.
Score 15 p.
From the ballet composed 1938.

VERNON, ASHLEY. pseudonym.
See: MANSCHINGER, KURT.

VERRALL, JOHN.   Britt, Iowa 17 June 1908

1895s Concert piece
1.Maestoso - Non troppo allegro 2.Molto calmo

quasi adagio 3.Allegro scherzando 4.Intro-
duction - Finale
2Hn.-Str.
Ms.
Score 43 p.
Originally composed as Sinfonietta, for small
orchestra; revised and enlarged, 1940. First
performance of revised version New York, 8
January 1941, New York Philharmonic, Dimitri
Mitropoulos conductor.

6166 Dark night of St. John   14'
1.Invocation 2.Night visions 3.Meditation
4.Song of praise
2(2nd alt. Picc.),1,2,1-2,1-Str.
Ms. ^c1957 by John Verrall
Score 30 p. Large folio
Inspired by the Dark Night of the Soul of St.
John of the Cross. Composed 1949. First
performance Seattle, 2 August 1949, University
of Washington Sinfonietta, Stanley Chapple
conductor.

4145 Portrait of man, symphonic suite   17'
for orchestra (1940)
1.Prelude (Ambition) 2.Canon (Pride) 3.Song
form (Compassion) 4.Scherzo (Joy) 5.Fugue
(Struggle) 6.Invention (Knowledge) 7.Passa-
caglia (Renunciation)
2,2,2,2-4,3,3,1-Timp.,Perc.-Pno.-Str.
Ms.
Score 71 p.
Inspired by Biblical passages. Composed 1941
at the request of Dimitri Mitropoulos. First
performance Minneapolis, 14 March 1941,
Minneapolis Symphony Orchestra, Dimitri
Mitropoulos conductor.

VERRIMST, VICTOR FRÉDÉRIC. Paris 29 November 1825

896m [Fantasy, trombone and strings]
Solo Tbn.-Str.
Ms.
Score 10 p.

VICTORIA, TOMÁS LUIS DE.   Avila ca.1549
                                 Madrid 27 August 1611

1699s O magnum mysterium, motet.   5'
Arranged for strings by Isadore Freed
Str.
Ms.
Score 5 p.
First performance Philadelphia, 30 January
1935, Chamber Orchestra of Philadelphia and
Composers' Laboratory, Isadore Freed con-
ductor.

1698s O vos omnes, motet. Arranged for   5'
strings by Isadore Freed
Str.
Ms.
Score 4 p.
First performance Philadelphia, 30 January
1935, Chamber Orchestra of Philadelphia and
Composers' Laboratory, Isadore Freed con-
ductor.

COLLECTION OF ORCHESTRAL MUSIC

Vieuxtemps, Henri

VIDAL, PAUL ANTOINE.   Toulouse 16 June 1863
                              Paris 9 April 1931

   822s Mélodie, D major
      Solo Bn.(or Vc., or Vn.)-Str.
      Leduc, Paris [n.d.]
      Score 6 p.

VIERLING, GEORG.
            Frankenthal, Bavaria 5 September 1820
                  Wiesbaden 1 May 1901

   1041v Fantasiestück, Op. 59
      Solo Vn.-1,1,1,1-2Hn.-Str.
      Score: Ms. 21 p.
      Parts: Challier, Berlin [n.d.]

VIEU, JANE.   b. 1871

   638s Minuetto, G major
      Pno.(ad lib.)-Str.(without Cb.)
      Ricordi, Milan, c1901
      Score 6 p.

VIEUXTEMPS, HENRI.
            Verviers, Belgium 17 February 1820
                  Mustapha, Algiers 6 June 1881

   1171v [Andante and rondo, Op. 29]
      Solo Vn.-2,2,2,2-2,2-Timp.-Str.
      Schuberth, Hamburg [1853]
      Score in reduction 23 p.

   464v Ballade et polonaise, Op. 38   10'
      Solo Vn.-1,2,2,2-2,2-Timp.-Str.
      G. Schirmer, New York, c1895
      Score in reduction 23 p.

   1053v [Concerto, violin, no. 1, Op. 10, E major]
      1.Allegro moderato 2.Adagio 3.Rondo
      Solo Vn.-2,2,2,2-4,2,3-Timp.,Perc.-Str.
      Score: Ms. 271 p.
      Parts: B. Schott, London [n.d.]

   458v [Concerto, violin, no. 2, Op. 8,   14'
      F-sharp minor]
      1.Allegro 2.Andante 3.Rondo
      Solo Vn.-2,2,2,2-4,2,3-Timp.,B.Dr.-Str.
      C. Joubert, Paris [n.d.]
      Score in reduction 21 p.
      Also published as Op. 19.

   436v [Concerto, violin, no. 3, Op. 25,   20'
      A major]
      1.Allegro 2.Adagio 3.Rondo
      Solo Vn.-2(2nd alt. Picc.),2,2,2-4,2,3-Timp.,
      Dr.-Str.
      Fr. Kistner, Leipzig [n.d.]
      No score published. Solo Violin part 23 p.
      First performance Brussels, January 1845, the
      composer as soloist.

   558v [Concerto, violin, no. 4, Op. 31,   25'
      D minor] Revised by Aug. Wilhelmj
      1.Andante 2.Scherzo 3.Finale
      Solo Vn.-2,2,2,2-4,2,3-Timp.-Hp.-Str.
      Joh. André, Offenbach a.M. [n.d.]
      Score 179 p.

Composed 1849-50. First performance Paris,
1851, the composer as soloist.

   459v [Concerto, violin, no. 5, Op. 37,   18'
      A minor]
      1.Allegro non troppo 2.Adagio - Allegro con
      fuoco
      Solo Vn.-1,2,2,2-2,2-Timp.-Str.
      Score: Luck's, Detroit [n.d.] 48 p.
      Parts: Kalmus, New York [n.d.]
      Composed 1860-61. First performance Brussels,
      September 1861, the composer as soloist.

   930v [Concerto, violin, no. 6, Op. 47,   20'
      G major]
      1.Allegro moderato 2.Pastorale 3.Intermezzo
      4.Rondo
      Solo Vn.-2,2,2,2-2,2-Timp.-Str.
      Score: Ms. 138 p.
      Parts: Brandus, Paris [n.d.]
      First performance by Mme. Norman-Néruda.

   1059v [Concerto, violin, no. 7, Op. 49, A minor]
      1.Moderato 2.Melancolie 3.Finale
      Solo Vn.-2,2,2,2-2,2,3-Timp.-Hp.-Str.
      Score: Ms. 133 p.
      Parts: Breitkopf & Härtel, Leipzig [n.d.]

   705c [Concerto, violoncello, no. 1, Op. 46,
      A minor]
      1.Allegro moderato 2.Andante 3.Finale
      Solo Vc.-2,2,2,2-2,2-Timp.-Str.
      Score: Ms. 179 p.
      Parts: B. Schott's Söhne, Mainz [n.d.]

   657c [Concerto, violoncello, no. 2, Op. 50,
      B minor]
      1.Allegro 2.Adagio 3.Finale
      Solo Vc.-2,2,2,2-4,2-Timp.-Str.
      Score: Ms. 156 p.
      Parts: Brandus, Paris [n.d.]

   1167v Fantaisie-caprice, Op. 11   15'
      Solo Vn.-1,2,2,2-2,2-Timp.-Str.
      Score in reduction: Peters, Leipzig [n.d.] 19 p.
      Parts: B. Schott's Söhne, Mainz [1842?]
      Composed 1840. First performance St. Peters-
      burg, 16 March 1840, the composer as soloist.

   463v [Fantasia-Appassionata, violin,   16'
      Op. 35, in G]
      Solo Vn.-1,2,2,2-2,2-Timp.-Str.
      Edition Peters, Leipzig [n.d.]
      Score 87 p.

   1042v Hommage à Paganini, caprice sur des
      thèmes du célèbre maestro, Op. 9
      Solo Vn.-1,0,1,1-Hn.-Str.
      Score: Ms. 25 p.
      Parts: E. Troupenas, Paris [n.d.]

      Morceaux de salon, Op. 22
   1001v No. 2. Air varié   7'
   562v No. 3. Rêverie   5'
   1010v No. 5. Tarantelle   4'
      Solo Vn.-2,2,2,2-2,2-Timp.,Perc.-Str.
      Scores: Ms. 48 p., 18 p., 53 p.
      Parts: Bote & Bock, Berlin/No. 1 G. Schirmer,
      New York, c1910

839

Vieuxtemps, Henri

Yankee Doodle, souvenir d'Amérique, Op. 17
273v Solo Vn.-Str.
381c Solo Vc.-Str. Solo transcribed by Robert
E. Bockmühl
C.F. Peters, Leipzig [1891?]
Score in reduction 11 p.
Composed for violin and string orchestra ca.
1845, after the composer's first American
tour in 1844.

VILLA, RICARDO.   Madrid 23 October 1873
                             Madrid 10 April 1935

555p Fantasia española   17'
Solo Pno.-2(2nd alt. Picc.),2(1st alt. E.H.),
2,2-2,2,3-Timp.,Perc.-Str.
J.H. Zimmermann, Leipzig, ᶜ1909
Score 62 p.

686v Rapsodia asturiana
Solo Vn.-2(2nd alt. Picc.),2(2nd alt. E.H.),
2,2-2,2,3,1-Timp.,Perc.-Str.
Breitkopf & Härtel, Leipzig, ᶜ1906
Score 62 p.

VILLA-LOBOS, HEITOR.   Rio de Janeiro 5 March 1887
                        Rio de Janeiro 17 November 1959

742c Bachianas brasileiras no. 1   17'
[for violoncelli]
1.Introdução (Embolada) 2.Preludio (Modinha)
3.Fuga (Conversa)
Str.(Vc. only)
Ms.
Score 63 p.
Composed 1930 for the Philharmonic Orchestra
of Rio de Janeiro. First performance Rio de
Janeiro, 12 September 1932, Philharmonic
Orchestra of Rio de Janeiro, Burle Marx con-
ductor.

3501 Bachianas brasileiras no. 2   20'
1.Preludio 2.Aria 3.Dansa 4.Tocata
1(alt. Picc.),1,1,1(alt. C.Bn.)-Bar.Sax.(alt.
Ten.Sax.)-2,0,1-Timp.,Perc.-Pno.,Cel.-Str.
Ms.
Score 127 p.
Composed 1930. First performance Venice,
September 1937.

Bachianas brasileiras no. 4   16'
1865s No. 1 Preludio
3735   No. 2 Coral (Canto do Sertão)
3736   No. 3 Aria (Cantiga)
3737   No. 4 Dansa (Mindinho)
3*,3*,3*,3*-4,3,2,1-Timp.,Perc.-Cel.(in no.
2 only)-Str.(only in no. 1)
Ms.
Scores: 8 p., 22 p., 32 p., 42 p.
No. 4 composed 1930. Nos. 1-3 composed 1941.
Nos. 2 and 3 first performed New York, 6 June
1942, NBC Symphony Orchestra, Burle Marx con-
ductor.

457c Bachianas brasileiras no. 5, for   11'
soprano and orchestra of violoncelli
1.Aria (Cantilena) 2.Dansa (Martelo)
Sop. Voice Solo-4Vc.

Associated Music Publishers, New York, ᶜ1947
Miniature score 30 p.
Aria lyrics by Ruth Valadares Corrêa; Dansa
lyrics by Manuel Bandeira. Aria composed
1938. First performance Rio de Janeiro, 25
March 1939, Ruth Valadares Corrêa soloist.
Dansa composed 1945. First performance Paris,
10 October 1947, Hilda Ohlin soloist.

3510 Caixinha de bôas-festas, ou Vitrine   17'
encantada [Small holiday box, or The magic
window (Children's ballet)]
3*,3*,3*,3*-4,4,2,1-Timp.,Perc.-Cel.,Hp.-Str.
Ms.
Score 87 p.
Composed 1932. First performance Rio de
Janeiro, 8 December 1932, Philharmonic Orches-
tra of Rio de Janeiro, Burle Marx conductor.

3733 Chôros no. 7   8'
1,1,1,1-Alto Sax.-Tam-tam-Vn.,Vc.
M. Eschig, Paris, ᶜ1928
Score 22 p.
Composed 1924.

4876 Chôros no. 10, Rasga o coração   20'
3*,2,2,3*-Alto Sax.-3,0,2Cnt.,2-Timp.,Perc.-
Pno.,Hp.-Chorus-Str.
M. Eschig, Paris, ᶜ1928
Score 92 p.
After the popular song Rasga o Coração, based
on Catullo Cearence's poem. Composed 1925.
First performance Rio de Janeiro, 15 December
1926.

289m Concerto for harmonica and   20'
orchestra
1.Allegro moderato 2.Andante 3.Allegro
Solo Harmonica-1,1,1,1-2,0,1-Timp.,Perc.-Cel.,
Hp.-Str.
Ms. [Controlled by Associated, New York]
Score 91 p. Large folio
Commissioned by John Sebastian, Sr. Composed
1955. First performance Jerusalem, October
1959, Jerusalem Radio Symphony Orchestra,
Jacques Singer conductor, John Sebastian, Sr.
soloist.

751c [Concerto, violoncello, Op. 50]   20'
In one movement
Solo Vc.-3*,2,2,2-4,3,3,1-Timp.-Hp.-Str.
Ms.
Score 123 p.
Composed 1915.

3747 Impressão moura [Moorish   5'
impression, from the 3rd suite of Descobri-
mento do Brasil]
3*,3*,3*,3*-4,3,3,1-Timp.,Perc.-Pno.,Hp.-Str.
Ms.
Score 30 p.
Composed 1937; also titled Canção Moura.

4717 Magdalena suite no. 1   15'
1.My bus and I 2.Scene de Paris 3.Food for
thought
1,1,1,1-Alto Sax.-3,0,Cnt.,3,1-Timp.,Perc.-
Cel.,Hp.-Str.

Vinci, Leonardo

Villa-Lobos Music Corp., New York, c1948
Score 65 p. Large folio
From the operetta composed 1947. Commissioned and produced by Edwin Lester. First performance Los Angeles, 26 July 1948.

4771 Magdalena suite no. 2 16'
1.The singing tree 2.The emerald song 3.Valse d'Espagne
1(alt. Picc.),1(alt. E.H.),1,1-Alto Sax.-3,1,
Cnt.,3,1-Timp.,Perc.-Pno.,Cel.,Hp.-Str.
Villa-Lobos Music Corp., New York, c1948
Score 69 p. Large folio

6483 Sinfonietta no. 1 ca.16'
1.Allegro giusto 2.Andante non troppo
3.Andantino
2,2,2,2-2,2,2-Timp.-Str.
Ms. [Southern Music, New York, c1955]
Score 66 p. Large folio
Based on two themes of Mozart. Composed 1916.

1831s Suite [for string orchestra]
1.Musica timida 2.Musica mysteriosa
3.Musica inquieta
Str.
Ms.
Score 29 p.
Composed 1912.

6474 [Suite no. 1, Memories of youth] 11'
In 10 movements
3*,3*,2,2-Alto Sax.-4,1,2,1-Timp.,Perc.-Str.
Ms. c1941 by Heitor Villa-Lobos [Controlled by Associated, New York]
Score 66 p.
Composed 1940. First performance 18 June 1950.

6686 Uirapurú (The magic bird) 18'
3*,3*,3*,3*-Sop.Sax.-4,0,3Cnt.-,3,1-Timp.,Perc.-Pno.,Cel.,2Hp.-Violinophone-Str.
Ms. [Associated, New York, c1948]
Score 90 p. Large folio
The ballet with book and music by Villa-Lobos. Composed 1917. First performance Buenos Aires, 25 May 1935, Orchestra of the Teatro Colón, the composer conducting, choreography by Ricardo Nemanoff.

VILLANUEVA GALEANO, IGNACIO.
See: GALEANO, IGNACIO VILLANUEVA.

VILLERMIN, LOUIS. Baccarat, France 16 July 1877

1671s Sérénade orientale
Str.
Score: Ms. 4 p.
Parts: E. Gaudet, Paris [n.d.]

VINCENT, JOHN. Birmingham, Alabama 17 May 1902

5334 Symphony in D, a festival piece 18'30"
in one movement
2(both alt. Picc.),2,2,2-4,2,3-Timp.,Perc.-Str.
Ms.
Score 81 p.
Commissioned by the Louisville Orchestra, 1954.

Composed 1954. Revised 1955. First performance Louisville, 5 February 1955, Louisville Orchestra, Robert Whitney conductor.

5026 Three Jacks, ballet in three 16'
tableaux [original version]
1.Jack be nimble 2.Jack Spratt 3.The house that Jack built
2(2nd alt. Picc.),2(2nd alt. E.H.),3*,2-4,3,3,1-Timp.,Perc.-Hp.-Str.
Ms.
Score 79 p. Large folio
Ballet on the popular rhymes. Composed 1941-42. First performance Rochester, October 1943, Eastman-Rochester Symphony Orchestra, Howard Hanson conductor.

5346 [Three Jacks, ballet. Revised 29'
version]
1.Fanfare 2.Jack be nimble 3.Jack Spratt
4.The house that Jack built
2(2nd alt. Picc.),2(2nd alt. E.H.),2(2nd alt. B.Cl.),2-2,1,1-Timp.,Perc.-Str.
Ms.
Score 117 p.
This version 1953. First performance Los Angeles, 16 March 1954, Los Angeles Chamber Symphony with the Lazar Galpern Ballet Company, Jan Popper conductor, choreography by Lazar Galpern.

5355 [Three Jacks. Suite from the 15'
ballet]
1.Fanfare [and Jack be nimble] 2.Jack Spratt
3.The house that Jack built
2(both alt. Picc.),2(2nd alt. E.H.),2(2nd alt. B.Cl.),2-2,2,2-Timp.,Perc.-Str.
Ms.
Score 79 p.
Extracted 1954, at the request of Alfred Wallenstein for the opening concert of the Los Angeles Philharmonic's 1954-55 season. First performance Los Angeles, 4 November 1954, Los Angeles Philharmonic Orchestra, Alfred Wallenstein conductor.

VINCI, LEONARDO. Strongoli, Calabria ?1690
Naples 27 May 1730

2130s [Six ancient dances, violin and harpsichord. Transcribed for strings by Guido Guerrini]
1.Allemanda 2.Quasi sarabanda 3.Gavotta
4.Minuetto 5.Siciliana 6.Furlana
Str.(Cb. ad lib.)
Bongiovanni, Bologna, c1941
Score 12 p.

841

Viotta, Henri

VIOTTA, HENRI.   Amsterdam 16 July 1848
                                  Montreux 17 February 1933

  623c Concert-fantasie
    Solo Vc.-2,2,2,2-4,2-Timp.-Str.
    van Eck, The Hague [n.d.]
    Score 62 p.

VIOTTI, GIOVANNI BATTISTA.
                                  Fontanetto da Po 12 May 1755
                                  London 3 March 1824

  292p [Concerto, piano, G minor. Giazotto   41'
  no. 91] Revised by Remo Giazotto
    1.Allegro maestoso 2.Adagio non troppo
    3.Rondò
    Solo Pno.-2,2,2,2-2,2-Timp.-Str.
    Ricordi, Milan, c1960
    Score 98 p.
    Composed 1792-94. First published by Naderman, Paris.

  940m [Concerto, violin, Op. 3, A major.   14'
  Giazotto no. 51. Transcribed anonymously for
  violin, piano and orchestra]
    1.Allegro 2.[No tempo indicated] 3.Rondo
    Solo Pno., Solo Vn.-2Fl.-2Hn.-Str.
    Ms.
    Score 70 p.
    Originally composed ca.1784.

  461v [Concerto, violin, no. 22, A minor.   27'
  Giazotto no. 97]
    1.Moderato 2.Adagio 3.Agitato assai
    Solo Vn.-1,2,2,2-2,2-Timp.-Str.
    Kalmus, New York [n.d.]
    Score 92 p.
    Composed 1793.

  478v [Concerto, violin, no. 23, G major.   16'
  Giazotto no. 98] Edited by Hans Sitt
    1.Allegro 2.Andante 3.Allegro
    Solo Vn.-2,0,0,1-2Hn.-Str.
    Joh. André, Offenbach a.M., c1904
    Score in reduction 37 p.
    Composed 1793.

  973v [Concerto, violin, no. 24, B minor.   20'
  Giazotto no. 105]
    1.Maestoso 2.Andante sostenuto 3.Allegretto
    Solo Vn.-2,2,0,2-2,2-Timp.-Str.
    Score: Ms. 87 p.
    Parts: J. André, Offenbach a.M. [n.d.]
    Composed 1795.

  963v [Concerto, violin, no. 25, A minor.   21'
  Giazotto no. 124]
    1.Andante - Allegro vivo assai 2.Andante
    sostenuto 3.Allegretto
    Solo Vn.-1(alt. Picc.),2,2,2-2,2-Timp.,Trgl.-
    Str.
    Score: Ms. 108 p.
    Parts: Chérubini, Méhul [et al.] Paris [n.d.]
    Composed 1805.

  1047v [Concerto, violin, no. 26, B-flat minor.
  Giazotto no. 131]
    1.Allegro con un poco di moto 2.Andante più

tosto adagio - Allegretto con moto
    Solo Vn.-1,2,2,2-2Hn.-Str.
    Score: Ms. 77 p.
    Parts: Chérubini, Méhul [et al.] Paris [n.d.]
    Composed ca.1810.

  1048v [Concerto, violin, no. 27, C major.
  Giazotto no. 142]
    1.Piùttosto lento - Allegro vivace 2.Adagio
    non troppo 3.Allegretto, ma non troppo
    Solo Vn.-1,2,0,2-2Hn.-Str.
    Ms. c1976 by The Fleisher Collection of Orches-
    tral Music, Free Library of Philadelphia
    Score 129 p. Large folio
    *Composed 1813. First published by Janet et
    Cotelle, Paris. Also published by Simrock,
    Berlin, 1815. This edition based on parts
    published by A. Offenbach, Mainz.*

  1049v [Concerto, violin, no. 28, A minor.
  Giazotto no. 143]
    1.Moderato 2.Andante sostenuto 3.Allegretto
    vivo
    Solo Vn.-1,2,2,2-2,2-Str.
    Score: Ms. 191 p.
    Parts: H.A. Probst, Leipzig [n.d.]
    Composed 1814.

  1050v [Concerto, violin, no. 29, E minor.
  Giazotto no. 144]
    1.Allegro maestoso 2.Andante 3.Andante -
    Allegretto
    Solo Vn.-2,2,2,2-2,2-Timp.-Str.
    Score: Ms. 174 p.
    Parts: J. André, Offenbach a.M.
    Composed 1815.

  1175v [Sinfonia concertante, 2 violins   20'
  and chamber orchestra, no. 1, F major.
  Giazotto no. 76] Edited by Felice Quaranta
    1.Allegro brillante 2.Adagio, non tanto
    3.Rondò: Allegro
    Solo Vn.I & II-2Ob.-2Hn.-Str.
    Carisch, Milan, c1960
    Score 72 p.
    *Composed 1786. First performance before Marie
    Antoinette, ca.1786, the composer and J.J.
    Imbault soloists. First published by Imbault,
    Paris, 1786.*

  1177v [Sinfonia concertante, 2 violins and
  chamber orchestra, no. 2, B-flat major.
  Giazotto no. 77]
    1.Allegro maestoso [2nd movement lacking]
    Solo Vn.I & II-2Ob.-2Hn.-Str.
    Ms.
    Score 22 p.
    *Composed 1786. First published Naderman,
    Paris, 1786. First performance before Marie
    Antoinette, ca.1787, the composer and J.J.
    Imbault soloists.*

VIRKHAUS, TAAVO.   Tartu, Estonia 29 June 1934

  309v [Concerto, violin]   21'
    1.Andante, molto rubato, quasi recitativo
    2.Rondo 3.Chorale
    Solo Vn.-2(2nd alt. Picc.),2,3*,2-4,3,3,1-

Timp.,Perc.-Hp.-Str.
Ms.
Score 73 p. Large folio
*Composed 1966. First performance Rochester,
5 May 1966, Eastman-Rochester Orchestra,
Howard Hanson conductor, Norma Auzin soloist.
Awarded Howard Hanson Prize, April 1966.*

5618 Overture to Kalevipoeg   *12'*
3*,2,3*,3*-4,2,3,1-Timp.,Perc.-Str.
Ms.
Score 39 p. Large folio
*Suggested by F. R. Kreutzwald's compilation of
Estonian mythology. Composed 1957. First
performance Rochester, 1 May 1971, Rochester
Philharmonic Orchestra, the composer con-
ducting.*

VISCARDINI, CARLO.

1281s Preludio lento
Str.
Score: Ms. 4 p.
Parts: Otto Junne, Leipzig, [c]1909
Awarded the silver medal at Bordeaux, 1907.

VISKI, JÁNOS.   Kolozsvár, Hungary 10 June 1906
                     Budapest 16 January 1961

5111 Enigma   *17'*
3(all alt. Picc.),2(2nd alt. E.H.),2,2-4,3,3,
1-Timp.,Perc.-Cel.,Hp.-Str.
Universal Edition, Vienna, [c]1941
Score 66 p.
*Inspired by a poem by Balassa Bálint (ca.1551-
1594). Composed 1939.*

4967 [Two Hungarian dances]   *6'*
1.[Palace] 2.[Lively]
2(2nd alt. Picc.),2(2nd alt. E.H.),2,2-4,3,3,1
-Timp.,Perc.-Hp.-Str.
Universal Edition, Vienna, [c]1944
Score 52 p.
Composed 1938.

VITALI, GIOVANNI BATTISTA.   Cremona ca.1644
                                  Modena 12 October 1692

952s Capriccio. Edited by Gustav Lenzewski, Sr.
Str.(without Cb.)
Chr. Fr. Vieweg, Berlin [n.d.]
Score 5 p.

771v Chaconne. Transcribed by Ottorino
Respighi
Solo Vn.-Org.-Str.
C. Schmidl, Leipzig, [c]1911
Score 23 p.

709v [Same as above] Abridged edition, arranged
by Felice Togni
Solo Vn.-Str.
Maurice Senart, Paris, [c]1926
Score 16 p.

VĪTOLIŅŠ, JĀNIS OTTOWITSCH.
                        Litena, Latvia 20 April 1886
                        Riga 14 May 1955

Also published as: Janis Wihtolin

4978 [Latvian rhapsody no. 1]   *16'*
2(2nd alt. Picc.),2,2,2-4,2,3,1-Timp.,Perc.-
Cel.,Hp.-Str.
Universal Edition, Vienna, [c]1937
Score 72 p.
Composed 1932.

VITOLS, JĀZEPS.
See: WIHTOL, JOSEPH.

VITTORIA, TOMÁS LUIS DE.
See: VICTORIA, TOMÁS LUIS DE.

VIVALDI, ANTONIO LUCIO.   Venice 4 March 1678
                               Vienna buried 28 July 1741

Vivaldi's works are entered in the following
order:
   CONCERTOS without opus numbers, by Fanna
      thematic catalog numbers
   CONCERTOS with opus numbers
   OPERA EXCERPTS alphabetically by title
   SONATAS by opus number
The concertos which have individual descriptive
titles are listed here with their respective
opus or Fanna numbers:
   Alla rustica. Fanna catalog no. F.XI n.11
   L'autunno. Op. VIII no. 3
   L'estate. Op. VIII no. 2
   Il gardellino. Op. X no. 3
   L'inverno. Op. VIII no. 4
   La notte. Fanna catalog no. F.VI n.13
   La primavera. Op. VIII no. 1
   Le quattro stagione. Op. VIII nos. 1-4
   La tempesta di mare. Two concerti: Fanna
      catalog no. F.XII n.28 *and* Op. X no. 1

293v [Concerto, 3 violins, strings and   *12'*
cembalo, F major. Fanna no. F.I n.34] Edited
by Ettore Bonelli
1.Allegro 2.Andante 3.Allegro
Solo Vn.I, Solo Vn.II, Solo Vn.III-Str.
Zanibon, Padua, [c]1960
Score 24 p.

710v [Same as above] Edited by Felice   *9'*
Togni
1.Allegro 2.Adagio 3.Allegro
Solo Vn.I, Solo Vn.II, Solo Vn.III-Cemb.-Str.

Vivaldi, Antonio

Maurice Senart, Paris, [c]1926
Score 24 p.

1141v [Same as above] Transcribed for   9'
3 violins and orchestra by Armand Balendonck
1.Allegro 2.Andante 3.Allegro
3 Solo Vn.-2,2,2,2-4,2,3,1-Timp.-Str.
Ms.
Score 72 p.
First performance of this transcription
Philadelphia, 25 April 1937, Civic Symphony
Orchestra, Armand Balendonck conductor.

286v [Concerto, 2 violins, strings and   11'
cembalo, B-flat major. Fanna no. F.I n.40]
Edited by Melinda Berlász
1.Allegro 2.Andante 3.Allegro
2 Solo Vn.-Cemb.-Str.
Editio Musica, Budapest/Edition Eulenburg,
Zurich, [c]1971
Score 21 p.

324v [Concerto, violin, strings and   10'
cembalo, G minor. Fanna no. F.I n.165.
2nd version, with woodwinds] Edited by Rudolf
Eller
1.Allegro 2.Largo 3.Allegro
Solo Vn.-2Ob.,Bn.-Cemb.-Str.
Breitkopf & Härtel, Leipzig [1960?]
Score 26 p.

540v [Concerto, violin, strings and   11'
cembalo, A major. Fanna no. F.I n.224]
Realized by F. de Guarnieri
1.Allegro mosso 2.Largo 3.Allegro
Solo Vn.-Cemb.-Str.
Ricordi, Milan, [c]1918
Score 22 p.
First modern performance Venice, 1918.

1143v [Concerto, viola d'amore, strings   9'
and cembalo, A minor. Fanna no. F.II n.6]
Edited by Alfred Einstein
1.[Vivaldi: Allegro] 2.Largo 3.Allegro
Solo Va.d'Amore-Str.
Ms.
Score 24 p.

206m [Concerto, oboe, strings and   10'
cembalo, F major. Fanna no. F.VII n.2] Edited
by György Balla
1.Allegro non molto 2.Andante 3.Allegro
molto
Solo Ob.-Cemb.-Str.
Editio Musica, Budapest/Edition Eulenburg,
Zurich, [c]1973
Score 21 p.

205m [Concerto, oboe, strings and   14'30"
cembalo, C major. Fanna no. F.VII n.6] Edited
by Vera Lampert
1.Allegro non molto 2.Larghetto 3.Minuetto
Solo Ob.-Cemb.-Str.
Editio Musica, Budapest/Edition Eulenburg,
Zurich, [c]1973
Score 36 p.

252m [Concerto, 2 trumpets, cembalo and   7'
strings, C major. Fanna no. F.IX n.1] Edited
by Felix Schroeder
1.Allegro 2.Largo 3.[Allegro]
2 Solo Tpt.-Cemb.-Str.
Eulenburg, Zurich, [c]1965
Miniature score 37 p.

2131s [Concerto, strings and cembalo,   5'
Alla rustica, G major. Fanna no. F.XI n.11]
Revised by Alfredo Casella
1.Presto 2.Andante 3.Allegro
Cemb.-Str.
Carisch, Milan, [c]1940
Score 7 p.
First modern performance Siena, 16 September
1940, Antonio Vivaldi Week sponsored by the
Accademia Musicale Chigiana, Fernando Pre-
vitala conductor.

1024v [Concerto, violin, 2 oboes,   13'
bassoon, 2 horns, strings and cembalo, F major.
Fanna no. F.XII n.10] Edited by Karl Straube
1.Allegro moderato 2.Adagio 3.Allegretto
commodo
Solo Vn.-0,2,0,1-2Hn.-Cemb.-Str.
Breitkopf & Härtel, Leipzig, [c]1930
Score 35 p.

248m [Concerto, flute, oboe, bassoon,   8'
strings and cembalo, La tempesta di mare, F
major. Fanna no. F.XII n.28] Edited by Felix
Schroeder
Solo Fl., Solo Ob., Solo Bn.-Cemb.-Str.
1.[Allegro] 2.Largo 3.Presto
Eulenburg, London, [c]1965
Miniature score 25 p.
This work constitutes essentially the same
music as the composer's concerto La Tempesta
di Mare, Catalog no. 492m (Fanna no. F.VI
n.12).

320m [Concerto, 2 flutes, 3 oboes,   11'
bassoon, violin, strings and cembalo, G minor.
Fanna no. F.XII n.33] Edited by Fausto
Torrefranca
1.Allegro maestoso, ma vivo 2.Larghetto
3.Allegro
Solo Ob., Solo Vn.-2,2,0,1-2Cemb.-Str.
Carisch, Milan, [c]1937
Score 75 p.

6379 [Concerto, 2 flutes, 2 salmò,   10'
2 mandolins, 2 theorbos, 2 violins, 2 violon-
celli, strings and cembalo, C major. Fanna no.
F.XII n.37] Transcribed by Alfredo Casella
1.Allegro molto 2.Andante molto 3.Allegro
2Fl.,Salmò(Bass Ob. or Heckelphone)-2Tpt.-
Cemb.,2Hp.,2Mand.-Str.
Carisch, Milan, [c]1943
Score 58 p.
Composed ca.1740.

966m [Concerto, viola d'amore, lute,   9'
strings and cembalo, D minor. Fanna no. F.XII
n.38] Edited by Alfred Einstein
1.Allegro 2.Largo 3.Allegro
Solo Va.d'Amore, Solo Lute-Str.

Ms.
Score 23 p.

348v [Concerto, 4 violins, violoncello, *10'*
strings and cembalo, L'estro armonico, Op. III
no. 1, D major. Fanna no. F.IV n.7] Edited by
Walter Upmeyer after parts published by Walsh
& Hare, London, ca.1723
1.Allegro 2.Largo e spiccato 3.Allegro
4Solo Vn.-Cemb.-Str.
Bärenreiter, Kassel, c1953
Score 27 p.
Op. III probably composed ca.1703. First
published 1712 by Estienne Roger, Amsterdam.

955s [Concerto, violin, string orchestra and
cembalo, L'estro armonico, Op. III no. 3, G
major. Fanna no. F.I n.173. Movements 1 *and*
3, *with* Marcello, Alessandro, Concerto, oboe
or violin and string orchestra, C minor. Movement 2. Transcribed for string orchestra and
cembalo by Arthur Egidi from the J.S. Bach
transcriptions for harpsichord, BWV 978 &
974]
1.Allegro [Vivaldi/Bach] 2.Adagio [Alessan-
dro Marcello/Bach] 3.Allegro [Vivaldi/Bach]
Cemb.(or Pno.)-Str.
Chr. Friedrich Vieweg, Berlin, c1926
Score 19 p.
For Alessandro Marcello's complete oboe con-
certo, formerly attributed to Benedetto Mar-
cello or Vivaldi, see Catalog nos. 464m and
618m.

341v [Concerto, 4 violins, strings and *8'*
cembalo, L'estro armonico, Op. III no. 4,
E minor. Fanna no. F.I n.174] Edited by Walter
Upmeyer after parts published by Walsh & Hare,
London, ca.1723
1.Andante 2.Allegro assai 3.Adagio
4.Allegro
4 Solo Vn.-Cemb.-Str.
Bärenreiter, Kassel, c1953
Score 24 p.

340v [Concerto, 2 violins, strings and *7'*
cembalo, L'estro armonico, Op. III no. 5,
A major. Fanna no. F.I n.175] Edited by Walter
Upmeyer after parts published by Walsh & Hare,
London, ca.1730
1.Allegro 2.Largo 3.Allegro
Solo Vn.I, Solo Vn.II-Cemb.-Str.
Bärenreiter, Kassel, c1960
Score 24 p.
This edition 1952.

386v [Concerto, violin, strings and *5'*
cembalo, L'estro armonico, Op. III no. 6,
A minor. Fanna no. F.I n.176] Edited by Alfred
Einstein
1.Allegro (moderato e deciso) 2.Largo
3.Presto
Solo Vn.-Cemb.-Str.
Eulenburg, London [c1952]
Miniature score 20 p.

484v [Same as above] Edited by Tivadar *5'*
Nachèz

1.Allegro 2.Largo 3.Presto
Solo Vn.-Org.-Str.
B. Schott's Söhne, Mainz, c1912
Score in reduction 14 p.

339v [Concerto, 4 violins, violoncello, *10'*
strings and cembalo, L'estro armonico, Op. III
no. 7, F major. Fanna no. F.IV n.9] Edited by
Walter Upmeyer
1.Andante - Adagio 2.Allegro - Adagio
3.Allegro
4 Solo Vn.-Cemb.-Str.
Bärenreiter, Kassel, c1954
Score 19 p.
This edition 1952. Based on parts published
ca.1723 by Walsh & Hare, London, in which this
concerto is Op. III no. 9.

72s [Concerto, 2 violins, strings and *10'*
cembalo, L'estro armonico, Op. III no. 8,
A minor. Fanna no. F.I n.177] Arranged by
Sam Franko
1.Allegro moderato 2.Adagio 3.Allegro
Solo Vn.I, Solo Vn.II-Str.
G. Schirmer, New York, c1909
Score 24 p.
Third movement is not the same as that listed
in the Fanna catalog and has not been identi-
fied.

764c [Same as above] Transcribed for *10'*
violoncello and string orchestra by Feder
1.Allegro moderato 2.Adagio 3.Allegro
Solo Vc.-Pno.(Continuo)-Str.
Ms.
Score 23 p.

2344s [Same as above] Transcribed for *12'*
string orchestra by Paul Glass from the J.S.
Bach transcription for organ, BWV 593.
Further editing by Norman Black
1.Allegro 2.Adagio 3.Allegro
Pno.(optional)-Str.
BMI, New York, c1942
Score 31 p.

342v [Concerto, violin, strings and *7'*
cembalo, L'estro armonico, Op. III no. 9,
D major. Fanna no. F.I n.178] Edited by Walter
Upmeyer after parts published by Walsh & Hare,
London, ca.1730
1.Allegro 2.Larghetto 3.Allegro
Solo Vn.-Cemb.-Str.
Bärenreiter, Kassel, c1953
Score 19 p.

579v [Concerto, 4 violins, violoncello, *11'*
strings and cembalo, L'estro armonico,
Op. III no. 10, B minor. Fanna no. F.IV n.10]
Edited by Charles Bouvet
1.Allegro 2.Largo 3.Allegro
4 Solo Vn.-Cemb.-Str.
Eschig, Paris, c1910 by E. Demets
Score 28 p.
First performance in this version, Paris, 28
February 1906, Fondation J. S. Bach.

Vivaldi, Antonio

1383s [Same as above] Transcribed for   *11'*
string orchestra by Michele Esposito
1.Allegro 2.Largo - Larghetto 3.Allegro
Str.
Oxford University Press, London, ^c1927
Score 31 p.

1622s [Concerto, 2 violins, violoncello,   *9'*
strings and cembalo, L'estro armonico, Op. III
no. 11, D minor. Fanna no. F.IV n.11] Edited
by Günter Raphael
1.Allegro 2.Largo e spiccato 3.Allegro
Solo Vn. I, Solo Vn. II, Solo Vc.-Cemb.-Str.
Breitkopf & Härtel, Leipzig, ^c1930
Score 15 p.

4767 [Same as above] Transcribed by   *12'*
Vittorio Giannini
1.Allegro non troppo 2.Largo 3.Allegro
3(3rd alt. Picc.),3(3rd alt. E.H.),3,3*-4,3,3,
1-Timp.,Cym.-Str.
Ms.
Score 37 p. Large folio

3897 [Same as above] Transcribed by   *9'*
Leslie Hodge from the J.S. Bach transcription
for organ, BWV 596
1.Andante maestoso - Adagio - Allegro
2.Andante 3.Allegro
3*,3*,3*,3*-4,4,3,1-Timp.,Perc.-Org.-Str.
Ms.
Score 44 p. Large folio

515 [Same as above] Transcribed by   *9'*
Alexander Siloti
1.Maestoso 2.Largo 3.Allegro
2,2,2,3*-Org.-Str.
Edition Russe de Musique, Berlin [1913?]
Score 25 p.

387v [Concerto, violin, strings and   *12'*
cembalo, L'estro armonico, Op. III no. 12,
E major. Fanna no. F.I n.179]
1.Allegro 2.Largo 3.Allegro
Solo Vn.-Cemb.-Str.
Edition Eulenburg, London [^c1951]
Miniature score 16 p.
This edition 1939.

338v [Concerto, violin, strings, cembalo   *12'*
and organ, La stravaganza, Op. IV no. 1,
B-flat major. Fanna no. F.I n.180] Edited by
Walter Upmeyer
1.Allegro 2.Largo e cantabile 3.Allegro
Solo Vn.-Cemb.-Str.
Bärenreiter, Kassel, 1960
Score 18 p.
Op. IV composed soon after 1703. First pub-
lished 1712-1713 by Estienne Roger, Amsterdam.
This edition 1949.

487s [Concerto, violin, strings and   *10'*
cembalo, La stravaganza, Op. IV no. 2, E minor.
Fanna no. F.I n.181] Transcribed for string
orchestra by A. Mistowski
1.Vigoroso [Fanna: Allegro] 2.Largo 3.Allegro
Str.
Oxford University Press, London, ^c1925
Score 15 p.

343v [Concerto, violin, strings,   *12'*
cembalo and organ, La stravaganza, Op. IV no. 3,
G major. Fanna no. F.I n.182] Edited by Walter
Upmeyer
1.Allegro 2.Largo 3.Allegro assai
Solo Vn.-Cemb.-Str.
Bärenreiter, Kassel, 1949
Score 18 p.

819v [Concerto, violin, strings, cembalo   *10'*
and organ, La stravaganza, Op. IV no. 6,
G minor. Fanna no. F.I n.185] Arranged by Sam
Franko
1.Allegro 2.Largo cantabile 3.Allegro
Solo Vn.-Pno.-Str.
Ries & Erler, Berlin, ^c1929
Score 31 p.

1382s [Same as above] Transcribed for   *10'*
string orchestra by A. Mistowski
1.Moderato 2.Largo 3.Allegro
Pno.(ad lib.)-Str.
Oxford University Press, London, ^c1929
Score 20 p.

552v [Concerto, violin, strings, cembalo   *12'*
and organ, La stravaganza, Op. IV no. 12,
G major. Fanna no. F.I n.191] Edited by
Tivadar Nachèz
1.Spiritoso e non presto 2.Largo 3.Allegro
Solo Vn.-Org.-Str.
B. Schott's Söhne, Mainz, ^c1921
Score in reduction 18 p.

385v [Concerto, violin, strings and   *10'*
organ (or cembalo), Op. VI no. 1, G minor.
Fanna no. F.I n.192] Edited by Alfred Einstein
1.Allegro [ma con forza] 2.Grave 3.Allegro
Solo Vn.-Cemb.-Str.
Ernst Eulenberg, London [n.d.]
Miniature score 16 p.
Op. VI first published ca.1716-17 by Jeanne
Roger, Amsterdam.

1128v [Concerto, violin, strings and   *9'*
organ (or cembalo), Op. VII no. 4, A minor.
Fanna no. F.I n.200] Edited by Alfred Einstein
1.Allegro 2.Adagio 3.Allegro
Solo Vn.-Str.
Ms.
Score 24 p.
Op. VII first published ca.1716-17 by Jeanne
Roger, Amsterdam.

267v [Concerto, violin, strings and   *10'*
organ or cembalo, La primavera, Op. VIII no. 1
E major. Fanna no. F.I n.22]
1.Giunt'é la Primavera 2.Largo e pianissimo
sempre 3.Danza pastorale
Solo Vn.-Org.-Str.
Kalmus, New York [n.d.]
Score 31 p.
Op. VIII, Il Cimento dell'Armonia e dell'
Inventione, first published ca.1725 by Michel
Le Cène, Amsterdam. The first four concertos
of Op. VIII are named for the seasons, each
preceded by a descriptive sonnet probably writ-
ten by the composer. First modern performance

Vivaldi, Antonio

of all four works, Augusteo, Rome, November 1927, Bernardino Molinari conductor.

1163s [Same as above] Elaborated by   *10'*
Bernardino Molinari
1.Giunt'è la primavera e festosetti 2.Largo
3.Danza pastorale
Solo Vn.-Cemb.,Org.-Str.
Ricordi, Milan, c1927
Score 27 p.

266v [Concerto, violin, strings and   *10'*
organ or cembalo, L'estate, Op. VIII no. 2,
G minor. Fanna no. F.I n.23]
1.Allegro non molto - Allegro 2.Adagio
3.Presto, Tempo impetuoso d'Estate
Solo Vn.-Org.-Str.
Kalmus, New York [n.d.]
Score 33 p.

1164s [Same as above] Elaborated by   *10'*
Bernardino Molinari
1.Andantino mosso 2.Adagio 3.Presto, tempo
impetuoso d'estate
Solo Vn.-Cemb.,Org.-Str.
Ricordi, Milan, c1927
Score 37 p.

265v [Concerto, violin, strings and organ *10'*
or cembalo, L'autunno, Op. VIII no. 3, F major.
Fanna no. F.I n.24]
1.Ballo e canto di villanelli 2.Adagio
3.Allegro
Solo Vn.-Pno.(Cemb.)-Str.
Kalmus, New York [n.d.]
Score 31 p.

1165s [Same as above] Elaborated by   *10'*
Bernardino Molinari
1.Allegro 2.Adagio 3.Allegro
Solo Vn.-Cemb.,Org.-Str.
Ricordi, Milan, c1927
Score 97 p.

264v [Concerto, violin, strings and organ *10'*
or cembalo, L'inverno, Op. VIII no. 4, F minor.
Fanna no. F.I n.25]
1.Allegro non molto 2.Largo 3.Allegro
Solo Vn.-Org.-Str.
Kalmus, New York [n.d.]
Score 31 p.

1166s [Same as above] Elaborated by   *10'*
Bernardino Molinari
1.Allegro non molto 2.Largo 3.Allegro
Solo Vn.-Cemb.,Org.-Str.
Ricordi, Milan, c1927
Score 28 p.

294v [Concerto, violin, strings and organ *12'*
(or cembalo), La cetra, Op. IX no. 12, B minor.
Fanna no. F.I n.50] Edited by Pina Carmirelli
1.Allegro non molto 2.Largo 3.Allegro
Solo Vn.-Cemb.(or Org.)-Str.
Zanibon, Padua, c1961
Score 30 p.
Op. IX, La Cetra, first published ca.1717-18
by Michel Le Cène, Amsterdam.

492m [Concerto, flute, strings and   *8'*
cembalo (or organ), La tempesta di mare,
Op. X no. 1, F major. Fanna no. F.VI n.12]
Edited by Wolfgang Fortner
1.Allegro 2.Largo 3.Presto
Solo Fl.-Cemb.-Str.
B. Schott's Söhne, Mainz, c1938
Score 16 p.
Op. X, first published ca.1729-30, by Michel
Le Cène, Amsterdam. This work constitutes
essentially the same music as the composer's
concerto La Tempesta di Mare in F major, Cata-
log no. 248m (Fanna no. F.XII n.28).

491m [Concerto, flute, strings and   *10'*
cembalo (or organ), La notte, Op. X no. 2,
G minor. Fanna no. F.VI n.13] Edited by Wolfgang Fortner
1.Largo 2.Fantasmi: Presto 3.Largo 4.Presto
5.Il sonno: Largo 6.Allegro
Solo Fl.-Cemb.-Str.
B. Schott's Söhne, Mainz, c1938
Score 15 p.

591m [Concerto, flute, strings and organ *11'*
or cembalo, Il gardellino, Op. X no. 3,
D major. Fanna no. F.VI n.14] Edited by Gustav
Lenzewski, Sr.
1.Allegro 2.Larghetto cantabile 3.Allegro
Solo Fl.-Cemb.-Str.
Chr. Friedrich Vieweg, Berlin [1930?]
Score 19 p.

1107m [Concerto, flute, strings and   *8'*
cembalo (or organ), Op. X no. 4, G major.
Fanna no. F.VI n.15] Edited by Wolfgang
Fortner
1.Allegro 2.Largo 3.Allegro
Solo Fl.-Cemb.-Str.
B. Schott's Söhne, Mainz, c1960
Score 12 p.

489m [Concerto, flute, strings and   *10'*
cembalo, Op. X no. 5, F major. Fanna no. F.VI
n.1] Edited by Wolfgang Fortner
1.Allegro ma non tanto 2.Largo cantabile
3.Allegro
Solo Fl.-Cemb.-Str.
B. Schott's Söhne, Mainz, c1936
Score 11 p.

495m [Concerto, flute, strings and   *10'*
cembalo (or organ), Op. X no. 6, G major.
Fanna no. F.VI n.16] Edited by Wolfgang
Fortner
1.Allegro 2.Largo 3.Allegro
Solo Fl.-Cemb.-Str.
Schott & Co., Ltd., London, c1950
Score 16 p.

1126v [Concerto, violin, strings and organ *14'*
(or cembalo), Il favorito, Op. XI no. 2,
E minor. Fanna no. F.I n.208] Edited by Alfred
Einstein
1.Allegro 2.Andante 3.Allegro
Solo Vn.-Org.-Str.
Ms.
Score 30 p.

Vivaldi, Antonio

Op. XI first published ca.1729-30 by Michel Le Cène, Amsterdam.

786v [Concerto, violin, strings and organ   *14'*
or cembalo, Op. XI no. 5, C minor. Fanna no.
F.I n.210] Edited by Alfred Moffat
1.Allegro ma non troppo 2.Largo molto espressivo 3.Allegro non molto
Solo Vn.-Str.
Score: Ms. 47 p.
Parts: B. Schott's Söhne, Mainz, ^c1920

485v [Concerto, violin, strings and organ   *13'*
or cembalo, Op. XII no. 1, G minor. Fanna no.
F.I n.211] Edited by Tivadar Nachèz
1.Allegro 2.Adagio 3.Allegro
Solo Vn.-Org.-Str.
Schott & Co., London, ^c1912
Score in reduction 19 p.
Op. XII first published ca.1729-30 by Michel Le Cène, Amsterdam.

861v [Concerto, violin, strings and   *9'30"*
organ or cembalo, Op. XII no. 2, D minor.
Fanna no. F.I n.212] Edited by Tivadar Nachèz
1.Allegro moderato 2.Larghetto 3.Allegretto grazioso
Solo Vn.-Str.
Score: Ms. 22 p.
Parts: B. Schott's Söhne, ^c1926

983v [Concerto, violin, strings and   *12'30"*
cembalo, Op. XII no. 5, B-flat major.
Fanna no. F.I n.86] Edited by Tivadar Nachèz
1.Allegro 2.Largo 3.Allegro
Solo Vn.-Org.-Str.
B. Schott's Söhne, Mainz, ^c1921
Score in reduction 20 p.

6384 Ercole sul Termodonte [Hercules at   *7'*
the river Thermodon. Two arias. Revised by
Alfredo Casella]
1.Chiare onde 2.Da due venti
Sop. Voice Solo-2 Solo Vn.-Cemb.-Str.
Carisch, Milan, ^c1940
Score 10 p.
From the opera. First modern performance Siena, 17 September 1939, Vivaldi Week organized by the Accademia Musicale Chigiana, Roberto Lupi conductor, Maria Teresa Pedicoli soloist.

2236s [Il Giustino. Sinfonia] Transcribed   *6'*
by Massimo Bruni
1.Allegro 2.Andante 3.Allegro
Cemb.-Str.
Carisch, Milan, ^c1959
Score 12 p.
From the opera based on the life of Justin I, Byzantine emperor from 518 to 527. First performance Rome, Carnival of 1724.

2235s [L'Olimpiade. Sinfonia] Elaborated   *6'*
by Virgilio Mortari
Str.
Carisch, Milan, ^c1939
Score 6 p.

From the opera in three acts with libretto by Pietro Metastasio. First performance Venice, Carnival of 1734.

635s [Sonata, 2 violins and violoncello   *8'*
or cembalo, Op. I no. 2, E minor. Fanna no.
F.XIII n.18. Transcribed for string orchestra
and piano by James Brown]
1.Preludio 2.Corrente 3.Giga 4.Tempo di gavotta
Pno.-Str.
Stainer & Bell, London, ^c1921
Score 8 p.
Op. 1 first published 1705 by Giuseppe Sala, Venice. Reissued by Estienne Roger, Amsterdam, ca.1712-13.

543c [Sonata, violoncello and continuo,   *16'*
Op. XIV(?) no. 4, B-flat major. Fanna no.
F.XIV n.4. Transcribed for violoncello and
string orchestra by Vincent d'Indy] Edited by
Marguerite Chaigneau
1.Largo 2.Allegro 3.Largo 4.Allegro
Solo Vc.-Str.
Maurice Senart, Paris, ^c1927
Score 12 p.
The six sonatas in this series were published without opus number ca.1740 by Le Clerc & Boivin, Paris.

447c [Sonata, violoncello and continuo,   *12'*
Op. XIV(?) no. 5, E minor. Fanna no. F.XIV
n.5. Transcribed for violoncello and string
orchestra by Paul Bazelaire]
1.Large 2.Allègre 3.Lent et expressif (alla siciliana) 4.Vif
Solo Vc.-Str.
Alphonse Leduc, Paris, ^c1942
Score 8 p.

531c [Same as above] Transcribed for   *12'*
violoncello and string orchestra by Vincent
d'Indy
1.Largo - Allegro 2.Largo (alla siciliana)
3.Allegro vivace
Solo Vc.-Str.
Maurice Senart, Paris, ^c1922
Score 8 p.

556c [Sonata, violoncello and continuo,   *16'*
Op. XIV(?) no. 6, B-flat major. Fanna no.
F.XIV n.6. Transcribed for violoncello and
string orchestra by Vincent d'Indy]
1.Largo - Allegro 2.Largo espressivo
3.Allegro giocoso
Solo Vc.-Str.
Maurice Senart, Paris, ^c1926
Score 9 p.

VLADIGEROV, PANTCHO.   Zurich 13 March 1899

2433 Vardar, Bulgarian rhapsody, Op. 16   *8'*
3*,3*,2,2-4,3,3,1-Timp.,Perc.-Hp.-Str.
Universal Edition, Vienna [n.d.]
Score 60 p.

VLAHOPOULOS, SOTIREOS.   St. Louis 1 June 1926

277m Elegy for oboe and strings
Solo Ob.-Str.
Ms.
Score 18 p.
Composed 1951.

2263s The moon pool   5'
Str.
Ms.
Score 11 p.
Inspired by Abraham Merritt's short story.
Composed 1958. First performance West Chester,
16 August 1963, Pennsylvania String Teachers
Association Youth String Symphony Orchestra,
Constantine Johns conductor.

VOGLER, GEORG JOSEPH (ABBÉ).
      Pleichach near Würzberg, Germany 15 June 1749
                        Darmstadt 6 May 1814

680p [Concerto, cembalo and strings, C major]
Edited by Gustav Lenzewski, Sr.
1.Allegro moderato 2.Andante
Cemb.(or Pno.)-Str.(Vn.I,Vn.II,Vc.,Cb.)
Chr. Fr. Vieweg, Berlin [n.d.]
Score 19 p.

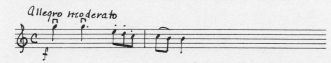

2330s [Mannheim ballet suite] Arranged by
Wolfgang Hofmann
1.Allegretto 2.Andantino 3.Largo 4.Contre-
dance 5.Allegretto – Allegro con spirito
Str.
Henry Litolff, Frankfurt, ᶜ1965
Score 19 p.

VOGLER, JOHANN KASPAR.   Arnstadt May 1696
                                  d. 1765

1724s Jesu Leiden, Pein und Tod [for   4'
organ. Transcribed by Leonid Leonardi]
Str.
Ms.
Score 4 p.
First performance of this transcription Bever-
ly Hills, 9 May 1940, Pollack String Ensemble,
Leonardi conductor. Bound with Walther, Lobe
den Herren den Mächtigen König der Ehren.

VOGLER, MARK. Dover, New Jersey 30 September 1952

7305 Symphony no. 1 [in 3 movements]
2,2,3*,2-4,2,3-Timp.,Perc.-Str.
Ms. ᶜ1976 by Mark Vogler

Score 108 p. Large folio
Composed 1976. Selected for performance by the
Orchestra Society of Philadelphia as part of
its Pennsylvania Composers Project 1977, made
possible by grants from the National Endow-
ment for the Arts and the Pennsylvania Council
on the Arts with performance materials pre-
pared by the Fleisher Collection of Orchestral
Music. First performance Drexel University,
Philadelphia, 27 March 1977, Orchestra Society
of Philadelphia, William Smith conductor.

VOGT, JOHANN (or JEAN).
        Gross-Tinz, near Liegnitz 17 January 1823
                      Eberswalde 31 July 1888

434p Andante et allegro de concert, Op. 33
Solo Pno.-2,2,2,2-2,2,1-Timp.-Str.
Score: Ms. 93 p.
Parts: Fr. Kistner, Leipzig [n.d.]

503s Nachtgesang [Night song]
Str.
Fr. Kistner, Leipzig [n.d.]
Score 3 p.

VOIGT, G. BERNHARD.

779m Albumblatt, Vergiss mein nicht!
Solo Ob.-Str.
Ms.
Score 6 p.

777m Heimaths-Sehnen [Longing for home,
romance]
Solo Ob.-Str.
Score: Ms. 7 p.
Parts: C.F. Kahnt, Leipzig [n.d.]

VOIGT, HERMANN.   Driesen 26 June 1851

1197s Schätzchen mein! [My darling]
Str.
Raabe & Plothow, Berlin, ᶜ1905
Score 5 p.

VOLBACH, FRITZ.
        Wipperfürth, near Cologne 17 December 1861
                    Wiesbaden 30 November 1940

5205 [Easter, symphonic poem, Op. 16]   17'
2,2(2nd alt. E.H.),2,2-4,2,3,1-Timp.,Perc.-
Org.,2Hp.-Str.
Schott's Söhne, Mainz, ᶜ1895
Score 65 p.

5206 Es waren zwei Königskinder, symphon-   15'
isches Dichtung, Op. 21
3*,3*,3*,2-4,3,3,1-Timp.,Perc.-2Hp.-Str.
Breitkopf & Härtel, Leipzig, ᶜ1900
Score 61 p.

5700 [Symphony, Op. 33, B minor]   30'
1.Lebhaft und trotzig 2.Scherzo 3.Adagio
molto 4.Finale
3(3rd alt. Picc.),3*,3*,3*-4,3,3,1-Timp.,Perc.
-Org.,Hp.-Str.
Hug, Leipzig, ᶜ1909
Score 142 p.

Volkmann, Friedrich Robert

VOLKMANN, FRIEDRICH ROBERT.
                    Lommatzsch, Saxony 6 April 1815
                    Budapest 29 October 1883

1017 Concert-Ouverture, C dur   5'
      2,2,2,2-2,2-Timp.-Str.
      Breitkopf & Härtel, Leipzig, ^c1895
      Score 19 p.
      Published posthumously, 1895.

477c [Concerto, violoncello, Op. 33,   10'
      A minor] Edited by Hugo Becker
      In one movement
      Solo Vc.-2,2,2,2-2,2-Timp.-Str.
      B. Schott's Söhne, Mainz, ^c1905
      Score 32 p.
      Composed 1854-57. First performance, Vienna,
      22 November 1857, Carl Schlesinger soloist.

      Musikalisches Bilderbuch, Op. 11. Arranged by
      Richard Hofmann (nos. 2-5) and J.M. Barnes
      (no. 1)
106s No. 1 In der Mühle [In the mill]
292s No. 2 Der Postillon
293s No. 3 Die Russen kommen
130s No. 4 Auf dem See [On the lake]
294s No. 5 Der Kukuk und der Wandersmann
           [The cuckoo and the wanderer]
      Str.
      Fr. Kistner, Leipzig [n.d.]
      Scores: 5 p., 9 p., 7 p., 5 p., 5 p.
      Originally composed for piano 4-hands.

5900 [Richard III. Complete music to
      Shakespeare's play, Op. 73]
      2(2nd alt. Picc.),2,2,2-4,2,3,1-Timp.,Perc.-
      Hp.(optional)-Str.
      Scores: B. Schott's Söhne, Mainz [1879] 79 p.
      Parts: Ms.
      Composed and first performed 1871.

5716 [Richard III. Overture, Op. 68]   14'
      2(2nd alt. Picc.),2,2,2-4,2,3,1-Timp.,Perc.-
      Str.
      B. Schott's Söhne, Mainz [1879]
      Score 43 p.
      Composed and first performed 1871.

131s [Serenade no. 1, Op. 62, C major]
      Str.
      B. Schott's Söhne, Mainz [n.d.]
      Score 23 p.

146s [Serenade no. 2, Op. 63, F major]   10'
      Str.
      Schott's Söhne, Mainz [1879]
      Score 31 p.

74s   [Serenade no. 3, Op. 69, D minor]
      Str.
      B. Schott's Söhne, Mainz [n.d.]
      Score 23 p.

5678 [Symphony no. 1, Op. 44, D minor]   30'
      1.Allegro patetico 2.Andante 3.Scherzo
      4.Finale
      2(2nd alt. Picc.),2,2,2-4,2,3-Timp.-Str.
      G. Heckenast, Pest [187-?]
      Score 187 p.

977   [Three Hungarian sketches, piano, Op. 24.
      Arranged by Akos von Buttykay]
      3*,3*,3*,2-4,3,3,1-Timp.,Perc.-Str.
      Rózsavölgyi, Budapest, ^c1803
      Score 45 p.

5656 [Wanderskizzen, Op. 23. In the tavern.
      Transcribed by Karl Schulz-Schwerin]
      2*,2(ad lib.),2(1Cl. in A,1Cl. in D),2-2,2,1
      (ad lib.)-Timp.,Perc.-Str.
      Fr. Kistner, Leipzig [1882?]
      Score 23 p.
      Originally composed for piano.

VOLLSTEDT, ROBERT.   Meldorf 19 December 1854
                           Hamburg 22 November 1919

1139s In Balletschuhen [In dancing-shoes] Op. 93
       Str.
       A.J. Benjamin, Hamburg [n.d.]
       Score 3 p.

1318s Ein Kuss in Ehren, kann niemand wehren!
       [There's nothing amiss in an honest kiss]
       Op. 30
       Str.
       Score: Ms. 4 p.
       Parts: Louis Oertel, Hannover [n.d.]

VOLPATTI, F.

1665s Minuetto, A major
       Str.
       Score: Ms. 11 p.
       Parts: E. Gaudet, Paris, ^c1915

1639s Rêverie, E major
       Solo Vn.-Str.
       Score: Ms. 4 p.
       Parts: E. Gaudet, Paris, ^c1915

VOORMOLEN, ALEXANDER NICOLAS.
                         b. Rotterdam 3 March 1895

5819 [The three knights, variations on a   16'
      Dutch tune]
      3(3rd alt. Picc.),3*,3*,3*-4,3,3,1-Timp.,Perc.
      -Cel.,2Hp.-Str.
      G. Alsbach, Amsterdam, ^c1932
      Score 60 p.
      Theme is from the Antwerps Liedboek, a 16th-
      century song collection. Composed 1927.

VORBERGER, FRIEDRICH.

808m [Concertino, 3 trumpets, E-flat major]
      Arranged by J. Schückel
      1.Allegro 2.Largo 3.Allegro brillante
      Solo Tpt.-1,2,2,2-2,2,1-Timp.-Str.
      Score: Ms. 48 p.
      Parts: Bellman & Thümer, Dresden [n.d.]

VOTICHENKO, SACHA.   Megene, Russia 1888

2485 Easter-chimes in Little Russia.   9'
      Orchestrated by Modest Altschuler
      3(3rd alt. Picc.),3*,2,2-4,3,3,1-Timp.,Perc.-
      Cel.,Hp.-Str.

C. Fischer, New York, ^c1922
Score 72 p.
Originally composed for tympanon and piano,
1916; orchestrated 1917. First performance
New York, 23 February 1919, Russian Symphony
Orchestra, Modest Altschuler conductor.

VREULS, VICTOR-JEAN-LÉONARD.
                        Verviers, Belgium 4 February 1876
                        Saint-Josse-ten-Noode,
                                near Brussels 26 July 1944

5579 [A midsummer night's dream. Fairy dances
      from Act 3]
      3(2nd&3rd alt. Picc.),3*,3(3rd alt. B.Cl.),2-
      4,3,3,1-Timp.,Perc.-Pno.,Cel.,Hp.-Chorus(SA)-
      Str.
      Cranz, Brussels, ^c1933
      Score 72 p.
      From the opera after Shakespeare's Midsummer
      Night's Dream. First performance Brussels,
      17 December 1925.

931v Romance pour violon et orchestre
      Solo Vn.-1,1,2,1-2Hn.-Timp.,Perc.-Str.
      Score: Ms. 11 p.
      Parts: Alph. Darimont, Bruxelles, ^c1924

5577 [The werewolf, choreographic legend]
      3(3rd alt. Picc.),3(3rd alt. E.H.),3(3rd alt.
      B.Cl.),3*-4,4,3,1-Timp.,Perc.-Pno.,Cel.,Hp.-
      Str.
      Cranz, Brussels, ^c1936
      Score 240 p.
      For the ballet in one act choreographed by
      François Ambrosiny. First performance Ghent,
      1937.

5576 [Werther, symphonic poem after Goethe's
      novel]
      3(3rd alt. Picc.),3*,3*,4*-3Sax.(all ad lib.)-
      4,3,Bugle,3,1-Timp.,Perc.-Cel.,2Hp.-Str.
      Cranz, Brussels, ^c1932
      Score 102 p.
      Composed 1908.

VUIDET, GASTON.

1527s Musiciens ambulants
       1*,0,1-Str.
       Paul Decourcelle, Nice [n.d.]
       Score 3 p.

1528s Les petites Saintes Marie
       Str.
       Paul Decourcelle, Nice [n.d.]
       Score 3 p.

625v Troubadour passant, Op. 35
      Solo Vn.-1,1,2,1-2Hn.-Str.
      Paul Decourcelle, Nice [n.d.]
      Score 4 p.

1530s Vénitienne, Op. 27
       Str.
       Paul Decourcelle, Nice [n.d.]
       Score 3 p.

1529s Un premier bal, Op. 42
       Str.
       Paul Decourcelle, Nice [n.d.]
       Score 3 p.

1526s Ave Maria
       Solo Fl., Solo Vn.-Str.
       Paul Decourcelle, Nice [n.d.]
       Score 3 p.

VUILLEMIN, LOUIS.   Nantes 1873
                                Paris 3 April 1929

1241 En Kernéo [In Cornwall] suite,   *16'*
      Op. 23
      3*,3*,2(1Cl. in E-flat),2,Sarrus.-4,3,3-Timp.,
      Perc.-Cel.,Hp.-Str.
      A. Durand, Paris, ^c1925
      Score 69 p.
      Composed 1908. First performance Paris 1910.

      Quatre danses, Op. 16
1999 No. 1 Bourrée   *4'*
      2,2,2,2-4,3,3,1-Timp.,Perc.-Pno.,Hp.-Str.
2000 No. 2 Gigue   *2'30"*
      3*,2,2,2-4,3,3-Timp.,Perc.-Hp.-Str.
2001 No. 3 Pavane   *6'*
      3(3rd alt. Picc.),2(2nd alt. E.H.),2,3*-4,3,3,
      1-Timp.,Perc.-Hp.-Str.
2002 No. 4 Passepied   *3'*
      3*,2,2,2-4,2,3,1-Timp.,Perc.-Pno.,Hp.-Str.
      A. Durand, Paris, ^c1924
      Scores: 28 p., 23 p., 28 p., 28 p.
      Composed 1923. First performance Paris, 1924.

VYNER, LOUIS.   Pittsburgh 1907

2672 Nocturne, for chamber orchestra   *6'*
      1,1,1,1-Hn.-Str.
      Ms.
      Score 10 p.
      Composed 1931. First performance, 1931, Curtis
      Institute of Music Symphony Orchestra, the
      composer conducting.

1717s Preludes   *11'*
       Str.(without Cb.)
       Ms.
       Score 25 p.
       Composed 1930. First performance Wilmington,
       Delaware, 27 January 1936, Wilmington Music
       School String Orchestra, the composer con-
       ducting.

913m Suite   *12'*
      1.Allemande 2.Corrente 3.Sarabande 4.Giga
      Soli: Fl.,Ob.,Cl.,Bn.,Hn.-2,2,2,2-4,2-Timp.-
      Str.
      Ms.
      Score 58 p.
      Originally composed 1932 for harp as The
      Rosamond Suite. Transcribed 1932.

Wachs, Paul

W

WACHS, PAUL ÉTIENNE VICTOR.
Paris 19 September 1851
St. Mandé, France 6 July 1915

205s Extase [Ecstasy]
Str.
Score: Ms. 7 p.
Parts: J. Hamelle, Paris [n.d.]

1509s Myosotis [Forget-me-not] Arranged by
L. Grus
Solo Vn.-Str.
Score: Ms. 5 p.
Parts: L. Grus, Paris [n.d.]

WAËL-MUNK, F.

932v Berceuse
Solo Vn.-1,1,1,1-Hn.-Hp.-Str.
Score: Ms. 11 p.
Parts: Evette & Schaeffer, Paris, ᶜ1923

WAELPUT, HENDRIK.
Ghent 26 October 1845
Ghent 8 July 1885

578m Serenade [A minor]
Solo Fl.-0,1,2,2-2,2-Timp.-Str.
Ms.
Score 19 p.

WAGENAAR, BERNARD.
Arnheim, Netherlands 18 July 1894
York Harbor, Maine 19 May 1971

2668 Divertimento in four movements   20'
1.Cortège 2.Paspy 3.Pastorale 4.Rondo
3*,2,3*,3*-4,3,3,1-Timp.,Perc.-Cel.,Hp.-Str.
C.C. Birchard, Boston, ᶜ1931 by Eastman School
of Music
Score 99 p.
Commissioned by Artur Bodanzky, for the
Society of the Friends of Music, 1927. Com-
posed 1928. First performance Detroit, 28
November 1929, Detroit Symphony Orchestra,
Ossip Gabrilovitch conductor.

4271 Fanfare for Airmen
See: TEN FANFARES BY TEN COMPOSERS FOR BRASS
AND PERCUSSION.

6289 Preamble for orchestra   5'
3*(2nd alt. Picc.II),3*,3*,3*-4,3,3,1-Timp.,
Perc.-Hp.-Str.
Ms.
Score 37 p. Large folio
Commissioned by the Juilliard School of Music
for the American Festival for its 50th anniversary, 1956. Composed 1955. First performance New York City, 10 February 1956,
Juilliard School Orchestra, Jean Morel conductor.

2669 Sinfonietta   12'
1.Con spirito 2.Adagietto 3.Finale
1,1,1,1-1,1,1,1-Timp.,Perc.-Pno.,Hp.-Str.
Cos-Cob-Press, New York, ᶜ1930
Score 47 p.
Composed 1929. First performance New York, 16
January 1930, New York Philharmonic, Willem
Mengelberg conductor. Chosen to represent
the U.S. at the Eighth Festival of the Inter-
national Society for Contemporary Music,
Liège, September 1930.

4839 Song of mourning: a reflection   6'
upon the slain Dutch patriots
1,1,1-2,2-B.Dr.,S.Dr.-Hp.-Str.
Ms. [C. Fischer, New York, ᶜ1944]
Score 13 p.
Commissioned by Netherlands America Founda-
tion. Composed 1944. First performance New
York, 1944, Hans Kindler conductor.

2698 [Symphony no. 1]   30'
1.Prologue 2.Allegro molto 3.Scherzo
4.Epilogue
3(3rd alt. Picc.),3*,4*(1Cl. in E-flat),4*-4,
3,3,1-Timp.,Perc.-Cel.,2Hp.-Str.
Ms.
Score 151 p.
Composed 1922-26. First performance New York,
7 October 1928, New York Philharmonic, Willem
Mengelberg conductor.

2776 Symphony no. 2   25'
1.Andante - Allegro 2.In modo di notturno
3.Scherzo 4.Finale
4(3rd alt. Picc.,Alto Fl.),4*,5*(1Cl. in E-
flat),4*-Ten.Sax.-6,Ten.Hn.,3,3,1-Timp.,
Perc.-Pno.,Cel.,2Hp.,Guit.-Str.
Ms.
Score 185 p.
Composed 1930. First performance New York,
10 November 1932, New York Philharmonic,
Arturo Toscanini conductor.

3680 [Symphony no. 3]   22'
1.Allegro 2.Intermezzo 3.Finale
3(3rd alt. Picc.),3*,4*,3*-4,3,3,1-Timp.,Perc.
-Pno.,Cel.,Hp.-Str.
Ms.
Score 87 p. Large folio
Completed 1935. First performance New York,
23 January 1937, Juilliard Graduate School
Orchestra, the composer conducting. Received
the Juillard Publication Award, 1942.

WAGENAAR, JOHAN.
Utrecht 1 November 1862
The Hague 17 June 1941

1323 Overture, Cyrano de Bergerac, Op. 23   12'
3(3rd alt. Picc.),2,2,2-4,3,3,1-Timp.,Trgl.-
Str.
F.E.C. Leuckart, Leipzig, ᶜ1906
Score 87 p.
Inspired by Edmond Rostand's play. Composed
1905.

WAGENSEIL, GEORG CHRISTOPH.   Vienna 15 January 1715
                                Vienna 1 March 1777

279p [Concerto, cembalo and strings,   16'
D major]
1.Allegro 2.Andante moderato 3.Allegro
Solo Cemb.-Str.(without Va.)
Breitkopf & Härtel, Leipzig [1964]
Score 43 p.
*Listed in Part IV of the Breitkopf Thematic
Catalog, 1763.*

431c [Concerto, violoncello, strings   ca.19'
and cembalo, A major] Edited by Enrico
Mainardi and Fritz Racek
1.Allegro 2.Largo 3.Allegro moderato
Solo Vc.-Cemb.-Str.
Doblinger, Vienna, C1960
Score 28 p.
Composed 1752.

414c [Concerto, violoncello and orchestra,
C major] Edited by Fritz Racek
1.Moderato 2.Larghetto 3.Allegro
Solo Vc.-2Ob.-2,2(optional)-Cemb.-Str.
Doblinger, Vienna, C1963
Score 58 p.
Composed 1763.

6336 [Symphony for orchestra, D major]
1.Allegro 2.Andante 3.Tempo di menuetto
2,2-2,2-Timp.-Cemb.-Str.
Score: Denkmäler der Tonkunst in Österreich,
Vol. XV/2. Artaria, Vienna, and Breitkopf &
Härtel, Leipzig, 1908. Edited by Karl
Horwitz and Karl Riedel. 12 p.
Parts: Ms. C1976 by The Fleisher Collection of
Orchestral Music, Free Library of Philadelphia
Composed 1746.

2299s [Symphony, string orchestra, D major]
1.Allegro molto 2.Menuetto 3.Andante
4.Allegro
Cemb.-Str.(without Va.)
Score: Denkmäler der Tonkunst in Österreich,
Vol. XV/2. Artaria, Vienna, and Breitkopf &
Härtel, Leipzig, 1908. Edited by Karl Horwitz
and Karl Riedel. 9 p.
Parts: Ms. C1976 by The Fleisher Collection of
Orchestral Music, Free Library of Philadelphia

WAGHALTER, IGNATZ.   Warsaw 15 March 1882
                            New York 7 April 1949

687v [Concerto, violin, Op. 15, A major]
1.Allegro moderato 2.Andante sostenuto
3.Allegro giocoso, con spirito
Solo Vn.-2(2nd alt. Picc.),2,2,2-4,2-Timp.-Str.
Simrock, Berlin, C1911
Score 47 p.

1011v Rhapsodie, Op. 9 [A-flat major]
Solo Vn.-2,2,2,2-2,2-Timp.-Str.
Mitteldeutscher Musikverlag, Leipzig [n.d.]
Score 19 p.

WAGNER, FRANZ THEODOR.
  See: WAGNER, THEODOR.

WAGNER, FRIEDRICH.   Kipsdorf 8 October 1889

1541s Am Abend [In the evening] Idylle, Op. 106
Str.(Cb. optional)
[J.G. Seeling, Dresden, n.d.]
Score 2 p.

WAGNER, JOSEF FRANZ.   Vienna 20 March 1856
                           Vienna June 1908

1291s [Murmuring seashells, Op. 325]
Perc.-Str.
J. Eberle [Vienna, n.d.]
Score 7 p.

WAGNER, JOSEPH FREDERICK.
        Springfield, Massachusetts 9 January 1900
                Los Angeles 12 October 1974

5104 American jubilee, a concert   5'30"
overture for band
2,2,6*(1Cl. in E-flat,1Alto Cl.),2-4Sax.-4,3,2
Cnt.,3,2Bar.,2-Timp.,Perc.
Ms. [M. Witmark, New York, C1945?]
Score 21 p. Large folio
*Composed 1943. First performance New York,
June 1945, Goldman Band, the composer con-
ducting.*

5140 American jubilee, a concert overture   6'
3*,2,2,2-4,3,3,1-Timp.,Perc.-Hp.-Str.

Wagner, Joseph

Ms. [Remick Music, New York, ^C1948?]
Score 24 p. Large folio
Originally composed for band, 1943. Transcribed 1946. First performance Grant Park Concerts, Chicago, 1948, Nicolai Malko conductor.

1051m Concertino for harp and orchestra   15'
1.Moderate - quietly 2.Rather slowly 3.Fast
Solo Hp.-2,2,2,2-2,2-Timp.,Perc.-Cel.-Str.
Ms. [Lyra Music, New York, ^Cn.d.]
Score 43 p.
Composed 1945-47. First performance Baltimore, 2 February 1949, National Symphony Orchestra, Howard Mitchell conductor, Sylvia Meyer soloist. Awarded First Prize in the Northern California Harpists' Association's Annual Competition, 1963.

714p [Concerto, piano, G minor]   12'
1.Allegro moderato 2.Intermezzo 3.Allegro moderato
Solo Pno.-1,1,2,1-2Hn.,2Cnt.-Timp.,Perc.-Str.
M. Witmark, New York, ^C1935
Score 56 p.
Originally composed 1920 as Miniature Concerto for piano and orchestra. Rewritten 1929. First performance Rutgers University, New Brunswick, New Jersey, 3 August 1930, the composer conducting, Minnie Kahn soloist.

1053m Concerto grosso for symphonic   17'30"
band
1.Introduction and Allegro moderato
2.Passacaglia 3.Gavotte 4.Gigue
3 Solo Cnt., 1 Solo Bar.-3*,2,6*(1Cl. in E-flat, 1Alto Cl.),2-4Sax.-4,2,3Cnt.,3,Bar.,2-Timp.,Perc.-Cb.
Ms. [M. Witmark, New York, ^C1949]
Score 56 p. Large folio
Composed 1949. First performance Washington, D.C., July 1953, United States Marine Corps Band, Lt. Col. William F. Santelmann conductor.

4582 Dance divertissement, 5   14'
abstractions with a prologue
2,2,2,2-2,2,2-Timp.,Perc.-Str.
Ms. [Robert B. Brown Music, New York, ^Cn.d.]
Score 37 p. Large folio
Composed 1942. First performance Boston, 1943, Boston Civic Symphony Orchestra with Jan Veen and His Dancers, the composer conducting.

800p Fantasy in technicolor [1960]   13'
Solo Pno.-3*,2,3*,2-2Alto Sax.,Ten.Sax.-4,3,
3,Bar.(optional),1-Timp.,Perc.-Cb.
Ms.
Score 63 p. Large folio
Originally composed for piano and orchestra, 1948. This version, 1960. First performance Los Angeles, 17 January 1963, Cal Arts Symphonic Wind Ensemble, the composer conducting, Carl Matthes soloist.

3301 Four miniatures   12'
1.Preface 2.A sarabande for the Infanta

3.A berceuse for a princess 4.March humoresque
2(2nd alt. Picc.),2,2,2-2,2-Timp.,Perc.-Str.
Ms.
Score 18 p. Large folio
Originally composed for piano, 1935. Transcribed 1939. First performance broadcast from New York, 15 May 1941, NBC Symphony Orchestra, Frank Black conductor.

1871s From the North Shore, two sea   7'
pieces
1.Andante con moto, ma mistirioso 2.Allegro con brio e agitato
Str.
Ms.
Score 14 p.
Written for Alexander Thiede. Composed 1942. First performance Boston, 10 March 1942, Women's Symphony Society, Alexander Thiede conductor.

715p A fugal triptych [original version]   12'
1.Scherzo dramatico 2.Sarabande 3.Introduction and fugue
Solo Pno.-Timp.,Perc.-Str.
Ms.
Score 28 p. Large folio
Composed 1936-37. First performance Boston, 25 May 1941, Women's Symphony Society, Alexander Thiede conductor, Leonard Bernstein soloist.

345p A fugal triptych, for piano, per-   17'
cussion and strings [revised version]
1.Allegro con brio 2.Andante con moto
3.Allegro animato
Solo Pno.-Timp.,Perc.-Cel.,Hp.-Str.
Ms.
Score 53 p. Large folio
Revised with celesta and harp parts added, 1954.

4135 Hudson River legend. Complete ballet *and*
Suite from the ballet, in 5 movements
3*,2,2,2-4,3,3,1-Timp.,Perc.-Pno.,Cel.-Str.
Complete ballet: Ms. Score 214 p.
Suite: E.B. Marks, New York, ^C1944   8'
Composed 1941-43. First performance of ballet, Boston, 1 March 1944, Boston Civic Symphony Orchestra with Jan Veen and His Dancers, Arthur Fiedler conductor.

1056m Introduction and rondo   8'
Solo Tpt.-2,2,2,2-2Hn.-Timp.,Perc.-Str.
Ms. [Chappell, Toronto, ^C1950?]
Score 35 p. Large folio
Composed 1950.

461m Introduction and scherzo   10'
Solo Bn.-Str.
Ms.
Score 17 p. Large folio
Composed 1950-54. First performance New York, 1958, Howard Shanet conductor.

2110s Litany for peace [revised version]   12'
Str.
Ms.

Score 9 p.
Transcribed 1956 from String Quartet in C minor, composed 1940. Revised 1959. First performance Oklahoma City, 20 January 1963, Oklahoma City Symphony, Guy Fraser Harrison conductor.

2114s Music of the sea (1954)   ca.10'
Str.
Ms.
Score 22 p.
A reworking (1954) of From the North Shore. First performance Philadelphia, 13 December 1958, University of Pennsylvania Gallery Concert Orchestra, Joseph Primavera conductor.

4532 Northland evocation, a landscape   13'
3(3rd alt. Picc.),2,3(3rd alt. B.Cl.),2-4,3,
3-Timp.,Perc.-Cel.-Sop. Voice(s) or Tpt.-Str.
Ms. [Southern, New York, c1950?]
Score 26 p. Large folio
Original title: Northern Saga. Composed 1949. First performance Helsinki, 19 August 1949, Finnish Radio Orchestra, the composer conducting.

5613 Panorama   8'
3*,2,2,2-4,3,3,1-Timp.,Perc.-Pno.(alt. Cel., optional)-Str.
Ms.
Score 39 p. Large folio
Composed 1948-56 using themes from the ballet Hudson River Legend. First performance Buffalo, 1 March 1957, Buffalo Philharmonic, Willis Page conductor.

5593 Pastoral costarricense, un recuerdo   10'
sentimental
1,1,1,1-2Hn.-Timp.,Perc.-Cel. or Pno.-Str.
Ms.
Score 15 p.
Composed 1955. First performance in an MBC radio broadcast, 24 January 1960, Oklahoma City Symphony, Guy Fraser Harrison conductor. Received the Benjamin Award Special Honorarium, 1956.

4046 Processions medieval, a choreo-   7'30"
graphic episode
3*,3*,3*,2(or 3*,2,2,2)-4,3,3,1-Timp.,Perc.-Pno.-Str.
Ms.
Score 40 p. Large folio
Originally composed for two pianos, 1935. This version 1937. First performance, under the title Festival Processions, Columbus, Ohio, 16 December 1946, Columbus Symphony Orchestra, Izler Solomon conductor.

4581 Radio City snapshots   7'
1.Just looking around 2.Waldteufel takes a look at the skaters 3.Round trip to the Rainbow Room 4.Resting in the Plaza 5.The Rockettes do a Can-Can
3*,2,2,2-3Sax.(2Alto,Ten.)-4,3,3,1-Timp., Perc.-Cel.,Hp.-Str.
Ms. [Mills Music, New York, c1946?]
Score 40 p. Large folio

Composed 1945. First performance St. Paul, 6 August 1947, St. Paul Pops, the composer conducting.

4005 Rhapsody, two themes with   9'30"
variations [revised version]
Cl.-Pno.-Str.
Boosey & Hawkes, New York, c1942
Score 16 p.
Composed 1928; revised 1937. First performance of this version Boston, 14 May 1941, Boston Civic Symphony Orchestra, the composer conducting, Victor Polatschek clarinetist.

4488 Sinfonietta no. 1 [revised version]   15'
1.Calmly 2.Gay 3.Calmly
2(2nd alt. Picc.),2,2,2-2,2-Timp.,Perc.-Pno.-Str.
Ms. [Southern Music, New York, c1945?]
Score 62 p.
Composed 1931. First performance Boston, 1932, Boston Civic Symphony Orchestra, the composer conducting. Revised 1944.

1872s Sinfonietta no. 2   15'
1.Allegro energico 2.Allegro risoluto
3.Andante mestoso
Str.
Ms.
Score 24 p.
Commissioned by the Boston String Orchestra, 1941. Composed 1941. First performance Boston, 22 February 1942, Boston String Orchestra, Jules Wolffers conductor.

5781 Symphonic transitions   9'
3*,2,6*(1Cl. in E-flat,1Alto Cl.),2-4Sax.-4, 2,3Cnt.,3,Bar.,Tuba-Timp.,Perc.-Cb.
Ms. [Mills Music, New York, c1960]
Score 42 p. Large folio
A reworking of Variations on an Old Form (Catalog no. 4047). This version 1958-59. First performance 26 March 1961, University of Wisconsin Concert Band, Raymond F. Dvorak conductor.

2864 [Symphony no. 1]   22'
1.Lento, molto sostenuto 2.Vivace 3.Lento - Allegro con spirito
3(3rd alt. Picc.),3(3rd alt. E.H.),3(3rd alt. B.Cl.),3(3rd alt. C.Bn.)-4,3,3,1-Timp.,Perc.-Pno.,Hp.-Str.
Ms.
Score 120 p.
Composed 1934. First performance Rochester, 19 October 1944, Rochester Symphony Orchestra, Howard Hanson conductor.

4646 Symphony no. 2 [revised version]   30'
1.With dramatic intensity 2.With continuous restless energy 3.With dignified - noble symplicity 4.With strong drive and power
3(3rd alt. Picc.),2,2,2-4,3,3,1-Timp.,Perc.-Pno.-Str.
Ms.
Score 103 p. Large folio
Composed 1945. Revised 1960. First performance Providence, 12 February 1963, Rhode

Wagner, Joseph

Island Philharmonic Orchestra, Francis Madeira conductor.

4897 Symphony no. 3, in one movement   25'
3*,2,2,2-4,3,3,1-Timp.,Perc.-Str.
Ms.
Score 88 p. Large folio
Composed 1950-51.

1769s Two moments musical   9'
1.Nocturne 2.Motion
Str.
A. Cranz, Brussels, ᶜ1938
Score 16 p.
Alternate title: Two Miniatures. Composed 1935. First performance Peterborough, New Hampshire, 7 July 1940, Women's Symphony Society of Boston, Alexander Thiede conductor.

4047 Variations on an old form   9'
3*,2,2,2-4,4,3,1-Timp.,Perc.-Org.(ad lib.)-Str.
C.C. Birchard, Boston, ᶜ1941
Score 43 p.
Composed 1940. First performance Washington, D.C., 1941, National Symphony Orchestra, Hans Kindler conductor. Rewritten for band as Symphonic Transitions (Catalog no. 5781).

WAGNER, RICHARD.   Leipzig 22 May 1813
    Venice 13 February 1883

Full name: Wilhelm Richard Wagner

674m Adagio   4'
Solo Cl.-Str.
Breitkopf & Härtel, Leipzig, ᶜ1926
Score 4 p.
Attribution uncertain.

6925 [Album sonata for Mathilde Wesendonk, E-flat major. Transcribed by K. Müller-Berghaus]
3,3*,3*,2-4,2,3,1-Timp.-Hp.-Str.
B. Schott's Söhne, Mainz [1878 or 1879]
Score 37 p.
Originally composed for piano, 1853.

611m Ein Albumblatt. Transcribed by   3'
F. Gumbert
Solo Hn.-1,0,2,2-2Hn.-Str.
E.W. Fritzsch, Leipzig [n.d.]
Score 15 p.
Originally composed for piano, 1861.

238 [Same as above] Transcribed by   3'
C. Reichelt
1,1,2,2-2,2-Timp.-Str.
C.F.W. Siegel, Leipzig [n.d.]
Score 15 p.

487v [Same as above] Transcribed by   3'
August Wilhelmj
Solo Vn.-1,0,2,2-2Hn.-Str.
C.F.W. Siegel, Leipzig [n.d.]
Score 19 p.

239 [American Centennial march]   12'
4*,3,3,4*-4,4,3,1-Timp.,Perc.-Str.
B. Schott's Söhne, Mainz [1876]

Score 47 p.
Composed 1876 for the opening of the American Centennial celebration. First performance Philadelphia, 10 May 1876, Theodore Thomas conductor.

5232 [Christopher Columbus overture] Edited by Felix Mottl
3*,2,2,2-4,6,3,1-Timp.-Str.
Breitkopf & Härtel, Leipzig, ᶜ1908
Score 44 p.
Composed for Theodor Apel's drama Columbus, 1835. First performance Magdeburg, 1835.

949 [Concert overture, C major]   9'
2,2,2,2-4,2,3-Timp.-Str.
Breitkopf & Härtel, Leipzig, ᶜ1926
Score 25 p.
Composed 1832. First performance Leipzig, 13 April 1833.

927 [Concert overture, D minor]   7'
2,2,2,2-4,2-Timp.-Str.
Breitkopf & Härtel, Leipzig, ᶜ1926
Score 23 p.
Composed 1831. First performance Leipzig, 23 February 1832.

190 [A Faust overture. Revised version]   12'
3*,2,2,3-4,2,3,1-Timp.-Str.
Kalmus, New York [n.d.]
Score 69 p.
Composed 1839-40. Revised 1855. First performance Zurich, 23 January 1855.

1053 Die Feen [overture]   12'
2,2,2,2-4,2,3-Timp.-Str.
Breitkopf & Härtel, Leipzig, ᶜ1912
Score 27 p.
Composed 1833-34. First performance Magdeburg, 1834, the composer conducting.

481 Der fliegende Holländer. Ouverture   11'
3*,3*,2,2-4,2,3,1-Timp.-Hp.-Str.
Luck's, Detroit [n.d.]
Score 51 p.
From the opera based on Heinrich Heine's story. Composed 1841. First performance Dresden, 2 January 1843, the composer conducting.

694 [Götterdämmerung. Prologue.   10'
Siegfried's Rhine journey] Edited by E. Humperdinck
2*(or3*),2,2,2-4,3(or 2),3,1-Timp.,Perc.-Hp.-Str.
Kalmus, New York [n.d.]
Score 22 p.
From the opera composed 1870-72. First performance Bayreuth, 17 August 1876, Hans Richter conductor.

692 [Götterdämmerung. Act III. Funeral   8'
march]
4*,4*,4*,3-4,4,4,5-Timp.,Perc.-6Hp.-Str.
B. Schott's Söhne, Mainz [1876]
Score 15 p.

Wagner, Richard

237 [Götterdämmerung. Act III. Song of   10'
the Rhinedaughters] Edited by H. Zumpe
2,2,2,2-4,2,3-Timp.,Perc.-Hp.-Str.
B. Schott's Söhne, Mainz [1879]
Score 53 p.

257 Huldigungs-Marsch [March of homage]   5'
3*,2,3*,2-4,3,3,1-Timp.,Perc.-Str.
B. Schott's Söhne, Mainz [1871]
Score 23 p.
Originally composed for band, 1864.

1018 Kaisermarsch   9'
3*,3,3,3-4,3,3,1-Timp.,Perc.-Str.
C.F. Peters, Leipzig [1894?]
Score 35 p.
*Composed 1871. First performance Berlin, 5
May 1871.*

2425 König Enzio Ouvertüre. Edited by   7'
Felix Mottl
2,2,2,2-4,2-Timp.-Str.
Breitkopf & Härtel, Leipzig, C1908
Score 36 p.
*Inspired by Ernst Raupach's play. Composed
1832. First performance Leipzig, March 1832.*

1163 Das Liebesverbot. Ouvertüre   9'
3*,2,2,2-4,4,3,Ophicl.-Timp.,Perc.-Str.
Breitkopf & Härtel, Leipzig, C1922
Score 53 p.
*From the opera based on Shakespeare's Measure
for Measure. Composed 1835-36. First performance Magdeburg, 29 March 1836, the composer conducting.*

53 [Lohengrin. Prelude]   7'
3,3*,3*,3-4,3,3,1-Timp.,Cym.-Str.
Breitkopf & Härtel, Leipzig [n.d.]
Score 12 p.
*From the opera composed 1845-48. First per-
formance Weimar, 28 August 1850, Franz Liszt
conductor.*

924 [Lohengrin. Act III, Introduction]   3'
3,3,3,3-4,3,3,1-Timp.,Perc.-Str.
Kalmus, New York [n.d.]
Score 12 p.

1490 [Lohengrin. Act III. Procession to   3'
the cathedral]
3,3*,3*,3-4,3,3,1-Timp.-Men's Chorus-Str.
Breitkopf & Härtel, Leipzig [n.d.]
Score 8 p.

697 [Die Meistersinger von Nürnberg.   9'
Prelude]
3*,2,2,2-4,3,3,1-Timp.,Perc.-Hp.-Str.
Breitkopf & Härtel, Wiesbaden, C1969
Score 40 p.
*From the opera composed 1862-67. First per-
formance of Prelude Leipzig, 1 November 1862,
the composer conducting. First performance of
opera Munich, 21 June 1868, Hans von Bülow
conductor.*

5737 [Die Meistersinger von Nürnberg.   13'
Act III. 1.Prelude 2.Dance of the apprentices

3.Procession of the mastersingers 4.Greetings
to Hans Sachs]
3*,2,2,2-4,3,3,1-Timp.,Perc.-Hp.-Str.
Schott's Söhne, Mainz [187-?]
Score 33 p.

1424s [Die Meistersinger von Nürnberg. Act III:
Quintet. Transcribed by G. Sandre]
Str.
B. Schott's Söhne, Mainz [n.d.]
Score 3 p.

691 [Parsifal. Prelude *and* Act III: 13'
Closing scene]
3,4*,4*,4-4,3,3,1-Timp.-2Hp.-Str.
B. Schott's Söhne, Mainz [1883]
Score 29 p.
*From the opera composed 1877-82. First per-
formance Bayreuth, 26 July 1882, Hermann Levi
conductor.*

1522 [Parsifal. Act I: Scene-change   28'
music and closing scene]
2,2,2,2-4,2,3,1-Timp.,Perc.-Str.
B. Schott's Söhne, Mainz [1887?]
Score 61 p.

690 [Parsifal. Act III. Good Friday   12'
spell] Arranged by Wouter Hutschenruyter
3,4*,4*,4-4,3,3,1-Timp.-Str.
Breitkopf & Härtel, New York, C1914
Score 15 p.

1145 Polonia Ouvertüre. Edited by Felix   11'
Mottl
4(2 are Picc.),2,2,2-4,4,3,1-Timp.,Perc.-Str.
Breitkopf & Härtel, Leipzig, C1908
Score 64 p.
*Completed 1836. First performance Palermo, 24
or 25 December 1881, the composer conducting.*

696 [Das Rheingold. Finale: Entrance of   9'
the gods into Valhalla] Edited by H. Zumpe
2,2,2,2-4,3,3,1-Timp.,Cym.-Hp.-Str.
Kalmus, New York [n.d.]
Score 37 p.
*From the opera composed 1853-54. First per-
formed Munich, 22 September 1869, Franz
Wüllner conductor.*

96 [Rienzi. Overture]   12'
3*(2nd alt. Picc.II),2,2,2,Serpent-4,4,3,1-
Timp.,Perc.-Str.
Luck's, Detroit [n.d.]
Score 62 p.
*From the opera composed 1838-40. First per-
formance Dresden, 20 October 1842, Karl Gott-
lieb Reissiger conductor.*

1233 [Rienzi. Act II. Peace march]   6'
3*,2,2,2,Serpent-4,3,3,Ophicl.-Timp.-Str.
A. Fürstner, Berlin [n.d.]
Score 11 p.

1466 [Rienzi. Act II. Pantomime]   15'
3*,2,2,3-4,4,3,1-Timp.,Perc.-Hp.-Str.
A. Fürstner, Berlin [n.d.]
Score 39 p.

Wagner, Richard

5222 [Rule Britannia overture] Edited by   10'
Felix Mottl
4*(2Picc.),2,3(1Cl. in F,2Cl. in C),3*-4,
4,3,Ophicl.-Timp.,Perc.-Str.
Breitkopf & Härtel, Leipzig, c1908
Score 48 p.
*Composed 1836 as a tribute to the English
people; never performed. Manuscript lost;
rediscovered among papers from the Leicester
Opera House band, 1904.*

693 [Siegfried. Act III. Forest murmurs]   8'
2(2nd alt. Picc.),2,2,2-4,2,3,1-Timp.,Perc.-
Str.
B. Schott's Söhne, Mainz [1878]
Score 34 p.
*From the opera composed 1856-69. First per-
formance Bayreuth, 16 August 1876, Hans
Richter conductor.*

99 Siegfried-Idyll   17'
1,1,2,1-2,1-Str.
Breitkopf & Härtel, Wiesbaden [n.d.]
Score 21 p.
*Composed 1870 to honor the composer's son.
First performance in Wagner's home, Trieb-
schen, 25 December 1870 (Cosima Wagner's
birthday).*

891 [Symphony, C major]   26'
1.Sostenuto e maestoso - Allegro con brio
2.Andante ma non troppo 3.Allegro assai
4.Allegro molto e vivace
2,2,2,3*-4,2,3-Timp.-Str.
M. Brockhaus, Leipzig, c1911
Score 87 p.
*Composed 1832. First public performance
Leipzig, 15 December 1832, Ch. Gottlieb
Müller conductor.*

98 [Tannhäuser. Overture]   14'
3(3rd alt. Picc.),2,2,2-4,3,3,1-Timp.,Perc.-
Str.
Breitkopf & Härtel, London [n.d.]
Score 68 p.
*From the opera composed 1843-44. First per-
formance Dresden, 19 October 1845, the com-
poser conducting. First concert performance
of overture Leipzig, 12 February 1846, Felix
Mendelssohn conductor. Opera revised and
Venusberg music added, 1860. First perform-
ance Paris, 13 March 1861.*

6942 [Tannhäuser. Act I. Venusberg   12'
music (Bacchanale)]
3*,2,2,2-4,3,3,1-Timp.,Perc.-Hp.-Str.
Kalmus, New York [n.d.]
Score 42 p.

473 [Tannhäuser. Act II. Entrance of the   5'
guests into the Wartburg]
3(3rd alt. Picc.),2,2,2-4,3,3,1-Timp.,Perc.-
Str.
A. Fürstner, Berlin [1891?]
Score 32 p.

935 [Tannhäuser. Act III. Introduction]   4'
Edited by Wouter Hutschenruyter

3*,2,2,2-4,3,3,1-Timp.-Str.
Breitkopf & Härtel, Leipzig, c1914
Score 7 p.

35 Träume [Dreams] Transcribed by Johan   4'
Svendsen
2,2,2,2-2Hn.-Timp.-Str.
B. Schott's Söhne, Mainz [1894]
Score 5 p.

97 [Tristan und Isolde. Prelude *and*   16'
Act III. Isolda's love death]
3(3rd alt. Picc.),3*,3*,3-4,3,3,1-Timp.-Hp.-
Str.
Kalmus, New York [n.d.]
Score 28 p.
*From the opera composed 1857-59. First per-
formance Munich, 10 June 1865, Hans von Bülow
conductor.*

1541 [Tristan und Isolde. Act III. Introduction.
Arranged by Arthur Seidel]
Solo E.H.-0,1,2,2-4Hn.-Timp.-Str.
Breitkopf & Härtel, Leipzig [n.d.]
Score 7 p.

352 Tristan und Isolde. Act III. Tristan's   3'
vision. Edited by Arthur Seidel
2,3*,3*,2-4,2,3,1-Timp.-Hp.-Str.
Breitkopf & Härtel, Leipzig [1894?]
Score 11 p.

353 [Tristan und Isolde. Excerpts   15'
arranged as tone pictures by Fritz Hoffmann]
8 excerpts, played without pause
2(2nd alt. Picc.),2(2nd alt. E.H.),3*,2-4,2,
3,1-Timp.-Hp.-Str.
Breitkopf & Härtel, Leipzig, c1908
Score 84 p.

1078 [Die Walküre. Act I. Siegmund's   3'
love song]
2,2,2,2-4,2,3,1-Hp.-Str.
B. Schott's Söhne, Mainz [1897?]
Score 15 p.
*From the opera composed 1854-56. First per-
formance Munich, 26 June 1870, Franz Wüllner
conductor.*

4001 [Die Walküre. Act III. The ride   5'
of the Valkyries]
4(2 are Picc.),4*,4*,3-8,3,4,Cb. Tuba-Timp.,
Perc.-Str.
B. Schott's Söhne, Mainz [1877?]
Score 47 p.

354 [Same as above] Edited by Wouter   5'
Hutschenruyter
3*,3*,4*,3-6,3,3,1-Timp.,Perc.-Str.
Breitkopf & Härtel, Leipzig, c1916
Score 45 p.

695 [Die Walküre. Act III. Wotan's   18'
farewell to Brünnhilde and magic fire music]
2(2nd alt. Picc.),2,2,2-4,2,3,1-Timp.,Perc.-
Hp.-Str.
B. Schott's Söhne, Mainz [1878?]
Score 67 p.

WAGNER, SIEGFRIED.
Triebschen, Switzerland 6 June 1869
Bayreuth, Germany 4 August 1930

896v [Concerto, violin, G major]
In one movement
Solo Vn.-2(2nd alt. Picc.),2,2,2-4,2-Timp.,
Perc.-Str.
C. Giessel, Bayreuth, ^c1915
Score 83 p.
Composed 1915.

616m Conzert-Stück [F major]
Solo Fl.-0,2,2,2-4Hn.-Timp.-Str.
C. Giessel, Bayreuth, ^c1913, 1914
Score 39 p.
Composed 1913.

WAGNER, THEODOR.
Loeberschütz 17 May 1870
Eisenach 7 May 1931

Also known as: Franz Theodor Wagner; Theodor
Wagner-Loeberschütz

[Two pieces, Op. 17]
608s No. 1 Elegie
718s No. 2 Tanz
Str.
C.F. Schmidt, Heilbronn a.N. [n.d.]
Scores: 2p., 2 p.

WAHLBERG, RUNE.   Gävle, Sweden 15 March 1910

395v Meditation, F-dur   *5'*
Solo Vn.-1,1,2,2-2Hn.-Str.
C. Gehrmans, Stockholm, ^c1944
Score 8 p.

5032 [Nordic suite]   *21'*
1.Preludium 2.[Herdsman's song and night
tune] 3.[Away over the meadows] 4.[And the
trees are in bloom]
2(2nd alt. Picc.),2,2,2-2,2,3,1-Timp.,Perc.-
Str.
Ms.
Score 87 p.
*First performance Sandviken, Sweden, 5 March
1944, Orchestra Society of Sandviken, Eric
Bengtson conductor.*

5024 [Symphony no. 1, F major]   *33'*
1.Allegro moderato 2.Lento 3.Scherzo
(Papillons) 4.Andante - Allegro
3*,2,2,3*-2Alto Sax.-4,3,3,1-Timp.,Perc.-Hp.-
Str.
Ms.
Score 167 p.
*First performance Gävle, Sweden, 10 October
1948, Orchestra Society of Gävle, the com-
poser conducting.*

WAILLY, LOUIS AUGUSTE PAUL DE.   Amiens 16 May 1854
Paris 18 June 1933

871 Sous un balcon, sérénade   *4'*
1,1,1,1-2Hn.-Str.
[n.p., n.d.]
Score 11 p.
Composed 1893.

WALD, MAX.   Litchfield, Illinois 14 July 1889
Dowagiac, Michigan 14 August 1954

2882 The dancer dead (pagan epitaph)   *14'*
3(3rd alt. Picc.),3*,3*,3-4,3,3,1-Timp.,Perc.
-Cel.,Hp.-Str.
Ms.
Score 55 p.
*Inspired by an epitaph from the Greek Anthol-
ogy. Composed 1931. First performance over
radio, New York, 1 May 1932, NBC Symphony
Orchestra, Eugene Goossens conductor.
Awarded second prize in the NBC Competition,
1932.*

3020 Overture, the streets of spring   *8'*
3(3rd alt. Picc.),3*,3*,3-4,3,3,1-Timp.,Perc.-
Cel.,Hp.-Str.
Ms.
Score 68 p.
Composed 1937-38.

3023 Retrospective, two orchestral   *10'*
pieces
1.In the Albaicin (nocturne) 2.Northern
gardens
3,3*,3*,3-4Hn.-Timp.,Perc.-2Hp.-Str.
Ms.
Score 34 p.
*The Albaicin is a Moorish quarter of Granada.
Composed 1923-24. First performance Chicago,
15 January 1926, Chicago Symphony Orchestra,
Frederick Stock conductor.*

WALDEN, OTTO VON. pseudonym.
See: SCHINDLER, FRITZ.

WALDROP, GIDEON WILLIAM.
b. Haskell County, Texas 2 September 1919

[From Old Double Mountain, suite]   *12'*
3370 1. Scene of desolation
3371 2.Rancher's whistling song 3.Primitive
dance
3*,2(2nd alt. E.H.),2,2-4,2,3,1-Timp.,Perc.-
Pno.,Hp.-Str.
Ms.
Scores: 16 p., 25 p. Large folios
*First performance Rochester, 1945-46, Roches-
ter Civic Orchestra, Howard Hanson conductor.*

WALDTEUFEL, ÉMILE.   Strasbourg 9 December 1837
Paris 12 February 1915

Real name: Charles Émile Lévy

6279 Braun oder Blond? Walzer, Op. 162
2,2,2,2-2,2,3,Ophicl.-Perc.-Str.
Henry Litolff, Braunschweig [188-?]
Score in reduction 9 p.

6267 Siesta-Walzer (La Berceuse), Op. 161
2,2,2,2-4,2,3,Euph.-Timp.,Perc.-Str.
Henry Litolff, Braunschweig [188-?]
Score in reduction 9 p.

Wall, Alfred Michael

WALL, ALFRED MICHAEL.   London 29 September 1875

971s Pastorale and bourrée
Str.
Oxford University Press, London, ^C1927
Score 6 p.

556s Recreations
1.Overture 2.Siciliano 3.Idyll 4.Minuet
and rigadoon
Str.
Oxford University Press, London, ^C1925
Score 18 p.

WALLENSTEIN, MARTIN.   Frankfurt a.M. 22 July 1843
                        Frankfurt a.M. 29 November 1896

667p [Concerto, piano, Op. 7, D minor]   *18'*
1.Allegro con moto 2.Andante religioso
3.Allegro vivace e con fuoco
Solo Pno.-2,2,2,2-2,2,1-Timp.-Str.
Score: Ms. 192 p.
Parts: Breitkopf & Härtel, Leipzig [1871?]

WALTER, ARNOLD.   Hannsdorf, Moravia 30 August 1902
                    Toronto 6 October 1973

5977 Concerto for orchestra   *22'*
1.Allegro deciso 2.Lento - Andante cantabile
3.Allegro vivace
3(3rd alt. Picc.),3(3rd alt. E.H.),3(3rd alt.
B.Cl.),3*-4,2,3,1-Timp.,Perc.-Str.
Ms.
Score 113 p. Large folio
Composed 1956. First performance Munich,
March 1958, Munich Philharmonic Orchestra,
Rudolph Albert conductor.

WALTER, EDUARD.

1664s [Spring awakening, violin and piano,
Op. 1. Transcribed by Gustav Blasser]
Solo Vn.-Hp.(optional)-Str.(Cb. optional)
A. Robitschek, Vienna [n.d.]
Score 5 p.

WALTHER, JOHANN GOTTFRIED. Erfurt 18 September 1684
                           Weimar 23 March 1748

1724s Lobe den Herren, den mächtigen König der
Ehren. Transcribed by Leonid Leonardi
Str.
Ms.
Score 4 p.
First performance Beverly Hills, 9 May 1940,
Pollack String Ensemble, Leonid Leonardi con-
ductor. Bound with Johann Kaspar Vogler,
Jesu Leiden, Pein und Tod.

WALTON, WILLIAM TURNER.
                b. Oldham, Lancashire 29 March 1902

1094v Concerto for viola and orchestra   *23'*
1.Andante comodo 2.Vivo, con molto preciso
3.Allegro moderato
Solo Va.-3(3rd alt. Picc.),3*,3*,3*-4,3,3,1-
Timp.-Str.
Oxford University Press, London, ^C1930
Score 71 p.

Composed 1928. First performance at a Prome-
nade Concert, London, 3 October 1929, New
Queen's Hall Orchestra, Henry Wood conductor,
Paul Hindemith soloist.

6960 Crown imperial, a coronation   *8'30"*
march (1937). Reduction for small orchestra
by Hyam Greenbaum
1,1,2,1-3Sax.-2,2,1-Perc.-Str.
Oxford University Press, London, ^C1937
Score in reduction 17 p.
Commissioned by the BBC. Composed 1937.
First performance 9 May 1937, BBC Symphony
Orchestra, Adrian Boult conductor.

3685 [Façade. Suite no. 1 for   *15'*
orchestra]
1.Polka 2.Valse 3.Swiss yodelling song
4.Tango - Pasodoblé 5.Tarantella, Sevillana
2(alt. 2 Picc.),2(2nd alt. E.H.),2,2-4(3rd&4th
ad lib.),2,1,1-Timp.,Perc.-Str.
Oxford University Press, London, ^C1936
Score 72 p.
From the entertainment for reciting voice and
six instruments, composed 1922-26 as accom-
paniment to poems by Edith Sitwell. Suite
extracted and transcribed, 1926. First per-
formance London, 1927.

3686 [Façade. Suite no. 2 for orchestra]   *9'*
1.Fanfare 2.Scotch rhapsody 3.Country dance
4.Noche espagnola 5.Popular song 6.Old Sir
Faulk
2(2nd alt. Picc.),3*,2,2-Alto Sax.-2,2,1-Perc.
-Str.
Oxford University Press, London, ^C1938
Score 43 p.
This suite extracted and transcribed 1938.
First performance New York, 30 March 1938, New
York Philharmonic, John Barbirolli conductor.
See also Suite no. 1 above.

3822 Portsmouth Point, an overture   *6'*
3*(2nd alt. 2nd Picc.),3*,3*,3*-4,3,3,1-Timp.,
Perc.-Str.
Oxford University Press, London, ^C1928
Miniature score 40 p.
Inspired by a print by Thomas Rowlandson
(1756-1827). Composed 1925. First perform-
ance Zurich, 22 June 1926, Fourth Festival of
the International Society for Contemporary
Music, Volkmar Andreae conductor.

2986 Siesta   *7'*
1(alt. Picc.),1,2,1-2Hn.-Str.
Oxford University Press, London, ^C1929
Score 12 p.

2991 [Symphony no. 1, B-flat minor]   *43'*
1.Allegro assai 2.Presto, con malizia 3.
Andante 4.Maestoso - Brioso ed ardamente -
Vivacissimo
2(2nd alt. Picc.),2,2,2-4,3,3,1-Timp.,Perc.-
Str.
Oxford University Press, London, ^C1936
Score 193 p.
Composed 1932-35. First complete performance
London, 6 November 1935, BBC Orchestra, Ham-
ilton Harty conductor.

WAMBACH, EMILE XAVER.
                    Arlon, Luxembourg 26 November 1854
                    Antwerp 6 May 1924

897m Concert aria [B-flat major]
      Solo Tbn.-Str.
      Ms.
      Score 13 p.

914m Edelweiss, melancoly
      Solo Ob.-Str.
      Ms.
      Score 7 p.

WANHAL, JOHANN BAPTIST.
      See: VAŇHAL, JAN KŘTITEL.

WAPPÄUS, KARL.   Berlin 5 March 1872

829s [Meadow saffron, intermezzo, Op. 463]
      Str.
      Score: Ms. 12 p.
      Parts: L. Oertel, Hanover [n.d.]

WARCHAVSKY, O.

1512s Danse russe
       Fl.-Str.
       Score: Ms. 6 p.
       Parts: [Ricordi, Paris, n.d.]

WARD, R. D. (RONALD DAVID).
                    b. Savannah, Georgia 26 November 1932

7279 George Washington tunes. Tran-   7'
      scribed for voices and small orchestra
      1.March 2.Minuet danced before Mrs.
      Washington 3.The toast
      1,2,0,2-2Hn.-SATB Voices(in no. 3 only)-Str.
      Ms. ᶜ1975 by R.D. Ward
      Score 27 p.
      Text and music of The Toast and probably the
      March as well, by Francis Hopkinson. Minuet
      by Pierre Duport, an 18th century French set-
      tler in Philadelphia. This transcription
      commissioned by the Richmond Sinfonia. Tran-
      scribed 1975. First performance Richmond,
      Virginia, 15 December 1975, Richmond Sinfonia,
      Jacques Houtmann conductor.

7277 Lafayette medley. Arranged for   6'
      small orchestra
      1.March 2.Waltz 3.Quickstep
      1,2,0,2-2Hn.-Str.
      Ms. ᶜ1975 by R.D. Ward
      Score 24 p.
      Based on themes from Blake's Evening Com-
      panion for the Flute, Clarinet, Violin or
      Flagelet [sic], published by George E. Blake,
      Philadelphia, ca.1825. This arrangement com-
      missioned by the Richmond Sinfonia. Arranged
      1975. First performance Richmond, Virginia,
      15 December 1975, Richmond Sinfonia, Jacques
      Houtmann conductor.

7278 Two Revolutionary hymns. Tran-   5'
      scribed for voices and small orchestra
      1.Bunker Hill 2.Chester

1(alt. Picc.),2,0,2-2Hn.-SATB Voices-Str.
Ms. ᶜ1975 by R.D. Ward
Score 14 p.
Bunker Hill originally composed by Andrew Law,
with lyrics by Nathaniel Miles, and published
in Law's A Select Number of Plain Tunes
Adapted to Congregational Worship, 1767. Text
and music of Chester by William Billings,
first published in his New England Psalm-
Singer, 1770. This arrangement commissioned
by the Richmond Sinfonia. Arranged 1975.
First performance Richmond, Virginia, 15
December 1975, Richmond Sinfonia, Jacques
Houtmann conductor.

WARD, ROBERT EUGENE.
                b. Cleveland, Ohio 13 September 1917

4921 Adagio and allegro   12'
      2(2nd alt. Picc.),2(2nd alt. E.H.),2,2-4,3,3,1
      -Timp.,Cym.-Str.
      Ms. [Peer International, New York, ᶜ1953]
      Score 48 p.
      Composed 1943. First performance New York, 5
      May 1945, Juilliard Graduate School Orchestra,
      Richard Bales conductor.

1793s Andante and scherzo   7'
       Str.
       Ms.
       Score 9 p. Large folio
       Originally composed for string quartet, 1937;
       arranged 1937-40. First performance Detroit,
       July 1941, Merrill String Ensemble, Celia
       Merrill conductor.

3120 Slow music for orchestra   10'
      3,3*,3*,3*-4,3,3,1-Timp.-Str.
      Ms.
      Score 40 p.
      Composed 1937 for a symphony in E minor, not
      completed. First performance Rochester, April
      1938, Rochester Civic Orchestra, Howard Hanson
      conductor.

3670 Symphony no. 1   15'
      1.Allegro pesante 2.Andante 3.Allegro
      3(3rd alt. Picc.),3*,3*,3(3rd alt. C.Bn.)-4,3,
      3,1-Timp.-Str.
      Ms. ᶜ1939 by Independent Music Publishers
      Score 65 p. Large folio
      Completed 1941. First complete performance,
      New York, 10 May 1941, Juilliard Graduate
      School Orchestra, the composer conducting.
      Received the Juilliard Publication Award, 1942.

WARLOCK, PETER. pseudonym.
      See: HESELTINE, PHILIP.

WARNECKE, MAX.
                b. Ottensen, near Hamburg 13 February 1878

653m Albumblatt, Op. 26   5'
      Solo Tbn.-1,1,2,1-2,2,1-Timp.-Str.
      J.H. Zimmermann, Leipzig [n.d.]
      Score in reduction 7 p.
      Composed 1898. First performance Stockholm,
      1900, the composer as soloist.

Warnecke, Max

668m Concertstück, Op. 28 [B-flat major] 5'
Solo Tbn.-1,1,2,1-2,2,1-Timp.-Str.
Score in reduction: Ms. 8 p.
Parts: [J.H. Zimmerman, Leipzig, n.d.]
*Composed 1899. First performance Stockholm,
1900, the composer as soloist.*

654m Nocturne, Op. 27 4'
Solo Tbn.-1,1,2,1-2,2,1-Timp.-Str.
J.H. Zimmermann, Leipzig [n.d.]
Score in reduction 7 p.
*Composed 1899. First performance Stockholm,
1900, the composer as soloist.*

WARNER, HARRY WALDO.
Northampton, England 4 January 1874
London 1 June 1945

2484 Hampton Wick, tone picture, Op. 38 22'
3(3rd alt. Picc.),3*,3*,3*-4,3,3,1-Timp.,Perc.
-Pno.,2Hp.-Str.
Ms. [J. Fischer, New York, n.d.]
Score 70 p.
*Inspired by Onslow Frampton's poem. Com-
posed 1930. First performance Cincinnati, 30
November 1934, Cincinnati Symphony Orchestra,
Eugene Goossens conductor. Won the Hollywood
Bowl Competition, 1932.*

1749s Suite in the olden style, Op. 34 15'
1.Prelude (Fughetta) 2.Sarabande 3.Bourrée
and chorale 4.Introduction and gigue
String Quartet or String Orchestra
Score: Ms. 29 p.
Parts: J. Fischer, New York, C1929
*Composed 1928. First performance London, 22
September 1928, London String Quartet.*

1750s Three arias in the olden style, 7'
Op. 39
1.Lento 2.Grave 3.Adagio
Str.
Score: Ms. 12 p.
Parts: J. Fischer, New York, C1931
*Originally composed for string quartet, 1929.
Transcribed 1931.*

WARREN, ELINOR REMICK. Los Angeles 23 February 1906

5229 The fountain 5'
2,2,2,2-3,2,3-Timp.,Perc.-Cel.,Hp.-Str.
Ms.
Score 19 p.
*Suggested by Sara Teasdale's poem. Originally
composed for piano, 1934. Transcribed, 1940.
First performance Pasadena, June 1940, Pasa-
dena Civic Orchestra, Richard Lert conductor.*

5230 [The legend of King Arthur. 4'30"
Intermezzo]
3,3*,3*,2-4,3,3,1-Timp.-Str.
Belwin-Mills, New York, C1974
Score 21 p.
*From a setting for chorus and orchestra of
part of Tennyson's Idylls of the King. Com-
posed 1939-40. First separate performance of*

*Intermezzo, Los Angeles, 8 August 1941, Holly-
wood Bowl Orchestra, John Barbirolli conductor.*

5031 Scherzo 1'30"
2(2nd alt. Picc.),2,2,2-3,2,3-Timp.,Perc.-
Cel.,Hp.-Str.
Ms. C1956 by Elinor Remick Warren
Score 32 p.
*Originally composed for piano, 1937. First
performance of this transcription Los Angeles,
1937, KHJ Radio Orchestra.*

6038 Suite for orchestra (revised 17'30"
version)
1.Black cloud horses 2.Cloud peaks 3.Ballet
of the midsummer sky 4.Pageant across the sky
2(2nd alt. Picc.),2,2,2-4,2,3,1-Timp.,Perc.-
Cel.,Hp.-Str.
Ms. [C. Fischer, New York, C1954]
Score 121 p. Large folio
*Inspired by poems of John Gould Fletcher.
Composed 1954. First performance Los Angeles,
3 March 1955, Los Angeles Philharmonic,
Alfred Wallenstein conductor. Revised 1960.*

WASHBURN, ROBERT.
b. Bouckville, New York 11 July 1928

6273 St. Lawrence overture 5'
2,2,2,2-2,2,2,1-Timp.,Perc.-Str.
Ms. [Boosey & Hawkes, Oceanside, N.Y., C1962]
Score 30 p.
*Composed 1961. First performance State Uni-
versity of New York at Potsdam, 28 November
1961, Crane Symphony Orchestra, Maurice Bari-
taud conductor.*

5849 Symphony no. 1 20'
1.Allegro con spirito 2.Adagio non tanto
3.Allegro marziale
2(2nd alt. Picc.),2,2,2-4,2,3,1-Timp.,Perc.-
Str.
Ms.
Score 89 p. Large folio
*Composed 1959. First performance Rochester,
26 March 1959, Eastman-Rochester Symphony,
Howard Hanson conductor.*

6290 Three pieces for orchestra 6'
1.Moderate 2.Adagio (Str. only) 3.Allegro
2*,2,2,2-2,2,1-Timp.,Perc.-Str.
Ms. [Oxford University Press, New York, C1961]
Score 19 p.
*Composed 1959. First performance Redlands,
California, University of Redlands Symposium
of American Orchestral Music, 18 April 1961,
University of Redlands Civic Symphony, Edward
Tritt conductor.*

WASSIL, BRUNO.

823p Tema con variazioni 15'
Solo Pno.-2(2nd alt. Picc.),3*,2,2-2,3,2,1-
Timp.,Perc.-Cel.,Hp.-Str.
Edizioni Cora, Milan, C1945
Score 76 p.
*First performance Venice, 17 August 1943,
Vincenzo Manno conductor.*

WEAVER, POWELL.
        Clearfield, Pennsylvania 10 June 1890
        Kansas City, Missouri 22 December 1951

1963s Fugue for strings   8'
Str.
Ms.
Score 10 p.
*Composed 1947. First performance Kansas City,
Missouri, 14 October 1947, Kansas City Phil-
harmonic, Efrem Kurtz conductor.*

2709 The little faun   4'
2,2,3*,1-Hn.-Perc.-Pno.,Hp.-Str.
Ms.
Score 35 p.
*Composed 1925. First performance Boston, 14
April 1929, Boston Women's Symphony Orches-
tra, Ethel Leginska conductor.*

5456 The sand dune cranes (ballet suite) 15'
2,3*,2,2-4,3,3,1-Timp.,Perc.-Pno.,Cel.,Hp.-Str.
Ms.
Score 96 p. Large folio
*Originally composed for solo piano and orches-
tra. Transcribed 1949-50. First performance
Kansas City, 21 or 22 November 1950, Kansas
City Philharmonic, Hans Schweiger conductor.*

5534 The squirrel, for orchestra   3'
2,2,2,1-3Hn.-S.Dr.-Hp.-Str.
Ms. J. Fischer, New York, ᶜ1926, ᶜ1940
Score 17 p.
*Originally composed for organ, 1925. This
version 1943; first performance Kansas City,
Missouri, April 1943, Kansas City Philharmonic,
Karl Kreuger conductor.*

2670 The vagabond, a symphonic poem   14'
3(3rd alt. Picc.),3(3rd alt. E.H.),3(3rd alt.
B.Cl.),3*-4,3,3,1-Timp.,Perc.-Pno.,Cel.,2Hp.-
Str.
Ms.
Score 59 p.
*Composed 1930. First performance Minneapolis,
6 March 1931, Minneapolis Symphony Orchestra,
Henri Verbrugghen conductor.*

WEBER, BEN.   St. Louis 23 July 1916

5875 Prelude and passacaglia, Op. 42 11'
2(2nd alt. Picc.),2(2nd alt. E.H.),2,2-4,2,3,
1-Timp.,Perc.-Pno.,Cel.,Hp.-Str.
Associated Music Publishers, New York, ᶜ1955
Score 51 p. Large folio
*Commissioned by the Louisville Orchestra under
a grant from the Rockefeller Foundation. Composed 1954. First performance Louisville,
1 January 1955, Louisville Orchestra, Robert
Whitney conductor.*

WEBER, CARL MARIA VON.
        Eutin near Lübeck, Germany 18 November 1786
                  London 5 June 1826

941 [Abu Hassan. Overture]   4'
2*,2,2,2-2,2,1-Timp.,Perc.-Str.
A.D. Schlesinger, Berlin [n.d.]

Score 28 p.
*From the opera composed 1811. First perform-
ance of opera Munich, 4 June 1811.*

625m Andante e rondo ongarese, Op. 35 5'
Solo Bn.-2,2,0,2-2,2-Timp.-Str.
Ms.
Score 56 p.
*Originally composed 1809 for viola and orches-
tra. Rewritten and first performed Prague, 18
February 1813, G. Fr. Brandt soloist.*

623m [Concertino, clarinet, Op. 26,   8'
E-flat major]
Solo Cl.-1,2,0,2-2,2-Timp.-Str.
Luck's Music, Detroit [n.d.]
Score 31 p.
*Composed 1811. First performance Munich, 5
April 1811, Heinrich Bärmann soloist.*

627m [Concertino, horn, Op. 45, in E]
Solo Hn.-1,0,2,2-2,2-Timp.-Str.
Score: Ms. 73 p.
Parts: Schlesinger [n.p., n.d.]

604m [Concerto, bassoon, Op. 75, F major] 12'
1.Allegro ma non troppo 2.Adagio 3.Rondo-
allegro
Solo Bn.-2,2,0,2-2,2-Timp.-Str.
Kalmus, New York [n.d.]
Score 51 p.
*Composed 1811. First performance Prague, 19
February 1813, G. Fr. Brandt soloist. Revised
1822.*

602m [Concerto, clarinet, no. 1, Op. 73, 12'
F minor]
1.Allegro 2.Adagio ma non troppo 3.Rondo
Solo Cl.-2,2,0,2-2,2-Timp.-Str.
Score: Ms. 136 p.
Parts: Breitkopf & Härtel, Leipzig [n.d.]
*Composed 1811. First performance Munich, 13
June 1811, Heinrich Bärmann soloist.*

606m [Concerto, clarinet, no. 2,   14'
Op. 74, E-flat major]
1.Allegro 2.Romanza 3.Alla polacca
Solo Cl.-2,2,0,2-2,2-Timp.-Str.
Kalmus, New York [n.d.]
Score 53 p.
*Composed 1811. First performance Munich, 25
November 1811, Heinrich Bärmann soloist.*

608p [Concerto, piano, no. 1, Op. 11, 18'
C major]
1.Allegro 2.Adagio 3.Presto
Solo Pno.-2,2,0,2-2,2-Timp.-Str.
Score: Ms. 193 p.
Parts: Schlesinger, Berlin [n.d.]
*Composed 1810. First performance Mannheim, 19
November 1810, the composer as soloist.*

562p [Concerto, piano, no. 2, Op. 32, 20'
E-flat major]
1.Allegro maestoso 2.Adagio 3.Presto
Solo Pno.-2,0,2,2-2,2-Timp.-Str.
Score: Ms. 168 p.
Parts: Schlesinger, Berlin [n.d.]

Weber, Carl Maria Von

*Composed 1812. First performance, Leipzig, 1
January 1813, the composer as soloist.*

1194 [Die drei Pintos. Entr'acte]   3'
2,2,2,2-4,2,1,1-Timp.,Trgl.-Str.
C.F. Kahnt, Leipzig [n.d.]
Score 16 p.
*From the unfinished comic opera composed 1821.
Completed by Gustav Mahler 1887. First per-
formance Leipzig, 20 January 1888, Gustav
Mahler conductor.*

148 [Euryanthe. Overture]   8'
2,2,2,2-4,2,3-Timp.-Str.
Kalmus, New York [n.d.]
Score 35 p.
*From the opera composed 1823. First perform-
ance Vienna, 25 October 1823, the composer
conducting.*

58 [Der Freischütz. Overture]   10'
2,2,2,2-4,2,3-Timp.-Str.
Kalmus, New York [n.d.]
Score 39 p.
*From the opera composed 1820. First perform-
ance of opera, Berlin, 18 June 1821.*

54 [Invitation to the dance, piano,   9'
Op. 65] Transcribed by Hector Berlioz
2*,2,2,4-4,2,2Cnt.,3-Timp.-2Hp.-Str.
Breitkopf & Härtel, Leipzig [n.d.]
Score 41 p.
*Transcribed 1841. First performance Paris, 7
June 1881, Battu conductor.*

1270 [Same as above] Transcribed by   12'
Felix Weingartner
3*,3,3,3-4,3,3,1-Timp.,Perc.-Hp.-Str.
A. Fürstner, Berlin, ᶜ1896
Score 46 p.
*Transcribed 1896. First performance Berlin,
1897, Felix Weingartner conductor.*

55 Jubel-Ouvertüre, Op. 59   7'
4(2 are Picc.),2,2,2-4,2,3-Timp.,Perc.-Str.
Breitkopf & Härtel, Leipzig [n.d.]
Score 42 p.
*Composed 1818. First performed Dresden, 20
September 1818.*

397p [Konzertstück, piano, Op. 79,   17'
F minor]
Solo Pno.-2,2,2,2-2,2,1-Timp.-Str.
Breitkopf & Härtel, Leipzig [n.d.]
Score 36 p.
*Composed 1821. First performance Berlin, 25
June 1821, the composer as soloist.*

2 [Oberon. Overture]   8'
2,2,2,2-4,2,3-Timp.-Str.
Breitkopf & Härtel, Wiesbaden [n.d.]
Score 20 p.
*From the opera composed 1826. First per-
formance London, 12 April 1826.*

905 Ouvertüre zum Beherrscher der Geister   5'
2*,2,2,2-4,2,3-Timp.-Str.
Breitkopf & Härtel, Leipzig [n.d.]

Score 33 p.
*A reworking, 1811, of the Rübezahl Overture
of 1805. First performance Munich, 11 November 1811.*

2423 [Peter Schmoll. Overture]   5'
2,2,2,2-2,2,1-Timp.-Str.
Schlesinger, Berlin [n.d.]
Score 53 p.
*From the opera composed 1802. First perform-
ance Augsburg, March 1803.*

585p [Polonaise brillante, piano, Op. 72,   8'
E major] Transcribed by Franz Liszt
Solo Pno.-2,2,2,2-2,2,3-Timp.,Perc.-Str.
Schlesinger, Berlin [n.d.]
Score 40 p.
Composed for piano 1819. Transcribed 1840.

925 [Preciosa. Overture]   6'
2,2,2,2-2,2-Timp.,Perc.-Str.
Breitkopf & Härtel, Leipzig [n.d.]
Score 35 p.
*From the opera composed 1820, after P. A.
Wolff's play. First performance Berlin, 14
March 1821.*

2422 [Silvana. Overture]   3'
2,2,0,2-2,2,1-Timp.-Str.
Schlesinger, Berlin [n.d.]
Score 44 p.
*From the opera composed 1810. First perform-
ance Frankfurt a.M., 17 September 1810.*

1111s Six ecossaises. Arranged for   5'
strings by Géza de Kresz
Str.(Cb. ad lib.)
J.&W. Chester, London, ᶜ1929
Miniature score 12 p.
Composed for piano 1802.

6071 [Symphony no. 1, Op. 19, C major]   23'
Edited by Fritz Oeser
1.Allegro con fuoco 2.Andante 3.Scherzo
4.Finale
1,2,0,2-2-2,2-Timp.-Str.
Brucknerverlag, Wiesbaden, ᶜ1948
Score 52 p.
Composed 1806-07.

1380 [Symphony no. 2, C major]   21'
1.Allegro 2.Adagio 3.Menuetto 4.Scherzo
1,2,0,2-2,2-Timp.-Str.
Score: Ms. 122 p.
Parts: Schlesinger, Berlin [n.d.]
*Composed 1807. First performance Karlsruhe,
1807.*

2574 [Turandot, Op. 37. Overture and march]
2*,2,2,2-2,2,1-Timp.,Perc.-Str.
Ms.
Score 38 p.
From music to Schiller's play, composed 1809.

WEBER, JOSEF MIROSLAW.   Prague 9 November 1854
                             Munich 2 January 1906

845m Dramatische Scene (in italienischer Weise)
Solo Tbn.-2,1,2,1-2,2-Perc.-Str.

Score: Ms. 46 p.
Parts: C.F. Schmidt, Heilbronn [n.d.]

WEBERN, ANTON (VON).   Vienna 3 December 1883
    Mittersill, near Salzburg 15 September 1945

5983 [Concerto for 9 instruments, Op. 24]   6'
1.Etwas lebhaft 2.Sehr langsam 3.Sehr rasch
1,1,1-1,1,1-Pno.-Vn.,Va.
Universal Edition, Vienna, c1948
Score 14 p.
*Composed 1934. First performance Prague, 4
September 1935, Festival of the International
Society for Contemporary Music.*

3980 Fünf Stücke, Op. 10   10'
1(alt. Picc.),1,2(1Cl. in E-flat, 2nd alt.
B.Cl.)-1,1,1-Perc.-Cel.,Hp.,Harm.,Mand.,Guit.-
Str.
Universal Edition, Vienna, c1923
Score 15 p.
*Composed 1911-13. First performance Fourth
Festival of the International Society for
Contemporary Music, Zurich, 23 June 1926.*

6746 Im Sommerwind, Idylle   12'
3,3*,5*,2-6,2-Timp.,Perc.-2Hp.-Str.
Carl Fischer, New York, c1962, 1966
Score 32 p. Large folio
*Composed 1904. First performance Philadelphia,
25 May 1962, The Philadelphia Orchestra,
Eugene Ormandy conductor.*

1749 Passacaglia, Op. 1   15'
3*,3*,3*,3*-4,3,3,1-Timp.,Perc.-Hp.-Str.
Universal Edition [n.p.] c1922
Score 50 p.
*Composed and first performed Vienna, 1908,
the composer conducting.*

1944s Sechs Bagatellen für Streich-   3'31"
quartett, Op. 9
Vn.I,Vn.II,Va.,Vc.
Ms. [Universal Edition, Vienna, c1924]
Score 6 p.
*Composed 1911-13. First public performance
Donaueschingen, Bavaria, July 1924, Amar-
Hindemith Quartet.*

3971 Symphonie, Op. 21   10'
1.Ruhig schreitend 2.Variationen
0,0,2*-2Hn.-Hp.-Str.(without Cb.)
Universal Edition [n.p.] c1929
Score 15 p.
*Commissioned by the League of Composers. Com-
posed 1928. First performance New York, 18
December 1929, League of Composers.*

WEHRS, ALBERT VON.

1499s Romanze, Op. 4 [G major]
Str.
Score: Ms. 9 p.
Parts: Chr. Bachmann, Hannover [n.d.]

WEIDIG, ADOLF.   Hamburg 28 November 1867
    Hinsdale, Illinois 23 September 1931

1368 Drei Episoden, Op. 38   25'
1.Im Freien 2.Trauer 3.Liebesglück
3(3rd alt. Picc.),2(2nd alt. E.H.),2,3*-4,2,
3,1-Timp.,Perc.-Org.(ad lib.),Hp.-Str.
B. Schott's Söhne, Mainz [n.d.]
Score 119 p.
*Composed 1909. First performance Berlin, 5
April 1909, Berlin Philharmonic, Arthur
Nikisch conductor.*

WEIGL, KARL.   Vienna 6 February 1881
    New York City 11 August 1949

5423 [Comedy overture, Op. 32]   10'
2(2nd alt. Picc.),2,2,2-4,2-Timp.,Perc.-Str.
Universal Edition, Vienna, c1935
Score 61 p.
*First performance Vienna, ca.1935. First per-
formance in the United States, Rochester,
1946-47 season, Eastman School of Music,
Howard Hanson conductor.*

379v [Concerto, violin and orchestra]   22'
1.Allegro 2.Largo 3.Allegro molto
Solo Vn.-2(2nd alt. Picc.),2,2,2-4,2-Timp.,
Perc.-Hp.-Str.
Ms. [Controlled by Boosey & Hawkes, New York]
Score 171 p.
*Composed 1928. First performance Vienna,
1931, Nikolai Malko conductor, Josef Wolfsthal
soloist.*

744c [Concerto, violoncello and   20'
orchestra]
1.Allegro moderato 2.Larghetto 3.Allegro ma
non troppo
Solo Vc.-2(2nd alt. Picc.),2,2,2-4,2-Timp.,
Perc.-Str.
Ms.
Score 190 p.
Composed 1934.

6659 Fanciful intermezzo, Op. 18   14'
3(3rd alt. Picc.),3(3rd alt. E.H.),3(3rd alt.
B.Cl.),3(3rd alt. C.Bn.)-4,3,3,1-Timp.,Perc.-
Cel.,Hp.-Str.
Ms. Schott, Mainz [c1924?]
Score 129 p.
*Inspired by Heinrich Heine's poem Frühlings-
feier. Originally composed in 1922 as the
fourth movement of the composer's Symphony
no. 2, Op. 19. Deleted from the symphony
after its first performance in 1924. First
separate performance of Intermezzo, Krefeld,
Rhineland, 19 January 1925, Krefeld Municipal
Orchestra, Rudolf Siegel conductor.*

3255 Festival prelude   9'
3(3rd alt. Picc.),3(3rd alt. E.H.),3(2nd alt.
Cl. in D,3rd alt. B.Cl.),3(3rd alt. C.Bn.)-
4,3,3,1-Timp.,Perc.-Hp.-Str.
Ms.
Score 96 p.
Composed 1938.

3456 Old Vienna [City that was]   13'
2(2nd alt. Picc.),2,2,2-4,2,3,1-Timp.,Perc.-
Hp.(ad lib.)-Str.

Weigl, Karl

Ms.
Score 103 p.
Composed 1939. Original title Tänze Aus Dem Alten Wien.

3218 Pictures and tales, suite, Op. 2   *13'*
1.Once upon a time 2.Snow White and the seven dwarfs 3.Stork, stork, clatter 4.Sleep, baby, sleep 5.At the grave of the sleeping beauty 6.Elves dance in the moonlight
2(2nd alt. Picc.),2,2,2-2,2-Timp.,Trgl.-Hp.-Str.
Ms.
Score 84 p.
Originally composed for piano 1909; orchestrated, 1922. First performance Vienna, 1924, Vienna Philharmonic Chamber Orchestra, Rudolf Nilius conductor.

6829 [The pied piper of Hamelin, Op. 24.   *21'*
Suite]
1.Prelude 2.The rats' enchantment 3.Ballet 4.Finale
1(alt. Picc.),1,1,1-Hn.-Timp.(2 players), Perc.-Pno.,Harm.-Str.
Universal Edition, Vienna, C1932
Score 132 p.
Originally a children's operetta. Composed 1932. First performance of suite, St. Paul, Minnesota, October 1977, St. Paul Chamber Orchestra, Denis Russell Davies conductor.

764p Rhapsody for piano and orchestra   *10'*
Solo Pno.-2(2nd alt. Picc.),2,2,2-4,2,3,1-Timp.,Perc.-Str.
Ms.
Score 72 p. Large folio
Composed 1940.

2232s [Rhapsody for strings, Op. 30]   *30-35'*
Str.
Universal Edition, Vienna, C1935
Score 65 p.
Originally composed as Sextet for Strings in D minor. Transcribed and retitled, 1931.

3846 Spring overture   *6'*
2(2nd alt. Picc.),2,2,2-2,1-Timp.,Perc.-Str.
Ms.
Score 27 p. Large folio
Composed 1939.

1811s Summer evening music   *7'*
Str.
Ms.
Score 16 p. Large folio
Composed 1940.

4042 [Symphonic prelude to a tragedy]   *18'*
3*(2nd alt. 2nd Picc.),3(3rd alt. E.H.),3(2nd alt. Cl. in E-flat,3rd alt. B.Cl.),3(3rd alt. C.Bn.)-4,3,3,1-Timp.,Perc.-Hp.-Str.
Ms.
Score 70 p.
Inspired by H. Chleunberg's drama Miracles around Verdun. Composed 1933.

3334 [Symphony no. 1, Op. 5, E major]   *50'*
1.Leicht bewegt 2.Sehr lebhaft 3.Langsam 4.Lebhaft
3(alt. 3Picc.),2,2,2-4,3,3,1-Timp.,Perc.-Hp.-Str.
Universal Edition, Vienna, C1911
Score 185 p.
Composed 1908. First performance Zurich, May 1910, Tonhalle Orchestra, Volkmar Andreae conductor.

6385 [Symphony no. 2, Op. 19, D minor] *50-55'*
1.Mässig 2.Lebhaft 3.Pro defunctis - Sehr langsam 4.Sehr mässig
4(3rd&4th alt. 2Picc.),4(4th alt. E.H.),5 (1Cl. in E-flat,3rd alt. B.Cl.,5th alt. Cl. in E-flat),4(4th alt. C.Bn.)-8(5th,6th,7th,8th alt. Tuba),4,4,2-Timp.(4 players),Perc.-Cel., 2Hp.-Str.
Ms. [Mercury Music, New York, n.d.]
Score in 4 volumes: 189 p., 110 p., 82 p., 220 p.
Originally composed in five movements, 1912-22. First performance Bochum, Ruhr, Germany, 2 May 1924, Bochum Municipal Orchestra, Rudolf Schulz-Dornburg conductor. Fourth movement later deleted from symphony and performed separately as Fanciful Intermezzo, Op. 18. First performance in present form, Vienna, probably 1925, Gesellschaft der Musikfreunde Orchester, Robert Heger conductor.

3583 [Symphony no. 3, B-flat major]   *40'*
1.Allegro molto 2.Adagio 3.Allegro
3(3rd alt. Picc.),3(3rd alt. E.H.),3(3rd alt. B.Cl.),3(3rd alt. C.Bn.)-4,3,3,1-Timp.,Perc.-Hp.-Str.
Ms.
Score 281 p.
Composed 1931.

3124 Symphony no. 4   *40'*
1.Allegro moderato 2.Allegro moderato 3.Adagio
3(3rd alt. Picc.),3(3rd alt. E.H.),3(2nd alt. Cl. in E-flat,3rd alt. B.Cl.),3(3rd alt. C.Bn.)-4,3,3,1-Timp.,Perc.-Hp.-Str.
Ms.
Score 164 p.
Composed 1936.

4470 [Symphony no. 5, Apocalyptic,   *48'*
C minor]
1.Evocation 2.The dance around the golden calf 3.Paradise lost 4.The four horsemen
3(3rd alt. Picc.),3(3rd alt. E.H.),4(3rd alt. B.Cl.,1Cl. in E-flat),3(3rd alt. C.Bn.)-4,3, 3,1-Timp.,Perc.-Hp.-Str.
Ms. [Now Associated Music, New York]
Score 174 p. Large folio
Inspired by the Old Testament and the Book of Revelation. Composed 1942-45. First performance New York, 27 October 1968, American Symphony Orchestra, Leopold Stokowski conductor.

4850 [Symphony no. 6, A minor]   *28'*
1.Andante mosso 2.Allegro 3.Adagio 4.Allegro

3(3rd alt. Picc.),3(3rd alt. E.H.),3(2nd alt.
Cl. in E-flat,3rd alt. B.Cl.),3(3rd alt. C.Bn.)
-4,3,3,1-Timp.,Perc.-Hp.-Str.
Ms. [Now Boosey & Hawkes, New York]
Score 101 p. Large folio
Composed 1947.

WEILL, KURT.   Dessau 2 March 1900
                 New York 3 April 1950

1750 Kleine Dreigroschenmusik [Suite   22'
      from Dreigroschenoper]
      1.Ouverture 2.[The murderous deed of Mackie
      Messer] 3.[Instead-of song] 4.[The ballad of
      pleasant life] 5.[Polly's song] 5a.Tango-
      Ballade 6.Kanonen-Song 7.Dreigroschen-Finale
      2(1st alt. Picc.),0,2,2-Alto Sax.,Ten.Sax.(alt.
      Sop.Sax.)-0,2,1,1-Timp.,Perc.-Pno.,Banjo,
      Guit.(ad lib.),Bandoneon(ad lib.)
      Universal Edition, Vienna, c1929
      Score 54 p.
      From the opera composed 1928. First perform-
      ance of this suite Berlin, 7 February 1929,
      State Opera Orchestra, Otto Klemperer con-
      ductor.

2344 Quodlibet, Op. 9   20'
      1.Andante non troppo 2.Molto vivace 3.Un
      poco sostenuto 4.Molto agitato - Molto vivo
      2(2nd alt. Picc.),2,2,2-2,2,2-Timp.,Perc.-Str.
      Universal Edition, Vienna, c1926
      Score 107 p.
      Composed 1924. First performance Coburg, 6
      February, 1926, Albert Bing conductor.

WEILLER, ERNEST.

479v Malagueña, danse espagnole
      Solo Vn.-Cast.-Str.
      Score: Ms. 12 p.
      Parts: Durand, Paris, c1929

949s Souffrance, mélodie
      Solo Vn.,Va.,Vc.-Str.
      Score: Ms. 4 p.
      Parts: Durand, Paris, c1929

WEINBERG, JACOB.   Odessa 5 July 1879
                New York 2 November 1956

6976 The Gettysburg address, Op. 36.   11'
      Small orchestra version
      Bar. Voice Solo,Chorus(SATB)-3(3rd Fl. or
      Picc.),2,2,2-4,4,3,1-Timp.,Perc.-Pno.,Org.,
      Theremin,2Hp.-Str.
      M. Witmark & Sons, New York, c1936
      Score 32 p. Large folio
      Composed 1935.

1926 Ora, Palestinian folk-dance
      2(1st alt. Picc.),2,2,2-4,3,3,1-Timp.,Perc.-
      Hp.-Chorus(SATB)-Str.
      Ms.
      Score 38 p.

1889 Palestine, rhapsody, Op. 18
      2(1st alt. Picc.),2,2,2-4,3,3,1-Timp.,Perc.-
      Hp.-Str.

Ms.
Score 42 p.

WEINBERGER, JAROMIR.   Prague 8 January 1896
        St. Petersburg, Florida 8 August 1967

[Bohemian songs and dances]   24'
2067   I G minor: Andante rubato - Con moto   5'
2068   II A major: Andantino   4'
2069 III G major: Con moto   4'
2070 IV A major: Allegretto   4'
2071   V D minor: Vivo   4'
2072 VI G major: Con moto   3'
      Solo Vn.(no. I only)-2(2nd alt. Picc. in no. V),
      2,2,2-4,2,3-Timp.,Perc.-Cel.,Hp.-Str.
      Universal Edition, Vienna, c1930
      Scores: 17 p., 13 p., 18 p., 16 p., 20 p., 10 p.
      Composed 1929. First performance Darmstadt,
      10 March 1930, Karl Böhm conductor.

1963 [Christmas]   20'
      3(3rd alt. Picc.),3*,3*,3*-4,3,3,1-Timp.,Perc.-
      Pno.,Cel.,Org.,2Hp.-Str.
      Universal Edition, Vienna, c1929
      Score 79 p.
      Composed 1929. First performance Munich, 7
      November 1929, Clemens von Franckenstein con-
      ductor.

944m Concerto for the timpani   8'
      1.Allegro 2.Andante sostenuto 3.Vivace
      Solo Timp.-4Tpt.,4Tbn.(or 3Tbn.,Tuba)
      Boosey & Hawkes, New York, c1939
      Score 16 p.
      Composed 1939.

317v The devil in the belfry   4'
      Solo Vn.-Bells,Tam-tam-Cel.-Str.
      Associated Music Publishers, New York, c1942
      Score 13 p.
      Suggested by Edgar Allan Poe's short story.
      Composed 1940.

3448 The Lincoln symphony   45'
      1.The hand on the plough 2.Scherzo héroique
      3.O Captain! My Captain! 4.Finale: Deep River
      3(2nd&3rd alt. Picc.),3*,3*,3(3rd alt. C.Bn.)-
      4,3,3,1-Timp.(3 players),Perc.-Org.,Hp.-Str.
      C. Fischer, New York, c1940
      Score 204 p. Large folio
      Composed 1940. First performance Cincinnati,
      17 October 1941, Cincinnati Symphony Orchestra,
      Eugene Goossens conductor.

1751 Overture to a marionette play   12'
      3(2nd&3rd alt. 2Picc.),2,2,2-4,3,3-Timp.,Perc.-
      Cel.,Hp.-Str.
      Universal Edition, Vienna, c1924
      Score 52 p.
      Composed 1922. First performance Vienna, 1923,
      Oskar Nedbal conductor.

6464 Prelude and fugue on Dixie   5'
      3(3rd alt. Picc.),2,2,2-4,3,3,1-Timp.,Perc.-
      Org.(ad lib.),Hp.-Str.
      Optional stage band: 2Hn.,2Tpt.,2Tbn.,Perc.
      Associated Music Publishers, New York, c1941
      Score 42 p.

Weinberger, Jaromir

Commissioned by the Symphony Society of San Antonio, Texas. Composed 1939. First performance San Antonio, 12 April 1940, Symphony Society of San Antonio, Max Reiter conductor.

400c The raven [after Edgar Allan Poe]   5'
Solo Vc.-B.Cl.-Hp.-Str.
Associated Music Publishers, New York, ^c1942
Score 10 p.
Composed 1940.

2074 [Schwanda the bagpiper. Overture]   20'
3(2nd&3rd alt. 2Picc.),2,2,2-4,3,3,1-Timp.,
Perc.-Cel.,2Hp.-Str.
Universal Edition, Vienna, ^c1929
Score 91 p.
From the opera based on J. K. Tyl's legend. First performance Prague, 27 April 1927, Otakar Ostrčil conductor.

2073 [Schwanda the bagpiper. Polka and   11'
fugue]
3(3rd alt. Picc.),2,2,2-4,7(4 backstage),3,1-
Timp.,Perc.-Org.(ad lib.),Hp.-Str.
Universal Edition, Vienna, ^c1930
Score 57 p.
First concert performance of this excerpt from the opera, Halle, 9 February 1930, Erich Band conductor.

3574 Song of the high seas   10'
3(3rd alt. Picc.),3*,3*,3*-4,3,3,1-Timp.,Perc.
-Org.(ad lib.),Hp.-Str.
Hawkes & Son, London, ^c1940
Score 26 p.
Composed 1940. First performance New York, 9 November 1940, New York Philharmonic, John Barbirolli conductor.

3131 Under the spreading chestnut   20'
tree, variations and fugue on an old English
tune
3(2nd&3rd alt. Picc.),2,2,2-4,3,3-Timp.,Perc.-
Pno.,Org.(ad lib.),Hp.-Str.
Boosey & Hawkes, New York, ^c1939
Score 56 p.
Composed 1939. First performance New York, 12 October 1939, New York Philharmonic, John Barbirolli conductor.

Wallenstein. Suite
3357   I [Praeludium and tambourin]   7'
3,2,2,2-4,3,3,1-Perc.-Hp.-Str.
3358   II [Sarabande and fugue]   7'
2,2*,2,2-2Hn.-Cel.,Hp.-Str.
3359   III The Bohemian grenadiers, march   4'
3(3rd alt. Picc.),2,2,2-4,3,3,1-Timp.,Perc.-
Str.
Ms. ^c1939 by Associated, New York
Scores: 24 p., 19 p., 43 p.
From the opera based on Schiller's trilogy, composed 1936. First performance Vienna, 18 November 1937, Wolfgang Martin conductor.

WEINER, LAZAR. Cherkassy, near Kiev 27 October 1897

3092 Prelude and fugue   10'
3(3rd alt. Picc.),3(3rd alt. E.H.),3(3rd alt.

B.Cl.),3*-3,3,3,1-Timp.,Perc.-Str.
Ms.
Score 36 p.
Composed 1938.

WEINER, LEO.   Budapest 16 April 1885
Budapest 13 September 1960

619p [Concertino, piano, Op. 15, in E]   18'
1.Allegro amabile, quasi allegretto 2.Vivace
Solo Pno.-2(2nd alt. Picc.),2,2,2-2,2-Timp.-
Str.
Universal Edition, Vienna, ^c1926
Score 102 p.
Composed 1924. First performance Budapest, December 1925, Philharmonic Society.

1676s [Divertimento no. 1, on old   9'
Hungarian dances, Op. 20]
1.[A real czardas] 2.[Fox-dance] 3.[Round
dance of Marosszék] 4.[Soldiers' dance]
5.[Swineherds' dance]
Picc.,Hn.,Tpt.(all optional, no. 4 only)-Str.
Rózsavölgyi, Budapest, ^c1934
Score 27 p.
First performance Rochester, 11 January 1934, Rochester Philharmonic Orchestra, Fritz Reiner conductor.

1788s Divertimento no. 2, Hungarian   13'
folk melodies, Op. 24
1.[Festive] 2.[Comedy] 3.[Plaintive song]
4.[Swineherd's song]
Str.
Rózsavölgyi, Budapest, ^c1939
Score 28 p.
Composed 1933.

1417 Fasching [Carnival, humoresque] Op. 5   7'
2(2nd alt. Picc.),1,2,1-2,2,1-Timp.,Trgl.-Str.
Lauterbach & Kuhn, Leipzig, ^c1908
Score 28 p.
Composed 1907. First performance Budapest, 20 January 1908, David Popper conductor.

2159 [Prince Csongor and the goblins,   9'
Op. 10. Introduction and scherzo]
2(2nd alt. Picc.),2,2,2-4,2,3-Timp.-Hp.-Str.
W. Hansen, Copenhagen, ^c1927
Score 63 p.
From the incidental music to Mihaly Vörösmarty's play. Composed 1913. First performance Budapest, 8 February 1914, Fritz Reiner conductor.

1291 Serenade, Op. 3 [F minor]   21'
1.Allegretto, quasi andantino 2.Lebhaft
3.Rubato 4.Allegro molto
2(2nd alt. Picc.),2,2,2-2,2-Timp.,Trgl.-Str.
Lauterbach & Kuhn, Leipzig, ^c1907
Score 48 p.
Composed 1905. First performance Budapest, 22 October 1906, Philharmonic Society, Stefan Kerner conductor.

3309 Soldatenspiel [Playing soldiers]   4'
Op. 16
2(2nd alt. Picc.),2,2,2-4,2,3-Timp.,Perc.-Str.

Universal Edition, Vienna, ^c1931
Score 34 p.

2495 Suite (Ungarische Volkstänze), Op. 18
1.Allegro risoluto e ben marcato 2.Andante
poco sostenuto - Allegro con fuoco 3.Andante
poco sostenuto 4.Presto
2(2nd alt. Picc.),2(2nd alt. E.H.),2,2-4,2,
3,1-Timp.,Perc.-Cel.,Hp.-Str.
Rózsavölgyi, Budapest, ^c1933
Score 158 p.
*Composed 1931. First performance Rochester,
19 January 1933, Rochester Philharmonic
Orchestra, Fritz Reiner conductor.*

WEINGARTNER, FELIX.　　　Zara, Dalmatia 2 June 1863
　　　　　　　　　　　Winterthur, Switzerland 7 May 1942

798v [Concerto, violin, Op. 52, G major]　　*18'*
1.Allegro placido 2.Andantino quasi allegretto
3.Caprice savoyard
Solo Vn.-2,2(2nd alt. E.H.),2,2-4,2-Timp.-Str.
Breitkopf & Härtel, Leipzig, ^c1912
Score 74 p.
*Composed 1911. First performance Vienna, 28
October 1912, the composer conducting, Fritz
Kreisler soloist.*

613c [Concerto, violoncello, Op. 60,　　*30'*
A minor]
1.Allegro 2.Cavatine 3.Allegro ma non troppo
Solo Vc.-2,2,2,2-3,2-Timp.-Str.
Universal Edition, Vienna, ^c1917
Score 82 p.
*Composed 1916. First performance Vienna,
1917, Konzertverein.*

4525 [The Elysian fields, symphonic　　*17'*
poem, Op. 21]
4(3rd alt. Picc.,1Alto Fl.),3*,3*,4*-4,4,3,1-
Timp.,Perc.-2(or 1)Hp.-Str.
Breitkopf & Härtel, Leipzig, ^c1897
Score 75 p.
*Suggested by Arnold Böcklin's painting. First
performance Mannheim, ca.1890, Allgemeine
Deutsche Musikverein.*

4513 [King Lear, symphonic poem, Op. 20]　*20'*
4*(3rd alt. Picc.II),3,3,4*-4,4,3,1-Timp.(2
players),Perc.-Str.
Breitkopf & Härtel, Leipzig, ^c1897
Score 91 p.
*First performance Cologne, ca.1889, Gürzenich
Concerts, Franz Wüllner conductor.*

266s Serenade [F major]
1.Andante, quasi allegretto 2.Intermezzo
3.Andante sostenuto 4.Molto vivace
Str.
Ries & Erler, Berlin [n.d.]
Score 14 p.

4526 [Symphony no. 2, Op. 29, E-flat　　*50'*
major]
1.Lento 2.Allegro giocoso 3.Adagio, ma non
troppo, cantabile 4.Lento - Allegro risoluto
3(3rd alt. Picc.),3(3rd alt. E.H.),3,3(3rd
alt. C.Bn.)-4,3,3,1-Timp.(3 players)-1(or 2)
Hp.-Str.

Breitkopf & Härtel, Leipzig, ^c1901
Score 177 p.
Composed ca.1898.

5523 [Symphony no. 3, Viennese, Op. 49,　*55'*
E major]
[1]Allegro con brio [2]Allegro un poco
moderato [3] Adagio, ma non troppo [4]Allegro
moderato
4(4th alt. Picc.),3*,Heckelphone,4*(1Cl. in
E-flat,alt. Cl. in D),4*-6,4,3,1-Timp.,Perc.-
Org.(ad lib.),Cel.,2Hp.-Str.
Breitkopf & Härtel, Leipzig, ^c1910, ^c1911
Score 241 p.
*Composed 1909. First performance Vienna, 1909
or 1910, Vienna Philharmonic.*

1754 [Symphony no. 4, Op. 61, F major]　*35'*
1.Allegro un poco moderato 2.Andante con moto
3.Comodo, grazioso 4.Allegro quasi pastorale
2(2nd alt. Picc.),2(2nd alt. E.H.),2,3*-4,2,
3,1-Timp.-Hp.-Str.
Universal Edition, Vienna, ^c1917
Score 108 p.
*Composed 1916. First performance Cologne,
1917, Hermann Abendroth conductor.*

1835 [Symphony no. 5, Op. 71, C minor]　*30'*
1.Allegro agitato 2.Allegro scherzando
3.Andante solenne 4.Fuga di due temi
3(3rd alt. Picc.),3*,3(2nd alt. Basset Hn.,1Cl.
in E-flat),3(3rd alt. C.Bn.)-4,3,3,1-Timp.,
Perc.-Str.
Simrock, Berlin, ^c1926
Score 90 p.
*Composed 1923. First performance Edinburgh,
1924, the composer conducting.*

1756 [The tempest, Op. 65. Overture]　　*13'*
2(2nd alt. Picc.),2(2nd alt. E.H.),2,2-4,2,3,
1-Timp.,Perc.-Hp.-Str.
Universal Edition, Vienna, ^c1919
Score 52 p.
*From the incidental music to Shakespeare's
play, composed 1918. First performance Darmstadt, 1919, Erich Kleiber conductor.*

1755 [The tempest, Op. 65. Interlude,　*12'*
scherzettino, and finale]
2(2nd alt. Picc.),2,2,2(2nd alt. C.Bn.)-4,2,3,
1-Timp.,Perc.-Org. or Harm.,Hp.-Str.
Universal Edition, New York, ^c1923
Score 59 p.

WEINREIS, HEINRICH.　　　　　　　19 August 1874

555s Wiegenlied [Cradle song] Op. 28
Hp.(optional)-Str.
Chr. Fr. Vieweg, Berlin, ^c1910
Score 5 p.

WEINZWEIG, JOHN JACOB.　　　Toronto 11 March 1913

1028m [Divertimento no. 1]　　　*10'30"*
1.Fast and playful 2.Slow 3.Moderately fast
Solo Fl.-Str.
Ms. [Boosey & Hawkes, London, ^c1950]
Score 22 p.

Weinzweig, John Jacob

Composed 1945-46. First performance over radio, Vancouver, 29 December 1946, CBC Orchestra, Albert Steinberg conductor, Nicholas Fiore soloist. First concert performance Prague, 26 July 1947, Ivan Romanoff conductor. Received second prize (highest awarded) in chamber music competition, Olympic Games, London, 1948.

2898 The enchanted hill   10'
3*,3*,3*,3*-4,3,3,1-Timp.,Perc.-Hp.-Str.
Ms.
Score 52 p. Large folio
Inspired by Walter de la Mare's poem. Composed 1938. First performance Rochester, 6 April 1938, Rochester Civic Orchestra, Howard Hanson conductor.

4319 Fanfare   2'
3Tpt.,3Tbn.
Ms.
Score 4 p.
Composed 1943. First performance Toronto, 13 November 1943, CBC Orchestra, Ernest MacMillan conductor.

1925s Interlude in an artist's life   7'30"
Str.
Ms.
Score 13 p.
Composed 1943. First performance Toronto, 1944, CBC Orchestra, Ettore Mazzoleni conductor.

1795s Spectre
Timp.-Str.
Ms.
Score 5 p. Large folio
Composed 1938. First performance broadcast over CBC radio, Toronto, 1 January 1939, Melodic Strings, Alexander Chuhaldin conductor.

3258 Suite for orchestra   7'30"
1.Pulsation 2.Introspection 3.Fugando
3*,3*,2,2-4,2,3-Timp.,Perc.-Hp.-Str.
Ms.
Score 35 p.
Composed 1938. First performance Rochester, 18 October 1938, Rochester Civic Orchestra, Howard Hanson conductor.

965m A tale of Tuamotu   25'
Solo Bn.-3(3rd alt. Picc.),2,3*-4,3,3,1-Timp.,
Perc.-Pno.-Str.
Ms.
Score 70 p.
Composed 1939.

WEIS, KAREL.   Prague 13 February 1862
                      Prague 4 April 1944

[Dramatic dances]
1757   I 1.Gavotta 2.Polka   5'
1,1,1,1-2,1-Trgl.-Str.
1758   II 3.Mazurka 4.Kvapík   5'
2*,2,2,2-4,2,3-Perc.-Str.
1759   III 5.[Waltz] 6.Polka   5'
1,1,1,1-2,1-Trgl.-Str.

Fr. A. Urbânek, Prague [n.d.]
Scores: 11 p., 15 p., 11 p.
Composed 1894.

WEISGALL, HUGO.
        b. Ivancice, Czechoslovakia 13 October 1912

3905 [Quest. Suite from the ballet]
1.Allegro molto (The woman of the world) 2.
Scherzo (The dance of the jealous ladies) 3.
Molto adagio 4.Slow, tempo di valse
3(3rd alt. Picc.),2,2,2-4,3,3,1-Timp.,Perc.-
Hp.-Str.
Ms.
Score 47 p. Large folio
Ballet commissioned by the Baltimore Ballet. Composed 1938. First performance of this suite New York, 21 March 1942, New York Philharmonic, John Barbirolli conductor.

WEISMANN, JULIUS.
        Freiburg-im-Breisgau, Germany 26 December 1879
                Singen, Germany 22 December 1950

662v [Concerto, violin, Op. 36, D minor]
1.Allegro appassionato 2.Adagio espressivo
3.Allegro vivace
Solo Vn.-2(2nd alt. Picc.),3*,3*,3*-4,2,3-
Timp.,Perc.-Str.
F.E.C. Leuckart, Leipzig [n.d.]
Score 102 p.

272 Tanz-Fantasie, Op. 35a
2(2nd alt. Picc.),2,2,2-4,2,3-Timp.,Perc.-Str.
Tischer & Jagenberg, Cologne, ᶜ1911
Score 60 p.

WEIS-OSTBORN, RUDOLPH VON.   Graz 8 November 1876

395s Melodie, Op. 3
Str.
Ries & Erler, Berlin [n.d.]
Score 13 p.

WEISS, ADOLPH.   Baltimore 12 September 1891
                Van Nuys, California 21 February 1971

2671 American life, scherzoso jazzoso   5'
3(3rd alt. Picc.),3*,3*,3*-3Sax.(SAT)-4,3,3,1-
Timp.,Perc.-Str.
New Music, San Francisco, ᶜ1932
Score 28 p.
Composed 1929. First performance New York, 21 February 1930, Conductorless Orchestra.

3052 I segreti, tone poem   12'
3*,3*,3*,3*-4,4,3,1-Timp.,Perc.-Cel.,Hp.-Str.
Ms.
Score 57 p.
Composed 1922. First performance Rochester, 1 May 1925, Rochester Philharmonic Orchestra, Howard Hanson conductor.

WEISSBERG, JULIA LAZAREVNA.
                Orenburg, Russia 25 December 1878
                Leningrad 1 March 1942

2148 Ballade, Op. 12   12'
3*,3*,3*,3*-4,3,3,1-Timp.,Perc.-Hp.-Str.

Mussektor, Moscow/Universal, Vienna, 1930
Score 55 p.
*Inspired by Heinrich Heine's poem Harald
Harfagar. Composed 1915-16. First performance
Pavlovsk, near Leningrad, 7 June 1916,
Asslanov conductor.*

4887 [A fairytale: Fingerhütchen, Op. 13] *17'*
3*,3*,3,2-4,2,3,1-Timp.,Perc.-Cel.,2Hp.-Str.
Universal Edition, Vienna, ᶜ1928
Score 59 p.
Inspired by Conrad Ferdinand Meyer's poem.

2987 In der Nacht, Op. 10 [after Feodor
Tuchev's poem]
3(3rd alt. Picc.),3*,3*,3*-4,3,3,1-Timp.,Bells
-Hp.-Str.
Mussektor, Moscow/Universal, Vienna, 1929
Score 31 p.

3400 [The mermaid. Sailors' dance]
3*,2,2,2-4,2,3,1-Timp.,Perc.-Str.
[Mussektor, Moscow] 1936
Score 31 p.
*From the opera based on Hans Christian Ander-
sen's The Little Mermaid. Composed 1923.*

WEISSENBORN, ERNST.
d. Nordhausen, Germany 6 December 1900

781m Impromptu, Op. 104
Solo Cl.-1,1,0,1-2Hn.-Str.
Score: Ms. 35 p.
Parts: [n.p., n.d.]

WEISSENBORN, JULIUS.
Friedrichstanneck, Thuringia 13 April 1837
Leipzig 21 April 1888

480m Ballade, Op. 9 no. 6 *3'*
Solo Bn.-1,1,1,1-Hn.-Str.
Ms.
Score 10 p.

476m Scherzo, Op. 9 no. 5 *3'*
Solo Bn.-1,1,1,1-Hn.-Str.
Ms.
Score 11 p.

WELANDER, WALDEMAR. Gödelöv, Sweden 26 August 1899

819p Concerto da camera [for piano and *22'*
orchestra]
1.Allegro risoluto 2.Andante espressivo
3.Allegro molto
Solo Pno.-1,1,2,1-2Hn.-Timp.-Str.
Ms.
Score 145 p.
*Composed 1948. First performance Malmö, 23
March 1948, Chamber Orchestra of Malmö, Carl-
Olof Anderberg conductor, Signe Hansson
soloist.*

2047s Sinfonia piccola för stråkorkester *27'*
1.Andante 2.Adagio 3.Presto 4.Moderato
Str.
Ms.
Score 57 p.

*Composed 1949. First performance Malmö, 4
December 1949, Orchestra Society of Malmö,
Sten-Åke Axelson conductor.*

WELLESZ, EGON. Vienna 21 October 1885
Oxford 9 November 1974

3977 Fanfare
6Tpt.-Timp.
Ms.
Score 2 p.
*Based on a motive from the composer's opera
Die Prinzessin Girnara.*

833v Suite für Violine und Kammer- *20'*
orchester, Op. 38
1.Moderato 2.Adagio 3.Largo 4.Allegretto
Solo Vn.-1,1*,1,1-Va.,Vc.
Universal Edition, Vienna, ᶜ1924
Score 20 p.
*Composed 1924. First performance Salzburg
Music Festival, August 1924, Hermann Scherchen
conductor.*

WENDLAND, WALDEMAR. Liegnitz, Prussia 10 May 1873
Zeitz 15 August 1947

4541 Das vergessene Ich [The forgotten I.
Act I: Intermezzo, Rümelin's dream]
2(2nd alt. Picc.),2,2,2-4,2,3-Timp.,Perc.-Hp.-
Str.
Bote & Bock, Berlin [ᶜ1911?]
Score 36 p.
*From the opera with libretto by Richard
Schott. First performance Berlin, 1911.*

WENINGER, LEOPOLD. Feistritz a.W. 13 October 1879

Also known as: Leo Minor

1019v [Air in Ionian style] *6'30"*
Solo Vn.-Str.
W. Ehrler, Leipzig, ᶜ1931
Score 7 p.

WENNER, E.

1502s Chanson d'avril, Op. 22
Solo Va.-Str.
Score: Ms. 7 p.
Parts: Costallat, Paris [n.d.]

WEPRIK, ALEXANDER.
See: VEPRIK, ALEXANDER.

WERNER, AUGUSTE. St. Petersburg 15 April 1841
Geneva 4 April 1900

5635 Introduction et gavotte, Op. 20
2,2,2,2-2Hn.-Timp.-Str.
J. Hamelle, Paris [188-?]
Score 11 p.
Originally composed for piano.

WERNER, GREGORIUS JOSEPH. (?) 1695
Eisenstadt 3 March 1766

1803s [Six fugues, organ. Transcribed and
preludes added by Joseph Haydn]

Wernicke, Alfred

Str.(without Cb.)
Ms.
Score 43 p.

WERNICKE, ALFRED.   Barth, Germany 2 December 1856
                                    d. ca.1916

  641m [Concertino, flute, Op. 12, C minor]   *6'*
  Solo Fl.-1,1,2,2-2Hn.-Timp.-Str.
  J.H. Zimmermann, Leipzig, ᶜ1903
  Score in reduction 13 p.
  Composed 1901. First performance Mannheim,
  1902, the composer conducting.

  613v [Gypsy serenade, Op. 28]
  Solo Vn.-2,1,2,2-2,2-Timp.-Hp.-Str.
  C.F. Kahnt, Leipzig, ᶜ1904
  Score 19 p.

WESSEL, MARK.   Coldwater, Michigan 26 March 1894
                                    d. 1973

  1777s Ballade   *10'*
  Solo Ob., Solo Vn.-Str.
  Ms.
  Score 23 p.
  Composed 1931. First performance Rochester,
  25 July 1932, Eastman School Orchestra,
  Samuel Belov conductor, Mitchell Miller oboist,
  Harry Friedman violinist.

  3127 Holiday   *6'*
  3*,3*,3*,3*-4,2,2,1-Timp.,Perc.-Pno.-Str.
  Ms.
  Score 42 p.
  Composed 1932. First performance Rochester,
  3 May 1934, Rochester Philharmonic Orchestra,
  Howard Hanson conductor.

  733p Scherzo burlesque   *16'*
  Solo Pno.-1,1,2,1-2,2,1-Timp.-Str.
  Ms.
  Score 80 p.
  Composed 1926. First performance Rochester,
  30 December 1926, Rochester Little Symphony,
  Howard Hanson conductor, the composer as
  soloist.

  3152 Song and dance   *10'*
  3*,3*,3*,3*-Bar.Sax.-2,2,2-Timp.,Perc.-Pno.-
  Str.
  Ms.
  Score 46 p.
  Composed 1932. First performance Rochester,
  3 May 1934, Rochester Philharmonic Orchestra,
  Howard Hanson conductor.

WESSELY, JOHANN.   Frauenberg 27 June 1762
                                    Ballenstedt 1814

  931m Ten Variations, Op. 15
  Solo Hn., Solo Vn.-2Ob.-2Hn.-Str.
  Ms.
  Score 27 p.

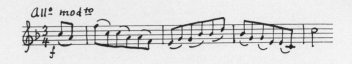

WESTBERG, ERIC.   Hudiksvall, Sweden 9 May 1892
                                    Stockholm 16 October 1944

  4963 [Symphony no. 3, Swedish   *32'*
  fiddling tunes and ballads]
  1.Allegro moderato 2.Allegro 3.Larghetto
  4.Allegro non troppo
  2,2,2,2-4,2,3,1-Timp.,Perc.-Hp.-Str.
  Ms.
  Score 112 p.

WESTERHOUT, NICCOLÒ VAN.
  See: VAN WESTERHOUT, NICCOLÒ.

WETZ, RICHARD.   Gleiwitz 26 February 1875
                                    Erfurt 16 January 1935

  1800 [Symphony no. 1, Op. 40, C minor]
  1.Ruhig bewegt 2.Scherzo 3.Sehr langsam und
  ausdrucksvoll 4.Kräftig und entschieden
  bewegt
  2(2nd alt. Picc.),3*,2,2-4,3,3,1-Timp.-Hp.-Str.
  Simrock, Berlin, ᶜ1924
  Score 174 p.

WETZLER, HERMANN HANS.   Frankfurt 8 September 1870
                                    New York 29 May 1943

  2156 [As you like it, Op. 7. Suite from   *20'*
  the music to Shakespeare's play]
  1.Pagenduett 2.Liebesszene 3.[First shepherd
  dance] 4.[Rosalind's farewell] 5.[Second
  shepherd dance]
  3(3rd alt. Picc.),2(2nd alt. E.H.),2,2-4,3,3,
  1-Timp.,Perc.-Hp.-Str.
  F.E.C. Leuckart, Leipzig [n.d.]
  Score 50 p.
  Completed 1917. First performance Lübeck,
  1918, the composer conducting.

  2515 [Assisi, legend for orchestra, Op. 13]
  In one movement
  3(3rd alt. Picc.),3*,4*(3rd alt. Cl. in E-flat),
  3(3rd alt. C.Bn.)-4,3,3,1-Timp.(3 players),
  Perc.-Pno.,Cel.,Org.(optional),1 or 2Hp.-Str.
  C.F. Peters, Leipzig, ᶜ1926
  Score 50 p.
  Composed 1924. First performance, under the
  title Legend of St. Francis, Chicago North
  Shore Festival, Evanston, Illinois, 30 May
  1925, Chicago Symphony Orchestra, Frederick
  Stock conductor. Awarded a prize by the
  Festival.

  5591 [The Basque Venus, Op. 14.   *15'*
  Symphonic dance from Act II]
  3(2nd&3rd alt. Picc.),3*,4*(3rd alt. Cl. in
  E-flat),3(3rd alt. C.Bn.)-4,3,3,1-Timp.,Perc.-
  Cel.,1(or 2)Hp.-Str.
  Brockhaus, Leipzig, ᶜ1928
  Score 99 p.

Inspired by Basque dances. From the opera based on Prosper Mérimée's short story La Vénus d'Ille. First performance Leipzig, 18 November 1928.

1497 Visionen, Op. 12   40'
1.Introduzione 2.Adagio 3.Scherzo demoniaco
4.Intermezzo ironico 5.Fugato risoluto
5.Risonanza estrema
3(alt. 3Picc.),3*,3*,3(3rd alt. C.Bn.)-4,6,6,
1(or 4,3,3,1)-Timp.,Perc.-Pno.,Cel.,Org.,
2Hp.-Str.
M. Brockhaus, Leipzig, c1924
Score 124 p.
Composed 1923. First performance Cologne, November 1923, Hermann Abendroth conductor.

WEWELER, AUGUST.   Reike, Germany 20 October 1868
                        Detmold, Germany 8 December 1952

4539 [Sleeping Beauty. Overture]
2(2nd alt. Picc.),2,2,2-4,2,3,1-Timp.,S.Dr.-
Str.
Bote & Bock, Berlin, c1904
Score 34 p.
From the opera. First performance Kassel, 1903.

WEYL, MAURICE.   Philadelphia 1869
                          Philadelphia 23 July 1936

1716s Allegro agitato   6'
Str.
Ms.
Score 16 p.
Composed 1935.

2466 4-4-4-4 [C minor]   9'
2,3*,2,2-4,2,3,1-Timp.,Cym.-Str.
Ms.
Score 47 p.
Composed 1932.

WEYSE, CHRISTOPH ERNST FRIEDRICH.
                   Altona, Germany 5 March 1774
                   Copenhagen 8 October 1842

7058 [Symphony no. 6, C minor]   ca.22'
1.Maestoso - Allegro con brio 2.Largo
3.Menuetto and Trio 4.Vivace
2,2,0,2-2,2-Timp.-Str.
Samfundet til Udgivelse af Dansk Musik,
Copenhagen, c1972
Score 145 p.
Completed 3 March 1798. First published in Copenhagen ca.1800 as Opus 1.

WHITE, CHARLES L.

7236 A fanfare for drums
Timp.orTpt.(either or both),B.Dr.,S.Dr.,T.Dr.
(any number of players),Cym.

Charles L. White, Los Angeles [n.d.]
Score 4 p.

7237 Nipponese miniatures for   5'
percussion
1.Miya-Sama 2.Kazumichi 3.Kishiko 4.Nippon
Bashi 5.Sho, Sho, Shojoji 6.Kojo no Tsuki
7.Coda: Kazumichi and Kishiko
Timp.,Perc.(7 players)
Charles L. White, Los Angeles [n.d.]
Score 8 p.
Based on popular Japanese songs.

7235 Three little pieces from the Far East,
petite suite for percussion with solos for the
kettledrums
1.Allegro 2.Andante 3.Scherzo
Timp.,Perc.(4 or more players)
Charles L. White, Los Angeles [n.d.]
Score 4 p.

WHITE, DONALD H.
        b. Narberth, Pennsylvania 28 February 1921

6696 Recitative, air, and dance, for band   7'
3*,2,8*(1Cl. in E-flat,1Alto Cl. in E-flat,
1Cb.Cl. in E-flat,1Cb.Cl. in B-flat)-4Sax.-4,
2,3Cnt.,3,2Bar.,1-Timp.,Perc.-Cb.
Ms. [Franco Colombo, New York, c1966]
Score 30 p.
Composed 1965. First performance Rochester, 6 May 1966, Eastman Wind Ensemble, Donald Hunsberger conductor. First runner-up in 1966 American Bandmasters Association competition.

WHITE, FELIX HAROLD.   London 27 April 1884
                            London 31 January 1945

3869 Fanfare for a challenge to   30"
accepted ideas. Arranged by Arthur Cohn
0,0,0,0-4,3,2,1-B.Dr.,Sn.Dr.,2Cym.
Ms.
Score 6 p.
Arranged 1943.

496s To Miranda, serenade. Edited by James
Brown
Str.
Stainer & Bell, London, c1928
Score 18 p.
Composed 1921.

WHITE, JOHN D.
        b. Rochester, Minnesota 28 November 1931

439c Dialogue concertante   14'
Solo Vc.-2,2,2,2-4,3,3-Timp.,Perc.-Str.
Ms.
Score 85 p. Large folio
Composed 1959. First reading Rochester, New York, 23 April 1959, Symposium of the Eastman School of Music, Howard Hanson conductor, the composer as soloist.

6165 Symphony no. II   22'
1.Allegretto 2.Andante 3.Theme and variations
2(2nd alt. Picc.),2(2nd alt. E.H.),2,2-4,3,3,
1-Timp.,Perc.-Str.

White, John Jesse

Rochester Music, Fairport, New York, ᶜ1961
Score 116 p. Large folio
*Composed 1960. First performance Rochester,
New York, 25 March 1960, Eastman-Rochester
Symphony Orchestra, Howard Hanson conductor.
Andante movement was awarded the Edward Ben-
jamin First Prize for music of a tranquil
nature, 1960.*

WHITE, JOHN JESSE.   Bermondsey, London 1830

724v [Concerto, violin, Hedwig, D minor]
1.Allegro appassionato 2.Andante espressivo
3.Allegro brillante
Solo Vn.-2,2,2,2-2,2,3,1-Timp.-Str.
Breitkopf & Härtel, Leipzig [1884?]
Score 154 p.

WHITE, MICHAEL.   Chicago 6 March 1931

2416s Renaissance suite for strings
1.Saltarello 2.Hymn to St. Magnus 3.Chanson
4.Cancion de cuna
Str.
Ms.
Score 21 p.
*Composed 1974. First performance Philadelphia,
27 October 1975, Mostovoy Soloists, Marc
Mostovoy conductor.*

7048 Tensions   20'
1.D and A vs. the rest 2.Percussion vs. the
rest 3.Row I vs. Row II 4.$\frac{6}{8}$ vs. $\frac{2}{4}$
2(both alt. Picc.),2,2,2-2,2,2-Perc.-Hp.-Str.
Ms. [ᶜ1971 by Michael White]
Score 20 p. Large folio
*Composed 1968. Selected for performance by
the Orchestra Society of Philadelphia as
part of its Pennsylvania Composers Project
1974, made possible by a grant from the Pennsylvania Council for the Arts with performance
materials prepared by The Fleisher Collection.
First performance Drexel University, Philadelphia, 22 June 1974, Orchestra Society of
Philadelphia, Sidney Rothstein conductor.*

WHITE, PAUL.   Bangor, Maine 22 August 1895
                      Henrietta, New York 31 May 1973

419c Andante and rondo, Op. 18   10'
Solo Vc.-2(2nd alt. Picc.),1,1,1-Hn.-Timp.,
Perc.-Cel.,Hp.-Str.
Ms. [ᶜ1945 by Elkan-Vogel, Philadelphia]
Score 24 p.
*Composed 1944. First performance Rochester,
23 October 1945, Eastman-Rochester Symphony
Orchestra, Howard Hanson conductor, Luigi
Silva soloist.*

3312 College caprice, on the Maine   5'
Y.M.C.A. (Son of a gambolier), Op. 15
3(3rd alt. Picc.),2,2,2(2nd alt. C.Bn. ad lib.)
-4,3,3,1-Timp.,Perc.-Hp.-Str.
Ms.
Score 17 p. Large folio
*Composed 1939. First performance Rochester,
4 January 1940, Rochester Civic Orchestra,
Howard Hanson conductor.*

2508 Five miniatures, Op. 7   6'
1.By the lake 2.Caravan song 3.Waltz for
Teenie's doll 4.Hippo dance 5.Mosquito dance
1(alt. Picc.),1(alt. E.H.),1,1-2,2,3-Perc.-
Hp.(or Cel.)-Str.
Elkan-Vogel, Philadelphia, ᶜ1934
Score 9 p.
*Composed for piano 1924. Transcribed 1933.
First performance Rochester, 14 January 1934,
Rochester Civic Orchestra, the composer con-
ducting.*

3000 Four spokes from the hub (Boston   9'
sketches), Op. 14
1.Boston Harbor 2.In the Fenway 3.North End
4.Gainsborough Street
3(3rd alt. Picc.),2,2,2-4,3,3,1-Timp.,Perc.-
Pno.,Cel.,Hp.-Str.
Ms.
Score 27 p. Large folio
*Written at the suggestion of Arthur Fiedler.
Composed 1938. First performance Boston, 18
June 1938, Boston Pops Orchestra, Arthur
Fiedler conductor.*

5265 Lake Placid scenes   16'
1.Sentinels 2.Mirror Lake 3.Slumber song
and pixie dance 4.Iroquois council fire
scene and war dance
3(3rd alt. Picc.),2(2nd alt. E.H.),2,3*-4,3,
3,1-Timp.,Perc.-Cel.,Hp.-Str.
Elkan-Vogel, Philadelphia, ᶜ1944
Score 57 p.
*Originally composed for smaller orchestra.
This version, 1942-43. First performance
Lake Placid, New York, ca.1943, Lake Placid
Club Sinfonietta, the composer conducting.*

3006 Lake spray, Op. 13   8'
3(3rd alt. Picc.),2,2,2-4,4,3,1-Timp.,Perc.-
Cel.,Hp.-Str.
Ms.
Score 47 p.
*Composed 1936. First performance Rochester,
22 November 1939, Rochester Philharmonic
Orchestra, José Iturbi conductor.*

2792 Little romance, Op. 5 no. 2   4'
1,1,1,1-2Hn.-Hp.(or Pno.)-Str.
Ms.
Score 7 p.
*Originally composed for piano, 1923; orches-
trated 1924. First performance Bangor, Maine,
20 April 1925, Bangor Symphony Orchestra,
A. W. Sprague conductor.*

2791 Little tune and variations, Op. 5   6'
no. 1
2,1,2,2-2,2-Timp.,Trgl.-Hp.-Str.
Ms.
Score 14 p.

5696 Lyric overture, Op. 1   8'
2,2,3*,3*-4,3,3,1-Timp.,Perc.-Hp.-Str.
Ms.
Score 36 p.
*Composed 1919. First performance Cincinnati,
18 April 1920, Cincinnati Symphony Orchestra,
the composer conducting.*

2733 Pagan festival overture, Op. 10   *4'30"*
4*,2,2,2-4,3,3,1-Timp.,Perc.-Cel.,Hp.-Str.
Ms.
Score 38 p.
Composed 1927. First performance Rochester, 28 April 1936, Eastman School Symphony Orchestra, Howard Hanson conductor.

981m Sea chanty [harp and strings]   *15'*
Solo Hp.-Str.(Cb. ad lib.)
Ms. [^c1943 by Elkan-Vogel, Philadelphia]
Score 28 p. Large folio
Commissioned by Samuel R. Rosenbaum. Composed 1941-42. First performance Rochester, 4 March 1942, Rochester Philharmonic Orchestra, José Iturbi conductor, Edna Phillips soloist.

1725s Sinfonietta, for strings, Op. 8   *18'*
1.Allegro 2.Andante 3.Allegro
Str.
Ms. [^c1935 by Elkan-Vogel, Philadelphia]
Score 17 p. Large folio
Originally composed for string quartet, 1925; revised for string orchestra, 1934. First performance Rochester, 11 November 1937, Eastman School Symphony Orchestra, broadcast over NBC, the composer conducting.

2711 Symphony, Op. 12, E minor   *18'*
1.Andante - Allegro con spirito 2.Andante
3.Allegro giusto
3(2nd&3rd alt. Picc.),2(2nd alt. E.H.),2,2-4, 3,3,1-Timp.,Perc.-Cel.,Hp.-Str.
Ms.
Score 94 p.
Composed 1931-32. First performance Rochester, 28 March 1934, Rochester Philharmonic Orchestra, Howard Hanson conductor.

3320 To youth (overture for orchestra),   *6'30"*
Op. 6
3(3rd alt. Picc.),2,2,2-4,3,3,1-Timp.,Perc.-Hp.-Str.
Ms.
Score 53 p.
Composed 1924. First performance Rochester, 1925, Eastman Theatre Orchestra, Guy Fraser Harrison conductor.

WHITHORNE, EMERSON.   Cleveland 6 September 1884
                         Lyme, Connecticut 25 March 1958

Born: Emerson Whittern

2717 The aeroplane, Op. 38 no. 2   *5'*
3*,3*,4*,3*-4,3,3,1-Timp.,Perc.-Cel.,Hp.-Str.
Ms.
Score 29 p.
Originally composed for piano, 1921. Transcribed 1925. First performance Birmingham, England, 31 January 1926, Birmingham City Orchestra, Adrian Boult conductor.

316v [Concerto, violin, Op. 46, D major]
1.Larghetto - Cadenza - Allegro moderato
2.Adagio 3.Allegro giocoso
Solo Vn.-2,3*,3*,3*-4,3,3,1-Timp.,Perc.-Hp.-Str.

Ms.
Score 98 p.
Composed 1928-31. First performance Chicago, 12 November 1931, Frederick Stock conductor, Jacques Gordon soloist.

2673 The dream pedlar, Op. 50   *16'*
4*,4*,4*,4*-4,3,3,1-Timp.,Perc.-Cel.,Hp.-Str.
Cos-Cob-Press, New York, ^c1933
Score 65 p.
Composed 1930. First performance Los Angeles, 15 January 1931, Los Angeles Philharmonic Orchestra, Artur Rodzinski conductor.

3671 Fandango, Op. 54   *6'*
3(3rd alt. Picc.),3*,3*,3*-4,3,3,1-Timp., Perc.-Cel.,Hp.-Str.
Ms.
Score 57 p.
Composed 1931. First performance New York, 19 April 1932, Musicians Symphony Orchestra, Thomas Beecham conductor.

2176 Fata Morgana, Op. 44   *20'*
3(3rd alt. Picc.),3*,3*,3*-4,3,3,1-Timp.,Perc.-Cel.,Hp.-Str.
Cos-Cob-Press, New York, ^c1930
Score 65 p.
Composed 1927. First performance New York, 11 October 1928.

2700 Moon trail, Op. 53   *16'*
1.Death Valley 2.The Devil's Kitchen 3.Palos Verdes 4.Surf at Malibu
4(3rd&4th alt. Picc.),4*,4*,4*-4,3,3,1-Timp., Perc.-Cel.,Hp.-Str.
Ms.
Score 89 p.
Originally composed for piano, 1930; orchestrated 1933. First performance Boston, 15 December 1933, Boston Symphony Orchestra, Serge Koussevitzky conductor.

2723 New York days and nights, Op. 40   *15'*
1.On the ferry 2.Chimes of St. Patrick's
3.Pell St. (Chinatown) 4.A Greenwich Village tragedy 5.Times Square
3(3rd alt. Picc.),3*,3*,3*-4,3,4,1-Timp.,Perc.-Cel.,Hp.-Str.
Ms.
Score 89 p.
Originally composed for piano, 1920; orchestrated 1922-23. First performance at the Sesqui-Centennial International Exposition, Philadelphia, 30 July 1926, The Philadelphia Orchestra, Alexander Smallens conductor.

699p Poem, for piano and orchestra,   *20'*
Op. 43
Solo Pno.-3*,3*,3*,3*-4,3,3,1-Timp.,Perc.-Str.
C. Fischer, New York, ^c1928
Score 62 p.
Composed 1926. First performance Chicago, 4 February 1927, Chicago Symphony Orchestra, Frederick Stock conductor, Walter Gieseking soloist.

Whithorne, Emerson

3833 Sierra Morena, Op. 59   6'
3(3rd alt. Picc.),3*,3*,3*-4,3,3,1-Timp.,Perc.
-Cel.,Hp.-Str.
Ms.
Score 26 p. Large folio
*Inspired by the Spanish bandits who hid in
the Sierra Morena. Composed 1938. First per-
formance over radio, New York, 7 May 1938,
NBC Symphony Orchestra, Pierre Monteux con-
ductor.*

1996s Strollers' serenade
Str.
Associated, New York, ᶜ1943 by composer
Score 16 p.

WHITMER, THOMAS CARL.
                    Altoona, Pennsylvania 24 June 1873
                    Poughkeepsie, New York 30 May 1959

5761 I walk by the three rivers, a   20-23'
tone poem
3(3rd alt. Picc.),3*,3*,3*-4,4,4,1-Timp.,Perc.
-Pno.,Org.(optional),Cel.,Hp.,Banjo-Bass
Speaking Voice-Str.
Ms.
Score 63 p. Large folio
*The three rivers are the Allegheny, Mononga-
hela, and Ohio which converge at Pittsburgh.
Originally composed 1945, at the request of
William Gibson, as Sarabande and Perpetual
Motion for brass ensemble, timpani and piano.
This version 1957.*

5755 Miniature suite   6'30"
1.Prelude 2.Old dance (Sarabande) 3.Promenade
with torches
1,1,2-2Alto Sax.-1,1,1-Timp.-Pno.,Org.(ad lib.)
-Str.
Ms.
Score 28 p.
*Composed 1950 at the request of Mihail Sto-
larewski. First performance Pittsburgh, May
1950, Chatham College Orchestra, Mihail Sto-
larewski conductor.*

2674 A Syrian night, ballet   17'
1.The night lights 2.The asp death 3.The
sucking bees 4.Sunrise
3(3rd alt. Picc.),3*,3*,3*-4,2,3,1-Timp.,Perc.
-Cel.,Hp.-Str.
C.C. Birchard, Boston, ᶜ1932 by Dramamount
Association
Score 110 p. Large folio
*Intended as part of a music drama about Mary
Magdalene. Composed 1918. First performance
Pittsburgh, 17 February 1919, Philadelphia
Orchestra, Leopold Stokowski conductor.*

WHITNEY, MAURICE C.
          b. Glens Falls, New York 25 March 1909

5701 Gavotto staccato   3'
2,2,2,2-4,2,3,1-Timp.,Perc.-Str.
Bourne, New York, ᶜ1953
Score 16 p.
*Composed 1952. First performance Glens Falls,
New York, November 1952, Glens Falls Junior*

*High School Orchestra, the composer con-
ducting.*

4747 River Jordan, fantasy on Negro   5'30"
spirituals
3*,2,6*(1Cl. in E-flat,1Alto Cl. in E-flat),
2-4Sax.-4,2,3Cnt.,3,Euph.,Bar.,1-Timp.,Perc.
G. Schirmer, New York, ᶜ1950
Score 26 p.
*Composed 1947. First performance Central
Park, New York, 20 June 1951, The Goldman
Band, Edwin Franko Goldman conductor.*

WHITTINGHAM, W. H.   New Berlin, New York 1852

3361 Symphony (second movement)
3*,Alto Fl.,3*,2,3*-4,2,3,1-Timp.-Str.
Ms.
Score 54 p.
Composed 1828; symphony perhaps not completed.

WICKENHAUSSER, Richard   Brünn 7 February 1867
                                Vienna 1 July 1936

6s [Suite, string orchestra, Op. 24, F major]
1.Praeludium 2.Air 3.Gavotte 4.Sarabande
5.Gigue
Str.
Fr. Kistner, Leipzig [n.d.]
Score 46 p.

WIDOR, CHARLES-MARIE.   Lyons 21 February 1844
                                Paris 12 March 1937

521m Choral et variations, Op. 74
Solo Hp.-2(2nd alt. Picc.),2,2,2-4,2,3,1-
Timp.,Perc.-Str.
Heugel, Paris, ᶜ1901
Score 73 p.
*Composed 1899. First performance Paris, 12
March 1900.*

506p [Concerto, piano, no. 1, Op. 39, in F]
1.Allegro con fuoco 2.Andante religioso
3.Final: Allegro
Solo Pno.-2,2,2,2-4,2,3-Timp.-Str.
J. Hamelle, Paris [n.d.]
Score 172 p.
*First performance Paris, 19 November 1876,
Louis Diemer soloist.*

521p [Concerto, piano, no. 2, Op. 77, in C]
1.Allegro con moto e patetico 2.Andante -
Allegro
Solo Pno.-3*,2,2,2-4,4,3,1-Timp.,Perc.-Str.
Heugel, Paris, ᶜ1906
Score 117 p.

610c [Concerto, violoncello, Op. 41, E minor]
1.Allegro 2.Andantino 3.Allegro vivace
Solo Vc.-2,2,2,2-4,2,3-Timp.,Trgl.-Hp.-Str.
J. Hamelle, Paris [n.d.]
Score 156 p.
*First performance Paris, 12 March 1882, Jules
Delsart soloist.*

527p Fantaisie, Op. 62
Solo Pno.-2,2,2,2-4,2,2Cnt.,3,1-Timp.,Perc.-
Str.

COLLECTION OF ORCHESTRAL MUSIC

Wieniawski, Henri

Durand, Paris [n.d.]
Score 116 p.

6991 [The fishermen of Saint John. Christmas march]
2(both alt. Picc.),2,2,2-4,2-Timp.,Perc.-Str.
Heugel, Paris, c1904
Score 26 p.
From the opera. First performance Paris, 26 December 1905.

6992 [The fishermen of Saint John. Act II. Prelude: Tranquillity of the sea]
2,2,2,2-4,2,2Cnt.,3,1-Timp.,Perc.-Hp.-Str.
Heugel, Paris, c1904
Score 21 p.

6990 Ouverture espagnole
2(2nd alt. Picc.),2,2,2-4,2,2Cnt.,3-Timp., Perc.-Str.
Heugel, Paris, c1896 and c1897
Score 58 p.

972 Sérénade, Op. 10 [B-flat major]   7'
2(2nd alt. Picc.),2,2,2-2,2-Timp.-Hp.-Str.
J. Hamelle, Paris [n.d.]
Score 44 p.
Composed 1877. First performance Paris, 1879.

592c [Suite, violoncello, Op. 21, E minor]
1.Meditation 2.Appassionato 3.Canzonetta 4.Final
Solo Vc.-2(2nd alt. Picc.),2,2,2-4,2-Timp., Perc.-Hp.-Str.
Heugel, Paris, c1913
Score 67 p.

392 [Symphony no. 2, Op. 54, A major]
1.Allegro vivace 2.Moderato 3.Andante con moto 4.Vivace
3*,2,2,2-4,2,2Cnt.,3,1-Timp.,Perc.-Str.
Durand, Paris [n.d.]
Score 169 p.

WIECK, CLARA JOSEPHINE.
See: SCHUMANN, CLARA JOSEPHINE WIECK.

WIEDEMANN, LUDWIG.

793m Auf den Lagunen, barcarole, Op. 12
Solo Bn.-1,2,0,2-2Hn.-Timp.-Str.
Score: 18 p.
Parts: A.E. Fischer, Bremen [n.d.]

834m [Concertino, clarinet, Op. 4, C minor]
1.Moderato 2.Romanze 3.Rondo
Solo Cl.-2,2,0,2-2,2,1-Timp.-Str.
Score: Ms. 74 p.
Parts: [n.p., n.d.]

784m Jägers Abschied [Hunter's farewell] Op. 13
Soli: Cl.,Hn.-0,1,1,2-Hn.-Timp.-Str.
Score: Ms. 15 p.
Parts: A.E. Fischer, Bremen [n.d.]

761m Souvenir de Wittekind, nocturne
Solo Fl.-0,0,2,1-2Hn.-Str.
Score: Ms. 20 p.
Parts: A.E. Fischer, Bremen [n.d.]

WIENER, KARL.   Vienna 27 March 1891

2528 Kammerstück, Op. 7   10'
0,1,1*,1-2Hn.-Timp.-Hp.-Str.
Adler, Berlin, c1932
Score 12 p.
Composed 1918.

WIENIAWSKI, HENRI (*or* HENRYK).
Lublin, Poland 10 July 1835
Moscow 12 April 1880

477v [Concerto, violin, no. 1, Op. 14,   22'
F-sharp minor]
1.Allegro moderato 2.Preghiera [Prayer] 3.Rondo
Solo Vn.-2,2,2,2-2,2,3-Timp.-Str.
[F. Hofmeister, Leipzig, n.d.]
Score 94 p.

438v [Concerto, violin, no. 2, Op. 22,   12'
D minor]
1.Allegro moderato 2.Romance 3.Allegro con fuoco - Allegro moderato (à la zingara)
Solo Vn.-2,2,2,2-2,2,3-Timp.-Str.
Luck's, Detroit [n.d.]
Score 118 p.

439v Fantaisie brillante, Op. 20 [on   18'
themes from Gounod's opera Faust]
Solo Vn.-3*,2,2,2-2,2,3-Timp.-Str.
Kistner, Leipzig [n.d.]
No score. Solo part 13 p.

525v Kuyawiak, 2me mazurka   3'
Solo Vn.-1,1,2,1-2Hn.-Str.
Jurgenson, Moscow [n.d.]
Score 13 p.

407v Légende, Op. 17   8'
Solo Vn.-2,2,2,2-2Hn.-Timp.-Str.
C. Fischer, New York [n.d.]
Score in reduction 11 p.

1057v [Polonaise brillante, violin, no. 2, Op. 21, A major]
Solo Vn.-2,2,2,2-2,2,3-Timp.-Str.
Score: Ms. 57 p.
Parts: B. Schott's Söhne, Mainz [n.d.]

997v Polonaise de concert, Op. 4   5'30"
Solo Vn.-2,2,2,2-2,2,1-Timp.-Str.
Score: Ms. 42 p.
Parts: H. Litolff, Brunswick [n.d.]

769v [Scherzo-tarantella, violin and piano, Op. 16. Transcribed by Paul Gilson]
Solo Vn.-2,2,2,2-2,2(ad lib.)-Timp.,Perc.-Str.
Kistner, Leipzig [n.d.]
Score 45 p.

777v Souvenir de Moscou, deux airs russes,   9'
Op. 6
Solo Vn.-2,2,2,2-2,2,3-Timp.-Str.
Jurgenson, Moscow [1878]
Score 19 p.

877

Wieniawski, Joseph

WIENIAWSKI, JOSEPH.   Lublin 23 May 1837
                            Brussels 11 November 1912

    656p [Concerto, piano, Op. 20, G minor.
    Revised edition]
    1.Allegro moderato 2.Andante 3.Allegro
    molto vivace
    Solo Pno.-2,2,2,2-4,2,3-Timp.-Str.
    A. Cranz, Leipzig [n.d.]
    Score 85 p.

WIGGERT, PAUL.

    839m Ungarische Rhapsodie no. 2, Op. 27.
    Arranged by Franz Herbst
    Solo Tpt.-1(alt. Picc.),2,2,1-4,2,3-Timp.-Str.
    Score: Ms. 37 p.
    Parts: Rühle & Wendling, Leipzig, C1928

WIHTOL, JOSEPH.   Volmar, Latvia 26 July 1863
                  Lübeck, Germany 24 April 1948

    Born: Jāzeps Vītols

    598v [Fantasy on Latvian folksongs, Op. 42]
    1.Allegro non troppo 2.Molto moderato, mesto
    3.Allegro
    Solo Vn.-2,2,2,2-4,2-Timp.,Perc.-Str.
    Belaieff, Leipzig, 1910
    Score 43 p.

    969 La fête Lihgo, Op. 4   16'
    3*,2,2,2-4,2,3,1-Timp.,Perc.-Hp.-Str.
    Belaieff, Leipzig, 1890
    Score 67 p.
    *Lihgo was a Latvian god. Composed 1889 on
    Latvian popular themes. First performance St.
    Petersburg, 1890.*

    759 [Seven Latvian folksongs, little   6'
    suite, Op. 29a]
    3(3rd alt. Picc.),3*,2,2-4Hn.-Timp.,Perc.-Str.
    Belaieff, Leipzig, 1905
    Score 17 p.
    *Composed 1904. First performance St. Peters-
    burg, 1905.*

WIHTOLIN, JANIS.
    See: VĪTOLIŅŠ, JĀNIS OTTOWITSCH.

WIKLUND, ADOLF.   Långserud, Sweden 5 June 1879
                      Stockholm 3 April 1950

    7241 [Song to the spring]   6'30"
    2,2,2,2-4,2,3-Timp.,Perc.-Hp.-Str.
    Edition Suecia, Stockholm, C1947
    Score 20 p.

    5047 [Summer night and sunrise, Op. 19] 14'
    3(3rd alt. Picc.),2,4*,3*-4,3,3,1-Timp.,Perc.-
    Hp.-Str.
    Ms.
    Score 78 p.
    Composed 1918.

    5048 Symfonisk prolog   10'
    3(3rd alt. Picc.),3(3rd alt. E.H.),3(3rd alt.
    B.Cl.),3*-4,3,3,1-Timp.-Str.

Ms.
Score 54 p.
Composed 1934.

    2291s [Three pieces for strings and harp] 20'
    1.I folkton 2.Andante espressivo 3.Molto
    ritmico
    Hp.-Str.
    Edition Suecia, Stockholm, C1945
    Score 21 p.
    Composed 1924.

WILCOX, A. GORDON.
        b. Revere, Massachusetts 26 February 1909

    6374 Ricercar and fugue (1963)   10'
    3*,3*,3*,2-4,3,3,1-Timp.-Pno.-Str.
    Ms. C1963 by A. Gordon Wilcox
    Score 54 p. Large folio
    *Composed 1963. First performance Erie, Penn-
    sylvania, 14 January 1964, Erie Philharmonic
    Orchestra, James Sample conductor.*

WILDER, ALEC.   Rochester, New York 16 February 1907

    Full name: Alexander Lafayette Chew Wilder

    6507 Carl Sandburg suite [4 movements] 16'
    2(2nd alt. Picc.),2(2nd alt. E.H.),2,2-2,2,2-
    Timp.,Perc.-Hp.-Str.
    Associated Music Publishers, New York, C1960
    Score 63 p.
    *Based on melodies from Carl Sandburg's com-
    pilation The American Songbag. Commissioned
    by Carl Havelin. Composed 1960. First per-
    formance, Twentieth Century Concert Hour
    broadcast, 20 December 1963, CBS Symphony,
    Alfredo Antonini conductor.*

    281m Concerto for oboe, string orchestra 24'
    and percussion
    1.Broadly 2.Slowly 3.Slow bounce 4.Quasi
    lento, freely
    Solo Ob.-Timp.,Perc.-Str.
    Associated Music Publishers, New York, C1957
    Score 48 p.
    *Commissioned by Mitch Miller, 1949. First per-
    formance New York, 15 February 1950, Saidenberg
    Little Symphony, Daniel Saidenberg conductor,
    Mitch Miller soloist.*

    3102 Symphonic piece
    3*,2(2nd alt. E.H.),3*,2-4,3,3,1-Timp.,Perc.-
    Hp.-Str.
    Ms.
    Score 40 p.
    Composed ca.1928.

WILHELMJ, AUGUST EMIL DANIEL FERDINAND.
              Usingen, Germany 21 September 1845
                   London 22 January 1908

    762v Alla polacca, Concertstück
    Solo Vn.-2,2,2,2-4,2,3-Timp.-Str.
    Schlesinger, Berlin [n.d.]
    Score 72 p.

765v All'ungherese, nach Franz Liszt
Solo Vn.-2,2,2,2-4,2,1-Timp.,Trgl.-Str.
Schlesinger, Berlin [n.d.]
Score 35 p.

664v In memoriam, Concertstück
Solo Vn.-2,2,2,2-2,B.Tbn.-Timp.-Str.
Schlesinger, Berlin [n.d.]
Score 39 p.

654v Italienische Suite nach Nicolo Paganini
1.Air 2.Marsch 3.Barcarole 4.Romanze
5.Moto perpetuo
Solo Vn.-2,2,2,2-2,2-Timp.-Str.
Schlesinger, Berlin [n.d.]
Score 111 p.

526v Parsifal-Paraphrase   6'
Solo Vn.-2,2,2,2-4,2,3-Timp.-Hp.-Str.
B. Schott's Söhne, Mainz [c1909]
Score 36 p.
Based on themes from Wagner's opera.

722v Romanze [revised version]
Solo Vn.-1,1,2,2-2Hn.-Str.
Schlesinger, Berlin [n.d.]
Score 15 p.

1445s Siciliano, nach Joh. Seb. Bach
2Ob.-Str.
Schlesinger, Berlin [1886?]
Score 7 p.
*Arranged from J. S. Bach's Sonata
no. 4 in C minor for piano and violin,
BWV 1017.*

534v Siegfried-Paraphrase   6'
Solo Vn.-2,1,2,2-2,2-Timp.-Str.
B. Schott's Söhne, Mainz [c1909]
Score in reduction 11 p.
Based on themes from Wagner's opera.

443v [Walther's prize song. Paraphrase]   4'
Solo Vn.-2,2,2,2-4Hn.-Hp.-Str.
B. Schott's Söhne, Mainz [n.d.]
Score 30 p.
*Arranged 1907 from Act III of Wagner's opera
Die Meistersinger von Nürnberg. First per-
formance London, 1908, August Wilhelmj
soloist.*

WILKINS, MARGARET LUCY.
          b. Surrey, England 13 November 1939

7106 Hymn to creation, Op. 24   8'
3(1st alt. Picc.),3,3,3-4,3,3-Timp.,Perc.-Str.
Ms. cby Margaret Lucy Wilkins
Score 50 p.
*Composed 1973. First performance Edinburgh,
7 September 1973, The Rehearsal Orchestra,
Harry Legge conductor.*

WILLEY, JAMES.   Lynn, Massachusetts 1 October 1939

6319 Two mood pieces for orchestra   12'
1.Adagio 2.Molto allegro
2,2(2nd alt. E.H.),2(2nd alt. B.Cl.),2(2nd
alt. C.Bn.)-4,3,3,1-Timp.,Perc.-Pno.(alt.

Cel.),Hp.-Str.
Ms.
Score 55 p. Large folio
*Composed 1962-63. Received the Louis Lane
Award, 1963.*

WILLIAMS, ALBERTO.   Buenos Aires 23 November 1862
                     Buenos Aires 17 June 1952

[Argentine suites]
1837s No. 1 Hueya, Milonga, Vidalita, Gato
1838s No. 2 Vidalita, Arrorró, Milonga, Cielito
1781s No. 3 Vidalita, Milonga, Arrorró con
variaciones, Cielito
Str.
Gurina, Buenos Aires [n.d.]
Scores: 16 p., 16 p., 20 p.

3682 [Concert overture no. 1, Op. 15, A minor]
3*,2,2,2-4,2,3,1-Timp.,Cym.-Str.
Gurina, Buenos Aires [n.d.]
Score 59 p.
Composed 1889.

3720 [Concert overture no. 2, Op. 18,   15'
G minor]
3*,2,2,2-4,2,3,1-Timp.,Cym.-Str.
Gurina, Buenos Aires [n.d.]
Score 55 p.
Composed 1892.

3786 Milongas [five Argentine dances]   12'
Op. 63
2,3*,3*,2-4,2,3,1-Timp.,Perc.-Hp.-Str.
Gurina, Buenos Aires [n.d.]
Score 40 p.
*First performance Paris, 24 February 1930,
Société des Concerts de Conservatoire, Philippe
Gaubert conductor.*

3785 [Poem of the bells, Op. 60]   20'
1.[Bells at twilight] 2.[Bells at dawn]
3.[Festival bells in the village]
3(3rd alt. Picc.),3*,3*,3*-4,3,3,1-Timp.,Perc.
-Cel.,Hp.-Str.
Gurina, Buenos Aires [n.d.]
Score 68 p.
*Composed 1913. First performance Buenos Aires,
1913, the composer conducting.*

3828 [Symphony no. 1, Op. 44, B minor]
1.Allegro assai 2.&3.Andante sostenuto -
Scherzo - Andante sostenuto 4.Allegro con
brio
3*,2,2,2-4,2,3,1-Timp.,Cym.-Hp.-Str.
Gurina, Buenos Aires [n.d.]
Score 87 p.
*Composed 1907. First performance Buenos Aires,
25 November 1907, the composer conducting.*

3807 [Symphony no. 2, The witch of the   30'
mountains, Op. 55, C minor]
1.[Echoes of the mountain] 2.[Prayer of the
monks] 3.[The white doves at prayer]
4.[The witch of the mountains]
3(3rd alt. Picc.),3*,3*,3*-4,2,3,1-Timp.,Perc.
-2Hp.-Str.
Gurina, Buenos Aires [n.d.]

Williams, Alberto

Score 127 p.
*Composed 1910. First performance Buenos
Aires, 9 September 1910, the composer con-
ducting.*

3873 [Symphony no. 9, Los batracios   20'
(tadpoles), Op. 108, B-flat major]
1.[Tadpoles' wedding procession] 2.[In the
lakes and ponds] 3.Finale
3*,3*,3*,3*-4,4,4,2-Timp.,Perc.-Cel.,Hp.-Str.
Ms.
Score 113 p.
Composed 1939.

WILLIAMS, DAVID RUSSELL.
                b. Indianapolis 21 October 1932

293p Concerto, piano 4-hands and   17'
orchestra
1.Buoyantly 2.Ponderously 3.Brightly
Solo Pno. 4-hands-3*,2,2,2-2,2,1-Timp.,Perc.-
Str.
Ms.
Score 90 p. Large folio
*Composed 1963-64. First performance Royal
Conservatory of the University of Toronto, 27
February 1965, Ettore Mazzolini conductor,
Ralph Elsaesser and Paul Helmer soloists.*

6321 In the still of the bayou, Op. 38   6'
2(2nd alt. Picc.),2,3,2-2Hn.-Str.
Ms. ^C1963 by David Russell Williams
Score 18 p.
*Composed 1963. First performance Rochester, 1
May 1963, Eastman-Rochester Symphony Orches-
tra, Howard Hanson conductor. Winner of
Edward B. Benjamin Award, third prize, for
music of a tranquil nature.*

2227s March and fugue, Op. 17   12'
Str.
Ms. ^C1963 by David Russell Williams
Score 13 p.
Composed 1956.

6322 Sinfonia in E, Op. 14   12'
1.Slowly - Moderately 2.Slowly
2(2nd alt. Picc.),2(2nd alt. E.H.),2,2-2,2,2-
Timp.,Perc.-Str.
Ms. ^C1963 by David Russell Williams
Score 35 p.
Composed 1956.

WILLIAMS, ERNEST S.   Richmond, Indiana 1881
                Kingston, New York 8 February 1947

3663 America   7'
2(2nd alt. Picc.),2,2,2-4,3,3,1-Timp.,Dr.-
Org.(ad lib.)-Str.
E. Williams School of Music, Brooklyn, ^C1941
Score 25 p.
*Composed 1940. First performance New York,
20 November 1940, New York University Orches-
tra, the composer conducting.*

3668 [Rip van Winkle. Revolutionary   6'
fantasy]
4*,2,2,2-4,3,3,1-Timp.,Perc.-Str.

E. Williams School of Music, Brooklyn, ^C1940
Score 43 p.
*From the opera based on Washington Irving's
story. Composed 1938. First performance
Saugerties, New York, 23 August 1938, E.
Williams School of Music Summer Music Camp
Orchestra, Pierre Henrotte conductor.*

3771 [Symphony, C minor. Movement 2,   11'
for orchestra]
2,2,2,2-4,3,3,1-Timp.,Perc.-Str.
E. Williams School of Music, Brooklyn, ^C1941
Score 29 p.
*Inspired by the life of Joan of Arc. Sym-
phony originally composed for band, 1938.
First performance of this excerpt transcribed
for orchestra, Kingston, New York, 14 August
1940, E. Williams School of Music Symphony
Orchestra, the composer conducting.*

WILLIAMS, GRACE.
        b. Barry, Glamorgan, Wales 19 February 1906

2336s Sea sketches, for string orchestra   17'
1.High wind 2.Sailing song 3.Channel sirens
4.Breakers 4.Calm sea in summer
Str.
Oxford University Press, London, ^C1951
Score 44 p.
*Composed 1944. First performance BBC (Wales)
network, 31 March 1947, BBC Welsh Orchestra,
Mansel Thomas conductor.*

WILLIAMS, JOHN EDWARD.

5137 Fanfare for a meeting of taxpayers.
Arranged by William J. Schinstine
3*,2,2,2-4,3,3,1-Timp.
Ms.
Score 6 p.
*Score inscribed 8 September 1921. This
arrangement ca.1953. First performance pro-
bably San Antonio, 1953, San Antonio Symphony
Orchestra, Victor Alessandro conductor.*

WILLIAMS, JOHN GERRARD.   London 10 December 1888
                Oxted, Surrey 7 March 1947

1144s Four traditional tunes
1.Fairest Jenny 2.The humours of Bath, or The
Bath medley 3.The sheep under the snow
4.The fits come on me now
2(2nd alt. Picc.),0,2-Cnt.-Perc.-Pno.(all ad
lib.)-Str.
Oxford University Press, London, ^C1926
Score 20 p.

1760 Pot-pourri, a cycle of fragments   11'
1.Lavender 2.Thyme 3.Pinks 4.Cassia
5.Roses 6.Musk 7.Rosemary and rue 7.Lilies
of the valley 8.Pot-pourri
3(3rd alt. Picc.),3*,3*,3*-4,2-Timp.,Perc.-
Cel.,2Hp.-Str.
Novello, London, ^C1921
Score 41 p.
*Inspired by Isobel Scott-Bremner's poems.
Composed 1919-20. First performance London,
9 March 1921, Albert Coates conductor.*

2386 Three miniatures   9'
  1.Dawn 2.The isle 3.Time
  2,2,2,3*-4,2,3,1-Timp.,Perc.-Hp.-Str.
  Ms.
  Score 47 p.
  Inspired by poems of Shelley. Composed 1918.
  First performance London, 5 November 1920.

1367s Three traditional Scottish tunes
  1.Green grow the rashes, oh 2.My faithful
  fond one 3.Kate Dalrymple
  2,0,2-Cnt.-Perc.-Pno.(all ad lib.)-Str.
  Oxford University Press, London, C1927
  Score 16 p.

WILLIAMS, NEAL S.
        b. Asheville, North Carolina 10 April 1954

7104 A tiger in the grass and his hair   7'
  2,2,2,2-2,2,3,1-3Perc.-Str. divisi
  Ms. C1975 by Neal S. Williams
  Score 1 p.
  Composed 1974.

WILLIAMS, RALPH VAUGHAN.
  See: VAUGHAN WILLIAMS, RALPH.

WILLIS, RICHARD MURAT.
            b. Mobile, Alabama 21 April 1929

5857 Prelude and dance   15'
  Andante mesto - Giocoso
  1,2,2,1-2,2-Timp.,Perc.-Pno.-Str.
  Ms.
  Score 72 p.
  Commissioned by a private donor through the
  Provincetown Symphony. Composed 1956. First
  performance Provincetown, Massachusetts,
  August 1956, Provincetown Symphony, Joseph
  Hawthorne conductor.

6572 Symphony no. 2 [revised]   25'
  1.Lento 2.Adagio 3.Energico
  3*,2,2,2-4,3,3,1-Timp.,Perc.-Hp.-Str.
  Ms.
  Score 118 p. Large folio
  Composed 1964. First performance Roches-
  ter, 29 April 1964, Eastman-Rochester Sym-
  phony Orchestra, Howard Hanson conductor.
  Awarded the Howard Hanson Prize, 1964.
  Revised 1965.

WILLMAN, ALLAN.   Hinckley, Illinois 11 May 1909

3094 Solitude, symphonic poem   10'
  2,2(2nd alt. E.H.),2,2-4,1-Timp.-Hp.-Str.
  Ms.
  Score 49 p.
  Composed 1931. First performance Boston, 20
  April 1936, Boston Symphony Orchestra, Serge
  Koussevitzky conductor. Awarded the Paderew-
  ski Prize, 1935.

WILLNER, ARTHUR.   Teplice, Bohemia 5 March 1881
                     London 7 April 1959

915s Concerto for string orchestra, Op. 37
  1.Adagio maestoso 2.Vivo assai

Str.
Universal Edition, Leipzig, C1927
Score 23 p.

3852 [Symphony, Op. 103, A minor]   25'
  1.Allegro risoluto 2.Andante espressivo
  3.Scherzo 4.Allegro con spirito
  2,2,3*,2-4,2,3,1-Timp.,Perc.-Str.
  Ms.
  Score 121 p.
  Composed 1940.

2382 Tanzsuite [Dance suite]   12'
  1.Maestoso 2.Sostenuto 3.Allegro molto con
  brio 4.Allegretto 5.Tempo di valse
  3*,2,2,2-4,2,3,1-Timp.,Perc.-Str.
  Ms. [Universal Edition, New York, n.d.]
  Score 30 p.
  Originally composed for piano, 1924; orches-
  trated 1929. First performance over radio,
  Leipzig, 7 September 1931, Theodor Blumer
  conductor.

1889s Through the centuries, suite
  1.Pavane 2.Gaillarde 3.Allemande 4.Courante
  5.Adagio cantabile 6.Finale burlesco
  Str.
  Ms.
  Score 10 p.

WILLSON, MEREDITH.   Mason City, Iowa 18 May 1902

3496 [Symphony no. 1, F minor]   38'
  1.Andante - Allegro moderato 2.Andante
  3.Presto 4.Allegro
  3(3rd alt. Picc.),3(3rd alt. E.H.),3(3rd alt.
  B.Cl.),3-4Sax.(AATB alt. BBTT)-Timp.,Perc.-Hp.
  -Str.
  Ms.
  Score 198 p.
  Inspired by the city of San Francisco. Com-
  posed 1934-36. First performance San Fran-
  cisco, 19 April 1936, San Francisco Symphony
  Orchestra, the composer conducting.

3497 [Symphony no. 2, The missions of   36'
  California, E minor]
  1.Junipero Serra 2.San Juan Bautista 3.San
  Juan Capistrano 4.El Camino Real
  3(2nd alt. Picc.,3rd alt. Picc.&Alto Fl.),3
  (3rd alt. E.H.),3(3rd alt. B.Cl.),3(3rd alt.
  C.Bn.)-4,4,3,1-Timp.,Perc.-Pno.(alt. Cel.),Hp.
  -Str.
  Ms.
  Score 151 p. Large folio
  Composed 1936-40. First performance Hollywood,
  4 April 1940, Los Angeles Philharmonic Orches-
  tra, Albert Coates conductor.

WILM, NIKOLAI VON.   Riga, Latvia 4 March 1834
                       Wiesbaden, Germany 20 February 1911

1030s [Character pieces, Op. 24. No. 6, At
  night]
  Str.
  F.E.C. Leuckart, Leipzig [n.d.]
  Score 3 p.
  Originally composed for piano.

Wilm, Nikolai von

613m Konzertstück, Op. 122   *14'*
Solo Hp.-2,2,2,2-4,2,3(ad lib.)-Timp.-Str.
Kistner, Leipzig [1893?]
Score in reduction 31 p.
First performance Wiesbaden, 1892.

WILMS, JAN WILLEM.
                Witzhelden, Germany 30 March 1772
                Amsterdam 19 July 1847

681p [Concerto, piano, Op. 26, D major]
1.Allegro 2.Poco adagio 3.Rondo alla polacca
Solo Pno.-1,2-2Hn.-Str.
Score: Ms. 144 p.
Parts: Hofmeister, Leipzig [181-?]

WILSON, CHRISTOPHER.   Melbourne 1874
                London 1919

253s [Suite, string orchestra, G major]
1.Prelude 2.Air 3.Scherzo 4.Bourrée
5.Romance 6.Rigaudon
Str.
B. Schott's Söhne, Mainz [1899]
Score 35 p.

WILSON, MORTIMER.   Chariton, Iowa 6 August 1876
             New York City 27 January 1932

3270 Overture, New Orleans, (Mardi Gras),   *6'*
Op. 64
2(2nd alt. Picc.),2,2,2-4,3,3-Timp.,Perc.-Hp.-
Str.
Score: Ms. 56 p.
Parts: G. Schirmer, New York, ᶜ1921
*Awarded the Riesenfeld Prize for an American
overture, 1920.*

WILTBERGER, HEINRICH.   Sobernheim 17 August 1841
             Colmar 26 May 1916

1236s Märchen [Fairy tale] Op. 58
Str.
Hug, Leipzig [n.d.]
Score 2 p.

WINDING, AUGUST HENRIK.
             Taaro, Denmark 24 March 1835
             Copenhagen 16 June 1899

450p [Concerto, piano, Op. 16, A minor]   *20'*
1.Allegro con fuoco 2.Andantino 3.Allegro
Solo Pno.-2,2,2,2-4,2-Timp.-Str.
Score: Ms. 128 p.
Parts: C.F.W. Siegel, Leipzig [1877?]

WINDSPERGER, LOTHAR.   Ampfing 22 October 1885
             Wiesbaden 29 May 1935

1546 Konzert-Ouverture, Lebenstanz, G-dur *18'*
3(3rd alt. Picc.),3*3rd alt. E.H.),3(3rd alt.
B.Cl.),3(3rd alt. C.Bn.)-4,3,3,3-Timp.-Str.
B.Schott's Söhne, Mainz, ᶜ1919
Score 41 p.
*Composed 1918.   First performance Wiesbaden,
1920.*

WINGAR, ALFRED ANDERSEN.
See: ANDERSEN-WINGAR, ALFRED.

WINKLER, ALEXANDER ADOLFOVICH.
             Kharkov 3 March 1865
             Besançon 6 August 1935

638v Air finnois varié, Op. 18
Solo Vn.-2,2,2,2-2,2-Timp.,Perc.-Str.
Belaieff, Leipzig, 1913
Score 36 p.

WINKLER, GERHARD.   Berlin 12 September 1906

4695 [Clouds over Samland]   *5'*
1,1,1-0,1,Cnt.,1-Timp.,Perc.-Pno.,Harm.-Str.
(without Va.)
B. Schott's Söhne, Mainz, ᶜ1941
Score in reduction 5 p.
*Samland was a region of East Prussia, now in
Poland.*

WINTER, PETER VON. Mannheim baptized 28 August 1754
             Munich 17 October 1825

431m [Concertante, violin, viola, oboe,
clarinet, bassoon, violoncello, and chamber
orchestra, Op. 20, B-flat major] Edited by
Thor Johnson and Donald M. McCorkle
1.Allegro 2.Rondo: Tempo giusto
Concertino: Ob.,Cl.,Bn.,Vn.,Va.,Vc.
Ripieno: 1,2,2,2-2Hn.-Str.
Ms.
Score 127 p. Large folio
*First published by Breitkopf & Härtel, Leip-
zig, ca.1815.   This edition based on a manu-
script in the Archives of the Moravian Church
in America, Bethlehem, Pennsylvania.   First
modern performance, Fifth Early American
Moravian Music Festival and Seminar, Salem
College, Winston-Salem, North Carolina, 27
June 1959, Thor Johnson conductor.*

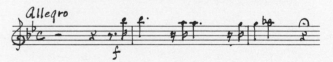

4114 I fratelli rivali [The rival brothers.
Overture]
2,2,2,2-2,1-Timp.-Str.
Ms.
Score 46 p.
*From the opera first performed Venice, Novem-
ber 1793.*

4115 [Maria von Montalban. Overture]
2,2,0,2-2Hn.-Str.
Ms.
Score 44 p.
*From the opera based on J. N. Komareck's
tragedy.   First performance Munich, 28 January 1800.*

3040 [Il ratto di Proserpina. Overture]
1,2,2,2-2,2,1-Timp.-Str.
Score: Ms. 20 p.
Parts: Breitkopf & Härtel, Leipzig [180-?]
*From the opera first performed London, 3 May
1804.*

4116 [Symphony no. 1, D major]
1.Allegro 2.Andante 3.Allegro
2,2-2Hn.-Str.
Ms.
Score 111 p.

4113 Das unterbrochene Opferfest [The
interrupted sacrifice]
2,2,2,2-2Hn.-Str.
Ms.
Score 38 p.
*From the opera first performed Vienna, 14
June 1796.*

WINTERLING, WILLIAM.

642m The two blackbirds, fantasie polka,   *4'*
Op. 38. Edited by Julius Hermann Matthey
2 Soli Picc.-0,2,2,2-2,2,3-Timp.,Perc.-Str.
J.H. Zimmermann, Leipzig, ^c1897
Piano transcription in lieu of score 7 p.

WINTERS, GEOFFREY.
                b. Chingford, Essex 17 October 1928

245p Concertino for piano, horns and   *13'*
strings, Op. 18
1.Andante 2.Allegro giocoso - Presto
Solo Pno.-2Hn.-Str.
Ms. ^c1959 by Geoffrey Winters
Score 33 p.
*Composed 1959. First performance Walthamstow,
England, 31 January 1961, South West Essex
Symphony Orchestra, John Auton conductor,
James Gibb soloist.*

281v Concerto for violin and orchestra,   *17'*
Op. 51 (1974)
1.Lento espressivo - Allegro moderato
2.Allegro scherzando
Solo Vn.-2(2nd alt. Picc.),2,2,2-4,2,3,1-Timp.,
Perc.-Hp.-Str.
Ms. ^c1974 by Geoffrey Winters
Score 57 p. Large folio
In memory of the composer's brother Eric.

7123 Intermezzo for orchestra - River   *7'*
Pastoral, Op. 7 (1954)
2,2,2,2-2Hn.-Str.
Ms. ^c1954 by Geoffrey Winters
Score 12 p. Large folio
*Inspired by the Thames River. Composed 1954.
First performance Manchester, England, 20
January 1961, Hallé Orchestra, Maurice Hand-
ford conductor.*

7304 [Symphony no. 1, Op. 23]   *14'30"*
1.Allegro molto 2.Allegro moderato 3.Adagio
molto e tranquillo 4.Allegro vivace
3(3rd alt. Picc.),2,2,2-4,3,3,1-Timp.,Perc.-
Str.

Ms. ^c1961 by Geoffrey Winters
Score 90 p.
*Composed 1961. First performance London, 4
October 1973, New Philharmonia, Owain Arwel
Hughes conductor.*

WIRÉN, DAG IVAR.   Striberg, Sweden 15 October 1905

5040 [Concert overture no. 2, Op. 16]   *5'*
2(2nd alt. Picc.),2,2,2-4,2,3,1-Timp.,Perc.-
Str.
Ms.
Score 53 p.
*Composed 1940. First performance Stockholm,
1941, Broadcasting Corporation Orchestra, Tor
Mann conductor.*

771c [Concerto, violoncello, Op. 10]   *16'*
1.Tempo moderato 2.Andante espressivo
3.Allegro
Solo Vc.-2(2nd alt. Picc.),2,2,2-2,2,1-Timp.-
Str.
Ms.
Score 72 p.
*Composed 1936. First performance Stockholm,
1940, Concert Society Symphony Orchestra, Fritz
Busch conductor, Gustav Gröndahl soloist.*

4348 [Little suite for orchestra,   *11'*
Op. 17]
1.Uvertyr 2.Burlesk 3.Final: Molto vivace
2(2nd alt. Picc.),2,2,2-2,2,1-Timp.,Perc.-Str.
Carl Gehrman, Stockholm, ^c1944
Score 32 p.
Composed 1941.

5049 [The merchant of Venice. Romantic   *12'*
suite, Op. 22]
1.[In sooth, I know not why I am so sad] 2.
[We journey to Venice] 3.Serenad för Jessica
4.[Playful dance] 5.[Portia's palace orches-
tra]
1,1,1,1-Hn.-Str.
Ms. [STIM, Stockholm, ^c1943]
Score 30 p.
*From the incidental music to Shakespeare's
play. Composed 1943. First performance
Stockholm, ca.1945, Small Chamber Orchestra of
the Broadcasting Orchestra of Stockholm, Lars-
Erik Larsson conductor.*

1929s [Serenade for string orchestra,   *16'*
Op. 11]
1.Preludium 2.Andante espressivo 3.Scherzo
4.Marcia
Str.
STIM, Stockholm, ^c1939; Carl Gehrman, Stock-
holm, ^c1944
Score 32 p.
*Composed 1937. First performance Stockholm,
1937, Stockholm Chamber Orchestra, Tobias
Wilhelmi conductor.*

WIRTH, CARL ANTON.
            b. Rochester, New York 24 January 1912

2116s Diversions in denim   *20'*
1.Excursion 2.Idlewood 3.Gallumphery

Wirth, Carl Anton

4.Lornsome 5.Shindig
Str.(Cb. ad lib.)
Ms.
Score 31 p. Large folio
Composed 1956.

5497 Elegy on an Appalachian folk song   *9'*
2,2,2,2-4,2,3,1-Timp.,Perc.-Str.
Ms.
Score 28 p. Large folio
*Based on Black Is the Color of My True Love's
Hair. Composed 1949. First performance
Rochester, 21 October 1949, Eastman-Rochester
Symphony Orchestra, Howard Hanson conductor.*

5379 Episodes from the life of Ichabod   *14'*
Crane, a set of variations
2(2nd alt. Picc.),2,3*,2-4,3,3,1-Timp.,Perc.-
Str.
Ms.
Score 53 p.
*Suggested by Washington Irving's The Legend
of Sleepy Hollow. Composed 1942. First per-
formance Rochester, 30 October 1942, Eastman-
Rochester Symphony Orchestra, Howard Hanson
conductor.*

328m Idlewood concerto for alto   *20'*
saxophone and orchestra
1.Vista 2.Scherzando 3.Ballad and finale
Solo Alto Sax.-2(2nd alt. Picc.),2,2,2-4,3,3,1
-Timp.,Perc.-Str.
Ms. c1954 by Carl Anton Wirth
Score 99 p. Large folio
*Composed Idlewood, New York, 1954. First per-
formance Chattanooga, Tennessee, 22 October
1956, Chattanooga Symphony, Julius Hegyi conductor, Sigurd Rascher soloist.*

433m Jephthah: invocation and dance   *10'*
[revised version]
Soli Sop. Sax.,Alto Sax.-Tamb.-Pno.-Str.
Ms.
Score 33 p.
*Suggested by Judges 11:30-40. Commissioned by
Sigurd Rascher. Originally composed for saxo-
phones and piano, 1958. This version 1959.
First performed during an Australian tour by
Sigurd Rascher, September-December 1959.*

2090s Portals, a prelude   *4'*
Str.
Ms.
Score 8 p.
*Inspired by Walt Whitman's poem. Originally
composed for organ, 1942. This version, 1943.
First performance St. Joseph, Michigan, 19
April 1950, Twin City Symphony, the composer
conducting.*

353p Rhapsody for piano and orchestra   *10'*
Solo Pno.-2,2,2,2-4,3,3,1-Timp.,Perc.-Str.
Ms.
Score 59 p. Large folio
*Composed 1947. First performance Rochester,
21 October 1948, Eastman-Rochester Symphony
Orchestra, Howard Hanson conductor, Alfred
Moulédous soloist.*

225m Serenade for solo woodwinds and strings
1(alt. Picc.),1,1,1-Str.
Ms.
Score 63 p.
Composed 1962.

WIRTZ, WARREN.   Keokuk, Iowa 1916

3681 Overture for orchestra   *6'30"*
2(2nd alt. Picc.),2(2nd alt. E.H.),2,2-4,3,3,
1-Timp.,Perc.-Hp.-Str.
Ms.
Score 46 p. Large folio
*Composed 1941. First performance Rochester,
24 April 1941, Rochester Civic Orchestra,
Howard Hanson conductor.*

WISCHNEGRADSKI, A.

970 La nonne, poème symphonique   *15'*
3*,3*,3,3*-4,3,3,1-Timp.,Perc.-Cel.,2Hp.-Str.
Belaieff, Leipzig, 1912
Score 125 p.
Inspired by Sergei Gorodetski's poem.

2184 [Suite. Andante, valse, tarantelle]
3(3rd alt. Picc.),3*,3,3*-4,3,3,1-Timp.,Perc.-
Cel.,Hp.-Str.
J.H. Zimmermann, St. Petersburg [n.d.]
Score 117 p.

1056 [Symphony no. 2, Op. 7, B-flat minor] *35'*
1.Largo - Allegro 2.Andante 3.Allegretto
4.Allegro
3(3rd alt. Picc.),2*,3,3*-4,3,3,1-Timp.,Perc.-
Hp.-Str.
Bote & Bock, Berlin [1914?]
Score 149 p.
Composed 1913.

5124 [Symphony no. 4, C minor, Op. 12]
1.Maestoso 2.Scherzo 3.Andante 4.Finale
3(3rd alt. Picc.),3*,3,3*-4,3,3,1-Timp.,Perc.-
Cel.,Hp.-Str.
Belaieff, Leipzig, 1922
Score 220 p.

WISSMER, PIERRE.   Geneva 30 October 1915

2035s [Movement for string orchestra]   *8'*
1.Maestoso 2.Andantino 3.Allegro
Str.
Durand, Paris, c1939
Score 14 p.
*Composed 1937. First performance Geneva, 1
February 1940, Orchestre Jane Evrard, Jane
Evrard conductor.*

WITKOWSKI, GEORGES-MARTIN.
        Mostaganem, Algeria 6 January 1867
        Lyons 12 August 1943

533p Mon lac, prélude, variations et   *23'*
final
Solo Pno.-3(3rd alt. Picc.),3*,3(3rd alt.
B.Cl.),3(3rd alt. C.Bn.)-4,3,4-Timp.,Perc.-Cel.,
Hp.-Str.
Rouart Lerolle, Paris, c1923

Score 138 p.
*Composed 1921. First performance Lyons, 20
November 1921, Blanche Selva soloist.*

6988 [Symphony no. 1, D minor]
1.Lent et solennel - Animé - Modéré 2.Très
lent 3.Animé
3*,3*,3*,2-4,3,3,1-Timp.,Perc.-2Hp.-Str.
Durand, Paris [1898]
Score 140 p.
Composed 1900.

WITT, JEREMIAS FRIEDRICH.
Hallenbergstetten, Württemberg 8 November 1770
Würzburg 1837

4117 [Symphony no. 1, B-flat major]
1.Adagio - Allegro vivace 2.Adagio 3.Menu-
etto 4.Finale: Allegro
1,2,2,1-2Hn.-Str.
Ms.
Score 124 p.
*First published by J. André, Offenbach a.M.,
ca.1804.*

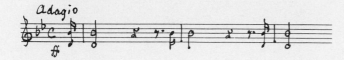

4118 [Symphony no. 2, D major]
1.Grave - Allegro non tanto 2.Adagio
3.Menuetto 4.Finale: Allegro non tanto
1,2,0,1-2Hn.-Str.
Ms.
Score 146 p.
*First published by J. André, Offenbach a.M.,
ca.1804.*

6608 [Symphony, A major] Edited by   28'
Gerhard Staar
1.Adagio 2.Menuetto allegro 3.Andante
4.Allegretto
1,2,0,2-2Hn.-Str.
Breitkopf & Härtel, Leipzig [c1963]
Score 68 p.

146 [Symphony, Jena, C major] Edited by   25'
Fritz Stein
1.Adagio - Allegro vivace 2.Adagio cantabile
3.Menuetto: Maestoso - Trio 4.Finale: Allegro
1,2,0,2-2,2-Timp.-Str.

Breitkopf & Härtel, Leipzig [1911]
Score 44 p.
*Edited from Ms. parts found in the archives of
the Akademisches Konzert, Jena, in 1909; long
misattributed to Beethoven. First modern performance Jena, 17 January 1910, Fritz Stein
conductor. This work appears in Kinsky's
thematic catalog of Beethoven's works
(Kinsky Anh.1).*

WITT, LEOPOLD FRIEDRICH.
Königsberg, 17 August 1811
Kiel 1 January 1891

1261s [Love's sorrow, romance, Op. 59]
Str.
O. Forberg, Leipzig [n.d.]
Score 9 p.

847s [Sunday rest, melody, Op. 69]
Str.
F. Schuberth, Hamburg [n.d.]
Score 3 p.

WITTE, GEORG HENDRIK.
Utrecht, Holland 16 November 1843
Essen, Germany 1 February 1929

911v [Concerto, violin, Op. 18, D major]
1.Allegro non troppo 2.Andante cantabile
3.Allegro con fuoco
Solo Vn.-2,2,2,2-2,2-Timp.,Trgl.-Str.
Tischer & Jagenberg, Cologne, c1914
Score 55 p.
*Composed 1889. First performance Essen, 1
December 1889, the composer conducting, Gustav
Holländer soloist.*

683c [Concerto, violoncello, Op. 12, A minor]
1.Allegro appassionato - Andante 2.Allegro
giojoso
Solo Vc.-2,2,2,2-2,2,B.Tbn.-Timp.-Str.
C. Kühle, Leipzig [n.d.]
Score 45 p.

WITTEBORN, OTTO.   Polleben 23 March 1874

636s Herzliebchen, Intermezzo, Op. 22
Str.
Apollo, Berlin, c1905
Score 7 p.

WITTELL, CHESTER.   Cordelia,
near Columbia, Pennsylvania 20 September 1893

7327 Algerian suite   25'
1.Dance of the Ouled Naels 2.Moghrebian
serenade 3.Scene Berber
2(2nd alt. Picc.),2(2nd alt. E.H.),2,2-4,2,3,1
-Timp.,Perc.-Hp.-Str.
Ms.

Wittell, Chester

Score 74 p. Large folio
Composed 1940. First performance Reading,
Pennsylvania, ca.1945, Reading Symphony Orches-
tra, Walter Pfeiffer, conductor.

7093 From the lips of Memnon, overture-   20'
fantasy
3*,3*,2,2-4,3,3,1-Timp.,Perc.-Str.
Ms.
Score 111 p. Large folio
Memnon is the famous singing statue of Egypt.
Composed ca.1952. First performance Reading,
1955, Reading Symphony Orchestra, Alexander
Hillsberg conductor.

7091 Heroic symphony, Op. 70 [revised]   30'
1.Maestoso - Allegro moderato 2.Andante con
moto 3.Allegro risoluto
3*,3*,2,2-4,3,3,1-Timp.,Perc.-Str.
Ms.
Score 151 p. Large folio
Composed 1954. Revised 1974.

246p Symphonic variations for piano and   35'
orchestra, Op. 60
Solo Pno.-3(3rd alt. Picc.),3*,2,2-4,2,3-Timp.,
Cym.-Str.
Ms.
Score 168 p. Large folio
Composed ca.1935. First performance Colum-
bia, Pennsylvania, 1950, Columbia Symphony
Orchestra, the composer conducting.

WITTMANN, G.

651c Prière du soir, nocturne
Solo Vc.-2,2,2,3*-4,2,3,Ophicl.-Timp.,Bells-
Hp.-Str.
Score: Ms. 9 p.
Parts: Evette & Schaeffer, Paris [n.d.]

WITTMANN, R.

805m [Concerto, two trumpets, E-flat major]
1.Allegro marciale 2.Allegretto - 3 variations 3.Marcia lugubre
2Soli Tpt.-1,1,2,1-2,0,1-Timp.-Str.
Score: Ms. 52 p.
Parts: J.G. Seeling, Dresden [n.d.]

WITTMER, EBERHARD LUDWIG.
            b. Freiburg, Germany 20 April 1905

4494 [Suite for band]
1.[Prelude] 2.[Song] 3.[Happy play]
4.[Dance]
1(ad lib.),0,3(1Cl. in E-flat ad lib.),1(ad
lib.)-0,2,2Fluegelhn.,2Ten.Hn.(or 2B.Fluegel-
hn.),2Waldhn.(or Tpt.&B.Tpt.),2,Bar.,2-Timp.,
Perc.
Chr. Friedrich Vieweg, Berlin, C1941
Score 23 p.
Composed 1940.

WOEBER, OTTOKAR.   Vienna 23 January 1859

31 Japanese war pictures. Orchestrated   5'
by Ottokar Woeber

1.Drill song 2.Transition 3.National hymn
4.My prince; rider's song
2(2nd alt. Picc.),2,2,2-4,3,3,1-Perc.-Str.
Breitkopf & Härtel, Leipzig, C1904
Score 27 p.
From Shogaku Shoka, Japanese popular songs
arranged for piano by Georg Capellen.

WOLF, BERNHARD.
   See: WOLFF, BERNHARD.

WOLF, HUGO.   Windischgraz, Styria 13 March 1860
                  Vienna 22 February 1903

1431 [Der Corregidor. Prelude *and*   6'
Entr'acte]
3*,2,2,2-4,3,3,1-Timp.-Str.
Bote & Bock, Berlin [n.d.]
Score 20 p.
From the opera composed 1895. First perform-
ance Mannheim, 7 June 1896.

195 Italienische Serenade   7'
Solo Va.-2,2,2,2-2Hn.-Str.
Lauterbach & Kuhn, Leipzig [n.d.]
Score 30 p.
Composed 1893-94. First performance Graz, 29
January 1904.

5869 [Penthesilea, symphonic poem] Edited   35'
by Robert Haas
1.[March of the Amazons on Troy] 2.[Penthe-
silea's dream of the Rose-Festival] 3.[Strife,
fury, frenzy, destruction]
3*,3*,2,3-4,4,3,1-Timp.,Perc.-Hp.-Str.
Hugo Wolf: Nachgelassene Werke, III/2. Musikwissenschaftlicher Verlag, Leipzig, C1937
Score 143 p.
Inspired by Heinrich von Kleist's tragic drama.
Composed 1883-85. Revised 1897. This first
publication of entire original version with
the revisions of 1897 is based on Wolf's auto-
graph in the Nationalbibliothek, Vienna.

5898 [Symphony, unfinished, G minor.   16'
2.Scherzo *and* 4.Finale] Edited and orchestration
completed by Helmut Schultz
3*,2,2,2-4,3,3,1-Timp.(2 players),Perc.-Str.
Hugo Wolf: Nachgelassene Werke, III/3. Musikwissenschaftlicher Verlag, Leipzig, C1940.
Score 107 p.
Symphony originally planned in B-flat major.
Scherzo sketched 1876; revised and completed,
1877. Finale originally composed as Rondo
Capriccioso for piano in B-flat major, Op. 15,
1876. Wolf later replaced the Finale with a
new movement which is now lost.

WOLF, KARL LEOPOLD.   Meerane 1 November 1859
                           Berlin 15 August 1932

280s Serenade, Op. 30, F major
Str.
Reinecke, Leipzig [n.d.]
Score 31 p.

WOLF, OTTO.   Bernburg, Germany 7 November 1874
                           d. ca.1930

608v Romance, Op. 34
Solo Vn.-2,2,2,2-2Hn.-Str.
Kahnt, Leipzig, ᶜ1905
Score 27 p.

528c Romance, Op. 64
Solo Vc.-1,0,2,2-2Hn.-Timp.-Str.
Kahnt, Leipzig, ᶜ1905
Score 24 p.

WOLFERMANN, ALBERT.   Altenburg 25 April 1844
                             Dresden 10 January 1908

750m Notturno, Op. 5
Solo Hn.(or Vc.),Solo Vn.(or Fl.)-1,1,2,2-
Timp.-Str.
Score: Ms. 17 p.
Parts: Hoffarth, Dresden [n.d.]

WOLFF, ALBERT LOUIS.   Paris 19 January 1884
                              Paris 20 February 1970

4943 [Wandering of the deceased soul,   18'
symphonic poem]
3*,3*,3*,3*-4,3,3,1-Timp.,Perc.-Hp.-Str.
Durand, Paris, ᶜ1928
Score 60 p.

WOLFF, BERNHARD.   Rakowitz 23 April 1835
                          Berlin 11 March 1906

742m Adagio, Op. 205 no. 4. Arranged by Otto
Brinkmann
Solo Tpt.-2,2,2,2-2,2,3-Timp.-Str.
Score: Ms. 9 p.
Parts: Bote & Bock, Berlin, ᶜ1900

WOLFF, ÉDOUARD.   Warsaw 15 September 1816
                         Paris 16 October 1880

802m [Concerto, trumpet, Op. 40, F minor]
In one movement
Solo Tpt.-2(2nd alt. Picc.),2,2,2-4,2,3-Timp.
-Str.
Score: Ms. 72 p.
Parts: Rühle & Wendling, Leipzig [n.d.]

WOLFF, KURT VON.
See: WOLFURT, KURT VON.

WOLF-FERRARI, ERMANNO.   Venice 12 January 1876
                                Venice 21 January 1948

19 [L'amore medico. Overture]   10'
3*,3*,3*,2-4,3,3,1-Timp.,Perc.-Hp.-Str.
Weinberger, Leipzig, ᶜ1913
Score 34 p.
*Composed 1912. First performance as Der
Liebhaber als Arzt, Dresden, December 1913.*

20 [L'amore medico. Intermezzo]   3'
2,3*,3*,2-4,1-Timp.-Hp.-Str.
Weinberger, Leipzig, ᶜ1913
Score 10 p.

4762 La dama boba [Miss Simpleton.   8'
Overture]
3*,2,2,2-4,3,3,1-Timp.,Trgl.-Hp.-Str.

Ricordi, Milan, ᶜ1938
Score 28 p. Large folio
*From the opera based on Lope de Vega's comedy.
First performance Milan, 1 February 1939.*

987m [Idillio-concertino, Op. 15,   20'
A major]
1.Preambolo 2.Scherzo 3.Adagio 4.Rondo
Solo Ob.-2Hn.-Str.
Ricordi, Milan, ᶜ1932
Miniature score 35 p.
*First performance Venice, September 1932,
Franco Ghione conductor.*

1752 [The jewels of the Madonna.   3'
Intermezzo II]
3*,3*,3*,3-4,3,3,1-Timp.,Trgl.-Hp.-Str.
Weinberger, Leipzig, ᶜ1911
Score 18 p.
*Composed 1909. First performance Charlotten-
burg, 1911.*

2298 Kammersymphonie, Op. 8
1.Allegro moderato 2.Adagio 3.Vivace con
spirito 4.Finale
1,1,1,1-Hn.-Pno.-Str. Quintet
Rahter, Hamburg, ᶜ1903
Score 81 p.

607s Das neue Leben, Op. 9. No. 3, Engelreigen
Timp.-Pno.,2Hp.-Str.
Rahter, Hamburg, ᶜ1904
Score 7 p.
Inspired by Dante's La Vita Nuova.

1753 [Il segreto di Susanna. Overture]   3'
3*,2,2,2-4,2,3-Timp.-Hp.-Str.
Kalmus, New York [n.d.]
Score 22 p.
*Composed 1908. First performance Munich,
December 1909.*

167s Serenade [E-flat major]
1.Allegro 2.Andante 3.Scherzo 4.Finale
Str.
Steingräber, Leipzig [n.d.]
Score 27 p.

989m [Suite-concertino, Op. 16, F major]   20'
1.Notturno 2.Strimpellata 3.Canzone 4.Finale
Solo Bn.-2Hn.-Str.
Ricordi, Milan, ᶜ1932
Miniature score 34 p.
*First performance Rome, 26 March 1933, M.
Rossi conductor.*

2990 [Venetian suite, Op. 18]   14'
1.[On the lagoon] 2.[Barcarolle] 3.[At night
(Deserted canals)] 4.[Festival morning]
1,1,2,2-2,2(2nd ad lib.),2(ad lib.)-Hp.(ad
lib.)-Str.
Leuckart, Leipzig, ᶜ1936
Score 43 p.
*Composed 1936. First performance Baden-Baden,
5 April 1936, Baden-Baden Kurorchester, H.
Albert conductor.*

Wolfurt, Kurt von

WOLFURT, KURT VON. Lettin, Latvia 7 September 1880
                                          Munich 25 February 1957

Real name: Kurt von Wolff

4848 [Triple fugue for orchestra, Op. 16]   *14'*
3*,2(2nd alt. E.H.),2,2-4,3,3,1-Timp.,Perc.-
Hp.-Str.
Eulenburg, Leipzig, c1929
Miniature score 68 p.
First performance Schwerin, 20 May 1928, Musi-
cians' Festival of the Universal German Music
Society.

WOLTMANN, FREDERICK.
                              b. Flushing, New York 13 May 1908

921m Poem for flute and small orchestra   *6'*
Solo Fl.-0,3*,2,2-2Hn.-Timp.-Str.
Ms.
Score 20 p.
Composed 1935. First performance Rochester,
17 November 1935, Rochester Civic Orchestra,
Guy Fraser Harrison conductor, Joseph Mari-
ano soloist.

919m Poem for horn and strings   *4'30"*
Solo Hn.-Str.
Ms.
Score 5 p.
Originally composed for horn and string
quartet; transcribed, 1936.

918m Rhapsody for horn and orchestra   *8'*
Solo Hn.-3(3rd alt. Picc.),3*,3*,2-0,2,3,1-
Timp.,Perc.-Str.
Ms.
Score 28 p.
Composed 1934. First performance Rochester,
12 December 1935, Rochester Philharmonic
Orchestra, Howard Hanson conductor, Edward
Murphy soloist.

WOOD, HAYDN.   Slaithwaite, England 25 March 1882
                              London 11 March 1959

3227 Apollo overture   *8'*
2,2,2,2-4(or 2),2,3-Timp.,Cym.-Str.
Boosey & Hawkes, London, c1935
Score 48 p.

3449 King Orry rhapsody   *10'*
2(2nd alt. Picc.),2,2,2-4(3rd&4th ad lib.),2,3
-Timp.,Cym.-Org.,Hp.-Str.
Boosey & Hawkes, London, c1939
Score 41 p.

3248 A Manx overture   *9'*
2(2nd alt. Picc.),2,2,2-4(3rd&4th ad lib.),2,3
-Timp.,Cym.-Str.
Boosey & Hawkes, London, c1937
Score 40 p.

WOOD, RALPH WALTER.
                              b. Plumstead, Kent 31 May 1902

158m Concerto per oboe ed archi   *18'30"*
1.Andantino 2.Allegro, ma non troppo

3.Andante 4.Moderato
Solo Ob.-Str.
Ms. c1973 by R. W. Wood
Score 23 p.
Composed 1973.

7306 Symphony no. 2 [revised version]   *26'*
1.Allegro moderato 2.Lento 3.Allegro
moderato 4.Allegro moderato
2(2nd alt. Picc.),2,2,2-4,2,3-Timp.,Perc.-
Cel.,Hp.-Str.
Ms. c1974 by R.W. Wood
Score 112 p.
Composed 1949-51. Revised 1974.

WOODGATE, LESLIE.

1333s English dance suite, Op. 12
1.Pastoral dance 2.Country dance 3.Hornpipe
Pno.(ad lib.)-Str.
Goodwin & Tabb, London, c1929
Score 16 p.

WOOD-HILL, MABEL.   Brooklyn 12 March 1870
                              Stamford, Connecticut 1 March 1954

3034 Reactions to Prose Rhythms of   *10'*
Fiona Macleod [revised version]
1.Nocturne 2.Lances of gold 3.The reed
player 4.The white merle
1,1,1,1-Hn.-Timp.-Hp.-Str.
Ms.
Score 34 p.
Fiona Macleod is a pseudonym for William
Sharp (1856-1905).

WOODS, FRANCIS CUNNINGHAM.   London 29 August 1862
                              London 21 September 1929

1292s The Gressenhall, suite
1.Preamble 2.A Norfolk folk tune 3.Slow air
4.Jig and finale
Pno.-Str.
Score: Ms. 40 p.
Parts: Hawkes & Son, London, c1915

1071 [Suite, F major]   *30'*
1.Prelude 2.Allemande 3.Slow air
4.Minuet and trio 5.Scherzo and trio
2,2,2,2-2Hn.-Timp.-Str.
Breitkopf & Härtel, Leipzig, c1901
Score 57 p.

WOOLLETT, HENRI ÉDOUARD.   Le Havre 13 August 1864
                              Le Havre 9 October 1936

2091 Petite suite
1.[Rustic dance] 2.[Morning song] 3.[Choral]
4.[Old popular song from Poitiers] 5.[Foolish
scherzo]
2,2(2nd alt. E.H.),2,2-4(Tpt. in D ad lib.),3-
Timp.,Cym.-Str.
Leduc, Paris [n.d.]
Score 40 p.

2286 Sentier couvert [The hidden path]   *6'*
2,3*,4(2 ad lib.),2-4,3-Timp.,Trgl.-Pno.,Hp.-
Str.

Senart, Paris, c1930
Score 18 p.
Composed 1912. First performance Paris, May 1914.

WORK, FREDERICK J.   Nashville 1885
                        Philadelphia 20 January 1942

Suite negre
3081   I. From my window   5'
3082   II. Idyl   5'
3083   III. Serenade   6'
3084   IV. Dance   6'
3*,2,2,2-4,2,3,1-Timp.,Perc.-Hp.-Str.
Ms.
Scores: 36 p., 21 p., 52 p., 31 p
Composed 1935. First performance Trenton, 28 April 1936, Trenton Symphony Orchestra, Max Jacobs conductor.

WORMSER, ANDRÉ ALPHONSE TOUSSAINT.
                        Paris 1 November 1851
                        Paris 4 November 1926

464s Les violins de Mr. de Conty
Str.
Lemoine, Paris, c1913
Score 8 p.

WOYRSCH, FELIX.
        Troppau, Austrian Silesia 8 October 1860
        Altona-Hamburg 20 March 1944

810v [Concerto, violin, Scaldic rhapsody, Op. 50, D minor]
1.Heldensage 2.Ballade 3.Heimfahrt
Solo Vn.-2,2,2,2-4,2,3,1-Timp.,Cym.-Hp.-Str.
Vieweg, Berlin, c1904
Score 100 p.
First performance Altona, Germany, Willy Hess soloist.

Drei Böcklin-Fantasien, Op. 53
2525 No. 1. Die Toteninsel [Isle of the dead]
3,3*,3*,3*-4,3,3,1-Timp.,Perc.-Hp.-Str.
2524 No. 2. Der Eremit [The hermit]
2,2,2,2-2,3,3,1-Timp.,Perc.-Org.(ad lib.),Hp.-Str.
794   No. 3. Im Spiel der Wellen [In the play of the waves]
3(3rd alt. Picc.),3*,3*,3*-4,3,3,1-Timp.,Perc.-Hp.-Str.
Breitkopf & Härtel, Leipzig, c1910
Scores: 19 p., 15 p., 48 p.
Composed 1909. First performance Altona, Germany, 1910, the composer conducting.

4572 [Overture to Shakespeare's Hamlet,   12'
Op. 56]
3(3rd alt. Picc.),3*,3*,2-4,3,3,1-Timp.,Perc.-Hp.-Str.
Leuckart, Leipzig, c1913
Score 59 p.
Composed 1913.

4202 [Symphonic prologue to Dante's Divine Comedy, Op. 40]
3*,2,2,2-4,2,3,1-Timp.-Hp.-Str.

Martin Oberdörffer, Leipzig [189-?]
Score 87 p.
Composed 1892.

4512 [Symphony no. 2, Op. 60, C major]   48'
1.Belebt 2.Sehr langsam und getragen 3.Einfach und schlicht; etwas gemächliches Zeitmass
4.Lebhaft und feurig
3(3rd alt. Picc.),3*,3*,3*-4,3,3,1-Timp.-Str.
Simrock, Berlin, c1927
Score 150 p.
Composed 1914.

4509 [Symphony no. 3, Op. 70, E-flat   38'
minor]
1.Bewegt, doch nicht übereilt 2.Mässig schnell
3.Langsam 4.Lebhaft und feurig
3(3rd alt. Picc.),3*,3*,3*-4,3,3,1-Timp.-Hp.-Str.
Simrock, Berlin, c1928
Score 130 p.
Composed 1921.

WRANITZKY, PAUL.
        Neureisch, Moravia 30 December 1756
        Vienna 28 September 1808

4119 [Symphony, Op. 37, D major]
1.Larghetto - Allegro molto 2.Andante
3.Presto 4.Allegro
2,2,2,2-2Hn.-Str.
Ms.
Score 224 p.

4120 [Symphony, Op. 50, G major]
1.Poco adagio - Allegro molto 2.Andante
3.Allegretto vivace - Alternativo 4.Allegro vivace
2,2,2,2-2Hn.-Str.
Ms.
Score 98 p.

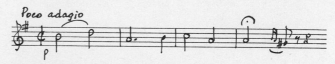

4121 [Symphony, Op. 51, A major]
1.Adagio - Allegro molto vivace 2.Andante
3.Allegretto 4.Allegro vivace assai
2,2,2,2-2Hn.-Str.
Ms.
Score 125 p.

Wranitzky, Paul

4122 [Symphony, Op. 52, D major]
1.Adagio maestoso - Allegro molto 2.Adagio
3.Allegretto vivace 4.Vivace assai
2,2,2,2-2Hn.-Str.
Ms.
Score 133 p.

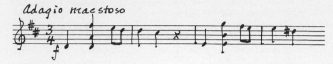

WRIGHT, KENNETH.   Hastings, Nebraska 1913

4286 Concerto grosso
1.Allegro 2.Andante 3.Allegro
2,2,2,2-4,3,3-Timp.,Perc.-Str.
Ms.
Score 131 p. Large folio
Composed 1940-41.

WRIGHTSON, HERBERT JAMES.
            Sunderland, England 20 December 1869
            West Lebanon, New York 24 December 1949

455m Concerto for organ and orchestra
1.Allegro moderato e maestoso 2.Andante molto
3.Con brio, non troppo allegro
Solo Org.-2,2,2,2-4,2,3,1-Timp.-Str.
Ms.
Score 106 p.
Composed 1902.

5630 [Symphony, E minor]
1.Allegro ma non troppo 2.Andante, molto
sostenuto 3.Allegretto scherzoso 4.Moderato
con moto e risoluto
3*,2,2,2-4,4,3,1-Timp.-Str.
Ms.
Score 166 p.
Composed 1901.

WÜERST, RICHARD FERDINAND. Berlin 22 February 1824
                            Berlin 9 October 1881

993v [Concerto, violin, Op. 37, in A]
1.Allegro animato 2.Adagio 3.Allegro con
moto
Solo Vn.-2,2,2,2-2,2-Timp.-Str.
Ms.
Score 174 p.

4508 [A fairytale, Op. 44]
2,2,2,2-4,3,3-Timp.,Perc.-Str.
Bote & Bock, Berlin [1866]
Score 90 p.

296s Intermezzo, Op. 53 [D major]
Str.
Bote & Bock, Berlin [n.d.]
Score 8 p.

174s Russische Suite, Op. 81 [in E]
1.[Prelude] 2.[Reverie] 3.Intermezzo
4.Trepak
Solo Vn.-Str.

H. Erler, Berlin [n.d.]
Score 15 p.

4511 [Symphony no. 2, Op. 52, D minor]
1.Largo - Allegro con impeto 2.Andante
quasi allegretto 3.Allegro con moto
4.Allegro con fuoco
2,2,2,2-2,2,3-Timp.-Str.
Bote & Bock, Berlin [1870]
Score 202 p.

2090 Tanz der Mücken, Fliegen und Käfer   4'
[Dance of the gnats, flies and beetles] Op. 87
2*,2(1st alt. E.H.),2,2-4Hn.-Timp.,Perc.-Str.
Ries & Erler, Berlin [n.d.]
Score 17 p.
Composed 1880. First performance Berlin, 1881.

265s Unterm Balkon [Under the balcony] Op. 78
Solo Vc.-Str.
Ries & Erler, Berlin [n.d.]
Score 7 p.

WUNSCH, HERMANN.   Neuss, Germany 9 August 1884
                       Berlin 21 December 1954

558p [Chamber concerto, piano, Op. 22]   20'
In one movement
Solo Pno.-1,1,1,1-2Hn.-Str.
B. Schott's Söhne, Mainz, c1925
Score 89 p.
Composed 1923. First performance Kiel, June
1925, Tonkünstler Festival.

3927 Fest auf Monbijou, Op. 50   14'
1.Intrada 2.Sarabanda 3.Menuett 4.Gavotte
5.Halali
2,2,2,2-2,2-Timp.-Str.
Eulenburg, Leipzig, c1933
Miniature score 46 p.
First performance Bonn, 26 January 1933.

4232 Kleine Lustspiel-Suite, Op. 37   10'
1.Heldische Fabel 2.Rührszene 3.Intrigen-
spiel 4.Finale
2(2nd alt. Picc.),2,2,2-4,2,3-Timp.,Perc.-Str.
Eulenburg, Leipzig, c1930
Miniature score 40 p.

907s Serenade, Op. 41
1.[March] 2.[Song] 3.[Minuet] 4.Polonaise
5.[March]
2Fl.(ad lib.)-Str.(Cb. ad lib.)
Kistner & Siegel, Leipzig, 1932
Score 16 p.

WUORINEN, CHARLES.   New York 9 June 1938

257p [Concerto, piano, no. 1]   18'
Solo Pno.-3,3,3,3-4,3,3,1-Timp.,Perc.-Hp.-Str.
Composers Facsimile Edition, New York, c1966
by Charles Wuorinen [Now published by C.F.
Peters, New York]
Score 190 p. Large folio
Commissioned by the University of Iowa. Com-
posed 1965-66. First performance Iowa City,
1966, University of Iowa Orchestra, James
Dixon conductor, the composer as soloist.

Y

6882 [Symphony no. 3]   17'
In 2 parts
3(3rd alt. Picc.),3,3,3-4,3,3,1-Timp.,Perc.-
Pno.-Str.
Ms. Composers Facsimile Edition, New York,
c1960 by Charles Wuorinen
Score 85 p. Large folio
*Commissioned by the Orchestra of America.
Composed 1959. First performance New York, 11
November 1959, Orchestra of America, Richard
Korn conductor.*

WURM, MARY.   Southampton, England 18 May 1860
                     Munich 21 January 1938

217s Estera gavotte
Str.
Augener, London [n.d.]
Score 5 p.
Originally composed for piano.

WURMB, RUDOLF.

1462s Sérénade provençale, Op. 18
Fl.-Str.
J. André, Offenbach a.M. [n.d.]
Score 6 p.

1290s Ständchen [Serenade] Op. 8
Pno.-Str.
J. André, Offenbach a.M. [n.d.]
Score 7 p.

1451s Wiegenlied [Cradle song] Op. 10
Fl.-Str.
J. André, Offenbach a.M. [n.d.]
Score 7 p.

WYKES, ROBERT. Aliquippa, Pennsylvania 19 May 1926

4959 Concert overture
3*,2,3*,2-4,2,3,1-Timp.,Perc.-Str.
Ms.
Score 70 p. Large folio
*Composed 1951. First performance Austin,
Texas, 23 March 1953, Southwestern Symposium
of Contemporary Music, Clifton Williams con-
ductor.*

WYLIE, RUTH SHAW.   Cincinnati 24 June 1916

3788 Suite for orchestra   12'
1.The green pears 2.Quicksilver boy (scherzo)
3.Nocturne
2,2(2nd alt. E.H.),3,2-4,3,3,1-Timp.,Perc.-Cel.
(optional),Hp.-Str.
Ms.
Score 47 p.
*Based on poems by Jeanne E. Wylie. Composed
1940. First performance Rochester, 24
April 1941, Rochester Civic Orchestra, Howard
Hanson conductor.*

YARDUMIAN, RICHARD.   Philadelphia 5 April 1917

5214 Armenian suite   16'
1.Introduction 2.Song 3.Lullaby 4.Dance I
5.Interlude 6.Dance II 7.Finale
4*,4*,4*(1Cl. in D),4*-6,4,4,1-Timp.,Perc.-Hp.
-Str.
Ms. [Elkan-Vogel, Philadelphia, c1953]
Score 42 p. Large folio
*Composed 1936-37. Finale added 1954. First
performance Philadelphia, 5 March 1954, The
Philadelphia Orchestra, Eugene Ormandy conductor.*

YELLOW RIVER CONCERTO.
See: CENTRAL PHILHARMONIC SOCIETY OF THE
PEOPLE'S REPUBLIC OF CHINA.
[Concerto for piano and orchestra...]

YOUNG, VICTOR.   Bristol, Tennessee 9 April 1889
                        Ossining, New York 2 September 1968

5285 Charm assembly line (a ballet)   15'
1.Opening - Cosmetician and machine music
2.Beauty pageant music 3.Shadows and sunshine
4.Parade of charm
1,1,2,1-2,2,1-Timp.,Perc.-Hp.-Str.
Ms. c1954 by Victor Young
Score 113 p.

5257 In the Great Smokies
1,1,2,1-2,2,1-Timp.,Perc.-Hp.-Str.
Ms.
Score 32 p.

5256 Jeep
3,2,3,2-4,2,3,1-Timp.,Perc.-Str.
Ms.
Score 29 p. Large folio

5254 Scherzetto   5'
3*,3*,3*,3*-4,3,3,1-Timp.,Perc.-Cel.,Hp.-Str.
Ms.
Score 52 p. Large folio

YRADIER, SEBASTIAN.
                     Sauciego, Spain 20 January 1809
                     Vitoria 6 December 1865

938s La paloma [The dove, Mexican song.   4'
Arranged by Carl Stix]
2Fl.-Glock.-Hp.(ad lib.)-Str.
J. André, Offenbach a.M. [1897]
Score 7 p.

YSAŸE, EUGÈNE.   Liège, Belgium 16 July 1858
                        Brussels 12 May 1931

528v [Caprice on Saint-Saëns' Op. 52 no. 6,
Etude en forme de valse]
Solo Vn.-2(2nd alt. Picc.),2,2,2-2,2-Timp.,
Trgl.-Str.
A. Durand, Paris [n.d.]
Score 68 p.

Ysaÿe, Eugène

446v Chant d'hiver [Song of winter] Op. 15
Solo Vn.-2,2,2,2-2Hn.-Timp.-Str.
Enoch, Paris, c1902
Score 53 p.

1038v Divertimento, Op. 24
1.Molto moderato 2.Allegretto poco scherzando
3.Vivace non troppo
Solo Vn.-2,3*,2,2-4,2,3-Timp.-Hp.-Str.
Ms. [c1921 by Schott Frères, Brussels]
Score 51 p.

1626s Harmonies du soir, Op. 31
Soli: 2Vn.,Va.,Vc.-Str.
Ms.
Score 23 p.
*Copied by special permission from the original
Ms. owned by the composer's son Antoine.*

681c Méditation, Op. 16
Solo Vc.-2,3*,2,2-4,2,3,1-Timp.,Cym.-Hp.-Str.
Ms. [c1921 by Schott Frères, Brussels]
Score 33 p.
*Copied by special permission from the original
Ms. owned by the composer's son Antoine.*

614v Les neiges d'antan, Op. 23 [The snows of
yesteryear]
Solo Vn.-Str.
Ms. [c1921 by Schott Frères, Brussels]
Score 21 p.
*Inspired by François Villon's Ballade des
Dames du Temps Jadis.*

662c Sérénade, Op. 22
Solo Vc.-2,2,2,2-2Hn.-Str.
Ms. [c1921 by Schott Frères, Brussels]
Score 27 p.
*Copied by special permission from the original
Ms. owned by the composer's son Antoine.*

YUFEROV, SERGEI VLADIMIROVICH.   Odessa 1865

1164 [Antony and Cleopatra. Suite,   *36'*
Op. 24a]
1.Prologue 2.Danses 3.Entr'acte 4.Mort
d'Antoine
3(3rd alt. Picc.),2*,3*,2-4,3,3,1-Timp.,Perc.
-2Hp.-Str.
J.H. Zimmermann, Leipzig [n.d.]
Score 162 p.
From the opera after Shakespeare.

589c Chant de cygne [Swan song] Op. 43   *4'*
no. 1
Solo Vc.-2,2,2,2-4Hn.-Hp.-Str.
B. Schott's Söhne, Mainz, c1910
Score 21 p.

2240 [Elegy beside a grave, Op. 48]
3(3rd alt. Picc.),3*,3*,3*-4,3,3,1-Timp.-Hp.-
Str.
F. Hofmeister, Leipzig [n.d.]
Score 31 p.

770v Fantaisie de concert, Op. 34
Solo Vn.-2(2nd alt. Picc),2*,2,2-2Hn.-Hp.-Str.
B. Schott's Söhne, Mainz [n.d.]
Score 39 p.

1511 Fantaisie funèbre, Op. 42   *16'*
3(3rd alt. Picc.),3*,3*,3*-4,3,3,1-Timp.,
Perc.-Hp.-Str.
B. Schott's Söhne, Mainz [1911?]
Score 30 p.

733v Mélancolie, Op. 43 no. 2   *4'*
Solo Va.-2,2,2,2-2Hn.-Hp.-Str.
B. Schott's Söhne, Mainz [1910?]
Score 19 p.
Composed 1908.

1357 Suite de ballet, Op. 49   *60'*
In 7 movements
3*,3*,3*,3*-4,2,2Cnt.,3,1-Timp.,Perc.-Pno.,
2Hp.-Str.
B. Schott's Söhne, Mainz [n.d.]
Score 123 p.
*Composed 1910. First performance Dresden,
22 October 1913, Blüthner Orchestra, the composer conducting.*

1326 Symphoniette, Op. 29   *25'*
2,2*,2,2-4,2,3,1-Timp.,Perc.-Hp.-Str.
B. Schott's Söhne, Mainz [n.d.]
Score 59 p.
Composed 1909.

Z

ZABEL, ALBERT HEINRICH.   Berlin 22 February 1834
                  St. Petersburg 16 February 1910

669m [Concerto, harp, Op. 35, C minor]   *14'*
Orchestrated by Eugen Reiche
1.Allegro risoluto 2.Andante 3.Allegro con
brio
Solo Hp.-2,2,2,2-2,2,3-Timp.,Perc.-Str.
J.H. Zimmermann, Leipzig, c1905
Score 188 p.
*Composed 1902. First performance St. Peters-
burg 1903, the composer as soloist.*

ZACHAU, FRIEDRICH WILHELM.
              Leipzig 19 November 1663
              Halle 14 August 1712
Also spelled: Zachow

958s [Fantasia, cembalo, D major. Transcribed
by Gustav Lenzewski, Sr.]
Str.
Chr. Fr. Vieweg, Berlin [n.d.]
Score 7 p.

ZÁDOR, EUGENE.   Bátaszék, Hungary 5 November 1894
                  (not 1895)

2171s Divertimento for strings   *13'*
1.Allegro moderato 2.Andantino 3.Moderato,

energico - Vivo
Str.
Eulenburg, London [1956]
Score 46 p.
*Commissioned by the La Jolla Music Festival,
1955. Composed 1955. First performance La
Jolla, California, July 1955, La Jolla Festi-
val Orchestra, Nicolai Sokoloff conductor.*

6082 Fugue fantasia   9'
3(3rd alt. Picc.),2,3*,3*-4,4,3,1-Timp.,Gong-
Str.
Eulenburg, London, ^c1960
Score 49 p. Large folio
*Composed 1959. First performance Hollywood,
July 1959, Los Angeles Philharmonic Orchestra,
Izler Solomon conductor.*

6103 Suite for brass instruments   12'
1.Allegretto moderato 2.Andante 3.Allegro
4Hn.,4Tpt.,3Tbn.,Tuba
Eulenburg, Zurich, ^c1961
Score 22 p.
*Composed 1960. First performance Los Angeles,
January 1961, Hollywood Symphony Orchestra,
Ernst Gebert conductor.*

6151 [Symphony no. 3, Dance symphony]   20'
1.Allegro moderato 2.Andante cantabile -
Allegretto 3.Allegro 4.Andantino - Rondo
3(3rd alt. Picc.),3(3rd alt. E.H.),3(3rd alt.
B.Cl.),3(3rd alt. C.Bn.)-4,3,3,1-Timp.,Perc.-
Hp.(1 or 2)-Str.
Eulenburg, Leipzig, ^c1937
Score 173 p.
*Composed 1936. First performance
Budapest, 8 February 1937, Budapest
Philharmonic Orchestra, Hans Knapperts-
busch conductor.*

1767 Variationen über ein ungarisches   22'
Volkslied
3(3rd alt. Picc.),3*,3*,3*-4,3,3,1-Timp.,Perc.
-Pno.,Hp.(1 or 2)-Str.
Ries & Erler, Berlin, ^c1929
Score 106 p.
*Composed 1924. First performance Vienna, 9
February 1928, Rudolf Nilius conductor.*

ZANDONAI, RICCARDO.
Sacco, Trentino, Italy 28 May 1883
Pesaro, Italy 5 June 1944

4765 Biancaneve [Snow White, impressions   19'
from a fairy tale]
1.Andante con moto 2.Andante mosso 3.Alle-
gretto piuttosto mosso 4.Andante mosso
5.Allegro giusto
3*,3*,3*,3*-4,4,3,1-Timp.,Perc.-Pno.,Cel.,Hp.-
Str.
Ricordi, Milan, ^c1943
Score 84 p.
First performance Rome, 4 January 1940.

4810 Colombina, ouvertura sopra un tema   8'
popolare veneziano
3*,2,2,2-4,3,4-Timp.,Perc.-Cel.,Hp.-Str.
Ricordi, Milan, ^c1935

Score 71 p.
First performance Rome, March 1934.

1063m Il flauto notturno (poemetto)   11'
Solo Fl.-Cl.-2Hn.-Tam-tam-Pno.,Hp.-Str.
Ricordi, Milan, ^c1933
Score 26 p.
First performance Venice, 3 September 1932.

1925 Giulietta e Romeo. Episodio sinfonico   14'
3*,3*,3*,2-6,4,4-Timp.,Perc.-Pno.,Cel.,Hp.-Str.
Ricordi, Milan, ^c1928
Score 83 p.
*From the opera composed 1920. First separate
performance Rome, 11 December 1927, the composer conducting.*

4828 [Musical comments on Sophocles'   20'
Ajax]
1.Preludio 2.Canto bacchico 3.Danza rituale
propiziatrice 4.[The death of Ajax] 5.Finale:
[Exaltation of the hero]
3*,3*,3*,3*-4,4,4-Timp.,Perc.-Pno.,Cel.,2Hp.-
Str.
Ricordi, Milan, ^c1940
Score 81 p.
*Composed 1939. First performed as incidental
music to the play, Syracuse, Italy, 1939.*

4867 Rapsodia Trentina   12'
3*,3*,3*,2-4,3,4-Timp.,Perc.-Cel.,Hp.-Str.
Ricordi, Milan, ^c1936
Score 86 p.
First performance Palermo, 10 January 1937.

621c Serenata medioevale   12'
Solo Vc.-2Hn.-Hp.-Str.
Ricordi, Milan, ^c1912
Score 19 p.
*Composed 1909. First performance Trento, Jan-
uary 1911, Vincenzo Gianferrari conductor.*

ZANELLA, AMILCARE.
Monticelli d'Ongina, Italy 26 September 1873
Pesaro 9 January 1949

1860 Festa campestre [A rustic festival]   5'
3*,3*,3*,2-4,3,3,1-Timp.,Perc.-Hp.-Str.
C. Schmidl, Trieste/Hofmeister, Leipzig, ^c1907
Score 29 p.
*Originally composed for piano 1894; orches-
trated 1915. First performance Pesaro, 1916,
the composer conducting.*

ZARZYCKI, ALEXANDER. Łwów, Poland 21 February 1834
Warsaw 1 November 1895

629p [Concerto, piano, Op. 17, A-flat major]
1.Andante 2.Allegro non troppo
Solo Pno.-2(2nd alt. Picc.),2,2,2-2,2,3-Timp.-
Str.
Bote & Bock, Berlin [1880]
Score 65 p.

678p Grande polonaise, Op. 7   8'
Solo Pno.-2*,2,2,2-2,2-Timp.-Str.
Score: Ms. 83 p.
Parts: Breitkopf & Härtel, Leipzig [1867?]

Zarzycki, Alexander

716v Introduction et cracovienne, Op. 35
Solo Vn.-2,2,2,2-2,2-Timp.,Trgl.-Str.
N. Simrock, Berlin, ᶜ1893
Score 22 p.

968v Mazourka, Op. 26
Solo Vn.-2,2,2,2-2,2-Timp.-Str.
Score: Ms. 48 p.
Parts: Bote & Bock, Berlin [1884]

988 Suite polonaise, Op. 37
1.À la polonaise 2.À la mazourka 3.Inter-
mezzo cantabile 4.À la cracovienne
3*,2,2,2-2,2,3-Timp.,Perc.-Str.
N. Simrock, Berlin, 1893
Score 95 p.

ZECKWER, CAMILLE.   Philadelphia 26 June 1875
                 Southampton, New York 7 August 1924

735p [Concerto, piano, Op. 8, E minor]
Edited by Arthur Cohn
1.Allegro energico 2.Élégie 3.Tarantelle
Solo Pno.-3*,2,2,2-2,2,3-Timp.,Perc.-Str.
Ms.
Score 269 p.
*Composed 1897. First performance Musical Fund
Hall, Philadelphia, 10 March 1899, the com-
poser as soloist.*

3095 Jade butterflies, Op. 50   21'
1.Dance rhythm 2.Silence 3.Balance 4.Return
5.Motion
2,3*,2,2-4Hn.-Cel.,Hp.-Str.
Ms.
Score 60 p.
*Inspired by Japanese poems. Composed 1921.
First performance Chicago North Shore Festival, Evanston, Illinois, 30 May 1922, Chicago
Symphony Orchestra, Frederick Stock conductor. Won the Chicago North Shore Festival
competition, 1922.*

3037 Sohrab and Rustum, Op. 30, after a   29'
poem by Matthew Arnold
3*,3*,3*,3*-4,3,3,1-Timp.,Perc.-Hp.-Str.
Ms.
Score 134 p.
*Composed 1915. First performance Philadel-
phia, 4 February 1916, Philadelphia Orchestra,
the composer conducting.*

ZEDTWITZ, CURT, FREIHERR VON.

2086 [In pursuit of happiness, symphonic   30'
poem, Op. 12]
3*,3*,3*,3*-4,2,3,1-Timp.,Perc.-2Hp.-Str.
Ries & Erler, Berlin [n.d.]
Score 43 p.
Composed 1895.

2087 [Regatta scenes, Op. 11]   30'
1.Start 2.Meteor 3.Windstille 4.[Flower
boat in the harbor] 5.[The victor]
3*,2,2,2-4,2,3,1-Timp.,Perc.-Hp.-Str.
Ries & Erler, Berlin [n.d.]
Score 58 p.
Composed 1894.

249s Serenade, Op. 6 [A major]
1.Allegro moderato 2.Andante 3.Allegro
vivace 4.Allegro non troppo
Str.
Challier, Berlin [n.d.]
No score. Vn.I part 9 p.

ŻELEŃSKI, WŁADISŁAW.
                 Grodkowice, near Cracow 6 July 1837
                 Cracow 23 January 1921

1033 [In the Tatra Mountains, Op. 27]   12'
3*,2,2,2-4,2,3,1-Timp.,Perc.-Str.
Kistner, Leipzig [1883]
Score 55 p.
Composed 1881. First performance Warsaw, 1882.

588c Romanze, Op. 40
Solo Vc.-2,2,2,2-2Hn.-Timp.-Str.
Kistner, Leipzig [1885?]
Score 44 p.

1937 Suite de danses polonaises, Op. 47
1.Polonaise 2.[Krakoviak] 3.Masovienne
3*,2,2,2-4,2,3,1-Timp.,Perc.-Str.
Jurgenson, Moscow [1903]
Score 73 p.

2061 Trauerklänge, elegisches Andante,   6'
Op. 36
2,2,2,2-4,2,3-Timp.-Str.
Kistner, Leipzig [1884]
Score 35 p.
Composed 1883. First performance Warsaw, 1884.

ZEMACHSON, ARNOLD.   Vilna, Lithuania 1892

3535 Chorale et fugue en re mineur, Op. 4 12'
3,3*,2,3*-4,3,3,1-Timp.,Perc.-Org.,2Hp.-Str.
Ms.
Score 36 p.
*Composed 1928. First performance Philadelphia,
21 November 1930, Philadelphia Orchestra, Leopold Stokowski conductor.*

3441 [Concerto grosso, Op. 8, E minor]   30'
1.Andante molto - Allegro ma non troppo
2.Gavotte 3.Largo - Vivace
4*,4*,3,4*-4,3,3,1-Timp.,Perc.-2Hp.-Str.
Ms.
Score 140 p.
*Composed 1932-33. First performance Chicago,
29 November 1934, Chicago Symphony Orchestra,
Frederick Stock conductor.*

1810s [Suite, strings, Op. 11, F major]   30'
1.Overture 2.Gavotte 3.Sarabande 4.Menuet
5.Gigue
Str.
Ms.
Score 84 p.
*Composed 1936-38. First performance over MBC,
New York, 9 May 1941, WOR Sinfonietta, Alfred
Wallenstein conductor.*

ZENGER, MAX.   Munich 2 February 1837
                 16 November 1911

642c Adagio concertante, Op. 65
Solo Vc.-2,2,2,2-2,2-Timp.-Str.
J. Rieter-Biedermann, Leipzig, 1889
Score 30 p.

ZERLETT, JOHANN BAPTIST.   Geistingen 29 July 1859
                           Berlin 24 June 1935

614s Bitte [Entreaty] Op. 144 no. 1
Str.
L. Oertel, Hanover [n.d.]
Score 3 p.

1267s Elegie, Meditation über ein Adagio von
A. Corelli
Solo Vn.-Str.(Cb. ad lib.)
Lehne, Hanover [n.d.]
Score 1 p.

ZEUMER, CL.

1550s [Two intermezzi: Gentle breeze, Op. 100,
and Alianni, Op. 136]
Str.
Scores: Ms. Op. 100, 5 p.; Op. 136, 5 p.
Parts: J.G. Seeling, Dresden [n.d.]

ZHITOMIRSKI, ALEXANDER MATVEIEVICH.
                  Kherson, Ukraine 23 May 1881
                  Leningrad 16 December 1937

Also transliterated: Jitomirsky

3182 Poème héroique, Op. 19
3(3rd alt. Picc.),3*,3(3rd alt. B.Cl.),3*-6,3,
3,1-Timp.(2 players),Perc.-Pno.,Cel.(ad lib.),
2Hp.-Str.
Musgiz, Moscow, 1937
Score 183 p.
Composed 1932.

2486 Poème symphonique, Op. 10   16'
4*,3*,4*,3*-6,4,3,1-Timp.,Perc.-Cel.,2Hp.-Str.
Mussektor/Universal Edition, 1929
Score 83 p.
Composed 1915. First performance Leningrad, 5
May 1926, Leningrad Philharmonic Orchestra,
Jacques Samossoud conductor.

2179 Prélude, Op. 7
3(3rd alt. Picc.),3*,3*,3*-4,2,3,1-Timp.,Perc.
-Cel.,2Hp.-Str.
Mussektor, Moscow, 1925
Score 23 p.
Composed 1911.

ZILCHER, HERMANN KARL JOSEF.
                  Frankfurt-am-Main 18 August 1881
                  Würzburg, Germany 1 January 1948

611p [Concerto, piano, Op. 20, B minor]   28'
1.Ziemlich bewegt 2.Langsam, ausdrucksvoll
Solo Pno.-3(3rd alt. Picc.),2,2,2-4,2,3,1-
Timp.,Perc.-Str.
Breitkopf & Härtel, Leipzig, C1925
Score 105 p.
Composed 1918. First performance Dresden, 27
February 1920, the composer conducting.

886v [Concerto, violin, Op. 11, B minor]   30'
1.Frisch 2.Leicht bewegt, sehr ausdrucksvoll
3.Schnell
Solo Vn.-2,2,2,2-2,2-Timp.,Perc.-Str.
Breitkopf & Härtel, Leipzig, C1906
Score 61 p.
Composed 1902. First performance Berlin, 1903,
Alexander Petchnikov soloist.

899v [Concerto, two violins, Op. 9,   30'
D minor]
1.Bewegt 2.Ruhig, sehr frei im Zeitmass
3.Sehr lebhaft
2 Solo Vn.-3(3rd alt. Picc.),2,2,3*(C.Bn. ad
lib.)-4,3,3-Timp.,Perc.-Str.
Breitkopf & Härtel, Leipzig, C1925
Score 79 p.
Composed 1902. First performance Berlin, 1902,
Alexander and Lily Petchnikov soloists.

898v [Lament, violin, Op. 22, F-sharp   16'
minor]
Solo Vn.-2,2,2,2-2,2-Timp.-Hp.(ad lib.)-Str.
Breitkopf & Härtel, Leipzig, C1926
Score 32 p.
Composed 1906. First performance Berlin, 1907,
Felix Berber soloist.

645p Nacht und Morgen, Op. 24   18'
2 Solo Pno.-Timp.-Str.
Breitkopf & Härtel, Leipzig, C1919
Score 81 p.
Composed 1917. First performance Munich, 11
December 1918, the composer conducting.

848v [Sketches from the Orient, Op. 18]   16'
1.[Muezzin's song] 2.[Dance of the dervishes]
Solo Vn.-2(2nd alt. Picc.),2,2,2-2,2-Timp.,
Perc.-Str.
O. Halbreiter, Munich, C1917
Score 39 p.
Composed 1902-04. First performance Berlin,
1904, Alexander Petchnikov soloist.

1768 [Suite, orchestra, Op. 4, G major]   25'
1.Frisch 2.Ballade 3.Marsch 4.[Serenade]
5.Carneval
3*,2,2,2-4,2,3-Timp.,Perc.-Str.
Ries & Erler, Berlin [n.d.]
Score 58 p.
Composed 1900. First performance Frankfurt,
1901, the composer conducting.

541v [Suite, two violins, Op. 15, G major]   30'
1.Pastorale 2.[Dialogue] 3.[Round dance]
4.Burleske
2 Solo Vn.-2,2,2,2-2,2-Timp.,Perc.-Str.
Breitkopf & Härtel, Leipzig, C1920
Score 53 p.
Composed 1901-02. First performance Berlin,
1903, Alexander and Lily Petchnikov soloists.

403c [Variations on a theme of W.A. Mozart, 20'
Op. 95]
Solo Vc.-2(2nd alt. Picc.),2,2,2-2,2-Timp.,
Perc.-Str.
Breitkopf & Härtel, Leipzig, C1942
Score 52 p.

Zilcher, Paul

*The theme does not appear in Köchel's Thematic
Catalog. Composed 1942. First performance
1943.*

ZILCHER, PAUL.   Frankfurt 9 July 1855

839s Serenade, Op. 15 [F major]
Solo Vn., Solo Vc.-Str.
F. Hofmeister, Leipzig [1900?]
Score 11 p.

9s Serenade, Op. 25 no. 1 [D major]
Fl.(ad lib.)-Str.
D. Rahter, Leipzig, ᶜ1900
Score 3 p.

ZILLMANN, EDUARD.   Dresden 8 October 1834
                               Dresden 26 May 1909

1483s Berceuse, Op. 71
Solo Vn.-Str.
Kahnt, Leipzig [n.d.]
Score 7 p.

ZIMBALIST, EFREM.
         b. Rostov on the Don, Russia 9 April 1889

334p [Concerto, piano, E-flat major]   23'
1.Allegro ma non troppo 2.Canzone 3.Rondo
Solo Pno.-3*,2,2,2-4,3,3-Timp.,Perc.-Str.
Ms. [Elkan-Vogel, Philadelphia, ᶜ1960]
Score 138 p. Large folio
*Originally composed for William Kapell; the
music lost in his fatal airplane accident,
1953. Reconstructed by the composer. First
performance New Orleans, 19 February 1959,
New Orleans Philharmonic Symphony Orchestra,
Alexander Hilsberg conductor, Lee Luvisi
soloist.*

ZIMMER, CARL.   Guben, Germany 7 June 1869
                           Berlin 28 August 1935

1315s [Tryst under the lilac bush, intermezzo]
Bells-Str.
Score: Ms. 5 p.
Parts: P. Westphal, Karlshorst-Berlin [n.d.]

598s [Two string quintets]
1.[Spell of love] 2.[Round dance]
Glock.-Str.
C.F. Schmidt, Heilbronn a.N. [n.d.]
Score 6 p.

ZIMMER, EDWARD.   New York 1893

3133 Great Smoky   10'
3(3rd alt. Picc.),3*,4*,2-4,3,3,1-Timp.,Perc.-
Cel.,Hp.-Str.
Ms.
Score 62 p.
*Composed 1940. First performance Los Angeles,
19 March 1941, Los Angeles Symphony Orchestra
of the WPA, Nathan Abas conductor.*

3134 Night witchery, a short tone poem   6'
2,2,3*,2-4,2,3-Timp.,Bells-Hp.-Str.
Ms.

Score 32 p.
*Inspired by Shakespeare's The Merchant of Ven-
ice. Composed 1939. First performance West
Chester, Pennsylvania, 10 May 1939, State
Teachers College Symphony Orchestra, the com-
poser conducting.*

3150 Ships   24'30"
1.Galleon 2.Those who go down to the sea in
ships
3(3rd alt. Picc.),3*,4*,4*-4,3,3,1-Timp.,Perc.
-Cel.,Hp.-Str.
Ms.
Score 122 p.
*Composed 1937. First performance Los Angeles,
19 March 1941, Los Angeles Symphony Orchestra
of the WPA, Nathan Abas conductor.*

ZIMMERMANS, A.

733c Serenade espagnole
Solo Vc.-Str.
Ms.
Score 9 p.

ZINNEN, J. A.

2079s Marche silencieuse et sérénade, Op. 80
Str.
Durdilly, Paris [n.d.]
Score 12 p.

ZIPOLI, DOMENICO.   Prato, Tuscany 16 October 1688
                       Cordoba, Argentina 2 January 1726

2072s [Suite, organ or cembalo, B minor.   13'
Transcribed by Leon Stein]
1.Preludio 2.Corrente 3.Aria 4.Gavotta
Str.
Ms.
Score 12 p.
*This transcription, 1954. First performance
on the NBC Radio Network program New Dimen-
sions, 26 September 1954, Chicago NBC Orches-
tra, Joseph Gallichio conductor.*

ZIPPEL, HERMANN.

688c Mit ihr allein [With her alone] Romanze
Solo Vc.-1,0,1-Hn.-Str.
Score: Ms. 16 p.
Parts: A.E. Fischer, Bremen [n.d.]

ZÖLLNER, HEINRICH.   Leipzig 4 July 1854
                            Freiburg-im-Breisgau 4 May 1941

1176v Elegie, Op. 46
Solo Vn.-2,1,2,1-Hn.-Str.
Rieter-Biedermann, Leipzig, 1889
Score 7 p.

1454s [Serenade, flute and strings, Op. 95,
C major]
1.Allegretto 2.Allegro con fuoco 3.Sehr
langsam 4.Presto
Solo Fl.-Str.
Ries & Erler, Berlin [n.d.]
Score 39 p.

159s [A summer excursion, Op. 15]
1.[Morning greeting] 2.[Mill song] 3.[Rest-
ful woods] 4.[Departure] 5.[Peasants' dance]
Str.
C.F.W. Siegel, Leipzig [1882]
Score 19 p.

1842 Under the star-spangled banner, overture,
Op. 88
3(3rd alt. Picc.),2,2,2-4,3,3,1-Timp.,Perc.-
Str.
R. Forberg, Leipzig, c1906
Score 65 p.

ZÖLLNER, RICHARD.   Metz, Germany 16 March 1896

240s [A little chamber symphony, Op. 4]
1.Andantino fugale 2.Scherzo 3.Musica sacra
4.Allegro moderato
Str.
Hug, Leipzig, c1922
Score 12 p.

ZOLOTAREV, VASSILI ANDREIEVICH.
                         Taganrog 7 March 1873
                         Moscow 25 May 1964

1069 Fête villageoise, ouverture, Op. 4
3(3rd alt. Picc.),2,2,2-4,2,3,1-Timp.,Perc.-
Str.
Belaieff, Leipzig, 1901
Score 51 p.

1369 Ouverture-Fantaisie, Op. 22
3(3rd alt. Picc.),2*,3,2-4,2,3,1-Timp.,Perc.-
Hp.-Str.
Belaieff, Leipzig, 1907
Score 59 p.

4834 [Phrygian march]
2*,2,2,2-4,2,3,1-Timp.,Perc.-Hp.-Str.
State Publisher, Moscow, 1935
Score 51 p.
Composed 1931.

331 Rhapsodie hébraïque, Op. 7
3*,2,2,2-4,2,3,1-Timp.,Perc.-Hp.-Str.
Belaieff, Leipzig, 1903
Score 99 p.

1441 [Symphony no. 1, Op. 8, F-sharp minor]
1.Introduction 2.Scherzo 3.Andante cantabile 4.Finale: Allegro agitato
3*,2,2,2-4,2,3,1-Timp.,Perc.-Str.
Belaieff, Leipzig, 1903
Score 134 p.

ZOPFF, HERMANN.   Glogau, Silesia 1 June 1826
                       Leipzig 12 July 1883

1389s [Idyll no. 3, Rustling linden-tree,
Op. 35]
Str.
Score: Ms. 7 p.
Parts: International, New York [n.d.]

ZUEHN, JOSEPH CARL.

494m [Concertino in the form of a choral scene]
Solo Bn.-2,2,2,2-2,2,3-Timp.-Str.
Ms.
Score 42 p.

ZUSCHNEID, KARL.   Oberglogau, Silesia 29 May 1854
                        Weimar 1 August 1926

396s Zwei Improvisationen, Op. 78
1.[Slumbersong] 2.Träumerei
Str.
Chr. Fr. Vieweg, Berlin [n.d.]
Score 5 p.

ZWEERS, BERNARD.   Amsterdam 18 May 1854
                        Amsterdam 9 December 1924

5633 [Symphony no. 3, To my fatherland] ca.90'
1.[In Holland's woods] 2.[In the country]
3.[At the seaside and on the sea] 4.[In the
capital]
4*(3rd alt. Picc.II),4*,4*,4*-6,3,2Alto Hn.,
2Ten.Hn.,4,1(alt. B.Tuba)-Timp.,Perc.-2Hp.-
Str.
A.A. Noske, Middleburg, Netherlands [1890]
Score 304 p. Large folio
First performance Amsterdam, 10 April 1890,
Concertgebouw Orchestra, Willem Kes conductor.

Index

This index is designed to provide access to:
(1) ensembles other than the standard orchestra,
and selected types of works, such as fanfares;
(2) works requiring one or more solo or featured
instruments; and (3) works requiring voices.

Within each category the arrangement is alphabetical.
Multiple entries are made for works featuring more
than one solo instrument.

Index entries are followed by the composer's name,
the page number in brackets, and the call number
appropriate to that entry. Thus #473p, J. S. Bach's
Concerto, Three Cembali, no. 1, D minor, BWV 1063,
entered on page 41 in the catalog appears in the
index under: THREE CEMBALI-STRING ORCHESTRA

        BACH, J. S. [41]473p

            ENSEMBLES OTHER THAN THE STANDARD ORCHESTRA

BAND (WIND ORCHESTRA, SYMPHONIC BAND)

AGUIRRE [7]5933; 5934
ALTEMARK [15]4357; 4363

BACH, J. S. [48]4699
BALENDONCK [55]3782
BECKRATH [70]4354
BEETHOVEN [72]6918 [73]2522; 6845; 6817; 6919
BERGER, P. [82]7179
BIRD [92]7207
BOLLMACHER [104]4484
BOTTJE [112]5747; 5746

CAMPO [143]7148; 7133

CAZDEN [153]3376 [154]3908; 4497; 4739; 4740; 4741
CHERNETSKY [166]4734
CHESLOCK [167]5758
CHRISTIANSEN [170]5144
CLAPP [172]5377
CODAVILLA [175]3812
COWELL [191]4864 [193]4865
CRESTON [196]7072; 4746

DAHL [200]4862

END [246]5918; 5786

FINNEY [265]7076
FOSTER, S. C. [273]7336
FRACKENPOHL [274]5452
FRANCESCHINI [275]7127; 6911; 7206 [276]7337

GALIMANY [289]4350
GIANNEO [301]3796
GILSON [305]5220
GOOSSENS [326]2120
GRABNER [330]2220
GRAINGER [333]4752
GROSS [343]7067
GRUNDMAN [344]7066

HARRIS, R. [373]4491
HARTLEY [375]5738
HAUFRECHT [380]7078
HENRY [398]3649
HINDEMITH [405]1544 [406]6024
HÖFFER, P. [407]4355; 4649
HOLZMANN [413]5097
HONEGGER [414] 5103

IVES [430]3196 [431]6453 [432]7096 [433]6456

JADASSOHN [436]6012
JAMES [437]5668

KAEMPFERT [448]4778
KAZDIN [456]7191

STRIEGLER [796]2473
STRINGHAM [797]2810
STÜRMER [798]4328

TAKÁCS [804]6586
TANSMAN [806]1747
TAYLOR, D. [811]2665
TCHEREPNIN, A. [812]1773
TOCH [821]3775
TOWNSEND [824]4896
TRAPP [824]2535
TUTHILL [827]4586

VUIDET [851]1527s
VYNER [851]2672

WEBERN [865]5983; 3971
WIENER [877]2528
WIRÉN [883] 5049
WIRTH [884]225m
WOLF-FERRARI [887]2298

CONCERTO GROSSO

BACH, J. S. [41]965v; 1356s; 712m; 1445; 78s; 991v
    [42]743m; 825m; 535s; 2363s
BENNETT, R. R. [79]3239
BEVERSDORF [88]1105m
BLOCH, E. [97]1117s; 2311s
BOŘKOVEC [108]439m

CASTRO, JOSE [151]3631
COHN, A. [176]1000m
CORELLI [186]1553s; 989s; 2376s; 616s; 1689s;
    1690s [187]1691s; 650s; 2329s; 212s; 601s;
    2361s; 1411s; 1696s; 1697s; 24s; 90s; 913s

DAVISON [205]2359s
DONATO, V. [223]755s

EMBORG [245]551m
EPPERT [248]972m

FIORILLO [265]3537

GEMINIANI [296]1045s; 1241s; 1494s; 171s; 2242s;
    2238s; 321m
GIANNINI [301]1990s

HANDEL, G. F. [363]2312; 2313; 1032m; 2314; 2315
    [364]1091s; 2316; 2317; 1585s; 545s; 922s;
    1586s; 1587s; 1588s; 923s; 1589s; 1146s; 1590s;
    1591s [365]1592s; 1593s; 1113s; 1594s; 1090s;
    1595s; 1596s; 1381s; 2318; 2325; 409v; 1380s
HEIDEN [394]1044m

KŘENEK [478]1673

LAZAR [497]2211

MARKEVITCH [541]3809
MITCHELL [564]334m

MUFFAT [590]490m; 488m; 487m; 485m; 484m; 474m
MÜLLER, S. [593]391m

ROMAN [687]2071s; 384m

SAMMARTINI, GIUSEPPE [712]2050s
SCARLATTI, A. [718]1243s; 2306s [719]957s
SHAFFER [749]2147s
STÖLZEL [786]434m
SZABELSKI [803]6283

TORELLI [823]1031s; 908s

WAGNER, JOSEPH FREDERICK [854]1053m

ELECTRONICS

FRANCESCHINI [275]7218

SPIER [771]440m

FANFARES

ANDREWS [20]3862

BANTOCK [57]3975
BEAUMONT [68]5226
BEHREND [76]7136
BLISS [97]3865; 6022
BUSH, I. [137]7182

CAMPO [143]7182
CATURLA [153]3814
CLAPP [172]5377
COPLAND [183]4271
COPPOLA [185]386g
COWELL [191]4271
CRESTON [196]4271

DEBUSSY [207]2973
DUBENSKY [227]3591
DUKAS [230]2303
DUTTON [233]7182

FALLA [253]3667
FANFARES [254]7182
FOGG [269]3863

GILSON [305]4542
GLAZUNOV [308]2302
GOOSSENS [326]3410; 3411; 4271

HANSON, H. [371]3628; 4271
HARRISON, J. [373]3973
HARTY [377]3662
HENRY [398]3649
HOLBROOKE [409]3864

MALIPIERO [535]3982
MILHAUD [561]3964
MOURET [576]6916

TOY INSTRUMENTS

CHWATAL [170]6180

GRENZEBACH [338]4668

MÉHUL [550]6172
MOZART, L. [577]4647

ROMBERG, B. [688]3613
RYAN [703]4529

SLONIMSKY [763]3804

WOODWIND ENSEMBLE

ALFVÉN [14]226m

BACH, C. P. E. [33]3321
BACH, JOHANN CHRISTIAN [35]3402; 3403; 3404
BACH, J. S. [46]5853
BEETHOVEN [74]2460
BENOIT, G. [79]4375
BERNARD [87]2338
BLACKWOOD [95]6331
BOEHM, Y. [102]6484
BONVIN [107]2449; 2471
BURGMEIN [134]2108

CAPLET [144]6585
CARR [146]7320
CONVERSE, F. S. [180]5820

DANCLA [201]306
DANIELS [202]7318
DONIZETTI [224]6867
DUBENSKY [228]969m
DUBOIS [229]6937; 6940
DVOŘÁK [236]520

ENESCO [246]5797

GOUNOD [330]2378
GOUVY [330]1778

HABERT [352]2390
HAYDN, J. [383]5959 [384]5957; 4392; 5958; 5960
    [385]3485
HOFFMEISTER [408]4205

INDY [426]2339

JADASSOHN [436]6012

LAMPE [489]2301
LESSARD [504]6673

MILHAUD [561]1801
MOSER, F. [574]1694
MOZART, W. A. [581]2365; 2330; 2332; 2333 [582]
    2439; 2334; 2335; 2336

NOVÁČEK, R. [605]2387

OTTERLOO [611]6539

PÉRILHOU [623]2292
PETYREK [626]2112

RAFF [653]2392
RAVEL [658]4955
ROSETTI [693]7062; 7289

SCARLATTI, D. [720]2337; 2472; 7130
STRAUSS, R. [793]2293

WOODWIND ENSEMBLE AND PERCUSSION

LELEU [501]2458

ONE SOLO OR FEATURED INSTRUMENT

ACCORDION

FOSTER, S. C. [273]7336

KLUCEVSEK [464]198m; 197m; 7149

SHCHEDRIN [749]6587

THOMSON [819]6947

BALALAIKA

RIMSKY-KORSAKOV [678]2057

BANDONEON

WEILL [867]1750

BASS CLARINET
    See: CLARINET

BASSET HORN - ORCHESTRA

IVES [430]199m

BASSOON - ORCHESTRA

BACH, J. C. [34]332m; 322m
BIELFELD [90]875m

DAVID, FERDINAND [203]791m
DONOVAN [224] 344m

ELGAR [243]544m
ERIKSSON [249]1086m

GIPPS [306]224m (Contrabassoon)

HÄSSLER [378]813m
HUMAN [421]482m

FREDERIKSEN [280]1093m
FÜRSTENAU [286]726m; 765m; 901m; 766m

GODARD [319]599m
GOOSSENS [327]1027m

GRANT [335]1082m
GRÉTRY [339]318m
GRIFFES [341]313m

HALLNÄS [357]399m
HASSE, J. [378]684m
HEUER [401]760m; 769m
HOFFMEISTER [408]331m
HOFMANN, H. [408]552m
HOLLAENDER, G. [410]554m
HÜE [420]562m; 685m; 686m
HUNRATH [423]638m

JACOBI, F. [435]979m

KALLIWODA [449]655m
KELLY, F. [457]869m
KEMPTER [458]664m; 657m; 656m
KÖHLER, E. [468]635m; 630m; 663m; 636m; 634m
       [469]629m; 628m; 632m; 631m; 633m

LANGER [491]564m
LUENING [519]932m

MANIGOLD [538]660m
MANNS, F. [539]759m
MOLIQUE [566]223m
MOUQUET [576]531m
MOZART, W. A. [577]522m; 1054m [578]519m; 520m
MÜLLER-OLDENBURG [593]767m

NIELSEN, C. [601]329m

PARTOS [620]295m
PÉRILHOU [623]538m
POPP [639]639m; 763m; 567m; 764m [640]579m; 568m
PRILL [644] 640m

REINECKE [665]645m; 762m

SAINT-SAËNS [706]582m [708]510m; 509m
SCHNEIDER, G. [731]862m; 884m
SCHUMANN, CAMILLO [739]829m
STAMITZ, J. [776]245m

TANNER, PETER [806]425m
TARP [806]413m
TERSCHAK [816]728m; 752m; 751m; 828m; 753m; 729m
TILLMETZ [820]644m; 584m
TULUO [825]827m; 572m
TUTHILL [827]446m

VAN VACTOR [832]929m
VERHEY [838]662m; 670m
VIVALDI [847]492m; 491m; 591m; 1107m; 489m; 495m;
       1126v

WAELPUT [852]578m
WAGNER, S. [859]616m
WERNICKE [872]641m
WIEDEMANN [877]761m
WOLTMANN [888]921m

ZANDONAI [893]1063m

FLUTE - PERCUSSION

HARRISON, L. [374]1009m

FLUTE - STRING ORCHESTRA

AMBERG [16]1341s
ANDERSEN [18]583m

BACH, J. S. [38]558s [43]1770s [44]1449s; 565m
BAIRD [52]184m
BARTELS [62]681m
BORDIER [107]690m
BOUGHTON [112]948m
BRUNNER [131]1095m
BURGMEIN [135]1497s

CAMPAGNOLI [142]1025m
CIARDI [170]576m
COUPERIN [190]1377s

FACCIO [252]1457s
FLETCHER, G. [267]468m
FOOTE [270]466m
FRACKENPOHL [274]469m
FREDERICK II (THE GREAT) [279]820m; 821m; 714m
       715m
FRUMERIE [282]1098m

GERNSHEIM [299]574m
GERVASIO [300]1561s
GLUCK [315]674s [316]1350s; 1351s
GNAGA [317]1180s
GOUVY [330]590m
GRAUN, C.H. [335]409m
GRÉTRY [338]1978s

HAINES [355]935m
HANSEN [370]1029m
HANSON, H. [371]1012m
HARRIS, R. [373]986m
HASSE, J. [378]684m
HAUBIEL [379]1041m
HAYDN, J. [383]356m
HELM [397]1038m
HENNEBERG [398]1088m
HILLMANN, K. [404]2s
HINDEMITH [406]500m
HOFMANN, H. [408]824m
HOVHANESS [415]1080m

IVERSEN [430]1285s

JADASSOHN [436]1456s

HARP - STRING ORCHESTRA

BENNETT, G. J. [79]1052s
BLASSER [95]400s [96]800s
BORTKIEVICH [110]1797s
BRANSCOMBE [118]152s
BRUNETTI [131]1678s
BURLEIGH [135]428s; 474s; 473s [136]153s
BUSSER [138]607m

CESTI [156]2043s
CHESLOCK [167]1765s
CZIBULKA [200]659s

DEBUSSY [206]573m

FRITZSCH [282]1280s

GOTTSCHEER [329]870s
GRAENER [332]916s
GRAZIANI-WALTER [336]1565s

HARRISON, J. [373]454s
HARTMANN, E. [376]408s
HELMBURG [397]196s
HUMPERDINCK [422]18s

JACOBI, F. [435]1070m
JOKL [443]1415s
JUNGMANN [445]575s [446]596s

KIENZL [459]150s; 111s
KOMZÁK [470]1252s; 595s
KORGANOV [471]154s
KRUG [481]62s

LAIGRE [487]1662s
LEMBA [501]330s
LOHSE [516]457s
LOMBARD [516]631s; 1578s

MANNFRED [538]1012s; 1198s
MISKOW [564]415s
MRACZEK [589]2371

NERUDA [599]1345s
NEWMAN, T. [600]2233s

PERAGALLO [622]740s
PIERNÉ [631]61s
PINTO [633]847m

REIFF [664]2062s
ROUSSEAU, S. A. [696]614m

SAMET [710]777s
STAHL [773]2051s

VALCÁRCEL [829]1855s

WEINREIS [869]555s
WHITE, P. [875]981m
WIKLUND [878]2291s

HARP - WIND ENSEMBLE

GRUNDMAN [344]195m

HARPSICHORD
  See also: CEMBALO

HARPSICHORD - ORCHESTRA

BACH, J. C. [34]566p

CARTER [147]280p

FALLA [253]579p

HOFFMEISTER [408]270p
HUNT [423]282p

MANFREDINI, V. [538]301p

ROESGEN-CHAMPION [683]796p

HARPSICHORD - STRING ORCHESTRA

BACH, J. C. [34]347p; 646p
BACH, W. F. [49]330p

GIORDANI [306]291p; 294p
GRAUN, C. H. [336]328p

LÖHLEIN [515]261p;260p [516]259p

MOLTER [566]1416s
MONN, G. [567]827p [568]618c
MOZART, W. A. [578]254p

PURCELL [649]2368s

SATUREN [717]2355s; 2354s
STANLEY [778]2401s

HORN - ORCHESTRA

ATTERBERG [27]626m

BECKER, JOHN J. [69]930m
BRUNEAU [131]541m
BUSCEMI [136]1040m

CARRAUD [146]798m
CHABRIER [156]516m
CHESLOCK [167]937m

DAUPRAT [202]703m; 881m
DENNISON [216]155m
DUBOIS [228]530m

FUCHS, H. [283]857m; 882m

GERVASIO [300]799m
GLAZUNOV [310]539m; 218m
GOEDICKE [321]673m

EILENBERG [241]771s

GILLET [304]2352s
GRUNEWALD [345]225s

HALFFTER, R. [356]2136s
HALLNÄS [357]7198
HECHT [394]1695s
HELLMESBERGER [396]1242s
HOVHANESS [415]2025s
HUMPERDINCK [422]19s

JOHNSON, HORACE [442]2003s

KAEMPFERT [448]1006s
KELLER, G. [457]1033s
KÖHLER, O. [469]611s; 782s; 879s; 824s
KRAFT, L. [475]2274s
KREMSER [477]994s
KRENZ [478]6282

LÁNYI [492]1401s
LA VIOLETTE [496]1885s
LINNALA [509]2040s
LÖSCHHORN [517]572s

MARTINU [542]2028s
MEYER-HELMUND [557]836s
MOESCHINGER [565]5266
MOZART [585]52s

NOELTE [604]902s

OELSCHLEGEL [608]416s

RICCI-SIGNORINI [672]433s

SCHLEGEL [727]730s
SCHOENEFELD [732]346s
SIBELIUS [753]2077s [755]364s
SPINDLER [771]1412s
STÖHR [786]1835s

THOMÉ [818]1500s

WAGNER, JOSEF FRANZ [853]1291s
WOLF-FERRARI [887]607s

ZIMMER, C. [896]1315s; 598s

PIANO - BAND

WAGNER, JOSEPH FREDERICK [854]800p

PIANO - ORCHESTRA

ABSIL [3]814p
AISBERG [7]721p
ALBÉNIZ [9]255p
ALBERT [9]600p; 498p
ALEXANDER, J. [12]755p
ARCHER [21]339p

ARENSKY [22]404p;425p
ARNELL [25]829p
ATTERBERG [27]285p
AUBERT [29]513p
AVSHALOMOV, A. [31]722p

BACH, J. C. [34]566p
BACON [51]303p
BAINTON [52]648p
BALAKIREV [53]583p
BALLOU [56]268p
BARTH [62]706p; 707p
BARTÓK [62]620p [63]359p; 830p [64]441p
BATE [65]785p
BEACH, H. H. A. [67]320p
BECKER, JOHN J. [69]700p; 771p
BEETHOVEN [71]366p; 377p; 368p; 369p; 363p; 795p;
    452p [72]590p [74]591p
BENEDICT [77]689p
BEN-HAIM [77]281p
BENNETT, W. S. [79]668p; 669p
BERNARD [87]538p
BILOTTI [90]724p
BINDER [90]826p
BLACHER [94]326p
BLANCHET [95]491p
BLITZSTEIN [97]769p
BLOCH, E. [98]264p
BLUMENFELD [100]517p
BOBINSKY [100]606p
BORCHARD [107]514p
BORDES [107]512p
BORGSTRØM [108]657p
BORTKIEVICH [111]436p
BOYLE [114]708p; 720p
BRAHMS [115]405p; 386p
BRANDTS-BUYS [118]601p; 541p
BRASSIN [119]428p
BRAUNFELS [120]580p
BRINDEL [122]727p
BRITTEN [124]765p; 780p
BRONSART [126]564p
BROOKS [126]757p
BRÜLL [130]573p; 569p; 572p; 551p
BUNIN [133]284p
BUSONI [137]529p [138]349p

CADMAN [140]356p; 719p
CASELLA, A. [148]637p [149]615p; 625p
CASTELNUOVO-TEDESCO [150]743p
CASTRO, R. [152]597p
CATOIRE [152]531p
CENTRAL PHILHARMONIC SOCIETY OF THE PEOPLE'S
    REPUBLIC OF CHINA [155]247p
CHAIKOVSKY [158]387p; 384p; 400p; 581p [159]414p
CHAJES [163]346p; 821p
CHAMINADE [163]373p
CHASINS [164]693p; 694p; 734p
CHOPIN [168]378p; 298p; 395p [169]455p; 453p; 448p
    [170]495p
CLEVE [175]509p; 570p
COHN, J. [177]235p

COLE, U. [178]748p
CONVERSE, F. S. [180]323p [181]337p
COPLAND [183]738p
COSMAN [189]747p
COWELL [191]758p; 273p [194]787p
COWEN [195]528p
CSONKA [197]276p

DEBUSSY [206]507p
DELIUS [213]609p
DIAMOND [217]806p
DIÉMER, L. [220]578p
DOHNÁNYI [222]408p [223]845
DRAESEKE [226]556p
DUBOIS [228]565p; 523p
DUMAS [231]653p
DUVERNOY [234]524p
DVOŘÁK [234]407p

EARLS [238]338p
EK [241]818p
EVETT [252]309p

FALLA [253]579p; 564
FARWELL [255]702p
FAURÉ [256]525p; 458p
FEINBERG [257]705p
FIELD [262]487p; 503p; 481p; 504p; 547p
FINE, V. [264]267p
FINNEY [264]770p
FLORIO [268]258p
FOSS [272]828p
FRANÇAIX [275]822p
FRANCK, C. [276]393p [277]394p
FRANCO [278]761p; 760p
FRUMERIE [283]817p; 324p

GAUDIOSI [294]824p
GEDALGE [294]520p
GERSHWIN [299]244p; 559p
GILCHRIST [304]695p
GINASTERA [306]777p
GLANVILLE-HICKS [307]275p
GLASS, L. [307]665p
GLAZUNOV [308]411p; 412p
GODARD [318]682p; 631p; 482p; 661p
GOEB [320]269p
GOEDICKE [321]589p
GOETZ [322]552p
GOLDSCHMIDT, O. [324]655p
GOTTSCHALK [328]283p
GRÄDENER, H. [331]613p
GRAENER [331]630p
GRIEG [339]376p
GRIFFIN [341]262p
GROSZ [343]454p
GRUENBERG [344]263p
GUARNIERI, C. [345]274p
GUTCHË [348]272p [349]285m; 278p

HAARKLOU [351]647p
HAIEFF [354]277p
HALFFTER, R. [356]773p

HANSON, H. [371]352p
HARSÁNYI [374]779p
HARTLEY [375]357p
HAYDN, J. [382]670p; 331p; 312p; 671p
HELM [397]325p; 358p
HENSELT [398]660p
HILL, E. B. [403]712p
HILLER [404]662p; 546p
HINDEMITH [405]342p
HOCHBERG [407]486p
HOFFMEISTER [408]270p
HONEGGER [413]424p
HOVHANESS [415]240p
HRUBY, F. [417]782p
HUBER, H. [419]574p; 429p
HUMMEL, JOHANN [421]622p; 518p
HURÉ [423]238p

INDY [428]667

JACOBI, F. [434]296p
JADASSOHN [436]644p; 484p
JOUBERT [445]289p

KAHN, R. [448]598p
KALKBRENNER [449]248p
KALLSTENIUS [450]820p
KAPLAN [451]772p
KAUFFMANN [453]577p
KAUN, H. [454]627p; 664p
KELLER, H. [457]808p
KENNAN [458]781p
KIRCHNER [460]266p
KRONKE [481]607p
KUBIK [482]717p
KUHLAU [483]286p
KULLAK [483]673p

LABUNSKI [485]766p
LALO [488]391p
LANGGAARD, S. [491]672p
LAPHAM [492]728p
LÁSZLÓ, ALEXANDER [494]759p
LA VIOLETTE [496]723p
LEONARD, C. [502]740p
LEWIS, A. [505]751p
LEWIS, J. [505]318p
LIAPUNOV [506]463p; 515p [507]443p
LILJEFORS [508]816p; 327p
LIMBERT [508]651p
LISZT [510]380p; 381p; 379p; 444p; 440p [512]437p
    [513]396p
LITOLFF [513]485p; 496p
LOTH [518]737p
LOUIS FERDINAND [518]799p
LUCA, E. DE [519]726p

MAAS [522]480p
MACCOLL [524]736p
MACDOWELL [526]409p; 365p
MACKENZIE [529]626p
MAJOR [535]567p

PIANO - STRING ORCHESTRA

TROMBONE - ORCHESTRA

BOHM, K. [102]542m [103]543m

CARL [145]814m
CLAPP [172]479m

DAVID, FERDINAND [203]749m

FLEISCHMANN, O. [267]842m

GRÄFE [332]852m

HÄSSLER [378]813m

JEHMLICH [440]851m

KAISER [448]811m
KARKOFF [452]402m
KÜHNE [483]846m
KUNKEL [484]809m

LASSEN [494]597m (Bass Trombone)

MCCULLOH [524]160m (Bass Trombone); 159m
MÜHLFELD [592]850m
MÜLLER-BERGHAUS [593]880m

NOWAKOWSKI [606]861m

RADOUX [652]812m
RASSE [657]748m
REICHE [664]652m
ROPARTZ [690]747m
RÜHLMANN [703]878m

SABATHIL [704]844m
SACHSE [705]810m
SERLY [746]1101m
STARK [779]843m

WARNECKE [861]653m; [862]668m; 654m
WEBER, J. [864]845m

TROMBONE - STRING ORCHESTRA

BENOÎT, P. [80]864m

MILHAUD [562]200m

PARRIS [618]350m

STEENEBRUGEN [780]865m

VERRIMST [838]896m

WAMBACH [861]897m

TRUMPET - ORCHESTRA

APITIUS [21]804m

BLÄTTERMANN [96]803m

BOHM, K. [102]542m [103]543m
BÖHME, O. [103]666m; 895m; 649m

CAHNBLEY [141]860m
CARL [145]876m
CASADESUS, F. [147]620m
CHOU WEN-CHUNG [170]227m
COPLAND [184]959m

EICHBERGER [240]676m

GILLET [304]708m
GOCK [318]859m
GOEDICKE [321]886m
GROSSMANN, E. [343]902m

HAYDN, J. [382]1024m [383]156m
HERFURTH [399]877m

IVES [430]199m

KENNAN [458]954m
KIETZER [460]665m
KÖHLER, E. [469]646m

LAPARRA [492]671m
LEUSCHNER [504]647m
LIESERING [508]841m

MAGANINI [532]2788
MAYER, W. [549]367m
MOZART, L. [577]757m
MÜLLER, S. [593]391m

SALMHOFER [710]679m

TELEMANN [813]243m
TORELLI [823]232m
TROGNÉE [825]667m; 648m

VORBERGER [850]808m

WAGNER, JOSEPH FREDERICK [854]1056m
WIGGERT [878]839m
WOLFF, B. [887]742m
WOLFF, E. [887]802m

TRUMPET - STRING ORCHESTRA

ALPAERTS [15]758m

CHAPELLE [163]707m
COPLAND [184]959m

HOVHANESS [416]1081m; 221m; 238m

LATHAM [495]467m

MALER [535]1959s
MOORE, T. [571]203m

PARRIS [619]387m
PERSICHETTI [624]1066m

SKRIABIN [763]1108s

TELEMANN [814]398v

WENNER [871]1502s

VIOLA - WOODWIND AND BRASS ENSEMBLE

GOEB [320]313v; 312v

VIOLA ALTA - ORCHESTRA

LISZT [512]909v

VIOLA DA GAMBA - STRING ORCHESTRA

BACH, C. P. E. [33]388c

VIOLA D'AMORE - STRING ORCHESTRA

BOISDEFFRE [104]1179v

VIVALDI [844]1143v

VIOLIN - ORCHESTRA

ABSIL [3]1195v
ACHRON [4]1071v; 1129v
ALARD [8]999v
ALBINONI [10]732v [11]940v; 331v
ALDAY [12]1106v
ALLEN [14]1073v
ALLENDE [15]1149v
AMANI [16]1067v
AMBROSIO [16]639v; 961v; 437v; 493v; 960v [17]495v;
    612v; 494v; 971v
ANDREAE [20]748v
ARENSKY [22]768v; 776v
ARNELL [25]1132v; 391v
ARNOLD, G. [25]1015v; 1008v
ATTERBERG [27]601v
ATTRUP [28]781v
AUBER [28]289v
AUBERT [29]621v
AUER [29]714v
AULIN [29]604v
AVSHALOMOV, A. [31]353v

BACH, J. S. [38]6896 [39]510s [40]787v; 574v [41]
    1445 [42]754v [45]803v [47]522v; 967v
BACHELET [50]622v
BAILLE [52]933v
BAILLOT [52]1103v; 1101v; 1105v; 1083v; 1104v;
    1084v; 1085v; 1090v; 1109v; 1099v; 1164v
BALTHASAR-FLORENCE [57]937v
BARTÓK [63]1159v [64]935v; 624v; 1573
BAZZINI [67]863v; 996v; 949v
BECKER, A. [68]414v; 415v
BECKER, JEAN [69]1009v
BECKER, JOHN J. [69]361v
BECKER, R. [70]1058v
BEETHOVEN [71]419v; 938v [73]417v; 279v [74]278v

BEN-HAIM [77]333v
BEREZOWSKY [81]1081v
BERG, A. [82]397v
BÉRIOT [83]354v [84]504v; 1169v; 505v; 506v; 1173v
BERLIOZ [86]462v
BERLYN [87]990v
BERNARD [87]1033v
BERWALD [88]842v
BEZEKIRSKY [90]1029v
BLEYLE [96]795v
BLOCH, E. [97]1120v; 1113v [98]304v
BLOCH, J. [98]816v [99]822v
BLUMER [100]700v
BOCCHERINI [100]743v
BOËLLMANN [102]954v
BOHM, K. [103]518v; 546v; 429v
BOISDEFFRE [104]649v
BORCH [107]870v
BORDIER [107]804v; 702v
BORGHINI [107]569m [108]917v
BORGSTRØM [108]684v
BORODIN [109]413v
BØRRESEN [110]610v
BORTKIEVICH [111]905v
BRAHMS [115]425v [117]424v
BRINK [122]962v
BRITTEN [124]1156v
BROCKWAY [125]704v
BRUCH, M. [127]547v [128]519v; 418v; 428v; 452v;
    450v; 520v; 1165v; 553v; 531v
BRUNETTI [131]975v
BULL, O. [133]1186v
BURLEIGH [135]1069v; 1080v
BUSONI [137]543v

CALLAERTS [142]936v
CAMPA [142]591v
CANTU [144]657v
CAPANNA [144]268v
CARL [145]1065v
CASELLA, A. [149]873v
CASTELNUOVO-TEDESCO [150]866v
CENTOLA [154]958v
CHAIKOVSKY [158]411v [160]834v [161]523v; 542v;
    550v [162]524v
CHAJES [163]1185v
CHAUSSON [164]433v
CHESLOCK [167]1121v
CHOPIN [168]766v [169]740v
CLEMENT [174]1112v; 1107v; 1110v
COLERIDGE-TAYLOR [178]831v
COLIN [179]695v
CONUS, J. [179]475v
COQUARD [185]939v
CORDERO [186]321v
CORELLI [188]272v [189]879v
CUI [197]901v [198]557v

DAVID, FERDINAND [203]1192v; 594v; 538v; 862v; 994v;
    992v; 718v; 499v; 1172v [204]1045v; 1020v
DELIUS [213]820v
DIAMOND [217]1082v
DIEMER, L. [220]801v

DIETRICH [220]1064v
DOHNÁNYI [222]556v; 315v
DUBOIS [228]517v [229]681v; 682v
DUPUIS, A. [232]922v
DVOŘÁK [234]427v [235]551v [236]521v

EBERHARDT [238]919v [239]918v
ECKHOLD [239]1086v
EHRENBERG [240]772v
EK [241]1206v
ELGAR [242]544v
ERLANGER, F. [249]964v
ERNST [250]404v; 507v; 1063v; 405v
ESPÉJO [251]1178v

FAIRCHILD [253]618v; 773v; 668v
FARAGO [254]363v
FAURÉ [256]592v [257]578v
FERNÁNDEZ [258]1148v
FIAMINGO [260]1062v
FIBICH [261]808v
FICHER [261]1145v
FOERSTER, J. B. [269]821v
FORSYTH [272]719v
FORT [272]976v
FOURDRAIN [274]944v
FRANCO [278]1138v
FREED [280]1136v
FUCHS, A. [283]629v

GADE, N. [287]693v; 925v
GALLINI [290]952v
GANDOLFO [290]467v
GAUBERT [293]620v
GAUBERT-ELGÉ [293]1018v
GEMINIANI [296]321m
GENG [297]627v
GERKE [297]376v
GERNSHEIM [298]764v; 595v [299]672v
GERVASIO [300]496v
GIANNEO [301]1144v
GIGOUT [302]953v
GILLET [304]947v; 977v [305]972v
GLAZUNOV [308]420v [309]1066v
GODARD [318]515v; 676v; 738v; 555v 739v; 560v
GOEB [320]310v
GOETINCK [322]529v
GOETZ [322]666v
GOHLISCH [323]876v
GOLDMARK, C. [323]469v
GOOSSENS [327]982v
GOUNOD [329]1180v [330]751v
GRÄDENER, H. [331]830v
GRAM [333]869v; 880v
GRUENBERG [344]307v
GRUND [344]1005v
GRÜTZMACHER, F. [345]946v
GUARNIERI, C. [345]1153v
GUIRAUD [347]527v
GUTCHË [348]345v
GYRING [350]1124v

HAARKLOU [352]897v

HALLNÄS [357]302v
HALVORSEN [358]1002v; 742v; 903v
HARRIS, R. [373]4944
HARTMANN, E. [376]1025v
HAUBIEL [378]384v
HAUSER [380]1012v; 476v
HEGAR [394]675v; 887v
HELM [397]1181v
HEURTEUR [401]979v; 1016v
HILLER [404]447v
HILLMANN, K. [404]635v
HOLLAENDER, G. [410]1031v; 586v; 611v; 841v; 448v
HOLLANDER [411]908v
HOLTER [412]784v
HOTH [414]790v
HOVHANESS [416]1194v; 390v
HUBAY [418]665v; 516v; 571v; 583v; 980v; 744v;
        619v; 605v; 587v; 850v; 589v [419]690v; 580v;
        728v; 907v; 817v; 726v; 846v
HÜE [420]916v; 615v
HUNT [423]1188v
HURLEBUSCH [423]299v [424]300v

INGHELBRECHT [428]532c

JACOBI, F. [434]330v
JADASSOHN [435]735v
JAQUES-DALCROZE [438]741v; 652v
JENSEN, G. [440]737v
JOACHIM [441]998v; 606v; 783v; 536v; 554v; 584v
JOAN [442]1108v
JONGEN [444]617v
JOUBERT [445]325v
JUON [446]802v; 727v; 813v; 1209v

KABALEVSKY [447]369v
KÄHLER [448]653v
KALOMIRIS [450]368v
KARLOWICZ [452]489v
KAUFFMANN [453]720v; 706v
KAUN, H. [454]890v
KERR [458]305v
KES [459]970v
KHRENNIKOV [459]285v
KINAPENNE [460]941v
KISTLER [461]636v
KLEIN, J. [462]1187v
KLEMM [463]823s
KLETZKI [463]1182v
KLUGHARDT [464]677v
KOCH, F. [466]871v
KOSTAKOWSKY [473]1202v
KOUTZEN [474]374v; 1130v
KRAMER, A. [475]1070v
KREISLER [476]712v [477]4226; 423v; 4225
KRENEK [478]812v
KREUTZ [479]1160v
KREUTZER, R. [480]1111v; 1087v; 1096v; 1088v
        1027v; 1046v; 1097v
KRUG [481]792v
KRYZHANOVSKI [482]599v; 582v
KUBIK [482]1078v; 1174v
KUNC, A. [484]763v

VIOLIN - STRING ORCHESTRA

ALARD [8]1574s
ALBINONI [10]2101s [11]940v; 283v; 331v
AMBROSIO [16]1066s; 511v; 895v [17]1131; 1077s;
    1154s
ARBEAU [21]297v

BACH, J. B. [34]942s
BACH, J. CHRISTOPH [36]1721s
BACH, J. S. [37]1149s [38]1149s; 558s [40]787v
    [41]572v; 573v [42]209m; 508s; 504s [43]466v
    [44]1353s; 824v
BAILLOT [52]984v
BAUSSART [66]1642s
BEAUME [68]1080s
BEHR, F. [76]1481s
BENDA, JAN J. [76]392v
BLOMDAHL [99]1200v
BOISDEFFRE [104]1179v
BONINCONTRO [105]1187s
BONPORTI [106]2237s; 326v; 336v; 334v; 358v
BRANDTS-BUYS [118]1496s
BROUSTET [126]1522s
BRUCH [128]1165v
BULL, O. [133]351v
BURGMEIN [134]720s; 776s; 1362s; 1363s;

CASTRUCCI [152]731v
CENTOLA [155]1132s; 1073s
CLEMENT [174]1098v
CODA [175]1079s
COHN, J. [177]172m
COLERIDGE-TAYLOR [178]540s
COLIN [179]1649s
CUI [197]902v

DELANEY [210]1116v
DESJOYEAUX [217]792s
DITTERSDORF [220]943v
DORET [225]1486s
DUNKLER [231]1657s
DURAND [232]1137s

EHRENBERG [240]312s
EHRLICH [240]350v
ENESCO [246]1155v
ERNST [250]633v; 892v; 893v
ESPOSITO [251]602s
ETCHECOPAR [251]1429s

FARKAS [255]796s
FENNEY [258]1597s
FORTERRE [272]1651s
FRANZOT [279]1283s
FRENKEL [280]864v
FUNCK [286]1640s

GAAL [287]1583s
GANNE [291]1488s
GEMINIANI [296]2238s
GERIN [297]1219s
GERVASIO [301]1458s; 1151s; 1074s

GILLET [305]1472s; 140s
GODARD [318]1128s
GOENS [322]1515s; 840s
GOUNOD [329]1517s
GRANDJEAN [334]1153s; 1056s; 1224s
GROLNIC [343]295v
GROTE [343]1394s
GUERRI [346]1644s
GUIRAUD [347]1479s
GUNGL [347]1095s

HALVORSEN [358]1273s; 1482s
HANDEL [367]851v
HAUCK [380]1656s
HAVE [381]1014v
HAYDN, J. [383]512v; 513v; 514v
HECK [394]946s; 1571s
HENRI [398]1487s
HENRIQUES, F. [398]1491s
HERRMANN, E. [400]791v
HEURTEUR [401]1217s
HILLE [404]327s
HUSSLA [424]1646s

IMELMANN [426]1397s

JEANJEAN [439]1493s
JÜTTNER [446]1547s

KAMINSKI [451]932s
KLASSERT [462]793s
KLING [464]1663s
KRUG [481]623v

LACOMBE, P. [486]1478s
LANDEAU [490]1135s
LAPORTE [493]1507s
LAUBER [495]658v
LEBERT [498]1645s
LEBLANC [498]1133s
LECLAIRE [498]296v; 311v
LEDERER [499]1510s
LÉONARD, H. [502]1021v; 1168v
LEONBRO [503]1567s
LIPIŃSKI [509]303v
LOVREGLIO [518]1653s

MA'AYANI [523]320v
MANÉN [537]827v
MARCELLO, A. [539]464m
MARCELLO, B. [539]867v
MASSENET [546]722s
MILANOLLO [560]632v
MISTOWSKI [564]917s
MOLÉ [565]1524s; 1525s
MONTI [570]1096s
MOOR [570]172v
MOZART, W. A. [585]399v

NACHÈZ [595]681s
NICK [600]679s
NIELSEN, L. [602]1484s

TARTINI [807]310m
TELEMANN [814]1085m

VIVALDI [847]492m; 491m; 591m; 1107m; 489m; 495m

2 CLARINETS - ORCHESTRA

STAMITZ, C. [774]222m

TUTHILL [826]271m

2 CLARINETS - STRING ORCHESTRA

BENOÎT, P. [80]756m

CLARINET, BASSOON - STRING ORCHESTRA

MASSENET [546]5060

RHODEN [672]3538

STAMITZ, C. [774]462m
STRAUSS, R. [792]1117m

CLARINET, FLUTE - ORCHESTRA

SAINT-SAËNS [709]517m

CLARINET, FLUTE - STRING ORCHESTRA

BERTOLYS [88]1606s
BOLZONI [104]772s
BONINCONTRO [105]941s
BOZI [115]1212s

CAPRI [144]1308s; 1409s

HENRI [398]179s

KAAN-ALBEST [447]918s

OLSEN, S. [609]6097

PICQUET [629]1551s

SANDRÉ [713]823m

CLARINET, HARP - STRING ORCHESTRA

JAMES, D. [436]946m

CLARINET, HORN - ORCHESTRA

BOHNE [103]814m

WIEDEMANN [877]784m

CLARINET, PIANO - STRING ORCHESTRA

HARRIS, R. [373]912m

WAGNER, JOSEPH FREDERIC [855]4005

CLARINET (BASS), TRUMPET - BAND

FRANCESCHINI [275]6911

CLARINET, VIOLIN - STRING ORCHESTRA

DELAUNAY [211]799s

CLARINET, VIOLONCELLO - STRING ORCHESTRA

BEVERSDORF [88]1102m

CONTRABASS, VIOLA - ORCHESTRA

DITTERSDORF [221]235m

2 CORNETS - ORCHESTRA

RICCIUS [673]806m

ENGLISH HORN, OBOE - STRING ORCHESTRA

SCHOECK [731]278m

ENGLISH HORN, TRUMPET - STRING ORCHESTRA

COPLAND [184]959m

2 FLUTES - ORCHESTRA

ANDERSEN [18]903m

BECKER, JOHN J. [69]923m

FÜRSTENAU [286]370m

HAYDN, J. [382]343m
HEINICHEN [395]5332

TULOU [826]905m

2 FLUTES - STRING ORCHESTRA

BACH, J. S. [38]2323s
BACH, W. F. [49]976m; 1419s

FESTING [260]178m

GLUCK [316]684s
GOUNOD [330]1446s

2 FLUTES - STRING ORCHESTRA

SCARLATTI, A. [719]6357; 6361
SIBELIUS [755]1455s

WUNSCH [890]907s

FLUTE, BARITONE HORN - BAND

TAYLOR, CLIFFORD [810]7116

FLUTE, BASSOON - STRING ORCHESTRA

COUPERIN [190]1379s; 1376s

FRESCOBALDI [281]1373s

FLUTE, CEMBALO - STRING ORCHESTRA

PERGOLESI [623]303m

SCARLATTI, A. [719]207m

TARTINI [807]310m
TELEMANN [814]1085m

VIVALDI [847]492m; 491m; 591m; 1107m; 489m; 495m

FLUTE, CLARINET - ORCHESTRA

SAINT-SAËNS [709]517m

FLUTE, CLARINET - STRING ORCHESTRA

BERTOLYS [88]1606s
BOLZONI [104]772s
BONINCONTRO [105]941s
BOZI [115]1212s

CAPRI [144]1308s; 1409s

HENRI [398]179s

KAAN-ALBEST [447]918s

OLSEN, S. [609]6097

PICQUET [629]1551s

SANDRÉ [713]823m

FLUTE, HARP - ORCHESTRA

COWELL [191]264m

HARTY [377]952m

MOZART, W. A. [578]524m

FLUTE, HARP - STRING ORCHESTRA

BERGÉ [82]773s

DONOVAN [225]961m

RAPOPORT [656]956m
RUDIN, H. [701]963m

FLUTE, HORN - ORCHESTRA

MÜLLER, B. [592]598m

FLUTE, HORN - STRING ORCHESTRA

KERVÉGUEN [459]1659s

FLUTE, OBOE - ORCHESTRA

HAYDN, J. [382]342m; 978m; 341m; 340m; 339m

FLUTE, OBOE - STRING ORCHESTRA

BACH, J. C. [34]3507

COLLINO [179]1306s

DEGEN [209]4330

HOLST [411]596m

KLAAS [461] 1600s

LACOMBE, P. [487]571m

FLUTE, PIANO - STRING ORCHESTRA

KLEPPER [463]293m

FLUTE, TRUMPET - ORCHESTRA

BOTTJE [112]420m

FLUTE, VIOLA - ORCHESTRA

ROGERS [684]938m

FLUTE, VIOLIN - ORCHESTRA

HOLMBOE [411]414m

TCHEREPNIN, A. [811]608m

FLUTE, VIOLIN - STRING ORCHESTRA

BAINTON [52]561s

CRESTON [196]922m

VUIDET [851]1526s

HARMONIUM, PIANO - STRING ORHCESTRA

DORNHECKTER [226]993s

GIOVANELLI [306]1102s; 1104s; 1103s

SKOP [762]357s

2 HARPS - ORCHESTRA

FREDERIKSEN [280]1091m

2 HARPS - STRING ORCHESTRA

FÉVRIER [260]480s

RICCI-SIGNORINI [672]435s

VAUGHAN WILLIAMS [836]1834s

VIOLA, VIOLIN - ORCHESTRA

BENJAMIN [79]1018m

HOLMBOE [411]257m

MOZART, W. A. [586]716m

STAMITZ, C. [775]256m

VIOLA, VIOLIN - STRING ORCHESTRA

ATTERBERG [27]605m

GRAUN, J. [336]283m

VIOLA, VIOLONCELLO - ORCHESTRA

RADOUX [652]815m

VIOLA D'AMORE, LUTE - STRING ORCHESTRA

VIVALDI [844]966m

2 VIOLINS - ORCHESTRA

BLOCH, J. [99]822v

BORNSCHEIN [109]2608

HOFMANN, K. [409]840v

KALLIWODA [449]357v

MANFREDINI, F. [538]80s
MAURER [548]362v; 1026v
MOZART, W. A. [580]872v

REICHA, J. [664]288v
ROMAN [687]2071s; 384m

SPOHR [772]473v
STAMITZ, C. [775]383v

TORELLI [823]908s

VIOTTI [842]1175v; 1177v
VIVALDI [844]286v [845]340v [848]6384

ZILCHER, H. [895]899v; 541v

2 VIOLINS - STRING ORCHESTRA

ALBINONI [11]2293s
ANDRÉ, L. [19]1272s

BACH, J. S. [38]2323s [40]575v [41]576v

ERSFELD [250]1189s

HOLST [411]596m
HUMPHRIES [423]1050s

JARNACH [438]280v

LANGEY [491]1002s
LOCATELLI [514]2402s

MANFREDINI, F. [538]80s
MOLIQUE [566]537v

NAGLER [596]1207s; 1387s

REINHARDT [666]1296s
ROMAN [687]2071s; 384m

SCARLATTI, A. [719]2255s
SCHINDLER [727]1492s

TORELLI [823]908s

VIVALDI [844]286v [845]340v; 72s [848]6384

VIOLIN, CLARINET - STRING ORCHESTRA

DELAUNAY [211]799s

VIOLIN, FLUTE - ORCHESTRA

HOLMBOE [411]414m

TCHEREPNIN, A. [811]608m

VIOLIN, FLUTE - STRING ORCHESTRA

BAINTON [52]561s

CRESTON [196]922m

VUIDET [851]1526s

VIOLIN, HARP - ORCHESTRA

HUBER, G. [419]610m

VIOLIN, HARP - STRING ORCHESTRA

BRANDTS-BUYS [118]1496s
BURGMEIN [134]1363s

HARTY [378]453s

VIOLIN, HORN - ORCHESTRA

WESSELY [872]931m
WOLFERMANN [887]750m

VIOLIN, OBOE - ORCHESTRA

BACH, J. S. [48]1543

VIVALDI [844]320m

VIOLIN, OBOE - STRING ORCHESTRA

BARLOW [61]933m

VALENTINI [830]365m

WESSEL [872]1777s

VIOLIN, PIANO - ORCHESTRA

HARRISON, L. [374]338m
HUMMEL, JOHANN [421]237m

LEBORNE [498]721m

MANÉN [538]720m

PLEYEL [636]229m

VIOTTI [842]940m

VIOLIN, PIANO - STRING ORCHESTRA

FAIRCHILD [253]718m

HAYDN, J. [383]463m

VIOLIN, VIOLA - ORCHESTRA

BENJAMIN [79]1018m

HOLMBOE [411]257m

MOZART, W. A. [586]716m

STAMITZ, C. [775]256m

VIOLIN, VIOLA - STRING ORCHESTRA

ATTERBERG [27]605m

GRAUN, J. [336]283m

VIOLIN, VIOLONCELLO - ORCHESTRA

ADOLPHUS [6]916m

BACH, J. C. [34]358m
BRAHMS [115]745m

DELIUS [213]722m

FLORIO [268]290m; 6448

HANDEL, G. F. [365]409v

KIRCHNER [460]319m
KLENGEL [463]717m
KRETSCHMER, P. [479]1573s; 1575s

REICHARDT [664]1258s
RIBIOLLET [672]617m

SAINT-SAËNS [708]724m
SKÖLD [762]396m
STANLEY [778]2401s

VIOLIN, VIOLONCELLO - PERCUSSION

GAILLARD [289]181m

VIOLIN, VIOLONCELLO - STRING ORCHESTRA

BANÈS [57]1518s
BÉHAULT [75]1216s
BRANDTS-BUYS [118]1495s

EMERSCHITZ [245]1289s

GAUL [294]1702s
GILLET [304]1413s

KRETSCHMER [479]1573s; 1575s

LOEWENTHAL [515]1277s

STANLEY [778]2401s
STECK [780]648s

ZILCHER, P. [896]839s

2 VIOLONCELLOS - ORCHESTRA

GILBERT [303]2614

MOÓR [570]561c

VIOLONCELLO, CLARINET - STRING ORCHESTRA

BEVERSDORF [88]1102m

VIOLONCELLO, VIOLA - ORCHESTRA

RADOUX [652]815m

VIOLONCELLO, VIOLIN - ORCHESTRA

ADOLPHUS [6]916m

BACH, J. C. [34]358m
BRAHMS [115]745m

DELIUS [213]722m

FLORIO [268]290m; 6448

HANDEL, G. F. [365]409v

KIRCHNER [460]319m
KLENGEL [463]717m
KRETSCHMER, P. [479]1573s; 1575s

REICHARDT [664]1258s
RIBIOLLET [672]617m

SAINT-SAËNS [708]724m
SKÖLD [762]396m
STANLEY [778]2401s

VIOLONCELLO, VIOLIN - PERCUSSION

GAILLARD [289]181m

FLUTE, OBOE, BASSOON - ORCHESTRA

CANNABICH [143]208m

FLUTE, OBOE, BASSOON - STRING ORCHESTRA

BURNHAM [136]458m

VIVALDI [844]248m

FLUTE, OBOE, CLARINET - STRING ORCHESTRA

GOEB [320]6658

FLUTE, OBOE, TRUMPET - STRING ORCHESTRA

BARBER [59]1072m

FLUTE, PIANO, VIOLIN - STRING ORCHESTRA

EMBORG [245]415m

FLUTE, PIANO, VIOLONCELLO - STRING ORCHESTRA

INDY [426]563m

FLUTE, VIOLIN, VIOLONCELLO - STRING ORCHESTRA

MASSENET [545]1447s

GLOCKENSPIEL, 2 FLUTES - STRING ORCHESTRA

STROHBACH [797]393m

HARMONIUM, FLUTE, CLARINET - STRING ORCHESTRA

MYDDLETON [595]1003s

HARP, PIANO, HARMONIUM - STRING ORCHESTRA

MULÉ [592]5112

STRAUSS, R. [793]1347s

HARPSICHORD, PIANO, CELESTA - STRING ORCHESTRA

MARTIN, F. [542]5279

HARPSICHORD, 2 RECORDERS - ORCHESTRA

NAGAN [595]276m

HARPSICHORD, VIOLA, VIOLONCELLO - STRING ORCHESTRA

FRANCESCHINI [275]254m

3 HORNS - ORCHESTRA

TELEMANN [813]247m

3 HORNS - STRING ORCHESTRA

LUENING [519]973m

TELEMANN[813]247m

HORN, CLARINET, BASSOON - ORCHESTRA

CRUSELL [197]266m

HORN, CLARINET, BASSOON - STRING ORCHESTRA

BRÉVAL [121]234m

HORN, CLARINET, VIOLIN - STRING ORCHESTRA

MERIKANTO [555]505m

HORN, OBOE, VIOLA - STRING ORCHESTRA

LEPLIN [503]239m

HORN, TRUMPET, TROMBONE - ORCHESTRA

CHEMBERDZHI [165]945m

HORN, VIOLIN, VIOLONCELLO - STRING ORCHESTRA

SCHUBERT [737]1452s

3 KAZOOS

MÉHUL [550]6172

2 OBOES, BASSOON - STRING ORCHESTRA

BACH, J. S. [37]1147s [43]1246
BOYCE [113]6830; 774s

STANLEY [778]2200s

OBOE, BASSOON, TRUMPET - ORCHESTRA

HEIDEN [394]1044m

OBOE, FLUTE, BASSOON - ORCHESTRA

CANNABICH [143]208m

VIVALDI [844]248m

OBOE, FLUTE, BASSOON - STRING ORCHESTRA

BURNHAM [136]458m

OBOE, FLUTE, CLARINET - STRING ORCHESTRA

GOEB [320]6658

OBOE, FLUTE, TRUMPET - STRING ORCHESTRA

BARBER [59]1072m

OBOE, HORN, VIOLA - STRING ORCHESTRA

LEPLIN [503]239m

OBOE, OBOE D'AMORE, ENGLISH HORN - STRING ORCHESTRA

MARIOTTE [541]826m

OBOE, VIOLIN, VIOLONCELLO - STRING ORCHESTRA

EMBORG [245]551m

ORGAN, VIOLIN, VIOLONCELLO - STRING ORCHESTRA

RHEINBERGER [671]335m

3 PIANOS - ORCHESTRA

CESANA, O. [155]754p

MOZART, W. A. [579]592p

PIANO, CELESTA, HARPSICHORD - STRING ORCHESTRA

MARTIN, F. [542]5279

PIANO, CLARINET, VIOLA - ORCHESTRA

PHILLIPS [628]1097m

PIANO, FLUTE, VIOLIN - STRING ORCHESTRA

EMBORG [245]415m

PIANO, FLUTE, VIOLONCELLO - STRING ORCHESTRA

INDY [426]563m

PIANO, HARP, HARMONIUM - STRING ORCHESTRA

MULÈ [592]5112

STRAUSS, R. [793]1347s

PIANO, TRUMPET, VIOLIN - STRING ORCHESTRA

HOVHANESS [416]478m

PIANO, VIOLIN, VIOLONCELLO - ORCHESTRA

BEETHOVEN [71]603m

CASELLA, A. [148]1076m

JUON [446]719m

MOÓR [570]816m

PIANO, VIOLIN, VIOLONCELLO - STRING ORCHESTRA

VEGA [836]369m

2 RECORDERS, HARPSICHORD - ORCHESTRA

NAGAN [595]276m

3 TROMBONES - ORCHESTRA

MITCHELL [564]334m

TUTHILL [827]262m

TROMBONE, HORN, TRUMPET - ORCHESTRA

CHEMBERDZHI [165]945m

3 TRUMPETS - BAND

STRAUSS, R. [792]3717

TRUMPET, FLUTE, OBOE - STRING ORCHESTRA

BARBER [59]1072m

TRUMPET, HORN, TROMBONE - ORCHESTRA

CHEMBERDZHI [165]945m

TRUMPET, OBOE, BASSOON - ORCHESTRA

HEIDEN [394]1044m

TRUMPET, PIANO, VIOLIN - STRING ORCHESTRA

HOVHANESS [416]478m

3 VIOLAS - STRING ORCHESTRA

DAVISON [205]2359s

VIOLA, CLARINET, PIANO - ORCHESTRA

PHILLIPS [628]1097m

VIOLA, HARPSICHORD, VIOLONCELLO - STRING ORCHESTRA

FRANCESCHINI [275]254m

VIOLA, OBOE, HORN - STRING ORCHESTRA

LEPLIN [503]239m

VIOLA, VIOLIN, VIOLONCELLO - ORCHESTRA

BACARISSE [32]962m

CAZDEN [154]1046m

KAMINSKI [451]1648
KIRCHBACH [460]723m
KRENEK [478]1673

ROSENBERG [691]397m

VIOLA, VIOLIN, VIOLONCELLO - STRING ORCHESTRA

LEKEU [500]204s

WEILLER [867]949s

3 CORNETS, BARITONE HORN - BAND

WAGNER, JOSEPH FREDERICK [854]1053m

3 FLUTES, HARP - ORCHESTRA

VAN VACTOR [832]926m

2 FLUTES, 2 OBOES - STRING ORCHESTRA

BACH, J. S. [37]1232s

FLUTE, OBOE, BASSOON, HORN - ORCHESTRA

DANZI [202]1047m

HARP, 3 FLUTES - ORCHESTRA

VAN VACTOR [832]926m

HARPSICHORD, 2 VIOLINS, VIOLONCELLO - STRING
ORCHESTRA

CORELLI [187]2361s

4 HORNS - ORCHESTRA

HÜBLER [420]325m

SCHUMANN, R. [740]518m

4 HORNS - STRING ORCHESTRA
HAYDN, J. [381]6036

SANDBY [712]6371

HORN, FLUTE, OBOE, BASSOON - ORCHESTRA

DANZI [202]1047m

HORN, OBOE, CLARINET, BASSOON - ORCHESTRA

MOZART, W. A. [585]619m

2 OBOES, 2 FLUTES - STRING ORCHESTRA

BACH, J. S. [37]1232s

2 OBOES, VIOLONCELLO, BASSOON - STRING ORCHESTRA

MUFFAT [590]490m; 485m

OBOE, CLARINET, BASSOON, HORN - ORCHESTRA

MOZART, W. A. [585]619m

OBOE, FLUTE, BASSOON, HORN - ORCHESTRA

DANZI [202]1047m

OBOE, VIOLIN, VIOLA, VIOLONCELLO -
ORCHESTRA

BEETHOVEN [73]844

4 RECORDERS

NEWMAN, J. [600]7107

STRING QUARTET - ORCHESTRA

BAUTISTA [66]1021m
BECK, C. [68]1031m
BEREZOWSKY [81]928m

FENNER [258]7300
FULEIHAN [285]939m

HAUBIEL [379]2690

LA VIOLETTE [496]984m

PHILLIPS [627]1099m

POOT [639]1106m

SPOHR [772]288m

STRAVINSKY [794]459p

VALLS [830]1104m

STRING QUARTET - STRING ORCHESTRA

BLOCH, E. [97]2311s

COOKE [182]1952s
CORELLI [186]2376s

ELGAR [243]533s
ETLER [251]268m

GEMINIANI [296]171s; 2242s

HANDEL, G. F. [365]1380s

JEHIN, L. [440]420s

SCALERO [718]258s

VAUGHAN WILLIAMS [835]502s

YSAŸE [892]1626s

VIOLA, OBOE, VIOLIN, VIOLONCELLO - ORCHESTRA

BEETHOVEN [73]844

4 VIOLINS - ORCHESTRA

VIVALDI [845]348v; 341v; 339v; 579v

2 VIOLINS, VIOLONCELLO, CONTRABASS - STRING
ORCHESTRA

MUFFAT [590]490m; 488m; 487m; 485m; 484m; 474m

SCHUBERT [735]2292s
SESSIONS [748]6428
SHAPEY [749]6334; 6333
SHOSTAKOVICH [753]6980
STEINBERG [781]5002

VAUGHN WILLIAMS [836]1019
VEGA [836]6614
VILLA-LOBOS [840]457c
VIVALDI [848]6384

WAGNER, JOSEPH FREDERICK [855]4532

MEZZO-SOPRANO

BACH, J. S. [38]6896
BERLIOZ [85]6596

ELGAR [242]1420

FANELLI [254]5592

HUMPERDINCK [422]7120

PARKER, H. [618]6579

ROGERS [685]2650

SKRIABIN [762]859

ALTO

BEETHOVEN [75]164
BERLIOZ [86]768

KLENAU [463]1662

MAHLER [533]6431

STEINBERG [781]5002

VEGA [836]6614

CONTRALTO

BAVICCHI [66]6196
BERLIOZ [85]6596

HOVEY [415]5890

KOHS [469]6328

MAHLER [533]6576; 6627
MOZART, W. A. [584]3661

SCHICKELE [726]7125
SICCARDI [757]3881

COUNTER TENOR

SCHICKELE [726]7125

TENOR

ALEXANDROV [13]6125

BEETHOVEN [75]164
BERLIOZ [85]6596 [86]768
BRANSCOMBE [118]7302

CASELLA, A. [149]1589
CHESLOCK [167]3605
CHOU WEN-CHUNG [170]6724
COHN, J. [177]2382s
CZERNIK [199]4653

FAURÉ [257]6003

GLANVILLE-HICKS [307]6638
GOLDSCHMIDT, A. [324]5223

HENNEBERG [398]6010
HOVEY [415]5890

IPPOLITOV-IVANOV [429]1914

LARSSON [494]5050
LISZT [510]1551

MAHLER [533]6576

ROCHBERG [681]5970

SKRIABIN [762]859
STRUTT [798]7299
SZYMANOWSKI [803]1744

TAL [804]297p

VAUGHAN WILLIAMS [836]1019

BARITONE

BAXTER [66]7321
BEACH, J. P. [67]3189
BERLIOZ [85]6569

CHESLOCK [167]3605

EVETT [252]6548

FLORIDIA [268]7015
FOSS [272]6329

MAHLER [533]6576

NABOKOV [595]5362
NIELSEN, C. [602]1230

PARKER, H. [617]6476
PORTER [641]6412

SCHOENBERG [732]5219
SHOSTAKOVICH [753]6966
SIEGMEISTER [757]741c

WEINBERG [867]6976

BASS-BARITONE

FLORIDIA [268]7015

SHOSTAKOVICH [753]6966
SCHOENBERG [732]5219

BASS

BEETHOVEN [75]164
BERLIOZ [86]768
BLOCH, E. [98]6771

FLORIDIA [268]7015

RODRIGO [683]6865

SCHOENBERG [732]5219
SHOSTAKOVICH [753]6966; 6980

HIGH RANGE

BERG, A. [82]6894

CARR [146]7044; 7043
CHAJES [162]417c

GARCÍA ESTRADA [291]5860

HEWITT, J. [402]7045
HOPKINSON [414]7042

REINAGLE [664]7040

SELBY [745]7041
SOWERBY [769]967m

MEDIUM RANGE

AVIDOM [30]6563

UNSPECIFIED RANGE

BECKER, JOHN J. [69]1061m; 6823
BIEBL [90]4648
BLANTER [95]5139
BOWLES [113]3151
BUCK [132]6819

COQUARD [185]445s

EICHBERGER [240]676m

FALLA [253]1594
FOSS [273]6299
FRANCK, C. [277]1617

GOMES [326]1118v
GRUENBERG [344]7002

IPPOLITOV-IVANOV [429]1965
IVES [430]199m; 3970 [431]6674

JAMES, P. [436]2849

KLETZKI [464]4527

LOEFFLER [514]4206

MAHLER [532]6206; 6617; 6618; 6619 [533]6620;
    6621; 6622; 6623; 6624; 6625; 6626
MALER [535]1959s
MAYER, W. [549]6201
MUSSORGSKY [595]7004

OLSEN, P. [609]6884

PITTALUGA [635]6880

RODRIGO [683]6132

SIBELIUS [753]2177s
SPENDIAROV [770]1806
SUPPÉ [800]4666

FEMALE

EICHHEIM [240]6139

LISZT [512]1172

MACCOLL [524]3559
MCKAY [528]3477
MARINUZZI [540]1916

NYSTROEM [607]5221

POHLIG [637]1510

REINECKE [665]5224

STEINBERG [781]5002
SUK [799]5757

MALE

SUPPÉ [800]4666

CHORUS

ALLENDE SARÓN [15]261

BACH, J. S. [37]571s; 862s
BECKER, JOHN J. [70]3856; 4760
BEETHOVEN [72]590p [75]164
BERLIOZ [85]5651 [86]768; 7146; 4254; 734
BLOCH, E. [97]1956 [98]6771
BORODIN [109]413
BRUNEAU [131]1643; 1550

CAPANNA [144]268v

DEBUSSY [207]409; 2350
DELIBES [212]405
DELIUS [214]2537
DONIZETTI [224]4291

2nd SYMPHONY by BRAHMS

I. Allegro non troppo

II. Adagio non troppo